CONNECT FEATURES

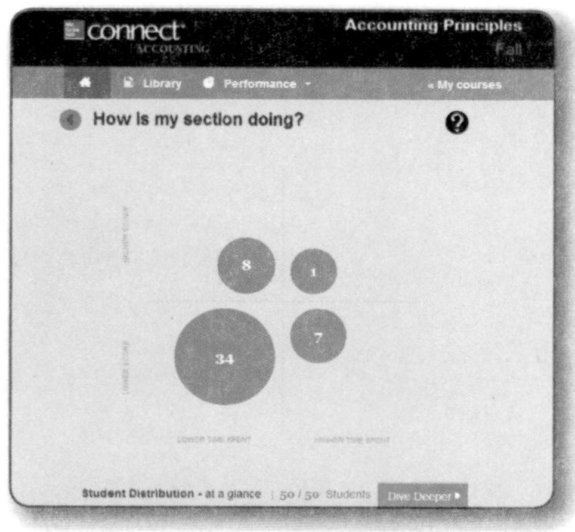

Connect Insight

The first and only analytics tool of its kind, Connect Insight is a series of visual data displays, each of which is framed by an intuitive question and provides at-a-glance information regarding how an instructor's class is performing. Connect Insight is available through Connect titles.

End-of-Chapter Material

McGraw-Hill Education redesigned the student interface for our end-of-chapter assessment content. The new interface provides improved answer acceptance to reduce students' frustration with formatting issues (such as rounding), and, for select questions, provides an expanded table that guides students through the process of solving the problem. Many questions have been redesigned to more fully test students' mastery of the content.

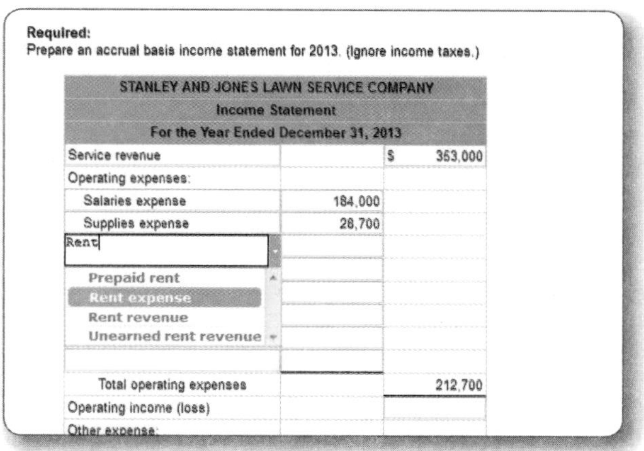

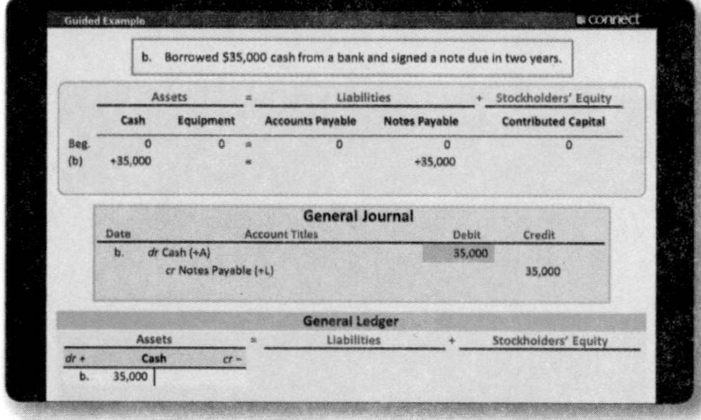

Guided Examples

Guided Examples provide narrated and animated step-by-step walkthroughs of algorithmic versions of assigned exercises. This allows students to identify, review, or reinforce the concepts and activities covered in class. Guided Examples provide immediate feedback and focus on the areas where students need the most guidance.

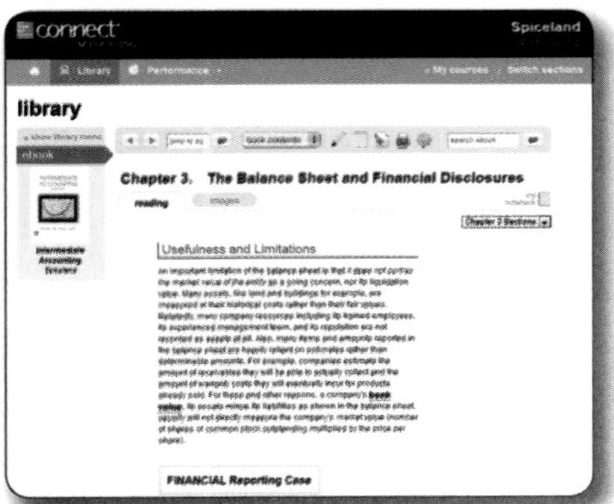

eBook

Connect includes a media-rich eBook that allows you to share your notes with your students. Your students can insert and review their own notes, highlight the text, search for specific information, and interact with media resources. Using an eBook with Connect gives your students a complete digital solution that allows them to access their materials from any computer.

EASY TO USE

Learning Management System Integration

McGraw-Hill Campus is a one-stop teaching and learning experience available to use with any learning management system. McGraw-Hill Campus provides single sign-on to faculty and students for all McGraw-Hill material and technology from within the school website. McGraw-Hill Campus also allows instructors instant access to all supplements and teaching materials for all McGraw-Hill products.

Blackboard users also benefit from McGraw-Hill's industry-leading integration, providing single sign-on to access all Connect assignments and automatic feeding of assignment results to the Blackboard grade book.

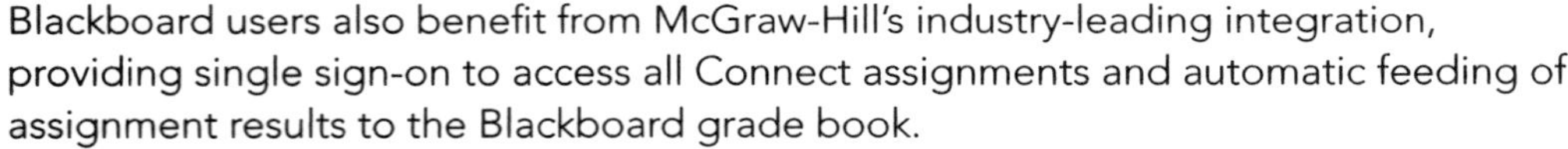

POWERFUL REPORTING

Connect generates comprehensive reports and graphs that provide instructors with an instant view of the performance of individual students, a specific section, or multiple sections. Since all content is mapped to learning objectives, Connect reporting is ideal for accreditation or other administrative documentation.

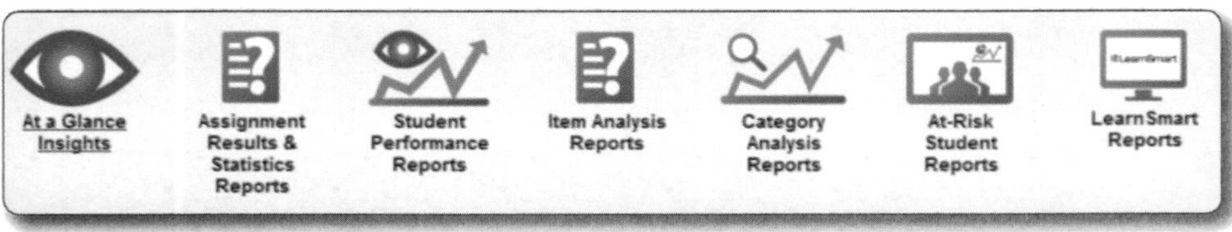

Intermediate Accounting

EIGHTH EDITION

J. DAVID SPICELAND
University of Memphis

JAMES F. SEPE
Santa Clara University

MARK W. NELSON
Cornell University

WAYNE B. THOMAS
University of Oklahoma

Dedicated to:

David's wife Charlene, daughters Denise and Jessica, and sons Michael David, Michael and David

Jim's wife Barbara, children Kristina, Matt, and Dave, daughter-in-law Donna, and grandchildren, Kaitlyn, Meghan, and Michael

Mark's wife Cathy, and daughters Liz and Clara

Wayne's wife Julee, daughter Olivia, and three sons Jake, Eli, and Luke

INTERMEDIATE ACCOUNTING, EIGHTH EDITION

Published by McGraw-Hill Education, 2 Penn Plaza, New York, NY 10121.

This book is printed on acid-free paper.

2 3 4 5 6 7 8 9 0 DOW/DOW 1 0 9 8 7 6 5

ISBN 978-0-07-8025839
MHID 0-07-8025834

Senior Vice President, Products & Markets: *Kurt L. Strand*
Vice President, General Manager, Products & Markets: *Marty Lange*
Vice President, Content Design & Delivery: *Kimberly Meriwether David*
Managing Director: *Tim Vertovec*
Marketing Director: *Brad Parkins*
Senior Brand Manager: *Natalie King*
Director, Product Development: *Rose Koos*
Director of Digital Content: *Patricia Plumb*
Lead Product Developer: *Ann Torbert*
Senior Product Developer: *Rebecca Mann*
Senior Marketing Manager: *Kathleen Klehr*
Digital Product Analyst: *Xin Lin*
Director, Content Design & Delivery: *Linda Avenarius*
Program Manager: *Daryl Horrocks*
Content Project Managers: *Pat Frederickson and Angela Norris*
Buyer: *Michael R. McCormick*
Design: *Srdjan Savanovic*
Content Licensing Specialists: *Keri Johnson* and *Ann Marie Jannette*
Cover Image: ©*Piriya Photography/Getty Images*
Compositor: *SPI-Global*
Printer: *R. R. Donnelley*

Library of Congress Cataloging-in-Publication Data

Spiceland, J. David, 1949-
Intermediate accounting / J. David Spiceland, James F. Sepe, Mark W. Nelson, Wayne B. Thomas.—Eighth edition.
pages cm
ISBN 978-0-07-802583-9 (alk. paper)
1. Accounting. I. Sepe, James F. II. Nelson, Mark (Mark W.) III. Thomas, Wayne, 1969- IV. Title.
HF5636.S773 2015
657'.044—dc23

2014028264

About the Authors

DAVID SPICELAND

David Spiceland is professor of accounting at the University of Memphis, where he teaches intermediate accounting and other financial accounting courses at the undergraduate and master's levels. He received his BS degree in finance from the University of Tennessee, his MBA from Southern Illinois University, and his PhD in accounting from the University of Arkansas.

Professor Spiceland's primary research interests are in earnings management and educational research. He has published articles in a variety of journals including *The Accounting Review, Accounting and Business Research, Journal of Financial Research,* and *Journal of Accounting Education,* and is an author of McGraw-Hill's *Financial Accounting* with Wayne Thomas and Don Herrmann. David has received university and college awards and recognition for his teaching, research, and technological innovations in the classroom.

JIM SEPE

Jim Sepe is an associate professor of accounting at Santa Clara University where he teaches primarily intermediate accounting in both the undergraduate and graduate programs. He previously taught at California Poly State University–San Luis Obispo and the University of Washington and has visited at Stanford University and the Rome campus of Loyola University of Chicago.

Professor Sepe received his BS from Santa Clara University, MBA from the University of California–Berkeley, and PhD from the University of Washington. His research interests concern financial reporting issues and the use of financial information by capital markets. He has published articles in *The Accounting Review,* the *Journal of Business Finance and Accounting, Financial Management,* the *Journal of Forensic Accounting,* the *Journal of Applied Business Research,* and the *Journal of Accounting Education.* He is a past recipient of the American Accounting Association's Competitive Manuscript Award and has served as a member of the editorial board of *The Accounting Review.*

Jim has received numerous awards for his teaching excellence and innovations in the classroom, including Santa Clara University's Brutocao Award for Excellence in Curriculum Innovation.

MARK NELSON

Mark Nelson is the Eleanora and George Landew Professor of Accounting at Cornell University's Johnson Graduate School of Management, where he teaches intermediate accounting at the MBA level. He received his BBA degree from Iowa State University and his MA and PhD degrees from Ohio State University. Professor Nelson has won eight teaching awards at Ohio State and Cornell.

Professor Nelson's research is focused on decision making in financial accounting and auditing. His research has been published in *The Accounting Review,* the *Journal of Accounting Research, Contemporary Accounting Research, Accounting Organizations and Society,* and several other journals. He has won the American Accounting Association's Notable Contribution to Accounting Literature Award, and also the AAA's Wildman Medal for work judged to make the most significant contribution to the advancement of the public practice of accountancy. He has served three times as an editor or associate editor of *The Accounting Review,* and serves on the editorial boards of several journals. Professor Nelson also served for four years on the FASB's Financial Accounting Standards Advisory Council.

WAYNE THOMAS

Wayne Thomas is the John T. Steed Chair and Professor of Accounting at the University of Oklahoma's Price College of Business. He received his BS degree from Southwestern Oklahoma State University and his MS and PhD from Oklahoma State University. He has received teaching awards at the university, college, and departmental levels, and has received the Outstanding Educator Award from the Oklahoma Society of CPAs. He is an author of McGraw-Hill's *Financial Accounting* with David Spiceland and Don Herrmann.

His research focuses on various financial reporting issues and has been published in *The Accounting Review, Journal of Accounting Research, Journal of Accounting and Economics, Contemporary Accounting Research, Review of Accounting Studies, Accounting Organizations and Society,* and others. He has served as an editor for *The Accounting Review* and has won the American Accounting Association's Competitive Manuscript Award and Outstanding International Accounting Dissertation.

Professor Thomas enjoys various activities such as tennis, basketball, golf, and crossword puzzles, and most of all he enjoys spending time with his wife and kids.

What Stands Out in the Eighth Edition?

The FASB and IASB have been working together to issue converged accounting standards that will dramatically change key reporting areas, but important differences remain between U.S. GAAP and IFRS. To help instructors navigate this challenging environment, the Spiceland team is committed to providing a complete learning system, encompassing the text, key ancillaries, and online content that guide students to a deeper understanding of intermediate accounting topics. All of that content is written by authors Spiceland, Sepe, Nelson, and Thomas.

1 The *Intermediate Accounting* learning system is built around three key attributes: current, comprehensive, and clear.

"An excellent textbook that covers accounting procedures thoroughly from a real-world perspective. It is very current and is accompanied by a great variety of learning aids to help students succeed."
—Kathy Hsiao Yu Hsu, *University of Louisiana-Lafayette*

Current: Few disciplines see the rapid changes that accounting experiences. The Spiceland team is committed to keeping your course up to date. The eighth edition fully integrates the latest FASB and IFRS updates, including:

- **NEW** Chapter 5 covering the latest standard on Revenue Recognition (ASU No. 2014-09—Revenue from Contracts with Customers (Topic 606)). Part A introduces the five-step process for recognizing revenue at a point in time, over a period of time, and for contracts with multiple performance obligations. Part B provides comprehensive coverage of specific topics within each of the five steps. Part C applies the five-step process to accounting for long-term contracts, and Part D considers the role of revenue recognition in profitability analysis.
- ASU No. 2014-08—Presentation of Financial Statements (Topic 205) and Property, Plant, and Equipment (Topic 360): Reporting Discontinued Operations and Disclosures of Disposals of Components of an Entity
- ASU No. 2012-02—Intangibles–Goodwill and Other (Topic 350): Testing Indefinite-Lived Intangible Assets for Impairment
- Exclusion of extraordinary items and valuation of inventory at the lower of cost and net realizable value
- Amendments to IFRS No. 9 with respect to classification, measurement and impairment of financial instruments.

In addition, current events have focused public attention on the key role of accounting in providing information useful to decision makers. The CPA exam, too, is redirecting its focus to emphasize the professional skills needed to critically evaluate accounting method alternatives. *Intermediate Accounting* provides a **decision maker's perspective** to emphasize the professional judgment and critical thinking skills required of accountants in today's business environment.

Comprehensive: Authors Spiceland, Sepe, Nelson, and Thomas ensure comprehensive coverage and quality throughout the learning system by writing *every major supplement*: study guide, instructor's resource manual, solutions manual, test bank, and website content. *All end-of-chapter material*, too, is written by the author team and tested in their classrooms before being included in *Intermediate Accounting.*

"This textbook is written in a way that is easy to read, provides clear examples, includes thorough coverage of necessary topics, and provides ample opportunity for practice and mastery of the material through end of chapter problems."

—Terra Brown, *University of Texas at Arlington*

"This is one of the most comprehensive and up-to-date texts for teaching intermediate accounting. It has a good balance of discussion, examples, problem solving and analytical case material, in addition to good integration of IFRS."

— Shailendra Pandit, *University of Illinois at Chicago*

Current, Comprehensive, Clear

Comprehensive coverage and quality of Spiceland's learning system continues in its **flexible technology** package. As today's accounting students continue to learn in a digital world, the eighth edition of Spiceland's learning system features: McGraw-Hill *Connect® Accounting*, SmartBook's adaptive learning and reading experience, Guided Examples, and Tegrity Campus. See pages viii–xv for more details!

Clear: Reviewers, instructors, and students all have hailed *Intermediate Accounting's* ability to explain both simple and complex topics in language that is clear and approachable. Its highly acclaimed conversational writing style establishes a friendly dialogue between the text and each individual student—creating the impression of speaking with the student, as opposed to teaching to the student. *Intermediate Accounting* is written to be the most complete and student-friendly book on the market.

2 **New Coauthor Wayne Thomas**
A new coauthor, Wayne Thomas of the University of Oklahoma, has joined the Spiceland team for the eighth edition. Wayne is an award-winning professor and a coauthor on the highly successful *Financial Accounting* with David Spiceland and Don Herrmann.

3 Added additional algorithmic questions to *Connect Accounting*—over **2,500 questions** available for assignment including more than 1,125 algorithmic questions.

4 New to *Connect Accounting*—**CPA and CMA exam multiple choice questions** are now available for assignment. These questions are automatically graded and can be assigned to your students along with Kaplan CPA simulations as a way to help your students prep for the CPA exam.

5 **PetSmart** financial statements for the year ended February 2, 2014, are used throughout each chapter to illustrate key accounting concepts. PetSmart is a company that will be familiar to most students and whose operations are easily understood. Its financial statements offer a comprehensive set of material that is presented in a clear manner.

"Very well written in a streamlined 21 chapter approach with IFRS incorporated throughout and excellent end of chapter materials."

—Michael Slaubaugh, *Indiana University/Purdue University*

Spiceland's Financial Accounting Series

To allow *Intermediate Accounting* to be part of a complete learning system, authors David Spiceland and Wayne Thomas have teamed up with Don Herrmann to offer *Financial Accounting*. Now in its third edition, *Financial Accounting* uses the same approach that makes *Intermediate Accounting* a success—conversational writing style with a real-world focus and author-prepared supplements, combined with McGraw-Hill *Connect Accounting*.

"If you like Spiceland's intermediate text, you will be thrilled with the financial accounting text. It is written in the same conversational style, addresses topics directly and clearly, and the illustrations are terrific too.

—Nancy Snow, *University of Toledo.*

What Keeps SPICELAND Users Coming Back?

Where We're Headed

These boxes describe the potential financial reporting effects of many of the FASB and IASB joint projects intended to further align U.S. GAAP and IFRS, as well as other projects the Boards are pursuing separately. Where We're Headed boxes allow instructors to deal with ongoing projects to the extent they desire.

Where We're Headed

The FASB is working on a project that could have a dramatic impact on the format of financial statements.

In 2004, the FASB and IASB began working together on a project, Financial Statement Presentation, to establish a common standard for presenting information in the financial statements, including classifying and displaying line items and aggregating line items into subtotals and totals. This project could have a dramatic impact on the format of financial statements. An important part of the proposal involves the organization of elements of the balance sheet (statement of financial position), statement of comprehensive income (including the in[...] classifications.

Progress was [...] concentrate on [...] FASB's agenda. [...] all of the financi[...] book was publis[...]

"Where We're Headed" boxes allow the students to be updated with the most current accounting changes without inundating them with needless technical specifications. A perfect balance!"

—Cheryl Bartlett, *Indiana University—South Bend*

Financial Reporting Cases

Each chapter opens with a Financial Reporting Case that places the student in the role of the decision maker, engaging the student in an interesting situation related to the accounting issues to come. Then, the cases pose questions for the student in the role of decision maker. Marginal notations throughout the chapter point out locations where each question is addressed. The case questions are answered at the end of the chapter.

Financial Reporting Case Solution

1. **What purpose do adjusting entries serve?** *(p. 67)* Adjusting entries help ensure that all revenues are recognized in the period goods or services are transferred to customers, regardless of when cash is received. In this instance, for example, $13,000 cash has been received for services that haven't yet been performed. Also, adjusting entries enable a company to recognize all expenses incurred during a period, regardless of when cash is paid. Without depreciation, the friends' cost of using the equipment is not taken into account. Conversely, without adjustment, the cost of rent is overstated by $3,000 paid in advance for part of next year's rent.

With adjustments, we get an accru[...] plete measure of a company's operatin[...] ing future operating cash flows. Simila[...] assessment of assets and liabilities as so[...]

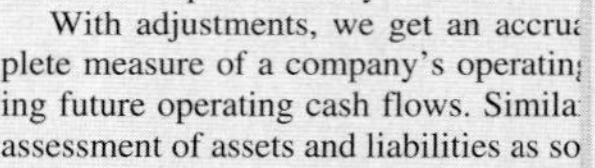

"The case at the beginning of each chapter is very captivating. After I read the case, I wanted to get paper and pencil and answer the questions."

—Carol Shaver, *Louisiana Tech University*

Decision Makers' Perspective

These sections appear throughout the text to illustrate how accounting information is put to work in today's firms. With the CPA exam placing greater focus on application of skills in realistic work settings, these discussions help your students gain an edge that will remain with them as they enter the workplace.

Decision Makers' Perspective

Cash often is referred to as a *nonearning* asset because it earns no interest. For this reason, managers invest idle cash in either cash equivalents or short-term investments, both of which provide a return. Management's goal is to hold the minimum amount of cash necessary to conduct normal business operations, meet its obligations, and take advantage of opportunities. Too much cash reduces profits through lost returns, while too little cash increases risk. This trade-off between risk and return is a[...] decision makers). Whether the choice m[...] by investors and creditors (external decis[...]

A company must have cash available [...] previous section as well as for planned [...] ing, and financing cash flows. However, [...] planned amounts, a company needs an a[...] prises. The size of the cushion depends o[...]

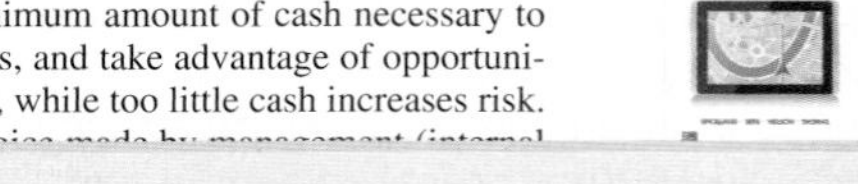

"This is an excellent feature of the book. It is so important to know why and how information is used and not just memorizing the "right" answers."

—Jeff Mankin, *Lipscomb University*

In talking with so many intermediate accounting faculty, we heard more than how to improve the book—there was much, much more that both users and nonusers insisted we not change. Here are some of the features that have made Spiceland such a phenomenal success in its previous editions.

Additional Consideration

Discounts in Contracts with Multiple Performance Obligations. Note that Illustration 5–7 shows that Tri-Box systems are sold at a discount—TrueTech sells the system for a transaction price ($250) that's less than the $300 sum of the stand-alone selling prices of the Tri-Box module ($240) and the subscription to Tri-Net ($60). Because there is no evidence that the discount relates to only one of the performance obligations, it is spread between them in the allocation process. If TrueTech had clear evidence from sales of those goods and services that the discount related to only one of them, the entire discount would be allocated to that good or service.

"This is a good technique that I actually use in my class and it's good to see it in a book!"

—Ramesh Narasimhan, *Montclair State University*

Ethical Dilemma

You recently have been employed by a large retail chain that sells sporting goods. One of your tasks is to help prepare periodic financial statements for external distribution. The chain's largest creditor, National Savings & Loan, requires quarterly financial statements, and you are currently working on the statements for the three-month period ending June 30, 2016.

During the months of May ar and TV advertising campaign. Tl commercials as well as the radic costs were charged to advertisir has asked you to prepare a June expense and to set up an asset The CFO explained that "This a and June and I think it will conti By recording the ad costs as an additional July sales. Besides, if

"Having ethical dilemma boxes in every chapter is much more significant than having a separate chapter devoted to ethics. Students can relate to the importance of being ethical in every aspect of business dealings."

—Gloria Worthy, *Southwest Tennessee Community College*

Broaden Your Perspective

Apply your critical-thinking ability to the knowledge you've gained. These cases will provide you an opportunity to develop your research, analysis, judgment, and communication skills. You also will work with other students, integrate what you've learned, apply it in real-world situations, and consider its global and ethical ramifications. This practice will broaden your knowledge and further develop your decision-making abilities.

Judgment Case 4–1
Earnings quality
● LO4–2, LO4–3

The financial community in the United States has become increasingly concerned with the quality of reported company earnings.

Required:
1. Define the tern

"I think students would benefit tremendously from the cases."

—Joyce Njoroge, *Drake University*

Additional Consideration Boxes

These are "on the spot" considerations of important, but incidental or infrequent aspects of the primary topics to which they relate. Their parenthetical nature, highlighted by enclosure in Additional Consideration boxes, helps maintain an appropriate level of rigor of topic coverage without sacrificing clarity of explanation.

Ethical Dilemmas

Because ethical ramifications of business decisions impact so many individuals as well as the core of our economy, Ethical Dilemmas are incorporated within the context of accounting issues as they are discussed. These features lend themselves very well to impromptu class discussions and debates.

Broaden Your Perspective Cases

Finish each chapter with these powerful and effective cases, a great way to reinforce and expand concepts learned in the chapter.

Star Problems

In each chapter, particularly challenging problems, designated by a ★, require students to combine multiple concepts or require significant use of judgment.

Easy to Use. Proven Effective

McGraw-Hill *CONNECT® ACCOUNTING*

McGraw-Hill *Connect Accounting* is a digital teaching and learning environment that gives students the means to better connect with their coursework, with their instructors, and with the important concepts that they will need to know for success now and in the future. With *Connect Accounting,* instructors can deliver assignments, quizzes and tests easily online. Students can review course material and practice important skills.

Connect Accounting provides all the following features:

- SmartBook and LearnSmart
- Auto-graded online homework
- Powerful learning resources including guided examples to pinpoint and connect key concepts for review.

In short, *Connect Accounting* offers students powerful tools and features that optimize their time and energy, enabling them to focus on learning.

SMARTBOOK, POWERED BY LEARNSMART

SMARTBOOK®

LearnSmart® is the market-leading adaptive study resource that is proven to strengthen memory recall, increase class retention, and boost grades. LearnSmart allows students to study more efficiently because they are made aware of what they know and don't know.

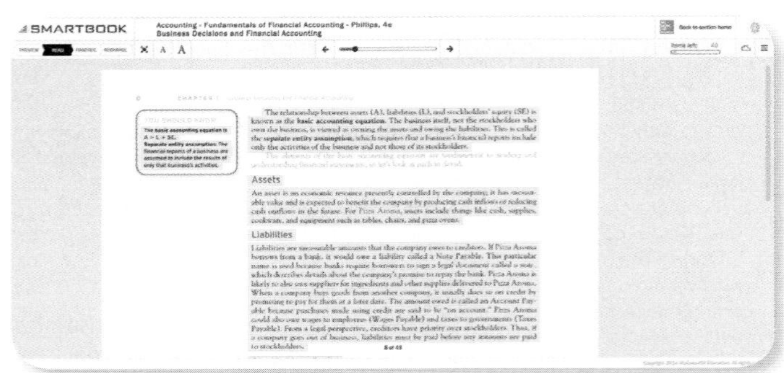

SmartBook, which is powered by LearnSmart, is the first and only adaptive reading experience designed to change the way students read and learn. It creates a personalized reading experience by highlighting the most impactful concepts a student needs to learn at that moment in time. As a student engages with SmartBook, the reading experience continuously adapts by highlighting content based on what the student knows and doesn't know. This ensures that the focus is on the content he or she needs to learn, while simultaneously promoting long-term retention of material. Use SmartBook's real-time reports to quickly identify the concepts that require more attention from individual students—or the entire class. The end result? Students are more engaged with course content, can better prioritize their time, and come to class ready to participate.

> "Using *Connect Accounting* and *LearnSmart* is great in any class, but really enhances online and hybrid sections. We are having better success with our online and hybrid classes as a result of having these tools available to us."
>
> —Patti Lopez, *Valencia College*

ailored to You.

ONLINE ASSIGNMENTS

Connect Accounting helps students learn more efficiently by providing feedback and practice material when they need it, where they need it. *Connect* grades homework automatically and gives immediate feedback on any questions students may have missed. Our assignable, gradable end-of-chapter content includes a general journal application that looks and feels more like what you would find in a general ledger software package. Also, select questions have been redesigned to test students' knowledge more fully. They now include tables for students to work through rather than requiring that all calculations be done offline.

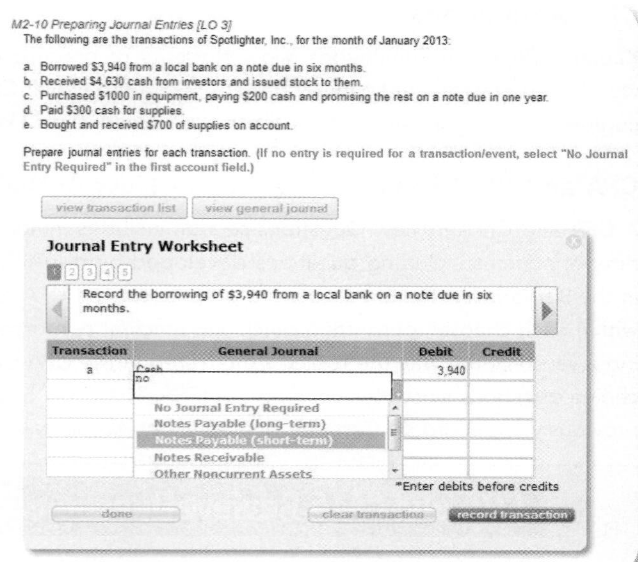

GUIDED EXAMPLES

The guided examples in *Connect Accounting* provide a narrated, animated, step-by-step walk-through of select exercises in *Intermediate Accounting* similar to those assigned. These short presentations can be turned on or off by instructors and provide reinforcement when students need it most.

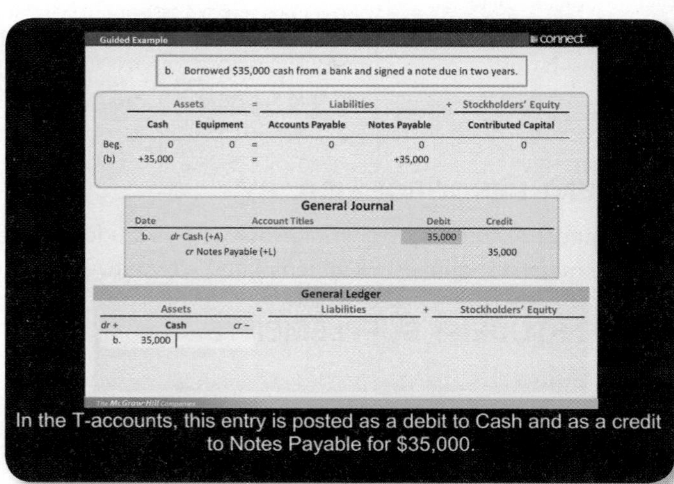

> "Great for an online class [and] for students that need the extra help in learning a process."
>
> —Terry Elliott, *Morehead State University*

CPA Simulations

Kaplan CPA Exam Simulations allow students to practice intermediate accounting concepts in a web-based environment similar to that used in the actual CPA exam. There will be no hesitation or confusion when your students sit for the real exam: they'll know exactly what they need to do.

CPA and CMA Review Questions—Now Available in *Connect Accounting!*

A CPA and CMA Review Questions section includes multiple-choice questions adapted from a variety of sources including questions developed by the AICPA Board of Examiners and those used in the Kaplan CPA Review Course to prepare for the CPA examination and focus on the key topics within each chapter, permitting quick and efficient reinforcement of those topics as well as conveying a sense of the way the topics are covered in the CPA exam. Also, a special section of multiple-choice questions illustrates coverage of IFRS. The CMA questions are adapted from questions that previously appeared on Certified Management Accountant (CMA) exams.

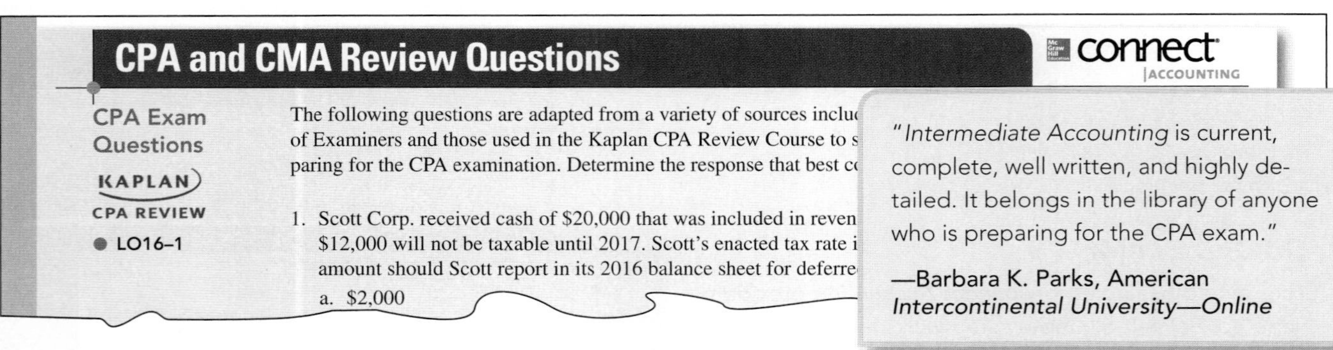

STUDENT RESOURCE LIBRARY

The *Connect Accounting* Student Resources give students access to additional resources such as recorded lectures, online practice materials, quizzes, Excel templates, alternative exercises and problems, an eBook, and more.

OTHER STUDENT SUPPLEMENTS

Study Guide

Volume 1: ISBN-13: 9780078095276 (MHID: 0078095271)
Volume 2: ISBN-13: 9780078127403 (MHID: 0078127408)

The Study Guide, written by the text authors, provides chapter summaries, detailed illustrations, and a wide variety of self-study questions, exercises, and multiple-choice problems (with solutions).

Understanding Corporate Annual Reports

Seventh Edition, by William R. Pasewark
ISBN-13: 9780073526935 (ISBN-10: 0073526932)

This project provides students with instruction for obtaining an annual report from a publicly traded corporation and for making an industry or competitor comparison.

McGRAW-HILL *CONNECT ACCOUNTING* FEATURES

Connect Accounting offers powerful tools, resources, and features to make managing assignments easier, so faculty can spend more time teaching.

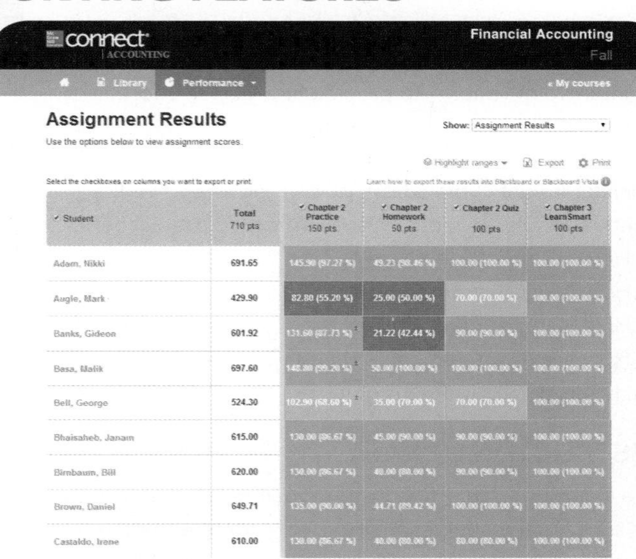

SIMPLE ASSIGNMENT MANAGEMENT AND SMART GRADING

With *Connect Accounting*, creating assignments is easier than ever, so instructors can spend more time teaching and less time managing.

- Create and deliver assignments easily with selectable end-of-chapter questions and test bank items.
- Have assignments scored automatically, giving students immediate feedback on their work and side-by-side comparisons with correct answers.
- Access and review each response; manually change grades or leave comments for students to review.
- Reinforce classroom concepts with practice assignments, instant quizzes, and exams.

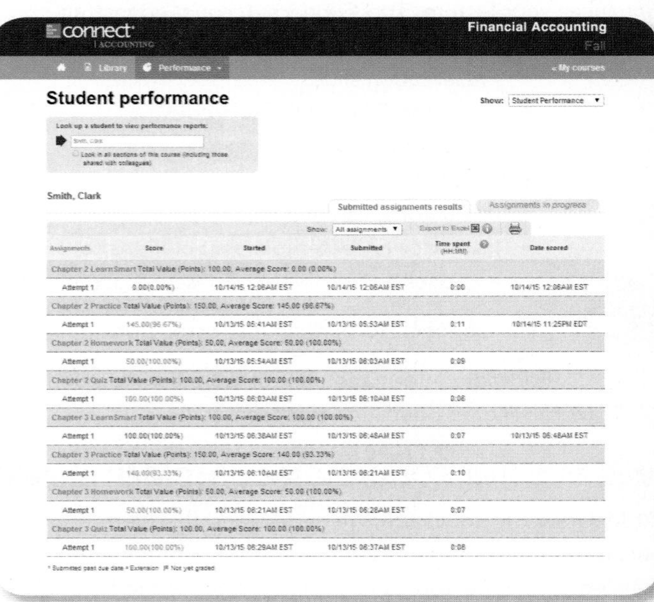

POWERFUL INSTRUCTOR AND STUDENT REPORTS

Connect Accounting keeps instructors informed about how each student, section, and class is performing, allowing for more productive use of lecture and office hours. The progress-tracking function enables you to:

- View scored work immediately and track individual or group performance with assignment and grade reports.
- Access an instant view of student or class performance relative to learning objectives.
- Collect data and generate reports required by many accreditation organizations, such as AACSB and AICPA.

> Students like the flexibility that *Connect* offers. It has made a major difference in the student athletes' participation and performance. They can complete their work and catch up on lectures anytime and anywhere.
>
> —Professor Lisa McKinney, M.T.A., CPA, *University of Alabama*

CONNECT INSIGHT

The first and only analytics tool of its kind, Connect Insight™ is a series of visual data displays—each framed by an intuitive question—to provide at-a-glance information regarding how your class is doing.

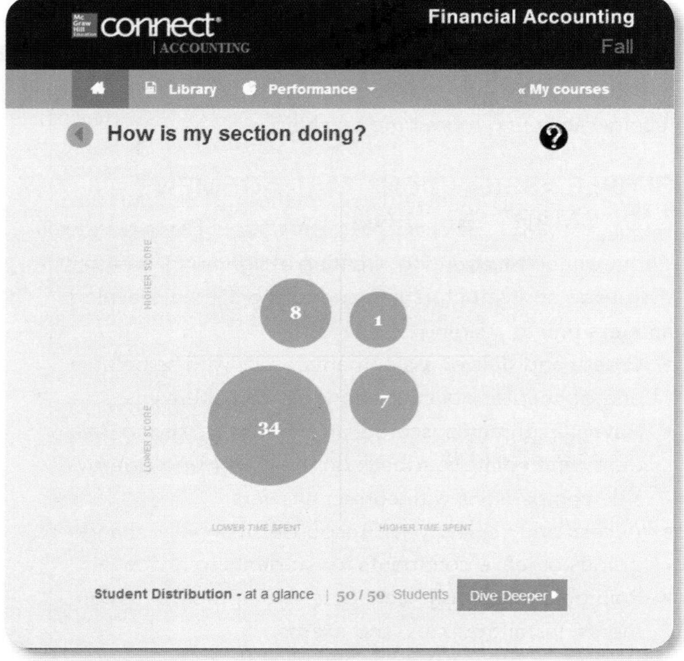

Connect Insight™ provides a quick analysis on five key insights, available at a moment's notice from your tablet device.

- How are my students doing?
- How is my section doing?
- How is this student doing?
- How are my assignments doing?
- How is this assignment going?

INSTRUCTOR LIBRARY

The *Connect Accounting* Instructor Library is a repository for additional resources to improve student engagement in and out of class. You can select and use any asset that enhances your lecture. The *Connect Accounting* Instructor Library includes

- Presentation slides
- Animated PowerPoint exercises
- Solutions manual
- Test bank
- Instructor's resource manual
- Instructor Excel templates. Solutions to the student Excel Templates used to solve selected end-of-chapter exercises and problems. These assignments are designated by the Excel icon.

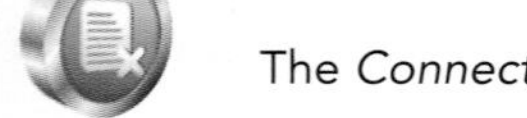

The *Connect Accounting* Instructor Library also allows you to upload your own files.

For more information about *Connect Accounting,* go to www.connect.mheducation.com, or contact your local McGraw-Hill Higher Education representative.

McGRAW-HILL EDUCATION CUSTOMER EXPERIENCE GROUP CONTACT INFORMATION

At McGraw-Hill Education, we understand that getting the most from new technology can be challenging. That's why our services don't stop after you purchase our products. You can contact our Product Specialists 24 hours a day to get product training online. Or you can search the knowledge bank of Frequently Asked Questions on our support website. For Customer Support, call **800-331-5094,** or visit www.mhhe.com/support. One of our Technical Support Analysts will be able to assist you in a timely fashion.

TEGRITY CAMPUS: LECTURES 24/7

Tegrity Campus is a service that makes class time available 24/7 by automatically capturing every lecture. With a simple one-click start-and-stop process, you capture all computer screens and corresponding audio in a format that is easily searchable, frame by frame. Students can replay any part of any class with easy-to-use browser-based viewing on a PC, Mac, or mobile device.

Help turn your students' study time into learning moments immediately supported by your lecture. With Tegrity Campus, you also increase intent listening and class participation by easing students' concerns about note-taking. Tegrity Campus will make it more likely you will see students' faces, not the tops of their heads.

To learn more about Tegrity, watch a 2-minute Flash demo at http://tegritycampus.mhhe.com.

MCGRAW-HILL CAMPUS

McGraw-Hill Campus™ is a new one-stop teaching and learning experience available to users of any learning management system. This institutional service allows faculty and students to enjoy single sign-on (SSO) access to all McGraw-Hill Higher Education materials, including the award-winning McGraw-Hill *Connect* platform, from directly within the institution's website. To learn more about MH Campus, visit http://mhcampus.mhhe.com.

CUSTOM PUBLISHING THROUGH CREATE

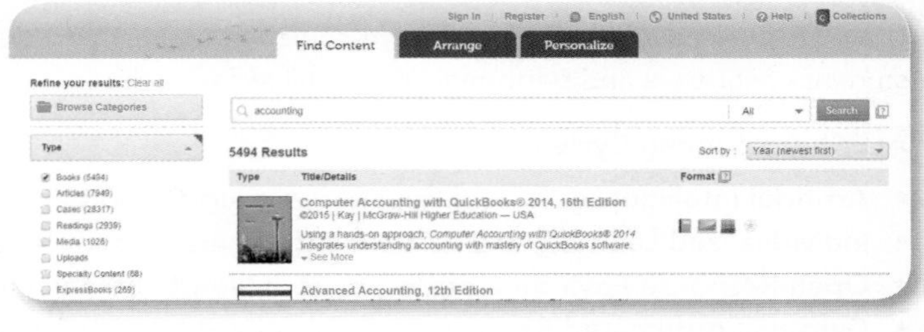

McGraw-Hill Create™ is a new, self-service website that allows instructors to create custom course materials by drawing upon McGraw-Hill's comprehensive, cross-disciplinary content. Instructors can add their own content quickly and easily and tap into other rights-secured third party sources as well, then arrange the content in a way that makes the most sense for their course. Instructors can even personalize their book with the course name and information and choose the best format for their students—color print, black-and-white print, or an eBook.

Through Create, instructors can

- Select and arrange the content in a way that makes the most sense for their course.
- Combine material from different sources and even upload their own content.
- Choose the best format for their students—print or eBook.
- Edit and update their course materials as often as they'd like.

Begin creating now at www.mcgrawhillcreate.com.

ALEKS®

ALEKS Accounting Cycle

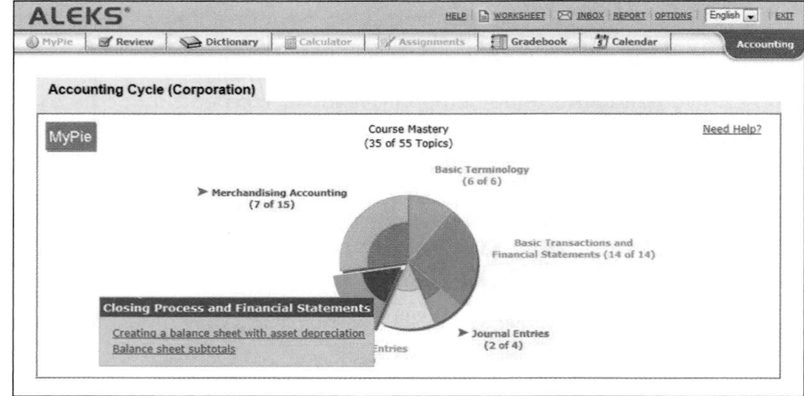

ALEKS Accounting Cycle is a web-based program that provides targeted coverage of prerequisite and introductory material necessary for student success in Intermediate Accounting. ALEKS uses artificial intelligence and adaptive questioning to assess precisely a student's preparedness and deliver personalized instruction on the exact topics the student is **most ready to learn**. Through comprehensive explanations, practice, and immediate feedback, ALEKS enables students to quickly fill individual knowledge gaps in order to build a strong foundation of critical accounting skills. Better prepared students saves you valuable time at the beginning of your course!

Use ALEKS Accounting Cycle as a pre-course assignment or during the first three weeks of the term to see improved student confidence and performance, as well as fewer drops.

ALEKS Accounting Cycle Features:

- **Artificial Intelligence:** Targets Gaps in Prerequisite Knowledge
- **Individualized Learning and Assessment:** Ensure Student Preparedness
- **Open-Response Environment:** Avoids Multiple-Choice and Ensures Mastery
- **Dynamic, Automated Reports:** Easily Identify Struggling Students

For more information, please visit:
www.aleks.com/highered/business.

Read ALEKS Success Stories:
www.aleks.com/highered/business/success_stories.

ALEKS is a registered trademark of ALEKS Corporation.

"With ALEKS, the issues that our finance majors were having with Intermediate Accounting have practically disappeared."

—Eric Kelley, *University of Arizona*

COURSESMART

Learn Smart. Choose Smart.

CourseSmart is a way for faculty to find and review eTextbooks. It's also a great option for students who are interested in accessing their course materials digitally and saving money.

CourseSmart offers thousands of the most commonly adopted textbooks across hundreds of courses from a wide variety of higher education publishers. With the CourseSmart eTextbook, students can save up to 45 percent off the cost of a print book, reduce their impact on the environment, and access powerful Web tools for learning. CourseSmart is an online eTextbook, which means users access and view their textbook online when connected to the Internet. Students can also print sections of the book for maximum portability. CourseSmart eTextbooks are available in one standard online reader with full text search, notes and highlighting, and e-mail tools for sharing notes between classmates. For more information on CourseSmart, go to www.coursesmart.com.

EZ TEST ONLINE

The comprehensive test bank includes more than 1,500 true/false, multiple-choice, problems, and matching questions—each tagged by learning objective; topic area; difficulty level; and AACSB, Bloom's, and AICPA categories.

McGraw-Hill's EZ Test Online is a flexible and easy-to-use electronic testing program that allows instructors to create tests from book-specific items. EZ Test Online accommodates a wide range of question types and allows instructors to add their own questions. Multiple versions of the test can be created and any test can be exported for use with course management systems such as BlackBoard/WebCT. EZ Test Online gives instructors a place to easily administer exams and quizzes online. The program is available for Windows and Macintosh environments.

ASSURANCE OF LEARNING READY

Many educational institutions today are focused on the notion of *assurance of learning,* an important element of some accreditation standards. *Intermediate Accounting* is designed specifically to support your assurance of learning initiatives with a simple, yet powerful solution.

Each test bank question for *Intermediate Accounting* maps to a specific chapter learning objective listed in the text. You can use our test bank software, EZ Test Online, or *Connect Accounting* to easily query for learning outcomes/objectives that directly relate to the learning objectives for your course. You can then use the reporting features of EZ Test Online or *Connect Accounting* to aggregate student results in a similar fashion, making the collection and presentation of assurance of learning data simple and easy.

AACSB STATEMENT

McGraw-Hill Education is a proud corporate member of AACSB International. Understanding the importance and value of AACSB accreditation, *Intermediate Accounting* recognizes the curricula guidelines detailed in the AACSB standards for business accreditation by connecting selected questions in the test bank to the eight general knowledge and skill guidelines in the AACSB standards.

The statements contained in *Intermediate Accounting* are provided only as a guide for the users of this textbook. The AACSB leaves content coverage and assessment within the purview of individual schools, the mission of the school, and the faculty. While *Intermediate Accounting* and the teaching package make no claim of any specific AACSB qualification or evaluation, within the Test Bank to accompany *Intermediate Accounting* we have labeled selected questions according to the six general knowledge and skill areas.

What's New in the Eighth Edition?

Revising a program as successful as *Intermediate Accounting* takes careful consideration and a strong vision of what a textbook and digital solution should be. New features aren't piled on for their own sake; the Spiceland team only implements changes that constitute real improvements that have been identified through extensive research with users. The result is a program that never loses its original strengths as it gains in usefulness and flexibility with each revision.

Pervasive changes throughout the program include updating and revising all real-world illustrations, amounts and discussions involving Dell to PetSmart; revising the Air France-KLM IFRS case to reflect financial statements for the year ended December 31, 2013; and updating and revising all real-world illustrations, amounts and discussions involving other companies in the text and end-of-chapter material.

Chapter 1

ENVIRONMENT AND THEORETICAL STRUCTURE OF FINANCIAL ACCOUNTING

- Changed opening case to introduce PetSmart, and featured PetSmart throughout chapter.
- Updated discussion of the convergence process to reflect latest SEC reports and decisions.
- Included Additional Consideration box introducing the Private Company Council and private company exceptions to GAAP.
- Modified the discussion of financial reporting concepts to reflect the new revenue recognition standard.
- Added Where We're Headed box to discuss the FASB's exposure draft on disclosure.
- Revised Real World Case to show current financial statements from The Gap, Inc.

Chapter 2

REVIEW OF THE ACCOUNTING PROCESS

- Added assignment materials on adjusting entries.

Chapter 3

THE BALANCE SHEET AND FINANCIAL DISCLOSURES

- All real-world illustrations, amounts, and discussion throughout involving other companies were updated to include most recent amounts.
- Revised the section on usefulness and limitations of the balance sheet.
- Revised the section on classification of balance sheet elements—assets, liabilities, and equity.
- Redesigned Illustration 3–1 to show basic elements and their subclassifications.
- Redesigned Illustration 3–2 to make the flow of the operating cycle more apparent.
- Expanded the discussion of restricted cash in the section on cash and cash equivalents.
- Updated the Where We're Headed box on the FASB's Financial Statement Presentation project.
- Updated references throughout to AICPA Professional Standards related to auditor's responsibilities with respect to financial statements.
- Replaced term "irregularities" with "fraud" in the section on noteworthy events and transactions and in the glossary.
- Modified the appendix on reporting segment information to include real-world analyses of Abbott Laboratories, Inc.
- Modified Ethics Case 3–16 to include geographic disclosure of operations in politically sensitive areas and in tax haven areas.

Chapter 4

THE INCOME STATEMENT, COMPREHENSIVE INCOME, AND THE STATEMENT OF CASH FLOWS

- Revised the chapter and assignment materials to incorporate the change in GAAP eliminating the extraordinary item classification.
- Revised the section on discontinued operations to reflect the new FASB Accounting Standards Update.
- Moved the Interim Reporting Appendix from Chapter 5 to Chapter 4 for better placement.
- Added assignment materials on operating versus nonoperating income and the indirect method of presenting cash flows from operating activities in the statement of cash flows.
- Added a PetSmart Analysis Case related to income statement information.

Chapter 5

REVENUE RECOGNITION AND PROFITABILITY ANALYSIS

- Created Parts A and B to provide comprehensive coverage of the new revenue recognition standard. Part A introduces revenue recognition at a point in time, over a period of time, and for contracts with multiple performance obligations. Part B provides in-depth coverage of the five-step revenue recognition process and how it relates to various common sales arrangements.
- Created all new assignment material to support coverage of the new revenue recognition standard.
- Modified coverage of long-term contracts, and included that material as Part C.
- Modified profitability analysis discussion to analyze Costco and Walmart, and included that material as Part D.
- Created an Appendix that covers GAAP that is superseded by the new revenue recognition standard, including installment and cost-recovery methods, accounting for software and other multiple-element contracts, and accounting for franchises.

Chapter 6

TIME VALUE OF MONEY CONCEPTS

- Replaced the introductory Financial Reporting Case to feature the role of the time value of money on Powerball winnings.
- Enhanced explanations throughout the chapter on the distinction between interest rates and discount rates.

We received an incredible amount of feedback prior to writing the eighth edition of *Intermediate Accounting.* The following list of changes and improvements is a testament to our users and their commitment to making *Intermediate Accounting* the best book of its kind.

- Added an Additional Consideration box that considers the effect of the time value of money when a customer prepays for a purchase rather than buying on credit.
- Revised Real World Case related to zero-coupon bonds of Johnson & Johnson.
- Added a Real World Case dealing with the present value of Southwest Airline's leases.

Chapter 7

CASH AND RECEIVABLES

- Revised accounts receivable analysis of Symantec Corp. and CA, Inc.
- Revised coverage of sales discounts and sales returns to reflect new revenue recognition standard and supported that coverage with new assignment materials.
- Added coverage of long-term notes receivable to complement existing coverage of short-term notes receivable and supported that coverage with new assignment materials.
- Added Where We're Headed boxes discussing the FASB and IASB projects concerning impairment of notes receivable, providing shorter coverage in the text and a numerical example in Appendix 7B.
- Revised Real World cases considering Nike and Del Monte v. Smithfield.

Chapter 8

INVENTORIES: MEASUREMENT

- Added assignment materials on LIFO liquidation and dollar-value LIFO.
- Added a PetSmart Analysis Case related to inventory method and ratio analysis.

Chapter 9

INVENTORIES: ADDITIONAL ISSUES

- Revised the chapter and assignment materials to incorporate the change in GAAP that now requires inventory to be valued at the lower of cost and net realizable value.
- Revised the section on changes in inventory method for greater clarity.

Chapter 10

PROPERTY, PLANT, AND EQUIPMENT AND INTANGIBLE ASSETS: ACQUISITION AND DISPOSITION

- Added an Additional Consideration box on contract acquisition costs to reflect the new Accounting Standards Update on revenue recognition.
- Added assignment materials on interest capitalization, research and development, and software development costs.
- Added a PetSmart Analysis Case related to the reporting of property, plant, and equipment and intangible assets.

Chapter 11

PROPERTY, PLANT, AND EQUIPMENT AND INTANGIBLE ASSETS: UTILIZATION AND IMPAIRMENT

- Added an Additional Consideration box on the new Accounting Standards Update on the subsequent measurement of goodwill for private companies.
- Added a Concept Review Exercise that covers impairment of property, plant, and equipment and goodwill.
- Added a Trueblood Accounting Case that deals with the measurement of impairment losses for property, plant, and equipment.
- Added a PetSmart Analysis Case related to depreciation and amortization.

Chapter 12

INVESTMENTS

- Revised opening financial reporting case
- Replaced the Where We're Headed Supplement with Where We're Headed boxes discussing the FASB and IASB projects concerning classification, measurement and impairment of investments.
- Added new assignment material on IFRS treatment of investments.
- Added new assignment material on equity method.
- Revised assignment material with real-world cases involving Intel, Unilever, and Microsoft.

Chapter 13

CURRENT LIABILITIES AND CONTINGENCIES

- Added Additional Consideration box to provide coverage on accounting for interest on advanced collections from customers, as required in the new revenue recognition standard.
- Revised coverage of warranties to be consistent with new revenue recognition standard.
- Added Additional Consideration box detailing coverage of rebates, premiums and coupons to be consistent with new revenue recognition standard.
- Added new assignment material with respect to contingent liabilities and unasserted claims,
- Revised assignment material with real-world cases involving Dow Chemical, Morgan Stanley, PetSmart, AU Optronics, B Communications LTD.
- Added Trueblood Accounting Cases involving loss contingencies for litigation and subsequent events.

Chapter 14

BONDS AND LONG-TERM NOTES

- Added an illustration of Microsoft's disclosure of debt payment commitments.
- Revised illustration of Pepsi and Coca Cola and the related financial statement analysis comparing their debt-equity ratios, return on assets, return on equity, and interest coverage.
- Added an example of Lakeland Bancorp's gain on early extinguishment of debt.
- Revised the section describing the fair value option to reflect the FASB's new requirement to report related gains and losses in other comprehensive income. Also revised related assignment material.
- Revised Appendix A on When Bonds are Issued between Interest Dates to include bonds issued at a discount between interest dates as well as related assignment material.
- Added assignment material on notes issued for cash from the borrower's and lender's perspectives, notes issued for a noncash asset from the lender's perspective, installment notes from the lender's perspective, and an IFRS-based problem on transaction costs.

- Revised Problem focusing on Microsoft's zero coupon notes and the FASB codification system.
- Revised Real World Cases involving Hewlett-Packard's zero coupon notes, Walmart's stock option plan.
- Added a Real World Case dealing with analyzing PetSmart's financial statements

Chapter 15

LEASES

- Revised illustration of leased asset disclosure by Kroger.
- Added an illustration of Hewlett-Packard's disclosure of using leases to sell products.
- Added an illustration of Walmart's disclosure of lease payments.
- Revised an illustration of IBM's disclosure of sales-type leases.
- Revised an illustration of Walmart's disclosure of lease payment commitments and capitalizing operating leases.
- Revised Brief Exercise focusing on Sonic Corporation's net investment in leases.
- Added an Analysis Case designed to see the financial statement effects of capitalizing PetSmart's operating leases.
- Revised a Walmart Real World Case involving lease concepts.
- Added Trueblood Accounting Cases dealing with the lease classification issues.
- Extensively revised the Where We're Headed Chapter Supplement on the proposed lease accounting standards update as well as all the related assignment materials.

Chapter 16

ACCOUNTING FOR INCOME TAXES

- Revised numerical illustrations to highlight relationships and provide T-accounts.
- Added Shoe Carnival real-world example to show how to extract summary tax journal entry from disclosure notes and how to tie that entry to changes in deferred tax accounts.
- Added Additional Consideration box for accounting for taxes on unrepatriated foreign earnings.
- Added Additional Consideration providing a template for applying the balance-sheet focus of tax accounting.
- Revised assignment material with real-world cases involving Delta Air Lines, Ford Motor Company, Dominion Resources, Walmart, Kroger, and Macy's.
- Added Trueblood case involving valuation allowances against deferred tax assets.
- Revised Air France–KLM IFRS case.

Chapter 17

PENSIONS AND OTHER POSTRETIREMENT BENEFIT PLANS

- Revised illustration of Microsoft's 401K plan disclosure.
- Added an illustration of General Mills' disclosure of the components of pension expense.
- Enhanced the example of amortizing prior service cost and net gains and losses.
- Revised Problem focusing on Toys "R" Us's pension plan.
- Added a Real World Case involving PetSmart's pension plan.

Chapter 18

SHAREHOLDERS' EQUITY

- Replaced the introductory Financial Reporting Case to feature MasterCard's share-based compensation plans.
- Enhanced the discussion of stock splits and included Apple Inc.'s rare 7–for–1 stock split.
- Added an illustration of Abercrombie & Fitch's disclosure of shareholders' equity.
- Revised Brief Exercise focusing on Microsoft's cash dividends.
- Added an Exercise dealing with Ford Motor Company's buyback of stock to offset stock grant issued to executives.
- Revised Problem focusing on Cisco System's reporting of shareholders' equity.
- Revised Research Case related to the FASB codification system and Cisco System's reporting of comprehensive income.

Chapter 19

SHARE-BASED COMPENSATION AND EARNINGS PER SHARE

- Added extensive discussion of accounting for restricted stock units (RSUs), now the most popular form of share-based compensation.
- Added an illustration of Apple Inc.'s disclosure of restricted stock units.
- Revised illustration of restricted stock accounting to include restricted stock units.
- Revised the section describing the declining popularity of stock options to emphasize the role of restricted stock units in that decline.
- Revised the Additional Consideration box for the effect of the actual exercise of stock options in EPS calculations.
- Added a discussion of including the effect of restricted stock units (RSUs) in EPS calculations.
- Added an illustration of Foundation Healthcare Inc.'s EPS disclosure.
- Added to Appendix B a discussion and illustration of accounting for restricted stock units (RSUs that are payable in cash and treated as a liability.
- Added a brief exercise and three exercises (including one based on Facebook) dealing with accounting for restricted stock units.
- Revised a Real World Case involving Walmart's stock option plan.
- Added a Trueblood Accounting Case dealing with the accounting treatment for different aspects of a share-based payment awards.
- Added Real World Cases involving PetSmart's restricted stock awards and employee stock purchase plan; Best Buy's EPS and antidilutive securities; Kaman Corporation's reporting of EPS and discontinued operations.
- Revised an Analysis Case involving AIG's earnings per share.
- Added an Analysis Case involving PetSmart's earnings per share.
- Revised a Research Case involving Kellogg's EPS, PE ratio, and dividend payout ratio.

Chapter 20

ACCOUNTING CHANGES AND ERROR CORRECTIONS

- Added an Abercrombie & Fitch illustration of disclosure of a change in inventory methods.
- Added Barnes & Noble illustration of a correction of an error.

Chapter 21

STATEMENT OF CASH FLOWS REVISITED

- Enhanced the discussion of accounting for gains and losses on cash equivalent transactions.
- Added a CVS Caremark Corp illustration of presenting cash flows from operating activities by the direct method.
- Added a Toys "R" Us illustration of presenting cash flows from operating activities by the indirect method.
- Added a Trueblood Accounting Case involving presentation issues related to the statement of cash flows.
- Added a PetSmart Real World Case involving presentation issues related to a disparity between net income and cash flows.
- Revised a Research Case involving researching the way cash flows are reported.
- Added a PetSmart Analysis Case for using free cash flows to analyze cash flow information.
- Revised an IFRS Case involving British Telecommunications.

Appendix A

Derivatives

- Added a discussion of the immense size of the derivatives market and the danger that size poses for the global financial system.
- Added an Additional Consideration box on the new Accounting Standards Update on private company accounting for derivatives and hedging.
- Revised a Real World Case related to the Chicago Mercantile Exchange.
- Revised a Johnson & Johnson Real World Case on hedging transactions.

Acknowledgments

Intermediate Accounting is the work not just of its talented authors, but of the more than 625 faculty reviewers who shared their insights, experience, and opinions with us. Our reviewers helped us to build *Intermediate Accounting* into the very best learning system available. A blend of Spiceland users and nonusers, these reviewers explained how they use texts and technology in their teaching, and many answered detailed questions about every one of Spiceland's 21 chapters. The work of improving *Intermediate Accounting* is ongoing—even now, we're scheduling new symposia and reviewers' conferences to collect even more opinions from faculty.

We want to recognize the valuable input of all those who helped guide our developmental decisions for the eight edition.

Eighth Edition Reviewers

Jagadison Aier, *George Mason University*

Matthew Anderson, *Michigan State University*

Abhijit Barua, *Florida International University*

Ira Bates, *Florida A&M University*

Sheila Bedford, *American University*

Carol Bishop, *Georgia Southwestern State University*

Terra Brown, *University of Texas at Arlington*

Helen Brubeck, *San Jose State University*

Nancy Cassidy, *Texas A&M University*

David DeBoskey, *San Diego State University*

David Doyon, *Southern New Hampshire University*

Jan Duffy, *Iowa State University*

Barbara Durham, *University of central Florida*

Dennis Elam, *Texas A&M Univeristy - San Antonio*

Terry Elliott, *Morehead State University*

Patrick Fan, *Virginia Tech*

Rita Grant, *Grand Valley State University*

Pamela Graybeal, *University of Central Florida*

Robert Hartman, *University of Iowa*

Lori Hatchell, *Aims Community College*

John Hathorn, *Metropolitan State College - Denver*

Dana Hollie, *Louisiana State University - Baton Rouge*

Thomas Hrubec, *Franklin University*

Ying Huang, *University of Louisville*

Mark Jackson, *University of Nevada - Reno*

Ching-Lih Jan, *California State University, East Bay*

Jerry Kreuze, *Western Michigan University*

Timothy Krumwiede, *Bryant University*

Dave Law, *Youngstown State University*

Howard Lawrence, *University of Mississippi*

Janice Lawrence, *University of Nebraska-Lincoln*

Mark Leininger, *University of North Florida*

Lisa Murawa, *Mott Community College*

Brian Nagle, *Duquesne University*

Ramesh Narasimhan, *Montclair State University*

Sewon O, *Texas Southern University*

Emeka O Ofobike, *The University of Akron*

Hong Pak, *California State Polytechnic University, Pomona*

Shailendra Pandit, *University of Illinois at Chicago*

Doug Parker, *York Technical College*

K.K. Raman, *University of North Texas*

MaryAnn Reynolds, *Western Washington University*

Paul Schwin, *Cleveland State University*

Vic Stanton, *Unversity of California, Berkeley*

Daniel Stubbs, *Rutgers University - Nwk/NB*

Pamela Stuerke, *University of Missouri - St. Louis*

William Wilcox, *University of Colorado*

Wendy Wilson *Southern Methodist University*

Suzanne Wright, *Pennsylvania State University*

Yan Xiong, *California State University Sacramento*

Michael Yampuler, *University of Houston*

Dan Zeiler, *Columbus State Community College*

As you know if you've read this far, *Intermediate Accounting* would not be what it is without the passionate feedback of our colleagues. Through your time and effort, we were able to create a learning system that truly responds to the needs of the market, and for that, we sincerely thank each of you.

Seventh Edition Reviewers

Patricia Abels, *University of Findlay*

John Abernathy, *Oklahoma State University–Stillwater*

Dawn Addington, *Central New Mexico Community College*

Noel Addy, *Mississippi State University*

Peter Aghimien, *Indiana University–South Bend*

John Ahern, *Depaul University*

John G. Ahmad, *Nova Cc Annandale*

Akinloye Akindayomi, *University of Massachusettes-Dartmouth*

Matt Anderson, *Michigan State University–East Lansing*

Charles P. Baril, *James Madison University*

Cheryl Bartlett, *Central New Mexico Community College*

Homer Bates, *University of North Florida*

Ira Bates, *Florida A & M University*

Sheila Bedford, *American University*

Yoel Beniluz, *Rutgers University–New Brunswick*

Scott Boylan, *Washington & Lee University*

Brian Bratten, *University of Kentucky–Lexington*

John Brozovsky, *Virginia Tech*

Phillip Buchanan, *George Mason University*

Mary Calegari, *San Jose State University*

Ronald L. Campbell, *North Carolina A & T University*

Charles Carslaw, *University of Nevada-Reno*

Joan Cezair, *Fayetteville State University*

Chiaho Chang, *Montclair State University*

Lynette Chapman-Vasill, *Texas A & M University*

Linda G. Chase, *Baldwin–Wallace College*

Nancy Christie, *Virginia Tech*

Stan Chu, *Borough of Manhattan Community College*

Kwang Chung, *Pace University Nyc*

Christie Comunale, *Long Island University–Cw Post*

Elizabeth C. Conner, *University of Colorado-Denver*

John Dallmus, *Arizona State University–West*

Johnny Deng, *California State University Sacramento*

Emily Drogt, *Grand Valley State University*

Jan Duffy, *Iowa State University*

Tim Eaton, *University of Miami Ohio*

Dennis Elam, *Texas A & M University*

Ed Etter, *Eastern Michigan University*

Anita Feller, *University of Illinois–Champaign*

Mark Felton, *University of Saint Thomas*

Gary Freeman, *Northeastern State University*

Clyde Galbraith, *West Chester University of Pa*

John Giles, *Nc State University-Raleigh*

Kathrine Glass, *Indiana University–Bloomington*

Robert T. Gregrich, *Brevard Community College*

Amy Haas, *Kingsborough Community College*

Abo-El-Yazeed T. Habib, *Minnesota State University–Mankato*

John Hathorn, *Metropolitan State College of Denver*

Frank Heflin, *Florida State University*

John Hoffer, *Stark State College of Tech*

Travis Holt, *University of Tennessee–Chattanooga*

Donald Hoppa, *Roosevelt University–Schaumburg*

Tom Hrubec, *Franklin University*

Kathy Hsiao Yu Hsu, *University of Louisiana–Lafayette*

Mark Jackson, *University of Nevada–Reno*

Ching-Lih Jan, *California State University–East Bay*

Randy Johnston, *University of Colorado–Boulder*

Christopher Jones, *California State University–Northridge*

Jessica Jones, *Chandler-Gilbert Community College*

Celina Jozsi, *University of South Florida–Tampa*

Beth Kane, *Columbia College–Columbia*

Shannon Knight, *Texas A & M University*

Adam Koch, *University of Virginia*

John Krahel, *Rutgers University–Newark*

Jerry G. Kreuze, *Western Michigan University–Kalamazoo*

Lisa Kutcher, *Colorado State University*
Brad Lail, *Nc State University–Raleigh*
Sheldon Langsam, *Western Mich University–Kalamazoo*
Howard Lawrence, *University of Mississippi*
Janice Lawrence, *University of Nebraska–Lincoln*
Gerald P. Lehman, *Madison Area Technical College–Truax*
Wei Li, *Kent State University-Kent*
Terry Lindenberg, *University of Maryland–University College*
Henock Louis, *Penn State University–University Park*
Steven Lustgarten, *Bernard M. Baruch College*
Victoria Mahan, *Clark State Community College*
Bob Maust, *West Virginia University–Morgantown*
Katie Maxwell, *University of Arizona*
Alan Mayer-Sommer, *Georgetown University*
John Mills, *University of Nevada-Reno*
Gary Mingle, *Golden Gate University*
Tommy Moores, *University of Nevada–Las Vegas*
John Murphy, *Iowa State University*
Ramesh Narasimhan, *Montclair State University*
Sia Nassiripour, *William Paterson University*
Siva Nathan, *Georgia State University*
Linda Nichols, *Texas Tech University*
Sewon O, *Texas Southern University*
Emeka Ofobike, *University of Akron*
Stevan Olson, *Missouri State University*
William Padley, *Madison Area Technical College–Truax*
Hong Pak, *California State Polytechnic University–Pomona*
Moses Pava, *Yeshiva University*
Alee Phillips, *University of Kansas–Lawrence*
Byron Pike, *Minnesota State University–Mankato*
Kevin Poirier, *Johnson & Wales University*
Atul Rai, *Wichita State University*
Philip M Reckers, *Arizona State University–Tempe*
Barbara Reider, *University of Montana*
Eric Rothenburg, *Kingsborough Community College*
Anwar Salimi, *California State Polytechnic University–Pomona*
Timothy Sigler, *Stark State College of Tech*
Kathleen Simons, *Bryant University*
Craig Sisneros, *Wichita State University*
Kevin Smith, *Utah Valley University–Orem*
Sheldon R. Smith, *Utah Valley University–Orem*
Victor Stanton, *University of Calif–Berkeley*
Dan Stubbs, *Rutgers University–New Brunswick*
Pamela S. Stuerke, *University of Missouri–St Louis*
Domenic Tavella, *Pittsburgh Technical Institute*
Kathy Terrell, *University of Central Oklahoma*
Paula B. Thomas, *Middle Tennessee State University*
Samuel Tiras, *Louisiana State University–Baton Rouge*
Ingrid Ulstad, *University of Wisconsin–Eau Claire*
Rishma Vedd, *California State University–Northridge*
Marcia Veit, *University of Central Florida*
Bruce Wampler, *University of Tennessee–Chattanooga*
Isabel Wang, *Michigan State University–East Lansing*
Kun Wang, *Texas Southern University*
Nancy Wilburn, *Northern Arizona*
Mike Wilson, *Metropolitan State University*
Jennifer Winchel, *University of South Carolina*
Joni J. Young, *University of New Mexico–Albuquerque*

We Are Grateful

We would like to acknowledge Ilene Persoff, Long Island University Post, for her detailed accuracy check of the Testbank. In addition, we thank Kathrine Glass of Indiana University, Marianne James of California State University–Los Angeles, Kevin Smith of Utah Valley University, Beth Woods of Accuracy Counts, and Teri Zuccaro of Clarke University who contributed new content and accuracy checks of Connect and LearnSmart. We greatly appreciate everyone's hard work on these products!

Ilene Persoff, Long Island University Post, and Mark McCarthy, East Carolina University, made significant contributions to the accuracy of the text, end-of-chapter material, and solutions manual.

We are most grateful for the talented assistance and support from the many people at McGraw-Hill Education. We would particularly like to thank Tim Vertovec, managing director; Brad Parkins, marketing director; James Heine, executive brand manager; Rebecca Mann, senior product developer; Kathleen Klehr, senior marketing manager; Pat Plumb, director of digital content; Xin Lin, digital product analyst; Daryl Horrocks, program manager; Pat Frederickson, lead content project manager; Angela Norris, content project manager; Michael McCormick, buyer; Srdjan Savanovic, designer; Keri Johnson and Ann Marie Jannette, content licensing specialists.

Finally, we extend our thanks to Kaplan CPA Review for their assistance developing simulations for our inclusion in the end-of-chapter material, as well as PetSmart and Air France–KLM for allowing us to use their Annual Reports throughout the text. We also acknowledge permission from the AICPA to adapt material from the Uniform CPA Examination, the IMA for permission to adapt material from the CMA Examination, and Dow Jones & Co., Inc., for permission to excerpt material from *The Wall Street Journal*.

David Spiceland *Jim Sepe* *Mark Nelson* *Wayne Thomas*

Contents in Brief

Contents

1 The Role of Accounting as an Information System

1 CHAPTER Environment and Theoretical Structure of Financial Accounting 2

2 CHAPTER Review of the Accounting Process 50

3 CHAPTER The Balance Sheet and Financial Disclosures 112

4 CHAPTER The Income Statement, Comprehensive Income, and the Statement of Cash Flows 170

5 CHAPTER Revenue Recognition and Profitability Analysis 230

2 Economic Resources

3 Financial Instruments and Liabilities

12 CHAPTER Investments 654

13 CHAPTER Current Liabilities and Contingencies 730

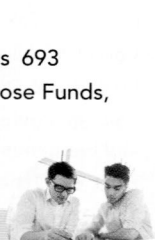

14 CHAPTER Bonds and Long-Term Notes 788

17 CHAPTER Pensions and Other Postretirement Benefits 996

18 CHAPTER Shareholders' Equity 1066

4 Additional Financial Reporting Issues

19 CHAPTER Share-Based Compensation and Earnings Per Share 1126

20 CHAPTER Accounting Changes and Error Corrections 1194

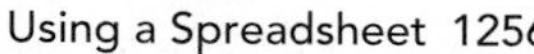

21 CHAPTER The Statement of Cash Flows Revisited 1242

CHAPTER

1 Environment and Theoretical Structure of Financial Accounting

OVERVIEW

The primary function of financial accounting is to provide useful financial information to users who are external to the business enterprise, particularly investors and creditors. These users make critical resource allocation decisions that affect the global economy. The primary means of conveying financial information to external users is through financial statements and related notes.

In this chapter you explore important topics, such as the reason why financial accounting is useful, the process by which accounting standards are produced, and the conceptual framework that underlies financial accounting. The perspective you gain in this chapter serves as a foundation for a more detailed study of financial statements, the way the statement elements are measured, and the concepts underlying these measurements and related disclosures.

LEARNING OBJECTIVES

After studying this chapter, you should be able to:

- **LO1–1** Describe the function and primary focus of financial accounting. (*p. 4*)
- **LO1–2** Explain the difference between cash and accrual accounting. (*p. 6*)
- **LO1–3** Define generally accepted accounting principles (GAAP) and discuss the historical development of accounting standards, including convergence between U.S. and international standards. (*p. 8*)
- **LO1–4** Explain why establishing accounting standards is characterized as a political process. (*p. 13*)
- **LO1–5** Explain factors that encourage high-quality financial reporting. (*p. 16*)
- **LO1–6** Explain the purpose of the conceptual framework. (*p. 20*)
- **LO1–7** Identify the objective and qualitative characteristics of financial reporting information, and the elements of financial statements. (*p. 21*)
- **LO1–8** Describe the four basic assumptions underlying GAAP. (*p. 26*)
- **LO1–9** Describe the recognition, measurement and disclosure concepts that guide accounting practice. (*p. 27*)
- **LO1–10** Contrast a revenue/expense approach and an asset/liability approach to accounting standard setting. (*p. 34*)
- **LO1–11** Discuss the primary differences between U.S. GAAP and IFRS with respect to the development of accounting standards and the conceptual framework underlying accounting standards. (*pp. 15* and *20*)

FINANCIAL REPORTING CASE

Misguided Marketing Major

During a class break in your investments class, a marketing major tells the following story to you and some friends:

The chief financial officer (CFO) of a large company is interviewing three candidates for the top accounting position with his firm. He asks each the same question:

CFO:	What is two plus two?
First candidate:	Four.
CFO:	What is two plus two?
Second candidate:	Four.
CFO:	What is two plus two?
Third candidate:	What would you like it to be?
CFO:	You're hired.

After you take some good-natured ribbing from the non-accounting majors, your friend says, "Seriously, though, there must be ways the accounting profession prevents that kind of behavior. Aren't there some laws, or rules, or something? Is accounting based on some sort of theory, or is it just arbitrary?"

QUESTIONS

By the time you finish this chapter, you should be able to respond appropriately to the questions posed in this case. Compare your response to the solution provided at the end of the chapter.

1. What should you tell your friend about the presence of accounting standards in the United States and the rest of the world? Who has the authority for standard setting? Who has the responsibility? (*p. 8*)
2. What is the economic and political environment in which standard setting occurs? (*p. 13*)
3. What is the relationship among management, auditors, investors, and creditors that tends to preclude the "What would you like it to be?" attitude? (*p. 16*)
4. In general, what is the conceptual framework that underlies accounting principles? (*p. 20*)

Financial Accounting Environment

PART A

Jim and Janice Dougherty opened their first Pet Food Warehouse store in 1986. Their idea was to sell pet food in bulk at discount prices—a concept that evolved to include offering pet accessories and supplies, pet training, pet grooming, veterinary centers, and pet boarding services. Today, the company the Dougherty's founded, now called **PetSmart, Inc.**, has grown to include more than 1,300 stores, almost 200 PetsHotels, and over 800 in-store veterinary hospitals, generating over $6 billion in annual sales. PetSmart Charities, created to help save the lives of homeless pets, recently celebrated its 5 millionth pet adoption.[1]

PetSmart

Many factors contributed to the success of PetSmart. The Doughertys were visionary in terms of their approach to providing pet owners with a more economical way to care for and feed their pets. The ability to raise money from investors and lenders at various times in PetSmart's history also was critical to the company's evolution. PetSmart funded its early

[1]PetSmart Company History (**PetSmart.com**).

growth with investments from venture capitalists, and later sold stock to the general public to finance its rapid expansion. Creditors (lenders) also supplied needed capital.

Investors and creditors use many different kinds of information before supplying capital to businesses like PetSmart. They use the information to predict the future risk and potential return of their prospective investments or loans.[2] For example, information about the enterprise's products and its management is key to this assessment. Investors and creditors also rely on various kinds of accounting information.

● LO1–1

The primary focus of *financial accounting* is on the information needs of investors and creditors.

Think of accounting as a special "language" that companies like PetSmart use to communicate financial information to people inside and outside of the business who need it to make decisions. This textbook focuses on **financial accounting**, which is chiefly concerned with providing financial information to various *external* users.[3] The chart in Illustration 1–1 lists a number of financial information supplier groups as well as several external user groups. Of these groups, the primary focus of financial accounting is on the financial information provided by *profit-oriented companies to their present and potential investors and creditors.* The reason for this focus is discussed in a later section of this chapter. One external user group, often referred to as *financial intermediaries,* includes financial analysts, stockbrokers, mutual fund managers, and credit rating organizations. These users provide advice to investors and creditors and/or make investment-credit decisions on their behalf.

The primary means of conveying financial information to investors, creditors, and other external users is through financial statements and related disclosure notes. The financial statements most frequently provided are (1) the balance sheet, also called the statement of financial position, (2) the income statement, also called the statement of operations, (3) the statement of cash flows, and (4) the statement of shareholders' equity. Also, companies must either provide a statement of other comprehensive income immediately following the income statement, or present a combined statement of comprehensive income that includes the information normally contained in both the income statement and the statement of other comprehensive income.[4] As you progress through this text, you

Illustration 1–1

Financial Information Providers and External User Groups

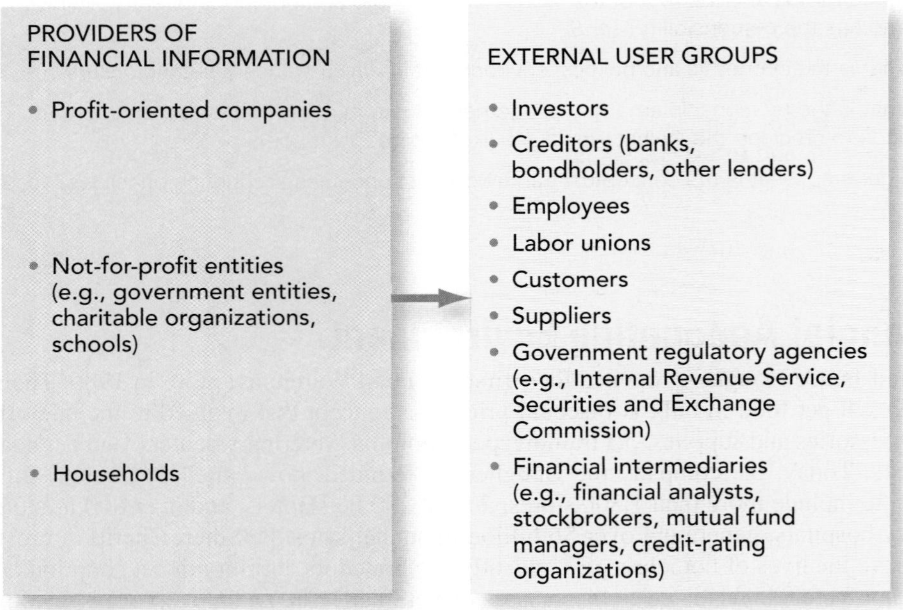

PROVIDERS OF FINANCIAL INFORMATION	→	EXTERNAL USER GROUPS
• Profit-oriented companies • Not-for-profit entities (e.g., government entities, charitable organizations, schools) • Households	→	• Investors • Creditors (banks, bondholders, other lenders) • Employees • Labor unions • Customers • Suppliers • Government regulatory agencies (e.g., Internal Revenue Service, Securities and Exchange Commission) • Financial intermediaries (e.g., financial analysts, stockbrokers, mutual fund managers, credit-rating organizations)

[2]Risk refers to the variability of possible outcomes from an investment. Return is the amount received over and above the investment.

[3]In contrast, *managerial* accounting deals with the concepts and methods used to provide information to an organization's *internal users,* that is, its managers. You study managerial accounting elsewhere in your curriculum.

[4]FASB ASC 220-45: Comprehensive Income—Other Presentation Matters (originally "Presentation of Comprehensive Income," *Accounting Standards Update No. 2011–05* (Norwalk, CT: FASB, June 2011)).

will review and expand your knowledge of the information in these financial statements, the way the elements in these statements are measured, and the concepts underlying these measurements and related disclosures. We use the term **financial reporting** to refer to the process of providing this information to external users. Keep in mind, though, that external users receive important financial information in a variety of other formats as well, including news releases and management forecasts, prospectuses, and reports filed with regulatory agencies.

PetSmart

PetSmart's financial statements for the fiscal year ended February 2, 2014, and related disclosure notes are provided in Appendix B, located at the back of the text. You also can access these statements and notes online at **PetSmart.com**. We will occasionally refer to PetSmart's financial statements and notes to provide context for our discussion. Also, as new topics are introduced in later chapters, you might want to refer to the information to see how PetSmart reported the items being discussed.

The Economic Environment and Financial Reporting

In the United States, we have a highly developed free-enterprise economy with the majority of productive resources privately owned rather than government owned. For the economy to operate efficiently, these resources should be allocated to private enterprises that will use them best to provide the goods and services desired by society, and not to enterprises that will waste them. The mechanisms that foster this efficient allocation of resources are the **capital markets**. We can think of the capital markets simply as a composite of all investors and creditors.

The *capital markets* provide a mechanism to help our economy allocate resources efficiently.

Businesses go to the capital markets to get the cash necessary for them to function. The three primary forms of business organization are the sole proprietorship, the partnership, and the corporation. In the United States, sole proprietorships and partnerships outnumber corporations. However, the dominant form of business organization, in terms of the ownership of productive resources, is the **corporation**. Investors provide resources, usually cash, to a corporation in exchange for an ownership interest, that is, shares of stock. Creditors lend cash to the corporation, either by making individual loans or by purchasing publicly traded debt such as bonds.

***Corporations* acquire capital from investors in exchange for ownership interest and from creditors by borrowing.**

Stocks and bonds usually are traded on organized security markets such as the New York Stock Exchange and the NASDAQ. New cash is provided by **initial market transactions** in which the corporation sells shares of stock or bonds to individuals or other entities that want to invest in it. For example, **PetSmart** first "went public" in 1993, selling shares to finance its expansion, and in later years issued additional shares for various purposes. Subsequent transfers of these stocks and bonds between investors and creditors are referred to as **secondary market transactions**. Corporations receive no new cash from secondary market transactions. Nevertheless, secondary market transactions are extremely important to the efficient allocation of resources in our economy. These transactions help establish market prices for additional shares and for bonds that corporations may wish to issue in the future to acquire additional capital. Also, many shareholders and bondholders might be unwilling to initially provide resources to corporations if there were no available mechanism for the future sale of their stocks and bonds to others.

***Initial market* transactions involve issuance of stocks and bonds by the corporation.**

PetSmart

***Secondary market* transactions involve the transfer of stocks and bonds between individuals and institutions.**

What information do investors and creditors need when determining which companies will receive capital? We explore that question next.

The Investment-Credit Decision—A Cash Flow Perspective

While the decisions made by investors and by creditors are somewhat different, they are similar in at least one important way. Investors and creditors are willing to provide capital to a corporation (buy stocks or bonds) only if they expect to receive more cash in return at some time in the future. A corporation's shareholders will receive cash from their investment through the ultimate sale of the ownership shares of stock. In addition, many corporations distribute cash to their shareholders in the form of periodic dividends. For example, if an investor provides a company with $10,000 cash by purchasing stock at the end of 2015, receives $400 in dividends from the company during 2016, and sells the ownership interest

Investors and creditors are interested in earning a fair return on the resources they provide.

(shares) at the end of 2016 for $10,600, the investment would have generated a **rate of return** of 10% for 2016, calculated as follows:

$$\frac{\$400 \text{ dividends} + \$600 \text{ share price appreciation}}{\$10{,}000 \text{ initial investment}} = 10\%$$

The expected rate of return and the uncertainty, or risk, of that return are key variables in the investment decision.

All else equal, investors and creditors would like to invest in stocks or bonds that provide the highest expected rate of return. However, there are many factors to consider before making an investment decision. For example, the *uncertainty,* or *risk,* of that expected return also is important. To illustrate, consider the following two investment options:

1. Invest $10,000 in a savings account insured by the U.S. government that will generate a 5% rate of return.
2. Invest $10,000 in a profit-oriented company.

A company will be able to provide a return to investors and creditors only if it can generate a profit from selling its products or services.

While the rate of return from option 1 is known with virtual certainty, the return from option 2 is uncertain. The amount and timing of the cash to be received in the future from option 2 are unknown. The company in option 2 will be able to provide investors with a return only if it can generate a profit. That is, it must be able to use the resources provided by investors and creditors to generate cash receipts from selling a product or service that exceed the cash disbursements necessary to provide that product or service. Therefore, potential investors require information about the company that will help them estimate the potential for future profits, as well as the return they can expect on their investment and the risk that is associated with it. If the potential return is high enough, investors will prefer to invest in the profit-oriented company, even if that return has more risk associated with it.

The objective of financial accounting is to provide investors and creditors with useful information for decision making.

In summary, the primary objective of financial accounting is to provide investors and creditors with information that will help them make investment and credit decisions. More specifically, the information should help investors and creditors evaluate the *amounts, timing,* and *uncertainty* of the enterprise's future cash receipts and disbursements. The better this information is, the more efficient will be investor and creditor resource allocation decisions. But financial accounting doesn't only benefit companies and their investors and creditors. By providing key elements of the information set used by capital market participants, financial accounting plays a vital role by providing information that helps direct society's resources to the companies that utilize those resources most effectively.

Cash versus Accrual Accounting

● LO1–2

Even though predicting future cash flows is the primary goal of many users of financial reporting, the model best able to achieve that goal is the **accrual accounting** model. A competing model is **cash basis accounting**. Each model produces a periodic measure of performance that could be used by investors and creditors for predicting future cash flows.

***Net operating cash flow* is the difference between cash receipts and cash disbursements from providing goods and services.**

CASH BASIS ACCOUNTING. Cash basis accounting produces a measure called **net operating cash flow**. This measure is the difference between cash receipts and cash payments from transactions related to providing goods and services to customers during a reporting period.

Over the life of a company, net operating cash flow definitely is the variable of concern. However, over short periods of time, operating cash flows may not be indicative of the company's long-run cash-generating ability. Sometimes a company pays or receives cash in one period that relates to performance in multiple periods. For example, in one period a company receives cash that relates to prior period sales, or makes advance payments for costs related to future periods. Therefore, net operating cash flow may not be a good predictor of long-run cash-generating ability.

To see this more clearly, consider Carter Company's net operating cash flows during its first three years of operations, shown in Illustration 1–2. Over this three-year period Carter generated a positive net operating cash flow of **$60,000**. At the end of the three-year period, Carter has no outstanding debts. Because total sales and cash receipts over the three-year

Illustration 1–2
Cash Basis Accounting

	Year 1	Year 2	Year 3	Total
Sales (on credit)	$100,000	$100,000	$100,000	$300,000
Net Operating Cash Flows				
Cash receipts from customers	$ 50,000	$125,000	$125,000	$300,000
Cash disbursements:				
Prepayment of three years' rent	(60,000)	–0–	–0–	(60,000)
Salaries to employees	(50,000)	(50,000)	(50,000)	(150,000)
Utilities	(5,000)	(15,000)	(10,000)	(30,000)
Net operating cash flow	$ (65,000)	$ 60,000	$ 65,000	$ 60,000

period were each $300,000, nothing is owed to Carter by customers. Also, there are no uncompleted transactions at the end of the three-year period. In that sense, we can view this three-year period as a micro version of the entire life of a company.

At the beginning of the first year, Carter prepaid $60,000 for three years' rent on the facilities. The company also incurred utility costs of $10,000 per year over the period. However, during the first year only $5,000 actually was paid, with the remainder being paid the second year. Employee salary costs of $50,000 were paid in full each year.

Over short periods of time, operating cash flow may not be an accurate predictor of future operating cash flows.

Is net operating cash flow for year 1 (negative $65,000) an accurate indicator of future cash-generating ability?[5] Clearly not, given that the next two years show positive net cash flows. Is the three-year pattern of net operating cash flows indicative of the company's year-by-year performance? No, because the years in which Carter paid for rent and utilities are not the same as the years in which Carter actually consumed those resources. Similarly, the amounts collected from customers are not the same as the amount of sales each period.

Net income is the difference between _revenues_ and _expenses_.

ACCRUAL ACCOUNTING. If we measure Carter's activities by the accrual accounting model, we get a more accurate prediction of future operating cash flows and a more reasonable portrayal of the periodic operating performance of the company. The accrual accounting model doesn't focus only on cash flows. Instead, it also reflects other resources provided and consumed by operations during a period. The accrual accounting model's measure of resources provided by business operations is called *revenues,* and the measure of resources sacrificed to produce revenues is called *expenses.* The difference between revenues and expenses is *net income,* or net loss if expenses are greater than revenues.[6]

Illustration 1–3 shows how we would measure revenues and expenses in this very simple situation.

Net income is considered a better indicator of future operating cash flows than is current net operating cash flow.

Revenue for year 1 is the $100,000 sales. Given that sales eventually are collected in cash, the year 1 revenue of $100,000 is a better measure of the inflow of resources from company operations than is the $50,000 cash collected from customers. Also, net income of $20,000 for year 1 appears to be a reasonable predictor of the company's cash-generating ability, as total net operating cash flow for the three-year period is a positive $60,000. Comparing the three-year pattern of net operating cash flows in Illustration 1–2 to the three-year pattern of net income in Illustration 1–3, the net income pattern is more representative of Carter Company's steady operating performance over the three-year period.[7]

While this example is somewhat simplistic, it allows us to see the motivation for using the accrual accounting model. Accrual income attempts to measure the resource inflows and

[5]A negative cash flow is possible only if invested capital (i.e., owners contributed cash to the company in exchange for ownership interest) is sufficient to cover the cash deficiency. Otherwise, the company would have to either raise additional external funds or go bankrupt.

[6]Net income also includes gains and losses, which are discussed later in the chapter.

[7]Empirical evidence that accrual accounting provides a better measure of short-term performance than cash flows is provided by Patricia DeChow, "Accounting Earnings and Cash Flows as Measures of Firm Performance: The Role of Accrual Accounting," *Journal of Accounting and Economics* 18 (1994), pp. 3–42.

Illustration 1–3
Accrual Accounting

The accrual accounting model provides a measure of periodic performance called *net income,* the difference between revenues and expenses.

CARTER COMPANY
Income Statements

	Year 1	Year 2	Year 3	Total
Revenues	$100,000	$100,000	$100,000	$300,000
Expenses:				
Rent	20,000	20,000	20,000	60,000
Salaries	50,000	50,000	50,000	150,000
Utilities	10,000	10,000	10,000	30,000
Total expenses	80,000	80,000	80,000	240,000
Net Income	$ 20,000	$ 20,000	$ 20,000	$ 60,000

outflows generated by operations during the reporting period, which may not correspond to cash inflows and outflows. Does this mean that information about cash flows from operating activities is not useful? No. Indeed, one of the basic financial statements—the statement of cash flows—reports information about cash flows from operating, investing and financing activities, and provides important information to investors and creditors.[8] The key point is that focusing on accrual accounting as well as cash flows provides a more complete view of a company and its operations.

The Development of Financial Accounting and Reporting Standards

● LO1–3

FINANCIAL Reporting Case

Q1, p. 3

Accrual accounting is the financial reporting model used by the majority of profit-oriented companies and by many not-for-profit companies. The fact that companies use the same model is important to investors and creditors, allowing them to *compare* financial information among companies. To facilitate these comparisons, financial accounting employs a body of standards known as **generally accepted accounting principles**, often abbreviated as **GAAP** (and pronounced *gap*). GAAP is a dynamic set of both broad and specific guidelines that companies should follow when measuring and reporting the information in their financial statements and related notes. The more important broad principles underlying GAAP are discussed in a subsequent section of this chapter and revisited throughout the text in the context of accounting applications for which they provide conceptual support. Specific standards, such as how to measure and report a lease transaction, receive more focused attention in subsequent chapters.

Historical Perspective and Standards

The *Securities and Exchange Commission (SEC)* was created by Congress with the 1934 Securities Exchange Act.

Pressures on the accounting profession to establish uniform accounting standards began to surface after the stock market crash of 1929. Some felt that insufficient and misleading financial statement information led to inflated stock prices and that this contributed to the stock market crash and the subsequent depression.

The 1933 Securities Act and the 1934 Securities Exchange Act were designed to restore investor confidence. The 1933 Act sets forth accounting and disclosure requirements for initial offerings of securities (stocks and bonds). The 1934 Act applies to secondary market transactions and mandates reporting requirements for companies whose securities are publicly traded on either organized stock exchanges or in over-the-counter markets.[9]

The SEC has the authority to set accounting standards for companies, but has delegated the task to the private sector.

The 1934 Act also created the **Securities and Exchange Commission (SEC)**. Congress gave the SEC the authority to set accounting and reporting standards for companies whose securities are publicly traded. However, the SEC, a government appointed body, has

[8]The statement of cash flows is discussed in detail in Chapters 4 and 21.

[9]Reporting requirements for SEC registrants include Form 10-K, the annual report form, and Form 10-Q, the report that must be filed for the first three quarters of each fiscal year.

delegated the task of setting accounting standards to the private sector. It is important to understand that the power still lies with the SEC. If the SEC does not agree with a particular standard issued by the private sector, it can force a change in the standard. In fact, it has done so in the past.[10]

EARLY U.S. STANDARD SETTING. The first private sector body to assume the task of setting accounting standards was the **Committee on Accounting Procedure (CAP)**. The CAP was a committee of the **American Institute of Accountants (AIA)**. The AIA, which was renamed the **American Institute of Certified Public Accountants (AICPA)** in 1957, is the national professional organization for certified professional public accountants. From 1938 to 1959, the CAP issued 51 *Accounting Research Bulletins (ARBs)* which dealt with specific accounting and reporting problems. No theoretical framework for financial accounting was established. This piecemeal approach of dealing with individual issues without a framework led to criticism.

In 1959 the **Accounting Principles Board (APB)** replaced the CAP. The APB operated from 1959 through 1973 and issued 31 *Accounting Principles Board Opinions (APBOs)*, various *Interpretations,* and four *Statements.* The *Opinions* also dealt with specific accounting and reporting problems. Many *ARBs* and *APBOs* have not been superseded and still represent authoritative GAAP.

The *Accounting Principles Board (APB)* followed the CAP.

The APB suffered from a variety of problems. It was never able to establish a conceptual framework for financial accounting and reporting that was broadly accepted. Also, members served on the APB on a voluntary, part-time basis, so the APB was not able to act quickly enough to keep up with financial reporting issues as they developed. Perhaps the most important flaw of the APB was a perceived lack of independence. Because the APB was composed almost entirely of certified public accountants and supported by the AICPA, critics charged that the clients of the represented public accounting firms exerted self-interested pressure on the board and inappropriately influenced decisions. A related complaint was that other interest groups lacked an ability to provide input to the standard-setting process.

THE FASB. Criticism of the APB led to the creation in 1973 of the **Financial Accounting Standards Board (FASB)** and its supporting structure. There are seven full-time members of the FASB. FASB members represent various constituencies concerned with accounting standards, and have included representatives from the auditing profession, profit-oriented companies, accounting educators, financial analysts, and government. The FASB is supported by its parent organization, the **Financial Accounting Foundation (FAF)**, which is responsible for selecting the members of the FASB and its Financial Accounting Standards Advisory Council (FASAC), ensuring adequate funding of FASB activities and exercising general oversight of the FASB's activities.[11] The FASB is, therefore, an independent, private sector body whose members represent a broad constituency of interest groups.[12]

The *FASB* was established to set U.S. accounting standards.

In 1984, the FASB's **Emerging Issues Task Force (EITF)** was formed to improve financial reporting by resolving narrowly defined financial accounting issues within the framework of existing GAAP. The EITF primarily addresses implementation issues, thereby speeding up the standard-setting process and allowing the FASB to focus on pervasive long-term problems. EITF rulings are ratified by the FASB and are considered part of GAAP.

The *Emerging Issues Task Force (EITF)* identifies financial reporting issues and attempts to resolve them without involving the FASB.

[10]The SEC issues *Financial Reporting Releases (FRRs),* which regulate what information companies must report to it. The SEC also issues *Staff Accounting Bulletins* that provide the SEC's interpretation of standards previously issued by the private sector. To learn more about the SEC, consult its Internet site at www.sec.gov.

[11]The FAF's primary sources of funding are fees assessed against issuers of securities under the *Public Company Accounting Reform and Investor Protection Act of 2002,* commonly referred to as the *Sarbanes-Oxley Act.* The FAF is governed by trustees, the majority of whom are appointed from the membership of eight sponsoring organizations. These organizations represent important constituencies involved with the financial reporting process. For example, one of the founding organizations is the Association of Investment Management and Research (formerly known as the Financial Analysts Federation) which represents financial information users, and another is the Financial Executives International which represents financial information preparers. The FAF also raises funds to support the activities of the Government Accounting Standards Board (GASB).

[12]The major responsibility of the FASAC is to advise the FASB on the priorities of its projects, including the suitability of new projects that might be added to its agenda. FASAC includes approximately 35 representatives from auditing firms, private companies, various user groups, and academia.

Illustration 1–4

Accounting Standard Setting

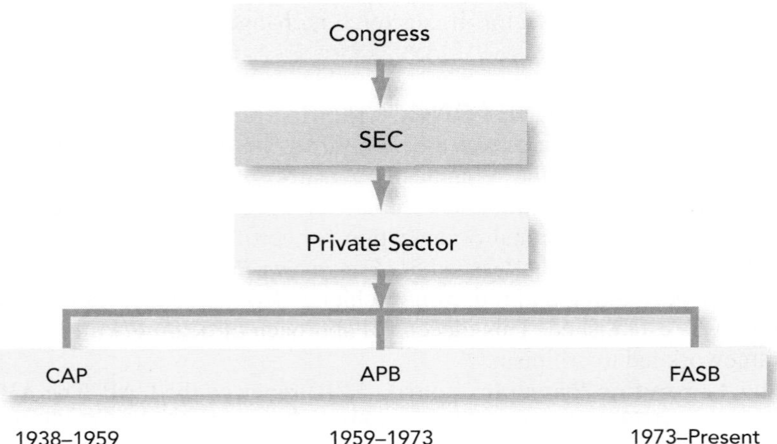

Illustration 1–4 summarizes this discussion on accounting standards. The graphic shows the hierarchy of accounting standard setting in order of authority.

CODIFICATION. Present-day GAAP includes a huge amount of guidance. The FASB has developed a **conceptual framework** (discussed in Part B of this chapter) that is not authoritative GAAP but provides an underlying structure for the development of accounting standards. The FASB also has issued over 160 specific accounting standards, called *Statements of Financial Accounting Standards (SFASs),* as well as numerous FASB *Interpretations, Staff Positions, Technical Bulletins* and *EITF Issue Consensuses.*[13] The SEC also has issued various important pronouncements. Until 2009, determining the appropriate accounting treatment for a particular event or transaction might require an accountant to research several of these sources.

The *FASB Accounting Standards Codification* is now the only source of authoritative U.S. GAAP, other than rules and interpretive releases of the SEC.

To simplify the task of researching an accounting topic, in 2009 the FASB implemented its *FASB Accounting Standards Codification.* The Codification integrates and topically organizes all relevant accounting pronouncements comprising GAAP in a searchable, online database. It represents the single source of authoritative nongovernmental U.S. GAAP, and also includes portions of SEC accounting guidance that are relevant to financial reports filed with the SEC. When the FASB issues a new standard, it is called an Accounting Standards Update (ASU) and becomes authoritative when it is entered into the Codification. The Codification is organized into nine main topics and approximately 90 subtopics. The main topics and related numbering system are presented in Illustration 1–5.[15] The Codification can be located at **www.fasb.org**.

The Codification does not change GAAP; instead it reorganizes the thousands of U.S. GAAP pronouncements into roughly 90 accounting topics, and displays all topics using a consistent structure.[14]

Throughout the text, we use the Accounting Standards Codification System (ASC) in footnotes when referencing generally accepted accounting principles (FASB ASC followed by the appropriate number). Each footnote also includes a reference to the original accounting standard that is codified in ASC. Your instructor may assign end-of-chapter exercises and cases that ask you to research the FASB's Accounting Standards Codification.

[13]For more information, go to the FASB's Internet site at www.fasb.org.

[14]"FASB Accounting Standards Codification™ Expected to Officially Launch on July 1, 2009," *FASB News Release* (Norwalk, Conn.: FASB, December 4, 2008).

[15]FASB ASC 105–10: Generally Accepted Accounting Principles—Overall (previously "The FASB Accounting Standards Codification™ and the Hierarchy of Generally Accepted Accounting Principles—a replacement of FASB Statement No. 162," *Statement of Financial Accounting Standards No. 168* (Norwalk, Conn.: FASB: 2009)).

Illustration 1–5
FASB Accounting Standards Codification Topics

FASB Accounting Standards Codification Topics

Topic	Numbered
General Principles	100–199
Presentation	200–299
Assets	300–399
Liabilities	400–499
Equity	500–599
Revenues	600–699
Expenses	700–799
Broad Transactions	800–899
Industry	900–999

Additional Consideration

Accounting standards and the standard-setting process discussed above relate to profit-oriented organizations and nongovernmental not-for-profit entities. In 1984, the Government Accounting Standards Board (GASB) was created to develop accounting standards for governmental units such as states and cities. The FAF oversees and funds the GASB, and the Governmental Accounting Standards Advisory Council (GASAC) provides input to it.

INTERNATIONAL STANDARD SETTING. Most industrialized countries have organizations responsible for determining accounting and reporting standards. In some countries, the United Kingdom, for instance, the responsible organization is a private sector body similar to the FASB in the United States. In other countries, such as France, the organization is a governmental body.

Accounting standards issued by these various groups are not the same. Standards differ from country to country for many reasons, including different legal systems, levels of inflation, culture, degrees of sophistication and use of capital markets, use of financial reports by taxing authorities or government planners, and political and economic ties with other countries. These differences can cause problems for multinational corporations. A company doing business in more than one country may find it difficult to comply with more than one set of accounting standards if there are important differences among the sets. These differences also cause problems for investors who must struggle to compare companies whose financial statements are prepared under different standards. It has been argued that different national accounting standards impair the ability of companies to raise capital in international markets.

The *International Accounting Standards Board (IASB)* is dedicated to developing a single set of global accounting standards.

In response to this problem, the International Accounting Standards Committee (IASC) was formed in 1973 to develop global accounting standards. The IASC reorganized itself in 2001 and created a new standard-setting body called the International Accounting Standards Board (IASB). The IASB's main objective is to develop a single set of high-quality, understandable, and enforceable global accounting standards to help participants in the world's capital markets and other users make economic decisions.[16]

As shown in Illustration 1–6, the way international standard setting is structured is similar in many respects to the way standard setting is structured in the U.S.

***International Financial Reporting Standards* are gaining support around the globe.**

The IASC issued 41 International Accounting Standards (IASs), and the IASB endorsed these standards when it was formed in 2001. Since then, the IASB has revised many IASs and has issued new standards of its own, called International Financial Reporting Standards (IFRSs). More and more countries are basing their national accounting

[16]www.iasb.org.

Illustration 1–6

Comparison of Organizations of U.S. and International Standard Setters

	U.S. GAAP	IFRS
Regulatory oversight provided by:	Securities Exchange Commission (SEC)	International Organization of Securities Commissions (IOSCO)*
Foundation providing oversight, appointing members, raising funds:	Financial Accounting Foundation (FAF): 20 trustees	International Accounting Standards Committee Foundation (IASCF): 22 trustees
Standard-setting board:	Financial Accounting Standards Board (FASB): 7 members	International Accounting Standards Board (IASB): 16 members
Advisory council providing input on agenda and projects:	Financial Accounting Standards Advisory Council (FASAC): 30–40 members	Standards Advisory Council (SAC): 30–40 members
Group to deal with emerging issues:	Emerging Issues Task Force (EITF): 15 members	International Financial Reporting Interpretations Committee (IFRIC): 14 members

*Each country's security regulator has authority. IOSCO includes representatives from numerous regulators, including the SEC, to facilitate coordination among those regulators and other organizations and encourage effective capital markets.

standards on IFRS. By 2014, over 115 jurisdictions, including Hong Kong, Egypt, Canada, Australia, and the countries in the European Union (EU), require or permit the use of IFRS or a local variant of IFRS.[17]

EFFORTS TO CONVERGE U.S. AND INTERNATIONAL STANDARDS. Should the U.S. also adopt IFRS? Many argue that a single set of global standards will improve comparability of financial reporting and facilitate access to capital. However, others argue that U.S. standards should remain customized to fit the stringent legal and regulatory requirements of the U.S. business environment. There also is concern that differences in implementation and enforcement from country to country will make accounting under IFRS appear more uniform and comparable than actually is the case. Another argument is that competition between alternative standard-setting regimes is healthy and can lead to improved standards.[18]

Regardless, the FASB and IASB have been working for many years to converge to one global set of accounting standards. Here are some important steps along the path to convergence:

- **September 2002:** The FASB and IASB sign the Norwalk Agreement, pledging to remove existing differences between their standards and to coordinate their future standard-setting agendas so that major issues are worked on together.
- **December 2007:** The SEC signaled its view that IFRS are of high quality by eliminating the requirement for foreign companies that issue stock in the United States to include in their financial statements a reconciliation of IFRS to U.S. GAAP. As a consequence, those companies have access to U.S. capital markets with IFRS-based financial statements.
- **April 2008:** The FASB and IASB agreed to accelerate the convergence process and focus on a subset of key convergence projects. Already-converged standards that you

[17]See **www.iasplus.com/country/useias.htm**.

[18]For a comprehensive analysis of the pros and cons of U.S. adoption of IFRS, see L. Hail, C. Leuz and P. Wysocki, "Global Accounting Convergence and the Potential Adoption of IFRS in the US (Part 1): An Analysis of Economic and Policy Factors", *Accounting Horizons 24* (No 3.), September 2010, pp. 355–394, and ". . . (Part 2): Political Factors and Future Scenarios for U.S. Accounting Standards", *Accounting Horizons* 24 (No. 4), December 2010, pp. 567–588.

will encounter later in this textbook deal with such topics as earnings per share, share-based compensation, nonmonetary exchanges, inventory costs, and the calculation of fair value. **Where We're Headed** boxes throughout the text describe additional projects that are ongoing, and a **Where We're Headed** supplement to Chapter 15 describes ongoing efforts to develop a converged standard relevant to accounting for leases.

- **November 2008:** The SEC issues a *Roadmap* that listed necessary conditions (called "milestones") that must be achieved before the U.S. will shift to requiring use of IFRS by public companies. Milestones include completion of key convergence projects, improving the structure and funding of the IASB, and updating the education and licensing of U.S. accountants.
- **November 2011:** The SEC issues two studies comparing U.S. GAAP and IFRS and analyzing how IFRS are applied globally. In these studies, the SEC identifies key differences between U.S. GAAP and IFRS, and notes that U.S. GAAP provides significantly more guidance about particular transactions or industries. The SEC also notes some diversity in the application of IFRS that suggests the potential for non-comparability of financial statements across countries and industries.
- **July 2012:** The SEC staff issues its Final Staff Report in which it concludes that it is not feasible for the U.S. to simply adopt IFRS, given (1) a need for the U.S. to have strong influence on the standard-setting process and ensure that standards meet U.S. needs, (2) the high costs to companies of converting to IFRS, and (3) the fact that many laws, regulations, and private contracts reference U.S. GAAP.[19] Therefore, the staff recommends that the SEC consider other approaches, such as developing a mechanism to consider endorsing individual IFRS standards for incorporation into U.S. GAAP, or to just maintain the current approach in which the FASB and IASB work together to converge standards.

At the time this textbook is being written, the SEC still has not made a final ruling on whether or how IFRS will be incorporated into U.S. GAAP. Although some convergence already has occurred through cooperation between the FASB and the IASB, recent events suggest that convergence efforts are waning. For example, as discussed further in Chapter 12, the FASB and IASB eventually concluded that full convergence was not possible with respect to accounting for recognition, measurement, and impairment of financial instruments, and instead have worked toward issuing separate standards that differ from each other in important ways.

In the meantime, although U.S. companies continue to follow U.S. GAAP, you should be aware of important differences that exist between U.S. GAAP and IFRS. Therefore, **International Financial Reporting Standards** boxes are included throughout the text to highlight circumstances in which IFRS differs from U.S. GAAP. Your instructor may assign end-of-chapter IFRS questions, exercises, problems, and cases that explore these differences. Throughout the remainder of the text, IFRS-related material is marked with the globe icon that you see beside this paragraph.

The Standard-Setting Process

LO1–4

DUE PROCESS. When developing accounting standards, a standard setter must understand the nuances of the economic transactions the standards address and the views of key constituents concerning how accounting would best capture that economic reality. Therefore, the FASB undertakes a series of elaborate information-gathering steps before issuing an Accounting Standards Update. These steps include open hearings, deliberations, and requests for written comments from interested parties. Illustration 1–7 outlines the FASB's standard-setting process.[20]

FINANCIAL Reporting Case

Q2, p. 3

[19]"Work Plan for the Consideration of Incorporating International Financial Reporting Standards into the Financial Reporting System for U.S. Issuers: Final Staff Report." Office of the Chief Accountant, United States Securities and Exchange Commission, July 13, 2012, available at www.sec.gov.

[20]www.FASB.org.

Illustration 1–7

The FASB's Standard-Setting Process

The FASB undertakes a series of information-gathering steps before issuing an Accounting Standards Update.

Step	Explanation
1.	The Board identifies financial reporting issues based on requests/recommendations from stakeholders or through other means.
2.	The Board decides whether to add a project to the technical agenda based on a staff-prepared analysis of the issues.
3.	The Board deliberates at one or more public meetings the various issues identified and analyzed by the staff.
4.	The Board issues an Exposure Draft. (In some projects, a Discussion Paper may be issued to obtain input at an early stage that is used to develop an Exposure Draft.)
5.	The Board holds a public roundtable meeting on the Exposure Draft, if necessary.
6.	The staff analyzes comment letters, public roundtable discussion, and any other information. The Board redeliberates the proposed provisions at public meetings.
7.	The Board issues an Accounting Standards Update describing amendments to the Accounting Standards Codification.

These steps help the FASB acquire information to determine the preferred method of accounting. However, as a practical matter this information gathering also exposes the FASB to much political pressure by various interest groups who want an accounting treatment that serves their economic best interest. As you will see later in this chapter, the FASB's concepts statements indicate that standards should present information in a neutral manner, rather than being designed to favor particular economic consequences, but sometimes politics intrudes on the standard-setting process.

POLITICS IN STANDARD SETTING. A change in accounting standards can result in a substantial redistribution of wealth within our economy. Therefore, it is no surprise that the FASB has had to deal with intense political pressure over controversial accounting standards, and sometimes has changed standards in response to that pressure.

One example of the effect of politics on standard setting occurred in the mid-1990's with respect to accounting for employee stock options. The accounting standards in place at that time typically did not recognize compensation expense if a company paid their employees with stock options rather than cash. Yet, the company was sacrificing something of value to compensate its employees. Therefore, the FASB proposed that companies recognize compensation expense in an amount equal to the fair value of the options, with some of the expense recognized in each of the periods in which the employee earned the options. Numerous companies (particularly in California's Silicon Valley, where high-tech companies had been compensating employees with stock options to a great extent) applied intense political pressure against this proposal, and eventually the FASB backed down and required only disclosure of options-related compensation expense in the notes to the financial statements. Nearly a decade later, this contentious issue resurfaced in a more amenable political climate, and the FASB issued a standard requiring expense recognition as originally proposed. This issue is discussed at greater length in Chapter 19.

Another example of politics in standard setting relates to accounting for business combinations. GAAP previously allowed two separate and distinct methods of accounting for business combinations: the pooling of interests method and the purchase method. A key issue involved goodwill, an intangible asset that arises only in business combinations accounted for using the purchase method. Under the then-existing standards, goodwill was amortized (expensed) over its estimated useful life. To avoid that amortization expense, many companies incurred costs to structure their business combinations as a pooling of interests. The FASB proposed eliminating the pooling method. As you can guess, that proposal met with strong opposition. Companies that were actively engaged in business acquisitions argued that they would not undertake business combinations important to economic growth if they were required to use the purchase method, due to the negative impact on earnings caused by goodwill amortization. Eventually the FASB compromised.[21] In the final standard issued in 2001, only the purchase method, now called the acquisition method, is acceptable, but to soften the impact, the resulting goodwill is *not* amortized.[22] We discuss goodwill and its measurement in Chapters 10 and 11.

A recent example of the political process at work in standard setting is the controversy surrounding the implementation of the fair value accounting standard issued in 2007. Many financial assets and liabilities are reported at fair value in the balance sheet, and many types of fair value changes are included in net income. Some have argued that fair values were estimated in a manner that exacerbated the financial crisis of 2008–2009 by forcing financial institutions to take larger than necessary write-downs of financial assets in the illiquid markets that existed at that time. As discussed further in Chapter 12, pressure from lobbyists and politicians influenced the FASB to revise its guidance on recognizing investment losses in these situations, and ongoing pressure remains to reduce the extent to which fair value changes are included in the determination of net income.

International Financial Reporting Standards

● LO1–11

Politics in International Standard Setting. Political pressures on the IASB's standard-setting process are severe. One source of pressure comes from the international business community. Unlike the FASB, which is funded through fees paid by companies listing securities on stock exchanges, the IASB receives much of its funding through voluntary donations by accounting firms and corporations, and there is concern that this financial support may compromise the IASB's independence.

Another source of political pressure arises from the fact that politicians from countries that use IFRS lobby for the standards they prefer. The European Union (EU) is a particularly important adopter of IFRS and utilizes a formal evaluation process for determining whether an IFRS standard will be endorsed for use in EU countries. Economic consequences for EU member nations are an important consideration in that process. For example, in 2003 and 2004 French banks lobbied against some aspects of accounting for financial instruments stridently enough that the EU eventually "carved out" two key provisions before endorsing the relevant accounting standard (IAS 39).[24] Similarly, in 2008 the EU successfully pressured the IASB to suspend its due process and immediately allow reclassification of investments so that EU banks could avoid recognizing huge losses during a financial crisis.[25] Highlighting the importance of politics in the IASB, the chairman of the IASB is Hans Hoogervorst, a Dutch securities regulator with much diplomatic experience but no formal accounting background. Although the IASB's vice-chairman, Ian Mackintosh, has a long career in accounting and standard setting, the appointment of a nonaccountant as IASB Chairman perhaps signals a priority on political considerations.

Charlie McCreevy, European Commissioner for Internal Markets and Services

Accounting is now far too important to be left solely to . . . accountants![23]

---

[21]Jonathan Weil, "FASB Backs Down on Goodwill-Accounting Rules," *The Wall Street Journal* (December 7, 2000).

[22]FASB ASC 805: Business Combinations (previously "Business Combinations," *Statement of Financial Accounting Standards No. 141 (revised)* (Norwalk, Conn.: FASB, 2007)), and FASB ASC 350: Intangibles—Goodwill and Other (previously "Goodwill and Other Intangible Assets," *Statement of Financial Accounting Standards No. 142* (Norwalk, Conn.: FASB, 2001)).

[23]Charlie McCreevy, Keynote Address, "Financial Reporting in a Changing World" Conference, Brussels, 5/7/2009.

[24]Stephen A. Zeff, "IFRS Developments in the USA and EU, and Some Implications for Australia," *Australian Accounting Review* 18 (2008), pp. 275–282.

[25]Sarah Deans and Dane Mott, "Lowering Standards," **www.morganmarkets.com**, 10/14/2008.

Additional Consideration

Private Company Council (PCC). Are the complex, comprehensive standards that are necessary to reflect the activities of a huge multinational conglomerate like **General Electric** also appropriate for a private company that, say, just needs to provide financial statements to its bank to get a loan? Private companies might be able to avoid much of that complexity. They don't sell securities like stocks and bonds to the general public, and they usually can identify the information needs of the specific users who rely on their financial statements and provide direct access to management to answer questions. Private companies typically also have a smaller accounting staff than do public companies. For those reasons, private companies have long sought a version of GAAP that is less costly to apply and better meets the information needs of the users of their financial statements.

In 2012, the Financial Accounting Foundation responded to this concern by establishing the Private Company Council (PCC). The ten-member PCC determines whether changes to existing GAAP are necessary to meet the needs of users of private company financial statements. But, a proposed exception or modification for private companies must be endorsed by the FASB before being issued as an Accounting Standards Update and added to the Codification. The PCC also advises the FASB about its current projects that affect private companies. In its short history the PCC already has published a decision-making framework that guides its decisions and has made progress on projects that address accounting for goodwill, other intangible assets acquired as part of business combinations, and interest-rate swaps. We discuss these private company exceptions to GAAP in "Additional Consideration" boxes in later chapters in this text.

Encouraging High-Quality Financial Reporting

● LO1–5

Numerous factors affect the quality of financial reporting. In this section, we discuss the role of the auditor, recent reforms in financial reporting, and the debate about whether accounting standards should emphasize rules or underlying principles.

The Role of the Auditor

FINANCIAL Reporting Case

Q3, p. 3

Auditors offer credibility to financial statements.

It is the responsibility of management to apply GAAP appropriately. Another group, **auditors**, serves as an independent intermediary to help ensure that management has in fact appropriately applied GAAP in preparing the company's financial statements. Auditors examine (audit) financial statements to express a professional, independent opinion about whether the statements fairly present the company's financial position, its results of operations, and its cash flows in compliance with GAAP. Audits add credibility to the financial statements, increasing the confidence of those who rely on the information. Auditors, therefore, play an important role in the capital markets.

PetSmart

The report of the independent auditors of **PetSmart Inc.**'s financial statements is in the annual report information in Appendix B located at the back of the text. In that report, the accounting firm of **Deloitte & Touche LLP** stated that "In our opinion, such consolidated financial statements present fairly . . . , in conformity with accounting principles generally accepted in the United States of America." This is known as a clean opinion. Had there been any material departures from GAAP or other problems that caused the auditors to question the fairness of the statements, the report would have been modified to inform readers. Normally, companies correct any material misstatements that auditors identify in the course of an audit, so companies usually receive clean opinions. The audit report for public companies also provides the auditors' opinion on the effectiveness of the company's internal control over financial reporting. We discuss this second opinion in the next section.

Auditors express an opinion on the compliance of financial statements with GAAP.

In most states, only individuals licensed as **certified public accountants (CPAs)** can represent that the financial statements have been audited in accordance with generally accepted auditing standards. Requirements to be licensed as a CPA vary from state to state, but all states specify education, testing, and experience requirements. The testing requirement is to pass the Uniform CPA Examination.

Certified public accountants (CPAs) are licensed by states to provide audit services.

Financial Reporting Reform

Sarbanes-Oxley

The dramatic collapse of **Enron** in 2001 and the dismantling of the international public accounting firm of **Arthur Andersen** in 2002 severely shook U.S. capital markets. The credibility of the accounting profession itself as well as of corporate America was called into question. Public outrage over accounting scandals at high-profile companies like **WorldCom**, **Xerox**, **Merck**, **Adelphia Communications**, and others increased the pressure on lawmakers to pass measures that would restore credibility and investor confidence in the financial reporting process.

Paul Sarbanes—U.S. Senator
We confront an increasing crisis of confidence with the public's trust in our markets. If this continues, I think it poses a real threat to our economic health.[26]

Driven by these pressures, Congress acted swiftly and passed the *Public Company Accounting Reform and Investor Protection Act of 2002,* commonly referred to as the *Sarbanes-Oxley Act* or *SOX* for the two congressmen who sponsored the bill. SOX applies to public securities-issuing entities. It provides for the regulation of auditors and the types of services they furnish to clients, increases accountability of corporate executives, addresses conflicts of interest for securities analysts, and provides for stiff criminal penalties for violators. Illustration 1–8 outlines key provisions of the Act.

Section 404 is perhaps the most controversial provision of SOX. It requires that company management document internal controls and report on their adequacy. Auditors also must express an opinion on whether the company has maintained effective control over financial reporting.

Key Provisions of the Sarbanes-Oxley Act:

- **Oversight board.** The five-member (two accountants) Public Company Accounting Oversight Board has the authority to establish standards dealing with auditing, quality control, ethics, independence and other activities relating to the preparation of audit reports, or can choose to delegate these responsibilities to the AICPA. Prior to the act, the AICPA set auditing standards. The SEC has oversight and enforcement authority.
- **Corporate executive accountability.** Corporate executives must personally certify the financial statements and company disclosures with severe financial penalties and the possibility of imprisonment for fraudulent misstatement.
- **Nonaudit services.** The law makes it unlawful for the auditors of public companies to perform a variety of nonaudit services for audit clients. Prohibited services include bookkeeping, internal audit outsourcing, appraisal or valuation services, and various other consulting services. Other nonaudit services, including tax services, require preapproval by the audit committee of the company being audited.
- **Retention of work papers.** Auditors of public companies must retain all audit or review work papers for seven years or face the threat of a prison term for willful violations.
- **Auditor rotation.** Lead audit partners are required to rotate every five years. Mandatory rotation of audit firms came under consideration.
- **Conflicts of interest.** Audit firms are not allowed to audit public companies whose chief executives worked for the audit firm and participated in that company's audit during the preceding year.
- **Hiring of auditor.** Audit firms are hired by the audit committee of the board of directors of the company, not by company management.
- **Internal control.** Section 404 of the act requires that company management document and assess the effectiveness of all internal control processes that could affect financial reporting. The PCAOB's *Auditing Standard No. 2* (since replaced by *Auditing Standard No. 5*) requires that the company auditors express an opinion on whether the company has maintained effective internal control over financial reporting.

Illustration 1–8
Public Company Accounting Reform and Investor Protection Act of 2002 (Sarbanes-Oxley)

[26]James Kuhnhenn, "Bush Vows to Punish Corporate Lawbreakers," *San Jose Mercury News* (July 9, 2002), p. 8A.

No one argues the importance of adequate internal controls, but many argued that the benefits of Section 404 did not justify the costs of complying with it. Research provides evidence that 404 reports affect investors' risk assessments and companies' stock prices, indicating these reports are seen as useful by investors.[27] Unfortunately, it is not possible to quantify the more important benefit of potentially avoiding business failures like Enron by focusing attention on the implementation and maintenance of adequate internal controls.

The costs of 404 compliance initially were quite steep. For example, one survey of Fortune 1,000 companies estimated that large companies spent, on average, approximately $8.5 million and $4.8 million (including internal costs and auditor fees) during the first two years of the act to comply with 404 reporting requirements.[28] As expected, the costs dropped significantly in the second year, and continued to drop as the efficiency of internal control audits increased. Many companies now perceive that the benefits of these internal control reports exceed their costs.[29]

We revisit Section 404 in Chapter 7 in the context of an introduction to internal controls.

A Move Away from Rules-Based Standards?

A principles-based, or objectives-oriented, approach to standard-setting stresses professional judgment, as opposed to following a list of rules.

The accounting scandals at Enron and other companies involved managers using elaborately structured transactions to try to circumvent specific rules in accounting standards. One consequence of those scandals was a rekindled debate over **principles-based**, or more recently termed **objectives-oriented**, versus **rules-based** accounting standards. In fact, a provision of the Sarbanes-Oxley Act required the SEC to study the issue and provide a report to Congress on its findings. That report, issued in July 2003, recommended that accounting standards be developed using an objectives-oriented approach.[30]

An objectives-oriented approach to standard setting emphasizes using professional judgment, as opposed to following a list of rules, when choosing how to account for a transaction. Proponents of an objectives-oriented approach argue that a focus on professional judgment means that there are few rules to sidestep, and we are more likely to arrive at an appropriate accounting treatment. Detractors, on the other hand, argue that the absence of detailed rules opens the door to even more abuse, because management can use the latitude provided by objectives to justify their preferred accounting approach. Even in the absence of intentional misuse, reliance on professional judgment might result in different interpretations for similar transactions, raising concerns about comparability. Also, detailed rules help auditors withstand pressure from clients who want a more favorable accounting treatment, and help companies ensure that they are complying with GAAP and avoid litigation or SEC inquiry. For these reasons, it's challenging to avoid providing detailed rules in the U.S. reporting environment. Given ongoing efforts to converge FASB and IASB standards, it is likely that this debate will continue.

Regardless of whether accounting standards are based more on rules or on objectives, prior research highlights that there is some potential for abuse, either by structuring transactions around precise rules or opportunistically interpreting underlying principles.[31] The key is whether management is dedicated to high-quality financial reporting. It appears that poor ethical values on the part of management are at the heart of accounting abuses and scandals, so we now turn to a discussion of ethics in the accounting profession.

Ethics in Accounting

***Ethics* deals with the ability to distinguish right from wrong.**

Ethics is a term that refers to a code or moral system that provides criteria for evaluating right and wrong. An ethical dilemma is a situation in which an individual or group is faced with a decision that tests this code. Many of these dilemmas are simple to recognize and resolve.

[27]Hollis Ashbaugh Skaife, Daniel W. Collins, William R. Kinney, Jr., and Ryan LaFond. "The Effect of SOX Internal Control Deficiencies on Firm Risk and Cost of Equity," *Journal of Accounting Research* 47 (2009), pp. 1–43.

[28]"Sarbanes-Oxley 404 Costs and Implementation Issues: Spring 2006 Survey Update," CRA International (April 17, 2006).

[29]Protiviti, Inc., *2011 Sarbanes-Oxley Compliance Survey* (June, 2011).

[30]"Study Pursuant to Section 108 (d) of the Sarbanes-Oxley Act of 2002 on the Adoption by the United States Financial Reporting System of a Principles-Based Accounting System," Securities and Exchange Commission (July 2003).

[31]Mark W. Nelson, John A. Elliott, and Robin L. Tarpley, "Evidence From Auditors About Managers' and Auditors Earnings Management Decisions," *The Accounting Review* 77 (2002), pp. 175–202.

For example, have you ever been tempted to call your professor and ask for an extension on the due date of an assignment by claiming a pretended illness? Temptation like this will test your personal ethics.

Accountants, like others in the business world, are faced with many ethical dilemmas, some of which are complex and difficult to resolve. For instance, the capital markets' focus on near-term profits may tempt a company's management to bend or even break accounting rules to inflate reported net income. In these situations, technical competence is not enough to resolve the dilemma.

ETHICS AND PROFESSIONALISM. One characteristic that distinguishes a profession from other occupations is the acceptance by its members of a responsibility for the interests of those it serves. Ethical behavior is expected of those engaged in a profession. That expectation often is articulated in a code of ethics. For example, law and medicine are professions that have their own codes of professional ethics. These codes provide guidance and rules to members in the performance of their professional responsibilities.

Public accounting has achieved widespread recognition as a profession. The AICPA, the national organization of certified public accountants, has its own Code of Professional Conduct that prescribes the ethical conduct members should strive to achieve. Similarly, the Institute of Management Accountants (IMA)—the primary national organization of accountants working in industry and government—has its own code of ethics, as does the Institute of Internal Auditors—the national organization of accountants providing internal auditing services for their own organizations.

ANALYTICAL MODEL FOR ETHICAL DECISIONS. Ethical codes are informative and helpful, but the motivation to behave ethically must come from within oneself and not just from the fear of penalties for violating professional codes. Presented below is a sequence of steps that provide a framework for analyzing ethical issues. These steps can help you apply your own sense of right and wrong to ethical dilemmas:[32]

Step 1. Determine the facts of the situation. This involves determining the who, what, where, when, and how.

Step 2. Identify the ethical issue and the stakeholders. Stakeholders may include shareholders, creditors, management, employees, and the community.

Step 3. Identify the values related to the situation. For example, in some situations confidentiality may be an important value that might conflict with the right to know.

Step 4. Specify the alternative courses of action.

Step 5. Evaluate the courses of action specified in step 4 in terms of their consistency with the values identified in step 3. This step may or may not lead to a suggested course of action.

Step 6. Identify the consequences of each possible course of action. If step 5 does not provide a course of action, assess the consequences of each possible course of action for all of the stakeholders involved.

Step 7. Make your decision and take any indicated action.

Ethical dilemmas are presented throughout the text. These dilemmas are designed to raise your awareness of accounting issues with ethical ramifications. The analytical steps outlined above provide a framework you can use to evaluate these situations. In addition, your instructor may assign end-of-chapter ethics cases for further discussion and application.

[32]Adapted from Harold Q. Langenderfer and Joanne W. Rockness, "Integrating Ethics into the Accounting Curriculum: Issues, Problems, and Solutions," *Issues in Accounting Education* (Spring 1989). These steps are consistent with those provided by the American Accounting Association's Advisory Committee on Professionalism and Ethics in their publication *Ethics in the Accounting Curriculum: Cases and Readings, 1990.*

Ethical Dilemma

You recently have been employed by a large retail chain that sells sporting goods. One of your tasks is to help prepare periodic financial statements for external distribution. The chain's largest creditor, National Savings & Loan, requires quarterly financial statements, and you are currently working on the statements for the three-month period ending June 30, 2016.

During the months of May and June, the company spent $1,200,000 on a hefty radio and TV advertising campaign. The $1,200,000 included the costs of producing the commercials as well as the radio and TV time purchased to air the commercials. All of the costs were charged to advertising expense. The company's chief financial officer (CFO) has asked you to prepare a June 30 adjusting entry to remove the costs from advertising expense and to set up an asset called *prepaid advertising* that will be expensed in July. The CFO explained that "This advertising campaign has led to significant sales in May and June and I think it will continue to bring in customers through the month of July. By recording the ad costs as an asset, we can match the cost of the advertising with the additional July sales. Besides, if we expense the advertising in May and June, we will show an operating loss on our income statement for the quarter. The bank requires that we continue to show quarterly profits in order to maintain our loan in good standing."

PART B

The Conceptual Framework

● LO1–6

FINANCIAL Reporting Case

Q4, p. 3

The conceptual framework does not prescribe GAAP. It provides an underlying foundation for accounting standards.

Sturdy buildings are built on sound foundations. The U.S. Constitution is the foundation for the laws of our land. The **conceptual framework** has been described as an "Accounting Constitution" because it provides the underlying foundation for U.S. accounting standards. More formally, it is a coherent system of interrelated objectives and fundamentals that is intended to lead to consistent standards and that prescribes the nature, function, and limits of financial accounting and reporting. The fundamentals are the underlying concepts of accounting that guide the selection of events to be accounted for, the measurement of those events, and the means of summarizing and communicating them to interested parties.[33] The conceptual framework provides structure and direction to financial accounting and reporting but does not directly prescribe GAAP.

The FASB disseminates this framework through Statements of Financial Accounting Concepts *(SFACs)*. *SFAC 8* discusses the objective of financial reporting and the qualitative characteristics of useful financial information. *SFAC 7* describes how cash flows and present values are used when making accounting measurements. *SFAC 6* defines the accounts and accrual accounting concepts that appear in financial statements, and *SFAC 5* discusses recognition and measurement concepts. Earlier *SFAC*s either have been superseded or involve nonbusiness organizations that aren't considered in this text.

In the remainder of this section we discuss the components of the conceptual framework, as depicted in Illustration 1–9. The financial statements and their elements are most informative when they possess specific qualitative characteristics. Proper recognition and measurement of financial information rely on several assumptions and principles that underlie the financial reporting process.

International Financial Reporting Standards

● LO1–11

Role of the conceptual framework. The conceptual frameworks in U.S. GAAP and IFRS are very similar, and are converging even more with ongoing efforts by the FASB and IASB. However, in U.S. GAAP, the conceptual framework primarily provides guidance to

(continued)

[33]"Conceptual Framework for Financial Accounting and Reporting: Elements of Financial Statements and Their Measurement," *Discussion Memorandum* (Stamford, Conn.: FASB, 1976), p. 2.

(concluded)

standard setters to help them develop high-quality standards. In IFRS the conceptual framework guides standard setting, but in addition it provides a basis for practitioners to make accounting judgments when another IFRS standard does not apply. Also, IFRS emphasizes the overarching concept of the financial statements providing a "true and fair representation" of the company. U.S. GAAP does not include a similar requirement, but U.S. auditing standards require this consideration.

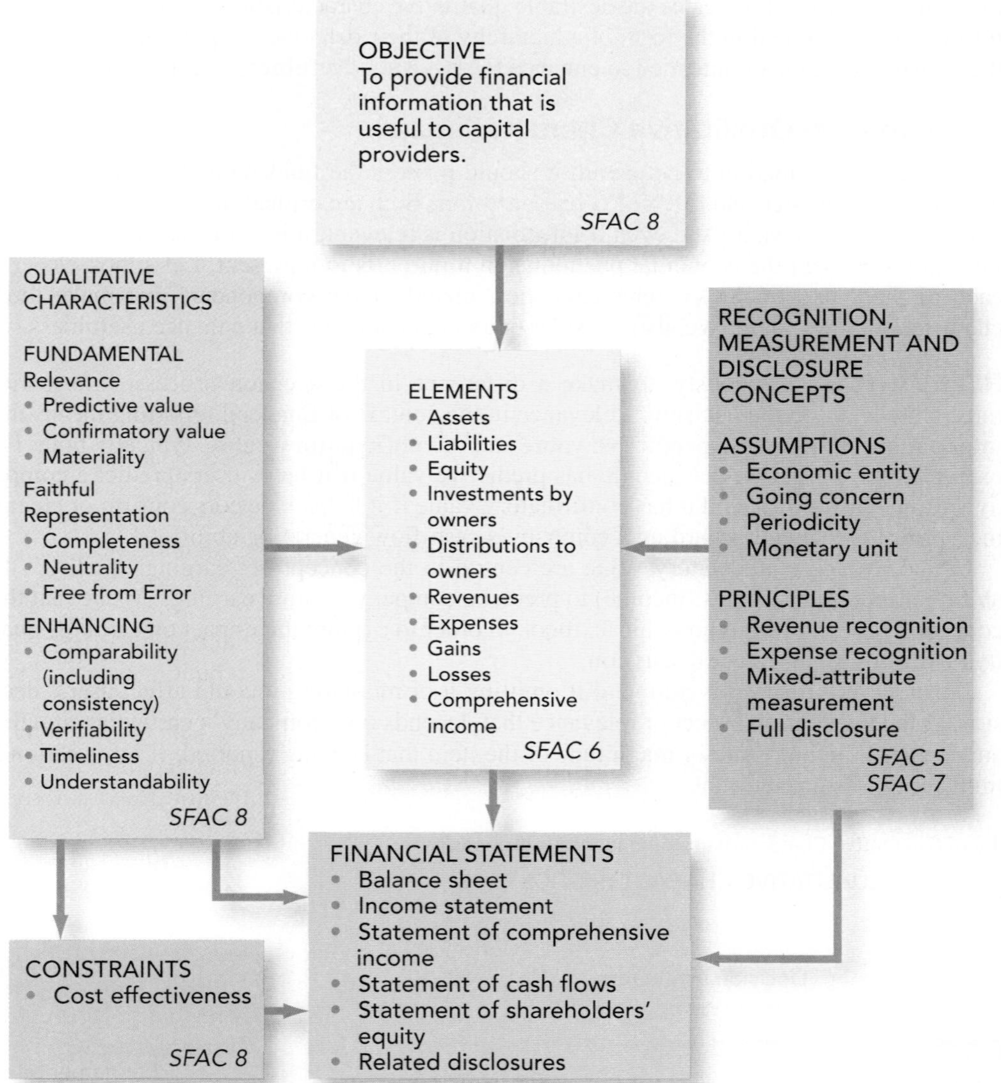

Illustration 1–9
The Conceptual Framework

Objective of Financial Reporting

● LO1–7

As indicated in Part A of this chapter, the objective of general purpose financial reporting is to provide financial information about companies that is useful to capital providers in making decisions. For example, investors decide whether to buy, sell, or hold equity or debt securities, and creditors decide whether to provide or settle loans.[34] Information that is useful to capital providers may also be useful to other users of financial reporting information, such as regulators or taxing authorities.

[34]Ibid., par. OB2.

Both investors and creditors are interested in the amount, timing, and uncertainty of a company's future cash flows. Information about a company's economic resources (assets) and claims against resources (liabilities) also is useful. Not only does this information about resources and claims provide insight into future cash flows, it also helps decision makers identify the company's financial strengths and weaknesses and assess liquidity and solvency.

Qualitative Characteristics of Financial Reporting Information

What characteristics should information have to best meet the objective of financial reporting? Illustration 1–10 indicates the desirable qualitative characteristics of financial reporting information, presented in the form of a hierarchy of their perceived importance. Notice that these characteristics are intended to enhance the **decision usefulness** of information.

Fundamental Qualitative Characteristics

To be useful for decision making, information should possess the qualities of *relevance* and *faithful representation*.

For financial information to be useful, it should possess the fundamental decision-specific qualities of **relevance** and **faithful representation**. Both are critical. Information is of little value if it's not relevant. And even if information is relevant, it is not as useful if it doesn't faithfully represent the economic phenomenon it purports to represent. Let's look closer at each of these two qualitative characteristics, including the components that make those characteristics desirable. We also consider other characteristics that enhance usefulness.

RELEVANCE. Obviously, to make a difference in the decision process, information must be relevant to the decision. Relevance in the context of financial reporting means that information must possess **predictive value** and/or **confirmatory value**, typically both. For example, current-period net income has predictive value if it helps users predict a company's future cash flows, and it has confirmatory value if it helps investors confirm or change their prior assessments regarding a company's cash-flow generating ability.

Predictive and confirmatory value are central to the concept of "earnings quality," the ability of reported earnings (income) to predict a company's future earnings. We revisit this concept frequently throughout this textbook in order to explore the impact on earnings quality of various topics under discussion.

Information is *material* if it has an effect on decisions.

Financial information is **material** if omitting it or misstating it could affect users' decisions. Materiality is an aspect of relevance that depends on a company's particular situation and is based on the nature or magnitude of the item that is being reported. If information is immaterial, it's not relevant.

Illustration 1–10 Hierarchy of Qualitative Characteristics of Financial Information

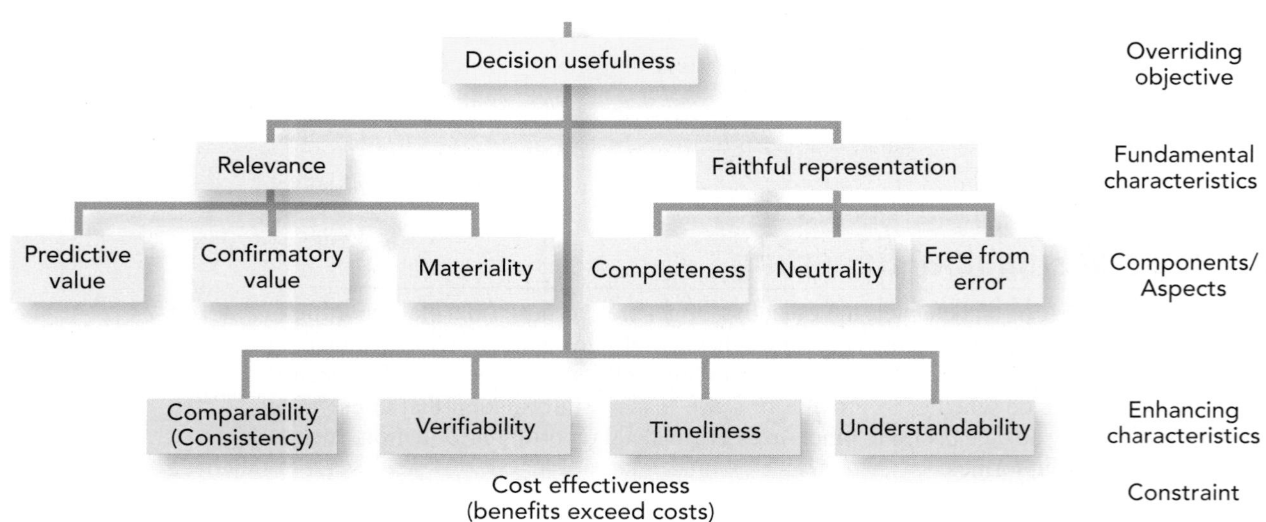

One consequence of considering materiality is that GAAP need not be followed if an item is immaterial. For example, GAAP requires that receivables be measured at their "net realizable value." If bad debts are anticipated, they should be estimated and subtracted from the face amount of receivables for balance sheet measurement, and the amount of the allowance for bad debts should be disclosed.[35] **PetSmart**'s February 2, 2014, balance sheet reports "Receivables, net" of $72,685. PetSmart's use of the term "net" implies that accounts receivable are stated at an amount reduced by an allowance for bad debts, but PetSmart does not disclose the amount of the allowance. Given that PetSmart received a "clean" audit opinion, we can infer that its auditor did not view the allowance to be material enough to require separate disclosure. Similarly, if the amount of anticipated bad debts is not considered material, it's OK to wait and just record the effects of bad debts when the receivable has gone bad rather than having to estimate bad debts for existing receivables.[36]

PetSmart

The threshold for materiality often depends on the *relative* dollar amount of the transaction. For example, $10,000 in total anticipated bad debts for a multibillion dollar company like **PetSmart** would not be considered material. This same $10,000 amount, however, might easily be material for a neighborhood pizza parlor. Because of the context-specific nature of materiality, the FASB has been reluctant to establish any quantitative materiality guidelines. The threshold for materiality has been left to the subjective judgment of the company preparing the financial statements and its auditors.

Materiality often relates to the nature of the item as well. It depends on qualitative as well as quantitative considerations. For example, an illegal payment of a $10,000 bribe to an official of a foreign government to secure a valuable contract probably would be considered material qualitatively even if the amount is small relative to the size of the company. Similarly, a small dollar amount that changes a net loss to a net income for the reporting period could be viewed as material to financial statement users for qualitative reasons.

Professional judgment determines what amount is material in each situation.

FAITHFUL REPRESENTATION. Faithful representation exists when there is agreement between a measure or description and the phenomenon it purports to represent. For example, the term *inventory* in the balance sheet of a retail company is understood by external users to represent items that are intended for sale in the ordinary course of business. If inventory includes, say, accounts receivable, it lacks faithful representation.

***Faithful representation* means agreement between a measure and a real-world phenomenon that the measure is supposed to represent.**

To break it down further, faithful representation requires that information be *complete, neutral,* and *free from error.* A depiction of an economic phenomenon is **complete** if it includes all the information necessary for faithful representation of the economic phenomenon that it purports to represent. Omitting a portion of that information can cause it to be false or misleading.

A depiction is *complete* if it includes all information necessary for faithful representation.

A financial accounting standard, and the standard-setting process, is "neutral" if it is free from bias. You learned earlier that changes in accounting standards can lead to adverse economic consequences for certain companies and that political pressure is sometimes brought to bear on the standard-setting process in hopes of achieving particular outcomes. Accounting standards should be established with the goal of providing high-quality information, and should try not to achieve particular social outcomes or favor particular groups or companies. The FASB faces a difficult task in maintaining **neutrality** in the face of economic consequences and resulting political pressures.

***Neutrality* implies freedom from bias.**

Representational faithfulness also is enhanced if information is **free from error**, meaning that there are no errors or omissions in the description of the amount or the process used to report the amount. Uncertainty is a fact of life when we measure many items of financial information included in financial statements. Estimates are common, and some inaccuracy is likely. An estimate is represented faithfully if it is described clearly and accurately as being an estimate, and financial statement users are given enough information to understand the potential for inaccuracy that exists.

Representational faithfulness is enhanced if information is *free from error*.

Many accountants have recommended that we deal with the potential for error by employing **conservatism**. Conservatism means that accountants require greater verification before recognizing good news than bad news. The result is that losses are reflected in net income more quickly than are gains, and net assets tend to be biased downwards.

***Conservatism* is inconsistent with neutrality.**

[35] This is called the *allowance method* of accounting for bad debts.

[36] This is called the *direct write-off method* of accounting for bad debts.

SFAC 8 explicitly rejects conservatism as a desirable characteristic of accounting information, stating that conservatism undermines representational faithfulness by being inconsistent with neutrality. Nevertheless, some accounting practices, such as the lower-of-cost-or-market method for measuring inventory (Chapter 9), appear to be generated by a desire to be conservative. One justification for these practices is that investors and creditors who lose money on their investments are less likely to sue the company if bad news has been exaggerated and good news underestimated. Another justification is that conservative accounting can trigger debt covenants that allow creditors to protect themselves from bad management. So, despite the lack of support for conservatism in the conceptual framework, it is likely to persist as an important consideration in accounting practice and in the application of some accounting standards.

Enhancing Qualitative Characteristics

Accounting information should be *comparable* across different companies and over different time periods.

Illustration 1–10 identifies four *enhancing* qualitative characteristics, *comparability (including consistency), verifiability, timeliness,* and *understandability.*

Accounting information is *consistent* if it is measured and reported the same way in each time period.

Comparability helps users see similarities and differences between events and conditions. We already have discussed the importance of investors and creditors being able to compare information *among companies* to make their resource allocation decisions. Closely related to comparability is the notion that **consistency** of accounting practices over time permits valid comparisons *among different reporting periods.* The predictive and confirmatory value of information is enhanced if users can compare the performance of a company over time.[37] In the **PetSmart** financial statements and disclosure notes, notice that disclosure Note 1 includes a summary of significant accounting policies. If PetSmart were to change one of these policies, new numbers might not be comparable to numbers measured under a previous policy. To be sure readers are aware of the change, PetSmart would need to provide full disclosure in the notes to the financial statements.

PetSmart

Information is *verifiable* if different measurers would reach consensus about whether it is representationally faithful.

Verifiability implies that different knowledgeable and independent measurers would reach consensus regarding whether information is a faithful representation of what it is intended to depict. Direct verification involves observing the item being depicted. For example, the historical cost of a parcel of land to be reported in a company's balance sheet usually is highly verifiable. The cost can be traced to an exchange transaction, the purchase of the land. On the other hand, the fair value of that land is much more difficult to verify. Appraisers could differ in their assessment of fair value. Verification of their estimates would be indirect, involving examination of their valuation models and assessments of the reasonableness of model inputs. The term *objectivity* often is linked to verifiability. The historical cost of the land is objective and easy to verify, but the land's fair value is subjective, and may be influenced by the measurer's past experience and biases. A measurement that is subjective is more difficult to verify, which may make users doubt its representational faithfulness.

Information is *timely* if it is available to users before a decision is made.

Timeliness also is important for information to be useful. Information is timely when it's available to users early enough to allow them to use it in their decision process. The need for timely information requires that companies provide information on a periodic basis. To enhance timeliness, the SEC requires its registrants to submit financial statement information on a quarterly as well as on an annual basis for each fiscal year.

Information is *understandable* if users can comprehend it.

Understandability means that users must be able to comprehend the information within the context of the decision being made. This is a user-specific quality because users will differ in their ability to comprehend any set of information. The overriding objective of financial reporting is to provide comprehensible information to those who have a *reasonable understanding* of business and economic activities and are diligent in studying the information.

Key Constraint: Cost Effectiveness

Information is *cost effective* only if the benefit of increased *decision usefulness* exceeds the costs of providing that information.

Most of us learn early in life that we can't get everything we want. The latest electronic gadget may have all the qualitative characteristics that current technology can provide, but limited resources may lead us to buy a model with fewer bells and whistles. **Cost effectiveness**

[37] Companies occasionally do change their accounting practices, which makes it difficult for users to make comparisons among different reporting periods. Chapter 4 and Chapter 20 describe the disclosures that a company makes in this situation to restore consistency among periods.

constrains the accounting choices we make. The benefits of endowing financial information with all the qualitative characteristics we've discussed must exceed the costs of doing so.

The costs of providing financial information include those of gathering, processing, and disseminating information. There also are costs to users when interpreting information. In addition, costs include possible adverse economic consequences of implementing accounting standards. For example, consider the requirement that companies having more than one operating segment must disclose certain disaggregated financial information.[38] In addition to the costs of information gathering, processing, and communicating that information, many companies feel that this reporting requirement imposes what could be called *competitive disadvantage costs.* These companies are concerned that their competitors will gain some advantage from having access to the disaggregated data.

The costs of providing financial information include any possible adverse economic consequences of accounting standards.

The perceived benefit from this or any accounting standard is increased *decision usefulness* of the information provided, which, ideally, improves the resource allocation process. It is inherently impossible to quantify this benefit. The elaborate information-gathering process undertaken by the FASB in setting accounting standards is an attempt to assess both costs and benefits of a proposed accounting standard, even if in a subjective, nonquantifiable manner.

Elements of Financial Statements

SFAC 6 defines 10 elements of financial statements. These elements are "the building blocks with which financial statements are constructed—the classes of items that financial statements comprise."[39] They focus directly on items related to reporting financial position and measuring performance. The *accrual accounting* model actually is embodied in the element definitions. For now, we list and define the elements in Illustration 1–11. You will learn much more about these elements in subsequent chapters.

The 10 elements of financial statements defined in *SFAC 6* describe financial position and periodic performance.

Illustration 1–11 Elements of Financial Statements

	Elements of Financial Statements
Assets	Probable future economic benefits obtained or controlled by a particular entity as a result of past transactions or events.
Liabilities	Probable future sacrifices of economic benefits arising from present obligations of a particular entity to transfer assets or provide services to other entities in the future as a result of past transactions or events.
Equity (or net assets)	Called shareholders' equity or stockholders' equity for a corporation, it is the residual interest in the assets of an entity that remains after deducting its liabilities.
Investments by owners	Increases in equity of a particular business enterprise resulting from transfers to it from other entities of something of value to obtain or increase ownership interests in it.
Distributions to owners	Decreases in equity of a particular enterprise resulting from transfers to owners.
Comprehensive income	The change in equity of a business enterprise during a period from transactions and other events and circumstances from nonowner sources. It includes all changes in equity during a period except those resulting from investments by owners and distributions to owners.
Revenues	Inflows or other enhancements of assets of an entity or settlements of its liabilities during a period from delivering or producing goods, rendering services, or other activities that constitute the entity's ongoing major or central operations.
Expenses	Outflows or other using up of assets or incurrences of liabilities during a period from delivering or producing goods, rendering services, or other activities that constitute the entity's ongoing major or central operations.
Gains	Increases in equity from peripheral or incidental transactions of an entity.
Losses	Represent decreases in equity arising from peripheral or incidental transactions of an entity.

[38]FASB ASC 280: Segment Reporting (previously "Disclosures about Segments of an Enterprise and Related Information," *Statement of Financial Accounting Standards No. 131* (Norwalk, Conn.: FASB, 1997)).

[39]"Elements of Financial Statements," *Statement of Financial Accounting Concepts No. 6* (Stamford, Conn.: FASB, 1985), par. 5.

Underlying Assumptions

LO1–8

Though not emphasized in the FASB's concepts statements, four basic assumptions underlie GAAP: (1) the economic entity assumption, (2) the going concern assumption, (3) the periodicity assumption, and (4) the monetary unit assumption. These assumptions identify the entity that is being reported on, the assumption that the entity will continue to exist, and the frequency and denomination in which reports occur.

Illustration 1–12 summaries the four assumptions underlying GAAP.

Illustration 1–12
Summary of Assumptions Underlying GAAP

Assumptions	Description
Economic entity	All economic events can be identified with a particular economic entity.
Going concern	In the absence of information to the contrary, it is anticipated that a business entity will continue to operate indefinitely.
Periodicity	The life of a company can be divided into artificial time periods to provide timely information to external users.
Monetary unit	In the United States, financial statement elements should be measured in terms of the U.S. dollar.

Economic Entity Assumption

The *economic entity assumption* presumes that economic events can be identified specifically with an economic entity.

An essential assumption is that all economic events can be identified with a particular economic entity. Investors desire information about an economic entity that corresponds to their ownership interest. For example, if you were considering buying some ownership stock in Google, you would want information on the various operating units that constitute Google. You would need information not only about its United States operations but also about its European and other international operations. The financial information for the various companies (subsidiaries) in which Google owns a controlling interest (greater than 50% ownership of voting stock) should be combined with that of Google (the parent) to provide a complete picture. The parent and its subsidiaries are separate *legal* entities but one *accounting* entity.

Another key aspect of this assumption is the distinction between the economic activities of owners and those of the company. For example, the economic activities of a sole proprietorship, Uncle Jim's Restaurant, should be separated from the activities of its owner, Uncle Jim. Uncle Jim's personal residence, for instance, is not an asset of the business.

Going Concern Assumption

Financial statements of a company presume the business is a *going concern*.

Another necessary assumption is that, in the absence of information to the contrary, we anticipate that a business entity will continue to operate indefinitely. Accountants realize that the going concern assumption does not always hold since there certainly are many business failures. However, this assumption is critical to many broad and specific accounting principles. For example, the assumption provides justification for measuring many assets based on their historical costs. If it were known that an enterprise would cease operations in the near future, assets and liabilities would be measured at their current liquidation values. Similarly, when we depreciate a building over an estimated life of 40 years, we assume the business will operate that long.

Periodicity Assumption

The *periodicity assumption* allows the life of a company to be divided into artificial time periods to provide timely information.

The periodicity assumption relates to the qualitative characteristic of *timeliness.* External users need *periodic* information to make decisions. This need for periodic information requires that the economic life of a company (presumed to be indefinite) be divided into artificial time periods for financial reporting. Corporations whose securities are publicly traded are required to provide financial information to the SEC on a quarterly and annual basis.[40] Financial statements often are prepared on a monthly basis for banks and others that might need more timely information.

For many companies, the annual time period (the fiscal year) is the calendar year. However, other companies have chosen a fiscal year that does not correspond to the calendar year. The accounting profession and the SEC advocate that companies adopt a fiscal year that corresponds to their natural business year. A natural business year is the 12-month period that ends when the business activities of a company reach their lowest point in the annual cycle. For example, many retailers, **Walmart** for example, have adopted a fiscal year ending on January 31. Business activity in January generally is quite slow following the very busy Christmas period. We can see from the **PetSmart** financial statements that the company's fiscal year ends at the end of January. The **Campbell Soup Company**'s fiscal year ends in July; **Clorox**'s in June; and **Monsanto**'s in August.

PetSmart

Monetary Unit Assumption

The **monetary unit** or measurement scale used in financial statements is nominal units of money, without any adjustment for changes in purchasing power. In the United States, the U.S. dollar is the monetary unit used in financial statements. In the EU, the euro is the monetary unit. Other countries use other currencies as their monetary units.

The *monetary unit assumption* states that financial statement elements should be measured in a particular monetary unit (in the United States, the U.S. dollar).

One problem with use of a monetary unit like the dollar or the euro is that it is presumed to be stable over time. That is, the value of the dollar, in terms of its ability to purchase certain goods and services, is assumed to be constant over time. This assumption obviously does not strictly hold. The U.S. economy has experienced periods of rapidly changing prices. To the extent that prices are unstable, and machines, trucks, and buildings were purchased at different times, the monetary unit used to measure them is not the same. The effect of changing prices on financial information generally is discussed elsewhere in your accounting curriculum, often in an advanced accounting course.

Recognition, Measurement, and Disclosure Concepts

● LO1–9

Now that we have identified the various elements and underlying assumptions of the financial statements, we discuss *when* the elements should be recognized (recorded) and how they should be *measured* and *disclosed.* For example, an asset was previously defined as a probable future economic benefit obtained or controlled by a company as a result of past transactions or events. But *when* should the asset be recorded, at *what* amount, and what other important information about the asset should be provided in the financial statements? *SFAC 5* addresses these issues. **Recognition** refers to the process of admitting information into the financial statements. **Measurement** is the process of associating numerical amounts with the elements. **Disclosure** refers to the process of including additional pertinent information in the financial statements and accompanying notes.

Recognition

GENERAL RECOGNITION CRITERIA. According to *SFAC 5,* an item should be recognized in the basic financial statements when it meets the following four criteria, subject to a cost effectiveness constraint and materiality threshold:

Recognition criteria

1. *Definition.* The item meets the definition of an element of financial statements.
2. *Measurability.* The item has a relevant attribute measurable with sufficient reliability.
3. *Relevance.* The information about it is capable of making a difference in user decisions.
4. *Reliability.* The information is representationally faithful, verifiable, and neutral.[41]

[40]The report that must be filed for the first three quarters of each fiscal year is Form 10-Q and the annual report is Form 10-K.

[41]"Recognition and Measurement in Financial Statements," *Statement of Financial Accounting Concepts No. 5* (Stamford, Conn.: FASB, 1984), par. 63. *SFAC 8* has replaced reliability with faithful representation as the second primary qualitative characteristic of financial information.

These obviously are very general guidelines. *SFAC 5* provides further guidance with respect to revenue and expense recognition, and you will learn about more specific guidelines throughout this book.

REVENUE RECOGNITION. Revenues are inflows of assets or settlements of liabilities resulting from providing a product or service to a customer. An income statement should report the results of these activities only for the time period specified in the financial statements. Therefore, the *timing* of revenue recognition is a key element of earnings measurement. Not adhering to revenue recognition criteria could result in overstating revenue and hence net income in one reporting period and, consequently, understating revenue and net income in another period.

Until recently, revenue recognition was guided by the *realization principle*, which requires that two criteria be satisfied before revenue can be recognized:

1. The earnings process is judged to be complete or virtually complete.
2. There is reasonable certainty as to the collectibility of the asset to be received (usually cash).

As discussed further in Chapter 5, the FASB recently issued ASU No. 2014-09, which changes how we determine the timing and measurement of revenue.[42] That standard requires that companies recognize revenue when goods or services are transferred to customers for the amount the company expects to be entitled to receive in exchange for those goods or services. Revenue is recognized at a point in time or over a period of time, depending on when goods or services are transferred to customers. For example, revenue for the sale of most goods is recognized upon delivery, but revenue for services like renting apartments or lending money is recognized over time as those services are provided. No revenue is recognized if it isn't probable that the seller will collect the amounts it's entitled to receive. While that standard doesn't rely on the realization principle, you can see that aspects of the realization principle remain—we still focus on the seller fulfilling its obligations to its customers, and before revenue can be recognized we still require a relatively high likelihood that the seller will be paid.

Notice that these criteria help implement the accrual accounting model. Revenue is recognized when the seller transfers goods and services to a customer, which isn't necessarily at the same time the seller is paid.

The timing of revenue recognition also affects the timing of asset recognition. When revenue is recognized by crediting a revenue account, the corresponding debit typically increases some asset, usually cash or an account receivable.

EXPENSE RECOGNITION. Expenses were defined earlier in the chapter as "outflows or other using up of assets or incurrences of liabilities." When are expenses recognized? In practice, expense recognition often matches revenues and expenses that arise from the same transactions or other events.[43] There is a cause-and-effect relationship between revenue and expense recognition implicit in this approach. The net result is a measure—net income—that identifies the amount of profit or loss for the period provided by operations.

Although these concepts are straightforward, their implementation can be difficult, because many expenses are not incurred *directly* to produce a particular amount of revenue. Instead, the association between revenue and many expenses is indirect. Therefore, expense recognition is implemented by one of four different approaches, depending on the nature of the specific expense:[44]

- **Based on an exact cause-and-effect relationship**. This approach is appropriate for *cost of goods sold,* as one example. There is a definite cause-and-effect relationship between

[42] "Revenue from Contracts with Customers (Topic 606)" *Accounting Standards Update 2014-09* (Norwalk, Conn: FASB, 2014).

[43] The term *matching principle* is sometimes used to refer to the practice of first recognizing revenue and then recognizing all expenses that were incurred to generate that revenue. However, the conceptual framework does not include that term. Rather, *SFACs 5* and *6* discuss matching as a result of recognizing expenses and revenues that arise from the same underlying transactions or events. Standard setters are reluctant to apply matching more broadly, because they are concerned that doing so could result in inappropriately recognizing as assets some amounts that do not provide "probable future economic benefits," and therefore don't meet the definition of an asset. We discuss this topic more in the "Evolving GAAP" section at the end of this chapter.

[44] "Elements of Financial Statements—a replacement of FASB Concepts Statement No. 3 (incorporating an amendment of FASB Concepts Statement No. 2)" *Statement of Financial Accounting Concepts No. 6* (Norwalk, Conn.: FASB, 1985).

PetSmart's revenue from selling dog food and its costs to purchase that dog food from suppliers. Commissions paid to salespersons for obtaining revenues also is an example of an expense recognized based on this approach.

- **By associating an expense with the revenues recognized in a specific time period.** Many expenses can be related only to periods of time during which revenue is earned. For example, the monthly salary paid to an office worker is not directly related to any specific revenue event. Instead, the employee provides benefits to the company for that one month that *indirectly* relate to the revenue recognized in that same period.
- **By a systematic and rational allocation to specific time periods.** Some costs are incurred to acquire assets that provide benefits to the company for more than one reporting period, so we recognize expenses over those time periods. For example, straight-line depreciation is a "systematical and rational" way to allocate the cost of equipment to the periods in which that equipment is used to produce revenue.
- **In the period incurred, without regard to related revenues.** Sometimes costs are incurred, but it is impossible to determine in which period or periods, if any, related revenues will occur. For example, let's say Google spends $1 million for a series of television commercials. It's difficult to determine when, how much, or even whether additional revenues occur as a result of that particular series of ads. As a result, we recognize advertising expenditures as expenses in the period incurred.

The timing of expense recognition also affects the timing of asset and liability recognition and de-recognition. When we debit an expense, the corresponding credit usually either decreases an asset (for example, decreasing cash because it was used to pay an employee's salary) or increases a liability (for example, increasing salaries payable to accrue wages that will be paid at a later date).

Measurement

If an amount is to be recognized, it also must be measured. As indicated in *SFAC 5,* GAAP currently employs a "mixed attribute" measurement model. If you look at a balance sheet, for instance, you might see land measured at historical cost, accounts receivable at net realizable value, a liability at the present value of cash payments, and an investment at fair value. The attribute chosen to measure a particular item should be the one that maximizes the combination of relevance and representational faithfulness. *SFAC 5* lists five measurement attributes employed in GAAP:

1. Historical cost
2. Net realizable value
3. Current cost
4. Present (or discounted) value of future cash flows
5. Fair value

These different measurement attributes often indicate the same amount, particularly when the amount is initially recognized. However, sometimes they differ in important ways.

Historical cost **bases measurements on the amount given or received in the exchange transaction.**

HISTORICAL COST. We often measure assets and liabilities based on their *original transaction value,* that is, their *historical cost.* Some accountants refer to this practice as applying the *historical cost principle.* For an asset, historical cost equals the value of what is given in exchange (usually cash) for the asset at its initial acquisition. For liabilities, it is the current cash equivalent received in exchange for assuming the liability. Historical cost for long-lived, revenue-producing assets such as equipment typically is adjusted subsequent to its initial measurement by recognizing depreciation or amortization.

Why base measurement on historical costs? First, historical cost provides important cash flow information as it represents the cash or cash equivalent paid for an asset or received in exchange for the assumption of a liability. Second, because historical cost valuation is the result of an exchange transaction between two independent parties, the agreed-upon exchange value is objective and highly verifiable.

Net realizable value **bases measurements on the amount of cash into which the asset or liability will be converted in the ordinary course of business.**

NET REALIZABLE VALUE. Some assets are measured at their *net realizable value,* which is the amount of cash into which an asset is expected to be converted in the ordinary course of business. For example, if customers purchased goods or services on account for $10,000, and if $2,000 in bad debts were anticipated, net receivables should be valued at $8,000, the net realizable value. Departures from historical cost measurement such as this provide useful information to aid in the prediction of future cash flows.

CURRENT COST. Companies sometimes report current costs, particularly if they operate in inflationary economies. The current cost of an asset is the cost that would be incurred to purchase or reproduce the asset.

Present value **bases measurement on future cash flows discounted for the time value of money.**

PRESENT VALUE. Because of its importance to many accounting measurements, *present value* is the focus of an FASB concept statement, *SFAC 7,* which provides a framework for using future cash flows as the basis for accounting measurement and also asserts that the objective in valuing an asset or liability using present value is to approximate its fair value.[45] We explore the topic of present value in more depth in Chapter 6 and the application of present value in accounting measurement in subsequent chapters.

FAIR VALUE. We measure many financial assets and liabilities at *fair value* (called *current market value* originally in *SFAC 5*). Also, we use fair values when determining whether the value of nonfinancial assets like property, plant, equipment and intangible assets has been impaired. Given the complexity and growing importance of this measurement attribute, we discuss it in some detail.

Fair value **bases measurements on the price that would be received to sell assets or transfer liabilities in an orderly market transaction.**

Fair value is defined as the price that would be received to sell assets or paid to transfer a liability in an orderly transaction between market participants at the measurement date. A key aspect of this definition is its focus on the perspective of *market participants.* For instance, if a company buys a competitor's patent, not intending to use it but merely to keep the competitor from using it, the company still will have to assign a value to the asset because a market participant would find value in using the patent.

Fair value can be measured using:
1. Market approaches.
2. Income approaches.
3. Cost approaches.

The FASB has provided a framework for measuring fair value whenever fair value is called for in applying generally accepted accounting principles.[46] The IASB recently converged to use the same framework.[47] In the framework, three types of valuation techniques can be used to measure fair value. *Market approaches* base valuation on market information. For example, the value of a share of a company's stock that's not traded actively could be estimated by multiplying the earnings of that company by the P/E (price of shares/earnings) multiples of similar companies. *Income approaches* estimate fair value by first estimating future amounts (for example, earnings or cash flows) and then mathematically converting those amounts to a single present value. You will see how to apply such techniques in Chapter 6 when we discuss time value of money concepts. *Cost approaches* determine value by estimating the amount that would be required to buy or construct an asset of similar quality and condition. A firm can use one or more of these valuation approaches, depending on availability of information, and should try to use them consistently unless changes in circumstances require a change in approach.

To increase consistency and comparability in applying this definition, the framework provides a "hierarchy" that prioritizes the inputs companies should use when determining fair value. The priority is based on three broad preference levels. The higher the level (Level 1 is the highest), the more preferable the input. The framework encourages companies to strive to obtain the highest level input available for each situation. Illustration 1–13 describes the type of inputs and provides an example for each level.

[45]"Using Cash Flow Information and Present Value in Accounting Measurements," *Statement of Financial Accounting Concepts No. 7* (Norwalk, Conn.: FASB, 2000).

[46]FASB ASC 820: Fair Value Measurements and Disclosures (previously "Fair Value Measurements," *Statement of Financial Accounting Standards No. 157* (Norwalk, Conn.: FASB, 2006)).

[47]"Fair Value Measurement," *International Financial Reporting Standard No. 13* (London, UK: IASCF, 2011).

Illustration 1–13 Fair Value Hierarchy

Fair Value Hierarchy

Level	Inputs	Example
1 **Most Desirable**	Quoted market prices in active markets for identical assets or liabilities.	In Chapter 12 you will learn that certain investments in marketable securities are reported at their *fair values*. Fair value in this case would be measured using the quoted market price from the NYSE, NASDAQ, or other exchange on which the security is traded.
2	Inputs other than quoted prices that are *observable* for the asset or liability. These inputs include quoted prices for *similar* assets or liabilities in active or inactive markets and inputs that are derived principally from or corroborated by observable related market data.	In Chapter 10 we discuss how companies sometimes acquire assets with consideration other than cash. In any noncash transaction, each element of the transaction is recorded at its *fair value*. If one of the assets in the exchange is a building, for instance, then quoted market prices for similar buildings recently sold could be used to value the building or, if there were no similar buildings recently exchanged from which to obtain a comparable market price, valuation could be based on the price per square foot derived from observable market data.
3 **Least Desirable**	*Unobservable* inputs that reflect the entity's own assumptions about the assumptions market participants would use in pricing the asset or liability developed based on the best information available in the circumstances.	Asset retirement obligations (AROs), discussed in Chapter 10, are measured at *fair value*. Neither Level 1 nor Level 2 inputs would be possible in most ARO valuation situations. Fair value would be estimated using Level 3 inputs to include the present value of expected cash flows estimated using the entity's own data if there is no information that indicates that market participants would use different assumptions.

Companies also must provide detailed disclosures about their use of fair value measurements. The disclosures include a description of the inputs used to measure fair value. For recurring fair value measurements that rely on significant *unobservable* inputs (within Level 3 of the fair value hierarchy), companies should disclose the effect of the measurements on earnings (or changes in net assets) for the period.

You are not yet familiar with some of the examples mentioned in Illustration 1–13, but as you progress through the book you will encounter many instances in which we use fair value for valuation purposes. Refer back to this discussion and speculate on the level of input that would be available to a company in these situations. When a company has the option to measure financial assets or liabilities at fair value (discussed next), we address the choices available to the company in those situations.

The use of the fair value measurement attribute is increasing, both under U.S GAAP and IFRS. This trend, though, is controversial. Proponents of fair value cite its relevance and are convinced that historical cost information may not be useful for many types of decisions. Opponents of fair value counter that estimates of fair value may lack representational faithfulness, particularly when based on inputs from Level 3 in the fair value hierarchy, and that managers might be tempted to exploit the unverifiability of such inputs to manipulate earnings. They argue that accounting should emphasize verifiability by recognizing only those gains and other increases in fair value that actually have been realized in transactions or are virtually certain to exist.

FAIR VALUE OPTION. Usually the measurement attribute we use for a particular financial statement item is not subject to choice. However, GAAP gives a company the option to report some *financial* assets and liabilities at fair value.[48] For example, in Chapter 14 you

GAAP **gives a company the option to value financial assets and liabilities at fair value.**

[48]FASB ASC 825–10–25–1: Financial Instruments—Overall—Recognition—Fair Value Option (previously "The Fair Value Option for Financial Assets and Financial Liabilities," *Statement of Financial Accounting Standards No. 159* (Norwalk, Conn.: FASB, 2007)).

will learn that a company normally would report bonds payable at historical cost (adjusted for unamortized premium or discount), but the fair value option allows that company to choose instead to report the bonds payable at fair value. If a company chooses the fair value option, future changes in fair value are reported as gains and losses in the income statement.

Why allow the fair value option for financial assets and liabilities, and not for, say, buildings or land? Financial assets and liabilities are cash and other assets and liabilities that convert directly into known amounts of cash. These include investments in stocks and bonds of other entities, notes receivable and payable, bonds payable, and derivative securities.[49] Some of these financial assets and liabilities currently are *required* under GAAP to be reported at fair value, and others are not, leading to some potential inconsistencies in how similar or related items are treated. The fair value option provides companies a way to reduce volatility in reported earnings without having to comply with complex hedge accounting standards. It also helps in the convergence with international accounting standards we discussed earlier in the chapter as the IASB also has adopted a fair value option for financial instruments.

We will revisit the fair value option in subsequent chapters that address the key financial assets and liabilities that now can be measured at fair value. You'll find it easier to understand the concepts introduced in this chapter in the context of the financial assets and liabilities affected: investments (Chapter 12) and bonds payable (Chapter 14).[50]

Disclosure

Remember, the purpose of accounting is to provide information that is useful to decision makers. So, naturally, if there is accounting information not included in the primary financial statements that would benefit users, that information should be provided too. The **full-disclosure principle** means that the financial reports should include any information that could affect the decisions made by external users. Of course, the benefits of that information, as noted earlier, should exceed the costs of providing the information. Such information is disclosed in a variety of ways, including:

The *full-disclosure principle* requires that any information useful to decision makers be provided in the financial statements, subject to the cost effectiveness constraint.

1. **Parenthetical comments** or **modifying comments** placed on the face of the financial statements.
2. **Disclosure notes** conveying additional insights about company operations, accounting principles, contractual agreements, and pending litigation.
3. **Supplemental schedules and tables** that report more detailed information than is shown in the primary financial statements.

PetSmart

We find examples of these disclosures in the **PetSmart** financial statements in Appendix B located at the back of the text. We discuss and illustrate disclosure requirements as they relate to specific financial statement elements in later chapters as those elements are discussed.

Illustration 1–14 provides an overview of key recognition, measurement and disclosure concepts.

Where We're Headed

"Disclosure overload" is a frequent complaint by companies and investors alike. The notes to the financial statements can be very useful, but they are costly for companies to prepare and difficult for many users to sift through and understand. In response to that concern, the FASB has been developing a framework intended to make disclosures more effective and less redundant.

(continued)

[49]The fair value option does not apply to certain specified financial instruments, including pension obligations and assets or liabilities arising from leases.

[50]As discussed in further detail in the Addendum to Chapter 12, the overhaul of accounting for financial instruments being completed by the FASB and IASB includes removal of the fair value option.

(concluded)

As part of that project, in March 2014 the FASB issued an exposure draft of a proposed addition to Concepts Statement No. 8, titled *Chapter 8: Notes to Financial Statements.*[51] The exposure draft describes three types of information that should be included in the notes to financial statements:

1. General information about the nature of the company, its activities, and any special advantages it enjoys or restrictions it faces.
2. Additional information that explains or amplifies financial statement line items.
3. Information about past events and current circumstances that might affect the company's future cash flows but don't yet appear in the financial statements.

The exposure draft also suggests a series of questions that the FASB and its staff should consider when determining what notes should be required by new standards. A separate part of the project will develop further guidance to help companies apply judgment when meeting disclosure requirements.

Illustration 1–14

Summary of Recognition, Measurement, and Disclosure Concepts

Concept	**Description**
Recognition	General criteria: 1. Meets the definition of an element 2. Has a measurement attribute 3. Is relevant 4. Is reliable (representationally faithful) Examples of recognition timing: 1. Revenues 2. Expenses
Measurement	Mixed attribute model in which the attribute used to measure an item is chosen to maximize relevance and representational faithfulness. These attributes include: 1. Historical cost 2. Net realizable value 3. Current cost 4. Present (or discounted) value of future cash flows 5. Fair value
Disclosure	Financial reports should include all information that could affect the decisions made by external users. Examples of disclosures: 1. Parenthetical amounts 2. Notes to the financial statements 3. Supplemental schedules and tables

Evolving GAAP

Earlier in this chapter you learned that the convergence of accounting standards with international standards is having a profound effect on financial reporting in the United States. More broadly, U.S. and international GAAP have been evolving over time from an emphasis on revenues and expenses to an emphasis on assets and liabilities. Of course, you know from introductory accounting that the balance sheet and income statement are intertwined and must reconcile with each other. For example, the revenues reported in the income statement depict inflows of assets whose balances at a particular point in time are reported in the balance sheet. But which comes first, identifying revenues and expenses, or identifying

[51] *Proposed Statement of Financial Accounting Concepts: Chapter 8: Notes to Financial Statements* (Norwalk, Conn: FASB, March 4, 2014).

assets and liabilities? That emphasis can affect accounting standards in important ways. To help you understand the changes taking place, we start by discussing the revenue/expense approach and then discuss the asset/liability approach.

● LO1–10

With the *revenue/expense approach*, recognition and measurement of revenues and expenses are emphasized.

With the *asset/liability approach*, recognition and measurement of assets and liabilities drives revenue and expense recognition.

Under the **revenue/expense approach**, we emphasize principles for recognizing revenues and expenses, with some assets and liabilities recognized as necessary to make the balance sheet reconcile with the income statement. For example, when accounting for a sales transaction our focus would be on whether revenue has been earned, and if we determine that to be the case, we would record an asset (usually cash or accounts receivable) that is associated with the revenue.[52] We would identify the expenses necessary to earn that revenue, and then would adjust assets and liabilities accordingly.

Under the **asset/liability approach**, on the other hand, we first recognize and measure the assets and liabilities that exist at a balance sheet date and, secondly, recognize and measure the revenues, expenses, gains and losses needed to account for the changes in these assets and liabilities from the previous measurement date. Proponents of this approach point out that, since revenues and expenses are defined in terms of inflows and outflows of assets and liabilities, the fundamental concepts underlying accounting are assets and liabilities. Therefore, we should try to recognize and measure assets and liabilities appropriately, and as a result will also capture their inflows and outflows in a manner that provides relevant and representationally faithful information about revenues and expenses.

For example, when accounting for a sales transaction, our focus would be on whether a potential accounts receivable meets the definition of an asset (a probable future economic benefit). We would consider such factors as whether the receivable is supported by an enforceable contract and whether the seller has performed its obligations enough to be able to expect receipt of cash flows. The key would be determining if the seller has an asset, and then recognizing whatever amount of revenue is implied by the inflow of that asset. Also, we would not attempt to match expenses to revenues. Rather, we would determine those net assets that had decreased as part of operations during the period, and recognize those decreases as expenses. In subsequent chapters you will see that recent standards involving accounting for revenue, investments, and income taxes follow this asset/liability approach.

These changes are controversial. It may seem like it shouldn't matter whether standard setters use the revenue/expense or asset/liability approach, given that both approaches affect both the income statement and balance sheet, and it is true that these approaches often will result in the same accounting outcomes. For example, whether matching is a principle used to determine when expenses are recognized, or a result of recognizing that assets were consumed as part of the economic activity that occurred in a particular period in which revenue was also recognized, we typically still will see expenses recognized in the periods in which they are incurred to produce revenues. However, the particular approach used by a standard setter can affect recognition and measurement in important ways. In particular, the asset/liability approach encourages us to focus on accurately measuring assets and liabilities. It perhaps is not surprising, then, that a focus on assets and liabilities has led standard setters to lean more and more toward fair value measurement. The future changes to the conceptual framework discussed in the following Where We're Headed box are likely to continue this emphasis on the asset/liability approach.

Where We're Headed

The FASB and IASB worked together to issue *SFAC 8* in 2010 and had planned to revisit concepts related to financial statement elements, recognition, measurement, and the reporting entity. But, progress stalled as the Boards focused on other projects. Starting in 2012, the IASB pursued an independent conceptual framework project, and the FASB plans to do so as well.

[52]Some assets and liabilities aren't related to revenue or expense. For example, issuance of shares of stock increases cash as well as shareholders' equity. The treatment of these sorts of transactions is not affected by whether GAAP emphasizes revenues and expenses or assets and liabilities.

Financial Reporting Case Solution

1. **What should you tell your friend about the presence of accounting standards in the United States? Who has the authority for standard setting? Who has the responsibility?** *(p. 8)* In the United States we have a set of standards known as generally accepted accounting principles (GAAP). GAAP is a dynamic set of both broad and specific guidelines that companies should follow when measuring and reporting the information in their financial statements and related notes. The Securities and Exchange Commission has the authority to set accounting standards for companies whose securities are publicly traded but always has delegated the primary responsibility to the accounting profession. At present, the Financial Accounting Standards Board is the private sector body responsible for standard setting.
2. **What is the economic and political environment in which standard setting occurs?** *(p. 13)* The setting of accounting and reporting standards often has been characterized as a *political process.* Standards, particularly changes in standards, can have significant differential effects on companies, investors and creditors, and other interest groups. A change in an accounting standard or the introduction of a new standard can result in a substantial redistribution of wealth within our economy. The FASB's due process is designed to obtain information from all interested parties to help determine the appropriate accounting approach, but standards are supposed to be neutral with respect to the interests of various parties. Nonetheless, both the FASB and IASB sometimes come under political pressure that sways the results of the standard-setting process.
3. **What is the relationship among management, auditors, investors, and creditors that tends to preclude the "What would you like it to be?" attitude?** *(p. 16)* It is the responsibility of management to apply accounting standards when communicating with investors and creditors through financial statements. Auditors serve as independent intermediaries to help ensure that the management-prepared statements are presented fairly in accordance with GAAP. In providing this assurance, the auditor precludes the "What would you like it to be?" attitude.
4. **In general, what is the conceptual framework that underlies accounting principles?** *(p. 20)* The conceptual framework is a coherent system of interrelated objectives and fundamentals that can lead to consistent standards and that prescribe the nature, function, and limits of financial accounting and reporting. The fundamentals are the underlying concepts of accounting, concepts that guide the selection of events to be accounted for, the measurement of those events, and the means of summarizing and communicating them to interested parties. ●

The Bottom Line

- **LO1–1** Financial accounting is concerned with providing relevant financial information to various external users. However, the primary focus is on the financial information provided by profit-oriented companies to their present and potential investors and creditors. (*p. 4*)
- **LO1–2** Cash basis accounting provides a measure of periodic performance called *net operating cash flow,* which is the difference between cash receipts and cash disbursements from transactions related to providing goods and services to customers. Accrual accounting provides a measure of performance called *net income,* which is the difference between revenues and expenses. Periodic net income is considered a better indicator of future operating cash flows than is current net operating cash flows. (*p. 6*)
- **LO1–3** Generally accepted accounting principles (GAAP) comprise a dynamic set of both broad and specific guidelines that companies follow when measuring and reporting the information in their financial statements and related notes. The Securities and Exchange Commission (SEC) has the authority to set accounting standards in the United States. However, the SEC has always delegated the task to a private sector body, at this time the Financial Accounting Standards Board (FASB). The International Accounting

Standards Board (IASB) sets global accounting standards and works with national accounting standard setters to achieve convergence in accounting standards around the world. *(p. 8)*

- **LO1–4** Accounting standards can have significant differential effects on companies, investors, creditors, and other interest groups. Various interested parties sometimes lobby standard setters for their preferred outcomes. For this reason, the setting of accounting standards often has been characterized as a political process. *(p. 13)*
- **LO1–5** Factors encouraging high-quality financial reporting include conceptually based financial accounting standards, external auditors, financial reporting reforms (such as the Sarbanes-Oxley Act), ethical management, and professional accounting organizations that prescribe ethical conduct and license practitioners. *(p. 16)*
- **LO1–6** The FASB's conceptual framework is a set of cohesive objectives and fundamental concepts on which financial accounting and reporting standards can be based. *(p. 20)*
- **LO1–7** The objective of financial reporting is to provide useful financial information to capital providers. The primary decision-specific qualities that make financial information useful are relevance and faithful representation. To be relevant, information must possess predictive value and/or confirmatory value, and all material information should be included. Completeness, neutrality, and freedom from error enhance faithful representation. The 10 elements of financial statements are assets, liabilities, equity, investments by owners, distributions to owners, revenues, expenses, gains, losses, and comprehensive income. *(p. 21)*
- **LO1–8** The four basic assumptions underlying GAAP are (1) the economic entity assumption, (2) the going concern assumption, (3) the periodicity assumption, and (4) the monetary unit assumption. *(p. 26)*
- **LO1–9** Recognition determines whether an item is reflected in the financial statements, and measurement determines the amount of the item. Measurement involves choice of a monetary unit and choice of a measurement attribute. In the United States, the monetary unit is the dollar. Various measurement attributes are used in GAAP, including historical cost, net realizable value, present value, and fair value. *(p. 27)*
- **LO1–10** A revenue/expense approach to financial reporting emphasizes recognition and measurement of revenues and expenses, while an asset/liability approach emphasizes recognition and measurement of assets and liabilities. *(p. 34)*
- **LO1–11** IFRS and U.S. GAAP are similar in the organizations that support standard setting and in the presence of ongoing political pressures on the standard-setting process. U.S. GAAP and IFRS also have similar conceptual frameworks, although the role of the conceptual framework in IFRS is to provide guidance to preparers as well as to standard setters, while the role of the conceptual framework in U.S. GAAP is more to provide guidance to standard setters. *(pp. 15 and 20)*

Questions For Review of Key Topics

Q 1–1 What is the function and primary focus of financial accounting?

Q 1–2 What is meant by the phrase *efficient allocation of resources?* What mechanism fosters the efficient allocation of resources in the United States?

Q 1–3 Identify two important variables to be considered when making an investment decision.

Q 1–4 What must a company do in the long run to be able to provide a return to investors and creditors?

Q 1–5 What is the primary objective of financial accounting?

Q 1–6 Define net operating cash flows. Briefly explain why periodic net operating cash flows may not be a good indicator of future operating cash flows.

Q 1–7 What is meant by GAAP? Why should all companies follow GAAP in reporting to external users?

Q 1–8 Explain the roles of the SEC and the FASB in the setting of accounting standards.

Q 1–9 Explain the role of the auditor in the financial reporting process.

Q 1–10 List three key provisions of the Sarbanes-Oxley Act of 2002. Order your list from most important to least important in terms of the likely long-term impact on the accounting profession and financial reporting.

Q 1–11 Explain what is meant by *adverse economic consequences* of new or changed accounting standards.

Q 1–12 Why does the FASB undertake a series of elaborate information-gathering steps before issuing a substantive accounting standard?

Q 1–13 What is the purpose of the FASB's conceptual framework?

Q 1–14 Discuss the terms *relevance* and *faithful representation* as they relate to financial accounting information.

Q 1–15 What are the components of relevant information? What are the components of faithful representation?

Q 1–16 Explain what is meant by: The benefits of accounting information must exceed the costs.

Q 1–17 What is meant by the term *materiality* in financial reporting?

Q 1–18 Briefly define the financial accounting elements: (1) assets, (2) liabilities, (3) equity, (4) investments by owners, (5) distributions to owners, (6) revenues, (7) expenses, (8) gains, (9) losses, and (10) comprehensive income.

Q 1–19 What are the four basic assumptions underlying GAAP?

Q 1–20 What is the going concern assumption?

Q 1–21 Explain the periodicity assumption.

Q 1–22 What are four key accounting practices that often are referred to as principles in current GAAP?

Q 1–23 What are two advantages to basing the valuation of assets and liabilities on their historical cost?

Q 1–24 Describe how revenue recognition relates to transferring goods and services.

Q 1–25 What are the four different approaches to implementing expense recognition? Give an example of an expense that is recognized under each approach.

Q 1–26 In addition to the financial statement elements arrayed in the basic financial statements, what are some other ways to disclose financial information to external users?

Q 1–27 Briefly describe the inputs that companies should use when determining fair value. Organize your answer according to preference levels, from highest to lowest priority.

Q 1–28 What measurement attributes are commonly used in financial reporting?

Q 1–29 Distinguish between the revenue/expense and the asset/liability approaches to setting financial reporting standards.

IFRS **Q 1–30** What are the functions of the conceptual framework under IFRS?

IFRS **Q 1–31** What is the standard-setting body responsible for determining IFRS? How does it obtain its funding?

IFRS **Q 1–32** In its Final Staff Report (issued in 2012), what type of convergence between U.S. GAAP and IFRS did the SEC staff argue was not feasible? What reasons did the SEC staff give for that conclusion?

Brief Exercises

BE 1–1
Accrual accounting
● LO1–2

Cash flows during the first year of operations for the Harman-Kardon Consulting Company were as follows: Cash collected from customers, $340,000; Cash paid for rent, $40,000; Cash paid to employees for services rendered during the year, $120,000; Cash paid for utilities, $50,000.

In addition, you determine that customers owed the company $60,000 at the end of the year and no bad debts were anticipated. Also, the company owed the gas and electric company $2,000 at year-end, and the rent payment was for a two-year period. Calculate accrual net income for the year.

BE 1–2
Financial statement elements
● LO1–7

For each of the following items, identify the appropriate financial statement element or elements: (1) probable future sacrifices of economic benefits; (2) probable future economic benefits owned by the company; (3) inflows of assets from ongoing, major activities; (4) decrease in equity from peripheral or incidental transactions.

BE 1–3
Basic assumptions and principles
● LO1–7 through LO1–9

Listed below are several statements that relate to financial accounting and reporting. Identify the accounting concept that applies to each statement.

1. **Sirius Satellite Radio Inc.** files its annual and quarterly financial statements with the SEC.
2. The president of **Applebee's International, Inc.**, travels on the corporate jet for business purposes only and does not use the jet for personal use.
3. Jackson Manufacturing does not recognize revenue for unshipped merchandise even though the merchandise has been manufactured according to customer specifications.
4. Lady Jane Cosmetics depreciates the cost of equipment over their useful lives.

BE 1–4
Basic assumptions and principles
● LO1–7 through LO1–9

Identify the accounting concept that was violated in each of the following situations.

1. Astro Turf Company recognizes an expense, cost of goods sold, in the period the product is manufactured.
2. McCloud Drug Company owns a patent that it purchased three years ago for $2 million. The controller recently revalued the patent to its approximate market value of $8 million.
3. Philips Company pays the monthly mortgage on the home of its president, Larry Crosswhite, and charges the expenditure to miscellaneous expense.

BE 1–5
Basic assumptions and principles
● LO1–7 through LO1–9

For each of the following situations, (1) indicate whether you agree or disagree with the financial reporting practice employed and (2) state the accounting concept that is applied (if you agree), or violated (if you disagree).

1. Winderl Corporation did not disclose that it was the defendant in a material lawsuit because the trial was still in progress.
2. Alliant Semiconductor Corporation files quarterly and annual financial statements with the SEC.
3. Reliant Pharmaceutical paid rent on its office building for the next two years and charged the entire expenditure to rent expense.
4. Rockville Engineering records revenue only after products have been shipped, even though customers pay Rockville 50% of the sales price in advance.

BE 1–6
IFRS
● LO1–11

IFRS

Indicate the organization related to IFRS that performs each of the following functions:

1. Obtains funding for the IFRS standard-setting process.
2. Determines IFRS.
3. Encourages cooperation among securities regulators to promote effective and efficient capital markets.
4. Provides input about the standard-setting agenda.
5. Provides implementation guidance about relatively narrow issues.

Exercises

An alternate exercise and problem set is available in the Connect library.

E 1–1
Accrual accounting
● LO1–2

Listed below are several transactions that took place during the first two years of operations for the law firm of Pete, Pete, and Roy.

	Year 1	Year 2
Amounts billed to customers for services rendered	$170,000	$220,000
Cash collected from customers	160,000	190,000
Cash disbursements		
Salaries paid to employees for services rendered during the year	90,000	100,000
Utilities	30,000	40,000
Purchase of insurance policy	60,000	–0–

In addition, you learn that the company incurred utility costs of $35,000 in year 1, that there were no liabilities at the end of year 2, no anticipated bad debts on receivables, and that the insurance policy covers a three-year period.

Required:

1. Calculate the net operating cash flow for years 1 and 2.
2. Prepare an income statement for each year similar to Illustration 1–3 on page 8 according to the accrual accounting model.
3. Determine the amount of receivables from customers that the company would show in its year 1 and year 2 balance sheets prepared according to the accrual accounting model.

E 1–2
Accrual accounting
● LO1–2

Listed below are several transactions that took place during the second and third years of operations for RPG Consulting.

	Year 2	Year 3
Amounts billed to customers for services rendered	$350,000	$450,000
Cash collected from credit customers	260,000	400,000
Cash disbursements:		
Payment of rent	80,000	–0–
Salaries paid to employees for services rendered during the year	140,000	160,000
Travel and entertainment	30,000	40,000
Advertising	15,000	35,000

In addition, you learn that the company incurred advertising costs of $25,000 in year 2, owed the advertising agency $5,000 at the end of year 1, and there were no liabilities at the end of year 3. Also, there were no anticipated bad debts on receivables, and the rent payment was for a two-year period, year 2 and year 3.

Required:
1. Calculate accrual net income for both years.
2. Determine the amount due the advertising agency that would be shown as a liability on RPG's balance sheet at the end of year 2.

E 1–3
FASB codification research
● LO1–3

Access the *FASB Accounting Standards Codification* at the FASB website (asc.fasb.org).

Required:
1. Identify the Codification topic number that provides guidance on fair value measurements.
2. What is the specific citation that lists the disclosures required in the notes to the financial statements for each major category of assets and liabilities measured at fair value?
3. List the disclosure requirements.

E 1–4
FASB codification research
● LO1–3

Access the *FASB Accounting Standards Codification* at the FASB website (asc.fasb.org). Determine the specific citation for each of the following items:
1. The topic number for business combinations.
2. The topic number for related party disclosures.
3. The topic, subtopic, and section number for the initial measurement of internal-use software.
4. The topic, subtopic, and section number for the subsequent measurement of asset retirement obligations.
5. The topic, subtopic, and section number for the recognition of stock compensation.

E 1–5
Participants in establishing GAAP
● LO1–3

Three groups that participate in the process of establishing GAAP are users, preparers, and auditors. These groups are represented by various organizations. For each organization listed below, indicate which of these groups it primarily represents.
1. Securities and Exchange Commission
2. Financial Executives International
3. American Institute of Certified Public Accountants
4. Institute of Management Accountants
5. Association of Investment Management and Research

E 1–6
Financial statement elements
● LO1–7

For each of the items listed below, identify the appropriate financial statement element or elements.
1. Obligation to transfer cash or other resources as a result of a past transaction.
2. Dividends paid by a corporation to its shareholders.
3. Inflow of an asset from providing a good or service.
4. The financial position of a company.
5. Increase in equity during a period from nonowner transactions.
6. Increase in equity from peripheral or incidental transaction.
7. Sale of an asset used in the operations of a business for less than the asset's book value.
8. The owners' residual interest in the assets of a company.
9. An item owned by the company representing probable future benefits.
10. Revenues plus gains less expenses and losses.
11. An owner's contribution of cash to a corporation in exchange for ownership shares of stock.
12. Outflow of an asset related to the production of revenue.

E 1–7
Concepts; terminology; conceptual framework
● LO1–7

Listed below are several terms and phrases associated with the FASB's conceptual framework. Pair each item from List A (by letter) with the item from List B that is most appropriately associated with it.

	List A	List B
____	1. Predictive value	a. Decreases in equity resulting from transfers to owners.
____	2. Relevance	b. Requires consideration of the costs and value of information.
____	3. Timeliness	c. Important for making interfirm comparisons.
____	4. Distribution to owners	d. Applying the same accounting practices over time.

(continued)

(concluded)

List A	List B
____ 5. Confirmatory value	e. Users understand the information in the context of the decision being made.
____ 6. Understandability	f. Agreement between a measure and the phenomenon it purports to represent.
____ 7. Gain	g. Information is available prior to the decision.
____ 8. Faithful representation	h. Pertinent to the decision at hand.
____ 9. Comprehensive income	i. Implies consensus among different measurers.
____ 10. Materiality	j. Information confirms expectations.
____ 11. Comparability	k. The change in equity from nonowner transactions.
____ 12. Neutrality	l. The process of admitting information into financial statements.
____ 13. Recognition	m. The absence of bias.
____ 14. Consistency	n. Results if an asset is sold for more than its book value.
____ 15. Cost effectiveness	o. Information is useful in predicting the future.
____ 16. Verifiability	p. Concerns the relative size of an item and its effect on decisions.

E 1–8
Qualitative characteristics
● LO1–7

The conceptual framework indicates the desired fundamental and enhancing qualitative characteristics of accounting information. Several constraints impede achieving these desired characteristics. Answer each of the following questions related to these characteristics and constraints.

1. Which component would allow a large company to record the purchase of a $120 printer as an expense rather than capitalizing the printer as an asset?
2. Donald Kirk, former chairman of the FASB, once noted that ". . . there must be public confidence that the standard-setting system is credible, that selection of board members is based on merit and not the influence of special interests . . ." Which characteristic is implicit in Mr. Kirk's statement?
3. Allied Appliances, Inc., changed its revenue recognition policies. Which characteristic is jeopardized by this change?
4. National Bancorp, a publicly traded company, files quarterly and annual financial statements with the SEC. Which characteristic is relevant to the timing of these periodic filings?
5. In general, relevant information possesses which qualities?
6. When there is agreement between a measure or description and the phenomenon it purports to represent, information possesses which characteristic?
7. Jeff Brown is evaluating two companies for future investment potential. Jeff's task is made easier because both companies use the same accounting methods when preparing their financial statements. Which characteristic does the information Jeff will be using possess?
8. A company should disclose information only if the perceived benefits of the disclosure exceed the costs of providing the information. Which constraint does this statement describe?

E 1–9
Basic assumptions, principles, and constraints
● LO1–7 through LO1–9

Listed below are several terms and phrases associated with the accounting concepts. Pair each item from List A (by letter) with the item from List B that is most appropriately associated with it.

List A	List B
____ 1. Expense recognition	a. The enterprise is separate from its owners and other entities.
____ 2. Periodicity	b. A common denominator is the dollar.
____ 3. Historical cost principle	c. The entity will continue indefinitely.
____ 4. Materiality	d. Record expenses in the period the related revenue is recognized.
____ 5. Revenue recognition	e. The original transaction value upon acquisition.
____ 6. Going concern assumption	f. All information that could affect decisions should be reported.
____ 7. Monetary unit assumption	g. The life of an enterprise can be divided into artificial time periods.
____ 8. Economic entity assumption	h. Criteria usually satisfied for products at point of sale.
____ 9. Full-disclosure principle	i. Concerns the relative size of an item and its effect on decisions.

E 1–10
Basic assumptions and principles
● LO1–7 through LO1–9

Listed below are several statements that relate to financial accounting and reporting. Identify the accounting concept that applies to each statement.

1. Jim Marley is the sole owner of Marley's Appliances. Jim borrowed $100,000 to buy a new home to be used as his personal residence. This liability was not recorded in the records of Marley's Appliances.
2. **Apple Inc.** distributes an annual report to its shareholders.
3. **Hewlett-Packard Corporation** depreciates machinery and equipment over their useful lives.
4. Crosby Company lists land on its balance sheet at $120,000, its original purchase price, even though the land has a current fair value of $200,000.

5. **Honeywell Corporation** records revenue when products are delivered to customers, even though the cash has not yet been received.
6. Liquidation values are not normally reported in financial statements even though many companies do go out of business.
7. **IBM Corporation**, a multibillion dollar company, purchased some small tools at a cost of $800. Even though the tools will be used for a number of years, the company recorded the purchase as an expense.

E 1–11
Basic assumptions and principles
● LO1–8, LO1–9

Identify the accounting concept that was violated in each of the following situations.

1. Pastel Paint Company purchased land two years ago at a price of $250,000. Because the value of the land has appreciated to $400,000, the company has valued the land at $400,000 in its most recent balance sheet.
2. Atwell Corporation has not prepared financial statements for external users for over three years.
3. The Klingon Company sells farm machinery. Revenue from a large order of machinery from a new buyer was recorded the day the order was received.
4. Don Smith is the sole owner of a company called Hardware City. The company recently paid a $150 utility bill for Smith's personal residence and recorded a $150 expense.
5. Golden Book Company purchased a large printing machine for $1,000,000 (a material amount) and recorded the purchase as an expense.
6. Ace Appliance Company is involved in a major lawsuit involving injuries sustained by some of its employees in the manufacturing plant. The company is being sued for $2,000,000, a material amount, and is not insured. The suit was not disclosed in the most recent financial statements because no settlement had been reached.

E 1–12
Basic assumptions and principles
● LO1–7 through LO1–9

For each of the following situations, indicate whether you agree or disagree with the financial reporting practice employed and state the accounting concept that is applied (if you agree) or violated (if you disagree).

1. Wagner Corporation adjusted the valuation of all assets and liabilities to reflect changes in the purchasing power of the dollar.
2. Spooner Oil Company changed its method of accounting for oil and gas exploration costs from successful efforts to full cost. No mention of the change was included in the financial statements. The change had a material effect on Spooner's financial statements.
3. Cypress Manufacturing Company purchased machinery having a five-year life. The cost of the machinery is being expensed over the life of the machinery.
4. Rudeen Corporation purchased equipment for $180,000 at a liquidation sale of a competitor. Because the equipment was worth $230,000, Rudeen valued the equipment in its subsequent balance sheet at $230,000.
5. Davis Bicycle Company received a large order for the sale of 1,000 bicycles at $100 each. The customer paid Davis the entire amount of $100,000 on March 15. However, Davis did not record any revenue until April 17, the date the bicycles were delivered to the customer.
6. Gigantic Corporation purchased two small calculators at a cost of $32.00. The cost of the calculators was expensed even though they had a three-year estimated useful life.
7. Esquire Company provides financial statements to external users every three years.

E 1–13
Basic assumptions and principles
● LO1–7 through LO1–9

For each of the following situations, state whether you agree or disagree with the financial reporting practice employed, and briefly explain the reason for your answer.

1. The controller of the Dumars Corporation increased the carrying value of land from its original cost of $2 million to its recently appraised value of $3.5 million.
2. The president of Vosburgh Industries asked the company controller to charge miscellaneous expense for the purchase of an automobile to be used solely for personal use.
3. At the end of its 2016 fiscal year, Dower, Inc., received an order from a customer for $45,350. The merchandise will ship early in 2017. Because the sale was made to a long-time customer, the controller recorded the sale in 2016.
4. At the beginning of its 2016 fiscal year, Rossi Imports paid $48,000 for a two-year lease on warehouse space. Rossi recorded the expenditure as an asset to be expensed equally over the two-year period of the lease.
5. The Reliable Tire Company included a note in its financial statements that described a pending lawsuit against the company.

6. The Hughes Corporation, a company whose securities are publicly traded, prepares monthly, quarterly, and annual financial statements for internal use but disseminates to external users only the annual financial statements.

E 1–14
Basic assumptions and principles
● LO1–7 through LO1–9

Listed below are accounting concepts discussed in this chapter.

a. Economic entity assumption
b. Going concern assumption
c. Periodicity assumption
d. Monetary unit assumption
e. Historical cost principle
f. Conservatism
g. Matching
h. Full-disclosure principle
i. Cost effectiveness
j. Materiality

Identify by letter the accounting concept that relates to each statement or phrase below.

_____ 1. Inflation causes a violation of this assumption.
_____ 2. Information that could affect decision making should be reported.
_____ 3. Recognizing expenses in the period they were incurred to produce revenue.
_____ 4. The basis for measurement of many assets and liabilities.
_____ 5. Relates to the qualitative characteristic of timeliness.
_____ 6. All economic events can be identified with a particular entity.
_____ 7. The benefits of providing accounting information should exceed the cost of doing so.
_____ 8. A consequence is that GAAP need not be followed in all situations.
_____ 9. Not a qualitative characteristic, but a practical justification for some accounting choices.
_____10. Assumes the entity will continue indefinitely.

E 1–15
Multiple choice; concept statements, basic assumptions, principles
● LO1–6 through LO1–9

Determine the response that best completes the following statements or questions.

1. The primary objective of financial reporting is to provide information
   a. About a firm's management team.
   b. Useful to capital providers.
   c. Concerning the changes in financial position resulting from the income-producing efforts of the entity.
   d. About a firm's financing and investing activities.

2. *Statements of Financial Accounting Concepts* issued by the FASB
   a. Represent GAAP.
   b. Have been superseded by *SFAS*s.
   c. Are subject to approval of the SEC.
   d. Identify the conceptual framework within which accounting standards are developed.

3. In general, revenue is recognized when
   a. The sales price has been collected.
   b. A purchase order has been received.
   c. A good or service has been delivered to a customer.
   d. A contract has been signed.

4. In depreciating the cost of an asset, accountants are most concerned with
   a. Conservatism.
   b. Recognizing revenue in the appropriate period.
   c. Full disclosure.
   d. Recognizing expense in the appropriate period.

5. The primary objective of the matching principle is to
   a. Provide full disclosure.
   b. Record expenses in the period that related revenues are recognized.
   c. Provide timely information to decision makers.
   d. Promote comparability between financial statements of different periods.

6. The separate entity assumption states that, in the absence of contrary evidence, all entities will survive indefinitely.
   a. True
   b. False

CPA and CMA Exam Questions

CPA Exam Questions

KAPLAN CPA REVIEW

The following questions are adapted from a variety of sources including questions developed by the AICPA Board of Examiners and those used in the Kaplan CPA Review Course to study the environment and theoretical structure of financial accounting while preparing for the CPA examination. Determine the response that best completes the statements or questions.

● LO1–7

1. Which of the following is *not* a qualitative characteristic of accounting information according to the FASB's conceptual framework?
   a. Auditor independence.
   b. Neutrality.
   c. Timeliness.
   d. Predictive value.

● LO1–7

2. According to the conceptual framework, neutrality is a characteristic of
   a. Understandability.
   b. Faithful representation.
   c. Relevance.
   d. Both relevance and faithful representation.

● LO1–3

3. The Financial Accounting Standards Board (FASB)
   a. Is a division of the Securities and Exchange Commission (SEC).
   b. Is a private body that helps set accounting standards in the United States.
   c. Is responsible for setting auditing standards that all auditors must follow.
   d. Consists entirely of members of the American Institute of Certified Public Accountants.

● LO1–7

4. Confirmatory value is an ingredient of the primary quality of

	Relevance	Faithful Representation
a.	Yes	No
b.	No	Yes
c.	Yes	Yes
d.	No	No

● LO1–7

5. Predictive value is an ingredient of

	Faithful Representation	Relevance
a.	Yes	No
b.	No	No
c.	Yes	Yes
d.	No	Yes

● LO1–7

6. Completeness is an ingredient of the primary quality of
   a. Verifiability.
   b. Faithful representation.
   c. Relevance.
   d. Understandability.

● LO1–1

7. The objective of financial reporting for business enterprises is based on
   a. Generally accepted accounting principles.
   b. The needs of the users of the information.
   c. The need for conservatism.
   d. None of above.

● LO1–7

8. According to the FASB's conceptual framework, comprehensive income includes which of the following?

	Operating Income	Investments by Owners
a.	No	Yes
b.	No	No
c.	Yes	Yes
d.	Yes	No

are International Financial Reporting Standards tested on the CPA exam along with U.S. GAAP. The following questions deal with the application of IFRS.

● LO1–11
IFRS

9. The equivalent to the FASB's Financial Accounting Standards Advisory Council (FASAC) for the IASB is:
   a. International Financial Reporting Interpretations Committee (IFRIC).
   b. International Organization of Securities Commissions (IOSCO).
   c. International Financial Accounting Advisory Council (IFAAC).
   d. Standards Advisory Council (SAC).

● LO1–11
IFRS

10. Which of the following is not a function of the IASB's conceptual framework?
   a. The conceptual framework provides guidance to standard setters to help them develop high quality standards.
   b. The conceptual framework provides guidance to practitioners when individual standards to not apply.
   c. The conceptual framework includes specific implementation guidance to enable consistent application of particular complex standards.
   d. The conceptual framework emphasizes a "true and fair representation" of the company.

CMA Exam Questions

The following questions dealing with the environment and theoretical structure of financial accounting are adapted from questions that previously appeared on Certified Management Accountant (CMA) examinations. The CMA designation sponsored by the Institute of Management Accountants (www.imanet.org) provides members with an objective measure of knowledge and competence in the field of management accounting. Determine the response that best completes the statements or questions.

● LO1–3

1. Accounting standard setting in the United States is
   a. Done primarily by the Securities and Exchange Commission.
   b. Done primarily by the private sector.
   c. The responsibility of the public sector.
   d. Done primarily by the International Accounting Standards Committee.

● LO1–7

2. Verifiability as used in accounting includes
   a. Determining the revenue first, then determining the costs incurred in earning that revenue.
   b. The entity's giving the same treatment to comparable transactions from period to period.
   c. Similar results being obtained by both the accountant and an independent party using the same measurement methods.
   d. The disclosure of all facts that may influence the judgment of an informed reader.

● LO1–7

3. Recognition is the process of formally recording and reporting an item in the financial statements. In order for a revenue item to be recognized, it must be all of the following except
   a. Measurable.
   b. Relevant.
   c. Material.
   d. Realized or realizable.

Broaden Your Perspective

Apply your critical-thinking ability to the knowledge you've gained. These cases will provide you an opportunity to develop your research, analysis, judgment, and communication skills. You will also work with other students, integrate what you've learned, apply it in real-world situations, and consider its global and ethical ramifications. This practice will broaden your knowledge and further develop your decision-making abilities.

Judgment Case 1–1
The development of accounting standards
● LO1–3

In 1934, Congress created the Securities and Exchange Commission (SEC) and gave the commission both the power and responsibility for setting accounting and reporting standards in the United States.

Required:

1. Explain the relationship between the SEC and the various private sector standard-setting bodies that have, over time, been delegated the responsibility for setting accounting standards.
2. Can you think of any reasons why the SEC has delegated this responsibility rather than set standards directly?

Research Case 1–2
Accessing SEC information through the Internet
● LO1–3

Internet access to the World Wide Web has provided a wealth of information accessible with our personal computers. Many chapters in this text contain Real World Cases that require you to access the web to research an accounting issue. The purpose of this case is to introduce you to the Internet home page of the Securities and Exchange Commission (SEC) and its EDGAR database.

Required:

1. Access the SEC home page on the Internet. The web address is www.sec.gov.
2. Choose the subaddress "About the SEC." What are the two basic objectives of the 1933 Securities Act?
3. Return to the SEC home page and access EDGAR. Describe the contents of the database.

Research Case 1–3
Accessing FASB information through the Internet
● LO1–4

The purpose of this case is to introduce you to the information available on the website of the Financial Accounting Standards Board (FASB).

Required:

Access the FASB home page on the Internet. The web address is www.fasb.org. Answer the following questions.

1. Describe the mission of the FASB.
2. Who are the current Board members of the FASB? Briefly describe their backgrounds.
3. How are topics added to the FASB's technical agenda?

Research Case 1–4
Accessing IASB information through the Internet
● LO1–3

The purpose of this case is to introduce you to the information available on the website of the International Accounting Standards Board (IASB).

Required:

Access the IASB home page on the Internet. The web address is www.iasb.org. Answer the following questions.

1. Describe the mission of the IASB.
2. The IASB has how many board members?
3. Who is the current chairman of the IASB?
4. Where is the IASB located?

Research Case 1–5
Accounting standards in China
● LO1–3, LO1–4

Economic reforms in the People's Republic of China are moving that nation toward a market-driven economy. China's accounting practices must also change to accommodate the needs of potential investors. In an article entitled "Institutional Factors Influencing China's Accounting Reforms and Standards," Professor Bing Xiang analyzes the changes in the accounting environment of China during the recent economic reforms and their implications for the development of accounting reforms.

Required:

1. In your library or from some other source, locate the indicated article in *Accounting Horizons,* June 1998.
2. Briefly describe the economic reforms that led to the need for increased external financial reporting in China.
3. Conformity with International Accounting Standards was specified as an overriding objective in formulating China's accounting standards. What is the author's opinion of this objective?

Communication Case 1–6
Relevance and reliability
● LO1–7

Some theorists contend that companies that create pollution should report the social cost of that pollution in income statements. They argue that such companies are indirectly subsidized as the cost of pollution is borne by society while only production costs (and perhaps minimal pollution fines) are shown in the income statement. Thus, the product sells for less than would be necessary if all costs were included.

Assume that the FASB is considering a standard to include the social costs of pollution in the income statement. The process would require considering both relevance and faithful representation of the information produced by the new standard. Your instructor will divide the class into two to six groups depending on the size of the class. The mission of your group is to explain how the concepts of relevance and faithful representation relate to this issue.

Required:

Each group member should consider the question independently and draft a tentative answer prior to the class session for which the case is assigned.

In class, each group will meet for 10 to 15 minutes in different areas of the classroom. During that meeting, group members will take turns sharing their suggestions for the purpose of arriving at a single group treatment.

After the allotted time, a spokesperson for each group (selected during the group meetings) will share the group's solution with the class. The goal of the class is to incorporate the views of each group into a consensus answer to the question.

Communication Case 1–7
Accounting standard setting
● LO1–4

One of your friends is a financial analyst for a major stock brokerage firm. Recently she indicated to you that she had read an article in a weekly business magazine that alluded to the political process of establishing accounting standards. She had always assumed that accounting standards were established by determining the approach that conceptually best reflected the economics of a transaction.

Required:

Write a one to two-page article for a business journal explaining what is meant by the political process for establishing accounting standards. Be sure to include in your article a discussion of the need for the FASB to balance accounting considerations and economic consequences.

Ethics Case 1–8
The auditors' responsibility
● LO1–4

It is the responsibility of management to apply accounting standards when communicating with investors and creditors through financial statements. Another group, auditors, serves as an independent intermediary to help ensure that management has in fact appropriately applied GAAP in preparing the company's financial statements. Auditors examine (audit) financial statements to express a professional, independent opinion. The opinion reflects the auditors' assessment of the statements' fairness, which is determined by the extent to which they are prepared in compliance with GAAP.

Some feel that it is impossible for an auditor to give an independent opinion on a company's financial statements because the auditors' fees for performing the audit are paid by the company. In addition to the audit fee, quite often the auditor performs other services for the company such as preparing the company's income tax returns.

Required:

How might an auditor's ethics be challenged while performing an audit?

Judgment Case 1–9
Qualitative characteristics
● LO1–7

Generally accepted accounting principles do not require companies to disclose forecasts of any financial variables to external users. A friend, who is a finance major, is puzzled by this and asks you to explain why such relevant information is not provided to investors and creditors to help them predict future cash flows.

Required:

Explain to your friend why this information is not routinely provided to investors and creditors.

Judgment Case 1–10
GAAP, comparability, and the role of the auditor
● LO1–4, LO1–7

Mary McQuire is trying to decide how to invest her money. A friend recommended that she buy the stock of one of two corporations and suggested that she should compare the financial statements of the two companies before making a decision.

Required:

1. Do you agree that Mary will be able to compare the financial statements of the two companies?
2. What role does the auditor play in ensuring comparability of financial statements between companies?

Judgment Case 1–11
Cost effectiveness
● LO1–7

Concepts Statement 8 includes a discussion of the cost effectiveness constraint. Assume that the FASB is considering revising an important accounting standard.

Required:

1. What is the desired benefit from revising an accounting standard?
2. What are some of the possible costs that could result from a revision of an accounting standard?
3. What does the FASB do in order to assess possible benefits and costs of a proposed revision of an accounting standard?

Judgment Case 1–12
Revenue recognition
● LO1–9

A new client, the Wolf Company, asks your advice concerning the point in time that the company should recognize revenue from the rental of its office buildings. Renters usually pay rent on a quarterly basis at the beginning of the quarter. The owners contend that the critical event that motivates revenue recognition should be the date the cash is received from renters. After all, the money is in hand and is very seldom returned.

Required:

Do you agree or disagree with the position of the owners of Wolf Company? Support your answer.

Analysis Case 1–13
Expense recognition
● LO1–9

Revenues measure the accomplishments of a company during the period. Expenses are then matched with revenues to produce a periodic measure of performance called *net income.*

Required:

1. Explain what is meant by the phrase *matched with revenues.*
2. Describe the four approaches used to implement the matching principle and label them 1 through 4.
3. For each of the following, identify which matching approach should be used to recognize the cost as expense.
   a. The cost of producing a product.
   b. The cost of advertising.
   c. The cost of monthly rent on the office building.
   d. The salary of an office employee.
   e. Depreciation on an office building.

Judgment Case 1–14
Capitalize or expense?
● LO1–9

When a company makes an expenditure that is neither a payment to a creditor nor a distribution to an owner, management must decide if the expenditure should be capitalized (recorded as an increase in an asset) or expensed (recorded as an expense thereby decreasing owners' equity).

Required:

1. Which factor or factors should the company consider when making this decision?
2. Are there any constraints that could cause the company to alter its decision?

Real World Case 1–15
Elements; disclosures; The Gap Inc.
● LO1–7, LO1–9

Real World Financials

Selected financial statements from a recent annual report of **The Gap Inc.** follow. Use these statements to answer the following questions.

Required:

1. What amounts did The Gap report for the following items for the fiscal year ended February 1, 2014?
   a. Total net revenues
   b. Total operating expenses
   c. Net income (earnings)
   d. Total assets
   e. Total stockholders' equity
2. How many shares of common stock did The Gap have issued on February 1, 2014?
3. Why do you think The Gap reports more than one year of data in its financial statements?

THE GAP, INC.
Consolidated Balance Sheets

($ and shares in millions except par value)	February 1, 2014	February 2, 2013
Assets		
Current assets:		
Cash and cash equivalents	$ 1,510	$ 1,460
Short-term investments	—	50
Merchandise inventory	1,928	1,758
Other current assets	992	864
Total current assets	4,430	4,132
Property and equipment, net	2,758	2,619
Other long-term assets	661	719
Total assets	$ 7,849	$ 7,470
Liabilities and Stockholders' Equity		
Current liabilities:		
Current maturities of debt	$ 25	$ —
Accounts payable	1,242	1,144
Accrued expenses and other current liabilities	1,142	1,092
Income taxes payable	36	108
Total current liabilities	2,445	2,344
Long-term liabilities:		
Long-term debt	1,369	1,246
Lease incentives and other long-term liabilities	973	986
Total long-term liabilities	2,342	2,232
Commitments and contingencies (see Notes 11 and 15)		
Stockholders' equity:		
Common stock $0.05 par value		
Authorized 2,300 shares and Issued 1,106 shares for all periods presented; Outstanding 463 and 485 shares	55	55
Additional paid-in capital	2,899	2,864
Retained earnings	14,218	13,259
Accumulated other comprehensive income	135	181
Treasury stock at cost (643 and 621 shares)	(14,245)	(13,465)
Total stockholders' equity	3,062	2,894
Total liabilities and stockholders' equity	$ 7,849	$ 7,470

THE GAP, INC.
Consolidated Statements of Income

	For the Fiscal Year Ended		
($ and shares in millions except par value)	**February 1, 2014**	**February 2, 2013**	**January 28, 2012**
Net sales	$16,148	$15,651	$14,549
Cost of goods sold and occupancy expenses	9,855	9,480	9,275
Gross profit	6,293	6,171	5,274
Operating expenses	4,144	4,229	3,836
Operating income	2,149	1,942	1,438
Interest expense (reversal)	61	87	74
Interest income	(5)	(6)	(5)
Income before income taxes	2,093	1,861	1,369
Income taxes	813	726	536
Net income	$ 1,280	$ 1,135	$ 833
Weighted-average number of shares—basic	461	482	529
Weighted-average number of shares—diluted	467	488	533
Earnings per share—basic	$ 2.78	$ 2.35	$ 1.57
Earnings per share—diluted	$ 2.74	$ 2.33	$ 1.56

Judgment Case 1–16
Convergence
● LO1–11

Consider the question of whether the United States should converge accounting standards with IFRS.

Required:

1. Make a list of arguments that favor convergence.
2. Make a list of arguments that favor nonconvergence.
3. Indicate your own conclusion regarding whether the United States should converge with IFRS, and indicate the primary considerations that determined your conclusion.

Air France–KLM Case

● LO1–11

Air France–KLM (AF), a Franco-Dutch company, prepares its financial statements according to International Financial Reporting Standards. AF's financial statements and disclosure notes for the year ended December 31, 2013, are provided with all new textbooks. This material also is available at **http://www.airfranceklm-finance.com**.

Required:

1. What amounts did AF report for the following items for the year ended December 31, 2013?
   a. Total revenues
   b. Income from current operations
   c. Net income or net loss (AF equity holders)
   d. Total assets
   e. Total equity
2. What was AF's basic earnings or loss per share for the year ended December 31, 2013?
3. Examine Note 4.1.1 of AF's annual report. What accounting principles were used to prepare AF's financial statements? Under those accounting principles, could AF's financial information differ from that of a company that exactly followed IFRS as published by the IASB? Explain.

CHAPTER

2

Review of the Accounting Process

OVERVIEW

Chapter 1 explained that the primary means of conveying financial information to investors, creditors, and other external users is through financial statements and related notes. The purpose of this chapter is to review the fundamental accounting process used to produce the financial statements. This review establishes a framework for the study of the concepts covered in intermediate accounting.

Actual accounting systems differ significantly from company to company. This chapter focuses on the many features that tend to be common to any accounting system.

LEARNING OBJECTIVES

After studying this chapter, you should be able to:

- **LO2–1** Analyze routine economic events—transactions—and record their effects on a company's financial position using the accounting equation format. *(p. 52)*
- **LO2–2** Record transactions using the general journal format. *(p. 56)*
- **LO2–3** Post the effects of journal entries to general ledger accounts and prepare an unadjusted trial balance. *(p. 63)*
- **LO2–4** Identify and describe the different types of adjusting journal entries. *(p. 66)*
- **LO2–5** Record adjusting journal entries in general journal format, post entries, and prepare an adjusted trial balance. *(p. 67)*
- **LO2–6** Describe the four basic financial statements. *(p. 75)*
- **LO2–7** Explain the closing process. *(p. 79)*
- **LO2–8** Convert from cash basis net income to accrual basis net income. *(p. 83)*

FINANCIAL REPORTING CASE

Engineering Profits

After graduating from college last year, two of your engineering-major friends started an Internet consulting practice. They began operations on July 1 and felt they did quite well during their first year. Now they would like to borrow $20,000 from a local bank to buy new computing equipment and office furniture. To support their loan application, the friends presented the bank with the following income statement for their first year of operations ending June 30:

Consulting revenue		$96,000
Operating expenses:		
Salaries	$32,000	
Rent	9,000	
Supplies	4,800	
Utilities	3,000	
Advertising	1,200	(50,000)
Net income		$46,000

The bank officer noticed that there was no depreciation expense in the income statement and has asked your friends to revise the statement after making year-end adjustments. After agreeing to help, you discover the following information:

a. The friends paid $80,000 for equipment when they began operations. They think the equipment will be useful for five years.

b. They pay $500 a month to rent office space. In January, they paid a full year's rent in advance. This is included in the $9,000 rent expense.

c. Included in consulting revenue is $13,000 they received from a customer in June as a deposit for work to be performed in August.

QUESTIONS

By the time you finish this chapter, you should be able to respond appropriately to the questions posed in this case. Compare your response to the solution provided at the end of the chapter.

1. What purpose do adjusting entries serve? (*p. 67*)
2. What year-end adjustments are needed to revise the income statement? Did your friends do as well their first year as they thought? (*p. 67*)

A solid foundation is vital to a sound understanding of intermediate accounting. So, we review the fundamental accounting process here to serve as a framework for the new concepts you will learn in this course.

Chapter 1 introduced the theoretical structure of financial accounting and the environment within which it operates. The primary function of financial accounting—to provide financial information to external users that possesses the fundamental decision-specific qualities of relevance and faithful representation—is accomplished by periodically disseminating financial statements and related notes. In this chapter we review the *process* used to identify, analyze, record, summarize, and then report the economic events affecting a company's financial position.

Keep in mind as you study this chapter that the accounting information systems businesses actually use are quite different from company to company. Larger companies generally use more complex systems than smaller companies use. The types of economic events affecting companies also cause differences in systems. We focus on the many features that tend to be common to all accounting systems.

Computers are used to process accounting information. In this chapter we provide an overview of the basic model that underlies computer software programs.

It is important to understand that this chapter and its appendixes are not intended to describe actual accounting systems. In most business enterprises, the sheer volume of data that must be processed precludes a manual accounting system. Fortunately, the computer provides a solution. *We describe and illustrate a manual accounting information system to provide an overview of the basic model that underlies the computer software programs actually used to process accounting information.*

Electronic data processing is fast, accurate, and affordable. Many large and medium-sized companies own or rent their own mainframe computers and company-specific data processing systems. Smaller companies can take advantage of technology with relatively inexpensive desktop and laptop computers and generalized data software packages such as QuickBooks and Peachtree Accounting Software. Enterprise Resource Planning (ERP) systems are now being installed in companies of all sizes. The objective of ERP is to create a customized software program that integrates all departments and functions across a company onto a single computer system that can serve the information needs of those different departments, including the accounting department.

The Basic Model

Economic events **cause changes in the financial position of the company.**

The first objective of any accounting system is to identify the **economic events** that can be expressed in financial terms by the system.[1] An economic event for accounting purposes is any event that *directly* affects the financial position of the company. Recall from Chapter 1 that financial position comprises assets, liabilities, and owners' equity. Broad and specific accounting principles determine which events should be recorded, when the events should be recorded, and the dollar amount at which they should be measured.

External events **involve an exchange between the company and another entity.**

Economic events can be classified as either external events or internal events. **External events** involve an exchange between the company and a separate economic entity. Examples are purchasing merchandise inventory for cash, borrowing cash from a bank, and paying salaries to employees. In each instance, the company receives something (merchandise, cash, and services) in exchange for something else (cash, assumption of a liability, and cash).

Internal events **do not involve an exchange transaction but do affect the company's financial position.**

On the other hand, **internal events** directly affect the financial position of the company but don't involve an exchange transaction with another entity. Examples are the depreciation of equipment and the use of supplies. As we will see later in the chapter, these events must be recorded to properly reflect a company's financial position and results of operations in accordance with the accrual accounting model.

The Accounting Equation

● LO2–1

The **accounting equation** underlies the process used to capture the effect of economic events.

Assets = Liabilities + Owners' Equity

This general expression portrays the equality between the total economic resources of an entity (its assets)—shown on the left side of the equation—and the total claims against the entity (liabilities and equity)—shown on the right side. In other words, the resources of an enterprise are provided by creditors and owners.

Each event, or *transaction*, has a dual effect on the accounting equation.

The equation also implies that each economic event affecting this equation will have a dual effect because resources always must equal claims. For illustration, consider the events (we refer to these throughout the text as **transactions**) in Illustration 2–1.

[1]There are many economic events that affect a company *indirectly* and are not recorded. For example, when the Federal Reserve changes its discount rate, it is an important economic event that can affect the company in many ways, but it is not recorded by the company.

Illustration 2–1

Transaction Analysis

1. **An attorney invested $50,000 to open a law office.**
   An investment by the owner causes both assets and owners' equity to increase.

Assets	=	Liabilities	+	Owners' Equity
+$50,000 (cash)				+$50,000 (investment by owner)

2. **$40,000 was borrowed from a bank and a note payable was signed.**
   This transaction causes assets and liabilities to increase. A bank loan increases cash and creates an obligation to repay it.

Assets	=	Liabilities	+	Owners' Equity
+$40,000 (cash)		+$40,000 (note payable)		

3. **Supplies costing $3,000 were purchased on account.**
   Buying supplies on credit also increases both assets and liabilities.

Assets	=	Liabilities	+	Owners' Equity
+$3,000 (supplies)		+$3,000 (accounts payable)		

Transactions 4, 5, and 6 are revenue and expense transactions. Revenues and expenses (and gains and losses) are events that cause owners' equity to change. Revenues and gains describe inflows of assets, causing owners' equity to increase. Expenses and losses describe outflows of assets (or increases in liabilities), causing owners' equity to decrease.

4. **Services were performed on account for $10,000.**

Assets	=	Liabilities	+	Owners' Equity
+$10,000 (accounts receivable)				+$10,000 (revenue)

5. **Salaries of $5,000 were paid to employees.**

Assets	=	Liabilities	+	Owners' Equity
−$5,000 (cash)				−$5,000 (expense)

6. **$500 of supplies were used.**

Assets	=	Liabilities	+	Owners' Equity
−$500 (supplies)				−$500 (expense)

7. **$1,000 was paid on account to the supplies vendor.**
   This transaction causes assets and liabilities to decrease.

Assets	=	Liabilities	+	Owners' Equity
−$1,000 (cash)		−$1,000 (accounts payable)		

Each transaction is analyzed to determine its effect on the equation and on the specific financial position elements.

Owners' equity for a corporation, called *shareholders' equity,* is classified by source as either *paid-in capital* or *retained earnings.*

The accounting equation can be expanded to include a column for each type of asset and liability and for each type of change in owners' equity.

As discussed in Chapter 1, owners of a corporation are its shareholders, so owners' equity for a corporation is referred to as shareholders' equity. Shareholders' equity for a corporation arises primarily from two sources: (1) amounts *invested* by shareholders in the corporation and (2) amounts *earned* by the corporation (on behalf of its shareholders). These are reported as (1) **paid-in capital** and (2) **retained earnings**. Retained earnings equals net income less distributions to shareholders (primarily dividends) since the inception of the corporation. Illustration 2–2 shows the basic accounting equation for a corporation with shareholders' equity expanded to highlight its composition. We use the corporate format throughout the remainder of the chapter.

The *double-entry system* is used to process transactions.

Illustration 2–2

Accounting Equation for a Corporation

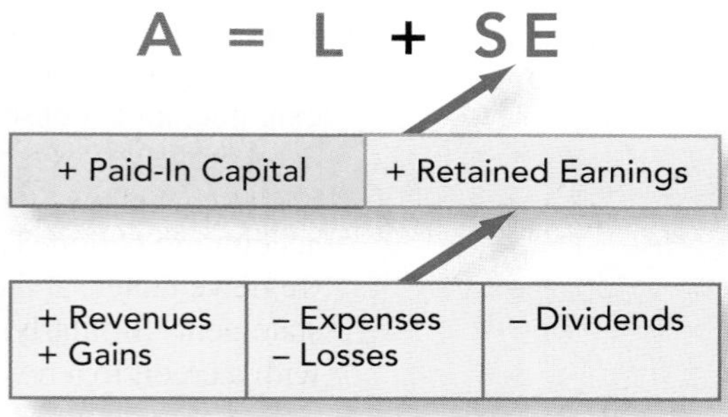

Account Relationships

All transactions could be recorded in columnar fashion as increases or decreases to elements of the accounting equation. However, even for a very small company with few transactions, this would become cumbersome. So, most companies use a process called the **double-entry system**. The term *double-entry* refers to the dual effect that each transaction has on the accounting equation.

A *general ledger* is a collection of storage areas, called *accounts,* used to keep track of increases and decreases in financial position elements.

Elements of the accounting equation are represented by **accounts** which are contained in a **general ledger**. Increases and decreases in each element of a company's financial position are recorded in these accounts. A separate account is maintained for individual assets and liabilities, retained earnings, and paid-in capital. Also, to accumulate information needed for the income statement, we use separate accounts to keep track of the changes in retained earnings caused by revenues, expenses, gains, and losses. The number of accounts depends on the complexity of the company's operations.

An account includes the account title, an account number to aid the processing task, and columns or fields for increases, decreases, the cumulative balance, and the date. For instructional purposes we use **T-accounts** instead of formal ledger accounts. A T-account has space at the top for the account title and two sides for recording increases and decreases.

In the double-entry system, *debit* means *left* side of an account and *credit* means *right* side of an account.

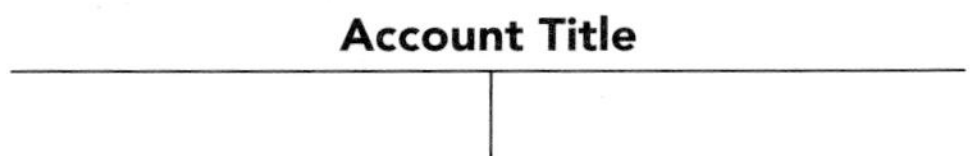

Asset *increases* are entered on the *debit* side of accounts and *decreases* are entered on the *credit* side. Liability and equity account *increases* are *credits* and *decreases* are *debits.*

For centuries, accountants have effectively used a system of **debits** and **credits** to increase and decrease account balances in the ledger. Debits merely represent the *left* side of the account and credits the *right* side, as shown below.

Account Title	
debit side	credit side

Whether a debit or a credit represents an increase or a decrease depends on the type of account. Accounts on the left side of the accounting equation (assets) are *increased* (+) by *debit* entries and *decreased* (−) by *credit* entries. Accounts on the right side of the accounting equation (liabilities and shareholders' equity) are *increased* (+) by *credit* entries and *decreased* (−) by *debit* entries. This arbitrary, but effective, procedure ensures that for each transaction the net impact on the left sides of accounts always equals the net impact on the right sides of accounts.

For example, consider the bank loan in our earlier illustration. An asset, cash, increased by $40,000. Increases in assets are *debits.* Liabilities also increased by $40,000. Increases in liabilities are *credits.*

Assets		=	**Liabilities**		+	**Owners' Equity**
Cash			**Note Payable**			
debit	credit		debit	credit		
+ 40,000				40,000 +		

The debits equal the credits in every transaction (dual effect), so both before and after a transaction the accounting equation is in balance.

Prior exposure to the terms debit and credit probably comes from your experience with a bank account. For example, when a bank debits your checking account for service charges, it decreases your account balance. When you make a deposit, the bank credits your account, increasing your account balance. You must remember that from the bank's perspective, your bank account balance is a liability—it represents the amount that the bank owes you. Therefore, when the bank debits your account, it is decreasing its liability. When the bank credits your account, its liability increases.

Illustration 2–3 demonstrates the relationship among the accounting equation, debits and credits, and the increases and decreases in financial position elements.

Notice that increases and decreases in retained earnings are recorded *indirectly.* For example, an expense represents a decrease in retained earnings, which requires a debit. That debit, however, is recorded in an appropriate expense account rather than in retained earnings itself. This allows the company to maintain a separate record of expenses incurred during an accounting period. The debit to retained earnings for the expense is recorded in a closing entry (reviewed later) at the end of the period, only after the expense total is reflected in the income statement. Similarly, an increase in retained earnings due to revenue is recorded indirectly with a credit to a revenue account, which is later reflected as a credit to retained earnings.

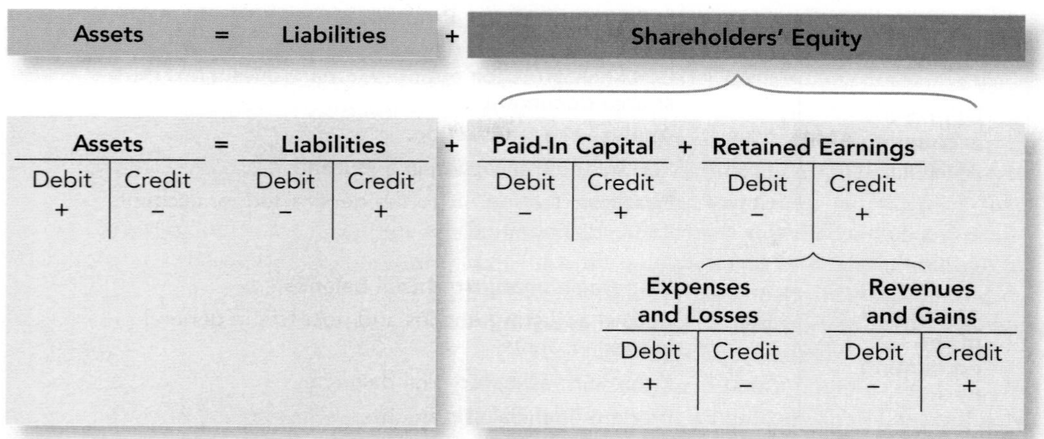

Illustration 2–3
Accounting Equation, Debits and Credits, Increases and Decreases

The general ledger accounts serve as control accounts. Subsidiary accounts associated with a particular general ledger control account are maintained in separate subsidiary ledgers. For example, a subsidiary ledger for accounts receivable contains individual account receivable accounts for each of the company's credit customers and the total of all subsidiary accounts would equal the amount in the control account. Subsidiary ledgers are discussed in more detail in Appendix 2C.

Permanent accounts represent the basic financial position elements of the accounting equation.

Temporary accounts keep track of the changes in the retained earnings component of shareholders' equity.

Each general ledger account can be classified as either *permanent* or *temporary*. **Permanent accounts** represent assets, liabilities, and shareholders' equity at a point in time. **Temporary accounts** represent changes in the retained earnings component of shareholders' equity for a corporation caused by revenue, expense, gain, and loss transactions. It would be cumbersome to record each revenue/expense, gain/loss transaction directly into the retained earnings account. The different types of events affecting retained earnings should be kept separate to facilitate the preparation of the financial statements. The balances in these temporary accounts are periodically, usually once a year, closed (zeroed out), and the net effect is recorded in the permanent retained earnings account. The temporary accounts need to be zeroed out to measure income on an annual basis. This closing process is discussed in a later section of this chapter.

The Accounting Processing Cycle

Now that we've reviewed the basics of the double-entry system, let's look closer at the process used to identify, analyze, record, and summarize transactions and prepare financial statements. This section deals only with *external transactions,* those that involve an exchange transaction with another entity. Internal transactions are discussed in a later section.

The 10 steps in the accounting processing cycle are listed in Illustration 2–4. Steps 1–4 take place during the accounting period while steps 5–8 occur at the end of the accounting period. Steps 9 and 10 are required only at the end of the year.

We now discuss these steps in order.

STEP 1
Obtain information about transactions from *source documents.*

The first step in the process is to *identify* external transactions affecting the accounting equation. An accountant usually does not directly witness business transactions. A mechanism is needed to relay the essential information about each transaction to the accountant. **Source documents** such as sales invoices, bills from suppliers, and cash register tapes serve this need.

STEP 2
Analyze the transaction.

These source documents usually identify the date and nature of each transaction, the participating parties, and the monetary terms. For example, a sales invoice identifies the date of sale, the customer, the specific goods sold, the dollar amount of the sale, and the payment terms. With this information, the second step in the processing cycle, **transaction analysis**, can be accomplished. Transaction analysis is the process of reviewing the source documents to determine the dual effect on the accounting equation and the specific elements involved.

Illustration 2–4

The Accounting Processing Cycle

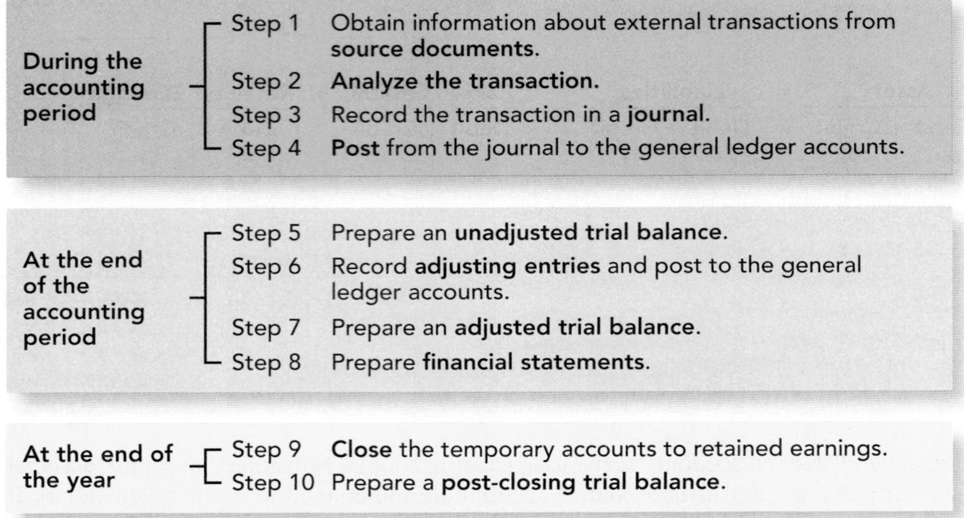

The Steps of the Accounting Processing Cycle

During the accounting period	Step 1	Obtain information about external transactions from **source documents.**
	Step 2	**Analyze the transaction.**
	Step 3	Record the transaction in a **journal.**
	Step 4	**Post** from the journal to the general ledger accounts.
At the end of the accounting period	Step 5	Prepare an **unadjusted trial balance.**
	Step 6	Record **adjusting entries** and post to the general ledger accounts.
	Step 7	Prepare an **adjusted trial balance.**
	Step 8	Prepare **financial statements.**
At the end of the year	Step 9	**Close** the temporary accounts to retained earnings.
	Step 10	Prepare a **post-closing trial balance.**

This process is summarized on the next page in Illustration 2–5 for the seven transactions described previously in Illustration 2–1. The item in each T-account is numbered to show the related transaction.

STEP 3

Record the transaction in a *journal.*

The third step in the process is to record the transaction in a **journal**. Journals provide a chronological record of all economic events affecting a firm. Each journal entry is expressed in terms of equal debits and credits to accounts affected by the transaction being recorded. Debits and credits represent increases or decreases to specific accounts, depending on the type of account, as explained earlier. For example, for credit sales, a debit to accounts receivable and a credit to sales revenue is recorded in a sales journal.

A sales journal is an example of a **special journal** used to record a repetitive type of transaction. Appendix 2C discusses the use of special journals in more depth. In this chapter and throughout the text, we use the **general journal** format to record all transactions.

● LO2–2

Any type of transaction can be recorded in a general journal. It has a place for the date of the transaction, a place for account titles, account numbers, and supporting explanations, as well as a place for debit entries, and a place for credit entries. A simplified journal entry is used throughout the text that lists the account titles to be debited and credited and the dollar amounts. A common convention is to list the debited accounts first, indent the credited accounts, and use the first of two columns for the debit amounts and the second column for the credit amounts. An explanation is entered for each journal entry (for ease in this example the explanation is located in the margin). For example, the **journal entry** for the bank loan in Illustration 2–1, which requires a debit to cash and a credit to note payable, is recorded as follows:

To record the borrowing of cash and the signing of a note payable.

Cash	40,000	
Note payable		40,000

STEP 4

Post from the journal to the general ledger accounts.

Step 4 is to periodically transfer or *post* the debit and credit information from the journal to individual ledger accounts. Recall that a ledger is simply a collection of all of the company's various accounts. Each account provides a summary of the effects of all events and transactions on that individual account. This process is called **posting**. Posting involves transferring debits and credits recorded in individual journal entries to the specific accounts affected. As discussed earlier in the chapter, most accounting systems today are computerized. For these systems, the journal input information creates a stored journal and simultaneously posts each entry to the ledger accounts.

Illustration 2–5 Transaction Analysis, the Accounting Equation, and Debits and Credits

Transaction	Transaction Analysis	Assets	=	Liabilities	+	Owners' Equity	Account Entry
		Accounting Equation					
1. An attorney invested $50,000 to open a law office.	Assets (cash) and owners' equity each increased by $50,000.	+50,000				+50,000	**Cash**: 1. 50,000 ‖ **Owners' Equity**: ‖ 50,000 1.
	Cumulative balances	50,000	=			50,000	
2. $40,000 was borrowed from a bank and a note payable was signed.	Assets (cash) and liabilities (note payable) each increased by $40,000.	+40,000		+40,000			**Cash**: 1. 50,000; 2. 40,000 ‖ **Note Payable**: ‖ 40,000 2.
	Cumulative balances	90,000	=	40,000	+	50,000	
3. Supplies costing $3,000 were purchased on account.	Assets (supplies) and liabilities (accounts payable) each increased by $3,000.	+3,000		+3,000			**Supplies**: 3. 3,000 ‖ **Accounts Payable**: ‖ 3,000 3.
	Cumulative balances	93,000	=	43,000	+	50,000	
4. Services were performed on account for $10,000.	Assets (accounts receivable) and owners' equity (revenue) each increased by $10,000.	+10,000				+10,000	**Accounts Receivable**: 4. 10,000 ‖ **Owners' Equity (Revenue)**: ‖ 10,000 4.
	Cumulative balances	103,000	=	43,000	+	60,000	
5. Salaries of $5,000 were paid to employees.	Assets (cash) decreased and owners' equity decreased (salaries expense increased) by $5,000.	−5,000				−5,000	**Cash**: 1. 50,000; 2. 40,000 ‖ 5,000 5. **Owners' Equity (Salaries Expense)**: 5. 5,000 ‖
	Cumulative balances	98,000	=	43,000	+	55,000	
6. $500 of supplies were used.	Assets (supplies) decreased and owners' equity decreased (supplies expense increased) by $500.	−500				−500	**Supplies**: 3. 3,000 ‖ 500 6. **Owners' Equity (Supplies Expense)**: 6. 500 ‖
	Cumulative balances	97,500	=	43,000	+	54,500	
7. $1,000 was paid on account to the supplies vendor.	Assets (cash) and liabilities (accounts payable) each decreased by $1,000.	−1,000		−1,000			**Cash**: 1. 50,000; 2. 40,000 ‖ 5,000 5.; 1,000 7. **Accounts Payable**: 7. 1,000 ‖ 3,000 3.
	Cumulative balances	96,500	=	42,000	+	54,500	

These first four steps in the processing cycle are illustrated using the external transactions in Illustration 2–6 which occurred during the month of July 2016, the first month of operations for Dress Right Clothing Corporation. The company operates a retail store that sells men's and women's clothing. Dress Right is organized as a corporation so owners' equity is classified by source as either paid-in capital or retained earnings.

Illustration 2–6
External Transactions for July 2016

July	1	Two individuals each invested $30,000 in the corporation. Each investor was issued 3,000 shares of common stock.
	1	Borrowed $40,000 from a local bank and signed two notes. The first note for $10,000 requires payment of principal and 10% interest in six months. The second note for $30,000 requires the payment of principal in two years. Interest at 10% is payable each year on July 1, 2017, and July 1, 2018.
	1	Paid $24,000 in advance for one year's rent on the store building.
	1	Purchased furniture and fixtures from Acme Furniture for $12,000 cash.
	3	Purchased $60,000 of clothing inventory on account from the Birdwell Wholesale Clothing Company.
	6	Purchased $2,000 of supplies for cash.
	4–31	During the month, sold merchandise costing $20,000 for $35,000 cash.
	9	Sold clothing on account to St. Jude's School for Girls for $3,500. The clothing cost $2,000.
	16	Subleased a portion of the building to a jewelry store. Received $1,000 in advance for the first two months' rent beginning on July 16.
	20	Paid Birdwell Wholesale Clothing $25,000 on account.
	20	Paid salaries to employees for the first half of the month, $5,000.
	25	Received $1,500 on account from St. Jude's.
	30	The corporation paid its shareholders a cash dividend of $1,000.

The local bank requires that Dress Right furnish financial statements on a monthly basis. The transactions listed in the illustration are used to demonstrate the accounting processing cycle for the month of July 2016.

For each transaction, a source document provides the necessary information to complete steps two and three in the processing cycle, transaction analysis, and recording the appropriate journal entry. Each transaction listed in Illustration 2–6 is analyzed below, preceded by the necessary journal entry.

To record the issuance of common stock.

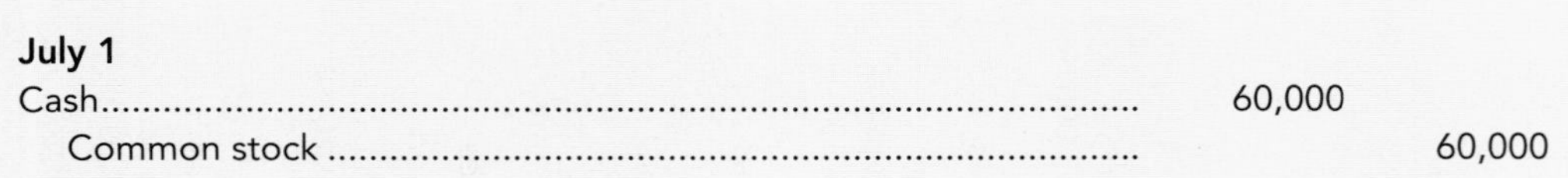

July 1		
Cash	60,000	
Common stock		60,000

This first transaction is an investment by owners that increases an asset, cash, and also increases shareholders' equity. Increases in assets are recorded as debits and increases in shareholders' equity are recorded as credits. We use the paid-in capital account called common stock because stock was issued in exchange for cash paid in.[2]

To record the borrowing of cash and the signing of notes payable.

July 1		
Cash	40,000	
Notes payable		40,000

This transaction causes increases in both cash and the liability, notes payable. Increases in assets are debits and increases in liabilities are credits. The notes require payment of $40,000 in principal and $6,500 ([$10,000 × 10% × $^6/_{12}$ = $500] + [$30,000 × 10% × 2 years = $6,000]) in interest. However, at this point we are concerned only with the

[2]The different types of stock are discussed in Chapter 18.

external transaction that occurs when the cash is borrowed and the notes are signed. Later we discuss how the interest is recorded.

July 1		
Prepaid rent	24,000	
Cash		24,000

To record the payment of one year's rent in advance.

This transaction increased an asset called prepaid rent, which is debited, and decreased the asset cash (a credit). Dress Right acquired the right to use the building for one full year. This is an asset because it represents a future benefit to the company. As we will see later, this asset expires over the one-year rental period.

July 1		
Furniture and fixtures	12,000	
Cash		12,000

To record the purchase of furniture and fixtures.

This transaction increases one asset, furniture and fixtures, and decreases another, cash.

July 3		
Inventory	60,000	
Accounts payable		60,000

To record the purchase of merchandise inventory.

This purchase of merchandise on account is recorded by a debit to inventory, an asset, and a credit to accounts payable, a liability. Increases in assets are debits, and increases in liabilities are credits.

The Dress Right Clothing Company uses the *perpetual inventory system* to keep track of its merchandise inventory. This system requires that the cost of merchandise purchased be recorded in inventory, an asset account. When inventory is sold, the inventory account is decreased by the cost of the item sold. The alternative method, the periodic system, is briefly discussed on the next page, and Chapters 8 and 9 cover the topic of inventory in depth.

July 6		
Supplies	2,000	
Cash		2,000

To record the purchase of supplies.

The acquisition of supplies is recorded as a debit to the asset account supplies (an increase) and a credit to the asset cash (a decrease). Supplies are recorded as an asset because they represent future benefits.

July 4–31		
Cash	35,000	
Sales revenue		35,000
Cost of goods sold (expense)	20,000	
Inventory		20,000

To record the month's cash sales and the cost of those sales.

During the month of July, cash sales to customers totaled $35,000. The company's assets (cash) increase by this amount as does shareholders' equity. This increase in equity is recorded by a credit to the temporary account sales revenue.

At the same time, an asset, inventory, decreases and retained earnings decreases. Recall that expenses are outflows or using up of assets from providing goods and services. Dress Right incurred an expense equal to the cost of the inventory sold. The temporary account cost of goods sold increases. However, this increase in an expense represents a *decrease* in shareholders' equity—retained earnings—and accordingly the account is debited. Both of these transactions are *summary* transactions. Normally each sale made during the month requires a separate and similar entry in a special journal which is discussed in Appendix 2C.

To record a credit sale and the cost of that sale.

July 9

Accounts receivable	3,500	
Sales revenue		3,500
Cost of goods sold	2,000	
Inventory		2,000

This transaction is similar to the cash sale on the previous page. The only difference is that the asset acquired in exchange for merchandise is accounts receivable rather than cash.

Additional Consideration

Periodic Inventory System

The principal alternative to the perpetual inventory system is the periodic system. This system requires that the cost of merchandise purchased be recorded in a temporary account called *purchases*. When inventory is sold, the inventory account is not decreased and cost of goods sold is not recorded. Cost of goods sold for a period is determined and the inventory account is adjusted only at the end of a reporting period.

For example, the purchase of $60,000 of merchandise on account by Dress Right Clothing is recorded as follows:

Purchases	60,000	
Accounts payable		60,000

No cost of goods sold entry is recorded when sales are made in the periodic system. At the end of July, the amount of ending inventory is determined (either by means of a physical count of goods on hand or by estimation) to be $38,000 and cost of goods sold for the month is determined as follows:

Beginning inventory	$ –0–
Plus: Purchases	60,000
Less: Ending inventory	(38,000)
Cost of goods sold	$22,000

The following journal entry records cost of goods sold for the period and adjusts the inventory account to the actual amount on hand (in this case from zero to $38,000):

Cost of goods sold	22,000	
Inventory	38,000	
Purchases		60,000

Inventory is discussed in depth in Chapters 8 and 9.

To record the receipt of rent in advance.

July 16

Cash	1,000	
Deferred rent revenue (liability)		1,000

Cash increases by $1,000 so the cash account is debited. At this point, Dress Right does not recognize revenue even though cash has been received. Dress Right does not recognize the revenue until it has provided the jewelry store with the use of facilities; that is, as the rental period expires. On receipt of the cash, a liability called *deferred rent revenue* increases and is credited. This liability represents Dress Right's obligation to provide the use of facilities to the jewelry store.

July 20		
Accounts payable	25,000	
Cash		25,000

To record the payment of accounts payable.

This transaction decreases both an asset (cash) and a liability (accounts payable). A debit decreases, the liability and a credit decreases the asset.

July 20		
Salaries expense	5,000	
Cash		5,000

To record the payment of salaries for the first half of the month.

Employees were paid for services rendered during the first half of the month. The cash expenditure did not create an asset since no future benefits resulted. Cash decreases and is credited; shareholders' equity decreases and is debited. The debit is recorded in the temporary account salaries expense.

July 25		
Cash	1,500	
Accounts receivable		1,500

To record receipt of cash on account.

This transaction is an exchange of one asset, accounts receivable, for another asset, cash.

July 30		
Retained earnings	1,000	
Cash		1,000

To record the payment of a cash dividend.

The payment of a cash dividend is a distribution to owners that reduces both cash and retained earnings.

Additional **Consideration**

An alternative method of recording a cash dividend is to debit a temporary account called dividends. In that case, the dividends account is later closed (transferred) to retained earnings along with the other temporary accounts at the end of the fiscal year. The journal entry to record the dividend using this approach is as follows:

Dividends	1,000	
Cash		1,000

We discuss and illustrate the closing process later in the chapter.

Illustration 2–7 summarizes each of the transactions just discussed as they would appear in a general journal. In addition to the date, account titles, and debit and credit columns, the journal also has a column titled Post Ref. (Posting Reference). This usually is a number assigned to the general ledger account that is being debited or credited. For purposes of this illustration, all asset accounts have been assigned numbers in the 100s, all liabilities are 200s, permanent shareholders' equity accounts are 300s, revenues are 400s, and expenses are 500s.

Illustration 2–7
The General Journal

General Journal — **Page 1**

Date 2016	Account Title and Explanation	Post Ref.	Debit	Credit
July 1	Cash	100	60,000	
	Common stock	300		60,000
	To record the issuance of common stock.			
1	Cash	100	40,000	
	Notes payable	220		40,000
	To record the borrowing of cash and the signing of notes payable.			
1	Prepaid rent	130	24,000	
	Cash	100		24,000
	To record the payment of one year's rent in advance.			
1	Furniture and fixtures	150	12,000	
	Cash	100		12,000
	To record the purchase of furniture and fixtures.			
3	Inventory	140	60,000	
	Accounts payable	210		60,000
	To record the purchase of merchandise inventory.			
6	Supplies	125	2,000	
	Cash	100		2,000
	To record the purchase of supplies.			
4–31	Cash	100	35,000	
	Sales revenue	400		35,000
	To record cash sales for the month.			
4–31	Cost of goods sold	500	20,000	
	Inventory	140		20,000
	To record the cost of cash sales.			
9	Accounts receivable	110	3,500	
	Sales revenue	400		3,500
	To record credit sale.			
9	Cost of goods sold	500	2,000	
	Inventory	140		2,000
	To record the cost of a credit sale.			
16	Cash	100	1,000	
	Deferred rent revenue	230		1,000
	To record the receipt of rent in advance.			
20	Accounts payable	210	25,000	
	Cash	100		25,000
	To record the payment of accounts payable.			
20	Salaries expense	510	5,000	
	Cash	100		5,000
	To record the payment of salaries for the first half of the month.			
25	Cash	100	1,500	
	Accounts receivable	110		1,500
	To record the receipt of cash on account.			
30	Retained earnings	310	1,000	
	Cash	100		1,000
	To record the payment of a cash dividend.			

The ledger accounts also contain a posting reference, usually the page number of the journal in which the journal entry was recorded. This allows for easy cross-referencing between the journal and the ledger. Page 1 is used for Illustration 2–7.

Step 4 in the processing cycle is to transfer (post) the debit/credit information from the journal to the general ledger accounts. Illustration 2–8 contains the ledger accounts (in T-account form) for Dress Right *after* all the general journal transactions have been posted. The reference GJ1 next to each of the posted amounts indicates that the source of the entry is page 1 of the general journal. An alternative is to number each of the entries in chronological order and reference them by number.

● LO2-3

Illustration 2–8

General Ledger Accounts

Balance Sheet Accounts

Cash 100

	Debit	Credit	
July 1 GJ1	60,000	24,000	July 1 GJ1
1 GJ1	40,000	12,000	1 GJ1
4–31GJ1	35,000	2,000	6 GJ1
16 GJ1	1,000	25,000	20 GJ1
25 GJ1	1,500	5,000	20 GJ1
		1,000	30 GJ1
July 31 Bal.	**68,500**		

Prepaid Rent 130

	Debit	Credit	
July 1 GJ1	24,000		
July 31 Bal.	**24,000**		

Accounts Receivable 110

	Debit	Credit	
July 9 GJ1	3,500	1,500	July 25 GJ1
July 31 Bal.	**2,000**		

Inventory 140

	Debit	Credit	
July 3 GJ1	60,000	20,000	July 4–31
		2,000	9 GJ1
July 31 Bal.	**38,000**		

Supplies 125

	Debit	Credit	
July 6 GJ1	2,000		
July 31 Bal.	**2,000**		

Furniture and Fixtures 150

	Debit	Credit	
July 1 GJ1	12,000		
July 31 Bal.	**12,000**		

Accounts Payable 210

	Debit	Credit	
July 20 GJ1	25,000	60,000	July 3 GJ1
		35,000	**July 31 Bal.**

Notes Payable 220

	Debit	Credit	
		40,000	July 1 GJ1
		40,000	**July 31 Bal.**

Deferred Rent Revenue 230

	Debit	Credit	
		1,000	July 16 GJ1
		1,000	**July 31 Bal.**

Common Stock 300

	Debit	Credit	
		60,000	July 1 GJ1
		60,000	**July 31 Bal.**

Retained Earnings 310

	Debit	Credit	
July 30 GJ1	1,000		
July 31 Bal.	**1,000**		

Income Statement Accounts

Sales Revenue 400

	Debit	Credit	
		35,000	July 4–31 GJ1
		3,500	9 GJ1
		38,500	**July 31 Bal.**

Cost of Goods Sold 500

	Debit	Credit	
July 4–31 GJ1	20,000		
9 GJ1	2,000		
July 31 Bal.	**22,000**		

Salaries Expense 510

	Debit	Credit	
July 20 GJ1	5,000		
July 31 Bal.	**5,000**		

STEP 5

Prepare an unadjusted trial balance.

Before financial statements are prepared and before adjusting entries (internal transactions) are recorded at the end of an accounting period, an **unadjusted trial balance** usually is prepared—step 5. A trial balance is simply a list of the general ledger accounts, listed in the order that they appear in the ledger, along with their balances at a particular date. Its purpose is to allow us to check for completeness and to prove that the sum of the accounts with debit balances equals the sum of the accounts with credit balances, that is, the accounting equation is in balance. The fact that the debits and credits are equal, though, does not necessarily ensure that the equal balances are correct. The trial balance could contain offsetting errors. As we will see later in the chapter, this trial balance also facilitates the preparation of adjusting entries.

The unadjusted trial balance at July 31, 2016, for the Dress Right Clothing Corporation appears in Illustration 2–9. Notice that retained earnings has a debit balance of $1,000. This reflects the payment of the cash dividend to shareholders. The increases and decreases in retained earnings from revenue, expense, gain and loss transactions are recorded indirectly in temporary accounts. Before the start of the next year, these increases and decreases are transferred to the retained earnings account.

Illustration 2–9

Unadjusted Trial Balance

DRESS RIGHT CLOTHING CORPORATION
Unadjusted Trial Balance
July 31, 2016

Account Title	Debits	Credits
Cash	68,500	
Accounts receivable	2,000	
Supplies	2,000	
Prepaid rent	24,000	
Inventory	38,000	
Furniture and fixtures	12,000	
Accounts payable		35,000
Notes payable		40,000
Deferred rent revenue		1,000
Common stock		60,000
Retained earnings	1,000	
Sales revenue		38,500
Cost of goods sold	22,000	
Salaries expense	5,000	
Totals	174,500	174,500

At any time, the total of all debit balances should equal the total of all credit balances.

Concept Review Exercise

JOURNAL ENTRIES FOR EXTERNAL TRANSACTIONS

The Wyndham Wholesale Company began operations on August 1, 2016. The following transactions occur during the month of August.

a. Owners invest $50,000 cash in the corporation in exchange for 5,000 shares of common stock.
b. Equipment is purchased for $20,000 cash.
c. On the first day of August, $6,000 rent on a building is paid for the months of August and September.
d. Merchandise inventory costing $38,000 is purchased on account. The company uses the perpetual inventory system.
e. $30,000 is borrowed from a local bank, and a note payable is signed.
f. Credit sales for the month are $40,000. The cost of merchandise sold is $22,000.
g. $15,000 is collected on account from customers.
h. $20,000 is paid on account to suppliers of merchandise.
i. Salaries of $7,000 are paid to employees for August.

j. A bill for $2,000 is received from the local utility company for the month of August.
k. $20,000 cash is loaned to another company, evidenced by a note receivable.
l. The corporation pays its shareholders a cash dividend of $1,000.

Required:

1. Prepare a journal entry for each transaction.
2. Prepare an unadjusted trial balance as of August 31, 2016.

Solution:

1. Prepare a journal entry for each transaction.
   a. The issuance of common stock for cash increases both cash and shareholders' equity (common stock).

Cash	50,000	
Common stock		50,000

   b. The purchase of equipment increases equipment and decreases cash.

Equipment	20,000	
Cash		20,000

   c. The payment of rent in advance increases prepaid rent and decreases cash.

Prepaid rent	6,000	
Cash		6,000

   d. The purchase of merchandise on account increases both inventory and accounts payable.

Inventory	38,000	
Accounts payable		38,000

   e. Borrowing cash and signing a note increases both cash and note payable.

Cash	30,000	
Note payable		30,000

   f. The sale of merchandise on account increases both accounts receivable and sales revenue. Also, cost of goods sold increases and inventory decreases.

Accounts receivable	40,000	
Sales revenue		40,000
Cost of goods sold	22,000	
Inventory		22,000

   g. The collection of cash on account increases cash and decreases accounts receivable.

Cash	15,000	
Accounts receivable		15,000

   h. The payment to suppliers on account decreases both accounts payable and cash.

Accounts payable	20,000	
Cash		20,000

i. The payment of salaries for the period increases salaries expense (decreases retained earnings) and decreases cash.

Salaries expense	7,000	
Cash		7,000

j. The receipt of a bill for services rendered increases both an expense (utilities expense) and accounts payable. The expense decreases retained earnings.

Utilities expense	2,000	
Accounts payable		2,000

k. The lending of cash to another entity and the signing of a note increases note receivable and decreases cash.

Note receivable	20,000	
Cash		20,000

l. Cash dividends paid to shareholders reduce both retained earnings and cash.

Retained earnings[3]	1,000	
Cash		1,000

2. Prepare an unadjusted trial balance as of August 31, 2016.

Account Title	Debits	Credits
Cash	21,000	
Accounts receivable	25,000	
Prepaid rent	6,000	
Inventory	16,000	
Note receivable	20,000	
Equipment	20,000	
Accounts payable		20,000
Note payable		30,000
Common stock		50,000
Retained earnings	1,000	
Sales revenue		40,000
Cost of goods sold	22,000	
Salaries expense	7,000	
Utilities expense	2,000	
Totals	140,000	140,000

● LO2–4

Adjusting Entries

STEP 6

Record *adjusting entries* and post to the ledger accounts.

Step 6 in the processing cycle is to record in the general journal and post to the ledger accounts the effect of *internal events* on the accounting equation. These transactions do not involve an exchange transaction with another entity and, therefore, are not initiated by a source document. They are recorded *at the end of any period when financial statements are prepared.* These transactions are commonly referred to as **adjusting entries**.

Even when all transactions and events are analyzed, corrected, journalized, and posted to appropriate ledger accounts, some account balances will require updating. Adjusting entries

[3]An alternative is to debit a temporary account—dividends—that is closed to retained earnings at the end of the fiscal year along with the other temporary accounts.

are required to implement the *accrual accounting model.* More specifically, these entries help ensure that all revenues are recognized in the period goods or services are transferred to customers, regardless of when the cash is received. Also, they enable a company to recognize all expenses incurred during a period, regardless of when cash payment is made. As a result, a period's income statement provides a more complete measure of a company's operating performance and a better measure for predicting future operating cash flows. The balance sheet also provides a more complete assessment of assets and liabilities as sources of future cash receipts and disbursements. You might think of adjusting entries as a method of bringing the company's financial information up to date before preparing the financial statements.

FINANCIAL Reporting Case

Q1, p. 51

Adjusting entries are necessary for three situations:

1. **Prepayments**, sometimes referred to as *deferrals.*
2. **Accruals.**
3. **Estimates.**

FINANCIAL Reporting Case

Q2, p. 51

Prepayments

Prepayments occur when the cash flow *precedes* either expense or revenue recognition. For example, a company may buy supplies in one period but use them in a later period. The cash outflow creates an asset (supplies) which then must be expensed in a future period as the asset is used up. Similarly, a company may receive cash from a customer in one period but provide the customer with a good or service in a future period. For instance, magazine publishers usually receive cash in advance for magazine subscriptions. The cash inflow creates a liability (deferred revenue) that is recognized as revenue in a future period when the goods or services are transferred to customers.

***Prepayments* are transactions in which the cash flow *precedes* expense or revenue recognition.**

PREPAID EXPENSES. **Prepaid expenses** are the costs of assets acquired in one period and expensed in a future period. Whenever cash is paid, and it is not to (1) satisfy a liability or (2) pay a dividend or return capital to owners, it must be determined whether or not the payment creates future benefits or whether the payment benefits only the current period. The purchase of buildings, equipment, or supplies or the payment of rent in advance are examples of payments that create future benefits and should be recorded as assets. The benefits provided by these assets expire in future periods and their cost is expensed in future periods as related revenues are recognized.

***Prepaid expenses* represent assets recorded when a cash disbursement creates benefits beyond the current reporting period.**

To illustrate this concept, assume that a company paid a radio station $2,000 in July for advertising. If that $2,000 were for advertising provided by the radio station during the month of July, the entire $2,000 would be expensed in the same period as the cash disbursement. If, however, the $2,000 was a payment for advertising to be provided in a future period, say the month of August, then the cash disbursement creates an asset called *prepaid advertising.* An adjusting entry is required at the end of August to increase advertising expense (decrease shareholders' equity) and to decrease the asset prepaid advertising by $2,000. Assuming that the cash disbursement records a debit to an asset, as in this example, the adjusting entry for a prepaid expense is, therefore, a *debit to an expense* and a *credit to an asset.*

The adjusting entry required for a prepaid expense is a *debit to an expense* and a *credit to an asset.*

The unadjusted trial balance can provide a starting point for determining which adjusting entries are required for a period, particularly for prepayments. Review the July 31, 2016, unadjusted trial balance for the Dress Right Clothing Corporation in Illustration 2–9 on page 64 and try to anticipate the required adjusting entries for prepaid expenses.

The first asset that requires adjustment is supplies, $2,000 of which were purchased during July. This transaction created an asset as the supplies will be used in future periods. The company could either track the supplies used or simply count the supplies at the end of the period and determine the dollar amount of supplies remaining. Assume that Dress Right determines that at the end of July, $1,200 of supplies remain. The following adjusting journal entry is required.

● LO2–5

July 31		
Supplies expense	800	
Supplies		800

To record the cost of supplies used during the month of July.

Supplies

	Debit	Credit
Beg. bal.	0	
	2,000	800
End bal.	1,200	

Supplies Expense

	Debit	Credit
Beg. bal.	0	
	800	
End bal.	800	

After this entry is recorded and posted to the ledger accounts, the supplies (asset) account is reduced to a $1,200 debit balance, and the supplies expense account will have an $800 debit balance.

The next prepaid expense requiring adjustment is rent. Recall that at the beginning of July, the company paid $24,000 to its landlord representing one year's rent in advance. As it is reasonable to assume that the rent services provided each period are equal, the monthly rent is $2,000. At the end of July 2016, one month's prepaid rent has expired and must be recognized as expense.

To record the cost of expired rent for the month of July.

July 31		
Rent expense ($24,000 ÷ 12)	2,000	
Prepaid rent		2,000

Prepaid Rent

	Debit	Credit
Beg. bal.	0	
	24,000	2,000
End bal.	22,000	

Rent Expense

	Debit	Credit
Beg. bal.	0	
	2,000	
End bal.	2,000	

After this entry is recorded and posted to the ledger accounts, the prepaid rent account will have a debit balance of $22,000, representing 11 remaining months at $2,000 per month, and the rent expense account will have a $2,000 debit balance.

The final prepayment involves the asset represented by furniture and fixtures that was purchased for $12,000. This asset has a long life but nevertheless will expire over time. For the previous two adjusting entries, it was fairly straightforward to determine the amount of the asset that expired during the period.

However, it is difficult, if not impossible, to determine how much of the benefits from using the furniture and fixtures expired during any particular period. Recall from Chapter 1 that one approach is to recognize an expense "by a systematic and rational allocation to specific time periods."

Assume that the furniture and fixtures have a useful life of five years (60 months) and will be worthless at the end of that period, and that we choose to allocate the cost equally over the period of use. The amount of monthly expense, called *depreciation expense,* is $200 ($12,000 ÷ 60 months = $200), and the following adjusting entry is recorded.

To record depreciation of furniture and fixtures for the month of July.

July 31		
Depreciation expense	200	
Accumulated depreciation—furniture and fixtures		200

The entry reduces an asset, furniture and fixtures, by $200. However, the asset account is not reduced directly. Instead, the credit is to an account called *accumulated depreciation.* This is a contra account to furniture and fixtures. The normal balance in a contra asset account will be a credit, that is, "contra," or opposite, to the normal debit balance in an asset account. The purpose of the contra account is to keep the original cost of the asset intact while reducing it indirectly. In the balance sheet, furniture and fixtures is reported net of accumulated depreciation. This topic is covered in depth in Chapter 11.

After this entry is recorded and posted to the ledger accounts, the accumulated depreciation account will have a credit balance of $200 and the depreciation expense account will have a $200 debit balance. If a required adjusting entry for a prepaid expense is not recorded, net income, assets, and shareholders' equity (retained earnings) will be overstated.

Deferred revenues represent liabilities recorded when cash is received from customers in advance of providing a good or service.

DEFERRED REVENUES. Deferred revenues are created when a company receives cash from a customer in one period for goods or services that are to be provided in a future period. The cash receipt, an external transaction, is recorded as a debit to cash and a credit to a liability. This liability reflects the company's obligation to provide goods or services in the future.

To illustrate a deferred revenue transaction, assume that during the month of June a magazine publisher received $24 in cash for a 24-month subscription to a monthly magazine. The subscription begins in July. On receipt of the cash, the publisher records a liability, deferred subscription revenue, of $24. Subsequently, revenue of $1 is recognized as each monthly magazine is published and mailed to the customer. An adjusting entry is required each month to increase shareholders' equity (revenue) to recognize the $1 in revenue and to decrease the liability. Assuming that the cash receipt entry included a credit to a liability, the adjusting entry for deferred revenues, therefore, is a *debit to a liability,* in this case deferred subscription revenue, and a *credit to revenue.*

The adjusting entry required when deferred revenues are recognized is a *debit to a liability* and a *credit to revenue.*

Once again, the unadjusted trial balance provides information concerning deferred revenues. For Dress Right Clothing Corporation, the only deferred revenue in the trial balance is deferred rent revenue. Recall that the company subleased a portion of its building to a jewelry store for $500 per month. On July 16, the jewelry store paid Dress Right $1,000 in advance for the first two months' rent. The transaction was recorded as a debit to cash and a credit to deferred rent revenue.

At the end of July, how much of the $1,000 must be recognized? Approximately one-half of one month's rent service has been provided, or $250, requiring the following adjusting journal entry.

July 31		
Deferred rent revenue	250	
Rent revenue		250

To record previously deferred rent revenue recognized during July.

Deferred Rent Revenue

	0 Beg. bal.
250	1,000
	750 End bal.

Rent Revenue

	0 Beg. bal.
	250
	250 End bal.

After this entry is recorded and posted to the ledger accounts, the deferred rent revenue account is reduced to a credit balance of $750 for the remaining one and one-half months' rent, and the rent revenue account will have a $250 credit balance. If this entry is not recorded, net income and shareholders' equity (retained earnings) will be understated, and liabilities will be overstated.

ALTERNATIVE APPROACH TO RECORD PREPAYMENTS. The same end result can be achieved for prepayments by recording the external transaction directly into an expense or revenue account. In fact, many companies prefer this approach. For simplicity, bookkeeping instructions may require all cash payments for expenses to be debited to the appropriate expense account and all cash receipts for revenues to be credited to the appropriate revenue account. The adjusting entry then records the *unexpired* prepaid expense (asset) or *deferred* revenue (liability) as of the end of the period.

For example, on July 1, 2016, Dress Right paid $24,000 in cash for one year's rent on its building. The entry included a debit to prepaid rent. The company could have debited rent expense instead.

Alternative Approach July 1		
Rent expense	24,000	
Cash		24,000

Rent Expense

Beg. bal. 0	
24,000	22,000
End bal. 2,000	

The adjusting entry then records the amount of prepaid rent as of the end of July, $22,000, and reduces rent expense to $2,000, the cost of rent for the month of July.

Alternative Approach July 31		
Prepaid rent	22,000	
Rent expense		22,000

Prepaid Rent

Beg. bal. 0	
22,000	
End bal. 22,000	

The net effect of handling the transactions in this manner is the same as the previous treatment. Either way, the prepaid rent account will have a debit balance at the end of July of $22,000, and the rent expense account will have a debit balance of $2,000. What's important is that an adjusting entry is recorded to ensure the appropriate amounts are reflected in both the expense and asset *before financial statements are prepared.*

Similarly, the July 16 cash receipt from the jewelry store representing an advance for two months' rent could have been recorded by Dress Right as a credit to rent revenue instead of deferred rent revenue (a liability).

Rent Revenue

Debit	Credit
	0 Beg. bal.
750	1,000
	250 End bal.

Alternative Approach
July 16

	Debit	Credit
Cash	1,000	
Rent revenue		1,000

If Dress Right records the entire $1,000 as rent revenue in this way, it would then use the adjusting entry to record the amount of deferred revenue as of the end of July, $750, and reduce rent revenue to $250, the amount of revenue recognized during the month of July.

Deferred Rent Revenue

Debit	Credit
	0 Beg. bal.
	750
	750 End bal.

Alternative Approach
July 31

	Debit	Credit
Rent revenue	750	
Deferred rent revenue		750

Accruals

***Accruals* involve transactions where the cash outflow or inflow takes place in a period subsequent to expense or revenue recognition.**

Accruals occur when the cash flow comes *after* either expense or revenue recognition. For example, a company often uses the services of another entity in one period and pays for them in a subsequent period. An expense must be recognized in the period incurred and an accrued liability recorded. Also, goods and services often are provided to customers on credit. In such instances, a revenue is recognized in the period goods or services are transferred to customers and an asset, a receivable, is recorded.

Many accruals involve external transactions that automatically are recorded from a source document. For example, a sales invoice for a credit sale provides all the information necessary to record the debit to accounts receivable and the credit to sales revenue. However, there are some accruals that involve internal transactions and thus require adjusting entries. Because accruals involve recognition of expense or revenue before cash flow, the unadjusted trial balance will not be as helpful in identifying required adjusting entries as with prepayments.

***Accrued liabilities* represent liabilities recorded when an expense has been incurred prior to cash payment.**

The adjusting entry required to record an accrued liability is a *debit to an expense* and a *credit to a liability*.

ACCRUED LIABILITIES. For **accrued liabilities**, we are concerned with expenses incurred but not yet paid. Dress Right Clothing Corporation requires two adjusting entries for accrued liabilities at July 31, 2016.

The first entry is for employee salaries for the second half of July. Recall that on July 20 the company paid employees $5,000 for salaries for the first half of the month. Salaries for the second half of July will probably be paid in early August. Nevertheless, the company incurred an expense in July for services provided to it by its employees. Also, there exists an obligation at the end of July to pay the salaries earned by employees. An adjusting entry is required to increase salaries expense (decrease shareholders' equity) and to increase liabilities for the salaries payable. The adjusting entry for an accrued liability always includes a *debit to an expense,* and a *credit to a liability.* Assuming that salaries for the second half of July are $5,500, the following adjusting entry is recorded.

To record accrued salaries at the end of July.

Salaries Payable

Debit	Credit
	0 Beg. bal.
	5,500
	5,500 End bal.

Salaries Expense

Debit	Credit
Beg. bal. 0	
July 20 5,000	
5,500	
End bal. 10,500	

July 31

	Debit	Credit
Salaries expense	5,500	
Salaries payable		5,500

After this entry is recorded and posted to the general ledger, the salaries expense account will have a debit balance of $10,500 ($5,000 + 5,500), and the salaries payable account will have a credit balance of $5,500.

The unadjusted trial balance does provide information about the second required accrued liability entry. In the trial balance we can see a balance in the notes payable account of $40,000. The company borrowed this amount on July 1, 2016, evidenced by two notes, each requiring the payment of 10% interest. Whenever the trial balance reveals interest-bearing debt, and interest is not paid on the last day of the period, an adjusting entry is required for the amount of interest that has built up (accrued) since the last payment date or the last date interest was accrued. In this case, we calculate interest as follows:

Principal ×	Interest rate ×	Time =	Interest
$40,000 ×	10%	× 1/12 =	$333 (rounded)

Interest rates always are stated as the annual rate. Therefore, the above calculation uses this annual rate multiplied by the principal amount multiplied by the amount of time outstanding, in this case one month or one-twelfth of a year.

July 31		
Interest expense	333	
Interest payable		333

To accrue interest expense for July on notes payable.

After this entry is recorded and posted to the ledger accounts, the interest expense account will have a debit balance of $333, and the interest payable account will have a credit balance of $333. Failure to record a required adjusting entry for an accrued liability will cause net income and shareholders' equity (retained earnings) to be overstated, and liabilities to be understated.[4]

ACCRUED RECEIVABLES. Accrued receivables involve the recognition of revenue for goods or services transferred to customers *before* cash is received. An example of an internal accrued revenue event is the recognition of interest earned on a loan to another entity. For example, assume that Dress Right loaned another corporation $30,000 at the beginning of August, evidenced by a note receivable. Terms of the note call for the payment of principal, $30,000, and interest at 8% in three months. An external transaction records the cash disbursement—a debit to note receivable and a credit to cash of $30,000.

Accrued receivables **involve situations when the revenue is recognized in a period prior to the cash receipt.**

What adjusting entry would be required at the end of August? Dress Right needs to record the interest revenue earned but not yet received along with the corresponding receivable. Interest receivable increases and interest revenue (shareholders' equity) also increases. The adjusting entry for accrued receivables always includes a *debit to an asset,* a receivable, and a *credit to revenue.* In this case, at the end of August Dress Right recognizes $200 in interest revenue ($30,000 × 8% × 1/12) and makes the following adjusting entry. If this entry is not recorded, net income, assets, and shareholders' equity (retained earnings) will be understated.

The adjusting entry required to record an accrued revenue is a *debit to an asset,* a receivable, and a *credit to revenue.*

August 31		
Interest receivable	200	
Interest revenue		200

To accrue interest revenue earned in August on note receivable.

There are no accrued revenue adjusting entries required for Dress Right at the end of July.

The required adjusting entries for prepayments and accruals are recapped with the aid of T-accounts in Illustration 2–10. In each case an expense or revenue is recognized in a period that differs from the period in which cash was paid or received. These adjusting entries are necessary to properly measure operating performance and financial position on an accrual basis.

[4]Dress Right Clothing is a corporation. Corporations are income-tax-paying entities. Income taxes—federal, state, and local—are assessed on an annual basis and payments are made throughout the year. An additional adjusting entry would be required for Dress Right to accrue the amount of estimated income taxes payable that are applicable to the month of July. Accounting for income taxes is introduced in Chapter 4 and covered in depth in Chapter 16.

Illustration 2–10
Adjusting Entries

Adjusting Entries

		Financial Statement Effects: Income Statement	Financial Statement Effects: Balance Sheet
Prepayments	**Prepaid Expenses** — Asset: Credit ⇔ Expense: Debit	Income ↓	Assets ↓
Prepayments	**Deferred Revenues** — Liability: Debit; Revenues: Credit	Income ↑	Liabilities ↓
Accruals	**Accrued Expenses** — Expense: Debit; Liability: Credit	Income ↓	Liabilities ↑
Accruals	**Accrued Receivables** — Asset: Debit; Revenues: Credit	Income ↑	Assets ↑

Estimates

Accountants often must make *estimates* in order to comply with the accrual accounting model.

A third classification of adjusting entries is **estimates**. Accountants often must make estimates of future events to comply with the accrual accounting model. For example, the calculation of depreciation expense requires an estimate of expected useful life of the asset being depreciated as well as its expected residual value. We discussed the adjusting entries for depreciation expense in the context of its being a prepayment, but it also could be thought of as an estimate.

One adjusting-entry situation involving an estimate that does not fit neatly into either the prepayment or accrual classification is bad debts. Accounting for bad debts requires a company to estimate the amount of accounts receivable that ultimately will prove to be uncollectible and to reduce accounts receivable by that estimated amount. This is neither a prepayment nor an accrual because it does not involve the payment of cash either before or after income is reduced. We explore accounts receivable and bad debts in depth in Chapter 7.

Illustration 2–11 recaps the July 31, 2016, adjusting entries for Dress Right Clothing Corporation as they would appear in a general journal. The journal entries are numbered (1) to (6) corresponding to the number used in the worksheet illustrated in Appendix 2A.

After the adjusting entries are posted to the general ledger accounts, the next step—step 7—in the processing cycle is to prepare an **adjusted trial balance**. The term adjusted refers to the fact that adjusting entries have now been posted to the accounts. Recall that the column titled Post Ref. (Posting Reference) is the number assigned to the general ledger account that is being debited or credited. Illustration 2–12 shows the July 31, 2016, adjusted trial balance for Dress Right Clothing Corporation.

Illustration 2–11

The General Journal—Adjusting Entries

DRESS RIGHT CLOTHING CORPORATION
General Journal **Page 2**

Date 2016		Account Title and Explanation	Post. Ref.	Debit	Credit
July	31	Supplies expense	520	800	
(1)		Supplies	125		800
		To record the cost of supplies used during the month of July.			
(2)	31	Rent expense	530	2,000	
		Prepaid rent	130		2,000
		To record the cost of expired rent for the month of July.			
(3)	31	Depreciation expense	540	200	
		Accumulated depreciation—furniture and fixtures	155		200
		To record depreciation of furniture and fixtures for the month of July.			
(4)	31	Deferred rent revenue	230	250	
		Rent revenue	410		250
		To record previously deferred rent revenue recognized during July.			
(5)	31	Salaries expense	510	5,500	
		Salaries payable	230		5,500
		To record accrued salaries at the end of July.			
(6)	31	Interest expense	550	333	
		Interest payable	240		333
		To accrue interest expense for July on notes payable.			

Illustration 2–12

Adjusted Trial Balance

STEP 7

Prepare an *adjusted trial balance.*

DRESS RIGHT CLOTHING CORPORATION
Adjusted Trial Balance
July 31, 2016

Account Title	Debits	Credits
Cash	68,500	
Accounts receivable	2,000	
Supplies	1,200	
Prepaid rent	22,000	
Inventory	38,000	
Furniture and fixtures	12,000	
Accumulated depreciation—furniture and fixtures		200
Accounts payable		35,000
Notes payable		40,000
Deferred rent revenue		750
Salaries payable		5,500
Interest payable		333
Common stock		60,000
Retained earnings	1,000	
Sales revenue		38,500
Rent revenue		250
Cost of goods sold	22,000	
Salaries expense	10,500	
Supplies expense	800	
Rent expense	2,000	
Depreciation expense	200	
Interest expense	333	
Totals	180,533	180,533

Concept Review Exercise

ADJUSTING ENTRIES

The Wyndham Wholesale Company needs to prepare financial statements at the end of August 2016 for presentation to its bank. An unadjusted trial balance as of August 31, 2016, was presented in a previous concept review exercise on page 66.

The following information also is available:

a. The note payable requires the entire $30,000 in principal plus interest at 10% to be paid on July 31, 2017. The date of the loan is August 1, 2016.

b. Depreciation on the equipment for the month of August is $500.

c. The note receivable is dated August 16, 2016. The note requires the entire $20,000 in principal plus interest at 12% to be repaid in four months (the loan was outstanding for one-half month during August).

d. The prepaid rent of $6,000 represents rent for the months of August and September.

Required:

1. Prepare any necessary adjusting entries at August 31, 2016.
2. Prepare an adjusted trial balance as of August 31, 2016.
3. What is the total net effect on income (overstated or understated) if the adjusting entries are not recorded?

Solution:

1. Prepare any necessary adjusting entries at August 31, 2016.

   a. An adjusting entry is required to accrue the interest expense on the note payable for the month of August. Accrued interest is calculated as follows:

$$\$30,000 \times 10\% \times 1/12 = \$250$$

Interest expense	250	
Interest payable		250

   b. Depreciation expense on the equipment must be recorded.

Depreciation expense	500	
Accumulated depreciation—equipment		500

   c. An adjusting entry is required for the one-half month of accrued interest revenue earned on the note receivable. Accrued interest is calculated as follows:

$$\$20,000 \times 12\% \times 1/12 \times 1/2 = \$100$$

Interest receivable	100	
Interest revenue		100

   d. An adjusting entry is required to recognize the amount of prepaid rent that expired during August.

Rent expense	3,000	
Prepaid rent		3,000

2. Prepare an adjusted trial balance as of August 31, 2016.

Account Title	Debits	Credits
Cash	21,000	
Accounts receivable	25,000	
Prepaid rent	3,000	
Inventory	16,000	
Interest receivable	100	

(continued)

(concluded)

Account Title	Debits	Credits
Note receivable	20,000	
Equipment	20,000	
Accumulated depreciation—equipment		500
Accounts payable		20,000
Interest payable		250
Note payable		30,000
Common stock		50,000
Retained earnings	1,000	
Sales revenue		40,000
Interest revenue		100
Cost of goods sold	22,000	
Salaries expense	7,000	
Utilities expense	2,000	
Interest expense	250	
Depreciation expense	500	
Rent expense	3,000	
Totals	140,850	140,850

3. What is the effect on income (overstated or understated), if the adjusting entries are not recorded?

Adjusting Entry	Income overstated (understated)
Interest expense	$ 250
Depreciation expense	500
Interest revenue	(100)
Rent expense	3,000
Net effect, income overstated by	$3,650

We now turn our attention to the preparation of financial statements.

Preparing the Financial Statements

● LO2–6

STEP 8

Preparation of financial statements.

The purpose of each of the steps in the processing cycle to this point is to provide information for step 8—preparation of the **financial statements**. The adjusted trial balance contains the necessary information. After all, the financial statements are the primary means of communicating financial information to external parties.

The Income Statement

The *income statement* is a *change* statement that summarizes the profit-generating transactions that caused shareholders' equity (retained earnings) to change during the period.

The purpose of the **income statement** is to summarize the profit-generating activities of a company that occurred during a particular period of time. It is a *change* statement in that it reports the changes in shareholders' equity (retained earnings) that occurred during the period as a result of revenues, expenses, gains, and losses. Illustration 2–13 shows the income statement for Dress Right Clothing Corporation for the month of July 2016.

The income statement indicates a profit for the month of July of $2,917. During the month, the company was able to increase its net assets (equity) from activities related to selling its product. Dress Right is a corporation and subject to the payment of income tax on its profits. We ignore this required accrual here and address income taxes in a later chapter.

The components of the income statement usually are classified, that is, grouped according to common characteristics. A common classification scheme is to separate operating items from nonoperating items, as we do in Dress Right's income statement. Operating items include revenues and expenses directly related to the principal revenue-generating activities of the company. For example, operating items for a manufacturing company include sales

Illustration 2–13
Income Statement

DRESS RIGHT CLOTHING CORPORATION Income Statement For the Month of July 2016		
Sales revenue		$38,500
Cost of goods sold		22,000
Gross profit		16,500
Operating expenses:		
Salaries	$10,500	
Supplies	800	
Rent	2,000	
Depreciation	200	
Total operating expenses		13,500
Operating income		3,000
Other income (expense):		
Rent revenue	250	
Interest expense	(333)	(83)
Net income		$ 2,917

revenues from the sale of products and all expenses related to this activity. Companies that sell products like Dress Right often report a subtotal within operating income, sales less cost of goods sold, called *gross profit.* Nonoperating items include certain gains and losses and revenues and expenses from peripheral activities. For Dress Right Clothing, rent revenue and interest expense are nonoperating items because they do not relate to the principal revenue-generating activity of the company, selling clothes. In Chapter 4 we discuss the format and content of the income statement in more depth.

The Statement of Comprehensive Income

The purpose of the **statement of comprehensive income** is to report the changes in shareholders' equity during the period that were not a result of transactions with owners. A few types of gains and losses, called **other comprehensive income (OCI) or loss** items, are excluded from the determination of net income and the income statement, but are included in the broader concept of **comprehensive income**. Comprehensive income can be reported in one of two ways: (1) in a single, continuous statement of comprehensive income, or (2) in two separate, but consecutive statements.[5]

In the single statement approach, net income is a subtotal within the statement followed by these OCI items, culminating in a final total of comprehensive income. In the two statement approach, a company presents an income statement immediately followed by a statement of comprehensive income. The statement of comprehensive income begins with net income as the first component followed by OCI items to arrive at comprehensive income. Obviously, the approaches are quite similar; in the separate statement approach, we separate the continuous statement into two parts, but the content is the same.

Dress Right Clothing has no OCI items so the company presents only an income statement in Illustration 2–13. An entity that has no OCI items is not required to report OCI or comprehensive income. We discuss comprehensive income and the alternative approaches to its presentation in more depth in Chapter 4.

The *balance sheet* is a position statement that presents an organized list of assets, liabilities and equity at a particular point in time.

The Balance Sheet

The purpose of the **balance sheet** is to present the financial position of the company on a particular date. Unlike the income statement, which is a change statement reporting events

[5]FASB ASC 220-10-45-1: Comprehensive Income—Overall—Other Presentation Matters [Accounting Standards Update No. 2011-05 (Norwalk, Conn.: FASB, June 2011)].

that occurred *during a period of time,* the balance sheet is a statement that presents an organized list of assets, liabilities, and shareholders' equity *at a point in time.* To provide a quick overview, Illustration 2–14 shows the balance sheet for Dress Right at July 31, 2016.

Illustration 2–14
Balance Sheet

DRESS RIGHT CLOTHING CORPORATION
Balance Sheet
At July 31, 2016

Assets		
Current assets:		
Cash		$ 68,500
Accounts receivable		2,000
Supplies		1,200
Inventory		38,000
Prepaid rent		22,000
Total current assets		131,700
Property and equipment:		
Furniture and fixtures	$12,000	
Less: Accumulated depreciation	200	11,800
Total assets		$143,500
Liabilities and Shareholders' Equity		
Current liabilities:		
Accounts payable		$ 35,000
Salaries payable		5,500
Deferred rent revenue		750
Interest payable		333
Note payable		10,000
Total current liabilities		51,583
Long-term liabilities:		
Note payable		30,000
Shareholders' equity:		
Common stock, 6,000 shares issued and outstanding	$60,000	
Retained earnings	1,917*	
Total shareholders' equity		61,917
Total liabilities and shareholders' equity		$143,500

*Beginning retained earnings + Net income − Dividends
$0 + 2,917 − 1,000 = $1,917

As we do in the income statement, we group the balance sheet elements into meaningful categories. For example, most balance sheets include the classifications of **current assets** and **current liabilities**. Current assets are those assets that are cash, will be converted into cash, or will be used up within one year or the operating cycle, whichever is longer. Current liabilities are those liabilities that will be satisfied within one year or the operating cycle, whichever is longer. For a manufacturing company, the operating cycle refers to the period of time necessary to convert cash to raw materials, raw materials to a finished product, the finished product to receivables, and then finally receivables back to cash. For most companies, this period is less than a year.

Balance sheet items usually are classified (grouped) according to common characteristics.

Examples of assets not classified as current include property and equipment and long-term receivables and investments. The only noncurrent asset that Dress Right has at July 31, 2016, is furniture and fixtures, which is classified under the property and equipment category.

All liabilities not classified as current are listed as long term. Dress Right's liabilities at July 31, 2016, include the $30,000 note payable due to be paid in 23 months. This liability is classified as long term.

Shareholders' equity lists the *paid-in capital* portion of equity—common stock—and *retained earnings*. Notice that the income statement we looked at in Illustration 2–13 ties in to the balance sheet through retained earnings. Specifically, the revenue, expense, gain, and loss transactions that make up net income in the income statement ($2,917) become the major components of retained earnings. Later in the chapter we discuss the closing process we use to transfer, or close, these *temporary* income statement accounts to the *permanent* retained earnings account.

During the month, retained earnings, which increased by the amount of net income, also decreased by the amount of the cash dividend paid to shareholders, $1,000. The net effect of these two changes is an increase in retained earnings from zero at the beginning of the period to $1,917 ($2,917 − 1,000) at the end of the period and also is reported in the statement of shareholders' equity in Illustration 2–16 on page 79.

The Statement of Cash Flows

The purpose of the *statement of cash flows* is to summarize the transactions that caused cash to change during the period.

Similar to the income statement, the statement of cash flows also is a change statement. The purpose of the statement is to report the events that caused cash to change during the period. The statement classifies all transactions affecting cash into one of three categories: (1) operating activities, (2) investing activities, and (3) financing activities. Operating activities are inflows and outflows of cash related to transactions entering into the determination of net income. Investing activities involve the acquisition and sale of (1) long-term assets used in the business and (2) nonoperating investment assets. Financing activities involve cash inflows and outflows from transactions with creditors and owners.

The statement of cash flows for Dress Right for the month of July 2016 is shown in Illustration 2–15. As this is the first period of operations for Dress Right, the cash balance at the beginning of the period is zero. The net increase in cash of $68,500, therefore, equals the ending balance of cash disclosed in the balance sheet.

Illustration 2–15
Statement of Cash Flows

DRESS RIGHT CLOTHING CORPORATION
Statement of Cash Flows
For the Month of July 2016

Cash Flows from Operating Activities		
Cash inflows:		
From customers	$36,500	
From rent	1,000	
Cash outflows:		
For rent	(24,000)	
For supplies	(2,000)	
To suppliers of merchandise	(25,000)	
To employees	(5,000)	
Net cash flows from operating activities		$(18,500)
Cash Flows from Investing Activities		
Purchase of furniture and fixtures		(12,000)
Cash Flows from Financing Activities		
Issue of common stock	$60,000	
Increase in notes payable	40,000	
Payment of cash dividend	(1,000)	
Net cash flows from financing activities		99,000
Net increase in cash		$ 68,500

There are two generally accepted formats that can be used to report operating activities, the direct method and the indirect method. In Illustration 2–15 we use the direct method. These two methods are discussed and illustrated in subsequent chapters.

The Statement of Shareholders' Equity

The final statement, the statement of shareholders' equity, also is a change statement. Its purpose is to disclose the sources of the changes in the various permanent shareholders' equity accounts that occurred during the period from investments by owners, distributions to owners, net income, and other comprehensive income. Illustration 2–16 shows the statement of shareholders' equity for Dress Right for the month of July 2016.[6]

The *statement of shareholders' equity* discloses the sources of changes in the permanent shareholders' equity accounts.

Illustration 2–16

Statement of Shareholders' Equity

DRESS RIGHT CLOTHING CORPORATION
Statement of Shareholders' Equity
For the Month of July 2016

	Common Stock	Retained Earnings	Total Shareholders' Equity
Balance at July 1, 2016	$ –0–	$ –0–	$ –0–
Issue of common stock	60,000		60,000
Net income for July 2016		2,917	2,917
Less: Dividends		(1,000)	(1,000)
Balance at July 31, 2016	$60,000	$1,917	$61,917

The individual profit-generating transactions causing retained earnings to change are summarized in the income statement. Therefore, the statement of shareholders' equity only shows the net effect of these transactions on retained earnings, in this case an increase of $2,917. In addition, the company paid its shareholders a cash dividend that reduced retained earnings.

The Closing Process

STEP 9

Close the temporary accounts to retained earnings (at year-end only).

At the end of any interim reporting period, the accounting processing cycle is now complete. An interim reporting period is any period when financial statements are produced other than at the end of the fiscal year. However, at the end of the fiscal year, two final steps are necessary, closing the temporary accounts—step 9—and preparing a post-closing trial balance—step 10.

● LO2–7

The closing process serves a *dual purpose:* (1) the temporary accounts (revenues, expenses, gains and losses) are reduced to *zero balances,* ready to measure activity in the upcoming accounting period, and (2) these temporary account balances are *closed (transferred) to retained earnings* to reflect the changes that have occurred in that account during the period. Often, an intermediate step is to close revenues and expenses to income summary, and then income summary is closed to retained earnings. The use of the income summary account is just a bookkeeping convenience that provides a check that all temporary accounts have been properly closed (that is, the balance equals net income or loss).

To illustrate the closing process, assume that the fiscal year-end for Dress Right Clothing Corporation is July 31. Using the adjusted trial balance in Illustration 2–12, we can prepare the following general journal entries.

To close the revenue accounts to income summary.

July 31		
Sales revenue	38,500	
Rent revenue	250	
Income summary		38,750

[6]Some companies choose to disclose the changes in the retained earnings component of shareholders' equity in a separate statement or in a combined statement of income and retained earnings.

The first closing entry transfers the revenue account balances to income summary. Because revenue accounts have credit balances, they are debited to bring them to zero. After this entry is posted to the accounts, both revenue accounts have a zero balance.

To close the expense accounts to income summary.

July 31		
Income summary	35,833	
Cost of goods sold		22,000
Salaries expense		10,500
Supplies expense		800
Rent expense		2,000
Depreciation expense		200
Interest expense		333

The second closing entry transfers the expense account balances to income summary. As expense accounts have debit balances, they are credited to bring them to zero. After this entry is posted to the accounts, the expense accounts have a zero balance and the income summary account has a credit balance equal to net income for the period, in this case $2,917.

Income Summary

	Debit	Credit	
Expenses	35,833	38,750	Revenues
		2,917	Net income

The third entry closes the income summary account to retained earnings.

To close the income summary account to retained earnings.

July 31		
Income summary	2,917	
Retained earnings		2,917

After this entry is posted to the accounts, the temporary accounts have zero balances and retained earnings has increased by the amount of the net income. It is important to remember that the temporary accounts are closed only at year-end and not at the end of any interim period. Closing the temporary accounts during the year would make it difficult to prepare the annual income statement.

Additional Consideration

A previous additional consideration indicated that an alternative method of recording a cash dividend is to debit a temporary account called dividends, rather than debiting retained earnings. If this approach is used, an additional closing entry is required to close the dividend account to retained earnings, as follows:

Retained earnings	1,000	
Dividends		1,000

As you can see, the net result of a cash dividend is the same—a reduction in retained earnings and a reduction in cash.

STEP 10

Prepare a *post-closing trial balance* (at year-end only).

After the closing entries are posted to the ledger accounts, a **post-closing trial balance** is prepared. The purpose of this trial balance is to verify that the closing entries were prepared and posted correctly and that the accounts are now ready for next year's transactions. Illustration 2–17 shows the post-closing trial balance for Dress Right at July 31, 2016, assuming a July 31 fiscal year-end.

Illustration 2–17
Post-Closing Trial Balance

DRESS RIGHT CLOTHING CORPORATION
Post-Closing Trial Balance
July 31, 2016

Account Title	Debits	Credits
Cash	68,500	
Accounts receivable	2,000	
Supplies	1,200	
Prepaid rent	22,000	
Inventory	38,000	
Furniture and fixtures	12,000	
Accumulated depreciation—furniture and fixtures		200
Accounts payable		35,000
Notes payable		40,000
Deferred rent revenue		750
Salaries payable		5,500
Interest payable		333
Common stock		60,000
Retained earnings		1,917
Totals	143,700	143,700

Concept Review Exercise

FINANCIAL STATEMENT PREPARATION AND CLOSING

Refer to the August 31, 2016, adjusted trial balance of the Wyndham Wholesale Company presented in a previous concept review exercise on pages 74 and 75.

Required:

1. Prepare an income statement and a statement of shareholders' equity for the month ended August 31, 2016, and a classified balance sheet as of August 31, 2016.
2. Assume that August 31 is the company's fiscal year-end. Prepare the necessary closing entries and a post-closing trial balance.

Solution:

1. Prepare an income statement and a statement of shareholders' equity for the month ended August 31, 2016, and a classified balance sheet as of August 31, 2016.

WYNDHAM WHOLESALE COMPANY
Income Statement
For the Month of August 2016

Sales revenue		$40,000
Cost of goods sold		22,000
Gross profit		18,000
Operating expenses:		
Salaries	$7,000	
Utilities	2,000	
Depreciation	500	
Rent	3,000	
Total operating expenses		12,500
Operating income		5,500
Other income (expense):		
Interest revenue	100	
Interest expense	(250)	(150)
Net income		$ 5,350

WYNDHAM WHOLESALE COMPANY
Statement of Shareholders' Equity
For the Month of August 2016

	Common Stock	Retained Earnings	Total Shareholders' Equity
Balance at August 1, 2016	$ –0–	$ –0–	$ –0–
Issue of common stock	50,000		50,000
Net income for August 2016		5,350	5,350
Less: Dividends		(1,000)	(1,000)
Balance at August 31, 2016	$50,000	$4,350	$54,350

WYNDHAM WHOLESALE COMPANY
Balance Sheet
At August 31, 2016

Assets

Current assets:		
Cash		$ 21,000
Accounts receivable		25,000
Inventory		16,000
Interest receivable		100
Note receivable		20,000
Prepaid rent		3,000
Total current assets		85,100
Property and equipment:		
Equipment	$20,000	
Less: Accumulated depreciation	500	19,500
Total assets		$104,600
Liabilities and Shareholders' Equity		
Current liabilities:		
Accounts payable		$ 20,000
Interest payable		250
Note payable		30,000
Total current liabilities		50,250
Shareholders' equity:		
Common stock, 5,000 shares issued and outstanding	$50,000	
Retained earnings	4,350	
Total shareholders' equity		54,350
Total liabilities and shareholders' equity		$104,600

2. Assume that August 31 is the company's fiscal year-end. Prepare the necessary closing entries and a post-closing trial balance.

To close the revenue accounts to income summary.

August 31		
Sales revenue	40,000	
Interest revenue	100	
Income summary		40,100

To close the expense accounts to income summary.

August 31		
Income summary	34,750	
Cost of goods sold		22,000
Salaries expense		7,000
Utilities expense		2,000
Depreciation expense		500
Rent expense		3,000
Interest expense		250

(continued)

(concluded)

August 31

Income summary	5,350		To close the income summary account to retained earnings.
Retained earnings		5,350	

Post-Closing Trial Balance

Account Title	Debits	Credits
Cash	21,000	
Accounts receivable	25,000	
Prepaid rent	3,000	
Inventory	16,000	
Interest receivable	100	
Note receivable	20,000	
Equipment	20,000	
Accumulated depreciation—equipment		500
Accounts payable		20,000
Interest payable		250
Note payable		30,000
Common stock		50,000
Retained earnings		4,350
Totals	105,100	105,100

Conversion from Cash Basis to Accrual Basis

LO2–8

In Chapter 1, we discussed and illustrated the differences between cash and accrual accounting. Cash basis accounting produces a measure called *net operating cash flow*. This measure is the difference between cash receipts and cash disbursements during a reporting period from transactions related to providing goods and services to customers. On the other hand, the accrual accounting model measures an entity's accomplishments and resource sacrifices during the period, regardless of when cash is received or paid. At this point, you might wish to review the material in Chapter 1 on pages 6 through 8 to reinforce your understanding of the motivation for using the accrual accounting model.

Adjusting entries, for the most part, are conversions from cash basis to accrual basis. Prepayments and accruals occur when cash flow precedes or follows expense or revenue recognition.

Accountants sometimes are called upon to convert cash basis financial statements to accrual basis financial statements, particularly for small businesses. You now have all of the tools you need to make this conversion. For example, if a company paid $20,000 cash for insurance during the fiscal year and you determine that there was $5,000 in prepaid insurance at the beginning of the year and $3,000 at the end of the year, then you can determine (accrual basis) *insurance expense* for the year. Prepaid insurance decreased by $2,000 during the year, so insurance expense must be $22,000 ($20,000 in cash paid *plus* the decrease in prepaid insurance). You can visualize as follows:

	Prepaid Insurance
Balance, beginning of year	$ 5,000
Plus: Cash paid	20,000
Less: Insurance expense	?
Balance, end of year	$ 3,000

Insurance expense of $22,000 completes the explanation of the change in the balance of prepaid insurance. Prepaid insurance of $3,000 is reported as an asset in an accrual basis balance sheet.

Suppose a company paid $150,000 for salaries to employees during the year and you determine that there were $12,000 and $18,000 in salaries payable at the beginning and end of the year, respectively. What was salaries expense for the year?

	Salaries Payable
Balance, beginning of year	$ 12,000
Plus: Salaries expense	?
Less: Cash paid	150,000
Balance, end of year	$ 18,000

Salaries payable increased by $6,000 during the year, so *salaries expense* must be $156,000 ($150,000 in cash paid *plus* the increase in salaries payable). Salaries payable of $18,000 is reported as a liability in an accrual basis balance sheet.

Using T-accounts is a convenient approach for converting from cash to accrual accounting.

Salaries Payable

		12,000	Beg. balance
Cash paid	150,000		
		?	Salaries expense
		18,000	End balance

Salaries Expense

Debit	Credit
?	

The debit to salaries expense and credit to salaries payable must have been $156,000 to balance the salaries payable account.

For another example using T-accounts, assume that the amount of cash collected from customers during the year was $220,000, and you know that accounts receivable at the beginning of the year was $45,000 and $33,000 at the end of the year. You can use T-accounts to determine that *sales revenue* for the year must have been $208,000, the necessary debit to accounts receivable and credit to sales revenue to balance the accounts receivable account.

Accounts Receivable

Beg. balance	45,000		
Credit sales	?		
		220,000	Cash collections
End balance	33,000		

Sales Revenue

Debit	Credit	
	?	Credit sales

Now suppose that, on occasion, customers pay in advance of receiving a product or service. Recall from our previous discussion of adjusting entries that this event creates a liability called deferred revenue. Assume the same facts in the previous example except you also determine that deferred revenues were $10,000 and $7,000 at the beginning and end of the year, respectively. A $3,000 decrease in deferred revenues means that the company recognized an additional $3,000 in sales revenue for which the cash had been collected in a previous year. So, *sales revenue* for the year must have been $211,000, the $208,000 determined in the previous example *plus* the $3,000 decrease in deferred revenue.

Illustration 2–18 provides another example of converting from cash basis net income to accrual basis net income.

Notice a pattern in the adjustments to cash net income. When converting from cash to accrual income, we add increases and deduct decreases in assets. For example, an increase in accounts receivable means that the company recognized more revenue than cash collected, requiring the addition to cash basis income. Conversely, we add decreases and deduct increases in accrued liabilities. For example, a decrease in interest payable means that the company incurred less interest expense than the cash interest it paid, requiring the addition to cash basis income. These adjustments are summarized in Illustration 2–19.

Most companies must convert from an accrual basis to a cash basis when preparing the statement of cash flows.

Most companies keep their books on an accrual basis.[7] A more important conversion for these companies is from the accrual basis to the cash basis. This conversion, essential for the

[7]Generally accepted accounting principles require the use of the accrual basis. Some small, nonpublic companies might use the cash basis in preparing their financial statements as an other comprehensive basis of accounting.

The Krinard Cleaning Services Company maintains its records on the cash basis, with one exception. The company reports equipment as an asset and records depreciation expense on the equipment. During 2016, Krinard collected $165,000 from customers, paid $92,000 in operating expenses, and recorded $10,000 in depreciation expense, resulting in net income of $63,000. The owner has asked you to convert this $63,000 in net income to full accrual net income. You are able to determine the following information about accounts receivable, prepaid expenses, accrued liabilities, and deferred revenues:

	January 1, 2016	December 31, 2016
Accounts receivable	$16,000	$25,000
Prepaid expenses	7,000	4,000
Accrued liabilities (for operating expenses)	2,100	1,400
Deferred revenues	3,000	4,200

Accrual net income is $68,500, determined as follows:

Cash basis net income		$63,000
Add:	Increase in accounts receivable	9,000
Deduct:	Decrease in prepaid expenses	(3,000)
Add:	Decrease in accrued liabilities	700
Deduct:	Increase in deferred revenues	(1,200)
Accrual basis net income		$68,500

Illustration 2–18

Cash to Accrual

Converting Cash Basis Income to Accrual Basis Income

	Increases	Decreases
Assets	Add	Deduct
Liabilities	Deduct	Add

Illustration 2–19

Converting Cash Basis to Accrual Basis Income

preparation of the statement of cash flows, is discussed and illustrated in Chapters 4 and 21. The lessons learned here, though, will help you with that conversion. For example, if sales revenue for the period is $120,000 and beginning and ending accounts receivable are $20,000 and $24,000, respectively, how much cash did the company collect from its customers during the period? The answer is $116,000. An increase in accounts receivable of $4,000 means that the company collected $4,000 less from customers than accrual sales revenue, and cash basis income is $4,000 less than accrual basis income.

Financial Reporting Case Solution

1. **What purpose do adjusting entries serve?** *(p. 67)* Adjusting entries help ensure that all revenues are recognized in the period goods or services are transferred to customers, regardless of when cash is received. In this instance, for example, $13,000 cash has been received for services that haven't yet been performed. Also, adjusting entries enable a company to recognize all expenses incurred during a period, regardless of when cash is paid. Without depreciation, the friends' cost of using the equipment is not taken into account. Conversely, without adjustment, the cost of rent is overstated by $3,000 paid in advance for part of next year's rent.

   With adjustments, we get an accrual income statement that provides a more complete measure of a company's operating performance and a better measure for predicting future operating cash flows. Similarly, the balance sheet provides a more complete assessment of assets and liabilities as sources of future cash receipts and disbursements.

2. What year-end adjustments are needed to revise the income statement? Did your friends do as well their first year as they thought? *(p. 67)* Three year-end adjusting entries are needed:

	Debit	Credit
1. Depreciation expense ($80,000 ÷ 5 years)	16,000	
Accumulated depreciation—equipment		16,000
2. Prepaid rent ($500 × 6 months [July–Dec.])	3,000	
Rent expense		3,000
3. Consulting revenue	13,000	
Deferred consulting revenue		13,000

No, your friends did not fare as well as their cash based statement would have indicated. With appropriate adjustments, their net income is actually only $20,000:

Consulting revenue ($96,000 − 13,000)		$83,000
Operating expenses:		
Salaries	$32,000	
Rent ($9,000 − 3,000)	6,000	
Supplies	4,800	
Utilities	3,000	
Advertising	1,200	
Depreciation	16,000	63,000
Net income		$20,000

The Bottom Line

- **LO2–1** The accounting equation underlies the process used to capture the effect of economic events. The equation (Assets = Liabilities + Owners' Equity) implies an equality between the total economic resources of an entity (its assets) and the total claims against the entity (liabilities and equity). It also implies that each economic event affecting this equation will have a dual effect because resources always must equal claims. *(p. 52)*
- **LO2–2** After determining the dual effect of external events on the accounting equation, the transaction is recorded in a journal. A journal is a chronological list of transactions in debit/credit form. *(p. 56)*
- **LO2–3** The next step in the processing cycle is to periodically transfer, or *post,* the debit and credit information from the journal to individual general ledger accounts. A general ledger is simply a collection of all of the company's various accounts. Each account provides a summary of the effects of all events and transactions on that individual account. The process of entering items from the journal to the general ledger is called *posting.* An unadjusted trial balance is then prepared. *(p. 63)*
- **LO2–4** The next step in the processing cycle is to record the effect of *internal events* on the accounting equation. These transactions are commonly referred to as *adjusting entries.* Adjusting entries can be classified into three types: (1) prepayments, (2) accruals, and (3) estimates. Prepayments are transactions in which the cash flow *precedes* expense or revenue recognition. Accruals involve transactions where the cash outflow or inflow takes place in a period *subsequent* to expense or revenue recognition. Estimates for items such as future bad debts on receivables often are required to comply with the accrual accounting model. *(p. 66)*
- **LO2–5** Adjusting entries are recorded in the general journal and posted to the ledger accounts at the end of any period when financial statements must be prepared for external use. After these entries are posted to the general ledger accounts, an adjusted trial balance is prepared. *(p. 67)*
- **LO2–6** The adjusted trial balance is used to prepare the financial statements. The basic financial statements are: (1) the income statement, (2) the statement of comprehensive income, (3) the balance sheet, (4) the statement of cash flows, and (5) the statement of shareholders' equity. The purpose of the income statement is to summarize the profit-generating activities of the company that occurred during a particular period of time. A company also must report its other comprehensive income (OCI) or loss items either in a single, continuous statement or in a separate statement of comprehensive income. In the single statement approach, net income is a subtotal within the statement followed by these OCI items, culminating

in a final total of comprehensive income. In the two statement approach, a company presents an income statement immediately followed by a statement of comprehensive income. The statement of comprehensive income begins with net income as the first component followed by OCI items to arrive at comprehensive income. The balance sheet presents the financial position of the company on a particular date. The statement of cash flows discloses the events that caused cash to change during the reporting period. The statement of shareholders' equity discloses the sources of the changes in the various permanent shareholders' equity accounts that occurred during the period. (*p. 75*)

● **LO2–7** At the end of the fiscal year, a final step in the accounting processing cycle, closing, is required. The closing process serves a *dual purpose:* (1) the temporary accounts (revenues and expenses) are reduced to *zero balances,* ready to measure activity in the upcoming accounting period, and (2) these temporary account balances are *closed (transferred) to retained earnings* to reflect the changes that have occurred in that account during the period. Often, an intermediate step is to close revenues and expenses to *income summary;* then *income summary* is closed to *retained earnings.* (*p. 79*)

● **LO2–8** Cash basis accounting produces a measure called *net operating cash flow.* This measure is the difference between cash receipts and cash disbursements during a reporting period from transactions related to providing goods and services to customers. On the other hand, the accrual accounting model measures an entity's accomplishments and resource sacrifices during the period, regardless of when cash is received or paid. Accountants sometimes are called upon to convert cash basis financial statements to accrual basis financial statements, particularly for small businesses. (*p. 83*) ●

APPENDIX 2A

Use of a Worksheet

A **worksheet** often is used to organize the accounting information needed to prepare adjusting and closing entries and the financial statements. It is an informal tool only and is not part of the accounting system. There are many different ways to design and use worksheets. We will illustrate a representative method using the financial information for the Dress Right Clothing Corporation presented in the chapter. Computerized programs such as Lotus 1-2-3 and Excel facilitate the use of worksheets.

A *worksheet* can be used as a tool to facilitate the preparation of adjusting and closing entries and the financial statements.

Illustration 2A–1 presents the completed worksheet. The worksheet is utilized in conjunction with step 5 in the processing cycle, preparation of an unadjusted trial balance.

Illustration 2A–1 Worksheet, Dress Right Clothing Corporation, July 31, 2016

	A	B	C	D	E	F	G	H	I	J	K	L	M
1	Worksheet, Dress Right Clothing Corporation, July 31, 2016												
2		Unadjusted Trial Balance		Adjusting Entries				Adjusted Trial Balance		Income Statement		Balance Sheet	
3	Account Title	Dr.	Cr.	Dr.		Cr.		Dr.	Cr.	Dr.	Cr.	Dr.	Cr.
4													
5	Cash	68,500						68,500				68,500	
6	Accounts receivable	2,000						2,000				2,000	
7	Supplies	2,000				(1)	800	1,200				1,200	
8	Prepaid rent	24,000				(2)	2,000	22,000				22,000	
9	Inventory	38,000						38,000				38,000	
10	Furniture & fixtures	12,000						12,000				12,000	
11	Accumulated depreciation -												
12	furniture & fixtures		0			(3)	200		200				200
13	Accounts payable		35,000						35,000				35,000
14	Note payable		40,000						40,000				40,000
15	Deferred rent revenue		1,000	(4)	250				750				750
16	Salaries payable		0			(5)	5,500		5,500				5,500
17	Interest payable		0			(6)	333		333				333
18	Common stock		60,000						60,000				60,000
19	Retained earnings	1,000						1,000				1,000	
20	Sales revenue		38,500						38,500		38,500		
21	Rent revenue		0			(4)	250		250		250		
22	Cost of goods sold	22,000						22,000		22,000			
23	Salaries expense	5,000		(5)	5,500			10,500		10,500			
24	Supplies expense	0		(1)	800			800		800			
25	Rent expense	0		(2)	2,000			2,000		2,000			
26	Depreciation expense	0		(3)	200			200		200			
27	Interest expense	0		(6)	333			333		333			
28	Totals	174,500	174,500		9,083		9,083	180,533	180,533				
29													
30	Net Income									2,917			2,917
31	Totals									38,750	38,750	144,700	144,700
32													

Sheet1 Sheet2 Sheet3

The first step is to enter account titles in column A and the unadjusted account balances in columns B and C.

Step 1. The account titles as they appear in the general ledger are entered in column A and the balances of these accounts are copied onto columns B and C, entitled Unadjusted Trial Balance. The accounts are copied in the same order as they appear in the general ledger, which usually is assets, liabilities, shareholders' equity permanent accounts, revenues, and expenses. The debit and credit columns are totaled to make sure that they balance. This procedure is repeated for each set of columns in the worksheet to check for accuracy.

The second step is to determine end-of-period adjusting entries and enter them in columns E and G.

Step 2. The end-of-period adjusting entries are determined and entered directly on the worksheet in columns E and G, entitled Adjusting Entries. The adjusting entries for Dress Right Clothing Corporation were discussed in detail in the chapter and exhibited in general journal form in Illustration 2–11 on page 73. You should refer back to this illustration and trace each of the entries to the worksheet. For worksheet purposes, the entries have been numbered from (1) to (6) for easy referencing.

For example, entry (1) records the cost of supplies used during the month of July with a debit to supplies expense and a credit to supplies for $800. A (1) is placed next to the $800 in the debit column in the supplies expense row as well as next to the $800 in the credit column in the supplies row. This allows us to more easily reconstruct the entry for general journal purposes and locate errors if the debit and credit columns do not balance.

The third step adds or deducts the effects of the adjusting entries on the account balances.

Step 3. The effects of the adjusting entries are added to or deducted from the account balances listed in the Unadjusted Trial Balance columns and copied across to columns H and I, entitled Adjusted Trial Balance. For example, supplies had an unadjusted balance of $2,000. Adjusting entry (1) credited this account by $800, reducing the balance to $1,200.

The fourth step is to transfer the temporary retained earnings account balances to columns J and K.

Step 4. The balances in the temporary retained earnings accounts, revenues and expenses, are transferred to columns J and K, entitled Income Statement. The difference between the total debits and credits in these columns is equal to net income or net loss. In this case, because credits (revenues) exceed debits (expenses), a net income of $2,917 results. To balance the debits and credits in this set of columns, a $2,917 debit entry is made in the line labeled Net income.

The fifth step is to transfer the balances in the permanent accounts to columns L and M.

Step 5. The balances in the permanent accounts are transferred to columns L and M, entitled Balance Sheet. To keep the debits and credits equal in the worksheet, a $2,917 credit must be recorded to offset the $2,917 debit recorded in step 4 and labeled as net income. This credit represents the fact that when the temporary accounts are closed out to retained earnings, a $2,917 credit to retained earnings will result. The credit in column M, therefore, represents an increase in retained earnings for the period, that is, net income.

After the worksheet is completed, the financial statements can be prepared directly from columns J–M. The financial statements for Dress Right Clothing Corporation are shown in Illustrations 2–13 through 2–16. The accountant must remember to then record the adjusting entries in the general journal and post them to the general ledger accounts. An adjusted trial balance should then be prepared, which should be identical to the one in the worksheet. At fiscal year-end, the income statement columns can then be used to prepare closing entries.

APPENDIX 2B Reversing Entries

Accountants sometimes use **reversing entries** at the beginning of a reporting period. These optional entries remove the effects of some of the adjusting entries recorded at the end of the previous reporting period for the sole purpose of simplifying journal entries recorded during the new period. If the accountant does use reversing entries, these entries are recorded in the general journal and posted to the general ledger accounts on the first day of the new period.

Reversing entries are used most often with accruals. For example, the following adjusting entry for accrued salaries was recorded at the end of July 2016 for the Dress Right Clothing Corporation in the chapter:

To record accrued salaries at the end of July.

July 31		
Salaries expense	5,500	
Salaries payable		5,500

If reversing entries are not used, when the salaries actually are paid in August, the accountant needs to remember to debit salaries payable and not salaries expense.

The account balances before and after salary payment can be seen below with the use of T-accounts.

Salaries Expense

	Debit	Credit
Bal. July 31	10,500	

Salaries Payable

	Debit	Credit	
		5,500	Bal. July 31
(Cash Payment)	5,500		
		–0–	Balance

If the accountant for Dress Right employs reversing entries, the following entry is recorded on August 1, 2016:

August 1

	Debit	Credit
Salaries payable	5,500	
Salaries expense		5,500

To reverse accrued salaries expense recorded at the end of July.

This entry reduces the salaries payable account to zero and reduces the salary expense account by $5,500. When salaries actually are paid in August, the debit is to salaries expense, thus increasing the account by $5,500.

Salaries Expense

	Debit	Credit	
Bal. July 31	10,500		
		5,500	(Reversing entry)
(Cash payment)	5,500		
Balance	10,500		

Salaries Payable

	Debit	Credit	
		5,500	Bal. July 31
(Reversing entry)	5,500		
		–0–	Balance

We can see that balances in the accounts after cash payment is made are identical. The use of reversing entries for accruals, which is optional, simply allows cash payments or cash receipts to be entered directly into the temporary expense or revenue accounts without regard to the accruals recorded at the end of the previous period.

Reversing entries also can be used with prepayments and deferred revenues. For example, earlier in the chapter Dress Right Clothing Corporation used the following entry to record the purchase of supplies on July 6:

July 6

	Debit	Credit
Supplies	2,000	
Cash		2,000

To record the purchase of supplies.

If reversing entries are not used, an adjusting entry is needed at the end of July to record the amount of supplies consumed during the period. In the illustration, Dress Right recorded this adjusting entry at the end of July:

July 31

	Debit	Credit
Supplies expense	800	
Supplies		800

To record the cost of supplies used during the month of July.

T-accounts help us visualize the account balances before and after the adjusting entry.

Supplies

	Debit	Credit	
(Cash payment)	2,000		
		800	(Adjusting entry)
Bal. July 31	1,200		

Supplies Expense

	Debit	Credit
(Adjusting entry)	800	
Bal. July 31	800	

If the accountant for Dress Right employs reversing entries, the purchase of supplies is recorded as follows:

To record the purchase of supplies.

July 6		
Supplies expense	2,000	
Cash		2,000

The adjusting entry then is used to establish the balance in the supplies account at $1,200 (amount of supplies still on hand at the end of the month) and reduce the supplies expense account from the amount purchased to the amount used.

To record the cost of supplies on hand at the end of July.

July 31		
Supplies (balance on hand)	1,200	
Supplies expense ($2,000 − 800)		1,200

T-accounts make the process easier to see before and after the adjusting entry:

Supplies

	Debit	Credit
(Adjusting entry)	1,200	
Bal. July 31	1,200	

Supplies Expense

	Debit	Credit
(Cash payment)	2,000	
(Adjusting entry)		1,200
Bal. July 31	800	

Notice that the ending balances in both accounts are the same as when reversing entries are not used. Up to this point, this approach is the alternate approach to recording prepayments discussed on page 69. The next step is an optional expediency.

On August 1, the following reversing entry can be recorded:

To reverse the July adjusting entry for supplies on hand.

August 1		
Supplies expense	1,200	
Supplies		1,200

This entry reduces the supplies account to zero and increases the supplies expense account to $2,000. Subsequent purchases would then be entered into the supplies expense account and future adjusting entries would record the amount of supplies still on hand at the end of the period. At the end of the fiscal year, the supplies expense account, along with all other temporary accounts, is closed to retained earnings.

Using reversing entries for prepayments, which is optional, simply allows cash payments to be entered directly into the temporary expense accounts without regard to whether only the current, or both the current and future periods, are benefitted by the expenditure. Adjustments are then recorded at the end of the period to reflect the amount of the unexpired benefit (asset).

APPENDIX 2C Subsidiary Ledgers and Special Journals

Subsidiary Ledgers

Accounting systems employ a *subsidiary ledger* which contains a group of subsidiary accounts associated with particular general ledger control accounts.

The general ledger contains what are referred to as *control accounts.* In addition to the general ledger, a **subsidiary ledger** contains a group of subsidiary accounts associated with a particular general ledger control account. For example, there will be a subsidiary ledger for accounts receivable that keeps track of the increases and decreases in the account receivable balance for each of the company's customers purchasing goods or services on credit. After all of the postings are made from the appropriate journals, the balance in the accounts receivable control account should equal the sum of the balances in the accounts receivable subsidiary ledger accounts. Subsidiary ledgers also are used for accounts payable, property and equipment, investments, and other accounts.

Special Journals

An actual accounting system employs many different types of journals. The purpose of each journal is to record, in chronological order, the dual effect of a transaction in debit/credit form. The chapter used the general journal format to record each transaction. However, even for small companies with relatively few transactions, the general journal is used to record only a few types of transactions.[8]

For most external transactions, *special journals* are used to capture the dual effect of the transaction in debit/credit form.

The majority of transactions are recorded in **special journals**. These journals capture the dual effect of *repetitive* types of transactions. For example, cash receipts are recorded in a **cash receipts journal**, cash disbursements in a **cash disbursements journal**, credit sales in a **sales journal**, and the purchase of merchandise on account in a **purchases journal**.

Special journals simplify the recording process in the following ways:

1. Journalizing the effects of a particular transaction is made more efficient through the use of specifically designed formats.
2. Individual transactions are not posted to the general ledger accounts but are accumulated in the special journals and a summary posting is made on a periodic basis.
3. The responsibility for recording journal entries for the repetitive types of transactions is placed on individuals who have specialized training in handling them.

The concepts of subsidiary ledgers and special journals are illustrated using the *sales journal* and the *cash receipts journal.*

Sales Journal

The purpose of the **sales journal** is to record all credit sales. Cash sales are recorded in the cash receipts journal. Every entry in the sales journal has exactly the same effect on the accounts; the sales revenue account is credited and the accounts receivable control account is debited. Therefore, there is only one column needed to record the debit/credit effect of these transactions. Other columns are needed to capture information for updating the accounts receivable subsidiary ledger. Illustration 2C–1 presents the sales journal for Dress Right Clothing Corporation for the month of August 2016.

All credit sales are recorded in the sales journal.

Illustration 2C–1

Sales Journal, Dress Right Clothing Corporation, August 2016

Page 1

Date	Accounts Receivable Subsidiary Account No.	Customer Name	Sales Invoice No.	Cr. Sales Revenue (400) Dr. Accounts Receivable (110)
2016				
Aug. 5	801	Leland High School	10-221	1,500
9	812	Mr. John Smith	10-222	200
18	813	Greystone School	10-223	825
22	803	Ms. Barbara Jones	10-224	120
29	805	Hart Middle School	10-225	650
				3,295

During the month of August, the company made five credit sales, totaling $3,295. This amount is posted as a debit to the accounts receivable control account, account number 110, and a credit to the sales revenue account, account number 400. The T-accounts for accounts receivable and sales revenue appear below. The reference SJ1 refers to page 1 of the sales journal.

General Ledger

Accounts Receivable 110			
July 31 Balance	2,000		
Aug. 31 SJ1	3,295		

Sales Revenue 400			
		3,295	Aug. 31 SJ1

[8]For example, end-of-period adjusting entries would be recorded in the general journal.

In a computerized accounting system, as each transaction is recorded in the sales journal, the subsidiary ledger accounts for the customer involved will automatically be updated. For example, the first credit sale of the month is to Leland High School for **$1,500**. The sales invoice number for this sale is **10-221** and the customer's subsidiary account number is 801. As this transaction is entered, the subsidiary account **801** for Leland High School is debited for **$1,500**.

Accounts Receivable Subsidiary Ledger

Leland High School			801
August 5 SJ1	1,500		

As cash is collected from this customer, the cash receipts journal records the transaction with a credit to the accounts receivable control account and a debit to cash. At the same time, the accounts receivable subsidiary ledger account number 801 also is credited. After the postings are made from the special journals, the balance in the accounts receivable control account should equal the sum of the balances in the accounts receivable subsidiary ledger accounts.

Cash Receipts Journal

All cash receipts are recorded in the *cash receipts journal*.

The purpose of the **cash receipts journal** is to record all cash receipts, regardless of the source. Every transaction recorded in this journal produces a debit entry to the cash account with the credit to various other accounts. Illustration 2C–2 shows a cash receipts journal using transactions of the Dress Right Clothing Corporation for the month of August 2016.

Illustration 2C–2

Cash Receipts Journal, Dress Right Clothing Corporation, August 2016

Page 1

Date	Explanation or Account Name	Dr. Cash (100)	Cr. Accounts Receivable (110)	Cr. Sales Revenue (400)	Cr. Other	Other Accounts
2016						
Aug. 7	Cash sale	500		500		
11	Borrowed cash	10,000			10,000	Note payable (220)
17	Leland High School	750	750			
20	Cash sale	300		300		
25	Mr. John Smith	200	200			
		11,750	950	800	10,000	

Because every transaction results in a debit to the cash account, No. 100, a column is provided for that account. At the end of August, an $11,750 debit is posted to the general ledger cash account with the source labeled CR1, cash receipts journal, page 1.

Because cash and credit sales are common, separate columns are provided for these accounts. At the end of August, a **$950** credit is posted to the accounts receivable general ledger account, No. 110, and an **$800** credit is posted to the sales revenue account, No. 400. Two additional credit columns are provided for uncommon cash receipt transactions, one for the credit amount and one for the account being credited. We can see that in August, Dress Right borrowed **$10,000** requiring a credit to the note payable account, No. 220.

In addition to the postings to the general ledger control accounts, each time an entry is recorded in the accounts receivable column, a credit is posted to the accounts receivable subsidiary ledger account for the customer making the payment. For example, on August 17, Leland High School paid $750 on account. The subsidiary ledger account for Leland High School is credited for **$750**.

Accounts Receivable Subsidiary Ledger

Leland High School			801
August 5 SJ1	1,500		
		750	August 17 CR1

Questions For Review of Key Topics

Q 2–1 Explain the difference between external events and internal events. Give an example of each type of event.

Q 2–2 Each economic event or transaction will have a dual effect on financial position. Explain what is meant by this dual effect.

Q 2–3 What is the purpose of a journal? What is the purpose of a general ledger?

Q 2–4 Explain the difference between permanent accounts and temporary accounts. Why does an accounting system include both types of accounts?

Q 2–5 Describe how debits and credits affect assets, liabilities, and permanent owners' equity accounts.

Q 2–6 Describe how debits and credits affect temporary owners' equity accounts.

Q 2–7 What is the first step in the accounting processing cycle? What role do source documents fulfill in this step?

Q 2–8 Describe what is meant by transaction analysis.

Q 2–9 Describe what is meant by posting, the fourth step in the processing cycle.

Q 2–10 Describe the events that correspond to the following two journal entries:

1. Inventory	20,000	
Accounts payable		20,000
2. Accounts receivable	30,000	
Sales revenue		30,000
Cost of goods sold	18,000	
Inventory		18,000

Q 2–11 What is an unadjusted trial balance? An adjusted trial balance?

Q 2–12 Define adjusting entries and discuss their purpose.

Q 2–13 Define closing entries and their purpose.

Q 2–14 Define prepaid expenses and provide at least two examples.

Q 2–15 Deferred revenues represent liabilities recorded when cash is received from customers in advance of providing a good or service. What adjusting journal entry is required at the end of a period to recognize the amount of deferred revenues that were recognized during the period?

Q 2–16 Define accrued liabilities. What adjusting journal entry is required to record accrued liabilities?

Q 2–17 Describe the purpose of each of the five primary financial statements.

Q 2–18 [Based on Appendix A] What is the purpose of a worksheet? In a columnar worksheet similar to Illustration 2A–1, what would be the result of incorrectly transferring the balance in a liability account to column K, the credit column under income statement?

Q 2–19 [Based on Appendix B] Define reversing entries and discuss their purpose.

Q 2–20 [Based on Appendix C] What is the purpose of special journals? In what ways do they simplify the recording process?

Q 2–21 [Based on Appendix C] Explain the difference between the general ledger and a subsidiary ledger.

Brief Exercises

BE 2–1
Transaction analysis
● LO2–1

The Marchetti Soup Company entered into the following transactions during the month of June: (1) purchased inventory on account for $165,000 (assume Marchetti uses a perpetual inventory system); (2) paid $40,000 in salaries to employees for work performed during the month; (3) sold merchandise that cost $120,000 to credit customers for $200,000; (4) collected $180,000 in cash from credit customers; and (5) paid suppliers of inventory $145,000. Analyze each transaction and show the effect of each on the accounting equation for a corporation.

BE 2–2
Journal entries
● LO2–2

Prepare journal entries for each of the transactions listed in BE 2–1.

BE 2–3
T-accounts
● LO2–3

Post the journal entries prepared in BE 2–2 to T-accounts. Assume that the opening balances in each of the accounts is zero except for cash, accounts receivable, and accounts payable that had opening balances of $65,000, $43,000, and $22,000, respectively.

BE 2–4
Journal entries
● LO2–2

Prepare journal entries for each of the following transactions for a company that has a fiscal year-end of December 31: (1) on October 1, $12,000 was paid for a one-year fire insurance policy; (2) on June 30 the company lent its chief financial officer $10,000; principal and interest at 6% are due in one year; and (3) equipment costing $60,000 was purchased at the beginning of the year for cash.

BE 2–5
Adjusting entries
● LO2–5

Prepare the necessary adjusting entries at December 31 for each of the items listed in BE 2–4. Depreciation on the equipment is $12,000 per year.

BE 2–6
Adjusting entries; income determination
● LO2–4, LO2–5

If the adjusting entries prepared in BE 2–5 were not recorded, would net income be higher or lower and by how much?

BE 2–7
Adjusting entries
● LO2–5

Prepare the necessary adjusting entries at its year-end of December 31, 2016, for the Jamesway Corporation for each of the following situations. No adjusting entries were recorded during the year.

1. On December 20, 2016, Jamesway received a $4,000 payment from a customer for services to be rendered early in 2017. Service revenue was credited.
2. On December 1, 2016, the company paid a local radio station $2,000 for 40 radio ads that were to be aired, 20 per month, throughout December and January. Prepaid advertising was debited.
3. Employee salaries for the month of December totaling $16,000 will be paid on January 7, 2017.
4. On August 31, 2016, Jamesway borrowed $60,000 from a local bank. A note was signed with principal and 8% interest to be paid on August 31, 2017.

BE 2–8
Income determination
● LO2–4

If none of the adjusting journal entries prepared in BE 2–7 were recorded, would assets, liabilities, and shareholders' equity on the 12/31/16 balance sheet be higher or lower and by how much?

BE 2–9
Adjusting entries
● LO2–5

Prepare the necessary adjusting entries for Johnstone Controls at the end of its December 31, 2016, fiscal year-end for each of the following situations. No adjusting entries were recorded during the year.

1. On March 31, 2016, the company lent $50,000 to another company. A note was signed with principal and interest at 6% payable on March 31, 2017.
2. On September 30, 2016, the company paid its landlord $12,000 representing rent for the period September 30, 2016, to September 30, 2017.
3. Supplies on hand at the end of 2015 totaled $3,000. Additional supplies costing $5,000 were purchased during 2016 and debited to the supplies account. At the end of 2016, supplies costing $4,200 remain on hand.
4. Vacation pay of $6,000 for the year that had been earned by employees was not paid or recorded. The company records vacation pay as salaries and wages expense.

BE 2–10
Financial statements
● LO2–6

The following account balances were taken from the 2016 adjusted trial balance of the Bowler Corporation: sales revenue, $325,000; cost of goods sold, $168,000; salaries expense; $45,000; rent expense, $20,000; depreciation expense, $30,000; and miscellaneous expense, $12,000. Prepare an income statement for 2016.

BE 2–11
Financial statements
● LO2–6

The following account balances were taken from the 2016 post-closing trial balance of the Bowler Corporation: cash, $5,000; accounts receivable, $10,000; inventory, $16,000; equipment, $100,000; accumulated depreciation—equipment, $40,000; accounts payable, $20,000; salaries payable, $12,000; retained earnings, $9,000; and common stock, $50,000. Prepare a 12/31/16 balance sheet.

BE 2–12
Closing entries
● LO2–7

The year-end adjusted trial balance of the Timmons Tool and Die Corporation included the following account balances: retained earnings, $220,000; sales revenue, $850,000; cost of goods sold, $580,000; salaries expense, $180,000; rent expense, $40,000; and interest expense, $15,000. Prepare the necessary closing entries.

BE 2–13
Cash versus accrual accounting
● LO2–8

Newman Consulting Company maintains its records on a cash basis. During 2016 the following cash flows were recorded: cash received from customers, $420,000; and cash paid for salaries, utilities, and advertising, $240,000, $35,000, and $12,000, respectively. You also determine that customers owed the company $52,000 and $60,000 at the beginning and end of the year, respectively, and that the company owed the utility company $6,000 and $4,000 at the beginning and end of the year, respectively. Determine accrual net income for the year.

Exercises

An alternate exercise and problem set is available in the Connect library.

E 2–1
Transaction analysis
● LO2–1

The following transactions occurred during March 2016 for the Wainwright Corporation. The company owns and operates a wholesale warehouse.

1. Issued 30,000 shares of common stock in exchange for $300,000 in cash.
2. Purchased equipment at a cost of $40,000. $10,000 cash was paid and a note payable was signed for the balance owed.
3. Purchased inventory on account at a cost of $90,000. The company uses the perpetual inventory system.
4. Credit sales for the month totaled $120,000. The cost of the goods sold was $70,000.
5. Paid $5,000 in rent on the warehouse building for the month of March.
6. Paid $6,000 to an insurance company for fire and liability insurance for a one-year period beginning April 1, 2016.
7. Paid $70,000 on account for the merchandise purchased in 3.
8. Collected $55,000 from customers on account.
9. Recorded depreciation expense of $1,000 for the month on the equipment.

Required:

Analyze each transaction and show the effect of each on the accounting equation for a corporation.

Example:

	Assets	= Liabilities + Paid-In Capital + Retained Earnings
1.	+300,000 (cash)	+ 300,000 (common stock)

E 2–2
Journal entries
● LO2–2

Prepare journal entries to record each of the transactions listed in E2–1.

E 2–3
T-accounts and trial balance
● LO2–3

Post the journal entries prepared in E2–2 to T-accounts. Assume that the opening balances in each of the accounts is zero. Prepare a trial balance from the ending account balances.

E 2–4
Journal entries
● LO2–2

The following transactions occurred during the month of June 2016 for the Stridewell Corporation. The company owns and operates a retail shoe store.

1. Issued 100,000 shares of common stock in exchange for $500,000 cash.
2. Purchased furniture and fixtures at a cost of $100,000. $40,000 was paid in cash and a note payable was signed for the balance owed.
3. Purchased inventory on account at a cost of $200,000. The company uses the perpetual inventory system.
4. Credit sales for the month totaled $280,000. The cost of the goods sold was $140,000.
5. Paid $6,000 in rent on the store building for the month of June.
6. Paid $3,000 to an insurance company for fire and liability insurance for a one-year period beginning June 1, 2016.
7. Paid $120,000 on account for the merchandise purchased in 3.
8. Collected $55,000 from customers on account.
9. Paid shareholders a cash dividend of $5,000.
10. Recorded depreciation expense of $2,000 for the month on the furniture and fixtures.
11. Recorded the amount of prepaid insurance that expired for the month.

Required:

Prepare journal entries to record each of the transactions and events listed above.

E 2–5
The accounting processing cycle
● LO2–2 through LO2–7

Listed below are several terms and phrases associated with the accounting processing cycle. Pair each item from List A (by letter) with the item from List B that is most appropriately associated with it.

List A	List B
____ 1. Source documents	a. Record of the dual effect of a transaction in debit/credit form.
____ 2. Transaction analysis	b. Internal events recorded at the end of a reporting period.
____ 3. Journal	c. Primary means of disseminating information to external decision makers.

(continued)

(concluded)

List A	List B
____ 4. Posting	d. To zero out the owners' equity temporary accounts.
____ 5. Unadjusted trial balance	e. Determine the dual effect on the accounting equation.
____ 6. Adjusting entries	f. List of accounts and their balances before recording adjusting entries.
____ 7. Adjusted trial balance	g. List of accounts and their balances after recording closing entries.
____ 8. Financial statements	h. List of accounts and their balances after recording adjusting entries.
____ 9. Closing entries	i. A means of organizing information: not part of the formal accounting system.
____ 10. Post-closing trial balance	j. Transferring balances from the journal to the ledger.
____ 11. Worksheet	k. Used to identify and process external transactions.

E 2–6
Debits and credits
● LO2–2

Indicate whether a *debit* will increase (I) or decrease (D) each of the following accounts listed in items 1 through 16:

Increase (I) or Decrease (D)	Account
1. ____	Inventory
2. ____	Depreciation expense
3. ____	Accounts payable
4. ____	Prepaid rent
5. ____	Sales revenue
6. ____	Common stock
7. ____	Salaries and wages payable
8. ____	Cost of goods sold
9. ____	Utility expense
10. ____	Equipment
11. ____	Accounts receivable
12. ____	Utilities payable
13. ____	Rent expense
14. ____	Interest expense
15. ____	Interest revenue

E 2–7
Transaction analysis; debits and credits
● LO2–2

Some of the ledger accounts for the Sanderson Hardware Company are numbered and listed below. For each of the October 2016 transactions numbered 1 through 12 below, indicate by account number which accounts should be debited and which should be credited. The company uses the perpetual inventory system. Assume that appropriate adjusting entries were recorded at the end of September.

(1) Accounts payable	(2) Equipment	(3) Inventory
(4) Accounts receivable	(5) Cash	(6) Supplies
(7) Supplies expense	(8) Prepaid rent	(9) Sales revenue
(10) Retained earnings	(11) Note payable	(12) Common stock
(13) Deferred revenue	(14) Rent expense	(15) Salaries and wages payable
(16) Cost of goods sold	(17) Salaries and wages expense	(18) Interest expense

	Account(s) Debited	Account(s) Credited
Example: Purchased inventory for cash	3	5

1. Paid a cash dividend.
2. Paid rent for the next three months.
3. Sold goods to customers on account.
4. Purchased inventory on account.
5. Purchased supplies for cash.
6. Paid employee salaries and wages for September.
7. Issued common stock in exchange for cash.
8. Collected cash from customers for goods sold in 3.
9. Borrowed cash from a bank and signed a note.
10. At the end of October, recorded the amount of supplies that had been used during the month.

11. Received cash for advance payment from customer.
12. Accrued employee salaries and wages for October.

E 2–8
Adjusting entries
● LO2–5

Prepare the necessary adjusting entries at December 31, 2016, for the Falwell Company for each of the following situations. Assume that no financial statements were prepared during the year and no adjusting entries were recorded.

1. A three-year fire insurance policy was purchased on July 1, 2016, for $12,000. The company debited insurance expense for the entire amount.
2. Depreciation on equipment totaled $15,000 for the year.
3. Employee salaries of $18,000 for the month of December will be paid in early January 2017.
4. On November 1, 2016, the company borrowed $200,000 from a bank. The note requires principal and interest at 12% to be paid on April 30, 2017.
5. On December 1, 2016, the company received $3,000 in cash from another company that is renting office space in Falwell's building. The payment, representing rent for December and January, was credited to deferred rent revenue.

E 2–9
Adjusting entries
● LO2–5

Prepare the necessary adjusting entries at December 31, 2016, for the Microchip Company for each of the following situations. Assume that no financial statements were prepared during the year and no adjusting entries were recorded.

1. On October 1, 2016, Microchip lent $90,000 to another company. A note was signed with principal and 8% interest to be paid on September 30, 2017.
2. On November 1, 2016, the company paid its landlord $6,000 representing rent for the months of November through January. Prepaid rent was debited.
3. On August 1, 2016, collected $12,000 in advance rent from another company that is renting a portion of Microchip's factory. The $12,000 represents one year's rent and the entire amount was credited to rent revenue.
4. Depreciation on office equipment is $4,500 for the year.
5. Vacation pay for the year that had been earned by employees but not paid to them or recorded is $8,000. The company records vacation pay as salaries expense.
6. Microchip began the year with $2,000 in its asset account, supplies. During the year, $6,500 in supplies were purchased and debited to supplies. At year-end, supplies costing $3,250 remain on hand.

E 2–10
Adjusting entries; solving for unknowns
● LO2–4, LO2–5

The Eldorado Corporation's controller prepares adjusting entries only at the end of the fiscal year. The following adjusting entries were prepared on December 31, 2016:

	Debit	Credit
Interest expense	7,200	
Interest payable		7,200
Rent expense	35,000	
Prepaid rent		35,000
Interest receivable	500	
Interest revenue		500

Additional information:

1. The company borrowed $120,000 on March 31, 2016. Principal and interest are due on March 31, 2017. This note is the company's only interest-bearing debt.
2. Rent for the year on the company's office space is $60,000. The rent is paid in advance.
3. On October 31, 2016, Eldorado lent money to a customer. The customer signed a note with principal and interest at 6% due in one year.

Required:

Determine the following:

1. What is the interest rate on the company's note payable?
2. The 2016 rent payment was made at the beginning of which month?
3. How much did Eldorado lend its customer on October 31?

E 2–11
Adjusting entries
● LO2–5

The Mazzanti Wholesale Food Company's fiscal year-end is June 30. The company issues quarterly financial statements requiring the company to prepare adjusting entries at the end of each quarter. Assuming all quarterly adjusting entries were properly recorded, prepare the necessary year-end adjusting entries at the end of June 30, 2016, for the following situations.

1. On December 1, 2015, the company paid its annual fire insurance premium of $6,000 for the year beginning December 1.

2. On August 31, 2015, the company borrowed $80,000 from a local bank. The note requires principal and interest at 8% to be paid on August 31, 2016.
3. Mazzanti owns a warehouse that it rents to another company. On January 1, 2016, Mazzanti collected $24,000 representing rent for the 2016 calendar year.
4. Depreciation on the office building is $20,000 for the fiscal year.
5. Employee salaries and wages for the month of June 2016 of $16,000 will be paid on July 20, 2016.

E 2–12
Financial statements and closing entries
● LO2–6, LO2–7

The December 31, 2016, adjusted trial balance for the Blueboy Cheese Corporation is presented below.

Account Title	Debits	Credits
Cash	21,000	
Accounts receivable	300,000	
Prepaid rent	10,000	
Inventory	50,000	
Office equipment	600,000	
Accumulated depreciation—office equipment		250,000
Accounts payable		60,000
Note payable (due in six months)		60,000
Salaries payable		8,000
Interest payable		2,000
Common stock		400,000
Retained earnings		100,000
Sales revenue		800,000
Cost of goods sold	480,000	
Salaries expense	120,000	
Rent expense	30,000	
Depreciation expense	60,000	
Interest expense	4,000	
Advertising expense	5,000	
Totals	1,680,000	1,680,000

Required:
1. Prepare an income statement for the year ended December 31, 2016, and a classified balance sheet as of December 31, 2016.
2. Prepare the necessary closing entries at December 31, 2016.

E 2–13
Closing entries
● LO2–7

American Chip Corporation's fiscal year-end is December 31. The following is a partial adjusted trial balance as of December 31, 2016.

Account Title	Debits	Credits
Retained earnings		80,000
Sales revenue		750,000
Interest revenue		3,000
Cost of goods sold	420,000	
Salaries expense	100,000	
Rent expense	15,000	
Depreciation expense	30,000	
Interest expense	5,000	
Insurance expense	6,000	

Required:
Prepare the necessary closing entries at December 31, 2016.

E 2–14
Closing entries
● LO2–7

Presented below is income statement information of the Schefter Corporation for the year ended December 31, 2016.

Sales revenue	$492,000	Cost of goods sold	$284,000
Salaries expense	80,000	Insurance expense	12,000
Interest revenue	6,000	Interest expense	4,000
Advertising expense	10,000	Income tax expense	30,000
Gain on sale of investments	8,000	Depreciation expense	20,000

Required:
Prepare the necessary closing entries at December 31, 2016.

E 2–15
Cash versus accrual accounting; adjusting entries
● LO2–4, LO2–5, LO2–8

The Righter Shoe Store Company prepares monthly financial statements for its bank. The November 30 and December 31, 2016, trial balances contained the following account information:

	Nov. 30		Dec. 31	
	Dr.	Cr.	Dr.	Cr.
Supplies	1,500		3,000	
Prepaid insurance	6,000		4,500	
Salaries and wages payable		10,000		15,000
Deferred rent revenue		2,000		1,000

The following information also is known:

a. The December income statement reported $2,000 in supplies expense.
b. No insurance payments were made in December.
c. $10,000 was paid to employees during December for salaries and wages.
d. On November 1, 2016, a tenant paid Righter $3,000 in advance rent for the period November through January. Deferred rent revenue was credited.

Required:

1. What was the cost of supplies purchased during December?
2. What was the adjusting entry recorded at the end of December for prepaid insurance?
3. What was the adjusting entry recorded at the end of December for accrued salaries and wages?
4. What was the amount of rent revenue recognized in December? What adjusting entry was recorded at the end of December for deferred rent?

E 2–16
External transactions and adjusting entries
● LO2–2, LO2–5

The following transactions occurred during 2016 for the Beehive Honey Corporation:

Feb. 1	Borrowed $12,000 from a bank and signed a note. Principal and interest at 10% will be paid on January 31, 2017.
Apr. 1	Paid $3,600 to an insurance company for a two-year fire insurance policy.
July 17	Purchased supplies costing $2,800 on account. The company records supplies purchased in an asset account. At the year-end on December 31, 2016, supplies costing $1,250 remained on hand.
Nov. 1	A customer borrowed $6,000 and signed a note requiring the customer to pay principal and 8% interest on April 30, 2017.

Required:

1. Record each transaction in general journal form. Omit explanations.
2. Prepare any necessary adjusting entries at the year-end on December 31, 2016. No adjusting entries were recorded during the year for any item.

E 2–17
Accrual accounting income determination
● LO2–4, LO2–8

During the course of your examination of the financial statements of the Hales Corporation for the year ended December 31, 2016, you discover the following:

a. An insurance policy covering three years was purchased on January 1, 2016, for $6,000. The entire amount was debited to insurance expense and no adjusting entry was recorded for this item.
b. During 2016, the company received a $1,000 cash advance from a customer for merchandise to be manufactured and shipped in 2017. The $1,000 was credited to sales revenue. No entry was recorded for the cost of merchandise.
c. There were no supplies listed in the balance sheet under assets. However, you discover that supplies costing $750 were on hand at December 31.
d. Hales borrowed $20,000 from a local bank on October 1, 2016. Principal and interest at 12% will be paid on September 30, 2017. No accrual was recorded for interest.
e. Net income reported in the 2016 income statement is $30,000 before reflecting any of the above items.

Required:

Determine the proper amount of net income for 2016.

E 2–18
Cash versus accrual accounting
● LO2–8

Stanley and Jones Lawn Service Company (S&J) maintains its books on a cash basis. However, the company recently borrowed $100,000 from a local bank and the bank requires S&J to provide annual financial statements prepared on an accrual basis. During 2016, the following cash flows were recorded:

Cash collected from customers		$320,000
Cash paid for:		
Salaries	$180,000	
Supplies	25,000	
Rent	12,000	
Insurance	6,000	
Miscellaneous	20,000	243,000
Net operating cash flow		$ 77,000

You are able to determine the following information about accounts receivable, prepaid expenses, and accrued liabilities:

	January 1, 2016	December 31, 2016
Accounts receivable	$32,000	$27,000
Prepaid insurance	–0–	2,000
Supplies	1,000	1,500
Accrued liabilities (for miscellaneous expenses)	2,400	3,400

In addition, you learn that the bank loan was dated September 30, 2016, with principal and interest at 6% due in one year. Depreciation on the company's equipment is $10,000 for the year.

Required:
Prepare an accrual basis income statement for 2016. (Ignore income taxes.)

E 2–19
Cash versus accrual accounting
● LO2–8

Haskins and Jones, Attorneys-at-Law, maintain its books on a cash basis. During 2016, the company collected $545,000 in fees from its clients and paid out $412,000 in expenses. You are able to determine the following information about accounts receivable, prepaid expenses, deferred fee revenue, and accrued liabilities:

	January 1, 2016	December 31, 2016
Accounts receivable	$62,000	$55,000
Prepaid insurance	4,500	6,000
Prepaid rent	9,200	8,200
Deferred fee revenue	9,200	11,000
Accrued liabilities (for various expenses)	12,200	15,600

In addition, 2016 depreciation expense on furniture and fixtures is $22,000.

Required:
Determine accrual basis net income for 2016.

E 2–20
Worksheet
● Appendix 2A

The December 31, 2016, unadjusted trial balance for the Wolkstein Drug Company is presented below. December 31 is the company's fiscal year-end.

Account Title	Debits	Credits
Cash	20,000	
Accounts receivable	35,000	
Prepaid rent	5,000	
Inventory	50,000	
Equipment	100,000	
Accumulated depreciation—equipment		30,000
Accounts payable		25,000
Salaries and wages payable		–0–
Common stock		100,000
Retained earnings		29,000
Sales revenue		323,000
Cost of goods sold	180,000	
Salaries and wages expense	71,000	
Rent expense	30,000	
Depreciation expense	–0–	
Utility expense	12,000	
Advertising expense	4,000	
Totals	507,000	507,000

The following year-end adjusting entries are required:

a. Depreciation expense for the year on the equipment is $10,000.

b. Accrued salaries and wages payable at year-end should be $4,000.

Required:

1. Prepare and complete a worksheet similar to Illustration 2A–1.
2. Prepare an income statement for 2016 and a balance sheet as of December 31, 2016.

E 2–21
Reversing entries
● Appendix 2B

The employees of Xitrex, Inc., are paid each Friday. The company's fiscal year-end is June 30, which falls on a Wednesday for the current year. Salaries and wages are earned evenly throughout the five-day workweek, and $10,000 will be paid on Friday, July 2.

Required:

1. Prepare an adjusting entry to record the accrued salaries and wages as of June 30, a reversing entry on July 1, and an entry to record the payment of salaries and wages on July 2.
2. Prepare journal entries to record the accrued salaries and wages as of June 30 and the payment of salaries and wages on July 2 assuming a reversing entry is not recorded.

E 2–22
Reversing entries
● Appendix 2B

Refer to E2–9 and respond to the following requirements.

Required:

1. If Microchip's accountant employed reversing entries for accruals, which adjusting entries would she likely reverse at the beginning of the following year?
2. Prepare the adjusting entries at the end of 2016 for the adjustments you identified in requirement 1.
3. Prepare the appropriate reversing entries at the beginning of 2017.

E 2–23
Reversing entries
● Appendix 2B

Refer to E2–9 and respond to the following requirements.

Required:

1. If Microchip's accountant employed reversing entries for prepaid expenses, which transactions would be affected?
2. Prepare the original transactions creating the prepaid expenses and the adjusting entries at the end of 2016 for the transactions you identified in requirement 1.
3. Prepare the appropriate reversing entries at the beginning of 2017.

E 2–24
Special journals
● Appendix 2C

The White Company's accounting system consists of a general journal (GJ), a cash receipts journal (CR), a cash disbursements journal (CD), a sales journal (SJ), and a purchases journal (PJ). For each of the following, indicate which journal should be used to record the transaction.

Transaction	Journal
1. Purchased merchandise on account.	______
2. Collected an account receivable.	______
3. Borrowed $20,000 and signed a note.	______
4. Recorded depreciation expense.	______
5. Purchased equipment for cash.	______
6. Sold merchandise for cash (the sale only, not the cost of the merchandise).	______
7. Sold merchandise on credit (the sale only, not the cost of the merchandise).	______
8. Recorded accrued salaries and wages payable.	______
9. Paid employee salaries and wages.	______
10. Sold equipment for cash.	______
11. Sold equipment on credit.	______
12. Paid a cash dividend to shareholders.	______
13. Issued common stock in exchange for cash.	______
14. Paid accounts payable.	______

E 2–25
Special journals
● Appendix 2C

The accounting system of K and M Manufacturing consists of a general journal (GJ), a cash receipts journal (CR), a cash disbursements journal (CD), a sales journal (SJ), and a purchases journal (PJ). For each of the following, indicate which journal should be used to record the transaction.

Transaction	Journal
1. Paid interest on a loan.	______
2. Recorded depreciation expense.	______
3. Purchased furniture for cash.	______

(continued)

(concluded)

Transaction	Journal
4. Purchased merchandise on account.	______
5. Sold merchandise on credit (the sale only, not the cost of the merchandise).	______
6. Sold merchandise for cash (the sale only, not the cost of the merchandise).	______
7. Paid rent.	______
8. Recorded accrued interest payable.	______
9. Paid advertising bill.	______
10. Sold equipment on credit.	______
11. Collected cash from customers on account.	______
12. Paid employee salaries and wages.	______
13. Collected interest on a note receivable.	______

CPA Review Questions

CPA Exam Questions

KAPLAN CPA REVIEW

The following questions are adapted from a variety of sources including questions developed by the AICPA Board of Examiners and those used in the Kaplan CPA Review Course to study accounting changes and errors processing while preparing for the CPA examination. Determine the response that best completes the statements or questions.

● LO2–1

1. JME Corporation bills its customers when services are rendered and recognizes revenue at the same time. This event causes an
   a. Increase in assets.
   b. Increase in net income.
   c. Increase in retained earnings.
   d. All of the above.

● LO2–5

2. Fay Corp. pays its outside salespersons fixed monthly salaries as well as commissions on net sales. Sales commissions are paid in the month following the month of sale, while the fixed salaries are expensed but considered advances against commissions. However, if salespersons' fixed salaries exceed their sales commissions earned for a month, such excess is not returned to the company. Pertinent data for the month of March for the three salespersons are as follows:

Salesperson	Fixed Salary	Net Sales	Commission Rate
A	$10,000	$ 200,000	4%
B	14,000	400,000	6%
C	18,000	600,000	6%
Totals	$42,000	$1,200,000	

What amount should Fay accrue as a debit to sales commissions expense and a credit to sales commissions payable at March 31?
   a. $26,000
   b. $28,000
   c. $68,000
   d. $70,000

● LO2–8

3. Compared to the accrual basis of accounting, the cash basis of accounting produces a lower amount of income by the net decrease during the accounting period of

	Accounts Receivable	Accrued Liabilities
a.	Yes	No
b.	No	Yes
c.	Yes	Yes
d.	No	No

● LO2–8

4. On April 1 Ivy Corp. began operating a service company with an initial cash investment by shareholders of $1,000,000. The company provided $3,200,000 of services in April and received full payment in May. Ivy also incurred expenses of $1,500,000 in April that were paid in June. During May, Ivy paid its shareholders

cash dividends of $500,000. What was the company's income before income taxes for the two months ended May 31 under the following methods of accounting?

	Cash Basis	Accrual Basis
a.	$3,200,000	$1,700,000
b.	$2,700,000	$1,200,000
c.	$1,700,000	$1,700,000
d.	$3,200,000	$1,200,000

● LO2–8

5. Under East Co.'s accounting system, all insurance premiums paid are debited to prepaid insurance. During the year, East records monthly estimated charges to insurance expense with credits to prepaid insurance. Additional information for the year ended December 31 is as follows:

Prepaid insurance at January 1	$105,000
Insurance expense recognized during the year	437,500
Prepaid insurance at December 31	122,500

What was the total amount of cash paid by East for insurance premiums during the year?
a. $332,500
b. $420,000
c. $437,500
d. $455,000

Problems

An alternate exercise and problem set is available in the Connect library.

P 2–1
Accounting cycle through unadjusted trial balance
● LO2–2, LO2–3

Halogen Laminated Products Company began business on January 1, 2016. During January, the following transactions occurred:

Jan.	1	Issued common stock in exchange for $100,000 cash.
	2	Purchased inventory on account for $35,000 (the perpetual inventory system is used).
	4	Paid an insurance company $2,400 for a one-year insurance policy.
	10	Sold merchandise on account for $12,000. The cost of the merchandise was $7,000.
	15	Borrowed $30,000 from a local bank and signed a note. Principal and interest at 10% is to be repaid in six months.
	20	Paid employees $6,000 salaries and wages for the first half of the month.
	22	Sold merchandise for $10,000 cash. The cost of the merchandise was $6,000.
	24	Paid $15,000 to suppliers for the merchandise purchased on January 2.
	26	Collected $6,000 on account from customers.
	28	Paid $1,000 to the local utility company for January gas and electricity.
	30	Paid $4,000 rent for the building. $2,000 was for January rent, and $2,000 for February rent.

Required:
1. Prepare general journal entries to record each transaction. Omit explanations.
2. Post the entries to T-accounts.
3. Prepare an unadjusted trial balance as of January 30, 2016.

P 2–2
Accounting cycle through unadjusted trial balance
● LO2–2, LO2–3

The following is the post-closing trial balance for the Whitlow Manufacturing Corporation as of December 31, 2015.

Account Title	Debits	Credits
Cash	5,000	
Accounts receivable	2,000	
Inventory	5,000	
Equipment	11,000	
Accumulated depreciation—equipment		3,500
Accounts payable		3,000

(continued)

(concluded)

Account Title	Debits	Credits
Common stock		10,000
Retained earnings		6,500
Sales revenue		–0–
Cost of goods sold	–0–	
Salaries and wages expense	–0–	
Rent expense	–0–	
Advertising expense	–0–	
Totals	23,000	23,000

The following transactions occurred during January 2016:

Jan.	1	Sold merchandise for cash, $3,500. The cost of the merchandise was $2,000. The company uses the perpetual inventory system.
	2	Purchased equipment on account for $5,500 from the Strong Company.
	4	Received a $150 bill from the local newspaper for an advertisement that appeared in the paper on January 2.
	8	Sold merchandise on account for $5,000. The cost of the merchandise was $2,800.
	10	Purchased merchandise on account for $9,500.
	13	Purchased equipment for cash, $800.
	16	Paid the entire amount due to the Strong Company.
	18	Received $4,000 from customers on account.
	20	Paid $800 to the owner of the building for January's rent.
	30	Paid employees $3,000 for salaries and wages for the month of January.
	31	Paid a cash dividend of $1,000 to shareholders.

Required:

1. Set up T-accounts and enter the beginning balances as of January 1, 2016.
2. Prepare general journal entries to record each transaction. Omit explanations.
3. Post the entries to T-accounts.
4. Prepare an unadjusted trial balance as of January 31, 2016.

P 2–3
Adjusting entries
 LO2–5

Pastina Company sells various types of pasta to grocery chains as private label brands. The company's fiscal year-end is December 31. The unadjusted trial balance as of December 31, 2016, appears below.

Account Title	Debits	Credits
Cash	30,000	
Accounts receivable	40,000	
Supplies	1,500	
Inventory	60,000	
Note receivable	20,000	
Interest receivable	–0–	
Prepaid rent	2,000	
Prepaid insurance	–0–	
Office equipment	80,000	
Accumulated depreciation—office equipment		30,000
Accounts payable		31,000
Salaries and wages payable		–0–
Note payable		50,000
Interest payable		–0–
Deferred revenue		–0–
Common stock		60,000
Retained earnings		24,500
Sales revenue		148,000
Interest revenue		–0–
Cost of goods sold	70,000	
Salaries and wages expense	18,900	
Rent expense	11,000	
Depreciation expense	–0–	

(continued)

(concluded)

Interest expense	–0–	
Supplies expense	1,100	
Insurance expense	6,000	
Advertising expense	3,000	
Totals	343,500	343,500

Information necessary to prepare the year-end adjusting entries appears below.

1. Depreciation on the office equipment for the year is $10,000.
2. Employee salaries and wages are paid twice a month, on the 22nd for salaries and wages earned from the 1st through the 15th, and on the 7th of the following month for salaries and wages earned from the 16th through the end of the month. Salaries and wages earned from December 16 through December 31, 2016, were $1,500.
3. On October 1, 2016, Pastina borrowed $50,000 from a local bank and signed a note. The note requires interest to be paid annually on September 30 at 12%. The principal is due in 10 years.
4. On March 1, 2016, the company lent a supplier $20,000 and a note was signed requiring principal and interest at 8% to be paid on February 28, 2017.
5. On April 1, 2016, the company paid an insurance company $6,000 for a two-year fire insurance policy. The entire $6,000 was debited to insurance expense.
6. $800 of supplies remained on hand at December 31, 2016.
7. A customer paid Pastina $2,000 in December for 1,500 pounds of spaghetti to be delivered in January 2017. Pastina credited sales revenue.
8. On December 1, 2016, $2,000 rent was paid to the owner of the building. The payment represented rent for December 2016 and January 2017, at $1,000 per month.

Required:

Prepare the necessary December 31, 2016, adjusting journal entries.

P 2–4
Accounting cycle; adjusting entries through post-closing trial balance
● LO2–3, LO2–5 through LO2–7

Refer to P2–3 and complete the following steps:

1. Enter the unadjusted balances from the trial balance into T-accounts.
2. Post the adjusting entries prepared in P2–3 to the accounts.
3. Prepare an adjusted trial balance.
4. Prepare an income statement and a statement of shareholders' equity for the year ended December 31, 2016, and a classified balance sheet as of December 31, 2016. Assume that no common stock was issued during the year and that $4,000 in cash dividends were paid to shareholders during the year.
5. Prepare closing entries and post to the accounts.
6. Prepare a post-closing trial balance.

P 2–5
Adjusting entries
● LO2–5

Howarth Company's fiscal year-end is December 31. Below are the unadjusted and adjusted trial balances for December 31, 2016.

	Unadjusted		Adjusted	
Account Title	**Debits**	**Credits**	**Debits**	**Credits**
Cash	50,000		50,000	
Accounts receivable	35,000		35,000	
Prepaid rent	2,000		1,200	
Supplies	1,500		800	
Inventory	60,000		60,000	
Note receivable	30,000		30,000	
Interest receivable	–0–		1,500	
Office equipment	45,000		45,000	
Accumulated depreciation		15,000		21,500
Accounts payable		34,000		34,000
Salaries and wages payable		–0–		6,200
Note payable		50,000		50,000
Interest payable		–0–		2,500
Deferred rent revenue		–0–		2,000
Common stock		46,000		46,000
Retained earnings		20,000		20,000

(continued)

(concluded)

	Unadjusted		Adjusted	
Account Title	**Debits**	**Credits**	**Debits**	**Credits**
Sales revenue		244,000		244,000
Rent revenue		6,000		4,000
Interest revenue		–0–		1,500
Cost of goods sold	126,000		126,000	
Salaries and wages expense	45,000		51,200	
Rent expense	11,000		11,800	
Depreciation expense	–0–		6,500	
Supplies expense	1,100		1,800	
Interest expense	5,400		7,900	
Advertising expense	3,000		3,000	
Totals	415,000	415,000	431,700	431,700

Required:

Prepare the adjusting journal entries that were recorded at December 31, 2016.

P 2–6
Accounting cycle
● LO2–2 through LO2–7

The general ledger of the Karlin Company, a consulting company, at January 1, 2016, contained the following account balances:

Account Title	Debits	Credits
Cash	30,000	
Accounts receivable	15,000	
Equipment	20,000	
Accumulated depreciation		6,000
Salaries payable		9,000
Common stock		40,500
Retained earnings		9,500
Total	65,000	65,000

The following is a summary of the transactions for the year:

a. Sales of services, $100,000, of which $30,000 was on credit.
b. Collected on accounts receivable, $27,300.
c. Issued shares of common stock in exchange for $10,000 in cash.
d. Paid salaries, $50,000 (of which $9,000 was for salaries payable).
e. Paid miscellaneous expenses, $24,000.
f. Purchased equipment for $15,000 in cash.
g. Paid $2,500 in cash dividends to shareholders.

Required:

1. Set up the necessary T-accounts and enter the beginning balances from the trial balance.
2. Prepare a general journal entry for each of the summary transactions listed above.
3. Post the journal entries to the accounts.
4. Prepare an unadjusted trial balance.
5. Prepare and post adjusting journal entries. Accrued salaries at year-end amounted to $1,000. Depreciation for the year on the equipment is $2,000.
6. Prepare an adjusted trial balance.
7. Prepare an income statement for 2016 and a balance sheet as of December 31, 2016.
8. Prepare and post closing entries.
9. Prepare a post-closing trial balance.

P 2–7
Adjusting entries and income effects
● LO2–4, LO2–5

The information necessary for preparing the 2016 year-end adjusting entries for Vito's Pizza Parlor appears below. Vito's fiscal year-end is December 31.

a. On July 1, 2016, purchased $10,000 of IBM Corporation bonds at face value. The bonds pay interest twice a year on January 1 and July 1. The annual interest rate is 12%.

b. Vito's depreciable equipment has a cost of $30,000, a five-year life, and no salvage value. The equipment was purchased in 2014. The straight-line depreciation method is used.

c. On November 1, 2016, the bar area was leased to Jack Donaldson for one year. Vito's received $6,000 representing the first six months' rent and credited deferred rent revenue.

d. On April 1, 2016, the company paid $2,400 for a two-year fire and liability insurance policy and debited insurance expense.

e. On October 1, 2016, the company borrowed $20,000 from a local bank and signed a note. Principal and interest at 12% will be paid on September 30, 2017.

f. At year-end, there is a $1,800 debit balance in the supplies (asset) account. Only $700 of supplies remain on hand.

Required:

1. Prepare the necessary adjusting journal entries at December 31, 2016.
2. Determine the amount by which net income would be misstated if Vito's failed to record these adjusting entries. (Ignore income tax expense.)

P 2–8
Adjusting entries
● LO2–5

Excalibur Corporation sells video games for personal computers. The unadjusted trial balance as of December 31, 2016, appears below. December 31 is the company's fiscal year-end. The company uses the perpetual inventory system.

Account Title	Debits	Credits
Cash	23,300	
Accounts receivable	32,500	
Supplies	–0–	
Prepaid rent	–0–	
Inventory	65,000	
Office equipment	75,000	
Accumulated depreciation—office equipment		10,000
Accounts payable		26,100
Salaries and wages payable		3,000
Note payable		30,000
Common stock		80,000
Retained earnings		16,050
Sales revenue		180,000
Cost of goods sold	95,000	
Interest expense	–0–	
Salaries and wages expense	32,350	
Rent expense	14,000	
Supplies expense	2,000	
Utility expense	6,000	
Totals	345,150	345,150

Information necessary to prepare the year-end adjusting entries appears below.

1. The office equipment was purchased in 2014 and is being depreciated using the straight-line method over an eight-year useful life with no salvage value.
2. Accrued salaries and wages at year-end should be $4,500.
3. The company borrowed $30,000 on September 1, 2016. The principal is due to be repaid in 10 years. Interest is payable twice a year on each August 31 and February 28 at an annual rate of 10%.
4. The company debits supplies expense when supplies are purchased. Supplies on hand at year-end cost $500.
5. Prepaid rent at year-end should be $1,000.

Required:

Prepare the necessary December 31, 2016, adjusting entries.

P 2–9
Accounting cycle; unadjusted trial balance through closing
● LO2–3, LO2–5, LO2–7

The unadjusted trial balance as of December 31, 2016, for the Bagley Consulting Company appears below. December 31 is the company's fiscal year-end.

Account Title	Debits	Credits
Cash	8,000	
Accounts receivable	9,000	
Prepaid insurance	3,000	
Land	200,000	
Buildings	50,000	
Accumulated depreciation—buildings		20,000
Office equipment	100,000	
Accumulated depreciation—office equipment		40,000
Accounts payable		35,050
Salaries and wages payable		–0–
Deferred rent revenue		–0–
Common stock		200,000
Retained earnings		56,450
Sales revenue		90,000
Interest revenue		3,000
Rent revenue		7,500
Salaries and wages expense	37,000	
Depreciation expense	–0–	
Insurance expense	–0–	
Utility expense	30,000	
Maintenance expense	15,000	
Totals	452,000	452,000

Required:

1. Enter the account balances in T-accounts.
2. From the trial balance and information given, prepare adjusting entries and post to the accounts.
   a. The buildings have an estimated useful life of 50 years with no salvage value. The company uses the straight-line depreciation method.
   b. The office equipment is depreciated at 10 percent of original cost per year.
   c. Prepaid insurance expired during the year, $1,500.
   d. Accrued salaries and wages at year-end, $1,500.
   e. Deferred rent revenue at year-end should be $1,200.
3. Prepare an adjusted trial balance.
4. Prepare closing entries.
5. Prepare a post-closing trial balance.

P 2–10
Accrual accounting; financial statements
● LO2–4, LO2–6, LO2–8

McGuire Corporation began operations in 2016. The company purchases computer equipment from manufacturers and then sells to retail stores. During 2016, the bookkeeper used a check register to record all cash receipts and cash disbursements. No other journals were used. The following is a recap of the cash receipts and disbursements made during the year.

Cash receipts:	
Sale of common stock	$ 50,000
Collections from customers	320,000
Borrowed from local bank on April 1, note signed requiring principal and interest at 12% to be paid on March 31, 2017	40,000
Total cash receipts	$410,000
Cash disbursements:	
Purchase of merchandise	$220,000
Payment of salaries and wages	80,000
Purchase of office equipment	30,000
Payment of rent on building	14,000
Miscellaneous expenses	10,000
Total cash disbursements	$354,000

You are called in to prepare financial statements at December 31, 2016. The following additional information was provided to you:

1. Customers owed the company $22,000 at year-end.
2. At year-end, $30,000 was still due to suppliers of merchandise purchased on credit.
3. At year-end, merchandise inventory costing $50,000 still remained on hand.
4. Salaries and wages owed to employees at year-end amounted to $5,000.
5. On December 1, $3,000 in rent was paid to the owner of the building used by McGuire. This represented rent for the months of December through February.
6. The office equipment, which has a 10-year life and no salvage value, was purchased on January 1, 2016. Straight-line depreciation is used.

Required:

Prepare an income statement for 2016 and a balance sheet as of December 31, 2016.

P 2–11
Cash versus accrual accounting
● LO2–8

Selected balance sheet information for the Wolf Company at November 30, and December 31, 2016, is presented below. The company uses the perpetual inventory system and all sales to customers are made on credit.

	Nov. 30		Dec. 31	
	Dr.	Cr.	Dr.	Cr.
Accounts receivable	10,000		3,000	
Prepaid insurance	5,000		7,500	
Inventory	7,000		6,000	
Accounts payable		12,000		15,000
Salaries and wages payable		5,000		3,000

The following cash flow information also is available:

a. Cash collected from credit customers, $80,000.
b. Cash paid for insurance, $5,000.
c. Cash paid to suppliers of inventory, $60,000 (the entire accounts payable amounts relate to inventory purchases).
d. Cash paid to employees for salaries and wages, $10,000.

Required:

1. Determine the following for the month of December:
   a. Sales revenue.
   b. Cost of goods sold.
   c. Insurance expense.
   d. Salaries and wages expense.
2. Prepare summary journal entries to record the month's sales and cost of those sales.

P 2–12
Cash versus accrual accounting
● LO2–8

Zambrano Wholesale Corporation maintains its records on a cash basis. At the end of each year the company's accountant obtains the necessary information to prepare accrual basis financial statements. The following cash flows occurred during the year ended December 31, 2016:

Cash receipts:	
From customers	$675,000
Interest on note	4,000
Loan from a local bank	100,000
Total cash receipts	$779,000
Cash disbursements:	
Purchase of merchandise	$390,000
Annual insurance payment	6,000
Payment of salaries and wages	210,000
Dividends paid to shareholders	10,000
Annual rent payment	24,000
Total cash disbursements	$640,000

Selected balance sheet information:

	12/31/15	12/31/16
Cash	$25,000	$164,000
Accounts receivable	62,000	92,000
Inventory	80,000	62,000
Prepaid insurance	2,500	?
Prepaid rent	11,000	?
Interest receivable	3,000	?
Note receivable	50,000	50,000
Equipment	100,000	100,000
Accumulated depreciation—equipment	(40,000)	(50,000)
Accounts payable (for merchandise)	110,000	122,000
Salaries and wages payable	20,000	24,000
Note payable	–0–	100,000
Interest payable	–0–	?

Additional information:

1. On March 31, 2015, Zambrano lent a customer $50,000. Interest at 8% is payable annually on each March 31. Principal is due in 2019.
2. The annual insurance payment is paid in advance on April 30. The policy period begins on May 1.
3. On October 31, 2016, Zambrano borrowed $100,000 from a local bank. Principal and interest at 6% are due on October 31, 2017.
4. Annual rent on the company's facilities is paid in advance on June 30. The rental period begins on July 1.

Required:

1. Prepare an accrual basis income statement for 2016 (ignore income taxes).
2. Determine the following balance sheet amounts on December 31, 2016:
   a. Prepaid insurance.
   b. Prepaid rent.
   c. Interest receivable.
   d. Interest payable.

P 2–13
Worksheet
● Appendix 2A

Using the information from P2–8, prepare and complete a worksheet similar to Illustration 2A–1. Use the information in the worksheet to prepare an income statement and a statement of shareholders' equity for 2016 and a balance sheet as of December 31, 2016. Cash dividends paid to shareholders during the year amounted to $6,000. Also prepare the necessary closing entries assuming that adjusting entries have been correctly posted to the accounts.

Broaden Your Perspective

Apply your critical-thinking ability to the knowledge you've gained. These cases will provide you an opportunity to develop your research, analysis, judgment, and communication skills. You also will work with other students, integrate what you've learned, apply it in real-world situations, and consider its global and ethical ramifications. This practice will broaden your knowledge and further develop your decision-making abilities.

Judgment Case 2–1
Cash versus accrual accounting; adjusting entries; Chapters 1 and 2
● LO2–4, LO2–8

You have recently been hired by Davis & Company, a small public accounting firm. One of the firm's partners, Alice Davis, has asked you to deal with a disgruntled client, Mr. Sean Pitt, owner of the city's largest hardware store. Mr. Pitt is applying to a local bank for a substantial loan to remodel his store. The bank requires accrual based financial statements but Mr. Pitt has always kept the company's records on a cash basis. He does not see the purpose of accrual based statements. His most recent outburst went something like this: "After all, I collect cash from customers, pay my bills in cash, and I am going to pay the bank loan with cash. And, I already show my building and equipment as assets and depreciate them. I just don't understand the problem."

Required:

1. Explain the difference between a cash basis and an accrual basis measure of performance.
2. Why, in most cases, does accrual basis net income provide a better measure of performance than net operating cash flow?
3. Explain the purpose of adjusting entries as they relate to the difference between cash and accrual accounting.

Judgment Case 2–2
Cash versus accrual accounting
● LO2–8

Refer to Case 2–1 above. Mr. Pitt has relented and agrees to provide you with the information necessary to convert his cash basis financial statements to accrual basis statements. He provides you with the following transaction information for the fiscal year ending December 31, 2016:

1. A comprehensive insurance policy requires a payment every year for the upcoming year. The last payment of $12,000 was made on September 1, 2016.
2. Mr. Pitt allows customers to pay using a credit card. At the end of the current year, various credit card companies owed Mr. Pitt $6,500. At the end of last year, customer credit card charges outstanding were $5,000.
3. Employees are paid once a month, on the 10th of the month following the work period. Cash disbursements to employees were $8,200 and $7,200 for January 10, 2017, and January 10, 2016, respectively.
4. Utility bills outstanding totaled $1,200 at the end of 2016 and $900 at the end of 2015.
5. A physical count of inventory is always taken at the end of the fiscal year. The merchandise on hand at the end of 2016 cost $35,000. At the end of 2015, inventory on hand cost $32,000.
6. At the end of 2015, Mr. Pitt did not have any bills outstanding to suppliers of merchandise. However, at the end of 2016, he owed suppliers $4,000.

Required:

1. Mr. Pitt's 2016 cash basis net income (including depreciation expense) is $26,000. Determine net income applying the accrual accounting model.
2. Explain the effect on Mr. Pitt's balance sheet of converting from cash to accrual. That is, would assets, liabilities, and owner's equity be higher or lower and by what amounts?

Communication Case 2–3
Adjusting entries
● LO2–4

"I don't understand," complained Chris, who responded to your bulletin board posting in your responsibilities as a tutor. The complaint was in response to your statements that recording adjusting entries is a critical step in the accounting processing cycle, and the two major classifications of adjusting entries are prepayments and accruals.

Required:

Respond to Chris.

1. When do prepayments occur? Accruals?
2. Describe the appropriate adjusting entry for prepaid expenses and for deferred revenues. What is the effect on net income, assets, liabilities, and shareholders' equity of not recording a required adjusting entry for prepayments?
3. Describe the required adjusting entry for accrued liabilities and for accrued receivables. What is the effect on net income, assets, liabilities, and shareholders' equity of not recording a required adjusting entry for accruals?

CHAPTER

3 The Balance Sheet and Financial Disclosures

OVERVIEW

Chapter 1 stressed the importance of the financial statements in helping investors and creditors predict future cash flows. The balance sheet, along with accompanying disclosures, provides relevant information useful in helping investors and creditors not only to predict future cash flows, but also to make the related assessments of liquidity and long-term solvency.

The purpose of this chapter is to provide an overview of the balance sheet and financial disclosures and to explore how this information is used by decision makers.

LEARNING OBJECTIVES

After studying this chapter, you should be able to:

- **LO3–1** Describe the purpose of the balance sheet and understand its usefulness and limitations. (*p. 114*)
- **LO3–2** Identify and describe the various balance sheet asset classifications. (*p. 116*)
- **LO3–3** Identify and describe the two balance sheet liability classifications. (*p. 120*)
- **LO3–4** Explain the purpose of financial statement disclosures. (*p. 124*)
- **LO3–5** Explain the purpose of the management discussion and analysis disclosure. (*p. 127*)
- **LO3–6** Explain the purpose of an audit and describe the content of the audit report. (*p. 129*)
- **LO3–7** Describe the techniques used by financial analysts to transform financial information into forms more useful for analysis. (*p. 132*)
- **LO3–8** Identify and calculate the common liquidity and financing ratios used to assess risk. (*p. 134*)
- **LO3–9** Discuss the primary differences between U.S. GAAP and IFRS with respect to the balance sheet, financial disclosures, and segment reporting. (*pp. 122* and *141*)

FINANCIAL REPORTING CASE

What's It Worth?

"I can't believe it. Why don't you accountants prepare financial statements that are relevant?" Your friend Jerry is a finance major and is constantly badgering you about what he perceives to be a lack of relevance of financial statements prepared according to generally accepted accounting principles. "For example, take a look at this balance sheet for **Electronic Arts** that I just downloaded off the Internet. Electronic Arts is the company in California that produces all those cool video games like Battlefield, NBA Live, and Madden NFL. Anyway, the shareholders' equity of the company according to the 2014 balance sheet is about $2.4. billion. But if you multiply the number of outstanding shares by the stock price per share at the same point in time, the company's market value is nearly four times that amount. I thought financial statements were supposed to help investors and creditors value a company." You decide to look at the company's balance sheet and try to set Jerry straight.

QUESTIONS

By the time you finish this chapter, you should be able to respond appropriately to the questions posed in this case. Compare your response to the solution provided at the end of the chapter.

1. Respond to Jerry's criticism that shareholders' equity does not represent the market value of the company. What information does the balance sheet provide? (*p. 115*)
2. The usefulness of the balance sheet is enhanced by classifying assets and liabilities according to common characteristics. What are the classifications used in Electronic Arts' balance sheets and what elements do those categories include? (*p. 116*)

The balance sheet, along with accompanying disclosures, provides a wealth of information to external decision makers. The information provided is useful not only in the prediction of future cash flows but also in the related assessments of liquidity and long-term solvency.

This chapter begins our discussion of the financial statements by providing an overview of the balance sheet and the financial disclosures that accompany the financial statements. The first part of the chapter describes the usefulness and limitations of the balance sheet and illustrates the content of the statement. The second part illustrates financial statement disclosures presented to external users in addition to the basic financial statements. In the third part we discuss how this information can be used by decision makers to assess business risk. That discussion introduces some common financial ratios used to assess liquidity and long-term solvency.

Chapter 4 continues this discussion of the financial statements with its coverage of the income statement, statement of comprehensive income, and the statement of cash flows.

Real World Financials

ELECTRONIC ARTS INC.
AND SUBSIDIARIES
Consolidated Balance Sheets
(In millions, except par value data)

	March 31, 2014	March 31, 2013
Assets		
Current assets:		
Cash and cash equivalents	$1,782	$1,292
Short-term investments	583	388
Receivables, net of allowances of $186 and $200, respectively	327	312
Inventories	56	42
Deferred income taxes, net	74	52
Other current assets	316	239
Total current assets	3,138	2,325
Property and equipment, net	510	548
Goodwill	1,723	1,721
Acquisition-related intangibles, net	177	253
Deferred income taxes, net	28	53
Other assets	140	170
Total Assets	$5,716	$5,070
Liabilities and Stockholders' Equity		
Current liabilities:		
Accounts payable	$ 119	$ 136
Accrued and other current liabilities	781	737
Deferred net revenue (online-enabled games)	1490	1,044
Total current liabilities	2,390	1,917
0.75% convertible senior notes due 2016, net	580	559
Income tax obligations	189	205
Deferred income taxes, net	18	1
Other liabilities	117	121
Total liabilities	3,294	2,803
Commitments and contingencies (See Note 13)		
Stockholders' equity:		
Preferred stock, $0.01 par value. 10 shares authorized	—	—
Common stock, $0.01 par value. 1,000 shares authorized: 311 and 302 shares issued and outstanding, respectively	3	3
Paid-in capital	2,353	2,174
Retained earnings (accumulated deficit)	29	21
Accumulated other comprehensive income	37	69
Total stockholders' equity	2,422	2,267
Total Liabilities and Stockholders' Equity	$5,716	$5,070

PART A

The Balance Sheet

● LO3–1

The purpose of the **balance sheet**, sometimes referred to as the **statement of financial position**, is to report a company's financial position on a particular date. Unlike the income statement, which is a change statement reporting events that occurred *during a period of time,* the balance sheet presents an organized array of assets, liabilities, and shareholders' equity *at a point in time.* It is a freeze frame or snapshot of financial position at the end of a particular day marking the end of an accounting period.

Usefulness and Limitations

The balance sheet does not simply list assets and liabilities. Instead, assets and liabilities are classified (grouped) according to common characteristics. These classifications, which we explore in the next section, along with related disclosure notes, help the balance sheet to provide useful information about liquidity and long-term solvency. **Liquidity** refers to the period of time before an asset is converted to cash or until a liability is paid. This information is useful in assessing a company's ability to pay its *current* obligations. **Long-term solvency** refers to the riskiness of a company with regard to the amount of liabilities in its capital structure. Other things being equal, the risk to an investor or creditor increases as the percentage of liabilities, relative to equity, increases.

The balance sheet provides information useful for assessing future cash flows, liquidity, and long-term solvency.

Solvency also provides information about *financial flexibility*—the ability of a company to alter cash flows in order to take advantage of unexpected investment opportunities and needs. For example, the higher the percentage of a company's liabilities to its equity, the more difficult it typically will be to borrow additional funds either to take advantage of a promising investment opportunity or to meet obligations. In general, the less financial flexibility, the more risk there is that an enterprise will fail. In Part C of this chapter, we introduce some common ratios used to assess liquidity and long-term solvency.

Another way the balance sheet is useful is in combination with income statement items. For example, the relation between net income and assets provides a measure of return that is useful in predicting future profitability. In fact, many of the amounts reported in either of the two statements are more informative when viewed relative to an amount from the other statement.[1]

Despite its usefulness, the balance sheet has limitations. One important limitation is that *it does not portray the market value of the entity* as a going concern, nor its liquidation value. Many assets, like land and buildings for example, are measured at their historical costs rather than their fair values. Relatedly, many company resources including its trained employees, its experienced management team, and its reputation are not recorded as assets at all. Another limitation is that many items and amounts reported in the balance sheet are heavily reliant on estimates rather than determinable amounts. For example, companies estimate the amount of receivables they will be able to actually collect and the amount of warranty costs they will eventually incur for products already sold. For these and other reasons, a company's **book value**, its assets minus its liabilities as shown in the balance sheet, usually will not directly measure the company's market value (number of shares of common stock outstanding multiplied by the price per share).

FINANCIAL Reporting Case

Q1, p. 113

Assets minus liabilities, measured according to GAAP, is not likely to be representative of the market value of the entity.

Consider for example that early in 2014, the 30 companies constituting the Dow Jones Industrial Average had an average ratio of market value to book value of approximately 3.25. The ratio for **IBM**, one of the world's largest technology companies, was almost 9.0. Can you think of a reason why IBM's market value would be nine times higher than its book value? A significant reason is the way we account for research and development costs. IBM invests considerable amounts, over $6 billion in 2013 alone, on research and development of new products. Quite a few of these products that the company has developed over the years have been market successes, and yet the costs to discover and develop them are not represented in the balance sheet. We expense research and development costs in the period incurred rather than capitalize them as assets for the balance sheet.

During the financial crisis of 2007–2008 we saw stock prices plummet resulting in historic declines in the market to book ratio for most companies. For example, by the end of 2008, the average market to book ratio of the companies in the Dow Jones Industrial Average average fell to 2.27. Particularly hard hit were financial services companies. At the end of 2008, both **Bank of America** and **Citigroup** had market to book ratios significantly less than 1.0. Then, during 2009, Citigroup was removed from the list of the Dow Jones Industrial 30 companies.

In summary, even though the balance sheet does not *directly measure* the market value of the entity, it provides valuable information that can be used to help *judge* market value.

[1]We explore some of these relationships in Chapter 5.

Classification of Elements

FINANCIAL Reporting Case

Q2, p. 113

The key classification of assets and liabilities in the balance sheet is the current versus long-term distinction.

The usefulness of the balance sheet is enhanced when assets and liabilities are grouped according to common characteristics. *The broad distinction made in the balance sheet is the current versus noncurrent (long-term) classification of both assets and liabilities.* The remainder of Part A provides an overview of the balance sheet. We discuss each of the three primary elements of the balance sheet (assets, liabilities, and shareholders' equity) in the order they are reported in the statement as well as the classifications typically made within the elements. The balance sheet elements were defined in Chapter 1 as follows:

> **Assets** are probable future economic benefits obtained or controlled by a particular entity as a result of past transactions or events. Simply, these are the economic resources of a company.
>
> **Liabilities** are probable future sacrifices of economic benefits arising from present obligations of a particular entity to transfer assets or provide services to other entities in the future as a result of past transactions or events. Simply, these are the obligations of a company.
>
> **Equity** (or net assets), called **shareholders' equity** or **stockholders' equity** for a corporation, is the residual interest in the assets of an entity that remains after deducting liabilities. Stated another way, equity equals total assets minus total liabilities.

Illustration 3–1 lists the balance sheet elements along with their subclassifications.

Illustration 3–1
Classification of Elements within a Balance Sheet

Assets	=	Liabilities	+	Shareholders' Equity
1. Current assets		1. Current liabilities		1. Paid-in capital
2. Long-term assets:		2. Long-term liabilities		2. Retained earnings
• Investments				
• Property, plant, and equipment				
• Intangible assets				
• Other assets				

Assets

● LO3–2

CURRENT ASSETS. Current assets include cash and other assets that are reasonably expected to be converted to cash or consumed within the coming year, or within the normal operating cycle of the business if that's longer than one year. The **operating cycle** for a typical manufacturing company refers to the period of time necessary to convert cash to raw materials, raw materials to a finished product, the finished product to receivables, and then finally receivables back to cash. This concept is illustrated in Illustration 3–2.

Illustration 3–2 Operating Cycle of a Typical Manufacturing Company

In some businesses, such as shipbuilding or distilleries, the operating cycle extends far beyond one year. For example, if it takes two years to build an oil-carrying supertanker, then the shipbuilder will classify as current those assets that will be converted to cash or consumed within two years. But for most businesses the operating cycle will be shorter than one year. In these situations the one-year convention is used to classify both assets and liabilities. Where a company has no clearly defined operating cycle, the one-year convention is used.

Illustration 3–3 presents the current asset sections of **PetSmart**'s balance sheets for the years ended February 2, 2014, and February 3, 2013. The complete balance sheet can be seen in the company's financial statements in Appendix B at the back of the text. In

(In thousands)	February 2, 2014	February 3, 2013
Current assets:		
Cash and cash equivalents	$ 285,622	$ 335,155
Short-term investments	—	9,150
Restricted cash	71,226	71,916
Receivables, net	72,685	72,198
Merchandise inventories	740,302	679,090
Deferred income taxes	71,945	62,859
Prepaid expenses and other current assets	76,463	86,768
Total current assets	$1,318,243	$1,317,136

Illustration 3–3

Current Assets—PetSmart, Inc.

Real World Financials

PetSmart

Current assets include cash and all other assets expected to become cash or be consumed within one year or the *operating cycle,* whichever is longer.

keeping with common practice, the individual current assets are listed in the order of their liquidity (estimated amount of time it would take to convert the asset to cash).

Cash and Cash Equivalents. The most liquid asset, cash, is listed first. Cash includes cash on hand and in banks that is available for use in the operations of the business and such items as bank drafts, cashier's checks, and money orders. **Cash equivalents** frequently include certain negotiable items such as commercial paper, money market funds, and U.S. treasury bills. These are highly liquid investments that can be quickly converted into cash. Most companies draw a distinction between investments classified as cash equivalents and the next category of current assets, short-term investments, according to the scheduled maturity of the investment. *It is common practice to classify investments that have a maturity date of three months or less from the date of purchase as cash equivalents.* **PetSmart**'s policy follows this practice and is disclosed in the summary of significant accounting policies disclosure note. The portion of the note from the company's financial statements is shown in Illustration 3–4.

Note 1—Description of Business and Summary of Significant Accounting Policies

Cash and Cash Equivalents

We consider any liquid investments with a maturity of three months or less at purchase to be cash equivalents. Included in cash and cash equivalents are credit and debit card receivables from banks, which typically settle within five business days, of $61.5 million and $58.9 million as of February 2, 2014, and February 3, 2013, respectively.

Illustration 3–4

Disclosure of Cash Equivalents—PetSmart, Inc.

Real World Financials

PetSmart

Cash that is restricted for a special purpose and not available for current operations should not be included in the primary balance of cash and cash equivalents. These restrictions could include future plans to repay debt, purchase equipment, or make investments. Restricted cash is classified as a current asset if it is expected to be used within one year. Otherwise, restricted cash is classified as a noncurrent asset.

Short-Term Investments. Liquid investments not classified as cash equivalents are reported as either **short-term investments**, sometimes called *temporary investments* or *short-term marketable securities.* Investments in stock and debt securities of other corporations are included as short-term investments *if* the company has the ability and intent to sell those securities within the next 12 months or operating cycle, whichever is longer. If, for example, a company owns 1,000 shares of **IBM Corporation** stock and intends to hold those shares for several years, the stock is a long-term investment and should be classified as a noncurrent asset, investments.

***Investments* are classified as current if management has the ability and intent to liquidate the investment in the near term.**

For reporting purposes, investments in debt and equity securities are classified in one of three categories: (1) held to maturity, (2) trading securities, or (3) securities available for sale. We discuss these different categories and their accounting treatment in Chapter 12.

Accounts Receivable. Accounts receivable result from the sale of goods or services on credit. Notice in Illustration 3–3 that PetSmart's receivables (discussed in Chapter 7) are valued net, that is, less an allowance for uncollectible accounts (the amount not expected to be collected). Accounts receivable often are referred to as *trade receivables* because they arise in the course of a company's normal trade. *Nontrade receivables* result from loans or advances by the company to individuals and other entities. When receivables are supported by a formal agreement or note that specifies payment terms they are called notes receivable.

Accounts receivable usually are due in 30 to 60 days, depending on the terms offered to customers and are, therefore, classified as current assets. Any receivable, regardless of the source, not expected to be collected within one year or the operating cycle, whichever is longer, is classified as a noncurrent asset, investments.

Inventories. Inventories include goods awaiting sale (finished goods), goods in the course of production (work in process), and goods to be consumed directly or indirectly in production (raw materials). Inventory for a wholesale or retail company consists only of finished goods, but the inventory of a manufacturer will include all three types of goods. Occasionally, a manufacturing company will report all three types of inventory directly in the balance sheet. More often, only the total amount of inventories is shown in the balance sheet and the balances of each type are shown in a disclosure note. For example, the note shown in Illustration 3–5 lists the components of inventory in the 2013 financial statements of Intel Corp.

***Inventories* consist of assets that a retail or wholesale company acquires for resale or goods that manufacturers produce for sale.**

Illustration 3–5

Inventories Disclosure—Intel Corp.

Real World Financials

	December 28, 2013	December 29, 2012
(In millions)		
Raw materials	$ 458	$ 478
Work in process	1,998	2,219
Finished goods	1,716	2,037
Total inventories	$4,172	$4,734

Inventories are reported as current assets because they normally are sold within the operating cycle.

Prepaid Expenses. Recall from Chapter 2 that a prepaid expense represents an asset recorded when an expense is paid in advance, creating benefits beyond the current period. Examples are prepaid rent and prepaid insurance. Even though these assets are not converted to cash, they would involve an outlay of cash if not prepaid.

Whether a prepaid expense is current or noncurrent depends on when its benefits will be realized. For example, if rent on an office building were prepaid for one year, then the entire prepayment is classified as a current asset. However, if rent were prepaid for a period extending beyond the coming year, a portion of the prepayment is classified as an other asset, a noncurrent asset.[2] PetSmart includes prepaid expenses along with other current assets. Other current assets also include assets—such as nontrade receivables—that, because their amounts are not material, did not warrant separate disclosure.

When assets are expected to provide economic benefits beyond the next year, or operating cycle, they are reported as *noncurrent assets*. Typical classifications of noncurrent assets are (1) investments, (2) property, plant, and equipment, and (3) intangible assets.

[2]Companies often include prepayments for benefits extending beyond one year as current assets when the amounts are not material.

INVESTMENTS. Most companies occasionally acquire assets that are not used directly in the operations of the business. These assets include investments in equity and debt securities of other corporations, land held for speculation, noncurrent receivables, and cash set aside for special purposes (such as for future plant expansion). These assets are classified as noncurrent because management does not intend to convert the assets into cash in the next year (or the operating cycle if that's longer).

***Investments* are assets not used directly in operations.**

PROPERTY, PLANT, AND EQUIPMENT. Virtually all companies own assets classified as **property, plant, and equipment**. The common characteristics these assets share are that they are *tangible, long-lived,* and *used in the operations of the business.* Property, plant, and equipment, along with intangible assets, often are the primary revenue-generating assets of the business.

Tangible, long-lived assets used in the operations of the business are classified as *property, plant, and equipment.*

Property, plant, and equipment includes land, buildings, equipment, machinery, and furniture, as well as natural resources, such as mineral mines, timber tracts, and oil wells. These various assets usually are reported as a single amount in the balance sheet, with details provided in a note. They are reported at original cost less accumulated depreciation (or depletion for natural resources) to date. Quite often, a company will present only the net amount of property, plant, and equipment in the balance sheet and provide details in a disclosure note. Land often is listed as a separate item in this classification because it has an unlimited useful life and thus is not depreciated.

INTANGIBLE ASSETS. Some assets used in the operations of a business have no physical substance. These are appropriately called **intangible assets**. Generally, these represent the ownership of an exclusive right to something such as a product, a process, or a name. This right can be a valuable resource in generating future revenues. Patents, copyrights, and franchises are examples. They are reported in the balance sheet net of accumulated amortization. Some companies include intangible assets as part of property, plant, and equipment, while others report them either in a separate intangible asset classification or as other noncurrent assets.

***Intangible assets* generally represent exclusive rights that a company can use to generate future revenues.**

Quite often, much of the value of intangibles is not reported in the balance sheet. For example, it would not be unusual for the historical cost of a patent to be significantly lower than its market value. As we discuss in Chapter 10, for internally developed intangibles, the costs that are included as part of historical cost are limited. Specifically, none of the research and development costs incurred in developing the intangible asset are included in cost.

OTHER ASSETS. Balance sheets often include a catch-all classification of noncurrent assets called **other assets**. This classification includes long-term prepaid expenses, called *deferred charges,* and any noncurrent asset not falling in one of the other classifications. For instance, if a company's noncurrent investments are not material in amount, they might be reported in the other asset classification rather than in a separate investments category.

Illustration 3–6 reproduces the noncurrent asset section of PetSmart's balance sheets. For PetSmart, noncurrent assets include property and equipment, an equity investment in a company called Banfield, deferred income taxes, goodwill (an intangible asset), and other noncurrent assets. You'll learn more about each of these types of noncurrent assets in the chapters to come.

Illustration 3–6

Noncurrent Assets—PetSmart, Inc.

Real World Financials

	February 2, 2014	February 3, 2013
(In thousands)		
Noncurrent assets:		
Property and equipment, net	$ 952,955	$ 985,707
Equity investment in Banfield	33,577	39,934
Deferred income taxes	110,408	102,992
Goodwill	41,140	44,242
Other noncurrent assets	65,645	46,970
Total noncurrent assets	$1,203,725	$1,219,845

We've seen how assets are grouped into current and noncurrent categories and that noncurrent assets always are subclassified further. Let's now turn our attention to liabilities. These, too, are separated into current and noncurrent (long-term) categories.

Liabilities

● LO3–3

Liabilities represent obligations to other entities. The information value of reporting these amounts is enhanced by classifying them as current liabilities and long-term liabilities. Illustration 3–7 shows the liability section of PetSmart's balance sheets.

Illustration 3–7
Liabilities—PetSmart, Inc.

Real World Financials

PetSmart

	February 2, 2014	February 3, 2013
(In thousands)		
Liabilities:		
Accounts payable and bank overdraft	$ 255,251	$ 202,122
Accrued payroll, bonus, and employee benefits	160,008	176,082
Accrued occupancy expenses and deferred rents	81,867	70,671
Current maturities of capital lease obligations	66,887	61,581
Other current liabilities	230,332	244,436
Total current liabilities	794,345	754,892
Capital lease obligations	451,597	464,578
Deferred rents	65,932	73,855
Other noncurrent liabilities	116,312	120,064
Total liabilities	1,428,186	1,413,389

Current liabilities are expected to be satisfied within one year or the operating cycle, whichever is longer.

CURRENT LIABILITIES. Current liabilities are those obligations that are expected to be satisfied through the use of current assets or the creation of other current liabilities. So, this classification includes all liabilities that are expected to be satisfied within one year or the operating cycle, whichever is longer. An exception is a liability that management intends to refinance on a long-term basis. For example, if management intends to refinance a six-month note payable by substituting a two-year note payable and has the ability to do so, then the liability would not be classified as current even though it's due within the coming year. This exception is discussed in more detail in Chapter 13.

Current liabilities usually include *accounts* and *notes payable, deferred revenues, accrued liabilities,* and the *current maturities of long-term debt.*

The most common current liabilities are accounts payable, notes payable (short-term borrowings), deferred revenues, accrued liabilities, and the currently maturing portion of long-term debt. Accounts payable are obligations to suppliers of merchandise or of services purchased on open account, with payment usually due in 30 to 60 days. Notes payable are written promises to pay cash at some future date (I.O.U.s). Unlike accounts payable, notes usually require the payment of explicit interest in addition to the original obligation amount. Notes maturing in the next year or operating cycle, whichever is longer, will be classified as current liabilities. Deferred revenues, sometimes called unearned revenues, represent cash received from a customer for goods or services to be provided in a future period. PetSmart records deferred revenue when it sells gift cards and then waits to record the (actual) revenue until the cards are redeemed or expire.

Accrued liabilities represent obligations created when expenses have been incurred but will not be paid until a subsequent reporting period. Examples are accrued salaries payable, accrued interest payable, and accrued taxes payable. PetSmart's accrued liabilities include accrued compensation, accrued rent, accrued taxes, and accrued interest.

Long-term notes, loans, mortgages, and bonds payable usually are reclassified and reported as current liabilities as they become payable within the next year (or operating cycle if that's longer).[3] Likewise, when long-term debt is payable in installments, the

[3] Payment can be with current assets or the creation of other current liabilities.

installment payable currently is reported as a current liability. For example, a $1,000,000 note payable requiring $100,000 in principal payments to be made in each of the next 10 years is classified as a $100,000 current liability—**current maturities of long-term debt**—and a $900,000 long-term liability. PetSmart classifies the current portion of its capital lease obligations as a current liability.

Chapter 13 provides a more detailed analysis of current liabilities.

LONG-TERM LIABILITIES. Long-term liabilities are obligations that will *not* be satisfied in the next year or operating cycle, whichever is longer. They do not require the use of current assets or the creation of current liabilities for payment. Examples are long-term notes, bonds, pension obligations, and lease obligations.

Noncurrent, or long-term liabilities, usually are those payable beyond the current year.

But simply classifying a liability as long-term doesn't provide complete information to external users. For instance, long-term could mean anything from 2 to 20, 30, or 40 years. Payment terms, interest rates, and other details needed to assess the impact of these obligations on future cash flows and long-term solvency are reported in a disclosure note.

PetSmart reports long-term liabilities related to long-term capital lease obligations and deferred rents. Other noncurrent liabilities include amounts expected to be paid in the future for workers' compensation, employee health care, and store closings.

Shareholders' Equity

Recall from our discussions in Chapters 1 and 2 that owners' equity is simply a residual amount derived by subtracting liabilities from assets. For that reason, it's sometimes referred to as *net assets* or *book value.* Also recall that owners of a corporation are its shareholders, so owners' equity for a corporation is referred to as shareholders' equity or stockholders' equity. Shareholders' equity for a corporation arises primarily from two sources: (1) amounts *invested* by shareholders in the corporation, and (2) amounts *earned* by the corporation (on behalf of its shareholders). These are reported as (1) **paid-in capital** and (2) **retained earnings**. Retained earnings represents the accumulated net income reported since the inception of the corporation and not (yet) paid to shareholders as dividends.

Shareholders' equity is composed of *paid-in capital* (invested capital) and *retained earnings* (earned capital).

Illustration 3–8 presents the shareholders' equity section of PetSmart's balance sheets.

Illustration 3–8

Shareholders' Equity—PetSmart, Inc.

Real World Financials

(In thousands)	February 2, 2014	February 3, 2013
Stockholders' equity:		
Common stock; $.0001 par value; 625,000 shares authorized, 169,178 and 167,209 shares issued	$ 17	$ 17
Additional paid-in capital	1,515,333	1,418,411
Retained earnings	2,173,005	1,827,996
Accumulated other comprehensive (loss) income	(2,159)	5,506
Less: Treasury stock, at cost, 68,520 and 61,879 shares	(2,592,414)	(2,128,338)
Total stockholders' equity	$ 1,093,782	$ 1,123,592

From the inception of the corporation through February 2, 2014, PetSmart has accumulated net income, less dividends, of $2,173,005 thousand which is reported as *retained earnings.* The company's *paid-in capital* is represented by common stock and additional paid-in capital less treasury stock (PetSmart's purchases of its own common stock), which collectively represent cash invested by shareholders in exchange for ownership interests. Information about the number of shares the company has authorized and how many shares have been issued and are outstanding also must be disclosed.

In addition to paid-in capital and retained earnings, shareholders' equity may include a few other equity components. For example, PetSmart reports accumulated other comprehensive (loss) income. Accumulated other comprehensive (loss) income is discussed in Chapters 4, 12, and 18. Other equity components are addressed in later chapters, Chapter 18 in particular. We also discuss the concept of par value in Chapter 18.

International Financial Reporting Standards

● LO3–9

Balance Sheet Presentation. There are more similarities than differences in balance sheets prepared according to U.S. GAAP and those prepared applying IFRS. Some of the differences are:

- International standards specify a minimum list of items to be presented in the balance sheet. U.S. GAAP has no minimum requirements.
- *IAS No. 1, revised,*[4] changed the title of the balance sheet to *statement of financial position,* although companies are not required to use that title. Some U.S. companies use the statement of financial position title as well.
- Under U.S. GAAP, we present current assets and liabilities before noncurrent assets and liabilities. *IAS No. 1* doesn't prescribe the format of the balance sheet, but balance sheets prepared using IFRS often report noncurrent items first. A recent survey of large companies that prepare their financial statements according to IFRS reports that 73% of the surveyed companies list noncurrent items first.[5] For example, **H&M**, a Swedish-based clothing company, reported assets, liabilities, and shareholders' equity in its balance sheet in the following order:

(SEK in millions)	
Noncurrrent assets (including property, plant, and equipment)	26,488
Current assets	39,188
Total assets	65,676
Shareholders' equity	45,248
Long-term liabilities	3,031
Current liabilities	17,397
Total liabilities and equity	65,676

Where We're Headed

The FASB is working on a project that could have a dramatic impact on the format of financial statements.

In 2004, the FASB and IASB began working together on a project, Financial Statement Presentation, to establish a common standard for presenting information in the financial statements, including classifying and displaying line items and aggregating line items into subtotals and totals. This project could have a dramatic impact on the format of financial statements. An important part of the proposal involves the organization of elements of the balance sheet (statement of financial position), statement of comprehensive income (including the income statement), and statement of cash flows into a common set of classifications.

Progress was slow, and in 2011 both Boards suspended activity on the project to concentrate on other convergence projects. In 2014, the project was moved back on the FASB's agenda. It is not known if the project will retain its original scope of encompassing all of the financial statements or if it will focus on one or two statements. At the time this book was published, no timetable for completion of the project had been announced.

[4] "Financial Statement Presentation," *International Accounting Standard No. 1* (IASCF), as amended effective January 1, 2014.
[5] *IFRS Accounting Trends and Techniques*—2011 (New York, AICPA, 2011), p.133.

Concept Review Exercise

BALANCE SHEET CLASSIFICATION

The following is a post-closing trial balance for the Sepia Paint Corporation at December 31, 2016, the end of the company's fiscal year:

Account Title	Debits	Credits
Cash	$ 80,000	
Accounts receivable	200,000	
Allowance for uncollectible accounts		$ 20,000
Inventories	300,000	
Prepaid expenses	30,000	
Note receivable (due in one month)	60,000	
Investments	50,000	
Land	120,000	
Buildings	550,000	
Machinery	500,000	
Accumulated depreciation—buildings and machinery		450,000
Patent (net of amortization)	50,000	
Accounts payable		170,000
Salaries payable		40,000
Interest payable		10,000
Note payable		100,000
Bonds payable (due in 10 years)		500,000
Common stock, no par		400,000
Retained earnings		250,000
Totals	$1,940,000	$1,940,000

The $50,000 balance in the investment account consists of marketable equity securities of other corporations. The company's intention is to hold the securities for at least three years. The $100,000 note payable is an installment loan. $10,000 of the principal, plus interest, is due on each July 1 for the next 10 years. At the end of the year, 100,000 shares of common stock were issued and outstanding. The company has 500,000 shares of common stock authorized.

Required:

Prepare a classified balance sheet for the Sepia Paint Corporation at December 31, 2016.

Solution:

SEPIA PAINT CORPORATION
Balance Sheet
At December 31, 2016

Assets

Current assets:		
Cash		$ 80,000
Accounts receivable	$ 200,000	
Less: Allowance for uncollectible accounts	(20,000)	180,000
Note receivable		60,000
Inventories		300,000
Prepaid expenses		30,000
Total current assets		650,000
Investments		50,000
Property, plant, and equipment:		
Land	120,000	
Buildings	550,000	
Machinery	500,000	
	1,170,000	
Less: Accumulated depreciation	(450,000)	
Net property, plant, and equipment		720,000
Intangible assets:		
Patent		50,000
Total assets		$1,470,000

SEPIA PAINT CORPORATION
Balance Sheet
At December 31, 2016

Liabilities and Shareholders' Equity

Current liabilities:		
Accounts payable		$ 170,000
Salaries payable		40,000
Interest payable		10,000
Current maturities of long-term debt		10,000
Total current liabilities		230,000
Long-term liabilities:		
Note payable	$ 90,000	
Bonds payable	500,000	
Total long-term liabilities		590,000
Shareholders' equity:		
Common stock, no par, 500,000 shares authorized, 100,000 shares issued and outstanding	400,000	
Retained earnings	250,000	
Total shareholders' equity		650,000
Total liabilities and shareholders' equity		$1,470,000

The usefulness of the balance sheet, as well as the other financial statements, is significantly enhanced by financial statement disclosures. We now turn our attention to these disclosures.

PART B

Financial Disclosures

● LO3–4

Financial statements are included in the annual report a company reports to its shareholders. They are, though, only part of the information provided. Critical to understanding the financial statements and to evaluating a firm's performance and financial health are additional disclosures included as part of the financial statements.

The full-disclosure principle requires that financial statements provide all material relevant information concerning the reporting entity.

Financial statement disclosures are provided (1) by including additional information, often parenthetically, on the face of the statement following a financial statement item and (2) in disclosure notes that often include supporting schedules. Common examples of disclosures included on the face of the balance sheet are the allowance for uncollectible accounts and information about common stock. Disclosure notes, discussed and illustrated in the next section, are the most common means of providing these additional disclosures. The specific format of disclosure is generally not important, only that the information is, in fact, disclosed.

Disclosure Notes

Disclosure notes typically span several pages and either explain or elaborate upon the data presented in the financial statements themselves, or provide information not directly related to any specific item in the statements. Throughout this text you will encounter examples of items that usually are disclosed this way. For instance, the fair values of financial instruments and "off-balance-sheet" risk associated with financial instruments are disclosed in notes. Information providing details of many financial statement items is provided using disclosure notes. Some examples include:

- Pension plans
- Leases
- Long-term debt
- Investments
- Income taxes

- Property, plant, and equipment
- Employee benefit plans

Disclosure notes must include certain specific notes such as a summary of significant accounting policies, descriptions of subsequent events, and related third-party transactions, but many notes are fashioned to suit the disclosure needs of the particular reporting enterprise. Actually, any explanation that contributes to investors' and creditors' understanding of the results of operations, financial position, and cash flows of the company should be included. Let's take a look at just a few disclosure notes.

Summary of Significant Accounting Policies

There are many areas where management chooses from among equally acceptable alternative accounting methods. For example, management chooses whether to use accelerated or straight-line depreciation, whether to use FIFO, LIFO, or average cost to measure inventories, and whether to measure certain financial investments at fair value or cost. The company also defines which securities it considers to be cash equivalents and its policies regarding the timing of recognizing revenues. Typically, the first disclosure note consists of a summary of significant accounting policies that discloses the choices the company makes.[6] Illustration 3–9 shows a portion of a typical summary note from a recent annual report of the **Starbucks Corporation**.

The *summary of significant accounting policies* conveys valuable information about the company's choices from among various alternative accounting methods.

Studying this note is an essential step in analyzing financial statements. Obviously, knowing which methods were used to derive certain accounting numbers is critical to assessing the adequacy of those amounts.

Illustration 3–9 Summary of Significant Accounting Policies—Starbucks Corporation

Note 1: Summary of Accounting Policies (in part)

Principles of Consolidation

The consolidated financial statements reflect the financial position and operating results of Starbucks, including wholly owned subsidiaries and investees that we control.

Cash and Cash Equivalents

We consider all highly liquid instruments with a maturity of three months or less at the time of purchase to be cash equivalents.

Inventories

Inventories are stated at the lower of cost (primarily moving average cost) or market. We record inventory reserves for obsolete and slow-moving inventory and for estimated shrinkage between physical inventory counts.

Property, Plant, and Equipment

Property, plant, and equipment are carried at cost less accumulated depreciation. Cost includes all direct costs necessary to acquire and prepare assets for use, including internal labor and overhead in some cases. Depreciation of property, plant, and equipment, which includes assets under capital leases, is provided on the straight-line method over estimated useful lives, generally ranging from 2 to 15 years for equipment and 30 to 40 years for buildings. Leasehold improvements are amortized over the shorter of their estimated useful lives or the related lease life, generally 10 years.

Revenue Recognition

Company-operated stores' revenues are recognized when payment is tendered at the point of sale. Revenues from our stored value cards, primarily Starbucks Cards, are recognized when redeemed or when the likelihood of redemption, based on historical experience, is deemed to be remote. Outstanding customer balances are included in deferred revenue on the consolidated balance sheets.

Real World Financials

Subsequent Events

When an event that has a material effect on the company's financial position occurs after the fiscal year-end but before the financial statements are issued or "available to be issued," the

[6]FASB ASC 235–10–50: Notes to Financial Statements—Overall—Disclosure (previously "Disclosure of Accounting Policies," *Accounting Principles Board Opinion No. 22* (New York: AICPA, 1972)).

A *subsequent event* is a significant development that occurs after a company's fiscal year-end but before the financial statements are issued or available to be issued.

event is described in a **subsequent event** disclosure note.[7] Examples include the issuance of debt or equity securities, a business combination or the sale of a business, the sale of assets, an event that sheds light on the outcome of a loss contingency, or any other event having a material effect on operations. Illustration 3–10 illustrates the required disclosure by showing a note that **Marriott Vacations Worldwide Corp.**, included in its 2013 financial statements.

We cover subsequent events in more depth in Chapter 13.

Illustration 3–10
Subsequent Event—Marriott Vacations Worldwide Corp.

Real World Financials

Subsequent Events

Subsequent to year-end, we disposed of a golf course and adjacent undeveloped land for $24 million of cash proceeds. As a condition of the sale, we will continue to operate the golf course until mid-2015 at our own risk. We will utilize the performance of services method to record a gain of approximately $2 million over the period in which we will operate the golf course.

Noteworthy Events and Transactions

Some transactions and events occur only occasionally but, when they do occur, they are potentially important to evaluating a company's financial statements. In this category are related-party transactions, errors and fraud, and illegal acts. The more frequent of these is related-party transactions.

Sometimes a company will engage in transactions with owners, management, families of owners or management, affiliated companies, and other parties that can significantly influence or be influenced by the company. The potential problem with **related-party transactions** is that their economic substance may differ from their legal form. For instance, borrowing or lending money at an interest rate that differs significantly from the market interest rate is an example of a transaction that could result from a related-party involvement. As a result of the potential for misrepresentation, financial statement users are particularly interested in more details about these transactions.

The economic substance of *related-party* transactions should be disclosed, including dollar amounts involved.

When related-party transactions occur, companies must disclose the nature of the relationship, provide a description of the transactions, and report the dollar amounts of transactions and any amounts due from or to related parties.[8] Illustration 3–11 shows a disclosure note from a recent annual report of **Guess**, the contemporary apparel and accessories company. The note describes the charter of aircraft from a trust organized for the benefit of executives of the company.

Less frequent events are errors and **fraud**. The distinction between these two terms is that errors are unintentional while fraud is intentional misappropriation of assets or fraudulent financial reporting.[9] Errors and fraud may require disclosure (e.g., of assets lost through either errors or fraud). Obviously, the existence of fraud involving management might cause a user to approach financial analysis from an entirely different and more cautious viewpoint.

Closely related to fraud are **illegal acts** such as bribes, kickbacks, illegal contributions to political candidates, and other violations of the law. Accounting for illegal practices has been influenced by the Foreign Corrupt Practices Act passed by Congress in 1977. The Act is intended to discourage illegal business practices through tighter controls and also encourage better disclosure of those practices when encountered. The nature of such

[7]Financial statements are viewed as issued if they have been widely distributed to financial statement users in a format consistent with GAAP. Some entities (for example, private companies) don't widely distribute their financial statements to users. For those entities, the key date for subsequent events is not the date of issuance but rather the date upon which the financial statements are "available to be issued," which occurs when the financial statements are complete, in a format consistent with GAAP, and have obtained the necessary approvals for issuance. Companies must disclose the date through which subsequent events have been evaluated. (FASB ASC 855: Subsequent Events (previously "Subsequent Events," *Statement of Financial Accounting Standards No. 165* (Stamford, Conn.: FASB, 2009))).

[8]FASB ASC 850–10–50: Related Party Disclosures—Overall—Disclosure (previously "Related Party Disclosures," *Statement of Financial Accounting Standards No. 57* (Stamford, Conn.: FASB, 1982)).

[9]"Consideration of Fraud in a Financial Statement Audit," *AICPA Professional Standards AU 240* (New York: AICPA, 2012).

(13) Related-Party Transactions (in part)

The Company and its subsidiaries periodically enter into transactions with other entities or individuals that are considered related parties, including certain transactions with entities affiliated with trusts for the respective benefit of Paul Marciano, who is an executive of the Company, Maurice Marciano, Chairman of the Board, Armand Marciano, their brother and former executive of the Company, and certain of their children (the "Marciano Trusts").

Aircraft Arrangements

The Company periodically charters aircraft owned by MPM Financial, LLC ("MPM Financial"), an entity affiliated with the Marciano Trusts, through independent third party management companies contracted by MPM Financial to manage its aircraft. Under an informal arrangement with MPM Financial and the third party management companies, the Company has chartered and may from time to time continue to charter aircraft owned by MPM Financial at a discount from the third party management companies' preferred customer hourly charter rates. The total fees paid under these arrangements for fiscal 2014, fiscal 2013, and fiscal 2012 were approximately $0.8 million, $1.3 million, and $0.8 million, respectively.

Illustration 3–11

Related-Party Transactions Disclosure—Guess, Inc.

Real World Financials

disclosures should be influenced by the materiality of the impact of illegal acts on amounts disclosed in the financial statements.[10] However, the SEC issued guidance expressing its view that exclusive reliance on quantitative benchmarks to assess materiality in preparing financial statements is inappropriate.[11] A number of other factors, including whether the item in question involves an unlawful transaction, should also be considered when determining materiality.

As you might expect, any disclosures of related-party transactions, fraud, and illegal acts can be quite sensitive. Although auditors must be considerate of the privacy of the parties involved, that consideration cannot be subordinate to users' needs for full disclosure.

We've discussed only a few of the disclosure notes most frequently included in annual reports. Other common disclosures include details concerning earnings per share calculations, income taxes, property and equipment, contingencies, long-term debt, leases, pensions, stock options, changes in accounting methods, fair values of financial instruments, and exposure to market risk and credit risk. We discuss and illustrate these in later chapters in the context of related financial statement elements.

Disclosure notes for some financial statement elements are required. Others are provided when required by specific situations in the interest of full disclosure.

Management Discussion and Analysis

In addition to the financial statements and accompanying disclosure notes, each annual report of a public company requires a fairly lengthy discussion and analysis provided by the company's management. In this section, which precedes the financial statements and the auditor's report, management provides its views on significant events, trends, and uncertainties pertaining to the company's (a) operations, (b) liquidity, and (c) capital resources. Although the **management discussion and analysis (MD&A)** section may embody management's biased perspective, it can offer an informed insight that might not be available elsewhere. As an example, Illustration 3–12 contains a portion of **PetSmart**'s MD&A regarding liquidity and capital resources that is in its annual report for the fiscal year ended February 2, 2014.

● LO3–5

The management discussion and analysis provides a biased but informed perspective of a company's
(a) operations,
(b) liquidity, and
(c) capital resources.

[10] "Consideration of Laws and Regulations in an Audit of Financial Statements," *AICPA Professional Standards AU 250* (New York: AICPA, 2012).

[11] FASB ASC 250–10–S99–1, SAB Topic 1.M: Assessing Materiality (originally "Materiality," *Staff Accounting Bulletin No. 99* (Washington, D.C.: SEC, August 1999)).

Illustration 3–12

Management Discussion and Analysis—PetSmart, Inc.

Real World Financials

PetSmart

Management Discussion and Analysis of Financial Condition and Results of Operations
(In part: Liquidity and Capital Resources only)

Cash Flow

We believe that our operating cash flow and cash on hand will be adequate to meet our operating, investing, and financing needs in the foreseeable future. In addition, we have access to our $100.0 million revolving credit facility, which expires on March 23, 2017. However, there can be no assurance of our ability to access credit markets on commercially acceptable terms in the future. We continuously assess the economic environment and market conditions to guide our decisions regarding our uses of cash, including capital expenditures, investments, dividends, and the purchase of treasury stock.

Share Purchase Programs

In September 2013, the Board of Directors approved a share purchase program authorizing the purchase of up to $535.0 million through January 31, 2015. The $535.0 million program commenced on October 1, 2013, and was in addition to any unused amount remaining under the previous $525.0 million program. We completed the $525.0 million program during the thirteen weeks ended February 2, 2014. As of February 2, 2014, $417.9 million remained available under the $535.0 million program.

Common Stock Dividends

We believe our ability to generate cash allows us to invest in the growth of the business and, at the same time, distribute a quarterly dividend. Our revolving credit facility and stand-alone letter of credit facility permit us to pay dividends, as long as we are not in default and the payment of dividends would not result in default. During 2013, 2012, and 2011, we paid aggregate dividends of $0.525 per share, $0.775 per share, and $0.53 per share, respectively. The decrease in dividends paid during 2013 was the result of the dividend declared in the fourth quarter of 2012, which was paid in December of 2012, rather than in February of 2013.

Operating Capital and Capital Expenditure Requirements

All our stores are leased facilities. We opened 60 new stores and closed 5 stores in 2013. Generally, each new store requires capital expenditures of approximately $0.7 million for fixtures, equipment, and leasehold improvements, approximately $0.3 million for inventory, and approximately $0.1 million for preopening costs. We expect total capital spending to be $150 million to $160 million for 2014, based on our plan to continue our store growth, remodel or replace certain store assets, enhance our supply chain, continue our investment in the development of our information systems, and improve our infrastructure.

Management's Responsibilities

Management prepares and is responsible for the financial statements and other information in the annual report. To enhance the awareness of the users of financial statements concerning the relative roles of management and the auditor, annual reports of public companies include a management's responsibilities section that asserts the responsibility of management for the information contained in the annual report as well as an assessment of the company's internal control procedures.

Illustration 3–13 contains the statement of responsibility disclosure for **The Home Depot**, included with the company's financial statements for the year ended February 2, 2014. Recall from our discussion of financial reporting reform in Chapter 1, that the *Sarbanes-Oxley Act of 2002* requires corporate executives to personally certify the financial statements. Submission of false statements carries a penalty of up to 20 years in jail. The illustration also contains Management's Report on Internal Control Over Financial Reporting. Francis S. Blake, Home Depot's chairman and chief executive officer, and Carol B. Tomé, the company's chief financial officer and executive vice president, signed the required certifications as well as these statements of responsibility.

Illustration 3–13

Management's Responsibilities—The Home Depot, Inc.

Real World Financials

Management's Responsibility for Financial Statements

The financial statements presented in this Annual Report have been prepared with integrity and objectivity and are the responsibility of the management of The Home Depot, Inc. These financial statements have been prepared in conformity with U.S. generally accepted accounting principles and properly reflect certain estimates and judgments based upon the best available information.

The financial statements of the Company have been audited by KPMG LLP, an independent registered public accounting firm. Their accompanying report is based upon an audit conducted in accordance with the standards of the Public Company Accounting Oversight Board (United States).

The Audit Committee of the Board of Directors, consisting solely of outside directors, meets five times a year with the independent registered public accounting firm, the internal auditors and representatives of management to discuss auditing and financial reporting matters. In addition, a telephonic meeting is held prior to each quarterly earnings release. The Audit Committee retains the independent registered public accounting firm and regularly reviews the internal accounting controls, the activities of the independent registered public accounting firm and internal auditors and the financial condition of the Company. Both the Company's independent registered public accounting firm and the internal auditors have free access to the Audit Committee.

Management's Report on Internal Control over Financial Reporting

Our management is responsible for establishing and maintaining adequate internal control over financial reporting, as such term is defined in Rules 13a–15(f) promulgated under the Securities Exchange Act of 1934, as amended (the "Exchange Act"). Under the supervision and with the participation of our management, including our Chief Executive Officer and Chief Financial Officer, we conducted an evaluation of the effectiveness of our internal control over financial reporting as of February 2, 2014 based on the framework in *Internal Control—Integrated Framework* issued by the Committee of Sponsoring Organizations of the Treadway Commission (COSO). Based on our evaluation, our management concluded that our internal control over financial reporting was effective as of February 2, 2014, in providing reasonable assurance regarding the reliability of financial reporting and the preparation of financial statements for external purposes in accordance with generally accepted accounting principles. The effectiveness of our internal control over financial reporting as of February 2, 2014, has been audited by KPMG LLP, an independent registered public accounting firm, as stated in their report which is included on page 28 in this Form 10-K.

Francis S. Blake
Chairman & Chief Executive Officer

Carol B. Tomé
Chief Financial Officer & Executive Vice President

The *management's responsibilities* section acknowledges the responsibility of management for the company's *financial* statements and internal control system.

Auditors' Report

● LO3–6

Auditors examine financial statements and the internal control procedures designed to support the content of those statements. Their role is to attest to the fairness of the financial statements based on that examination. The auditors' attest function results in an opinion stated in the **auditors' report**.

The auditors' report provides the financial statement user with an independent and professional opinion about the fairness of the representations in the financial statements and about the effectiveness of internal controls.

One step in financial analysis should be an examination of the auditors' report, which is issued by the CPA firm that audits the financial statements and informs users of the audit findings. Every audit report of a public company looks similar to the one prepared by **KPMG LLP** for the financial statements of **The Home Depot**, as shown in Illustration 3–14.

The reason for the similarities is that auditors' reports of public companies must be in compliance with the specifications of the PCAOB.[12] In most cases, including the report for Home Depot, the auditors will be satisfied that the financial statements "present fairly" the

[12] "An Audit of Internal Control over Financial Reporting That Is Integrated with An Audit of Financial Statements," *Auditing Standard No. 5* (Washington, D.C., PCAOB, 2007).

Illustration 3–14
Auditors' Report—The Home Depot, Inc.

Real World Financials

Report of Independent Registered Public Accounting Firm
The Board of Directors and Stockholders
The Home Depot, Inc.:

We have audited the accompanying Consolidated Balance Sheets of The Home Depot, Inc. and subsidiaries as of February 2, 2014 and February 3, 2013, and the related Consolidated Statements of Earnings, Comprehensive Income, Stockholders' Equity, and Cash Flows for each of the fiscal years in the three-year period ended February 2, 2014. These Consolidated Financial Statements are the responsibility of the Company's management. Our responsibility is to express an opinion on these Consolidated Financial Statements based on our audits.

We conducted our audits in accordance with the standards of the Public Company Accounting Oversight Board (United States). Those standards require that we plan and perform the audit to obtain reasonable assurance about whether the financial statements are free of material misstatement. An audit includes examining, on a test basis, evidence supporting the amounts and disclosures in the financial statements. An audit also includes assessing the accounting principles used and significant estimates made by management, as well as evaluating the overall financial statement presentation. We believe that our audits provide a reasonable basis for our opinion.

In our opinion, the Consolidated Financial Statements referred to above present fairly, in all material respects, the financial position of The Home Depot, Inc. and subsidiaries as of February 2, 2014 and February 3, 2013, and the results of their operations and their cash flows for each of the fiscal years in the threeyear period ended February 2, 2014, in conformity with U.S. generally accepted accounting principles.

We also have audited, in accordance with the standards of the Public Company Accounting Oversight Board (United States), The Home Depot, Inc.'s internal control over financial reporting as of February 2, 2014, based on criteria established in *Internal Control—Integrated Framework (1992)* issued by the Committee of Sponsoring Organizations of the Treadway Commission (COSO), and our report dated March 27, 2014, expressed an unqualified opinion on the effectiveness of the Company's internal control over financial reporting.

KPMG LLP
Atlanta, Georgia
March 27, 2014

financial position, results of operations, and cash flows and are "in conformity with U.S. generally accepted accounting principles." These situations prompt an unqualified opinion. Notice that the last paragraph in Home Depot's report references the auditors' separate report on the effectiveness of the company's internal control over financial reporting.

Sometimes circumstances cause the auditors' report to include an explanatory paragraph in addition to the standard wording, even though the report is unqualified. Most notably, these include:

- *Lack of consistency* due to a change in accounting principle such that comparability is affected even though the auditor concurs with the desirability of the change.
- *Uncertainty* as to the ultimate resolution of a contingency for which a loss is material in amount but not necessarily probable or probable but not estimable.
- *Emphasis* of a matter concerning the financial statements that does not affect the existence of an unqualified opinion but relates to a significant event such as a related-party transaction.

The auditors' report calls attention to problems that might exist in the financial statements.

Some audits result in the need to issue other than an unqualified opinion due to exceptions such as (a) nonconformity with generally accepted accounting principles, (b) inadequate disclosures, and (c) a limitation or restriction of the scope of the examination. In these situations the auditor will issue a (an):

- *Qualified opinion* This contains an exception to the standard unqualified opinion but not of sufficient seriousness to invalidate the financial statements as a whole.

- *Adverse opinion* This is necessary when the exceptions (a) and (b) are so serious that a qualified opinion is not justified. Adverse opinions are rare because auditors usually are able to persuade management to rectify problems to avoid this undesirable report.
- *Disclaimer* An auditor will disclaim an opinion for item (c) such that insufficient information has been gathered to express an opinion.

During the course of each audit, the auditor is required to evaluate the company's ability to continue for a reasonable time as a going concern. If the auditor determines there is significant doubt, an explanation of the potential problem must be included in the auditors' report.[13]

The auditor should assess the firm's ability to continue as a going concern.

Obviously, the auditors' report is most informative when any of these deviations from the standard unqualified opinion are present. These departures from the norm should raise a red flag to a financial analyst and prompt additional search for information.

As an example, the 2013 auditors' report of iBio included a going concern paragraph shown in Illustration 3–15.

Illustration 3–15

Going Concern Paragraph—iBio Inc.

Real World Financials

> The accompanying financial statements have been prepared assuming that the Company will continue as a going concern. As discussed in Note 2 to the financial statements, the Company has incurred net losses and negative cash flows from operating activities for the years ended June 30, 2013 and 2012 and has an accumulated deficit as of June 30, 2013. These matters, among others, raise substantial doubt about the Company's ability to continue as a going concern. Management's plans regarding these matters are also described in Note 2. The accompanying financial statements do not include any adjustments that might result from the outcome of this uncertainty.

Compensation of Directors and Top Executives

The compensation large U.S. corporations pay their top executives is an issue of considerable public debate and controversy. Shareholders, employees, politicians, and the public in general sometimes question the huge pay packages received by company officials at the same time that more and more rank-and-file employees are being laid off as a result of company cutbacks. Contributing to the debate is the realization that the compensation gap between executives and lower-level employees is much wider in the United States than in most other industrialized countries.

Historically, disclosures related to executive compensation were not clear. In addition, a substantial portion of executive pay often is in the form of stock options, further confusing the total compensation paid to executives. Executive stock options give their holders the right to buy stock at a specified price, usually equal to the market price when the options are granted. When stock prices rise, executives can exercise their options and realize a profit. In some cases, options have made executive compensation extremely high. Stock options are discussed in depth in Chapter 19.

To help shareholders and others sort out the content of executive pay packages and better understand the commitments of the company in this regard, SEC requirements provide for disclosures on compensation to directors and executives, and in particular, concerning stock options. The proxy statement that must be reported each year to all shareholders, usually along with the annual report, invites shareholders to the meeting to elect board members and to vote on issues before the shareholders or to vote by proxy. The proxy statement also includes compensation and stock option information for directors and top executives. Illustration 3–16 shows a portion of Best Buy's summary compensation table included in a recent proxy statement.

The *proxy statement* contains disclosures on compensation to directors and executives.

[13]"The Auditor's Consideration of an Entity's Ability to Continue as a Going Concern (Redrafted)," *Statement on Auditing Standards No. 126, AICPA Professional Standards AU 570* (New York: AICPA, 2012).

Illustration 3–16 Summary Compensation Table—Best Buy Co. Inc.

Summary Compensation Table (in part)

Name and Title	Fiscal Year	Salary and Bonus	Stock Awards	Option Awards	Non-Equity Incentive Plan Companesation	All Other Compensation	Total Compensation
Hubert Joly Chief Executive Officer	2013	$3,992,596	$11,801,306	$3,750,002	—	$ 6,788	$19,550,692
Sharon L. McCollam Executive VP and Chief Financial Officer	2013	873,558	2,666,672	1,333,334	—	38,618	4,912,182
Shari L. Ballard Executive VP & President, International	2013	1,146,154	2,307,793	226,911	—	8,512	3,689,370
Keith J. Nelsen Executive VP – General Counsel, Chief Risk Officer & Secretary	2013	794,327	1,791,312	204,207	—	8,027	2,797,873
Carol A. Surface Executive VP and President, International	2013	952,308	2,267,435	204,207	—	13,301	3,437,251

Real World Financials

PART C

Risk Analysis

Using Financial Statement Information

● LO3–7

The overriding objective of financial reporting is providing information that investors and creditors can use to make decisions. Nevertheless, it's sometimes easy to lose sight of that objective while dealing with the intricacies that specific concepts and procedures can involve. In this part of the chapter we provide an overview of financial statement analysis and then demonstrate the use of ratios, a popular financial statement analysis technique, to analyze risk.

Investors, creditors, and others use information that companies provide in corporate financial reports to make decisions. Although the financial reports focus primarily on the past performance and the present financial condition of the reporting company, information users are most interested in the outlook for the future. Trying to gain a glimpse of the future from past and present data entails using various tools and techniques to formulate predictions. This is the goal of financial statement analysis.

Comparative financial statements allow financial statement users to compare year-to-year financial position, results of operations, and cash flows.

Financial statements are not presented in isolation. Every financial statement issued is accompanied by the corresponding financial statement of the preceding year, and often the previous two years. These are called **comparative financial statements**. They enable investors, creditors, and other users to compare year-to-year financial position, results of operations, and cash flows. These comparative data help an analyst detect and predict trends. Because operations often expand and contract in a cyclical fashion, analysis of any one year's data may not provide an accurate picture of a company.

Some analysts enhance their comparison by expressing each item as a percentage of that same item in the financial statements of another year (base amount) in order to more easily see year-to-year changes. This is referred to as **horizontal analysis**. Similarly, **vertical analysis** involves expressing each item in the financial statements as a percentage of an appropriate corresponding total, or base amount, but within the same year. For example, cash, inventory, and other assets can be restated as a percentage of total assets; net income and each expense can be restated as a percentage of revenues.

Regardless of the specific technique used, the essential point is that accounting numbers are virtually meaningless in isolation. Their value derives from comparison with other numbers. The most common way of comparing accounting numbers to evaluate the performance and risk of a firm is **ratio analysis**.

No accounting numbers are meaningful in and of themselves.

We use ratios every day. Batting averages indicate how well our favorite baseball players are performing. We evaluate basketball players by field goal percentage and rebounds per game. Speedometers measure the speed of our cars in terms of miles per hour. We compare grocery costs on the basis of price per pound or ounce. In each of these cases, the ratio is more meaningful than a single number by itself. Do 45 hits indicate satisfactory performance? It depends on the number of at-bats. Is $2 a good price for cheese? It depends on how many ounces the $2 buys. Ratios make these measurements meaningful.

Likewise, we can use ratios to help evaluate a firm's performance and financial position. Is net income of $4 million a cause for shareholders to celebrate? Probably not if shareholders' equity is $10 billion. But if shareholders equity is $10 million, that's a 40% return on equity! Although ratios provide more meaningful information than absolute numbers alone, the ratios are most useful when analyzed relative to some standard of comparison. That standard of comparison may be previous performance of the same company, the performance of a competitor company, or an industry average for the particular ratio.

Evaluating information in ratio form allows analysts to control for size differences over time and among firms.

Accountants should be conversant with ratio analysis for at least three reasons. First, when preparing financial statements, accountants should be familiar with the ways users will use the information provided to make better decisions concerning what and how to report. Second, when accountants participate in company decisions concerning operating and financing alternatives, they may find ratio analysis helpful in evaluating available choices. Third, during the planning stages of an audit, independent auditors often use ratio analysis. This analysis assists in identifying potential audit problems and determining the specific audit procedures that should be performed.

We introduce ratios related to risk analysis in this chapter and ratios related to profitability analysis in Chapter 5. You will also employ ratios in Decision Makers' Perspective sections of many of the chapters in this text. Analysis cases that benefit from ratio analysis are included in many of these chapters as well.

Investors and creditors use financial information to assess the future risk and return of their investments in business enterprises. The balance sheet provides information useful to this assessment. A key element of risk analysis is investigating a company's ability to pay its obligations when they come due. This type of risk often is referred to as **default risk**. Another aspect of risk is **operational risk**, which relates more to how adept a company is at withstanding various events and circumstances that might impair its ability to earn profits. Obviously, these two types of risk are not completely independent of one another. Inability to earn profits certainly increases a company's chances of defaulting on its obligations. Conversely, regardless of a company's long-run prospects for generating profits, if it can't meet its obligations, the company's operations are at risk.

Assessing risk necessarily involves consideration of a variety of economywide risk factors such as inflation, interest rates, and the general business climate. Industrywide influences including competition, labor conditions, and technological forces also affect a company's risk profile. Still other risk factors are specific to the company itself. Financial ratios often are used in risk analysis to investigate a company's **liquidity** and **long-term solvency**. As we discuss some of the more common ratios in the following paragraphs, keep in mind the inherent relationship between risk and return and thus between our risk analysis in this chapter and our profitability analysis in Chapter 5.

Liquidity Ratios

● LO3–8

Liquidity refers to the readiness of assets to be converted to cash. By comparing a company's liquid assets with its short-term obligations, we can obtain a general idea of the firm's ability to pay its short-term debts as they come due. Usually, current assets are thought of as the most liquid of a company's assets. Obviously, though, some are more liquid than others, so it's important also to evaluate the specific makeup of current assets. Two common measures of liquidity are (1) the current ratio and (2) the acid-test ratio (or quick ratio) calculated as follows:

$$\text{Current ratio} = \frac{\text{Current assets}}{\text{Current liabilities}}$$

$$\text{Acid-test ratio (or quick ratio)} = \frac{\text{Quick assets}}{\text{Current liabilities}}$$

Working capital, the difference between current assets and current liabilities, is a popular measure of a company's ability to satisfy its short-term obligations.

CURRENT RATIO. Implicit in the definition of a current liability is the relationship between current assets and current liabilities. The difference between current assets and current liabilities is called working capital. By comparing a company's obligations that will shortly become due with the company's cash and other assets that, by definition, are expected to shortly be converted to cash, the analysis offers some indication as to ability to pay those debts. Although used in a variety of decisions, it is particularly useful to those considering whether to extend short-term credit. The current ratio is computed by dividing current assets by current liabilities. A current ratio of 2 indicates that the company has twice as many current assets available as current liabilities.

PetSmart

PetSmart's working capital (in thousands) at the end of its February 2, 2014, fiscal year is \$523,898, consisting of current assets of \$1,318,243 (Illustration 3–3 on page 117) minus current liabilities of \$794,345 (Illustration 3–7 on page 120). The current ratio can be computed as follows:

$$\text{Current ratio} = \frac{\$1,318,243}{\$794,345} = 1.66$$

Care should be taken, however, in assessing liquidity based solely on working capital. Liabilities usually are paid with cash, not other components of working capital. A company could have difficulty paying its liabilities even with a current ratio significantly greater than 1.0. For example, if a significant portion of current assets consisted of inventories, and inventories usually are not converted to cash for several months, there could be a problem in paying accounts payable due in 30 days. On the other hand, a current ratio of less than 1.0 doesn't necessarily mean the company will have difficulty meeting its current obligations. A line of credit, for instance, which the company can use to borrow funds, provides financial flexibility. That also must be considered in assessing liquidity.

The *acid-test ratio* provides a more stringent indication of a company's ability to pay its current obligations.

ACID-TEST RATIO (OR QUICK RATIO). Some analysts like to modify the current ratio to consider only current assets that are readily available to pay current liabilities. One such variation in common use is the acid-test ratio. This ratio excludes inventories, prepaid

Ethical Dilemma

The Raintree Cosmetic Company has several loans outstanding with a local bank. The debt agreements all contain a covenant stipulating that Raintree must maintain a current ratio of at least 0.9. Jackson Phillips, company controller, estimates that the 2016 year-end current assets and current liabilities will be \$2,100,000 and \$2,400,000, respectively. These estimates provide a current ratio of only 0.875. Violation of the debt agreement will increase Raintree's borrowing costs as the loans are renegotiated at higher rates.

Jackson proposes to the company president that Raintree purchase inventory of \$600,000 on credit before year-end. This will cause both current assets and current liabilities to increase by the same amount, but the current ratio will increase to 0.9. The extra \$600,000 in inventory will be used over the later part of 2017. However, the purchase will cause warehousing costs and financing costs to increase.

Jackson is concerned about the ethics of his proposal. What do you think?

items, restricted cash, and deferred taxes from current assets before dividing by current liabilities. The numerator, then, consists of (unrestricted) cash, short-term investments, and accounts receivable, the "quick assets." By eliminating current assets less readily convertible into cash, the acid-test ratio provides a more rigorous indication of liquidity than does the current ratio.

PetSmart's quick assets at the end of its February 2, 2014, fiscal year (in thousands) total 358,307 (285,622 + 72,685). The acid-test ratio can be computed as follows:

PetSmart

$$\text{Acid-test ratio} = \frac{\$358{,}307}{\$794{,}345} = 0.45$$

Are these liquidity ratios adequate? It's generally difficult to say without some point of comparison. As indicated previously, common standards for such comparisons are industry averages for similar ratios or ratios of the same company in prior years. Industry averages for the above two ratios are as follows:

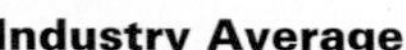

Industry Average

Current ratio = 1.27

Acid-test ratio = 0.33

PetSmart's ratios are higher than the industry average. What if the ratios were lower? Would that indicate a liquidity problem? Not necessarily, but it would raise a red flag that calls for caution in analyzing other areas. Remember that each ratio is but one piece of the entire puzzle. For instance, profitability is perhaps the best indication of liquidity in the long run. We discuss ratios that measure profitability in Chapter 5.

Liquidity ratios should be assessed in the context of both profitability and efficiency of managing assets.

Also, management may be very efficient in managing current assets so that, let's say, receivables are collected faster than normal or inventory is sold faster than normal, making those assets more liquid than they otherwise would be. Higher turnover ratios, relative to those of a competitor or the industry, generally indicate a more liquid position for a given level of the current ratio. We discuss these turnover ratios in Chapter 5.

Financing Ratios

Investors and creditors, particularly long-term creditors, are vitally interested in a company's long-term solvency and stability. Financing ratios provide some indication of the riskiness of a company with regard to its ability to pay its long-term debts. Two common financing ratios are (1) the debt to equity ratio and (2) the times interest earned ratio. These ratios are calculated as follows:

$$\text{Debt to equity ratio} = \frac{\text{Total liabilities}}{\text{Shareholders' equity}}$$

$$\text{Times interest earned ratio} = \frac{\text{Net income} + \text{Interest expense} + \text{Income taxes}}{\text{Interest expense}}$$

The *debt to equity ratio* indicates the extent of reliance on creditors, rather than owners, in providing resources.

DEBT TO EQUITY RATIO. The debt to equity ratio compares resources provided by creditors with resources provided by owners. It is calculated by dividing total liabilities (current and long-term) by total shareholders' equity (including retained earnings).[14]

The ratio provides a measure of creditors' protection in the event of insolvency. Other things being equal, the higher the ratio, the higher the risk. The higher the ratio, the greater the creditor claims on assets, so the higher the likelihood an individual creditor would not be paid in full if the company is unable to meet its obligations. Relatedly, a high ratio indicates not only more fixed interest obligations, but probably a higher *rate* of interest as well because lenders tend to charge higher rates as the level of debt increases.

PetSmart's liabilities at the end of its February 2, 2014, fiscal year (in thousands) total $1,428,186 (Illustration 3–7 on page 120), and stockholders' equity totals $1,093,782 (Illustration 3–8 on page 121). The debt to equity ratio can be computed as follows:

PetSmart

$$\text{Debt to equity ratio} = \frac{\$1{,}428{,}186}{\$1{,}093{,}782} = 1.31$$

[14]A commonly used variation of the debt to equity ratio is found by dividing total liabilities by *total assets*, rather than by shareholders' equity only. Of course, in this configuration the ratio measures precisely the same attribute of the firm's capital structure but can be interpreted as the percentage of a company's total assets provided by funds from creditors, rather than by owners.

As with all ratios, the debt to equity ratio is more meaningful if compared to some standard such as an industry average or a competitor. For example, the industry average debt to equity ratio of 2.36 is significantly higher than PetSmart's ratio, indicating that PetSmart has fewer liabilities in its capital structure than does the average firm in its industry. Does this mean that PetSmart's default risk is lower? Other things equal—yes. Is that good? Not necessarily. As discussed in the next section, it may be that debt is being underutilized by PetSmart. More debt might increase the potential for return to shareholders, but with higher debt comes higher risk. This is a fundamental trade-off faced by virtually all firms when trying to settle on the optimal amount of debt versus equity in its capital structure.

The makeup of liabilities also is important. For example, liabilities could include deferred services revenue. Recall that deferred revenues are liabilities recorded when cash is received from customers in advance of providing a good or service. Companies satisfy these liabilities not by paying cash, but by providing a service to their customers.

The debt to equity ratio indicates the extent of trading on the equity by using *financial leverage*.

Relationship Between Risk and Profitability. The proportion of debt in the capital structure also is of interest to shareholders. After all, shareholders receive no return on their investments until after all creditor claims are paid. Therefore, the higher the debt to equity ratio, the higher the risk to shareholders. On the other hand, by earning a return on borrowed funds that exceeds the cost of borrowing the funds, a company can provide its shareholders with a total return higher than it could achieve by employing equity funds alone. This is referred to as favorable **financial leverage**.

For illustration, consider a newly formed corporation attempting to determine the appropriate mix of debt and equity. The initial capitalization goal is $50 million. The capitalization mix alternatives have been narrowed to two: (1) $10 million in debt and $40 million in equity and (2) $30 million in debt and $20 million in equity.

Also assume that regardless of the capitalization mix chosen, the corporation will be able to generate a 16% annual return, *before payment of interest and income taxes,* on the $50 million in assets acquired. In other words, income before interest and taxes will be $8 million (16% × $50 million). If the interest rate on debt is 8% and the income tax rate is 40%, comparative net income for the first year of operations for the two capitalization alternatives can be calculated as follows:

	Alternative 1	Alternative 2
Income before interest and income taxes	$8,000,000	$8,000,000
Less: Interest expense	(800,000)[a]	(2,400,000)[b]
Income before income taxes	$7,200,000	$5,600,000
Less: Income tax expense (40%)	(2,880,000)	(2,240,000)
Net income	$4,320,000	$3,360,000

[a]8% × $10,000,000
[b]8% × $30,000,000

Favorable financial leverage means earning a return on borrowed funds that exceeds the cost of borrowing the funds.

Choose alternative 1? Probably not. Although alternative 1 provides a higher net income, the return on the shareholders' equity (net income divided by shareholders' equity) is higher for alternative 2. Here's why:

	Alternative 1	Alternative 2
Return on shareholders' equity[15] =	$\frac{\$4,320,000}{\$40,000,000}$	$\frac{\$3,360,000}{\$20,000,000}$
=	10.8%	16.8%

[15]If return is calculated on *average* shareholders' equity, we're technically assuming that all income is paid to shareholders in cash dividends, so that beginning, ending, and average shareholders' equity are the same. If we assume *no* dividends are paid, rates of return would be

	Alternative 1	Alternative 2
Return on shareholders' equity =	$\frac{\$4,320,000}{(\$44,320,000 + 40,000,000)/2}$	$\frac{\$3,360,000}{(\$20,000,000 + 23,360,000)/2}$
=	10.25%	15.50%

In any case our conclusions are the same.

Alternative 2 generated a higher return for each dollar invested by shareholders. This is because the company leveraged its $20 million equity investment with additional debt. Because the cost of the additional debt (8%) is less than the return on assets invested (16%), the return to shareholders is higher. This is the essence of favorable financial leverage.

Be aware, though, leverage is not always favorable; the cost of borrowing the funds might exceed the returns they provide. If the return on assets invested turned out to be less than expected, the additional debt could result in a lower return on equity for alternative 2. If, for example, the return on assets invested (before interest and income taxes) had been 6% of $50,000,000 (or $3,000,000), rather than 16%, alternative 1 would have provided the better return on equity:

	Alternative 1	Alternative 2
Income before interest and income taxes	$3,000,000	$3,000,000
Less: Interest expense	(800,000)[a]	(2,400,000)[b]
Income before income taxes	$2,200,000	$ 600,000
Less: Income tax expense (40%)	(880,000)	(240,000)
Net income	$1,320,000	$ 360,000

[a]8% × $10,000,000
[b]8% × $30,000,000

	Alternative 1	Alternative 2
Return on shareholders' equity[16] =	$\frac{\$1{,}320{,}000}{\$40{,}000{,}000}$	$\frac{\$360{,}000}{\$20{,}000{,}000}$
=	3.3%	1.8%

So, shareholders typically are faced with a trade-off between the risk that high debt denotes and the potential for a higher return from having the higher debt. In any event, the debt to equity ratio offers a basis for making the choice.

TIMES INTEREST EARNED RATIO. Another way to gauge the ability of a company to satisfy its fixed debt obligations is by comparing interest charges with the income available to pay those charges. The **times interest earned ratio** is designed to do this. It is calculated as income before subtracting interest expense and income taxes divided by interest expense.

The *times interest earned ratio* indicates the margin of safety provided to creditors.

Bondholders, noteholders, and other creditors can measure the margin of safety they are accorded by a company's earnings. If income is many times greater than interest expense, creditors' interests are more protected than if income just barely covers this expense. For this purpose, income should be the amount available to pay interest, which is income before subtracting interest and income taxes, calculated by adding back to net income the interest and income taxes that were deducted.

As an example, **PetSmart**'s financial statements for the fiscal year ended February 2, 2014, report the following:

PetSmart

	($ in thousands)
Net income	$419,520
Interest expense	52,479
Income taxes	239,444
Income before interest and taxes	$711,443

The times interest earned ratio can be computed as follows:

$$\text{Times interest earned ratio} = \frac{\$711{,}443}{\$52{,}479} = 13.6$$

[16]If we assume *no* dividends are paid, rates of return would be

	Alternative 1	Alternative 2
Return on shareholders' equity =	$\frac{\$1{,}320{,}000}{(\$41{,}320{,}000 + 40{,}000{,}000)/2}$	$\frac{\$360{,}000}{(\$20{,}000{,}000 + 20{,}360{,}000)/2}$
=	3.25%	1.78%

In any case our conclusions are the same.

The ratio of 13.6 times indicates a considerable margin of safety for creditors. Income could decrease many times and the company would still be able to meet its interest payment obligations.[17] PetSmart is a highly profitable company with little interest-bearing debt. However, in comparison, the average times interest earned ratio for its industry is approximately 24.1 times; even higher than PetSmart's ratio.

Especially when viewed alongside the debt-equity ratio, the coverage ratio seems to indicate a comfortable safety cushion for creditors. It also indicates a degree of financial mobility if the company were to decide to raise new debt funds to "trade on the equity" and attempt to increase the return to shareholders through favorable financial leverage.

[17]Of course, interest is paid with cash, not with "income." The times interest earned ratio often is calculated by using cash flow from operations before subtracting either interest payments or tax payments as the numerator and interest payments as the denominator.

Financial Reporting Case Solution

1. **Respond to Jerry's criticism that shareholders' equity does not represent the market value of the company. What information does the balance sheet provide?** *(p. 115)* Jerry is correct. The financial statements are supposed to help investors and creditors value a company. However, the balance sheet is not intended to portray the market value of the entity. The assets of a company minus its liabilities as shown in the balance sheet (shareholders' equity) usually will not equal the company's market value for several reasons. For example, many assets are measured at their historical costs rather than their fair values. Also, many company resources, including its trained employees, its experienced management team, and its reputation are not recorded as assets at all. The balance sheet must be used in conjunction with other financial statements, disclosure notes, and other publicly available information.

   The balance sheet does, however, provide valuable information that can be used by investors and creditors to help determine market value. After all, it is the balance sheet that describes many of the resources a company has available for generating future cash flows. The balance sheet also provides important information about liquidity and long-term solvency.

2. **The usefulness of the balance sheet is enhanced by classifying assets and liabilities according to common characteristics. What are the classifications used in Electronic Arts' balance sheets and what elements do those categories include?** *(p. 116)* Electronic Arts' balance sheets contain the following classifications:

   Assets:

   - *Current assets* include cash and several other assets that are reasonably expected to be converted to cash or consumed within the coming year, or within the normal operating cycle of the business if that's longer than one year.
   - *Property and equipment* are the tangible long-lived assets used in the operations of the business. This category includes land, buildings, equipment, machinery, and furniture, as well as natural resources.
   - *Goodwill* is a unique intangible asset in that its cost can't be directly associated with any specifically identifiable right and is not separable from the company as a whole. It represents the unique value of the company as a whole over and above all identifiable tangible and intangible assets.
   - *Acquisition-related intangibles* are assets that represent exclusive rights to something such as a product, a process, or a name. Patents, copyrights, and franchises are examples. These intangible assets were acquired by purchasing other companies.
   - *Deferred income taxes* result from temporary differences between taxable income and accounting income.
   - *Other assets* is a "catch-all" classification of noncurrent assets and could include long-term prepaid expenses and any noncurrent asset not included in one of the other categories.

Liabilities:

- *Current liabilities* are those obligations that are expected to be satisfied through the use of current assets or the creation of other current liabilities. Usually, this means liabilities that are expected to be paid within one year, or the operating cycle if that's longer than one year.
- *Long-term liabilities* are payable further in the future and include bonds, deferred income taxes, and pension obligations. Electronic Arts lists *income tax obligations, deferred income taxes,* and *other liabilities* as its long-term liabilities.

Shareholders' equity:

- *Common stock* and *paid-in capital* collectively equal the amounts invested by shareholders in the corporation.
- *Retained earnings (accumulated deficit)* represents the accumulated net income or net loss reported since inception of the corporation less dividends paid out to shareholders. If this amount is negative, it is called *accumulated deficit.*
- *Accumulated other comprehensive income* is the cumulative amount of other comprehensive income items. This topic is addressed in subsequent chapters. ●

The Bottom Line

- **LO3–1** The balance sheet is a position statement that presents an organized array of assets, liabilities, and shareholders' equity at a particular point in time. The statement does not portray the market value of the entity. However, the information in the statement can be useful in assessing market value, as well as in providing important information about liquidity and long-term solvency. *(p. 114)*
- **LO3–2** Current assets include cash and other assets that are reasonably expected to be converted to cash or consumed during one year or within the normal operating cycle of the business if the operating cycle is longer than one year. All other assets are classified as various types of noncurrent assets. In addition to cash and cash equivalents, current assets include short-term investments, accounts receivable, inventories, and prepaid expenses. Other asset classifications include investments; property, plant, and equipment; intangible assets; and other assets. *(p. 116)*
- **LO3–3** Current liabilities are those obligations that are expected to be satisfied through the use of current assets or the creation of other current liabilities. All other liabilities are classified as long term. Current liabilities include notes and accounts payable, deferred revenues, accrued liabilities, and the current maturities of long-term debt. Long-term liabilities include long-term notes, loans, mortgages, bonds, pension and lease obligations, as well as deferred income taxes. *(p. 120)*
- **LO3–4** Financial statement disclosures are used to convey additional information about the account balances in the basic financial statements as well as to provide supplemental information. This information is disclosed, often parenthetically in the basic financial statements, or in disclosure notes that often include supporting schedules. *(p. 124)*
- **LO3–5** Annual reports of public companies will include management's discussion and analysis of key aspects of the company's business. The purpose of this disclosure is to provide external parties with management's insight into certain transactions, events, and circumstances that affect the enterprise, including their financial impact. *(p. 127)*
- **LO3–6** The purpose of an audit is to provide a professional, independent opinion as to whether or not the financial statements are prepared in conformity with generally accepted accounting principles. The standard audit report of a public company contains four paragraphs; the first two deal with the scope of the audit and the third paragraph states the auditors' opinion regarding the financial statements. The fourth paragraph provides the auditors' opinion on the effectiveness of the company's internal control. *(p. 129)*
- **LO3–7** Financial analysts use various techniques to transform financial information into forms more useful for analysis. Horizontal analysis and vertical analysis provide a useful way of analyzing year-to-year changes. Ratio analysis allows analysts to control for size differences over time and among firms while investigating important relationships among financial variables. *(p. 132)*

- **LO3–8** The balance sheet provides information that can be useful in assessing risk. A key element of risk analysis is investigating a company's ability to pay its obligations when they come due. Liquidity ratios and financing ratios provide information about a company's ability to pay its obligations. (*p. 134*)
- **LO3–9** There are more similarities than differences in balance sheets and financial disclosures prepared according to U.S. GAAP and those prepared applying IFRS. Balance sheet presentation is one important difference. Under U.S. GAAP, we present current assets and liabilities before noncurrent assets and liabilities. IFRS doesn't prescribe the format of the balance sheet, but balance sheets prepared using IFRS often report noncurrent items first. Reportable segment disclosures also are similar. However, IFRS requires an additional disclosure, the amount of segment liabilities (Appendix 3). (*pp. 122* and *141*)

APPENDIX 3 Reporting Segment Information

Many companies operate in several business segments as a strategy to achieve growth and to reduce operating risk through diversification.

Financial analysis of diversified companies is especially difficult. Consider, for example, a company that operates in several distinct business segments including computer peripherals, home health care systems, textiles, and consumer food products. The results of these distinctly different activities will be aggregated into a single set of financial statements, making difficult an informed projection of future performance. It may well be that the five-year outlook differs greatly among the areas of the economy represented by the different segments. To make matters worse for an analyst, the integrated financial statements do not reveal the relative investments in each of the business segments nor the success the company has had within each area. Given the fact that so many companies these days have chosen to balance their operating risks through diversification, aggregated financial statements pose a widespread problem for analysts, lending and credit officers, and other financial forecasters.

Reporting by Operating Segment

Segment reporting facilitates the financial statement analysis of diversified companies.

To address the problem, the accounting profession requires companies engaged in more than one significant business to provide supplemental information concerning individual operating segments. The supplemental disaggregated data do not include complete financial statements for each reportable segment, only certain specified items.

WHAT IS A REPORTABLE OPERATING SEGMENT?

According to U.S. GAAP guidelines, a *management approach* is used in determining which segments of a company are reportable. This approach is based on the way that management organizes the segments within the enterprise for making operating decisions and assessing performance. The segments are, therefore, evident from the structure of the enterprise's internal organization.

More formally, the following characteristics define an **operating segment**:[18]

An operating segment is a component of an enterprise:

- That engages in business activities from which it may recognize revenues and incur expenses (including revenues and expenses relating to transactions with other components of the same enterprise).
- Whose operating results are regularly reviewed by the enterprise's chief operating decision maker to make decisions about resources to be allocated to the segment and assess its performance.
- For which discrete financial information is available.

The FASB hopes that this approach provides insights into the risk and opportunities management sees in the various areas of company operations. Also, reporting information based on the enterprise's internal organization should reduce the incremental cost to companies of providing the data. In addition, there are quantitative thresholds for the definition of an

[18]FASB ASC 280–10–50–1: Segment Reporting—Overall—Disclosure (previously "Disclosures about Segments of an Enterprise and Related Information," *Statement of Financial Accounting Standards No. 131* (Norwalk, Conn.: FASB, 1997), par. 10).

operating segment to limit the number of reportable segments. Only segments of certain size (10% or more of total company revenues, assets, or net income) must be disclosed. However, a company must account for at least 75% of consolidated revenue through segment disclosures.

WHAT AMOUNTS ARE REPORTED BY AN OPERATING SEGMENT?

For areas determined to be reportable operating segments, the following disclosures are required:

a. General information about the operating segment.
b. Information about reported segment profit or loss, including certain revenues and expenses included in reported segment profit or loss, segment assets, and the basis of measurement.
c. Reconciliations of the totals of segment revenues, reported profit or loss, assets, and other significant items to corresponding enterprise amounts.
d. Interim period information.[19]

Illustration 3A–1 shows the business segment information reported by Abbott Laboratories, in its 2013 annual report.

Illustration 3A–1

Business Segment Information Disclosure—Abbott Laboratories, Inc.

Real World Financials

Business Segment Information
($ in millions)

Segments	Net Sales	Operating Earnings	Identifiable Assets	Depr. and Amort.	Capital Expenditures
Established Pharmaceuticals	$ 4,974	$1,182	$ 2,637	$ 84	$ 128
Nutritionals	6,740	1,263	3,518	190	340
Diagnostics	4,545	1,008	3,312	368	394
Vascular	3,012	962	1,711	122	62
Other	2,577	(1,894)	31,775[a]	164	982
Total	$21,848	$2,521	$42,953	$928	$1,906

[a]This amount includes assets not identified with a specific segment, such as restricted cash, deferred income taxes, goodwill and other intangible assets, and other non-reportable segments.

International Financial Reporting Standards

Segment Reporting. U.S. GAAP requires companies to report information about reported segment profit or loss, including certain revenues and expenses included in reported segment profit or loss, segment assets, and the basis of measurement. The international standard on segment reporting, *IFRS No. 8*,[20] requires that companies also disclose total *liabilities* of its reportable segments.

● LO3–9

REPORTING BY GEOGRAPHIC AREA

In today's global economy it is sometimes difficult to distinguish domestic and foreign companies. Most large U.S. firms conduct significant operations in other countries in addition to having substantial export sales from this country. Differing political and economic

[19]FASB ASC 280–10–50–20 through 26 and 280–10–50–32: Segment Reporting—Overall—Disclosure (previously "Disclosures about Segments of an Enterprise and Related Information," *Statement of Financial Accounting Standards No. 131* (Norwalk, Conn.: FASB, 1997), par. 25).

[20]"Operating Segments," *International Financial Reporting Standard No. 8* (IASCF), as amended effective January 1, 2014.

environments from country to country means risks and associated rewards sometimes vary greatly among the various operations of a single company. For instance, manufacturing facilities in a South American country embroiled in political unrest pose different risks from having a plant in Vermont, or even Canada. Without disaggregated financial information, these differences cause problems for analysts.

U.S. GAAP requires an enterprise to report certain geographic information unless it is impracticable to do so. This information includes:

a. Revenues from external customers (1) attributed to the enterprise's country of domicile and (2) attributed to all foreign countries in total from which the enterprise derives revenues, and
b. Long-lived assets other than financial instruments, long-term customer relationships of a financial institution, mortgage and other servicing rights, deferred policy acquisition costs, and deferred tax assets (1) located in the enterprise's country of domicile and (2) located in all foreign countries in total in which the enterprise holds assets.[21]

Abbott Laboratories reports its geographic area information by separate countries in 2013, as shown in Illustration 3A–2. Notice that both the business segment (Illustration 3A–1) and geographic information disclosures include a reconciliation to company totals. For example, in both illustrations, net sales of both the business segments and the geographic areas are reconciled to the company's total net sales of $21,848 ($ in millions).

Illustration 3A–2
Geographic Area Information Disclosure—Abbott Laboratories, Inc.

Real World Financials

Geographic Areas
($ in millions)

Net Sales				**Long-Term Assets**			
U.S.	$6,269	Canada	734	U.S	$7,884	Canada	368
Japan	1,442	Italy	726	Japan	902	Italy	100
Germany	1,070	France	680	Germany	1,040	France	213
Netherlands	960	Russia	525	Netherlands	560	Russia	30
China	1,083	Spain	413	China	356	Spain	326
India	922	U.K.	479	India	3,080	U.K.	1,380
Brazil	470	All Others	5,283	Brazil	216	All Others	6,133
Switzerland	792	Total	$21,848	Switzerland	1,117	Total	$23,705

Revenues from major customers must be disclosed.

INFORMATION ABOUT MAJOR CUSTOMERS

Some companies in the defense industry derive substantial portions of their revenues from contracts with the Defense Department. When cutbacks occur in national defense or in specific defense systems, the impact on a company's operations can be considerable. Obviously, financial analysts are extremely interested in information concerning the extent to which a company's prosperity depends on one or more major customers such as in the situation described here. For this reason, if 10% or more of the revenue of an enterprise is derived from transactions with a single customer, the enterprise must disclose that fact, the total amount of revenue from each such customer, and the identity of the operating segment or segments reporting the revenue. The identity of the major customer or customers need not be disclosed, although companies routinely provide that information. In its 2013 annual report, Abbott Laboratories did not report any major customer information. In its 2013 segment disclosures, Lockheed Martin Corp. reports that the U.S. government accounts for 82% of its revenues. ●

[21]FASB ASC 280–10–50–41: Segment Reporting—Overall—Disclosure (previously "Disclosures about Segments of an Enterprise and Related Information," *Statement of Financial Accounting Standards No. 131* (Norwalk, Conn.: FASB, 1997), par. 38).

Questions For Review of Key Topics

Q 3–1 Describe the purpose of the balance sheet.

Q 3–2 Explain why the balance sheet does not portray the market value of the entity.

Q 3–3 Define current assets and list the typical asset categories included in this classification.

Q 3–4 Define current liabilities and list the typical liability categories included in this classification.

Q 3–5 Describe what is meant by an operating cycle for a typical manufacturing company.

Q 3–6 Explain the difference(s) between investments in equity securities classified as current assets versus those classified as noncurrent assets.

Q 3–7 Describe the common characteristics of assets classified as property, plant, and equipment and identify some assets included in this classification.

Q 3–8 Distinguish between property, plant, and equipment and intangible assets.

Q 3–9 Explain how each of the following liabilities would be classified in the balance sheet:

- A note payable of $100,000 due in five years.
- A note payable of $100,000 payable in annual installments of $20,000 each, with the first installment due next year.

Q 3–10 Define the terms *paid-in-capital* and *retained earnings.*

Q 3–11 Disclosure notes are an integral part of the information provided in financial statements. In what ways are the notes critical to understanding the financial statements and to evaluating the firm's performance and financial health?

Q 3–12 A summary of the company's significant accounting policies is a required disclosure. Why is this disclosure important to external financial statement users?

Q 3–13 Define a subsequent event.

Q 3–14 Every annual report of a public company includes an extensive discussion and analysis provided by the company's management. Specifically, which aspects of the company must this discussion address? Isn't management's perspective too biased to be of use to investors and creditors?

Q 3–15 The auditors' report provides the analyst with an independent and professional opinion about the fairness of the representations in the financial statements. What are the four main types of opinion an auditor might issue? Describe each.

Q 3–16 What is a proxy statement? What information does it provide?

Q 3–17 Define the terms *working capital, current ratio,* and *acid-test ratio*(or *quick ratio*).

Q 3–18 Show the calculation of the following financing ratios: (1) the debt to equity ratio, and (2) the times interest earned ratio.

IFRS **Q 3–19** Where can we find authoritative guidance for balance sheet presentation under IFRS?

IFRS **Q 3–20** Describe at least two differences between U.S. GAAP and IFRS in balance sheet presentation.

Q 3–21 (Based on Appendix 3) Segment reporting facilitates the financial statement analysis of diversified companies. What determines whether an operating segment is a reportable segment for this purpose?

Q 3–22 (Based on Appendix 3) For segment reporting purposes, what amounts are reported by each operating segment?

IFRS **Q 3–23** (Based on Appendix 3) Describe any differences in segment disclosure requirements between U.S. GAAP and IFRS.

Brief Exercises

BE 3–1
Current versus noncurrent classification
● LO3–2, LO3–3

Indicate whether each of the following assets and liabilities should be classified as current or noncurrent: (a) accounts receivable; (b) prepaid rent for the next six months; (c) note receivable due in two years; (d) note payable due in 90 days; (e) note payable due in five years; and (f) patent.

BE 3–2
Balance sheet classification
● LO3–2, LO3–3

The trial balance for K and J Nursery, Inc., listed the following account balances at December 31, 2016, the end of its fiscal year: cash, $16,000; accounts receivable, $11,000; inventories, $25,000; equipment (net), $80,000; accounts payable, $14,000; wages payable, $9,000; interest payable, $1,000; note payable (due in 18 months), $30,000; common stock, $50,000. Calculate total current assets and total current liabilities that would appear in the company's year-end balance sheet.

BE 3–3
Balance sheet classification
● LO3–2, LO3–3

Refer to the situation described in BE 3–2. Determine the year-end balance in retained earnings for K and J Nursery, Inc.

BE 3–4
Balance sheet classification
● LO3–2, LO3–3

Refer to the situation described in BE 3–2. Prepare a classified balance sheet for K and J Nursery, Inc. The equipment originally cost $140,000.

BE 3–5
Balance sheet classification
● LO3–2, LO3–3

The following is a December 31, 2016, post-closing trial balance for Culver City Lighting, Inc. Prepare a classified balance sheet for the company.

Account Title	Debits	Credits
Cash	55,000	
Accounts receivable	39,000	
Inventories	45,000	
Prepaid insurance	15,000	
Equipment	100,000	
Accumulated depreciation—equipment		34,000
Patent, net	40,000	
Accounts payable		12,000
Interest payable		2,000
Note payable (due in 10, equal annual installments)		100,000
Common stock		70,000
Retained earnings		76,000
Totals	294,000	294,000

BE 3–6
Balance sheet classification
● LO3–2, LO3–3

You have been asked to review the December 31, 2016, balance sheet for Champion Cleaning. After completing your review, you list the following three items for discussion with your superior:

1. An investment of $30,000 is included in current assets. Management has indicated that it has no intention of liquidating the investment in 2017.
2. A $100,000 note payable is listed as a long-term liability, but you have determined that the note is due in 10, equal annual installments with the first installment due on March 31, 2017.
3. Deferred revenue of $60,000 is included as a current liability even though only two-thirds will be recognized as revenue in 2017, and the other one-third in 2018.

Determine the appropriate classification of each of these items.

BE 3–7
Balance sheet preparation; missing elements
● LO3–2, LO3–3

The following information is taken from the balance sheet of Raineer Plumbing: cash and cash equivalents, $40,000; accounts receivable, $120,000; inventories, ?; total current assets, $235,000; property, plant, and equipment (net), ?; total assets, $400,000; accounts payable, $32,000; note payable (due in two years), $50,000; common stock; $100,000; and retained earnings, ?. Determine the missing amounts.

BE 3–8
Financial statement disclosures
● LO3–4

For each of the following note disclosures, indicate whether the disclosure would likely appear in (A) the summary of significant accounts policies or (B) a separate note: (1) depreciation method; (2) contingency information; (3) significant issuance of common stock after the fiscal year-end; (4) cash equivalent designation; (5) long-term debt information; and (6) inventory costing method.

BE 3–9
Calculating ratios
● LO3–8

Refer to the trial balance information in BE 3–5. Calculate the (a) current ratio, (b) acid-test ratio, and (c) debt to equity ratio.

BE 3–10
Effect of decisions on ratios
● LO3–8

At the end of 2016, Barker Corporation's preliminary trial balance indicated a current ratio of 1.2. Management is contemplating paying some of its accounts payable balance before the end of the fiscal year. Explain the effect this transaction would have on the current ratio. Would your answer be the same if the preliminary trial balance indicated a current ratio of 0.8?

BE 3–11
Calculating ratios; solving for unknowns
● LO3–8

The current asset section of Stibbe Pharmaceutical Company's balance sheet included cash of $20,000 and accounts receivable of $40,000. The only other current asset is inventories. The company's current ratio is 2.0 and its acid-test ratio is 1.5. Determine the ending balance in inventories and total current liabilities.

Exercises

An alternate exercise and problem set is available in the Connect library.

E 3–1
Balance sheet; missing elements
● LO3–2, LO3–3, LO3–8

The following December 31, 2016, fiscal year-end account balance information is available for the Stonebridge Corporation:

Cash and cash equivalents	$ 5,000
Accounts receivable (net)	20,000
Inventories	60,000
Property, plant, and equipment (net)	120,000
Accounts payable	44,000
Wages payable	15,000
Paid-in-capital	100,000

The only asset not listed is short-term investments. The only liabilities not listed are a $30,000 note payable due in two years and related accrued interest of $1,000 due in four months. The current ratio at year-end is 1.5:1.

Required:

Determine the following at December 31, 2016:

1. Total current assets
2. Short-term investments
3. Retained earnings

E 3–2
Balance sheet classification
● LO3–2, LO3–3

The following are the typical classifications used in a balance sheet:

a. Current assets
b. Investments and funds
c. Property, plant, and equipment
d. Intangible assets
e. Other assets
f. Current liabilities
g. Long-term liabilities
h. Paid-in-capital
i. Retained earnings

Required:

For each of the following balance sheet items, use the letters above to indicate the appropriate classification category. If the item is a contra account, place a minus sign before the chosen letter.

1. ____ Equipment
2. ____ Accounts payable
3. ____ Allowance for uncollectible accounts
4. ____ Land, held for investment
5. ____ Note payable, due in 5 years
6. ____ Deferred rent revenue
7. ____ Note payable, due in 6 months
8. ____ Income less dividends, accumulated
9. ____ Investment in XYZ Corp., long-term
10. ____ Inventories
11. ____ Patent
12. ____ Land, in use
13. ____ Accrued liabilities
14. ____ Prepaid rent
15. ____ Common stock
16. ____ Building, in use
17. ____ Cash
18. ____ Taxes payable

E 3–3
Balance sheet classification
● LO3–2, LO3–3

The following are the typical classifications used in a balance sheet:

a. Current assets
b. Investments and funds
c. Property, plant, and equipment
d. Intangible assets
e. Other assets
f. Current liabilities
g. Long-term liabilities
h. Paid-in-capital
i. Retained earnings

Required:

For each of the following 2016 balance sheet items, use the letters above to indicate the appropriate classification category. If the item is a contra account, place a minus sign before the chosen letter.

1. ____ Accrued interest payable
2. ____ Franchise
3. ____ Accumulated depreciation
4. ____ Prepaid insurance, for 2017
5. ____ Bonds payable, due in 10 years
6. ____ Current maturities of long-term debt
7. ____ Note payable, due in three months
8. ____ Long-term receivables
9. ____ Restricted cash, will be used to retire bonds in 10 years
10. ____ Supplies
11. ____ Machinery
12. ____ Land, in use
13. ____ Deferred revenue
14. ____ Copyrights
15. ____ Preferred stock
16. ____ Land, held for speculation
17. ____ Cash equivalents
18. ____ Wages payable

E 3–4
Balance sheet preparation
● LO3–2, LO3–3

The following is a December 31, 2016, post-closing trial balance for the Jackson Corporation.

Account Title	Debits	Credits
Cash	40,000	
Accounts receivable	34,000	
Inventories	75,000	
Prepaid rent	16,000	
Marketable securities (short term)	10,000	
Machinery	145,000	
Accumulated depreciation—machinery		11,000
Patent (net of amortization)	83,000	
Accounts payable		8,000
Wages payable		4,000
Taxes payable		32,000
Bonds payable (due in 10 years)		200,000
Common stock		100,000
Retained earnings		48,000
Totals	403,000	403,000

Required:
Prepare a classified balance sheet for Jackson Corporation at December 31, 2016.

E 3–5
Balance sheet preparation
● LO3–2, LO3–3

The following is the ending balances of accounts at December 31, 2016 for the Valley Pump Corporation.

Account Title	Debits	Credits
Cash	25,000	
Accounts receivable	56,000	
Inventories	81,000	
Interest payable		10,000
Marketable securities	44,000	
Land	120,000	
Buildings	300,000	
Accumulated depreciation—buildings		100,000
Equipment	75,000	
Accumulated depreciation—equipment		25,000
Copyright (net of amortization)	12,000	
Prepaid expenses	32,000	
Accounts payable		65,000
Deferred revenues		20,000
Notes payable		250,000
Allowance for uncollectible accounts		5,000
Common stock		200,000
Retained earnings		70,000
Totals	745,000	745,000

Additional Information:

1. The $120,000 balance in the land account consists of $100,000 for the cost of land where the plant and office buildings are located. The remaining $20,000 represents the cost of land being held for speculation.
2. The $44,000 in the marketable securities account represents an investment in the common stock of another corporation. Valley intends to sell one-half of the stock within the next year.
3. The notes payable account consists of a $100,000 note due in six months and a $150,000 note due in three annual installments of $50,000 each, with the first payment due in August of 2017.

Required:
Prepare a classified balance sheet for the Valley Pump Corporation at December 31, 2016.

E 3–6
Balance sheet; Current versus noncurrent classification
● LO3–2, LO3–3

Presented below is the ending balances of accounts for the Kansas Instruments Corporation at December 31, 2016.

Account Title	Debits	Credits
Cash	20,000	
Accounts receivable	130,000	
Raw materials	24,000	
Note receivable	100,000	
Interest receivable	3,000	
Interest payable		5,000
Marketable securities	32,000	
Land	50,000	
Buildings	1,300,000	
Accumulated depreciation—buildings		620,000
Work in process	42,000	
Finished goods	89,000	
Equipment	300,000	
Accumulated depreciation—equipment		130,000
Patent (net of amortization)	120,000	
Prepaid rent (for the next two years)	60,000	
Deferred revenue		36,000
Accounts payable		180,000
Note payable		400,000
Cash restricted for payment of note payable	80,000	
Allowance for uncollectible accounts		13,000
Sales revenue		800,000
Cost of goods sold	450,000	
Rent expense	28,000	

Additional Information:

1. The note receivable, along with any accrued interest, is due on November 22, 2017.
2. The note payable is due in 2020. Interest is payable annually.
3. The marketable securities consist of treasury bills, all of which mature in the next year.
4. Deferred revenue will be recognized as revenue equally over the next two years.

Required:

Determine the company's working capital (current assets minus current liabilities) at December 31, 2016.

E 3–7
Balance sheet preparation; errors
● LO3–2, LO3–3

The following balance sheet for the Los Gatos Corporation was prepared by a recently hired accountant. In reviewing the statement you notice several errors.

LOS GATOS CORPORATION
Balance Sheet
At December 31, 2016
Assets

Cash	$ 40,000
Accounts receivable	80,000
Inventories	55,000
Machinery (net)	120,000
Franchise (net)	30,000
Total assets	$325,000
Liabilities and Shareholders' Equity	
Accounts payable	$ 50,000
Allowance for uncollectible accounts	5,000
Note payable	55,000
Bonds payable	110,000
Shareholders' equity	105,000
Total liabilities and shareholders' equity	$325,000

Additional Information:

1. Cash includes a $20,000 restricted amount to be used for repayment of the bonds payable in 2020.
2. The cost of the machinery is $190,000.
3. Accounts receivable includes a $20,000 note receivable from a customer due in 2019.

4. The note payable includes accrued interest of $5,000. Principal and interest are both due on February 1, 2017.
5. The company began operations in 2011. Income less dividends since inception of the company totals $35,000.
6. 50,000 shares of no par common stock were issued in 2011. 100,000 shares are authorized.

Required:
Prepare a corrected, classified balance sheet.

E 3–8
Balance sheet; current versus noncurrent classification
● LO3–2, LO3–3

Cone Corporation is in the process of preparing its December 31, 2016, balance sheet. There are some questions as to the proper classification of the following items:

a. $50,000 in cash restricted in a savings account to pay bonds payable. The bonds mature in 2020.
b. Prepaid rent of $24,000, covering the period January 1, 2017, through December 31, 2018.
c. Note payable of $200,000. The note is payable in annual installments of $20,000 each, with the first installment payable on March 1, 2017.
d. Accrued interest payable of $12,000 related to the note payable.
e. Investment in marketable securities of other corporations, $80,000. Cone intends to sell one-half of the securities in 2017.

Required:
Prepare a partial classified balance sheet to show how each of the above items should be reported.

E 3–9
Balance sheet preparation
● LO3–2, LO3–3

The following is the balance sheet of Korver Supply Company at December 31, 2015.

KORVER SUPPLY COMPANY
Balance Sheet
At December 31, 2015

Assets	
Cash	$120,000
Accounts receivable	300,000
Inventories	200,000
Furniture and fixtures, net	150,000
Total assets	$770,000
Liabilities and Shareholders' Equity	
Accounts payable (for merchandise)	$190,000
Note payable	200,000
Interest payable	6,000
Common stock	100,000
Retained earnings	274,000
Total liabilities and shareholders' equity	$770,000

Transactions during 2016 were as follows:

1. Sales to customers on account	$800,000
2. Cash collected from customers	780,000
3. Purchase of merchandise on account	550,000
4. Cash payment to suppliers	560,000
5. Cost of merchandise sold	500,000
6. Cash paid for operating expenses	160,000
7. Cash paid for interest on note	12,000

The note payable is dated June 30, 2015 and is due on June 30, 2017. Interest at 6% is payable annually on June 30. Depreciation on the furniture and fixtures for the year is $20,000. The furniture and fixtures originally cost $300,000.

Required:
Prepare a classified balance sheet at December 31, 2016 (ignore income taxes).

E 3–10
Financial statement disclosures
● LO3–4

The following are typical disclosures that would appear in the notes accompanying financial statements. For each of the items listed, indicate where the disclosure would likely appear—either in (A) the significant accounting policies note or (B) a separate note.

1. Inventory costing method	A
2. Information on related party transactions	___
3. Composition of property, plant, and equipment	___
4. Depreciation method	___
5. Subsequent event information	___
6. Measurement basis for certain financial instruments	___
7. Important merger occurring after year-end	___
8. Composition of receivables	___

E 3–11
Disclosure notes
● LO3–4

Hallergan Company produces car and truck batteries that it sells primarily to auto manufacturers. Dorothy Hawkins, the company's controller, is preparing the financial statements for the year ended December 31, 2016. Hawkins asks for your advice concerning the following information that has not yet been included in the statements. The statements will be issued on February 28, 2017.

1. Hallergan leases its facilities from the brother of the chief executive officer.
2. On January 8, 2017, Hallergan entered into an agreement to sell a tract of land that it had been holding as an investment. The sale, which resulted in a material gain, was completed on February 2, 2017.
3. Hallergan uses the straight-line method to determine depreciation on all of the company's depreciable assets.
4. On February 8, 2017, Hallergan completed negotiations with its bank for a $10,000,000 line of credit.
5. Hallergan uses the first-in, first-out (FIFO) method to value inventory.

Required:
For each of the above items, discuss any additional disclosures that Hawkins should include in Hallergan's financial statements.

E 3–12
Financial statement disclosures
● LO3–4

Parkman Sporting Goods is preparing its annual report for its 2016 fiscal year. The company's controller has asked for your help in determining how best to disclose information about the following items:

1. A related-party transaction.
2. Depreciation method.
3. Allowance for uncollectible accounts.
4. Composition of investments.
5. Composition of long-term debt.
6. Inventory costing method.
7. Number of shares of common stock authorized, issued, and outstanding.
8. Employee benefit plans.

Required:
Indicate whether the above items should be disclosed (A) in the summary of significant accounting policies note, (B) in a separate disclosure note, or (C) on the face of the balance sheet.

E 3–13
FASB codification research
● LO3–4
CODE

The *FASB Accounting Standards Codification* represents the single source of authoritative U.S. generally accepted accounting principles.

Required:
1. Obtain the relevant authoritative literature on the disclosure of accounting policies using the *FASB Accounting Standards Codification* at the FASB website (asc.fasb.org). Identify the topic number that provides guidance on information contained in the notes to the financial statements.
2. What is the specific citation that requires a company to identify and describe in the notes to the financial statements the accounting principles and methods used to prepare the financial statements?
3. Describe the disclosure requirements.

E 3–14
FASB codification research
● LO3–2, LO3–4
CODE

Access the *FASB Accounting Standards Codification* at the FASB website (asc.fasb.org). Determine the specific citation for each of the following items:

1. What is the balance sheet classification for a note payable due in six months that was used to purchase a building?
2. Which assets may be excluded from current assets?
3. Should a note receivable from a related party be included in the balance sheet with notes receivable or accounts receivable from customers?
4. What items are nonrecognized subsequent events that require a disclosure in the notes to the financial statements?

E 3–15
Concepts; terminology
● LO3–2 through LO3–4, LO3–6

Listed below are several terms and phrases associated with the balance sheet and financial disclosures. Pair each item from List A (by letter) with the item from List B that is most appropriately associated with it.

List A	List B
____ 1. Balance sheet	a. Will be satisfied through the use of current assets.
____ 2. Liquidity	b. Items expected to be converted to cash or consumed within one year or the operating cycle, whichever is longer.
____ 3. Current assets	c. The statements are presented fairly in conformity with GAAP.
____ 4. Operating cycle	d. An organized array of assets, liabilities, and equity.
____ 5. Current liabilities	e. Important to a user in comparing financial information across companies.
____ 6. Cash equivalent	f. Scope limitation or a departure from GAAP.
____ 7. Intangible asset	g. Recorded when an expense is incurred but not yet paid.
____ 8. Working capital	h. Relates to the amount of time before an asset is converted to cash or a liability is paid.
____ 9. Accrued liabilities	i. Occurs after the fiscal year-end but before the statements are issued.
____ 10. Summary of significant accounting policies	j. Cash to cash.
____ 11. Subsequent events	k. One-month U.S. Treasury bill.
____ 12. Unqualified opinion	l. Current assets minus current liabilities.
____ 13. Qualified opinion	m. Lacks physical substance.

E 3–16
Calculating ratios
● LO3–8

The 2016 balance sheet for Hallbrook Industries, Inc., is shown below.

HALLBROOK INDUSTRIES, INC.
Balance Sheet
December 31, 2016
($ in 000s)

Assets	
Cash	$ 200
Short-term investments	150
Accounts receivable	200
Inventories	350
Property, plant, and equipment (net)	1,000
Total assets	$1,900
Liabilities and Shareholders' Equity	
Current liabilities	$ 400
Long-term liabilities	350
Paid-in capital	750
Retained earnings	400
Total liabilities and shareholders' equity	$1,900

The company's 2016 income statement reported the following amounts ($ in 000s):

Net sales	$4,600
Interest expense	40
Income tax expense	100
Net income	160

Required:

Determine the following ratios for 2016:

1. Current ratio
2. Acid-test ratio
3. Debt to equity ratio
4. Times interest earned ratio

E 3–17
Calculating ratios; Best Buy
● LO3–8

Best Buy Co, Inc., is a leading retailer specializing in consumer electronics. A condensed income statement and balance sheet for the fiscal year ended February 1, 2014, are shown below.

Real World Financials

Best Buy Co., Inc.
Balance Sheet
At February 1, 2014
($ in millions)

Assets

Current assets:	
Cash and cash equivalents	$ 2,678
Short-term investments	223
Accounts receivable, net	1,308
Merchandise inventories	5,376
Other current assets	900
Total current assets	10,485
Noncurrent assets	3,528
Total assets	$14,013
Liabilities and Shareholders' Equity	
Current liabilities:	
Accounts payable	$ 5,122
Other current liabilities	2,314
Total current liabilities	7,436
Long-term liabilities	2,588
Shareholders' equity	3,989
Total liabilities and shareholders' equity	$14,013

Best Buy Co., Inc.
Income Statement
For the Year Ended February 1, 2014
($ in millions)

Revenues	$42,410
Costs and expenses	41,270
Operating income	1,140
Other income (expense)*	(53)
Income before income taxes	1,087
Income tax expense	398
Net income	$ 689

*Includes $100 of interest expense.

Liquidity and financing ratios for the industry are as follows:

	Industry Average
Current ratio	1.23
Acid-test ratio	0.60
Debt to equity	0.70
Times interest earned	5.66 times

Required:

1. Determine the following ratios for Best Buy for its fiscal year ended February, 1, 2014:
   a. Current ratio
   b. Acid-test ratio
   c. Debt to equity ratio
   d. Times interest earned ratio
2. Using the ratios from requirement 1, assess Best Buy's liquidity and solvency relative to its industry.

E 3–18
Calculating ratios; solve for unknowns
● LO3–8

The current asset section of the Excalibur Tire Company's balance sheet consists of cash, marketable securities, accounts receivable, and inventories. The December 31, 2016, balance sheet revealed the following:

Inventories	$ 840,000
Total assets	$2,800,000
Current ratio	2.25
Acid-test ratio	1.2
Debt to equity ratio	1.8

Required:

Determine the following 2016 balance sheet items:

1. Current assets
2. Shareholders' equity
3. Noncurrent assets
4. Long-term liabilities

E 3–19
Calculating ratios; solve for unknowns
● LO3–8

The current asset section of Guardian Consultant's balance sheet consists of cash, accounts receivable, and prepaid expenses. The 2016 balance sheet reported the following: cash, $1,300,000; prepaid expenses, $360,000; noncurrent assets, $2,400,000; and shareholders' equity, $2,500,000. The current ratio at the end of the year was 2.0 and the debt to equity ratio was 1.4.

Required:

Determine the following 2016 amounts and ratios:

1. Current liabilities.
2. Long-term liabilities.
3. Accounts receivable.
4. The acid-test ratio.

E 3–20
Effect of management decisions on ratios
● LO3–8

Most decisions made by management impact the ratios analysts use to evaluate performance. Indicate (by letter) whether each of the actions listed below will immediately increase (I), decrease (D), or have no effect (N) on the ratios shown. Assume each ratio is less than 1.0 before the action is taken.

Action	Current Ratio	Acid-Test Ratio	Debt to Equity Ratio
1. Issuance of long-term bonds	____	____	____
2. Issuance of short-term notes	____	____	____
3. Payment of accounts payable	____	____	____
4. Purchase of inventory on account	____	____	____
5. Purchase of inventory for cash	____	____	____
6. Purchase of equipment with a 4-year note	____	____	____
7. Retirement of bonds	____	____	____
8. Sale of common stock	____	____	____
9. Write-off of obsolete inventory	____	____	____
10. Purchase of short-term investment for cash	____	____	____
11. Decision to refinance on a long-term basis some currently maturing debt	____	____	____

E 3–21
Segment reporting
● Appendix 3

The Canton Corporation operates in four distinct business segments. The segments, along with 2016 information on revenues, assets and net income, are listed below ($ in millions):

Segment	Revenues	Assets	Net Income
Pharmaceuticals	$2,000	$1,000	$200
Plastics	3,000	1,500	270
Farm equipment	2,500	1,250	320
Electronics	500	250	40
Total company	$8,000	$4,000	$830

Required:

1. For which segments must Canton report supplementary information according to U.S. GAAP?
2. What amounts must be reported for the segments you identified in requirement 1?

E 3–22
Segment reporting
● Appendix 3
LO3–9

IFRS

Refer to E3–21.

Required:

How might your answers differ if Canton Corporation prepares its segment disclosure according to International Financial Reporting Standards?

CPA and CMA Review Questions

CPA Exam Questions

KAPLAN CPA REVIEW

The following questions are adapted from a variety of sources including questions developed by the AICPA Board of Examiners and those used in the Kaplan CPA Review Course to study balance sheet presentation, financial disclosures, and liquidity ratios while preparing for the CPA examination. Determine the response that best completes the statements or questions.

● LO3–2

1. In Merf's April 30, 2016, balance sheet, a note receivable was reported as a noncurrent asset and the related accrued interest for eight months was reported as a current asset. Which of the following descriptions would fit Merf's receivable classification?
   a. Both principal and interest amounts are due on August 31, 2016, and August 31, 2017.
   b. Principal is due August 31, 2017, and interest is due August 31, 2016, and August 31, 2017.
   c. Principal and interest are due December 31, 2016.
   d. Both principal and interest amounts are due on December 31, 2016, and December 31, 2017.

● LO3–3

2. Mill Co.'s trial balance included the following account balances at December 31, 2016:

Accounts payable	$15,000
Bond payable, due 2017	22,000
Dividends payable 1/31/17	8,000
Notes payable, due 2018	20,000

   What amount should be included in the current liability section of Mill's December 31, 2016, balance sheet?
   a. $45,000
   b. $51,000
   c. $65,000
   d. $78,000

● LO3–4

3. Which of the following would be disclosed in the summary of significant accounting policies disclosure note?

	Composition of Plant Assets	Inventory Pricing
a.	No	Yes
b.	Yes	No
c.	Yes	Yes
d.	No	No

● LO3–6

4. How are management's responsibility and the auditor's report represented in the standard auditor's report?

	Management's Responsibility	Auditor's Responsibility
a.	Implicitly	Explicitly
b.	Implicitly	Implicitly
c.	Explicitly	Explicitly
d.	Explicitly	Implicitly

● LO3–8

5. At December 30, Vida Co. had cash of $200,000, a current ratio of 1.5:1, and a quick ratio of 0.5:1. On December 31, all the cash was used to reduce accounts payable. How did this cash payment affect the ratios?

	Current Ratio	Quick Ratio
a.	Increased	No effect
b.	Increased	Decreased
c.	Decreased	Increased
d.	Decreased	No effect

● LO3–8

6. Zenk Co. wrote off obsolete inventory of $100,000 during 2016. What was the effect of this write-off on Zenk's ratio analysis?
   a. Decrease in the current ratio but not the quick ratio.
   b. Decrease in the quick ratio but not in the current ratio.
   c. Increase in the current ratio but not in the quick ratio.
   d. Increase in the quick ratio but not in the current ratio.

International Financial Reporting Standards are tested on the CPA exam along with U.S. GAAP. The following questions deal with the application of IFRS.

● LO3–9

IFRS

7. Noncurrent assets must be reported before current assets in a balance sheet reported by a company using:
   a. IFRS.
   b. U.S. GAAP.
   c. Both U.S. GAAP and IFRS.
   d. Neither U.S. GAAP nor IFRS.

● LO3–9
● Appendix 3

IFRS

8. Total liabilities of a company's reportable segments must be reported when the company provides supplemental information on operating segments using:
   a. IFRS.
   b. U.S. GAAP.
   c. Both U.S. GAAP and IFRS.
   d. Neither U.S. GAAP nor IFRS.

CMA Exam Questions

The following questions dealing with balance sheet presentation, financial disclosures, and liquidity ratios are adapted from questions that previously appeared on Certified Management Accountant (CMA) examinations. The CMA designation sponsored by the Institute of Management Accountants (**www.imanet.org**) provides members with an objective measure of knowledge and competence in the field of management accounting. Determine the response that best completes the statements or questions.

● LO3–4

1. The Financial Accounting Standards Board has provided guidance on disclosures of transactions between related parties, for example, transactions between subsidiaries of a common parent. GAAP regarding related-party transactions requires all of the following disclosures except
   a. The nature of the relationship involved.
   b. A description of the transactions for each period an income statement is presented.
   c. The dollar amounts of transactions for each period an income statement is presented.
   d. The effect on the cash flow statement for each period a cash flow statement is presented.

● LO3–5

2. The Management's Discussion and Analysis (MD&A) section of an annual report
   a. Includes the company president's letter.
   b. Covers three financial aspects of a firm's business: liquidity, capital resources, and results of operations.
   c. Is a technical analysis of past results and a defense of those results by management.
   d. Covers marketing and product line issues.

● LO3–8

3. Windham Company has current assets of $400,000 and current liabilities of $500,000. Windham Company's current ratio would be increased by
   a. The purchase of $100,000 of inventory on account.
   b. The payment of $100,000 of accounts payable.
   c. The collection of $100,000 of accounts receivable.
   d. Refinancing a $100,000 long-term loan with short-term debt.

Problems

An alternate exercise and problem set is available in the Connect library.

P 3–1
Balance sheet preparation
● LO3–2, LO3–3

Presented below is a list of balance sheet accounts.

Accounts payable	Cash
Accounts receivable	Common stock
Accumulated depreciation—buildings	Copyright
Accumulated depreciation—equipment	Equipment
Allowance for uncollectible accounts	Interest receivable (due in three months)
Restricted cash (to be used in 10 years)	Inventories
Bonds payable (due in 10 years)	Land (in use)
Buildings	Long-term investments
Notes payable (due in 6 months)	Rent payable (current)
Notes receivable (due in 2 years)	Retained earnings
Patent	Short-term investments
Preferred stock	Taxes payable
Prepaid expenses	Wages payable

Required:
Prepare a classified balance sheet ignoring monetary amounts.

P 3–2
Balance sheet preparation; missing elements
● LO3–2, LO3–3

The data listed below are taken from a balance sheet of Trident Corporation at December 31, 2016. Some amounts, indicated by question marks, have been intentionally omitted.

	($ in 000s)
Cash and cash equivalents	$ 239,186
Short-term investments	353,700
Accounts receivable (net of allowance)	504,944
Inventories	?
Prepaid expenses (current)	83,259
Total current assets	1,594,927
Long-term receivables	110,800
Property and equipment (net)	?
Total assets	?
Notes payable and short-term debt	31,116
Accounts payable	?
Accrued liabilities	421,772
Other current liabilities	181,604
Total current liabilities	693,564
Long-term debt and deferred taxes	?
Total liabilities	956,140
Shareholders' equity	1,370,627

Required:
1. Determine the missing amounts.
2. Prepare Trident's classified balance sheet.

P 3–3
Balance sheet preparation
● LO3–2, LO3–3

The following is a December 31, 2016, post-closing trial balance for Almway Corporation.

Account Title	Debits	Credits
Cash	45,000	
Investments	110,000	
Accounts receivable	60,000	
Inventories	200,000	
Prepaid insurance	9,000	
Land	90,000	
Buildings	420,000	
Accumulated depreciation—buildings		100,000
Equipment	110,000	
Accumulated depreciation—equipment		60,000
Patents (net of amortization)	10,000	
Accounts payable		75,000
Notes payable		130,000
Interest payable		20,000
Bonds payable		240,000
Common stock		300,000
Retained earnings		129,000
Totals	1,054,000	1,054,000

Additional Information:
1. The investment account includes an investment in common stock of another corporation of $30,000 which management intends to hold for at least three years. The balance of these investments is intended to be sold in the coming year.
2. The land account includes land which cost $25,000 that the company has not used and is currently listed for sale.
3. The cash account includes $15,000 restricted in a fund to pay bonds payable that mature in 2019 and $23,000 restricted in a three-month Treasury bill.
4. The notes payable account consists of the following:
   a. a $30,000 note due in six months.
   b. a $50,000 note due in six years.
   c. a $50,000 note due in five annual installments of $10,000 each, with the next installment due February 15, 2017.

5. The $60,000 balance in accounts receivable is net of an allowance for uncollectible accounts of $8,000.
6. The common stock account represents 100,000 shares of no par value common stock issued and outstanding. The corporation has 500,000 shares authorized.

Required:
Prepare a classified balance sheet for the Almway Corporation at December 31, 2016.

P 3–4
Balance sheet preparation
● LO3–2, LO3–3

The following is the ending balances of accounts at December 31, 2016 for the Weismuller Publishing Company.

Account Title	Debits	Credits
Cash	65,000	
Accounts receivable	160,000	
Inventories	285,000	
Prepaid expenses	148,000	
Machinery and equipment	320,000	
Accumulated depreciation—equipment		110,000
Investments	140,000	
Accounts payable		60,000
Interest payable		20,000
Deferred revenue		80,000
Taxes payable		30,000
Notes payable		200,000
Allowance for uncollectible accounts		16,000
Common stock		400,000
Retained earnings		202,000
Totals	1,118,000	1,118,000

Additional Information:
1. Prepaid expenses include $120,000 paid on December 31, 2016, for a two-year lease on the building that houses both the administrative offices and the manufacturing facility.
2. Investments include $30,000 in Treasury bills purchased on November 30, 2016. The bills mature on January 30, 2017. The remaining $110,000 includes investments in marketable equity securities that the company intends to sell in the next year.
3. Deferred revenue represents customer prepayments for magazine subscriptions. Subscriptions are for periods of one year or less.
4. The notes payable account consists of the following:
   a. a $40,000 note due in six months.
   b. a $100,000 note due in six years.
   c. a $60,000 note due in three annual installments of $20,000 each, with the next installment due August 31, 2017.
5. The common stock account represents 400,000 shares of no par value common stock issued and outstanding. The corporation has 800,000 shares authorized.

Required:
Prepare a classified balanced sheet for the Weismuller Publishing Company at December 31, 2016.

P 3–5
Balance sheet preparation
● LO3–2, LO3–3

The following is the ending balances of accounts at June 30, 2016 for Excell Company.

Account Title	Debits	Credits
Cash	83,000	
Short-term investments	65,000	
Accounts receivable	280,000	
Prepaid expenses	32,000	
Land	75,000	
Buildings	320,000	
Accumulated depreciation—buildings		160,000
Equipment	265,000	
Accumulated depreciation—equipment		120,000
Accounts payable		173,000
Accrued expenses		45,000
Notes payable		100,000

(continued)

(concluded)

Mortgage payable		250,000
Common stock		100,000
Retained earnings		172,000
Totals	1,120,000	1,120,000

Additional Information:

1. The short-term investments account includes $18,000 in U.S. treasury bills purchased in May. The bills mature in July.
2. The accounts receivable account consists of the following:

a. Amounts owed by customers	$225,000
b. Allowance for uncollectible accounts—trade customers	(15,000)
c. Nontrade note receivable (due in three years)	65,000
d. Interest receivable on note (due in four months)	5,000
Total	$280,000

3. The notes payable account consists of two notes of $50,000 each. One note is due on September 30, 2016, and the other is due on November 30, 2017.
4. The mortgage payable is payable in *semiannual* installments of $5,000 each plus interest. The next payment is due on October 31, 2016. Interest has been properly accrued and is included in accrued expenses.
5. Five hundred thousand shares of no par common stock are authorized, of which 200,000 shares have been issued and are outstanding.
6. The land account includes $50,000 representing the cost of the land on which the company's office building resides. The remaining $25,000 is the cost of land that the company is holding for investment purposes.

Required:

Prepare a classified balance sheet for the Excell Company at June 30, 2016.

P 3–6
Balance sheet preparation; disclosures
● **LO3–2 through LO3–4**

The following is the ending balances of accounts at December 31, 2016 for the Vosburgh Electronics Corporation.

Account Title	Debits	Credits
Cash	67,000	
Short-term investments	182,000	
Accounts receivable	123,000	
Long-term investments	35,000	
Inventories	215,000	
Loans to employees	40,000	
Prepaid expenses (for 2017)	16,000	
Land	280,000	
Building	1,550,000	
Machinery and equipment	637,000	
Patent	152,000	
Franchise	40,000	
Note receivable	250,000	
Interest receivable	12,000	
Accumulated depreciation—building		620,000
Accumulated depreciation—equipment		210,000
Accounts payable		189,000
Dividends payable (payable on 1/16/17)		10,000
Interest payable		16,000
Taxes payable		40,000
Deferred revenue		60,000
Notes payable		300,000
Allowance for uncollectible accounts		8,000
Common stock		2,000,000
Retained earnings		146,000
Totals	3,599,000	3,599,000

Additional Information:

1. The common stock represents 1 million shares of no par stock authorized, 500,000 shares issued and outstanding.
2. The loans to employees are due on June 30, 2017.

3. The note receivable is due in installments of $50,000, payable on each September 30. Interest is payable annually.
4. Short-term investments consist of marketable equity securities that the company plans to sell in 2017 and $50,000 in treasury bills purchased on December 15 of the current year that mature on February 15, 2017. Long-term investments consist of marketable equity securities that the company does not plan to sell in the next year.
5. Deferred revenue represents customer payments for extended service contracts. Eighty percent of these contracts expire in 2017, the remainder in 2018.
6. Notes payable consists of two notes, one for $100,000 due on January 15, 2018, and another for $200,000 due on June 30, 2019.

Required:
1. Prepare a classified balance sheet for Vosburgh at December 31, 2016.
2. Identify the items that would require additional disclosure, either on the face of the balance sheet or in a disclosure note.

P 3–7
Balance sheet preparation; errors
● LO3–2, LO3–3

The following balance sheet for the Hubbard Corporation was prepared by the company:

HUBBARD CORPORATION
Balance Sheet
At December 31, 2016

Assets	
Buildings	$ 750,000
Land	250,000
Cash	60,000
Accounts receivable (net)	120,000
Inventories	240,000
Machinery	280,000
Patent (net)	100,000
Investment in marketable equity securities	60,000
Total assets	$1,860,000
Liabilities and Shareholders' Equity	
Accounts payable	$ 215,000
Accumulated depreciation	255,000
Notes payable	500,000
Appreciation of inventories	80,000
Common stock, authorized and issued 100,000 shares of no par stock	430,000
Retained earnings	380,000
Total liabilities and shareholders' equity	$1,860,000

Additional Information:
1. The buildings, land, and machinery are all stated at cost except for a parcel of land that the company is holding for future sale. The land originally cost $50,000 but, due to a significant increase in market value, is listed at $120,000. The increase in the land account was credited to retained earnings.
2. Marketable equity securities consist of stocks of other corporations and are recorded at cost, $20,000 of which will be sold in the coming year. The remainder will be held indefinitely.
3. Notes payable are all long-term. However, a $100,000 note requires an installment payment of $25,000 due in the coming year.
4. Inventories are recorded at current resale value. The original cost of the inventories is $160,000.

Required:
Prepare a corrected classified balance sheet for the Hubbard Corporation at December 31, 2016.

P 3–8
Balance sheet; errors; missing amounts
● LO3–2, LO3–3

The following incomplete balance sheet for the Sanderson Manufacturing Company was prepared by the company's controller. As accounting manager for Sanderson, you are attempting to reconstruct and revise the balance sheet.

Sanderson Manufacturing Company
Balance Sheet
At December 31, 2016
($ in 000s)

Assets		
Current assets:		
Cash		$ 1,250
Accounts receivable		3,500
Allowance for uncollectible accounts		(400)
Finished goods inventory		6,000
Prepaid expenses		1,200
Total current assets		11,550
Noncurrent assets:		
Investments		3,000
Raw materials and work in process inventory		2,250
Equipment		15,000
Accumulated depreciation—equipment		(4,200)
Patent		?
Total assets		$?
Liabilities and Shareholders' Equity		
Current liabilities:		
Accounts payable		$ 5,200
Note payable		4,000
Interest payable—note		100
Deferred revenue		3,000
Total current liabilities		12,300
Long-term liabilities:		
Bonds payable		5,500
Interest payable—bonds		200
Shareholders' equity:		
Common stock	$?	
Retained earnings	?	?
Total liabilities and shareholders' equity		?

Additional Information ($ in 000s):

1. Certain records that included the account balances for the patent and shareholders' equity items were lost. However, the controller told you that a complete, preliminary balance sheet prepared before the records were lost showed a debt to equity ratio of 1.2. That is, total liabilities are 120% of total shareholders' equity. Retained earnings at the beginning of the year was $4,000. Net income for 2016 was $1,560 and $560 in cash dividends were declared and paid to shareholders.
2. Management intends to sell the investments in the next six months.
3. Interest on both the note and the bonds is payable annually.
4. The note payable is due in annual installments of $1,000 each.
5. Deferred revenue will be recognized as revenue equally over the next two fiscal years.
6. The common stock represents 400,000 shares of no par stock authorized, 250,000 shares issued and outstanding.

Required:

Prepare a complete, corrected, classified balance sheet.

P 3–9
Balance sheet preparation
● LO3–2, LO3–3

Presented below is the balance sheet for HHD, Inc., at December 31, 2016.

Current assets	$ 600,000	Current liabilities	$ 400,000
Investments	500,000	Long-term liabilities	1,100,000
Property, plant, and equipment	2,000,000	Shareholders' equity	1,800,000
Intangible assets	200,000		
Total assets	$3,300,000	Total liabilities and shareholders' equity	$3,300,000

The captions shown in the summarized statement above include the following:

a. Current assets: cash, $150,000; accounts receivable, $200,000; inventories, $225,000; and prepaid insurance, $25,000.

b. Investments: investments in common stock, short term, $90,000, and long term, $160,000; and restricted cash, long term, $250,000.

c. Property, plant, and equipment: buildings, $1,500,000 less accumulated depreciation, $600,000; equipment, $500,000 less accumulated depreciation, $200,000; and land, $800,000.
d. Intangible assets: patent, $110,000; and copyright, $90,000.
e. Current liabilities: accounts payable, $100,000; notes payable, short term, $150,000, and long term, $90,000; and taxes payable, $60,000.
f. Long-term liabilities: bonds payable due 2021.
g. Shareholders' equity: common stock, $1,000,000; retained earnings, $800,000. Five hundred thousand shares of no par common stock are authorized, of which 200,000 shares were issued and are outstanding.

Required:
Prepare a corrected classified balance sheet for HHD, Inc., at December 31, 2016.

P 3–10
Balance sheet preparation
● LO3–2, LO3–3

Melody Lane Music Company was started by John Ross early in 2016. Initial capital was acquired by issuing shares of common stock to various investors and by obtaining a bank loan. The company operates a retail store that sells records, tapes, and compact discs. Business was so good during the first year of operations that John is considering opening a second store on the other side of town. The funds necessary for expansion will come from a new bank loan. In order to approve the loan, the bank requires financial statements.

John asks for your help in preparing the balance sheet and presents you with the following information for the year ending December 31, 2016:

a. Cash receipts consisted of the following:

From customers	$360,000
From issue of common stock	100,000
From bank loan	100,000

b. Cash disbursements were as follows:

Purchase of inventory	$300,000
Rent	15,000
Salaries	30,000
Utilities	5,000
Insurance	3,000
Purchase of equipment and furniture	40,000

c. The bank loan was made on March 31, 2016. A note was signed requiring payment of interest and principal on March 31, 2017. The interest rate is 12%.
d. The equipment and furniture were purchased on January 3, 2016, and have an estimated useful life of 10 years with no anticipated salvage value. Depreciation per year is $4,000.
e. Inventories on hand at the end of the year cost $100,000.
f. Amounts owed at December 31, 2016, were as follows:

To suppliers of inventory	$20,000
To the utility company	1,000

g. Rent on the store building is $1,000 per month. On December 1, 2016, four months' rent was paid in advance.
h. Net income for the year was $76,000. Assume that the company is not subject to federal, state, or local income tax.
i. One hundred thousand shares of no par common stock are authorized, of which 20,000 shares were issued and are outstanding.

Required:
Prepare a balance sheet at December 31, 2016.

Broaden Your Perspective

Apply your critical-thinking ability to the knowledge you've gained. These cases will provide you an opportunity to develop your research, analysis, judgment, and communication skills. You also will work with other students, integrate what you've learned, apply it in real-world situations, and consider its global and ethical ramifications. This practice will broaden your knowledge and further develop your decision-making abilities.

Communication Case 3–1
Current versus noncurrent classification
● LO3–2

A first-year accounting student is confused by a statement made in a recent class. Her instructor stated that the assets listed in the balance sheet of the IBM Corporation include computers that are classified as current assets as well as computers that are classified as noncurrent assets. In addition, the instructor stated that investments in marketable securities of other corporations could be classified in the balance sheet as either current or noncurrent assets.

Required:

Explain to the student the distinction between current and noncurrent assets pertaining to the IBM computers and the investments in marketable securities.

Analysis Case 3–2
Current versus noncurrent classification
● LO3–2, LO3–3

The usefulness of the balance sheet is enhanced when assets and liabilities are grouped according to common characteristics. The broad distinction made in the balance sheet is the current versus noncurrent classification of both assets and liabilities.

Required:

1. Discuss the factors that determine whether an asset or liability should be classified as current or noncurrent in a balance sheet.
2. Identify six items that under different circumstances could be classified as either current or noncurrent. Indicate the factors that would determine the correct classification.

Communication Case 3–3
FASB codification research; inventory or property, plant, and equipment
● LO3–2

The Red Hen Company produces, processes, and sells fresh eggs. The company is in the process of preparing financial statements at the end of its first year of operations and has asked for your help in determining the appropriate treatment of the cost of its egg-laying flock. The estimated life of a laying hen is approximately two years, after which they are sold to soup companies.

The controller considers the company's operating cycle to be two years and wants to present the cost of the egg-producing flock as inventory in the current asset section of the balance sheet. He feels that the hens are "goods awaiting sale." The chief financial officer does not agree with this treatment. He thinks that the cost of the flock should be classified as property, plant, and equipment because the hens are used in the production of product—the eggs.

The focus of this case is the balance sheet presentation of the cost of the egg-producing flock. Your instructor will divide the class into two to six groups depending on the size of the class. The mission of your group is to reach consensus on the appropriate presentation.

Required:

1. Each group member should deliberate the situation independently and draft a tentative argument prior to the class session for which the case is assigned.
2. In class, each group will meet for 10 to 15 minutes in different areas of the classroom. During that meeting, group members will take turns sharing their suggestions for the purpose of arriving at a single group treatment.
3. After the allotted time, a spokesperson for each group (selected during the group meetings) will share the group's solution with the class. The goal of the class is to incorporate the views of each group into a consensus approach to the situation.

IFRS Case 3–4
Balance sheet presentation; Vodafone Group, Plc.
● LO3–2, LO3–3, LO3–9

Real World Financials

Vodafone Group, Plc., a U.K. company, is the largest mobile telecommunications network company in the world. The company prepares its financial statements in accordance with International Financial Reporting Standards. Below are partial company balance sheets (statements of financial position) included in a recent annual report:

Vodafone Group, Plc.
Consolidated Statements of Financial Position
At March 31

	2013	2012
	£m	£m
Noncurrent assets		
Goodwill	30,372	38,350
Other intangible assets	22,025	21,164
Property, plant and equipment	20,331	18,655
Investments in associates	38,635	35,108
Other investments	774	791
Deferred tax assets	2,920	1,970
Post employment benefits	52	31
Trade and other receivables	4,302	3,482
	119,411	119,551

(continued)

(concluded)	2013	2012
	£m	£m
Current assets		
Inventory	450	486
Taxation recoverable	452	334
Trade and other receivables	9,412	10,744
Other investments	5,350	1,323
Cash and cash equivalents	7,623	7,138
	23,287	**20,025**
Total assets	142,698	139,576
Equity (details provided in complete statements)	72,488	78,202
Noncurrent liabilities		
Long-term borrowings	29,108	28,362
Taxation liabilities	150	250
Deferred tax liabilities	6,698	6,597
Post employment benefits	629	337
Provisions	907	479
Trade and other payables	1,494	1,324
	38,986	**37,349**
Current liabilities		
Short-term borrowings	12,289	6,258
Taxation liabilities	1,919	1,898
Provisions	818	633
Trade and other payables	16,198	15,236
	31,224	**24,025**
Total equity and liabilities	142,698	139,576

Required:

1. Describe the differences between Vodafone's balance sheets and a typical U.S. company balance sheet.
2. What type of liabilities do you think are included in the *provisions* category in Vodafone's balance sheets?

Judgment Case 3–5
Balance sheet; errors
● LO3–2 through LO3–4

You recently joined the internal auditing department of Marcus Clothing Corporation. As one of your first assignments, you are examining a balance sheet prepared by a staff accountant.

MARCUS CLOTHING CORPORATION
Balance Sheet
At December 31, 2016

Assets

Current assets:		
Cash		$ 137,000
Accounts receivable, net		80,000
Note receivable		53,000
Inventories		240,000
Investments		66,000
Total current assets		576,000
Other assets:		
Land	$200,000	
Equipment, net	320,000	
Prepaid expenses	27,000	
Patent	22,000	
Total other assets		569,000
Total assets		$1,145,000

Liabilities and Shareholders' Equity

Current liabilities:	
Accounts payable	$ 125,000
Salaries payable	32,000
Total current liabilities	157,000

(continued)

(concluded)			
	Long-term liabilities:		
	Note payable	$100,000	
	Bonds payable	300,000	
	Interest payable	20,000	
	Total long-term liabilities		420,000
	Shareholders' equity:		
	Common stock	500,000	
	Retained earnings	68,000	
	Total shareholders' equity		568,000
	Total liabilities and shareholders' equity		$1,145,000

In the course of your examination you uncover the following information pertaining to the balance sheet:

1. The company rents its facilities. The land that appears in the statement is being held for future sale.
2. The note receivable is due in 2018. The balance of $53,000 includes $3,000 of accrued interest. The next interest payment is due in July 2017.
3. The note payable is due in installments of $20,000 per year. Interest on both the notes and bonds is payable annually.
4. The company's investments consist of marketable equity securities of other corporations. Management does not intend to liquidate any investments in the coming year.

Required:

Identify and explain the deficiencies in the statement prepared by the company's accountant. Include in your answer items that require additional disclosure, either on the face of the statement or in a note.

Judgment Case 3–6
Financial disclosures
● LO3–4

You recently joined the auditing staff of Best, Best, and Krug, CPAs. You have been assigned to the audit of Clearview, Inc., and have been asked by the audit senior to examine the balance sheet prepared by Clearview's accountant.

CLEARVIEW, INC.
Balance Sheet
At December 31, 2016
($ in millions)

Assets		
Current assets:		
Cash		$ 10.5
Accounts receivable		112.1
Inventories		220.6
Prepaid expenses		5.5
Total current assets		348.7
Investments		22.0
Property, plant, and equipment, net		486.9
Total assets		$857.6
Liabilities and Shareholders' Equity		
Current liabilities:		
Accounts payable		$ 83.5
Accrued taxes and interest		25.5
Current maturities of long-term debt		20.0
Total current liabilities		129.0
Long-term liabilities:		420.0
Total liabilities		549.0
Shareholders' equity:		
Common stock	$100.0	
Retained earnings	208.6	
Total shareholders' equity		308.6
Total liabilities and shareholders' equity		$857.6

Required:

Identify the items in the statement that most likely would require further disclosure either on the face of the statement or in a note. Further identify those items that would require disclosure in the significant accounting policies note.

Real World Case 3–7
Balance sheet and significant accounting policies disclosure; Walmart

● LO3–2 through LO3–4, LO3–8

Real World Financials

The balance sheet and disclosure of significant accounting policies taken from the 2014 annual report of **Wal-Mart Stores, Inc.**, appear below. Use this information to answer the following questions:

1. What are the asset classifications contained in Walmart's balance sheet?
2. What amounts did Walmart report for the following items for 2014:
   a. Total assets
   b. Current assets
   c. Current liabilities
   d. Total equity
   e. Retained earnings
   f. Inventories
3. What is Walmart's largest current asset? What is its largest current liability?
4. Compute Walmart's current ratio for 2014.
5. Identify the following items:
   a. The company's inventory valuation method.
   b. The definition of cash equivalents.

WAL-MART STORES, INC.
Consolidated Balance Sheets
(Amounts in millions except per share data)

	As of January 31,	
(Amounts in millions)	**2014**	**2013**
Assets		
Current assets:		
Cash and cash equivalents	$ 7,281	$ 7,781
Receivables, net	6,677	6,768
Inventories	44,858	43,803
Prepaid expenses and other	1,909	1,551
Current assets of discontinued operations	460	37
Total current assets	61,185	59,940
Property and equipment:		
Property and equipment	173,089	165,825
Less accumulated depreciation	(57,725)	(51,896)
Property and equipment, net	115,364	113,929
Property under capital leases:		
Property under capital leases	5,589	5,899
Less accumulated amortization	(3,046)	(3,147)
Property under capital leases, net	2,543	2,752
Goodwill	19,510	20,497
Other assets and deferred charges	6,149	5,987
Total assets	$204,751	$203,105
Liabilities, Redeemable Noncontrolling Interest and Equity		
Current liabilities:		
Short-term borrowings	$ 7,670	$ 6,805
Accounts payable	37,415	38,080
Accrued liabilities	18,793	18,808
Accrued income taxes	966	2,211
Long-term debt due within one year	4,103	5,587
Obligations under capital leases due within one year	309	327
Current liabilities of discontinued operations	89	—
Total current liabilities	69,345	71,818
Long-term debt	41,771	38,394
Long-term obligations under capital leases	2,788	3,023
Deferred income taxes and other	8,017	7,613
Redeemable noncontrolling interest	1,491	519

(continued)

(concluded)

Commitments and contingencies		
Equity:		
Common stock	323	332
Capital in excess of par value	2,362	3,620
Retained earnings	75,566	72,978
Accumulated other comprehensive income (loss)	(2,996)	(587)
Total Walmart shareholders' equity	75,255	76,343
Nonredeemable noncontrolling interest	5,084	5,395
Total equity	81,339	81,738
Total liabilities, redeemable noncontrolling interest and equity	$204,751	$203,105

NOTES TO CONSOLIDATED FINANCIAL STATEMENTS
WAL-MART STORES, INC.

1 Summary of Significant Accounting Policies (in part)

Cash and Cash Equivalents

The Company considers investments with a maturity of three months or less when purchased to be cash equivalents.

Inventories

The Company values inventories at the lower of cost or market as determined primarily by the retail method of accounting, using the last-in, first-out ("LIFO") method for substantially all of the Walmart U.S. segment's merchandise inventories. Inventories for the Walmart International operations are primarily valued by the retail method of accounting, using the first-in, first-out ("FIFO") method. At January 31, 2014 and 2013, our inventories valued at LIFO approximate those inventories as if they were valued at FIFO.

Revenue Recognition

The Company recognizes sales revenue net of sales taxes and estimated sales returns at the time it sells merchandise to the customer. Customer purchases of shopping cards are not recognized as revenue until the card is redeemed and the customer purchases merchandise by using the shopping card. The Company also recognizes revenue from service transactions at the time the service is performed. Generally, revenue from services is classified as a component of net sales on our consolidated statements of income.

Judgment Case 3–8
Post fiscal year-end events
● LO3–4

The fiscal year-end for the Northwest Distribution Corporation is December 31. The company's 2016 financial statements were issued on March 15, 2017. The following events occurred between December 31, 2016, and March 15, 2017.

1. On January 22, 2017, the company negotiated a major merger with Blandon Industries. The merger will be completed by the middle of 2017.
2. On February 3, 2017, Northwest negotiated a $10 million long-term note with the Credit Bank of Ohio. The amount of the note is material.
3. On February 25, 2017, a flood destroyed one of the company's manufacturing plants causing $600,000 of uninsured damage.

Required:

Determine the appropriate treatment of each of these events in the 2016 financial statements of Northwest Distribution Corporation.

Research Case 3–9
FASB codification; locate and extract relevant information and cite authoritative support for a financial reporting issue; related-party disclosures; Enron Corporation
● LO3–4

Enron Corporation was a darling in the energy-provider arena, and in January 2001 its stock price rose above $100 per share. A collapse of investor confidence in 2001 and revelations of accounting fraud led to one of the largest bankruptcies in U.S. history. By the end of the year, Enron's stock price had plummeted to less than $1 per share. Investigations and lawsuits followed. One problem area concerned transactions with related parties that were not adequately disclosed in the company's financial statements. Critics stated that the lack of information about these transactions made it difficult for analysts following Enron to identify problems the company was experiencing.

Required:

1. Obtain the relevant authoritative literature on related-party transactions using the *FASB Accounting Standards Codification* at the FASB website (**asc.fasb.org**). What is the specific citation that outlines the required information on related-party disclosures that must be included in the notes to the financial statements?
2. Describe the disclosures required for related-party transactions.

Real World Financials

3. Use EDGAR (www.sec.gov) or another method to locate the December 31, 2000, financial statements of Enron. Search for the related-party disclosure. Briefly describe the relationship central to the various transactions described.
4. Why is it important that companies disclose related-party transactions? Use the Enron disclosure of the sale of dark fiber inventory in your answer.

Real World Case 3–10
Disclosures; proxy statement; Coca-Cola
● LO3–4, LO3–6
Real World Financials

EDGAR, the Electronic Data Gathering, Analysis, and Retrieval system, performs automated collection, validation, indexing, and forwarding of submissions by companies and others who are required by law to file forms with the SEC. All publicly traded domestic companies use EDGAR to make the majority of their filings. (Some foreign companies file voluntarily.) Form 10-K, which includes the annual report, is required to be filed on EDGAR. The SEC makes this information available on the Internet.

Required:

1. Access EDGAR on the Internet. The web address is www.sec.gov.
2. Search for The Coca-Cola Company. Access the 10-K for the year ended December 31, 2013. Search or scroll to find the disclosure notes and audit report.
3. Answer the following questions:
   a. Describe the subsequent events disclosed by the company.
   b. Which firm is the company's auditor? What type of audit opinion did the auditor render?
4. Access the proxy statement filed with the SEC on March 7, 2014 (the proxy statement designation is Def 14A), locate the executive officers summary compensation table and answer the following questions:
   a. What is the principal position of Muhtar Kent?
   b. What was the salary paid to Mr. Kent during the year ended December 31, 2013?

Judgment Case 3–11
Debt versus equity
● LO3–7

A common problem facing any business entity is the debt versus equity decision. When funds are required to obtain assets, should debt or equity financing be used? This decision also is faced when a company is initially formed. What will be the mix of debt versus equity in the initial capital structure? The characteristics of debt are very different from those of equity as are the financial implications of using one method of financing as opposed to the other.

Cherokee Plastics Corporation is formed by a group of investors to manufacture household plastic products. Their initial capitalization goal is $50,000,000. That is, the incorporators have decided to raise $50,000,000 to acquire the initial assets of the company. They have narrowed down the financing mix alternatives to two:

1. All equity financing.
2. $20,000,000 in debt financing and $30,000,000 in equity financing.

No matter which financing alternative is chosen, the corporation expects to be able to generate a 10% annual return, before payment of interest and income taxes, on the $50,000,000 in assets acquired. The interest rate on debt would be 8%. The effective income tax rate will be approximately 50%.

Alternative 2 will require specified interest and principal payments to be made to the creditors at specific dates. The interest portion of these payments (interest expense) will reduce the taxable income of the corporation and hence the amount of income tax the corporation will pay. The all-equity alternative requires no specified payments to be made to suppliers of capital. The corporation is not legally liable to make distributions to its owners. If the board of directors does decide to make a distribution, it is not an expense of the corporation and does not reduce taxable income and hence the taxes the corporation pays.

Required:

1. Prepare abbreviated income statements that compare first-year profitability for each of the two alternatives.
2. Which alternative would be expected to achieve the highest first-year profits? Why?
3. Which alternative would provide the highest rate of return on shareholders' equity? Why?
4. What other related implications of the decision should be considered?

Analysis Case 3–12
Obtain and critically evaluate an actual annual report
● LO3–4, LO3–6 through LO3–8
Real World Financials

Financial reports are the primary means by which corporations report their performance and financial condition. Financial statements are one component of the annual report mailed to their shareholders and to interested others.

Required:

Obtain an annual report from a corporation with which you are familiar. Using techniques you learned in this chapter and any analysis you consider useful, respond to the following questions:

1. Do the firm's auditors provide a clean opinion on the financial statements?
2. Has the company made changes in any accounting methods it uses?
3. Have there been any subsequent events, errors and fraud, illegal acts, or related-party transactions that have a material effect on the company's financial position?

4. What are two trends in the company's operations or capital resources that management considers significant to the company's future?
5. Is the company engaged in more than one significant line of business? If so, compare the relative profitability of the different segments.
6. How stable are the company's operations?
7. Has the company's situation deteriorated or improved with respect to liquidity, solvency, asset management, and profitability?

Note: You can obtain a copy of an annual report from a local company, from a friend who is a shareholder, from the investor relations department of the corporation, from a friendly stockbroker, or from EDGAR (Electronic Data Gathering, Analysis, and Retrieval) on the Internet (www.sec.gov).

Analysis Case 3–13
Obtain and compare annual reports from companies in the same industry
● LO3–4, LO3–7, LO3–8
Real World Financials

Insight concerning the performance and financial condition of a company often comes from evaluating its financial data in comparison with other firms in the same industry.

Required:
Obtain annual reports from three corporations in the same primary industry. Using techniques you learned in this chapter and any analysis you consider useful, respond to the following questions:

1. Are there differences in accounting methods that should be taken into account when making comparisons?
2. How do earnings trends compare in terms of both the direction and stability of income?
3. Which of the three firms had the greatest earnings relative to resources available?
4. Which corporation has made most effective use of financial leverage?
5. Of the three firms, which seems riskiest in terms of its ability to pay short-term obligations? Long-term obligations?

Note: You can obtain copies of annual reports from friends who are shareholders, from the investor relations department of the corporations, from a friendly stockbroker, or from EDGAR (Electronic Data Gathering, Analysis, and Retrieval) on the Internet (www.sec.gov).

Analysis Case 3–14
Balance sheet information
● LO3–2 through LO3–4

PetSmart

Refer to the financial statements and related disclosure notes of PetSmart in Appendix B located at the back of the text.

Required:

1. What categories does the company use to classify its assets? Its liabilities?
2. Why are investments shown as a current asset?
3. Explain the current liability "Accrued payroll, bonus, and employee benefits."
4. What purpose do the disclosure notes serve?
5. What method does the company use to depreciate its property and equipment?
6. Does the company report any subsequent events or related party transactions in its disclosure notes?

Analysis Case 3–15
Segment reporting concepts
● Appendix 3, LO3–9

IFRS

Levens Co. operates in several distinct business segments. The company does not have any reportable foreign operations or major customers.

Required:

1. What is the purpose of operating segment disclosures?
2. Define an operating segment.
3. List the amounts to be reported by operating segment.
4. How would your answer to requirement 3 differ if Levens Co. prepares its segment disclosure according to International Financial Reporting Standards?

Ethics Case 3–16
Segment reporting
● Appendix 3

You are in your third year as an accountant with McCarver-Lynn Industries, a multidivisional company involved in the manufacturing, marketing, and sales of surgical prosthetic devices. After the fiscal year-end, you are working with the controller of the firm to prepare geographic area disclosures. Yesterday you presented her with the following summary information:

	($ in millions)					
	Domestic	Libya	Egypt	France	Cayman Islands	Total
Revenues	$ 845	$222	$265	$343	$2,311	$3,986
Operating income	145	76	88	21	642	972
Assets	1,005	301	290	38	285	1,919

Upon returning to your office after lunch, you find the following memo:

Nice work. Let's combine the data this way:

	($ in millions)			
	Domestic	**Africa**	**Europe and Other Foreign**	**Total**
Revenues	$ 845	$487	$2,654	$3,986
Capital expenditures	145	164	663	972
Assets	1,005	591	323	1,919

Because of political instability in North Africa, let's not disclose specific countries. In addition, we restructured most of our French sales and some of our U.S. sales to occur through our offices in the Cayman Islands. This allows us to avoid paying higher taxes in those countries. The Cayman Islands has a 0% corporate income tax rate. We don't want to highlight our ability to shift profits to avoid taxes.

Required:

Do you perceive an ethical dilemma? What would be the likely impact of following the controller's suggestions? Who would benefit? Who would be injured?

Air France–KLM Case

AIRFRANCE / KLM

● LO3–9

IFRS

Air France-KLM (AF), a Franco-Dutch company, prepares its financial statements according to International Financial Reporting Standards. AF's financial statements and disclosure notes for the year ended December 31, 2013, are provided with all new textbooks. This material also is available at **www.airfranceklm-finance.com**.

Required:

Describe the apparent differences in the order of presentation of the components of the balance sheet between IFRS as applied by Air France–KLM (AF) and a typical balance sheet prepared in accordance with U.S. GAAP.

CHAPTER

4 The Income Statement, Comprehensive Income, and the Statement of Cash Flows

OVERVIEW

The purpose of the income statement is to summarize the profit-generating activities that occurred during a particular reporting period. Comprehensive income includes net income as well as a few gains and losses that are not part of net income and are considered other comprehensive income items instead.

The purpose of the statement of cash flows is to provide information about the cash receipts and cash disbursements of an enterprise that occurred during the period.

This chapter has a twofold purpose: (1) to consider important issues dealing with the content, presentation, and disclosure of net income and other components of comprehensive income and (2) to provide an *overview* of the statement of cash flows, which is covered in depth in Chapter 21.

LEARNING OBJECTIVES

After studying this chapter, you should be able to:

- **LO4–1** Discuss the importance of income from continuing operations and describe its components. (*p. 172*)
- **LO4–2** Describe earnings quality and how it is impacted by management practices to manipulate earnings. (*p. 177*)
- **LO4–3** Discuss the components of operating and nonoperating income and their relationship to earnings quality. (*p. 178*)
- **LO4–4** Define what constitutes discontinued operations and describe the appropriate income statement presentation for these transactions. (*p. 182*)
- **LO4–5** Define earnings per share (EPS) and explain required disclosures of EPS for certain income statement components. (*p. 188*)
- **LO4–6** Explain the difference between net income and comprehensive income and how we report components of the difference. (*p. 189*)
- **LO4–7** Describe the purpose of the statement of cash flows. (*p. 194*)
- **LO4–8** Identify and describe the various classifications of cash flows presented in a statement of cash flows. (*p. 194*)
- **LO4–9** Discuss the primary differences between U.S. GAAP and IFRS with respect to the income statement, statement of comprehensive income, and statement of cash flows. (*pp. 177, 190, 195,* and *204*)

FINANCIAL REPORTING CASE

Pfizer Inc.

Your friend, Becky Morgan, just received a generous gift from her grandfather. Accompanying a warm letter were 200 shares of stock of Pfizer Inc., a global biopharmaceutical company, along with the most recent annual financial statements of the company. Becky knows that you are an accounting major and pleads with you to explain some items in the company's income statement. "I remember studying the income statement in my introductory accounting course," says Becky, "but I am still confused. What is this item *discontinued operations?* How about *restructuring costs?* These don't sound good. Are they something I should worry about? We studied earnings per share briefly, but what does *earnings per common share—diluted* mean?" You agree to try to help.

PFIZER INC. AND SUBSIDIARY COMPANIES
Statements of Income
For the Year Ended December 31
($ in millions, except per share data)

	2013	2012
Revenues	$51,584	$54,657
Costs and expenses:		
Cost of sales	9,586	9,821
Selling, informational, and administrative expenses	14,355	15,171
Research and development expenses	6,678	7,482
Amortization of intangible assets	4,599	5,109
Restructuring costs	1,182	1,810
Other (income) deductions	(532)	4,022
Income from continuing operations before income taxes	15,716	11,242
Provision for taxes on income	4,306	2,221
Income from continuing operations	11,410	9,021
Income from discontinued operations, net of tax	10,662	5,577
Net income before allocation to noncontrolling interests	22,072	14,598
Less: Net income attributable to noncontrolling interests	69	28
Net income	$22,003	$14,570
Earnings per common share—basic:		
Continuing operations	$ 1.67	$ 1.21
Discontinued operations	1.56	0.75
Net income	$ 3.23	$ 1.96
Earnings per common share—diluted:		
Continuing operations	$ 1.65	$ 1.20
Discontinued operations	1.54	0.74
Net income	$ 3.19	$ 1.94

QUESTIONS

By the time you finish this chapter, you should be able to respond appropriately to the questions posed in this case. Compare your response to the solution provided at the end of the chapter.

1. How would you explain restructuring costs to Becky? Are restructuring costs something Becky should worry about? (*p. 179*)

(continued)

2. Explain to Becky what is meant by discontinued operations and describe to her how that item is reported in an income statement. (*p. 182*)
3. Describe to Becky the difference between basic and diluted earnings per share. (*p. 188*)

In Chapter 1 we discussed the critical role of financial accounting information in allocating resources within our economy. Ideally, resources should be allocated to private enterprises that will (1) provide the goods and services our society desires and (2) at the same time provide a fair rate of return to those who supply the resources. A company will be able to achieve these goals only if it can use the resources society provides to generate revenues from selling products and services that exceed the expenses necessary to provide those products and services (that is, generate a profit).

The income statement displays a company's operating performance, that is, its net profit or loss, during the reporting period.

The purpose of the **income statement**, sometimes called the **statement of operations** or **statement of earnings**, is to summarize the profit-generating activities that occurred during a particular reporting period. Many investors and creditors perceive it as the statement most useful for predicting future profitability (future cash-generating ability).

A few types of gains and losses are excluded from the determination of net income and the income statement but are included in the broader concept of **comprehensive income**. We refer to these as items of **other comprehensive income (OCI) or loss**. Comprehensive income can be reported in one of two ways: (1) in a single, continuous **statement of comprehensive income** or (2) in two separate but consecutive statements—an income statement and a statement of comprehensive income that begins with net income and then reports OCI items to combine for comprehensive income.

The purpose of the **statement of cash flows** is to provide information about the cash receipts and cash disbursements of an enterprise that occurred during a period. In describing cash flows, the statement provides valuable information about the operating, investing, and financing activities that occurred during the period.

The *income statement* and *statement of cash flows* report changes that occurred during a particular reporting period.

Unlike the balance sheet, which is a position statement, the income statement and the statement of cash flows are *change* statements. The income statement reports the changes in shareholders' equity (retained earnings) that occurred during the reporting period as a result of revenues, expenses, gains, and losses. The statement of cash flows also is a change statement, disclosing the events that caused cash to change during the period.

This chapter is divided into two parts. The first part describes the content and presentation of the income statement and comprehensive income as well as related disclosure issues. The second part provides an overview of the statement of cash flows.

PART A The Income Statement and Comprehensive Income

Before we discuss the specific components of an income statement in much depth, let's take a quick look at the general makeup of the statement. Illustration 4–1 offers a statement for a hypothetical manufacturing company that you can refer to as we proceed through the chapter. At this point, our objective is only to gain a general perspective on the items reported and classifications contained in corporate income statements.

Let's first look closer at the components of net income. At the end of this part, we'll see how net income fits within the concept of comprehensive income and how comprehensive income is reported.

● LO4–1

Income from Continuing Operations

Income from continuing operations includes the revenues, expenses, gains and losses that will probably continue in future periods.

The need to provide information to help analysts predict future cash flows emphasizes the importance of properly reporting the amount of income from the entity's continuing operations. Clearly, it is the operating transactions that probably will continue into the future that are the best predictors of future cash flows. The components of **income from continuing**

Illustration 4–1
Income Statement

Income Statements
(In millions, except per share data)

		Year Ended June 30	
		2016	**2015**
Income from Continuing Operations	Sales revenue	$1,450.6	$1,380.0
	Cost of goods sold	832.6	800.4
	Gross profit	618.0	579.6
	Operating expenses:		
	Selling	123.5	110.5
	General and administrative	147.8	139.1
	Research and development	55.0	65.0
	Restructuring costs	125.0	—
	Total operating expenses	451.3	314.6
	Operating income	166.7	265.0
	Other income (expense):		
	Interest income	12.4	11.1
	Interest expense	(25.9)	(24.8)
	Gain on sale of investments	18.0	19.0
	Income from continuing operations before income taxes	171.2	270.3
	Income tax expense	59.9	94.6
	Income from continuing operations	111.3	175.7
Discontinued Operations	Discontinued operations:		
	Loss from operations of discontinued component (including gain on disposal in 2016 of $47)	(7.6)	(45.7)
	Income tax benefit	2.0	13.0
	Loss on discontinued operations	(5.6)	(32.7)
	Net income	$ 105.7	$ 143.0
Earnings per Share	**Earnings per common share—basic:**		
	Income from continuing operations	$ 2.14	$ 3.38
	Discontinued operations	(0.11)	(0.63)
	Net income	$ 2.03	$ 2.75
	Earnings per common share—diluted:		
	Income from continuing operations	$ 2.06	$ 3.25
	Discontinued operations	(0.10)	(0.61)
	Net income	$ 1.96	$ 2.64

operations are revenues, expenses (including income taxes), gains, and losses, excluding those related to discontinued operations.[1]

Revenues, Expenses, Gains, and Losses

Revenues are inflows of resources resulting from providing goods or services to customers. For merchandising companies like **Walmart**, the main source of revenue is sales revenue derived from selling merchandise. Service firms such as **FedEx** and **State Farm Insurance** generate revenue by providing services.

Expenses are outflows of resources incurred while generating revenue. They represent the costs of providing goods and services. When recognizing expenses, we attempt to

[1]Discontinued operations are addressed in a subsequent section.

establish a causal relationship between revenues and expenses. If causality can be determined, expenses are reported in the same period that the related revenue is recognized. If a causal relationship cannot be established, we relate the expense to a particular period, allocate it over several periods, or expense it as incurred.

Gains and losses are increases or decreases in equity from peripheral or incidental transactions of an entity. In general, these gains and losses result from changes in equity that do not result directly from operations but nonetheless are related to those activities. For example, gains and losses from the routine sale of equipment, buildings, or other operating assets and from the sale of investment assets normally would be included in income from continuing operations. Later in the chapter we discuss certain gains and losses that are excluded from continuing operations.

Income Tax Expense

Income tax expense **is reported in a separate line in the income statement.**

Income taxes represent a major expense to a corporation, and accordingly, income tax expense is given special treatment in the income statement. Income taxes are levied on taxpayers in proportion to the amount of taxable income that is reported to taxing authorities. Like individuals, corporations are income-tax-paying entities.[2] Because of the importance and size of income tax expense (sometimes called *provision for income taxes*), it always is reported in a separate line in corporate income statements.

Federal, state, and sometimes local taxes are assessed annually and usually are determined by first applying a designated percentage (or percentages), the tax rate (or rates), to taxable income. Taxable income comprises revenues, expenses, gains, and losses as measured according to the regulations of the appropriate taxing authority.

While the actual measurement of income tax expense can be complex, at this point we can consider income tax expense to be a simple percentage of income before taxes.

Many of the components of taxable income and income reported in the income statement coincide. But sometimes tax rules and GAAP differ with respect to when and even whether a particular revenue or expense is included in income. When tax rules and GAAP differ regarding the timing of revenue or expense recognition, the actual payment of taxes may occur in a period different from when income tax expense is reported in the income statement. A common example is when a corporation takes advantage of tax laws by legally deducting more depreciation in the early years of an asset's life on its federal income tax return than it reports in its income statement. The amount of tax actually paid in the early years is less than the amount that is found by applying the tax rate to the reported GAAP income before taxes. We discuss this and other issues related to accounting for income taxes in Chapter 16. At this point, consider income tax expense to be simply a percentage of income before taxes.

Operating versus Nonoperating Income

A distinction often is made between *operating* and *nonoperating* income.

Many corporate income statements distinguish between operating income and nonoperating income. Operating income includes revenues and expenses directly related to the primary revenue-generating activities of the company. For example, operating income for a manufacturing company includes sales revenues from selling the products it manufactures as well as all expenses related to this activity. Similarly, operating income might also include gains and losses from selling equipment and other assets used in the manufacturing process.[3]

Nonoperating income relates to peripheral or incidental activities of the company. For example, a manufacturer would include interest and dividend revenue, gains and losses from selling investments, and interest expense in nonoperating income. *Other income (expense)* often is the classification heading companies use in the income statement for nonoperating items. On the other hand, a financial institution like a bank would consider those items to be

[2]Partnerships are not tax-paying entities. Their taxable income or loss is included in the taxable income of the individual partners.

[3]FASB ASC 360–10–45–5: Property, plant, and equipment—Overall—Other Presentation Matters (previously "Accounting for the Impairment of Long-Lived Assets and for Long-Lived Assets to Be Disposed Of," *Statement of Financial Accounting Standards No. 144* (Norwalk, Conn.: FASB, 2001)).

a part of operating income because they relate to the principal revenue-generating activities for that type of business.

Illustration 4–2 presents the 2014, 2013, and 2012 income statements for **Urban Outfitters, Inc.**, a leading lifestyle specialty retail company. Notice that Urban Outfitters distinguishes between operating income and nonoperating income. Nonoperating revenues, expenses, gains and losses, and income tax expense are added to or subtracted from operating income to arrive at net income.

Illustration 4–2

Income Statement—Urban Outfitters, Inc.

Real World Financials

Consolidated Statements of Income

(In thousands, except per share data)	Fiscal Year Ended January 31		
	2014	**2013**	**2012**
Net sales	$3,086,608	$2,794,925	$2,473,801
Cost of sales	1,925,266	1,763,394	1,613,265
Gross profit	1,161,342	1,031,531	860,536
Selling, general, and administrative expenses	734,511	657,246	575,811
Operating income	426,831	374,285	284,725
Interest income	2,713	2,126	5,120
Other income	1,088	862	553
Other expenses	(3,114)	(1,701)	(1,567)
Income before income taxes	427,518	375,572	288,831
Income tax expense	145,158	138,258	103,580
Net income	$ 282,360	$ 237,314	$ 185,251
Earnings per common share:			
Basic	$ 1.92	$ 1.63	$ 1.20
Diluted	$ 1.89	$ 1.62	$ 1.19

Now let's consider the formats used to report the components of net income.

Income Statement Formats

No specific standards dictate how income from continuing operations must be displayed, so companies have considerable latitude in how they present the components of income from continuing operations. This flexibility has resulted in a variety of income statement presentations. However, we can identify two general approaches, the single-step and the multiple-step formats, that might be considered the two extremes, with the income statements of most companies falling somewhere in between.

The **single-step** format first lists all the revenues and gains included in income from continuing operations. Then, expenses and losses are grouped, subtotaled, and subtracted—in a single step—from revenues and gains to derive income from continuing operations. In a departure from that, though, companies usually report income tax expense in a separate line in the statement. Operating and nonoperating items are not separately classified. **The Pfizer Inc.** income statements shown in the financial reporting case at the beginning of this chapter are examples of the single-step format. Illustration 4–3 shows another example of a single-step income statement, this time for a hypothetical manufacturing company, Maxwell Gear Corporation.

A *single-step* income statement format groups all revenues and gains together and all expenses and losses together.

The **multiple-step** format reports a series of intermediate subtotals such as gross profit, operating income, and income before taxes. The overview income statements presented in Illustration 4–1 and the **Urban Outfitters, Inc.**, income statements in Illustration 4–2 are variations of the multiple-step format. Illustration 4–4 presents a multiple-step income statement for the Maxwell Gear Corporation.

A *multiple-step* income statement format includes a number of intermediate subtotals before arriving at income from continuing operations.

Illustration 4–3
Single-Step Income Statement

MAXWELL GEAR CORPORATION
Income Statement
For the Year Ended December 31, 2016

Revenues and gains:		
Sales		$573,522
Interest and dividends		26,400
Gain on sale of investments		5,500
Total revenues and gains		605,422
Expenses and losses:		
Cost of goods sold	$302,371	
Selling	47,341	
General and administrative	24,888	
Research and development	16,300	
Interest	14,522	
Total expenses and losses		405,422
Income before income taxes		200,000
Income tax expense		80,000
Net income		$120,000

Illustration 4–4
Multiple-Step Income Statement

MAXWELL GEAR CORPORATION
Income Statement
For the Year Ended December 31, 2016

Sales revenue		$573,522
Cost of goods sold		302,371
Gross profit		271,151
Operating expenses:		
Selling	$47,341	
General and administrative	24,888	
Research and development	16,300	
Total operating expenses		88,529
Operating income		182,622
Other income (expense):		
Interest and dividend revenue	26,400	
Gain on sale of investments	5,500	
Interest expense	(14,522)	
Total other income, net		17,378
Income before income taxes		200,000
Income tax expense		80,000
Net income		$120,000

An advantage of the single-step format is its simplicity. Revenues and expenses are not classified or prioritized. A primary advantage of the multiple-step format is that, by separately classifying operating and nonoperating items, it provides information that might be useful in analyzing trends. Similarly, the classification of expenses by function also provides useful information. For example, reporting gross profit for merchandising companies highlights the important relationship between sales revenue and cost of goods sold. It is important to note that this issue is one of presentation. The bottom line, net income, is the same regardless of the format used. Most large companies use the multiple-step format. For example, 21 of the Dow Jones Industrial 30 companies use this format. We use the multiple-step format for illustration purposes throughout the remainder of this chapter.

International Financial Reporting Standards

Income Statement Presentation. There are more similarities than differences between income statements prepared according to U.S. GAAP and those prepared applying international standards. Some of the differences are:

- International standards require certain minimum information to be reported on the face of the income statement. U.S. GAAP has no minimum requirements.
- International standards allow expenses to be classified either by function (e.g., cost of goods sold, general and administrative, etc.), or by natural description (e.g., salaries, rent, etc.). SEC regulations require that expenses be classified by function.
- In the United States, the "bottom line" of the income statement usually is called either *net income* or *net loss*. The descriptive term for the bottom line of the income statement prepared according to international standards is either *profit* or *loss*.

● LO4–9

Before we investigate discontinued operations, let's take a closer look at the components of both operating and nonoperating income and their relationship to earnings quality.

Earnings Quality

● LO4–2

Financial analysts are concerned with more than just the bottom line of the income statement—net income. The presentation of the components of net income and the related supplemental disclosures provide clues to the user of the statement in an assessment of *earnings quality*. Earnings quality is used as a framework for more in-depth discussions of operating and nonoperating income.

Earnings quality refers to the ability of reported earnings (income) to predict a company's future earnings.

The term **earnings quality** refers to the ability of reported earnings (income) to predict a company's future earnings. After all, an income statement simply reports on events that already have occurred. The relevance of any historical-based financial statement hinges on its predictive value. To enhance predictive value, analysts try to separate a company's *transitory earnings* effects from its *permanent earnings*. Transitory earnings effects result from transactions or events that are not likely to occur again in the foreseeable future or that are likely to have a different impact on earnings in the future. Later in the chapter we address discontinued operations that, because of its nature, is required to be reported separately at the bottom of the income statement. Analysts begin their assessment of permanent earnings with income before discontinued operations, that is, income from continuing operations.

It would be a mistake, though, to assume income from continuing operations reflects permanent earnings entirely. In other words, there may be transitory earnings effects included in income from continuing operations. In a sense, the phrase *continuing* may be misleading.

Manipulating Income and Income Smoothing

An often-debated contention is that, within GAAP, managers have the power, to a limited degree, to manipulate reported company income. And the manipulation is not always in the direction of higher income. One author states that "Most executives prefer to report earnings that follow a smooth, regular, upward path. They hate to report declines, but they also want to avoid increases that vary wildly from year to year; it's better to have two years of 15% earnings increases than a 30% gain one year and none the next. As a result, some companies 'bank' earnings by understating them in particularly good years and use the banked profits to polish results in bad years."[4]

Many believe that manipulating income reduces earnings quality because it can mask permanent earnings. A 1998 *BusinessWeek* issue was devoted entirely to the topic of earnings management. The issue, entitled "Corporate Earnings: Who Can You Trust," contains articles that are highly critical of corporate America's earnings manipulation practices. Arthur Levitt,

[4]Ford S. Worthy, "Manipulating Profits: How It's Done," *Fortune*, June 25, 1984, p. 50.

Arthur Levitt, Jr.
While the problem of earnings management is not new, it has swelled in a market that is unforgiving of companies that miss their estimates. I recently read of one major U.S. company that failed to meet its so-called numbers by one penny and lost more than six percent of its stock value in one day.[5]

Many believe that corporate earnings management practices reduce the quality of reported earnings.

Jr., former Chairman of the Securities and Exchange Commission, has been outspoken in his criticism of corporate earnings management practices and their effect on earnings quality. In an article appearing in the *CPA Journal,* he states,

> Increasingly, I have become concerned that the motivation to meet Wall Street earnings expectations may be overriding commonsense business practices. Too many corporate managers, auditors, and analysts are participants in a game of nods and winks. In the zeal to satisfy consensus earnings estimates and project a smooth earnings path, wishful thinking may be winning the day over faithful representation. As a result, I fear that we are witnessing an erosion in the *quality of earnings,* and therefore, the quality of financial reporting. Managing may be giving way to manipulation; integrity may be losing out to illusion. (emphasis added)[6]

How do managers manipulate income? Two major methods are (1) income shifting and (2) income statement classification. Income shifting is achieved by accelerating or delaying the recognition of revenues or expenses. For example, a practice called "channel stuffing" accelerates revenue recognition by persuading distributors to purchase more of your product than necessary near the end of a reporting period. The most common income statement classification manipulation involves the inclusion of recurring operating expenses in "special charge" categories such as restructuring costs (discussed below). This practice sometimes is referred to as "big bath" accounting, a reference to cleaning up company balance sheets. Asset reductions, or the incurrence of liabilities, for these restructuring costs result in large reductions in income that might otherwise appear as normal operating expenses either in the current or future years.

Mr. Levitt called for changes by standard setters to improve the transparency of financial statements. He did not want to eliminate necessary flexibility in financial reporting, but wanted to make it easier for financial statement users to "see through the numbers" to the future. A key to a meaningful assessment of a company's future profitability is to understand the events reported in the income statement and their relationship with future earnings. Let's now revisit the components of operating income.

Operating Income and Earnings Quality

● LO4–3

Should all items of revenue and expense included in operating income be considered indicative of a company's permanent earnings? No, not necessarily. Sometimes, for example, operating expenses include some unusual items that may or may not continue in the future.

Until recently, GAAP distinguished between events that were both unusual *and* infrequent and those that were either unusual *or* infrequent. If an event that was judged unusual and infrequent caused a material gain or loss, it was considered "extraordinary" and reported just as we now report discontinued operations. As you will learn later in this chapter, discontinued operations are reported *after-tax* below income or loss from continuing operations. Separate earnings per share disclosure also is required.

The notion of extraordinary items has been eliminated from U.S. GAAP.

The extraordinary classification has now been eliminated from GAAP.[7] Very few extraordinary gains and losses were being reported in corporate income statements. An important factor, too, was the FASB's desire to converge U.S. GAAP with international accounting standards, which does not recognize extraordinary items.

Now, we report unusual *and* infrequent events that have a material impact on a company's financial statements the same way as we report an event that is unusual *or* infrequent. That is, the income statement reports the *before-tax* effect as a line item included in continuing operations with no separate earnings per share disclosure.

---

[5]Arthur Levitt, Jr., "The Numbers Game," *The CPA Journal,* December 1998, p. 16.

[6]Ibid., p. 14.

[7]Our discussion here is based on an Exposure Draft (ED) issued by the FASB in July 2014. At the time this text went to print, a final Accounting Standards Update (ASU) had not yet been issued. It is unlikely that the ASU will differ from the ED.

What kind of items might be included in this category? Look closely at the 2014 and 2013 partial income statements of GameStop Corp., the world's largest multichannel video game retailer, presented in Illustration 4–5. Which items appear unusual? Certainly not Net sales, Cost of sales, Selling, general and administrative expenses. But what about "Goodwill impairments" and "Asset impairments and restructuring costs"? Let's consider both.

Illustration 4–5

Partial Income Statement—GameStop Corp.

Real World Financials

Income Statements (in part) ($ in millions)	**Year Ended**	
	February 1, 2014	**February 2, 2013**
Net sales	$9,039.5	$8,886.7
Cost of sales	6,378.4	6,235.2
Gross profit	2,661.1	2,651.5
Selling, general, and administrative expenses	1,892.4	1,835.9
Depreciation and amortization	166.5	176.5
Goodwill impairments	10.2	627.0
Asset impairments and restructuring costs	18.5	53.7
Operating income (loss)	573.5	(41.6)

FINANCIAL Reporting Case

Q1, p. 171

RESTRUCTURING COSTS. It's not unusual for a company to reorganize its operations to attain greater efficiency. When this happens, the company often incurs significant associated restructuring costs. Facility closings and related employee layoffs translate into costs incurred for severance pay and relocation costs. Restructuring costs are incurred in connection with:

> A program that is planned and controlled by management, and materially changes either the scope of a business undertaken by an entity, or the manner in which that business is conducted.[8]

***Restructuring costs* include costs associated with shutdown or relocation of facilities or downsizing of operations.**

Restructuring costs appear frequently in corporate income statements. In fact, a recent survey reports that of the 500 companies surveyed, 40% included restructuring costs in their income statements.[9] For instance, consider again our GameStop Corp. example. A disclosure note accompanying the company's financial statements reported that recent restructuring costs were related to the exit of markets in Europe and the closure of underperforming stores in the international segments, as well as the consolidation of European home office sites and back-office functions.

GAAP requires that restructuring costs be recognized only in the period incurred.

Restructuring costs are recognized in the period the exit or disposal cost obligation actually is incurred. As an example, suppose terminated employees are to receive termination benefits, but only after they remain with the employer beyond a minimum retention period. In that case, a liability for termination benefits, and corresponding expense, should be accrued in the period(s) the employees render their service. On the other hand, if future service beyond a minimum retention period is not required, the liability and corresponding expense for benefits are recognized at the time the company communicates the arrangement to employees. In both cases, the liability and expense are recorded at the point they are deemed incurred. Similarly, costs associated with closing facilities and relocating employees are recognized when goods or services associated with those activities are received.

Fair value is the objective for the initial measurement of a liability associated with restructuring costs.

GAAP also establishes that fair value is the objective for initial measurement of the liability, and that a liability's fair value often will be measured by determining the present value of future estimated cash outflows. We discuss such present value calculations at length in later chapters, particularly in Chapters 6 and 14. Because some restructuring costs

[8]FASB ASC 420–10–20: Exit or Disposal Cost Obligations—Overall—Glossary (previously "Accounting for Costs Associated with Exit or Disposal Activities," *Statement of Financial Accounting Standards No. 146* (Norwalk, Conn.: FASB, 2002)).

[9]*U.S. GAAP Financial Statements—Best Practices in Presentation and Disclosure—2013* (New York: AICPA, 2013).

require estimation, actual costs could differ. Also, the costs might not occur until a subsequent reporting period. As we discuss later in this chapter and throughout the text, when an estimate is changed, the company should record the effect of the change in the period the estimate is changed rather than by restating prior years' financial statements to correct the estimate. On occasion, this process has resulted in a negative expense amount for restructuring costs due to the overestimation of costs in a prior reporting period.

Should restructuring costs be considered part of a company's permanent earnings stream?

Now that we understand the nature of restructuring costs, we can address the important question: Should financial statement users attempting to forecast future earnings consider these costs to be part of a company's permanent earnings stream, or are they transitory in nature? There is no easy answer. For example, GameStop incurred restructuring costs in both 2013 and 2012. Will the company incur these costs again in the near future? Consider the following facts. During the 10-year period from 2004 through 2013, the Dow Jones Industrial 30 companies reported 107 restructuring charges in their collective income statements. That's an average of 3.6 per company. But the average is deceiving. Six of the 30 companies reported no restructuring charges during that period, while three of the 30 companies reported restructuring charges in each of the 10 years. The inference: a financial statement user must interpret restructuring charges in light of a company's past history. In general, the more frequently these sorts of unusual charges occur, the more appropriate it is that financial statement users include them in the company's permanent earnings stream. Information in disclosure notes describing the restructuring and management plans related to the business involved also can be helpful.

Arthur Levitt, Jr.
When a company decides to restructure, management and employees, investors and creditors, customers and suppliers all want to understand the expected effects. We need, of course, to ensure that financial reporting provides this information. But this should not lead to flushing all the associated costs—and maybe a little extra—through the financial statements.[10]

OTHER UNUSUAL ITEMS. Two other expenses in GameStop's income statements that warrant additional scrutiny are *goodwill impairments* and *asset impairments.* These involve what is referred to as impairment losses or charges. Any long-lived asset, whether tangible or intangible, should have its balance reduced if there has been a significant impairment of value. We explore property, plant, and equipment and intangible assets in Chapters 10 and 11. After discussing this topic in more depth in those chapters, we revisit the concept of earnings quality as it relates to asset impairment.

Is it possible that financial analysts might look favorably at a company in the year it incurs a substantial restructuring charge or other unusual expense such as an asset impairment loss? Perhaps so, if they view management as creating higher profits in future years through operating efficiencies. Would analysts then reward that company again in future years when those operating efficiencies materialize? Certainly this double halo effect might provide an attractive temptation to the management of some companies.

Unusual items included in operating income require investigation to determine their permanent or transitory nature.

These aren't the only components of operating expenses that call into question this issue of earnings quality. For example, in Chapter 9 we discuss the write-down of inventory to comply with the lower of cost and net realizable value rule. Other possibilities include losses from natural disasters such as earthquakes and floods and gains and losses from litigation settlements. Earnings quality also is influenced by the way a company records income from investments (Chapter 12) and accounts for its pension plans (Chapter 17).

Earnings quality is affected by revenue issues as well. As an example, suppose that toward the end of its fiscal year, a company loses a major customer that can't be replaced. That would mean the current year's revenue numbers include a transitory component equal to the revenue generated from sales to the lost customer. Of course, in addition to its effect on revenues, losing the customer would have implications for the transitory/permanent nature of expenses and net income.

Another revenue issue affecting earnings quality is the timing of revenue recognition. Companies face continual pressure to meet their earnings expectations. That pressure often has led to premature revenue recognition, reducing the quality of reported earnings.

[10]Arthur Levitt, Jr. "The Numbers Game," *The CPA Journal,* December 1998, p. 16.

Accelerating revenue recognition has caused problems for many companies. For example, in 2008, **International Rectifier Corporation**, a manufacturer of power management products, was named defendant in a federal class action suit related to numerous irregularities including premature revenue recognition. The company admitted shipping products and recording sales with no obligation by customers to receive and pay for the products. In 2011, the SEC convinced **Groupon** to change its policy related to premature recognition of revenue from the sale of coupons and gift certificates.

Real World Financials

We explore these issues in Chapter 5, when we discuss revenue recognition in considerable depth, and in Chapter 13, when we discuss liabilities that companies must record when they receive payment prior to having actually recognized the related revenue. Now, though, let's discuss earnings quality issues related to *nonoperating* items.

Nonoperating Income and Earnings Quality

Most of the components of earnings in an income statement relate directly to the ordinary, continuing operations of the company. Some, though, such as interest and gains or losses are only tangentially related to normal operations. These we refer to as nonoperating items. Some nonoperating items have generated considerable discussion with respect to earnings quality, notably gains and losses generated from the sale of investments. For example, as the stock market boom reached its height late in the year 2000, many companies recorded large gains from sale of investments that had appreciated significantly in value. How should those gains be interpreted in terms of their relationship to future earnings? Are they transitory or permanent? Let's consider an example.

Gains and losses from the sale of investments often can significantly inflate or deflate current earnings.

Intel Corporation is the world's largest manufacturer of semiconductors. Illustration 4–6 shows the nonoperating section of Intel's income statements for the 2000 and 1999 fiscal years. In 2000, income before taxes increased by approximately 35% from the prior year. But notice that the *gains on investments, net* (net means net of losses) increased from $883 million to over $3.7 billion, accounting for a large portion of the increase in income. Some analysts questioned the quality of Intel's 2000 earnings because of these large gains.

Illustration 4–6

Income Statements (in part)—Intel Corporation

Real World Financials

Income Statements (in part)
(in millions)

	Years Ended December 30	
	2000	**1999**
Operating income	10,395	9,767
Gains on investments, net	3,759	883
Interest and other, net	987	578
Income before taxes	15,141	11,228

Consider **The New York Times Company**, a global media company. In a recent fiscal year, the company reported income before income taxes of $259 million. Included in this amount was a $220 million gain on the sale of investments, representing 85% of before-tax income. Can The New York Times Company sustain these gains? Should they be considered part of permanent earnings or are they transitory? There are no easy answers to these questions. It's interesting to note that in the subsequent fiscal year the company reported no investment gains.

Companies often voluntarily provide a **pro forma earnings** number when they announce annual or quarterly earnings. Supposedly, these pro forma earnings numbers are management's view of "permanent earnings," in the sense of being a better long-run performance measure. For example, in January 2014, **Google Inc.** announced that its income for the fourth quarter of 2013 was $3.38 billion or $9.90 per share. At the same time, the company announced that its *pro forma net income* (for which Google excluded stock-based compensation expense and restructuring costs) for the quarter was $4.1 billion or $12.01 per share. These pro forma earnings numbers are controversial because determining which items to exclude is at the discretion of management. Therefore, management could mislead

Many companies voluntarily provide *pro forma earnings*—management's assessment of permanent earnings.

Real World Financials

investors. Nevertheless, these disclosures do represent management's perception of what its permanent earnings are and provides additional information to the financial community.

The Sarbanes-Oxley Act requires reconciliation between pro forma earnings and earnings determined according to GAAP.

The Sarbanes-Oxley Act addressed pro forma earnings in its Section 401. One of the act's important provisions requires that if pro forma earnings are included in any periodic or other report filed with the SEC or in any public disclosure or press release, the company also must provide a reconciliation with earnings determined according to generally accepted accounting principles.[11]

We now turn our attention to discontinued operations, an item that is not part of a company's permanent earnings and, appropriately, is excluded from continuing operations.

Discontinued Operations

● LO4–4

The information in the income statement is useful if it can help users predict the future. So what if some of the operations reported in the income statement are operations the company has discontinued? Obviously, those items will be absent in the future and amounts related to the discontinued operations will be useless in predicting future profitability. It's logical, then, that if discontinued operations had a material effect[12] on the income statement, they should be reported separately to allow statement users to focus on continuing operations. So, discontinued operations must be reported separately, below income from continuing operations. Although a company has considerable flexibility in reporting income from *continuing operations,* the presentation of **discontinued operations** is mandated as follows:[13]

Income from continuing operations before income taxes	$xxx
Income tax expense	xx
Income from continuing operations	xxx
Discontinued operations, net of $xx tax (expense)/benefit	xx
Net income	**$xxx**

The objective is to report *all* of the income effects of a discontinued operation separately. That's why we include the income tax effect in this separate presentation rather than report it as part of income tax expense related to continuing operations. The process of associating income tax effects with the income statement components that create those effects is referred to as *intraperiod tax allocation*, something we discuss in depth in Chapter 16.

What are some examples of discontinued operations? **Pfizer Inc.** is a global biopharmaceutical company. In addition to its drug and consumer healthcare divisions, the company also operated a nutrition business prior to 2013 focusing primarily on infants. Late in 2012 the nutrition business was sold to **Nestlé** for $11.85 billion. **H. J. Heinz** is a food products company best known for its ketchup. In addition to its condiments, sauces, soups, and other packaged food products, the company operated a frozen desserts business that was sold in 2013. In 2013 **Google** sold its Motorola Mobility smartphone subsidiary to Lenovo for $2.9 billion. Pfizer's sale of its nutrition business, Heinz's sale of its frozen desserts business, and Google's sale of its smartphone subsidiary are examples of discontinued operations.

FINANCIAL Reporting Case

Q2, p. 172

What Constitutes an Operation?

Because we report income and loss from discontinued operations separate from continuing operations, it's important to know what we should consider to be an "operation" for this purpose. In 2001 the FASB issued a standard that defined an operation as a *component of an entity.* International standards also defined a discontinued operation as a *component of an entity.* However, what constitutes a "component" differed significantly between U.S. GAAP and *IFRS No. 5.*[14]

[11]The Congress of the United States of America, *The Sarbanes-Oxley Act of 2002,* Section 401 (b) (2), Washington, D.C., 2004.

[12]We discussed the concept of materiality in Chapter 1.

[13]The presentation of discontinued operations is the same for single-step and multiple-step income statement formats. The single-step versus multiple-step distinction applies to items included in income from continuing operations.

[14]"Noncurrent Assets Held for Sale and Discontinued Operations," *International Financial Reporting Standard No. 5* (IASCF), as amended effective January 1, 2014.

As part of the continuing process to converge U.S. GAAP and international standards, the FASB and IASB worked together to develop a common definition and a common set of disclosures for discontinued operations. As a result of this effort, in 2014 the FASB issued an Accounting Standards Update (ASU) that defines a discontinued operation as a component of an entity or a group of components.[15, 16]

Separate reporting as a discontinued operation is required when the disposal of a component represents a strategic shift that has, or will have, a major effect on a company's operations and financial results.

A *component* is any part of the company, such as an operating segment or subsidiary, that includes operations and cash flows that can be clearly distinguished, operationally and for financial reporting purposes, from the rest of the company. A component or group of components that has been sold or disposed of in some other way, or is considered held for sale, is reported as a discontinued operation if the disposal represents a *strategic shift* that has, or will have, a major effect on a company's operations and financial results. Company management needs to apply judgment when deciding if the disposal represents a strategic shift. Examples of possible strategic shifts include the disposal of operations in a major geographical area, a major line of business, a major equity method investment,[17] or other major parts of the company.

Many were critical of prior U.S. GAAP for its broader definition of a component. In addition to achieving convergence with international standards, the new ASU is expected to reduce the number of business segments that will require separate income statement presentation for discontinued operations.

Reporting Discontinued Operations

By definition, the income or loss stream from a discontinued operation no longer will continue. A financial statement user concerned with Pfizer's, H.J. Heinz's, and Google's future profitability is more interested in the results of their operations that will continue. It is informative, then, for companies to separate the effects of the discontinued operations from the results of operations that will continue. This information might have a significant impact on the financial statement user's assessment of future profitability.

The net-of-tax income effects of a discontinued operation are reported separately in the income statement, below income from continuing operations.

For this reason, the revenues, expenses, gains, losses, and income tax related to a *discontinued* operation must be removed from *continuing* operations and reported separately for all years presented.[18] A key for assessing profitability is comparing the company's performance from *continuing* operations from year to year and from company to company.

Sometimes a discontinued component actually has been sold by the end of a reporting period. Often, though, the component is being held for sale, but the disposal transaction has not yet been completed as of the end of the reporting period. We consider these two possibilities next.

WHEN THE COMPONENT HAS BEEN SOLD. When the discontinued component is sold before the end of the reporting period, the reported income effects of a discontinued operation will include two elements:

1. Income or loss from operations (revenues, expenses, gains, and losses) of the component from the beginning of the reporting period to the disposal date.
2. Gain or loss on disposal of the component's assets.

These two elements can be combined or reported separately, net of their tax effects. If combined, the gain or loss component must be indicated. In our illustrations to follow,

[15]*Accounting Standards Update No. 2014-08,* "Presentation of Financial Statements (Topic 205) and Property, Plant, and Equipment (Topic 360): Reporting Discontinued Operations and Disclosures of Disposals of Components of an Entity," (Norwalk, Conn.: FASB, April 2014).

[16]The ASU also requires reporting as a discontinued operation a business or nonprofit activity that is considered held for sale when acquired. A business is a set of activities and assets that is managed for purposes of providing economic benefits to the company. A nonprofit activity is similar to a business but is not intended to provide goods and services to customers at a profit.

[17]Under prior GAAP, equity method investments were not included under the scope of a discontinued operation. Equity method investments are discussed in Chapter 12.

[18]For example, even though Heinz did not sell its frozen desserts business until 2013, it's important for comparative purposes to separate the effects for any prior years presented. This allows an apples-to-apples comparison of income from *continuing* operations. So, in its 2013 three-year comparative income statements, the 2012 and 2011 income statements were reclassified and the income from discontinued operations presented as a separately reported item. In addition, there was a disclosure note to inform readers that prior years were reclassified.

we combine the income effects. Illustration 4–7 describes a situation in which the discontinued component is sold before the end of the reporting period.

Illustration 4–7
Discontinued Operations—Gain on Disposal

The Duluth Holding Company has several operating divisions. In October 2016, management decided to sell one of its divisions that qualifies as a separate component according to generally accepted accounting principles. The division was sold on December 18, 2016, for a net selling price of $14,000,000. On that date, the assets of the division had a book value of $12,000,000. For the period January 1 through disposal, the division reported a pretax loss from operations of $4,200,000. The company's income tax rate is 40% on all items of income or loss. Duluth generated after-tax profits of $22,350,000 from its continuing operations.

Duluth's income statement for the year 2016, beginning with income from continuing operations, would be reported as follows:

Income from continuing operations		$22,350,000
Discontinued operations:		
Loss from operations of discontinued component (including gain on disposal of **$2,000,000***)	$(2,200,000)†	
Income tax benefit	880,000‡	
Loss on discontinued operations		(1,320,000)
Net income		$21,030,000

*Net selling price of $14 million less book value of $12 million
†Loss from operations of $4.2 million less gain on disposal of $2 million
‡$2,200,000 × 40%

Notice that a tax *benefit* occurs because a *loss* reduces taxable income, saving the company $880,000. On the other hand, had there been *income* from operations of $2,200,000, the $880,000 income tax effect would have represented additional income tax expense.

For comparison purposes, the net of tax income or loss from operations of the discontinued component for any prior years included in the comparative income statements also are separately reported as discontinued operations.

If a component to be discontinued has not yet been sold, its income effects, including any impairment loss, usually still are reported separately as discontinued operations.

WHEN THE COMPONENT IS CONSIDERED HELD FOR SALE. What if a company has decided to discontinue a component but, when the reporting period ends, the component has not yet been sold? If the situation indicates that the component is likely to be sold within a year, the component is considered "held for sale."[19] In that case, the income effects of the discontinued operation still are reported, but the two components of the reported amount are modified as follows:

1. Income or loss from operations (revenues, expenses, gains and losses) of the component from the beginning of the reporting period *to the end of the reporting period.*
2. An "impairment loss" if the book value, sometimes called carrying value or carrying amount, of the assets of the component is more than fair value minus cost to sell.

The two income elements can be combined or reported separately, net of their tax effects. In addition, if the amounts are combined and there is an impairment loss, the loss must be disclosed, either parenthetically on the face of the statement or in a disclosure note. Consider the example in Illustration 4–8.

Also, the net-of-tax income or loss from operations of the component being discontinued is reported separate from continuing operations for any prior year that is presented for comparison purposes along with the 2016 income statement. Then, in the year of actual disposal, the discontinued operations section of the income statement will include the final gain or loss on the sale of the discontinued segment's assets. The gain or loss is determined relative to the revised book values of the assets after the impairment writedown.

Important information about discontinued operations, whether sold or held for sale, is reported in a disclosure note. The note provides additional details about the discontinued

[19]Six criteria are used to determine whether the component is likely to be sold and therefore considered "held for sale." You can find these criteria in FASB ASC 360–10–45–9: Property, Plant, and Equipment—Overall—Other Presentation Matters—Long-Lived Assets Classified as Held for Sale (previously "Accounting for the Impairment or Disposal of Long-Lived Assets," *Statement of Financial Accounting Standards No. 144* (Norwalk, Conn.: FASB, 2001), par. 30).

Illustration 4–8

Discontinued Operations—Impairment Loss

The Duluth Holding Company has several operating divisions. In October 2016, management decided to sell one of its divisions that qualifies as a separate component according to generally accepted accounting principles. On December 31, 2016, the end of the company's fiscal year, the division had not yet been sold. On that date, the assets of the division had a book value of $12,000,000 and a fair value, minus anticipated cost to sell, of $9,000,000. For the year, the division reported a pre-tax loss from operations of $4,200,000. The company's income tax rate is 40% on all items of income or loss. Duluth generated after-tax profits of $22,350,000 from its continuing operations.

Duluth's income statement for 2016, beginning with income from continuing operations, would be reported as follows:

Income from continuing operations		$22,350,000
Discontinued operations:		
Loss from operations of discontinued component (including impairment loss of $3,000,000*)	$(7,200,000)†	
Income tax benefit	2,880,000‡	
Loss on discontinued operations		(4,320,000)
Net income		$18,030,000

*Book value of $12 million less fair value net of cost to sell of $9 million
†Loss from operations of $4.2 million plus impairment loss of $3 million
‡$7,200,000 × 40%

component, including its identity, its major classes of assets and liabilities, the major revenues and expenses constituting pretax income or loss from operations, the reason for the discontinuance, and the expected manner of disposition if held for sale.[20]

In Illustration 4–8, if the fair value of the division's assets minus cost to sell exceeded the book value of $12,000,000, there is no impairment loss and the income effects of the discontinued operation would include only the loss from operations of $4,200,000, less the income tax benefit.[21]

The balance sheet is affected, too. The assets and liabilities of the component considered held for sale are reported at the lower of their book value or fair value minus cost to sell. And, because it's not in use, an asset classified as held for sale is no longer reported as part of property, plant, and equipment or intangible assets and is not depreciated or amortized.

Eastman Kodak Company provides an example. The company is best known for its photographic film products. Recently, it sold its digital capture and devices business, Kodak Gallery, and other businesses. The sales were completed by the end of 2013, but some assets and liabilities of the sold businesses had not yet been transferred. The current asset and current liability sections of the 2013 year-end balance sheet reported $95 million in "Assets held for sale," and $38 million in "Liabilities held for sale." Information about the discontinued operations was included in the disclosure note shown in Illustration 4–9.

Notice that the assets and liabilities held for sale are classified as *current* because the company expects to complete the transfer of these assets and liabilities in the next fiscal year.

INTERIM REPORTING. Remember that companies whose ownership shares are publicly traded in the United States must file quarterly reports with the Securities and Exchange Commission. If a component of an entity is considered held for sale at the end of a quarter, the income effects of the discontinued component must be separately reported in the quarterly income statement. These effects would include the income or loss from operations for the quarter as well as an impairment loss if the component's assets have a book value more than fair value minus cost to sell. If the assets are impaired and written down, any gain or loss on disposal in a subsequent quarter is determined relative to the new, written-down book value.

In the next section, we briefly discuss the way various types of accounting changes are reported.

[20]For a complete list of disclosure requirements, see FASB ASC 205-20-50: Presentation of Financial Statements—Discontinued Operations—Disclosure.

[21]In the following year when the component is sold, the income effects also must be reported as a discontinued operation.

Illustration 4–9
Discontinued Operations Disclosure—Eastman Kodak Company

Real World Financials

Note 26. Discontinued Operations (in part)
The following table summarizes the major classes of assets and liabilities related to the disposition of businesses which have been segregated and included in assets held for sale and liabilities held for sale in the consolidated balance sheet.

($ in millions)	December 31, 2013
Receivables, net	$16
Inventories	62
Property, plant, and equipment, net	10
Other assets	7
Current assets held for sale	$95
Trade payables	$24
Miscellaneous payable and accruals	14
Current liabilities held for sale	$38

Accounting Changes

Accounting changes fall into one of three categories: (1) a change in an accounting principle, (2) a change in estimate, or (3) a change in reporting entity. The correction of an error is another adjustment that is accounted for in the same way as certain accounting changes. A brief overview of a change in accounting principle, a change in estimate, and correction of errors is provided here. We cover accounting changes in detail, including changes in reporting entities, in subsequent chapters, principally in Chapter 20.

Change in Accounting Principle

A change in accounting principle refers to a change from one acceptable accounting method to another. There are many situations that allow alternative treatments for similar transactions. Common examples of these situations include the choice among FIFO, LIFO, and average cost for the measurement of inventory and among alternative revenue recognition methods. New accounting standard updates issued by the FASB also may require companies to change their accounting methods.

VOLUNTARY CHANGES IN ACCOUNTING PRINCIPLES. Occasionally, a company will change from one generally accepted treatment to another. When these changes in accounting principles occur, information lacks consistency, hampering the ability of external users to compare financial information among reporting periods. If, for example, inventory and cost of goods sold are measured in one reporting period using the LIFO method, but are measured using the FIFO method in a subsequent period, inventory, cost of goods sold, and hence net income for the two periods are not comparable. Difficulties created by inconsistency and lack of comparability are alleviated by the way we report voluntary accounting changes.

Voluntary changes in accounting principles are accounted for retrospectively by revising prior years' financial statements.

GAAP requires that voluntary accounting changes be accounted for retrospectively.[22] That is, we recast prior years' financial statements when we report those statements again (in comparative statements, for example) to appear as if the new accounting method had been used in those periods. For each year in the comparative statements reported, we revise the balance of each account affected to make those statements appear as if the newly adopted accounting method had been applied all along. Then, a journal entry is created to adjust all account balances affected to what those amounts would have been. An adjustment is made to the beginning balance of retained earnings for the earliest period reported in the comparative statements of shareholders' equity to account for the cumulative income effect of changing to the new principle in periods prior to those reported.[23]

[22]FASB ASC 250–10–45–5: Accounting Changes and Error Corrections—Overall—Other Presentation Matters (previously "Accounting Changes and Error Corrections—a replacement of APB Opinion No. 20 and FASB Statement No. 3," *Statement of Financial Accounting Standard No. 154* (Norwalk, Conn.: FASB, 2005)).

[23]Sometimes a lack of information makes it impracticable to report a change retrospectively so the new method is simply applied prospectively, that is, we simply use the new method from now on. Also, if a new standard specifically requires prospective accounting, that requirement is followed.

We will see these aspects of accounting for the change in accounting principle demonstrated in Chapter 9 in the context of our discussion of inventory methods. We'll also discuss changes in accounting principles in depth in Chapter 20.

MANDATED CHANGES IN ACCOUNTING PRINCIPLES. When a new FASB accounting standard update mandates a change in accounting principle, the board often allows companies to choose among multiple ways of accounting for the changes. One approach generally allowed is to account for the change retrospectively, exactly as we account for voluntary changes in principles. The FASB may also allow companies to report the cumulative effect on the income of previous years from having used the old method rather than the new method in the income statement of the year of change as a separately reported item below discontinued operations. Other approaches might also be allowed. Therefore, when a mandated change in accounting principle occurs, it is important to check the accounting standards update to determine how companies might account for the change.

Change in Depreciation, Amortization, or Depletion Method

A change in depreciation, amortization, or depletion method is considered to be a change in accounting estimate that is achieved by a change in accounting principle. We account for this change prospectively, almost exactly as we would any other change in estimate. One difference is that most changes in estimate don't require a company to justify the change. However, this change in estimate is a result of changing an accounting principle and therefore requires a clear justification as to why the new method is preferable. Chapter 11 provides an illustration of a change in depreciation method.

Changes in depreciation, amortization, or depletion methods are accounted for the same way as a change in an accounting estimate.

Change in Accounting Estimate

Estimates are a necessary aspect of accounting. A few of the more common accounting estimates are the amount of future bad debts on existing accounts receivable, the useful life and residual value of a depreciable asset, and future warranty expenses.

A *change in accounting estimate* is reflected in the financial statements of the current period and future periods.

Because estimates require the prediction of future events, it's not unusual for them to turn out to be wrong. When an estimate is modified as new information comes to light, accounting for the change in estimate is quite straightforward. We do not revise prior years' financial statements to reflect the new estimate. Instead, we merely incorporate the new estimate in any related accounting determinations from that point on, that is, we account for a change in accounting estimate prospectively.[24] If the effect of the change is material, a disclosure note is needed to describe the change and its effect on both net income and earnings per share. Chapters 11 and 20 provide illustrations of changes in accounting estimates.

Correction of Accounting Errors

Errors occur when transactions are either recorded incorrectly or not recorded at all. We briefly discuss the correction of errors here as an overview and in later chapters in the context of the effect of errors on specific chapter topics. In addition, Chapter 20 provides comprehensive coverage of the correction of errors.

Accountants employ various control mechanisms to ensure that transactions are accounted for correctly. In spite of this, errors occur. When errors do occur, they can affect any one or several of the financial statement elements on any of the financial statements a company prepares. In fact, many kinds of errors simultaneously affect more than one financial statement. When errors are discovered, they should be corrected.

Most errors are discovered in the same year that they are made. These errors are simple to correct. The original erroneous journal entry is reversed and the appropriate entry is recorded. If an error is discovered in a year subsequent to the year the error is made, the accounting treatment depends on whether or not the error is material with respect to its effect on the financial statements. In practice, the vast majority of errors are not material and are, therefore, simply corrected in the year discovered. However, material errors that are discovered in subsequent periods require a prior period adjustment.

[24]If the original estimate had been based on erroneous information or calculations or had not been made in good faith, the revision of that estimate would constitute the correction of an error.

Prior Period Adjustments

Assume that after its financial statements are published and distributed to shareholders, Roush Distribution Company discovers a material error in the statements. What does it do? Roush must make a **prior period adjustment**.[25] Roush would record a journal entry that adjusts any balance sheet accounts to their appropriate levels and would account for the income effects of the error by increasing or decreasing the beginning retained earnings balance in a statement of shareholders' equity. Remember, net income in prior periods was closed to retained earnings so, by adjusting retained earnings, the prior period adjustment accounts for the error's effect on prior periods' net income.

Simply reporting a corrected retained earnings amount might cause misunderstanding for someone familiar with the previously reported amount. Explicitly reporting a prior period adjustment in the statement of shareholders' equity (or statement of retained earnings if that's presented instead) highlights the adjustment and avoids this confusion.

In addition to reporting the prior period adjustment to retained earnings, previous years' financial statements that are incorrect as a result of the error are retrospectively restated to reflect the correction. Also, a disclosure note communicates the impact of the error on prior periods' net income.

Earnings per Share Disclosures

LO4–5

As we discussed in Chapter 3, financial statement users often use summary indicators, called *ratios,* to more efficiently make comparisons among different companies and over time for the same company. Besides highlighting important relationships among financial statement variables, ratios also accommodate differences in company size.

FINANCIAL Reporting Case

Q3, p. 172

All corporations whose common stock is publicly traded must disclose EPS.

One of the most widely used ratios is **earnings per share (EPS)**, which shows the amount of income earned by a company expressed on a per share basis. Public companies report basic EPS and, if there are certain potentially dilutive securities, **diluted** EPS, on the face of the income statement. Basic EPS is computed by dividing income available to common shareholders (net income less any preferred stock dividends) by the weighted-average number of common shares outstanding (weighted by time outstanding) for the period. For example, suppose the Fetzer Corporation reported net income of $600,000 for its fiscal year ended December 31, 2016. Preferred stock dividends of $75,000 were declared during the year. Fetzer had one million shares of common stock outstanding at the beginning of the year and issued an additional one million shares on March 31, 2016. Basic EPS of $.30 per share for 2016 is computed as follows:

$$\frac{\$600{,}000 - 75{,}000}{\underset{\text{Shares at Jan. 1}}{1{,}000{,}000} + \underset{\text{New shares}}{1{,}000{,}000\,(9/12)}} = \frac{\$525{,}000}{1{,}750{,}000} = \$0.30$$

Diluted EPS reflects the potential dilution that could occur for companies that have certain securities outstanding that are convertible into common shares or stock options that could create additional common shares if the options were exercised. These items could cause EPS to decrease (become diluted) because there would be more shares in the denominator of the EPS calculation. Because of the complexity of the calculation and the importance of EPS to investors, we devote a substantial portion of Chapter 19 to this topic. At this point, we focus on the financial statement presentation of EPS. In Illustration 4–2 on page 175, **Urban Outfitters, Inc.**, discloses both basic and diluted EPS in its income statements for all years presented.

When the income statement includes discontinued operations, we report per-share amounts for both income (loss) from continuing operations and for net income (loss), as well as for the discontinued operations. We see this demonstrated in recent quarterly income statements of **Big Lots, Inc.**, the largest closeout retailer in the U.S., partially reproduced in Illustration 4–10.

[25]FASB ASC 250–10–45–23: Accounting Changes and Error Corrections—Overall—Other Presentation Matters (previously "Prior Period Adjustments," *Statement of Financial Accounting Standards No. 16* (Norwalk, Conn.: FASB, 1977)).

BIG LOTS, INC.
Consolidated Statements of Operations (in part)

	Thirteen Weeks Ended	
(In thousands, except per share amounts)	May 3, 2014	May 4, 2013
Income from continuing operations	$28,581	$37,065
Loss from discontinued operations, net of tax	(25,233)	(4,732)
Net income	$ 3,348	$32,333
Earnings per common share—basic:		
Continuing operations	$ 0.50	$ 0.65
Discontinued operations	(0.44)	(0.08)
Net income	$ 0.06	$ 0.57
Earnings per common share—diluted:		
Continuing operations	$ 0.50	$ 0.64
Discontinued operations	(0.44)	(0.08)
Net income	$ 0.06	$ 0.56

Illustration 4–10

EPS Disclosures—Big Lots, Inc.

Real World Financials

Comprehensive Income

● LO4–6

Accounting professionals have engaged in an ongoing debate concerning which transactions should be included as components of periodic income. For instance, some argue that certain changes in shareholders' equity besides those attributable to traditional net income should be included in the determination of income. In what might be viewed as a compromise, the FASB decided to maintain the traditional view of net income, but to require companies also to report an expanded version of income called comprehensive income to include four types of gains and losses that traditionally hadn't been included in income statements. Let's consider what that means.

Other Comprehensive Income

Comprehensive income **is the total change in equity for a reporting period other than from transactions with owners.**

The calculation of net income omits certain types of gains and losses that are instead included in comprehensive income. As one example, in Chapter 12 you will learn that certain investments are reported in the balance sheet at their fair values, but that the gains and losses resulting from adjusting those investments to fair value might not be included in net income. Instead, they are reported as a separate component of shareholders' equity, other comprehensive income (OCI) (loss).

Companies must report both net income and comprehensive income and reconcile the difference between the two.[26] Be sure to remember that net income actually is a part of comprehensive income. The reconciliation simply extends net income to include other comprehensive income items, reported net of tax, as shown in Illustration 4–11.

The actual terminology used by companies for the four items of other comprehensive income varies considerably. For instance, deferred gains (losses) from derivatives are sometimes called *derivative mark-to-market adjustments* or *changes in fair value of derivatives,* and gains (losses) from foreign currency translation are often identified as *foreign currency translation adjustments.*

Flexibility in Reporting

Reporting comprehensive income can be accomplished with a single, continuous statement or in two separate, but consecutive statements.

The information in the income statement and other comprehensive income items shown in Illustration 4–11 can be presented either (1) in a single, continuous statement of comprehensive income or (2) in two separate, but consecutive statements, an income statement and a statement of comprehensive income. Each component of other comprehensive income can be displayed net of tax, as in Illustration 4–11, or alternatively, before tax with one amount shown for the aggregate income tax expense (or benefit).[27]

[26]FASB ASC 220-10-45-1A and 1B: Comprehensive Income–Overall–Other Presentation Matters (previously "Reporting Comprehensive Income," *Statement of Financial Accounting Standards No. 130* (Norwalk, Conn.: FASB, 1997)).

[27]GAAP does not require the reporting of comprehensive earnings per share.

Illustration 4–11
Comprehensive Income

Comprehensive income includes net income as well as other gains and losses that change shareholders' equity but are not included in traditional net income.

		($ in millions)
Net income		$xxx
Other comprehensive income:		
Net unrealized holding gains (losses) on investments (net of tax)*	$x	
Gains (losses) from and amendments to postretirement benefit plans (net of tax)†	(x)	
Deferred gains (losses) from derivatives (net of tax)‡	(x)	
Gains (losses) from foreign currency translation (net of tax)§	x	xx
Comprehensive income		$xxx

*Changes in the market value of certain investments (described in Chapter 12).
†Gains and losses due to revising assumptions or market returns differing from expectations and prior service cost from amending the plan (described in Chapter 17).
‡When a derivative designated as a cash flow hedge is adjusted to fair value, the gain or loss is deferred as a component of comprehensive income and included in earnings later, at the same time as earnings are affected by the hedged transaction (described in the Derivatives Appendix to the text).
§Gains or losses from changes in foreign currency exchange rates. The amount could be an addition to or reduction in shareholders' equity. (This item is discussed elsewhere in your accounting curriculum.)

PetSmart

Companies such as **PetSmart, Inc.**, choose to present comprehensive income in a single statement. On the other hand, in its 2014 financial statements, **Astro-Med Inc.**, a manufacturer of a broad range of specialty technology products, chose to use the separate statement approach, as shown in Illustration 4–12.

Illustration 4–12
Comprehensive Income Presented as a Separate Statement—Astro-Med Inc.

Real World Financials

ASTRO-MED, INC.
Consolidated Statements of Comprehensive Income
For the Years Ended January 31,

($ in thousands)	2014	2013
Net income	$3,212	$10,767
Other comprehensive income (loss), net of taxes		
Foreign currency translation adjustments	(14)	60
Unrealized gain (loss) on securities available for sale	17	(8)
Other comprehensive income	3	52
Comprehensive income	$3,215	$10,819

International Financial Reporting Standards

● LO4–9

Comprehensive Income. Both U.S. GAAP and IFRS allow companies to report comprehensive income in either a single statement of comprehensive income or in two separate statements.

Other comprehensive income items are similar under the two sets of standards. However, an additional OCI item, *changes in revaluation surplus,* is possible under IFRS. In Chapter 11 you will learn that *IAS No. 16*[28] permits companies to value property, plant, and equipment at (1) cost less accumulated depreciation or (2) fair value (revaluation). *IAS No. 38*[29] provides a similar option for the valuation of intangible assets. U.S. GAAP prohibits revaluation.

If the revaluation option is chosen and fair value is higher than book value, the difference, changes in revaluation surplus, is reported as *other comprehensive income* and then accumulates in a revaluation surplus account in equity.

[28]"Property, Plant and Equipment," *International Accounting Standard No. 16* (IASCF), as amended effective January 1, 2014.
[29]"Intangible Assets," *International Accounting Standard No. 38* (IASCF), as amended effective January 1, 2014.

Accumulated Other Comprehensive Income

In addition to reporting OCI that occurs in the current reporting period, we must also report these amounts on a cumulative basis in the balance sheet. This is consistent with the way we report net income that occurs in the current reporting period in the income statement and also report accumulated net income (that hasn't been distributed as dividends) in the balance sheet as retained earnings. Similarly, we report OCI as it occurs in the current reporting period and also report **accumulated other comprehensive income (AOCI)** in the balance sheet. This is demonstrated in Illustration 4–13 for Astro-Med Inc.

The cumulative total of OCI (or comprehensive loss) is reported as accumulated other comprehensive income (AOCI), an additional component of shareholders' equity that is displayed separately.

Illustration 4–13

Shareholders' Equity—Astro-Med Inc.

Real World Financials

ASTRO-MED, INC.
Consolidated Balance Sheets (in part)
For the Years ended January 31

($ in thousands)	2014	2013
Shareholders' equity:		
Common stock	465	452
Additional paid-in capital	41,235	38,786
Retained earnings	37,201	36,092
Treasury stock, at cost	(12,463)	(11,666)
Accumulated other comprehensive income	176	173
Total shareholders' equity	$66,614	$63,837

Supplementing information in Illustration 4–13 with numbers reported in Illustration 4–12 along with dividends declared by Astro-Med, we can reconcile the changes in both retained earnings and AOCI:

($ in thousands)	Retained Earnings	Accumulated Other Comprehensive Income
Balance, 1/31/13	$36,092	$173
Add: Net income	3,212	
Deduct: Dividends	(2,103)	
Other comprehensive income		3
Balance, 1/31/14	$37,201	$176

AOCI increased by $3 thousand, from $173 thousand to $176 thousand.

To further understand the relationship between net income and other comprehensive income, consider another example. Suppose Philips Corporation began 2016 with retained earnings of $600 million and accumulated other comprehensive income of $34 million. Let's also assume that net income for 2016, before considering the gain discussed below, is $100 million, of which $40 million was distributed to shareholders as dividends. Now assume that Philips purchased shares of IBM stock for $90 million during the year and sold them at year-end for $100 million. In that case, Philips would include the realized gain of $10 million in determining net income. If the income tax rate is 40%, net income includes a $6 million net-of-tax gain from the sale. This means that shareholders' equity, specifically retained earnings, also will include the $6 million.

($ in millions)	Retained Earnings	Accumulated Other Comprehensive Income
Balance, 12/31/15	$600	$34
Net income ($100 + 6)	106	
Dividends	(40)	
Other comprehensive income		–0–
Balance, 12/31/16	$666	$34

$700

If the shares are not sold, the *unrealized* gain is part of other comprehensive income.

On the other hand, what if the shares are not sold before the end of the fiscal year but the year-end fair value is $100 million and Philips accounts for the shares as an other comprehensive income item? In that case, the *unrealized* gain of $10 million is not included in net income. Instead, $6 million net-of-tax gain is considered a component of *other comprehensive income (loss)* for 2016 and results in an increase in *accumulated other comprehensive income (loss)*, rather than retained earnings, in the 2016 balance sheet. The total of retained earnings and accumulated other comprehensive income is $700 million either way, as demonstrated below.

($ in millions)	Retained Earnings	Accumulated Other Comprehensive Income
Balance, 12/31/15	$600	$34
Net income	100	
Dividends	(40)	
Other comprehensive income		6
Balance, 12/31/16	$660	$40

$700

Net income and comprehensive income are identical for an enterprise that has no other comprehensive income items. When this occurs for all years presented, a statement of comprehensive income is not required. Components of other comprehensive income are described in subsequent chapters.

Concept Review Exercise

INCOME STATEMENT PRESENTATION; COMPREHENSIVE INCOME

The Barrington Construction Company builds office buildings. It also owns and operates a chain of motels throughout the Northwest. On September 30, 2016, the company decided to sell the entire motel business for $40 million. The sale was completed on December 15, 2016. Income statement information for 2016 is provided below for the two components of the company.

	($ in millions)	
	Construction Component	Motel Component
Sales revenue	$450.0	$200.0
Operating expenses	226.0	210.0
Other income (loss)*	16.0	(30.0)
Income (loss) before income taxes	$240.0	$ (40.0)
Income tax expense (benefit)†	96.0	(16.0)
Net income (loss)	$144.0	$ (24.0)

*For the motel component, the entire Other income (loss) amount represents the loss on sale of assets of the component for $40 million when their book value was $70 million.
†A 40% tax rate applies to all items of income or loss.

In addition, in 2016 the company had pretax net unrealized holding gains on investment securities of $3 million and a foreign currency translation adjustment gain of $1 million.

Required:

1. Prepare a single, continuous 2016 statement of comprehensive income for the Barrington Construction Company including EPS disclosures. There were 100 million shares of common stock outstanding throughout 2016. The company had no potentially dilutive

securities outstanding or stock options that could cause additional common shares. Use the multiple-step approach for the income statement portion of the statement.

2. Prepare a separate 2016 statement of comprehensive income.

Solution:

1. Prepare a single, continuous 2016 statement of comprehensive income.

BARRINGTON CONSTRUCTION COMPANY
Statement of Comprehensive Income
For the Year Ended December 31, 2016
($ in millions, except per share amounts)

Sales revenue		$450.0
Operating expenses		226.0
Operating income		224.0
Other income		16.0
Income from continuing operations before income taxes		240.0
Income tax expense		96.0
Income from continuing operations		144.0
Discontinued operations:		
Loss from operations of discontinued motel component (including loss on disposal of $30)	$(40)	
Income tax benefit	16	
Loss on discontinued operations		(24.0)
Net income		120.0
Other comprehensive income:		
Unrealized gains on investment securities, net of tax	1.8	
Foreign currency translation gain, net of tax	0.6	
Total other comprehensive income		2.4
Comprehensive income		$122.4
Earnings per share:		
Income from continuing operations		$ 1.44
Discontinued operations		(0.24)
Net income		$ 1.20

2. Prepare a separate 2016 statement of comprehensive income.

BARRINGTON CONSTRUCTION COMPANY
Statement of Comprehensive Income
For the Year Ended December 31, 2016
($ in millions)

Net income		$120.0
Other comprehensive income:		
Unrealized gains on investment securities, net of tax	1.8	
Foreign currency translation gain, net of tax	0.6	
Total other comprehensive income		2.4
Comprehensive income		$122.4

Now that we have discussed the presentation and content of the income statement, we turn our attention to the statement of cash flows.

PART B

The Statement of Cash Flows

● LO4–7

A statement of cash flows is presented for each period for which results of operations are provided.

In addition to the income statement and the balance sheet, a statement of cash flows (SCF) is an essential component within the set of basic financial statements.[30] Specifically, when a balance sheet and an income statement are presented, a statement of cash flows is required for each income statement period. The purpose of the SCF is to provide information about the cash receipts and cash disbursements of an enterprise that occurred during a period. Similar to the income statement, it is a *change* statement, summarizing the transactions that caused cash to change during a reporting period. The term *cash* refers to *cash plus cash equivalents*. Cash equivalents, discussed in Chapter 3, include highly liquid (easily converted to cash) investments such as Treasury bills. Chapter 21 is devoted exclusively to the SCF. A brief overview is provided here.

Usefulness of the Statement of Cash Flows

We discussed the difference between cash and accrual accounting in Chapter 1. It was pointed out and illustrated that over short periods of time, operating cash flows may not be indicative of the company's long-run cash-generating ability, and that accrual-based net income provides a more accurate prediction of future operating cash flows. Nevertheless, information about cash flows from operating activities, when combined with information about cash flows from other activities, can provide information helpful in assessing future profitability, liquidity, and long-term solvency. After all, a company must pay its debts with cash, not with income.

Of particular importance is the amount of cash generated from operating activities. In the long run, a company must be able to generate positive cash flow from activities related to selling its product or service. These activities must provide the necessary cash to pay debts, provide dividends to shareholders, and provide for future growth.

Classifying Cash Flows

● LO4–8

A list of cash flows is more meaningful to investors and creditors if they can determine the type of transaction that gave rise to each cash flow. Toward this end, the statement of cash flows classifies all transactions affecting cash into one of three categories: (1) operating activities, (2) investing activities, and (3) financing activities.

Operating Activities

Operating activities are inflows and outflows of cash related to the transactions entering into the determination of net operating income.

The inflows and outflows of cash that result from activities reported in the income statement are classified as cash flows from operating activities. In other words, this classification of cash flows includes the elements of net income reported on a cash basis rather than an accrual basis.[31]

Cash inflows include cash received from:

1. Customers from the sale of goods or services.
2. Interest and dividends from investments.

These amounts may differ from sales and investment income reported in the income statement. For example, sales revenue measured on the accrual basis reflects revenue earned during the period, not necessarily the cash actually collected. Revenue will not equal cash collected from customers if receivables from customers or deferred revenue changed during the period.

Cash outflows include cash paid for:

1. The purchase of inventory.
2. Salaries, wages, and other operating expenses.
3. Interest on debt.
4. Income taxes.

[30]FASB ASC 230–10–45: Statement of Cash Flows—Overall—Other Presentation Matters (previously "Statement of Cash Flows," *Statement of Financial Accounting Standards No. 95* (Norwalk, Conn.: FASB, 1987)).

[31]Cash flows related to gains and losses from the sale of assets shown in the income statement are reported as investing activities in the SCF.

Likewise, these amounts may differ from the corresponding accrual expenses reported in the income statement. Expenses are reported when incurred, not necessarily when cash is actually paid for those expenses. Also, some revenues and expenses, like depreciation expense, don't affect cash at all and aren't included as cash outflows from operating activities.

The difference between the inflows and outflows is called *net cash flows from operating activities.* This is equivalent to net income if the income statement had been prepared on a cash basis rather than an accrual basis.

International Financial Reporting Standards

LO4–9

Classification of Cash Flows. Like U.S. GAAP, international standards also require a statement of cash flows. Consistent with U.S. GAAP, cash flows are classified as operating, investing, or financing. However, the U.S. standard designates cash outflows for interest payments and cash inflows from interest and dividends received as operating cash flows. Dividends paid to shareholders are classified as financing cash flows.

IAS No. 7,[32] on the other hand, allows more flexibility. Companies can report interest and dividends paid as either operating or financing cash flows and interest and dividends received as either operating or investing cash flows. Interest and dividend payments usually are reported as financing activities. Interest and dividends received normally are classified as investing activities.

Typical Classification of Cash Flows from Interest and Dividends

U.S. GAAP	IFRS
Operating Activities	*Operating Activities*
Dividends received	
Interest received	
Interest paid	
Investing Activities	*Investing Activities*
	Dividends received
	Interest received
Financing Activities	*Financing Activities*
Dividends paid	Dividends paid
	Interest paid

Real World Financials

Siemens AG, a German company, prepares its financial statements according to IFRS. In its statement of cash flows for the first three months of the 2014 fiscal year, the company reported interest and dividends received as operating cash flows, as would a U.S. company. However, Siemens classified interest paid as a financing cash flow.

SIEMENS AG
Statement of Cash Flows (partial)
For the First Three Months of Fiscal 2014

(€ in millions)	
Cash flows from financing activities:	
Transactions with owners	(6)
Repayment of long-term debt	(5)
Change in short-term debt and other financing activities	1,138
Interest paid	(78)
Dividends paid	(4)
Financing discontinued operations	(107)
Cash flows from financing activities—continuing operations	938

[32]"Statement of Cash Flows," *International Accounting Standard No. 7* (IASCF), as amended effective January 1, 2014.

By the *direct method,* the cash effect of each operating activity is reported directly in the SCF.

DIRECT AND INDIRECT METHODS OF REPORTING. Two generally accepted formats can be used to report operating activities, the direct method and the indirect method. Under the **direct method**, the cash effect of each operating activity is reported directly in the statement. For example, *cash received from customers* is reported as the cash effect of sales activities. Income statement transactions that have no cash flow effect, such as depreciation, are simply not reported.

By the *indirect method,* cash flow from operating activities is derived indirectly by starting with reported net income and adding or subtracting items to convert that amount to a cash basis.

By the **indirect method**, on the other hand, we arrive at net cash flow from operating activities indirectly by starting with reported net income and working backwards to convert that amount to a cash basis. Two types of adjustments to net income are needed. First, components of net income that do not affect cash are reversed. That means that noncash revenues and gains are subtracted, while noncash expenses and losses are added. For example, depreciation expense does not reduce cash, but it is subtracted in the income statement. To reverse this, then, we add back depreciation expense to net income to arrive at the amount that we would have had if depreciation had not been subtracted.

Second, we make adjustments for changes in operating assets and liabilities during the period that indicate that amounts included as components of net income are not the same as cash flows for those components. For instance, suppose accounts receivable increases during the period because cash collected from customers is less than sales revenue. This increase in accounts receivable would then be subtracted from net income to arrive at *cash flow from operating activities.* In the indirect method, positive adjustments to net income are made for decreases in related assets and increases in related liabilities, while negative adjustments are made for increases in those assets and decreases in those liabilities.

To contrast the direct and indirect methods further, consider the example in Illustration 4–14.

Illustration 4–14

Contrasting the Direct and Indirect Methods of Presenting Cash Flows from Operating Activities

Arlington Lawn Care (ALC) began operations at the beginning of 2016. ALC's 2016 income statement and its year-end balance sheet are shown below ($ in thousands).

Net income is $35,000, but cash flow from these same activities is not necessarily the same amount.

ARLINGTON LAWN CARE
Income Statement
For the Year Ended December 31, 2016

Service revenue		$90
Operating expenses:		
General and administrative	$32*	
Depreciation	8	
Total operating expenses		40
Income before income taxes		50
Income tax expense		15
Net income		$35

*Includes $6 in insurance expense

ARLINGTON LAWN CARE
Balance Sheet
At December 31, 2016

Changes in assets and liabilities can indicate that cash inflows are different from revenues and cash outflows are different from expenses.

Assets		**Liabilities and Shareholders' Equity**	
Current assets:		Current liabilities:	
Cash	$ 54	Accounts payable**	$ 7
Accounts receivable	12	Income taxes payable	15
Prepaid insurance	4	Total current liabilities	22
Total current assets	70	Shareholders' equity:	
Equipment	40	Common stock	50
Less: Accumulated depreciation	(8)	Retained earnings	30***
Total assets	$102	Total liabilities and shareholders' equity	$102

**For general and administrative expenses

***Net income of $35 less $5 in cash dividends paid

DIRECT METHOD. Let's begin with the direct method of presentation. We illustrated this method previously in Chapter 2. In that chapter, specific cash transactions were provided and we simply included them in the appropriate cash flow category in the SCF. Here, we start with account balances, so the direct method requires a bit more reasoning.

From the income statement, we see that ALC's net income has four components. Three of those—service revenue, general and administrative expenses, and income tax expense—affect cash flows, but not by the accrual amounts reported in the income statement. One component—depreciation—reduces net income but not cash; it's simply an allocation over time of a prior year's expenditure for a depreciable asset. So, to report these operating activities on a cash basis, rather than an accrual basis, we take the three items that affect cash and adjust the amounts to reflect cash inflow rather than revenue earned and cash outflows rather than expenses incurred. Let's start with service revenue.

Service revenue is $90,000, but ALC did not collect that much cash from its customers. We know that because accounts receivable increased from $0 to $12,000, ALC must have collected to date only $78,000 of the amount earned.

Accounts receivable		
Beg. bal. 0		
Revenue 90		
	78	Cash
End bal. 12		

Similarly, general and administrative expenses of $32,000 were incurred, but $7,000 of that hasn't yet been paid. We know that because accounts payable increased by $7,000. Also, prepaid insurance increased by $4,000 so ALC must have paid $4,000 more cash for insurance coverage than the amount that expired and was reported as insurance expense. That means cash paid thus far for general and administrative expenses was only $29,000 ($32,000 less the $7,000 increase in accounts payable plus the $4,000 increase in prepaid insurance). The other expense, income tax, was $15,000, but that's the amount by which income taxes payable increased so no cash has yet been paid for income taxes.

We can report ALC's cash flows from operating activities using the direct method as shown in Illustration 4–14A.

Illustration 4–14A

Direct Method of Presenting Cash Flows from Operating Activities

ARLINGTON LAWN CARE
Statement of Cash Flows
For the Year Ended December 31, 2016

	($ in thousands)
Cash Flows from Operating Activities	
Cash received from customers*	$78
Cash paid for general and administrative expenses**	(29)
Net cash flows from operating activities	$49

*Service revenue of $90 thousand, less increase of $12 thousand in accounts receivable.

**General and administrative expenses of $32 thousand, less increase of $7 thousand in accounts payable, plus increase of $4 thousand in prepaid insurance.

By the direct method, we report the components of net income on a cash basis.

INDIRECT METHOD. To report operating cash flows using the indirect method, we take a different approach. We start with ALC's net income but realize that the $35,000 includes both cash and noncash components. We need to adjust net income, then, to eliminate the noncash effects so that we're left with only the cash flows. We start by eliminating the only noncash component of net income in our illustration—depreciation expense. Depreciation of $8,000 was subtracted in the income statement, so we simply add it back in to eliminate it.

Depreciation expense does not reduce cash, but is subtracted in the income statement. So, we add back depreciation expense to net income to eliminate it.

That leaves us with the three components that do affect cash but not by the amounts reported. For those, we need to make adjustments to net income to cause it to reflect cash flows rather than accrual amounts. For instance, we saw earlier that only $78,000 cash was received from customers even though $90,000 in revenue is reflected in net income. That means we need to include an adjustment to reduce net income by $12,000, the increase in accounts receivable. In a similar manner, we include adjustments for the changes in accounts payable, income taxes payable, and prepaid insurance to cause net income to reflect cash payments rather than expenses incurred. For accounts payable and taxes payable, because more was subtracted in the income statement than cash paid for the expenses related to these two liabilities, we need to add back the differences. Note that if these liabilities had decreased, we would have subtracted, rather

We make adjustments for changes in assets and liabilities that indicate that components of net income are not the same as cash flows.

than added, the changes. For prepaid insurance, because less was subtracted in the income statement than cash paid, we need to subtract the difference—the increase in prepaid insurance. If this asset had decreased, we would have added, rather than subtracted, the change.

Cash flows from operating activities using the indirect method are shown in Illustration 4–14B.

Illustration 4–14B
Indirect Method of Presenting Cash Flows from Operating Activities

By the indirect method, we start with net income and work backwards to convert that amount to a cash basis.

ARLINGTON LAWN CARE
Statement of Cash Flows
For the Year Ended December 31, 2016

		($ in thousands)
Cash Flows from Operating Activities		
Net income		$35
Adjustments for noncash effects:		
Depreciation expense	$ 8	
Changes in operating assets and liabilities:		
Increase in prepaid insurance	(4)	
Increase in accounts receivable	(12)	
Increase in accounts payable	7	
Increase in income taxes payable	15	14
Net cash flows from operating activities		$49

Both the direct and the indirect methods produce the same net cash flows from operating activities ($49 thousand in our illustration); they are merely alternative approaches to reporting the cash flows. The FASB, in promulgating GAAP for the statement of cash flows, stated its preference for the direct method. However, while both methods are used in practice, the direct method is infrequently used.

The choice of presentation method for cash flow from operating activities has no effect on how investing activities and financing activities are reported. We now look at how cash flows are classified into those two categories.

Investing Activities

***Investing activities* involve the acquisition and sale of (1) long-term assets used in the business and (2) nonoperating investment assets.**

Cash flows from **investing activities** include inflows and outflows of cash related to the acquisition and disposition of long-lived assets used in the operations of the business (such as property, plant, and equipment) and investment assets (except those classified as cash equivalents and trading securities). The purchase and sale of inventories are not considered investing activities. Inventories are purchased for the purpose of being sold as part of the company's operations, so their purchase and sale are included with operating activities rather than investing activities.

Cash outflows from investing activities include cash paid for:

1. The purchase of long-lived assets used in the business.
2. The purchase of investment securities like stocks and bonds of other entities (other than those classified as cash equivalents and trading securities).
3. Loans to other entities.

Later, when the assets are disposed of, cash inflow from the sale of the assets (or collection of loans and notes) also is reported as cash flows from investing activities. As a result, cash inflows from these transactions are considered investing activities:

1. The sale of long-lived assets used in the business.
2. The sale of investment securities (other than cash equivalents and trading securities).
3. The collection of a nontrade receivable (excluding the collection of interest, which is an operating activity).

Net cash flows from investing activities represents the difference between the inflows and outflows. The only investing activity indicated in Illustration 4–14 is ALC's investment of $40,000 cash for equipment.

Financing Activities

Financing activities relate to the external financing of the company. Cash inflows occur when cash is borrowed from creditors or invested by owners. Cash outflows occur when cash is paid back to creditors or distributed to owners. The payment of interest to a creditor, however, is classified as an operating activity.

Financing activities **involve cash inflows and outflows from transactions with creditors (excluding trade creditors) and owners.**

Cash inflows include cash received from:

1. Owners when shares are sold to them.
2. Creditors when cash is borrowed through notes, loans, mortgages, and bonds.

Cash outflows include cash paid to:

1. Owners in the form of dividends or other distributions.
2. Owners for the reacquisition of shares previously sold.
3. Creditors as repayment of the principal amounts of debt (excluding trade payables that relate to operating activities).

Net cash flows from financing activities is the difference between the inflows and outflows. The only financing activities indicated in Illustration 4–14 are ALC's receipt of $50,000 cash from issuing common stock and the payment of $5,000 in cash dividends.

Noncash Investing and Financing Activities

As we just discussed, the statement of cash flows provides useful information about the investing and financing activities in which a company is engaged. Even though these primarily result in cash inflows and cash outflows, there may be significant investing and financing activities occurring during the period that do not involve cash flows at all. In order to provide complete information about these activities, any significant noncash investing and financing activities (that is, noncash exchanges) are reported either on the face of the SCF or in a disclosure note. An example of a significant noncash investing and financing activity is the acquisition of equipment (an investing activity) by issuing either a long-term note payable or equity securities (a financing activity).

The 2016 statement of cash flows for ALC, beginning with net cash flows from operating activities, is shown in Illustration 4–15.

Illustration 4–15

Statement of Cash Flows (beginning with net cash flows from operating activities)

ARLINGTON LAWN CARE
Statement of Cash Flows (in part)
For the Year Ended December 31, 2016

		($ in thousands)
Net cash flows from operating activities		$49
Cash flows from investing activities:		
Purchase of equipment		(40)
Cash flows from financing activities:		
Sale of common stock	$50	
Payment of cash dividends	(5)	
Net cash flows from financing activities		45
Net increase in cash		54
Cash balance, January 1		0
Cash balance, December 31		$54

We know $40 thousand was paid to buy equipment because that balance sheet account increased from no balance to $40 thousand. Likewise, because common stock increased from zero to $50 thousand, we include that amount as a cash inflow from financing activities. Finally, Illustration 4–14 told us that $5 thousand was paid as a cash dividend, also a financing activity.

Concept Review Exercise

STATEMENT OF CASH FLOWS

Dublin Enterprises, Inc. (DEI), owns a chain of retail electronics stores located in shopping malls. The following are the company's 2016 income statement and comparative balance sheets ($ in millions):

Income Statement
For the Year Ended December 31, 2016

Revenue		$2,100
Cost of goods sold		1,400
Gross profit		700
Operating expenses:		
Selling and administrative	$ 355	
Depreciation	85	
Total operating expenses		440
Income before income taxes		260
Income tax expense		78
Net income		$ 182

Comparative Balance Sheets	12/31/16	12/31/15
Assets:		
Cash	$ 300	$ 220
Accounts receivable (net)	227	240
Inventory	160	120
Property, plant, and equipment	960	800
Less: Accumulated depreciation	(405)	(320)
Total assets	$1,242	$1,060
Liabilities and shareholders' equity:		
Accounts payable	$ 145	$ 130
Payables for selling and admin. expenses	147	170
Income taxes payable	95	50
Long-term debt	–0–	100
Common stock	463	400
Retained earnings	392	210
Total liabilities and shareholders' equity	$1,242	$1,060

Required:

1. Prepare DEI's 2016 statement of cash flows using the direct method.
2. Prepare the cash flows from operating activities section of DEI's 2016 statement of cash flows using the indirect method.

Solution:

1. Prepare DEI's 2016 statement of cash flows using the direct method.

DUBLIN ENTERPRISES, INC.
Statement of Cash Flows
For the Year Ended December 31, 2016
($ in millions)

Cash Flows from Operating Activities	
Collections from customers[1]	$2,113
Purchase of inventory[2]	(1,425)

[1]Sales revenue of $2,100 million, plus $13 million decrease in accounts receivable (net).
[2]Cost of goods sold of $1,400 million, plus $40 million increase in inventory, less $15 million increase in accounts payable.

(continued)

(concluded)

Payment of selling and administrative expenses[3]	(378)	
Payment of income taxes[4]	(33)	
Net cash flows from operating activities		$277
Cash Flows from Investing Activities		
Purchase of property, plant, and equipment		(160)
Cash Flows from Financing Activities		
Issuance of common stock	63	
Payment on long-term debt	(100)	
Net cash flows from financing activities		(37)
Net increase in cash		80
Cash, January 1		220
Cash, December 31		$300

[3]Selling and administrative expenses of $355 million, plus $23 million decrease in payables for selling and administrative expenses.
[4]Income tax expense of $78 million, less $45 million increase in income taxes payable.

2. Prepare the cash flows from operating activities section of DEI's 2016 statement of cash flows using the indirect method.

DUBLIN ENTERPRISES, INC.
Statement of Cash Flows
For the Year Ended December 31, 2016
($ in millions)

Cash Flows from Operating Activities		
Net Income	$182	
Adjustments for noncash effects:		
Depreciation expense	85	
Changes in operating assets and liabilities:		
Decrease in accounts receivable (net)	13	
Increase in inventory	(40)	
Increase in accounts payable	15	
Increase in income taxes payable	45	
Decrease in payables for selling and administrative expenses	(23)	
Net cash flows from operating activities		$277

Financial Reporting Case Solution

1. **How would you explain restructuring costs to Becky? Are restructuring costs something Becky should worry about?** *(p. 179)* Restructuring costs include employee severance and termination benefits plus other costs associated with the shutdown or relocation of facilities or downsizing of operations. Restructuring costs are not necessarily bad. In fact, the objective is to make operations more efficient. The costs are incurred now in hopes of better earnings later.
2. **Explain to Becky what is meant by discontinued operations and describe to her how that item is reported in an income statement.** *(p. 182)* Separate reporting as a discontinued operation is required when the disposal of a component represents a strategic shift that has, or will have, a major effect on a company's operations and financial results. The net-of-tax effect of discontinued operations is separately reported below income from continuing operations. If the component has been disposed of by the end

of the reporting period, the income effects include: (1) income or loss from operations of the discontinued component from the beginning of the reporting period through the disposal date and (2) gain or loss on disposal of the component's assets. If the component has not been disposed of by the end of the reporting period, the income effects include: (1) income or loss from operations of the discontinued component from the beginning of the reporting period through the end of the reporting period, and (2) an impairment loss if the fair value minus cost to sell of the component's assets is less than their book value.

3. **Describe to Becky the difference between basic and diluted earnings per share.** *(p. 188)* Basic earnings per share is computed by dividing net income available to common shareholders (net income less any preferred stock dividends) by the weighted-average number of common shares outstanding for the period. Diluted earnings per share reflects the potential dilution that could occur for companies that have certain securities outstanding that are convertible into common shares or stock options that could create additional common shares if the options were exercised. These items could cause earnings per share to decrease (become diluted). Because of the complexity of the calculation and the importance of earnings per share to investors, the text devotes a substantial portion of Chapter 19 to this topic. ●

The Bottom Line

- **LO4–1** The components of income from continuing operations are revenues, expenses (including income taxes), gains, and losses, excluding those related to discontinued operations. Companies often distinguish between operating and nonoperating income within continuing operations. *(p. 172)*
- **LO4–2** The term *earnings quality* refers to the ability of reported earnings (income) to predict a company's future earnings. The relevance of any historical-based financial statement hinges on its predictive value. To enhance predictive value, analysts try to separate a company's *transitory earnings* effects from its *permanent earnings.* Many believe that manipulating income reduces earnings quality because it can mask permanent earnings. Two major methods used by managers to manipulate earnings are (1) income shifting and (2) income statement classification. *(p. 177)*
- **LO4–3** Analysts begin their assessment of permanent earnings with income from continuing operations. It would be a mistake to assume income from continuing operations reflects permanent earnings entirely. In other words, there may be transitory earnings effects included in both operating and nonoperating income. *(p. 178)*
- **LO4–4** A discontinued operation refers to the disposal or planned disposal of a component of the entity. The net-of-tax effect of discontinued operations is separately reported below income from continuing operations. *(p. 182)*
- **LO4–5** Earnings per share (EPS) is the amount of income achieved during a period expressed per share of common stock outstanding. The EPS must be disclosed for income from continuing operations and for each item below continuing operations. *(p. 188)*
- **LO4–6** The FASB's Concept Statement 6 defines the term *comprehensive income* as the change in equity from nonowner transactions. The calculation of net income, however, excludes certain transactions that are included in comprehensive income. To convey the relationship between the two measures, companies must report both net income and comprehensive income and reconcile the difference between the two. The presentation can be (1) in a single, continuous statement of comprehensive income, or (2) in two separate, but consecutive statements—an income statement and a statement of comprehensive income. *(p. 189)*
- **LO4–7** When a company provides a set of financial statements that reports both financial position and results of operations, a statement of cash flows is reported for each period for which results of operations are

provided. The purpose of the statement is to provide information about the cash receipts and cash disbursements that occurred during the period. (*p. 194*)

● LO4–8 To enhance the usefulness of the information, the statement of cash flows classifies all transactions affecting cash into one of three categories: (1) operating activities, (2) investing activities, or (3) financing activities. (*p. 194*)

● LO4–9 There are more similarities than differences between income statements and statements of cash flows prepared according to U.S. GAAP and those prepared applying international standards. In a statement of cash flows, some differences are possible in the classifications of interest and divided revenue, interest expense, and dividends paid. (*pp. 177, 190, 195, and 204*) ●

APPENDIX 4

Interim Reporting

Financial statements covering periods of less than a year are called *interim reports.* Companies registered with the SEC, which includes most public companies, must submit quarterly reports, and you will see excerpts from these reports throughout this book.[33] Though there is no requirement to do so, most also send quarterly reports to their shareholders and typically include abbreviated, unaudited interim reports as supplemental information within their annual reports. For instance, Illustration 4A–1 shows the quarterly information disclosed in the annual report of **PetSmart, Inc.**, for the fiscal year ended February 2, 2014.

***Interim reports* are issued for periods of less than a year, typically as quarterly financial statements.**

PetSmart

For accounting information to be useful to decision makers, it must be available on a timely basis. One of the objectives of interim reporting is to enhance the timeliness of financial

Illustration 4A–1

Interim Data in Annual Report—PetSmart, Inc.

Real World Financials

Note 13—Selected Quarterly Financial Data (Unaudited)

Year Ended February 2, 2014	First Quarter (13 weeks)	Second Quarter (13 weeks)	Third Quarter (13 weeks)	Fourth Quarter (13 weeks)
	(In thousands, except per share data)			
Merchandise sales	$1,509,372	$1,492,457	$1,500,443	$1,609,430
Services sales	191,577	204,707	184,190	185,532
Other revenue	9,647	8,833	10,535	9,904
Net sales	1,710,596	1,705,997	1,695,168	1,804,866
Gross profit	529,746	515,220	504,973	565,998
Operating income	167,518	156,550	152,669	216,581
Income before income tax expense and equity income from Banfield	154,350	143,722	139,739	203,728
Net income	102,415	93,368	92,221	131,516
Earnings per common share:				
Basic	$ 0.99	$ 0.90	$ 0.89	$ 1.29
Diluted	$ 0.98	$ 0.89	$ 0.88	$ 1.28
Weighted average shares outstanding:				
Basic	103,305	103,474	103,957	102,076
Diluted	104,583	104,512	104,753	102,992

[33]Quarterly reports are filed with the SEC on Form 10-Q. Annual reports to the SEC are on Form 10-K.

The fundamental debate regarding interim reporting centers on the choice between the *discrete* and *integral part* approaches.

information. In addition, quarterly reports provide investors and creditors with additional insight on the seasonality of business operations that might otherwise get lost in annual reports.

However, the downside to these benefits is the relative unreliability of interim reporting. With a shorter reporting period, questions associated with estimation and allocation are magnified. For example, certain expenses often benefit an entire year's operations and yet are incurred primarily within a single interim period. Similarly, should smaller companies use lower tax rates in the earlier quarters and higher rates in later quarters as higher tax brackets are reached? Another result of shorter reporting periods is the intensified effect of unusual events such as material gains and losses. A second quarter casualty loss, for instance, that would reduce annual profits by 10% might reduce second quarter profits by 40% or more. Is it more realistic to allocate such a loss over the entire year? These and similar questions tend to hinge on the way we view an interim period in relation to the fiscal year. More specifically, should each interim period be viewed as a *discrete* reporting period or as an *integral part* of the annual period?

Reporting Revenues and Expenses

With only a few exceptions, the same accounting principles applicable to annual reporting are used for interim reporting.

Existing practice and current reporting requirements for interim reporting generally follow the viewpoint that interim reports are an integral part of annual statements, although the discrete approach is applied to some items. Most revenues and expenses are recognized using the same accounting principles applicable to annual reporting. Some modifications are necessary to help cause interim statements to relate better to annual statements. This is most evident in the way costs and expenses are recognized. Most are recognized in interim periods as incurred. But when an expenditure clearly benefits more than just the period in which it is incurred, the expense should be allocated among the periods benefited on an allocation basis consistent with the company's annual allocation procedures. For example, annual repair expenses, property tax expense, and advertising expenses incurred in the first quarter that clearly benefit later quarters are assigned to each quarter through the use of accruals and deferrals. Costs and expenses subject to year-end adjustments, such as depreciation expense, are estimated and allocated to interim periods in a systematic way. Similarly, income tax expense at each interim date should be based on estimates of the effective tax rate for the whole year. This would mean, for example, that if the estimated effective rate has changed since the previous interim period(s), the tax expense period would be determined as the new rate times the cumulative pretax income to date, less the total tax expense reported in previous interim periods.

Reporting Unusual Items

Discontinued operations and unusual items are reported entirely within the interim period in which they occur.

On the other hand, major events such as discontinued operations should be reported separately in the interim period in which they occur. That is, these amounts should not be allocated among individual quarters within the fiscal year. The same is true for items that are unusual. Treatment of these items is more consistent with the discrete view than the integral part view.

International Financial Reporting Standards

● LO4–9

Interim Reporting. *IAS No. 34* requires that a company apply the same accounting policies in its interim financial statements as it applies in its annual financial statements. Therefore, IFRS takes much more of a discrete-period approach than does U.S. GAAP. For example, costs for repairs, property taxes, and advertising that do not meet the definition of an asset at the end of an interim period are expensed entirely in the period in which they occur under IFRS, but are accrued or deferred and then charged to each of the periods they benefit under U.S. GAAP. This difference would tend to make interim period income more volatile under IFRS than under U.S. GAAP. However, as in U.S. GAAP, income taxes are accounted for based on an estimate of the tax rate expected to apply for the entire year.[43]

[43] "Interim Financial Reporting," *International Accounting Standard No. 34* (IASCF), as amended effective January 1, 2014, par. 28–30.

Earnings Per Share

A second item that is treated in a manner consistent with the discrete view is earnings per share. EPS calculations for interim reports follow the same procedures as annual calculations that you will study in Chapter 19. The calculations are based on conditions actually existing during the particular interim period rather than on conditions estimated to exist at the end of the fiscal year.

Quarterly EPS calculations follow the same procedures as annual calculations.

Reporting Accounting Changes

Recall that we account for a change in accounting principle retrospectively, meaning we recast prior years' financial statements when we report those statements again in comparative form. In other words, we make those statements appear as if the newly adopted accounting method had been used in those prior years. It's the same with interim reporting. We retrospectively report a change made during an interim period in similar fashion. Then in financial reports of subsequent interim periods of the same fiscal year, we disclose how that change affected (a) income from continuing operations, (b) net income, and (c) related per share amounts for the postchange interim period.

Accounting changes made in an interim period are reported by retrospectively applying the changes to prior financial statements.

Minimum Disclosures

Complete financial statements are not required for interim period reporting, but certain minimum disclosures are required as follows:[44]

- Sales, income taxes, and net income.
- Earnings per share.
- Seasonal revenues, costs, and expenses.
- Significant changes in estimates for income taxes.
- Discontinued operations and unusual items.
- Contingencies.
- Changes in accounting principles or estimates.
- Information about fair value of financial instruments and the methods and assumptions used to estimate fair values.
- Significant changes in financial position.

When fourth quarter results are not separately reported, material fourth quarter events, including year-end adjustments, should be reported in disclosure notes to annual statements.

Questions For Review of Key Topics

Q 4–1 The income statement is a change statement. Explain what is meant by this.

Q 4–2 What transactions are included in income from continuing operations? Briefly explain why it is important to segregate income from continuing operations from other transactions affecting net income.

Q 4–3 Distinguish between operating and nonoperating income in relation to the income statement.

Q 4–4 Briefly explain the difference between the single-step and multiple-step income statement formats.

Q 4–5 Explain what is meant by the term *earnings quality*.

Q 4–6 What are restructuring costs and where are they reported in the income statement?

Q 4–7 Define intraperiod tax allocation. Why is the process necessary?

Q 4–8 How are discontinued operations reported in the income statement?

Q 4–9 What is meant by a change in accounting principle? Describe the accounting treatment for a voluntary change in accounting principle.

[44]FASB ASC 270–10–50: Interim Reporting–Overall–Disclosure (previously "Interim Financial Reporting," *Accounting Principles Board Opinion No 28* (New York: AICPA, 1973)).

Q 4–10 Accountants very often are required to make estimates, and very often those estimates prove incorrect. In what period(s) is the effect of a change in an accounting estimate reported?

Q 4–11 The correction of a material error discovered in a year subsequent to the year the error was made is considered a prior period adjustment. Briefly describe the accounting treatment for prior period adjustments.

Q 4–12 Define earnings per share (EPS). For which income statement items must EPS be disclosed?

Q 4–13 Define comprehensive income. What are the two ways companies can present comprehensive income?

Q 4–14 Describe the purpose of the statement of cash flows.

Q 4–15 Identify and briefly describe the three categories of cash flows reported in the statement of cash flows.

Q 4–16 Explain what is meant by noncash investing and financing activities pertaining to the statement of cash flows. Give an example of one of these activities.

Q 4–17 Distinguish between the direct method and the indirect method for reporting the results of operating activities in the statement of cash flows.

Q 4–18 [Based on Appendix 4] Interim reports are issued for periods of less than a year, typically as quarterly financial statements. Should these interim periods be viewed as separate periods or integral parts of the annual period?

IFRS Q 4–19 Describe the potential statement of cash flows classification differences between U.S. GAAP and IFRS.

IFRS Q 4–20 [Based on Appendix 4] What is the primary difference between interim reports under IFRS and U.S. GAAP?

Brief Exercises

BE 4–1 Single-step income statement ● LO4–1

The adjusted trial balance of Pacific Scientific Corporation on December 31, 2016, the end of the company's fiscal year, contained the following income statement items ($ in millions): sales revenue, $2,106; cost of goods sold, $1,240; selling expenses, $126; general and administrative expenses, $105; interest expense, $35; and gain on sale of investments, $45. Income tax expense has not yet been recorded. The income tax rate is 40%. Prepare a single-step income statement for 2016. Ignore EPS disclosures.

BE 4–2 Multiple-step income statement ● LO4–1, LO4–3

Refer to the situation described in BE 4–1. If the company's accountant prepared a multiple-step income statement, what amount would appear in that statement for (a) operating income and (b) nonoperating income?

BE 4–3 Multiple-step income statement ● LO4–1, LO4–3

Refer to the situation described in BE 4–1. Prepare a multiple-step income statement for 2016. Ignore EPS disclosures.

BE 4–4 Multiple-step income statement ● LO4–1, LO4–3

The following is a partial year-end adjusted trial balance.

Account Title	Debits	Credits
Sales revenue		300,000
Loss on sale of investments	22,000	
Interest revenue		4,000
Cost of goods sold	160,000	
General and administrative expenses	40,000	
Restructuring costs	50,000	
Selling expenses	25,000	
Income tax expense	0	

Income tax expense has not yet been recorded. The income tax rate is 40%. Determine the following: (a) operating income (loss), (b) income (loss) before income taxes, and (c) net income (loss).

BE 4–5
Income from continuing operations
● LO4–3, LO4–5

The following are partial income statement account balances taken from the December 31, 2016, year-end trial balance of White and Sons, Inc.: restructuring costs, $300,000; interest revenue, $40,000; before-tax loss on discontinued operations, $400,000; and loss on sale of investments, $50,000. Income tax expense has not yet been recorded. The income tax rate is 40%. Prepare the lower portion of the 2016 income statement beginning with $850,000 income from continuing operations before income taxes. Include appropriate EPS disclosures. The company had 100,000 shares of common stock outstanding throughout the year.

BE 4–6
Discontinued operations
● LO4–4

On December 31, 2016, the end of the fiscal year, California Microtech Corporation completed the sale of its semiconductor business for $10 million. The business segment qualifies as a component of the entity according to GAAP. The book value of the assets of the segment was $8 million. The loss from operations of the segment during 2016 was $3.6 million. Pretax income from continuing operations for the year totaled $5.8 million. The income tax rate is 30%. Prepare the lower portion of the 2016 income statement beginning with pretax income from continuing operations. Ignore EPS disclosures.

BE 4–7
Discontinued operations
● LO4–4

Refer to the situation described in BE 4–6. Assume that the semiconductor segment was not sold during 2016 but was held for sale at year-end. The estimated fair value of the segment's assets, less costs to sell, on December 31 was $10 million. Prepare the lower portion of the 2016 income statement beginning with pretax income from continuing operations. Ignore EPS disclosures.

BE 4–8
Discontinued operations
● LO4–4

Refer to the situation described in BE 4–7. Assume instead that the estimated fair value of the segment's assets, less costs to sell, on December 31 was $7 million rather than $10 million. Prepare the lower portion of the 2016 income statement beginning with pretax income from continuing operations. Ignore EPS disclosures.

BE 4–9
Comprehensive income
● LO4–6

O'Reilly Beverage Company reported net income of $650,000 for 2016. In addition, the company deferred a $60,000 pretax loss on derivatives and had pretax net unrealized holding gains on investment securities of $40,000. Prepare a separate statement of comprehensive income for 2016. The company's income tax rate is 40%.

BE 4–10
Statement of cash flows; direct method
● LO4–8

The following are summary cash transactions that occurred during the year for Hilliard Healthcare Co. (HHC):

Cash received from:	
Customers	$660,000
Interest on note receivable	12,000
Collection of note receivable	100,000
Sale of land	40,000
Issuance of common stock	200,000
Cash paid for:	
Interest on note payable	18,000
Purchase of equipment	120,000
Operating expenses	440,000
Dividends to shareholders	30,000

Prepare the cash flows from operating activities section of HHC's statement of cash flows using the direct method.

BE 4–11
Statement of cash flows; investing and financing activities
● LO4–8

Refer to the situation described in BE 4–10. Prepare the cash flows from investing and financing activities sections of HHC's statement of cash flows.

BE 4–12
Statement of cash flows; indirect method
● LO4–8

Net income of Mansfield Company was $45,000. The accounting records reveal depreciation expense of $80,000 as well as increases in prepaid rent, salaries payable, and income taxes payable of $60,000, $15,000, and $12,000, respectively. Prepare the cash flows from operating activities section of Mansfield's statement of cash flows using the indirect method.

BE 4–13
IFRS; Statement of cash flows
● LO4–8, LO4–9

IFRS

Refer to the situation described in BE 4–10 and BE 4–11. How might your solution to those brief exercises differ if Hilliard Healthcare Co. prepares its statement of cash flows according to International Financial Reporting Standards?

Exercises

An alternate exercise and problem set is available in the Connect library.

E 4–1
Operating versus nonoperating income
● LO4–1

Pandora Corporation operates several factories in the Midwest that manufacture consumer electronics. The December 31, 2016, year-end trial balance contained the following income statement items:

Account Title	Debits	Credits
Sales revenue		12,500,000
Interest revenue		50,000
Loss on sale of investments	100,000	
Cost of goods sold	6,200,000	
Selling expenses	620,000	
General and administrative expenses	1,520,000	
Interest expense	40,000	
Research and development expense	1,200,000	
Income tax expense	900,000	

Required:
Calculate the company's operating income for the year.

E 4–2
Income statement format; single step and multiple step
● LO4–1, LO4–5

The following is a partial trial balance for the Green Star Corporation as of December 31, 2016:

Account Title	Debits	Credits
Sales revenue		1,300,000
Interest revenue		30,000
Gain on sale of investments		50,000
Cost of goods sold	720,000	
Selling expenses	160,000	
General and administrative expenses	75,000	
Interest expense	40,000	
Income tax expense	130,000	

100,000 shares of common stock were outstanding throughout 2016.

Required:
1. Prepare a single-step income statement for 2016, including EPS disclosures.
2. Prepare a multiple-step income statement for 2016, including EPS disclosures.

E 4–3
Income statement format; single step and multiple step
● LO4–1, LO4–3, LO4–5

The following is a partial trial balance for General Lighting Corporation as of December 31, 2016:

Account Title	Debits	Credits
Sales revenue		2,350,000
Interest revenue		80,000
Loss on sale of investments	22,500	
Cost of goods sold	1,200,300	
Loss from write-down of inventory due to obsolescence	200,000	
Selling expenses	300,000	
General and administrative expenses	150,000	
Interest expense	90,000	

300,000 shares of common stock were outstanding throughout 2016. Income tax expense has not yet been recorded. The income tax rate is 40%.

Required:
1. Prepare a single-step income statement for 2016, including EPS disclosures.
2. Prepare a multiple-step income statement for 2016, including EPS disclosures.

E 4–4
Multiple-step continuous statement of comprehensive income
● LO4–1, LO4–5, LO4–6

The trial balance for Lindor Corporation, a manufacturing company, for the year ended December 31, 2016, included the following income accounts:

Account Title	Debits	Credits
Sales revenue		2,300,000
Cost of goods sold	1,400,000	
Selling and administrative expenses	420,000	
Interest expense	40,000	
Unrealized holding gains on investment securities		80,000

The trial balance does not include the accrual for income taxes. Lindor's income tax rate is 30%. One million shares of common stock were outstanding throughout 2016.

Required:
Prepare a single, continuous multiple-step statement of comprehensive income for 2016, including appropriate EPS disclosures.

E 4–5
Income statement presentation
● LO4–1, LO4–5

The following *incorrect* income statement was prepared by the accountant of the Axel Corporation:

AXEL CORPORATION
Income Statement
For the Year Ended December 31, 2016

Revenues and gains:		
Sales		$592,000
Interest and dividends		32,000
Gain on sale of investments		86,000
Total revenues and gains		710,000
Expenses and losses:		
Cost of goods sold	$325,000	
Selling expenses	67,000	
Administrative expenses	87,000	
Interest	26,000	
Restructuring costs	55,000	
Income taxes	60,000	
Total expenses and losses		620,000
Net Income		$ 90,000
Earnings per share		$ 0.90

Required:
Prepare a multiple-step income statement for 2016 applying generally accepted accounting principles. The income tax rate is 40%.

E 4–6
Discontinued operations
● LO4–4, LO4–5

Chance Company had two operating divisions, one manufacturing farm equipment and the other office supplies. Both divisions are considered separate components as defined by generally accepted accounting principles. The farm equipment component had been unprofitable, and on September 1, 2016, the company adopted a plan to sell the assets of the division. The actual sale was completed on December 15, 2016, at a price of $600,000. The book value of the division's assets was $1,000,000, resulting in a before-tax loss of $400,000 on the sale.

The division incurred a before-tax operating loss from operations of $130,000 from the beginning of the year through December 15. The income tax rate is 40%. Chance's after-tax income from its continuing operations is $350,000.

Required:
Prepare an income statement for 2016 beginning with income from continuing operations. Include appropriate EPS disclosures assuming that 100,000 shares of common stock were outstanding throughout the year.

E 4–7
Income statement presentation; discontinued operations; restructuring costs
● LO4–1, LO4–3, LO4–4

Esquire Comic Book Company had income before tax of $1,000,000 in 2016 *before* considering the following material items:

1. Esquire sold one of its operating divisions, which qualified as a separate component according to generally accepted accounting principles. The before-tax loss on disposal was $350,000. The division generated before-tax income from operations from the beginning of the year through disposal of $500,000. Neither the loss on disposal nor the operating income is included in the $1,000,000 before-tax income the company generated from its other divisions.
2. The company incurred restructuring costs of $80,000 during the year.

Required:
Prepare a 2016 income statement for Esquire beginning with income from continuing operations. Assume an income tax rate of 40%. Ignore EPS disclosures.

E 4–8
Discontinued operations; disposal in subsequent year
● LO4–4

Kandon Enterprises, Inc., has two operating divisions; one manufactures machinery and the other breeds and sells horses. Both divisions are considered separate components as defined by generally accepted accounting principles. The horse division has been unprofitable, and on November 15, 2016, Kandon adopted a formal plan to sell the division. The sale was completed on April 30, 2017. At December 31, 2016, the component was considered held for sale.

On December 31, 2016, the company's fiscal year-end, the book value of the assets of the horse division was $250,000. On that date, the fair value of the assets, less costs to sell, was $200,000. The before-tax loss from operations of the division for the year was $140,000. The company's effective tax rate is 40%. The after-tax income from continuing operations for 2016 was $400,000.

Required:
1. Prepare a partial income statement for 2016 beginning with income from continuing operations. Ignore EPS disclosures.
2. Repeat requirement 1 assuming that the estimated net fair value of the horse division's assets was $400,000, instead of $200,000.

E 4–9
Discontinued operations; disposal in subsequent year; solving for unknown
● LO4–4

On September 17, 2016, Ziltech, Inc., entered into an agreement to sell one of its divisions that qualifies as a component of the entity according to generally accepted accounting principles. By December 31, 2016, the company's fiscal year-end, the division had not yet been sold, but was considered held for sale. The net fair value (fair value minus costs to sell) of the division's assets at the end of the year was $11 million. The pretax income from operations of the division during 2016 was $4 million. Pretax income from continuing operations for the year totaled $14 million. The income tax rate is 40%. Ziltech reported net income for the year of $7.2 million.

Required:
Determine the book value of the division's assets on December 31, 2016.

E 4–10
Earnings per share
● LO4–5

The Esposito Import Company had 1 million shares of common stock outstanding during 2016. Its income statement reported the following items: income from continuing operations, $5 million; loss from discontinued operations, $1.6 million. All of these amounts are net of tax.

Required:
Prepare the 2016 EPS presentation for the Esposito Import Company.

E 4–11
Comprehensive income
● LO4–6

The Massoud Consulting Group reported net income of $1,354,000 for its fiscal year ended December 31, 2016. In addition, during the year the company experienced a foreign currency translation adjustment gain of $240,000 and had unrealized losses on investment securities of $80,000. The company's effective tax rate on all items affecting comprehensive income is 30%. Each component of other comprehensive income is displayed net of tax.

Required:
Prepare a separate statement of comprehensive income for 2016.

E 4–12
Statement of cash flows; classifications
● LO4–8

The statement of cash flows classifies all cash inflows and outflows into one of the three categories shown below and lettered from a through c. In addition, certain transactions that do not involve cash are reported in the statement as noncash investing and financing activities, labeled d.

a. Operating activities
b. Investing activities
c. Financing activities
d. Noncash investing and financing activities

Required:
For each of the following transactions, use the letters above to indicate the appropriate classification category.

1. _____ Purchase of equipment for cash.
2. _____ Payment of employee salaries.
3. _____ Collection of cash from customers.
4. _____ Cash proceeds from a note payable.
5. _____ Purchase of common stock of another corporation for cash.

6._____ Issuance of common stock for cash.
7._____ Sale of equipment for cash.
8._____ Payment of interest on note payable.
9._____ Issuance of bonds payable in exchange for land and building.
10._____ Payment of cash dividends to shareholders.
11._____ Payment of principal on note payable.

E 4–13
Statement of cash flows preparation
● LO4–8

The following summary transactions occurred during 2016 for Bluebonnet Bakers:

Cash Received from:	
Customers	$380,000
Interest on note receivable	6,000
Principal on note receivable	50,000
Sale of investments	30,000
Proceeds from note payable	100,000
Cash Paid for:	
Purchase of inventory	160,000
Interest on note payable	5,000
Purchase of equipment	85,000
Salaries to employees	90,000
Principal on note payable	25,000
Payment of dividends to shareholders	20,000

The balance of cash and cash equivalents at the beginning of 2016 was $17,000.

Required:
Prepare a statement of cash flows for 2016 for Bluebonnet Bakers. Use the direct method for reporting operating activities.

E 4–14
IFRS; statement of cash flows
● LO4–8, LO4–9

IFRS

Refer to the situation described in E 4–13.

Required:
Prepare the statement of cash flows assuming that Bluebonnet prepares its financial statements according to International Financial Reporting Standards. Where IFRS allows flexibility, use the classification used most often in IFRS financial statements.

E 4–15
Indirect method; reconciliation of net income to net cash flows from operating activities
● LO4–8

The accounting records of Hampton Company provided the data below ($ in 000s).

Net income	$17,300
Depreciation expense	7,800
Increase in accounts receivable	4,000
Decrease in inventory	5,500
Decrease in prepaid insurance	1,200
Decrease in salaries payable	2,700
Increase in interest payable	800

Required:
Prepare a reconciliation of net income to net cash flows from operating activities.

E 4–16
Statement of cash flows; directly from transactions
● LO4–8

The following transactions occurred during March 2016 for the Wainwright Corporation. The company owns and operates a wholesale warehouse. [These are the same transactions analyzed in Exercise 2–1, when we determined their effect on elements of the accounting equation.]

1. Issued 30,000 shares of capital stock in exchange for $300,000 in cash.
2. Purchased equipment at a cost of $40,000. $10,000 cash was paid and a note payable was signed for the balance owed.
3. Purchased inventory on account at a cost of $90,000. The company uses the perpetual inventory system.
4. Credit sales for the month totaled $120,000. The cost of the goods sold was $70,000.
5. Paid $5,000 in rent on the warehouse building for the month of March.
6. Paid $6,000 to an insurance company for fire and liability insurance for a one-year period beginning April 1, 2016.
7. Paid $70,000 on account for the merchandise purchased in 3.
8. Collected $55,000 from customers on account.
9. Recorded depreciation expense of $1,000 for the month on the equipment.

Required:

1. Analyze each transaction and classify each as a financing, investing, and/or operating activity (a transaction can represent more than one type of activity). In doing so, also indicate the cash effect of each, if any. If there is no cash effect, simply place a check mark (√) in the appropriate column(s).

   Example:

Operating	Investing	Financing
1.		$300,000

2. Prepare a statement of cash flows, using the direct method to present cash flows from operating activities. Assume the cash balance at the beginning of the month was $40,000.

E 4–17
Statement of cash flows; indirect method
● LO4–8

Cemptex Corporation prepares its statement of cash flows using the indirect method to report operating activities. Net income for the 2016 fiscal year was $624,000. Depreciation and amortization expense of $87,000 was included with operating expenses in the income statement. The following information describes the changes in current assets and liabilities other than cash:

Decrease in accounts receivable	$22,000
Increase in inventories	9,200
Increase prepaid expenses	8,500
Increase in salaries payable	10,000
Decrease in income taxes payable	14,000

Required:

Prepare the operating activities section of the 2016 statement of cash flows.

E 4–18
Statement of cash flows; indirect method
● LO4–8

Chew Corporation prepares its statement of cash flows using the indirect method of reporting operating activities. Net income for the 2016 fiscal year was $1,250,000. Depreciation expense of $140,000 was included with operating expenses in the income statement. The following information describes the changes in current assets and liabilities other than cash:

Increase in accounts receivable	$152,000
Decrease in inventories	108,000
Decrease prepaid expenses	62,000
Decrease in salaries payable	30,000
Increase in income taxes payable	44,000

Required:

Calculate cash flows from operating activities for 2016.

E 4–19
IFRS; statement of cash flows
● LO4–8, LO4–9

The statement of cash flows for the year ended December 31, 2016, for Bronco Metals is presented below.

BRONCO METALS
Statement of Cash Flows
For the Year Ended December 31, 2016

Cash flows from operating activities:		
Collections from customers	$ 353,000	
Interest on note receivable	4,000	
Dividends received from investments	2,400	
Purchase of inventory	(186,000)	
Payment of operating expenses	(67,000)	
Payment of interest on note payable	(8,000)	
Net cash flows from operating activities		$ 98,400
Cash flows from investing activities:		
Collection of note receivable	100,000	
Purchase of equipment	(154,000)	
Net cash flows from investing activities		(54,000)

(continued)

(concluded)

Cash flows from financing activities:		
Proceeds from issuance of common stock	200,000	
Dividends paid	(40,000)	
Net cash flows from financing activities		160,000
Net increase in cash		204,400
Cash and cash equivalents, January 1		28,600
Cash and cash equivalents, December 31		$233,000

Required:

Prepare the statement of cash flows assuming that Bronco prepares its financial statements according to International Financial Reporting Standards. Where IFRS allows flexibility, use the classification used most often in IFRS financial statements.

E 4–20
Statement of cash flows; indirect method
● LO4–8

Presented below is the 2016 income statement and comparative balance sheet information for Tiger Enterprises.

TIGER ENTERPRISES
Income Statement
For the Year Ended December 31, 2016

($ in thousands)		
Sales revenue		$7,000
Operating expenses:		
Cost of goods sold	$3,360	
Depreciation	240	
Insurance	100	
Administrative and other	1,800	
Total operating expenses		5,500
Income before income taxes		1,500
Income tax expense		600
Net income		$ 900

Balance Sheet Information ($ in thousands)	**Dec. 31, 2016**	**Dec. 31, 2015**
Assets:		
Cash	$ 300	$ 200
Accounts receivable	750	830
Inventory	640	600
Prepaid insurance	50	20
Plant and equipment	2,100	1,800
Less: Accumulated depreciation	(840)	(600)
Total assets	$3,000	$2,850
Liabilities and Shareholders' Equity:		
Accounts payable	$ 300	$ 360
Payables for administrative and other expenses	300	400
Income taxes payable	200	150
Note payable (due 12/31/2017)	800	600
Common stock	900	800
Retained earnings	500	540
Total liabilities and shareholders' equity	$3,000	$2,850

Required:

Prepare Tiger's statement of cash flows, using the indirect method to present cash flows from operating activities. (Hint: You will have to calculate dividend payments.)

E 4–21
Statement of cash flows; direct method
● LO4–8

Refer to the situation described in E 4–20.

Required:

Prepare the cash flows from operating activities section of Tiger's 2016 statement of cash flows using the direct method. Assume that all purchases and sales of inventory are on account, and that there are no anticipated bad debts for accounts receivable. (Hint: Use T-accounts for the pertinent items to isolate the information needed for the statement.)

E 4–22
FASB codification research
● LO4–5

The *FASB Accounting Standards Codification* represents the single source of authoritative U.S. generally accepted accounting principles.

Required:

1. Obtain the relevant authoritative literature on earnings per share using the *FASB Accounting Standards Codification* at the FASB website (asc.fasb.org). Identify the Codification topic number that provides the accounting for earnings per share.
2. What is the specific citation that describes the additional information for earnings per share that must be included in the notes to the financial statements?
3. Describe the required disclosures.

E 4–23
FASB codification research
● LO4–5, LO4–6, LO4–8

Access the *FASB Accounting Standards Codification* at the FASB website (asc.fasb.org). Determine the specific citation for each of the following items:

1. The calculation of the weighted average number of shares for basic earnings per share purposes.
2. The alternative formats permissible for reporting comprehensive income.
3. The classifications of cash flows required in the statement of cash flows.

E 4–24
Concepts; terminology
● LO4–1 through LO4–4, LO4–5 through LO4–8

Listed below are several terms and phrases associated with income statement presentation and the statement of cash flows. Pair each item from List A (by letter) with the item from List B that is most appropriately associated with it.

List A	List B
_____ 1. Intraperiod tax allocation	a. An other comprehensive income item.
_____ 2. Comprehensive income	b. Starts with net income and works backwards to convert to cash.
_____ 3. Unrealized holding gain on investments	c. Reports the cash effects of each operating activity directly on the statement.
_____ 4. Operating income	d. Correction of a material error of a prior period.
_____ 5. A discontinued operation	e. Related to the external financing of the company.
_____ 6. Earnings per share	f. Associates tax with income statement item.
_____ 7. Prior period adjustment	g. Total nonowner change in equity.
_____ 8. Financing activities	h. Related to the transactions entering into the determination of net income.
_____ 9. Operating activities (SCF)	i. Related to the acquisition and disposition of long-term assets.
_____10. Investing activities	j. Required disclosure for publicly traded corporation.
_____11. Direct method	k. A component of an entity.
_____12. Indirect method	l. Directly related to principal revenue-generating activities.

E 4–25
Interim financial statements; income tax expense
● Appendix 4

Joplin Laminating Corporation reported income before income taxes during the first three quarters, and management's estimates of the annual effective tax rate at the end of each quarter as shown below:

	Quarter		
	First	**Second**	**Third**
Income before income taxes	$50,000	$40,000	$100,000
Estimated annual effective tax rate	34%	30%	36%

Required:

Determine the income tax expense to be reported in the income statement in each of the three quarterly reports.

E 4–26
Interim reporting; recognizing expenses
● Appendix 4

Security-Rand Corporation determines executive incentive compensation at the end of its fiscal year. At the end of the first quarter, management estimated that the amount will be $300 million. Depreciation expense for the year is expected to be $60 million. Also during the quarter, the company realized a gain of $23 million from selling two of its manufacturing plants.

Required:

What amounts for these items should be reported in the first quarter's income statement?

E 4–27
Interim financial statements; reporting expenses
● Appendix 4

Shields Company is preparing its interim report for the second quarter ending June 30. The following payments were made during the first two quarters:

Required:

Expenditure	Date	Amount
Annual advertising	January	$800,000
Property tax for the fiscal year	February	350,000
Annual equipment repairs	March	260,000
One-time research and development fee to consultant	May	96,000

For each expenditure, indicate the amount that would be reported in the quarterly income statements for the periods ending March 31, June 30, September 30, and December 31.

E 4–28
Interim financial statements
● Appendix 4

Assume the same facts as in E 4–27, but that Shields Company reports under IFRS. For each expenditure, indicate the amount that would be reported in the quarterly income statements for the periods ending March 31, June 30, September 30, and December 31.

CPA and CMA Review Questions

CPA Exam Questions

KAPLAN CPA REVIEW

The following questions are adapted from a variety of sources including questions developed by the AICPA Board of Examiners and those used in the Kaplan CPA Review Course to study the income statement and statement of cash flows while preparing for the CPA examination. Determine the response that best completes the statements or questions.

● LO4–4

1. Roco Company manufactures both industrial and consumer electronics. Due to a change in its strategic focus, the company decided to exit the consumer electronics business, and in 2016 sold the division to Sunny Corporation. The consumer electronics division qualifies as a component of the entity according to GAAP. How should Roco report the sale in its 2016 income statement?
   a. Include in income from continuing operations as a nonoperating gain or loss.
   b. As restructuring costs.
   c. As a discontinued operation, reported below income from continuing operations.
   d. None of the above.

● LO4–3, LO4–4

2. Bridge Company's results for the year ended December 31, 2016, include the following material items:

Sales revenue	$5,000,000
Cost of goods sold	3,000,000
Administrative expenses	1,000,000
Gain on sale of equipment	200,000
Loss on discontinued operations	400,000
Understatement of depreciation expense in 2015 caused by mathematical error	250,000

   Bridge Company's income from continuing operations before income taxes for 2016 is:
   a. $700,000
   b. $950,000
   c. $1,000,000
   d. $1,200,000

● LO4–4

3. In Baer Food Co.'s 2016 single-step income statement, the section titled "Revenues" consisted of the following:

Net sales revenue	$187,000
Income on discontinued operations, including gain on disposal of $21,000, and tax expense of $6,000	13,500
Interest revenue	10,200
Gain on sale of equipment	4,700
Total revenues	$215,400

   In the revenues section of the 2016 income statement, Baer Food should have reported total revenues of
   a. $201,900
   b. $203,700
   c. $215,400
   d. $216,300

● LO4–4

4. On November 30, 2016, Pearman Company committed to a plan to sell a division that qualified as a component of the entity according to GAAP, and was properly classified as held for sale on December 31, 2016, the end of the company's fiscal year. The division was tested for impairment and a $400,000 loss was indicated. The division's loss from operations for 2016 was $1,000,000. The final sale was expected to occur on February 15, 2017. What before-tax amount(s) should Pearman report as loss on discontinued operations in its 2016 income statement?
   a. $1,400,000 loss.
   b. $400,000 loss.

c. None.
d. $400,000 impairment loss included in continuing operations and a $1,000,000 loss from discontinued operations.

● LO4–8

5. Which of the following items is *not* considered an operating cash flow in the statement of cash flows?
a. Dividends paid to stockholders.
b. Cash received from customers.
c. Interest paid to creditors.
d. Cash paid for salaries.

● LO4–8

6. Which of the following items is *not* considered an investing cash flow in the statement of cash flows?
a. Purchase of equipment.
b. Purchase of securities.
c. Issuing common stock for cash.
d. Sale of land.

International Financial Reporting Standards are tested on the CPA exam along with U.S. GAAP. The following questions deal with the application of IFRS.

● LO4–9

IFRS

7. In a statement of cash flows prepared under IFRS, interest paid
a. Must be classified as an operating cash flow.
b. Can be classified as either an operating cash flow or an investing cash flow.
c. Can be classified as either an operating cash flow or a financing cash flow.
d. Can be classified as either an investing cash flow or a financing cash flow.

CMA Exam Questions

The following questions dealing with the income statement are adapted from questions that previously appeared on Certified Management Accountant (CMA) examinations. The CMA designation sponsored by the Institute of Management Accountants (www.imanet.org) provides members with an objective measure of knowledge and competence in the field of management accounting. Determine the response that best completes the statements or questions.

● LO4–1

1. Which one of the following items is not included in the determination of income from continuing operations?
a. Discontinued operations.
b. Restructuring costs.
c. Long-lived asset impairment loss.
d. Unusual loss from a write-down of inventory.

● LO4–3

2. In a multiple-step income statement for a retail company, all of the following are included in the operating section except
a. Sales.
b. Cost of goods sold.
c. Dividend revenue.
d. Administrative and selling expenses.

Problems

An alternate exercise and problem set is available in the Connect library.

P 4–1
Comparative income statements; multiple-step format
● LO4–1, LO4–3, LO4–4, LO4–5

Selected information about income statement accounts for the Reed Company is presented below (the company's fiscal year ends on December 31):

	2016	2015
Sales	$4,400,000	$3,500,000
Cost of goods sold	2,860,000	2,000,000
Administrative expenses	800,000	675,000
Selling expenses	360,000	312,000
Interest revenue	150,000	140,000
Interest expense	200,000	200,000
Loss on sale of assets of discontinued component	50,000	—

On July 1, 2016, the company adopted a plan to discontinue a division that qualifies as a component of an entity as defined by GAAP. The assets of the component were sold on September 30, 2016, for $50,000 less than their book value. Results of operations for the component (*included* in the above account balances) were as follows:

	1/1/16–9/30/16	2015
Sales	$400,000	$500,000
Cost of goods sold	(290,000)	(320,000)
Administrative expenses	(50,000)	(40,000)
Selling expenses	(20,000)	(30,000)
Operating income before taxes	$ 40,000	$110,000

In addition to the account balances above, several events occurred during 2016 that have *not* yet been reflected in the above accounts:

1. A fire caused $50,000 in uninsured damages to the main office building. The fire was considered to be an infrequent but not unusual event.
2. Inventory that had cost $40,000 had become obsolete because a competitor introduced a better product. The inventory was sold as scrap for $5,000.
3. Income taxes have not yet been recorded.

Required:
Prepare a multiple-step income statement for the Reed Company for 2016, showing 2015 information in comparative format, including income taxes computed at 40% and EPS disclosures assuming 300,000 shares of common stock.

P 4–2
Discontinued operations
● LO4–4

The following condensed income statements of the Jackson Holding Company are presented for the two years ended December 31, 2016 and 2015:

	2016	2015
Sales	$15,000,000	$9,600,000
Cost of goods sold	9,200,000	6,000,000
Gross profit	5,800,000	3,600,000
Operating expenses	3,200,000	2,600,000
Operating income	2,600,000	1,000,000
Gain on sale of division	600,000	—
	3,200,000	1,000,000
Income tax expense	1,280,000	400,000
Net income	$ 1,920,000	$ 600,000

On October 15, 2016, Jackson entered into a tentative agreement to sell the assets of one of its divisions. The division qualifies as a component of an entity as defined by GAAP. The division was sold on December 31, 2016, for $5,000,000. Book value of the division's assets was $4,400,000. The division's contribution to Jackson's operating income before-tax for each year was as follows:

2016	$400,000 loss
2015	$300,000 loss

Assume an income tax rate of 40%.

Required:

1. Prepare revised income statements according to generally accepted accounting principles, beginning with income from continuing operations before income taxes. Ignore EPS disclosures.
2. Assume that by December 31, 2016, the division had not yet been sold but was considered held for sale. The fair value of the division's assets on December 31 was $5,000,000. How would the presentation of discontinued operations be different from your answer to requirement 1?
3. Assume that by December 31, 2016, the division had not yet been sold but was considered held for sale. The fair value of the division's assets on December 31 was $3,900,000. How would the presentation of discontinued operations be different from your answer to requirement 1?

P 4–3
Income statement presentation
● LO4–4

For the year ending December 31, 2016, Micron Corporation had income from continuing operations before taxes of $1,200,000 before considering the following transactions and events. All of the items described below are before taxes and the amounts should be considered material.

1. In November 2016, Micron sold its Waffle House restaurant chain that qualified as a component of an entity. The company had adopted a plan to sell the chain in May 2016. The income from operations of the chain from January 1, 2016, through November was $160,000 and the loss on sale of the chain's assets was $300,000.

2. In 2016, Micron sold one of its six factories for $1,200,000. At the time of the sale, the factory had a book value of $1,100,000. The factory was not considered a component of the entity.
3. In 2014, Micron's accountant omitted the annual adjustment for patent amortization expense of $120,000. The error was not discovered until December 2016.

Required:
Prepare Micron's income statement, beginning with income from continuing operations before taxes, for the year ended December 31, 2016. Assume an income tax rate of 30%. Ignore EPS disclosures.

P 4–4
Income statement presentation; unusual items
● LO4–3, LO4–4

The preliminary 2016 income statement of Alexian Systems, Inc., is presented below:

ALEXIAN SYSTEMS, INC.
Income Statement
For the Year Ended December 31, 2016
($ in millions, except earnings per share)

Revenues and gains:	
Net sales	$ 425
Interest	3
Other income	126
Total revenues and gains	554
Expenses:	
Cost of goods sold	270
Selling and administrative	154
Income taxes	52
Total expenses	476
Net Income	$ 78
Earnings per share	$3.90

Additional Information:
1. Selling and administrative expenses include $26 million in restructuring costs.
2. Included in other income is $120 million in income from a discontinued operation. This consists of $90 million in operating income and a $30 million gain on disposal. The remaining $6 million is from the gain on sale of investments.
3. Cost of goods sold was increased by $5 million to correct an error in the calculation of 2015's ending inventory. The amount is material.

Required:
For each of the three additional facts listed in the additional information, discuss the appropriate presentation of the item described. Do not prepare a revised statement.

P 4–5
Income statement presentation; unusual items
● LO4–1, LO4–3, LO4–4, LO4–5

[This is a variation of the previous problem focusing on income statement presentation.]

Required:
Refer to the information presented in P 4–4. Prepare a revised income statement for 2016 reflecting the additional facts. Use a multiple-step format. Assume that an income tax rate of 40% applies to all income statement items, and that 20 million shares of common stock were outstanding throughout the year.

P 4–6
Income statement presentation
● LO4–1, LO4–3, LO4–4, LO4–5

Rembrandt Paint Company had the following income statement items for the year ended December 31, 2016 ($ in 000s):

Net sales	$18,000	Cost of goods sold	$10,500
Interest income	200	Selling and administrative expenses	2,500
Interest expense	350	Restructuring costs	800

In addition, during the year the company completed the disposal of its plastics business and incurred a loss from operations of $1.6 million and a gain on disposal of the component's assets of $2 million. 500,000 shares of common stock were outstanding throughout 2016. Income tax expense has not yet been recorded. The income tax rate is 30% on all items of income (loss).

Required:

Prepare a multiple-step income statement for 2016, including EPS disclosures.

P 4–7
Income statement presentation; statement of comprehensive income; unusual items
● LO4–1, LO4–3 through LO4–6

The following income statement items appeared on the adjusted trial balance of Schembri Manufacturing Corporation for the year ended December 31, 2016 ($ in 000s): sales revenue, $15,300; cost of goods sold, $6,200; selling expenses, $1,300; general and administrative expenses, $800; interest revenue, $85; interest expense, $180. Income taxes have not yet been recorded. The company's income tax rate is 40% on all items of income or loss. These revenue and expense items appear in the company's income statement every year. The company's controller, however, has asked for your help in determining the appropriate treatment of the following nonrecurring transactions that also occurred during 2016 ($ in 000s). All transactions are material in amount.

1. Investments were sold during the year at a loss of $220. Schembri also had unrealized gains of $320 for the year on investments.
2. One of the company's factories was closed during the year. Restructuring costs incurred were $1,200.
3. During the year, Schembri completed the sale of one of its operating divisions that qualifies as a component of the entity according to GAAP. The division had incurred a loss from operations of $560 in 2016 prior to the sale, and its assets were sold at a gain of $1,400.
4. In 2016, the company's accountant discovered that depreciation expense in 2015 for the office building was understated by $200.
5. Foreign currency translation losses for the year totaled $240.

Required:

1. Prepare Schembri's single, continuous multiple-step statement of comprehensive income for 2016, including earnings per share disclosures. One million shares of common stock were outstanding at the beginning of the year and an additional 400,000 shares were issued on July 1, 2016.
2. Prepare a separate statement of comprehensive income for 2016.

P 4–8
Multiple-step statement of income and comprehensive income
● LO4–1, LO4–3, LO4–6

Duke Company's records show the following account balances at December 31, 2016:

Sales	$15,000,000
Cost of goods sold	9,000,000
General and administrative expenses	1,000,000
Selling expenses	500,000
Interest expense	700,000

Income tax expense has not yet been determined. The following events also occurred during 2016. All transactions are material in amount.

1. $300,000 in restructuring costs were incurred in connection with plant closings.
2. Inventory costing $400,000 was written off as obsolete. Material losses of this type are considered to be unusual.
3. It was discovered that depreciation expense for 2015 was understated by $50,000 due to a mathematical error.
4. The company experienced a foreign currency translation adjustment loss of $200,000 and had unrealized gains on investments of $180,000.

Required:

Prepare a single, continuous multiple-step statement of comprehensive income for 2016. The company's effective tax rate on all items affecting comprehensive income is 40%. Each component of other comprehensive income should be displayed net of tax. Ignore EPS disclosures.

P 4–9
Statement of cash flows
● LO4–8

The Diversified Portfolio Corporation provides investment advice to customers. A condensed income statement for the year ended December 31, 2016, appears below:

Service revenue	$900,000
Operating expenses	700,000
Income before income taxes	200,000
Income tax expense	80,000
Net income	$120,000

The following balance sheet information also is available:

	12/31/16	12/31/15
Cash	$275,000	$ 70,000
Accounts receivable	120,000	100,000
Accounts payable (operating expenses)	70,000	60,000
Income taxes payable	10,000	15,000

In addition, the following transactions took place during the year:

1. Common stock was issued for $100,000 in cash.
2. Long-term investments were sold for $50,000 in cash. The original cost of the investments also was $50,000.
3. $80,000 in cash dividends was paid to shareholders.
4. The company has no outstanding debt, other than those payables listed above.
5. Operating expenses include $30,000 in depreciation expense.

Required:

1. Prepare a statement of cash flows for 2016 for the Diversified Portfolio Corporation. Use the direct method for reporting operating activities.
2. Prepare the cash flows from operating activities section of Diversified's 2016 statement of cash flows using the indirect method.

P 4–10
Integration of financial statements; Chapters 3 and 4
● LO4–8

The chief accountant for Grandview Corporation provides you with the company's 2016 statement of cash flows and income statement. The accountant has asked for your help with some missing figures in the company's comparative balance sheets. These financial statements are shown next ($ in millions).

GRANDVIEW CORPORATION
Statement of Cash Flows
For the Year Ended December 31, 2016

Cash Flows from Operating Activities:		
Collections from customers	$71	
Payment to suppliers	(30)	
Payment of general & administrative expenses	(18)	
Payment of income taxes	(9)	
Net cash flows from operating activities		$14
Cash Flows from Investing Activities:		
Sale of investments		65
Cash Flows from Financing Activities:		
Issuance of common stock	10	
Payment of dividends	(3)	
Net cash flows from financing activities		7
Net increase in cash		$86

GRANDVIEW CORPORATION
Income Statement
For the Year Ended December 31, 2016

Sales revenue		$80
Cost of goods sold		32
Gross profit		48
Operating expenses:		
General and administrative	$18	
Depreciation	10	
Total operating expenses		28
Operating income		20
Other income:		
Gain on sale of investments		15
Income before income taxes		35
Income tax expense		7
Net income		$28

GRANDVIEW CORPORATION
Balance Sheets
At December 31

	2016	2015
Assets:		
Cash	$145	$?
Accounts receivable	?	84
Investments	—	50
Inventory	60	?
Property, plant & equipment	150	150
Less: Accumulated depreciation	(65)	?
Total assets	?	?

(continued)

(concluded)

Liabilities and Shareholders' Equity:		
Accounts payable to suppliers	$ 40	$ 30
Payables for selling & admin. expenses	9	9
Income taxes payable	22	?
Common stock	240	230
Retained earnings	?	47
Total liabilities and shareholders' equity	?	?

Required:

1. Calculate the missing amounts.
2. Prepare the operating activities section of Grandview's 2016 statement of cash flows using the indirect method.

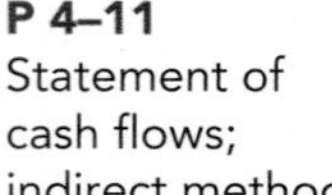

P 4–11
Statement of cash flows; indirect method
● LO4–8

Presented below are the 2016 income statement and comparative balance sheets for Santana Industries.

SANTANA INDUSTRIES
Income Statement
For the Year Ended December 31, 2016
($ in thousands)

Sales revenue	$14,250	
Service revenue	3,400	
Total revenue		$17,650
Operating expenses:		
Cost of goods sold	7,200	
Selling	2,400	
General and administrative	1,500	
Total operating expenses		11,100
Operating income		6,550
Interest expense		200
Income before income taxes		6,350
Income tax expense		2,500
Net income		$ 3,850

Balance Sheet Information ($ in thousands)	**Dec. 31, 2016**	**Dec. 31, 2015**
Assets:		
Cash	$ 7,350	$ 2,200
Accounts receivable	2,500	2,200
Inventory	4,000	3,000
Prepaid rent	150	300
Plant and equipment	14,500	12,000
Less: Accumulated depreciation	(5,100)	(4,500)
Total assets	$23,400	$15,200
Liabilities and Shareholders' Equity:		
Accounts payable	$ 1,400	$ 1,100
Interest payable	100	0
Deferred service revenue	800	600
Income taxes payable	550	800
Loan payable (due 12/31/2015)	5,000	0
Common stock	10,000	10,000
Retained earnings	5,550	2,700
Total liabilities and shareholders' equity	$23,400	$15,200

Additional information for the 2016 fiscal year ($ in thousands):

1. Cash dividends of $1,000 were declared and paid.
2. Equipment costing $4,000 was purchased with cash.
3. Equipment with a book value of $500 (cost of $1,500 less accumulated depreciation of $1,000) was sold for $500.
4. Depreciation of $1,600 is included in operating expenses.

Required:

Prepare Santana Industries' 2016 statement of cash flows, using the indirect method to present cash flows from operating activities.

P 4–12
Interim financial reporting
● Appendix 4

Branson Electronics Company is a small, publicly traded company preparing its first quarter interim report to be mailed to shareholders. The following information for the quarter has been compiled:

Revenues		$180,000
Cost of goods sold		35,000
Operating expenses:		
Fixed	$59,000	
Variable	48,000	107,000

Fixed operating expenses include payments of $50,000 to an advertising firm to promote Branson through various media throughout the year. The income tax rate for Branson's level of operations in the first quarter is 30%, but management estimates the effective rate for the entire year will be 36%.

Required:
Prepare the income statement to be included in Branson's first quarter interim report.

Broaden Your Perspective

Apply your critical-thinking ability to the knowledge you've gained. These cases will provide you an opportunity to develop your research, analysis, judgment, and communication skills. You also will work with other students, integrate what you've learned, apply it in real-world situations, and consider its global and ethical ramifications. This practice will broaden your knowledge and further develop your decision-making abilities.

Judgment Case 4–1
Earnings quality
● LO4–2, LO4–3

The financial community in the United States has become increasingly concerned with the quality of reported company earnings.

Required:
1. Define the term *earnings quality.*
2. Explain the distinction between permanent and transitory earnings as it relates to the concept of earnings quality.
3. How do earnings management practices affect the quality of earnings?
4. Assume that a manufacturing company's annual income statement included a large gain from the sale of investment securities. What factors would you consider in determining whether or not this gain should be included in an assessment of the company's permanent earnings?

Judgment Case 4–2
Restructuring costs
● LO4–3

The appearance of restructuring costs in corporate income statements increased significantly in the 1980s and 1990s and continues to be relevant today.

Required:
1. What types of costs are included in restructuring costs?
2. When are restructuring costs recognized?
3. How would you classify restructuring costs in a multi-step income statement?
4. What factors would you consider in determining whether or not restructuring costs should be included in an assessment of a company's permanent earnings?

Judgment Case 4–3
Earnings management
● LO4–2, LO4–3

Companies often are under pressure to meet or beat Wall Street earnings projections in order to increase stock prices and also to increase the value of stock options. Some resort to earnings management practices to artificially create desired results.

Required:
Is *earnings management* always intended to produce higher income? Explain.

Real World Case 4–4
Earnings quality and pro forma earnings
● LO4–3

Companies often voluntarily provide a pro forma earnings number when they announce annual or quarterly earnings.

Required:
1. What is meant by the term *pro forma earnings* in this context?
2. How do pro forma earnings relate to the concept of earnings quality?

Research Case 4–5
FASB codification; locate and extract relevant information and cite authoritative support for a financial reporting issue; restructuring costs; exit or disposal cost obligations
● LO4–2, LO4–3

The accrual of restructuring costs creates obligations (liabilities) referred to as *exit or disposal cost obligations.*

Required:

1. Obtain the relevant authoritative literature on exit or disposal cost obligations using the *FASB Accounting Standards Codification*. You might gain access at the FASB website (asc.fasb.org). What is the Codification topic number that addresses this issue?
2. What is the specific citation that addresses the initial measurement of these obligations?
3. How are these obligations and related costs to be measured?
4. What is the specific citation that describes the disclosure requirements in the notes to the financial statements for exit or disposal obligations?
5. List the required disclosures.

Judgment Case 4–6
Income statement presentation
● LO4–3, LO4–4

Each of the following situations occurred during 2016 for one of your audit clients:

1. The write-off of inventory due to obsolescence.
2. Discovery that depreciation expenses were omitted by accident from 2015's income statement.
3. The useful lives of all machinery were changed from eight to five years.
4. The depreciation method used for all equipment was changed from the declining-balance to the straight-line method.
5. Restructuring costs were incurred.
6. The Stridewell Company, a manufacturer of shoes, sold all of its retail outlets. It will continue to manufacture and sell its shoes to other retailers. A loss was incurred in the disposition of the retail stores. The retail stores are considered a component of the entity.
7. The inventory costing method was changed from FIFO to average cost.

Required:

1. For each situation, identify the appropriate reporting treatment from the list below (consider each event to be material):
   a. As an unusual gain or loss.
   b. As a prior period adjustment.
   c. As a change in accounting principle.
   d. As a discontinued operation.
   e. As a change in accounting estimate.
   f. As a change in accounting estimate achieved by a change in accounting principle.
2. Indicate whether each situation would be included in the income statement in continuing operations (CO) or below continuing operations (BC), or if it would appear as an adjustment to retained earnings (RE). Use the format shown below to answer requirements 1 and 2.

Situation	Treatment (a–f)	Financial Statement Presentation (CO, BC, or RE)
1.		
2.		
3.		
4.		
5.		
6.		
7.		

Judgment Case 4–7
Income statement presentation
● LO4–3, LO4–4

The following events occurred during 2016 for various audit clients of your firm. Consider each event to be independent and the effect of each event to be material.

1. A manufacturing company recognized a loss on the sale of investments.
2. An automobile manufacturer sold all of the assets related to its financing component. The operations of the financing business is considered a component of the entity.

3. A company changed its depreciation method from the double-declining-balance method to the straight-line method.
4. Due to obsolescence, a company engaged in the manufacture of high-technology products incurred a loss on the write-down of inventory.
5. One of your clients discovered that 2015's depreciation expense was overstated. The error occurred because of a miscalculation of depreciation for the office building.
6. A cosmetics company decided to discontinue the manufacture of a line of women's lipstick. Other cosmetic lines will be continued. A loss was incurred on the sale of assets related to the lipstick product line. The operations of the discontinued line is not considered a component of the entity.

Required:

Discuss the 2016 financial statement presentation of each of the above events. Do not consider earnings per share disclosures.

IFRS Case 4–8
Statement of cash flows; GlaxoSmithKline Plc.
● LO4–8, LO4–9

IFRS

Real World Financials

GlaxoSmithKline Plc. (GSK) is a global pharmaceutical and consumer health-related products company located in the United Kingdom. The company prepares its financial statements in accordance with International Financial Reporting Standards. Below is a portion of the company's statements of cash flows included in recent financial statements:

GLAXOSMITHKLINE PLC.
Consolidated Cash Flow Statement
For the Year Ended 31 December 2013

	Notes	2013 £m	2012 (restated) £m	2011 (restated) £m
Cash flow from operating activities				
Profit after taxation for the year		5,628	4,678	5,405
Adjustments reconciling profit after tax to operating cash flows	36	2,871	1,370	2,308
Cash generated from operations		8,499	6,048	7,713
Taxation paid		(1,277)	(1,673)	(1,463)
Net cash inflow from operating activities		7,222	4,375	6,250
Cash flow from investing activities				
Purchase of property, plant and equipment		(1,188)	(1,051)	(923)
Proceeds from sale of property, plant and equipment		46	68	100
Purchase of intangible assets		(513)	(469)	(405)
Proceeds from sale of intangible assets		136	1,056	237
Purchase of equity investments		(133)	(229)	(76)
Proceeds from sale of equity investments		59	28	68
Purchase of businesses, net of cash acquired	38	(247)	(2,235)	(264)
Disposal of businesses	38	1,851	—	—
Investments in associates and joint ventures	20	(8)	(99)	(35)
Proceeds from disposal of subsidiary and interest in associate		429	—	1,034
Decrease in liquid investments		15	224	30
Interest received		59	30	97
Dividends from associates and joint ventures		18	46	25
Net cash inflow/(outflow) from investing activities		524	(2,631)	(112)
Cash flow from financing activities				
Proceeds from own shares for employee share options		—	58	45
Shares acquired by ESOP Trusts		(45)	(37)	(36)
Issue of share capital	33	585	356	250
Purchase of own shares for cancellation or to be held as Treasury shares		(1,504)	(2,493)	(2,191)
Purchase of non-controlling interests		(588)	(14)	—
Increase in long-term loans		1,913	4,430	—
Increase in short-term loans		-	1,743	45
Repayment of short-term loans		(1,872)	(2,559)	(8)
Net repayment of obligations under finance leases		(31)	(35)	(38)
Interest paid		(749)	(779)	(769)
Dividends paid to shareholders		(3,680)	(3,814)	(3,406)
Distributions to non-controlling interests		(238)	(171)	(234)
Other financing cash flows		(64)	(36)	110
Net cash outflow from financing activities		(6,273)	(3,351)	(6,232)

(continued)

(concluded)

Increase/(decrease) in cash and bank overdrafts	37	1,473	(1,607)	(94)
Cash and bank overdrafts at beginning of year		3,906	5,605	5,807
Exchange adjustments		(148)	(92)	(108)
Increase/(decrease) in cash and bank overdrafts		1,473	(1,607)	(94)
Cash and bank overdrafts at end of year		5,231	3,906	5,605
Cash and bank overdrafts at end of year comprise:				
Cash and cash equivalents		5,534	4,184	5,714
Overdrafts		(303)	(278)	(109)
		5,231	3,906	5,605

Required:

Identify the items in the above statements that would be reported differently if GlaxoSmithKline prepared its financial statements according to U.S. GAAP rather than IFRS.

Judgment Case 4–9
Income statement presentation; unusual items; comprehensive income
● LO4–3, LO4–4, LO4–6

Norse Manufacturing Inc. prepares an annual single, continuous statement of income and comprehensive income. The following situations occurred during the company's 2016 fiscal year:

1. Restructuring costs were incurred due to the closing of a factory.
2. Investments were sold, and a loss was recognized.
3. Gains from foreign currency translation were recognized.
4. Interest expense was incurred.
5. A division was sold that qualifies as a separate component of the entity according to GAAP.
6. Obsolete inventory was written off.
7. The controller discovered an error in the calculation of 2015's patent amortization expense.

Required:

1. For each situation, identify the appropriate reporting treatment from the list below (consider each event to be material).
   a. As a component of operating income.
   b. As a nonoperating income item (other income or expense).
   c. As a discontinued operation.
   d. As an other comprehensive income item.
   e. As an adjustment to retained earnings.
2. Identify the situations that would be reported net-of-tax.

Judgment Case 4–10
Management incentives for change
● LO4–2

It has been suggested that not all accounting choices are made by management in the best interest of fair and consistent financial reporting.

Required:

What motivations can you think of for management's choice of accounting methods?

Research Case 4–11
Pro forma earnings
● LO4–3

Companies often voluntarily provide a pro forma earnings number when they announce annual or quarterly earnings. These pro forma earnings numbers are controversial as they represent management's view of permanent earnings. The Sarbanes-Oxley Act (SOX), issued in 2002, requires that if pro forma earnings are included in any periodic or other report filed with the SEC or in any public disclosure or press release, the company also must provide a reconciliation with earnings determined according to GAAP.

Professors Entwistle, Feltham, and Mbagwu, in "Financial Reporting Regulation and the Reporting of Pro Forma Earnings," examine whether firms changed their reporting practice in response to the pro forma regulations included in SOX.

Required:

1. In your library or from some other source, locate the indicated article in *Accounting Horizons,* March 2006.
2. What sample of firms did the authors use in their examination?
3. What percent of firms reported pro forma earnings in 2001? In 2003?
4. What percent of firms had pro forma earnings greater than GAAP earnings in 2001? In 2003?
5. What was the most frequently reported adjusting item in 2001? In 2003?
6. What are the authors' main conclusions of the impact of SOX on pro forma reporting?

Integrating Case 4–12
Balance sheet and income statement; Chapters 3 and 4
● LO4–3

Rice Corporation is negotiating a loan for expansion purposes and the bank requires financial statements. Before closing the accounting records for the year ended December 31, 2016, Rice's controller prepared the following financial statements:

RICE CORPORATION
Balance Sheet
At December 31, 2016
($ in 000s)

Assets	
Cash	$ 275
Marketable securities	78
Accounts receivable	487
Inventories	425
Allowance for uncollectible accounts	(50)
Property and equipment, net	160
Total assets	$1,375
Liabilities and Shareholders' Equity	
Accounts payable and accrued liabilities	$ 420
Notes payable	200
Common stock	260
Retained earnings	495
Total liabilities and shareholders' equity	$1,375

RICE CORPORATION
Income Statement
For the Year Ended December 31, 2016
($ in 000s)

Net sales		$1,580
Expenses:		
Cost of goods sold	$755	
Selling and administrative	385	
Miscellaneous	129	
Income taxes	100	
Total expenses		1,369
Net income		$ 211

Additional Information:

1. The company's common stock is traded on an organized stock exchange.
2. The investment portfolio consists of short-term investments valued at $57,000. The remaining investments will not be sold until the year 2018.
3. Notes payable consist of two notes:

   Note 1: $80,000 face value dated September 30, 2016. Principal and interest at 10% are due on September 30, 2017.

   Note 2: $120,000 face value dated April 30, 2016. Principal is due in two equal installments of $60,000 plus interest on the unpaid balance. The two payments are scheduled for April 30, 2017, and April 30, 2018.

   Interest on both loans has been correctly accrued and is included in accrued liabilities on the balance sheet and selling and administrative expenses on the income statement.
4. Selling and administrative expenses include $90,000 representing costs incurred by the company in restructuring some of its operations. The amount is material.

Required:

Identify and explain the deficiencies in the presentation of the statements prepared by the company's controller. Do not prepare corrected statements. Include in your answer a list of items which require additional disclosure, either on the face of the statement or in a note.

Analysis Case 4–13
Income statement information
● LO4–1

PetSmart

Refer to the income statements of PetSmart, Inc., included in the company's financial statements in Appendix B at the back of the text.

Required:

1. What was the percentage increase or decrease in the company's net income from the fiscal year ended February 3, 2013, to the fiscal year ended February 2, 2014? From 2012 to 2013?
2. Using data from the fiscal year ended February 2, 2014, what is the company's approximate income tax rate?
3. Using data from the fiscal year ended February 2, 2014, what is the percentage of net income relative to net sales?

All revenue recognition starts with a contract between a seller and a customer. You may not have realized it, but you have been a party to several such contracts very recently. Maybe you bought a cup of Starbucks coffee or a breakfast biscuit at McDonalds this morning. Or maybe you bought this textbook through Amazon or had a checkup at your doctor's office. Even though these transactions weren't accompanied by written and signed agreements, they are considered contracts for purposes of revenue recognition. The key is that, implicitly or explicitly, you entered into an arrangement that specifies the legal rights and obligations of a seller and a customer.

Contracts between a seller and a customer contain one or more performance obligations, which are promises by the seller to transfer goods or services to a customer. The seller recognizes revenue when it satisfies a performance obligation by transferring the promised good or service. We consider transfer to have occurred when the customer has *control* of the good or service. *Control* means that the customer has direct influence over the use of the good or service and obtains its benefits.

***Performance obligations* are promises to transfer goods or services to a customer.**

For many contracts, following this approach is very straightforward. In particular, if a contract includes only one performance obligation, we typically just have to decide when the seller delivers the good or provides the service to a customer, and then make sure that the seller recognizes revenue at that time.

Performance obligations are satisfied when the seller transfers *control* of goods or services to the customer.

As a simple example, assume Macy's sells a skirt to Susan for $75 that Macy's previously purchased from a wholesaler for $40. How would Macy's account for the sale to Susan?

1. **Identify the contract with a customer:** In this case, the contract may not be written, but it is clear—Macy's delivers the skirt to Susan, and Susan agrees to pay $75 to Macy's.
2. **Identify the performance obligation(s) in the contract:** Macy's has only a single performance obligation—to deliver the skirt.
3. **Determine the transaction price:** Macy's is entitled to receive $75 from Susan.
4. **Allocate the transaction price to each performance obligation:** With only one performance obligation, Macy's allocates the full transaction price of $75 to delivery of the skirt.
5. **Recognize revenue when (or as) each performance obligation is satisfied:** Macy's satisfies its performance obligation when it delivers the skirt to Susan, so Macy's records the following journal entries at that time:

Cash	75	
Sales revenue		75
Cost of goods sold[6]	40	
Inventory		40

Revenue recognition gets more complicated when a contract contains more than one performance obligation. For example, when Verizon signs up a new cell phone customer, the sales contract might require Verizon to provide (1) a smartphone, (2) related software, (3) a warranty on the phone, (4) ongoing network access, and (5) optional future upgrades. Verizon must determine which of these goods and services constitute performance obligations, allocate the transaction price to those performance obligations, and recognize revenue when (or as) each performance obligation is satisfied.

In Part A of this chapter, we apply the five steps for recognizing revenue to various types of contracts. First we'll focus on contracts that have only one performance obligation to deliver a good or service at a single point in time, like Macy's sale of a skirt to Susan. Then we'll consider situations in which one performance obligation to deliver goods and services is satisfied over time, like a landlord renting an apartment or a bank lending money. For those contracts, we recognize revenue over a period of time. After that, we'll consider contracts that contain multiple performance obligations, like the Verizon example we just discussed. Illustration 5–2 summarizes some key considerations we will return to throughout this chapter.

[6]This second journal entry assumes that Macy's uses a "perpetual" inventory system, by which we record increases and decreases in inventory as they occur ("perpetually"). We reviewed this method briefly in Chapter 2 and explore it in more depth in Chapter 8.

Illustration 5–2 Key Considerations When Applying the Five Steps to Revenue Recognition

Five Steps to Recognizing Revenue	For Transactions Involving Single and Multiple Performance Obligations		
Step 1 Identify the contract	Legal rights of seller and customer established		
Step 2 Identify the performance obligation(s)	***Single*** performance obligation		***Multiple*** performance obligations
Step 3 Determine the transaction price	Amount seller is entitled to receive from customer		Amount seller is entitled to receive from customer
Step 4 Allocate the transaction price	No allocation required		Allocate a portion to each performance obligation
Step 5 Recognize revenue when (or as) each performance obligation is satisfied	At a point in time	Over a period of time	At whatever time is appropriate for each performance obligation

Recognizing Revenue at a Single Point in Time

● LO5–2

FINANCIAL Reporting Case

Q1, p. 231

First we consider a simple contract that includes only one performance obligation and is satisfied at a single point in time when goods or services are transferred to a customer. The performance obligation is satisfied when control of the goods or services is transferred from the seller to the customer, and usually it's obvious that transfer occurs at the time of delivery. In our Macy's example above, for instance, the performance obligation is satisfied at the time of the sale when the skirt is transferred to Susan.

In other cases transfer of control can be harder to determine. Illustration 5–3 lists five key indicators we use to decide whether control has passed from the seller to the customer. Sellers should evaluate these indicators individually and in combination to decide whether control has been transferred and revenue can be recognized.

Illustration 5–3
Indicators that Control Has Been Transferred from the Seller to the Customer

The customer is more likely to control a good or service if the customer has:
- An obligation to pay the seller.
- Legal title to the asset.
- Physical possession of the asset.
- Assumed the risks and rewards of ownership.
- Accepted the asset.[7]

In Illustration 5–4 we apply these indicators to TrueTech Industries, a company we will revisit throughout this chapter to illustrate revenue recognition.

Illustration 5–4
Recognizing Revenue at a Point in Time

TrueTech Industries sells the Tri-Box, a gaming console that allows users to play video games individually or in multiplayer environments over the Internet. A Tri-Box is only a gaming module and includes no other goods or services. When should TrueTech recognize revenue for the following sale of 1,000 Tri-Boxes to CompStores?

- **December 20, 2015: CompStores orders 1,000 Tri-Boxes at a price of $240 each, promising payment within 30 days after delivery.** TrueTech has received the order but hasn't fulfilled its performance obligation to deliver Tri-Boxes. In light of this and other indicators, TrueTech's judgment is that control has not been transferred and revenue should not be recognized.

(continued)

[7]These indicators apply to both goods and services. It may seem strange to talk about the customer accepting an asset with respect to a service, but think of a service as an asset that is consumed as the customer receives it.

Illustration 5–4

(concluded)

- **January 1, 2016: TrueTech delivers 1,000 Tri-Boxes to CompStores, and title to the Tri-Boxes transfers to CompStores.** TrueTech has delivered the Tri-Boxes, and CompStores has accepted delivery, so CompStores has physical possession, legal title, the risks and rewards of ownership, and an obligation to pay TrueTech. TrueTech's performance obligation has been satisfied, so TrueTech can recognize revenue and a related account receivable of $240,000.[8]

Accounts receivable ($240 × 1,000)	240,000	
Sales revenue		240,000

- **January 25, 2016: TrueTech receives $240,000 from CompStores.** This transaction does not affect revenue. We recognize revenue when performance obligations are satisfied, not when cash is received. TrueTech simply records collection of the account receivable.

Cash	240,000	
Accounts receivable		240,000

Recognizing Revenue over a Period of Time

● LO5–3

Services such as lending money, performing audits, and providing consulting advice are performed over a period of time. Some construction contracts require construction over months or even years. In these situations, should a company recognize revenue continuously over time as a product or service is being provided, or wait to recognize revenue at the single point in time when the company has finished providing the product or service? As we'll see next, in most situations like these, companies should recognize revenue over time as the service or product is being provided.

Criteria for Recognizing Revenue over Time

Let's assume once again that we have a contract with a customer that includes a single performance obligation and a known transaction price. As indicated in Illustration 5–5, we recognize revenue over time if any one of three criteria is met.

Illustration 5–5

Criteria for Recognizing Revenue over Time

Revenue is recognized over time if either:

1. **The customer consumes the benefit of the seller's work as it is performed,** as when a company provides cleaning services to a customer for a period of time, or
2. **The customer controls the asset as it is created,** as when a contractor builds an extension onto a customer's existing building, or
3. **The seller is creating an asset that has no alternative use to the seller, and the seller has the legal right to receive payment for progress to date,** as when a company manufactures customized fighter jets for the U.S. Air Force.

We recognize revenue over time if one of three criteria is met.

If a performance obligation meets at least one of these criteria, we recognize revenue over time, in proportion to the amount of the performance obligation that has been satisfied. If, say, one-third of a service has been performed, then one-third of the performance obligation has been satisfied, so one-third of the revenue should be recognized. For example, **Gold's Gym** recognizes revenue from a two-year membership over the 24-month membership period, and **Six Flags Entertainment** recognizes revenue for season passes over the operating season. As another example, consider Illustration 5–6 on the next page.

When a performance obligation is satisfied over time, revenue is recognized in proportion to the amount of the performance obligation that has been satisfied.

Most long-term construction contracts qualify for revenue recognition over time. For example, many long-term construction contracts are structured such that the customer owns the work-in-process (WIP) as it is constructed, which satisfies the second criterion in Illustration 5–5. Also, the third criterion is satisfied if the asset the seller is constructing has no alternate use to the seller and the contract stipulates that the seller is paid for performance. We discuss accounting for long-term construction contracts in more detail in Part C of this chapter.

Most long-term contracts qualify for revenue recognition over time.

[8] TrueTech also would debit cost of goods sold and credit inventory to recognize the cost of inventory sold.

Illustration 5–6

Recognizing Revenue over a Period of Time

Deferred Revenue

	Debit	Credit
1/1		60,000
1/31	5,000	
2/28	5,000	
. . .	. . .	
12/31	5,000	
12/31		-0-

Service Revenue

	Debit	Credit
1/1		-0-
1/31		5,000
2/28		5,000
. . .		. . .
12/31		5,000
12/31		60,000

TrueTech Industries sells one-year subscriptions to the Tri-Net multiuser platform of Internet-based games. TrueTech sells 1,000 subscriptions for $60 each on January 1, 2016. TrueTech has a single performance obligation—to provide a service to subscribers by allowing them access to the gaming platform for one year. Because Tri-Net users consume the benefits of access to that service over time, under the first criterion in Illustration 5–5 TrueTech recognizes revenue from the subscriptions over the one-year time period.

On January 1, 2016, TrueTech records the following journal entry:

Cash ($60 × 1,000)	60,000	
Deferred revenue		60,000

TrueTech recognizes no revenue on January 1. Rather, TrueTech recognizes a deferred revenue liability for $60,000 associated with receiving cash prior to satisfying its performance obligation to provide customers with access to the Tri-Net games for a year.

Tri-Net subscribers receive benefits each day they have access to the Tri-Net network, so TrueTech uses "proportion of time" as its measure of progress toward completion. At the end of each of the 12 months following the sale, TrueTech would record the following entry to recognize Tri-Net subscription revenue:

Deferred revenue ($60,000 ÷ 12)	5,000	
Service revenue		5,000

After 12 months TrueTech will have recognized the entire $60,000 of Tri-Net subscription revenue, and the deferred revenue liability will be reduced to zero.

If a performance obligation doesn't meet any of the three criteria for recognizing revenue over time, we recognize revenue at the point in time when the performance obligation has been completely satisfied, which usually occurs at the end of the long-term contract.

Many services are so short term in nature that companies don't bother with recognizing revenue over time even if they qualify for doing so. For example, **FedEx** picks up a package and delivers it to its destination within a few days. The company's summary of significant accounting policies disclosure note indicates that "Revenue is recognized upon delivery of shipments." In other words, FedEx recognizes revenue at the end of the service period rather than over time. This departure from GAAP is immaterial given the short duration of FedEx's services and the lack of additional useful information that would be provided by more precise timing of revenue recognition.

Determining Progress toward Completion

Because progress toward completion is the basis for recognizing revenue over time, the seller needs to estimate that progress in a way that reflects when the control of goods or services is transferred to the customer.

Input **or** ***output*** **methods can be used to estimate progress toward completion when performance obligations are satisfied over time.**

Sellers sometimes use an *output-based* estimate of progress toward completion, measured as the proportion of the goods or services transferred to date. For our Tri-Net example in Illustration 5–6, output is measured by the passage of time, because the performance obligation being satisfied is to provide access to the Tri-Net gaming platform. Other times sellers use an *input-based* estimate of progress toward completion, measured as the proportion of effort expended thus far relative to the total effort expected to satisfy the performance obligation. For example, sellers often use the ratio of costs incurred to date compared to total costs estimated to complete the job.[9] In Part C of this chapter, we continue our discussion of output- and input-based measures of progress toward completion, and also consider how to deal with changes in estimates of progress toward completion.

[9]If for some reason the seller can't make a reasonable estimate of progress to completion using either input or output methods, the seller must wait to recognize revenue until the performance obligation has been completely satisfied. However, if the seller expects to be able to at least recover its costs from the customer, the seller can recognize an amount of revenue equal to the costs incurred until it can make a reasonable estimate of progress toward completion.

Recognizing Revenue for Contracts that Contain Multiple Performance Obligations

● LO5–4

Revenue recognition becomes more complicated when a contract contains multiple performance obligations. As an example, in Illustration 5–7 we combine the two TrueTech examples we already have discussed. In the first example (Illustration 5–4), TrueTech sold Tri-Box modules and recognized revenue at a single point in time (upon delivery). In the second example (Illustration 5–6), TrueTech sold one-year subscriptions to the Tri-Net platform and recognized revenue over time (one-twelfth each month over the year). Now, let's consider how TrueTech would recognize revenue if these two items were sold as a package deal for a single price.

FINANCIAL Reporting Case

Q2, p. 231

Illustration 5–7

Contract Containing Multiple Performance Obligations

TrueTech Industries manufactures the Tri-Box System, a multiplayer gaming system allowing players to compete with each other over the Internet.

- The Tri-Box System includes the physical Tri-Box module as well as a one-year subscription to the Tri-Net multiuser platform of Internet-based games and other applications.
- TrueTech sells individual one-year subscriptions to the Tri-Net platform for $60.
- TrueTech sells individual Tri-Box modules for $240.
- As a package deal, TrueTech sells the Tri-Box System (module plus subscription) for $250.

On January 1, 2016, TrueTech delivers 1,000 Tri-Box Systems to CompStores at a price of $250 per system. TrueTech receives $250,000 from CompStores on January 25, 2016.

We'll assume TrueTech has concluded that it has a contract with CompStores, so step 1 of revenue recognition is satisfied. We'll start with step 2.

Step 2: Identify the Performance Obligation(s)

Promises to provide goods and services are performance obligations when the goods and services are *distinct*.

Sellers account for a promise to provide a good or service as a performance obligation if the good or service is **distinct** from other goods and services in the contract. The idea is to separate contracts into parts that can be viewed on a stand-alone basis. That way the financial statements can better reflect the timing of the transfer of separate goods and services and the profit generated on each one. Goods or services that are not distinct are combined and treated as a single performance obligation.

A good or service is distinct if it is both:

1. *Capable of being distinct.* The customer could use the good or service on its own or in combination with other goods and services it could obtain elsewhere, and
2. *Separately identifiable from other goods or services in the contract.* The good or service is distinct in the context of the contract because it is not highly interrelated with other goods and services in the contract.

The first criterion is clear, but the second, "separately identifiable from other goods and services in the contract," needs some explanation. In some contracts, performance obligations are so intertwined that it doesn't make sense to view them separately. For example, in most long-term construction contracts, the seller's role is to combine many products and services, such as lumber, concrete, design, electrical, plumbing, and actual construction, to provide a single completed building or other constructed asset to the customer. Therefore, each of these separate products and services are *not* considered distinct in the context of a contract. As we discuss further in Part C of this chapter, most long-term construction contracts are viewed as including a single performance obligation because the individual goods and services needed to construct the asset are highly interrelated. Even though these goods and services might be capable of being distinct outside the context of the contract, the contract itself causes them to be more appropriately thought of as being provided together as a single performance obligation.[11]

In Illustration 5–8 we apply these criteria to identify the performance obligations for our TrueTech example.

Illustration 5–8

Determining Whether Goods and Services Are Distinct

Assume the same facts as in Illustration 5–7. Do the Tri-Box module and the Tri-Net subscription qualify as performance obligations in TrueTech's contract with CompStores?

Which of the goods and services promised in the contract are distinct? Both the Tri-Box module and the Tri-Net subscription can be used on their own by a customer, so they are capable of being distinct and are separately identifiable.

Conclusion: The module and subscription are distinct so the contract has two performance obligations: (1) delivery of Tri-Box modules and (2) fulfillment of one-year Tri-Net subscriptions.

Step 3: Determine the Transaction Price

The *transaction price* is the amount the seller expects to be entitled to receive from the customer in exchange for providing goods and services.

The **transaction price** is the amount the seller expects to be entitled to receive from the customer in exchange for providing goods and services.[12] Determining the transaction price is simple if the customer pays a fixed amount immediately or soon after the sale. That's the case with our TrueTech example. The transaction price is $250,000, equal to $250 per system × 1,000 systems.

Step 4: Allocate the Transaction Price to Each Performance Obligation

We allocate the transaction price to performance obligations in proportion to their relative *stand-alone selling prices.*

If a contract includes more than one performance obligation, the seller allocates the transaction price to each one in proportion to the stand-alone selling prices of the goods or services underlying all the performance obligations in the contract. The **stand-alone selling price** is the amount at which the good or service is sold separately under similar circumstances.[13] If a stand-alone selling price can't be directly observed, the seller should estimate it.

Look at Illustration 5–9 to see how we allocate the transaction price to each of the performance obligations in our TrueTech example.

Illustration 5–9

Allocating Transaction Price to Performance Obligations Based on Relative Selling Prices

Assume the same facts as in Illustration 5–7. Because the stand-alone price of the Tri-Box module ($240) represents 80% of the total of all the stand-alone selling prices ($240 ÷ [$240 + 60]), and the Tri-Net subscription comprises 20% of the total ($60 ÷ [$240 + 60]), we allocate 80% of the transaction price to the Tri-Box modules and 20% of the transaction price to the Tri-Net subscriptions, as follows:

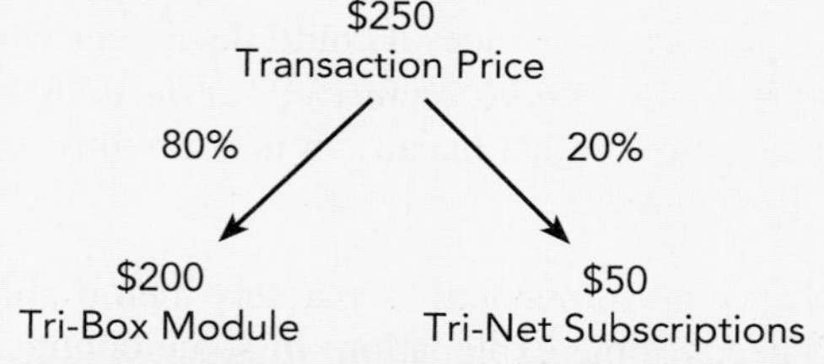

[11]Sellers also treat as a single performance obligation a series of distinct goods or services that are substantially the same and have the same pattern of transfer.

[12]Normally, sellers are immediately or eventually paid in cash, but sometimes sellers are paid with other assets like property. In that case, the seller measures the assets received at fair value.

[13]A contractually stated "list price" doesn't necessarily represent a stand-alone selling price, because the seller might actually sell the good or service for a different amount. The seller has to reference actual stand-alone selling prices, or estimate those prices.

Additional Consideration

Discounts in Contracts with Multiple Performance Obligations. Note that Illustration 5–7 shows that Tri-Box systems are sold at a discount—TrueTech sells the system for a transaction price ($250) that's less than the $300 sum of the stand-alone selling prices of the Tri-Box module ($240) and the subscription to Tri-Net ($60). Because there is no evidence that the discount relates to only one of the performance obligations, it is spread between them in the allocation process. If TrueTech had clear evidence from sales of those goods and services that the discount related to only one of them, the entire discount would be allocated to that good or service.

Step 5: Recognize Revenue When (Or As) Each Performance Obligation Is Satisfied

As we discussed earlier, performance obligations can be satisfied either at a point in time or over a period of time, and revenue with respect to a performance obligation is recognized when (or as) the performance obligation is satisfied. That timing doesn't depend on whether a performance obligation is the only one in a contract or is one of several performance obligations in a contract. We determine the timing of revenue recognition for each performance obligation individually.

Revenue with respect to each performance obligation is recognized when (or as) that performance obligation is satisfied.

Returning to our TrueTech example, the $200,000 of revenue associated with the Tri-Box modules is recognized when those modules are delivered to CompStores on January 1, but the $50,000 of revenue associated with the Tri-Net subscriptions is recognized over the one-year subscription term. The timing of revenue recognition for each performance obligation is shown in Illustration 5–10.

Assume the same facts as in Illustration 5–7. TrueTech records the following journal entry at the time of the sale to CompStores (ignoring any entry to record the reduction in inventory and the corresponding cost of goods sold):

January 1, 2016:		
Accounts receivable	250,000	
Sales revenue ($250,000 × 80%)........................		200,000
Deferred revenue ($250,000 × 20%)		50,000

In each of the 12 months following the sale, TrueTech records the following entry to recognize Tri-Net subscription revenue:

Deferred revenue ($50,000 ÷ 12)	4,167	
Service revenue		4,167

After 12 months TrueTech will have recognized the entire $50,000 of Tri-Net subscription revenue, and the deferred revenue liability will have been reduced to zero.

Illustration 5–10

Recognizing Revenue for Multiple Performance Obligations

Deferred Revenue

	Debit	Credit
1/1		50,000
1/31	4,167	
2/28	4,167	
. . .	. . .	
12/31	4,167	
12/31		-0-

Service Revenue

	Debit	Credit
1/1		-0-
1/31		4,167
2/28		4,167
. . .		. . .
12/31		4,167
12/31		50,000

Illustration 5–11 summarizes Part A's discussion of the fundamental issues related to recognizing revenue.

Illustration 5–11 Summary of Fundamental Issues Related to Recognizing Revenue

Revenue Recognition	Fundamental Issues	
Step 1 Identify the contract	A contract establishes the legal rights and obligations of the seller and customer with respect to one or more performance obligations.	
Step 2 Identify the performance obligation(s)	A performance obligation is a promise to transfer a good or service that is distinct, which is the case if the good or service is both (a) capable of being distinct and (b) separately identifiable.	
Step 3 Determine the transaction price	The transaction price is the amount the seller is entitled to receive from the customer.	
Step 4 Allocate the transaction price	The seller allocates the transaction price to performance obligations based on the relative stand alone selling prices of the goods or services in each performance obligation.	
Step 5 Recognize revenue when (or as) each performance obligation is satisfied	The seller recognizes revenue **at a single point in time** when control passes to the customer, which is more likely if the customer has: • Obligation to pay the seller. • Legal title to the asset. • Possession of the asset. • Assumed the risks and rewards of ownership. • Accepted the asset.	The seller recognizes revenue **over a period of time** if: • Customer consumes benefit as work performed, • Customer controls asset as it's created, or • Seller is creating an asset that has no alternative use and the seller has right to receive payment for work completed.

Concept Review Exercise

REVENUE RECOGNITION FOR CONTRACTS WITH MULTIPLE PERFORMANCE OBLIGATIONS

Macrovision sells a variety of satellite TV packages. The popular $600 Basic Package includes a hardware component (consisting of a satellite dish and receiver) along with a twelve-month subscription to 130 TV channels. Macrovision sells the hardware component without a subscription for $180, and sells a twelve-month subscription to the same 130 channels without hardware for $540/year. Let's account for the sale of one Basic Package for $600 on January 1, 2016.

Required:

1. Identify the performance obligations in the Basic Package contract, and determine when revenue for each should be recognized.
2. For the single Basic Package sold on January 1, 2016, allocate the $600 transaction price to the performance obligations in the contract, and prepare a journal entry to record the sale (ignoring any entry to record the reduction in inventory and the corresponding cost of goods sold).
3. Prepare any journal entry necessary to record revenue related to the same contract on January 31, 2016.

Solution:

1. Identify the performance obligations in the Basic Package contract, and determine when revenue for each should be recognized.

   The hardware component and the twelve-month subscription are *capable of being distinct* (they are sold separately) and are *separately identifiable* (the hardware and services are not highly intertwined so it makes sense to consider them separately). Therefore, the hardware component and the twelve-month subscription are distinct from each other and should be treated as separate performance obligations. Revenue for the hardware component should be recognized on January 1, 2016, because transfer of control of the hardware occurs when the hardware is delivered to the customer. Revenue for the subscription should be recognized over the next twelve months as the customer receives the benefit of having access to TV channels.

2. For the single Basic Package sold on January 1, 2016, allocate the $600 transaction price to the performance obligations in the contract, and prepare a journal entry to record the sale (ignoring any entry to record the reduction in inventory and the corresponding cost of goods sold).

   Because the stand-alone price of the hardware component ($180) represents 25% of the total of all the stand-alone selling prices ($180 ÷ [$180 + 540]), and the stand-alone price of the twelve-month subscription comprises 75% of the total ($540 ÷ [$180 + 540]), we allocate 25% of the transaction price to the hardware component and 75% of the transaction price to the twelve-month subscription. The transaction price of $600 would be allocated as follows:

   Hardware Component: $600 × 25% = $150.
   Twelve-Month Subscription: $600 × 75% = $450.

   The journal entry recorded on January 1, 2016, would be:

Cash	600	
Sales revenue (for delivery of hardware)		150
Deferred revenue (for subscription)		450

3. Prepare any journal entry necessary to record revenue for the same contract on January 31, 2016.

Deferred revenue ($450 ÷ 12)	37.50	
Service revenue		37.50

Special Topics in Revenue Recognition

PART B

Now that we've covered the basics, let's consider some important issues that occur in practice with respect to each of the five steps. We'll cover each step in turn.

LO5–5

Special Issues for Step 1: Identify the Contract

A **contract** is an agreement that creates legally enforceable rights and obligations. We normally think of a contract as being specified in a written document, but contracts can be oral rather than written. Contracts also can be *implicit* based on the typical business practices that a company follows. Remember from our example in Part A, just buying a skirt from Macy's implies a contract for purposes of recognizing revenue. The key is that all parties to the contract are committed to performing their obligations and enforcing their rights.[14]

A *contract* is an agreement that creates legally enforceable rights and obligations.

A contract only exists for purposes of revenue recognition if the seller believes it's probable that it will collect the amount it's entitled to receive under the contract. This collectibility threshold makes sure that revenue really reflects an inflow of net assets from the customer.[15]

A seller must believe collectibility is probable for a contract to exist for purposes of revenue recognition.

[14]Specifically, ASU No. 2014–09 indicates that a contract exists for purposes of revenue recognition only if it (a) has commercial substance, affecting the risk, timing or amount of the seller's future cash flows, (b) has been approved by both the seller and the customer, indicating commitment to fulfilling their obligations, (c) specifies the seller's and customer's rights regarding the goods or services to be transferred, (d) specifies payment terms, and (e) is probable that the seller will collect the amount it is entitled to receive. These criteria are very similar to requirements previously indicated by the SEC in the Staff Accounting Bulletins No. 101 and No. 104 mentioned earlier in this chapter.

[15]ASU No. 2014–09 defines "probable" as "likely to occur." Similarly, *SFAC No. 6* defines "probable" to mean an amount can "reasonably be expected or believed on the basis of available evidence or logic but is neither certain nor proved," which implies a relatively high likelihood of occurrence. IFRS defines "probable" as a likelihood that is greater than 50%, which is lower than the definition in U.S. GAAP. Therefore, some contracts might not meet this threshold under U.S. GAAP that do meet it under IFRS.

A contract does not exist if (a) neither the seller nor the customer has performed any obligations under the contract and (b) both the seller and the customer can terminate the contract without penalty. In other words, either the seller or the customer must have done something that has commercial substance for the seller to start accounting for revenue. Illustration 5–12 provides an example.

Illustration 5–12
Determining Whether a Contract Exists for Revenue Recognition Purposes

Recall from Illustration 5–7 that CompStores ordered 1,000 Tri-Box systems on December 20, 2015, at a price of $250 per unit. Assume that CompStores and TrueTech can cancel the order without penalty prior to delivery. TrueTech made delivery on January 1, 2016, and received $250,000 on January 25, 2016. When does TrueTech's arrangement with CompStores qualify as a contract for purposes of revenue recognition?

The arrangement qualifies as a contract on January 1, 2016. That's the date TrueTech makes delivery to CompStores. Prior to delivery, neither TrueTech nor CompStores had performed an obligation under the contract, and both parties could cancel the order without penalty, so the arrangement didn't qualify as a contract for purposes of revenue recognition.

Additional Consideration

Contract Modifications. A customer and seller might agree to modify a contract in some way. For instance, they might change the transaction price, change the performance obligations, or add another performance obligation. The way we account for a contract modification depends on the nature of the modification:

1. Sometimes a modification is really just a separate new contract. That happens when the modification adds another distinct good or service and requires the customer to pay an additional amount equal to the stand-alone selling price of the added good or service. In that case, we view the modification as a separate contract.
2. Other times a modification adds a distinct performance obligation, but that new performance obligation isn't priced at its stand-alone selling price. In that case, the seller needs to update the existing contract to reflect the modification. The modified contract includes whatever performance obligations remain after the modification, and its transaction price is equal to the amount that hasn't yet been recognized under the old contract plus or minus any change in price required by the modification. We allocate the revised transaction price to all performance obligations remaining in the contract based on their stand-alone selling prices at that time.
3. Finally, sometimes we modify a contract that includes a performance obligation that is being satisfied over time. In that case, we need to update our assessment of progress toward completion and adjust revenue as appropriate to reflect progress to date, just like we treat other changes in estimates.

Special Issues for Step 2: Identify the Performance Obligation(s)

Previously we saw that promises to provide goods and services are treated as performance obligations when the goods and services are distinct. Now let's consider several aspects of contracts we often encounter and whether they qualify as performance obligations. We discuss prepayments, warranties, and options.

A *prepayment* is not a performance obligation.

PREPAYMENTS. Some contracts require non-refundable up-front fees for particular activities (for example, **Bally Total Fitness** charges up-front registration fees for gym memberships). We don't consider such *prepayments* to be performance obligations because they aren't a promise to transfer a product or service to a customer. Instead, the up-front fee is an advance payment by the customer for future products or services and should be included in the transaction price, allocated to the various performance obligations in the contract, initially recorded as deferred revenue, and recognized as revenue when (or as) each performance obligation is satisfied.

WARRANTIES. Most products are sold with a warranty that obligates the seller to make repairs or replace products that later are found to be defective or unsatisfactory. These warranties are not sold separately, and either can be stated explicitly or be implicit based on normal business practice. We call these **quality-assurance warranties**. A quality-assurance warranty (sometimes called an "assurance-type warranty") is not a performance obligation. Rather, it is a cost of satisfying the performance obligation to deliver products of acceptable quality. The seller recognizes this cost in the period of sale as a warranty expense and related contingent liability. Because the exact amount of the cost usually is not known at the time of the sale, it must be estimated. For example, **Lenovo**, which manufactures personal computers and other technology products, reported a quality-assurance warranty liability of $279 million at the end of its 2013 fiscal year.

A *quality-assurance warranty* is not a performance obligation.

Extended warranties, on the other hand, are offered as an additional service that covers new problems arising after the customer takes control of the product. It's unusual these days to buy a phone, digital tablet, car, or almost any durable consumer product without being asked to buy an extended warranty. An extended warranty (sometimes called a "service-type warranty") provides protection beyond the manufacturer's quality-assurance warranty. Because an extended warranty usually is priced and sold separately from the product, it constitutes a performance obligation and can be viewed as a separate sales transaction. The price is recorded as a deferred revenue liability and then recognized as revenue over the extended warranty period. However, if an extended warranty is included along with the related product as part of a single contract, the extended warranty still is treated as a separate performance obligation, allocated a portion of the transaction price, and that portion of the transaction price is recorded as deferred revenue. **Lenovo** reported a liability for deferred extended warranty revenue of $404 million at the end of its 2013 fiscal year.

An *extended warranty* is a separate performance obligation.

How can you tell if a warranty should be treated as a quality-assurance warranty or an extended warranty? A warranty should be treated as an extended warranty if either (a) the customer has the option to purchase the warranty separately from the seller or (b) the warranty provides a service to the customer beyond only assuring that the seller delivered a product or service that was free from defects. The specifics of the warranty have to be considered when making this determination. For example, if the warranty period is very long, it's likely the warranty is covering more than just the quality of the product at the date of delivery, so it likely would represent an extended warranty.

We discuss accounting for warranties more in Chapter 13.

CUSTOMER OPTIONS FOR ADDITIONAL GOODS OR SERVICES. In some contracts the seller grants to the customer an *option* to receive additional goods or services at no cost or at a discount. Examples include software upgrades, customer loyalty programs (frequent flier miles, credit card points), discounts on future goods or services, and contract renewal options. Options for additional goods or services are considered performance obligations if they provide a *material right* to the customer that the customer would not receive otherwise.[16] For example, if a shoe seller normally discounts its products by 5%, but customers who purchase a pair of shoes receive a 20% discount off the next pair of shoes purchased at the same store, the extra discount of 15% (20% − 5%) is a material right, as it is a discount customers would not receive otherwise.

An *option* for additional goods or services is a performance obligation if it confers a material right to the customer.

When a contract includes an option that provides a material right, the seller must allocate part of the contract's transaction price to the option. Just like for other performance obligations, that allocation process requires the seller to estimate the stand-alone selling price of the option, taking into account the likelihood that the customer will actually exercise the

[16]Be careful not to confuse these types of options with stock options, which are financial instruments that allow purchase of shares of stock at a specific price at a future date.

option. The seller recognizes revenue associated with the option when the option is exercised or expires. Illustration 5–13 provides an example.

Illustration 5–13

Customer options for additional goods or services.

As a promotion, TrueTech Industries offers a 50% coupon for a gaming headset with the purchase of a Tri-Box for its normal price of $240. The headset costs $120 without a coupon (and $60 with a coupon), and the coupon must be exercised within one year of the Tri-Box purchase. TrueTech estimates that 80% of customers will take advantage of the coupon. How would TrueTech account for the cash sale of 100 Tri-Boxes sold under this promotion on January 1, 2016?

The coupon provides a material right to the customer, because it provides a discount of $120 × 50% = $60, so it is a performance obligation. Therefore, TrueTech must allocate the $240 transaction price to two performance obligations: the Tri-Box and the coupon.

Because TrueTech expects only 80% of the coupons to be used, it estimates the stand-alone selling price of a coupon to be $60 × 80% = $48.[17] The sum of the stand-alone selling prices of the performance obligations is $288, equal to the Tri-Box module ($240) plus the coupon ($48). The Tri-Box module ($240) represents five-sixths (or 83.33%) of the total ($240 ÷ $288), and the coupon comprises one-sixth (or 16.67%) of the total ($48 ÷ $288), so TrueTech allocates five-sixths of the $240 transaction price to the Tri-Box module and one-sixth to the coupon, as follows:

January 1, 2016:		
Cash	24,000	
Sales revenue ($240 × 5/6 × 100 units)		20,000
Deferred revenue—coupons ($240 × 1/6 × 100 units)		4,000

When the coupons are later redeemed or expire, TrueTech will debit deferred revenue—coupons and credit revenue.

Special Issues for Step 3: Determine the Transaction Price

● LO5–6

The transaction price is the amount the seller expects to be entitled to receive from the customer.

Until now we've assumed that contracts indicate a fixed transaction price that will be paid at or soon after delivery. However, in some contracts the transaction price is less clear. Specific situations affecting the transaction price are (a) variable consideration and the constraint on its recognition, (b) sales with a right of return, (c) identifying whether the seller is acting as a principal or an agent, (d) the time value of money, and (e) payments by the seller to the customer. Let's consider these one at a time.

VARIABLE CONSIDERATION. Sometimes a transaction price is uncertain because some of the price depends on the outcome of future events. Contracts that include this variable consideration are commonplace in many industries, including construction (incentive payments), entertainment and media (royalties), health care (Medicare and Medicaid reimbursements), manufacturing (volume discounts and product returns), and telecommunications (rebates).

***Variable consideration* is estimated as either the expected value or the most likely amount.**

Estimating Variable Consideration. When an amount to be received depends on some uncertain future event, the seller still should include the uncertain amount in the transaction price by estimating it. A seller estimates variable consideration as either (a) the *expected value* (calculated as the sum of each possible amount multiplied by its probability), or (b) the *most likely amount,* depending on which estimation approach better predicts the amount that the seller will receive. If there are several possible outcomes, the expected value will be more appropriate. On the other hand, if only two outcomes are possible, the most likely amount might be the best indication of the amount the seller will likely receive. Illustration 5–14 provides an example.

[17]It may seem strange that we consider the likelihood that the customer will use the coupon when estimating the coupon's stand-alone selling price, but think about it from TrueTech's perspective. Each coupon saves a customer $60, but on average TrueTech will only have to provide discounts of $48, so $48 is its estimate of the average stand-alone value of its performance obligation.

Illustration 5–14

Accounting for Variable Consideration

TrueTech enters into a contract with ProSport Gaming to add ProSport's online games to the Tri-Net network. ProSport offers popular games like Brawl of Bands, and wants those games offered on the Tri-Net so ProSport can sell gems, weapons, health potions, and other game features that allow players to advance more quickly in a game.

On January 1, 2016, ProSport pays TrueTech an up-front fixed fee of $300,000 for six months of featured access. ProSport also will pay TrueTech a bonus of $180,000 if Tri-Net users access ProSport games for at least 15,000 hours during the six-month period. TrueTech estimates a 75% chance that it will achieve the usage target and receive the $180,000 bonus.

TrueTech would record the following entry for the receipt of the cash on January 1, 2016:

Cash	300,000	
Deferred revenue		300,000

Subsequent entries to recognize revenue depend on whether TrueTech estimates the transaction price as the expected value or the most likely amount.

Alternative 1: Expected Value

The expected value would be calculated as a probability-weighted transaction price:

Possible Amounts	Probabilities		Expected Amounts
$480,000 ($300,000 fixed fee + 180,000 bonus)	× 75%	=	$ 360,000
$300,000 ($300,000 fixed fee + 0 bonus)	× 25%	=	75,000
Expected value of the contract price at inception			**$435,000**

Alternative 2: Most Likely Amount

Because there is a greater chance of qualifying for the bonus than of not qualifying for the bonus, a transaction price based on the most likely amount would be $300,000 + $180,000, or **$480,000**.

Let's assume that TrueTech bases the estimate on the most likely amount, **$480,000.** In each successive month TrueTech would recognize one month's revenue based on a total transaction price of $480,000. Because it previously recorded $300,000 as deferred revenue, at the end of each month TrueTech would reduce deferred revenue by one-sixth of the $300,000 as well as recognizing a bonus receivable for one-sixth of the $180,000 bonus it expects to receive:

Deferred revenue ($300,000 ÷ 6 months)	50,000	
Bonus receivable ($180,000 ÷ 6 months)	30,000	
Service revenue (**$480,000** ÷ 6 months)[18]		80,000

After six months, TrueTech's deferred revenue account would have been reduced to a zero balance, and the bonus receivable account would have a balance of $180,000 ($30,000 × 6). At that point, TrueTech would know if the usage of ProSport products had reached the bonus threshold and would record one of the following two journal entries:

If TrueTech receives the bonus:			If TrueTech does not receive the bonus:		
Cash	180,000		Service revenue	180,000	
Bonus receivable		180,000	Bonus receivable		180,000

Bonus Receivable

	Debit	Credit
1/1	-0-	
1/31	30,000	
2/28	30,000	
3/31	30,000	
4/30	30,000	
5/31	30,000	
6/30	30,000	180,000
6/30	-0-	

Service Revenue

	Debit	Credit
1/1		-0-
1/31		80,000
2/28		80,000
3/31		80,000
4/30		80,000
5/31		80,000
6/30		80,000
6/30		480,000

The seller must reassess its estimate of the transaction price in each period to determine whether circumstances have changed. If the seller revises its estimate of the amount of variable consideration it will receive, it must revise any receivable it has recorded and reflect the adjustment in that period's revenue, as we see in Illustration 5–15.

[18]If TrueTech instead used the expected value as its estimate of the transaction price, the journal entries would be the same except that the amount of revenue recognized each month would be $72,500 (**$435,000** ÷ 6 months). The reduction in the deferred revenue liability each month would still be $50,000, and the amount of bonus receivable accrued each month would be $22,500 ($135,000 ÷ 6 months).

Illustration 5–15

Accounting for Variable Consideration

Bonus Receivable

	Debit	Credit
1/1	-0-	
1/31	30,000	
2/28	30,000	
3/31	30,000	
4/30		90,000
4/30	-0-	

Service Revenue

	Debit	Credit
1/1		-0-
1/31		80,000
2/28		80,000
3/31		80,000
4/30	90,000	50,000
5/31		50,000
6/30		50,000
6/30		300,000

Assume the same facts as in Illustration 5–14, but that after three months TrueTech concludes that, due to low usage of ProSport's games, the most likely outcome is that TrueTech will *not* receive the $180,000 bonus. TrueTech would record the following entry in April to reduce its bonus receivable to zero and reflect the adjustment in revenue:

Service revenue	90,000	
Bonus receivable (reducing the account to zero)		90,000

For the remainder of the contract, TrueTech only recognizes revenue in each month associated with the up-front fixed payment of $300,000.

Deferred revenue ($300,000 ÷ 6 months)	50,000	
Service revenue		50,000

Constraint on Recognizing Variable Consideration. Sometimes sellers lack sufficient information to make a good estimate of variable consideration. The concern is that a seller might overestimate variable consideration, recognize revenue based on a transaction price that is too high, and later have to reverse that revenue (and reduce net income) to correct the estimate. To guard against this, sellers only include an estimate of variable consideration in the transaction price to the extent it is "probable" that a significant reversal of revenue recognized to date will not occur when the uncertainty associated with the variable consideration is resolved in the future.[19]

Sellers are limited to recognizing variable consideration to the extent that it is probable that a significant revenue reversal will not occur in the future.

Applying this constraint requires judgment on the part of the seller, taking into account all information available. Indicators that a significant revenue reversal could occur include (a) poor evidence on which to base an estimate, (b) dependence of the estimate on factors outside the seller's control, (c) a history of the seller changing payment terms on similar contracts, (d) a broad range of outcomes that could occur, and (e) a long delay before uncertainty resolves.

If a seller changes its opinion regarding whether a constraint on variable consideration is necessary, the seller should update the transaction price in the current reporting period, just as the seller would do for other changes in estimated variable consideration. Illustration 5–16 provides an example.

Illustration 5–16

Constraint on Recognizing Variable Consideration

Assume the same facts as in Illustration 5–14, but that initially TrueTech can't conclude that it is probable that a significant revenue reversal will not occur in the future. In that case, TrueTech is constrained from recognizing revenue associated with variable consideration. It includes only the up-front fixed payment of $300,000 in the transaction price, and recognizes revenue of $50,000 each month.

Deferred revenue ($300,000 ÷ 6 months)	50,000	
Service revenue		50,000

On March 31, after three months of the contract have passed, TrueTech concludes it can make an accurate enough bonus estimate for it to be probable that a significant revenue reversal will not occur. As in Illustration 5–14, TrueTech estimates a 75% likelihood it will receive the bonus and bases its estimate on the "most likely amount" of $180,000. Since on March 31 the contract is one-half finished (3 of the 6 months have passed), TrueTech records a bonus receivable and service revenue for $90,000 ($180,000 × 3/6), the amount that would

(continued)

[19]IFRS uses the term "highly probable" instead of "probable" in this case. Because IFRS defines "probable" to mean a likelihood greater than 50%, its use of "highly probable" is intended to convey the same likelihood as is conveyed by "probable" in U.S. GAAP.

(concluded)

have been recognized over the first three months of the contract if an estimate of variable consideration had been included in the transaction price to begin with:

Bonus receivable ($180,000 × 3/6)	90,000	
Service revenue		90,000

In the final three months of the contract, TrueTech recognizes the remaining revenue assuming a transaction price of $480,000, exactly as if it had included an estimate of variable consideration in the transaction price all along:

Deferred revenue ($300,000 ÷ 6 months)	50,000	
Bonus receivable ($180,000 ÷ 6 months)	30,000	
Service revenue ($480,000 ÷ 6 months)		80,000

Bonus Receivable

Date	Debit	Credit
1/1	-0-	
3/31	90,000	
4/30	30,000	
5/31	30,000	
6/30	30,000	
6/30	180,000	

Service Revenue

Date	Debit	Credit
1/1		-0-
1/31		50,000
2/28		50,000
3/31		50,000
3/31		90,000
4/30		80,000
5/31		80,000
6/30		80,000
6/30		480,000

RIGHT OF RETURN. Retailers usually give customers the right to return merchandise if customers are not satisfied or are unable to resell it. For example, manufacturers of semiconductors like **Motorola Corporation** usually sell their products through independent distributor companies. Economic factors, competition among manufacturers, and rapid obsolescence of the product motivate these manufacturers to grant the distributors the **right of return** if they are unable to sell the semiconductors.

The right to return merchandise does not create a performance obligation for the seller. Instead, it represents a potential failure to satisfy the original performance obligation to provide goods that the customer wants to keep.

A *right of return* is not a performance obligation.

Because the total amount of cash received from the customer depends on the amount of returns, a right of return creates a situation involving variable consideration. Based on past experience, a seller usually can estimate the returns that will result for a given volume of sales, so the seller reduces revenue by the estimated returns and records a liability for cash the seller anticipates refunding to customers. For example, assume that TrueTech sold 1,000 Tri-Boxes to CompStores for $240 each. TrueTech would record the following entry:

Cash ($240 × 1,000)	240,000	
Sales revenue		240,000

If TrueTech estimates that CompStores will return five percent of the Tri-Boxes purchased, TrueTech would record a liability for that amount:

Sales returns ($240,000 × 5% estimated returns)	12,000	
Refund liability		12,000

The sales returns account is a "contra revenue" account that has the effect of reducing revenue. As a result, we report sales revenues net of the amount expected to be returned.[20] Along with the entries above, TrueTech also would need to reduce cost of goods sold and record an asset, "inventory—estimated returns," to reflect the cost of inventory expected to be returned.

Sales revenue
Less: Sales returns
Net sales

In practice, most companies find it impractical to record an estimated refund liability each time they make a sale. Instead, they debit sales returns and credit cash as returns occur

[20]Alternatively, the seller could combine the journal entries and record net revenue as:

Cash	240,000	
Sales revenue (net)		228,000
Refund liability		12,000

and then, at the end of each reporting period, make appropriate adjustments to sales returns and a refund liability to account for their estimate of remaining returns. We discuss these and other aspects of accounting for returns in more detail in Chapter 7.

What if TrueTech had sold the Tri-Boxes on account rather than for cash? When TrueTech accounts for estimated returns, it wouldn't make sense to record a refund liability to return cash it hadn't yet received. So, instead of crediting a refund liability, TrueTech typically would credit a contra asset, *allowance for sales returns,* that reduces the book value, sometimes called the carrying value or carrying amount, of accounts receivable to $218,000 ($240,000 − 12,000).

If the seller lacks sufficient information to be able to accurately estimate returns, the constraint on recognizing variable consideration we discussed earlier applies, and the seller should recognize revenue only to the extent it is probable that a significant revenue reversal will not occur later if the estimate of returns changes. In fact, the seller might postpone recognizing any revenue until the uncertainty about returns is resolved. Illustration 5–17 provides an example.

Illustration 5–17

Disclosure of Revenue Recognition Policy—Intel Corporation.

Real World Financials

Revenue Recognition

Because of frequent sales price reductions and rapid technology obsolescence in the industry, we defer product revenue and related costs of sales from component sales made to distributors under agreements allowing price protection or right of return until the distributors sell the merchandise.

IS THE SELLER A PRINCIPAL OR AGENT? Sometimes more than one company is involved in providing goods or services to a customer. In those situations, we need to determine whether a company is acting as a **principal** and providing the good or service to the customer, or an **agent** and only arranging for another company to provide the good or service.

A *principal* controls goods or services and is responsible for providing them to the customer.

An *agent* doesn't control goods or services, but rather facilitates transfers between sellers and customers.

We view the seller as a principal if it obtains control of the goods or services before they are transferred to the customer. Control is evident if the principal has primary responsibility for delivering a product or service and is vulnerable to risks associated with holding inventory, delivering the product or service, and collecting payment from the customer. A principal's performance obligation is to deliver goods and services. In contrast, an agent doesn't primarily deliver goods or services, but acts as a facilitator that receives a commission for helping sellers provide goods and services to buyers. An agent's performance obligation is to facilitate a transaction between a principal and a customer.

Many examples of agents occur in business. One you're familiar with is a real estate agent. Real estate agents don't own the houses they sell, but rather charge a commission to help home owners transact with home buyers. Similarly, online auction houses like **eBay**, travel facilitators like **Expedia, Inc.** and **priceline.com**, and broad web-based retailers like **Amazon.com** act as agents for a variety of sellers. Complicating matters, these same companies also act as principals on some other arrangements, selling their own products and services directly to customers. For example, eBay acts as an agent by linking sellers with buyers, but acts as a principal when selling its PayPal transaction-processing service.

An agent only records its commission as revenue.

The distinction between a principal and an agent is important because it affects the amount of revenue that a company can record. If the company is a principal, it records revenue equal to the total sales price paid by customers as well as cost of goods sold equal to the cost of the item to the company. On the other hand, if the company is an agent, it records as revenue only the commission it receives on the transaction. In Illustration 5–18 we see the difference in accounting by principals and agents.

We see from Illustration 5–18 that whether the seller is a principal or an agent can have a significant effect on its revenue. This is particularly important for start-ups or growth-oriented companies that may be valued more for growth in revenue, than for growth in net income.

Illustration 5–18

Comparison of Revenue Recognition by Principals and Agents

Mike buys a Tri-Box module from an online retailer for $290. Let's consider accounting for that sale by two retailers: PrinCo and AgenCo:

- PrinCo purchases Tri-Box modules directly from TrueTech for $240, has the modules shipped to its distribution center in Kansas, and then ships individual modules to buyers when a sale is made. PrinCo offers occasional price discounts according to its marketing strategy. Because PrinCo is responsible for fulfilling the contract, bears the risk of holding inventory, and has latitude in setting sales prices, the evidence suggests that PrinCo is a principal in this transaction.
- AgenCo serves as a web portal by which multiple game module manufacturers like TrueTech can offer their products for sale. The manufacturers ship directly to buyers when a sale is made. AgenCo receives a $50 commission on each sale that occurs via its web portal. Given that AgenCo is not primarily responsible for fulfilling the contract, bears no inventory risk, has no latitude in setting sales prices, and is paid on commission, the evidence suggests AgenCo is an agent in this transaction.

The first part of the income statement for each retailer is shown below. Notice that the same amount of gross profit, $50, is recognized by the principal and the agent. What differ are the amounts of revenue and expense that are recognized and reported.

A Principal Records Gross Revenue (PrinCo)		An Agent Records Net Revenue (AgenCo)	
Revenue	$290	Revenue	$50
Less: Cost of goods sold	240	Less: Cost of goods sold	0
Gross profit	$ 50	Gross profit	$50

THE TIME VALUE OF MONEY. It's common for contracts to specify that payment occurs either before or after delivery. We recognize an account receivable when payment occurs after delivery, and we recognize deferred revenue when payment occurs before delivery. We can think of these arrangements in part as financing transactions. In the case of an account receivable, the seller is making a loan to the customer between delivery and payment. In the case of a payment prior to delivery, the customer is making a loan to the seller by paying in advance. As with any other loan, there is an interest charge (a "time value of money") implicit in these arrangements.

If delivery and payment occur relatively near each other, the time value of money is not significant and can be ignored. As a practical matter, a seller can assume the time value of money is not significant if the period between delivery and payment is less than a year. However, if the time value of money is significant, the seller views the transaction price as consisting of (a) the cash price of the good or service and (b) a "financing component" representing the interest for the time between the sale and the cash payment. The seller then adjusts the transaction price to remove the financing component. That way, the seller recognizes the same amount of revenue for goods and services that it would recognize if the customer paid cash at the time the seller delivers those goods and services. The seller separately accounts for the financing component of the contract by recognizing interest revenue (in the case of an account receivable) or interest expense (in the case of a customer prepayment) over time. We discuss the time value of money in detail in Chapter 6. We discuss how sellers make adjustments for the time value of money for accounts receivable in Chapter 7 and for prepayments in Chapter 13.

Sellers must account for the financing component of transactions when it is significant.

PAYMENTS BY THE SELLER TO THE CUSTOMER. Usually it's the customer who pays the seller for goods or services. Occasionally, though, a *seller* also makes payments to a *customer*. For example, **Samsung** sells TVs, smartphones, tablets, and other products to **BestBuy**. However, Samsung also might pay BestBuy for dedicated space in BestBuy stores or to conduct special Samsung-focused advertising programs. The question is whether a payment by Samsung is a purchase of goods or services from BestBuy, or really just a refund of some of the price paid by BestBuy to purchase Samsung products.

The way we account for payments by a seller to a customer depends on the specifics of the arrangement. If the seller is purchasing distinct goods or services from the customer at the fair value of those goods or services, we account for that purchase as a separate transaction. If a seller pays more for distinct goods or services purchased from its customer than the fair value of those goods or services, those excess payments are viewed as a refund. They are subtracted from the amount the seller is entitled to receive when calculating the transaction price of the sale to the customer. In our Samsung example, if Samsung pays more for dedicated floor space at BestBuy than the fair value of that floor space, Samsung should treat that excess payment as a refund to BestBuy of part of the price paid by BestBuy for Samsung products.

Special Issues for Step 4: Allocate the Transaction Price to the Performance Obligations

We already discussed the need for the seller to allocate the transaction price to each performance obligation in a contract in proportion to the stand-alone selling prices of the goods or services. We also noted that when goods and services aren't normally sold separately, sellers must estimate those stand-alone selling prices. Various approaches are available to estimate stand-alone selling prices. Examples include the following:

1. **Adjusted market assessment approach:** The seller considers what it could sell the product or services for in the market in which it normally conducts business, perhaps referencing prices charged by competitors.
2. **Expected cost plus margin approach:** The seller estimates its costs of satisfying a performance obligation and then adds an appropriate profit margin.
3. **Residual approach:** The seller estimates an unknown (or highly uncertain) stand-alone selling price by subtracting the sum of the known or estimated stand-alone selling prices of other goods and services in the contract from the total transaction price of the contract. The residual approach is allowed only if the stand-alone selling price is highly uncertain, either because the seller hasn't previously sold the good or service and hasn't yet determined a price for it, or because the seller provides the same good or service to different customers at substantially different prices. Illustration 5–19 provides an example of the residual approach.

The *residual approach* is used to estimate a stand-alone selling price that is very uncertain.

Illustration 5–19

Allocating Transaction Price to Performance Obligations Using the Residual Approach

Assume the same facts as Illustration 5–7, except that the stand-alone selling price of the one-year Tri-Net subscription is highly uncertain because TrueTech hasn't sold that service previously and hasn't established a price for it. Under the residual approach, the value of the subscription would be estimated as follows:

Total price of Tri-Box with Tri-Net subscription ($250 × 1,000)	$250,000
Stand-alone price of Tri-Box sold without subscription ($240 × 1,000)	240,000
Estimated stand-alone price of Tri-Net subscription	$ 10,000

Based on these relative stand-alone selling prices, if CompStores orders 1,000 Tri-Box Systems at the normal wholesale price of $250 each, TrueTech records the following journal entry (ignoring any entry to record the reduction in inventory and corresponding cost of goods sold):

Accounts receivable	250,000	
Sales revenue		240,000
Deferred revenue		10,000

TrueTech would convert the $10,000 of deferred revenue to revenue (debit deferred revenue; credit service revenue) over the one-year term of the Tri-Net subscription.

Additional Consideration

Allocating Variable Consideration. What if a contract that has variable consideration includes multiple performance obligations? Typically the seller would include the variable consideration in the transaction price that is allocated to each of those performance obligations according to their relative stand-alone selling prices. Also, changes in estimated variable consideration are allocated to performance obligations on the same basis. However, if the variable consideration relates only to one performance obligation, it is allocated to only that performance obligation.

Special Issues for Step 5: Recognize Revenue When (Or As) Each Performance Obligation Is Satisfied

● LO5–7

Previously, we discussed recognizing revenue at a point in time and over a period of time. Now let's look at a few commonplace arrangements that occur in practice that make it more difficult to determine when revenue should be recognized. In particular, we discuss licenses, franchises, bill-and-hold sales, consignment arrangements, and gift cards.

LICENSES. Customers sometimes pay a licensing fee to use a company's intellectual property. Licenses are common in the software, technology, media, and entertainment (including motion pictures and music) industries.

Licenses allow the customer to use the seller's intellectual property.

Some licenses transfer a right to use the seller's intellectual property as it exists when the license is granted. Examples include software like Microsoft Office, music CDs, and movie DVDs. For these licenses, subsequent activity by the seller doesn't affect the benefit that the customer receives. For example, once you download a Beyoncé hit from Apple's iTunes, you can enjoy listening to that song as often as you like, regardless of future actions by Beyoncé or iTunes. If a license transfers such a *right of use*, revenue is recognized at the point in time the right is transferred.

If a seller's activities during the license period are *not* expected to affect the intellectual property being licensed to the customer, revenue is recognized at the start of the license period.

Other licenses provide the customer with access to the seller's intellectual property with the understanding that the seller will undertake ongoing activities during the license period that affect the benefit the customer receives. Examples include licenses to use a company's brand or trademark. For instance, if the NBA sells Adidas a five-year license to manufacture jerseys with NBA team logos, Adidas would expect that the value of that right is affected by whether the NBA continues to play games and provide advertising during that license period. If a license provides such a *right of access* to the seller's intellectual property, the seller satisfies its performance obligation over time as the customer benefits from the seller's ongoing activities, so revenue is recognized over the period of time for which access is provided.

If a seller's activities during the license period *are* expected to affect the intellectual property being licensed to the customer, revenue is recognized over the license period.

Finally, sometimes a license isn't distinct from other promised goods or services. For example, an online service might grant a license to customers to access content at a website. In that case, the license isn't distinct from the content, because the point of the license is to access the content, so they would be treated as a single performance obligation and revenue would be recognized as appropriate for that performance obligation.

Additional Consideration

Variable Consideration and Licenses. Previously you learned about sellers being able to recognize revenue associated with variable consideration. There's an exception for sales-based or usage-based royalties on licenses. Those royalties are only included in the transaction price when they are no longer variable (which happens when the customer's sales or usage has actually occurred).

In a *franchise* arrangement, a franchisor grants to the franchisee the right to sell the franchisor's products and use its name.

FRANCHISES. Many retail outlets for fast food, restaurants, hotels, and auto rental agencies are operated as franchises. In franchise arrangements, the franchisor, such as **Subway**, grants to the franchisee, quite often an individual, a right to sell the franchisor's products and use its name for a specified period of time. The franchisor also typically provides initial start-up services (such as identifying locations, remodeling or constructing facilities, selling equipment, and providing training to the franchisee) as well as providing ongoing products and services (such as franchise-branded products and advertising and administrative services). So, a franchise involves a *license* to use the franchisor's intellectual property, but also involves *initial sales* of products and services as well as *ongoing sales* of products and services. The franchisor must evaluate each part of the franchise arrangement to identify the performance obligations. Illustration 5–20 gives an example.

Illustration 5–20

Franchise Arrangements

Assume that TrueTech starts selling TechStop franchises. TrueTech charges franchisees an initial fee in exchange for (a) the exclusive right to operate the only TechStop in a particular area for a five-year period, (b) the equipment necessary to distribute and repair TrueTech products, and (c) training services to be provided over a two-year period. Similar equipment and training can be purchased elsewhere. What are the performance obligations in this arrangement, and when would TrueTech recognize revenue for each of them?

1. The exclusive five-year right to operate the only TechStop in a particular area is distinct because it can be used with other goods or services (furnishings, equipment, products) that the customer could obtain elsewhere.
2. The equipment is distinct because similar equipment is sold separately.
3. The training is distinct because similar training could be acquired elsewhere.

TrueTech would allocate the initial franchise fee to three separate performance obligations based on their relative stand-alone prices: (1) the right to operate a TechStop, (2) equipment, and (3) training. TrueTech would recognize revenue for the right to operate a TechStop over the five-year license period, because TrueTech's ongoing activities over the license period affect the value of the right to run a TechStop. TrueTech would recognize revenue for the equipment at the time the equipment is delivered to the franchisee, and would recognize revenue for the training over the two-year period that the training is provided.

What if TrueTech also charges franchisees an additional fee for ongoing services provided by TrueTech? In that case, TrueTech would recognize revenue associated with that fee over time as it provides the ongoing services.

BILL-AND-HOLD ARRANGEMENTS. A bill-and-hold arrangement exists when a customer purchases goods but requests that the seller not ship the product until a later date. For example, a customer might buy equipment and ask the seller to store the equipment until an installation site has been prepared.

For bill-and-hold arrangements, the key issue is that the customer doesn't have physical possession of the asset until the seller has delivered it. Remember, physical possession is one of the indicators that control may have been transferred as listed in Illustration 5–3. Bill-and-hold arrangements might arise normally in the course of business, but they also have been abused by some companies in the past. Managers at companies like **Sunbeam**, **NutraCea**, and **Nortel Networks** are alleged to have overstated revenue by falsely claiming that unsold inventory has been sold under a bill-and-hold arrangement.

Revenue recognition usually occurs at delivery for a *bill-and-hold* arrangement.

The physical possession indicator normally overshadows other control indicators in a bill-and-hold arrangement, so sellers usually conclude that control has not been transferred and revenue should not be recognized until actual delivery to the customer occurs.

Consistent with SEC guidance, sellers can recognize revenue prior to delivery only if (a) they conclude that the customer controls the product, (b) there is a good reason for the bill-and-hold arrangement, and (c) the product is specifically identified as belonging to the customer and is ready for shipment.[21]

Ethical Dilemma

The Precision Parts Corporation manufactures automobile parts. The company has reported a profit every year since the company's inception in 1980. Management prides itself on this accomplishment and believes one important contributing factor is the company's incentive plan that rewards top management a bonus equal to a percentage of operating income if the operating income goal for the year is achieved. However, 2016 has been a tough year, and prospects for attaining the income goal for the year are bleak.

Tony Smith, the company's chief financial officer, has determined a way to increase December sales by an amount sufficient to boost operating income over the goal for the year and secure bonuses for all top management. A reputable customer ordered $120,000 of normally stocked parts to be shipped on January 15, 2017. Tony told the rest of top management "I know we can get that order ready by December 31. We can then just leave the order on the loading dock until shipment. I see nothing wrong with recognizing the sale in 2016, since the parts will have been manufactured and we do have a firm order from a reputable customer." The company's normal procedure is to ship goods f.o.b. destination and to recognize sales revenue when the customer receives the parts.

CONSIGNMENT ARRANGEMENTS. Sometimes a company arranges for another company to sell its product under **consignment**. In these arrangements, the "consignor" physically transfers the goods to the other company (the consignee), but the consignor retains legal title. If a buyer is found, the consignee remits the selling price (less commission and approved expenses) to the consignor. If the consignee can't find a buyer within an agreed-upon time, the consignee returns the goods to the consignor.

When does control transfer from the consignor, allowing the consignor to recognize revenue? Referring to the indicators listed in Illustration 5–3, the consignor still has title and retains many of the risks and rewards of ownership for goods it has placed on consignment. Therefore, it's likely that the consignor would be judged to retain control after transfer to the consignee and would postpone recognizing revenue until sale to an end customer occurs. Illustration 5–21 provides an example of a consignment arrangement by **Boston Scientific Corporation** from a recent annual report.

Revenue recognition occurs upon sale to an end customer in a *consignment* arrangement.

Note 1: Business and Summary of Significant Accounting Policies: Revenue Recognition (in part)

We generally meet these criteria at the time of shipment, unless a consignment arrangement exists or we are required to provide additional services. We recognize revenue from consignment arrangements based on product usage, or implant, which indicates that the sale is complete.

Illustration 5–21

Disclosure of Revenue Recognition Policy for Consignment Arrangements—Boston Scientific Corporation

Real World Financials

[21]FASB ASC 605–10–S99: Revenue Recognition–Overall–SEC Materials (originally "Revenue Recognition in Financial Statements," *Staff Accounting Bulletin No. 101* (Washington, D.C.: SEC, 1999) and *Staff Accounting Bulletin No. 104* (Washington, D.C.: SEC, 2003)).

Sales of gift cards are recognized as deferred revenue.

GIFT CARDS Let's assume you received an iTunes gift card that allows you to download songs or audiobooks later. When your friend bought that gift card, Apple recorded a deferred revenue liability in anticipation of recording revenue when you used your gift card to get songs. But, what if you lose the card or fail to redeem it for some other reason? Sellers like Apple, Target, Amazon, and others will recognize revenue at the point when they have concluded based on past experience that there is only a "remote likelihood" that customers will use the cards.[22] We discuss accounting for gift card liabilities further in Chapter 13.

Disclosures

● LO5–8

INCOME STATEMENT DISCLOSURE. Of course, a seller reports revenue in its income statement. In addition, that seller is required to either include in its income statement or disclosure notes any bad debt expense and any interest revenue or interest expense associated with significant financing components of long-term contracts.

The seller recognizes *contract liabilities, contract assets,* and *accounts receivable* on separate lines of its balance sheet.

BALANCE SHEET DISCLOSURE. A seller reports accounts receivable, "contract liabilities," and "contract assets" on separate lines of its balance sheet. We discuss each in turn.

If a customer pays the seller before the seller has satisfied a performance obligation, we saw earlier that the seller records deferred revenue. For example, we recorded deferred revenue in Illustration 5–6 when TrueTech received payment for Tri-Net subscriptions prior to providing that service. A contract liability is a label we give to deferred revenue (or unearned revenue) accounts.

On the other hand, if the seller satisfies a performance obligation *before* the customer has paid for it, the seller records either a contract asset or accounts receivable. The seller recognizes an account receivable if the seller has an unconditional right to receive payment, which is the case if only the passage of time is required before the payment is due. In other words, the seller has satisfied all of its performance obligations and is just waiting to be paid.

If, instead, the seller satisfies a performance obligation but payment depends on something other than the passage of time, the seller recognizes a contract asset. For example, construction companies sometimes complete a significant amount of work prior to when the construction contract indicates they can bill their clients for progress payments. As we will see in Part C of this chapter, a construction company in that situation reports a contract asset called "construction-in-progress in excess of billings" to reflect that the company will be able to bill its client in the future for the work that has been completed.

DISCLOSURE NOTES. Several important aspects of revenue recognition must be disclosed in the notes to the financial statements. For example, sellers must separate their revenue into categories that help investors understand the nature, amount, timing, and uncertainty of revenue and cash flows. Categories might include product lines, geographic regions, types of customers, or types of contracts. Sellers also must disclose amounts included in revenue that were previously recognized as deferred revenue or that resulted from changes in transaction prices.

Companies provide detailed disclosures about revenues.

Sellers also must describe their outstanding performance obligations, discuss how performance obligations typically are satisfied, and describe important contractual provisions like payment terms and policies for refunds, returns, and warranties. They also must disclose any significant judgments used to estimate transaction prices, to allocate transaction prices to performance obligations, and to determine when performance obligations have been satisfied.

Sellers also must explain significant changes in contract assets and contract liabilities that occurred during the period.

The objective of these disclosures is to help users of financial statements understand the revenue and cash flows arising from contracts with customers. Of course, the downside of these disclosures is that sellers also are providing information to competitors, suppliers, and customers.

Illustration 5–22 provides a summary of both Parts A and Parts B of this chapter to provide a comprehensive review of revenue recognition.

[22]This is sometimes referred to as "breakage" of the gift card.

Illustration 5–22 Summary of Fundamental and Special Issues Related to Recognizing Revenue

Revenue Recognition	Fundamental Issues (Part A)		Special Issues (Part B)	
Step 1 Identify the contract	A contract establishes the legal rights and obligations of the seller and customer with respect to one or more performance obligations.		A contract exists if it (a) has commercial substance, (b) has been approved by both the seller and the customer, (c) specifies the seller's and customer's rights and obligations, (d) specifies payment terms, and (e) is probable that the seller will collect the amounts it is entitled to receive. A contract does ***not*** exist if (a) neither the seller nor the customer has performed any obligations under the contract, and (b) both the seller and the customer can terminate the contract without penalty.	
Step 2 Identify the performance obligation(s)	A performance obligation is a promise to transfer a good or service that is distinct, which is the case if the good or service is both (a) capable of being distinct and (b) separately identifiable.		The following ***do not*** qualify as performance obligations: • Quality assurance warranties • Customer prepayments	The following ***do*** qualify as performance obligations: • Extended warranties • Customer options for additional goods and services that provide a material right
Step 3 Determine the transaction price	The transaction price is the amount the seller is entitled to receive from the customer.		The seller adjusts the transaction price for: • Variable consideration (estimated as either the expected value or the most likely amount). Constraint: Variable consideration is recognized only to the extent it is probable that a significant revenue reversal will not occur in the future. • Whether the seller is acting as a principal or agent • A significant financing component • Any payments by the seller to the customer	
Step 4 Allocate the transaction price	The seller allocates the transaction price to performance obligations based on relative stand alone selling prices of the goods or services in each performance obligation.		Various approaches are available to estimate stand-alone selling prices: • Adjusted market assessment approach • Expected cost plus margin approach • Residual approach	
Step 5 Recognize revenue when (or as) each performance obligation is satisfied	The seller recognizes revenue **at a single point in time** when control passes to the customer, which is more likely if the customer has: • Obligation to pay seller. • Legal title to the asset. • Possession of the asset. • Assumed the risks and rewards of ownership. • Accepted the asset.	The seller recognizes revenue **over a period of time** if: • Customer consumes benefit as work performed, • Customer controls asset as it's created, or • Seller is creating an asset that has no alternative use and the seller has right to receive payment for work completed.	The seller must determine the timing of revenue recognition for: • Licenses (if the seller's activity over the license period is expected to affect the benefits the customer receives, recognize revenue over time; otherwise, recognize revenue at the time the license is transferred). • Franchises (initial fees recognized when goods and services are transferred; continuing fees recognized over time). • Bill-and-hold arrangements (typically do not transfer control, so recognize upon delivery of goods to customer). • Consignment arrangements (do not transfer control, so recognize after sale to end customer occurs). • Gift cards (initially deferred and then recognized as redeemed or expire).	

PART C

Accounting for Long-Term Contracts

● LO5–9

A recent survey of reporting practices of 500 large public companies indicates that approximately one in every eight companies participates in long-term contracts.[23] These are not only construction companies. Illustration 5–23 lists just a sampling of companies that use long-term contracts, many of which you might recognize.

Illustration 5–23
Companies Engaged in Long-Term Contracts

Company	Type of Industry or Product
Oracle Corp.	Computer software, license and consulting fees
Lockheed Martin Corporation	Aircraft, missiles, and spacecraft
Hewlett-Packard	Information technology
Northrop Grumman Newport News	Shipbuilding
Nortel Networks Corp.	Networking solutions and services to support the Internet
SBA Communications Corp.	Telecommunications
Layne Christensen Company	Water supply services and geotechnical construction
Kaufman & Broad Home Corp.	Commercial and residential construction
Raytheon Company	Defense electronics
Foster Wheeler Corp.	Construction, petroleum and chemical facilities
Halliburton	Construction, energy services
Allied Construction Products Corp.	Large metal stamping presses

The five-step process for recognizing revenue described in Parts A and B of this chapter also applies to long-term contracts. However, steps 2 and 5 merit special attention.

Step 2, "Identify the performance obligation(s) in the contract," is important because long-term contracts typically include many products and services that could be viewed as separate performance obligations. For example, constructing a building requires the builder to deliver many different materials and other products (concrete, lumber, furnace, bathroom fixtures, carpeting) and to provide many different services (surveying, excavating, construction, fixture installation, painting, landscaping). These products and services are capable of being distinct, but they are not separately identifiable, because the seller's role is to combine those products and services for purposes of delivering a completed building to the customer. Therefore, it's the bundle of products and services that comprise a single performance obligation. Most long-term contracts should be viewed as including a single performance obligation.

Step 5, "Recognize revenue when (or as) each performance obligation is satisfied," is important because there can be a considerable difference for long-term contracts between recognizing revenue over time and recognizing revenue only when the contract has been completed. Imagine a builder who spends years constructing a skyscraper but only gets to recognize revenue at the end of the contract. Such delayed revenue recognition would do a poor job of informing financial statement users about the builder's economic activity. Fortunately, most long-term contracts qualify for revenue recognition over time. Often the customer owns the seller's work in process, such that the seller is creating an asset that the customer controls as it is completed. Also, often the seller is creating an asset that is customized for the customer, so the seller has no other use for the asset and has the right to be paid for progress even if the customer cancels the contract. In either of those cases, the seller recognizes revenue over time.

Long-term contracts are complex, and specialized accounting approaches have been developed to handle that complexity. For many years, long-term contracts that qualified for revenue recognition over time were accounted for using an approach called the *percentage-of-completion method*, which recognized revenue in each year of the contract according to

[23]*U.S. GAAP Financial Statements—Best Practices in Presentation and Disclosure–2013* (New York: AICPA, 2013).

the progress toward completion that occurred during that year. Long-term contracts that didn't qualify for revenue recognition over time were accounted for using an approach called the *completed contract method*, because all revenue was recognized at a single point in time—upon completion of the contract.

ASU No. 2014–09 removes the terms "percentage-of-completion method" and "completed contract method" from the Accounting Standards Codification, and changes the criteria that determine whether revenue should be recognized over a period of time or at a point in time. However, the journal entries necessary to account for revenue over time are the same as those that were used under the percentage-of-completion method, and those used to account for revenue at a point in time are the same as those used under the completed contract method. We demonstrate those journal entries next.

Accounting for a Profitable Long-Term Contract

FINANCIAL Reporting Case

Q3, p. 231

Much of the accounting for long-term contracts is the same regardless of whether we recognize revenue over the contract period or upon completion of the contract. So, we start by discussing the similarities between the two approaches, and then the differences. You'll see that we recognize the same total amounts of revenue and profit over the life of the contract either way. Only the timing of recognition differs.

Illustration 5–24 provides information for a typical long-term construction contract that we'll use to consider accounting for long-term contracts.

Illustration 5–24

Example of Long-Term Construction Contract

At the beginning of 2016, the Harding Construction Company received a contract to build an office building for $5 million. Harding will construct the building according to specifications provided by the buyer, and the project is estimated to take three years to complete. According to the contract, Harding will bill the buyer in installments over the construction period according to a prearranged schedule. Information related to the contract is as follows:

	2016	2017	2018
Construction costs incurred during the year	$1,500,000	$1,000,000	$1,600,000
Construction costs incurred in prior years	-0-	1,500,000	2,500,000
Cumulative actual construction costs	1,500,000	2,500,000	4,100,000
Estimated costs to complete at end of year	2,250,000	1,500,000	-0-
Total estimated and actual construction costs	$3,750,000	$4,000,000	$4,100,000
Billings made during the year	$1,200,000	$2,000,000	$1,800,000
Cash collections during year	1,000,000	1,400,000	2,600,000

Construction costs include the labor, materials, and overhead costs directly related to the construction of the building. Notice how the total of estimated and actual construction costs changes from period to period. Cost revisions are typical in long-term contracts because costs are estimated over long periods of time.

ACCOUNTING FOR THE COST OF CONSTRUCTION AND ACCOUNTS RECEIVABLE. Summary journal entries are shown in Illustration 5–24A for actual construction costs, billings, and cash receipts. These journal entries are not affected by the timing of revenue recognition.

The first journal entry shows Harding incurring various costs during the construction process and recording them in an asset account called **construction in progress** (or "CIP" for short). This asset account is equivalent to work-in-process inventory in a manufacturing company. This is logical because the construction project is essentially an inventory item in process for the contractor.

***Construction in progress* (CIP) is the contractor's work-in-process inventory.**

Illustration 5–24A Journal Entries—Costs, Billings, and Cash Collections

	2016		2017		2018	
Construction in progress (CIP)	1,500,000		1,000,000		1,600,000	
Cash, materials, etc.		1,500,000		1,000,000		1,600,000
To record construction costs.						
Accounts receivable	1,200,000		2,000,000		1,800,000	
Billings on construction contract ...		1,200,000		2,000,000		1,800,000
To record progress billings.						
Cash..	1,000,000		1,400,000		2,600,000	
Accounts receivable		1,000,000		1,400,000		2,600,000
To record cash collections.						

Accounting for costs, billings, and cash receipts does not depend on the timing of revenue recognition.

The second journal entry occurs when Harding bills its customer according to whatever schedule the contract permits. Notice that periodic billings are credited to **billings on construction contract**. This account is a contra account to the CIP asset. At the end of each period, the balances in these two accounts are compared. If the net amount is a debit, it is reported in the balance sheet as a contract asset. Conversely, if the net amount is a credit, it is reported as a contract liability.[24]

To understand why we use the billings on construction contract account (or "billings" for short), consider a key difference between accounting for a long-term contract and accounting for a more normal sale of inventory to a customer. In the normal case, the seller debits an account receivable and credits revenue, and also debits cost of goods sold and credits inventory. Thus, the seller gives up its physical asset (inventory) and recognizes cost of goods sold at the same time it gets a financial asset (an account receivable) and recognizes revenue. First the physical asset is in the balance sheet, and then the financial asset, but the two are not in the balance sheet at the same time.

The *billings on construction contract* account prevents "double counting" assets by reducing CIP whenever an account receivable is recognized.

Now consider our Harding Construction example. Harding is creating a physical asset (CIP) in the same periods it recognizes a financial asset (first recognizing accounts receivable when the customer is billed and then recognizing cash when the receivable is collected). Having both the physical asset and the financial asset in the balance sheet at the same time constitutes double counting the same arrangement. The billings account solves this problem. Whenever an account receivable is recognized, the other side of the journal entry increases the billings account, which is contra to (and thus reduces) CIP. As a result, the financial asset (accounts receivable) increases and the physical asset (the net amount of CIP and billings) decreases, and no double counting occurs.

Remember, we recognize accounts receivable when the seller has an unconditional right to receive payment, which is the case if only the passage of time is required before the payment is due, and we recognize a contract asset when the seller's right to receive payment depends on something other than the passage of time. Consistent with those definitions, Harding will report an account receivable for amounts it has billed the client and not yet been paid, and will report a contract asset (CIP – Billings) for the remaining amount of work completed, for which it eventually will be paid once it is able to bill the client.

REVENUE RECOGNITION—GENERAL APPROACH. Now let's consider revenue recognition. The top portion of Illustration 5–24B shows the single journal entry to recognize revenue, cost of construction (think of this as cost of goods sold), and gross profit when recognizing revenue upon completion of the contract, while the bottom portion shows the journal entries that achieve this when recognizing revenue over the term of the contract. At this point focus on the structure of the journal entries (what is debited and credited). We'll discuss how to calculate the specific amounts later in the chapter.

[24]If the company is engaged in more than one long-term contract, all contracts for which construction in progress exceeds billings are reported in the balance sheet as contract assets, and all contracts for which billings exceed construction in progress are reported as contract liabilities.

Illustration 5–24B Journal Entries—Revenue Recognition

	2016		2017		2018	
Recognizing Revenue upon Completion						
Construction in progress (CIP)					900,000	
Cost of construction					4,100,000	
Revenue from long-term contracts...						5,000,000
To record gross profit.						
Recognizing Revenue Over Time According to Percentage of Completion						
Construction in progress (CIP)	500,000		125,000		275,000	
Cost of construction	1,500,000		1,000,000		1,600,000	
Revenue from long-term contracts...		2,000,000		1,125,000		1,875,000
To record gross profit.						

It's important to understand two key aspects of Illustration 5–24B. First, the same amounts of revenue (the $5 million contract price), cost, and gross profit are recognized whether it's over the term of the contract or only upon completion. The only difference is timing. To check this, we can add together all of the revenue recognized for both methods over the three years:

The same total amount of revenue is recognized whether it's over the term of the contract or only upon completion, but the timing of recognition differs.

	Revenue Recognition:	
	Over Time	**Upon Completion**
Revenue recognized:		
2016	$2,000,000	-0-
2017	1,125,000	-0-
2018	1,875,000	$5,000,000
Total revenue	$5,000,000	$5,000,000

Second, notice that, regardless of the timing of revenue recognition, we add gross profit (the difference between revenue and cost) to the CIP asset. That seems odd—why add profit to what is essentially an inventory account? The key here is that, when Harding recognizes gross profit, Harding is acting like it has sold some portion of the asset to the customer, but Harding keeps the asset in Harding's own balance sheet (in the CIP account) until delivery to the customer. Putting recognized gross profit into the CIP account just updates that account to reflect the total value (cost + gross profit = sales price) of the customer's asset. But don't forget that the billings account is contra to the CIP account. Over the life of the construction project, Harding will bill the customer for the entire sales price of the asset. Therefore, at the end of the contract, the CIP account (containing total cost and gross profit) and the billings account (containing all amounts billed to the customer) will have equal balances that exactly offset to create a net value of zero.

CIP includes profits and losses on the contract that have been recognized to date.

Now let's discuss the timing of revenue recognition in more detail.

REVENUE RECOGNITION UPON THE COMPLETION OF THE CONTRACT. If a contract doesn't qualify for revenue recognition over time, revenue is recognized at the point in time that control transfers from the seller to the customer, which typically occurs when the contract has been completed. At that time, the seller views itself as selling the asset and recognizes revenues and expenses associated with the sale. As shown in Illustration 5–24B and in the T-accounts on the next page, completion occurs in 2018 for our Harding example. Prior to then, CIP includes only costs, showing a cumulative balance of $1,500,000 and $2,500,000 at the end of 2016 and 2017, respectively, and totaling $4,100,000 ($1,500,000 + 1,000,000 + 1,600,000) when the project is completed in 2018. Upon completion, Harding recognizes revenue of $5,000,000 and cost of construction (similar to cost of goods sold) of $4,100,000, because the asset is viewed as "sold" on that date. Harding includes the resulting $900,000 gross profit in CIP, increasing its balance to the $5,000,000 total cost + gross profit for the project.

If a contract doesn't qualify for revenue recognition over time, revenue is recognized when the project is completed.

Recognizing Revenue upon Completion

If revenue is recognized upon completion of the contract, CIP is updated to include gross profit at that point in time.

	Construction in Progress (CIP)			Billings on Construction Contract	
2016 construction costs	1,500,000			1,200,000	2016 billings
End balance, 2016	1,500,000			1,200,000	End balance, 2016
2017 construction costs	1,000,000			2,000,000	2017 billings
End balance, 2017	2,500,000			3,200,000	End balance, 2017
2018 construction costs	1,600,000			1,800,000	2018 billings
Total gross profit	900,000				
Balance, before closing	5,000,000			5,000,000	Balance, before closing

RECOGNIZING REVENUE OVER TIME ACCORDING TO PERCENTAGE OF COMPLETION. If a contract qualifies for revenue recognition over time, revenue is recognized based on progress towards completion. How should progress to date be estimated?

If a contract qualifies for revenue recognition over time, revenue is recognized over time as the project is completed.

As discussed in Part A of this chapter, one approach to estimating progress towards completion is to use output-based measures, like number of units produced or delivered, achievement of milestones, and surveys or appraisals of performance completed to date. A shortcoming of output measures is that they may provide a distorted view of actual progress to date.[25] For example, an output measure for highway construction might be finished miles of road, but that measure could be deceptive if not all miles of road require the same effort. A highway contract for the state of Arizona would likely pay the contractor more for miles of road blasted through the mountains than for miles paved across flat dessert. Another shortcoming of some output measures is that the information they require, such as surveys or appraisals, might be costly to obtain.

Another way to estimate progress is to base it on the seller's *input,* measured as the proportion of effort expended thus far relative to the total effort expected to satisfy the performance obligation. Measures of effort include costs incurred, labor hours expended, machine hours used, or time lapsed. The most common approach to estimating progress toward completion is to use a "cost-to-cost ratio" that compares total cost incurred to date to the total estimated cost to complete the project.[26] When using that approach, sellers have to make sure to exclude from the ratio costs that don't reflect progress toward completion. For example, inefficiencies in production could lead to wasted materials, labor, or other resources. Those costs must be expensed as incurred, but not included in the cost-to-cost ratio.

Regardless of the specific approach used to estimate progress towards completion, we determine the amount of revenue recognized in each period using the following logic:

$$\text{Revenue recognized this period} = \underbrace{\left(\text{Total estimated revenue} \times \text{Percentage completed to date}\right)}_{\text{Cumulative revenue to be recognized to date}} - \text{Revenue recognized in prior periods}$$

Illustration 5–24C shows the calculation of revenue for each of the years for our Harding Construction Company example, with progress to date estimated using the cost-to-cost ratio. Notice that this approach automatically includes changes in estimated cost to complete the job, and therefore in estimated percentage completion, by first calculating the cumulative amount of revenue to be recognized to date and then subtracting revenue recognized in prior periods to determine revenue recognized in the current period. Refer to the T-accounts that follow Illustration 5–24C to see that the gross profit recognized in each period is added to the CIP account.

[25]Number of units produced or delivered is not an appropriate basis for measuring progress toward completion if these measures are distorted by the seller having material amounts of work-in-progress or finished-goods inventory at the end of the period.

[26]R. K. Larson and K. L. Brown, 2004, "Where Are We with Long-Term Contract Accounting?" *Accounting Horizons,* September, pp. 207–219.

Illustration 5–24C

Allocation of Revenue to Each Period

	2016	2017	2018
Construction costs:			
Construction costs incurred during the year	$ 1,500,000	$ 1,000,000	$ 1,600,000
Construction costs incurred in prior years	–0–	1,500,000	2,500,000
Actual costs to date	$ 1,500,000	$ 2,500,000	$ 4,100,000
Estimated remaining costs to complete	2,250,000	1,500,000	–0–
Total cost (estimated + actual)	$ 3,750,000	$ 4,000,000	$ 4,100,000
Contract price	$5,000,000	$ 5,000,000	$ 5,000,000
Multiplied by:	×	×	×
Percentage of completion	$1,500,000	$2,500,000	$4,100,000
Actual costs to date / Total cost (est. + actual)	$3,750,000	$4,000,000	$4,100,000
	= 40%	= 62.5%	= 100%
Equals:			
Cumulative revenue to be recognized to date	$2,000,000	$ 3,125,000	$5,000,000
Less:			
Revenue recognized in prior periods	–0–	(2,000,000)	(3,125,000)
Equals:			
Revenue recognized in the current period	$2,000,000	$1,125,000	$1,875,000
Journal entries to recognize revenue:			
Construction in progress (CIP)	500,000	125,000	275,000
Cost of construction	1,500,000	1,000,000	1,600,000
Revenue from long-term contracts	2,000,000	1,125,000	1,875,000

Recognizing Revenue Over the Term of the Contract

	Construction in Progress (CIP)			Billings on Construction Contract	
2016 construction costs	1,500,000			1,200,000	2016 billings
2016 gross profit	500,000				
End balance, 2016	2,000,000			1,200,000	End balance, 2016
2017 construction costs	1,000,000			2,000,000	2017 billings
2017 gross profit	125,000				
End balance, 2017	3,125,000			3,200,000	End balance, 2017
2018 construction costs	1,600,000			1,800,000	2018 billings
2018 gross profit	275,000				
Balance, before closing	5,000,000			5,000,000	Balance, before closing

When recognizing revenue over the term of the contract, CIP is updated each period to include gross profit.

If a contract qualifies for revenue recognition over time, the income statement for each year will report the appropriate revenue and cost of construction amounts. For example, in 2016, the income statement will report revenue of $2,000,000 (40% of the $5,000,000 contract price) less $1,500,000 cost of construction, yielding gross profit of $500,000.[27] The table in Illustration 5–24D shows the revenue, cost of construction, and gross profit recognized in each of the three years of our example.

The income statement includes revenue, cost of construction and gross profit.

COMPLETION OF THE CONTRACT. After the job is finished, the only task remaining is for Harding to officially transfer title to the finished asset to the customer. At that time, Harding will prepare a journal entry that removes the contract from its balance sheet by debiting billings and crediting CIP for the entire value of the contract. As shown in Illustration 5–24E, the same journal entry is recorded to close out the billings on construction contract and CIP accounts whether revenue is recognized over the term of the contract or at the completion of the contract.

We record the same journal entry to close out the billings and CIP accounts regardless of whether revenue is recognized over time or upon completion.

[27] In most cases, cost of construction also equals the construction costs incurred during the period. Cost of construction does not equal the construction costs incurred during the year when a loss is projected on the entire project. This situation is illustrated later in the chapter.

Illustration 5–24D

Recognition of Revenue and Cost of Construction in Each Period

2016		
Revenue recognized ($5,000,000 × 40%)		$2,000,000
Cost of construction		(1,500,000)
Gross profit		$ 500,000
2017		
Revenue recognized to date ($5,000,000 × 62.5%)	$3,125,000	
Less: Revenue recognized in 2016	2,000,000	
Revenue recognized		$1,125,000
Cost of construction		(1,000,000)
Gross profit		$ 125,000
2018		
Revenue recognized to date ($5,000,000 × 100%)	$5,000,000	
Less: Revenue recognized in 2016 and 2017	3,125,000	
Revenue recognized		$1,875,000
Cost of construction		(1,600,000)
Gross profit		$ 275,000

Illustration 5–24E

Journal Entry to Close Billings and CIP Accounts Upon Contract Completion

	2016	2017	2018	
Billings on construction contract			5,000,000	
Construction in progress (CIP)				5,000,000
To close accounts.				

A Comparison of Revenue Recognized Over the Term of the Contract and at the Completion of Contract

INCOME RECOGNITION. Illustration 5–24B (page 261) shows the journal entries that would determine the amount of revenue, cost, and therefore gross profit that would appear in the income statement when we recognize revenue over the term of the contract and at the completion of contract. Comparing the gross profit patterns produced by each method of revenue recognition demonstrates the essential difference between them:

Timing of revenue recognition does not affect the total amount of profit or loss recognized.

	Revenue Recognition	
	Over Time	**Upon Completion**
Gross profit recognized:		
2016	$500,000	–0–
2017	125,000	–0–
2018	275,000	$900,000
Total gross profit	$ 900,000	$900,000

Whether revenue is recognized over time or upon completion does not affect the total gross profit of $900,000 recognized over the three-year contract, but the timing of gross profit recognition is affected. When the contract does not qualify for recognizing revenue over time, we defer all gross profit to 2018, when the project is completed. Obviously, recognizing revenue over the term of the contract provides a better measure of the company's economic activity and progress over the three-year term. As indicated previously, most long-term contracts qualify for revenue recognition over time.[28] Revenue is deferred

[28]For income tax purposes, revenue can be recognized at completion for home construction contracts and certain other real estate construction contracts. All other contracts must recognize revenue over time according to percentage of completion.

until the completion of the contract only if the seller doesn't qualify for revenue recognition over time according to the criteria listed in Illustration 5–5.

BALANCE SHEET RECOGNITION. The balance sheet presentation for the construction-related accounts for both methods is shown in Illustration 5–24F.

Illustration 5–24F

Balance Sheet Presentation

Balance Sheet (End of Year)	2016	2017
Projects for which Revenue Recognized Upon Completion:		
Current assets:		
Accounts receivable	$200,000	$800,000
Costs ($1,500,000) in excess of billings ($1,200,000)	300,000	
Current liabilities:		
Billings ($3,200,000) in excess of costs ($2,500,000)		$700,000
Projects for which Revenue Recognized Over Time:		
Current assets:		
Accounts receivable	$200,000	$800,000
Costs and profit ($2,000,000) in excess of billings ($1,200,000)	800,000	
Current liabilities:		
Billings ($3,200,000) in excess of costs and profit ($3,125,000)		$ 75,000

Billings on construction contracts are subtracted from CIP to determine balance sheet presentation.

In the balance sheet, the construction in progress (CIP) account is offset against the billings on construction contract account, with CIP > Billings shown as a contract asset and Billings > CIP shown as a contract liability. Rather than referring to CIP, companies sometimes refer to what the CIP account contains, as is done in Illustration 5–24F. When revenue is recognized over the term of the contract, CIP contains cost and gross profit; if revenue is recognized upon the completion of the contract, CIP typically contains only costs. Because a company may have some contracts that have a net asset position and others that have a net liability position, it is not unusual to see both contract assets and contract liabilities shown in a balance sheet at the same time.

CIP in excess of billings is treated as a contract asset rather than an accounts receivable because something other than the passage of time must occur for the company to be paid for that amount. Although Harding has incurred construction costs (and is recognizing gross profit over the term of the contract) for which it will be paid by the buyer, those amounts are not yet billable according to the construction contract. Once Harding has made progress sufficient to bill the customer, it will debit accounts receivable and credit billings, which will increase the accounts receivable asset and reduce CIP in excess of billings (by increasing billings).

On the other hand, *Billings in excess of CIP* is treated as a contract liability. It reflects that Harding has billed its customer for more work than it actually has done. This is similar to the deferred revenue liability that is recorded when a customer pays for a product or service in advance. The advance is properly shown as a liability that represents the obligation to provide the good or service in the future.

Long-Term Contract Losses

The Harding Construction Company example above involves a situation in which an overall profit was anticipated at each stage of the contract. Unfortunately, losses sometimes occur on long-term contracts. As facts change, sellers must update their estimates and recognize losses if necessary to properly account for the amount of revenue that should have been recognized to date. How we treat losses in any one period depends on whether the contract is profitable overall.

PERIODIC LOSS OCCURS FOR PROFITABLE PROJECT. When a project qualifies for revenue recognition over time, a loss sometimes must be recognized in at least one period along the way, even though the project as a whole is expected to be profitable. We determine the loss in precisely the same way we determine the profit in profitable years. For example, assume the same $5 million contract for Harding Construction Company described earlier in Illustration 5–24 but with the following cost information:

	2016	2017	2018
Construction costs incurred during the year	$1,500,000	$1,260,000	$1,840,000
Construction costs incurred in prior years	–0–	1,500,000	2,760,000
Cumulative construction costs	1,500,000	2,760,000	4,600,000
Estimated costs to complete at end of year	2,250,000	1,840,000	–0–
Total estimated and actual construction costs	$3,750,000	$4,600,000	$4,600,000

At the end of 2016, 40% of the project is complete ($1,500,000 ÷ 3,750,000). Revenue of $2,000,000 – cost of construction of $1,500,000 = gross profit of $500,000 is recognized in 2016, as previously determined.

At the end of 2017, though, the company now forecasts a total profit of $400,000 ($5,000,000 – 4,600,000) on the project and, at that time, the project is estimated to be 60% complete ($2,760,000 ÷ 4,600,000). Applying this percentage to the anticipated revenue of $5,000,000 results in revenue *to date* of $3,000,000. This implies that gross profit recognized to date should be $240,000 ($3,000,000 – 2,760,000). But remember, gross profit of $500,000 was recognized the previous year.

We treat a situation like this as a *change in accounting estimate* because it results from a change in the estimation of costs to complete at the end of 2016. Total estimated costs to complete the project at the end of 2017—$4,600,000—were much higher than the 2016 year-end estimate of $3,750,000. Recall from our discussion of changes in accounting estimates in Chapter 4 that we don't go back and restate the prior year's income statement. Instead, the 2017 income statement reports *a loss of $260,000* ($500,000 – 240,000) so that the cumulative amount of gross profit recognized to date is $240,000. The loss consists of 2017 revenue of $1,000,000 (computed as $5,000,000 × 60% = $3,000,000 revenue to be recognized by end of 2017 less 2016 revenue of $2,000,000) less cost of construction of $1,260,000 (cost incurred in 2017). The following journal entry records the loss in 2017:

Recognized losses on long-term contracts reduce the CIP account.

Cost of construction	1,260,000	
Revenue from long-term contracts (below)		1,000,000
Construction in progress (CIP)		260,000

In 2018 the company recognizes $2,000,000 in revenue ($5,000,000 less revenue of $3,000,000 recognized in 2016 and 2017) and $1,840,000 in cost of construction (cost incurred in 2018), yielding a gross profit of $160,000:

Revenue	$2,000,000
Less: Cost of construction	(1,840,000)
Gross profit	$ 160,000

Of course, if revenue is instead recognized upon the completion of the contract, rather than over time, no profit or loss is recorded in 2016 or 2017. Instead, revenue of $5,000,000, cost of construction of $4,600,000, and gross profit of $400,000 are recognized in 2018.

LOSS IS PROJECTED ON THE ENTIRE PROJECT. If an overall loss is projected on the entire contract, the total loss must be recognized in the period in which that loss becomes evident, regardless of whether revenue is recognized over the term of the contract or only upon the completion of the contract. Again, consider the Harding Construction Company example but with the following cost information:

	2016	2017	2018
Construction costs incurred during the year	$1,500,000	$ 1,260,000	$2,440,000
Construction costs incurred in prior years	–0–	1,500,000	2,760,000
Cumulative construction costs	1,500,000	2,760,000	5,200,000
Estimated costs to complete at end of year	2,250,000	2,340,000	–0–
Total estimated and actual construction costs	$3,750,000	$5,100,000	$5,200,000

An estimated loss on a long-term contract is fully recognized in the first period the loss is anticipated, regardless of the whether revenue is recognized over time or upon completion.

At the end of 2017, revised costs indicate an estimated loss of $100,000 for the entire project (contract revenue of $5,000,000 less estimated construction costs of $5,100,000). In this situation, the *total* anticipated loss must be recognized in 2017 regardless of whether revenue is recognized over the term of the contract or only upon the completion of the contract. If revenue is being recognized over the term of the contract, a gross profit of $500,000 was recognized in 2016, so a *$600,000 loss is recognized in 2017* to make the cumulative amount recognized to date total a $100,000 loss. Once again, this situation is treated as a change in accounting estimate, with no restatement of 2016 income. On the other hand, if revenue is being recognized only upon the completion of the contract, no gross profit is recognized in 2016, and the $100,000 loss for the project is recognized in 2017. This is accomplished by debiting a loss from long-term contracts and crediting CIP for $100,000.

Why recognize the estimated overall loss of $100,000 in 2017, rather than at the end of the contract? If the loss is not recognized in 2017, CIP would be valued at an amount greater than the company expects to realize from the contract. To avoid that problem, the loss reduces the CIP account to $2,660,000 ($2,760,000 in costs to date less $100,000 estimated total loss). This amount combined with the estimated costs to complete of $2,340,000 equals the contract price of $5,000,000. Recognizing losses on long-term contracts in the period the losses become known is equivalent to measuring inventory at the lower of cost or market, a concept we will study in Chapter 9.

The pattern of gross profit (loss) over the contract term is summarized in the following table. Notice that in 2018 an additional unanticipated increase in costs of $100,000 causes a further loss of $100,000 to be recognized.

	Revenue Recognition:	
	Over Time	**Upon Completion**
Gross profit (loss) recognized:		
2016	$500,000	–0–
2017	(600,000)	$(100,000)
2018	(100,000)	(100,000)
Total project loss	$(200,000)	$(200,000)

The table in Illustration 5–24G shows the revenue and cost of construction recognized in each of the three years, assuming the contract qualifies for recognizing revenue over time. Revenue is recognized in the usual way by multiplying a percentage of completion by the total contract price. In situations where a loss is expected on the entire project, cost of construction for the period will no longer be equal to cost incurred during the period. The easiest way to compute the cost of construction is to add the amount of the loss recognized to the amount of revenue recognized. For example, in 2017 revenue recognized of $706,000 is added to the loss of $600,000 to arrive at the cost of construction of $1,306,000.[29]

[29]The cost of construction also can be determined as follows:

Loss to date (100% recognized)		$ 100,000
Add:		
Remaining total project cost, not including the loss ($5,100,000 − 100,000)	$5,000,000	
Multiplied by the percentage of completion	× .5412*	2,706,000
Total		2,806,000
Less: Cost of construction recognized in 2016		(1,500,000)
Cost of construction recognized in 2017		$1,306,000

*$2,760,000 ÷ 5,100,000

Illustration 5–24G

Allocation of Revenue and Cost of Construction to Each Period—Loss on Entire Project

2016		
Revenue recognized ($5,000,000 × 40%)		$2,000,000
Cost of construction		(1,500,000)
Gross profit		$ 500,000
2017		
Revenue recognized to date ($5,000,000 × 54.12%)*	$2,706,000	
Less: Revenue recognized in 2016	(2,000,000)	
Revenue recognized		$ 706,000
Cost of construction†		(1,306,000)
Loss		$ (600,000)
2018		
Revenue recognized to date ($5,000,000 × 100%)	$5,000,000	
Less: Revenue recognized in 2016 and 2017	(2,706,000)	
Revenue recognized		$2,294,000
Cost of construction†		(2,394,000)
Loss		$ (100,000)

*$2,760,000 ÷ $5,100,000 = 54.12%
†The difference between revenue and loss

The journal entries to record the losses in 2017 and 2018 are as follows:

Recognized losses on long-term contracts reduce the CIP account.

2017		
Cost of construction	1,306,000	
Revenue from long-term contracts		706,000
Construction in progress (CIP)		600,000
2018		
Cost of construction	2,394,000	
Revenue from long-term contracts		2,294,000
Construction in progress (CIP)		100,000

Recognizing revenue over time in this case produces a large overstatement of income in 2016 and a large understatement in 2017 because of a change in the estimation of future costs. These estimate revisions happen occasionally when revenue is recognized over time.

When the contract does not qualify for recognizing revenue over time, no revenue or cost of construction is recognized until the contract is complete. In 2017, a loss on long-term contracts (an income statement account) of $100,000 is recognized. In 2018, the income statement will report revenue of $5,000,000 and cost of construction of $5,100,000, combining for an additional loss of $100,000. The journal entries to record the losses in 2017 and 2018 are as follows:

2017		
Loss on long-term contracts	100,000	
Construction in progress (CIP)		100,000
2018		
Cost of construction	5,100,000	
Revenue from long-term contracts		5,000,000
Construction in progress (CIP)		100,000

Concept Review Exercise

LONG-TERM CONSTRUCTION CONTRACTS

During 2016, the Samuelson Construction Company began construction on an office building for the City of Gernon. The contract price is $8,000,000 and the building will take approximately 18 months to complete. Completion is scheduled for early in 2018. The company's fiscal year ends on December 31.

The following is a year-by-year recap of construction costs incurred and the estimated costs to complete the project as of the end of each year. Progress billings and cash collections also are indicated.

	2016	2017	2018
Actual costs incurred during the year	$1,500,000	$4,500,000	$1,550,000
Actual costs incurred in prior years	–0–	1,500,000	6,000,000
Cumulative actual costs incurred to date	1,500,000	6,000,000	7,550,000
Estimated costs to complete at end of year	4,500,000	1,500,000	–0–
Total costs (actual + estimated)	$6,000,000	$7,500,000	$7,550,000
Billings made during the year	$1,400,000	$5,200,000	$1,400,000
Cash collections during year	1,000,000	4,000,000	3,000,000

Required:

1. Determine the amount of construction revenue, construction cost, and gross profit or loss to be recognized in each of the three years assuming (a) the contract qualifies for recognizing revenue over time and (b) the contract does *not* qualify for recognizing revenue over time.
2. Assuming the contract qualifies for recognizing revenue over time, prepare the necessary summary journal entries for each of the three years to account for construction costs, construction revenue, contract billings, and cash collections, and to close the construction accounts in 2018.
3. Assuming the contract qualifies for recognizing revenue over time, prepare a partial balance sheet for 2016 and 2017 that includes all construction-related accounts.

Solution:

1. Determine the amount of construction revenue, construction cost, and gross profit or loss to be recognized in each of the three years assuming (a) the contract qualifies for recognizing revenue over time and (b) the contract does *not* qualify for recognizing revenue over time.

	The Contract Qualifies for Recognizing Revenue Over Time		
	2016	2017	2018
Contract price	$8,000,000	$8,000,000	$8,000,000
Multiplied by % of completion*	25%	80%	100%
Cumulative revenue to be recognized to date	2,000,000	6,400,000	8,000,000
Less revenue recognized in prior years	–0–	(2,000,000)	(6,400,000)
Revenue recognized this year	2,000,000	4,400,000	1,600,000
Less actual costs incurred this year	(1,500,000)	(4,500,000)	1,550,000
Gross profit (loss) recognized this year	$ 500,000	$ (100,000)	$ 50,000

*Estimated percentage of completion:

2016	2017	2018
$\frac{1,500,000}{6,000,000} = 25\%$	$\frac{6,000,000}{7,500,000} = 80\%$	Project complete = 100%

	The Contract Does *Not* Qualify for Recognizing Revenue Over Time		
	2016	2017	2018
Revenue recognized	–0–	–0–	$8,000,000
Less cost of construction recognized	–0–	–0–	(7,550,000)
Gross profit recognized	–0–	–0–	$ 450,000

2. Assuming the contract qualifies for recognizing revenue over time, prepare the necessary summary journal entries for each of the three years to account for construction costs, construction revenue, contract billings, and cash collections, and to close the construction accounts in 2018.

	2016		2017		2018	
Construction in progress (CIP)	1,500,000		4,500,000		1,550,000	
Cash, materials, etc.		1,500,000		4,500,000		1,550,000
To record construction costs.						
Construction in progress (CIP)	500,000				50,000	
Cost of construction	1,500,000				1,550,000	
Revenue		2,000,000				1,600,000
To record revenue and gross profit.						
Cost of construction			4,500,000			
Revenue				4,400,000		
Construction in progress (CIP)				100,000		
To record revenue and gross loss.						
Accounts receivable	1,400,000		5,200,000		1,400,000	
Billings on construction contract		1,400,000		5,200,000		1,400,000
To record progress billings.						
Cash	1,000,000		4,000,000		3,000,000	
Accounts receivable		1,000,000		4,000,000		3,000,000
To record cash collections.						
Billings on construction contract					8,000,000	
Construction in progress (CIP)						8,000,000
To close accounts.						

3. Assuming the contract qualifies for recognizing revenue over time, prepare a partial balance sheet for 2016 and 2017 that includes all construction-related accounts.

Balance Sheet
(End of Year)

	2016	2017
Current assets:		
Accounts receivable	$400,000	$1,600,000
Costs and profit ($2,000,000) in excess of billings ($1,400,000)	600,000	
Current liabilities:		
Billings ($6,600,000) in excess of costs and profit ($6,400,000)		200,000

Profitability Analysis

PART D

● LO5–10

Chapter 3 provided an overview of financial statement analysis and introduced some of the common ratios used in risk analysis to investigate a company's liquidity and long-term solvency. We now look at ratios related to profitability analysis.

Activity Ratios

Activity ratios **measure a company's efficiency in managing its assets.**

One key to profitability is how well a company manages and utilizes its assets. Some ratios are designed to evaluate a company's effectiveness in managing assets. Of particular interest are the activity, or turnover ratios, of certain assets. The greater the number of times an asset turns over—the higher the ratio—the fewer assets are required to maintain a given level of activity (revenue). Given that a company incurs costs to finance its assets with debt (paying interest) or equity (paying dividends), high turnovers are usually attractive.

Although, in concept, the activity or turnover can be measured for any asset, activity ratios are most frequently calculated for total assets, accounts receivable, and inventory. These ratios are calculated as follows:

$$\text{Asset turnover ratio} = \frac{\text{Net sales}}{\text{Average total assets}}$$

$$\text{Receivables turnover ratio} = \frac{\text{Net sales}}{\text{Average accounts receivable (net)}}$$

$$\text{Inventory turnover ratio} = \frac{\text{Cost of goods sold}}{\text{Average inventory}}$$

ASSET TURNOVER. A broad measure of asset efficiency is the **asset turnover ratio**. The ratio is computed by dividing a company's net sales or revenues by the average total assets available for use during a period. The denominator, average assets, is determined by adding beginning and ending total assets and dividing by two. The asset turnover ratio provides an indication of how efficiently a company utilizes all of its assets to generate revenue.

The *asset turnover ratio* measures a company's efficiency in using assets to generate revenue.

RECEIVABLES TURNOVER. The **receivables turnover ratio** is calculated by dividing a period's net credit sales by the average net accounts receivable. Because income statements seldom distinguish between cash sales and credit sales, this ratio usually is computed using total net sales as the numerator. The denominator, average accounts receivable, is determined by adding beginning and ending net accounts receivable (gross accounts receivable less allowance for uncollectible accounts) and dividing by two.[30]

The *receivables turnover ratio* offers an indication of how quickly a company is able to collect its accounts receivable.

The receivables turnover ratio provides an indication of a company's efficiency in collecting receivables. The ratio shows the number of times during a period that the average accounts receivable balance is collected. The higher the ratio, the shorter the average time between credit sales and cash collection.

A convenient extension is the **average collection period**. This measure is computed simply by dividing 365 days by the receivables turnover ratio. The result is an approximation of the number of days the average accounts receivable balance is outstanding.

The *average collection period* indicates the average age of accounts receivable.

$$\text{Average collection period} = \frac{365}{\text{Receivables turnover ratio}}$$

Monitoring the receivables turnover ratio (and average collection period) over time can provide useful information about a company's future prospects. For example, a decline in the receivables turnover ratio (an increase in the average collection period) could be an indication that sales are declining because of customer dissatisfaction with the company's products. Another possible explanation is that the company has changed its credit policy and is granting extended credit terms in order to maintain customers. Either explanation could

[30]Although net accounts receivable typically is used in practice for the denominator of receivables turnover, some prefer to use gross accounts receivable. Why? As the allowance for bad debts increases, net accounts receivable decreases, so if net accounts receivable is in the denominator, more bad debts have the effect of decreasing the denominator and therefore increasing receivables turnover. All else equal, an analyst would rather see receivables turnover improve because of more sales or less gross receivables, and not because of an increase in the allowance for bad debts.

signal a future increase in bad debts. Ratio analysis does not explain what is wrong. It does provide information that highlights areas for further investigation.

The *inventory turnover ratio* measures a company's efficiency in managing its investment in inventory.

INVENTORY TURNOVER. An important activity measure for a merchandising company (a retail, wholesale, or manufacturing company) is the **inventory turnover ratio**. The ratio shows the number of times the average inventory balance is sold during a reporting period. It indicates how quickly inventory is sold. The more frequently a business is able to sell, or turn over, its inventory, the lower its investment in inventory must be for a given level of sales. The ratio is computed by dividing the period's cost of goods sold by the average inventory balance. The denominator, average inventory, is determined by adding beginning and ending inventory and dividing by two.[31]

A relatively high ratio, say compared to a competitor, usually is desirable. A high ratio indicates comparative strength, perhaps caused by a company's superior sales force or maybe a successful advertising campaign. However, it might also be caused by a relatively low inventory level, which could mean either very efficient inventory management or stockouts and lost sales in the future.

On the other hand, a relatively low ratio, or a decrease in the ratio over time, usually is perceived to be unfavorable. Too much capital may be tied up in inventory. A relatively low ratio may result from overstocking, the presence of obsolete items, or poor marketing and sales efforts.

Similar to the receivables turnover, we can divide the inventory turnover ratio into 365 days to compute the **average days in inventory**. This measure indicates the number of days it normally takes to sell inventory.

$$\text{Average days in inventory} = \frac{365}{\text{Inventory turnover ratio}}$$

Profitability Ratios

Profitability ratios assist in evaluating various aspects of a company's profit-making activities.

A fundamental element of an analyst's task is to develop an understanding of a firm's profitability. Profitability ratios attempt to measure a company's ability to earn an adequate return relative to sales or resources devoted to operations. Resources devoted to operations can be defined as total assets or only those assets provided by owners, depending on the evaluation objective.

Three common profitability measures are (1) the profit margin on sales, (2) the return on assets, and (3) the return on shareholders' equity. These ratios are calculated as follows:

$$\text{Profit margin on sales} = \frac{\text{Net income}}{\text{Net sales}}$$

$$\text{Return on assets} = \frac{\text{Net income}}{\text{Average total assets}}$$

$$\text{Return on shareholder's equity} = \frac{\text{Net income}}{\text{Average shareholders' equity}}$$

Notice that for all of the profitability ratios, our numerator is net income. Recall our discussion in Chapter 4 on earnings quality. The relevance of any historical-based financial statement hinges on its predictive value. To enhance predictive value, analysts often adjust net income in these ratios to separate a company's *transitory earnings* effects from its *permanent earnings.* Analysts begin their assessment of permanent earnings with income from continuing operations. Then, adjustments are made for any unusual, one-time gains or losses included in income from continuing operations. It is this adjusted number that they use as the numerator in these ratios.

When calculating profitability ratios, analysts often adjust net income for any transitory income effects.

The *profit margin on sales* measures the amount of net income achieved per sales dollar.

PROFIT MARGIN ON SALES. The **profit margin on sales** is simply net income divided by net sales. The ratio measures an important dimension of a company's profitability. It indicates the portion of each dollar of revenue that is available after all expenses have been covered. It offers a measure of the company's ability to withstand either higher expenses or lower revenues.

[31]Notice the consistency in the measure used for the numerator and denominator of the two turnover ratios. For the receivables turnover ratio, both numerator and denominator are based on sales dollars, whereas they are both based on cost for the inventory turnover ratio.

What is considered to be a desirable profit margin is highly sensitive to the nature of the business activity. For instance, you would expect a specialty shop to have a higher profit margin than, say, **Walmart**. A low profit margin can be compensated for by a high asset turnover rate, and vice versa, which brings us to considering the trade-offs inherent in generating return on assets.

RETURN ON ASSETS. The **return on assets (ROA)** ratio expresses income as a percentage of the average total assets available to generate that income. Because total assets are partially financed with debt and partially by equity funds, this is an inclusive way of measuring earning power that ignores specific sources of financing.

A company's return on assets is related to both profit margin and asset turnover. Specifically, profitability can be achieved by either a high profit margin, high turnover, or a combination of the two. In fact, the return on assets can be calculated by multiplying the profit margin and the asset turnover.

Profit margin and asset turnover combine to yield *return on assets,* which measures the return generated by a company's assets.

$$\textbf{Return on assets} = \textbf{Profit margin} \times \textbf{Asset turnover}$$

$$\frac{\text{Net income}}{\text{Average total assets}} = \frac{\text{Net income}}{\text{Net sales}} \times \frac{\text{Net sales}}{\text{Average total assets}}$$

Industry standards are particularly important when evaluating asset turnover and profit margin. Some industries are characterized by low turnover but typically make up for it with higher profit margins. Others have low profit margins but compensate with high turnover. Grocery stores typically have relatively low profit margins but relatively high asset turnover. In comparison, a manufacturer of specialized equipment will have a higher profit margin but a lower asset turnover ratio.

Additional Consideration

The return on assets ratio often is computed as follows:

$$\text{Return on assets} = \frac{\text{Net income} + \text{Interest expense } (1 - \text{Tax rate})}{\text{Average total assets}}$$

The reason for adding back interest expense (net of tax) is that interest represents a return to suppliers of debt capital and should not be deducted in the computation of net income when computing the return on total assets. In other words, the numerator is the total amount of income available to both debt and equity capital.

RETURN ON SHAREHOLDERS' EQUITY. Equity investors typically are concerned about the amount of profit that management can generate from the resources that owners provide. A closely watched measure that captures this concern is **return on equity (ROE)**, calculated by dividing net income by average shareholders' equity.

The *return on shareholders' equity* measures the return to suppliers of equity capital.

In addition to monitoring return on equity, investors want to understand how that return can be improved. The **DuPont framework** provides a convenient basis for analysis that breaks return on equity into three key components:[32]

The DuPont framework shows that return on equity depends on profitability, activity, and financial leverage.

- **Profitability,** measured by the profit margin (Net income ÷ Sales). As discussed already, a higher profit margin indicates that a company is generating more profit from each dollar of sales.
- **Activity,** measured by asset turnover (Sales ÷ Average total assets). As discussed already, higher asset turnover indicates that a company is using its assets efficiently to generate more sales from each dollar of assets.
- **Financial Leverage,** measured by the equity multiplier (Average total assets ÷ Average total equity). A high equity multiplier indicates that relatively more of the company's assets have been financed with debt. As indicated in Chapter 3, leverage can provide additional return to the company's equity holders.

[32]DuPont analysis is so named because the basic model was developed by F. Donaldson Brown, an electrical engineer who worked for DuPont in the early part of the 20th century.

In equation form, the DuPont framework looks like this:

$$\textbf{Return on equity} = \textbf{Profit margin} \times \textbf{Asset turnover} \times \textbf{Equity multiplier}$$

$$\frac{\text{Net income}}{\text{Avg. total equity}} = \frac{\text{Net income}}{\text{Total sales}} \times \frac{\text{Total sales}}{\text{Avg. total assets}} \times \frac{\text{Avg. total assets}}{\text{Avg. total equity}}$$

Notice that total sales and average total assets appear in the numerator of one ratio and the denominator of another, so they cancel to yield net income ÷ average total equity, or ROE.

We have already seen that ROA is determined by profit margin and asset turnover, so another way to compute ROE is by multiplying ROA by the equity multiplier:

$$\textbf{Return on equity} = \textbf{Return on assets} \times \textbf{Equity multiplier}$$

$$\frac{\text{Net income}}{\text{Avg. total equity}} = \frac{\text{Net income}}{\text{Avg. total assets}} \times \frac{\text{Avg. total assets}}{\text{Avg. total equity}}$$

We can see from this equation that an equity multiplier of greater than 1 will produce a return on equity that is higher than the return on assets. However, as with all ratio analysis, there are trade-offs. If leverage is too high, creditors become concerned about the potential for default on the company's debt and require higher interest rates. Because interest is recognized as an expense, net income is reduced, so at some point the benefits of a higher equity multiplier are offset by a lower profit margin. Part of the challenge of managing a company is to identify the combination of profitability, activity, and leverage that produces the highest return for equity holders.

Additional Consideration

Sometimes when return on equity is calculated, shareholders' equity is viewed more narrowly to include only common shareholders. In that case, preferred stock is excluded from the denominator, and preferred dividends are deducted from net income in the numerator. The resulting rate of return on common shareholders' equity focuses on profits generated on resources provided by common shareholders.

Illustration 5–25 provides a recap of the ratios we have discussed.

Illustration 5–25
Summary of Profitability Analysis Ratios

Activity ratios		
Asset turnover	=	$\frac{\text{Net sales}}{\text{Average total assets}}$
Receivables turnover	=	$\frac{\text{Net sales}}{\text{Average accounts receivable (net)}}$
Average collection period	=	$\frac{365}{\text{Receivables turnover ratio}}$
Inventory turnover	=	$\frac{\text{Cost of goods sold}}{\text{Average inventory}}$
Average days in inventory	=	$\frac{365}{\text{Inventory turnover ratio}}$
Profitability ratios		
Profit margin on sales	=	$\frac{\text{Net income}}{\text{Net sales}}$
Return on assets	=	$\frac{\text{Net income}}{\text{Average total assets}}$
Return on shareholders' equity	=	$\frac{\text{Net income}}{\text{Average shareholders' equity}}$
Leverage ratio		
Equity multiplier	=	$\frac{\text{Average total assets}}{\text{Average total equity}}$

Profitability Analysis — An Illustration

To illustrate the application of the DuPont framework and the computation of the activity and profitability ratios, we analyze the 2013 financial statements of two well-known retailers, **Costco Wholesale Corporation** and **Walmart Stores, Inc.**[33] The operations of these two companies are similar in their focus on operating large general merchandising and food discount stores. Illustration 5–26A presents selected financial statement information for the two companies (all numbers are in millions of dollars).

Illustration 5–26A

Selected Financial Information for Costco Wholesale Corporation and Wal-Mart Stores, Inc.

Real World Financials

	Costco		Walmart	
	2013	2012	2013	2012
Accounts receivable (net)	$ 1,201	$ 1,026	$ 6,677	$ 6,768
Inventories	$ 7,894	$ 7,096	$ 44,858	$ 43,803
Total assets	$30,283	$27,140	$204,751	$203,105
Total liabilities	$19,271	$14,622	$123,412	$121,367
Total shareholders' equity	$11,012	$12,518	$ 81,339	$ 81,738
Average for 2013:				
Accounts receivable (net)	$ 1,114		$ 6,723	
Inventories	$ 7,495		$ 44,331	
Total assets	$ 28,712		$203,928	
Total shareholders' equity	$ 11,765		$ 81,539	
Income Statement—2013				
Net sales	$102,870		$473,076	
Cost of goods sold	$ 91,948		$358,069	
Net Income	$ 2,061		$ 16,551	

On the surface, it appears that Walmart is far more profitable than Costco. As shown in Illustration 5–26A, Walmart's 2013 net income was $16.551 billion, compared to Costco's $2.061 billion. But that's not the whole story. Even though both are very large companies, Walmart is more than six times the size of Costco in terms of total assets, so how can they be compared? Focusing on financial ratios helps adjust for size differences, and the DuPont framework helps identify the determinants of profitability from the perspective of shareholders.

Illustration 5–26B includes the DuPont analysis for Walmart and Costco, as well as some additional activity ratios we've discussed. Walmart's return on assets (ROA) is higher than Costco's (8.12% for Walmart compared to 7.18% for Costco). Why? Remember that both profitability and activity combine to determine return on assets. Costco's asset turnover is much higher than Walmart's (3.58 compared to 2.32), but its profit margin is much lower than Walmart's (2.00% compared to 3.50%). So, even though Costco makes significantly more sales with each dollar of its assets, Walmart makes more profit on each dollar of sales, and Walmart ends up coming out ahead on return on assets.

The average days in inventory provides insight into Costco's higher asset turnover. Inventory takes only 30 days on average before being sold by Costco, compared with 79 for the industry average and 45 days for Walmart. Costco also turns over its accounts receivable faster than Walmart does, but accounts receivable are relatively small so attention would be focused on other ratios for both companies.

[33] Walmart's financial statements are for the fiscal year ended January 31, 2014. Walmart refers to this as its 2014 fiscal year. Costco's financial statements are for the fiscal year ended September 1, 2013. For consistency with Costco, we refer to Walmart's fiscal year as 2013.

Illustration 5–26B

DuPont Framework and Activity Ratios—Costco Wholesale Corporation and Wal-Mart Stores, Inc.

DuPont analysis:	Costco		Walmart		Industry Average*
Profit margin on sales	= $\frac{\$2{,}061}{\$102{,}870}$	= 2.00%	$\frac{\$16{,}551}{\$473{,}076}$	= 3.50%	3.76%
×		×		×	
Asset turnover	= $\frac{\$102{,}870}{\$28{,}712}$	= 3.58	$\frac{\$473{,}076}{\$203{,}928}$	= 2.32	2.51
=		=		=	
Return on assets	= $\frac{\$2{,}061}{\$28{,}712}$	= 7.18%	$\frac{\$16{,}551}{\$203{,}928}$	= 8.12%	9.33%
×		×		×	
Equity Multiplier	= $\frac{\$28{,}712}{\$11{,}765}$	= 2.44	$\frac{\$203{,}928}{\$81{,}539}$	= 2.50	2.24
=		=		=	
Return on equity	= $\frac{\$2{,}061}{\$11{,}765}$	= 17.52%	$\frac{\$16{,}551}{\$81{,}539}$	= 20.30%	20.56%
Other activity ratios:					
Receivables turnover	= $\frac{\$102{,}870}{\$1{,}114}$	= 92.34	$\frac{\$473{,}076}{\$6{,}723}$	= 70.37	176.36
Average collection period	= $\frac{365}{92.34}$	= 3.95 days	$\frac{365}{70.37}$	= 5.19 days	4.60 days
Inventory turnover	= $\frac{\$91{,}948}{\$7{,}495}$	= 12.27	$\frac{\$358{,}069}{\$44{,}331}$	= 8.08	5.53
Average days in inventory	= $\frac{365}{12.27}$	= 29.75 days	$\frac{365}{8.08}$	= 45.17 days	78.92 days

*Industry average based on sample of eleven discount retail companies.

What matters most to the shareholders of these companies is not return on assets, but the return on equity (ROE). Both fall short of the industry average, but Walmart wins over Costco on this measure, with an ROE of 20.3% compared to Costco's 17.5%. Walmart's equity multiplier also is a bit higher than Costco's (2.5 for Walmart compared to 2.4 for Costco), which causes the two companies' ROEs to be even farther apart than their ROAs.

A Costco shareholder looking at these numbers might wonder how best to increase Costco's ROE. Should Costco attempt to increase operational efficiency on the asset turnover dimension? That might be tough, given its already high asset turnover. Or, should Costco attempt to increase profit margin? Given competitive pressures on retail pricing, can Costco generate a much higher profit margin with its current product mix and low-price strategy, or should it consider including more upscale, high-margin items in its inventory? Or, should Costco attempt to increase leverage and improve its equity multiplier, so that debt holders are financing a greater percentage of its assets?

The essential point of our discussion here, and in Part C of Chapter 3, is that raw accounting numbers alone mean little to decision makers. The numbers gain value when viewed in relation to other numbers. Similarly, the financial ratios formed by those relationships provide even greater perspective when compared with similar ratios of other companies, or with averages for several companies in the same industry. Accounting information is useful in making decisions. Financial analysis that includes comparisons of financial ratios enhances the value of that information.

Financial Reporting Case Solution

1. **Under what circumstances do companies recognize revenue at a point in time? Over a period of time?** *(p. 234)* A seller recognizes revenue when it satisfies a performance obligation, which happens when the seller transfers control of a good or service to the customer. Indicators that transfer of control has occurred include customer acceptance and physical possession of the good or service as well as the seller having a right to receive payment. Some performance obligations are satisfied at a point in time, when the seller has finished transferring the good or service to the customer. Other performance obligations are satisfied over time. For example, the customer might consume the benefit of the seller's work as it is performed, or the customer might control an asset as the seller creates it.
2. **When do companies break apart a sale and treat its parts differently for purposes of recognizing revenue?** *(p. 237)* Sellers must break apart a contract if the contract contains more than one performance obligation. Goods and services are viewed as performance obligations if they are both capable of being distinct (for example, if the goods and services could be sold separately) and if they are separately identifiable (which isn't the case if the point of the contract is to combine various goods and services into a completed product, as occurs with construction contracts). To account for contracts with multiple performance obligations, the seller allocates the contract's transaction price to the performance obligations according to their stand-alone selling prices and then recognizes revenue for each performance obligation when it is satisfied.
3. **How do companies account for long-term contracts that qualify for revenue recognition over time?** *(p. 257)* When contracts qualify for revenue recognition over time, the seller recognizes revenue each period as the contract is being fulfilled. The amount recognized is based on progress to date, which usually is estimated as the fraction of the project's cost incurred to date divided by total estimated costs. To calculate the total amount of revenue that should be recognized up to a given date, the estimated percentage of completion is multiplied by the contract price. To calculate the amount of revenue to be recognized in the current period, the amount of revenue recognized in prior periods is subtracted from the total amount of revenue that should be recognized as of the end of the current period. ●

The Bottom Line

- **LO5–1** Companies recognize revenue when goods or services are transferred to customers for the amount the company expects to be entitled to receive in exchange for those goods or services. That core principle is implemented by (1) identifying a contract with a customer, (2) identifying the performance obligations in the contract, (3) determining the transaction price of the contract, (4) allocating that price to the performance obligations, and (5) recognizing revenue when (or as) each performance obligation is satisfied. *(p. 232)*
- **LO5–2** Revenue should be recognized *at a single point in time* when control of a good or service is transferred to the customer on a specific date. Indicators that transfer has occurred and that revenue should be recognized include the seller having the right to receive payment, the customer having legal title and physical possession of the asset, the customer formally accepting the asset, and the customer assuming the risks and rewards of ownership. *(p. 234)*
- **LO5–3** Revenue should be recognized *over time* when a performance obligation is satisfied over time. That occurs if (1) the customer consumes the benefit of the seller's work as it is performed, (2) the customer controls the asset as the seller creates it, or (3) the asset has no alternative use to the seller and the seller can be paid for its progress even if the customer cancels the contract. *(p. 235)*

● **LO5–4** A contract's transaction price is allocated to its performance obligations. The allocation is based on the *stand-alone selling prices* of the goods and services underlying those performance obligations. The stand-alone selling price must be estimated if a good or service is not sold separately. (*p. 237*)

● **LO5–5** A contract exists when it has commercial substance and all parties to the contract are committed to performing the obligations and enforcing the rights that it specifies. Performance obligations are promises by the seller to transfer goods or services to a customer. A promise to transfer a good or service is a performance obligation if it is *distinct,* which is the case if it is both *capable of being distinct* (meaning that the customer could use the good or service on its own or in combination with other goods and services it could obtain elsewhere), and *it is separately identifiable* (meaning that the good or service is not highly interrelated with other goods and services in the contract, so it is distinct in the context of the contract). Prepayments, rights to return merchandise, and normal quality-assurance warrantees do not qualify as performance obligations, because they don't transfer a good or service to the customer. On the other hand, extended warranties and customer options to receive goods or services in some preferred manner (for example, at a discount) qualify as performance obligations. (*p. 241*)

● **LO5–6** When a contract includes consideration that depends on the outcome of future events, sellers estimate that variable consideration and include it in the contract's transaction price. The seller's estimate is based either on the most likely outcome or the expected value of the outcome. However, a constraint applies—variable consideration only should be included in the transaction price to the extent it is probable that a significant revenue reversal will not occur. The estimate of variable consideration is updated each period to reflect changes in circumstances. A seller also needs to determine if it is a principal (and recognizes as revenue the amount received from the customer) or an agent (and recognizes its commission as revenue), consider time value of money, and consider the effect of any payments by the seller to the customer. Once the transaction price is estimated, we allocate it to performance obligations according to their stand-alone selling prices, which can be estimated using the adjusted market assessment approach, the expected cost plus margin approach, or the residual approach. (*p. 244*)

● **LO5–7** If the seller's activity over the license period is expected to affect the benefits the customer receives from the intellectual property being licensed, the seller recognizes revenue over the license period. Otherwise, the seller recognizes revenue at the point in time that the customer obtains access to the seller's intellectual property. Franchises are an example of contracts that typically include licenses as well as other performance obligations. Revenue for bill-and-hold sales should be recognized when goods are delivered to the customer, and for consignment sales when goods are delivered to the end customer. Revenue for gift cards should be recognized when the gift card is redeemed, expires, or viewed as broken. (*p. 251*)

● **LO5–8** Much disclosure is required for revenue recognition. For example, a seller recognizes contract liabilities, contract assets, and accounts receivable on separate lines of its balance sheet. If the customer makes payment to the seller before the seller has satisfied performance obligations, the seller records a contract liability, such as deferred revenue. If the seller satisfies a performance obligation before the customer has paid for it, the seller records either a contract asset or an account receivable. The seller recognizes an account receivable if only the passage of time is required before the payment is due. If instead the seller's right to payment depends on something other than the passage of time, the seller recognizes a contract asset. (*p. 254*)

● **LO5–9** Long-term contracts usually qualify for revenue recognition over time. We recognize revenue over time by assigning a share of the project's revenues and costs to each reporting period over the life of the project according to percentage of the project completed to date. If long-term contracts don't qualify for revenue recognition over time, we recognize revenues and expenses at the point in time when the project is complete. (*p. 256*)

● **LO5–10** Activity and profitability ratios provide information about a company's profitability. Activity ratios include the receivables turnover ratio, the inventory turnover ratio, and the asset turnover ratio. Profitability ratios include the profit margin on sales, the return on assets, and the return on shareholders' equity. DuPont analysis explains return on stockholders' equity as determined by profit margin, asset turnover, and the extent to which assets are financed with equity versus debt. (*p. 269*) ●

Questions For Review of Key Topics

Q 5–1 What are the five key steps a company follows to apply the core revenue recognition principle?

Q 5–2 What indicators suggest that a performance obligation has been satisfied at a single point in time?

Q 5–3 What criteria determine whether a company can recognize revenue over time?

Q 5–4 We recognize service revenue either at one point in time or over a period of time. Explain the rationale for recognizing service revenue using these two approaches.

Q 5–5 What characteristics make a good or service a performance obligation?

Q 5–6 How does a seller allocate a transaction price to a contract's performance obligations?

Q 5–7 What must a contract include for the contract to exist for purposes of revenue recognition?

Q 5–8 When a contract includes an option to buy additional goods or services, when does that option give rise to a performance obligation?

Q 5–9 Is variable consideration included in the calculation of a contract's transaction price? If so, how is the amount of variable consideration estimated?

Q 5–10 How are sellers constrained from recognizing variable consideration, and under what circumstances does the constraint apply?

Q 5–11 Is a customer's right to return merchandise a performance obligation of the seller? How should sellers account for a right of return?

Q 5–12 What is the difference between a principal and an agent for determining the amount of revenue to recognize?

Q 5–13 Under what circumstances should sellers consider the time value of money when recognizing revenue?

Q 5–14 When should a seller view a payment to its customer as a refund of part of the price paid by the customer for the seller's products or services?

Q 5–15 What are three methods for estimating stand-alone selling prices of goods and services that normally are not sold separately?

Q 5–16 When is revenue recognized with respect to licenses?

Q 5–17 In a franchise arrangement, what are a franchisor's typical performance obligations?

Q 5–18 When does a company typically recognize revenue for a bill-and-hold sale?

Q 5–19 When does a consignor typically recognize revenue for a consignment sale?

Q 5–20 When does a company recognize revenue for a sale of a gift card?

Q 5–21 Must bad debt expense be reported on its own line on the income statement? If not, how should it be disclosed?

Q 5–22 Explain the difference between contract assets, contract liabilities, and accounts receivable.

Q 5–23 Explain how to account for revenue on a long-term contract over time as opposed to at a point in time. Under what circumstances should revenue be recognized at the point in time a contract is completed?

Q 5–24 Periodic billings to the customer for a long-term construction contract are recorded as billings on construction contract. How is this account reported in the balance sheet?

Q 5–25 When is an estimated loss on a long-term contract recognized, both for contracts that recognize revenue over time and those that recognize revenue at the point in time the contract is completed?

Q 5–26 Show the calculation of the following activity ratios: (1) the receivables turnover ratio, (2) the inventory turnover ratio, and (3) the asset turnover ratio. What information about a company do these ratios offer?

Q 5–27 Show the calculation of the following profitability ratios: (1) the profit margin on sales, (2) the return on assets, and (3) the return on shareholders' equity. What information about a company do these ratios offer?

Q 5–28 Show the DuPont framework's calculation of the three components of return on shareholders' equity. What information about a company do these ratios offer?

Brief Exercises

BE 5–1
Revenue recognition at a point in time
● LO5–2

On July 1, 2016, Apache Company, a real estate developer, sold a parcel of land to a construction company for \$3,000,000. The book value of the land on Apache's books was \$1,200,000. Terms of the sale required a down payment of \$150,000 and 19 annual payments of \$150,000 plus interest at an appropriate interest rate due on each July 1 beginning in 2017. How much revenue will Apache recognize for the sale (ignoring interest), assuming that it recognizes revenue at the point in time at which it transfers the land to the construction company?

BE 5–2
Timing of revenue recognition
● LO5–3

Estate Construction is constructing a building for CyberB, an online retailing company. Under the construction agreement, if for any reason Estate can't complete construction, CyberB would own the partially completed building and could hire another construction company to complete the job. When should Estate recognize revenue: as the building is constructed, or after construction is completed?

BE 5–3
Timing of revenue recognition
● LO5–3

On May 1, 2016, Varga Tech Services signed a $6,000 consulting contract with Shaffer Holdings. The contract requires Varga to provide computer technology support services whenever requested over the period from May 1, 2016, to April 30, 2017, with Shaffer paying the entire $6,000 on May 1, 2016. How much revenue should Varga recognize in 2016?

BE 5–4
Allocating the transaction price
● LO5–4

Sarjit Systems sold software to a customer for $80,000. As part of the contract, Sarjit promises to provide "free" technical support over the next six months. Sarjit sells the same software without technical support for $70,000 and a stand-alone six-month technical support contract for $30,000, so these products would sell for $100,000 if sold separately. Prepare Sarjit's journal entry to record the sale of the software.

BE 5–5
Performance obligations; prepayments
● LO5–5

eLean is an online fitness community, offering access to workout routines, nutrition advice, and eLean coaches. Customers pay a $50 fee to become registered on the website, and then pay $5 per month for access to all eLean services. How many performance obligations exist in the implied contract when a customer registers for the services?

BE 5–6
Performance obligations; warranties
● LO5–5

Vroom Vacuums sells the Tornado vacuum cleaner. Each Tornado has a one-year warranty that covers any product defects. When customers purchase a Tornado, they also have the option to purchase an extended three-year warranty that covers any breakage or maintenance. The extended warranty sells for the same amount regardless of whether it is purchased at the same time as the Tornado or at some other time. How many performance obligations exist in the implied contract for the purchase of a vacuum cleaner?

BE 5–7
Performance obligations; warranties
● LO5–5

Assume the same facts as in BE 5–6 but that customers pay 20% less for the extended warranty if they buy it at the same time they buy a Tornado. How many performance obligations exist in the implied contract for the purchase of a vacuum cleaner?

BE 5–8
Performance obligations; options
● LO5–5

McAfee sells a subscription to its anti-virus software along with a subscription renewal option that allows renewal at half the prevailing price for a new subscription. How many performance obligations exist in this contract?

BE 5–9
Performance obligations; construction
● LO5–5

Precision Equipment, Inc., specializes in designing and installing customized manufacturing equipment. On February 1, 2016, it signs a contract to design a fully automated wristwatch assembly line for $2 million, which will be settled in cash upon completion of construction. Precision Equipment will install the equipment on the client's property, furnish it with a customized software package that is integral to operations, and provide consulting services that integrate the equipment with Precision's other assembly lines. How many performance obligations exist in this contract?

BE 5–10
Performance obligations; construction
● LO5–5

On January 1, 2016, Lego Construction Company signed a contract to build a custom garage for a customer and received $10,000 in advance for the job. The new garage will be built on the customer's land. To complete this project, Lego must first build a concrete floor, construct wooden pillars and walls, and finally install a roof. Lego normally charges stand-alone prices of $3,000, $4,000, and $5,000, respectively, for each of these three smaller tasks if done separately. How many performance obligations exist in this contract?

BE 5–11
Performance obligations; right of return
● LO5–5, LO5–6

Aria Perfume, Inc., sold 3,210 boxes of white musk soap during January of 2016 at the price of $90 per box. The company offers a full refund for any product returned within 30 days from the date of purchase. Based on historical experience, Aria expects that 3% of sales will be returned. How many performance obligations are there in each sale of a box of soap? How much revenue should Aria recognize in January?

BE 5–12
Variable consideration
● LO5–6

Leo Consulting enters into a contract with Highgate University to restructure Highgate's processes for purchasing goods from suppliers. The contract states that Leo will earn a fixed fee of $25,000 and earn an additional $10,000 if Highgate achieves $100,000 of cost savings. Leo estimates a 50% chance that Highgate will achieve $100,000 of cost savings. Assuming that Leo determines the transaction price as the expected value of expected consideration, what transaction price will Leo estimate for this contract?

BE 5–13
Variable consideration
● LO5–6

In January 2016, Continental Fund Services, Inc., enters into a one-year contract with a client to provide investment advisory services. The company will receive a management fee, prepaid at the beginning of the contract, that is calculated as 1% of the client's $150 million total assets being managed. In addition, the contract specifies that Continental will receive a performance bonus of 20% of any returns in excess of the return on the Dow Jones Industrial Average market index. Continental estimates that it will earn a $2 million performance bonus, but is very uncertain of that estimate, given that the bonus depends on a highly volatile stock market. On what transaction price should Continental base revenue recognition?

BE 5–14
Right of return
● LO5–6

Finerly Corporation sells cosmetics through a network of independent distributors. Finerly shipped cosmetics to its distributors and is considering whether it should record $300,000 of revenue upon shipment of a new line of cosmetics. Finerly expects the distributors to be able to sell the cosmetics, but is uncertain because it has little experience with selling cosmetics of this type. Finerly is committed to accepting the cosmetics back from the distributors if the cosmetics are not sold. How much revenue should Finerly recognize upon delivery to its distributors?

BE 5–15
Principal or agent
● LO5–6

Assume that **Amazon.com** sells the MacBook Pro, a computer brand produced by **Apple**, for a retail price of $1,500. Amazon arranges its operations such that customers receive products directly from Apple Stores rather than Amazon. Customers purchase from Amazon using credit cards, and Amazon forwards cash to Apple equal to the retail price minus a $150 commission that Amazon keeps. In this arrangement, how much revenue will Amazon recognize for the sale of one MacBook Pro?

BE 5–16
Payments by the seller to the customer
● LO5–6

Lewis Co. sold merchandise to AdCo for $60,000 and received $60,000 for that sale one month later. One week prior to receiving payment from AdCo, Lewis made a $10,000 payment to AdCo for advertising services that have a fair value of $7,500. After accounting for any necessary adjustments, how much revenue should Lewis Co. record for the merchandise sold to AdCo?

BE 5–17
Estimating stand-alone selling prices: adjusted market assessment approach
● LO5–6

O'Hara Associates sells golf clubs and, with each sale of a full set of clubs, provides complementary club-fitting services. A full set of clubs with the fitting services sells for $1,500. Similar club-fitting services are offered by other vendors for $110, and O'Hara generally charges approximately 10% more than do other vendors for similar services. Estimate the stand-alone selling price of the club-fitting services using the adjusted market assessment approach.

BE 5–18
Estimating stand-alone selling prices: expected cost plus margin approach
● LO5–6

O'Hara Associates sells golf clubs and with each sale of a full set of clubs provides complementary club-fitting services. A full set of clubs with the fitting services sells for $1,500. O'Hara estimates that it incurs $60 of staff compensation and other costs to provide the fitting services, and normally earns 30% over cost on similar services. Assuming that the golf clubs and the club fitting services are separate performance obligations, estimate the stand-alone selling price of the club-fitting services using the expected cost plus margin approach.

BE 5–19
Estimating stand-alone selling prices; residual approach
● LO5–6

O'Hara Associates sells golf clubs, and with each sale of a full set of clubs provides complementary club-fitting services. A full set of clubs with the fitting services sells for $1,500. O'Hara sells the same clubs without the fitting service for $1,400. Assuming that the golf clubs and the club-fitting services are separate performance obligations, estimate the stand-alone selling price of the club fitting services using the residual approach.

BE 5–20
Timing of revenue recognition; licenses
● LO5–7

Saar Associates sells two licenses to Kim & Company on September 1, 2016. First, in exchange for $100,000, Saar provides Kim with a copy of its proprietary investment management software, which Saar does not anticipate updating and which Kim can use permanently. Second, in exchange for $90,000, Saar provides Kim with a three-year right to market Kim's financial advisory services under the name of Saar Associates, which Saar advertises on an ongoing basis. How much revenue will Saar recognize in 2016 under this arrangement?

BE 5–21
Timing of revenue recognition; franchises
● LO5–7

TopChop sells hairstyling franchises. TopChop receives $50,000 from a new franchisee for providing initial training, equipment and furnishings that have a stand-alone selling price of $50,000. TopChop also receives $30,000 per year for use of the TopChop name and for ongoing consulting services (starting on the date the franchise is purchased). Carlos became a TopChop franchisee on July 1, 2016, and on August 1, 2016, had completed training and was open for business. How much revenue in 2016 will TopChop recognize for its arrangement with Carlos?

BE 5–22
Timing of revenue recognition; bill-and-hold
● LO5–7

Dowell Fishing Supply, Inc., sold $50,000 of Dowell Rods on December 15, 2016, to Bassadrome. Because of a shipping backlog, Dowell held the inventory in Dowell's warehouse until January 12, 2017 (having assured Bassadrome that it would deliver sooner if necessary). How much revenue should Dowell recognize in 2016 for the sale to Bassadrome?

BE 5–23
Timing of revenue recognition; consignment
● LO5–7

Kerianne paints landscapes, and in late 2016 placed four paintings with a retail price of $250 each in the Holmstrom Gallery. Kerianne's arrangement with Holmstrom is that Holmstrom will earn a 20% commission on paintings sold to gallery patrons. As of December 31, 2016, one painting had been sold by Holmstrom to gallery patrons. How much revenue with respect to these four paintings should Kerianne recognize in 2016?

BE 5–24
Timing of revenue recognition; gift card
● LO5–7

GoodBuy sells gift cards redeemable for GoodBuy products either in store or online. During 2016, GoodBuy sold $1,000,000 of gift cards, and $840,000 of the gift cards were redeemed for products. As of December 31, 2016, $30,000 of the remaining gift cards had passed the date at which GoodBuy concludes that the cards will never be redeemed. How much gift card revenue should GoodBuy recognize in 2016?

BE 5–25
Contract assets and contract liabilities
● LO5–8

Holt Industries received a $2,000 prepayment from the Ramirez Company for the sale of new office furniture. Holt will bill Ramirez an additional $3,000 upon delivery of the furniture to Ramirez. Upon receipt of the $2,000 prepayment, how much should Holt recognize for a contract asset, a contract liability, and accounts receivable?

BE 5–26
Contract assets and contract liabilities
● LO5–8, LO5–9

As of December 31, 2016, Cady Construction has one construction job for which the construction in progress (CIP) account has a balance of $20,000 and the billings on construction contract account has a balance of $14,000. Cady has another construction job for which the construction in progress account has a balance of $3,000 and the billings on construction contract account has a balance of $5,000. Indicate the amount of contract asset and/or contract liability that Cady would show in its December 31, 2016, balance sheet.

BE 5–27
Long-term contract; revenue recognition over time; profit recognition
● LO5–9

A construction company entered into a fixed-price contract to build an office building for $20 million. Construction costs incurred during the first year were $6 million and estimated costs to complete at the end of the year were $9 million. The company recognizes revenue over time according to percentage of completion. How much revenue and gross profit or loss will appear in the company's income statement in the first year of the contract?

BE 5–28
Long-term contract; revenue recognition over time; balance sheet
● LO5–9

Refer to the situation described in BE 5–27. During the first year the company billed its customer $7 million, of which $5 million was collected before year-end. What would appear in the year-end balance sheet related to this contract?

BE 5–29
Long-term contract; revenue recognition upon completion
● LO5–9

Refer to the situation described in BE 5–27. The building was completed during the second year. Construction costs incurred during the second year were $10 million. How much revenue and gross profit or loss will the company recognize in the first and second year if it recognizes revenue upon contract completion?

BE 5–30
Long-term contract; revenue recognition; loss on entire project
● LO5–9

Franklin Construction entered into a fixed-price contract to build a freeway-connecting ramp for $30 million. Construction costs incurred in the first year were $16 million and estimated remaining costs to complete at the end of the year were $17 million. How much gross profit or loss will Franklin recognize in the first year if it recognizes revenue over time according to percentage of completion? What if instead Franklin recognizes revenue upon contract completion?

BE 5–31
Receivables and inventory turnover ratios
● LO5–10

Universal Calendar Company began the year with accounts receivable (net) and inventory balances of $100,000 and $80,000, respectively. Year-end balances for these accounts were $120,000 and $60,000, respectively. Sales for the year of $600,000 generated a gross profit of $200,000. Calculate the receivables and inventory turnover ratios for the year.

BE 5–32
Profitability ratios
● LO5–10

The 2016 income statement for Anderson TV and Appliance reported sales revenue of $420,000 and net income of $65,000. Average total assets for 2016 was $800,000. Shareholders' equity at the beginning of the year was $500,000 and $20,000 was paid to shareholders as dividends. There were no other shareholders' equity transactions that occurred during the year. Calculate the profit margin on sales, return on assets, and return on shareholders' equity for 2016.

BE 5–33
Profitability ratios
● LO5–10

Refer to the facts described in BE 5–32. Show the DuPont framework's calculation of the three components of the 2016 return on shareholders' equity for Anderson TV and Appliance.

BE 5–34
Inventory turnover ratio
● LO5–10

During 2016, Rogue Corporation reported sales revenue of $600,000. Inventory at both the beginning and end of the year totaled $75,000. The inventory turnover ratio for the year was 6.0. What amount of gross profit did the company report in its 2016 income statement?

Exercises

An alternate exercise and problem set is available in the Connect library.

E 5–1
FASB codification research
● LO5–1, LO5–2, LO5–3

Access the *FASB's Accounting Standards Codification* at the FASB website (asc.fasb.org).

Required:

Determine the specific citation for accounting for each of the following items:

1. What are the five key steps to applying the revenue recognition principle?
2. What are indicators that control has passed from the seller to the buyer, such that it is appropriate to recognize revenue at a point in time?
3. Under what circumstances can sellers recognize revenue over time?

E 5–2
Service revenue
● LO5–3

Ski West, Inc., operates a downhill ski area near Lake Tahoe, California. An all-day adult lift ticket can be purchased for $85. Adult customers also can purchase a season pass that entitles the pass holder to ski any day during the season, which typically runs from December 1 through April 30. Ski West expects its season pass holders to use their passes equally throughout the season. The company's fiscal year ends on December 31.

On November 6, 2016, Jake Lawson purchased a season pass for $450.

Required:

1. When should Ski West recognize revenue from the sale of its season passes?
2. Prepare the appropriate journal entries that Ski West would record on November 6 and December 31.
3. What will be included in the Ski West 2016 income statement and balance sheet related to the sale of the season pass to Jake Lawson?

E 5–3
Allocating transaction price
● LO5–4

Video Planet ("VP") sells a big screen TV package consisting of a 60-inch plasma TV, a universal remote, and on-site installation by VP staff. The installation includes programming the remote to have the TV interface with other parts of the customer's home entertainment system. VP concludes that the TV, remote, and installation service are separate performance obligations. VP sells the 60-inch TV separately for $1,700, sells the remote separately for $100, and offers the installation service separately for $200. The entire package sells for $1,900.

Required:
How much revenue would be allocated to the TV, the remote, and the installation service?

E 5–4
FASB codification research
● LO5–4, LO5–5

Access the *FASB Standards Codification* at the FASB website (**asc.fasb.org**).

Required:
Determine the specific citation for accounting for each of the following items:

1. On what basis is a contract's transaction price allocated to its performance obligations?
2. What are indicators that a promised good or service is separately identifiable from other goods and services promised in the contract?
3. Under what circumstances is an option viewed as a performance obligation?

E 5–5
Performance obligations
● LO5–2, LO5–4, LO5–5

On March 1, 2016, Gold Examiner receives $147,000 from a local bank and promises to deliver 100 units of certified 1-oz. gold bars on a future date. The contract states that ownership passes to the bank when Gold Examiner delivers the products to Brink's, a third-party carrier. In addition, Gold Examiner has agreed to provide a replacement shipment at no additional cost if the product is lost in transit. The stand-alone price of a gold bar is $1,440 per unit, and Gold Examiner estimates the stand-alone price of the replacement insurance service to be $60 per unit. Brink's picked up the gold bars from Gold Examiner on March 30, and delivery to the bank occurred on April 1.

Required:

1. How many performance obligations are in this contract?
2. Prepare the journal entry Gold Examiner would record on March 1.
3. Prepare the journal entry Gold Examiner would record on March 30.
4. Prepare the journal entry Gold Examiner would record on April 1.

E 5–6
Performance obligations; customer option for additional goods or services
● LO5–2, LO5–4, LO5–5

Clarks Inc., a shoe retailer, sells boots in different styles. In early November the company starts selling "SunBoots" to customers for $70 per pair. When a customer purchases a pair of SunBoots, Clarks also gives the customer a 30% discount coupon for any additional future purchases made in the next 30 days. Customers can't obtain the discount coupon otherwise. Clarks anticipates that approximately 20% of customers will utilize the coupon, and that on average those customers will purchase additional goods that normally sell for $100.

Required:

1. How many performance obligations are in a contract to buy a pair of SunBoots?
2. Prepare a journal entry to record revenue for the sale of 1,000 pairs of SunBoots, assuming that Clarks uses the residual method to estimate the stand-alone selling price of SunBoots sold without the discount coupon.

E 5–7
Performance obligations; customer option for additional goods or services; prepayment
● LO5–3, LO5–4, LO5–5

A New York City daily newspaper called "Manhattan Today" charges an annual subscription fee of $135. Customers prepay their subscriptions and receive 260 issues over the year. To attract more subscribers, the company offered new subscribers the ability to pay $130 for an annual subscription that also would include a coupon to receive a 40% discount on a one-hour ride through Central Park in a horse-drawn carriage. The list price of a carriage ride is $125 per hour. The company estimates that approximately 30% of the coupons will be redeemed.

Required:

1. How much revenue should Manhattan Today recognize upon receipt of the $130 subscription price?
2. How many performance obligations exist in this contract?
3. Prepare the journal entry to recognize sale of 10 new subscriptions, clearly identifying the revenue or deferred revenue associated with each performance obligation.

E 5–8
Performance obligations; customer option for additional goods or services
● LO5–4, LO5–5

On May 1, 2016, Meta Computer, Inc., enters into a contract to sell 5,000 units of Comfort Office Keyboard to one of its clients, Bionics, Inc., at a fixed price of $95,000, to be settled by a cash payment on May 1. Delivery is scheduled for June 1, 2016. As part of the contract, the seller offers a 25% discount coupon to Bionics for any purchases in the next six months. The seller will continue to offer a 5% discount on all sales during the same time period, which will be available to all customers. Based on experience, Meta Computer estimates a 50% probability that Bionics will redeem the 25% discount voucher, and that the coupon will be applied to $20,000 of purchases. The stand-alone selling price for the Comfort Office Keyboard is $19.60 per unit.

Required:

1. How many performance obligations are in this contract?
2. Prepare the journal entry that Meta would record on May 1, 2016.
3. Assume the same facts and circumstances as above, except that Meta gives a 5% discount option to Bionics instead of 25%. In this case, what journal entry would Meta record on May 1, 2016?

E 5–9
Variable consideration; estimation and constraint
● LO5–6

Thomas Consultants provided Bran Construction with assistance in implementing various cost-savings initiatives. Thomas' contract specifies that it will receive a flat fee of $50,000 and an additional $20,000 if Bran reaches a prespecified target amount of cost savings. Thomas estimates that there is a 20% chance that Bran will achieve the cost-savings target.

Required:

1. Assuming Thomas uses the expected value as its estimate of variable consideration, calculate the transaction price.
2. Assuming Thomas uses the most likely value as its estimate of variable consideration, calculate the transaction price.
3. Assume Thomas uses the expected value as its estimate of variable consideration, but is very uncertain of that estimate due to a lack of experience with similar consulting arrangements. Calculate the transaction price.

E5–10
Variable consideration—most likely amount; change in estimate
● LO5–3, LO5–6

Rocky Guide Service provides guided 1–5 day hiking tours throughout the Rocky Mountains. Wilderness Tours hires Rocky to lead various tours that Wilderness sells. Rocky receives $1,000 per tour day, and shortly after the end of each month Rocky learns whether it will receive a $100 bonus per tour day it guided during the previous month if its service during that month received an average evaluation of "excellent" by Wilderness customers. The $1,000 per day and any bonus due are paid in one lump payment shortly after the end of each month.

- On July 1, based on prior experience, Rocky estimated that there is a 30% chance that it will earn the bonus for July tours. It guided a total of 10 days from July 1–July 15.
- On July 16, based on Rocky's view that it had provided excellent service during the first part of the month, Rocky revised its estimate to an 80% chance it would earn the bonus for July tours. Rocky also guided customers for 15 days from July 16–July 31.
- On August 5 Rocky learned that it did not receive an average evaluation of "excellent" for its July tours, so it would not receive any bonus for July, and received all payment due for the July tours.

Rocky bases estimates of variable consideration on the most likely amount it expects to receive.

Required:

1. Prepare Rocky's July 15 journal entry to record revenue for tours given from July 1–July 15.
2. Prepare Rocky's July 31 journal entry to record revenue for tours given from July 16–July 31.
3. Prepare Rocky's August 5 journal entry to record any necessary adjustments to revenue and receipt of payment from Wilderness.

E5–11
Variable consideration–expected value; change in estimate
● LO5–3, LO5–6

Assume the same facts as in E5–10.

Required:

Complete the requirements of E5–10 assuming that Rocky bases estimates of variable consideration on the expected value it expects to receive.

E 5–12
Consideration payable to customer; collectibility of transaction price
● LO5–2, LO5–5, LO5–6

Furtastic manufactures imitation fur garments. On June 1, 2016, Furtastic made a sale to Willett's Department Store under terms that require Willett to pay $150,000 to Furtastic on June 30, 2016. In a separate transaction on June 15, 2016, Furtastic purchased brand advertising services from Willett for $12,000. The fair value of those advertising services is $5,000. Furtastic expects that 3% of all sales will prove uncollectible.

Required:

1. Prepare the journal entry to record Furtastic's sale on June 1, 2016.
2. Prepare the journal entry to record Furtastic's purchase of advertising services from Willett on June 15, 2016. Assume all of the advertising services are delivered on June 15, 2016.
3. Prepare the journal entry to record Furtastic's receipt of $150,000 from Willett on June 30, 2016.
4. How would Furtastic's expectation regarding uncollectible accounts affect its recognition of revenue from the sale to Willett's Department Store on June 1, 2016? Explain briefly.

E 5–13
Approaches for estimating stand-alone selling prices
● LO5–6

(This exercise is a variation of E 5–3.)

Video Planet ("VP") sells a big screen TV package consisting of a 60-inch plasma TV, a universal remote, and on-site installation by VP staff. The installation includes programming the remote to have the TV interface with other parts of the customer's home entertainment system. VP concludes that the TV, remote, and installation service are separate performance obligations. VP sells the 60-inch TV separately for $1,750 and sells the remote separately for $100, and offers the entire package for $1,900. VP does not sell the installation service separately. VP is aware that other similar vendors charge $150 for the installation service. VP also estimates that it incurs approximately $100 of compensation and other costs for VP staff to provide the installation service. VP typically charges 40% above cost on similar sales.

Required:

1. Estimate the stand-alone selling price of the installation service using the adjusted market assessment approach.
2. Estimate the stand-alone selling price of the installation service using the expected cost plus margin approach.
3. Estimate the stand-alone selling price of the installation service using the residual approach.

E 5–14
FASB codification research
● LO5–6, LO5–7

Access the *FASB Accounting Standards Codification* at the FASB website (**asc.fasb.org**).

Required:

Determine the specific citation for accounting for each of the following items:

1. What alternative approaches can be used to estimate variable consideration?
2. What alternative approaches can be used to estimate the stand-alone selling price of performance obligations that are not sold separately?
3. What determines the timing of revenue recognition with respect to licenses?

E 5–15
Franchises; residual method
● LO5–6, LO5–7

Monitor Muffler sells franchise arrangements throughout the United States and Canada. Under a franchise agreement, Monitor receives $600,000 in exchange for satisfying the following separate performance obligations: (1) franchisees have a five-year right to operate as a Monitor Muffler retail establishment in an exclusive sales territory, (2) franchisees receive initial training and certification as a Monitor Mechanic, and (3) franchisees receive a Monitor Muffler building and necessary equipment. The stand-alone selling price of the initial training and certification is $15,000, and $450,000 for the building and equipment. Monitor estimates the stand-alone selling price of the five-year right to operate as a Monitor Muffler establishment using the residual approach.

Monitor received $75,000 on July 1, 2016, from Perkins and accepted a note receivable for the rest of the franchise price. Monitor will construct and equip Perkins' building and train and certify Perkins by September 1, and Perkins' five-year right to operate as a Monitor Muffler establishment will commence on September 1 as well.

Required:

1. What amount would Monitor calculate as the stand-alone selling price of the five-year right to operate as a Monitor Muffler retail establishment?
2. What journal entry would Monitor record on July 1, 2016, to reflect the sale of a franchise to Dan Perkins?
3. How much revenue would Monitor recognize in the year ended December 31, 2016, with respect to its franchise arrangement with Perkins? (Ignore any interest on the note receivable.)

E 5–16
FASB codification research
● LO5–8

Access the *FASB Accounting Standards Codification* at the FASB website (**asc.fasb.org**).

Required:

Determine the specific citation for accounting for each of the following items:

1. What disclosures are required with respect to performance obligations that the seller is committed to satisfying but that are not yet satisfied?
2. What disclosures are required with respect to uncollectible accounts receivable, also called impairments of receivables?
3. What disclosures are required with respect to significant changes in contract assets and contract liabilities?

E 5–17
Long-term contract; revenue recognition over time and at a point in time
● LO5–9

Assume **Nortel Networks** contracted to provide a customer with Internet infrastructure for $2,000,000. The project began in 2016 and was completed in 2017. Data relating to the contract are summarized below:

	2016	2017
Costs incurred during the year	$ 300,000	$1,575,000
Estimated costs to complete as of 12/31	1,200,000	–0–
Billings during the year	380,000	1,620,000
Cash collections during the year	250,000	1,750,000

Required:

1. Compute the amount of revenue and gross profit or loss to be recognized in 2016 and 2017 assuming Nortel recognizes revenue over time according to percentage of completion.
2. Compute the amount of revenue and gross profit or loss to be recognized in 2016 and 2017 assuming this project does not qualify for revenue recognition over time.
3. Prepare a partial balance sheet to show how the information related to this contract would be presented at the end of 2016 assuming Nortel recognizes revenue over time according to percentage of completion.
4. Prepare a partial balance sheet to show how the information related to this contract would be presented at the end of 2016 assuming this project does not qualify for revenue recognition over time.

E 5–18
Long-term contract; revenue recognition over time vs. upon project completion
● LO5–9

On June 15, 2016, Sanderson Construction entered into a long-term construction contract to build a baseball stadium in Washington, D.C., for $220 million. The expected completion date is April 1, 2018, just in time for the 2018 baseball season. Costs incurred and estimated costs to complete at year-end for the life of the contract are as follows ($ in millions):

	2016	2017	2018
Costs incurred during the year	$ 40	$80	$50
Estimated costs to complete as of December 31	120	60	—

Required:

1. How much revenue and gross profit will Sanderson report in its 2016, 2017, and 2018 income statements related to this contract assuming Sanderson recognizes revenue over time according to percentage of completion?
2. How much revenue and gross profit will Sanderson report in its 2016, 2017, and 2018 income statements related to this contract assuming this project does not qualify for revenue recognition over time?
3. Suppose the estimated costs to complete at the end of 2017 are $80 million instead of $60 million. Determine the amount of revenue and gross profit or loss to be recognized in 2017 assuming Sanderson recognizes revenue over time according to percentage of completion.

E 5–19
Long-term contract; revenue recognition over time; loss projected on entire project
● LO5–9

On February 1, 2016, Arrow Construction Company entered into a three-year construction contract to build a bridge for a price of $8,000,000. During 2016, costs of $2,000,000 were incurred with estimated costs of $4,000,000 yet to be incurred. Billings of $2,500,000 were sent, and cash collected was $2,250,000.

In 2017, costs incurred were $2,500,000 with remaining costs estimated to be $3,600,000. 2017 billings were $2,750,000, and $2,475,000 cash was collected. The project was completed in 2018 after additional costs of $3,800,000 were incurred. The company's fiscal year-end is December 31. Arrow recognizes revenue over time according to percentage of completion.

Required:

1. Calculate the amount of revenue and gross profit or loss to be recognized in each of the three years.
2. Prepare journal entries for 2016 and 2017 to record the transactions described (credit "various accounts" for construction costs incurred).
3. Prepare a partial balance sheet to show the presentation of the project as of December 31, 2016 and 2017.

E 5–20
Long-term contract; revenue recognition upon project completion; loss projected on entire project
● LO5–8, LO5–9

[This is a variation of Exercise 5–19 focusing on the revenue recognition upon project completion.]

On February 1, 2016, Arrow Construction Company entered into a three-year construction contract to build a bridge for a price of $8,000,000. During 2016, costs of $2,000,000 were incurred, with estimated costs of $4,000,000 yet to be incurred. Billings of $2,500,000 were sent, and cash collected was $2,250,000.

In 2017, costs incurred were $2,500,000 with remaining costs estimated to be $3,600,000. 2017 billings were $2,750,000, and $2,475,000 cash was collected. The project was completed in 2018 after additional costs of $3,800,000 were incurred. The company's fiscal year-end is December 31. This project does not qualify for revenue recognition over time.

Required:

1. Calculate the amount of gross profit or loss to be recognized in each of the three years.
2. Prepare journal entries for 2016 and 2017 to record the transactions described (credit "various accounts" for construction costs incurred).
3. Prepare a partial balance sheet to show the presentation of the project as of December 31, 2016 and 2017. Indicate whether any of the amounts shown are contract assets or contract liabilities.

E 5–21
Income (loss) recognition; Long-term contract; revenue recognition over time vs. upon project completion
● LO5–9

Brady Construction Company contracted to build an apartment complex for a price of $5,000,000. Construction began in 2016 and was completed in 2018. The following is a series of independent situations, numbered 1 through 6, involving differing costs for the project. All costs are stated in thousands of dollars.

	Costs Incurred During Year			Estimated Costs to Complete (As of the End of the Year)		
Situation	2016	2017	2018	2016	2017	2018
1	1,500	2,100	900	3,000	900	—
2	1,500	900	2,400	3,000	2,400	—
3	1,500	2,100	1,600	3,000	1,500	—
4	500	3,000	1,000	3,500	875	—
5	500	3,000	1,300	3,500	1,500	—
6	500	3,000	1,800	4,600	1,700	—

Required:
Copy and complete the following table.

	Gross Profit (Loss) Recognized					
	Revenue Recognized Over Time			Revenue Recognized Upon Completion		
Situation	2016	2017	2018	2016	2017	2018
1						
2						
3						
4						
5						
6						

E 5–22
Long-term contract; revenue recognition over time; solve for unknowns
● LO5–9

In 2016, Long Construction Corporation began construction work under a three-year contract. The contract price is $1,600,000. Long recognizes revenue over time according to percentage of completion for financial reporting purposes. The financial statement presentation relating to this contract at December 31, 2016, is as follows:

Balance Sheet

Accounts receivable (from construction progress billings)		$30,000
Construction in progress	$100,000	
Less: Billings on construction contract	(94,000)	
Cost and profit of uncompleted contracts in excess of billings		6,000

Income Statement

Income (before tax) on the contract recognized in 2016	$20,000

Required:
1. What was the cost of construction actually incurred in 2016?
2. How much cash was collected in 2016 on this contract?
3. What was the estimated cost to complete as of the end of 2016?
4. What was the estimated percentage of completion used to calculate revenue in 2016? *(AICPA adapted)*

E 5–23
Inventory turnover; calculation and evaluation
● LO5–10

The following is a portion of the condensed income statement for Rowan, Inc., a manufacturer of plastic containers:

Net sales		$2,460,000
Less: Cost of goods sold:		
Inventory, January 1	$ 630,000	
Net purchases	1,900,000	
Inventory, December 31	(690,000)	1,840,000
Gross profit		$ 620,000

Required:
1. Determine Rowan's inventory turnover.
2. What information does this ratio provide?

E 5–24
Evaluating efficiency of asset management
● LO5–10

The 2016 income statement of Anderson Medical Supply Company reported net sales of $8 million, cost of goods sold of $4.8 million, and net income of $800,000. The following table shows the company's comparative balance sheets for 2016 and 2015:

	($ in 000s)	
	2016	2015
Assets		
Cash	$ 300	$ 380
Accounts receivable	700	500
Inventory	900	700
Property, plant, and equipment (net)	2,400	2,120
Total assets	$4,300	$3,700
Liabilities and Shareholders' Equity		
Current liabilities	$ 960	$ 830
Bonds payable	1,200	1,200
Paid-in capital	1,000	1,000
Retained earnings	1,140	670
Total liabilities and shareholders' equity	$4,300	$3,700

Some industry averages for Anderson's line of business are

Inventory turnover	5 times
Average collection period	25 days
Asset turnover	1.8 times

Required:
Assess Anderson's asset management relative to its industry.

E 5–25
Profitability ratios
● LO5–10

The following condensed information was reported by Peabody Toys, Inc., for 2016 and 2015:

	($ in 000s)	
	2016	**2015**
Income statement information		
Net sales	$5,200	$4,200
Net income	180	124
Balance sheet information		
Current assets	$ 800	$ 750
Property, plant, and equipment (net)	1,100	950
Total assets	$1,900	$1,700
Current liabilities	$ 600	$ 450
Long-term liabilities	750	750
Paid-in capital	400	400
Retained earnings	150	100
Liabilities and shareholders' equity	$1,900	$1,700

Required:
1. Determine the following ratios for 2016:
   a. Profit margin on sales.
   b. Return on assets.
   c. Return on shareholders' equity.
2. Determine the amount of dividends paid to shareholders during 2016.

E 5–26
DuPont analysis
● LO5–10

This exercise is based on the Peabody Toys, Inc., data from Exercise 5–25.

Required:
1. Determine the following components of the DuPont framework for 2016:
   a. Profit margin on sales.
   b. Asset turnover.
   c. Equity multiplier.
   d. Return on shareholders' equity.
2. Write an equation that relates these components in calculating ROE. Use the Peabody Toys data to show that the equation is correct.

CPA and CMA Review Questions

CPA Exam Questions

KAPLAN CPA REVIEW

The following questions are adapted from a variety of sources including questions developed by the AICPA Board of Examiners and those used in the Kaplan CPA Review Course to study revenue recognition while preparing for the CPA examination. Determine the response that best completes the statements or questions.

● LO5–2

1. On October 1, 2016, Acme Fuel Co. sold 100,000 gallons of heating oil to Karn Co. at $3 per gallon. Fifty thousand gallons were delivered on December 15, 2016, and the remaining 50,000 gallons were delivered on January 15, 2017. Payment terms were 50% due on October 1, 2016, 25% due on first delivery, and the remaining 25% due on second delivery. What amount of revenue should Acme recognize from this sale during 2017?
   a. $ 75,000
   b. $150,000
   c. $225,000
   d. $300,000

LO5–4

2. Elmo Painting Service signed a contract charging a customer $3,000 to paint the customer's house. The contract includes all paint and all painting labor. Elmo would charge $1,200 for the paint if sold separately, and $2,800 for the labor if done using the customer's paint. How much of the transaction price would Elmo allocate to its performance obligation to provide paint to the customer?

   a. $0
   b. $900
   c. $1,200
   d. $3,000

LO5–4

3. Triangle Travel offers their normal Bahama Get-Away travel package for $2,000, and offers their special Bahama Elite package (with additional guided tours) for $2,500. Triangle hasn't offered the Elite package previously, and is unsure what it would charge for the additional guided tours absent the basic Bahama Get-Away package. How much of the Elite transaction price should Triangle assign to the basic Bahama Get-Away portion of the Elite package?

   a. $2,500
   b. $2,000
   c. $1,250
   d. $0

LO5–5

4. Perkins Appliances offers a contract in which customers receive the following:
   - A new Perkins Pro washing machine,
   - a warranty that protects against product defects for the first six months of use,
   - an option to purchase a Perkins Pro dryer for a 30% discount (Perkins typically discounts that brand of dryer 10%), and
   - a coupon to purchase an extended warranty for $150 (extended warranties regularly sell for $150).

   How many performance obligations are included in the contract?

   a. 4
   b. 3
   c. 2
   d. 1

LO5–7

5. Mowry Maintenance signs a one-year contract to provide janitorial services for a new amusement park. The contract will pay Mowry $10,000 per month as a base fee, and will pay an additional bonus of $60,000 if attendance at the park for the year exceeds a specified threshold. Mowry believes it has a 75% chance of meeting the threshold, and uses an expected value estimate to account for variable consideration. After eight months of the contract, how much revenue will Mowry have recognized?

   a. $0
   b. $80,000
   c. $110,000
   d. $120,000

LO5–8

6. Which of the following statements is FALSE regarding recognizing revenue over time on long-term contracts? The construction-in-progress account:

   a. is shown net of billings as a liability if the amount is less than the amount of billings.
   b. is an asset.
   c. is shown net of billings in the balance sheet.
   d. does not include the cumulative effect of gross profit recognition.

LO5–8

7. The following data relates to a construction job started by Syl Co. during 2016:

Total contract price	$100,000
Actual costs incurred during 2016	20,000
Estimated remaining costs	40,000
Billed to customer during 2016	30,000
Received from customer during 2016	10,000

   Assuming that Syl recognizes revenue over time according to percentage of completion, how much should Syl recognize as gross profit for 2016?

   a. $26,667
   b. $0
   c. $13,333
   d. $33,333

● LO5–8

8. Hansen Construction Inc. has consistently recognized revenue over time according to percentage of completion. During 2016, Hansen started work on a $3,000,000 fixed-price construction contract. The accounting records disclosed the following data for the year ended December 31, 2016:

Costs incurred	$ 930,000
Estimated cost to complete	2,170,000
Progress billings	1,100,000
Collections	700,000

How much loss should Hansen have recognized in 2016?

a. $180,000
b. $230,000
c. $ 30,000
d. $100,000

CMA Exam Questions

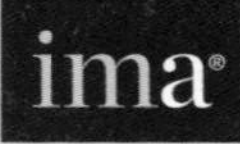

The following question dealing with income measurement is adapted from questions that previously appeared on Certified Management Accountant (CMA) examinations. The CMA designation sponsored by the Institute of Management Accountants (**www.imanet.org**) provides members with an objective measure of knowledge and competence in the field of management accounting. Determine the response that best completes the statements or questions.

● LO5–8

1. Roebling Construction signed a $24 million contract on August 1, 2015, with the city of Candu to construct a bridge over the Vine River. Roebling's estimated cost of the bridge on that date was $18 million. The bridge was to be completed by April 2018. Roebling recognizes revenue over time according to percentage of completion. Roebling's fiscal year ends May 31. Data regarding the bridge contract are presented in the schedule below.

	At May 31 ($000 omitted)	
	2016	**2017**
Actual costs to date	$ 6,000	$15,000
Estimated costs to complete	12,000	5,000
Progress billings to date	5,000	14,000
Cash collected to date	4,000	12,000

The gross profit or loss recognized in the fiscal year ended May 31, 2016, from this bridge contract is

a. $6,000,000 gross profit.
b. $2,000,000 gross profit.
c. $3,000,000 gross profit.
d. $1,000,000 gross profit.

Problems

An alternate exercise and problem set is available in the Connect library.

P 5–1
Upfront fees; performance obligations
● LO5–4, LO5–5

Fit & Slim (F&S) is a health club that offers members various gym services.

Required:

1. Assume F&S offers a deal whereby enrolling in a new membership for $700 provides a year of unlimited access to facilities and also entitles the member to receive a voucher redeemable for 25% off yoga classes for one year. The yoga classes are offered to gym members as well as to the general public. A new membership normally sells for $720, and a one-year enrollment in yoga classes sells for an additional $500. F&S estimates that approximately 40% of the vouchers will be redeemed. F&S offers a 10% discount on all one-year enrollments in classes as part of its normal promotion strategy.
   a. How many performance obligations are included in the new member deal?
   b. How much of the contract price would be allocated to each performance obligation? Explain your answer.
   c. Prepare the journal entry to recognize revenue for the sale of a new membership. Clearly identify revenue or deferred revenue associated with each performance obligation.

2. Assume F&S offers a "Fit 50" coupon book with 50 prepaid visits over the next year. F&S has learned that Fit 50 purchasers make an average of 40 visits before the coupon book expires. A customer purchases a Fit 50 book by paying $500 in advance, and for any additional visits over 50 during the year after the book is purchased, the customer can pay a $15 visitation fee per visit. F&S typically charges $15 to nonmembers who use the facilities for a single day.
   a. How many separate performance obligations are included in the Fit 50 member deal? Explain your answer.
   b. How much of the contract price would be allocated to each separate performance obligation? Explain your answer.
   c. Prepare the journal entry to recognize revenue for the sale of a new Fit 50 book.

P 5–2
Performance obligations; warranties; option
● LO5–2, LO5–4, LO5–5

Creative Computing sells a tablet computer called the Protab. The $780 sales price of a Protab Package includes the following:

- One Protab computer.
- A 6-month limited warranty. This warranty guarantees that Creative will cover any costs that arise due to repairs or replacements associated with defective products for up to six months.
- A coupon to purchase a Creative Probook e-book reader for $200, a price that represents a 50% discount from the regular Probook price of $400. It is expected that 20% of the discount coupons will be utilized.
- A coupon to purchase a one-year extended warranty for $50. Customers can buy the extended warranty for $50 at other times as well. Creative estimates that 40% of customers will purchase an extended warranty.
- Creative does not sell the Protab without the limited warranty, option to purchase a Probook, and the option to purchase an extended warranty, but estimates that if it did so, a Protab alone would sell for $760.

Required:

1. How many performance obligations are included in a Protab Package? Explain your answer.
2. List the performance obligations in the Protab Package in the following table, and complete it to allocate the transaction price of 100,000 Protab Packages to the performance obligations in the contract.

Performance obligation:	Stand-alone selling price of the performance obligation:	Percentage of the sum of the stand-alone selling prices of the performance obligations (to two decimal places):	Allocation of total transaction price to the performance obligation:

3. Prepare a journal entry to record sales of 100,000 Protab Packages (ignore any sales of extended warranties).

P 5–3
Performance obligations; warranties; option
● LO5–2, LO5–4, LO5–5

Assume the same facts as in P5–2, except that customers must pay $75 to purchase the extended warranty if they don't purchase it with the $50 coupon that was included in the Protab Package. Creative estimates that 40% of customers will use the $50 coupon to purchase an extended warranty. Complete the same requirements as in P5–2.

P 5–4
Performance obligations; customer options for additional goods and services
● LO5–2, LO5–4, LO5–5

Supply Club, Inc., sells a variety of paper products, office supplies, and other products used by businesses and individual consumers. During July 2016 it started a loyalty program through which qualifying customers can accumulate points and redeem those points for discounts on future purchases. Redemption of a loyalty point reduces the price of one dollar of future purchases by 20% (equal to 20 cents). Customers do not earn additional loyalty points for purchases on which loyalty points are redeemed. Based on past experience, Supply Club estimates a 60% probability that any point issued will be redeemed for the discount. During July 2016, the company records $135,000 of revenue and awards 125,000 loyalty points. The aggregate stand-alone selling price of the purchased products is $135,000. Eighty percent of sales were cash sales, and the remainder were credit sales.

Required:

1. Prepare Supply Club's journal entry to record July sales.
2. During August, customers redeem loyalty points on $60,000 of merchandise. Seventy-five percent of those sales were for cash, and the remainder were credit sales. Prepare Supply Club's journal entry to record those sales.

P 5–5
Variable consideration
● LO5–3, LO5–6

On January 1 Revis Consulting entered into a contract to complete a cost reduction program for Green Financial over a six-month period. Revis will receive $20,000 from Green at the end of each month. If total cost savings reach a specific target, Revis will receive an additional $10,000 from Green at the end of the contract, but if total cost savings fall short, Revis will refund $10,000 to Green. Revis estimates an 80% chance that cost savings will reach the target and calculates the contract price based on the expected value of future payments to be received.

Required:
Prepare the following journal entries for Revis:

1. Prepare the journal entry on January 31 to record the collection of cash and recognition of the first month's revenue.
2. Assuming total cost savings exceed target, prepare the journal entry on June 30 to record receipt of the bonus.
3. Assuming total cost savings fall short of target, prepare the journal entry on June 30 to record payment of the penalty.

P 5–6
Variable consideration; change of estimate
● LO5–3, LO5–6

Since 1970, Super Rise, Inc., has provided maintenance services for elevators. On January 1, 2016, Super Rise obtains a contract to maintain an elevator in a 90-story building in New York City for 10 months and receives a fixed payment of $80,000. The contract specifies that Super Rise will receive an additional $40,000 at the end of the 10 months if there is no unexpected delay, stoppage, or accident during the year. Super Rise estimates variable consideration to be the most likely amount it will receive.

Required:

1. Assume that, because the building sees a constant flux of people throughout the day, Super Rise is allowed to access the elevators and related mechanical equipment only between 3am and 5am on any given day, which is insufficient to perform some of the more time-consuming repair work. As a result, Super Rise believes that unexpected delays are likely and that it will not earn the bonus. Prepare the journal entry Super Rise would record on January 1.
2. Assume instead that Super Rise knows at the inception of the contract that it will be given unlimited access to the elevators and related equipment each day, with the right to schedule repair sessions any time. When given these terms and conditions, Super Rise has never had any delays or accidents in the past. Prepare the journal entry Super Rise would record on January 31 to record one month of revenue.
3. Assume the same facts as requirement 1. In addition assume that, on May 31, Super Rise determines that it does not need to spend more than two hours on any given day to operate the elevator safely because the client's elevator is relatively new. Therefore, Super Rise believes that unexpected delays are very unlikely. Prepare the journal entry Super Rise would record on May 31 to recognize May revenue and any necessary revision in its estimated bonus receivable.

P 5–7
Variable consideration; constraint and change of estimate
● LO5–3, LO5–6

Assume the same facts as P5–6.

Required:

1. Assume that Super Rise anticipates it will earn the performance bonus, but is highly uncertain about its estimate given unfamiliarity with the building and uncertainty about its access to the elevators and related equipment. Prepare the journal entry Super Rise would record on January 1.
2. Assume the same facts as requirement 1. In addition assume that, on May 31, Super Rise determines that it has sufficient experience with the company to make an accurate estimate of the likelihood that it will earn the performance bonus, and concludes that it is likely to earn the performance bonus. Prepare the journal entry Super Rise would record on May 31 to recognize May revenue and any necessary revision in its estimated bonus receivable.

P 5–8
Variable transaction price
● LO5–3, LO5–6

Velocity, a consulting firm, enters into a contract to help Burger Boy, a fast-food restaurant, design a marketing strategy to compete with **Burger King**. The contract spans eight months. Burger Boy promises to pay $60,000 at the beginning of each month. At the end of the contract, Velocity either will give Burger Boy a refund of $20,000 or will be entitled to an additional $20,000 bonus, depending on whether sales at Burger Boy at year-end have increased to a target level. At the inception of the contract, Velocity estimates an 80% chance that it will earn the $20,000 bonus and calculates the contract price based on the expected value of future payments to be received. After four months, circumstances change, and Velocity revises to 60% its estimate of the probability that it will earn the bonus. At the end of the contract, Velocity receives the additional consideration of $20,000.

Required:

1. Prepare the journal entry to record revenue each month for the first four months of the contract.
2. Prepare the journal entry that the Velocity Company would record after four months to recognize the change in estimate associated with the reduced likelihood that the $20,000 bonus will be received.

3. Prepare the journal entry to record the revenue each month for the second four months of the contract.
4. Prepare the journal entry after eight months to record receipt of the $20,000 cash bonus.

P 5–9
Variable transaction price
● LO5–3, LO5–6, LO5–7

Tran Technologies licenses its intellectual property to Lyon Industries. Terms of the arrangement require Lyon to pay Tran $500,000 on April 1, 2016, when Lyon first obtains access to Tran's intellectual property, and then to pay Tran a royalty of 4% of future sales of products that utilize that intellectual property. Tran anticipates receiving sales-based royalties of $1,000,000 during 2016 and $1,500,000/year for the years 2017–2021. Assume Tran accounts for the Lyon license as a right of use, because Tran's actions subsequent to April 1, 2016, will affect the benefits that Lyon receives from access to Tran's intellectual property.

Required:

1. Access the *FASB Accounting Standards Codification* at the FASB website (**asc.fasb.org**). Identify the specific citation for accounting for variable consideration arising from sales-based royalties on licenses of intellectual property, and consider the relevant GAAP. When can Tran recognize revenue from sales-based royalties associated with the Lyon license?
2. What journal entry would Tran record on April 1, 2016, when it receives the $500,000 payment from Lyon?
3. Assume on December 31, 2016, Tran receives $1,000,000 for all sales-based royalties earned from Lyon in 2016. What journal entry would Tran record on December 31, 2016, to recognize any revenue that should be recognized in 2016 with respect to the Lyon license that it has not already recognized?
4. Assume Tran accounts for the Lyon license as a five-year right to access Tran's intellectual property from April 1, 2016, through March 31, 2021. Tran expects that its ongoing marketing efforts will affect the value of the license to Lyon during the five-year license period. Repeat requirements 2 and 3.

P 5–10
Long-term contract; revenue recognition over time
● LO5–8, LO5–9

In 2016, the Westgate Construction Company entered into a contract to construct a road for Santa Clara County for $10,000,000. The road was completed in 2018. Information related to the contract is as follows:

	2016	2017	2018
Cost incurred during the year	$2,400,000	$3,600,000	$2,200,000
Estimated costs to complete as of year-end	5,600,000	2,000,000	–0–
Billings during the year	2,000,000	4,000,000	4,000,000
Cash collections during the year	1,800,000	3,600,000	4,600,000

Westgate recognizes revenue over time according to percentage of completion.

Required:

1. Calculate the amount of revenue and gross profit to be recognized in each of the three years.
2. Prepare all necessary journal entries for each of the years (credit "various accounts" for construction costs incurred).
3. Prepare a partial balance sheet for 2016 and 2017 showing any items related to the contract. Indicate whether any of the amounts shown are contract assets or contract liabilities.
4. Calculate the amount of revenue and gross profit to be recognized in each of the three years assuming the following costs incurred and costs to complete information:

	2016	2017	2018
Costs incurred during the year	$2,400,000	$3,800,000	$3,200,000
Estimated costs to complete as of year-end	5,600,000	3,100,000	–0–

5. Calculate the amount of revenue and gross profit to be recognized in each of the three years assuming the following costs incurred and costs to complete information:

	2016	2017	2018
Costs incurred during the year	$2,400,000	$3,800,000	$3,900,000
Estimated costs to complete as of year-end	5,600,000	4,100,000	–0–

P 5–11
Long-term contract; revenue recognition upon completion
● LO5–9

[This is a variation of Problem 5–10 modified to focus on revenue recognition upon project completion.]

Required:

Complete the requirements of Problem 5–10 assuming that Westgate Construction's contract with Santa Clara County does *not* qualify for revenue recognition over time.

P 5–12
Long-term contract; revenue recognized over time; loss projected on entire project
● LO5–9

Curtiss Construction Company, Inc., entered into a fixed-price contract with Axelrod Associates on July 1, 2016, to construct a four-story office building. At that time, Curtiss estimated that it would take between two and three years to complete the project. The total contract price for construction of the building is $4,000,000. Curtiss concludes that the contract does not qualify for revenue recognition over time. The building was completed on December 31, 2018. Estimated percentage of completion, accumulated contract costs incurred, estimated costs to complete the contract, and *accumulated* billings to Axelrod under the contract were as follows:

	At 12-31-2016	At 12-31-2017	At 12-31-2018
Percentage of completion	10%	60%	100%
Costs incurred to date	$ 350,000	$2,500,000	$4,250,000
Estimated costs to complete	3,150,000	1,700,000	–0–
Billings to Axelrod, to date	720,000	2,170,000	3,600,000

Required:

1. For each of the three years, prepare a schedule to compute total gross profit or loss to be recognized as a result of this contract.
2. Assuming Curtiss recognizes revenue over time according to percentage of completion, compute gross profit or loss to be recognized in each of the three years.
3. Assuming Curtiss recognizes revenue over time according to percentage of completion, compute the amount to be shown in the balance sheet at the end of 2016 and 2017 as either cost in excess of billings or billings in excess of costs.

(AICPA adapted)

P 5–13
Long-term contract; revenue recognition over time vs. upon project completion
● LO5–9

Citation Builders, Inc., builds office buildings and single-family homes. The office buildings are constructed under contract with reputable buyers. The homes are constructed in developments ranging from 10–20 homes and are typically sold during construction or soon after. To secure the home upon completion, buyers must pay a deposit of 10% of the price of the home with the remaining balance due upon completion of the house and transfer of title. Failure to pay the full amount results in forfeiture of the down payment. Occasionally, homes remain unsold for as long as three months after construction. In these situations, sales price reductions are used to promote the sale.

During 2016, Citation began construction of an office building for Altamont Corporation. The total contract price is $20 million. Costs incurred, estimated costs to complete at year-end, billings, and cash collections for the life of the contract are as follows:

	2016	2017	2018
Costs incurred during the year	$ 4,000,000	$ 9,500,000	$4,500,000
Estimated costs to complete as of year-end	12,000,000	4,500,000	—
Billings during the year	2,000,000	10,000,000	8,000,000
Cash collections during the year	1,800,000	8,600,000	9,600,000

Also during 2016, Citation began a development consisting of 12 identical homes. Citation estimated that each home will sell for $600,000, but individual sales prices are negotiated with buyers. Deposits were received for eight of the homes, three of which were completed during 2016 and paid for in full for $600,000 each by the buyers. The completed homes cost $450,000 each to construct. The construction costs incurred during 2016 for the nine uncompleted homes totaled $2,700,000.

Required:

1. Briefly explain the difference between recognizing revenue over time and upon project completion when accounting for long-term construction contracts.
2. Answer the following questions assuming that Citation concludes it does not qualify for revenue recognition over time for its office building contracts:
   a. How much revenue related to this contract will Citation report in its 2016 and 2017 income statements?
   b. What is the amount of gross profit or loss to be recognized for the Altamont contract during 2016 and 2017?
   c. What will Citation report in its December 31, 2016, balance sheet related to this contract? (Ignore cash.)
3. Answer requirements 2a through 2c assuming that Citation recognizes revenue over time according to percentage of completion for its office building contracts.
4. Assume the same information for 2016 and 2017, but that as of year-end 2017 the estimated cost to complete the office building is $9,000,000. Citation recognizes revenue over time according to percentage of completion for its office building contracts.
   a. How much revenue related to this contract will Citation report in the 2017 income statement?

b. What is the amount of gross profit or loss to be recognized for the Altamont contract during 2017?
c. What will Citation report in its 2017 balance sheet related to this contract? (Ignore cash.)

5. When should Citation recognize revenue for the sale of its single-family homes?
6. What will Citation report in its 2016 income statement and 2016 balance sheet related to the single-family home business (ignore cash in the balance sheet)?

P 5–14
Calculating activity and profitability ratios
● LO5–10

Financial statements for Askew Industries for 2016 are shown below (in $000's):

2016 Income Statement

Sales	$ 9,000
Cost of goods sold	(6,300)
Gross profit	2,700
Operating expenses	(2,000)
Interest expense	(200)
Tax expense	(200)
Net income	$ 300

Comparative Balance Sheets

	Dec. 31	
	2016	**2015**
Assets		
Cash	$ 600	$ 500
Accounts receivable	600	400
Inventory	800	600
Property, plant, and equipment (net)	2,000	2,100
	$4,000	$3,600
Liabilities and Shareholders' Equity		
Current liabilities	$1,100	$ 850
Bonds payable	1,400	1,400
Paid-in capital	600	600
Retained earnings	900	750
	$4,000	$3,600

Required:
Calculate the following ratios for 2016.

1. Inventory turnover ratio
2. Average days in inventory
3. Receivables turnover ratio
4. Average collection period
5. Asset turnover ratio
6. Profit margin on sales
7. Return on assets
8. Return on shareholders' equity
9. Equity multiplier
10. Return on shareholders' equity (using the DuPont framework)

P 5–15
Use of ratios to compare two companies in the same industry
● LO5–10

Presented on the next page are condensed financial statements adapted from those of two actual companies competing in the pharmaceutical industry—**Johnson and Johnson (J&J)** and **Pfizer, Inc.** ($ in millions, except per share amounts).

Required:
Evaluate and compare the two companies by responding to the following questions.

Note: Because two-year comparative statements are not provided, you should use year-end balances in place of average balances as appropriate.

1. Which of the two companies appears more efficient in collecting its accounts receivable and managing its inventory?
2. Which of the two firms had greater earnings relative to resources available?
3. Have the two companies achieved their respective rates of return on assets with similar combinations of profit margin and turnover?
4. From the perspective of a common shareholder, which of the two firms provided a greater rate of return?
5. From the perspective of a common shareholder, which of the two firms appears to be using leverage more effectively to provide a return to shareholders above the rate of return on assets?

Balance Sheets
($ in millions, except per share data)

	J&J	Pfizer
Assets:		
Cash	$ 5,377	$ 1,520
Short-term investments	4,146	10,432
Accounts receivable (net)	6,574	8,775
Inventories	3,588	5,837
Other current assets	3,310	3,177
Current assets	22,995	29,741
Property, plant, and equipment (net)	9,846	18,287
Intangibles and other assets	15,422	68,747
Total assets	$48,263	$116,775
Liabilities and Shareholders' Equity:		
Accounts payable	$ 4,966	$ 2,601
Short-term notes	1,139	8,818
Other current liabilities	7,343	12,238
Current liabilities	13,448	23,657
Long-term debt	2,955	5,755
Other long-term liabilities	4,991	21,986
Total liabilities	21,394	51,398
Capital stock (par and additional paid-in capital)	3,120	67,050
Retained earnings	30,503	29,382
Accumulated other comprehensive income (loss)	(590)	195
Less: Treasury stock and other equity adjustments	(6,164)	(31,250)
Total shareholders' equity	26,869	65,377
Total liabilities and shareholders' equity	$48,263	$116,775

Income Statements

	J&J	Pfizer
Net sales	$41,862	$ 45,188
Cost of goods sold	12,176	9,832
Gross profit	29,686	35,356
Operating expenses	19,763	28,486
Other (income) expense—net	(385)	3,610
Income before taxes	10,308	3,260
Tax expense	3,111	1,621
Net income	$ 7,197	$ 1,639*
Basic net income per share	$ 2.42	$ .22

*This is before income from discontinued operations.

P 5–16
Creating a balance sheet from ratios; Chapters 3 and 5
● LO5–10

Cadux Candy Company's income statement for the year ended December 31, 2016, reported interest expense of $2 million and income tax expense of $12 million. Current assets listed in its balance sheet include cash, accounts receivable, and inventories. Property, plant, and equipment is the company's only noncurrent asset. Financial ratios for 2016 are listed below. Profitability and turnover ratios with balance sheet items in the denominator were calculated using year-end balances rather than averages.

Debt to equity ratio	1.0
Current ratio	2.0
Acid-test ratio	1.0
Times interest earned ratio	17 times
Return on assets	10%
Return on shareholders' equity	20%
Profit margin on sales	5%
Gross profit margin (gross profit divided by net sales)	40%
Inventory turnover	8 times
Receivables turnover	20 times

Required:
Prepare a December 31, 2016, balance sheet for the Cadux Candy Company.

P 5–17
Compare two companies in the same industry; Chapters 3 and 5
● LO5–10

Presented below are condensed financial statements adapted from those of two actual companies competing as the primary players in a specialty area of the food manufacturing and distribution industry. ($ in millions, except per share amounts.)

Balance Sheets

	Metropolitan	Republic
Assets:		
Cash	$ 179.3	$ 37.1
Accounts receivable (net)	422.7	325.0
Short-term investments	—	4.7
Inventories	466.4	635.2
Prepaid expenses and other current assets	134.6	476.7
Current assets	$1,203.0	$1,478.7
Property, plant, and equipment (net)	2,608.2	2,064.6
Intangibles and other assets	210.3	464.7
Total assets	$4,021.5	$4,008.0
Liabilities and Shareholders' Equity		
Accounts payable	$ 467.9	$ 691.2
Short-term notes	227.1	557.4
Accruals and other current liabilities	585.2	538.5
Current liabilities	$1,280.2	$1,787.1
Long-term debt	535.6	542.3
Deferred tax liability	384.6	610.7
Other long-term liabilities	104.0	95.1
Total liabilities	$2,304.4	$3,035.2
Common stock (par and additional paid-in capital)	144.9	335.0
Retained earnings	2,476.9	1,601.9
Less: Treasury stock	(904.7)	(964.1)
Total liabilities and shareholders' equity	$4,021.5	$4,008.0

Income Statements

	Metropolitan	Republic
Net sales	$5,698.0	$7,768.2
Cost of goods sold	(2,909.0)	(4,481.7)
Gross profit	$2,789.0	$3,286.5
Operating expenses	(1,743.7)	(2,539.2)
Interest expense	(56.8)	(46.6)
Income before taxes	$ 988.5	$ 700.7
Tax expense	(394.7)	(276.1)
Net income	$ 593.8	$ 424.6
Net income per share	$ 2.40	$ 6.50

Required:
Evaluate and compare the two companies by responding to the following questions.
Note: Because comparative statements are not provided you should use year-end balances in place of average balances as appropriate.

1. Which of the two firms had greater earnings relative to resources available?
2. Have the two companies achieved their respective rates of return on assets with similar combinations of profit margin and turnover?
3. From the perspective of a common shareholder, which of the two firms provided a greater rate of return?
4. Which company is most highly leveraged and which has made most effective use of financial leverage?
5. Of the two companies, which appears riskier in terms of its ability to pay short-term obligations?
6. How efficiently are current assets managed?
7. From the perspective of a creditor, which company offers the most comfortable margin of safety in terms of its ability to pay fixed interest charges?

Broaden Your Perspective

Apply your critical-thinking ability to the knowledge you've gained. These cases will provide you an opportunity to develop your research, analysis, judgment, and communication skills. You also will work with other students, integrate what you've learned, apply it in real-world situations, and consider its global and ethical ramifications. This practice will broaden your knowledge and further develop your decision-making abilities.

Research Case 5–1
Earnings management with respect to revenues
● LO5–1

An article published in *Accounting Horizons* describes various techniques that companies use to manage their earnings.

Required:

In your library, on the Internet, or from some other source, locate the article "How Are Earnings Managed? Evidence from Auditors" in *Accounting Horizons,* 2003 (Supplement), and answer the following questions:

1. What are the four most common revenue-recognition abuses identified by auditors in that article? From the examples provided in the article, briefly explain each abuse.
2. What is the revenue-recognition abuse identified in the article related to the percentage-of-completion method?
3. Did revenue-recognition abuses tend to increase or decrease net income in the year they occurred?
4. Did auditors tend to require their clients to make adjustments that reduced the revenue-recognition abuses they detected?

Judgment Case 5–2
Satisfaction of performance obligations
● LO5–2

Assume McDonald's enters into a contract to sell Billy Bear dolls for Toys4U Stores. Based on the contract, McDonald's displays the dolls in selected stores. Toys4U is not paid until the dolls have been sold by McDonald's, and unsold dolls are returned to Toys4U.

Required:

Determine whether Toys4U has satisfied its performance obligation when it delivers the dolls to McDonald's. Explain your answer.

Judgment Case 5–3
Satisfaction of performance obligations
● LO5–2

Cutler Education Corporation developed a software product to help children under age 12 learn mathematics. The software contains two separate parts: Basic Level (Level I) and Intermediate Level (Level II). Parents purchase each level separately and are eligible to purchase the access code for Level II only if their children pass the Level I exam.

Kerry purchases the Level I software at a price of $50 for his son, Tom, on December 1. Suppose Tom passed the Level I test on December 10, and Kerry immediately purchased the access code for Level II for an additional $30. Cutler provided Kerry with the access code to Level II on December 20.

Required:

When would Cutler recognize revenue for the sale of Level I and Level II software?

Ethics Case 5–4
Revenue recognition
● LO5–2

Horizon Corporation manufactures personal computers. The company began operations in 2011 and reported profits for the years 2011 through 2014. Due primarily to increased competition and price slashing in the industry, 2015's income statement reported a loss of $20 million. Just before the end of the 2016 fiscal year, a memo from the company's chief financial officer to Jim Fielding, the company controller, included the following comments:

If we don't do something about the large amount of unsold computers already manufactured, our auditors will require us to write them off. The resulting loss for 2016 will cause a violation of our debt covenants and force the company into bankruptcy. I suggest that you ship half of our inventory to J.B. Sales, Inc., in Oklahoma City. I know the company's president and he will accept the merchandise and acknowledge the shipment as a purchase. We can record the sale in 2016 which will boost profits to an acceptable level. Then J.B. Sales will simply return the merchandise in 2017 after the financial statements have been issued.

Required:

Discuss the ethical dilemma faced by Jim Fielding.

Judgment Case 5–5
Satisfying performance obligations
● LO5–2, LO5–3

Consider each of the following scenarios separately:

Scenario 1: Crown Construction Company entered into a contract with Star Hotel for building a highly sophisticated, customized conference room to be completed for a fixed price of $400,000. Nonrefundable progress payments are made on a monthly basis for work completed during the month. Legal title to the conference room equipment is held by Crown until the end of the construction project, but if the contract is terminated before the conference room is finished, Star retains the partially completed job and must pay for any work completed to date.

Scenario 2: Regent Company entered into a contract with Star Hotel for constructing and installing a standard designed gym for a fixed price of $400,000. Nonrefundable progress payments are made on a monthly basis for work completed during the month. Legal title to the gym passes to Star upon completion of the building process. If Star cancels the contract before the gym construction is completed, Regent removes all the installed equipment and Star must compensate Regent for any loss of profit on sale of the gym to another customer.

Scenario 3: On January 1, the CostDriver Company, a consulting firm, entered into a three-month contract with Coco Seafood Restaurant to analyze its cost structure in order to find a way to reduce operating costs and increase profits. CostDriver promises to share findings with the restaurant every two weeks and to provide the restaurant with a final analytical report at the end of the contract. This service is customized to Coco, and CostDriver would need to start from scratch if it provided a similar service to another client. Coco promises to pay $5,000 per month. If Coco chooses to terminate the contract, it is entitled to receive a report detailing analyses to that stage.

Scenario 4: Assume Trump International Tower (Phase II) is developing luxury residential real estate and begins to market individual apartments during their construction. The Tower entered into a contract with Edwards for the sale of a specific apartment. Edwards pays a deposit that is refundable only if the Tower fails to deliver the completed apartment in accordance with the contract. The remainder of the purchase price is paid on completion of the contract when Edwards obtains possession of the apartment.

Required:

For each of the scenarios, determine whether the seller should recognize revenue (a) over time or (b) when the product or service is completed. Explain your answer.

Judgment Case 5–6
Performance obligation; licensing
● LO5–5, LO5–7

Assume that **Pfizer**, a large research-based pharmaceutical company, enters into a contract with a start-up biotechnology company called HealthPro and promises to:

1. Grant HealthPro the exclusive rights to use Pfizer's Technology A for the life of its patent. The license gives HealthPro the exclusive right to market, distribute, and manufacture Drug B as developed using Technology A.
2. Assign four full-time equivalent employees to perform research and development services for HealthPro in a specially designated Pfizer lab facility. The primary objective of these services is to receive regulatory approval to market and distribute Drug B using Technology A.

HealthPro is required to use Pfizer's lab to perform the research and development services necessary to develop Drug B using Technology A, because the expertise related to Technology A is proprietary to Pfizer and not available elsewhere.

Required:

What parts of this contract are separate performance obligations? Explain your reasoning for each obligation.

Communication Case 5–7
Performance obligations; loyalty program
● LO5–5

Jerry's Ice Cream Parlor is considering a marketing plan to increase sales of ice cream cones. The plan will give customers a free ice cream cone if they buy 10 ice cream cones at regular prices. Customers will be issued a card that will be punched each time an ice cream cone is purchased. After 10 punches, the card can be turned in for a free cone.

Jerry Donovan, the company's owner, is not sure how the new plan will affect accounting procedures. He realizes that the company will be incurring costs each time a free ice cream cone is awarded, but there will be no corresponding revenue or cash inflow.

The focus of this case is on how to account for revenue if the new plan is adopted. Your instructor will divide the class into two to six groups depending on the size of the class. The mission of your group is to reach consensus on the appropriate accounting treatment for the new plan. That treatment should describe when revenue is recognized and how it will be calculated.

Required:

1. Each group member should deliberate the situation independently and draft a tentative argument prior to the class session for which the case is assigned.
2. In class, each group will meet for 10–15 minutes in different areas of the classroom. During that meeting, group members will take turns sharing their suggestions for the purpose of arriving at a single group treatment.
3. After the allotted time, a spokesperson for each group (selected during the group meetings) will share the group's solution with the class. The goal of the class is to incorporate the views of each group into a consensus approach to the situation.

Judgment Case 5–8
Principal or agent
● LO5–6

AuctionCo.com sells used products collected from different suppliers. Assume a customer purchases a used bicycle through AuctionCo.com for $300. AuctionCo.com agrees to pay the supplier $200 for the bicycle. The bicycle will be shipped to the customer by the original bicycle owner.

Required:

1. Assume AuctionCo.com takes control of this used bicycle before the sale and pays $200 to the supplier. Under this assumption, how much revenue would AuctionCo.com recognize at the time of the sale to the customer?

2. Assume AuctionCo.com never takes control of this used bicycle before the sale. Instead, the bicycle is shipped directly to the customer by the original bicycle owner, and then AuctionCo.com pays $200 to the supplier. Under this assumption, how much revenue would AuctionCo.com recognize at the time of the sale to the customer?
3. Assume AuctionCo.com promises to pay $200 to the supplier regardless of whether the bicycle is sold, but the bicycle will continue to be shipped directly from the supplier to the customer. Under this assumption, how much revenue would Auction.com recognize at the time of the sale to the customer?

Real World Case 5–9
Principal agent considerations
● LO5–6

EDGAR, the Electronic Data Gathering, Analysis, and Retrieval system, performs automated collection, validation, indexing, and forwarding of submissions by companies and others who are required by law to file forms with the U.S. Securities and Exchange Commission (SEC). All publicly traded domestic companies use EDGAR to make the majority of their filings. (Some foreign companies file voluntarily.) Form 10-K, which includes the annual report, is required to be filed on EDGAR. The SEC makes this information available on the Internet.

Required:

1. Access EDGAR on the Internet. The web address is www.sec.gov.
2. Search for the most recent 10-K's of Orbitz and priceline.com. Search or scroll to find the revenue recognition note in the financial statements.
3. For each of the following types of revenue, indicate whether the amount shown in the income statement is "net" or "gross" (the terms used with respect to revenue recognition in the chapter), and briefly explain your answer.
   a. Orbitz's "merchant model" revenues.
   b. Orbitz's "retail model" revenues.
   c. Priceline.com's "merchant revenues for 'Name Your Own Price'® services."
   d. Priceline.com's "merchant retail services."
   e. Priceline.com's agency revenues.
4. Consider your responses to 3a through 3e. Does it look like there is the potential for noncomparability when readers consider Orbitz and priceline.com? Indicate "yes" or "no," and briefly explain your answer.

Research Case 5–10
FASB codification; locate and extract relevant information and authoritative support for a financial reporting issue; reporting revenue as a principal or as an agent
● LO5–6

The birth of the Internet in the 1990s led to the creation of a new industry of online retailers such as Amazon, Overstock.com, and PC Mall, Inc. Many of these companies often act as intermediaries between the manufacturer and the customer without ever taking possession of the merchandise sold. Revenue recognition for this type of transaction has been controversial.

Assume that Overstock.com sold you a product for $200 that cost $150. The company's profit on the transaction clearly is $50. Should Overstock recognize $200 in revenue and $150 in cost of goods sold (the gross method), or should it recognize only the $50 in gross profit (the net method) as commission revenue?

Required:

1. Access the *FASB Accounting Standards Codification* at the FASB website (asc.fasb.org). Determine the specific Codification citation that indicates the key consideration determining whether revenue gross versus net. (hint: this is related to principal versus agent considerations).
2. What indicators does the Codification list that suggest a net presentation is appropriate? Determine the specific Codification citation.
3. Using EDGAR (www.sec.gov), access Google, Inc.'s 2013 10-K. Locate the disclosure note that discusses the company's revenue recognition policy.
4. Does Google discuss determining whether they should report revenue on a gross versus net basis with respect to any of their products or services? What is the reason Google provides for its choices? Do you agree with Google's reasoning?

Real World Case 5–11
Chainsaw Al; revenue recognition and earnings management
● LO5–7

In May 2001, the Securities and Exchange Commission sued the former top executives at Sunbeam, charging the group with financial reporting fraud that allegedly cost investors billions in losses. Sunbeam Corporation is a recognized designer, manufacturer, and marketer of household and leisure products, including Coleman, Eastpak, First Alert, Grillmaster, Mixmaster, Mr. Coffee, Oster, Powermate, and Campingaz. In the mid-1990s, Sunbeam needed help: its profits had declined by over 80% percent, and in 1996, its stock price was down over 50% from its high. To the rescue: Albert Dunlap, also known as "Chainsaw Al" based on his reputation as a ruthless executive known for his ability to restructure and turn around troubled companies, largely by eliminating jobs.

The strategy appeared to work. In 1997, Sunbeam's revenues had risen by 18 percent. However, in April 1998, the brokerage firm of Paine Webber downgraded Sunbeam's stock recommendation. Why the downgrade? Paine Webber had noticed unusually high accounts receivable, massive increases in sales of electric blankets in the third quarter 1997, which usually sell best in the fourth quarter, as well as unusually high sales of barbeque grills for the fourth quarter. Soon after, Sunbeam announced a first quarter loss of $44.6 million, and Sunbeam's stock price fell 25 percent.

It eventually came to light that Dunlap and Sunbeam had been using a "bill and hold" strategy with retail buyers. This involved selling products at large discounts to retailers before they normally would buy and then holding the products in third-party warehouses, with delivery at a later date.

Many felt Sunbeam had deceived shareholders by artificially inflating earnings and the company's stock price. A class-action lawsuit followed, alleging that Sunbeam and Dunlap violated federal securities laws, suggesting the motivation to inflate the earnings and stock price was to allow Sunbeam to complete hundreds of millions of dollars of debt financing in order to complete some ongoing mergers. Shareholders alleged damages when Sunbeam's subsequent earnings decline caused a huge drop in the stock price.

Required:

1. How might Sunbeam's 1997 "bill and hold" strategy have contributed to artificially high earnings in 1997?
2. How would the strategy have led to the unusually high accounts receivable Paine Webber noticed?
3. How might Sunbeam's 1997 "bill and hold" strategy have contributed to a 1998 earnings decline?
4. How does earnings management of this type affect earnings quality?

Judgment Case 5–12
Revenue recognition; long-term construction contracts
● LO5–9

Two accounting students were discussing the timing of revenue recognition for long-term construction contracts. The discussion focused on which method was most like the typical revenue recognition method of recognizing revenue at the point of product delivery. Bill argued that recognizing revenue upon project completion was preferable because it was analogous to recognizing revenue at the point of delivery. John disagreed and supported recognizing revenue over time, stating that it was analogous to accruing revenue as a performance obligation was satisfied. John also pointed out that an advantage of recognizing revenue over time is that it provides information sooner to users.

Required:

Discuss the arguments made by both students. Which argument do you support? Why?

Communication Case 5–13
Long-term contract; revenue recognition over time vs. upon project completion
● LO5–9

Willingham Construction is in the business of building high-priced, custom, single-family homes. The company, headquartered in Anaheim, California, operates throughout the Southern California area. The construction period for the average home built by Willingham is six months, although some homes have taken as long as nine months.

You have just been hired by Willingham as the assistant controller and one of your first tasks is to evaluate the company's revenue recognition policy. The company presently recognizes revenue upon completion for all of its projects and management is now considering whether revenue recognition over time is appropriate.

Required:

Write a 1- to 2-page memo to Virginia Reynolds, company controller, describing the differences between the effects of recognizing revenue over time and upon project completion on the income statement and balance sheet. Indicate any criteria specifying when revenue should be recognized. Be sure to include references to GAAP as they pertain to the choice of method. Do not address the differential effects on income taxes nor the effect on the financial statements of switching between methods.

Analysis Case 5–14
Evaluating profitability and asset management; obtain and compare annual reports from companies in the same industry
● LO5–10

Performance and profitability of a company often are evaluated using the financial information provided by a firm's annual report in comparison with other firms in the same industry. Ratios are useful in this assessment.

Required:

Obtain annual reports from two corporations in the same primary industry. Using techniques you learned in this chapter and any analysis you consider useful, respond to the following questions:

1. How do earnings trends compare in terms of both the direction and stability of income?
2. Which of the two firms had greater earnings relative to resources available?
3. How efficiently are current assets managed?
4. Has each of the companies achieved its respective rate of return on assets with similar combinations of profit margin and turnover?
5. Are there differences in accounting methods that should be taken into account when making comparisons?

Note: You can obtain copies of annual reports from friends who are shareholders, the investor relations department of the corporations, from a friendly stockbroker, or from EDGAR (Electronic Data Gathering, Analysis, and Retrieval) on the Internet (www.sec.gov).

Judgment Case 5–15
Relationships among ratios; Chapters 3 and 5
● LO5–10

You are a part-time financial advisor. A client is considering an investment in common stock of a waste recycling firm. One motivation is a rumor the client heard that the company made huge investments in a new fuel creation process. Unable to confirm the rumor, your client asks you to determine whether the firm's assets had recently increased significantly.

Because the firm is small, information is sparse. Last quarter's interim report showed total assets of $324 million, approximately the same as last year's annual report. The only information more current than that is a press release last week in which the company's management reported "record net income for the year of $21 million, representing a 14.0% return on shareholders' equity. Performance was enhanced by the Company's judicious use of financial leverage on a debt/equity ratio of 2 to 1."

Required:

Use the information available to provide your client with an opinion as to whether the waste recycling firm invested in the new fuel creation process during the last quarter of the year.

Integrating Case 5–16
Using ratios to test reasonableness of data; Chapters 3 and 5
● LO5–10

You are a new staff accountant with a large regional CPA firm, participating in your first audit. You recall from your auditing class that CPAs often use ratios to test the reasonableness of accounting numbers provided by the client. Since ratios reflect the relationships among various account balances, if it is assumed that prior relationships still hold, prior years' ratios can be used to estimate what current balances should approximate. However, you never actually performed this kind of analysis until now. The CPA in charge of the audit of Covington Pike Corporation brings you the list of ratios shown below and tells you these reflect the relationships maintained by Covington Pike in recent years.

Profit margin on sales = 5%
Return on assets = 7.5%
Gross profit margin = 40%
Inventory turnover ratio = 6 times
Receivables turnover ratio = 25 times
Acid-test ratio = .9 to one
Current ratio = 2 to 1
Return on shareholders' equity = 10%
Debt to equity ratio = 1/3
Times interest earned ratio = 12 times

Jotted in the margins are the following notes:

- Net income $15,000
- Only one short-term note ($5,000); all other current liabilities are trade accounts
- Property, plant, and equipment are the only noncurrent assets
- Bonds payable are the only noncurrent liabilities
- The effective interest rate on short-term notes and bonds is 8%
- No investment securities
- Cash balance totals $15,000

Required:

You are requested to approximate the current year's balances in the form of a balance sheet and income statement, to the extent the information allows. Accompany those financial statements with the calculations you use to estimate each amount reported.

Air France–KLM Case

AIRFRANCE / KLM
● LO5–2, LO5–4, LO5–5
IFRS

Air France–KLM (AF), a Franco-Dutch company, prepares its financial statements according to International Financial Reporting Standards. AF's financial statements and disclosure notes for the year ended December 31, 2013, are provided with all new textbooks. This material also is available at **www.airfranceklm-finance.com**.

Required:

1. In note 4.6, AF indicates that "Sales related to air transportation are recognized when the transportation service is provided," and "both passenger and cargo tickets are consequently recorded as 'Deferred revenue on ticket sales'."
   a. Examine AF's balance sheet. What is the total amount of deferred revenue on ticket sales as of December 31, 2013?
   b. When transportation services are provided with respect to the deferred revenue on ticket sales, what journal entry would AF make to reduce deferred revenue?
   c. Does AF's treatment of deferred revenue under IFRS appear consistent with how these transactions would be handled under U.S. GAAP? Explain.
2. AF has a frequent flyer program, "Flying Blue," which allows members to acquire "miles" as they fly on Air France or partner airlines that are redeemable for free flights or other benefits.
   a. How does AF account for these miles?
   b. Does AF report any liability associated with these miles as of December 31, 2013?
   c. Although AF's 2013 annual report was issued prior to the effective date of ASU No. 2014-09, consider whether the manner in which AF accounts for its frequent flier program appears consistent with the revenue recognition guidelines included in the ASU.

REVENUE RECOGNITION

GAAP in Effect Prior to ASU No. 2014-09

A Chapter Appendix

PREFACE

Chapter 5 is based on the revenue recognition approach established in ASU No. 2014-09, which is effective for companies issuing reports under U.S. GAAP for periods beginning after December 15, 2016, and for companies issuing reports under IFRS for periods beginning January 1, 2017. This appendix discusses GAAP that is eliminated by the ASU but that is traditionally covered in intermediate accounting courses. GAAP covered in this appendix will be relevant until the ASU becomes effective, and students taking the CPA or CMA exams will be responsible for this GAAP until six months after the effective date of the ASU.

Summary of GAAP Changes

Over 200 specific items of revenue recognition guidance were replaced by ASU No. 2014-09 (hereafter "the ASU"). Illustration 5–A1 summarizes some important changes in GAAP that occurred.

The rest of this appendix discusses some of these changes in more detail, focusing on aspects of GAAP that usually are featured in intermediate accounting courses but that are eliminated by the ASU. We start by discussing the realization principle, which guided revenue recognition prior to the ASU. Then we discuss the installment sales and cost recovery methods, which were used when collectibility of receivables was very uncertain. We

Additional Consideration

Transitioning to ASU No. 2014-09. Given the importance of revenue recognition and the changes in information systems and reporting practices necessary to implement the new ASU, the FASB gave companies over two years before requiring that it be adopted. The FASB also allowed companies to choose between two alternatives to transition to the ASU.

- Retroactive Restatement: This approach restates prior years to appear as if the ASU had been used all along, similar to the approach used for other accounting changes. For example, prior-year revenue, net income, and retained earnings are adjusted to reflect the ASU.
- Prospective: This approach applies the ASU only to new contracts and to contracts that have not been completed as of the date the ASU is initially adopted by the company. Under this approach, the company only adjusts the opening balance of retained earnings in the year the ASU is adopted to account for the cumulative effect of the ASU on net income recognized in prior years with respect to uncompleted contracts.

Allowing two approaches for adopting the ASU reduces comparability between companies.

Illustration 5–A1 Some Important Changes in Revenue Recognition GAAP Resulting from ASU No. 2014-09

	Previous GAAP	New GAAP Under ASU No. 2014-09
Key concept underlying revenue recognition	The realization principle: Recognize revenue when both the earnings process is complete and there is reasonable certainty as to collectibility of the asset(s) to be received.	The core revenue recognition principle: Recognize revenue when goods or services are transferred to customers for the amount the company expects to be entitled to receive in exchange for those goods and services.
Role of collectibility in determining whether revenue is recognized.	Defer revenue recognition if cash collection is not reasonably certain. Use installment method or cost-recovery method to tie revenue recognition to subsequent cash collection.	Defer revenue recognition until cash collection is probable. Installment and cost-recovery methods eliminated.
Criteria for recognizing revenue over time	Depends on the earnings process. For long-term contracts, recognizing revenue over time is generally required unless reliable estimates can't be made.	Depends on characteristics of the contract and of the performance obligations being satisfied.
Accounting for multiple performance obligations	Depends on the industry. Sometimes performance obligations are ignored (e.g., "free" smartphones in cell phone contracts); sometimes revenue recognition is constrained (e.g., software for which there is not sufficient evidence of stand-alone prices).	Regardless of industry, apply criteria for determining whether goods and services are distinct to identify performance obligations, allocate transaction price to performance obligations, and recognize revenue when each performance obligation is satisfied.
Treatment of customer options for additional goods or services	Depends on the industry. Sometimes treated as a separate deliverable (e.g., software upgrades), other times ignored (e.g., frequent flyer miles).	Regardless of industry, treat an option as a separate performance obligation if it provides a material right to the customer that the customer would not otherwise have.
Treatment of variable consideration	Typically only recognize revenue associated with variable consideration when uncertainty has been resolved.	Include estimated variable consideration in the transaction price, but only to the extent it is probable that a significant revenue reversal will not occur in the future.
Treatment of time value of money	Interest revenue recognized for long-term receivables but interest expense typically not recognized for long-term customer prepayments.	Interest revenue or expense recognized for both long-term receivables and long-term customer prepayments if amount is significant.

conclude with coverage of revenue recognition practices particular to software contracts, other multiple-deliverable arrangements, and franchises.

The Realization Principle

Revenue recognition used to be based on the **realization principle**. As shown in Illustration 5–A2, the realization principle required that two criteria be satisfied before revenue can be recognized (recorded).

The *realization principle* bases revenue recognition on completion of the earnings process and reasonable certainty about collectibility.

The realization principle may sound similar to the approach discussed in Chapter 5, which bases revenue recognition on satisfaction of performance obligations and which requires that it be probable that receivables will be collected. However, it differs in important ways.

First, the idea of completion of the earnings process was interpreted and applied differently in various industries and for various types of products and services. As a consequence, revenue recognition standards and other guidance became very complicated, and sometimes transactions that were relatively similar were treated very differently. The ASU eliminates

Illustration 5–A2
The Realization Principle

The Realization Principle[34]

Revenue should only be recognized when *both:*

1. The earnings process is judged to be complete or virtually complete (the earnings process refers to the activity or activities performed by the company to generate revenue).
2. There is reasonable certainty as to the collectibility of the asset to be received (usually cash).

much of that industry-specific guidance, including special treatment of software sales and franchise arrangements. We cover that guidance in a later section of this appendix.

Second, the realization principle's requirement that there be reasonable certainty as to collectibility meant that revenue recognition sometimes was delayed until cash had been collected. As discussed in the next section of this appendix, the installment sales method and the cost recovery method were used to tie revenue recognition to cash collection. Those methods aren't allowed by the ASU.[35] Instead, the ASU only requires that collectibility be probable, and ties subsequent revenue recognition to satisfying performance obligations rather than cash collection.

International Financial Reporting Standards

Revenue Recognition Concepts. The IFRS version of ASU No. 2014-09, called IFRS No. 15, replaces preexisting IFRS. Prior to IFRS No. 15, IAS No. 18 governed most revenue recognition under IFRS. It allowed revenue to be recognized when the following conditions had been satisfied:

(a) The amount of revenue and costs associated with the transaction can be measured reliably,

(b) it is probable that the economic benefits associated with the transaction will flow to the seller,

(c) (for sales of goods) the seller has transferred to the buyer the risks and rewards of ownership, and doesn't effectively manage or control the goods, and

(d) (for sales of services) the stage of completion can be measured reliably.

These general conditions typically led to revenue recognition at the same time and in the same amount as would occur under U.S. GAAP, but there were exceptions. Also, IFRS had much less industry-specific guidance than did U.S. GAAP, leading to fewer exceptions to applying these revenue recognition conditions.

Installment Sales

Customers sometimes are allowed to pay for purchases in installments over a long period of time. Many large retail stores, such as Sears and J.C. Penney, sell products on such installment plans. In most situations, the increased uncertainty concerning the collection of cash from installment sales can be accommodated satisfactorily by estimating uncollectible amounts. However, if it is not possible to make a reasonable assessment of future bad debts, the seller lacks reasonable certainty as to collectibility, and the realization principle requires that revenue recognition be delayed.

The *installment sales* and *cost recovery* methods are only used when extreme uncertainty exists regarding future cash collections.

These circumstances occur relatively rarely in practice, because sellers typically don't want to enter into transactions when they can't estimate how much cash they will be paid. However, exceptions do occur. For example, real estate sales often are made on an installment

[34]These criteria are addressed in *SFAC 5,* "Recognition and Measurement in Financial Statements," *Statement of Financial Accounting Concepts No. 5* (Stamford, Conn.: FASB, 1984).

[35]The tax law still requires the use of the installment sales method for certain types of properties unless a taxpayer elects not to use the method.

basis with relatively small down payments and long payment periods, perhaps 25 years or more. These payment characteristics, combined with the general speculative nature of many of these transactions, may translate into extreme uncertainty concerning the collectibility of the installment receivable.[36]

When extreme uncertainty exists regarding the ultimate collectibility of cash, GAAP previously required the use of one of two accounting techniques, the installment sales method or the cost recovery method. We discuss each in turn.

Installment Sales Method. The installment sales method recognizes revenue and costs only when cash payments are received. Each payment is assumed to be composed of two components: (1) a partial recovery of the cost of the item sold and (2) a gross profit component. These components are determined by the gross profit percentage applicable to the sale. For example, if the gross profit percentage (gross profit ÷ sales price) is 40%, then 40% of each dollar collected represents gross profit and the remaining 60% represents cost recovery. Consider the example in Illustration 5–A3.

Illustration 5–A3
Installment Sales Method

On November 1, 2016, the Belmont Corporation, a real estate developer, sold a tract of land for $800,000. The sales agreement requires the customer to make four equal annual payments of $200,000 plus interest on each November 1, beginning November 1, 2016. The land cost $560,000 to develop. The company's fiscal year ends on December 31.

The *installment sales method* recognizes the gross profit by applying the gross profit percentage on the sale to the amount of cash actually received.

The gross profit of $240,000 ($800,000 − 560,000) represents 30% of the sales price ($240,000 ÷ $800,000). The collection of cash and the recognition of gross profit under the installment method are summarized below. In this example, we ignore the collection of interest charges and the recognition of interest revenue to concentrate on the collection of the $800,000 sales price and the recognition of gross profit on the sale.

		Amount Allocated to:	
Date	Cash Collected	Cost (70%)	Gross Profit (30%)
Nov. 1, 2016	$200,000	$140,000	$ 60,000
Nov. 1, 2017	200,000	140,000	60,000
Nov. 1, 2018	200,000	140,000	60,000
Nov. 1, 2019	200,000	140,000	60,000
Totals	$800,000	$560,000	$240,000

The gross profit recognized in a period will be equal to the gross profit percentage multiplied by the period's cash collection. The following journal entries are recorded (interest charges ignored):

Make Installment Sale:
November 1, 2016

Installment receivables	800,000	
Inventory		560,000
Deferred gross profit		240,000

To record installment sale.

The first entry records the installment receivable and the reduction of inventory. The difference between the $800,000 selling price and the $560,000 cost of sales represents the gross profit on the sale of $240,000. As gross profit will be recognized in net income only as collections are received, it is recorded initially in an account called deferred gross profit.

[36]In fact, the installment sales method was required for retail land sales that met certain conditions. FASB ASC 360–20: Property, Plant, and Equipment—Real Estate Sales (previously "Accounting for Sales of Real Estate," *Statement of Financial Accounting Standards No. 66* (Stamford, Conn.: FASB, 1982)).

This is a contra account to the installment receivable. The deferred gross profit account will be reduced as collections are received until all profit has been recognized.[37]

Collect Cash:
November 1, 2016

Cash	200,000	
Installment receivables		200,000
To record cash collection from installment sale.		
Deferred gross profit	60,000	
Realized gross profit		60,000
To recognize gross profit from installment sale.		

The second set of entries records the collection of the first installment and recognizes the gross profit component of the payment, $60,000. Realized gross profit gets closed to income summary as part of the normal year-end closing process and is included in net income in the income statement. Journal entries to record the remaining three payments on November 1, 2017, 2018, and 2019, are identical.

At the end of 2016, the balance sheet would report the following:

Installment receivables ($800,000 – 200,000)	$600,000
Less: Deferred gross profit ($240,000 – 60,000)	(180,000)
Installment receivables (net)	$420,000

The net amount of the receivable reflects the portion of the remaining payments to be received that represents cost recovery (70% × $600,000). The installment receivables are classified as current assets if they will be collected within one year (or within the company's operating cycle, if longer); otherwise, they are classified as noncurrent assets.

The income statement for 2016 would report gross profit from installment sales of $60,000. Sales and cost of goods sold associated with installment sales usually are not reported in the income statement under the installment method, just the resulting gross profit. However, if those amounts aren't included in the income statement in the period in which the installment sale is made, they need to be included in the notes to the financial statements, along with the amount of gross profit that has not yet been recognized.

Additional Consideration

A company uses the installment method because it can't reliably estimate bad debts. Therefore, the company doesn't explicitly recognize bad debts or create an allowance for uncollectible accounts in the installment method. Rather, bad debts are dealt with

(continued)

[37]Accountants sometimes initially record installment sales in separate entries:

Installment receivables	800,000	
Installment sales		800,000
To record installment sales.		
Cost of installment sales	560,000	
Inventory		560,000
To record the cost of installment sales.		

Then at the end of the period, the following adjusting/closing entry is needed:

Installment sales	800,000	
Cost of installment sales		560,000
Deferred gross profit on installment sales		240,000

The text entries concentrate on the effect of the transactions and avoid this unnecessary procedural complexity.

(concluded)

implicitly by deferring gross profit until cash is collected. If the cash never is collected, the related deferred gross profit never gets included in net income. To illustrate, assume that in the example described in Illustration 5–A3, the Belmont Corporation collected the first payment but the customer was unable to make the remaining payments. Typically, the seller would repossess the item sold and make the following journal entry:

Repossessed inventory	420,000	
Deferred gross profit	180,000	
Installment receivable		600,000

This entry removes the receivable and the remaining deferred gross profit and records the repossessed land in an inventory account. This example assumes that the repossessed land's current fair value is equal to the net receivable of $420,000. If the land's fair value at the date of repossession is less than $420,000, a loss on repossession is recorded (debited).

Cost Recovery Method. In situations where there is an extremely high degree of uncertainty regarding the ultimate cash collection on an installment sale, an even more conservative approach, the **cost recovery method**, can be used. This method defers all gross profit recognition until the cost of the item sold has been recovered. The gross profit recognition pattern applying the cost recovery method to the Belmont Corporation situation used in Illustration 5–A3 is shown below.

The *cost recovery method* defers all gross profit recognition until cash equal to the cost of the item sold has been received.

Date	Cash Collected	Cost Recovery	Gross Profit Recognized
Nov. 1, 2016	$200,000	$200,000	$ –0–
Nov. 1, 2017	200,000	200,000	–0–
Nov. 1, 2018	200,000	160,000	40,000
Nov. 1, 2019	200,000	–0–	200,000
Totals	$800,000	$560,000	$240,000

The journal entries using this method are similar to those for the installment sales method except that $40,000 in gross profit is recognized in 2018 and $200,000 in 2019.

The cost recovery method's initial journal entry is identical to the installment sales method.

Make Installment Sale:
November 1, 2016

Installment receivables	800,000	
Inventory		560,000
Deferred gross profit		240,000

To record installment sale.

Collect Cash:
November 1, 2016, 2017, 2018, and 2019

Cash	200,000	
Installment receivables		200,000

To record cash collection from installment sale.

November 1, 2016 and 2017
No entry for gross profit.

When payments are received, gross profit is recognized only after cost has been fully recovered.

November 1, 2018

Deferred gross profit	40,000	
Realized gross profit		40,000

To recognize gross profit from installment sale.

November 1, 2019

Deferred gross profit	200,000	
Realized gross profit		200,000

To recognize gross profit from installment sale.

Concept Review Exercise

INSTALLMENT SALES

Boatwright Implements, Inc., manufactures and sells farm machinery. For most of its sales, revenue and cost of sales are recognized at the delivery date. In 2016 Boatwright sold a cotton baler to a new customer for $100,000. The cost of the baler was $60,000. Payment will be made in five annual installments of $20,000 each, with the first payment due in 2016. Boatwright usually does not allow its customers to pay in installments. Due to the unusual nature of the payment terms and the uncertainty of collection of the installment payments, Boatwright is considering alternative methods of recognizing profit on this sale.

Required:

Ignoring interest charges, prepare a table showing the gross profit to be recognized from 2016 through 2020 on the cotton baler sale using the following three methods:

1. Revenue recognition upon delivery.
2. The installment sales method.
3. The cost recovery method.

Solution:

	At Delivery	Installment Sales Method (40% × cash collection)	Cost Recovery Method
2016	$40,000	$ 8,000	$ -0-
2017	-0-	8,000	-0-
2018	-0-	8,000	-0-
2019	-0-	8,000	20,000
2020	-0-	8,000	20,000
Totals	$40,000	$40,000	$40,000

Industry-Specific Revenue Issues

SOFTWARE AND OTHER MULTIPLE-ELEMENT ARRANGEMENTS

The software industry is a key economic component of our economy. Microsoft alone reported revenues of almost $78 billion for its 2013 fiscal year. Yet, the recognition of software revenues has been a controversial accounting issue because of the way software vendors typically package their products. It is not unusual for these companies to sell multiple software elements in a bundle for a lump-sum contract price. The bundle often includes product, upgrades, post-contract customer support, and other services. The critical accounting question concerns the timing of revenue recognition.

Revenue for bundled software contracts was allocated based on vendor-specific objective evidence (VSOE).

Prior to ASU No. 2014-09, GAAP required that the revenue associated with a software contract that included multiple elements be allocated to the elements based on "vendor-specific objective evidence" ("VSOE") of fair values of the individual elements. The VSOE of fair values are the sales prices of the elements when sold separately by that vendor. If VSOE didn't exist, revenue recognition was deferred until VSOE became available or until all elements of the contract had been delivered.[38]

For example, suppose that a vendor sold software to a customer for $90,000. As part of the contract, the vendor promises to provide "free" technical support over the next six months. However, the vendor sells the same software without technical support for $80,000, and the vendor sells a stand-alone six-month technical support contract for $20,000, so those products would sell for $100,000 if sold separately. Based on that VSOE, the software comprises 80% of the total fair values, and the technical support 20%. Therefore, the seller would recognize $72,000 ($90,000 × 80%) in revenue up front when the software is delivered, and defer the remaining $18,000 ($90,000 × 20%) and recognize it ratably over

[38]FASB ASC 985–605–25: Software–Revenue Recognition–Recognition (previously "Software Revenue Recognition," *Statement of Position 97-2* (New York: AICPA, 1997), p. 14).

the next six months as the technical support service is provided. If VSOE was not available, the vendor couldn't recognize any revenue initially, and instead would recognize the entire $90,000 ratably over the six-month period.

These revenue deferrals can be material. For example, in its 2013 balance sheet, **Microsoft** reported a liability for unearned (deferred) software revenue of over $22 billion.

In 2009, the FASB's Emerging Issues Task Force (EITF) issued guidance to broaden the application of this basic perspective to other arrangements that involve "multiple deliverables."[39] Examples of such arrangements are sales of appliances with maintenance contracts and even painting services that include sales of paint as well as labor. Other examples are products that contain both hardware and software essential to the functioning of the product, such as computers and smartphones that are always sold with an operating system. The new guidance required that sellers allocate total revenue to the various parts of a multiple-deliverable arrangement on the basis of the relative stand-alone selling prices of the parts, similar to how software contracts were handled. Sellers had to defer revenue recognition for parts that don't have stand-alone value, or whose value was contingent upon other undelivered parts. However, unlike software-only arrangements, sellers offering other multiple-deliverable contracts were allowed to estimate selling prices when they lacked VSOE from stand-alone sales prices. Using estimated selling prices allowed earlier revenue recognition than would be allowed if sellers had to have VSOE in order to recognize revenue.

Revenue for multiple-deliverable contracts was allocated based on actual or estimated stand-alone selling prices.

For some sellers this change had a huge effect. As an example, consider **Apple Inc.** and the highly successful iPhone. Prior to the change, Apple deferred revenue on iPhones and other products because it didn't have VSOE of the sales price of future software upgrades included with the phones. This practice resulted in over $12 billion of unearned (deferred) revenue in its balance sheet at the end of the company's 2009 fiscal year. After this accounting change, Apple recognized almost all of the revenue associated with an iPhone at the time of sale. The only amount deferred was the small amount of revenue estimated for future software upgrade rights.

The ASU requires a similar process as was used to account for revenue on contracts that include multiple deliverables. Sellers allocate a contract's transaction price to the contract's performance obligations based on the stand-alone selling prices of those performance obligations. Important differences are that the ASU provides much more guidance concerning how to identify performance obligation and eliminates the need for VSOE for software contracts.

FRANCHISE SALES

The use of franchise arrangements is popular throughout the world. Many retail outlets for fast food, restaurants, motels, and auto rental agencies are operated as franchises. In franchise arrangements, the **franchisor**, such as **McDonald's Corporation**, grants to the **franchisee**, quite often an individual, the right to sell the franchisor's products and use its name for a specified period of time. The fees to be paid by the franchisee to the franchisor usually comprise (1) an *initial franchise fee* and (2) *continuing franchise fees.*

Initial franchise fees compensate the franchisor for the right to use its name and sell its products, as well as for such services as assistance in finding a location, constructing the facilities, and training employees. The initial franchise fee usually is a fixed amount, but it may be payable in installments.

In the early 1960s and 1970s, many franchisors recognized the entire initial franchise fee as revenue in the period in which the contract was signed. However, in many cases the fee included payment for significant services to be performed after that period and the fee was collectible in installments over an extended period of time, creating uncertainty as to cash collection. GAAP was modified to require that substantially all of the initial services of the franchisor required by the franchise agreement be performed before the initial franchise fee could be recognized as revenue. If the initial franchise fee was collectible in installments, and if a reasonable estimate of bad debts could not be made, the installment sales or cost recovery methods were required.

[39]FASB ASC 605-25-25: Revenue Recognition—Multiple-Element Arrangements-Recognition (Originally *EITF 08-1: Revenue Arrangements with Multiple Deliverables* (Stamford, Conn.: FASB, 2009)), and *EITF 09-3: Applicability of AICPA Statement of Position 97-2 to Certain Arrangements that Include Software Elements* (Stamford, Conn.: FASB, 2009)).

Unlike initial franchise fees, continuing franchise fees compensate the franchisor for ongoing rights and services provided over the life of the franchise agreement. These fees sometimes are a fixed annual or monthly amount, a percentage of the volume of business done by the franchise, or a combination of both. They usually do not present any accounting difficulty and previous GAAP required that they be recognized by the franchisor as revenue over time in the periods the services are performed by the franchisor, which generally corresponded to the periods they are received.

Consider the example in Illustration 5–A4.

Illustration 5–A4
Franchise Sales

On March 31, 2016, the Red Hot Chicken Wing Corporation entered into a franchise agreement with Thomas Keller. In exchange for an initial franchise fee of $50,000, Red Hot will provide initial services to include the selection of a location, construction of the building, training of employees, and consulting services over several years. $10,000 is payable on March 31, 2016, with the remaining $40,000 payable in annual installments that include interest at an appropriate rate. In addition, the franchisee will pay continuing franchise fees of $1,000 per month for advertising and promotion provided by Red Hot, beginning immediately after the franchise begins operations. Thomas Keller opened his Red Hot franchise for business on September 30, 2016.

Initial Franchise Fee. Assuming that the initial services to be performed by Red Hot subsequent to the contract signing are substantial but that collectibility of the installment note receivable is reasonably certain, the following journal entry is recorded:

March 31, 2016		
Cash	10,000	
Note receivable	40,000	
Unearned franchise fee revenue		50,000
To record franchise agreement and down payment.		

Unearned franchise fee revenue is a liability. It would be reduced to zero and revenue would be recognized when the initial services have been performed. This could occur in increments or at one point in time, depending on the circumstances.[40] For example, in our illustration, if substantial performance was deemed to have occurred when the franchise began operations, the following entry would be recorded:

Sept. 30, 2016		
Unearned franchise fee revenue	50,000	
Franchise fee revenue		50,000
To recognize franchise fee revenue.		

If collectibility of the installment note receivable is uncertain and there is no basis for estimating uncollectible amounts, the September 30 entry would record a credit to deferred franchise fee revenue, which is then recognized as being earned using either the installment sales or cost recovery methods.

Continuing Franchise Fees. Continuing franchise fee revenue is recognized on a monthly basis as follows:

Cash (or accounts receivable)	1,000	
Service revenue		1,000
To recognize continuing franchise fee revenue.		

[40]Franchise agreements sometimes require that any payments made to the franchisor will be refunded if the franchise fails to open. If this condition is present, it would be an important factor in deciding whether to recognize revenue before the franchise opens.

Expenses incurred by the franchisor in providing these continuing franchise services should be recognized in the same periods as the service revenue.

Accounting for franchise revenue under ASU No. 2014-09 is similar to revenue recognition under previous GAAP. To the extent that the services underlying initial franchise fees constitute separate performance obligations, revenue associated with those fees is recognized when those services have been performed. Similarly, to the extent that continuing franchise fees constitute payments for services that are provided over time, revenue recognition over time is likely to be appropriate. However, the justification for the amount and timing of revenue recognition is based on the ASU, rather than on special guidance provided for franchise arrangements. Also, ASU 2014-09 includes new guidance for recognizing licensing revenue.

Other unique industry-specific revenue recognition situations exist besides those we have discussed. The FASB and AICPA previously issued detailed revenue recognition guidance for such industries as insurance, record and music, cable television, and motion pictures. All of that guidance was replaced by ASU No. 2014-09.[41]

Additional Differences Between U.S. GAAP and IFRS

ASU No. 2014-09 is a converged standard, providing virtually identical guidance for U.S. GAAP and IFRS. However, prior to issuance of the ASU, there was incomplete convergence between U.S. GAAP and IFRS. In addition to differences in revenue recognition concepts discussed earlier in this appendix, key differences involved accounting for revenue on long-term contracts and multiple-deliverable arrangements. We provide an IFRS Box for each of these issues below.

International Financial Reporting Standards

Long-Term Construction Contracts. Prior to issuance of the ASU, *IAS No. 11* governed revenue recognition for long-term construction contracts.[42] Like U.S. GAAP, that standard required the use of the percentage-of-completion method when reliable estimates can be made. However, unlike U.S. GAAP, *IAS No. 11* required the use of the cost recovery method rather than the completed contract method when reliable estimates couldn't be made.[43] Under the cost recovery method, contract costs are expensed as incurred, and an offsetting amount of contract revenue is recognized to the extent that it is probable that costs will be recoverable from the customer. No gross profit is recognized until all costs have been recovered, which is why this method is also sometimes called the "zero-profit method." Note that under both the completed contract and cost recovery methods no gross profit is recognized until the contract is near completion, but revenue and construction costs will be recognized earlier under the cost recovery method than under the completed contract method. Also, under both methods an expected loss is recognized immediately.

(continued)

[41]FASB ASC 944: Financial Services–Insurance (previously "Accounting and Reporting by Insurance Enterprises," *Statement of Financial Accounting Standards No. 60* (Stamford, Conn.: FASB, 1982)); FASB ASC 928—Entertainment–Music (previously "Financial Reporting in the Record and Music Industry," *Statement of Financial Accounting Standards No. 50* (Stamford, Conn.: FASB, 1981)); FASB ASC 922: Entertainment—Cable Television (previously "Financial Reporting by Cable Television Companies," *Statement of Financial Accounting Standards No. 51* (Stamford, Conn.: FASB, 1981)); FASB ASC 928: Entertainment–Films (previously "Accounting by Producers or Distributors of Films," *Statement of Position 00-2* (New York: AICPA, 2000)).

[42]"Construction Contracts," *International Accounting Standard No. 11* (IASCF), as amended, effective January 1, 2011.

[43]Earlier in this appendix we referred to the "cost recovery method" in a different circumstance—when a company had already delivered a product to a customer but had to delay gross profit recognition until a point after delivery because of an inability to make reliable estimates of uncollectible accounts. In that case, gross profit only could be recognized after costs had been recovered (and cash collections exceeded cost of goods sold). IFRS' use of "cost recovery method" is similar, in that gross profit recognition is delayed until after cost has been recovered, but note that in this case the product is being constructed for the customer and therefore has not yet been delivered.

(concluded)

To see this difference between the completed contract and cost recovery methods, here is a version of Illustration 5–24B that compares revenue, cost, and gross profit recognition under the two methods:

	2016		2017		2018	
Completed Contract						
Construction in progress (CIP)					900,000	
Cost of construction					4,100,000	
Revenue from long-term contracts						5,000,000
To record gross profit.						
Cost Recovery						
Construction in progress (CIP)					900,000	
Cost of construction	1,500,000		1,000,000		1,600,000	
Revenue from long-term contracts		1,500,000		1,000,000		2,500,000
To record gross profit.						

Revenue recognition occurs earlier under the cost recovery method than under the completed contract method, but gross profit recognition occurs near the end of the contract for both methods. As a result, gross profit as a percentage of revenue differs between the two methods at various points in the life of the contract.

International Financial Reporting Standards

Multiple-Deliverable Arrangements. IFRS contained very little guidance about multiple-deliverable arrangements. *IAS No. 18* simply states that: ". . . in certain circumstances, it is necessary to apply the recognition criteria to the separately identifiable components of a single transaction in order to reflect the substance of the transaction" and gives a couple of examples.[44] Allocations of total revenue to individual components were based on fair value, with no requirements to focus on VSOE. Also, IFRS tended to encourage focus on the underlying economics of revenue transactions, so particular contractual characteristics like contingencies mattered less under IFRS than they do under U.S. GAAP.

Questions For Review of Key Topics

Q 5–29 What are the two general criteria that must be satisfied before a company can recognize revenue?

Q 5–30 Explain why, in most cases, a seller recognizes revenue when it delivers its product rather than when it produces the product.

Q 5–31 Revenue recognition for most installment sales occurs at the point of delivery of the product or service. Under what circumstances would a seller delay revenue recognition for installment sales beyond the delivery date?

[44]"Revenue," *International Accounting Standards No. 18* (IASCF), as amended effective January 1, 2014, par. 13.

Q 5–32 Distinguish between the installment sales method and the cost recovery method of accounting for installment sales.

Q 5–33 How does a company report deferred gross profit resulting from the use of the installment sales method in its balance sheet?

IFRS Q 5–34 When percentage-of-completion accounting is not appropriate, U.S. GAAP requires the use of the completed contract method, while IFRS requires the use of the cost recovery method. Explain how the two methods affect recognition of revenue, cost of construction, and gross profit over the life of a profitable contract.

Q 5–35 Briefly describe the guidelines for recognizing revenue from the sale of software and other multiple-deliverable arrangements.

IFRS Q 5–36 Briefly describe how IFRS guidelines for recognizing revenue from multiple-deliverable arrangements differ from U.S. GAAP guidelines.

Q 5–37 Briefly describe the guidelines provided by GAAP for the recognition of revenue by a franchisor for an initial franchise fee.

Brief Exercises

BE 5–35
Installment sales method

On July 1, 2016, Apache Company sold a parcel of undeveloped land to a construction company for $3,000,000. The book value of the land on Apache's books was $1,200,000. Terms of the sale required a down payment of $150,000 and 19 annual payments of $150,000 plus interest at an appropriate interest rate due on each July 1 beginning in 2017. Apache has no significant obligations to perform services after the sale. How much gross profit will Apache recognize in both 2016 and 2017 applying the installment sales method?

BE 5–36
Installment sales method

Refer to the situation described in BE 5–35. What should be the balance in the deferred gross profit account at the end of 2017 applying the installment sales method?

BE 5–37
Cost recovery method

Refer to the situation described in BE 5–35. How much gross profit will Apache recognize in both 2016 and 2017 applying the cost recovery method?

BE 5–38
IFRS; long-term contracts; cost recovery method
IFRS

A construction company entered into a fixed-price contract to build an office building for $20 million. Construction costs incurred during the first year were $6 million and estimated costs to complete at the end of the year were $9 million. The building was completed during the second year. Construction costs incurred during the second year were $10 million. How much revenue, cost, and gross profit will the company recognize in the first and second year of the contract applying the cost recovery method that is required by IFRS?

BE 5–39
Revenue recognition; software contracts

Orange, Inc., sells a LearnIt-Plus software package that consists of their normal LearnIt math tutorial program along with a one-year subscription to the online LearnIt Office Hours virtual classroom. LearnIt-Plus retails for $200. When sold separately, the LearnIt math tutorial sells for $150, and access to the LearnIt Office Hours sells for $100 per year. When should Orange recognize revenue for the parts of this arrangement? Would your answer change if Orange did not sell the LearnIt Office Hours separately, but believed it would price it at $100 per year if they ever decided to do so?

BE 5–40
Revenue recognition; software contracts under IFRS
IFRS

Refer to the situation described in BE 5–39. How would your answer change if Orange reported under IFRS?

BE 5–41
Revenue recognition; franchise sales

Collins, Inc., entered into a 10-year franchise agreement with an individual. For an initial franchise fee of $40,000, Collins agrees to assist in design and construction of the franchise location and in all other necessary start-up activities. Also, in exchange for advertising and promotional services, the franchisee agrees to pay continuing franchise fees equal to 5% of revenue generated by the franchise. When should Collins recognize revenue for the initial and continuing franchise fees?

Exercises

An alternate exercise and problem set is available in the Connect library.

E 5–27
Installment sales method

Charter Corporation, which began business in 2016, appropriately uses the installment sales method of accounting for its installment sales. The following data were obtained for sales made during 2016 and 2017:

	2016	2017
Installment sales	$360,000	$350,000
Cost of installment sales	234,000	245,000
Cash collections on installment sales during:		
2016	150,000	100,000
2017	—	120,000

Required:

1. How much gross profit should Charter recognize in 2016 and 2017 from installment sales?
2. What should be the balance in the deferred gross profit account at the end of 2016 and 2017?

E 5–28
Installment sales method; journal entries

[This is a variation of Exercise 5–27 focusing on journal entries.]
Charter Corporation, which began business in 2016, appropriately uses the installment sales method of accounting for its installment sales. The following data were obtained for sales during 2016 and 2017:

	2016	2017
Installment sales	$360,000	$350,000
Cost of installment sales	234,000	245,000
Cash collections on installment sales during:		
2016	150,000	100,000
2017	—	120,000

Required:

Prepare summary journal entries for 2016 and 2017 to account for the installment sales and cash collections. The company uses the perpetual inventory system.

E 5–29
Installment sales; alternative recognition methods

On July 1, 2016, the Foster Company sold inventory to the Slate Corporation for $300,000. Terms of the sale called for a down payment of $75,000 and three annual installments of $75,000 due on each July 1, beginning July 1, 2017. Each installment also will include interest on the unpaid balance applying an appropriate interest rate. The inventory cost Foster $120,000. The company uses the perpetual inventory system.

Required:

1. Compute the amount of gross profit to be recognized from the installment sale in 2016, 2017, 2018, and 2019 if revenue was recognized upon delivery. Ignore interest charges.
2. Repeat requirement 1 applying the installment sales method.
3. Repeat requirement 1 applying the cost recovery method.

E 5–30
Journal entries; point of delivery, installment sales, and cost recovery methods

[This is a variation of Exercise 5–29 focusing on journal entries.]
On July 1, 2016, the Foster Company sold inventory to the Slate Corporation for $300,000. Terms of the sale called for a down payment of $75,000 and three annual installments of $75,000 due on each July 1, beginning July 1, 2017. Each installment also will include interest on the unpaid balance applying an appropriate interest rate. The inventory cost Foster $120,000. The company uses the perpetual inventory system.

Required:

1. Prepare the necessary journal entries for 2016 and 2017 assuming revenue recognition upon delivery. Ignore interest charges.
2. Repeat requirement 1 applying the installment sales method.
3. Repeat requirement 1 applying the cost recovery method.

E 5–31
Installment sales and cost recovery methods; solve for unknowns

Wolf Computer Company began operations in 2016. The company allows customers to pay in installments for many of its products. Installment sales for 2016 were $1,000,000. If revenue is recognized at the point of delivery, $600,000 in gross profit would be recognized in 2016. If the company instead uses the cost recovery method, $100,000 in gross profit would be recognized in 2016.

Required:

1. What was the amount of cash collected on installment sales in 2016?
2. What amount of gross profit would be recognized if the company uses the installment sales method?

E 5–32
Installment sales; default and repossession

Sanchez Development Company uses the installment sales method to account for some of its installment sales. On October 1, 2016, Sanchez sold a parcel of land to the Kreuze Corporation for $4 million. This amount was not considered significant relative to Sanchez's other sales during 2016. The land had cost Sanchez $1.8 million to acquire and develop. Terms of the sale required a down payment of $800,000 and four annual payments of $800,000 plus interest at an appropriate interest rate, with payments due on each October 1 beginning in 2017. Kreuze paid the down payment, but on October 1, 2017, defaulted on the remainder of the contract. Sanchez repossessed the land. On the date of repossession the land had a fair value of $1.3 million.

Required:

Prepare the necessary entries for Sanchez to record the sale, receipt of the down payment, and the default and repossession applying the installment sales method. Ignore interest charges.

E 5–33
Real estate sales; gain recognition

On April 1, 2016, the Apex Corporation sold a parcel of underdeveloped land to the Applegate Construction Company for $2,400,000. The book value of the land on Apex's books was $480,000. Terms of the sale required a down payment of $120,000 and 19 annual payments of $120,000 plus interest at an appropriate interest rate due on each April 1 beginning in 2017. Apex has no significant obligations to perform services after the sale.

Required:

1. Prepare the necessary entries for Apex to record the sale, receipt of the down payment, and receipt of the first installment assuming that Apex is able to make a reliable estimate of possible uncollectible amounts (that is, profit is recognized upon delivery). Ignore interest charges.
2. Repeat requirement 1 assuming that Apex cannot make a reliable estimate of possible uncollectible amounts and decides to use the installment sales method for profit recognition.

E 5–34
FASB codification research

Access the *FASB Accounting Standards Codification* at the FASB website (**asc.fasb.org**).

Required:

Determine the specific citation for accounting for each of the following items: Circumstances indicating when the installment method or cost recovery method is appropriate for revenue recognition.

E 5–35
Long-term contracts, Cost recovery method

Assume the same information as in Exercise E 5–18.

Required:

Determine the amount of revenue, cost, and gross profit or loss to be recognized in each of the three years under IFRS, assuming that using the percentage-of-completion method is not appropriate.

E 5–36
Revenue recognition; software

Easywrite Software Company shipped software to a customer on July 1, 2016. The arrangement with the customer also requires the company to provide technical support over the next 12 months and to ship an expected software upgrade on January 1, 2017. The total contract price is $243,000, and Easywrite estimates that the individual fair values of the components of the arrangement if sold separately would be:

Software	$210,000
Technical support	30,000
Upgrade	30,000

Required:

1. Determine the timing of revenue recognition for the $243,000.
2. Assume that the $243,000 contract price was paid on July 1, 2016. Prepare a journal entry to record the cash receipt. Disregard the cost of the items sold.

E 5–37
Multiple-deliverable arrangements

Richardson Systems sells integrated bottling manufacturing systems that involve a conveyer, a labeler, a filler, and a capper. All of this equipment is sold separately by other vendors, and the fair values of the separate equipment are as follows:

Conveyer	$20,000
Labeler	10,000
Filler	15,000
Capper	5,000
Total	$50,000

Richardson sells the integrated system for $45,000. Each of the components is shipped separately to the customer for the customer to install.

Required:

1. Assume that each of the components can be used independently, even though Richardson sells them as an integrated system. How much revenue should be allocated to each component?
2. Now assume that the labeler, filler, and capper can't be used in production without the conveyer, and that the conveyer is the last component installed. How much revenue should be recognized at the time the conveyer is installed?

E 5–38
Multiple-deliverable arrangements under IFRS

IFRS

Assume the same facts as in E5–37, but that Richardson Systems reports under IFRS. How would your answers change? (Assume for requirement 2 that separate shipment is part of the normal course of Richardson's operations, and successful customer installation is highly probable.)

E 5–39
Revenue recognition; franchise sales

On October 1, 2016, the Submarine Sandwich Company entered into a franchise agreement with an individual. In exchange for an initial franchise fee of $300,000, Submarine will provide initial services to the franchisee to include assistance in design and construction of the building, help in training employees, and help in obtaining financing. Ten percent of the initial franchise fee is payable on October 1, 2016, with the remaining $270,000 payable in nine equal annual installments beginning on October 1, 2017. These installments will include interest at an appropriate rate. The franchise opened for business on January 15, 2017.

Required:

Assume that the initial services to be performed by Submarine Sandwich subsequent to October 1, 2016, are substantial and that collectibility of the installment receivable is reasonably certain. Substantial performance of the initial services is deemed to have occurred when the franchise opened. Prepare the necessary journal entries for the following dates (ignoring interest charges):

1. October 1, 2016
2. January 15, 2017

CPA and CMA Review Questions

CPA Exam Questions

The following questions are adapted from a variety of sources including questions developed by the AICPA Board of Examiners and those used in the Kaplan CPA Review Course to study revenue recognition while preparing for the CPA examination. Determine the response that best completes the statements or questions.

Installment method

9. Since there is no reasonable basis for estimating the degree of collectibility, Astor Co. uses the installment sales method of revenue recognition for the following sales:

	2016	2017
Sales	$600,000	$900,000
Collections from:		
2016 sales	200,000	100,000
2017 sales	—	300,000
Accounts written off:		
2016 sales	50,000	150,000
2017 sales	—	50,000
Gross profit percentage	30%	40%

What amount should Astor report as deferred gross profit in its December 31, 2017, balance sheet for the 2016 and 2017 sales?

a. $225,000
b. $150,000
c. $160,000
d. $250,000

Installment method

10. Dolce Co., which began operations on January 1, 2016, appropriately uses the installment sales method of accounting to record revenues. The following information is available for the years ended December 31, 2016 and 2017:

	2016	2017
Sales	$1,000,000	$2,000,000
Gross profit realized on sales made in:		
2016	150,000	90,000
2017	—	200,000
Gross profit percentages	30%	40%

What amount of installment accounts receivable should Dolce report in its December 31, 2017, balance sheet?

a. $1,700,000
b. $1,225,000
c. $1,300,000
d. $1,775,000

Beginning in 2011, International Financial Reporting Standards are tested on the CPA exam along with U.S. GAAP. The following questions deal with the application of IFRS.

Revenue recognition for services

11. Which of the following is NOT a condition that must be satisfied under IFRS before revenue for a service can be recognized?

a. The stage of completion can be measured reliably.
b. It is probable that the economic benefits associated with the transaction will flow to the seller.
c. Cash collection is at least reasonably possible.
d. The amount of revenue and costs associated with the transaction can be measured reliably.

Long-term contracts

12. O'Hara Company recognizes revenue on long-term construction contracts under IFRS. It cannot estimate progress toward completion accurately, and so uses the cost recovery method (also called the "zero profit method") to estimate revenue. O'Hara writes a contract to deliver an automated assembly line to Easley Motors. Easley will pay $2,000,000 to O'Hara, and O'Hara estimates the line will cost $1,500,000 to construct. The job is estimated to take three years to complete. In the first year of its contract with Easley Motors, O'Hara incurs $1,000,000 of cost, which O'Hara believes will eventually be recovered in the contract. How much revenue will O'Hara recognize in the first year of the contract?

a. $1,000,000
b. $0
c. $1,333,333
d. $666,667

Multiple-deliverable arrangements

13. Which of the following is NOT true about revenue recognition for multiple deliverable contracts under IFRS?

a. *IAS No. 18* provides extensive guidance determining how contracts are to be separated into components for purposes of revenue recognition.
b. IFRS encourages focus on the economic substance of transactions, so some arrangements are likely to be accounted for differently than under U.S. GAAP.
c. Unlike U.S. GAAP, IFRS does not require VSOE for software contracts in order to separate contracts into multiple deliverables.
d. IFRS focuses on fair values to allocate total revenue to components.

CMA Exam Questions

The following question dealing with income measurement is adapted from questions that previously appeared on Certified Management Accountant (CMA) examinations. The CMA designation sponsored by the Institute of Management Accountants (**www.imanet.org**) provides members with an objective measure of knowledge and competence in the field of management accounting. Determine the response that best completes the statements or questions.

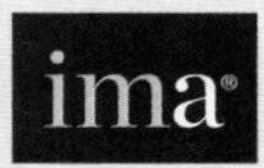

Installment method

2. On May 28, Markal Company purchased a tooling machine from Arens and Associates for $1,000,000 payable as follows: 50 percent at the transaction closing date and 50 percent due June 28. The cost of the machine to Arens is $800,000. Markal paid Arens $500,000 at the transaction closing date and took possession of the machine. On June 10, Arens determined that a change in the business environment has created a great deal of uncertainty regarding the collection of the balance due from Markal, and the amount is probably

uncollectible. Arens and Markal have a fiscal year-end of May 31. The revenue recognized by Arens and Associates on May 28 is

a. $200,000
b. $800,000
c. $1,000,000
d. $0

Problems

An alternate exercise and problem set is available in the Connect library.

P 5–18
Income statement presentation; installment sales method (Chapters 4 and 5)

Reagan Corporation computed income from continuing operations before income taxes of $4,200,000 for 2016. The following material items have not yet been considered in the computation of income:

1. The company sold equipment and recognized a gain of $50,000. The equipment had been used in the manufacturing process and was replaced by new equipment.
2. In December, the company received a settlement of $1,000,000 for a lawsuit it had filed based on antitrust violations of a competitor. The settlement was considered to be an unusual and infrequent event.
3. Inventory costing $400,000 was written off as obsolete. Material losses of this type were incurred twice in the last eight years.
4. It was discovered that depreciation expense on the office building of $50,000 per year was not recorded in either 2015 or 2016.

In addition, you learn that included in revenues is $400,000 from installment sales made during the year. The cost of these sales is $240,000. At year-end, $100,000 in cash had been collected on the related installment receivables. Because of considerable uncertainty regarding the collectibility of receivables from these sales, the company's accountant should have used the installment sales method to recognize revenue and gross profit on these sales.

Also, the company's income tax rate is 40% and there were 1 million shares of common stock outstanding throughout the year.

Required:
Prepare an income statement for 2016 beginning with income from continuing operations before income taxes. Include appropriate EPS disclosures.

P 5–19
Installment sales and cost recovery methods

Ajax Company appropriately accounts for certain sales using the installment sales method. The perpetual inventory system is used. Information related to installment sales for 2016 and 2017 is as follows:

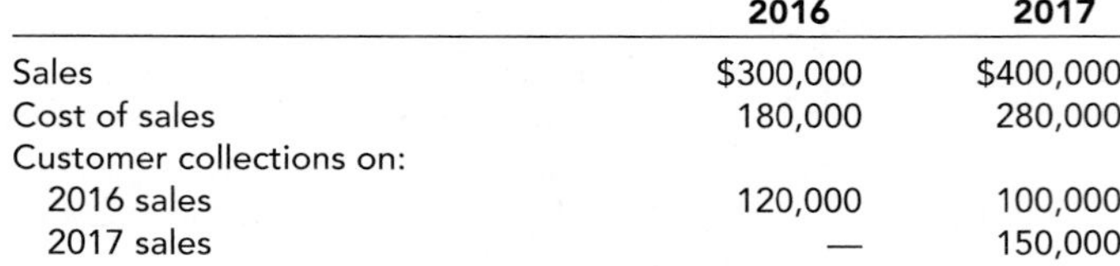

	2016	2017
Sales	$300,000	$400,000
Cost of sales	180,000	280,000
Customer collections on:		
2016 sales	120,000	100,000
2017 sales	—	150,000

Required:
1. Calculate the amount of gross profit that would be recognized each year from installment sales.
2. Prepare all necessary journal entries for each year.
3. Repeat requirements 1 and 2 assuming that Ajax uses the cost recovery method to account for its installment sales.

P 5–20
Installment sales; alternative recognition methods

On August 31, 2016, the Silva Company sold merchandise to the Bendix Corporation for $500,000. Terms of the sale called for a down payment of $100,000 and four annual installments of $100,000 due on each August 31, beginning August 31, 2017. Each installment also will include interest on the unpaid balance applying an appropriate interest rate. The book value of the merchandise on Silva's books on the date of sale was $300,000. The perpetual inventory system is used. The company's fiscal year-end is December 31.

Required:
1. Prepare a table showing the amount of gross profit to be recognized in each of the five years of the installment sale applying each of the following methods:
   a. Point of delivery revenue recognition.

b. Installment sales method.
c. Cost recovery method.

2. Prepare journal entries for each of the five years applying the three revenue recognition methods listed in requirement 1. Ignore interest charges.
3. Prepare a partial balance sheet as of the end of 2016 and 2017 listing the items related to the installment sale applying each of the three methods listed in requirement 1.

P 5–21
Installment sales and cost recovery methods

Mulcahey Builders (MB) remodels office buildings in low-income urban areas that are undergoing economic revitalization. MB typically accepts a 25% down payment when they complete a job and a note that requires that the remainder be paid in three equal installments over the next three years, plus interest. Because of the inherent uncertainty associated with receiving these payments, MB has historically used the cost recovery method to recognize revenue.

As of January 1, 2016, MB's outstanding gross installment accounts receivable (not net of deferred gross profit) consist of the following:

1. $400,000 due from the Bluebird Motel. MB completed the Bluebird job in 2014, and estimated gross profit on that job is 25%.
2. $150,000 due from the PitStop Gas and MiniMart. MB completed the PitStop job in 2013, and estimated gross profit on that job is 35%.

Dan Mulcahey has been considering switching from the cost recovery method to the installment sales method, because he wants to show the highest possible gross profit in 2016 and he understands that the installment sales method recognizes gross profit sooner than does the cost recovery method.

Required:

1. Calculate how much gross profit is expected to be earned on these jobs in 2016 under the cost recovery method, and how much would be earned if MB instead used the installment sales method. Ignore interest.
2. If Dan is primarily concerned about 2016, do you think he would be happy with a switch to the installment sales method? Explain.

P 5–22
Construction accounting under IFRS

[This is a variation of Problem 5–10 modified to focus on IFRS.]

Required:

Complete the requirements of Problem 5–10 assuming that Westgate Construction reports under IFRS and concludes that the percentage-of-completion method is not appropriate.

P 5–23
Franchise sales; installment sales method

Olive Branch Restaurant Corporation sells franchises throughout the western states. On January 30, 2016, the company entered into the following franchise agreement with Jim and Tammy Masters:

1. The initial franchise fee is $1.2 million. $200,000 is payable immediately and the remainder is due in ten, $100,000 installments plus 10% interest on the unpaid balance each January 30, beginning January 30, 2017. The 10% interest rate is an appropriate market rate.
2. In addition to allowing the franchisee to use the franchise name for the 10-year term of the agreement, in exchange for the initial fee Olive Branch agrees to assist the franchisee in selecting a location, obtaining financing, designing and constructing the restaurant building, and training employees.
3. All of the initial down payment of $200,000 is to be refunded by Olive Branch and the remaining obligation canceled if, for any reason, the franchisee fails to open the franchise.
4. In addition to the initial franchise fee, the franchisee is required to pay a monthly fee of 3% of franchise sales for advertising, promotion, menu planning, and other continuing services to be provided by Olive Branch over the life of the agreement. This fee is payable on the 10th of the following month.

Substantial performance of the initial services provided by Olive Branch, which are significant, is deemed to have occurred when the franchise opened on September 1, 2016. Franchise sales for the month of September 2016 were $40,000.

Required:

1. Assuming that collectibility of the installment receivable is reasonably certain, prepare the necessary journal entries for Olive Branch on the following dates (ignore interest charges on the installment receivable and the costs of providing franchise services):
   a. January 30, 2016
   b. September 1, 2016
   c. September 30, 2016
   d. January 30, 2017

2. Assume that significant uncertainty exists as to the collection of the installment receivable and that Olive Branch elects to recognize initial franchise fee revenue using the installment sales method. Prepare the necessary journal entries for the dates listed in requirement 1 (ignore interest charges on the installment receivable and the costs of providing franchise services).
3. Examine your answer to requirement 1a of this problem (the January 30, 2016, journal entry under the installment sales method). What is the effect of that journal entry on Olive Branch's balance sheet? (Ignore cash.) Briefly explain your answer.

Broaden Your Perspective

Apply your critical-thinking ability to the knowledge you've gained. These cases will provide you an opportunity to develop your research, analysis, judgment, and communication skills. You also will work with other students, integrate what you've learned, apply it in real-world situations, and consider its global and ethical ramifications. This practice will broaden your knowledge and further develop your decision-making abilities.

Judgment Case 5–17
Revenue recognition; installment sale

On October 1, 2016, the Marshall Company sold a large piece of machinery to the Hammond Construction Company for $80,000. The cost of the machine was $40,000. Hammond made a down payment of $10,000 and agreed to pay the remaining balance in seven equal monthly installments of $10,000, plus interest at 12% on the unpaid balance, beginning November 1.

Required:

1. Identify three alternative methods for recognizing revenue and costs for the situation described and compute the amount of gross profit that would be recognized in 2016 using each method.
2. Discuss the circumstances under which each of the three methods would be used.

IFRS Case 5–18
Comparison of revenue recognition in Sweden and the United States

Vodafone Group, Plc, headquartered in the United Kingdom, is one of the world's largest telecommunications companies. Excerpts from the revenue recognition disclosure included in its 2013 annual report are reproduced below.

Note A1: Significant accounting policies

Revenue

Revenue is recognised to the extent the Group has delivered goods or rendered services under an agreement, the amount of revenue can be measured reliably and it is probable that the economic benefits associated with the transaction will flow to the Group. Revenue is measured at the fair value of the consideration received, exclusive of sales taxes and discounts.

The Group principally obtains revenue from providing the following telecommunication services: access charges, airtime usage, messaging, interconnect fees, data services and information provision, connection fees and equipment sales. Products and services may be sold separately or in bundled packages.

Revenue for access charges, airtime usage and messaging by contract customers is recognised as services are performed, with unbilled revenue resulting from services already provided accrued at the end of each period and deferred revenue from services to be provided in future periods deferred. Revenue from the sale of prepaid credit is deferred until such time as the customer uses the airtime, or the credit expires.

Revenue from interconnect fees is recognised at the time the services are performed.

Revenue from data services and information provision is recognised when the Group has performed the related service and, depending on the nature of the service, is recognised either at the gross amount billed to the customer or the amount receivable by the Group as commission for facilitating the service.

Customer connection revenue is recognised together with the related equipment revenue to the extent that the aggregate equipment and connection revenue does not exceed the fair value of the equipment delivered to the customer. Any customer connection revenue not recognised together with related equipment revenue is deferred and recognised over the period in which services are expected to be provided to the customer.

Revenue for device sales is recognised when the device is delivered to the end customer and the sale is considered complete. For device sales made to intermediaries, revenue is recognised if the significant risks associated with the device are transferred to the intermediary and the intermediary has no general right of return. If the significant risks are not transferred, revenue recognition is deferred until sale of the device to an end customer by the intermediary or the expiry of the right of return.

In revenue arrangements including more than one deliverable, the arrangements are divided into separate units of accounting. Deliverables are considered separate units of accounting if the following two conditions are met: (1) the deliverable has value to the customer on a stand-alone basis and (2) there is evidence of the fair value of the item. The arrangement consideration is allocated to each separate unit of accounting based on its relative fair value.

Required:

On the basis of the information the disclosures provide, compare revenue recognition under IFRS (as applied by Vodafone) with that in the United States.

IFRS Case 5–19
Comparison of revenue recognition for construction contracts

ThyssenKrupp AG, headquartered in Germany, is one of the world's largest technology companies, with almost 160,000 employees worldwide and primary segments in steel, technology, and capital goods and services.

Required:

1. Access ThyssenKrupp's most recent annual report using the Internet. Find the footnote describing significant accounting policies. Indicate the methods that ThyssenKrupp uses to account for long-term construction contracts when they can and cannot make an accurate estimate of the income on a construction contract.
2. If ThyssenKrupp was a U.S. company, how would you expect its accounting for these contracts to differ?

Trueblood Accounting Case 5–20
Revenue recognition for long-term contracts

The following Trueblood case is recommended for use with this chapter. The case provides an excellent opportunity for class discussion, group projects, and writing assignments. The case, along with Professor's Discussion Material, can be obtained from the Deloitte Foundation at its website www.deloitte.com/us/truebloodcases.

Case 12.5: *Aren't We Done Yet?*

This case concerns the appropriate timing of revenue recognition for a long-term construction contract, including percentage-of-completion, completed contract, and zero-profit methods used pre-ASU No. 2014-09 under U.S. GAAP and IFRS.

Trueblood Accounting Case 5–21
Revenue recognition for multiple-deliverable contracts.

The following Trueblood case is recommended for use with this chapter. The case provides an excellent opportunity for class discussion, group projects, and writing assignments. The case, along with Professor's Discussion Material, can be obtained from the Deloitte Foundation at its website www.deloitte.com/us/truebloodcases.

Case 12-4: *Hemo-Tech*

This case concerns indentifying multiple deliverables and their sales prices in a multiple-deliverable contract, as well as identifying the relevant standard used pre-ASU No. 2014-09 under U.S. GAAP and IFRS.

Trueblood Accounting Case 5–22
Revenue recognition for multiple-deliverable contracts involving software

The following Trueblood case is recommended for use with this chapter. The case provides an excellent opportunity for class discussion, group projects, and writing assignments. The case, along with Professor's Discussion Material, can be obtained from the Deloitte Foundation at its website www.deloitte.com/us/truebloodcases.

Case 10-11: *Eye Vision*

This case concerns the appropriate timing of revenue recognition for a bundled product and service used pre-ASU No. 2014-09 under U.S. GAAP and IFRS.

Real World Case 5–23
Revenue recognition; franchise sales

EDGAR, the Electronic Data Gathering, Analysis, and Retrieval system, performs automated collection, validation, indexing, and forwarding of submissions by companies and others who are required by law to file forms with the U.S. Securities and Exchange Commission (SEC). All publicly traded domestic companies use EDGAR to make the majority of their filings. (Some foreign companies file voluntarily.) Form 10-K which includes the annual report, is required to be filed on EDGAR. The SEC makes this information available on the Internet.

Required:

1. Access EDGAR on the Internet. The web address is www.sec.gov.
2. Search for Jack in the Box, Inc. Access the most recent 10-K filing. Search or scroll to find the financial statements and related notes.
3. Answer the following questions related to the company's revenue recognition policies:
   a. When does the company recognize initial franchise license fee revenue?
   b. How are continuing fees determined?
4. Repeat requirements 2 and 3 for two additional companies that you suspect also earn revenues through the sale of franchise rights. Compare their revenue recognition policies with the policies of Jack in the Box.

CHAPTER

Time Value of Money Concepts

OVERVIEW

Time value of money concepts, specifically future value and present value, are essential in a variety of accounting situations. These concepts and the related computational procedures are the subjects of this chapter. Present values and future values of *single amounts* and present values and future values of *annuities* (series of equal periodic payments) are described separately but shown to be interrelated.

LEARNING OBJECTIVES

After studying this chapter, you should be able to:

- **LO6–1** Explain the difference between simple and compound interest. (*p. 324*)
- **LO6–2** Compute the future value of a single amount. (*p. 325*)
- **LO6–3** Compute the present value of a single amount. (*p. 326*)
- **LO6–4** Solve for either the interest rate or the number of compounding periods when present value and future value of a single amount are known. (*p. 327*)
- **LO6–5** Explain the difference between an ordinary annuity and an annuity due situation. (*p. 333*)
- **LO6–6** Compute the future value of both an ordinary annuity and an annuity due. (*p. 334*)
- **LO6–7** Compute the present value of an ordinary annuity, an annuity due, and a deferred annuity. (*p. 335*)
- **LO6–8** Solve for unknown values in annuity situations involving present value. (*p. 340*)
- **LO6–9** Briefly describe how the concept of the time value of money is incorporated into the valuation of bonds, long-term leases, and pension obligations. (*p. 343*)

FINANCIAL REPORTING CASE

The Winning Ticket

Pedro Quezada, a former shop owner from a working-class suburb, had been in the United States for 26 years. On Monday, March 25, 2013, he walked out of a local liquor store with a lottery ticket. The next day the New Jersey resident learned he had won the $338 million Powerball lottery, the fourth-largest jackpot in Powerball history. "I felt pure joy, just happiness," he said. Imagine his surprise, though, when he was told that, having chosen a lump-sum payout rather than 30-year installment payments, he would get a check for "only" $152 million. Sure, federal tax was withheld at a 25% rate and New Jersey added another 3%, but this difference was far more than the amount of the tax.

(Source: This case is adapted from an actual situation.)

QUESTIONS

By the time you finish this chapter, you should be able to respond appropriately to the questions posed in this case. Compare your response to the solution provided at the end of the chapter.

1. Why was Quezada to receive $152 million rather than the $338 million lottery prize? (*p. 336*)
2. What interest rate did the state of New Jersey use to calculate the $152 million lump-sum payment? (*p. 341*)
3. What are some of the accounting applications that incorporate the time value of money into valuation? (*p. 344*)

Basic Concepts

PART A

Time Value of Money

The key to solving the problem described in the financial reporting case is an understanding of the concept commonly referred to as the **time value of money**. This concept means that money invested today will grow to a larger dollar amount in the future. For example, $100 invested in a savings account at your local bank yielding 6% annually will grow to $106 in one year. The difference between the $100 invested now—the present value of the investment—and its $106 future value represents the time value of money.

The *time value of money* means that money can be invested today to earn interest and grow to a larger dollar amount in the future.

This concept has nothing to do with the worth or buying power of those dollars. Prices in our economy can change. If the inflation rate were higher than 6%, then the $106 you would have in the savings account actually would be worth less than the $100 you had a year earlier. The time value of money concept concerns only the growth in the dollar amounts of money.

The concepts you learn in this chapter are useful in solving business decisions such as the determination of the lottery award presented in the financial reporting case. More important, the concepts are necessary when valuing assets and liabilities for financial reporting purposes. Most accounting applications that incorporate the time value of money involve the concept of present value. The valuation of leases, bonds, pension obligations, and certain notes receivable and payable are a few prominent examples. It is important that you master the concepts and tools we review here as it is essential for the remainder of your accounting education.

Time value of money concepts are useful in valuing several assets and liabilities.

Simple versus Compound Interest

● LO6–1

Interest is the amount of money paid or received in excess of the amount borrowed or lent.

Interest is the "rent" paid for the use of money for some period of time. In dollar terms, it is the amount of money paid or received in excess of the amount of money borrowed or lent. If you lent the bank $100 today and "received" $106 a year from now, your interest earned would be $6. Interest also can be expressed as a rate at which money will grow. In this case, that rate is 6%. It is this interest that gives money its time value.

Simple interest is computed by multiplying an initial investment times both the applicable interest rate and the period of time for which the money is used. For example, simple interest earned each year on a $1,000 investment paying 10% is $100 ($1,000 × 10%).

Compound interest includes interest not only on the initial investment but also on the accumulated interest in previous periods.

Compound interest results in increasingly larger interest amounts for each period of the investment. The reason is that interest is now being earned not only on the initial investment amount but also on the accumulated interest earned in previous periods.

For example, Cindy Johnson invested $1,000 in a savings account paying 10% interest *compounded* annually. How much interest will she earn each year, and what will be her investment balance after three years?

Date	Interest (Interest rate × Outstanding balance = Interest)	Balance
Initial deposit		$1,000
End of year 1	10% × $1,000 = $100	$1,100
End of year 2	10% × $1,100 = $110	$1,210
End of year 3	10% × $1,210 = $121	**$1,331**

With compound interest at 10% annually, the $1,000 investment would grow to **$1,331** at the end of the three-year period. If Cindy withdrew the interest earned each year, she would earn only $100 in interest each year (the amount of simple interest). If the investment period had been 20 years, 20 calculations would be needed. However, calculators, computer programs, and compound interest tables make these calculations easier.

Interest rates are typically stated as annual rates.

Most banks compound interest more frequently than once a year. Daily compounding is common for savings accounts. More rapid compounding has the effect of increasing the actual rate, which is called the **effective rate**, at which money grows per year. It is important to note that interest is typically stated as an annual rate regardless of the length of the compounding period involved. In situations when the compounding period is less than a year, the interest rate per compounding period is determined by dividing the annual rate by the number of periods. Assuming an annual rate of 12%:

Compounded	Interest Rate Per Compounding Period
Semiannually	12% ÷ 2 = 6%
Quarterly	12% ÷ 4 = 3%
Monthly	12% ÷ 12 = 1%

As an example, now let's assume Cindy Johnson invested $1,000 in a savings account paying 10% interest *compounded* twice a year. There are two six-month periods paying interest at 5% (the annual rate divided by two periods). How much interest will she earn the first year, and what will be her investment balance at the end of the year?

Date	Interest (Interest rate × Outstanding balance = Interest)	Balance
Initial deposit		$ 1,000.00
After six months	5% × $1,000 = $50.00	$ 1,050.00
End of year 1	5% × $1,050 = $52.50	**$1,102.50**

The *effective interest rate* is the rate at which money actually will grow during a full year.

The $1,000 would grow by $102.50, the interest earned, to **$1,102.50**, $2.50 more than if interest were compounded only once a year. The effective annual interest rate, often referred to as the annual *yield,* is 10.25% ($102.50 ÷ $1,000).

Valuing a Single Cash Flow Amount

Future Value of a Single Amount

In the first Cindy example, in which $1,000 was invested for three years at 10% compounded annually, the **$1,331** is referred to as the **future value (FV)**. A time diagram is a useful way to visualize this relationship, with 0 indicating the date of the initial investment.

● LO6–2

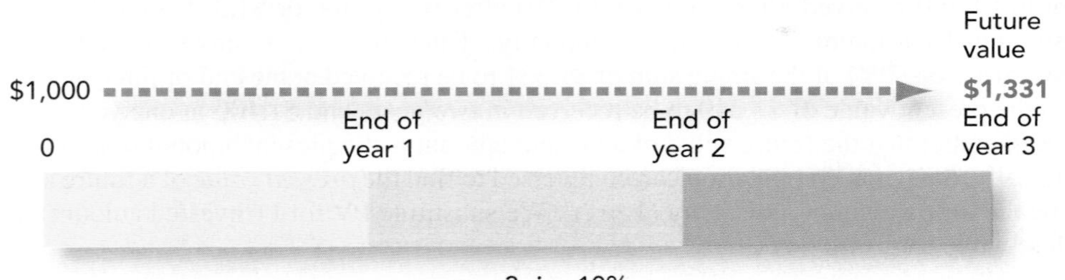

$n = 3, i = 10\%$

Future value of a single amount.

The future value after one year can be calculated as $1,000 × 1.10 (1.00 + .10) = $1,100. After three years, the future value is $1,000 × 1.10 × 1.10 × 1.10 = $1,331. In fact, the future value of any invested amount can be determined as follows:

$$FV = I(1 + i)^n$$

where:
FV = Future value of the invested amount
I = Amount invested at the beginning of the period
i = Interest rate
n = Number of compounding periods

The *future value* of a single amount is the amount of money that a dollar will grow to at some point in the future.

The future value can be determined by using Table 1, Future Value of $1, located at the end of this textbook. The table contains the future value of $1 invested for various periods of time, n, and at various rates, i.

Use this table to determine the future value of any invested amount simply by multiplying it by the table value at the *intersection* of the column for the desired rate and the row for the number of compounding periods. Illustration 6–1 contains an excerpt from Table 1.

Illustration 6–1

Future Value of $1 (excerpt from Table 1 located at the end of this textbook)

	Interest Rates (*i*)					
Periods (*n*)	**7%**	**8%**	**9%**	**10%**	**11%**	**12%**
1	1.07000	1.08000	1.09000	1.10000	1.11000	1.12000
2	1.14490	1.16640	1.18810	1.21000	1.23210	1.25440
3	1.22504	1.25971	1.29503	1.33100	1.36763	1.40493
4	1.31080	1.36049	1.41158	1.46410	1.51807	1.57352
5	1.40255	1.46933	1.53862	1.61051	1.68506	1.76234

The table shows various values of $(1 + i)^n$ for different combinations of i and n. From the table you can find the future value factor for three periods at 10% to be **1.331**. This means that $1 invested at 10% compounded annually will grow to approximately $1.33 in three years. So, the future value of $1,000 invested for three years at 10% is **$1,331**:

FV = I × FV factor
FV = $1,000 × **1.331*** = **$1,331**
*Future value of $1; $n = 3$, $i = 10\%$

The future value function in financial calculators or in computer spreadsheet programs calculates future values in the same way. Determining future values (and present values) electronically avoids the need for tables such as those in the chapter appendix. It's important to remember that the n in the future value formula refers to the number of compounding periods, not necessarily the number of years. For example, suppose you wanted to know the future value *two* years from today of $1,000 invested at 12% with *quarterly* compounding.

The number of periods is therefore eight and the compounding rate is 3% (12% annual rate divided by four, the number of quarters in a year). The future value factor from Table 1 is 1.26677, so the future value is $1,266.77 ($1,000 × 1.26677).[1]

Present Value of a Single Amount

LO6–3

The present value of a single amount is today's equivalent to a particular amount in the future.

The example used to illustrate future value reveals that $1,000 invested today is equivalent to $1,100 received after one year, $1,210 after two years, or $1,331 after three years, assuming 10% interest compounded annually. Thus, the **$1,000** investment (I) is the **present value (PV)** of the single sum of $1,331 to be received at the end of three years. It is also the present value of $1,210 to be received in two years and $1,100 in one year.

Remember that the future value of a present amount is the present amount *times* $(1 + i)^n$. Logically, then, that computation can be reversed to find the *present value* of a future amount to be the future amount *divided* by $(1 + i)^n$. We substitute PV for I (invested amount) in the future value formula above.

$$FV = PV\,(1 + i)^n$$

$$PV = \frac{FV}{(1 + i)^n}$$

In our example,

$$PV = \frac{\$1{,}331}{(1 + .10)^3} = \frac{\$1{,}331}{1.331} = \$1{,}000$$

Of course, dividing by $(1 + i)^n$ is the same as multiplying by its reciprocal, $1/(1 + i)^n$.

$$PV = \$1{,}331 \times \frac{1}{(1 + .10)^3} = \$1{,}331 \times .75131 = \$1{,}000$$

As with future value, these computations are simplified by using calculators, computer programs, or present value tables. Table 2, Present Value of $1, located at the end of this textbook provides the solutions of $1/(1 + i)^n$ for various interest rates (i) and compounding periods (n). These amounts represent the present value of $1 to be received at the *end* of the different periods. The table can be used to find the present value of any single amount to be received in the future by *multiplying* that amount by the value in the table that lies at the *intersection* of the column for the appropriate rate and the row for the number of compounding periods.[2] Illustration 6–2 contains an excerpt from Table 2.

Notice that the farther into the future the $1 is to be received, the less valuable it is now. This is the essence of the concept of the time value of money. Given a choice between $1,000 now and $1,000 three years from now, you would choose to have the money now. If you have

Illustration 6–2

Present Value of $1 (excerpt from Table 2 located at the end of this textbook)

	Interest Rates (i)					
Periods (n)	**7%**	**8%**	**9%**	**10%**	**11%**	**12%**
1	.93458	.92593	.91743	.90909	.90090	.89286
2	.87344	.85734	.84168	.82645	.81162	.79719
3	.81630	.79383	.77218	.75131	.73119	.71178
4	.76290	.73503	.70843	.68301	.65873	.63552
5	.71299	.68058	.64993	.62092	.59345	.56743

[1]When interest is compounded more frequently than once a year, the effective annual interest rate, or yield, can be determined using the following equation:

$$\text{Yield} = (1 + \tfrac{i}{p})^p - 1$$

with i being the annual interest rate and p the number of compounding periods per year. In this example, the annual yield would be 12.55%, calculated as follows:

$$\text{Yield} = (1 + \tfrac{.12}{4})^4 - 1 = 1.1255 - 1 = .1255$$

Determining the yield is useful when comparing returns on investment instruments with different compounding period length.

[2]The factors in Table 2 are the reciprocals of those in Table 1. For example, the future value factor for 10%, three periods is 1.331, while the present value factor is .75131. $1 ÷ 1.331 = $.75131, and $1 ÷ .75131 = $1.331.

it now, you could put it to use. But the choice between, say, $740 now and $1,000 three years from now would depend on your time value of money. If your time value of money is 10%, you would choose the $1,000 in three years, because the $740 invested at 10% for three years would grow to only $984.94 [$740 × 1.331 (FV of $1, $i = 10\%$, $n = 3$)]. On the other hand, if your time value of money is 11% or higher, you would prefer the $740 now.[3] Presumably, you would invest the $740 now and have it grow to $1,012.05 ($740 × 1.36763) in three years.

Using the present value table above, the present value of $1,000 to be received in three years assuming a time value of money of 10% is $751.31 [$1,000 × .75131 (PV of $1, $i = 10\%$ and $n = 3$)]. Because the present value of the future amount, $1,000, is higher than $740 we could have today, we again determine that with a time value of money of 10%, the $1,000 in three years is preferred to the $740 now.

In our earlier example, $1,000 now is equivalent to $1,331 in three years, assuming the time value of money is 10%. Graphically, the relation between the present value and the future value can be viewed this way:

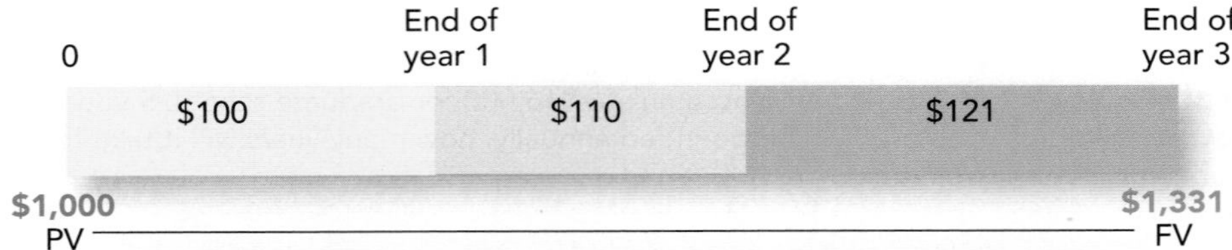

While the calculation of future value of a single sum invested today requires the *inclusion* of compound interest, present value problems require the *removal* of compound interest. The process of computing present value *removes* the $331 of interest earned over the three-year period from the future value of $1,331, just as the process of computing future value *adds* $331 of interest to the present value of $1,000 to arrive at the future value of $1,331.

The calculation of future value requires the addition of interest, while the calculation of present value requires the removal of interest.

As we demonstrate later in this chapter and in subsequent chapters, present value calculations are incorporated into accounting valuation much more frequently than future value.

Accountants use PV calculations much more frequently than FV.

Solving for Other Values When FV and PV are Known

● LO6–4

There are four variables in the process of adjusting single cash flow amounts for the time value of money: the present value (PV), the future value (FV), the number of compounding periods (n), and the interest rate (i). If you know any three of these, the fourth can be determined. Illustration 6–3 solves for an unknown interest rate and Illustration 6–4 determines an unknown number of periods.

DETERMINING THE UNKNOWN INTEREST RATE

Illustration 6–3

Determining i When PV, FV, and n are Known

Suppose a friend asks to borrow $500 today and promises to repay you $605 two years from now. What is the annual interest rate you would be agreeing to?

The following time diagram illustrates the situation:

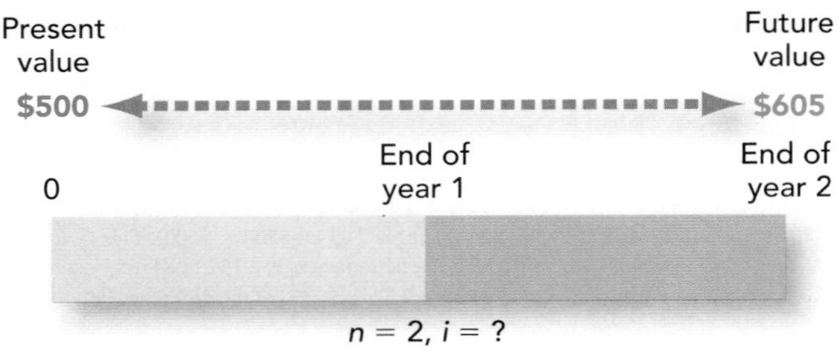

[3]The interest rate used to find the present value sometimes is called the *discount rate,* and finding the present value is sometimes called "discounting" a future amount to its present value.

The interest rate is the rate that will provide a present value of $500 when determining present value of the $605 to be received in two years:

$500 (present value) = $605 (future value) × ?*

*Present value of $1: $n = 2$, $i = ?$

Rearranging algebraically, we find that the present value table factor is .82645.

$500 (present value) ÷ $605 (future value) = .82645*

*Present value of $1: $n = 2$, $i = ?$

The unknown variable is the interest rate.

When you consult the present value table, Table 2, you search row two ($n = 2$) for this value and find it in the 10% column. So the effective interest rate is 10%. Notice that the computed factor value exactly equals the table factor value.[4]

DETERMINING THE UNKNOWN NUMBER OF PERIODS

Illustration 6–4

Determining n When PV, FV, and i are Known

You want to invest $10,000 today to accumulate $16,000 for graduate school. If you can invest at an interest rate of 10% compounded annually, how many years will it take to accumulate the required amount?

The following time diagram illustrates the situation:

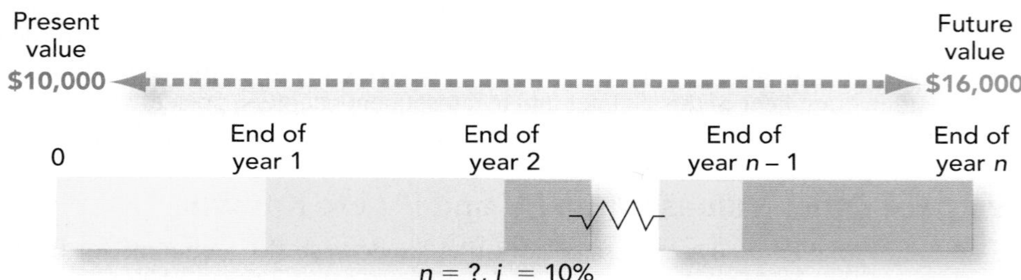

The number of years is the value of n that will provide a present value of $10,000 when finding the present value of $16,000 at a rate of 10%:

The unknown variable is the number of periods.

$10,000 (present value) = $16,000 (future value) × ?*

*Present value of $1; $n = ?$, $i = 10\%$

Rearranging algebraically, we find that the present value table factor is .625.

$10,000 (present value) ÷ $16,000 (future value) = .625*

*Present value of $1: $n = ?$, $i = 10\%$

When you consult the present value table, Table 2, you search the 10% column ($i = 10\%$) for this value and find .62092 in row five. So it would take approximately five years to accumulate $16,000 in the situation described.

[4]If the calculated factor lies between two table factors, interpolation is useful in finding the unknown value. For example, if the future value in our example is $600, instead of $605, the calculated PV factor is .83333 ($500 ÷ $600). This factor lies between the 9% factor of .84168 and the 10% factor of .82645. The total difference between these factors is .01523 (.84168 − .82645). The difference between the calculated factor of .83333 and the 10% factor of .82645 is .00688. This is 45% of the difference between the 9% and 10% factors:

$$\frac{.00688}{.01523} = .45$$

Therefore, the interpolated interest rate is 9.55% (10 − .45).

Additional Consideration

Solving for the unknown factor in either of these examples could just as easily be done using the future value tables. The number of years is the value of n that will provide a present value of \$10,000 when \$16,000 is the future amount and the interest rate is 10%.

$16,000 (future value) = $10,000 (present value) × ?*

*Future value of \$1: $n = ?$, $i = 10\%$

Rearranging algebraically, the future value table factor is 1.6.

$16,000 (future value) ÷ $10,000 (present value) = 1.6*

*Future value of \$1: $n = ?$, $i = 10\%$

When you consult the future value table, Table 1, you search the 10% column ($i = 10\%$) for this value and find 1.61051 in row five. So it would take approximately five years to accumulate \$16,000 in the situation described.

Concept Review Exercise

VALUING A SINGLE CASH FLOW AMOUNT

Using the appropriate table, answer each of the following independent questions.

1. What is the future value of \$5,000 at the end of six periods at 8% compound interest?
2. What is the present value of \$8,000 to be received eight periods from today assuming a compound interest rate of 12%?
3. What is the present value of \$10,000 to be received two *years* from today assuming an annual interest rate of 24% and *monthly* compounding?
4. If an investment of \$2,000 grew to \$2,520 in three periods, what is the interest rate at which the investment grew? Solve using both present and future value tables.
5. Approximately how many years would it take for an investment of \$5,250 to accumulate to \$15,000, assuming interest is compounded at 10% annually? Solve using both present and future value tables.

Solution:

1. FV = \$5,000 × 1.58687* = \$7,934

   *Future value of \$1: $n = 6$, $i = 8\%$ (from Table 1)
2. PV = \$8,000 × .40388* = \$3,231

   *Present value of \$1: $n = 8$, $i = 12\%$ (from Table 2)
3. PV = \$10,000 × .62172* = \$6,217

   *Present value of \$1: $n = 24$, $i = 2\%$ (from Table 2)
4. Using present value table,

   $$\frac{\$2{,}000}{\$2{,}520} = .7937^*$$

   *Present value of \$1: $n = 3$, $i = ?$ (from Table 2, i approximately **8%**)

   Using future value table,

   $$\frac{\$2{,}520}{\$2{,}000} = 1.260^*$$

   *Future value of \$1: $n = 3$, $i = ?$ (from Table 1, i approximately **8%**)
5. Using present value table,

   $$\frac{\$5{,}250}{\$15{,}000} = .35^*$$

   *Present value of \$1: $n = ?$, $i = 10\%$ (from Table 2, n approximately **11 years**)

   Using future value table,

   $$\frac{\$15{,}000}{\$5{,}250} = 2.857^*$$

   *Future value of \$1: $n = ?$. $i = 10\%$ (from Table 1, n approximately **11 years**)

Preview of Accounting Applications of Present Value Techniques—Single Cash Amount

Kile Petersen switched off his television set immediately after watching the Super Bowl game and swore to himself that this would be the last year he would watch the game on his 10-year-old 20-inch TV set. “Next year, a big screen TV,” he promised himself. Soon after, he saw an advertisement in the local newspaper from Slim Jim’s TV and Appliance offering a Philips 60-inch large screen television on sale for $1,800. And the best part of the deal was that Kile could take delivery immediately but would not have to pay the $1,800 for one whole year! “In a year, I can easily save the $1,800,” he thought.

In the above scenario, the seller, Slim Jim’s TV and Appliance, records a sale when the TV is delivered to Kile. How should the company value its receivable and corresponding sales revenue? We provide a solution to this question at the end of this section on page 331. The following discussion will help you to understand that solution.

Most *monetary assets* and *monetary liabilities* are valued at the present value of future cash flows.

Many assets and most liabilities are monetary in nature. **Monetary assets** include money and claims to receive money, the amount of which is fixed or determinable. Examples include cash and most receivables. **Monetary liabilities** are obligations to pay amounts of cash, the amount of which is fixed or determinable. Most liabilities are monetary. For example, if you borrow money from a bank and sign a note payable, the amount of cash to be repaid to the bank is fixed. Monetary receivables and payables are valued based on the fixed amount of cash to be received or paid in the future with proper reflection of the time value of money. In other words, we value most receivables and payables at the present value of future cash flows, reflecting an appropriate time value of money.[5]

The example in Illustration 6–5 demonstrates this concept.

Illustration 6–5

Valuing a Note: One Payment, Explicit Interest

Explicit Interest

The Stridewell Wholesale Shoe Company manufactures athletic shoes for sale to retailers. The company recently sold a large order of shoes to Harmon Sporting Goods for $50,000. Stridewell agreed to accept a note in payment for the shoes requiring payment of $50,000 in one year plus interest at 10%.

How should Stridewell value the note receivable and corresponding sales revenue earned? How should Harmon value the note payable and corresponding inventory purchased? As long as the interest rate explicitly stated in the agreement properly reflects the time value of money, the answer is $50,000, the face value of the note. It’s important to realize that this amount also equals the present value of future cash flows at 10%. Future cash flows equal $55,000, $50,000 in note principal plus $5,000 in interest ($50,000 × 10%). Using a time diagram:

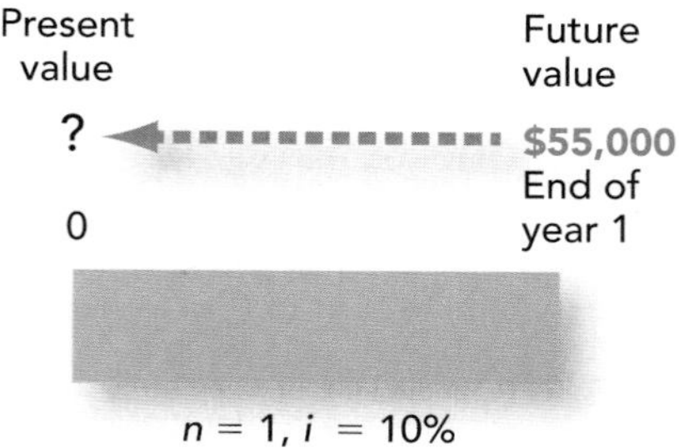

In equation form, we can solve for present value as follows:

$55,000 (future value) × .90909* = $50,000 (present value)

*Present value of $1: $n = 1$, $i = 10\%$

[5]FASB ASC 835–30: Interest—Imputation of Interest (previously “Interest on Receivables and Payables,” *Accounting Principles Board Opinion No. 21* (New York: AICPA, 1971)). As you will learn in Chapter 7, we value normal trade accounts receivable and accounts payable at the amounts expected to be received or paid, not the present value of those amounts. The difference between the amounts expected to be received or paid and present values often is immaterial.

By calculating the present value of $55,000 to be received in one year, the interest of $5,000 is removed from the future value, resulting in a proper note receivable/sales revenue value of $50,000 for Stridewell and a $50,000 note payable/inventory value for Harmon.

While most notes, loans, and mortgages explicitly state an interest rate that will properly reflect the time value of money, there can be exceptions. Consider the example in Illustration 6–6.

No Explicit Interest
The Stridewell Wholesale Shoe Company recently sold a large order of shoes to Harmon Sporting Goods. Terms of the sale require Harmon to sign a noninterest-bearing note of $60,500 with payment due in two years.

Illustration 6–6
Valuing a Note: One Payment, No Explicit Interest

How should Stridewell and Harmon value the note receivable/payable and corresponding sales revenue/inventory? Even though the agreement states a noninterest-bearing note, the $60,500 does, in fact, include interest for the two-year period of the loan. We need to remove the interest portion of the $60,500 to determine the portion that represents the sales price of the shoes. We do this by computing the present value. The following time diagram illustrates the situation assuming that a rate of 10% reflects the appropriate interest rate for a loan of this type:

Present value ? ← Future value $60,500

0 | End of year 1 | End of year 2

$n = 2, i = 10\%$

Again, using the present value of $1 table,

$60,500 (future value) × .82645* = $50,000 (present value)

*Present value of $1: $n = 2, i = 10\%$

Both the note receivable for Stridewell and the note payable for Harmon initially will be valued at $50,000. The difference of $10,500 ($60,500 − 50,000) represents interest revenue/expense to be recognized over the life of the note. The appropriate journal entries are illustrated in later chapters.

Now can you answer the question posed in the scenario at the beginning of this section? Assuming that a rate of 10% reflects the appropriate interest rate in this situation, Slim Jim's TV and Appliance records a receivable and sales revenue of $1,636 which is the present value of the $1,800 to be received from Kile Petersen one year from the date of sale.

$1,800 (future value) × .90909* = $1,636 (present value)

*Present value of $1: $n = 1, i = 10\%$ (from Table 2)

Additional Consideration

In Illustration 6–6, if Harmon Sporting Goods had prepaid Stridewell for delivery of the shoes in two years, rather than buying now and paying later, Harmon would be viewed as providing a two-year loan to Stridewell. Assuming that Harmon pays Stridewell $41,323, the present value of $50,000 for two-periods at 10%, Stridewell would record interest expense and Harmon interest revenue of $8,677 ($50,000 − 41,323) over the two-year period. When delivery occurs in two years, Stridewell records sales revenue of $50,000 and Harmon values the inventory acquired at $50,000.

Expected Cash Flow Approach

SFAC No. 7 provides a framework for using future cash flows in accounting measurements.

Present value measurement has long been integrated with accounting valuation and is specifically addressed in several accounting standards. Because of its increased importance, the FASB issued *Statement of Financial Accounting Concepts No. 7,* "Using Cash Flow Information and Present Value in Accounting Measurements."[6] This statement provides a framework for using future cash flows as the basis for accounting measurement and asserts that the objective in valuing an asset or liability using present value is to approximate the fair value of that asset or liability. Key to that objective is determining the present value of future cash flows associated with the asset or liability, *taking into account any uncertainty concerning the amounts and timing of the cash flows.* Although future cash flows in many instances are contractual and certain, the amounts and timing of cash flows are less certain in other situations.

For example, lease payments are provided in the contract between lessor and lessee. On the other hand, the future cash flows to be paid to settle a pending lawsuit may be highly uncertain. Traditionally, the way uncertainty has been considered in present value calculations has been by finding the present value of the "best estimate" of future cash flows applying an interest rate that has been adjusted to reflect the uncertainty or risk of those cash flows. With the approach described by *SFAC No. 7,* though, the adjustment for uncertainty or risk of cash flows is applied to the cash flows, not the interest rate. This new *expected cash flow approach* incorporates specific probabilities of cash flows into the analysis. Consider Illustration 6–7.

Illustration 6–7

Expected Cash Flow Approach

LDD Corporation faces the likelihood of having to pay an uncertain amount in five years in connection with an environmental cleanup. The future cash flow estimate is in the range of $100 million to $300 million with the following estimated probabilities:

Loss Amount	Probability
$100 million	10%
$200 million	60%
$300 million	30%

The expected cash flow, then, is $220 million:

$100 × 10% = $ 10 million
200 × 60% = 120 million
300 × 30% = 90 million
$220 million

If the company's credit-adjusted risk-free rate of interest is 5%, LDD will report a liability of $172,376,600, the present value of the expected cash outflow:

$220,000,000
× .78353*
$172,376,600

*Present value of $1, n = 5, i = 5% (from Table 2)

The company's credit-adjusted risk-free rate of interest is used when applying the expected cash flow approach to the calculation of present value.

Compare the approach described in Illustration 6–7 to the traditional approach that uses the present value of the most likely estimate of $200 million and ignores information about cash flow probabilities.

The interest rate used to determine present value when applying the expected cash flow approach should be the company's *credit-adjusted risk-free rate of interest.* Other elements of uncertainty are incorporated into the determination of the probability-weighted

[6] "Using Cash Flow Information and Present Value in Accounting Measurements," *Statement of Financial Accounting Concepts No. 7* (Norwalk, Conn.: FASB, 2000). Recall that Concept Statements do not directly prescribe GAAP, but instead provide structure and direction to financial accounting.

expected cash flows. In the traditional approach, elements of uncertainty are incorporated into a risk-adjusted interest rate.

The FASB expects that the traditional approach to calculating present value will continue to be used in many situations, particularly those where future cash flows are contractual. The board also believes that the expected cash flow approach is more appropriate in more complex situations. In fact, the board has incorporated the concepts developed in *SFAC No. 7* into standards on asset retirement obligations, impairment losses, and business combinations. In Chapter 10 we illustrate the use of the expected cash flow approach as it would be applied to the measurement of an asset retirement obligation. In Chapter 13, we use the approach to measure the liability associated with a loss contingency.

SFAC No. 7
"While many accountants do not routinely use the expected cash flow approach, expected cash flows are inherent in the techniques used in some accounting measurements, like pensions, other postretirement benefits, and some insurance obligations."[7]

Basic Annuities

PART B

● LO6–5

The previous examples involved the receipt or payment of a single future amount. Financial instruments frequently involve multiple receipts or payments of cash. If the same amount is to be received or paid each period, the series of cash flows is referred to as an **annuity**. A common annuity encountered in practice is a loan on which periodic interest is paid in equal amounts. For example, bonds typically pay interest semiannually in an amount determined by multiplying a stated rate by a fixed principal amount. Some loans and most leases are paid in equal installments during a specified period of time.

In an *ordinary annuity* cash flows occur at the end of each period.

An agreement that creates an annuity can produce either an **ordinary annuity** or an **annuity due** (sometimes referred to as an annuity in advance) situation. The first cash flow (receipt or payment) of an ordinary annuity is made one compounding period *after* the date on which the agreement begins. The final cash flow takes place on the *last* day covered by the agreement. For example, an installment note payable dated December 31, 2016, might require the debtor to make three equal annual payments, with the first payment due on December 31, 2017, and the last one on December 31, 2019. The following time diagram illustrates an ordinary annuity:

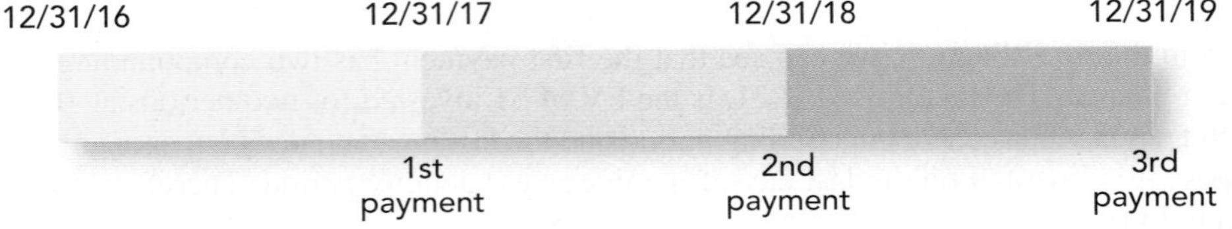

Ordinary annuity.

In an *annuity due* cash flows occur at the *beginning* of each period.

The first payment of an annuity due is made on the *first* day of the agreement, and the last payment is made one period *before* the end of the agreement. For example, a three-year lease of a building that begins on December 31, 2016, and ends on December 31, 2019, may require the first year's lease payment in advance on December 31, 2016. The third and last payment would take place on December 31, 2018, the beginning of the third year of the lease. The following time diagram illustrates this situation:

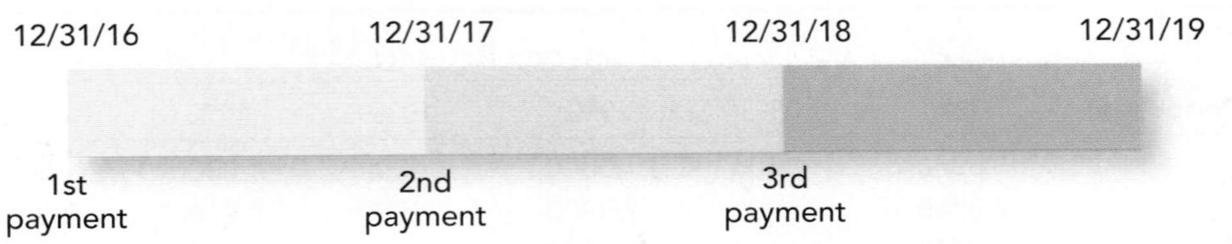

Annuity due.

[7]Ibid., para. 48.

Future Value of an Annuity

Future Value of an Ordinary Annuity

Let's first consider the future value of an ordinary annuity in Illustration 6–8.

Illustration 6–8
Future Value of an Ordinary Annuity

Sally Rogers wants to accumulate a sum of money to pay for graduate school. Rather than investing a single amount today that will grow to a future value, she decides to invest $10,000 a year over the next three years in a savings account paying 10% interest compounded annually. She decides to make the first payment to the bank one year from today.

The following time diagram illustrates this ordinary annuity situation. Time 0 is the start of the first period.

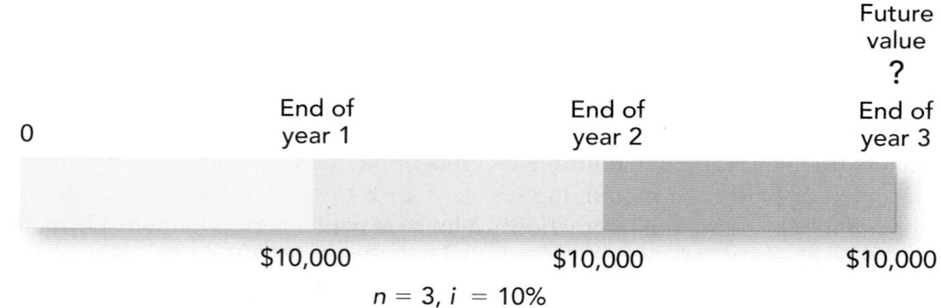

Using the FV of $1 factors from Table 1, we can calculate the future value of this annuity by calculating the future value of each of the individual payments as follows:

	Payment		FV of $1 $i = 10\%$		Future Value (at the end of year 3)	*n*
First payment	$10,000	×	1.21	=	$12,100	2
Second payment	10,000	×	1.10	=	11,000	1
Third payment	10,000	×	1.00	=	10,000	0
Total			3.31		$33,100	

In the future value of an ordinary annuity, the last cash payment will not earn any interest.

From the time diagram, we can see that the first payment has two compounding periods to earn interest. The factor used, 1.21, is the FV of $1 invested for two periods at 10%. The second payment has one compounding period and the last payment does not earn any interest because it is invested on the last day of the three-year annuity period. Therefore, the factor used is 1.00.

● LO6–6

This illustration shows that it's possible to calculate the future value of the annuity by separately calculating the FV of each payment and then adding these amounts together. Fortunately, that's not necessary. Table 3, Future Value of an Ordinary Annuity of $1, located at the end of this textbook, simplifies the computation by summing the individual FV of $1 factors for various factors of *n* and *i*. Illustration 6–9 contains an excerpt from Table 3.

Illustration 6–9
Future Value of an Ordinary Annuity of $1 (excerpt from Table 3 located at the end of this textbook)

	Interest Rates (*i*)					
Periods (*n*)	7%	8%	9%	10%	11%	12%
1	1.0000	1.0000	1.0000	1.0000	1.0000	1.0000
2	2.0700	2.0800	2.0900	2.1000	2.1100	2.1200
3	3.2149	3.2464	3.2781	3.3100	3.3421	3.3744
4	4.4399	4.5061	4.5731	4.6410	4.7097	4.7793
5	5.7507	5.8666	5.9847	6.1051	6.2278	6.3528

The future value of \$1 at the end of each of three periods invested at 10% is shown in Table 3 to be \$3.31. We can simply multiply this factor by \$10,000 to derive the FV of our ordinary annuity (FVA):

FVA = \$10,000 (annuity amount) × 3.31* = \$33,100

*Future value of an ordinary annuity of \$1: $n = 3$, $i = 10\%$

Future Value of an Annuity Due

Let's modify the previous illustration to create an annuity due in Illustration 6–10.

Illustration 6–10
Future Value of an Annuity Due

> Sally Rogers wants to accumulate a sum of money to pay for graduate school. Rather than investing a single amount today that will grow to a future value, she decides to invest \$10,000 a year over the next three years in a savings account paying 10% interest compounded annually. She decides to make the first payment to the bank immediately. How much will Sally have available in her account at the end of three years?

The following time diagram depicts the situation. Again, note that 0 is the start of the first period.

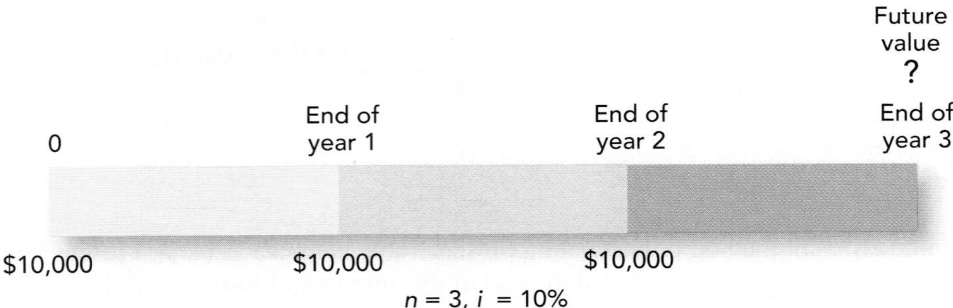

The future value can be found by separately calculating the FV of each of the three payments and then summing those individual future values:

	Payment		FV of \$1 $i = 10\%$		Future Value (at the end of year 3)	n
First payment	\$10,000	×	1.331	=	\$13,310	3
Second payment	10,000	×	1.210	=	12,100	2
Third payment	10,000	×	1.100	=	11,000	1
Total			3.641		\$36,410	

In the future value of an annuity due, the last cash payment will earn interest.

And, again, this same future value can be found by using the future value of an annuity due (FVAD) factor from Table 5, Future Value of an Annuity Due of \$1, located at the end of this textbook, as follows:

FVAD = \$10,000 (annuity amount) × 3.641* = \$36,410

*Future value of an annuity due of \$1: $n = 3$, $i = 10\%$

Of course, if *unequal* amounts are invested each year, we can't solve the problem by using the annuity tables. The future value of each payment would have to be calculated separately.

Present Value of an Annuity

Present Value of an Ordinary Annuity

● LO6–7

You will learn in later chapters that liabilities and receivables, with the exception of certain trade receivables and payables, are reported in financial statements at their present values. Most of these financial instruments specify equal periodic interest payments or installment payments. As a result, the most common accounting applications of the time value of money involve determining present value of annuities. As in the future value applications we discussed above, an annuity can be either an ordinary annuity or an annuity due. Let's look at an ordinary annuity first.

FINANCIAL Reporting Case

Q1, p. 323

In Illustration 6–8 on page 334, we determined that Sally Rogers could accumulate $33,100 for graduate school by investing $10,000 at the end of each of three years at 10%. The $33,100 is the future value of the ordinary annuity described. Another alternative is to invest one single amount at the beginning of the three-year period. (See Illustration 6–11.) This single amount will equal the present value at the beginning of the three-year period of the $33,100 future value. It will also equal the present value of the $10,000 three-year annuity.

Illustration 6–11

Present Value of an Ordinary Annuity

Sally Rogers wants to accumulate a sum of money to pay for graduate school. She wants to invest a single amount today in a savings account earning 10% interest compounded annually that is equivalent to investing $10,000 at the end of each of the next three years.

The present value can be found by separately calculating the PV of each of the three payments and then summing those individual present values:

	Payment		PV of $1 i = 10%		Present Value (at the beginning of year 1)	n
First payment	$10,000	×	.90909	=	$ 9,091	1
Second payment	10,000	×	.82645	=	8,264	2
Third payment	10,000	×	.75131	=	7,513	3
Total			2.48685		$24,868	

A more efficient method of calculating present value is to use Table 4, Present Value of an Ordinary Annuity of $1, located at the end of this textbook. Illustration 6–12 contains an excerpt from Table 4.

Illustration 6–12

Present Value of an Ordinary Annuity of $1 (excerpt from Table 4 located at the end of this textbook)

	Interest Rates (i)					
Periods (n)	7%	8%	9%	10%	11%	12%
1	0.93458	0.92593	0.91743	0.90909	0.90090	0.89286
2	1.80802	1.78326	1.75911	1.73554	1.71252	1.69005
3	2.62432	2.57710	2.53129	2.48685	2.44371	2.40183
4	3.38721	3.31213	3.23972	3.16987	3.10245	3.03735
5	4.10020	3.99271	3.88965	3.79079	3.69590	3.60478

Using Table 4, we calculate the PV of the ordinary annuity (PVA) as follows:

PVA = $10,000 (annuity amount) × 2.48685* = $24,868

*Present value of an ordinary annuity of $1: n = 3, i = 10%

The relationship between the present value and the future value of the annuity can be depicted graphically as follows:

Relationship between present value and future value—ordinary annuity.

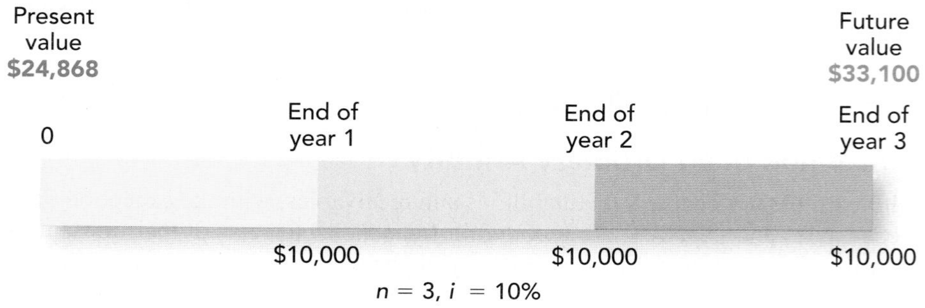

This can be interpreted in several ways:

1. \$10,000 invested at 10% at the end of each of the next three years will accumulate to \$33,100 at the end of the third year.
2. \$24,868 invested at 10% now will grow to \$33,100 after three years.
3. Someone whose time value of money is 10% would be willing to pay \$24,868 now to receive \$10,000 at the end of each of the next three years.
4. If your time value of money is 10%, you should be indifferent with respect to paying/receiving (a) \$24,868 now, (b) \$33,100 three years from now, or (c) \$10,000 at the end of each of the next three years.

Additional Consideration

We also can verify that these are the present value and future value of the same annuity by calculating the present value of a single cash amount of \$33,100 three years hence:

PV = \$33,100 (future value) × .75131* = \$24,868

*Present value of \$1: $n = 3$, $i = 10\%$

Present Value of an Annuity Due

Illustration 6–13
Present Value of an Annuity Due

In the previous illustration, suppose that the three equal payments of \$10,000 are to be made at the *beginning* of each of the three years. Recall from Illustration 6–10 on page 335 that the future value of this annuity is \$36,410. What is the present value?

The following time diagram depicts this situation:

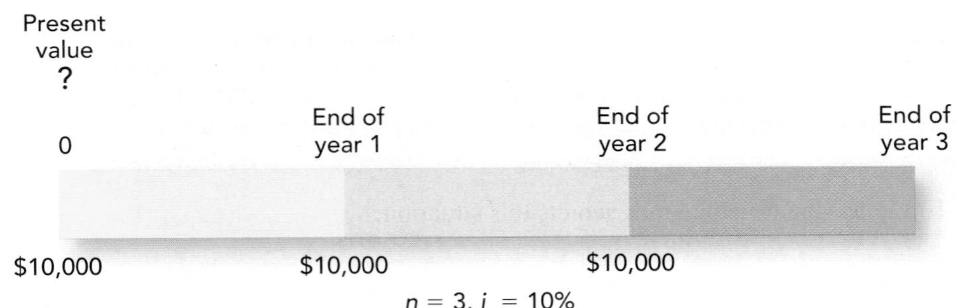

Present value of an annuity due.

Once again, using individual PV factors of \$1 from Table 2, the PV of the annuity due can be calculated as follows:

	Payment		PV of \$1 $i = 10\%$		Present Value (at the beginning of year 1)	n
First payment	\$10,000	×	1.00000	=	\$ 10,000	0
Second payment	10,000	×	.90909	=	9,091	1
Third payment	10,000	×	.82645	=	8,264	2
Total			2.73554		\$27,355	

The first payment does not contain any interest since it is made on the first day of the three-year annuity period. Therefore, the factor used is 1.00. The second payment has one compounding period and the factor used of .90909 is the PV factor of \$1 for one period and 10%, and we need to remove two compounding periods of interest from the third payment. The factor used of .82645 is the PV factor of \$1 for two periods and 10%.

In the present value of an annuity due, no interest needs to be removed from the first cash payment.

The relationship between the present value and the future value of the annuity can be depicted graphically as follows:

Relationship between present value and future value—annuity due.

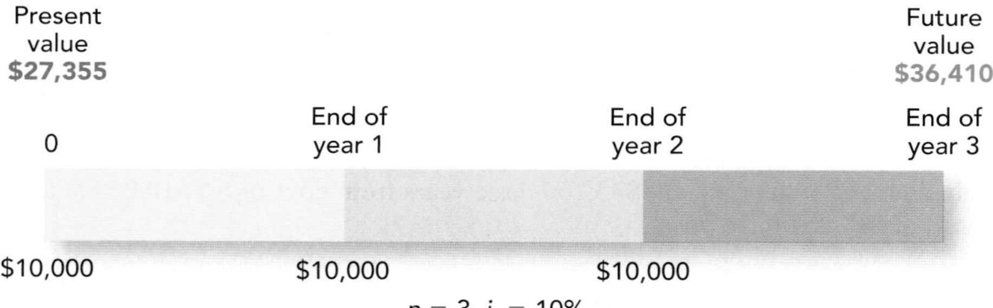

Using Table 6, Present Value of an Annuity Due, located at the end of this book, we can more efficiently calculate the PV of the annuity due (PVAD):

PVAD = \$10,000 (annuity amount) × 2.73554* = \$27,355

*Present value of an annuity due of \$1: $n = 3$, $i = 10\%$

To better understand the relationship between Tables 4 and 6, notice that the PVAD factor for three periods, 10%, from Table 6 is 2.73554. This is simply the PVA factor for two periods, 10%, of 1.73554, plus 1.0. The addition of 1.0 reflects the fact that the first payment does not require the removal of any interest.

Present Value of a Deferred Annuity

A *deferred annuity* exists when the first cash flow occurs more than one period after the date the agreement begins.

Accounting valuations often involve the present value of annuities in which the first cash flow is expected to occur more than one time period after the date of the agreement. As the inception of the annuity is deferred beyond a single period, this type of annuity is referred to as a **deferred annuity**.[8]

Illustration 6–14
Deferred Annuity

> At January 1, 2016, you are considering acquiring an investment that will provide three equal payments of \$10,000 each to be received at the end of three consecutive years. However, the first payment is not expected until *December 31, 2018*. The time value of money is 10%. How much would you be willing to pay for this investment?

The following time diagram depicts this situation:

Cash flows for a deferred annuity.

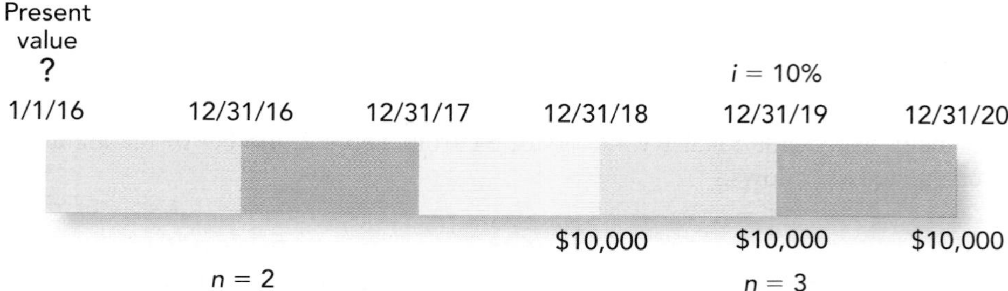

The present value of the deferred annuity can be calculated by summing the present values of the three individual cash flows, as of today:

	Payment		PV of \$1 $i = 10\%$		Present Value	n
First payment	\$10,000	×	.75131	=	\$ 7,513	3
Second payment	10,000	×	.68301	=	6,830	4
Third payment	10,000	×	.62092	=	6,209	5
					\$20,552	

[8] The future value of a deferred annuity is the same as the future amount of an annuity not deferred. That is because there are no interest compounding periods prior to the beginning of the annuity period.

A more efficient way of calculating the present value of a deferred annuity involves a two-step process:

1. Calculate the PV of the annuity *as of the beginning of the annuity period.*
2. Reduce the single amount calculated in (1) to its present value *as of today.*

In this case, we compute the present value of the annuity as of December 31, 2017, by multiplying the annuity amount by the three-period ordinary annuity factor:

$$PVA = \$10,000 \text{ (annuity amount)} \times 2.48685^{*} = \$24,868$$

*Present value of an ordinary annuity of $1: $n = 3, i = 10\%$

This is the present value as of December 31, 2017. This single amount is then reduced to present value as of January 1, 2016, by making the following calculation:

$$PV = \$24,868 \text{ (future amount)} \times .82645^{*} = \$20,552$$

*Present value of $1: $n = 2, i = 10\%$

The following time diagram illustrates this two-step process:

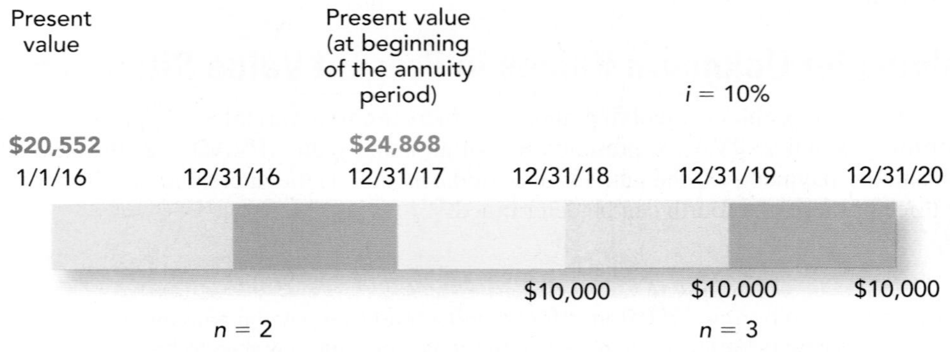

Present value of a deferred annuity—two-step process.

If you recall the concepts you learned in this chapter, you might think of other ways the present value of a deferred annuity can be determined. Among them:

1. Calculate the PV of an annuity due, rather than an ordinary annuity, and then reduce that amount **three** periods rather than two:

$$PVAD = \$10,000 \text{ (annuity amount)} \times 2.73554^{*} = \$27,355$$

*Present value of an annuity due of $1: $n = 3, i = 10\%$

This is the present value as of December 31, 2018. This single amount is then reduced to present value as of January 1, 2016 by making the following calculation:

$$PV = \$27,355 \times .75131^{*} = \$20,552$$

*Present value of $1: $n = 3, i = 10\%$

2. From Table 4, subtract the two-period PVA factor (1.73554) from the five-period PVA factor (3.79079) and multiply the difference (2.05525) by $10,000 to get $20,552.

Financial Calculators and Excel

As previously mentioned, financial calculators can be used to solve future and present value problems. For example, a Texas Instruments model BA-35 has the following pertinent keys:

N   %I   PV   FV   PMT   CPT

These keys are defined as follows:

N = number of periods
%I = interest rate
PV = present value

FV = future value
PMT = annuity payments
CPT = compute button

Using a calculator:
Enter: N 10 I 10
PMT 200
Output: PV 1,229

Using Excel, enter:
= PV(.10,10,200)
Output: 1,229

To illustrate its use, assume that you need to determine the present value of a 10-period ordinary annuity of $200 using a 10% interest rate. You would enter N 10, %I 10, PMT −200, then press CPT and PV to obtain the answer of $1,229.

Many professionals choose to use spreadsheet software, such as Excel, to solve time value of money problems. These spreadsheets can be used in a variety of ways. A template can be created using the formulas shown in Illustration 6–22 on page 346. An alternative is to use the software's built-in financial functions. For example, Excel has a function called PV that calculates the present value of an ordinary annuity. To use the function, you would select the pull-down menu for "Insert," click on "Function" and choose the category called "Financial." Scroll down to PV and double-click. You will then be asked to input the necessary variables—interest rate, the number of periods, and the payment amount.

In subsequent chapters we illustrate the use of both a calculator and Excel in addition to present value tables to solve present value calculations for selected examples and illustrations.

Solving for Unknown Values in Present Value Situations

LO6–8

In present value problems involving annuities, there are four variables: (1) present value of an ordinary annuity (PVA) or present value of an annuity due (PVAD), (2) the amount of each annuity payment, (3) the number of periods, *n*, and (4) the interest rate, *i*. If you know any three of these, the fourth can be determined.

Illustration 6–15

Determining the Annuity Amount When Other Variables Are Known

Assume that you borrow $700 from a friend and intend to repay the amount in four equal annual installments beginning one year from today. Your friend wishes to be reimbursed for the time value of money at an 8% annual rate. What is the required annual payment that must be made (the annuity amount), to repay the loan in four years?

The following time diagram illustrates the situation:

Determining the unknown annuity amount—ordinary annuity.

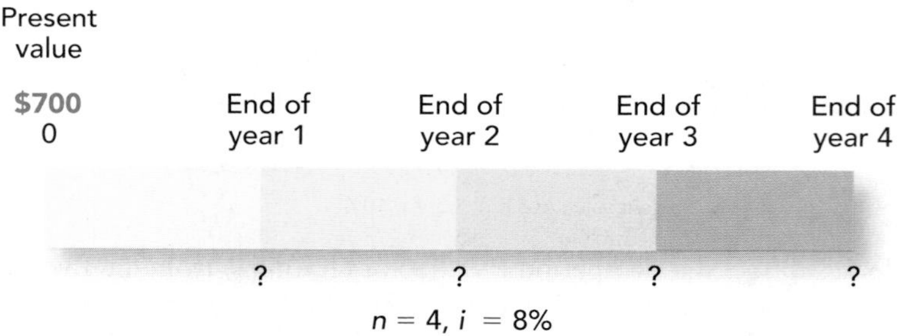

The required payment is the annuity amount that will provide a present value of $700 when using an interest rate of 8%:

The unknown variable is the annuity amount.

$$\$700 \text{ (present value)} = 3.31213^{*} \times \text{annuity amount}$$

Rearranging algebraically, we find that the annuity amount is $211.34.

$$\$700 \text{ (present value)} \div 3.31213^{*} = \$211.34 \text{ (annuity amount)}$$

*Present value of an ordinary annuity of $1: $n = 4$, $i = 8\%$

You would have to make four annual payments of $211.34 to repay the loan. Total payments of $845.36 (4 × $211.34) would include $145.36 in interest ($845.36 − 700.00).

Illustration 6–16

Determining n When Other Variables Are Known

> Assume that you borrow $700 from a friend and intend to repay the amount in equal installments of $100 per year over a period of years. The payments will be made at the end of each year beginning one year from now. Your friend wishes to be reimbursed for the time value of money at a 7% annual rate. How many years would it take before you repaid the loan?

Once again, this is an ordinary annuity situation because the first payment takes place one year from now. The following time diagram illustrates the situation:

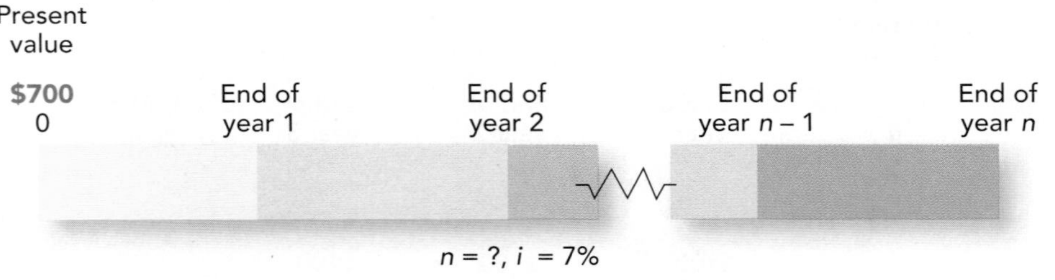

Determining the unknown number of periods—ordinary annuity.

The number of years is the value of n that will provide a present value of $700 when finding the present value of $100 payments using an interest rate of 7%:

$700 (present value) = $100 (annuity amount) × ?*

*Present value of an ordinary annuity of $1: n = ?, i = 7%

The unknown variable is the number of periods.

Rearranging algebraically, we find that the PVA table factor is 7.0.

$700 (present value) ÷ $100 (annuity amount) = 7.0*

*Present value of an ordinary annuity of $1: n = ?, i = 7%

When you consult the PVA table, Table 4, you search the 7% column (i = 7%) for this value and find 7.02358 in row 10. So it would take approximately 10 years to repay the loan in the situation described.

Illustration 6–17

Determining i When Other Variables Are Known

> Suppose that a friend asked to borrow $331 today (present value) and promised to repay you $100 (the annuity amount) at the end of each of the next four years. What is the annual interest rate implicit in this agreement?

FINANCIAL Reporting Case

Q2, p. 323

First of all, we are dealing with an ordinary annuity situation as the payments are at the end of each period. The following time diagram illustrates the situation:

Present value
$331
0
End of year 1 — $100
End of year 2 — $100
End of year 3 — $100
End of year 4 — $100
n = 4, i = ?

Determining the unknown interest rate—ordinary annuity.

The interest rate is the rate that will provide a present value of $331 when finding the present value of the $100 four-year ordinary annuity:

$331 (present value) = $100 (annuity amount) × ?*

*Present value of an ordinary annuity of $1: n = 4, i = ?

The unknown variable is the interest rate.

Rearranging algebraically, we find that the PVA table factor is 3.31.

$331 (present value) ÷ $100 (annuity amount) = 3.31*

*Present value of an ordinary annuity of $1: n = 4, i = ?

When you consult the PVA table, Table 4, you search row four ($n = 4$) for this value and find it in the 8% column. So the effective interest rate is 8%.

Illustration 6–18

Determining i When Other Variables Are Known—Unequal Cash Flows

Suppose that you borrowed $400 from a friend and promised to repay the loan by making three annual payments of $100 at the end of each of the next three years plus a final payment of $200 at the end of year four. What is the interest rate implicit in this agreement?

The following time diagram illustrates the situation:

Determining the unknown interest rate—unequal cash flow.

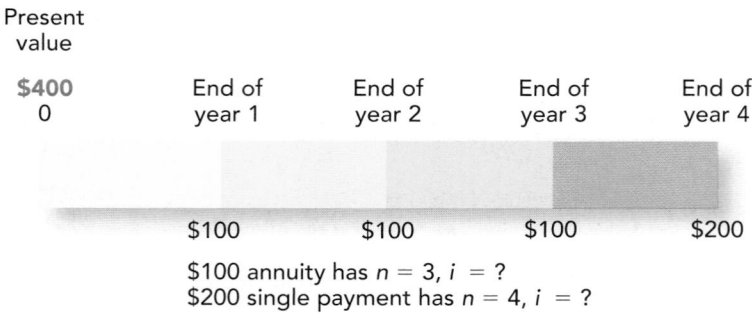

Present value	End of year 1	End of year 2	End of year 3	End of year 4
$400 0				
	$100	$100	$100	$200

$100 annuity has $n = 3$, $i = ?$
$200 single payment has $n = 4$, $i = ?$

The interest rate is the rate that will provide a present value of $400 when finding the present value of the $100 three-year ordinary annuity plus the $200 to be received in four years:

The unknown variable is the interest rate.

$400 (present value) = $100 (annuity amount) × ?* + $200 (single payment) × ?†

*Present value of an ordinary annuity of $1: $n = 3$, $i = ?$
†Present value of $1: $n = 4$, $i = ?$

This equation involves two unknowns and is not as easily solved as the two previous examples. One way to solve the problem is to trial-and-error the answer. For example, if we assumed i to be 9%, the total PV of the payments would be calculated as follows:

PV = $100 (2.53129*) + $200 (.70843†) = $395

*Present value of an ordinary annuity of $1: $n = 3$, $i = 9\%$
†Present value of $1: $n = 4$, $i = 9\%$

Because the present value computed is less than the $400 borrowed, using 9% removes too much interest. Recalculating PV with $i = 8\%$ results in a PV of $405. This indicates that the interest rate implicit in the agreement is between 8% and 9%.

Concept Review Exercise

ANNUITIES

Using the appropriate table, answer each of the following independent questions.

1. What is the future value of an annuity of $2,000 invested at the *end* of each of the next six periods at 8% interest?
2. What is the future value of an annuity of $2,000 invested at the *beginning* of each of the next six periods at 8% interest?
3. What is the present value of an annuity of $6,000 to be received at the *end* of each of the next eight periods assuming an interest rate of 10%?
4. What is the present value of an annuity of $6,000 to be received at the *beginning* of each of the next eight periods assuming an interest rate of 10%?
5. Jane bought a $3,000 audio system and agreed to pay for the purchase in 10 equal annual installments of $408 beginning one year from today. What is the interest rate implicit in this agreement?
6. Jane bought a $3,000 audio system and agreed to pay for the purchase in 10 equal annual installments beginning one year from today. The interest rate is 12%. What is the amount of the annual installment?

7. Jane bought a $3,000 audio system and agreed to pay for the purchase by making nine equal annual installments beginning one year from today plus a lump-sum payment of $1,000 at the end of 10 periods. The interest rate is 10%. What is the required annual installment?
8. Jane bought an audio system and agreed to pay for the purchase by making four equal annual installments of $800 beginning one year from today plus a lump-sum payment of $1,000 at the end of five years. The interest rate is 12%. What was the cost of the audio system? (Hint: What is the present value of the cash payments?)
9. Jane bought an audio system and agreed to pay for the purchase by making five equal annual installments of $1,100 beginning four years from today. The interest rate is 12%. What was the cost of the audio system? (Hint: What is the present value of the cash payments?)

Solution:

1. $\text{FVA} = \$2{,}000 \times 7.3359^{*} = \$14{,}672$

   *Future value of an ordinary annuity of $1: $n = 6$, $i = 8\%$ (from Table 3)

2. $\text{FVAD} = \$2{,}000 \times 7.9228^{*} = \$15{,}846$

   *Future value of an annuity due of $1: $n = 6$, $i = 8\%$ (from Table 5)

3. $\text{PVA} = \$6{,}000 \times 5.33493^{*} = \$32{,}010$

   *Present value of ordinary annuity of $1: $n = 8$, $i = 10\%$ (from Table 4)

4. $\text{PVAD} = \$6{,}000 \times 5.86842^{*} = \$35{,}211$

   *Present value of an annuity due of $1: $n = 8$, $i = 10\%$ (from Table 6)

5. $\dfrac{\$3{,}000}{\$408} = 7.35^{*}$

   *Present value of an ordinary annuity of $1: $n = 10$, $i = ?$ (from Table 4, i approximately 6%)

6. $\text{Each annuity payment} = \dfrac{\$3{,}000}{5.65022^{*}} = \$531$

   *Present value of an ordinary annuity of $1: $n = 10$, $i = 12\%$ (from Table 4)

7. $\text{Each annuity payment} = \dfrac{\$3{,}000 - [\text{PV of } \$1{,}000\ (n = 10,\ i = 10\%)]}{5.75902^{*}}$

   $\text{Each annuity payment} = \dfrac{\$3{,}000 - (\$1{,}000 \times .38554^{\dagger})}{5.75902^{*}}$

   $\text{Each annuity payment} = \dfrac{\$2{,}614}{5.75902^{*}} = \$454$

   *Present value of an ordinary annuity of $1: $n = 9$, $i = 10\%$ (from Table 4)
   †Present value of $1: $n = 10$, $i = 10\%$ (from Table 2)

8. $\text{PV} = \$800 \times 3.03735^{*} + \$1{,}000 \times .56743^{\dagger} = \$2{,}997$

   *Present value of an ordinary annuity of $1: $n = 4$, $i = 12\%$ (from Table 4)
   †Present value of $1: $n = 5$, $i = 12\%$ (from Table 2)

9. $\text{PVA} = \$1{,}100 \times 3.60478^{*} = \$3{,}965$

   *Present value of an ordinary annuity of $1: $n = 5$, $i = 12\%$ (from Table 4)

   This is the present value three years from today (the beginning of the five-year ordinary annuity). This single amount is then reduced to present value as of today by making the following calculation:

   $\text{PV} = \$3{,}965 \times .71178^{\dagger} = \$2{,}822$

   †Present value of $1: $n = 3$, $i = 12\%$, (from Table 2)

Preview of Accounting Applications of Present Value Techniques—Annuities

The time value of money has many applications in accounting. Most of these applications involve the concept of present value. Because financial instruments typically specify equal periodic payments, these applications quite often involve annuity situations. For example, let's consider one accounting situation using both an ordinary annuity and the present value of a single amount (long-term bonds), one using an annuity due (long-term leases), and a third using a deferred annuity (pension obligations). LO6–9

Valuation of Long-Term Bonds

FINANCIAL Reporting Case

Q3, p. 323

You will learn in Chapter 14 that a long-term bond usually requires the issuing (borrowing) company to repay a specified amount at maturity and make periodic stated interest payments over the life of the bond. The *stated* interest payments are equal to the contractual stated rate multiplied by the face value of the bonds. At the date the bonds are issued (sold), the marketplace will determine the price of the bonds based on the *market* rate of interest for investments with similar characteristics. The market rate at date of issuance may not equal the bonds' stated rate in which case the price of the bonds (the amount the issuing company actually is borrowing) will not equal the bonds' face value. Bonds issued at more than face value are said to be issued at a premium, while bonds issued at less than face value are said to be issued at a discount. Consider the example in Illustration 6–19.

Illustration 6–19

Valuing a Long-term Bond Liability

On June 30, 2016, Fumatsu Electric issued 10% stated rate bonds with a face amount of $200 million. The bonds mature on June 30, 2036 (20 years). The market rate of interest for similar issues was 12%. Interest is paid semiannually (5%) on June 30 and December 31, beginning December 31, 2016. The interest payment is $10 million (5% × $200 million). What was the price of the bond issue? What amount of interest expense will Fumatsu record for the bonds in 2016?

To determine the price of the bonds, we calculate the present value of the 40-period annuity (40 semiannual interest payments of $10 million) and the lump-sum payment of $200 million paid at maturity using the semiannual market rate of interest of 6%. In equation form,

PVA = $10 million (annuity amount) × 15.04630* =	$150,463,000
PV = $200 million (lump-sum) × .09722† =	19,444,000
Price of the bond issue =	$169,907,000

*Present value of an ordinary annuity of $1: n = 40, i = 6%
†Present value of $1: n = 40, i = 6%

The bonds will sell for $169,907,000, which represents a discount of $30,093,000 ($200,000,000 − 169,907,000). The discount results from the difference between the semiannual stated rate of 5% and the market rate of 6%. Fumatsu records a $169,907,000 increase in cash and a corresponding liability for bonds payable.

Interest expense for the first six months is determined by multiplying the carrying value (book value) of the bonds ($169,907,000) by the semiannual effective rate (6%) as follows:

$169,907,000 × 6% = $10,194,420

The difference between interest expense ($10,194,420) and interest paid ($10,000,000) increases the carrying value of the bond liability. Interest for the second six months of the bond's life is determined by multiplying the new carrying value by the 6% semiannual effective rate.[9]

We discuss the specific accounts used to record these transactions in Chapters 12 and 14.

Valuation of Long-Term Leases

Companies frequently acquire the use of assets by leasing rather than purchasing them. Leases usually require the payment of fixed amounts at regular intervals over the life of the lease. You will learn in Chapter 15 that certain leases are treated in a manner similar to an installment purchase by the lessee. In other words, the lessee records an asset and corresponding lease liability at the present value of the lease payments. Consider the example in Illustration 6–20.

Leases require the recording of an asset and corresponding liability at the present value of future lease payments.

Once again, by computing the present value of the lease payments, we remove the portion of the payments that represents interest, leaving the portion that represents payment for the asset itself. Because the first payment is due immediately, as is common for leases, this is an annuity due situation. In equation form:

PVAD = $10,000 (annuity amount) × 9.98474* = $99,847

*Present value of an annuity due of $1: n = 25, i = 10%

[9]In Chapters 12 and 14 we refer to the process of determining interest as the effective interest rate times the loan balance as the *effective interest method*.

Illustration 6–20
Valuing a Long-Term Lease Liability

On January 1, 2016, the Stridewell Wholesale Shoe Company signed a 25-year lease agreement for an office building. Terms of the lease call for Stridewell to make annual lease payments of $10,000 at the beginning of each year, with the first payment due on January 1, 2016. Assuming an interest rate of 10% properly reflects the time value of money in this situation, how should Stridewell value the asset acquired and the corresponding lease liability?

Stridewell initially will value the leased asset and corresponding lease liability at $99,847.

Journal entry at the inception of a lease.

Leased office building	99,847	
Lease payable		99,847

The difference between this amount and total future cash payments of $250,000 ($10,000 × 25) represents the interest that is implicit in this agreement. That difference is recorded as interest over the life of the lease.

Valuation of Pension Obligations

Pension plans are important compensation vehicles used by many U.S. companies. These plans are essentially forms of deferred compensation as the pension benefits are paid to employees after they retire. You will learn in Chapter 17 that some pension plans create obligations during employees' service periods that must be paid during their retirement periods. These obligations are funded during the employment period. This means companies contribute cash to pension funds annually with the intention of accumulating sufficient funds to pay employees the retirement benefits they have earned. The amounts contributed are determined using estimates of retirement benefits. The actual amounts paid to employees during retirement depend on many factors including future compensation levels and length of life. Consider Illustration 6–21.

Illustration 6–21
Valuing a Pension Obligation

On January 1, 2016, the Stridewell Wholesale Shoe Company hired Sammy Sossa. Sammy is expected to work for 25 years before retirement on December 31, 2040. Annual retirement payments will be paid at the end of each year during his retirement period, expected to be 20 years. The first payment will be on December 31, 2041. During 2016 Sammy earned an annual retirement benefit estimated to be $2,000 per year. The company plans to contribute cash to a pension fund that will accumulate to an amount sufficient to pay Sammy this benefit. Assuming that Stridewell anticipates earning 6% on all funds invested in the pension plan, how much would the company have to contribute at the end of 2016 to pay for pension benefits earned in 2016?

To determine the required contribution, we calculate the present value on December 31, 2016, of the deferred annuity of $2,000 that begins on December 31, 2041, and is expected to end on December 31, 2060.

The following time diagram depicts this situation:

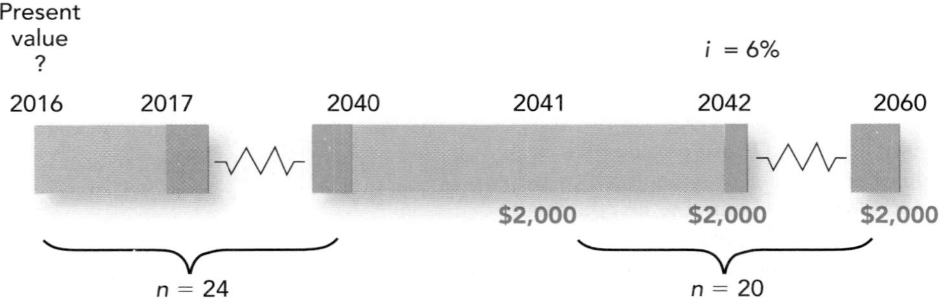

We can calculate the present value of the annuity using a two-step process. The first step computes the present value of the annuity as of December 31, 2040, by multiplying the annuity amount by the 20-period ordinary annuity factor:

$$PVA = \$2{,}000 \text{ (annuity amount)} \times 11.46992^{*} = \$22{,}940$$

*Present value of an ordinary annuity of $1: $n = 20$, $i = 6\%$

This is the present value as of December 31, 2040. This single amount is then reduced to present value as of December 31, 2016, by a second calculation:

$$PV = \$22{,}940 \text{ (future amount)} \times .24698^{*} = \$5{,}666$$

*Present value of $1: $n = 24$, $i = 6\%$

Stridewell would have to contribute $5,666 at the end of 2016 to fund the estimated pension benefits earned by its employee in 2016. Viewed in reverse, $5,666 invested now at 6% will accumulate a fund balance of $22,940 at December 31, 2040. If the fund balance remains invested at 6%, $2,000 can be withdrawn each year for 20 years before the fund is depleted.

Among the other situations you'll encounter using present value techniques are valuing notes (Chapters 10 and 14) and other postretirement benefits (Chapter 17).

Summary of Time Value of Money Concepts

Illustration 6–22 summarizes the time value of money concepts discussed in this chapter.

Illustration 6–22

Summary of Time Value of Money Concepts

Concept	Summary	Formula	Table
Future value (FV) of $1	The amount of money that a dollar will grow to at some point in the future.	$FV = \$1\,(1 + i)^n$	1
Present value (PV) of $1	The amount of money today that is equivalent to a given amount to be received or paid in the future.	$PV = \dfrac{\$1}{(1 + i)^n}$	2
Future value of an ordinary annuity (FVA) of $1	The future value of a series of equal-sized cash flows with the first payment taking place at the end of the first compounding period.	$FVA = \dfrac{(1 + i)^n - 1}{i}$	3
Present value of an ordinary annuity (PVA) of $1	The present value of a series of equal-sized cash flows with the first payment taking place at the end of the first compounding period.	$PVA = \dfrac{1 - \dfrac{1}{(1 + i)^n}}{i}$	4
Future value of an annuity due (FVAD) of $1	The future value of a series of equal-sized cash flows with the first payment taking place at the beginning of the annuity period.	$FVAD = \left[\dfrac{(1 + i)^n - 1}{i}\right] \times (1 + i)$	5
Present value of an annuity due (PVAD) of $1	The present value of a series of equal-sized cash flows with the first payment taking place at the beginning of the annuity period.	$PVAD = PVA = \left[\dfrac{1 - \dfrac{1}{(1 + i)^n}}{i}\right] \times (1 + i)$	6

Financial Reporting Case Solution

1. **Why was Quezada to receive $152 million rather than the $338 million lottery prize?** *(p. 336)* Quezada chose to receive his lottery winnings in one lump payment immediately rather than in 30 installment payments. The state calculates the present value of the payments, withholds the necessary federal and state income tax, and pays Quezada the remainder.
2. **What interest rate did the state of New Jersey use to calculate the $152 million lump-sum payment** *(p. 341)* Assuming equal annual installment payments beginning immediately, the amount of the payments is determined by dividing $338 million by 30 periods:

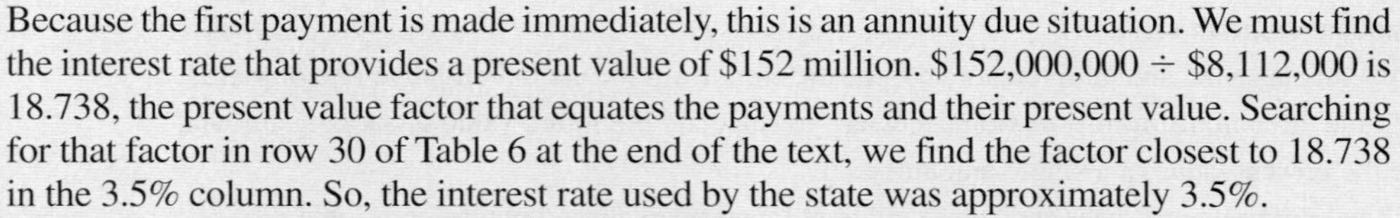

$338 million ÷ 30 =	$11,266,667
Less: 28% income tax	(3,154,667)
Net-of-tax payment	$ 8,112,000

Because the first payment is made immediately, this is an annuity due situation. We must find the interest rate that provides a present value of $152 million. $152,000,000 ÷ $8,112,000 is 18.738, the present value factor that equates the payments and their present value. Searching for that factor in row 30 of Table 6 at the end of the text, we find the factor closest to 18.738 in the 3.5% column. So, the interest rate used by the state was approximately 3.5%.

3. **What are some of the accounting applications that incorporate the time value of money into valuation?** *(p. 344)* Accounting applications that incorporate the time value of money techniques into valuation include the valuation of long-term notes receivable and various long-term liabilities that include bonds, notes, leases, pension obligations, and other postretirement benefits. We study these in detail in later chapters. ●

The Bottom Line

- **LO6–1** A dollar today is worth more than a dollar to be received in the future. The difference between the present value of cash flows and their future value represents the time value of money. Interest is the rent paid for the use of money over time. (*p. 324*)
- **LO6–2** The future value of a single amount is the amount of money that a dollar will grow to at some point in the future. It is computed by *multiplying* the single amount by $(1 + i)^n$, where i is the interest rate and n the number of compounding periods. The Future Value of $1 table allows for the calculation of future value for any single amount by providing the factors for various combinations of i and n. (*p. 325*)
- **LO6–3** The present value of a single amount is the amount of money today that is equivalent to a given amount to be received or paid in the future. It is computed by *dividing* the future amount by $(1 + i)^n$. The Present Value of $1 table simplifies the calculation of the present value of any future amount. (*p. 326*)
- **LO6–4** There are four variables in the process of adjusting single cash flow amounts for the time value of money: present value (PV), future value (FV), i and n. If you know any three of these, the fourth can be computed easily. (*p. 327*)
- **LO6–5** An annuity is a series of equal-sized cash flows occurring over equal intervals of time. An ordinary annuity exists when the cash flows occur at the end of each period. An annuity due exists when the cash flows occur at the beginning of each period. (*p. 333*)
- **LO6–6** The future value of an ordinary annuity (FVA) is the future value of a series of equal-sized, cash flows with the first payment taking place at the end of the first compounding period. The last payment will not earn any interest since it is made at the end of the annuity period. The future value of an annuity due (FVAD) is the future value of a series of equal-sized cash flows with the first payment taking place at the beginning of the annuity period (the beginning of the first compounding period). (*p. 334*)
- **LO6–7** The present value of an ordinary annuity (PVA) is the present value of a series of equal-sized cash flows with the first payment taking place at the end of the first compounding period. The present value of an annuity due (PVAD) is the present value of a series of equal-sized cash flows with the first payment taking

place at the beginning of the annuity period. The present value of a deferred annuity is the present value of a series of equal-sized cash flows with the first payment taking place more than one time period after the date of the agreement. (*p. 335*)

● LO6–8 In present value problems involving annuities, there are four variables: PVA or PVAD, the annuity amount, the number of compounding periods (n) and the interest rate (i). If you know any three of these, you can determine the fourth. (*p. 340*)

● LO6–9 Most accounting applications of the time value of money involve the present values of annuities. The initial valuation of long-term bonds is determined by calculating the present value of the periodic stated interest payments and the present value of the lump-sum payment made at maturity. Certain leases require the lessee to compute the present value of future lease payments to value the leased asset and corresponding lease obligation. Also, pension plans require the payment of deferred annuities to retirees. (*p. 343*) ●

Questions For Review of Key Topics

Q 6–1 Define interest.

Q 6–2 Explain compound interest.

Q 6–3 What would cause the annual interest rate to be different from the annual effective rate or yield?

Q 6–4 Identify the three items of information necessary to calculate the future value of a single amount.

Q 6–5 Define the present value of a single amount.

Q 6–6 Explain the difference between monetary and nonmonetary assets and liabilities.

Q 6–7 What is an annuity?

Q 6–8 Explain the difference between an ordinary annuity and an annuity due.

Q 6–9 Explain the relationship between Table 2, Present Value of $1, and Table 4, Present Value of an Ordinary Annuity of $1.

Q 6–10 Prepare a time diagram for the present value of a four-year ordinary annuity of $200. Assume an interest rate of 10% per year.

Q 6–11 Prepare a time diagram for the present value of a four-year annuity due of $200. Assume an interest rate of 10% per year.

Q 6–12 What is a deferred annuity?

Q 6–13 Assume that you borrowed $500 from a friend and promised to repay the loan in five equal annual installments beginning one year from today. Your friend wants to be reimbursed for the time value of money at an 8% annual rate. Explain how you would compute the required annual payment.

Q 6–14 Compute the required annual payment in Question 6–13.

Q 6–15 Explain how the time value of money concept is incorporated into the valuation of certain leases.

Brief Exercises

BE 6–1
Simple versus compound interest
● LO6–1

Fran Smith has two investment opportunities. The interest rate for both investments is 8%. Interest on the first investment will compound annually while interest on the second will compound quarterly. Which investment opportunity should Fran choose? Why?

BE 6–2
Future value; single amount
● LO6–2

Bill O'Brien would like to take his wife, Mary, on a trip three years from now to Europe to celebrate their 40th anniversary. He has just received a $20,000 inheritance from an uncle and intends to invest it for the trip. Bill estimates the trip will cost $23,500 and he believes he can earn 5% interest, compounded annually, on his investment. Will he be able to pay for the trip with the accumulated investment amount?

BE 6–3
Future value; solving for unknown; single amount
● LO6–4

Refer to the situation described in BE 6–2. Assume that the trip will cost $26,600. What interest rate, compounded annually, must Bill earn to accumulate enough to pay for the trip?

BE 6–4
Present value; single amount
● LO6–3

John has an investment opportunity that promises to pay him $16,000 in four years. He could earn a 6% annual return investing his money elsewhere. What is the maximum amount he would be willing to invest in this opportunity?

BE 6–5
Present value; solving for unknown; single amount
● LO6–4

Refer to the situation described in BE 6–4. Suppose the opportunity requires John to invest $13,200 today. What is the interest rate John would earn on this investment?

BE 6–6
Future value; ordinary annuity
● LO6–6

Leslie McCormack is in the spring quarter of her freshman year of college. She and her friends already are planning a trip to Europe after graduation in a little over three years. Leslie would like to contribute to a savings account over the next three years in order to accumulate enough money to take the trip. Assuming an interest rate of 4%, compounded quarterly, how much will she accumulate in three years by depositing $500 at the *end* of each of the next 12 quarters, beginning three months from now?

BE 6–7
Future value; annuity due
● LO6–6

Refer to the situation described in BE 6–6. How much will Leslie accumulate in three years by depositing $500 at the *beginning* of each of the next 12 quarters?

BE 6–8
Present value; ordinary annuity
● LO6–7

Canliss Mining Company borrowed money from a local bank. The note the company signed requires five annual installment payments of $10,000 beginning one year from today. The interest rate on the note is 7%. What amount did Canliss borrow?

BE 6–9
Present value; annuity due
● LO6–7

Refer to the situation described in BE 6–8. What amount did Canliss borrow assuming that the first $10,000 payment was due immediately?

BE 6–10
Deferred annuity
● LO6–7

Refer to the situation described in BE 6–8. What amount did Canliss borrow assuming that the first of the five annual $10,000 payments was not due for three years?

BE 6–11
Solve for unknown; annuity
● LO6–8

Kingsley Toyota borrowed $100,000 from a local bank. The loan requires Kingsley to pay 10 equal annual installments beginning one year from today. Assuming an interest rate of 8%, what is the amount of each annual installment payment?

BE 6–12
Price of a bond
● LO6–9

On December 31, 2016, Interlink Communications issued 6% stated rate bonds with a face amount of $100 million. The bonds mature on December 31, 2046. Interest is payable annually on each December 31, beginning in 2017. Determine the price of the bonds on December 31, 2016, assuming that the market rate of interest for similar bonds was 7%.

BE 6–13
Lease payment
● LO6–9

On September 30, 2016, Ferguson Imports leased a warehouse. Terms of the lease require Ferguson to make 10 annual lease payments of $55,000 with the first payment due immediately. Accounting standards require the company to record a lease liability when recording this type of lease. Assuming an 8% interest rate, at what amount should Ferguson record the lease liability on September 30, 2016, before the first payment is made?

Exercises

An alternate exercise and problem set is available in the Connect library.

E 6–1
Future value; single amount
● LO6–2

Determine the future value of the following single amounts:

	Invested Amount	Interest Rate	No. of Periods
1.	$15,000	6%	12
2.	20,000	8	10
3.	30,000	12	20
4.	50,000	4	12

E 6–2
Future value; single amounts
● LO6–2

Determine the future value of $10,000 under each of the following sets of assumptions:

	Annual Rate	Period Invested	Interest Compounded
1.	10%	10 years	Semiannually
2.	12	5 years	Quarterly
3.	24	30 months	Monthly

E 6–3
Present value; single amounts
● LO6–3

Determine the present value of the following single amounts:

	Future Amount	Interest Rate	No. of Periods
1.	$20,000	7%	10
2.	14,000	8	12
3.	25,000	12	20
4.	40,000	10	8

E 6–4
Present value; multiple, unequal amounts
● LO6–3

Determine the combined present value as of December 31, 2016, of the following four payments to be received at the end of each of the designated years, assuming an annual interest rate of 8%.

Payment	Year Received
$5,000	2017
6,000	2018
8,000	2020
9,000	2022

E 6–5
Noninterest-bearing note; single payment
● LO6–3

The Field Detergent Company sold merchandise to the Abel Company on June 30, 2016. Payment was made in the form of a noninterest-bearing note requiring Abel to pay $85,000 on June 30, 2018. Assume that a 10% interest rate properly reflects the time value of money in this situation.

Required:
Calculate the amount at which Field should record the note receivable and corresponding sales revenue on June 30, 2016.

E 6–6
Solving for unknowns; single amounts
● LO6–4

For each of the following situations involving single amounts, solve for the unknown (?). Assume that interest is compounded annually. (i = interest rate, and n = number of years)

	Present Value	Future Value	i	n
1.	?	$ 40,000	10%	5
2.	$36,289	65,000	?	10
3.	15,884	40,000	8	?
4.	46,651	100,000	?	8
5.	15,376	?	7	20

E 6–7
Future value; annuities
● LO6–6

Wiseman Video plans to make four annual deposits of $2,000 each to a special building fund. The fund's assets will be invested in mortgage instruments expected to pay interest at 12% on the fund's balance. Using the appropriate annuity table, determine how much will be accumulated in the fund on December 31, 2019, under each of the following situations:

1. The first deposit is made on December 31, 2016, and interest is compounded annually.
2. The first deposit is made on December 31, 2015, and interest is compounded annually.
3. The first deposit is made on December 31, 2015, and interest is compounded quarterly.
4. The first deposit is made on December 31, 2015, interest is compounded annually, *and* interest earned is withdrawn at the end of each year.

E 6–8
Present value; annuities
● LO6–7

Using the appropriate present value table and assuming a 12% annual interest rate, determine the present value on December 31, 2016, of a five-period annual annuity of $5,000 under each of the following situations:

1. The first payment is received on December 31, 2017, and interest is compounded annually.
2. The first payment is received on December 31, 2016, and interest is compounded annually.
3. The first payment is received on December 31, 2017, and interest is compounded quarterly.

E 6–9
Solving for unknowns; annuities
● LO6–8

For each of the following situations involving annuities, solve for the unknown (?). Assume that interest is compounded annually and that all annuity amounts are received at the *end* of each period. (i = interest rate, and n = number of years)

	Present Value	Annuity Amount	*i*	*n*
1.	?	$ 3,000	8%	5
2.	$242,980	75,000	?	4
3.	161,214	20,000	9	?
4.	500,000	80,518	?	8
5.	250,000	?	10	4

E 6–10
Future value; solving for annuities and single amount
● LO6–4, LO6–8

John Rider wants to accumulate $100,000 to be used for his daughter's college education. He would like to have the amount available on December 31, 2021. Assume that the funds will accumulate in a certificate of deposit paying 8% interest compounded annually.

Required:
Answer each of the following independent questions.
1. If John were to deposit a single amount, how much would he have to invest on December 31, 2016?
2. If John were to make five equal deposits on each December 31, beginning on December 31, 2017, what is the required amount of each deposit?
3. If John were to make five equal deposits on each December 31, beginning on December 31, 2016, what is the required amount of each deposit?

E 6–11
Future and present value
● LO6–3, LO6–6, LO6–7

Answer each of the following independent questions.
1. Alex Meir recently won a lottery and has the option of receiving one of the following three prizes: (1) $64,000 cash immediately, (2) $20,000 cash immediately and a six-period annuity of $8,000 beginning one year from today, or (3) a six-period annuity of $13,000 beginning one year from today. Assuming an interest rate of 6%, which option should Alex choose?
2. The Weimer Corporation wants to accumulate a sum of money to repay certain debts due on December 31, 2025. Weimer will make annual deposits of $100,000 into a special bank account at the end of each of 10 years beginning December 31, 2016. Assuming that the bank account pays 7% interest compounded annually, what will be the fund balance after the last payment is made on December 31, 2025?

E 6–12
Deferred annuities
● LO6–7

Lincoln Company purchased merchandise from Grandville Corp. on September 30, 2016. Payment was made in the form of a noninterest-bearing note requiring Lincoln to make six annual payments of $5,000 on each September 30, beginning on September 30, 2019.

Required:
Calculate the amount at which Lincoln should record the note payable and corresponding purchases on September 30, 2016, assuming that an interest rate of 10% properly reflects the time value of money in this situation.

E 6–13
Solving for unknown annuity payment
● LO6–8

Don James purchased a new automobile for $20,000. Don made a cash down payment of $5,000 and agreed to pay the remaining balance in 30 monthly installments, beginning one month from the date of purchase. Financing is available at a 24% *annual* interest rate.

Required:
Calculate the amount of the required monthly payment.

E 6–14
Solving for unknown interest rate
● LO6–8

Lang Warehouses borrowed $100,000 from a bank and signed a note requiring 20 annual payments of $13,388 beginning one year from the date of the agreement.

Required:
Determine the interest rate implicit in this agreement.

E 6–15
Solving for unknown annuity amount
● LO6–8

Sandy Kupchack just graduated from State University with a bachelor's degree in history. During her four years at the university, Sandy accumulated $12,000 in student loans. She asks for your help in determining the amount of the *quarterly* loan payment. She tells you that the loan must be paid back in five years and that the annual interest rate is 8%. Payments begin in three months.

Required:
Determine Sandy's quarterly loan payment.

E 6–16
Deferred annuities; solving for annuity amount
● LO6–7, LO6–8

On April 1, 2016, John Vaughn purchased appliances from the Acme Appliance Company for $1,200. In order to increase sales, Acme allows customers to pay in installments and will defer any payments for six months. John will make 18 equal monthly payments, beginning October 1, 2016. The annual interest rate implicit in this agreement is 24%.

Required:
Calculate the monthly payment necessary for John to pay for his purchases.

E 6–17
Price of a bond
● LO6–9

On September 30, 2016, the San Fillipo Corporation issued 8% stated rate bonds with a face amount of $300 million. The bonds mature on September 30, 2036 (20 years). The market rate of interest for similar bonds was 10%. Interest is paid semiannually on March 31 and September 30.

Required:
Determine the price of the bonds on September 30, 2016.

E 6–18
Price of a bond; interest expense
● LO6–9

On June 30, 2016, Singleton Computers issued 6% stated rate bonds with a face amount of $200 million. The bonds mature on June 30, 2031 (15 years). The market rate of interest for similar bond issues was 5% (2.5% semiannual rate). Interest is paid semiannually (3%) on June 30 and December 31, beginning on December 31, 2016.

Required:
1. Determine the price of the bonds on June 30, 2016.
2. Calculate the interest expense Singleton reports in 2016 for these bonds.

E 6–19
Lease payments
● LO6–9

On June 30, 2016, Fly-By-Night Airlines leased a jumbo jet from Boeing Corporation. The terms of the lease require Fly-By-Night to make 20 annual payments of $400,000 on each June 30. Generally accepted accounting principles require this lease to be recorded as a liability for the present value of scheduled payments. Assume that a 7% interest rate properly reflects the time value of money in this situation.

Required:
1. At what amount should Fly-By-Night record the lease liability on June 30, 2016, assuming that the first payment will be made on June 30, 2017?
2. At what amount should Fly-By-Night record the lease liability on June 30, 2016, *before* any payments are made, assuming that the first payment will be made on June 30, 2016?

E 6–20
Lease payments; solve for unknown interest rate
● LO6–8, LO6–9

On March 31, 2016, Southwest Gas leased equipment from a supplier and agreed to pay $200,000 annually for 20 years beginning March 31, 2017. Generally accepted accounting principles require that a liability be recorded for this lease agreement for the present value of scheduled payments. Accordingly, at inception of the lease, Southwest recorded a $2,293,984 lease liability.

Required:
Determine the interest rate implicit in the lease agreement.

E 6–21
Concepts; terminology
● LO6–1 through LO6–3, LO6–5

Listed below are several terms and phrases associated with concepts discussed in the chapter. Pair each item from List A with the item from List B (by letter) that is most appropriately associated with it.

List A	List B
____ 1. Interest	a. First cash flow occurs one period after agreement begins.
____ 2. Monetary asset	b. The rate at which money will actually grow during a year.
____ 3. Compound interest	c. First cash flow occurs on the first day of the agreement.
____ 4. Simple interest	d. The amount of money that a dollar will grow to.
____ 5. Annuity	e. Amount of money paid/received in excess of amount borrowed/lent.
____ 6. Present value of a single amount	
____ 7. Annuity due	f. Obligation to pay a sum of cash, the amount of which is fixed.
____ 8. Future value of a single amount	g. Money can be invested today and grow to a larger amount.
____ 9. Ordinary annuity	h. No fixed dollar amount attached.
____10. Effective rate or yield	i. Computed by multiplying an invested amount by the interest rate.
____11. Nonmonetary asset	j. Interest calculated on invested amount plus accumulated interest.
____12. Time value of money	k. A series of equal-sized cash flows.
____13. Monetary liability	l. Amount of money required today that is equivalent to a given future amount.
	m. Claim to receive a fixed amount of money.

CPA and CMA Review Questions

CPA Exam Questions

KAPLAN CPA REVIEW

● LO6–3

The following questions are used in the Kaplan CPA Review Course to study the time value of money while preparing for the CPA examination. Determine the response that best completes the statements or questions.

1. An investment product promises to pay $25,458 at the end of nine years. If an investor feels this investment should produce a rate of return of 14 percent, compounded annually, what's the most the investor should be willing to pay for the investment?

n	PV of $1 @ 14%
8	0.3506
9	0.3075
10	0.2697

a. $6,866
b. $7,828
c. $8,926
d. $9,426

● LO6–7

2. On January 1, 2016, Ott Company sold goods to Fox Company. Fox signed a noninterest-bearing note requiring payment of $60,000 annually for seven years. The first payment was made on January 1, 2016. The prevailing rate of interest for this type of note at date of issuance was 10%. Information on present value factors is as follows:

Periods	Present Value of 1 at 10%	Present Value of Ordinary Annuity of 1 at 10%
6	.56	4.36
7	.51	4.87

Ott should record sales revenue in January 2016 of

a. $214,200
b. $261,600
c. $292,600
d. $321,600

● LO6–7

3. An annuity will pay eight annual payments of $100, with the first payment to be received one year from now. If the interest rate is 12 percent per year, what is the present value of this annuity? Use the appropriate table located at the end of the textbook to solve this problem.

a. $497
b. $556
c. $801
d. $897

● LO6–7

4. An annuity will pay four annual payments of $100, with the first payment to be received three years from now. If the interest rate is 12 percent per year, what is the present value of this annuity? Use the appropriate table located at the end of the textbook to solve this problem.

a. $181
b. $242
c. $304
d. $400

● LO6–7

5. Justin Banks just won the lottery and is trying to decide between the annual cash flow payment option of $100,000 per year for 15 years beginning today, and the lump-sum option. Justin can earn 8 percent investing his money. At what lump-sum payment amount would he be indifferent between the two alternatives? Use the appropriate table located at the end of the textbook to solve this problem.

a. $824,424
b. $855,948
c. $890,378
d. $924,424

● LO6–9

6. An investor purchases a 10-year, $1,000 par value bond that pays *annual* interest of $100. If the market rate of interest is 12 percent, what is the current market value of the bond?

a. $887
b. $950
c. $1,000
d. $1,100

● LO6–8

7. You borrow $15,000 to buy a car. The loan is to be paid off in monthly installments over five years at 12 percent interest annually. The first payment is due one month from today. If the present value of an ordinary annuity of $1 for 5 years @12% with monthly compounding is 44.955, what is the amount of each monthly payment?

a. $334
b. $456
c. $546
d. $680

CMA Exam Questions

The following questions dealing with the time value of money are adapted from questions that previously appeared on Certified Management Accountant (CMA) examinations. The CMA designation sponsored by the Institute of Management Accountants (www.imanet.org) provides members with an objective measure of knowledge and competence in the field of management accounting. Determine the response that best completes the statements or questions.

● LO6–2

1. Janet Taylor Casual Wear has $75,000 in a bank account as of December 31, 2016. If the company plans on depositing $4,000 in the account at the end of each of the next 3 years (2017, 2018, and 2019) and all amounts in the account earn 8% per year, what will the account balance be at December 31, 2019? Ignore the effect of income taxes.

	8% Interest Rate Factors	
Period	Future Value of an Amount of $1	Future Value of an Ordinary Annuity of $1
1	1.08	1.00
2	1.17	2.08
3	1.26	3.25
4	1.36	4.51

   a. $ 87,000
   b. $ 88,000
   c. $ 96,070
   d. $107,500

● LO6–5, LO6–9

2. Essex Corporation is evaluating a lease that takes effect on March 1. The company must make eight equal payments, with the first payment due on March 1. The concept most relevant to the evaluation of the lease is
   a. The present value of an annuity due.
   b. The present value of an ordinary annuity.
   c. The future value of an annuity due.
   d. The future value of an ordinary annuity.

Problems

An alternate exercise and problem set is available in the Connect library.

P 6–1
Analysis of alternatives
● LO6–3, LO6–7

Esquire Company needs to acquire a molding machine to be used in its manufacturing process. Two types of machines that would be appropriate are presently on the market. The company has determined the following:

Machine A could be purchased for $48,000. It will last 10 years with annual maintenance costs of $1,000 per year. After 10 years the machine can be sold for $5,000.

Machine B could be purchased for $40,000. It also will last 10 years and will require maintenance costs of $4,000 in year three, $5,000 in year six, and $6,000 in year eight. After 10 years, the machine will have no salvage value.

Required:

Determine which machine Esquire should purchase. Assume an interest rate of 8% properly reflects the time value of money in this situation and that maintenance costs are paid at the end of each year. Ignore income tax considerations.

P 6–2
Present and future value
● LO6–6, LO6–7, LO6–9

Johnstone Company is facing several decisions regarding investing and financing activities. Address each decision independently.

1. On June 30, 2016, the Johnstone Company purchased equipment from Genovese Corp. Johnstone agreed to pay Genovese $10,000 on the purchase date and the balance in five annual installments of $8,000 on each June 30 beginning June 30, 2017. Assuming that an interest rate of 10% properly reflects the time value of money in this situation, at what amount should Johnstone value the equipment?
2. Johnstone needs to accumulate sufficient funds to pay a $400,000 debt that comes due on December 31, 2021. The company will accumulate the funds by making five equal annual deposits to an account paying 6% interest compounded annually. Determine the required annual deposit if the first deposit is made on December 31, 2016.
3. On January 1, 2016, Johnstone leased an office building. Terms of the lease require Johnstone to make 20 annual lease payments of $120,000 beginning on January 1, 2016. A 10% interest rate is implicit in the lease agreement. At what amount should Johnstone record the lease liability on January 1, 2016, *before* any lease payments are made?

P 6–3
Analysis of alternatives
● LO6–3, LO6–7

Harding Company is in the process of purchasing several large pieces of equipment from Danning Machine Corporation. Several financing alternatives have been offered by Danning:

1. Pay $1,000,000 in cash immediately.
2. Pay $420,000 immediately and the remainder in 10 annual installments of $80,000, with the first installment due in one year.
3. Make 10 annual installments of $135,000 with the first payment due immediately.
4. Make one lump-sum payment of $1,500,000 five years from date of purchase.

Required:
Determine the best alternative for Harding, assuming that Harding can borrow funds at an 8% interest rate.

P 6–4
Investment analysis
● LO6–3, LO6–7

John Wiggins is contemplating the purchase of a small restaurant. The purchase price listed by the seller is $800,000. John has used past financial information to estimate that the net cash flows (cash inflows less cash outflows) generated by the restaurant would be as follows:

Years	Amount
1–6	$80,000
7	70,000
8	60,000
9	50,000
10	40,000

If purchased, the restaurant would be held for 10 years and then sold for an estimated $700,000.

Required:
Assuming that John desires a 10% rate of return on this investment, should the restaurant be purchased? (Assume that all cash flows occur at the end of the year.)

P 6–5
Investment decision; varying rates
● LO6–3, LO6–7

John and Sally Claussen are contemplating the purchase of a hardware store from John Duggan. The Claussens anticipate that the store will generate cash flows of $70,000 per year for 20 years. At the end of 20 years, they intend to sell the store for an estimated $400,000. The Claussens will finance the investment with a variable rate mortgage. Interest rates will increase twice during the 20-year life of the mortgage. Accordingly, the Claussens' desired rate of return on this investment varies as follows:

Years 1–5	8%
Years 6–10	10%
Years 11–20	12%

Required:
What is the maximum amount the Claussens should pay John Duggan for the hardware store? (Assume that all cash flows occur at the end of the year.)

P 6–6
Solving for unknowns
● LO6–3, LO6–8

The following situations should be considered independently.

1. John Jamison wants to accumulate $60,000 for a down payment on a small business. He will invest $30,000 today in a bank account paying 8% interest compounded annually. Approximately how long will it take John to reach his goal?
2. The Jasmine Tea Company purchased merchandise from a supplier for $28,700. Payment was a noninterest-bearing note requiring Jasmine to make five annual payments of $7,000 beginning one year from the date of purchase. What is the interest rate implicit in this agreement?
3. Sam Robinson borrowed $10,000 from a friend and promised to pay the loan in 10 equal annual installments beginning one year from the date of the loan. Sam's friend would like to be reimbursed for the time value of money at a 9% annual rate. What is the annual payment Sam must make to pay back his friend?

P 6–7
Solving for unknowns
● LO6–8

Lowlife Company defaulted on a $250,000 loan that was due on December 31, 2016. The bank has agreed to allow Lowlife to repay the $250,000 by making a series of equal annual payments beginning on December 31, 2017.

Required:

1. Calculate the required annual payment if the bank's interest rate is 10% and four payments are to be made.
2. Calculate the required annual payment if the bank's interest rate is 8% and five payments are to be made.
3. If the bank's interest rate is 10%, how many annual payments of $51,351 would be required to repay the debt?
4. If three payments of $104,087 are to be made, what interest rate is the bank charging Lowlife?

P 6–8
Deferred annuities
● LO6–7

On January 1, 2016, the Montgomery Company agreed to purchase a building by making six payments. The first three are to be $25,000 each, and will be paid on December 31, 2016, 2017, and 2018. The last three are to be $40,000 each and will be paid on December 31, 2019, 2020, and 2021. Montgomery borrowed other money at a 10% annual rate.

Required:

1. At what amount should Montgomery record the note payable and corresponding cost of the building on January 1, 2016?
2. How much interest expense on this note will Montgomery recognize in 2016?

P 6–9
Deferred annuities
● LO6–7

John Roberts is 55 years old and has been asked to accept early retirement from his company. The company has offered John three alternative compensation packages to induce John to retire:

1. $180,000 cash payment to be paid immediately.
2. A 20-year annuity of $16,000 beginning immediately.
3. A 10-year annuity of $50,000 beginning at age 65.

Required:

Which alternative should John choose assuming that he is able to invest funds at a 7% rate?

P 6–10
Noninterest-bearing note; annuity and lump-sum payment
● LO6–3, LO6–7

On January 1, 2016, The Barrett Company purchased merchandise from a supplier. Payment was a noninterest-bearing note requiring five annual payments of $20,000 on each December 31 beginning on December 31, 2016, and a lump-sum payment of $100,000 on December 31, 2020. A 10% interest rate properly reflects the time value of money in this situation.

Required:

Calculate the amount at which Barrett should record the note payable and corresponding merchandise purchased on January 1, 2016.

P 6–11
Solving for unknown lease payment
● LO6–8, LO6–9

Benning Manufacturing Company is negotiating with a customer for the lease of a large machine manufactured by Benning. The machine has a cash price of $800,000. Benning wants to be reimbursed for financing the machine at an 8% annual interest rate.

Required:

1. Determine the required lease payment if the lease agreement calls for 10 equal annual payments beginning immediately.
2. Determine the required lease payment if the first of 10 annual payments will be made one year from the date of the agreement.
3. Determine the required lease payment if the first of 10 annual payments will be made immediately and Benning will be able to sell the machine to another customer for $50,000 at the end of the 10-year lease.

P 6–12
Solving for unknown lease payment; compounding periods of varying length
● LO6–8, LO6–9

(This is a variation of P6–11 focusing on compounding periods of varying length.)

Benning Manufacturing Company is negotiating with a customer for the lease of a large machine manufactured by Benning. The machine has a cash price of $800,000. Benning wants to be reimbursed for financing the machine at a 12% annual interest rate over the five-year lease term.

Required:

1. Determine the required lease payment if the lease agreement calls for 10 equal semiannual payments beginning six months from the date of the agreement.
2. Determine the required lease payment if the lease agreement calls for 20 equal quarterly payments beginning immediately.
3. Determine the required lease payment if the lease agreement calls for 60 equal monthly payments beginning one month from the date of the agreement. The present value of an ordinary annuity factor for $n = 60$ and $i = 1\%$ is 44.9550.

P 6–13
Lease vs. buy alternatives
● LO6–3, LO6–7, LO6–9

Kiddy Toy Corporation needs to acquire the use of a machine to be used in its manufacturing process. The machine needed is manufactured by Lollie Corp. The machine can be used for 10 years and then sold for $10,000 at the end of its useful life. Lollie has presented Kiddy with the following options:

1. *Buy machine.* The machine could be purchased for $160,000 in cash. All maintenance and insurance costs, which approximate $5,000 per year, would be paid by Kiddy.
2. *Lease machine.* The machine could be leased for a 10-year period for an annual lease payment of $25,000 with the first payment due immediately. All maintenance and insurance costs will be paid for by the Lollie Corp. and the machine will revert back to Lollie at the end of the 10-year period.

Required:

Assuming that a 12% interest rate properly reflects the time value of money in this situation and that all maintenance and insurance costs are paid at the end of each year, determine which option Kiddy should choose. Ignore income tax considerations.

P 6–14
Deferred annuities; pension obligation
● LO6–7, LO6–9

Three employees of the Horizon Distributing Company will receive annual pension payments from the company when they retire. The employees will receive their annual payments for as long as they live. Life expectancy for each employee is 15 years beyond retirement. Their names, the amount of their annual pension payments, and the date they will receive their first payment are shown below:

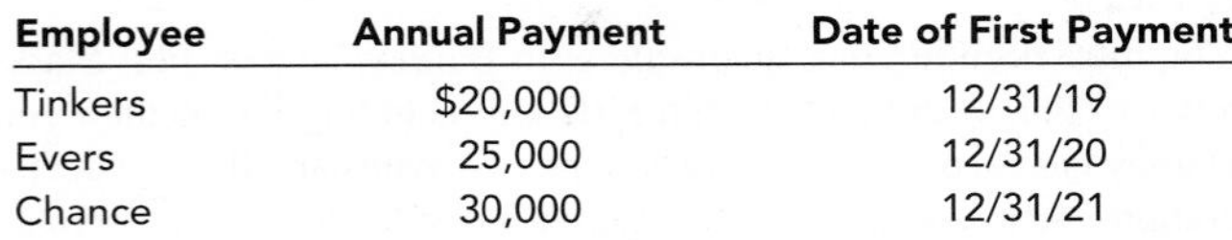

Employee	Annual Payment	Date of First Payment
Tinkers	$20,000	12/31/19
Evers	25,000	12/31/20
Chance	30,000	12/31/21

Required:

1. Compute the present value of the pension obligation to these three employees as of December 31, 2016. Assume an 11% interest rate.
2. The company wants to have enough cash invested at December 31, 2019, to provide for all three employees. To accumulate enough cash, they will make three equal annual contributions to a fund that will earn 11% interest compounded annually. The first contribution will be made on December 31, 2016. Compute the amount of this required annual contribution.

P 6–15
Bonds and leases; deferred annuities
● LO6–3, LO6–7, LO6–9

On the last day of its fiscal year ending December 31, 2016, the Sedgwick & Reams (S&R) Glass Company completed two financing arrangements. The funds provided by these initiatives will allow the company to expand its operations.

1. S&R issued 8% stated rate bonds with a face amount of $100 million. The bonds mature on December 31, 2036 (20 years). The market rate of interest for similar bond issues was 9% (4.5% semiannual rate). Interest is paid semiannually (4%) on June 30 and December 31, beginning on June 30, 2017.
2. The company leased two manufacturing facilities. Lease A requires 20 annual lease payments of $200,000 beginning on January 1, 2017. Lease B also is for 20 years, beginning January 1, 2017. Terms of the lease require 17 annual lease payments of $220,000 beginning on January 1, 2020. Generally accepted accounting principles require both leases to be recorded as liabilities for the present value of the scheduled payments. Assume that a 10% interest rate properly reflects the time value of money for the lease obligations.

Required:

What amounts will appear in S&R's December 31, 2016, balance sheet for the bonds and for the leases?

Broaden Your Perspective

Apply your critical-thinking ability to the knowledge you've gained. These cases will provide you an opportunity to develop your research, analysis, judgment, and communication skills. You also will work with other students, integrate what you've learned, apply it in real-world situations, and consider its global and ethical ramifications. This practice will broaden your knowledge and further develop your decision-making abilities.

Ethics Case 6–1
Rate of return
● LO6–1

The Damon Investment Company manages a mutual fund composed mostly of speculative stocks. You recently saw an ad claiming that investments in the funds have been earning a rate of return of 21%. This rate seemed quite high so you called a friend who works for one of Damon's competitors. The friend told you that the 21% return figure was determined by dividing the two-year appreciation on investments in the fund by the average investment. In other words, $100 invested in the fund two years ago would have grown to $121 ($21 ÷ $100 = 21%).

Required:

Discuss the ethics of the 21% return claim made by the Damon Investment Company.

Analysis Case 6–2
Bonus alternatives; present value analysis
● LO6–3, LO6–7

Sally Hamilton has performed well as the chief financial officer of the Maxtech Computer Company and has earned a bonus. She has a choice among the following three bonus plans:

1. A $50,000 cash bonus paid now.
2. A $10,000 annual cash bonus to be paid each year over the next six years, with the first $10,000 paid now.
3. A three-year $22,000 annual cash bonus with the first payment due three years from now.

Required:

Evaluate the three alternative bonus plans. Sally can earn a 6% annual return on her investments.

Communication Case 6–3
Present value of annuities
● LO6–7

Harvey Alexander, an all-league professional football player, has just declared free agency. Two teams, the San Francisco 49ers and the Dallas Cowboys, have made Harvey the following offers to obtain his services:

49ers: $1 million signing bonus payable immediately and an annual salary of $1.5 million for the five-year term of the contract.

Cowboys: $2.5 million signing bonus payable immediately and an annual salary of $1 million for the five-year term of the contract.

With both contracts, the annual salary will be paid in one lump sum at the end of the football season.

Required:
You have been hired as a consultant to Harvey's agent, Phil Marks, to evaluate the two contracts. Write a short letter to Phil with your recommendation including the method you used to reach your conclusion. Assume that Harvey has no preference between the two teams and that the decision will be based entirely on monetary considerations. Also assume that Harvey can invest his money and earn an 8% annual return.

Analysis Case 6–4
Present value of an annuity
● LO6–7

On a rainy afternoon two years ago, John Smiley left work early to attend a family birthday party. Eleven minutes later, a careening truck slammed into his SUV on the freeway causing John to spend two months in a coma. Now he can't hold a job or make everyday decisions and is in need of constant care. Last week, the 40-year-old Smiley won an out-of-court settlement from the truck driver's company. He was awarded payment for all medical costs and attorney fees, plus a lump-sum settlement of $2,330,716. At the time of the accident, John was president of his family's business and earned approximately $200,000 per year. He had anticipated working 25 more years before retirement.[10]

John's sister, an acquaintance of yours from college, has asked you to explain to her how the attorneys came up with the settlement amount. "They said it was based on his lost future income and a 7% rate of some kind," she explained. "But it was all 'legal-speak' to me."

Required:
How was the amount of the lump-sum settlement determined? Create a calculation that might help John's sister understand.

Judgment Case 6–5
Replacement decision
● LO6–3, LO6–7

Hughes Corporation is considering replacing a machine used in the manufacturing process with a new, more efficient model. The purchase price of the new machine is $150,000 and the old machine can be sold for $100,000. Output for the two machines is identical; they will both be used to produce the same amount of product for five years. However, the annual operating costs of the old machine are $18,000 compared to $10,000 for the new machine. Also, the new machine has a salvage value of $25,000, but the old machine will be worthless at the end of the five years.

Required:
Should the company sell the old machine and purchase the new model? Assume that an 8% rate properly reflects the time value of money in this situation and that all operating costs are paid at the end of the year. Ignore the effect of the decision on income taxes.

Real World Case 6–6
Zero-coupon bonds; Johnson & Johnson
● LO6–3, LO6–9
Real World Financials

Johnson & Johnson is one of the world's largest manufacturers of health care products. The company's December 31, 2013, financial statements included the following information in the long-term debt disclosure note:

	($ in millions) 2013
Zero-coupon convertible subordinated debentures, due 2020	$179

The bonds were issued at the beginning of 2000. The disclosure note stated that the effective interest rate for these bonds is 3% annually. Some of the original convertible bonds have been converted into Johnson & Johnson shares of stock. The $179 million is the present value of the bonds not converted and thus reported in the financial statements. Each individual bond has a maturity value (face amount) of $1,000. The maturity value indicates the amount that Johnson & Johnson will pay bondholders at the beginning of 2020. Zero-coupon bonds pay no cash interest during the term to maturity. The company is "accreting" (gradually increasing) the issue price to maturity value using the bonds' effective interest rate computed on a semiannual basis.

Required:
1. Determine the maturity value of the zero-coupon bonds that Johnson & Johnson will pay bondholders at the beginning of 2020.
2. Determine the issue price at the beginning of 2000 of a single, $1,000 maturity-value bond.

[10]This case is based on actual events.

Real World Case 6–7
Leases; Southwest Airlines
● LO6–3, LO6–9

Real World Financials

Southwest Airlines provides scheduled air transportation services in the United States. Like many airlines, Southwest leases many of its planes from **Boeing Company**. In its long-term debt disclosure note included in the financial statements for the year ended December 31, 2013, the company listed $56 million in lease obligations. The existing leases had an approximate eight-year remaining life and future lease payments average approximately $8 million per year.

Required:

1. Determine the effective interest rate the company used to determine the lease liability assuming that lease payments are made at the end of each fiscal year.
2. Repeat requirement 1 assuming that lease payments are made at the beginning of each fiscal year.

CHAPTER

7 Cash and Receivables

OVERVIEW

We begin our study of assets by looking at cash and receivables—the two assets typically listed first in a balance sheet. For cash, the key issues are internal control and classification in the balance sheet. For receivables, the key issues are valuation and the related income statement effects of transactions involving accounts receivable and notes receivable.

LEARNING OBJECTIVES

After studying this chapter, you should be able to:

- **LO7–1** Define what is meant by internal control and describe some key elements of an internal control system for cash receipts and disbursements. (*p. 362*)
- **LO7–2** Explain the possible restrictions on cash and their implications for classification in the balance sheet. (*p. 364*)
- **LO7–3** Distinguish between the gross and net methods of accounting for cash discounts. (*p. 367*)
- **LO7–4** Describe the accounting treatment for merchandise returns. (*p. 368*)
- **LO7–5** Describe the accounting treatment of anticipated uncollectible accounts receivable. (*p. 371*)
- **LO7–6** Describe the two approaches to estimating bad debts. (*p. 371*)
- **LO7–7** Describe the accounting treatment of notes receivable. (*p. 376*)
- **LO7–8** Differentiate between the use of receivables in financing arrangements accounted for as a secured borrowing and those accounted for as a sale. (*p. 382*)
- **LO7–9** Describe the variables that influence a company's investment in receivables and calculate the key ratios used by analysts to monitor that investment. (*p. 391*)
- **LO7–10** Discuss the primary differences between U.S. GAAP and IFRS with respect to cash and receivables. (*pp. 365, 382, 390,* and *401*)

FINANCIAL REPORTING CASE

What Does It All Mean?

Your roommate, Todd Buckley, was surfing the net looking for information about his future employer, **Cisco Systems**. Todd, an engineering major, recently accepted a position with Cisco, the world's largest provider of hardware, software, and services that drive the Internet. He noticed an article on TheStreet.com entitled "Cisco Triples Bad-Account Provision." "This doesn't look good," Todd grumbled. "The article says that my new employer's deadbeat account column has more than tripled in the span of a year. I guess all those dot-com companies are not paying their bills. But this sentence is confusing. 'For the fiscal first quarter Cisco moved $275 million from operating cash to cover potential nonpayments from failed customers.' Did they actually move cash and if so, where did they move it and why?"

You studied accounting for bad debts in your intermediate accounting class and are confident you can help. After reading the article, you comfort Todd. "First of all, the term *provision* just means expense, and no, Cisco didn't move any cash. The company uses what is called the *allowance method* to account for its bad debts, and it looks like it simply recorded $275 million in expense for the quarter and increased the allowance for uncollectible accounts." Todd was not happy with your answer. "Provisions! Allowance method! Uncollectible accounts! I want you to help me understand, not make things worse." "Okay," you offer, "let's start at the beginning."

QUESTIONS

By the time you finish this chapter, you should be able to respond appropriately to the questions posed in this case. Compare your response to the solution provided at the end of the chapter.

1. Explain the allowance method of accounting for bad debts. (*p. 371*)
2. What approaches might Cisco have used to arrive at the $275 million bad debt provision? (*p. 372*)
3. Are there any alternatives to the allowance method? (*p. 375*)

In the earlier chapters of this text, we studied the underlying measurement and reporting concepts for the basic financial statements presented to external decision makers. Now we turn our attention to the elements of those financial statements. Specifically, we further explore the elements of the balance sheet, and also consider the income statement effects of transactions involving these elements. We first address assets, then liabilities, and finally shareholders' equity. This chapter focuses on the current assets **cash and cash equivalents** and **receivables**.

PART A

Cash and Cash Equivalents

Cash includes currency and coins, balances in checking accounts, and items acceptable for deposit in these accounts, such as checks and money orders received from customers. These forms of cash represent amounts readily available to pay off debt or to use in operations, without any legal or contractual restriction.

Managers typically invest temporarily idle cash to earn interest on those funds rather than keep an unnecessarily large checking account. These amounts are essentially equivalent to cash because they can quickly become available for use as cash. So, short-term, highly liquid investments that can be readily converted to cash with little risk of loss are viewed as cash equivalents. For financial reporting we make no distinction between cash in the form of currency or bank account balances and amounts held in cash-equivalent investments.

A company's policy concerning which short-term, highly liquid investments it classifies as cash equivalents should be described in a disclosure note.

Cash equivalents include money market funds, treasury bills, and commercial paper. To be classified as cash equivalents, these investments must have a maturity date no longer than three months *from the date of purchase.* Companies are permitted flexibility in designating cash equivalents and must establish individual policies regarding which short-term, highly liquid investments are classified as cash equivalents. A company's policy should be consistent with the usual motivation for acquiring these investments. The policy should be disclosed in the notes to the financial statements.

Illustration 7–1 shows a note from the 2013 annual report of Walgreen Co., which operates the largest drugstore chain in the United States.

Illustration 7–1

Disclosure of Cash Equivalents—Walgreen Co.

Real World Financials

> **Note 1: Summary of Major Accounting Policies (in part) Cash and Cash Equivalents**
> Cash and cash equivalents include cash on hand and all highly liquid investments with an original maturity of three months or less. Credit and debit card receivables from banks, which generally settle within two business days, of $160 million and $88 million were included in cash and cash equivalents at August 31, 2013 and 2012, respectively. At August 31, 2013 and 2012, the Company had $1.6 billion and $820 million, respectively, in money market funds, all of which was included in cash and cash equivalents.

PetSmart

Similarly, PetSmart's balance of cash and cash equivalents for the fiscal year ended February 2, 2014, includes $61.5 million of credit card and debit card receivables from banks that typically settle within five business days.

Credit and debit card receivables often are included in cash equivalents.

The measurement and reporting of cash and cash equivalents are largely straightforward because cash generally presents no measurement problems. It is the standard medium of exchange and the basis for measuring assets and liabilities. Cash and cash equivalents usually are combined and reported as a single amount in the balance sheet. However, cash that is not available for use in current operations because it is restricted for a special purpose usually is classified in one of the noncurrent asset categories. Restricted cash is discussed later in this chapter.

All assets must be safeguarded against possible misuse. However, cash is the most liquid asset and the asset most easily expropriated. As a result, a system of internal control of cash is a key accounting issue.

Internal Control

The success of any business enterprise depends on an effective system of **internal control**. Internal control refers to a company's plan to (a) encourage adherence to company policies and procedures, (b) promote operational efficiency, (c) minimize errors and theft, and (d) enhance the reliability and accuracy of accounting data. From a financial accounting perspective, the focus is on controls intended to improve the accuracy and reliability of accounting information and to safeguard the company's assets.

● LO7–1

The Sarbanes-Oxley Act requires a company to document and assess its internal controls. Auditors express an opinion on management's assessment.

Recall from our discussion in Chapter 1 that Section 404 of the *Sarbanes-Oxley Act of 2002* requires that companies document their internal controls and assess their adequacy. The Public Company Accounting Oversight Board's *Auditing Standard No. 5* further requires the auditor to express its own opinion on whether the company has maintained effective internal control over financial reporting.

Many companies have incurred significant costs in an effort to comply with the requirements of Section 404.[1] A framework for designing an internal control system is provided

[1] *Auditing Standard No. 5* emphasizes audit efficiency with a focused, risk-based testing approach that is intended to reduce the total costs of 404 compliance.

by the Committee of Sponsoring Organizations (COSO) of the Treadway Commission.[2] Formed in 1985, the organization is dedicated to improving the quality of financial reporting through, among other things, effective internal controls.

COSO defines internal control as a process, undertaken by an entity's board of directors, management and other personnel, designed to provide reasonable assurance regarding the achievement of objectives in the following categories:

- Effectiveness and efficiency of operations.
- Reliability of financial reporting.
- Compliance with applicable laws and regulations.[3]

Internal Control Procedures—Cash Receipts

As cash is the most liquid of all assets, a well-designed and functioning system of internal control must surround all cash transactions. Separation of duties is critical. Individuals that have physical responsibility for assets should not also have access to accounting records. So, employees who handle cash should not be involved in or have access to accounting records nor be involved in the reconciliation of cash book balances to bank balances.

Employees involved in recordkeeping should not also have physical access to the assets.

Consider the cash receipt process. Most nonretail businesses receive payment for goods by checks received through the mail. An approach to internal control over cash receipts that utilizes separation of duties might include the following steps:

1. Employee A opens the mail each day and prepares a multicopy listing of all checks including the amount and payor's name.
2. Employee B takes the checks, along with one copy of the listing, to the person responsible for depositing the checks in the company's bank account.
3. A second copy of the check listing is sent to the accounting department where Employee C enters receipts into the accounting records.

Good internal control helps ensure accuracy as well as safeguard against theft. The bank-generated deposit slip can be compared with the check listing to verify that the amounts received were also deposited. And, because the person opening the mail is not the person who maintains the accounting records, it's impossible for one person to steal checks and alter accounting records to cover up their theft.

Internal Control Procedures—Cash Disbursements

Proper controls for cash disbursements should be designed to prevent any unauthorized payments and ensure that disbursements are recorded in the proper accounts. Important elements of a cash disbursement control system include:

1. All disbursements, other than very small disbursements from petty cash, should be made by check. This provides a permanent record of all disbursements.
2. All expenditures should be *authorized* before a check is prepared. For example, a vendor invoice for the purchase of inventory should be compared with the purchase order and receiving report to ensure the accuracy of quantity, price, part numbers, and so on. This process should include verification of the proper ledger accounts to be debited.
3. Checks should be signed only by authorized individuals.

Once again, separation of duties is important. Responsibilities for check signing, check writing, check mailing, cash disbursement documentation, and recordkeeping should be separated whenever possible. That way, a single person can't write checks to himself and disguise that theft as a payment to an approved vendor.

[2]The sponsoring organizations include the AICPA, the Financial Executives International, the Institute of Internal Auditors, the American Accounting Association, and the Institute of Management Accountants.

[3]www.coso.org.

An important part of any system of internal control of cash is the periodic reconciliation of book balances and bank balances to the correct balance. In addition, a petty cash system is employed by many business enterprises. We cover these two topics in Appendix 7A.

Restricted Cash and Compensating Balances

● LO7–2

We discussed the classification of assets and liabilities in Chapter 3. You should recall that only cash available for current operations or to satisfy current liabilities is classified as a current asset. Cash that is restricted in some way and not available for current use usually is reported as a noncurrent asset such as *investments and funds* or *other assets*.

Restrictions on cash can be informal, arising from management's intent to use a certain amount of cash for a specific purpose. For example, a company may set aside funds for future plant expansion. This cash, if material, should be classified as investments and funds or other assets. Sometimes restrictions are contractually imposed. Debt instruments, for instance, frequently require the borrower to set aside funds (often referred to as a sinking fund) for the future payment of a debt. In these instances, the restricted cash is classified as noncurrent investments and funds or other assets if the debt is classified as noncurrent. On the other hand, if the liability is current, the restricted cash also is classified as current. Disclosure notes should describe any material restrictions of cash.

Banks frequently require cash restrictions in connection with loans or loan commitments (lines of credit). Typically, the borrower is asked to maintain a specified balance in a low interest or noninterest-bearing account at the bank (creditor). The required balance usually is some percentage of the committed amount (say 2% to 5%). These are known as **compensating balances** because they compensate the bank for granting the loan or extending the line of credit.

The effect of a *compensating balance* is a higher effective interest rate on the debt.

A compensating balance results in the borrower's paying an effective interest rate higher than the stated rate on the debt. For example, suppose that a company borrows $10,000,000 from a bank at an interest rate of 12%. If the bank requires a compensating balance of $2,000,000 to be held in a noninterest-bearing checking account, the company really is borrowing only $8,000,000 (the loan less the compensating balance). This means an effective interest rate of 15% ($1,200,000 interest divided by $8,000,000 cash available for use).

A material compensating balance must be disclosed regardless of the classification of the cash.

The classification and disclosure of a compensating balance depends on the nature of the restriction and the classification of the related debt.[4] If the restriction is legally binding, the cash is classified as either current or noncurrent (investments and funds or other assets) depending on the classification of the related debt. In either case, note disclosure is appropriate.

If the compensating balance arrangement is informal with no contractual agreement that restricts the use of cash, the compensating balance can be reported as part of cash and cash equivalents, with note disclosure of the arrangement.

PetSmart

Illustration 7–2 provides an example of a note disclosure from **PetSmart**'s February 2, 2014, annual report.

Illustration 7–2
Disclosure of Cash Equivalents—PetSmart, Inc.
Real World Financials

Note 11: Financing Arrangements and Lease Obligations
***Credit Facilities* (in part)**
We also have a $100.0 million stand-alone letter of credit facility agreement, or "Stand-alone Letter of Credit Facility," which expires on March 23, 2017. . . . we are required to maintain a cash deposit with the lender equal to 103% of the amount of outstanding letters of credit. We had $69.2 million and $69.8 million in outstanding letters of credit . . . as of February 2, 2014, and February 3, 2013, respectively. We had $71.2 million and $71.9 million in restricted cash on deposit as of February 2, 2014, and February 3, 2013, respectively.

[4]FASB ASC 210–10–S99–2: SAB Topic 6.H–Balance Sheet—Overall—SEC Materials, *Accounting Series Release 148* (originally "Amendments to Regulations S-X and Related Interpretations and Guidelines Regarding the Disclosure of Compensating Balances and Short-Term Borrowing Arrangements," *Accounting Series Release No. 148*, Securities and Exchange Commission (November 13, 1973)).

International Financial Reporting Standards

Cash and Cash Equivalents. In general, cash and cash equivalents are treated similarly under IFRS and U.S. GAAP. One difference relates to bank overdrafts, which occur when withdrawals from a bank account exceed the available balance. U.S. GAAP requires that overdrafts typically be treated as liabilities. In contrast, *IAS No. 7* allows bank overdrafts to be offset against other cash accounts when overdrafts are payable on demand and fluctuate between positive and negative amounts as part of the normal cash management program that a company uses to minimize its cash balance.[5] For example, LaDonia Company has two cash accounts with the following balances as of December 31, 2016:

● LO7–10

IFRS ILLUSTRATION

National Bank:	$300,000
Central Bank:	(15,000)

Under U.S. GAAP, LaDonia's 12/31/16 balance sheet would report a cash asset of $300,000 and an overdraft current liability of $15,000. Under IFRS, LaDonia would report a cash asset of $285,000.

Decision Makers' Perspective

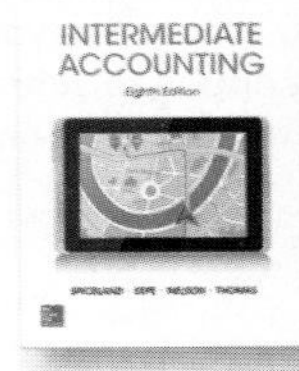

Cash often is referred to as a *nonearning* asset because it earns no interest. For this reason, managers invest idle cash in either cash equivalents or short-term investments, both of which provide a return. Management's goal is to hold the minimum amount of cash necessary to conduct normal business operations, meet its obligations, and take advantage of opportunities. Too much cash reduces profits through lost returns, while too little cash increases risk. This trade-off between risk and return is an ongoing choice made by management (internal decision makers). Whether the choice made is appropriate is an ongoing assessment made by investors and creditors (external decision makers).

A company must have cash available for the compensating balances we discussed in the previous section as well as for planned disbursements related to normal operating, investing, and financing cash flows. However, because cash inflows and outflows can vary from planned amounts, a company needs an additional cash cushion as a precaution against surprises. The size of the cushion depends on the company's ability to convert cash equivalents and short-term investments into cash quickly, along with its short-term borrowing capacity.

Companies hold cash to pay for planned and unplanned transactions and to satisfy compensating balance requirements.

Liquidity is a measure of a company's cash position and overall ability to obtain cash in the normal course of business. A company is assumed to be liquid if it has sufficient cash or is capable of converting its other assets to cash in a relatively short period of time so that current needs can be met. Frequently, liquidity is measured with respect to the ability to pay currently maturing debt. The current ratio is one of the most common ways of measuring liquidity and is calculated by dividing current assets by current liabilities. By comparing liabilities that must be satisfied in the near term with assets that either are cash or will be converted to cash in the near term we have a base measure of a company's liquidity. We can refine the measure by adjusting for the implicit assumption of the current ratio that all current assets are equally liquid. In the acid-test or quick ratio, the numerator consists of "quick assets," which include only cash and cash equivalents, short-term investments, and accounts receivable. By eliminating inventories and prepaid expenses, the current assets that are less readily convertible into cash, we get a more precise indication of a company's short-term liquidity than with the current ratio. We discussed and illustrated these liquidity ratios in Chapter 3.

We should evaluate the adequacy of any ratio in the context of the industry in which the company operates and other specific circumstances. Bear in mind, though, that industry averages are only one indication of acceptability and any ratio is but one indication of liquidity. Profitability, for instance, is perhaps the best long-run indication of liquidity. And

[5] "Statement of Cash Flows," *International Accounting Standard No. 7* (IASCF), as amended effective January 1, 2014, par. 8.

a company may be very efficient in managing its current assets so that, say, receivables are more liquid than they otherwise would be. The receivables turnover ratio we discuss in Part B of this chapter offers a measure of management's efficiency in this regard.

A manager should actively monitor the company's cash position.

There are many techniques that a company can use to manage cash balances. A discussion of these techniques is beyond the scope of this text. However, it is sufficient here to understand that management must make important decisions related to cash that have a direct impact on a company's profitability and risk. Because the lack of prudent cash management can lead to the failure of an otherwise sound company, it is essential that managers as well as outside investors and creditors maintain close vigil over this facet of a company's health. ●

PART B

Current Receivables

Receivables represent a company's claims to the future collection of cash, other assets, or services. Receivables resulting from the sale of goods or services on account are called **accounts receivable** and often are referred to as *trade receivables. Nontrade receivables* are those other than trade receivables and include tax refund claims, interest receivable, and loans by the company to other entities including stockholders and employees. When a receivable, trade or nontrade, is accompanied by a formal promissory note, it is referred to as a note receivable. We consider notes receivable after first discussing accounts receivable.

An account receivable and an account payable reflect opposite sides of the same transaction.

As you study receivables, realize that one company's claim to the future collection of cash corresponds to another company's (or individual's) obligation to pay cash. One company's account receivable will be the mirror image of another company's account payable. Chapter 13 addresses accounts payable and other current liabilities.

Accounts Receivable

Accounts receivable are current assets because, by definition, they will be converted to cash within the normal operating cycle.

Most businesses provide credit to their customers, either because it's not practical to require immediate cash payment or to encourage customers to purchase the company's product or service. Accounts receivable are *informal* credit arrangements supported by an invoice and normally are due in 30 to 60 days after the sale. They almost always are classified as *current* assets because their normal collection period, even if longer than a year, is part of, and therefore less than, the operating cycle.

Typically, revenue and related accounts receivable are recognized at the point of delivery of the product or service.

Accounts receivable are created when sellers recognize revenue associated with a credit sale. We discussed revenue recognition in Chapter 5. Recall that revenue is recognized when a seller satisfies a performance obligation. For most products or services, the performance obligation is satisfied at the point of delivery of the product or service, so revenue and the related receivable are recognized at that time.

Initial Valuation of Accounts Receivable

We know from prior discussions that receivables should be recorded at the present value of future cash receipts using a realistic interest rate. So, a $10,000 sale on credit due in 30 days should result in a receivable valued at the present value of the $10,000. In other words, the interest portion of the $10,000 due in 30 days should be removed and recognized as interest revenue over the 30-day period, not as sales revenue at date of delivery of the product. If the monthly interest rate is 2%, the receivable would be valued at $9,804, calculated by multiplying the future cash payment of $10,000 by the present value of $1 factor for one period at 2% (.98039).

The typical account receivable is valued at the amount expected to be received, not the present value of that amount.

However, because the difference between the future and present values of accounts receivable often is immaterial, GAAP specifically excludes accounts receivable from the general rule that receivables be recorded at present value.[6] Therefore, accounts receivable initially are valued at the exchange price agreed on by the buyer and seller. In our example, both the account receivable and sales revenue would be recorded at $10,000. Let's discuss two aspects of accounts receivable related to their initial valuation—trade discounts and cash discounts.

[6]FASB ASC 835–30–15–3: Interest—Imputation of Interest—Scope and Scope Exceptions (previously "Interest on Receivables and Payables," *Accounting Principles Board Opinion No. 21* (New York: AICPA, 1971)).

TRADE DISCOUNTS. Companies frequently offer **trade discounts** to customers, usually a percentage reduction from the list price. Trade discounts can be a way to change prices without publishing a new catalog or to disguise real prices from competitors. They also are used to give quantity discounts to large customers. For example, a manufacturer might list a machine part at $2,500 but sell it to a customer at a 10% discount. The trade discount of $250 is not recognized directly when recording the transaction. The discount is recognized indirectly by recording the sale at the net of discount price of $2,250, not at the list price.

***Trade discounts* allow a customer to pay an amount that is below the list price.**

CASH DISCOUNTS. Be careful to distinguish a *trade* discount from a *cash* discount. **Cash discounts**, often called *sales discounts*, represent reductions not in the selling price of a good or service but in the amount to be paid by a credit customer if paid within a specified period of time. It is a discount intended to provide incentive for quick payment.

***Cash discounts* reduce the amount to be paid if remittance is made within a specified short period of time.**

● LO7–3

The amount of the discount and the time period within which it's available usually are conveyed by terms like 2/10, n/30 (meaning a 2% discount if paid within 10 days, otherwise full payment within 30 days). There are two ways to record cash discounts, the gross method and the net method. Conceptually, the **gross method** views a discount not taken by the customer as part of sales revenue. On the other hand, the **net method** considers sales revenue to be the net amount, after discount, and any discounts not taken by the customer as interest revenue. The discounts are viewed as compensation to the seller for providing financing to the customer. With both methods, sales revenue only ends up being reduced by sales discounts that are actually taken. Consider the example in Illustration 7–3.

The *gross method* views cash discounts not taken to be part of sales revenue.

Illustration 7–3

Cash Discounts

The Hawthorne Manufacturing Company offers credit customers a 2% cash discount if the sales price is paid within 10 days. Any amounts not paid within 10 days are due in 30 days. These repayment terms are stated as 2/10, n/30. On October 5, 2016, Hawthorne sold merchandise at a price of $20,000. The customer paid $13,720 ($14,000 less the 2% cash discount) on October 14 and the remaining balance of $6,000 on November 4.

The appropriate journal entries to record the sale and cash collection, comparing the gross and net methods are as follows:

Gross Method			Net Method		
October 5, 2016			**October 5, 2016**		
Accounts receivable	20,000		Accounts receivable	19,600	
Sales revenue		20,000	Sales revenue		19,600
October 14, 2016			**October 14, 2016**		
Cash	13,720		Cash	13,720	
Sales discounts	280		Accounts receivable		13,720
Accounts receivable		14,000			
November 4, 2016			**November 4, 2016**		
Cash	6,000		Cash	6,000	
Accounts receivable		6,000	Accounts receivable		5,880
			Interest revenue		120

By either method, net sales is reduced by discounts *taken.*

Discounts *not* taken are included in sales revenue using the gross method and interest revenue using the net method.

Notice that by using the gross method we initially record the revenue and related receivable at the full **$20,000** price. On remittance within the discount period, the $280 discount is recorded as a debit to an account called *sales discounts.* This is a contra account to sales revenue and is deducted from sales revenue to derive the net sales reported in the income statement. For payments made after the discount period, cash is simply increased and accounts receivable decreased by the gross amount originally recorded.

Under the net method, we record revenue and the related accounts receivable at the agreed-on price *less* the 2% discount applied to the entire price. Payments made within the discount period are recorded as debits to cash and credits to accounts receivable for the amount received. If a customer loses a discount by failing to pay within the discount period, the discount not taken is recorded as interest revenue. In this case, **$120** in cash ($6,000 × 2%) is interest.[7]

The *net method* considers cash discounts not taken as interest revenue.

[7]In Chapter 5 you learned that when the price of a good or service can vary depending upon future events, sellers must estimate the variable consideration and reduce revenue to account for it at the time of sale. Cash discounts are a form of variable consideration so, technically, sellers should estimate the discounts that will be taken and base revenue on that estimate. Typically, that approach will provide an outcome very similar to the net method because customers usually pay quickly enough to receive the discount.

Total revenue in the 2016 income statement would be the same using either method:

Revenue comparison of the gross method and the net method.

	Gross Method	Net Method
Sales	$20,000	$19,600
Less: Sales discounts	(280)	–0–
Net sales revenue	19,720	19,600
Interest revenue	0	120
Total revenue	$19,720	$19,720

Which is correct? Conceptually, the net method usually reflects the reality of the situation—the real price is $19,600 and $120 is an interest penalty for not paying promptly. The net price usually is the price expected by the seller because the discount usually reflects a hefty interest cost that prudent buyers are unwilling to bear. Consider Illustration 7–3. Although the discount rate is stated as 2%, the effective rate really is 37.23%. In order to save $2, the buyer must pay $98 twenty days earlier than otherwise due, effectively "investing" $98 to "earn" $2, a rate of return of 2.04% ($2/$98) for a 20-day period. To convert this 20-day rate to an annual rate, we multiply by 365/20:

$$2.04\% \times 365/20 = 37.23\% \text{ effective rate}$$

Understandably, most buyers try to take the discount if at all possible.

The difference between the two methods, in terms of the effect of the transactions on income, is in the timing of the recognition of any discounts not taken. The gross method recognizes discounts not taken as revenue when the sale is made. The net method recognizes them as revenue after the discount period has passed and the cash is collected. These two measurement dates could be in different reporting periods. From a practical standpoint, the effect on the financial statements of the difference between the two methods usually is immaterial.

Subsequent Valuation of Accounts Receivable

Following the initial valuation of an account receivable, two situations possibly could cause the cash ultimately collected to be less than the initial valuation of the receivable: (1) the customer could return the product, or (2) the customer could default and not pay the agreed-upon sales price. When accounting for sales and accounts receivable, we anticipate these possibilities.

● LO7–4

SALES RETURNS. Customers frequently are given the right to return the merchandise they purchase if they are not satisfied. We discussed how this policy affects revenue recognition in Chapter 5. We now discuss it from the perspective of accounts receivable.

Recognizing *sales returns* when they occur could result in an overstatement of income in the period of the related sale.

When merchandise is returned for a refund or for credit to be applied to other purchases, the situation is called a **sales return**. When practical, a dissatisfied customer might be given a special price reduction as an incentive to keep the merchandise purchased.[8] Returns are common and often substantial in some industries such as food products, publishing, and retailing. In these cases, recognizing returns and allowances only as they occur could cause profit to be overstated in the period of the sale and understated in the return period. For example, assume merchandise is sold to a customer for $10,000 in December 2016, the last month in the selling company's fiscal year, and that the merchandise cost $6,000. If all of the merchandise is returned in 2017 after financial statements for 2016 are issued, gross profit will be overstated in 2016 and understated in 2017 by $4,000. Assets at the end of 2016 also will be overstated by $4,000 because a $10,000 receivable would be recorded instead of $6,000 in inventory.

In Chapter 5 you learned that sales returns are a form of "variable consideration" because the eventual consideration received will vary depending on the amount of goods that are returned. The seller must estimate sales returns and reduce revenue accordingly.

[8]Price reductions sometimes are referred to as *sales allowances* and are distinguished from situations when the products actually are returned for a refund or credit (sales returns).

Technically, the seller should estimate returns at the time of sale and adjust the transaction price to reflect them at that time. However, as noted in Chapter 5, it is impractical for most sellers to estimate returns every time they make a sale. For that reason, sellers typically account for returns as they occur, and then at the end of an accounting period make an adjusting entry for any remaining returns they expect to occur in the future. That is the approach we demonstrate.

To account for returns, we debit a contrarevenue account, *sales returns,* which reduces sales revenue to reflect only the sales that aren't returned (referred to as *net sales* in the income statement). As shown in Illustration 7–4, the account that we credit depends on whether cash has already been collected or we have an outstanding receivable.

Sales revenue
Less: Sales returns
Net sales

Illustration 7–4 Accounting for Sales Returns

During 2016, its first year of operations, the Hawthorne Manufacturing Company sold merchandise for $2,000,000. This merchandise cost Hawthorne $1,200,000 (60% of the selling price). Industry experience indicates that 10% of all sales will be returned, which equals $200,000 ($2,000,000 × 10%) in this case. Customers returned $130,000 of sales during 2016. Hawthorne uses a perpetual inventory system.

	Assuming Hawthorne received cash at the time of sales:			Assuming Hawthorne recorded accounts receivable at the time of sales that have not yet been collected:		
Sales of $2,000,000 occurred in 2016, with cost of goods sold of $1,200,000.	Cash	2,000,000		Accounts receivable	2,000,000	
	Sales revenue		2,000,000	Sales revenue		2,000,000
	Cost of goods sold	1,200,000		Cost of goods sold	1,200,000	
	Inventory		1,200,000	Inventory		1,200,000
Sales returns of $130,000 occurred during 2016. The cost of returned inventory is $78,000 ($130,000 × 60%)	Sales returns	130,000		Sales returns	130,000	
	Cash		130,000	Accounts receivable		130,000
	Inventory	78,000		Inventory	78,000	
	Cost of goods sold		78,000	Cost of goods sold		78,000
At the end of 2016, an additional $70,000 of sales returns are expected. The cost of the inventory expected to be returned is $42,000 ($70,000 × 60%)	Sales returns	70,000		Sales returns	70,000	
	Refund liability		70,000	Allow. for sales returns		70,000
	Inventory—est. returns	42,000		Inventory—est. returns	42,000	
	Cost of goods sold		42,000	Cost of goods sold		42,000
Sales returns of $70,000 occurred during 2017. The cost of returned inventory is $42,000.	Refund liability	70,000		Allow. for sales returns	70,000	
	Cash		70,000	Accounts receivable		70,000
	Inventory	42,000		Inventory	42,000	
	Inventory—est. returns		42,000	Inventory—est. returns		42,000

As shown in Illustration 7–4, if a customer has paid cash for a returned item, Hawthorne refunds the cash when the return occurs, and then at the end of the period records a **refund liability** for its estimate of any remaining cash that may be refunded in the future. On the other hand, if Hawthorne has an account receivable outstanding, it reduces the account receivable when the return occurs, and then at the end of the period credits an **allowance for sales returns** account, which is a contra account to accounts receivable, to reduce the net balance of accounts receivable for estimated returns. Of course, Hawthorne also would reduce accounts receivable as it receives payments from customers. And, regardless of whether cash has been collected, the 2016 income statement reports net sales revenue of $1,800,000, which is gross sales revenue of $2,000,000 reduced by actual and estimated returns of $200,000 ($130,000 + 70,000).

Accounts receivable
Less: Allow. for sales returns
Net accounts receivable

Because it's inventory that's being returned, Hawthorne also must adjust inventory when returns occur. Using a perpetual inventory system we record increases (debits) and decreases (credits) in the inventory account as they occur. So, when actual returns do occur, Hawthorne increases inventory to include the $78,000 of returned items. Later, when Hawthorne estimates returns at the end of the period, the $42,000 of inventory *expected* to be returned is included in an asset, "inventory—estimated returns," in Hawthorne's balance sheet, even though the actual merchandise still belongs to customers, because ownership of the goods is expected to revert back to the company. As a result, cost of goods sold equals $1,080,000, which is $1,200,000 reduced by the cost of actual and estimated returns of $120,000 ($78,000 + $42,000).[9]

Sometimes a customer will return merchandise because it has been damaged during shipment or is defective. This possibility is included in a company's estimate of returns. As you will see in Chapter 9, inventory is valued at the lower of cost and net realizable value. By that process, damaged or defective merchandise returned from a customer is written down to the amount the company expects to receive when it sells or disposes of the merchandise.

If the estimate of future sales returns turns out to be wrong, the new estimate is incorporated into accounting determinations in the next period.

What happens if the estimate of future returns turns out to be more or less than $70,000? Remember from previous discussions that when an estimate turns out to be wrong, we don't revise prior years' financial statements to reflect the new estimate. Instead, as you learned in Chapter 5, we adjust the accounts to reflect the change in estimated returns. Suppose in our illustration that in 2017 actual returns from 2016 sales are $60,000 instead of $70,000, and Hawthorne estimates that no more returns will occur. In that case, the allowance for sales returns still has $10,000 remaining from 2016 sales. Likewise, inventory—estimated returns still has 60% × $10,000 = $6,000 remaining from 2016 sales. In 2017, Hawthorne would record its change in estimated returns of 2016 sales as follows:

Account	Debit	Credit
Allowance for sales returns	10,000	
Sales returns ($70,000 – 60,000)		10,000
Cost of goods sold (60% × $10,000)	6,000	
Inventory—estimated returns		6,000

These adjustments remove the remaining 2016 balance from the allowance for sales returns and inventory—estimated returns, and increases sales revenue (by reducing sales returns) and cost of goods sold in the period in which the change in estimate occurs.

Experience guides firms when estimating returns.

How do companies estimate returns? Principally they rely on past history, taking into account any changes that might affect future experience. For example, changes in customer base, payment terms offered to customers, and overall economic conditions might suggest that future returns will differ from past returns. The task of estimating returns is made easier for many large retail companies whose fiscal year-end is the end of January. Since retail companies generate a large portion of their annual sales during the Christmas season, most returns from these sales would already have been accounted for by the end of January.

AVX Corporation is a leading manufacturer of electronic components. Illustration 7–5, drawn from AVX's recent annual report, describes the company's approach to estimating returns.

If sales returns are immaterial, they can be recorded as they occur.

In some industries, returns typically are small and infrequent. Companies in these industries usually record returns in the period they occur because the effect on income measurement and asset valuation is immaterial. Also, companies sometimes lack sufficient information to make a good estimate of returns. As you learned in Chapter 5, companies must recognize only the amount of revenue that is probable to not require reversal in the future, so difficulty estimating returns likely will require a larger estimate of returns (and

[9]As indicated in Chapter 5, companies technically should estimate all variable consideration, including sales returns, at the time a sale is made. The financial statement outcomes of that approach are the same as those shown in Illustration 7–4, but the journal entries that get us there are somewhat different. To adapt our example to account for estimated returns at the time of sale, look at the journal entries that Hawthorne makes at the end of 2016 to account for estimated future returns. Hawthorne would record the same journal entries at the time of sale, but for the full amount of estimated sales returns ($200,000) and estimated inventory to be returned ($200,000 × 60% = $120,000). After recording the estimated returns at the time of the sale, all *actual* returns would be accounted for as shown in our example for actual returns occurring in 2017, reducing the refund liability for cash sales or reducing the allowance for sales returns for credit sales.

Revenue Recognition and Accounts Receivable (in part): Returns

Sales revenue and cost of sales reported in the income statement are reduced to reflect estimated returns. We record an estimated sales allowance for returns at the time of sale based on using historical trends, current pricing and volume information, other market specific information and input from sales, marketing and other key management personnel. The amount accrued reflects the return of value of the customer's inventory. These procedures require the exercise of significant judgments. We believe that these procedures enable us to make reliable estimates of future returns. Our actual results have historically approximated our estimates. When the product is returned and verified, the customer is given credit against their accounts receivable.

Illustration 7–5

Disclosure of Sales Returns Policy—AVX Corporation

Real World Financials

therefore a smaller amount of net sales revenue recognized) than would be the case if a more precise estimate was possible.

UNCOLLECTIBLE ACCOUNTS RECEIVABLE. Companies that extend credit to customers know that it's unlikely that all customers will fully pay their accounts. **Bad debt expense** is an inherent cost of granting credit. It's an operating expense incurred to make sales. As a result, even when specific customer accounts haven't been proven uncollectible by the end of the reporting period, the expense should be matched with sales revenue in the income statement for that period. Likewise, as it's not expected that all accounts receivable will be collected, the balance sheet should report only the expected **net realizable value** of the asset, that is, the amount of cash the company expects to actually collect from customers.

● LO7–5

FINANCIAL Reporting Case

Q1, p. 361

Recognizing bad debt expense results in accounts receivable being reported at their *net realizable value*.

Companies account for bad debts by recording an adjusting entry that debits bad debt expense and reduces accounts receivable indirectly by crediting a contra account to accounts receivable (allowance for uncollectible accounts) for an estimate of the amount that eventually will prove uncollectible. This approach to accounting for bad debts is known as the **allowance method**. Quite often, companies report the allowance for uncollectible accounts (often called the *allowance for doubtful accounts*) parenthetically or alongside the accounts receivable account title separated by a dash or a comma. For example, Illustration 7–6 shows how **Johnson & Johnson**, the large pharmaceutical company, reported accounts receivable in its comparative balance sheets for 2013 and 2012:

The *allowance method* is an application of matching in accounting for bad debts.

	($ in millions)	
	December 29, 2013	**December 30, 2012**
Accounts receivable trade, less allowances for doubtful accounts $333 (2012, $466)	11,713	11,309

Illustration 7–6

Disclosure of Accounts Receivable—Johnson & Johnson

Real World Financials

J&J's balance sheet communicates that, as of December 29, 2013, it had net accounts receivable of $11,713 and an allowance for doubtful accounts of $333, which implies a gross accounts receivable of $11,713 + 333 = $12,046.

Sometimes companies simply show the net balance in the balance sheet, and then describe the allowance for uncollectible accounts in a note to the financial statements if it is material. That's the approach that **PetSmart** uses. Its balance sheet lists "Accounts Receivable, net" as $72,685 as of February 2, 2014, and doesn't disclose the amount in the allowance account, which implies that the allowance is not material.

PetSmart

There are two ways commonly used to arrive at this estimate of future bad debts—the income statement approach and the balance sheet approach. Illustration 7–7 is used to demonstrate both approaches. As you proceed through the illustration, remember that the two approaches represent alternative ways to estimate the *amount* of future bad debts. Except for the amounts, the accounting entries are identical.

● LO7–6

Illustration 7–7
Bad Debts

The Hawthorne Manufacturing Company sells its products offering 30 days' credit to its customers. During 2016, its first year of operations, the following events occurred:

Sales on credit	$1,200,000
Cash collections from credit customers	(895,000)
Accounts receivable, end of year	$ 305,000

There were no specific accounts determined to be uncollectible in 2016. The company anticipates that 2% of all credit sales will ultimately become uncollectible.

Using the *income statement approach,* the balance sheet amount is an incidental result of estimating bad debt expense as a percentage of net credit sales.

Income statement approach. Using the **income statement approach**, we estimate bad debt expense as a percentage of each period's net credit sales. This percentage usually is determined by reviewing the company's recent history of the relationship between credit sales and actual bad debts. For a relatively new company, this percentage may be obtained by referring to other sources such as industry averages.

Under the income statement approach, the Hawthorne Manufacturing Company would make the following adjusting journal entry at the end of 2016:

FINANCIAL Reporting Case

Q2, p. 361

Bad debt expense (2% × $1,200,000)	24,000	
Allowance for uncollectible accounts		24,000

In the current asset section of the 2016 balance sheet, accounts receivable would be reported net of the allowance, as follows:

Accounts receivable	$305,000
Less: Allowance for uncollectible accounts	(24,000)
Net accounts receivable	$281,000

It's important to notice that the income statement approach focuses on the current year's credit sales. The effect on the balance sheet—the allowance for uncollectible accounts and hence net accounts receivable—is an incidental result of estimating the expense. An alternative is to focus on the balance sheet amounts instead. We look at this approach next.

Using the *balance sheet approach,* bad debt expense is an incidental result of estimating the net realizable value of accounts receivable.

Balance sheet approach. Using the **balance sheet approach** to estimate future bad debts, we determine bad debt expense by estimating the net realizable value of accounts receivable to be reported in the balance sheet. Specifically, we determine what the ending balance of the allowance for uncollectible accounts should be, and then we record the amount of bad debt expense that's necessary to adjust the allowance to that desired balance.

For the Hawthorne Manufacturing Company example in Illustration 7–7, the company would estimate the amount of uncollectible accounts that will result from the $305,000 in accounts receivable outstanding at the end of 2016. This could be done by analyzing each customer account, by applying a percentage to the entire outstanding receivable balance, or by applying different percentages to accounts receivable balances depending on the length of time outstanding. This latter approach normally employs an **accounts receivable aging schedule**. For example, the aging schedule for Hawthorne's 2016 year-end accounts receivable is shown in Illustration 7–7A.

The schedule classifies the year-end receivable balances according to their length of time outstanding. Presumably, the longer an account has been outstanding the more likely it will prove uncollectible. Based on past experience or other sources of information, a percentage is applied to age group totals.

The 2016 entry to record bad debts adjusts the balance in the allowance for uncollectible accounts to this required amount of **$25,500**. Because it is the first year of operations for Hawthorne and the beginning balance in the allowance account is zero, the adjusting entry would debit bad debt expense and credit allowance for uncollectible accounts for $25,500.

Illustration 7–7A
Accounts Receivable Aging Schedule

Customer	Accounts Receivable 12/31/2016	0–60 Days	61–90 Days	91–120 Days	Over 120 Days
Axel Manufacturing Co.	$ 20,000	$ 14,000	$ 6,000		
Banner Corporation	33,000		20,000	$10,000	$ 3,000
Dando Company	60,000	50,000	10,000		
"	"	"	"	"	"
"	"	"	"	"	"
Xicon Company	18,000	10,000	4,000	3,000	1,000
Totals	$305,000	$220,000	$50,000	$25,000	$10,000

Summary

Age Group	Amount	Estimated Percent Uncollectible	Estimated Allowance
0–60 days	$220,000	5%	$11,000
61–90 days	50,000	10%	5,000
91–120 days	25,000	20%	5,000
Over 120 days	10,000	45%	4,500
Allowance for uncollectible accounts			$25,500

The schedule assumes older accounts are more likely to prove uncollectible.

Higher estimated default percentages are applied to groups of older receivables.

To illustrate the concept further, let's suppose that this was not the first year of operations and the allowance account prior to the adjusting entry had a *credit* balance of $4,000. Then the amount of the entry would be $21,500—the amount necessary to adjust a credit balance of $4,000 to a credit balance of $25,500. Similarly, if the allowance account prior to the adjusting entry had a *debit* balance[10] of $4,000, then the amount of the entry would be $29,500.

Allowance		
Beg. bal.		4,000
Adj. entry		21,500
Bal.		25,500

Some companies use a combination of approaches in estimating bad debts. For example, Hawthorne could decide to accrue bad debts on a monthly basis using the income statement approach and then employ the balance sheet approach at the end of the year based on an aging of receivables. Each month an adjusting entry would record a debit to bad debt expense and a credit to allowance for uncollectible accounts equal to 2% of credit sales. In our illustration, the monthly accruals for 2016 would result in the following account balances at the end of 2016:

Accounts Receivable	
305,000	

Bad Debt Expense	
24,000	

Allowance for Uncollectible Accounts	
	24,000

At the end of the year, if the aging revealed a required allowance of $25,500, the following adjusting entry would be recorded:

Bad debt expense	1,500	
Allowance for uncollectible accounts		1,500

Allowance	
	24,000
	1,500
	25,500

[10]A debit balance could result if the amount of receivables actually written off (discussed in the next section) during the period exceeds the beginning credit balance in the allowance account.

This entry adjusts the allowance account to the required amount.

In the 2016 balance sheet, accounts receivable would be reported net of the allowance, as follows:

Accounts receivable	$305,000
Less: Allowance for uncollectible accounts	(25,500)
Net accounts receivable	$279,500

When accounts are deemed uncollectible. The actual write-off of a receivable occurs when it is determined that all or a portion of the amount due will not be collected. Using the allowance method, the write-off is recorded as a debit to allowance for uncollectible accounts and a credit to accounts receivable. In our illustration, assume that actual bad debts in 2017 were $25,000. These write-offs would be recorded (in a summary journal entry) as follows:

Allowance	
	25,500
25,000	
	500

Allowance for uncollectible accounts	25,000	
Accounts receivable		25,000

The write-off of an account receivable reduces both receivables and the allowance, thus having no effect on income or financial position.

Net realizable value is not affected directly by the write-offs.

Accounts receivable	$280,000
Less: Allowance for uncollectible accounts	(500)
Net accounts receivable	$279,500

Of course, actual bad debts will tend to differ from estimates. However, the year in which the estimate is made, 2016 in this case, is not adjusted to correct the estimate. Rather, changes in estimate are made in whatever future year the estimate is revised. If the prior year's estimate of bad debts is too low, bad debt expense in the subsequent year will be increased. If the estimate is too high, bad debt expense in the subsequent year will be decreased. For example, in our illustration, the allowance at the end of 2016 is $25,500. Actual bad debts related to 2016 receivables are $25,000. 2016's financial information cannot be changed. Instead, the $500 credit balance in allowance for uncollectible accounts will cause 2017's bad debt expense to be less than if 2016's estimate of bad debts had been correct.

Ethical Dilemma

The management of the Auto Parts Division of the Santana Corporation receives a bonus if the division's income achieves a specific target. For 2016 the target will be achieved by a wide margin. Mary Beth Williams, the controller of the division, has been asked by Philip Stanton, the head of the division's management team, to try to reduce this year's income and "bank" some of the profits for future years. Mary Beth suggests that the division's bad debt expense as a percentage of net credit sales for 2016 be increased from 3% to 5%. She believes that 3% is the more accurate estimate but knows that both the corporation's internal auditors as well as the external auditors allow some flexibility when estimates are involved. Does Mary Beth's proposal present an ethical dilemma?

Recoveries of accounts receivable previously written off require the reinstatement of both the receivable and the allowance.

When previously written-off accounts are collected. Occasionally, a receivable that has been written off will be collected in part or in full. When this happens, the receivable and the allowance should be reinstated. To make that happen, the entry to write off the account simply is reversed. The collection is then recorded the usual way as a debit to cash and a credit to accounts receivable. This process ensures that the company will have a complete record of the payment history of the customer. For example, assume that in our illustration, $1,200 that was previously written off is collected. The following journal entries record the event:

Accounts receivable	1,200	
Allowance for uncollectible accounts		1,200
To reinstate the receivable previously written off.		

To reinstate the receivable previously written off.

Cash	1,200	
Accounts receivable		1,200
To record the cash collection.		

To record the cash collection.

Direct write-off of uncollectible accounts. If uncollectible accounts are not anticipated or are immaterial, an allowance for uncollectible accounts is not appropriate. In these few cases, adjusting entries are not recorded and any bad debts that do arise simply are written off as bad debt expense. A $750 uncollectible account would be recorded as follows:

FINANCIAL Reporting Case

Q3, p. 361

Bad debt expense	750	
Accounts receivable		750

This approach is known as the **direct write-off method**. Of course, if the sale that generated this receivable occurred in a previous reporting period, failure to record bad debt expense would have resulted in a mismatching of expenses and revenues. Also, operating expenses would have been understated and assets overstated in that period. This is why the direct write-off method of accounting for uncollectible accounts is not permitted by GAAP except in limited circumstances. Specifically, the allowance method must be used if it is probable that a material amount of receivables will not be collected and the amount can be reasonably estimated.[11] For federal income tax purposes, however, the direct write-off method is the required method for most companies and the allowance method is not permitted.

The *direct write-off method* is used only rarely for financial reporting, but it is the required method for income tax purposes.

Illustration 7–8 summarizes the key issues involving measuring and reporting accounts receivable.

Illustration 7–8

Measuring and Reporting Accounts Receivable

Recognition	Depends on revenue recognition; for most credit sales, revenue and the related receivables are recognized at the point of delivery.
Initial valuation	Initially recorded at the exchange price agreed upon by the buyer and seller.
Subsequent valuation	Initial valuation reduced by: 1. Allowance for sales returns 2. Allowance for uncollectible accounts: —The income statement approach —The balance sheet approach
Classification	Almost always classified as a current asset.

Concept Review Exercise

UNCOLLECTIBLE ACCOUNTS RECEIVABLE

The Hawthorne Manufacturing Company offers 30 days' credit to its customers. Uncollectible amounts are estimated by accruing a monthly charge to bad debt expense equal to 2% of credit sales. At the end of the year, the allowance for uncollectible accounts is adjusted based on an aging of accounts receivable. The company began 2017 with the following balances in its accounts:

Accounts receivable	$305,000
Allowance for uncollectible accounts	(25,500)

[11]FASB ASC 450–20–25–2: Contingencies—Loss Contingencies—Recognition (previously "Accounting for Contingencies," *Statement of Financial Accounting Standards No. 5* (Stamford, Conn.: FASB, 1975), par. 8).

During 2017, sales on credit were $1,300,000, cash collections from customers were $1,250,000, and actual write-offs of accounts were $25,000. An aging of accounts receivable at the end of 2017 indicates a required allowance of $30,000.

Required:

1. Determine the balances in accounts receivable and allowance for uncollectible accounts at the end of 2017.
2. Determine bad debt expense for 2017.
3. Prepare journal entries for the accrual of bad debts (in summary form, with one entry covering all twelve months of the year), the write-off of receivables, and the year-end adjusting entry for bad debts.

Solution:

Accounts Receivable

Debit	Credit
305,000	
1,300,000	1,250,000
	25,000
330,000	

Allowance for Uncollectible Accounts

Debit	Credit
	25,500
25,000	26,000
	3,500
	30,000

1. Determine the balances in accounts receivable and allowance for uncollectible accounts at the end of 2017.

Accounts receivable	
Beginning balance	$ 305,000
Add: Credit sales	1,300,000
Less: Cash collections	(1,250,000)
Write-offs	(25,000)
Ending balance	$ 330,000

Allowance for uncollectible accounts:	
Beginning balance	$ 25,500
Add: Bad debt expense recorded monthly (2% × $1,300,000)	26,000
Less: Write-offs	(25,000)
Balance before year-end adjustment	26,500
Year-end adjustment	3,500*
Ending balance	$ 30,000

*Required allowance of $30,000 less $26,500 already in allowance account.

2. Determine bad debt expense for 2017.

   Bad debt expense would be $29,500 (accrual of $26,000 plus year-end adjustment of an additional $3,500).

3. Prepare journal entries for the accrual of bad debts (in summary form), the write-off of receivables, and the year-end adjusting entry for bad debts.

Account	Debit	Credit
Bad debt expense (2% × $1,300,000)	26,000	
Allowance for uncollectible accounts		26,000
Monthly accrual of 2% of credit sales—summary entry.		
Allowance for uncollectible accounts	25,000	
Accounts receivable		25,000
Write-off of accounts receivable as they are determined uncollectible.		
Bad debt expense	3,500	
Allowance for uncollectible accounts		3,500
Year-end adjusting entry for bad debts.		

Notes Receivable

Notes receivable are formal credit arrangements between a creditor (lender) and a debtor (borrower). Notes arise from loans to other entities including affiliated companies and to stockholders and employees, from the extension of the credit period to trade customers, and occasionally from the sale of merchandise, other assets, or services. Notes receivable are classified as either current or noncurrent depending on the expected collection date(s).

LO7–7

Our examples below illustrate short-term notes. When the term of a note is longer than a year, it is reported as a long-term note. Long-term notes receivable are discussed in conjunction with long-term notes payable in Chapter 14.

Interest-Bearing Notes

The typical note receivable requires payment of a specified face amount, also called *principal,* at a specified maturity date or dates. In addition, interest is paid at a stated percentage of the face amount. Interest on notes is calculated as:

Face amount × Annual rate × Fraction of the annual period

For an example, consider Illustration 7–9.

Illustration 7–9

Note Receivable

The Stridewell Wholesale Shoe Company manufactures athletic shoes that it sells to retailers. On May 1, 2016, the company sold shoes to Harmon Sporting Goods. Stridewell agreed to accept a $700,000, 6-month, 12% note in payment for the shoes. Interest is payable at maturity. Assume that an interest rate of 12% is appropriate for a note of this type.

Stridewell would account for the note as follows:*

May 1, 2016		
Note receivable	700,000	
Sales revenue		700,000
To record the sale of goods in exchange for a note receivable.		
November 1, 2016		
Cash ($700,000 + $42,000)	742,000	
Interest revenue ($700,000 × 12% × 6/12)		42,000
Note receivable		700,000
To record the collection of the note at maturity.		

*To focus on recording the note we intentionally omit the entry required for the cost of the goods sold if the perpetual inventory system is used.

If the sale in the illustration occurs on August 1, 2016, and the company's fiscal year-end is December 31, a year-end adjusting entry accrues interest earned.

December 31, 2016		
Interest receivable	35,000	
Interest revenue ($700,000 × 12% × 5/12)		35,000

The February 1 collection is then recorded as follows:

February 1, 2017		
Cash ($700,000 + [$700,000 × 12% × 6/12])	742,000	
Interest revenue ($700,000 × 12% × 1/12)		7,000
Interest receivable (accrued at December 31)		35,000
Note receivable		700,000

Noninterest-Bearing Notes

Sometimes a receivable assumes the form of a so-called **noninterest-bearing note**. The name is a misnomer, though. Noninterest-bearing notes actually do bear interest, but the interest is deducted (or *discounted*) from the face amount to determine the cash proceeds made available to the borrower at the outset. For example, consider a six-month, $700,000 noninterest-bearing note with a 12% discount rate. In that case, $42,000 ($700,000 × 12% × ½ year) interest would be discounted at the outset rather than explicitly stated, and the selling price of the shoes would be only $658,000.[12] Assuming a May 1, 2016 sale, the transaction is recorded as follows:[13]

The discount becomes interest revenue in a noninterest-bearing note.

May 1, 2016		
Note receivable (face amount)	700,000	
Discount on note receivable ($700,000 × 12% × 6/12)		42,000
Sales revenue (difference)		658,000
November 1, 2016		
Discount on note receivable	42,000	
Interest revenue		42,000
Cash	700,000	
Note receivable (face amount)		700,000

When interest is discounted from the face amount of a note, the effective interest rate is higher than the stated discount rate.

The discount on note receivable is a contra account to the note receivable account. That is, the note receivable would be reported in the balance sheet net (less) any remaining discount. The discount represents future interest revenue that will be recognized as it is earned over time. The sales revenue under this arrangement is only $658,000, but the total amount of interest is calculated as the discount rate times the $700,000 face amount. This causes the *effective* interest rate to be higher than the 12% discount rate.

$ 42,000	Interest for 6 months
÷ $658,000	Sales price
= 6.383%	Rate for 6 months
× 2*	To annualize the rate
= 12.766%	Effective interest rate

*Two 6-month periods

Using a calculator:
Enter: N 1 I .06383
PMT – 700000
Output: PV 658,000

Using Excel, enter:
= PV(.06383,1,700000)
Output: 658,000

This note should be valued at the present value of future cash receipts. The present value of $700,000 to be received in six months using an effective interest rate of 6.383% is $658,000 ($700,000 ÷ 1.06383 = $658,000). The use of present value techniques for valuation purposes was introduced in Chapter 6, and we'll use these techniques extensively in subsequent chapters to value various long-term notes receivable, investments, and liabilities.

In the illustration, if the sale occurs on August 1, the December 31, 2016, adjusting entry and the entry to record the cash collection on February 1, 2017, are recorded as follows:

December 31, 2016		
Discount on note receivable	35,000	
Interest revenue ($700,000 × 12% × 5/12)*		35,000
February 1, 2017		
Discount on note receivable	7,000	
Interest revenue ($700,000 × 12% × 1/12)		7,000
Cash	700,000	
Note receivable (face amount)		700,000

*We also can calculate interest revenue by multiplying the net note receivable balance by the effective interest rate ($658,000 × 12.766% × 5/12 = $35,000).

[12]Sometimes the terms *discount rate* and *effective interest rate* are used interchangeably, so don't be confused by the different use of the term *discount rate* with respect to noninterest-bearing notes. Here, *discount rate* refers only to a rate that is multiplied by the face amount of the note (in Stridewell's case, $700,000) to calculate how much interest is included in the note (in Stridewell's case, $42,000). As shown later in this section, that discount rate is different from the *effective interest rate* that Stridewell earns on the outstanding receivable balance, and that Stridewell would use to calculate the present value of future cash flows.

[13]The entries shown assume the note is recorded by the gross method. By the net method, the interest component is netted against the face amount of the note as follows:

May 1, 2016		
Note receivable	658,000	
Sales revenue		658,000
November 1, 2016		
Cash	700,000	
Note receivable		658,000
Interest revenue ($700,000 × 12% × 6/12)		42,000

In the December 31, 2016 balance sheet, the note receivable is shown at $693,000: the face amount ($700,000) less remaining discount ($7,000).

Long-Term Notes Receivable

We account for long-term notes receivable the same way we account for short-term notes receivable, but the time value of money has a larger effect. To provide an example, Illustration 7–10 modifies the facts in Illustration 7–9 to have Stridewell agree on January 1, 2016, to accept a two-year noninterest-bearing note.

Illustration 7–10
Long-Term Noninterest-Bearing Note Receivable

The Stridewell Wholesale Shoe Company manufactures athletic shoes that it sells to retailers. On January 1, 2016, the company sold shoes to Harmon Sporting Goods. Stridewell agreed to accept a $700,000, two-year note in payment for the shoes. Assuming a 12% effective interest rate, Stridewell would account for the note as follows:*

January 1, 2016		
Notes receivable	700,000	
Discount on note receivable		141,964
Sales revenue**		558,036
To record the sale of goods in exchange for a two-year note receivable.		
December 31, 2016		
Discount on note receivable	66,964	
Interest revenue ($558,036 × 12%)		66,964
To record interest revenue in 2016.		
December 31, 2017		
Cash	700,000	
Discount on note receivable	75,000	
Interest revenue (($558,036 + $66,964) × 12%)		75,000
Notes receivable		700,000
To record interest revenue in 2017 and collection of the note		

*To focus on recording the note we intentionally omit the entry required for the cost of the goods sold if the perpetual inventory system is used.
** $700,000 × Present value of $1; $n = 2$, $i = 12\%$

It's useful to consider a couple of aspects of Illustration 7–10. First, notice that the sales revenue in 2016 is not recorded for the full $700,000. Instead, sales revenue is calculated as the present value of $700,000 *to be received in two years* ($558,036). The net amount of the note receivable equals its present value ($558,036), which is the note receivable of $700,000 less the discount on note receivable of $141,964. Recall from Chapter 5 that sellers need to recognize the financing component of a contract when the time value of money is significant. That is what Stridewell is doing. It earns sales revenue of $558,036 from selling shoes, and interest revenue totaling $141,964 ($66,964 + 75,000) for financing the transaction.

Using a calculator:
Enter: N 2 I .12
PMT −700000
Output: PV 558,036

Using Excel, enter:
= PV(.12,2,700000)
Output: 558,036

Second, interest revenue each period is calculated based on the *net* note receivable as of the beginning of that period. As a consequence, interest revenue differs between periods because the net note receivable increases over time. In our example, Stridewell's 2016 interest revenue of $66,964 is calculated based on the initial net note receivable balance ($558,036 × 12%). We reduce the discount on note receivable for 2016 interest revenue, which increases the net note receivable balance to $625,000 ($558,036 + $66,964). So, Stridewell's 2017 interest revenue of $75,000 is calculated based on that higher net note receivable balance ($625,000 × 12%), reducing the discount on note receivable to zero by the end of 2017. At that point, the book value of the note, sometimes called the carrying value or carrying amount, is $700,000, and that is the amount of cash that is collected. The effective interest rate stays the same over time, but interest revenue increases as that rate is multiplied by a receivable balance that increases over time. This is an application of the **effective interest method**, by which we calculate interest revenue or interest expense by

In the *effective interest method*, interest is determined by multiplying the outstanding balance by the effective interest rate.

multiplying the outstanding balance of a long-term receivable or liability by the effective interest rate. As you will see in later chapters, that method is used for all long-term receivables and liabilities.

We discuss long-term notes receivable in much greater detail in Chapter 14 at the same time we discuss accounting for long-term notes payable. That discussion provides more examples of accounting for long-term noninterest-bearing notes, as well as long-term interest-bearing notes, and also considers accounting for notes receivable that are collected in equal installment payments.

Marriott International accepts both interest-bearing and noninterest-bearing notes from developers and franchisees of new hotels. The 2013 disclosure note shown in Illustration 7–11 describes the company's accounting policy for these notes.

Illustration 7–11
Disclosure of Notes Receivable—Marriott International

Real World Financials

Summary of Significant Accounting Policies (in part) Senior, Mezzanine, and Other Loans

We may make loans to owners of hotels that we operate or franchise, generally to facilitate the development of a hotel and sometimes to facilitate brand programs or initiatives. We expect the owners to repay the loans in accordance with the loan agreements, or earlier as the hotels mature and capital markets permit.

Note 9: Notes Receivable (in part)

Notes Receivable Principal Payments (net of reserves and unamortized discounts) and Interest Rates ($ in millions)	**Amount**
Balance at year-end 2013	$178
Range of stated interest rates at year-end 2013	0 to 8.0%

When a noninterest-bearing note is received solely in exchange for cash, the amount of cash exchanged is the basis for valuing the note.

NOTES RECEIVED SOLELY FOR CASH. If a note with an unrealistic interest rate—even a noninterest-bearing note—is received *solely* in exchange for cash, the cash paid to the issuer is considered to be the note's present value.[14] Even if this means recording interest at a ridiculously low or zero rate, the amount of cash exchanged is the basis for valuing the note. When a non-cash asset is exchanged for a note with a low stated rate, we can argue that its real value is less than it's purported to be, but we can't argue that the present value of a sum of cash currently exchanged is less than that sum. If the noninterest-bearing note in the previous example had been received solely in exchange for $700,000 cash, the transaction would be recorded as follows:

Note receivable (face amount)	700,000	
Cash (given)		700,000

Subsequent Valuation of Notes Receivable

Similar to accounts receivable, if a company anticipates bad debts on short-term notes receivable, it uses an allowance account to reduce the receivable to net realizable value. The process of recording bad debt expense is the same as with accounts receivable.

Long-term notes present a more significant measurement problem. The longer the duration of the note, the more likely are bad debts. One of the more difficult measurement problems facing banks and other lending institutions is the estimation of bad debts on their long-term notes (loans). As an example, **Wells Fargo & Company**, a large bank

[14]This assumes that no other present or future considerations are included in the agreement. For example, a noninterest-bearing note might be given to a vendor in exchange for cash *and* a promise to provide future inventories at prices lower than anticipated market prices. The issuer values the note at the present value of cash payments using a realistic interest rate, and the difference between present value and cash payments is recognized as interest revenue over the life of the note. This difference also increases future inventory purchases to realistic market prices.

holding company, reported the following in the asset section of its December 31, 2013, balance sheet:

(in millions)	December 31, 2013	December 31, 2012
Loans	$825,799	$799,574
Allowance for loan losses	14,502	17,060
Net loans	$811,297	$782,514

A disclosure note, reproduced in Illustration 7–12, describes Wells Fargo's loan loss policy.

Allowance for Credit Losses (ACL) (in part)
The allowance for credit losses is management's estimate for credit losses inherent in the loan portfolio, including unfunded credit commitments, at the balance sheet date. We have an established process to determine the appropriateness of the allowance for credit losses that assesses the losses inherent in our portfolio and related unfunded credit commitments. While we attribute portions of the allowance to our respective commercial and consumer portfolio segments, the entire allowance is available to absorb credit losses inherent in the total loan portfolio and unfunded credit commitments.

Illustration 7–12
Disclosure of Allowance for Loan Losses—Wells Fargo & Company

Real World Financials

GAAP requires that companies disclose the fair value of their notes receivable in the disclosure notes (they don't have to disclose the fair value of accounts receivable when the book value of the receivables approximates their fair value).[15] Also, companies can choose to carry receivables at fair value in their balance sheets, with changes in fair value recognized as gains or losses in the income statements.[16] This "fair value option" is discussed in Chapter 12.

When it becomes probable that a creditor will be unable to collect all amounts due according to the contractual terms of a note, the receivable is considered **impaired**. When a creditor's investment in a note receivable becomes impaired for any reason, the receivable is remeasured as the present value of currently expected cash flows, discounted at the loan's original effective rate. Impairments of receivables are discussed in Appendix 7B.

Where We're Headed

As of the date this text was written, it appears that, starting as early as 2017, companies will use the *CECL ("Current Expected Credit Loss") model* to account for bad debts ("credit losses") on long-term notes receivable. The CECL model differs from current GAAP in two important ways.[17] First, the "probable" threshold for identifying impaired receivables is removed. Starting on day 1 of the long-term receivable, even if the likelihood of bad debts is very low, the creditor estimates bad debts by comparing the balance in the receivable to the present value of the cash flows expected to be received, discounted at the interest rate that was effective when the receivable was initially recognized. Second, while current practice tends to focus on events that already have occurred when considering the potential for bad debts, the CECL model broadens the information that creditors should consider and explicitly requires creditors to estimate bad debts based on predictions about the future, even if no events have occurred that indicate a problem. An example applying the CECL model is included in Appendix 7B.

[15] FASB ASC 825–10–50–10: Financial Instruments—Overall—Disclosure—Fair Value of Financial Instruments (previously "Disclosures about Fair Value of Financial Instruments" *Statement of Financial Accounting Standards No. 107* (Norwalk, Conn.: FASB, 1991)).
[16] FASB ASC 825–10–25: Financial Instruments—Overall—Recognition Fair Value Option (previously "The Fair Value Option for Financial Assets and Financial Liabilities" *Statement of Financial Accounting Standards No. 159* (Norwalk, Conn.: FASB, 2007)).
[17] *Proposed Accounting Standards Update*, "Financial Instruments—Credit Losses (Subtopic 825-15)" (Norwalk, Conn: FASB, December 20, 2012).

International Financial Reporting Standards

LO7–10

Accounts Receivable. Until recently, *IAS No. 39*[18] was the standard that specified appropriate accounting for accounts and notes receivables, under the category of Loans and Receivables. However, *IFRS No. 9*[19] currently is scheduled to be required after January 1, 2018, and earlier adoption is allowed. Therefore, until 2018 either standard could be in effect for a particular company that reports under IFRS (although countries in the European Union may not report under *IFRS No. 9*, as the European Commission has not yet ratified it). Still, both of the IFRS standards are very similar to U.S. GAAP with respect to accounting for accounts and notes receivable, with similar treatment of trade and cash discounts, sales returns, recognizing interest on notes receivable, and using an allowance for uncollectible accounts (which typically is called a "provision for bad debts" under IFRS).

A few key differences remain. IFRS and U.S. GAAP both allow a "fair value option" for accounting for receivables, but the IFRS standards restrict the circumstances in which that option is allowed (we discuss this more in Chapter 12). Also, *IAS No. 39* permits accounting for receivables as "available for sale" investments if that approach is elected upon initial recognition of the receivable. *IFRS No. 9* does not allow that option for receivables, and U.S. GAAP only allows "available for sale" accounting for investments in securities (we also discuss that approach further in Chapter 12). Also, U.S. GAAP requires more disaggregation of accounts and notes receivable in the balance sheet or notes. For example, companies need to separately disclose accounts receivable from customers, from related parties, and from others. IFRS recommends but does not require separate disclosure.

A final important difference relates to estimating bad debts. As of the date this text was written, it appears that IFRS requirements are moving to an ECL ("Expected Credit Loss") model. Similar to U.S. GAAP's CECL model, bad debts are estimated by comparing the balance in the receivable to the present value of cash flows expected to be received. However, for most receivables, the ECL model reports a "12-month ECL," which bases expected credit losses only on defaults that could occur within the next twelve months. Only if a receivable's credit quality has deteriorated significantly does the creditor instead report the "lifetime ECL," which also includes credit losses expected to occur from defaults after twelve months, as is done for all receivables under the CECL model likely to be used in U.S. GAAP. As a result of this lack of convergence, it is likely that bad debts accruals under IFRS will be lower, and occur later, than under U.S. GAAP.

Financing with Receivables

LO7–8

Financial institutions have developed a wide variety of ways for companies to use their receivables to obtain immediate cash. Companies can find this attractive because it shortens their operating cycles by providing cash immediately rather than having to wait until credit customers pay the amounts due. Also, many companies avoid the difficulties of servicing (billing and collecting) receivables by having financial institutions take on that role. Of course, financial institutions require compensation for providing these services, usually interest and/or a finance charge.

The various approaches used to finance with receivables differ with respect to which rights and risks are retained by the *transferor* (the company who was the original holder of the receivables) and which are passed on to the *transferee* (the new holder, the financial institution). Despite this diversity, any of these approaches can be described as either:

1. A *secured borrowing.* Under this approach, the transferor (borrower) simply acts like it borrowed money from the transferee (lender), with the receivables remaining in the transferor's balance sheet and serving as collateral for the loan. On the other side of the transaction, the transferee recognizes a note receivable.

[18]"Financial Instruments: Recognition and Measurement," *International Accounting Standard No. 39* (IASCF), as amended effective January 1, 2014.

[19]"Financial Instruments," *International Financial Reporting Standard No. 9* (IASCF), as amended effective January 1, 2014.

2. *A sale of receivables.* Under this approach, the transferor (seller) "derecognizes" (removes) the receivables from its balance sheet, acting like it sold them to the transferee (buyer). On the other side of the transaction, the transferee recognizes the receivables as assets in its balance sheet and measures them at their fair value.

As you will see in the examples that follow, the transferor (borrower) debits cash regardless of whether the transaction is treated as a secured borrowing or a sale of receivables. What differs is whether the borrower credits a liability (for a secured borrowing) or credits the receivable asset (for a sale of receivables). Let's discuss each of these approaches in more detail as they apply to accounts receivable and notes receivable. Then we'll discuss the circumstances under which GAAP requires each approach.

Secured Borrowing

Sometimes companies **pledge** accounts receivable as collateral for a loan. No particular receivables are associated with the loan. Rather, the entire receivables balance serves as collateral. The responsibility for collection of the receivables remains solely with the company. No special accounting treatment is needed for pledged receivables, but the arrangement should be described in a disclosure note. For example, Illustration 7–13 shows a portion of the long-term debt disclosure note included in the January 31, 2013 annual report of **Virco Mfg. Corporation**, a manufacturer of office furniture.

When companies *pledge* accounts receivable as collateral for debt, a disclosure note describes the arrangement.

Illustration 7–13

Disclosure of Receivables Used as Collateral—Virco Mfg. Corporation

Real World Financials

Liquidity and Capital Resources (in part) Working Capital Requirements (in part)
The Revolving Credit Facility is an asset-based line of credit that is subject to a borrowing base limitation and generally provides for advances of up to 85% of eligible accounts receivable . . .

Alternatively, financing arrangements can require that companies **assign** particular receivables to serve as collateral for loans. You already may be familiar with the concept of assigning an asset as collateral if you or someone you know has a mortgage on a home. The bank or other financial institution holding the mortgage will require that, if the homeowner defaults on the mortgage payments, the home be sold and the proceeds used to pay off the mortgage debt. Similarly, in the case of an assignment of receivables, nonpayment of a debt will require the proceeds from collecting the assigned receivables to go directly toward repayment of the debt.

In these arrangements, the lender typically lends an amount of money that is less than the amount of receivables assigned by the borrower. The difference provides some protection for the lender to allow for possible uncollectible accounts. Also, the lender (sometimes called an *assignee*) usually charges the borrower (sometimes called an *assignor*) an up-front finance charge in addition to stated interest on the loan. The receivables might be collected either by the lender or the borrower, depending on the details of the arrangement. Illustration 7–14 provides an example.

Illustration 7–14

Assignment of Accounts Receivable

On December 1, 2016, the Santa Teresa Glass Company borrowed $500,000 from Finance Bank and signed a promissory note. Interest at 12% is payable monthly. The company assigned $620,000 of its receivables as collateral for the loan. Finance Bank charges a finance fee equal to 1.5% of the accounts receivable assigned.

Santa Teresa Glass records the borrowing as follows:

Cash (difference)	490,700	
Finance charge expense* (1.5% × $620,000)	9,300	
Liability—financing arrangement		500,000

*In theory, this fee should be allocated over the entire period of the loan rather than recorded as an expense in the initial period. However, amounts usually are small and the loan period usually is short. For expediency, then, we expense the entire fee immediately.

(continued)

Accounts Receivable

620,000	
	400,000
220,000	

Note Payable

	500,000
400,000	
	100,000

(concluded)

Santa Teresa will continue to collect the receivables, and will record any discounts, sales returns, and bad debt write-offs, but will remit the cash to Finance Bank, usually on a monthly basis. If $400,000 of the receivables assigned are collected in December, Santa Teresa Glass records the following entries:

Cash	400,000	
Accounts receivable		400,000
Interest expense ($500,000 × 12% × 1⁄12)	5,000	
Liability—financing arrangement	400,000	
Cash		405,000

In Santa Teresa's December 31, 2016, balance sheet, the company would report the receivables and note payable together as net accounts receivable:

When companies *assign* particular accounts receivable as collateral for debt, the balances of the receivables and the debt are offset in the balance sheet.

Current assets:	
Accounts receivable assigned	$220,000
Less: Liability—financing arrangement	(100,000)
Equity in accounts receivable assigned	$ 120,000

Netting a liability against a related asset, also called offsetting, usually is not allowed by GAAP. However, in this case, we deduct the note payable from the accounts receivable assigned because, by contractual agreement, the note will be paid with cash collected from the receivables. In Santa Teresa's financial statements, the arrangement also is described in a disclosure note.

Sale of Receivables

Accounts and notes receivable, like any other assets, can be sold at a gain or a loss. The basic accounting treatment for the sale of receivables is similar to accounting for the sale of other assets. The seller (transferor) (a) removes from the accounts the receivables (and any allowance for bad debts associated with them), (b) recognizes at fair value any assets acquired or liabilities assumed by the seller in the transaction, and (c) records the difference as a gain or loss.

The sale of accounts receivable is a popular method of financing. A technique once used by companies in a few industries or with poor credit ratings, the sale of receivables is now a common occurrence for many different types of companies. For example, General Motors, Deere & Co., and Bank of America all sell receivables. The two most common types of selling arrangements are **factoring** and **securitization**. We'll now discuss each type.

Two popular arrangements used for the sale of receivables are *factoring* and *securitization*.

In a factoring arrangement, the company sells its accounts receivable to a financial institution. The financial institution typically buys receivables for cash, handles the billing and collection of the receivables, and charges a fee for this service. Actually, credit cards like VISA and Mastercard are forms of factoring arrangements. The seller relinquishes all rights to the future cash receipts in exchange for cash from the buyer (the *factor*).

As an example, Illustration 7–15 shows an excerpt from the website of BusinessCash .Com, a financial institution that offers factoring as one of its services.

Illustration 7–15
Advertisement of Factoring Service—BusinessCash.Com
Real World Financials

Accounts Receivable Factoring
Accounts receivable factoring is the selling of your invoices (accounts receivable) for cash versus waiting 30–60 days to be paid by your customer. Factoring will get you the working capital you need now and improve your cash flow. We will advance 75%–90% against the invoice you generate and pay you the balance less our fee (typically 2%–4%) when the invoice is paid.

Notice that the factor, BusinessCash.com, advances only between 75%–90% of the factored receivables. The remaining balance is retained as security until all of the receivables are collected and then remitted to the transferor, net of the factor's fee. The fee charged by this factor ranges from 2%–4%. The range depends on, among other things, the quality of the receivables and the length of time before payment is required.

Another popular arrangement used to sell receivables is **securitization**. In a typical accounts receivable securitization, the company creates a "special purpose entity" (SPE), usually a trust or a subsidiary. The SPE buys a pool of trade receivables, credit card receivables, or loans from the company, and then sells related securities, typically debt such as bonds or commercial paper, that are backed (collateralized) by the receivables. Securitizing receivables using an SPE can provide significant economic advantages, allowing companies to reach a large pool of investors and to obtain more favorable financing terms.[20]

As an example of a securitization, Illustration 7–16 shows a portion of the disclosure note included in the 2013 annual report of **Flextronics International Limited**, a worldwide leader in design, manufacturing and logistics services, describing the securitization of its trade accounts receivables.

Note 8: TRADE RECEIVABLES SECURITIZATION

The Company continuously sells designated pools of trade receivables . . . to affiliated special purpose entities, each of which in turns sells 100% of the receivables to unaffiliated financial institutions . . . The company services, administers and collects the receivables on behalf of the special purpose entities and receives a servicing fee of 0.5% to 1.00% of serviced receivables per annum.

Illustration 7–16

Description of Securitization Program—Flextronics International Limited

Real World Financials

The specifics of sale accounting vary depending on the particular arrangement between the seller and buyer (transferee).[21] One key feature is whether the receivables are transferred **without recourse** or **with recourse**.

The buyer assumes the risk of uncollectibility when accounts receivable are sold *without recourse*.

SALE WITHOUT RECOURSE. If a factoring arrangement is made **without recourse**, the buyer can't ask the seller for more money if the receivables prove to be uncollectible. Therefore, the buyer assumes the risk of bad debts. Illustration 7–17 provides an example of receivables factored without recourse.

In December 2016, the Santa Teresa Glass Company factored accounts receivable that had a book value of \$600,000 to Factor Bank. The transfer was made without recourse. Under this arrangement, Santa Teresa transfers the \$600,000 of receivables to Factor, and Factor immediately remits to Santa Teresa cash equal to 90% of the factored amount (90% × \$600,000 = \$540,000). Factor retains the remaining 10% to cover its factoring fee (equal to 4% of the total factored amount; 4% × \$600,000 = \$24,000) and to provide a cushion against potential sales returns and allowances. After Factor has collected cash equal to the amount advanced to Santa Teresa plus their factoring fee, Factor remits the excess to Santa Teresa. Therefore, under this arrangement Factor provides Santa Teresa with cash up-front and a "beneficial interest" in the transferred receivables equal to the fair value of the last 10% of the receivables to be collected (which management estimates to equal \$50,000), less the 4% factoring fee.[22]

Santa Teresa Glass records the transfer as follows:

Cash (90% × \$600,000)	540,000	
Loss on sale of receivables (to balance)	34,000	
Receivable from factor (\$50,000 − 24,000 fee)	26,000	
Accounts receivable (book value sold)		600,000

Illustration 7–17

Accounts Receivable Factored without Recourse

[20]Because the SPE is a separate legal entity, it typically is viewed as "bankruptcy remote," meaning that the transferor's creditors can't access the receivables if the transferor goes bankrupt. This increases the safety of the SPE's assets and typically allows it to obtain more favorable financing terms than could the transferor.

[21]FASB ASC 860: Transfers and Servicing (previously "Accounting for Transfers of Financial Assets, an amendment of FASB Statement No. 140," *Statement of Financial Accounting Standards No. 166* (Norwalk, Conn.: FASB, 2009)).

[22]Illustration 7–17 depicts an arrangement in which the factor's fee is paid out of the 10% of receivables retained by the factor. Alternatively, a factoring arrangement could be structured to have the factor's fee withheld from the cash advanced to the company at the start of the arrangement. In that case, in Illustration 7–17 the journal entry recorded by Santa Teresa would be:

Cash ([90% × \$600,000] − \$24,000 fee)	516,000	
Loss on sale of receivables (to balance)	34,000	
Receivable from factor	50,000	
Accounts receivable (book value sold)		600,000

Note that, in Illustration 7–17, the fair value ($50,000) of the last 10% of the receivables to be collected is less than 10% of the total book value of the receivables (10% × $600,000 = $60,000). That's typical, because the last receivables to be collected are likely to be reduced by sales returns and allowances, and therefore have a lower fair value.

The seller retains the risk of uncollectibility when accounts receivable are sold *with recourse*.

SALE WITH RECOURSE. When a company sells accounts receivable **with recourse**, the seller retains all of the risk of bad debts. In effect, the seller guarantees that the buyer will be paid even if some receivables prove to be uncollectible. To compensate the seller for retaining the risk of bad debts, the buyer usually charges a lower factoring fee when receivables are sold with recourse.

In Illustration 7–17, even if the receivables were sold with recourse, Santa Teresa Glass still could account for the transfer as a sale so long as the conditions for sale treatment are met. The only difference is the additional requirement that Santa Teresa record the estimated fair value of its recourse obligation as a liability. The recourse obligation is the estimated amount that Santa Teresa will have to pay Factor Bank as a reimbursement for uncollectible receivables. Illustration 7–18 provides an example of receivables factored with recourse.

Illustration 7–18
Accounts Receivable Factored with Recourse

Assume the same facts as in Illustration 7–17, except that Santa Teresa sold the receivables to Factor *with recourse* and estimates the fair value of the recourse obligation to be $5,000. Santa Teresa records the transfer as follows:

	Debit	Credit
Cash (90% × $600,000)	540,000	
Loss on sale of receivables (to balance)	39,000	
Receivable from factor ($50,000 − 24,000 fee)	26,000	
Recourse liability		5,000
Accounts receivable (book value sold)		600,000

When comparing Illustrations 7–17 and 7–18, notice that the estimated recourse liability of $5,000 increases the loss on sale by $5,000. If the factor eventually collects all of the receivables, Santa Teresa eliminates the recourse liability and recognizes a gain.

Transfers of Notes Receivable

We handle transfers of notes receivable in the same manner as transfers of accounts receivable. A note receivable can be used to obtain immediate cash from a financial institution either by pledging the note as collateral for a loan or by selling the note. Notes also can be securitized.

The transfer of a note receivable to a financial institution is called *discounting*.

The transfer of a note to a financial institution is referred to as **discounting**. The financial institution accepts the note and gives the seller cash equal to the maturity value of the note reduced by a discount. The discount is computed by applying a discount rate to the maturity value and represents the financing fee the financial institution charges for the transaction. Illustration 7–19 provides an example of the calculation of the proceeds received by the transferor.

Illustration 7–19
Discounting a Note Receivable

On December 31, 2016, the Stridewell Wholesale Shoe Company sold land in exchange for a nine-month, 10% note. The note requires the payment of $200,000 plus interest on September 30, 2017. The company's fiscal year-end is December 31. The 10% rate properly reflects the time value of money for this type of note. On March 31, 2017, Stridewell discounted the note at the Bank of the East. The bank's discount rate is 12%.

Because the note had been outstanding for three months before it's discounted at the bank, Stridewell first records the interest that has accrued prior to being discounted:

STEP 1: Accrue interest earned on the note receivable prior to its being discounted.

March 31, 2017

	Debit	Credit
Interest receivable	5,000	
Interest revenue ($200,000 × 10% × 3/12)		5,000

(continued)

(concluded)

Next, the value of the note if held to maturity is calculated. Then the discount for the time remaining to maturity is deducted to determine the cash proceeds from discounting the note:

$ 200,000	Face amount
15,000	Interest to maturity ($200,000 × 10% × 9/12)
215,000	Maturity value
(12,900)	Discount ($215,000 × 12% × 6/12)
$202,100	Cash proceeds

STEP 2: Add interest to maturity to calculate maturity value.

STEP 3: Deduct discount to calculate cash proceeds.

Similar to accounts receivable, Stridewell potentially could account for the transfer as a sale or a secured borrowing. For example, Illustration 7–20 shows the appropriate journal entries to account for the transfer as a sale without recourse.

Cash (proceeds determined above)	202,100	
Loss on sale of note receivable (to balance)	2,900	
Note receivable (face amount)		200,000
Interest receivable (accrued interest determined above)		5,000

Illustration 7–20

Discounted Note Treated as a Sale

Deciding Whether to Account for a Transfer as a Sale or a Secured Borrowing

Transferors usually prefer to use the sale approach rather than the secured borrowing approach to account for the transfer of a receivable, because the sale approach makes the transferor seem less leveraged, more liquid, and perhaps more profitable than does the secured borrowing approach. Illustration 7–21 explains why by describing particular effects on key accounting metrics.

	Transfer of Receivables Accounted for as a:		
Does the Accounting Approach:	**Sale**	**Secured Borrowing**	**Why Sales Approach is Preferred by the Transferor:**
Derecognize A/R, reducing assets?	Yes	No	Sale approach produces lower total assets and higher return on assets (ROA)
Recognize liability for cash received?	No	Yes	Sale approach produces lower liabilities and less leverage (debt/equity)
Where is cash received shown in the statement of cash flows?	May be in operating or financing sections	Always in financing section	Sale approach can produce higher cash flow from operations at time of transfer
Recognize gain on transfer?	More likely	Less likely	Sale approach can produce higher income at time of transfer.

Illustration 7–21

Why Do Transferors of Receivables Generally Want to Account for the Transfer as a Sale?

So, when is a company allowed to account for the transfer of receivables as a sale? The most critical element is the extent to which the company (the transferor) *surrenders control over the assets transferred.* For some arrangements, surrender of control is clear (e.g., when a receivable is sold without recourse and without any other involvement by the transferor). However, for other arrangements this distinction is not obvious. Indeed, some companies appear to structure transactions in ways that qualify for sale treatment but retain enough involvement to have control. This led the FASB to provide guidelines designed to constrain inappropriate use of the sale approach. Specifically, the transferor (defined to include the company, its consolidated affiliates, and people acting on behalf of the company) is determined to have surrendered control over the receivables if and only if all of the following conditions are met:[23]

If the transferor is deemed to have surrendered control over the transferred receivables, the arrangement is accounted for as a sale; otherwise as a secured borrowing.

a. The transferred assets have been isolated from the transferor—beyond the reach of the transferor and its creditors.
b. Each transferee has the right to pledge or exchange the assets it received.
c. The transferor does not maintain *effective control* over the transferred assets, for example, by structuring the transfer such that the assets are likely to end up returned to the transferor.

If all of these conditions are met, the transferor accounts for the transfer as a sale. If any of the conditions are *not* met, the transferor treats the transaction as a secured borrowing.

It is not surprising that some companies have aggressively tried to circumvent these conditions by creating elaborate transactions to qualify for sale treatment. The most famous recent case was Lehman Brothers' use of "Repo 105" transactions, discussed in Illustration 7–22.

Illustration 7–22

Repo 105 Transactions—Lehman Brothers

Real World Financials

Lehman Brothers' bankruptcy in 2008 was the largest ever to occur in the United States. One factor that likely contributed to investor losses was Lehman's use of "Repo 105" transactions that concealed how overburdened with liabilities the company had become. Here is how a Repo 105 transaction worked. Near the end of each quarter, Lehman would transfer financial assets like receivables to a bank or other financial institution in exchange for cash, and would account for that transfer as a sale of the financial assets. Lehman would use the cash obtained from the transfer to pay down liabilities, so the net effect of the transaction was to reduce assets, reduce liabilities, and therefore make Lehman appear less leveraged and less risky. Lehman also agreed to repurchase ("repo") the assets in the next quarter for an amount of cash that exceeded the amount it initially received.

In substance, this transaction is a loan, since Lehman ended up retaining the financial assets and paying amounts equivalent to principal and interest. However, Lehman argued that the assets were beyond its *effective control,* because the cash it received for transferring the assets was insufficient to enable Lehman to repurchase those assets (the "105" in "Repo 105" refers to the assets being worth at least 105% of the cash Lehman was getting for them). Although Lehman's interpretation was supported by the GAAP in effect at the time, these transactions were very poorly disclosed, and when they eventually came to light, the financial markets and investing public reacted very negatively. In response to the Lehman debacle, the FASB has taken steps to close the loophole that allowed Repo 105 transactions to be accounted for as sales.[24]

Additional Consideration

Participating Interests. What if, rather than transferring all of a particular receivable, a company transfers only part of it? For example, what if a company transfers the right to receive future interest payments on a note, but retains the right to receive the loan principal? Recent changes in U.S. GAAP require that a partial transfer be treated as a secured borrowing unless the amount transferred qualifies as a "participating interest" as well as meeting the "surrender of control" requirements described above. Participating interests are defined as having a proportionate ownership interest in the receivable and sharing proportionally in the cash flows of the receivable. Many common securitization arrangements do not qualify as participating interests, so this change in GAAP makes it harder for partial transfers to qualify for the sale approach.

[23]FASB ASC 860–10–40: Transfers and Servicing—Overall—Derecognition (previously "Accounting for Transfers and Servicing of Financial Assets and Extinguishments of Liabilities," *Statement of Financial Accounting Standards No. 140* (Norwalk, Conn.: FASB, 2000), as amended by *SFAS No. 166*).

[24]FASB ASC 860–10–55: Transfers and Servicing—Overall—Implementation Guidance and Illustrations (previously ASU 2011-03: Transfers and Servicing (Topic 860): *Reconsideration of Effective Control for Repurchase Agreements* (Norwalk, Conn.: FASB 2011)).

Illustration 7–23 summarizes the decision process that is used to determine whether a transfer of a receivable is accounted for as a secured borrowing or a sale.

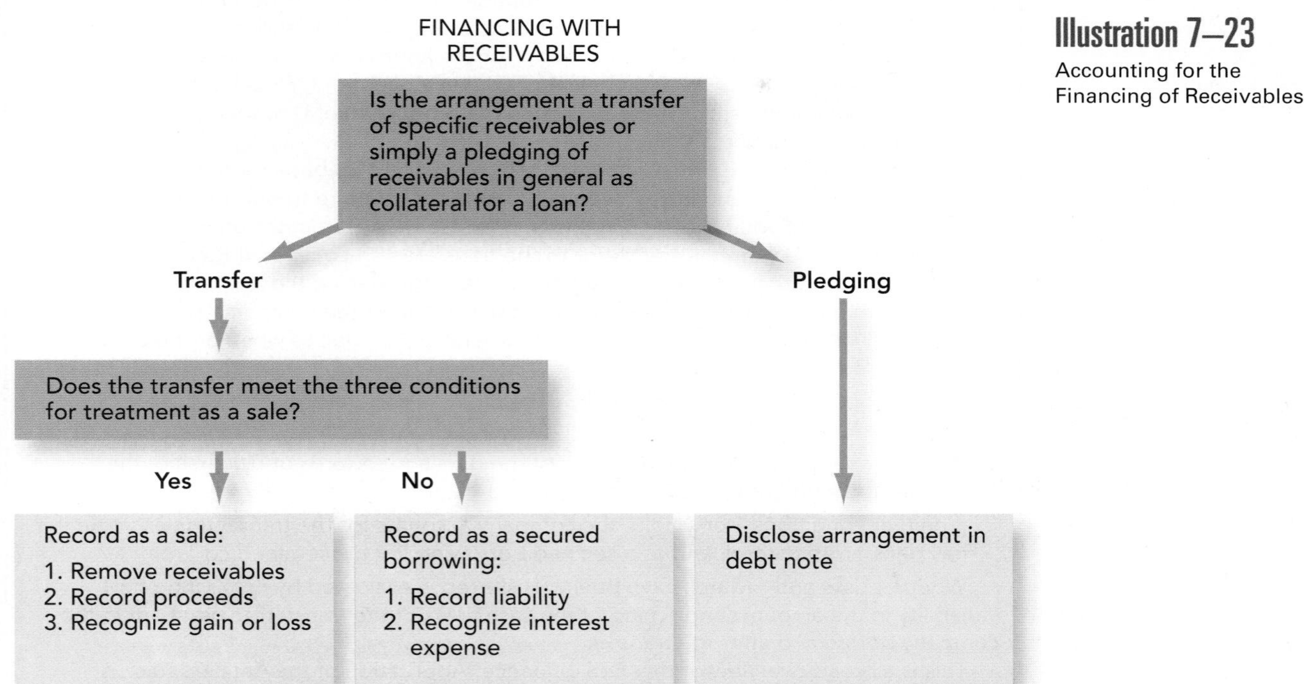

Illustration 7–23
Accounting for the Financing of Receivables

Disclosures

The amount of disclosures relevant to asset transfers increased dramatically in response to the 2008/2009 financial crisis. In particular, much disclosure is required when the transferor has continuing involvement in the transferred assets but accounts for the transfer as a sale. Why? Those are the circumstances under which it's most likely that the transferor may still bear significant risk associated with the arrangement, so those are the arrangements that analysts often view instead as a secured borrowing. As a result, transferors must provide enough information about the transfer to allow financial statement users to fully understand (a) the transfer, (b) any continuing involvement with the transferred assets, and (c) any ongoing risks to the transferor.

The company also has to provide information about the quality of the transferred assets. For example, for transferred receivables, the company needs to disclose the amount of receivables that are past due and any credit losses occurring during the period. Among the other information the company must disclose are:

- How fair values were estimated when recording the transaction.
- Any cash flows occurring between the transferor and the transferee.
- How any continuing involvement in the transferred assets will be accounted for on an ongoing basis.[25]

[25]FASB ASC 860–10–40: Transfers and Servicing—Overall—Derecognition (previously "Accounting for Transfers of Financial Assets, an amendment of FASB Statement No. 140," *Statement of Financial Accounting Standards No. 166* (Norwalk, Conn.: FASB, 2009), par. 17).

International Financial Reporting Standards

LO7–10

Transfers of Receivables. *IAS No. 39*[26] and FASB ASC Topic 860[27] cover financing with receivables under IFRS and U.S. GAAP, respectively. The international and U.S. guidance often lead to similar accounting treatments. Both seek to determine whether an arrangement should be treated as a secured borrowing or a sale, and, having concluded which approach is appropriate, both account for the approaches in a similar fashion. Also, the recent change in U.S. GAAP that eliminated the concept of QSPEs is a big step toward convergence with IFRS, and is likely to reduce the proportion of U.S. securitizations that qualify for sale accounting.

Where IFRS and U.S. GAAP most differ is in the conceptual basis for their choice of accounting approaches and in the decision process they require to determine which approach to use. As you have seen in this chapter, U.S. GAAP focuses on whether control of assets has shifted from the transferor to the transferee. In contrast, IFRS requires a more complex decision process. The company has to have transferred the rights to receive the cash flows from the receivable, and then considers whether the company has transferred "substantially all of the risks and rewards of ownership," as well as whether the company has transferred control. Under IFRS:

1. If the company *transfers* substantially all of the risks and rewards of ownership, the transfer is treated as a sale.
2. If the company *retains* substantially all of the risks and rewards of ownership, the transfer is treated as a secured borrowing.
3. If neither conditions 1 or 2 hold, the company accounts for the transaction as a sale if it has transferred control, and as a secured borrowing if it has retained control.

Whether risks and rewards have been transferred is evaluated by comparing how variability in the amounts and timing of the cash flows of the transferred asset affect the company before and after the transfer.

This is a broad overview of the IFRS guidance. Application of the detailed rules is complex, and depending on the specifics of an arrangement, a company could have different accounting under IFRS and U.S. GAAP.

Where We're Headed

LO7–10

As indicated previously in this chapter, the FASB recently modified accounting for transfers of receivables. The board also indicated that those changes were a short-term solution and that it intended to work with the IASB to produce a standard that comprehensively addressed derecognition of assets and liabilities (which would include determining when transfers of receivables can be accounted for as sales). However, in 2010 the boards decided to focus on other convergence projects and so have not made recent progress on this one. Many differences between current IFRS and U.S. GAAP remain to be resolved before full convergence is achieved in this area.

Concept Review Exercise

FINANCING WITH RECEIVABLES

The Hollywood Lumber Company obtains financing from the Midwest Finance Company by factoring (or discounting) its receivables. During June 2016, the company factored $1,000,000 of accounts receivable to Midwest. The transfer was made *without* recourse. The

[26] "Financial Instruments: Recognition and Measurement," *International Accounting Standard No. 39* (IASCF), as amended effective January 1, 2014.

[27] FASB ASC 860: Transfers and Servicing (previously "Accounting for Transfers of Financial Assets, an amendment of FASB Statement No. 140," *Statement of Financial Accounting Standards No. 166* (Norwalk, Conn.: FASB, 2009)).

factor, Midwest Finance, remits 80% of the factored receivables and retains 20%. When the receivables are collected by Midwest, the retained amount, less a 3% fee (3% of the total factored amount), will be remitted to Hollywood Lumber. Hollywood estimates that the fair value of the amount retained by Midwest is $180,000.

In addition, on June 30, 2016, Hollywood discounted a note receivable without recourse. The note, which originated on March 31, 2016, requires the payment of $150,000 *plus* interest at 8% on March 31, 2017. Midwest's discount rate is 10%. The company's fiscal year-end is December 31.

Required:

Prepare journal entries for Hollywood Lumber for the factoring of accounts receivable and the note receivable discounted on June 30. Assume that the required criteria are met and the transfers are accounted for as sales.

Solution:

The Factoring of Receivables		
Cash (80% × $1,000,000)	800,000	
Loss on sale of receivables (to balance)	50,000	
Receivable from factor ($180,000 − 30,000 fee)	150,000	
Accounts receivable (balance sold)		1,000,000
The Note Receivable Discounted		
Interest receivable	3,000	
Interest revenue ($150,000 × 8% × 3/12)		3,000
Cash (proceeds determined below)	149,850	
Loss on sale of note receivable (difference)	3,150	
Note receivable (face amount)		150,000
Interest receivable (accrued interest determined above)		3,000

$150,000	Face amount
12,000	Interest to maturity ($150,000 × 8%)
162,000	Maturity value
(12,150)	Discount ($162,000 × 10% × 9/12)
$149,850	Cash proceeds

Add interest to maturity to calculate maturity value.

Deduct discount to calculate cash proceeds.

Decision Makers' Perspective

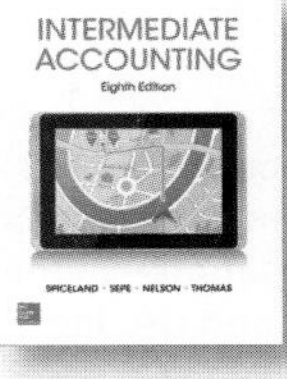

RECEIVABLES MANAGEMENT. A company's investment in receivables is influenced by several variables, including the level of sales, the nature of the product or service sold, and credit and collection policies. These variables are, of course, related. For example, a change in credit policies could affect sales. In fact, more liberal credit policies—allowing customers a longer time to pay or offering cash discounts for early payment—often are initiated with the specific objective of increasing sales volume.

● LO7–9

Management's choice of credit and collection policies often involves trade-offs. For example, offering cash discounts may increase sales volume, accelerate customer payment, and reduce bad debts. These benefits are not without cost. The cash discounts reduce the amount of cash collected from customers who take advantage of the discounts. Extending payment terms also may increase sales volume. However, this creates an increase in the required investment in receivables and may increase bad debts.

Management must evaluate the costs and benefits of any change in credit and collection policies.

The ability to use receivables as a method of financing also offers management alternatives. Assigning, factoring, and discounting receivables are alternative methods of financing operations that must be evaluated relative to other financing methods such as lines of credit or other types of short-term borrowing.

Investors, creditors, and financial analysts can gain important insights by monitoring a company's investment in receivables. Chapter 5 introduced the receivables turnover ratio and the related average collection period, ratios designed to monitor receivables. Recall that these ratios are calculated as follows:

$$\text{Receivables turnover ratio} = \frac{\text{Net sales}}{\text{Average accounts receivable (net)}}$$

$$\text{Average collection period} = \frac{365 \text{ days}}{\text{Receivables turnover ratio}}$$

The turnover ratio shows the number of times during a period that the average accounts receivable balance is collected, and the average collection period is an approximation of the number of days the average accounts receivable balance is outstanding.

As a company's sales grow, receivables also will increase. If the percentage increase in receivables is greater than the percentage increase in sales, the receivables turnover ratio will decline (the average collection period will increase). This could indicate customer dissatisfaction with the product or that the company has extended too generous payment terms in order to attract new customers, which, in turn, could increase sales returns and bad debts.

These ratios also can be used to compare the relative effectiveness of companies in managing the investment in receivables. Of course, it would be meaningless to compare the receivables turnover ratio of a computer products company such as **IBM** with that of, say, a food products company like **Hershey**. A company selling high-priced, low-volume products like mainframe computers generally will grant customers longer payment terms than a company selling lower priced, higher volume food products. Illustration 7–24 lists the 2013 receivables turnover ratio for some well-known companies. The differences are as expected, given the nature of the companies' products and operations. In particular, companies designing expensive products for medical and business applications turn over their receivables less frequently than do consumer-goods manufacturers and wholesalers.

Illustration 7–24
Receivables Turnover Ratios

Company	2013 Receivables Turnover Ratio
Medtronic (medical technology)	4.28
Autodesk (design software)	5.19
General Mills (wholesale consumer foods)	12.83

To illustrate receivables analysis in more detail, let's compute the 2013 receivables turnover ratio and the average collection period for two companies in the software industry, **Symantec Corp.** and **CA, Inc.** (formerly Computer Associates, Inc.).

Balance sheet and income statement information—Symantec Corp. and CA, Inc.

	($ in millions)			
	Symantec Corp.		CA, Inc.	
	2013	2012	2013	2012
Accounts receivable (net)	$1,031	$940	$856	$902
Two-year averages	$985.5		$ 879	
Net sales—2013	$6,906		$4,643	

Receivables turnover and average collection period—Symantec Corp. and CA, Inc.

	Symantec Corp.	CA, Inc.	Industry Average
Receivables Turnover	$= \frac{\$6,906}{\$985.5} = 7.01$ times	$\frac{\$4,643}{\$879} = 5.28$ times	7.16 times
Average Collection Period	$= \frac{365}{7.01} = 52.07$ days	$\frac{365}{5.28} = 69.13$ days	50.98 days

On average, Symantec collects its receivables 17 days sooner than does CA, and 1 day slower than the industry average. A major portion of Symantec's sales of products like Norton antivirus software are made directly to consumers online who pay immediately with credit cards, significantly accelerating payment. CA, on the other hand, sells primarily to businesses, who take longer to pay.

EARNINGS QUALITY. Recall our discussion in Chapter 4 concerning earnings quality. We learned that managers have the ability, to a limited degree, to manipulate reported income and that many observers believe this practice diminishes earnings quality because it can mask "permanent" earnings. Former SEC Chairman Arthur Levitt listed discretionary accruals, which he called "Miscellaneous Cookie Jar Reserves," as one of the most popular methods companies use to manipulate income.

> **Arthur Levitt, Jr.**
> A third illusion played by some companies is using unrealistic assumptions to estimate . . . such items as sales returns, loan losses or warranty costs. In doing so, they stash accruals in cookie jars during good times and reach into them when needed in the bad times.[28]

Bad debt expense is one of a variety of discretionary accruals that provide management with the opportunity to manipulate income.

Sometimes financial statement users can examine accounts receivable, the allowance for bad debts, and other accounts to detect low earnings quality. For example, **PaineWebber Inc.** downgraded its stock recommendation for **Sunbeam, Inc.**, after noticing unusually high accounts receivable and unexpected increases in sales of certain products. Also, Sunbeam's allowance for uncollectible accounts had shown large increases in prior periods. It eventually came to light that Sunbeam had been manipulating its income by using a "bill and hold" strategy with retail buyers. This involved selling products at large discounts to retailers before they normally would buy and then holding the products in third-party warehouses, with delivery at a later date.

Another area for accounting-quality concern is the sale method used to account for transfers of receivables. Research suggests that some companies manage earnings by distorting the fair value estimates that are made as part of recording securitizations.[29] Also, some firms classify cash flows associated with selling their accounts receivable in the operating section of the statement of cash flows, such that changes in the extent to which accounts receivable are sold can be used to manipulate cash flow from operations. In fact, evidence suggests that sophisticated investors and bond-rating agencies undo sales accounting to treat transfers of receivables as secured borrowings before assessing the riskiness of a company's debt.[30] As noted earlier in this chapter, recent changes in GAAP have made it more difficult for transfers to qualify for sales accounting, but Wall Street is very good at identifying clever ways to structure transactions around accounting standards, so it is important to be vigilant regarding the accounting for these transactions. ●

Financial Reporting Case Solution

1. **Explain the allowance method of accounting for bad debts.** *(p. 371)* The allowance method estimates future bad debts in order to (1) match bad debt expense with related revenues and (2) report accounts receivable in the balance sheet at net realizable value. In an adjusting entry, we record bad debt expense and reduce accounts receivable indirectly by crediting a contra account to accounts receivable for an estimate of the amount that eventually will prove uncollectible.
2. **What approaches might Cisco have used to arrive at the $275 million bad debt provision?** *(p. 372)* There are two ways commonly used to arrive at an estimate of future bad debts: the income statement approach and the balance sheet approach. Using the income statement approach, we estimate bad debt expense as a percentage of each period's net credit sales. The balance sheet approach determines bad debt expense by

[28] Arthur Levitt, Jr., "The Numbers Game," *The CPA Journal*, December 1998, p. 16.

[29] P. M. Dechow, L. A. Myers, and C. Shakespeare, "Fair Value Accounting and Gains from Asset Securitizations: A Convenient Earnings Management Tool with Compensation Side-Benefits," *Journal of Accounting and Economics* 49, No. 2 (2010): 2–25.

[30] Other recent research provides evidence that investors treat securitizations as loans rather than asset sales, suggesting that they are unconvinced that a sale has truly taken place. For example, see W. R. Landsman, K. Peasnell, and C. Shakespeare, "Are Asset Securitizations Sales or Loans?" *The Accounting Review* 83, No. 5 (2008), pp. 1251–72.

estimating the net realizable value of accounts receivable. In other words, the allowance for uncollectible accounts is determined and bad debt expense is an indirect outcome of adjusting the allowance account to the desired balance.

3. **Are there any alternatives to the allowance method?** *(p. 375)* An alternative to the allowance method is the direct write-off method. Using this method, adjusting entries are not recorded and any bad debt that does arise simply is written off as bad debt expense. Of course, if the sale that generated this receivable occurred in a previous reporting period, this violates the matching principle. Operating expenses would have been understated and assets overstated that period. This is why the direct write-off method is not permitted by GAAP except in limited circumstances. ●

The Bottom Line

- **LO7–1** Internal control refers to the plan designed to encourage adherence to company policies and procedures; promote operational efficiency; minimize errors, thefts or fraud; and maximize the reliability and accuracy of accounting data. Key elements of an internal control system for cash receipts and disbursements include separation of record keeping from control of cash duties and the periodic preparation of a bank reconciliation. *(p. 362)*
- **LO7–2** Cash can be informally restricted by management for a particular purpose. Restrictions also can be contractually imposed. If restricted cash is available for current operations or to pay current liabilities, it's classified as a current asset; otherwise, it's classified as investments and funds or other assets. *(p. 364)*
- **LO7–3** The gross method of accounting for cash discounts considers a discount not taken as part of sales revenue. The net method considers a discount not taken as interest revenue. *(p. 367)*
- **LO7–4** When merchandise returns are anticipated, an allowance for sales returns should be recorded as a contra account to accounts receivable and sales revenue also should be reduced by the anticipated sales returns. *(p. 368)*
- **LO7–5** Uncollectible accounts receivable should be anticipated in order to match bad debt expense with revenues generated. Likewise, accounts receivable should be reduced by an allowance for uncollectible accounts to report accounts receivable at net realizable value. *(p. 371)*
- **LO7–6** There are two approaches to estimating future bad debts. The income statement approach estimates bad debt expense based on the notion that a certain percentage of each period's credit sales will prove to be uncollectible. The balance sheet approach to estimating future bad debts indirectly determines bad debt expense by directly estimating the net realizable value of accounts receivable at the end of the period. *(p. 371)*
- **LO7–7** Notes receivable are formal credit arrangements between a creditor (lender) and a debtor (borrower). The typical note receivable requires the payment of a specified face amount, also called principal, at a specified maturity date or dates. In addition, interest is paid at a stated percentage of the face amount. Interest on notes is calculated by multiplying the face amount by the annual rate by the fraction of the annual period. *(p. 376)*
- **LO7–8** A wide variety of methods exists for companies to use their receivables to obtain immediate cash. These methods can be described as either a secured borrowing or a sale of receivables. If three conditions indicating surrender of control are met, the transferor accounts for the transfer of receivables as a sale; otherwise as a secured borrowing. *(p. 382)*
- **LO7–9** A company's investment in receivables is influenced by several related variables, to include the level of sales, the nature of the product or service, and credit and collection policies. Investors, creditors, and financial analysts can gain important insights by monitoring a company's investment in receivables. The receivables turnover and average collection period ratios are designed to monitor receivables. *(p. 391)*
- **LO7–10** Accounting for cash and accounts receivable are similar under U.S. GAAP and IFRS. Other than some differences in terminology and balance sheet classifications, the most important differences involve accounting for transfers of receivables. Both IFRS and U.S. GAAP seek to distinguish between determining whether a sales treatment or secured borrowing treatment is appropriate, but they use different conceptual frameworks to guide that choice. U.S. GAAP focuses on whether control of the receivables is transferred, while IFRS use a more complex decision process that also considers whether substantially all of the risks and rewards of ownership have been transferred. Convergence efforts in this area are proceeding slowly and, in fact, U.S. GAAP and IFRS are diverging in the models they are developing for accounting for bad debts on long-term receivables. *(pp. 365, 382, 390,* and *401)* ●

APPENDIX 7A

Cash Controls

Bank Reconciliation

One of the most important tools used in the control of cash is the **bank reconciliation**. Since all cash receipts are deposited into the bank account and cash disbursements are made by check, the bank account provides a separate record of cash. It's desirable to periodically compare the bank balance with the balance in the company's own records and reconcile any differences.

You probably know from your own personal experience that the ending balance in your checking account reported on your monthly bank statement rarely equals the balance you have recorded in your checkbook. Differences arise from two types of items: timing differences and errors.

Differences between the cash book and bank balance occur due to differences in the timing of recognition of certain transactions and errors.

Timing differences occur when the company and the bank record transactions at different times. At any point in time the company may have adjusted the cash balance for items of which the bank is not yet aware. Likewise, the bank may have adjusted its record of that balance by items of which the company is not yet aware. For example, checks written and cash deposits are not all processed by the bank in the same month that they are recorded by the company. Also, the bank may adjust the company's account for items such as service charges that the company is not aware of until the bank statement is received.

Errors can be made either by the company or the bank. For example, a check might be written for $210 but recorded on the company's books as a $120 disbursement; a deposit of $500 might be processed incorrectly by the bank as a $50 deposit. In addition to serving as a safeguard of cash, the bank reconciliation also uncovers errors such as these and helps ensure that the proper cash balance is reported in the balance sheet.

STEP 1: Adjust the bank balance to the corrected cash balance.

Bank reconciliations include adjustments to the balance per bank for timing differences involving transactions already reflected in the company's accounting records that have not yet been processed by the bank. These adjustments usually include *checks outstanding* and *deposits outstanding* (also called *deposits in transit*). In addition, the balance per bank would be adjusted for any bank errors discovered. These adjustments produce an adjusted bank balance that represents the corrected cash balance.

STEP 2: Adjust the book balance to the corrected cash balance.

The balance per books is similarly adjusted for timing differences involving transactions already reflected by the bank of which the company is unaware until the bank statement is received. These would include service charges, charges for NSF (nonsufficient funds) checks, and collections made by the bank on the company's behalf. In addition, the balance per books is adjusted for any company errors discovered, resulting in an adjusted book balance that will also represent the corrected cash balance. *Each of these adjustments requires a journal entry to correct the book balance.* Only adjustments to the book balance require journal entries. Illustration 7A-1 recaps these reconciling items.

Step 1: Adjustments to Bank Balance:

1. *Add deposits outstanding.* These represent cash amounts received by the company and debited to cash that have not been deposited in the bank by the bank statement cutoff date and cash receipts deposited in the bank near the end of the period that are not recorded by the bank until after the cutoff date.
2. *Deduct checks outstanding.* These represent checks written and recorded by the company as credits to cash that have not yet been processed by the bank before the cutoff date.
3. *Bank errors.* These will either be increases or decreases depending on the nature of the error.

Step 2: Adjustments to Book Balance:

1. *Add collections made by the bank* on the company's behalf and other increases in cash that the company is unaware of until the bank statement is received.
2. *Deduct service and other charges* made by the bank that the company is unaware of until the bank statement is received.
3. *Deduct NSF (nonsufficient funds) checks.* These are checks previously deposited for which the payors do not have sufficient funds in their accounts to cover the amount of the checks. The checks are returned to the company whose responsibility it is to seek payment from payors.
4. *Company errors.* These will either be increases or decreases depending on the nature of the error.

Illustration 7A–1
Bank Reconciliation—Reconciling Items

Bank balance
+ Deposits outstanding
− Checks outstanding
± Errors
Corrected balance

Book balance
+ Collections by bank
− Service charges
− NSF checks
± Errors
Corrected balance

The two corrected balances must equal.

To demonstrate the bank reconciliation process, consider Illustration 7A–2.

Illustration 7A–2
Bank Reconciliation

The Hawthorne Manufacturing Company maintains a general checking account at the First Pacific Bank. First Pacific provides a bank statement and canceled checks once a month. The cutoff date is the last day of the month. The bank statement for the month of May is summarized as follows:

Balance, May 1, 2016	$32,120
Deposits	82,140
Checks processed	(78,433)
Service charges	(80)
NSF checks	(2,187)
Note payment collected by bank (includes $120 interest)	1,120
Balance, May 31, 2016	$34,680

The company's general ledger cash account has a balance of $35,276 at the end of May. A review of the company records and the bank statement reveals the following:

1. Cash receipts not yet deposited totaled $2,965.
2. A deposit of $1,020 was made on May 31 that was not credited to the company's account until June.
3. All checks written in April have been processed by the bank. Checks written in May that had not been processed by the bank total $5,536.
4. A check written for $1,790 was incorrectly recorded by the company as a $790 disbursement. The check was for payment to a supplier of raw materials.

The bank reconciliation prepared by the company appears as follows:

Step 1: Bank Balance to Corrected Balance	
Balance per bank statement	$34,680
Add: Deposits outstanding	3,985*
Deduct: Checks outstanding	(5,536)
Corrected cash balance	$33,129

Step 2: Book Balance to Corrected Balance	
Balance per books	$35,276
Add: Note collected by bank	1,120
Deduct:	
Service charges	(80)
NSF checks	(2,187)
Error—understatement of check	(1,000)
Corrected cash balance	$33,129

*$2,965 + 1,020 = $3,985

The next step is to prepare adjusting journal entries to reflect each of the adjustments to the balance per books. These represent amounts the company was not previously aware of until receipt of the bank statement. No adjusting entries are needed for the adjustments to the balance per bank because the company has already recorded these items. However, the bank needs to be notified of any errors discovered.

To record the receipt of principal and interest on note collected directly by the bank.

Cash	1,120	
Notes receivable		1,000
Interest revenue		120

Miscellaneous expense (bank service charges)	80	
Accounts receivable (NSF checks)	2,187	
Accounts payable (error in check to supplier)	1,000	
Cash		3,267

To record credits to cash revealed by the bank reconciliation.

After these entries are posted, the general ledger cash account will equal the corrected balance of $33,129.

Petty Cash

Most companies keep a small amount of cash on hand to pay for low-cost items such as postage, office supplies, delivery charges, and entertainment expenses. It would be inconvenient, time consuming, and costly to process a check each time these small payments are made. A petty cash fund provides a more efficient way to handle these payments.

A petty cash fund is established by transferring a specified amount of cash from the company's general checking account to an employee designated as the petty cash custodian. The amount of the fund should approximate the expenditures made from the fund during a relatively short period of time (say a week or a month). The custodian disburses cash from the fund when the appropriate documentation is presented, such as a receipt for the purchase of office supplies. At any point in time, the custodian should be in possession of cash and appropriate receipts that sum to the amount of the fund. The receipts serve as the basis for recording appropriate expenses each time the fund is replenished. Consider the example in Illustration 7A–3.

The petty cash fund always should have cash and receipts that together equal the amount of the fund.

Illustration 7A–3

Petty Cash Fund

On May 1, 2016, the Hawthorne Manufacturing Company established a $200 petty cash fund. John Ringo is designated as the petty cash custodian. The fund will be replenished at the end of each month. On May 1, 2016, a check is written for $200 made out to John Ringo, petty cash custodian. During the month of May, John paid bills totaling $160 summarized as follows:

Postage	$ 40
Office supplies	35
Delivery charges	55
Entertainment	30
Total	$160

In journal entry form, the transaction to establish the fund would be recorded as follows:

May 1, 2016		
Petty Cash	200	
Cash (checking account)		200

A petty cash fund is established by writing a check to the custodian.

No entries are recorded at the time the actual expenditures are made from the fund. The expenditures are recorded when reimbursement is requested at the end of the month. At that time, a check is written to John Ringo, petty cash custodian, for the total of the fund receipts, $160 in this case. John cashes the check and replenishes the fund to $200. In journal entry form, replenishing the fund would be recorded as follows:

May 31, 2016		
Postage expense	40	
Office supplies expense	35	
Delivery expense	55	
Entertainment expense	30	
Cash (checking account)		160

The appropriate expense accounts are debited when the petty cash fund is reimbursed.

The petty cash account is not debited when replenishing the fund. If, however, the size of the fund is increased at time of replenishment, the account is debited for the increase. Similarly, petty cash would be credited if the size of the fund is decreased.

To maintain the control objective of separation of duties, the petty cash custodian should not be involved in the process of writing or approving checks, nor in recordkeeping. In addition, management should arrange for surprise counts of the fund.

APPENDIX 7B Accounting for Impairment of a Receivable and a Troubled Debt Restructuring[31]

Impairment of a Receivable

Earlier in this chapter you learned about the allowance method of accounting for bad debts. Because it is difficult to determine which individual receivables will ultimately prove uncollectible, the allowance method recognizes bad debt expense for a large group of receivables and reduces the book value of that group of receivables by establishing an allowance for uncollectible accounts. Later, when an individual receivable proves uncollectible, the receivable and the allowance are both reduced. The allowance method is used for many types of receivables, including normal trade receivables, notes receivable, and loans receivable.

However, for long-term receivables like notes receivable and loans receivable, companies also can consider information specific to the receivable when estimating whether bad debts will occur. For example, a bank might learn that one of its borrowers is having financial difficulties, or a bank might realize that borrowers in particular industries or countries are facing economic instability. In that case, a more precise estimate of an impairment loss for that receivable can be made.

Under current GAAP, an impairment loss on a receivable is recognized if the creditor (lender) believes it is probable that it will not receive all of the cash flows (principal and any interest payments) that have been promised by the debtor (borrower). In that case, the creditor remeasures the receivable based on the present value of currently expected cash flows, discounted at the loan's original effective interest rate.[32] The adjustment necessary to record the impaired receivable should seem familiar—a loss is included in current income by debiting bad debt expense (or a separate impairment loss account) and crediting the allowance for uncollectible accounts. Illustration 7B–1 provides an example.

In the future, if additional information indicates that conditions have changed, bad debt expense and the allowance for uncollectible accounts are increased or decreased as necessary to reflect the change.

You may be wondering whether recognizing an impairment loss leads to a double counting of bad debt expense. After all, the receivable first was included in a group of receivables for which bad debt expense was estimated, and then was singled out for recognition of an impairment loss. Creditors have to be careful to avoid this problem by excluding an impaired receivable from the rest of the receivables and estimating bad debt expense as appropriate for the rest of the receivables. That way, bad debt expense for the impaired receivable and the rest of the receivables is calculated separately, and there is no double counting.

---

[31]This appendix discusses accounting for the impairment of individual accounts and notes receivable, as specified in ASC 310–10–35: Receivables—Overall—Subsequent Measurement (previously "Accounting by Creditors for Impairment of a Loan–An amendment of FASB Statements No. 5 and 15," *Statement of Financial Accounting Standards No. 114* (Norwalk, Conn.: FASB, 1993)). When a receivable has been securitized, or when a company has elected to account for a receivable under the fair value option, the receivable is viewed as an investment and different GAAP applies, as described in Appendix 12B.

[32]Rather than calculating the present value of the loan, as a practical expediency the creditor can base the new value of the loan on the loan's market price or the fair value of collateral that supports the loan.

Illustration 7B–1

Receivable Impairment

Brillard Properties owes First Prudent Bank $30 million under a 10% note with two years remaining to maturity. Due to Brillard's financial difficulties, the previous year's interest ($3 million) was not paid. First Prudent estimates that it will not receive the $3 million of accrued interest, that it will receive only $2 million of interest in each of the next two years, and that it will receive only $25 million of principal at the end of two years.

Analysis

Previous Value			
Accrued interest (10% × $30,000,000)		$ 3,000,000	
Principal		30,000,000	
Book value of the receivable			$ 33,000,000
New Value (based on estimated cash flows to be received)			
Present value of accrued interest to be received	=	$ 0	
Present value of future interest	$ 2 million × 1.73554* =	3,471,080	
Present value of estimated principal	$25 million × 0.82645† =	20,661,250	
Present value of the receivable			(24,132,330)
Loss			$ 8,867,670

*Present value of an ordinary annuity of $1: $n = 2$, $i = 10\%$

†Present value of $1: $n = 2$, $i = 10\%$

The discounted present value of the cash flows prior to the impairment is the same as the receivable's book value.

The discounted present value of the cash flows after the impairment is less than book value.

The difference is a loss, debited to bad debt expense.

Journal Entry

Bad debt expense (to balance)	8,867,670	
Accrued interest receivable		3,000,000
Allowance for uncollectible accounts ($30,000,000 − 24,132,330)		5,867,670

Where We're Headed 

A concern about recognizing impairments of receivables in current GAAP is that it doesn't provide timely information—impairment recognition is delayed until losses are probable, and tends to focus on historical rather than forward-looking information when making that determination. To provide more timely impairment recognition, the FASB has developed the CECL ("Current Expected Credit Loss") model.[33] Under the CECL model, the "probable" threshold is removed, so the creditor accounts for potential impairments even when the probability of their occurrence is very low. The creditor adjusts its estimate of impairment losses (and therefore the allowance for bad debts) up or down over the life of the receivable as new information becomes available. The CECL model explicitly requires creditors to estimate impairments based on predictions about the future as well as current and past events, so impairments may be recognized even if no past information or current conditions suggest a problem.

To consider how the CECL model would be applied, let's modify Illustration 7B–1 to consider a long-term receivable for which there is a relatively lower likelihood of impairment.

Brillard Properties owes First Prudent Bank $30 million under a 10% note with two years remaining to maturity. The previous year's interest ($3 million) was not paid. Based on its experience with similar loans and its projections regarding Brillard's ability to generate cash in the future, First Prudent estimates that there is a 75% chance it will be paid in full and a 25% chance that it will (a) not receive the $3 million of accrued interest, (b) receive only $2 million of interest in each of the next two years, and (c) receive only $25 million of principal at the end of two years.

(continued)

[33] *Proposed Accounting Standards Update*, "Financial Instruments—Credit Losses (Subtopic 825–15)" (Norwalk, Conn: FASB, December 20, 2012).

(concluded)

Because a loss is not probable, current GAAP would not recognize an impairment. In contrast, the CECL model *does* recognize an impairment, calculated as follows:

Book value of the receivable (see Illustration 7B–1)		$33,000,000
Expected loss		
(25%) × $8,867,670 (see Illustration 7B–1)	$2,216,918	
(75%) × $0 loss	0	
Expected loss		$ 2,216,918
Revised book value of the receivable		$30,783,082

First Prudent would account for the expected loss as bad debts expense, adjusting upward or downward its allowance for bad debts with respect to the Brillard loan as necessary to state the net receivable at $30,783,082.

Troubled Debt Restructurings

A ***troubled debt restructuring*** **occurs when the creditor makes concessions to the debtor in response to the debtor's financial difficulties.**

Sometimes a creditor changes the original terms of a debt agreement in response to the debtor's financial difficulties. The creditor makes concessions to the debtor that make it easier for the debtor to pay, with the goal of maximizing the amount of cash that the creditor can collect. In that case, the new arrangement is referred to as a **troubled debt restructuring**. Because identifying an arrangement as a troubled debt restructuring requires recognizing any impairment loss associated with the arrangement, creditors might be reluctant to conclude that a troubled debt restructuring has occurred. The FASB recently provided clarification to help ensure that all troubled debt restructurings are properly identified.[34]

WHEN THE RECEIVABLE IS CONTINUED, BUT WITH MODIFIED TERMS. In a troubled debt restructuring, it's likely that the bank allows the receivable to continue but with the terms of the debt agreement modified to make it easier for the debtor to comply. The lender might agree to reduce or delay the scheduled interest payments. Or, it may agree to reduce or delay the maturity amount. Often a troubled debt restructuring will call for some combination of these concessions.

Consider again Illustration 7B–1. What if First Prudent Bank and Brillard Properties actually *renegotiated* Brillard's debt to (1) forgive the interest accrued from last year, (2) reduce the two remaining interest payments from $3 million each to $2 million each, and (3) reduce the face amount from $30 million to $25 million? In that case, First Prudent would account for its impairment loss in exactly the same way as shown in Illustration 7B–1. The only difference would be that, whereas we originally based calculations on First Prudent's estimates of future cash flows, we now base calculations on the cash flows that were specified in the restructured debt agreement.

WHEN THE RECEIVABLE IS SETTLED OUTRIGHT. Sometimes a receivable in a troubled debt restructuring is actually settled at the time of the restructuring by the debtor making a payment of cash, some other noncash assets, or even shares of the debtor's stock. In that case, the creditor simply records a loss for the difference between the book amount of the receivable and the fair value of the asset(s) or equity securities received. Illustration 7B–2 provides an example.

[34]A troubled debt restructuring occurs when a creditor makes concessions in response to a debtor's financial difficulties. These terms have been clarified recently (ASC 310–40–15: Receivables—Troubled Debt Restructurings by Creditors—Scope and Scope Exceptions; previously "A Creditor's Determination of Whether a Restructuring is a Troubled Debt Restructuring," *Accounting Standards Update No. 2011–02* (Norwalk, Conn.: FASB, 2011)). A debtor is viewed as experiencing *financial difficulties* if it is probable that the debtor will default on any of its liabilities unless the creditor restructures the debt. A *concession* has occurred if, as a result of the restructuring, the creditor does not expect to collect all amounts due, including accrued interest. A concession also can occur if the creditor restructures the terms of the debt in a way that provides the debtor with funds at a better rate of interest than the debtor could receive if the debtor tried to obtain new debt with similar terms (for example, a similar payment schedule, collateral, and guarantees) as the restructured debt. But, not all changes are concessions. For example, a restructuring that results in an insignificant delay of payment is not a concession.

Illustration 7B–2
Debt Settled at the Time of a Restructuring

First Prudent Bank is owed $30 million by Brillard Properties under a 10% note with two years remaining to maturity. Due to Brillard's financial difficulties, the previous year's interest ($3 million) was not received. The bank agrees to settle the receivable (and accrued interest receivable) in exchange for property having a fair value of $20 million.

	($ in millions)	
Land (fair value)	20	
Bad debt expense (to balance)*	13	
Accrued interest receivable (10% × $30 million)		3
Note receivable (account balance)		30

*Rather than debiting bad debt expense, First Prudent might debit Loss on troubled debt restructuring.

International Financial Reporting Standards

● LO7–10

Impairments. IFRS (IAS 39)[35] and current U.S. GAAP (ASC 310)[36] generally provide similar treatments of impairments of receivables, but the specific impairment evaluation process and criteria are somewhat different regarding:

- Level of analysis:
  - Under U.S. GAAP we examine impairment of individual receivables. If impairment isn't indicated, we group the receivables with other receivables of similar risk characteristics when estimating bad debts for the group.
  - Under IFRS we first consider whether individually significant receivables are impaired. If impairment isn't indicated, the individually significant receivables are grouped with other receivables of similar risk characteristics to test impairment.
- Impairment indicators:
  - U.S. GAAP provides an illustrative list of information we might consider when evaluating receivables for impairment, and requires measurement of potential impairment if impairment (a) is viewed as probable and (b) can be estimated reliably.
  - IFRS provides an illustrative list of "loss events" and requires measurement of an impairment if there is objective evidence that a loss event has occurred that has an impact on the future cash flows to be collected and that can be estimated reliably. Requiring the occurrence of a loss event may result in recognizing a loss later under IFRS than U.S. GAAP.
- Reversal of impairments: Under both U.S. GAAP and IFRS, if an impaired receivable's estimated future cash flows improve, the creditor recalculates the impairment and adjusts the valuation allowance up or down as appropriate. The net book value of the receivable can't exceed the original amount of the receivable (as adjusted for any normal amortization of any discount or premium). Reversals increase income (for example, by crediting bad debt expense in the period of reversal).

Also, as indicated earlier in this chapter, IFRS requirements are moving to an ECL ("Expected Credit Loss") model for recognizing impairment of long-term receivables, while U.S. GAAP is moving to the CECL model. The primary difference between the two approaches is that the ECL model used in IFRS does not accrue post-twelve-month credit losses for receivables that have not as yet deteriorated in credit quality. Therefore, U.S. GAAP will tend to recognize bad debt accruals earlier, and in higher amounts, than are recognized under IFRS. Further convergence in this area is unlikely in the near future.

In this appendix we have focused on creditors' accounting for impairments and troubled debt restructurings. We discuss those topics from the standpoint of the debtor in Chapter 14, Appendix B. ●

[35]"Financial Instruments: Recognition and Measurement," *International Accounting Standard No. 39* (IASCF), as amended effective January 1, 2014.

[36]FASB ASC 310–10–35: Receivables—Overall—Subsequent Measurement.

Questions For Review of Key Topics

Q 7–1 Define cash equivalents.

Q 7–2 Explain the primary functions of internal controls procedures in the accounting area. What is meant by separation of duties?

Q 7–3 What are the responsibilities of management described in Section 404 of the Sarbanes-Oxley Act? What are the responsibilities of the company's auditor?

Q 7–4 Define a compensating balance. How are compensating balances reported in financial statements?

IFRS **Q 7–5** Do U.S. GAAP and IFRS differ in how bank overdrafts are treated? Explain.

Q 7–6 Explain the difference between a trade discount and a cash discount.

Q 7–7 Distinguish between the gross and net methods of accounting for cash discounts.

Q 7–8 Briefly explain the accounting treatment for sales returns.

Q 7–9 Explain the typical way companies account for uncollectible accounts receivable (bad debts). When is it permissible to record bad debt expense only at the time when receivables actually prove uncollectible?

Q 7–10 Briefly explain the difference between the income statement approach and the balance sheet approach to estimating bad debts.

IFRS **Q 7–11** If a company has accounts receivable from ordinary customers and from related parties, can they combine those receivables in their financial statements under U.S. GAAP? Under IFRS?

Q 7–12 Is any special accounting treatment required for the assigning of accounts receivable in general as collateral for debt?

Q 7–13 Explain any possible differences between accounting for an account receivable factored with recourse compared with one factored without recourse.

IFRS **Q 7–14** Do U.S. GAAP and IFRS differ in the criteria they use to determine whether a transfer of receivables is treated as a sale? Explain.

Q 7–15 What is meant by the discounting of a note receivable? Describe the four-step process used to account for discounted notes.

Q 7–16 What are the key variables that influence a company's investment in receivables? Describe the two ratios used by financial analysts to monitor a company's investment in receivables.

Q 7–17 (Based on Appendix 7A) In a two-step bank reconciliation, identify the items that might be necessary to adjust the bank balance to the corrected cash balance. Identify the items that might be necessary to adjust the book balance to the corrected cash balance.

Q 7–18 (Based on Appendix 7A) How is a petty cash fund established? How is the fund replenished?

Q 7–19 (Based on Appendix 7B) Marshall Companies, Inc., holds a note receivable from a former subsidiary. Due to financial difficulties, the former subsidiary has been unable to pay the previous year's interest on the note. Marshall agreed to restructure the debt by both delaying and reducing remaining cash payments. The concessions impair the creditor's investment in the receivable. How is this impairment recorded?

IFRS **Q 7–20** (Based on Appendix 7B) Do U.S. GAAP and IFRS differ in the ability of a company to recognize in net income the recovery of impairment losses of accounts and notes receivable?

Brief Exercises

BE 7–1
Internal control
● LO7–1

Janice Dodds opens the mail for the Ajax Plumbing Company. She lists all customer checks on a spreadsheet that includes the name of the customer and the check amount. The checks, along with the spreadsheet, are then sent to Jim Seymour in the accounting department who records the checks and deposits them daily in the company's checking account. How could the company improve its internal control procedure for the handling of its cash receipts?

BE 7–2
Bank overdrafts
● LO7–2, LO7–10

IFRS

Cutler Company has a cash account with a balance of $250,000 with Wright Bank and a cash account with an overdraft of $5,000 at Lowe Bank. What would the current assets section of Cutler's balance sheet include for "cash" under IFRS? Under U.S. GAAP?

BE 7–3
Cash and cash equivalents
● LO7–2

The following items appeared on the year-end trial balance of Consolidated Freight Corporation: cash in a checking account, U.S. Treasury bills that mature in six months, undeposited customer checks, cash in a savings account, and currency and coins. Which of these items would be included in the company's balance sheet as cash and cash equivalents?

BE 7–4
Cash discounts; gross method
● LO7–3

On December 28, 2016, Tristar Communications sold 10 units of its new satellite uplink system to various customers for $25,000 each. The terms of each sale were 1/10, n/30. Tristar uses the gross method to account for sales discounts. In what year will income before tax be affected by discounts, assuming that all customers paid the net-of-discount amount on January 6, 2017? By how much?

BE 7–5
Cash discounts; net method
● LO7–3

Refer to the situation described in BE 7–4. Answer the questions assuming that Tristar uses the net method to account for sales discounts.

BE 7–6
Sales returns
● LO7–4

During 2016, its first year of operations, Hollis Industries recorded sales of $10,600,000 and experienced returns of $720,000. Cost of goods sold totaled $6,360,000 (60% of sales). The company estimates that 8% of all sales will be returned. Prepare the year-end adjusting journal entries to account for anticipated sales returns, assuming that all sales are made on credit and all accounts receivable are outstanding.

BE 7–7
Sales returns
● LO7–4

Refer to the situation described in BE 7–6. Prepare the year-end adjusting journal entries to account for anticipated sales returns under the assumption that all sales are made for cash (no accounts receivable are outstanding).

BE 7–8
Accounts receivable classification
● LO7–5, LO7–10

 IFRS

Singletary Associates has accounts receivable due from normal credit customers, and also has an account receivable due from a director of the company. Singletary would like to combine both of those receivables on one line in the current assets section of their balance sheet and in the disclosure notes. Is that permissible under U.S. GAAP? Under IFRS? Explain.

BE 7–9
Uncollectible accounts; income statement approach
● LO7–5, LO7–6

The following information relates to a company's accounts receivable: accounts receivable balance at the beginning of the year, $300,000; allowance for uncollectible accounts at the beginning of the year, $25,000 (credit balance); credit sales during the year, $1,500,000; accounts receivable written off during the year, $16,000; cash collections from customers, $1,450,000. Assuming the company estimates bad debts at an amount equal to 2% of credit sales, calculate (1) bad debt expense for the year and (2) the year-end balance in the allowance for uncollectible accounts.

BE 7–10
Uncollectible accounts; balance sheet approach
● LO7–5, LO7–6

Refer to the situation described in BE 7–9. Answer the two questions assuming the company estimates that future bad debts will equal 10% of the year-end balance in accounts receivable.

BE 7–11
Uncollectible accounts; solving for unknown
● LO7–5, LO7–6

A company's year-end balance in accounts receivable is $2,000,000. The allowance for uncollectible accounts had a beginning-of-year credit balance of $30,000. An aging of accounts receivable at the end of the year indicates a required allowance of $38,000. If bad debt expense for the year was $40,000, what was the amount of bad debts written off during the year?

BE 7–12
Uncollectible accounts; solving for unknown
● LO7–5, LO7–6

Refer to the situation described in BE 7–11. If credit sales for the year were $8,200,000 and $7,950,000 was collected from credit customers, what was the beginning-of-year balance in accounts receivable?

BE 7–13
Note receivable
● LO7–7

On December 1, 2016, Davenport Company sold merchandise to a customer for $20,000. In payment for the merchandise, the customer signed a 6% note requiring the payment of interest and principal on March 1, 2017. How much interest revenue will the company recognize during 2016? In 2017?

BE 7–14
Long-term notes receivable
● LO7–4

On April 19, 2016, Millipede Machinery sold a tractor to Thomas Hartwood, accepting a note promising payment of $120,000 in five years. The applicable effective interest rate is 7%. What amount of sales revenue would Millipede recognize on April 19, 2016, for the Hartwood transaction?

BE 7–15
Factoring of accounts receivable
● LO7–8

Logitech Corporation transferred $100,000 of accounts receivable to a local bank. The transfer was made without recourse. The local bank remits 85% of the factored amount to Logitech and retains the remaining 15%. When the bank collects the receivables, it will remit to Logitech the retained amount less a fee equal to 3% of the total amount factored. Logitech estimates a fair value of its 15% interest in the receivables of $11,000 (not including the 3% fee). What is the effect of this transaction on the company's assets, liabilities, and income before income taxes?

BE 7–16
Factoring of accounts receivable
● LO7–8

Refer to the situation described in BE 7–15. Assuming that the sale criteria are not met, describe how Logitech would account for the transfer.

BE 7–17
Transfers of accounts receivable
● LO7–8, LO7–10

 IFRS

Huling Associates plans to transfer $300,000 of accounts receivable to Mitchell Inc. in exchange for cash. Huling has structured the arrangement so that it retains substantially all the risks and rewards of ownership but shifts control over the receivables to Mitchell. Assuming all other criteria are met for recognizing the transfer as a sale, how would Huling account for this transaction under IFRS? Under U.S. GAAP?

BE 7–18
Discounting a note
● LO7–8

On March 31, Dower Publishing discounted a $30,000 note at a local bank. The note was dated February 28 and required the payment of the principal amount and interest at 6% on May 31. The bank's discount rate is 8%. How much cash will Dower receive from the bank on March 31?

BE 7–19
Receivables turnover
● LO7–8

Camden Hardware's credit sales for the year were $320,000. Accounts receivable at the beginning and end of the year were $50,000 and $70,000, respectively. Calculate the accounts receivable turnover ratio and the average collection period for the year.

BE 7–20
Bank Reconciliation
● Appendix 7A

Marin Company's general ledger indicates a cash balance of $22,340 as of September 30, 2016. Early in October Marin received a bank statement indicating that during September Marin had an NSF check of $1,500 returned to a customer and incurred service charges of $45. Marin also learned it had incorrectly recorded a check received from a customer on September 15 as $500 when in fact the check was for $550. Calculate Marin's correct September 30, 2016, cash balance.

BE 7–21
Bank Reconciliation
● Appendix 7A

Shan Enterprises received a bank statement listing its May 31, 2016, bank balance as $47,582. Shan determined that as of May 31 it had cash receipts of $2,500 that were not yet deposited and checks outstanding of $7,224. Calculate Shan's correct May 31, 2016, cash balance.

Exercises

An alternate exercise and problem set is available in the Connect library.

E 7–1
Cash and cash equivalents; restricted cash
● LO7–2

The controller of the Red Wing Corporation is in the process of preparing the company's 2016 financial statements. She is trying to determine the correct balance of cash and cash equivalents to be reported as a current asset in the balance sheet. The following items are being considered:

a. Balances in the company's accounts at the First National Bank; checking $13,500, savings $22,100.
b. Undeposited customer checks of $5,200.
c. Currency and coins on hand of $580.
d. Savings account at the East Bay Bank with a balance of $400,000. This account is being used to accumulate cash for future plant expansion (in 2018).
e. $20,000 in a checking account at the East Bay Bank. The balance in the account represents a 20% compensating balance for a $100,000 loan with the bank. Red Wing may not withdraw the funds until the loan is due in 2019.
f. U.S. Treasury bills; 2-month maturity bills totaling $15,000, and 7-month bills totaling $20,000.

Required:

1. Determine the correct balance of cash and cash equivalents to be reported in the current asset section of the 2016 balance sheet.
2. For each of the items not included in your answer to requirement 1, explain the correct classification of the item.

E 7–2
Cash and cash equivalents
● LO7–2

Delta Automotive Corporation has the following assets listed in its 12/31/2016 trial balance:

Cash in bank—checking account	$22,500
U.S. Treasury bills (mature in 60 days)*	5,000
Cash on hand (currency and coins)	1,350
U.S. Treasury bills (mature in six months)*	10,000
Undeposited customer checks	1,840

*Purchased on 11/30/2016

Required:

1. Determine the correct balance of cash and cash equivalents to be reported in the current asset section of the 2016 balance sheet.
2. For each of the items not included in your answer to requirement 1, explain the correct classification of the item.

E 7–3
FASB codification research
● LO7–2, LO7–6, LO7–7

Access the *FASB Accounting Standards Codification* at the FASB website (**asc.fasb.org**).

Required:

Determine the specific citation for accounting for each of the following items:

1. Accounts receivables from related parties should be shown separately from trade receivables.
2. The definition of cash equivalents.
3. The requirement to value notes exchanged for cash at the cash proceeds.
4. The two conditions that must be met to accrue a loss on an accounts receivable.

E 7–4
Bank overdrafts
● LO7–2, LO7–10

Parker Inc. has the following cash balances:

First Bank:	$150,000
Second Bank:	(10,000)
Third Bank:	25,000
Fourth Bank:	(5,000)

Required:

1. Prepare the current assets and current liabilities section of Parker's 2016 balance sheet, assuming Parker reports under U.S. GAAP.
2. Prepare the current assets and current liabilities section of Parker's 2016 balance sheet, assuming Parker reports under IFRS.

E 7–5
Trade and cash discounts; the gross method and the net method compared
● LO7–3

Tracy Company, a manufacturer of air conditioners, sold 100 units to Thomas Company on November 17, 2016. The units have a list price of $600 each, but Thomas was given a 30% trade discount. The terms of the sale were 2/10, n/30.

Required:

1. Prepare the journal entries to record the sale on November 17 (ignore cost of goods) and collection on November 26, 2016, assuming that the gross method of accounting for cash discounts is used.
2. Prepare the journal entries to record the sale on November 17 (ignore cost of goods) and collection on December 15, 2016, assuming that the gross method of accounting for cash discounts is used.
3. Repeat requirements 1 and 2 assuming that the net method of accounting for cash discounts is used.

E 7–6
Cash discounts; the gross method
● LO7–3

Harwell Company manufactures automobile tires. On July 15, 2016, the company sold 1,000 tires to the Nixon Car Company for $50 each. The terms of the sale were 2/10, n/30. Harwell uses the gross method of accounting for cash discounts.

Required:

1. Prepare the journal entries to record the sale on July 15 (ignore cost of goods) and collection on July 23, 2016.
2. Prepare the journal entries to record the sale on July 15 (ignore cost of goods) and collection on August 15, 2016.

E 7–7
Cash discounts; the net method
● LO7–3

[This is a variation of E 7–6 modified to focus on the net method of accounting for cash discounts.]
Harwell Company manufactures automobile tires. On July 15, 2016, the company sold 1,000 tires to the Nixon Car Company for $50 each. The terms of the sale were 2/10, n/30. Harwell uses the net method of accounting for cash discounts.

Required:

1. Prepare the journal entries to record the sale on July 15 (ignore cost of goods) and payment on July 23, 2016.
2. Prepare the journal entries to record the sale on July 15 (ignore cost of goods) and payment on August 15, 2016.

E 7–8
Sales returns
● LO7–4

Halifax Manufacturing allows its customers to return merchandise for any reason up to 90 days after delivery and receive a credit to their accounts. All of Halifax's sales are for credit (no cash is collected at the time of sale). The company began 2016 with an allowance for sales returns of $300,000. During 2016, Halifax sold merchandise on account for $11,500,000. This merchandise cost Halifax $7,475,000 (65% of selling prices). Also during the year, customers returned $450,000 in sales for credit. Sales returns, estimated to be 4% of sales, are recorded as an adjusting entry at the end of the year.

Required:

1. Prepare the entry to record the merchandise returns and the year-end adjusting entry for estimated returns.
2. What is the amount of the year-end allowance for sales returns after the adjusting entry is recorded?

E 7–9
FASB codification research
● LO7–5

The *FASB Accounting Standards Codification* represents the single source of authoritative U.S. generally accepted accounting principles.

Required:

1. Obtain the relevant authoritative literature on accounting for accounts receivable using the FASB's Codification Research System at the FASB website (www.fasb.org). What is the specific citation that describes disclosure of accounting policies for credit losses and doubtful accounts?
2. List the disclosure requirements.

E 7–10
Uncollectible accounts; allowance method vs. direct write-off method
● LO7–5, LO7–6

Johnson Company uses the allowance method to account for uncollectible accounts receivable. Bad debt expense is established as a percentage of credit sales. For 2016, net credit sales totaled $4,500,000, and the estimated bad debt percentage is 1.5%. The allowance for uncollectible accounts had a credit balance of $42,000 at the beginning of 2016 and $40,000, after adjusting entries, at the end of 2016.

Required:

1. What is bad debt expense for 2016?
2. Determine the amount of accounts receivable written off during 2016.
3. If the company uses the direct write-off method, what would bad debt expense be for 2016?

E 7–11
Uncollectible accounts; allowance method; balance sheet approach
● LO7–5, LO7–6

Colorado Rocky Cookie Company offers credit terms to its customers. At the end of 2016, accounts receivable totaled $625,000. The allowance method is used to account for uncollectible accounts. The allowance for uncollectible accounts had a credit balance of $32,000 at the beginning of 2016 and $21,000 in receivables were written off during the year as uncollectible. Also, $1,200 in cash was received in December from a customer whose account previously had been written off. The company estimates bad debts by applying a percentage of 10% to accounts receivable at the end of the year.

Required:

1. Prepare journal entries to record the write-off of receivables, the collection of $1,200 for previously written off receivables, and the year-end adjusting entry for bad debt expense.
2. How would accounts receivable be shown in the 2016 year-end balance sheet?

E 7–12
Uncollectible accounts; allowance method and direct write-off method compared; solving for unknown
● LO7–6

Castle Company provides estimates for its uncollectible accounts. The allowance for uncollectible accounts had a credit balance of $17,280 at the beginning of 2016 and a $22,410 credit balance at the end of 2016 (after adjusting entries). If the direct write-off method had been used to account for uncollectible accounts (bad debt expense equals actual write-offs), the income statement for 2016 would have included bad debt expense of $17,100 and revenue of $2,200 from the collection of previously written off bad debts.

Required:

Determine bad debt expense for 2016 according to the allowance method.

E 7–13
Uncollectible accounts; allowance method; solving for unknowns; General Mills
● LO7–5, LO7–6
Real World Financials

General Mills reported the following information in its 2013 financial statements ($ in millions):

	2013	2012
Balance Sheet:		
Accounts receivable, net	$ 1,446.4	$1,323.6
Income statement:		
Sales revenue	$17,774.1	

A note disclosed that the allowance for uncollectible accounts had a balance of $19.9 million and $21.7 million at the end of 2013 and 2012, respectively. Bad debt expense for 2013 was $12.0 million.

Required:

Determine the amount of cash collected from customers during 2013.

E 7–14
Note receivable
● LO7–7

On June 30, 2016, the Esquire Company sold some merchandise to a customer for $30,000. In payment, Esquire agreed to accept a 6% note requiring the payment of interest and principal on March 31, 2017. The 6% rate is appropriate in this situation.

Required:

1. Prepare journal entries to record the sale of merchandise (omit any entry that might be required for the cost of the goods sold), the December 31, 2016 interest accrual, and the March 31, 2017 collection.
2. If the December 31 adjusting entry for the interest accrual is not prepared, by how much will income before income taxes be over- or understated in 2016 and 2017?

E 7–15
Noninterest-bearing note receivable
● LO7–7

[This is a variation of E 7–14 modified to focus on a noninterest-bearing note.]

On June 30, 2016, the Esquire Company sold some merchandise to a customer for $30,000 and agreed to accept as payment a noninterest-bearing note with an 8% discount rate requiring the payment of $30,000 on March 31, 2017. The 8% rate is appropriate in this situation.

Required:

1. Prepare journal entries to record the sale of merchandise (omit any entry that might be required for the cost of the goods sold), the December 31, 2016 interest accrual, and the March 31, 2017 collection.
2. What is the *effective* interest rate on the note?

E 7–16
Long-term notes receivable
● LO7–7

On January 1, 2016, Wright Transport sold four school buses to the Elmira School District. In exchange for the buses, Wright received a note requiring payment of $515,000 by Elmira on December 31, 2018. The effective interest rate is 8%.

Required:

1. How much sales revenue would Wright recognize on January 1, 2016, for this transaction?
2. Prepare journal entries to record the sale of merchandise on January 1, 2016 (omit any entry that might be required for the cost of the goods sold), the December 31, 2016, interest accrual, the December 31, 2017, interest accrual, and receipt of payment of the note on December 31, 2018.

E 7–17
Interest-bearing note receivable; solving for unknown rate
● LO7–7

On January 1, 2016, the Apex Company exchanged some shares of common stock it had been holding as an investment for a note receivable. The note principal plus interest is due on January 1, 2017. The 2016 income statement reported $2,200 in interest revenue from this note and a $6,000 gain on sale of investment in stock. The stock's book value was $16,000. The company's fiscal year ends on December 31.

Required:

1. What is the note's effective interest rate?
2. Reconstruct the journal entries to record the sale of the stock on January 1, 2016, and the adjusting entry to record interest revenue at the end of 2016. The company records adjusting entries only at year-end.

E 7–18
Assigning of specific accounts receivable
● LO7–8

On June 30, 2016, the High Five Surfboard Company had outstanding accounts receivable of $600,000. On July 1, 2016, the company borrowed $450,000 from the Equitable Finance Corporation and signed a promissory note. Interest at 10% is payable monthly. The company assigned specific receivables totaling $600,000 as collateral for the loan. Equitable Finance charges a finance fee equal to 1.8% of the accounts receivable assigned.

Required:

Prepare the journal entry to record the borrowing on the books of High Five Surfboard.

E 7–19
Factoring of accounts receivable without recourse
● LO7–8

Mountain High Ice Cream Company transferred $60,000 of accounts receivable to the Prudential Bank. The transfer was made *without recourse.* Prudential remits 90% of the factored amount to Mountain High and retains 10%. When the bank collects the receivables, it will remit to Mountain High the retained amount (which Mountain estimates has a fair value of $5,000) less a 2% fee (2% of the total factored amount).

Required:

Prepare the journal entry to record the transfer on the books of Mountain High assuming that the sale criteria are met.

E 7–20
Factoring of accounts receivable with recourse
● LO7–8

[This is a variation of E 7–19 modified to focus on factoring with recourse.]
Mountain High Ice Cream Company transferred $60,000 of accounts receivable to the Prudential Bank. The transfer was made *with recourse.* Prudential remits 90% of the factored amount to Mountain High and retains 10% to cover sales returns and allowances. When the bank collects the receivables, it will remit to Mountain High the retained amount (which Mountain estimates has a fair value of $5,000). Mountain High anticipates a $3,000 recourse obligation. The bank charges a 2% fee (2% of $60,000), and requires that amount to be paid at the start of the factoring arrangement.

Required:
Prepare the journal entry to record the transfer on the books of Mountain High assuming that the sale criteria are met.

E 7–21
Factoring of accounts receivable with recourse under IFRS
● LO7–8, LO7–10

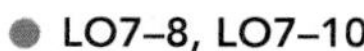

IFRS

[This is a variation of E 7–20 modified to focus on factoring with recourse under IFRS.]
Mountain High Ice Cream Company reports under IFRS. Mountain High transferred $60,000 of accounts receivable to the Prudential Bank. The transfer was made *with recourse.* Prudential remits 90% of the factored amount to Mountain High and retains 10% to cover sales returns and allowances. When the bank collects the receivables, it will remit to Mountain High the retained amount (which Mountain estimates has a fair value of $5,000). Mountain High anticipates a $3,000 recourse obligation. The bank charges a 2% fee (2% of $60,000), and requires that amount to be paid at the start of the factoring arrangement. Mountain High has transferred control over the receivables, but determines that it still retains substantially all risks and rewards associated with them.

Required:
Prepare the journal entry to record the transfer on the books of Mountain High, considering whether the sale criteria under IFRS have been met.

E 7–22
Discounting a note receivable
● LO7–8

Selkirk Company obtained a $15,000 note receivable from a customer on January 1, 2016. The note, along with interest at 10%, is due on July 1, 2016. On February 28, 2016, Selkirk discounted the note at Unionville Bank. The bank's discount rate is 12%.

Required:
Prepare the journal entries required on February 28, 2016, to accrue interest and to record the discounting (round all calculations to the nearest dollar) for Selkirk. Assume that the discounting is accounted for as a sale.

E 7–23
Concepts; terminology
● LO7–1 through LO7–8

Listed below are several terms and phrases associated with cash and receivables. Pair each item from List A (by letter) with the item from List B that is most appropriately associated with it.

List A	List B
____ 1. Internal control	a. Restriction on cash.
____ 2. Trade discount	b. Cash discount not taken is sales revenue.
____ 3. Cash equivalents	c. Includes separation of duties.
____ 4. Allowance for uncollectibles	d. Bad debt expense a % of credit sales.
____ 5. Cash discount	e. Recognizes bad debts as they occur.
____ 6. Balance sheet approach	f. Sale of receivables to a financial institution.
____ 7. Income statement approach	g. Include highly liquid investments.
____ 8. Net method	h. Estimate of bad debts.
____ 9. Compensating balance	i. Reduction in amount paid by credit customer.
____ 10. Discounting	j. Reduction below list price.
____ 11. Gross method	k. Cash discount not taken is interest revenue.
____ 12. Direct write-off method	l. Bad debt expense determined by estimating realizable value.
____ 13. Factoring	m. Sale of note receivable to a financial institution.

E 7–24
Receivables; transaction analysis
● LO7–3, LO7–5 through LO7–8

Weldon Corporation's fiscal year ends December 31. The following is a list of transactions involving receivables that occurred during 2016:

Mar. 17	Accounts receivable of $1,700 were written off as uncollectible. The company uses the allowance method.
30	Loaned an officer of the company $20,000 and received a note requiring principal and interest at 7% to be paid on March 30, 2017.
May 30	Discounted the $20,000 note at a local bank. The bank's discount rate is 8%. The note was discounted without recourse and the sale criteria are met.
June 30	Sold merchandise to the Blankenship Company for $12,000. Terms of the sale are 2/10, n/30. Weldon uses the gross method to account for cash discounts.

July 8	The Blankenship Company paid its account in full.
Aug. 31	Sold stock in a nonpublic company with a book value of $5,000 and accepted a $6,000 noninterest-bearing note with a discount rate of 8%. The $6,000 payment is due on February 28, 2017. The stock has no ready market value.
Dec. 31	Bad debt expense is estimated to be 2% of credit sales for the year. Credit sales for 2016 were $700,000.

Required:

1. Prepare journal entries for each of the above transactions (round all calculations to the nearest dollar).
2. Prepare any additional year-end adjusting entries indicated.

E 7–25
Ratio analysis; Microsoft
● LO7–9

Real World Financials

Microsoft Corporation reported the following information in its financial statements for three successive quarters during the 2014 fiscal year ($ in millions):

	Three Months Ended		
	3/31/2014 (Q3)	**12/31/2013 (Q2)**	**9/30/2013 (Q1)**
Balance sheets:			
Accounts receivable, net	$13,497	$15,986	$11,007
Income statements:			
Sales revenue	$20,403	$24,519	$18,529

Required:

Compute the receivables turnover ratio and the average collection period for the second and third quarters. Assume that each quarter consists of 91 days.

E 7–26
Ratio analysis; solve for unknown
● LO7–9

The current asset section of the Moorcroft Outboard Motor Company's balance sheet reported the following amounts:

	12/31/2016	**12/31/2015**
Accounts receivable, net	$400,000	$300,000

The average collection period for 2016 is 50 days.

Required:

Determine net sales for 2016.

E 7–27
Petty cash
● Appendix 7A

Loucks Company established a $200 petty cash fund on October 2, 2016. The fund is replenished at the end of each month. At the end of October 2016, the fund contained $37 in cash and the following receipts:

Office supplies	$76
Lunch with client	48
Postage	20
Miscellaneous	19

Required:

Prepare the necessary general journal entries to establish the petty cash fund on October 2 and to replenish the fund on October 31.

E 7–28
Petty cash
● Appendix 7A

The petty cash fund of Ricco's Automotive contained the following items at the end of September 2016:

Currency and coins		$ 58
Receipts for the following expenditures:		
Delivery charges	$16	
Printer paper	11	
Paper clips and rubber bands	8	35
An I.O.U. from an employee		25
Postage		32
Total		$150

The petty cash fund was established at the beginning of September with a transfer of $150 from cash to the petty cash account.

Required:

Prepare the journal entry to replenish the fund at the end of September.

E 7–29
Bank reconciliation
● Appendix 7A

Jansen Company's general ledger showed a checking account balance of $23,820 at the end of May 2016. The May 31 cash receipts of $2,340, included in the general ledger balance, were placed in the night depository at the bank on May 31 and were processed by the bank on June 1. The bank statement dated May 31, 2016, showed bank service charges of $38. All checks written by the company had been processed by the bank by May 31 and were listed on the bank statement except for checks totaling $1,890.

Required:

Prepare a bank reconciliation as of May 31, 2016. [*Hint:* You will need to compute the balance that would appear on the bank statement.]

E 7–30
Bank reconciliation and adjusting entries
● Appendix 7A

Harrison Company maintains a checking account at the First National City Bank. The bank provides a bank statement along with canceled checks on the last day of each month. The July 2016 bank statement included the following information:

Balance, July 1, 2016	$ 55,678
Deposits	179,500
Checks processed	(192,610)
Service charges	(30)
NSF checks	(1,200)
Monthly loan payment deducted directly by bank from account (includes $320 in interest)	(3,320)
Balance, July 31, 2016	$ 38,018

The company's general ledger account had a balance of $38,918 at the end of July. Deposits outstanding totaled $6,300 and all checks written by the company were processed by the bank except for those totaling $8,420. In addition, a $2,000 July deposit from a credit customer was recorded as a $200 debit to cash and credit to accounts receivable, and a check correctly recorded by the company as a $30 disbursement was incorrectly processed by the bank as a $300 disbursement.

Required:

1. Prepare a bank reconciliation for the month of July.
2. Prepare the necessary journal entries at the end of July to adjust the general ledger cash account.

E 7–31
Impairment of securities available-for-sale; troubled debt restructuring
● Appendix 7B

At January 1, 2016, Clayton Hoists Inc. owed Third BancCorp $12 million, under a 10% note due December 31, 2017. Interest was paid last on December 31, 2014. Clayton was experiencing severe financial difficulties and asked Third BancCorp to modify the terms of the debt agreement. After negotiation Third BancCorp agreed to:

- Forgive the interest accrued for the year just ended.
- Reduce the remaining two years' interest payments to $1 million each.
- Reduce the principal amount to $11 million.

Required:

Prepare the journal entries by Third BancCorp necessitated by the restructuring of the debt at

1. January 1, 2016.
2. December 31, 2016.
3. December 31, 2017.

E 7–32
Impairment of securities available-for-sale; troubled debt restructuring
● Appendix 7B

At January 1, 2016, NCI Industries, Inc. was indebted to First Federal Bank under a $240,000, 10% unsecured note. The note was signed January 1, 2014, and was due December 31, 2017. Annual interest was last paid on December 31, 2014. NCI was experiencing severe financial difficulties and negotiated a restructuring of the terms of the debt agreement. First Federal agreed to reduce last year's interest and the remaining two years' interest payments to $11,555 each and delay all payments until December 31, 2017, the maturity date.

Required:

Prepare the journal entries by First Federal Bank necessitated by the restructuring of the debt at

1. January 1, 2016.
2. December 31, 2016.
3. December 31, 2017.

CPA and CMA Review Questions

CPA Exam Questions
KAPLAN CPA REVIEW

The following questions are adapted from a variety of sources including questions developed by the AICPA Board of Examiners and those used in the Kaplan CPA Review Course to study receivables while preparing for the CPA examination. Determine the response that best completes the statements or questions.

● LO7–5

1. At January 1, 2016, Simpson Co. had a credit balance of $260,000 in its allowance for uncollectible accounts. Based on past experience, 2 percent of Simpson's credit sales have been uncollectible. During 2016, Simpson

wrote off $325,000 of accounts receivable. Credit sales for 2016 were $9,000,000. In its December 31, 2016, balance sheet, what amount should Simpson report as allowance for uncollectible accounts?

a. $115,000
b. $180,000
c. $245,000
d. $440,000

● LO7–5, LO7–6

2. The balance in accounts receivable at the beginning of 2016 was $600. During 2016, $3,200 of credit sales were recorded. If the ending balance in accounts receivable was $500 and $200 in accounts receivable were written off during the year, the amount of cash collected from customers was

a. $3,100
b. $3,200
c. $3,300
d. $3,800

● LO7–5

3. A company uses the allowance method to account for bad debts. What is the effect on each of the following accounts of the collection of an account previously written off?

	Allowance for Uncollectible Accounts	Bad Debt Expense
a.	Increase	Decrease
b.	No effect	Decrease
c.	Increase	No effect
d.	No effect	No effect

● LO7–4, LO7–5

4. The following information relates to Jay Co.'s accounts receivable for 2016:

Accounts receivable balance, 1/1/2016	$ 650,000
Credit sales for 2016	2,700,000
Sales returns during 2016	75,000
Accounts receivable written off during 2016	40,000
Collections from customers during 2016	2,150,000
Allowance for uncollectible accounts balance, 12/31/2016	110,000

What amount should Jay report for accounts receivable, before allowances, at December 31, 2016?

a. $925,000
b. $1,085,000
c. $1,125,000
d. $1,200,000

● LO7–8

5. Gar Co. factored its receivables without recourse with Ross Bank. Gar received cash as a result of this transaction, which is best described as a

a. Loan from Ross collateralized by Gar's accounts receivable.
b. Loan from Ross to be repaid by the proceeds from Gar's accounts receivables.
c. Sale of Gar's accounts receivable to Ross, with the risk of uncollectible accounts transferred to Ross.
d. Sale of Gar's accounts receivable to Ross, with the risk of uncollectible accounts retained by Gar.

● LO7–5, LO7–6

6. The following information pertains to Tara Co.'s accounts receivable at December 31, 2016:

Days Outstanding	Amount	Estimated % Uncollectible
0–60	$120,000	1%
61–120	90,000	2%
Over 120	100,000	6%
	$310,000	

During 2016, Tara wrote off $7,000 in receivables and recovered $4,000 that had been written off in prior years. Tara's December 31, 2015, allowance for uncollectible accounts was $22,000. Under the aging method, what amount of allowance for uncollectible accounts should Tara report at December 31, 2016?

a. $9,000
b. $10,000
c. $13,000
d. $19,000

● LO7–5, LO7–6

7. West Company had the following account balances at December 31, 2016, before recording bad debt expense for the year:

Accounts receivable	$ 900,000
Allowance for uncollectible accounts (credit balance)	16,000
Credit sales for 2016	1,750,000

West is considering the following methods of estimating bad debts for 2016:

- Based on 2% of credit sales
- Based on 5% of year-end accounts receivable

What amount should West charge to bad debt expense at the end of 2016 under each method?

	Percentage of Credit Sales	Percentage of Accounts Receivable
a.	$35,000	$29,000
b.	$35,000	$45,000
c.	$51,000	$29,000
d.	$51,000	$45,000

International Financial Reporting Standards are tested on the CPA exam along with U.S. GAAP. The following questions deal with the application of IFRS to accounting for cash and receivables.

● LO7–10
IFRS

8. Shaefer Company prepares its financial statements according to International Financial Reporting Standards (IFRS). Shaefer sometimes has bank overdrafts that are payable on demand and that fluctuate as part of its cash management program. At the most recent financial reporting date, Shaefer had a €500,000 overdraft in one cash account and a positive balance of €3,000,000 in another cash account. Shaefer should report its cash balances as:
   a. A cash asset of €3,000,000 and an overdraft liability of €500,000.
   b. A cash asset of €2,500,000.
   c. An overdraft liability of (€2,500,000).
   d. None of the above.

● LO7–10
IFRS

9. Under IFRS, accounts receivable can be accounted for as "available for sale" investments if that approach is elected upon initial recognition of the receivable under:
   a. *IASB No. 1.*
   b. *IFRS No. 9.*
   c. *IAS No. 39.*
   d. None of the above.

● LO7–10
IFRS

10. Under IFRS, measurement of an impairment of a receivable is required if:
   a. Cash payments have not been received for more than twelve months.
   b. It is at least more likely than not that a future loss will occur, and the amount of discounted loss is measurable.
   c. It is reasonably possible that prior events will give rise to a future loss that can be estimated with moderate reliability.
   d. There is objective evidence that a loss event has occurred that has an impact on the future cash flows to be collected and that can be estimated reliably.

CMA Exam Questions

The following questions dealing with receivables are adapted from questions that previously appeared on Certified Management Accountant (CMA) examinations. The CMA designation sponsored by the Institute of Management Accountants (**www.imanet.org**) provides members with an objective measure of knowledge and competence in the field of management accounting. Determine the response that best completes the statements or questions.

● LO7–5, LO7–6

1. Bad debt expense must be estimated in order to satisfy the matching principle when expenses are recorded in the same periods as the related revenues. In estimating bad debt expense for a period, companies generally accrue
   a. Either an amount based on a percentage of total sales or an amount based on a percentage of accounts receivable after adjusting for any balance in the allowance for doubtful accounts.
   b. A percentage of total sales.
   c. Either an amount based on a percentage of credit sales or an amount based on a percentage of accounts receivable after adjusting for any balance in the allowance for doubtful accounts.
   d. An amount equal to last year's bad debt expense.

Questions 2 and 3 are based on the following information:

Madison Corporation uses the allowance method to value its accounts receivable and is making the annual adjustments at fiscal year-end, November 30. The proportion of uncollectible accounts is estimated based on past experience, which indicates 1.5% of net credit sales will be uncollectible. Total sales for the year were $2,000,000, of which $200,000 were cash transactions. Madison has determined that the Norris Corporation accounts receivable balance of $10,000 is uncollectible and will write off this account before year-end adjustments are made. Listed below are Madison's account balances at November 30 prior to any adjustments and the $10,000 write-off.

Sales	$2,000,000
Accounts receivable	750,000
Sales discounts	125,000
Allowance for doubtful accounts	16,500
Sales returns and allowances	175,000
Bad debt expense	0

● LO7–5

2. The entry to write off Norris Corporation's accounts receivable balance of $10,000 will
   a. Increase total assets and decrease net income.
   b. Decrease total assets and net income.
   c. Have no effect on total assets and decrease net income.
   d. Have no effect on total assets and net income.

● LO7–5

3. As a result of the November 30 adjusting entry to provide for bad debts, the allowance for doubtful accounts will
   a. Increase by $30,000.
   b. Increase by $25,500.
   c. Increase by $22,500.
   d. Decrease by $22,500.

Problems

An alternate exercise and problem set is available in the Connect library.

P 7–1
Uncollectible accounts; allowance method; income statement and balance sheet approach

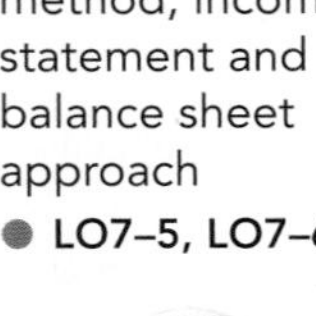

● LO7–5, LO7–6

Swathmore Clothing Corporation grants its customers 30 days' credit. The company uses the allowance method for its uncollectible accounts receivable. During the year, a monthly bad debt accrual is made by multiplying 3% times the amount of credit sales for the month. At the fiscal year-end of December 31, an aging of accounts receivable schedule is prepared and the allowance for uncollectible accounts is adjusted accordingly.

At the end of 2015, accounts receivable were $574,000 and the allowance account had a credit balance of $54,000. Accounts receivable activity for 2016 was as follows:

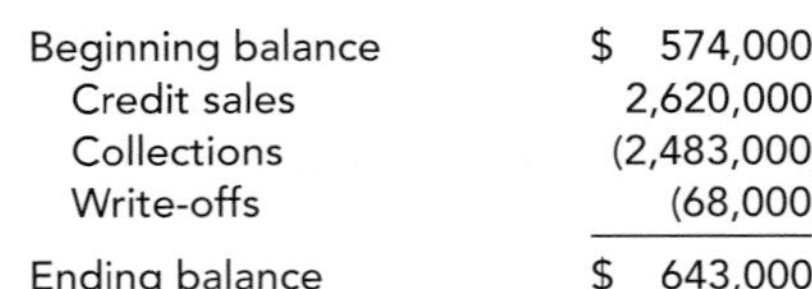

Beginning balance	$ 574,000
Credit sales	2,620,000
Collections	(2,483,000)
Write-offs	(68,000)
Ending balance	$ 643,000

The company's controller prepared the following aging summary of year-end accounts receivable:

	Summary	
Age Group	**Amount**	**Percent Uncollectible**
0–60 days	$430,000	4%
61–90 days	98,000	15
91–120 days	60,000	25
Over 120 days	55,000	40
Total	$643,000	

Required:

1. Prepare a summary journal entry to record the monthly bad debt accrual and the write-offs during the year.
2. Prepare the necessary year-end adjusting entry for bad debt expense.
3. What is total bad debt expense for 2016? How would accounts receivable appear in the 2016 balance sheet?

P 7–2
Uncollectible accounts; Amdahl
● LO7–5

Real World Financials

Amdahl Corporation manufactures large-scale, high performance computer systems. In a recent annual report, the balance sheet included the following information (dollars in thousands):

	Current Year	Previous Year
Current assets:		
Receivables, net of allowances of $5,042 and $6,590 in the previous year	$504,944	$580,640

In addition, the income statement reported sales revenue of $2,158,755 ($ in thousands) for the current year. All sales are made on a credit basis. The statement of cash flows indicates that cash collected from customers during the current year was $2,230,065 ($ in thousands). There were no recoveries of accounts receivable previously written off.

Required:

1. Compute the following (dollar amounts in thousands):
   a. The amount of uncollectibles written off by Amdahl during the current year.
   b. The amount of bad debt expense that Amdahl would include in its income statement for the current year.
   c. The approximate percentage that Amdahl used to estimate uncollectibles for the current year, assuming that it uses the income statement approach.
2. Suppose that Amdahl had used the direct write-off method to account for uncollectibles. Compute the following (dollars in thousands):
   a. The accounts receivable information that would be included in the year-end balance sheet.
   b. The amount of bad debt expense that Amdahl would include in its income statement for the current year.

P 7–3
Bad debts; Nike, Inc.
● LO7–5

Real World Financials

Nike, Inc., is a leading manufacturer of sports apparel, shoes, and equipment. The company's 2013 financial statements contain the following information (in millions):

	2013	2012
Balance sheets:		
Accounts receivable, net	$ 3,117	$ 3,132
Income statements:		
Sales revenue	$25,313	$23,331

A note disclosed that the allowance for uncollectible accounts had a balance of $104 million and $91 million at the end of 2013 and 2012, respectively. Bad debt expense for 2013 was $32 million. Assume that all sales are made on a credit basis.

Required:

1. What is the amount of gross (total) accounts receivable due from customers at the end of 2013 and 2012?
2. What is the amount of bad debt write-offs during 2013?
3. Analyze changes in the gross accounts receivable account to calculate the amount of cash received from customers during 2013.
4. Analyze changes in net accounts receivable to calculate the amount of cash received from customers during 2013.

P 7–4
Uncollectible accounts
● LO7–5, LO7–6

Raintree Cosmetic Company sells its products to customers on a credit basis. An adjusting entry for bad debt expense is recorded only at December 31, the company's fiscal year-end. The 2015 balance sheet disclosed the following:

Current assets:	
Receivables, net of allowance for uncollectible accounts of $30,000	$432,000

During 2016, credit sales were $1,750,000, cash collections from customers $1,830,000, and $35,000 in accounts receivable were written off. In addition, $3,000 was collected from a customer whose account was written off in 2015. An aging of accounts receivable at December 31, 2016, reveals the following:

Age Group	Percentage of Year-End Receivables in Group	Percent Uncollectible
0–60 days	65%	4%
61–90 days	20	15
91–120 days	10	25
Over 120 days	5	40

Required:

1. Prepare summary journal entries to account for the 2016 write-offs and the collection of the receivable previously written off.
2. Prepare the year-end adjusting entry for bad debts according to each of the following situations:
   a. Bad debt expense is estimated to be 3% of credit sales for the year.
   b. Bad debt expense is estimated by computing net realizable value of the receivables. The allowance for uncollectible accounts is estimated to be 10% of the year-end balance in accounts receivable.
   c. Bad debt expense is estimated by computing net realizable value of the receivables. The allowance for uncollectible accounts is determined by an aging of accounts receivable.
3. For situations (a)–(c) in requirement 2 above, what would be the net amount of accounts receivable reported in the 2016 balance sheet?

P 7–5
Receivables; bad debts and returns; Symantec
● LO7–4, LO7–5

Real World Financials

Symantec Corp., located in Cupertino, California, is one of the world's largest producers of security and systems management software. The company's consolidated balance sheets for the 2009 and 2008 fiscal years included the following ($ in thousands):

	2009	2008
Current assets:		
Receivables, less allowances of $20,991 in 2009 and $23,314 in 2008	$837,010	$758,200

A disclosure note accompanying the financial statements reported the following ($ in thousands):

	Year Ended	
	2009	2008
	(In thousands)	
Trade accounts receivable, net:		
Receivables	$858,001	$781,514
Less: allowance for doubtful accounts	(8,863)	(8,915)
Less: reserve for product returns	(12,128)	(14,399)
Trade accounts receivable, net:	$837,010	$758,200

Assume that the company reported bad debt expense in 2009 of $1,500 and had products returned for credit totaling $3,155 (sales price). Net sales for 2009 were $6,149,800 (all numbers in thousands).

Required:

1. What is the amount of accounts receivable due from customers at the end of 2009 and 2008?
2. What amount of accounts receivable did Symantec write off during 2009?
3. What is the amount of Symantec's gross sales for the 2009 fiscal year?
4. Assuming that all sales are made on a credit basis, what is the amount of cash Symantec collected from customers during the 2009 fiscal year?

P 7–6
Notes receivable; solving for unknowns
● LO7–7

Cypress Oil Company's December 31, 2016, balance sheet listed $645,000 of notes receivable and $16,000 of interest receivable included in current assets. The following notes make up the notes receivable balance:

Note 1	Dated 8/31/2016, principal of $300,000 and interest at 10% due on 2/28/2017.
Note 2	Dated 6/30/2016, principal of $150,000 and interest due 3/31/2017.
Note 3	$200,000 face value noninterest-bearing note dated 9/30/2016, due 3/31/2017. Note was issued in exchange for merchandise.

The company records adjusting entries only at year-end. There were no other notes receivable outstanding during 2016.

Required:

1. Determine the rate used to discount the noninterest-bearing note.
2. Determine the explicit interest rate on Note 2.
3. What is the amount of interest revenue that appears in the company's 2016 income statement related to these notes?

P 7–7
Factoring versus assigning of accounts receivable
● LO7–8

Lonergan Company occasionally uses its accounts receivable to obtain immediate cash. At the end of June 2016, the company had accounts receivable of $780,000. Lonergan needs approximately $500,000 to capitalize on a unique investment opportunity. On July 1, 2016, a local bank offers Lonergan the following two alternatives:

a. Borrow $500,000, sign a note payable, and assign the entire receivable balance as collateral. At the end of each month, a remittance will be made to the bank that equals the amount of receivables collected plus 12% interest on the unpaid balance of the note at the beginning of the period.

b. Transfer $550,000 of specific receivables to the bank without recourse. The bank will charge a 2% factoring fee on the amount of receivables transferred. The bank will collect the receivables directly from customers. The sale criteria are met.

Required:

1. Prepare the journal entries that would be recorded on July 1 for each of the alternatives.
2. Assuming that 80% of all June 30 receivables are collected during July, prepare the necessary journal entries to record the collection and the remittance to the bank.
3. For each alternative, explain any required note disclosures that would be included in the July 31, 2016, financial statements.

P 7–8
Factoring of accounts receivable; without recourse
● LO7–8

Samson Wholesale Beverage Company regularly factors its accounts receivable with the Milpitas Finance Company. On April 30, 2016, the company transferred $800,000 of accounts receivable to Milpitas. The transfer was made without recourse. Milpitas remits 90% of the factored amount and retains 10%. When Milpitas collects the receivables, it remits to Samson the retained amount less a 4% fee (4% of the total factored amount). Samson estimates the fair value of the last 10% of its receivables to be $60,000.

Required:

Prepare journal entries for Samson Wholesale Beverage for the transfer of accounts receivable on April 30 assuming the sale criteria are met.

P 7–9
Cash and accounts receivable under IFRS
● LO7–2, LO7–5, LO7–8, LO7–10
IFRS

The following facts apply to Walken Company during December 2016:

a. Walken began December with an accounts receivable balance (net of bad debts) of €25,000.
b. Walken had credit sales of €85,000.
c. Walken had cash collections of €30,000.
d. Walken factored €20,000 of net accounts receivable with Reliable Factor Company, transferring all risks and rewards associated with the receivable, and otherwise meeting all criteria necessary to qualify for treating the transfer of receivables as a sale.
e. Walken factored €15,000 of net accounts receivable with Dependable Factor Company, retaining all risks and rewards associated with the receivable, and otherwise meeting all criteria necessary to qualify for treating the transfer of receivables as a sale.
f. Walken did not recognize any additional bad debts expense, and had no write-offs of bad debts during the month.
g. At December 31, 2016, Walken had a balance of €40,000 of cash at M&V Bank and an overdraft of (€5000) at First National Bank. (That cash balance includes any effects on cash of the other transactions described in this problem.)

Required:

Prepare the cash and accounts receivable lines of the current assets section of Walken's balance sheet, as of December 31, 2016.

P 7–10
Miscellaneous receivable transactions
● LO7–3, LO7–4, LO7–7, LO7–8

Evergreen Company sells lawn and garden products to wholesalers. The company's fiscal year-end is December 31. During 2016, the following transactions related to receivables occurred:

Feb. 28	Sold merchandise to Lennox, Inc. for $10,000 and accepted a 10%, 7-month note. 10% is an appropriate rate for this type of note.
Mar. 31	Sold merchandise to Maddox Co. and accepted a noninterest-bearing note with a discount rate of 10%. The $8,000 payment is due on March 31, 2017.
Apr. 3	Sold merchandise to Carr Co. for $7,000 with terms 2/10, n/30. Evergreen uses the gross method to account for cash discounts.
11	Collected the entire amount due from Carr Co.
17	A customer returned merchandise costing $3,200. Evergreen reduced the customer's receivable balance by $5,000, the sales price of the merchandise. Sales returns are recorded by the company as they occur.
30	Transferred receivables of $50,000 to a factor without recourse. The factor charged Evergreen a 1% finance charge on the receivables transferred. The sale criteria are met.
June 30	Discounted the Lennox, Inc., note at the bank. The bank's discount rate is 12%. The note was discounted without recourse.
Sep. 30	Lennox, Inc., paid the note amount plus interest to the bank.

Required:

1. Prepare the necessary journal entries for Evergreen for each of the above dates. For transactions involving the sale of merchandise, ignore the entry for the cost of goods sold (round all calculations to the nearest dollar).

2. Prepare any necessary adjusting entries at December 31, 2016. Adjusting entries are only recorded at year-end (round all calculations to the nearest dollar).
3. Prepare a schedule showing the effect of the journal entries in requirements 1 and 2 on 2016 income before taxes.

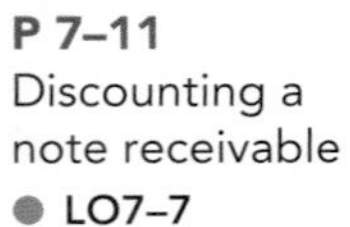

P 7–11
Discounting a note receivable
● LO7–7

Descriptors are provided below for six situations involving notes receivable being discounted at a bank. In each case, the maturity date of the note is December 31, 2016, and the principal and interest are due at maturity. For each, determine the proceeds received from the bank on discounting the note.

Note	Note Face Value	Date of Note	Interest Rate	Date Discounted	Discount Rate
1	$50,000	3/31/2016	8%	6/30/2016	10%
2	50,000	3/31/2016	8	9/30/2016	10
3	50,000	3/31/2016	8	9/30/2016	12
4	80,000	6/30/2016	6	10/31/2016	10
5	80,000	6/30/2016	6	10/31/2016	12
6	80,000	6/30/2016	6	11/30/2016	10

P 7–12
Accounts and notes receivable; discounting a note receivable; receivables turnover ratio
● LO7–5, LO7–6, LO7–7, LO7–8, LO7–9

Chamberlain Enterprises Inc. reported the following receivables in its December 31, 2016, year-end balance sheet:

Current assets:	
Accounts receivable, net of $24,000 in allowance for uncollectible accounts	$218,000
Interest receivable	6,800
Notes receivable	260,000

Additional Information:

1. The notes receivable account consists of two notes, a $60,000 note and a $200,000 note. The $60,000 note is dated October 31, 2016, with principal and interest payable on October 31, 2017. The $200,000 note is dated June 30, 2016, with principal and 6% interest payable on June 30, 2017.
2. During 2017, sales revenue totaled $1,340,000, $1,280,000 cash was collected from customers, and $22,000 in accounts receivable were written off. All sales are made on a credit basis. Bad debt expense is recorded at year-end by adjusting the allowance account to an amount equal to 10% of year-end accounts receivable.
3. On March 31, 2017, the $200,000 note receivable was discounted at the Bank of Commerce. The bank's discount rate is 8%. Chamberlain accounts for the discounting as a sale.

Required:

1. In addition to sales revenue, what revenue and expense amounts related to receivables will appear in Chamberlain's 2017 income statement?
2. What amounts will appear in the 2017 year-end balance sheet for accounts receivable?
3. Calculate the receivables turnover ratio for 2017.

P 7–13
Bank reconciliation and adjusting entries; cash and cash equivalents
● Appendix 7A

The bank statement for the checking account of Management Systems Inc. (MSI) showed a December 31, 2016, balance of $14,632.12. Information that might be useful in preparing a bank reconciliation is as follows:

a. Outstanding checks were $1,320.25.
b. The December 31, 2016, cash receipts of $575 were not deposited in the bank until January 2, 2017.
c. One check written in payment of rent for $246 was correctly recorded by the bank but was recorded by MSI as a $264 disbursement.
d. In accordance with prior authorization, the bank withdrew $450 directly from the checking account as payment on a mortgage note payable. The interest portion of that payment was $350. MSI has made no entry to record the automatic payment.
e. Bank service charges of $14 were listed on the bank statement.
f. A deposit of $875 was recorded by the bank on December 13, but it did not belong to MSI. The deposit should have been made to the checking account of MIS, Inc.
g. The bank statement included a charge of $85 for an NSF check. The check was returned with the bank statement and the company will seek payment from the customer.
h. MSI maintains a $200 petty cash fund that was appropriately reimbursed at the end of December.
i. According to instructions from MSI on December 30, the bank withdrew $10,000 from the account and purchased U.S. Treasury bills for MSI. MSI recorded the transaction in its books on December 31 when it received notice from the bank. Half of the Treasury bills mature in two months and the other half in six months.

Required:

1. Prepare a bank reconciliation for the MSI checking account at December 31, 2016. You will have to compute the balance per books.
2. Prepare any necessary adjusting journal entries indicated.
3. What amount would MSI report as cash and cash equivalents in the current asset section of the December 31, 2016, balance sheet?

P 7–14
Bank reconciliation and adjusting entries
● Appendix 7A

El Gato Painting Company maintains a checking account at American Bank. Bank statements are prepared at the end of each month. The November 30, 2016, reconciliation of the bank balance is as follows:

Balance per bank, November 30		$3,231
Add: Deposits outstanding		1,200
Less: Checks outstanding		
#363	$123	
#365	201	
#380	56	
#381	86	
#382	340	(806)
Adjusted balance per bank, November 30		$3,625

The company's general ledger checking account showed the following for December:

Balance, December 1	$ 3,625
Receipts	42,650
Disbursements	(41,853)
Balance, December 31	$ 4,422

The December bank statement contained the following information:

Balance, December 1	$ 3,231
Deposits	43,000
Checks processed	(41,918)
Service charges	(22)
NSF checks	(440)
Balance, December 31	$ 3,851

The checks that were processed by the bank in December include all of the outstanding checks at the end of November except for check #365. In addition, there are some December checks that had not been processed by the bank by the end of the month. Also, you discover that check #411 for $320 was correctly recorded by the bank but was incorrectly recorded on the books as a $230 disbursement for advertising expense. Included in the bank's deposits is a $1,300 deposit incorrectly credited to the company's account. The deposit should have been posted to the credit of the Los Gatos Company. The NSF checks have not been redeposited and the company will seek payment from the customers involved.

Required:

1. Prepare a bank reconciliation for the El Gato checking account at December 31, 2016.
2. Prepare any necessary adjusting journal entries indicated.

P 7–15
Impairment of securities available-for-sale; troubled debt restructuring
● Appendix 7B

Rothschild Chair Company, Inc., was indebted to First Lincoln Bank under a $20 million, 10% unsecured note. The note was signed January 1, 2008, and was due December 31, 2019. Annual interest was last paid on December 31, 2014. At January 1, 2016, Rothschild Chair Company was experiencing severe financial difficulties and negotiated a restructuring of the terms of the debt agreement.

Required:

Prepare all journal entries by First Lincoln Bank to record the restructuring and any remaining transactions, for current and future years, relating to the debt under each of the independent circumstances below:

1. First Lincoln Bank agreed to settle the debt in exchange for land having a fair value of $16 million but carried on Rothschild Chair Company's books at $13 million.
2. First Lincoln Bank agreed to (a) forgive the interest accrued from last year, (b) reduce the remaining four interest payments to $1 million each, and (c) reduce the principal to $15 million.
3. First Lincoln Bank agreed to defer all payments (including accrued interest) until the maturity date and accept $27,775,000 at that time in settlement of the debt.

Broaden Your Perspective

Apply your critical-thinking ability to the knowledge you've gained. These cases will provide you an opportunity to develop your research, analysis, judgment, and communication skills. You also will work with other students, integrate what you've learned, apply it in real-world situations, and consider its global and ethical ramifications. This practice will broaden your knowledge and further develop your decision-making abilities.

Judgment Case 7–1
Accounts and notes receivable
● LO7–5, LO7–6, LO7–8

Magrath Company has an operating cycle of less than one year and provides credit terms for all of its customers. On April 1, 2016, the company factored, without recourse, some of its accounts receivable. Magrath transferred the receivables to a financial institution, and will have no further association with the receivables.

Magrath uses the allowance method to account for uncollectible accounts. During 2016, some accounts were written off as uncollectible and other accounts previously written off as uncollectible were collected.

Required:

1. How should Magrath account for and report the accounts receivable factored on April 1, 2016? Why is this accounting treatment appropriate?
2. How should Magrath account for the collection of the accounts previously written off as uncollectible?
3. What are the two basic approaches to estimating uncollectible accounts under the allowance method? What is the rationale for each approach?

(AICPA Adapted)

Communication Case 7–2
Uncollectible accounts
● LO7–5

You have been hired as a consultant by a parts manufacturing firm to provide advice as to the proper accounting methods the company should use in some key areas. In the area of receivables, the company president does not understand your recommendation to use the allowance method for uncollectible accounts. She stated, "Financial statements should be based on objective data rather than the guesswork required for the allowance method. Besides, since my uncollectibles are fairly constant from period to period, with significant variations occurring infrequently, the direct write-off method is just as good as the allowance method."

Required:

Draft a one-page response in the form of a memo to the president in support of your recommendation for the company to use the allowance method.

Judgment Case 7–3
Accounts receivable
● LO7–3, LO7–7, LO7–8

Hogan Company uses the net method of accounting for sales discounts. Hogan offers trade discounts to various groups of buyers.

On August 1, 2016, Hogan factored some accounts receivable on a without recourse basis. Hogan incurred a finance charge.

Hogan also has some notes receivable bearing an appropriate rate of interest. The principal and total interest are due at maturity. The notes were received on October 1, 2016, and mature on September 30, 2017. Hogan's operating cycle is less than one year.

Required:

1. a. Using the net method, how should Hogan account for the sales discounts at the date of sale? What is the rationale for the amount recorded as sales under the net method?
   b. Using the net method, what is the effect on Hogan's sales revenues and net income when customers do not take the sales discounts?
2. What is the effect of trade discounts on sales revenues and accounts receivable? Why?
3. How should Hogan account for the accounts receivable factored on August 1, 2016? Why?
4. How should Hogan report the effects of the interest-bearing notes receivable in its December 31, 2016, balance sheet and its income statement for the year ended December 31, 2016? Why?

(AICPA Adapted)

Real World Case 7–4
Sales returns; Green Mountain Coffee Roasters
● LO7–4

Real World Financials

The following is an excerpt from Antar, Sam, "Is Green Mountain Coffee Roasters Shuffling the Beans to Beat Earnings Expectations?" *Phil's Stock World delivered by Newstex,* May 9, 2011.

> On May 3, 2011, Green Mountain Coffee Roasters (NASDAQ: GMCR) beat analysts' earnings estimates by \$0.10 per share for the thirteen-week period ended March 26, 2011. The next day, the stock price had risen to \$11.91 per share to close at \$75.98 per share, a staggering 18.5% increase over the previous day's closing stock price. CNBC Senior Stocks Commentator Herb Greenberg raised questions about the quality of Green Mountain Coffees earnings because its provision for sales returns dropped \$22 million in the thirteen-week period. He wanted to know if there was a certain adjustment to reserves ("a reversal") that helped Green Mountain Coffee beat analysts' earnings estimates. . . .

During the thirteen-week period ended March 26, 2011, it was calculated that Green Mountain Coffee had a negative $22.259 million provision for sales returns. In its latest 10-Q report, Green Mountain Coffee disclosed that its provision for sales returns was $5.262 million for the twenty-six week period ending March 26, 2011, but the company did not disclose amounts for the thirteen-week period ended March 26, 2011. In its previous 10-Q report for the thirteen-week period ended December 25, 2010, Green Mountain Coffee disclosed that its provision for sales returns was $27.521 million. Therefore, the provision for sales returns for the thirteen-week period ended March 26, 2011 was a negative $22.259 million ($5.262 million minus $27.521 million).

Required:

1. Access EDGAR on the Internet. The web address is **www.sec.gov**.
2. Search for **Green Mountain Coffee Roasters, Inc.**'s 10-K for the fiscal year ended September 25, 2010 (filed December 9, 2010). Answer the following questions related to the company's 2010 accounting for sales returns:
   a. What type of an account (for example, asset, contraliability) is Sales Returns Reserve? Explain.
   b. Prepare a T-account for fiscal 2010's sales returns reserve. Include entries for the beginning and ending balance, acquisitions, amounts charged to cost and expense, and deductions.
   c. Prepare journal entries for amounts charged to cost and expense and for deductions. Provide a brief explanation of what each of those journal entries represents.
   d. For any of the amounts included in your journal entries that appear in Green Mountain's statement of cash flows on page F-8, explain why the amount appears as an increase or decrease to cash flows.
3. Now consider the information provided by Antar in the excerpt at the beginning of this case.
   a. Prepare a T-account for the first quarter of fiscal 2011's sales returns reserve. Assume amounts associated with acquisitions and deductions are zero, such that the only entry affecting the account during the first quarter of fiscal 2011 is to record amounts charged or recovered from cost and expense. Compute the ending balance of the account.
   b. Prepare a T-account for the second quarter of fiscal 2011's sales returns reserve. Assume amounts associated with acquisitions and deductions are zero, such that the only entry affecting the account during the first quarter of fiscal 2011 is to record amounts charged or recovered from cost and expense. Compute the ending balance of the account.
   c. Assume that actual returns were zero during the second quarter of fiscal 2011. Prepare a journal entry to record amounts charged or recovered from cost and expense during the second quarter of fiscal 2011. How would that journal entry affect 2011 net income?
   d. Speculate as to what might have caused the activity in Green Mountain's sales returns account during the second quarter of fiscal 2011. Consider how this result could occur unintentionally, or why it might occur intentionally as a way to manage earnings.

Ethics Case 7–5
Uncollectible accounts
● LO7–5

You have recently been hired as the assistant controller for Stanton Industries, a large, publicly held manufacturing company. Your immediate superior is the controller who, in turn, is responsible to the vice president of finance.

The controller has assigned you the task of preparing the year-end adjusting entries. In the receivables area, you have prepared an aging of accounts receivable and have applied historical percentages to the balances of each of the age categories. The analysis indicates that an appropriate balance for the allowance for uncollectible accounts is $180,000. The existing balance in the allowance account prior to any adjusting entry is a $20,000 credit balance.

After showing your analysis to the controller, he tells you to change the aging category of a large account from over 120 days to current status and to prepare a new invoice to the customer with a revised date that agrees with the new aging category. This will change the required allowance for uncollectible accounts from $180,000 to $135,000. Tactfully, you ask the controller for an explanation for the change and he tells you "We need the extra income, the bottom line is too low."

Required:

1. What is the effect on income before taxes of the change requested by the controller?
2. Discuss the ethical dilemma you face. Consider your options and responsibilities along with the possible consequences of any action you might take.

Judgment Case 7–6
Internal control
● LO7–1

For each of the following independent situations, indicate the apparent internal control weaknesses and suggest alternative procedures to eliminate the weaknesses.

1. John Smith is the petty cash custodian. John approves all requests for payment out of the $200 fund, which is replenished at the end of each month. At the end of each month, John submits a list of all accounts and amounts to be charged and a check is written to him for the total amount. John is the only person ever to tally the fund.
2. All of the company's cash disbursements are made by check. Each check must be supported by an approved voucher, which is in turn supported by the appropriate invoice and, for purchases, a receiving document. The

vouchers are approved by Dean Leiser, the chief accountant, after reviewing the supporting documentation. Betty Hanson prepares the checks for Leiser's signature. Leiser also maintains the company's check register (the cash disbursements journal) and reconciles the bank account at the end of each month.

3. Fran Jones opens the company's mail and makes a listing of all checks and cash received from customers. A copy of the list is sent to Jerry McDonald who maintains the general ledger accounts. Fran prepares and makes the daily deposit at the bank. Fran also maintains the subsidiary ledger for accounts receivable, which is used to generate monthly statements to customers.

Real World Case 7–7
Receivables; bad debts; Avon Products
● LO7–5

Real World Financials

EDGAR, the Electronic Data Gathering, Analysis, and Retrieval system, performs automated collection, validation, indexing, and forwarding of submissions by companies and others who are required by law to file forms with the U.S. Securities and Exchange Commission (SEC). All publicly traded domestic companies use EDGAR to make the majority of their filings. (Some foreign companies file voluntarily.) Form 10-K or 10-KSB, which include the annual report, is required to be filed on EDGAR. The SEC makes this information available on the Internet.

Required:

1. Access EDGAR on the Internet. The web address is **www.sec.gov**.
2. Search for **Avon Products, Inc.** Access the 10-K filing for the most recent fiscal year. Search or scroll to find the financial statements.
3. Answer the following questions related to the company's accounts receivable and bad debts:
   a. What is the amount of gross trade accounts receivable at the end of the year?
   b. What is the amount of bad debt expense for the year? (*Hint:* check the statement of cash flows.)
   c. Determine the amount of actual bad debt write-offs made during the year. Assume that all bad debts relate only to trade accounts receivable.
   d. Using only information from the balance sheets, income statements, and your answer to requirement 3(c), determine the amount of cash collected from customers during the year. Assume that all sales are made on a credit basis, that the company provides no allowances for sales returns, that no previously written-off receivables were collected, and that all sales relate to trade accounts receivable.

Integrating Case 7–8
Change in estimate of bad debts
● LO7–5

McLaughlin Corporation uses the allowance method to account for bad debts. At the end of the company's fiscal year, accounts receivable are analyzed and the allowance for uncollectible accounts is adjusted. At the end of 2016, the company reported the following amounts:

Accounts receivable	$10,850,000
Less: Allowance for uncollectible accounts	(450,000)
Accounts receivable, net	$10,400,000

In 2017, it was determined that $1,825,000 of year-end 2016 receivables had to be written off as uncollectible. This was due in part to the fact that Hughes Corporation, a long-standing customer that had always paid its bills, unexpectedly declared bankruptcy in 2017. Hughes owed McLaughlin $1,400,000. At the end of 2016, none of the Hughes receivable was considered uncollectible.

Required:

Describe the appropriate accounting treatment and required disclosures for McLaughlin's underestimation of bad debts at the end of 2016.

Analysis Case 7–9
Financing with receivables
● LO7–8

Financial institutions have developed a wide variety of methods for companies to use their receivables to obtain immediate cash. The methods differ with respect to which rights and risks are retained by the transferor (the original holder of the receivable) and those passed on to the transferee (the new holder, usually a financial institution).

Required:

1. Describe the alternative methods available for companies to use their receivables to obtain immediate cash.
2. Discuss the alternative accounting treatments for these methods.

Real World Case 7–10
Financing with receivables; Sanofi-Aventis
● LO7–5, LO7–8, LO7–10

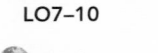

 IFRS

Search on the Internet for the 2013 annual report for **Sanofi-Aventis**. Find the accounts receivable disclosure note.

Required:

1. Sanofi-Aventis subtracts "impairment" from the gross value of accounts receivable to obtain the net value. Interpret the impairment of (€137) in 2013 in terms of how that amount would typically be described in U.S. GAAP.
2. To what extent does Sanofi-Aventis factor or securitize accounts receivable? How do you know?

3. Assume that Sanofi-Aventis decided to increase the extent to which it securitizes its accounts receivable, changing to a policy of securitizing accounts receivable immediately upon making a sale and treating the securitization as a sale of accounts receivable. Indicate the likely effect of that change in policy on:
   a. Accounts receivable in the period of the change.
   b. Cash flow from operations in the period of the change.
   c. Accounts receivable in subsequent periods.
   d. Cash flow from operations in subsequent periods.
4. Given your answers to requirement 3, could a company change the extent to which it factors or securitizes receivables to create one-time changes in its cash flow? Explain.

Research Case 7–11
Locate and extract relevant information and authoritative support for a financial reporting issue; financing with receivables
● LO7–8

CODE

You are spending the summer working for a local wholesale furniture company, Samson Furniture, Inc. The company is considering a proposal from a local financial institution, Old Reliant Financial, to factor Samson's receivables. The company controller is unfamiliar with the prevailing GAAP that deals with accounting for the transfer of financial assets and has asked you to do some research. The controller wants to make sure the arrangement with the financial institution is structured in such a way as to allow the factoring to be accounted for as a sale.

Old Reliant has offered to factor all of the company's receivables on a "without recourse" basis. Old Reliant will remit to Samson 90% of the factored amount, collect the receivables from Samson's customers, and retain the remaining 10% until all of the receivables have been collected. When Old Reliant collects all of the receivables, it will remit to Samson the retained amount, less a 4% fee (4% of the total factored amount).

Required:
1. Explain the meaning of the term *without recourse*.
2. Access the relevant authoritative literature on accounting for the transfer of financial assets using the *FASB Accounting Standards Codification*. You might gain access at the FASB website (www.fasb.org), from your school library, or some other source. What conditions must be met for a transfer of receivables to be accounted for as a sale (or in accounting terms, "derecognized")? What is the specific citation that Samson would rely on in applying that accounting treatment?
3. Assuming that the conditions for treatment as a sale are met, prepare Samson's journal entry to record the factoring of $400,000 of receivables. Assume that the fair value of the last 10% of Samson's receivables is equal to $25,000.
4. An agreement that both entitles and obligates the transferor, Samson, to repurchase or redeem transferred assets from the transferee, Old Reliant, maintains the transferor's effective control over those assets and the transfer is accounted for as a secured borrowing, not a sale, if and only if what conditions are met?

Analysis Case 7–12
Compare receivables management using ratios; Del Monte Foods and Smithfield Foods
● LO7–9

Real World Financials

The table below contains selected financial information included in the 2013 financial statements of Del Monte Foods Co. and Smithfield Foods Inc.

	($ in millions)			
	Del Monte		Smithfield	
	2013	2012	2013	2012
Balance sheets:				
Accounts receivable, net	$ 191.7	$ 195.3	$ 663.2	$ 624.7
Income statements:				
Net sales	3,819.4	3,676.2	13,221.1	13,094.3

Required:
1. Calculate the 2013 receivables turnover ratio and average collection period for both companies. Evaluate the management of each company's investment in receivables.
2. Obtain annual reports from three corporations in the same primary industry and compare the management of each company's investment in receivables.

Note: You can obtain copies of annual reports from your library, from friends who are shareholders, from the investor relations department of the corporations, from a friendly stockbroker, or from EDGAR (Electronic Data Gathering, Analysis, and Retrieval) on the Internet (www.sec.gov).

Analysis Case 7–13
Reporting cash and receivables
● LO7–2, LO7–5

Refer to the financial statements and related disclosure notes of PetSmart, Inc., included with all new copies of the text.

PetSmart

Required:

1. What is PetSmart's policy for designating investments as cash equivalents?
2. As of February 2, 2014, how much cash was included in cash and cash equivalents?
3. Determine the gross and net amount of accounts receivable outstanding at February 2, 2014, and February 3, 2013.

Air France–KLM Case

● LO7–8

IFRS

Air France–KLM (AF), a Franco-Dutch company, prepares its financial statements according to International Financial Reporting Standards. AF's financial statements and disclosure notes for the year ended December 31, 2013, are provided with all new textbooks. This material also is available at **www.airfranceklm-finance.com**.

Required:

1. In note 4.10.1, AF describes how it values trade receivables. How does the approach used by AF compare to U.S. GAAP?
2. In note 26, AF reconciles the beginning and ending balances of its valuation allowances for trade accounts receivable. Prepare a T-account for the valuation allowance and include entries for the beginning and ending balances as well as any reconciling items that affected the account during 2013.
3. Examine note 28. Does AF have any bank overdrafts? If so, are the overdrafts shown in the balance sheet the same way they would be shown under U.S. GAAP?

CHAPTER

8 Inventories: Measurement

OVERVIEW

The next two chapters continue our study of assets by investigating the measurement and reporting issues involving inventories and the related expense—cost of goods sold. Inventory refers to the assets a company (1) intends to sell in the normal course of business, (2) has in production for future sale, or (3) uses currently in the production of goods to be sold.

LEARNING OBJECTIVES

After studying this chapter, you should be able to:

- **LO8–1** Explain the difference between a perpetual inventory system and a periodic inventory system. (*p. 427*)
- **LO8–2** Explain which physical quantities of goods should be included in inventory. (*p. 430*)
- **LO8–3** Determine the expenditures that should be included in the cost of inventory. (*p. 431*)
- **LO8–4** Differentiate between the specific identification, FIFO, LIFO, and average cost methods used to determine the cost of ending inventory and cost of goods sold. (*p. 434*)
- **LO8–5** Discuss the factors affecting a company's choice of inventory method. (*p. 441*)
- **LO8–6** Understand supplemental LIFO disclosures and the effect of LIFO liquidations on net income. (*p. 442*)
- **LO8–7** Calculate the key ratios used by analysts to monitor a company's investment in inventories. (*p. 448*)
- **LO8–8** Determine ending inventory using the dollar-value LIFO inventory method. (*p. 451*)
- **LO8–9** Discuss the primary difference between U.S. GAAP and IFRS with respect to determining the cost of inventory. (*p. 441*)

FINANCIAL REPORTING CASE

Inventory Measurement at Phillips 66

A recent article in the financial section of your local newspaper reported record profits generated by U.S. oil and gas companies. When you showed the article to a friend, he laughed, "I'll bet U.S. oil and gas companies use LIFO to value their inventories. That way they can report lower profits than they would if using another inventory method. If the profits are too high it could cause the government to jump in and impose an excess profits tax as it did in the 1980s." Curiosity aroused, you downloaded from the Internet a recent annual report of **Phillips 66**, one of the large U.S. oil and gas companies. The report included the following disclosure:

Note 4—Inventories (in part)

Inventories at December 31 consisted of the following ($ in millions):

	2013	2012
Crude oil and petroleum products	$3,093	$3,138
Materials and supplies	261	292
Total inventories	$3,354	$3,430

Inventories valued on a LIFO basis totaled $2,945 million and $2,987 million at December 31, 2013, and December 31, 2012, respectively. The estimated excess of current replacement cost over LIFO cost of inventories amounted to approximately $7,600 million and $7,700 million at December 31, 2013 and 2012, respectively.

The company's summary of significant accounting policies reports that the LIFO method is used to value crude oil and petroleum products inventories and materials and supplies inventories are valued using the weighted-average cost method.

QUESTIONS

By the time you finish this chapter, you should be able to respond appropriately to the questions posed in this case. Compare your response to the solution provided at the end of the chapter.

1. What inventory methods does Phillips 66 use to value its inventories? Is this permissible according to GAAP? *(p. 442)*
2. What is the purpose of disclosing the difference between the reported LIFO inventory amounts and replacement cost, assuming that replacement cost is equivalent to a FIFO basis? *(p. 444)*
3. Is your friend correct in his assertion that, by using LIFO, Phillips 66 was able to report lower profits for the year ended December 31, 2013? *(p. 450)*

Recording and Measuring Inventory

PART A

Inventory refers to the assets a company (1) intends to sell in the normal course of business, (2) has in production for future sale (work in process), or (3) uses currently in the production of goods to be sold (raw materials). The computers produced by **Dell, Inc.**, that are intended for sale to customers are inventory, as are partially completed components in the assembly lines of Dell's Texas facility, and the computer chips and memory modules that will go into

Inventories consist of assets that a retail or wholesale company acquires for resale or goods that manufacturers produce for sale.

computers produced later. The computers *used* by Dell to maintain its accounting system, however, are classified and accounted for as plant and equipment. Similarly, the stocks and bonds a securities dealer holds for sale are inventory, whereas Dell would classify the securities it holds as investments.

Proper accounting for inventories is essential for manufacturing, wholesale, and retail companies (enterprises that earn revenue by selling goods). Inventory usually is one of the most valuable assets listed in the balance sheet for these firms. Cost of goods sold—the expense recorded when inventory is sold—typically is the largest expense in the income statement. For example, a recent balance sheet for **The Hillshire Brands Company**, formerly Sara Lee Corporation, reported inventories of $300 million, which represented 27% of current assets. The company's income statement for the nine months ended March 29, 2014, reported cost of goods sold of $2,150 million representing 78% of operating expenses.

An important objective in inventory accounting is to match the appropriate cost of goods sold with sales revenue.

In this and the following chapter we discuss the measurement and reporting issues involving **inventory**, an asset, and the related expense, **cost of goods sold**. Inventory represents *quantities* of goods acquired, manufactured, or in the process of being manufactured. The inventory amount in the balance sheet at the end of an accounting period represents the cost of the inventory still on hand, and cost of goods sold in the income statement represents the cost of the inventory sold during the period. The historical cost principle and the desire to match expenses with revenues offers guidance for measuring inventory and cost of goods sold, but as we will see in this and the next chapter, it's usually difficult to measure inventory (cost of goods sold) at the exact cost of the actual physical quantities on hand (sold). Fortunately, accountants can use one of several techniques to approximate the desired result and satisfy our measurement objectives.

Types of Inventory

Merchandising Inventory

Wholesale and retail companies purchase goods that are primarily in finished form. These companies are intermediaries in the process of moving goods from the manufacturer to the end-user. They often are referred to as merchandising companies and their inventory as merchandise inventory. *The cost of merchandise inventory includes the purchase price plus any other costs necessary to get the goods in condition and location for sale.* We discuss the concept of condition and location and the types of costs that typically constitute inventory later in this chapter.

Manufacturing Inventories

Inventory for a manufacturing company consists of *raw materials*, work in process, and finished goods.

Unlike merchandising companies, manufacturing companies actually produce the goods they sell to wholesalers, retailers, or other manufacturers. Inventory for a manufacturer consists of (1) raw materials, (2) work in process, and (3) finished goods. **Raw materials** represent the cost of components purchased from other manufacturers that will become part of the finished product. For example, Dell's raw materials inventory includes semiconductors, circuit boards, plastic, and glass that go into the production of personal computers.

The cost of *work in process* and *finished goods* includes the cost of raw materials, direct labor, and an allocated portion of manufacturing overhead.

Work-in-process inventory refers to the products that are not yet complete. The cost of work in process includes the cost of raw materials used in production, the cost of labor that can be directly traced to the goods in process, and an allocated portion of other manufacturing costs, called *manufacturing overhead.* Overhead costs include electricity and other utility costs to operate the manufacturing facility, depreciation of manufacturing equipment, and many other manufacturing costs that cannot be directly linked to the production of specific goods. Once the manufacturing process is completed, these costs that have accumulated in work in process are transferred to **finished goods**.

Manufacturing companies generally disclose, either in a note or directly in the balance sheet, the dollar amount of each inventory category. For example, **The Hillshire Brands Company** reports inventory categories directly in the balance sheet, as shown in recent quarterly financial statements in Illustration 8–1.

Illustration 8–1
Inventories Disclosure—The Hillshire Brands Company

Real World Financials

Balance Sheets

	($ in millions)	
	March 29, 2014	**June 29, 2013**
Current assets:		
Inventories		
Finished goods	$198	$207
Work in process	16	15
Materials and supplies	86	91
Total	$300	$313

The inventory accounts and the cost flows for a typical manufacturing company are shown using T-accounts in Illustration 8–2. The costs of raw materials used, direct labor applied, and manufacturing overhead applied flow into work in process and then to finished goods. When the goods are sold, the cost of those goods flows to cost of goods sold.

Illustration 8–2
Inventory Components and Cost Flow for a Manufacturing Company

The costs of inventory units follow their physical movement from one stage of activity to another.

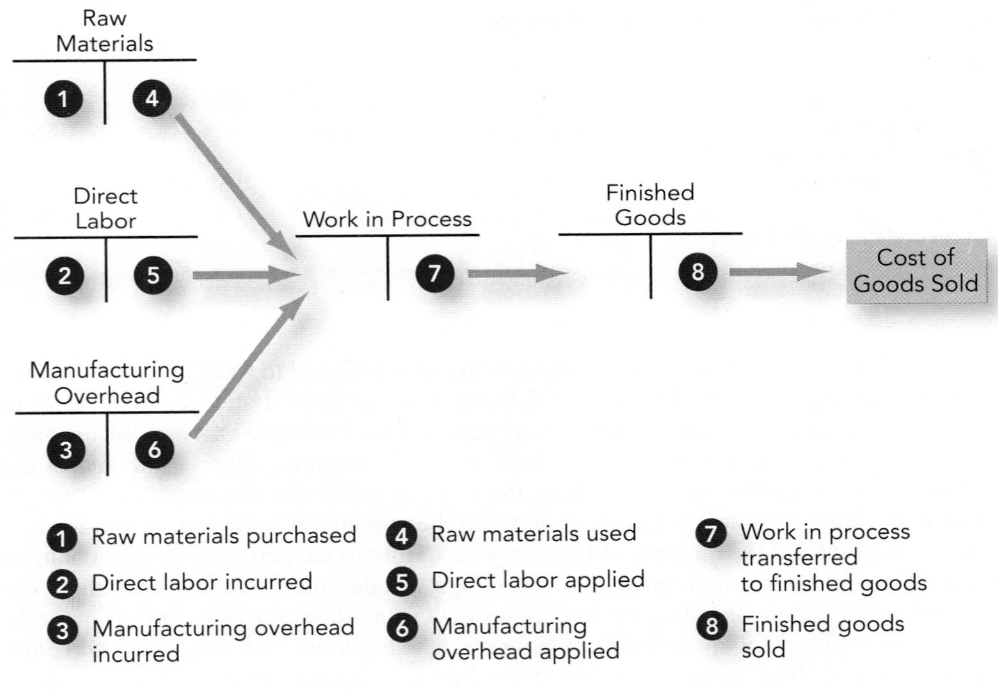

We focus in this text primarily on merchandising companies (wholesalers and retailers). Still, most of the accounting principles and procedures discussed here also apply to manufacturing companies. The unique problems involved with accumulating the direct costs of raw materials and labor and with allocating manufacturing overhead are addressed in managerial and cost accounting textbooks.

Types of Inventory Systems

Perpetual Inventory System

● LO8–1

Two accounting systems are used to record transactions involving inventory: the **perpetual inventory system** and the **periodic inventory system**. The perpetual system was introduced in Chapter 2. The system is aptly termed perpetual because the account *inventory* is continually adjusted for each change in inventory, whether it's caused by a purchase, a sale, or a return of merchandise by the company to its supplier (a *purchase return* for the buyer,

A *perpetual inventory system* continuously records both changes in inventory quantity and inventory cost.

a *sales return* for the seller).[1] The cost of goods sold account, along with the inventory account, is adjusted each time goods are sold or are returned by a customer. This concept is applied to the Lothridge Wholesale Beverage Company for which inventory information is provided in Illustration 8–3. This hypothetical company also will be used in the next several illustrations.

Illustration 8–3
Perpetual Inventory System

The Lothridge Wholesale Beverage Company purchases soft drinks from producers and then sells them to retailers. The company begins 2016 with merchandise inventory of $120,000 on hand. During 2016 additional merchandise is purchased on account at a cost of $600,000. Sales for the year, all on account, totaled $820,000. The cost of the soft drinks sold is $540,000. Lothridge uses the perpetual inventory system to keep track of both inventory quantities and inventory costs. The system indicates that the cost of inventory on hand at the end of the year is $180,000.

The following summary journal entries record the inventory transactions for the Lothridge Company:

2016		
Inventory	600,000	
Accounts payable		600,000
To record the purchase of merchandise inventory.		
2016		
Accounts receivable	820,000	
Sales revenue		820,000
To record sales on account.		
Cost of goods sold	540,000	
Inventory		540,000
To record the cost of sales.		

An important feature of a perpetual system is that it is designed to track inventory quantities from their acquisition to their sale. If the system is accurate, it allows management to determine how many goods are on hand on any date without having to take a physical count. However, physical counts of inventory usually are made anyway, either at the end of the fiscal year or on a sample basis throughout the year, to verify that the perpetual system is correctly tracking quantities. Differences between the quantity of inventory determined by the physical count and the quantity of inventory according to the perpetual system could be caused by system errors, theft, breakage, or spoilage. In addition to keeping up with inventory, a perpetual system also directly determines how many items are sold during a period.

Barcode tracking systems are used to control and measure inventory.

You probably are familiar with the scanning mechanisms used at grocery stores and other checkout counters. The scanners not only record each item sold but also track the sale of merchandise for inventory management purposes. Inventory software and barcode tracking systems are used to control and measure inventory in many industries. Barcoding also lessens the burden of physical inventory counts.

A perpetual inventory system tracks both inventory quantities and inventory costs.

When a company uses a perpetual inventory system to record inventory and cost of goods sold transactions, merchandise cost data also is included in the system. That way, when merchandise is purchased/sold, the system records not only the addition/reduction in inventory quantity but also the addition/reduction in the *cost* of the inventory.

Periodic Inventory System

A *periodic inventory system* adjusts inventory and records cost of goods sold only at the end of each reporting period.

A **periodic inventory system** is not designed to track either the quantity or cost of merchandise. The merchandise inventory account balance is not adjusted as purchases and sales are made but only periodically at the end of a reporting period. A physical count of the period's ending inventory is made and costs are assigned to the quantities determined. Merchandise

[1]We discussed accounting for sales returns in Chapter 7.

purchases, purchase returns, purchase discounts, and freight-in (purchases plus freight-in less returns and discounts equals net purchases) are recorded in temporary accounts and the period's cost of goods sold is determined at the end of the period by combining the temporary accounts with the inventory account:

Beginning inventory + Net purchases − Ending inventory = Cost of goods sold

Cost of goods sold equation

The cost of goods sold equation assumes that all inventory quantities not on hand at the end of the period were sold. This may not be the case if inventory items were either damaged or stolen. If damaged and stolen inventory are identified, they must be removed from beginning inventory or purchases before calculating cost of goods sold and then classified as a separate expense item.

Illustration 8–4 looks at the periodic system using the Lothridge Wholesale Beverage Company example.

Illustration 8–4

Periodic Inventory System

The Lothridge Wholesale Beverage Company purchases soft drinks from producers and then sells them to retailers. The company begins 2016 with merchandise inventory of $120,000 on hand. During 2016, additional merchandise was purchased on account at a cost of $600,000. Sales for the year, all on account, totaled $820,000. Lothridge uses a periodic inventory system. A physical count determined the cost of inventory at the end of the year to be $180,000.

The following summary journal entries record the inventory transactions for 2016. Of course, each individual transaction would actually be recorded as incurred:

2016		
Purchases	600,000	
Accounts payable		600,000
To record the purchase of merchandise inventory.		

2016		
Accounts receivable	820,000	
Sales revenue		820,000
To record sales on account.		

No entry is recorded for the cost of inventory sold.

Because cost of goods sold isn't determined automatically and continually by the periodic system, it must be determined indirectly after a physical inventory count. Cost of goods sold for 2016 is determined as follows:

Beginning inventory	$120,000
Plus: Purchases	600,000
Cost of goods available for sale	720,000
Less: Ending inventory (per physical count)	(180,000)
Cost of goods sold	$540,000

The following journal entry combines the components of cost of goods sold into a single expense account and updates the balance in the inventory account:

December 31, 2016		
Cost of goods sold	540,000	
Inventory (ending)	180,000	
Inventory (beginning)		120,000
Purchases		600,000
To adjust inventory, close the purchases account, and record cost of goods sold.		

This entry adjusts the inventory account to the correct period-end amount, closes the temporary purchases account, and records the residual as cost of goods sold. Now let's compare the two inventory accounting systems.

A Comparison of the Perpetual and Periodic Inventory Systems

Beginning inventory plus net purchases during the period is the *cost of goods available for sale.* The main difference between a perpetual and a periodic system is that the periodic system allocates cost of goods available for sale between ending inventory and cost of goods sold (periodically) *at the end of the period.* In contrast, the perpetual system performs this allocation by decreasing inventory and increasing cost of goods sold (perpetually) *each time goods are sold.*

The impact on the financial statements of choosing one system over the other generally is not significant. The choice between the two approaches usually is motivated by management control considerations as well as the comparative costs of implementation. Perpetual systems can provide more information about the dollar amounts of inventory levels on a continuous basis. They also facilitate the preparation of interim financial statements by providing fairly accurate information without the necessity of a physical count of inventory.

A perpetual system provides more timely information but generally is more costly.

On the other hand, a perpetual system may be more expensive to implement than a periodic system. This is particularly true for inventories consisting of large numbers of low-cost items. Perpetual systems are more workable with inventories of high-cost items such as construction equipment or automobiles. However, with the help of computers and electronic sales devices such as cash register systems with barcode scanners, the perpetual inventory system is now available to many small businesses that previously could not afford them and is economically feasible for a broader range of inventory items than before.

The periodic system is less costly to implement during the period but requires a physical count before ending inventory and cost of goods sold can be determined. This makes the preparation of interim financial statements more costly unless an inventory estimation technique is used.[2] And, perhaps most importantly, the inventory monitoring features provided by a perpetual system are not available. However, it is important to remember that a perpetual system involves the tracking of both inventory quantities *and* costs. Many companies that determine costs only periodically employ systems to constantly monitor inventory quantities.

What is Included in Inventory?

Physical Quantities Included in Inventory

LO8–2

Regardless of the system used, the measurement of inventory and cost of goods sold starts with determining the physical quantities of goods. Typically, determining the physical quantity that should be included in inventory is a simple matter because it consists of items in the possession of the company. However, in some situations the identification of items that should be included in inventory is more difficult. Consider, for example, goods in transit, goods on consignment, and sales returns.

GOODS IN TRANSIT. At the end of a reporting period, it's important to ensure a proper inventory cutoff. This means determining the ownership of goods that are in transit between the company and its customers as well as between the company and its suppliers. For example, in December 2016, the Lothridge Wholesale Beverage Company sold goods to the Jabbar Company. The goods were shipped on December 29, 2016, and arrived at Jabbar's warehouse on January 3, 2017. The fiscal year-end for both companies is December 31.

Should the merchandise shipped to Jabbar be recorded as a sale by Lothridge and a purchase by Jabbar in 2016 and thus included in Jabbar's 2016 ending inventory? Should recording the sale/purchase be delayed until 2017 and the merchandise be included in Lothridge's 2016 ending inventory? The answer depends on who owns the goods at December 31. Ownership depends on the terms of the agreement between the two companies. If the goods

[2]In Chapter 9 we discuss inventory estimation techniques that avoid the necessity of a physical count to determine ending inventory and cost of goods sold.

are shipped **f.o.b. (free on board) shipping point**, then legal title to the goods changes hands at the point of shipment when the seller delivers the goods to the common carrier (for example, a trucking company), and the purchaser is responsible for shipping costs and transit insurance. In that case, Lothridge records the sale and inventory reduction in 2016 and Jabbar records a 2016 purchase and includes the goods in 2016 ending inventory even though the company is not in physical possession of the goods on the last day of the fiscal year.

Inventory shipped *f.o.b. shipping point* is included in the purchaser's inventory as soon as the merchandise is shipped.

On the other hand, if the goods are shipped **f.o.b. destination**, the seller is responsible for shipping and legal title does not pass until the goods arrive at their destination (the customer's location). In our example, if the goods are shipped f.o.b. destination, Lothridge includes the merchandise in its 2016 ending inventory and the sale is recorded in 2017. Jabbar records the purchase in 2017.

Inventory shipped *f.o.b. destination* is included in the purchaser's inventory only after it reaches the purchaser's destination.

GOODS ON CONSIGNMENT. Sometimes a company arranges for another company to sell its product under **consignment**. The goods are physically transferred to the other company (the consignee), but the transferor (consignor) retains legal title. If the consignee can't find a buyer, the goods are returned to the consignor. If a buyer is found, the consignee remits the selling price (less commission and approved expenses) to the consignor.

Goods held on *consignment* are included in the inventory of the consignor until sold by the consignee.

As we discussed in Chapter 5, because risk is retained by the consignor, the sale is not complete (revenue is not recognized) until an eventual sale to a third party occurs. As a result, goods held on consignment generally are not included in the consignee's inventory. While in stock, they belong to the consignor and should be included in inventory of the consignor even though not in the company's physical possession. A sale is recorded by the consignor only when the goods are sold by the consignee and title passes to the customer.

SALES RETURNS. Recall from our discussions in Chapters 5 and 7 that when the right of return exists, a seller must be able to estimate those returns before revenue can be recognized. The adjusting entry for estimated sales returns reduces sales revenue and accounts receivable. At the same time, cost of goods sold is reduced and inventory is increased (see Illustration 7–4 on page 369). As a result, a company includes in inventory the cost of merchandise it anticipates will be returned.

Now that we've considered which goods are part of inventory, let's examine the types of costs that should be associated with those inventory quantities.

Expenditures Included in Inventory

● LO8–3

As mentioned earlier, the cost of inventory includes all necessary expenditures to acquire the inventory and bring it to its desired *condition* and *location* for sale or for use in the manufacturing process. Obviously, the cost includes the purchase price of the goods. But usually the cost of acquiring inventory also includes freight charges on incoming goods borne by the buyer; insurance costs incurred by the buyer while the goods are in transit (if shipped f.o.b. shipping point); and the costs of unloading, unpacking, and preparing merchandise inventory for sale or raw materials inventory for use.[3] The costs included in inventory are called **product costs**. They are associated with products and *expensed as cost of goods sold only when the related products are sold.*[4]

Expenditures necessary to bring inventory to its *condition* and *location* for sale or use are included in its cost.

FREIGHT-IN ON PURCHASES. Freight-in on purchases is commonly included in the cost of inventory. These costs clearly are necessary to get the inventory in location for sale or use and can generally be associated with particular goods. Freight costs are added to the inventory account in a perpetual system. In a periodic system, freight costs generally are added to a temporary account called **freight-in** or **transportation-in**, which is added to purchases in determining net purchases. The account is closed to cost of goods sold along with purchases and other components of cost of goods sold at the end of the reporting period. (See Illustration 8–6 on page 433.) From an accounting system perspective, freight-in also

The cost of *freight-in* paid by the purchaser generally is part of the cost of inventory.

[3]Generally accepted accounting principles require that abnormal amounts of certain costs be recognized as current period expenses rather than being included in the cost of inventory, specifically idle facility costs, freight, handling costs, and waste materials (spoilage). FASB ASC 330–10–30: Inventory–Overall–Initial Measurement (previously "Inventory Costs—An Amendment of *ARB No. 43,* Chapter 4," *Statement of Financial Accounting Standards No. 151* (Norwalk, Conn.: FASB, 2004)).

[4]For practical reasons, though, some of these expenditures often are not included in inventory cost and are treated as **period costs.** They often are immaterial or it is impractical to associate the expenditures with particular units of inventory (for example, unloading and unpacking costs). Period costs are not associated with products and are expensed in the *period* incurred.

could be added to the purchases account. From a control perspective, by recording freight-in as a separate item, management can more easily track its freight costs. The same perspectives pertain to purchases returns and purchase discounts, which are discussed next.

Shipping charges on outgoing goods are reported either as part of cost of goods sold or as an operating expense, usually among selling expenses.

Shipping charges on outgoing goods (freight-out) are not included in the cost of inventory. They are reported in the income statement either as part of cost of goods sold or as an operating expense, usually among selling expenses. If a company adopts a policy of not including shipping charges in cost of goods sold, both the amounts incurred during the period as well as the income statement classification of the expense must be disclosed.[5]

A *purchase return* represents a reduction of net purchases.

PURCHASE RETURNS. In Chapter 7 we discussed merchandise returns from the perspective of the selling company. We now address returns from the buyer's point of view. You may recall that the seller views a return as a reduction of net sales. Likewise, a buyer views a return as a reduction of net purchases. When the buyer returns goods to the seller, a **purchase return** is recorded. In a perpetual inventory system, this means a reduction in both inventory and accounts payable (if the account has not yet been paid) at the time of the return. In a periodic system an account called *purchase returns* temporarily accumulates these amounts. Purchase returns are subtracted from purchases when determining net purchases. The account is closed to cost of goods sold at the end of the reporting period.

Purchase discounts represent reductions in the amount to be paid if remittance is made within a designated period of time.

PURCHASE DISCOUNTS. Cash discounts also were discussed from the seller's perspective in Chapter 7. These discounts really are quick-payment discounts because they represent reductions in the amount to be paid by the buyer in the event payment is made within a specified period of time. The amount of the discount and the time period within which it's available are conveyed by terms like 2/10, n/30 (meaning a 2% discount if paid within 10 days, otherwise full payment within 30 days). As with the seller, the purchaser can record these **purchase discounts** using either the **gross method** or the **net method**. Consider Illustration 8–5, which is similar to the cash discount illustration in Chapter 7.

Illustration 8–5

Purchase Discounts

On October 5, 2016, the Lothridge Wholesale Beverage Company purchased merchandise at a price of $20,000. The repayment terms are stated as 2/10, n/30. Lothridge paid $13,720 ($14,000 less the 2% cash discount) on October 14 and the remaining balance of $6,000 on November 4. Lothridge employs a periodic inventory system.

The gross and net methods of recording the purchase and cash payment are compared as follows:

By either method, net purchases are reduced by discounts taken.

Discounts not taken are included as purchases using the gross method and as interest expense using the net method.

Gross Method			Net Method		
October 5, 2016			**October 5, 2016**		
Purchases*	20,000		Purchases*	19,600	
Accounts payable		20,000	Accounts payable		19,600
October 14, 2016			**October 14, 2016**		
Accounts payable	14,000		Accounts payable	13,720	
Purchase discounts*		280	Cash		13,720
Cash		13,720			
November 4, 2016			**November 4, 2016**		
Accounts payable	6,000		Accounts payable	5,880	
Cash		6,000	Interest expense	120	
			Cash		6,000

*The inventory account is used in a perpetual system.

Conceptually, the gross method views a discount not taken as part of the cost of inventory. The net method considers the cost of inventory to include the net, after-discount amount, and any discounts not taken are reported as *interest expense*.[6] The discount is viewed as compensation to the seller for providing financing to the buyer.

[5]FASB ASC 605–45–50–2: Revenue Recognition–Principal Agent Considerations–Disclosure–Shipping and Handling Fees and Costs (previously "Accounting for Shipping and Handling Fees and Costs," *EITF Issue No. 00–10* (Norwalk, Conn.: FASB, 2000), par. 6).

[6]An alternative treatment is to debit an expense account called *purchase discounts lost* rather than interest expense. This enables a company to more easily identify the forgone discounts.

Purchase discounts recorded under the gross method are subtracted from purchases when determining net purchases. The account is a temporary account that is closed to cost of goods sold at the end of the reporting period. Under the perpetual inventory system, purchase discounts are treated as a reduction in the inventory account.

The effect on the financial statements of the difference between the two methods usually is immaterial. Net income over time will be the same using either method. There will, however, be a difference in gross profit between the two methods equal to the amount of discounts not taken. In the preceding illustration, $120 in discounts not taken is included as interest expense using the net method and cost of goods sold using the gross method.

Illustration 8–6 compares the perpetual and periodic inventory systems, using the net method.

Illustration 8–6

Inventory Transactions—Perpetual and Periodic Systems

The Lothridge Wholesale Beverage Company purchases soft drinks from producers and then sells them to retailers. The company began 2016 with merchandise inventory of $120,000 on hand. During 2016, additional merchandise is purchased on account at a cost of $600,000. Lothridge's suppliers offer credit terms of 2/10, n/30. All discounts were taken. Lothridge uses the net method to record purchase discounts. All purchases are made f.o.b. shipping point. Freight charges paid by Lothridge totaled $16,000. Merchandise with a net of discount cost of $20,000 was returned to suppliers for credit. Sales for the year, all on account, totaled $830,000. The cost of the soft drinks sold is $550,000. $154,000 of inventory remained on hand at the end of 2016.

The above transactions are recorded in summary form according to both the perpetual and periodic inventory systems as follows:

($ in 000s)

Perpetual System			Periodic System		
Purchases					
Inventory ($600 × 98%)	588		Purchases ($600 × 98%)	588	
Accounts payable		588	Accounts payable		588
Freight					
Inventory	16		Freight-in	16	
Cash		16	Cash		16
Returns					
Accounts payable	20		Accounts payable	20	
Inventory		20	Purchase returns		20
Sales					
Accounts receivable	830		Accounts receivable	830	
Sales revenue		830	Sales revenue		830
Cost of goods sold	550		No entry		
Inventory		550			
End of period					
No entry			Cost of goods sold (below)	550	
			Inventory (ending)	154	
			Purchase returns	20	
			Inventory (beginning)		120
			Purchases		588
			Freight-in		16

Supporting Schedule:

Cost of goods sold:		
Beginning inventory		$120
Purchases	$588	
Less: Returns	(20)	
Plus: Freight-in	16	
Net purchases		584
Cost of goods available		704
Less: Ending inventory		(154)
Cost of goods sold		$550

Inventory Cost Flow Assumptions

LO8–4

Regardless of whether the perpetual or periodic system is used, it's necessary to assign dollar amounts to the physical quantities of goods sold and goods remaining in ending inventory. Unless each item of inventory is specifically identified and traced through the system, assigning dollars is accomplished by making an assumption regarding how units of goods (and their associated costs) flow through the system. We examine the common cost flow assumptions next. In previous illustrations, dollar amounts of the cost of goods sold and the cost of ending inventory were assumed known. However, if various portions of inventory are acquired at different costs, we need a way to decide which units were sold and which remain in inventory. Illustration 8–7 will help explain.

Illustration 8–7
Cost Flow

Goods available for sale include beginning inventory plus purchases.

The Browning Company began 2016 with $22,000 of inventory. The cost of beginning inventory is composed of 4,000 units purchased for $5.50 each. Merchandise transactions during 2016 were as follows:

Purchases

Date of Purchase	Units	Unit Cost*	Total Cost
Jan. 17	1,000	$6.00	$ 6,000
Mar. 22	3,000	7.00	21,000
Oct. 15	3,000	7.50	22,500
Totals	7,000		$49,500

Sales

Date of Sale	Units
Jan. 10	2,000
Apr. 15	1,500
Nov. 20	3,000
Total	6,500

*Includes purchase price and cost of freight.

As the data show, 7,000 units were purchased during 2016 at various prices and 6,500 units were sold. What is the cost of the 6,500 units sold? If all units, including beginning inventory, were purchased at the same price, then the answer would be simple. However, that rarely is the case.

The year started with 4,000 units, 7,000 units were purchased, and 6,500 units were sold. This means 4,500 units remain in ending inventory. This allocation of units available for sale is depicted in Illustration 8–7A.

Illustration 8–7A
Allocation of Units Available

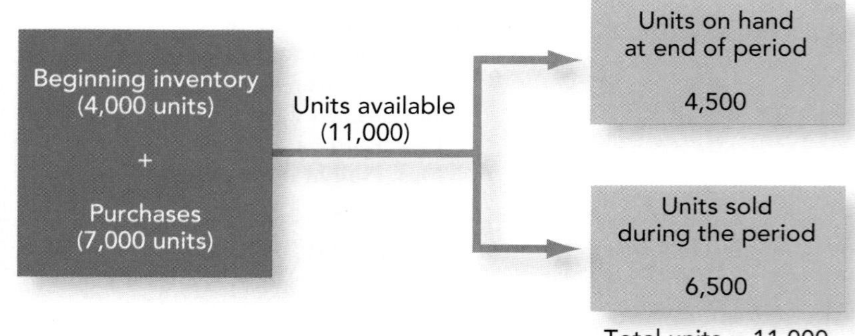

If a periodic system is used, what is the cost of the 4,500 units in ending inventory? In other words, which of the 11,000 (4,000 + 7,000) units available for sale were sold? Are they the more expensive ones bought toward the end of the year, or the less costly ones acquired before prices increased? Using the numbers given, let's consider the question as follows:

Beginning inventory (4,000 units @ $5.50)	$22,000
Plus: Purchases (7,000 units @ various prices)	49,500
Cost of goods available for sale (11,000 units)	$71,500
Less: Ending inventory (4,500 units @ ?)	?
Cost of goods sold (6,500 units @ ?)	?

The $71,500 in cost of goods available for sale must be allocated to ending inventory and cost of goods sold. The allocation decision is depicted in Illustration 8–7B.

Illustration 8–7B

Allocation of Cost of Goods Available

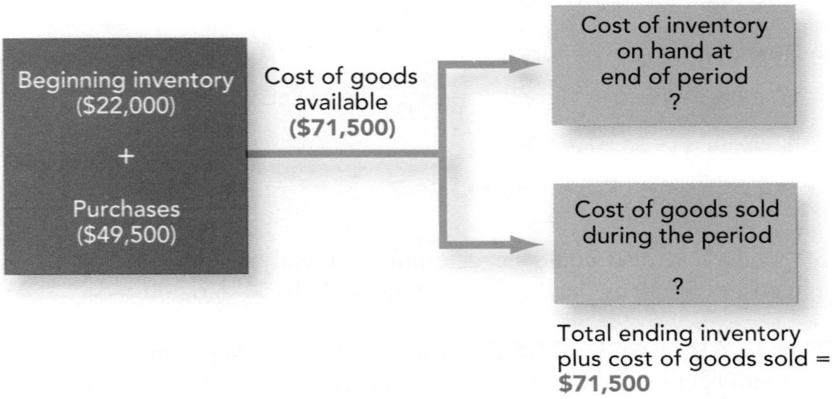

Let's turn our attention now to the various inventory methods that can be used to achieve this allocation.

Specific Identification

It's sometimes possible for each unit sold during the period or each unit on hand at the end of the period to be matched with its actual cost. Actual costs can be determined by reference to the invoice representing the purchase of the item. This method is used frequently by companies selling unique, expensive products with low sales volume which makes it relatively easy and economically feasible to associate each item with its actual cost. For example, automobiles have unique serial numbers that can be used to match a specific auto with the invoice identifying the actual purchase price.

The **specific identification method**, however, is not feasible for many types of products either because items are not uniquely identifiable or because it is too costly to match a specific purchase price with each item sold or each item remaining in ending inventory. Most companies use cost flow methods to determine cost of goods sold and ending inventory. Cost flow methods are based on assumptions about how inventory might flow in and out of a company. However, it's important to note that the actual flow of a company's inventory does not have to correspond to the cost flow assumed. The various motivating factors that influence management's choice among alternative methods are discussed later in this chapter. We now explore the three most common cost flow methods: average cost, first-in, first-out (FIFO) and last-in, first-out (LIFO).

Average Cost

The **average cost method** assumes that cost of goods sold and ending inventory consist of a mixture of all the goods available for sale. The average unit cost applied to goods sold or to ending inventory is not simply an average of the various unit costs of purchases during the period but an average unit cost *weighted* by the number of units acquired at the various unit costs.

The *average cost method* assumes that items sold and items in ending inventory come from a mixture of all the goods available for sale.

In a periodic inventory system, the average cost is computed only at the end of the period.

PERIODIC AVERAGE COST. In a periodic inventory system, this weighted average is calculated only at the end of the period as follows:

$$\text{Weighted-average unit cost} = \frac{\text{Cost of goods available for sale}}{\text{Quantity available for sale}}$$

The calculation of average cost is demonstrated in Illustration 8–7C using data from Illustration 8–7.

Illustration 8–7C

Average Cost—Periodic Inventory System

Beginning inventory (4,000 units @ $5.50)	$22,000
Plus: Purchases (7,000 units @ various prices)	49,500
Cost of goods available for sale (11,000 units)	71,500
Less: Ending inventory (determined below)	(29,250)
Cost of goods sold (6,500 units)	$42,250

Cost of Ending Inventory:

$$\text{Weighted-average unit cost} = \frac{\$71{,}500}{11{,}000 \text{ units}} = \$6.50$$

4,500 units × $6.50 = $29,250

Cost of goods sold also could be determined directly by multiplying the weighted-average unit cost of $6.50 by the number of units sold ($6.50 × 6,500 = **$42,250**).

In a perpetual inventory system, the average cost method is applied by computing a moving-average unit cost each time additional inventory is purchased.

PERPETUAL AVERAGE COST. The weighted-average unit cost in a perpetual inventory system becomes a moving-average unit cost. A new weighted-average unit cost is calculated each time additional units are *purchased.* The new average is determined after each purchase by (1) summing the cost of the previous inventory balance and the cost of the new purchase, and (2) dividing this new total cost (cost of goods available for sale) by the number of units on hand (the inventory units that are available for sale). This average is then used to cost any units sold before the next purchase is made. The moving-average concept is applied in Illustration 8–7D.

Illustration 8–7D

Average Cost—Perpetual Inventory System

	Date	Purchased	Sold	Balance
	Beginning inventory	4,000 @ $5.50 = $22,000		4,000 @ $5.50 = $22,000
	Jan. 10		2,000 @ $5.50 = $ 11,000	2,000 @ $5.50 = $11,000
	Jan. 17	1,000 @ $6.00 = $6,000		$11,000 + $6,000 = $17,000 2,000 + 1,000 = 3,000 units
Average cost per unit	→	[$17,000 / 3,000 units] = $5.667/unit		
	Mar. 22	3,000 @ $7.00 = $21,000		$17,000 + $21,000 = $38,000
Average cost per unit	→	[$38,000 / 6,000 units] = $6.333/unit		3,000 + 3,000 = 6,000 units
	Apr. 15		1,500 @ $6.333 = $ 9,500	4,500 @ $6.333 = $28,500
	Oct. 15	3,000 @ $7.50 = $22,500		$28,500 + $22,500 = $51,000
Average cost per unit	→	[$51,000 / 7,500 units] = $6.80/unit		4,500 + 3,000 = 7,500 units
	Nov. 20		3,000 @ $6.80 = $ 20,400	4,500 @ $6.80 = **$30,600**
		Total cost of goods sold	= **$40,900**	

On January 17 the new average of $5.667 (rounded) is calculated by dividing the $17,000 cost of goods available ($11,000 from beginning inventory + $6,000 purchased on January 17) by the 3,000 units available (2,000 units from beginning inventory + 1,000 units acquired on January 17). The average is updated to $6.333 (rounded) with the March 22 purchase. The 1,500 units sold on April 15 are then costed at the average cost of $6.333.

Periodic average cost and perpetual average cost generally produce different allocations to cost of goods sold and ending inventory.

First-In, First-Out (FIFO)

The first-in, first-out (FIFO) method assumes that units sold are the first units acquired. Beginning inventory is sold first, followed by purchases during the period in the chronological order of their acquisition. In our illustration, 6,500 units were sold during 2016. Applying FIFO, these would be the 4,000 units in beginning inventory, the 1,000 units purchased on January 17, and 1,500 of the 3,000 units from the March 22 purchase. By default, ending inventory consists of the most recently acquired units. In this case, the 4,500 units in ending inventory consist of the 3,000 units purchased on October 15, and 1,500 of the 3,000 units purchased on March 22. Graphically, the flow is as follows:

The *first-in, first-out (FIFO) method* assumes that items sold are those that were acquired first.

Ending inventory applying FIFO consists of the most recently acquired items.

FIFO flow

Units Available		
Beg. inv.	4,000	6,500 units sold
Jan. 17	1,000	
Mar. 22	1,500	
Mar. 22	1,500	4,500 units in ending inventory
Oct. 15	3,000	
Total	11,000	

PERIODIC FIFO. Recall that we determine physical quantities on hand in a periodic inventory system by taking a physical count. Costing the 4,500 units in ending inventory this way automatically gives us the cost of goods sold as well. Using the numbers from our illustration, we determine cost of goods sold to be $38,500 by subtracting the $33,000 ending inventory from $71,500 cost of goods available for sale as shown in Illustration 8–7E.

Illustration 8–7E

FIFO—Periodic Inventory System

Beginning inventory (4,000 units @ $5.50)	$22,000
Plus: Purchases (7,000 units @ various prices)	49,500
Cost of goods available for sale (11,000 units)	71,500
Less: Ending inventory (determined below)	(33,000)
Cost of goods sold (6,500 units)	$38,500

Cost of Ending Inventory:

Date of Purchase	Units	Unit Cost	Total Cost
Mar. 22	1,500	$7.00	$10,500
Oct. 15	3,000	7.50	22,500
Total	4,500		$33,000

Of course, the 6,500 units sold could be costed directly as follows:

Date of Purchase	Units	Unit Cost	Total Cost
Beg. inv.	4,000	$5.50	$22,000
Jan. 17	1,000	6.00	6,000
Mar. 22	1,500	7.00	10,500
Total	6,500		$38,500

PERPETUAL FIFO. The same ending inventory and cost of goods sold amounts are always produced in a perpetual inventory system as in a periodic inventory system when FIFO is used. This is because the same units and costs are first in and first out whether cost of goods sold is determined as each sale is made or at the end of the period as a residual amount. The application of FIFO in a perpetual system is shown in Illustration 8–7F.

Illustration 8–7F
FIFO—Perpetual Inventory System

Date	Purchased	Sold	Balance	
Beginning inventory	4,000 @ $5.50 = $22,000		4,000 @ $5.50	= $22,000
Jan. 10		2,000 @ $5.50 = $ 11,000	2,000 @ $5.50	= $11,000
Jan. 17	1,000 @ $6.00 = $ 6,000		2,000 @ $5.50 1,000 @ $6.00	$17,000
Mar. 22	3,000 @ $7.00 = $21,000		2,000 @ $5.50 1,000 @ $6.00 3,000 @ $7.00	$38,000
Apr. 15		1,500 @ $5.50 = $ 8,250	500 @ $5.50 1,000 @ $6.00 3,000 @ $7.00	$29,750
Oct. 15	3,000 @ $7.50 = $22,500		500 @ $5.50 1,000 @ $6.00 3,000 @ $7.00 3,000 @ $7.50	$52,250
Nov. 20		500 @ $5.50 + 1,000 @ $6.00 + 1,500 @ $7.00 = $ 19,250	1,500 @ $7.00 3,000 @ $7.50	**$33,000**
	Total cost of goods sold	= **$38,500**		

Last-In, First-Out (LIFO)

The *last-in, first-out (LIFO) method* assumes that items sold are those that were most recently acquired.

The **last-in, first-out (LIFO) method** assumes that the units sold are the most recent units purchased. In our illustration, the 6,500 units assumed sold would be the 6,500 units acquired most recently: the 3,000 units acquired on October 15, the 3,000 units acquired on March 22, and 500 of the 1,000 units purchased on January 17. Ending inventory, then, consists of the units acquired first; in this case, the 4,000 units from beginning inventory and 500 of the 1,000 units purchased on January 17. Graphically, the flow is as follows:

Ending inventory applying LIFO consists of the items acquired first.

LIFO flow

	Units Available	
Beg. inv.	4,000	4,500 units in ending inventory
Jan. 17	500	
Jan. 17	500	6,500 units sold
Mar. 22	3,000	
Oct. 15	3,000	
Total	11,000	

PERIODIC LIFO. The cost of ending inventory determined to be $25,000 (calculated below) by the LIFO assumption and using a periodic system is subtracted from cost of goods available for sale to arrive at the cost of goods sold of $46,500 as shown in Illustration 8–7G.

Illustration 8–7G
LIFO—Periodic Inventory System

Beginning inventory (4,000 units @ $5.50)			$22,000
Plus: Purchases (7,000 units @ various prices)			49,500
Cost of goods available for sale (11,000 units)			71,500
Less: Ending inventory (determined below)			(25,000)
Cost of goods sold (6,500 units)			$46,500
Cost of Ending Inventory:			
Date of Purchase	**Units**	**Unit Cost**	**Total Cost**
Beginning inventory	4,000	$5.50	$22,000
Jan. 17	500	6.00	3,000
Total	4,500		$25,000

The 6,500 sold could be costed directly as follows:

Date of Purchase	Units	Unit Cost	Total Cost
Jan. 17	500	$6.00	$ 3,000
Mar. 22	3,000	7.00	21,000
Oct. 15	3,000	7.50	22,500
Total	6,500		$46,500

PERPETUAL LIFO. The application of LIFO in a perpetual system is shown in Illustration 8–7H. Each time inventory is purchased or sold, the LIFO layers are adjusted. For example, after the March 22 purchase, we have three layers of inventory at different unit costs listed in the chronological order of their purchase. When 1,500 units are sold on April 15, we assume they come from the most recent layer of 3,000 units purchased at $7.00.

Illustration 8–7H
LIFO—Perpetual Inventory System

Date	Purchased	Sold	Balance	
Beginning inventory	4,000 @ $5.50 = $22,000		4,000 @ $5.50 = $22,000	
Jan. 10		2,000 @ $5.50 = $11,000	2,000 @ $5.50 = $11,000	
Jan. 17	1,000 @ $6.00 = $6,000		2,000 @ $5.50 1,000 @ $6.00	$17,000
Mar. 22	3,000 @ $7.00 = $21,000		2,000 @ $5.50 1,000 @ $6.00 3,000 @ $7.00	$38,000
Apr. 15		1,500 @ $7.00 = $10,500	2,000 @ $5.50 1,000 @ $6.00 1,500 @ $7.00	$27,500
Oct. 15	3,000 @ $7.50 = $22,500		2,000 @ $5.50 1,000 @ $6.00 1,500 @ $7.00 3,000 @ $7.50	$50,000
Nov. 20		3,000 @ $7.50 = $22,500	2,000 @ $5.50 1,000 @ $6.00 1,500 @ $7.00	$27,500
	Total cost of goods sold	= $44,000		

Notice that the total cost of goods available for sale is allocated $44,000 to cost of goods sold by perpetual LIFO and $27,500 to ending inventory (the balance after the last transaction), which is different from the periodic LIFO result of $46,500 and $25,000. Unlike

Perpetual LIFO generally results in cost of goods sold and inventory amounts that are different from those obtained by applying periodic LIFO.

FIFO, applying LIFO in a perpetual inventory system will generally result in an ending inventory and cost of goods sold different from the allocation arrived at when applying LIFO in a periodic system. Periodic LIFO applies the last-in, first-out concept to total sales and total purchases only at the conclusion of the reporting period. Perpetual LIFO applies the same concept, but several times during the period—every time a sale is made.

For example, when 2,000 units are sold on January 10, perpetual LIFO costs those units at $5.50, the beginning inventory unit cost, because those were the last units acquired before the sale. Periodic LIFO, by contrast, would be applied at year-end. By the end of the year, enough purchases have been made that the beginning inventory would be assumed to remain intact, and the January 10 units sold would be costed at a price from the most recent acquisition before the end of the year.

Comparison of Cost Flow Methods

Comparison of cost flow methods

The three cost flow methods are compared below assuming a periodic inventory system.

	Average	FIFO	LIFO
Cost of goods sold	$42,250	$38,500	$46,500
Ending inventory	29,250	33,000	25,000
Total	$71,500	$71,500	$71,500

Notice that the average cost method in this example produces amounts that fall in between the FIFO and LIFO amounts for both cost of goods sold and ending inventory. This will usually be the case. Whether it will be FIFO or LIFO that produces the highest or lowest value of cost of goods sold and ending inventory depends on the pattern of the actual unit cost changes during the period.

If unit costs are increasing, LIFO will result in a higher cost of goods sold and lower ending inventory than FIFO.

During periods of generally rising costs, as in our example, FIFO results in a lower cost of goods sold than LIFO because the lower costs of the earliest purchases are assumed sold. LIFO cost of goods sold will include the more recent higher cost purchases. On the other hand, FIFO ending inventory includes the most recent higher cost purchases which results in a higher ending inventory than LIFO. LIFO ending inventory includes the lower costs of the earliest purchases. Conversely, if costs are declining, then FIFO will result in a higher cost of goods sold and lower ending inventory than LIFO.[7]

FINANCIAL Reporting Case

Q1, p. 425

A company must disclose the inventory method(s) it uses.

Each of the three methods is permissible according to generally accepted accounting principles and frequently is used. Also, a company need not use the same method for its entire inventory. For example, **International Paper Company** uses LIFO for its raw materials and finished pulp and paper products, and both the FIFO and average cost methods for other inventories. Because of the importance of inventories and the possible differential effects of different methods on the financial statements, a company must identify in a disclosure note the method(s) it uses. The chapter's opening case included an example of this disclosure for **Phillips 66**, and you will encounter additional examples later in the chapter.

Illustration 8–8 shows the results of a survey of inventory methods used by 500 large public companies.[8] FIFO is the most popular method, but both LIFO and average cost are used

Illustration 8–8
Inventory Cost Flow Methods Used in Practice

	# of Companies	% of Companies
FIFO	312	47%
LIFO	163	24
Average	133	20
Other* and not disclosed	61	9
Total	669	100%

*"Other" includes the specific identification method and miscellaneous less popular methods.

[7]The differences between the various methods also hold when a perpetual inventory system is used.

[8]*U.S. GAAP Financial Statements—Best Practices in Presentation and Disclosure—2013* (New York, New York: AICPA, 2013).

by many companies. Notice that the column total for the number of companies is greater than 500, indicating that many companies included in this sample do use multiple methods.

International Financial Reporting Standards

Inventory Cost Flow Assumptions. *IAS No. 2*[9] does not permit the use of LIFO. Because of this restriction, many U.S. multinational companies use LIFO only for their domestic inventories and FIFO or average cost for their foreign subsidiaries. A disclosure note included in a recent annual report of General Mills provides an example:

● LO8–9

Real World Financials

Inventories (in part)

All inventories in the United States other than grain are valued at the lower of cost, using the last-in, first-out (LIFO) method, or market. . . . Inventories outside of the United States generally are valued at the lower of cost, using the first-in, first-out (FIFO) method, or market.

This difference could prove to be a significant impediment to U.S. convergence to international standards. Unless the U.S. Congress repeals the LIFO conformity rule (see page 442), convergence would cause many corporations to lose a valuable tax shelter, the use of LIFO for tax purposes. If these companies were immediately taxed on the difference between LIFO inventories and inventories valued using another method, it would cost companies billions of dollars. Some industries would be particularly hard hit. Most oil companies and auto manufacturers, for instance, use LIFO. The government estimates that the repeal of the LIFO method would increase federal tax revenues by $59 billion over a ten-year period.[10] The companies affected most certainly will lobby heavily to retain the use of LIFO for tax purposes.

Decision Makers' Perspective—Factors Influencing Method Choice

● LO8–5

What factors motivate companies to choose one method over another? What factors have caused the increased popularity of LIFO? Choosing among alternative accounting methods is a complex issue. Often such choices are not made in isolation but in such a way that the combination of inventory cost flow assumptions, depreciation methods, pension assumptions, and other choices meet a particular objective. Also, many believe managers sometimes make these choices to maximize their own personal benefits rather than those of the company or its external constituents. But regardless of the motive, the impact on reported numbers is an important consideration in each choice of method. The inventory choice determines (a) how closely reported costs reflect the actual physical flow of inventory, (b) the timing of reported income and income tax expense, and (c) how well costs are matched with associated revenues.

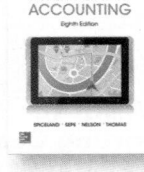

PHYSICAL FLOW. If a company wanted to choose a method that most closely approximates specific identification, then the actual physical flow of inventory in and out of the company would motivate the choice of method.

For example, companies often attempt to sell the oldest goods in inventory first for some of their products. This certainly is the case with perishable goods such as many grocery items. The FIFO method best mirrors the physical flow in these situations. The average cost method might be used for liquids such as chemicals where items sold are taken from a mixture of inventory acquired at different times and different prices. There are very few inventories that actually flow in a LIFO manner. It is important for you to understand that there is no requirement that companies choose an inventory method that approximates actual physical flow and few companies make the choice on this basis. In fact, as we discuss next, the

A company is not required to choose an inventory method that approximates actual physical flow.

[9] "Inventories," *International Accounting Standard No. 2* (IASCF), as amended effective January 1, 2014.

[10] Marie Leone, "Sucking the LIFO Out of Inventory," *CFO Magazine*, July 15, 2010.

effect of inventory method on income and income taxes is the primary motivation that influences method choice.

INCOME TAXES AND NET INCOME. If the unit cost of inventory changes during a period, the inventory method chosen can have a significant effect on the amount of income reported by the company to external parties and also on the amount of income taxes paid to the Internal Revenue Service (IRS) and state and local taxing authorities. Over the entire life of a company, cost of goods sold for all years will equal actual costs of items sold regardless of the inventory method used. However, as we have discussed, different inventory methods can produce significantly different results in each particular year.

Many companies choose LIFO in order to reduce income taxes in periods when prices are rising.

When prices rise and inventory quantities are not decreasing, LIFO produces a higher cost of goods sold and therefore lower net income than the other methods. The company's income tax returns will report a lower taxable income using LIFO and lower taxes will be paid currently. Taxes are not reduced permanently, only deferred. The reduced amount will be paid to the taxing authorities when either the unit cost of inventory or the quantity of inventory subsequently declines. However, we know from our discussion of the time value of money that it is advantageous to save a dollar today even if it must be paid back in the future. In the past, high inflation (increasing prices) periods motivated many companies to switch to LIFO in order to gain this tax benefit.

If a company uses LIFO to measure its taxable income, IRS regulations require that LIFO also be used to measure income reported to investors and creditors (the *LIFO conformity rule*).

A corporation's taxable income comprises revenues, expenses (including cost of goods sold), gains, and losses measured according to the regulations of the appropriate taxing authority. Income before tax as reported in the income statement does not always equal taxable income. In some cases, differences are caused by the use of different measurement methods.[11] However, IRS regulations, which determine federal taxable income, require that if a company uses LIFO to measure taxable income, the company also must use LIFO for external financial reporting. This is known as the **LIFO conformity rule** with respect to inventory methods.

Because of the LIFO conformity rule, to obtain the tax advantages of using LIFO in periods of rising prices, lower net income is reported to shareholders, creditors, and other external parties. The income tax motivation for using LIFO may be offset by a desire to report higher net income. Reported net income could have an effect on a corporation's share price,[12] on bonuses paid to management, or on debt agreements with lenders. For example, research has indicated that the managers of companies with bonus plans tied to income measures are more likely to choose accounting methods that maximize their bonuses (often those that increase net income).[13]

FINANCIAL Reporting Case

Q2, p. 425

The LIFO conformity rule permits LIFO users to report non-LIFO inventory valuations in a disclosure note, but not on the face of the income statement. For example, Illustration 8–9 shows the notes provided in a recent annual report of **Rite Aid Corporation**, a large drugstore chain, disclosing its use of LIFO to value its inventories and also its non-LIFO inventory valuations.

● LO8–6

LIFO RESERVES. Many companies use LIFO for external reporting and income tax purposes but maintain their internal records using FIFO or average cost. There is a variety of reasons, including: (1) the high recordkeeping costs for LIFO, (2) contractual agreements such as bonus or profit sharing plans that calculate net income with a method other than LIFO, and (3) using FIFO or average cost information for pricing decisions.

[11]For example, a corporation can take advantage of incentives offered by Congress by deducting more depreciation in the early years of an asset's life in its federal income tax return than it reports in its income statement.

[12]The concept of capital market efficiency has been debated for many years. In an efficient capital market, the market is not fooled by differences in accounting method choice that do not translate into real cash flow differences. The only apparent cash flow difference caused by different inventory methods is the amount of income taxes paid currently. In an efficient market, we would expect the share price of a company that switched its method to LIFO and saved tax dollars to increase even though it reported lower net income than if LIFO had not been adopted. Research on this issue is mixed. For example, see William E. Ricks, "Market's Response to the 1974 LIFO Adoptions," *Journal of Accounting Research* (Autumn 1982); and Robert Moren Brown, "Short-Range Market Reaction to Changes to LIFO Using Preliminary Earnings Announcement Dates," *Journal of Accounting Research* (Spring 1980).

[13]For example, see P. M. Healy, "The Effect of Bonus Schemes on Accounting Decisions," *Journal of Accounting and Economics* (April 1985); and D. Dhaliwal, G. Salamon, and E. Smith, "The Effect of Owner Versus Management Control on the Choice of Accounting Methods," *Journal of Accounting and Economics* (July 1982).

Illustration 8–9

Inventories Disclosures—Rite Aid Corporation

Real World Financials

Summary of Significant Accounting Policies (in part)

Inventories

Inventories are stated at the lower of cost or market. The Company uses the last-in, first-out ("LIFO") cost flow assumption for substantially all of its inventories.

7. Inventory (in part) ($ in thousands)

At March 1, 2014, and March 2, 2013, inventories were $1,018,581 and $915,241, respectively, lower than the amounts that would have been reported using the first-in, first-out ("FIFO") cost flow assumption.

Generally, the conversion to LIFO from the internal records occurs at the end of the reporting period without actually entering the adjustment into the company's records. Some companies, though, enter the conversion adjustment—the difference between the internal method and LIFO—directly into the records as a "contra account" to inventory. This contra account is called either the **LIFO reserve** or the **LIFO allowance**.

For illustration, let's say that the Doubletree Corporation began 2016 with a balance of $475,000 in its LIFO reserve account, the difference between inventory valued internally using FIFO and inventory valued using LIFO. At the end of 2016, assume this difference increased to $535,000. The entry to record the increase in the reserve is:

Cost of goods sold ($535,000 − 475,000)	60,000	
LIFO reserve		60,000

If the difference between inventory valued internally using FIFO and inventory valued using LIFO had decreased, this entry would be made in reverse. Companies such as Doubletree often use a disclosure note to show the difference between ending inventory valued using the internal method and the LIFO inventory amount reported in the balance sheet.

As an example, **Books-A-Million, Inc.**, is a leading book retailer primarily located in the eastern United States and operates both superstores and traditional bookstores. Illustration 8–10 is a disclosure note from a recent annual report that showed the company's inventories valued at FIFO, the internal method, less the LIFO reserve, to arrive at the LIFO amount reported in the company's balance sheet.

Illustration 8–10

Inventories Disclosure—Books-A-Million

Real World Financials

Inventories (in part)

($ in thousands)	2014	2013
Inventories (at FIFO)	$204,220	$205,853
Less: LIFO reserve	(4,636)	(4,326)
Net inventories	$199,584	$201,527

Proponents of LIFO argue that it results in a better match of revenues and expenses.

LIFO LIQUIDATIONS. Earlier in the text, we demonstrated the importance of matching revenues and expenses in creating an income statement that is useful in predicting future cash flows. If prices change during a period, then LIFO generally will provide a better match of revenues and expenses. Sales reflect the most recent selling prices, and cost of goods sold includes the costs of the most recent purchases.

For the same reason, though, inventory costs in the balance sheet with LIFO generally are out of date because they reflect old purchase transactions. It is not uncommon for a company's LIFO inventory balance to be based on unit costs actually incurred several years earlier.

This distortion sometimes carries over to the income statement as well. When inventory quantities decline during a period, then these out-of-date inventory layers are liquidated and cost of goods sold will partially match noncurrent costs with current selling prices. If costs have been increasing (decreasing), LIFO liquidations produce higher (lower) net income than would have resulted if the liquidated inventory were included in cost of goods sold at current costs. The paper profits (losses) caused by including out of date, low (high) costs in cost of goods sold is referred to as the effect on income of liquidations of LIFO inventory.

To illustrate this problem, consider the example in Illustration 8–11.

Illustration 8–11
LIFO Liquidation

National Distributors, Inc. uses the LIFO inventory method. The company began 2016 with inventory of 10,000 units that cost $20 per unit. During 2016, 30,000 units were purchased for $25 each and 35,000 units were sold.

National's LIFO cost of goods sold for 2016 consists of:

30,000 units @ $25 per unit =	$750,000
5,000 units @ $20 per unit =	$100,000
35,000	$850,000

Included in cost of goods sold are 5,000 units from beginning inventory that have now been liquidated. If the company had purchased at least 35,000 units, no liquidation would have occurred. Then cost of goods sold would have been $875,000 (35,000 units × $25 per unit) instead of $850,000. The difference between these two cost of goods sold figures is $25,000 ($875,000 − 850,000). This is the before-tax income effect of the LIFO liquidation. We also can determine the $25,000 before-tax LIFO liquidation profit by multiplying the 5,000 units liquidated by the difference between the $25 *current cost* per unit and the $20 *acquisition cost* per unit we included in cost of goods sold (5,000 units × [$25 − 20] = $25,000). Assuming a 40% income tax rate, the net effect of the liquidation is to increase net income by $15,000 [$25,000 × (1 − .40)]. The lower the costs of the units liquidated, the more severe the effect on income.

A company must disclose in a note any material effect of **LIFO liquidation** on net income. For example, Illustration 8–12 shows the disclosure note included with recent financial statements of **Genuine Parts Company**, a distributor of automotive replacement parts, industrial replacement parts, office products, and electrical parts.

Illustration 8–12
LIFO Liquidation Disclosure—Genuine Parts Company

Real World Financials

Summary of Significant Accounting Policies (in part)

Merchandise Inventories

During 2013, 2012, and 2011, reductions in inventory levels in automotive parts inventories (2013 and 2012), industrial parts inventories (2013, 2012, and 2011), and electrical parts inventories (2012 and 2011) resulted in liquidations of LIFO inventory layers. The effect of the LIFO liquidation in 2013, 2012, and 2013 was to reduce cost of goods sold by approximately $5,000,000, $6,000,000, and $16,000,000, respectively.

In our illustration, National Distributors, Inc. would disclose that LIFO liquidations increased income by $15,000 in 2016, assuming that this effect on income is considered material.

We've discussed several factors that influence companies in their choice of inventory method. A company could be influenced by the actual physical flow of its inventory, by the effect of inventory method on reported net income and the amount of income taxes payable currently, or by a desire to provide a better match of expenses with revenues. You've seen that the direction of the change in unit costs determines the effect of using different methods on net income and income taxes. While the United States has experienced persistent inflation for many years (increases in the general price-level), the prices of many goods and services have experienced periods of declining prices (for example, personal computers). ●

Concept Review Exercise

INVENTORY COST FLOW METHODS

The Rogers Company began 2016 with an inventory of 10 million units of its principal product. These units cost $5 each. The following inventory transactions occurred during the first six months of 2016.

Date	Transaction
Feb. 15	Purchased, on account, 5 million units at a cost of $6.50 each.
Mar. 20	Sold, on account, 8 million units at a selling price of $12 each.
Apr. 30	Purchased, on account, 5 million units at a cost of $7 each.

On June 30, 2016, 12 million units were on hand.

Required:

1. Prepare journal entries to record the above transactions. The company uses a periodic inventory system.
2. Prepare the required adjusting entry on June 30, 2016, applying each of the following inventory methods:
   a. Average
   b. FIFO
   c. LIFO
3. Repeat requirement 1 assuming that the company uses a perpetual inventory system.

Solution:

1. Prepare journal entries to record the above transactions. The company uses a periodic inventory system.

	($ in millions)	
February 15		
Purchases (5 million × $6.50)	32.5	
Accounts payable		32.5
To record the purchase of inventory.		
March 20		
Accounts receivable (8 million × $12)	96	
Sales revenue		96
To record sales on account.		
No entry is recorded for the cost of inventory sold.		
April 30		
Purchases (5 million × $7)	35	
Accounts payable		35
To record the purchase of inventory.		

2. Prepare the required adjusting entry on June 30, 2016, applying each method.

Date	Journal entry	Average		FIFO		LIFO	
		($ in millions)					
June 30	Cost of goods sold (determined below)	47.0		40.0		54.5	
	Inventory (ending—determined below)	70.5		77.5		63.0	
	Inventory (beginning—[10 million @ $5])		50.0		50.0		50.0
	Purchases ($32.5 million + 35 million)		67.5		67.5		67.5

Calculation of ending inventory and cost of goods sold:

a. Average:

	($ in millions)
Beginning inventory (10 million units @ $5.00)	$ 50.0
Plus: Purchases (10 million units @ various prices)	67.5
Cost of goods available for sale (20 million units)	117.5
Less: Ending inventory (determined below)	(70.5)
Cost of goods sold	$ 47.0

Cost of ending inventory:

$$\text{Weighted-average unit cost} = \frac{\$117.5}{20 \text{ million units}} = \$5.875$$

12 million units × \$5.875 = **\$70.5 million**

b. FIFO:

Cost of goods available for sale (20 million units)	\$117.5
Less: Ending inventory (determined below)	(77.5)
Cost of goods sold	\$ 40.0

Cost of ending inventory:

Date of Purchase	Units	Unit Cost	Total Cost
Beg. inv.	2 million	\$5.00	10.0
Feb. 15	5 million	6.50	32.5
April 30	5 million	7.00	35.0
Total	12 million		\$77.5

c. LIFO:

Cost of goods available for sale (20 million units)	\$117.5
Less: Ending inventory (determined below)	(63.0)
Cost of goods sold	\$ 54.5

Cost of ending inventory:

Date of Purchase	Units	Unit Cost	Total Cost
Beg. inv.	10 million	\$5.00	\$50.0
Feb. 15	2 million	6.50	13.0
Total	12 million		\$63.0

3. Repeat requirement 1 assuming that the company uses a perpetual inventory system.

	(\$ in millions)	
February 15		
Inventory (5 million × \$6.50)	32.5	
Accounts payable		32.5
To record the purchase of inventory.		
April 30		
Inventory (5 million × \$7.00)	35.0	
Accounts payable		35.0
To record the purchase of inventory.		

	(\$ in millions)					
Journal Entries—March 20	**Average**		**FIFO**		**LIFO**	
Accounts receivable (8 million × \$12)	96.0		96.0		96.0	
Sales revenue		96.0		96.0		96.0
To record sales on account.						
Cost of goods sold (determined below)	44.0		40.0		47.5	
Inventory		44.0		40.0		47.5
To record cost of goods sold.						

Calculation of cost of goods sold:

a. Average:

Cost of goods sold:

	($, except unit costs, in millions)		
Date	**Purchased**	**Sold**	**Balance**
Beg. inv.	10 million @ \$5.00 = \$50.0		10 million @ \$5.00 = \$50.0
Feb. 15	5 million @ \$6.50 = \$32.5		\$50 + \$32.5 = \$82.5
	$\frac{\$82.5}{15 \text{ million units}} = \$5.50/\text{unit}$		
Mar. 20		8 million @ \$5.50 = \$44.0	

b. FIFO:

Cost of goods sold:

Units Sold	Cost of Units Sold	Total Cost
8 million (from Beg. inv.)	\$5.00	\$40.0

c. LIFO:

Cost of goods sold:

Units Sold	Cost of Units Sold	Total Cost
5 million (from Feb. 15 purchase)	\$6.50	\$32.5
3 million (from Beg. inv.)	5.00	15.0
8 million		\$47.5

Decision Makers' Perspective

INVENTORY MANAGEMENT. Managers closely monitor inventory levels to (1) ensure that the inventories needed to sustain operations are available, and (2) hold the cost of ordering and carrying inventories to the lowest possible level.[14] Unfortunately, these objectives often conflict with one another. Companies must maintain sufficient quantities of inventory to meet customer demand. However, maintaining inventory is costly. Fortunately, a variety of tools are available, including computerized inventory control systems and the outsourcing of inventory component production, to help balance these conflicting objectives.[15]

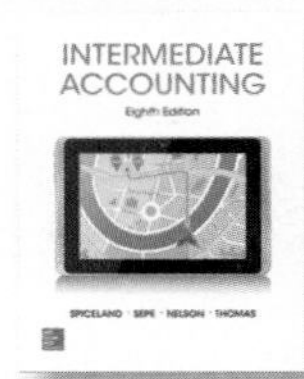

A company should maintain sufficient inventory quantities to meet customer demand while at the same time minimizing inventory ordering and carrying costs.

A **just-in-time (JIT) system** is another valuable technique that many companies have adopted to assist them with inventory management. JIT is a system used by a manufacturer to coordinate production with suppliers so that raw materials or components arrive just as they are needed in the production process. Have you ever ordered a personal computer from **Dell Inc.**? If so, the PC you received was not manufactured until you placed your order, and many of the components used in the production of your PC were not even acquired by Dell until then as well. This system enables Dell to maintain relatively low inventory balances. At the same time, the company's efficient production techniques, along with its excellent relationships with suppliers ensuring prompt delivery of components, enables Dell to quickly meet customer demand. For the quarter ended August 2, 2013, Dell reported an inventory balance of \$1.4 billion. With this relatively low investment in inventory, Dell was able to generate \$11 billion in revenue

[14]The cost of carrying inventory includes the possible loss from the write-down of obsolete inventory. We discuss inventory write-downs in Chapter 9. There are analytical models available to determine the appropriate amount of inventory a company should maintain. A discussion of these models is beyond the scope of this text.

[15]Eugene Brigham and Joel Houston, *Fundamentals of Financial Management,* 12th ed. (Florence, Kentucky: South-Western, 2010).

Real World Financials

from the sale of products. To appreciate the advantage this provides, compare these numbers with **Hewlett Packard (HP)**, a company that includes PCs among its wide variety of technology products. For its quarter ended July 31, 2013, HP reported product revenue of $17 billion. However, to achieve this level of sales, HP's investment in inventory was over $6 billion.

It is important for a financial analyst to evaluate a company's effectiveness in managing its inventory. As we discussed in Chapter 5, one key to profitability is how well a company utilizes its assets. This evaluation is influenced by the company's inventory method choice. The choice of inventory method is an important and complex management decision. The many factors affecting this decision were discussed in a previous section. The inventory method also affects the analysis of a company's liquidity and profitability by investors, creditors, and financial analysts. Analysts must make adjustments when evaluating companies that use different inventory methods. During periods of rising prices, we would expect a company using FIFO to report higher income than a LIFO or average cost company. If one of the companies being analyzed uses LIFO, precise adjustments can often be made using the supplemental disclosures provided by many LIFO companies. Recall that the LIFO conformity rule allows LIFO users to report in a note the effect of using a method other than LIFO for inventory valuation.

FINANCIAL Reporting Case

Q3, p. 425

For example, the disclosure note shown in Illustration 8–9 on page 443 reveals that the **Rite Aid Corporation** uses the LIFO method. Additional information from the company's recent financial statements is provided below.

Real World Financials

	For the Year Ended	
($ in thousands)	March 1, 2014	March 2, 2013
Balance sheets:		
Inventories	$ 2,993,948	$ 3,154,742
Income statements:		
Net sales	$25,526,413	25,392,263
Cost of goods sold	18,202,679	18,073,987

Supplemental LIFO disclosures can be used to convert LIFO inventories and cost of goods sold amounts.

Suppose an analyst wanted to compare Rite Aid with a competitor that used all FIFO, or that used both LIFO and FIFO but with different percentages of LIFO and FIFO. To compare apples with apples, we can convert Rite Aid's inventories and cost of goods sold (and the competitor's if necessary) to a 100% FIFO basis before comparing the two companies by using the information provided in Illustration 8–9. Inventories recorded at LIFO were lower by $1,018,581 thousand at March 1, 2014, and $915,241 thousand at March 2, 2013, than if they had been valued at FIFO:

	2014	2013
Inventories (as reported)	$2,993,948	$3,154,742
Add: conversion to FIFO	1,018,581	915,241
Inventories (100% FIFO)	$4,012,529	$4,069,983

If Rite Aid had used FIFO instead of LIFO, 2014 beginning inventory would have been $915,241 thousand higher, and ending inventory would have been higher by $1,018,581 thousand. As a result, cost of goods sold for the 2014 fiscal year would have been $103,340 ($1,018,581 − 915,241) thousand lower. This is because an increase in beginning inventory causes an *increase* in cost of goods sold, but an increase in ending inventory causes a *decrease* in cost of goods sold. Purchases for 2014 are the same regardless of the inventory valuation method used. Cost of goods sold, then, would have been $18,099,339 thousand (18,202,679 − 103,340) if FIFO had been used for all inventories.

We can now use the 100% FIFO amounts to compare the two companies. Because cost of goods sold would be lower by $103,340 thousand, income taxes and net income require similar adjustments before calculating a profitability ratio. Also, the converted inventory amounts can be used to compute liquidity ratios.

● LO8–7

One useful profitability indicator that involves cost of goods sold is **gross profit** sometimes called **gross margin**, which highlights the important relationship between net sales revenue and cost of goods sold. The **gross profit ratio** is computed as follows:

$$\text{Gross profit ratio} = \frac{\text{Gross profit}}{\text{Net sales}}$$

The higher the ratio, the higher the markup a company is able to achieve on its products. For example, a product that costs $100 and sells for $150 provides a gross profit of $50 ($150 − 100) and the gross profit ratio is 33% ($50 ÷ $150). If that same product can be sold for $200, the gross profit increases to $100 and the gross profit ratio increases to 50% ($100 ÷ $200), so more dollars are available to cover expenses other than cost of goods sold.

The ***gross profit ratio*** indicates the percentage of each sales dollar available to cover expenses other than cost of goods sold and to provide a profit.

The 2014 gross profit ($ in thousands), for Rite Aid, using the 100% FIFO amounts, is $7,427,074 ($25,526,413 − 18,099,339), and the gross profit ratio is 29.1% ($7,427,074 ÷ $25,526,413). The same ratio for the drugstore industry is 17%, indicating that Rite Aid is able to sell its products at significantly higher markups than the average for its competitors. Rite Aid's percentage of each sales dollar available to cover remaining expenses and to provide a profit is over 12% higher than the industry average.

Monitoring this ratio over time can provide valuable insights. For example, a declining ratio might indicate that the company is unable to offset rising costs with corresponding increases in selling price, or perhaps that sales prices are declining without a commensurate reduction in costs. In either case, the decline in the ratio has important implications for future profitability.

In Chapter 5 we were introduced to an important ratio, the **inventory turnover ratio**, which is designed to evaluate a company's effectiveness in managing its investment in inventory. The ratio shows the number of times the average inventory balance is sold during a reporting period. The more frequently a business is able to sell or turn over its inventory, the lower its investment in inventory must be for a given level of sales. Usually, the higher the ratio the more profitable a company will be. Monitoring the inventory turnover ratio over time can highlight potential problems. A declining ratio generally is unfavorable and could be caused by the presence of obsolete or slow-moving products, or poor marketing and sales efforts.

Recall that the ratio is computed as follows:

$$\text{Inventory turnover ratio} = \frac{\text{Cost of goods sold}}{\text{Average inventory}}$$

If the analysis is prepared for the fiscal year reporting period, we can divide the inventory turnover ratio into 365 days to calculate the **average days in inventory**, which indicates the average number of days it normally takes the company to sell its inventory.

For Rite Aid, the inventory turnover ratio for the 2014 fiscal year, using the 100% FIFO amounts, is 4.48 ($18,099,339 ÷ [($4,012,529 + 4,069,983) ÷ 2]) and the average days in inventory is 81 days (365 ÷ 4.48). This compares to an industry average of 33 days. Rite Aid's products command a higher markup (higher gross profit ratio) but the inventory turns over much slower (higher average days in inventory) than the industry average.

Inventory increases that outrun increases in cost of goods sold might indicate difficulties in generating sales. These inventory buildups may also indicate that a company has obsolete or slow-moving inventory. This proposition was tested in an important academic research study. Professors Lev and Thiagarajan empirically demonstrated the importance of a set of 12 fundamental variables in valuing companies' common stock. The set of variables included inventory (change in inventory minus change in sales). The inventory variable was found to be a significant indicator of returns on investments in common stock, particularly during high and medium inflation years.[16]

EARNINGS QUALITY. Changes in the ratios we discussed above often provide information about the quality of a company's current period earnings. For example, a slowing turnover ratio combined with higher than normal inventory levels may indicate the potential for decreased production, obsolete inventory, or a need to decrease prices to sell inventory (which will then decrease gross profit ratios and net income).

[16]B. Lev and S. R. Thiagarajan, "Fundamental Information Analysis," *Journal of Accounting Research* (Autumn 1993). The main conclusion of the study was that fundamental variables, not just earnings, are useful in firm valuation, particularly when examined in the context of macroeconomic conditions such as inflation.

The choice of which inventory method to use also affects earnings quality, particularly in times of rapidly changing prices. Earlier in this chapter we discussed the effect of a LIFO liquidation on company profits. A LIFO liquidation profit (or loss) reduces the quality of current period earnings. Fortunately for analysts, companies must disclose these profits or losses, if material. In addition, LIFO cost of goods sold determined using a periodic inventory system is more susceptible to manipulation than is FIFO. Year-end purchases can have a dramatic effect on LIFO cost of goods sold in rapid cost-change environments. Recall again our discussion in Chapter 4 concerning earnings quality. Many believe that manipulating income reduces earnings quality because it can mask permanent earnings. Inventory write-downs and changes in inventory method are two additional inventory-related techniques a company could use to manipulate earnings. We discuss these issues in the next chapter. ●

PART B Methods of Simplifying LIFO

The LIFO method described and illustrated to this point is called *unit LIFO*[17] because the last-in, first-out concept is applied to individual units of inventory. One problem with unit LIFO is that it can be very costly to implement. It requires records of each unit of inventory. The costs of maintaining these records can be significant, particularly when a company has numerous individual units of inventory and when unit costs change often during a period.

The recordkeeping costs of unit LIFO can be significant.

In the previous section, a second disadvantage of unit LIFO was identified—the possibility that LIFO layers will be liquidated if the quantity of a particular inventory unit declines below its beginning balance. Even if a company's total inventory quantity is stable or increasing, if the quantity of any particular inventory unit declines, unit LIFO will liquidate all or a portion of a LIFO layer of inventory. When inventory quantity declines in a period of rising costs, noncurrent lower costs will be included in cost of goods sold and matched with current selling prices, resulting in LIFO liquidation profit.

Another disadvantage of unit LIFO is the possibility of LIFO liquidation.

This part of the chapter discusses techniques that can be used to significantly reduce the recordkeeping costs of LIFO and to minimize the probability of LIFO inventory layers being liquidated. Specifically, we discuss the use of inventory pools and the dollar-value LIFO method.

LIFO Inventory Pools

The objectives of using **LIFO inventory pools** are to simplify recordkeeping by grouping inventory units into pools based on physical similarities of the individual units and to reduce the risk of LIFO layer liquidation. For example, a glass company might group its various grades of window glass into a single window pool. Other pools might be auto glass and sliding door glass. A lumber company might pool its inventory into hardwood, framing lumber, paneling, and so on.

A pool consists of inventory units grouped according to natural physical similarities.

This allows a company to account for a few inventory pools rather than every specific type of inventory separately. Within pools, all purchases during a period are considered to have been made at the same time and at the same cost. Individual unit costs are converted to an average cost for the pool. If the quantity of ending inventory for the pool increases, then ending inventory will consist of the beginning inventory plus a single layer added during the period at the average acquisition cost for that pool.

The average cost for all of the pool purchases during the period is applied to the current year's LIFO layer.

Here's an example. Let's say Diamond Lumber Company has a rough-cut lumber inventory pool that includes three types: oak, pine, and maple. The beginning inventory consisted of the following:

[17]Unit LIFO sometimes is called *specific goods LIFO*.

	Quantity (Board Feet)	Cost (Per Foot)	Total Cost
Oak	16,000	$2.20	$35,200
Pine	10,000	3.00	30,000
Maple	14,000	2.40	33,600
	40,000		$98,800

The average cost for this pool is $2.47 per board foot ($98,800 ÷ 40,000 board feet). Now assume that during the next reporting period Diamond purchased 50,000 board feet of lumber as follows:

	Quantity (Board Feet)	Cost (Per Foot)	Total Cost
Oak	20,000	$2.25	$ 45,000
Pine	14,000	3.00	42,000
Maple	16,000	2.50	40,000
	50,000		$127,000

The average cost for this pool is $2.54 per board foot ($127,000 ÷ 50,000 board feet). Assuming that Diamond sold 46,000 board feet during this period, the quantity of inventory for the pool increased by 4,000 board feet (50,000 purchased less 46,000 sold). The ending inventory will include the beginning inventory and a LIFO layer consisting of the 4,000 board feet increase. We would add this LIFO layer at the average cost of purchases made during the period, $2.54. The ending inventory of $108,960 now consists of two layers:

	Quantity (Board Feet)	Cost (Per Foot)	Total Cost
Beginning inventory	40,000	$2.47	$ 98,800
LIFO layer added	4,000	2.54	10,160
Ending inventory	44,000		$108,960

Despite the advantages of LIFO inventory pools, it's easy to imagine situations in which its benefits are not achieved. Suppose, for instance, that a company discontinues a certain product included in one of its pools. The old costs that existed in prior layers of inventory would be recognized as cost of goods sold and produce LIFO liquidation profit. Even if the product is replaced with another product, the replacement may not be similar enough to be included in the same inventory pool. In fact, the process itself of having to periodically redefine pools as changes in product mix occur can be expensive and time consuming. Next we discuss the dollar-value LIFO approach which helps overcome these problems.

Dollar-Value LIFO

Dollar-value LIFO (DVL) gained such widespread popularity during the 1960s and 1970s that many LIFO applications are now based on this approach. DVL extends the concept of inventory pools by allowing a company to combine a large variety of goods into one pool. Physical units are not used in calculating ending inventory. Instead, the inventory is viewed as a quantity of value instead of a physical quantity of goods. Instead of layers of units from different purchases, the DVL inventory pool is viewed as comprising layers of dollar value from different years. LO8–8

Because the physical characteristics of inventory items are not relevant to DVL, an inventory pool is identified in terms of economic similarity rather than physical similarity. Specifically, a pool should consist of those goods that are likely to be subject to the same cost change pressures.

A DVL pool is made up of items that are likely to face the same cost change pressures.

Advantages of DVL

The DVL method has important advantages. First, it simplifies the recordkeeping procedures compared to unit LIFO because no information is needed about unit flows. Second, it minimizes the probability of the liquidation of LIFO inventory layers, even more so than the use of pools alone, through the aggregation of many types of inventory into larger pools. In addition, the method can be used by firms that do not replace units sold with new units of the same kind. For firms whose products are subject to annual model changes, for example, the items in one year's inventory are not the same as those of the prior year. Under pooled LIFO, however, the new replacement items must be substantially identical to previous models to be included in the same pool. Under DVL, no distinction is drawn between the old and new merchandise on the basis of their physical characteristics, so a much broader range of goods can be included in the pool. That is, the acquisition of the new items is viewed as replacement of the dollar value of the old items. Because the old layers are maintained, this approach retains the benefits of LIFO by matching the most recent acquisition cost of goods with sales measured at current selling prices.

Cost Indexes

In either the unit LIFO approach or the pooled LIFO approach, we determine whether a new LIFO layer was added by comparing the ending quantity with the beginning quantity. The focus is on *units* of inventory. Under DVL, we determine whether a new LIFO layer was added by comparing the ending dollar amount with the beginning dollar amount. The focus is on inventory *value,* not units. However, if the price level has changed, we need a way to determine whether an observed increase is a real increase (an increase in the quantity of inventory) or one caused by an increase in prices. So before we compare the beginning and ending inventory amounts, we need to deflate inventory amounts by any increase in prices so that both the beginning and ending amounts are measured in terms of the same price level. We accomplish this by using cost indexes. A cost index for a particular layer year is determined as follows:

$$\text{Cost index in layer year} = \frac{\text{Cost in layer year}}{\text{Cost in base year}}$$

The cost index for the base year (the year DVL is initially adopted) is set at 1.00.

The base year is the year in which the DVL method is adopted and the layer year is any subsequent year in which an inventory layer is created. The cost index for the base year is set at 1.00. Subsequent years' indexes reflect cost changes relative to the base year. For example, if a "basket" of inventory items cost \$120 at the end of the current year, and \$100 at the end of the base year, the cost index for the current year would be: \$120 ÷ \$100 = 120%, or 1.20. This index simply tells us that costs in the layer year are 120% of what they were in the base year (i.e., costs increased by 20%).

There are several techniques that can be used to determine an index for a DVL pool. An external index like the Consumer Price Index (CPI) or the Producer Price Index (PPI) can be used. For example, assume that a company adopted the DVL method on January 1, 2016, when the CPI was 200. This amount is set equivalent to 1.00, the base year index. Then, the index in the layer year, say the end of 2016, would be determined relative to 200. So, if the CPI is 210 at the end of 2016, the 2016 index for DVL purposes would be 1.05 (210 ÷ 200).

However, in most cases these indexes would not properly reflect cost changes for any individual DVL pool. Instead, most companies use an internally generated index. These indexes can be calculated using one of several techniques such as the *double-extension method* or the *link-chain method.* A discussion of these methods is beyond the scope of this text. In our examples and illustrations, we assume cost indexes are given.

The DVL Inventory Estimation Technique

The starting point in DVL is determining the current year's ending inventory valued at year-end costs.

DVL estimation begins with the determination of the current year's ending inventory valued in terms of year-end costs. It's not necessary for a company using DVL to track the item-by-item cost of purchases during the year. All that's needed is to take the physical quantities of goods on hand at the end of the year and apply year-end costs. Let's say the Hanes Company adopted the dollar-value LIFO method on January 1, 2016, when the inventory value was $400,000. The 2016 ending inventory valued at year-end costs is $441,000, and the cost index for the year is 1.05 (105%).

What is the 2016 ending inventory valued at DVL cost? The first step is to convert the ending inventory from year-end costs to base year costs so we can see if there was a real increase in inventory rather than an illusory one caused by price increases. We divide the ending inventory by the year's cost index to get an amount that can be compared directly with beginning inventory.

STEP 1: Convert ending inventory valued at year-end cost to base year cost.

$$\text{Ending inventory at } \textit{base year} \text{ cost} = \frac{\$441{,}000}{1.05} = \$420{,}000$$

The $420,000 reflects the 2016 ending inventory deflated to base year cost.

Next we compare the $420,000 ending inventory at base year cost to the beginning inventory, also at base year cost, of $400,000. The $20,000 increase in base-year dollars signifies a real increase in inventory quantity during the year. Applying the LIFO concept, ending inventory at base year cost consists of the beginning inventory layer of $400,000 plus a $20,000 2016 layer. These are the hypothetical costs of the layers as if each was acquired at base year prices.

STEP 2: Identify the layers of ending inventory and the years they were created.

Once the layers are identified, each is restated to prices existing when the layers were acquired. Each layer is multiplied by the cost index for the year it was acquired. The costs are totaled to obtain ending inventory at DVL cost.[18]

Date	Ending Inventory at Base Year Cost	×	Cost Index	=	Ending Inventory at DVL Cost
1/1/16	$400,000		1.00		$400,000
2016 layer	20,000		1.05		21,000
Totals	$420,000				$421,000

STEP 3: Convert each layer's base year cost to layer year cost using the cost index for the year it was acquired.

If we determined that inventory quantity had decreased during the year, then there would have been no 2016 layer added. The most recently added layer, in this case the beginning inventory layer, would be decreased to the inventory valuation determined in step 1. Once a layer of inventory or a portion of a layer is used (that is, sold) it cannot be replaced. In our example, if the base year layer is reduced to $380,000, it will never be increased. Future increases in inventory quantity will result in new layers being added. This situation is illustrated in the concept review exercise that follows.

Concept Review Exercise

DOLLAR-VALUE LIFO

On January 1, 2016, the Johnson Company adopted the dollar-value LIFO method. The inventory value on this date was $500,000. Inventory data for 2016 through 2019 are as follows:

Date	Ending Inventory at Year-End Costs	Cost Index
12/31/16	$556,500	1.05
12/31/17	596,200	1.10
12/31/18	615,250	1.15
12/31/19	720,000	1.25

Required:

Calculate Johnson's ending inventory for the years 2016 through 2019.

[18]It is important to note that the costs of the year's layer are only an approximation of actual acquisition cost. DVL assumes that all inventory quantities added during a particular year were acquired at a single cost.

Solution:

JOHNSON COMPANY

Date	Ending Inventory at Year-End Cost	Step 1 Ending Inventory at Base Year Cost	Step 2 Inventory Layers at Base Year Cost	Step 3 Inventory Layers Converted to Acquisition Year Cost	Ending Inventory at DVL Cost
1/1/16	$500,000 (base year)	$\frac{\$500,000}{1.00} = \$500,000$	$500,000 (base)	$500,000 × 1.00 = $500,000	$500,000
12/31/16	556,500	$\frac{\$556,500}{1.05} = \$530,000$	$500,000 (base) 30,000 (2016)	$500,000 × 1.00 = $500,000 30,000 × 1.05 = 31,500	531,500
12/31/17	596,200	$\frac{\$596,200}{1.10} = \$542,000$	$500,000 (base) 30,000 (2016) 12,000 (2017)	$500,000 × 1.00 = $500,000 30,000 × 1.05 = 31,500 12,000 × 1.10 = 13,200	544,700
12/31/18	615,250	$\frac{\$615,250}{1.15} = \$535,000$*	$500,000 (base) 30,000 (2016) 5,000 (2017)	$500,000 × 1.00 = $500,000 30,000 × 1.05 = 31,500 5,000 × 1.10 = 5,500	537,000
12/31/19	720,000	$\frac{\$720,000}{1.25} = \$576,000$	$500,000 (base) 30,000 (2016) 5,000 (2017) 41,000 (2019)	$500,000 × 1.00 = $500,000 30,000 × 1.05 = 31,500 5,000 × 1.10 = 5,500 41,000 × 1.25 = 51,250	588,250

*Since inventory declined during 2018 (from $542,000 to $535,000 at base year costs), no new layer is added. Instead the most recently acquired layer, 2017, is reduced to arrive at the $535,000 ending inventory at base year cost.

Financial Reporting Case Solution

1. **What inventory methods does Phillips 66 use to value its inventories? Is this permissible according to GAAP?** *(p. 440)* Phillips 66 uses the LIFO inventory method to value its crude oil and petroleum products inventories and the weighted-average cost method for materials and supplies inventories. Yes, each of these methods is permissible according to generally accepted accounting principles. A company need not use the same method for all of its inventories.
2. **What is the purpose of disclosing the difference between the reported LIFO inventory amounts and replacement cost, assuming that replacement cost is equivalent to a FIFO basis?** *(p. 442)* The LIFO conformity rule requires that if a company uses LIFO to measure taxable income, it also must use LIFO for external financial reporting. Phillips 66 does this. However, the LIFO conformity rule allows LIFO users to report non-LIFO inventory valuations in a disclosure note, but not on the face of the income statement. The company's disclosure note offers this additional information.
3. **Is your friend correct in his assertion that, by using LIFO, Phillips 66 was able to report lower profits for the year ended December 31, 2013?** *(p. 448)* No. If Phillips 66 had used FIFO instead of LIFO for its LIFO inventories, income before taxes for all prior years, including 2013, would have been higher by $7,600 million (the increase in December 31, 2013, ending inventory). For the year ended December 31, 2013, alone, income before taxes would have been *lower* by $100 million. Here's why. The increase in ending inventory of $7,600 million *decreases* cost of goods sold, but the increase in beginning inventory of $7,700 million *increases* cost of goods sold, resulting in a net increase in cost of goods sold of $100 million. ●

The Bottom Line

- **LO8–1** In a perpetual inventory system, inventory is continually adjusted for each change in inventory. Cost of goods sold is adjusted each time goods are sold or returned by a customer. A periodic inventory system adjusts inventory and records cost of goods sold only at the end of a reporting period. *(p. 427)*
- **LO8–2** Generally, determining the physical quantity that should be included in inventory is a simple matter, because it consists of items in the possession of the company. However, at the end of a reporting period it's important to determine the ownership of goods that are in transit between the company and its customers as well as between the company and its suppliers. Also, goods on consignment should be included in inventory of the consignor even though the company doesn't have physical possession of the goods. In addition, a company anticipating sales returns includes in inventory the cost of merchandise it estimates will be returned. *(p. 430)*
- **LO8–3** The cost of inventory includes all expenditures necessary to acquire the inventory and bring it to its desired condition and location for sale or use. Generally, these expenditures include the purchase price of the goods reduced by any returns and purchase discounts, plus freight-in charges. *(p. 431)*
- **LO8–4** Once costs are determined, the cost of goods available for sale must be allocated between cost of goods sold and ending inventory. Unless each item is specifically identified and traced through the system, the allocation requires an assumption regarding the flow of costs. First-in, first-out (FIFO) assumes that units sold are the first units acquired. Last-in, first-out (LIFO) assumes that the units sold are the most recent units purchased. The average cost method assumes that cost of goods sold and ending inventory consist of a mixture of all the goods available for sale. *(p. 434)*
- **LO8–5** A company's choice of inventory method will be influenced by (a) how closely cost flow reflects the actual physical flow of its inventory, (b) the timing of income tax expenses, and (c) how costs are matched with revenues. *(p. 441)*
- **LO8–6** The LIFO conformity rule requires that if a company uses LIFO to measure taxable income, it also must use LIFO for external financial reporting. LIFO users often provide a disclosure note describing the effect on inventories of using another method for inventory valuation rather than LIFO. If a company uses LIFO and inventory quantities decline during a period, then out-of-date inventory layers are liquidated and the cost of goods sold will partially match noncurrent costs with current selling prices. If costs have been increasing (decreasing), LIFO liquidations produce higher (lower) net income than would have resulted if the liquidated inventory were included in cost of goods sold at current costs. The paper profits (losses) caused by including out-of-date, low (high) costs in cost of goods sold is referred to as the effect on income of liquidations of LIFO inventory. *(p. 442)*
- **LO8–7** Investors, creditors, and financial analysts can gain important insights by monitoring a company's investment in inventories. The gross profit ratio, inventory turnover ratio, and average days in inventory are designed to monitor inventories. *(p. 448)*
- **LO8–8** The dollar-value LIFO method converts ending inventory at year-end cost to base year cost using a cost index. After identifying the layers in ending inventory with the years they were created, each year's base year cost measurement is converted to layer year cost measurement using the layer year's cost index. The layers are then summed to obtain total ending inventory at cost. *(p. 451)*
- **LO8–9** The primary difference between U.S. GAAP and IFRS with respect to determining the cost of inventory is that IFRS does not allow the use of the LIFO method to value inventory. *(p. 441)*

Questions For Review of Key Topics

Q 8–1 Describe the three types of inventory of a manufacturing company.

Q 8–2 What is the main difference between a perpetual inventory system and a periodic inventory system?

Q 8–3 The Cloud Company employs a perpetual inventory system and the McKenzie Corporation uses a periodic system. Describe the differences between the two systems in accounting for the following events: (1) purchase of merchandise, (2) sale of merchandise, (3) return of merchandise to supplier, and (4) payment of freight charge on merchandise purchased. Indicate which inventory-related accounts would be debited or credited for each event.

Q 8–4 The Bockner Company shipped merchandise to Laetner Corporation on December 28, 2016. Laetner received the shipment on January 3, 2017. December 31 is the fiscal year-end for both companies. The merchandise was shipped f.o.b. shipping point. Explain the difference in the accounting treatment of the merchandise if the shipment had instead been designated f.o.b. destination.

Q 8–5 What is a consignment arrangement? Explain the accounting treatment of goods held on consignment.

Q 8–6 Distinguish between the gross and net methods of accounting for purchase discounts.

Q 8–7 The Esquire Company employs a periodic inventory system. Indicate the effect (increase or decrease) of the following items on cost of goods sold:

1. Beginning inventory
2. Purchases
3. Ending inventory
4. Purchase returns
5. Freight-in

Q 8–8 Identify four methods of assigning cost to ending inventory and cost of goods sold and briefly explain the difference in the methods.

Q 8–9 It's common in the electronics industry for unit costs of raw materials inventories to decline over time. In this environment, explain the difference between LIFO and FIFO, in terms of the effect on income and financial position. Assume that inventory quantities remain the same for the period.

Q 8–10 Explain why proponents of LIFO argue that it provides a better match of revenue and expenses. In what situation would it not provide a better match?

Q 8–11 Explain what is meant by the Internal Revenue Service conformity rule with respect to the inventory method choice.

Q 8–12 Describe the ratios used by financial analysts to monitor a company's investment in inventories.

Q 8–13 What is a LIFO inventory pool? How is the cost of ending inventory determined when pools are used?

Q 8–14 Identify two advantages of dollar-value LIFO compared with unit LIFO.

Q 8–15 The Austin Company uses the dollar-value LIFO inventory method with internally developed price indexes. Assume that ending inventory at year-end cost has been determined. Outline the remaining steps used in the dollar-value LIFO computations.

IFRS Q 8–16 Identify any differences between U.S. GAAP and International Financial Reporting Standards in the methods allowed to value inventory.

Brief Exercises

BE 8–1
Determining ending inventory; periodic system
● LO8–1

A company began its fiscal year with inventory of $186,000. Purchases and cost of goods sold for the year were $945,000 and $982,000, respectively. What was the amount of ending inventory?

BE 8–2
Perpetual system; journal entries
● LO8–1

Litton Industries uses a perpetual inventory system. The company began its fiscal year with inventory of $267,000. Purchases of merchandise on account during the year totaled $845,000. Merchandise costing $902,000 was sold on account for $1,420,000. Prepare the journal entries to record these transactions.

BE 8–3
Goods in transit
● LO8–2

Kelly Corporation shipped goods to a customer f.o.b. destination on December 29, 2016. The goods arrived at the customer's location in January. In addition, one of Kelly's major suppliers shipped goods to Kelly f.o.b. shipping point on December 30. The merchandise arrived at Kelly's location in January. Which shipments should be included in Kelly's December 31 inventory?

BE 8–4
Purchase discounts; gross method
● LO8–3

On December 28, 2016, Videotech Corporation (VTC) purchased 10 units of a new satellite uplink system from Tristar Communications for $25,000 each. The terms of each sale were 1/10, n/30. VTC uses the gross method to account for purchase discounts and a perpetual inventory system. VTC paid the net-of-discount amount on January 6, 2017. Prepare the journal entries on December 28 and January 6 to record the purchase and payment.

BE 8–5
Purchase discounts; net method
● LO8–3

Refer to the situation described in BE 8–4. Prepare the necessary journal entries assuming that VTC uses the net method to account for purchase discounts.

BE 8–6
Inventory cost flow methods; periodic system
● LO8–4

Samuelson and Messenger (S&M) began 2016 with 200 units of its one product. These units were purchased near the end of 2015 for $25 each. During the month of January, 100 units were purchased on January 8 for $28 each and another 200 units were purchased on January 19 for $30 each. Sales of 125 units and 100 units were made on January 10 and January 25, respectively. There were 275 units on hand at the end of the month. S&M uses a *periodic* inventory system. Calculate ending inventory and cost of goods sold for January using (1) FIFO, and (2) average cost.

BE 8–7
Inventory cost flow methods; perpetual system
● LO8–4

Refer to the situation described in BE 8–6. S&M uses a *perpetual* inventory system. Calculate ending inventory and cost of goods sold for January using (1) FIFO, and (2) average cost.

BE 8–8
LIFO method
● LO8–4

Esquire Inc. uses the LIFO method to value its inventory. Inventory at January 1, 2016, was $500,000 (20,000 units at $25 each). During 2016, 80,000 units were purchased, all at the same price of $30 per unit. 85,000 units were sold during 2016. Esquire uses a periodic inventory system. Calculate the December 31, 2016, ending inventory and cost of goods sold for 2016.

BE 8–9
LIFO method
● LO8–4

AAA Hardware uses the LIFO method to value its inventory. Inventory at the beginning of the year consisted of 10,000 units of the company's one product. These units cost $15 each. During the year, 60,000 units were purchased at a cost of $18 each and 64,000 units were sold. Near the end of the fiscal year, management is considering the purchase of an additional 5,000 units at $18. What would be the effect of this purchase on income before income taxes? Would your answer be the same if the company used FIFO instead of LIFO?

BE 8–10
LIFO liquidation
● LO8–6

Refer to the situation described in BE 8–8. Assuming an income tax rate of 40%, what is LIFO liquidation profit or loss that the company would report in a disclosure note accompanying its financial statements?

BE 8–11
Supplemental LIFO disclosures; Walgreen
● LO8–6
Real World Financials

Walgreen Co., the largest drug store chain in the United States, reported inventories of $7,213 million and $6,852 million in its February 28, 2014, and August 31, 2013, balance sheets, respectively. Cost of goods sold for the six months ended February 28, 2014, was $27,132 million. The company uses primarily the LIFO inventory method. A disclosure note reported that if FIFO had been used instead of LIFO, inventory would have been higher by $2,200 million and $2,100 million at the end of the February 28, 2014, and August 31, 2013, periods, respectively. Calculate cost of goods sold for the six months ended February 28, 2014, assuming Walgreen used FIFO instead of LIFO.

BE 8–12
Ratio analysis
● LO8–7

Selected financial statement data for Schmitzer Inc. is shown below:

	2016	2015
Balance sheet:		
Inventories	60,000	48,000
Ratios:		
Gross profit ratio for 2016	40%	
Inventory turnover ratio for 2016	5	

What was the amount of net sales for 2016?

BE 8–13
Dollar-value LIFO
● LO8–8

At the beginning of 2016, a company adopts the dollar-value LIFO inventory method for its one inventory pool. The pool's value on that date was $1,400,000. The 2016 ending inventory valued at year-end costs was $1,664,000 and the year-end cost index was 1.04. Calculate the inventory value at the end of 2016 using the dollar-value LIFO method.

Exercises

An alternate exercise and problem set is available in the Connect library.

E 8–1
Perpetual inventory system; journal entries
● LO8–1

John's Specialty Store uses a perpetual inventory system. The following are some inventory transactions for the month of May 2016:

1. John's purchased merchandise on account for $5,000. Freight charges of $300 were paid in cash.
2. John's returned some of the merchandise purchased in (1). The cost of the merchandise was $600 and John's account was credited by the supplier.
3. Merchandise costing $2,800 was sold for $5,200 in cash.

Required:
Prepare the necessary journal entries to record these transactions.

E 8–2
Periodic inventory system; journal entries
● LO8–1

[This is a variation of E 8–1 modified to focus on the periodic inventory system.]

John's Specialty Store uses a periodic inventory system. The following are some inventory transactions for the month of May 2016:

1. John's purchased merchandise on account for $5,000. Freight charges of $300 were paid in cash.
2. John's returned some of the merchandise purchased in (1). The cost of the merchandise was $600 and John's account was credited by the supplier.
3. Merchandise costing $2,800 was sold for $5,200 in cash.

Required:
Prepare the necessary journal entries to record these transactions.

E 8–3
Determining cost of goods sold; periodic inventory system
● LO8–1

Askew Company uses a periodic inventory system. The June 30, 2016, year-end trial balance for the company contained the following information:

Account	Debit	Credit
Merchandise inventory, 7/1/15	32,000	
Sales		380,000
Sales returns	12,000	
Purchases	240,000	
Purchase discounts		6,000
Purchase returns		10,000
Freight-in	17,000	

In addition, you determine that the June 30, 2016, inventory balance is $40,000.

Required:
1. Calculate the cost of goods sold for the Askew Company for the year ending June 30, 2016.
2. Prepare the year-end adjusting entry to record cost of goods sold.

E 8–4
Perpetual and periodic inventory systems compared
● LO8–1

The following information is available for the Johnson Corporation for 2016:

Beginning inventory	$ 25,000
Merchandise purchases (on account)	155,000
Freight charges on purchases (paid in cash)	10,000
Merchandise returned to supplier (for credit)	12,000
Ending inventory	30,000
Sales (on account)	250,000
Cost of merchandise sold	148,000

Required:
Applying both a perpetual and a periodic inventory system, prepare the journal entries that summarize the transactions that created these balances. Include all end-of-period adjusting entries indicated.

E 8–5
Periodic inventory system; missing data
● LO8–1

The Playa Company uses a periodic inventory system. The following information is taken from Playa's records. Certain data have been intentionally omitted. ($ in thousands)

	2016	2017	2018
Beginning inventory	?	?	225
Cost of goods sold	627	621	?
Ending inventory	?	225	216
Cost of goods available for sale	876	?	800
Purchases (gross)	630	?	585
Purchase discounts	18	15	?
Purchase returns	24	30	14
Freight-in	13	32	16

Required:
Determine the missing numbers. Show computations where appropriate.

E 8–6
Goods in transit
● LO8–2

The Kwok Company's inventory balance on December 31, 2016, was $165,000 (based on a 12/31/16 physical count) *before* considering the following transactions:

1. Goods shipped to Kwok f.o.b. destination on December 20, 2016, were received on January 4, 2017. The invoice cost was $30,000.
2. Goods shipped to Kwok f.o.b. shipping point on December 28, 2016, were received on January 5, 2017. The invoice cost was $17,000.
3. Goods shipped from Kwok to a customer f.o.b. destination on December 27, 2016, were received by the customer on January 3, 2017. The sales price was $40,000 and the merchandise cost $22,000.
4. Goods shipped from Kwok to a customer f.o.b. destination on December 26, 2016, were received by the customer on December 30, 2016. The sales price was $20,000 and the merchandise cost $13,000.
5. Goods shipped from Kwok to a customer f.o.b. shipping point on December 28, 2016, were received by the customer on January 4, 2017. The sales price was $25,000 and the merchandise cost $12,000.

Required:
Determine the correct inventory amount to be reported in Kwok's 2016 balance sheet.

E 8–7
Goods in transit; consignment
● LO8–2

The December 31, 2016, year-end inventory balance of the Raymond Corporation is $210,000. You have been asked to review the following transactions to determine if they have been correctly recorded.

1. Goods shipped to Raymond f.o.b. destination on December 26, 2016, were received on January 2, 2017. The invoice cost of $30,000 *is* included in the preliminary inventory balance.
2. At year-end, Raymond held $14,000 of merchandise on consignment from the Harrison Company. This merchandise *is* included in the preliminary inventory balance.
3. On December 29, merchandise costing $6,000 was shipped to a customer f.o.b. shipping point and arrived at the customer's location on January 3, 2017. The merchandise is *not* included in the preliminary inventory balance.
4. At year-end, Raymond had merchandise costing $15,000 on consignment with the Joclyn Corporation. The merchandise is *not* included in the preliminary inventory balance.

Required:
Determine the correct inventory amount to be reported in Raymond's 2016 balance sheet.

E 8–8
Physical quantities and costs included in inventory
● LO8–2

The Phoenix Corporation's fiscal year ends on December 31. Phoenix determines inventory quantity by a physical count of inventory on hand at the close of business on December 31. The company's controller has asked for your help in deciding if the following items should be included in the year-end inventory count.

1. Merchandise held on consignment for Trout Creek Clothing.
2. Goods shipped f.o.b. destination on December 28 that arrived at the customer's location on January 4.
3. Goods purchased from a vendor shipped f.o.b. shipping point on December 26 that arrived on January 3.
4. Goods shipped f.o.b. shipping point on December 28 that arrived at the customer's location on January 5.
5. Phoenix had merchandise on consignment at Lisa's Markets, Inc.
6. Goods purchased from a vendor shipped f.o.b. destination on December 27 that arrived on January 3.
7. Freight charges on goods purchased in 3.

Required:
Determine if each of the items above should be included or excluded from the company's year-end inventory.

E 8–9
Purchase discounts; the gross method
● LO8–3

On July 15, 2016, the Nixon Car Company purchased 1,000 tires from the Harwell Company for $50 each. The terms of the sale were 2/10, n/30. Nixon uses a periodic inventory system and the *gross* method of accounting for purchase discounts.

Required:

1. Prepare the journal entries to record the purchase on July 15 and payment on July 23, 2016.
2. Prepare the journal entry to record the payment on August 15, 2016.
3. If Nixon instead uses a perpetual inventory system, explain any changes to the journal entries created in requirements 1 and 2.

E 8–10
Purchase discounts; the net method
● LO8–3

[This is a variation of E 8–9 modified to focus on the net method of accounting for purchase discounts.]
On July 15, 2016, the Nixon Car Company purchased 1,000 tires from the Harwell Company for $50 each. The terms of the sale were 2/10, n/30. Nixon uses a periodic inventory system and the *net* method of accounting for purchase discounts.

Required:

1. Prepare the journal entries to record the purchase on July 15 and payment on July 23, 2016.
2. Prepare the journal entry to record the payment on August 15, 2016.
3. If Nixon instead uses a perpetual inventory system, explain any changes to the journal entries created in requirements 1 and 2.

E 8–11
Trade and purchase discounts; the gross method and the net method compared
● LO8–3

Tracy Company, a manufacturer of air conditioners, sold 100 units to Thomas Company on November 17, 2016. The units have a list price of $500 each, but Thomas was given a 30% trade discount. The terms of the sale were 2/10, n/30. Thomas uses a periodic inventory system.

Required:

1. Prepare the journal entries to record the purchase by Thomas on November 17 and payment on November 26, 2016, using the gross method of accounting for purchase discounts.
2. Prepare the journal entry to record the payment on December 15, 2016, using the gross method of accounting for purchase discounts.
3. Repeat requirements 1 and 2 using the net method of accounting for purchase discounts.

E 8–12
FASB codification research
● LO8–2, LO8–3

Access the *FASB Accounting Standards Codification* at the FASB website (asc.fasb.org). Determine the specific citation for each of the following items:

1. Define the meaning of cost as it applies to the initial measurement of inventory.
2. Indicate the circumstances when it is appropriate to initially measure agricultural inventory at fair value.
3. What is a major objective of accounting for inventory?
4. Are abnormal freight charges included in the cost of inventory?

E 8–13
Inventory cost flow methods; periodic system
● LO8–1, LO8–4

Altira Corporation uses a periodic inventory system. The following information related to its merchandise inventory during the month of August 2016 is available:

Aug. 1	Inventory on hand—2,000 units; cost $6.10 each.
8	Purchased 10,000 units for $5.50 each.
14	Sold 8,000 units for $12.00 each.
18	Purchased 6,000 units for $5.00 each.
25	Sold 7,000 units for $11.00 each.
31	Inventory on hand—3,000 units.

Required:

Determine the inventory balance Altira would report in its August 31, 2016, balance sheet and the cost of goods sold it would report in its August 2016 income statement using each of the following cost flow methods:

1. First-in, first-out (FIFO)
2. Last-in, first-out (LIFO)
3. Average cost

E 8–14
Inventory cost flow methods; perpetual system
● LO8–1, LO8–4

[This is a variation of E 8–13 modified to focus on the perpetual inventory system and alternative cost flow methods.]

Altira Corporation uses a perpetual inventory system. The following transactions affected its merchandise inventory during the month of August 2016:

Aug. 1	Inventory on hand—2,000 units; cost $6.10 each.
8	Purchased 10,000 units for $5.50 each.
14	Sold 8,000 units for $12.00 each.
18	Purchased 6,000 units for $5.00 each.
25	Sold 7,000 units for $11.00 each.
31	Inventory on hand—3,000 units.

Required:

Determine the inventory balance Altira would report in its August 31, 2016, balance sheet and the cost of goods sold it would report in its August 2016 income statement using each of the following cost flow methods:

1. First-in, first-out (FIFO)
2. Last-in, first-out (LIFO)
3. Average cost

E 8–15
Comparison of FIFO and LIFO; periodic system
● LO8–1, LO8–4

Alta Ski Company's inventory records contained the following information regarding its latest ski model. The company uses a periodic inventory system.

Beginning inventory, January 1, 2016	600 units @ $80 each
Purchases:	
January 15	1,000 units @ $95 each
January 21	800 units @ $100 each
Sales:	
January 5	400 units @ $120 each
January 22	800 units @ $130 each
January 29	400 units @ $135 each
Ending inventory, January 31, 2016	800 units

Required:
1. Which method, FIFO or LIFO, will result in the highest cost of goods sold figure for January 2016? Why? Which method will result in the highest ending inventory balance? Why?
2. Compute cost of goods sold for January and the ending inventory using both the FIFO and LIFO methods.

E 8–16
Average cost method; periodic and perpetual systems
● LO8–1, LO8–4

The following information is taken from the inventory records of the CNB Company for the month of September:

Beginning inventory, 9/1/16	5,000 units @ $10.00
Purchases:	
9/7	3,000 units @ $10.40
9/25	8,000 units @ $10.75
Sales:	
9/10	4,000 units
9/29	5,000 units
7,000 units were on hand at the end of September.	

Required:
1. Assuming that CNB uses a periodic inventory system and employs the average cost method, determine cost of goods sold for September and September's ending inventory.
2. Repeat requirement 1 assuming that the company uses a perpetual inventory system.

E 8–17
FIFO, LIFO, and average cost methods
● LO8–1, LO8–4

Causwell Company began 2016 with 10,000 units of inventory on hand. The cost of each unit was $5.00. During 2016 an additional 30,000 units were purchased at a single unit cost, and 20,000 units remained on hand at the end of 2016 (20,000 units therefore were sold during 2016). Causwell uses a periodic inventory system. Cost of goods sold for 2016, applying the average cost method, is $115,000. The company is interested in determining what cost of goods sold would have been if the FIFO or LIFO methods were used.

Required:
1. Determine the cost of goods sold for 2016 using the FIFO method. [*Hint:* Determine the cost per unit of 2016 purchases.]
2. Determine the cost of goods sold for 2016 using the LIFO method.

E 8–18
Supplemental LIFO disclosures; LIFO reserve; AEP Industries
● LO8–6

Real World Financials

AEP Industries Inc. is a leading manufacturer of plastic packing films. The company uses the LIFO inventory method for external reporting but maintains its internal records using FIFO. The following disclosure note was included in a recent quarterly report:

4. Inventories (in part)

Inventories are comprised of the following ($ in thousands):

	January 31, 2014	October 31, 2013
Raw materials	$ 49,883	$48,467
Finished goods	93,483	83,363
Supplies	5,865	6,322
	149,231	138,152
Less: LIFO reserve	(42,935)	(41,061)
	$106,296	$97,091

The company's income statements reported cost of goods sold of $247,933 thousand for the quarter ended January 31, 2014.

Required:

1. Assume that AEP adjusts the LIFO reserve at the end of its quarter. Prepare the January 31, 2014, adjusting entry to record the cost of goods sold adjustment.
2. If AEP had used FIFO to value its inventories, what would cost of goods sold have been for the quarter ended January 31, 2014?

E 8–19
LIFO liquidation
● LO8–1, LO8–4, LO8–6

The Reuschel Company began 2016 with inventory of 10,000 units at a cost of $7 per unit. During 2016, 50,000 units were purchased for $8.50 each. Sales for the year totaled 54,000 units leaving 6,000 units on hand at the end of 2016. Reuschel uses a periodic inventory system and the LIFO inventory cost method.

Required:

1. Calculate cost of goods sold for 2016.
2. From a financial reporting perspective, what problem is created by the use of LIFO in this situation? Describe the disclosure required to report the effects of this problem.

E 8–20
LIFO liquidation
● LO8–4, LO8–6

The Churchill Corporation uses a periodic inventory system and the LIFO inventory cost method for its one product. Beginning inventory of 20,000 units consisted of the following, listed in chronological order of acquisition:

12,000 units at a cost of $8.00 per unit = $96,000
8,000 units at a cost of $9.00 per unit = 72,000

During 2016, inventory quantity declined by 10,000 units. All units purchased during 2016 cost $12.00 per unit.

Required:

Calculate the before-tax LIFO liquidation profit or loss that the company would report in a disclosure note, assuming the amount determined is material.

E 8–21
FASB codification research
● LO8–6

The *FASB Accounting Standards Codification* represents the single source of authoritative U.S. generally accepted accounting principles.

Required:

1. Obtain the relevant authoritative literature on the disclosure of accounting policies using the *FASB Accounting Standards Codification* at the FASB website (asc.fasb.org).
2. What is the specific citation that describes the disclosure requirements that must be made by publicly traded companies for a LIFO liquidation?
3. Describe the disclosure requirements.

E 8–22
Ratio analysis; Home Depot and Lowe's
● LO8–7

Real World Financials

The table below contains selected information from recent financial statements of **The Home Depot, Inc.**, and **Lowe's Companies, Inc.**, two companies in the home improvement retail industry ($ in millions):

	Home Depot		Lowe's	
	2/2/14	2/3/13	1/31/14	2/1/13
Net sales	$78,812	$74,754	$53,417	$50,521
Cost of goods sold	51,422	48,912	34,941	33,194
Year-end inventory	11,057	10,710	9,127	8,600
Industry averages:				
Gross profit ratio	33%			
Inventory turnover ratio	3.7 times			
Average days in inventory	99 days			

Required:

Calculate the gross profit ratio, the inventory turnover ratio, and the average days in inventory for the two companies for their fiscal years ending in 2014. Compare your calculations for the two companies, taking into account the industry averages.

E 8–23
Dollar-value LIFO
● LO8–8

On January 1, 2016, the Haskins Company adopted the dollar-value LIFO method for its one inventory pool. The pool's value on this date was $660,000. The 2016 and 2017 ending inventory valued at year-end costs were $690,000 and $760,000, respectively. The appropriate cost indexes are 1.04 for 2016 and 1.08 for 2017.

Required:

Calculate the inventory value at the end of 2016 and 2017 using the dollar-value LIFO method.

E 8–24
Dollar-value LIFO
● LO8–8

Mercury Company has only one inventory pool. On December 31, 2016, Mercury adopted the dollar-value LIFO inventory method. The inventory on that date using the dollar-value LIFO method was $200,000. Inventory data are as follows:

Year	Ending Inventory at Year-End Costs	Ending Inventory at Base Year Costs
2017	$231,000	$220,000
2018	299,000	260,000
2019	300,000	250,000

Required:
Compute the inventory at December 31, 2017, 2018, and 2019, using the dollar-value LIFO method.
(AICPA adapted)

E 8–25
Dollar-value LIFO
● LO8–8

Carswell Electronics adopted the dollar-value LIFO method on January 1, 2016, when the inventory value of its one inventory pool was $720,000. The company decided to use an external index, the Consumer Price Index (CPI), to adjust for changes in the cost level. On January 1, 2016, the CPI was 240. On December 31, 2016, inventory valued at year-end cost was $880,000 and the CPI was 264.

Required:
Calculate the inventory value at the end of 2016 using the dollar-value LIFO method.

E 8–26
Concepts; terminology
● LO8–1 through LO8–5

Listed below are several terms and phrases associated with inventory measurement. Pair each item from List A with the item from List B (by letter) that is most appropriately associated with it.

List A	List B
____ 1. Perpetual inventory system	a. Legal title passes when goods are delivered to common carrier.
____ 2. Periodic inventory system	b. Goods are transferred to another company but title remains with transferor.
____ 3. F.o.b. shipping point	c. Purchase discounts not taken are included in inventory cost.
____ 4. Gross method	d. If LIFO is used for taxes, it must be used for financial reporting.
____ 5. Net method	e. Assumes items sold are those acquired first.
____ 6. Cost index	f. Assumes items sold are those acquired last.
____ 7. F.o.b. destination	g. Purchase discounts not taken are considered interest expense.
____ 8. FIFO	h. Used to convert ending inventory at year-end cost to base year cost.
____ 9. LIFO	i. Continuously records changes in inventory.
____ 10. Consignment	j. Assumes items sold come from a mixture of goods acquired during the period.
____ 11. Average cost	k. Legal title passes when goods arrive at location.
____ 12. IRS conformity rule	l. Adjusts inventory at the end of the period.

CPA and CMA Review Questions

CPA Exam Questions
KAPLAN
CPA REVIEW

The following questions are adapted from a variety of sources including questions developed by the AICPA Board of Examiners and those used in the Kaplan CPA Review Course to study inventory while preparing for the CPA examination. Determine the response that best completes the statements or questions.

● LO8–2

1. Herc Co.'s inventory at December 31, 2016, was $1,500,000 based on a physical count priced at cost, and before any necessary adjustment for the following:
   - Merchandise costing $90,000, shipped f.o.b shipping point from a vendor on December 30, 2016, was received and recorded on January 5, 2017.
   - Goods in the shipping area were excluded from inventory although shipment was not made until January 4, 2017. The goods, billed to the customer f.o.b. shipping point on December 30, 2016, had a cost of $120,000.

   What amount should Herc report as inventory in its December 31, 2016, balance sheet?

   a. $1,500,000
   b. $1,590,000
   c. $1,700,000
   d. $1,710,000

● LO8–3

2. Dixon Menswear Shop regularly buys shirts from Colt Company. Dixon purchased shirts from Colt on May 27, and received an invoice with a list price amount of $3,600 and payment terms of 2/10, n/30. Dixon uses the net method to record purchases. Dixon should record the purchase at
   a. $3,430
   b. $3,500
   c. $3,528
   d. $3,600

● LO8–4

Questions 3 through 5 are based on the following information. Esquire Corp. uses the periodic inventory system. During its first year of operations, Esquire made the following purchases (list in chronological order of acquisition):

- 20 units at $50
- 35 units at $40
- 85 units at $30

Sales for the year totaled 135 units, leaving 5 units on hand at the end of the year.

3. Ending inventory using the average cost method is
   a. $ 150
   b. $ 177
   c. $ 250
   d. $1,540
4. Ending inventory using the FIFO method is
   a. $ 150
   b. $ 177
   c. $ 250
   d. $1,540
5. Ending inventory using the LIFO method is
   a. $ 150
   b. $ 177
   c. $ 250
   d. $1,540

● LO8–4, LO8–5

6. Jamison Corporation's inventory cost in its balance sheet is lower using the first-in, first-out method than it would have been had it used the last-in, first-out method. Assuming no beginning inventory, what direction did the cost of purchases move during the period?
   a. Up.
   b. Down.
   c. Unchanged.
   d. Can't be determined.

● LO8–8

7. Dalton Company adopted the dollar-value LIFO inventory method on January 1, 2016. In applying the LIFO method, Dalton uses internal price indexes and the multiple-pools approach. The following data were available for Inventory Pool No. 1 for the two years following the adoption of LIFO:

	Ending Inventory		
	At Current Year Cost	At Base Year Cost	Cost Index
1/1/16	$100,000	$100,000	1.00
12/31/16	126,000	120,000	1.05
12/31/17	140,800	128,000	1.10

Under the dollar-value LIFO method the inventory at December 31, 2017, should be
   a. $128,000
   b. $129,800
   c. $130,800
   d. $140,800

International Financial Reporting Standards are tested on the CPA exam along with U.S. GAAP. The following question deals with the application of IFRS.

● LO8–9

IFRS

8. Under IFRS, which of the following methods is not acceptable for the valuation of inventory?
   a. LIFO.
   b. FIFO.

c. Average cost.
d. Specific identification.

CMA Exam Questions

ima®

The following questions dealing with inventory are adapted from questions that previously appeared on Certified Management Accountant (CMA) examinations. The CMA designation sponsored by the Institute of Management Accountants (www.imanet.org) provides members with an objective measure of knowledge and competence in the field of management accounting. Determine the response that best completes the statements or questions.

● LO8–1, LO8–4

Questions 1 through 3 are based on the following information. Thomas Engine Company is a wholesaler of marine engine parts. The activity of carburetor 2642J during the month of March is presented below.

Date	Balance or Transaction	Units	Unit Cost	Unit Sales Price
Mar 1	Inventory	3,200	$64.30	$86.50
4	Purchase	3,400	64.75	87.00
14	Sales	3,600		87.25
25	Purchase	3,500	66.00	87.25
28	Sales	3,450		88.00

1. If Thomas uses a first-in, first-out perpetual inventory system, the total cost of the inventory for carburetor 2642J at March 31 is
   a. $196,115
   b. $197,488
   c. $201,300
   d. $263,825
2. If Thomas uses a last-in, first-out periodic inventory system, the total cost of the inventory for carburetor 2642J at March 31 is
   a. $196,115
   b. $197,488
   c. $201,300
   d. $268,400
3. If Thomas uses a last-in, first-out perpetual inventory system, the total cost of the inventory for carburetor 2642J at March 31 is
   a. $196,200
   b. $197,488
   c. $263,863
   d. $268,400

Problems

An alternate exercise and problem set is available in the Connect library.

P 8–1
Various inventory transactions; journal entries
● LO8–1 through LO8–3

James Company began the month of October with inventory of $15,000. The following inventory transactions occurred during the month:

a. The company purchased merchandise on account for $22,000 on October 12, 2016. Terms of the purchase were 2/10, n/30. James uses the net method to record purchases. The merchandise was shipped f.o.b. shipping point and freight charges of $500 were paid in cash.
b. On October 31, James paid for the merchandise purchased on October 12.
c. During October merchandise costing $18,000 was sold on account for $28,000.
d. It was determined that inventory on hand at the end of October cost $19,060.

Required:

1. Assuming that the James Company uses a periodic inventory system, prepare journal entries for the above transactions including the adjusting entry at the end of October to record cost of goods sold.
2. Assuming that the James Company uses a perpetual inventory system, prepare journal entries for the above transactions.

P 8–2
Items to be included in inventory
● LO8–2

The following inventory transactions took place near December 31, 2016, the end of the Rasul Company's fiscal year-end:

1. On December 27, 2016, merchandise costing $2,000 was shipped to the Myers Company on consignment. The shipment arrived at Myers's location on December 29, but none of the merchandise was sold by the end of the year. The merchandise was *not* included in the 2016 ending inventory.
2. On January 5, 2017, merchandise costing $8,000 was received from a supplier and recorded as a purchase on that date and *not* included in the 2016 ending inventory. The invoice revealed that the shipment was made f.o.b. shipping point on December 28, 2016.
3. On December 29, 2016, the company shipped merchandise costing $12,000 to a customer f.o.b. destination. The goods, which arrived at the customer's location on January 4, 2017, were *not* included in Rasul's 2016 ending inventory. The sale was recorded in 2016.
4. Merchandise costing $4,000 was received on December 28, 2016, on consignment from the Aborn Company. A purchase was *not* recorded and the merchandise was *not* included in 2016 ending inventory.
5. Merchandise costing $6,000 was received and recorded as a purchase on January 8, 2017. The invoice revealed that the merchandise was shipped from the supplier on December 28, 2016, f.o.b. destination. The merchandise was *not* included in 2016 ending inventory.

Required:
State whether Rasul correctly accounted for each of the above transactions. Give the reason for your answer.

P 8–3
Costs included in inventory
● LO8–2, LO8–3

Reagan Corporation is a wholesale distributor of truck replacement parts. Initial amounts taken from Reagan's records are as follows:

Inventory at December 31 (based on a physical count of goods in Reagan's warehouse on December 31)		$1,250,000
Accounts payable at December 31:		
Vendor	**Terms**	**Amount**
Baker Company	2%, 10 days, net 30	$ 265,000
Charlie Company	Net 30	210,000
Dolly Company	Net 30	300,000
Eagler Company	Net 30	225,000
Full Company	Net 30	—
Greg Company	Net 30	—
Accounts payable, December 31		$1,000,000
Sales for the year		$9,000,000

Additional Information:

1. Parts held by Reagan on consignment from Charlie, amounting to $155,000, were included in the physical count of goods in Reagan's warehouse and in accounts payable at December 31.
2. Parts totaling $22,000, which were purchased from Full and paid for in December, were sold in the last week of the year and *appropriately* recorded as sales of $28,000. The parts were included in the physical count of goods in Reagan's warehouse on December 31 because the parts were on the loading dock waiting to be picked up by customers.
3. Parts in transit on December 31 to customers, shipped f.o.b. shipping point on December 28, amounted to $34,000. The customers received the parts on January 6 of the following year. Sales of $40,000 to the customers for the parts were recorded by Reagan on January 2.
4. Retailers were holding goods on consignment from Reagan, which had a cost of $210,000 and a retail value of $250,000.
5. Goods were in transit from Greg to Reagan on December 31. The cost of the goods was $25,000, and they were shipped f.o.b. shipping point on December 29.
6. A freight bill in the amount of $2,000 specifically relating to merchandise purchased in December, all of which was still in the inventory at December 31, was received on January 3. The freight bill was not included in either the inventory or in accounts payable at December 31.
7. All the purchases from Baker occurred during the last seven days of the year. These items have been recorded in accounts payable and accounted for in the physical inventory at cost before discount. Reagan's policy is to pay invoices in time to take advantage of all discounts, adjust inventory accordingly, and record accounts payable net of discounts.

Required:
Prepare a schedule of adjustments to the initial amounts using the format shown below. Show the effect, if any, of each of the transactions separately and if the transactions would have no effect on the amount shown, state *none*.

	Inventory	Accounts Payable	Sales
Initial amounts	$1,250,000	$1,000,000	$ 9,000,000
Adjustments—increase (decrease):			
1.			
2.			
3.			
4.			
5.			
6.			
7.			
Total adjustments			
Adjusted amounts	$	$	$

(AICPA adapted)

P 8–4
Various inventory transactions; determining inventory and cost of goods
● LO8–1 through LO8–4

Johnson Corporation began 2016 with inventory of 10,000 units of its only product. The units cost $8 each. The company uses a periodic inventory system and the LIFO cost method. The following transactions occurred during 2016:

a. Purchased 50,000 additional units at a cost of $10 per unit. Terms of the purchases were 2/10, n/30, and 100% of the purchases were paid for within the 10-day discount period. The company uses the gross method to record purchase discounts. The merchandise was purchased f.o.b. shipping point and freight charges of $.50 per unit were paid by Johnson.
b. 1,000 units purchased during the year were returned to suppliers for credit. Johnson was also given credit for the freight charges of $.50 per unit it had paid on the original purchase. The units were defective and were returned two days after they were received.
c. Sales for the year totaled 45,000 units at $18 per unit.
d. On December 28, 2016, Johnson purchased 5,000 additional units at $10 each. The goods were shipped f.o.b. destination and arrived at Johnson's warehouse on January 4, 2017.
e. 14,000 units were on hand at the end of 2016.

Required:
1. Determine ending inventory and cost of goods sold for 2016.
2. Assuming that operating expenses other than those indicated in the above transactions amounted to $150,000, determine income before income taxes for 2016.

P 8–5
Various inventory costing methods
● LO8–1, LO8–4

Ferris Company began 2016 with 6,000 units of its principal product. The cost of each unit is $8. Merchandise transactions for the month of January 2016 are as follows:

		Purchases	
Date of Purchase	Units	Unit Cost*	Total Cost
Jan. 10	5,000	$ 9	$ 45,000
Jan. 18	6,000	10	60,000
Totals	11,000		$105,000

*Includes purchase price and cost of freight.

Sales

Date of Sale	Units
Jan. 5	3,000
Jan. 12	2,000
Jan. 20	4,000
Total	9,000

8,000 units were on hand at the end of the month.

Required:
Calculate January's ending inventory and cost of goods sold for the month using each of the following alternatives:
1. FIFO, periodic system
2. LIFO, periodic system

3. LIFO, perpetual system
4. Average cost, periodic system
5. Average cost, perpetual system

P 8–6
Various inventory costing methods; gross profit ratio
● LO8–1, LO8–4, LO8–7

Topanga Group began operations early in 2016. Inventory purchase information for the quarter ended March 31, 2016, for Topanga's only product is provided below. The unit costs include the cost of freight. The company uses a periodic inventory system.

Date of Purchase	Units	Unit Cost	Total Cost
Jan. 7	5,000	$4.00	$ 20,000
Feb. 16	12,000	4.50	54,000
March 22	17,000	5.00	85,000
Totals	34,000		$159,000

Sales for the quarter, all at $7.00 per unit, totaled 20,000 units leaving 14,000 units on hand at the end of the quarter.

Required:

1. Calculate the Topanga's gross profit ratio for the first quarter using:
   a. FIFO
   b. LIFO
   c. Average cost
2. Comment on the relative effect of each of the three inventory methods on the gross profit ratio.

P 8–7
Various inventory costing methods
● LO8–1, LO8–4

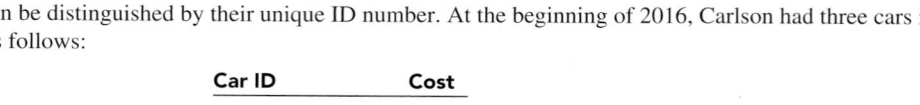

Carlson Auto Dealers Inc. sells a handmade automobile as its only product. Each automobile is identical; however, they can be distinguished by their unique ID number. At the beginning of 2016, Carlson had three cars in inventory, as follows:

Car ID	Cost
203	$60,000
207	60,000
210	63,000

During 2016, each of the three autos sold for $90,000. Additional purchases (listed in chronological order) and sales for the year were as follows:

Car ID	Cost	Selling Price
211	$63,000	$ 90,000
212	63,000	93,000
213	64,500	not sold
214	66,000	96,000
215	69,000	100,500
216	70,500	not sold
217	72,000	105,000
218	72,300	106,500
219	75,000	not sold

Required:

1. Calculate 2016 ending inventory and cost of goods sold assuming the company uses the specific identification inventory method.
2. Calculate ending inventory and cost of goods sold assuming FIFO and a periodic inventory system.
3. Calculate ending inventory and cost of goods sold assuming LIFO and a periodic inventory system.
4. Calculate ending inventory and cost of goods sold assuming the average cost method and a periodic inventory system.

P 8–8
Supplemental LIFO disclosures; Caterpillar
● LO8–4, LO8–6

Caterpillar, Inc., is one of the world's largest manufacturers of construction, mining, and forestry machinery. The following disclosure note is included in the company's 2013 financial statements:

Real World Financials

D. Inventories ($ in millions)

Inventories are stated at the lower of cost or market. Cost is principally determined using the last-in, first-out, (LIFO) method. The value of inventories on the LIFO basis represented about 60% of total inventories at December 31, 2013, and 2012, and about 65% at December 31, 2011.

If the FIFO (first-in, first-out) method had been in use, inventories would have been $2,504 million, $2,750 million, and $2,422 million higher than reported at December 31, 2013, 2012, and 2011, respectively.

If inventories valued at LIFO cost had been valued at FIFO cost, net income would have been $184.5 million lower in 2013 and $246 million higher in 2012.

Required:

1. Approximate the company's effective income tax rate for the year ended December 31, 2013.
2. Why might the information contained in the disclosure note be useful to a financial analyst?
3. Using the income tax rate calculated in 1, how much higher (lower) would retained earnings have been at the end of 2013 if Caterpillar had used the FIFO inventory method for all of its inventory?

P 8–9
LIFO liquidation
● LO8–4, LO8–6

Taylor Corporation has used a periodic inventory system and the LIFO cost method since its inception in 2009. The company began 2016 with the following inventory layers (listed in chronological order of acquisition):

10,000 units @ $15	$150,000
15,000 units @ $20	300,000
Beginning inventory	$450,000

During 2016, 30,000 units were purchased for $25 per unit. Due to unexpected demand for the company's product, 2016 sales totaled 40,000 units at various prices, leaving 15,000 units in ending inventory.

Required:

1. Calculate cost of goods sold for 2016.
2. Determine the amount of LIFO liquidation profit that the company must report in a disclosure note to its 2016 financial statements. Assume an income tax rate of 40%.
3. If the company decided to purchase an additional 10,000 units at $25 per unit at the end of the year, how much income tax currently payable would be saved?

P 8–10
LIFO liquidation
● LO8–4, LO8–6

Cansela Corporation uses a periodic inventory system and the LIFO method to value its inventory. The company began 2016 with inventory of 4,500 units of its only product. The beginning inventory balance of $64,000 consisted of the following layers:

2,000 units at $12 per unit	=	$24,000
2,500 units at $16 per unit	=	40,000
Beginning inventory		$64,000

During the three years 2016–2018 the cost of inventory remained constant at $18 per unit. Unit purchases and sales during these years were as follows:

	Purchases	Sales
2016	10,000	11,000
2017	13,000	14,500
2018	12,000	13,000

Required:

1. Calculate cost of goods sold for 2016, 2017, and 2018.
2. Disregarding income tax, determine the LIFO liquidation profit or loss, if any, for each of the three years.
3. Prepare the company's LIFO liquidation disclosure note that would be included in the 2018 financial statements to report the effects of any liquidation on cost of goods sold and net income. Assume any liquidation effects are material and that Cansela's effective income tax rate is 40%. Cansela's 2018 financial statements include income statements for two prior years for comparative purposes.

P 8–11
Inventory cost flow methods: LIFO liquidation; ratios
● LO8–4, LO8–6, LO8–7

Cast Iron Grills, Inc., manufactures premium gas barbecue grills. The company uses a periodic inventory system and the LIFO cost method for its grill inventory. Cast Iron's December 31, 2016, fiscal year-end inventory consisted of the following (listed in chronological order of acquisition):

Units	Unit Cost
5,000	$700
4,000	800
6,000	900

The replacement cost of the grills throughout 2017 was $1,000. Cast Iron sold 27,000 grills during 2017. The company's selling price is set at 200% of the current replacement cost.

Required:

1. Compute the gross profit (sales minus cost of goods sold) and the gross profit ratio for 2017 assuming that Cast Iron purchased 28,000 units during the year.
2. Repeat requirement 1 assuming that Cast Iron purchased only 15,000 units.
3. Why does the number of units purchased affect your answers to the above requirements?
4. Repeat requirements 1 and 2 assuming that Cast Iron uses the FIFO inventory cost method rather than the LIFO method.
5. Why does the number of units purchased have no effect on your answers to requirements 1 and 2 when the FIFO method is used?

P 8–12
Integrating problem; inventories and accounts receivable; Chapters 7 and 8
● LO8–4, LO8–6, LO8–7

Inverness Steel Corporation is a producer of flat-rolled carbon, stainless and electrical steels, and tubular products. The company's income statement for the 2016 fiscal year reported the following information ($ in millions):

Sales	$6,255
Cost of goods sold	5,190

The company's balance sheets for 2016 and 2015 included the following information ($ in millions):

	2016	2015
Current assets:		
Accounts receivable, net	$703	$583
Inventories	880	808

The statement of cash flows reported bad debt expense for 2016 of $8 million. The summary of significant accounting policies included the following notes ($ in millions):

Accounts Receivable (in part)

The allowance for uncollectible accounts was $10 and $7 at December 31, 2016 and 2015, respectively. All sales are on credit.

Inventories

Inventories are valued at the lower of cost or market. The cost of the majority of inventories is measured using the last in, first out (LIFO) method. Other inventories are measured principally at average cost and consist mostly of foreign inventories and certain raw materials. If the entire inventory had been valued on an average cost basis, inventory would have been higher by $480 and $350 at the end of 2016 and 2015, respectively.

During 2016, 2015, and 2014, liquidation of LIFO layers generated income of $6, $7, and $25, respectively.

Required:

Using the information provided:

1. Determine the amount of accounts receivable Inverness wrote off during 2016.
2. Calculate the amount of cash collected from customers during 2016.
3. Calculate what cost of goods sold would have been for 2016 if the company had used average cost to value its entire inventory.

4. Calculate the following ratios for 2016:
   a. Receivables turnover ratio
   b. Inventory turnover ratio
   c. Gross profit ratio
5. Explain briefly what caused the income generated by the liquidation of LIFO layers. Assuming an income tax rate of 35%, what was the effect of the liquidation of LIFO layers on cost of goods sold in 2016?

P 8–13
Dollar-value LIFO
● LO8–8

On January 1, 2016, the Taylor Company adopted the dollar-value LIFO method. The inventory value for its one inventory pool on this date was $400,000. Inventory data for 2016 through 2018 are as follows:

Date	Ending Inventory at Year-End Costs	Cost Index
12/31/16	$441,000	1.05
12/31/17	487,200	1.12
12/31/18	510,000	1.20

Required:
Calculate Taylor's ending inventory for 2016, 2017, and 2018.

P 8–14
Dollar-value LIFO
● LO8–8

Kingston Company uses the dollar-value LIFO method of computing inventory. An external price index is used to convert ending inventory to base year. The company began operations on January 1, 2016, with an inventory of $150,000. Year-end inventories at year-end costs and cost indexes for its one inventory pool were as follows:

Year Ended December 31	Ending Inventory at Year-End Costs	Cost Index (Relative to Base Year)
2016	$200,000	1.08
2017	245,700	1.17
2018	235,980	1.14
2019	228,800	1.10

Required:
Calculate inventory amounts at the end of each year.

P 8–15
Dollar-value LIFO
● LO8–8

On January 1, 2016, Avondale Lumber adopted the dollar-value LIFO inventory method. The inventory value for its one inventory pool on this date was $260,000. An internally generated cost index is used to convert ending inventory to base year. Year-end inventories at year-end costs and cost indexes for its one inventory pool were as follows:

Year Ended December 31	Inventory Year-End Costs	Cost Index (Relative to Base Year)
2016	$340,000	1.02
2017	350,000	1.06
2018	400,000	1.07
2019	430,000	1.10

Required:
Calculate inventory amounts at the end of each year.

P 8–16
Dollar-value LIFO; solving for unknowns
● LO8–8

At the beginning of 2016, Quentin and Kopps (Q&K) adopted the dollar-value LIFO (DVL) inventory method. On that date the value of its one inventory pool was $84,000. The company uses an internally generated cost index to convert ending inventory to base year. Inventory data for 2016 through 2019 are as follows:

Year Ended December 31	Ending Inventory at Year-End Costs	Ending Inventory at Base-Year Costs	Cost Index	Ending Inventory at DVL cost
2016	$100,800	$ 96,000	1.05	?
2017	136,800	?	1.14	?
2018	150,000	125,000	?	?
2019	?	?	1.25	$133,710

Required:
Determine the missing amounts.

Broaden Your Perspective

Apply your critical-thinking ability to the knowledge you've gained. These cases will provide you an opportunity to develop your research, analysis, judgment, and communication skills. You also will work with other students, integrate what you've learned, apply it in real-world situations, and consider its global and ethical ramifications. This practice will broaden your knowledge and further develop your decision-making abilities.

Judgment Case 8–1
Riding the Merry-Go-Round
● LO8–7

Real World Financials

Merry-Go-Round Enterprises, the clothing retailer for dedicated followers of young men's and women's fashion, was looking natty as a company. It was March 1993, and the Joppa, Maryland-based outfit had just announced the acquisition of Chess King, a rival clothing chain, a move that would give it the biggest share of the young men's clothing market. Merry-Go-Round told brokerage firm analysts that the purchase would add $13 million, or 15 cents a share, to profits for the year. So some Wall Street analysts raised their earnings estimates for Merry-Go-Round. The company's stock rose $2.25, or 15 percent, to $17 on the day of the Chess King news. Merry-Go-Round was hot—$100 of its stock in January 1988 was worth $804 five years later. In 1993 the chain owned 1,460 stores in 44 states, mostly under the Cignal, Chess King, and Merry-Go-Round names.

Merry-Go-Round's annual report for the fiscal year ended January 30, 1993, reported a 15% sales growth, to $877.5 million from $761.2 million. A portion of the company's balance sheet is reproduced below:

	Jan. 30, 1993	Feb. 1, 1992
Assets		
Cash and cash equivalents	$40,115,000	$29,781,000
Marketable securities	—	9,703
Receivables	6,466,000	6,195
Merchandise inventories	82,197,000	59,971,000

But Merry-Go-Round spun out. The company lost $544,000 in the first six months of 1993, compared with earnings of $13.5 million in the first half of 1992. In the fall of 1992, Leonard "Boogie" Weinglass, Merry-Go-Round's flamboyant founder and chairman who had started the company in 1968, boarded up his Merry-Go-Ranch in Aspen, Colorado, and returned to management after a 12-year hiatus. But the pony-tailed, shirtsleeved entrepreneur—the inspiration for the character Boogie in the movie *Diner*—couldn't save his company from bankruptcy. In January 1994, the company filed for Chapter 11 protection in Baltimore. Shares crumbled below $3.

Required:
In retrospect, can you identify any advance warning at the date of the financial statements of the company's impending bankruptcy?
[Adapted from Jonathan Burton, "Due Diligence," *Worth,* June 1994, pp. 89–96.]

Real World Case 8–2
Physical quantities and costs included in inventory; Sport Chalet
● LO8–2

Real World Financials

Determining the physical quantity that should be included in inventory normally is a simple matter because that amount consists of items in the possession of the company. The cost of inventory includes all necessary expenditures to acquire the inventory and bring it to its desired *condition* and *location* for sale or for use in the manufacturing process.

Required:
1. Identify and describe the situations in which physical quantity included in inventory is more difficult than simply determining items in the possession of the company.
2. In addition to the direct acquisition costs such as the price paid and transportation costs to obtain inventory, what other expenditures might be necessary to bring the inventory to its desired condition and location?
3. Access EDGAR on the Internet. The web address is www.sec.gov. Search for Sport Chalet Inc., a leading operator of full-service, specialty sporting goods stores in California and Nevada. Access the 10-K filing for the most recent fiscal year. Search or scroll to find the disclosure notes (footnotes). What costs does Sport Chalet include in its inventory?

Judgment Case 8–3
The specific identification inventory method; inventoriable costs
● LO8–3, LO8–4

Happlia Co. imports household appliances. Each model has many variations and each unit has an identification number. Happlia pays all costs for getting the goods from the port to its central warehouse in Des Moines. After repackaging, the goods are consigned to retailers. A retailer makes a sale, simultaneously buys the appliance from Happlia, and pays the balance due within one week.

To alleviate the overstocking of refrigerators at a Minneapolis retailer, some were reshipped to a Kansas City retailer where they were still held in inventory at December 31, 2016. Happlia paid the costs of this reshipment. Happlia uses the specific identification inventory costing method.

Required:

1. In regard to the specific identification inventory costing method:
   a. Describe its key elements.
   b. Discuss why it is appropriate for Happlia to use this method.
2. a. What general criteria should Happlia use to determine inventory carrying amounts at December 31, 2016?
   b. Give four examples of costs included in these inventory carrying amounts.
3. What costs should be reported in Happlia's 2016 income statement? Ignore lower of cost or market considerations.

(AICPA adapted)

Communication Case 8–4
LIFO versus FIFO
● LO8–4, LO8–5

You have just been hired as a consultant to Tangier Industries, a newly formed company. The company president, John Meeks, is seeking your advice as to the appropriate inventory method Tangier should use to value its inventory and cost of goods sold. Mr. Meeks has narrowed the choice to LIFO and FIFO. He has heard that LIFO might be better for tax purposes, but FIFO has certain advantages for financial reporting to investors and creditors. You have been told that the company will be profitable in its first year and for the foreseeable future.

Required:

Prepare a report for the president describing the factors that should be considered by Tangier in choosing between LIFO and FIFO.

Communication Case 8–5
LIFO versus FIFO
● LO8–4, LO8–5

An accounting intern for a local CPA firm was reviewing the financial statements of a client in the electronics industry. The intern noticed that the client used the FIFO method of determining ending inventory and cost of goods sold. When she asked a colleague why the firm used FIFO instead of LIFO, she was told that the client used FIFO to minimize its income tax liability. This response puzzled the intern because she thought that LIFO would minimize income tax liability.

Required:

What would you tell the intern to resolve the confusion?

Judgment Case 8–6
Goods in transit
● LO8–2

At the end of 2016, the Biggie Company performed its annual physical inventory count. John Lawrence, the manager in charge of the physical count, was told that an additional $22,000 in inventory that had been sold and was in transit to the customer should be included in the ending inventory balance. John was of the opinion that the merchandise shipped should be excluded from the ending inventory since Biggie was not in physical possession of the merchandise.

Required:

Discuss the situation and indicate why John's opinion might be incorrect.

Ethics Case 8–7
Profit manipulation
● LO8–4

In 2015 the Moncrief Company purchased from Jim Lester the right to be the sole distributor in the western states of a product called Zelenex. In payment, Moncrief agreed to pay Lester 20% of the gross profit recognized from the sale of Zelenex in 2016.

Moncrief uses a periodic inventory system and the LIFO inventory method. Late in 2016, the following information is available concerning the inventory of Zelenex:

Beginning inventory, 1/1/16 (10,000 units @ $30)	$ 300,000
Purchases (40,000 units @ $30)	1,200,000
Sales (35,000 units @ $60)	$2,100,000

By the end of the year, the purchase price of Zelenex had risen to $40 per unit. On December 28, 2016, three days before year-end, Moncrief is in a position to purchase 20,000 additional units of Zelenex at the $40 per unit price. Due to the increase in purchase price, Moncrief will increase the selling price in 2017 to $80 per unit. Inventory on hand before the purchase, 15,000 units, is sufficient to meet the next six months' sales and the company does not anticipate any significant changes in purchase price during 2017.

Required:

1. Determine the effect of the purchase of the additional 20,000 units on the 2016 gross profit from the sale of Zelenex and the payment due to Jim Lester.
2. Discuss the ethical dilemma Moncrief faces in determining whether or not the additional units should be purchased.

Real World Case 8–8
Effects of inventory valuation methods; supplemental LIFO disclosures; The Kroger Company
● LO8–4, LO8–6

Real World Financials

Income statement and balance sheet information abstracted from a recent annual report of **The Kroger Company**, one of the world's largest retailers, appears below:

Balance Sheets
($ in millions)

	February 2, 2014	February 2, 2013
Current assets:		
Inventories	$5,651	$5,146

Income Statements
($ in millions)

	For the Year Ended	
	February 2, 2014	February 2, 2013
Net sales	$98,375	$96,619
Cost of goods sold	78,138	76,726
Gross profit	$20,237	$19,893

The significant accounting policies note disclosure contained the following:

Inventories (in part)

Inventories are stated at the lower of cost (principally on a last-in, first out "LIFO" basis) or market. In total, approximately 95% of inventories were valued using the LIFO method. Cost for the balance of the inventories, including substantially all fuel inventories, was determined using the first-in, first-out ("FIFO") method. Replacement cost was higher than the carrying amount by $1,150 million at February 2, 2014, and $1,098 million at February 2, 2013.

Required:

1. Why is Kroger disclosing the replacement cost of its LIFO inventory?
2. Assuming that year-end replacement cost figures approximate FIFO inventory values, estimate what the beginning and ending inventory balances for the fiscal year ended February 2, 2014, would have been if Kroger had used FIFO for all of its inventories.
3. Estimate the effect on cost of goods sold (that is, would it have been greater or less and by how much?) for the fiscal year ended February 2, 2014, if Kroger had used FIFO for all of its inventories.

Real World Case 8–9
Effects of inventory valuation methods; Whole Foods Market
● LO8–4, LO8–5, LO8–7

Real World Financials

EDGAR, the Electronic Data Gathering, Analysis, and Retrieval system, performs automated collection, validation, indexing, and forwarding of submission by companies and others who are required by law to file forms with the U.S. Securities and Exchange Commission (SEC). All publicly traded domestic companies use EDGAR to make the majority of their filings. (Some foreign companies file voluntarily.) Form 10-K, which includes the annual report, is required to be filed on EDGAR. The SEC makes this information available on the Internet.

Required:

1. Access EDGAR on the Internet. The web address is **www.sec.gov**.
2. Search for **Whole Foods Market, Inc.** Access the 10-K filing for the most recent fiscal year. Search or scroll to find the financial statements and related notes.
3. Answer the following questions related to the company's inventories:
   a. What method(s) does the company use to value its inventories?
   b. Calculate what cost of sales would have been for the year if the company had used FIFO to value its inventories.
   c. Calculate inventory turnover for the year using the reported numbers.

Communication Case 8–10
Dollar-value LIFO method
● LO8–8

Maxi Corporation uses the unit LIFO inventory method. The costs of the company's products have been steadily rising since the company began operations in 2006 and cost increases are expected to continue. The chief financial officer of the company would like to continue using LIFO because of its tax advantages. However, the controller, Sally Hamel, would like to reduce the recordkeeping costs of LIFO that have steadily increased over the years as new products have been added to the company's product line. Sally suggested the use of the dollar-value LIFO method. The chief financial officer has asked Sally to describe the dollar-value LIFO procedure.

Required:
Describe the dollar-value LIFO procedure.

Research Case 8–11
FASB codification; locate and extract relevant information and authoritative support for a financial reporting issue; product financing arrangement
● LO8–2, LO8–3

You were recently hired to work in the controller's office of the Balboa Lumber Company. Your boss, Alfred Eagleton, took you to lunch during your first week and asked a favor. "Things have been a little slow lately, and we need to borrow a little cash to tide us over. Our inventory has been building up and the CFO wants to pledge the inventory as collateral for a short-term loan. But I have a better idea." Mr. Eagleton went on to describe his plan. "On July 1, 2016, the first day of the company's third quarter, we will sell $100,000 of inventory to the Harbaugh Corporation for $160,000. Harbaugh will pay us immediately and then we will agree to repurchase the merchandise in two months for $164,000. The $4,000 is Harbaugh's fee for holding the inventory and for providing financing. I already checked with Harbaugh's controller and he has agreed to the arrangement. Not only will we obtain the financing we need, but the third quarter's before-tax profits will be increased by $56,000, the gross profit on the sale less the $4,000 fee. Go research the issue and make sure we would not be violating any specific accounting standards related to product financing arrangements."

Required:
1. Obtain the relevant authoritative literature on product financing arrangements using the *FASB Accounting Standards Codification*. You might gain access at the FASB website (asc.fasb.org). What is the specific citation that provides guidance for determining whether an arrangement involving the sale of inventory is "in substance" a financing arrangement?
2. What is the specific citation that addresses the recognition of a product financing arrangement?
3. Determine the appropriate treatment of product financing arrangements like the one proposed by Mr. Eagleton.
4. Prepare the journal entry for Balboa Lumber to record the "sale" of the inventory and subsequent repurchase.

Analysis Case 8–12
Compare inventory management using ratios; Kohl's and Dillards
● LO8–7

The table below contains selected financial information included in the 2014 financial statements of Kohl's Corporation, and Dillards, Inc., two companies in the department store industry.

	($ in millions)			
	Kohl's Corp.		Dillards, Inc.	
	2014	2013	2014	2013
Balance sheet:				
Inventories	$ 3,874	$3,748	$1,345	$1,295
Income statement—2014:				
Net sales	$19,031		$6,532	
Cost of goods sold	12,087		4,224	

Required:
1. Calculate the 2014 gross profit ratio, inventory turnover ratio, and average days in inventory for both companies. Evaluate the management of each company's investment in inventory.
2. Obtain annual reports from three corporations in an industry other than department stores and compare the management of each company's investment in inventory.

Note: You can obtain copies of annual reports from your library, from friends who are shareholders, from the investor relations department of the corporations, from a friendly stockbroker, or from EDGAR (Electronic Data Gathering, Analysis, and Retrieval) on the Internet (www.sec.gov).

Analysis Case 8–13
Costs included in inventory; inventory cost flow methods; ratio analysis
● LO8–3, LO8–4, LO8–7

PetSmart

Refer to the financial statements and related disclosure notes of PetSmart in Appendix B located at the back of the text.

Required:
1. What inventory method(s) does PetSmart use to value its inventories?
2. In addition to the purchase price, what additional expenditures does the company include in the initial cost of merchandise?
3. Calculate the gross profit ratio and the inventory turnover ratio for the fiscal year ended February 2, 2014. Compare PetSmart's ratios with the industry averages of 41% and 7.7 times.

Air France–KLM Case

AIRFRANCE / KLM

● LO8–9

IFRS

Air France–KLM (AF), a Franco-Dutch company, prepares its financial statements according to International Financial Reporting Standards. AF's financial statements and disclosure notes for the year ended December 31, 2013, are provided with all new textbooks. This material also is available at **www.airfranceklm-finance.com**.

Required:

What method does the company use to value its inventory? What other alternatives are available under IFRS? Under U.S. GAAP?

CPA Simulation 8–1

Johnson Company

Physical quantities and costs included in inventory.

KAPLAN CPA REVIEW

Test your knowledge of the concepts discussed in this chapter, practice critical professional skills necessary for career success, and prepare for the computer-based CPA exam by accessing our CPA simulations in the Connect library.

The Johnson Company simulation tests your knowledge of the physical quantities and costs that should be included in inventory.

CHAPTER

9

Inventories: Additional Issues

OVERVIEW

We covered most of the principal measurement and reporting issues involving the asset inventory and the corresponding expense cost of goods sold in the previous chapter. In this chapter we complete our discussion of inventory measurement by explaining that inventories are valued at the lower of cost and net realizable value. In addition, we investigate inventory estimation techniques, methods of simplifying LIFO, changes in inventory method, and inventory errors.

LEARNING OBJECTIVES

After studying this chapter, you should be able to:

- **LO9–1** Understand and apply the lower of cost and net realizable value rule used to value inventories. (*p. 479*)
- **LO9–2** Estimate ending inventory and cost of goods sold using the gross profit method. (*p. 484*)
- **LO9–3** Estimate ending inventory and cost of goods sold using the retail inventory method, applying the various cost flow methods. (*p. 486*)
- **LO9–4** Explain how the retail inventory method can be made to approximate the lower of cost and net realizable value rule. (*p. 489*)
- **LO9–5** Determine ending inventory using the dollar-value LIFO retail inventory method. (*p. 494*)
- **LO9–6** Explain the appropriate accounting treatment required when a change in inventory method is made. (*p. 497*)
- **LO9–7** Explain the appropriate accounting treatment required when an inventory error is discovered. (*p. 500*)
- **LO9–8** Discuss the primary differences between U.S. GAAP and IFRS with respect to the lower of cost and net realizable value rule for valuing inventory. (*p. 482*)

FINANCIAL REPORTING CASE

Does It Count?

Today you drove over to **Sears** to pick up a few items. Yesterday, your accounting professor had discussed inventory measurement issues and the different methods (FIFO, LIFO, and average) used by companies to determine ending inventory and cost of goods sold. You can't imagine actually counting the inventory in all of the Sears stores around the country. "There must be some way Sears can avoid counting all of that inventory every time they want to produce financial statements," you tell your dog when you get home. "I think I'll go check their financial statements on the Internet to see what kind of inventory method they use." You find the following in the summary of significant accounting policies included in Sears's most recent financial statements:

Merchandise Inventories (in part):

For Kmart and Sears Domestic, cost is primarily determined using the retail inventory method (RIM). Approximately 47% of consolidated merchandise inventories are valued using LIFO. To estimate the effects of inflation on inventories, we utilize external price indices determined by an outside source, the Bureau of Labor Statistics.

QUESTIONS

By the time you finish this chapter, you should be able to respond appropriately to the questions posed in this case. Compare your response to the solution provided at the end of the chapter.

1. How does Sears avoid counting all its inventory every time it produces financial statements? *(p. 494)*
2. What are external price indices used for? *(p. 494)*

Reporting—Lower of Cost and Net Realizable Value

PART A

● LO9–1

In the previous chapter you learned that several methods are available for a company to determine the *cost* of inventory at the end of a period and the corresponding cost of goods sold for the period. However, valuing inventory requires an additional important step because GAAP requires companies to report inventory at the **lower of cost and net realizable value**.

Inventory is valued at the lower of cost and net realizable value.

The utility, or benefit, a company receives from inventory results from the ultimate sale of that inventory. So deterioration, obsolescence, changes in price levels, or any situation that might compromise the inventory's salability impairs that utility. That's the reason for the lower of cost and net realizable value approach to valuing inventory. It avoids reporting inventory at an amount greater than the benefits it can provide. Reporting inventories this way causes losses to be recognized in the period the value of inventory declines below its cost rather than in the period in which the goods ultimately are sold.

On the other hand, critics of this approach contend that the method causes losses to be recognized that haven't actually occurred. Others maintain that it introduces needless inconsistency in order to be conservative. Inconsistency is created because decreases in value are recognized as they occur, but not increases. So, why not record increases as well? The practice of recognizing decreases but not increases is consistent with conservatism, but a more compelling reason not to recognize increases is rooted in our revenue recognition guidance. Recognizing increases in the value of inventory prior to sale would, in most cases, result in premature revenue recognition. Let's say that merchandise costing $100 now has a net realizable value of $150. Recognizing a gain for the increase in value would increase pretax income by $50. This is equivalent to recognizing revenue of $150, cost of goods sold of $100, and gross profit of $50. The effect is to increase pretax income in a period prior to sale of the product.

Until recently, U.S. GAAP required inventory to be valued at the *lower of cost or market (LCM)*. "Market" was defined as replacement cost, except that market could not exceed net realizable value and could not be less than net realizable value reduced by a normal profit margin. The LCM rule was intended as a guide rather than a literal rule. In practice, companies frequently defined market as net realizable value. This is a number that usually is easier to determine than replacement cost.

In a move to bring GAAP more in line with practice, we now value inventory at the *lower of cost and net realizable value*.[1] This change is part of what the FASB is calling its "simplification initiative", an effort to target parts of GAAP that are difficult to apply. Another advantage is the convergence of U.S. GAAP with international accounting standards in this area, because IFRS also values inventory at the lower of cost and net realizable value.

Determining Net Realizable Value

Net realizable value (NRV) is selling price less any costs of completion, disposal, and transportation.

What is net realizable value (NRV)? It is the estimated selling price of the product in the ordinary course of business reduced by reasonably predictable costs of completion, disposal, and transportation. These costs could include things such as sales commissions and shipping costs. In other words, it's the *net* amount a company expects to *realize* from the sale of the inventory. Companies often estimate these "costs to sell" by applying a predetermined percentage to the selling price. For example, if the selling price of Product A is $10 per unit, and the company estimates that sales commissions and shipping costs average approximately 10% of selling price, NRV would be $9 ($10 − [10% × $10]).

Let's see how the lower of cost and NRV approach is applied in Illustration 9–1.

Illustration 9–1

Lower of Cost and Net Realizable Value (NRV)

The Collins Company has five inventory items on hand at the end of 2016. The year-end unit costs (determined by applying the average cost method), current unit selling prices, and estimated costs to sell for each of the items are presented below:

Item	Cost	Selling Price	Estimated Costs To Sell
A	$ 50	$100	$15
B	100	120	30
C	80	85	10
D	90	100	15
E	95	120	24

For each item we first compute NRV, selling price less estimated costs to sell, and then compare it with cost. The item is valued at the lower of these two amounts.

Item	Cost	NRV	Inventory Value
A	$ 50	$85*	$50
B	100	90	90
C	80	75	75
D	90	85	85
E	95	96	95

*$100 − 15

For items A and E, cost is lower than NRV. For each of the other items, NRV is lower than cost, requiring an adjustment to the book value, sometimes called carrying value or carrying amount, of the inventory. We discuss the adjustment procedure later in the chapter. First though, let's consider the various ways of applying the lower of cost and net realizable value rule.

[1]Our discussion here is based on an Exposure Draft (ED) issued by the FASB in July 2014. At the time this text went to print, a final Accounting Standards Update (ASU) had not yet been issued. It is unlikely that the ASU will differ from the ED.

Ethical Dilemma

The Hartley Paper Company, owned and operated by Bill Hartley, manufactures and sells different types of computer paper. The company has reported profits in the majority of years since the company's inception in 1972 and is projecting a profit in 2016 of $65,000, down from $96,000 in 2015.

Near the end of 2016, the company is in the process of applying for a bank loan. The loan proceeds will be used to replace manufacturing equipment necessary to modernize the manufacturing operation. In preparing the financial statements for the year, the chief accountant, Don Davis, mentioned to Bill Hartley that approximately $40,000 of paper inventory has become obsolete and should be written off as a loss in 2016. Bill is worried that the write-down would lower 2016 income to a level that might cause the bank to refuse the loan. Without the loan, it would be difficult for the company to compete. This could cause decreased future business and employees might have to be laid off. Bill is considering waiting until 2017 to write down the inventory. Don Davis is contemplating his responsibilities in this situation.

Applying Lower of Cost and Net Realizable Value

Lower of cost and net realizable value can be applied to individual inventory items, to logical categories of inventory, or to the entire inventory. A major product line can be considered a logical category of inventory. For income tax purposes, the rule must be applied on an individual item basis.

Lower of Cost and Net Realizable Value Application
Depending on the character and composition of the inventory, the rule of lower of cost and net realizable value may properly be applied either directly to each item or to the total of the inventory (or, in some cases, to the total of the components of each major category). The method shall be that which most clearly reflects periodic income.[2]

The lower of cost and net realizable value rule can be applied to individual inventory items, logical inventory categories, or the entire inventory.

Let's return to our illustration and assume the unit amounts pertain to 1,000 units of each inventory item. Also, let's say items A–B and items C–E are two collections of similar items that can be considered logical categories of inventory. Illustration 9–2 demonstrates the lower of cost and net realizable value approach with each of the three possible applications.

Illustration 9–2
Lower of Cost and Net Realizable Value-Application at Different Levels of Aggregation

			Lower of Cost and NRV		
Item	**Cost**	**Net Realizable Value**	**By Individual Items**	**By Product Line**	**By Total Inventory**
A	$ 50,000	$ 85,000	$ 50,000		
B	100,000	90,000	90,000		
Total A + B	$150,000	$175,000		$150,000	
C	$ 80,000	$ 75,000	75,000		
D	90,000	85,000	85,000		
E	95,000	96,000	95,000		
Total C, D, & E	$265,000	$256,000		256,000	
Total	$415,000	$431,000	$395,000	$406,000	$415,000

The final inventory value is different for each of the three applications. The inventory value is $395,000 if applied to each item, $406,000 if it is applied to product line categories, and $415,000 if applied to the entire inventory. Applying the lower of cost and net realizable value rule to groups of inventory items usually will cause a higher inventory valuation than if applied on an item-by-item basis because group application permits decreases in the net realizable value of some items to be offset by increases in others. Each approach is acceptable but should be applied consistently from one period to another.

[2]FASB ASC 330–10–35–8: Inventory—Overall—Subsequent Measurement.

Adjusting Cost to Net Realizable Value

If inventory write-downs are commonplace for a company, losses usually are included in cost of goods sold. However, when a write-down is substantial and unusual, GAAP requires that the loss be expressly disclosed. This could be accomplished with a disclosure note or, instead of including the loss in cost of goods sold, by reporting the loss in a separate line in the income statement, usually among operating expenses. Even with separate line item reporting, a disclosure note still would be appropriate. The journal entries for these two alternatives are as follows:

Cost of goods sold	xx		or	Loss on write-down of inventory.........	xx	
Inventory*		xx		Inventory*		xx

*Or, inventory can be reduced indirectly with a credit to an allowance or reserve account.

Regardless of which approach we use to report the write-down, the reduced inventory value becomes the new cost basis for subsequent reporting, and if the inventory value later recovers prior to its sale, we do not write it back up.[3]

International Financial Reporting Standards

Lower of cost and net realizable value. You just learned that in the United States inventory is valued at the lower of cost and net realizable value. International standards also value inventories this way.

LO9–8 However, there are some differences between U.S. GAAP and IFRS in this area. *IAS No. 2*[4] specifies that if circumstances indicate that an inventory write-down is no longer appropriate, it must be reversed. Reversals are not permitted under U.S. GAAP.

Under U.S. GAAP, the lower of cost and net realizable value rule can be applied to individual items, logical inventory categories, or the entire inventory. Using the international standard, the assessment usually is applied to individual items, although using logical inventory categories is allowed under certain circumstances.

Real World Financials

Siemens AG, a German electronics and electrical engineering company, prepares its financial statements according to IFRS. The following disclosure note illustrates the valuation of inventory at the lower of cost and net realizable value.

Inventories (in part)

Inventory is valued at the lower of acquisition or production cost and net realizable value, cost being generally determined on the basis of an average or first-in, first-out method.

Concept Review Exercise

LOWER OF COST AND NET REALIZABLE VALUE

The Strand Company sells four products that can be grouped into two major categories. Information necessary to apply the lower of cost and net realizable value rule at the end of 2016 for each of the four products is presented below. Commissions and transportation costs average 10% of selling price.

Product	Cost	Selling Price
101	$120,000	$160,000
102	175,000	180,000
201	160,000	160,000
202	45,000	60,000

[3]The SEC, in *Staff Accounting Bulletin* No. 100, "Restructuring and Impairment Charges" (Washington, D.C.: SEC, November, 1999), paragraph B.B., [FASB ASC 330–10–S35–1: SAB Topic 5.BB], reaffirmed the provisions of GAAP literature on this issue. For interim reporting purposes, however, recoveries of losses on the same inventory in subsequent interim periods of the same fiscal year through market price recoveries should be recognized as gains in the later interim period, not to exceed the previously recognized losses.

[4]"Inventories," *International Accounting Standard No. 2* (IASCF), as amended effective January 1, 2014.

Products 101 and 102 are in category A, and products 201 and 202 are in category B.

Required:

1. Determine the inventory value for each of the four products according to the lower of cost and net realizable value approach.
2. Determine the amount of the loss from write-down of inventory that would be required, applying the lower of cost and net realizable value approach to:
   a. Individual items
   b. Major categories
   c. The entire inventory

Solution:

1. Determine the inventory value for each of the four products according to the lower of cost and net realizable value rule.

Product	(1) Cost	(2) NRV (Selling Price Less Selling Costs)	Inventory Value [Lower of (1) and (2)]
101	$120,000	$144,000*	$120,000
102	175,000	162,000	162,000
201	160,000	144,000	144,000
202	45,000	54,000	45,000

*$160,000 − (10% × $160,000)

2. Determine the amount of the loss from write-down of inventory that would be required, applying the lower of cost and net realizable value rule.

			Lower of Cost and NRV		
Product	Cost	NRV	By Individual Products	By Category	By Total Inventory
101	$120,000	$144,000	$120,000		
102	175,000	162,000	162,000		
Total 101 + 102	$295,000	$306,000		$295,000	
201	$160,000	$144,000	144,000		
202	45,000	54,000	45,000		
Total 201 + 202	$205,000	198,000		198,000	
Total	$500,000	$504,000	$471,000	$493,000	$500,000

The net realizable values for both the individual product and category applications are lower than cost so inventory write-downs are needed. On the other hand, cost is lower than net realizable value at the entire inventory level of aggregation.

Amount of loss from write-down using individual items:

$500,000 − 471,000 = **$29,000**

Amount of loss from write-down using categories:

$500,000 − 493,000 = **$7,000**

Amount of loss from write-down using entire inventory:

$500,000 < 504,000 so **no loss**

Inventory Estimation Techniques

PART B

The Southern Wholesale Company distributes approximately 100 products throughout the state of Mississippi. Southern uses a periodic inventory system and takes a physical count of inventory once a year at the end of the year. A recent fire destroyed the entire inventory in one of Southern's warehouses. How can the company determine the dollar amount of inventory destroyed when submitting an insurance claim to obtain reimbursement for the loss?

Home Improvement Stores, Inc., sells over 1,000 different products to customers in each of its 17 retail stores. The company uses a periodic inventory system and takes a physical count of inventory once a year at its fiscal year-end. Home Improvement's bank has asked for monthly financial statements as a condition attached to a recent loan. Can the company avoid the costly procedure of counting inventory at the end of each month to determine ending inventory and cost of goods sold?

These are just two examples of situations when it is either impossible or infeasible to determine the dollar amount of ending inventory by taking a count of the physical quantity of inventory on hand at the end of a period. Fortunately, companies can estimate inventory in these situations by either the gross profit method or the retail inventory method.

The Gross Profit Method

The **gross profit method**, also known as the **gross margin method**, is useful in situations where estimates of inventory are desirable. The technique is valuable in a variety of situations:

LO9–2

1. In determining the cost of inventory that has been lost, destroyed, or stolen.
2. In estimating inventory and cost of goods sold for interim reports, avoiding the expense of a physical inventory count.
3. In auditors' testing of the overall reasonableness of inventory amounts reported by clients.
4. In budgeting and forecasting.

The *gross profit method* is not acceptable for the preparation of annual financial statements.

However, the gross profit method provides only an approximation of inventory and is not acceptable according to generally accepted accounting principles for annual financial statements.

The technique relies on a relationship you learned in the previous chapter—ending inventory and cost of goods sold always equal the cost of goods available for sale. Even when inventory is unknown, we can estimate it because accounting records usually indicate the cost of goods available for sale (beginning inventory plus net purchases), and the cost of goods sold can be estimated from available information. So by subtracting the cost of goods sold estimate from the cost of goods available for sale, we obtain an estimate of ending inventory. Let's compare that with the way inventory and cost of goods sold normally are determined.

Usually, in a periodic inventory system, ending inventory is known from a physical count and cost of goods sold is *derived* as follows:

Beginning inventory	(from the accounting records)
Plus: Net purchases	(from the accounting records)
Goods available for sale	
Less: Ending inventory	(from a physical count)
Cost of goods sold	

However, when using the gross profit method, the ending inventory is *not* known. Instead, the amount of sales is known—from which we can estimate the cost of goods sold—and ending inventory is the amount calculated.

Beginning inventory	(from the accounting records)
Plus: Net purchases	(from the accounting records)
Goods available for sale	
Less: Cost of goods sold	(estimated)
Ending inventory	(estimated)

So, a first step in estimating inventory is to estimate cost of goods sold. This estimate relies on the historical relationship among (a) net sales, (b) cost of goods sold, and (c) gross profit. Gross profit, you will recall, is simply net sales minus cost of goods sold. So, if we know what net sales are, and if we know what percentage of net sales the gross profit is, we can fairly accurately estimate cost of goods sold. Companies often sell products that have similar gross profit ratios. As a result, accounting records usually provide the information necessary to estimate the cost of ending inventory, even when a physical count is impractical. Let's use the gross profit method to solve the problem of Southern Wholesale Company introduced earlier in the chapter. Suppose the company began 2016 with inventory of $600,000, and on March 17 a warehouse fire destroyed the entire inventory. Company records indicate net purchases of $1,500,000 and net sales of $2,000,000 prior to the fire. The gross profit ratio in each of the previous three years has been very close to 40%. Illustration 9–3 shows how Southern can estimate the cost of the inventory destroyed for its insurance claim.

Illustration 9–3
Gross Profit Method

Beginning inventory (from records)		$ 600,000
Plus: Net purchases (from records)		1,500,000
Goods available for sale		2,100,000
Less: Cost of goods sold:		
Net sales	$2,000,000	
Less: Estimated gross profit of 40%	(800,000)	
Estimated cost of goods sold*		(1,200,000)
Estimated ending inventory		$ 900,000

*Alternatively, cost of goods sold can be calculated as $2,000,000 × (1 − .40) = $1,200,000.

A Word of Caution

The key to obtaining good estimates is the reliability of the gross profit ratio.

The gross profit method provides only an estimate. The key to obtaining good estimates is the reliability of the gross profit ratio. The ratio usually is estimated from relationships between sales and cost of goods sold. However, the current relationship may differ from the past. In that case, all available information should be used to make necessary adjustments. For example, the company may have made changes in the markup percentage of some of its products. Very often different products have different markups. In these situations, a blanket ratio should not be applied across the board. The accuracy of the estimate can be improved by grouping inventory into pools of products that have similar gross profit relationships rather than using one gross profit ratio for the entire inventory.

The company's cost flow assumption should be implicitly considered when estimating the gross profit ratio. For example, if LIFO is used and the relationship between cost and selling price has changed for recent acquisitions, this would suggest a ratio different from one where the average cost method was used. Another difficulty with the gross profit method is that it does not explicitly consider possible theft or spoilage of inventory. The method assumes that if the inventory was not sold, then it must be on hand at the end of the period. Suspected theft or spoilage would require an adjustment to estimates obtained using the gross profit method.

Additional Consideration

The gross profit ratio is, by definition, a percentage of sales. Sometimes, though, the gross profit is stated as a percentage of cost instead. In that case, it is referred to as the markup on cost. For instance, a 66% markup on cost is equivalent to a gross profit ratio of 40%. Here's why:

A gross profit ratio of 40% can be formulated as:

Sales	=	Cost	+	Gross profit
100%	=	60%	+	40%

Now, expressing gross profit as a percentage of cost we get:

Gross profit %	÷	Cost %	=	Gross profit as a % of cost
40%	÷	60%	=	66⅔%

(continued)

(concluded)

Conversely, gross profit as a percentage of cost can be converted to gross profit as a percentage of sales (the gross profit ratio) as follows:

$$\text{Gross profit as a \% of sales} = \frac{\text{Gross profit as a \% of cost}}{1 + \text{Gross profit as a \% of cost}}$$

$$\frac{66\frac{2}{3}\%}{1 + 66\frac{2}{3}\%} = 40\%$$

Be careful to note which way the percentage is being stated. If stated as a markup on cost, it can be converted to the gross profit ratio, and the gross profit method can be applied the usual way.

The Retail Inventory Method

The retail inventory method is similar to the gross profit method in that it relies on the relationship between cost and selling price to estimate ending inventory and cost of goods sold.

● LO9–3

As the name implies, the method is used by many retail companies such as **Target**, **Walmart**, **Sears Holding Corporation**, **J.C. Penney**, and **Macy's**. Certain retailers like auto dealers and jewelry stores, whose inventory consists of few, high-priced items, can economically use the specific identification inventory method. However, high-volume retailers selling many different items at low unit prices find the retail inventory method ideal, although with the advent of bar coding on more and more retail merchandise, use of the method is declining. Similar to the gross profit method, its principal benefit is that a physical count of inventory is not required to estimate ending inventory and cost of goods sold.

The *retail inventory method* uses the *cost-to-retail percentage* based on a current relationship between cost and selling price.

The retail method tends to provide a more accurate estimate than the gross profit method because it's based on the current **cost-to-retail percentage** rather than on a historical gross profit ratio.

The increased reliability in the estimate of the cost percentage is achieved by comparing cost of goods available for sale with goods available for sale *at current selling prices.* So, to use the technique, a company must maintain records of inventory and purchases not only at cost, but also at current selling price. We refer to this as *retail information.* In its simplest form, the retail inventory method estimates the amount of ending inventory (at retail) by subtracting sales (at retail) from goods available for sale (at retail). This estimated ending inventory at retail is then converted to cost by multiplying it by the cost-to-retail percentage. This ratio is found by dividing goods available for sale at *cost* by goods available for sale at *retail.*

Let's use the retail inventory method to solve the problem of the Home Improvement Store introduced earlier in the chapter. Suppose the company's bank has asked for monthly financial statements as a condition attached to a loan dated May 31, 2016. To avoid a physical count of inventory, the company intends to use the retail inventory method to estimate ending inventory and cost of goods sold for the month of June. Using data available in its accounting records, Illustration 9–4 shows how Home Improvement can estimate ending inventory and cost of goods sold for June.

The retail inventory method can be used for financial reporting and income tax purposes.

Unlike the gross profit method, the retail inventory method is acceptable for external financial reporting if the results of applying the method are sufficiently close to what would have been achieved using a more rigorous determination of the cost of ending inventory. Also, it's allowed by the Internal Revenue Service as a method that can be used to determine cost of goods sold for income tax purposes.[5] Another advantage of the method is that different cost flow methods can be explicitly incorporated into the estimation technique. In other words, we can modify the application of the method to estimate ending inventory and cost of goods sold using FIFO, LIFO, or average cost. Just a couple of retail method companies

[5]The retail method is acceptable for external reporting and for tax purposes because it tends to provide a better estimate than the gross profit method. The retail method uses a current cost-to-retail percentage rather than a historical gross profit ratio.

	Cost	Retail
Beginning inventory	$ 60,000	$100,000
Plus: Net purchases	287,200	460,000
Goods available for sale	$347,200	$560,000
Cost-to-retail percentage: $\frac{\$347,200}{\$560,000} = 62\%$		
Less: Net sales		(400,000)
Estimated ending inventory at retail		$160,000
Estimated ending inventory at cost (62% × $160,000)	(99,200)	
Estimated cost of goods sold—goods available for sale (at cost) minus ending inventory (at cost) equals cost of goods sold	$248,000	

Illustration 9–4
Retail Method

Goods available for sale (at retail) minus net sales equals estimated ending inventory (at retail).

that use FIFO are **Family Dollar Stores** and **Home Depot**; those using LIFO include **Dillards**, **Target**, and **The Bon-Ton Stores**; and a few average cost users are **Pacific Sunwear of California**, **TJX Companies**, and **Ingles Markets**.

As shown in Illustration 9–5, **American Eagle Outfitters** uses the retail method in concert with average cost to value its inventory.

Summary of Significant Accounting Policies (in part)
Merchandise Inventory
Merchandise inventory is valued at the lower of average cost and net realizable value, utilizing the retail method.

Illustration 9–5
Inventory Method Disclosure—American Eagle Outfitters

Real World Financials

Later in the chapter we illustrate average cost including variations to approximate the lower of cost and net realizable value (conventional retail method) and LIFO. We do not illustrate the FIFO method because it is used infrequently in practice.

Like the gross profit method, the retail inventory method also can be used to estimate the cost of inventory lost, stolen, or destroyed; for testing the overall reasonableness of physical counts; in budgeting and forecasting as well as in generating information for interim financial statements. Even though the retail method provides fairly accurate estimates, a physical count of inventory usually is performed at least once a year to verify accuracy and detect spoilage, theft, and other irregularities.[6]

Retail Terminology

Our example above is simplified in that we implicitly assumed that the selling prices of beginning inventory and of merchandise purchased did not change from date of acquisition to the end of the period. This frequently is an unrealistic assumption. The terms in Illustration 9–6 are associated with changing retail prices of merchandise inventory.

Changes in the selling prices must be included in the determination of ending inventory at retail.

Initial markup	Original amount of markup from cost to selling price.
Additional markup	Increase in selling price subsequent to initial markup.
Markup cancellation	Elimination of an additional markup.
Markdown	Reduction in selling price below the original selling price.
Markdown cancellation	Elimination of a markdown.

Illustration 9–6
Terminology Used in Applying the Retail Method

[6]The retail inventory method also is allowable under IFRS. "Inventories," International Accounting Standard No. 2 (IASCF), as amended effective January 1, 2014, par. 22.

To illustrate, assume that a product purchased for $6 is initially marked up $4, from $6 to $10, the original selling price. If the selling price is subsequently increased to $12, the additional markup is $2. If the selling price is then subsequently decreased to **$10.50**, the markup cancellation is $1.50. We refer to the net effect of the additional changes ($2.00 − 1.50 = $.50) as the **net markup**. Illustration 9–7A depicts these events.

Illustration 9–7A
Retail Inventory Method Terminology

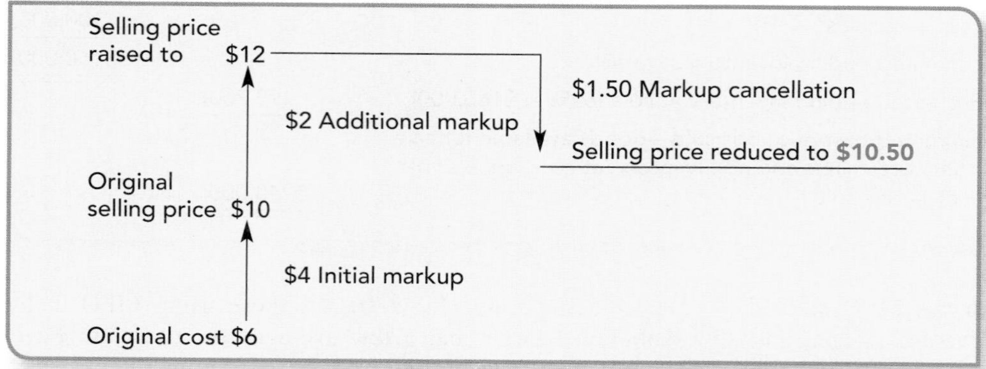

Now let's say the selling price of the product purchased for $6 and initially marked up to $10, is reduced to $7. The markdown is $3. If the selling price is later increased to **$8**, the markdown cancellation is $1. The net effect of the change ($3 − 1 = $2) is the **net markdown**. Illustration 9–7B depicts this possibility.

Illustration 9–7B
Retail Inventory Method Terminology

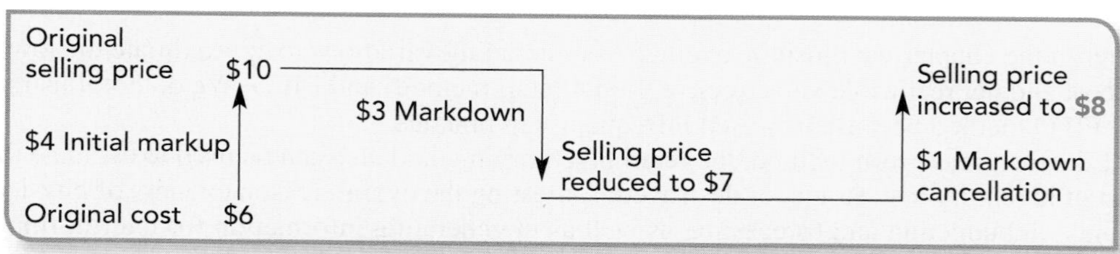

***Net markups* and *net markdowns* are included in the retail column to determine ending inventory at retail.**

When applying the retail inventory method, *net markups and net markdowns must be included in the determination of ending inventory at retail.* We now continue our illustration of the retail inventory method, but expand it to incorporate markups and markdowns as well as to approximate cost by each of the alternative inventory cost flow methods.

Cost Flow Methods

Let's continue the Home Improvement Stores example into July with Illustration 9–8 and see how the retail inventory method can be used to approximate different cost flow assumptions. We'll also use the same illustration to see how the retail method can be modified to approximate lower of cost and net realizable value.

To approximate average cost, the cost-to-retail percentage is determined for *all* goods available for sale.

APPROXIMATING AVERAGE COST. Recall that the average cost method assumes that cost of goods sold and ending inventory each consist of a *mixture* of all the goods available for sale. So when we use the retail method to approximate average cost, the cost-to-retail percentage should be based on the weighted averages of the costs and retail amounts for *all* goods available for sale. This is achieved by calculating the cost-to-retail percentage by dividing the total cost of goods available for sale by total goods available for sale at

Illustration 9–8
The Retail Inventory Method—Various Cost Flow Methods

Home Improvement Stores, Inc., uses a periodic inventory system and the retail inventory method to estimate ending inventory and cost of goods sold. The following data are available from the company's records for the month of July 2016:

	Cost	Retail
Beginning inventory	$ 99,200	$160,000
Net purchases	305,280[1]	470,000[2]
Net markups		10,000
Net markdowns		8,000
Net sales		434,000[3]

[1]Purchases at cost less returns, plus freight-in.
[2]Original selling price of purchased goods less returns at retail.
[3]Gross sales less returns.

retail. When this average percentage is applied to ending inventory at retail, we get an estimate of ending inventory at average cost. If you look back to our simplified example for the month of June, you'll notice that we used this approach there. So, our ending inventory and cost of goods sold estimates for June were estimates of average cost.[7]

Now, we use the retail inventory method to approximate average costs for July. Notice in Illustration 9–9 that both markups and markdowns are included in the determination of goods available for sale at retail.

Illustration 9–9
Retail Method—Average Cost

	Cost	Retail
Beginning inventory	$ 99,200	$160,000
Plus: Net purchases	305,280	470,000
Net markups		10,000
Less: Net markdowns		(8,000)
Goods available for sale	404,480	632,000
Cost-to-retail percentage: $\frac{\$404,480}{\$632,000} = 64\%$		
Less: Net sales		(434,000)
Estimated ending inventory at retail		$198,000
Estimated ending inventory at cost (64% × $198,000)	(126,720)	
Estimated cost of goods sold	$277,760	

● LO9–4

APPROXIMATING AVERAGE LOWER OF COST AND NRV—THE CONVENTIONAL RETAIL METHOD. Recall from our discussion earlier in the chapter that, however costs are determined, inventory should be reported in the balance sheet at the lower of cost and net realizable value. Fortunately, we can apply the retail inventory method in such a way that the lower of average cost and net realizable value is approximated. This method often is referred to as the **conventional retail method**. We apply the method by *excluding markdowns from the calculation of the cost-to-retail percentage.* Markdowns still are subtracted in the retail column but only after the percentage is calculated. To approximate lower of average cost and net realizable value, the retail method is modified as shown in Illustration 9–10.

To approximate the lower of average cost and net realizable value, markdowns are not included in the calculation of the cost-to-retail percentage.

Notice that by not subtracting net markdowns from the denominator, the cost-to-retail percentage is lower than it was previously (63.2% versus 64%). This always will be the case when markdowns exist. As a result, the cost approximation of ending inventory always will be less when markdowns exist. To understand why this lower amount approximates the

[7]We also implicitly assumed no net markups or markdowns.

Illustration 9–10
Retail Method—Conventional

	Cost	Retail
Beginning inventory	$ 99,200	$160,000
Plus: Net purchases	305,280	470,000
Net markups		10,000
		640,000
Cost-to-retail percentage: $\frac{\$404,480}{\$640,000} = 63.2\%$		
Less: Net markdowns		(8,000)
Goods available for sale	404,480	632,000
Less: Net sales		(434,000)
Estimated ending inventory at retail		$198,000
Estimated ending inventory at cost (63.2% × $198,000)	(125,136)	
Estimated cost of goods sold	$279,344	

The logic for using this approximation is that a markdown is evidence of a reduction in the utility of inventory.

lower of average cost and net realizable value, we need to realize that markdowns usually occur when obsolescence, spoilage, overstocking, price declines, or competition has lessened the utility of the merchandise. To recognize this decline in utility in the period it occurs, we exclude net markdowns from the calculation of the cost-to-retail percentage. It should be emphasized that this approach provides only an *approximation* of what ending inventory might be as opposed to applying the lower of cost and net realizable value rule in the more exact way described earlier in the chapter.

Also notice that the ending inventory at retail is the same using both approaches (**$198,000**). This will be the case regardless of the cost flow method used because in all approaches this amount reflects the ending inventory at current retail prices.

The conventional retail variation is not generally used in combination with LIFO. This does not mean that a company using LIFO ignores the lower of cost and net realizable value rule. Any obsolete or slow-moving inventory that has not been marked down by year-end can be written down to net realizable value after the estimation of inventory using the retail method. This is usually not a significant problem. If prices are rising, LIFO ending inventory includes old lower priced items whose costs are likely to be lower than current net realizable value. The conventional retail variation could be applied to the FIFO method.

THE LIFO RETAIL METHOD. The last-in, first-out (LIFO) method assumes that units sold are those most recently acquired. When there's a net increase in inventory quantity during a period, the use of LIFO results in ending inventory that includes the beginning inventory as well as one or more additional layers added during the period. When there's a net decrease in inventory quantity, LIFO layer(s) are liquidated. In applying LIFO to the retail method in the simplest way, we assume that the retail prices of goods remained stable during the period. This assumption, which is relaxed later in the chapter, allows us to look at the beginning and ending inventory in dollars to determine if inventory quantity has increased or decreased.

If inventory at retail increases during the year, a new layer is added.

We'll use the numbers from our previous example to illustrate using the retail method to approximate LIFO so we can compare the results with those of the conventional retail method. Recall that beginning inventory at retail is $160,000 and ending inventory at retail is $198,000. If we assume stable retail prices, inventory quantity must have increased during the year. This means ending inventory includes the beginning inventory layer of $160,000 ($99,200 at cost) as well as some additional merchandise purchased during the period. To estimate total ending inventory at LIFO cost, we also need to determine the inventory layer added during the period. When using the LIFO retail method, we assume no more than one inventory layer is added per year if inventory increases.[8] Each layer will carry its own cost-to-retail percentage.

Illustration 9–11 shows how Home Improvement Stores would estimate total ending inventory and cost of goods sold for the period using the LIFO retail method. The beginning inventory layer carries a cost-to-retail percentage of **62%** ($99,200 ÷ $160,000). The layer

[8]Of course, any number of layers at different costs can actually be added through the years. When using the regular LIFO method, rather than LIFO retail, we would keep track of each of those layers.

Illustration 9–11
LIFO Retail Method

	Cost	Retail
Beginning inventory	$ 99,200	$160,000
Plus: Net purchases	305,280	470,000
Net markups		10,000
Less: Net markdowns		(8,000)
Goods available for sale (excluding beginning inventory)	305,280	472,000
Goods available for sale (including beginning inventory)	404,480	632,000

Beginning inventory cost-to-retail percentage: $\frac{\$99,200}{\$160,000} = 62\%$

July cost-to-retail percentage: $\frac{\$305,280}{\$472,000} = 64.68\%$

		Retail
Less: Net sales		(434,000)
Estimated ending inventory at retail		$198,000

Estimated ending inventory at cost:

	Retail	Cost	
Beginning inventory	$160,000 × 62.00% =	$ 99,200	
Current period's layer	38,000 × 64.68% =	24,578	
Total	$ 198,000	$123,778	(123,778)
Estimated cost of goods sold			$280,702

Beginning inventory is excluded from the calculation of the cost-to-retail percentage.

Each layer has its own cost-to-retail percentage.

of inventory added during the period is $38,000 at retail, which is determined by subtracting beginning inventory at retail from ending inventory at retail ($198,000 − 160,000). This layer will be converted to cost by multiplying it by its own cost-to-retail percentage reflecting the *current* period's ratio of cost to retail amounts, in this case 64.68%.

The next period's (August's) beginning inventory will include the two distinct layers (June and July), each of which carries its own unique cost-to-retail percentage. Notice in the illustration that both net markups and net markdowns are included in the calculation of the current period's cost-to-retail percentage.

Other Issues Pertaining to the Retail Method

To focus on the key elements of the retail method, we've so far ignored some of the details of the retail process. Fundamental elements such as returns and allowances, discounts, freight, spoilage, and shortages can complicate the retail method.

Recall that net purchases is found by adding freight-in to purchases and subtracting both purchase returns and purchase discounts. When these components are considered separately in the retail method, purchase returns are deducted from purchases on both the cost and retail side (at different amounts) and freight-in is added only to the cost side in determining net purchases. If the gross method is used to record purchases, purchase discounts taken also are deducted in determining the cost of net purchases.

Likewise, net sales is determined by subtracting sales returns from sales. However, sales discounts are *not* subtracted because to do so would cause the inventory to be overstated. Sales discounts do not represent an adjustment in selling price but a financial incentive for customers to pay early. On the other hand, when sales are recorded net of employee discounts, the discounts are *added* to net sales before sales are deducted in the retail column.

If sales are recorded net of employee discounts, the discounts are added to sales.

For example, suppose an item of merchandise purchased for $6 is initially marked up to $10. Original selling price is therefore $10. When the item is sold, we deduct sales of $10 from the retail column. But if the item is sold to an employee for $7 (a $3 employee discount) and recorded as a $7 sale, the $3 employee discount must be added back to sales so the full $10 is deducted from goods available at retail to arrive at ending inventory at retail.

We also need to consider spoilage, breakage, and theft. So far we've assumed that by subtracting goods sold from goods available for sale, we find ending inventory. It's possible, though, that some of the goods available for sale were lost to such shortages and therefore do not remain in ending inventory.

Normal shortages are deducted in the retail column *after* the calculation of the cost-to-retail percentage.

To take these shortages into account when using the retail method, we deduct the retail value of inventory lost due to spoilage, breakage, or theft in the retail column. These losses are expected for most retail ventures so they are referred to as *normal shortages* (spoilage, breakage, etc.), and are deducted in the retail column *after* the calculation of the cost-to-retail percentage. Because these losses are anticipated, they are included implicitly in the determination of selling prices. Including normal spoilage in the calculation of the percentage would distort the normal relationship between cost and retail. *Abnormal shortages* should be deducted in both the cost and retail columns *before* the calculation of the cost-to-retail percentage. These losses are not anticipated and are not included in the determination of selling prices.

Abnormal shortages are deducted in both the cost and retail columns *before* the calculation of the cost-to-retail percentage.

We recap the treatment of special elements in the application of the retail method in Illustration 9–12 and illustrate the use of some of them in the concept review exercise that follows.

Illustration 9–12

Recap of Other Retail Method Elements

Element	Treatment
Before calculating the cost-to-retail percentage:	
Freight-in	*Added* in the cost column.
Purchase returns	*Deducted* in both the cost and retail columns.
Purchase discounts taken (if gross method used to record purchases)	*Deducted* in the cost column.
Abnormal shortages (spoilage, breakage, theft)	*Deducted* in both the cost and retail columns.
After calculating the cost-to-retail percentage:	
Normal shortages (spoilage, breakage, theft)	*Deducted* in the retail column.
Employee discounts (if sales recorded net of discounts)	*Added* to net sales.

Concept Review Exercise

RETAIL INVENTORY METHOD

The Henderson Company uses the retail inventory method to estimate ending inventory and cost of goods sold. The following data for 2016 are available in Henderson's accounting records:

	Cost	Retail
Beginning inventory	$ 8,000	$12,000
Purchases	68,000	98,000
Freight-in	3,200	
Purchase returns	3,000	4,200
Net markups		6,000
Net markdowns		2,400
Normal spoilage		1,800
Net sales		92,000

The company records sales net of employee discounts. These discounts for 2016 totaled $2,300.

Required:

1. Estimate Henderson's ending inventory and cost of goods sold for the year using the average cost method.
2. Estimate Henderson's ending inventory and cost of goods sold for the year using the conventional retail method.
3. Estimate Henderson's ending inventory and cost of goods sold for the year using the LIFO retail method.

Solution:

1. Estimate Henderson's ending inventory and cost of goods sold for the year using the average cost method.

		Cost	Retail
Beginning inventory		$ 8,000	$ 12,000
Plus: Purchases		68,000	98,000
Freight-in		3,200	
Less: Purchase returns		(3,000)	(4,200)
Plus: Net markups			6,000
Less: Net markdowns			(2,400)
Goods available for sale		$76,200	$109,400
Cost-to-retail percentage: $\frac{\$76,200}{\$109,400} = 69.65\%$			
Less: Normal spoilage			(1,800)
Sales:			
Net sales	$92,000		
Add back employee discounts	2,300		(94,300)
Estimated ending inventory at retail			$ 13,300
Estimated ending inventory at cost (69.65% × $13,300)		(9,263)	
Estimated cost of goods sold		$66,937	

2. Estimate Henderson's ending inventory and cost of goods sold for the year using the conventional retail method.

		Cost	Retail
Beginning inventory		$ 8,000	$ 12,000
Plus: Purchases		68,000	98,000
Freight-in		3,200	
Less: Purchase returns		(3,000)	(4,200)
Plus: Net markups			6,000
			111,800
Cost-to-retail percentage: $\frac{\$76,200}{\$111,800} = 68.16\%$			
Less: Net markdowns			(2,400)
Goods available for sale		76,200	109,400
Less: Normal spoilage			(1,800)
Sales:			
Net sales	$92,000		
Add back employee discounts	2,300		(94,300)
Estimated ending inventory at retail			$ 13,300
Estimated ending inventory at cost (68.16% × $13,300)		(9,065)	
Estimated cost of goods sold		$67,135	

3. Estimate Henderson's ending inventory and cost of goods sold for the year using the LIFO retail method.

	Cost	Retail
Beginning inventory	$ 8,000	$ 12,000
Plus: Purchases	68,000	98,000
Freight-in	3,200	
Less: Purchase returns	(3,000)	(4,200)
Plus: Net markups		6,000
Less: Net markdowns		(2,400)
Goods available for sale (excluding beginning inventory)	68,200	97,400
Goods available for sale (including beginning inventory)	76,200	109,400

(continued)

(concluded)

			Cost	Retail
Cost-to-retail percentage: $\frac{\$68,200}{\$97,400} = 70.02\%$				
Less: Normal spoilage				(1,800)
Sales:				
Net sales	$92,000			
Add back employee discounts	2,300			(94,300)
Estimated ending inventory at retail				$ 13,300
Estimated ending inventory at cost:				

	Retail	Cost	
Beginning inventory	$12,000 × 66.67%* =	$8,000	
Current period's layer	1,300 × 70.02% =	910	
Total	$13,300	$8,910	(8,910)
Estimated cost of goods sold			$67,290

*$8,000 ÷ $12,000 = 66.67%

PART C

Dollar-Value LIFO Retail

● LO9–5

FINANCIAL Reporting Case

Q1, p. 479

In our earlier illustration of the LIFO retail method, we assumed that the retail prices of the inventory remained stable during the period. If you recall, we compared the ending inventory (at retail) with the beginning inventory (at retail) to see if inventory had increased. If the dollar amount of ending inventory exceeded the beginning amount, we assumed a new LIFO layer had been added. But this isn't necessarily true. It may be that the dollar amount of ending inventory exceeded the beginning amount simply because prices increased, without an actual change in the quantity of goods. So, to see if there's been a "real" increase in quantity, we need a way to eliminate the effect of any price changes before we compare the ending inventory with the beginning inventory. Fortunately, we can accomplish this by combining two methods we've already discussed—the LIFO retail method (Part B of this chapter) and dollar-value LIFO (previous chapter). The combination is called the **dollar-value LIFO retail method**.

Using the retail method to approximate LIFO is referred to as the *dollar-value LIFO retail method.*

FINANCIAL Reporting Case

Q2, p. 479

To illustrate, we return to the Home Improvement Stores situation (Illustration 9–11) in which we applied LIFO retail. We keep the same inventory data, but change the illustration from the month of July to the fiscal year 2016. This allows us to build into Illustration 9–11A a significant change in retail prices over the year of 10% (an increase in the retail price index from 1 to 1.10). We follow the LIFO retail procedure up to the point of comparing the ending inventory with the beginning inventory. However, because prices have risen, the apparent increase in inventory is only partly due to an additional layer of inventory and partly due to the increase in retail prices. The real increase is found by deflating the ending inventory amount to beginning of the year prices before comparing beginning and ending amounts. We did this with the dollar-value LIFO technique discussed in the previous chapter.[9]

Each layer year carries its unique retail price index and its unique cost-to-retail percentage.

In this illustration, a $20,000 year 2016 layer is added to the base layer. Two adjustments are needed to convert this amount to LIFO cost. Multiplying by the 2016 price index (1.10) converts it from its base year retail to 2016 retail. Multiplying by the 2016 cost-to-retail percentage (.6468) converts it from its 2016 retail to 2016 cost. The two steps are combined in our illustration. The base year inventory also is converted to cost. The two layers are added to derive ending inventory at dollar-value LIFO retail cost.

When additional layers are added in subsequent years, their LIFO amounts are determined the same way. For illustration, let's assume ending inventory in 2017 is $226,200 at current retail prices and the price level has risen to 1.16. Also assume that the cost-to-retail

[9]The index used here is analogous to the cost index used in regular DVL except that it reflects the change in retail prices rather than in acquisition costs.

Illustration 9–11A
The Dollar-Value LIFO Retail Method

	Cost	Retail
Beginning inventory	$ 99,200	$160,000
Plus: Net purchases	305,280	470,000
Net markups		10,000
Less: Net markdowns		(8,000)
Goods available for sale (excluding beginning inventory)	305,280	472,000
Goods available for sale (including beginning inventory)	404,480	632,000
Base layer cost-to-retail percentage: $\frac{\$99,200}{\$160,000} = 62\%$		
2016 layer cost-to-retail percentage: $\frac{\$305,280}{\$472,000} = 64.68\%$		
Less: Net sales		(434,000)
Ending inventory at current year retail prices		$198,000
Estimated ending inventory at cost (calculated below)	(113,430)	
Estimated cost of goods sold	$291,050	

Ending Inventory at Year-End Retail Prices	Step 1 Ending Inventory at Base Year Retail Prices	Step 2 Inventory Layers at Base Year Retail Prices	Step 3 Inventory Layers Converted to Cost
$198,000 (determined above) →	$\frac{\$198,000}{1.10}$ = $180,000 →	$180,000	
		160,000 (base) × 1.00 × .62	= $ 99,200
		20,000 (2016) × 1.10 × .6468 =	14,230
Total ending inventory at dollar-value LIFO retail cost			$113,430

Base year retail amounts are converted to layer year retail and then to cost.

percentage for 2017 net purchases is 63%. In Illustration 9–11B, the ending inventory is converted to base year retail (step 1). This amount is apportioned into layers, each at base year retail (step 2). Layers then are converted to layer year costs (step 3).

Illustration 9–11B
The Dollar-Value LIFO Retail Inventory Method

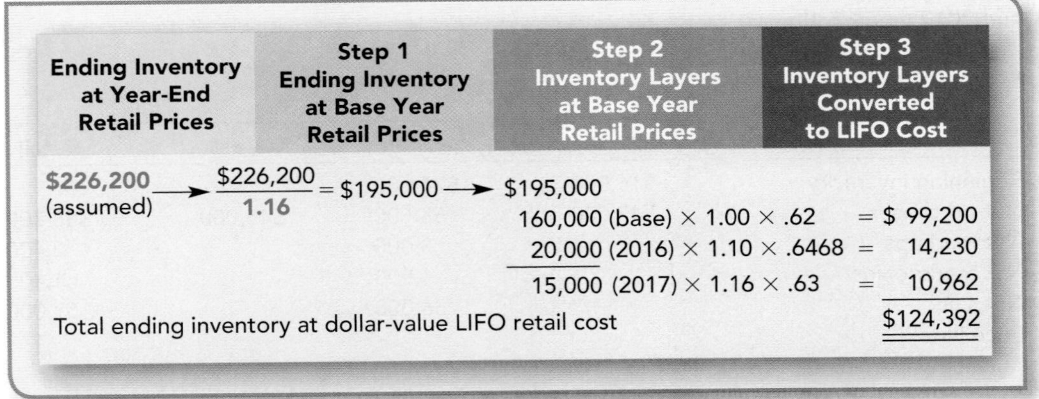

Ending Inventory at Year-End Retail Prices	Step 1 Ending Inventory at Base Year Retail Prices	Step 2 Inventory Layers at Base Year Retail Prices	Step 3 Inventory Layers Converted to LIFO Cost
$226,200 (assumed) →	$\frac{\$226,200}{1.16}$ = $195,000 →	$195,000	
		160,000 (base) × 1.00 × .62	= $ 99,200
		20,000 (2016) × 1.10 × .6468 =	14,230
		15,000 (2017) × 1.16 × .63 =	10,962
Total ending inventory at dollar-value LIFO retail cost			$124,392

Base year retail amounts are converted to layer year retail and then to cost.

Now, let's assume that ending inventory in 2017 is **$204,160** at current retail prices (instead of $226,200) and the price level has risen to 1.16. Also assume that the cost-to-retail percentage for 2017 net purchases is 63%. Step 1 converts the ending inventory to a base year price of $176,000 ($204,160 ÷ 1.16). A comparison to the beginning inventory at base year prices of $180,000 ($160,000 base year layer + $20,000 2016 layer) indicates that inventory *decreased* during 2017. In this case, no 2017 layer is added and 2017 ending inventory at dollar-value LIFO retail of $110,584 is determined in Illustration 9–11C.

Illustration 9–11C
The Dollar-Value LIFO Retail Inventory Method

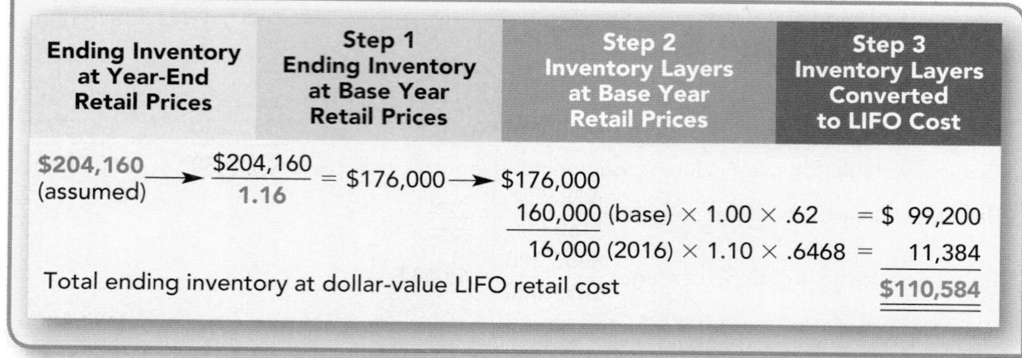

Ending Inventory at Year-End Retail Prices	Step 1 Ending Inventory at Base Year Retail Prices	Step 2 Inventory Layers at Base Year Retail Prices	Step 3 Inventory Layers Converted to LIFO Cost
$204,160 (assumed) →	$204,160 / 1.16 = $176,000 →	$176,000	
		160,000 (base) × 1.00 × .62	= $ 99,200
		16,000 (2016) × 1.10 × .6468 =	11,384
Total ending inventory at dollar-value LIFO retail cost			$110,584

A portion of the 2016 inventory layer has been liquidated—reduced from $20,000 to $16,000 at base year prices—to reduce total inventory at base year prices to $176,000.

As we mentioned earlier in this section, many high-volume retailers selling many different items use the retail method. **Target Corporation**, for example, uses the dollar-value LIFO variation of the retail method. Illustration 9–13 shows the inventory disclosure note included in the company's recent financial statements.

Illustration 9–13
Disclosure of Inventory Method—Target Corporation

Real World Financials

10. Inventory (in part)
The majority of our inventory is accounted for under the retail inventory accounting method (RIM) using the last-in, first-out (LIFO) method. The LIFO provision is calculated based on inventory levels, markup rates and internally measured retail price indices.

Notice that Target uses internal indices to adjust for changing prices.

Concept Review Exercise

DOLLAR-VALUE LIFO RETAIL METHOD

On January 1, 2016, the Nicholson Department Store adopted the dollar-value LIFO retail inventory method. Inventory transactions at both cost and retail and cost indexes for 2016 and 2017 are as follows:

	2016		2017	
	Cost	Retail	Cost	Retail
Beginning inventory	$16,000	$24,000		
Net purchases	42,000	58,500	$45,000	$58,700
Net markups		3,000		2,400
Net markdowns		1,500		1,100
Net sales		56,000		57,000
Price index:				
January 1, 2016	1.00			
December 31, 2016	1.08			
December 31, 2017	1.15			

Required:

Estimate the 2016 and 2017 ending inventory and cost of goods sold using the dollar-value LIFO retail inventory method.

Solution:

	2016		2017	
	Cost	**Retail**	**Cost**	**Retail**
Beginning inventory	$16,000	$24,000	$17,456	$28,000
Plus: Net purchases	42,000	58,500	45,000	58,700
Net markups		3,000		2,400
Less: Net markdowns		(1,500)		(1,100)
Goods available for sale (excluding beg. inv.)	42,000	60,000	45,000	60,000
Goods available for sale (including beg. inv.)	58,000	84,000	62,456	88,000

Base layer

Cost-to-retail percentage: $\frac{\$16,000}{\$24,000} = 66.67\%$

2016

Cost-to-retail percentage: $\frac{\$42,000}{\$60,000} = 70\%$

2017

Cost-to-retail percentage: $\frac{\$45,000}{\$60,000} = 75\%$

	2016 Cost	2016 Retail	2017 Cost	2017 Retail
Less: Net sales		(56,000)		(57,000)
Estimated ending inv. at current year retail prices		$28,000		$31,000
Less: Estimated ending inventory at cost (below)	(17,456)		(18,345)	
Estimated cost of goods sold	$40,544		$44,111	

2016

Ending Inventory at Year-End Retail Prices	Step 1 Ending Inventory at Base Year Retail Prices	Step 2 Inventory Layers at Base Year Retail Prices	Step 3 Inventory Layers Converted to Cost
$28,000 (above)	$\frac{\$28,000}{1.08} = 25,926$	$24,000 (base) × 1.00 × 66.67% =	$16,000
		1,926 (2016) × 1.08 × 70.00% =	1,456
Total ending inventory at dollar-value LIFO retail cost			$17,456

2017

Ending Inventory at Year-End Retail Prices	Step 1 Ending Inventory at Base Year Retail Prices	Step 2 Inventory Layers at Base Year Retail Prices	Step 3 Inventory Layers Converted to Cost
$31,000 (above)	$\frac{\$31,000}{1.15} = \$26,957$	$24,000 (base) × 1.00 × 66.67% =	$16,000
		1,926 (2016) × 1.08 × 70.00% =	1,456
		1,031 (2017) × 1.15 × 75.00% =	889
Total ending inventory at dollar-value LIFO retail cost			$18,345

Change in Inventory Method and Inventory Errors

PART D

Change in Inventory Method

LO9–6

Accounting principles should be applied consistently from period to period to allow for comparability of operating results. However, changes within a company as well as changes in the external economic environment may require a company to change an accounting method. As we mentioned in Chapter 8, in the past, high inflation periods motivated many companies to switch to LIFO for the tax benefit.

Specific accounting treatment and disclosures are prescribed for companies that change accounting principles. Chapter 4 introduced the subject of accounting changes and Chapter 20 provides in-depth coverage of the topic. Here we provide an overview of how changes in inventory methods are reported.

Most Inventory Changes

Changes in inventory methods, other than a change to LIFO, are accounted for retrospectively.

Recall from our brief discussion in Chapter 4 that most voluntary changes in accounting principles are reported retrospectively. This means reporting all previous periods' financial statements as if the new method had been used in all prior periods. Changes in inventory methods, other than a change to LIFO, are treated this way. We discuss the *to LIFO* exception in the next section. In Chapter 4 we briefly discussed the steps a company undertakes to account for a change in accounting principle. We demonstrate those steps in Illustration 9–14.

Illustration 9–14

Change in Inventory Method

> Autogeek, Inc., a wholesale distributor of auto parts, began business in 2013. Inventory reported in the 2015 year-end balance sheet, determined using the average cost method, was $123,000. In 2016, the company decided to change its inventory method to FIFO. If the company had used the FIFO method in 2015, ending inventory would have been $146,000. What steps should Autogeek take to report this change?

Step 1: Revise comparative financial statements.

The first step is to revise prior years' financial statements. That is, for each year reported in the comparative statements, Autogeek makes those statements appear as if the newly adopted inventory method, FIFO, had been applied all along. In its balance sheets, assuming that the company presents balance sheets for two years for comparative purposes, the company would report 2016 inventory by its newly adopted method, FIFO, and also would revise the amounts it reported last year for its 2015 inventory. In its 2016 and prior year income statements, cost of goods sold would also reflect the new method.

In its statements of shareholders' equity, Autogeek would report retained earnings each year as if it had used FIFO all along. And, for the earliest year reported, the company would revise beginning retained earnings that year to reflect the cumulative income effect of the difference in inventory methods for all prior years. You will see this step illustrated in Chapter 20 after you have studied the statement of shareholders' equity in more depth.

Step 2: The affected accounts are adjusted.

Autogeek also would record a journal entry to adjust the book balances from their current amounts to what those balances would have been using FIFO. Because differences in cost of goods sold and income are reflected in retained earnings, as are the income tax effects, the journal entry updates inventory, retained earnings, and the appropriate income tax account. We ignore the income tax effects here but include those effects in an illustration in Chapter 20. The journal entry below, *ignoring income taxes,* increases the 2016 beginning inventory to the FIFO basis amount of $146,000 and increases retained earnings by the same amount, because that's what the increase in prior years' income would have been had FIFO been used.

Inventory ($146,000 − 123,000)	23,000	
Retained earnings		23,000

Step 3: A disclosure note provides additional information.

Autogeek must provide in a disclosure note clear justification that the change to FIFO is appropriate. The note also would indicate the effects of the change on (a) items not reported on the face of the primary statements, (b) any per share amounts affected for the current period and all prior periods, and (c) the cumulative effect of the change on retained earnings or other components of equity as of the beginning of the earliest period presented.

We see in Illustration 9–15 an example of such a note in a recent annual report of **CVS Caremark Corporation**, the largest integrated pharmacy health care provider in the United States, when it changed its inventory method for prescription drug inventories to the average cost method.

2. Change in Accounting Principle (in part)

Prior to 2012, the Company valued prescription drug inventories on a first-in, first-out ("FIFO") basis in retail pharmacies using the retail inventory method and in distribution centers using the FIFO cost method. Effective January 1, 2012, all prescription drug inventories in the Retail Pharmacy Segment have been valued using the weighted average cost method.

These changes were made primarily to bring all of the pharmacy operations of the Company to a common inventory valuation methodology and to provide the Company with better information to manage its retail pharmacy operations.

The effect of these changes in accounting principle as of January 1, 2012, was a decrease in inventories of $146 million, an increase in current deferred income tax assets of $57 million, and a decrease in retained earnings of $89 million.

Illustration 9–15

Disclosure of Change in Inventory Method—CVS Caremark Corporation

Real World Financials

CVS Caremark's note also disclosed the effect of the change on the current year's income from continuing operations, net income, and earnings per share.

Change to the LIFO Method

Accounting records usually are inadequate for a company changing to *LIFO* to report the change retrospectively.

When a company changes *to the LIFO inventory method* from any other method, it usually is impossible to calculate the income effect on prior years. To do so would require assumptions as to when specific LIFO inventory layers were created in years prior to the change. As a result, a company changing to LIFO usually does not report the change retrospectively. Instead, the LIFO method simply is used from that point on. The base year inventory for all future LIFO determinations is the beginning inventory in the year the LIFO method is adopted.[10]

A disclosure note is needed to explain (a) the nature of and justification for the change, (b) the effect of the change on current year's income and earnings per share, and (c) why retrospective application was impracticable. When **Seneca Foods Corporation** adopted the LIFO inventory method, it reported the change in the note shown in Illustration 9–16.

10. Inventories (in part)

The Company decided to change its inventory valuation method from the FIFO method to the LIFO method. In the high inflation environment that the Company is experiencing, the Company believes that the LIFO inventory method is preferable over the FIFO method because it better compares the cost of current production to current revenue. Selling prices are established to reflect current market activity, which recognizes the increasing costs. Under FIFO, revenue and costs are not aligned. Under LIFO, the current cost of sales is matched to the current revenue.

The Company determined that retrospective application of LIFO for periods prior to the current fiscal year was impracticable because the period-specific information necessary to analyze inventories, including inventories acquired as part of the prior fiscal year's Signature acquisition, were not readily available and could not be precisely determined at the appropriate level of detail, including the commodity, size and item code information necessary to perform the detailed calculations required to retrospectively compute the internal LIFO indices applicable to prior fiscal years. The effect of this change was to reduce net earnings by $37,917,000 and $18,307,000 in the current and prior fiscal year, respectively, below that which would have been reported using the Company's previous inventory method. The reduction in earnings per share was $3.12 ($3.09 diluted) and $1.50 per share ($1.49 diluted) in the current and prior fiscal year, respectively.

Illustration 9–16

Change in Inventory Method Disclosure—Seneca Foods Corporation

Real World Financials

[10]A change to LIFO is handled the same way for income tax purposes.

As we discussed in Chapter 8, an important motivation for using LIFO in periods of rising costs is that it produces higher cost of goods sold and lowers income and income taxes. Notice in the Seneca Foods disclosure note that the switch to LIFO did cause a decrease in income and therefore income taxes in the year of the switch indicating an environment of increasing costs.

Additional Consideration

When changing from one generally accepted accounting principle to another, a company must justify that the change results in financial information that more properly portrays operating results and financial position. For income tax purposes, a company generally must obtain consent from the Internal Revenue Service before changing an accounting method. A special form also must be filed with the IRS when a company intends to adopt the LIFO inventory method. When a company changes from LIFO for tax purposes, it can't change back to LIFO until five tax returns have been filed using the non-LIFO method.

Inventory Errors

LO9–7

Accounting errors must be corrected when they are discovered. In Chapter 4 we briefly discussed the correction of accounting errors and Chapter 20 provides in-depth coverage. Here we provide an overview of the accounting treatment and disclosures in the context of inventory errors. Inventory errors include the over- or understatement of ending inventory due to a mistake in physical count or a mistake in pricing inventory quantities. Also, errors include the over- or understatement of purchases which could be caused by the cutoff errors described in Chapter 8.

If an inventory error is discovered in the same accounting period it occurred, the original erroneous entry should simply be reversed and the appropriate entry recorded. This situation presents no particular reporting problem.

For material errors, previous years' financial statements are retrospectively restated.

Incorrect balances are corrected.

A correction of retained earnings is reported as a prior period adjustment.

A disclosure note describes the nature and the impact of the error.

If a *material* inventory error is discovered in an accounting period subsequent to the period in which the error was made, any previous years' financial statements that were incorrect as a result of the error are retrospectively restated to reflect the correction.[11] And, of course, any account balances that are incorrect as a result of the error are corrected by journal entry. If, due to an error affecting net income, retained earnings is one of the incorrect accounts, the correction is reported as a prior period adjustment to the beginning balance on the statement of shareholders' equity.[12] In addition, a disclosure note is needed to describe the nature of the error and the impact of its correction on net income, income before extraordinary items, and earnings per share.

When analyzing inventory errors, it's helpful to visualize the way cost of goods sold, net income, and retained earnings are determined (see Illustration 9–17). Beginning inventory and net purchases are *added* in the calculation of cost of goods sold. If either of these is overstated (understated) then cost of goods sold would be overstated (understated). On the other hand, ending inventory is *deducted* in the calculation of cost of goods sold, so if ending inventory is overstated (understated) then cost of goods sold is understated (overstated). Of course, errors that affect income also will affect income taxes. In the illustration that follows, we ignore the tax effects of the errors and focus on the errors themselves rather than their tax aspects.

Let's look at an example in Illustration 9–18.

---

[11]If the effect of the error is not material, it is simply corrected in the year of discovery.

[12]The prior period adjustment is applied to beginning retained earnings for the year following the error, or for the earliest year being reported in the comparative financial statements when the error occurs prior to the earliest year presented. The retained earnings balances in years after the first year also are adjusted to what those balances would be if the error had not occurred, but a company may choose not to explicitly report those adjustments as separate line items.

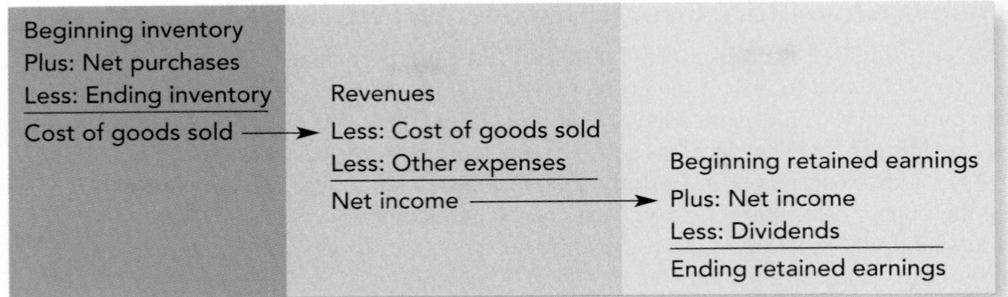

Illustration 9–17
Visualizing the Effect of Inventory Errors

Illustration 9–18
Inventory Error Correction

The Barton Company uses a periodic inventory system. At the end of 2015, a mathematical error caused an $800,000 overstatement of ending inventory. Ending inventories for 2016 and 2017 are correctly determined.

The way we correct this error depends on when the error is discovered. Assuming that the error is not discovered until after 2016, the 2015 and 2016 effects of the error, ignoring income tax effects, are shown below. The overstated and understated amounts are $800,000 in each instance.

Analysis: U = Understated O = Overstated

2015		2016	
Beginning inventory		Beginning inventory	O – 800,000
Plus: Net purchases		Plus: Net purchases	
Less: Ending inventory	O – 800,000	Less: Ending inventory	
Cost of goods sold	U – 800,000	Cost of goods sold	O – 800,000
Revenues		Revenues	
Less: Cost of goods sold	U – 800,000	Less: Cost of goods sold	O – 800,000
Less: Other expenses		Less: Other expenses	
Net income	O – 800,000	Net income	U – 800,000
↓		↓	
Retained earnings	O – 800,000	Retained earnings	*corrected*

When the Inventory Error Is Discovered the Following Year

First, let's assume the error is discovered in 2016. The 2015 financial statements that were incorrect as a result of the error are retrospectively restated to reflect the correct inventory amount, cost of goods sold, net income, and retained earnings when those statements are reported again for comparative purposes in the 2016 annual report. The following journal entry, *ignoring income taxes*, corrects the error.

Previous years' financial statements are retrospectively restated.

Retained earnings	800,000	
Inventory		800,000

A journal entry corrects any incorrect account balance.

Because retained earnings is one of the accounts that is incorrect, when the error is discovered in 2016, the correction to that account is reported as a *prior period adjustment* to the 2016 beginning retained earnings balance in Barton's statement of shareholders' equity (or statement of retained earnings). Prior period adjustments do not flow through the income statement but directly adjust retained earnings. This adjustment is illustrated in Chapter 20.

When retained earnings requires correction, a *prior period adjustment* is made on the statement of shareholders' equity.

When the Inventory Error Is Discovered Two Years Later

If the error in 2015 isn't discovered until 2017, the 2016 financial statements also are retrospectively restated to reflect the correct cost of goods sold and net income even though no correcting entry would be needed at that point. Inventory and retained earnings would not require adjustment. The error has self-corrected and no prior period adjustment is needed.

A disclosure note describes the nature of the error and the impact of the correction on income.

Also, a disclosure note in Barton's annual report should describe the nature of the error and the impact of its correction on each year's net income (overstated by $800,000 in 2015; understated by $800,000 in 2016), income before extraordinary items (same as net income in this case), and earnings per share.

Concept Review Exercise

INVENTORY ERRORS

In 2016, the controller of the Fleischman Wholesale Beverage Company discovered the following material errors related to the 2014 and 2015 financial statements:

a. Inventory at the end of 2014 was understated by $50,000.
b. Late in 2015, a $3,000 purchase was incorrectly recorded as a $33,000 purchase. The invoice has not yet been paid.
c. Inventory at the end of 2015 was overstated by $20,000.

The company uses a periodic inventory system.

Required:

1. Assuming that the errors were discovered after the 2015 financial statements were issued, analyze the effect of the errors on 2014 and 2015 cost of goods sold, net income, and retained earnings. Ignore income taxes.
2. Prepare a journal entry to correct the errors.

Solution:

1. **Analysis: U = Understated O = Overstated**

2014		2015	
Beginning inventory		Beginning inventory	U – 50,000
Plus: Net purchases		Plus: Net purchases	O – 30,000
Less: Ending inventory	U – 50,000	Less: Ending inventory	O – 20,000
Cost of goods sold	O – 50,000	Cost of goods sold	U – 40,000
Revenues		Revenues	
Less: Cost of goods sold	O – 50,000	Less: Cost of goods sold	U – 40,000
Less: Other expenses		Less: Other expenses	
Net income	U – 50,000	Net income	O – 40,000
↓		↓	
Retained earnings	U – 50,000	Retained earnings	U – 10,000

2. Prepare a journal entry to correct the errors.

Accounts payable	30,000	
Inventory		20,000
Retained earnings		10,000

Earnings Quality

A change in the accounting method a company uses to value inventory is one way managers can artificially manipulate income. However, this method of income manipulation is transparent. As we learned in a previous section, the effect on income of switching from one inventory method to another must be disclosed. That disclosure restores comparability between periods and enhances earnings quality.

William Schaff—Bay Isle Financial
I have nothing on which to base these theories other than the fact that writing off a whole quarter's inventory seems a bit much to just shrug off. It's very disturbing.[13]

On the other hand, inventory write-downs are included in the broader category of "big bath" accounting techniques some companies use to manipulate earnings. By overstating the write-down, profits are increased in future periods as the inventory is used or sold. When the demand for many high technology products decreased significantly in late 2000 and early 2001, several companies, including **Sycamore Networks**, **Cisco Systems**, **Lucent Technologies**, and **JDS Uniphase**, recorded large inventory write-offs, some in the billions of dollars. Certainly, these write-offs reflected the existing economic environment. However, some analysts questioned the size of some of the write-offs. For example, William Schaff, an investment officer at Bay Isle Financial, noted that Cisco's $2 billion write-off was approximately equal to the balance of inventory on hand at the end of the previous quarter and about equal to the cost of goods actually sold during the quarter.

Inventory write-downs often are cited as a method used to shift income between periods.

A financial analyst must carefully consider the effect of any significant asset write-down on the assessment of a company's permanent earnings.

[13]William Schaff, "What Is the Definition of an Earnings Bath," *Information Week Online*, April 24, 2001.

Financial Reporting Case Solution

1. **How does Sears avoid counting all its inventory every time it produces financial statements?** *(p. 494)* Sears uses the dollar-value LIFO retail inventory method. The retail inventory estimation technique avoids the counting of ending inventory by keeping track of goods available for sale not only at cost but also at retail prices. Each period's sales, at sales prices, are deducted from the retail amount of goods available for sale to arrive at ending inventory at retail. This amount is then converted to cost using a cost-to-retail percentage.
2. **What are external price indices used for?** *(p. 494)* The dollar-value LIFO retail method uses a price index to first convert ending inventory at retail to base year prices. Yearly LIFO layers are then determined and each layer is converted to that year's current year retail prices using the year's price index and then to cost using the layer's cost-to-retail percentage. For the price index, Sears uses external indices rather than internally generated price indices. ●

The Bottom Line

- **LO9–1** Inventory is valued at the lower of cost and net realizable value (NRV). Net realizable value is selling price less costs to sell. *(p. 479)*
- **LO9–2** The gross profit method estimates cost of goods sold which is then subtracted from cost of goods available for sale to estimate ending inventory. The estimate of cost of goods sold is determined by subtracting an estimate of gross profit from net sales. The estimate of gross profit is determined by multiplying the historical gross profit ratio times net sales. *(p. 484)*

- **LO9–3** The retail inventory method determines the amount of ending inventory at retail by subtracting sales for the period from goods available for sale at retail. Ending inventory at retail is then converted to *cost* by multiplying it by the cost-to-retail percentage, which is based on a current relationship between cost and selling price. (*p. 486*)
- **LO9–4** By the conventional retail method, we estimate average cost at lower of cost and net realizable value. Average cost is estimated by including beginning inventory in the calculation of the cost-to-retail percentage. The lower of average cost and net realizable value is estimated by excluding markdowns from the calculation. Markdowns are subtracted in the retail column after the percentage is calculated. (*p. 489*)
- **LO9–5** By the LIFO retail method, ending inventory includes the beginning inventory plus the current year's layer. To determine layers, we compare ending inventory at retail to beginning inventory at retail and assume that no more than one inventory layer is added if inventory increases. Each layer carries its own cost-to-retail percentage which is used to convert each layer from retail to cost. The dollar-value LIFO retail inventory method combines the LIFO retail method and the dollar-value LIFO method (Chapter 8) to estimate LIFO from retail prices when the price level has changed. (*p. 494*)
- **LO9–6** Most changes in inventory methods are reported retrospectively. This means revising all previous periods' financial statements to appear as if the newly adopted inventory method had been applied all along. An exception is a change to the LIFO method. In this case, it usually is impossible to calculate the income effect on prior years. To do so would require assumptions as to when specific LIFO inventory layers were created in years prior to the change. As a result, a company changing to LIFO usually does not report the change retrospectively. Instead, the LIFO method simply is used from that point on. (*p. 497*)
- **LO9–7** If a material inventory error is discovered in an accounting period subsequent to the period in which the error is made, previous years' financial statements that were incorrect as a result of the error are retrospectively restated to reflect the correction. Account balances are corrected by journal entry. A correction of retained earnings is reported as a prior period adjustment to the beginning balance in the statement of shareholders' equity. In addition, a disclosure note is needed to describe the nature of the error and the impact of its correction on income. (*p. 500*)
- **LO9–8** *IAS No. 2* specifies that if circumstances reveal that an inventory write-down is no longer appropriate, it must be reversed. Reversals are not permitted under U.S. GAAP. Under U.S. GAAP, the lower of cost and net realizable value rule can be applied to individual items, logical inventory categories, or the entire inventory. Using the international standard, the assessment usually is applied to individual items, although using logical inventory categories is allowed under certain circumstances. (*p. 482*)

APPENDIX 9 Purchase Commitments

Purchase commitments protect the buyer against price increases and provide a supply of product.

Purchase commitments are contracts that obligate a company to purchase a specified amount of merchandise or raw materials at specified prices on or before specified dates. Companies enter into these agreements to make sure they will be able to obtain important inventory as well as to protect against increases in purchase price. However, if the purchase price decreases before the agreement is exercised, the commitment has the disadvantage of requiring the company to purchase inventory at a higher than market price. If this happens, a loss on the purchase commitment is recorded.

Purchases made pursuant to a purchase commitment are recorded at the lower of contract price or market price on the date the contract is executed.

Because purchase commitments create the possibility of this kind of loss, the loss occurs when the market price falls below the commitment price rather than when the inventory eventually is sold. This means recording the loss when the product is purchased or, if the commitment is still outstanding, at the end of the reporting period. In other words, purchases are recorded at market price when that price is lower than the contract price, and a loss is recognized for the difference. Also, losses are recognized for any purchase commitments outstanding at the end of a reporting period when market price is less than contract price. In effect, the lower of cost and net realizable value rule is applied to purchase commitments. This is best understood by the example in Illustration 9A–1.

Illustration 9A–1
Purchase Commitments

In July 2016, the Lassiter Company signed two purchase commitments. The first requires Lassiter to purchase inventory for $500,000 by November 15, 2016. The second requires the company to purchase inventory for $600,000 by February 15, 2017. Lassiter's fiscal year-end is December 31. The company uses a perpetual inventory system.

Contract Period within Fiscal Year

The contract period for the first commitment is contained within a single fiscal year. Lassiter would record the purchase at the contract price if the market price at date of acquisition is at least *equal to* the contract price of $500,000.[14]

Inventory (contract price)	500,000	
Cash (or accounts payable)		500,000

If market price on purchase date declines from year-end price, the purchase is recorded at the market price.

If the market price at acquisition is *less* than the contract price, inventory is recorded at the market price and a loss is recognized.[15] For example, if the market price is $425,000, the following entry records the purchase:

Inventory (market price)	425,000	
Loss on purchase commitment	75,000	
Cash (or accounts payable)		500,000

If market price is less than the contract price, the purchase is recorded at the market price.

The objective of this treatment is to associate the loss with the period in which the price declines rather than with the period in which the company eventually sells the inventory. This is the same objective as the lower of cost and net realizable value rule you studied in the chapter.

Contract Period Extends beyond Fiscal Year

Now let's consider Lassiter's second purchase commitment that is outstanding at the end of the fiscal year 2016 (that is, the purchases have not yet been made). If the market price at the end of the year is at least *equal* to the contract price of $600,000, no entry is recorded. However, if the market price at year-end is *less* than the contract price, a loss must be recognized to satisfy the lower of cost and net realizable value objective of associating the loss with the period in which the price declines rather than with the period in which the company eventually sells the inventory. Let's say the year-end market price of the inventory for Lassiter's second purchase commitment is $540,000. The following adjusting entry is recorded:

December 31, 2016		
Estimated loss on purchase commitment ($600,000 − 540,000)	60,000	
Estimated liability on purchase commitment		60,000

If the market price at year-end is less than the contract price a loss is recorded for the difference.

At this point, the loss is an *estimated* loss. The actual loss, if any, will not be known until the inventory actually is purchased. The best estimate of the market price on date of purchase is the current market price, in this case $540,000. Because no inventory has been acquired, we can't credit inventory for the lower of cost and net realizable value loss. Instead, a liability is credited because, in a sense, the loss represents an obligation to the seller of the inventory to purchase inventory above market price.

A liability is credited for estimated losses on purchase commitments.

The entry to record the actual purchase on or before February 15, 2017, will vary depending on the market price of the inventory at date of purchase. If the market price is unchanged or has increased from the year-end price, the following entry is made:

Inventory (accounting cost)	540,000	
Estimated liability on purchase commitment	60,000	
Cash (or accounts payable)		600,000

If market price on purchase date has not declined from year-end price, the purchase is recorded at the year-end market price.

[14] In each of the following situations, if a periodic inventory system is used purchases is debited instead of inventory.

[15] Recall from the lower of cost and net realizable value rule discussion in the chapter that one method of recording losses from inventory write-downs is to report the loss as a line item in the income statement.

Even if the market price of the inventory increases, there is no recovery of the $60,000 loss recognized in 2016. Remember that when the lower of cost and net realizable value rule is applied, the reduced inventory value, in this case the reduced value of purchases, is considered to be the new cost and any recovery of value is ignored.

If market price on purchase date has not declined from year-end price, the purchase is recorded at the year-end market price.

If the market price declines even further from year-end levels, an additional loss is recognized. For example, if the market price of the inventory covered by the commitment declines to $510,000, the following entry is recorded:

Inventory (market price)	510,000	
Loss on purchase commitment ($540,000 − 510,000)	30,000	
Estimated liability on purchase commitment	60,000	
Cash (or accounts payable)		600,000

The total loss on this purchase commitment of $90,000 is thus allocated between 2016 and 2017 according to when the decline in value of the inventory covered by the commitment occurred.

If there are material amounts of purchase commitments outstanding at the end of a reporting period, the contract details are disclosed in a note. This disclosure is required even if no loss estimate has been recorded. ●

Questions For Review of Key Topics

Q 9–1 Explain the lower of cost and net realizable value approach to valuing inventory.

Q 9–2 What are the various levels of aggregation to which the lower of cost and net realizable value rule can be applied?

Q 9–3 Describe the alternative approaches for recording inventory write-downs.

Q 9–4 Explain the gross profit method of estimating ending inventory.

Q 9–5 The Rider Company uses the gross profit method to estimate ending inventory and cost of goods sold. The cost percentage is determined based on historical data. What factors could cause the estimate of ending inventory to be overstated?

Q 9–6 Explain the retail inventory method of estimating ending inventory.

Q 9–7 Both the gross profit method and the retail inventory method provide a way to estimate ending inventory. What is the main difference between the two estimation techniques?

Q 9–8 Define each of the following retail terms: initial markup, additional markup, markup cancellation, markdown, markdown cancellation.

Q 9–9 Explain how to estimate the average cost of inventory when using the retail inventory method.

Q 9–10 What is the conventional retail method?

Q 9–11 Explain the LIFO retail inventory method.

Q 9–12 Discuss the treatment of freight-in, net markups, normal spoilage, and employee discounts in the application of the retail inventory method.

Q 9–13 Explain the difference between the retail inventory method using LIFO and the dollar-value LIFO retail method.

Q 9–14 Describe the accounting treatment for a change in inventory method other than to LIFO.

Q 9–15 When a company changes its inventory method to LIFO, an exception is made for the way accounting changes usually are reported. Explain the difference in the accounting treatment of a change *to* the LIFO inventory method from other inventory method changes.

Q 9–16 Explain the accounting treatment of material inventory errors discovered in an accounting period subsequent to the period in which the error is made.

Q 9–17 It is discovered in 2016 that ending inventory in 2014 was understated. What is the effect of the understatement on the following:

2014:	Cost of goods sold
	Net income
	Ending retained earnings
2015:	Net purchases
	Cost of goods sold
	Net income
	Ending retained earnings

 **IFRS** **Q 9–18** Identify any differences between U.S. GAAP and IFRS when applying the lower of cost and net realizable value rule to inventory valuation.

Q 9–19 (Based on Appendix 9) Define purchase commitments. What is the advantage(s) of these agreements to buyers?

Q 9–20 (Based on Appendix 9) Explain how the lower of cost and net realizable value rule is applied to purchase commitments.

Brief Exercises

BE 9–1
Lower of cost and net realizable value
● LO9–1

Ross Electronics has one product in its ending inventory. Per unit data consist of the following: cost, $20; selling price, $30; selling costs, $4. What unit value should Ross use when applying the lower of cost and net realizable value rule to ending inventory?

BE 9–2
Lower of cost and net realizable value
● LO9–1

SLR Corporation has 1,000 units of each of its two products in its year-end inventory. Per unit data for each of the products are as follows:

	Product 1	Product 2
Cost	$50	$34
Selling price	70	36
Costs to sell	6	4

Determine the book value of SLR's inventory assuming that the lower of cost and net realizable value rule is applied to individual products. What is the before-tax income effect of the adjustment?

BE 9–3
Gross profit method
● LO9–2

On February 26 a hurricane destroyed the entire inventory stored in a warehouse owned by the Rockford Corporation. The following information is available from the records of the company's periodic inventory system: beginning inventory, $220,000; purchases and net sales from the beginning of the year through February 26, $400,000 and $600,000, respectively; gross profit ratio, 30%. Estimate the cost of the inventory destroyed by the hurricane using the gross profit method.

BE 9–4
Gross profit method; solving for unknown
● LO9–2

Adams Corporation estimates that it lost $75,000 in inventory from a recent flood. The following information is available from the records of the company's periodic inventory system: beginning inventory, $150,000; purchases and net sales from the beginning of the year through the date of the flood, $450,000 and $700,000, respectively. What is the company's gross profit ratio?

BE 9–5
Retail inventory method; average cost
● LO9–3

Kiddie World uses a periodic inventory system and the retail inventory method to estimate ending inventory and cost of goods sold. The following data are available for the quarter ending September 30, 2016:

	Cost	Retail
Beginning inventory	$300,000	$ 450,000
Net purchases	861,000	1,210,000
Freight-in	22,000	
Net markups		48,000
Net markdowns		18,000
Net sales		1,200,000

Estimate ending inventory and cost of goods sold (average cost).

BE 9–6
Retail inventory method; LIFO
● LO9–3

Refer to the situation described in BE 9–5. Estimate ending inventory and cost of goods sold (LIFO).

BE 9–7
Conventional retail method
● LO9–4

Refer to the situation described in BE 9–5. Estimate ending inventory and cost of goods sold using the conventional method.

BE 9–8
Conventional retail method
● LO9–4

Roberson Corporation uses a periodic inventory system and the retail inventory method. Accounting records provided the following information for the 2016 fiscal year:

	Cost	Retail
Beginning inventory	$220,000	$ 400,000
Net purchases	640,000	1,180,000
Freight-in	17,800	
Net markups		16,000
Net markdowns		6,000
Normal spoilage		3,000
Net sales		1,300,000

The company records sales to employees net of discounts. These discounts totaled $15,000 for the year. Estimate ending inventory and cost of goods sold using the conventional method.

BE 9–9
Dollar-value LIFO retail
● LO9–5

On January 1, 2016, Sanderson Variety Store adopted the dollar-value LIFO retail inventory method. Accounting records provided the following information:

	Cost	Retail
Beginning inventory	$ 40,800	$ 68,000
Net purchases	155,440	270,000
Net markups		6,000
Net markdowns		8,000
Net sales		250,000
Retail price index, end of year		1.02

Calculate the inventory value at the end of the year using the dollar-value LIFO retail method.

BE 9–10
Dollar-value LIFO retail
● LO9–5

This exercise is a continuation of BE 9–9. During 2017, purchases at cost and retail were $168,000 and $301,000, respectively. Net markups, net markdowns, and net sales for the year were $3,000, $4,000, and $280,000, respectively. The retail price index at the end of 2017 was 1.06. Calculate the inventory value at the end of 2017 using the dollar-value LIFO retail method.

BE 9–11
Change in inventory costing methods
● LO9–6

In 2016, Hopyard Lumber changed its inventory method from LIFO to FIFO. Inventory at the end of 2015 of $127,000 would have been $145,000 if FIFO had been used. Inventory at the end of 2016 is $162,000 using the new FIFO method but would have been $151,000 if the company had continued to use LIFO. Describe the steps Hopyard should take to report this change. What is the effect of the change on 2016 cost of goods sold?

BE 9–12
Change in inventory costing methods
● LO9–6

In 2016, Wade Window and Glass changed its inventory method from FIFO to LIFO. Inventory at the end of 2015 is $150,000. Describe the steps Wade Window and Glass should take to report this change.

BE 9–13
Inventory error
● LO9–7

In 2016, Winslow International, Inc.'s controller discovered that ending inventories for 2014 and 2015 were overstated by $200,000 and $500,000, respectively. Determine the effect of the errors on retained earnings at January 1, 2016. (Ignore income taxes.)

BE 9–14
Inventory error
● LO9–7

Refer to the situation described in BE 9–13. What steps would be taken to report the error in the 2016 financial statements?

Exercises

An alternate exercise and problem set is available in the Connect library.

E 9–1
Lower of cost and net realizable value
● LO9–1

Herman Company has three products in its ending inventory. Specific per unit data for each of the products are as follows:

	Product 1	Product 2	Product 3
Cost	$20	$ 90	$50
Selling price	40	120	70
Costs to sell	6	40	10

Required:

What unit values should Herman use for each of its products when applying the lower of cost net realizable value rule to ending inventory?

E 9–2
Lower of cost and net realizable value
● LO9–1

Tatum Company has four products in its inventory. Information about the December 31, 2016, inventory is as follows:

Product	Total Cost	Total Net Realizable Value
101	$120,000	$100,000
102	90,000	110,000
103	60,000	50,000
104	30,000	50,000

Required:

1. Determine the book value of inventory at December 31, 2016, assuming the lower of cost and net realizable value rule is applied to individual products.
2. Assuming that Tatum reports an inventory write-down as a line item in the income statement, determine the amount of the loss.

E 9–3
Lower of cost and net realizable value
● LO9–1

The inventory of Royal Decking consisted of five products. Information about the December 31, 2016, inventory is as follows:

	Per Unit	
Product	Cost	Selling Price
A	$ 40	$ 60
B	90	100
C	40	80
D	100	130
E	20	30

Costs to sell consist only of a sales commission equal to 10% of selling price and shipping costs equal to 5% of cost.

Required:

What unit value should Royal Decking use for each of its products when applying the lower of cost and net realizable value rule to units of inventory?

E 9–4
FASB codification research
● LO9–3, LO9–6, LO9–7

Access the *FASB Accounting Standards Codification* at the FASB website (**asc.fasb.org**). Determine the specific citation for each of the following items:

1. The accounting treatment required for a correction of an inventory error in previously issued financial statements.
2. The use of the retail method to value inventory.

E 9–5
Gross profit method
● LO9–2

On September 22, 2016, a flood destroyed the entire merchandise inventory on hand in a warehouse owned by the Rocklin Sporting Goods Company. The following information is available from the records of the company's periodic inventory system:

Inventory, January 1, 2016	$140,000
Net purchases, January 1 through September 22	370,000
Net sales, January 1 through September 22	550,000
Gross profit ratio	25%

Required:

Estimate the cost of inventory destroyed in the flood using the gross profit method.

E 9–6
Gross profit method
● LO9–2

On November 21, 2016, a fire at Hodge Company's warehouse caused severe damage to its entire inventory of Product Tex. Hodge estimates that all usable damaged goods can be sold for $12,000. The following information was available from the records of Hodge's periodic inventory system:

Inventory, November 1	$100,000
Net purchases from November 1, to the date of the fire	140,000
Net sales from November 1, to the date of the fire	220,000

Based on recent history, Hodge's gross profit ratio on Product Tex is 35% of net sales.

Required:

Calculate the estimated loss on the inventory from the fire, using the gross profit method.

(AICPA adapted)

E 9–7
Gross profit method
● LO9–2

A fire destroyed a warehouse of the Goren Group, Inc., on May 4, 2016. Accounting records on that date indicated the following:

Merchandise inventory, January 1, 2016	$1,900,000
Purchases to date	5,800,000
Freight-in	400,000
Sales to date	8,200,000

The gross profit ratio has averaged 20% of sales for the past four years.

Required:

Use the gross profit method to estimate the cost of the inventory destroyed in the fire.

E 9–8
Gross profit method
● LO9–2

Royal Gorge Company uses the gross profit method to estimate ending inventory and cost of goods sold when preparing monthly financial statements required by its bank. Inventory on hand at the end of October was $58,500. The following information for the month of November was available from company records:

Purchases	$110,000
Freight-in	3,000
Sales	180,000
Sales returns	5,000
Purchases returns	4,000

In addition, the controller is aware of $8,000 of inventory that was stolen during November from one of the company's warehouses.

Required:

1. Calculate the estimated inventory at the end of November, assuming a gross profit ratio of 40%.
2. Calculate the estimated inventory at the end of November, assuming a markup on cost of 100%.

E 9–9
Gross profit method; solving for unknown cost percentage
● LO9–2

National Distributing Company uses a periodic inventory system to track its merchandise inventory and the gross profit method to estimate ending inventory and cost of goods sold for interim periods. Net purchases for the month of August were $31,000. The July 31 and August 31, 2016, financial statements contained the following information:

Income Statements
For the Months Ending

	August 31, 2016	July 31, 2016
Net sales	$50,000	$40,000

Balance Sheets
At

	August 31, 2016	July 31, 2016
Assets:		
Merchandise inventory	$28,000	$27,000

Required:

Determine the company's cost percentage.

E 9–10
Retail inventory method; average cost
● LO9–3

San Lorenzo General Store uses a periodic inventory system and the retail inventory method to estimate ending inventory and cost of goods sold. The following data are available for the month of October 2016:

	Cost	Retail
Beginning inventory	$35,000	$50,000
Net purchases	19,120	31,600
Net markups		1,200
Net markdowns		800
Net sales		32,000

Required:

Estimate the average cost of ending inventory and cost of goods sold for October.

E 9–11
Conventional retail method
● LO9–4

Campbell Corporation uses the retail method to value its inventory. The following information is available for the year 2016:

	Cost	Retail
Merchandise inventory, January 1, 2016	$190,000	$280,000
Purchases	600,000	840,000
Freight-in	8,000	
Net markups		20,000
Net markdowns		4,000
Net sales		800,000

Required:
Determine the December 31, 2016, inventory that approximates average cost, lower of cost and net realizable value.

E 9–12
Retail inventory method; LIFO
● LO9–3

Crosby Company owns a chain of hardware stores throughout the state. The company uses a periodic inventory system and the retail inventory method to estimate ending inventory and cost of goods sold. The following data are available for the three months ending March 31, 2016:

	Cost	Retail
Beginning inventory	$160,000	$280,000
Net purchases	607,760	840,000
Net markups		20,000
Net markdowns		4,000
Net sales		800,000

Required:
Estimate the LIFO cost of ending inventory and cost of goods sold for the three months ending March 31, 2016. Assume stable retail prices during the period.

E 9–13
Conventional retail method; normal spoilage
● LO9–4

Almaden Valley Variety Store uses the retail inventory method to estimate ending inventory and cost of goods sold. Data for 2016 are as follows:

	Cost	Retail
Beginning inventory	$ 12,000	$ 20,000
Purchases	102,600	165,000
Freight-in	3,480	
Purchase returns	4,000	7,000
Net markups		6,000
Net markdowns		3,000
Normal spoilage		4,200
Net sales		152,000

Required:
Estimate the ending inventory and cost of goods sold for 2016, applying the conventional retail method.

E 9–14
Conventional retail method; employee discounts
● LO9–3, LO9–4

LeMay Department Store uses the retail inventory method to estimate ending inventory for its monthly financial statements. The following data pertain to one of its largest departments for the month of March 2016:

	Cost	Retail
Beginning inventory	$ 40,000	$ 60,000
Purchases	207,000	400,000
Freight-in	14,488	
Purchase returns	4,000	6,000
Net markups		5,800
Net markdowns		3,500
Normal breakage		6,000
Net sales		280,000
Employee discounts		1,800

Sales are recorded net of employee discounts.

Required:
1. Compute estimated ending inventory and cost of goods sold for March applying the conventional retail method.
2. Recompute the cost-to-retail percentage using the average cost method.

E 9–15
Retail inventory method; solving for unknowns
● LO9–3

Adams Corporation uses a periodic inventory system and the retail inventory method to estimate ending inventory and cost of goods sold. The following data are available for the month of September 2016:

	Cost	Retail
Beginning inventory	$21,000	$35,000
Net purchases	10,500	?
Net markups		4,000
Net markdowns		1,000
Net sales		?

The company used the average cost flow method and estimated inventory at the end of September to be $17,437.50. If the company had used the LIFO cost flow method, the cost-to-retail percentage would have been 50%.

Required:
Compute net purchases at retail and net sales for the month of September.

E 9–16
Dollar-value LIFO retail
● LO9–5

On January 1, 2016, the Brunswick Hat Company adopted the dollar-value LIFO retail method. The following data are available for 2016:

	Cost	Retail
Beginning inventory	$ 71,280	$132,000
Net purchases	112,500	255,000
Net markups		6,000
Net markdowns		11,000
Net sales		232,000
Retail price index, 12/31/16		1.04

Required:
Calculate the estimated ending inventory and cost of goods sold for 2016.

E 9–17
Dollar-value LIFO retail
● LO9–5

Canova Corporation adopted the dollar-value LIFO retail method on January 1, 2016. On that date, the cost of the inventory on hand was $15,000 and its retail value was $18,750. Information for 2016 and 2017 is as follows:

Date	Ending Inventory at Retail	Retail Price Index	Cost-to-Retail Percentage
12/31/16	$25,000	1.25	82%
12/31/17	28,600	1.30	85

Required:
1. What is the cost-to-retail percentage for the inventory on hand at 1/1/16?
2. Calculate the inventory value at the end of 2016 and 2017 using the dollar-value LIFO retail method.

E 9–18
Dollar-value LIFO retail
● LO9–5

Lance-Hefner Specialty Shoppes decided to use the dollar-value LIFO retail method to value its inventory. Accounting records provide the following information:

	Cost	Retail
Merchandise inventory, January 1, 2016	$160,000	$250,000
Net purchases	350,200	510,000
Net markups		7,000
Net markdowns		2,000
Net sales		380,000

Pertinent retail price indexes are as follows:

January 1, 2016	1.00
December 31, 2016	1.10

Required:
Determine ending inventory and cost of goods sold.

E 9–19
Dollar-value LIFO retail; solving for unknowns
● LO9–5

Bosco Company adopted the dollar-value LIFO retail method at the beginning of 2016. Information for 2016 and 2017 is as follows, with certain data intentionally omitted:

	Inventory			
Date	**Cost**	**Retail**	**Retail Price Index**	**Cost-to-Retail Percentage**
Inventory, 1/1/16	$21,000	$28,000	1.00	?
Inventory, 12/31/16	22,792	33,600	1.12	?
2017 net purchases	60,000	88,400		
2017 net sales		80,000		
Inventory, 12/31/17	?	?	1.20	

Required:
Determine the missing data.

E 9–20
Change in inventory costing methods
● LO9–6

In 2016, CPS Company changed its method of valuing inventory from the FIFO method to the average cost method. At December 31, 2015, CPS's inventories were $32 million (FIFO). CPS's records indicated that the inventories would have totaled $23.8 million at December 31, 2015, if determined on an average cost basis.

Required:
1. Prepare the journal entry to record the adjustment. (Ignore income taxes.)
2. Briefly describe other steps CPS should take to report the change.

E 9–21
Change in inventory costing methods
● LO9–6

Goddard Company has used the FIFO method of inventory valuation since it began operations in 2013. Goddard decided to change to the average cost method for determining inventory costs at the beginning of 2016. The following schedule shows year-end inventory balances under the FIFO and average cost methods:

Year	FIFO	Average Cost
2013	$45,000	$54,000
2014	78,000	71,000
2015	83,000	78,000

Required:
1. Ignoring income taxes, prepare the 2016 journal entry to adjust the accounts to reflect the average cost method.
2. How much higher or lower would cost of goods sold be in the 2015 revised income statement?

E 9–22
Error correction; inventory error
● LO9–7

During 2016, WMC Corporation discovered that its ending inventories reported in its financial statements were misstated by the following material amounts:

2014	understated by	$120,000
2015	overstated by	150,000

WMC uses a periodic inventory system and the FIFO cost method.

Required:
1. Determine the effect of these errors on retained earnings at January 1, 2016, before any adjustments. Explain your answer. (Ignore income taxes.)
2. Prepare a journal entry to correct the errors.
3. What other step(s) would be taken in connection with the correction of the errors?

E 9–23
Inventory errors
● LO9–7

For each of the following inventory errors occurring in 2016, determine the effect of the error on 2016's cost of goods sold, net income, and retained earnings. Assume that the error is not discovered until 2017 and that a periodic inventory system is used. Ignore income taxes.

U = understated O = overstated NE = no effect

	Cost of Goods Sold	Net Income	Retained Earnings
1. Overstatement of ending inventory	U	O	O
2. Overstatement of purchases			
3. Understatement of beginning inventory			
4. Freight-in charges are understated			
5. Understatement of ending inventory			
6. Understatement of purchases			
7. Overstatement of beginning inventory			
8. Understatement of purchases plus understatement of ending inventory by the same amount			

E 9–24
Inventory error
● LO9–7

In 2016, the internal auditors of Development Technologies, Inc. discovered that a $4 million purchase of merchandise in 2016 was recorded in 2015 instead. The physical inventory count at the end of 2015 was correct.

Required:

Prepare the journal entry needed in 2016 to correct the error. Also, briefly describe any other measures Development Technologies would take in connection with correcting the error. (Ignore income taxes.)

E 9–25
Inventory errors
● LO9–7

In 2016, the controller of Sytec Corporation discovered that $42,000 of inventory purchases were incorrectly charged to advertising expense in 2015. In addition, the 2015 year-end inventory count failed to include $30,000 of company merchandise held on consignment by Erin Brothers. Sytec uses a periodic inventory system. Other than the omission of the merchandise on consignment, the year-end inventory count was correct. The amounts of the errors are deemed to be material.

Required:

1. Determine the effect of the errors on retained earnings at January 1, 2016. Explain your answer. (Ignore income taxes.)
2. Prepare a journal entry to correct the errors.
3. What other step(s) would be taken in connection with the correction of the errors?

E 9–26
Concepts; terminology
● LO9–1 through LO9–7

Listed below are several terms and phrases associated with inventory measurement. Pair each item from List A with the item from List B (by letter) that is most appropriately associated with it.

List A	List B
____ 1. Gross profit ratio	a. Reduction in selling price below the original selling price.
____ 2. Cost-to-retail percentage	b. Beginning inventory is not included in the calculation of the cost-to-retail percentage.
____ 3. Additional markup	c. Deducted in the retail column after the calculation of the cost-to-retail percentage.
____ 4. Markdown	d. Requires base year retail to be converted to layer year retail and then to cost.
____ 5. Net markup	e. Gross profit divided by net sales.
____ 6. Retail method, FIFO and LIFO	f. Material inventory error discovered in a subsequent year.
____ 7. Conventional retail method	g. Must be added to sales if sales are recorded net of discounts.
____ 8. Change from LIFO	h. Deducted in the retail column to arrive at goods available for sale at retail.
____ 9. Dollar-value LIFO retail	i. Divide cost of goods available for sale by goods available at retail.
____ 10. Normal spoilage	j. Average cost, lower of cost and NRV.
____ 11. Requires retrospective restatement	k. Added to the retail column to arrive at goods available for sale.
____ 12. Employee discounts	l. Increase in selling price subsequent to initial markup.
____ 13. Net markdowns	m. Selling price less costs of completion, disposal, and transportation.
____ 14. Net realizable value	n. Accounting change requiring retrospective treatment.

E 9–27
Purchase commitments
● Appendix

On October 6, 2016, the Elgin Corporation signed a purchase commitment to purchase inventory for $60,000 on or before March 31, 2017. The company's fiscal year-end is December 31. The contract was exercised on March 21, 2017, and the inventory was purchased for cash at the contract price. On the purchase date of March 21, the market price of the inventory was $54,000. The market price of the inventory on December 31, 2016, was $56,000. The company uses a perpetual inventory system.

Required:

1. Prepare the necessary adjusting journal entry (if any is required) on December 31, 2016.
2. Prepare the journal entry to record the purchase on March 21, 2017.

E 9–28
Purchase commitments
● Appendix

In March 2016, the Phillips Tool Company signed two purchase commitments. The first commitment requires Phillips to purchase inventory for $100,000 by June 15, 2016. The second commitment requires the company to purchase inventory for $150,000 by August 20, 2016. The company's fiscal year-end is June 30. Phillips uses a periodic inventory system.

The first commitment is exercised on June 15, 2016, when the market price of the inventory purchased was $85,000. The second commitment was exercised on August 20, 2016, when the market price of the inventory purchased was $120,000.

Required:

Prepare the journal entries required on June 15, June 30, and August 20, 2016, to account for the two purchase commitments. Assume that the market price of the inventory related to the outstanding purchase commitment was $140,000 at June 30.

CPA and CMA Review Questions

CPA Exam Questions

KAPLAN CPA REVIEW

The following questions are adapted from a variety of sources including questions developed by the AICPA Board of Examiners and those used in the Kaplan CPA Review Course to study inventory while preparing for the CPA examination. Determine the response that best completes the statements or questions.

● LO9–1

1. Moss Co. has determined its year-end inventory on a FIFO basis to be $400,000. Information pertaining to that inventory is as follows:

Estimated selling price	$408,000
Estimated costs to sell	20,000

What should be the book value of Moss's inventory?

a. $408,000
b. $380,000
c. $388,000
d. $400,000

● LO9–2

2. On May 2, a fire destroyed the entire merchandise inventory on hand of Sanchez Wholesale Corporation. The following information is available:

Sales, January 1 through May 2	$360,000
Inventory, January 1	80,000
Merchandise purchases, January 1 through May 2 (including $40,000 of goods in transit on May 2, shipped f.o.b. shipping point)	330,000
Markup percentage on cost	20%

What is the estimated inventory on May 2 immediately prior to the fire?

a. $ 70,000
b. $ 82,000
c. $110,000
d. $122,000

● LO9–4

3. Hutch, Inc., uses the conventional retail inventory method to account for inventory. The following information relates to current year's operations:

	Average	
	Cost	Retail
Beginning inventory and purchases	$600,000	$920,000
Net markups		40,000
Net markdowns		60,000
Sales		780,000

What amount should be reported as cost of sales for the year?

a. $480,000
b. $487,500
c. $500,000
d. $525,000

● LO9–7

4. Bren Co.'s beginning inventory on January 1 was understated by $26,000, and its ending inventory on December 31 was overstated by $52,000. As a result, Bren's cost of goods sold for the year was

a. Understated by $26,000.
b. Overstated by $78,000.
c. Understated by $78,000.
d. Overstated by $26,000.

International Financial Reporting Standards are tested on the CPA exam along with U.S. GAAP. The following questions deal with the application of IFRS.

● LO9–8

IFRS

5. If circumstances indicate that an inventory write-down is no longer appropriate:

a. The write-down can be reversed under U.S. GAAP.
b. The write-down can be reversed under IFRS.
c. The write-down can be reversed under both U.S. GAAP and IFRS.
d. The write-down can't be reversed under either U.S. GAAP or IFRS.

CMA Exam Questions

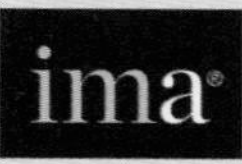

The following questions dealing with inventory are adapted from questions that previously appeared on Certified Management Accountant (CMA) examinations. The CMA designation sponsored by the Institute of Management Accountants (www.imanet.org) provides members with an objective measure of knowledge and competence in the field of management accounting. Determine the response that best completes the statements or questions.

● LO9–4

1. The following FCL Corporation inventory information is available for the year ended December 31:

	Cost	Retail
Beginning inventory at 1/1	$35,000	$100,000
Net purchases	55,000	110,000
Net markups		15,000
Net markdowns		25,000
Net sales		150,000

The December 31 ending inventory at cost using the conventional retail inventory method equals
   a. $17,500
   b. $20,000
   c. $27,500
   d. $50,000

● LO9–7

2. All sales and purchases for the year at Ross Corporation are credit transactions. Ross uses a perpetual inventory system. During the year, it shipped certain goods that were correctly excluded from ending inventory although the sale was not recorded. Which one of the following statements is correct?
   a. Accounts receivable was not affected, inventory was not affected, sales were understated, and cost of goods sold was understated.
   b. Accounts receivable was understated, inventory was not affected, sales were understated, and cost of goods sold was understated.
   c. Accounts receivable was understated, inventory was overstated, sales were understated, and cost of goods sold was overstated.
   d. Accounts receivable was understated, inventory was not affected, sales were understated, and cost of goods sold was not affected.

● LO9–7

3. During the year 1 year-end physical inventory count at Tequesta Corporation, $40,000 worth of inventory was counted twice. Assuming that the year 2 year-end inventory was correct, the result of the year 1 error was that
   a. Year 1 retained earnings was understated, and year 2 ending inventory was correct.
   b. Year 1 cost of goods sold was overstated, and year 2 income was understated.
   c. Year 1 income was overstated, and year 2 ending inventory was overstated.
   d. Year 1 cost of goods sold was understated, and year 2 retained earnings was correct.

Problems

An alternate exercise and problem set is available in the Connect library.

P 9–1
Lower of cost and net realizable value
● LO9–1

Decker Company has five products in its inventory. Information about the December 31, 2016, inventory follows.

Product	Quantity	Unit Cost	Unit Selling Price
A	1,000	$10	$16
B	800	15	18
C	600	3	8
D	200	7	6
E	600	14	13

The cost to sell for each product consists of a 15 percent sales commission.

Required:

1. Determine the book value of inventory at December 31, 2016, assuming the lower of cost and net realizable value rule is applied to individual products.

2. Determine the book value of inventory at December 31, 2016, assuming the lower of cost and net realizable value rule is applied to the entire inventory. Also, assuming that Decker reports an inventory write-down as a line item in the income statement, determine the amount of the loss.

P 9–2
Lower of cost and net realizable value
● LO9–1

Almaden Hardware Store sells two distinct types of products, tools and paint products. Information pertaining to its 2016 year-end inventory is as follows:

Inventory, by Product Type	Quantity	Per Unit Cost	Net Realizable Value
Tools:			
Hammers	100	$ 5.00	$5.50
Saws	200	10.00	9.00
Screwdrivers	300	2.00	2.60
Paint products:			
1-gallon cans	500	6.00	5.00
Paint brushes	100	4.00	4.50

Required:
1. Determine the book value of inventory at year-end, assuming the lower of cost and net realizable value rule is applied to (a) individual products, (b) product type, and (c) total inventory.
2. Assuming that the company reports an inventory write-down as a line item in the income statement, for each of the lower of cost and net realizable value applications determine the amount of the loss.

P 9–3
Gross profit method
● LO9–2

Smith Distributors, Inc., supplies ice cream shops with various toppings for making sundaes. On November 17, 2016, a fire resulted in the loss of all of the toppings stored in one section of the warehouse. The company must provide its insurance company with an estimate of the amount of inventory lost. The following information is available from the company's accounting records:

	Fruit Toppings	Marshmallow Toppings	Chocolate Toppings
Inventory, January 1, 2016	$ 20,000	$ 7,000	$ 3,000
Net purchases through Nov. 17	150,000	36,000	12,000
Net sales through Nov. 17	200,000	55,000	20,000
Historical gross profit ratio	20%	30%	35%

Required:
1. Calculate the estimated cost of each of the toppings lost in the fire.
2. What factors could cause the estimates to be over-or understated?

P 9–4
Retail inventory method; various cost methods
● LO9–3, LO9–4

Sparrow Company uses the retail inventory method to estimate ending inventory and cost of goods sold. Data for 2016 are as follows:

	Cost	Retail
Beginning inventory	$ 90,000	$180,000
Purchases	355,000	580,000
Freight-in	9,000	
Purchase returns	7,000	11,000
Net markups		16,000
Net markdowns		12,000
Normal spoilage		3,000
Abnormal spoilage	4,800	8,000
Sales		540,000
Sales returns		10,000

The company records sales net of employee discounts. Discounts for 2016 totaled $4,000.

Required:
Estimate Sparrow's ending inventory and cost of goods sold for the year using the retail inventory method and the following applications:
1. Average cost
2. Conventional

P 9–5
Retail inventory method; conventional and LIFO
● LO9–3, LO9–4

Alquist Company uses the retail method to estimate its ending inventory. Selected information about its year 2016 operations is as follows:

a. January 1, 2016, beginning inventory had a cost of $100,000 and a retail value of $150,000.
b. Purchases during 2016 cost $1,387,500 with an original retail value of $2,000,000.
c. Freight costs were $10,000 for incoming merchandise.
d. Net additional markups were $300,000 and net markdowns were $150,000.
e. Based on prior experience, shrinkage due to shoplifting was estimated to be $15,000 of retail value.
f. Merchandise is sold to employees at a 20% of selling price discount. Employee sales are recorded in a separate account at the net selling price. The balance in this account at the end of 2016 is $250,000.
g. Sales to customers totaled $1,750,000 for the year.

Required:

1. Estimate ending inventory and cost of goods sold using the conventional retail method.
2. Estimate ending inventory and cost of goods sold using the LIFO retail method. (Assume stable prices.)

P 9–6
Retail inventory method; conventional
● LO9–4

Grand Department Store, Inc., uses the retail inventory method to estimate ending inventory for its monthly financial statements. The following data pertain to a single department for the month of October 2016:

Inventory, October 1, 2016:	
At cost	$ 20,000
At retail	30,000
Purchases (exclusive of freight and returns):	
At cost	100,151
At retail	146,495
Freight-in	5,100
Purchase returns:	
At cost	2,100
At retail	2,800
Additional markups	2,500
Markup cancellations	265
Markdowns (net)	800
Normal spoilage and breakage	4,500
Sales	135,730

Required:

1. Using the conventional retail method, prepare a schedule computing estimated lower of cost and net realizable value inventory for October 31, 2016.
2. A department store using the conventional retail inventory method estimates the cost of its ending inventory as $29,000. An accurate physical count reveals only $22,000 of inventory at lower of cost and net realizable value. List the factors that may have caused the difference between computed inventory and the physical count.

(AICPA adapted)

P 9–7
Retail method—average cost and conventional
● LO9–3, LO9–4

Smith-Kline Company maintains inventory records at selling prices as well as at cost. For 2016, the records indicate the following data:

	($ in 000s)	
	Cost	**Retail**
Beginning inventory	$ 80	$ 125
Purchases	671	1,006
Freight-in on purchases	30	
Purchase returns	1	2
Net markups		4
Net markdowns		8
Net sales		916

Required:

Use the retail method to approximate cost of ending inventory in each of the following ways:

1. Average cost
2. Conventional

P 9–8
Dollar-value LIFO retail method
● LO9–5

[This is a variation of P9–7, modified to focus on the dollar-value LIFO retail method.] Smith-Kline Company maintains inventory records at selling prices as well as at cost. For 2016, the records indicate the following data:

	($ in 000s)	
	Cost	**Retail**
Beginning inventory	$ 80	$ 125
Purchases	671	1,006
Freight-in on purchases	30	
Purchase returns	1	2
Net markups		4
Net markdowns		8
Net sales		916

Required:
Assuming the price level increased from 1.00 at January 1 to 1.10 at December 31, 2016, use the dollar-value LIFO retail method to approximate cost of ending inventory and cost of goods sold.

P 9–9
Dollar-value LIFO retail
● LO9–5

On January 1, 2016, HGC Camera Store adopted the dollar-value LIFO retail inventory method. Inventory transactions at both cost and retail, and cost indexes for 2016 and 2017 are as follows:

	2016		2017	
	Cost	**Retail**	**Cost**	**Retail**
Beginning inventory	$28,000	$ 40,000		
Net purchases	85,000	108,000	$90,000	$114,000
Freight-in	2,000		2,500	
Net markups		10,000		8,000
Net markdowns		2,000		2,200
Net sales to customers		100,000		104,000
Sales to employees (net of 20% discount)		2,400		4,000
Price Index:				
January 1, 2016				1.00
December 31, 2016				1.06
December 31, 2017				1.10

Required:
Estimate the 2016 and 2017 ending inventory and cost of goods sold using the dollar-value LIFO retail inventory method.

P 9–10
Retail inventory method; various applications
● LO9–3 through LO9–5

Raleigh Department Store converted from the conventional retail method to the LIFO retail method on January 1, 2014, and is now considering converting to the dollar-value LIFO retail inventory method. Management requested, during your examination of the financial statements for the year ended December 31, 2016, that you furnish a summary showing certain computations of inventory costs for the past three years. Available information follows:

a. The inventory at January 1, 2014, had a retail value of $45,000 and a cost of $27,500 based on the conventional retail method.

b. Transactions during 2014 were as follows:

	Cost	**Retail**
Gross purchases	$282,000	$490,000
Purchase returns	6,500	10,000
Purchase discounts	5,000	
Gross sales		492,000
Sales returns		5,000
Employee discounts		3,000
Freight-in	26,500	
Net markups		25,000
Net markdowns		10,000

Sales to employees are recorded net of discounts.

c. The retail value of the December 31, 2015, inventory was $56,100, the cost-to-retail percentage for 2015 under the LIFO retail method was 62%, and the appropriate price index was 102% of the January 1, 2015, price level.

d. The retail value of the December 31, 2016, inventory was $48,300, the cost-to-retail percentage for 2016 under the LIFO retail method was 61%, and the appropriate price index was 105% of the January 1, 2015, price level.

Required:

1. Prepare a schedule showing the computation of the cost of inventory at December 31, 2014, based on the conventional retail method.
2. Prepare a similar schedule as in requirement 1 based on the LIFO retail method.
3. Same requirement as (1) for December 31, 2015 and 2016, based on the dollar-value LIFO retail method.

(AICPA adapted)

P 9–11
Retail inventory method; various applications
● LO9–3 through LO9–5

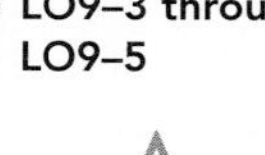

On January 1, 2016, Pet Friendly Stores adopted the retail inventory method. Inventory transactions at both cost and retail, and cost indexes for 2016 and 2017 are as follows:

	2016		2017	
	Cost	**Retail**	**Cost**	**Retail**
Beginning inventory	$ 90,000	$150,000		
Purchases	478,000	730,000	$511,000	$760,000
Purchase returns	2,500	3,500	2,200	4,000
Freight-in	6,960		8,000	
Net markups		8,500		10,000
Net markdowns		4,000		6,000
Net sales to customers		650,000		680,000
Sales to employees (net of 30% discount)		14,000		17,500
Normal spoilage		5,000		6,600
Price Index:				
January 1, 2016	1.00			
December 31, 2016	1.03			
December 31, 2017	1.06			

Required:

1. Estimate the 2016 and 2017 ending inventory and cost of goods sold using the dollar-value LIFO retail method.
2. Estimate the 2016 ending inventory and cost of goods sold using the average cost method.
3. Estimate the 2016 ending inventory and cost of goods sold using the conventional retail method.

P 9–12
Change in methods
● LO9–6

Rockwell Corporation uses a periodic inventory system and has used the FIFO cost method since inception of the company in 1979. In 2016, the company decided to switch to the average cost method. Data for 2016 are as follows:

Beginning inventory, FIFO (5,000 units @ $30)		$150,000
Purchases:		
5,000 units @ $36	$180,000	
5,000 units @ $40	200,000	380,000
Cost of goods available for sale		$530,000
Sales for 2016 (8,000 units @ $70)		$560,000

Additional Information:

a. The company's effective income tax rate is 40% for all years.
b. If the company had used the average cost method prior to 2016, ending inventory for 2015 would have been $130,000.
c. 7,000 units remained in inventory at the end of 2016.

Required:

1. Ignoring income taxes, prepare the 2016 journal entry to adjust the accounts to reflect the average cost method.
2. What is the effect of the change in methods on 2016 net income?

P 9–13
Inventory errors
● LO9–7

You have been hired as the new controller for the Ralston Company. Shortly after joining the company in 2016, you discover the following errors related to the 2014 and 2015 financial statements:

a. Inventory at 12/31/14 was understated by $6,000.
b. Inventory at 12/31/15 was overstated by $9,000.
c. On 12/31/15, inventory was purchased for $3,000. The company did not record the purchase until the inventory was paid for early in 2016. At that time, the purchase was recorded by a debit to purchases and a credit to cash.

The company uses a periodic inventory system.

Required:

1. Assuming that the errors were discovered after the 2015 financial statements were issued, analyze the effect of the errors on 2015 and 2014 cost of goods sold, net income, and retained earnings. (Ignore income taxes.)
2. Prepare a journal entry to correct the errors.
3. What other step(s) would be taken in connection with the errors?

P 9–14
Inventory errors
● LO9–7

The December 31, 2016, inventory of Tog Company, based on a physical count, was determined to be $450,000. Included in that count was a shipment of goods received from a supplier at the end of the month that cost $50,000. The purchase was recorded and paid for in 2017. Another supplier shipment costing $20,000 was correctly recorded as a purchase in 2016. However, the merchandise, shipped FOB shipping point, was not received until 2017 and was incorrectly omitted from the physical count. A third purchase, shipped from a supplier FOB shipping point on December 28, 2016, did not arrive until January 3, 2017. The merchandise, which cost $80,000, was not included in the physical count and the purchase has not yet been recorded.

The company uses a periodic inventory system.

Required:

1. Determine the correct December 31, 2016, inventory balance and, assuming that the errors were discovered after the 2016 financial statements were issued, analyze the effect of the errors on 2016 cost of goods sold, net income, and retained earnings. (Ignore income taxes.)
2. Prepare a journal entry to correct the errors.

P 9–15
Integrating problem; Chapters 8 and 9; inventory errors
● LO9–7

Capwell Corporation uses a periodic inventory system. The company's ending inventory on December 31, 2016, its fiscal-year end, based on a physical count, was determined to be $326,000. Capwell's unadjusted trial balance also showed the following account balances: Purchases, $620,000; Accounts payable; $210,000; Accounts receivable, $225,000; Sales revenue, $840,000.

The internal audit department discovered the following items:

1. Goods valued at $32,000 held on consignment from Dix Company were included in the physical count but not recorded as a purchase.
2. Purchases from Xavier Corporation were incorrectly recorded at $41,000 instead of the correct amount of $14,000. The correct amount was included in the ending inventory.
3. Goods that cost $25,000 were shipped from a vendor on December 28, 2016, terms f.o.b. destination. The merchandise arrived on January 3, 2017. The purchase and related accounts payable were recorded in 2016.
4. One inventory item was incorrectly included in ending inventory as 100 units, instead of the correct amount of 1,000 units. This item cost $40 per unit.
5. The 2015 balance sheet reported inventory of $352,000. The internal auditors discovered that a mathematical error caused this inventory to be understated by $62,000. This amount is considered to be material.
6. Goods shipped to a customer f.o.b. destination on December 25, 2016, were received by the customer on January 4, 2017. The sales price was $40,000 and the merchandise cost $22,000. The sale and corresponding accounts receivable were recorded in 2016.
7. Goods shipped from a vendor f.o.b. shipping point on December 27, 2016, were received on January 3, 2017. The merchandise cost $18,000. The purchase was not recorded until 2017.

Required:

1. Determine the correct amounts for 2016 ending inventory, purchases, accounts payable, sales revenue, and accounts receivable.
2. Calculate cost of goods sold for 2016.
3. Describe the steps Capwell would undertake to correct the error in the 2015 ending inventory. What was the effect of the error on 2015 before-tax income?

P 9–16
Purchase commitments
● **Appendix**

In November 2016, the Brunswick Company signed two purchase commitments. The first commitment requires Brunswick to purchase 10,000 units of inventory at $10 per unit by December 15, 2016. The second commitment requires the company to purchase 20,000 units of inventory at $11 per unit by March 15, 2017. Brunswick's fiscal year-end is December 31. The company uses a periodic inventory system. Both contracts were exercised on their expiration date.

Required:

1. Prepare the journal entry to record the December 15 purchase for cash assuming the following alternative unit market prices on that date:
   a. $10.50
   b. $ 9.50
2. Prepare any necessary adjusting entry at December 31, 2016, for the second purchase commitment assuming the following alternative unit market prices on that date:
   a. $12.50
   b. $10.30
3. Assuming that the unit market price on December 31 was $10.30, prepare the journal entry to record the purchase on March 15, 2017, assuming the following alternative unit market prices on that date:
   a. $11.50
   b. $10.00

Broaden Your Perspective

Apply your critical-thinking ability to the knowledge you've gained. These cases will provide you an opportunity to develop your research, analysis, judgment, and communication skills. You also will work with other students, integrate what you've learned, apply it in real-world situations, and consider its global and ethical ramifications. This practice will broaden your knowledge and further develop your decision-making abilities.

Judgment Case 9–1
Inventoriable costs; lower of cost and net realizable value; retail inventory method
● LO9–1, LO9–3, LO9–4

Hudson Company, which is both a wholesaler and a retailer, purchases its inventories from various suppliers. Additional facts for Hudson's wholesale operations are as follows:

a. Hudson incurs substantial warehousing costs.
b. Hudson values inventory at the lower of cost and net realizable value. Net realizable value is below cost of the inventories.

Additional facts for Hudson's retail operations are as follows:

a. Hudson determines the estimated cost of its ending inventories held for sale at retail using the conventional retail inventory method, which approximates lower of average cost and net realizable value.
b. Hudson incurs substantial freight-in costs.
c. Hudson has net markups and net markdowns.

Required:

1. Theoretically, how should Hudson account for the warehousing costs related to its wholesale inventories? Why?
2. a. In general, why is inventory valued at the lower of cost and net realizable value?
   b. At which amount should Hudson's wholesale inventories be reported in the balance sheet?
3. In the calculation of the cost-to-retail percentage used to determine the estimated cost of its ending retail inventories, how should Hudson treat
   a. Freight-in costs?
   b. Net markups?
   c. Net markdowns?
4. Why does Hudson's retail inventory method approximate lower of average cost and net realizable value?

(AICPA adapted)

Communication Case 9–2
Lower of cost and net realizable value
● LO9–1

The lower of cost and net realizable value approach to valuing inventory is a departure from the accounting principle of reporting assets at their historical costs. There are those who believe that inventory, as well as other assets, should be valued at market, regardless of whether market is above or below cost.

The focus of this case is the justification for the lower of cost and net realizable value rule for valuing inventories. Your instructor will divide the class into two to six groups depending on the size of the class. The mission of your group is to defend the lower of cost and net realizable value approach against the alternatives of valuing inventory at either historical cost or market value.

Required:

1. Each group member should consider the situation independently and draft a tentative argument prior to the class session for which the case is assigned.
2. In class, each group will meet for 10 to 15 minutes in different areas of the classroom. During that meeting, group members will take turns sharing their suggestions for the purpose of arriving at a single group argument.
3. After the allotted time, a spokesperson for each group (selected during the group meetings) will share the group's solution with the class. The goal of the class is to incorporate the views of each group into a consensus approach to the situation.

Integrating Case 9–3
Unit LIFO and lower of cost and net realizable value
● LO9–1

York Co. sells one product, which it purchases from various suppliers. York's trial balance at December 31, 2016, included the following accounts:

Sales (33,000 units @ $16)	$528,000
Sales discounts	7,500
Purchases	368,900
Purchase discounts	18,000
Freight-in	5,000
Freight-out	11,000

York Co.'s inventory purchases during 2016 were as follows:

	Units	Cost per Unit	Total Cost
Beginning inventory	8,000	$8.20	$ 65,600
Purchases, quarter ended March 31	12,000	8.25	99,000
Purchases, quarter ended June 30	15,000	7.90	118,500
Purchases, quarter ended September 30	13,000	7.50	97,500
Purchases, quarter ended December 31	7,000	7.70	53,900
	55,000		$434,500

Additional Information:

a. York's accounting policy is to report inventory in its financial statements at the lower of cost and net realizable value, applied to total inventory. Cost is determined under the last-in, first-out (LIFO) method.

b. York has determined that, at December 31, 2016, the net realizable value was $8.00 per unit.

Required:

1. Prepare York's schedule of cost of goods sold, with a supporting schedule of ending inventory. York includes inventory write-down losses in cost of goods sold.
2. Explain the rule of lower of cost and net realizable value and its application in this situation.

(AICPA adapted)

Judgment Case 9–4
The dollar-value LIFO method; the retail inventory method
● LO9–3, LO9–4

Huddell Company, which is both a wholesaler and retailer, purchases merchandise from various suppliers. The dollar-value LIFO method is used for the wholesale inventories.

Huddell determines the estimated cost of its retail ending inventories using the conventional retail inventory method, which approximates lower of average cost and net realizable value.

Required:

1. a. What are the advantages of using the dollar-value LIFO method as opposed to the traditional LIFO method?
   b. How does the application of the dollar-value LIFO method differ from the application of the traditional LIFO method?
2. a. In the calculation of the cost-to-retail percentage used to determine the estimated cost of its ending inventories, how should Huddell use
      - Net markups?
      - Net markdowns?
   b. Why does Huddell's retail inventory method approximate lower of average cost and net realizable value?

(AICPA adapted)

Communication Case 9–5
Retail inventory method
● LO9–3, LO9–4

The Brenly Paint Company, your client, manufactures paint. The company's president, Mr. Brenly, decided to open a retail store to sell paint as well as wallpaper and other items that would be purchased from other suppliers. He has asked you for information about the retail method of estimating inventories at the retail store.

Required:

Prepare a report to the president explaining the retail method of estimating inventories.

Analysis Case 9–6
Change in inventory method
● LO9–6

Generally accepted accounting principles should be applied consistently from period to period. However, changes within a company, as well as changes in the external economic environment, may force a company to change an accounting method. The specific reporting requirements when a company changes from one generally accepted inventory method to another depend on the methods involved.

Required:

Explain the accounting treatment for a change in inventory method (a) not involving LIFO, (b) from the LIFO method, and (c) to the LIFO method. Explain the logic underlying those treatments. Also, describe how disclosure requirements are designed to address the departure from consistency and comparability of changes in accounting principle.

Real World Case 9–7
Change in inventory method; Abercrombie & Fitch Co.
● LO9–6
Real World Financials

Abercrombie & Fitch Co. is a specialty retail company operating over 1,000 stores globally. The following disclosure note was included in recent financial statements:

> **4. Change in Accounting Principle**
>
> The Company elected to change its method of accounting for inventory from the retail method to the weighted average cost method effective February 2, 2013. In accordance with generally accepted accounting principles, all periods have been retroactively adjusted to reflect the period-specific effects of the change to the weighted average cost method. The Company believes that accounting under the weighted average cost method is preferable as it better aligns with the Company's focus on realized selling margin and improves the comparability of the Company's financial results with those of its competitors. Additionally, it will improve the matching of cost of goods sold with the related net sales and reflect the acquisition cost of inventory outstanding at each balance sheet date. The cumulative adjustment as of January 30, 2010, was an increase in its inventory of $73.6 million and an increase in retained earnings of $47.3 million.

Required:

Why does GAAP require Abercrombie to retroactively adjust all prior periods for this type of accounting change?

Real World Case 9–8
Various inventory issues; Chapters 8 and 9; Fred's Inc.
● LO9–1, LO9–5, LO9–6
Real World Financials

Fred's Inc. operates general merchandise retail discount stores and full-service pharmacies in the Southeastern United States. Access the company's 10-K for the fiscal year ended February 1, 2014. You can find the 10-K by using EDGAR at www.sec.gov. Answer the following questions.

Required:

1. What inventory methods does Fred's use to value its inventory?
2. Which price index does the company use in applying the retail inventory method?
3. A company that uses LIFO is allowed to provide supplemental disclosures reporting the effect of using another inventory method rather than LIFO. Using the supplemental LIFO disclosures provided by Fred's, determine the income effect of using LIFO versus another method for the current fiscal year.
4. Calculate the company's inventory turnover ratio for the fiscal year ended February 1, 2014.
5. Assume that in the next fiscal year the company decides to switch to the average cost method. Describe the accounting treatment required for the switch.

Communication Case 9–9
Change in inventory method; disclosure note
● LO9–6

Mayfair Department Stores, Inc., operates over 30 retail stores in the Pacific Northwest. Prior to 2016, the company used the FIFO method to value its inventory. In 2016, Mayfair decided to switch to the dollar value LIFO retail inventory method. One of your responsibilities as assistant controller is to prepare the disclosure note describing the change in method that will be included in the company's 2016 financial statements. Kenneth Meier, the controller, provided the following information:

a. Internally developed retail price indexes are used to adjust for the effects of changing prices.
b. If the change had not been made, cost of goods sold for the year would have been $22 million lower. The company's income tax rate is 40% and there were 100 million shares of common stock outstanding during 2016.
c. The cumulative effect of the change on prior years' income is not determinable.
d. The reasons for the change were (a) to provide a more consistent matching of merchandise costs with sales revenue, and (b) the new method provides a more comparable basis of accounting with competitors that also use the LIFO method.

Required:

1. Prepare for Kenneth Meier the disclosure note that will be included in the 2016 financial statements.
2. Explain why the "cumulative effect of the change on prior years' income is not determinable."

Judgment Case 9–10
Inventory errors
● LO9–7

Some inventory errors are said to be self-correcting in that the error has the opposite financial statement effect in the period following the error, thereby correcting the original account balance errors.

Required:

Despite this self-correcting feature, discuss why these errors should not be ignored and describe the steps required to account for the error correction.

Ethics Case 9–11
Overstatement of ending inventory
● LO9–7

Danville Bottlers is a wholesale beverage company. Danville uses the FIFO inventory method to determine the cost of its ending inventory. Ending inventory quantities are determined by a physical count. For the fiscal year-end June 30, 2016, ending inventory was originally determined to be $3,265,000. However, on July 17, 2016, John Howard, the company's controller, discovered an error in the ending inventory count. He determined that the correct ending inventory amount should be $2,600,000.

Danville is a privately owned corporation with significant financing provided by a local bank. The bank requires annual audited financial statements as a condition of the loan. By July 17, the auditors had completed their review of the financial statements which are scheduled to be issued on July 25. They did not discover the inventory error.

John's first reaction was to communicate his finding to the auditors and to revise the financial statements before they are issued. However, he knows that his and his fellow workers' profit-sharing plans are based on annual pretax earnings and that if he revises the statements, everyone's profit-sharing bonus will be significantly reduced.

Required:

1. Why will bonuses be negatively affected? What is the effect on pretax earnings?
2. If the error is not corrected in the current year and is discovered by the auditors during the following year's audit, how will it be reported in the company's financial statements?
3. Discuss the ethical dilemma John Howard faces.

Analysis Case 9–12
Purchase commitments
● Appendix

The management of the Esquire Oil Company believes that the wholesale price of heating oil that they sell to homeowners will increase again as the result of increased political problems in the Middle East. The company is currently paying $.80 a gallon. If they are willing to enter an agreement in November 2016 to purchase a million gallons of heating oil during the winter of 2017, their supplier will guarantee the price at $.80 per gallon. However, if the winter is a mild one, Esquire would not be able to sell a million gallons unless they reduced their retail price and thereby increase the risk of a loss for the year. On the other hand, if the wholesale price did increase substantially, they would be in a favorable position with respect to their competitors. The company's fiscal year-end is December 31.

Required:

Discuss the accounting issues related to the purchase commitment that Esquire is considering.

Air France–KLM Case

● LO9–8

IFRS

Air France–KLM (AF), a Franco-Dutch company, prepares its financial statements according to International Financial Reporting Standards. AF's financial statements and disclosure notes for the year ended December 31, 2013, are provided with all new textbooks. This material also is available at **www.airfranceklm-finance.com**.

Required:

AF's inventories are valued at the lower of cost and net realizable value. Does this approach differ from U.S. GAAP?

CHAPTER

10 Property, Plant, and Equipment and Intangible Assets: Acquisition and Disposition

OVERVIEW

This chapter and the one that follows address the measurement and reporting issues involving property, plant, and equipment and intangible assets, the tangible and intangible long-lived assets that are used in the production of goods and services. This chapter covers the valuation at date of acquisition and the disposition of these assets. In Chapter 11 we discuss the allocation of the cost of property, plant, and equipment and intangible assets to the periods benefited by their use, the treatment of expenditures made over the life of these assets to maintain and improve them, and impairment.

LEARNING OBJECTIVES

After studying this chapter, you should be able to:

- **LO10–1** Identify the various costs included in the initial cost of property, plant, and equipment, natural resources, and intangible assets. (*p. 530*)
- **LO10–2** Determine the initial cost of individual property, plant, and equipment and intangible assets acquired as a group for a lump-sum purchase price. (*p. 539*)
- **LO10–3** Determine the initial cost of property, plant, and equipment and intangible assets acquired in exchange for a deferred payment contract. (*p. 540*)
- **LO10–4** Determine the initial cost of property, plant, and equipment and intangible assets acquired in exchange for equity securities or through donation. (*p. 542*)
- **LO10–5** Calculate the fixed-asset turnover ratio used by analysts to measure how effectively managers use property, plant, and equipment. (*p. 544*)
- **LO10–6** Explain how to account for dispositions and exchanges for other nonmonetary assets. (*p. 544*)
- **LO10–7** Identify the items included in the cost of a self-constructed asset and determine the amount of capitalized interest. (*p. 549*)
- **LO10–8** Explain the difference in the accounting treatment of costs incurred to purchase intangible assets versus the costs incurred to internally develop intangible assets. (*p. 554*)
- **LO10–9** Discuss the primary differences between U.S. GAAP and IFRS with respect to the acquisition and disposition of property, plant, and equipment and intangible assets. (*pp. 543, 559,* and 560)

FINANCIAL REPORTING CASE

A Disney Adventure

"Now I'm really confused," confessed Stan, your study partner, staring blankly at the Walt Disney Company balance sheet that your professor handed out last week. "I thought that interest is always expensed in the income statement. Now I see that Disney is capitalizing interest. I'm not even sure what *capitalize* means! And what about this other account called *goodwill?* What's that all about?" "If you hadn't missed class today, we wouldn't be having this conversation. Let's take a look at the Disney financial statements and the disclosure note on capitalized interest and I'll try to explain it all to you."

Borrowings (in part):
The Company capitalizes interest on assets constructed for its theme parks, resort and other property, and on theatrical and television productions. In 2013, 2012, and 2011, total interest capitalized was $77 million, $92 million, and $91 million, respectively.

QUESTIONS

By the time you finish this chapter, you should be able to respond appropriately to the questions posed in this case. Compare your response to the solution provided at the end of the chapter.

1. Describe to Stan what it means to capitalize an expenditure. What is the general rule for determining which costs are capitalized when property, plant, and equipment or an intangible asset is acquired? (*p. 530*)
2. Which costs might be included in the initial cost of equipment? (*p. 530*)
3. In what situations is interest capitalized rather than expensed? (*p. 549*)
4. What is the three-step process used to determine the amount of interest capitalized? (*p. 550*)
5. What is goodwill and how is it measured? (*p. 537*)

General Motors Corporation has significant investments in the production facilities it uses to manufacture the automobiles it sells. On the other hand, the principal revenue-producing assets of **Microsoft Corporation** are the copyrights on its computer software that permit it the exclusive rights to earn profits from those products. Timber reserves provide major revenues to **International Paper**. From a reporting perspective, we classify GM's production facilities as property, plant, and equipment;[1] Microsoft's copyrights as intangible assets; and International Paper's timber reserves as natural resources. Together, these three noncurrent assets constitute the *long-lived, revenue-producing assets* of a company. Unlike manufacturers, many service firms and merchandising companies rely primarily on people or investments in inventories rather than on property, plant, and equipment and intangible assets to generate revenues. Even nonmanufacturing firms, though, typically have at least modest investments in buildings and equipment.

[1]These are sometimes called *plant assets* or *fixed assets*.

The measurement and reporting issues pertaining to this group of assets include valuation at date of acquisition, disposition, the treatment of expenditures made over the life of these assets to maintain and improve them, the allocation of cost to reporting periods that benefit from their use, and impairment. The allocation of asset cost over time is called *depreciation* for plant and equipment, *amortization* for intangible assets, and *depletion* for natural resources. We focus on initial valuation and disposition in this chapter, and subsequent expenditures, cost allocation, and impairment in the next chapter.

PART A Valuation at Acquisition

Types of Assets

For financial reporting purposes, long-lived, revenue-producing assets typically are classified in two categories:

1. **Property, plant, and equipment.** Assets in this category include land, buildings, equipment, machinery, furniture, autos, and trucks. **Natural resources** such as oil and gas deposits, timber tracts, and mineral deposits also are included.
2. **Intangible assets.** Unlike property, plant, and equipment and natural resources, these lack physical substance and the extent and timing of their future benefits typically are highly uncertain. They include patents, copyrights, trademarks, franchises, and goodwill.

Of course, every company maintains its own unique mix of these assets. The way these assets are classified and combined for reporting purposes also varies from company to company. As an example, a recent balance sheet of **Semtech Corporation**, a leading supplier of analog and mixed-signal semiconductor products, reported net property, plant, and equipment of **$110,121** thousand and **$101,837** thousand at the end of fiscal 2014 and 2013, respectively. A disclosure note, shown in Illustration 10–1, provided the details.

Illustration 10–1
Property, Plant, and Equipment—Semtech Corporation

Real World Financials

Note 7. Property, Plant, and Equipment (in part):
The following is a summary of property and equipment, at cost less accumulated depreciation:

	January 26, 2014	January 27, 2013
(In thousands)		
Property	$ 9,022	$ 9,050
Buildings	18,633	18,627
Leasehold improvements	10,109	8,881
Machinery and equipment	132,549	130,595
Furniture and office equipment	34,263	30,120
Construction in progress	18,155	6,330
Property, plant, and equipment, gross	222,731	203,603
Less: accumulated depreciation and amortization	(112,610)	(101,766)
Property, plant, and equipment, net	$ 110,121	$ 101,837

In practice, some companies report intangibles as part of property, plant, and equipment. Some include intangible assets in the other asset category in the balance sheet, and others show intangibles as a separate balance sheet category.

For example, **Layne Christensen Company**, a leading construction and exploration company, reported goodwill of $8,915 thousand and other intangible assets of **$11,558** thousand in a recent balance sheet. A disclosure note, shown in Illustration 10–2, provided the details of the other intangible assets. We discuss goodwill, tradenames, patents, and other traditional intangible assets later in this part of the chapter. Technology and capitalized software are addressed in Part C of the chapter.

Before we examine in detail specific assets, you should find it helpful to study the overview provided by Illustration 10–3 on page 529.

Illustration 10–2
Intangible Assets—Layne Christensen Company

Real World Financials

(5) Other Intangible Assets (in part)
Other intangible assets consisted of the following as of January 31:

	2014		2013	
(in thousands)	Gross Carrying Amount	Accumulated Amortization	Gross Carrying Amount	Accumulated Amortization
Amortizable intangible assets:				
Tradenames	$ 6,260	$(3,215)	$ 8,008	$ (3,798)
Customer/contract-related	—	—	3,340	(3,215)
Patents	905	(503)	3,012	(1,634)
Software and licenses	2,747	(1,794)	2,747	(919)
Non-competition agreements	680	(368)	680	(255)
Other	966	(528)	1,600	(726)
Total amortizable intangible assets	$11,558	$(6,408)	$19,387	$(10,547)

Illustration 10–3 Property, Plant, and Equipment and Intangible Assets and Their Acquisition Costs

Asset	Description	Typical Acquisition Costs
Property, plant, and equipment	Productive assets that derive their value from long-term use in operations rather than from resale.	All expenditures necessary to get the asset in condition and location for its intended use.
Equipment	Broad term that includes machinery, computers and other office equipment, vehicles, furniture, and fixtures.	Purchase price (less discounts), taxes, transportation, installation, testing, trial runs, and reconditioning.
Land	Real property used in operations (land held for speculative investment or future use is reported as investments or other assets).	Purchase price, attorney's fees, title, recording fees, commissions, back taxes, mortgages, liens, clearing, filling, draining, and removing old buildings.
Land improvements	Enhancements to property such as parking lots, driveways, private roads, fences, landscaping, and sprinkler systems.	Separately identifiable costs.
Buildings	Structures that include warehouses, plant facilities, and office buildings.	Purchase price, attorney's fees, commissions, and reconditioning.
Natural resources	Productive assets that are physically consumed in operations such as timber, mineral deposits, and oil and gas reserves.	Acquisition, exploration, development, and restoration costs.
Intangible Assets	Productive assets that lack physical substance and have long-term but typically uncertain benefits.	All expenditures necessary to get the asset in condition and location for its intended use.
Patents	Exclusive 20-year right to manufacture a product or use a process.	Purchase price, legal fees, filing fees, not including internal R&D.
Copyrights	Exclusive right to benefit from a creative work such as a song, film, painting, photograph, or book.	Purchase price, legal fees, filing fees, not including internal R&D.
Trademarks (tradenames)	Exclusive right to display a word, a slogan, a symbol, or an emblem that distinctively identifies a company, product, or a service.	Purchase price, legal fees, filing fees, not including internal R&D.
Franchises	A contractual arrangement under which a franchisor grants the franchisee the exclusive right to use the franchisor's trademark or tradename and certain product rights.	Franchise fee plus any legal fees.
Goodwill	The unique value of the company as a whole over and above all identifiable assets.	Excess of the fair value of the consideration exchanged for the company over the fair value of the net assets acquired.

Costs to Be Capitalized

LO10–1

FINANCIAL Reporting Case

Q1, p. 527

The initial cost of property, plant, and equipment and intangible assets includes the purchase price and all expenditures necessary to bring the asset to its desired condition and location for use.

Property, plant, and equipment and intangible assets can be acquired through purchase, exchange, lease, donation, self-construction, or a business combination. We address acquisitions through leasing in Chapter 15 and acquisitions through business combinations later in this chapter and in Chapter 12.

The initial valuation of property, plant, and equipment and intangible assets usually is quite simple. We know from prior study that assets are valued on the basis of their original costs. In Chapter 8 we introduced the concept of condition and location in determining the cost of inventory. For example, if Thompson Company purchased inventory for $42,000 and incurred $1,000 in freight costs to have the inventory shipped to its location, the initial cost of the inventory is $43,000. This concept applies to the valuation of property, plant, and equipment and intangible assets as well. The initial cost of these assets includes the purchase price and all expenditures necessary to bring the asset to its desired condition and location for use. We discuss these additional expenditures in the next section.

Our objective in identifying the costs of an asset is to distinguish the expenditures that produce future benefits from those that produce benefits only in the current period. The costs in the second group are recorded as expenses, but those in the first group are *capitalized;* that is, they are recorded as an asset and expensed in future periods.[2] For example, the cost of a major improvement to a delivery truck that extends its useful life generally would be capitalized. On the other hand, the cost of an engine tune-up for the delivery truck simply allows the truck to continue its productive activity but does not increase future benefits. These maintenance costs would be expensed. Subsequent expenditures for these assets are discussed in Chapter 11.

The distinction is not trivial. This point was unmistakably emphasized in the summer of 2002 when WorldCom, Inc. disclosed that it had improperly capitalized nearly $4 billion in expenditures related to the company's telecom network. This massive fraud resulted in one of the largest financial statement restatements in history and triggered the collapse of the once powerful corporation. Capitalizing rather than expensing these expenditures caused a substantial overstatement of reported income for 2001 and the first quarter of 2002, in fact, producing impressive profits where losses should have been reported. If the deception had not been discovered, not only would income for 2001 and 2002 have been overstated, but also income for many years into the future would have been understated as the fraudulent capitalized assets were depreciated. Of course, the balance sheet also would have overstated the assets and equity of the company.

Property, Plant, and Equipment

FINANCIAL Reporting Case

Q2, p. 527

COST OF EQUIPMENT. Equipment is a broad term that encompasses machinery used in manufacturing, computers and other office equipment, vehicles, furniture, and fixtures. The cost of equipment includes the purchase price plus any sales tax (less any discounts received from the seller), transportation costs paid by the buyer to transport the asset to the location in which it will be used, expenditures for installation, testing, legal fees to establish title, and any other costs of bringing the asset to its condition and location for use. To the extent that these costs can be identified and measured, they should be included in the asset's initial valuation rather than expensed currently.

Although most costs can be identified easily, others are more difficult. For example, the costs of training personnel to operate machinery could be considered a cost necessary to make the asset ready for use. However, because it is difficult to measure the amount of training costs associated with specific assets, these costs usually are expensed. Consider Illustration 10–4.

[2]Exceptions are land and certain intangible assets that have indefinite useful lives. Costs to acquire these assets also produce future benefits and therefore are capitalized, but unlike other property, plant, and equipment and intangible assets, their costs are not systematically expensed in future periods as depreciation or amortization.

Illustration 10–4
Initial Cost of Equipment

Central Machine Tools purchased an industrial lathe to be used in its manufacturing process. The purchase price was $62,000. Central paid a freight company $1,000 to transport the machine to its plant location plus $300 shipping insurance. In addition, the machine had to be installed and mounted on a special platform built specifically for the machine at a cost of $1,200. After installation, several trial runs were made to ensure proper operation. The cost of these trials including wasted materials was $600. At what amount should Central capitalize the lathe?

Purchase price	$62,000
Freight and handling	1,000
Insurance during shipping	300
Special foundation	1,200
Trial runs	600
	$65,100

Each of the expenditures described was necessary to bring the machine to its condition and location for use and should be capitalized and then expensed in the future periods in which the asset is used.

COST OF LAND. The cost of land also should include expenditures needed to get the land ready for its intended use. These include the purchase price plus closing costs such as fees for the attorney, real estate agent commissions, title and title search, and recording. If the property is subject to back taxes, liens, mortgages, or other obligations, these amounts are included also. In addition, any expenditures such as clearing, filling, draining, and even removing (razing) old buildings that are needed to prepare the land for its intended use are part of the land's cost. Proceeds from the sale of salvaged materials from old buildings torn down after purchase reduce the cost of land. Illustration 10–5 provides an example.

Illustration 10–5
Initial Cost of Land

The Byers Structural Metal Company purchased a six-acre tract of land and an existing building for $500,000. The company plans to raze the old building and construct a new office building on the site. In addition to the purchase price, the company made the following expenditures at closing of the purchase:

Title insurance	$ 3,000
Commissions	16,000
Property taxes	6,000

Shortly after closing, the company paid a contractor $10,000 to tear down the old building and remove it from the site. An additional $5,000 was paid to grade the land. The $6,000 in property taxes included $4,000 of delinquent taxes paid by Byers on behalf of the seller and $2,000 attributable to the portion of the current fiscal year after the purchase date. What should be the capitalized cost of the land?

Capitalized cost of land:	
Purchase price of land (and building to be razed)	$500,000
Title insurance	3,000
Commissions	16,000
Delinquent property taxes	4,000
Cost of removing old building	10,000
Cost of grading	5,000
Total cost of land	$538,000

Two thousand dollars of the property taxes relate only to the current period and should be expensed. Other costs were necessary to acquire the land and are capitalized.

The costs of *land improvements* are capitalized and depreciated.

LAND IMPROVEMENTS. It's important to distinguish between the cost of land and the cost of land improvements because land has an indefinite life and land improvements usually have useful lives that are estimable. Examples of land improvements include the cost of parking lots, driveways, and private roads and the costs of fences and lawn and garden sprinkler systems. Costs of these assets are separately identified and capitalized. We depreciate their cost over periods benefited by their use.

COST OF BUILDINGS. The cost of acquiring a building usually includes realtor commissions and legal fees in addition to the purchase price. Quite often a building must be refurbished, remodeled, or otherwise modified to suit the needs of the new owner. These reconditioning costs are part of the building's acquisition cost. When a building is constructed rather than purchased, unique accounting issues are raised. We discuss these in the "Self-Constructed Assets" section of this chapter.

COST OF NATURAL RESOURCES. Natural resources that provide long-term benefits are reported as property, plant, and equipment. These include timber tracts, mineral deposits, and oil and gas deposits. They can be distinguished from other assets by the fact that their benefits are derived from their physical consumption. For example, mineral deposits are physically diminishing as the minerals are extracted from the ground and either sold or used in the production process.[3] On the contrary, equipment, land, and buildings produce benefits for a company through their *use* in the production of goods and services. Unlike those of natural resources, their physical characteristics usually remain unchanged during their useful lives.

Sometimes a company buys natural resources from another company. In that case, initial valuation is simply the purchase price plus any other costs necessary to bring the asset to condition and location for use. More frequently, though, the company will develop these assets. In this situation, the initial valuation can include (a) acquisition costs, (b) exploration costs, (c) development costs, and (d) restoration costs. Acquisition costs are the amounts paid to acquire the rights to explore for undiscovered natural resources or to extract proven natural resources. Exploration costs are expenditures such as drilling a well, or excavating a mine, or any other costs of searching for natural resources. Development costs are incurred after the resource has been discovered but before production begins. They include a variety of costs such as expenditures for tunnels, wells, and shafts. It is not unusual for the cost of a natural resource, either purchased or developed, also to include estimated restoration costs. These are costs to restore land or other property to its original condition after extraction of the natural resource ends. Because restoration expenditures occur later—after production begins—they initially represent an obligation incurred in conjunction with an asset retirement. Restoration costs are one example of *asset retirement obligations,* the topic of the next subsection.

The cost of a natural resource includes the *acquisition costs* for the use of land, the *exploration* and *development costs* incurred before production begins, and *restoration costs* incurred during or at the end of extraction.

On the other hand, the costs of heavy equipment and other assets a company uses during drilling or excavation usually are not considered part of the cost of the natural resource itself. Instead, they are considered depreciable plant and equipment. However, if an asset used in the development of a natural resource cannot be moved and has no alternative use, its depreciable life is limited by the useful life of the natural resource.

ASSET RETIREMENT OBLIGATIONS. Sometimes a company incurs obligations associated with the disposition of property, plant, and equipment and natural resources, often as a result of acquiring those assets. For example, an oil and gas exploration company might be required to restore land to its original condition after extraction is completed. Before 2001, there was considerable diversity in the ways companies accounted for these obligations. Some companies recognized these asset retirement obligations (AROs) gradually over the life of the asset while others did not recognize the obligations until the asset was retired or sold.

An asset retirement obligation (ARO) is measured at fair value and is recognized as a liability and corresponding increase in asset valuation.

Generally accepted accounting principles now require that an existing legal obligation associated with the retirement of a tangible, long-lived asset be recognized as a liability and

[3]Because of this characteristic, natural resources sometimes are called *wasting assets.*

measured at fair value, if value can be reasonably estimated. When the liability is credited, the offsetting debit is to the related asset.[4] These retirement obligations could arise in connection with several types of assets. We introduce the topic here because it often arises with natural resources. Let's consider some of the provisions of the standard that addresses these obligations.

Scope. AROs arise only from *legal* obligations associated with the retirement of a tangible long-lived asset that result from the acquisition, construction, or development and (or) normal operation of a long-lived asset.

Recognition. A retirement obligation might arise at the inception of an asset's life or during its operating life. For instance, an offshore oil-and-gas production facility typically incurs its removal obligation when it begins operating. On the other hand, a landfill or a mining operation might incur a reclamation obligation gradually over the life of the asset as space is consumed with waste or as the mine is excavated.

Measurement. A company recognizes the fair value of an ARO in the period it's incurred. The amount of the liability increases the valuation of the related asset. Usually, the fair value is estimated by calculating the present value of estimated future cash outflows.

Present value calculations. Traditionally, the way uncertainty has been considered in present value calculations has been by discounting the "best estimate" of future cash flows applying a discount rate that has been adjusted to reflect the uncertainty or risk of those cash flows. That's not the approach we take here. Instead, we follow the approach described in the FASB's *Concept Statement No. 7*[5] which is to adjust the cash flows, not the discount rate, for the uncertainty or risk of those cash flows. This **expected cash flow approach** incorporates specific probabilities of cash flows into the analysis. We use a discount rate equal to the *credit-adjusted risk free rate.* The higher a company's credit risk, the higher will be the discount rate. All other uncertainties or risks are incorporated into the cash flow probabilities. We first considered an illustration of this approach in Chapter 6. Illustration 10–6 on the next page demonstrates the approach in connection with the acquisition of a natural resource.

As we discuss in Chapter 11, the cost of the coal mine is allocated to future periods as *depletion* using a depletion rate based on the estimated amount of coal discovered. The $600,000 cost of the excavation equipment, less any anticipated residual value, is allocated to future periods as *depreciation.*

Additionally, the difference between the asset retirement liability of **$468,360** and the probability-weighted expected cash outflow of **$590,000** is recognized as **accretion expense**, an additional expense that accrues as an operating expense, over the three-year excavation period. This process increases the liability to $590,000 by the end of the excavation period.

Year	Accretion Expense	Increase in Balance	Asset Retirement Obligation
			468,360
1	8% (468,360) = 37,469	37,469	505,829
2	8% (505,829) = 40,466	40,466	546,295
3	8% (546,295) = 43,705*	43,705	590,000

*rounded

The journal entry to record accretion expense for the first year is:

Accretion expense	37,469	
Asset retirement liability		37,469

[4]FASB ASC 410–20–25: Asset Retirement and Environmental Obligations–Asset Retirement Obligations–Recognition (previously "Accounting for Asset Retirement Obligations," *Statement of Financial Accounting Standards No. 143* (Norwalk, Conn.: FASB, 2001)).

[5]"Using Cash Flow Information and Present Value in Accounting Measurements," *Statement of Financial Accounting Concepts No. 7* (Norwalk, Conn.: FASB, 2000).

Illustration 10–6
Cost of Natural Resources

The Jackson Mining Company paid $1,000,000 for the right to explore for a coal deposit on 500 acres of land in Pennsylvania. Costs of exploring for the coal deposit totaled $800,000 and intangible development costs incurred in digging and erecting the mine shaft were $500,000. In addition, Jackson purchased new excavation equipment for the project at a cost of $600,000. After the coal is removed from the site, the equipment will be sold.

Jackson is required by its contract to restore the land to a condition suitable for recreational use after it extracts the coal. The company has provided the following three cash flow possibilities (A, B, and C) for the restoration costs to be paid in three years, after extraction is completed:

	Cash Outflow	Probability
A	$500,000	30%
B	600,000	50%
C	700,000	20%

The company's credit-adjusted risk free interest rate is 8%.
Total capitalized cost for the coal deposit is:

Purchase of rights to explore	$1,000,000
Exploration costs	800,000
Development costs	500,000
Restoration costs	468,360*
Total cost of coal deposit	$2,768,360

*Present value of expected cash outflow for restoration costs (asset retirement obligation):
$500,000 × 30% = $150,000
600,000 × 50% = 300,000
700,000 × 20% = 140,000
$590,000 × .79383 = $468,360
(.79383 is the present value of $1, $n = 3$, $i = 8\%$)

Journal Entries:

Coal mine (determined above)	2,768,360	
Cash ($1,000,000 + 800,000 + 500,000)		2,300,000
Asset retirement liability (determined above)		468,360
Excavation equipment	600,000	
Cash (cost)		600,000

If the actual restoration costs are more (less) than the $590,000, we recognize a loss (gain) on retirement of the obligation for the difference. For example, if the actual restoration costs were $625,000, we would record the transaction as:

Asset retirement liability	590,000	
Loss ($625,000 − 590,000)	35,000	
Cash		625,000

Real World Financials

SM Energy Company is engaged in the exploration, development, acquisition, and production of natural gas and crude oil. For the six months ended June 30, 2014, SM reported $121 million in asset retirement obligations in its balance sheet. A disclosure note included in a recent annual report shown in Illustration 10–7 describes the company's policy and provides a summary of disclosure requirements.

Asset retirement obligations could result from the acquisition of many different types of tangible assets, not just natural resources.

It is important to understand that asset retirement obligations could result from the acquisition of many different types of tangible assets, not just natural resources. For example, **Dow Chemical Company** reported an $89 million asset retirement liability in its 2013 balance sheet related to anticipated demolition and remediation activities at its manufacturing sites in the United States, Canada, Brazil, China, Argentina, Australia, Japan, India, and Europe.

Note 9—Asset Retirement Obligations (in part)
The Company recognizes an estimated liability for future costs associated with the abandonment of its oil and gas properties. A liability for the fair value of an asset retirement obligation and a corresponding increase to the carrying value of the related long-lived asset are recorded at the time a well is completed or acquired. The increase in carrying value is included in proved oil and gas properties in the consolidated balance sheets. The Company depletes the amount added to proved oil and gas property costs and recognizes accretion expense in connection with the discounted liability over the remaining estimated economic lives of the respective oil and gas properties. Cash paid to settle asset retirement obligations is included in the operating section of the Company's consolidated statement of cash flows.

The Company's estimated asset retirement obligation liability is based on historical experience in abandoning wells, estimated economic lives, estimates as to the cost to abandon the wells in the future and federal, and state regulatory requirements. The liability is discounted using a credit-adjusted risk-free rate estimated at the time the liability is incurred or revised. The credit-adjusted risk-free rates used to discount the Company's abandonment liabilities range from 5.5 percent to 12.0 percent. Revisions to the liability could occur due to changes in estimated abandonment costs or well economic lives, or if federal or state regulators enact new requirements regarding the abandonment of wells.

Illustration 10–7
Disclosure of Asset Retirement Obligations—SM Energy Company

Real World Financials

Sometimes, after exploration or development, it becomes apparent that continuing the project is economically infeasible. If that happens, any costs incurred are expensed rather than capitalized. An exception is in the oil and gas industry, where we have two generally accepted accounting alternatives for accounting for projects that prove unsuccessful. We discuss these alternatives in Appendix 10.

Intangible Assets

Intangible assets **generally represent exclusive rights that provide benefits to the owner.**

Intangible assets are assets, other than financial assets, that lack physical substance. They include such items as patents, copyrights, trademarks, franchises, and goodwill. Despite their lack of physical substance, these assets can be extremely valuable resources for a company. For example, **Interbrand Sampson**, the world's leading branding consulting company, recently estimated the value of the **Coca-Cola** trademark to be $79 billion.[6] In general, intangible assets refer to the ownership of exclusive rights that provide benefits to the owner in the production of goods and services.

The issues involved in accounting for intangible assets are similar to those of property, plant, and equipment. One key difference, though, is that the future benefits that we attribute to intangible assets usually are much less certain than those attributed to tangible assets. For example, will the new toy for which a company acquires a patent be accepted by the market? If so, will it be a blockbuster like Silly Bandz or Rubik's Cube, or will it be only a moderate success? Will it have lasting appeal like Barbie dolls, or will it be a short-term fad? In short, it's often very difficult to anticipate the timing, and even the existence, of future benefits attributable to many intangible assets. In fact, this uncertainty is a discriminating characteristic of intangible assets that perhaps better distinguishes them from tangible assets than their lack of physical substance. After all, other assets, too, do not exist physically but are not considered intangible assets. Accounts receivable and prepaid expenses, for example, have no physical substance and yet are reported among tangible assets.

Intangible assets with finite useful lives are amortized; intangible assets with indefinite useful lives are not amortized.

Companies can either (1) *purchase* intangible assets from other entities (existing patent, copyright, trademark, or franchise rights) or (2) *develop* intangible assets internally (say, develop a new product or process that is then patented). In either case, we amortize its cost, unless it has an indefinite useful life.[7] Also, just like property, plant, and equipment, intangibles are subject to asset impairment rules. We discuss amortization and impairment in Chapter 11. In this chapter, we consider the acquisition cost of intangible assets.

[6]This $79 billion represents an estimate of the fair value to the company at the time the estimate was made, not the historical cost valuation that appears in the balance sheet of Coca-Cola.

[7]FASB ASC 350–30–35–1: Intangibles–Goodwill and Other–General Intangibles Other Than Goodwill–Subsequent Measurement, and FASB ASC 350–20–35–1: Intangibles–Goodwill and Other–Goodwill–Subsequent Measurement (previously "Goodwill and Other Intangible Assets," *Statement of Financial Accounting Standards No. 142* (Norwalk, Conn.: FASB, 2001)).

Purchased intangible assets are valued at their original cost.

The initial valuation of purchased intangible assets usually is quite simple. We value a purchased intangible at its original cost, which includes its purchase price and all other costs necessary to bring it to condition and location for intended use. For example, if a company purchases a patent from another entity, it might pay legal fees and filing fees in addition to the purchase price. We value intangible assets acquired in exchange for stock, or for other nonmonetary assets, or with deferred payment contracts exactly as we do property, plant, and equipment. Let's look briefly at the costs of purchasing some of the more common intangible assets.

PATENTS. A **patent** is an exclusive right to manufacture a product or to use a process. This right is granted by the U.S. Patent Office for a period of 20 years. In essence, the holder of a patent has a monopoly on the use, manufacture, or sale of the product or process. If a patent is purchased from an inventor or another individual or company, the amount paid is its initial valuation. The cost might also include such other costs as legal and filing fees to secure the patent. Holders of patents often need to defend a patent in court against infringement. Any attorney fees and other costs of successfully defending a patent are added to the patent account.

When a patent is *developed internally,* the research and development costs of doing so are expensed as incurred. We discuss research and development in more detail in a later section. We capitalize legal and filing fees to secure the patent, even if internally developed.

COPYRIGHTS. A **copyright** is an exclusive right of protection given to a creator of a published work, such as a song, film, painting, photograph, or book. Copyrights are protected by law and give the creator the exclusive right to reproduce and sell the artistic or published work for the life of the creator plus 70 years. Accounting for the costs of copyrights is virtually identical to that of patents.

Trademarks or tradenames often are considered to have indefinite useful lives.

TRADEMARKS. A **trademark**, also called **tradename**, is an exclusive right to display a word, a slogan, a symbol, or an emblem that distinctively identifies a company, a product, or a service. The trademark can be registered with the U.S. Patent Office which protects the trademark from use by others for a period of 10 years. The registration can be renewed for an indefinite number of 10-year periods, so a trademark is an example of an intangible asset whose useful life could be indefinite.

Real World Financials

Trademarks or tradenames often are acquired through a business combination. As an example, in 2002, **Hewlett-Packard Company (HP)** acquired all of the outstanding stock of **Compaq Computer Corporation** for $24 billion. Of that amount, $1.4 billion was assigned to the Compaq tradename. HP stated in a disclosure note that this ". . . intangible asset will not be amortized because it has an indefinite remaining useful life based on many factors and considerations, including the length of time that the Compaq name has been in use, the Compaq brand awareness and market position and the plans for continued use of the Compaq brand within a portion of HP's overall product portfolio."

Trademarks or tradenames can be very valuable. The estimated value of $79 billion for the Coca-Cola trademark mentioned previously is a good example. Note that the cost of the trademark reported in the balance sheet is far less than the estimate of its worth to the company. The Coca-Cola Company's balance sheet at March 28, 2014, the end of the company's first quarter, disclosed all trademarks at a cost of only $6.7 billion.

FRANCHISES. A **franchise** is a contractual arrangement under which the franchisor grants the franchisee the exclusive right to use the franchisor's trademark or tradename and may include product and formula rights, within a geographical area, usually for a specified period of time. Many popular retail businesses such as fast food outlets, automobile dealerships, and motels are franchises. For example, the last time you ordered a hamburger at McDonald's, you were probably dealing with a franchise.

***Franchise* operations are among the most common ways of doing business.**

The owner of that McDonald's outlet paid **McDonald's Corporation** a fee in exchange for the exclusive right to use the McDonald's name and to sell its products within a specified geographical area. In addition, many franchisors provide other benefits to the franchisee, such as participating in the construction of the retail outlet, training of employees, and national advertising.

Payments to the franchisor usually include an initial payment plus periodic payments over the life of the franchise agreement. The franchisee capitalizes as an intangible asset the initial franchise fee plus any legal costs associated with the contract agreement. The franchise asset is then amortized over the life of the franchise agreement. The periodic payments usually relate to services provided by the franchisor on a continuing basis and are expensed as incurred.

Most purchased intangibles are *specifically identifiable.* That is, cost can be directly associated with a specific intangible right. An exception is goodwill, which we discuss next.

GOODWILL. Goodwill is a unique intangible asset in that its cost can't be directly associated with any specifically identifiable right and it is not separable from the company itself. It represents the unique value of a company as a whole over and above its identifiable tangible and intangible assets. Goodwill can emerge from a company's clientele and reputation, its trained employees and management team, its favorable business location, and any other unique features of the company that can't be associated with a specific asset.

***Goodwill* can only be purchased through the acquisition of another company.**

Because goodwill can't be separated from a company, it's not possible for a buyer to acquire it without also acquiring the whole company or a portion of it. Goodwill will appear as an asset in a balance sheet only when it was purchased in connection with the acquisition of control over another company. In that case, the capitalized cost of goodwill equals the fair value of the consideration exchanged (acquisition price) for the company less the fair value of the net assets acquired. The fair value of the net assets equals the fair value of all identifiable tangible and intangible assets less the fair value of any liabilities of the selling company assumed by the buyer. Goodwill is a residual asset; it's the amount left after other assets are identified and valued. Consider Illustration 10–8.

FINANCIAL Reporting Case

Q5, p. 527

***Goodwill* is the excess of the fair value of the consideration exchanged over the fair value of the net assets acquired.**

Illustration 10–8
Goodwill

The Smithson Corporation acquired all of the outstanding common stock of the Rider Corporation in exchange for $18 million cash.* Smithson assumed all of Rider's long-term debts which have a fair value of $12 million at the date of acquisition. The fair values of all identifiable assets of Rider are as follows ($ in millions):

Receivables	$ 5
Inventory	7
Property, plant, and equipment	9
Patent	4
Total	$25

The cost of the goodwill resulting from the acquisition is $5 million:

Fair value of consideration exchanged		$18
Less: Fair value of net assets acquired		
Assets	$25	
Less: Fair value of liabilities assumed	(12)	(13)
Goodwill		$ 5

The following journal entry captures the effect of the acquisition on Smithson's assets and liabilities:

Receivables (fair value)	5	
Inventory (fair value)	7	
Property, plant, and equipment (fair value)	9	
Patent (fair value)	4	
Goodwill (difference)	5	
Liabilities (fair value)		12
Cash (acquisition price)		18

*Determining the amount an acquirer is willing to pay for a company in excess of the identifiable net assets is a question of determining the value of a company as a whole. This question is addressed in most introductory and advanced finance textbooks.

Of course, a company can develop its own goodwill through advertising, training, and other efforts. In fact, most do. However, a company must expense all such costs incurred in the internal generation of goodwill. By not capitalizing these items, accountants realize that this results in an improper match of expenses with revenues because many of these expenditures do result in significant future benefits. Also, it's difficult to compare two companies when one has acquired goodwill and the other has not. But imagine how difficult it would be to associate these expenditures with any objective measure of goodwill. In essence, we have a situation where the characteristic of faithful representation overshadows relevance.

Goodwill, along with other intangible assets with indefinite useful lives, is not amortized.

Just like for other intangible assets that have indefinite useful lives, *we do not amortize goodwill.* This makes it imperative that companies make every effort to identify specific intangibles other than goodwill that they acquire in a business combination since goodwill is the amount left after other assets are identified.

Additional Consideration

It's possible for the fair value of net assets to exceed the fair value of the consideration exchanged for those net assets. A "bargain purchase" situation could result from an acquisition involving a "forced sale" in which the seller is acting under duress. The FASB previously required this excess, deemed *negative goodwill,* to be allocated as a pro rata reduction of the amounts that otherwise would have been assigned to particular assets acquired. This resulted in assets acquired being recorded at amounts less than their fair values. However, current GAAP makes it mandatory that assets and liabilities acquired in a business combination be valued at their fair values.[8] Any negative goodwill is reported as a gain in the year of the combination.

In a business combination, an intangible asset must be recognized as an asset apart from goodwill if it arises from contractual or other legal rights or is separable.

In keeping with that goal, GAAP provides guidelines for determining which intangibles should be separately recognized and valued. Specifically, an intangible should be recognized as an asset apart from goodwill if it arises from contractual or other legal rights or is capable of being separated from the acquired entity. Possibilities are patents, trademarks, copyrights, and franchise agreements, and such items as customer lists, license agreements, order backlogs, employment contracts, and noncompetition agreements.[9] In past years, some of these intangibles, if present in a business combination, often were included in the cost of goodwill.[10]

Additional Consideration

Contract Acquisition Costs. Chapter 5 introduced you to the new guidance on revenue recognition issued by the FASB in 2014. Under the new standard, sellers of goods and services are required to capitalize, as an intangible asset, the incremental costs of obtaining and fulfilling a long-term (longer than one year) contract. A sales commission is an example of a contract acquisition cost that could be capitalized, rather than expensed, under this new guidance.

If capitalized, the cost of the resulting intangible asset is amortized on a systematic basis that is consistent with the pattern of transfer of the goods or services to which the asset relates. The intangible asset also is evaluated for impairment using the same approach used for other intangible assets. We discuss amortization and impairment testing of intangible assets in Chapter 11.

[8]FASB ASC 805: Business Combinations (previously "Business Combinations," *Statement of Financial Accounting Standards No. 141 (revised)* (Norwalk, Conn.: FASB, 2007)).

[9]Ibid.

[10]An assembled workforce is an example of an intangible asset that is not recognized as a separate asset. A workforce does not represent a contractual or legal right, nor is it separable from the company as a whole.

Lump-Sum Purchases

It's not unusual for a group of assets to be acquired for a single sum. If these assets are indistinguishable, for example 10 identical delivery trucks purchased for a lump-sum price of $150,000, valuation is obvious. Each of the trucks would be valued at $15,000 ($150,000 ÷ 10). However, if the lump-sum purchase involves different assets, it's necessary to allocate the lump-sum acquisition price among the separate items. The assets acquired may have different characteristics and different useful lives. For example, the acquisition of a factory may include assets that are significantly different such as land, building, and equipment.

● LO10–2

The allocation is made in proportion to the individual assets' relative fair values. This process is best explained by an example in Illustration 10–9.

Illustration 10–9
Lump-Sum Purchase

The Smyrna Hand & Edge Tools Company purchased an existing factory for a single sum of $2,000,000. The price included title to the land, the factory building, and the manufacturing equipment in the building, a patent on a process the equipment uses, and inventories of raw materials. An independent appraisal estimated the fair values of the assets (if purchased separately) at $330,000 for the land, $550,000 for the building, $660,000 for the equipment, $440,000 for the patent and $220,000 for the inventories. The lump-sum purchase price of $2,000,000 is allocated to the separate assets as follows:

	Fair Values	
Land	$ 330,000	15%
Building	550,000	25
Equipment	660,000	30
Patent	440,000	20
Inventories	220,000	10
Total	$2,200,000	100%

Land	(15% × $2,000,000)	300,000	
Building	(25% × $2,000,000)	500,000	
Equipment	(30% × $2,000,000)	600,000	
Patent	(20% × $2,000,000)	400,000	
Inventories	(10% × $2,000,000)	200,000	
Cash			2,000,000

The total purchase price is allocated in proportion to the relative fair values of the assets acquired.

The relative fair value percentages are multiplied by the lump-sum purchase price to determine the initial valuation of each of the separate assets. Notice that the lump-sum purchase includes inventories. The procedure used here to allocate the purchase price in a lump-sum acquisition pertains to any type of asset mix, not just to property, plant, and equipment and intangible assets.

Ethical Dilemma

Grandma's Cookie Company purchased a factory building. The company controller, Don Nelson, is in the process of allocating the lump-sum purchase price between land and building. Don suggests to the company's chief financial officer, Judith Prince, that they fudge a little by allocating a disproportionately higher share of the price to land. Don reasons that this will reduce depreciation expense, boost income, increase their profit-sharing bonus, and hopefully, increase the price of the company's stock. Judith has some reservations about this because the higher reported income will also cause income taxes to be higher than they would be if a correct allocation of the purchase price is made.

What are the ethical issues? What stakeholders' interests are in conflict?

Noncash Acquisitions

Assets acquired in noncash transactions are valued at the fair value of the assets given or the fair value of the assets received, whichever is more clearly evident.

Companies sometimes acquire assets without paying cash but instead by issuing debt or equity securities, receiving donated assets, or exchanging other assets. *The controlling principle in each of these situations is that in any noncash transaction (not just those dealing with property, plant, and equipment and intangible assets), the components of the transaction are recorded at their fair values.* The first indicator of fair value is the fair value of the assets, debt, or equity securities given. Sometimes the fair value of the assets received is used when their fair value is more clearly evident than the fair value of the assets given.

Deferred Payments

● LO10–3

A company can acquire an asset by giving the seller a promise to pay cash in the future and thus creating a liability, usually a note payable. The initial valuation of the asset is, again, quite simple as long as the note payable explicitly requires the payment of interest at a realistic interest rate. For example, suppose a machine is acquired for $15,000 and the buyer signs a note requiring the payment of $15,000 sometime in the future *plus* interest in the meantime at a realistic interest rate. The machine would be valued at $15,000 and the transaction recorded as follows:

Machine	15,000	
Note payable		15,000

We know from our discussion of the time value of money in Chapter 6 that most liabilities are valued at the present value of future cash payments, reflecting an appropriate time value of money. As long as the note payable explicitly contains a realistic interest rate, the present value will equal the face value of the note, $15,000 in our previous example. This also should be equal to the fair value of the machine purchased. On the other hand, when an interest rate is not specified or is unrealistic, determining the cost of the asset is less straightforward. In that case, the accountant should look beyond the form of the transaction and record its substance. Consider Illustration 10–10.

Illustration 10–10

Asset Acquired with Debt—Present Value of Note Indicative of Fair Value

> On January 2, 2016, the Midwestern Steam Gas Corporation purchased an industrial furnace. In payment, Midwestern signed a noninterest-bearing note requiring $50,000 to be paid on December 31, 2017. If Midwestern had borrowed cash to buy the furnace, the bank would have required an interest rate of 10%.

Some portion of the payment(s) required by a noninterest-bearing note in reality is interest.

On the surface, it might appear that Midwestern is paying $50,000 for the furnace, the eventual cash payment. However, when you recognize that the agreement specifies no interest even though the payment won't be made for two years, it becomes obvious that a portion of the $50,000 payment is not actually payment for the furnace, but instead is interest on the note. At what amount should Midwestern value the furnace and the related note payable?

Noncash transactions are recorded at the fair value of the items exchanged.

The answer is fair value, as it is for any noncash transaction. This might be the fair value of the furnace or the fair value of the note. Let's say, in this situation, that the furnace is custom-built, so its cash price is unavailable. But Midwestern can determine the fair value of the note payable by computing the present value of the cash payments at the appropriate interest rate of 10%. The amount actually paid for the machine, then, is the present value of the cash flows called for by the loan agreement, discounted at the market rate—10% in this case.

$$PV = \$50{,}000\ (.82645^{*}) = \$41{,}323$$

*Present value of $1: $n = 2$, $i = 10\%$ (from Table 2)

So the furnace should be recorded at its *real* cost, $41,323, as follows:[11]

Furnace (determined above)	41,323	
Discount on note payable (difference)	8,677	
Note payable (face amount)		50,000

The economic essence of a transaction should prevail over its outward appearance.

Notice that the note also is recorded at $41,323, its present value, but this is accomplished by using a contra account, called *discount on note payable,* for the difference between the face amount of the note ($50,000) and its present value ($41,323). The difference of $8,677 is the portion of the eventual $50,000 payment that represents interest and is recognized as interest expense over the life of the note.

Assuming that Midwestern's fiscal year-end is December 31 and that adjusting entries are recorded only at the end of each year, the company would record the following entries at the end of 2016 and 2017 to accrue interest and the payment of the note:

December 31, 2016		
Interest expense ($41,323 × 10%)	4,132	
Discount on note payable		4,132
December 31, 2017		
Interest expense ([$41,323 + 4,132]* × 10%)	4,545	
Discount on note payable		4,545
Note payable (face amount)	50,000	
Cash		50,000

*The 2016 unpaid interest increases the amount owed by $4,132.

Note payable

Jan. 1, 2016	50,000
50,000	Dec. 31, 2017
Bal. 12/31/17	0

Discount on note payable

8,677	Jan. 1, 2016
Dec. 31, 2016	4,132
Dec. 31, 2017	4,545
0	Bal. 12/31/17

Sometimes, the fair value of an asset acquired in a noncash transaction is readily available from price lists, previous purchases, or otherwise. In that case, this fair value may be more clearly evident than the fair value of the note and it would serve as the best evidence of the exchange value of the transaction. As an example, let's consider Illustration 10–11.

Illustration 10–11

Noninterest-Bearing Note—Fair Value of Asset Is Known

On January 2, 2016, Dennison, Inc., purchased a machine and signed a noninterest-bearing note in payment. The note requires the company to pay $100,000 on December 31, 2018. Dennison is not sure what interest rate appropriately reflects the time value of money. However, price lists indicate the machine could have been purchased for cash at a price of $79,383.

Dennison records both the asset and liability at $79,383 on January 2:

Machine (cash price)	79,383	
Discount on note payable (difference)	20,617	
Note payable (face amount)		100,000

In this situation, we infer the present value of the note from the fair value of the asset. Again, the difference between the note's $79,383 present value and the cash payment of $100,000 represents interest. We can determine the interest rate that is implicit in the agreement as follows:

$$\$79{,}383 \text{ (present value)} = \$100{,}000 \text{ (face amount)} \times \text{PV factor}$$

$$\$79{,}383 \div \$100{,}000 = .79383^*$$

*Present value of $1: $n = 3$, $i = ?$ (from Table 2, $i = 8\%$)

We refer to the 8% rate as the *implicit rate of interest.* Dennison records interest each year at 8% in the same manner as demonstrated in Illustration 10–10 and discussed in greater depth in Chapter 14.

[11] The entry shown assumes the note is recorded using the gross method. By the net method, a discount account is not used and the note is simply recorded at present value.

Machine	41,323	
Note payable		41,323

We now turn our attention to the acquisition of assets acquired in exchange for equity securities and through donation.

Issuance of Equity Securities

● LO10–4

The most common situation in which equity securities are issued for property, plant, and equipment and intangible assets occurs when small companies incorporate and the owner or owners contribute assets to the new corporation in exchange for ownership securities, usually common stock. Because the common shares are not publicly traded, it's difficult to determine their fair value. In that case, the fair value of the assets received by the corporation is probably the better indicator of the transaction's exchange value. In other situations, particularly those involving corporations whose stock is actively traded, the market value of the shares is the best indication of fair value. Consider Illustration 10–12.

Illustration 10–12
Asset Acquired by Issuing Equity Securities

On March 31, 2016, the Elcorn Company issued 10,000 shares of its nopar common stock in exchange for land. On the date of the transaction, the fair value of the common stock, evidenced by its market price, was $20 per share. The journal entry to record this transaction is:

Land	200,000	
Common stock (10,000 shares × $20)		200,000

Assets acquired by issuing common stock are valued at the fair value of the securities or the fair value of the assets, whichever is more clearly evident.

If the fair value of the common stock had not been reliably determinable, the value of the land as determined through an independent appraisal would be used as the cost of the land and the value of the common stock.

Donated Assets

***Donated assets* are recorded at their fair values.**

On occasion, companies acquire assets through donation. The donation usually is an enticement to do something that benefits the donor. For example, the developer of an industrial park might pay some of the costs of building a manufacturing facility to entice a company to locate in its park. Companies record assets donated by unrelated parties at their fair values based on either an available market price or an appraisal value. This should not be considered a departure from historical cost valuation. Instead, it is equivalent to the donor contributing cash to the company and the company using the cash to acquire the asset.

Revenue is credited for the amount paid by an unrelated party.

As the recipient records the asset at its fair value, what account receives the offsetting credit? Over the years, there has been disagreement over this question. Should the recipient increase its paid-in capital—the part of shareholders' equity representing investments in the firm? Or, should the donated asset be considered revenue? GAAP requires that donated assets be recorded as *revenue*.[12] Recall that revenues generally are inflows of assets from delivering or producing goods, rendering services, or from other activities that constitute the entity's ongoing major or central operations. The rationale is that the company receiving the donation is performing a service for the donor in exchange for the asset donated.

Corporations occasionally receive donations from governmental units. A local governmental unit might provide land or pay all or some of the cost of a new office building or manufacturing plant to entice a company to locate within its geographical boundaries. For example, the city of San Jose, California, paid a significant portion of the cost of a new office building for **IBM Corporation**. The new office building, located in downtown San Jose, brought jobs to a revitalized downtown area and increased revenues to the city. The City of San Jose did not receive an equity interest in IBM through its donation, but significantly benefited nevertheless.

Illustration 10–13 provides an example.

[12]FASB ASC 958–605–15–2 and FASB ASC 958–605–15–4: Not-for-Profit Entities–Revenue Recognition–Scope and Scope Exceptions–Contributions Received (previously "Accounting for Contributions Received and Contributions Made," *Statement of Financial Accounting Standards No. 116* (Norwalk, Conn.: FASB, 1993)).

Illustration 10–13
Asset Donation

Elcorn Enterprises decided to relocate its office headquarters to the city of Westmont. The city agreed to pay 20% of the $20 million cost of building the headquarters in order to entice Elcorn to relocate. The building was completed on May 3, 2016. Elcorn paid its portion of the cost of the building in cash. Elcorn records the transaction as follows:

Building	20,000,000	
Cash		16,000,000
Revenue—donation of asset (20% × $20 million)		4,000,000

International Financial Reporting Standards

● LO10–9

IFRS requires government grants to be recognized in income over the periods necessary to match them on a systematic basis with the related costs that they are intended to compensate.

IFRS ILLUSTRATION

Government Grants. Both U.S. GAAP and IFRS require that companies value donated assets at their fair values. For government grants, though, the way that value is recorded is different under the two sets of standards. Unlike U.S. GAAP, donated assets are not recorded as revenue under IFRS. *IAS No. 20*[13] requires that government grants be recognized in income over the periods necessary to match them on a systematic basis with the related costs that they are intended to compensate. So, for example, *IAS No. 20* allows two alternatives for grants related to assets:

1. Deduct the amount of the grant in determining the initial cost of the asset.
2. Record the grant as a liability, deferred income, in the balance sheet and recognize it in the income statement systematically over the asset's useful life.

In Illustration 10–13, if a company chose the first option, the building would be recorded at $16 million. If instead the company chose the second option, the building would be recorded at $20 million, but rather than recognizing $4 million in revenue as with U.S. GAAP, a $4 million credit to deferred income would be recorded and recognized as income over the life of the building.

Real World Financials

Siemens, a global electronics and electrical engineering company based in Germany, prepares its financial statements according to IFRS, and sometimes receives government grants for the purchase or production of fixed assets. The following disclosure note included with recent financial statements indicates that Siemens uses the first option, deducting the amount of the grant from the initial cost of the asset.

Government Grants (in part)
Grants awarded for the purchase or the production of fixed assets (grants related to assets) are generally offset against the acquisition or production costs of the respective assets and reduce future depreciations accordingly.

Property, plant, and equipment and intangible assets also can be acquired in an exchange. Because an exchange transaction inherently involves a disposition of one asset as it is given up in exchange for another, we cover these transactions in Part B, Dispositions and Exchanges.

Decision Makers' Perspective

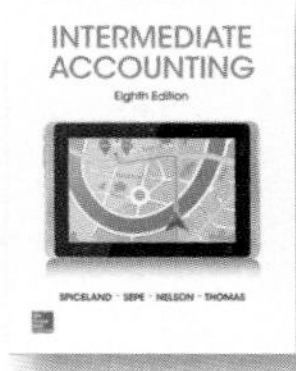

The property, plant, and equipment and intangible asset acquisition decision is among the most significant decisions that management must make. A decision to acquire a new fleet of airplanes or to build or purchase a new office building or manufacturing plant could influence a company's performance for many years.

These decisions, often referred to as **capital budgeting** decisions, require management to forecast all future net cash flows (cash inflows minus cash outflows) generated by the asset(s). These cash flows are then used in a model to determine if the future cash flows are sufficient to warrant the capital expenditure. One such model, the net present value model,

[13] "Government Grants," *International Accounting Standard No. 20* (IASCF), as amended effective January 1, 2014.

compares the present value of future net cash flows with the required initial acquisition cost of the asset(s). If the present value is higher than the acquisition cost, the asset is acquired. You have studied or will study capital budgeting in considerable depth in a financial management course. The introduction to the time value of money concept in Chapter 6 provided you with important tools necessary to evaluate capital budgeting decisions.

● LO10–5

A key to profitability is how well a company manages and utilizes its assets. Financial analysts often use activity, or turnover, ratios to evaluate a company's effectiveness in managing assets. This concept was illustrated with receivables and inventory in previous chapters. Property, plant, and equipment (PP&E) usually are a company's primary revenue-generating assets. Their efficient use is critical to generating a satisfactory return to owners. One ratio analysts often use to measure how effectively managers use PP&E is the **fixed-asset turnover ratio**. This ratio is calculated as follows:

The *fixed-asset turnover ratio* measures a company's effectiveness in managing property, plant, and equipment.

$$\text{Fixed-asset turnover ratio} = \frac{\text{Net sales}}{\text{Average fixed assets}}$$

The ratio indicates the level of sales generated by the company's investment in fixed assets. The denominator usually is the book value, sometimes called carrying value or carrying amount (cost less accumulated depreciation and depletion) of property, plant, and equipment.[14]

As with other turnover ratios, we can compare a company's fixed-asset turnover with that of its competitors, with an industry average, or with the same company's ratio over time. Let's compare the fixed-asset turnover ratios for **The Gap, Inc.**, and **Ross Stores, Inc.**, two companies in the retail apparel industry.

Real World Financials

	($ in millions)			
	Gap		**Ross Stores**	
	2014	**2013**	**2014**	**2013**
Property, plant, and equipment (net)	$2,758	$2,619	$1,875	$1,493
Net sales—2014	$16,148		$10,230	

The 2014 fixed-asset turnover for GAP is 6.01 ($16,148 ÷ [($2,758 + 2,619) ÷ 2]) compared to the turnover for Ross Stores of 6.07 ($10,230 ÷ [($1,875 + 1,493) ÷ 2]). Ross Stores is able to generate $.06 more in sales dollars than GAP for each dollar invested in fixed assets. ●

PART B

Dispositions and Exchanges

● LO10–6

After using property, plant, and equipment and intangible assets, companies will sell, retire, or exchange those assets. Accounting for exchanges differs somewhat from accounting for sales and retirements because they involve both an acquisition and a disposition. So let's look first at sales and retirements and then we'll address accounting for exchanges. Be sure to note that in each case, the companies should record depreciation, depletion, or amortization up to the date of disposition or exchange.

Dispositions

When selling property, plant, and equipment and intangible assets for monetary consideration (cash or a receivable), the seller recognizes a gain or loss for the difference between the consideration received and the book value of the asset sold. Let's look at Illustration 10–14.

Retirements (or abandonments) are treated similarly. The only difference is that there will be no monetary consideration received. A loss is recorded for the remaining book value of the asset.

When property, plant, and equipment or an intangible asset is to be disposed of by sale in the near future, we classify it as "held for sale" and report it at the lower of its book value or

[14]If intangible assets are significant, their book value could be added to the denominator to produce a turnover that reflects all long-lived, revenue-producing assets. The use of book value provides an approximation of the company's current investment in these assets.

The Robosport Company sold for $6,000 equipment that originally cost $20,000. Depreciation of $12,000 had been recorded up to the date of sale. Since the $8,000 book value of the asset ($20,000 − 12,000) exceeds the $6,000 consideration Robosport received, the company recognizes a $2,000 loss. The sale is recorded as follows:

Cash (selling price)	6,000	
Accumulated depreciation (account balance)	12,000	
Loss on disposal of equipment (difference)	2,000	
Equipment (account balance)		20,000

Illustration 10–14

Sale of Property, Plant, and Equipment

A gain or loss is recognized for the difference between the consideration received and the asset's book value.

fair value less any cost to sell.[15] If the fair value less cost to sell is below book value, we recognize an impairment loss. Assets classified as held for sale are not depreciated or amortized. Recall from your study of discontinued operations in Chapter 4 that this treatment is the same one we employed in accounting for a component of an entity that is held for sale. We cover this topic in more depth in the impairment section of Chapter 11.

Property, plant, and equipment and intangible assets to be disposed of by sale are classified as held for sale and measured at the lower of book value or fair value less cost to sell.

Additional Consideration

Involuntary Conversions

Occasionally companies dispose of property, plant, and equipment and intangible assets unintentionally. These so-called involuntary conversions include destruction by fire, earthquake, flood, or other catastrophe and expropriation by a governmental body.

Usually, the company receives a cash settlement from an insurance company for destroyed assets or from the governmental body for expropriated assets. The company often immediately reinvests this cash in similar assets. Nevertheless, involuntary conversions are treated precisely the same as voluntary conversions. That is, the proceeds are recorded, the book value of the lost assets is removed, and a gain or loss is recognized for the difference.

Exchanges

Sometimes a company will acquire an asset in exchange for an asset other than cash. This frequently involves a trade-in by which a new asset is acquired in exchange for an old asset, and cash is given to equalize the fair values of the assets exchanged. The basic principle followed in these nonmonetary asset[16] exchanges is to value the asset received at fair value. This can be the fair value of the asset(s) given up or the fair value of the asset(s) received plus (or minus) any cash exchanged. We first look to the fair value of the asset given up. However, in a trade-in, quite often the fair value of the new asset is more clearly evident than the second-hand value of the asset traded in. We recognize a gain or loss for the difference between the fair value of the asset given up and its book value. See the example in Illustration 10–15A.

Let's modify the illustration slightly by assuming that the fair value of the old equipment is $75,000 instead of $150,000. Illustration 10–15B shows the journal entry to record the transaction.

It's important to understand that the gain or loss recognized in these transactions is the difference between the fair value and book value of the asset given. *The amount of cash given or received has no effect on the amount of gain or loss recognized.* The cash given or received simply serves to equalize the fair value of the assets exchanged.

Gain or loss is the difference between fair value and book value of the asset given.

[15]FASB ASC 360–10–35–15: Property, Plant, and Equipment–Overall–Subsequent Measurement–Impairment or Disposal of Long-Lived Assets (previously "Accounting for the Impairment or Disposal of Long-lived Assets," *Statement of Financial Accounting Standards No. 144* (Norwalk, Conn.: FASB, 2001)).

[16]Monetary items are assets and liabilities whose *amounts are fixed*, by contract or otherwise, in terms of a specific number of dollars. Others are considered nonmonetary.

Illustration 10–15A

Nonmonetary Asset Exchange

An asset received in an exchange of nonmonetary assets generally is valued at fair value.

A gain is recognized when the fair value of an asset given is more than its book value.

The Elcorn Company traded its laser equipment for the newer air-cooled ion lasers manufactured by American Laser Corporation. The old equipment had a book value of $100,000 (cost of $500,000 less accumulated depreciation of $400,000) and a fair value of $150,000. To equalize the fair values of the assets exchanged, in addition to the old equipment, Elcorn paid American Laser $430,000 in cash. This means that the fair value of the new laser equipment is $580,000. We know this because American Laser was willing to trade the new lasers in exchange for old lasers worth $150,000 plus $430,000 cash. The following journal entry records the transaction:

Laser equipment—new (fair value: $150,000 + 430,000) ...	580,000	
Accumulated depreciation (account balance)	400,000	
Laser equipment—old (account balance)		500,000
Cash (amount paid)..		430,000
Gain (to balance; also: $150,000 − 100,000)		50,000

The new laser equipment is recorded at $580,000, the fair value of the old equipment, $150,000, plus the cash given of $430,000. This also equals the fair value of the new lasers. Elcorn recognizes a gain of $50,000, which is simply the difference between the old equipment's fair value of $150,000 and its $100,000 book value as well as the amount needed to allow the debits to equal credits in the journal entry.

Illustration 10–15B

Nonmonetary Asset Exchange

A loss is recognized when the fair value of an asset given is less than its book value.

The Elcorn Company traded its laser equipment for the newer air-cooled ion lasers manufactured by American Laser Corporation. The old equipment had a book value of $100,000 (cost of $500,000 less accumulated depreciation of $400,000) and a fair value of $75,000. To equalize the fair values of the assets exchanged, in addition to the old equipment, Elcorn paid American Laser $430,000 in cash. This means that the fair value of the new laser equipment is $505,000. We know this because American Laser was willing to trade the new lasers in exchange for old lasers worth $75,000 plus $430,000 in cash. The following journal entry records the transaction:

Laser equipment—new (fair value: $75,000 + 430,000)	505,000	
Accumulated depreciation (account balance)	400,000	
Loss (to balance; also: $100,000 − 75,000)	25,000	
Laser equipment—old (account balance)		500,000
Cash (amount paid)		430,000

The $25,000 difference between the equipment's fair value of $75,000 and its book value of $100,000 is recognized as a loss. The new equipment is valued at $505,000, the fair value of the old equipment of $75,000 plus the $430,000 cash given.

Until 2005, the accounting treatment of nonmonetary asset exchanges depended on a number of factors including (1) whether the assets exchanged were similar or dissimilar, (2) whether a gain or loss was indicated in the exchange, and (3) whether cash was given or received. A new accounting standard[17] simplified accounting for exchanges by requiring the use of fair value except in rare situations in which the fair value can't be determined or the exchange lacks commercial substance.[18]

Let's discuss these two rare situations.

Fair Value Not Determinable

It would be unusual for a company to be unable to reasonably determine fair value of either asset in an exchange. Nevertheless, if the situation does occur, the company would simply use the book value of the asset given up, plus (minus) any cash given (received) to value the

[17]FASB ASC 845: Nonmonetary Transactions (previously "Exchanges of Nonmonetary Assets an amendment of APB Opinion No. 29," *Statement of Financial Accounting Standards No. 153* (Norwalk, Conn.: FASB, 2004)).

[18]There is a third situation which precludes the use of fair value in a nonmonetary exchange. The transaction is an exchange of inventories to facilitate sales to customers other than the parties to the exchange.

asset acquired. For example, if fair value had not been determinable in Illustration 10–15A, Elcorn would have recorded the exchange as follows:

Equipment—new (book value + cash: $100,000 + 430,000)	530,000	
Accumulated depreciation (account balance)	400,000	
Equipment—old (account balance)		500,000
Cash (amount paid)		430,000

If we can't determine the fair value of either asset in the exchange, the asset received is valued at the book value of the asset given.

The new equipment is valued at the book value of the old equipment ($100,000) plus the cash given ($430,000). No gain or loss is recognized.

Exchange Lacks Commercial Substance

If we record an exchange at fair value, we recognize a gain or loss for the difference between the fair value and book value of the asset(s) given up. To preclude the possibility of a company exchanging appreciated assets solely to recognize a gain, fair value can be used only in gain situations that have "commercial substance."

A nonmonetary exchange is considered to have commercial substance if future cash flows will change as a result of the exchange. Most exchanges are for business reasons and would not be transacted if there were no anticipated change in future cash flows. For example, newer models of equipment can increase production or improve manufacturing efficiency, causing an increase in revenue or a decrease in operating costs with a corresponding increase in future cash flows. The exchange of old laser equipment for the *newer* model in Illustration 10–15A is an example of an exchange transacted for business reasons.

Commercial substance is present when future cash flows change as a result of the exchange.

GAIN SITUATION. Suppose a company owned a tract of land that had a book value of $1 million and a fair value of $5 million. The only ways to recognize the $4 million appreciation are to either sell the land or to exchange the land for another nonmonetary asset for a genuine business purpose. For example, if the land were exchanged for a different type of asset, say an office building, then future cash flows most likely will change, the exchange has commercial substance, fair value is used and the $4 million gain can be recognized. On the other hand, if the land were exchanged for a tract of land that has the identical characteristics as the land given, then it is unlikely that future cash flows would change. In this case, the exchange lacks commercial substance and the new land is valued at the book value of the old land. Illustration 10–16 provides an example.

Illustration 10–16
Nonmonetary Asset Exchange—Exchange Lacks Commercial Substance

The Elcorn Company traded a tract of land to Sanchez Development for a similar tract of land. The old land had a book value of $2,500,000 and a fair value of $4,500,000. To equalize the fair values of the assets exchanged, in addition to the land, Elcorn paid Sanchez $500,000 in cash. This means that the fair value of the land acquired is $5,000,000. The following journal entry records the transaction, *assuming that the exchange lacks commercial substance:*

Land—new (book value + cash: $2,500,000 + 500,000)	3,000,000	
Land—old (account balance)		2,500,000
Cash (amount paid)		500,000

The new land is recorded at $3,000,000, the book value of the old land, $2,500,000, plus the cash given of $500,000. No gain is recognized.

LOSS SITUATION. In Illustration 10–16, what if the fair value of the land given was less than its book value? It's unlikely that a company would enter into this type of transaction unless there was a good reason. The FASB's intent in including the commercial substance requirement for the use of fair value was to avoid companies' trading *appreciated* property for no business reason other than to recognize the gain. This means that when a loss is indicated in a nonmonetary exchange, it's okay to record the loss and we use fair value to value the asset acquired.

When the fair value of the asset given is less than its book value, we always use fair value to record the exchange.

Additional Consideration

In Illustration 10–16, cash was given to equalize the fair values of the assets exchanged. What if cash was received? Suppose that $500,000 cash was *received* instead of given and that the fair value of the old land was $5,000,000. This means that the fair value of the land received is $4,500,000. In that case, part of the transaction is considered monetary and we would recognize a portion of the $2,500,000 gain ($5,000,000 − 2,500,000). The amount of gain recognized is equal to the proportion of cash received relative to total received:[19]

$$\frac{\$500,000}{\$500,000 + 4,500,000} = 10\%$$

Elcorn would recognize a $250,000 gain (10% × $2,500,000) and would value the land received at **$2,250,000**, the book value of the land given ($2,500,000), plus the gain recognized ($250,000), less the cash received ($500,000). The following journal entry records the transaction:

	Debit	Credit
Land—new ($2,500,000 + 250,000 − 500,000)	2,250,000	
Cash	500,000	
Land—old		2,500,000
Gain		250,000

Concept Review Exercise

EXCHANGES

The MD Corporation recently acquired new equipment to be used in its production process. In exchange, the company traded in an existing asset that had an original cost of $60,000 and accumulated depreciation on the date of the exchange of $45,000. In addition, MD paid $40,000 cash to the equipment manufacturer. The fair value of the old equipment is $17,000.

Required:

1. Prepare the journal entry MD would use to record the exchange transaction assuming that the transaction has commercial substance.
2. Prepare the journal entry MD would use to record the exchange transaction assuming that the transaction does *not* have commercial substance.

Solution:

1. Prepare the journal entry MD would use to record the exchange transaction assuming that the transaction has commercial substance.

	Debit	Credit
Equipment—new ($17,000 + 40,000)	57,000	
Accumulated depreciation (account balance)	45,000	
Cash (amount paid)		40,000
Equipment—old (account balance)		60,000
Gain ($17,000 fair value − $15,000 book value)		2,000

2. Prepare the journal entry MD would use to record the exchange transaction assuming that the transaction does not have commercial substance.

	Debit	Credit
Equipment—new ($15,000 + 40,000)	55,000	
Accumulated depreciation (account balance)	45,000	
Cash (amount paid)		40,000
Equipment—old (account balance)		60,000

[19] If the amount of monetary consideration received is deemed significant, the transaction is considered to be monetary and the entire gain is recognized. In other words, the transaction is accounted for as if it had commercial substance. GAAP defines "significance" in this situation as 25% or more of the fair value of the exchange. FASB ASC 845–10–25–6: Nonmonetary transactions–Overall–Recognition (previously "Interpretations of *APB Opinion No. 29*," *EITF Abstracts No. 01–02* (Norwalk, Conn.: FASB, 2002)).

PART C

Self-Constructed Assets and Research and Development

Two types of expenditures relating to property, plant, and equipment and intangible assets whose accounting treatment has generated considerable controversy are interest costs pertaining to self-constructed assets and amounts spent for research and development. We now consider those expenditures and why those controversies have developed.

Self-Constructed Assets

● LO10–7

A company might decide to construct an asset for its own use rather than buy an existing one. For example, a retailer like **Nordstrom** might decide to build its own store rather than purchase an existing building. A manufacturing company like **Intel** could construct its own manufacturing facility. In fact, Nordstrom and Intel are just two of the many companies that self-construct assets. Other recognizable examples include **Walt Disney**, **Sears**, and **Caterpillar**. Quite often these companies act as the main contractor and then subcontract most of the actual construction work.

The critical accounting issue in these instances is identifying the cost of the self-constructed asset. The task is more difficult than for purchased assets because there is no external transaction to establish an exchange price. Actually, two difficulties arise in connection with assigning costs to self-constructed assets: (1) determining the amount of the company's indirect manufacturing costs (overhead) to be allocated to the construction and (2) deciding on the proper treatment of interest (actual or implicit) incurred during construction.

Overhead Allocation

One difficulty of associating costs with self-constructed assets is the same difficulty encountered when determining cost of goods manufactured for sale. The costs of material and direct labor usually are easily identified with a particular construction project and are included in cost. However, the treatment of manufacturing overhead cost and its allocation between construction projects and normal production is a controversial issue.

The cost of a self-constructed asset includes identifiable materials and labor and a portion of the company's manufacturing overhead costs.

Some accountants advocate the inclusion of only the *incremental* overhead costs in the total cost of construction. That is, the asset's cost would include only those additional costs that are incurred because of the decision to construct the asset. This would exclude such indirect costs as depreciation and the salaries of supervisors that would be incurred whether or not the construction project is undertaken. If, however, a new construction supervisor was hired specifically to work on the project, then that salary would be included in asset cost.

Others advocate assigning overhead on the same basis that is used for a regular manufacturing process. That is, all overhead costs are allocated both to production and to self-constructed assets based on the relative amount of a chosen cost driver (for example, labor hours) incurred. This is known as the *full-cost approach* and is the generally accepted method used to determine the cost of a self-constructed asset.

Interest Capitalization

FINANCIAL Reporting Case

Q3, p. 527

To reiterate, the cost of an asset includes all costs necessary to get the asset ready for its intended use. Unlike one purchased from another company, a self-constructed asset requires time to create it. During this construction period, the project must be financed in some way. This suggests the question as to whether interest costs during the construction period are one of the costs of acquiring the asset itself or simply costs of financing the asset. On the one hand, we might point to interest charges to finance inventories during their period of manufacture or to finance the purchase of plant assets from others and argue that construction period interest charges are merely costs of financing the asset that should be expensed as incurred like all other interest costs. On the other hand, we might argue that self-constructed assets are different in that during the construction period, they are not yet ready for their intended use for producing revenues. And, so, in keeping with both the historical cost principle and the matching concept, all costs during this period, including interest, should be capitalized and then allocated as depreciation during later periods when the assets are providing benefits.

Only assets that are constructed as discrete projects qualify for interest capitalization.

Only interest incurred during the construction period is eligible for capitalization.

QUALIFYING ASSETS. Generally accepted accounting principles are consistent with the second argument. Specifically, interest is capitalized during the construction period for (a) assets built for a company's own use as well as for (b) assets constructed *as discrete projects* for sale or lease (a ship or a real estate development, for example). This excludes from interest capitalization consideration inventories that are routinely manufactured in large quantities on a repetitive basis and assets that already are in use or are ready for their intended use.[20] Interest costs incurred during the productive life of the asset are expensed as incurred.

The interest capitalization period begins when construction begins and the first expenditure is made as long as interest costs are actually being incurred.

PERIOD OF CAPITALIZATION. The capitalization period for a self-constructed asset starts with the first expenditure (materials, labor, or overhead) and ends either when the asset is substantially complete and ready for use or when interest costs no longer are being incurred. Interest costs incurred can pertain to borrowings other than those obtained specifically for the construction project. However, interest costs can't be imputed; actual interest costs must be incurred.

Average accumulated expenditures approximates the average debt necessary for construction.

AVERAGE ACCUMULATED EXPENDITURES. Because we consider interest to be a necessary cost of getting a self-constructed asset ready for use, the amount capitalized is only that portion of interest cost incurred during the construction period that *could have been avoided* if expenditures for the asset had not been made. In other words, if construction had not been undertaken, debt incurred for the project would not have been necessary and/or other interest-bearing debt could have been liquidated or employed elsewhere.

As a result, interest should be determined for only the construction expenditures *actually incurred* during the capitalization period. And unless all expenditures are made at the outset of the period, it's necessary to determine the *average* amount outstanding during the period. This is the amount of debt that would be required to finance the expenditures and thus the amount on which interest would accrue. For instance, if a company accumulated $1,500,000 of construction expenditures fairly evenly throughout the construction period, the average expenditures would be:

Total accumulated expenditures incurred evenly throughout the period	$1,500,000
	÷2
Average accumulated expenditures	$ 750,000

Average accumulated expenditures is determined by time-weighting individual expenditures made during the construction period.

At the beginning of the period, no expenditures have accumulated, so no interest has accrued (on the equivalent amount of debt). But, by the end of the period interest is accruing on the total amount, $1,500,000. On average, then, interest accrues on half the total or $750,000.

If expenditures are not incurred evenly throughout the period, a simple average is insufficient. In that case, a *weighted average* is determined by time-weighting individual expenditures or groups of expenditures by the number of months from their incurrence to the end of the construction period. This is demonstrated in Illustration 10–17.

The weighted-average accumulated expenditures by the end of 2016 are:

FINANCIAL Reporting Case

Q4, p. 527

	Actual Expenditures	Time-Weighted Expenditures
January 1, 2016	$500,000 × 12/12 =	$500,000
March 31, 2016	400,000 × 9/12 =	300,000
September 30, 2016	600,000 × 3/12 =	150,000
Average accumulated expenditures for 2016	=	$950,000

STEP 1: Determine the average accumulated expenditures.

Again notice that the average accumulated expenditures are less than the total accumulated expenditures of $1,500,000. If Mills had borrowed exactly the amount necessary to finance the project, it would not have incurred interest on a loan of $1,500,000 for the whole year but only on an average loan of $950,000. The next step is to determine the interest to be capitalized for the average accumulated expenditures.

[20]FASB ASC 835–20–25: Interest–Capitalization of Interest–Recognition (previously "Capitalization of Interest Costs," *Statement of Financial Accounting Standards No. 34* (Stamford, Conn.: FASB, 1979)).

Illustration 10–17
Interest Capitalization

On January 1, 2016, the Mills Conveying Equipment Company began construction of a building to be used as its office headquarters. The building was completed on June 30, 2017. Expenditures on the project, mainly payments to subcontractors, were as follows:

January 1, 2016	$ 500,000
March 31, 2016	400,000
September 30, 2016	600,000
Accumulated expenditures at December 31, 2016 (before interest capitalization)	$1,500,000
January 31, 2017	600,000
April 30, 2017	300,000

On January 1, 2016, the company obtained a $1 million construction loan with an 8% interest rate. The loan was outstanding during the entire construction period. The company's other interest-bearing debt included two long-term notes of $2,000,000 and $4,000,000 with interest rates of 6% and 12%, respectively. Both notes were outstanding during the entire construction period.

STEP 2: Calculate the amount of interest to be capitalized.

INTEREST RATES. In this situation, debt financing was obtained specifically for the construction project, and the amount borrowed is sufficient to cover the average accumulated expenditures. To determine the interest capitalized, then, we simply multiply the construction loan rate of 8% by the average accumulated expenditures.

The amount of interest capitalized is determined by multiplying an interest rate by the average accumulated expenditures.

Interest capitalized for 2016 = $950,000 × 8% = **$76,000**

Notice that this is the same answer we would get by assuming separate 8% construction loans were made for each expenditure at the time each expenditure was made:

Loans		Annual Rate		Portion of Year Outstanding		Interest
$500,000	×	8%	×	12/12	=	$40,000
400,000	×	8%	×	9/12	=	24,000
600,000	×	8%	×	3/12	=	12,000
Interest capitalized for 2016						$76,000

The interest of **$76,000** is added to the cost of the building, bringing accumulated expenditures at December 31, 2016, to $1,576,000 ($1,500,000 + **76,000**). The remaining interest cost incurred but not capitalized is expensed.

It should be emphasized that interest capitalization does not require that funds actually be borrowed for this specific purpose, only that the company does have outstanding debt. The presumption is that even if the company doesn't borrow specifically for the project, funds from other borrowings must be diverted to finance the construction. Either way—directly or indirectly—interest costs are incurred. In our illustration, for instance, even without the construction loan, interest would be capitalized because other debt was outstanding. The capitalized interest would be the average accumulated expenditures multiplied by the weighted-average rate on these other loans. The weighted-average interest rate on all debt other than the construction loan would be 10%, calculated as follows:[21]

Loans		Rate		Interest
$2,000,000	×	6%	=	$120,000
4,000,000	×	12%	=	480,000
$6,000,000				$600,000

[21]The same result can be obtained simply by multiplying the individual debt interest rates by the relative amount of debt at each rate. In this case, one-third of total debt is at 6% and two-thirds of the total debt is at 12% [(1/3 × 6%) + (2/3 × 12%) = 10%].

$$\text{Weighted-average rate: } \frac{\$600{,}000}{\$6{,}000{,}000} = 10\%$$

This is a weighted average because total interest is $600,000 on total debt of $6,000,000. Therefore, in our illustration, without any specific construction loan, interest capitalized for 2016 would have been $95,000 ($950,000 × 10%).

Additional Consideration

The weighted-average rate isn't used for 2016 in our illustration because the specific construction loan is sufficient to cover the average accumulated expenditures. If the specific construction loan had been insufficient to cover the average accumulated expenditures, its 8% interest rate would be applied to the average accumulated expenditures up to the amount of the specific borrowing, and any remaining average accumulated expenditures in excess of specific borrowings would be multiplied by the weighted-average rate on all other outstanding interest-bearing debt. Suppose, for illustration, that the 8% construction loan had been only $500,000 rather than $1,000,000. We would calculate capitalized interest using both the specific rate and the weighted-average rate:

	Average Accumulated Expenditures		Rate		Interest
Total	$950,000				
Specific borrowing	500,000	×	8%	=	$40,000
Excess	$450,000	×	10%	=	45,000
Capitalized interest					$85,000

In our illustration, it's necessary to use this approach in 2017.

Interest capitalized is limited to interest incurred.

It's possible that the amount of interest calculated to be capitalized exceeds the amount of interest actually incurred. If that's the case, we limit the interest capitalized to the actual interest incurred. In our illustration, total interest cost incurred during 2016 far exceeds the $76,000 of capitalized interest calculated, so it's not necessary to limit the capitalized amount.

STEP 3: Compare calculated interest with actual interest incurred.

Loans		Annual Rate		Actual Interest	Calculated Interest
$1,000,000	×	8%	=	$ 80,000	
2,000,000	×	6%	=	120,000	
4,000,000	×	12%	=	480,000	
				$680,000	$76,000

Use lower amount ↑ ($76,000)

Continuing the example based on the information in Illustration 10–17, let's determine the amount of interest capitalized during 2017 for the building. The total accumulated expenditures by the end of the project are:

Accumulated expenditures at the beginning of 2017 (including interest capitalization)	$1,576,000
January 31, 2017 expenditures	600,000
April 30, 2017 expenditures	300,000
Accumulated expenditures at June 30, 2017 (before 2017 interest capitalization)	$2,476,000

The weighted-average accumulated expenditures by the end of the project are:

	Actual Expenditures	Time-Weighted Expenditures
January 1, 2017	$1,576,000 × 6/6 =	$1,576,000
January 31, 2017	600,000 × 5/6 =	500,000
April 30, 2017	300,000 × 2/6 =	100,000
Average accumulated expenditures for 2017		$2,176,000

STEP 1: Determine the average accumulated expenditures.

Notice that the 2017 expenditures are weighted relative to the construction period of six months because the project was finished on June 30, 2017. Interest capitalized for 2017 would be **$98,800**, calculated as follows:

	Average Accumulated Expenditures		Annual Rate		Fraction of Year		
	$2,176,000						
Specific borrowing	1,000,000	×	8%	×	6/12	=	$40,000
Excess	$1,176,000	×	10%	×	6/12	=	58,800
Capitalized interest							$98,800

STEP 2: Calculate the amount of interest to be capitalized.

Multiplying by six-twelfths reflects the fact that the interest rates are annual rates (12-month rates) and the construction period is only 6 months.

Loans		Annual Rate	Actual Interest	Calculated Interest
$1,000,000	×	8% × 6/12 =	$ 40,000	
2,000,000	×	6% × 6/12 =	60,000	
4,000,000	×	12% × 6/12 =	240,000	
			$340,000	$98,800
				↑ Use lower amount

STEP 3: Compare calculated interest with actual interest incurred.

For the first six months of 2017, **$98,800** of interest would be capitalized, bringing the total capitalized cost of the building to $2,574,800 ($2,476,000 + 98,800), and $241,200 in interest would be expensed ($340,000 − 98,800).

Additional Consideration

To illustrate how the actual interest limitation might come into play, let's assume the nonspecific borrowings in our illustration were $200,000 and $400,000 (instead of $2,000,000 and $4,000,000). Our comparison would change as follows:

Loans		Annual Rate	Actual Interest	Calculated Interest
$1,000,000	×	8% × 6/12 =	$40,000	
200,000	×	6% × 6/12 =	6,000	
400,000	×	12% × 6/12 =	24,000	
			$70,000	$98,800
			↑ Use lower amount	

The method of determining interest to capitalize that we've discussed is called the **specific interest method** because we use rates from specific construction loans to the extent of specific borrowings before using the average rate of other debt. Sometimes, though, it's difficult to associate specific borrowings with projects. In these situations, it's acceptable to just use the weighted-average rate on all interest-bearing debt, including all construction loans. This is known as the **weighted-average method**. In our illustration, for example, if the $1,000,000, 8% loan had not been specifically related to construction, we would calculate a single weighted-average rate as shown below.

Weighted-average method

Loans		Rate		Interest
$1,000,000	×	8%	=	$ 80,000
2,000,000	×	6%	=	120,000
4,000,000	×	12%	=	480,000
$7,000,000				$680,000

$$\text{Weighted-average rate: } \frac{\$680,000}{\$7,000,000} = 9.7\%$$

If we were using the weighted-average method rather than the specific interest method, we would simply multiply this single rate times the average accumulated expenditures to determine capitalizable interest.

If material, the amount of interest capitalized during the period must be disclosed.

DISCLOSURE. For an accounting period in which interest costs are capitalized, the total amount of interest costs capitalized, if the amount is material, should be disclosed. Illustration 10–18 shows an interest capitalization disclosure note that was included in a recent annual report of **Wal-Mart Stores, Inc.**, the world's largest retailer.

Illustration 10–18

Capitalized Interest Disclosure—Wal-Mart Stores, Inc.

Real World Financials

Property and equipment (in part)

Interest costs capitalized on construction projects were $78 million, $74 million, and $60 million in fiscal 2014, 2013, and 2012, respectively.

Research and Development (R&D)

● LO10–8

Prior to 1974, the practice was to allow companies to either expense or capitalize R&D costs, but GAAP now requires all research and development costs to be charged to expense when incurred.[22] This was a controversial change opposed by many companies that preferred delaying the recognition of these expenses until later years when presumably the expenditures bear fruit.

R&D costs are expensed in the periods incurred.

A company undertakes an R&D project because it believes the project will eventually provide benefits that exceed the current expenditures. Unfortunately, though, it's difficult to predict which individual research and development projects will ultimately provide benefits. In fact, only 1 in 10 actually reaches commercial production. Moreover, even for those projects that pan out, a direct relationship between research and development costs and specific future revenue is difficult to establish. In other words, even if R&D costs do lead to future benefits, it's difficult to objectively determine the size of the benefits and in which periods the costs should be expensed if they are capitalized. These are the issues that prompted the FASB to require immediate expensing.

R&D costs entail a high degree of uncertainty of future benefits and are difficult to match with future revenues.

The FASB's approach is certain in many cases to understate assets and overstate current expense because at least some of the R&D expenditures will likely produce future benefits.

[22]FASB ASC 730–10–25–1: Research and Development–Overall–Recognition (previously "Accounting for Research and Development Costs," *Statement of Financial Accounting Standards No. 2* (Stamford, Conn.: FASB, 1974), par. 12).

Determining R&D Costs

GAAP distinguishes research and development as follows:

Research is planned search or critical investigation aimed at discovery of new knowledge with the hope that such knowledge will be useful in developing a new product or service or a new process or technique or in bringing about a significant improvement to an existing product or process.
Development is the translation of research findings or other knowledge into a plan or design for a new product or process or for a significant improvement to an existing product or process whether intended for sale or use.[23]

R&D costs include salaries, wages, and other labor costs of personnel engaged in R&D activities, the costs of materials consumed, equipment, facilities, and intangibles used in R&D projects, the costs of services performed by others in connection with R&D activities, and a reasonable allocation of indirect costs related to those activities. General and administrative costs should not be included unless they are clearly related to the R&D activity.

If an asset is purchased specifically for a single R&D project, its cost is considered R&D and expensed immediately even though the asset's useful life extends beyond the current year. However, the cost of an asset that has an alternative future use beyond the current R&D project is *not* a current R&D expense. Instead, the depreciation or amortization of these alternative-use assets is included as R&D expenses in the current and future periods the assets are used for R&D activities.

R&D expense includes the depreciation and amortization of assets used in R&D activities.

In general, R&D costs pertain to activities that occur prior to the start of commercial production, and costs of starting commercial production and beyond are not R&D costs. Illustration 10–19 captures this concept with a time line beginning with the start of an R&D project and ending with the ultimate sale of a developed product or the use of a developed process. The illustration also provides examples of activities typically included as R&D and examples of activities typically excluded from R&D.[24]

Illustration 10–19
Research and Development Expenditures

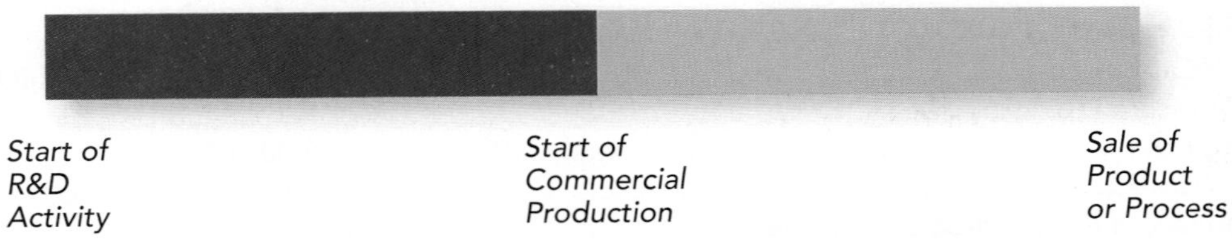

Start of R&D Activity	*Start of Commercial Production*	*Sale of Product or Process*

Examples of R&D Costs:	*Examples of Non-R&D Costs:*
• Laboratory research aimed at discovery of new knowledge	• Engineering follow-through in an early phase of commercial production
• Searching for applications of new research findings or other knowledge	• Quality control during commercial production including routine testing of products
• Design, construction, and testing of preproduction prototypes and models	• Routine ongoing efforts to refine, enrich, or otherwise improve on the qualities of an existing product
• Modification of the formulation or design of a product or process	• Adaptation of an existing capability to a particular requirement or customer's need as a part of a continuing commercial activity

Costs incurred *before* the start of commercial production are all expensed as R&D.

Costs incurred *after* commercial production begins would be either expensed or included in the cost of inventory.

[23]Ibid., section 730–10–20 (previously par. 8 of *SFAS No.* 2).
[24]Ibid., section 730–10–55 (previously par. 9 of *SFAS No.* 2).

Costs incurred before the start of commercial production are all expensed as R&D. The costs incurred after commercial production begins would be either expensed or treated as manufacturing overhead and included in the cost of inventory. Let's look at an example in Illustration 10–20.

Illustration 10–20
Research and Development Costs

The Askew Company made the following cash expenditures during 2016 related to the development of a new industrial plastic:

R&D salaries and wages	$10,000,000
R&D supplies consumed during 2016	3,000,000
Purchase of R&D equipment	5,000,000
Patent filing and legal costs	100,000
Payments to others for services performed in connection with R&D activities	1,200,000
Total	$19,300,000

The project resulted in a new product to be manufactured in 2017. A patent was filed with the U.S. Patent Office. The equipment purchased will be employed in other projects. Depreciation on the equipment for 2016 was $500,000.

Filing and legal costs for patents, copyrights, and other developed intangibles are capitalized and amortized in future periods.

The salaries and wages, supplies consumed, and payments to others for R&D services are expensed in 2016 as R&D. The equipment is capitalized and the 2016 depreciation is expensed as R&D. Even though the costs to develop the patented product are expensed, the filing and legal costs for the patent are capitalized and amortized in future periods just as similar costs are capitalized for purchased intangibles. Amortization of the patent is discussed in Chapter 11.

The various expenditures would be recorded as follows:

	Debit	Credit
R&D expense ($10,000,000 + 3,000,000 + 1,200,000)	14,200,000	
Cash		14,200,000
To record R&D expenses.		
Equipment	5,000,000	
Cash		5,000,000
To record the purchase of equipment.		
R&D expense	500,000	
Accumulated depreciation—equipment		500,000
To record R&D depreciation.		
Patent	100,000	
Cash		100,000
To capitalize the patent filing and legal costs.		

Expenditures reconciliation:	
Recorded as R&D	$14,200,000
Capitalized as equipment	5,000,000
Capitalized as patent	100,000
Total expenditures	$19,300,000

GAAP requires disclosure of total R&D expense incurred during the period.

GAAP requires that total R&D expense incurred must be disclosed either as a line item in the income statement or in a disclosure note. For example, **Microsoft** reported over $11 billion of R&D expense on the face of its 2014 income statement. In our illustration, total R&D expense disclosed in 2016 would be $14,700,000 ($14,200,000 in expenditures and $500,000 in depreciation). Note that if Askew later sells this patent to another company for, say, $15 million, the buyer would capitalize the entire purchase price rather than only the filing and legal costs. Once again, the reason for the apparent inconsistency in accounting treatment of internally generated intangibles and externally purchased intangibles is the difficulty of associating costs and benefits.

R&D Performed for Others

The principle requiring the immediate expensing of R&D does not apply to companies that perform R&D for other companies under contract. In these situations, the R&D costs are capitalized as inventory and carried forward into future years until the project is completed. Of course, justification is that the benefits of these expenditures are the contract fees that are determinable and are earned over the term of the project. Income from these contracts can be recognized over time or at a point in time, depending on the specifics of the contract. We discussed these alternatives in Chapter 5.

Another exception pertains to a company that develops computer software. Expenditures made after the software is determined to be technologically feasible but before it is ready for commercial production are capitalized. Costs incurred before technological feasibility is established are expensed as incurred. We discuss software development costs below.

Start-Up Costs

For the six months ended June 30, 2014, **Chipotle Mexican Grill, Inc.**, opened 89 new restaurants. The company incurred a variety of one-time preopening costs for wages, benefits and travel for the training and opening teams, food and other restaurant operating costs totaling $7.7 million. In fact, whenever a company introduces a new product or service, or commences business in a new territory or with a new customer, it incurs similar **start-up costs**. As with R&D expenditures, a company must expense all the costs related to a company's start-up activities in the period incurred, rather than capitalize those costs as an asset. Start-up costs also include **organization costs** related to organizing a new entity, such as legal fees and state filing fees to incorporate.[25]

Start-up costs are expensed in the period incurred.

Additional Consideration

Development Stage Enterprises

A development stage enterprise is a new business that has either not commenced its principal operations or has begun its principal operations but has not generated significant revenues. Years ago, many of these companies recorded an asset for the normal operating costs incurred during the development stage. This asset was then expensed over a period of time beginning with the commencement of operations.

GAAP requires that these enterprises comply with the same generally accepted accounting principles that apply to established operating companies in determining whether a cost is to be charged to expense when incurred or capitalized and expensed in future periods.[26] Therefore, normal operating costs incurred during the development stage are expensed, not capitalized. Development stage enterprises are allowed to provide items of supplemental information to help financial statement readers more readily assess their future cash flows.

Software Development Costs

The computer software industry has become a large and important U.S. business over the last two decades. Relative newcomers such as **Microsoft** and **Adobe Systems**, as well as traditional hardware companies like **IBM**, are leaders in this multibillion dollar industry. A significant expenditure for these companies is the cost of developing software. In the early years of the software industry, some software companies were capitalizing software development costs and expensing them in future periods and others were expensing these costs in the period incurred.

GAAP requires the capitalization of software development costs incurred after technological feasibility is established.

[25]FASB ASC 720–15–25–1: Other Expenses–Start-Up Costs–Recognition (previously "Reporting on the Costs of Start-Up Activities," *Statement of Position 98-5* (New York: AICPA, 1998)).

[26]FASB ASC 915: Development Stage Entities (previously "Accounting and Reporting by Development Stage Enterprises," *Statement of Financial Accounting Standards No. 7* (Stamford, Conn.: FASB, 1975)).

Now GAAP requires that companies record R&D as an expense, until **technological feasibility** of the software has been established, for costs they incur to develop or purchase computer software to be sold, leased, or otherwise marketed.[27] We account for the costs incurred to develop computer software *to be used internally* in a similar manner. Costs incurred during the preliminary project stage are expensed as R&D. After the application development stage is reached (for example, at the coding stage or installation stage), we capitalize any further costs.[28] We generally capitalize the costs of computer software *purchased* for internal use.

Technological feasibility is established "when the enterprise has completed all planning, designing, coding, and testing activities that are necessary to establish that the product can be produced to meet its design specifications including functions, features, and technical performance requirements."[29] Costs incurred after technological feasibility but before the software is available for general release to customers are capitalized as an intangible asset. These costs include coding and testing costs and the production of product masters. Costs incurred after the software release date usually are not R&D expenditures. Illustration 10–21 shows the R&D time line introduced earlier in the chapter modified to include the point at which technological feasibility is established. Only the costs incurred between technological feasibility and the software release date are capitalized.

Illustration 10–21

Research and Development Expenditures—Computer Software

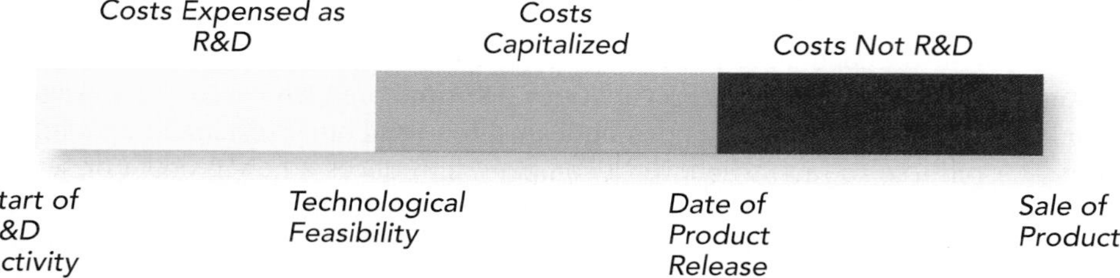

The amortization of capitalized computer software development costs begins when the product is available for general release to customers. The periodic amortization percentage is the greater of (1) the ratio of current revenues to current and anticipated revenues (percentage-of-revenue method) or (2) the straight-line percentage over the useful life of the asset, as shown in Illustration 10–22.

Illustration 10–22

Software Development Costs

The Astro Corporation develops computer software graphics programs for sale. A new development project begun in 2015 reached technological feasibility at the end of June 2016, and the product was available for release to customers early in 2017. Development costs incurred in 2016 prior to June 30 were $1,200,000 and costs incurred from June 30 to the product availability date were $800,000. 2017 revenues from the sale of the new product were $3,000,000 and the company anticipates an additional $7,000,000 in revenues. The economic life of the software is estimated at four years.

Astro Corporation would expense the $1,200,000 in costs incurred prior to the establishment of technological feasibility and capitalize the $800,000 in costs incurred between technological feasibility and the product availability date. 2017 amortization of the intangible asset, software development costs, is calculated as follows:

1. Percentage-of-revenue method:

$$\frac{\$3{,}000{,}000}{\$3{,}000{,}000 + 7{,}000{,}000} = 30\% \times \$800{,}000 = \$240{,}000$$

2. Straight-line method:

$$\tfrac{1}{4} \text{ or } 25\% \times \$800{,}000 = \$200{,}000.$$

The percentage-of-revenue method is used because it produces the greater amortization, $240,000.

[27]FASB ASC 985–20–25–1: Software–Costs of Software to be Sold, Leased, or Marketed–Recognition (previously "Accounting for the Costs of Computer Software to be Sold, Leased, or Otherwise Marketed," *Statement of Financial Accounting Standards No. 86* (Stamford, Conn.: FASB, 1985)).

[28]FASB ASC 350–40–25: Intangibles–Goodwill and Other–Internal-Use Software–Recognition (previously "Accounting for the Costs of Computer Software Developed or Obtained for Internal Use," *Statement of Position 98-1* (New York: AICPA, 1998)).

[29]FASB ASC 985–20–25–2: Software–Costs of Software to be Sold, Leased, or Marketed–Recognition (previously "Accounting for the Costs of Computer Software to be Sold, Leased, or Otherwise Marketed," *Statement of Financial Accounting Standards No. 86* (Stamford, Conn.: FASB, 1985), par. 4).

Illustration 10–23 shows the software disclosure included in a recent annual report of **CA, Inc.** The note provides a good summary of the accounting treatment of software development costs.

Illustration 10–23
Software Disclosure—CA, Inc.

Real World Financials

> **Capitalized Development Costs (in part)**
> Capitalized development costs in the accompanying Consolidated Balance Sheets include costs associated with the development of computer software to be sold, leased or otherwise marketed. Software development costs associated with new products and significant enhancements to existing software products are expensed as incurred until technological feasibility, as defined in FASB ASC Topic 985-20, has been established. Costs incurred thereafter are capitalized until the product is made generally available. Annual amortization of capitalized software costs is the greater of the amount computed using the ratio that current gross revenues for a product bear to the total of current and anticipated future gross revenues for that product or the straight-line method over the remaining estimated economic life of the software product, generally estimated to be five years from the date the product became available for general release to customers.

Why do generally accepted accounting principles allow this exception to the general rule of expensing all R&D? We could attribute it to the political process. Software is a very important industry to our economy and perhaps its lobbying efforts resulted in the standard allowing software companies to capitalize certain R&D costs.

We could also attribute the exception to the nature of the software business. Recall that R&D costs in general are expensed in the period incurred for two reasons: (1) they entail a high degree of uncertainty of future benefits, and (2) they are difficult to match with future benefits. With software, there is an important identifiable engineering milestone, technological feasibility. When this milestone is attained, the probability of the software product's success increases significantly. And because the useful life of software is fairly short (one to four years in most cases), it is much easier to determine the periods of increased revenues than for R&D projects in other industries. Compare this situation with, say, the development of a new drug. Even after the drug has been developed, it must go through

International Financial Reporting Standards

● LO10–9

IFRS requires companies to capitalize development expenditures that meet specified criteria.

Research and Development Expenditures. Except for software development costs incurred after technological feasibility has been established, U.S. GAAP requires all research and development expenditures to be expensed in the period incurred. *IAS No. 38*[30] draws a distinction between research activities and development activities. Research expenditures are expensed in the period incurred. However, development expenditures that meet specified criteria are capitalized as an intangible asset. Under both U.S. GAAP and IFRS, any direct costs to secure a patent, such as legal and filing fees, are capitalized.

Heineken, a company based in Amsterdam, prepares its financial statements according to IFRS. The following disclosure note describes the company's adherence to *IAS No. 38*. The note also describes the criteria for capitalizing development expenditures as well as the types of expenditures capitalized.

Real World Financials

> **Software, Research and Development and Other Intangible Assets (in part)**
> Expenditures on research activities, undertaken with the prospect of gaining new technical knowledge and understanding, are recognized in the income statement when incurred. Development activities involve a plan or design for the production of new or substantially improved products and processes. Development expenditures are capitalized only if development costs can be measured reliably, the product or process

(continued)

[30]"Intangible Assets," *International Accounting Standard No. 38* (IASCF), as amended effective January 1, 2014.

(concluded)

is technically and commercially feasible, future economic benefits are probable, and Heineken intends to and has sufficient resources to complete development and to use or sell the asset. The expenditures capitalized include the cost of materials, direct labor and overhead costs that are directly attributable to preparing the asset for its intended use, and capitalized borrowing costs.

Amortization of capitalized development costs begins when development is complete and the asset is available for use. Heineken disclosed that it amortizes its capitalized development costs using the straight-line method over an estimated 3-year useful life.

extensive testing to meet FDA (Food and Drug Administration) approval, which may never be attained. If attained, the useful life of the drug could be anywhere from a few months to many years.

Purchased Research and Development

It's not unusual for one company to buy another company in order to obtain technology that the acquired company has developed or is in the process of developing. Any time a company buys another, it values the tangible and intangible assets acquired at fair value. When technology is involved, we distinguish between *developed technology* and *in-process research and development.* To do that, we borrow a criterion used in accounting for software development costs, and determine whether *technological feasibility* has been achieved. If so, the value of that technology is considered "developed," and we capitalize its fair value (record it as an asset) and amortize that amount over its useful life just like any other finite-life intangible asset.

In business acquisitions, the fair value of in-process research and development is capitalized as an indefinite-life intangible asset.

We treat in-process R&D differently. GAAP requires the capitalization of the fair value of in-process R&D. But, unlike developed technology, we view it as an *indefinite-life* intangible asset.[31] As you will learn in Chapter 11, we don't amortize indefinite-life intangibles. Instead, we monitor these assets and test them for impairment when required by GAAP. If the R&D project is completed successfully, we switch to the way we account for developed technology and amortize the capitalized amount over the estimated period the product or process developed will provide benefits. If the project instead is abandoned, we expense the entire balance immediately. Research and development costs incurred after the acquisition to complete the project are expensed as incurred, consistent with the treatment of any other R&D expenditure not acquired in an acquisition.

Real World Financials

As an example, in 2013 **Cisco Systems, Inc.**, the global networking equipment giant, acquired **Sourcefire, Inc.**, a leader in intelligent cybersecurity solutions for $2,449 million. The fair values assigned included $577 million for finite-life intangible assets (including $400 million in developed technology), $22 million for in-process R&D, and $1,791 million for goodwill.

International Financial Reporting Standards

● LO10–9

Software Development Costs. The percentage we use to amortize computer software development costs under U.S. GAAP is the greater of (1) the ratio of current revenues to current and anticipated revenues or (2) the straight-line percentage over the useful life of the software. This approach is allowed under IFRS, but not required.

[31]FASB ASC 805: Business Combinations (previously "Business Combinations," *Statement of Financial Accounting Standards No. 141 (revised)* (Norwalk, Conn.: FASB, 2007)).

Financial Reporting Case Solution

1. **Describe to Stan what it means to capitalize an expenditure. What is the general rule for determining which costs are capitalized when property, plant, and equipment or an intangible asset is acquired?** *(p. 530)* To capitalize an expenditure simply means to record it as an asset. All expenditures other than payments to shareholders and debt repayments are either expensed as incurred or capitalized. In general, the choice is determined by whether the expenditure benefits more than just the current period. Exceptions to this general principle are discussed in the chapter. The initial cost of an asset includes all expenditures necessary to bring the asset to its desired condition and location for use.
2. **Which costs might be included in the initial cost of equipment?** *(p. 530)* In addition to the purchase price, the cost of equipment might include the cost of transportation, installation, testing, and legal fees to establish title.
3. **In what situations is interest capitalized rather than expensed?** *(p. 549)* Interest is capitalized only for assets constructed for a company's own use or for assets constructed as discrete products for sale or lease. For example, **Walt Disney** capitalizes interest on assets constructed for its theme parks, resorts and other property, and on theatrical and television productions. During the construction period, interest is considered a cost necessary to get the asset ready for its intended use.
4. **What is the three-step process used to determine the amount of interest capitalized?** *(p. 550)* The first step is to determine the average accumulated expenditures for the period. The second step is to multiply the average accumulated expenditures by an appropriate interest rate or rates to determine the amount of interest capitalized. A final step compares the interest determined in step two with actual interest incurred. Interest capitalized is limited to the amount of interest incurred.
5. **What is goodwill and how is it measured?** *(p. 537)* Goodwill represents the unique value of a company as a whole over and above its identifiable tangible and intangible assets. Because goodwill can't be separated from a company, it's not possible for a buyer to acquire it without also acquiring the whole company or a controlling portion of it. Goodwill will appear as an asset in a balance sheet only when it was purchased in connection with the acquisition of another company. In that case, the capitalized cost of goodwill equals the fair value of the consideration exchanged for the company less the fair value of the net assets acquired. Goodwill is a residual asset; it's the amount left after other assets are identified and valued. Just like for other intangible assets that have indefinite useful lives, we do not amortize goodwill. ●

The Bottom Line

- **LO10–1** The initial cost of property, plant, and equipment and intangible assets acquired in an exchange transaction includes the purchase price and all expenditures necessary to bring the asset to its desired condition and location for use. The cost of a natural resource includes the acquisition costs for the use of land, the exploration and development costs incurred before production begins, and restoration costs incurred during or at the end of extraction. Purchased intangible assets are valued at their original cost to include the purchase price and legal and filing fees. *(p. 530)*
- **LO10–2** If a lump-sum purchase involves different assets, it is necessary to allocate the lump-sum acquisition price among the separate items according to some logical allocation method. A widely used allocation method is to divide the lump-sum purchase price according to the individual assets' relative fair values. *(p. 539)*
- **LO10–3** Assets acquired in exchange for deferred payment contracts are valued at their fair value or the present value of payments using a realistic interest rate. *(p. 540)*

- **LO10–4** Assets acquired through the issuance of equity securities are valued at the fair value of the securities if known; if not known, the fair value of the assets received is used. Donated assets are valued at their fair value. *(p. 542)*
- **LO10–5** A key to profitability is how well a company manages and utilizes its assets. Financial analysts often use activity, or turnover, ratios to evaluate a company's effectiveness in managing its assets. Property, plant, and equipment (PP&E) usually are a company's primary revenue-generating assets. Their efficient use is critical to generating a satisfactory return to owners. One ratio that analysts often use to measure how effectively managers use PP&E is the fixed-asset turnover ratio. This ratio is calculated by dividing net sales by average fixed assets. *(p. 544)*
- **LO10–6** When an item of property, plant, and equipment or an intangible asset is sold, a gain or loss is recognized for the difference between the consideration received and the asset's book value. The basic principle used for nonmonetary exchanges is to value the asset(s) received based on the fair value of the asset(s) given up. In certain situations, the valuation of the asset(s) received is based on the book value of the asset(s) given up. *(p. 544)*
- **LO10–7** The cost of a self-constructed asset includes identifiable materials and labor and a portion of the company's manufacturing overhead costs. In addition, GAAP provides for the capitalization of interest incurred during construction. The amount of interest capitalized is equal to the average accumulated expenditures for the period multiplied by the appropriate interest rates, not to exceed actual interest incurred. *(p. 549)*
- **LO10–8** Research and development costs incurred to internally develop an intangible asset are expensed in the period incurred. Filing and legal costs for developed intangibles are capitalized. *(p. 554)*
- **LO10–9** *IAS No. 20* requires that government grants be recognized in income over the periods necessary to match them on a systematic basis with the related costs that they are intended to compensate. Other than software development costs incurred after technological feasibility has been established, U.S. GAAP requires all research and development expenditures to be expensed in the period incurred. *IAS No. 38* draws a distinction between research activities and development activities. Research expenditures are expensed in the period incurred. However, development expenditures that meet specified criteria are capitalized as an intangible asset. *(pp. 543, 559,* and *560)*

APPENDIX 10 Oil And Gas Accounting

There are two generally accepted methods that companies can use to account for oil and gas exploration costs. The **successful efforts method** requires that exploration costs that are known *not* to have resulted in the discovery of oil or gas (sometimes referred to as *dry holes*) be included as expenses in the period the expenditures are made. The alternative, the **full-cost method**, allows costs incurred in searching for oil and gas within a large geographical area to be capitalized as assets and expensed in the future as oil and gas from the successful wells are removed from that area. Both of these methods are widely used. Illustration 10A–1 compares the two alternatives.

Illustration 10A–1
Oil and Gas Accounting

The Shannon Oil Company incurred $2,000,000 in exploration costs for each of 10 oil wells drilled in 2016 in west Texas. Eight of the 10 wells were dry holes.

The accounting treatment of the $20 million in total exploration costs will vary significantly depending on the accounting method used. The summary journal entries using each of the alternative methods are as follows:

Successful Efforts			**Full Cost**		
Oil deposit	4,000,000		Oil deposit	20,000,000	
Exploration expense	16,000,000		Cash		20,000,000
Cash		20,000,000			

Using the full-cost method, Shannon would capitalize the entire $20 million which is expensed as oil from the two successful wells is depleted. On the other hand, using the successful efforts method, the cost of the unsuccessful wells is expensed in 2016, and only the $4 million cost related to the successful wells is capitalized and expensed in future periods as the oil is depleted.

Chapter 1 characterized the establishment of accounting and reporting standards as a political process. Standards, particularly changes in standards, can have significant differential effects on companies, investors and creditors, and other interest groups. The FASB must consider potential economic consequences of a change in an accounting standard or the introduction of a new standard. The history of oil and gas accounting provides a good example of this political process and the effect of possible adverse economic consequences on the standard-setting process.

In 1977 the FASB attempted to establish uniformity in the accounting treatment of oil and gas exploration costs. An accounting standard was issued requiring all companies to use the successful efforts method.[32]

This Standard met with criticism from the oil and gas companies that were required to switch from full cost to successful efforts accounting. These companies felt that the switch would seriously depress their reported income over time. As a result, they argued, their ability to raise capital in the securities markets would be inhibited, which would result in a cutback of new exploration. The fear that the Standard would cause domestic companies to significantly reduce oil and gas exploration and thus increase our dependence on foreign oil was compelling to the U.S. Congress, the SEC, and the Department of Energy.

Many feared that the requirement to switch to successful efforts accounting would cause a significant cutback in the exploration for new oil and gas in the United States.

Extensive pressure from Congress, the SEC, and affected companies forced the FASB to rescind the Standard. Presently, oil and gas companies can use either the successful efforts or full-cost method to account for oil and gas exploration costs. Of course, the method used must be disclosed. For example, Illustration 10A–2 shows how **Chevron Corp**. disclosed its use of the successful efforts method in a note to recent financial statements.

Properties, Plant and Equipment (in part)
The successful efforts method is used for crude oil and gas exploration and production activities.

Illustration 10A–2
Oil and Gas Accounting Disclosure—Chevron Corp.

Real World Financials

[32]The rescinded standard was "Financial Accounting and Reporting by Oil and Gas Producing Companies," *Statement of Financial Accounting Standards No. 19* (Stamford, Conn.: FASB, 1977). Authoritative guidance on this topic can now be found at FASB ASC 932: Extractive Activities–Oil and Gas.

Questions For Review of Key Topics

Q 10–1 Explain the difference between tangible and intangible long-lived, revenue-producing assets.

Q 10–2 What is included in the original cost of property, plant, and equipment and intangible assets acquired in an exchange transaction?

Q 10–3 Identify the costs associated with the initial valuation of a developed natural resource.

Q 10–4 Briefly summarize the accounting treatment for intangible assets, explaining the difference between purchased and internally developed intangible assets.

Q 10–5 What is goodwill and how is it measured?

Q 10–6 Explain the method generally used to allocate the cost of a lump-sum purchase to the individual assets acquired.

Q 10–7 When an asset is acquired and a note payable is assumed, explain how acquisition cost of the asset is determined when the interest rate for the note is less than the current market rate for similar notes.

Q 10–8 Explain how assets acquired in exchange for equity securities are valued.

Q 10–9 Explain how property, plant, and equipment and intangible assets acquired through donation are valued.

Q 10–10 When an item of property, plant, and equipment is disposed of, how is gain or loss on disposal computed?

Q 10–11 What is the basic principle for valuing property, plant, and equipment and intangible assets acquired in exchange for other nonmonetary assets?

Q 10–12 Identify the two exceptions to valuing property, plant, and equipment and intangible assets acquired in nonmonetary exchanges at the fair value of the asset(s) given up.

Q 10–13 In what situations is interest capitalized?

Q 10–14 Define average accumulated expenditures and explain how the amount is computed.

Q 10–15 Explain the difference between the specific interest method and the weighted-average method in determining the amount of interest to be capitalized.

Q 10–16 Define R&D according to U.S. GAAP.

Q 10–17 Explain the accounting treatment of equipment acquired for use in R&D projects.

Q 10–18 Explain the accounting treatment of costs incurred to develop computer software.

Q 10–19 Explain the difference in the accounting treatment of the cost of developed technology and the cost of in-process R&D in an acquisition.

IFRS **Q 10–20** Identify any differences between U.S. GAAP and International Financial Reporting Standards in accounting for government grants received.

IFRS **Q 10–21** Identify any differences between U.S. GAAP and International Financial Reporting Standards in the treatment of research and development expenditures.

IFRS **Q 10–22** Identify any differences between U.S. GAAP and International Financial Reporting Standards in the treatment of software development costs.

Q 10–23 (Based on Appendix 10) Explain the difference between the successful efforts and the full-cost methods of accounting for oil and gas exploration costs.

Brief Exercises

BE 10–1
Acquisition cost; machine
● LO10–1

Beaverton Lumber purchased a milling machine for $35,000. In addition to the purchase price, Beaverton made the following expenditures: freight, $1,500; installation, $3,000; testing, $2,000; personal property tax on the machine for the first year, $500. What is the initial cost of the machine?

BE 10–2
Acquisition cost; land and building
● LO10–1

Fullerton Waste Management purchased land and a warehouse for $600,000. In addition to the purchase price, Fullerton made the following expenditures related to the acquisition: broker's commission, $30,000; title insurance, $3,000; miscellaneous closing costs, $6,000. The warehouse was immediately demolished at a cost of $18,000 in anticipation of the building of a new warehouse. Determine the amounts Fullerton should capitalize as the cost of the land and the building.

BE 10–3
Lump-sum acquisition
● LO10–2

Refer to the situation described in BE 10–2. Assume that Fullerton decides to use the warehouse rather than demolish it. An independent appraisal estimates the fair values of the land and warehouse at $420,000 and $280,000, respectively. Determine the amounts Fullerton should capitalize as the cost of the land and the building.

BE 10–4
Cost of a natural resource; asset retirement obligation
● LO10–1

Smithson Mining operates a silver mine in Nevada. Acquisition, exploration, and development costs totaled $5.6 million. After the silver is extracted in approximately five years, Smithson is obligated to restore the land to its original condition, including constructing a wildlife preserve. The company's controller has provided the following three cash flow possibilities for the restoration costs: (1) $500,000, 20% probability; (2) $550,000, 45% probability; and (3) $650,000, 35% probability. The company's credit-adjusted, risk-free rate of interest is 6%. What is the initial cost of the silver mine?

BE 10–5
Asset retirement obligation
● LO10–1

Refer to the situation described in BE 10–4. What is the book value of the asset retirement liability at the end of one year? Assuming that the actual restoration costs incurred after extraction is completed are $596,000, what amount of gain or loss will Smithson recognize on retirement of the liability?

BE 10–6
Goodwill
● LO10–1

Pro-tech Software acquired all of the outstanding stock of Reliable Software for $14 million. The book value of Reliable's net assets (assets minus liabilities) was $8.3 million. The fair values of Reliable's assets and liabilities equaled their book values with the exception of certain intangible assets whose fair values exceeded book values by $2.5 million. Calculate the amount paid for goodwill.

BE 10–7
Acquisition cost; noninterest-bearing note
● LO10–3

On June 30, 2016, Kimberly Farms purchased custom-made harvesting equipment from a local producer. In payment, Kimberly signed a noninterest-bearing note requiring the payment of $60,000 in two years. The fair value of the equipment is not known, but an 8% interest rate properly reflects the time value of money for this type of loan agreement. At what amount will Kimberly initially value the equipment? How much interest expense will Kimberly recognize in its income statement for this note for the year ended December 31, 2016?

BE 10–8
Acquisition cost; issuance of equity securities
● LO10–4

Shackelford Corporation acquired a patent from its founder, Jim Shackelford, in exchange for 50,000 shares of the company's nopar common stock. On the date of the exchange, the common stock had a fair value of $22 per share. Determine the cost of the patent.

BE 10–9
Fixed-asset turnover ratio; solve for unknown
● LO10–5

The balance sheets of Pinewood Resorts reported net fixed assets of $740,000 and $940,000 at the end of 2015 and 2016, respectively. The fixed-asset turnover ratio for 2016 was 3.25. Calculate Pinewood's net sales for 2016.

BE 10–10
Disposal of property, plant, and equipment
● LO10–6

Lawler Clothing sold manufacturing equipment for $16,000. Lawler originally purchased the equipment for $80,000, and depreciation through the date of sale totaled $71,000. What was the gain or loss on the sale of the equipment?

BE 10–11
Nonmonetary exchange
● LO10–6

Calaveras Tire exchanged equipment for two pickup trucks. The book value and fair value of the equipment were $20,000 (original cost of $65,000 less accumulated depreciation of $45,000) and $17,000, respectively. To equalize fair values, Calaveras paid $8,000 in cash. At what amount will Calaveras value the pickup trucks? How much gain or loss will the company recognize on the exchange? Assume the exchange has commercial substance.

BE 10–12
Nonmonetary exchange
● LO10–6

Refer to the situation described in BE 10–11. Answer the questions assuming that the fair value of the equipment was $24,000, instead of $17,000.

BE 10–13
Nonmonetary exchange
● LO10–6

Refer to the situation described in BE 10–12. Answer the questions assuming that the exchange lacks commercial substance.

BE 10–14
Interest capitalization
● LO10–7

A company constructs a building for its own use. Construction began on January 1 and ended on December 30. The expenditures for construction were as follows: January 1, $500,000; March 31, $600,000; June 30, $400,000; October 30, $600,000. To help finance construction, the company arranged a 7% construction loan on January 1 for $700,000. The company's other borrowings, outstanding for the whole year, consisted of a $3 million loan and a $5 million note with interest rates of 8% and 6%, respectively. Assuming the company uses the *specific interest method,* calculate the amount of interest capitalized for the year.

BE 10–15
Interest capitalization
● LO10–7

Refer to the situation described in BE 10–14. Assuming the company uses the *weighted-average method,* calculate the amount of interest capitalized for the year.

BE 10–16
Research and development
● LO10–8

Maxtor Technology incurred the following costs during the year related to the creation of a new type of personal computer monitor:

Salaries	$220,000
Depreciation on R&D facilities and equipment	125,000
Utilities and other direct costs incurred for the R&D facilities	66,000
Patent filing and related legal costs	22,000
Payment to another company for performing a portion of the development work	120,000
Costs of adapting the new monitor for the specific needs of a customer	80,000

What amount should Maxtor report as research and development expense in its income statement?

Exercises

An alternate exercise and problem set is available in the Connect library.

E 10–1
Acquisition costs; land and building
● LO10–1

On March 1, 2016, Beldon Corporation purchased land as a factory site for $60,000. An old building on the property was demolished, and construction began on a new building that was completed on December 15, 2016. Costs incurred during this period are listed below:

Demolition of old building	$ 4,000
Architect's fees (for new building)	12,000
Legal fees for title investigation of land	2,000
Property taxes on land (for period beginning March 1, 2016)	3,000
Construction costs	500,000
Interest on construction loan	5,000

Salvaged materials resulting from the demolition of the old building were sold for $2,000.

Required:
Determine the amounts that Beldon should capitalize as the cost of the land and the new building.

E 10–2
Acquisition cost; equipment
● LO10–1

Oaktree Company purchased new equipment and made the following expenditures:

Purchase price	$45,000
Sales tax	2,200
Freight charges for shipment of equipment	700
Insurance on the equipment for the first year	900
Installation of equipment	1,000

The equipment, including sales tax, was purchased on open account, with payment due in 30 days. The other expenditures listed above were paid in cash.

Required:
Prepare the necessary journal entries to record the above expenditures.

E 10–3
Acquisition costs; lump-sum acquisition
● LO10–1, LO10–2

Samtech Manufacturing purchased land and building for $4 million. In addition to the purchase price, Samtech made the following expenditures in connection with the purchase of the land and building:

Title insurance	$16,000
Legal fees for drawing the contract	5,000
Pro-rated property taxes for the period after acquisition	36,000
State transfer fees	4,000

An independent appraisal estimated the fair values of the land and building, if purchased separately, at $3.3 and $1.1 million, respectively. Shortly after acquisition, Samtech spent $82,000 to construct a parking lot and $40,000 for landscaping.

Required:
1. Determine the initial valuation of each asset Samtech acquired in these transactions.
2. Repeat requirement 1, assuming that immediately after acquisition, Samtech demolished the building. Demolition costs were $250,000 and the salvaged materials were sold for $6,000. In addition, Samtech spent $86,000 clearing and grading the land in preparation for the construction of a new building.

E 10–4
Cost of a natural resource; asset retirement obligation
● LO10–1

Jackpot Mining Company operates a copper mine in central Montana. The company paid $1,000,000 in 2016 for the mining site and spent an additional $600,000 to prepare the mine for extraction of the copper. After the copper is extracted in approximately four years, the company is required to restore the land to its original condition, including repaving of roads and replacing a greenbelt. The company has provided the following three cash flow possibilities for the restoration costs:

	Cash Outflow	Probability
1	$300,000	25%
2	400,000	40%
3	600,000	35%

To aid extraction, Jackpot purchased some new equipment on July 1, 2016, for $120,000. After the copper is removed from this mine, the equipment will be sold. The credit-adjusted, risk-free rate of interest is 10%.

Required:

1. Determine the cost of the copper mine.
2. Prepare the journal entries to record the acquisition costs of the mine and the purchase of equipment.

E 10–5
Intangibles
● LO10–1

Freitas Corporation was organized early in 2016. The following expenditures were made during the first few months of the year:

Attorneys' fees in connection with the organization of the corporation	$ 12,000
State filing fees and other incorporation costs	3,000
Purchase of a patent	20,000
Legal and other fees for transfer of the patent	2,000
Purchase of furniture	30,000
Pre-opening salaries	40,000
Total	$107,000

Required:

Prepare a summary journal entry to record the $107,000 in cash expenditures.

E 10–6
Goodwill
● LO10–1

On March 31, 2016, Wolfson Corporation acquired all of the outstanding common stock of Barney Corporation for $17,000,000 in cash. The book values and fair values of Barney's assets and liabilities were as follows:

	Book Value	Fair Value
Current assets	$ 6,000,000	$ 7,500,000
Property, plant, and equipment	11,000,000	14,000,000
Other assets	1,000,000	1,500,000
Current liabilities	4,000,000	4,000,000
Long-term liabilities	6,000,000	5,500,000

Required:

Calculate the amount paid for goodwill.

E 10–7
Goodwill
● LO10–1

Johnson Corporation acquired all of the outstanding common stock of Smith Corporation for $11,000,000 in cash. The book value of Smith's net assets (assets minus liabilities) was $7,800,000. The fair values of all of Smith's assets and liabilities were equal to their book values with the following exceptions:

	Book Value	Fair Value
Receivables	$1,300,000	$1,100,000
Property, plant, and equipment	8,000,000	9,400,000
Intangible assets	200,000	1,200,000

Required:

Calculate the amount paid for goodwill.

E 10–8
Lump-sum acquisition
● LO10–2

Pinewood Company purchased two buildings on four acres of land. The lump-sum purchase price was $900,000. According to independent appraisals, the fair values were $450,000 (building A) and $250,000 (building B) for the buildings and $300,000 for the land.

Required:

Determine the initial valuation of the buildings and the land.

E 10–9
Acquisition cost; noninterest-bearing note
● LO10–3

On January 1, 2016, Byner Company purchased a used tractor. Byner paid $5,000 down and signed a noninterest-bearing note requiring $25,000 to be paid on December 31, 2018. The fair value of the tractor is not determinable. An interest rate of 10% properly reflects the time value of money for this type of loan agreement. The company's fiscal year-end is December 31.

Required:

1. Prepare the journal entry to record the acquisition of the tractor. Round computations to the nearest dollar.
2. How much interest expense will the company include in its 2016 and 2017 income statements for this note?
3. What is the amount of the liability the company will report in its 2016 and 2017 balance sheets for this note?

E 10–10
Acquisition costs; noninterest-bearing note
● LO10–1, LO10–3

Teradene Corporation purchased land as a factory site and contracted with Maxtor Construction to construct a factory. Teradene made the following expenditures related to the acquisition of the land, building, and equipment for the factory:

Purchase price of the land	$1,200,000
Demolition and removal of old building	80,000
Clearing and grading the land before construction	150,000
Various closing costs in connection with acquiring the land	42,000
Architect's fee for the plans for the new building	50,000
Payments to Maxtor for building construction	3,250,000
Equipment purchased	860,000
Freight charges on equipment	32,000
Trees, plants, and other landscaping	45,000
Installation of a sprinkler system for the landscaping	5,000
Cost to build special platforms and install wiring for the equipment	12,000
Cost of trial runs to ensure proper installation of the equipment	7,000
Fire and theft insurance on the factory for the first year of use	24,000

In addition to the above expenditures, Teradene purchased four forklifts from **Caterpillar**. In payment, Teradene paid $16,000 cash and signed a noninterest-bearing note requiring the payment of $70,000 in one year. An interest rate of 7% properly reflects the time value of money for this type of loan.

Required:
Determine the initial valuation of each of the assets Teradene acquired in the above transactions.

E 10–11
IFRS; acquisition cost; issuance of equity securities and donation
● LO10–4, LO10–9

 IFRS

On February 1, 2016, the Xilon Corporation issued 50,000 shares of its nopar common stock in exchange for five acres of land located in the city of Monrovia. On the date of the acquisition, Xilon's common stock had a fair value of $18 per share. An office building was constructed on the site by an independent contractor. The building was completed on November 2, 2016, at a cost of $6,000,000. Xilon paid $4,000,000 in cash and the remainder was paid by the city of Monrovia.

Required:
1. Prepare the journal entries to record the acquisition of the land and the building.
2. Assuming that Xilon prepares its financial statements according to International Financial Reporting Standards, explain the alternatives the company has for recording the acquisition of the office building.

E 10–12
IFRS; acquisition cost; acquisition by donation; government grant
● LO10–9

 IFRS

Cranston LTD. prepares its financial statements according to International Financial Reporting Standards. In October 2016, the company received a $2 million government grant. The grant represents 20% of the total cost of equipment that will be used to improve the roads in the local area. Cranston recorded the grant and the purchase of the equipment as follows:

Cash................................	2,000,000	
Revenue		2,000,000
Equipment.......................	10,000,000	
Cash		10,000,000

Required:
1. Explain the alternative accounting treatments available to Cranston for accounting for this government grant.
2. Prepare any necessary correcting entries under each of the alternatives described in requirement 1.

E 10–13
Fixed-asset turnover ratio; Nvidia
● LO10–5

Real World Financials

Nvidia Corporation, a global technology company located in Santa Clara, California, reported the following information in its 2014 financial statements ($ in thousands):

	2014	2013
Balance sheets		
Property, plant, and equipment (net)	$ 582,740	$576,144
Income statement		
Net sales for 2014	$4,130,162	

Required:
1. Calculate the company's 2014 fixed-asset turnover ratio.
2. How would you interpret this ratio?

E 10–14
Disposal of property, plant, and equipment
● LO10–6

Funseth Farms Inc. purchased a tractor in 2013 at a cost of $30,000. The tractor was sold for $3,000 in 2016. Depreciation recorded through the disposal date totaled $26,000.

Required:
1. Prepare the journal entry to record the sale.
2. Assuming that the tractor was sold for $10,000, prepare the journal entry to record the sale.

E 10–15
Disposal of property, plant, and equipment and intangible assets
● LO10–6

On July 15, 2016, Cottonwood Industries sold a patent and equipment to Roquemore Corporation for $750,000 and $325,000, respectively. The book value of the patent and equipment on the date of sale were $120,000 and $400,000 (cost of $550,000 less accumulated depreciation of $150,000), respectively.

Required:
Prepare the journal entries to record the sales of the patent and equipment.

E 10–16
Nonmonetary exchange
● LO10–6

Cedric Company recently traded in an older model computer for a new model. The old model's book value was $180,000 (original cost of $400,000 less $220,000 in accumulated depreciation) and its fair value was $200,000. Cedric paid $60,000 to complete the exchange which has commercial substance.

Required:
Prepare the journal entry to record the exchange.

E 10–17
Nonmonetary exchange
● LO10–6

[This is a variation of the previous exercise.]

Required:
Assume the same facts as in Exercise 10–16, except that the fair value of the old equipment is $170,000. Prepare the journal entry to record the exchange.

E 10–18
Nonmonetary exchange
● LO10–6

The Bronco Corporation exchanged land for equipment. The land had a book value of $120,000 and a fair value of $150,000. Bronco paid the owner of the equipment $10,000 to complete the exchange which has commercial substance.

Required:
1. What is the fair value of the equipment?
2. Prepare the journal entry to record the exchange.

E 10–19
Nonmonetary exchange
● LO10–6

[This is a variation of the previous exercise.]

Required:
Assume the same facts as in Exercise 10–18 except that Bronco *received* $10,000 from the owner of the equipment to complete the exchange.
1. What is the fair value of the equipment?
2. Prepare the journal entry to record the exchange.

E 10–20
Nonmonetary exchange
● LO10–6

The Tinsley Company exchanged land that it had been holding for future plant expansion for a more suitable parcel located farther from residential areas. Tinsley carried the land at its original cost of $30,000. According to an independent appraisal, the land currently is worth $72,000. Tinsley paid $14,000 in cash to complete the transaction.

Required:
1. What is the fair value of the new parcel of land received by Tinsley?
2. Prepare the journal entry to record the exchange assuming the exchange has commercial substance.
3. Prepare the journal entry to record the exchange assuming the exchange lacks commercial substance.

E 10–21
Acquisition cost; multiple methods
● LO10–1, LO10–3, LO10–4, LO10–6

Connors Corporation acquired manufacturing equipment for use in its assembly line. Below are four *independent* situations relating to the acquisition of the equipment.
1. The equipment was purchased on account for $25,000. Credit terms were 2/10, n/30. Payment was made within the discount period and the company records the purchases of equipment net of discounts.
2. Connors gave the seller a noninterest-bearing note. The note required payment of $27,000 one year from date of purchase. The fair value of the equipment is not determinable. An interest rate of 10% properly reflects the time value of money in this situation.
3. Connors traded in old equipment that had a book value of $6,000 (original cost of $14,000 and accumulated depreciation of $8,000) and paid cash of $22,000. The old equipment had a fair value of $2,500 on the date of the exchange. The exchange has commercial substance.
4. Connors issued 1,000 shares of its nopar common stock in exchange for the equipment. The market value of the common stock was not determinable. The equipment could have been purchased for $24,000 in cash.

Required:
For each of the above situations, prepare the journal entry required to record the acquisition of the equipment. Round computations to the nearest dollar.

E 10–22
FASB codification research
● LO10–6

The *FASB Accounting Standards Codification* represents the single source of authoritative U.S. generally accepted accounting principles.

Required:
1. Obtain the relevant authoritative literature on nonmonetary exchanges using the *FASB Accounting Standards Codification* at the FASB website (asc.fasb.org). Identify the Codification topic number for nonmonetary transactions.
2. What are the specific citations that list the disclosure requirements for nonmonetary transactions?
3. Describe the disclosure requirements.

E 10–23
FASB codification research
● LO10–1, LO10–6, LO10–7, LO10–8

Access the *FASB Accounting Standards Codification* at the FASB website (asc.fasb.org). Determine the specific citation for each of the following items:
1. The disclosure requirements in the notes to the financial statements for depreciation on property, plant, and equipment.
2. The criteria for determining commercial substance in a nonmonetary exchange.
3. The disclosure requirements for interest capitalization.
4. The elements of costs to be included as R&D activities.

E 10–24
Interest capitalization
● LO10–7

On January 1, 2016, the Marjlee Company began construction of an office building to be used as its corporate headquarters. The building was completed early in 2017. Construction expenditures for 2016, which were incurred evenly throughout the year, totaled $6,000,000. Marjlee had the following debt obligations which were outstanding during all of 2016:

Construction loan, 10%	$1,500,000
Long-term note, 9%	2,000,000
Long-term note, 6%	4,000,000

Required:
Calculate the amount of interest capitalized in 2016 for the building using the specific interest method.

E 10–25
Interest capitalization
● LO10–7

On January 1, 2016, the Shagri Company began construction on a new manufacturing facility for its own use. The building was completed in 2017. The only interest-bearing debt the company had outstanding during 2016 was long-term bonds with a book value of $10,000,000 and an effective interest rate of 8%. Construction expenditures incurred during 2016 were as follows:

January 1	$500,000
March 1	600,000
July 31	480,000
September 30	600,000
December 31	300,000

Required:
Calculate the amount of interest capitalized for 2016.

E 10–26
Interest capitalization
● LO10–7

On January 1, 2016, the Highlands Company began construction on a new manufacturing facility for its own use. The building was completed in 2017. The company borrowed $1,500,000 at 8% on January 1 to help finance the construction. In addition to the construction loan, Highlands had the following debt outstanding throughout 2016:

$5,000,000, 12% bonds
$3,000,000, 8% long-term note

Construction expenditures incurred during 2016 were as follows:

January 1	$ 600,000
March 31	1,200,000
June 30	800,000
September 30	600,000
December 31	400,000

Required:
Calculate the amount of interest capitalized for 2016 using the specific interest method.

E 10–27
Interest capitalization; multiple periods
● LO10–7

Thornton Industries began construction of a warehouse on July 1, 2016. The project was completed on March 31, 2017. No new loans were required to fund construction. Thornton does have the following two interest-bearing liabilities that were outstanding throughout the construction period:

$2,000,000, 8% note
$8,000,000, 4% bonds

Construction expenditures incurred were as follows:

July 1, 2016	$400,000
September 30, 2016	600,000
November 30, 2016	600,000
January 30, 2017	540,000

The company's fiscal year-end is December 31.

Required:
Calculate the amount of interest capitalized for 2016 and 2017.

E 10–28
Research and development
● LO10–8

In 2016, Space Technology Company modified its model Z2 satellite to incorporate a new communication device. The company made the following expenditures:

Basic research to develop the technology	$2,000,000
Engineering design work	680,000
Development of a prototype device	300,000
Acquisition of equipment	60,000
Testing and modification of the prototype	200,000
Legal and other fees for patent application on the new communication system	40,000
Legal fees for successful defense of the new patent	20,000
Total	$3,300,000

The equipment will be used on this and other research projects. Depreciation on the equipment for 2016 is $10,000.

During your year-end review of the accounts related to intangibles, you discover that the company has capitalized all of the above as costs of the patent. Management contends that the device simply represents an improvement of the existing communication system of the satellite and, therefore, should be capitalized.

Required:
Prepare correcting entries that reflect the appropriate treatment of the expenditures.

E 10–29
Research and development
● LO10–8

Delaware Company incurred the following research and development costs during 2016:

Salaries and wages for lab research	$ 400,000
Materials used in R&D projects	200,000
Purchase of equipment	900,000
Fees paid to outsiders for R&D projects	320,000
Patent filing and legal costs for a developed product	65,000
Salaries, wages, and supplies for R&D work performed for another company under a contract	350,000
Total	$2,235,000

The equipment has a seven-year life and will be used for a number of research projects. Depreciation for 2016 is $120,000.

Required:
Calculate the amount of research and development expense that Delaware should report in its 2016 income statement.

E 10–30
IFRS; research and development
● LO10–8, LO10–9

Janson Pharmaceuticals incurred the following costs in 2016 related to a new cancer drug:

Research for new formulas	$2,425,000
Development of a new formula	1,600,000
Legal and filing fees for a patent for the new formula	60,000
Total	$4,085,000

The development costs were incurred after technological and commercial feasibility was established and after the future economic benefits were deemed probable. The project was successfully completed and the new drug was patented before the end of the 2016 fiscal year.

Required:

1. Calculate the amount of research and development expense Janson should report in its 2016 income statement related to this project.
2. Repeat requirement 1 assuming that Janson prepares its financial statements according to International Financial Reporting Standards.

E 10–31
IFRS; research and development
● LO10–9
IFRS

NXS Semiconductor prepares its financial statements according to International Financial Reporting Standards. The company incurred the following expenditures during 2016 related to the development of a chip to be used in mobile devices:

Salaries and wages for basic research	$3,450,000
Materials used in basic research	330,000
Other costs incurred for basic research	1,220,000
Development costs	1,800,000
Legal and filing fees for a patent for the new technology	50,000

The development costs were incurred after NXS established technological and commercial feasibility and after NXS deemed the future economic benefits to be probable. The project was successfully completed, and the new chip was patented near the end of the 2016 fiscal year.

Required:

1. Which of the expenditures should NXS expense in its 2016 income statement?
2. Explain the accounting treatment of the remaining expenditures.

E 10–32
Concepts; terminology
● LO10–1, LO10–4, LO10–6, LO10–7

Listed below are several terms and phrases associated with property, plant, and equipment and intangible assets. Pair each item from List A with the item from List B (by letter) that is most appropriately associated with it.

List A	List B
____ 1. Depreciation	a. Exclusive right to display a word, a symbol, or an emblem.
____ 2. Depletion	b. Exclusive right to benefit from a creative work.
____ 3. Amortization	c. Assets that represent rights.
____ 4. Average accumulated expenditures	d. The allocation of cost for natural resources.
____ 5. Revenue—donation of asset	e. Purchase price less fair value of net identifiable assets.
____ 6. Nonmonetary exchange	f. The allocation of cost for plant and equipment.
____ 7. Natural resources	g. Approximation of average amount of debt if all construction funds were borrowed.
____ 8. Intangible assets	h. Account credited when assets are donated to a corporation.
____ 9. Copyright	i. The allocation of cost for intangible assets.
____10. Trademark	j. Basic principle is to value assets acquired using fair value of assets given.
____11. Goodwill	k. Wasting assets.

E 10–33
Software development costs
● LO10–8

Early in 2016, the Excalibur Company began developing a new software package to be marketed. The project was completed in December 2016 at a cost of $6 million. Of this amount, $4 million was spent before technological feasibility was established. Excalibur expects a useful life of five years for the new product with total revenues of $10 million. During 2017, revenue of $3 million was recognized.

Required:

1. Prepare a journal entry to record the 2016 development costs.
2. Calculate the required amortization for 2017.
3. At what amount should the computer software costs be reported in the December 31, 2017, balance sheet?

E 10–34
Software development costs
● LO10–8

On September 30, 2016, Athens Software began developing a software program to shield personal computers from malware and spyware. Technological feasibility was established on February 28, 2017, and the program was available for release on April 30, 2017. Development costs were incurred as follows:

September 30 through December 31, 2016	$2,200,000
January 1 through February 28, 2017	800,000
March 1 through April 30, 2017	400,000

Athens expects a useful life of four years for the software and total revenues of $5,000,000 during that time. During 2017, revenue of $1,000,000 was recognized.

Required:

1. Prepare the journal entries to record the development costs in 2016 and 2017.
2. Calculate the required amortization for 2017.

E 10–35
Full-cost and successful efforts methods compared
● Appendix

The Manguino Oil Company incurred exploration costs in 2016 searching and drilling for oil as follows:

Well 101	$ 50,000
Well 102	60,000
Well 103	80,000
Wells 104–108	260,000
Total	$450,000

It was determined that Wells 104–108 were dry holes and were abandoned. Wells 101, 102, and 103 were determined to have sufficient oil reserves to be commercially successful.

Required:

1. Prepare a summary journal entry to record the indicated costs assuming that the company uses the full-cost method of accounting for exploration costs. All of the exploration costs were paid in cash.
2. Prepare a summary journal entry to record the indicated costs assuming that the company uses the successful efforts method of accounting for exploration costs. All of the exploration costs were paid in cash.

CPA and CMA Review Questions

CPA Exam Questions
KAPLAN CPA REVIEW

The following questions are adapted from a variety of sources including questions developed by the AICPA Board of Examiners and those used in the Kaplan CPA Review Course to study property, plant, and equipment and intangible assets while preparing for the CPA examination. Determine the response that best completes the statements or questions.

● LO10–1

1. Simons Company purchased land to build a new factory. The following expenditures were made in conjunction with the land purchase:
   - Purchase price of the land, $150,000
   - Real estate commissions of 7% of the purchase price
   - Land survey, $5,000
   - Back taxes, $5,000

   What is the initial value of the land?
   a. $160,000
   b. $160,500
   c. $165,500
   d. $170,500

● LO10–2

2. During 2016, Burr Co. made the following expenditures related to the acquisition of land and the construction of a building:

Purchase price of land	$ 60,000
Legal fees for contracts to purchase land	2,000
Architects' fees	8,000
Demolition of old building on site	5,000
Sale of scrap from old building	3,000
Construction cost of new building (fully completed)	350,000

   What amounts should be recorded as the initial values of the land and the building?

	Land	Building
a.	$60,000	$360,000
b.	$62,000	$360,000
c.	$64,000	$358,000
d.	$65,000	$362,000

● LO10–3

3. On December 31, 2016, Bart Inc. purchased a machine from Fell Corp. in exchange for a noninterest-bearing note requiring eight payments of $20,000. The first payment was made on December 31, 2016, and the remaining seven payments are due annually on each December 31, beginning in 2017. At the date of the transaction, the prevailing rate of interest for this type of note was 11%. Present value factors are as follows:

Period	Present value of ordinary annuity of 1 at 11%	Present value of an annuity due of 1 at 11%
7	4.712	5.231
8	5.146	5.712

The initial value of the machine is

a. $ 94,240
b. $102,920
c. $104,620
d. $114,240

LO10–6

4. Amble Inc. exchanged a truck with a book value of $12,000 and a fair value of $20,000 for a truck and $5,000 cash. The exchange has commercial substance. At what amount should Amble record the truck received?

a. $12,000
b. $15,000
c. $20,000
d. $25,000

LO10–7

5. Dahl Corporation has just built a machine to produce car doors. Dahl had to build this machine because it couldn't purchase one that met its specifications. The following are the costs related to the machine's construction and the first month of operations:

- Construction materials, $20,000
- Labor, $9,000 (construction, $3,000; testing, $1,000; operations, $5,000)
- Engineering fees, $5,000
- Utilities, $4,000 (construction, $1,000; testing, $1,000; operations, $2,000)

What is the initial value of the machine?

a. $28,000
b. $29,000
c. $31,000
d. $38,000

LO10–7

6. Cole Co. began constructing a building for its own use in January 2016. During 2016, Cole incurred interest of $50,000 on specific construction debt, and $20,000 on other borrowings. Interest computed on the weighted-average amount of accumulated expenditures for the building during 2016 was $40,000. What amount of interest should Cole capitalize?

a. $20,000
b. $40,000
c. $50,000
d. $70,000

LO10–8

7. On December 31, 2015, Bit Co. had capitalized costs for a new computer software product with an economic life of five years. Sales for 2016 were 30 percent of expected total sales of the software. At December 31, 2016, the software had a fair value equal to 90 percent of the capitalized cost. What percentage of the original capitalized cost should be reported as the net amount in Bit's December 31, 2016, balance sheet?

a. 70%
b. 72%
c. 80%
d. 90%

LO10–8

8. During the current year, Orr Company incurred the following costs:

Research and development services performed by Key Corp. for Orr	$150,000
Design, construction, and testing of preproduction prototypes and models	200,000
Testing in search for new products or process alternatives	175,000

In its income statement for the current year, what amount should Orr report as research and development expense?

a. $150,000
b. $200,000
c. $350,000
d. $525,000

International Financial Reporting Standards are tested on the CPA exam along with U.S. GAAP. The following questions deal with the application of IFRS to accounting for property, plant, and equipment.

LO10–9

IFRS

9. Under IFRS

a. research and development expenditures are expensed in the period incurred.
b. research and development expenditures are capitalized and amortized.

c. development expenditures that meet certain criteria are capitalized and amortized; research expenditures are expensed in the period incurred.
d. research expenditures that meet certain criteria are capitalized and amortized; development expenditures are expensed in the period incurred.

● LO10–9

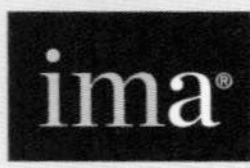
IFRS

10. In 2016 Sanford LTD. received a government grant of $100,000 to be used for the purchase of a machine. Sanford prepares its financial statements using IFRS. The grant must be recognized
a. as revenue in 2016.
b. as a reduction in the cost of the machine.
c. as deferred income in the balance sheet and then recognized in the income statement systematically over the asset's useful life.
d. either b or c.

CMA Exam Questions

ima®

The following questions dealing with property, plant, and equipment and intangible assets are adapted from questions that previously appeared on Certified Management Accountant (CMA) examinations. The CMA designation sponsored by the Institute of Management Accountants (www.imanet.org) provides members with an objective measure of knowledge and competence in the field of management accounting. Determine the response that best completes the statements or questions.

● LO10–1

1. Pearl Corporation acquired manufacturing machinery on January 1 for $9,000. During the year, the machine produced 1,000 units, of which 600 were sold. There was no work-in-process inventory at the beginning or at the end of the year. Installation charges of $300 and delivery charges of $200 were also incurred. The machine is expected to have a useful life of five years with an estimated salvage value of $1,500. Pearl uses the straight-line depreciation method. The original cost of the machinery to be recorded in Pearl's books is
a. $9,500
b. $9,300
c. $9,200
d. $9,000

● LO10–6

Questions 2 and 3 are based on the following information. Harper is contemplating exchanging a machine used in its operations for a similar machine on May 31. Harper will exchange machines with either Austin Corporation or Lubin Company. The data relating to the machines are presented below. Assume that the exchanges would have commercial substance.

	Harper	Austin	Lubin
Original cost of the machine	$162,500	$180,000	$150,000
Accumulated depreciation thru May 31	98,500	70,000	65,000
Fair value at May 31	80,000	95,000	60,000

2. If Harper exchanges its used machine and $15,000 cash for Austin's used machine, the gain that Harper should recognize from this transaction for financial reporting purposes would be
a. $0
b. $2,526
c. $15,000
d. $16,000

3. If Harper exchanges its used machine for Lubin's used machine and also receives $20,000 cash, the gain that Harper should recognize from this transaction for financial reporting purposes would be
a. $0
b. $4,000
c. $16,000
d. $25,000

Problems

An alternate exercise and problem set is available in the Connect library.

P 10–1
Acquisition costs
● LO10–1 through LO10–4

Tristar Production Company began operations on September 1, 2016. Listed below are a number of transactions that occurred during its first four months of operations.

1. On September 1, the company acquired five acres of land with a building that will be used as a warehouse. Tristar paid $100,000 in cash for the property. According to appraisals, the land had a fair value of $75,000 and the building had a fair value of $45,000.

2. On September 1, Tristar signed a $40,000 noninterest-bearing note to purchase equipment. The $40,000 payment is due on September 1, 2017. Assume that 8% is a reasonable interest rate.
3. On September 15, a truck was donated to the corporation. Similar trucks were selling for $2,500.
4. On September 18, the company paid its lawyer $3,000 for organizing the corporation.
5. On October 10, Tristar purchased equipment for cash. The purchase price was $15,000 and $500 in freight charges also were paid.
6. On December 2, Tristar acquired various items of office equipment. The company was short of cash and could not pay the $5,500 normal cash price. The supplier agreed to accept 200 shares of the company's nopar common stock in exchange for the equipment. The fair value of the stock is not readily determinable.
7. On December 10, the company acquired a tract of land at a cost of $20,000. It paid $2,000 down and signed a 10% note with both principal and interest due in one year. Ten percent is an appropriate rate of interest for this note.

Required:

Prepare journal entries to record each of the above transactions.

P 10–2
Acquisition costs; land and building
● LO10–1, LO10–2, LO10–7

On January 1, 2016, the Blackstone Corporation purchased a tract of land (site number 11) with a building for $600,000. Additionally, Blackstone paid a real estate broker's commission of $36,000, legal fees of $6,000, and title insurance of $18,000. The closing statement indicated that the land value was $500,000 and the building value was $100,000. Shortly after acquisition, the building was razed at a cost of $75,000.

Blackstone entered into a $3,000,000 fixed-price contract with Barnett Builders, Inc., on March 1, 2016, for the construction of an office building on land site 11. The building was completed and occupied on September 30, 2017. Additional construction costs were incurred as follows:

Plans, specifications, and blueprints	$12,000
Architects' fees for design and supervision	95,000

To finance the construction cost, Blackstone borrowed $3,000,000 on March 1, 2016. The loan is payable in 10 annual installments of $300,000 plus interest at the rate of 14%. Blackstone's average amounts of accumulated building construction expenditures were as follows:

For the period March 1 to December 31, 2016	$ 900,000
For the period January 1 to September 30, 2017	2,300,000

Required:

1. Prepare a schedule that discloses the individual costs making up the balance in the land account in respect of land site 11 as of September 30, 2017.
2. Prepare a schedule that discloses the individual costs that should be capitalized in the office building account as of September 30, 2017.

(AICPA adapted)

P 10–3
Acquisition costs
● LO10–1, LO10–4, LO10–6

The plant asset and accumulated depreciation accounts of Pell Corporation had the following balances at December 31, 2015:

	Plant Asset	Accumulated Depreciation
Land	$ 350,000	$ —
Land improvements	180,000	45,000
Building	1,500,000	350,000
Machinery and equipment	1,158,000	405,000
Automobiles	150,000	112,000

Transactions during 2016 were as follows:

a. On January 2, 2016, machinery and equipment were purchased at a total invoice cost of $260,000, which included a $5,500 charge for freight. Installation costs of $27,000 were incurred.
b. On March 31, 2016, a machine purchased for $58,000 in 2012 was sold for $36,500. Depreciation recorded through the date of sale totaled $24,650.
c. On May 1, 2016, expenditures of $50,000 were made to repave parking lots at Pell's plant location. The work was necessitated by damage caused by severe winter weather.
d. On November 1, 2016, Pell acquired a tract of land with an existing building in exchange for 10,000 shares of Pell's common stock that had a market price of $38 per share. Pell paid legal fees and title insurance totaling $23,000. Shortly after acquisition, the building was razed at a cost of $35,000 in anticipation of new building construction in 2017.

e. On December 31, 2016, Pell purchased a new automobile for $15,250 cash and trade-in of an old automobile purchased for $18,000 in 2012. Depreciation on the old automobile recorded through December 31, 2016, totaled $13,500. The fair value of the old automobile was $3,750.

Required:

1. Prepare a schedule analyzing the changes in each of the plant assets during 2016, with detailed supporting computations.
2. Prepare a schedule showing the gain or loss from each asset disposal that would be recognized in Pell's income statement for the year ended December 31, 2016.

(AICPA adapted)

P 10–4
Intangibles
● LO10–1, LO10–8

The Horstmeyer Corporation commenced operations early in 2016. A number of expenditures were made during 2016 that were debited to one account called *intangible asset.* A recap of the $144,000 balance in this account at the end of 2016 is as follows:

Date	Transaction	Amount
2/3/16	State incorporation fees and legal costs related to organizing the corporation	$ 7,000
3/1/16	Fire insurance premium for three-year period	6,000
3/15/16	Purchased a copyright	20,000
4/30/16	Research and development costs	40,000
6/15/16	Legal fees for filing a patent on a new product resulting from an R&D project	3,000
9/30/16	Legal fee for successful defense of patent developed above	12,000
10/13/16	Entered into a 10-year franchise agreement with franchisor	40,000
Various	Advertising costs	16,000
	Total	$144,000

Required:

Prepare the necessary journal entry to clear the intangible asset account and to set up accounts for separate intangible assets, other types of assets, and expenses indicated by the transactions.

P 10–5
Acquisition costs; journal entries
● LO10–1, LO10–3, LO10–6, LO10–8

Consider each of the transactions below. All of the expenditures were made in cash.

1. The Edison Company spent $12,000 during the year for experimental purposes in connection with the development of a new product.
2. In April, the Marshall Company lost a patent infringement suit and paid the plaintiff $7,500.
3. In March, the Cleanway Laundromat bought equipment. Cleanway paid $6,000 down and signed a noninterest-bearing note requiring the payment of $18,000 in nine months. The cash price for this equipment was $23,000.
4. On June 1, the Jamsen Corporation installed a sprinkler system throughout the building at a cost of $28,000.
5. The Mayer Company, plaintiff, paid $12,000 in legal fees in November, in connection with a successful infringement suit on its patent.
6. The Johnson Company traded its old machine with an original cost of $7,400 and a book value of $3,000 plus cash of $8,000 for a new one that had a fair value of $10,000. The exchange has commercial substance.

Required:

Prepare journal entries to record each of the above transactions.

P 10–6
Nonmonetary exchange
● LO10–6

Southern Company owns a building that it leases to others. The building's fair value is $1,400,000 and its book value is $800,000 (original cost of $2,000,000 less accumulated depreciation of $1,200,000). Southern exchanges this for a building owned by the Eastern Company. The building's book value on Eastern's books is $950,000 (original cost of $1,600,000 less accumulated depreciation of $650,000). Eastern also gives Southern $140,000 to complete the exchange. The exchange has commercial substance for both companies.

Required:

Prepare the journal entries to record the exchange on the books of both Southern and Eastern.

P 10–7
Nonmonetary exchange
● LO10–6

On September 3, 2016, the Robers Company exchanged equipment with Phifer Corporation. The facts of the exchange are as follows:

	Robers' Asset	Phifer's Asset
Original cost	$120,000	$140,000
Accumulated depreciation	55,000	63,000
Fair value	75,000	70,000

To equalize the exchange, Phifer paid Robers $5,000 in cash.

Required:
Record the exchange for both Robers and Phifer. The exchange has commercial substance for both companies.

P 10–8
Nonmonetary exchange
● LO10–6

Case A. Kapono Farms exchanged an old tractor for a newer model. The old tractor had a book value of $12,000 (original cost of $28,000 less accumulated depreciation of $16,000) and a fair value of $9,000. Kapono paid $20,000 cash to complete the exchange. The exchange has commercial substance.

Required:
1. What is the amount of gain or loss that Kapono would recognize on the exchange? What is the initial value of the new tractor?
2. Repeat requirement 1 assuming that the fair value of the old tractor is $14,000 instead of $9,000.

Case B. Kapono Farms exchanged 100 acres of farmland for similar land. The farmland given had a book value of $500,000 and a fair value of $700,000. Kapono paid $50,000 cash to complete the exchange. The exchange has commercial substance.

Required:
1. What is the amount of gain or loss that Kapono would recognize on the exchange? What is the initial value of the new land?
2. Repeat requirement 1 assuming that the fair value of the farmland given is $400,000 instead of $700,000.
3. Repeat requirement 1 assuming that the exchange lacked commercial substance.

P 10–9
Interest capitalization; specific interest method
● LO10–7

On January 1, 2016, the Mason Manufacturing Company began construction of a building to be used as its office headquarters. The building was completed on September 30, 2017.

Expenditures on the project were as follows:

January 1, 2016	$1,000,000
March 1, 2016	600,000
June 30, 2016	800,000
October 1, 2016	600,000
January 31, 2017	270,000
April 30, 2017	585,000
August 31, 2017	900,000

On January 1, 2016, the company obtained a $3 million construction loan with a 10% interest rate. The loan was outstanding all of 2016 and 2017. The company's other interest-bearing debt included two long-term notes of $4,000,000 and $6,000,000 with interest rates of 6% and 8%, respectively. Both notes were outstanding during all of 2016 and 2017. Interest is paid annually on all debt. The company's fiscal year-end is December 31.

Required:
1. Calculate the amount of interest that Mason should capitalize in 2016 and 2017 using the specific interest method.
2. What is the total cost of the building?
3. Calculate the amount of interest expense that will appear in the 2016 and 2017 income statements.

P 10–10
Interest capitalization; weighted-average method
● LO10–7

[This is a variation of the previous problem, modified to focus on the weighted-average interest method.]

Required:
Refer to the facts in Problem 10–9 and answer the following questions:
1. Calculate the amount of interest that Mason should capitalize in 2016 and 2017 using the weighted-average method.
2. What is the total cost of the building?
3. Calculate the amount of interest expense that will appear in the 2016 and 2017 income statements.

P 10–11
Research and development
● LO10–8

In 2016, Starsearch Corporation began work on three research and development projects. One of the projects was completed and commercial production of the developed product began in December. The company's fiscal year-end is December 31. All of the following 2016 expenditures were included in the R&D expense account:

Salaries and wages for:	
Lab research	$ 300,000
Design and construction of preproduction prototype	160,000
Quality control during commercial production	20,000
Materials and supplies consumed for:	
Lab research	60,000
Construction of preproduction prototype	30,000
Purchase of equipment	600,000
Patent filing and legal fees for completed project	40,000
Payments to others for research	120,000
Total	$1,330,000

$200,000 of equipment was purchased solely for use in one of the projects. After the project is completed, the equipment will be abandoned. The remaining $400,000 in equipment will be used on future R&D projects. The useful life of equipment is five years. Assume that all of the equipment was acquired at the beginning of the year.

Required:
Prepare journal entries, reclassifying amounts in R&D expense, to reflect the appropriate treatment of the expenditures.

P 10–12
Acquisition costs; lump-sum acquisition; noninterest-bearing note; interest capitalization
● LO10–1, LO10–2, LO10–3, LO10–7

Early in its fiscal year ending December 31, 2016, San Antonio Outfitters finalized plans to expand operations. The first stage was completed on March 28 with the purchase of a tract of land on the outskirts of the city. The land and existing building were purchased for $800,000. San Antonio paid $200,000 and signed a noninterest-bearing note requiring the company to pay the remaining $600,000 on March 28, 2018. An interest rate of 8% properly reflects the time value of money for this type of loan agreement. Title search, insurance, and other closing costs totaling $20,000 were paid at closing.

During April, the old building was demolished at a cost of $70,000, and an additional $50,000 was paid to clear and grade the land. Construction of a new building began on May 1 and was completed on October 29. Construction expenditures were as follows:

May 1	$1,200,000
July 30	1,500,000
September 1	900,000
October 1	1,800,000

San Antonio borrowed $3,000,000 at 8% on May 1 to help finance construction. This loan, plus interest, will be paid in 2017. The company also had the following debt outstanding throughout 2016:

$2,000,000, 9% long-term note payable
$4,000,000, 6% long-term bonds payable

In November, the company purchased 10 identical pieces of equipment and office furniture and fixtures for a lump-sum price of $600,000. The fair values of the equipment and the furniture and fixtures were $455,000 and $245,000, respectively. In December, San Antonio paid a contractor $285,000 for the construction of parking lots and for landscaping.

Required:
1. Determine the initial values of the various assets that San Antonio acquired or constructed during 2016. The company uses the specific interest method to determine the amount of interest capitalized on the building construction.
2. How much interest expense will San Antonio report in its 2016 income statement?

Broaden Your Perspective

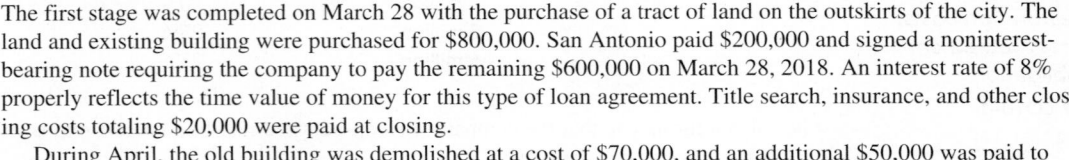

Apply your critical-thinking ability to the knowledge you've gained. These cases will provide you an opportunity to develop your research, analysis, judgment, and communication skills. You also will work with other students, integrate what you've learned, apply it in real-world situations, and consider its global and ethical ramifications. This practice will broaden your knowledge and further develop your decision-making abilities.

Judgment Case 10–1
Acquisition costs
● LO10–1, LO10–3, LO10–6

A company may acquire property, plant, and equipment and intangible assets for cash, in exchange for a deferred payment contract, by exchanging other assets, or by a combination of these methods.

Required:

1. Identify six types of costs that should be capitalized as the cost of a parcel of land. For your answer, assume that the land has an existing building that is to be removed in the immediate future in order that a new building can be constructed on the site.
2. At what amount should a company record an asset acquired in exchange for a deferred payment contract?
3. In general, at what amount should assets received in exchange for other nonmonetary assets be valued? Specifically, at what amount should a company value a new machine acquired by exchanging an older, similar machine and paying cash?

(AICPA adapted)

Research Case 10–2
FASB codification; locate and extract relevant information and cite authoritative support for a financial reporting issue; restoration costs; asset retirement obligation
● LO10–1

Your client, Hazelton Mining, recently entered into an agreement to obtain the rights to operate a coal mine in West Virginia for $15 million. Hazelton incurred development costs of $6 million in preparing the mine for extraction, which began on July 1, 2016. The contract requires Hazelton to restore the land and surrounding area to its original condition after extraction is complete in three years.

The company controller, Alice Cushing, is not sure how to account for the restoration costs and has asked your advice. Alice is aware of an accounting standard addressing this issue, but is not sure of its provisions. She has narrowed down the possible cash outflows for the restoration costs to four possibilities:

Cash Outflow	Probability
$3 million	20%
4 million	30%
5 million	25%
6 million	25%

Alice also informs you that the company's credit-adjusted risk-free interest rate is 9%. Before responding to Alice, you need to research the issue.

Required:

1. Obtain the relevant authoritative literature on accounting for asset retirement obligations using the *FASB Accounting Standards Codification*. You might gain access at the FASB website (asc.fasb.org). Explain the basic treatment of asset retirement obligations. What are the specific citations that you would rely on to determine (a) the accounting treatment for an asset retirement obligation and (b) how to measure the obligation?
2. Determine the capitalized cost of the coal mine.
3. Prepare a summary journal entry to record the acquisition costs of the mine.
4. How much accretion expense will the company record in its income statement for the 2016 fiscal year, related to this transaction? What are the specific citations from the *FASB Accounting Standards Codification* that address (a) the calculation of accretion expense and (b) the classification of accretion expense in the income statement?
5. Explain to Alice how Hazelton would account for the restoration if the restoration costs differed from the recorded liability in three years. By way of explanation, prepare the journal entry to record the payment of the retirement obligation in three years assuming that the actual restoration costs were $4.7 million.
6. Describe to Alice the necessary disclosure requirements for the obligation. What is the specific citation from the *FASB Accounting Standards Codification* that contains these disclosure requirements?

Judgment Case 10–3
Self-constructed assets
● LO10–7

Chilton Peripherals manufactures printers, scanners, and other computer peripheral equipment. In the past, the company purchased equipment used in manufacturing from an outside vendor. In March 2016, Chilton decided to design and build equipment to replace some obsolete equipment. A section of the manufacturing plant was set aside to develop and produce the equipment. Additional personnel were hired for the project. The equipment was completed and ready for use in September.

Required:

1. In general, what costs should be capitalized for a self-constructed asset?
2. Discuss two alternatives for the inclusion of overhead costs in the cost of the equipment constructed by Chilton. Which alternative is generally accepted for financial reporting purposes?
3. Under what circumstance(s) would interest be included in the cost of the equipment?

Judgment Case 10–4
Interest capitalization
● LO10–7

GAAP provides guidelines for the inclusion of interest in the initial cost of a self-constructed asset.

Required:

1. What assets qualify for interest capitalization? What assets do not qualify for interest capitalization?
2. Over what period should interest be capitalized?

3. Explain average accumulated expenditures.
4. Explain the two methods that could be used to determine the appropriate interest rate(s) to be used in capitalizing interest.
5. Describe the three steps used to determine the amount of interest capitalized during a reporting period.

Research Case 10–5
Goodwill
● LO10–1

Accounting for acquired goodwill has been a controversial issue for many years. In the United States, the amount of acquired goodwill is capitalized and not amortized. Globally, the treatment of goodwill varies significantly, with some countries not recognizing goodwill as an asset. Professors Johnson and Petrone, in "Is Goodwill an Asset?" discuss this issue.

Required:
1. In your library or from some other source, locate the indicated article in Accounting Horizons, September 1998.
2. Does goodwill meet the FASB's definition of an asset?
3. What are the key concerns of those that believe goodwill is not an asset?

Real World Case 10–6
Property, plant, and equipment; intangibles; Chico's FAS
● LO10–1

Real World Financials

Chico's FAS, a major U.S. retailer, reported the following amounts in the asset section of its balance sheets for the years ended February 1, 2014, and February 2, 2013:

	($ in thousands)	
	February 1, 2014	**February 2, 2013**
Property and equipment, net	$631,050	$608,120

In addition, the 2014 statement of cash flows reported the following items ($ in thousands):

Depreciation	$113,800
Additions to property and equipment	138,510
Loss on disposal of property and equipment	1,736

Required:
What were the proceeds Chico's received in the year ended February 1, 2014, from the sale of property and equipment?

Judgment Case 10–7
Goodwill
● LO10–1

Athena Paper Corporation acquired for cash 100% of the outstanding common stock of Georgia, Inc., a supplier of wood pulp. The $4,500,000 amount paid was significantly higher than the book value of Georgia's net assets (assets less liabilities) of $2,800,000. The Athena controller recorded the difference of $1,700,000 as an asset, goodwill.

Required:
1. Discuss the meaning of the term goodwill.
2. In what situation would the Athena controller be correct in her valuation of goodwill?

Judgment Case 10–8
Research and development
● LO10–8

Prior to 1974, accepted practice was for companies to either expense or capitalize R&D costs. In 1974, the FASB issued a Standard that requires all research and development costs to be charged to expense when incurred. This was a controversial standard, opposed by many companies who preferred delaying the recognition of these expenses until later years when presumably the expenditures bear fruit.

Several research studies have been conducted to determine if the Standard had any impact on the behavior of companies. One interesting finding was that, prior to 1974, companies that expensed R&D costs were significantly larger than those companies that capitalized R&D costs.

Required:
1. Explain the FASB's logic in deciding to require all companies to expense R&D costs in the period incurred.
2. Identify possible reasons to explain why, prior to 1974, companies that expensed R&D costs were significantly larger than those companies that capitalized R&D costs.

Judgment Case 10–9
Research and development
● LO10–8

Clonal, Inc., a biotechnology company, developed and patented a diagnostic product called Trouver. Clonal purchased some research equipment to be used exclusively for Trouver and subsequent research projects. Clonal defeated a legal challenge to its Trouver patent, and began production and marketing operations for the project.

Corporate headquarters' costs were allocated to Clonal's research division as a percentage of the division's salaries.

Required:

1. How should the equipment purchased for Trouver be reported in Clonal's income statements and statements of financial position?
2. a. Describe the matching concept.
   b. Describe the accounting treatment of research and development costs and consider whether this is consistent with the matching concept. What is the justification for the accounting treatment of research and development costs?
3. How should corporate headquarters' costs allocated to the research division be classified in Clonal's income statements? Why?
4. How should the legal expenses incurred in defending Trouver's patent be reported in Clonal's financial statements?

(AICPA adapted)

Communication Case 10–10
Research and development
● LO10–8

The focus of this case is the situation described in Case 10–9. What is the appropriate accounting for R&D costs? Do you believe that (1) capitalization is the correct treatment of R&D costs, (2) expensing is the correct treatment of R&D costs, or (3) that companies should be allowed to choose between expensing and capitalizing R&D costs?

Required:

1. Develop a list of arguments in support of your view prior to the class session for which the case is assigned. Do not be influenced by the method required by the FASB. Base your opinion on the conceptual merit of the options.
2. In class, your instructor will pair you (and everyone else) with a classmate who also has independently developed a position.
   a. You will be given three minutes to argue your view to your partner. Your partner likewise will be given three minutes to argue his or her view to you. During these three-minute presentations, the listening partner is not permitted to speak.
   b. Then after each person has had a turn attempting to convince his or her partner, the two partners will have a three-minute discussion in which they will decide which alternative is more convincing and arguments will be merged into a single view for each pair.
3. After the allotted time, a spokesperson for each of the three alternatives will be selected by the instructor. Each spokesperson will field arguments from the class as to the appropriate alternative. The class will then discuss the merits of the alternatives and attempt to reach a consensus view, though a consensus is not necessary.

Communication Case 10–11
Research and development
● LO10–8

Thomas Plastics is in the process of developing a revolutionary new plastic valve. A new division of the company was formed to develop, manufacture, and market this new product. As of year-end (December 31, 2016), the new product has not been manufactured for sale; however, prototype units were built and are in operation.

Throughout 2016, the new division incurred a variety of costs. These costs included expenses (including salaries of administrative personnel) and market research costs. In addition, approximately $500,000 in equipment (estimated useful life of 10 years) was purchased for use in developing and manufacturing the new valve. Approximately $200,000 of this equipment was built specifically for developing the design of the new product; the remaining $300,000 of the equipment was used to manufacture the preproduction prototypes and will be used to manufacture the new product once it is in commercial production.

The president of the company, Sally Rogers, has been told that research and development costs must be expensed as incurred, but she does not understand this treatment. She believes the research will lead to a profitable product and to increased future revenues. Also, she wonders how to account for the $500,000 of equipment purchased by the new division. "I thought I understood accounting," she growled. "Explain to me why expenditures that benefit our future revenues are expensed rather than capitalized!"

Required:

Write a one-to two-page report to Sally Rogers explaining the generally accepted accounting principles relevant to this issue. The report should also address the treatment of the equipment purchases.

(AICPA adapted)

Ethics Case 10–12
Research and development
● LO10–8

Mayer Biotechnical, Inc., develops, manufactures, and sells pharmaceuticals. Significant research and development (R&D) expenditures are made for the development of new drugs and the improvement of existing drugs. During 2016, $220 million was spent on R&D. Of this amount, $30 million was spent on the purchase of equipment to be used in a research project involving the development of a new antibiotic.

The controller, Alice Cooper, is considering capitalizing the equipment and depreciating it over the five-year useful life of the equipment at $6 million per year, even though the equipment likely will be used on only one project. The company president has asked Alice to make every effort to increase 2016 earnings because in 2017 the company will be seeking significant new financing from both debt and equity sources. "I guess we might use the equipment in other projects later," Alice wondered to herself.

Required:

1. Assuming that the equipment was purchased at the beginning of 2016, by how much would Alice's treatment of the equipment increase before tax earnings as opposed to expensing the equipment cost?
2. Discuss the ethical dilemma Alice faces in determining the treatment of the $30 million equipment purchase.

IFRS Case 10–13
Research and development; comparison of U.S. GAAP and IFRS; Siemens AG
● LO10–8, LO10–9

IFRS

Siemens AG, a German company, is Europe's largest engineering and electronics company. The company prepares its financial statements according to IFRS.

Required:

1. Use the Internet to locate the most recent financial report for Siemens. The address is **www.siemens.com**. Locate the significant accounting policies disclosure note.
2. How does the company account for research and development expenditures? Does this policy differ from U.S. GAAP?

Analysis Case 10–14
Fixed-asset turnover ratio; Pier 1 Imports, Inc.
● LO10–5

Real World Financials

Pier 1 Imports, Inc., is a leading retailer of domestic merchandise and home furnishings. The company's 2014 fixed-asset turnover ratio, using the average book value of property, plant, and equipment (PP&E) as the denominator, was approximately 10.61. Additional information taken from the company's 2014 annual report is as follows:

	($ in thousands)
Book value of PP&E—beginning of 2014	$150,615
Purchases of PP&E during 2014	80,306
Depreciation of PP&E for 2014	38,873

Equipment having a book value of $8,696 thousand was sold during 2014.

Required:

1. How is the fixed-asset turnover ratio computed? How would you interpret Pier 1's ratio of 10.61?
2. Use the data to determine Pier 1's net sales for 2014.
3. Obtain annual reports from three corporations in the same primary industry as Pier 1 Imports, Inc. (Bed Bath & Beyond and Williams-Sonoma, Inc., are two well-known companies in the same industry) and compare the management of each company's investment in property, plant, and equipment.

Note: You can obtain copies of annual reports from your library, from friends who are shareholders, from the investor relations department of the corporations, from a friendly stockbroker, or from EDGAR (Electronic Data Gathering, Analysis, and Retrieval) on the Internet (**www.sec.gov**).

Judgment Case 10–15
Computer software costs
● LO10–8

The Elegant Software Company recently completed the development and testing of a new software program that provides the ability to transfer data from among a variety of operating systems. The company believes this product will be quite successful and capitalized all of the costs of designing, developing, coding, and testing the software. These costs will be amortized over the expected useful life of the software on a straight-line basis.

Required:

1. Was Elegant correct in its treatment of the software development costs? Why?
2. Explain the appropriate method for determining the amount of periodic amortization for any capitalized software development costs.

Real World Case 10–16
Property, plant, and equipment; Home Depot
● LO10–1, LO10–7

Real World Financials

EDGAR, the Electronic Data Gathering, Analysis, and Retrieval system, performs automated collection, validation, indexing, and forwarding of submissions by companies and others who are required by law to file forms with the U.S. Securities and Exchange Commission (SEC). All publicly traded domestic companies use EDGAR to make the majority of their filings. (Some foreign companies file voluntarily.) Form 10-K, which includes the annual report, is required to be filed on EDGAR. The SEC makes this information available on the Internet.

Required:

1. Access EDGAR on the Internet. The web address is **www.sec.gov**.
2. Search for **Home Depot, Inc.** Access the 10-K filing for the most recent fiscal year. Search or scroll to find the financial statements and related notes.

3. Answer the following questions related to the company's property, plant, and equipment:
   a. Name the different types of assets the company lists in its balance sheet under property, plant, and equipment.
   b. How much cash was used for the acquisition of property, plant, and equipment during the year?
   c. What was the amount of interest capitalized during the year?
   d. Compute the fixed-asset turnover ratio for the fiscal year.

Analysis Case 10–17
Reporting property, plant, and equipment and intangible assets
● LO10–1, LO10–5

PetSmart

Refer to the financial statements and related disclosure notes of PetSmart Inc. in Appendix B located at the back of the text.

Required:

1. What categories of property, plant, and equipment and intangible assets does PetSmart report in its February 2, 2014 balance sheet?
2. How much cash was used in the fiscal year ended February 2, 2014, to purchase property and equipment? How does this compare with purchases in previous years?
3. What is PetSmart's fixed-asset turnover ratio for the fiscal year ended February 2, 2014? What is the ratio intended to measure?

Air France–KLM Case

● LO10–9

IFRS

Air France–KLM (AF), a Franco-Dutch company, prepares its financial statements according to International Financial Reporting Standards. AF's financial statements and disclosure notes for the year ended December 31, 2013, are provided with all new textbooks. This material also is available at www.airfranceklm-finance.com.

Required:

1. What method does Air France-KLM use to amortize the cost of computer software development costs? How does this approach differ from U.S. GAAP?
2. AF does not report any research and development expenditures. If it did, its approach to accounting for research and development would be significantly different from U.S. GAAP. Describe the differences between IFRS and U.S. GAAP in accounting for research and development expenditures.
3. AF does not report the receipt of any governments grants. If it did, its approach to accounting for government grants would be significantly different from U.S. GAAP. Describe the differences between IFRS and U.S. GAAP in accounting for government grants. If AF received a grant for the purchase of assets, what alternative accounting treatments are available under IFRS?

CPA Simulation 10–1

Yamashita Corporation
Interest capitalization

KAPLAN CPA REVIEW

Test your knowledge of the concepts discussed in this chapter, practice critical professional skills necessary for career success, and prepare for the computer-based CPA exam by accessing our CPA simulations in the Connect library.

The Yamashita Corporation simulation tests your knowledge of accounting for interest capitalization.

CHAPTER

11 Property, Plant, and Equipment and Intangible Assets: Utilization and Impairment

OVERVIEW

This chapter completes our discussion of accounting for property, plant, and equipment and intangible assets. We address the allocation of the cost of these assets to the periods benefited by their use.

The usefulness of most of these assets is consumed as the assets are applied to the production of goods or services. Cost allocation corresponding to this consumption of usefulness is known as *depreciation* for plant and equipment, *depletion* for natural resources, and *amortization* for intangibles.

We also consider impairment of these assets, and the treatment of expenditures incurred subsequent to acquisition.

LEARNING OBJECTIVES

After studying this chapter, you should be able to:

- **LO11–1** Explain the concept of cost allocation as it pertains to property, plant, and equipment and intangible assets. (*p. 587*)
- **LO11–2** Determine periodic depreciation using both time-based and activity-based methods. (*p. 590*)
- **LO11–3** Calculate the periodic depletion of a natural resource. (*p. 600*)
- **LO11–4** Calculate the periodic amortization of an intangible asset. (*p. 601*)
- **LO11–5** Explain the appropriate accounting treatment required when a change is made in the service life or residual value of property, plant, and equipment and intangible assets. (*p. 607*)
- **LO11–6** Explain the appropriate accounting treatment required when a change in depreciation, amortization, or depletion method is made. (*p. 608*)
- **LO11–7** Explain the appropriate treatment required when an error in accounting for property, plant, and equipment and intangible assets is discovered. (*p. 610*)
- **LO11–8** Identify situations that involve a significant impairment of the value of property, plant, and equipment and intangible assets and describe the required accounting procedures. (*p. 611*)
- **LO11–9** Discuss the accounting treatment of repairs and maintenance, additions, improvements, and rearrangements to property, plant, and equipment and intangible assets. (*p. 622*)
- **LO11–10** Discuss the primary differences between U.S. GAAP and IFRS with respect to the utilization and impairment of property, plant, and equipment and intangible assets. (*pp. 595, 598, 602, 604, 614, 615, 618, 621, and 625*)

FINANCIAL REPORTING CASE

What's in a Name?

"I don't understand this at all," your friend Penny Lane moaned. "Depreciation, depletion, amortization; what's the difference? Aren't they all the same thing?" Penny and you are part of a class team working on a case involving **Weyerhaeuser Company**, a large forest products company. Part of the project involves comparing reporting methods over a three-year period. "Look at these disclosure notes from last year's annual report. Besides mentioning those three terms, they also talk about asset impairment. How is that different?" Penny showed you the disclosure notes.

Property and Equipment and Timber and Timberlands (in part)

Depreciation is calculated using a straight-line method at rates based on estimated service lives. Logging roads are generally amortized—as timber is harvested—at rates based on the volume of timber estimated to be removed. We carry timber and timberlands at cost less depletion.

Depletion (in part)

To determine depletion rates, we divide the net carrying value by the related volume of timber estimated to be available over the growth cycle.

Impairment of Long-Lived Assets (in part)

We review long-lived assets—including certain identifiable intangibles—for impairment whenever events or changes in circumstances indicate that the carrying amount of the assets may not be recoverable.

QUESTIONS

By the time you finish this chapter, you should be able to respond appropriately to the questions posed in this case. Compare your response to the solution provided at the end of the chapter.

1. Is Penny correct? Do the terms *depreciation, depletion,* and *amortization* all mean the same thing? (*p. 588*)
2. Weyerhaeuser determines depletion based on the "volume of timber estimated to be available." Explain this approach. (*p. 592*)
3. Explain how asset impairment differs from depreciation, depletion, and amortization. How do companies measure impairment losses for property, plant, and equipment and intangible assets with finite useful lives? (*p. 611*)

Depreciation, Depletion, and Amortization

PART A

Cost Allocation—an Overview

● LO11–1

Property, plant, and equipment and intangible assets are purchased with the expectation that they will provide future benefits, usually for several years. Specifically, they are acquired to be used as part of the revenue-generating operations. Logically, then, the costs of acquiring the assets should be allocated to expense during the reporting periods benefited by their use. That is, their costs are matched with the revenues they help generate.

Let's suppose that a company purchases a used delivery truck for $8,200 to be used to deliver product to customers. The company estimates that five years from the acquisition date the truck will be sold for $2,200. It is estimated, then, that $6,000 ($8,200 − 2,200) of the truck's purchase price will be used up (consumed) during a five-year useful life. The situation is portrayed in Illustration 11–1.

Illustration 11–1
Cost Allocation

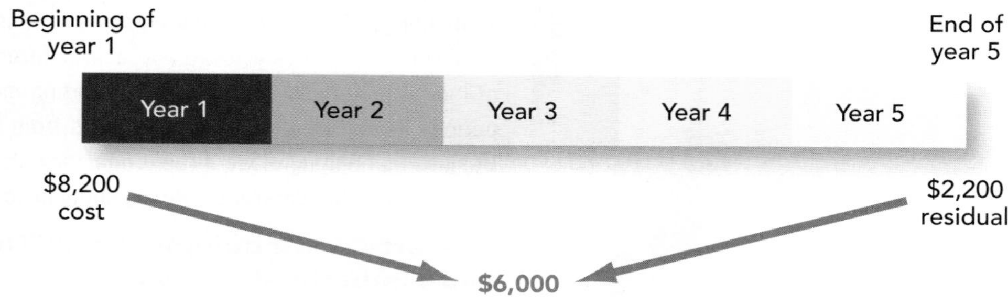

Theoretically, the matching concept requires that the $6,000 be allocated to the five individual years of asset use in direct proportion to the role the asset played in revenue production. However, very seldom is there a clear-cut relationship between the use of the asset and revenue production. In other words, we can't tell precisely the portion of the total benefits of the asset that was consumed in any particular period. As a consequence, we must resort to arbitrary allocation methods to approximate a matching of expense with revenue. Contrast this situation with the $24,000 prepayment of one year's rent on an office building at $2,000 per month. In that case, we know precisely that the benefits of the asset, prepaid rent, are consumed at a rate of $2,000 per month.

FINANCIAL Reporting Case

Q1, p. 587

Cost allocation is known as **depreciation** for plant and equipment, **depletion** for natural resources, and **amortization** for intangibles. The process often is confused with measuring a decline in fair value of an asset. For example, let's say our delivery truck purchased for $8,200 can be sold for $5,000 at the end of one year but we intend to keep it for the full five-year estimated life. It has experienced a decline in value of $3,200 ($8,200 − 5,000). However, *depreciation is a process of cost allocation, not valuation.* We would not record depreciation expense of $3,200 for year one of the truck's life. Instead, we would distribute the cost of the asset, less any anticipated residual value, over the estimated useful life in a systematic and rational manner that attempts to match revenues with the *use* of the asset, not the decline in its value. After all, the truck is purchased to be used in operations, not to be sold.

Depreciation, depletion, and amortization are processes that attempt to satisfy the matching concept.

The specific accounting treatment depends on the intended use of the asset. For assets used in the manufacture of a product, for example, depreciation, depletion, or amortization is considered a product cost to be included as part of the cost of inventory. Eventually, when the product is sold, it becomes part of the cost of goods sold. For assets *not* used in production, primarily plant and equipment and certain intangibles used in the selling and administrative functions of the company, periodic depreciation or amortization is reported as expense in the income statement. You might recognize this distinction as the difference between a product cost and a period cost. When a product cost is reported as an expense (cost of goods sold) depends on when the product is sold; when a period cost is reported as an expense depends on the reporting period in which it is incurred.

Depreciation, depletion, and amortization for an asset used to manufacture a product are included in the cost of inventory.

Measuring Cost Allocation

The process of cost allocation requires that three factors be established at the time the asset is put into use. These factors are:

1. **Service life**—the estimated use that the company expects to receive from the asset.
2. **Allocation base**—the value of the usefulness that is expected to be consumed.
3. **Allocation method**—the pattern in which the usefulness is expected to be consumed.

Let's consider these one at a time.

Service Life

The **service life**, or **useful life**, is the amount of use that the company expects to obtain from the asset before disposing of it. This use can be expressed in units of time or in units of activity. For example, the estimated service life of a delivery truck could be expressed in terms of years or in terms of the number of miles that the company expects the truck to be driven before disposition. We use the terms service life and useful life interchangeably throughout the chapter.

The *service life*, or *useful life*, can be expressed in units of time or in units of activity.

Physical life provides the upper bound for service life of tangible, long-lived assets. Physical life will vary according to the purpose for which the asset is acquired and the environment in which it is operated. For example, a diesel powered electric generator may last for many years if it is used only as an emergency backup or for only a few years if it is used regularly.

Expected obsolescence can shorten service life below physical life.

The service life of a tangible asset may be less than physical life for a variety of reasons. For example, the expected rate of technological change may shorten service life. If suppliers are expected to develop new technologies that are more efficient, the company may keep an asset for a period of time much shorter than physical life. Likewise, if the company sells its product in a market that frequently demands new products, the machinery and equipment used to produce products may be useful only for as long as its output can be sold. Similarly, a mineral deposit might be projected to contain 4 million tons of a mineral, but it may be economically feasible with existing extraction methods to mine only 2 million tons. For intangible assets, legal or contractual life often is a limiting factor. For instance, a patent might be capable of providing enhanced profitability for 50 years, but the legal life of a patent is only 20 years.

Management intent also may shorten the period of an asset's usefulness below its physical, legal, or contractual life. For example, a company may have a policy of using its delivery trucks for a three-year period and then trading the trucks for new models.

Companies quite often disclose the range of service lives for different categories of assets. For example, Illustration 11–2 shows how **IBM Corporation** disclosed its service lives in a note accompanying recent financial statements.

Summary of Significant Accounting Policies (in part)
Depreciation and Amortization
The estimated useful lives of certain depreciable assets are as follows: buildings, 30 to 50 years; building equipment, 10 to 20 years; land improvements, 20 years; plant, laboratory and office equipment, 2 to 20 years; and computer equipment, 1.5 to 5 years.

Illustration 11–2
Service Life Disclosure—International Business Machines Corporation

Real World Financials

Allocation Base

The total amount of cost to be allocated over an asset's service life is called its **allocation base**. The amount is the difference between the initial value of the asset at its acquisition (its cost) and its **residual value**. Residual or **salvage value** is the amount the company expects to receive for the asset at the end of its service life less any anticipated disposal costs. In our delivery truck example above, the allocation base is $6,000 ($8,200 cost less $2,200 anticipated residual value).

Allocation base is the difference between the cost of the asset and its anticipated _residual value_.

In certain situations, residual value can be estimated by referring to a company's prior experience or to publicly available information concerning resale values of various types of assets. For example, if a company intends to trade its delivery trucks in three years for the new model, approximations of the three-year residual value for that type of truck can be obtained from used truck values.

However, estimating residual value for many assets can be very difficult due to the uncertainty about the future. For this reason, along with the fact that residual values often are immaterial, many companies simply assume a residual value of zero. Companies usually do not disclose estimated residual values.

Allocation Method

The *allocation method* used should be systematic and rational and correspond to the pattern of asset use.

In determining how much cost to allocate to periods of an asset's use, a method should be selected that corresponds to the pattern of the loss of the asset's usefulness. Generally accepted accounting principles state that the chosen method should allocate the asset's cost "as equitably as possible to the periods during which services are obtained from [its] use." GAAP further specifies that the method should produce a cost allocation in a "systematic and rational manner."[1] The objective is to try to allocate cost to the period in an amount that is proportional to the amount of benefits generated by the asset during the period relative to the total benefits provided by the asset during its life.

In practice, there are two general approaches that attempt to obtain this systematic and rational allocation. The first approach allocates the cost base according to the *passage of time*. Methods following this approach are referred to as time-based methods. The second approach allocates an asset's cost base using a measure of the asset's *input* or *output*. This is an activity-based method. We compare these approaches first in the context of depreciation. Later we see that depletion of natural resources typically follows an activity-based approach and the amortization of intangibles typically follows a time-based approach.

Depreciation

● LO11–2

To demonstrate and compare the most common depreciation methods, we refer to the situation described in Illustration 11–3.

Illustration 11–3
Depreciation Methods

The Hogan Manufacturing Company purchased a machine for $250,000. The company expects the service life of the machine to be five years. During that time, it is expected that the machine will produce 140,000 units. The anticipated residual value is $40,000. The machine was disposed of after five years of use. Actual production during the five years of the asset's life was:

Year	Units Produced
1	24,000
2	36,000
3	46,000
4	8,000
5	16,000
Total	130,000

Time-Based Depreciation Methods

The *straight-line depreciation method* allocates an equal amount of depreciable base to each year of the asset's service life.

STRAIGHT-LINE METHOD. By far the most easily understood and widely used depreciation method is straight line. By this approach, an equal amount of depreciable base is allocated to each year of the asset's service life. The depreciable base is simply divided by the number of years in the asset's life to determine annual depreciation. In our illustration, the straight-line annual depreciation is $42,000, calculated as follows:

$$\frac{\$250{,}000 - 40{,}000}{5 \text{ years}} = \$42{,}000 \text{ per year}$$

ACCELERATED METHODS. Using the straight-line method implicitly assumes that the benefits derived from the use of the asset are the same each year. In some situations it might be more appropriate to assume that the asset will provide greater benefits in the early years of its life than in the later years. In these cases, a more appropriate matching of depreciation with revenues is achieved with a declining pattern of depreciation, with higher

[1]FASB ASC 360–10–35–4: Property, Plant, and Equipment—Overall—Subsequent Measurement (previously "Restatement and Revision of Accounting Research Bulletins," *Accounting Research Bulletin No. 43* (New York: AICPA, 1953), Ch. 9).

depreciation in the early years of the asset's life and lower depreciation in later years. An accelerated depreciation method also would be appropriate when benefits derived from the asset are approximately equal over the asset's life, but repair and maintenance costs increase significantly in later years. The early years incur higher depreciation and lower repairs and maintenance expense, while the later years have lower depreciation and higher repairs and maintenance. Two ways to achieve such a declining pattern are the sum-of-the-years'-digits method and declining balance methods.

***Accelerated depreciation methods* are appropriate when the asset is more useful in its earlier years.**

Sum-of-the-years'-digits method. The **sum-of-the-years'-digits (SYD) method** has no logical foundation other than the fact that it accomplishes the objective of accelerating depreciation in a systematic manner. This is achieved by multiplying the depreciable base by a fraction that declines each year and results in depreciation that decreases by the same amount each year. The denominator of the fraction remains constant and is the sum of the digits from one to n, where n is the number of years in the asset's service life. For example, if there are five years in the service life, the denominator is the sum of 1, 2, 3, 4, and 5, which equals 15.[2] The numerator decreases each year; it begins with the value of n in the first year and decreases by one each year until it equals one in the final year of the asset's estimated service life. The annual fractions for an asset with a five-year life are: 5/15, 4/15, 3/15, 2/15, and 1/15. We calculate depreciation for the five years of the machine's life using the sum-of-the-years'-digits method in Illustration 11–3A.

The *SYD method* multiplies depreciable base by a declining fraction.

Illustration 11–3A Sum-of-the-Years'-Digits Depreciation

Year	Depreciable Base ($250,000 – 40,000)	×	Depreciation Rate per Year	=	Depreciation	Accumulated Depreciation	Book Value End of Year ($250,000 less Accum. Depreciation)
1	$210,000		5/15*		$ 70,000	$ 70,000	$180,000
2	210,000		4/15		56,000	126,000	124,000
3	210,000		3/15		42,000	168,000	82,000
4	210,000		2/15		28,000	196,000	54,000
5	210,000		1/15		14,000	210,000	40,000
Totals			15/15		$210,000		

$*\frac{n(n+1)}{2} = \frac{5(5+1)}{2} = 15$

Declining balance methods. As an alternative, an accelerated depreciation pattern can be achieved by various declining balance methods. Rather than multiplying a constant balance by a declining fraction as we do in SYD depreciation, we multiply a constant fraction by a declining balance each year. Specifically, we multiply a constant percentage rate times the decreasing book value (cost less accumulated depreciation), sometimes called carrying value or carrying amount, of the asset (not depreciable base) at the beginning of the year. Because the rate remains constant while the book value declines, annual depreciation is less each year.

***Declining balance depreciation methods* multiply beginning-of-year book value, not depreciable base, by an annual rate that is a multiple of the straight-line rate.**

The rates used are multiples of the straight-line rate. The straight-line rate is calculated as one, divided by the number of years in the asset's service life. For example, the straight-line rate for an asset with a five-year life is one-fifth, or 20%. Various multiples used in practice are 125%, 150%, or 200% of the straight-line rate. When 200% is used as the multiplier, the method is known as the **double-declining-balance (DDB) method** because the rate used is twice the straight-line rate.

In our illustration, the double-declining-balance rate would be 40% (two times the straight-line rate of 20%). Depreciation is calculated in Illustration 11–3B for the five years of the machine's life using the double-declining-balance method.

[2]A formula useful when calculating the denominator is $n(n + 1)/2$.

Illustration 11–3B
Double-Declining-Balance Depreciation

Year	Book Value Beginning of Year	×	Depreciation Rate per Year	=	Depreciation	Accumulated Depreciation	Book Value End of Year ($250,000 less Accum. Depreciation)
1	$250,000		40%		$100,000	$100,000	$150,000
2	150,000		40%		60,000	160,000	90,000
3	90,000		40%		36,000	196,000	54,000
4	54,000				14,000*	210,000	40,000
5	40,000				—		40,000
Total					$210,000		

*Amount necessary to reduce book value to residual value.

Notice that in the fourth year depreciation is a plug amount that reduces book value to the expected residual value (book value beginning of year, $54,000, minus expected residual value, $40,000 = $14,000). There is no depreciation in year 5 since book value has already been reduced to the expected residual value. Declining balance methods often allocate the asset's depreciable base over fewer years than the expected service life.

It is not uncommon for a company to switch from accelerated to straight line approximately halfway through an asset's useful life as part of the company's planned depreciation approach.

SWITCH FROM ACCELERATED TO STRAIGHT LINE. The result of applying the double-declining-balance method in our illustration produces an awkward result in the later years of the asset's life. By using the double-declining-balance method in our illustration, no depreciation is recorded in year 5 even though the asset is still producing benefits. In practice, many companies switch to the straight-line method approximately halfway through an asset's useful life.

In our illustration, the company would switch to straight line in either year 3 or year 4. Assuming the switch is made at the beginning of year 4, and the book value at the beginning of that year is $54,000, an additional $14,000 ($54,000 − 40,000 in residual value) of depreciation must be recorded. Applying the straight-line concept, $7,000 ($14,000 divided by two remaining years) in depreciation is recorded in both year 4 and year 5.

It should be noted that this switch to straight line is not a change in depreciation method. The switch is part of the company's planned depreciation approach. However, as you will learn later in the chapter, the accounting treatment is the same as a change in depreciation method.

Activity-Based Depreciation Methods

Activity-based depreciation methods estimate service life in terms of some measure of productivity.

The most logical way to allocate an asset's cost to periods of an asset's use is to measure the usefulness of the asset in terms of its productivity. For example, we could measure the service life of a machine in terms of its *output* (for example, the estimated number of units it will produce) or in terms of its *input* (for example, the number of hours it will operate). We have already mentioned that one way to measure the service life of a vehicle is to estimate the number of miles it will operate. The most common activity-based method is called the **units-of-production method**.

FINANCIAL Reporting Case

Q2, p. 587

The *units-of-production method* computes a depreciation rate per measure of activity and then multiplies this rate by actual activity to determine periodic depreciation.

The measure of output used is the estimated number of units (pounds, items, barrels, etc.) to be produced by the machine. We could also use a measure of input such as the number of hours the machine is expected to operate. By the units-of-production method, we first compute the average depreciation rate per unit by dividing the depreciable base by the number of units expected to be produced. This per unit rate is then multiplied by the number of units produced each period. In our illustration, the depreciation rate per unit is $1.50, computed as follows:

$$\frac{\$250{,}000 - 40{,}000}{140{,}000 \text{ units}} = \$1.50 \text{ per unit}$$

Each unit produced will require $1.50 of depreciation to be recorded. As we are estimating service life based on units produced rather than in years, depreciation is not constrained by time. However, total depreciation is constrained by the asset's cost and the anticipated residual value. In our illustration, suppose the company intended to dispose of the asset at the end of five years. Depreciation for year five must be modified. Depreciation would be an amount necessary to bring the book value of the asset down to residual value. Depreciation for the five years is determined in Illustration 11–3C using the units-of-production method. Notice that the last year's depreciation is a plug amount that reduces book value to the expected residual value.

Illustration 11–3C
Units-of-Production Depreciation

Year	Units Produced	×	Depreciation Rate per Unit	=	Depreciation	Accumulated Depreciation	Book Value End of Year ($250,000 less Accum. Depreciation)
1	24,000		$1.50		$ 36,000	$ 36,000	$214,000
2	36,000		1.50		54,000	90,000	160,000
3	46,000		1.50		69,000	159,000	91,000
4	8,000		1.50		12,000	171,000	79,000
5	16,000				39,000*	210,000	40,000
Totals	130,000				$210,000		

*Amount necessary to reduce book value to residual value.

Decision Makers' Perspective—Selecting A Depreciation Method

Illustration 11–3D compares periodic depreciation calculated using each of the alternatives we discussed and illustrated.

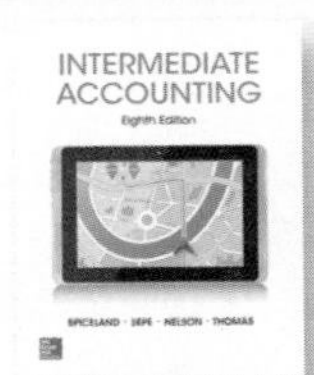

Illustration 11–3D Comparison of Various Depreciation Methods

Year	Straight Line	Sum-of-the-Years'-Digits	Double-Declining Balance	Units of Production
1	$ 42,000	$ 70,000	$100,000	$ 36,000
2	42,000	56,000	60,000	54,000
3	42,000	42,000	36,000	69,000
4	42,000	28,000	14,000	12,000
5	42,000	14,000	0	39,000
Total	$210,000	$210,000	$210,000	$210,000

All methods provide the same total depreciation over an asset's life.

Theoretically, using an activity-based depreciation method provides a better matching of revenues and expenses. Clearly, the productivity of a plant asset is more closely associated with the benefits provided by that asset than the mere passage of time. Also, these methods allow for random patterns of depreciation to correspond with the random patterns of asset use.

However, activity-based methods quite often are either infeasible or too costly to use. For example, buildings don't have an identifiable measure of productivity. Even for machinery, there may be an identifiable measure of productivity such as machine hours or units produced, but it frequently is more costly to determine each period than it is to simply measure the passage of time. For these reasons, most companies use time-based depreciation methods.

Activity-based methods are theoretically superior to time-based methods but often are impractical to apply in practice.

Illustration 11–4 shows the results of a recent survey of depreciation methods used by large public companies.[3]

Illustration 11–4
Use of Various Depreciation Methods

Depreciation Method	Number of Companies
Straight line	490
Declining balance	9
Sum-of-the-years'-digits	2
Accelerated method—not specified	9
Units of production	12
Group/composite	17

Why do so many companies use the straight-line method as opposed to other time-based methods? Many companies perhaps consider the benefits derived from the majority of plant assets to be realized approximately evenly over these assets' useful lives. Certainly a contributing factor is that straight-line is the easiest method to understand and apply.

Another motivation is the positive effect on reported income. Straight-line depreciation produces a higher net income than accelerated methods in the early years of an asset's life. In Chapter 8 we pointed out that reported net income can affect bonuses paid to management or debt agreements with lenders.

A company does not have to use the same depreciation method for both financial reporting and income tax purposes.

Conflicting with the desire to report higher profits is the desire to reduce taxes by reducing taxable income. An accelerated method serves this objective by reducing taxable income more in the early years of an asset's life than straight line. You probably recall a similar discussion from Chapter 8 in which the benefits of using the LIFO inventory method during periods of increasing costs were described. However, remember that the LIFO conformity rule requires companies using LIFO for income tax reporting to also use LIFO for financial reporting. *No such conformity rule exists for depreciation methods.* Income tax regulations allow firms to use different approaches to computing depreciation in their tax returns and in their financial statements. The method used for tax purposes is therefore not a constraint in the choice of depreciation methods for financial reporting. As a result, most companies use the straight-line method for financial reporting and the Internal Revenue Service's prescribed accelerated method (discussed in Appendix 11A) for income tax purposes. For example, Illustration 11–5 shows **Merck & Co.**'s depreciation policy as reported in a disclosure note accompanying recent financial statements.

Illustration 11–5
Depreciation Method Disclosure—Merck & Co.

Real World Financials

> **Summary of Accounting Policies (in part): Depreciation**
>
> Depreciation is provided over the estimated useful lives of the assets, principally using the straight-line method. For tax purposes, accelerated methods are used.

It is not unusual for a company to use different depreciation methods for different classes of assets. For example, Illustration 11–6 illustrates the **International Paper Company** depreciation policy disclosure contained in a note accompanying recent financial statements.

Illustration 11–6
Depreciation Method Disclosure—International Paper Company

Real World Financials

> **Summary of Accounting Policies (in part): Plants, Properties, and Equipment**
>
> Plants, properties, and equipment are stated at cost, less accumulated depreciation. The units-of-production method of depreciation is used for major pulp and paper mills and the straight-line method is used for other plants and equipment. ●

[3]*U.S. GAAP Financial Statements—Best Practices in Presentation and Disclosure—2013* (New York: AICPA, 2013).

International Financial Reporting Standards

● LO11–10

Depreciation. *IAS No. 16* requires that each component of an item of property, plant, and equipment must be depreciated separately if its cost is significant in relation to the total cost of the item.[4] In the United States, component depreciation is allowed but is not often used in practice.

Consider the following illustration:

IFRS ILLUSTRATION

Cavandish LTD. purchased a delivery truck for $62,000. The truck is expected to have a service life of six years and a residual value of $12,000. At the end of three years, the oversized tires, which have a cost of $6,000 (included in the $62,000 purchase price), will be replaced.

Under U.S. GAAP, the typical accounting treatment is to depreciate the $50,000 ($62,000 − 12,000) depreciable base of the truck over its six-year useful life. Using IFRS, the depreciable base of the truck is $44,000 ($62,000 − 12,000 − 6,000) and is depreciated over the truck's six-year useful life, and the $6,000 cost of the tires is depreciated separately over a three-year useful life.

U.S. GAAP and IFRS determine depreciable base in the same way, by subtracting estimated residual value from cost. However, IFRS requires a review of residual values at least annually.

Real World Financials

Sanofi-Aventis, a French pharmaceutical company, prepares its financial statements using IFRS. In its property, plant, and equipment note, the company discloses its use of the component-based approach to accounting for depreciation.

Property, plant, and equipment (in part)

The component-based approach to accounting for property, plant, and equipment is applied. Under this approach, each component of an item of property, plant, and equipment with a cost which is significant in relation to the total cost of the item and which has a different useful life from the other components must be depreciated separately.

Depreciation Methods. *IAS No. 16* specifically mentions three depreciation methods: straight-line, units-of-production, and the diminishing balance method. The diminishing balance method is similar to the declining balance method sometimes used by U.S. companies. As in the U.S., the straight-line method is used by most companies. A recent survey of large companies that prepare their financial statement according to IFRS reports 93% of the surveyed companies used the straight-line method.[5]

Concept Review Exercise

DEPRECIATION METHODS

The Sprague Company purchased a fabricating machine on January 1, 2016, at a net cost of $130,000. At the end of its four-year useful life, the company estimates that the machine will be worth $30,000. Sprague also estimates that the machine will run for 25,000 hours during its four-year life. The company's fiscal year ends on December 31.

Required:

Compute depreciation for 2016 through 2019 using each of the following methods:

1. Straight line.
2. Sum-of-the-years'-digits.

[4]"Property, Plant and Equipment," *International Accounting Standard No. 16* (IASCF), par. 42, as amended effective January 1, 2014.

[5]"*IFRS Accounting Trends and Techniques*" (New York, AICPA, 2011), p. 328.

3. Double-declining balance.
4. Units of production (using machine hours). Actual production was as follows:

Year	Machine Hours
2016	6,000
2017	8,000
2018	5,000
2019	7,000

Solution:

1. Straight line.

$$\frac{\$130{,}000 - 30{,}000}{4 \text{ years}} = \$25{,}000 \text{ per year}$$

2. Sum-of-the-years'-digits.

Year	Depreciable Base	×	Depreciation Rate per Year	=	Depreciation
2016	$100,000		4⁄10		$ 40,000
2017	100,000		3⁄10		30,000
2018	100,000		2⁄10		20,000
2019	100,000		1⁄10		10,000
Total					$100,000

3. Double-declining balance.

Year	Book Value Beginning of Year	×	Depreciation Rate per Year	=	Depreciation	Book Value End of Year
2016	$130,000		50%		$ 65,000	$65,000
2017	65,000		50		32,500	32,500
2018	32,500				2,500*	30,000
2019	30,000				—	30,000
Total					$100,000	

*Amount necessary to reduce book value to residual value.

4. Units of production (using machine hours).

Year	Machine Hours	×	Depreciation Rate per Hour	=	Depreciation	Book Value End of Year
2016	6,000		$4*		$ 24,000	$106,000
2017	8,000		4		32,000	74,000
2018	5,000		4		20,000	54,000
2019	7,000				24,000†	30,000
Total					$100,000	

*($130,000 − 30,000)/25,000 hours = $4 per hour.
†Amount necessary to reduce book value to residual value.

Group and Composite Depreciation Methods

Group and composite depreciation methods **aggregate assets to reduce the recordkeeping costs of determining periodic depreciation.**

As you might imagine, depreciation records could become quite cumbersome and costly if a company has hundreds, or maybe thousands, of depreciable assets. However, the burden can be lessened if the company uses the group or composite method to depreciate assets collectively rather than individually. The two methods are the same except for the way the collection of assets is aggregated for depreciation. The **group depreciation method** defines the collection as depreciable assets that share similar service lives and other attributes. For example, group depreciation could be used for fleets of vehicles or collections of machinery. The **composite depreciation method** is used when assets are physically dissimilar but are aggregated anyway to gain the convenience of a collective depreciation calculation. For instance, composite depreciation can be used for all of the depreciable assets in one manufacturing plant, even though individual assets in the composite may have widely diverse service lives.

Both approaches are similar in that they involve applying a single straight-line rate based on the average service lives of the assets in the group or composite.[6] The process is demonstrated using Illustration 11–7.

Illustration 11–7
Group Depreciation

The Express Delivery Company began operations in 2016. It will depreciate its fleet of delivery vehicles using the group method. The cost of vehicles purchased early in 2016, along with residual values, estimated lives, and straight-line depreciation per year by type of vehicle, are as follows:

Asset	Cost	Residual Value	Depreciable Base	Estimated Life (yrs.)	Depreciation per Year (straight line)
Vans	$150,000	$30,000	$120,000	6	$ 20,000
Trucks	120,000	16,000	104,000	5	20,800
Wagons	60,000	12,000	48,000	4	12,000
Totals	$330,000	$58,000	$272,000		$52,800

The *group depreciation* rate is determined by dividing the depreciation per year by the total cost. The group's *average service* life is calculated by dividing the depreciable base by the depreciation per year:

$$\text{Group depreciation rate} = \frac{\$52,800}{\$330,000} = 16\%$$

$$\text{Average service life} = \frac{\$272,000}{\$52,800} = 5.15 \text{ years (rounded)}$$

If there are no changes in the assets contained in the group, depreciation of $52,800 per year (16% × $330,000) will be recorded for 5.15 years. This means the depreciation in the sixth year will be $7,920 (.15 of a full year's depreciation = 15% × $52,800), which depreciates the cost of the group down to its estimated residual value. In other words, the group will be depreciated over the average service life of the assets in the group.

The depreciation rate is applied to the total cost of the group or composite for the period.

In practice, there very likely will be changes in the assets constituting the group as new assets are added and others are retired or sold. Additions are recorded by increasing the group asset account for the cost of the addition. Depreciation is determined by multiplying the group rate by the total cost of assets in the group for that period. Once the group or composite rate and the average service life are determined, they normally are continued despite the addition and disposition of individual assets. This implicitly assumes that the service lives of new assets approximate those of individual assets they replace.

Because depreciation records are not kept on an individual asset basis, dispositions are recorded under the assumption that the book value of the disposed item exactly equals any proceeds received and no gain or loss is recorded. For example, if a delivery truck in the above illustration that cost $15,000 is sold for $3,000 in the year 2019, the following journal entry is recorded:

No gain or loss is recorded when a group or composite asset is retired or sold.

Cash	3,000	
Accumulated depreciation (difference)	12,000	
Vehicles		15,000

[6] A declining balance method could also be used with either the group or composite method by applying a multiple (e.g., 200%) to the straight-line group or composite rate.

Any actual gain or loss is included in the accumulated depreciation account. This practice generally will not distort income as the unrecorded gains tend to offset unrecorded losses.

The group and composite methods simplify the recordkeeping of depreciable assets. This simplification justifies any immaterial errors in income determination. Illustration 11–8 shows a disclosure note accompanying recent financial statements of the **El Paso Natural Gas Company (EPNG)** describing the use of the group depreciation method for its property that is regulated by federal statutes.

Illustration 11–8
Disclosure of Depreciation Method—El Paso Natural Gas Company

Real World Financials

Summary of Significant Accounting Policies (in part)
Property, Plant, and Equipment (in part)

We use the group method to depreciate property, plant, and equipment. Under this method, assets with similar lives and characteristics are grouped and depreciated as one asset. We apply the depreciation rate approved in our rate settlements to the total cost of the group until its net book value equals its salvage value. The majority of our property, plant, and equipment are on our El Paso Natural Gas Company (EPNG) system, which has depreciation rates ranging from one percent to 50 percent.

When we retire property, plant, and equipment, we charge accumulated depreciation and amortization for the original cost of the assets in addition to the cost to remove, sell, or dispose of the assets, less their salvage value. We do not recognize a gain or loss unless we sell an entire operating unit.

Additional group-based depreciation methods, the retirement and replacement methods, are discussed in Appendix 11B.

International Financial Reporting Standards

● LO11–10

Valuation of Property, Plant, and Equipment. As we've discussed, under U.S. GAAP a company reports property, plant, and equipment (PP&E) in the balance sheet at cost less accumulated depreciation (book value). *IAS No. 16*[7] allows a company to report property, plant, and equipment at that amount or, alternatively, at its fair value (revaluation). If a company chooses revaluation, all assets within a class of PP&E must be revalued on a regular basis. U.S. GAAP prohibits revaluation.

If the revaluation option is chosen, the way the company reports the difference between fair value and book value depends on which amount is higher:

- If fair value is higher than book value, the difference is reported as *other comprehensive income (OCI)* which then accumulates in a "revaluation surplus" (sometimes called revaluation reserve) account in equity.
- If book value is higher than fair value, the difference is reported as an *expense in the income statement*. An exception is when a revaluation surplus account relating to the same asset has a balance from a previous *increase* in fair value, that balance is eliminated before debiting revaluation expense.

Consider the following illustration:

IFRS ILLUSTRATION

Candless Corporation prepares its financial statements according to IFRS. At the beginning of its 2016 fiscal year, the company purchased equipment for $100,000. The equipment is expected to have a five-year useful life with no residual value, so depreciation for 2016 is $20,000. At the end of the year, Candless chooses to revalue the equipment as permitted by *IAS No. 16*. Assuming that the fair value of the equipment at year-end is $84,000, Candless records depreciation and the revaluation using the following journal entries:

(a) Depreciation expense ($100,000 ÷ 5 years)	20,000	
Accumulated depreciation		20,000

(continued)

[7] "Property, Plant and Equipment," *International Accounting Standard No. 16* (IASCF), as amended effective January 1, 2014.

(concluded)

After this entry, the book value of the equipment is $80,000; the fair value is $84,000. We use the ratio of the two amounts to adjust both the equipment and the accumulated depreciation accounts (and thus the book value) to fair value ($ in thousands):

December 31, 2016	Before Revaluation				After Revaluation
Equipment	$100	×	84/80	=	$105
Accumulated depreciation	20	×	84/80	=	21
Book value	$ 80	×	84/80	=	$ 84

The entries to revalue the equipment and the accumulated depreciation accounts (and thus the book value) are:

To record the revaluation of equipment to its fair value.

(b) Equipment ($105,000 − 100,000)	5,000	
Accumulated depreciation ($21,000 − 20,000)		1,000
Revaluation surplus—OCI ($84,000 − 80,000)		4,000

The new basis for the equipment is its fair value of $84,000 ($105,000 − 21,000), and the following years' depreciation is based on that amount. Thus, 2017 depreciation would be $84,000 divided by the four remaining years, or $21,000:[8]

(a) Depreciation expense ($84,000 ÷ 4 years)	21,000	
Accumulated depreciation		21,000

After this entry, the accumulated depreciation is $42,000 and the book value of the equipment is $63,000. Let's say the fair value now is $57,000. We use the ratio of the two amounts (fair value of $57,000 divided by book value of $63,000) to adjust both the equipment and the accumulated depreciation accounts (and thus the book value) to fair value ($ in thousands):

December 31, 2017	Before Revaluation				After Revaluation
Equipment	$105	×	57/63	=	$95
Accumulated depreciation	42	×	57/63	=	38
Book value	$ 63	×	57/63	=	$57

The entries to revalue the equipment and the accumulated depreciation accounts (and thus the book value) are:

(b) Revaluation surplus—OCI ($57,000 − 63,000 = $6,000; limit: $4,000 balance)	4,000	
Revaluation expense (to balance)	2,000	
Accumulated depreciation ($38,000 − 42,000)	4,000	
Equipment ($95,000 − 105,000)		10,000

A decrease in fair value, as occurred in 2017, is expensed unless it reverses a revaluation surplus account relating to the same asset, as in this illustration. So, of the $6,000 decrease in value ($63,000 book value less $57,000 fair value), $4,000 is debited to the previously created revaluation surplus and the remaining $2,000 is recorded as revaluation expense in the income statement.

Real World Financials

Investcorp, a provider and manager of alternative investment products headquartered in London, prepares its financial statements according to IFRS. The following disclosure

(continued)

[8] *IAS No. 16* allows companies to choose between the method illustrated here and an alternative. The second method eliminates the entire accumulated depreciation account and adjusts the asset account (equipment in this illustration) to fair value. Using either method the revaluation surplus (or expense) would be the same.

(concluded)

note included in a recent annual report discusses the company's method of valuing its building and certain operating assets.

Premises and Equipment (in part)

The Bank carries its building on freehold land and certain operating assets at revalued amounts, being the fair value of the assets at the date of revaluation less any subsequent accumulated depreciation and subsequent accumulated impairment losses. Any revaluation surplus is credited to the asset revaluation reserve included in equity, except to the extent that it reverses a revaluation decrease of the same asset previously recognized in profit and loss, in which case the increase is recognized in profit or loss. A revaluation deficit is recognized directly in profit or loss, except that a deficit directly offsetting a previous surplus on the same asset is directly offset against the surplus in the asset revaluation reserve.

The revaluation alternative is used infrequently. A recent survey of large companies that prepare their financial statements according to IFRS reports that only 10 of the 160 surveyed companies used the revaluation alternative for at least one asset class.[9]

Depletion of Natural Resources

LO11–3

Allocation of the cost of natural resources is called **depletion**. Because the usefulness of natural resources generally is directly related to the amount of the resources extracted, the activity-based units-of-production method is widely used to calculate periodic depletion. Service life is therefore the estimated amount of natural resource to be extracted (for example, tons of mineral or barrels of oil).

Depletion base is cost less any anticipated residual value. Residual value could be significant if cost includes land that has a value after the natural resource has been extracted.

The example in Illustration 11–9 was first introduced in Chapter 10.

Illustration 11–9
Depletion of Natural Resources

The Jackson Mining Company paid $1,000,000 for the right to explore for a coal deposit on 500 acres of land in Pennsylvania. Costs of exploring for the coal deposit totaled $800,000 and intangible development costs incurred in digging and erecting the mine shaft were $500,000. In addition, Jackson purchased new excavation equipment for the project at a cost of $600,000. After the coal is removed from the site, the equipment will be sold for an anticipated residual value of $60,000.

The company geologist estimates that 1 million tons of coal will be extracted over the three-year period. During 2016, 300,000 tons were extracted. Jackson is required by its contract to restore the land to a condition suitable for recreational use after it extracts the coal.

In Illustration 10–6 on page 534 we determined that the capitalized cost of the natural resource, coal mine, including the restoration costs, is **$2,768,360**. Since there is no residual value to the land, the depletion base equals cost and the depletion rate per ton is calculated as follows:

Depletion of the cost of natural resources usually is determined using the units-of-production method.

$$\text{Depletion per ton} = \frac{\text{Depletion base}}{\text{Estimated extractable tons}}$$

$$\text{Depletion per ton} = \frac{\$2{,}768{,}360}{1{,}000{,}000 \text{ tons}} = \$2.76836 \text{ per ton}$$

For each ton of coal extracted, $2.76836 in depletion is recorded. In 2016, the following journal entry records depletion.

Depletion ($2.76836 × 300,000 tons)	830,508	
Coal mine		830,508

[9]"*IFRS Accounting Trends and Techniques*" (New York, AICPA, 2011), p. 171.

Notice that the credit is to the asset, coal mine, rather than to a contra account, accumulated depletion. Although this approach is traditional, the use of a contra account is acceptable.

Depletion is a product cost and is included in the cost of the inventory of coal, just as the depreciation on manufacturing equipment is included in inventory cost. The depletion is then included in cost of goods sold in the income statement when the coal is sold.

What about depreciation on the $600,000 cost of excavation equipment? If the equipment can be moved from the site and used on future projects, the equipment's depreciable base should be allocated over its useful life. If the asset is not movable, as in our illustration, then it should be depreciated over its useful life or the life of the natural resource, whichever is shorter.

Quite often, companies use the units-of-production method to calculate depreciation and amortization on assets used in the extraction of natural resources. The activity base used is the same as that used to calculate depletion, the estimated recoverable natural resource. In our illustration, the depreciation rate would be $.54 per ton, calculated as follows.

The units-of-production method often is used to determine depreciation and amortization on assets used in the extraction of natural resources.

$$\text{Depreciation per ton} = \frac{\$600{,}000 - 60{,}000}{1{,}000{,}000 \text{ tons}} = \$.54 \text{ per ton}$$

In 2016, $162,000 in depreciation ($.54 × 300,000 tons) is recorded and also included as part of the cost of the coal inventory.

The summary of significant accounting policies disclosure accompanying recent financial statements of ConocoPhilips shown in Illustration 11–10 provides a good summary of depletion, amortization, and depreciation for natural resource properties.

Summary of Significant Accounting Policies (in part)

Depletion and Amortization—Leasehold costs of producing properties are depleted using the units-of-production method based on estimated proved oil and gas reserves. Amortization of intangible development costs is based on the units-of-production method using estimated proved developed oil and gas reserves.
Depreciation and Amortization—Depreciation and amortization of PP&E on producing hydrocarbon properties and certain pipeline assets (those which are expected to have a declining utilization pattern), are determined by the units-of-production method. Depreciation and amortization of all other PP&E are determined by either the individual-unit-straight-line method or the group-straight-line method (for those individual units that are highly integrated with other units).

Illustration 11–10

Depletion Method Disclosure—ConocoPhilips

Real World Financials

Additional Consideration

Percentage Depletion

Depletion of cost less residual value required by GAAP should not be confused with percentage depletion (also called *statutory depletion*) allowable for income tax purposes for oil, gas, and most mineral natural resources. Under these tax provisions, a producer is allowed to deduct the greater of cost-based depletion or a fixed percentage of gross income as depletion expense. Over the life of the asset, depletion could exceed the asset's cost. The percentage allowed for percentage-based depletion varies according to the type of natural resource.

Because percentage depletion usually differs from cost depletion, a difference between taxable income and financial reporting income before tax results. Differences between taxable income and financial reporting income are discussed in Chapter 16.

Amortization of Intangible Assets

Let's turn now to a third type of long-lived asset—intangible assets. As with other assets we have discussed, we allocate the cost of an intangible asset over its service or useful life. However, for the few intangible assets with indefinite useful lives, amortization is inappropriate.

● LO11–4

International Financial Reporting Standards

● LO11–10

Biological Assets. Living animals and plants, including the trees in a timber tract or in a fruit orchard, are referred to as *biological assets*. Under U.S. GAAP, a timber tract is valued at cost less accumulated depletion and a fruit orchard at cost less accumulated depreciation. Under IFRS, biological assets are valued at their fair value less estimated costs to sell, with changes in fair value included in the calculation of net income.[10]

Real World Financials

Mondi Limited, an international paper and packing group headquartered in Johannesburg, South Africa, prepares its financial statements according to IFRS. The following disclosure note included in a recent annual report discusses the company's policy for valuing its forestry assets.

Owned Forestry Assets (in part)

Owned forestry assets are measured at fair value, calculated by applying the expected selling price, less costs to harvest and deliver, to the estimated volume of timber on hand at each reporting date.

Changes in fair value are recognized in the combined and consolidated income statement within other net operating expenses.

Intangible Assets Subject to Amortization

The cost of an intangible asset with a *finite* useful life is *amortized*.

Allocating the cost of intangible assets is called amortization. For an intangible asset with a finite useful life, we allocate its capitalized cost less any estimated residual value to periods in which the asset is expected to contribute to the company's revenue-generating activities. This requires that we determine the asset's useful life, its amortization base (cost less estimated residual value), and the appropriate allocation method, similar to our depreciating tangible assets.

USEFUL LIFE. Legal, regulatory, or contractual provisions often limit the useful life of an intangible asset. On the other hand, useful life might sometimes be less than the asset's legal or contractual life. For example, the useful life of a patent would be considerably less than its legal life of 20 years if obsolescence were expected to limit the longevity of a protected product.

RESIDUAL VALUE. We discussed the cost of intangible assets in Chapter 10. The expected residual value of an intangible asset usually is zero. This might not be the case, though, if at the end of its useful life to the reporting entity the asset will benefit another entity. For example, if Quadra Corp. has a commitment from another company to purchase one of Quadra's patents at the end of its useful life at a determinable price, we use that price as the patent's residual value.

ALLOCATION METHOD. The method of amortization should reflect the pattern of use of the asset in generating benefits. Most companies use the straight-line method. We discussed and illustrated a unique approach to determining the periodic amortization of software development costs in Chapter 10. Recall that the periodic amortization percentage for software development costs is the *greater* of (1) the ratio of current revenues to current and anticipated revenues (percentage of revenue method), or (2) the straight-line percentage over the useful life of the asset.

Intel Corporation reported several intangible assets in a recent balance sheet. A note, shown in Illustration 11–11, disclosed the range of estimated useful lives.

Like depletion, amortization expense traditionally is credited to the asset account itself rather than to accumulated amortization. However, the use of a contra account is acceptable. Let's look at an example in Illustration 11–12.

[10]"Agriculture," *International Accounting Standard No. 41* (IASCF), as amended effective January 1, 2014.

Summary of Significant Accounting Policies (in part)
Identified Intangible Assets (in part)

The estimated useful life ranges for identified intangible assets that are subject to amortization are as follows:

(In Years)	Estimated Useful Life
Acquisition-related developed technology	3–13
Acquisition-related customer relationships	5–8
Acquisition-related trade names	5–7
Licensed technology and patents	5–17

Illustration 11–11

Intangible Asset Useful Life Disclosure—Intel Corporation

Real World Financials

Illustration 11–12

Amortization of Intangibles

Hollins Corporation began operations in 2016. Early in January, the company purchased a franchise from Ajax Industries for $200,000. The franchise agreement is for a period of 10 years. In addition, Hollins purchased a patent for $50,000. The remaining legal life of the patent is 13 years. However, due to expected technological obsolescence, the company estimates that the useful life of the patent is only 8 years. Hollins uses the straight-line amortization method for all intangible assets. The company's fiscal year-end is December 31.

The journal entries to record a full year of amortization for these intangibles are as follows:

Amortization expense ($200,000 ÷ 10 years)	20,000	
Franchise		20,000
To record amortization of franchise.		
Amortization expense ($50,000 ÷ 8 years)	6,250	
Patent		6,250
To record amortization of patent.		

Similar to depreciation, amortization is either a product cost or a period cost depending on the use of the asset. For intangibles used in the manufacture of a product, amortization is a product cost and is included in the cost of inventory (and doesn't become an expense until the inventory is sold). For intangible assets not used in production, such as the franchise cost in our illustration, periodic amortization is expensed in the period incurred.

Intangible Assets Not Subject to Amortization

An intangible asset that is determined to have an indefinite useful life is not subject to periodic amortization. Useful life is considered indefinite if there is no foreseeable limit on the period of time over which the asset is expected to contribute to the cash flows of the entity.[11]

The cost of an intangible asset with an *indefinite* useful life is *not* amortized

Indefinite does not necessarily mean permanent. For example, suppose Collins Corporation acquired a trademark in conjunction with the acquisition of a tire company. Collins plans to continue to produce the line of tires marketed under the acquired company's trademark. Recall from our discussion in Chapter 10 that trademarks have a legal life of 10 years, but the registration can be renewed for an indefinite number of 10-year periods. The life of the purchased trademark is initially considered to be indefinite and the cost of the trademark is not amortized. However, if after several years management decides to phase out production of the tire line over the next three years, Collins would amortize the remaining book value over a three-year period.

Trademarks or tradenames often are considered to have indefinite useful lives.

Recall the **Hewlett-Packard Company (HP)** acquisition of **Compaq Computer Corporation** discussed in Chapter 10. HP allocated $1.4 billion of the purchase price to Compaq's tradename, which is not being amortized. Illustration 11–13 provides another example in a disclosure made by **The Estee Lauder Companies Inc.**, in a recent annual report.

[11]FASB ASC 350–30–35–4: Intangibles–Goodwill and Other—General Intangibles Other than Goodwill—Subsequent Measurement (previously "Goodwill and Other Intangible Assets," *Statement of Financial Accounting Standards No. 142* (Norwalk, Conn.: FASB, 2001), par. B45).

Illustration 11–13
Indefinite-Life Intangibles Disclosure—The Estee Lauder Companies Inc.

Real World Financials

Other Intangible Assets

Indefinite-lived intangible assets (e.g. trademarks) are not subject to amortization and are assessed at least annually for impairment during the fiscal fourth quarter, or more frequently if certain events or circumstances warrant.

Goodwill is an intangible asset whose cost is *not* expensed through periodic amortization.

Goodwill is the most common intangible asset with an indefinite useful life. Recall that goodwill is measured as the difference between the purchase price of a company and the fair value of all of the identifiable net assets acquired (tangible and intangible assets minus the fair value of liabilities assumed). Does this mean that goodwill and other intangible assets with indefinite useful lives will remain in a company's balance sheet at their original capitalized values indefinitely? Not necessarily. Like other assets, intangibles are subject to the impairment of value rules we discuss in a subsequent section of this chapter.

International Financial Reporting Standards

● LO11–10

Valuation of Intangible Assets. *IAS No. 38*[12] allows a company to value an intangible asset subsequent to initial valuation at (1) cost less accumulated amortization or (2) fair value, if fair value can be determined by reference to an active market. If revaluation is chosen, all assets within that class of intangibles must be revalued on a regular basis. Goodwill, however, cannot be revalued. U.S. GAAP prohibits revaluation of any intangible asset.

Notice that the revaluation option is possible only if fair value can be determined by reference to an active market, making the option relatively uncommon. However, the option possibly could be used for intangibles such as franchises and certain license agreements.

If the revaluation option is chosen, the accounting treatment is similar to the way we applied the revaluation option for property, plant, and equipment earlier in this chapter. Recall that the way the company reports the difference between fair value and book value depends on which amount is higher. If fair value is higher than book value, the difference is reported as other comprehensive income (OCI) and then accumulates in a revaluation surplus account in equity. On the other hand, if book value is higher than fair value, the difference is expensed after reducing any existing revaluation surplus for that asset.

Consider the following illustration:

IFRS ILLUSTRATION

Amershan LTD. prepares its financial statements according to IFRS. At the beginning of its 2016 fiscal year, the company purchased a franchise for $500,000. The franchise has a 10-year contractual life and no residual value, so amortization in 2016 is $50,000. The company does not use an accumulated amortization account and credits the franchise account directly when amortization is recorded. At the end of the year, Amershan chooses to revalue the franchise as permitted by *IAS No. 38*. Assuming that the fair value of the franchise at year-end, determined by reference to an active market, is $600,000, Amershan records amortization and the revaluation using the following journal entries:

To record the revaluation of franchise to its fair value.

Amortization expense ($500,000 ÷ 10 years)	50,000	
Franchise		50,000
Franchise ($600,000 − 450,000)	150,000	
Revaluation surplus—OCI		150,000

With the second entry Amershan increases the book value of the franchise from $450,000 ($500,000 − 50,000) to its fair value of $600,000 and records a revaluation surplus for the difference. The new basis for the franchise is its fair value of $600,000, and the following years' amortization is based on that amount. Thus, 2017 amortization would be $600,000 divided by the nine remaining years, or $66,667.

[12] "Intangible Assets," *International Accounting Standard No. 38* (IASCF), as amended effective January 1, 2014.

Concept Review Exercise

DEPLETION AND AMORTIZATION

Part A:

On March 29, 2016, the Horizon Energy Corporation purchased the mineral rights to a coal deposit in New Mexico for $2 million. Development costs and the present value of estimated land restoration costs totaled an additional $3.4 million. The company removed 200,000 tons of coal during 2016 and estimated that an additional 1,600,000 tons would be removed over the next 15 months.

Required:

Compute depletion on the mine for 2016.

Solution:

Cost of Coal Mine:	($ in millions)
Purchase price of mineral rights	$2.0
Development and restoration costs	3.4
	$5.4

Depletion:

$$\text{Depletion per ton} = \frac{\$5.4 \text{ million}}{1.8 \text{ million tons}^*} = \$3 \text{ per ton}$$

*200,000 + 1,600,000

$$\text{2016 depletion} = \$3 \times 200{,}000 \text{ tons} = \$600{,}000$$

Part B:

On October 1, 2016, Advanced Micro Circuits, Inc., completed the purchase of Zotec Corporation for $200 million. Included in the allocation of the purchase price were the following identifiable intangible assets ($ in millions), along with the fair values and estimated useful lives:

Intangible Asset	Fair value	Useful Life (in years)
Patent	$10	5
Developed technology	50	4
Customer list	10	2

In addition, the fair value of acquired tangible assets was $100 million. Goodwill was valued at $30 million. Straight-line amortization is used for all purchased intangibles.

During 2016, Advanced finished work on a software development project. Development costs incurred after technological feasibility was achieved and before the product release date totaled $2 million. The software was available for release to the general public on September 29, 2016. During the last three months of the year, revenue from the sale of the software was $4 million. The company estimates that the software will generate an additional $36 million in revenue over the next 45 months.

Required:

Compute amortization for purchased intangibles and software development costs for 2016.

Solution:

Amortization of Purchased Intangibles:	
Patent	$10 million / 5 = $2 million × 3/12 year = $.5 million
Developed technology	$50 million / 4 = $12.5 million × 3/12 year = $3.125 million
Customer list	$10 million / 2 = $5 million × 3/12 year = $1.25 million
Goodwill	The cost of goodwill is not amortized.

Amortization of Software Development Costs:

(1) Percentage-of-revenue method:

$$\frac{\$4 \text{ million}}{(\$4 \text{ million} + 36 \text{ million})} = 10\% \times \$2 \text{ million} = \$200{,}000$$

(2) Straight-line:

$$\frac{3 \text{ months}}{48 \text{ months}} \text{ or } 6.25\% \times \$2 \text{ million} = \$125{,}000$$

Advanced will use the percentage-of-revenue method since it produces the greater amortization, $200,000.

PART B Additional Issues

In this part of the chapter, we discuss the following issues related to cost allocation:

1. Partial periods.
2. Changes in estimates.
3. Change in depreciation method.
4. Error correction.
5. Impairment of value.

Partial Periods

Only in textbooks are property, plant, and equipment and intangible assets purchased and disposed of at the very beginning or very end of a company's fiscal year. When acquisition and disposal occur at other times, a company theoretically must determine how much depreciation, depletion, and amortization to record for the part of the year that each asset actually is used.

Let's repeat the Hogan Manufacturing Company illustration used earlier in the chapter but modify it in Illustration 11–14 to assume that the asset was acquired *during* the company's fiscal year.

Illustration 11–14
Depreciation Methods—Partial Year

On April 1, 2016, the Hogan Manufacturing Company purchased a machine for $250,000. The company expects the service life of the machine to be five years and the anticipated residual value is $40,000. The machine was disposed of after five years of use. The company's fiscal year-end is December 31. Partial-year depreciation is recorded based on the number of months the asset is in service.

Notice that no information is provided on the estimated output of the machine. Partial-year depreciation presents a problem only when time-based depreciation methods are used. In an activity-based method, the rate per unit of output simply is multiplied by the actual output for the period, regardless of the length of that period.

Depreciation per year of the asset's life calculated earlier in the chapter for the various time-based depreciation methods is shown in Illustration 11–14A.

Illustration 11–14A
Yearly Depreciation

Year	Straight Line	Sum-of-the-Years'-Digits	Double-Declining Balance
1	$ 42,000	$ 70,000	$100,000
2	42,000	56,000	60,000
3	42,000	42,000	36,000
4	42,000	28,000	14,000
5	42,000	14,000	0
Total	$210,000	$210,000	$210,000

Illustration 11–14B shows how Hogan would depreciate the machinery by these three methods assuming an April 1 acquisition date.

Illustration 11–14B Partial-Year Depreciation

Year	Straight Line	Sum-of-the-Years'-Digits	Double-Declining Balance
2016	$42,000 × ¾ = $ 31,500	$70,000 × ¾ = $ 52,500	$100,000 × ¾ = $ 75,000
2017	$ 42,000	$70,000 × ¼ = $ 17,500	$100,000 × ¼ = $ 25,000
		+56,000 × ¾ = 42,000	+60,000 × ¾ = 45,000
		$ 59,500	$ 70,000*
2018	$ 42,000	$56,000 × ¼ = $ 14,000	$60,000 × ¼ = $ 15,000
		+42,000 × ¾ = 31,500	+36,000 × ¾ = 27,000
		$ 45,500	$ 42,000
2019	$ 42,000	$42,000 × ¼ = $ 10,500	$36,000 × ¼ = $ 9,000
		+28,000 × ¾ = 21,000	+14,000 × ¾ = 10,500
		$ 31,500	$ 19,500
2020	$ 42,000	$28,000 × ¼ = $ 7,000	$14,000 × ¼ = $ 3,500
		+14,000 × ¾ = 10,500	
		$ 17,500	
2021	$42,000 × ¼ = $ 10,500	$14,000 × ¼ = $ 3,500	
	Totals $210,000	$210,000	$210,000

*Could also be determined by multiplying the book value at the beginning of the year by twice the straight-line rate: ($250,000 − 75,000) × 40% = $70,000.

Notice that 2016 depreciation is three-quarters of the full year's depreciation for the first year of the asset's life, because the asset was used nine months, or ¾ of the year. The remaining one-quarter of the first year's depreciation is included in 2017's depreciation along with ¾ of the depreciation for the second year of the asset's life. This calculation is not necessary for the straight-line method because a full year's depreciation is the same for each year of the asset's life.

Usually, the above procedure is impractical or at least cumbersome. As a result, most companies adopt a simplifying assumption, or convention, for computing partial year's depreciation and use it consistently. A common convention is to record one-half of a full year's depreciation in the year of acquisition and another half year in the year of disposal. This is known as the **half-year convention.**[13]

Changes in Estimates

The calculation of depreciation, depletion, or amortization requires estimates of both service life and residual value. It's inevitable that at least some estimates will prove incorrect. Chapter 4 briefly introduced the topic of changes in estimates along with coverage of changes in accounting principles and the correction of errors. Here and in subsequent sections of this chapter, we provide overviews of the accounting treatment and disclosures required for these changes and errors when they involve property, plant, and equipment and intangible assets.

● LO11–5

Changes in estimates are accounted for prospectively. When a company revises a previous estimate based on new information, prior financial statements are not restated. Instead, the company merely incorporates the new estimate in any related accounting determinations from then on. So, it usually will affect some aspects of both the balance sheet and the income statement in the current and future periods. A disclosure note should describe the effect of a change in estimate net income, and related per share amounts for the current period.

A change in estimate should be reflected in the financial statements of the current period and future periods.

[13]Another common method is the modified half-year convention. This method records a full year's depreciation when the asset is acquired in the first half of the year or sold in the second half. No depreciation is recorded if the asset is acquired in the second half of the year or sold in the first half. These half-year conventions are simple and, in most cases, will not result in material differences from a more precise calculation.

Consider the example in Illustration 11–15.

Illustration 11–15
Change in Accounting Estimate

On January 1, 2014, the Hogan Manufacturing Company purchased office furniture and fixtures for $250,000. The company expects the service life of the office furniture and fixtures to be five years and the anticipated residual value to be $40,000. The company's fiscal year-end is December 31 and the straight-line depreciation method is used for all depreciable assets. During 2016, the company revised its estimate of service life from five to eight years and also revised estimated residual value to $22,000.

For 2014 and 2015, depreciation is $42,000 per year [($250,000 − 40,000) ÷ 5 years] or $84,000 for the two years. However, with the revised estimate, depreciation for 2016 and subsequent years is determined by allocating the book value remaining at the beginning of 2016 less the revised residual value equally over the remaining service life of six years (8 − 2). The remaining book value at the beginning of 2016 is $166,000 ($250,000 − 84,000) and depreciation for 2016 and subsequent years is recorded as follows:

Depreciation expense (below)	24,000	
Accumulated depreciation		24,000

	$250,000	Cost
$42,000		Previous annual depreciation ($210,000 ÷ 5 years)
× 2 years	84,000	Depreciation to date (2014–2015)
	166,000	Book value as of 1/1/16
	22,000	Less revised residual value
	144,000	Revised depreciable base
	÷ 6	Estimated remaining life (8 years − 2 years)
	$ 24,000	New annual depreciation

The asset's book value is depreciated down to the anticipated residual value of $22,000 at the end of the revised eight-year service life. In addition, a note discloses the effect of the change in estimate on income, if material. The before-tax effect is an increase in income of $18,000 (depreciation of $42,000 if the change had not been made, less $24,000 depreciation after the change).

CHC Helicopter is a world-leading commercial operator of medium and heavy helicopters. The company recently revised its estimates of the service lives and residual values of certain aircraft types. Illustration 11–16 shows the note that disclosed the change.

Illustration 11–16
Change in Estimate Disclosure—CHC Helicopter

Real World Financials

(k) Property and Equipment (in part)
Flying Assets (in part)

As a result of the depreciation review we reduced the remaining useful lives and residual values of certain aircraft types. The decrease in the estimated useful life and change in residual value was accounted for as a change in estimate and resulted in an increase to depreciation of $11.3 million and a decrease in property and equipment in the year ended April 30, 2013.

Change in Depreciation, Amortization, or Depletion Method

● LO11–6

Changes in depreciation, amortization, or depletion methods are accounted for the same way as a change in accounting estimate.

Generally accepted accounting principles require that a change in depreciation, amortization, or depletion method be considered a change in accounting estimate that is achieved by a change in accounting principle. We account for these changes prospectively, exactly as we would any other change in estimate. One difference is that most changes in estimate do not require a company to justify the change. However, this change in estimate is a result of changing an accounting principle and therefore requires a clear justification as to why the new method is preferable. Consider the example in Illustration 11–17.

Illustration 11–17
Change in Depreciation Method

On January 1, 2014, the Hogan Manufacturing Company purchased office equipment for $250,000. The company expects the service life of the office equipment to be five years and its anticipated residual value to be $30,000. The company's fiscal year-end is December 31 and the double-declining-balance (DDB) depreciation method is used. During 2016, the company switched from the DDB to the straight-line method. In 2016, the adjusting entry is:

Depreciation expense (below)	20,000	
Accumulated depreciation		20,000

DDB depreciation:

2014	$100,000 ($250,000 × 40%*)
2015	60,000 ([$250,000 − 100,000] × 40%*)
Total	$160,000

*Double the straight-line rate for 5 years ([1/5 = 20%] × 2 = 40%)

$250,000	Cost
160,000	Depreciation to date, DDB (2014–2015)
90,000	Undepreciated cost as of 1/1/16
30,000	Less residual value
60,000	Depreciable base
÷ 3 yrs.	Remaining life (5 years − 2 years)
$ 20,000	New annual depreciation

A disclosure note reports the effect of the change on net income and earnings per share along with clear justification for changing depreciation methods.

Weis Markets, Inc., operates a chain of grocery stores in Pennsylvania and surrounding states. Illustration 11–18 shows a disclosure note describing a recent change in depreciation method made by the company.

Illustration 11–18
Change in Depreciation Method—Weis Markets, Inc.

Real World Financials

Note 1 Summary of Significant Accounting Policies (in part)
(j) Property and Equipment (in part)

In the first quarter of 2012, the Company changed its accounting policy for property and equipment. Property and equipment continue to be recorded at cost. Prior to January 1, 2012, the Company provided for depreciation of buildings and improvements and equipment using accelerated methods. Effective January 1, 2012, the Company changed its method of depreciation for this group of assets from the accelerated methods to straight-line. Management deemed the change preferable because the straight-line method will more accurately reflect the pattern of usage and the expected benefits of such assets. Management also considered that the change will provide greater consistency with the depreciation methods used by other companies in the Company's industry. The change was accounted for as a change in accounting estimate effected by a change in accounting principle. The net book value of assets acquired prior to January 1, 2012, with useful lives remaining will be depreciated using the straight-line method prospectively. If the Company had continued using accelerated methods, depreciation expense would have been $11.5 million greater in 2012. Had accelerated methods continued to be used, after considering the impact of income taxes, the effect would decrease net income by $6.8 million or $.25 per share in 2012.

Frequently, when a company changes depreciation method, the change will be effective only for assets placed in service after that date. Of course, that means depreciation schedules do not require revision because the change does not affect assets depreciated in prior periods. A disclosure note still is required to provide justification for the change and to report the effect of the change on the current year's income.

Error Correction

LO11–7

Errors involving property, plant, and equipment and intangible assets include computational errors in the calculation of depreciation, depletion, or amortization and mistakes made in determining whether expenditures should be capitalized or expensed. These errors can affect many years. For example, let's say a major addition to equipment should be capitalized but incorrectly is expensed. Not only is income in the year of the error understated, but subsequent years' income is overstated because depreciation is omitted.

Recall from our discussion of inventory errors in Chapter 9 that if a material error is discovered in an accounting period subsequent to the period in which the error is made, any previous years' financial statements that were incorrect as a result of the error are retrospectively restated to reflect the correction. Any account balances that are incorrect as a result of the error are corrected by journal entry. If retained earnings is one of the incorrect accounts, the correction is reported as a *prior period adjustment* to the beginning balance in the statement of shareholders' equity.[14] In addition, a disclosure note is needed to describe the nature of the error and the impact of its correction on net income and earnings per share.

Here is a summary of the treatment of material errors occurring in a previous year:

- Previous years' financial statements are retrospectively restated.
- Account balances are corrected.
- If retained earnings requires correction, the correction is reported as a prior period adjustment.
- A note describes the nature of the error and the impact of the correction on income.

Consider Illustration 11–19. The 2014 and 2015 financial statements that were incorrect as a result of the error are *retrospectively restated* to report the addition to the patent and to

Illustration 11–19
Error Correction

In 2016, the controller of the Hathaway Corporation discovered an error in recording $300,000 in legal fees to successfully defend a patent infringement suit in 2014. The $300,000 was charged to legal fee expense but should have been capitalized and amortized over the five-year remaining life of the patent. Straight-line amortization is used by Hathaway for all intangibles.

Analysis

($ in thousands)

	Correct (Should Have Been Recorded)			**Incorrect (As Recorded)**		
2014	Patent	300		Expense	300	
	Cash		300	Cash		300
2014	Expense	60		Amortization entry omitted		
	Patent		60			
2015	Expense	60		Amortization entry omitted		
	Patent		60			

During the two-year period, amortization expense was *understated* by $120 thousand, but other expenses were *overstated* by $300 thousand, so net income during the period was *understated* by $180 thousand (ignoring income taxes). This means retained earnings is currently *understated* by that amount.

Patent is understated by $180 thousand.

	($ in thousands)	
Patent	180	
Retained earnings		180
To correct incorrect accounts.		

Sometimes, the analysis is easier if you re-create the entries actually recorded incorrectly and those that would have been recorded if the error hadn't occurred, and then compare them.

[14]The prior period adjustment is applied to beginning retained earnings for the year following the error, or for the earliest year being reported in the comparative financial statements when the error occurs prior to the earliest year presented. The retained earnings balances in years after the first year also are adjusted to what those balances would be if the error had not occurred, but a company may choose not to explicitly report those adjustments as separate line items.

reflect the correct amount of amortization expense, assuming both statements are reported again for comparative purposes in the 2016 annual report.

Because retained earnings is one of the accounts incorrect as a result of the error, a correction to that account of **$180,000** is reported as a prior period adjustment to the 2016 beginning retained earnings balance in Hathaway's comparative statements of shareholders' equity. Assuming that 2015 is included with 2016 in the comparative statements, a correction would be made to the 2015 beginning retained earnings balance as well. That prior period adjustment, though, would be for the pre-2015 difference: $300,000 − 60,000 = $240,000.

Also, a disclosure note accompanying Hathaway's 2016 financial statements should describe the nature of the error and the impact of its correction on each year's net income (understated by $240,000 in 2014 and overstated by $60,000 in 2015), and earnings per share.

Chapter 20 provides in-depth coverage of changes in estimates and methods, and of accounting errors. We cover the tax effect of these changes and errors in that chapter.

Impairment of Value

● LO11–8

Depreciation, depletion, and amortization reflect a gradual consumption of the benefits inherent in property, plant, and equipment and intangible assets. An implicit assumption in allocating the cost of an asset over its useful life is that there has been no significant reduction in the anticipated total benefits or service potential of the asset. Situations can arise, however, that cause a significant decline or impairment of those benefits or service potentials. An extreme case would be the destruction of a plant asset—say a building destroyed by fire—before the asset is fully depreciated. The remaining book value of the asset in that case should be written off as a loss. Sometimes, though, the impairment of future value is more subtle.

FINANCIAL Reporting Case

Q3, p. 587

The way we recognize and measure an impairment loss differs depending on whether the assets are to be held and used or are being held to be sold. Accounting is different, too, for assets with finite lives and those with indefinite lives. We consider those differences now.

Assets to Be Held and Used

An increasingly common occurrence in practice is the partial write-down of property, plant, and equipment and intangible assets that remain in use. For example, in the second quarter of 2001, **American Airlines** reduced the book value of certain aircraft by $685 million. The write-down reflected the significant reduction in demand for air travel that occurred even before the September 11, 2001, terrorist attacks on the World Trade Center and the Pentagon.

An asset held for use should be written down if there has been a significant impairment of value.

Conceptually, there is considerable merit for a policy requiring the write-down of an asset when there has been a significant decline in value. A write-down can provide important information about the future cash flows that a company can generate from using the asset. However, in practice, this process is very subjective. Even if it appears certain that significant impairment of value has occurred, it often is difficult to measure the amount of the required write-down.

For example, let's say a company purchased $2,000,000 of equipment to be used in the production of a new type of laser printer. Depreciation is determined using the straight-line method over a useful life of six years and the residual value is estimated at $200,000. At the beginning of year 3, the machine's book value has been reduced by accumulated depreciation to $1,400,000 [$2,000,000 − ($300,000 × 2)]. At that time, new technology is developed causing a significant reduction in the selling price of the new laser printer as well as a reduction in anticipated demand for the product. Management estimates that the equipment will be useful for only two more years and will have no significant residual value.

This situation is not simply a matter of a change in the estimates of useful life and residual value. Management must decide if the events occurring in year 3 warrant a write-down of the asset below $1,400,000. A write-down would be appropriate if the company decided that it would be unable to fully recover this amount through future use.

For assets to be held and used, different guidelines apply to (1) property, plant, and equipment and intangible assets with finite useful lives (subject to depreciation, depletion, or amortization) and (2) intangible assets with indefinite useful lives (not subject to amortization).

PROPERTY, PLANT, AND EQUIPMENT AND FINITE-LIFE INTANGIBLE ASSETS. Generally accepted accounting principles provide guidelines for when to recognize and how to measure impairment losses of long-lived tangible assets and intangible assets with finite useful lives.[15] For purposes of this recognition and measurement, assets are grouped at the lowest level for which identifiable cash flows are largely independent of the cash flows of other assets.

Property, plant, and equipment and finite-life intangible assets are tested for impairment only when events or changes in circumstances indicate book value may not be recoverable.

When to Test for Impairment. It would be impractical to test all assets or asset groups for impairment at the end of every reporting period. GAAP requires investigation of possible impairment only if events or changes in circumstances indicate that the book value of the asset or asset group may not be recoverable. This might happen from:

a. A significant decrease in market price.
b. A significant adverse change in how the asset is being used or in its physical condition.
c. A significant adverse change in legal factors or in the business climate.
d. An accumulation of costs significantly higher than the amount originally expected for the acquisition or construction of an asset.
e. A current-period loss combined with a history of losses or a projection of continuing losses associated with the asset.
f. A realization that the asset will be disposed of significantly before the end of its estimated useful life.[16]

STEP 1—An impairment loss is required only when the undiscounted sum of future cash flows is less than book value.

Measurement. Determining whether an impairment loss has occurred and actually recording the loss is a two-step process. The first step is a *recoverability* test—an impairment loss is required only when the undiscounted sum of estimated future cash flows from an asset is less than the asset's book value. The *measurement* of impairment loss—step 2—is the difference between the asset's book value and its fair value. If an impairment loss is recognized, the written-down book value becomes the new cost base for future cost allocation. Later recovery of an impairment loss is prohibited.

STEP 2—The impairment loss is the excess of book value over fair value.

Let's look closer at the measurement process (step two). Fair value is the amount at which the asset could be bought or sold in a current transaction between willing parties. Quoted market prices could be used if they're available. If fair value is not determinable, it must be estimated.

The process is best described by an example. Consider Illustration 11–20.

In the entry in Illustration 11–20, we reduce accumulated depreciation to zero and decrease the cost of the assets to their fair value of $135 million ($300 − 165). This adjusted amount serves as the revised basis for subsequent depreciation over the remaining useful life of the assets, just as if the assets had been acquired on the impairment date for their fair values.

The present value of future cash flows often is used as a measure of fair value.

Because the fair value of the factory assets was not readily available to Dakota in Illustration 11–20, the $135 million had to be estimated. One method that can be used to estimate fair value is to compute the discounted present value of future cash flows expected from the asset. Keep in mind that we use *undiscounted* estimates of cash flows in step one to determine whether an impairment loss is indicated, but *discounted* estimates of cash flows to determine the amount of the loss. In calculating present value, either a traditional approach or an expected cash flow approach can be used. The traditional approach is to incorporate risk and uncertainty into the discount rate. Recall from discussions in previous chapters that the expected cash flow approach incorporates risk and uncertainty instead into a determination of a probability-weighted cash flow expectation, and then discounts this expected cash flow using a risk-free interest rate. We discussed and illustrated the expected cash flow approach in previous chapters.

A disclosure note is needed to describe the impairment loss. The note should include a description of the impaired asset or asset group, the facts and circumstances leading to the impairment, the amount of the loss if not separately disclosed on the face of the income statement, and the method used to determine fair value.

---

[15]FASB ASC 360–10–35–15 through 20: Property, Plant, and Equipment—Overall—Subsequent Measurement—Impairment or Disposal of Long-Lived Assets (previously "Accounting for the Impairment of Long-Lived Assets and for Long-Lived Assets to Be Disposed Of," *Statement of Financial Accounting Standards No. 144* (Norwalk, Conn.: FASB, 2001)).

[16]FASB ASC 360–10–35–21: Property, Plant, and Equipment—Overall—Subsequent Measurement—Impairment or Disposal of Long-Lived Assets (previously "Accounting for the Impairment of Long-Lived Assets and for Long-Lived Assets to Be Disposed Of," *Statement of Financial Accounting Standards No. 144* (Norwalk, Conn.: FASB, 2001), par.8).

Illustration 11–20

Impairment Loss—Property, Plant, and Equipment

The Dakota Corporation operates several factories that manufacture medical equipment. Near the end of the company's 2016 fiscal year, a change in business climate related to a competitor's innovative products indicated to management that the $170 million book value (original cost of $300 million less accumulated depreciation of $130 million) of the assets of one of Dakota's factories may not be recoverable.

Management is able to identify cash flows from this factory and estimates that future cash flows over the remaining useful life of the factory will be $150 million. The fair value of the factory's assets is not readily available but is estimated to be $135 million.

Change in circumstances. A change in the business climate related to a competitor's innovative products requires Dakota to investigate for possible impairment.

Step 1. Recoverability. Because the book value of $170 million exceeds the $150 million undiscounted future cash flows, an impairment loss is indicated.

Step 2. Measurement of impairment loss. The impairment loss is $35 million, determined as follows:

Book value	$170 million
Fair value	135 million
Impairment loss	$ 35 million

The entry to record the loss is ($ in millions):

Loss on impairment	35	
Accumulated depreciation	130	
Factory assets		165

The loss normally is reported in the income statement as a separate component of operating expenses.

Sears Holding Corporation, the parent company of Sears and Kmart, is one of the largest retail chains in the world. Illustration 11–21 shows the company's disclosure notes describing recent impairment losses. The notes also provide a summary of the process used to identify and measure impairment losses for property, plant, and equipment and finite-life intangible assets.

Illustration 11–21

Asset Impairment Disclosure—Sears Holding Corporation

Real World Financials

Impairment of Long-Lived Assets (in part)

In accordance with accounting standards governing the impairment or disposal of long-lived assets, the carrying value of long-lived assets, including property and equipment and definite-lived intangible assets, is evaluated whenever events or changes in circumstances indicate that a potential impairment has occurred relative to a given asset or assets. Factors that could result in an impairment review include, but are not limited to, a current period cash flow loss combined with a history of cash flow losses, current cash flows that may be insufficient to recover the investment in the property over the remaining useful life, or a projection that demonstrates continuing losses associated with the use of a long-lived asset, significant changes in the manner of use of the assets or significant changes in business strategies. An impairment loss is recognized when the estimated undiscounted cash flows expected to result from the use of the asset plus net proceeds expected from disposition of the asset (if any) are less than the carrying value of the asset. When an impairment loss is recognized, the carrying amount of the asset is reduced to its estimated fair value as determined based on quoted market prices or through the use of other valuation techniques.

Note 13—Store Closing Charges, Severance Costs and Impairments (in part)
Long-Lived Assets

In accordance with accounting standards governing the impairment or disposal of long-lived assets, we performed an impairment test of certain of our long-lived assets (principally the value of buildings and other fixed assets associated with our stores) due to events and changes in circumstances during 2013, 2012, and 2011 that indicated an impairment might have occurred. As a result of this impairment testing, the Company recorded impairment charges of $220 million, $35 million, and $16 million during 2013, 2012, and 2011, respectively.

International Financial Reporting Standards

LO11–10

Impairment of Value: Property, Plant, and Equipment and Finite-Life Intangible Assets. Highlighted below are some important differences in accounting for impairment of value for property, plant, and equipment and finite-life intangible assets between U.S. GAAP and *IAS No. 36*.[17]

	U.S. GAAP	IFRS
When to Test	When events or changes in circumstances indicate that book value may not be recoverable.	Assets must be assessed for indicators of impairment at the end of each reporting period. Indicators of impairment are similar to U.S. GAAP.
Recoverability	An impairment loss is required when an asset's book value exceeds the undiscounted sum of the asset's estimated future cash flows.	There is no equivalent recoverability test. An impairment loss is required when an asset's book value exceeds the higher of the asset's value-in-use (present value of estimated future cash flows) and fair value less costs to sell.
Measurement	The impairment loss is the difference between book value and fair value.	The impairment loss is the difference between book value and the "recoverable amount" (the higher of the asset's value-in-use and fair value less costs to sell).
Subsequent Reversal of Loss	Prohibited.	Required if the circumstances that caused the impairment are resolved.

IFRS ILLUSTRATION

Let's look at an illustration highlighting the important differences described above. The Jasmine Tea Company has a factory that has significantly decreased in value due to technological innovations in the industry. Below are data related to the factory's assets:

	($ in millions)
Book value	$18.5
Undiscounted sum of estimated future cash flows	19.0
Present value of future cash flows	16.0
Fair value less cost to sell (determined by appraisal)	15.5

What amount of impairment loss should Jasmine Tea recognize, if any, under U.S. GAAP? Under IFRS?

U.S. GAAP There is no impairment loss. The sum of undiscounted estimated future cash flows exceeds the book value.

IFRS Jasmine should recognize an impairment loss of $2.5 million. Indicators of impairment are present and book value exceeds both value-in-use (present value of cash flows) and fair value less costs to sell. The recoverable amount is $16 million, the higher of value-in-use ($16 million) and fair value less costs to sell ($15.5 million). The impairment loss is the difference between book value of $18.5 million and the $16 million recoverable amount.

Real World Financials

Nokia, a Finnish company, prepares its financial statements according to IFRS. The following disclosure note describes the company's impairment policy:

> **Assessment of the Recoverability of Long-Lived Assets, Intangible Assets, and Goodwill (in part)**
> The carrying value of identifiable intangible assets and long-lived assets is assessed if events or changes in circumstances indicate that such carrying value may not be recoverable. Factors that trigger an impairment review include, but are not limited to, underperformance relative to historical or projected future results, significant changes in the manner of the use of the acquired assets or the strategy for the overall business and significant negative industry or economic trends.

(continued)

[17]"Impairment of Assets," *International Accounting Standard No. 36* (IASCF), as amended effective January 1,2014.

(concluded)

The Group conducts its impairment testing by determining the recoverable amount for the asset. The recoverable amount of an asset is the higher of its fair value less costs to sell and its value-in-use. The recoverable amount is then compared to the asset's carrying amount and an impairment loss is recognized if the recoverable amount is less than the carrying amount. Impairment losses are recognized immediately in the income statement.

INDEFINITE-LIFE INTANGIBLE ASSETS OTHER THAN GOODWILL. Intangible assets with indefinite useful lives, other than goodwill, should be tested for impairment annually and more frequently if events or changes in circumstances indicate that it is more likely than not that the asset is impaired.

A company has the option of first undertaking a qualitative assessment. Companies selecting this option will evaluate relevant events and circumstances to determine whether it is "more likely than not" (a likelihood of more than 50 percent) that the fair value of the asset is less than its book value. Only if that's determined to be the case will the company perform the quantitative impairment test described in the next paragraph.

If book value exceeds fair value, an impairment loss is recognized for the difference.

The measurement of an impairment loss for indefinite-life intangible assets other than goodwill is a one-step process. We compare the fair value of the asset with its book value. If book value exceeds fair value, an impairment loss is recognized for the difference. Notice that we omit the recoverability test with these assets. Because we anticipate cash flows to continue indefinitely, recoverability is not a good indicator of impairment.

Similar to property, plant, and equipment and finite-life intangible assets, if an impairment loss is recognized, the written-down book value becomes the new cost base for future cost allocation. Recovery of the impairment loss is prohibited. Disclosure requirements also are similar.

International Financial Reporting Standards

● LO11–10

Impairment of Value: Indefinite-Life Intangible Assets Other than Goodwill. Similar to U.S. GAAP, IFRS requires indefinite-life intangible assets other than goodwill to be tested for impairment at least annually. However, under U.S. GAAP, a company has the option to avoid annual testing by making qualitative evaluations of the likelihood of asset impairment. Also, under U.S. GAAP, the impairment loss is measured as the difference between book value and fair value, while under IFRS the impairment loss is the difference between book value and the recoverable amount. The recoverable amount is the higher of the asset's value-in-use (present value of estimated future cash flows) and fair value less costs to sell.

IFRS requires the reversal of an impairment loss if the circumstances that caused the impairment are resolved. Reversals are prohibited under U.S. GAAP.

Also, indefinite-life intangible assets may not be combined with other indefinite-life intangible assets for the required annual impairment test. Under U.S. GAAP, though, if certain criteria are met, indefinite-life intangible assets should be combined for the required annual impairment test.

GOODWILL. Recall that goodwill is a unique intangible asset. Unlike other assets, its cost (a) can't be directly associated with any specific identifiable right and (b) is not separable from the company as a whole. Because of these unique characteristics, we can't measure the impairment of goodwill the same way as we do other assets. GAAP provides guidelines for impairment, which, while similar to general impairment guidelines, are specific to goodwill.[18] Let's compare the two-step process for measuring goodwill impairment with the two-step process for measuring impairment for property, plant, and equipment and finite-life intangible assets.

[18]FASB ASC 350–20–35: Intangibles—Goodwill and Other—Goodwill—Subsequent Measurement (previously "Goodwill and Other Intangible Assets," *Statement of Financial Accounting Standards No. 142* (Norwalk, Conn.: FASB, 2001)).

STEP 1—A goodwill impairment loss is indicated when the fair value of the reporting unit is less than its book value.

In Step 1, for all classifications of assets, we decide whether a write-down due to impairment is required by determining whether the value of an asset has fallen below its book value. However, in this comparison, the value of assets for property, plant, and equipment and finite-life intangible assets is considered to be value-in-use as measured by the sum of undiscounted cash flows expected from the asset. But due to its unique characteristics, the value of goodwill is not associated with any specific cash flows and must be measured in a unique way. By its very nature, goodwill is inseparable from a particular *reporting unit.* So, for this step, we compare the value of the reporting unit itself with its book value. If the fair value of the reporting unit is less than its book value, an impairment loss is indicated. A reporting unit is an operating segment of a company or a component of an operating segment for which discrete financial information is available and segment management regularly reviews the operating results of that component.

If goodwill is tested for impairment at the same time as other assets of the reporting unit, the other assets must be tested first and any impairment loss and asset write-down recorded prior to testing goodwill.

STEP 2—A goodwill impairment loss is measured as the excess of the book value of the goodwill over its "implied" fair value.

In Step 2, for all classifications of property, plant, and equipment and intangible assets, if impairment is indicated from step 1, we measure the amount of impairment as the excess of the book value of the asset over its fair value. However, unlike for most other assets, the fair value of goodwill cannot be measured directly (market value, present value of associated cash flows, etc.) and so must be "implied" from the fair value of the reporting unit that acquired the goodwill.

The implied fair value of goodwill is calculated in the same way that goodwill is determined in a business combination. That is, it's a residual amount measured by subtracting the fair value of all identifiable net assets from the purchase price using the unit's previously determined fair value as the purchase price.[19]

When to test for impairment. Prior to 2012, companies were required to perform *step one* of the two-step test for goodwill impairment at least once a year, as well as in between annual test dates if something occurred that would indicate that the fair value of the reporting unit was below its book value. Then, if the first step indicated that the fair value of the reporting unit was indeed below book value, the company would perform *step two* to measure the amount of goodwill impairment.

In response to concerns about the cost and complexity of performing step one every year, the FASB issued an Accounting Standards Update (ASU) in 2011 that allows companies the option to decide whether step one is necessary.[20] Companies selecting this option will perform a qualitative assessment by evaluating relevant events and circumstances to determine whether it is "more likely than not" (a likelihood of more than 50 percent) that the fair value of a reporting unit is now less than its book value. Only if that's determined to be the case will the company perform the first step of the two-step goodwill impairment test. A list of possible events and circumstances that a company should consider in this qualitative assessment is provided in the ASU.

A goodwill impairment example is provided in Illustration 11–22.

The acquiring company in a business combination often pays for the acquisition using its own stock. In the late 1990s, the stock prices of many companies were unusually high. These often-inflated stock prices meant high purchase prices for many acquisitions and, in many cases, incredibly high values allocated to goodwill. When stock prices retreated in 2000 and 2001, it became obvious that the book value of goodwill for many companies would never be recovered. Some examples of multibillion dollar goodwill impairment losses are shown in Illustration 11–23.

Alcoa Inc., a world leader in the production of aluminum and other lightweight metals, provides a more recent example. In Illustration 11–24 we see the disclosure note that describes a $1.731 billion goodwill impairment charge.

---

[19]The impairment loss recognized can't exceed the book value of goodwill.

[20]FASB ASC 350–20–35–3: Intangibles—Goodwill and Other—Goodwill—Subsequent Measurement (previously "Goodwill and Other Intangible Assets," *Statement of Financial Accounting Standards No. 142* (Norwalk, Conn.: FASB, 2001)).

Illustration 11–22
Impairment Loss—Goodwill

In 2015, the Upjane Corporation acquired Pharmacopia Corporation for $500 million. Upjane recorded $100 million in goodwill related to this acquisition because the fair value of the net assets of Pharmacopia was $400 million. After the acquisition, Pharmacopia continues to operate as a separate company and is considered a reporting unit.

At the end of 2016, events and circumstances indicated that it is more likely than not that the fair value of Pharmacopia is less than its book value requiring Upjane to perform step one of the goodwill impairment test. The book value of Pharmacopia's net assets at the end of 2016 is $440 million, including the $100 million in goodwill. On that date, the fair value of Pharmacopia is estimated to be $360 million and the fair value of all of its identifiable tangible and intangible assets, excluding goodwill, is estimated to be $335 million.

Step 1. Recoverability. Because the book value of the net assets of $440 million exceeds the $360 million fair value of the reporting unit, an impairment loss is indicated.

Step 2. Measurement of impairment loss. The impairment loss is **$75** million, determined as follows:

Determination of implied fair value of goodwill:	
Fair value of Pharmacopia	$360 million
Fair value of Pharmacopia's net assets (excluding goodwill)	335 million
Implied fair value of goodwill	$ 25 million
Measurement of impairment loss:	
Book value of goodwill	$100 million
Implied fair value of goodwill	25 million
Impairment loss	$ 75 million

The entry to record the loss is ($ in millions):

Loss on impairment of goodwill	75	
Goodwill		75

The loss normally is reported in the income statement as a separate component of operating expenses.

The "implied" fair value of goodwill is a residual amount measured by subtracting the fair value of all identifiable net assets from the unit's fair value.

Illustration 11–23
Goodwill Impairment Losses

Company	Goodwill Impairment Loss
AOL Time Warner	$99 billion
JDS Uniphase	50 billion
Nortel Networks	12 billion
Lucent Technologies	4 billion
Vivendi Universal SA	15 billion (Euros)

Illustration 11–24
Goodwill Impairment Disclosure—Alcoa Inc.

Real World Financials

Goodwill and Other Intangible Assets (in part)

For Primary Metals, the estimated fair value as determined by the discounted cash flow model was lower than the associated carrying value. As a result, management performed the second step of the impairment analysis in order to determine the implied fair value of Primary Metal's goodwill. The result of the second-step analysis showed that the implied fair value of goodwill was zero. Therefore, in the fourth quarter, Alcoa recorded a goodwill impairment of $1.731 billion. As a result of the goodwill impairment, there is no goodwill remaining for the Primary Metals reporting unit.

Additional Consideration

Private Company GAAP—Accounting for Goodwill. The Private Company Council (PCC) sought feedback from private company stakeholders on the issue of goodwill accounting and found that most users of private company financial statements disregard goodwill and goodwill impairment losses. As a result, the PCC concluded that the cost and complexity of goodwill accounting outweigh the benefits for private companies.

In response to the PCC's conclusion, the FASB issued an Accounting Standards Update in 2014 that allows an accounting alternative for the subsequent measurement of goodwill for private companies that is quite different from what is required for public companies.[21] This alternative calls for goodwill to be amortized and also simplifies the goodwill impairment test.

The main provisions of the alternative are

1. amortizing goodwill on a straight-line basis over a maximum of 10 years,
2. testing goodwill for impairment at either the company level or the reporting unit level,
3. testing goodwill for impairment only when a triggering event occurs indicating that goodwill may be impaired,
4. the option of determining whether a quantitative impairment test is necessary when a triggering event occurs, and
5. if a quantitative test is necessary, measuring the goodwill impairment loss as the excess of the book value of the company (or reporting unit) over its fair value, not to exceed the book value of goodwill.

This alternative should significantly reduce the cost and complexity of accounting for goodwill after its initial measurement for private companies.

Where We're Headed for Public Companies. The FASB's research on goodwill accounting for *private* companies also revealed that many *public* companies also are concerned about the cost of annual goodwill impairment testing. As a result, the Board added a project to its agenda with the objective of reducing the cost and complexity of accounting for goodwill for public companies. The four alternatives being considered are: (1) the PCC alternative discussed above, (2) the amortization of goodwill over its useful life not to exceed some maximum number of years, (3) the direct write-off of goodwill, and (4) a simplified impairment test.

At the time this text was published, the FASB had not yet reached any tentative or final conclusions on the project.

International Financial Reporting Standards

● LO11–10

Impairment of Value—Goodwill. Highlighted below are some important differences in accounting for the impairment of goodwill between U.S. GAAP and *IAS No. 36.*

	U.S. GAAP	IFRS
Level of Testing	*Reporting unit*—a segment or a component of an operating segment for which discrete financial information is available.	*Cash-generating unit (CGU)*—the lowest level at which goodwill is monitored by management. A CGU can't be lower than a segment.
Measurement	*A two-step process:* 1. Compare the fair value of the reporting unit with its book value. A loss is indicated if fair value is less than book value. 2. The impairment loss is the excess of book value over implied fair value.	*A one-step process:* Compare the recoverable amount of the CGU to book value. If the recoverable amount is less, reduce goodwill first, then other assets. The recoverable amount is the higher of fair value less costs to sell and value-in-use (present value of estimated future cash flows).

(continued)

[21] *Accounting Standards Update No. 2014–02,* "Intangibles-Goodwill and Other (Topic 350): Accounting for Goodwill," (Norwalk, Conn.: FASB, January 2014).

(concluded)

IAS No. 36 requires goodwill to be tested for impairment at least annually. U.S. GAAP allows a company to avoid annual testing by making qualitative evaluations of the likelihood of goodwill impairment to determine if step one is necessary. Both U.S. GAAP and *IAS No. 36* prohibit the reversal of goodwill impairment losses.

Let's look at an illustration highlighting these differences.

IFRS ILLUSTRATION

Canterbury LTD. has $38 million of goodwill in its balance sheet from the 2014 acquisition of Denton, Inc. At the end of 2016, Canterbury's management provided the following information for the year-end goodwill impairment test ($ in millions):

Fair value of Denton (determined by appraisal)	$132
Fair value of Denton's net assets (excluding goodwill)	120
Book value of Denton's net assets (including goodwill)	150
Present value of Denton's estimated future cash flows	135

Assume that Denton is considered a reporting unit under U.S. GAAP and a cash-generating unit under IFRS, and that its fair value approximates fair value less costs to sell. What is the amount of goodwill impairment loss that Canterbury should recognize, if any, under U.S. GAAP? Under IFRS?

U.S. GAAP	Fair value of Denton	$132
	Fair value of Denton's net assets (excluding goodwill)	120
	Implied fair value of goodwill	$ 12
	Book value of goodwill	$ 38
	Implied fair value of goodwill	12
	Impairment loss	$ 26

IFRS The recoverable amount is $135 million, the higher of the $135 million value-in-use (present value of estimated future cash flows) and the $132 million fair value less costs to sell.

Denton's book value	$150
Recoverable amount	135
Impairment loss	$ 15

Real World Financials

Nestle SA, a Swiss company, is one of the largest food and nutrition companies in the world. The company prepares its financial statements according to IFRS. The following disclosures describe the company's goodwill impairment policy as well as a $105 million Swiss franc goodwill impairment loss related to its Sports Nutrition unit.

Impairment of Goodwill (in part)

Goodwill is tested for impairment at least annually and upon the occurrence of an indication of impairment.

The impairment tests are performed annually at the same time each year at the cash-generating unit (CGU) level. . . . The impairment tests are performed by comparing the carrying value of the amount of assets of these CGU with their recoverable amount, based on their future projected cash flows discounted at an appropriate pre-tax rate.

Impairment charge during the period (in part)

Goodwill related to the acquisition of PowerBar in 2000 has been allocated for the impairment test to the Cash-Generating Unit (CGU) Sports Nutrition Worldwide. . . . Competitive environment and economic conditions in the USA led to lower than anticipated sales demand, resulting in downward revision of projected cash flows since the last impairment test and the recoverable amount of the CGU is lower than its carrying amount. An impairment of goodwill amounting to CHF 105 million has been recognized.

Assets to Be Sold

We have been discussing the recognition and measurement for the impairment of value of assets to be held and used. We also test for impairment of assets held for sale. These are assets management has actively committed to immediately sell in their present condition and for which sale is probable.

For assets held for sale, if book value exceeds fair value less cost to sell, an impairment loss is recognized for the difference.

An asset or group of assets classified as held for sale is measured at the lower of its book value, or fair value less cost to sell. An impairment loss is recognized for any write-down to fair value less cost to sell.[22] Except for including the cost to sell, notice the similarity to impairment of assets to be held and used. We don't depreciate or amortize these assets while classified as held for sale and we report them separately in the balance sheet. Recall from our discussion of discontinued operations in Chapter 4 that similar rules apply for a component of an entity that is classified as held for sale.

Illustration 11–25 summarizes the guidelines for the recognition and measurement of impairment losses.

Illustration 11–25
Summary of Asset Impairment Guidelines

Type of Asset	When to Test for Impairment	Impairment Test
To Be Held and Used		
Property, plant, and equipment and finite-life intangible assets	When events or circumstances indicate book value may not be recoverable.	Step 1—An impairment loss is required only when book value is not recoverable (undiscounted sum of estimated future cash flows less than book value). Step 2—The impairment loss is the excess of book value over fair value.
Indefinite-life intangible assets (other than goodwill)	At least annually, and more frequently if indicated. Option to avoid annual testing by making qualitative evaluations of the likelihood of asset impairment.	If book value exceeds fair value, an impairment loss is recognized for the difference.
Goodwill	At least annually, and more frequently if indicated. Option to avoid annual testing by making qualitative evaluations of the likelihood of goodwill impairment to determine if step one is necessary.	Step 1—A loss is indicated when the fair value of the reporting unit is less than its book value. Step 2—An impairment loss is measured as the excess of book value over implied fair value.
To Be Sold	When considered held for sale	If book value exceeds fair value less cost to sell, an impairment loss is recognized for the difference.

Impairment Losses and Earnings Quality

What do losses from the write-down of inventory and restructuring costs have in common? The presence of these items in a corporate income statement presents a challenge to an analyst trying to determine a company's permanent earnings—those likely to continue in the future. We discussed these issues in prior chapters.

[22] If the asset is unsold at the end of a subsequent reporting period, a gain is recognized for any increase in fair value less cost to sell, but not in excess of the loss previously recognized.

We now can add asset impairment losses to the list of "big bath" accounting techniques some companies use to manipulate earnings. By writing off large amounts of assets, companies significantly reduce earnings in the year of the write-off but are able to increase future earnings by lowering future depreciation, depletion, or amortization. Here's how. We measure the impairment loss as the difference between an asset's book value and its fair value. However, in most cases, fair value must be estimated, and the estimation process usually involves a forecast of future net cash flows the company expects to generate from the asset's use. If a company underestimates future net cash flows, fair value is understated. This has two effects: (1) current year's income is unrealistically low due to the impairment loss being overstated and (2) future income is unrealistically high because depreciation, depletion, and amortization are based on understated asset values.

An analyst must decide whether to consider asset impairment losses as transitory in nature or as a part of permanent earnings.

Where We're Headed

In their 2006 *Memorandum of Understanding*, the FASB and IASB included impairment as one of their short-term convergence projects. However, in 2008 the Boards agreed to defer work on impairment. Early in 2009, the Boards identified impairment as a topic for longer term convergence. When this text was published, no specific impairment project had been proposed.

● LO11–10

The FASB and IASB have identified impairment as a topic for longer-term convergence.

Concept Review Exercise

IMPAIRMENT

Part A:

Illumination Inc. owns a factory in Wisconsin that makes light bulbs. During 2016, due to increased competition from LED light bulb manufacturers, the company determined that an impairment test was appropriate. Management has prepared the following information for the assets of the factory ($ in millions):

Cost	$345
Accumulated depreciation	85
Estimated future undiscounted cash flows to be generated by the factory	230
Estimated fair value of the factory assets	170

Required:

1. Determine the amount of impairment loss Illumination should recognize, if any.
2. If a loss is indicated, prepare the journal entry to record the loss.
3. Repeat requirement 1 assuming that the estimated undiscounted future cash flows are $270 million instead of $230 million.

Solution:

1. Determine the amount of impairment loss Illumination should recognize, if any.

   Recoverability: Because the book value of $260 ($345 − 85) million exceeds the $230 million undiscounted future cash flows, an impairment loss is indicated.

   Measurement: The impairment loss is $90 million, determined as follows:

	($ in millions)
Book value	$260
Fair value	170
Impairment loss	$ 90

2. If a loss is indicated, prepare the journal entry to record the loss.

	($ in millions)	
Loss on impairment (determined above)	90	
Accumulated depreciation (balance)	85	
Factory assets ($345 − 170)		175

3. Repeat requirement 1 assuming that the estimated undiscounted future cash flows are $270 million instead of $230 million.

   Because the undiscounted sum of future cash flows of $270 million exceeds book value of $260 million, there is no impairment loss.

Part B:

In 2014, Illumination Inc. acquired Zapo Lighting Company for $620 million, of which $80 million was allocated to goodwill. After the acquisition, Zapo continues to operate a separate company and is considered a reporting unit. At the end of 2016, management provided the following information for a required goodwill impairment test ($ in millions):

Fair value of Zapo Lighting	$540
Fair value of Zapo's net assets (excluding goodwill)	510
Book value of Zapo's net assets (including goodwill)	600

Required:

Determine the amount of goodwill impairment loss that Illumination should recognize at the end of 2016, if any.

Solution:

Recoverability: Because the book value of the net assets of $600 million exceeds the $540 million fair value of the reporting unit, an impairment loss is indicated.

Measurement: The impairment loss is $50 million, determined as follows:

Determination of implied fair value of goodwill:	($ in millions)
Fair value of Zapo	$540
Fair value of Zapo's net assets (excluding goodwill)	510
Implied fair value of goodwill	$ 30
Measurement of impairment loss:	
Book value of goodwill	$ 80
Implied fair value of goodwill	30
Impairment loss	$ 50

PART C

Subsequent Expenditures

Now that we have acquired and measured assets, we can address accounting issues incurred subsequent to their acquisition. This part of the chapter deals with the treatment of expenditures made over the life of these assets to maintain and/or improve them.

Expenditures Subsequent to Acquisition

LO11–9

Many long-lived assets require expenditures to repair, maintain, or improve them. These expenditures can present accounting problems if they are material. In general, a choice must be made between capitalizing the expenditures by either increasing the asset's book value or creating a new asset, or expensing them in the period in which they are incurred. Conceptually, we can refer to the matching concept that requires the capitalization of expenditures that are expected to produce benefits beyond the current fiscal year. Expenditures that simply maintain a given level of benefits are expensed in the period they are incurred.

Expenditures related to assets can increase future benefits in the following ways:

1. An extension of the *useful life* of the asset.
2. An increase in the *operating efficiency* of the asset resulting in either an increase in the quantity of goods or services produced or a decrease in future operating costs.
3. An increase in the *quality* of the goods or services produced by the asset.

Theoretically, expenditures that cause any of these results should be capitalized initially and then expensed in future periods through depreciation, depletion, or amortization. This permits the matching of the expenditure with the future benefits. Of course, materiality is an important factor in the practical application of this approach.

For expediency, many companies set materiality thresholds for the capitalization of any expenditure. For example, a company might decide to expense all expenditures under $200 regardless of whether or not future benefits are increased. Judgment is required to determine the appropriate materiality threshold as well as the appropriate treatment of expenditures over $200. There often are practical problems in capitalizing these expenditures. For example, even if future benefits are increased by the expenditure, it may be difficult to determine how long the benefits will last. It's important for a company to establish a policy for treating these expenditures and apply it consistently.

Many companies do not capitalize any expenditure unless it exceeds a predetermined amount that is considered material.

We classify subsequent expenditures as (1) repairs and maintenance, (2) additions, (3) improvements, or (4) rearrangements.

Repairs and Maintenance

These expenditures are made to *maintain* a given level of benefits provided by the asset and do not *increase* future benefits. For example, the cost of an engine tune-up or the repair of an engine part for a delivery truck allows the truck to continue its productive activity. If the maintenance is not performed, the truck will not provide the benefits originally anticipated. In that sense, future benefits are provided; without the repair, the truck will no longer operate. The key, though, is that future benefits are not provided *beyond those originally anticipated.* Expenditures for these activities should be expensed in the period incurred.

Expenditures for *repairs and maintenance* generally are expensed when incurred.

Additional Consideration

If repairs and maintenance costs are seasonal, interim financial statements may be misstated. For example, suppose annual maintenance is performed on a company's fleet of delivery trucks. The annual income statement correctly includes one year's maintenance expense. However, for interim reporting purposes, if the entire expenditure is made in one quarter, should that quarter's income statement include as expense the entire cost of the annual maintenance? If these expenditures can be anticipated, they should be accrued evenly throughout the year by crediting an allowance account. The allowance account is then debited when the maintenance is performed.

Additions

As the term implies, **additions** involve adding a new major component to an existing asset and should be capitalized because future benefits are increased. For example, adding a refrigeration unit to a delivery truck increases the capability of the truck, thus increasing its future benefits. Other examples include the construction of a new wing on a building and the addition of a security system to an existing building.

The costs of *additions* usually are capitalized.

The capitalized cost includes all necessary expenditures to bring the addition to a condition and location for use. For a building addition, this might include the costs of tearing down and removing a wall of the existing building. The capitalized cost of additions is depreciated over the remaining useful life of the original asset or its own useful life, whichever is shorter.

Improvements

Expenditures classified as **improvements** involve the replacement of a major component of an asset. The replacement can be a new component with the same characteristics as the old component or a new component with enhanced operating capabilities. For example, an existing refrigeration unit in a delivery truck could be replaced with a new but similar unit or with a new and improved refrigeration unit. In either case, the cost of the improvement usually increases future benefits and should be capitalized by increasing the book value of the related asset (the delivery truck) and depreciated over the useful life of the improved asset. There are three methods used to record the cost of improvements.

The costs of *improvements* usually are capitalized.

1. *Substitution.* The improvement can be recorded as both (1) a disposition of the old component and (2) the acquisition of the new component. This approach is conceptually appealing but it is practical only if the original cost and accumulated depreciation of the old component can be separately identified.
2. *Capitalization of new cost.* Another way to record an improvement is to include the cost of the improvement (net of any consideration received from the disposition of the old component) as a debit to the related asset account, without removing the original cost and accumulated depreciation of the original component. This approach is acceptable only if the book value of the original component has been reduced to an immaterial amount through prior depreciation.
3. *Reduction of accumulated depreciation.* Another way to increase an asset's book value is to leave the asset account unaltered but decrease its related accumulated depreciation. The argument for this method is that many improvements extend the useful life of an asset and are equivalent to a partial recovery of previously recorded depreciation. This approach produces the same book value as the capitalization of cost to the asset account. However, cost and accumulated depreciation amounts will differ under the two methods.

The three methods are compared in Illustration 11–26.

Illustration 11–26
Improvements

The Palmer Corporation replaced the air conditioning system in one of its office buildings that it leases to tenants. The cost of the old air conditioning system, $200,000, is included in the cost of the building. However, the company has separately depreciated the air conditioning system. Depreciation recorded up to the date of replacement totaled $160,000. The old system was removed and the new system installed at a cost of $230,000, which was paid in cash. Parts from the old system were sold for $12,000.

Accounting for the improvement differs depending on the alternative chosen.

1. Substitution (a) Disposition of old component.	Cash	12,000	
	Accumulated depreciation—buildings	160,000	
	Loss on disposal (difference)	28,000	
	Buildings		200,000
(b) Acquisition of new component.	Buildings	230,000	
	Cash		230,000
2. Capitalization of new cost.	Buildings	218,000	
	Cash ($230,000 − 12,000)		218,000
3. Reduction of accumulated depreciation.	Accumulated depreciation—buildings	218,000	
	Cash ($230,000 − 12,000)		218,000

Rearrangements

The costs of material *rearrangements* should be capitalized if they clearly increase future benefits.

Expenditures made to restructure an asset without addition, replacement, or improvement are termed **rearrangements**. The objective is to create a new capability for the asset and not necessarily to extend its useful life. Examples include the rearrangement of machinery on the production line to increase operational efficiency and the relocation of a company's operating plant or office building. If these expenditures are material and they clearly increase future benefits, they should be capitalized and expensed in the future periods benefited. If the expenditures are not material or if it's not certain that future benefits have increased, they should be expensed in the period incurred.

Illustration 11–27 provides a summary of the accounting treatment for the various types of expenditures related to property, plant, and equipment.

Costs of Defending Intangible Rights

The costs incurred to *successfully* defend an intangible right should be capitalized.

Repairs, additions, improvements, and rearrangements generally relate to property, plant, and equipment. A possible significant expenditure incurred subsequent to the acquisition of intangible assets is the cost of defending the right that gives the asset its value. If an intangible right is *successfully* defended, the litigation costs should be capitalized and amortized over the remaining useful life of the related intangible. This is the appropriate treatment of these expenditures even if the intangible asset was originally developed internally rather than purchased.

If the defense of an intangible right is *unsuccessful,* then the litigation costs should be expensed as incurred because they provide no future benefit. In addition, the book value of any intangible asset should be reduced to realizable value. For example, if a company is unsuccessful in defending a patent infringement suit, the patent's value may be eliminated. The book value of the patent should be written off as a loss.

The costs incurred to *unsuccessfully* defend an intangible right should be expensed.

Illustration 11–27
Expenditures Subsequent to Acquisition

Type of Expenditure	Definition	Usual Accounting Treatment
Repairs and maintenance	Expenditures to maintain a given level of benefits	Expense in the period incurred
Additions	The addition of a new major component to an existing asset	Capitalize and depreciate over the remaining useful life of the *original asset or its own useful* life, whichever is shorter
Improvements	The replacement of a major component	Capitalize and depreciate over the useful life of the improved asset
Rearrangements	Expenditures to restructure an asset without addition, replacement, or improvement	If expenditures are material and clearly increase future benefits, capitalize and depreciate over the future periods benefited

International Financial Reporting Standards

Costs of Defending Intangible Rights. Under U.S. GAAP, litigation costs to successfully defend an intangible right are capitalized and amortized over the remaining useful life of the related intangible. Under IFRS, these costs are expensed, except in rare situations when an expenditure increases future benefits.[23]

● LO11–10

Financial Reporting Case Solution

1. **Is Penny correct? Do the terms *depreciation, depletion,* and *amortization* all mean the same thing?** *(p. 588)* Penny is correct. Each of these terms refers to the cost allocation of assets over their service lives. The term *depreciation* is used for plant and equipment, *depletion* for natural resources, and *amortization* for intangible assets.
2. **Weyerhaeuser determines depletion based on the "volume of timber estimated to be available." Explain this approach.** *(p. 592)* Weyerhaeuser is using the units-of-production method to determine depletion. The units-of-production method is an activity-based method that computes a depletion (or depreciation or amortization) rate per measure of activity and then multiplies this rate by actual activity to determine periodic cost allocation. The method is used by Weyerhaeuser to measure depletion of the cost of timber harvested and the amortization of logging roads. Logging roads are intangible assets because the company does not own the roads.

[23]"Intangible Assets," *International Accounting Standard No. 38* (IASCF), par. 20, as amended effective January 1, 2014.

3. **Explain how asset impairment differs from depreciation, depletion, and amortization. How do companies measure impairment losses for property, plant, and equipment and intangible assets with finite useful lives?** *(p. 611)* Depreciation, depletion, and amortization reflect a gradual consumption of the benefits inherent in a long-lived asset. An implicit assumption in allocating the cost of an asset over its useful life is that there has been no significant reduction in the anticipated total benefits or service potential of the asset. Situations can arise, however, that cause a significant decline or *impairment* of those benefits or service potentials. Determining whether to record an impairment loss for an asset and actually recording the loss is a two-step process. The first step is a recoverability test—an impairment loss is required only when the undiscounted sum of estimated future cash flows from an asset is less than the asset's book value. The measurement of impairment loss—step 2—is the difference between the asset's book value and its fair value. If an impairment loss is recognized, the written-down book value becomes the new cost base for future cost allocation. ●

The Bottom Line

- **LO11–1** The use of property, plant, and equipment and intangible assets represents a consumption of benefits, or service potentials, inherent in the assets. The matching concept requires that the cost of these inherent benefits or service potentials that were consumed be recognized as an expense. As there very seldom is a direct relationship between the use of assets and revenue production, accounting resorts to arbitrary allocation methods to achieve a matching of expenses with revenues. *(p. 587)*
- **LO11–2** The allocation process for plant and equipment is called *depreciation.* Time-based depreciation methods estimate service life in years and then allocate depreciable base, cost less estimated residual value, using either a straight-line or accelerated pattern. Activity-based depreciation methods allocate the depreciable base by estimating service life according to some measure of productivity. *(p. 590)*
- **LO11–3** The allocation process for natural resources is called *depletion.* The activity-based method called units-of-production usually is employed to determine periodic depletion. *(p. 600)*
- **LO11–4** The allocation process for intangible assets is called *amortization.* For an intangible asset with a finite useful life, the capitalized cost less any estimated residual value must be allocated to periods in which the asset is expected to contribute to the company's revenue-generating activities. An intangible asset that is determined to have an indefinite useful life is not subject to periodic amortization. Goodwill is perhaps the most typical intangible asset with an indefinite useful life. *(p. 601)*
- **LO11–5** A change in either the service life or residual value of property, plant, and equipment and intangible assets should be reflected in the financial statements of the current period and future periods by recalculating periodic depreciation, depletion, or amortization. *(p. 607)*
- **LO11–6** A change in depreciation, depletion, or amortization method is considered a change in accounting estimate that is achieved by a change in accounting principle. We account for these changes prospectively, exactly as we would any other change in estimate. One difference is that most changes in estimate do not require a company to justify the change. However, this change in estimate is a result of changing an accounting principle and therefore requires a clear justification as to why the new method is preferable. *(p. 608)*
- **LO11–7** A material error in accounting for property, plant, and equipment and intangible assets that is discovered in a year subsequent to the year of the error requires that previous years' financial statements that were incorrect as a result of the error are retrospectively restated to reflect the correction. Any account balances that are incorrect as a result of the error are corrected by journal entry. If retained earnings is one of the incorrect accounts, the correction is reported as a prior period adjustment to the beginning balance in the statement of shareholders' equity. In addition, a disclosure note is needed to describe the nature of the error and the impact of its correction on income. *(p. 610)*
- **LO11–8** Conceptually, there is considerable merit for a policy requiring the write-down of an asset when there has been a *significant* decline in value below book value. The write-down provides important information about the future cash flows to be generated from the use of the asset. However, in practice this policy is very subjective. GAAP [FASB ASC 360] establishes guidance for when to recognize and how to measure

impairment losses of property, plant, and equipment and intangible assets that have finite useful lives. GAAP [FASB ASC 350] also provides guidance for the recognition and measurement of impairment for indefinite-life intangibles and goodwill. *(p. 611)*

- **LO11–9** Expenditures for repairs and maintenance generally are expensed when incurred. The costs of additions and improvements usually are capitalized. The costs of material rearrangements should be capitalized if they clearly increase future benefits. *(p. 622)*
- **LO11–10** Among the several differences between U.S. GAAP and IFRS with respect to the utilization and impairment of property, plant, and equipment and intangible assets pertains to reporting assets in the balance sheet. IFRS allows a company to value property, plant, and equipment (PP&E) and intangible assets subsequent to initial valuation at (1) cost less accumulated depreciation/amortization or (2) fair value (revaluation). U.S. GAAP prohibits revaluation. There also are significant differences in accounting for the impairment of property, plant, and equipment and intangible assets. *(pp. 595, 598, 602, 604, 614, 615, 618, 621, and 625)*

APPENDIX 11A

Comparison with MACRS (Tax Depreciation)

Depreciation for financial reporting purposes is an attempt to distribute the cost of the asset, less any anticipated residual value, over the estimated useful life in a systematic and rational manner that attempts to match revenues with the use of the asset. Depreciation for income tax purposes is influenced by the revenue needs of government as well as the desire to influence economic behavior. For example, accelerated depreciation schedules currently allowed are intended to provide incentive for companies to expand and modernize their facilities thus stimulating economic growth.

The federal income tax code allows taxpayers to compute depreciation for their tax returns on assets acquired after 1986 using the **modified accelerated cost recovery system (MACRS)**.[24] Key differences between the calculation of depreciation for financial reporting and the calculation using MACRS are:

1. Estimated useful lives and residual values are not used in MACRS.
2. Firms can't choose among various accelerated methods under MACRS.
3. A half-year convention is used in determining the MACRS depreciation amounts.

Under MACRS, each asset generally is placed within a recovery period category. The six categories for personal property are 3, 5, 7, 10, 15, and 20 years. For example, the 5-year category includes automobiles, light trucks, and computers.

Depending on the category, fixed percentage rates are applied to the original cost of the asset. The rates for the 5-year asset category are as follows:

Year	Rate
1	20.00%
2	32.00
3	19.20
4	11.52
5	11.52
6	5.76
Total	100.00%

These rates are equivalent to applying the double-declining-balance method with a switch to straight-line in the year straight-line yields an equal or higher deduction than DDB. In most cases, the half-year convention is used regardless of when the asset is placed in service.[25]

[24]For assets acquired between 1981 and 1986, tax depreciation is calculated using the accelerated cost recovery system (ACRS), which is similar to MACRS. For assets acquired before 1981, tax depreciation can be calculated using any of the depreciation methods discussed in the chapter. Residual values are used in the calculation of depreciation for pre-1981 assets.

[25]In certain situations, mid-quarter and mid-month conventions are used.

The first-year rate of 20% for the five-year category is one-half of the DDB rate for an asset with a five-year life (2 × 20%). The sixth year rate of 5.76% is one-half of the straight-line rate established in year 4, the year straight-line depreciation exceeds DDB depreciation.

Companies have the option to use the straight-line method for the entire tax life of the asset, applying the half-year convention, rather than using MACRS depreciation schedules. Because of the differences discussed above, tax depreciation for a given year will likely be different from GAAP depreciation.

APPENDIX 11B Retirement and Replacement Methods of Depreciation

Retirement and replacement depreciation methods occasionally are used to depreciate relatively low-valued assets with short service lives. Under either approach, an aggregate asset account that represents a group of similar assets is increased at the time the initial collection is acquired.

Retirement Method

The *retirement depreciation method records* depreciation when assets are disposed of and measures depreciation as the difference between the proceeds received and cost.

Using the retirement depreciation method, the asset account also is increased for the cost of subsequent expenditures. When an item is disposed of, the asset account is credited for its cost, and depreciation expense is recorded for the difference between cost and proceeds received, if any. No other entries are made for depreciation. As a consequence, one or more periods may pass without any expense recorded. For example, the following entry records the purchase of 100 handheld calculators at $50 acquisition cost each:

Calculators (100 × $50)	5,000	
Cash		5,000
To record the acquisition of calculators.		

If 20 new calculators are acquired at $45 each, the asset account is increased.

Calculators (20 × $45)	900	
Cash		900
To record additional calculator acquisitions.		

Thirty calculators are disposed of (retired) by selling them secondhand to a bookkeeping firm for $5 each. The following entry reflects the retirement method:

Cash (30 × $5)	150	
Depreciation expense (difference)	1,350	
Calculators (30 × $50)		1,500
To record the sale/depreciation of calculators.		

Notice that the retirement system assumes a FIFO cost flow approach in determining the cost of assets, $50 each, that were disposed.

Replacement Method

By the *replacement method, depreciation* is recorded when assets are replaced.

By the replacement depreciation method, the initial acquisition of assets is recorded the same way as by the retirement method; that is, the aggregate cost is increased. However, depreciation expense is the amount paid for new or replacement assets. Any proceeds received from asset dispositions reduces depreciation expense. For our example, the acquisition of 20 new calculators at $45 each is recorded as depreciation as follows:

Depreciation expense (20 × $45)	900	
Cash		900
To record the replacement/depreciation of calculators.		

The sale of the old calculators is recorded as a reduction of depreciation:

Cash (30 × $5)	150	
Depreciation expense		150
To record the sale of calculators.		

The asset account balance remains the same throughout the life of the aggregate collection of assets.

Because these methods are likely to produce aggregate expense measurements that differ from individual calculations, retirement and replacement methods are acceptable only in situations where the distortion in depreciation expense does not have a material effect on income. These methods occasionally are encountered in regulated industries such as utilities.

Questions For Review of Key Topics

Q 11–1 Explain the similarities in and differences among depreciation, depletion, and amortization.

Q 11–2 Depreciation is a process of cost allocation, not valuation. Explain this statement.

Q 11–3 Identify and define the three characteristics of an asset that must be established to determine periodic depreciation, depletion, or amortization.

Q 11–4 Discuss the factors that influence the estimation of service life for a depreciable asset.

Q 11–5 What is meant by depreciable base? How is it determined?

Q 11–6 Briefly differentiate between activity-based and time-based allocation methods.

Q 11–7 Briefly differentiate between the straight-line depreciation method and accelerated depreciation methods.

Q 11–8 Why are time-based depreciation methods used more frequently than activity-based methods?

Q 11–9 What are some factors that could explain the predominant use of the straight-line depreciation method?

Q 11–10 Briefly explain the differences and similarities between the group approach and composite approach to depreciating aggregate assets.

Q 11–11 Define depletion and compare it with depreciation.

Q 11–12 Compare and contrast amortization of intangible assets with depreciation and depletion.

Q 11–13 What are some of the simplifying conventions a company can use to calculate depreciation for partial years?

Q 11–14 Explain the accounting treatment required when a change is made to the estimated service life of a machine.

Q 11–15 Explain the accounting treatment and disclosures required when a change is made in depreciation method.

Q 11–16 Explain the steps required to correct an error in accounting for property, plant, and equipment and intangible assets that is discovered in a year subsequent to the year the error was made.

Q 11–17 Explain what is meant by the impairment of the value of property, plant, and equipment and intangible assets. How should these impairments be accounted for?

Q 11–18 Explain the differences in the accounting treatment of repairs and maintenance, additions, improvements, and rearrangements.

IFRS **Q 11–19** Identify any differences between U.S. GAAP and International Financial Reporting Standards in the subsequent valuation of property, plant, and equipment and intangible assets.

IFRS **Q 11–20** Briefly explain the difference between U.S. GAAP and IFRS in the *measurement* of an impairment loss for property, plant, and equipment and finite-life intangible assets.

IFRS **Q 11–21** Briefly explain the differences between U.S. GAAP and IFRS in the measurement of an impairment loss for goodwill.

IFRS **Q 11–22** Under U.S. GAAP, litigation costs to successfully defend an intangible right are capitalized and amortized over the remaining useful life of the related intangible. How are these costs typically accounted for under IFRS?

Brief Exercises

BE 11–1
Cost allocation
LO11–1

At the beginning of its fiscal year, Koeplin Corporation purchased a machine for $50,000. At the end of the year, the machine had a fair value of $32,000. Koeplin's controller recorded depreciation of $18,000 for the year, the decline in the machine's value. Why is this an incorrect approach to measuring periodic depreciation?

BE 11–2
Depreciation methods
● LO11–2

On January 1, 2016, Canseco Plumbing Fixtures purchased equipment for $30,000. Residual value at the end of an estimated four-year service life is expected to be $2,000. The company expects the machine to operate for 10,000 hours. Calculate depreciation expense for 2016 and 2017 using each of the following depreciation methods: (a) straight line, (b) sum-of-the-years'-digits, (c) double-declining balance, and (d) units-of-production using machine hours. The machine operated for 2,200 and 3,000 hours in 2016 and 2017, respectively.

BE 11–3
Depreciation methods; partial years
● LO11–2

Refer to the situation described in BE 11–2. Assume the machine was purchased on March 31, 2016, instead of January 1. Calculate depreciation expense for 2016 and 2017 using each of the following depreciation methods: (a) straight line, (b) sum-of-the-years'-digits, and (c) double-declining balance.

BE 11–4
Group depreciation
● LO11–2

Mondale Winery depreciates its equipment using the group method. The cost of equipment purchased in 2016 totaled $425,000. The estimated residual value of the equipment was $40,000 and the group depreciation rate was determined to be 18%. What is the annual depreciation for the group? If equipment that cost $42,000 is sold in 2017 for $35,000, what amount of gain or loss will the company recognize for the sale?

BE 11–5
Depletion
● LO11–3

Fitzgerald Oil and Gas incurred costs of $8.25 million for the acquisition and development of a natural gas deposit. The company expects to extract 3 million cubic feet of natural gas during a four-year period. Natural gas extracted during years 1 and 2 were 700,000 and 800,000 cubic feet, respectively. What was the depletion for year 1 and year 2?

BE 11–6
Amortization
● LO11–4

On June 28 Lexicon Corporation acquired 100% of the common stock of Gulf & Eastern. The purchase price allocation included the following items: $4 million, patent; $3 million, developed technology; $2 million, in-process research and development; $5 million, goodwill. Lexicon's policy is to amortize intangible assets using the straight-line method, no residual value, and a five-year useful life. What is the total amount of expenses (ignoring taxes) that would appear in Lexicon's income statement for the year ended December 31 related to these items?

BE 11–7
Change in estimate; useful life of equipment
● LO11–5

At the beginning of 2014, Robotics Inc. acquired a manufacturing facility for $12 million. $9 million of the purchase price was allocated to the building. Depreciation for 2014 and 2015 was calculated using the straight-line method, a 25-year useful life, and a $1 million residual value. In 2016, the estimates of useful life and residual value were changed to 20 years and $500,000, respectively. What is depreciation on the building for 2016?

BE 11–8
Change in principle; change in depreciation method
● LO11–6

Refer to the situation described in BE 11–7. Assume that instead of changing the useful life and residual value, in 2016 the company switched to the double-declining-balance depreciation method. How should Robotics account for the change? What is depreciation on the building for 2016?

BE 11–9
Error correction
● LO11–7

Refer to the situation described in BE 11–7. Assume that 2014 depreciation was incorrectly recorded as $32,000. This error was discovered in 2016. How should Robotics account for the error? What is depreciation on the building for 2016 assuming no change in estimate of useful life or residual value?

BE 11–10
Impairment; property, plant, and equipment
● LO11–8

Collison and Ryder Company (C&R) has been experiencing declining market conditions for its sportswear division. Management decided to test the assets of the division for possible impairment. The test revealed the following: book value of division's assets, $26.5 million; fair value of division's assets, $21 million; sum of estimated future cash flows generated from the division's assets, $28 million. What amount of impairment loss should C&R recognize?

BE 11–11
Impairment; property, plant, and equipment
● LO11–8

Refer to the situation described in BE 11–10. Assume that the sum of estimated future cash flows is $24 million instead of $28 million. What amount of impairment loss should C&R recognize?

BE 11–12
IFRS; impairment; property, plant, and equipment
● LO11–8, LO11–10

IFRS

Refer to the situation described in BE 11–10. Assume that the present value of the estimated future cash flows generated from the division's assets is $22 million and that their fair value approximates fair value less costs to sell. What amount of impairment loss should C&R recognize if the company prepares its financial statements according to IFRS?

BE 11–13
Impairment; goodwill
● LO11–8

WebHelper Inc. acquired 100% of the outstanding stock of Silicon Chips Corporation (SCC) for $45 million, of which $15 million was allocated to goodwill. At the end of the current fiscal year, an impairment test revealed the following: fair value of SCC, $40 million; fair value of SCC's net assets (excluding goodwill), $31 million; book value of SCC's net assets (including goodwill), $42 million. What amount of impairment loss should WebHelper recognize?

BE 11–14
Impairment; goodwill
● LO11–8

Refer to the situation described in BE 11–13. Assume that the fair value of SCC is $44 million instead of $40 million. What amount of impairment loss should WebHelper recognize?

BE 11–15
IFRS; impairment; goodwill
● LO11–10

IFRS

Refer to the situation described in BE 11–13. Assume that SCC's fair value of $40 million approximates fair value less costs to sell and that the present value of SCC's estimated future cash flows is $41 million. If WebHelper prepares its financial statements according to IFRS and SCC is considered a cash-generating unit, what amount of impairment loss, if any, should WebHelper recognize?

BE 11–16
Subsequent expenditures
● LO11–9

Demmert Manufacturing incurred the following expenditures during the current fiscal year: annual maintenance on its machinery, $5,400; remodeling of offices, $22,000; rearrangement of the shipping and receiving area resulting in an increase in productivity, $35,000; addition of a security system to the manufacturing facility, $25,000. How should Demmert account for each of these expenditures?

Exercises

An alternate exercise and problem set is available in the Connect library.

E 11–1
Depreciation methods
● LO11–2

On January 1, 2016, the Excel Delivery Company purchased a delivery van for $33,000. At the end of its five-year service life, it is estimated that the van will be worth $3,000. During the five-year period, the company expects to drive the van 100,000 miles.

Required:

Calculate annual depreciation for the five-year life of the van using each of the following methods. Round all computations to the nearest dollar.

1. Straight line.
2. Sum-of-the-years'-digits.
3. Double-declining balance.
4. Units of production using miles driven as a measure of output, and the following actual mileage:

Year	Miles
2016	22,000
2017	24,000
2018	15,000
2019	20,000
2020	21,000

E 11–2
Depreciation methods
● LO11–2

On January 1, 2016, the Allegheny Corporation purchased machinery for $115,000. The estimated service life of the machinery is 10 years and the estimated residual value is $5,000. The machine is expected to produce 220,000 units during its life.

Required:
Calculate depreciation for 2016 and 2017 using each of the following methods. Round all computations to the nearest dollar.

1. Straight line.
2. Sum-of-the-years'-digits.
3. Double-declining balance.
4. One hundred fifty percent declining balance.
5. Units of production (units produced in 2016, 30,000; units produced in 2017, 25,000).

E 11–3
Depreciation methods; partial years
● LO11–2

[This is a variation of Exercise 11–2 modified to focus on depreciation for partial years.]
On October 1, 2016, the Allegheny Corporation purchased machinery for $115,000. The estimated service life of the machinery is 10 years and the estimated residual value is $5,000. The machine is expected to produce 220,000 units during its life.

Required:
Calculate depreciation for 2016 and 2017 using each of the following methods. Partial-year depreciation is calculated based on the number of months the asset is in service. Round all computations to the nearest dollar.

1. Straight line.
2. Sum-of-the-years'-digits.
3. Double-declining balance.
4. One hundred fifty percent declining balance.
5. Units of production (units produced in 2016, 10,000; units produced in 2017, 25,000).

E 11–4
Depreciation methods; asset addition
● LO11–2, LO11–9

Funseth Company purchased a five-story office building on January 1, 2014, at a cost of $5,000,000. The building has a residual value of $200,000 and a 30-year life. The straight-line depreciation method is used. On June 30, 2016, construction of a sixth floor was completed at a cost of $1,650,000.

Required:
Calculate the depreciation on the building and building addition for 2016 and 2017 assuming that the addition did not change the life or residual value of the building.

E 11–5
Depreciation methods; solving for unknowns
● LO11–2

For each of the following depreciable assets, determine the missing amount (?). Abbreviations for depreciation methods are SL for straight line, SYD for sum-of-the-years'-digits, and DDB for double-declining balance.

Asset	Cost	Residual Value	Service Life (Years)	Depreciation Method	Depreciation (Year 2)
A	?	$ 20,000	5	DDB	$ 24,000
B	$ 40,000	?	8	SYD	7,000
C	65,000	5,000	?	SL	6,000
D	230,000	10,000	10	?	22,000
E	200,000	20,000	8	150%DB	?

E 11–6
Depreciation methods; partial periods
● LO11–2

On April 29, 2016, Quality Appliances purchased equipment for $260,000. The estimated service life of the equipment is six years and the estimated residual value is $20,000. Quality's fiscal year ends on December 31.

Required:
Calculate depreciation for 2016 and 2017 using each of the three methods listed. Quality calculates partial year depreciation based on the number of months the asset is in service. Round all computations to the nearest dollar.

1. Straight-line.
2. Sum-of-the-years'-digits.
3. Double-declining balance.

E 11–7
Depreciation methods; partial periods
● LO11–2

On March 31, 2016, Susquehanna Insurance purchased an office building for $12,000,000. Based on their relative fair values, one-third of the purchase price was allocated to the land and two-thirds to the building. Furniture and fixtures were purchased separately from office equipment on the same date for $1,200,000 and $700,000, respectively. The company uses the straight-line method to depreciate its buildings and the double-declining-balance method to depreciate all other depreciable assets. The estimated useful lives and residual values of these assets are as follows:

	Service Life	Residual Value
Building	30	10% of cost
Furniture and fixtures	10	10% of cost
Office equipment	5	$30,000

Required:
Calculate depreciation for 2016 and 2017.

E 11–8
IFRS; depreciation
● LO11–2, LO11–10

On June 30, 2016, Rosetta Granite purchased a machine for $120,000. The estimated useful life of the machine is eight years and no residual value is anticipated. An important component of the machine is a specialized high-speed drill that will need to be replaced in four years. The $20,000 cost of the drill is included in the $120,000 cost of the machine. Rosetta uses the straight-line depreciation method for all machinery.

Required:
1. Calculate depreciation for 2016 and 2017 applying the typical U.S. GAAP treatment.
2. Repeat requirement 1 applying IFRS.

E 11–9
IFRS; revaluation of machinery; depreciation
● LO11–10

Dower Corporation prepares its financial statements according to IFRS. On March 31, 2016, the company purchased equipment for $240,000. The equipment is expected to have a six-year useful life with no residual value. Dower uses the straight-line depreciation method for all equipment. On December 31, 2016, the end of the company's fiscal year, Dower chooses to revalue the equipment to its fair value of $220,000.

Required:
1. Calculate depreciation for 2016.
2. Prepare the journal entry to record the revaluation of the equipment. Round calculations to the nearest thousand.
3. Calculate depreciation for 2017.
4. Repeat requirement 2 assuming that the fair value of the equipment at the end of 2016 is $195,000.

E 11–10
Group depreciation
● LO11–2

Highsmith Rental Company purchased an apartment building early in 2016. There are 20 apartments in the building and each is furnished with major kitchen appliances. The company has decided to use the group depreciation method for the appliances. The following data are available:

Appliance	Cost	Residual Value	Service Life (in Years)
Stoves	$15,000	$3,000	6
Refrigerators	10,000	1,000	5
Dishwashers	8,000	500	4

In 2019, three new refrigerators costing $2,700 were purchased for cash. The old refrigerators, which originally cost $1,500, were sold for $200.

Required:
1. Calculate the group depreciation rate, group life, and depreciation for 2016.
2. Prepare the journal entries to record the purchase of the new refrigerators and the sale of the old refrigerators.

E 11–11
Double-declining-balance method; switch to straight line
● LO11–2, LO11–6

On January 2, 2016, the Jackson Company purchased equipment to be used in its manufacturing process. The equipment has an estimated life of eight years and an estimated residual value of $30,625. The expenditures made to acquire the asset were as follows:

Purchase price	$154,000
Freight charges	2,000
Installation charges	4,000

Jackson's policy is to use the double-declining-balance (DDB) method of depreciation in the early years of the equipment's life and then switch to straight line halfway through the equipment's life.

Required:
1. Calculate depreciation for each year of the asset's eight-year life.
2. Discuss the accounting treatment of the depreciation on the equipment.

E 11–12
Depletion
● LO11–3

On April 17, 2016, the Loadstone Mining Company purchased the rights to a coal mine. The purchase price plus additional costs necessary to prepare the mine for extraction of the coal totaled $4,500,000. The company expects to extract 900,000 tons of coal during a four-year period. During 2016, 240,000 tons were extracted and sold immediately.

Required:

1. Calculate depletion for 2016.
2. Discuss the accounting treatment of the depletion calculated in requirement 1.

E 11–13
Depreciation and depletion
● LO11–2, LO11–3

At the beginning of 2016, Terra Lumber Company purchased a timber tract from Boise Cantor for $3,200,000. After the timber is cleared, the land will have a residual value of $600,000. Roads to enable logging operations were constructed and completed on March 30, 2016. The cost of the roads, which have no residual value and no alternative use after the tract is cleared, was $240,000. During 2016, Terra logged 500,000 of the estimated five million board feet of timber.

Required:

Calculate the 2016 depletion of the timber tract and depreciation of the logging roads assuming the units-of-production method is used for both assets.

E 11–14
Cost of a natural resource; depletion and depreciation; Chapters 10 and 11
● LO11–2, LO11–3

[This exercise is a continuation of Exercise 10–4 in Chapter 10 focusing on depletion and depreciation.]

Jackpot Mining Company operates a copper mine in central Montana. The company paid $1,000,000 in 2016 for the mining site and spent an additional $600,000 to prepare the mine for extraction of the copper. After the copper is extracted in approximately four years, the company is required to restore the land to its original condition, including repaving of roads and replacing a greenbelt. The company has provided the following three cash flow possibilities for the restoration costs:

	Cash Outflow	Probability
1	$300,000	25%
2	400,000	40%
3	600,000	35%

To aid extraction, Jackpot purchased some new equipment on July 1, 2016, for $120,000. After the copper is removed from this mine, the equipment will be sold for an estimated residual amount of $20,000. There will be no residual value for the copper mine. The credit-adjusted risk-free rate of interest is 10%.

The company expects to extract 10 million pounds of copper from the mine. Actual production was 1.6 million pounds in 2016 and 3 million pounds in 2017.

Required:

1. Compute depletion and depreciation on the mine and mining equipment for 2016 and 2017. The units-of-production method is used to calculate depreciation.
2. Discuss the accounting treatment of the depletion and depreciation on the mine and mining equipment.

E 11–15
Amortization
● LO11–4, LO11–5

Janes Company provided the following information on intangible assets:

a. A patent was purchased from the Lou Company for $700,000 on January 1, 2014. Janes estimated the remaining useful life of the patent to be 10 years. The patent was carried on Lou's accounting records at a net book value of $350,000 when Lou sold it to Janes.

b. During 2016, a franchise was purchased from the Rink Company for $500,000. The contractual life of the franchise is 10 years and Janes records a full year of amortization in the year of purchase.

c. Janes incurred research and development costs in 2016 as follows:

Materials and supplies	$140,000
Personnel	180,000
Indirect costs	60,000
Total	$380,000

d. Effective January 1, 2016, based on new events that have occurred, Janes estimates that the remaining life of the patent purchased from Lou is only five more years.

Required:

1. Prepare the entries necessary for years 2014 through 2016 to reflect the above information.
2. Prepare a schedule showing the intangible asset section of Janes's December 31, 2016, balance sheet.

E 11–16
Patent amortization; patent defense
● LO11–4, LO11–9

On January 2, 2016, David Corporation purchased a patent for $500,000. The remaining legal life is 12 years, but the company estimated that the patent will be useful only for eight years. In January 2018, the company incurred legal fees of $45,000 in successfully defending a patent infringement suit. The successful defense did not change the company's estimate of useful life.

Required:
Prepare journal entries related to the patent for 2016, 2017, and 2018.

E 11–17
Change in estimate; useful life of patent
● LO11–4, LO11–5

Van Frank Telecommunications has a patent on a cellular transmission process. The company has amortized the patent on a straight-line basis since 2012, when it was acquired at a cost of $9 million at the beginning of that year. Due to rapid technological advances in the industry, management decided that the patent would benefit the company over a total of six years rather than the nine-year life being used to amortize its cost. The decision was made at the end of 2016 (before adjusting and closing entries).

Required:
Prepare the appropriate adjusting entry for patent amortization in 2016 to reflect the revised estimate.

E 11–18
IFRS; revaluation of patent; amortization
● LO11–10

IFRS

Saint John Corporation prepares its financial statements according to IFRS. On June 30, 2016, the company purchased a franchise for $1,200,000. The franchise is expected to have a 10-year useful life with no residual value. Saint John uses the straight-line amortization method for all intangible assets. On December 31, 2016, the end of the company's fiscal year, Saint John chooses to revalue the franchise. There is an active market for this particular franchise and its fair value on December 31, 2016, is $1,180,000.

Required:
1. Calculate amortization for 2016.
2. Prepare the journal entry to record the revaluation of the patent.
3. Calculate amortization for 2017.

E 11–19
Change in estimate; useful life and residual value of equipment
● LO11–2, LO11–5

Wardell Company purchased a minicomputer on January 1, 2014, at a cost of $40,000. The computer was depreciated using the straight-line method over an estimated five-year life with an estimated residual value of $4,000. On January 1, 2016, the estimate of useful life was changed to a total of 10 years, and the estimate of residual value was changed to $900.

Required:
1. Prepare the appropriate adjusting entry for depreciation in 2016 to reflect the revised estimate.
2. Repeat requirement 1 assuming that the company uses the sum-of-the-years'-digits method instead of the straight-line method.

E 11–20
Change in principle; change in depreciation methods
● LO11–2, LO11–6

Alteran Corporation purchased office equipment for $1.5 million in 2013. The equipment is being depreciated over a 10-year life using the sum-of-the-years'-digits method. The residual value is expected to be $300,000. At the beginning of 2016, Alteran decided to change to the straight-line depreciation method for this equipment.

Required:
Prepare the 2016 depreciation adjusting entry.

E 11–21
Change in principle; change in depreciation methods
● LO11–2, LO11–6

For financial reporting, Clinton Poultry Farms has used the declining-balance method of depreciation for conveyor equipment acquired at the beginning of 2013 for $2,560,000. Its useful life was estimated to be six years, with a $160,000 residual value. At the beginning of 2016, Clinton decides to change to the straight-line method. The effect of this change on depreciation for each year is as follows:

	($ in 000s)		
Year	**Straight Line**	**Declining Balance**	**Difference**
2013	$ 400	$ 853	$453
2014	400	569	169
2015	400	379	(21)
	$1,200	$1,801	$601

Required:
1. Briefly describe the way Clinton should report this accounting change in the 2014–2016 comparative financial statements.
2. Prepare any 2016 journal entry related to the change.

E 11–22
Error correction
● LO11–2, LO11–7

In 2016, internal auditors discovered that PKE Displays, Inc., had debited an expense account for the $350,000 cost of equipment purchased on January 1, 2013. The equipment's life was expected to be five years with no residual value. Straight-line depreciation is used by PKE.

Required:

1. Prepare the appropriate correcting entry assuming the error was discovered in 2016 before the adjusting and closing entries. (Ignore income taxes.)
2. Assume the error was discovered in 2018 after the 2017 financial statements are issued. Prepare the appropriate correcting entry.

E 11–23
Impairment; property, plant, and equipment
● LO11–8

Chadwick Enterprises, Inc., operates several restaurants throughout the Midwest. Three of its restaurants located in the center of a large urban area have experienced declining profits due to declining population. The company's management has decided to test the assets of the restaurants for possible impairment. The relevant information for these assets is presented below.

Book value	$6.5 million
Estimated undiscounted sum of future cash flows	4.0 million
Fair value	3.5 million

Required:

1. Determine the amount of the impairment loss, if any.
2. Repeat requirement 1 assuming that the estimated undiscounted sum of future cash flows is $6.8 million and fair value is $5 million.

E 11–24
IFRS; impairment; property, plant, and equipment
● LO11–10

Refer to the situation described in Exercise 11–23.

Required:

How might your solution differ if Chadwick Enterprises, Inc., prepares its financial statements according to International Financial Reporting Standards? Assume that the fair value amount given in the exercise equals both (a) the fair value less costs to sell and (b) the present value of estimated future cash flows.

E 11–25
IFRS; Impairment; property, plant, and equipment
● LO11–8, LO11–10

Collinsworth LTD., a U.K. company, prepares its financial statements according to International Financial Reporting Standards. Late in its 2016 fiscal year, a significant adverse change in business climate indicated to management that the assets of its appliance division may be impaired. The following data relate to the division's assets:

	(£ in millions)
Book value	£220
Undiscounted sum of estimated future cash flows	210
Present value of future cash flows	150
Fair value less cost to sell (determined by appraisal)	145

Required:

1. What amount of impairment loss, if any, should Collinsworth recognize?
2. Assume that Collinsworth prepares its financial statements according to U.S. GAAP and that fair value less cost to sell approximates fair value. What amount of impairment loss, if any, should Collinsworth recognize?

E 11–26
Impairment; property, plant, and equipment
● LO11–8

General Optic Corporation operates a manufacturing plant in Arizona. Due to a significant decline in demand for the product manufactured at the Arizona site, an impairment test is deemed appropriate. Management has acquired the following information for the assets at the plant:

Cost	$32,500,000
Accumulated depreciation	14,200,000
General's estimate of the total cash flows to be generated by selling the products manufactured at its Arizona plant, not discounted to present value	15,000,000

The fair value of the Arizona plant is estimated to be $11,000,000.

Required:

1. Determine the amount of impairment loss, if any.
2. If a loss is indicated, where would it appear in General Optic's multiple-step income statement?
3. If a loss is indicated, prepare the entry to record the loss.

4. Repeat requirement 1 assuming that the estimated undiscounted sum of future cash flows is $12,000,000 instead of $15,000,000.
5. Repeat requirement 1 assuming that the estimated undiscounted sum of future cash flows is $19,000,000 instead of $15,000,000

E 11–27
Impairment; goodwill
● LO11–8

In 2014, Alliant Corporation acquired Centerpoint Inc. for $300 million, of which $50 million was allocated to goodwill. At the end of 2016, management has provided the following information for a required goodwill impairment test:

Fair value of Centerpoint, Inc.	$220 million
Fair value of Centerpoint's net assets (excluding goodwill)	200 million
Book value of Centerpoint's net assets (including goodwill)	250 million

Required:
1. Determine the amount of the impairment loss.
2. Repeat requirement 1 assuming that the fair value of Centerpoint is $270 million.

E 11–28
IFRS; impairment; goodwill
● LO11–10
IFRS

Refer to the situation described in Exercise 11–27, requirement 1. Alliant prepares its financial statements according to IFRS, and Centerpoint is considered a cash-generating unit. Assume that Centerpoint's fair value of $220 million approximates fair value less costs to sell and that the present value of Centerpoint's estimated future cash flows is $225 million.

Required:
Determine the amount of goodwill impairment loss Alliant should recognize.

E 11–29
Goodwill valuation and impairment; Chapters 10 and 11
● LO11–8

On May 28, 2016, Pesky Corporation acquired all of the outstanding common stock of Harman, Inc., for $420 million. The fair value of Harman's identifiable tangible and intangible assets totaled $512 million, and the fair value of liabilities assumed by Pesky was $150 million.

Pesky performed a goodwill impairment test at the end of its fiscal year ended December 31, 2016. Management has provided the following information:

Fair value of Harman, Inc.	$400 million
Fair value of Harman's net assets (excluding goodwill)	370 million
Book value of Harman's net assets (including goodwill)	410 million

Required:
1. Determine the amount of goodwill that resulted from the Harman acquisition.
2. Determine the amount of goodwill impairment loss that Pesky should recognize at the end of 2016, if any.
3. If an impairment loss is required, prepare the journal entry to record the loss.

E 11–30
FASB codification research
● LO11–8
CODE

The *FASB Accounting Standards Codification* represents the single source of authoritative U.S. generally accepted accounting principles.

Required:
1. Obtain the relevant authoritative literature on the impairment or disposal of long-lived assets using the *FASB Accounting Standards Codification* at the FASB website (**asc.fasb.org**). Indicate the Codification topic number that provides guidance on accounting for the impairment of long-lived assets.
2. What is the specific citation that discusses the disclosures required in the notes to the financial statements for the impairment of long-lived assets classified as held and used?
3. Describe the disclosure requirements.

E 11–31
FASB codification research
● LO11–2, LO11–1, LO11–6, LO11–8
CODE

Access the *FASB Accounting Standards Codification* at the FASB website (**asc.fasb.org**). Determine the specific citation for each of the following items:
1. Depreciation involves a systematic and rational allocation of cost rather than a process of valuation.
2. The calculation of an impairment loss for property, plant, and equipment.
3. Accounting for a change in depreciation method.
4. Goodwill should not be amortized.

E 11–32
Subsequent expenditures
● LO11–9

Belltone Company made the following expenditures related to its 10-year-old manufacturing facility:

1. The heating system was replaced at a cost of $250,000. The cost of the old system was not known. The company accounts for improvements as reductions of accumulated depreciation.
2. A new wing was added at a cost of $750,000. The new wing substantially increases the productive capacity of the plant.
3. Annual building maintenance was performed at a cost of $14,000.
4. All of the equipment on the assembly line in the plant was rearranged at a cost of $50,000. The rearrangement clearly increases the productive capacity of the plant.

Required:
Prepare journal entries to record each of the above expenditures.

E 11–33
IFRS; amortization; cost to defend a patent
● LO11–4, LO11–9, LO11–10
IFRS

On September 30, 2014, Leeds LTD. acquired a patent in conjunction with the purchase of another company. The patent, valued at $6 million, was estimated to have a 10-year life and no residual value. Leeds uses the straight-line method of amortization for intangible assets. At the beginning of January 2016, Leeds successfully defended its patent against infringement. Litigation costs totaled $500,000.

Required:
1. Calculate amortization of the patent for 2014 and 2015.
2. Prepare the journal entry to record the 2016 litigation costs.
3. Calculate amortization for 2016.
4. Repeat requirements 2 and 3 assuming that Leeds prepares its financial statements according to IFRS.

E 11–34
Depreciation methods; disposal; Chapters 10 and 11
● LO11–2

Howarth Manufacturing Company purchased a lathe on June 30, 2012, at a cost of $80,000. The residual value of the lathe was estimated to be $5,000 at the end of a five-year life. The lathe was sold on March 31, 2016, for $17,000. Howarth uses the straight-line depreciation method for all of its plant and equipment. Partial-year depreciation is calculated based on the number of months the asset is in service.

Required:
1. Prepare the journal entry to record the sale.
2. Assuming that Howarth had instead used the sum-of-the-years'-digits depreciation method, prepare the journal entry to record the sale.

E 11–35
Concepts; terminology
● LO11–1 through LO11–6, LO11–8

Listed below are several items and phrases associated with depreciation, depletion, and amortization. Pair each item from List A with the item from List B (by letter) that is most appropriately associated with it.

List A	List B
____ 1. Depreciation	a. Cost allocation for natural resource.
____ 2. Service life	b. Accounted for prospectively.
____ 3. Depreciable base	c. When there has been a significant decline in value.
____ 4. Activity-based methods	d. The amount of use expected from plant and equipment and finite-life intangible assets.
____ 5. Time-based methods	e. Estimates service life in units of output.
____ 6. Double-declining balance	f. Cost less residual value.
____ 7. Group method	g. Cost allocation for plant and equipment.
____ 8. Composite method	h. Does not subtract residual value from cost.
____ 9. Depletion	i. Accounted for in the same way as a change in estimate.
____ 10. Amortization	j. Aggregates assets that are similar.
____ 11. Change in useful life	k. Aggregates assets that are physically unified.
____ 12. Change in depreciation method	l. Cost allocation for an intangible asset.
____ 13. Write-down of asset	m. Estimates service life in years.

E 11–36
Retirement and replacement depreciation
● Appendix B

Cadillac Construction Company uses the retirement method to determine depreciation on its small tools. During 2014, the first year of the company's operations, tools were purchased at a cost of $8,000. In 2016, tools originally costing $2,000 were sold for $250 and replaced with new tools costing $2,500.

Required:
1. Prepare journal entries to record each of the above transactions.
2. Repeat requirement 1 assuming that the company uses the replacement depreciation method instead of the retirement method.

CPA and CMA Review Questions

CPA Exam Questions

KAPLAN CPA REVIEW

The following questions are adapted from a variety of sources including questions developed by the AICPA Board of Examiners and those used in the Kaplan CPA Review Course to study property, plant, and equipment and intangible assets while preparing for the CPA examination. Determine the response that best completes the statements or questions.

● LO11–2

1. Slovac Company purchased a machine that has an estimated useful life of eight years for $7,500. Its salvage value is estimated at $500. What is the depreciation for the second year of the asset's life, assuming Slovac uses the double-declining-balance method of depreciation?
   a. $1,406
   b. $1,438
   c. $1,875
   d. $3,750

● LO11–2

2. Calculate depreciation for year 2 based on the following information:

   Historical cost $40,000
   Useful life 5 years
   Salvage value $3,000
   Year 1 depreciation $7,400

   a. $7,000
   b. $7,400
   c. $8,000
   d. $8,600

● LO11–3

3. A company pays $20,000 for the rights to a well with 5 million gallons of water. If the company extracts 250,000 gallons of water in the first year, what is the total depletion in year 1?
   a. $ 400
   b. $1,000
   c. $1,250
   d. $5,000

● LO11–4

4. Black, Inc., acquired another company for $5,000,000. The fair value of all identifiable tangible and intangible assets was $4,500,000. Black will amortize any goodwill over the maximum number of years allowed. What is the annual amortization of goodwill for this acquisition?
   a. $12,500
   b. $20,000
   c. $25,000
   d. 0

● LO11–4

5. On January 2, 2016, Rafa Company purchased a franchise with a useful life of 10 years for $50,000. An additional franchise fee of 3% of franchise operating revenues also must be paid each year to the franchisor. Revenues during 2016 totaled $400,000. In its December 31, 2016, balance sheet, what net amount should Rafa report as an intangible asset-franchise?
   a. $33,000
   b. $43,800
   c. $45,000
   d. $50,000

● LO11–5

6. JME acquired a depreciable asset on January 1, 2014, for $60,000 cash. At that time JME estimated the asset would last 10 years and have no salvage value. During 2016, JME estimated the remaining life of the asset to be only three more years with a salvage value of $3,000. If JME uses straight-line depreciation, what is the depreciation for 2016?
   a. $ 6,000
   b. $12,000
   c. $15,000
   d. $16,000

● LO11–8

7. The following information concerns Franklin Inc.'s stamping machine:

   Acquired: January 1, 2010
   Cost: $22 million
   Depreciation: straight-line method
   Estimated useful life: 12 years
   Salvage value: $4 million

As of December 31, 2016, the stamping machine is expected to generate $1,500,000 per year for five more years and will then be sold for $1,000,000. The stamping machine is

a. Impaired because expected salvage value has declined.
b. Not impaired because annual expected revenue exceeds annual depreciation.
c. Not impaired because it continues to produce revenue.
d. Impaired because its book value exceeds expected future cash flows.

● LO11–9

8. During 2015, Yvo Corp. installed a production assembly line to manufacture furniture. In 2016, Yvo purchased a new machine and rearranged the assembly line to install this machine. The rearrangement did not increase the estimated useful life of the assembly line, but it did result in significantly more efficient production. The following expenditures were incurred in connection with this project:

Machine	$75,000
Labor to install machine	14,000
Parts added in rearranging the assembly line to provide future benefits	40,000
Labor and overhead to rearrange the assembly line	18,000

What amount of the above expenditures should be capitalized in 2016?

a. $ 75,000
b. $ 89,000
c. $107,000
d. $147,000

International Financial Reporting Standards are tested on the CPA exam along with U.S. GAAP. The following questions deal with the application of IFRS.

● LO11–10

IFRS

9. On January 1, 2016, D Company acquires for $100,000 a new machine with an estimated useful life of 10 years and no residual value. The machine has a drum that must be replaced every five years and costs $20,000 to replace. The company uses straight-line depreciation. Under IFRS, what is depreciation for 2016?

a. $10,000.
b. $10,800.
c. $12,000.
d. $13,200.

● LO11–10

IFRS

10. Under IFRS, when a company chooses the revaluation model as its accounting policy for measuring property, plant, and equipment, which of the following statements is correct?

a. When an asset is revalued, the entire class of property, plant, and equipment to which the asset belongs must be revalued.
b. When an asset is revalued, individual assets within a class of property, plant, and equipment to which that asset belongs can be revalued.
c. Revaluations of property, plant, and equipment must be made every three years.
d. An increase in an asset's book value as a result of the first revaluation must be recognized as a component of profit and loss.

● LO11–10

IFRS

11. Under IFRS, the initial revaluation of equipment when book value exceeds fair value results in

a. An increase in net income.
b. A decrease in net income.
c. An increase in other comprehensive income.
d. A decrease in other comprehensive income.

● LO11–10

IFRS

12. Under IFRS, a company that acquires an intangible asset may use the revaluation model for subsequent measurement only if

a. The useful life of the intangible asset can be readily determined.
b. An active market exists for the intangible asset.
c. The cost of the intangible asset can be measured reliably.
d. The intangible asset is a monetary asset.

● LO11–10

IFRS

13. The management of Clayton LTD. determined that the cost of one of its factories may be impaired. Below are data related to the assets of the factory ($ in millions):

Book value	$400
Undiscounted sum of future estimated cash flows	420
Present value of future cash flows	320
Fair value less costs to sell (determined by appraisal)	330

Under IFRS, what amount of impairment loss, if any, should Clayton recognize?

a. $90 million.
b. $80 million.
c. $70 million.
d. No impairment loss is required.

● LO11–10

14. Blankbank Corporation has $150 million of goodwill on its books from the 2014 acquisition of Walsh Technology. Walsh is considered a cash-generating unit under IFRS. At the end of its 2016 fiscal year, management provided the following information for its annual goodwill impairment test ($ in millions):

Fair value of Walsh less costs to sell	$455
Fair value of Walsh's net assets (excluding goodwill)	400
Book value of Walsh's net assets (including goodwill)	500
Present value of estimated future cash flows	440

Under IFRS, what amount of goodwill impairment loss, if any, should Blankbank recognize?

a. $100 million.
b. $60 million.
c. $50 million.
d. $45 million.

CMA Exam Questions

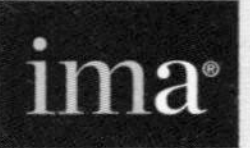

The following questions dealing with property, plant, and equipment and intangible assets are adapted from questions that previously appeared on Certified Management Accountant (CMA) examinations. The CMA designation sponsored by the Institute of Management Accountants (**www.imanet.org**) provides members with an objective measure of knowledge and competence in the field of management accounting. Determine the response that best completes the statements or questions.

● LO11–3

1. WD Mining Company purchased a section of land for $600,000 in 2006 to develop a zinc mine. The mine began operating in 2008. At that time, management estimated that the mine would produce 200,000 tons of quality ore. A total of 100,000 tons of ore was mined and processed from 2008 through December 31, 2015. During January 2016, a very promising vein was discovered. The revised estimate of ore still to be mined was 250,000 tons. Estimated salvage value for the mine land was $100,000 in both 2008 and 2016. Assuming that 10,000 tons of ore was mined in 2016, the computation WD Mining Company should use to determine the amount of depletion to record in 2016 would be

a. (($600,000 − $100,000)/450,000 tons) × 10,000 tons.
b. (($600,000 − $100,000)/350,000 tons) × 10,000 tons.
c. (($600,000 − $100,000 − $250,000)/350,000 tons) × 10,000 tons.
d. (($600,000 − $100,000 − $250,000)/250,000 tons) × 10,000 tons.

● LO11–4

2. On September 1, year 1, for $4,000,000 cash and $2,000,000 notes payable, Norbend Corporation acquired the net assets of Crisholm Company, which had a fair value of $5,496,000 on that date. Norbend's management is of the opinion that the goodwill generated has an indefinite life. During the year-end audit for year 3 after all adjusting entries have been made, the goodwill is determined to be worthless. The amount of the write-off as of December 31, year 3 should be

a. $504,000.
b. $478,800.
c. $466,200.
d. $474,600.

● LO11–9

3. Costs that are capitalized with regard to a patent include

a. Legal fees of obtaining the patent, incidental costs of obtaining the patent, and costs of successful patent infringement suits.
b. Legal fees of obtaining the patent, incidental costs of obtaining the patent, and research and development costs incurred on the invention that is patented.
c. Legal fees of obtaining the patent, costs of successful patent infringement suits, and research and development costs incurred on the invention that is patented.
d. Incidental costs of obtaining the patent, costs of successful and unsuccessful patent infringement suits, and the value of any signed patent licensing agreement.

Problems

An alternate exercise and problem set is available in the Connect library.

P 11–1
Depreciation methods; change in methods
● LO11–2, LO11–6

The fact that generally accepted accounting principles allow companies flexibility in choosing between certain allocation methods can make it difficult for a financial analyst to compare periodic performance from firm to firm.

Suppose you were a financial analyst trying to compare the performance of two companies. Company A uses the double-declining-balance depreciation method. Company B uses the straight-line method. You have the following information taken from the 12/31/16 year-end financial statements for Company B:

Income Statement

Depreciation expense	$ 10,000

Balance Sheet

Assets:	
Plant and equipment, at cost	$200,000
Less: Accumulated depreciation	(40,000)
Net	$160,000

You also determine that all of the assets constituting the plant and equipment of Company B were acquired at the same time, and that all of the $200,000 represents depreciable assets. Also, all of the depreciable assets have the same useful life and residual values are zero.

Required:

1. In order to compare performance with Company A, estimate what B's depreciation expense would have been for 2016 if the double-declining-balance depreciation method had been used by Company B since acquisition of the depreciable assets.
2. If Company B decided to switch depreciation methods in 2016 from the straight line to the double-declining-balance method, prepare the 2016 adjusting journal entry to record depreciation for the year, assuming no journal entry for depreciation in 2016 has been recorded.

P 11–2
Comprehensive problem; Chapters 10 and 11
● LO11–2, LO11–4

At December 31, 2015, Cord Company's plant asset and accumulated depreciation and amortization accounts had balances as follows:

Category	Plant Asset	Accumulated Depreciation and Amortization
Land	$ 175,000	$ —
Buildings	1,500,000	328,900
Machinery and equipment	1,125,000	317,500
Automobiles and trucks	172,000	100,325
Leasehold improvements	216,000	108,000
Land improvements	—	—

Depreciation methods and useful lives:
Buildings—150% declining balance; 25 years.
Machinery and equipment—Straight line; 10 years.
Automobiles and trucks—150% declining balance; 5 years, all acquired after 2012.
Leasehold improvements—Straight line.
Land improvements—Straight line.

Depreciation is computed to the nearest month and residual values are immaterial. Transactions during 2016 and other information:

a. On January 6, 2016, a plant facility consisting of land and building was acquired from King Corp. in exchange for 25,000 shares of Cord's common stock. On this date, Cord's stock had a fair value of $50 a share. Current assessed values of land and building for property tax purposes are $187,500 and $562,500, respectively.
b. On March 25, 2016, new parking lots, streets, and sidewalks at the acquired plant facility were completed at a total cost of $192,000. These expenditures had an estimated useful life of 12 years.
c. The leasehold improvements were completed on December 31, 2012, and had an estimated useful life of eight years. The related lease, which would terminate on December 31, 2018, was renewable for an additional four-year term. On April 29, 2016, Cord exercised the renewal option.
d. On July 1, 2016, machinery and equipment were purchased at a total invoice cost of $325,000. Additional costs of $10,000 for delivery and $50,000 for installation were incurred.

e. On August 30, 2016, Cord purchased a new automobile for $12,500.

f. On September 30, 2016, a truck with a cost of $24,000 and a book value of $9,100 on date of sale was sold for $11,500. Depreciation for the nine months ended September 30, 2016, was $2,650.

g. On December 20, 2016, a machine with a cost of $17,000 and a book value of $2,975 at date of disposition was scrapped without cash recovery.

Required:

1. Prepare a schedule analyzing the changes in each of the plant asset accounts during 2016. This schedule should include columns for beginning balance, increase, decrease, and ending balance for each of the plant asset accounts. Do not analyze changes in accumulated depreciation and amortization.
2. For each asset category, prepare a schedule showing depreciation or amortization expense for the year ended December 31, 2016. Round computations to the nearest whole dollar.

(AICPA adapted)

P 11–3
Depreciation methods; Chapters 10 and 11
● LO11–2

[This problem is a continuation of Problem 10–3 in Chapter 10 focusing on depreciation.]

Required:

For each asset classification, prepare a schedule showing depreciation for the year ended December 31, 2016, using the following depreciation methods and useful lives:

Land improvements—Straight line; 15 years.
Building—150% declining balance; 20 years.
Machinery and equipment—Straight line; 10 years.
Automobiles—150% declining balance; 3 years.

Depreciation is computed to the nearest month and no residual values are used.

(AICPA adapted)

P 11–4
Partial-year depreciation; asset addition; increase in useful life
● LO11–2, LO11–5, LO11–9

On April 1, 2014, the KB Toy Company purchased equipment to be used in its manufacturing process. The equipment cost $48,000, has an eight-year useful life, and has no residual value. The company uses the straight-line depreciation method for all manufacturing equipment.

On January 4, 2016, $12,350 was spent to repair the equipment and to add a feature that increased its operating efficiency. Of the total expenditure, $2,000 represented ordinary repairs and annual maintenance and $10,350 represented the cost of the new feature. In addition to increasing operating efficiency, the total useful life of the equipment was extended to 10 years.

Required:

Prepare journal entries for the following:

1. Depreciation for 2014 and 2015.
2. The 2016 expenditure.
3. Depreciation for 2016.

P 11–5
Property, plant, and equipment and intangible assets; comprehensive
● LO11–2

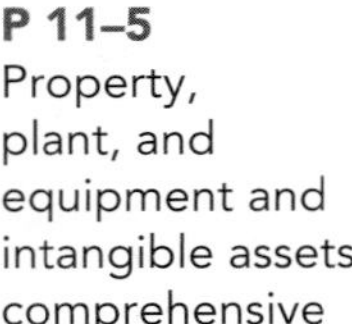

The Thompson Corporation, a manufacturer of steel products, began operations on October 1, 2014. The accounting department of Thompson has started the fixed-asset and depreciation schedule presented below. You have been asked to assist in completing this schedule. In addition to ascertaining that the data already on the schedule are correct, you have obtained the following information from the company's records and personnel:

a. Depreciation is computed from the first of the month of acquisition to the first of the month of disposition.

b. Land A and Building A were acquired from a predecessor corporation. Thompson paid $812,500 for the land and building together. At the time of acquisition, the land had a fair value of $72,000 and the building had a fair value of $828,000.

c. Land B was acquired on October 2, 2014, in exchange for 3,000 newly issued shares of Thompson's common stock. At the date of acquisition, the stock had a par value of $5 per share and a fair value of $25 per share. During October 2014, Thompson paid $10,400 to demolish an existing building on this land so it could construct a new building.

d. Construction of Building B on the newly acquired land began on October 1, 2015. By September 30, 2016, Thompson had paid $210,000 of the estimated total construction costs of $300,000. Estimated completion and occupancy are July 2017.

e. Certain equipment was donated to the corporation by the city. An independent appraisal of the equipment when donated placed the fair value at $16,000 and the residual value at $2,000.

f. Machine A's total cost of $110,000 includes installation charges of $550 and normal repairs and maintenance of $11,000. Residual value is estimated at $5,500. Machine A was sold on February 1, 2016.

g. On October 1, 2015, Machine B was acquired with a down payment of $4,000 and the remaining payments to be made in 10 annual installments of $4,000 each beginning October 1, 2016. The prevailing interest rate was 8%.

THOMPSON CORPORATION
Fixed Asset and Depreciation Schedule
For Fiscal Years Ended September 30, 2015, and September 30, 2016

Assets	Acquisition Date	Cost	Residual	Depreciation Method	Estimated Life in Years	Depreciation for Year Ended 9/30 2015	2016
Land A	10/1/14	$(1)	N/A	N/A	N/A	N/A	N/A
Building A	10/1/14	(2)	$47,500	SL	(3)	$14,000	$(4)
Land B	10/2/14	(5)	N/A	N/A	N/A	N/A	N/A
Building B	Under construction	210,000 to date	—	SL	30	—	(6)
Donated Equipment	10/2/14	(7)	2,000	150% Declining balance	10	(8)	(9)
Machine A	10/2/14	(10)	5,500	Sum-of-the-years'-digits	10	(11)	(12)
Machine B	10/1/15	(13)	—	SL	15	—	(14)

N/A = not applicable

Required:
Supply the correct amount for each numbered item on the schedule. Round each answer to the nearest dollar.

(AICPA adapted)

P 11–6
Depreciation methods; partial-year depreciation; sale of assets
● LO11–2

On March 31, 2016, the Herzog Company purchased a factory complete with machinery and equipment. The allocation of the total purchase price of $1,000,000 to the various types of assets along with estimated useful lives and residual values are as follows:

Asset	Cost	Estimated Residual Value	Estimated Useful Life in Years
Land	$ 100,000	N/A	N/A
Building	500,000	none	25
Machinery	240,000	10% of cost	8
Equipment	160,000	$13,000	6
Total	$1,000,000		

On June 29, 2017, machinery included in the March 31, 2016, purchase that cost $100,000 was sold for $80,000. Herzog uses the straight-line depreciation method for buildings and machinery and the sum-of-the-years'-digits method for equipment. Partial-year depreciation is calculated based on the number of months an asset is in service.

Required:
1. Compute depreciation expense on the building, machinery, and equipment for 2016.
2. Prepare the journal entries to record (1) depreciation on the machinery sold on June 29, 2017, and (2) the sale of machinery.
3. Compute depreciation expense on the building, remaining machinery, and equipment for 2017.

P 11–7
Depletion; change in estimate
● LO11–3, LO11–5

In 2016, the Marion Company purchased land containing a mineral mine for $1,600,000. Additional costs of $600,000 were incurred to develop the mine. Geologists estimated that 400,000 tons of ore would be extracted. After the ore is removed, the land will have a resale value of $100,000.

To aid in the extraction, Marion built various structures and small storage buildings on the site at a cost of $150,000. These structures have a useful life of 10 years. The structures cannot be moved after the ore has been removed and will be left at the site. In addition, new equipment costing $80,000 was purchased and installed at the site. Marion does not plan to move the equipment to another site, but estimates that it can be sold at auction for $4,000 after the mining project is completed.

In 2016, 50,000 tons of ore were extracted and sold. In 2017, the estimate of total tons of ore in the mine was revised from 400,000 to 487,500. During 2017, 80,000 tons were extracted, of which 60,000 tons were sold.

Required:
1. Compute depletion and depreciation of the mine and the mining facilities and equipment for 2016 and 2017. Marion uses the units-of-production method to determine depreciation on mining facilities and equipment.

2. Compute the book value of the mineral mine, structures, and equipment as of December 31, 2017.
3. Discuss the accounting treatment of the depletion and depreciation on the mine and mining facilities and equipment.

P 11–8
Amortization
● LO11–4

The following information concerns the intangible assets of Epstein Corporation:

a. On June 30, 2016, Epstein completed the acquisition of the Johnstone Corporation for $2,000,000 in cash. The fair value of the net identifiable assets of Johnstone was $1,700,000.
b. Included in the assets purchased from Johnstone was a patent that was valued at $80,000. The remaining legal life of the patent was 13 years, but Epstein believes that the patent will only be useful for another eight years.
c. Epstein acquired a franchise on October 1, 2016, by paying an initial franchise fee of $200,000. The contractual life of the franchise is 10 years.

Required:

1. Prepare year-end adjusting journal entries to record amortization expense on the intangibles at December 31, 2016.
2. Prepare the intangible asset section of the December 31, 2016, balance sheet.

P 11–9
Straight-line depreciation; change in useful life and residual value
● LO11–2, LO11–5

The property, plant, and equipment section of the Jasper Company's December 31, 2015, balance sheet contained the following:

Property, plant, and equipment:		
Land		$120,000
Building	$ 840,000	
Less: Accumulated depreciation	(200,000)	640,000
Equipment	180,000	
Less: Accumulated depreciation	?	?
Total property, plant, and equipment		?

The land and building were purchased at the beginning of 2011. Straight-line depreciation is used and a residual value of $40,000 for the building is anticipated.

The equipment is comprised of the following three machines:

Machine	Cost	Date Acquired	Residual Value	Life in Years
101	$70,000	1/1/13	$7,000	10
102	80,000	6/30/14	8,000	8
103	30,000	9/1/15	3,000	9

The straight-line method is used to determine depreciation on the equipment. On March 31, 2016, Machine 102 was sold for $52,500. Early in 2016, the useful life of machine 101 was revised to seven years in total, and the residual value was revised to zero.

Required:

1. Calculate the accumulated depreciation on the equipment at December 31, 2015.
2. Prepare the journal entry to record the sale of machine 102. Also prepare the journal entry to record 2016 depreciation on machine 102 up to the date of sale.
3. Prepare the 2016 year-end adjusting journal entries to record depreciation on the building and equipment.

P 11–10
Accounting changes; three accounting situations
● LO11–2, LO11–5, LO11–6

Described below are three independent and unrelated situations involving accounting changes. Each change occurs during 2016 before any adjusting entries or closing entries are prepared.

a. On December 30, 2012, Rival Industries acquired its office building at a cost of $10,000,000. It has been depreciated on a straight-line basis assuming a useful life of 40 years and no residual value. Early in 2016, the estimate of useful life was revised to 28 years in total with no change in residual value.
b. At the beginning of 2012, the Hoffman Group purchased office equipment at a cost of $330,000. Its useful life was estimated to be 10 years with no residual value. The equipment has been depreciated by the sum-of-the-years'-digits method. On January 1, 2016, the company changed to the straight-line method.
c. At the beginning of 2016, Jantzen Specialties, which uses the sum-of-the-years'-digits method, changed to the straight-line method for newly acquired buildings and equipment. The change increased current year net income by $445,000.

Required:

For each situation:

1. Identify the type of change.

2. Prepare any journal entry necessary as a direct result of the change as well as any adjusting entry for 2016 related to the situation described. (Ignore income tax effects.)
3. Briefly describe any other steps that should be taken to appropriately report the situation.

P 11–11
Error correction; change in depreciation method
● LO11–2, LO11–6, LO11–7

Collins Corporation purchased office equipment at the beginning of 2014 and capitalized a cost of $2,000,000. This cost figure included the following expenditures:

Purchase price	$1,850,000
Freight charges	30,000
Installation charges	20,000
Annual maintenance charge	100,000
Total	$2,000,000

The company estimated an eight-year useful life for the equipment. No residual value is anticipated. The double-declining-balance method was used to determine depreciation expense for 2014 and 2015.

In 2016, after the 2015 financial statements were issued, the company decided to switch to the straight-line depreciation method for this equipment. At that time, the company's controller discovered that the original cost of the equipment incorrectly included one year of annual maintenance charges for the equipment.

Required:

1. Ignoring income taxes, prepare the appropriate correcting entry for the equipment capitalization error discovered in 2016.
2. Ignoring income taxes, prepare any 2016 journal entry(s) related to the change in depreciation methods.

P 11–12
Depreciation and amortization; impairment
● LO11–2, LO11–4, LO11–8

At the beginning of 2014, Metatec Inc. acquired Ellison Technology Corporation for $600 million. In addition to cash, receivables, and inventory, the following assets and their fair values were also acquired:

Plant and equipment (depreciable assets)	$150 million
Patent	40 million
Goodwill	100 million

The plant and equipment are depreciated over a 10-year useful life on a straight-line basis. There is no estimated residual value. The patent is estimated to have a 5-year useful life, no residual value, and is amortized using the straight-line method.

At the end of 2016, a change in business climate indicated to management that the assets of Ellison might be impaired. The following amounts have been determined:

Plant and equipment:	
Undiscounted sum of future cash flows	$ 80 million
Fair value	60 million
Patent:	
Undiscounted sum of future cash flows	$ 20 million
Fair value	13 million
Goodwill:	
Fair value of Ellison Technology	$450 million
Fair value of Ellison's net assets (excluding goodwill)	390 million
Book value of Ellison's net assets (including goodwill)	470 million*

*After first recording any impairment losses on plant and equipment and the patent.

Required:

1. Compute the book value of the plant and equipment and patent at the end of 2016.
2. When should the plant and equipment and the patent be tested for impairment?
3. When should goodwill be tested for impairment?
4. Determine the amount of any impairment loss to be recorded, if any, for the three assets.

P 11–13
Depreciation and depletion; change in useful life; asset retirement obligation; Chapters 10 and 11
● LO11–2, LO11–3, LO11–5

On May 1, 2016, Hecala Mining entered into an agreement with the state of New Mexico to obtain the rights to operate a mineral mine in New Mexico for $10 million. Additional costs and purchases included the following:

Development costs in preparing the mine	$3,200,000
Mining equipment	140,000
Construction of various structures on site	68,000

After the minerals are removed from the mine, the equipment will be sold for an estimated residual value of $10,000. The structures will be torn down.

Geologists estimate that 800,000 tons of ore can be extracted from the mine. After the ore is removed the land will revert back to the state of New Mexico.

The contract with the state requires Hecala to restore the land to its original condition after mining operations are completed in approximately four years. Management has provided the following possible outflows for the restoration costs:

Cash Outflow	Probability
$600,000	30%
700,000	30%
800,000	40%

Hecala's credit-adjusted risk-free interest rate is 8%. During 2016, Hecala extracted 120,000 tons of ore from the mine. The company's fiscal year ends on December 31.

Required:

1. Determine the amount at which Hecala will record the mine.
2. Calculate the depletion of the mine and the depreciation of the mining facilities and equipment for 2016, assuming that Hecala uses the units-of-production method for both depreciation and depletion. Round depletion and depreciation rates to four decimals.
3. How much accretion expense will the company record in its income statement for the 2016 fiscal year?
4. Are depletion of the mine and depreciation of the mining facilities and equipment reported as separate expenses in the income statement? Discuss the accounting treatment of these items in the income statement and balance sheet.
5. During 2017, Hecala changed its estimate of the total amount of ore originally in the mine from 800,000 to 1,000,000 tons. Briefly describe the accounting treatment the company will employ to account for the change *and* calculate the depletion of the mine and depreciation of the mining facilities and equipment for 2017 assuming Hecala extracted 150,000 tons of ore in 2017.

Broaden Your Perspective

Apply your critical-thinking ability to the knowledge you've gained. These cases will provide you an opportunity to develop your research, analysis, judgment, and communication skills. You also will work with other students, integrate what you've learned, apply it in real-world situations, and consider its global and ethical ramifications. This practice will broaden your knowledge and further develop your decision-making abilities.

Analysis Case 11–1
Depreciation, depletion, and amortization
● LO11–1

The terms depreciation, depletion, and amortization all refer to the process of allocating the cost of an asset to the periods the asset is used.

Required:
Discuss the differences between depreciation, depletion, and amortization as the terms are used in accounting for property, plant, and equipment and intangible assets.

Communication Case 11–2
Depreciation
● LO11–1

At a recent luncheon, you were seated next to Mr. Hopkins, the president of a local company that manufactures bicycle parts. He heard that you were a CPA and made the following comments to you:

> Why is it that I am forced to recognize depreciation expense in my company's income statement when I know that I could sell many of my assets for more than I paid for them? I thought that the purpose of the balance sheet was to reflect the value of my business and that the purpose of the income statement was to report the net change in value or wealth of a company. It just doesn't make sense to penalize my profits when there hasn't been any loss in value from using the assets.

At the conclusion of the luncheon, you promised to send him a short explanation of the rationale for current depreciation practices.

Required:
Prepare a letter to Mr. Hopkins. Explain the accounting concept of depreciation and include a brief example in your explanation showing that over the life of the asset the change in value approach to depreciation and the allocation of cost approach will result in the same total effect on income.

Judgment Case 11–3
Straight-line method; composite depreciation
● LO11–1, LO11–2

Portland Co. uses the straight-line depreciation method for depreciable assets. All assets are depreciated individually except manufacturing machinery, which is depreciated by the composite method.

Required:

1. What factors should have influenced Portland's selection of the straight-line depreciation method?
2. a. What benefits should derive from using the composite method rather than the individual basis for manufacturing machinery?
   b. How should Portland have calculated the manufacturing machinery's annual depreciation in its first year of operation?

(AICPA adapted)

Judgment Case 11–4
Depreciation
● LO11–1, LO11–2

At the beginning of the year, Patrick Company acquired a computer to be used in its operations. The computer was delivered by the supplier, installed by Patrick, and placed into operation. The estimated useful life of the computer is five years, and its estimated residual value is significant.

Required:

1. a. What costs should Patrick capitalize for the computer?
   b. What is the objective of depreciation accounting?
2. What is the rationale for using accelerated depreciation methods?

(AICPA adapted)

Judgment Case 11–5
Capitalize or expense; materiality
● LO11–9

Redline Publishers, Inc. produces various manuals ranging from computer software instructional booklets to manuals explaining the installation and use of large pieces of industrial equipment. At the end of 2016, the company's balance sheet reported total assets of $62 million and total liabilities of $40 million. The income statement for 2016 reported net income of $1.1 million, which represents an approximate 3% increase from the prior year. The company's effective income tax rate is 30%.

Near the end of 2016, a variety of expenditures were made to overhaul the company's manufacturing equipment. None of these expenditures exceeded $750, the materiality threshold the company has set for the capitalization of any such expenditure. Even though the overhauls extended the service life of the equipment, the expenditures were expensed, not capitalized.

John Henderson, the company's controller, is worried about the treatment of the overhaul expenditures. Even though no individual expenditure exceeded the $750 materiality threshold, total expenditures were $70,000.

Required:

Should the overhaul expenditures be capitalized or expensed?

Communication Case 11–6
Capitalize or expense; materiality
● LO11–9

The focus of the case is the situation described in Case 11–5. Your instructor will divide the class into two to six groups depending on the size of the class. The mission of your group is to determine the treatment of the overhaul expenditures.

Required:

1. Each group member should deliberate the situation independently and draft a tentative argument prior to the class session for which the case is assigned.
2. In class, each group will meet for 10 to 15 minutes in different areas of the classroom. During the meeting, group members will take turns sharing their suggestions for the purpose of arriving at a single group treatment.
3. After the allotted time, a spokesperson for each group (selected during the group meetings) will share the group's solution with the class. The goal of the class is to incorporate the views of each group into a consensus approach to the situation.

Integrating Case 11–7
Errors; change in estimate; change in principle; inventory, patent, and equipment
● LO11–5 through LO11–7

Whaley Distributors is a wholesale distributor of electronic components. Financial statements for the year ended December 31, 2016, reported the following amounts and subtotals ($ in millions):

	Assets	Liabilities	Shareholders' Equity	Net Income	Expenses
2015	$640	$330	$310	$210	$150
2016	$820	$400	$420	$230	$175

In 2017 the following situations occurred or came to light:

a. Internal auditors discovered that ending inventories reported in the financial statements the two previous years were misstated due to faulty internal controls. The errors were in the following amounts:

2015 inventory	Overstated by $12 million
2016 inventory	Understated by $10 million

b. A patent costing $18 million at the beginning of 2015, expected to benefit operations for a total of six years, has not been amortized since acquired.

c. Whaley's conveyer equipment has been depreciated by the sum-of-the-years'-digits (SYD) method since constructed at the beginning of 2015 at a cost of $30 million. It has an expected useful life of five years and no expected residual value. At the beginning of 2017, Whaley decided to switch to straight-line depreciation.

Required:

For each situation:

1. Prepare any journal entry necessary as a direct result of the change or error correction as well as any adjusting entry for 2017 related to the situation described. (Ignore tax effects.)
2. Determine the amounts to be reported for each of the items shown above from the 2015 and 2016 financial statements when those amounts are reported again in the 2017, 2016, and 2015 comparative financial statements.

Judgment Case 11–8
Accounting changes
● LO11–5, LO11–6

There are various types of accounting changes, each of which is required to be reported differently.

Required:

1. What type of accounting change is a change from the sum-of-the-years'-digits method of depreciation to the straight-line method for previously recorded assets? Under what circumstances does this type of accounting change occur?
2. What type of accounting change is a change in the expected service life of an asset arising because of more experience with the asset? Under what circumstances does this type of accounting change occur?

(AICPA adapted)

Research Case 11–9
FASB codification; locate and extract relevant information and cite authoritative support for a financial reporting issue; impairment of property, plant, and equipment and intangible assets
● LO11–8

The company controller, Barry Melrose, has asked for your help in interpreting the authoritative accounting literature that addresses the recognition and measurement of impairment losses for property, plant, and equipment and intangible assets. "We have a significant amount of goodwill on our books from last year's acquisition of Churchill Corporation. Also, I think we may have a problem with the assets of some of our factories out West. And one of our divisions is currently considering disposing of a large group of depreciable assets."

Your task as assistant controller is to research the issue.

Required:

1. Obtain the relevant authoritative literature on accounting for the impairment of property, plant, and equipment and intangible assets using the *FASB Accounting Standards Codification*. You might gain access at the FASB website (asc.fasb.org). Cite the reference locations regarding impairment of property, plant, and equipment and intangible assets.
2. When should property, plant, and equipment and finite-life intangible assets be tested for impairment?
3. Explain the process for measuring an impairment loss for property, plant, and equipment and finite-life intangible assets to be held and used.
4. What are the specific criteria that must be met for an asset or asset group to be classified as held-for-sale? What is the specific citation reference from the *FASB Accounting Standards Codification* that contains these criteria?
5. Explain the process for measuring an impairment loss for property, plant, and equipment and finite-life intangible assets classified as held-for-sale.

Ethics Case 11–10
Asset impairment
● LO11–8

At the beginning of 2014, the Healthy Life Food Company purchased equipment for $42 million to be used in the manufacture of a new line of gourmet frozen foods. The equipment was estimated to have a 10-year service life and no residual value. The straight-line depreciation method was used to measure depreciation for 2014 and 2015.

Late in 2016, it became apparent that sales of the new frozen food line were significantly below expectations. The company decided to continue production for two more years (2017 and 2018) and then discontinue the line. At that time, the equipment will be sold for minimal scrap values.

The controller, Heather Meyer, was asked by Harvey Dent, the company's chief executive officer (CEO), to determine the appropriate treatment of the change in service life of the equipment. Heather determined that there has been an impairment of value requiring an immediate write-down of the equipment of $12,900,000. The remaining book value would then be depreciated over the equipment's revised service life.

The CEO does not like Heather's conclusion because of the effect it would have on 2016 income. "Looks like a simple revision in service life from 10 years to 5 years to me," Dent concluded. "Let's go with it that way, Heather."

Required:

1. What is the difference in before-tax income between the CEO's and Heather's treatment of the situation?
2. Discuss Heather Meyer's ethical dilemma.

Judgment Case 11–11
Earnings management and accounting changes; impairment
● LO11–5, LO11–6, LO11–8

Companies often are under pressure to meet or beat Wall Street earnings projections in order to increase stock prices and also to increase the value of stock options. Some resort to earnings management practices to artificially create desired results.

Required:

1. How can a company manage earnings by changing its depreciation method? Is this an effective technique to manage earnings?
2. How can a company manage earnings by changing the estimated useful lives of depreciable assets? Is this an effective technique to manage earnings?
3. Using a fictitious example and numbers you make up, describe in your own words how asset impairment losses could be used to manage earnings. How might that benefit the company?

Trueblood Accounting Case 11–12
Accounting for impairment losses; property, plant, and equipment
● LO11–8

The following Trueblood case is recommended for use with this chapter. The case provides an excellent opportunity for class discussion, group projects, and writing assignments. The case, along with Professor's Discussion Material, can be obtained from the Deloitte Foundation at its website **www.deloitte.com/us/truebloodcases**.

Case 12–9: *Rough Waters Ahead*
This case concerns the impairment test for a cruise ship.

Judgment Case 11–13
Subsequent expenditures
● LO11–9

The Cummings Company charged various expenditures made during 2016 to an account called repairs and maintenance expense. You have been asked by your supervisor in the company's internal audit department to review the expenditures to determine if they were appropriately recorded. The amount of each of the transactions included in the account is considered material.

1. Engine tune-up and oil change on the company's 12 delivery trucks—$1,300.
2. Rearrangement of machinery on the main production line—$5,500. It is not evident that the rearrangement will increase operational efficiency.
3. Installation of aluminum siding on the manufacturing plant—$32,000.
4. Replacement of the old air conditioning system in the manufacturing plant with a new system—$120,000.
5. Replacement of broken parts on three machines—$1,500.
6. Annual painting of the manufacturing plant—$11,000.
7. Purchase of new forklift to move finished product to the loading dock—$6,000.
8. Patching leaks in the roof of the manufacturing plant—$6,500. The repair work did not extend the useful life of the roof.

Required:

For each of the transactions listed above, indicate whether the expenditure is appropriately charged to the repair and maintenance expense account, and if not, indicate the proper account to be charged.

Real World Case 11–14
Disposition and depreciation; Chapters 10 and 11; Caterpillar
● LO11–1

Real World Financials

Caterpillar Inc. (CAT) is a world leader in the manufacture of construction and mining equipment, diesel and natural gas engines, and industrial gas turbines. CAT reported the following in a disclosure note accompanying its 2013 financial statements:

($ in millions)	2013	2012
Property, plant and equipment	$31,316	$29,932
Less: Accumulated depreciation	(14,241)	(13,471)
Property, plant and equipment - Net	$17,075	$16,461

Also, Note 8 disclosed that the total cost of property, plant, and equipment included $688 and $723 (dollars in millions) in land at the end of 2013 and 2012, respectively. In addition, the statement of cash flows for the year ended December 31, 2013, reported the following as cash flows from investing activities:

($ in millions)	
Payments for property, plant and equipment	$(4,446)
Proceeds from disposition of property, plant and equipment	844

The statement of cash flows also reported 2013 depreciation and amortization of $3,087 million (depreciation of $2,710 and amortization of $377).

Required:

1. Assume that all property, plant, and equipment acquired during 2013 were purchased for cash. Determine the amount of gain or loss from dispositions of property, plant, and equipment that Caterpillar recognized during 2013.
2. Assume that Caterpillar uses the straight-line method to depreciate plant and equipment. What is the approximate average service life of CAT's depreciable assets?

Real World Case 11–15
Depreciation and depletion method; asset impairment; subsequent expenditures; Chevron

● LO11–2, LO11–3, LO11–8, LO11–9

Real World Financials

EDGAR, the Electronic Data Gathering, Analysis, and Retrieval system, performs automated collection, validation, indexing, and forwarding of submissions by companies and others who are required by law to file forms with the U.S. Securities and Exchange Commission (SEC). All publicly traded domestic companies use EDGAR to make the majority of their filings. (Some foreign companies file voluntarily.) Form 10-K, which includes the annual report, is required to be filed on EDGAR. The SEC makes this information available on the Internet.

Required:

1. Access EDGAR on the Internet. The web address is www.sec.gov.
2. Search for Chevron Corporation. Access the 10-K filing for most recent fiscal year. Search or scroll to find the financial statements and related notes.
3. Answer the following questions related to the company's property, plant, and equipment and intangible assets:
   a. Describe the company's depreciation and depletion policies.
   b. Describe the company's policy for subsequent expenditures made for plant and equipment.

IFRS Case 11–16
Subsequent valuation of property, plant, and equipment; comparison of U.S. GAAP and IFRS; GlaxoSmithKline

● LO11–10

Real World Financials

GlaxoSmithKline is a global pharmaceutical and consumer health-related products company located in the United Kingdom. The company prepares its financial statements in accordance with International Financial Reporting Standards.

Required:

1. Use the Internet to locate GlaxoSmithKline's most recent annual report. The address is www.gsk.com/investors. Locate the significant accounting policies disclosure note.
2. How does the company value its property, plant, and equipment? Does the company have any other options under IFRS for valuing these assets? How do these options differ from U.S. GAAP?
3. What are the company's policies for possible reversals of impairment losses for goodwill and for other non-current assets? How do these policies differ from U.S. GAAP?

Analysis Case 11–17
Depreciation and amortization

● LO11–2, LO11–4

PetSmart

Refer to the financial statements and related disclosure notes of PetSmart in Appendix B located at the back of the text.

Required:

1. What amount of depreciation and amortization did the company report in the fiscal year ended February 2, 2014?
2. What depreciation method is used for financial reporting purposes and what are the service lives of depreciable assets?

Air France–KLM Case

● LO11–10

IFRS

Air France–KLM (AF), a Franco-Dutch company, prepares its financial statements according to International Financial Reporting Standards. AF's financial statements and disclosure notes for the year ended December 31, 2013, are provided with all new textbooks. This material also is available at www.airfranceklm-finance.com.

Required:

1. AF's property, plant, and equipment is reported at cost. The company has a policy of not revaluing property, plant, and equipment. Suppose AF decided to revalue its flight equipment on December 31, 2013, and that the fair value of the equipment on that date was €10,000 million. Prepare the journal entry to record the revaluation assuming that the journal entry to record annual depreciation had already been recorded. (*Hint:* you will need to locate the original cost and accumulated depreciation of the equipment at the end of the year in the appropriate disclosure note.)

2. Under U.S. GAAP, what alternatives do companies have to value their property, plant, and equipment?
3. AF calculates depreciation of plant and equipment on a straight-line basis, over the useful life of the asset. Describe any differences between IFRS and U.S. GAAP in the calculation of depreciation.
4. When does AF test for the possible impairment of fixed assets? How does this approach differ from U.S. GAAP?
5. Describe the approach AF uses to determine fixed asset impairment losses. (*Hint:* see Note 4.14) How does this approach differ from U.S. GAAP?
6. The following is included in AF's disclosure note 4.12: "Intangible assets are held at initial cost less accumulated amortization and any accumulated impairment losses." Assume that on December 31, 2013, AF decided to revalue its Other intangible assets (see Note 18) and that the fair value on that date was determined to be €580 million. Amortization expense for the year already has been recorded. Prepare the journal entry to record the revaluation.

CPA Simulation 11–1

Fukisan Inc.
Depreciation; change in estimate

Test your knowledge of the concepts discussed in this chapter, practice critical professional skills necessary for career success, and prepare for the computer-based CPA exam by accessing our CPA simulations in the Connect library.

The Fukisan Inc. simulation tests your knowledge of calculating depreciation using various methods and accounting for the change in the useful life of a depreciable asset.

CHAPTER

12

Investments

OVERVIEW

In this chapter you will learn about various approaches used to account for investments that companies make in the debt and equity of other companies. An investing company always has the option to account for these investments at fair value, with changes in fair values reported on the income statement. However, depending on the nature of an investment, investors can use alternative accounting approaches that ignore most fair value changes (e.g., *held-to-maturity* investments) or that include fair value changes only in other comprehensive income (e.g., *available-for-sale* investments). And, when an equity investor can significantly influence an investee but does not control it, the investor can use the *equity method* of accounting, which ignores fair value changes but includes the investee's income when reporting the investor's income. In appendices to this chapter, you will learn about other types of investments, and also about how to deal with other-than-temporarily impairments. Where We're Headed boxes in the chapter describe ongoing efforts by the FASB and IASB to improve accounting standards with respect to investments.

LEARNING OBJECTIVES

After studying this chapter, you should be able to:

- **LO12–1** Demonstrate how to identify and account for investments classified for reporting purposes as held-to-maturity. *(p. 658)*
- **LO12–2** Demonstrate how to identify and account for investments classified for reporting purposes as trading securities. *(p. 661)*
- **LO12–3** Demonstrate how to identify and account for investments classified for reporting purposes as available-for-sale securities. *(p. 665)*
- **LO12–4** Explain what constitutes significant influence by the investor over the operating and financial policies of the investee. *(p. 682)*
- **LO12–5** Demonstrate how to account for investments accounted for under the equity method. *(p. 682)*
- **LO12–6** Explain the adjustments made in the equity method when the fair value of the net assets underlying an investment exceeds their book value at acquisition. *(p. 684)*
- **LO12–7** Explain how electing the fair value option affects accounting for investments. (*pp. 674* and *690*)
- **LO12–8** Discuss the primary differences between U.S. GAAP and IFRS with respect to investments. (*pp. 674, 675, 676, 677, 690, 702,* and *704*)

FINANCIAL REPORTING CASE

A Case of Coke

You are the lone accounting major in your five-member group in your Business Policy class. A part of the case your group is working on is the analysis of the financial statements of the **Coca-Cola Company**.

The marketing major in the group is confused by the following disclosure note from Coca-Cola's 2013 annual report:

NOTE 3: INVESTMENTS (in part)

Investments in debt and marketable securities, other than investments accounted for under the equity method, are classified as trading, available-for-sale or held-to-maturity. Our marketable equity investments are classified as either trading or available-for-sale with their cost basis determined by the specific identification method. Our investments in debt securities are carried at either amortized cost or fair value. Investments in debt securities that the Company has the positive intent and ability to hold to maturity are carried at amortized cost and classified as held-to-maturity. Investments in debt securities that are not classified as held-to-maturity are carried at fair value and classified as either trading or available-for-sale. Realized and unrealized gains and losses on trading securities and realized gains and losses on available-for-sale securities are included in net income. Unrealized gains and losses, net of deferred taxes, on available-for-sale securities are included in our consolidated balance sheets as a component of AOCI, except for the change in fair value attributable to the currency risk being hedged.

"They say unrealized gains and losses on available-for-sale securities are reported as part of AOCI. What's that? I don't see these gains and losses on the income statement," he complained. "And held-to-maturity securities—why are they treated differently? And what about equity method investments? On the balance sheet they have over $10 billion of investments accounted for under the equity method. They made over $600 million on those investments in 2013! Is that cash they can use?"

QUESTIONS

By the time you finish this chapter, you should be able to respond appropriately to the questions posed in this case. Compare your response to the solution provided at the end of the chapter.

1. How should you respond? Why are held-to-maturity securities treated differently from other investment securities? *(p. 657)*
2. Why are unrealized gains and losses on trading securities reported in the income statement? *(p. 661)*
3. Why are unrealized gains and losses on available-for-sale securities not reported in the income statement, but instead are in other comprehensive income, and then shown in accumulated other comprehensive income (AOCI) in the balance sheet? *(p. 666)*
4. Explain why Coke accounts for some of its investments by the equity method and what that means. *(p. 683)*

To finance its operations, and often the expansion of those operations, a corporation raises funds by selling equity securities (common and preferred stock) and debt securities (bonds and notes). These securities, also called financial instruments, are purchased as investments by individual investors, mutual funds, and also by other corporations. In later chapters we discuss equity and debt securities from the perspective of the issuing company. Our focus in this chapter is on the corporations that invest in debt and equity securities issued by other corporations as well as debt securities issued by governmental units (bonds, Treasury bills, and Treasury bonds).

Most companies invest in financial instruments issued by other companies. For some investors, these investments represent ongoing affiliations with the companies whose securities are acquired. For instance, recent investments include **Berkshire Hathaway**'s $28 billion acquisition of **Heinz**, the largest ketchup producer in the world, and **Comcast**'s $17 billion acquisition of **NBCUniversal** from General Electric, which improved Comcast's position as a leading media company. Some investments, though, are made not to obtain a favorable business relationship with another firm but simply to earn a return from the dividends or interest the securities pay or from increases in the market prices of the securities—the same reasons that might motivate you to buy stocks, bonds, or other investment securities.

With such diversity in investment objectives, it's not surprising that there is diversity in the approaches used to account for investments. As you'll discover when reading this chapter, investments are accounted for in five primary ways, depending on the nature of the investment relationship and the preferences of the investor. Before we discuss the approaches in detail, see the quick overview in Illustration 12–1.

In Part A of this chapter we discuss accounting for investments when the investor lacks significant influence over the operating and financial policies of the investee. In Part B we discuss accounting for "significant influence" investments. In both Parts A and B, we first discuss specific reporting methods and then discuss how the reporting changes if the investor elects the fair value option.

Illustration 12–1
Reporting Categories for Investments

Control Characteristics of the Investment	Reporting Method Used by the Investor
The investor *lacks significant influence* over the operating and financial policies of the investee:	
Investments in debt securities for which the investor has the "positive intent and ability" to hold to maturity	**Held-to-maturity ("HTM")**—investment reported at amortized cost*
Investments held in an active trading account	**Trading securities ("TS")**—investment reported at fair value (with unrealized holding gains and losses included in net income)
Other	**Securities available-for-sale ("AFS")**—investment reported at fair value (with unrealized holding gains and losses excluded from net income and reported in other comprehensive income)*
The investor *has significant influence* over the operating and financial policies of the investee:	
Typically the investor owns between 20% and 50% of the voting stock of the investee	**Equity method**—investment cost adjusted for subsequent earnings and dividends of the investee*
The investor *controls* the investee:	
The investor owns more than 50% of the investee	**Consolidation**—the financial statements of the investor and investee are combined as if they are a single company

*If the investor elects the *fair value option*, this type of investment also can be accounted for using the same approach that's used for trading securities, with the investment reported at fair value and unrealized holding gains and losses included in net income.

PART A

Investor Lacks Significant Influence

The reporting approaches we use for investments differ according to how the approaches account for one or more of the four critical events that an investor experiences in the life of an investment:

1. Purchasing the investment.

2. Recognizing investment revenue (interest in the case of debt, dividends in the case of equity).
3. Holding the investment during periods in which the investment's fair value changes (and thus incurring *unrealized holding* gains and losses, since the security has not yet been sold).
4. Selling the investment (and thus incurring *realized* gains and losses, since the security has been sold and the gains or losses actually incurred).

As shown in Illustration 12–1, when the investor lacks significant influence over the investee, the investment is classified in one of three categories: held-to-maturity securities (HTM), trading securities (TS), and available-for-sale securities (AFS). Each type of investment has its own reporting method. However, regardless of the investment type, investors can elect the "fair value option" that we discuss later in the chapter and classify HTM and AFS securities as TS. The key difference among the reporting approaches is how we account for unrealized holding gains and losses (critical event number 3 above), as shown in Illustration 12–2.

Illustration 12–2
Accounting for Unrealized Holding Gains and Losses When Investor Lacks Significant Influence

Reporting Approach	Treatment of Unrealized Holding Gains and Losses	Investment Reported in the Balance Sheet at
Held-to-maturity (HTM): used for debt that is planned to be held for its entire life	Not recognized	Amortized Cost
Trading (TS): used for debt or equity that is held in an active trading account for immediate resale.	Recognized in net income, and therefore in retained earnings as part of shareholders' equity	Fair Value
Available-for-sale (AFS): used for debt or equity that does not qualify as held-to-maturity or trading	Recognized in other comprehensive income, and therefore in accumulated other comprehensive income in shareholders' equity	Fair Value

Illustration 12–3 provides a description from a 2013 annual report of how the Bank of America accounts for its debt investments in each of the three reporting categories.

Illustration 12–3
Disclosure about Investments—Bank of America

Real World Financials

Note 1 (in part): Securities
Debt securities bought principally with the intent to buy and sell in the short term as part of the Corporation's trading activities are reported at fair value in trading account assets with unrealized gains and losses included in trading account profits. Debt securities purchased for longer term investment purposes, as part of asset and liability management (ALM) and other strategic activities are generally reported at fair value as available-for-sale (AFS) securities with net unrealized gains and losses included in accumulated OCI. . . . Debt securities which management has the intent and ability to hold to maturity are reported at amortized cost.

FINANCIAL Reporting Case

Q1, p. 655

Why treat unrealized gains and losses differently depending on the type of investment? As you know, the primary purpose of accounting is to provide information useful for making decisions. What's most relevant for that purpose is not necessarily the same for each investment a company might make. For example, a company might invest in corporate bonds to provide a steady return until the bonds mature, in which case day-to-day changes in market value may not be viewed as very relevant, so the held-to-maturity approach is preferable. On the other hand, a company might invest in the same bonds because it plans to sell them at a profit in the near future, in which case the day-to-day changes in market value could be viewed as very relevant, and the trading security or available-for-sale approach is preferable.

Let's examine the three reporting classifications, one by one.

Securities to Be Held to Maturity

LO12–1

Unlike a share of stock, a bond or other debt security has a specified date on which it matures. On its maturity date, the principal (also called the "face amount") is paid to investors. In the meantime, interest equal to a specified percentage of the principal is paid to investors on specified interest dates. Think of the principal and interest payments of the bond as a stream of cash flows that an investor will receive in exchange for purchasing the bond. The investor values that stream of cash flows using the prevailing market interest rate for debt of similar risk and maturity. If the interest rate paid by the bond (the "stated rate") is higher than the market rate, the bond can be sold for more than its maturity value (so it is "sold at a premium"). If the stated rate is lower than the market rate, the bond must be sold for less than its maturity value (so it is "sold at a discount"). For an example of valuing a bond, see Illustration 12–4.

Illustration 12–4

Bonds Purchased at a Discount

On July 1, 2016, Masterwear Industries issued $700,000 of 12% bonds, dated July 1. Interest of $42,000 is payable semiannually on June 30 and December 31. The bonds mature in three years, on June 30, 2019. The market interest rate for bonds of similar risk and maturity is 14%. The entire bond issue was purchased by United Intergroup, Inc.*

Calculation of the Price of the Bonds

			Present Values
Interest	$ 42,000 × 4.76654**	=	$200,195
Principal (face amount)	$700,000 × 0.66634†	=	466,438
Present value (price) of the bonds			$666,633

*The numbers in this illustration are the same as those in Illustration 14–3 in Chapter 14 (except for some differences in dates between the two chapters). This helps us to better appreciate in Chapter 14 how Masterwear's accounting for its bond liability to United compares to United's accounting for its investment in Masterwear bonds. Illustration 14–3 explains why we calculate the bond price this way.
**Present value of an ordinary annuity of $1: $n = 6$, $i = 7\%$ (Table 4).
†Present value of $1: $n = 6$, $i = 7\%$ (Table 2).
Note: Present value tables are provided at the end of this textbook. If you need to review the concept of the time value of money, refer to the discussions in Chapter 6.

Because interest is paid semiannually, the present value calculations use:
a. one-half the stated rate (6%),
b. one-half the market rate (7%), and
c. 6 (= 3 × 2) semiannual periods.

The market value of a fixed-rate investment moves in the opposite direction of market rates of interest.

The fair value of a bond changes when market interest rates change because investors use the current market interest rate to calculate the present value of the bond's future cash flows. If market rates of interest *rise* after a fixed-rate security is purchased, the present value of the fixed-interest payments declines. So, the fair value of the investment falls. Conversely, if market rates of interest *fall* after a fixed-rate security is purchased, the present value of the fixed interest payments increases, so the fair value of the investment rises.

Changes in market value are less relevant to an investor who will hold a security to its maturity regardless of those changes.

Increases and decreases in fair value between the day a debt security is acquired and the day it matures to a prearranged maturity value are less important if sale before maturity isn't an alternative. For this reason, if an investor has the "positive intent and ability" to hold the securities to maturity, investments in debt securities can be classified as **held-to-maturity (HTM)** and reported at their *amortized cost* in the balance sheet.[1] A debt security cannot be classified as held-to-maturity if the investor might sell it before maturity in response to changes in market prices or interest rates, to meet the investor's liquidity needs, or similar factors.

Let's use the bond from Illustration 12–4 to see how we account for an investment in held-to-maturity debt securities.

PURCHASE OF INVESTMENT. The journal entry to record the *purchase* of the HTM investments is:

All investment securities are initially recorded at cost.

July 1		
Investment in bonds (face amount)	700,000	
Discount on bond investment (difference)		33,367
Cash (price paid for the bonds)		666,633

[1]FASB ASC 320–10–25–1: Investments–Debt and Equity Securities–Overall–Recognition (previously "Accounting for Certain Investments in Debt and Equity Securities," *Statement of Financial Accounting Standards No. 115* (Norwalk, Conn.: FASB, 1993)).

Discount on bond investment is a contra asset to the investment in bonds asset account that serves to reduce the carrying value of the bond asset to its cost at the date of purchase.

RECOGNIZE INVESTMENT REVENUE. The Masterwear bonds pay cash interest at a rate of 12%, but were issued at a time when the market rate of interest was 14%. As a result, the bonds were sold at a discount that was large enough to provide bond purchasers with the same effective rate of return on their investment (14%) that they could get elsewhere in the market. Think of it this way: a little piece of that initial discount serves each period to make up the difference between the relatively low rate of interest that the bond pays (12%) and the higher rate of interest that the market demands (14%). As you learned in Chapter 7, recording interest each period as the *effective market rate of interest multiplied by the outstanding balance of the investment* is referred to as the effective interest method. This simply is an application of the accrual concept, consistent with accruing all revenues as they are earned, regardless of when cash is received.

The effective interest method calculates interest revenue as the market rate of interest multiplied by the outstanding balance of the investment.

Continuing our example, the initial investment is $666,633. Since the effective interest rate is 14%, interest recorded as revenue to the investor for the first six-month interest period is $46,664:

$666,633	×	[14% ÷ 2]	=	$46,664
Outstanding balance		Effective rate		Effective interest

However, the bond calls for semiannual interest payments of only $42,000—the *stated* rate (12% ÷ 2 = 6%) times the *face amount* ($700,000). As always, when only a portion of revenue is received, the remainder becomes an asset (a receivable). In this case we increase the investment by $4,664 by reducing the discount to $28,703 ($33,367 − 4,664). The journal entry to record the interest received for the first six months as investment revenue is:

December 31		
Cash (stated rate × face amount)	42,000	
Discount on bond investment (difference)	4,664	
Investment revenue (market rate × outstanding balance)		46,664

The amortized cost of the investment now is $700,000 − $28,703 = $671,297.

Illustration 12–5 demonstrates interest being recorded at the effective rate over the life of this investment. As you can see, the amortization of discount gradually increases the carrying value of the investment, until the investment reaches its face amount of $700,000 at the time when the debt matures.

We discuss accounting for discounts and premiums in much greater detail in Chapter 14.

Illustration 12–5

Amortization Schedule—Discount

Date	Cash Interest	Effective Interest	Increase in Balance	Outstanding Balance
	(6% × Face amount)	(7% × Outstanding balance)	(Discount reduction)	
7/1/2016				666,633
12/31/2016	42,000	.07 (666,633) = 46,664	4,664	671,297
6/30/2017	42,000	.07 (671,297) = 46,991	4,991	676,288
12/31/2017	42,000	.07 (676,288) = 47,340	5,340	681,628
6/30/2018	42,000	.07 (681,628) = 47,714	5,714	687,342
12/31/2018	42,000	.07 (687,342) = 48,114	6,114	693,456
6/30/2019	42,000	.07 (693,456) = 48,544*	6,544	700,000
	252,000	285,367	33,367	

*Rounded.

If a bond is purchased at a discount, less cash is received each period than the effective interest earned by the investor, so the unpaid difference increases the outstanding balance of the investment.

DO NOT RECOGNIZE UNREALIZED HOLDING GAINS AND LOSSES FOR HTM INVESTMENTS. Suppose that, as of the end of the first reporting period, the market interest rate for similar securities has fallen to 11%. A market participant valuing the Masterwear bonds at that time would do so at the current market interest rate (11%) because that's the rate of return she or he could get from similar bonds. Calculating the present value of the bonds using a lower discount rate results in a higher present value. Let's say that checking market prices in *The Wall Street Journal* indicates that the fair value of the Masterwear bonds on that date is $714,943. How will United account for this increase in fair value? If United views the bonds as HTM investments, that change in fair value will be ignored so long as it is viewed as temporary.[2] The investment simply will be recorded at amortized cost (the amounts in the right-hand column of the amortization schedule in Illustration 12–5). United will *disclose* the fair value of its HTM investments in a note to the financial statements, but will not recognize any fair value changes in the income statement or balance sheet.[3]

Additional Consideration

Using Excel, enter:
=PV(.055,5,42000,700000)
Output: 714,946

Using a calculator:
enter: N 5 I 5.5
PMT −42000
FM −700000
Output: = PV 714,946

Suppose the bonds are not traded on an active exchange. How would you determine the fair value of the Masterwear bonds on December 31, 2016? Recall from Chapter 1 that GAAP identifies different ways that a firm can determine fair value. If the Masterwear bonds are publicly traded, United can find the fair value by looking up the current market price (this way of obtaining fair value is consistent with "level one" of the fair value hierarchy). On the other hand, if the bonds are not publicly traded, United can calculate the fair value by using the present value techniques shown in Illustration 12–1 (this way of obtaining fair value is consistent with "level two" of the fair value hierarchy). With five interest periods remaining, and a current market rate of 11% (5.5% semi-annually), the present value would be $714,943:

			Present Values
Interest	$ 42,000 × 4.27028*	=	$179,352
Principal	$700,000 × 0.76513†	=	535,591
Present value of the bonds			$714,943

*Present value of an ordinary annuity of $1: $n = 5$, $i = 5.5\%$. (Table 4)
†Present value of $1: $n = 5$, $i = 5.5\%$. (Table 2)

SELL HTM INVESTMENTS. Typically, held-to-maturity investments are—you guessed it—held to maturity. However, suppose that due to unforeseen circumstances the company decided to sell its debt investment for $725,000 on January 15, 2017.[4] United would record the sale as follows (for simplicity we ignore any interest earned during 2017):

January 15, 2017		
Cash	725,000	
Discount on bond investment	28,703	
Investment in Masterwear bonds		700,000
Gain on sale of investments (to balance)		53,703

[2]If an unrealized loss from holding an HTM investment is not viewed as temporary, an "other-than-temporary impairment" (OTT impairment) may have to be recorded. We discuss OTT impairments in more detail in Appendix 12B.

[3]If United had chosen the fair value option for this investment, it would classify the investment as a trading security rather than as an HTM security. We'll illustrate the fair value option when we discuss trading securities.

[4]GAAP [FASB ASC 320–10–25–6: Investments–Debt and Equity Securities–Overall–Recognition, previously *SFAS No. 115*] lists major unforeseen events that could justify sale of an HTM investment. Sale for other reasons could call into question whether the company actually had the intent and ability to hold the investment to maturity. In that case, the company's HTM classification is viewed as "tainted," and the company can be required to reclassify *all* of its HTM investments as AFS investments and avoid using the HTM classification for two years. Similar provisions exist under IFRS for public companies.

In other words, United would record this sale just like any other asset sale, with a gain or loss determined by comparing the cash received with the carrying value (in this case, the amortized cost) of the asset given up.

We will revisit our discussion of investments in debt securities to be "held to maturity" in Chapter 14, "Bonds and Long-Term Notes." You'll see that accounting by the company that issues bonds and by the company that invests in those bonds is opposite but parallel; that is, the debt issuer records a liability and recognizes interest expense, while the debt investor records an asset and recognizes interest revenue.

Obviously, not all investments are intended to be held to maturity. When an investment is acquired to be held for an *unspecified period of time,* we classify the investment as either (a) "trading securities" or (b) "securities available-for-sale." These include investments in *debt* securities that are not classified as held-to-maturity and *equity* securities that have *readily determinable fair values.* You'll notice that, unlike held-to-maturity securities, we report investments in the other two categories at their fair values.

Trading Securities

● LO12–2

Some companies—primarily financial institutions—actively and frequently buy and sell securities, expecting to earn profits on short-term differences in price. Investments in debt or equity securities acquired principally for the purpose of selling them in the near term are classified as **trading securities**. The holding period for trading securities generally is measured in hours and days rather than months or years. These investments typically are reported among the investor's current assets. Relatively few investments are classified this way, because usually only banks and other financial operations invest in securities in the manner and for the purpose necessary to be categorized as trading securities.

Trading securities are actively managed in a trading account for the purpose of profiting from short-term price changes.

Just like other investments, trading securities initially are recorded at cost—that is, the total amount paid for the securities, including any brokerage fees. However, when a balance sheet is prepared in subsequent periods, this type of investment is written up or down to its fair value, or "marked to market."

Be sure to notice that fair value accounting is a departure from amortized cost, which is the way most assets are reported in balance sheets. Why the difference? For these investments, fair value information is more relevant than for other assets intended primarily to be used in company operations, like buildings, land and equipment, or for investments to be *held to maturity.*[5]

Unrealized holding gains and losses for trading securities are included in net income in the period in which fair value changes.

For instance, consider an investment in debt. As interest rates rise or fall, the fair value of the investment will decrease or increase. Movements in fair values are less relevant if the investment is to be held to maturity; the investor receives the same contracted interest payments and principal at maturity, regardless of changes in fair value.

However, if the debt investment is held for active trading, changes in market values, and thus market returns, provide an indication of management's success in deciding when to acquire the investment, when to sell it, whether to invest in fixed-rate or variable-rate securities, and whether to invest in long-term or short-term securities. For that reason, it makes sense to report unrealized holding gains and losses on trading securities in net income during a period that fair values change, even though those gains and losses haven't yet been realized through the sale of the securities.

To see how we account for trading securities, let's modify the example we used for HTM securities. We'll assume that those debt investments are held in an active trading portfolio, with United intending to profit from short-term changes in price. In addition, let's add a couple of equity (stock) investments to highlight that, while the HTM approach applies only to debt securities, the TS approach applies to both debt and equity securities. The relevant facts are included in Illustration 12–6. Assuming all investments are classified as trading securities, the accounting would be as follows.

FINANCIAL Reporting Case

Q2, p. 655

[5]Investments to be held to maturity, of course, include only debt securities.

Illustration 12–6

Accounting for Trading Securities and Securities Available-for-Sale

United Intergroup, Inc., buys and sells both debt and equity securities of other companies as investments. United's fiscal year-end is December 31. The following events during 2016 and 2017 pertain to the investment portfolio.

Purchase Investments July 1, 2016	• Purchased Masterwear Industries' 12%, 3-year bonds for $666,633 to yield an effective interest rate of 14%. • Purchased $1,500,000 of Arjent, Inc., common stock. • Purchased $1,000,000 of Bendac common stock.
Receive Investment Revenue December 31, 2016	• Received a semi-annual cash interest payment of $42,000 from Masterwear. • Received a cash dividend of $75,000 from Arjent. (Bendac does not pay dividends)
Adjust Investments to Fair Value December 31, 2016	• Valued the Masterwear bonds at $714,943. • Valued the Arjent stock at $1,450,000. • Valued the Bendac stock at $990,000.
Sell Investments January 15, 2017	• Sold the Masterwear bonds for $725,000. • Sold the Arjent stock for $1,446,000.
Adjust Remaining Investments to Fair Value December 31, 2017	• Valued the Bendac stock at $985,000.

PURCHASE INVESTMENTS. The journal entry to record the purchase of the bond investment is the same as it is for HTM securities. The journal entries to record the equity investments are even simpler, just exchanging one asset (cash) for another (investment):

All investment securities are recorded initially at cost.

July 1, 2016		
Investment in Masterwear bonds	700,000	
Discount on bond investment		33,367
Cash		666,633
Investment in Arjent stock	1,500,000	
Cash		1,500,000
Investment in Bendac stock	1,000,000	
Cash		1,000,000

RECOGNIZE INVESTMENT REVENUE. The journal entry to record the receipt of bond interest is the same as it is for HTM securities, with the carrying value of the investment increasing due to amortization of $4,664 of discount. The journal entry to record the receipt of dividends related to the Arjent equity investment is straightforward. There is no entry for the Bendac equity investment, because Bendac doesn't pay dividends.

Dividend and interest income are included in net income.

December 31, 2016		
Cash (6% × $700,000)	42,000	
Discount on bond investment (difference)	4,664	
Investment revenue (interest: 7% × $666,633)		46,664
Cash	75,000	
Investment revenue (dividends received)		75,000

ADJUST TRADING SECURITY INVESTMENTS TO FAIR VALUE (2016). Unlike HTM securities, trading securities are carried at fair value in the balance sheet, so their carrying value must be adjusted to fair value at the end of every reporting period. Rather than increasing or decreasing the investment account itself, we use a valuation allowance, *fair value adjustment,* to increase or decrease the carrying value of the investment. At the same time, we record an unrealized holding gain or loss that is included in net income in the period

Trading securities are adjusted to their fair value at each reporting date.

in which fair value changes (the gain or loss is *unrealized* because the securities haven't actually been sold). The next table summarizes the relevant facts for United's investments.

December 31, 2016

Security	Amortized Cost	Fair Value	Fair Value Adjustment
Masterwear	$ 671,297	$ 714,943	$ 43,646
Arjent	1,500,000	1,450,000	(50,000)
Bendac	1,000,000	990,000	(10,000)
Total	$3,171,297	$3,154,943	$(16,354)
	Existing balance in fair value adjustment:		–0–
	Increase (decrease) needed in fair value adjustment:		($ 16,354)

Fair Value Adjustment	
	0
	16,354
	16,354

United has an unrealized loss of $16,354. Note that, to determine the amount of unrealized holding gain or loss on the Masterwear bonds, United first identifies the bonds' *amortized cost* and then determines the amount necessary to adjust them to fair value:

Face amount of the bond	$700,000
Less: Discount on bond investment	
$33,367 initial discount	
(4,664) accumulated amortization	
$28,703 discount at 12/31/2016	(28,703)
Amortized cost of the bonds	671,297
+/− Fair value adjustment (plug)	**+ 43,646**
Fair value of the bond at 12/31/2016	$714,943

There is no discount to amortize for the equity investments, so for the Arjent and Bendac investments, their amortized cost is simply their initial cost. The journal entry to record the unrealized loss in United's fair value adjustment is:

December 31, 2016[6]		
Net unrealized holding gains and losses—I/S[7]	16,354	
Fair value adjustment		16,354

For trading securities, *unrealized* gains or losses are included in net income.

Additional Consideration

Don't Shoot the Messenger

Or, as written in *The Economist*, "Messenger, Shot: Accounting rules are under attack. Standard-setters should defend them. Politicians and banks should back off."[8] Using fair values that are hard to estimate is controversial. For example, during the recent financial crisis many financial services companies had to recognize huge unrealized losses associated with their investments. Some blamed their losses on GAAP for requiring estimates of fair value that were driven by depressed current market prices, argued that those losses worsened the financial crisis, and lobbied for a move away from fair value accounting. Others countered that these companies were using GAAP's requirement for fair value accounting as a "scapegoat" for their bad investment decisions. "Fair value accounting . . . does not create losses but rather reflects a firm's present condition," says Georgene Palacky, director of the CFA's financial reporting group."[9]

[6] Sometimes companies don't bother with a separate fair value adjustment account and simply adjust the investment account to fair value. Also, sometimes companies set up separate fair value adjustment accounts for each investment.

[7] We title this account "Net unrealized holding gains and losses—I/S" to highlight that, for trading securities, unrealized holding gains and losses are included in the income statement (I/S) in the period in which they occur.

[8] "Messenger, Shot," *The Economist*, April 8, 2009.

[9] Sarah Johnson, "The Fair Value Blame Game," CFO.com, March 19, 2008.

SELL TRADING SECURITY INVESTMENTS. To record the gain or loss realized on the sale of the Masterwear and Arjent investments, United records the receipt of cash ($725,000 for Masterwear and $1,446,000 for Arjent), removes all balance sheet accounts that are directly associated with the investments, and calculates the difference to determine realized gain or loss.[10]

***Realized* gain or loss for the difference between carrying value and the cash received from selling a trading security is included in net income.**

January 15, 2017		
Cash (amount received)	725,000	
Discount on bond investment (account balance)	28,703	
Investment in Masterwear bonds (account balance)		700,000
Gain on sale of investments (to balance)		53,703
Cash (amount received)	1,446,000	
Loss on sale of investments (to balance)	54,000	
Investment in Arjent stock (account balance)		1,500,000

When trading securities are sold, *unrealized* gains or losses that were recorded previously are removed from the fair value adjustment and net income at the end of the accounting period.

For the Masterwear bonds, this journal entry is identical to what United used when recording the sale of held-to-maturity investments. However, United isn't done yet. Now that those investments are sold, United needs to remove the fair value adjustment from the balance sheet. Also, because United has recognized in this period's net income the entire gain or loss *realized* on sale of the investments, it must back out of this period's net income any *unrealized* gains and losses that were included in net income in prior periods. That way, this period's net income includes only the fair value changes arising since the last period, and United avoids double counting gains and losses (once when unrealized, and again when realized). United can accomplish all of this when it adjusts its investment portfolio to fair value at the end of the reporting period.

ADJUST TRADING SECURITY INVESTMENTS TO FAIR VALUE (2017). The following table summarizes the situation at the end of 2017:

December 31, 2017

Security	Amortized Cost	Fair Value	Fair Value Adjustment
Masterwear	(sold)	–0–	–0–
Arjent	(sold)	–0–	–0–
Bendac	$1,000,000	$985,000	($15,000)
Total	$1,000,000	$985,000	($15,000)
		Existing balance in fair value adjustment:	($16,354)
		Increase (decrease) needed in fair value adjustment:	$ 1,354

Fair Value Adjustment

Debit	Credit
	16,354
1,354	
	15,000

The journal entry necessary to show the appropriate balance in the fair value adjustment at the end of 2017 is

December 31, 2017		
Fair value adjustment	1,354	
Net unrealized holding gains and losses—I/S		1,354

This journal entry serves two purposes: it (a) accounts for changes in the fair value of investments that have not been sold (in this case, Bendac), and (b) removes from the fair value adjustment and net income any unrealized holding gains or losses that were recognized in prior periods and that are associated with investments that were sold during the period (in this case, Masterwear and Arjent). We discuss those purposes in more detail when we show later in this chapter how these investments would be accounted for as available-for-sale securities.

[10]For purposes of this example, we ignore any unpaid interest associated with the bonds. In practice, that amount would be added to the sales price of the bonds and included in investment revenue.

FINANCIAL STATEMENT PRESENTATION. We present trading securities in the financial statements as follows:

- **Income Statement and Statement of Comprehensive Income:** For trading securities, fair value changes are included in the income statement in the periods in which they occur, regardless of whether they are realized or unrealized. Investments in trading securities do not affect other comprehensive income.
- **Balance Sheet:** Investments in trading securities are reported at fair value, typically as current assets, and do not affect accumulated other comprehensive income in shareholders' equity.
- **Cash Flow Statement:** Cash flows from buying and selling trading securities typically are classified as operating activities, because the financial institutions that routinely hold trading securities consider them as part of their normal operations. However, as discussed in more detail later, it may be appropriate to classify cash flows from buying and selling some trading securities as investing activities if they are not held for sale in the near term (which is particularly likely when an investment is classified as a trading security as a result of electing the fair value option).[11]

United's 2016 and 2017 financial statements will include the amounts shown in Illustration 12–7.

Illustration 12–7
Reporting Trading Securities

Income Statement	**2016**	**2017**
Revenues	$ ♦	$ ♦
Expenses	♦	♦
Other income (expense):		
Interest and dividend income	121,664[a]	–0–
Realized and unrealized gains and losses on investments	(16,354)[b]	1,057[c]
Tax expense	♦	♦
Net income	♦	♦
Balance Sheet		
Assets:		
Trading securities	3,154,943	985,000
Statement of Cash Flows (direct method)		
Operating Activities:		
Cash from investment revenue	117,000	–0–
Purchase of trading securities	(3,166,633)	–0–
Sale of trading securities	–0–	2,171,000

[a]$121,664 is the sum of $46,664 interest revenue from Masterwear and $75,000 dividends from Arjent.
[b]$16,354 is the net unrealized loss from the 2016 fair value adjustment.
[c]$1,057 is the $1,354 net unrealized gain from the 2017 fair value adjustment minus the $297 loss realized on sale of investments during 2017 (the $297 net realized loss results from the $54,000 loss realized on sale of the Arjent stock and the $53,703 gain realized on sale of the Masterwear bonds).

For trading securities, fair value changes affect net income in the period in which they occur.

Trading securities are reported at fair value in the balance sheet.

Cash flows from buying and selling trading securities are classified as operating activities.

Securities Available-for-Sale

● LO12–3

When you or I buy stock in a corporation, say **Coca-Cola**, we hope the market value will rise before we sell it. We also may look forward to the cash dividends Coca-Cola pays its shareholders every three months. We may even have planned when we will sell the stock, or we may intend to wait and see what happens to market prices. In either case, we aren't planning to trade the investment actively, but our investment is available to sell given the right combination of market factors and our own cash situation. These same considerations apply to companies that invest in the securities of other corporations or governmental entities.

Investments in available-for-sale securities typically are reported at their fair values.

[11]FASB ASC 320: Investments (previously "The Fair Value Option for Financial Assets and Financial Liabilities," *Statement of Financial Accounting Standards No. 159* (Norwalk, Conn.: FASB, 2007, par. A42)). The relevant paragraphs from the original standard are not codified in the FASB Research System as they primarily provide a basis for conclusions.

When a company acquires an investment, not for an active trading account (as a financial institution might) or to be held to maturity (which of course couldn't be stock because it has no maturity date), the company classifies its investment as **securities available-for-sale (AFS)**. Like trading securities, we report investments in AFS securities in the balance sheet at fair value. Unlike trading securities, though, unrealized holding gains and losses on AFS securities are *not* included in net income. Instead, they are reported in the statement of comprehensive income as other comprehensive income (OCI).

Comprehensive income includes not only net income, but also other changes in equity that don't arise from transactions with owners.

COMPREHENSIVE INCOME. You may recall from Chapter 4 that comprehensive income is a more all-encompassing view of changes in shareholders' equity, including not only net income but also all other changes in equity that do not arise from transactions with owners.[12] Comprehensive income therefore includes net income and *other comprehensive income (OCI)*. Both net income and OCI accumulate in shareholders' equity in the balance sheet, but in different accounts. While net income accumulates in retained earnings, OCI accumulates in *accumulated other comprehensive income (AOCI)*.

FINANCIAL Reporting Case

Q3, p. 655

RATIONALE FOR AFS TREATMENT OF UNREALIZED HOLDING GAINS AND LOSSES. Why use an approach for accounting for AFS securities that differs from that used for trading securities? The big concern is that including in net income unrealized holding gains and losses on AFS investments might make income appear more volatile than it really is. For example, many companies purchase AFS investments for the purpose of having the changes in fair value of those investments offset changes in the fair value of liabilities. This *hedging* insulates the company from risk and ensures that earnings are stable. However, if fair value changes for investments were to be recognized in income (as is the case with trading securities), but the offsetting fair value changes for liabilities were not recognized in income as well, we could end up with income appearing very volatile when in fact the underlying assets and liabilities are hedged effectively.[13]

More generally, because AFS securities are likely to be held for multiple reporting periods, one could argue that there is sufficient time for unrealized holding gains in some periods to balance out with unrealized holding losses in other periods, so including unrealized holding gains and losses in income would confuse investors by making income appear more volatile than it really is over the long run. Of course, one could counter-argue that these unrealized holding gains and losses still are relevant, given that each period an investor has discretion over whether or not to continue holding the security or sell that security to realize a gain or loss.

To consider accounting for AFS investments, refer to the facts shown in Illustration 12–6. Let's assume now that United classifies its investments as AFS rather than trading securities.

PURCHASE INVESTMENTS. The journal entries to record the purchase of the investments are the same for AFS securities as they are for trading securities:

All investment securities are initially recorded at cost.

July 1, 2016		
Investment in Masterwear bonds	700,000	
Discount on bond investment		33,367
Cash		666,633
Investment in Arjent stock	1,500,000	
Cash		1,500,000
Investment in Bendac stock	1,000,000	
Cash		1,000,000

[12]Transactions with owners primarily include dividends and the sale or purchase of shares of the company's stock.

[13]The option to report in earnings changes in the fair value of liabilities was not permitted at the time the FASB wrote the initial standard (*SFAS No. 115*) that specified appropriate accounting for investments in debt and equity securities. As we will see in Chapter 14, that option now is allowed.

RECOGNIZE INVESTMENT REVENUE. The journal entries to record the receipt of investment revenue also are the same for AFS securities as they are for trading securities.

December 31, 2016		
Cash (6% × $700,000)	42,000	
Discount on bond investment	4,664	
Investment revenue (interest: 7% × $666,633)		46,664
Cash	75,000	
Investment revenue (dividends received)		75,000

Interest income and dividends on AFS investments are included in net income.

ADJUST AFS INVESTMENTS TO FAIR VALUE (2016). Let's first recall the facts:

December 31, 2016

Security	Amortized Cost	Fair Value	Fair Value Adjustment
Masterwear	$ 671,297	$ 714,943	$ 43,646
Arjent	1,500,000	1,450,000	(50,000)
Bendac	1,000,000	990,000	(10,000)
Total	$3,171,297	$3,154,943	$ (16,354)
	Existing balance in fair value adjustment:		–0–
	Increase (decrease) needed in fair value adjustment:		($ 16,354)

Fair Value Adjustment

	0
	16,354
	16,354

Like trading securities, AFS securities are adjusted to fair value at the end of each reporting period, which produces an unrealized holding gain or loss due to holding the securities while their fair values change. The journal entry to record United's unrealized holding loss is:

December 31, 2016		
Net unrealized holding gains and losses—OCI[14]	16,354	
Fair value adjustment		16,354

AFS securities are adjusted to their fair value at each reporting date.

Notice that the amount of unrealized holding loss is the same as with trading securities. What differs is that the net unrealized holding loss of $16,354 is included in net income for trading securities and in OCI for AFS securities.[15] At the end of the reporting period the net unrealized holding loss ends up being closed to a shareholders' equity account for both approaches. What differs is that it gets closed to retained earnings for trading securities and to AOCI for AFS securities.

For AFS securities, unrealized holding gains and losses from fair value changes are not included in net income, but instead are recorded as OCI.

SELL AFS INVESTMENTS. AFS investments require the same journal entry on the date of sale as is made to record the sale of trading securities. United simply records the receipt of cash, removes from the balance sheet any accounts that are directly associated with the investment, and calculates the difference to determine realized gain or loss.

January 15, 2017		
Cash (amount received)	725,000	
Discount on bond investment (account balance)	28,703	
Investment in Masterwear bonds (account balance)		700,000
Gain on sale of investments (to balance)		53,703
Cash (amount received)	1,446,000	
Loss on sale of investments (to balance)	54,000	
Investment in Arjent stock (account balance)		1,500,000

Realized gain or loss for the difference between carrying value and the cash received from selling an AFS investment is included in net income.

[14]We title this account "Net unrealized holding gains and losses—OCI" to highlight that, for available-for-sale securities, unrealized holding gains and losses are included in other comprehensive income (OCI) in the period in which they occur.

[15]As with trading securities, we could have not used a separate valuation allowance and simply adjusted the AFS investment account itself to fair value, and we also could set up separate valuation allowances and record separate journal entries for each AFS investment.

When AFS securities are sold, *unrealized* gains or losses that were recorded previously are removed from the fair value adjustment and OCI.

United also needs to adjust the fair value adjustment account and AOCI to remove any unrealized gains or losses previously recorded that relate to the sold investments. That is typically done at the end of the accounting period as part of the journal entry that adjusts the AFS investment portfolio to fair value, as we see below.

ADJUST AFS INVESTMENTS TO FAIR VALUE (2017). The following table summarizes the situation at the end of 2017:

Fair Value Adjustment

	16,354
1,354	
	15,000

December 31, 2017

Security	Amortized Cost	Fair Value	Fair Value Adjustment
Masterwear	(sold)	–0–	–0–
Arjent	(sold)	–0–	–0–
Bendac	$1,000,000	$985,000	($15,000)
Total	$1,000,000	$985,000	($15,000)
	Existing balance in fair value adjustment:		($16,354)
	Increase (decrease) needed in fair value adjustment:		$ 1,354

This analysis indicates that United needs to increase the fair value adjustment by $1,354 and record an unrealized gain of the same amount in OCI.

December 31, 2017		
Fair value adjustment	1,354	
Net unrealized holding gains and losses—OCI		1,354

As mentioned when we covered accounting for trading securities, this journal entry serves two purposes: it (a) accounts for changes in the fair value of investments that have not been sold (in this case, Bendac), and (b) removes from the fair value adjustment and net income any unrealized holding gains or losses that were recognized in prior periods and that are associated with investments that were sold during the period (in this case, Masterwear and Arjent).

($5,000)	to add 2017 unrealized loss associated with investments not sold
6,354	to remove 2016 net unrealized loss that's no longer unrealized
$1,354	2017 adjustment to OCI

Let's consider the two purposes separately.

New changes in the fair value of investments held. The first purpose of the journal entry is to record in OCI any new unrealized gains or losses associated with investments that have not been sold. For United, that's the Bendac stock. The new unrealized gain or loss equals whatever amount is necessary to report the Bendac investment at fair value as of the end of 2017.

$1,000,000	initial cost of Bendac stock
(985,000)	fair value at the end of 2017
$ 15,000	balance needed at end of 2017
(10,000)	balance at end of 2016
$ 5,000	new unrealized loss in 2017

If the 2017 journal entry had focused only on this first purpose, the journal entry would have been to recognize an unrealized holding loss of $5,000:

Net unrealized holding gains and losses—OCI	5,000	
Fair value adjustment		5,000

Reclassification adjustment. The second purpose of the journal entry is to remove from OCI any amounts associated with *sold* investments. What amounts must United consider? Last year, in 2016, United recorded a net unrealized loss of $6,354 on the Arjent and Masterwear investments as part of the $16,354 fair value adjustment made at the end of that year.

$50,000	2016 unrealized loss for the Arjent stock
43,646	2016 unrealized gain for the Masterwear bonds
$ 6,354	net unrealized loss in 2016

If the *2016* fair value adjustment had only included the net unrealized loss on the Arjent and Masterwear investments, it would have been:

For AFS securities, *unrealized* gains and losses affect OCI and accumulate in AOCI until such time as the investment is sold.

Net unrealized holding gains and losses—OCI	6,354	
Fair value adjustment		6,354

Because those investments have now been sold, United must reverse this entry in 2017 to remove their effects from OCI and the fair value adjustment. If the 2017 journal entry had focused only on this second purpose, it would have been:

Fair value adjustment	6,354	
Net unrealized holding gains and losses—OCI		6,354

See how the two purposes combine to create the single journal entry we use?

Fair value adjustment ($6,354 − 5,000)	1,354	
Net unrealized holding gains and losses—OCI		1,354

Now, why is this often referred to as a "reclassification adjustment"? Remember that United included a $6,354 unrealized loss in 2016 OCI (and therefore in AOCI). Then, in 2017, it backed out that amount from OCI (and AOCI) as part of the fair value adjustment entry, and included the realized gain or loss in net income (and therefore retained earnings) as part of the journal entry that recorded the sale of those investments. From the perspective of shareholders' equity, the amount was basically reclassified from AOCI to retained earnings in the period of sale.[16]

Note that we don't separately *record* this reclassification. That happens automatically as part of the fair value adjustment entry at the end of the period. What we do is *report* the reclassification in the statement of comprehensive income, as you will see in the next section.

Additional Consideration

Available-for-Sale Investments and Income Taxes

Regardless of whether an investment is classified as TS or AFS, the same amount of unrealized gain or loss is recognized each period. What differs is whether that unrealized gain or loss is reported in net income (for TS) or as OCI (for AFS securities). Regardless of whether the investment is TS or AFS, total shareholders' equity ends up equaling the same amount, because net income is closed to retained earnings and OCI is closed to AOCI. But what about taxes? Tax expense affects net income, so retained earnings includes after-tax amounts. For AOCI to be equivalent to retained earnings, it also should include only after-tax amounts. Therefore, adjustments must be made to OCI and AOCI to account for tax effects. Typically these adjustments also give rise to deferred tax assets and liabilities, as unrealized holding gains and losses rarely affect the current period's taxes payable. The effect of taxes on each component of OCI must be disclosed in the notes to the financial statements or presented in the statement in which OCI is presented.

[16]Reclassification also avoids double accounting with respect to comprehensive income and equity. If United didn't back out the 2016 unrealized loss from 2017 OCI, it would end up having included it in comprehensive income twice, once in OCI (2016) and once in net income (2017), thereby overstating total shareholders' equity.

FINANCIAL STATEMENT PRESENTATION. We present AFS securities in the financial statements as follows:

- **Income Statement and Statement of Comprehensive Income:** *Realized* gains and losses are shown in net income in the period in which securities are sold. *Unrealized* gains and losses are shown in OCI in the periods in which changes in fair value occur, and reclassified out of OCI in the periods in which securities are sold.
- **Balance Sheet:** Investments in AFS securities are reported at fair value. *Unrealized* gains and losses affect AOCI in shareholders' equity, and are reclassified out of AOCI in the periods in which securities are sold.
- **Cash Flow Statement:** Cash flows from buying and selling AFS securities typically are classified as investing activities.

United's 2016 and 2017 financial statements will include the amounts shown in Illustration 12–8.

Illustration 12–8

Reporting Available-for-Sale Securities

Only *realized* gains and losses are included in net income.

Other comprehensive income includes *unrealized* holding gains and losses *that occur during the reporting period.*

AFS securities are reported at fair value.

AOCI (in shareholders' equity) includes net unrealized holding gains or losses *accumulated over the current and prior periods.*

Cash flows from buying and selling AFS securities are classified as investing activities.

	2016	2017
Comprehensive Income Statement		
Revenues	$ ♦	$ ♦
Expenses	♦	♦
Other income (expense):		
Interest and dividend income	121,664[a]	–0–
Realized net loss on sale of investments	–0–	(297)[c]
Tax Expense	♦	♦
Net income	♦	♦
Other comprehensive income (loss) items (OCI):[17]		
Unrealized holding gains (losses) on investments	(16,354)[b]	(5,000)[d]
Reclassification adjustment for net gains and losses included in net income	–0–	6,354[e]
Total	(16,354)	1,354
Comprehensive income	♦	♦
Balance Sheet		
Assets:		
Available-for-sale securities	3,154,943	985,000
Stockholders' equity:		
Accumulated other comprehensive income (AOCI)	(16,354)	(15,000)
Statement of Cash Flows (direct method)		
Operating Activities:		
Cash from investment revenue	117,000	–0–
Investing Activities:		
Purchase of available-for-sale securities	(3,166,633)	–0–
Sale of available-for-sale securities	–0–	2,171,000

[a]$121,664 is the sum of $46,664 interest revenue from Masterwear and $75,000 dividends from Arjent.
[b]$16,354 is the net unrealized loss from the 2016 fair value adjustment.
[c]$297 is the loss realized on sale of investments during 2017, resulting from the $54,000 loss realized on sale of the Arjent stock and the $53,703 gain realized on sale of the Masterwear bonds.
[d]$5,000 is the new net unrealized loss included in the 2017 fair value adjustment for Bendac.
[e]$6,354 is the reclassification adjustment included in the 2017 fair value adjustment to remove from AOCI amounts associated with investments that now have been sold.

[17]This illustration follows ASU 2011-05 (Comprehensive Income (Topic 220): *Presentation of Comprehensive Income* (Norwalk, Conn.: FASB 2011)), which requires that, for items reclassified from OCI to net income, reclassification adjustments be presented on the face of the financial statement where the components of net income and OCI are presented. Prior to ASU 2011-05, reclassification adjustments typically were only disclosed in the notes.

Individual securities available for sale are classified as either current or noncurrent assets, depending on how long they're likely to be held. An example from the 2013 annual report of **Cisco Systems** is shown in Illustration 12–9.

Item 1A: Risk Factors (in part)
We maintain an investment portfolio of various holdings, types, and maturities. These securities are generally classified as available-for-sale and, consequently, are recorded on our Consolidated Balance Sheets at fair value with unrealized gains or losses reported as a component of accumulated other comprehensive income, net of tax.

Note 8: Investments (in part)
The following tables summarize the Company's available-for-sale investments (in millions):

July 27, 2013	Amortized Cost	Gross Unrealized Gains	Gross Unrealized Losses	Fair Value
Fixed income securities:				
U.S. Government securities	$ 27,814	$ 22	$ (13)	$ 27,823
U.S. Gov't agency securities	3,083	7	(1)	3,089
Non-U.S. Gov't agency securities	1,094	3	(2)	1,095
Corporate debt securities	7,876	55	(50)	7,881
Total fixed income securities	39,867	87	(66)	39,888
Publicly traded equity securities	2,063	738	(4)	2,797
Total	$ 41,930	$ 825	$ (70)	$ 42,685

Illustration 12–9
Investments in Securities Available-for-Sale—Cisco Systems

Real World Financials

Comparison of HTM, TS, and AFS Approaches

Illustration 12–10 compares accounting for the Masterwear bonds under the three different approaches used when an investor lacks significant influence.

Illustration 12–10 Comparison of HTM, TS, and AFS Approaches

	Held-to-Maturity (Htm)	Trading (TS)	Available-for-Sale (AFS)
Purchase bonds at a discount	Investments 700,000 Discount 33,367 Cash 666,633	Same as HTM	Same as HTM
Receive investment revenue	Cash 42,000 Discount 4,664 Invest. income 46,664	Same as HTM	Same as HTM
Adjust to fair value	No entry (unless impaired)	FV adjustment 43,646 Net unrealized gain/loss—I/S 43,646	FV adjustment 43,646 Net unrealized gain/loss—OCI 43,646
Sell bonds for a realized gain	Discount 28,703 Cash 725,000 Investments 700,000 Gain 53,703	Recognize gain or loss: Same as HTM Reverse out previously recorded unrealized gain or loss that's no longer unrealized (automatically part of next adjustment to fair value): Net unrealized gain/loss—I/S 43,646 FV adjustment 43,646	Recognize gain or loss: Same as HTM Reverse out previously recorded unrealized gain or loss that's no longer unrealized (automatically part of next adjustment to fair value): Net unrealized gain/loss—OCI 43,646* FV adjustment 43,646

*Reported as a reclassification adjustment in the statement of comprehensive income.

This side-by-side comparison highlights several aspects of these accounting approaches:

- To record the purchase of an investment and the receipt of investment revenue, we use identical entries in all three approaches.
- To record changes in fair value, the entries we use for TS and AFS securities have the same effect on the investment (via the fair value adjustment valuation allowance) and the same eventual effect on shareholders' equity. What differs is whether the unrealized gain or loss is recognized in the income statement and then in retained earnings (TS) or recognized in OCI and then in AOCI (AFS).
- To record the sale of the security, we use identical entries in all three approaches. For TS and AFS securities, the fair value adjustment and unrealized holding gains and losses associated with sold securities are dealt with automatically as part of the next adjustment to fair value.
- Regardless of approach, the cash flows are the same, and the same total amount of gain or loss is recognized in the income statement (TS: $43,646 in 2016 + [$53,703 − $43, 646] in 2017 = $53,703 total; AFS and HTM: $53,703 in 2017). Thus, the question is not how much total net income is recognized, but *when* that net income is recognized.

International Financial Reporting Standards

Accounting for Investments When Investor Lacks Significant Influence. Until recently, *IAS No. 39*[18] was the standard that specified appropriate accounting for investments under IFRS. The primary categories in *IAS No. 39* are similar to those in U.S. GAAP, consisting of "Fair Value through Profit & Loss" ("FVPL," similar to TS), HTM, and AFS.

IFRS No. 9,[19] amended July 24, 2014, will be required after January 1, 2018, and earlier adoption is allowed in some jurisdictions, so until 2018 either *IAS No. 39* or *IFRS No. 9* might be in effect for a particular company. *IFRS No. 9* eliminates the HTM and AFS classifications, replaced by new classifications that are more restrictive. Specifically, under *IFRS No. 9:*

- Investments in debt securities are classified either as amortized cost (accounted for like HTM investments in U.S. GAAP), fair value through other comprehensive income ("FVOCI," accounted for like AFS investments) or fair value through profit or loss ("FVPL," accounted for like trading securities). Classification depends on two criteria: (1) whether the investment's contractual cash flows consist solely of payments of principal and interest (this criterion is called "SPPI"), and (2) whether the business purpose of the investment is to collect contractual cash flows, sell investments, or both. If the investment qualifies as SPPI and is held only to collect cash flows, it is classified as amortized cost. If it qualifies as SPPI and is held both to collect cash flows and potentially be sold, it is classified as FVOCI. Otherwise it is classified as FVPL.
- Investments in equity securities are classified as either "FVPL" ("Fair Value through Profit & Loss") or "FVOCI" ("Fair Value through Other Comprehensive Income"). If the equity is held for trading, it must be classified as FVPL, but otherwise the company can irrevocably elect to classify it as FVOCI. The FVOCI classification is similar to AFS in U.S. GAAP. However, there is an important difference between accounting for AFS in U.S. GAAP and accounting for FVOCI under IFRS No. 9, which applies to equity (but not debt) investments. Like the AFS classification, the FVOCI category includes *unrealized* gains and losses in OCI. However, unlike AFS, *realized* gains and losses on equity investments are not reclassified out of OCI and into net income when the investment is later sold. Rather, the accumulated gain or loss associated with a sold investment is just transferred from AOCI to retained earnings (both shareholders' equity accounts), without passing through the income statement.

One other difference between U.S. GAAP and IFRS is worth noting. U.S. GAAP allows specialized accounting (beyond the scope of this textbook) for particular industries like securities brokers/dealers, investment companies, and insurance companies. IFRS does not.

[18] "Financial Instruments: Recognition and Measurement," *International Accounting Standard No. 39* (IASCF), as amended effective January 1, 2014.

[19] "Financial Instruments," *International Financial Reporting Standard No. 9* (IASCF), November 12, 2009, as amended effective July 24, 2014.

Where We're Headed

Classifying and Measuring Investments. For several years the FASB has collaborated with the IASB in an attempt to develop a converged approach to accounting for investments. The FASB issued two exposure drafts of proposed accounting standards updates, with the second exposure draft based on an approach that is similar to *IFRS No. 9* in many respects. However, based on feedback from U.S. constituents, the FASB concluded that the costs of making large changes in this area outweigh the benefits, so in early 2014 the FASB decided to abandon its efforts to converge accounting in this area and instead will work independently to improve existing U.S. GAAP. The most important change likely to occur in the near term is to stop allowing equity investments (investments in stock) to be accounted for as AFS.[20] If this change is implemented, investments in all publicly listed equity investments for which the investor lacks significant influence will be accounted for as TS, with unrealized gains and losses recognized in net income rather than OCI.

Transfers between Reporting Categories

At acquisition, an investor assigns debt and equity securities to one of the three reporting classifications—held-to-maturity, available-for-sale, or trading. At each reporting date, the appropriateness of the classification is reassessed. For instance, if the investor no longer has the ability to hold certain securities to maturity and will now hold them for resale, those securities would be reclassified from HTM to AFS. When a security is reclassified between two reporting categories, the security is transferred at its fair value on the date of transfer. Any unrealized holding gain or loss at reclassification should be accounted for *in a manner consistent with the classification into which the security is being transferred.* A summary is provided in Illustration 12–11.

A transfer of a security between reporting categories is accounted for at fair value and in accordance with *the new reporting classification*.

Illustration 12–11 Transfer between Investment Categories

Transfer from:	To:	Unrealized Gain or Loss from Transfer at Fair Value
Either HTM or AFS	Trading	Include in current net income the total unrealized gain or loss, as if it all occurred in the current period.
Trading	Either HTM or AFS	Include in current net income any unrealized gain or loss that occurred in the current period prior to the transfer. (Unrealized gains and losses that occurred in prior periods already were included in net income in those periods.)
Held-to-maturity	Available-for-sale	No current income effect. Report total unrealized gain or loss as a separate component of shareholders' equity (in AOCI).
Available-for-sale	Held-to-maturity	No current income effect. Don't write off any existing unrealized holding gain or loss in AOCI, but amortize it to net income over the remaining life of the security (fair value amount becomes the security's amortized cost basis).

[20]For the current status of this project, see "Accounting for Financial Instruments: Classification and Measurement" under "Projects" at www.fasb.org.

Reclassifications are quite unusual, so when they occur, disclosure notes should describe the circumstances that resulted in the transfers. Other note disclosures are described in a later section.

International Financial Reporting Standards

● LO12–8

Transfers Between Investment Categories. Until recently, IFRS did not allow transfers out of the "Fair Value through P&L" (FVPL) classification (which is roughly equivalent to the trading securities classification in U.S. GAAP). However, in October 2008 the IASB responded to the financial crisis underway at that time by amending *IAS No. 39* to allow transfers of debt investments out of the FVPL category into AFS or HTM in "rare circumstances," and indicated that the financial crisis qualified as one of those circumstances.[21] The change was justified as increasing convergence to U.S. GAAP, which also allows transfers out of the trading security category, but in fact reclassifications in U.S. GAAP continue to be rarer events than occurred under IFRS with this change.

IFRS ILLUSTRATION

This change allowed banks in October 2008 to transfer investments out of the FVPL category as of July 1, 2008, and thus avoid recognizing in earnings the losses they knew had already occurred during the third quarter of 2008. The effect on bank profits was substantial. A study by J. P. Morgan indicated that 32 of 43 West European banks it covered reclassified assets worth almost €620 billion, increasing pretax profits by almost €27 billion.[22]

Lloyds Banking Group of the United Kingdom wrote the following explanation:

Real World Financials

Note 49 Financial Risk Management (in part)

Reclassification of Financial Assets

In accordance with the amendment to IAS 39 as disclosed in note 2, the Group reviewed the categorisation of its assets classified as held for trading and available-for-sale financial assets. On the basis that there was no longer an active market for some of those assets, which are therefore more appropriately managed as loans, the Group reclassified £2,993 million of assets classified as held for trading (measured at fair value through profit or loss immediately prior to reclassification) to loans and receivables with effect from 1 July 2008 . . . If the assets had not been transferred and had been kept as held for trading, a loss of £347 million would have been recognised in the income statement for the six months to 31 December 2008 within net trading income.

Under *IFRS No. 9* (discussed earlier in this chapter), transfers of debt investments between the FVPL and the amortized cost categories can occur only if the company changes its business model with respect to the debt investment. No transfers of equity investments between the FVPL and FVOCI categories are allowed.

Fair Value Option

● LO12–7

TS already are accounted for at fair value, so there is no need to choose the fair value option for them.

You may recall from Chapter 1 that GAAP allows a fair value option that permits companies to elect to account for most financial assets and liabilities at fair value. Under the fair value option, unrealized gains and losses are recognized in net income in the period in which they occur. That accounting approach should sound familiar—it's the same approach we use to account for trading securities.

Choosing the fair value option for HTM and AFS investments just means reclassifying those investments as TS.

Here's how the fair value option works for these investments. When a security that qualifies for HTM or AFS treatment is purchased, the investor makes an irrevocable decision about whether to elect the fair value option. The company can elect the fair value option for some securities and not for identical others—it's entirely up to the company, but the company has to explain in the notes why it made a partial election. If the fair value option is elected for a security that would normally be accounted for as HTM or AFS, the company just classifies that security as a trading security, and that's how it appears in the financial

[21]"Reclassification of Financial Assets" *Amendments to IAS 39 Financial Instruments: Recognition and Measurement and IFRS 7 Financial Instruments: Disclosures,* IASB, October 2008.

[22]J.P. Morgan, *IAS 39 Reclassification: Impact on Banks' FY 08 Results and Equity,* May 11, 2009.

statements.[23] The only difference is that, unlike most trading securities, purchases and sale of investments accounted for under the fair value option are likely to be classified as investing activities in the statement of cash flows, because those investments are not held for sale in the near term and therefore are not operational in nature. Also, note that electing the fair value option is irrevocable. If a company elects the fair value option and later believes that the fair value of an investment is likely to decline, it can't change the election and discontinue use of fair value accounting.

Why allow the fair value option? Recall that a primary reason for creating the AFS approach was to allow companies to avoid excess earnings volatility that would result from reporting in earnings the fair value changes of only part of a hedging arrangement. As described in Appendix A of the text, other accounting rules apply to hedging arrangements that involve derivatives, but those rules are very complex and don't cover all forms of hedging arrangements. The fair value option simplifies this process by allowing companies to choose whether to use fair value for most types of financial assets and liabilities. Thus, when a company enters into a hedging arrangement, it just has to make sure to elect the fair value option for each asset and liability in the hedging arrangement, and fair value changes of those assets and liabilities will be included in earnings.

International Financial Reporting Standards

Fair Value Option. International accounting standards are more restrictive than U.S. standards for determining when firms are allowed to elect the fair value option. Under both *IAS No. 39* and *IFRS No. 9,* companies can elect the fair value option only in specific circumstances. For example, a firm could elect the fair value option for an asset or liability in order to avoid the "accounting mismatch" that occurs when some parts of a fair value risk-hedging arrangement are accounted for at fair value and others are not. Although U.S. GAAP indicates that the intent of the fair value option is to address these sorts of circumstances, it does not require that those circumstances exist.

● LO12–8

Impairment of Investments

An "other-than-temporary" impairment loss is recognized in net income even though the security hasn't been sold.

In this chapter we've seen that declines (as well as increases) in the fair value of some investments are reported in earnings. For instance, if the fair value of an investment in trading securities declines, we reduce the reported amount of that investment in the balance sheet and include the loss from the fair value decline in the income statement. Likewise, if the investor has elected the fair value option for HTM or AFS investments, those investments are accounted for as trading securities, so fair value changes always are recognized in earnings. Otherwise, fair value changes for HTM and AFS investment typically are not recognized in earnings.

However, there is an exception. If the fair value of an HTM or AFS investment declines below the amortized cost of the investment, and that decline is deemed to be *other-than-temporary (OTT),* the company recognizes an OTT impairment loss in earnings. The specific process for determining whether an investment has an OTT impairment differs between equity and debt investments.[24] For equity investments, the question is whether the company has the intent and ability to hold the investment until fair value recovers. If that isn't the case, the company recognizes an OTT impairment loss in earnings and reduces the carrying value of the investment in the balance sheet by that amount. For debt investments, the process is more complicated than for equity investments, both in determining whether an impairment is OTT and in determining the amount of the impairment to include in earnings. For both equity and debt investments, after an OTT impairment is recognized, the ordinary treatment of

[23]FASB ASC 825–10–25: Financial Instruments–Overall–Recognition (previously "The Fair Value Option for Financial Assets and Financial Liabilities," *Statement of Financial Accounting Standards No. 159* (Norwalk, Conn.: FASB, 2007, par. 29)).

[24]FASB ASC 320–10–35: Investments–Overall–Subsequent Measurement (previously "Recognition and Presentation of Other-Than-Temporary Impairments," *FASB Staff Position No. 115-2 and 124-2* (Norwalk, Conn.: FASB April 9, 2009)).

unrealized gains and losses is resumed; that is, further changes in fair value are reported in OCI for AFS investments and not recognized for HTM investments. An in-depth discussion of accounting for OTT impairments is provided in Appendix 12B to this chapter.

Where We're Headed

Impairments. As discussed in Chapter 7, as of the date this text is written it appears that U.S. GAAP will change the way we account for OTT impairments of debt investments.[25] Under the new approach, called the *current expected credit loss ("CECL") model*, the investor estimates impairment losses by comparing the amortized cost of the debt investment to the present value of the cash flows it's expected to provide, discounted at the interest rate that was effective when the investment was initially purchased. Those cash flows are estimated considering all information that's available about the potential for payment in the future.

Both the U.S. GAAP and IFRS models are discussed further in Appendix 12B to this chapter.

International Financial Reporting Standards

LO12–8

Impairments. IFRS No. 9, amended on July 24, 2014, will be required after January 1, 2018, and earlier adoption is permitted.[26] IFRS No. 9 calculates impairment of debt investments using the *expected credit loss ("ECL") model*, which is somewhat similar to the CECL model likely to be required soon in U.S. GAAP. Both the U.S. CECL model, and the IFRS ECL model calculate expected credit losses over the remaining life of the investment if there has been a significant increase in credit risk. The U.S. CECL model also does that if there has not been a significant increase in credit risk. In contrast, under the IFRS ECL model, if the credit risk of a debt investment has not increased, the estimate of credit losses only considers credit losses that result from default events that are possible within the *next twelve months*. For many debt investments, this approach accrues very little credit loss, because the credit risk of the investment hasn't changed and default within the next twelve months is very unlikely. That means that U.S. GAAP will tend to recognize impairment losses earlier, and in higher amounts, than are recognized under IFRS. Further convergence in this area is unlikely in the near future.

We discuss the U.S. GAAP and IFRS models further in Appendix 12B to this chapter.

Additional Consideration

What if the Fair Value Isn't "Readily Determinable"?

According to GAAP, the fair value of an equity security is considered readily determinable only if its selling price is currently available on particular securities exchanges or over-the-counter markets.[27] If the fair value of an equity security is *not* readily determinable, we use the *cost method* (except when the equity method described in Part B of this chapter is appropriate). The cost method is so named because the investment is carried in the balance sheet at cost, and temporary unrealized holding gains and losses are not recognized in either net income or other comprehensive income. Any dividends received are reported as investment revenue, and any gain or loss realized upon selling the investment is included in income. However, fair values still matter under the cost method, because the investment still is subject to testing for other-than-temporary impairments. Therefore, even if the fair value of an equity investment isn't viewed as readily determinable, companies have to determine it if there are indications that the investment has been impaired.

[25]For the current status of this project, see "Accounting for Financial Instruments: Impairment" uner "Projects" at www.fasb.org.

[26]"Financial Instruments," *International Financial Reporting Standard No. 9* (IASCF), November 12, 2009, as amended effective July 24, 2014.

[27]FASB ASC 320–10–20: Investments–Overall–Glossary–Readily Determinable Fair Value (previously "Accounting for Certain Investments in Debt and Equity Securities (as amended)," *Statement of Financial Accounting Standards No. 115* (Norwalk, Conn.: FASB 2008), par. 3a).

International Financial Reporting Standards

Cost Method. Under *IAS No. 39*, equity investments typically are measured at fair value, even if they are not listed on an exchange or over-the-counter market. The cost method is used only if fair value cannot be measured reliably, which occurs when the range of reasonable fair value estimates is significant and the probability of various estimates within the range cannot be reasonably estimated. *IFRS No. 9* does not allow the cost method, but may allow cost as an estimate of fair value in some circumstances. In general, use of the cost method is less prevalent under IFRS than under U.S. GAAP.

● LO12–8

Concept Review Exercise

VARIOUS INVESTMENT SECURITIES

Diversified Services, Inc., offers a variety of business services, including financial services through its escrow division. Diversified's fiscal year ends on December 31. The only securities held by Diversified at December 1 were 12 million common shares of Shelby Laminations, Inc., purchased in November for $50 million and classified as available-for-sale. Diversified entered into the following investment activities during the last month of 2016 and the first week of 2017:

2016

Dec. 1	Purchased $30 million of 12% bonds of Vince-Gill Amusement Corporation and $24 million of 10% bonds of Eastern Waste Disposal Corporation, both at face value and both to be held until they mature. Interest on each bond issue is payable semiannually on November 30 and May 31.
9	Sold one-half of the Shelby Laminations common shares for $26 million.
29	Received cash dividends of $1.5 million from the Shelby Laminations common shares.
30	Purchased U.S. Treasury bonds for $5.8 million as trading securities hoping to earn profits on short-term differences in prices.
31	Recorded the necessary adjusting entry(s) relating to the investments.

The year-end market price of the Shelby Laminations common stock was $4.25 per share. The fair values of the bond investments were $32 million for Vince-Gill Amusement Corporation and $20 million for Eastern Waste Disposal Corporation. A sharp rise in short-term interest rates on the last day of the year caused the fair value of the Treasury bonds to fall to $5.7 million.

2017

Jan. 7	Sold the remaining Shelby Laminations common shares for $27 million.

Required:

Prepare the appropriate journal entry for each transaction or event and show the amounts that would be reported in the company's 2016 income statement relative to these investments. Determine the effects of the Shelby Laminations investment on net income, other comprehensive income, and comprehensive income for 2016, 2017, and combined over both years.

2016

Dec. 1	Purchased $30 million of 12% bonds of Vince-Gill Amusement Corporation and $24 million of 10% bonds of Eastern Waste Disposal Corporation, both at face value and both to be held until they mature. Interest on each bond issue is payable semiannually on November 30 and May 31.

Investment in Vince-Gill Amusement bonds	30	
Investment in Eastern Waste Disposal bonds	24	
Cash		54

Dec. 9 Sold one-half of the Shelby Laminations common shares for $26 million.

Sale of one-half of the Shelby Laminations shares results in a $1 million gain ($26 million sales price − [$50 million cost ÷ 2]).

Cash (selling price)	26	
Investment in Shelby Laminations common shares ($50 × ½)		25
Gain on sale of investments (difference)		1

Dec. 29 Received cash dividends of $1.5 million from the Shelby Laminations common shares.

Cash	1.5	
Investment revenue		1.5

Dec. 30 Purchased U.S. Treasury bonds for $5.8 million as trading securities, hoping to earn profits on short-term differences in prices.

Investment in U.S. Treasury bonds	5.8	
Cash		5.8

Dec. 31 Recorded the necessary adjusting entry(s) relating to the investments.

Accrued Interest (one month)		
Investment revenue receivable—Vince-Gill Amusement ($30 million × 12% × 1⁄12)	0.3	
Investment revenue receivable—Eastern Waste Disposal ($24 million × 10% × 1⁄12)	0.2	
Investment revenue		0.5
Fair Value Adjustments		
Net unrealized holding gains and losses—I/S ($5.7 − 5.8)	0.1	
Fair value adjustment, TS investments		0.1
Fair value adjustment, AFS investments ([12 million shares × ½ × $4.25] − [$50 million × ½])	0.5	
Net unrealized holding gains and losses—OCI		0.5

Note: Securities held-to-maturity are not adjusted to fair value.

Reported in the 2016 Income Statement:	($ in millions)
Investment revenue ($1.5 dividends + 0.5 interest)	$2.0
Gain on sale of investments (Shelby)	1.0
Unrealized holding loss on investments (trading securities)	(0.1)

Note: The $0.5 million unrealized holding gain for the Shelby Laminations common shares is not included in income because it pertains to securities available-for-sale rather than trading securities, and so is reflected in OCI.

2017

Jan. 7 Sold the remaining Shelby Laminations common shares for $27 million.

The fair value of the Shelby shares at the time of sale is $27 million. Those shares were purchased for $25 million ($50 million × ½), so the gain realized on the sale is $2 million.

Cash (selling price)	27	
Investment in Shelby Laminations common shares (cost: ½ × $50)		25
Gain on sale of investments (difference)		2

Given that the fair value adjustment for the Shelby shares has a $0.5 million balance (recorded on 12/31/2016), we need to remove that amount and eliminate the corresponding unrecognized gain from AOCI. This happens automatically when we next adjust the portfolio to fair value. If we were to make the adjustment separately, the entry would be:

Net unrealized holding gains and losses—OCI	0.5	
Fair value adjustment, AFS investments		0.5

The Shelby investment's unrealized and realized gains and losses affected net income, other comprehensive income, and comprehensive income as follows ($ in millions):

2016	
$1.0	realized gain on sale of investments (in net income)
0.5	unrealized gain on investments (in OCI)
$1.5	total 2016 effect in comprehensive income
2017	
$2.0	realized gain on sale of investments (in net income)
(0.5)	reclassification out of OCI of previously recognized unrealized gain associated with sold investments
$1.5	total 2017 effect in comprehensive income
$3.0	grand total effect in comprehensive income ($1.5 + 1.5).
$3.0	grand total effect in net income ($1.0 + 2.0).
$0.0	grand total effect in other comprehensive income ($0.5 + (0.5)).

Note that the $3.0 grand total effect of the Shelby shares on comprehensive income and net income reconciles with the difference between their purchase price ($50) and their sales price ($53, which is equal to the sum of $26 for the half sold in 2016 and $27 for the half sold in 2017). The only difference between comprehensive income and net income is timing.

Financial Statement Presentation and Disclosure

Trading securities, held-to-maturity securities and available-for-sale securities are either current or noncurrent depending on when they are expected to mature or to be sold. However, it's not necessary that a company report individual amounts for the three categories of investments—held-to-maturity, available-for-sale, or trading—on the face of the balance sheet as long as that information is presented in the disclosure notes.[28]

On the statement of cash flows, inflows and outflows of cash from buying and selling trading securities typically are considered operating activities because, for companies that routinely transact in trading securities (financial institutions), trading in those securities constitutes an appropriate part of the companies' normal operations. But because held-to-maturity and available-for-sale securities are not purchased and held principally to be sold in the near term, cash flows from the purchase, sale, and maturity of these securities are considered investing activities. Also, if an investment that normally would be HTM or AFS is classified as a trading security because the company chose the fair value option, cash flows may be classified as investing, because they are viewed as nonoperating in nature.

Investors should disclose the following in the disclosure notes for each year presented:

- Aggregate fair value.
- Gross realized and unrealized holding gains.
- Gross realized and unrealized holding losses.
- Change in net unrealized holding gains and losses.
- Amortized cost basis by major security type.

Extensive footnote disclosure is provided to help financial statement users assess the quality of fair value measurements and understand where they affect the financial statements.

The notes also include disclosures designed to help financial statement users understand the quality of the inputs companies use when determining fair values and to identify parts of

[28]FASB ASC 320–10–45–13: Investments–Debt and Equity Securities–Overall–Other Presentation Matters (previously *Statement of Financial Accounting Standards No. 115,* "Accounting for Certain Investments in Debt and Equity Securities," (Norwalk, Conn.: FASB, 1993), par. 18).

the financial statements that are affected by those fair value estimates. For example, the notes should include the level of the fair value hierarchy (levels 1, 2, or 3) in which all fair value measurements fall. For fair value measurements that use unobservable inputs (level 3), the notes need to provide information about the effect of fair value measurements on earnings, including a reconciliation of beginning and ending balances of the investment that identifies:

- Total gains or losses for the period (realized and unrealized), unrealized gains and losses associated with assets and liabilities still held at the reporting date, and where those amounts are included in earnings or shareholders' equity.
- Purchases, sales, issuances and settlements.
- Transfers in and out of level 3 of the fair value hierarchy (for example, because of changes in the observability of inputs used to determine fair values).
- For instruments accounted for under the fair value option, an estimate of the gains or losses included in earnings that are attributable to changes in credit risk.

For example, as shown in Illustration 12–12, notes in GE's 2013 annual report include a discussion of fair values of investments in its pension plan.

Illustration 12–12 Fair Value Disclosure of Investment Securities—General Electric

Real World Financials

Fair Value Measurements

	December 31, 2013			
	Level 1	**Level 2**	**Level 3**	**Total**
	Quoted Prices in Active Markets for Identical Assets	**Significant Other Observable Inputs**	**Significant Unobservable Inputs**	
Equity securities				
U.S. equity securities	$11,067	$ 1,568	$ –	$12,635
Non-U.S. equity securities	7,832	1,292	–	9,124
Debt securities				
Fixed income and cash investment funds	–	2,078	–	2,078
U.S. corporate	–	4,555	–	4,555
Residential mortgage-backed	–	1,093	–	1,093
U.S. government and federal agency	–	5,253	–	5,253
Other debt securities	–	2,317	–	2,317
Private equities	–	–	6,269	6,269
Real estate	–	–	3,354	3,354
Other investments	–	169	1,622	1,791
Total investments	$18,899	$18,325	$11,245	48,469
Other				(172)
Total assets				$48,297

Changes in Level 3 investments for the Year Ended December 31, 2013 (condensed)

	Jan. 1, 2013	Net realized gains (losses)	Net unrealized gains (losses)	Purchases, issuances, and settlements	Transfers in and/or out of Level 3	Dec. 31, 2013
Debt securities	$ 75	$ (7)	$ –	$ (65)	$ (3)	$ –
Private equities	6,878	525	588	(1,675)	(47)	6,269
Real estate	3,356	23	330	(355)	–	3,354
Other investments	1,694	(1)	200	(77)	(194)	1,622
	$12,003	**$540**	**$1,118**	**$(2,172)**	**$(244)**	**$11,245**

We can see from Illustration 12–12 that GE has significant investments in all three levels of the fair value hierarchy. The second part of the illustration shows us that GE had unrealized gains of $1,118 million on its Level 3 investments. Because those gains relate to Level 3 investments, users of the financial statements might be concerned about their reliability.

Recent changes in U.S. GAAP and IFRS have only increased the amount of disclosure that is required about fair values.[29] For example, for level 2 or 3 fair values, the notes to the financial statements must include a description of the valuation technique(s) and the inputs used in the fair value measurement process, and for level 3 fair values, the notes must indicate the significant inputs used in the fair value measurement and the sensitivity of fair values to significant changes in those inputs. All of this disclosure is designed to provide financial statement users with information about those fair values that are most vulnerable to bias or error in the estimation process.

Investor Has Significant Influence

PART B

When a company invests in the equity securities (primarily common stock) of another company, the investing company can benefit either (a) *directly* through dividends and/or market price appreciation or (b) *indirectly* through the creation of desirable operating relationships with the investee. The way we report a company's investment in the stock of another company depends on the nature of the relationship between the investor and the investee.

For reporting purposes, we classify the investment relationship in one of three ways, and account for the investment differently depending on the classification, as shown in Illustration 12–13.

Illustration 12–13
Reporting Classifications for Investment Relationships

Relationship: How much does the investor influence the operating and financial policies of the investee?	Reporting Method
Lacks significant influence (usually < 20% equity ownership)	Varies by type of investment (see Part A of this chapter)
Has significant influence (usually 20%–50% equity ownership)	Equity method
Has control (usually > 50% equity ownership)	Consolidation

The *equity method* can be used when an investor can't control, but can significantly influence, the investee.

We focused on situations in which the investor lacks significant influence in Part A of this chapter. In Part B of this chapter we focus on situations in which the investor has significant influence and discuss the **equity method** and **fair value option** that are used to account for those investments.

A detailed discussion of the third classification—consolidated financial statements—is beyond the scope of this book. That discussion often is a focus of the advanced accounting course or is taught as a separate consolidations course. In this chapter, we'll briefly overview consolidation only to provide perspective to aspects of the equity method that purposely mimic some effects of consolidation. Let's do that now, before addressing the specifics of the equity method.

How the Equity Method Relates to Consolidated Financial Statements

If a company acquires more than 50% of the voting stock of another company, it's said to have a controlling interest, because by voting those shares, the investor actually can control the company acquired. The investor is referred to as the *parent;* the investee is termed the *subsidiary*. For reporting purposes (although not legally), the parent and subsidiary are

[29]FASB ASC 820–10–50: Fair Value Measurement–Overall–Disclosure (previously "Fair Value Measurement (Topic 820): Amendments to Achieve Common Fair Value Measurement and Disclosure Requirements in U.S. GAAP and IFRSs" *Accounting Standards Update No. 2011-04* (Norwalk, Conn.: FASB, May 2011)).

considered to be a single reporting entity, and their financial statements are *consolidated.* Both companies continue to operate as separate legal entities and the subsidiary reports separate financial statements. However, because of the controlling interest, the parent company reports consolidated financial statements.

Consolidated financial statements **combine the individual elements of the parent and subsidiary statements.**

Consolidated financial statements combine the separate financial statements of the parent and the subsidiary each period into a single aggregate set of financial statements as if there were only one company. This entails an item-by-item combination of the parent and subsidiary statements (after first eliminating any amounts that are shared by the separate financial statements).[30] For instance, if the parent has $8 million cash and the subsidiary has $3 million cash, the consolidated balance sheet would report $11 million cash.

The acquired company's assets are included in consolidated financial statements at their fair values as of the date of the acquisition, and the difference between the acquisition price and the sum of the fair values of the acquired net assets is recorded as goodwill.

Two aspects of the consolidation process are of particular interest to us in understanding the equity method. First, in consolidated financial statements, the acquired company's assets are included in the financial statements at their fair values as of the date of the acquisition, rather than their book values on that date. Second, if the acquisition price is more than the sum of the separate fair values of the acquired net assets (assets less liabilities), that difference is recorded as an intangible asset—goodwill.[31] We'll return to the discussion of these two aspects when we reach the point in our discussion of the equity method where their influence is felt. As we'll see, the equity method is in many ways a partial consolidation.

We use the equity method when the investor can't control the investee but can exercise significant influence over the operating and financial policies of an investee.

What Is Significant Influence?

● LO12–4

Usually an investor can exercise significant influence over the investee when it owns between 20% and 50% of the investee's voting shares.

When effective control is absent, the investor still may be able to exercise significant influence over the operating and financial policies of the investee. This would be the case if the investor owns a large percentage of the outstanding shares relative to other shareholders. By voting those shares as a block, decisions often can be swayed in the direction the investor desires. When significant influence exists, the investment should be accounted for by the equity method. It should be presumed, in the absence of evidence to the contrary, that the investor has the ability to exercise **significant influence** over the investee when it owns between 20% and 50% of the investee's voting shares.[32]

A Single Entity Concept

● LO12–5

The investor's ownership interest in individual assets and liabilities of the investee is represented by a single investment account.

Much like consolidation, the equity method views the investor and investee collectively as a special type of single entity (as if the two companies were one company). However, using the equity method, the investor doesn't include separate financial statement items of the investee on an item-by-item basis as in consolidation. Instead, the investor reports its equity interest in the investee as a single investment account. For that reason, the equity method sometimes is referred to as a "one-line consolidation," because it essentially collapses the consolidation approach into single lines in the balance sheet and income statement, while having the same effect on total income and shareholders' equity.

Under the equity method, the investor recognizes investment income equal to its percentage share (based on stock ownership) of the net income earned by the investee rather than the portion of that net income received as cash dividends. The rationale for this approach is the presumption of the equity method that the fortunes of the investor and investee are sufficiently intertwined that as the investee prospers, the investor prospers proportionately. Stated differently, as the investee earns additional net assets, the investor's share of those net assets increases.

[30]This avoids double counting those amounts in the consolidated statements. For example, amounts owed by one company to the other are represented by accounts payable in one set of financial statements and accounts receivable in the other. These amounts are not included in the statements of the consolidated entity because a company can't "owe itself."

[31]This is the usual case because most companies are worth more than the sum of the values of individual components of the company due to reputation, longevity, managerial expertise, customer loyalty, or a host of other possibilities. Accounting for goodwill in acquisitions is discussed in Chapter 10.

[32]Shareholders are the owners of the corporation. By voting their shares, it is they who determine the makeup of the board of directors—who, in turn, appoint officers—who, in turn, manage the company. Common stock usually is the class of shares that has voting privileges. However, a corporation can create classes of preferred shares that also have voting rights. This is discussed at greater length in Chapter 18.

Initially, the investment is recorded at cost. The carrying amount of this investment subsequently is:

- Increased by the investor's percentage share of the investee's net income (or decreased by its share of a loss).
- Decreased by dividends paid.

FINANCIAL Reporting Case

Q4, p. 655

Additional Consideration

It's possible that a company owns more than 20% of the voting shares but still cannot exercise significant influence over the investee. If, for instance, another company or a small group of shareholders owns 51% or more of the shares, they control the investee regardless of how other investors vote their shares. GAAP provides this and other examples of indications that an investor may be unable to exercise significant influence:

- The investee challenges the investor's ability to exercise significant influence (through litigation or complaints to regulators).
- The investor surrenders significant shareholder rights in a signed agreement.
- The investor is unable to acquire sufficient information about the investee to apply the equity method.
- The investor tries and fails to obtain representation on the board of directors of the investee.[33]

In such cases, the equity method would not be appropriate, and the investment would likely be treated as AFS.

Conversely, it's also possible that a company owns less than 20% of the voting shares but is able to exercise significant influence over the investee. Ability to exercise significant influence with less than 20% ownership might be indicated, for example, by having an officer of the investor corporation on the board of directors of the investee corporation or by having, say, 18% of the voting shares while no other single investor owns more than 50%. In such cases the equity method would be appropriate.

To see how the equity method works, let's assume that United Intergroup purchased 30% of Arjent, Inc.'s, common stock for $1,500,000 cash. Illustration 12–14 highlights that buying 30% of Arjent can be viewed as buying 30% of all of Arjent's assets and

Illustration 12–14
Equity Method

Account	Book Value on Arjent's Financial Statements	Fair Value at Time of United's Investment
Buildings (10-year remaining useful life, no salvage value)	$1,000,000	$ 2,000,000
Land	500,000	1,000,000
Other net assets*	600,000	600,000
Net assets	2,100,000	3,600,000
Goodwill		1,400,000 (to balance)
	Total fair value of Arjent	$ 5,000,000
		× 30% purchased
Other information:		**$1,500,000 purchase price**
Arjent's 2016 net income:	$500,000	
Arjent's 2016 dividends:	$250,000	

*Other net assets = other assets − liabilities

[33]FASB ASC 323–10–15–10: Investments–Equity Method and Joint Ventures–Overall–Scope and Scope Exceptions (previously "Criteria for Applying the Equity Method of Accounting for Investments in Common Stock," *FASB Interpretation No. 35* (Stamford, Conn.: FASB, 1981)).

liabilities. Those assets and liabilities likely have book values on Arjent's balance sheet that differ from their separate fair values. We can think of United as paying a price equal to 30% of the sum of the fair values of all of those assets and liabilities, plus an extra amount, goodwill, that captures 30% of the value of other attractive aspects of Arjent (e.g., loyal customers, well-trained workers) that GAAP doesn't capture as separate assets or liabilities. We will see that, under the equity method, all of those amounts are shown in a single investment account, but we still need to track their individual information to account for them correctly.

The cost principal governs the acquisition of assets.

PURCHASE OF INVESTMENT. Recording United's purchase of 30% of Arjent is straightforward. In fact, it requires the same entry used to record the purchase of the Arjent investment in Part A of this chapter.

Investment in Arjent stock	1,500,000	
Cash		1,500,000

As the investee earns additional net assets, the investor's investment in those net assets increases.

RECORDING INVESTMENT REVENUE. Under the equity method, the investor includes in net income its proportionate share of the investee's net income. The reasoning is that, as the investee earns additional net assets, the investor's equity interest in those net assets also increases, so the investor increases its investment by the amount of income recognized. United's entry would be:

As the investee prospers, the investor prospers proportionately.

Investment in Arjent stock	150,000	
Investment revenue (30% × $500,000)		150,000

Of course, if Argent had recorded a net loss rather than net income, United would *reduce* its investment in Arjent and recognize a *loss* on investment for its share of the loss. Note that you won't always see these amounts called "investment revenue" or "investment loss." Rather, United might call this line "equity in earnings (losses) of affiliate" or some other title that suggests it is using the equity method.

As the investee distributes net assets as dividends, the investor does not recognize revenue. Rather, the investor's investment in the investee's net assets is reduced.

RECEIVING DIVIDENDS. Because investment revenue is recognized as it is earned by the investee, it would be inappropriate to recognize revenue again when earnings are distributed as dividends. That would be double counting. Instead, we view the dividend distribution as a reduction of the investee's net assets. The rationale is that the investee is returning assets to its investors in the form of a cash payment, so each investor's equity interest in the remaining net assets declines proportionately.

Cash	75,000	
Investment in Arjent stock (30% × $250,000)		75,000

Further Adjustments

LO12–6

When the investor's expenditure to acquire an investment exceeds the book value of the underlying net assets acquired, additional adjustments to both the investment account and investment revenue might be needed. The purpose is to approximate the effects of consolidation, without actually consolidating financial statements. More specifically, after the date of acquisition, both the investment account and investment revenue are adjusted for differences between net income reported by the investee and what that amount would have been if consolidation procedures had been followed. This process is often referred to as "amortizing the differential," because it mimics the process of expensing some of the difference between the price paid for the investment and the book value of the investment.[34] Let's look closer at what that means.

[34]Adjustments also are made to eliminate the effects of any other transactions that occurred between the investor and the investee, such as sales of goods and services. Those adjustments are beyond the scope of this text.

As mentioned earlier, consolidated financial statements report (a) the acquired company's assets at their fair values on the date of acquisition rather than their book values, subsequently adjusted for amortization, and (b) goodwill for the excess of the acquisition price over the fair value of the identifiable net assets acquired.

The first of these two consequences of the consolidation process usually has an effect on income, and it's the income effect that we're interested in when applying the equity method. Increasing asset balances to their fair values usually will result in higher expenses in subsequent periods. For instance, if buildings, equipment, or other depreciable assets are written up to higher values, depreciation expense will be higher during their remaining useful lives. Likewise, if the recorded amount of inventory is increased, cost of goods sold will be higher when the inventory is sold. As a consequence of increasing these asset balances to fair value, expenses will rise and income will fall. It is this negative effect on income that the equity method seeks to imitate.

However, if it's land that's increased, there is no income effect because we don't depreciate land. Also, goodwill will not result in higher expenses. Goodwill is an intangible asset, but one whose cost usually is not charged to earnings.[35]

In our example, United needs to make adjustments for the fact that, at the time it purchased its investment in Arjent, the fair values of Arjent's assets and liabilities were higher than the book values of those assets and liabilities in Arjent's balance sheet. Illustration 12–15 highlights the portions of United's investment that may require adjustment:

Notice in Illustration 12–15 that United paid (in thousands) $1,500 for identifiable net assets that, sold separately, would be worth $1,080 and the $420 difference is attributable to goodwill. The identifiable net assets worth $1,080 have a book value of only $630, and we assumed the $450 difference is attributable to undervalued buildings ($300) and land ($150).

Illustration 12–15

Source of Differences between the Investment and the Book Value of Net Assets Acquired

	Investee Net Assets ↓	Net Assets Purchased ↓	($ in thousands) Difference Attributed to: ↓	
Cost	$5,000 × 30% =	$1,500	*Goodwill:*	$420
Fair value	$3,600 × 30% =	$1,080		
			Undervaluation of:	
			Buildings	$300
			Land	$150
Book value	$ 2,100 × 30% =	$630		

ADJUSTMENTS FOR ADDITIONAL DEPRECIATION. When Arjent determines its net income, it bases depreciation expense on the book value of its buildings, but United needs to depreciate its share of the *fair value* of those buildings at the time it made its investment. Therefore, United must adjust its investment revenue for additional depreciation expense. Over the life of the buildings, United will need to recognize its 30% share of a total of $1,000,000 of additional depreciation expense ($2,000,000 fair value less $1,000,000 book value), or $300,000. Assuming a 10-year life of the buildings and straight-line depreciation, United must recognize $30,000 of additional depreciation each year. Had Arjent recorded that additional depreciation, United's portion of Arjent's net income would have been lower by $30,000 (ignoring taxes). To act as if Arjent had recorded the additional

The investor adjusts its share of the investee's net income to reflect revenues and expenses associated with differences between the fair value and book value of the investee's assets and liabilities that existed at the time the investment was made.

[35]Goodwill is not amortized periodically to expense. Only if the asset's value is subsequently judged to be impaired is all or a portion of the recorded amount charged against earnings. FASB ASC 350–20–35: Intangibles–Goodwill and Other–Goodwill–Subsequent Measurement (previously "Goodwill and Other Intangible Assets," *Statement of Financial Accounting Standards No. 141* (Norwalk, Conn.: FASB, 2001)). For review, see Chapter 11.

depreciation, United adjusts the accounts to reduce investment revenue and reduce its investment in Arjent stock by $30,000.

Investment revenue	30,000	
Investment in Arjent stock (30% × [$2,000,000 − 1,000,000] ÷ 10 yrs.)		30,000

NO ADJUSTMENTS FOR LAND OR GOODWILL. United makes no adjustments for land or goodwill. Land, unlike buildings, is not an asset that we depreciate. As a result, the difference between the fair value and book value of the land would not cause higher expenses, and we have no need to adjust investment revenue or the investment in Arjent stock for the land.

Recall from Chapter 11 that goodwill, unlike most other intangible assets, is not amortized. In that sense, goodwill resembles land. Thus, acquiring goodwill will not cause higher expenses, so we have no need to adjust investment revenue or the investment in Arjent stock for goodwill.

If the fair value of purchased inventory exceeds its book value, we usually assume the inventory is sold in the next year and reduce investment revenue in the next year by the entire difference.

ADJUSTMENTS FOR OTHER ASSETS AND LIABILITIES. Also, because in our example there was no difference between the book value and fair value of the remaining net assets, we don't need an adjustment for them either. However, that often will not be the case.

For example, Arjent's inventory could have had a fair value that exceeded its book value at the time United purchased its Arjent investment. To recognize expense associated with that higher fair value, United would need to identify the period in which that inventory is sold (usually the next year) and, in that period, reduce its investment revenue and its investment in Arjent stock by its 30% share of the difference between the fair value and book value of the inventory. If, for instance, the $300,000 difference between fair value and book value had been attributable to inventory rather than buildings, and that inventory was sold by Arjent in the year following United's investment, United would reduce investment revenue by the entire $300,000 in the year following the investment. By so doing, United would be making an adjustment that yielded the same net investment revenue as if Arjent had carried the inventory on its books at fair value at the time the Arjent investment was made and therefore recorded higher cost of goods sold ($300,000) when it was sold in the next year. More generally, an equity method investor needs to make these sorts of adjustments whenever there are revenues or expenses associated with an asset or liability that had a difference between book value and fair value at the time the investment was made.

Additional Consideration

Effect on Deferred Income Taxes

Investment revenue is recorded by the equity method when income is earned by the investee, but that revenue is not taxed until it's actually received as cash dividends. This creates a temporary difference between book income and taxable income. You will learn in Chapter 16 that the investor must report a deferred tax liability for the income tax that ultimately will be paid when the income eventually is received as dividends.

Reporting the Investment

The carrying amount of the investment is its initial cost plus the investor's equity in the undistributed earnings of the investee.

The fair value of the investment shares at the end of the reporting period is not reported when using the equity method. The investment account is reported at its original cost, increased by the investor's share of the investee's net income (adjusted for additional expenses like depreciation), and decreased by the portion of those earnings actually received as dividends. In other words, the investment account represents the investor's share of the investee's net assets initially acquired, adjusted for the investor's share of the subsequent increase in the investee's net assets (net assets earned and not yet distributed as dividends).

The balance of United's 30% investment in Arjent at December 31, 2016, would be calculated as follows:

Investment in Arjent Stock

Cost	1,500,000		
Share of income	150,000		
		30,000	Depreciation adjustment
		75,000	Dividends
	1,545,000		

In the statement of cash flows, the purchase and sale of the investment are reported as outflows and inflows of cash in the investing activities section, and the receipt of dividends is reported as an inflow of cash in the operating activities section.[36]

WHEN THE INVESTEE REPORTS A NET LOSS. Our illustration assumed the investee earned net income. If the investee reports a *net loss* instead, the investment account would be *decreased* by the investor's share of the investee's net loss (adjusted for additional expenses).

Additional Consideration

It's possible that the investor's proportionate share of investee losses could exceed the carrying amount of the investment. If this happens, the investor should discontinue applying the equity method until the investor's share of subsequent investee earnings has equaled losses not recognized during the time the equity method was discontinued. This avoids reducing the investment account below zero.

WHEN THE INVESTMENT IS ACQUIRED IN MID-YEAR. Obviously, we've simplified the illustration by assuming the investment was acquired at the beginning of 2016, entailing a full year's income, dividends, and adjustments to account for the income effects of any differences between book value and fair value on the date the investment was acquired. In the more likely event that an investment is acquired sometime after the beginning of the year, the application of the equity method is easily modified to include the appropriate fraction of each of those amounts. For example, if United's purchase of 30% of Arjent had occurred on October 1 rather than January 2, we would simply record income, dividends, and adjustments for three months (3⁄12) of the year. This would result in the following entries to the investment account:

Investment in Arjent Stock

Cost	1,500,000		
Share of income (3⁄12 × $150,000)	37,500		
		7,500	Depreciation adjustment (3⁄12 × $30,000)
		18,750	Dividends (3⁄12 × $75,000)
	1,511,250		

Changes in the investment account the first year are adjusted for the fraction of the year the investor has owned the investment.

[36]Some companies prepare a statement of cash flows using the indirect method of reporting operating activities. In that case, the operating section begins with net income and adjustments are made to back out the effects of accrual accounting and calculate cash from operations. For companies with equity method investments, net income will include investment revenue and gains or losses associated with sold investments, but cash from operations should include only cash dividends. As an example, because United's 2016 net income includes $120,000 of investment revenue from Arjent ($150,000 portion of income − $30,000 depreciation adjustment), but United received only $75,000 of dividends from Arjent, an indirect method statement of cash flows would include an adjustment, often titled "undistributed earnings of investee," that reduces net income by $45,000 ($75,000 − $120,000) when determining cash flow from operating activities.

AT&T reported its 2013 investments in affiliated companies for which it exercised significant influence using the equity method as shown in Illustration 12–16.

Illustration 12–16
Equity Method Investments on the Balance Sheet—AT&T

Real World Financials

	Dec 31, 2013	Dec 31, 2012
Total current assets	$ 23,196	$ 22,706
Property, plant, and equipment—Net	110,968	109,767
Goodwill	69,273	69,773
Licenses	56,433	52,352
Customer lists and relationships—Net	763	1,391
Other intangible assets—Net	5,016	5,032
Investments in and advances to equity affiliates	3,860	4,581
Other assets	8,278	6,713
Total assets	$277,787	$272,315

What If Conditions Change?

Both the investment and retained earnings would be increased by the investor's share of the undistributed earnings in years prior to a change to the equity method.

A CHANGE FROM THE EQUITY METHOD TO ANOTHER METHOD. When the investor's level of influence changes, it may be necessary to change from the equity method to another method. When this situation happens, *no adjustment* is made to the remaining carrying amount of the investment. Instead, the equity method is simply discontinued and the new method applied from then on. The balance in the investment account when the equity method is discontinued would serve as the new cost basis for writing the investment up or down to fair value on the next set of financial statements.

For example, when Visa's influence over one of its investees was reduced during 2013, Visa changed from accounting for the investment by the equity method to accounting for the investment as available-for-sale. The investment had been carried at $12 million under the equity method, but its fair value was $99 million. So when Visa made the change it recognized an $87 million gain in other comprehensive income, just as if the investment had initially cost Visa $12 million and had appreciated $87 million in value during the year.

A CHANGE FROM ANOTHER METHOD TO THE EQUITY METHOD. Sometimes companies change from another method to the equity method. For example, recently the Mitsubishi UFJ Financial Group converted its investment in the convertible preferred stock of Morgan Stanley into common stock, and as a result started accounting for that investment under the equity method. When a change *to* the equity method is appropriate, the investment account should be retroactively adjusted to the balance that would have existed if the equity method always had been used. As income also would have been different, retained earnings would be adjusted as well. For example, assume it's determined that an investor's share of investee net income, reduced by dividends, was $4 million during a period when the equity method was not used, but additional purchases of shares cause the equity method to be appropriate now. The following journal entry would record the change (ignoring taxes):

	($ in millions)	
Investment in equity securities	4	
Retained earnings (investment revenue from the equity method)		4

In addition to the adjustment of account balances, financial statements would be restated to the equity method for each year reported in the annual report for comparative purposes. Also, the income effect for years prior to those shown in the comparative statements is reported on the statement of retained earnings as an adjustment to beginning retained earnings of the earliest year reported. A disclosure note also should describe the change. Reporting accounting changes is described in more detail in Chapter 20.

If an Equity Method Investment Is Sold

When an investment reported by the equity method is sold, a gain or loss is recognized if the selling price is more or less than the carrying amount (book value) of the investment. For example, let's continue our illustration and assume United sells its investment in Arjent on January 1, 2017, for $1,446,000. A journal entry would record a loss as follows:

When an equity method investment is sold, a gain or loss is recognized for the difference between its selling price and its carrying amount.

Cash	1,446,000	
Loss on sale of investments (to balance)	99,000	
Investment in Arjent stock (account balance)		1,545,000

If the sale of the equity-method investment meets the criteria for a discontinued operation (discussed in Chapter 4), it is reported in the financial statements as a discontinued operation.

Comparison of Fair Value and the Equity Method

Illustration 12–17 compares accounting for the Arjent investment at fair value (as trading securities or securities available for sale, discussed in Part A of this chapter) and under the equity method (covered in Part B of this chapter):

Illustration 12–17 Comparison of Fair Value and Equity Methods

	Fair Value			Equity Method		
Purchase equity investment	Investment in Arjent	1,500,000		Same as Fair Value Method		
	Cash		1,500,000			
Recognize proportionate share of investee's net income and any related adjustments	No entry			Investment in Arjent	150,000	
				Investment revenue		150,000
				Investment revenue	30,000	
				Investment in Arjent		30,000
Adjust investment to reflect changes in fair value from $1,500,000 to $1,450,000	Net unrealized gain/loss*	50,000		No entry		
	FV adjustment		50,000			
Receive dividend	Cash	75,000		Cash	75,000	
	Investment revenue		75,000	Investment in Arjent		75,000
Sell equity investment	Recognize gain or loss:			Cash	1,446,000	
	Cash	1,446,000		Loss (to balance)	99,000	
	Loss (to balance)	54,000		Investment in Arjent		1,545,000
	Investment in Arjent		1,500,000			
	Reverse out previously recorded unrealized gain or loss that's no longer unrealized (automatically part of next adjustment to fair value):					
	FV adjustment	50,000				
	Net unrealized gain/loss*		50,000			

*Net unrealized holding gains and losses are reported in net income for trading securities and in other comprehensive income for available-for-sale securities.

This side-by-side comparison highlights several aspects of these accounting approaches:

- To record the purchase of an investment, we use identical entries for both approaches.
- The two approaches differ in whether we record investment revenue when dividends are received and whether we recognize unrealized holding gains and losses associated with changes in the fair value of the investment.
- The differences in how the two approaches account for unrealized holding gains and losses result in different book values for the investment at the time the investment is sold, and therefore result in different realized gains or losses when the investment is sold.

- Regardless of approach, the same cash flows occur, and the same total amount of net income is recognized over the life of the investment. In the case of Arjent:
  - **Fair value method:** A total of $21,000 of net income is recognized over the life of the investment, equal to $75,000 of dividend revenue minus $54,000 realized loss on sale of investment.
  - **Equity method:** A total of $21,000 of net income is recognized over the life of the investment, equal to $150,000 of United's portion of Arjent's income minus $30,000 depreciation adjustment and minus $99,000 realized loss on sale of investment.
  - Thus, the question is not how much total net income is recognized, but *when* that net income is recognized.

Fair Value Option

● LO12–7

We learned in Part A of this chapter that GAAP allows a fair value option with respect to investments that otherwise would be accounted for using the held-to-maturity or available-for-sale approaches. Electing the fair value option for those investments is simple—the investments are reclassified as trading securities and accounted for in that manner.

If the fair value option is chosen for investments otherwise accounted for by the equity method, the amount that is reported at fair value is clearly indicated.

Companies also can choose the fair value option for "significant influence" investments that otherwise would be accounted for under the equity method. The company makes an irrevocable decision about whether to elect the fair value option, and can make that election for some investments and not for others. As shown for the fair value method in Illustration 12–17, the company carries the investment at fair value in the balance sheet and includes unrealized gains and losses in earnings.

However, investments that otherwise would be accounted for under the equity method but for which the fair value option has been elected are not reclassified as trading securities. Instead, these investments are shown on their own line in the balance sheet or are combined with equity method investments with the amount at fair value shown parenthetically. Still, they are reported at fair value with changes in fair value reported in earnings as if they were trading securities. Also, all of the disclosures that are required when reporting fair values as well as some of those that would be required under the equity method still must be provided.[37]

Exactly how a company does the bookkeeping necessary to comply with these broad requirements is up to the company. One alternative is to account for the investment using entries similar to those that would be used to account for trading securities. A second alternative is to record all of the accounting entries during the period under the equity method, and then record a fair value adjustment at the end of the period. Regardless of which alternative the company uses to account for the investment during the period, though, the same fair value is reported in the balance sheet at the end of the period, and the same total amount is shown on the income statement (the fair value adjustment amount plus the investment revenue recorded).

International Financial Reporting Standards

● LO12–8

Equity Method. Like U.S. GAAP, international accounting standards require the equity method for use with significant influence investees (which they call "associates"), but you should understand two important differences. First, *IAS No. 28* governs application of the equity method and requires that the accounting policies of investees be adjusted to correspond to those of the investor when applying the equity method.[38] U.S. GAAP has no such requirement.

Second, IFRS does not provide the fair value option for most investments that qualify for the equity method. U.S. GAAP provides the fair value option for all investments that qualify for the equity method.

---

[37]FASB ASC 825–10–50–28: Financial Instruments–Overall–Disclosure–Fair Value Option (previously "The Fair Value Option for Financial Assets and Financial Liabilities," *Statement of Financial Accounting Standards No. 159* (Norwalk, Conn.: FASB, 2007), paragraph 18.f).

[38]"Investments in Associates," *International Accounting Standard 28* (London, UK: IASCF, 2003), as amended effective January 1, 2014.

Concept Review Exercise

THE EQUITY METHOD

Delta Apparatus bought 40% of Clay Crating Corp.'s outstanding common shares on January 2, 2016, for $540 million. The carrying amount of Clay Crating's net assets (shareholders' equity) at the purchase date totaled $900 million. Book values and fair values were the same for all financial statement items except for inventory and buildings, for which fair values exceeded book values by $25 million and $225 million, respectively. All inventory on hand at the acquisition date was sold during 2016. The buildings have average remaining useful lives of 18 years. During 2016, Clay Crating reported net income of $220 million and paid an $80 million cash dividend.

Required:

1. Prepare the appropriate journal entries during 2016 for the investment.
2. Determine the amounts relating to the investment that Delta Apparatus should report in the 2016 financial statements:
   a. As an investment in the balance sheet.
   b. As investment revenue in the income statement.
   c. As investing and/or operating activities in the statement of cash flows (direct method).

Solution

1. Prepare the appropriate journal entries during 2016 for the investment.

	($ in millions)	
Purchase		
Investment in Clay Crating shares	540	
Cash		540
Net income		
Investment in Clay Crating shares (40% × $220 million)	88	
Investment revenue		88
Dividends		
Cash (40% × $80 million)	32	
Investment in Clay Crating shares		32
Inventory		
Investment revenue (as if 2016 cost of goods sold is higher because beginning inventory was adjusted to fair value)	10	
Investment in Clay Crating shares (40% × $25 million)		10
Buildings		
Investment revenue ([$225 million × 40%] ÷ 18 years)	5	
Investment in Clay Crating shares		5

	Investee Net Assets ↓	Net Assets Purchased ↓	Difference Attributed to ↓	
Cost		$540	Goodwill:	$80 [difference]
Fair value	$1,150† × 40% =	$460	Undervaluation of inventory	$10 [$25 × 40%]
Book value	$ 900 × 40% =	$360	Undervaluation of buildings	$90 [$225 × 40%]

†($900 + 25 + 225)

2. Determine the amounts that Delta Apparatus should report in the 2016 financial statements:

 a. As an investment in the balance sheet:

Investment in Clay Crating Shares

($ in millions)

Cost	540		
Share of income	88		
		32	Dividends
		10	Cost of goods sold adjustment for inventory
		5	Depreciation adjustment for buildings
Balance	581		

 b. As investment revenue in the income statement:

$88 million (share of income) − [$10 + 5] million (adjustments) = $73 million

 c. In the statement of cash flows (direct method):

- Investing activities: $540 million cash outflow
- Operating activities: $32 million cash inflow

Decision Makers' Perspective

The various approaches used to account for investments can have very different effects on an investor's income statement and balance sheet. Consequently, it's critical that both managers and external decision makers clearly understand those effects and make decisions accordingly.

To highlight key considerations, suppose that, on January 1, 2016, BigCo spent $5,000,000 to purchase 20% of TechStart, a small start-up company that is developing products that apply an exciting new technology. The purchase price included $500,000 for BigCo's share of the difference between the fair value and book value of TechStart's inventory, all of which was then sold in 2016. TechStart paid a small dividend of $100,000 in 2016, so BigCo received 20% of it, or $20,000. TechStart incurs and expenses large amounts of research and development costs as it develops new technology, so it had a net loss in 2016 of $1,000,000. Yet, the future income-generating potential of the products that TechStart is developing has made TechStart a hot stock, and the fair value of BigCo's 20% investment increased to $5,500,000 by the end of 2016. Illustration 12–18 shows how BigCo's investment would be accounted for under three alternative approaches.

Illustration 12–18
Comparison of Methods Used to Account for Investments

	Trading Security	Available-for-Sale	Equity Method
Share of investee net income[a]	–0–	–0–	($ 700,000)
Dividend income[b]	$ 20,000	$ 20,000	–0–
Increase in investee's fair value[c]	$ 500,000	–0–	–0–
Total 2016 effect on net income	$ 520,000	$ 20,000	($ 700,000)
12/31/2016 investment book value[d]	$5,500,000	$5,500,000	$4,280,000

[a]Not recognized for trading securities or available-for-sale securities. Under the equity method, investment revenue (loss) is 20% × ($1,000,000 loss) + ($500,000) additional expense for fair value inventory adjustment = ($700,000).
[b]Not recognized for equity method investments. Instead, dividends reduce book value of the investment.
[c]Recognized in net income for trading securities, in other comprehensive income for available-for-sale securities, and not recognized for equity method investments.
[d]Equals fair value for trading securities and available-for-sale securities. Equals initial cost plus income (or minus loss) and minus dividends for equity method.

The accounting method does not affect cash flows, but it has a big effect on net income in current and future periods. Also, because the accounting method affects the book value of the investment, it affects gain or loss on sale of that investment. In our example, if BigCo sold its TechStart investment at the beginning of 2017 for $5,000,000, it would recognize a $720,000 gain on sale if the investment was accounted for under the equity method, but a $500,000 loss if it was accounted for as a trading security or available-for-sale security. All of these income effects are predictable, but only if a user understands the relevant accounting methods and the fact that those methods all end up recognizing the same amount of total gain or loss over the life of an investment. Nevertheless, sometimes even experienced analysts get confused.[39]

The way an investment is accounted for affects net income, investment book value, and the amount of gain or loss recognized in the future when the investment is sold.

One strength of the equity method is that it prevents the income manipulation that would be possible if a company recognized income when it received dividends and could significantly influence an investee to pay dividends whenever the company needed an income boost. Remember, under the equity method dividends aren't income, but rather reduce the book value of the investment. Nevertheless, users still need to realize that managers may choose and apply methods in ways that make their company appear most attractive. For example, research suggests that investments sometimes are structured to avoid crossing the 20 to 25 percent threshold that typically requires using the equity method,[40] presumably to avoid the negative effect on earnings that comes from having to recognize the investor's share of investee losses and other income adjustments. Also, a company might smooth income by timing the sale of available-for-sale or equity method investments to realize gains in otherwise poor periods and realize losses in otherwise good periods. While consistent with GAAP, mixing these sorts of one-time gains and losses with operating income could encourage users to think that operating income is less volatile than it really is.

Managers may structure investments to include only the amount of equity that qualifies for their preferred accounting approach.

If investments are not accounted for at fair value, their sale can be timed to recognize gains or losses in particular accounting periods.

Of particular concern is the potential for inaccurate fair value estimates. Even if management is trying to provide the most accurate fair value estimate possible, there is much potential for error, particularly when making estimates at level 3 of the fair value hierarchy. Also, a company conceivably could use the discretion inherent in fair value estimation to manage earnings with respect to trading securities or other investments for which they have elected the fair value option. Given this potential for error and bias, it's not surprising that investors are nervous about the accuracy of fair value estimates. To address these sorts of concerns, the FASB has required extensive note disclosure about the quality of inputs associated with estimates of fair value, but financial statement users need to know to look for those disclosures and still must understand that they cannot assess fully the accuracy of fair value estimates. ●

A concern with fair value accounting is that management has much discretion over fair values, and may not be able to estimate fair values accurately.

Financial Instruments and Investment Derivatives

A **financial instrument** is defined as:

- Cash,
- Evidence of an *ownership interest* in an entity,[41]
- A contract that (a) imposes on one entity an obligation to *deliver* cash (say accounts payable) or another financial instrument and (b) conveys to the second entity a right to *receive* cash (say accounts receivable) or another financial instrument, or

[39]For example, in 2000, analysts were accustomed to including **Intel**'s investment gainss as ordinary income, because those amounts were not particularly large and could be viewed as part of Intel's business. However, in the 2nd quarter of 2000, Intel recorded a net $2.1 billion gain from selling securities in its available-for-sale portfolio. Analysts were surprised and confused, with some eliminating the gain from their earnings estimates but others including them ("Intel Says Net Jumped 79%; Analysts Upset," *The Wall Street Journal,* July 19, 2000, p. A3).

[40]E. E. Comiskey and C. W. Mulford, "Investment Decisions and the Equity Accounting Standard," *The Accounting Review* 61, no. 3 (July 1986), pp. 519–525.

[41]This category includes not just shares of stock, but also partnership agreements and stock options.

- A contract that (a) imposes on one entity an obligation to *exchange* financial instruments on potentially unfavorable terms (say the issuer of a stock option) and (b) conveys to a second entity a right to *exchange* other financial instruments on potentially favorable terms (say the holder of a stock option).[42]

***Derivatives* are financial instruments that "derive" their values from some other security or index.**

A complex class of financial instruments exists in financial markets in response to the desire of firms to manage risks. In fact, these financial instruments would not exist in their own right, but have been created solely to hedge against risks created by other financial instruments or by transactions that have yet to occur but are anticipated. Financial futures, interest rate swaps, forward contracts, and options have become commonplace. These financial instruments often are called **derivatives** because they "derive" their values or contractually required cash flows from some other security or index. For instance, an option to buy an asset in the future at a preset price has a value that is dependent on, or derived from, the value of the underlying asset. Their rapid acceptance as indispensable components of the corporate capital structure has left the accounting profession scrambling to keep pace.

The urgency to establish accounting standards for financial instruments has been accelerated by headline stories in the financial press reporting multibillion-dollar losses on exotic derivatives by **J.P. Morgan** and **UPS**, to mention a couple. The headlines have tended to focus attention on the misuse of these financial instruments rather than their legitimate use in managing risk.

The FASB's ongoing financial instruments project is expected to lead to a consistent framework for accounting for all financial instruments.

The FASB has for many years been involved in a project to provide a consistent framework for resolving financial instrument accounting issues, including those related to derivatives and other "off-balance-sheet" instruments. The financial instruments project has three separate but related parts: disclosure, recognition and measurement, and distinguishing between liabilities and equities. Unfortunately, issues to be resolved are extremely complex and will likely require several more years to resolve. To help fill the disclosure gap in the meantime, the FASB has offered a series of temporary, "patchwork" solutions. These are primarily in the form of additional disclosures for financial instruments. More recently, the FASB has tackled the issues of recognition and measurement. We discuss these requirements in Appendix A after we've spent some time with the measurement issues necessary to understand accounting for derivatives.

Financial Reporting Case Solution

1. **How should you respond? Why are held-to-maturity securities treated differently from other investment securities?** *(p. 657)* You should explain that if an investor has the positive intent and ability to hold the securities to maturity, investments in debt securities are classified as held-to-maturity and reported at amortized cost in the balance sheet. Increases and decreases in fair value are not reported in the financial statements. The reasoning is that the changes are not as relevant to an investor who will hold a security to its maturity regardless of those changes. Changes in the fair value between the time a debt security is acquired and the day it matures to a prearranged maturity value aren't as important if sale before maturity isn't an alternative.[43]
2. **Why are unrealized gains and losses on trading securities reported in the income statement?** *(p. 661)* Trading securities are acquired for the purpose of profiting from short-term market price changes, so gains and losses from holding these securities while prices change are often viewed as relevant performance measures that should be included in net income.

[42]FASB ASC Master Glossary: Financial Instrument (previously "Disclosure of Information about Financial Instruments with Off-Balance-Sheet Risk and Financial Instruments with Concentrations of Credit Risk," *Statement of Financial Accounting Standards No. 105* (Stamford, Conn.: FASB, 1990), par. 6).

[43]Interest rate futures were traded for the first time in 1975 on the Chicago Board of Trade. Interest rate swaps were invented in the early 1980s. They now comprise over 70% of derivatives in use.

3. **Why are unrealized gains and losses on available-for-sale securities not reported in the income statement, but instead are in other comprehensive income, and then shown in accumulated other comprehensive income (AOCI) on the balance sheet?** *(p. 666)* Available-for-sale securities are not acquired for the purpose of profiting from short-term market price changes, so gains and losses from holding these securities while prices change are viewed as insufficiently relevant performance measures to be included in net income. Instead, those amounts are shown in other comprehensive income (OCI) and accumulated in an owners' equity account (AOCI). It's likely that holding gains in some periods will be offset by holding losses in other periods. When the investment is sold, the net amount of gain or loss is removed from AOCI and recognized in net income.
4. **Explain why Coke accounts for some of its investments by the equity method and what that means.** *(p. 683)* When an investor does not have "control," but still is able to exercise *significant influence* over the operating and financial policies of the investee, the investment should be accounted for by the equity method. Apparently Coke owns between 20% and 50% of the voting shares of some of the companies it invests in. By the equity method, Coke recognizes investment income in an amount equal to its percentage share of the net income earned by those companies, instead of the amount of that net income it receives as cash dividends. The rationale is that as the investee earns additional net assets, Coke's share of those net assets increases. ●

The Bottom Line

- **LO12–1** When an investor lacks significant influence over the operating and financial policies of the investee, its investment is classified for reporting purposes as held-to-maturity (HTM), available-for-sale (AFS), or trading securities (TS). If an investor has the positive intent and ability to hold the securities to maturity, investments in debt securities are classified as HTM and reported at amortized cost in the balance sheet. These investments are recorded at cost, and holding gains or losses from fair value changes are ignored. (*p. 658*)
- **LO12–2** Investments in debt or equity securities acquired principally for the purpose of selling them in the near term are classified as trading securities. They are reported at their fair values. Holding gains and losses for trading securities are included in earnings. (*p. 661*)
- **LO12–3** Investments in debt and equity securities that don't fit the definitions of the other reporting categories are classified as available-for-sale. They are reported at their fair values. Holding gains and losses from retaining securities during periods of price change are not included in the determination of income for the period; they are reported as a separate component of shareholders' equity. (*p. 665*)
- **LO12–4** When an investor is able to exercise significant influence over the operating and financial policies of the investee, the investment should be accounted for by the equity method. Usually an investor is presumed to have the ability to exercise significant influence when it owns between 20% and 50% of the investee's voting shares. (*p. 682*)
- **LO12–5** By the equity method, the investor recognizes investment income equal to its percentage share (based on share ownership) of the net income earned by the investee, rather than the portion of that net income received as cash dividends. The investment account is adjusted for the investor's percentage share of net income or loss reported by the investee. When the investor actually receives dividends, the investment account is reduced accordingly. (*p. 682*)
- **LO12–6** When the cost of an investment exceeds the book value of the underlying net assets acquired, both the investment account and investment revenue are adjusted for differences between net income reported by the investee and what that amount would have been if consolidation procedures had been followed. (*p. 684*)
- **LO12–7** The fair value option allows companies to account for most financial assets and liabilities in the same way they account for trading securities, with unrealized holding gains and losses included in net income and the investment carried at fair value in the balance sheet. For HTM and AFS investments, this simply requires reclassifying those investments as trading securities. For equity method investments, this requires clearly identifying the portion of those investments classified in the significant-influence category that is

being accounted for at fair value. In all cases, additional disclosures are required that indicate the quality of inputs used to calculate fair values. (*pp. 674* and *690*)

● LO12–8 U.S. GAAP and IFRS are similar in most respects concerning how they account for investments, but accounting in this area is being overhauled by both the IASB and the FASB, and IFRS companies may report under two different standards (either *IAS No. 39* or *IFRS No. 9*) until 2018. Under both standards, IFRS is more restrictive in terms of the circumstances in which the fair value option can be used. IAS No. 39 recognizes different amounts of OTT impairment for HTM and AFS debt investments, and allows recovery of OTT impairments for debt investments (but not equity investments). IFRS No. 9 takes a different approach, adopting an "expected credit loss" model that should result in later and lower impairments than will exist under the impairment model likely to be adopted by U.S. GAAP. (*pp. 674, 675, 676, 677, 690, 702,* and *704*) ●

APPENDIX 12A Other Investments (Special Purpose Funds, Investments in Life Insurance Policies)

Special Purpose Funds

Some special purpose funds—like petty cash—are current assets.

It's often convenient for companies to set aside money to be used for specific purposes. You learned about one such special purpose fund in Chapter 7 when we discussed petty cash funds. Recall that a petty cash fund is money set aside to conveniently make small expenditures using currency rather than having to follow the time-consuming, formal procedures normally used to process checks. Similar funds sometimes are used to pay interest, payroll, or other short-term needs. Like petty cash, these short-term special purpose funds are reported as current assets.

A special purpose fund can be established for *virtually any purpose.*

Noncurrent special purpose funds are reported within the category *investments and funds.*

Special purpose funds also are sometimes established to serve longer-term needs. It's common, for instance, to periodically set aside cash into a fund designated to repay bonds and other long-term debt. Such funds usually accumulate cash over the debt's term to maturity and are composed of the company's periodic contributions plus interest or dividends from investing the money in various return-generating investments. In fact, some debt contracts require the borrower to establish such a fund to repay the debt. In similar fashion, management might voluntarily choose to establish a fund to accumulate money to expand facilities, provide for unexpected losses, buy back shares of stock, or any other special purpose that might benefit from an accumulation of funds. Of course, funds that won't be used within the upcoming operating cycle are noncurrent assets. They typically are reported as part of investments. The same criteria for classifying securities into reporting categories that we discussed previously should be used to classify securities in which funds are invested. Any investment revenue from these funds is reported as such on the income statement.

Investments in Life Insurance Policies

Certain life insurance policies can be surrendered while the *insured is still alive in* exchange for its *cash surrender value.*

Companies frequently buy life insurance policies on the lives of their key officers. Under normal circumstances, the company pays the premium for the policy and, as beneficiary, receives the proceeds when the officer dies. Of course, the objective is to compensate the company for the untimely loss of a valuable resource in the event the officer dies. However, some types of life insurance policies can be surrendered while the insured is still alive in exchange for a determinable amount of money, called the **cash surrender value**. In effect, a portion of each premium payment is not used by the insurance company to pay for life insurance coverage, but instead is invested on behalf of the insured company in a fixed-income investment. Accordingly, the cash surrender value increases each year by the portion of premiums invested plus interest on the previous amount invested. This is simply a characteristic of whole life insurance, unlike term insurance that has lower premiums and that provides death benefits only.

Part of the annual premium represents a build-up in the cash surrender value.

From an accounting standpoint, the periodic insurance premium should not be expensed in its entirety. Rather, part of each premium payment, the investment portion, is recorded as an asset. Illustration 12A–1 provides an example. ●

Illustration 12A–1
Cash Surrender Value

Several years ago, American Capital acquired a $1 million insurance policy on the life of its chief executive officer, naming American Capital as beneficiary. Annual premiums are $18,000, payable at the beginning of each year. In 2016, the cash surrender value of the policy increased according to the contract from $5,000 to $7,000. The CEO died at the end of 2016.

Insurance expense (difference)	16,000	
Cash surrender value of life insurance ($7,000 – 5,000)	2,000	
Cash (2016 premium)		18,000

To record insurance expense and the increase in the investment.

Part of each insurance premium represents an increase in the cash surrender value.

The cash surrender value is considered to be a noncurrent investment and would be reported in the investments and funds section of the balance sheet. Of course when the insured officer dies, the corporation receives the death benefit of the insurance policy, and the cash surrender value ceases to exist because canceling the policy no longer is an option. The corporation recognizes a gain for the amount of the death benefit less the cash surrender value:

Cash (death benefit)	1,000,000	
Cash surrender value of life insurance (balance)		7,000
Gain on life insurance settlement (difference)		993,000

To record the proceeds at death.

When the death benefit is paid, the cash surrender value becomes null and void.

APPENDIX 12B

Impairment of Investments

An "other-than-temporary" impairment loss is recognized in net income even though the security hasn't been sold.

We saw in Chapter 11 that intangible assets and property, plant, and equipment are subject to impairment losses that reduce earnings if a decline in fair value indicates that the assets' value has been impaired. The same is true for investments. As indicated in Chapter 12, if the fair value of an investment declines to a level below cost, and that decline is not viewed as temporary, companies typically have to recognize an other-than-temporary (OTT) impairment loss in earnings. We don't need to worry about OTT impairments for trading securities or other investments for which a company has chosen the fair value option, because all changes in the fair values of those investments (whether temporary or OTT) always are recognized in earnings. However, that is not the case for HTM and AFS investments. Declines in fair value typically are ignored for HTM investments and recorded in OCI for AFS investments. Therefore, companies need to evaluate HTM and AFS investments to determine whether an OTT impairment loss has occurred.

We use a three-step process to determine whether an OTT impairment loss must be recognized and how that loss is to be measured and recorded: (1) determine if the investment is impaired, (2) determine whether any impairment is OTT, (3) determine where to report the OTT impairment.[44] Illustration 12B–1 summarizes those steps. As you can see, the specifics of accounting for OTT impairments depend on whether the investment is in equity or debt, so we'll discuss each in turn.

Impairments of Equity Investments

Recall that OTT impairments don't apply to trading securities and that equity investments cannot be classified as held-to-maturity. Therefore, when we consider OTT impairments of equity investments, we are looking at available-for-sale investments. Here are the three steps:

1. ***Is the investment impaired?*** Impairment occurs when fair value has declined to a level below the investment's cost (which equals the investment's purchase price less previously recognized impairments and other adjustments).

[44]FASB ASC 320–10–35: Investments–Overall–Subsequent Measurement (originally "The Meaning of Other-Than-Temporary Impairment and Its Application to Certain Investments," *FASB Staff Position No. 115-1 and 124-1* (Norwalk, Conn.: FASB, November 3, 2005)).

Illustration 12B–1

Other-Than-Temporary Impairment of Equity Investments and Debt Investments Compared

	Equity Investment	Debt Investment
Is the investment impaired?	Yes, if the fair value is less than the investment's cost	Same (yes, if the fair value is less than the investment's amortized cost)
Is any of the impairment *other-than-temporary* (OTT)?	Yes, if the investor cannot assert that it has the intent and ability to hold the investment until fair value recovers	Yes, if the investor (a) intends to sell the investment, (b) believes it is "more likely than not" that the investor will be required to sell the investment prior to recovering the amortized cost of the investment, less any current-period credit loss, or (c) has incurred credit losses
Where is the OTT impairment reported?	In net income	In net income, if the investor intends to sell the security or is "more likely than not" to be required to sell it before recovery of its amortized cost. Otherwise: • Credit loss portion in net income. (Credit loss = amortized cost − PV of expected cash flows); • Noncredit loss portion in OCI (Noncredit loss portion = total impairment − credit loss)

Equity impairments are OTT if the investor cannot assert it has the intent and ability to hold the investment until fair value recovers.

2. ***Is any impairment other-than-temporary (OTT)?*** The impairment is temporary if the investing company can assert that it has the intent and ability to hold the investment until fair value recovers to a level that once again exceeds cost. That assertion is more difficult to defend if the expected recovery period is relatively long, the amount of impairment is large, or the financial condition of the investor or the issuer of the equity is weak.[45]

If an equity impairment is OTT:
- **Investment is written down to fair value**
- **All of the OTT impairment loss is included in net income**

3. ***Where is the OTT impairment reported?*** A *temporary* impairment of an equity investment is simply accounted for as an unrealized loss in OCI, as demonstrated previously for fair value declines in AFS securities in Illustration 12–6. However, if the impairment is viewed as OTT, the investor recognizes the loss in the income statement, just as if the loss had been realized by selling the investment. Also, because the equity investment is classified as AFS, recognizing an OTT impairment likely will involve reclassifying amounts out of OCI that were recorded previously as unrealized gains or losses.

Illustration 12B–2 provides a description of the OTT equity impairment process from **Bank of America**'s recent annual report.

Illustration 12B–2

Disclosure about OTT Impairments of Equity Investments—Bank of America

Real World Financials

Note 1 (in part): Securities

All AFS marketable equity securities are carried at fair value with net unrealized gains and losses included in accumulated OCI on an after-tax basis. If there is an other-than-temporary decline in the fair value of any individual AFS marketable equity security, the cost basis is reduced and the Corporation reclassifies the associated net unrealized loss out of accumulated OCI with a corresponding charge to equity investment income.

[45]FASB ASC 320–10–S99: Investments–Overall–SEC Materials (previously "Other-Than-Temporary Impairment of Certain Investments in Equity Securities," *Staff Accounting Bulletin Topic 5.M*).

For an example of an OTT impairment of an equity investment, Illustration 12B–3 modifies a portion of Illustration 12–6:

Illustration 12B–3
Other-Than-Temporary (OTT) Impairment of an Equity Investment

United Intergroup, Inc., buys and sells both debt and equity securities of other companies as investments. United's fiscal year-end is December 31. The following events during 2016 and 2017 pertain to the investment portfolio.

Purchase Investment

July 1, 2016	Purchased $1,000,000 of Bendac common stock.
Adjust Investment to Fair Value	
December 31, 2016	Valued the Bendac stock at $990,000 and determined that the decline in FV should *not* be treated as an OTT impairment.
December 31, 2017	Valued the Bendac stock at $985,000 and determined that the decline in FV should be treated as an OTT impairment.

The journal entries to record the adjustments of the Bendac stock investment to fair value are:

December 31, 2016		
Net unrealized holding gains and losses—OCI	10,000	
Fair value adjustment		10,000
December 31, 2017		
Other-than-temporary impairment loss—I/S	15,000	
Investment in Bendac		15,000
Fair value adjustment	10,000	
Net unrealized holding gains and losses—OCI		10,000

The first 2017 journal entry in Illustration 12B–3 reduces the Bendac investment to reflect the OTT impairment and recognizes the entire $15,000 in 2017 earnings. United adjusts the Bendac investment directly rather than using a fair value adjustment account because the OTT impairment cannot be recovered. The second 2017 journal entry reclassifies any previously recognized unrealized losses associated with the investment, the same as if the investment had been sold. In 2016 United debited OCI and credited the fair value adjustment for $10,000 to reflect the decline in Bendac's fair value to $990,000, so the second 2017 journal entry reverses the 2016 entry to remove those amounts.

Impairments of Debt Investments

As with equity investments, we use a three-step process to determine whether an impairment loss on debt investments must be recognized and how that loss is to be measured and recorded.[46] Debt investments can be classified either as HTM or AFS. We'll start with the assumption that the investment is AFS, and then indicate what is different if it is HTM.

1. ***Is the investment impaired?*** As with equity, impairment of a debt investment occurs when its fair value has declined to a level below amortized cost. For debt investments, though, it also may be necessary to split the total amount of impairment into credit losses and noncredit losses. *Credit losses* reflect expected reductions in future cash flows from anticipated defaults on interest or principal payments. We calculate credit losses as the difference between the amortized cost of the debt and the *present value of the cash flows* expected to be collected, using a discount rate equal to the effective interest rate that existed at the date the investment was acquired. *Noncredit losses* capture other reductions in fair value such as those due to changes in general economic conditions.

Debt impairments can be divided into credit losses and noncredit losses.

Credit losses **are due to anticipated reductions in cash flows from the debt investment; all others are** ***noncredit losses.***

[46]FASB ASC 320–10–35: Investments–Overall–Subsequent Measurement (previously "Recognition and Presentation of Other-Than-Temporary Impairments," *FASB Staff Position No. 115-2 and 124-2* (Norwalk, Conn.: FASB April 9, 2009)).

Debt impairments are OTT if the investor:
a. intends to sell the investment, or
b. believes it is more likely than not that they will sell the investment prior to fair value recovery, or
c. has suffered a credit loss.

2. ***Is any impairment other-than-temporary (OTT)?*** We view a debt impairment as OTT if one of three conditions holds:

   a. The investor intends to sell the investment,

   b. The investor believes it is "more likely than not" that the investor will be required to sell the investment prior to recovering the amortized cost of the investment less any current-period credit losses, or

   c. The investor determines that a credit loss exists on the investment.

   The rationale for 2a and 2b is that an impairment is OTT if the investor is likely to sell the investment before fair value can recover. The rationale for 2c is that an impairment is OTT if the company believes the cash flows provided by the investment won't be enough to allow it to recover the amortized cost of the investment over the life of the investment.

If a debt impairment is OTT:
- **Investment is written down to fair value.**
- **If OTT because of (a) or (b), all of the OTT impairment loss is recognized in net income.**
- **If OTT because of (c), only the credit loss is recognized in net income; noncredit loss in OCI.**

3. ***Where is the OTT impairment reported?*** If the debt impairment is considered OTT, the investor always writes the investment down to fair value in the balance sheet, but the amount included in net income or other comprehensive income depends on the reason the impairment is considered OTT:

   a. If the impairment is considered OTT due to reasons 2a or 2b above, the entire impairment loss is included in net income, because it is likely that the company will incur a loss equal to the entire difference between fair value and amortized cost.

   b. If the impairment is considered OTT due to reason 2c above, *only the credit loss* component is included in net income, as that amount of amortized cost is unlikely to be recovered. Any noncredit loss component reduces OCI, similar to how we normally account for unrealized gains and losses on AFS investments.

   Also, if the debt investment is classified as AFS, recognizing an OTT impairment may involve reclassifying amounts out of OCI that were recorded previously as unrealized gains or losses.

Illustration 12B–4 provides a description of the OTT debt impairment process from **Bank of America**'s recent annual report.

Illustration 12B–4

Disclosure about OTT Impairments of Debt Investments—Bank of America

Real World Financials

Note 1 (in part): Securities

The Corporation regularly evaluates each AFS and held-to-maturity (HTM) debt security where the value has declined below amortized cost to assess whether the decline in fair value is other than temporary. In determining whether an impairment is other than temporary, the Corporation considers the severity and duration of the decline in fair value, the length of time expected for recovery, the financial condition of the issuer, and other qualitative factors, as well as whether the Corporation either plans to sell the security or it is more-likely-than-not that it will be required to sell the security before recovery of the amortized cost. If the impairment of the AFS or HTM debt security is credit-related, an other-than-temporary impairment (OTTI) loss is recorded in earnings. For AFS debt securities, the non–credit-related impairment loss is recognized in accumulated OCI. If the Corporation intends to sell an AFS debt security or believes it will more-likely-than-not be required to sell a security, the Corporation records the full amount of the impairment loss as an OTTI loss.

For an example of an OTT impairment for a debt investment, we modify our Bendac example again in Illustration 12B–5. In both Cases 1 and 2 of Illustration 12B–5, the amortized cost of the investment is reduced by the amount of OTT impairment that is recognized in earnings. United achieves this by crediting a contra asset, discount on bond investment, which United amortizes over the remaining life of the debt the same way it would if it had initially purchased the debt at that discounted amount. In Case 2, the *noncredit loss* component of the impairment is recognized in OCI, the same way it would be if it were viewed as an unrealized loss under normal accounting for fair value declines of AFS investments. In both cases the carrying value of the debt becomes $950,000, reduced by the entire amount

Illustration 12B–5
Other-than-temporary Impairment of Debt Investment

United Intergroup, Inc., buys and sells both debt and equity securities of other companies as investments, and classifies these investments as AFS. United's fiscal year-end is December 31. The following events occurred during 2017.

Purchase Investment

July 1, 2017 — Purchased $1,000,000 of Bendac bonds, maturing on December 31, 2022.

Adjust Investment to Fair Value

December 31, 2017 — Valued the Bendac bonds at $950,000. Of the $50,000 impairment, $30,000 is credit loss and $20,000 is noncredit loss.

We'll consider two cases:

- Case 1: United either plans to sell the investment or believes it is more likely than not that it will have to sell the investment before fair value recovers (such that the impairment is viewed as OTT under 2a or 2b above).
- Case 2: United does *not* intend to sell the investment and does *not* believe it is more likely than not that it will have to sell the Bendac investment before fair value recovers, but estimates that $30,000 of credit losses have occurred (such that the impairment is viewed as OTT under 2c above).

	Case 1		Case 2	
December 31, 2017				
OTT impairment loss—I/S	50,000		30,000	
Discount on bond investment		50,000		30,000
OTT impairment loss—OCI			20,000	
Fair value adjustment—Noncredit loss				20,000

Note: if United had included unrealized gains or losses for this investment in OCI in a prior period, it also would have to make a reclassification entry, as demonstrated for an equity OTT impairment in Illustration 12B–3.

of the OTT impairment. In Case 1 this occurs via the $50,000 discount, and in Case 2 via the combination of the $30,000 discount and $20,000 fair value adjustment.

In both cases all of the OTT impairment is reflected in comprehensive income. The question is how much is reflected in net income as opposed to OCI. To clarify this distinction, GAAP requires that the entire OTT impairment be shown in the income statement, and then the portion attributed to noncredit losses backed out, such that only the credit loss portion reduces net income. That way, financial statement users are aware of the total amount as well as the amount included in net income. Continuing Illustration 12B–5, income statement presentation of the two cases would be as follows:

Income Statement Presentation, December 31, 2017	Case 1	Case 2
OTT impairment of AFS investments:		
Total OTT impairment loss	$50,000	$50,000
Less: portion recognized in OCI	–0–	20,000
Net impairment loss recognized in net income	$50,000	$30,000

Additional Consideration

A Little Credit Loss Goes a Long Way

Here's a twist: Consider Case 2 from Illustration 12B–5, in which United does *not* intend to sell its debt investment and does *not* consider it more likely than not that it will have to sell the investment prior to recovering fair value. According to GAAP, if the entire

(continued)

(concluded)

$50,000 impairment is due to noncredit loss, there is no credit loss, so the impairment is not viewed as OTT and does not show up on the income statement. On the other hand, if any of the impairment is due to credit loss, the impairment is viewed as OTT. Therefore, whether the impairment is OTT depends on whether it includes a credit loss, and a small amount of credit loss can matter a lot, as it makes the company show the entire impairment loss as OTT in the income statement and then back out the noncredit-loss portion to include in OCI.

What if a debt investment is classified as HTM rather than AFS? Most of the accounting is the same, but an important difference relates to the recognition of *noncredit* losses in OCI. HTM investments normally don't include unrealized gains and losses in OCI, so these won't routinely be adjusted up or down over time. Therefore, for HTM investments, GAAP requires that companies gradually remove from AOCI any noncredit losses associated with HTM investments. This is achieved by gradually amortizing the noncredit loss over the remaining life of the investment, debiting the fair value adjustment and crediting OCI each period. That way, when the HTM investment has matured, the fair value adjustment and any amount in AOCI have been reduced to zero.

After an OTT impairment is recorded, the usual treatment of unrealized gains or losses is resumed. Changes in fair value are reported in OCI for AFS investments, and are ignored for HTM investments. Reversals of impairments of debt and equity securities are prohibited under U.S. GAAP (except, as indicated in Chapter 7, a debt investment is classified as a note or loan receivable). ●

Additional Consideration

OTT Impairments: An Ongoing Debate

Other-than-temporary impairments of debt instruments previously were accounted for the same as OTT impairments of equity instruments; that is, the entire impairment was shown in net income if it was viewed as OTT. Then the recent credit crisis hit, financial institutions started having to recognize huge OTT impairments for their investments, and impairment accounting was blamed by many for worsening the crisis. Critics argued that it is inappropriate to recognize impairment losses in earnings when all of the cash flows associated with an investment still are anticipated to be collected despite current fair value declines. Proponents argued that fair value declines still are relevant and that critics were simply looking for an accounting fix to reduce their losses. This disagreement came to a head in Spring of 2009, when the FASB responded to pressure from Congress by changing OTT impairment accounting to provide more latitude and avoid including noncredit losses in net income. Firms were allowed to use that approach for OTT impairments occurring in the first quarter of 2009. This had a large effect for some firms; for example, increasing the pretax earnings of twenty banks and other financial institutions by an estimated $4.9 billion in that qarter.[47]

International Financial Reporting Standards

● LO12–8

Accounting for OTT impairments. Under *IAS No. 39*, companies recognize OTT impairments if there exists objective evidence of impairment. Objective evidence must relate to one or more events occurring after initial recognition of the asset that affect the future cash flows that are going to be generated by the asset. Examples of objective

(continued)

[47]Credit Suisse, *Focusing on Fair Value: An Update*, June 4, 2009.

(concluded)

evidence include significant financial difficulty of the issuer and default on interest or principal payments. For an equity security, a significant or prolonged decline in fair value below cost is viewed as objective evidence.

Calculation of the amount of impairment differs depending on the classification of an investment. For an HTM investment, the impairment is calculated as the difference between the amortized cost of the asset and the present value of expected future cash flows, estimated at the asset's original effective rate. So, the impairment is essentially equal to the amount that would be considered a credit loss in U.S. GAAP. For an AFS investment (debt or equity), the impairment is calculated as the difference between amortized cost and fair value. Thus, under *IAS No. 39,* an OTT impairment for a debt investment is likely to be larger if it is classified as AFS than if it is classified as HTM, because it includes the entire decline in fair value if classified as AFS but only the credit loss if classified as HTM. All OTT impairments are recognized in earnings (there is no equivalent to recognizing in OCI any non-credit losses on debt investments). Also, when an OTT impairment is recognized, either the investment account is reduced directly or an allowance account is used.

IAS No. 39 allows recoveries of impairments to be recognized in earnings for debt investments, but not for equity investments. This is a difference from U.S. GAAP, which does not allow recoveries of any OTT impairment of equity or debt (other than debt that is classified as a loan).

To illustrate, let's modify our Bendac debt example from Illustration 12B–5 to assume amortized cost of €1,000,000 and fair value of €950,000, with the €50,000 impairment consisting of €30,000 of credit losses and €20,000 of noncredit losses. If the investment was classified as AFS, IFRS would recognize a €50,000 OTT impairment:

Other-than-temporary impairment loss—I/S	50,000	
Investment in Bendac		50,000

If Bendac had recognized any cumulative unrealized losses in AOCI associated with these investments, it would also need to reclassify those amounts out of AOCI and recognize them in the income statement by debiting the OTT impairment loss and crediting OCI.

If the investment had been classified as HTM rather than AFS, IFRS would recognize an OTT impairment of €30,000:

Other-than-temporary impairment loss—I/S	30,000	
Investment in Bendac		30,000

If in a subsequent period the fair value of the debt investment improved by €15,000, IFRS would allow *reversal* of that amount of impairment charge:

Investment in Bendac	15,000	
Reversal of other-than-temporary impairment loss—I/S		15,000

Recent events highlight the judgmental nature of OTT impairments. A financial crisis in Greece prompted OTT impairments of Greek government bonds by various European banks. In late 2011 the chairman of the IASB, Hans Hoogervorst, complained to the EU's market regulator about inconsistency in how banks were valuing the bonds. Some banks took only a 21% impairment, while others took an impairment of over 50% on the exact same bonds![48]

[48]Jones, A., and J. Thompson. "IASB Criticises Greek Debt Writedowns", *FT.com,* 8/30/2011.

Where We're Headed

Impairments. As discussed earlier in this chapter, the FASB is planning to change the way we account for OTT impairments of debt investments.[49] Under the new approach, called the *current expected credit loss (CECL)* model, the investor estimates impairment losses by comparing the amortized cost of the debt investment to the present value of the cash flows that the investment is expected to provide, discounted at the interest rate that was effective when the investment was initially purchased. Investors will estimate potential "credit losses" (losses due to the borrower defaulting on interest or principal payments) starting on the first day of the investment, even if the likelihood of credit losses is very low. Those estimates will be based on all information that's available about the potential for payment in the future.

A limitation will apply for AFS investments: the carrying value of AFS investments can't be reduced below the fair value of the investment. That's because AFS investments are carried at fair value, so it would be inconsistent to recognize an impairment that reduces the investment to below fair value.

International Financial Reporting Standards

● LO12–8

Accounting for Impairments under IFRS No. 9. International standards also are changing in this area. Starting in 2018 companies using IFRS will calculate impairment of debt investments using the *expected credit loss (ECL)* model.[50] The big difference between the U.S. and IFRS approaches is that, under the IFRS approach, if the credit risk of a debt investment has not increased, the estimate of credit losses will only consider losses that are expected to arise from a default occurring within the next twelve months. Only if the borrower's credit quality has deteriorated significantly would companies report credit losses expected to occur from defaults after twelve months. For many debt investments, the credit risk of the investment hasn't increased, so this approach accrues very little credit loss, because default within the next twelve months is very unlikely. Also, under IFRS No. 9, OTT impairments of equity investments are not recognized, instead remaining in owners' equity.

As a result of this lack of convergence, it is likely that OTT impairments under IFRS will be lower, and recognized later, than under U.S. GAAP.

Questions For Review of Key Topics

Q 12–1 All investments in *debt* securities and investments in *equity* securities for which the investor lacks significant influence over the operation and financial policies of the investee are classified for reporting purposes in one of three categories, and can be accounted for differently depending on the classification. What are these three categories?

Q 12–2 When market rates of interest *rise* after a fixed-rate security is purchased, the value of the now-below-market, fixed-interest payments declines, so the market value of the investment falls. On the other hand, if market rates of interest *fall* after a fixed-rate security is purchased, the fixed-interest payments become relatively attractive, and the market value of the investment rises. Assuming these price changes are not viewed as giving rise to an other-than-temporary impairment, how are they reflected in the investment account for a security classified as held-to-maturity?

Q 12–3 Does GAAP distinguish between fair values that are readily determinable from a securities exchange versus those needing to be calculated based on the company's own assumptions? Explain how a user will know about the reliability of the inputs used to determine fair value.

Q 12–4 When an investment is acquired to be held for an unspecified period of time as opposed to being held to maturity, it is reported at the fair value of the investment securities on the reporting date. Why?

Q 12–5 Reporting an investment at its fair value means adjusting its carrying amount for changes in fair value after its acquisition (or since the last reporting date if it was held at that time). Such changes are called unrealized holding gains and losses because they haven't yet been realized through the sale of the security. If the security

[49] For the current status of this project, see "Accounting for Financial Instruments: Classification and Measurement" under "Projects" at www.fasb.org.

[50] "Financial Instruments," *International Financial Reporting Standard No. 9* (IASCF), November 12, 2009, as amended effective July 24, 2014.

is classified as available-for-sale, how are unrealized holding gains and losses reported if they are not viewed as giving rise to an other-than-temporary impairment?

Q 12–6 What is "comprehensive income"? Its composition varies from company to company but may include which investment-related items that are not included in net income?

Q 12–7 Why are holding gains and losses treated differently for trading securities and securities available-for-sale?

Q 12–8 Western Die-Casting Company holds an investment in unsecured bonds of LGB Heating Equipment, Inc. When the investment was acquired, management's intention was to hold the bonds for resale. Now management has the positive intent and ability to hold the bonds to maturity. How should the reclassification of the investment be accounted for?

Q 12–9 Is it necessary for an investor to report individual amounts for the three categories of investments—held-to-maturity, available-for-sale, or trading—in the financial statements? What information should be disclosed about these investments?

IFRS **Q 12–10** Under *IFRS No. 9,* which reporting categories are used to account for debt investments? What about for equity investments when the investor lacks the ability to significantly influence the operations of the investee?

IFRS **Q 12–11** Are there circumstances in which the cost method is required under U.S. GAAP but not under IFRS? Explain.

Q 12–12 What is the effect of a company electing the fair value option with respect to a held-to-maturity investment or an available-for-sale investment?

IFRS **Q 12–13** Do U.S. GAAP and IFRS differ in the amount of flexibility that companies have in electing the fair value option? Explain.

Q 12–14 Under what circumstances is the equity method used to account for an investment in stock?

Q 12–15 The equity method has been referred to as a *one-line consolidation.* What might prompt this description?

Q 12–16 In the application of the equity method, how should dividends from the investee be accounted for? Why?

Q 12–17 The fair value of depreciable assets of Penner Packaging Company exceeds their book value by $12 million. The assets' average remaining useful life is 10 years. They are being depreciated by the straight-line method. Finest Foods Industries buys 40% of Penner's common shares. When adjusting investment revenue and the investment by the equity method, how will the situation described affect those two accounts?

Q 12–18 Superior Company owns 40% of the outstanding stock of Bernard Company. During 2016, Bernard paid a $100,000 cash dividend on its common shares. What effect did this dividend have on Superior's 2016 financial statements?

Q 12–19 Sometimes an investor's level of influence changes, making it necessary to change from the equity method to another method. How should the investor account for this change in accounting method?

IFRS **Q 12–20** How does IFRS differ from U.S. GAAP with respect to using the equity method?

Q 12–21 What is the effect of a company electing the fair value option with respect to an investment that otherwise would be accounted for using the equity method?

Q 12–22 Define a financial instrument. Provide three examples of current liabilities that represent financial instruments.

Q 12–23 Some financial instruments are called derivatives. Why?

Q 12–24 (Based on Appendix 12A) Northwest Carburetor Company established a fund in 2016 to accumulate money for a new plant scheduled for construction in 2018. How should this special purpose fund be reported in Northwest's December 31, 2016 balance sheet?

Q 12–25 (Based on Appendix 12A) Whole-life insurance policies typically can be surrendered while the insured is still alive in exchange for a determinable amount of money called the *cash surrender value.* When a company buys a life insurance policy on the life of a key officer to protect the company against the untimely loss of a valuable resource in the event the officer dies, how should the company account for the cash surrender value?

Q 12–26 (Based on Appendix 12B) When market rates of interest *rise* after a fixed-rate security is purchased, the value of the now below-market, fixed-interest payments declines, so the market value of the investment falls. If that drop in fair value is viewed as giving rise to an other-than-temporary impairment, how would it be reflected in the investment account for a security classified as held-to-maturity?

Q 12–27 (Based on Appendix 12B) Reporting an investment at its fair value requires adjusting its carrying amount for changes in fair value after its acquisition (or since the last reporting date if it was held at that time). Such changes are called unrealized holding gains and losses because they haven't yet been realized through the sale of the security. If a security is classified as available-for-sale, and an unrealized holding loss is viewed as giving rise to an other-than-temporary (OTT) impairment, how is it reported in the financial statements?

Q 12–28 (Based on Appendix 12B) The market value of Helig Forestry and Mining Corporation common stock dropped 6 ⅛ points when the federal government passed new legislation banning one of the company's primary techniques for extracting ore. Harris Corporation owns shares of Helig and classifies its investment as securities available-for-sale. How should the decline in market value be handled by Harris?

IFRS **Q 12–29** (Based on Appendix 12B) Do U.S. GAAP and IFRS (under *IAS No. 39*) differ in how they account for other-than-temporary impairments? Explain.

Brief Exercises

BE 12–1
Securities held-to-maturity; bond investment; effective interest
● LO12–1

Lance Brothers Enterprises acquired $720,000 of 3% bonds, dated July 1, on July 1, 2016, as a long-term investment. Management has the positive intent and ability to hold the bonds until maturity. The market interest rate (yield) was 4% for bonds of similar risk and maturity. Lance Brothers paid $600,000 for the investment in bonds and will receive interest semiannually on June 30 and December 31. Prepare the journal entries (a) to record Lance Brothers' investment in the bonds on July 1, 2016, and (b) to record interest on December 31, 2016, at the effective (market) rate.

BE 12–2
Trading securities
● LO12–2

S&L Financial buys and sells securities expecting to earn profits on short-term differences in price. On December 27, 2016, S&L purchased Coca-Cola common shares for $875,000 and sold the shares on January 3, 2017, for $880,000. At December 31, the shares had a fair value of $873,000. What pretax amounts did S&L include in its 2016 and 2017 earnings as a result of this investment?

BE 12–3
Available-for-sale securities
● LO12–3

S&L Financial buys and sells securities which it classifies as available-for-sale. On December 27, 2016, S&L purchased Coca-Cola common shares for $875,000 and sold the shares on January 3, 2017, for $880,000. At December 31, the shares had a fair value of $873,000, and S&L has the intent and ability to hold the investment until fair value recovers. What pretax amounts did S&L include in its 2016 and 2017 earnings as a result of this investment?

BE 12–4
Securities available-for-sale; adjusting entry
● LO12–3

For several years Fister Links Products has held shares of Microsoft common stock, considered by the company to be securities available-for-sale. The shares were acquired at a cost of $500,000. Their fair value last year was $610,000 and is $670,000 this year. At what amount will the investment be reported in this year's balance sheet? What adjusting entry is required to accomplish this objective?

BE 12–5
Classification of securities; reporting
● LO12–3

Adams Industries holds 40,000 shares of FedEx common stock. On December 31, 2015, and December 31, 2016, the market value of the stock is $95 and $100 per share, respectively. What is the appropriate reporting category for this investment and at what amount will it be reported in the 2016 balance sheet?

BE 12–6
Fair value option; available-for-sale securities
● LO12–7

S&L Financial buys and sells securities that it typically classifies as available-for-sale. On December 27, 2016, S&L purchased Coca-Cola common shares for $875,000 and sold the shares on January 3, 2017, for $880,000. At December 31, the shares had a fair value of $873,000. When it purchased the Coca-Cola shares, S&L Financial decided to elect the fair value option for this investment. What pretax amounts did S&L include in its 2016 and 2017 earnings as a result of this investment?

BE 12–7
Trading securities, securities available-for-sale and dividends
● LO12–2, LO12–3

Turner Company owns 10% of the outstanding stock of ICA Company. During the current year, ICA paid a $5 million cash dividend on its common shares. What effect did this dividend have on Turner's 2016 financial statements? Explain the reasoning for this effect.

BE 12–8
Accounting for fair value changes in debt investments
● LO12–3, LO12–8

Fowler Inc. purchased $75,000 of bonds on January 1, 2018. The bonds pay interest semiannually and mature in 20 years, at which time the $75,000 principal will be paid. The bonds do not pay any amounts other than interest and principal. Fowler's intention is to collect contractual cash flows and eventually sell the bonds within the next couple of years if the price is right. During 2018, the fair value of the bonds increased to $80,000. Fowler reports investments under *IFRS No. 9*. How much unrealized gain or loss will Fowler include in 2018 net income with respect to the bonds?

BE 12–9
Accounting for fair value changes in debt investments
● LO12–1, LO12–8

IFRS

Assume the same facts as in BE12–8, but that Fowler intends to hold the bonds until maturity. How much unrealized gain or loss would Fowler include in 2018 net income with respect to the bonds?

BE 12–10
Equity method and dividends
● LO12–5

Turner Company owns 40% of the outstanding stock of ICA Company. During the current year, ICA paid a $5 million cash dividend on its common shares. What effect did this dividend have on Turner's 2016 financial statements? Explain the reasoning for this effect.

BE 12–11
Equity method
● LO12–6

The fair value of Wallis, Inc.'s depreciable assets exceeds their book value by $50 million. The assets have an average remaining useful life of 15 years and are being depreciated by the straight-line method. Park Industries buys 30% of Wallis's common shares. When Park adjusts its investment revenue and the investment by the equity method, how will the situation described affect those two accounts?

BE 12–12
Equity method investments
● LO12–6, LO12–8

Kim Company bought 30% of the shares of Phelps, Inc., at the start of 2016. Kim paid $10 million for the shares. Thirty percent of the book value of Phelps's net assets is $8 million, and the difference of $2 million is due to land that Phelps owns that has appreciated in value. During 2016, Phelps reported net income of $1 million and paid a cash dividend of $0.5 million. At what amount does Kim carry the Phelps investment on its balance sheet as of December 31, 2016?

BE 12–13
Change in principle; change to the equity method
● LO12–5

At the beginning of 2016, Pioneer Products' ownership interest in the common stock of LLB Co. increased to the point that it became appropriate to begin using the equity method of accounting for the investment. The balance in the investment account was $44 million at the time of the change but would have been $56 million if Pioneer had used the equity method and the account had been adjusted for investee net income and dividends. How should Pioneer report the change? Would your answer be the same if Pioneer is changing *from* the equity method rather than *to* the equity method?

BE 12–14
Fair value option; equity method investments
● LO12–7

Turner Company purchased 40% of the outstanding stock of ICA Company for $10,000,000 on January 2, 2016. Turner elects the fair value option to account for the investment. During 2016, ICA earns $750,000 of income and on December 30 pays a dividend of $500,000. On December 31, 2016, the fair value of Turner's investment has increased to $11,500,000. What journal entries would Turner make to account for this investment during 2016, assuming Turner will account for the investment similar to how it would account for a trading security?

BE 12–15
Available-for-sale securities and impairment (Appendix 12B)
● LO12–3

LED Corporation owns 100,000 shares of Branch Pharmaceuticals common stock and classifies its investment as securities available-for-sale. The market price of LED's investment in Branch's stock fell more than 30%, by $4.50 per share, due to concerns about one of the company's principal drugs. The concerns were justified when the FDA banned the drug. $1.00 per share of that decline in value already had been included in OCI as a temporary unrealized loss in a prior period. What journal entries should LED record to account for the decline in market value in the current period? How should the decline affect net income and comprehensive income?

BE 12–16
Available-for-sale securities and impairment (Appendix 12B)
● LO12–3

LED Corporation owns $1,000,000 of Branch Pharmaceuticals bonds and classifies its investment as securities available-for-sale. The market price of LED's investment in Branch's bonds fell by $450,000, due to concerns about one of the company's principal drugs. The concerns were justified when the FDA banned the drug. $100,000 of that decline in value already had been included in OCI as a temporary unrealized loss in a prior period. LED views $200,000 of the $450,000 loss as related to *credit* losses, and the other $250,000 as *noncredit* losses. LED thinks it is more likely than not that it will have to sell the investment before fair value recovers. What journal entries should LED record to account for the decline in market value in the current period? How should the decline affect net income and comprehensive income?

BE 12–17
Available-for-sale securities and impairment (Appendix 12B)
● LO12–3

LED Corporation owns $1,000,000 of Branch Pharmaceuticals bonds and classifies its investment as securities available-for-sale. The market price of Branch's bonds fell by $450,000, due to concerns about one of the company's principal drugs. The concerns were justified when the FDA banned the drug. $100,000 of that decline in value already had been included in OCI as a temporary unrealized loss in a prior period. LED views $200,000 of the $450,000 loss as related to *credit* losses, and the other $250,000 as *noncredit* losses. LED does not plan to sell the investment and does not think it is more likely than not that it will have to sell the investment before fair value recovers. What journal entries should LED record to account for the decline in market value in the current period? How should the decline affect net income and comprehensive income?

BE 12–18
Recovery of impairments under IFRS (Appendix 12B)
● LO12–1, LO12–8

Wickum Corporation reports under IFRS (according to *IAS No. 39*), and recognized a $500,000 other-than-temporary impairment of an HTM debt investment in Right Corporation. Subsequently, the fair value of Wickum's investment in Right increased by $300,000. How would Wickum account for that increase in fair value?

Exercises

An alternate exercise and problem set is available in the Connect library.

E 12–1
Securities held-to-maturity; bond investment; effective interest
● LO12–1

Tanner-UNF Corporation acquired as a long-term investment $240 million of 6% bonds, dated July 1, on July 1, 2016. Company management has the positive intent and ability to hold the bonds until maturity. The market interest rate (yield) was 8% for bonds of similar risk and maturity. Tanner-UNF paid $200 million for the bonds. The company will receive interest semiannually on June 30 and December 31. As a result of changing market conditions, the fair value of the bonds at December 31, 2016 was $210 million.

Required:

1. Prepare the journal entry to record Tanner-UNF's investment in the bonds on July 1, 2016.
2. Prepare the journal entry by Tanner-UNF to record interest on December 31, 2016, at the effective (market) rate.
3. At what amount will Tanner-UNF report its investment in the December 31, 2016, balance sheet? Why?
4. Suppose Moody's bond rating agency downgraded the risk rating of the bonds motivating Tanner-UNF to sell the investment on January 2, 2017, for $190 million. Prepare the journal entry to record the sale.

E 12–2
Securities held-to-maturity
● LO12–1

FF&T Corporation is a confectionery wholesaler that frequently buys and sells securities to meet various investment objectives. The following selected transactions relate to FF&T's investment activities during the last two months of 2016. At November 1, FF&T held $48 million of 20-year, 10% bonds of Convenience, Inc., purchased May 1, 2016, at face value. Management has the positive intent and ability to hold the bonds until maturity. FF&T's fiscal year ends on December 31.

Nov. 1	Received semiannual interest of $2.4 million from the Convenience, Inc., bonds.
Dec. 1	Purchased 12% bonds of Facsimile Enterprises at their $30 million face value, to be held until they mature in 2026. Semiannual interest is payable May 31 and November 30.
31	Purchased U.S. Treasury bills that mature in two months for $8.9 million.
31	Recorded any necessary adjusting entry(s) relating to the investments.

The fair values of the investments at December 31 were:

Convenience bonds	$44.7 million
Facsimile Enterprises bonds	30.9 million
U.S. Treasury bills	8.9 million

Required:

Prepare the appropriate journal entry for each transaction or event.

E 12–3
FASB codification research
● LO12–1

The *FASB Accounting Standards Codification* represents the single source of authoritative U.S. generally accepted accounting principles.

Required:

1. Obtain the relevant authoritative literature on accounting for investments in held-to-maturity securities using the FASB's Codification Research System at the FASB website (**www.fasb.org**).
2. What is the specific citation that describes examples of circumstances under which an investment in debt is available to be sold and therefore should not be classified as held-to-maturity?
3. List the circumstances and conditions.

E 12–4
Purchase and sale of investment securities
● LO12–2, LO12–3

Shott Farm Supplies Corporation purchased 800 shares of **General Motors** stock at $50 per share and paid a brokerage fee of $1,200. Two months later, the shares were sold for $53 per share. The brokerage fee on the sale was $1,300.

Required:
Prepare entries for the purchase and the sale.

E 12–5
Various transactions relating to trading securities
● LO12–2

Rantzow-Lear Company buys and sells securities expecting to earn profits on short-term differences in price. The company's fiscal year ends on December 31. The following selected transactions relating to Rantzow-Lear's trading account occurred during December 2016 and the first week of 2017.

2016

Dec. 17	Purchased 100,000 Grocers' Supply Corporation preferred shares for $350,000.
28	Received cash dividends of $2,000 from the Grocers' Supply Corporation preferred shares.
31	Recorded any necessary adjusting entry relating to the Grocers' Supply Corporation preferred shares. The market price of the stock was $4 per share.

2017

Jan. 5	Sold the Grocers' Supply Corporation preferred shares for $395,000.

Required:
1. Prepare the appropriate journal entry for each transaction.
2. Indicate any amounts that Rantzow-Lear Company would report in its 2016 balance sheet and income statement as a result of this investment.

E 12–6
FASB codification research
● LO12–2, LO12–3, LO12–5

Access the *FASB's Codification Research System* at the FASB website (**www.fasb.org**).

Required:
Determine the specific citation for accounting for each of the following items:
1. Unrealized holding gains for trading securities should be included in earnings.
2. Under the equity method, the investor accounts for its share of the earnings or losses of the investee in the periods they are reported by the investee in its financial statements.
3. Transfers of securities between categories are accounted for at fair value.
4. Disclosures for available-for-sale securities should include total losses for securities that have net losses included in accumulated other comprehensive income.

E 12–7
Securities available-for-sale; adjusting entries
● LO12–3

Loreal-American Corporation purchased several marketable securities during 2016. At December 31, 2016, the company had the investments in common stock listed below. None was held at the last reporting date, December 31, 2015, and all are considered securities available-for-sale.

	Cost	Fair Value	Unrealized Holding Gain (Loss)
Short term:			
Blair, Inc.	$ 480,000	$ 405,000	$(75,000)
ANC Corporation	450,000	480,000	30,000
Totals	$ 930,000	$ 885,000	$(45,000)
Long term:			
Drake Corporation	$ 480,000	$ 560,000	$ 80,000
Aaron Industries	720,000	660,000	(60,000)
Totals	$1,200,000	$1,220,000	$ 20,000

Required:
1. Prepare the appropriate adjusting entry at December 31, 2016.
2. What amounts would be reported in the income statement at December 31, 2016, as a result of the adjusting entry?

E 12–8
Classification of securities; adjusting entries
● LO12–3

On February 18, 2016, Union Corporation purchased 10,000 shares of **IBM** common stock as a long-term investment at $60 per share. On December 31, 2016, and December 31, 2017, the market value of IBM stock is $58 and $61 per share, respectively.

Required:
1. What is the appropriate reporting category for this investment? Why?
2. Prepare the adjusting entry for December 31, 2016.
3. Prepare the adjusting entry for December 31, 2017.

E 12–9
Various transactions related to securities available-for-sale
● LO12–3

Construction Forms Corporation buys securities to be available for sale when circumstances warrant, not to profit from short-term differences in price and not necessarily to hold debt securities to maturity. The following selected transactions relate to investment activities of Construction Forms whose fiscal year ends on December 31. No investments were held by Construction Forms at the beginning of the year.

2016

Mar. 2	Purchased 1 million Platinum Gauges, Inc., common shares for $31 million, including brokerage fees and commissions.
Apr. 12	Purchased $20 million of 10% bonds at face value from Zenith Wholesale Corporation.
July 18	Received cash dividends of $2 million on the investment in Platinum Gauges, Inc., common shares.
Oct. 15	Received semiannual interest of $1 million on the investment in Zenith bonds.
16	Sold the Zenith bonds for $21 million.
Nov. 1	Purchased 500,000 LTD International preferred shares for $40 million, including brokerage fees and commissions.
Dec. 31	Recorded the necessary adjusting entry(s) relating to the investments. The market prices of the investments are $32 per share for Platinum Gauges, Inc., and $74 per share for LTD International preferred shares.

2017

Jan. 23	Sold half the Platinum Gauges, Inc., shares for $32 per share.
Mar. 1	Sold the LTD International preferred shares for $76 per share.

Required:

1. Prepare the appropriate journal entry for each transaction or event.
2. Show the amounts that would be reported in the company's 2016 combined statement of net income and other comprehensive income relative to these investments.

E 12–10
Securities available-for-sale; journal entries
● LO12–3

On January 2, 2016, Sanborn Tobacco Inc. bought 5% of Jackson Industry's capital stock for $90 million as a temporary investment. Sanborn classified the securities acquired as available-for-sale. Jackson Industry's net income for the year ended December 31, 2016, was $120 million. The fair value of the shares held by Sanborn was $98 million at December 31, 2016. During 2016, Jackson declared a dividend of $60 million.

Required:

1. Prepare all appropriate journal entries related to the investment during 2016.
2. Indicate the effect of this investment on 2016 income before taxes.

E 12–11
Various investment securities
● LO12–1, LO12–2, LO12–3

At December 31, 2016, Hull-Meyers Corp. had the following investments that were purchased during 2016, its first year of operations:

	Cost	Fair Value
Trading Securities:		
Security A	$ 900,000	$ 910,000
Security B	105,000	100,000
Totals	$1,005,000	$1,010,000
Securities Available-for-Sale:		
Security C	$ 700,000	$ 780,000
Security D	900,000	915,000
Totals	$1,600,000	$1,695,000
Securities to Be Held-to-Maturity:		
Security E	$ 490,000	$ 500,000
Security F	615,000	610,000
Totals	$1,105,000	$1,110,000

No investments were sold during 2016. All securities except Security D and Security F are considered short-term investments. None of the fair value changes is considered permanent.

Required:

Determine the following amounts at December 31, 2016.

1. Investments reported as current assets.
2. Investments reported as noncurrent assets.
3. Unrealized gain (or loss) component of income before taxes.
4. Unrealized gain (or loss) component of accumulated other comprehensive income in shareholders' equity.

E 12–12
Securities available-for-sale; adjusting entries
● LO12–3

The accounting records of Jamaican Importers Inc. at January 1, 2016, included the following:

Assets:	
Investment in IBM common shares	$1,345,000
Less: Fair value adjustment	(145,000)
	$1,200,000
Shareholders' Equity:	
Accumulated unrealized holding gains and losses	$ 145,000

No changes occurred during 2016 in the investment portfolio.

Required:

Prepare appropriate adjusting entry(s) at December 31, 2016, assuming the fair value of the IBM common shares was:

1. $1,175,000
2. $1,275,000
3. $1,375,000

E 12–13
Securities available-for-sale; fair value adjustment
● LO12–3

The investments of Harlon Enterprises included the following cost and fair value amounts:

($ in millions)		Fair Value, Dec. 31	
Securities Available-for-Sale	**Cost**	**2016**	**2017**
A Corporation shares	$ 20	$14	na
B Corporation bonds	35	35	$ 37
C Corporation shares	15	na	14
D Industries shares	45	46	50
Totals	$115	$95	$101

Harlon Enterprises sold its holdings of A Corporation shares on June 1, 2017, for $15 million. On September 12, 2017, it purchased the C Corporation shares.

Required:

1. What is the effect of the sale of the A Corporation shares and the purchase of the C Corporation shares on Harlon's 2017 pretax earnings?
2. At what amount should Harlon's securities available-for-sale portfolio be reported in its 2017 balance sheet? What adjusting entry is needed to accomplish this? What is the effect of the adjustment on Harlon's 2017 pre-tax earnings?

E 12–14
Accounting for debt investments
● LO12–1, LO12–8

IFRS

Watney Inc. purchased $10,000 of 6% Hamel bonds at par on July 1, 2016. The bonds pay interest semiannually, and pay only interest and principal. Watney intends to hold the Hamel bonds for purposes of collecting the cash flows provided by interest and principal. During the second half of 2016, an increase in interest rates reduced the fair value of the bonds to $9,000. Watney reports investments under *IFRS No. 9*.

Required:

1. Prepare the December 31, 2016, journal entry to record Watney's interest revenue.
2. Prepare the December 31, 2016, journal entry (if any is required) to record unrealized gains or losses on the Hamel bonds during 2016. (Do not consider whether an impairment should be recorded.)

E 12–15
Accounting for debt investments
● LO12–3, LO12–8

IFRS

Assume the same facts as in E12–14, but that Watney also may sell the Hamel bonds if the price of the bonds appreciates sufficiently.

Required:

1. Prepare the December 31, 2016, journal entry to record Watney's interest revenue.
2. Prepare the December 31, 2016, journal entry (if any is required) to record unrealized gains or losses on the Hamel bonds during 2016. (Do not consider whether an impairment should be recorded.)

E 12–16
Investment securities and equity method investments compared
● LO12–3, LO12–4, LO12–5

As a long-term investment, Painters' Equipment Company purchased 20% of AMC Supplies Inc.'s 400,000 shares for $480,000 at the beginning of the fiscal year of both companies. On the purchase date, the fair value and book value of AMC's net assets were equal. During the year, AMC earned net income of $250,000 and distributed cash dividends of 25 cents per share. At year-end, the fair value of the shares is $505,000.

Required:

1. Assume no significant influence was acquired. Prepare the appropriate journal entries from the purchase through the end of the year.
2. Assume significant influence was acquired. Prepare the appropriate journal entries from the purchase through the end of the year.

E 12–17
Equity method; purchase; investee income; dividends
● LO12–4, LO12–5

As a long-term investment at the beginning of the fiscal year, Florists International purchased 30% of Nursery Supplies Inc.'s 8 million shares for $56 million. The fair value and book value of the shares were the same at that time. During the year, Nursery Supplies earned net income of $40 million and distributed cash dividends of $1.25 per share. At the end of the year, the fair value of the shares is $52 million.

Required:
Prepare the appropriate journal entries from the purchase through the end of the year.

E 12–18
Change in principle; change to the equity method
● LO12–5

The Trump Companies Inc. has ownership interests in several public companies. At the beginning of 2016, the company's ownership interest in the common stock of Milken Properties increased to the point that it became appropriate to begin using the equity method of accounting for the investment. The balance in the investment account was $31 million at the time of the change. Accountants working with company records determined that the balance would have been $48 million if the account had been adjusted for investee net income and dividends as prescribed by the equity method.

Required:
1. Prepare the journal entry to record the change in principle.
2. Briefly describe other steps Trump should take to report the change.
3. Suppose Trump is changing *from* the equity method rather than *to* the equity method. How would your answers to requirements 1 and 2 differ?

E 12–19
Error corrections; investment
● LO12–1, LO12–2, LO12–3

On December 12, 2016, an investment costing $80,000 was sold for $100,000. The total of the sale proceeds was credited to the investment account.

Required:
1. Prepare the journal entry to correct the error assuming it is discovered before the books are adjusted or closed in 2016. (Ignore income taxes.)
2. Prepare the journal entry to correct the error assuming it is not discovered until early 2017. (Ignore income taxes.)

E 12–20
Equity method; adjustment for depreciation
● LO12–5, LO12–6

Fizer Pharmaceutical paid $68 million on January 2, 2016, for 4 million shares of Carne Cosmetics common stock. The investment represents a 25% interest in the net assets of Carne and gave Fizer the ability to exercise significant influence over Carne's operations. Fizer received dividends of $1 per share on December 21, 2016, and Carne reported net income of $40 million for the year ended December 31, 2016. The fair value of Carne's common stock at December 31, 2016, was $18.50 per share.

- The book value of Carne's net assets was $192 million.
- The fair value of Carne's depreciable assets exceeded their book value by $32 million. These assets had an average remaining useful life of eight years.
- The remainder of the excess of the cost of the investment over the book value of net assets purchased was attributable to goodwill.

Required:
Prepare all appropriate journal entries related to the investment during 2016.

E 12–21
Equity method
● LO12–5, LO12–6

On January 1, 2016, Cameron Inc. bought 20% of the outstanding common stock of Lake Construction Company for $300 million cash. At the date of acquisition of the stock, Lake's net assets had a fair value of $900 million. Their book value was $800 million. The difference was attributable to the fair value of Lake's buildings and its land exceeding book value, each accounting for one-half of the difference. Lake's net income for the year ended December 31, 2016, was $150 million. During 2016, Lake declared and paid cash dividends of $30 million. The buildings have a remaining life of 10 years.

Required:
1. Prepare all appropriate journal entries related to the investment during 2016, assuming Cameron accounts for this investment by the equity method.
2. Determine the amounts to be reported by Cameron:
   a. As an investment in Cameron's 2016 balance sheet.
   b. As investment revenue in the income statement.
   c. Among investing activities in the statement of cash flows.

E 12–22
Equity method, partial year
● LO12–5, LO12–6

On July 1, 2016, Gupta Corporation bought 25% of the outstanding common stock of VB Company for $100 million cash. At the date of acquisition of the stock, VB's net assets had a total fair value of $350 million and a book value of $220 million. Of the $130 million difference, $20 million was attributable to the appreciated value of inventory that was sold during the last half of 2016, $80 million was attributable to buildings that had a remaining depreciable life of 10 years, and $30 million related to equipment that had a remaining depreciable life of 5 years. Between July 1, 2016, and December 31, 2016, VB earned net income of $32 million and declared and paid cash dividends of $24 million.

Required:

1. Prepare all appropriate journal entries related to the investment during 2016, assuming Gupta accounts for this investment by the equity method.
2. Determine the amounts to be reported by Gupta:
   a. As an investment in Gupta's December 31, 2016, balance sheet.
   b. As investment revenue or loss in Gupta's 2016 income statement.
   c. Among investing activities in Gupta's 2016 statement of cash flows.

E 12–23
Fair value option; held-to-maturity investments
● LO12–1, LO12–2, LO12–7

[This is a variation of Exercise 12–1 focusing on the fair value option.]
Tanner-UNF Corporation acquired as a long-term investment $240 million of 6% bonds, dated July 1, on July 1, 2016. Company management has the positive intent and ability to hold the bonds until maturity, but when the bonds were acquired Tanner-UNF decided to elect the fair value option for accounting for its investment. The market interest rate (yield) was 8% for bonds of similar risk and maturity. Tanner-UNF paid $200 million for the bonds. The company will receive interest semiannually on June 30 and December 31. As a result of changing market conditions, the fair value of the bonds at December 31, 2016, was $210 million.

Required:

1. Would this investment be classified on Tanner-UNF's balance sheet as held-to-maturity securities, trading securities, available-for-sale securities, significant-influence investments, or other? Explain.
2. Prepare the journal entry to record Tanner-UNF's investment in the bonds on July 1, 2016.
3. Prepare the journal entry used by Tanner-UNF to record interest on December 31, 2016, at the effective (market) rate.
4. Prepare any journal entry necessary to recognize fair value changes as of December 31, 2016.
5. At what amount will Tanner-UNF report its investment in the December 31, 2016, balance sheet? Why?
6. Suppose Moody's bond rating agency downgraded the risk rating of the bonds motivating Tanner-UNF to sell the investment on January 2, 2017, for $190 million. Prepare the journal entry to record the sale.

E 12–24
Fair value option; available-for-sale investments
● LO12–2, LO12–3, LO12–7

[This is a variation of Exercise 12–10 focusing on the fair value option.]
On January 2, 2016, Sanborn Tobacco, Inc., bought 5% of Jackson Industry's capital stock for $90 million as a temporary investment. Sanborn realized that these securities normally would be classified as available-for-sale, but elected the fair value option to account for the investment. Jackson Industry's net income for the year ended December 31, 2016, was $120 million. The fair value of the shares held by Sanborn was $98 million at December 31, 2016. During 2016, Jackson declared a dividend of $60 million.

Required:

1. Would this investment be classified on Sanborn's balance sheet as held-to-maturity securities, trading securities, available-for-sale securities, significant-influence investments, or other? Explain.
2. Prepare all appropriate journal entries related to the investment during 2016.
3. Indicate the effect of this investment on 2016 income before taxes.

E 12–25
Fair value option; equity method investments
● LO12–2, LO12–5, LO12–7

[This is a variation of Exercise 12–17 focusing on the fair value option.]
As a long-term investment at the beginning of the fiscal year, Florists International purchased 30% of Nursery Supplies Inc.'s 8 million shares for $56 million. The fair value and book value of the shares were the same at that time. The company realizes that this investment typically would be accounted for under the equity method, but instead chooses the fair value option. During the year, Nursery Supplies earned net income of $40 million and distributed cash dividends of $1.25 per share. At the end of the year, the fair value of the shares is $52 million.

Required:

1. Would this investment be classified on Florists' balance sheet as held-to-maturity securities, trading securities, available-for-sale securities, significant-influence investments, or other? Explain.
2. Prepare all appropriate journal entries related to the investment during 2016.
3. Indicate the effect of this investment on 2016 income before taxes.

E 12–26
Life insurance policy (Appendix 12A)

Edible Chemicals Corporation owns a $4 million whole life insurance policy on the life of its CEO, naming Edible Chemicals as beneficiary. The annual premiums are $70,000 and are payable at the beginning of each year. The cash surrender value of the policy was $21,000 at the beginning of 2016.

Required:

1. Prepare the appropriate 2016 journal entry to record insurance expense and the increase in the investment assuming the cash surrender value of the policy increased according to the contract to $27,000.
2. The CEO died at the end of 2016. Prepare the appropriate journal entry.

E 12–27
Life insurance policy (Appendix 12A)

Below are two unrelated situations relating to life insurance.

Required:

Prepare the appropriate journal entry for each situation.

1. Ford Corporation owns a whole life insurance policy on the life of its president. Ford Corporation is the beneficiary. The insurance premium is $25,000. The cash surrender value increased during the year from $2,500 to $4,600.
2. Petroleum Corporation received a $250,000 life insurance settlement when its CEO died. At that time, the cash surrender value was $16,000.

E 12–28
Held-to-maturity securities; impairments (Appendix 12B)
● LO12–1

Bloom Corporation purchased $1,000,000 of Taylor Company 5% bonds at par with the intent and ability to hold the bonds until they matured in 2020, so Bloom classifies its investment as HTM. Unfortunately, a combination of problems at Taylor Company and in the debt market caused the fair value of the Taylor investment to decline to $600,000 during 2016.

Required:

For each of the following scenarios, prepare appropriate entry(s) at December 31, 2016, and indicate how the scenario will affect the 2016 income statement (ignore income taxes).

1. Bloom now believes it is more likely than not that it will have to sell the Taylor bonds before the bonds have a chance to recover their fair value. Of the $400,000 decline in fair value, Bloom attributes $250,000 to credit losses, and $150,000 to noncredit losses.
2. Bloom does not plan to sell the Taylor bonds prior to maturity, and does not believe it is more likely than not that it will have to sell the Taylor bonds before the bonds have a chance to recover their fair value. Of the $400,000 decline in fair value, Bloom attributes $250,000 to credit losses, and $150,000 to noncredit losses.
3. Bloom does not plan to sell the Taylor bonds prior to maturity, and does not believe it is more likely than not that it will have to sell the Taylor bonds before the bonds have a chance to recover their fair value. Bloom attributes the entire $400,000 decline in fair value to noncredit losses.

E 12–29
Available-for-sale debt securities; impairments (Appendix 12B)
● LO12–3

(Note: This exercise is a variation of Exercise 12–28, modified to categorize the investment as securities available-for-sale.)

Assume all of the same facts and scenarios as E12–28, except that Bloom Corporation classifies their Taylor investment as AFS.

Required:

1. For each of the scenarios shown in E12–28, prepare the appropriate entry(s) at December 31, 2016. Indicate how the scenario will affect the 2016 income statement, OCI, and comprehensive income.
2. Repeat requirement 1, but now assume that, at the end of 2015, Bloom had recorded a temporary unrealized loss (not an OTT impairment) of $100,000 on the Taylor investment.

E 12–30
Available-for-sale equity securities; impairments (Appendix 12B)
● LO12–3

In early December of 2016, Kettle Corp purchased $50,000 of Icalc Company common stock, which constitutes less than 1% of Icalc's outstanding shares. By December 31, 2016, the value of Icalc's investment had fallen to $40,000, and Kettle recorded an unrealized loss. By December 31, 2017, the value of the Icalc investment had fallen to $25,000, and Kettle determined that it can no longer assert that it has both the intent and ability to hold the shares long enough for their fair value to recover, so Kettle recorded an OTT impairment. By December 31, 2018, fair value had recovered to $30,000.

Required:

Prepare appropriate entry(s) at December 31, 2016, 2017, and 2018, and for each year indicate how the scenario will affect net income, OCI, and comprehensive income.

E 12–31
Accounting for impairments under IFRS (Appendix 12B)
● LO12–1, LO12–3, LO12–8
IFRS

Flower Corporation uses IFRS (under *IAS No. 39*), and purchased €1,000,000 of James Company 5% bonds at face value during 2016. Unfortunately, a combination of problems at James Company and in the debt market caused the fair value of the James investment to decline to €600,000 by December 31, 2016. On December 31, 2016, Flower calculated the present value of the future cash flows expected to be collected from the James investment (using the interest rate effective when the investment was made) to equal €750,000. Flower recognized an OTT impairment. By December 31, 2017, the fair value of the investment increased to €875,000, and Flower calculated the present value of the future cash flows expected to be collected from the James investment (again using the interest rate effective when the investment was made) to equal €800,000.

Required:

1. Prepare appropriate entry(s) to account for the James investment at December 31, 2016, assuming Flower classifies its James investment as held to maturity.
2. Prepare appropriate entry(s) to account for the James investment at December 31, 2017, assuming Flower classifies its James investment as held to maturity.
3. Prepare appropriate entry(s) to account for the James investment at December 31, 2016, assuming Flower classifies its James investment as available for sale.
4. Prepare appropriate entry(s) to account for the James investment at December 31, 2017, assuming Flower classifies its James investment as available for sale.
5. How would your answer to requirement 4 change if the James investment was equity rather than debt?

CPA and CMA Review Questions

CPA Exam Questions

The following questions are adapted from a variety of sources including questions developed by the AICPA Board of Examiners and those used in the Kaplan CPA Review Course to study investments while preparing for the CPA examination. Determine the response that best completes the statements or questions.

● LO12–2

1. During year 4, Wall Co. purchased 2,000 shares of Hemp Corp. common stock for $31,500 as a short-term investment. The investment was appropriately classified as a trading security. The market value of this investment was $29,500 at December 31, year 4. Wall sold all of the Hemp common stock for $14 per share on January 15, year 5, incurring $1,400 in brokerage commissions and taxes. On the sale, Wall should report a realized loss of:
   a. $1,500
   b. $2,900
   c. $3,500
   d. $4,900

● LO12–3

2. The following information pertains to Lark Corp.'s long-term marketable equity securities portfolio:

	December 31	
	2016	**2015**
Cost	$200,000	$200,000
Fair value	240,000	180,000

Differences between cost and market values are considered to be temporary. The decline in market value was properly accounted for at December 31, 2015. At December 31, 2016, what is the net unrealized holding gain or loss to be reported as:

	Other Comprehensive Income	**Accumulated Other Comprehensive Income**
a.	$60,000 gain	$40,000 gain
b.	$40,000 gain	$60,000 gain
c.	$20,000 loss	$20,000 loss
d.	–0–	–0–

● LO12–3

3. The following information was extracted from Gil Co.'s December 31, 2016, balance sheet:

Noncurrent assets:	
Long-term investments in marketable equity securities (at fair value)	$96,450
Stockholders' equity:	
Accumulated other comprehensive income**	(25,000)

** Includes a net unrealized holding loss on long-term investments in marketable equity securities of $19,800.

The historical cost of the long-term investments in marketable equity securities was:
   a. $ 63,595
   b. $ 76,650
   c. $ 96,450
   d. $116,250

● LO12–3

4. On both December 31, 2015, and December 31, 2016, Kopp Co.'s only equity security investment had the same fair value, which was below its original cost. Kopp considered the decline in value to be temporary in 2015 but other-than-temporary in 2016. At the end of both years the security was classified as a noncurrent asset. Kopp could not exercise significant influence over the investee. What should be the effects of the determination that the decline was other-than-temporary on Kopp's 2016 net noncurrent assets and net income?
   a. Decrease in both net noncurrent assets and net income.
   b. No effect on both net noncurrent assets and net income.
   c. Decrease in net noncurrent assets and no effect on net income.
   d. No effect on net noncurrent assets and decrease in net income.

● LO12–5

5. When the equity method is used to account for investments in common stock, which of the following affect(s) the investor's reported investment income?

	A Change in Fair Value of Investee's Common Stock	Cash Dividends from Investee
a.	Yes	Yes
b.	No	Yes
c.	Yes	No
d.	No	No

● LO12–5

6. A corporation uses the equity method to account for its 40% ownership of another company. The investee earned $20,000 and paid $5,000 in dividends. The investor made the following entries:

Investment in affiliate	$8,000	
Equity in earnings of affiliate		$8,000
Cash	2,000	
Dividend revenue		2,000

What effect will these entries have on the investor's statement of financial position?
   a. Investment in affiliate overstated, retained earnings understated.
   b. Financial position will be fairly stated.
   c. Investment in affiliate overstated, retained earnings overstated.
   d. Investment in affiliate understated, retained earnings understated.

● LO12–6

7. Park Co. uses the equity method to account for its January 1, 2016, purchase of Tun Inc.'s common stock. On January 1, 2016, the fair values of Tun's FIFO inventory and land exceeded their carrying amounts. How do these excesses of fair values over carrying amounts affect Park's reported equity in Tun's 2016 earnings?

	Inventory Excess	Land Excess
a.	Decrease	Decrease
b.	Decrease	No effect
c.	Increase	No effect
d.	Increase	Increase

● LO12–4

8. On January 2, 2016, Well Co. purchased 10% of Rea Inc.'s outstanding common shares for $400,000. Well is the largest single shareholder in Rea, and Well's officers are a majority on Rea's board of directors. Rea reported net income of $500,000 for 2016, and paid dividends of $150,000. In its December 31, 2016, balance sheet, what amount should Well report as investment in Rea?
   a. $435,000
   b. $450,000
   c. $400,000
   d. $385,000

International Financial Reporting Standards are tested on the CPA exam along with U.S. GAAP. The following questions deal with the application of IFRS to accounting for investments.

● LO12–8

IFRS

9. Under *IFRS No. 9*, which of the following is *not* a category into which a debt investment can be classified?
   a. FVPL ("fair value through profit and loss").
   b. FVOCI ("fair value through other comprehensive income").
   c. Amortized cost.
   d. Parts a–c are all classifications in which a debt investment might be classified under *IFRS No. 9*.

● LO12–8

IFRS

10. Under *IFRS No. 9*, which of the following is *not* a category in which an equity investment can be classified?
   a. FVPL ("Fair Value through Profit and Loss").
   b. FVOCI ("Fair Value through Other Comprehensive Income").
   c. Amortized cost.
   d. Parts a–c are all classifications in which an equity investment is classified under *IFRS No. 9*.

● LO12–8 IFRS

11. Which of the following is *not* true about transfers between investment categories under IFRS?
   a. Under *IAS No. 39,* transfers of debt investments out of FVPL into AFS or HTM is permitted under rare circumstances.
   b. Under *IFRS No. 9,* transfers of debt investments out of FVPL to amortized cost are possible if the business model changes with respect to the debt investment.
   c. Under *IFRS No. 9,* transfers of equity investments out of FVOCI to amortized cost are possible if the business model changes with respect to the equity investment.
   d. Parts a–c are all true about transfers between investment categories under IFRS.

● LO12–8 IFRS

12. Which of the following is true about use of the equity method under IFRS?
   a. IFRS allows use of the fair value option under essentially the same circumstances as does U.S. GAAP for investments that otherwise would be accounted for under the equity method.
   b. *IFRS No. 11* allows proportionate consolidation rather than the equity method for investments that qualify as joint ventures.
   c. FVPL is preferred to the equity method when the investor can exercise significant influence over the operations of the investee.
   d. *IAS No. 28* requires that the accounting policies of investees be adjusted to correspond to those of the investor.

● LO12–8 IFRS

13. Which of the following is true about accounting for other-than-temporary impairments under *IAS No. 39*?
   a. Recoveries of OTT impairments for debt investments can be recognized in earnings.
   b. Recoveries of OTT impairments for equity investments can be recognized in earnings.
   c. The amount of OTT impairment calculated for a debt investment is the same regardless of whether the investment is classified as held-to-maturity or available-for-sale.
   d. Two of the three answers included in a-c are true.

CMA Exam Questions

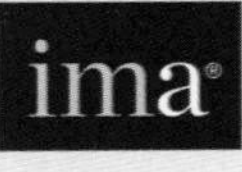

The following questions dealing with investments are adapted from questions that previously appeared on Certified Management Accountant (CMA) examinations. The CMA designation sponsored by the Institute of Management Accountants (**www.imanet.org**) provides members with an objective measure of knowledge and competence in the field of management accounting. Determine the response that best completes the statements or questions.

● LO12–3

1. An investment in available-for-sale securities is valued on the balance sheet at
   a. The cost to acquire the asset.
   b. Accumulated income minus accumulated dividends since acquisition.
   c. Fair value.
   d. The par or stated value of the securities.

Questions 2 and 3 are based on the following information concerning Monahan Company's portfolio of debt securities at May 31, year 2 and May 31, year 3. All of the debt securities were purchased by Monahan during June, year 1. Prior to June, year 1, Monahan had no investments in debt or equity securities.

As of May 31, Year 2	Amortized Cost	Fair Value
Cleary Company bonds	$164,526	$168,300
Beauchamp Industry bonds	204,964	205,200
Morrow Inc. bonds	305,785	285,200
Total	$675,275	$658,700

As of May 31, Year 3	Amortized Cost	Fair Value
Cleary Company bonds	$152,565	$147,600
Beauchamp Industry bonds	193,800	204,500
Morrow Inc. bonds	289,130	291,400
Total	$635,495	$643,500

● LO12–3

2. Assuming that the above securities are properly classified as available-for-sale securities under U.S. GAAP, the unrealized holding gain or loss as of May 31, year 3 would be
   a. recognized as an $8,005 unrealized holding gain on the income statement.
   b. recognized in accumulated other comprehensive income by a year-end credit balance of $8,005.
   c. recognized in accumulated other comprehensive income by a year-end debit balance of $8,005.
   d. not recognized.

● LO12–1

3. Assuming that the above securities are properly classified as held-to-maturity securities under U.S. GAAP, the unrealized holding gain or loss as of May 31, year 3 would be
   a. recognized as an $8,005 unrealized holding gain on the income statement.
   b. recognized in accumulated other comprehensive income by a year-end credit balance of $8,005.
   c. recognized in accumulated other comprehensive income by a year-end debit balance of $8,005.
   d. not recognized.

Problems

An alternate exercise and problem set is available in the Connect library.

P 12–1
Securities held-to-maturity; bond investment; effective interest
● LO12–1

Fuzzy Monkey Technologies, Inc., purchased as a long-term investment $80 million of 8% bonds, dated January 1, on January 1, 2016. Management has the positive intent and ability to hold the bonds until maturity. For bonds of similar risk and maturity the market yield was 10%. The price paid for the bonds was $66 million. Interest is received semiannually on June 30 and December 31. Due to changing market conditions, the fair value of the bonds at December 31, 2016, was $70 million.

Required:

1. Prepare the journal entry to record Fuzzy Monkey's investment on January 1, 2016.
2. Prepare the journal entry by Fuzzy Monkey to record interest on June 30, 2016 (at the effective rate).
3. Prepare the journal entry by Fuzzy Monkey to record interest on December 31, 2016 (at the effective rate).
4. At what amount will Fuzzy Monkey report its investment in the December 31, 2016, balance sheet? Why?
5. How would Fuzzy Monkey's 2016 statement of cash flows be affected by this investment?

P 12–2
Trading securities; bond investment; effective interest
● LO12–2

[This problem is a variation of Problem 12–1, modified to categorize the investment as trading securities.]

Fuzzy Monkey Technologies, Inc., purchased as a short-term investment $80 million of 8% bonds, dated January 1, on January 1, 2016. Management intends to include the investment in a short-term, active trading portfolio. For bonds of similar risk and maturity the market yield was 10%. The price paid for the bonds was $66 million. Interest is received semiannually on June 30 and December 31. Due to changing market conditions, the fair value of the bonds at December 31, 2016, was $70 million.

Required:

1. Prepare the journal entry to record Fuzzy Monkey's investment on January 1, 2016.
2. Prepare the journal entry by Fuzzy Monkey to record interest on June 30, 2016 (at the effective rate).
3. Prepare the journal entry by Fuzzy Monkey to record interest on December 31, 2016 (at the effective rate).
4. At what amount will Fuzzy Monkey report its investment in the December 31, 2016, balance sheet? Why? Prepare any entry necessary to achieve this reporting objective.
5. How would Fuzzy Monkey's 2016 statement of cash flows be affected by this investment?

P 12–3
Securities available-for-sale; bond investment; effective interest
● LO12–3

[This problem is a variation of Problem 12–1, modified to categorize the investment as securities available-for-sale.]

Fuzzy Monkey Technologies, Inc., purchased as a long-term investment $80 million of 8% bonds, dated January 1, on January 1, 2016. Management intends to have the investment available for sale when circumstances warrant. For bonds of similar risk and maturity the market yield was 10%. The price paid for the bonds was $66 million. Interest is received semiannually on June 30 and December 31. Due to changing market conditions, the fair value of the bonds at December 31, 2016, was $70 million.

Required:

1. Prepare the journal entry to record Fuzzy Monkey's investment on January 1, 2016.
2. Prepare the journal entry by Fuzzy Monkey to record interest on June 30, 2016 (at the effective rate).
3. Prepare the journal entry by Fuzzy Monkey to record interest on December 31, 2016 (at the effective rate).
4. At what amount will Fuzzy Monkey report its investment in the December 31, 2016, balance sheet? Why? Prepare any entry necessary to achieve this reporting objective.
5. How would Fuzzy Monkey's 2016 statement of cash flows be affected by this investment?

P 12–4
Fair value option; bond investment; effective interest
● LO12–1, LO12–2, LO12–3, LO12–7

[This problem is a variation of Problem 12–3, modified to cause the investment to be accounted for under the fair value option.]

Fuzzy Monkey Technologies, Inc., purchased as a long-term investment $80 million of 8% bonds, dated January 1, on January 1, 2016. Management intends to have the investment available for sale when circumstances warrant. When the company purchased the bonds, management elected to account for them under the fair value option. For bonds of similar risk and maturity the market yield was 10%. The price paid for the bonds was $66 million. Interest is received semiannually on June 30 and December 31. Due to changing market conditions, the fair value of the bonds at December 31, 2016, was $70 million.

Required:

1. Prepare the journal entry to record Fuzzy Monkey's investment on January 1, 2016.
2. Prepare the journal entry by Fuzzy Monkey to record interest on June 30, 2016 (at the effective rate).

3. Prepare the journal entries by Fuzzy Monkey to record interest on December 31, 2016 (at the effective rate).
4. At what amount will Fuzzy Monkey report its investment in the December 31, 2016, balance sheet? Why? Prepare any entry necessary to achieve this reporting objective.
5. How would Fuzzy Monkey's 2016 statement of cash flows be affected by this investment?
6. How would your answers to requirements 1–5 differ if management had the intent and ability to hold the investments until maturity?

P 12–5
Various transactions related to securities available-for-sale
● LO12–3

The following selected transactions relate to investment activities of Ornamental Insulation Corporation. The company buys securities, *not* intending to profit from short-term differences in price and *not* necessarily to hold debt securities to maturity, but to have them available for sale when circumstances warrant. Ornamental's fiscal year ends on December 31. No investments were held by Ornamental on December 31, 2015.

2016

Feb. 21	Acquired Distribution Transformers Corporation common shares costing $400,000.
Mar. 18	Received cash dividends of $8,000 on the investment in Distribution Transformers common shares.
Sep. 1	Acquired $900,000 of American Instruments' 10% bonds at face value.
Oct. 20	Sold the Distribution Transformers shares for $425,000.
Nov. 1	Purchased M&D Corporation common shares costing $1,400,000.
Dec. 31	Recorded any necessary adjusting entry(s) relating to the investments. The market prices of the investments are:

American Instruments bonds	$ 850,000
M&D Corporation shares	$1,460,000

(Hint: Interest must be accrued for the American Instruments' bonds.)

2017

Jan. 20	Sold the M&D Corporation shares for $1,485,000.
Mar. 1	Received semiannual interest of $45,000 on the investment in American Instruments bonds.
Aug. 12	Acquired Vast Communication common shares costing $650,000.
Sept. 1	Received semiannual interest of $45,000 on the investment in American Instruments bonds.
Dec. 31	Recorded any necessary adjusting entry(s) relating to the investments. The market prices of the investments are:

Vast Communication shares	$670,000
American Instruments bonds	$830,000

Required:
1. Prepare the appropriate journal entry for each transaction or event during 2016.
2. Indicate any amounts that Ornamental Insulation would report in its 2016 balance sheet and income statement as a result of these investments.
3. Prepare the appropriate journal entry for each transaction or event during 2017.
4. Indicate any amounts that Ornamental Insulation would report in its 2017 balance sheet and income statement as a result of these investments.

P 12–6
Various transactions relating to trading securities
● LO12–2

American Surety and Fidelity buys and sells securities expecting to earn profits on short-term differences in price. For the first 11 months of 2016, gains from selling trading securities totaled $8 million, losses were $11 million, and the company had earned $5 million in investment revenue. The following selected transactions relate to American's trading account during December 2016, and the first week of 2017. The company's fiscal year ends on December 31. No trading securities were held by American on December 1, 2016.

2016

Dec. 12	Purchased FF&G Corporation bonds for $12 million.
13	Purchased 2 million Ferry Intercommunications common shares for $22 million.
15	Sold the FF&G Corporation bonds for $12.1 million.
22	Purchased U.S. Treasury bills for $56 million and Treasury bonds for $65 million.
23	Sold half the Ferry Intercommunications common shares for $10 million.
26	Sold the U.S. Treasury bills for $57 million.
27	Sold the Treasury bonds for $63 million.

(continued)

(concluded)

28	Received cash dividends of $200,000 from the Ferry Intercommunications common shares.
31	Recorded any necessary adjusting entry(s) and closing entries relating to the investments. The market price of the Ferry Intercommunications stock was $10 per share.
2017	
Jan. 2	Sold the remaining Ferry Intercommunications common shares for $10.2 million.
5	Purchased Warehouse Designs Corporation bonds for $34 million.

Required:

1. Prepare the appropriate journal entry for each transaction or event during 2016, including the closing entry to income summary for the year.
2. Indicate any amounts that American would report in its 2016 balance sheet and income statement as a result of these investments.
3. Prepare the appropriate journal entry for each transaction or event during 2017. Assume the fair value of the Warehouse Designs bonds did not change during 2017.

P 12–7
Securities held-to-maturity, securities available for sale, and trading securities
● LO12–1, LO12–2, LO12–3

Amalgamated General Corporation is a consulting firm that also offers financial services through its credit division. From time to time the company buys and sells securities intending to earn profits on short-term differences in price. The following selected transactions relate to Amalgamated's investment activities during the last quarter of 2016 and the first month of 2017. The only securities held by Amalgamated at October 1 were $30 million of 10% bonds of Kansas Abstractors, Inc., purchased on May 1 at face value. The company's fiscal year ends on December 31.

2016	
Oct. 18	Purchased 2 million preferred shares of Millwork Ventures Company for $58 million as a speculative investment to be sold under suitable circumstances.
31	Received semiannual interest of $1.5 million from the Kansas Abstractors bonds.
Nov. 1	Purchased 10% bonds of Holistic Entertainment Enterprises at their $18 million face value, to be held until they mature in 2018. Semiannual interest is payable April 30 and October 31.
1	Sold the Kansas Abstractors bonds for $28 million because rising interest rates are expected to cause their fair value to continue to fall.
Dec. 1	Purchased 12% bonds of Household Plastics Corporation at their $60 million face value, to be held until they mature in 2028. Semiannual interest is payable May 31 and November 30.
20	Purchased U. S. Treasury bonds for $5.6 million as trading securities, hoping to earn profits on short-term differences in prices.
21	Purchased 4 million common shares of NXS Corporation for $44 million as trading securities, hoping to earn profits on short-term differences in prices.
23	Sold the Treasury bonds for $5.7 million.
29	Received cash dividends of $3 million from the Millwork Ventures Company preferred shares.
31	Recorded any necessary adjusting entry(s) and closing entries relating to the investments. The market price of the Millwork Ventures Company preferred stock was $27.50 per share and $11.50 per share for the NXS Corporation common. The fair values of the bond investments were $58.7 million for Household Plastics Corporation and $16.7 million for Holistic Entertainment Enterprises.
2017	
Jan. 7	Sold the NXS Corporation common shares for $43 million.

Required:

Prepare the appropriate journal entry for each transaction or event.

P 12–8
Securities available-for-sale; fair value adjustment; reclassification adjustment
● LO12–3

At December 31, 2016, the investments in securities available-for-sale of Beale Developments were reported at $78 million:

Securities available-for-sale	$74	
Plus: Fair value adjustment	4	$78

During 2017, Beale sold its investment in Schwab Pharmaceuticals, which had cost $25 million, for $28 million. Those shares had a fair value at December 31, 2016, of $27 million. No other investments were sold. At December 31, 2017, the investments in securities available-for-sale included the cost and fair value amounts shown below.

($ in millions) **Securities Available-for-Sale**	**Cost**	**Fair Value**	**Unrealized Gain (Loss)**
Daisy Theaters, Inc. shares	$40	$42	$2
Orpheum Entertainment bonds	9	12	3
Totals	$49	$54	$5

Required:

1. At what amount should Beale report its securities available-for-sale in its December 31, 2017, balance sheet?
2. What journal entry is needed to enable the investment to be reported at this amount?
3. What is the amount of the reclassification adjustment to 2017 other comprehensive income? Show how the reclassification adjustment should be reported.

P 12–9
Investment securities and equity method investments compared
● LO12–3, LO12–4, LO12–5, LO12–6

On January 4, 2016, Runyan Bakery paid $324 million for 10 million shares of Lavery Labeling Company common stock. The investment represents a 30% interest in the net assets of Lavery and gave Runyan the ability to exercise significant influence over Lavery's operations. Runyan received dividends of $2.00 per share on December 15, 2016, and Lavery reported net income of $160 million for the year ended December 31, 2016. The market value of Lavery's common stock at December 31, 2016, was $31 per share. On the purchase date, the book value of Lavery's net assets was $800 million and:

a. The fair value of Lavery's depreciable assets, with an average remaining useful life of six years, exceeded their book value by $80 million.
b. The remainder of the excess of the cost of the investment over the book value of net assets purchased was attributable to goodwill.

Required:

1. Prepare all appropriate journal entries related to the investment during 2016, assuming Runyan accounts for this investment by the equity method.
2. Prepare the journal entries required by Runyan, assuming that the 10 million shares represent a 10% interest in the net assets of Lavery rather than a 30% interest.

P 12–10
Fair value option; equity method investments
● LO12–2, LO12–4, LO12–7

[This problem is a variation of Problem 12–9 focusing on the fair value option.]

On January 4, 2016, Runyan Bakery paid $324 million for 10 million shares of Lavery Labeling Company common stock. The investment represents a 30% interest in the net assets of Lavery and gave Runyan the ability to exercise significant influence over Lavery's operations. Runyan chose the fair value option to account for this investment. Runyan received dividends of $2.00 per share on December 15, 2016, and Lavery reported net income of $160 million for the year ended December 31, 2016. The market value of Lavery's common stock at December 31, 2016, was $31 per share. On the purchase date, the book value of Lavery's net assets was $800 million and:

a. The fair value of Lavery's depreciable assets, with an average remaining useful life of six years, exceeded their book value by $80 million.
b. The remainder of the excess of the cost of the investment over the book value of net assets purchased was attributable to goodwill.

Required:

1. Prepare all appropriate journal entries related to the investment during 2016, assuming Runyan accounts for this investment under the fair value option in a manner similar to what it would use for trading securities.
2. What would be the effect of this investment on Runyan's 2016 net income?

P 12–11
Fair value option; equity method investments
● LO12–2, LO12–4, LO12–5, LO12–7

[This problem is an expanded version of Problem 12–10 that considers alternative ways in which a firm might apply the fair value option to account for significant-influence investments that would normally be accounted for under the equity method.]

Companies can choose the fair value option for investments that otherwise would be accounted for under the equity method. If the fair value option is chosen, the investment is shown at fair value in the balance sheet, and unrealized holding gains and losses are recognized in the income statement. However, exactly how a company complies with those broad requirements is up to the company. This problem requires you to consider alternative ways in which a company might apply the fair value option for investments that otherwise would be accounted for under the equity method.

On January 4, 2016, Runyan Bakery paid $324 million for 10 million shares of Lavery Labeling Company common stock. The investment represents a 30% interest in the net assets of Lavery and gave Runyan the ability to exercise significant influence over Lavery's operations. Runyan chose the fair value option to account for this investment. Runyan received dividends of $2.00 per share on December 15, 2016, and Lavery reported net income of $160 million for the year ended December 31, 2016. The market value of Lavery's common stock at December 31, 2016, was $31 per share. On the purchase date, the book value of Lavery's net assets was $800 million and:

a. The fair value of Lavery's depreciable assets, with an average remaining useful life of six years, exceeded their book value by $80 million.
b. The remainder of the excess of the cost of the investment over the book value of net assets purchased was attributable to goodwill.

Required:

1. Prepare all appropriate journal entries related to the investment during 2016, assuming Runyan accounts for this investment under the fair value option, and accounts for the Lavery investment in a manner similar to what it would use for trading securities. Indicate the effect of these journal entries on 2016 net income, and show the amount at which the investment is carried in the December 31, 2016, balance sheet.
2. Prepare all appropriate journal entries related to the investment during 2016, assuming Runyan accounts for this investment under the fair value option, but uses equity method accounting to account for Lavery's income and dividends, and then records a fair value adjustment at the end of the year that allows it to comply with GAAP. Indicate the effect of these journal entries on 2016 net income, and show the amount at which the investment is carried in the December 31, 2016, balance sheet. (Note: You should end up with the same total 2016 income effect and same carrying value on the balance sheet for requirements 1 and 2.)

P 12–12
Equity method
● LO12–5, LO12–6

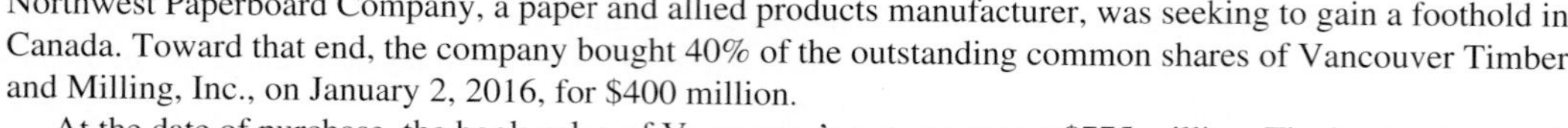

Northwest Paperboard Company, a paper and allied products manufacturer, was seeking to gain a foothold in Canada. Toward that end, the company bought 40% of the outstanding common shares of Vancouver Timber and Milling, Inc., on January 2, 2016, for $400 million.

At the date of purchase, the book value of Vancouver's net assets was $775 million. The book values and fair values for all balance sheet items were the same except for inventory and plant facilities. The fair value exceeded book value by $5 million for the inventory and by $20 million for the plant facilities.

The estimated useful life of the plant facilities is 16 years. All inventory acquired was sold during 2016.

Vancouver reported net income of $140 million for the year ended December 31, 2016. Vancouver paid a cash dividend of $30 million.

Required:

1. Prepare all appropriate journal entries related to the investment during 2016.
2. What amount should Northwest report as its income from its investment in Vancouver for the year ended December 31, 2016?
3. What amount should Northwest report in its balance sheet as its investment in Vancouver?
4. What should Northwest report in its statement of cash flows regarding its investment in Vancouver?

P 12–13
Equity method
● LO12–5, LO12–6

On January 2, 2016, Miller Properties paid $19 million for 1 million shares of Marlon Company's 6 million outstanding common shares. Miller's CEO became a member of Marlon's board of directors during the first quarter of 2016.

The carrying amount of Marlon's net assets was $66 million. Miller estimated the fair value of those net assets to be the same except for a patent valued at $24 million above cost. The remaining amortization period for the patent is 10 years.

Marlon reported earnings of $12 million and paid dividends of $6 million during 2016. On December 31, 2016, Marlon's common stock was trading on the NYSE at $18.50 per share.

Required:

1. When considering whether to account for its investment in Marlon under the equity method, what criteria should Miller's management apply?
2. Assume Miller accounts for its investment in Marlon using the equity method. Ignoring income taxes, determine the amounts related to the investment to be reported in its 2016
   a. Income statement.
   b. Balance sheet.
   c. Statement of cash flows.

P 12–14
Classifying investments
● LO12–1 through LO12–5

Indicate (by letter) the way each of the investments listed below most likely should be accounted for based on the information provided.

Item	Reporting Category
____ 1. 35% of the nonvoting preferred stock of American Aircraft Company.	T. Trading securities
____ 2. Treasury bills to be held to maturity.	M. Securities held-to-maturity
____ 3. Two-year note receivable from affiliate.	A. Securities available-for-sale
____ 4. Accounts receivable.	E. Equity method
____ 5. Treasury bond maturing in one week.	C. Consolidation
____ 6. Common stock held in trading account for immediate resale.	N. None of these
____ 7. Bonds acquired to profit from short-term differences in price.	
____ 8. 35% of the voting common stock of Computer Storage Devices Company.	

(continued)

(concluded)

____ 9. 90% of the voting common stock of Affiliated Peripherals, Inc.
____ 10. Corporate bonds of Primary Smelting Company to be sold if interest rates fall ½%.
____ 11. 25% of the voting common stock of Smith Foundries Corporation: 51% family-owned by Smith family; fair value determinable.
____ 12. 17% of the voting common stock of Shipping Barrels Corporation: Investor's CEO on the board of directors of Shipping Barrels Corporation.

P 12–15
Fair value option; held-to-maturity investments
● LO12–1, LO12–7

On January 1, 2016, Ithaca Corp. purchases Cortland Inc. bonds that have a face value of $150,000. The Cortland bonds have a stated interest rate of 6%. Interest is paid semiannually on June 30 and December 31, and the bonds mature in 10 years. For bonds of similar risk and maturity, the market yield on particular dates is as follows:

January 1, 2016	7.0%
June 30, 2016	8.0%
December 31, 2016	9.0%

Required:

1. Calculate the price Ithaca would have paid for the Cortland bonds on January 1, 2016 (ignoring brokerage fees), and prepare a journal entry to record the purchase.
2. Prepare all appropriate journal entries related to the bond investment during 2016, assuming Ithaca accounts for the bonds as a held-to-maturity investment. Ithaca calculates interest revenue at the effective interest rate as of the date it purchased the bonds.
3. Prepare all appropriate journal entries related to the bond investment during 2016, assuming that Ithaca chose the fair value option when the bonds were purchased, and that Ithaca determines fair value of the bonds semi-annually. Ithaca calculates interest revenue at the effective interest rate as of the date it purchased the bonds.

P 12–16
Accounting for debt and equity investments
● LO12–1, LO12–2, LO12–8

IFRS

Feherty, Inc., accounts for its investments under *IFRS No. 9* and purchased the following investments during December 2016:

1. **50 of Donald Company's $1,000 bonds.** The bonds pay semiannual interest, return principal in eight years, and include no other cash flows or other features. Feherty plans to hold 10 of the bonds to collect contractual cash flows over the life of the investment and to hold 40, both to collect contractual cash flows but also to sell them if their price appreciates sufficiently. Subsequent to Feherty's purchase of the bonds, but prior to December 31, the fair value of the bonds increased to $1,040 per bond, and Feherty sold 10 of the 40 bonds. Feherty also sold 5 of the 10 bonds it had planned to hold to collect contractual cash flows over the life of the investment. The fair value of the bonds remained at $1,040 as of December 31, 2016.
2. **$25,000 of Watson Company common stock.** Feherty does not have the ability to significantly influence the operations of Watson. Feherty elected to account for this equity investment at fair value through OCI (FVOCI). Subsequent to Feherty's purchase of the stock, the fair value of the stock investment increased to $30,000 as of December 31, 2016.

Required:

1. Indicate how Feherty would account for its investments when it acquired the Donald bonds and Watson stock.
2. Calculate the effect of realized and unrealized gains and losses associated with the Donald bonds and the Watson stock on Feherty's net income, other comprehensive income, and comprehensive income for the year ended December 31, 2016. Ignore interest revenue and taxes.

P 12–17
Accounting for other-than-temporary impairments (Appendix 12B)
● LO12–1, LO12–2, LO12–3

Stewart Enterprises has the following investments, all purchased prior to 2016:

1. Bee Company 5% bonds, purchased at face value, with an amortized cost of $4,000,000, and classified as held to maturity. At December 31, 2016, the Bee investment had a fair value of $3,500,000, and Stewart calculated that $240,000 of the fair value decline is a credit loss and $260,000 is a noncredit loss. At December 31, 2017, the Bee investment had a fair value of $3,700,000, and Stewart calculated that $140,000 of the difference between fair value and amortized cost was a credit loss and $160,000 was a noncredit loss.
2. Oliver Corporation 4% bonds, purchased at face value, with an amortized cost of $2,500,000, classified as a trading security. Because of unrealized losses prior to 2016, the Oliver bonds have a fair value adjustment account with a credit balance of $200,000, such that the carrying value of the Oliver investment is $2,300,000 prior to making any adjusting entries in 2016. At December 31, 2016, the Oliver investment had a fair value of $2,200,000, and Stewart calculated that $120,000 of the difference between amortized cost and fair value is a credit loss and $180,000 is a noncredit loss. At December 31, 2017, the Oliver investment had a fair value of $2,700,000.

3. Jones Inc. 6% bonds, purchased at face value, with an amortized cost of $3,500,000, and classified as an available-for-sale investment. Because of unrealized losses prior to 2016, the Jones bonds have a fair value adjustment account with a credit balance of $400,000, such that the carrying value of the Jones investment is $3,100,000 prior to making any adjusting entries in 2016. At December 31, 2016, the Jones investment had a fair value of $2,700,000, and Stewart calculated that $225,000 of the difference between amortized cost and fair value is a credit loss and $575,000 is a noncredit loss. At December 31, 2017, the Jones investment had a fair value of $2,900,000, and Stewart calculated that $125,000 of the difference between amortized cost and fair value is a credit loss and $475,000 is a noncredit loss.
4. Helms Corp. equity, purchased for $1,000,000, classified as available for sale. Because of unrealized gains prior to 2016, the Helms shares have a fair value adjustment account with a debit balance of $120,000, such that the carrying value of the Helms investment is $1,120,000 prior to making any adjusting entries in 2016. At December 31, 2016 and 2017, the Helms investment had a fair value of $600,000 and $700,000, respectively.

Stewart does not intend to sell any of these investments and does not believe it is more likely than not that it will have to sell any of the bond investments before fair value recovers. However, Stewart cannot assert that it has the ability to hold the Helms equity investment before fair value recovers.

Required:

Prepare the appropriate adjusting journal entries to account for fair value changes during 2016 and 2017, assuming that each investment is viewed as qualifying as an other-than-temporary (OTT) impairment as of December 31, 2016, and then is accounted for normally during 2017 (with no additional OTT impairment in 2017).

P 12–18
Accounting for other-than-temporary impairments under IFRS (Appendix 12B)
● LO12–1, LO12–2, LO12–3, LO12–8

[This problem is a variation of Problem 12–17, modified to consider accounting for impairments under IFRS.]

Required:

Consider the facts presented in P12–17, and assume that Stewart accounts for its investments under *IAS No. 39*. Prepare the appropriate adjusting journal entries to account for fair value changes during 2016 and 2017, assuming that Stewart views each investment as meeting any criteria necessary for recognizing an other-than-temporary (OTT) impairment as of December 31, 2016, and then is accounted for normally during 2017 (with no additional OTT impairment in 2017).

Broaden Your Perspective

Apply your critical-thinking ability to the knowledge you've gained. These cases will provide you an opportunity to develop your research, analysis, judgment, and communication skills. You also will work with other students, integrate what you've learned, apply it in real-world situations, and consider its global and ethical ramifications. This practice will broaden your knowledge and further develop your decision-making abilities.

Real World Case 12–1
Intel's investments
● LO12–3

The following disclosure note appeared in the December 28, 2013, annual financial statement of the Intel Corporation.

Note 5: Cash and Investments: Available-for-Sale Investments (in part)

Table 1: Available-for-sale investments as of December 28, 2013, and December 29, 2012, are shown at the top of the next page.

Table 2: The before-tax net unrealized holding gains (losses) on available-for-sale investments that have been included in accumulated other comprehensive income (loss) are shown after Table 1 on the next page.

Required:

1. Considering only Table 1, draw a T-account that shows the change between December 29, 2012, and December 28, 2013, in balances for the fair value adjustment associated with Intel's AFS investments. By how much did fair value change during 2013?

Table 1

(in millions)	December 28, 2013 Adjusted Cost	Gross Unrealized Gains	Gross Unrealized Losses	Fair Value	December 29, 2012 Adjusted Cost	Gross Unrealized Gains	Gross Unrealized Losses	Fair Value
Asset-backed securities	$ 11	$ —	$ (2)	$ 9	$ 14	$ —	$ (3)	$ 11
Bank deposits	2,951	6	(1)	2,956	1,417	1	—	1,418
Commercial paper	4,464	—	—	4,464	4,184	1	—	4,185
Corporate bonds	2,359	15	(3)	2,371	635	8	(1)	642
Government bonds	1,024	—	—	1,024	2,235	—	—	2,235
Marketable equity securities	3,340	2,881	—	6,221	3,356	1,069	(1)	4,424
Money market fund deposits	1,042	—	(1)	1,041	1,086	—	—	1,086
Total available-for-sale investments	**$15,191**	**$2,902**	**$ (7)**	**$18,086**	**$12,927**	**$1,079**	**$ (5)**	**$14,001**

Table 2

(in millions)	2013 Before tax	2013 Net of tax	2012 Before tax	2012 Net of tax
Change in unrealized holding gains (losses) on available-for-sale investments	$1,963	$1,276	$ 909	$ 591
Adjustment for (gains) losses on available-for-sale investments included in net income	$ (146)	$ (95)	$ (187)	$ (121)

2. Now also consider Table 2. Prepare a journal entry to recognize the "change in unrealized holding gains (losses) on available-for-sale investments", and determine how that journal entry would affect the T-account prepared in requirement 1.
3. Considering Table 2 again, how would the "adjustment for (gains) losses on available-for-sale investments included in net income" affect the T-account? Have you accounted for the entire change in the fair value adjustment that occurred during 2013? Speculate as to what might explain any difference.

Real World Case 12–2
Reporting securities available-for-sale; obtain and critically evaluate an annual report
● LO12–3

Investments in common stocks potentially affect each of the various financial statements as well as the disclosure notes that accompany those statements.

Required:

1. Locate a recent annual report of a public company that includes a disclosure note that describes an investment in securities available-for-sale. You can use EDGAR at www.sec.gov.
2. Under what caption are the investments reported in the comparative balance sheets? Are they reported as current or noncurrent assets?
3. Are realized gains or losses reported in the comparative income statements?
4. Where are unrealized gains or losses reported in the comparative financial statements?
5. Under what caption are unrealized gains or losses listed in the comparative balance sheets? Why are unrealized gains or losses reported here rather than in the income statements?
6. Are cash flow effects of these investments reflected in the company's comparative statements of cash flows? If so, what information is provided by this disclosure?
7. Does the disclosure note provide information not available in the financial statements?

International Case 12–3
Comparison of equity method between IFRS and U.S. GAAP
● LO12–4, LO12–5, LO12–6, LO12–8

The following are excerpts from the 2010 financial statements of Renault, a large French automobile manufacturer.

14–INVESTMENT IN NISSAN

A–Nissan consolidation method

Following the operations described in "Significant events," Renault's investment in Nissan was down slightly, from 44.3% in 2009 to 43.4% in 2010. Renault and Nissan have chosen to develop a unique type of alliance between two distinct companies with common interests, uniting forces to achieve optimum performance. The Alliance is organized so as to preserve individual brand identities and respect each company's corporate culture.

Consequently:

- Renault does not hold the majority of Nissan voting rights.
- The terms of the Renault-Nissan agreements do not entitle Renault to appoint the majority of Nissan directors, nor to hold the majority of voting rights at meetings of Nissan's Board of Directors; at December 31, 2010 as in 2009, Renault supplied four of the total nine members of Nissan's Board of Directors.
- Renault Nissan BV, owned 50% by Renault and 50% by Nissan, is the Alliance's joint decision-making body for strategic issues concerning either group individually. Its decisions are applicable to both Renault and Nissan. This entity does not enable Renault to direct Nissan's financial and operating strategies, and cannot therefore be considered to represent contractual control by Renault over Nissan. The matters examined by Renault Nissan BV since it was formed have remained strictly within this contractual framework, and are not an indication that Renault exercises control over Nissan.
- Renault can neither use nor influence the use of Nissan's assets in the same way as its own assets.
- Renault provides no guarantees in respect of Nissan's debt.

In view of this situation, Renault is considered to exercise significant influence in Nissan, and therefore uses the equity method to include its investment in Nissan in the consolidation.

F–Nissan financial information under IFRS (partial)

(When accounting for its investment in Nissan, Renault makes restatements that) include adjustments for harmonisation of accounting standards and the adjustments to fair value of assets and liabilities applied by Renault at the time of acquisitions in 1999 and 2002.

Required:

1. Go to Deloitte's IAS Plus website and examine the summary of the IASB's *IAS No. 28* (at **http://www.iasplus.com/en/standards**), which governs application of the equity method. Focus on two areas: Identification of Associates and Applying the Equity Method of Accounting.
2. Evaluate Renault's decision to use the equity method to account for its investment in Nissan. Does Renault have insignificant influence, significant influence, or control?
3. Evaluate the fact that, when accounting for its investment in Nissan under the equity method, Renault makes adjustments that take into account the fair value of assets and liabilities at the time Renault invested in Nissan. Give an example of the sorts of adjustments that might be made. Are such adjustments consistent with IFRS? With U.S. GAAP? Explain.
4. Evaluate the fact that, when accounting for its investment in Nissan under the equity method, Renault makes adjustments for harmonization of accounting standards. Are such adjustments consistent with IFRS? With U.S. GAAP? Explain.

Case 12–4
Accounting for debt and equity investments
● LO12–1, LO12–2, LO12–3, LO12–8

Obtain the 2013 annual report of Unilever (**www.Unilever.com**). Assume that Unilever accounts for its investments according to *IAS No. 39.*

Required:

1. Examine Unilever's Notes 17 and 18. Indicate the fair value and the carrying amount of investments that Unilever designates as held-to-maturity (HTM), fair value through profit or loss (FVPL), and available-for-sale (AFS) as of December 31, 2013, and discuss briefly how Unilever accounts for unrealized gains and losses on each of those categories of investments.
2. Examine Unilever's December 31, 2013, balance sheet and its Note 17A. On what lines do the HTM, FVPL, and AFS investments appear?
3. Consider Unilever's description of how it accounts for the HTM investments. Does it appear Unilever accounts for those investments as it describes? Explain.

Research Case 12–5
Researching the way investments are reported; retrieving information from the Internet
● LO12–1, LO12–2, LO12–3

All publicly traded domestic companies use EDGAR, the Electronic Data Gathering, Analysis, and Retrieval system, to make the majority of their filings with the SEC. You can access EDGAR at **www.sec.gov**.

Required:

1. Search for a public company with which you are familiar. Access its most recent 10-K filing. Search or scroll to find financial statements and related notes.
2. Answer the following questions. (If the chosen company does not report investments in the securities of other companies, choose another company.)
   a. What is the amount and classification of any investment securities reported in the balance sheet? Are unrealized gains or losses reported in the shareholders' equity section?
   b. Are any investments reported by the equity method?
   c. What amounts from these investments are reported in the comparative income statements? Has that income increased or decreased over the years reported?
   d. Are any acquisitions or disposals of investments reported in the statement of cash flows?

Real World Case 12–6
Merck's investments
● LO12–3, LO12–4, LO12–5

Corporations frequently invest in securities issued by other corporations. Some investments are acquired to secure a favorable business relationship with another company. On the other hand, others are intended only to earn an investment return from the dividends or interest the securities pay or from increases in the market prices of the securities—the same motivations that might cause you to invest in stocks, bonds, or other securities. This diversity in investment objectives means no single accounting method is adequate to report every investment.

Merck & Co., Inc., invests in securities of other companies. Access Merck's 2013 10-K (which includes financial statements) using EDGAR at **www.sec.gov**.

Required:

1. What is the amount and classification of any investment securities reported on the balance sheet? In which current and noncurrent asset categories are investments reported by Merck? What criteria are used to determine the classifications?
2. How are unrealized gains or losses reported? Realized gains and losses?
3. Are any investments reported by the equity method?
4. What amounts from equity method investments are reported in the comparative income statements?
5. Are cash flow effects of these investments reflected in the company's comparative statements of cash flows? If so, what information is provided by this disclosure?

Real World Case 12–7
Comprehensive income—Microsoft
● LO12–3

As required by GAAP [FASB ASC 320, previously *SFAS No. 115*], **Microsoft Corporation** reports its investments available-for-sale at the *fair value* of the investment securities. The *net* unrealized holding gain is not reported in the income statement. Instead, it's reported as part of Other comprehensive income and added to Accumulated other comprehensive income in shareholders' equity.

Comprehensive income is a broader view of the change in shareholders' equity than traditional net income, encompassing all changes in equity from nonowner transactions. Microsoft chose to report its Other comprehensive income as a separate statement in a disclosure note in its 2013 annual report.

NOTE 19 – Other Comprehensive Income (Loss)
The activity in other comprehensive income (loss) and related income tax effects were as follows:

(in millions)

Year Ended June 30	2013	2012	2011
Net Unrealized Gains (Losses) on Derivatives			
Unrealized gains (losses), net of tax effect of $54, $127, and $(340)	$101	$ 236	$ (632)
Reclassification adjustment for losses (gains) included in net income, net of tax effect of $(68), $10, and $2	(127)	19	5
Net unrealized gains (losses) on derivatives	$ (26)	$ 255	$ (627)
Net Unrealized Gains (Losses) on Investments			
Unrealized gains (losses), net of tax effect of $244, $(93), and $726	$453	$(172)	$1,349
Reclassification adjustment for gains included in net income, net of tax effects of $(49), $(117), and $(159)	(90)	(218)	(295)
Net unrealized gains (losses) on investments	363	(390)	1,054
Translation adjustments and other, net of tax effects of $(8), $(165) and $205	(16)	(306)	381
Other comprehensive income (loss)	$321	$(441)	$ 808

The components of accumulated other comprehensive income were as follows:

(In millions)

Year Ended June 30	2013	2012	2011
Net unrealized gains (losses) on derivatives	$ 66	$ 92	$ (163)
Net unrealized gains on investments	1,794	1,431	1,821
Translation adjustments and other	(117)	(101)	205
Accumulated other comprehensive income	$1,743	$1,422	$1,863

Required:

1. The note indicates Unrealized holding gains during 2013 in the amount of $453 million. Is this the balance of accumulated other comprehensive income that Microsoft would include as a separate component of shareholders' equity? Explain.
2. What does Microsoft mean by the term, "Reclassification adjustment for (losses) gains included in net income"?

Trueblood Accounting Case 12–8
Impairments (Appendix 12B)
● LO12–3

The following Trueblood case is recommended for use with this chapter. The case provides an excellent opportunity for class discussion, group projects, and writing assignments. The case, along with Professor's Discussion Material, can be obtained from the Deloitte Foundation at its website: www.deloitte.com/us/truebloodcases.

Case: 10–7: Impaired Abilities
This case gives students an opportunity to discuss accounting for other-than-temporary impairments.

Research Case 12–9
Changes in accounting for other-than-temporary impairments (Appendix 12B)
● LO12–1, LO12–3

Appendix 12B discusses accounting for other-than-temporary impairments In FASB deliberations on changing to this GAAP, these changes were controversial. In fact, two of the five members of the FASB voted against the changes and provided an explanation for their position when the standard that defined the changes was issued. That information isn't included in the FASB's Accounting Standards Codification, but you can find it in the original standard, "Recognition and Presentation of Other-Than-Temporary Impairments," FASB Staff Position (FSP) No. 115-2 and 124-2 (Norwalk, Conn.: FASB April 9, 2009), which is available under the "Standards" link at www.FASB.org.

Required:

Access the FSP and turn to p. 17, and read why FASB members Linsmeier and Siegel dissented. What were their major concerns with the new approach for accounting for OTT impairments? Do you find those concerns compelling?

Air France–KLM Case

● LO12–8

IFRS

Air France–KLM (AF), a Franco-Dutch company, prepares its financial statements according to International Financial Reporting Standards. AF's financial statements and disclosure notes for the year ended December 31, 2013, are provided with all new textbooks. This material also is available at www.airfranceklm-finance.com.

Required:

1. Read Notes 4.10.2, 4.10.5, 24, 34.3, and 34.4, focusing on investments accounted for at fair value through profit and loss (FVPL):
   a. As of December 31, 2013, what is the balance of those investments in the balance sheet? Be specific regarding which line of the balance sheet includes the balance.
   b. How much of that balance is classified as current and how much as noncurrent?
   c. Is that balance stated at fair value? How do you know?
   d. How much of the fair value of those investments is accounted for using level 1, level 2, and level 3 inputs of the fair value hierarchy? Given that information, assess the reliability (representational faithfulness) of this fair value estimate.
2. Complete requirement 1 again, but for investments accounted for as available-for-sale.
3. Read notes 4.3.2, 11, and 22.
   a. When AF can exercise significant influence over an investee, what accounting approach do they use to account for the investment? How does AF determine if it can exercise significant influence?

b. If AF exercises joint control over an investee by virtue of a contractual agreement, what accounting method does it use?

c. What is the carrying value of AF's equity-method investments in its December 31, 2013, balance sheet?

d. How did AF's equity-method investments affect AF's 2013 net income from continuing operations?

CPA Simulation 12–1

Barbados Investments

Investments

KAPLAN CPA REVIEW

Test your knowledge of the concepts discussed in this chapter, practice critical professional skills necessary for career success, and prepare for the computer-based CPA exam by accessing our CPA simulations in the Connect library.

The Barbados Investments simulation tests your knowledge of (a) the way we classify investment securities among the categories of trading securities, available-for-sale securities, and those held-to-maturity, (b) how we account for those investments, (c) the way accounting for investments affects comprehensive income, and (d) the appropriate use of the equity method.

As on the CPA exam itself, you will be asked to use tools including a spreadsheet, a calculator, and generally accepted accounting principles, to conduct research, derive solutions, and communicate conclusions related to these issues in a simulated environment.

Specific tasks in the simulation include:

- Analyzing various transactions involving investment securities and determining their appropriate balance sheet classification.
- Applying judgment in the application of the equity method.
- Determining the amount of interest revenue to be reported from a debt investment.
- Demonstrating an understanding of comprehensive income and how it is affected by investments in securities.
- Communicating the way we account for investments using the equity method.
- Researching the financial reporting ramifications of changing the classification of investment securities.

CHAPTER

13

Current Liabilities and Contingencies

OVERVIEW

Chapter 13 is the first of five chapters devoted to liabilities. In Part A of this chapter, we discuss liabilities that are classified appropriately as current. In Part B we turn our attention to situations in which there is uncertainty as to whether an obligation really exists. These are designated as loss contingencies. Some loss contingencies are accrued as liabilities, but others only are disclosed in the notes.

LEARNING OBJECTIVES

After studying this chapter, you should be able to:

- **LO13–1** Define liabilities and distinguish between current and long-term liabilities. (*p. 732*)
- **LO13–2** Account for the issuance and payment of various forms of notes and record the interest on the notes. (*p. 734*)
- **LO13–3** Characterize accrued liabilities and liabilities from advance collection and describe when and how they should be recorded. (*pp. 737* and *740*)
- **LO13–4** Determine when a liability can be classified as a noncurrent obligation. (*p. 743*)
- **LO13–5** Identify situations that constitute contingencies and the circumstances under which they should be accrued. (*p. 746*)
- **LO13–6** Demonstrate the appropriate accounting treatment for contingencies, including unasserted claims and assessments. (*p. 747*)
- **LO13–7** Discuss the primary differences between U.S. GAAP and IFRS with respect to current liabilities and contingencies. (*pp. 744, 755,* and *756*)

FINANCIAL REPORTING CASE

Dinstuhl's Dad

"My dad is confused," your friend Buzz Dinstuhl proclaimed at the office one morning. "You see, we're competing against each other in that investment game I told you about, and one of his hot investments is Syntel Microsystems. When he got their annual report yesterday afternoon, he started analyzing it, you know, really studying it closely. Then he asked me about this part here." Buzz pointed to the current liability section of the balance sheet and related disclosure note:

SYNTEL MICROSYSTEMS, INC.
Balance Sheet
December 31, 2016 and 2015
($ in millions)

Current Liabilities	**2016**	**2015**
Accounts payable	$233.5	$241.6
Short-term borrowings (Note 3)	187.0	176.8
Accrued liabilities	65.3	117.2
Accrued loss contingency	76.9	—
Other current liabilities	34.6	45.2
Current portion of long-term debt	44.1	40.3
Total current liabilities	$641.4	$621.1

Note 3: Short-Term Borrowings (in part)

The components of short-term borrowings and their respective weighted average interest rates at the end of the period are as follows:

$ in millions

	2016		**2015**	
	Amount	**Average Interest Rate**	**Amount**	**Average Interest Rate**
Commercial paper	$ 34.0	5.2%	$ 27.1	5.3%
Bank loans	218.0	5.5	227.7	5.6
Amount reclassified to long-term liabilities	(65.0)	—	(78.0)	—
Total short-term borrowings	$187.0		$176.8	

The Company maintains bank credit lines sufficient to cover outstanding short-term borrowings. As of December 31, 2016, the Company had $200.0 million fee-paid lines available. At December 31, 2016 and 2015, the Company classified $65.0 million and $78.0 million, respectively, of commercial paper and bank notes as long-term debt. The Company has the intent and ability, through formal renewal agreements, to renew these obligations into future periods.

Note 6: Contingencies (in part)

Between 2014 and 2015, the Company manufactured cable leads that, the Company has learned, contribute to corrosion of linked components with which they are installed. At December 31, 2016, the Company accrued $132.0 million in anticipation of remediation and claims settlement deemed probable, of which $76.9 million is considered a current liability.

"So, what's the problem?" you asked.

"Well, he thinks I'm some sort of financial wizard because I'm in business."

"And because you tell him so all the time," you interrupted.

(continued)

(continued)

"Maybe so, but he's been told that current liabilities are riskier than long-term liabilities, and now he's focusing on that. He can't see why some long-term debt is reported here in the current section. And it also looks like some is reported the other way around; some current liabilities reported as long term. Plus, the contingency amount seems like it's not even a contractual liability. Then he wants to know what some of those terms mean. Lucky for me, I had to leave before I had to admit I didn't know the answers. You're the accounting graduate; help me out."

QUESTIONS

By the time you finish this chapter, you should be able to respond appropriately to the questions posed in this case. Compare your response to the solution provided at the end of the chapter.

1. What are accrued liabilities? What is commercial paper? *(p. 737)*
2. Why did Syntel Microsystems include some long-term debt in the current liability section? *(p. 743)*
3. Did they also report some current amounts as long-term debt? Explain. *(p. 743)*
4. Must obligations be known contractual debts in order to be reported as liabilities? *(p. 747)*
5. Is it true that current liabilities are riskier than long-term liabilities? *(p. 759)*

PART A Current Liabilities

Liabilities and owners' equity accounts represent specific sources of a company's assets.

Before a business can invest in an asset it first must acquire the money to pay for it. This can happen in either of two ways—funds can be provided by owners or the funds must be borrowed. You may recognize this as a description of the basic accounting equation: Assets = Liabilities + Owners' Equity. Liabilities and owners' equity on the right-hand side of the equation represent the two basic sources of the assets on the left-hand side. You studied assets in the chapters leading to this one and you will study owners' equity later. This chapter and the next four describe the various liabilities that constitute creditors' claims on a company's assets.

Characteristics of Liabilities

Most liabilities obligate the debtor to pay cash at specified times and result from legally enforceable agreements.

You already know what liabilities are. You encounter them every day. If you are paying for a car or a home with monthly payments, you have a personal liability. Similarly, when businesses issue notes and bonds, their creditors are the banks, individuals, and organizations that exchange cash for those securities. Each of these obligations represents the most common type of liability—one to be paid in cash and for which the amount and timing are specified by a legally enforceable contract.

Entities routinely incur most liabilities to acquire the funds, goods, and services they need to operate and just as routinely settle the liabilities they incur.[1]

Some liabilities are not contractual obligations and may not be payable in cash.

However, to be reported as a **liability**, an obligation need not be payable in cash. Instead, it may require the company to transfer other assets or to provide services. A liability doesn't have to be represented by a written agreement nor be legally enforceable. Even the amount and timing of repayment need not be precisely known.

From a financial reporting perspective, a liability has three essential characteristics. Liabilities:

● LO13–1

1. Are *probable, future* sacrifices of economic benefits.
2. Arise from *present* obligations (to transfer assets or provide services) to other entities.
3. Result from *past* transactions or events.[2]

[1]"Elements of Financial Statements," *Statement of Financial Accounting Concepts No. 6* (Stamford, Conn.: FASB, 1985), par. 38.
[2]Ibid.

Notice that the definition of a liability involves the past, the present, and the future. It is a present responsibility to sacrifice assets in the future because of a transaction or other event that happened in the past.

Later in the chapter we'll discuss several liabilities that possess these characteristics but have elements of uncertainty regarding the amount and timing of payments and sometimes even whether an obligation exists.

What Is a Current Liability?

In a classified balance sheet, we categorize liabilities as either **current liabilities** or long-term liabilities. We often characterize current liabilities as obligations payable within one year or within the firm's operating cycle, whichever is longer. This general definition usually applies. However, a more discriminating definition identifies current liabilities as those expected to be satisfied with *current assets* or by the creation of other *current liabilities.*[3]

Current liabilities are **expected to require current assets and usually are payable within one year.**

Classifying liabilities as either current or long term helps investors and creditors assess the risk that the liabilities will require expenditure of cash or other assets in the near term. Is the due date years in the future, permitting resources to be used for other purposes without risking default? Or, will payment require the use of current assets and reduce the amount of liquid funds available for other uses? If so, are sufficient liquid funds available to make necessary payments of liabilities in addition to meeting current operating needs, or must additional funds be obtained by raising capital? The answers to these questions can have significant implications. For example, a major factor contributing to the collapse of the financial giant **Bear Stearns** in 2008 was its reliance on short-term liabilities that it couldn't refinance when lenders, clients, and trading partners grew concerned about the quality of Bear's investments.[4]

Classifying liabilities as either current or long term helps investors and creditors assess the relative risk of a business's liabilities.

Conceptually, liabilities should be recorded at their present values. In other words, the amount recorded is the present value of all anticipated future cash payments resulting from the debt (specifically, principal and interest payments).[5] However, in practice, liabilities payable within one year ordinarily are recorded instead at their maturity amounts.[6] This inconsistency usually is inconsequential because the relatively short-term maturity of current liabilities makes the interest or time value component immaterial.

Current liabilities ordinarily are reported at their maturity amounts.

The most common obligations reported as current liabilities are accounts payable, notes payable, commercial paper, income tax liability, dividends payable, and accrued liabilities. Liabilities related to income taxes are the subject of Chapter 16. We discuss the others here.

Before we examine specific current liabilities, let's use the current liability section of the balance sheet of **General Mills, Inc.**, and related disclosure notes to overview the chapter and to provide perspective on the liabilities we discuss (Illustration 13–1).

You may want to refer back to portions of Illustration 13–1 as corresponding liabilities are described later in the chapter. We discuss accounts payable and notes payable first.

Open Accounts and Notes

Many businesses buy merchandise or supplies on credit. Most also find it desirable to borrow cash from time to time to finance their activities. In this section we discuss the liabilities these borrowing activities create: namely, trade accounts and trade notes, bank loans, and commercial paper.

Accounts Payable and Trade Notes Payable

Buying merchandise on account in the ordinary course of business creates *accounts payable.*

Accounts payable are obligations to suppliers of merchandise or of services purchased on *open account.* Most trade credit is offered on open account. This means that the only formal

[3]FASB ASC Master Glossary (previously Committee on Accounting Procedure, American Institute of CPAs, *Accounting Research and Terminology Bulletin, Final Edition* (New York: AICPA, August 1961), p. 21).

[4]William D. Cohan, *House of Cards: A Tale of Hubris and Wretched Excess on Wall Street* (New York: Doubleday, 2009).

[5]The concepts of the time value of money and the mechanics of present value calculations are covered in Chapter 6.

[6]In fact, those arising in connection with suppliers in the normal course of business and due within a year are specifically exempted from present value reporting by FASB ASC 835–30–15–3: Interest—Imputation of Interest—Scope and Scope Exceptions (previously "Interest on Receivables and Payables," *Accounting Principles Board Opinion No. 21* (New York: AICPA, August 1971), par. 3).

Illustration 13–1
Current Liabilities—General Mills

In practice, there is little uniformity regarding precise captions used to describe current liabilities or in the extent to which accounts are combined into summary captions. The presentation here is representative and fairly typical.

Real World Financials

Amounts reported on the face of the balance sheet seldom are sufficient to adequately describe current liabilities. Additional descriptions are provided in disclosure notes.

GENERAL MILLS, INC.
Excerpt from Consolidated Balance Sheets ($ in millions)
May 26, 2013 and May 27, 2012
Liabilities

Current Liabilities:	**2013**	**2012**
Accounts payable	$1,423.2	$1,148.9
Current portion of long-term debt	1,443.3	741.2
Notes payable	599.7	526.5
Other current liabilities	1,827.7	1,426.6
Total current liabilities	$5,293.9	$3,843.2

Note 8. Debt

Notes Payable The components of notes payable and their respective weighted-average interest rates at the end of the periods were as follows:

	2013		**2012**	
Dollars in millions:	**Note Payable**	**Weighted Average Interest Rate**	**Note Payable**	**Weighted Average Interest Rate**
U.S. commercial paper	$515.5	0.2%	$412.0	0.2%
Financial institutions	84.2	13.0	114.5	10.0
Total notes payable	$599.7	2.0%	$526.5	2.4%

To ensure availability of funds, we maintain bank credit lines sufficient to cover our outstanding short-term borrowings. Commercial paper is a continuing source of short-term financing. We have commercial paper programs available to us in the United States and Europe. In April 2012, we entered into fee-paid committed credit lines, consisting of a $1.0 billion facility scheduled to expire in April 2015 and a $1.7 billion facility scheduled to expire in April 2017. We also have $332.8 million in uncommitted credit lines that support our foreign operations. As of May 26, 2013, there were no amounts outstanding on the fee-paid committed credit lines and $84.2 million was drawn on the uncommitted lines. The credit facilities contain several covenants, including a requirement to maintain a fixed charge coverage ratio of at least 2.5 times. We were in compliance with all credit facility covenants as of May 26, 2013.

credit instrument is the invoice. Because the time until payment usually is short (often 30, 45, or 60 days), these liabilities typically are noninterest-bearing and are reported at their face amounts. As shown in Illustration 13–1, General Mills' accounts payable in 2013 was $1,423 million. The key accounting considerations relating to accounts payable are determining their existence and ensuring that they are recorded in the appropriate accounting period. You studied these issues and learned how cash discounts are handled during your study of inventories in Chapter 8.

Trade notes payable differ from accounts payable in that they are formally recognized by a written promissory note. Often these are of a somewhat longer term than open accounts and bear interest.

Short-Term Notes Payable

● LO13–2

The most common way for a corporation to obtain temporary financing is to arrange a short-term bank loan. When a company borrows cash from a bank and signs a promissory note (essentially an IOU), the firm's liability is reported as *notes payable* (sometimes *bank loans* or *short-term borrowings*). About two-thirds of bank loans are short term, but because many are routinely renewed, some tend to resemble long-term debt. In fact, in some cases we report them as long-term debt (as you'll see later in the chapter).

Very often, smaller firms are unable to tap into the major sources of long-term financing to the extent necessary to provide for their capital needs. So they must rely heavily on short-term financing. Even large companies typically utilize short-term debt as a significant and indispensable component of their capital structure. One reason is that short-term funds usually offer lower interest rates than long-term debt. Perhaps most importantly, corporations desire flexibility. Managers want as many financing alternatives as possible.

CREDIT LINES. Usually short-term bank loans are arranged under an existing line of credit with a bank or group of banks. A line of credit is an agreement to provide short-term financing, with amounts withdrawn by the borrower only when needed. Even though the loans are short-term, with amounts borrowed and repayed frequently, the agreement to provide a line of credit typically lasts several years. Lines of credit can be noncommitted or committed. A *noncommitted* line of credit is an informal agreement that permits a company to borrow up to a prearranged limit without having to follow formal loan procedures and paperwork. Banks sometimes require the company to maintain a compensating balance on deposit with the bank, say, 5% of the line of credit.[7] A *committed* line of credit is a more formal agreement that usually requires the company to pay a commitment fee to the bank to keep a credit line amount available to the company. A typical annual commitment fee is ¼% of the total committed funds, and may also require a compensating balance. A recent annual report of IBM Corporation illustrates noncommitted lines of credit (Illustration 13–2).

A *line of credit* allows a company to borrow cash without having to follow formal loan procedures and paperwork.

Note J. Borrowings (in part)

LINES OF CREDIT: In 2013, the company extended the term of its five-year, $10 billion Credit Agreement (the "Credit Agreement") by one year to November 10, 2018. The total expense recorded by the company related to this global credit facility was $5.4 million in 2013, $5.3 million in 2012 and $5.0 million in 2011. The Credit Agreement permits the company and its Subsidiary Borrowers to borrow up to $10 billion on a revolving basis. Borrowings of the Subsidiary Borrowers will be unconditionally backed by the company. . . . As of December 31, 2013, there were no borrowings by the company, or its subsidiaries, under the Credit Agreement.

Illustration 13–2

Disclosure of Credit Lines—IBM Corporation

Real World Financials

General Mills' disclosure notes that we looked at in Illustration 13–1 indicate that the company has both noncommitted and committed lines of credit.

INTEREST. When a company borrows money, it pays the lender interest in return for using the lender's money during the term of the loan. You might think of the interest as the "rent" paid for using money. Interest is stated in terms of a percentage rate to be applied to the face amount of the loan. Because the stated rate typically is an annual rate, when calculating interest for a short-term note we must adjust for the fraction of the annual period the loan spans. Interest on notes is calculated as:

Face amount × Annual rate × Time to maturity

This is demonstrated in Illustration 13–3.

On May 1, Affiliated Technologies, Inc., a consumer electronics firm borrowed $700,000 cash from First BancCorp under a noncommitted short-term line of credit arrangement and issued a six-month, 12% promissory note. Interest was payable at maturity.

May 1		
Cash	700,000	
Notes payable		700,000
November 1		
Interest expense ($700,000 × 12% × 6⁄12)	42,000	
Notes payable	700,000	
Cash ($700,000 + 42,000)		742,000

Illustration 13–3

Note Issued for Cash

Interest on notes is calculated as:

Face amount × Annual rate × Time to maturity

[7]A compensating balance is a deposit kept by a company in a low-interest or noninterest-bearing account at the bank. The required deposit usually is some percentage of the committed amount or the amount used (say, 2% to 5%). The effect of the compensating balance is to increase the borrower's effective interest rate and the bank's effective rate of return.

Sometimes a bank loan assumes the form of a so-called **noninterest-bearing note**. Obviously, though, no bank will lend money without interest. Noninterest-bearing loans actually do bear interest, but the interest is deducted (or discounted) from the face amount to determine the cash proceeds made available to the borrower at the outset. For example, the preceding note could be packaged as a $700,000 noninterest-bearing note, with a 12% discount rate.[8] In that case, the $42,000 interest would be discounted at the outset, rather than explicitly stated:[9]

The proceeds of the note are reduced by the interest in a noninterest-bearing note.

May 1		
Cash (difference)	658,000	
Discount on notes payable ($700,000 × 12% × 6⁄12)	42,000	
Notes payable (face amount)		700,000
November 1		
Interest expense	42,000	
Discount on notes payable		42,000
Notes payable (face amount)	700,000	
Cash		700,000

Notice that the amount borrowed under this arrangement is only $658,000, but the interest is calculated as the discount rate times the $700,000 face amount. This causes the *effective* interest rate to be higher than the 12% stated rate:

When interest is discounted from the face amount of a note, the effective interest rate is higher than the stated discount rate.

$$\frac{\$42{,}000 \text{ Interest for 6 months}}{\$658{,}000 \text{ Amount borrowed}} = 6.38\% \text{ Rate for 6 months}$$

To annualize:

$$6.38\% \times {}^{12}\!/\!_{6} = 12.76\% \text{ Effective interest rate}$$

We studied short-term notes from the perspective of the lender (note receivable) in Chapter 7.

Inventory or accounts receivable often are pledged as security for short-term loans.

SECURED LOANS. Sometimes short-term loans are *secured,* meaning a specified asset of the borrower is pledged as collateral or security for the loan. Although many kinds of assets can be pledged, the secured loans most frequently encountered in practice are secured by inventory or accounts receivable. For example, **Smithfield Foods, Inc.**, disclosed the secured notes described in Illustration 13–4.

Illustration 13–4

Disclosure of Notes Secured by Inventory—Smithfield Foods, Inc.

Real World Financials

Note 7: Debt (in part)
Working Capital Facilities
We and our material U.S. subsidiaries are jointly and severally liable for, as primary obligors, the obligations under the Inventory Revolver, and those obligations are secured by a first priority lien on certain personal property, including cash and cash equivalents, deposit accounts, inventory, intellectual property, and certain equity interests. We incurred approximately $9.7 million in transaction fees in connection with the Inventory Revolver, which were being amortized over its five-year life.

[8]Sometimes the terms *discount rate* and *effective interest rate* are used interchangeably, so don't be confused by the different use of the term *discount rate* with respect to noninterest-bearing notes. Here *discount rate* refers only to a rate that is multiplied by the face amount of the note (in Affiliated's case, $700,000) to calculate how much interest is included in the note (in Affiliated's case, $42,000). That discount rate is different from the *effective interest rate* that Affiliated pays on the outstanding payable balance, and that Affiliated would use to calculate the present value of future cash flows.

[9]Be sure to understand that we are actually recording the note at 658,000, *not* 700,000, but are recording the interest portion separately in a contra-liability account, *discount on notes payable.* The entries shown reflect the gross method. By the net method, the interest component is netted against the face amount of the note as follows:

May 1		
Cash	658,000	
Notes payable		658,000
November 1		
Interest expense ($700,000 × 12% × 6⁄12)	42,000	
Notes payable	658,000	
Cash		700,000

When accounts receivable serve as collateral, we refer to the arrangement as *pledging* accounts receivable. Sometimes, the receivables actually are sold outright to a finance company as a means of short-term financing. This is called *factoring* receivables.[10]

Commercial Paper

Some large corporations obtain temporary financing by issuing **commercial paper**, often purchased by other companies as a short-term investment. Commercial paper refers to unsecured notes sold in minimum denominations of $25,000 with maturities ranging from 30 to 270 days (beyond 270 days the firm would be required to file a registration statement with the SEC). Interest often is discounted at the issuance of the note. Usually commercial paper is issued directly to the buyer (lender) and is backed by a line of credit with a bank. This allows the interest rate to be lower than in a bank loan. Commercial paper has become an increasingly popular way for large companies to raise funds, the total amount having expanded over fivefold in the last decade.

Large, highly rated firms sometimes sell *commercial paper* to borrow funds at a lower rate than through a bank loan.

Illustration 13–5 includes a disclosure note from the 2013 annual report of **Comcast Corporation** that describes Comcast's recently expanded commercial paper program.

Illustration 13–5

Disclosure of Commercial Paper—Comcast Corporation

Real World Financials

Note 9: (in part)
Commercial Paper Program
Our commercial paper program provides a lower cost source of borrowing to fund our short-term working capital requirements and is supported by our $6.25 billion revolving credit facility due June 2017. In September 2013, we increased the borrowing capacity of our commercial paper program from $2.25 billion to $6.25 billion.

The name *commercial paper* refers to the fact that a paper certificate traditionally is issued to the lender to signify the obligation, although there is a trend toward total computerization so that no paper is created. Since commercial paper is a form of notes payable, recording its issuance and payment is exactly the same as our earlier illustration.

In a statement of cash flows, the cash a company receives from using short-term notes to borrow funds as well as the cash it uses to repay the notes are reported among cash flows from financing activities. Most of the other liabilities we study in this chapter, such as accounts payable, interest payable, and bonuses payable, are integrally related to a company's primary operations and thus are part of operating activities. We discuss long-term notes in the next chapter.

FINANCIAL Reporting Case

Q1, p. 732

Accrued Liabilities

Accrued liabilities represent expenses already incurred but not yet paid (accrued expenses). These liabilities are recorded by adjusting entries at the end of the reporting period, prior to preparing financial statements. You learned how to record accrued liabilities in your study of introductory accounting and you reinforced your understanding in Chapter 2. Common examples are salaries and wages payable, income taxes payable, and interest payable. Although recorded in separate liability accounts, accrued liabilities usually are combined and reported under a single caption or perhaps two accrued liability captions in the balance sheet. General Mills includes accrued liabilities in other current liabilities (totaling $1,827.7 million as of May 26, 2013).

● LO13–3

Liabilities accrue for expenses that are incurred but not yet paid.

Accrued Interest Payable

Accrued interest payable arises in connection with notes like those discussed earlier in this chapter (as well as other forms of debt). For example, to continue Illustration 13–3, let's assume the fiscal period for Affiliated Technologies ends on June 30, two months after the six-month note is issued. The issuance of the note, intervening adjusting entry, and note payment would be recorded as shown in Illustration 13–6.

[10]Both methods of accounts receivable financing are discussed in Chapter 7, "Cash and Receivables."

Illustration 13–6

Note with Accrued Interest

At June 30, two months' interest has accrued and is recorded to avoid misstating expenses and liabilities on the June 30 financial statements.

Issuance of Note on May 1		
Cash	700,000	
Note payable		700,000
Accrual of Interest on June 30		
Interest expense ($700,000 × 12% × 2/12)	14,000	
Interest payable		14,000
Note Payment on November 1		
Interest expense ($700,000 × 12% × 4/12)	28,000	
Interest payable (from June 30 accrual)	14,000	
Note payable	700,000	
Cash ($700,000 + 42,000)		742,000

Salaries, Commissions, and Bonuses

Compensation for employee services can be in the form of hourly wages, salary, commissions, bonuses, stock compensation plans, and pensions.[11] Accrued liabilities arise in connection with compensation expense when employees have provided services but have not yet been paid as of a financial statement date. These accrued expenses/accrued liabilities are recorded by adjusting entries at the end of the reporting period, prior to preparing financial statements.

VACATIONS, SICK DAYS, AND OTHER PAID FUTURE ABSENCES. Suppose a firm grants two weeks of paid vacation each year to nonsalaried employees. Some employees take their vacations during the year in which the vacations are earned and are compensated then. Some wait. Should the firm recognize compensation expense during the year for only those employees who actually are paid that year for their absence? When you recall what you've learned about accrual accounting, you probably conclude otherwise.

An employer should accrue an expense and the related liability for employees' compensation for future absences (such as vacation pay) if the obligation meets *all* of the four conditions listed in Illustration 13–7.

Illustration 13–7

Conditions for Accrual of Paid Future Absences

1. The obligation is attributable to employees' services already performed.
2. The paid absence can be taken in a later year—the benefit vests (will be compensated even if employment is terminated) or the benefit can be accumulated over time.
3. Payment is probable.
4. The amount can be reasonably estimated.

If these conditions look familiar, it's because they are simply the characteristics of a liability we discussed earlier, adapted to relate to a potential obligation for future absences of employees. Also, these conditions are consistent with the requirement that we accrue loss contingencies only when the obligation is both (a) probable and (b) can be reasonably estimated, as discussed in Part B of this chapter.

The liability for paid absences usually is accrued at the existing wage rate rather than at a rate estimated to be in effect when absences occur.[12] So, if wage rates have risen, the difference between the accrual and the amount paid increases compensation expense that year. This situation is demonstrated in Illustration 13–8, in which vacation time carried over from 2016 is taken in 2017 and the actual amount paid to employees is $5,700,000.

Customary practice should be considered when deciding whether an obligation exists.

Company policy and actual practice should be considered when deciding whether the rights to payment for absences have been earned by services already rendered. For example, scientists in a private laboratory are eligible for paid sabbaticals every seven years. Should a liability be accrued at the end of a scientist's sixth year? No—if sabbatical leave is granted

[11]We discuss pensions in Chapter 17 and share-based compensation plans in Chapter 19.

[12]Actually, FASB ASC 710–10–25: Compensation–General–Overall–Recognition (previously *SFAS 43*, "Accounting for Compensated Absences") is silent on how the liability should be measured. In practice, most companies accrue at the current rate because it avoids estimates and usually produces a lower expense and liability. Then, later, they remeasure periodically at updated rates.

Illustration 13–8
Paid Future Absences

Davidson-Getty Chemicals has 8,000 employees. Each employee earns two weeks of paid vacation per year. Vacation time not taken in the year earned can be carried over to subsequent years. During 2016, 2,500 employees took both weeks' vacation, but at the end of the year, 5,500 employees had vacation time carryovers as follows:

Employees	Vacation Weeks Earned But Not Taken	Total Carryover Weeks
2,500	0	0
2,000	1	2,000
3,500	2	7,000
8,000		9,000

During 2016, compensation averaged $600 a week per employee.

When Vacations Were Taken in 2016

Salaries and wages expense (2,500 × 2 wks. × $600) + (2,000 × 1 wk. × $600)	4,200,000	
Cash (or wages payable)		4,200,000

December 31, 2016 (adjusting entry)

Salaries and wages expense (9,000 carryover weeks × $600)	5,400,000	
Liability—compensated future absences		5,400,000

When the necessary conditions are met, compensated future absences are accrued in the year the compensation is earned.

When Year 2016 Vacations Are Taken in 2017

Liability—compensated future absences (account balance)	5,400,000	
Salaries and wages expense (difference)	300,000	
Cash (or salaries and wages payable) (given)		5,700,000

only to perform research beneficial to the employer. Yes—if past practice indicates that sabbatical leave is intended to provide unrestricted compensated absence for past service and other conditions are met.

Custom and practice also influence whether unused rights to paid absences expire or can be carried forward. Obviously, if rights vest (payable even if employment is terminated) they haven't expired. But holiday time, military leave, maternity leave, and jury time typically do not accumulate if unused, so a liability for those benefits usually is not accrued. On the other hand, if it's customary that a particular paid absence, say holiday time, can be carried forward—if employees work on holidays, in this case—a liability is accrued if it's probable that employees will be compensated in a future year.

Accrual of sick pay is not required, but may be appropriate in some circumstances.

Interestingly, sick pay quite often meets the conditions for accrual, but accrual is not mandatory because future absence depends on future illness, which usually is not a certainty. Similar to other forms of paid absences, the decision of whether to accrue nonvesting sick pay should be based on actual policy and practice. If company policy or custom is that employees are paid sick pay even when their absences are not due to illness, it's appropriate to record a liability for unused sick pay. For example, some companies routinely allow unused sick pay benefits to be accumulated and paid at retirement (or to beneficiaries if death comes before retirement). If each condition is met except that the company finds it impractical to reasonably estimate the amount of compensation for future absences, a disclosure note should describe the situation.

A wide variety of bonus plans provide compensation tied to performance other than stock prices.

ANNUAL BONUSES. Sometimes compensation packages include annual bonuses tied to performance objectives designed to provide incentive to executives. The most common performance measures are earnings per share, net income, and operating income, each being used by about a quarter of firms having bonus plans. Nonfinancial performance measures, such as customer satisfaction and product or service quality, also are used.[13] Annual bonuses

Bonuses sometimes take the place of permanent annual raises.

[13] C. D. Ittner, D. F. Larcker, and M. V. Rajan, "The Choice of Performance Measures in Annual Bonus Contracts," *The Accounting Review*, vol. 72, No. 2 (April, 1997), pp. 231–255.

also are popular, not just for executives, but for nonmanagerial personnel as well. Unfortunately for employees, bonuses often take the place of annual raises. This allows a company to increase employee pay without permanently locking in the increases in salaries. Bonuses are compensation expense of the period in which they are earned.

Liabilities from Advance Collections

Liabilities are created when amounts are received that will be returned or remitted to others. Deposits and advances from customers and collections for third parties are cases in point.

LO13–3

Deposits and Advances from Customers

Collecting cash from a customer as a refundable deposit or as an advance payment for products or services creates a liability to return the deposit or to supply the products or services.[14]

REFUNDABLE DEPOSITS. In some businesses it's typical to require customers to pay cash as a deposit that will be refunded when a specified event occurs. You probably have encountered such situations. When apartments are rented, security or damage deposits often are collected. Utility companies frequently collect deposits when service is begun. Similarly, deposits sometimes are required on returnable containers, to be refunded when the containers are returned. That situation is demonstrated in Illustration 13–9.

Illustration 13–9
Refundable Deposits

Rancor Chemical Company sells combustible chemicals in expensive, reusable containers. Customers are charged a deposit for each container delivered and receive a refund when the container is returned. Deposits collected on containers delivered during the year were $300,000. Deposits are forfeited if containers are not returned within one year. Ninety percent of the containers were returned within the allotted time. Deposits charged are twice the actual cost of containers. The inventory of containers remains on the company's books until deposits are forfeited.

When Deposits Are Collected		
Cash	300,000	
Liability—refundable deposits		300,000
When Containers Are Returned*		
Liability—refundable deposits	270,000	
Cash		270,000
When Deposits Are Forfeited*		
Liability—refundable deposits	30,000	
Revenue—sale of containers		30,000
Cost of goods sold	15,000	
Inventory of containers		15,000

*Of course, not all containers are returned at the same time, nor does the allotted return period expire at the same time for all containers not returned. These entries summarize the several individual returns and forfeitures.

When a deposit becomes nonrefundable, inventory should be reduced to reflect the fact that the containers won't be returned.

ADVANCES FROM CUSTOMERS. At times, businesses require advance payments from customers that will be applied to the purchase price when goods are delivered or services provided. Gift certificates, magazine subscriptions, layaway deposits, special order deposits, and airline tickets are examples. These customer advances, also called *deferred revenue* or *unearned revenue,* represent liabilities until the related product or service is provided. For instance, the **New York Times Company** reports deferred revenue from unexpired subscriptions of over $58 million in its 2013 balance sheet. Advances are demonstrated in Illustration 13–10.

[14]*SFAC 6* specifically identifies customer advances and deposits as liabilities under the definition provided in that statement. "Elements of Financial Statements," *Statement of Financial Accounting Concepts No. 6* (Stamford, Conn.: FASB, 1985), par. 197.

Illustration 13–10
Customer Advance

Tomorrow Publications collects magazine subscriptions from customers at the time subscriptions are sold. Subscription revenue is recognized over the term of the subscription. Tomorrow collected $20 million in subscription sales during its first year of operations. At December 31, the average subscription was one-fourth expired.

	($ in millions)	
When Advance Is Collected		
Cash	20	
Deferred subscriptions revenue		20
When Product Is Delivered		
Deferred subscriptions revenue	5	
Subscriptions revenue		5

A customer advance produces an obligation that is satisfied when the product or service is provided.

This illustration highlights that deferred revenue gets reduced when the revenue associated with the advance has been recognized, either because the seller has delivered the goods or services as promised or because the buyer has forfeited the advance payment (for example, not redeeming a gift certificate before it expires). Less often, deferred revenue is reduced when an advance payment is returned by the seller to the buyer because the seller didn't deliver the goods or services as promised. This should sound familiar—recall from Chapter 5 that revenue recognition must be delayed until the seller has fulfilled its performance obligation. When revenue recognition is delayed, but some advanced payment is received, the seller reports a deferred revenue liability until delivery has occurred.

Additional Consideration

Accounting for Interest on Advances from Customers. Earlier in this chapter you saw that we calculate interest expense on "noninterest-bearing" notes. After all, there is a "time value of money," and nobody is willing to loan money for free. The same reasoning suggests that companies should calculate interest expense when a customer pays far in advance of delivery of a product or service. As indicated in Chapter 5, that's what GAAP for revenue recognition requires.[15]

For example, assume that on January 1, 2016, Lewis Manufacturing Co. enters into a contract to deliver to Williams Surgical Supply, Inc., on December 31, 2017. Williams pays $907 (in thousands) to Lewis at the start of the contract (January 1, 2016). In this arrangement, Williams pays Lewis significantly in advance of delivery, so Williams can be viewed as loaning money to Lewis, and Lewis should recognize interest expense on the loan. Assuming an effective interest rate of 5%, Lewis would recognize interest expense on its deferred revenue liability as follows:

January 1, 2016		
When prepayment occurs:		
Cash	907*	
Deferred revenue		907

*$907 = $1000 × .90703 (present value of $1, n = 2, I = 5%; from Table 2)

December 31, 2016		
Accrual of year 1 interest expense:		
Interest expense ($907 × 5%)	45	
Accrued interest payable		45

(continued)

[15]FASB ASC 606-10-32-16: Revenue from Contracts with Customers — Overall — Measurement — The Existence of a Significant Financing Component in the Contract (previously "Revenue from Contracts with Customers (Topic 606)" *Accounting Standards Update 2014-09* (Norwalk, Conn: FASB, 2014)).

(concluded)

December 31, 2017

When subsequent delivery occurs:

Interest expense (($907 + 45) × 5%)	48	
Accrued interest payable	45	
Deferred revenue	907	
Revenue		1,000

Lewis recognizes revenue of $1,000 rather than $907 because that is the fair value it received from Williams, including the $907 received up front and $45 + $48 = $93 of interest that Williams is allowing Lewis to not pay. Put differently, the equipment must be worth $1,000 for Williams to be willing to accept it in exchange for giving up $907 cash and $93 of interest it is owed by Lewis.

Payment so far in advance of delivery is rare. Also, as discussed in Chapter 5, companies can ignore the interest component of advance payments if it is not significant, which is assumed to be the case if the period between payment and delivery is less than one year.

Gift Cards

Gift cards or gift certificates are particularly common forms of advanced payments. As indicated in Chapter 5, when a company sells a gift card, it initially records the cash received as deferred revenue, and then recognizes revenue either when the gift card is redeemed or when the probability of redemption is viewed as remote (called *gift card breakage,* and based on expiration or the company's experience). The amounts involved can be significant. For example, **Best Buy**'s 2014 annual report lists a $406 million liability for unredeemed gift cards and $53 million of income from gift card breakage. Illustration 13–11 shows the journal entries used to account for gift cards.

Illustration 13–11
Accounting for Gift Cards

During May 2016, Great Buy, Inc., sold $2 million of gift cards. Also during May, $1.5 million of gift cards sold in May and in prior periods were redeemed by customers, and $1 million of gift cards sold in prior periods expired unused. Great Buy would make the following journal entries:

To record sale of gift cards

Cash	2,000,000	
Deferred gift card revenue		2,000,000

To record redemption of gift cards (ignoring entries to inventory and cost of sales)

Deferred gift card revenue	1,500,000	
Revenue—gift cards		1,500,000

To record expiration of gift cards

Deferred gift card revenue	1,000,000	
Revenue—gift cards		1,000,000

Liabilities for deferred revenue are classified as current or long-term depending on when the obligation is expected to be satisfied.

Collections for Third Parties

Companies often make collections for third parties from customers or from employees and periodically remit these amounts to the appropriate governmental (or other) units. Amounts collected this way represent liabilities until remitted.

An example is sales taxes. For illustration, assume a state sales tax rate of 4% and local sales tax rate of 3%. Adding the tax to a $100 sale creates a $7 liability until the tax is paid:

Sales taxes collected from customers represent liabilities until remitted.

Cash (or accounts receivable)	107	
Sales revenue		100
Sales taxes payable ([4% + 3%] × $100)		7

Payroll-related deductions such as withholding taxes, Social Security taxes, employee insurance, employee contributions to retirement plans, and union dues also create current liabilities until the amounts collected are paid to appropriate parties. These payroll-related liabilities are discussed further in the appendix to this chapter.

Amounts collected from employees in connection with payroll also represent liabilities until remitted.

A Closer Look at the Current and Noncurrent Classification

LO13–4

Given a choice, do you suppose management would prefer to report an obligation as a current liability or as a noncurrent liability? Other things being equal, most would choose the noncurrent classification. The reason is that in most settings outsiders (like banks, bondholders, and shareholders) consider debt that is payable currently to be riskier than debt that need not be paid for some time, because the current payable requires the company to be able to access the necessary cash relatively soon. Also, the long-term classification enables the company to report higher working capital (current assets minus current liabilities) and a higher current ratio (current assets/current liabilities). Working capital and the current ratio often are explicitly restricted in loan contracts. As you study this section, you should view the classification choice from this perspective. That is, a manager might not so much ask the question "What amount should I report as a current liability?" but rather "What amount can I exclude from classification as a current liability?"

Current Maturities of Long-Term Debt

FINANCIAL Reporting Case

Q2, p. 732

Long-term obligations (bonds, notes, lease liabilities, deferred tax liabilities) usually are reclassified and reported as current liabilities when they become payable within the upcoming year (or operating cycle, if longer than a year). For example, a 20-year bond issue is reported as a long-term liability for 19 years but normally is reported as a current liability on the balance sheet prepared during the 20th year of its term to maturity.[16] General Mills reported $1,443.3 million of its long-term debt as a current liability in 2013 (see Illustration 13–1), and PetSmart reported almost $67 million of current maturities of capital lease obligations in its February 2, 2014, balance sheet.

PetSmart

The currently maturing portion of a long-term debt must be reported as a current liability.

Obligations Callable by the Creditor

The requirement to classify currently maturing debt as a current liability includes debt that is *callable* (in other words, due on demand) *by the creditor* in the upcoming year (or operating cycle, if longer), even if the debt is not expected to be called. The current liability classification also is intended to include situations in which the creditor has the right to demand payment because an *existing violation* of a provision of the debt agreement makes it callable (say, working capital has fallen below a minimum covenant specified by a debt agreement). This also includes situations in which debt is not yet callable but will be callable within the year if an existing violation is not corrected within a specified grace period (unless it's probable the violation will be corrected within the grace period or waived by the creditor).[17]

When Short-Term Obligations Are Expected to Be Refinanced

FINANCIAL Reporting Case

Q3, p. 732

Reconsider the 20-year bond issue we discussed earlier. Normally we would reclassify it as a current liability on the balance sheet prepared during its 20th year. But suppose a second 20-year bond issue is sold specifically to refund the first issue when it matures. Do we have a long-term liability for 19 years, then a current liability in year 20, and then another long-term liability in years 21 and beyond? Or, do we have a single 40-year, long-term liability? If we look beyond the outward form of the transactions, the substance of the events obviously supports a single, continuing, noncurrent obligation. The concept of substance over form influences the classification of obligations expected to be refinanced.

[16]Debt to be refinanced is an exception we discuss later.

[17]FASB ASC 470–10–45: Debt–Overall–Other Presentation Matters (previously "Classification of Obligations That Are Callable by the Creditor," *Statement of Financial Accounting Standards No. 78* (Stamford, Conn.: FASB, 1983)).

Short-term obligations can be reported as noncurrent liabilities if the company (a) *intends* to refinance on a long-term basis and (b) demonstrates the *ability* to do so by a refinancing agreement or by actual financing.

Short-term obligations (including the callable obligations we discussed in the previous section) that are expected to be refinanced on a long-term basis can be reported as noncurrent, rather than current, liabilities only if two conditions are met:

(1) the firm must intend to refinance on a long-term basis, and

(2) the firm must actually have demonstrated the ability to refinance on a long-term basis.

Ability to refinance on a long-term basis can be demonstrated by either an existing refinancing agreement or by actual financing prior to the issuance of the financial statements.[18] Illustration 13–12 provides an example.

Illustration 13–12

Short-Term Obligations that Are Expected to Be Refinanced on a Long-Term Basis

Brahm Bros. Ice Cream had $12 million of notes that mature in May 2017 and also had $4 million of bonds issued in 1987 that mature in February 2017. On December 31, 2016, the company's fiscal year-end, management intended to refinance both on a long-term basis.

On February 7, 2017, the company issued $4 million of 20-year bonds, applying the proceeds to repay the bond issue that matured that month. In early March, prior to the actual issuance of the 2016 financial statements, Brahm Bros. negotiated a line of credit with a commercial bank for up to $7 million any time during 2017. Any borrowings will mature two years from the date of borrowing. Interest is at the prime London interbank borrowing rate.*

	December 31, 2016
Classification	($ in 000s)
Current Liabilities	
Notes payable	$5,000
Long-Term Liabilities	
Notes payable	$7,000
Bonds payable	4,000

Management's ability to refinance the $4 million of bonds on a long-term basis was demonstrated by actual financing prior to the issuance of the financial statements. Management's ability to refinance $7 million of the $12 million of notes was demonstrated by a refinancing agreement. The remaining $5 million must be reported as a current liability.

*This is a widely available rate often used as a basis for establishing interest rates on lines of credit and often abbreviated as LIBOR.

If shares of stock had been issued to refinance the bonds in the illustration, the bonds still would be excluded from classification as a current liability. The specific form of the long-term refinancing (bonds, bank loans, equity securities) is irrelevant when determining the appropriate classification. Requiring companies to actually demonstrate the ability to refinance on a long-term basis in addition to merely intending to do so avoids intentional or unintentional understatements of current liabilities.

It's important to remember that several weeks usually pass between the end of a company's fiscal year and the date the financial statements for that year actually are issued. Events occurring during that period can be used to clarify the nature of financial statement elements at the reporting date. Here we consider refinancing agreements and actual securities transactions to support a company's ability to refinance on a long-term basis. Later in the chapter we use information that becomes available during this period to decide how loss contingencies are reported.

International Financial Reporting Standards

LO13–7

Classification of Liabilities to be Refinanced. Under U.S. GAAP, liabilities payable within the coming year are classified as long-term liabilities if refinancing is completed before the date of issuance of the financial statements. Under IFRS, refinancing must be completed before the balance sheet date.[19]

[18]FASB ASC 470–10–45–14: Debt Overall–Other Presentation Matters (previously "Classification of Obligations Expected to Be Refinanced," *Statement of Financial Accounting Standards No. 6* (Stamford, Conn.: FASB, 1975)).

[19]"Presentation of Financial Statements" *International Accounting Standard No. 1* (IASCF), as amended effective January 1, 2014.

Concept Review Exercise

CURRENT LIABILITIES

The following selected transactions relate to liabilities of Southern Communications, Inc., for portions of 2016 and 2017. Southern's fiscal year ends on December 31.

Required:
Prepare the appropriate journal entries for these transactions.

2016

July 1	Arranged an uncommitted short-term line of credit with First City Bank amounting to \$25,000,000 at the bank's prime rate (11.5% in July). The company will pay no commitment fees for this arrangement.
Aug. 9	Received a \$30,000 refundable deposit from a major customer for copper-lined mailing containers used to transport communications equipment.
Oct. 7	Received most of the mailing containers covered by the refundable deposit and a letter stating that the customer will retain containers represented by \$2,000 of the deposit and forfeits that amount. The cost of the forfeited containers was \$1,500.
Nov. 1	Borrowed \$7 million cash from First City Bank under the line of credit arranged in July and issued a nine-month promissory note. Interest at the prime rate of 12% was payable at maturity.
Dec. 31	Recorded appropriate adjusting entries for the liabilities described above.

2017

Feb. 12	Using the unused portion of the credit line as support, issued \$9 million of commercial paper and issued a six-month promissory note. Interest was discounted at issuance at a 10% discount rate.
Aug. 1	Paid the 12% note at maturity.
12	Paid the commercial paper at maturity.

2016

July 1
No entry is made for a line of credit until a loan actually is made. The existence and terms of the line would be described in a disclosure note.

	Debit	Credit
August 9		
Cash	30,000	
Liability—refundable deposits		30,000
October 7		
Liability—refundable deposits	30,000	
Cash		28,000
Revenue—sale of containers		2,000
Cost of goods sold	1,500	
Inventory of containers		1,500
November 1		
Cash	7,000,000	
Notes payable		7,000,000
December 31		
Interest expense (\$7,000,000 × 12% × 2/12)	140,000	
Interest payable		140,000

2017

	Debit	Credit
February 12		
Cash (\$9,000,000 − [\$9,000,000 × 10% × 6/12])	8,550,000	
Discount on notes payable (difference)	450,000	
Note payable		9,000,000

Note that the effective interest rate is
[(\$9,000,000 × 10% × 6/12) ÷ \$8,550,000] × 12/6 = \$450,000 ÷ \$8,550,000 × 2 = 10.53%

August 1		
Interest expense ($7,000,000 × 12% × 7/12)	490,000	
Interest payable (from adjusting entry)	140,000	
Note payable (face amount)	7,000,000	
Cash ($7,000,000 + $630,000)		7,630,000
August 12		
Interest expense ($9,000,000 × 10% × 6/12)	450,000	
Discount on notes payable		450,000
Note payable (face amount)	9,000,000	
Cash ($8,550,000 + $450,000)		9,000,000

PART B

Contingencies

The feature that distinguishes the loss contingencies we discuss in this part of the chapter from the liabilities we discussed previously is uncertainty as to whether an obligation really exists. The circumstance giving rise to the contingency already has occurred, but there is uncertainty about whether a liability exists that will be resolved only when some future event occurs (or doesn't occur). We also discuss gain contingencies because of their similarity to loss contingencies.

Loss Contingencies

LO13–5

General Motors and Company's 2013 financial statements indicate a variety of potential obligations, as shown in Illustration 13–13.

Illustration 13–13
Disclosure of Potential Contingent Losses—General Motors Company

Real World Financials

17. Commitments and Contingencies (in part)
Various legal actions, governmental investigations, claims and proceedings are pending against us including matters arising out of alleged product defects; employment-related matters; governmental regulations relating to safety, emissions and fuel economy; product warranties; financial services; dealer, supplier and other contractual relationships; tax-related matters not recorded pursuant to ASC 740, "Income Taxes" (indirect tax-related matters) and environmental matters.

These "legal actions, governmental investigations, claims and proceedings" all relate to situations that already have occurred. However, it isn't clear that these situations have given rise to liabilities, because GM doesn't know if it will have to make future payments. How likely is an unfavorable outcome, and how much will GM have to pay if an unfavorable outcome occurs?

A *loss contingency* arises when there is uncertainty about whether a past event will result in a future loss. The uncertainty will be resolved only when some future event occurs.

A **loss contingency** is an existing, uncertain situation involving potential loss depending on whether some future event occurs. Whether a contingency is accrued and reported as a liability depends on (a) the likelihood that the confirming event will occur and (b) what can be determined about the amount of loss. For example, consider lawsuits filed against GM by customers who allege they suffered injuries as a result of faulty ignition switches in GM cars. Those lawsuits have been filed, but it may take several years for them to be settled or litigated. When considering how to account for those lawsuits prior to their resolution, GM must assess the likelihood that it eventually will have to pay damages, and if so, what the amount of those damages will be.

Note that we only account for a loss contingency when the event that gave rise to it occurred before the financial statement date. Otherwise, regardless of the likelihood of the eventual outcome, no liability existed at the statement date. Remember, one of the essential characteristics of a liability is that it results from past transactions or events. In our GM example, GM previously sold the cars to customers, so the event giving rise to potential litigation losses has occurred. The uncertainty relates not to that past event, but to the potential litigation losses that could occur in the future.

Generally accepted accounting principles require that the likelihood that the future event(s) will confirm the incurrence of the liability be (somewhat arbitrarily) categorized as probable, reasonably possible, or remote:[20]

FINANCIAL Reporting Case

Q4, p. 732

Likelihood That a Liability Exists

Probable	Confirming event is likely to occur.
Reasonably possible	The chance the confirming event will occur is more than remote but less than likely.
Remote	The chance the confirming event will occur is slight.

● LO13–6

Also key to reporting a contingent liability is its dollar amount. The amount of the potential loss is classified as either known, reasonably estimable, or not reasonably estimable.

A liability is accrued if it is both probable that the confirming event will occur and the amount can be at least reasonably estimated. A general depiction of the accrual of a loss contingency is:

Loss (or expense)	x,xxx	
Liability		x,xxx

Accrual of a Loss Contingency—Liability

If one amount within a range of possible loss appears better than other amounts within the range, that amount is accrued. When no amount within the range appears more likely than others, the minimum amount should be recorded and the possible additional loss should be disclosed.[21]

As an example, consider the following disclosure note from **Merck & Co.**'s 2013 financial statements (Illustration 13–14).

10. Contingencies and Environmental Liabilities (in part)
In management's opinion, the liabilities for all environmental matters that are probable and reasonably estimable have been accrued and totaled $213 million and $145 million at December 31, 2013 and 2012, respectively. . . . Although it is not possible to predict with certainty the outcome of these matters, or the ultimate costs of remediation, management does not believe that any reasonably possible expenditures that may be incurred in excess of the liabilities accrued should exceed $84 million in the aggregate.

Illustration 13–14

Accrual of a Loss Contingency—Merck & Co.

Real World Financials

Consistent with GAAP, Merck accrued and disclosed the $213 million loss that is probable and reasonably estimable, and then only disclosed the $84 million estimated range of reasonably possible losses above that amount.

It is important to note that some contingent losses don't involve liabilities at all. Rather, these contingencies, when resolved, cause a noncash asset to be impaired, so accruing the contingency means reducing the related asset rather than recording a liability:

Loss (or expense)	x,xxx	
Asset (or valuation account)		x,xxx

Accrual of a Loss Contingency—Asset Impairment

The most common loss contingency of this type is an uncollectible receivable. You have recorded these before without knowing you were accruing a loss contingency (*Debit:* bad debt expense; *Credit:* allowance for uncollectible accounts).[22]

A loss contingency is disclosed in notes to the financial statements if there is at least a reasonable possibility that the loss will occur.

Not all loss contingencies are accrued. If one or both criteria for accrual are not met, but there is at least a reasonable possibility that a loss will occur, a disclosure note should

[20]Because FASB ASC 740–10–25: Income Taxes–Overall–Recognition (previously "Accounting for Uncertainty in Income Taxes," *FASB Interpretation No. 48* (Norwalk, Conn.: FASB, 2006)) provides guidance on accounting for uncertainty in income taxes, FASB ASC 450–10: Contingencies–Loss Contingencies (previously *SFAS No. 5*) does not apply to income taxes. GAAP regarding uncertainty in income taxes changes the threshold for recognition of tax positions from the most probable amount to the amount that has a "more likely than not" chance of being sustained upon examination. We discuss accounting for uncertainty in income taxes in Chapter 16.

[21]FASB ASC 450–20–30: Contingencies–Loss Contingencies–Initial Measurement (previously "Reasonable Estimation of the Amount of the Loss," *FASB Interpretation No. 14* (Stamford, Conn.: FASB, 1976)).

[22]FASB ASC 310–10–35–7: Receivables–Overall–Subsequent Measurement–Losses from Uncollectible Receivables (previously "Accounting for Contingencies" *SFAS No. 5,* Norwalk, Conn: FASB 1975, para. 22).

describe the contingency. It also should provide an estimate of the potential loss or range of loss, if possible. If an estimate cannot be made, a statement to that effect is needed.

As an example of only disclosing a contingent loss, consider a disclosure note accompanying a 2013 annual report of **U.S. Steel Corporation**. As shown in Illustration 13–15, U.S. Steel considered its potential liability for carbon dioxide emissions to be impossible to estimate, and so only disclosed that contingent loss.

Illustration 13–15
Disclosure of Loss Contingency—U.S. Steel

Real World Financials

Note 20: Contingencies and Commitments (in part)
The regulation of carbon dioxide (CO_2) emissions has either become law or is being considered by legislative bodies of many nations, including countries where we have operating facilities. . . . It is impossible to estimate the timing or impact of these or other future government action on U.S. Steel, although it could be significant. Such impacts may include substantial capital expenditures, costs for emission allowances, restriction of production, and higher prices for coking coal, natural gas and electricity generated by carbon based systems.

Illustration 13–16 highlights the appropriate accounting treatment for each possible combination of (a) the likelihood of an obligation's being confirmed and (b) the determinability of its dollar amount.

Illustration 13–16
Accounting Treatment of Loss Contingencies

	Dollar Amount of Potential Loss		
Likelihood	**Known**	**Reasonably Estimable**	**Not Reasonably Estimable**
Probable	Liability accrued and disclosure note	Liability accrued and disclosure note	Disclosure note only
Reasonably possible	Disclosure note only	Disclosure note only	Disclosure note only
Remote	No disclosure required*	No disclosure required*	No disclosure required*

*Except for certain guarantees and other specified off-balance-sheet risk situations discussed in the next chapter.

Product Warranties and Guarantees

Most consumer products are accompanied by a guarantee.

MANUFACTURER'S QUALITY-ASSURANCE WARRANTY. Satisfaction guaranteed! Your money back if not satisfied! If anything goes wrong in the first five years or 100,000 miles . . . ! Three-year guarantee! These and similar promises accompany most consumer goods. In Chapter 5 we called this sort of guarantee a *quality-assurance warranty*. When this type of warranty is included in a contract between a seller and a customer, it isn't a separate performance obligation for the seller. Rather, it is a guarantee by the seller that the customer will be satisfied with the goods or services that the seller provided.

Why do sellers offer quality-assurance warranties? To boost sales. It follows, then, that any costs of making good on such guarantees should be estimated and recorded as expenses in the same accounting period the products are sold (matching expenses with revenues). Also, it is in the period of sale that the company becomes obligated to eventually make good on a guarantee, so it makes sense that it recognizes a liability in the period of sale. The challenge is that much of the cost of satisfying a guarantee usually occurs later, sometimes years later. So, this is a loss contingency. There may be a future sacrifice of economic benefits (cost of satisfying the guarantee) due to an existing circumstance (the guaranteed products have been sold) that depends on an uncertain future event (customer claim).

The contingent liability for product warranties almost always is accrued.

The criteria for accruing a contingent loss (rather than only disclosing it) almost always are met for product warranties (or product guarantees). While we usually can't predict the liability associated with an individual sale, reasonably accurate estimates of the *total* liability for a period usually are possible, because prior experience makes it possible to predict how many warrantees or guarantees (on average) will need to be satisfied. Illustration 13–17 demonstrates accrual of the contingent liability for warranties in the reporting period in which the product under warranty is sold.

Estimates of warranty costs cannot be expected to be precise. However, if the estimating method is monitored and revised when necessary, overestimates and underestimates should cancel each other over time. The estimated liability may be classified as current or as part current and part long-term, depending on when warranty claims are expected to be satisfied.

Illustration 13–17
Product Warranty

Caldor Health, a supplier of in-home health care products, introduced a new therapeutic chair carrying a two-year warranty against defects. Estimates based on industry experience indicate warranty costs of 3% of sales during the first 12 months following the sale and 4% the next 12 months. During December 2016, its first month of availability, Caldor sold $2 million of chairs.

During December

Cash (and accounts receivable)	2,000,000	
Sales revenue		2,000,000

December 31, 2016 (adjusting entry)

Warranty expense ([3% + 4%] × $2,000,000)	140,000	
Estimated warranty liability		140,000

When customer claims are made and costs are incurred to satisfy those claims, the liability is reduced (let's say $61,000 in 2017):

Estimated warranty liability	61,000	
Cash, wages payable, parts and supplies, etc		61,000

The costs of satisfying guarantees should be recorded as expenses in the same accounting period the products are sold.

EXPECTED CASH FLOW APPROACH. In Chapter 6, you learned of a framework for using future cash flows as the basis for measuring assets and liabilities, introduced by the FASB in 2000 with *Statement of Financial Accounting Concepts No. 7,* "Using Cash Flow Information and Present Value in Accounting Measurements."[23] The approach described in the Concept Statement offers a way to take into account *any uncertainty concerning the amounts and timing of the cash flows.* Although future cash flows in many instances are contractual and certain, the amounts and timing of cash flows are less certain in other situations, such as warranty obligations.

SFAC No. 7 provides a framework for using future cash flows in accounting measurements.

As demonstrated in Illustration 13–17, the traditional way of measuring a warranty obligation is to report the "best estimate" of future cash flows, ignoring the time value of money on the basis of immateriality. However, when the warranty obligation spans more than one year and we can associate probabilities with possible cash flow outcomes, the approach described by *SFAC No. 7* offers a more plausible estimate of the warranty obligation. This "expected cash flow approach" incorporates specific probabilities of cash flows into the analysis. In Chapter 6, we discussed the expected cash flow approach to determining present value. Illustration 13–18 provides an example.

EXTENDED WARRANTY CONTRACTS. It's difficult these days to buy a computer, a digital camera, a car, or almost any durable consumer product without being asked to buy an extended warranty agreement. An extended warranty provides warranty protection beyond the manufacturer's original warranty. As discussed in Chapter 5, because an extended warranty is priced and sold separately from the warranteed product, it constitutes a separate performance obligation. So, rather than only worrying about how to recognize the contingent liability associated with an extended warranty, we face another accounting question: When should the revenue from the sale of an extended warranty be recognized?

[23] "Using Cash Flow Information and Present Value in Accounting Measurements," *Statement of Financial Accounting Concepts No. 7* (Norwalk, Conn.: FASB, 2000). Recall that Concept Statements do not directly prescribe GAAP, but instead provide structure and direction to financial accounting.

Illustration 13–18
Product Warranty

Caldor Health, a supplier of in-home health care products, introduced a new therapeutic chair carrying a two-year warranty against defects. During December of 2016, its first month of availability, Caldor sold $2 million of the chairs. Industry experience indicates the following probability distribution for the potential warranty costs:

Probabilities are associated with possible cash outcomes.

Warranty Costs	Probability
2017	
$50,000	20%
$60,000	50%
$70,000	30%
2018	
$70,000	20%
$80,000	50%
$90,000	30%

An arrangement with a service firm requires that costs for the two-year warranty period be settled at the end of 2017 and 2018. The risk-free rate of interest is 5%. Applying the expected cash flow approach, at the end of the 2016 fiscal year, Caldor would record a warranty liability (and expense) of $131,564, calculated as follows:

The probability-weighted cash outcomes provide the expected cash flows.

The present value of the expected cash flows is the estimated liability.

$50,000 × 20% =	$10,000	
60,000 × 50% =	30,000	
70,000 × 30% =	21,000	
	$61,000	
	× .95238*	$ 58,095
$70,000 × 20% =	$14,000	
80,000 × 50% =	40,000	
90,000 × 30% =	27,000	
	$81,000	
	× .90703†	73,469
		$131,564

*Present value of $1, $n = 1$, $i = 5\%$ (from Table 2)
†Present value of $1, $n = 2$, $i = 5\%$ (from Table 2)

December 31, 2016 (adjusting entry)

Warranty expense	131,564	
Estimated warranty liability (calculated above)		131,564

Revenue is recognized when performance obligations are satisfied, not necessarily when cash is received. Because an extended warranty provides coverage over a period of time, these arrangements typically qualify for revenue recognition over the period of coverage. However, cash typically is received up front, when the extended warranty is sold. Similar to other advanced payments for future products and services, revenue from extended warranty contracts is not recognized immediately, but instead is recorded as a deferred revenue liability at the time of sale and recognized as revenue over the contract period, typically on a straight-line basis. We demonstrate accounting for extended warranties in Illustration 13–19.

The costs incurred to satisfy customer claims under the extended warranties also will be recorded during the same three-year period. That way, net income in each year of the extended warranty will reflect both the warranty revenue recognized and the costs associated with that revenue.

Illustration 13–19
Extended Warranty

Brand Name Appliances sells major appliances that carry a one-year manufacturer's warranty. Customers are offered the opportunity at the time of purchase to also buy a three-year extended warranty for an additional charge. On January 3, 2016, Brand Name sold a $60 extended warranty, covering years 2017, 2018, and 2019.

January 3, 2016		
Cash (or accounts receivable)	60	
Deferred revenue—extended warranties		60
December 31, 2017, 2018, 2019 (adjusting entries)		
Deferred revenue—extended warranties	20	
Revenue—extended warranties ($60 ÷ 3)		20

Revenue from the extended warranty is recognized during the three years of the contract period.

Additional Consideration

Accounting for Rebates, Premiums, and Coupons. Sometimes a company promotes its products in ways that obligate the company to do something in the future. For example, at the time of a sale, customers obtain cash register receipts, bar codes on the product, or other proofs of purchase that later can be mailed to the manufacturer for *cash rebates*. Also, customers sometimes can show proof of purchase to obtain noncash items (called *premiums*), like toys, small appliances, or dishes. Companies may also mail out *coupons*, which entice customers to buy a company's products and services at a discounted price at some point in the future. How should we account for the future obligations created by these promotions?

Until very recently, all of these promotions were viewed as creating a contingent liability. After all, they obligate the seller to transfer some uncertain amount of cash, goods, or services at a future date. However, with recent changes in accounting for revenue recognition, the accounting in this area has changed. Now we view promises to provide rebates and premiums to be part of agreements between sellers and customers. This means we account for them using the revenue recognition process we learned about in Chapter 5.

Cash rebates are an obligation to return cash in the future, so they represent a reduction in the net amount paid by the customer. To record these, we estimate the amount of cash rebates that customers will take and reduce revenue by the amount of that estimate in the period revenue is recognized. We also recognize a liability for the estimated rebate, similar to how we recognize a refundable deposit.

Premiums obligate a company to provide noncash items, and are treated as separate performance obligations. We allocate a portion of the original sales price to the premiums (based on their relative stand-alone selling prices), record that amount as deferred revenue, and recognize that portion as revenue when premiums are delivered. No contingent liability is recognized because, as with extended warranties, we recognize the cost of premiums in the period in which we deliver them and recognize revenue.

Coupons that aren't offered as part of a sales contract aren't accounted for as part of revenue recognition. Instead, issuing coupons creates a contingent liability that is recognized in the period the coupons are issued. In practice, firms typically either (a) recognize the entire expense associated with estimated coupon redemptions in the period the coupons are issued, or (b) recognize no liability in the period the coupons are issued and instead record the expense when coupons are redeemed. The difference between these approaches typically is not viewed as material.

Litigation Claims

PetSmart

Pending litigation is not unusual. In fact, the majority of medium and large corporations annually report multiple loss contingencies due to litigation. For example, **PetSmart**'s annual report for the year ended February 2, 2014, indicates litigation involving former employees as well as litigation with customers claiming their pets were injured by consuming defective jerky treats.

In practice, accrual of a loss from pending or ongoing litigation is rare. Can you guess why? Suppose you are chief financial officer of Feinz Foods. Feinz is the defendant in a $44 million class action suit. The company's legal counsel informally advises you that the chance the company will win the lawsuit is quite doubtful. Counsel feels the company might lose $30 million. Now suppose you decide to accrue a $30 million loss in your financial statements. Later, in the courtroom, your disclosure that Feinz management feels it is probable that the company will lose $30 million would be welcome ammunition for the opposing legal counsel. Understanding this, most companies rely on the knowledge that in today's legal environment the outcome of litigation is highly uncertain, making likelihood predictions difficult.

Therefore, while companies may accrue estimated lawyer fees and other legal costs, they usually do not record a loss until after the ultimate settlement has been reached or negotiations for settlement are substantially completed. While companies should provide extensive disclosure of these contingent liabilities, they do not always do so in practice.[25] In 2010 the SEC began pressuring firms for more complete disclosure of litigation, including better descriptions of the range of losses that are reasonably possible to occur. As an example, Illustration 13–20 provides a few excerpts from the eight pages of litigation note appearing in **JP Morgan Chase & Company**'s 2013 annual report.

Illustration 13–20

Disclosure of Litigation Contingencies—JP Morgan Chase & Company

Real World Financials

Note 31: Litigation (in part)

As of December 31, 2013, the Firm and its subsidiaries are defendants or putative defendants in numerous legal proceedings, including private, civil litigations and regulatory/government investigations. . . . The Firm believes the estimate of the aggregate range of reasonably possible losses, in excess of reserves established, for its legal proceedings is from $0 to approximately $5.0 billion at December 31, 2013. This estimated aggregate range of reasonably possible losses is based upon currently available information for those proceedings in which the Firm is involved, taking into account the Firm's best estimate of such losses for those cases for which such estimate can be made. For certain cases, the Firm does not believe that an estimate can currently be made.

Even after a firm loses in court, it may not make an accrual. As you can see in Illustration 13–21, the **Las Vegas Sands Corporation**, in a recent annual report, disclosed but did not accrue damages from a lawsuit it lost, because the company was appealing the verdict.

Illustration 13–21

Disclosure of a Lawsuit—Las Vegas Sands Corporation

Real World Financials

Note 13: Commitments and Contingencies (in part): Litigation

On May 28, 2013, a judgment was entered in the matter in the amount of $101.6 million (including pre-judgment interest). . . . On December 6, 2013, the Company filed a notice of appeal of the jury verdict with the Nevada Supreme Court. . . . The Company believes that it has valid bases in law and fact to appeal these verdicts. As a result, the Company believes that the likelihood that the amount of the judgments will be affirmed is not probable, and, accordingly, that the amount of any loss cannot be reasonably estimated at this time. Because the Company believes that this potential loss is not probable or estimable, it has not recorded any reserves or contingencies related to this legal matter.

Subsequent Events

It's important to remember that several weeks usually pass between the end of a company's fiscal year and the date the financial statements for that year actually are issued or available

[25]For research indicating incomplete disclosure of litigation-related contingent liabilities, see R. Desir, K. Fanning, and R. Pfeiffer, "Are Revisions to SFAS No. 5 Needed? *Accounting Horizons* 24(4): December, 2010: 525–546.

to be issued.[26] As shown on the following time line, events occurring during this period can be used to clarify the nature of financial statement elements at the report date.

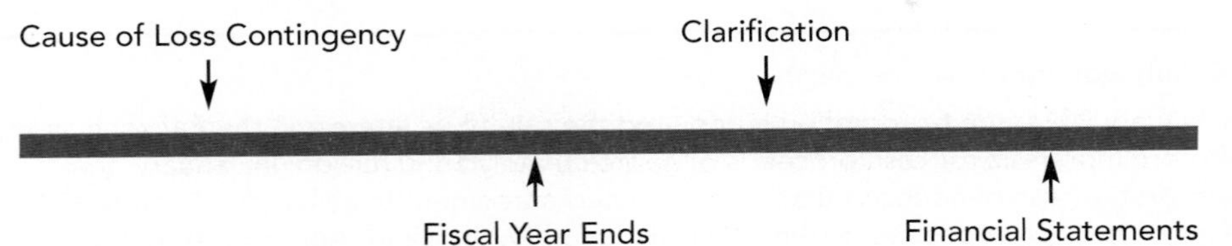

When the cause of a loss contingency occurs before the year-end, a clarifying event before financial statements are issued can be used to determine how the contingency is reported.

For instance, if information becomes available that sheds light on a claim that existed when the fiscal year ended, that information should be used in determining the probability of a loss contingency materializing and in estimating the amount of the loss.

The settlement of a lawsuit after **Starbucks**' September 29, 2013, fiscal year ended apparently influenced its accrual of a loss contingency (Illustration 13–22).

Illustration 13–22

Accrual of Litigation Contingencies—Starbucks

Real World Financials

Note 15: Commitments and Contingencies (in part)
Legal Proceedings
On December 6, 2010, Kraft commenced a federal court action against Starbucks, entitled Kraft Foods Global, Inc. v. Starbucks Corporation, in the U.S. District Court for the Southern District of New York. On November 12, 2013, the arbitrator ordered Starbucks to pay Kraft $2,227.5 million in damages plus prejudgment interest and attorney's fees. We have estimated prejudgment interest, which includes an accrual through the estimated payment date, and attorneys' fees to be approximately $556.6 million. As a result, we recorded a litigation charge of $2,784.1 million in our fiscal 2013 operating results.

For a loss contingency to be accrued, the cause of the lawsuit must have occurred before the accounting period ended. It's not necessary that the lawsuit actually was filed during that reporting period.

Sometimes, the cause of a loss contingency occurs after the end of the year but before the financial statements are issued:

If an event giving rise to a contingency occurs after the year-end, a liability should not be accrued.

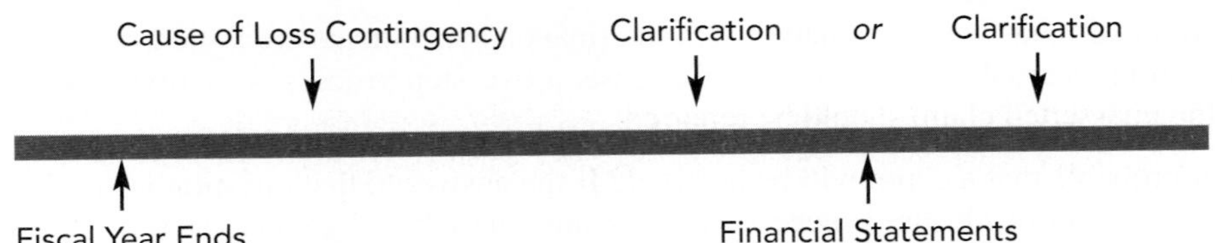

When a contingency comes into existence after the company's fiscal year-end, a liability cannot be accrued because it didn't exist at the end of the year. However, if the failure to disclose the possible loss would cause the financial statements to be misleading, the situation should be described in a disclosure note, including the effect of the possible loss on key accounting numbers affected.[27]

In fact, *any* event occurring after the fiscal year-end but before the financial statements are issued that has a material effect on the company's financial position must be disclosed in a subsequent events disclosure note. Examples are an issuance of debt or equity securities, a business combination, and discontinued operations.

[26]Financial statements are viewed as *issued* if they have been widely distributed to financial statement users in a format consistent with GAAP. Some entities (for example, private companies) do not widely distribute their financial statements to users. For those entities, the key date for subsequent events is not the date of issuance but rather the date upon which the financial statements are *available to be issued,* which occurs when the financial statements are complete, in a format consistent with GAAP, and have obtained the necessary approvals for issuance. Entities must disclose the date through which subsequent events have been evaluated (FASB ASC 855: Subsequent Events (previously "Subsequent Events," *Statement of Financial Accounting Standards No. 165* (Stamford, Conn.: FASB, 2009)).

[27]FASB ASC 450–20–50v9: Contingencies—Loss Contingencies—Disclosure (previously "Accounting for Contingencies," *Statement of Financial Accounting Standards No. 5* (Stamford, Conn.: FASB, 1975), par. 11).

A disclosure note of **Hess Corporation** from its 2013 annual report is shown in Illustration 13–23 and describes events that occurred in the first quarter of 2014.

Illustration 13–23
Subsequent Events—Hess Corporation

Real World Financials

24. Subsequent events (in part)

In January 2014, the Corporation completed the sale of its interest in the Pangkah asset, offshore Indonesia for cash proceeds of approximately $650 million. In January, the Corporation also announced that it had reached agreement to sell approximately 74,000 acres of its dry gas position in the Utical Shale for $924 million. Approximately two-thirds of these proceeds are expected at the end of the first quarter of 2014, with the balance to be received in the third quarter of 2014.

Additional Consideration

Contingent liabilities that a company takes on when it acquires another company may be treated differently from those that arise during the normal course of business. If the acquirer can determine the fair value of a contingent liability, the liability is measured at fair value. For example, the acquisition-date fair value of a warranty obligation often can be determined. If the acquirer cannot determine the fair value, then the acquirer uses the normal criteria that apply to contingent liabilities. That is, the contingent liability is accrued if (1) available information indicates that it is probable a liability has been incurred as of the acquisition date, and (2) the amount of the liability can be reasonably estimated. In periods subsequent to the acquisition, GAAP is vague about how the acquirer should account for these contingent liabilities, indicating that "An acquirer shall develop a systematic and rational basis for subsequently measuring and accounting for assets and liabilities arising from contingencies depending on their nature."[28] This lack of clear guidance suggests that there could be a lack of comparability between firms in how they account for acquired contingent liabilities.

Unasserted Claims and Assessments

It must be probable that an unasserted claim or assessment will be asserted before considering whether and how to report the possible loss.

Even if a claim has yet to be made when the financial statements are issued, a contingency may warrant accrual or disclosure. In this case, a two-step process is involved in deciding how the unasserted claim should be reported:

1. Is it probable that a claim will be asserted? If the answer to that question is "no," stop. No accrual or disclosure is necessary. If the answer is "yes," go on to step 2.
2. Treat the claim as if the claim has been asserted. That requires evaluating (a) the likelihood of an unfavorable outcome and (b) whether the dollar amount of loss can be estimated, just as we already have discussed for other loss contingencies for which a claim has already been asserted.

For example, suppose a trucking company frequently transports hazardous waste materials and is subject to environmental laws and regulations. Management has identified several sites at which it is or may be liable for remediation. For those sites for which no penalties have been asserted, management must assess the likelihood that a claim will be made, and if so, the likelihood that the company actually will be held liable. If management feels an assessment is probable, an estimated loss and contingent liability would be accrued only if an unfavorable outcome is probable and the amount can be reasonably estimated. However, a disclosure note alone would be appropriate if an unfavorable settlement is only reasonably possible or if the settlement is probable but cannot be reasonably estimated. No action is needed if chances of that outcome occurring are remote.

[28]FASB ASC 805-20-25: Business Combinations—Identifiable Assets and Liabilities, and Any Noncontrolling Interest—Recognition (previously "Accounting for Assets Acquired and Liabilities Assumed in a Business Combination that Arise from Contingencies," FASB Staff Position *No. 141R-1* (Norwalk, Conn.: FASB, 2009)).

As described in a December 31, 2013, disclosure note (see Illustration 13–24), **Union Pacific** concluded that some unasserted claims met the criteria for accrual under this two-step decision process.

Illustration 13–24
Unasserted Claims—Union Pacific Corporation

Real World Financials

> **15. Commitments and Contingencies (in part)**
>
> **Asserted and Unasserted Claims**—Various claims and lawsuits are pending against us and certain of our subsidiaries. We cannot fully determine the effect of all asserted and unasserted claims on our consolidated results of operations, financial condition, or liquidity; however, to the extent possible, where asserted and unasserted claims are considered probable and where such claims can be reasonably estimated, we have recorded a liability.

Notice that the treatment of contingent liabilities is consistent with the accepted definition of liabilities as (a) probable, future sacrifices of economic benefits (b) that arise from present obligations to other entities and (c) that result from past transactions or events.[29] The inherent uncertainty involved with contingent liabilities means additional care is required to determine whether future sacrifices of economic benefits are probable and whether the amount of the sacrifices can be quantified.

International Financial Reporting Standards

● LO13–7

Loss Contingencies. Accounting for contingencies is part of a broader international standard, *IAS No. 37,* "Provisions, Contingent Liabilities and Contingent Assets." Overall, accounting for contingent losses under IFRS is quite similar to accounting under U.S. GAAP. A contingent loss is accrued if it's both probable and can be reasonably estimated, and disclosed if it's of at least a remote probability. However, there are some important differences:

- IFRS refers to accrued liabilities as "provisions," and refers to possible obligations that are not accrued as "contingent liabilities." The term "contingent liabilities" is used for all of these obligations in U.S. GAAP.
- IFRS requires disclosure (but not accrual) of two types of contingent liabilities: (1) possible obligations whose existence will be confirmed by some uncertain future events that the company does not control, and (2) a present obligation for which either it is not probable that a future outflow will occur or the amount of the future outflow cannot be measured with sufficient reliability. U.S. GAAP does not make this distinction but typically would require disclosure of the same contingencies.
- IFRS defines "probable" as "more likely than not" (greater than 50%), which is a lower threshold than typically associated with "probable" in U.S. GAAP.
- If a liability is accrued, IFRS measures the liability as the best estimate of the expenditure required to settle the present obligation. If there is a range of equally likely outcomes, IFRS would use the midpoint of the range, while U.S. GAAP requires use of the low end of the range.
- If the effect of the time value of money is material, IFRS requires the liability to be stated at present value. U.S. GAAP allows using present values under some circumstances, but liabilities for loss contingencies like litigation typically are not discounted for time value of money.[30]
- IFRS recognizes provisions and contingencies for "onerous" contracts, defined as those in which the unavoidable costs of meeting the obligations exceed the expected

(continued)

[29] "Elements of Financial Statements," *Statement of Financial Accounting Concepts No. 6* (Stamford, Conn.: FASB, 1985).

[30] See, for example, FASB ASC 410–30–35–12: Asset Retirements and Environmental Obligations–Environmental Obligations–Subsequent Measurement.

(concluded)

benefits.[31] Under U.S. GAAP we generally don't disclose or recognize losses on such money-losing contracts, although there are some exceptions (for example, losses on long-term construction contracts are accrued, as are losses on contracts that have been terminated).

IFRS ILLUSTRATION

Real World Financials

Here's a portion of a note from the 2013 financial statements of Vodafone, which reports under IFRS:

Note A1: Significant Accounting Policies (in part)

Provisions are recognised when the Group has a present obligation (legal or constructive) as a result of a past event, it is probable that the Group will be required to settle that obligation and a reliable estimate can be made of the amount of the obligation. Provisions are measured at the directors' best estimate of the expenditure required to settle the obligation at the reporting date and are discounted to present value where the effect is material.

Where We're Headed

The controversy over accounting for contingencies and the mixture of approaches is likely to continue. The FASB recently removed from its agenda a project to reconsider the recognition and measurement of contingent losses, and has postponed further work on a project intended to enhance note disclosures of contingent losses. The IASB has a project ongoing, but progress on this project has been slow as the IASB has focused on more pressing convergence projects.

Gain Contingencies

Gain contingencies are not accrued.

A gain contingency is an uncertain situation that might result in a gain. For example, in a pending lawsuit, one side—the defendant—faces a loss contingency; the other side—the plaintiff—has a gain contingency. As we discussed earlier, loss contingencies are accrued when it's probable that an amount will be paid and the amount can reasonably be estimated. However, gain contingencies are not accrued. The nonparallel treatment of gain contingencies is an example of conservatism, following the reasoning that it's desirable to anticipate losses, but recognizing gains should await their realization.

Though gain contingencies are not recorded in the accounts, material ones are disclosed in notes to the financial statements. Care should be taken that the disclosure note not give "misleading implications as to the likelihood of realization."[32]

International Financial Reporting Standards

● LO13–7

Gain Contingencies. Under U.S. GAAP, gain contingencies are never accrued. Under IFRS, gain contingencies are accrued if their future realization is "virtually certain" to occur. Both U.S. GAAP and IFRS *disclose* contingent gains when future realization is probable, but under IFRS "probable" is defined as "more likely than not" (greater than 50 percent), and so has a lower threshold than it does under U.S. GAAP.

[31]Paragraph 10 of "Provisions, Contingent Liabilities and Contingent Assets", *International Accounting Standard 37* (London, UK: IASB, 2008.

[32]FASB ASC 450-30-50: Contingencies–Gain Contingencies–Disclosure (previously "Accounting For Contingencies," *Statement of Financial Accounting Standards No. 5* (Stamford, Conn.: FASB, 1975), par. 17).

Additional Consideration

Accounting for contingencies is controversial. Many accountants dislike the idea of only recognizing a liability for a contingent loss when it is probable, and then reporting the liability at the best estimate of the future expenditure. The obvious alternative is fair value, which does not incorporate probability into determining whether to *recognize* a loss but rather considers probability when *measuring* the amount of loss. Recent changes in GAAP have adopted fair value approaches for some types of events that are contingent losses (or appear to be close relatives). Consider the following examples:

- Illustration 13–18 uses a discounted expected cash flow approach to measure the contingent liability associated with a warranty. That approach approximates fair value.
- Recall from Chapter 10 that asset retirement obligations are recorded at fair value when an asset is acquired. The offsetting liability is similar to a contingent liability because it is an uncertain future amount arising from the past purchase of the asset but is recorded at fair value.
- Sometimes a company provides a guarantee that may require it to make payment to another party based on some future event. For example, a company might guarantee the debt of an affiliated company to make it easier for the affiliate to obtain financing. Recent GAAP views this sort of guarantee as having two parts: (1) a certain "stand ready obligation" to meet the terms of the guarantee, and (2) the uncertain contingent obligation to make future payments depending on future events (for example, the affiliate defaulting on their debt). The "stand ready obligation" is recorded initially at fair value, while the contingent obligation is handled as an ordinary contingent loss.[33]

Concept Review Exercise

CONTINGENCIES

Hanover Industries manufactures and sells food products and food processing machinery. While preparing the December 31, 2016, financial statements for Hanover, the following information was discovered relating to contingencies and possible adjustments to liabilities. Hanover's 2016 financial statements were issued on April 1, 2017.

a. On November 12, 2016, a former employee filed a lawsuit against Hanover alleging age discrimination and asking for damages of $750,000. At December 31, 2016, Hanover's attorney indicated that the likelihood of losing the lawsuit was possible but not probable. On March 5, 2017, Hanover agreed to pay the former employee $125,000 in return for withdrawing the lawsuit.

b. Hanover believes there is a possibility a service provider may claim that it has been undercharged for outsourcing a processing service based on verbal indications of the company's interpretation of a negotiated rate. The service provider has not yet made a claim for additional fees as of April 2017, but Hanover feels it will. Hanover's accountants and legal counsel believe the charges were appropriate but that if an assessment is made, there is a reasonable possibility that subsequent court action would result in an additional tax liability of $55,000.

c. Hanover grants a two-year warranty for each processing machine sold. Past experience indicates that the costs of satisfying warranties are approximately 2% of sales. During 2016, sales of processing machines totaled $21,300,000. 2016 expenditures for warranty repair costs were $178,000 related to 2016 sales and $220,000 related to 2015 sales. The January 1, 2016, balance of the warranty liability account was $250,000.

d. Hanover is the plaintiff in a $600,000 lawsuit filed in 2015 against Ansdale Farms for failing to deliver on contracts for produce. The suit is in final appeal. Legal counsel advises that it is probable that Hanover will prevail and will be awarded $300,000 (considered a material amount).

[33]FASB ASC 460–10–25: Guarantees–Overall–Recognition (previously "Guarantor's Accounting and Disclosure Requirements for Guarantees, Including Indirect Guarantees of Indebtedness of Others," *FASB Interpretation No. 45* (Stamford, Conn.: FASB, 2002)).

Required:

1. Determine the appropriate reporting for each situation. Briefly explain your reasoning.
2. Prepare any necessary journal entries and state whether a disclosure note is needed.

Solution:

a. This is a loss contingency. Hanover can use the information occurring after the end of the year in determining appropriate disclosure. The cause for the suit existed at the end of the year. Hanover should accrue the $125,000 loss because an agreement has been reached confirming the loss and the amount is known.

Loss—litigation	125,000	
Liability—litigation		125,000

A disclosure note also is appropriate.

b. At the time financial statements are issued, a claim is as yet unasserted. However, an assessment is probable. Thus, (a) the likelihood of an unfavorable outcome and (b) whether the dollar amount can be estimated are considered. No accrual is necessary because an unfavorable outcome is not probable. But because an unfavorable outcome is reasonably possible, a disclosure note is appropriate.

Note: If the likelihood of a claim being asserted is not probable, disclosure is not required even if an unfavorable outcome is thought to be probable in the event of an assessment and the amount is estimable.

c. The contingency for warranties should be accrued because it is probable that expenditures will be made and the amount can be estimated from past experience. When customer claims are made and costs are incurred to satisfy those claims the liability is reduced.

Warranty expense (2% × $21,300,000)	426,000	
Estimated warranty liability		426,000
Estimated warranty liability ($178,000 + 220,000)	398,000	
Cash, wages payable, parts and supplies, etc.		398,000

The liability at December 31, 2016, would be reported as $278,000:

Warranty Liability
(in 000s)

		250	Balance, Jan. 1
		426	2016 expense
2016 expenditures	398		
		278	Balance, Dec. 31

A disclosure note explaining the contingency also is appropriate.

d. This is a gain contingency. Gain contingencies cannot be accrued even if the gain is probable and reasonably estimable. The gain should be recognized only when realized. It can be disclosed, but care should be taken to avoid misleading language regarding the realizability of the gain.

Decision Makers' Perspective

Current liabilities impact a company's liquidity. Liquidity refers to a company's cash position and overall ability to obtain cash in the normal course of business. A company is said to be liquid if it has sufficient cash (or other assets convertible to cash in a relatively short time) to pay currently maturing debts. Because the lack of liquidity can cause the demise of an otherwise healthy company, it is critical that managers as well as outside investors and creditors maintain close scrutiny of this aspect of a company's well-being.

Keeping track of the current ratio is one of the most common ways of doing this. The current ratio is intended as a measure of short-term solvency and is determined by dividing current assets by current liabilities.

A risk analyst should be concerned with a company's ability to meet its short-term obligations.

When we compare liabilities that must be satisfied in the near term with assets that either are cash or will be converted to cash in the near term, we get a useful measure of a company's liquidity. A ratio of 1 to 1 or higher often is considered a rule-of-thumb standard, but like other ratios, acceptability should be evaluated in the context of the industry in which the company operates and other specific circumstances. Keep in mind, though, that industry averages are only one indication of adequacy and that the current ratio is but one indication of liquidity.

FINANCIAL Reporting Case

Q5, p. 732

We can adjust for the implicit assumption of the current ratio that all current assets are equally liquid. The acid-test, or quick, ratio is similar to the current ratio but is based on a more conservative measure of assets available to pay current liabilities. Specifically, the numerator, quick assets, includes only cash and cash equivalents, short-term investments, and accounts receivable. By eliminating current assets such as inventories and prepaid expenses that are less readily convertible into cash, the acid-test ratio provides a more rigorous indication of a company's short-term solvency than does the current ratio.

A manager should actively monitor a company's liquidity.

If either of these liquidity ratios is less than that of the industry as a whole, does that mean that liquidity is a problem? Not necessarily. It does, though, raise a red flag that suggests caution when assessing other areas. It's important to remember that each ratio is but one piece of the puzzle. For example, profitability is probably the best long-run indication of liquidity. Also, management may be very efficient in managing current assets so that some current assets—receivables or inventory—are converted to cash more quickly than they otherwise would be and are more readily available to satisfy liabilities. The turnover ratios discussed in earlier chapters help measure the efficiency of asset management in this regard.

A liquidity ratio is but one indication of a company's liquidity.

In fact, some companies view their accounts payable as a free loan from their suppliers, just as they view their accounts receivable as a free loan to their customers. These companies tend to pressure their customers to pay quickly, but try to obtain more extended terms with their suppliers. Although this would produce relatively low current assets and high current liabilities, and therefore a lower current ratio, it could be a very intelligent way to manage cash and decrease the overall amount of capital needed by the company to finance operations.

Some companies maintain relatively high current liabilities as part of a cash-management strategy.

Given the actual and perceived importance of a company's liquidity in the minds of analysts, it's not difficult to adopt a management perspective and imagine efforts to manipulate the ratios that measure liquidity. For instance, a company might use its economic muscle or persuasive powers to influence the timing of accounts payable recognition by asking suppliers to change their delivery schedules. Because accounts payable is included in the denominator in most measures of liquidity, such as the current ratio, the timing of their recognition could mean the difference between an unacceptable ratio and an acceptable one, or between violating a debt covenant and compliance. For example, suppose a company with a current ratio of 1.25 (current assets of $5 million and current liabilities of $4 million) is in violation of a debt covenant requiring a minimum current ratio of 1.3. By delaying the delivery of $1 million of inventory, the ratio would be 1.33 (current assets of $4 million and current liability of $3 million).

Analysts should be alert for efforts to manipulate measures of liquidity.

It is important for creditors and analysts to be attentive for evidence of activities that would indicate timing strategies, such as unusual variations in accounts payable levels. You might notice that such timing strategies are similar to earnings management techniques we discussed previously—specifically, manipulating the timing of revenue and expense recognition in order to "smooth" income over time.

Finally, all financial statement users need to keep in mind the relation between the recognition of deferred revenue associated with advance payments and the later recognition of revenue. On the one hand, increases in deferred revenue can signal future revenue recognition because the deferred revenue likely will eventually be recognized as revenue. On the

Changes in deferred revenue provide information about future revenue, and may be used to manipulate it.

other hand, research suggests that some firms that report deferred revenue may manipulate the timing of revenue recognition to manage their earnings.[34]

In the next chapter, we continue our discussion of liabilities. Our focus will shift from current liabilities to long-term liabilities in the form of bonds and long-term notes. ●

Financial Reporting Case Solution

1. **What are accrued liabilities? What is commercial paper?** *(p. 737)* Accrued liabilities are reported for expenses already incurred but not yet paid (accrued expenses). These include salaries and wages payable, income taxes payable, and interest payable. Commercial paper is a form of notes payable sometimes used by large corporations to obtain temporary financing. It is sold to other companies as a short-term investment. It represents unsecured notes sold in minimum denominations of $25,000 with maturities ranging from 30 to 270 days. Typically, commercial paper is issued directly to the buyer (lender) and is backed by a line of credit with a bank.
2. **Why did Syntel Microsystems include some long-term debt in the current liability section?** *(p. 743)* Syntel Microsystems did include some long-term debt in the current liability section. The currently maturing portion of a long-term debt must be reported as a current liability. Amounts are reclassified and reported as current liabilities when they become payable within the upcoming year.
3. **Did they also report some current amounts as long-term debt? Explain.** *(p. 743)* Yes they did. It is permissible to report short-term obligations as noncurrent liabilities if the company (a) intends to refinance on a long-term basis and (b) demonstrates the ability to do so by a refinancing agreement or by actual financing. As the disclosure note explains, this is the case for a portion of Syntel's currently payable debt.
4. **Must obligations be known contractual debts in order to be reported as liabilities?** *(p. 747)* No. From an accounting perspective, it is not necessary that obligations be known, legally enforceable debts to be reported as liabilities. They must only be probable and the dollar amount reasonably estimable.
5. **Is it true that current liabilities are riskier than long-term liabilities?** *(p. 759)* Other things being equal, current liabilities generally are considered riskier than longterm liabilities. For that reason, management usually would rather report a debt as long term. Current debt, though, is not necessarily risky. The liquidity ratios we discussed in the chapter attempt to measure liquidity. Remember, any such measure must be assessed in the context of other factors: industry standards, profitability, turnover ratios, and risk management activities, to name a few. ●

The Bottom Line

- **LO13–1** Liabilities are present obligations to sacrifice assets in the future because of something that already has occurred. Current liabilities are expected to require current assets (or the creation of other current liabilities) and usually are payable within one year. (*p. 732*)
- **LO13–2** Short-term bank loans usually are arranged under an existing line of credit with a bank or group of banks. When interest is discounted from the face amount of a note (a type of noninterest-bearing note), the effective interest rate is higher than the stated discount rate. Large, highly rated firms sometimes sell commercial paper directly to the buyer (lender) to borrow funds at a lower rate than through a bank loan. (*p. 734*)
- **LO13–3** Accrued liabilities are recorded by adjusting entries for expenses already incurred, but for which cash has yet to be paid (accrued expenses). Familiar examples are salaries and wages payable, income taxes payable, and interest payable. (*pp. 737* and *740*)

[34]Marcus Caylor, "Strategic Revenue Recognition to Achieve Earnings Benchmarks," *Journal of Accounting and Public Policy*, 2011 forthcoming.

- **LO13–4** Short-term obligations can be reported as noncurrent liabilities if the company (a) intends to refinance on a long-term basis and (b) demonstrates the ability to do so by actual financing or a formal agreement to do so. *(p. 743)*
- **LO13–5** A loss contingency is an existing, uncertain situation involving potential loss depending on whether some future event occurs. Whether a contingency is accrued and reported as a liability depends on (a) the likelihood that the confirming event will occur and (b) what can be determined about the amount of loss. It is accrued if it is both probable that the confirming event will occur and the amount can be at least reasonably estimated. *(p. 746)*
- **LO13–6** A clarifying event before financial statements are issued, but after the year-end, can be used to determine how a contingency is reported. An unasserted suit, claim, or assessment warrants accrual or disclosure if it is probable it will be asserted. A gain contingency is a contingency that might result in a gain. A gain contingency is not recognized until it actually is realized. *(p. 747)*
- **LO13–7** IFRS and U.S. GAAP are relatively similar with respect to current liabilities and contingencies. Relatively minor differences relate to when financing must be in place for a liability expected to be refinanced to be classified as long term. Also, with respect to contingent losses, IFRS defines "probable" at a lower threshold, requires the accrual of the expected value of loss, and requires the use of present values when measuring amounts to be accrued. Contingent gains are not accrued under U.S. GAAP, but are accrued under IFRS when they are considered to be virtually certain to occur *(pp. 744, 755,* and *756)*

APPENDIX 13

Payroll-Related Liabilities

All firms incur liabilities in connection with their payrolls. These arise primarily from legal requirements to withhold taxes from employees' paychecks and from payroll taxes on the firms themselves. Some payroll-related liabilities result from voluntary payroll deductions of amounts payable to third parties.

Employees' Withholding Taxes

Employers are required by law to withhold federal (sometimes state) income taxes and Social Security taxes from employees' paychecks and remit these to the Internal Revenue Service. The amount withheld for federal income taxes is determined by a tax table furnished by the IRS and varies according to the amount earned and the number of exemptions claimed by the employee. Also, the Federal Insurance Contributions Act (FICA) requires employers to withhold a percentage of each employee's earnings up to a specified maximum. Both the percentage and the maximum are changed intermittently. As this text went to print, the deduction for Social Security was 6.2% of the first $117,000 an employee earns, and this ceiling amount changes each year for cost-of-living adjustments. Additionally, a deduction for Medicare tax is 1.45% with no limit on the base amount. The employer also must pay an equal (matching) amount on behalf of the employee. Self-employed persons must pay both the employer and employee portions (12.4% for Social Security and 2.9% for Medicare).

Voluntary Deductions

Besides the required deductions for income taxes and Social Security taxes, employees often authorize their employers to deduct other amounts from their paychecks. These deductions might include union dues, contributions to savings or retirement plans, and insurance premiums. Amounts deducted this way represent liabilities until paid to the appropriate organizations.

Employers' Payroll Taxes

One payroll tax mentioned previously is the employer's matching amount of FICA taxes. The employer also must pay federal and state unemployment taxes on behalf of its employees. The Federal Unemployment Tax Act (FUTA) requires a tax of 6.0% of the first $7,000 earned by each employee. This amount is reduced by a 5.4% (maximum) credit for contributions to state unemployment programs, so the net federal rate often is 0.6%.[35] In many states the state rate is 5.4% but may be reduced if the employer maintains relatively low employee turnover.

Fringe Benefits

In addition to salaries and wages, withholding taxes, and payroll taxes, many companies provide employees a variety of fringe benefits. Most commonly, employers pay all or part of employees' insurance premiums and/or contributions to retirement income plans.

Representative payroll-related liabilities are presented in Illustration 13A–1.

Illustration 13A–1
Payroll-Related Liabilities

Crescent Lighting and Fixtures' payroll for the second week in January was $100,000. The following deductions, fringe benefits, and taxes apply:

Federal income taxes to be withheld	$20,000
State income taxes to be withheld	3,000
Medical insurance premiums (Blue Cross)—70% paid by employer	1,000
Employee contribution to voluntary retirement plan (Fidelity Investments)—contributions matched by employer	4,000
Union dues (Local No. 222)—paid by employees	100
Life insurance premiums (Prudential Life)—100% paid by employer	200
Social Security tax rate	6.2%
Medicare tax rate	1.45%
Federal unemployment tax rate (after state deduction)	0.60%
State unemployment tax rate	5.40%

Crescent's journal entries to record payroll:

Salaries and wages expense (total amount earned)	100,000	
Withholding taxes payable (federal income tax)		20,000
Withholding taxes payable (state income tax)		3,000
Social Security taxes payable (employees' portion, 6.2%)		6,200
Medicare taxes payable (employees' portion, 1.45%)		**1,450**
Payable to Blue Cross (employee's portion of insurance premiums—30%)		300
Payable to Fidelity Investments (employees' investment)		4,000
Payable to Local No. 222 (union dues)		100
Salaries and wages payable (net pay)		64,950
Payroll tax expense (total)	13,650	
Social Security taxes payable (employer's matching amount)		6,200
Medicare taxes payable (employer's matching amount)		1,450
FUTA payable (federal unemployment tax: 0.6%)		600
State unemployment tax payable (5.4%)		5,400
Salaries and wages expense (fringe benefits)	4,900	
Payable to Blue Cross (insurance premiums—70%)		700
Payable to Fidelity Investments (employer's matching amount)		4,000
Payable to Prudential life (insurance premiums)		200

Amounts withheld from paychecks represent liabilities until remitted to third parties.

The employer's share of FICA and unemployment taxes constitute the employer's payroll tax expense.

Fringe benefits are part of salaries and wages expense and represent liabilities until remitted to third parties.

[35]All states presently have unemployment tax programs.

As you study the illustration, you should note the similarity among all payroll-related liabilities. Amounts withheld from paychecks—voluntarily or involuntarily—are liabilities until turned over to appropriate third parties. Payroll taxes and expenses for fringe benefits are incurred as a result of services performed by employees and also are liabilities until paid to appropriate third parties. ●

Questions For Review of Key Topics

Q 13–1 What are the essential characteristics of liabilities for purposes of financial reporting?

Q 13–2 What distinguishes current liabilities from long-term liabilities?

Q 13–3 Bronson Distributors owes a supplier $100,000 on open account. The amount is payable in three months. What is the theoretically correct way to measure the reportable amount for this liability? In practice, how will it likely be reported? Why?

Q 13–4 Bank loans often are arranged under existing lines of credit. What is a line of credit? How does a noncommitted line of credit differ from a committed line?

Q 13–5 Banks sometimes loan cash under noninterest-bearing notes. Is it true that banks lend money without interest?

Q 13–6 How does commercial paper differ from a bank loan? Why is the interest rate often less for commercial paper?

Q 13–7 Salaries of $5,000 have been earned by employees by the end of the period but will not be paid to employees until the following period. How should the expense and related liability be recorded? Why?

Q 13–8 Under what conditions should an employer accrue an expense and the related liability for employees' compensation for future absences? How do company custom and practice affect the accrual decision?

Q 13–9 How are refundable deposits and customer advances similar? How do they differ?

Q 13–10 How do companies account for gift cards?

Q 13–11 Amounts collected for third parties represent liabilities until remitted. Provide several examples of this kind of collection.

Q 13–12 When companies have debt that is not due to be paid for several years but that is callable (due on demand) by the creditor, do they classify the debt as current or as long-term?

Q 13–13 Long-term obligations usually are reclassified and reported as current liabilities when they become payable within the upcoming year (or operating cycle, if longer than a year). So, a 25-year bond issue is reported as a long-term liability for 24 years but normally is reported as a current liability on the balance sheet prepared during the 25th year of its term to maturity. Name a situation in which this would not be the case.

IFRS **Q 13–14** How do IFRS and U.S. GAAP differ with respect to the classification of debt that is expected to be refinanced?

Q 13–15 Define a loss contingency. Provide three examples.

Q 13–16 List and briefly describe the three categories of likelihood that a future event(s) will confirm the incurrence of the liability for a loss contingency.

Q 13–17 Under what circumstances should a loss contingency be accrued?

IFRS **Q 13–18** What is the difference between the use of the term *contingent liability* in U.S. GAAP and IFRS?

Q 13–19 Suppose the analysis of a loss contingency indicates that an obligation is not probable. What accounting treatment if any is warranted?

Q 13–20 Name two loss contingencies that almost always are accrued.

Q 13–21 Distinguish between the accounting treatment of a manufacturer's warranty and an extended warranty. Why the difference?

Q 13–22 At December 31, the end of the reporting period, the analysis of a loss contingency indicates that an obligation is only reasonably possible, though its dollar amount is readily estimable. During February, before the financial statements are issued, new information indicates the loss is probable. What accounting treatment is warranted?

Q 13–23 After the end of the reporting period, a contingency comes into existence. Under what circumstances, if any, should the contingency be reported in the financial statements for the period ended?

IFRS **Q 13–24** How do U.S. GAAP and IFRS differ in their treatment of a range of equally likely losses?

IFRS **Q 13–25** How do U.S. GAAP and IFRS differ in their use of present values when measuring contingent liabilities?

Q 13–26 Suppose the Environmental Protection Agency is in the process of investigating Ozone Ruination Limited for possible environmental damage but has not proposed a penalty as of December 31, 2013, the company's fiscal year-end. Describe the two-step process involved in deciding how this unasserted assessment should be reported.

Q 13–27 You are the plaintiff in a lawsuit. Your legal counsel advises that your eventual victory is inevitable. "You will be awarded $12 million," your attorney confidently asserts. Describe the appropriate accounting treatment.

IFRS **Q 13–28** Answer Q 13-27, but assume that you report under IFRS.

Brief Exercises

BE 13–1
Bank loan; accrued interest
● LO13–2

On October 1, Eder Fabrication borrowed $60 million and issued a nine-month, 12% promissory note. Interest was payable at maturity. Prepare the journal entry for the issuance of the note and the appropriate adjusting entry for the note at December 31, the end of the reporting period.

BE 13–2
Non-interest-bearing note; accrued interest
● LO13–2

On October 1, Eder Fabrication borrowed $60 million and issued a nine-month promissory note. Interest was discounted at issuance at a 12% discount rate. Prepare the journal entry for the issuance of the note and the appropriate adjusting entry for the note at December 31, the end of the reporting period.

BE 13–3
Determining accrued interest
● LO13–2

On July 1, Orcas Lab issued a $100,000, 12%, 8-month note. Interest is payable at maturity. What is the amount of interest expense that should be recorded in a year-end adjusting entry if the fiscal year-end is (a) December 31? (b) September 30?

BE 13–4
Commercial paper
● LO13–2

Branch Corporation issued $12 million of commercial paper on March 1 on a nine-month note. Interest was discounted at issuance at a 9% discount rate. Prepare the journal entry for the issuance of the commercial paper and its repayment at maturity.

BE 13–5
Non-interest-bearing note; effective interest rate
● LO13–2

Life.com issued $10 million of commercial paper on April 1 on a nine-month note. Interest was discounted at issuance at a 6% discount rate. What is the effective interest rate on the commercial paper?

BE 13–6
Advance collection
● LO13–3

On December 12, 2016, Pace Electronics received $24,000 from a customer toward a cash sale of $240,000 of diodes to be completed on January 16, 2017. What journal entries should Pace record on December 12 and January 16?

BE 13–7
Advance collection
● LO13–3

In Lizzie Shoes' experience, gift cards that have not been redeemed within 12 months are not likely to be redeemed. Lizzie Shoes sold gift cards for $18,000 during August of 2016. $4,000 of cards were redeemed in September of 2016, $3,000 in October, $2,500 in November, and $2,000 in December of 2016. In 2017 an additional $1,000 of cards were redeemed in January and $500 in February. How much gift card revenue associated with the August 2016 gift card sales would Lizzie get to recognize in 2016 and 2017?

BE 13–8
Sales tax
● LO13–3

During December, Rainey Equipment made a $600,000 credit sale. The state sales tax rate is 6% and the local sales tax rate is 1.5%. Prepare the appropriate journal entry.

BE 13–9
Classifying debt
● LO13–4

Consider the following liabilities of Future Brands, Inc., at December 31, 2016, the company's fiscal year-end. Should they be reported as current liabilities or long-term liabilities?

1. $77 million of 8% notes are due on May 31, 2020. The notes are callable by the company's bank, beginning March 1, 2017.
2. $102 million of 8% notes are due on May 31, 2021. A debt covenant requires Future to maintain a current ratio (ratio of current assets to current liabilities) of at least 2 to 1. Future is in violation of this requirement but has obtained a waiver from the bank until May 2017, since both companies feel Future will correct the situation during the first half of 2017.

BE 13–10
Refinancing debt
● LO13–4

Coulson Company is in the process of refinancing some long-term debt. Its fiscal year ends on December 31, 2016, and its financial statements will be issued on March 15, 2017. Under current U.S. GAAP, how would the debt be classified if the refinancing is completed on December 15, 2016? What if instead it is completed on January 15, 2017?

BE 13–11
Refinancing debt
● LO13–4, LO13–7

Fleener Company is in the process of refinancing some long-term debt. Its fiscal year ends on December 31, 2016, and its financial statements will be issued on March 15, 2017. Under current IFRS, how would the debt be classified if the refinancing is completed on December 15, 2016? What if instead it is completed on January 15, 2017?

BE 13–12
Warranties
● LO13–5, LO13–6

Right Medical introduced a new implant that carries a five-year warranty against manufacturer's defects. Based on industry experience with similar product introductions, warranty costs are expected to approximate 1% of sales. Sales were $15 million and actual warranty expenditures were $20,000 for the first year of selling the product. What amount (if any) should Right report as a liability at the end of the year?

BE 13–13
Product recall
● LO13–5, LO13–6

Consultants notified management of Goo Goo Baby Products that a crib toy poses a potential health hazard. Counsel indicated that a product recall is probable and is estimated to cost the company $5.5 million. How will this affect the company's income statement and balance sheet this period?

BE 13–14
Contingency
● LO13–5, LO13–6

Skill Hardware is the plaintiff in a $16 million lawsuit filed against a supplier. The litigation is in final appeal and legal counsel advises that it is virtually certain that Skill will win the lawsuit and be awarded $12 million. How should Skill account for this event?

BE 13–15
Contingency
● LO13–5, LO13–6

Bell International can estimate the amount of loss that will occur if a foreign government expropriates some company property. Expropriation is considered reasonably possible. How should Bell report the loss contingency?

BE 13–16
Contingencies
● LO13–5, LO13–6

Household Solutions manufactures kitchen storage products. During the year, the company became aware of potential costs due to (1) a recently filed lawsuit for patent infringement for which the probability of loss is remote and damages can be reasonably estimated, (2) another recently filed lawsuit for food contamination by the plastics used in Household Solutions' products for which a loss is probable but the amount of loss cannot be reasonably estimated, and (3) a new product warranty that is probable and can be reasonably estimated. Which, if any, of these costs should be accrued?

BE 13–17
Contingencies
● LO13–5, LO13–6, LO13–7

IFRS

Quandary Corporation has a major customer who is alleging a significant product defect. Quandary engineers and attorneys have analyzed the claim and have concluded that there is a 51% chance that the customer would be successful in court and that a successful claim would result in a range of damages from $10 million to $20 million, with each part of the range equally likely to occur. The damages would need to be paid soon enough that time-value-of-money considerations are not material. Would a liability be accrued under U.S. GAAP? Under IFRS? If a liability were accrued, what amount would be accrued under U.S. GAAP? Under IFRS?

BE 13–18
Unasserted assessment
● LO13–5, LO13–6

At March 13, 2017, the Securities Exchange Commission is in the process of investigating a possible securities law violation by Now Chemical. The SEC has not yet proposed a penalty assessment. Now's fiscal year ends on December 31, 2016, and its financial statements are published in March 2017. Management feels an assessment is *reasonably possible,* and if an assessment is made an unfavorable settlement of $13 million is *probable.* What, if any, action should Now take for its financial statements?

Exercises

An alternate exercise and problem set is available in the Connect library.

E 13–1
Bank loan; accrued interest
● LO13–2

On November 1, 2016, Quantum Technology, a geothermal energy supplier, borrowed $16 million cash to fund a geological survey. The loan was made by Nevada BancCorp under a noncommitted short-term line of credit arrangement. Quantum issued a nine-month, 12% promissory note. Interest was payable at maturity. Quantum's fiscal period is the calendar year.

Required:

1. Prepare the journal entry for the issuance of the note by Quantum Technology.
2. Prepare the appropriate adjusting entry for the note by Quantum on December 31, 2016.
3. Prepare the journal entry for the payment of the note at maturity.

E 13–2
Determining accrued interest in various situations
● LO13–2

On July 1, 2016, Ross-Livermore Industries issued nine-month notes in the amount of $400 million. Interest is payable at maturity.

Required:

Determine the amount of interest expense that should be recorded in a year-end adjusting entry under each of the following independent assumptions:

	Interest Rate	Fiscal Year-End
1.	12%	December 31
2.	10%	September 30
3.	9%	October 31
4.	6%	January 31

E 13–3
Short-term notes
● LO13–2

The following selected transactions relate to liabilities of United Insulation Corporation. United's fiscal year ends on December 31.

Required:
Prepare the appropriate journal entries through the maturity of each liability.

2016	
Jan. 13	Negotiated a revolving credit agreement with Parish Bank that can be renewed annually upon bank approval. The amount available under the line of credit is $20 million at the bank's prime rate.
Feb. 1	Arranged a three-month bank loan of $5 million with Parish Bank under the line of credit agreement. Interest at the prime rate of 10% was payable at maturity.
May 1	Paid the 10% note at maturity.
Dec. 1	Supported by the credit line, issued $10 million of commercial paper on a nine-month note. Interest was discounted at issuance at a 9% discount rate.
31	Recorded any necessary adjusting entry(s).
2017	
Sept. 1	Paid the commercial paper at maturity.

E 13–4
Paid future absences
● LO13–3

JWS Transport Company's employees earn vacation time at the rate of 1 hour per 40-hour work period. The vacation pay vests immediately (that is, an employee is entitled to the pay even if employment terminates). During 2016, total wages paid to employees equaled $404,000, including $4,000 for vacations actually taken in 2016 but not including vacations related to 2016 that will be taken in 2017. All vacations earned before 2016 were taken before January 1, 2016. No accrual entries have been made for the vacations. No overtime premium and no bonuses were paid during the period.

Required:
Prepare the appropriate adjusting entry for vacations earned but not taken in 2016.

E 13–5
Paid future absences
● LO13–3

On January 1, 2016, Poplar Fabricators Corporation agreed to grant its employees two weeks' vacation each year, with the stipulation that vacations earned each year can be taken the following year. For the year ended December 31, 2016, Poplar Fabricators' employees each earned an average of $900 per week. Seven hundred vacation weeks earned in 2016 were not taken during 2016.

Required:
1. Prepare the appropriate adjusting entry for vacations earned but not taken in 2016.
2. Suppose that, by the time vacations actually are taken in 2017, wage rates for employees have risen by an average of 5 percent from their 2016 level. Also, assume wages earned in 2017 (including vacations earned and taken in 2017) were $31 million. Prepare a journal entry that summarizes 2017 wages and the payment for 2016 vacations taken in 2017.

E 13–6
Customer advances; sales taxes
● LO13–3

Bavarian Bar and Grill opened for business in November 2016. During its first two months of operation, the restaurant sold gift certificates in various amounts totaling $5,200, mostly as Christmas presents. They are redeemable for meals within two years of the purchase date, although experience within the industry indicates that 80% of gift certificates are redeemed within one year. Certificates totaling $1,300 were presented for redemption during 2016 for meals having a total price of $2,100. The sales tax rate on restaurant sales is 4%, assessed at the time meals (not gift certificates) are purchased. Sales taxes will be remitted in January.

Required:
1. Prepare the appropriate journal entries (in summary form) for the gift certificates sold during 2016 (keeping in mind that, in actuality, each sale of a gift certificate or a meal would be recorded individually).
2. Determine the liability for gift certificates to be reported on the December 31, 2016, balance sheet.
3. What is the appropriate classification (current or noncurrent) of the liabilities at December 31, 2016? Why?

E 13–7
Customer deposits
● LO13–3

Diversified Semiconductors sells perishable electronic components. Some must be shipped and stored in reusable protective containers. Customers pay a deposit for each container received. The deposit is equal to the container's cost. They receive a refund when the container is returned. During 2016, deposits collected on containers shipped were $850,000.

Deposits are forfeited if containers are not returned within 18 months. Containers held by customers at January 1, 2016, represented deposits of $530,000. In 2016, $790,000 was refunded and deposits forfeited were $35,000.

Required:
1. Prepare the appropriate journal entries for the deposits received and returned during 2016.
2. Determine the liability for refundable deposits to be reported on the December 31, 2016, balance sheet.

E 13–8
Various transactions involving advance collections
● LO13–3

The following selected transactions relate to liabilities of Interstate Farm Implements for December of 2016. Interstate's fiscal year ends on December 31.

Required:

Prepare the appropriate journal entries for these transactions.

1. On December 15, received $7,500 from Bradley Farms toward the purchase of a $98,000 tractor to be delivered on January 6, 2017.
2. During December, received $25,500 of refundable deposits relating to containers used to transport equipment parts.
3. During December, credit sales totaled $800,000. The state sales tax rate is 5% and the local sales tax rate is 2%. (This is a summary journal entry for the many individual sales transactions for the period.)

E 13–9
Gift Cards
● LO13–3

CircuitTown commenced a gift card program in January 2016 and sold $10,000 of gift cards in January, $15,000 in February, and $16,000 in March of 2016 before discontinuing further gift card sales. During 2016, gift card redemptions were $6,000 for the January gift cards sold, $4,500 for the February cards, and $4,000 for the March cards. CircuitTown considers gift cards to be "broken" (not redeemable) 10 months after sale.

Required:

1. How much revenue will CircuitTown recognize with respect to January gift card sales during 2016?
2. Prepare journal entries to record the sale of January gift cards, redemption of gift cards (ignore sales tax), and breakage (expiration) of gift cards.
3. How much revenue will CircuitTown recognize with respect to March gift card sales during 2016?
4. What liability for deferred revenue associated with gift card sales would CircuitTown show as of December 31, 2016?

E 13–10
FASB codification research
● LO13–3, LO13–4, LO13–5

Access the *FASB Accounting Standards Codification* at the FASB website (asc.fasb.org)

Required:

Determine the specific citation for accounting for each of the following items:

1. If it is only reasonably possible that a contingent loss will occur, the contingent loss should be disclosed.
2. Criteria allowing short-term liabilities expected to be refinanced to be classified as long-term liabilities.
3. Accounting for the revenue from separately priced extended warranty contracts.
4. The criteria to determine if an employer must accrue a liability for vacation pay.

E 13–11
Current–noncurrent classification of debt; Sprint Corporation
● LO13–1, LO13–4

An annual report of **Sprint Corporation** contained a rather lengthy narrative entitled "Review of Segmental Results of Operation." The narrative noted that short-term notes payable and commercial paper outstanding at the end of the year aggregated $756 million and that during the following year "This entire balance will be replaced by the issuance of long-term debt or will continue to be refinanced under existing long-term credit facilities."

Required:

How did Sprint report the debt in its balance sheet? Why?

E 13–12
Current-noncurrent classification of debt; Sprint Corporation
● LO13–1, LO13–4, LO13–7

Consider the information presented in E13–11.

Required:

1. How would Sprint report the debt in its balance sheet if it reported under IFRS? Why?
2. Would your answer to requirement 1 change if Sprint obtained its long-term credit facility after the balance sheet date? Why?

E 13–13
Current-noncurrent classification of debt
● LO13–1, LO13–4

At December 31, 2016, Newman Engineering's liabilities include the following:

1. $10 million of 9% bonds were issued for $10 million on May 31, 1997. The bonds mature on May 31, 2027, but bondholders have the option of calling (demanding payment on) the bonds on May 31, 2017. However, the option to call is not expected to be exercised, given prevailing market conditions.
2. $14 million of 8% notes are due on May 31, 2020. A debt covenant requires Newman to maintain current assets at least equal to 175% of its current liabilities. On December 31, 2016, Newman is in violation of this covenant. Newman obtained a waiver from National City Bank until June 2017, having convinced the bank that the company's normal 2 to 1 ratio of current assets to current liabilities will be reestablished during the first half of 2017.
3. $7 million of 11% bonds were issued for $7 million on August 1, 1987. The bonds mature on July 31, 2017. Sufficient cash is expected to be available to retire the bonds at maturity.

Required:

What portion of the debt can be excluded from classification as a current liability (that is, reported as a noncurrent liability)? Explain.

E 13–14
FASB codification research
● LO13–5

CODE

Access the *FASB Accounting Standards Codification* at the FASB website (asc.fasb.org)

Required:

1. Obtain the relevant authoritative literature on recognition of contingent losses. What is the specific citation that describes the guidelines for determining when an expense and liability should be accrued for a contingent loss?
2. List the guidelines.

E 13–15
Warranties
● LO13–5, LO13–6

Cupola Awning Corporation introduced a new line of commercial awnings in 2016 that carry a two-year warranty against manufacturer's defects. Based on their experience with previous product introductions, warranty costs are expected to approximate 3% of sales. Sales and actual warranty expenditures for the first year of selling the product were:

Sales	Actual Warranty Expenditures
$5,000,000	$37,500

Required:

1. Does this situation represent a loss contingency? Why or why not? How should Cupola account for it?
2. Prepare journal entries that summarize sales of the awnings (assume all credit sales) and any aspects of the warranty that should be recorded during 2016.
3. What amount should Cupola report as a liability at December 31, 2016?

E 13–16
Extended warranties
● LO13–5, LO13–6

Carnes Electronics sells consumer electronics that carry a 90-day manufacturer's warranty. At the time of purchase, customers are offered the opportunity to also buy a two-year extended warranty for an additional charge. During the year, Carnes received $412,000 for these extended warranties (approximately evenly throughout the year).

Required:

1. Does this situation represent a loss contingency? Why or why not? How should it be accounted for?
2. Prepare journal entries that summarize sales of the extended warranties (assume all credit sales) and any aspects of the warranty that should be recorded during the year.

E 13–17
Contingency; product recall
● LO13–5, LO13–6

Sound Audio manufactures and sells audio equipment for automobiles. Engineers notified management in December 2016 of a circuit flaw in an amplifier that poses a potential fire hazard. An intense investigation indicated that a product recall is virtually certain, estimated to cost the company $2 million. The fiscal year ends on December 31.

Required:

1. Should this loss contingency be accrued, only disclosed, or neither? Explain.
2. What loss, if any, should Sound Audio report in its 2016 income statement?
3. What liability, if any, should Sound Audio report in its 2016 balance sheet?
4. Prepare any journal entry needed.

E 13–18
Impairment of accounts receivable
● LO13–5, LO13–6

The Manda Panda Company uses the allowance method to account for bad debts. At the beginning of 2016, the allowance account had a credit balance of $75,000. Credit sales for 2016 totaled $2,400,000 and the year-end accounts receivable balance was $490,000. During this year, $73,000 in receivables were determined to be uncollectible. Manda Panda anticipates that 3% of all credit sales will ultimately become uncollectible. The fiscal year ends on December 31.

Required:

1. Does this situation describe a loss contingency? Explain.
2. What is the bad debt expense that Manda Panda should report in its 2016 income statement?
3. Prepare the appropriate journal entry to record the contingency.
4. What is the net realizable value (book value) Manda Panda should report in its 2016 balance sheet?

E 13–19
Unasserted assessment
● LO13–6

At April 1, 2017, the Food and Drug Administration is in the process of investigating allegations of false marketing claims by Hulkly Muscle Supplements. The FDA has not yet proposed a penalty assessment. Hulkly's fiscal year ends on December 31, 2016. The company's financial statements are issued in April 2017.

Required:

For each of the following scenarios, determine the appropriate way to report the situation. Explain your reasoning and prepare any necessary journal entry.

1. Management feels an assessment is *reasonably possible,* and if an assessment is made an unfavorable settlement of $13 million is *reasonably possible.*
2. Management feels an assessment is *reasonably possible,* and if an assessment is made an unfavorable settlement of $13 million is *probable.*
3. Management feels an assessment is *probable,* and if an assessment is made an unfavorable settlement of $13 million is *reasonably possible.*
4. Management feels an assessment is *probable,* and if an assessment is made an unfavorable settlement of $13 million is *probable.*

E 13–20
Various transactions involving contingencies
● LO13–5, LO13–6

The following selected transactions relate to contingencies of Classical Tool Makers, Inc., which began operations in July 2016. Classical's fiscal year ends on December 31. Financial statements are issued in April 2017.

Required:

Prepare the year-end entries for any amounts that should be recorded as a result of each of these contingencies and indicate whether a disclosure note is indicated.

1. Classical's products carry a one-year warranty against manufacturer's defects. Based on previous experience, warranty costs are expected to approximate 4% of sales. Sales were $2 million (all credit) for 2016. Actual warranty expenditures were $30,800 and were recorded as warranty expense when incurred.
2. Although no customer accounts have been shown to be uncollectible, Classical estimates that 2% of credit sales will eventually prove uncollectible.
3. In December 2016, the state of Tennessee filed suit against Classical, seeking penalties for violations of clean air laws. On January 23, 2017, Classical reached a settlement with state authorities to pay $1.5 million in penalties.
4. Classical is the plaintiff in a $4 million lawsuit filed against a supplier. The suit is in final appeal and attorneys advise that it is virtually certain that Classical will win the case and be awarded $2.5 million.
5. In November 2016, Classical became aware of a design flaw in an industrial saw that poses a potential electrical hazard. A product recall appears unavoidable. Such an action would likely cost the company $500,000.
6. Classical offered $25 cash rebates on a new model of jigsaw. Customers must mail in a proof-of-purchase seal from the package plus the cash register receipt to receive the rebate. Experience suggests that 60% of the rebates will be claimed. Ten thousand of the jigsaws were sold in 2016. Total rebates to customers in 2016 were $105,000 and were recorded as promotional expense when paid.

E 13–21
Various transactions involving contingencies
● LO13–5, LO13–6

The following selected circumstances relate to pending lawsuits for Erismus, Inc. Erismus's fiscal year ends on December 31. Financial statements are issued in March 2017. Erismus prepares its financial statements according to U.S. GAAP.

Required:

Indicate the amount of asset or liability that Erismus would record, and explain your answer.

1. Erismus is defending against a lawsuit. Erismus's management believes the company has a slightly worse than 50/50 chance of eventually prevailing in court, and that if it loses, the judgment will be $1,000,000.
2. Erismus is defending against a lawsuit. Erismus's management believes it is probable that the company will lose in court. If it loses, management believes that damages could fall anywhere in the range of $2,000,000 to $4,000,000, with any damage in that range equally likely.
3. Erismus is defending against a lawsuit. Erismus's management believes it is probable that the company will lose in court. If it loses, management believes that damages will eventually be $5,000,000, with a present value of $3,500,000.
4. Erismus is a plaintiff in a lawsuit. Erismus's management believes it is probable that the company eventually will prevail in court, and that if it prevails, the judgment will be $1,000,000.
5. Erismus is a plaintiff in a lawsuit. Erismus's management believes it is virtually certain that the company eventually will prevail in court, and that if it prevails, the judgment will be $500,000.

E 13–22
Various transactions involving contingencies; IFRS
● LO13–5, LO13–6, LO13–7

IFRS

[This exercise is a variation of E13–21 focusing on reporting under IFRS]. Refer to the circumstances listed in E13–21, but assume that Erismus prepares its financial statements according to International Financial Reporting Standards.

Required:
For each circumstance, indicate the amount of asset or liability that Erismus would record, and explain your answer.

E 13–23
Disclosures of liabilities
● LO13–1 through LO13–6

Indicate (by letter) the way each of the items listed below should be reported in a balance sheet at December 31, 2016.

Item	Reporting Method
____ 1. Commercial paper.	N. Not reported
____ 2. Noncommitted line of credit.	C. Current liability
____ 3. Customer advances.	L. Long-term liability
____ 4. Estimated quality-assurance warranty cost.	D. Disclosure note only
____ 5. Accounts payable.	A. Asset
____ 6. Long-term bonds that will be callable by the creditor in the upcoming year unless an existing violation is not corrected (there is a reasonable possibility the violation will be corrected within the grace period).	
____ 7. Note due March 3, 2017.	
____ 8. Interest accrued on note, Dec. 31, 2016.	
____ 9. Short-term bank loan to be paid with proceeds of sale of common stock.	
____ 10. A determinable gain that is contingent on a future event that appears extremely likely to occur in three months.	
____ 11. Unasserted assessment of back taxes that probably will be asserted, in which case there would probably be a loss in six months.	
____ 12. Unasserted assessment of back taxes with a reasonable possibility of being asserted, in which case there would probably be a loss in 13 months.	
____ 13. A determinable loss from a past event that is contingent on a future event that appears extremely likely to occur in three months.	
____ 14. Note payable due April 4, 2019.	
____ 15. Long-term bonds callable by the creditor in the upcoming year that are not expected to be called.	

E 13–24
Warranty expense; change in estimate
● LO13–5, LO13–6

Woodmier Lawn Products introduced a new line of commercial sprinklers in 2015 that carry a one-year warranty against manufacturer's defects. Because this was the first product for which the company offered a warranty, trade publications were consulted to determine the experience of others in the industry. Based on that experience, warranty costs were expected to approximate 2% of sales. Sales of the sprinklers in 2015 were $2.5 million. Accordingly, the following entries relating to the contingency for warranty costs were recorded during the first year of selling the product:

Accrued liability and expense		
Warranty expense (2% × $2,500,000)	50,000	
Estimated warranty liability		50,000
Actual expenditures (summary entry)		
Estimated warranty liability	23,000	
Cash, wages payable, parts and supplies, etc.		23,000

In late 2016, the company's claims experience was evaluated and it was determined that claims were far more than expected—3% of sales rather than 2%.

Required:

1. Assuming sales of the sprinklers in 2016 were $3.6 million and warranty expenditures in 2016 totaled $88,000, prepare any journal entries related to the warranty.
2. Assuming sales of the sprinklers were discontinued after 2015, prepare any journal entry(s) in 2016 related to the warranty.

E 13–25
Change in accounting estimate
● LO13–3

The Commonwealth of Virginia filed suit in October 2014 against Northern Timber Corporation, seeking civil penalties and injunctive relief for violations of environmental laws regulating forest conservation. When the 2015 financial statements were issued in 2016, Northern had not reached a settlement with state authorities, but legal counsel advised Northern Timber that it was probable the ultimate settlement would be $1,000,000 in penalties. The following entry was recorded:

Loss—litigation	1,000,000	
Liability—litigation		1,000,000

Late in 2016, a settlement was reached with state authorities to pay a total of $600,000 to cover the cost of violations.

Required:

1. Prepare any journal entries related to the change.
2. Briefly describe other steps Northern should take to report the change.

E 13–26
Contingency; Dow Chemical Company disclosure
● LO13–5, LO13–6

Real World Financials

The **Dow Chemical Company** provides chemical, plastic, and agricultural products and services to various consumer markets. The following excerpt is taken from the disclosure notes of Dow's 2013 annual report:

> In total, the Company's accrued liability for probable environmental remediation and restoration costs was $722 million at December 31, 2013, compared with $754 million at the end of 2012. This is management's best estimate of the costs for remediation and restoration with respect to environmental matters for which the Company has accrued liabilities, although it is reasonably possible that the ultimate cost with respect to these particular matters could range up to approximately two and a half times that amount.

Required:

Does the excerpt describe a loss contingency? Under what conditions would Dow accrue such a contingency? What journal entry would Dow use to record this amount of provision (loss)?

E 13–27
Payroll-related liabilities
● Appendix

Lee Financial Services pays employees monthly. Payroll information is listed below for January 2016, the first month of Lee's fiscal year. Assume that none of the employees exceeded any relevant wage base.

Salaries	$500,000
Federal income taxes to be withheld	100,000
Federal unemployment tax rate	0.60%
State unemployment tax rate (after FUTA deduction)	5.40%
Social Security tax rate	6.2%
Medicare tax rate	1.45%

Required:

Prepare the appropriate journal entries to record salaries and wages expense and payroll tax expense for the January 2016 pay period.

CPA and CMA Review Questions

CPA Exam Questions

KAPLAN CPA REVIEW

The following questions are adapted from a variety of sources including questions developed by the AICPA Board of Examiners and those used in the Kaplan CPA Review Course to study accounting for current liabilities and contingencies while preparing for the CPA examination. Determine the response that best completes the statements or questions.

● LO13–3

1. On March 1, 2015, Fine Co. borrowed $10,000 and signed a two-year note bearing interest at 12% per annum compounded annually. Interest is payable in full at maturity on February 28, 2017. What amount should Fine report as a liability for accrued interest at December 31, 2016?

a. $ 0
b. $1,000
c. $1,200
d. $2,320

● LO13–3

2. North Corp. has an employee benefit plan for compensated absences that gives employees 10 paid vacation days and 10 paid sick days. Both vacation and sick days can be carried over indefinitely. Employees can elect to receive payment in lieu of vacation days; however, no payment is given for sick days not taken. At December 31, 2016, North's unadjusted balance of liability for compensated absences was $21,000. North estimated that there were 150 vacation days and 75 sick days available at December 31, 2016. North's employees earn an average of $100 per day. In its December 31, 2016, balance sheet, what amount of liability for compensated absences is North required to report?

a. $15,000
b. $21,000
c. $22,500
d. $36,000

● LO13–4

3. On December 31, 2016, Largo, Inc., had a $750,000 note payable outstanding, due July 31, 2017. Largo borrowed the money to finance construction of a new plant. Largo planned to refinance the note by issuing long-term bonds. Because Largo temporarily had excess cash, it prepaid $250,000 of the note on January 12, 2017. In February 2017, Largo completed a $1,500,000 bond offering. Largo will use the bond offering proceeds to repay the note payable at its maturity and to pay construction costs during 2017. On March 3, 2017, Largo issued its 2016 financial statements. What amount of the note payable should Largo include in the current liabilities section of its December 31, 2016, balance sheet?

a. $250,000
b. $750,000
c. $500,000
d. $ 0

● LO13–5

4. In May 2013, Caso Co. filed suit against Wayne, Inc., seeking $1,900,000 in damages for patent infringement. A court verdict in November 2016 awarded Caso $1,500,000 in damages, but Wayne's appeal is not expected to be decided before 2018. Caso's counsel believes it is probable that Caso will be successful against Wayne for an estimated amount in the range between $800,000 and $1,100,000, with $1,000,000 considered the most likely amount. What amount should Caso record as income from the lawsuit in the year ended December 31, 2016?

a. $ 0
b. $ 800,000
c. $1,000,000
d. $1,500,000

● LO13–6

5. In March 2016, Emett Motors began selling extended warranties for the vehicles it sells. The extended warranties cover parts and labor for all repairs to brakes and powertrain. Emett sold $10,000 of the extended warranties in March, and estimates that it will incur $6,000 of cost over the five-year time period to fulfill them (the present value of the $6,000 is $5,000). In March 2016, Emett would record:

a. A contingent liability of $6,000
b. A contingent liability of $5,000
c. Deferred revenue of $10,000
d. Both (a) and (c) are correct.

● LO13–6

6. During 2016, Gum Co. introduced a new product carrying a two-year warranty against defects. The estimated warranty costs related to dollar sales are 2% within 12 months following the sale and 4% in the second 12 months following the sale. Sales and actual warranty expenditures for the years ended December 31, 2016, and 2017, are as follows:

	Sales	Actual Warranty Expenditures
2016	$150,000	$2,250
2017	250,000	7,500
	$400,000	$9,750

What amount should Gum report as estimated warranty liability in its December 31, 2017, balance sheet?

a. $ 2,500
b. $ 4,250
c. $11,250
d. $14,250

International Financial Reporting Standards are tested on the CPA exam along with U.S. GAAP. The following questions deal with the application of IFRS in accounting for current liabilities and contingencies.

● LO13–7 IFRS

7. Wilhelm Company prepares its financial statements according to International Accounting Standards (IFRS). It recently estimated that it has a 55 percent chance of losing a lawsuit. Assuming Wilhelm can reliably estimate the amount it would pay if it loses the lawsuit, it should.
   a. Accrue a liability for the lawsuit.
   b. Disclose the matter in the notes to the financial statements but not accrue a liability for the lawsuit.
   c. Make no mention of the lawsuit in the financial statements or notes.
   d. None of the above.

● LO13–7 IFRS

8. Tweedy Inc. prepares its financial statements according to International Accounting Standards (IFRS). It recently estimated that it has a 99 percent chance of winning a lawsuit. Assuming Tweedy can reliably estimate the amount it would receive if it wins the lawsuit, it should.
   a. Accrue an asset for the lawsuit.
   b. Disclose the matter in the notes to the financial statements but not accrue an asset for the lawsuit.
   c. Make no mention of the lawsuit in the financial statements or notes.
   d. None of the above.

● LO13–7 IFRS

9. Cline Inc. prepares its financial statements according to International Accounting Standards (IFRS). It recently concluded that it will lose a lawsuit, and that it will pay a range of damages falling somewhere between $10 million and $20 million. Cline should accrue a liability in the amount of.
   a. $0, as no specific amount is probable to be incurred.
   b. $10 million, the lower end of the range of probable amounts.
   c. $15 million, the expected value of the amount to be paid.
   d. $20 million, the upper end of the range of probable amounts.

CMA Exam Questions

ima®

The following questions dealing with current liabilities and contingencies are adapted from questions that previously appeared on Certified Management Accountant (CMA) examinations. The CMA designation sponsored by the Institute of Management Accountants (www.imanet.org) provides members with an objective measure of knowledge and competence in the field of management accounting. Determine the response that best completes the statements or questions.

● LO13–4

1. Lister Company intends to refinance a portion of its short-term debt next year and is negotiating a long-term financing agreement with a local bank. This agreement will be noncancelable and will extend for 2 years. The amount of short-term debt that Lister Company can exclude from its statement of financial position at December 31
   a. May exceed the amount available for refinancing under the agreement.
   b. Depends on the demonstrated ability to consummate the refinancing.
   c. Must be adjusted by the difference between the present value and the market value of the short-term debt.
   d. Is reduced by the proportionate change in the working capital ratio.

● LO13–5

2. An employee has the right to receive compensation for future paid leave, and the payment of compensation is probable. If the obligation relates to rights that vest but the amount cannot be reasonably estimated, the employer should
   a. Accrue a liability with proper disclosure.
   b. Not accrue a liability nor disclose the situation.
   c. Accrue a liability; however, the additional disclosure is not required.
   d. Not accrue a liability; however, disclosure is required.

● LO13–5

3. The accrual of a contingent liability and the related loss should be recorded when the
   a. Loss resulting from a future event may be material in relation to income.
   b. Future event that gives rise to the liability is unusual in nature and nonrecurring.
   c. Amount of the loss resulting from the event is reasonably estimated and the occurrence of the loss is probable.
   d. Event that gives rise to the liability is unusual and its occurrence is probable.

● LO13–6

4. For the past 3 months, Kenton Inc. has been negotiating a labor contract with potentially significant wage increases. Before completing the year-end financial statements on November 30, Kenton determined that the contract was likely to be signed in the near future. Kenton has estimated that the effect of the new contract will cost the company either $100,000, $200,000, or $300,000. Also Kenton believes that each estimate has an equal chance of occurring and that the likelihood of the new contract being retroactive to the fiscal year ended November 30 is probable. According to GAAP regarding contingencies, Kenton should
   a. Do nothing because no loss will occur if the contract is never signed.
   b. Disclose each loss contingency amount in the notes to the November 30 financial statements.
   c. Accrue $100,000 in the income statement, and disclose the nature of the contingency and the additional loss exposure.
   d. Follow conservatism and accrue $300,000 in the income statement, and disclose the nature of the contingency.

Problems

An alternate exercise and problem set is available in the Connect library.

P 13–1
Bank loan; accrued interest
● LO13–2

Blanton Plastics, a household plastic product manufacturer, borrowed $14 million cash on October 1, 2016, to provide working capital for year-end production. Blanton issued a four-month, 12% promissory note to L&T Bank under a prearranged short-term line of credit. Interest on the note was payable at maturity. Each firm's fiscal period is the calendar year.

Required:

1. Prepare the journal entries to record (a) the issuance of the note by Blanton Plastics and (b) L&T Bank's receivable on October 1, 2016.
2. Prepare the journal entries by both firms to record all subsequent events related to the note through January 31, 2017.
3. Suppose the face amount of the note was adjusted to include interest (a noninterest-bearing note) and 12% is the bank's stated discount rate. (a) Prepare the journal entries to record the issuance of the noninterest-bearing note by Blanton Plastics on October 1, 2016, the adjusting entry at December 31, and payment of the note at maturity. (b) What would be the effective interest rate?

P 13–2
Various transactions involving liabilities
● LO13–2 through LO13–4

Camden Biotechnology began operations in September 2016. The following selected transactions relate to liabilities of the company for September 2016 through March 2017. Camden's fiscal year ends on December 31. Its financial statements are issued in April.

2016

a. On September 5, opened checking accounts at Second Commercial Bank and negotiated a short-term line of credit of up to $15,000,000 at the bank's prime rate (10.5% at the time). The company will pay no commitment fees.

b. On October 1, borrowed $12 million cash from Second Commercial Bank under the line of credit and issued a five-month promissory note. Interest at the prime rate of 10% was payable at maturity. Management planned to issue 10-year bonds in February to repay the note.

c. Received $2,600 of refundable deposits in December for reusable containers used to transport and store chemical-based products.

d. For the September–December period, sales on account totaled $4,100,000. The state sales tax rate is 3% and the local sales tax rate is 3%. (This is a summary journal entry for the many individual sales transactions for the period.)

e. Recorded the adjusting entry for accrued interest.

2017

f. In February, issued $10 million of 10-year bonds at face value and paid the bank loan on the March 1 due date.

g. Half of the storage containers covered by refundable deposits were returned in March. The remaining containers are expected to be returned during the next six months.

Required:

1. Prepare the appropriate journal entries for these transactions.
2. Prepare the current and long-term liability sections of the December 31, 2016, balance sheet. Trade accounts payable on that date were $252,000.

P 13–3
Current–noncurrent classification of debt
● LO13–1, LO13–4

The balance sheet at December 31, 2016, for Nevada Harvester Corporation includes the liabilities listed below:

a. 11% bonds with a face amount of $40 million were issued for $40 million on October 31, 2007. The bonds mature on October 31, 2027. Bondholders have the option of calling (demanding payment on) the bonds on October 31, 2017, at a redemption price of $40 million. Market conditions are such that the call is not expected to be exercised.

b. Management intended to refinance $6 million of its 10% notes that mature in May 2017. In early March, prior to the actual issuance of the 2016 financial statements, Nevada Harvester negotiated a line of credit with a commercial bank for up to $5 million any time during 2017. Any borrowings will mature two years from the date of borrowing.

c. Noncallable 12% bonds with a face amount of $20 million were issued for $20 million on September 30, 1994. The bonds mature on September 30, 2017. Sufficient cash is expected to be available to retire the bonds at maturity.

d. A $12 million 9% bank loan is payable on October 31, 2022. The bank has the right to demand payment after any fiscal year-end in which Nevada Harvester's ratio of current assets to current liabilities falls below a contractual minimum of 1.7 to 1 and remains so for six months. That ratio was 1.45 on December 31, 2016, due primarily to an intentional temporary decline in inventory levels. Normal inventory levels will be reestablished during the first quarter of 2017.

Required:

1. Determine the amount that can be excluded from classification as a current liability (that is, reported as a noncurrent liability) for each. Explain the reasoning behind your classifications.
2. Prepare the liability section of a classified balance sheet and any necessary note disclosure for Nevada Harvester at December 31, 2016. Accounts payable and accruals are $22 million.

P 13–4
Various liabilities
● LO13–1 through LO13–4

The unadjusted trial balance of the Manufacturing Equitable at December 31, 2016, the end of its fiscal year, included the following account balances. Manufacturing's 2016 financial statements were issued on April 1, 2017.

Accounts receivable	$ 92,500
Accounts payable	35,000
Bank notes payable	600,000
Mortgage note payable	1,200,000

Other information:

a. The bank notes, issued August 1, 2016, are due on July 31, 2017, and pay interest at a rate of 10%, payable at maturity.

b. The mortgage note is due on March 1, 2017. Interest at 9% has been paid up to December 31 (assume 9% is a realistic rate). Manufacturing intended at December 31, 2016, to refinance the note on its due date with a new 10-year mortgage note. In fact, on March 1, Manufacturing paid $250,000 in cash on the principal balance and refinanced the remaining $950,000.

c. Included in the accounts receivable balance at December 31, 2016, were two subsidiary accounts that had been overpaid and had credit balances totaling $18,000. The accounts were of two major customers who were expected to order more merchandise from Manufacturing and apply the overpayments to those future purchases.

d. On November 1, 2016, Manufacturing rented a portion of its factory to a tenant for $30,000 per year, payable in advance. The payment for the 12 months ended October 31, 2017, was received as required and was credited to rent revenue.

Required:

1. Prepare any necessary adjusting journal entries at December 31, 2016, pertaining to each item of other information (a–d).
2. Prepare the current and long-term liability sections of the December 31, 2016, balance sheet.

P 13–5
Bonus compensation; algebra
● LO13–3

Sometimes compensation packages include bonuses designed to provide performance incentives to employees. The difficulty a bonus can cause accountants is not an accounting problem, but a math problem. The complication is that the bonus formula sometimes specifies that the calculation of the bonus is based in part on the bonus itself. This occurs anytime the bonus is a percentage of income because expenses are components of income, and the bonus is an expense.

Regalia Fashions has an incentive compensation plan through which a division manager receives a bonus equal to 10% of the division's net income. Division income in 2016 before the bonus and income tax was $150,000. The tax rate is 30%.

Required:

1. Express the bonus formula as one or more algebraic equation(s).*
2. Using these formulas calculate the amount of the bonus.
3. Prepare the adjusting entry to record the bonus compensation.
4. Bonus arrangements take many forms. Suppose the bonus specifies that the bonus is 10% of the division's income before tax, but after the bonus itself. Calculate the amount of the bonus.

P 13–6
Various contingencies
● LO13–5, LO13–6

Eastern Manufacturing is involved with several situations that possibly involve contingencies. Each is described below. Eastern's fiscal year ends December 31, and the 2016 financial statements are issued on March 15, 2017.

a. Eastern is involved in a lawsuit resulting from a dispute with a supplier. On February 3, 2017, judgment was rendered against Eastern in the amount of $107 million plus interest, a total of $122 million. Eastern plans to appeal the judgment and is unable to predict its outcome though it is not expected to have a material adverse effect on the company.

b. In November 2015, the State of Nevada filed suit against Eastern, seeking civil penalties and injunctive relief for violations of environmental laws regulating hazardous waste. On January 12, 2017, Eastern reached a

*Remember when you were studying algebra and you wondered if you would ever use it?

settlement with state authorities. Based upon discussions with legal counsel, the Company feels it is probable that $140 million will be required to cover the cost of violations. Eastern believes that the ultimate settlement of this claim will not have a material adverse effect on the company.

c. Eastern is the plaintiff in a $200 million lawsuit filed against United Steel for damages due to lost profits from rejected contracts and for unpaid receivables. The case is in final appeal and legal counsel advises that it is probable that Eastern will prevail and be awarded $100 million.

d. At March 15, 2017, Eastern knows a competitor has threatened litigation due to patent infringement. The competitor has not yet filed a lawsuit. Management believes a lawsuit is reasonably possible, and if a lawsuit is filed, management believes damages of up to $33 million are reasonably possible.

Required:

1. Determine the appropriate means of reporting each situation. Explain your reasoning.
2. Prepare any necessary journal entries and disclosure notes.

P 13–7
Various liabilities
● LO13–4, LO13–5 LO13–6, LO13–7

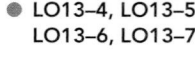

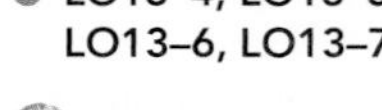

HolmesWatson (HW) is considering what the effect would be of reporting its liabilities under IFRS rather than U.S. GAAP. The following facts apply:

a. HW is defending against a lawsuit and believes it is virtually certain to lose in court. If it loses the lawsuit, management estimates it will need to pay a range of damages that falls between $5,000,000 and $10,000,000, with each amount in that range equally likely.

b. HW is defending against another lawsuit that is identical to item (a), but the relevant losses will only occur far into the future. The present values of the endpoints of the range are $3,000,000 and $8,000,000, with the timing of cash flow somewhat uncertain. HW considers these effects of the time value of money to be material.

c. HW is defending against another lawsuit for which management believes HW has a slightly worse than 50/50 chance of losing in court. If it loses the lawsuit, management estimates HW will need to pay a range of damages that falls between $3,000,000 and $9,000,000, with each amount in that range equally likely.

d. HW has $10,000,000 of short-term debt that it intends to refinance on a long-term basis. Soon after the balance sheet date, but before issuance of the financial statements, HW obtained the financing necessary to refinance the debt.

Required:

1. For each item, indicate how treatment of the amount would differ between U.S. GAAP and IFRS.
2. Consider the total effect of items a–d. If HW's goal is to show the lowest total liabilities, which set of standards, U.S. GAAP or IFRS, best helps it meet that goal?

P 13–8
Expected cash flow approach; product recall
● LO13–6

The Heinrich Tire Company recalled a tire in its subcompact line in December 2016. Costs associated with the recall were originally thought to approximate $50 million. Now, though, while management feels it is probable the company will incur substantial costs, all discussions indicate that $50 million is an excessive amount. Based on prior recalls in the industry, management has provided the following probability distribution for the potential loss:

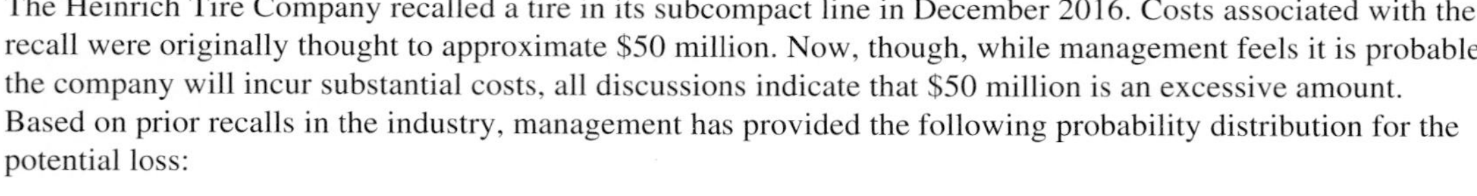

Loss Amount	Probability
$40 million	20%
$30 million	50%
$20 million	30%

An arrangement with a consortium of distributors requires that all recall costs be settled at the end of 2017. The risk-free rate of interest is 5%.

Required:

1. By the traditional approach to measuring loss contingencies, what amount would Heinrich record at the end of 2016 for the loss and contingent liability?
2. For the remainder of this problem, apply the expected cash flow approach of *SFAC No. 7*. Estimate Heinrich's liability at the end of the 2016 fiscal year.
3. Prepare the journal entry to record the contingent liability (and loss).
4. Prepare the journal entry to accrue interest on the liability at the end of 2017.
5. Prepare the journal entry to pay the liability at the end of 2017, assuming the actual cost is $31 million. Heinrich records an additional loss if the actual costs are higher or a gain if the costs are lower.

---

*Remember when you were studying algebra and you wondered if you would ever use it?

P 13–9
Subsequent events
● LO13–6

Lincoln Chemicals became involved in investigations by the U.S. Environmental Protection Agency in regard to damages connected to waste disposal sites. Below are four possibilities regarding the timing of (A) the alleged damage caused by Lincoln, (B) an investigation by the EPA, (C) the EPA assessment of penalties, and (D) ultimate settlement. In each case, assume that Lincoln is unaware of any problem until an investigation is begun. Also assume that once the EPA investigation begins, it is probable that a damage assessment will ensue and that once an assessment is made by the EPA, it is reasonably possible that a determinable amount will be paid by Lincoln.

Required:

For each case, decide whether (a) a loss should be accrued in the financial statements with an explanatory note, (b) a disclosure note only should be provided, or (c) no disclosure is necessary.

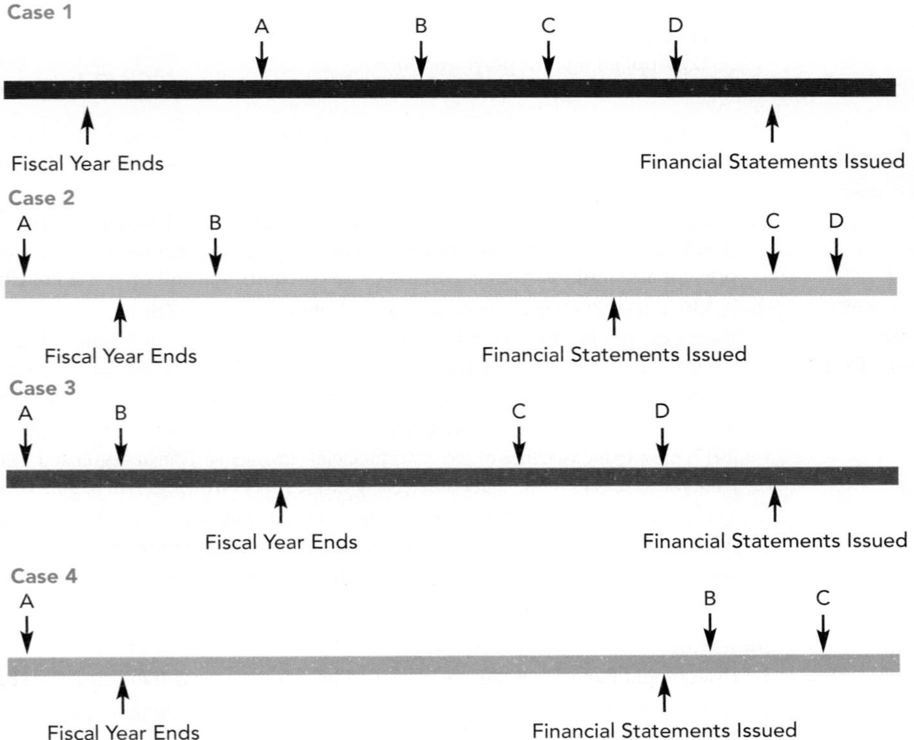

P 13–10
Subsequent events; classification of debt; loss contingency; financial statement effects
● LO13–4, LO13–5

Van Rushing Hunting Goods' fiscal year ends on December 31. At the end of the 2016 fiscal year, the company had notes payable of $12 million due on February 8, 2017. Rushing sold 2 million shares of its $0.25 par, common stock on February 3, 2017, for $9 million. The proceeds from that sale along with $3 million from the maturation of some 3-month CDs were used to pay the notes payable on February 8.

Through his attorney, one of Rushing's construction workers notified management on January 5, 2017, that he planned to sue the company for $1 million related to a work-site injury on December 20, 2016. As of December 31, 2016, management had been unaware of the injury, but reached an agreement on February 23, 2017, to settle the matter by paying the employee's medical bills of $75,000.

Rushing's financial statements were finalized on March 3, 2017.

Required:

1. What amount(s) if any, related to the situations described should Rushing report among current liabilities in its balance sheet at December 31, 2016? Why?
2. What amount(s) if any, related to the situations described should Rushing report among long-term liabilities in its balance sheet at December 31, 2016? Why?
3. How would your answers to requirements 1 and 2 differ if the settlement agreement had occurred on March 15, 2017, instead? Why?
4. How would your answers to requirements 1 and 2 differ if the work-site injury had occurred on January 3, 2017, instead? Why?

P 13–11
Concepts; terminology
● LO13–1 through LO13–4

Listed below are several terms and phrases associated with current liabilities. Pair each item from List A (by letter) with the item from List B that is most appropriately associated with it.

List A	List B
____ 1. Face amount × Interest rate × Time.	a. Informal agreement
____ 2. Payable with current assets.	b. Secured loan
____ 3. Short-term debt to be refinanced with common stock.	c. Refinancing prior to the issuance of the financial statements
____ 4. Present value of interest plus present value of principal.	d. Accounts payable
____ 5. Noninterest-bearing.	e. Accrued liabilities
____ 6. Noncommitted line of credit.	f. Commercial paper
____ 7. Pledged accounts receivable.	g. Current liabilities
____ 8. Reclassification of debt.	h. Long-term liability
____ 9. Purchased by other corporations.	i. Usual valuation of liabilities
____ 10. Expenses not yet paid.	j. Interest on debt
____ 11. Liability until refunded.	k. Customer advances
____ 12. Applied against purchase price.	l. Customer deposits

P 13–12
Various liabilities; balance sheet classification; prepare liability section of balance sheet; write notes
● LO13–4, LO13–5

Transit Airlines provides regional jet service in the Mid-South. The following is information on liabilities of Transit at December 31, 2016. Transit's fiscal year ends on December 31. Its annual financial statements are issued in April.

1. Transit has outstanding 6.5% bonds with a face amount of $90 million. The bonds mature on July 31, 2025. Bondholders have the option of calling (demanding payment on) the bonds on July 31, 2017, at a redemption price of $90 million. Market conditions are such that the call option is not expected to be exercised.
2. A $30 million 8% bank loan is payable on October 31, 2022. The bank has the right to demand payment after any fiscal year-end in which Transit's ratio of current assets to current liabilities falls below a contractual minimum of 1.9 to 1 and remains so for 6 months. That ratio was 1.75 on December 31, 2016, due primarily to an intentional temporary decline in parts inventories. Normal inventory levels will be reestablished during the sixth week of 2017.
3. Transit management intended to refinance $45 million of 7% notes that mature in May of 2017. In late February 2017, prior to the issuance of the 2016 financial statements, Transit negotiated a line of credit with a commercial bank for up to $40 million any time during 2017. Any borrowings will mature two years from the date of borrowing.
4. Transit is involved in a lawsuit resulting from a dispute with a food caterer. On February 13, 2017, judgment was rendered against Transit in the amount of $53 million plus interest, a total of $54 million. Transit plans to appeal the judgment and is unable to predict its outcome though it is not expected to have a material adverse effect on the company.

Required:

1. How should the 6.5% bonds be classified by Transit among liabilities in its balance sheet? Explain.
2. How should the 8% bank loan be classified by Transit among liabilities in its balance sheet? Explain.
3. How should the 7% notes be classified by Transit among liabilities in its balance sheet? Explain.
4. How should the lawsuit be reported by Transit? Explain.
5. Prepare the liability section of a classified balance sheet for Transit Airlines at December 31, 2016. Transit's accounts payable and accruals were $43 million.
6. Draft appropriate note disclosures for Transit's financial statements at December 31, 2016, for each of the five items described.

P 13–13
Payroll-related liabilities
● Appendix

Alamar Petroleum Company offers its employees the option of contributing retirement funds up to 5% of their wages or salaries, with the contribution being matched by Alamar. The company also pays 80% of medical and life insurance premiums. Deductions relating to these plans and other payroll information for the first biweekly payroll period of February are listed as follows:

Wages and salaries	$2,000,000
Employee contribution to voluntary retirement plan	84,000
Medical insurance premiums	42,000
Life insurance premiums	9,000
Federal income taxes to be withheld	400,000
Local income taxes to be withheld	53,000
Payroll taxes:	
Federal unemployment tax rate	0.60%
State unemployment tax rate (after FUTA deduction)	5.40%
Social Security tax rate	6.20%
Medicare tax rate	1.45%

Required:

Prepare the appropriate journal entries to record salaries and wages expense and payroll tax expense for the biweekly pay period. Assume that no employee's cumulative wages exceed the relevant wage bases for Social Security, and that all employees' cumulative wages do exceed the relevant unemployment wage bases.

Broaden Your Perspective

Apply your critical-thinking ability to the knowledge you've gained. These cases will provide you an opportunity to develop your research, analysis, judgment, and communication skills. You also will work with other students, integrate what you've learned, apply it in real-world situations, and consider its global and ethical ramifications. This practice will broaden your knowledge and further develop your decision-making abilities.

Research Case 13–1
Bank loan; accrued interest
● LO13–1, LO13–2

A fellow accountant has solicited your opinion regarding the classification of short-term obligations repaid prior to being replaced by a long-term security. Cheshire Foods, Inc., issued $5,000,000 of short-term commercial paper during 2015 to finance construction of a plant. At September 30, 2016, Cheshire's fiscal year-end, the company intends to refinance the commercial paper by issuing long-term bonds. However, because Cheshire temporarily has excess cash, in November 2016 it liquidates $2,000,000 of the commercial paper as the paper matures. In December 2016, the company completes a $10,000,000 long-term bond issue. Later during December, it issues its September 30, 2016, financial statements. The proceeds of the long-term bond issue are to be used to replenish $2,000,000 in working capital, to pay $3,000,000 of commercial paper as it matures in January 2017, and to pay $5,000,000 of construction costs expected to be incurred later that year to complete the plant.

You initially are hesitant because you don't recall encountering a situation in which short-term obligations were repaid prior to being replaced by a long-term security. However, you are encouraged by a vague memory that this general topic is covered by GAAP literature you came across when reading an Internet article.

Required:

Determine how the $5,000,000 of commercial paper should be classified by consulting the authoritative GAAP literature and citing the appropriate location in the FASB Codification. Before doing so, formulate your own opinion on the proper treatment.

Real World Case 13–2
Returnable containers
● LO13–1, LO13–3

Real World Financials

The **Zoo Doo Compost Company** processes a premium organic fertilizer made with the help of the animals at the Memphis Zoo. Zoo Doo is sold in a specially designed plastic pail that may be kept and used for household chores or returned to the seller. The fertilizer is sold for $12.50 per two-gallon pail (including the $1.76 cost of the pail). For each pail returned, Zoo Doo donates $1 to the Memphis Zoo and the pail is used again.[36]

Required:

The founder and president of this start-up firm has asked your opinion on how to account for the donations to be made when fertilizer pails are returned. (Ignore any tax implications.)

Research Case 13–3
Relationship of liabilities to assets and owners' equity
● LO13–1

SFAC No. 6, "Elements of Financial Statements," states that "an entity's assets, liabilities, and equity (net assets) all pertain to the same set of probable future economic benefits." Explain this statement.

Judgment Case 13–4
Paid future absences
● LO13–3

Cates Computing Systems develops and markets commercial software for personal computers and workstations. Three situations involving compensation for possible future absences of Cates's employees are described below.

a. Cates compensates employees at their regular pay rate for time absent for military leave, maternity leave, and jury time. Employees are allowed predetermined absence periods for each type of absence.
b. Members of the new product development team are eligible for three months' paid sabbatical leave every four years. Five members of the team have just completed their fourth year of participation.
c. Company policy permits employees four paid sick days each year. Unused sick days can accumulate and can be carried forward to future years.

Required:

1. What are the conditions that require accrual of an expense and related liability for employees' compensation for future absences?
2. For each of the three situations, indicate the circumstances under which accrual of an expense and related liability is warranted.

[36]Case based on Kay McCullen, "Take The Zoo Home With You!" *Head Lions,* July 1991; and a conversation with the Zoo Doo Compost Company president, Pierce Ledbetter.

Ethics Case 13–5
Outdoors R Us
● LO13–1

Outdoors R Us owns several membership-based campground resorts throughout the Southwest. The company sells campground sites to new members, usually during a get-acquainted visit and tour. The campgrounds offer a wider array of on-site facilities than most. New members sign a multiyear contract, pay a down payment, and make monthly installment payments. Because no credit check is made and many memberships originate on a spur-of-the-moment basis, cancellations are not uncommon.

Business has been brisk during its first three years of operations, and since going public in 2003, the market value of its stock has tripled. The first sign of trouble came in 2016 when the new sales dipped sharply.

One afternoon, two weeks before the end of the fiscal year, Diane Rice, CEO, and Gene Sun, controller, were having an active discussion in Sun's office.

Sun: I've thought more about our discussion yesterday. Maybe something can be done about profits.
Rice: I hope so. Our bonuses and stock value are riding on this period's performance.
Sun: We've been recording deferred revenues when new members sign up. Rather than recording liabilities at the time memberships are sold, I think we can justify reporting sales revenue for all memberships sold.
Rice: What will be the effect on profits?
Sun: I haven't run the numbers yet, but let's just say very favorable.

Required:

1. Why do you think liabilities had been recorded previously?
2. Is the proposal ethical?
3. Who would be affected if the proposal is implemented?

Trueblood Case 13–6
Contingencies
● LO13–5

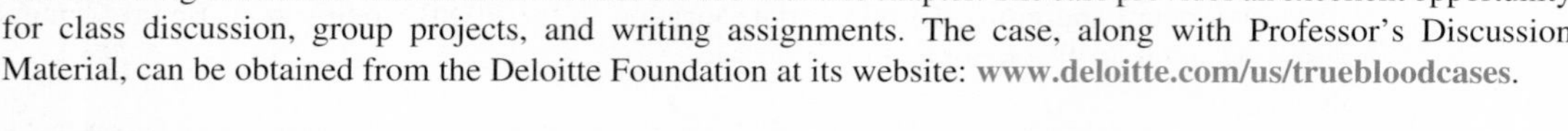

The following Trueblood case is recommended for use with this chapter. The case provides an excellent opportunity for class discussion, group projects, and writing assignments. The case, along with Professor's Discussion Material, can be obtained from the Deloitte Foundation at its website: **www.deloitte.com/us/truebloodcases**.

Case 13–8: Accounting for a Loss Contingency for a Verdict Overturned on Appeal

This case gives students the opportunity to apply GAAP regarding accrual and disclosure of contingencies with respect to a complex lawsuit. As an addition to the case, students should cite the appropriate location of relevant GAAP in the FASB Codification.

Communication Case 13–7
Exceptions to the general classification guideline; group interaction
● LO13–4

Domestic Transfer and Storage is a large trucking company headquartered in the Midwest. Rapid expansion in recent years has been financed in large part by debt in a variety of forms. In preparing the financial statements for 2017, questions have arisen regarding the way certain of the liabilities are to be classified in the company's classified balance sheet.

A meeting of several members of the accounting area is scheduled for tomorrow, April 8, 2017. You are confident that that meeting will include the topic of debt classification. You want to appear knowledgeable at the meeting, but realizing it's been a few years since you have dealt with classification issues, you have sought out information you think relevant. Questionable liabilities at the company's fiscal year-end (January 31, 2017) include the following:

a. $15 million of 9% commercial paper is due on July 31, 2017. Management intends to refinance the paper on a long-term basis. In early April 2017, Domestic negotiated a credit agreement with a commercial bank for up to $12 million any time during the next three years, any borrowings from which will mature two years from the date of borrowing.
b. $17 million of 11% notes were issued on June 30, 2014. The notes are due on November 30, 2017. The company has investments of $20 million classified as "available for sale."
c. $25 million of 10% notes were due on February 28, 2017. On February 21, 2017, the company issued 30-year, 9.4% bonds in a private placement to institutional investors.
d. Recently, company management has considered reducing debt in favor of a greater proportion of equity financing. $20 million of 12% bonds mature on July 31, 2017. Discussions with underwriters, which began on January 4, 2017, resulted in a contractual arrangement on March 15 under which new common shares will be sold in July for approximately $20 million.

In order to make notes to yourself in preparation for the meeting concerning the classification of these items, you decide to discuss them with a colleague. Specifically, you want to know what portion of the debt can be excluded from classification as a current liability (that is, reported as a noncurrent liability) and why.

Required:

1. What is the appropriate classification of each liability? Develop a list of arguments in support of your view prior to the class session for which the case is assigned.

2. In class, your instructor will pair you (and everyone else) with a classmate (who also has independently developed a position). You will be given three minutes to argue your view to your partner. Your partner likewise will be given three minutes to argue his or her view to you. During these three-minute presentations, the listening partner is not permitted to speak.
3. Then after each person has had a turn attempting to convince his or her partner, the two partners will have a three-minute discussion to decide which classifications are more convincing. Arguments will be merged into a single view for each pair.
4. After the allotted time, a spokesperson for each of the four liabilities will be selected by the instructor. Each spokesperson will field arguments from the class as to the appropriate classification. The class then will discuss the merits of the classification and attempt to reach a consensus view, though a consensus is not necessary.

Communication Case 13–8
Various contingencies
● LO13–5, LO13–6

"I see an all-nighter coming on," Gayle grumbled. "Why did Mitch just now give us this assignment?" Your client, Western Manufacturing, is involved with several situations that possibly involve contingencies. The assignment Gayle refers to is to draft appropriate accounting treatment for each situation described below in time for tomorrow's meeting of the audit group. Western's fiscal year is the calendar year 2016, and the 2016 financial statements are issued on March 15, 2017.

1. During 2016, Western experienced labor disputes at three of its plants. Management hopes an agreement will soon be reached. However negotiations between the Company and the unions have not produced an acceptable settlement and, as a result, strikes are ongoing at these facilities since March 1, 2017. It is virtually certain that material costs will be incurred but the amount of possible costs cannot be reasonably ascertained.
2. In accordance with a 2014 contractual agreement with A. J. Conner Company, Western is entitled to $37 million for certain fees and expense reimbursements. These were written off as bad debts in 2015. A. J. Conner has filed for bankruptcy. The bankruptcy court on February 4, 2017, ordered A. J. Conner to pay $23 million immediately upon consummation of a proposed merger with Garner Holding Group.
3. Western warrants most products it sells against defects in materials and workmanship for a period of a year. Based on their experience with previous product introductions, warranty costs are expected to approximate 2% of sales. A warranty liability of $39 million was reported at December 31, 2015. Sales of warranted products during 2016 were $2,100 million and actual warranty expenditures were $40 million.
4. Western is involved in a suit filed in January 2017 by Crump Holdings seeking $88 million, as an adjustment to the purchase price in connection with the Company's sale of its textile business in 2016. The suit alleges that Western misstated the assets and liabilities used to calculate the purchase price for the textile division. Legal counsel advises that it is reasonably possible that Western could end up losing an indeterminable amount not expected to have a material adverse effect on the Company's financial position.

Required:

1. Determine the appropriate means of reporting each situation.
2. In a memo to the audit manager, Mitch Riley, explain your reasoning. Include any necessary journal entries and drafts of appropriate disclosure notes.

Judgment Case 13–9
Loss contingency and full disclosure
● LO13–5, LO13–6

In the March 2017 meeting of Valleck Corporation's board of directors, a question arose as to the way a possible obligation should be disclosed in the forthcoming financial statements for the year ended December 31. A veteran board member brought to the meeting a draft of a disclosure note that had been prepared by the controller's office for inclusion in the annual report. Here is the note:

> On May 9, 2016, the United States Environmental Protection Agency (EPA) issued a Notice of Violation (NOV) to Valleck alleging violations of the Clean Air Act. Subsequently, in June 2016, the EPA commenced a civil action with respect to the foregoing violation seeking civil penalties of approximately $853,000. The EPA alleges that Valleck exceeded applicable volatile organic substance emission limits. The Company estimates that the cost to achieve compliance will be $190,000; in addition the Company expects to settle the EPA lawsuit for a civil penalty of $205,000 which will be paid in 2017.

"Where did we get the $205,000 figure?" he asked. On being informed that this is the amount negotiated last month by company attorneys with the EPA, the director inquires, "Aren't we supposed to report a liability for that in addition to the note?"

Required:

Explain whether Valleck should report a liability in addition to the note. Why or why not? For full disclosure, should anything be added to the disclosure note itself?

Communication Case 13–10
Change in loss contingency; write a memo
● LO13–5, LO13–6

Late in 2016, you and two other officers of Curbo Fabrications Corporation just returned from a meeting with officials of The City of Jackson. The meeting was unexpectedly favorable even though it culminated in a settlement with city authorities that required your company pay a total of $475,000 to cover the cost of violations of city construction codes. Jackson had filed suit in November 2014 against Curbo Fabrications Corporation, seeking civil penalties and injunctive relief for violations of city construction codes regulating earthquake damage standards. Alleged violations involved several construction projects completed during the previous three years. When the financial statements were issued in 2015, Curbo had not reached a settlement with state authorities, but legal counsel had advised the Company that it was probable the ultimate settlement would be $750,000 in penalties. The following entry had been recorded:

Loss—litigation	750,000	
Liability—litigation		750,000

The final settlement, therefore, was a pleasant surprise. While returning from the meeting, your conversation turned to reporting the settlement in the 2016 financial statements. You drew the short straw and were selected to write a memo to Janet Zeno, the financial vice president, advising the proper course of action.

Required:
Write the memo. Include descriptions of any journal entries related to the change in amounts. Briefly describe other steps Curbo should take to report the settlement.

Research Case 13–11
Researching the way contingencies are reported; retrieving information from the Internet
● LO13–5, LO13–6

CODE

EDGAR (Electronic Data Gathering, Analysis, and Retrieval system) performs automated collection, validation, indexing, acceptance, and forwarding of submissions by companies and others who are required by law to file forms with the U.S. Securities and Exchange Commission (SEC). All publicly traded domestic companies use EDGAR to make the majority of their filings. Form 10-K, which includes the annual report, is required to be filed on EDGAR. The SEC makes this information available on the Internet.

Required:
1. Access the *FASB Accounting Standards Codification* at the FASB website (asc.fasb.org). Identify the authoritative literature that provides guidance on accounting for contingent losses, and indicate the specific citations that describe the guidelines for determining when an expense and liability associated with a contingent loss should be accrued vs. only disclosed in the notes?
2. Access EDGAR on the Internet at: www.sec.gov.
3. Search for a public company with which you are familiar. Access its most recent 10-K filing. Search or scroll to find the financial statements and related notes.
4. Specifically, look for any contingency(s) reported in the disclosure notes. Identify the nature of the contingency(s) described and explain the reason(s) the loss or losses was or was not accrued.
5. Repeat requirements 2 and 3 for two additional companies.

Communication Case 13–12
Accounting changes
● LO13–5, LO13–6

Kevin Brantly is a new hire in the controller's office of Fleming Home Products. Two events occurred in late 2016 that the company had not previously encountered. The events appear to affect two of the company's liabilities, but there is some disagreement concerning whether they also affect financial statements of prior years. Each change occurred during 2016 before any adjusting entries or closing entries were prepared. The tax rate for Fleming is 40% in all years.

- Fleming Home Products introduced a new line of commercial awnings in 2015 that carry a one-year warranty against manufacturer's defects. Based on industry experience, warranty costs were expected to approximate 3% of sales. Sales of the awnings in 2015 were $3,500,000. Accordingly, warranty expense and a warranty liability of $105,000 were recorded in 2015. In late 2016, the company's claims experience was evaluated and it was determined that claims were far fewer than expected—2% of sales rather than 3%. Sales of the awnings in 2016 were $4,000,000 and warranty expenditures in 2016 totaled $91,000.
- In November 2014, the State of Minnesota filed suit against the company, seeking penalties for violations of clean air laws. When the financial statements were issued in 2015, Fleming had not reached a settlement with state authorities, but legal counsel advised Fleming that it was probable the company would have to pay $200,000 in penalties. Accordingly, the following entry was recorded:

Loss—litigation	200,000	
Liability—litigation		200,000

Late in 2016, a settlement was reached with state authorities to pay a total of $350,000 in penalties.

Required:
Kevin's supervisor, perhaps unsure of the answer, perhaps wanting to test Kevin's knowledge, e-mails the message, "Kevin, send me a memo on how we should handle our awning warranty and that clean air suit." Wanting to be accurate, Kevin consults his reference materials. What will he find? Prepare the memo requested.

Real World Case 13–13
Lawsuit settlement; Morgan Stanley
● LO13–5, LO13–6
Real World Financials

Morgan Stanley is a leading investment bank founded in 1935. The company's fiscal year ends December 31, 2013, and it filed its financial statements with the SEC on February 25, 2014. On February 5, 2014, *Bloomberg* reported that Morgan Stanley would make a $1.25 billion settlement with the Federal Housing Finance Agency:

> Morgan Stanley said yesterday it reached a $1.25 billion deal to end Federal Housing Finance Agency claims the bank sold faulty mortgage bonds to Fannie Mae (FNMA) and Freddie Mac (FMCC) before the firms' losses pushed them into U.S. conservatorship. . . . Morgan Stanley, which disclosed its settlement in a regulatory filing yesterday, was among 18 banks sued by the FHFA in 2011. Authorities sought to recoup some losses taxpayers covered when the government took control of the failing mortgage-finance companies in 2008.

Required:
1. From an accounting perspective, how should Morgan Stanley have treated the settlement?
2. Relying on the information provided by the news article, re-create the journal entry Morgan Stanley recorded for the settlement. Assume it had not made any prior liability accrual with respect to this litigation.
3. Suppose the settlement had occurred after February 25, 2014. How should Morgan Stanley have treated the settlement?

Ethics Case 13–14
Profits guaranteed
● LO13–5

This was Joel Craig's first visit to the controller's corner office since being recruited for the senior accountant position in May. Because he'd been directed to bring with him his preliminary report on year-end adjustments, Craig presumed he'd done something wrong in preparing the report. That he had not was Craig's first surprise. His second surprise was his boss's request to reconsider one of the estimated expenses.

S & G Fasteners was a new company, specializing in plastic industrial fasteners. All products carry a generous long-term warranty against manufacturer's defects. "Don't you think 4% of sales is a little high for our warranty expense estimate?" his boss wondered. "After all, we're new at this. We have little experience with product introductions. I just got off the phone with Blanchard (the company president). He thinks we'll have trouble renewing our credit line with the profits we're projecting. The pressure's on."

Required:
1. Should Craig follow his boss's suggestion?
2. Does revising the warranty estimate pose an ethical dilemma?
3. Who would be affected if the suggestion is followed?

IFRS Case 13–15
Current liabilities and contingencies; differences between U.S. GAAP and IFRS
● LO13–4, LO13–5, LO13–7
IFRS

As a second-year financial analyst for A.J. Straub Investments, you are performing an initial analysis on Fizer Pharmaceuticals. A difficulty you've encountered in making comparisons with its chief rival is that Fizer uses U.S. GAAP and the competing company uses International Financial Reporting Standards. Some areas of concern are the following:

1. Fizer has been designated as a potentially responsible party by the United States Environmental Protection Agency with respect to certain waste sites. These claims are in various stages of administrative or judicial proceedings and include demands for recovery of past governmental costs and for future investigations or remedial actions. Fizer accrues costs associated with environmental matters when they become probable and reasonably estimable. Counsel has advised that the likelihood of payments of about $70 million is slightly more than 50%. Accordingly, payment is judged reasonably possible and the contingency was disclosed in a note.
2. Fizer had $10 million of bonds issued in 1988 that mature in February 2017. On December 31, 2016, the company's fiscal year-end, management intended to refinance the bonds on a long-term basis. On February 7, 2017, Fizer issued $10 million of 20-year bonds, applying the proceeds to repay the bond issue that matured that month. The bonds were reported in Fizer's balance sheet as long-term debt.
3. Fizer reported in its 2016 financial statements a long-term contingency at its face amount rather than its present value even though the difference was considered material. The reason the cash flows were not discounted is that their timing is uncertain.

Required:
If Fizer used IFRS as does its competitor, how would the items described be reported differently?

Analysis Case 13–16
Analyzing financial statements; liquidity ratios
● LO13–1

IGF Foods Company is a large, primarily domestic, consumer foods company involved in the manufacture, distribution and sale of a variety of food products. Industry averages are derived from Troy's *The Almanac of Business and Industrial Financial Ratios.* Following are the 2016 and 2015 comparative balance sheets for IGF. (The financial data we use are from actual financial statements of a well-known corporation, but the company name used is fictitious and the numbers and dates have been modified slightly.)

IGF FOODS COMPANY
Comparative Balance Sheets Years Ended December 31, 2016 and 2015
($ in millions)

	2016	2015
Assets		
Current assets:		
Cash	$ 48	$ 142
Accounts receivable	347	320
Marketable securities	358	—
Inventories	914	874
Prepaid expenses	212	154
Total current assets	$1,879	$1,490
Property, plant, and equipment (net)	2,592	2,291
Intangibles (net)	800	843
Other assets	74	60
Total assets	$5,345	$4,684
Liabilities and Shareholders' Equity		
Current liabilities:		
Accounts payables	$ 254	$ 276
Accrued liabilities	493	496
Notes payable	518	115
Current portion of long-term debt	208	54
Total current liabilities	$1,473	$ 941
Long-term debt	534	728
Deferred income taxes	407	344
Total liabilities	$2,414	$2,013
Shareholders' equity:		
Common stock	180	180
Additional paid-in capital	21	63
Retained earnings	2,730	2,428
Total shareholders' equity	$2,931	$2,671
Total liabilities and shareholders' equity	$5,345	$4,684

Liquidity refers to a company's cash position and overall ability to obtain cash in the normal course of business. A company is said to be liquid if it has sufficient cash or is capable of converting its other assets to cash in a relatively short period of time so that currently maturing debts can be paid.

Required:

1. Calculate the current ratio for IGF for 2016. The average ratio for the stocks listed on the New York Stock Exchange in a comparable time period was 1.5. What information does your calculation provide an investor?
2. Calculate IGF's acid-test or quick ratio for 2016. The ratio for the stocks listed on the New York Stock Exchange in a comparable time period was .80. What does your calculation indicate about IGF's liquidity?

Analysis Case 13–17
Reporting current liabilities; liquidity
● LO13–1

PetSmart

Refer to the financial statements and related disclosure notes of PetSmart located in the company's 2013 annual report included with all new copies of the text. They also can be found at www.petsmart.com. At February 2, 2014, fiscal year, PetSmart reported current liabilities of $794.3 million in its balance sheet.

Required:

1. What are the five components of current liabilities?
2. Are current assets sufficient to cover current liabilities? What is the current ratio for the year ended February 2, 2014? How does the ratio compare with the prior year?
3. Why might a company want to avoid having its current ratio be too low? Too high?

Real World Case 13–18
Contingencies
● LO13–5

Real World Financials

The following is an excerpt from *USAToday.com:*

> Microsoft (MSFT) on Thursday extended the warranty on its Xbox 360 video game console and said it will take a charge of more than $1 billion to pay for "anticipated costs." Under the new warranty, Microsoft will pay for shipping and repairs for three years, worldwide, for consoles afflicted with what gamers call "the red ring of death." Previously, the warranty expired after a year for U.S. customers and two years for Europeans. The charge will be $1.05 billion to $1.15 billion for the quarter ended June 30. Microsoft reports its fourth-quarter results July 19.

Required:

1. Why must Microsoft report this charge of over $1 billion entirely in one quarter, the last quarter of the company's fiscal year?
2. When the announcement was made, analyst Richard Doherty stated that either a high number of Xbox 360s will fail or the company is being overly conservative in its warranty estimate. From an accounting standpoint, what will Microsoft do in the future if the estimate of future repairs is overly conservative (too high)?

Real World Case 13–19
Contingencies
● LO13–5

Real World Financials

IFRS

Reporting requirements for contingent liabilities under IFRS differ somewhat from those under U.S. GAAP.

Required:

For each of the following, access the online version of the indicated financial report and answer the question. Also compare reporting under IFRS to similar reporting under U.S. GAAP.

1. **AU Optronics** (Form 20-F, filed 3/21/2014): When there is a continuous range of possible outcomes, with each point in the range as likely as any other, what amount is accrued as the estimate of the obligation?
2. **B Communications LTD** (Form 20-F, filed 4/24/2013): With respect to legal claims, at what probability level would B Communications accrue a liability for a possible litigation loss?

Real World Case 13–20
Contingencies and Subsequent events
● LO13–5, LO13–6

Real World Financials

The following events are indicated in note 15 of **J. Crew**'s 10-K annual report for the fiscal year ended January 29, 2011, and its 10K was filed on March 21, 2011.

> **Acquisition**
>
> On November 23, 2010, the Company entered into an Agreement and Plan of Merger (the "Merger Agreement") with Chinos Holdings, Inc., a Delaware corporation ("Parent") . . . . At a special meeting of shareholders held in March 1, 2011, our shareholders voted to approve the Acquisition, and Parent acquired us on March 7, 2011 through a reverse subsidiary merger with J. Crew Group, Inc. being the surviving company. . . .
>
> **Litigation**
>
> In connection with the Acquisition, between November 24, 2010 and December 16, 2010, sixteen purported class action complaints were filed against some or all of the following: the Company, certain officers of the Company, members of the Company's Board of Directors, Holdings, the Issuer, TPG, TPG Fund VI and LGP. The plaintiffs in each of these complaints allege, among other things, (1) that certain officers of the Company and members of the Company's Board breached their fiduciary duties to the Company's public stockholders by authorizing the Acquisition for inadequate consideration and pursuant to an inadequate process, and (2) that the Company, TPG and LGP aided and abetted the other defendants' alleged breaches of fiduciary duty. The purported class action complaints sought, among other things, an order enjoining the consummation of the Acquisition or an order rescinding the Acquisition and an award of compensatory damages. Although the Company, the Company's Board, TPG, and LGP have entered into a memorandum of understanding to settle the actions filed in Delaware, they believe that the claims asserted in that action, as well as the claims asserted in New York and Federally, are without merit and intend to defend against the actions vigorously. The Company has notified its insurers of the actions and believes that any and all costs, expenses, and/or losses associated with the lawsuits are covered by its applicable insurance policies. The Company has recorded a reserve for litigation settlement of $10 million in the consolidated financial statements as of and for the fiscal year ended January 29, 2011.

Required:

1. Is the acquisition a subsequent event? What are J. Crew's responsibilities in its financial statements with respect to disclosing it?

2. With respect to litigation,
   a. Has J. Crew recorded any journal entry with respect to the litigation associated with the acquisition? If so, prepare the journal entry.
   b. Do you believe that there is some amount associated with the litigation that J. Crew considers to be probable and reasonably estimable? What about reasonably possible, or probable but not reasonably estimable? Explain your reasoning.

Trueblood Case 13–21
Subsequent Events
● LO13–5

The following Trueblood case is recommended for use with this chapter. The case provides an excellent opportunity for class discussion, group projects, and writing assignments. The case, along with Professor's Discussion Material, can be obtained from the Deloitte Foundation at its website: **www.deloitte.com/us/truebloodcases**.

Case 12-02: To Recognize or Not to Recognize, That is the Question
This case gives students the opportunity to apply GAAP regarding recognition of subsequent events. As an addition to the case, students should cite the appropriate location of relevant GAAP in the FASB Codification.

Air France–KLM Case

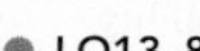

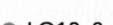

● LO13–8

IFRS

Air France-KLM (AF), a Franco-Dutch company, prepares its financial statements according to International Financial Reporting Standards. AF's annual report for the year ended December 31, 2013, which includes financial statements and disclosure notes, is provided with all new textbooks. This material also is included in AF's "Results" section of the company's website **www.airfranceklm-finance.com**.

Required:

1. Read Notes 4.6 and 33. What do you think gave rise to total deferred income of €126 as of the end of fiscal 2013? Would transactions of this type be handled similarly under U.S. GAAP?
2. Is the threshold for recognizing a provision under IFRS different than it is under U.S. GAAP? Explain.
3. Note 31 lists "provisions and retirement benefits."
   a. Do the beginning and ending balances of total provisions and retirement benefits shown in Note 31 for fiscal 2013 tie to the balance sheet? By how much has the total amount of the AF-KLM's "provisions and retirement benefits" increased or decreased during fiscal 2013?
   b. Prepare journal entries for the following changes in the litigation provision that occurred during fiscal 2013, assuming any amounts recorded on the income statement are recorded as "provision expense," and any use of provision is paid for in cash. In each case, provide a brief explanation of the event your journal entry is capturing.
      i. New provision
      ii. Use of provision
   c. Is AF-KLM's treatment of its litigation provision under IFRS similar to how it would be treated under U.S. GAAP?
4. Note 31.3 lists a number of contingent liabilities. Are amounts for those items recognized as a liability on AF-KLM's balance sheet? Explain.

CHAPTER

14 Bonds and Long-Term Notes

OVERVIEW

This chapter continues the presentation of liabilities. While the discussion focuses on the accounting treatment of long-term liabilities, the borrowers' side of the same transactions is presented as well. Long-term notes and bonds are discussed, as well as the extinguishment of debt and debt convertible into stock.

LEARNING OBJECTIVES

After studying this chapter, you should be able to:

- **LO14–1** Identify the underlying characteristics of debt instruments and describe the basic approach to accounting for debt. (*p. 789*)
- **LO14–2** Account for bonds issued at face value, at a discount, or at a premium, recording interest using the effective interest method or using the straight-line method. (*p. 791*)
- **LO14–3** Characterize the accounting treatment of notes, including installment notes, issued for cash or for noncash consideration. (*p. 802*)
- **LO14–4** Describe the disclosures appropriate to long-term debt in its various forms and calculate related financial ratios. (*p. 806*)
- **LO14–5** Record the early extinguishment of debt and its conversion into equity securities. (*p. 811*)
- **LO14–6** Understand the option to report liabilities at their fair values. (*p. 817*)
- **LO14–7** Discuss the primary differences between U.S. GAAP and IFRS with respect to accounting for bonds and long-term notes. (*pp. 793, 802, and 813*).

FINANCIAL REPORTING CASE

Service Leader, Inc.

The mood is both upbeat and focused on this cool October morning. Executives and board members of Service Leader, Inc., are meeting with underwriters and attorneys to discuss the company's first bond offering in its 20-year history. You are attending in the capacity of company controller and two-year member of the board of directors. The closely held corporation has been financed entirely by equity, internally generated funds, and short-term bank borrowings.

Bank rates of interest, though, have risen recently and the company's unexpectedly rapid, but welcome, growth has prompted the need to look elsewhere for new financing. Under consideration are 15-year, 6.25% first mortgage bonds with a principal amount of $70 million. The bonds would be callable at 103 any time after June 30, 2018, and convertible into Service Leader common stock at the rate of 45 shares per $1,000 bond.

Other financing vehicles have been discussed over the last two months, including the sale of additional stock, nonconvertible bonds, and unsecured notes. This morning *The Wall Street Journal* indicated that market rates of interest for debt similar to the bonds under consideration are about 6.5%.

QUESTIONS

By the time you finish this chapter, you should be able to respond appropriately to the questions posed in this case. Compare your response to the solution provided at the end of the chapter.

1. What does it mean that the bonds are "first mortgage" bonds? What effect does that have on financing? *(p. 791)*
2. From Service Leader's perspective, why are the bonds callable? What does that mean? *(p. 791)*
3. How will it be possible to sell bonds paying investors 6.25% when other, similar investments will provide the investors a return of 6.5%? *(p. 791)*
4. Would accounting differ if the debt were designated as notes rather than bonds? *(p. 802)*
5. Why might the company choose to make the bonds convertible into common stock? *(p. 812)*

The Nature of Long-Term Debt

LO14–1

A company must raise funds to finance its operations and often the expansion of those operations. Presumably, at least some of the necessary funding can be provided by the company's own operations, though some funds must be provided by external sources. Ordinarily, external financing includes some combination of equity and debt funding. We explore debt financing first.

Liabilities signify *borrowers'* interests in a company's assets.

In the present chapter, we focus on debt in the form of bonds and notes. The following three chapters deal with liabilities also, namely those arising in connection with leases (Chapter 15), deferred income taxes (Chapter 16), and pensions and employee benefits (Chapter 17). Some employee benefits create equity rather than debt, which are discussed in Chapter 19. In Chapter 18, we examine shareholders' interests arising from external *equity* financing. In Chapter 21, we see that cash flows from both debt and equity financing are reported together in a statement of cash flows as "cash flows from financing activities."

A note payable and a note receivable are two sides of the same coin.

As you read this chapter, you will find the focus to be on the liability side of the transactions we examine. Realize, though, that the mirror image of a liability is an asset (bonds payable/investment in bonds, note payable/note receivable, etc.). So as we discuss accounting for debts from the viewpoint of the issuers of the debt instruments (borrowers), we also will take the opportunity to see how the lender deals with the corresponding asset. Studying the two sides of the same transaction in tandem will emphasize their inherent similarities.

Accounting for a liability is a relatively straightforward concept. This is not to say that all debt instruments are unchallenging, "plain vanilla" loan agreements. Quite the contrary, the financial community continually devises increasingly exotic ways to flavor financial instruments in the attempt to satisfy the diverse and evolving tastes of both debtors and creditors.

Periodic interest is the effective interest rate times the amount of the debt outstanding during the interest period.

Packaging aside, a liability requires the future payment of cash in specified (or estimated) amounts, at specified (or projected) dates. As time passes, interest accrues on debt. As a general rule, the periodic interest is the effective interest rate times the amount of the debt outstanding during the period. This same principle applies regardless of the specific form of the liability—note payable, bonds payable, lease liability, pension obligation, or other debt instruments. Also, as a general rule, long-term liabilities are reported at their present values. The present value of a liability is the present value of its related cash flows (principal and/or interest payments), discounted at the effective rate of interest at issuance.

We begin our study of long-term liabilities by examining accounting for bonds. We follow that section with a discussion of debt in the form of notes in Part B. It's important to note that, although particulars of the two forms of debt differ, the basic approach to accounting for each type is precisely the same. In Part C, we look at various ways bonds and notes are retired or converted into other securities. Finally, in Part D we discuss the option companies have to report liabilities at their fair values.

PART A Bonds

A bond issue divides a large liability into many smaller liabilities.

A company can borrow cash from a bank or other financial institution by signing a promissory note. We discuss notes payable later in the chapter. Medium- and large-sized corporations often choose to borrow cash by issuing bonds to the public. In fact, the most common form of corporate debt is bonds. A bond issue, in effect, breaks down a large debt (large corporations often borrow hundreds of millions of dollars at a time) into manageable parts—usually $1,000 or $5,000 units. This avoids the necessity of finding a single lender who is both willing and able to loan a large amount of money at a reasonable interest rate. So rather than signing a $400 million note to borrow cash from a financial institution, a company may find it more economical to sell 400,000 $1,000 bonds to many lenders—theoretically up to 400,000 lenders.

Corporations issuing bonds are obligated to repay a stated amount at a specified *maturity date* and periodic *interest* between the issue date and maturity.

Bonds obligate the issuing corporation to repay a stated amount (variously referred to as the *principal, par value, face amount,* or *maturity value*) at a specified *maturity date*. Maturities for bonds typically range from 10 to 40 years. In return for the use of the money borrowed, the company also agrees to pay *interest* to bondholders between the issue date and maturity. The periodic interest is a stated percentage of face amount (variously referred to as the *stated rate, coupon rate,* or *nominal rate*). Ordinarily, interest is paid semiannually on designated interest dates beginning six months after the day the bonds are "dated."

The Bond Indenture

A *bond indenture* describes the specific promises made to bondholders.

The specific promises made to bondholders are described in a document called a **bond indenture**. Because it would be impractical for the corporation to enter into a direct agreement with each of the many bondholders, the bond indenture is held by a trustee, usually a commercial bank or other financial institution, appointed by the issuing firm to represent the rights of the bondholders. If the company fails to live up to the terms of the bond indenture, the trustee may bring legal action against the company on behalf of the bondholders.

Most corporate bonds are debenture bonds. A **debenture bond** is secured only by the "full faith and credit" of the issuing corporation. No specific assets are pledged as security. Investors in debentures usually have the same standing as the firm's other general creditors. So in case of bankruptcy, debenture holders and other general creditors would be treated equally. An exception is the **subordinated debenture**, which is not entitled to receive any liquidation payments until the claims of other specified debt issues are satisfied.

A **mortgage bond**, on the other hand, is backed by a lien on specified real estate owned by the issuer. Because a mortgage bond is considered less risky than debentures, it typically will command a lower interest rate.

FINANCIAL Reporting Case

Q1, p. 789

Today most corporate bonds are registered bonds. Interest checks are mailed directly to the owner of the bond, whose name is registered with the issuing company. Years ago, it was typical for bonds to be structured as **coupon bonds** (sometimes called *bearer bonds*). The name of the owner of a coupon bond was not registered. Instead, to collect interest on a coupon bond the holder actually clipped an attached coupon and redeemed it in accordance with instructions in the indenture. A carryover effect of this practice is that we still sometimes see the term *coupon rate* in reference to the stated interest rate on bonds.

FINANCIAL Reporting Case

Q2, p. 789

Most corporate bonds are **callable** (or redeemable). The call feature allows the issuing company to buy back, or call, outstanding bonds from bondholders before their scheduled maturity date. This feature affords the company some protection against being stuck with relatively high-cost debt in the event interest rates fall during the period before maturity. The call price must be pre-specified and often exceeds the bond's face amount (a call premium), sometimes declining as maturity is approached.

For example, financial statements of **Emhart Corporation** included this disclosure note:

Real World Financials

The Company's 9¼% (9.65% effective interest rate, after discount) sinking fund debentures are callable at prices decreasing from 105% of face amount currently to 100%.

Mandatory sinking fund redemptions retire a bond issue gradually over its term to maturity.

"No call" provisions usually prohibit calls during the first few years of a bond's life. Very often, calls are mandatory. That is, the corporation may be required to redeem the bonds on a pre-specified, year-by-year basis. Bonds requiring such **sinking fund** redemptions often are labeled *sinking fund debentures.*

Serial bonds provide a more structured (and less popular) way to retire bonds on a piecemeal basis. Serial bonds are retired in installments during all or part of the life of the issue. Each bond has its own specified maturity date. So for a typical 30-year serial issue, 25 to 30 separate maturity dates might be assigned to specific portions of the bond issue.

Convertible bonds are retired as a consequence of bondholders choosing to convert them into shares of stock. We look closer at convertible bonds a little later in the chapter.

Recording Bonds at Issuance

● LO14–2

Bonds represent a liability to the corporation that issues the bonds and an asset to an investor who buys the bonds as an investment. Each side of the transaction is the mirror image of the other.[1] This is demonstrated in Illustration 14–1.

Most bonds these days are issued on the day they are dated (date printed in the indenture contract). On rare occasions, there may be a delay in issuing bonds that causes them to be issued between interest dates, in which case the interest that has accrued since the day they are dated is added to the bonds' price. We discuss this infrequent event in Appendix 14A to this chapter.

Determining the Selling Price

FINANCIAL Reporting Case

Q3, p. 789

The price of a bond issue at any particular time is not necessarily equal to its face amount. The $700,000, 12% bond issue in the previous illustration, for example, may sell for more than face amount (at a **premium**) or less than face amount (at a **discount**), depending on how the 12% *stated* interest rate compares with the prevailing *market* or *effective rate* of interest (for securities of similar risk and maturity). For instance, if the 12% bonds are competing in a market in which similar bonds are providing a 14% return, the bonds could be

[1]You should recall from Chapter 12 that investments in bonds that are to be held to maturity by the investor are reported at amortized cost, which is the method described here. However, also remember that investments in debt securities *not* to be held to maturity are reported at the fair value of the securities held, as described in Chapter 12, with the interest determined by the effective interest method.

Illustration 14–1

Bonds Sold at Face Amount

On January 1, 2016, Masterwear Industries issued $700,000 of 12% bonds. Interest of $42,000 is payable semiannually on June 30 and December 31. The bonds mature in three years (an unrealistically short maturity to shorten the illustration). The entire bond issue was sold in a private placement to United Intergroup, Inc., at the face amount.

At Issuance (January 1)

Masterwear (Issuer)		
Cash	700,000	
Bonds payable (face amount)		700,000
United (Investor)		
Investment in bonds (face amount)	700,000	
Cash		700,000

sold only at a price less than $700,000. On the other hand, if the market rate is only 10%, the 12% stated rate would seem relatively attractive and the bonds would sell at a premium over face amount. The reason the stated rate often differs from the market rate, resulting in a *discount* or *premium,* is the inevitable delay between the date the terms of the issue are established and the date the issue comes to market.

Other things being equal, the lower the perceived riskiness of the corporation issuing bonds, the higher the price those bonds will command.

In addition to the characteristic terms of a bond agreement as specified in the indenture, the market rate for a specific bond issue is influenced by the creditworthiness of the company issuing the bonds. To evaluate the risk and quality of an individual bond issue, investors rely heavily on bond ratings provided by **Standard & Poor's Corporation** and by **Moody's Investors Service, Inc**. See the bond ratings in Illustration 14–2.

Illustration 14–2

Bond Ratings*

	S&P	Moody's
Investment Grades:		
Highest	AAA	Aaa
High	AA	Aa
Medium	A	A
Minimum investment grade	BBB	Baa
"Junk" Ratings:		
Speculative	BB	Ba
Very speculative	B	B
Default or near default	CCC	Caa
	CC	Ca
	C	C
	D	

*Adapted from *Bond Record* (New York: Moody's Investors Service, monthly) and *Bond Guide* (New York: Standard & Poor's Corporation, monthly).

A bond issue will be priced by the marketplace to yield the market rate of interest for securities of similar risk and maturity.

Forces of supply and demand cause a bond issue to be *priced to yield the market rate.* In other words, an investor paying that price will earn an effective rate of return on the investment equal to the market rate. The price is calculated as the present value of all the cash flows required of the bonds, where the discount rate used in the present value calculation is the market rate. Specifically, the price will be the present value of the periodic cash interest payments (face amount × stated rate) plus the present value of the principal payable at maturity, both discounted at the market rate.

Bonds priced at a discount are described in Illustration 14–3.

Illustration 14–3

Bonds Sold at a Discount

On January 1, 2016, Masterwear Industries issued $700,000 of 12% bonds, dated January 1. Interest of $42,000 is payable semiannually on June 30 and December 31. The bonds mature in three years. The market yield for bonds of similar risk and maturity is 14%. The entire bond issue was purchased by United Intergroup, Inc.

Calculation of the Price of the Bonds

	Present Values
Interest	$ 42,000 × 4.76654* = $200,195
Principal	$700,000 × 0.66634† = 466,438
Present value (price) of the bonds	$666,633

*Present value of an ordinary annuity of $1: $n = 6$, $i = 7\%$ (Table 4).
†Present value of $1: $n = 6$, $i = 7\%$ (Table 2).
Because interest is paid semiannually, the present value calculations use: (a) one-half the stated rate (6%) to determine cash payments, (b) one-half the market rate (7%) as the discount rate, and (c) six (3 × 2) semiannual periods.
Note: Present value tables are provided at the end of this textbook. If you need to review the concept of the time value of money, refer to the discussions in Chapter 6.
Rounding: Because present value tables truncate decimal places, the solution may be slightly different if you use a calculator or Excel.

Using a calculator:
Enter: N 6 I 7
PMT −42000 FV −700000
Output: PV 666,634

Using Excel, enter:
=PV(.07,6,42000,700000)
Output: 666,634

The calculation is illustrated in Illustration 14–4:

Illustration 14–4

Cash Flows from a Bond Issue

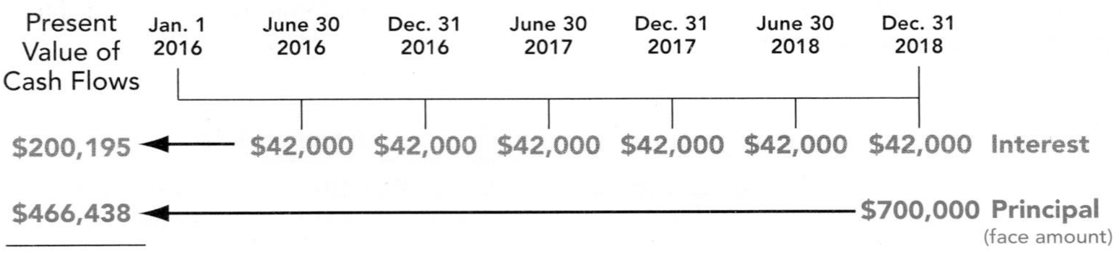

$666,633 Present value of interest and principal

Although the cash flows total $952,000, the present value of those future cash flows as of January 1, 2016, is only $666,633. This is due to the time value of money. These bonds are issued at a discount because the present value of the cash flows is less than the face amount of the bonds.

Journal Entries at Issuance—Bonds Sold at a Discount

Masterwear (Issuer)		
Cash (price calculated above)	666,633	
Discount on bonds payable (difference)	33,367	
Bonds payable (face amount)		700,000
United (Investor)		
Investment in bonds (face amount)	700,000	
Discount on bond investment (difference)		33,367
Cash (price calculated above)		666,633

Note: A sometimes-used alternative way to record bonds is the "net method," shown next, in which the discount is included directly in the book value.

Masterwear (Issuer)		
Cash	666,633	
Bonds payable		666,633
United (Investor)		
Investment in bonds	666,633	
Cash		666,633

The net method actually is the preferred method for companies that prepare financial statements according to International Financial Reporting Standards. It also is the common approach for an investor to record its investment.

● LO14–7

When bond prices are quoted in financial media, they typically are stated in terms of a percentage of face amounts. Thus, a price quote of 98 means a $1,000 bond will sell for $980; a bond priced at 101 will sell for $1,010.

Determining Interest—Effective Interest Method

The *effective interest* on debt is the market rate of interest multiplied by the outstanding balance of the debt.

Interest accrues on an outstanding debt at a constant percentage of the debt each period. Of course, under the concept of accrual accounting, the periodic effective interest is not affected by the time at which the cash interest actually is paid. Recording interest each period as the *effective market rate of interest multiplied by the outstanding balance of the debt* (during the interest period) is referred to as the **effective interest method**. Although giving this a label—the effective interest method—implies some specialized procedure, this simply is an application of the accrual concept, consistent with accruing all expenses as they are incurred.

Continuing our example, we determined that the amount of debt when the bonds are issued is $666,633. Since the effective interest rate is 14%, interest recorded (as expense to the issuer and revenue to the investor) for the first six-month interest period is $46,664:

$666,633	×	[14% ÷ 2]	=	$46,664
Outstanding balance		Effective rate		Effective interest

However, the bond indenture calls for semiannual interest payments of only $42,000—the *stated* rate (6%) times the *face amount* ($700,000). The remainder, $4,664, increases the liability and is reflected as a reduction in the discount (a contra-liability account). This is illustrated in Illustration 14–5.

Illustration 14–5
Change in Debt When Effective Interest Exceeds Cash Paid

The difference between the effective interest and the interest paid increases the existing liability.

			Account Balances		
	Outstanding Balance		**Bonds Payable (face amount)**		**Discount on Bonds Payable**
January 1	$666,633	=	$700,000	less	$33,367
Interest accrued at 7%	46,664				
Portion of interest paid	(42,000)				(4,664)
June 30	$671,297	=	$700,000	less	$28,703

Interest expense (issuer) and revenue (investor) are calculated on the outstanding debt balance at the effective (or market) rate. Interest *paid* is the amount specified in the bond indenture—the *stated* rate times the face amount. These amounts and the change in the outstanding debt are recorded as follows:

Journal Entries—The Interest Method

The effective interest is calculated each period as the market rate times the amount of the debt outstanding during the interest period.

At the First Interest Date (June 30)

Masterwear (Issuer)		
Interest expense (effective rate × outstanding balance)	46,664	
Discount on bonds payable (difference)		4,664
Cash (stated rate × face amount)		42,000
United (Investor)		
Cash (stated rate × face amount)	42,000	
Discount on bond investment (difference)	4,664	
Interest revenue (effective rate × outstanding balance)		46,664

In this example and others in the chapter we look at the investor's entries as well as the issuer's to see both sides of the same transactions.

Because the balance of the debt changes each period, the dollar amount of interest (balance × rate) also will change each period. To keep up with the changing amounts, it usually is convenient to prepare a schedule that reflects the changes in the debt over its term to maturity. An amortization schedule for the situation under discussion is shown in Illustration 14–6.

Illustration 14–6
Amortization Schedule—Discount

Date	Cash Interest	Effective Interest	Increase in Balance	Outstanding Balance
	(6% × Face amount)	(7% × Outstanding balance)	(Discount reduction)	
1/1/16				666,633
6/30/16	42,000	.07 (666,633) = 46,664	4,664	671,297
12/31/16	42,000	.07 (671,297) = 46,991	4,991	676,288
6/30/17	42,000	.07 (676,288) = 47,340	5,340	681,628
12/31/17	42,000	.07 (681,628) = 47,714	5,714	687,342
6/30/18	42,000	.07 (687,342) = 48,114	6,114	693,456
12/31/18	42,000	.07 (693,456) = 48,544*	6,544	700,000
	252,000	285,367	33,367	

*Rounded.

Amounts for the journal entries each interest date are found in the second, third, and fourth columns of the schedule. The essential point to remember is that the effective interest method is a straightforward application of the accrual concept, whereby interest expense (or revenue) is accrued periodically at the effective rate. We record that amount of interest expense or revenue accrued even though the cash interest is a different amount.

Determining interest in this manner has a convenient side effect. It results in reporting the liability at the present value of future cash payments—the appropriate valuation method for any liability. This is obvious at issuance; we actually calculated the present value to be $666,633. What perhaps is not quite as obvious is that the outstanding amount of debt each subsequent period (shown in the right-hand column of the amortization schedule) is still the present value of the remaining cash flows, discounted at the original rate. The outstanding amount of the debt is its book value, sometimes called carrying value or carrying amount, which is the face amount minus the balance in the discount.

Before moving on, notice some key characteristics of the amortization schedule. As mentioned earlier, the unpaid interest each period ($4,664 the first period) adds to the balance. Since this happens each period, the balance continually increases, eventually becoming the face amount at maturity. Conveniently, that's the amount to be paid at maturity. Also, because the balance increases each period, so does the effective interest. That's because effective interest is the same percentage rate times a higher balance each period.

Now look at the column totals. The total interest expense (from the issuer's perspective) is equal to the sum of the total cash interest plus the total change in the balance (the discount). One way we might view this is to say the total interest paid ($285,367) is the $252,000 cash interest paid during the term to maturity plus the "extra" amount paid at maturity. That $33,367 amount is extra in the sense that, by selling the bonds, we borrow $666,633 but must repay $700,000 at maturity. That's why the effective interest on the bonds is 14% even though the cash interest is only 12% annually; the extra interest at maturity makes up the difference.

Additional Consideration

Although the reported amount each period is the present value of the bonds, at any date after issuance this amount is not necessarily equal to the market value (fair value) of the bonds. This is because the market rate of interest will not necessarily remain the same as the rate implicit in the original issue price (the effective rate). Of course, for negotiable financial instruments, the issue price is the market price at any given time. Differences between market values and present values based on the original rate are holding gains and losses. If we were to use the market rate to revalue bonds on each reporting date—that is, recalculate the present value using the market rate—the reported amount always would be the market value. As we will see later, companies have the option to report their liabilities at fair value.

Zero-Coupon Bonds

A zero-coupon bond pays no interest. Instead, it offers a return in the form of a "deep discount" from the face amount. For illustration, let's look at the zero-coupon bonds issued by **General Mills, Inc.** Two billion, two hundred thirty million dollars face amount of the 20-year securities sold for one billion, five hundred one million dollars. As the amortization schedule in Illustration 14–7 demonstrates, they were priced to yield 2%.[2]

Illustration 14–7

Zero-Coupon Securities—General Mills, Inc.

Real World Financials

($ in millions)	Cash Interest	Effective Interest	Increase in Balance	Outstanding Balance*
	(0% × Face amount)	(2% × Outstanding debt)	(Discount reduction)	
				1,501
2002	0	.02 (1,501) = 30	30	1,531
2003	0	.02 (1,531) = 31	31	1,561
2004	0	.02 (1,561) = 31	31	1,593
◆	◆	◆	◆	◆
◆	◆	◆	◆	◆
◆	◆	◆	◆	◆
2021	0	.02 (2,143) = 43	43	2,186
2022	0	.02 (2,186) = 44	44	2,230
		729	729	

*Some numbers appear not to total because the underlying calculations are not rounded.
Note that the final number in the schedule ($2,230 million) is the face amount payable at maturity.

Zero-coupon bonds provide us with a convenient opportunity to reinforce a key concept we just learned: that we accrue the interest expense (or revenue) each period at the effective rate regardless of how much cash interest actually is paid (zero in this case). An advantage of issuing zero-coupon bonds or notes is that the corporation can deduct for tax purposes the annual interest expense (see schedule) but has no related cash outflow until the bonds mature. However, the reverse is true for investors in "zeros." Investors receive no periodic cash interest, even though annual interest revenue is reportable for tax purposes. So those who invest in zero-coupon bonds usually have tax-deferred or tax-exempt status, such as pension funds, individual retirement accounts (IRAs), and charitable organizations. Zero-coupon bonds and notes have popularity but still constitute a relatively small proportion of corporate debt.

Bonds Sold at a Premium

In Illustration 14–3, Masterwear Industries sold the bonds at a price that would yield an effective rate higher than the stated rate. The result was a discount. On the other hand, if the 12% bonds had been issued when the market yield for bonds of similar risk and maturity was *lower* than the stated rate, say 10%, the issue would have been priced at a *premium.* Because the 12% rate would seem relatively attractive in a 10% market, the bonds would command an issue price of more than $700,000, calculated in Illustration 14–8.

Interest on bonds issued at a premium is determined in precisely the same manner as on bonds issued at a discount. Again, interest is the effective interest rate applied to the debt

[2]The present value of $2,230M, discounted at 2% for 20 years, is $1,501M.

Illustration 14–8
Bonds Sold at a Premium

On January 1, 2016, Masterwear Industries issued $700,000 of 12% bonds, dated January 1. Interest of $42,000 is payable semiannually on June 30 and December 31. The bonds mature in three years. The market yield for bonds of similar risk and maturity is 10%. The entire bond issue was purchased by United Intergroup, Inc.

Calculation of the Price of the Bonds

	Present Values
Interest	$ 42,000 × 5.07569* = $213,179
Principal	$700,000 × 0.74622† = 522,354
Present value (price) of the bonds	$735,533

*Present value of an ordinary annuity of $1: $n = 6$, $i = 5\%$.
†Present value of $1: $n = 6$, $i = 5\%$.

Because interest is paid *semiannually*, the present value calculations use:

a. one-half the stated rate (6%),
b. one-half the market rate (5%), and
c. 6 (3 × 2) semiannual periods.

Journal Entries at Issuance—Bonds Sold at Premium

Masterwear (Issuer)		
Cash (price calculated above)	735,533	
Bonds payable (face amount)		700,000
Premium on bonds payable (difference)		35,533
United (Investor)		
Investment in bonds (face amount)	700,000	
Premium on bond investment (difference)	35,533	
Cash (price calculated above)		735,533

balance outstanding during each period (balance at the end of the previous interest period), and the cash paid is the stated rate times the face amount, as shown in Illustration 14–9. The difference between the two is the reduction (amortization) of the premium.

Illustration 14–9
Amortization Schedule—Premium

Date	Cash Interest	Effective Interest	Decrease in Balance	Outstanding Balance
	(6% × Face amount)	(5% × Outstanding balance)	(Premium reduction)	
1/1/16				735,533
6/30/16	42,000	.05 (735,533) = 36,777	5,223	730,310
12/31/16	42,000	.05 (730,310) = 36,516	5,484	724,826
6/30/17	42,000	.05 (724,826) = 36,241	5,759	719,067
12/31/17	42,000	.05 (719,067) = 35,953	6,047	713,020
6/30/18	42,000	.05 (713,020) = 35,651	6,349	706,671
12/31/18	42,000	.05 (706,671) = 35,329*	6,671	700,000
	252,000	**216,467**	**35,533**	

*Rounded.

Since *more* cash is paid each period than the effective interest, the debt outstanding is reduced by the overpayment.

Notice that the debt declines each period. As the premium is reduced by amortization, the book value of the bonds declines toward face value. This is because the effective interest each period is less than the cash interest paid. Remember, this is precisely the opposite of when the bonds are at a discount, when the effective interest each period is more than the cash paid. As the discount is reduced by amortization, the book value of the bonds increases toward face value. This is illustrated in Illustration 14–10.

Illustration 14–10

Premium and Discount Amortization Compared

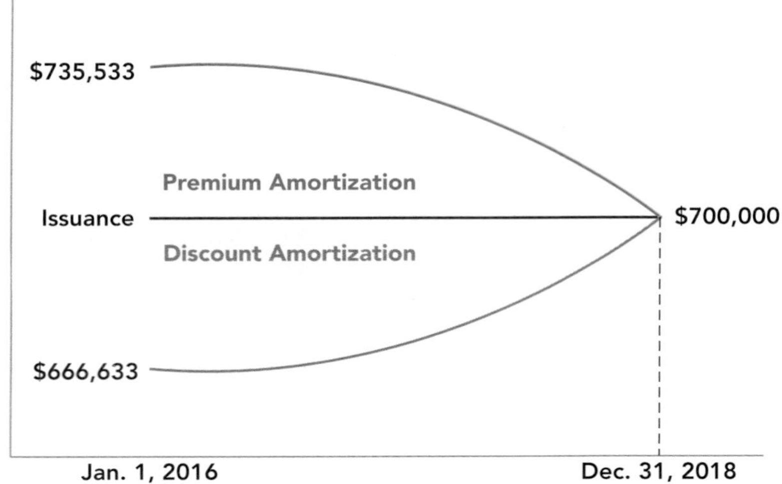

Whether bonds are issued at a premium or a discount, the outstanding balance becomes zero at maturity.

In practice, corporate bonds rarely are issued at a premium.[3] Because of the delay between the date the terms of the bonds are established and when the bonds are issued, it's difficult to set the stated rate equal to the ever-changing market rate. Knowing that, for marketing reasons, companies deliberately set the terms to more likely create a small discount rather than a premium at the issue date. Some investors are psychologically prone to prefer buying at a discount rather than a premium even if the yield is the same (the market rate).

Additional Consideration

The preceding illustrations describe bonds sold at a discount and at a premium. The same concepts apply to bonds sold at face amount. But some of the procedures would be unnecessary. For instance, calculating the present value of the interest and the principal always will give us the face amount when the effective rate and the stated rate are the same:

Calculation of the Price of the Bonds

	Present Values		
Interest	$ 42,000 × 4.91732*	=	$206,528
Principal	$700,000 × 0.70496†	=	493,472
Present value (price) of the bonds			$700,000

*Present value of an ordinary annuity of $1: $n = 6, i = 6\%$.
†Present value of $1: $n = 6, i = 6\%$.

When Financial Statements Are Prepared between Interest Dates

Any interest that has accrued since the last interest date must be recorded by an adjusting entry prior to preparing financial statements.

When an accounting period ends between interest dates, it is necessary to record interest that has accrued since the last interest date. As an example, refer again to Illustration 14–3 on page 793. If the fiscal years of Masterwear and United end on October 31 and interest was last paid and recorded on June 30, four months' interest must be accrued in a year-end adjusting entry. Because interest is recorded for only a portion of a semiannual period, amounts recorded are simply the amounts shown in the amortization schedule (Illustration 14–6, p. 795) times the appropriate fraction of the semiannual period (in this case 4/6).

[3]Only about 1% of corporate bonds are issued at a premium. Amiram, Dan, A. Kalay, and B Ozel, "The Bond Discount Puzzle," *Financial Accounting eJournal*, March 25, 2013.

At October 31		
Masterwear (Issuer)		
Interest expense (4/6 × 46,991)	31,327	
Discount on bonds payable (4/6 × 4,991)		3,327
Interest payable (4/6 × 42,000)		28,000
United (Investor)		
Interest receivable (4/6 × 42,000)	28,000	
Discount on bond investment (4/6 × 4,991)	3,327	
Interest revenue (4/6 × 46,991)		31,327

Adjusting Entries—To Accrue Interest

To avoid understating interest in the financial statements, four months' interest is recorded at the end of the reporting period.

Two months later, when semiannual interest is paid next, the remainder of the interest is allocated to the first two months of the next fiscal year—November and December:

At the December 31 Interest Date		
Masterwear (Issuer)		
Interest expense (2/6 × 46,991)	15,664	
Interest payable (from adjusting entry)	28,000	
Discount on bonds payable (2/6 × 4,991)		1,664
Cash (stated rate × face amount)		42,000
United (Investor)		
Cash (stated rate × face amount)	42,000	
Discount on bond investment (2/6 × 4,991)	1,664	
Interest receivable (from adjusting entry)		28,000
Interest revenue (2/6 × 46,991)		15,664

Of the six months' interest paid December 31, only the November and December interest is expensed in the new fiscal year.

The Straight-Line Method—A Practical Expediency

In some circumstances the profession permits an exception to the conceptually appropriate method of determining interest for bond issues. A company is allowed to determine interest indirectly by allocating a discount or a premium equally to each period over the term to maturity—if doing so produces results that are not materially different from the usual (and preferable) interest method. The decision should be guided by whether the **straight-line method** would tend to mislead investors and creditors in the particular circumstance.

By the straight-line method, the discount in Illustration 14–3 and Illustration 14–6 would be allocated equally to the six semiannual periods (three years):

$33,367 ÷ 6 periods = **$5,561** per period

At Each of the Six Interest Dates		
Masterwear (Issuer)		
Interest expense (to balance)	47,561	
Discount on bonds payable (discount ÷ 6 periods)		5,561
Cash (stated rate × face amount)		42,000
United (Investor)		
Cash (stated rate × face amount)	42,000	
Discount on bond investment (discount ÷ 6 periods)	5,561	
Interest revenue (to balance)		47,561

Journal Entries—Straight-Line Method

By the straight-line method, interest (expense and revenue) is a plug figure, resulting from calculating the amount of discount reduction.

Allocating the discount or premium equally over the life of the bonds by the straight-line method results in a constant dollar amount of interest each period. An amortization schedule, then, would serve little purpose. For example, if we prepared one for the straight-line method in this situation, it would provide the same amounts each period as shown in Illustration 14–11.

Illustration 14–11

Amortization Schedule—Straight-Line Method

By the straight-line method, the amount of the discount to be reduced periodically is calculated, and the recorded interest is the plug figure.

	Cash Interest	Recorded Interest	Increase in Balance	Outstanding Balance
	(6% × Face amount)	(Cash + Discount reduction)	($33,367 ÷ 6)	
1/1/16				666,633
6/30/16	42,000	(42,000 + 5,561) = 47,561	5,561	672,194
12/31/16	42,000	(42,000 + 5,561) = 47,561	5,561	677,755
6/30/17	42,000	(42,000 + 5,561) = 47,561	5,561	683,316
12/31/17	42,000	(42,000 + 5,561) = 47,561	5,561	688,877
6/30/18	42,000	(42,000 + 5,561) = 47,561	5,561	694,438
12/31/18	42,000	(42,000 + 5,561) = 47,561	5,561	700,000*
	252,000	285,366	33,366	

*Rounded.

Determining interest by allocating the discount (or premium) on a straight-line basis is a practical expediency permitted in some situations by the materiality concept.

Remember, constant dollar amounts are not produced when the effective interest method is used. By that method, the dollar amounts of interest vary over the term to maturity because the percentage rate of interest remains constant but is applied to a changing debt balance.

Also, be sure to realize that the straight-line method is not an alternative method of determining interest in a conceptual sense. Instead, it is an application of the materiality concept, by which an appropriate application of GAAP (e.g., the effective interest method) can be bypassed for reasons of practical expediency in situations when doing so has no material effect on the results. Based on the frequency with which the straight-line method is used in practice, we can infer that managers very frequently conclude that its use has no material impact on investors' decisions.

Concept Review Exercise

ISSUING BONDS AND RECORDING INTEREST

On January 1, 2016, the Meade Group issued $8,000,000 of 11% bonds, dated January 1. Interest is payable semiannually on June 30 and December 31. The bonds mature in four years. The market yield for bonds of similar risk and maturity is 10%.

Required:

1. Determine the price these bonds issued to yield the 10% market rate and record their issuance by the Meade Group.
2. Prepare an amortization schedule that determines interest at the effective rate and record interest on the first interest date, June 30, 2016.

Solution:

1. Determine the price these bonds sold for to yield the 10% market rate and record their issuance by the Meade Group.

Calculation of the Price of the Bonds

There are eight semiannual periods and one-half the market rate is 5%.

Interest	$ 440,000 × 6.46321* =	$2,843,812
Principal	$8,000,000 × 0.67684† =	5,414,720
Present value (price) of the bonds		$8,258,532

*Present value of an ordinary annuity of $1: $n = 8$, $i = 5\%$.
†Present value of $1: $n = 8$, $i = 5\%$.

Journal Entries at Issuance

Cash (price calculated above)	8,258,532	
Bonds payable (face amount)		8,000,000
Premium on bonds payable (difference)		258,532

2. Prepare an amortization schedule that determines interest at the effective rate and record interest on the first interest date, June 30, 2016.

Amortization Schedule

Date	Cash Interest	Effective Interest	Decrease in Balance	Outstanding Balance
	(5.5% × Face amount)	(5% × Outstanding balance)	(Premium reduction)	
1/1/16				8,258,532
6/30/16	440,000	.05 (8,258,532) = 412,927	27,073	8,231,459
12/31/16	440,000	.05 (8,231,459) = 411,573	28,427	8,203,032
6/30/17	440,000	.05 (8,203,032) = 410,152	29,848	8,173,184
12/31/17	440,000	.05 (8,173,184) = 408,659	31,341	8,141,843
6/30/18	440,000	.05 (8,141,843) = 407,092	32,908	8,108,935
12/31/18	440,000	.05 (8,108,935) = 405,447	34,553	8,074,382
6/30/19	440.000	.05 (8,074,382) = 403,719	36,281	8,038,101
12/31/19	440,000	.05 (8,038,101) = 401,899*	38,101	8,000,000
	3,520,000	3,261,468	258,532	

*Rounded.

More cash is paid each period than the effective interest, so the debt outstanding is reduced by the "overpayment."

Interest expense (5% × $8,258,532)	412,927	
Premium on bonds payable (difference)	27,073	
Cash (5.5% × $8,000,000)		440,000
To record interest for six months.		

Debt Issue Costs

Rather than sell bonds directly to the public, corporations usually sell an entire issue to an underwriter who then resells them to other security dealers and the public. By committing to purchase bonds at a set price, investment banks such as **JPMorgan Chase** and **Goldman Sachs** are said to underwrite any risks associated with a new issue. The underwriting fee is the spread between the price the underwriter pays and the resale price.

Alternatively, the issuing company may choose to sell the debt securities directly to a single investor (as we assumed in previous illustrations)—often a pension fund or an insurance company. This is referred to as *private placement.* Issue costs are less because privately placed securities are not subject to the costly and lengthy process of registering with the SEC that is required of public offerings. Underwriting fees also are avoided.[4]

With either publicly or privately sold debt, the issuing company will incur costs in connection with issuing bonds or notes, such as legal and accounting fees and printing costs, in addition to registration and underwriting fees. These **debt issue costs** are recorded *separately* and are amortized over the term of the related debt. GAAP requires a debit to an asset account—debt issue costs. The asset is allocated to expense, usually on a straight-line basis.

Costs of issuing debt securities are recorded as a debit to an asset account, "debt issue costs," and amortized to expense over the term to maturity.

For example, let's assume issue costs in Illustration 14–8 had been **$12,000**. The entries for the issuance of the bonds would include a separate asset account for the issue costs:

Cash ($735,533 minus $12,000 issue costs)	723,533	
Debt issue costs	12,000	
Bonds payable (face amount)		700,000
Premium on bonds payable ($735,533 minus face amount)		35,533

The premium (or discount) is unaffected by debt issue costs because they are recorded in a separate account.

[4]Rule 144A of the Securities Act of 1933, as amended, allows for the private resale of unregistered securities to "qualified institutional buyers," which are generally large institutional investors with assets exceeding $100 million.

Semiannual amortization of the asset would be:

Debt issue expense ($12,000 ÷ 6)	2,000	
Debt issue costs		2,000

International Financial Reporting Standards

● LO14–7

Debt Issue costs. Under U.S. GAAP, these costs are recorded separately as an asset. A conceptually more appealing treatment, and the one prescribed by IFRS, is to reduce the recorded amount of the debt by the debt issue costs (called transaction costs under IFRS). The cost of these services reduces the net cash the issuing company receives from the sale of the financial instrument. A lower [net] amount is borrowed at the same cost, increasing the effective interest rate. However, unless the debt is recorded net of the transaction costs, the higher rate is not reflected in a higher recorded interest expense. The actual increase in the effective interest rate is reflected in the interest expense only if the issue cost is allowed to reduce the book value of the debt:

Cash (price minus transaction costs)	723,533	
Bonds payable ($735,533 − 12,000)		723,533*

Also, this approach is consistent with the treatment of issue costs when equity securities are sold. You will see in Chapter 18 that the effect of share issue costs is to reduce the amount credited to stock accounts.

*Notice that the premium is combined with the face amount of the bonds. This is the "net method" that, as we saw earlier, is the preferred method under IFRS.

The corporate bond is the basic long-term debt instrument for most large companies. But for many firms, the debt instrument often used is a *note*. We discuss notes next.

PART B

Long-Term Notes

● LO14–3

FINANCIAL Reporting Case

Q4, p. 789

When a company borrows cash from a bank and signs a promissory note (essentially an IOU), the firm's liability is reported as a *note payable*. Or a note might be issued in exchange for a noncash asset—perhaps to purchase equipment on credit. In concept, notes are accounted for in precisely the same way as bonds. In fact, we could properly substitute notes payable for bonds payable in each of our previous illustrations. For comparison, we continue to also present the lenders' entries (in blue) in the illustrations to follow.

As we discuss accounting for the borrower's notes *payable*, we also will consider the lender's perspective and look at notes *receivable* at the same time. By considering both sides of each transaction at the same time, we will see that the two sides are essentially mirror images of one another. This coverage of long-term notes complements our Chapter 7 discussion of *short-term* notes receivable.

Note Issued for Cash

The interest rate stated in a note is likely to be equal to the market rate because the rate usually is negotiated at the time of the loan. So discounts and premiums are less likely for notes than for bonds. Accounting for a note issued for cash is demonstrated in Illustration 14–12.

Note Exchanged for Assets or Services

Occasionally the *stated* interest rate is not indicative of the *market* rate at the time a note is negotiated. The value of the asset (cash or noncash) or service exchanged for the note establishes the market rate.[5] For example, let's assume Skill Graphics purchased a package-labeling machine from Hughes–Barker Corporation by issuing a 12%, $700,000, three-year note that

[5]If the debt instrument is negotiable and a dependable exchange price is readily available, the market value of the debt may be better evidence of the value of the transaction than the value of a noncash asset, particularly if it has no established cash selling price. The value of the asset or the debt, whichever is considered more reliable, should be used to record the transaction.

Illustration 14–12
Note Issued for Cash

On January 1, 2016, Skill Graphics, Inc., a product-labeling and graphics firm, borrowed $700,000 cash from First BancCorp and issued a three-year, $700,000 promissory note. Interest of $42,000 was payable semiannually on June 30 and December 31.

At Issuance		
Skill Graphics (Borrower)		
Cash	700,000	
Notes payable (face amount)		700,000
First BancCorp (Lender)		
Notes receivable (face amount)	700,000	
Cash		700,000
At Each of the Six Interest Dates		
Skill Graphics (Borrower)		
Interest expense	42,000	
Cash (stated rate × face amount)		42,000
First BancCorp (Lender)		
Cash (stated rate × face amount)	42,000	
Interest revenue		42,000
At Maturity		
Skill Graphics (Borrower)		
Notes payable	700,000	
Cash (face amount)		700,000
First BancCorp (Lender)		
Cash (face amount)	700,000	
Notes receivable		700,000

requires interest to be paid semiannually. Let's also assume that the machine could have been purchased at a cash price of $666,633. You probably recognize this numerical situation as the one used earlier to illustrate bonds sold at a discount (Illustration 14–3). Reference to the earlier example will confirm that exchanging this $700,000 note for a machine with a cash price of $666,633 implies an annual market rate of interest of 14%. That is, 7% is one-half the discount rate that yields a present value of $666,633 for the note's cash flows (interest plus principal):

	Present Values		
Interest	$ 42,000 × 4.76654*	=	$200,195
Principal	$700,000 × 0.66634†	=	466,438
Present value of the note			$666,633

*Present value of an ordinary annuity of $1: $n = 6$, $i = 7\%$.
†Present value of $1: $n = 6$, $i = 7\%$.

This is referred to as the **implicit rate of interest**—the rate implicit in the agreement. It may be that the implicit rate is not apparent. Sometimes the value of the asset (or service) is not readily determinable, but the interest rate stated in the transaction is unrealistic relative to the rate that would be expected in a similar transaction under similar circumstances. Deciding what the appropriate rate should be is called *imputing* an interest rate.

For example, suppose the machine exchanged for the 12% note is custom-made for Skill Graphics so that no customary cash price is available with which to work backwards to find the implicit rate. In that case, the appropriate rate would have to be found externally. It might be determined, for instance, that a more realistic interest rate for a transaction of this type, at this time, would be 14%. Then it would be apparent that Skill Graphics actually paid less than $700,000 for the machine and that part of the face amount of the note in effect makes up for the lower than normal interest rate. You learned early in your study of accounting that the economic essence of a transaction should prevail over its outward appearance. In keeping with this basic precept, the accountant should look beyond the *form* of this transaction and record its *substance*. The amount actually paid for the machine is the present value of the cash flows called for by the loan agreement, discounted at the market rate—imputed in this case to be 14%. So both the asset acquired and the liability used to purchase it should be recorded at the real cost, $666,633.

A basic concept of accounting is *substance over form*.

Additional Consideration

For another example, let's assume the more realistic interest rate for a transaction of this type is, say, 16%. In that case we would calculate the real cost of the machine by finding the present value of both the interest and the principal, discounted at half the 16% rate (because interest is paid semiannually):

	Present Values		
Interest	$ 42,000 × 4.62288*	=	$194,161
Principal	$700,000 × 0.63017†	=	441,119
Present value of the note			$635,280

*Present value of an ordinary annuity of $1: $n = 6$, $i = 8\%$.
†Present value of $1: $n = 6$, $i = 8\%$.

Both the asset acquired and the liability used to purchase it would be recorded at $635,280.

The accounting treatment is the same whether the amount is determined directly from the market value of the machine (and thus the note) or indirectly as the present value of the note (and thus the value of the asset):[6]

Journal Entries at Issuance—Note with Unrealistic Interest Rate

Skill Graphics (Buyer/Issuer)		
Machinery (cash price)	666,633	
Discount on notes payable (difference)	33,367	
Notes payable (face amount)		700,000
Hughes–Barker (Seller/Lender)		
Notes receivable (face amount)	700,000	
Discount on notes receivable (difference)		33,367
Sales revenue (cash price)		666,633

Likewise, whether the effective interest rate is determined as the rate implicit in the agreement, given the asset's market value, or whether the effective rate is imputed as the appropriate interest rate if the asset's value is unknown, both parties to the transaction should record periodic interest (interest expense to the borrower, interest revenue to the lender) at the effective rate, rather than the stated rate.

Journal Entries—The Interest Method

The effective interest (expense to the issuer; revenue to the investor) is calculated each period as the effective rate times the amount of the debt outstanding during the interest period.

At the First Interest Date (June 30)		
Skill Graphics (Borrower)		
Interest expense (effective rate × outstanding balance)	46,664	
Discount on notes payable (difference)		4,664
Cash (stated rate × face amount)		42,000
Hughes–Barker (Seller/Lender)		
Cash (stated rate × face amount)	42,000	
Discount on notes receivable (difference)	4,664	
Interest revenue (effective rate × outstanding balance)		46,664

[6]The method shown is the *gross method.* Alternatively, the *net method* can be used as follows:

Skill Graphics (Buyer/Issuer)		
Machinery (cash price)	666,633	
Notes payable		666,633
Hughes–Barker (Seller/Lender)		
Notes receivable	666,633	
Sales revenue (cash price)		666,633

Under the net method, the note is recorded at the face amount reduced by the discount on notes payable, which is the difference between face value and present value. As cash interest is paid, the note balance increases by the difference between the cash interest payment and the interest revenue (and interest expense). After the last payment, the note account balance will be equal to the face amount of the note.

The interest expense (interest revenue for the lender) varies as the balance of the note changes over time. See the amortization schedule in Illustration 14–13.[7] Be sure to notice that this amortization schedule is identical to the one in Illustration 14–6 for bonds issued at a discount.

Illustration 14–13

Amortization Schedule—Note

Date	Cash Interest	Effective Interest	Increase in Balance	Outstanding Balance
	(6% × Face amount)	(7% × Outstanding balance)	(Discount reduction)	
1/1/16				666,633
6/30/16	42,000	.07 (666,633) = 46,664	4,664	671,297
12/31/16	42,000	.07 (671,297) = 46,991	4,991	676,288
6/30/17	42,000	.07 (676,288) = 47,340	5,340	681,628
12/31/17	42,000	.07 (681,628) = 47,714	5,714	687,342
6/30/18	42,000	.07 (687,342) = 48,114	6,114	693,456
12/31/18	42,000	.07 (693,456) = 48,544*	6,544	700,000
	252,000	285,367	33,367	

*Rounded.

Since less cash is paid each period than the effective interest, the unpaid difference (the discount reduction) increases the outstanding balance (book value) of the note.

Installment Notes

You may have recently purchased a car, or maybe a house. If so, unless you paid cash, you signed a note promising to pay a portion of the purchase price over, say, five years for the car, or 30 years for the house. Car and house notes usually call for payment in monthly installments rather than by a single amount at maturity. Corporations, too, often borrow using installment notes. Typically, installment payments are equal amounts each period. Each payment includes both an amount that represents interest and an amount that represents a reduction of the outstanding balance (principal reduction). The periodic reduction of the balance is sufficient that at maturity the note is completely paid. This amount is easily calculated by dividing the amount of the loan by the appropriate discount factor for the present value of an annuity. The installment payment amount that would pay the note described in the previous section is:

$666,633	÷	4.76654	=	**$139,857**
Amount of loan		(from Table 4 $n = 6, i = 7.0\%$)		Installment payment

Consider Illustration 14–14.

Illustration 14–14

Amortization Schedule—Installment Note

Date	Cash Payment	Effective Interest	Decrease in Debt	Outstanding Balance
		(7% × Outstanding balance)		
1/1/16				666,633
6/30/16	139,857	.07 (666,633) = 46,664	93,193	573,440
12/31/16	139,857	.07 (573,440) = 40,141	99,716	473,724
6/30/17	139,857	.07 (473,724) = 33,161	106,696	367,028
12/31/17	139,857	.07 (367,028) = 25,692	114,165	252,863
6/30/18	139,857	.07 (252,863) = 17,700	122,157	130,706
12/31/18	139,857	.07 (130,706) = 9,151*	130,706	0
	839,142	172,509	666,633	

*Rounded.

Each installment payment includes interest on the outstanding debt at the effective rate. The remainder of each payment reduces the outstanding balance.

[7]The creation of amortization schedules is simplified by an electronic spreadsheet such as Microsoft Excel.

For installment notes, the outstanding balance of the note does not eventually become its face amount as it does for notes with designated maturity amounts. Instead, at the maturity date the balance is zero. The procedure is the same as for a note whose principal is paid at maturity, but the periodic cash payments are larger and there is no lump-sum payment at maturity. We calculated the amount of the payments so that after covering the interest on the existing debt each period, the excess would exactly amortize the debt to zero at maturity (rather than to a designated maturity amount).

Consequently, the significance is lost of maintaining separate balances for the face amount (in a note account) and the discount (or premium). So an installment note typically is recorded at its net book value in a single note payable (or receivable) account:

Journal Entries at Issuance—Installment Note

Skill Graphics (Buyer/Issuer)		
Machinery	666,633	
Note payable		666,633
Hughes–Barker (Seller/Lender)		
Note receivable	666,633	
Sales revenue		666,633

Each payment includes both an amount that represents interest and an amount that represents a reduction of principal.

At the First Interest Date (June 30)		
Skill Graphics (Borrower)		
Interest expense (effective rate × outstanding balance)	46,664	
Notes payable (difference)	93,193	
Cash (installment payment calculated above)		139,857
Hughes–Barker (Seller/Lender)		
Cash (installment payment calculated above)	139,857	
Notes receivable (difference)		93,193
Interest revenue (effective rate × outstanding balance)		46,664

Additional Consideration

You will learn in the next chapter that the liability associated with a lease is accounted for the same way as this installment note. In fact, if the asset described above had been leased rather than purchased, the cash payments would be designated lease payments rather than installment loan payments, and a virtually identical amortization schedule would apply.

The reason for the similarity is that we view a lease as being, in substance, equivalent to an installment purchase of the right to use an asset. Naturally, then, accounting treatment of the two essentially identical transactions should be consistent. Be sure to notice the parallel treatment as you study leases in the next chapter.

Financial Statement Disclosures

● LO14–4

In the balance sheet, long-term debt (liability for the debtor; asset for the creditor) typically is reported as a single amount, net of any discount or increased by any premium, rather than at its face amount accompanied by a separate valuation account for the discount or premium. Any portion of the debt to be paid (received) during the upcoming year, or operating cycle if longer, should be reported as a current amount.

Note disclosure is required of the fair value of bonds, notes, and other financial instruments.

The fair value of financial instruments must be disclosed either in the body of the financial statements or in disclosure notes.[8] These fair values are available for bonds and other securities traded on market exchanges in the form of quoted market prices. On the other hand, financial instruments not traded on market exchanges require other evidence of

[8]FASB ASC 825–10–50–10: Financial Instruments–Overall–Disclosure (previously "Disclosures About Fair Values of Financial Instruments," *Statement of Financial Accounting Standards No. 107* (Norwalk, Conn.: FASB, 1991)).

market value. For example, the market value of a note payable might be approximated by the present value of principal and interest payments using a current discount rate commensurate with the risks involved.

The disclosure note for debt includes the nature of the company's liabilities, interest rates, maturity dates, call provisions, conversion options, restrictions imposed by creditors, and any assets pledged as collateral. For all long-term borrowings, disclosures also should include the aggregate amounts payable for each of the next five years. To comply, Microsoft's annual report for the fiscal year ended June 30, 2013, included the disclosure shown in Illustration 14–15:

Illustration 14–15

Debt Disclosures—Microsoft Corporation

Real World Financials

Maturities of our long-term debt for each of the next five years and thereafter are as follows:

(In millions) Year Ending June 30,	
2014	$ 3,000
2015	0
2016	2,500
2017	0
2018	1,050
Thereafter	9,115
Total	$15,665

Borrowing is a financing activity; lending is an investing activity.

Paying or receiving interest is an operating activity.

In a statement of cash flows, issuing bonds or notes are reported as cash flows from financing activities by the issuer (borrower) and cash flows from investing activities by the investor (lender). Similarly, as the debt is repaid, the issuer (borrower) reports a financing activity while the investor (lender) reports an investing activity. However, because both interest expense and interest revenue are components of the income statement, both parties to the transaction report interest among operating activities. We discuss the cash flow reporting process in more depth in Chapter 21.

Decision Makers' Perspective

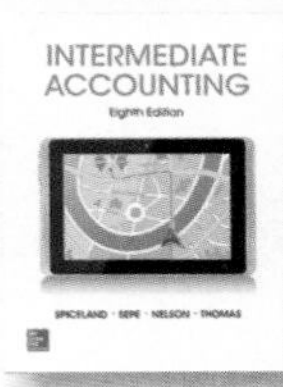

Business decisions involve risk. Failure to properly consider risk in those decisions is one of the most costly, yet one of the most common mistakes investors and creditors can make. Long-term debt is one of the first places decision makers should look when trying to get a handle on risk.

In general, debt increases risk. As an owner, debt would place you in a subordinate position relative to creditors because the claims of creditors must be satisfied first in case of liquidation. In addition, debt requires payment, usually on specific dates. Failure to pay debt interest and principal on a timely basis may result in default and perhaps even bankruptcy. The debt to equity ratio, total liabilities divided by shareholders' equity, often is calculated to measure the degree of risk. Other things being equal, the higher the debt to equity ratio, the higher the risk. The type of risk this ratio measures is called *default risk* because it presumably indicates the likelihood a company will default on its obligations.

Generally speaking, debt increases risk.

To evaluate a firm's risk, you might start by calculating its debt to equity ratio.

Debt also can be an advantage. It can be used to enhance the return to shareholders. This concept, known as leverage, was described and illustrated in Chapter 3. If a company earns a return on borrowed funds in excess of the cost of borrowing the funds, shareholders are provided with a total return greater than what could have been earned with equity funds alone. This desirable situation is called *favorable financial leverage.* Unfortunately, leverage is not always favorable. Sometimes the cost of borrowing the funds exceeds the returns they generate. This illustrates the typical risk-return trade-off faced by shareholders.

As a manager, you would try to create favorable financial leverage to earn a return on borrowed funds in excess of the cost of borrowing the funds.

Creditors demand interest payments as compensation for the use of their capital. Failure to pay interest as scheduled may cause several adverse consequences, including bankruptcy.

As an external analyst or a manager, you are concerned with a company's ability to repay debt.

Therefore, another way to measure a company's ability to pay its obligations is by comparing interest payments with income available to pay those charges. The times interest earned ratio does this by dividing income, before subtracting interest expense or income tax expense, by interest expense.

Two points about this ratio are important. First, because interest is deductible for income tax purposes, income before interest and taxes is a better indication of a company's ability to pay interest than is income after interest and taxes (i.e., net income). Second, income before interest and taxes is a rough approximation for cash flow generated from operations. The primary concern of decision makers is, of course, the cash available to make interest payments. In fact, this ratio often is computed by dividing cash flow generated from operations by interest payments.

For illustration, let's compare the ratios for **Coca-Cola** and **PepsiCo**. Illustration 14–16 provides condensed financial statements adapted from 2013 midyear reports of those companies.

The debt to equity ratio indicates the extent of trading on the equity, or financial leverage.

The debt to equity ratio is much higher for PepsiCo:

$$\text{Debt to equity ratio} = \frac{\text{Total liabilities}}{\text{Shareholders' equity}}$$

$$\text{Coca-Cola} = \frac{\$56,880}{\$32,631} = 1.74$$

$$\text{PepsiCo} = \frac{\$53,888}{\$22,765} = 2.37$$

Illustration 14–16

Condensed Financial Statements—Coca-Cola, PepsiCo

Real World Financials

Balance Sheets

	($ in millions)	
	Coca-Cola	**PepsiCo**
Assets		
Current assets	$32,572	$21,963
Property, plant, and equipment (net)	14,549	18,390
Intangibles and other assets	42,390	36,300
Total assets	$89,511	$76,653
Liabilities and Shareholders' Equity		
Current liabilities	$32,469	$19,162
Long-term liabilities	24,411	34,726
Total liabilities	$56,880	$53,888
Shareholders' equity	32,631	22,765
Total liabilities and shareholders' equity	$89,511	$76,653
Income Statements		
Net sales	$23,784	$29,388
Cost of goods sold	(9,313)	(13,732)
Gross profit	$14,471	$15,656
Operating and other expenses	(8,378)	(11,129)
Interest expense	(224)	(377)
Income before taxes	$ 5,869	$ 4,150
Tax expense	(1,406)	(1,040)
Net income	$ 4,463	$ 3,110

Remember, that's not necessarily a positive or a negative. Let's look closer. When the return on shareholders' equity is greater than the return on assets, management is using debt funds to enhance the earnings for shareholders. Both firms do this. We calculate return on assets for the first half of 2013 as follows:

$$\text{Rate of return on assets}^{9} = \frac{\text{Net income}}{\text{Total assets}}$$

$$\text{Coca-Cola} = \frac{\$4{,}463}{\$89{,}511} = 5.0\%$$

$$\text{PepsiCo} = \frac{\$3{,}110}{\$76{,}653} = 4.1\%$$

The rate of return on assets indicates profitability without regard to how resources are financed.

The return on assets indicates a company's overall profitability, ignoring specific sources of financing. In this regard, PepsiCo's profitability is slightly less than Coca-Cola's. That advantage, though, disappears when we compare the return to shareholders:

$$\frac{\text{Rate of return on}}{\text{shareholders' equity}} = \frac{\text{Net income}}{\text{Shareholders' equity}}$$

$$\text{Coca-Cola} = \frac{\$4{,}463}{\$32{,}631} = 13.7\%$$

$$\text{PepsiCo} = \frac{\$3{,}110}{\$22{,}765} = 13.7\%$$

The rate of return on shareholders' equity indicates the effectiveness of employing resources provided by owners.

Coca-Cola's return on assets is 22% higher than PepsiCo's, but its return on shareholders' equity is the same. The reason is that higher leverage has been used by Pepsi to provide a relatively greater return to shareholders. PepsiCo increased its return to shareholders 3.34 times (13.7%/4.1%) the return on assets. Coca-Cola increased its return to shareholders 2.74 times (13.7%/5.0%) the return on assets. Interpret this with caution, though. First, the difference is small. Second, PepsiCo's higher leverage means higher risk as well. In down times, PepsiCo's return to shareholders will suffer proportionally more than will Coca-Cola's.

From the perspective of a creditor, we might look at which company offers the most comfortable margin of safety in terms of its ability to pay fixed interest charges:

$$\text{Times interest earned ratio} = \frac{\text{Net income plus interest plus taxes}}{\text{Interest}}$$

$$\text{Coca-Cola} = \frac{\$4{,}463 + 224 + 1{,}406}{\$224} = 27.2 \text{ times}$$

$$\text{PepsiCo} = \frac{\$3{,}110 + 377 + 1{,}040}{\$377} = 12 \text{ times}$$

The times interest earned ratio indicates the margin of safety provided to creditors.

In this regard, Coca-Cola provides a greater margin of safety. And, Pepsi has more debt in its capital structure relative to Coca-Cola. However, Pepsi clearly is able to pay the cost of borrowing and provide an impressive return to its shareholders. Both firms, though, trade quite favorably on their leverage.

Liabilities also can have misleading effects on the income statement. Decision makers should look carefully at gains and losses produced by early extinguishment of debt. These have nothing to do with a company's normal operating activities. Unchecked, corporate management can be tempted to schedule debt buybacks to provide discretionary income in down years or even losses in up years to smooth income over time.

Decision makers should be alert to gains and losses that have nothing to do with a company's normal operating activities.

---

[9]A more accurate way to calculate this ratio is:

$$\text{Rate of return on assets} = \frac{\text{Net income} + \text{Interest expense } (1 - \text{tax rate})}{\text{Average total assets}}$$

The reason for adding back interest expense (net of tax) is that interest represents a return to suppliers of debt capital and should not be deducted in the computation of net income when computing the return on total assets. In other words, the numerator is the total amount of income available to both debt and equity capital.

Outside analysts as well as managers should actively monitor risk management activities.

Alert investors and lenders also look outside the financial statements for risks associated with "off-balance-sheet" financing and other commitments that don't show up on the face of financial statements but nevertheless expose a company to risk. Relatedly, most companies attempt to actively manage the risk associated with these and other obligations. It is important for top management to understand and closely monitor risk management strategies. Some of the financial losses that have grabbed headlines in recent years were permitted by a lack of oversight and scrutiny by senior management of companies involved. It is similarly important for investors and creditors to become informed about risks companies face and how well-equipped those companies are in managing that risk. The supplemental disclosures designed to communicate the degree of risk associated with the financial instruments we discuss in this chapter contribute to that understanding. We examine the significance of lease commitments in the next chapter. ●

Concept Review Exercise

NOTE WITH AN UNREALISTIC INTEREST RATE

Cameron-Brown, Inc., constructed for Harmon Distributors a warehouse that was completed and ready for occupancy on January 2, 2016. Harmon paid for the warehouse by issuing a $900,000, four-year note that required 7% interest to be paid on December 31 of each year. The warehouse was custom-built for Harmon, so its cash price was not known. By comparison with similar transactions, it was determined that an appropriate interest rate was 10%.

Required:

1. Prepare the journal entry for Harmon's purchase of the warehouse on January 2, 2016.
2. Prepare (a) an amortization schedule for the four-year term of the note and (b) the journal entry for Harmon's first interest payment on December 31, 2016.
3. Suppose Harmon's note had been an installment note to be paid in four equal payments. What would be the amount of each installment if payable (a) at the end of each year, beginning December 31, 2016? or (b) at the beginning of each year, beginning on January 2, 2016?

Solution:

1. Prepare the journal entry for Harmon's purchase of the warehouse on January 2, 2016.

	Present Values
Interest	$ 63,000 × 3.16987* = $199,702
Principal	$900,000 × 0.68301† = 614,709
Present value of the note	$814,411

*Present value of an ordinary annuity of $1: $n = 4$, $i = 10\%$.
†Present value of $1: $n = 4$, $i = 10\%$.

Warehouse (price determined above)	814,411	
Discount on notes payable (difference)	85,589	
Notes payable (face amount)		900,000

2. Prepare (a) an amortization schedule for the four-year term of the note and (b) the journal entry for Harmon's first interest payment on December 31, 2016.

Each period the unpaid interest increases the outstanding balance of the debt.

a.

Dec. 31	Cash	Effective Interest	Increase in Balance	Outstanding Balance
	(7% × Face amount)	(10% × Outstanding balance)	(Discount reduction)	
				814,411
2016	63,000	.10 (814,411) = 81,441	18,441	832,852

(continued)

(concluded)

2017	63,000	.10 (832,852) = 83,285	20,285	853,137
2018	63,000	.10 (853,137) = 85,314	22,314	875,451
2019	63,000	.10 (875,451) = 87,549*	24,549	900,000
	252,000	337,589	85,589	

*Rounded.

b.

Interest expense (effective rate × outstanding balance)	81,441	
Discount on notes payable (difference)		18,441
Cash (stated rate × face amount)		63,000

The effective interest is the market rate times the amount of the debt outstanding during the year.

3. Suppose Harmon's note had been an installment note to be paid in four equal payments. What would be the amount of each installment if payable (a) at the end of each year, beginning December 31, 2016? or (b) at the beginning of each year, beginning on January 2, 2016?

a.	$814,411	÷	3.16987	=	$256,923
	Amount of loan		(from Table 4 $n = 4, i = 10\%$)		Installment payment
b.	$814,411	÷	3.48685	=	$233,566
	Amount of loan		(from Table 6 $n = 4, i = 10\%$)		Installment payment

Because money has a time value, installment payments delayed until the end of each period must be higher than if the payments are made at the beginning of each period.

Debt Retired Early, Convertible Into Stock, or Providing an Option to Buy Stock

PART C

Early Extinguishment of Debt

● LO14–5

As we saw in the previous section, debt paid in installments is systematically retired over the term to maturity so that at the designated maturity date the outstanding balance is zero. On the other hand, when a maturity amount is specified as in our earlier illustrations, any discount or premium has been systematically reduced to zero as of the maturity date and the debt is retired simply by paying the maturity amount. Sometimes, though, companies choose to retire debt before its scheduled maturity. In that case, a gain or a loss may result.

Earlier we noted that a call feature accompanies most bonds to protect the issuer against declining interest rates. Even when bonds are not callable, the issuing company can retire bonds early by purchasing them on the open market. Regardless of the method, when debt of any type is retired prior to its scheduled maturity date, the transaction is referred to as **early extinguishment of debt**.

To record the extinguishment, the account balances pertinent to the debt obviously must be removed from the books. Of course cash is credited for the amount paid—the call price or market price. The difference between the book value of the debt and the reacquisition price represents either a gain or a loss on the early extinguishment of debt. When the debt is retired for less than book value, the debtor is in a favorable position and records a gain. The opposite occurs for a loss. Let's continue an earlier example to illustrate the retirement of debt prior to its scheduled maturity (Illustration 14–17).

Any difference between the outstanding debt and the amount paid to retire that debt represents either a gain or a loss.

For instance, in its 2013 income statement, **Lakeland Bancorp, Inc.**, reported a $1.2 million gain on the early extinguishment of debt.

Illustration 14–17
Early Extinguishment of Debt

On January 1, 2017, Masterwear Industries called its $700,000, 12% bonds when their book value was $676,288. The indenture specified a call price of $685,000. The bonds were issued previously at a price to yield 14%.

Bonds payable (face amount)	700,000	
Loss on early extinguishment ($685,000 − 676,288)	8,712	
Discount on bonds payable ($700,000 − 676,288)		23,712
Cash (call price)		685,000

Convertible Bonds

FINANCIAL Reporting Case

Q5, p. 789

Convertible bonds can be exchanged for shares of stock at the option of the investor.

Sometimes corporations include a convertible feature as part of a bond offering. **Convertible bonds** can be converted into (that is, exchanged for) shares of stock at the option of the bondholder. Among the reasons for issuing convertible bonds rather than straight debt are (a) to sell the bonds at a higher price (which means a lower effective interest cost),[10] (b) to use as a medium of exchange in mergers and acquisitions, and (c) to enable smaller firms or debt-heavy companies to obtain access to the bond market. Sometimes convertible bonds serve as an indirect way to issue stock when there is shareholder resistance to direct issuance of additional equity.

Convertible bonds have features of both debt and equity.

Central to each of these reasons for issuing convertible debt is that the conversion feature is attractive to investors. This hybrid security has features of both debt and equity. The owner has a fixed-income security that can become common stock if and when the firm's prosperity makes that feasible. This increases the investor's upside potential while limiting the downside risk. The conversion feature has monetary value. Just how valuable it is depends on both the conversion terms and market conditions. But from an accounting perspective the question raised is how to account for its value. To evaluate the question, consider Illustration 14–18.

Illustration 14–18
Convertible Bonds

On January 1, 2016, HTL Manufacturers issued $100 million of 8% convertible debentures due 2036 at 103 (103% of face value). The bonds are convertible at the option of the holder into no par common stock at a conversion ratio of 40 shares per $1,000 bond. HTL recently issued nonconvertible, 20-year, 8% debentures at 98.

Because of the inseparability of their debt and equity features, the entire issue price of convertible bonds is recorded as debt, as if they are nonconvertible bonds.

It would appear that the conversion feature is valued by the market at $5 million—the difference between the market value of the convertible bonds, $103 million, and the market value of the nonconvertible bonds, $98 million. Some accountants argue that we should record the value of the conversion option in a shareholders' equity account ($5 million in this case) and the debt value in the bond accounts ($100 million bonds payable less $2 million discount). However, counter to that intuitive argument, the currently accepted practice is to record the entire issue price as debt in precisely the same way as for nonconvertible bonds.[11] Treating the features as two inseparable parts of a single security avoids the practical difficulty of trying to measure the separate values of the debt and the conversion option.

Journal Entry at Issuance—Convertible Bonds

	($ in millions)	
Cash (103% × $100 million)	103	
Convertible bonds payable (face amount)		100
Premium on bonds payable (difference)		3

[10]Remember, there is an inverse relationship between bond prices and interest rates. When the price is higher, the rate (yield) is lower, and vice versa.

[11]FASB ASC 470–20–25: Debt–Debt with Conversion Options–Recognition (previously "Accounting for Convertible Debt and Debt Issued with Stock Purchase Warrants," *Accounting Principles Board Opinion No. 14* (New York: APB, 1969)).

Since we make no provision for the separate value of the conversion option, all subsequent entries, including the periodic reduction of the premium, are exactly the same as if these were nonconvertible bonds. So the illustrations and examples of bond accounting we discussed earlier would pertain equally to nonconvertible or convertible bonds.

The value of the conversion feature is not separately recorded.

Additional Consideration

While we normally don't separate the conversion option from the debt for convertible bonds, an exception is when the conversion option is deemed to be a "beneficial conversion feature." That's the case when the conversion option has a positive "intrinsic value" at the time the bonds are issued, meaning the fair value of the stock into which the bonds are convertible exceeds the face amount of the bonds.[12] Suppose, for instance, that HTL's stock in Illustration 14–18 has a fair value of $30 per share when the bonds are issued. This implies an intrinsic value of the conversion feature of $5 per share:

Price per share to convert: $1,000 ÷ 40 shares = $25 per share

Fair value of stock at issue date	$30
Conversion price for shares	25
Intrinsic value of beneficial conversion option per share	$ 5

Intrinsic value of beneficial conversion feature:

100,000 bonds × 40 shares = 4,000,000 shares × $5 per share = **$20,000,000**

The intrinsic value of the conversion option is recorded separately:

	($ in millions)	
Cash (103% × $100 million)	103	
Discount on bonds (to balance)	17	
Convertible bonds payable (face amount)		100
Equity—conversion option (intrinsic value)		20

Where We're Headed

● LO14–7

Accounting for convertible debt is likely to change. In fact, the FASB and IASB are working on a joint project on "Financial Instruments with Characteristics of Equity."[13] A pre-Codification FASB Staff Position gives us another hint, perhaps, of the direction the project might take. For a limited subset of convertible securities not within the scope of current GAAP—those that could possibly be settled in cash rather than shares—companies must divide the proceeds from convertible securities into its two components and record the fair value of the debt as a liability and the conversion option in an equity account. Lending credence to that projection is the fact that international standards already require that convertible debt be divided into its liability and equity elements, so moving in that direction would be a step closer to convergence of U.S. GAAP and IFRS.

[12]FASB ASC 470–20–25–5: Debt–Debt with Conversion and Other Options–Recognition–Beneficial Conversion Features (previously "Accounting for Convertible Securities with Beneficial Conversion Features or Contingently Adjustable Conversion Ratios," *EITF Issue No. 98-5* (Norwalk, Conn.: FASB, 1998)).

[13]The Boards are developing a classification model that includes consideration of which financial instruments might be divided into separate components of liabilities and equity. In its tentative decisions reached to date as of this writing, the Boards had decided that "A bond (or other debt instrument) should be separated into a liability component and an equity component if it is convertible at the option of the holder into a specified number of instruments that will be equity in their entirety when issued."

International Financial Reporting Standards

Convertible bonds. Under IFRS, unlike U.S. GAAP, convertible debt is divided into its liability and equity elements. In Illustration 14–18, if HTL prepared its financial statements in accordance with IFRS, it would record the convertible bonds as follows:

Journal Entry at Issuance—Convertible Bonds

	($ in millions)	
Cash (103% × $100 million)	103	
Convertible bonds payable (value of the debt only)		98*
Equity—conversion option (to balance)		5

*Notice that the discount is combined with the face amount of the bonds. This is the "net method" that we saw earlier and is the preferred method under IFRS.

The components of compound financial instruments such as convertible bonds are valued and reported separately under IFRS.

In essence, HTL is selling two securities—(1) bonds and (2) an option to convert to stock—for one package price. The bonds represent a liability; the option is shareholders' equity. Compound instruments such as this one are separated into their liability and equity components in accordance with *IAS No. 32*.[14] Because the bonds have a separate fair value of $98 million, we record that amount as the liability and the remaining $5 million (the difference between the fair value of the convertible bonds, $103 million, and the $98 million) as equity. If the fair value of the bonds cannot be determined from an active trading market, that value can be calculated as the present value of the bonds' cash flows, using the market rate of interest.

When the Conversion Option Is Exercised

If and when the bondholder exercises his or her option to convert the bonds into shares of stock, the bonds are removed from the accounting records and the new shares issued are recorded at the same amount (in other words, at the book value of the bonds). To illustrate, assume that half the convertible bonds issued by HTL Manufacturers are converted at a time when the remaining unamortized premium is $2 million:

Journal Entry at Conversion

The 2 million shares issued are recorded at the $51 million book value of the bonds retired.

	($ in millions)	
Convertible bonds payable (½ the account balance)	50	
Premium on bonds payable (½ the account balance)	1	
Common stock (to balance)		51

Additional Consideration

The method just described is referred to as the *book value method*, since the new shares are recorded at the book value of the redeemed bonds. It is by far the most popular method in practice. Another acceptable approach, the *market value method*, records the new shares at the market value of the shares themselves or of the bonds, whichever is more determinable. Because the market value most likely will differ from the book value of the bonds, a gain or loss on conversion will result. Assume for illustration that the market value of HTL's stock is $30 per share at the time of the conversion:

	($ in millions)	
Convertible bonds payable (½ the account balance)	50	
Premium on bonds payable (½ the account balance)	1	
Loss on conversion of bonds (to balance)	9	
Common stock [(50,000 bonds × 40 shares) × $30]		60

[14] "Financial Statements: Presentation," *International Accounting Standard (IAS) No. 32* (IASCF) as amended effective January 1, 2014.

If the 50,000 convertible bonds were held by a single investor, that company would record the conversion as follows:

	($ in millions)	
Investment in common stock	51	
Investment in convertible bonds (account balance)		50
Premium on bond investment (account balance)		1

Induced Conversion

Investors often are reluctant to convert bonds to stock, even when share prices have risen significantly since the convertible bonds were purchased. This is because the market price of the convertible bonds will rise along with market prices of the stock. So companies sometimes try to induce conversion. The motivation might be to reduce debt and become a better risk to potential lenders or achieve a lower debt-to-equity ratio.

One way is through the call provision. As we noted earlier, most corporate bonds are callable by the issuing corporation. When the specified call price is less than the conversion value of the bonds (the market value of the shares), calling the convertible bonds provides bondholders with incentive to convert. Bondholders will choose the shares rather than the lower call price.

Occasionally, corporations may try to encourage voluntary conversion by offering an added inducement in the form of cash, stock warrants, or a more attractive conversion ratio. When additional consideration is provided to induce conversion, the fair value of that consideration is considered an expense incurred to bring about the conversion.[15]

Any additional consideration provided to induce conversion of convertible debt is recorded as an expense of the period.

Bonds with Detachable Warrants

Another (less common) way to sweeten a bond issue is to include **detachable stock purchase warrants** as part of the security issue. A stock warrant gives the investor an option to purchase a stated number of shares of common stock at a specified *option price,* often within a given period of time. Like a conversion feature, warrants usually mean a lower interest rate and often enable a company to issue debt when borrowing would not be feasible otherwise.

However, unlike the conversion feature for convertible bonds, warrants can be separated from the bonds. This means they can be exercised independently or traded in the market separately from bonds, having their own market price. In essence, two different securities—the bonds and the warrants—are sold as a package for a single issue price. Accordingly, the issue price is allocated between the two different securities on the basis of their fair values. If the independent market value of only one of the two securities is reliably determinable, that value establishes the allocation. This is demonstrated in Illustration 14–19.

Illustration 14–19

Bonds with Detachable Warrants

On January 1, 2016, HTL Manufacturers issued $100 million of 8% debentures due 2020 at 103 (103% of face value). Accompanying each $1,000 bond were 20 warrants. Each warrant permitted the holder to buy one share of no par common stock at $25 per share. Shortly after issuance, the warrants were listed on the stock exchange at $3 per warrant.

	($ in millions)	
Cash (103% × $100 million)	103	
Discount on bonds payable (difference)	3	
Bonds payable (face amount)		100
Equity—stock warrants* (100,000 bonds × 20 warrants × $3)		6

*Reported as part of shareholders' equity rather than as a liability.

The issue price of bonds with detachable warrants is allocated between the two different securities on the basis of their fair values.

[15]FASB ASC 470–20–40: Debt–Debt with Conversion Options–Derecognition (previously "Induced Conversions of Convertible Debt," *Statement of Financial Accounting Standards No. 84* (Stamford, Conn.: FASB, 1985)).

Additional Consideration

Market imperfections may cause the separate market values not to sum to the issue price of the package. In this event, allocation is achieved on the basis of the relative market values of the two securities. Let's say the bonds have a separate market price of $940 per bond (priced at 94):

Market Values	Dollars ($ in millions)	Percent
Bonds (100,000 bonds × $940)	$ 94	94%
Warrants (100,000 bonds × 20 warrants × $3)	6	6
Total	$100	100%

Proportion of Issue Price Allocated to Bonds:
$103 million × 94% = $96,820,000

Proportion of Issue Price Allocated to Warrants:
$103 million × 6% = $6,180,000

	($ in millions)	
Cash (103% × $100 million)	103.00	
Discount on bonds payable ($100 million − $96.82 million)	3.18	
Bonds payable (face amount)		100.00
Equity—stock warrants ($103 million × 6% = $6,180,000)		6.18

Notice that this is the same approach we used in Chapter 10 to allocate a single purchase price to two or more assets bought for that single price. We also will allocate the total selling price of two equity securities sold for a single issue in proportion to their relative market values in Chapter 18.

If one-half of the warrants (1 million) in Illustration 14–19 are exercised when the market value of HTL's common stock is $30 per share, 1 million shares would be issued for one warrant each plus the exercise price of $25 per share.

Journal Entry at Exercise of Detachable Warrants

	($ in millions)	
Cash (1,000,000 warrants × $25)	25	
Equity—stock warrants (1,000,000 warrants × $3)	3	
Common stock (to balance)		28

The $30 market value at the date of exercise is not used in valuing the additional shares issued. The new shares are recorded at the total of the previously measured values of both the warrants and the shares.

Concept Review Exercise

ISSUANCE AND EARLY EXTINGUISHMENT OF DEBT

The disclosure notes to the 2016 financial statements of Olswanger Industries included the following:

Note 12: Bonds

On September 15, 2015, the Corporation sold bonds with an aggregate principal amount of $500,000,000 bearing a 14% interest rate. The bonds will mature on September 15, 2025, and are unsecured subordinated obligations of the Corporation. Interest is payable semiannually on March 15 and September 15. The Corporation may redeem the bonds at any time beginning September 15, 2015, as a whole or from time to time in part, through maturity, at specified redemption prices ranging from 112% of principal in declining percentages of principal amount through 2022 when the percentage is set at 100% of principal amount. The cost of issuing the bonds, totaling $11,000,000, and the discount of $5,000,000 are being amortized over the life of the bonds, using the straight-line method and the interest method, respectively. Amortization of these items for the year ended December 31, 2016, was $960,000 and $252,000, respectively.

During the year ended December 31, 2016, the Corporation repurchased, in open market transactions, $200,000,000 in face amount of the bonds for $219,333,000. The unamortized cost of issuing these bonds and the unamortized discount, $3,972,000 and $1,892,000, respectively, have been deducted in the current period.

From the information provided by Olswanger in Note 12, you should be able to recreate some of the journal entries the company recorded in connection with this bond issue.

Required:

1. Prepare the journal entry for the issuance of these bonds on September 15, 2015.
2. Prepare the journal entry for the repurchase of these bonds, assuming the date of repurchase was September 15, 2016. The cash paid to repurchase the bonds was $219,333,000.

Solution:

1. Prepare the journal entry for the issuance of these bonds on September 15, 2015.

	($ in 000s)	
Cash (to balance)	484,000	
Bond issue costs (given in note)	11,000	
Discount on bonds payable (given in note)	5,000	
Bonds payable (face amount—given in note)		500,000

2. Prepare the journal entry for the repurchase of these bonds, assuming the date of repurchase was September 15, 2016.

	($ in 000s)	
Bonds payable (face amount repurchased)	200,000	
Loss on early extinguishment (to balance)	25,197	
Discount on bonds payable (given in note)		1,892
Bond issue costs (given in note)		3,972
Cash (given in requirement 2)		219,333

Option to Report Liabilities at Fair Value

PART D

Companies are not required to, but have the option to, value some or all of their financial assets and liabilities at fair value.[16] In Chapter 12, we saw examples of the option applied to financial assets—specifically, companies reporting their investments in securities at fair value. Now, we see how liabilities, too, can be reported at fair value.

● LO14–6

A company has the option to value financial assets and liabilities at fair value.

How does a liability's fair value change? Remember that there are two sides to every investment. For example, if a company has an investment in General Motors' bonds, that investment is an asset to the investor, and the same bonds are a liability to GM. So, the same market forces that influence the fair value of an investment in debt securities (interest rates, credit risk, etc.) influence the fair value of liabilities. For bank loans or other debts that aren't traded on a market exchange, the mix of factors will differ, but in any case, changes in the current market rate of interest often are a major contributor to changes in fair value.

[16]FASB ASC 825–10–25–1: Financial Instruments–Overall–Recognition–Fair Value Option (previously "The Fair Value Option for Financial Assets and Financial Liabilities," *Statement of Financial Accounting Standards No. 159* (Norwalk, Conn.: FASB, 2007)).

Determining Fair Value

Changes in interest rates cause changes in the fair value of liabilities.

For demonstration, we revisit the Masterwear Industries bonds that sold at a discount in Illustration 14–3 on page 795. Now, suppose it's six months later, the market rate of interest has fallen to 11%, and June 30 is the end of Masterwear's fiscal year. A decline in market interest rates means bond prices rise. Let's say that checking market prices in *The Wall Street Journal* indicates that the fair value of the Masterwear bonds on June 30, 2016, is **$714,943**. Referring to the amortization schedule on page 797, we see that on the same date, with 5 periods remaining to maturity, the present value of the bonds—their price—would have been $671,297 if the market rate still had been 14% (7% semiannually).

Additional Consideration

If the bonds are not traded on an open-market exchange, their fair value would not be readily observable. In that case, the next most preferable way to determine fair value would be to calculate the fair value as the present value of the remaining cash flows discounted at the current interest rate. If the rate is 11% (5.5% semiannually),[17] as we're assuming now, that present value would be $714,943:

	Present Values	
Interest	$ 42,000 × 4.27028* =	$179,352
Principal	$700,000 × 0.76513† =	535,591
Present value of the bonds		$714,943

*Present value of an ordinary annuity of $1: $n = 5$, $i = 5.5\%$.
†Present value of $1: $n = 5$, $i = 5.5\%$

When the bonds were issued, Masterwear had a choice—report this liability (a) at its amortized initial measurement throughout the term to maturity or (b) at its current fair value on each reporting date. Had the company not elected the fair value option, on June 30 it would report the $671,297 we calculated earlier for the amortization schedule. On the other hand, if Masterwear had elected the fair value option, it would report the bonds at their current fair value, **$714,943**.

Reporting Changes in Fair Value

Electing the FVO means reporting unrealized holding gains and losses in OCI to the extent the change is due to credit risk.

If a company chooses the option to report at fair value, a change in fair value will create a gain or loss. Any portion of that gain or loss that is a result of a change in the "credit risk" of the debt, rather than a change in general interest rates, is reported, not as part of net income, but instead as other comprehensive income (OCI).[18] Credit risk is the risk that the investor in the bonds will not receive the promised interest and maturity amounts at the times they are due. Companies can assume that any change in fair value that exceeds the amount caused by a change in the general (risk-free) interest rate is the result of credit risk changes.

In our example, Masterwear would report the increase in fair value from $666,633 to **$714,943**, or $48,310. Note, though, that part of the change is due to the unpaid interest we discussed earlier. Here's a recap.

[17] The current market rate would consist of the general risk-free rate at the time, increased by a risk premium for the credit risk of the bonds.
[18] At the time this text was written, these unrealized gains and losses were reported as part of net income. But, the FASB had made a tentative decision to require unrealized gains and losses to be reported instead as other comprehensive income (OCI) to the extent they are attributable to credit risk beginning in 2015. The discussion and illustrations in this section are based on that decision.

At June 30, 2016, the interest that accrued during the first six months was $46,664, but only $42,000 of that was paid in cash; so the book value increased by the $4,664 unpaid interest. We recorded the following entry:

Interest expense	46,664	
Discount on bonds payable		4,664
Cash		42,000

Amortizing the discount in this entry increased the book value of the liability by $4,664 to $671,297:

January 1 book value and fair value	$666,633
Increase from discount amortization	4,664
June 30 book value (amortized initial amount)	$671,297

Bonds payable
Less: Discount
Book value

FAIR VALUE RISES. Comparing that book value with the fair value of the bonds on that date provides the amount needed to adjust the bonds to their fair value.

June 30 fair value	$714,943
June 30 book value (amortized initial amount)	671,297
Fair value adjustment needed	$ 43,646

Rather than increasing the bonds payable account itself, though, we instead adjust it *indirectly* with a credit to a valuation allowance (or contra) account. If general interest rates have not changed, we assume the change in fair value is due to the credit risk associated with the bonds and report the loss in OCI:

Unrealized holding loss—OCI	43,646	
Fair value adjustment ($714,943 − 671,297)		43,646

When the fair value option is elected, we report changes in fair value in OCI to the extent caused by changes in credit risk.

If any portion of the fair value change is due to a change in general interest rates, that portion would be reported in net income. For instance, if interest rate declines alone would have created a $20,000 increase in fair value, we would report $20,000 of the loss in in the income statement and $23,646 as OCI.

The new book value of the bonds is now the fair value:

The *credit* balance in the fair value adjustment *increases* the book value; the discount reduces it.

Bonds payable	$700,000
Less: Discount ($33,367 − 4,664)	(28,703)
Amortization schedule value	$671,297
Plus: Fair value adjustment	43,646
Book value, June 30	$714,943

FAIR VALUE FALLS. Suppose the fair value at June 30, 2016, had been $650,000 instead of $714,943. In that case, Masterwear would record a *reduction* in the liability from $671,297 to $650,000, or $21,297. Again assuming no change in interest rates, the entry would be:

Fair value adjustment ($671,297 − 650,000)	21,297	
Unrealized holding gain—OCI		21,297

The new book value of the bonds is the fair value:

The *debit* balance in the fair value adjustment *reduces* the book value; as does the discount.

Bonds payable	$ 700,000
Less: Discount ($33,367 − 4,664)	(28,703)
Amortization schedule value	$ 671,297
Less: Fair value adjustment	(21,297)
Book value, June 30	$650,000

The outstanding balance in the last column of the amortization schedule at any date up to and including the balance at maturity will be the bonds payable less the discount (for instance $671,297 at June 30, 2016, on page 795). But the amount we report in the balance sheet at any reporting date, the fair value, will be that amortized initial amount from the amortization schedule, plus or minus the fair value adjustment. That's the **$714,943** or the **$650,000** in the two scenarios above.

To understand why we report credit risk-related fair value changes as OCI, it's useful to consider the consequence of reporting them in the income statement, which was the prescribed treatment prior to the FASB mandating their classification as OCI beginning in 2015. Here's one example. As a result of adjusting for fair value changes in its debt, **J.P. Morgan Chase & Co.** reported an impressive $1.9 billion gain in its 2011 third-quarter income statement. This was reason for the company's shareholders and creditors to celebrate, right? Not so fast. It's true that the company followed the proper procedure for recording a decline in the fair value of its debt, which was to record a gain in the income statement. As it turned out, though, the reason the fair value declined was that the company's financial situation had worsened, resulting in increased credit risk, and the increased credit risk caused the fair value of liabilities to decline. This, in fact, is the reason for most if not all of J.P. Morgan's huge gain. Does it make sense to you that worsening credit ratings should result in higher net income? Most observers, including the FASB, saw that as counterintuitive, and as a result, credit risk-related fair value changes are now reported as part of OCI.

Mix and Match

Companies choose which financial instruments to report at fair value.

Remember from our discussions in prior chapters that if a company elects the fair value option, it's not necessary that the company elect the option to report all of its financial instruments at fair value or even all instruments of a particular type at fair value. They can "mix and match" on an instrument-by-instrument basis. So Masterwear, for instance, might choose to report these bonds at fair value but all its other liabilities at their amortized initial measurement. However, the company must make the election when the item originates, in this case when the bonds are issued, and is not allowed to switch methods once a method is chosen.

Financial Reporting Case Solution

1. **What does it mean that the bonds are "first mortgage" bonds? What effect does that have on financing?** *(p. 791)* A mortgage bond is backed by a lien on specified real estate owned by the issuer. This makes it less risky than unsecured debt, so Service Leader can expect to be able to sell the bonds at a higher price (lower interest rate).
2. **From Service Leader's perspective, why are the bonds callable? What does that mean?** *(p. 791)* The call feature gives Service Leader some protection against being stuck with relatively high-cost debt in case interest rates fall during the 15 years to maturity. Service Leader can buy back, or call, the bonds from bondholders before the 15-year maturity date, after June 30, 2015. The call price is prespecified at 103 percent of the face value—$1,030 per $1,000 bond.

3. **How will it be possible to sell bonds paying investors 6.25% when other, similar investments will provide the investors a return of 6.5%?** *(p. 791)* Service Leader will be able to sell its 6.25% bonds in a 6.5% market only by selling them at a discounted price, below face amount. Bonds are priced by the marketplace to yield the market rate of interest for securities of similar risk and maturity. The price will be the present value of all the periodic cash interest payments (face amount × stated rate) plus the present value of the principal payable at maturity, both discounted at the market rate.
4. **Would accounting differ if the debt were designated as notes rather than bonds?** *(p. 802)* No. Other things being equal, whether they're called bonds, notes, or some other form of debt, the same accounting principles apply. They will be recorded at present value and interest will be recorded at the market rate over the term to maturity.
5. **Why might the company choose to make the bonds convertible into common stock?** *(p. 812)* Convertible bonds can be converted at the option of the bondholders into shares of stock. Sometimes the motivation for issuing convertible bonds rather than straight debt is to use the bonds as a medium of exchange in mergers and acquisitions, as a way for smaller firms or debt-heavy companies to obtain access to the bond market, or as an indirect way to issue stock when there is shareholder resistance to direct issuance of additional equity. None of these seems pertinent to Service Leader. The most likely reason is to sell at a higher price. The conversion feature is attractive to investors. Investors have a fixed-income security that can become common stock if circumstances make that attractive. The investor has additional possibilities for higher returns, with downside risk limited by the underlying debt. ●

The Bottom Line

- **LO14–1** A liability requires the future payment of cash in specified amounts at specified dates. As time passes, interest accrues on debt at the effective interest rate times the amount of the debt outstanding during the period. This same principle applies regardless of the specific form of the liability. (*p. 789*)
- **LO14–2** Forces of supply and demand cause a bond to be priced to yield the market rate, calculated as the present value of all the cash flows required, where the discount rate is the market rate. Interest expense is calculated as the effective market rate of interest multiplied by the outstanding balance (during the interest period). A company is permitted to allocate a discount or a premium equally to each period over the term to maturity if doing so produces results that are not materially different from the interest method. (*p. 791*)
- **LO14–3** In concept, notes are accounted for in precisely the same way as bonds. When a note is issued with an unrealistic interest rate, the effective market rate is used both to determine the amount recorded in the transaction and to record periodic interest thereafter. (*p. 802*)
- **LO14–4** In the balance sheet, disclosure should include, for all long-term borrowings, the aggregate amounts maturing and sinking fund requirements (if any) for each of the next five years. Supplemental disclosures are needed for (a) off-balance-sheet credit or market risk, (b) concentrations of credit risk, and (c) the fair value of financial instruments. (*p. 806*)
- **LO14–5** A gain or loss on early extinguishment of debt should be recorded for the difference between the reacquisition price and the book value of the debt. Convertible bonds are accounted for as straight debt, but the value of the equity feature is recorded separately for bonds issued with detachable warrants. (*p. 811*)
- **LO14–6** Companies are not required to, but have the option to, value some or all of their liabilities at fair value. If the option is elected, an increase (or decrease) in fair value from one balance sheet to the next is reported as a loss (or gain) as other comprehensive income to the extent it's related to credit risk. Otherwise, it's reported in net income. It's a one-time election for each liability when the liability is created. (*p. 817*)
- **LO14–7** U.S. GAAP and IFRS are generally compatible with respect to accounting for bonds and long-term notes. Some differences exist in determining which securities are reported as debt, the way convertible securities and debt issuance costs are reported, and when the fair value option can be elected. (*pp. 793, 802, and 813*). ●

APPENDIX 14A Bonds Issued Between Interest Dates

In Part A of this chapter, we assumed that the bonds were issued on the day they were dated (date printed in the indenture contract). But suppose a weak market caused a delay in selling the bonds until two months after that date (four months before semiannual interest was to be paid). In that case, the buyer would be asked to pay the seller **accrued interest** for two months in addition to the price of the bonds.

When Bonds Are Issued at Face Amount between Interest Dates

For illustration, assume that in Illustration 14–1 on page 792, Masterwear was unable to sell the bonds in the previous example until March 1—two months after they are dated. This variation is shown in Illustration 14A–1. United would pay the price of the bonds ($700,000) plus **$14,000** accrued interest:

All bonds sell at their price plus any interest that has accrued since the last interest date.

$700,000	×	12%	×	2⁄12	=	**$14,000**
Face amount		Annual rate		Fraction of the annual period		Accrued interest

Illustration 14A–1
Bonds Sold at Face Amount between Interest Dates

At Issuance (March 1)

Masterwear (Issuer)		
Cash (price plus accrued interest)	714,000	
Bonds payable (face amount)		700,000
Interest payable (accrued interest determined above)		14,000
United (Investor)		
Investment in bonds (face amount)	700,000	
Interest receivable (accrued interest determined above)	14,000	
Cash (price plus accrued interest)		714,000

Since the investor will hold the bonds for only four months before receiving six months' interest, two months' accrued interest must be added to the price paid.

When Masterwear pays semiannual interest on June 30, a full six months' interest is paid. But having received two months' accrued interest in advance, Masterwear's net interest expense will be four months' interest, for the four months the bonds have been outstanding at that time. Likewise, when United receives six months' interest—after holding the bonds for only four months—United will net only the four months' interest to which it is entitled:

The issuer incurs interest expense, and the investor recognizes interest revenue, for only the four months the bonds are outstanding.

At the First Interest Date (June 30)

Masterwear (Issuer)		
Interest expense (6 mo. − 2 mo. = 4 mo.)	28,000	
Interest payable[19] (accrued interest determined above)	14,000	
Cash (stated rate × face amount)		42,000
United (Investor)		
Cash (stated rate × face amount)	42,000	
Interest receivable (accrued interest determined above)		14,000
Interest revenue (6 mo. − 2 mo. = 4 mo.)		28,000

[19]Some accountants prefer to credit interest expense, rather than interest payable, when the bonds are sold. When that is done, this entry would require a debit to interest expense and a credit to cash for $42,000. The interest expense account would then reflect the same *net* debit of four months' interest ($42,000 − $14,000).

Interest Expense

	2 months
6 months	
4 months	

Similarly, the investor could debit interest revenue, rather than interest receivable when buying the bonds.

When Bonds Are Issued at a Discount between Interest Dates

Our objective is the same when the bonds are not issued at their face amount. For instance, in Illustration 14–3 on page 793, the $700,000 of 12% bonds were issued when the market rate was 14% and thus were priced at a discount, $666,633. If those bonds were issued March 1, two months after they are dated, the investor would pay the price of the bonds ($666,633) plus $14,000 accrued interest:

All bonds sell at their price plus any interest that has accrued since the last interest date.

Illustration 14A–2

Bonds Sold at a Discount between Interest Dates

Masterwear (Issuer)		
Cash (price plus accrued interest)	680,633	
Discount on bonds payable (difference)	33,367	
Bonds payable (face amount)		700,000
Interest payable (accrued interest determined above)		14,000
United (Investor)		
Investment in bonds (face amount)	700,000	
Interest receivable (accrued interest determined above)	14,000	
Discount on bond investment (difference)		33,367
Cash (price plus accrued interest)		680,633

By contract, a full six months' interest is paid on June 30 at the *stated* rate times the face amount. But having received two months' accrued interest in advance, Masterwear's *net* interest expense will be four months' interest, for the four months the bonds have been outstanding at that time. Interest is calculated on the outstanding debt balance at the effective (or market) rate. Interest for the first six months, then, would be $666,633 × 14% × ½ = $46,664. But because on June 30 only four months have passed, only four months' interest, 4/6 × 46,664, or $31,109, is recorded as interest expense. Similarly, the reduction of the discount, which for a full six-month interest period would be $46,664 − 42,000, or $4,664, will be only 4/6 of that amount. These amounts are recorded as follows:

Journal Entries—Interest between Interest Dates

At the First Interest Date (June 30)		
Masterwear (Issuer)		
Interest expense (4/6 × 46,664)	31,109	
Interest payable (accrued interest determined above)	14,000	
Discount on bonds payable (4/6 × 4,664)		3,109
Cash (stated rate × face amount)		42,000
United (Investor)		
Cash (stated rate × face amount)	42,000	
Discount on bond investment (4/6 × 4,991)	3,109	
Interest receivable (accrued interest determined above)		14,000
Interest revenue (4/6 × 46,664)		31,109

Only four months' interest is recorded because the bonds were outstanding only four months.

APPENDIX 14B

Troubled Debt Restructuring

A respected real estate developer, Brillard Properties, was very successful developing and managing a number of properties in the southeastern United States. To finance these investments, the developer had borrowed hundreds of millions of dollars from several regional banks. For years, events occurred as planned. The investments prospered. Cash flow was high. Interest payments on the debt were timely and individual loans were repaid as they matured.

Almost suddenly, however, the real estate climate soured. Investments that had provided handsome profits now did not provide the cash flow necessary to service the debt. Bankers who had loaned substantial funds to Brillard now faced a dilemma. Because contractual interest payments were unpaid, the bankers had the legal right to demand payment, which would force the developer to liquidate all or a major part of the properties to raise the cash. Sound business practice? Not necessarily.

A sharp rise in debt restructurings accompanied the 2008/2009 economic crisis.

If creditors force liquidation, they then must share among themselves the cash raised from selling the properties—at forced sale prices. Believing the developer's financial difficulties were caused by temporary market forces, not by bad management, the bankers felt they could minimize their losses by *restructuring* the debt agreements, rather than by forcing liquidation.

When changing the original terms of a debt agreement is motivated by financial difficulties experienced by the debtor (borrower), the new arrangement is referred to as a **troubled debt restructuring**. By definition, a troubled debt restructuring involves some concessions on the part of the creditor (lender). In the first half of 2009, the economic crisis prompted nearly 40 companies to negotiate such deals with their creditors, a huge increase over the handful that normally would do so during a six-month period.[20] A troubled debt restructuring may be achieved in either of two ways:

1. The debt may be *settled* at the time of the restructuring.
2. The debt may be *continued,* but with *modified terms.*

Debt Is Settled

In the situation described above, one choice the bankers had was to try to actually settle the debt outright at the time of the troubled debt restructuring. For instance, a bank holding a $30 million note from the developer might agree to accept a property valued at, let's say, $20 million as final settlement of the debt. In that case, the developer has a $10 million gain equal to the difference between the book value of the debt and the fair value of the property transferred. The debtor may need to adjust the book value of an asset to its fair value prior to recording its exchange for a debt. The developer in our example, for instance, would need to change the recorded amount for the property specified in the exchange agreement if it is carried at an amount other than its $20 million fair value. In such an instance, an ordinary gain or loss on disposition of assets should be recorded as shown in Illustration 14B–1.

In all areas of accounting, a noncash transaction is recorded at fair value.

Illustration 14B–1
Debt Settled

An asset is adjusted to fair value prior to recording its exchange for a debt.

First Prudent Bank agrees to settle Brillard's $30 million debt in exchange for property having a fair value of $20 million. The book value of the property on Brillard's books is $17 million:

	($ in millions)	
Land ($20 million minus $17 million)	3	
Gain on disposition of assets		3
Note payable (book value)	30	
Gain on troubled debt restructuring		10
Land (fair value)		20

The payment to settle a debt in a troubled debt restructuring might be cash, or a noncash asset (as in the example here), or even shares of the debtor's stock. An example of shares of stock given in exchange for debt forgiveness is the celebrated reorganization of TWA in 1992 (since acquired by American Airlines), when creditors received a 55% stake in the company's common shares in return for forgiving about $1 billion of the airline's $1.5 billion debt. In any case, the debtor's gain is the difference between the book value of the debt and the fair value of the asset(s) or equity securities transferred.

Debt Is Continued, but with Modified Terms

We assumed in the previous example that First Prudent Bank agreed to accept property in full settlement of the debt. A more likely occurrence would be that the bank allows the debt to continue, but modifies the terms of the debt agreement to make it easier for

[20] David Henry, "The Time Bomb in Corporate Debt," *BusinessWeek*, July 15, 2009.

the debtor to comply. The bank might agree to reduce or delay the scheduled *interest payments*. Or, it may agree to reduce or delay the *maturity amount*. Often a troubled debt restructuring will call for some combination of these concessions. Distressed by the 2008/2009 economic downturn, amusement park operator **Six Flags** persuaded a group of creditors to trim its debt by 5%, or $130 million, a restructuring designed to give Six Flags a financial cushion going into its busy 2009 summer season and an opportunity to recover its interest-paying ability.

The book value of a debt is the current balance of the primary debt plus any accrued (unpaid) interest.

Let's say the stated interest rate on the note in question is 10% and annual interest payments of $3 million (10% × $30 million) are payable in December of each of two remaining years to maturity. Also assume that the developer was unable to pay the $3 million interest payment for the year just ended. This means that the amount owed—the carrying amount (or book value) of the debt—is $33 million ($30 million plus one year's accrued interest).

The way the debtor accounts for the restructuring depends on the extent of the reduction in cash payments called for by the restructured arrangement. More specifically, the accounting procedure depends on whether, under the new agreement, total cash payments (a) are *less than* the book value of the debt or (b) still *exceed* the book value of the debt.

Two quite different situations are created when the terms of a debt are modified, depending on whether the cash payments are reduced to the extent that interest is eliminated.

WHEN TOTAL CASH PAYMENTS ARE LESS THAN THE BOOK VALUE OF THE DEBT By the original agreement, the debtor was to pay at maturity the $30 million loaned, plus enough periodic interest to provide a 10% effective rate of return. If the new agreement calls for less cash than the $33 million now owed, interest is presumed to have been eliminated.

As one of many possibilities, suppose the bank agrees to (1) forgive the interest accrued from last year, (2) reduce the two remaining interest payments from $3 million each to $2 million each, and (3) reduce the face amount from $30 million to $25 million. Clearly, the debtor will pay less by the new agreement than by the original one. In fact, if we add up the total payments called for by the new agreement, the total [($2 million × 2) plus $25 million] is less than the $33 million book value. Because the $29 million does not exceed the amount owed, the restructured debt agreement no longer provides interest on the debt. Actually, the new payments are $4 million short of covering the debt itself. So, after the debt restructuring, no interest expense is recorded. All subsequent cash payments are considered to be payment of the debt itself. Consider Illustration 14B–2.

Illustration 14B–2

Cash Payments Less than the Debt

Brillard Properties owes First Prudent Bank $30 million under a 10% note with two years remaining to maturity. Due to financial difficulties of the developer, the previous year's interest ($3 million) was not paid. First Prudent Bank agrees to:

1. Forgive the interest accrued from last year.
2. Reduce the remaining two interest payments to $2 million each.
3. Reduce the principal to $25 million.

Analysis:		
Book value	$30 million + $3 million =	$33 million
Future payments	($2 million × 2) + $25 million =	29 million
Gain		$ 4 million

	($ in millions)	
Accrued interest payable (10% × $30 million)	3	
Note payable ($30 million − 29 million)	1	
Gain on debt restructuring		4

Book Value		
Before Restr.	Adj.	After Restr.
$30	(1)	$29
3	(3)	0
$33	(4)	$29

When the total future cash payments are less than the book value of the debt, the difference is recorded as a gain at the date of restructure. No interest should be recorded thereafter. That is, all subsequent cash payments result in reductions of principal.

After restructuring, no interest expense is recorded. All cash payments are considered to be payment of the note itself.

At Each of the Two Interest Dates	($ in millions)	
Note payable	2	
Cash (revised "interest" amount)		2
At Maturity		
Note payable	25	
Cash (revised principal amount)		25

The $25 million payment at maturity reduces the note to zero.

WHEN TOTAL CASH PAYMENTS EXCEED THE BOOK VALUE OF THE DEBT Let's modify the example in the previous section. Now suppose the bank agrees to delay the due date for all cash payments until maturity and accept $34,333,200 at that time in full settlement of the debt. Rather than just reducing the cash payments as in the previous illustration, the payments are delayed. It is not the nature of the change that creates the need to account differently for this situation, but the amount of the total cash payments under the agreement relative to the book value of the debt. This situation is demonstrated in Illustration 14B–3.

Illustration 14B–3

Cash Payments More than the Debt

The discount rate that equates the present value on the debt ($33 million) and its future value ($34,333,200) is the effective rate of interest.

Brillard Properties owes First Prudent Bank $30 million under a 10% note with two years remaining to maturity. Due to Brillard's financial difficulties, the previous year's interest ($3 million) was not paid. First Prudent Bank agrees to:

1. Delay the due date for all cash payments until maturity.
2. Accept $34,333,200 at that time in full settlement of the debt.

Analysis:	Future payments		$34,333,200
	Book value	$30 million + $3 million =	33,000,000
	Interest		$ 1,333,200

Calculation of the New Effective Interest Rate

- $33,000,000 ÷ 34,333,200 = .9612, the Table 2 value for $n = 2$, $i = ?$
- In row 2 of Table 2, the number .9612 is in the 2% column. So, this is the new effective interest rate.

As long as cash payments exceed the amount owed there will be interest—although at a lower effective rate.

Now the total payments called for by the new agreement, $34,333,200, exceed the $33 million book value. Because the payments exceed the amount owed, the restructured debt agreement still provides interest on the debt—but less than before the agreement was revised. No longer is the effective rate 10%. The accounting objective now is to determine what the new effective rate is and *record interest for the remaining term of the loan at that new, lower rate,* as shown in Illustration 14B–3.

Unpaid interest is accrued at the effective rate times the book value of the note.

Because the total future cash payments are not less than the book value of the debt, no reduction of the existing debt is necessary and no entry is required at the time of the debt restructuring. Even though no cash is paid until maturity under the restructured debt agreement, interest expense still is recorded annually—but at the new rate.

The book value of the debt is increased by the unpaid interest from the previous year.

The total of the accrued interest account plus the note account is equal to the amount scheduled to be paid at maturity.

At the End of the First Year		
Interest expense [2% × ($30,000,000 + 3,000,000)]	660,000	
Accrued interest payable		660,000
At the End of the Second Year		
Interest expense [2% × ($30,000,000 + 3,660,000)]	673,200	
Accrued interest payable		673,200
At Maturity (End of the Second Year)		
Note payable	30,000,000	
Accrued interest payable ($3,000,000 + 660,000 + 673,200)	4,333,200	
Cash (required by new agreement)		34,333,200

Additional Consideration

To keep up with the changing amounts, it may be convenient to prepare an amortization schedule for the debt.

Year	Cash Interest	Effective Interest		Increase in Balance	Outstanding Balance
		(2% × Outstanding balance)			
					33,000,000
1	0	.02 (33,000,000) =	660,000	660,000	33,660,000
2	0	.02 (33,660,000) =	673,200	673,200	34,333,200
	0		1,333,200	1,333,200	

An amortization schedule is particularly helpful if there are several years remaining to maturity.

In our example, the restructured debt agreement called for a single cash payment at maturity ($34,333,200). If more than one cash payment is required (as in the agreement in our earlier example), calculating the new effective rate is more difficult. The concept would remain straightforward: (1) determine the interest rate that provides a present value of all future cash payments that is equal to the current book value and (2) record the interest at that rate thereafter. Mechanically, though, the computation by hand would be cumbersome, requiring a time-consuming trial-and-error calculation. Since our primary interest is understanding the concepts involved, we will avoid the mathematical complexities of such a situation.

You also should be aware that when a restructuring involves modification of terms, accounting for a liability by the debtor, as described in this section, and accounting for a receivable by the creditor (essentially an impairment of a receivable), which was described in Chapter 7, are inconsistent. You may recall that when a creditor's investment in a receivable becomes impaired, due to a troubled debt restructuring or for any other reason, the receivable is remeasured based on the discounted present value of currently expected cash flows at the loan's original effective rate (regardless of the extent to which expected cash receipts have been reduced). For ease of comparison, the example in this chapter (Illustration 14B–3) describes the same situation as the example in Chapter 7 (Illustration 7B–2). There is no conceptual justification for the asymmetry between debtors' and creditors' accounting for troubled debt restructurings. The FASB will likely reconsider debtors' accounting in the future. ●

Questions For Review of Key Topics

Q 14–1 How is periodic interest determined for outstanding liabilities? For outstanding receivables? How does the approach compare from one form of debt instrument (say bonds payable) to another (say notes payable)?

Q 14–2 As a general rule, how should long-term liabilities be reported on the debtor's balance sheet?

Q 14–3 How are bonds and notes the same? How do they differ?

Q 14–4 What information is contained in a bond indenture? What purpose does it serve?

Q 14–5 On January 1, 2016, Brandon Electronics issued $85 million of 11.5% bonds, dated January 1. The market yield for bonds of maturity issued by similar firms in terms of riskiness is 12.25%. How can Brandon sell debt paying only 11.5% in a 12.25% market?

Q 14–6 How is the price determined for a bond (or bond issue)?

Q 14–7 A zero-coupon bond pays no interest. Explain.

Q 14–8 When bonds are issued at a premium the debt declines each period. Explain.

Q 14–9 Compare the two commonly used methods of determining interest on bonds.

Q 14–10 GAAP requires that debt issue costs be recorded separately and amortized over the term of the related debt. Describe a logical alternative to this accounting treatment.

Q 14–11 When a note's stated rate of interest is unrealistic relative to the market rate, the concept of substance over form should be employed. Explain.

Q 14–12 How does an installment note differ from a note for which the principal is paid as a single amount at maturity?

Q 14–13 Long-term debt can be reported either (a) as a single amount, net of any discount or increased by any premium or (b) at its face amount accompanied by a separate valuation account for the discount or premium. Any portion of the debt to be paid during the upcoming year, or operating cycle if longer, should be reported as a current amount. Regarding amounts to be paid in the future, what additional disclosures should be made in connection with long-term debt?

Q 14–14 Early extinguishment of debt often produces a gain or a loss. How is the gain or loss determined?

Q 14–15 Air Supply issued $6 million of 9%, 10-year convertible bonds at 101. The bonds are convertible into 24,000 shares of common stock. Bonds that are similar in all respects except that they are nonconvertible, currently are selling at 99 (that is, 99% of face amount). What amount should Air Supply record as equity and how much as a liability when the bonds are issued?

Q 14–16 Both convertible bonds and bonds issued with detachable warrants have features of both debt and equity. How does the accounting treatment differ for the two hybrid securities? Why is the accounting treatment different?

Q 14–17 At times, companies try to induce voluntary conversion by offering an added incentive—maybe cash, stock warrants, or a more favorable conversion ratio. How is such an inducement accounted for? How is it measured?

Q 14–18 Cordova Tools has bonds outstanding during a year in which the market rate of interest has risen. If Cordova has elected the fair value option for the bonds, will it report a gain or a loss on the bonds for the year? Explain.

IFRS **Q 14–19** If a company prepares its financial statements according to International Financial Reporting Standards, how would it account for convertible bonds it issues for $12.5 million? What is the conceptual justification?

Q 14–20 (Based on Appendix 14A) Why will bonds always sell at their price plus any interest that has accrued since the last interest date?

Q 14–21 (Based on Appendix 14B) When the original terms of a debt agreement are changed because of financial difficulties experienced by the debtor (borrower), the new arrangement is referred to as a *troubled debt restructuring.* Such a restructuring can take a variety of forms. For accounting purposes, these possibilities are categorized. What are the accounting classifications of troubled debt restructurings?

Q 14–22 (Based on Appendix 14B) Pratt Industries owes First National Bank $5 million but, due to financial difficulties, is unable to comply with the original terms of the loan. The bank agrees to settle the debt in exchange for land having a fair value of $3 million. The book value of the property on Pratt's books is $2 million. For the reporting period in which the debt is settled, what amount(s) will Pratt report on its income statement in connection with the troubled debt restructuring?

Q 14–23 (Based on Appendix 14B) The way a debtor accounts for the restructuring depends on the extent of the reduction in cash payments called for by the restructured arrangement. Describe, in general, the accounting procedure for the two basic cases: when, under the new agreement, total cash payments (a) are less than the book value of the debt or (b) still exceed the book value of the debt.

Brief Exercises

BE 14–1
Bond interest
● LO14–1

Holiday Brands issued $30 million of 6%, 30-year bonds for $27.5 million. What is the amount of interest that Holiday will pay semiannually to bondholders?

BE 14–2
Determining the price of bonds
● LO14–2

A company issued 5%, 20-year bonds with a face amount of $80 million. The market yield for bonds of similar risk and maturity is 6%. Interest is paid semiannually. At what price did the bonds sell?

BE 14–3
Determining the price of bonds
● LO14–2

A company issued 6%, 15-year bonds with a face amount of $75 million. The market yield for bonds of similar risk and maturity is 6%. Interest is paid semiannually. At what price did the bonds sell?

BE 14–4
Determining the price of bonds
● LO14–2

A company issued 5%, 20-year bonds with a face amount of $100 million. The market yield for bonds of similar risk and maturity is 4%. Interest is paid semiannually. At what price did the bonds sell?

BE 14–5
Effective interest on bonds
● LO14–2

On January 1, a company issued 7%, 15-year bonds with a face amount of $90 million for $82,218,585 to yield 8%. Interest is paid semiannually. What was interest expense at the effective interest rate on June 30, the first interest date?

BE 14–6
Effective interest on bonds
● LO14–2

On January 1, a company issued 3%, 20-year bonds with a face amount of $80 million for $69,033,776 to yield 4%. Interest is paid semiannually. What was the interest expense at the effective interest rate on the December 31 annual income statement?

BE 14–7
Straight-line interest on bonds
● LO14–2

On January 1, a company issued 3%, 20-year bonds with a face amount of $80 million for $69,033,776 to yield 4%. Interest is paid semiannually. What was the straight-line interest expense on the December 31 annual income statement?

BE 14–8
Investment in bonds
● LO14–2

On January 1, a company purchased 3%, 20-year corporate bonds for $69,033,776 as an investment. The bonds have a face amount of $80 million and are priced to yield 4%. Interest is paid semiannually. Prepare the journal entry to record revenue at the effective interest rate on December 31, the second interest payment date.

BE 14–9
Note issued for cash; borrower and lender
● LO14–3

On January 1, 2016, Nantucket Ferry borrowed $14,000,000 cash from BankOne and issued a four-year, $14,000,000, 6% note. Interest was payable annually on December 31. Prepare the journal entries for both firms to record interest at December 31, 2016.

BE 14–10
Note with unrealistic interest rate
● LO14–3

On January 1, Snipes Construction paid for earth-moving equipment by issuing a $300,000, 3-year note that specified 2% interest to be paid on December 31 of each year. The equipment's retail cash price was unknown, but it was determined that a reasonable interest rate was 5%. At what amount should Snipes record the equipment and the note? What journal entry should it record for the transaction?

BE 14–11
Installment note
● LO14–3

On January 1, a company borrowed cash by issuing a $300,000, 5%, installment note to be paid in three equal payments at the end of each year beginning December 31. What would be the amount of each installment? Prepare the journal entry for the second installment payment.

BE 14–12
Early extinguishment; effective interest
● LO14–5

A company retired $60 million of its 6% bonds at 102 ($61.2 million) before their scheduled maturity. At the time, the bonds had a remaining discount of $2 million. Prepare the journal entry to record the redemption of the bonds.

BE 14–13
Bonds with detachable warrants
● LO14–5

Hoffman Corporation issued $60 million of 5%, 20-year bonds at 102. Each of the 60,000 bonds was issued with 10 detachable stock warrants, each of which entitled the bondholder to purchase, for $20, one share of $1 par common stock. At the time of sale, the market value of the common stock was $25 per share and the market value of each warrant was $5. Prepare the journal entry to record the issuance of the bonds.

BE 14–14
Convertible bonds
● LO14–5

Hoffman Corporation issued $60 million of 5%, 20-year bonds at 102. Each of the 60,000 bonds was convertible into one share of $1 par common stock. Prepare the journal entry to record the issuance of the bonds.

BE 14–15
Reporting bonds at fair value
● LO14–6

AI Tool and Dye issued 8% bonds with a face amount of $160 million on January 1, 2016. The bonds sold for $150 million. For bonds of similar risk and maturity the market yield was 9%. Upon issuance, AI elected the option to report these bonds at their fair value. On June 30, 2016, the fair value of the bonds was $145 million as determined by their market value on the NASDAQ. Will AI report a gain or will it report a loss when adjusting the bonds to fair value? If the change in fair value is attributable to a change in the interest rate, did the rate increase or decrease? Will the gain or loss be reported in net income or as OCI?

Exercises

An alternate exercise and problem set is available in the Connect library.

E 14–1
Bond valuation
● LO14–2

Your investment department has researched possible investments in corporate debt securities. Among the available investments are the following $100 million bond issues, each dated January 1, 2016. Prices were determined by underwriters at different times during the last few weeks.

	Company	Bond Price	Stated Rate
1.	BB Corp.	$109 million	11%
2.	DD Corp.	$100 million	10%
3.	GG Corp.	$ 91 million	9%

Each of the bond issues matures on December 31, 2035, and pays interest semiannually on June 30 and December 31. For bonds of similar risk and maturity, the market yield at January 1, 2016, is 10%.

Required:
Other things being equal, which of the bond issues offers the most attractive investment opportunity if it can be purchased at the prices stated? The least attractive? Why?

E 14–2
Determine the price of bonds in various situations
● LO14–2

Determine the price of a $1 million bond issue under each of the following independent assumptions:

	Maturity	Interest Paid	Stated Rate	Effective (Market) Rate
1.	10 years	annually	10%	12%
2.	10 years	semiannually	10%	12%
3.	10 years	semiannually	12%	10%
4.	20 years	semiannually	12%	10%
5.	20 years	semiannually	12%	12%

E 14–3
Determine the price of bonds; issuance; effective interest
● LO14–2

The Bradford Company issued 10% bonds, dated January 1, with a face amount of $80 million on January 1, 2016. The bonds mature on December 31, 2025 (10 years). For bonds of similar risk and maturity, the market yield is 12%. Interest is paid semiannually on June 30 and December 31.

Required:
1. Determine the price of the bonds at January 1, 2016.
2. Prepare the journal entry to record their issuance by The Bradford Company on January 1, 2016.
3. Prepare the journal entry to record interest on June 30, 2016 (at the effective rate).
4. Prepare the journal entry to record interest on December 31, 2016 (at the effective rate).

E 14–4
Investor; effective interest
● LO14–2

(Note: This is a variation of E 14–3 modified to consider the investor's perspective.) The Bradford Company sold the entire bond issue described in the previous exercise to Saxton-Bose Corporation.

Required:
1. Prepare the journal entry to record the purchase of the bonds by Saxton-Bose on January 1, 2016.
2. Prepare the journal entry to record interest revenue on June 30, 2016 (at the effective rate).
3. Prepare the journal entry to record interest revenue on December 31, 2016 (at the effective rate).

E 14–5
Bonds; issuance; effective interest; financial statement effects
● LO14–2

Myriad Solutions, Inc., issued 10% bonds, dated January 1, with a face amount of $320 million on January 1, 2016 for $283,294,720. The bonds mature on December 31, 2025 (10 years). For bonds of similar risk and maturity the market yield is 12%. Interest is paid semiannually on June 30 and December 31.

Required:
1. What would be the net amount of the liability Myriad would report in its balance sheet at December 31, 2016?
2. What would be the amount related to the bonds that Myriad would report in its income statement for the year ended December 31, 2016?

3. What would be the amount(s) related to the bonds that Myriad would report in its statement of cash flows for the year ended December 31, 2016?

E 14–6
Bonds; issuance; effective interest
● LO14–2

The Gorman Group issued $900,000 of 13% bonds on June 30, 2016, for $967,707. The bonds were dated on June 30 and mature on June 30, 2036 (20 years). The market yield for bonds of similar risk and maturity is 12%. Interest is paid semiannually on December 31 and June 30.

Required:

1. Prepare the journal entry to record their issuance by The Gorman Group on June 30, 2016.
2. Prepare the journal entry to record interest on December 31, 2016 (at the effective rate).
3. Prepare the journal entry to record interest on June 30, 2017 (at the effective rate).

E 14–7
Determine the price of bonds; issuance; straight-line method
● LO14–2

Universal Foods issued 10% bonds, dated January 1, with a face amount of $150 million on January 1, 2016. The bonds mature on December 31, 2030 (15 years). The market rate of interest for similar issues was 12%. Interest is paid semiannually on June 30 and December 31. Universal uses the straight-line method.

Required:

1. Determine the price of the bonds at January 1, 2016.
2. Prepare the journal entry to record their issuance by Universal Foods on January 1, 2016.
3. Prepare the journal entry to record interest on June 30, 2016.
4. Prepare the journal entry to record interest on December 31, 2023.

E 14–8
Investor; straight-line method
● LO14–2

(Note: This is a variation of E 14–7 modified to consider the investor's perspective.) Universal Foods sold the entire bond issue described in the previous exercise to Wang Communications.

Required:

1. Prepare the journal entry to record the purchase of the bonds by Wang Communications on January 1, 2016.
2. Prepare the journal entry to record interest revenue on June 30, 2016.
3. Prepare the journal entry to record interest revenue on December 31, 2023.

E 14–9
Issuance of bonds; effective interest; amortization schedule; financial statement effects
● LO14–2

When Patey Pontoons issued 6% bonds on January 1, 2016, with a face amount of $600,000, the market yield for bonds of similar risk and maturity was 7%. The bonds mature December 31, 2019 (4 years). Interest is paid semiannually on June 30 and December 31.

Required:

1. Determine the price of the bonds at January 1, 2016.
2. Prepare the journal entry to record their issuance by Patey on January 1, 2016.
3. Prepare an amortization schedule that determines interest at the effective rate each period.
4. Prepare the journal entry to record interest on June 30, 2016.
5. What is the amount(s) related to the bonds that Patey will report in its balance sheet at December 31, 2016?
6. What is the amount(s) related to the bonds that Patey will report in its income statement for the year ended December 31, 2016? (Ignore income taxes.)
7. Prepare the appropriate journal entries at maturity on December 31, 2019.

E 14–10
Issuance of bonds; effective interest; amortization schedule
● LO14–2

National Orthopedics Co. issued 9% bonds, dated January 1, with a face amount of $500,000 on January 1, 2016. The bonds mature on December 31, 2019 (4 years). For bonds of similar risk and maturity the market yield was 10%. Interest is paid semiannually on June 30 and December 31.

Required:

1. Determine the price of the bonds at January 1, 2016.
2. Prepare the journal entry to record their issuance by National on January 1, 2016.
3. Prepare an amortization schedule that determines interest at the effective rate each period.
4. Prepare the journal entry to record interest on June 30, 2016.
5. Prepare the appropriate journal entries at maturity on December 31, 2019.

E 14–11
Bonds; effective interest; adjusting entry
● LO14–2

On February 1, 2016, Strauss-Lombardi issued 9% bonds, dated February 1, with a face amount of $800,000. The bonds sold for $731,364 and mature on January 31, 2036 (20 years). The market yield for bonds of similar risk and maturity was 10%. Interest is paid semiannually on July 31 and January 31. Strauss-Lombardi's fiscal year ends December 31.

Required:

1. Prepare the journal entry to record their issuance by Strauss-Lombardi on February 1, 2016.
2. Prepare the journal entry to record interest on July 31, 2016 (at the effective rate).
3. Prepare the adjusting entry to accrue interest on December 31, 2016.
4. Prepare the journal entry to record interest on January 31, 2017.

E 14–12
Bonds; straight-line method; adjusting entry
● LO14–2

On March 1, 2016, Stratford Lighting issued 14% bonds, dated March 1, with a face amount of $300,000. The bonds sold for $294,000 and mature on February 28, 2036 (20 years). Interest is paid semiannually on August 31 and February 28. Stratford uses the straight-line method and its fiscal year ends December 31.

Required:

1. Prepare the journal entry to record the issuance of the bonds by Stratford Lighting on March 1, 2016.
2. Prepare the journal entry to record interest on August 31, 2016.
3. Prepare the journal entry to accrue interest on December 31, 2016.
4. Prepare the journal entry to record interest on February 28, 2017.

E 14–13
Issuance of bonds; effective interest
● LO14–2

Federal Semiconductors issued 11% bonds, dated January 1, with a face amount of $800 million on January 1, 2016. The bonds sold for $739,814,813 and mature on December 31, 2035 (20 years). For bonds of similar risk and maturity the market yield was 12%. Interest is paid semiannually on June 30 and December 31.

Required:

1. Prepare the journal entry to record their issuance by Federal on January 1, 2016.
2. Prepare the journal entry to record interest on June 30, 2016 (at the effective rate).
3. Prepare the journal entry to record interest on December 31, 2016 (at the effective rate).
4. At what amount will Federal report the bonds among its liabilities in the December 31, 2016, balance sheet?

E 14–14
New debt issues; offerings announcements
● LO14–2

When companies offer new debt security issues, they publicize the offerings in the financial press and on Internet sites. Assume the following were among the debt offerings reported in December 2016:

New Securities Issues

Corporate

National Equipment Transfer Corporation—$200 million bonds via lead managers Second Tennessee Bank N.A. and Morgan, Dunavant & Co., according to a syndicate official. Terms: maturity, Dec. 15, 2022; coupon 7.46%; issue price, par; yield, 7.46%; noncallable, debt ratings: Ba-1 (Moody's Investors Service, Inc.), BBB+ (Standard & Poor's).

IgWig Inc.—$350 million of notes via lead manager Stanley Brothers, Inc., according to a syndicate official. Terms: maturity, Dec. 1, 2024; coupon, 6.46%; Issue price, 99; yield, 6.56%; call date, NC; debt ratings: Baa-1 (Moody's Investors Service, Inc.), A (Standard & Poor's).

Required:

1. Prepare the appropriate journal entries to record the sale of both issues to underwriters. Ignore share issue costs and assume no accrued interest.
2. Prepare the appropriate journal entries to record the first semiannual interest payment for both issues.

E 14–15
Error correction; accrued interest on bonds
● LO14–2

At the end of 2015, Majors Furniture Company failed to accrue $61,000 of interest expense that accrued during the last five months of 2015 on bonds payable. The bonds mature in 2029. The discount on the bonds is amortized by the straight-line method. The following entry was recorded on February 1, 2016, when the semiannual interest was paid:

Interest expense	73,200	
Discount on bonds payable		1,200
Cash		72,000

Required:

Prepare any journal entry necessary to correct the errors as of February 2, 2016 when the errors were discovered. Also, prepare any adjusting entry at December 31, 2016, related to the situation described. (Ignore income taxes.)

E 14–16
Error in amortization schedule
● LO14–3

Wilkins Food Products, Inc., acquired a packaging machine from Lawrence Specialists Corporation. Lawrence completed construction of the machine on January 1, 2014. In payment for the machine Wilkins issued a three-year installment note to be paid in three equal payments at the end of each year. The payments include interest at the rate of 10%.

Lawrence made a conceptual error in preparing the amortization schedule, which Wilkins failed to discover until 2016. The error had caused Wilkins to understate interest expense by $45,000 in 2014 and $40,000 in 2015.

Required:

1. Determine which accounts are incorrect as a result of these errors at January 1, 2016, before any adjustments. Explain your answer. (Ignore income taxes.)
2. Prepare a journal entry to correct the error.
3. What other step(s) would be taken in connection with the error?

E 14–17
Note with unrealistic interest rate; borrower; amortization schedule
● LO14–3

Amber Mining and Milling, Inc., contracted with Truax Corporation to have constructed a custom-made lathe. The machine was completed and ready for use on January 1, 2016. Amber paid for the lathe by issuing a $600,000, three-year note that specified 4% interest, payable annually on December 31 of each year. The cash market price of the lathe was unknown. It was determined by comparison with similar transactions that 12% was a reasonable rate of interest.

Required:

1. Prepare the journal entry on January 1, 2016, for Amber Mining and Milling's purchase of the lathe.
2. Prepare an amortization schedule for the three-year term of the note.
3. Prepare the journal entries to record (a) interest for each of the three years and (b) payment of the note at maturity.

E 14–18
Note with unrealistic interest rate; lender; amortization schedule
● LO14–3

Refer to the situation described in E14–17.

Required:

1. Prepare the journal entry on January 1, 2016, for Truax Corporation's sale of the lathe.
2. Prepare an amortization schedule for the three-year term of the note.
3. Prepare the journal entries to record (a) interest for each of the three years and (b) payment of the note at maturity for Truax.

E 14–19
Installment note; lender; amortization schedule
● LO14–3

FinanceCo lent $8 million to Corbin Construction on January 1, 2016, to construct a playground. Corbin signed a three-year, 6% installment note to be paid in three equal payments at the end of each year.

Required:

1. Prepare the journal entry for FinanceCo's lending the funds on January 1, 2016.
2. Prepare an amortization schedule for the three-year term of the installment note.
3. Prepare the journal entry for the first installment payment on December 31, 2016.
4. Prepare the journal entry for the third installment payment on December 31, 2018.

E 14–20
Installment note; amortization schedule
● LO14–3

American Food Services, Inc., acquired a packaging machine from Barton and Barton Corporation. Barton and Barton completed construction of the machine on January 1, 2016. In payment for the $4 million machine, American Food Services issued a four-year installment note to be paid in four equal payments at the end of each year. The payments include interest at the rate of 10%.

Required:

1. Prepare the journal entry for American Food Services' purchase of the machine on January 1, 2016.
2. Prepare an amortization schedule for the four-year term of the installment note.
3. Prepare the journal entry for the first installment payment on December 31, 2016.
4. Prepare the journal entry for the third installment payment on December 31, 2018.

E 14–21
Installment note
● LO14–3

LCD Industries purchased a supply of electronic components from Entel Corporation on November 1, 2016. In payment for the $24 million purchase, LCD issued a 1-year installment note to be paid in equal monthly payments at the end of each month. The payments include interest at the rate of 12%.

Required:

1. Prepare the journal entry for LCD's purchase of the components on November 1, 2016.
2. Prepare the journal entry for the first installment payment on November 30, 2016.
3. What is the amount of interest expense that LCD will report in its income statement for the year ended December 31, 2016?

E 14–22
FASB codification research
● LO14–2, LO14–3, LO14–4

Access the *FASB Accounting Standards Codification* at the FASB website (**www.fasb.org**). Determine the specific citation for accounting for each of the following items:

1. Disclosure requirements for maturities of long-term debt.
2. How to estimate the value of a note when a note having no ready market and no interest rate is exchanged for a noncash asset without a readily available fair value.
3. When the straight-line method can be used as an alternative to the interest method of determining interest.

E 14–23
Early extinguishment
● LO14–5

The balance sheet of Indian River Electronics Corporation as of December 31, 2015, included 12.25% bonds having a face amount of $90 million. The bonds had been issued in 2008 and had a remaining discount of $3 million at December 31, 2015. On January 1, 2016, Indian River Electronics called the bonds before their scheduled maturity at the call price of 102.

Required:
Prepare the journal entry by Indian River Electronics to record the redemption of the bonds at January 1, 2016.

E 14–24
Convertible bonds
● LO14–5

On January 1, 2016, Gless Textiles issued $12 million of 9%, 10-year convertible bonds at 101. The bonds pay interest on June 30 and December 31. Each $1,000 bond is convertible into 40 shares of Gless's no par common stock. Bonds that are similar in all respects, except that they are nonconvertible, currently are selling at 99 (that is, 99% of face amount). Century Services purchased 10% of the issue as an investment.

Required:

1. Prepare the journal entries for the issuance of the bonds by Gless and the purchase of the bond investment by Century.
2. Prepare the journal entries for the June 30, 2020, interest payment by both Gless and Century assuming both use the straight-line method.
3. On July 1, 2021, when Gless's common stock had a market price of $33 per share, Century converted the bonds it held. Prepare the journal entries by both Gless and Century for the conversion of the bonds (book value method).

E 14–25
IFRS; convertible bonds
● LO14–5, LO14–7

Refer to the situation described in the previous exercise.

Required:
How might your solution to requirement 1 for the issuer of the bonds differ if Gless Textiles prepares its financial statements according to International Financial Reporting Standards? Include any appropriate journal entry in your response.

E 14–26
Convertible bonds; induced conversion
● LO14–5

On January 1, 2016, Madison Products issued $40 million of 6%, 10-year convertible bonds at a net price of $40.8 million. Madison recently issued similar, but nonconvertible, bonds at 99 (that is, 99% of face amount). The bonds pay interest on June 30 and December 31. Each $1,000 bond is convertible into 30 shares of Madison's no par common stock. Madison records interest by the straight-line method.

On June 1, 2018, Madison notified bondholders of its intent to call the bonds at face value plus a 1% call premium on July 1, 2018. By June 30 all bondholders had chosen to convert their bonds into shares as of the interest payment date. On June 30, Madison paid the semiannual interest and issued the requisite number of shares for the bonds being converted.

Required:

1. Prepare the journal entry for the issuance of the bonds by Madison.
2. Prepare the journal entry for the June 30, 2016, interest payment.
3. Prepare the journal entries for the June 30, 2018, interest payment by Madison and the conversion of the bonds (book value method).

E 14–27
IFRS; convertible bonds
● LO14–5, LO14–7

Refer to the situation described in E 14–26.

Required:
How might your solution for the issuer of the bonds differ if Madison Products prepares its financial statements according to International Financial Reporting Standards? Include any appropriate journal entries in your response.

E 14–28
Bonds with detachable warrants
● LO14–5

On August 1, 2016, Limbaugh Communications issued $30 million of 10% nonconvertible bonds at 104. The bonds are due on July 31, 2036. Each $1,000 bond was issued with 20 detachable stock warrants, each of which entitled the bondholder to purchase, for $60, one share of Limbaugh Communications' no par common stock. Interstate Containers purchased 20% of the bond issue. On August 1, 2016, the market value of the common stock was $58 per share and the market value of each warrant was $8.

In February 2027, when Limbaugh's common stock had a market price of $72 per share and the unamortized discount balance was $1 million, Interstate Containers exercised the warrants it held.

Required:

1. Prepare the journal entries on August 1, 2016, to record (a) the issuance of the bonds by Limbaugh and (b) the investment by Interstate.
2. Prepare the journal entries for both Limbaugh and Interstate in February 2027, to record the exercise of the warrants.

E 14–29
Reporting bonds at fair value
● LO14–6

(Note: This is a variation of E14–13 modified to consider the fair value option for reporting liabilities.) Federal Semiconductors issued 11% bonds, dated January 1, with a face amount of $800 million on January 1, 2016. The bonds sold for $739,814,813 and mature on December 31, 2035 (20 years). For bonds of similar risk and maturity the market yield was 12%. Interest is paid semiannually on June 30 and December 31. Federal determines interest at the effective rate. Federal elected the option to report these bonds at their fair value. On December 31, 2016, the fair value of the bonds was $730 million as determined by their market value in the over-the-counter market.

Required:

1. Prepare the journal entry to adjust the bonds to their fair value for presentation in the December 31, 2016, balance sheet. Federal determined that none of the change in fair value was due to a decline in general interest rates.
2. Assume the fair value of the bonds on December 31, 2017, had risen to $736 million. Prepare the journal entry to adjust the bonds to their fair value for presentation in the December 31, 2017, balance sheet. Federal determined that one-half of the increase in fair value was due to a decline in general interest rates.

E 14–30
Reporting bonds at fair value
● LO14–6

On January 1, 2016, Rapid Airlines issued $200 million of its 8% bonds for $184 million. The bonds were priced to yield 10%. Interest is payable semiannually on June 30 and December 31. Rapid Airlines records interest at the effective rate and elected the option to report these bonds at their fair value. On December 31, 2016, the fair value of the bonds was $188 million as determined by their market value in the over-the-counter market. Rapid determined that $1,000,000 of the increase in fair value was due to a decline in general interest rates.

Required:

1. Prepare the journal entry to record interest on June 30, 2016 (the first interest payment).
2. Prepare the journal entry to record interest on December 31, 2016 (the second interest payment).
3. Prepare the journal entry to adjust the bonds to their fair value for presentation in the December 31, 2016, balance sheet.

E 14–31
Reporting bonds at fair value; calculate fair value
● LO14–6

On January 1, 2016, Essence Communications issued $800,000 of its 10-year, 8% bonds for $700,302. The bonds were priced to yield 10%. Interest is payable semiannually on June 30 and December 31. Essence Communications records interest at the effective rate and elected the option to report these bonds at their fair value. On December 31, 2016, the market interest rate for bonds of similar risk and maturity was 9%. The bonds are not traded on an active exchange. The increase in the market interest rate was due to a 1% increase in general (risk-free) interest rates.

Required:

1. Using the information provided, estimate the fair value of the bonds at December 31, 2016.
2. Prepare the journal entry to record interest on June 30, 2016 (the first interest payment).
3. Prepare the journal entry to record interest on December 31, 2016 (the second interest payment).
4. Prepare the journal entry to adjust the bonds to their fair value for presentation in the December 31, 2016, balance sheet.

E 14–32
Accrued interest
● Appendix A

On March 1, 2016, Brown-Ferring Corporation issued $100 million of 12% bonds, dated January 1, 2016, for $99 million (plus accrued interest). The bonds mature on December 31, 2035, and pay interest semiannually on June 30 and December 31. Brown-Ferring's fiscal period is the calendar year.

Required:

1. Determine the amount of accrued interest that was included in the proceeds received from the bond sale.
2. Prepare the journal entry for the issuance of the bonds by Brown-Ferring.

E 14–33
Troubled debt restructuring; debt settled
● Appendix B

At January 1, 2016, Transit Developments owed First City Bank Group $600,000, under an 11% note with three years remaining to maturity. Due to financial difficulties, Transit was unable to pay the previous year's interest.

First City Bank Group agreed to settle Transit's debt in exchange for land having a fair value of $450,000. Transit purchased the land in 2012 for $325,000.

Required:
Prepare the journal entry(s) to record the restructuring of the debt by Transit Developments.

E 14–34
Troubled debt restructuring; modification of terms
● Appendix B

At January 1, 2016, Brainard Industries, Inc., owed Second BancCorp $12 million under a 10% note due December 31, 2018. Interest was paid last on December 31, 2014. Brainard was experiencing severe financial difficulties and asked Second BancCorp to modify the terms of the debt agreement. After negotiation Second BancCorp agreed to:

a. Forgive the interest accrued for the year just ended.
b. Reduce the remaining two years' interest payments to $1 million each and delay the first payment until December 31, 2017.
c. Reduce the unpaid principal amount to $11 million.

Required:
Prepare the journal entries by Brainard Industries, Inc., necessitated by the restructuring of the debt at (1) January 1, 2016; (2) December 31, 2017; and (3) December 31, 2018.

E 14–35
Troubled debt restructuring; modification of terms; unknown effective rate
● Appendix B

At January 1, 2016, NCI Industries, Inc., was indebted to First Federal Bank under a $240,000, 10% unsecured note. The note was signed January 1, 2012, and was due December 31, 2017. Annual interest was last paid on December 31, 2014. NCI was experiencing severe financial difficulties and negotiated a restructuring of the terms of the debt agreement. First Federal agreed to reduce last year's interest and the remaining two years' interest payments to $11,555 each and delay all payments until December 31, 2017, the maturity date.

Required:
Prepare the journal entries by NCI Industries, Inc., necessitated by the restructuring of the debt at: (1) January 1, 2016; (2) December 31, 2016; and (3) December 31, 2017.

E 14–36
FASB codification research; legal fees in a troubled debt restructuring
● Appendix B

CODE

In negotiating and effecting a troubled debt restructuring, the creditor usually incurs various legal costs. The *FASB Accounting Standards Codification* represents the single source of authoritative U.S. generally accepted accounting principles.

Required:
1. Obtain the relevant authoritative literature on the accounting treatment of legal fees incurred by a creditor to effect a troubled debt restructuring using the *FASB Accounting Standards Codification* at the FASB website (**asc.fasb.org**).
2. What is the specific citation that describes the guidelines for reporting legal costs?
3. What is the appropriate accounting treatment?

CPA and CMA Review Questions

CPA Exam Questions

KAPLAN CPA REVIEW

The following questions are adapted from a variety of sources including questions developed by the AICPA Board of Examiners and those used in the Kaplan CPA Review Course to study long-term debt while preparing for the CPA examination. Determine the response that best completes the statements or questions.

● LO14–1

1. The market price of a bond issued at a discount is the present value of its principal amount at the market (effective) rate of interest
   a. Less the present value of all future interest payments at the rate of interest stated on the bond.
   b. Plus the present value of all future interest payments at the rate of interest stated on the bond.
   c. Plus the present value of all future interest payments at the market (effective) rate of interest.
   d. Less the present value of all future interest payments at the market (effective) rate of interest.

● LO14–2

2. A bond issue on June 1, 2016, has interest payment dates of April 1 and October 1. Bond interest expense for the year ended December 31, 2016, is for a period of
   a. Three months
   b. Four months
   c. Six months
   d. Seven months

● LO14–2

3. On July 1, 2016, Pell Co. purchased Green Corp. 10-year, 8% bonds with a face amount of $500,000 for $420,000. The bonds mature on June 30, 2026, and pay interest semiannually on June 30 and December 31.

Using the effective interest method, Pell recorded bond discount amortization of $1,800 for the six months ended December 31, 2016. From this long-term investment, Pell should report 2016 revenue of

a. $16,800
b. $18,200
c. $20,000
d. $21,800

● LO14–2

4. The following information pertains to Camp Corp.'s issuance of bonds on July 1, 2016:

Face amount	$800,000
Terms	10 years
Stated interest rate	6%
Interest payment dates	Annually on July 1
Yield	9%

	At 6%	At 9%
Present value of $1 for 10 periods	0.558	0.422
Future value of $1 for 10 periods	1.791	2.367
Present value of ordinary annuity of $1 for 10 periods	7.360	6.418

What should be the issue price for each $1,000 bond?

a. $ 700
b. $ 807
c. $ 864
d. $1,000

● LO14–2

5. For a bond issue that sells for less than its face value, the market rate of interest is

a. Higher than the rate stated on the bond.
b. Dependent on the rate stated on the bond.
c. Equal to the rate stated on the bond.
d. Less than the rate stated on the bond.

● LO14–2

6. On January 31, 2016, Beau Corp. issued $300,000 maturity value, 12% bonds for $300,000 cash. The bonds are dated December 31, 2015, and mature on December 31, 2025. Interest will be paid semiannually on June 30 and December 31. What amount of accrued interest payable should Beau report in its September 30, 2016, balance sheet?

a. $ 9,000
b. $18,000
c. $27,000
d. $24,000

● LO14–5

7. On January 1, 2011, Fox Corp. issued 1,000 of its 10%, $1,000 bonds for $1,040,000. These bonds were to mature on January 1, 2021, but were callable at 101 any time after December 31, 2013. Interest was payable semiannually on July 1 and January 1. On July 1, 2016, Fox called all of the bonds and retired them. Bond premium was amortized on a straight-line basis. Before income taxes, Fox's gain or loss in 2016 on this early extinguishment of debt was

a. $ 8,000 gain
b. $10,000 loss
c. $12,000 gain
d. $30,000 gain

● LO14–5

8. On April 30, 2016, Witt Corp. had outstanding 8%, $1,000,000 face amount, convertible bonds maturing on April 30, 2024. Interest is payable on April 30 and October 31. On April 30, 2016, all these bonds were converted into 40,000 shares of $20 par common stock. On the date of conversion:

- Unamortized bond discount was $30,000.
- Each bond had a market price of $1,080.
- Each share of stock had a market price of $28.

Using the book value method, how much of a gain or loss should be recognized?

a. $ 0
b. $150,000
c. $110,000
d. $ 30,000

● LO14–5

9. On June 30, 2016, King Co. had outstanding 9%, $5,000,000 face value bonds maturing on June 30, 2021. Interest was payable semiannually every June 30 and December 31. On June 30, 2016, after amortization was

recorded for the period, the unamortized bond premium and bond issuance costs were $30,000 and $50,000, respectively. On that date, King acquired all its outstanding bonds on the open market at 98 and retired them. At June 30, 2016, what amount should King recognize as gain before income taxes on redemption of bonds?

a. $ 20,000
b. $ 80,000
c. $120,000
d. $180,000

● LO14–5

10. Ray Corp. issued bonds with a face amount of $200,000. Each $1,000 bond contained detachable stock warrants for 100 shares of Ray's common stock. Total proceeds from the issue amounted to $240,000. The market value of each warrant was $2, and the market value of the bonds without the warrants was $196,000. The bonds were issued at a discount of (rounding the allocation percentage to two decimal places):

a. $ 0
b. $ 800
c. $ 4,000
d. $33,898

International Financial Reporting Standards are tested on the CPA exam along with U.S. GAAP. The following questions deal with the application of IFRS in accounting for long-term debt.

● LO14–7 IFRS

11. On May 1, 2016, Maine Co. issued 10-year convertible bonds at 103. During 2018, the bonds were converted into common stock. Maine prepares its financial statements according to International Accounting Standards (IFRS). On May 1, 2016, cash proceeds from the issuance of the convertible bonds should be reported as

a. A liability for the entire proceeds.
b. Paid-in capital for the entire proceeds.
c. Paid-in capital for the portion of the proceeds attributable to the conversion feature and as a liability for the balance.
d. A liability for the face amount of the bonds and paid-in capital for the premium over the par value.

● LO14–7 IFRS

12. When bonds and other debt securities are issued, payments such as legal costs, printing costs, and underwriting fees, are referred to as debt issuance costs (called transaction costs under IFRS). If Rushing International prepares its financial statements using IFRS:

a. the recorded amount of the debt is increased by the transaction costs.
b. the decrease in the effective interest rate caused by the transaction costs is reflected in the interest expense.
c. the transaction costs are recorded separately as an asset.
d. the increase in the effective interest rate caused by the transaction costs is reflected in the interest expense.

CMA Exam Questions

The following questions dealing with long-term liabilities are adapted from questions that previously appeared on Certified Management Accountant (CMA) examinations. The CMA designation sponsored by the Institute of Management Accountants (**www.imanet.org**) provides members with an objective measure of knowledge and competence in the field of management accounting. Determine the response that best completes the statements or questions.

Questions 1 and 2 are based on the following information. On January 1, Matthew Company issued 7% term bonds with a face amount of $1,000,000 due in 8 years. Interest is payable semiannually on January 1 and July 1. On the date of issue, investors were willing to accept an effective interest rate of 6%.

● LO14–1

1. The bonds were issued on January 1 at

a. a premium.
b. an amortized value.
c. book value.
d. a discount.

● LO14–2

2. Assume the bonds were issued on January 1 for $1,062,809. Using the effective interest amortization method, Matthew Company recorded interest expense for the 6 months ended June 30 in the amount of

a. $35,000
b. $70,000
c. $63,769
d. $31,884

● LO14–4

3. A bond issue sold at a premium is valued on the statement of financial position at the

a. maturity value.
b. maturity value plus the unamortized portion of the premium.
c. cost at the date of investment.
d. maturity value less the unamortized portion of the premium.

Problems

An alternate exercise and problem set is available in the Connect library.

P 14–1
Determining the price of bonds; discount and premium; issuer and investor
● LO14–2

On January 1, 2016, Instaform, Inc., issued 10% bonds with a face amount of $50 million, dated January 1. The bonds mature in 2035 (20 years). The market yield for bonds of similar risk and maturity is 12%. Interest is paid semiannually.

Required:

1. Determine the price of the bonds at January 1, 2016, and prepare the journal entry to record their issuance by Instaform.
2. Assume the market rate was 9%. Determine the price of the bonds at January 1, 2016, and prepare the journal entry to record their issuance by Instaform.
3. Assume Broadcourt Electronics purchased the entire issue in a private placement of the bonds. Using the data in requirement 2, prepare the journal entry to record the purchase by Broadcourt.

P 14–2
Effective interest; financial statement effects
● LO14–2

On January 1, 2016, Baddour, Inc., issued 10% bonds with a face amount of $160 million. The bonds were priced at $140 million to yield 12%. Interest is paid semiannually on June 30 and December 31. Baddour's fiscal year ends September 30.

Required:

1. What amount(s) related to the bonds would Baddour report in its balance sheet at September 30, 2016?
2. What amount(s) related to the bonds would Baddour report in its income statement for the year ended September 30, 2016?
3. What amount(s) related to the bonds would Baddour report in its statement of cash flows for the year ended September 30, 2016? In which section(s) should the amount(s) appear?

P 14–3
Straight-line and effective interest compared
● LO14–2

On January 1, 2016, Bradley Recreational Products issued $100,000, 9%, four-year bonds. Interest is paid semiannually on June 30 and December 31. The bonds were issued at $96,768 to yield an annual return of 10%.

Required:

1. Prepare an amortization schedule that determines interest at the effective interest rate.
2. Prepare an amortization schedule by the straight-line method.
3. Prepare the journal entries to record interest expense on June 30, 2018, by each of the two approaches.
4. Explain why the pattern of interest differs between the two methods.
5. Assuming the market rate is still 10%, what price would a second investor pay the first investor on June 30, 2018, for $10,000 of the bonds?

P 14–4
Bond amortization schedule
● LO14–2

On January 1, 2016, Tennessee Harvester Corporation issued debenture bonds that pay interest semiannually on June 30 and December 31. Portions of the bond amortization schedule appear below:

Payment	Cash Payment	Effective Interest	Increase in Balance	Outstanding Balance
				6,627,273
1	320,000	331,364	11,364	6,638,637
2	320,000	331,932	11,932	6,650,569
3	320,000	332,528	12,528	6,663,097
4	320,000	333,155	13,155	6,676,252
5	320,000	333,813	13,813	6,690,065
6	320,000	334,503	14,503	6,704,568
~	~	~	~	~
~	~	~	~	~
~	~	~	~	~
38	320,000	389,107	69,107	7,851,247
39	320,000	392,562	72,562	7,923,809
40	320,000	396,191	76,191	8,000,000

Required:

1. What is the face amount of the bonds?
2. What is the initial selling price of the bonds?
3. What is the term to maturity in years?

4. Interest is determined by what approach?
5. What is the stated annual interest rate?
6. What is the effective annual interest rate?
7. What is the total cash interest paid over the term to maturity?
8. What is the total effective interest expense recorded over the term to maturity?

P 14–5
Issuer and investor; effective interest; amortization schedule; adjusting entries
● LO14–2

On February 1, 2016, Cromley Motor Products issued 9% bonds, dated February 1, with a face amount of $80 million. The bonds mature on January 31, 2020 (4 years). The market yield for bonds of similar risk and maturity was 10%. Interest is paid semiannually on July 31 and January 31. Barnwell Industries acquired $80,000 of the bonds as a long-term investment. The fiscal years of both firms end December 31.

Required:

1. Determine the price of the bonds issued on February 1, 2016.
2. Prepare amortization schedules that indicate (a) Cromley's effective interest expense and (b) Barnwell's effective interest revenue for each interest period during the term to maturity.
3. Prepare the journal entries to record (a) the issuance of the bonds by Cromley and (b) Barnwell's investment on February 1, 2016.
4. Prepare the journal entries by both firms to record all subsequent events related to the bonds through January 31, 2018.

P 14–6
Issuer and investor; straight-line method; adjusting entries
● LO14–2, Appendix A

On April 1, 2016, Western Communications, Inc., issued 12% bonds, dated March 1, 2016, with face amount of $30 million. The bonds sold for $29.3 million and mature on February 28, 2019. Interest is paid semiannually on August 31 and February 28. Stillworth Corporation acquired $30,000 of the bonds as a long-term investment. The fiscal years of both firms end December 31, and both firms use the straight-line method.

Required:

1. Prepare the journal entries to record (a) issuance of the bonds by Western and (b) Stillworth's investment on April 1, 2016.
2. Prepare the journal entries by both firms to record all subsequent events related to the bonds through maturity.

P 14–7
Issuer and investor; effective interest
● LO14–2

McWherter Instruments sold $400 million of 8% bonds, dated January 1, on January 1, 2016. The bonds mature on December 31, 2035 (20 years). For bonds of similar risk and maturity, the market yield was 10%. Interest is paid semiannually on June 30 and December 31. Blanton Technologies, Inc., purchased $400,000 of the bonds as a long-term investment.

Required:

1. Determine the price of the bonds issued on January 1, 2016.
2. Prepare the journal entries to record (a) their issuance by McWherter and (b) Blanton's investment on January 1, 2016.
3. Prepare the journal entries by (a) McWherter and (b) Blanton to record interest on June 30, 2016 (at the effective rate).
4. Prepare the journal entries by (a) McWherter and (b) Blanton to record interest on December 31, 2016 (at the effective rate).

P 14–8
Bonds; effective interest; partial period interest; financial statement effects
● LO14–2

The fiscal year ends December 31 for Lake Hamilton Development. To provide funding for its Moonlight Bay project, LHD issued 5% bonds with a face amount of $500,000 on November 1, 2016. The bonds sold for $442,215, a price to yield the market rate of 6%. The bonds mature October 31, 2036 (20 years). Interest is paid semiannually on April 30 and October 31.

Required:

1. What amount of interest expense related to the bonds will LHD report in its income statement for the year ending December 31, 2016?
2. What amount(s) related to the bonds will LHD report in its balance sheet at December 31, 2016?
3. What amount of interest expense related to the bonds will LHD report in its income statement for the year ending December 31, 2017?
4. What amount(s) related to the bonds will LHD report in its balance sheet at December 31, 2017?

P 14–9
Zero-coupon bonds
● LO14–2

On January 1, 2016, Darnell Window and Pane issued $18 million of 10-year, zero-coupon bonds for $5,795,518.

Required:

1. Prepare the journal entry to record the bond issue.
2. Determine the effective rate of interest.

3. Prepare the journal entry to record annual interest expense at December 31, 2016.
4. Prepare the journal entry to record annual interest expense at December 31, 2017.
5. Prepare the journal entry to record the extinguishment at maturity.

P 14–10
Notes exchanged for assets; unknown effective rate
● LO14–3

At the beginning of the year, Lambert Motors issued the three notes described below. Interest is paid at year-end.

1. The company issued a two-year, 12%, $600,000 note in exchange for a tract of land. The current market rate of interest is 12%.
2. Lambert acquired some office equipment with a fair value of $94,643 by issuing a one-year, $100,000 note. The stated interest on the note is 6%.
3. The company purchased a building by issuing a three-year installment note. The note is to be repaid in equal installments of $1 million per year beginning one year hence. The current market rate of interest is 12%.

Required:
Prepare the journal entries to record each of the three transactions and the interest expense at the end of the first year for each.

P 14–11
Note with unrealistic interest rate
● LO14–3

At January 1, 2016, Brant Cargo acquired equipment by issuing a five-year, $150,000 (payable at maturity), 4% note. The market rate of interest for notes of similar risk is 10%.

Required:
1. Prepare the journal entry for Brant Cargo to record the purchase of the equipment.
2. Prepare the journal entry for Brant Cargo to record the interest at December 31, 2016.
3. Prepare the journal entry for Brant Cargo to record the interest at December 31, 2017.

P 14–12
Noninterest-bearing installment note
● LO14–3

At the beginning of 2016, VHF Industries acquired a machine with a fair value of $6,074,700 by issuing a four-year, noninterest-bearing note in the face amount of $8 million. The note is payable in four annual installments of $2 million at the end of each year.

Required:
1. What is the effective rate of interest implicit in the agreement?
2. Prepare the journal entry to record the purchase of the machine.
3. Prepare the journal entry to record the first installment payment at December 31, 2016.
4. Prepare the journal entry to record the second installment payment at December 31, 2017.
5. Suppose the market value of the machine was unknown at the time of purchase, but the market rate of interest for notes of similar risk was 11%. Prepare the journal entry to record the purchase of the machine.

P 14–13
Note and installment note with unrealistic interest rate
● LO14–3

Braxton Technologies, Inc., constructed a conveyor for A&G Warehousers that was completed and ready for use on January 1, 2016. A&G paid for the conveyor by issuing a $100,000, four-year note that specified 5% interest to be paid on December 31 of each year, and the note is to be repaid at the end of four years. The conveyor was custom-built for A&G, so its cash price was unknown. By comparison with similar transactions it was determined that a reasonable interest rate was 10%.

Required:
1. Prepare the journal entry for A&G's purchase of the conveyor on January 1, 2016.
2. Prepare an amortization schedule for the four-year term of the note.
3. Prepare the journal entry for A&G's third interest payment on December 31, 2018.
4. If A&G's note had been an installment note to be paid in four equal payments at the end of each year beginning December 31, 2016, what would be the amount of each installment?
5. Prepare an amortization schedule for the four-year term of the installment note.
6. Prepare the journal entry for A&G's third installment payment on December 31, 2018.

P 14–14
Early extinguishment of debt
● LO14–5

Three years ago American Insulation Corporation issued 10 percent, $800,000, 10-year bonds for $770,000. Debt issue costs were $3,000. American Insulation exercised its call privilege and retired the bonds for $790,000. The corporation uses the straight-line method both to determine interest and to amortize debt issue costs.

Required:
Prepare the journal entry to record the call of the bonds.

P 14–15
Early extinguishment; effective interest
● LO14–5

The long-term liability section of Twin Digital Corporation's balance sheet as of December 31, 2015, included 12% bonds having a face amount of $20 million and a remaining discount of $1 million. Disclosure notes indicate the bonds were issued to yield 14%.

Interest expense is recorded at the effective interest rate and paid on January 1 and July 1 of each year. On July 1, 2016, Twin Digital retired the bonds at 102 ($20.4 million) before their scheduled maturity.

Required:

1. Prepare the journal entry by Twin Digital to record the semiannual interest on July 1, 2016.
2. Prepare the journal entry by Twin Digital to record the redemption of the bonds on July 1, 2016.

P 14–16
Debt issue costs; issuance; expensing; early extinguishment; straight-line interest
● LO14–2, LO14–5

Cupola Fan Corporation issued 10%, $400,000, 10-year bonds for $385,000 on June 30, 2016. Debt issue costs were $1,500. Interest is paid semiannually on December 31 and June 30. One year from the issue date (July 1, 2017), the corporation exercised its call privilege and retired the bonds for $395,000. The corporation uses the straight-line method both to determine interest expense and to amortize debt issue costs.

Required:

1. Prepare the journal entry to record the issuance of the bonds.
2. Prepare the journal entries to record the payment of interest and amortization of debt issue costs on December 31, 2016.
3. Prepare the journal entries to record the payment of interest and amortization of debt issue costs on June 30, 2017.
4. Prepare the journal entry to record the call of the bonds.

P 14–17
IFRS; Transaction costs
● LO14–2, LO14–7

Refer to the situation described in P14–16.

Required:

How might your solution for the issuer of the bonds differ if Cupola prepares its financial statements according to International Financial Reporting Standards? Include any appropriate journal entries in your response.

P 14–18
Early extinguishment
● LO14–5

The long-term liability section of Eastern Post Corporation's balance sheet as of December 31, 2015, included 10% bonds having a face amount of $40 million and a remaining premium of $6 million. On January 1, 2016, Eastern Post retired some of the bonds before their scheduled maturity.

Required:

Prepare the journal entry by Eastern Post to record the redemption of the bonds under each of the independent circumstances below:

1. Eastern Post called half the bonds at the call price of 102 (102% of face amount).
2. Eastern Post repurchased $10 million of the bonds on the open market at their market price of $10.5 million.

P 14–19
Convertible bonds; induced conversion; bonds with detachable warrants
● LO14–5

Bradley-Link's December 31, 2016, balance sheet included the following items:

Long-Term Liabilities	($ in millions)
9.6% convertible bonds, callable at 101 beginning in 2017, due 2020 (net of unamortized discount of $2) [note 8]	$198
10.4% registered bonds callable at 104 beginning in 2026, due 2030 (net of unamortized discount of $1) [note 8]	49
Shareholders' Equity	
Equity—stock warrants	4

Note 8: Bonds (in part)

The 9.6% bonds were issued in 2003 at 97.5 to yield 10%. Interest is paid semiannually on June 30 and December 31. Each $1,000 bond is convertible into 40 shares of the Company's no par common stock.

The 10.4% bonds were issued in 2007 at 102 to yield 10%. Interest is paid semiannually on June 30 and December 31. Each $1,000 bond was issued with 40 detachable stock warrants, each of which entitles the holder to purchase one share of the Company's no par common stock for $25, beginning 2017.

On January 3, 2017, when Bradley-Link's common stock had a market price of $32 per share, Bradley-Link called the convertible bonds to force conversion. 90% were converted; the remainder were acquired at the call price. When the common stock price reached an all-time high of $37 in December of 2017, 40% of the warrants were exercised.

Required:

1. Prepare the journal entries that were recorded when each of the two bond issues was originally sold in 2003 and 2007.
2. Prepare the journal entry to record (book value method) the conversion of 90% of the convertible bonds in January 2017 and the retirement of the remainder.
3. Assume Bradley-Link induced conversion by offering $150 cash for each bond converted. Prepare the journal entry to record (book value method) the conversion of 90% of the convertible bonds in January 2017.
4. Assume Bradley-Link induced conversion by modifying the conversion ratio to exchange 45 shares for each bond rather than the 40 shares provided in the contract. Prepare the journal entry to record (book value method) the conversion of 90% of the convertible bonds in January 2017.
5. Prepare the journal entry to record the exercise of the warrants in December 2017.

P 14–20
Convertible bonds; zero coupon; potentially convertible into cash; FASB codification research
● LO14–5

Real World Financials

The June 30, 2012, annual report of **Microsoft Corporation** reports zero-coupon convertible notes that the company issued in June of 2010.

Required:

1. Access the **Microsoft** website: www.microsoft.com. Select "Investor Relations" and then "SEC Filings." Access the 10-K filing for the year ended June 30, 2012. (The debt was converted in June 2013.) Search or scroll to find the disclosure notes related to the zero-coupon convertible notes. What is the amount of the convertible notes issued?
2. Prepare the journal entry that was recorded when the notes were issued in 2010. Use the information in the financial statement note accessed in Requirement 1. The actual present value of the debt was $1,183,115 (PV of $1,250,000 discounted for 3 years at 1.85%). Consider the conversion component and the debt issue costs for the entry.
3. What amount of interest expense, if any, did Microsoft record the first year the notes were outstanding? Use the information from Requirement 2.
4. Normally, under U.S. GAAP, we record the entire issue price of convertible debt as a liability. However, Microsoft separately recorded the liability and equity components of the notes. Why?
5. Obtain the relevant authoritative literature on classification of debt expected to be financed using the *FASB Accounting Standards Codification*. You might gain access from the FASB website (www.fasb.org), from your school library, or some other source. Determine the criteria for reporting debt potentially convertible into cash. What is the specific codification citation that Microsoft would rely on in applying that accounting treatment?

P 14–21
Concepts; terminology
● LO14–1 through LO14–5

Listed below are several terms and phrases associated with long-term debt. Pair each item from List A with the item from List B (by letter) that is most appropriately associated with it.

	List A	List B
____	1. Effective rate times balance	a. Straight-line method
____	2. Promises made to bondholders	b. Discount
____	3. Present value of interest plus present value of principal	c. Liquidation payments after other claims satisfied
____	4. Call feature	d. Name of owner not registered
____	5. Debt issue costs	e. Premium
____	6. Market rate higher than stated rate	f. Checks are mailed directly
____	7. Coupon bonds	g. No specific assets pledged
____	8. Convertible bonds	h. Bond indenture
____	9. Market rate less than stated rate	i. Backed by a lien
____	10. Stated rate times face amount	j. Interest expense
____	11. Registered bonds	k. May become stock
____	12. Debenture bond	l. Legal, accounting, printing
____	13. Mortgage bond	m. Protection against falling rates
____	14. Materiality concept	n. Periodic cash payments
____	15. Subordinated debenture	o. Bond price

P 14–22
Determine bond price; record interest; report bonds at fair value
● LO14–6

On January 1, 2016, NFB Visual Aids issued $800,000 of its 20-year, 8% bonds. The bonds were priced to yield 10%. Interest is payable semiannually on June 30 and December 31. NFB Visual Aids records interest expense at the effective rate and elected the option to report these bonds at their fair value. On December 31, 2016, the fair value of the bonds was $668,000 as determined by their market value in the over-the-counter market.

Required:

1. Determine the price of the bonds at January 1, 2016, and prepare the journal entry to record their issuance.
2. Prepare the journal entry to record interest on June 30, 2016 (the first interest payment).
3. Prepare the journal entry to record interest on December 31, 2016 (the second interest payment).
4. Prepare the journal entry to adjust the bonds to their fair value for presentation in the December 31, 2016, balance sheet.

P 14–23
Report bonds at fair value; quarterly reporting
● LO14–6

Appling Enterprises issued 8% bonds with a face amount of $400,000 on January 1, 2016. The bonds sold for $331,364 and mature in 2035 (20 years). For bonds of similar risk and maturity the market yield was 10%. Interest is paid semiannually on June 30 and December 31. Appling determines interest expense at the effective rate. Appling elected the option to report these bonds at their fair value. The fair values of the bonds at the end of each quarter during 2016 as determined by their market values in the over-the-counter market were the following:

March 31	$350,000
June 30	340,000
September 30	335,000
December 31	342,000

General (risk-free) interest rates did not change during 2016.

Required:

1. By how much will Appling's comprehensive income be increased or decreased by the bonds (ignoring taxes) in the March 31 *quarterly* financial statements?
2. By how much will Appling's comprehensive income be increased or decreased by the bonds (ignoring taxes) in the June 30 *quarterly* financial statements?
3. By how much will Appling's comprehensive income be increased or decreased by the bonds (ignoring taxes) in the September 30 *quarterly* financial statements?
4. By how much will Appling's comprehensive income be increased or decreased by the bonds (ignoring taxes) in the December 31 *annual* financial statements?

P 14–24
Investments in bonds; accrued interest; sale; straight-line interest
● LO14–2
● Appendix A

The following transactions relate to bond investments of Livermore Laboratories. The company's fiscal year ends on December 31. Livermore uses the straight-line method to determine interest.

2016	
July 1	Purchased $16 million of Bracecourt Corporation 10% debentures, due in 20 years (June 30, 2036), for $15.7 million. Interest is payable on January 1 and July 1 of each year.
Oct. 1	Purchased $30 million of 12% Framm Pharmaceuticals debentures, due May 31, 2026, for $31,160,000 plus accrued interest. Interest is payable on June 1 and December 1 of each year.
Dec. 1	Received interest on the Framm bonds.
31	Accrued interest.
2017	
Jan. 1	Received interest on the Bracecourt bonds.
June 1	Received interest on the Framm bonds.
July 1	Received interest on the Bracecourt bonds.
Sept. 1	Sold $15 million of the Framm bonds at 101 plus accrued interest.
Dec. 1	Received interest on the remaining Framm bonds.
31	Accrued interest.
2018	
Jan. 1	Received interest on the Bracecourt bonds.
Feb. 28	Sold the remainder of the Framm bonds at 102 plus accrued interest.
Dec. 31	Accrued interest.

Required:

1. Prepare the appropriate journal entries for these long-term bond investments.
2. By how much will Livermore Labs' earnings increase in each of the three years as a result of these investments? (Ignore income taxes.)

P 14–25
Accrued interest; effective interest; financial statement effects
● Appendix A

On March 1, 2016, Baddour, Inc., issued 10% bonds, dated January 1, with a face amount of $160 million. The bonds were priced at $140 million (plus accrued interest) to yield 12%. Interest is paid semiannually on June 30 and December 31. Baddour's fiscal year ends September 30.

Required:

1. What would be the amount(s) related to the bonds Baddour would report in its balance sheet at September 30, 2016?

2. What would be the amount(s) related to the bonds that Baddour would report in its income statement for the year ended September 30, 2016?
3. What would be the amount(s) related to the bonds that Baddour would report in its statement of cash flows for the year ended September 30, 2016?

P 14–26
Troubled debt restructuring
● Appendix B

At January 1, 2016, Rothschild Chair Company, Inc., was indebted to First Lincoln Bank under a $20 million, 10% unsecured note. The note was signed January 1, 2013, and was due December 31, 2019. Annual interest was last paid on December 31, 2014. Rothschild Chair Company was experiencing severe financial difficulties and negotiated a restructuring of the terms of the debt agreement.

Required:
Prepare all journal entries by Rothschild Chair Company, Inc., to record the restructuring and any remaining transactions relating to the debt under each of the independent circumstances below:
1. First Lincoln Bank agreed to settle the debt in exchange for land having a fair value of $16 million but carried on Rothschild Chair Company's books at $13 million.
2. First Lincoln Bank agreed to (a) forgive the interest accrued from last year, (b) reduce the remaining four interest payments to $1 million each, and (c) reduce the principal to $15 million.
3. First Lincoln Bank agreed to defer all payments (including accrued interest) until the maturity date and accept $27,775,000 at that time in settlement of the debt.

Broaden Your Perspective

Apply your critical-thinking ability to the knowledge you've gained. These cases will provide you an opportunity to develop your research, analysis, judgment, and communication skills. You also will work with other students, integrate what you've learned, apply it in real-world situations, and consider its global and ethical ramifications. This practice will broaden your knowledge and further develop your decision-making abilities.

Communication Case 14–1
Convertible securities and warrants; concepts
● LO14–5

It is not unusual to issue long-term debt in conjunction with an arrangement under which lenders receive an option to buy common stock during all or a portion of the time the debt is outstanding. Sometimes the vehicle is convertible bonds; sometimes warrants to buy stock accompany the bonds and are separable. Interstate Chemical is considering these options in conjunction with a planned debt issue.

"You mean we have to report $7 million more in liabilities if we go with convertible bonds? Makes no sense to me," your CFO said. "Both ways seem pretty much the same transaction. Explain it to me, will you?"

Required:
Write a memo. Include in your explanation each of the following:
1. The differences in accounting for proceeds from the issuance of convertible bonds and of debt instruments with separate warrants to purchase common stock.
2. The underlying rationale for the differences.
3. Arguments that could be presented for the alternative accounting treatment.

Real World Case 14–2
Zero-coupon debt; Hewlett-Packard Company
● LO14–2

Real World Financials

The **Hewlett-Packard Company** issued zero-coupon notes at the end of its 1997 fiscal year that mature at the end of its 2017 fiscal year. One billion, eight hundred million dollars face amount of 20-year debt sold for $968 million, a price to yield 3.149%. In fiscal 2002, HP repurchased $257 million in face value of the notes for a purchase price of $127 million, resulting in a gain on the early extinguishment of debt.

Required:
1. What journal entry did Hewlett-Packard use to record the sale in 1997?
2. Using an electronic spreadsheet, prepare an amortization schedule for the notes. Assume interest is calculated annually and use numbers expressed in millions of dollars; that is, the face amount is $1,800.
3. What was the effect on HP's earnings in 1998? Explain.
4. From the amortization schedule, determine the book value of the debt at the end of 2002.
5. What journal entry did Hewlett-Packard use to record the early extinguishment of debt in 2002, assuming the purchase was made at the end of the year?
6. If none of the notes is repaid prior to maturity, what entry would HP use to record their repayment at the end of 2017?

Communication Case 14–3
Is convertible debt a liability or is it shareholders' equity? Group Interaction
● LO14–5

Some financial instruments can be considered compound instruments in that they have features of both debt and shareholders' equity. The most common example encountered in practice is convertible debt—bonds or notes convertible by the investor into common stock. A topic of debate for several years has been whether:

View 1: Issuers should account for an instrument with both liability and equity characteristics entirely as a liability or entirely as an equity instrument depending on which characteristic governs.

View 2: Issuers should account for an instrument as consisting of a liability component and an equity component that should be accounted for separately.

In considering this question, you should disregard what you know about the current position of the FASB on the issue. Instead, focus on conceptual issues regarding the practicable and theoretically appropriate treatment, unconstrained by GAAP. Also, focus your deliberations on convertible bonds as the instrument with both liability and equity characteristics.

Required:

1. Which view do you favor? Develop a list of arguments in support of your view prior to the class session for which the case is assigned.
2. In class, your instructor will pair you (and everyone else) with a classmate (who also has independently developed an argument).
   a. You will be given three minutes to argue your view to your partner. Your partner likewise will be given three minutes to argue his or her view to you. During these three-minute presentations, the listening partner is not permitted to speak.
   b. After each person has had a turn attempting to convince his or her partner, the two partners will have a three-minute discussion in which they will decide which view is more convincing. Arguments will be merged into a single view for each pair.
3. After the allotted time, a spokesperson for each of the two views will be selected by the instructor. Each spokesperson will field arguments from the class in support of that view's position and list the arguments on the board. The class then will discuss the merits of the two lists of arguments and attempt to reach a consensus view, though a consensus is not necessary.

Analysis Case 14–4
Issuance of bonds
● LO14–2

The following appeared in the October 15, 2016, issue of the *Financial Smarts Journal:*

This announcement is not an offer of securities for sale or an offer to buy securities.
New Issue
October 15, 2016

$750,000,000
CRAFT FOODS, INC.
7.75% Debentures Due October 1, 2026
Price 99.57%
plus accrued interest if any from date of issuance

Copies of the prospectus and the related prospectus supplement may be obtained from such of the undersigned as may legally offer these securities under applicable securities laws.

Keegan Morgan & Co. Inc.
Coldwell Bros. & Co.
Robert Stacks & Co.
Sherwin-William & Co.

Required:

1. Explain what is being described by the announcement.
2. Can you think of a psychological reason for the securities to be priced as they are?
3. What are the accounting considerations for Craft Foods, Inc.? Describe how Craft recorded the sale.

Judgment Case 14–5
Noninterest-bearing debt
● LO14–3

While reading a recent issue of *Health & Fitness*, a trade journal, Brandon Wilde noticed an ad for equipment he had been seeking for use in his business. The ad offered oxygen therapy equipment under the following terms:

Model BL 44582
$204,000 zero interest loan
Quarterly payments of $17,000 for only 3 years

The ad captured Wilde's attention, in part, because he recently had been concerned that the interest charges incurred by his business were getting out of line. The price, though, was somewhat higher than prices for this model he had seen elsewhere.

Required:

Advise Mr. Wilde on the purchase he is considering.

Judgment Case 14–6
Noninterest-bearing note exchanged for cash and other privileges
● LO14–3

The Jaecke Group, Inc., manufactures various kinds of hydraulic pumps. In June 2016, the company signed a four-year purchase agreement with one of its main parts suppliers, Hydraulics, Inc. Over the four-year period, Jaecke has agreed to purchase 100,000 units of a key component used in the manufacture of its pumps. The agreement allows Jaecke to purchase the component at a price lower than the prevailing market price at the time of purchase. As part of the agreement, Jaecke will lend Hydraulics $200,000 to be repaid after four years with no stated interest (the prevailing market rate of interest for a loan of this type is 10%).

Jaecke's chief accountant has proposed recording the note receivable at $200,000. The parts inventory purchase from Hydraulics over the next four years will then be recorded at the actual prices paid.

Required:
Do you agree with the accountant's valuation of the note and his intention to value the parts inventory acquired over the four-year period of the agreement at actual prices paid? If not, how would you account for the initial transaction and the subsequent inventory purchases?

Communication Case 14–7
Note receivable exchanged for cash and other services
● LO14–3

The Pastel Paint Company recently loaned $300,000 to KIX 96, a local radio station. The radio station signed a noninterest-bearing note requiring the $300,000 to be repaid in three years. As part of the agreement, the radio station will provide Pastel with a specified amount of free radio advertising over the three-year term of the note.

The focus of this case is the valuation of the note receivable by Pastel Paint Company and the treatment of the "free" advertising provided by the radio station. Your instructor will divide the class into two to six groups depending on the size of the class. The mission of your group is to reach consensus on the appropriate note valuation and accounting treatment of the free advertising.

Required:
1. Each group member should deliberate the situation independently and draft a tentative argument prior to the class session for which the case is assigned.
2. In class, each group will meet for 10 to 15 minutes in different areas of the classroom. During that meeting, group members will take turns sharing their suggestions for the purpose of arriving at a single group treatment.
3. After the allotted time, a spokesperson for each group (selected during the group meetings) will share the group's solution with the class. The goal of the class is to incorporate the views of each group into a consensus approach to the situation.

Ethics Case 14–8
Debt for equity swaps; have your cake and eat it too
● LO14–5

The cloudy afternoon mirrored the mood of the conference of division managers. Claude Meyer, assistant to the controller for Hunt Manufacturing, wore one of the gloomy faces that were just emerging from the conference room. "Wow, I knew it was bad, but not that bad," Claude thought to himself. "I don't look forward to sharing those numbers with shareholders."

The numbers he discussed with himself were fourth quarter losses which more than offset the profits of the first three quarters. Everyone had known for some time that poor sales forecasts and production delays had wreaked havoc on the bottom line, but most were caught off guard by the severity of damage.

Later that night he sat alone in his office, scanning and rescanning the preliminary financial statements on his computer monitor. Suddenly his mood brightened. "This may work," he said aloud, though no one could hear. Fifteen minutes later he congratulated himself, "Yes!"

The next day he eagerly explained his plan to Susan Barr, controller of Hunt for the last six years. The plan involved $300 million in convertible bonds issued three years earlier.

Meyer: By swapping stock for the bonds, we can eliminate a substantial liability from the balance sheet, wipe out most of our interest expense, and reduce our loss. In fact, the book value of the bonds is significantly more than the market value of the stock we'd issue. I think we can produce a profit.

Barr: But Claude, our bondholders are not inclined to convert the bonds.

Meyer: Right. But, the bonds are callable. As of this year, we can call the bonds at a call premium of 1%. Given the choice of accepting that redemption price or converting to stock, they'll all convert. We won't have to pay a cent. And, since no cash will be paid, we won't pay taxes either.

Required:
Do you perceive an ethical dilemma? What would be the impact of following up on Claude's plan? Who would benefit? Who would be injured?

Judgment Case 14–9
Analyzing financial statements; financial leverage; interest coverage
● LO14–1, LO14–4

AGF Foods Company is a large, primarily domestic, consumer foods company involved in the manufacture, distribution, and sale of a variety of food products. Industry averages are derived from Troy's *The Almanac of Business and Industrial Financial Ratios.* Following are the 2016 and 2015 comparative income statements and balance sheets for AGF. (The financial data we use are from actual financial statements of a well-known corporation, but the company name is fictitious and the numbers and dates have been modified slightly to disguise the company's identity.)

AGF FOODS COMPANY
Years Ended December 31, 2016 and 2015
($ in millions)

Comparative Income Statements	**2016**	**2015**
Net sales	$6,440	$5,800
Cost of goods sold	(3,667)	(3,389)
Gross profit	2,773	2,411
Operating expenses	(1,916)	(1,629)
Operating income	857	782
Interest expense	(54)	(53)
Income from operations before tax	803	729
Income taxes	(316)	(287)
Net income	$ 487	$ 442
Comparative Balance Sheets		
Assets		
Total current assets	$1,879	$1,490
Property, plant, and equipment (net)	2,592	2,291
Intangibles (net)	800	843
Other assets	74	60
Total assets	$5,345	$4,684
Liabilities and Shareholders' Equity		
Total current liabilities	$1,473	$ 941
Long-term debt	534	728
Deferred income taxes	407	344
Total liabilities	2,414	2,013
Shareholders' equity:		
Common stock	180	180
Additional paid-in capital	21	63
Retained earnings	2,730	2,428
Total shareholders' equity	2,931	2,671
Total liabilities and shareholders' equity	$5,345	$4,684

Long-term solvency refers to a company's ability to pay its long-term obligations. Financing ratios provide investors and creditors with an indication of this element of risk.

Required:

1. Calculate the debt to equity ratio for AGF for 2016. The average ratio for the stocks listed on the New York Stock Exchange in a comparable time period was 1.0. What information does your calculation provide an investor?
2. Is AGF experiencing favorable or unfavorable financial leverage?
3. Calculate AGF's times interest earned ratio for 2016. The coverage for the stocks listed on the New York Stock Exchange in a comparable time period was 5.1. What does your calculation indicate about AGF's risk?

Research Case 14–10
FASB codification research; researching the way long-term debt is reported; Macy's, Inc.
● LO14–1 through LO14–4

EDGAR, the Electronic Data Gathering. Analysis, and Retrieval system, performs automated collection, validation, indexing, acceptance and forwarding of submissions by companies and others who are required by law to file forms with the U.S. Securities and Exchange Commission (SEC). All publicly traded domestic companies use EDGAR to make the majority of their filings. (Some foreign companies do so voluntarily.) Form 10-K, including the annual report, is required to be filed on EDGAR. The SEC makes this information available on the Internet.

Required:

1. Access EDGAR on the Internet at www.sec.gov or the Macy's, Inc., website: www.macys.com.
2. Search for Macy's. Access its 10-K filing for the year ended February 1, 2014. Search or scroll to find the financial statements and related notes.
3. What is the total debt (including current liabilities and deferred taxes) reported in the balance sheet? How has that amount changed over the most recent two years?

Real World Financials

4. Compare the total liabilities (including current liabilities and deferred taxes) with the shareholders' equity and calculate the debt to equity ratio for the most recent two years. Has the proportion of debt financing and equity financing changed recently?
5. Does Macy's obtain more financing through notes, bonds, or commercial paper? Are required debt payments increasing or decreasing over time? Is any short-term debt classified as long-term? Why?
6. **Note 6: Financing** includes the following statement: "On November 20, 2012, the Company issued $750 million aggregate principal amount of 2.875% senior unsecured notes due 2023 and $250 million aggregate principal amount of 4.3% senior unsecured notes due 2043. This debt was used to pay for the notes repurchased on November 28, 2012 described above, and to retire $298 million of 5.875% senior unsecured notes that matured in January 2013." Under some circumstances, Macy's could have reported the amounts due in 2013 as long-term debt at the end of the previous year even though these amounts were due within the coming year. Obtain the relevant authoritative literature on classification of debt expected to be financed using the *FASB Accounting Standards Codification*. You might gain access from the FASB website (asc.fasb.org), from your school library, or some other source. Determine the criteria for reporting currently payable debt as long-term. What is the specific codification citation that Macy's would rely on in applying that accounting treatment?

Analysis Case 14–11
Bonds; conversion; extinguishment
● LO14–5

On August 31, 2013, Chickasaw Industries issued $25 million of its 30-year, 6% convertible bonds dated August 31, priced to yield 5%. The bonds are convertible at the option of the investors into 1,500,000 shares of Chickasaw's common stock. Chickasaw records interest expense at the effective rate. On August 31, 2016, investors in Chickasaw's convertible bonds tendered 20% of the bonds for conversion into common stock that had a market value of $20 per share on the date of the conversion. On January 1, 2015, Chickasaw Industries issued $40 million of its 20-year, 7% bonds dated January 1 at a price to yield 8%. On December 31, 2016, the bonds were extinguished early through acquisition in the open market by Chickasaw for $40.5 million.

Required:
1. Using the book value method, would recording the conversion of the 6% convertible bonds into common stock affect earnings? If so, by how much? Would earnings be affected if the market value method is used? If so, by how much?
2. Were the 7% bonds issued at face value, at a discount, or at a premium? Explain.
3. Would the amount of interest expense for the 7% bonds be higher in the first year or second year of the term to maturity? Explain.
4. How should gain or loss on early extinguishment of debt be determined? Does the early extinguishment of the 7% bonds result in a gain or loss? Explain.

Analysis Case 14–12
Analyzing financial statements; debt-to-equity; interest coverage
● LO14–1, LO14–4

PetSmart

Refer to the financial statements and related disclosure notes of PetSmart in Appendix B located at the back of this textbook. Long-term solvency refers to a company's ability to pay its long-term obligations. Financing ratios provide investors and creditors with an indication of this element of risk.

Required:
1. Calculate the debt to equity ratio for PetSmart at February 2, 2014. The average ratio for companies in the pet supplies industry in a comparable time period was 1.8. What information does your calculation provide an investor?
2. Calculate PetSmart's times interest earned ratio for the year ended February 2, 2014. The coverage for companies in the pet supplies industry in a comparable time period was 12. What does your calculation indicate about PetSmart's risk?

Air France–KLM Case

AIRFRANCE / KLM
● LO14–7

Air France–KLM (AF), a Franco-Dutch company, prepares its financial statements according to International Financial Reporting Standards. AF's financial statements and disclosure notes for the year ended December 31, 2013, are provided with all new textbooks. This material also is available at www.airfranceklm-finance.com.

Required:
1. Sealy Corporation reported the following line items in its statement of cash flows:

Amortization of discount on secured notes	382,000
Amortization of debt issuance costs and other	1,175,000

In AF's financial statements, Note 32: "Financial Debt" describes the company's long-term debt. Neither of the two items above is reported in the financial statements of Air France, and neither is likely to appear there in the future. Why?

2. Examine the long-term borrowings in AF's balance sheet and the related note (32.2.1). Note that AF has convertible bonds outstanding that it issued in 2005. Prepare the journal entry AF would use to record the issue of convertible bonds. Prepare the journal entry AF would use to record the issue of the convertible bonds if AF used U.S. GAAP.
3. AF does not elect the fair value option (FVO) to report its financial liabilities. Examine Note 34.3. "Market value of financial instruments." If the company had elected the FVO for all of its debt measured at amortized cost, what would be the balance at December 31, 2013, in the fair value adjustment account?

CPA Simulation 14–1

Ace
Early extinguishment of debt

KAPLAN
CPA REVIEW

Test your knowledge of the concepts discussed in this chapter, practice critical professional skills necessary for career success, and prepare for the computer-based CPA exam by accessing our CPA simulations in the Connect library.

The Ace Company simulation tests your knowledge of the way we account for early extinguishment of bonds.

CHAPTER

15 Leases

OVERVIEW

In the previous chapter, we saw how companies account for their long-term debt. The focus of that discussion was *bonds* and *notes.* In this chapter we continue our discussion of debt, but we now turn our attention to liabilities arising in connection with *leases.* Leases that produce such debtor/creditor relationships are referred to as *capital* leases by the lessee and as either *direct financing* or *sales-type* leases by the lessor. We also will see that some leases do not produce debtor/creditor relationships, but instead are accounted for as rental agreements. These are designated as *operating* leases. The chapter concludes with a Where We're Headed Supplement explaining a proposed Accounting Standards Update (hereafter, "the proposed ASU") that substantially changes how we account for leases.

LEARNING OBJECTIVES

After studying this chapter, you should be able to:

- **LO15–1** Identify and describe the operational, financial, and tax objectives that motivate leasing. (*p. 854*)
- **LO15–2** Explain why some leases constitute rental agreements and some represent purchases/sales accompanied by debt financing. (*p. 855*)
- **LO15–3** Explain the basis for each of the criteria and conditions used to classify leases. (*p. 856*)
- **LO15–4** Record all transactions associated with operating leases by both the lessor and lessee. (*p. 860*)
- **LO15–5** Describe and demonstrate how both the lessee and lessor account for a capital lease. (*p. 862*)
- **LO15–6** Describe and demonstrate how the lessor accounts for a sales-type lease. (*p. 867*)
- **LO15–7** Describe the way a bargain purchase option affects lease accounting. (*p. 870*)
- **LO15–8** Explain how lease accounting is affected by the residual value of a leased asset. (*p. 873*)
- **LO15–9** Explain the impact on lease accounting of executory costs, the discount rate, initial direct costs, and contingent rentals. (*p. 877*)
- **LO15–10** Explain sale-leaseback agreements and other special leasing arrangements and their accounting treatment. (*p. 888*)
- **LO15–11** Discuss the primary differences between U.S. GAAP and IFRS with respect to leases. (*pp. 859, 869, 880, 891,* and *892*)

FINANCIAL REPORTING CASE

It's a Hit!

"Don't get too comfortable with those big numbers," said Aaron Sanchez, controller for your new employer. "It's likely our revenues will take a hit over the next couple of years as more of our customers lease our machines rather than buy them."

You've just finished your first look at Higher Graphics' third quarter earnings report. Like most companies in your industry, HG leases its labeling machines to some customers and sells them to others. Eager to understand the implications of your new supervisor's concerns, you pull out your old intermediate accounting book and turn to the leases chapter.

QUESTIONS

By the time you finish this chapter, you should be able to respond appropriately to the questions posed in this case. Compare your response to the solution provided at the end of the chapter.

1. How would HG's revenues "take a hit" as a result of more customers leasing rather than buying labeling machines? (*p. 860*)
2. Under what kind of leasing arrangements would the "hit" not occur? (*p. 868*)

Accounting by the Lessor and Lessee

PART A

If you ever have leased an apartment, you know that a lease is a contractual arrangement by which a **lessor** (owner) provides a **lessee** (user) the right to use an asset for a specified period of time. In return for this right, the lessee agrees to make stipulated, periodic cash payments during the term of the lease. An apartment lease is a typical rental agreement in which the fundamental rights and responsibilities of ownership are retained by the lessor; the lessee merely uses the asset temporarily. Businesses, too, lease assets under similar arrangements. These are referred to as **operating leases**. Many contracts, though, are formulated outwardly as leases, but in reality are installment purchases/sales. These are called **capital leases** (**direct financing** or **sales-type leases** to the lessor). Illustration 15–1 compares the classification possibilities.

An apartment lease is a typical rental agreement referred to as an *operating lease*.

Illustration 15–1

Basic Lease Classifications

Lessee	Lessor
● Operating lease	● Operating lease
● Capital lease	● Capital lease: ➥ Direct financing lease ➥ Sales-type lease

After looking at some of the possible advantages of leasing assets rather than buying them in certain circumstances, we will explore differences in leases further.

Decision Makers' Perspective—Advantages of Leasing

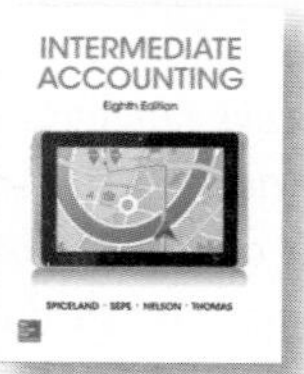

LO15–1

> The U.S. Navy once leased a fleet of tankers to avoid asking Congress for appropriations.

When a young entrepreneur started a computer training center a few years ago, she had no idea how fast her business would grow. Now, while she knows she needs computers, she doesn't know how many. Just starting out, she also has little cash with which to buy them.

The mutual funds department of a large investment firm often needs new computers and peripherals—fast. The department manager knows he can't afford to wait up to a year, the time it sometimes takes, to go through company channels to obtain purchase approval.

An established computer software publisher recently began developing a new line of business software. The senior programmer has to be certain he's testing the company's products on the latest versions of computer hardware. And yet he views large expenditures on equipment subject to rapid technological change and obsolescence as risky business.

Leasing can facilitate asset acquisition.

Each of these individuals is faced with different predicaments and concerns. The entrepreneur is faced with uncertainty and cash flow problems, the department manager with time constraints and bureaucratic control systems, the programmer with fear of obsolescence. Though their specific concerns differ, these individuals have all met their firms' information technology needs with the same solution: each has decided to lease the computers rather than buy them.

The number one method of external financing by U.S. businesses is leasing.

Computers are by no means the only assets obtained through leasing arrangements. To the contrary, leasing has grown to be the most popular method of external financing of corporate assets in America. The airplane in which you last flew probably was leased, as was the gate from which it departed. Your favorite retail outlet at the local shopping mall likely leases the space it operates. Many companies actually exist for the sole purpose of acquiring assets and leasing them to others. And, leasing often is a primary method of "selling" a firm's products. IBM and Boeing are familiar examples.

In light of its popularity, you may be surprised that leasing usually is more expensive than buying. Of course, the higher apparent cost of leasing is because the lessor usually shoulders at least some of the financial and risk burdens that a purchaser normally would assume. So, why the popularity?

Tax incentives often motivate leasing.

The lease decisions described above are motivated by operational incentives. Tax and market considerations also motivate firms to lease. Sometimes leasing offers tax saving advantages over outright purchases. For instance, a company with little or no taxable income—maybe a business just getting started, or one experiencing an economic downturn—will get little benefit from depreciation deductions. But the company can benefit *indirectly* by leasing assets rather than buying. By allowing the *lessor* to retain ownership and thus benefit from depreciation deductions, the lessee often can negotiate lower lease payments. Lessees with sufficient taxable income to take advantage of the depreciation deductions, but still in lower tax brackets than lessors, also can achieve similar indirect tax benefits.

Leasing sometimes is used as a means of off-balance-sheet financing.

The desire to obtain "off-balance-sheet financing" also is sometimes a leasing stimulus. When funds are borrowed to purchase an asset, the liability has a detrimental effect on the company's debt to equity ratio and other quantifiable indicators of riskiness. Similarly, the purchased asset increases total assets and correspondingly lowers calculations of the rate of return on assets. Despite research that indicates otherwise, management actions continue to reflect a belief that the financial market is naive and is fooled by off-balance-sheet financing. Managers continue to avoid reporting assets and liabilities by leasing rather than buying and by constructing lease agreements in such a way that capitalizing the assets and liabilities is not required.[1]

[1]You will learn later in the chapter that accounting standards are designed to identify lease arrangements that, despite their outward appearance, are in reality purchases of assets. Assets acquired by these arrangements, *capital leases,* are required to be recorded as well as the related lease liability. Managers often structure lease terms so that capitalization requirements are avoided.

Whether or not there is any real effect on security prices, sometimes off-balance-sheet financing helps a firm avoid exceeding contractual limits on designated financial ratios (like the debt to equity ratio, for instance).[2] When the operational, tax, and financial market advantages are considered, the *net* cost of leasing often is less than the cost of purchasing. ●

Operational, tax, and financial market incentives often make leasing an attractive alternative to purchasing.

Capital Leases and Installment Notes Compared

● LO15–2

You learned in the previous chapter how to account for an installment note. To a great extent, then, you already have learned how to account for a capital lease. To illustrate, let's recall the situation described in the previous chapter. We assumed that Skill Graphics purchased a package-labeling machine from Hughes–Barker Corporation by issuing a three-year installment note that required six semiannual installment payments of $139,857 each. That arrangement provided for the purchase of the $666,633 machine as well as interest at an annual rate of 14% (7% twice each year). Remember, too, that each installment payment consisted of part interest (7% times the outstanding balance) and part payment for the machine (the remainder of each payment).

Now let's suppose that Skill Graphics instead acquired the package-labeling machine from Hughes–Barker Corporation under a three-year *lease* that required six semiannual rental payments of $139,857 each. Obviously, the fundamental nature of the transaction remains the same regardless of whether it is negotiated as an installment purchase or as a lease. So, it would be inconsistent to account for this lease in a fundamentally different way than for an installment purchase:

Comparison of a Note and Capital Lease

In keeping with the basic accounting concept of substance over form, accounting for a capital lease parallels that for an installment purchase.

At Inception (January 1)		
Installment Note		
Machinery	666,633	
Note payable		666,633
Capital Lease		
Leased machinery	666,633	
Lease payable		666,633

Consistent with the nature of the transaction, interest expense accrues each period at the effective rate times the outstanding balance:

Interest Compared for a Note and Capital Lease

Each payment includes both an amount that represents interest and an amount that represents a reduction of principal.

At the First Semiannual Payment Date (June 30)		
Installment Note		
Interest expense (7% × $666,633)	46,664	
Note payable (difference)	93,193	
Cash (installment payment)		139,857
Capital Lease		
Interest expense (7% × $666,633)	46,664	
Lease payable (difference)	93,193	
Cash (rental payment)		139,857

Because the lease payable balance declines with each payment, the amount of interest expense decreases each period. An amortization schedule is convenient to track the changing amounts as shown in Illustration 15–2.

[2]It is common for debt agreements, particularly long-term ones, to include restrictions on the debtor as a way to provide some degree of protection to the creditor. Sometimes a minimum level is specified for current assets relative to current liabilities, net assets, debt as a ratio of equity, or many other financial ratios. Often a restriction is placed on dividend payments, share repurchases, or other activities that might impede the debtor's ability to repay the debt. Typically, the debt becomes due on demand when the debtor becomes in violation of such a debt covenant, often after a specified grace period.

Illustration 15–2

Lease Amortization Schedule

Each rental payment includes interest on the outstanding balance at the effective rate. The remainder of each payment reduces the outstanding balance.

Date	Payments	Effective Interest	Decrease in Balance	Outstanding Balance
		(7% × Outstanding balance)		
				666,633
1	139,857	.07(666,633) = 46,664	93,193	573,440
2	139,857	.07(573,440) = 40,141	99,716	473,724
3	139,857	.07(473,724) = 33,161	106,696	367,028
4	139,857	.07(367,028) = 25,692	114,165	252,863
5	139,857	.07(252,863) = 17,700	122,157	130,706
6	139,857	.07(130,706) = 9,151*	130,706	0
	839,142	172,509	666,633	

*Rounded

You should recognize this as essentially the same amortization schedule we used in the previous chapter in connection with our installment note example. The reason for the similarity is that we view a capital lease as being, in substance, equivalent to an installment purchase. So naturally the accounting treatment of the two essentially identical transactions should be consistent.

Lease Classification

A lease is accounted for as either a rental agreement or a purchase/sale accompanied by debt financing. The choice of accounting method hinges on the nature of the leasing arrangement.

A basic concept of accounting is substance over form.

Capital leases are agreements that we identify as being formulated outwardly as leases, but which are in reality essentially installment purchases. Sometimes the true nature of an arrangement is obvious. For example, a 10-year noncancelable lease of a computer with a 10-year useful life, by which title passes to the lessee at the end of the lease term, obviously more nearly represents a purchase than a rental agreement. But what if the terms of the contract do not transfer title, and the lease term is for only seven years of the asset's 10-year life? Suppose contractual terms permit the lessee to obtain title under certain prearranged conditions? What if compensation provided by the lease contract is nearly equal to the value of the asset under lease? These situations are less clear-cut.

Accounting for leases attempts to see through the legal form of the agreements to determine their economic substance.

Professional judgment is needed to differentiate between leases that represent rental agreements and those that in essence are installment purchases/sales. It's important to note that from an accounting perspective legal ownership is irrelevant in the decision. The essential question is whether the usual risks and rewards of ownership have been transferred to the lessee. But judgment alone is likely to lead to inconsistencies in practice. The desire to encourage consistency in practice motivated the FASB to provide guidance for distinguishing between two fundamental types of leases: capital leases and operating leases.[3] As you study the classification criteria in the following paragraphs, keep in mind that some leases clearly fit the classifications we give them, but others fall in a gray area somewhere between the two extremes. For those, we end up forcing them into one category or the other by somewhat arbitrary criteria.

Classification Criteria

● LO15–3

A lessee should classify a lease transaction as a *capital lease* if it includes a noncancelable lease term and one or more of the four criteria listed in Illustration 15–3 are met.[4] Otherwise, it is an *operating lease.*

[3]FASB ASC 840–10–15: Leases–Overall–Recognition (previously "Accounting for Leases," *Statement of Financial Accounting Standards No. 13* (Stamford, Conn.: FASB, 1980), par. 7).

[4]Noncancelable in this context does not preclude the agreement from specifying that the lease is cancelable after a designated noncancelable lease term. Unless some portion of the lease term is noncancelable, it is an operating lease. Later in this section, we discuss treatment of any cancelable portion of the lease term.

1. The agreement specifies that ownership of the asset transfers to the lessee.
2. The agreement contains a bargain purchase option.
3. The noncancelable lease term is equal to 75% or more of the expected economic life of the asset.
4. The present value of the "minimum lease payments"[5] is equal to or greater than 90% of the fair value of the asset.

Illustration 15–3

Criteria for Classification as a Capital Lease

Let's look closer at these criteria.

Criterion 1: Transfer of ownership.

Since our objective is to determine when the risks and rewards of ownership have been transferred to the lessee, the first criterion is self-evident. If legal title passes to the lessee during, or at the end of, the lease term, obviously ownership attributes are transferred.

Criterion 2: Bargain purchase option.

A **bargain purchase option (BPO)** is a provision in the lease contract that gives the lessee the option of purchasing the leased property at a bargain price. This is defined as a price sufficiently lower than the expected fair value of the property (when the option becomes exercisable) that the exercise of the option appears reasonably assured at the inception of the lease. Because exercise of the option appears reasonably assured, transfer of ownership is expected. So the logic of the second criterion is similar to that of the first. Applying criterion 2 in practice, though, often is more difficult because it is necessary to make a judgment now about whether a future option price will be a bargain.

Criterion 3: Lease term is 75% of economic life.

If an asset is leased for most of its useful life, then most of the benefits and responsibilities of ownership are transferred to the lessee. GAAP specifies, quite arbitrarily, that 75% or more of the **expected economic life** of the asset is an appropriate threshold point for this purpose.

Although the intent of this criterion is fairly straightforward, implementation sometimes is troublesome. First, the lease term may be uncertain. It may be renewable beyond its initial term. Or the lease may be cancelable after a designated noncancelable period. When either is an issue, we ordinarily consider the lease term to be the noncancelable[6] term of the lease plus any periods covered by **bargain renewal options**.[7] A bargain renewal option gives the lessee the option to renew the lease at a bargain rate. That is, the rental payment is sufficiently lower than the expected fair rental of the property at the date the option becomes exercisable that exercise of the option appears reasonably assured.

Additional Consideration

Periods covered by bargain renewal options are not included in the lease term if a **bargain purchase option** is present. This is because the lease term should not extend beyond the date a bargain purchase option becomes exercisable. For example, assume a BPO allows a lessee to buy a leased delivery truck at the end of the noncancelable five-year lease term. Even if an option to renew the lease beyond that date is considered to be a bargain renewal option, that extra period would not be included as part of the lease term. Remember, we presume the BPO will be exercised after the initial five-year term, making the renewal option irrelevant.

[5]Minimum lease payments are defined on the next page.

[6]Noncancelable in this context is a lease that is cancelable only by (a) the occurrence of some remote contingency, (b) permission of the lessor, (c) a new lease with the same lessor, or (d) payment by the lessee of a penalty in an amount such that continuation of the lease appears, at inception, reasonably assured. FASB ASC Master Glossary–Noncancelable Lease Term (previously "Accounting for Leases: Sale and Leaseback Transactions Involving Real Estate, Sales-Type Leases of Real Estate, Definition of the Lease Term, Initial Direct Costs of Direct Financing Leases," *Statement of Financial Accounting Standards No. 98* (Stamford, Conn.: FASB, 1988), par. 22).

[7]If applicable, the lease term also should include (a) periods for which failure to renew the lease imposes a penalty on the lessee in an amount such that renewal appears reasonably assured, (b) periods covered by ordinary renewal options during which a guarantee by the lessee of the lessor's debt directly or indirectly related to the leased property is expected to be in effect or a loan from the lessee to the lessor directly or indirectly related to the leased property is expected to be outstanding, (c) periods covered by ordinary renewal options preceding the date that a bargain purchase option is exercisable, or (d) periods representing renewals or extensions of the lease at the lessor's option. FASB ASC Master Glossary–Lease Term (previously "Accounting for Leases: Sale and Leaseback Transactions Involving Real Estate, Sales-Type Leases of Real Estate, Definition of the Lease Term, Initial Direct Costs of Direct Financing Leases," *Statement of Financial Accounting Standards No. 98* (Stamford, Conn.: FASB, 1988), par. 22).

Another implementation issue is estimating the economic life of the leased property. This is the estimated remaining time the property is expected to be economically usable for its intended purpose, with normal maintenance and repairs, at the inception of the lease. Estimates of the economic life of leased property are subject to the same uncertainty limitations of most estimates. This uncertainty presents the opportunity to arrive at estimates that cause this third criterion not to be met.

Finally, if the inception of the lease occurs during the last 25% of an asset's economic life, this third criterion does not apply. This is consistent with the basic premise of this criterion that most of the risks and rewards of ownership occur during the first 75% of an asset's life.

Criterion 4: Present value of payments is 90% of fair value.

If the lease payments required by a lease contract substantially pay for a leased asset, it is logical to identify the arrangement as a lease equivalent to an installment purchase. This situation is considered to exist when the present value of the **minimum lease payments** is equal to or greater than 90% of the fair value of the asset at the inception of the lease. In general, minimum lease payments are payments the lessee is required to make in connection with the lease and consist of:

- the total of periodic rental payments
- any guaranteed residual value
- any bargain purchase option price

We look closer at the make-up of minimum lease payments later in the chapter when we discuss residual values and bargain purchase options in more detail.

The 90% of fair value criterion often is the decisive one in identifying a capital lease. As mentioned earlier, lessees often try to avoid writing a lease agreement that will require recording an asset and liability. When this is an objective, it usually is relatively easy to avoid meeting the first three criteria. However, when the underlying motive for the lease agreement is that the lessee substantively acquire the asset, it is more difficult to avoid meeting the 90% recovery criterion without defeating that motive. New ways, though, continually are being devised to structure leases to avoid meeting this criterion. Later we will look at some popular devices that are used.

Again consistent with the basic premise that most of the risks and rewards of ownership occur during the first 75% of an asset's life, this fourth criterion does not apply if the inception of the lease occurs during the last 25% of an asset's economic life.

Additional Lessor Conditions

As we saw in the previous section, the lessee accounts for a capital lease as if an asset were purchased; that is, the lessee records both an asset and a liability at the inception of the lease. Consistency would suggest that the lessor in the same lease transaction should record the sale of an asset. Indeed, consistency is a goal of the FASB's lease accounting standards. The four classification criteria discussed in the previous section apply to both parties to the transaction, lessees and lessors. However, a fundamental difference is that for a lessor to record the sale side of the transaction, it is necessary also to satisfy the conditions of revenue recognition we discussed in Chapter 5. In particular, the FASB specifies that for the lessor to record a lease as a direct financing lease or a sales-type lease, two conditions must be met in addition to one of the four classification criteria. These are listed in Illustration 15–4.

Illustration 15–4

Additional Conditions for Classification as a Capital Lease by the Lessor

1. The collectibility of the lease payments must be reasonably predictable.
2. If any costs to the lessor have yet to be incurred, they are reasonably predictable. (Performance by the lessor is substantially complete.)

Although uniformity of classification is a goal of lease accounting standards, it is obvious that the additional conditions allow inconsistencies.[8] Indeed, in lease negotiations an

[8] "FASB ASC 840–10–25–42: Leases–Overall–Recognition (previously "Accounting for Leases," *Statement of Financial Accounting Standards No. 13* (Stamford, Conn.: FASB, 1980)).

objective of the parties involved often is to devise terms that will result in a sale by the lessor but an operating lease by the lessee.[9]

In the remaining sections of Part A of this chapter we consider, in order, operating leases, direct financing leases (capital leases to the lessee), and sales-type leases (capital leases to the lessee).

International Financial Reporting Standards

● LO15–11

Lease Classification.

Lease accounting under U.S. GAAP and IFRS provides a good general comparison of "rules-based accounting," as U.S. GAAP often is described, and "principles-based accounting," which often is the description assigned to IFRS. We discussed four classification criteria used under U.S. GAAP to determine whether a lease is a capital lease. Under IFRS, we don't have such bright-line rules. Instead, a lease is deemed a capital lease (called a **finance lease** under *IAS No. 17*, "Leases"[10]), if substantially all risks and rewards of ownership are judged to have been transferred. Judgment is made based on a number of "indicators" including some similar to the specific criteria of U.S. GAAP. Here is a comparison:

IFRS Illustration

IFRS	U.S. GAAP
Situations (individually or in combination) that ***normally would lead to*** classification as a finance lease are:	Situations that ***require*** classification as a capital lease if any one (or more) is met are:
• The agreement specifies that ownership of the asset transfers to the lessee.	Same as IFRS.
• The agreement contains a bargain purchase option.	Same as IFRS.
• The noncancelable lease term is for a "major portion" of the expected economic life of the asset.	"Major portion" is defined specifically as 75% or more.
• The present value of the minimum lease payments is equal to or greater than "substantially all" of the fair value of the asset.	"Substantially all" is defined specifically as 90%.
• The leased asset is of a specialized nature such that only the lessee can use it without major modifications being made.	No similar situation specified.
Other situations (individually or in combination) that ***might also lead to*** classification as a finance lease are:	
• The lessor's losses are borne by the lessee upon cancellation.	No similar situation specified.
• Gains or losses from changes in the fair value of the residual value go to the lessee (for instance, by means of a rebate of lease payments).	No similar situation specified.
• The lease contains a "bargain renewal option" whereby the lessee can continue the lease for substantially less than market rent.	No similar situation specified.

(continued)

[9]Later in the chapter we discuss ways this is done.

[10]"Leases," *International Accounting Standard No. 17* (IASCF), as amended effective January 1, 2014.

(concluded)

Ordinarily, it will not be a single indicator, but the combined implication of two or more indicators that will sway the classification decision under IFRS. Often the appropriate classification is obvious. At other times, careful consideration of all aspects of the agreement with reference to the classification indicators is needed. Substance over form is the goal. Professional judgment is key.

Operating Leases

FINANCIAL Reporting Case

Q1, p. 853

If a lease does not meet any of the criteria for a capital lease it is considered to be more in the nature of a rental agreement and is referred to as an **operating lease.**[11] We assume that the fundamental rights and responsibilities of ownership are retained by the lessor and that the lessee merely is using the asset temporarily. In keeping with that presumption, a sale is not recorded by the lessor; a purchase is not recorded by the lessee. Instead, the periodic rental payments are accounted for merely as rent by both parties to the transaction—*rent revenue* by the lessor; *rent expense* by the lessee.

LO15–4

Let's look at an example that illustrates the relatively straightforward accounting for operating leases. The earlier example comparing a capital lease to an installment purchase assumed rental payments at the *end* of each period. A more typical leasing arrangement requires rental payments at the *beginning* of each period. This more realistic payment schedule is assumed in Illustration 15–5.

Illustration 15–5

Application of Classification Criteria

Using Excel, enter:
= PV(.104,100000,1)
Output: 348685.2

Using a calculator:
enter: BEG mode N 4
I 10
PMT – 100000 FV
Output: PV 348685

On January 1, 2016, Sans Serif Publishers, Inc., a computer services and printing firm, leased printing equipment from First LeaseCorp.

The lease agreement specifies four annual payments of $100,000 beginning January 1, 2016, the inception of the lease, and at each January 1 thereafter through 2019. The useful life of the equipment is estimated to be six years.

Before deciding to lease, Sans Serif considered purchasing the equipment for its cash price of $479,079. If funds were borrowed to buy the equipment, the interest rate would have been 10%.

How should this lease be classified? We apply the four classification criteria:

1. Does the agreement specify that ownership of the asset transfers to the lessee? — No
2. Does this agreement contain a bargain purchase option? — No
3. Is the lease term equal to 75% or more of the expected economic life of the asset? — No (4yrs < 75% of 6 yrs)
4. Is the present value of the minimum lease payments equal to or greater than 90% of the fair value of the asset? — No ($348,685 < 90% of $479,079)

$100,000 (Lease payments) = 3.48685* = $348,685 (Present value)

Since none of the four classification criteria is met, this is an operating lease.

*Present value of an annuity due of $1: $n = 4$, $i = 10\%$. Recall from Chapter 6 that we refer to periodic payments at the beginning of each period as an *annuity due.*

[11] The term *operating lease* got its name long ago when a lessee routinely received from the lessor an operator along with leased equipment.

Journal entries for Illustration 15–5 are shown in Illustration 15–5A.

Illustration 15–5A

Journal Entries for an Operating Lease

The operating lease described in Illustration 15–5 is recorded as follows:

At Each of the Four Payment Dates		
Sans Serif Publishers, Inc. (Lessee)		
Prepaid rent	100,000	
Cash		100,000
CompuDec Corporation (Lessor)		
Cash	100,000	
Deferred rent revenue		100,000
At the End of Each Year		
Sans Serif Publishers, Inc. (Lessee)		
Rent expense	100,000	
Prepaid rent		100,000
CompuDec Corporation (Lessor)		
Deferred rent revenue	100,000	
Rent revenue		100,000
Depreciation expense	x,xxx	
Accumulated depreciation		x,xxx

At the beginning of the year, the rent payments are prepaid rent to the lessee and deferred rent to the lessor.

The lessor retains the asset on its books, and accordingly records depreciation on the asset.

In an operating lease, rent is recognized on a straight-line basis unless another systematic method more clearly reflects the benefits of the asset's use. So, if rental payments are uneven—for instance, if rent increases are scheduled—the total scheduled payments ordinarily would be expensed equally (straight-line basis) over the lease term.[12]

Advance Payments

Often lease agreements call for advance payments to be made at the inception of the lease that represent prepaid rent. For instance, it is common for a lessee to pay a bonus in return for negotiating more favorable lease terms. Such payments are recorded as prepaid rent and allocated (normally on a straight-line basis) to rent expense/rent revenue over the lease term. So the rent that is periodically reported in those cases consists of the periodic rent payments themselves plus an allocated portion of prepaid rent.

In the journal entries above and throughout the chapter, we look at the entries of the lessee and the lessor together. This way, we can be reminded that the entries for the lessor usually are essentially the mirror image of those for the lessee, the other side of the same coin.[13]

Sometimes advance payments include security deposits that are refundable at the expiration of the lease or prepayments of the last period's rent. A refundable security deposit is recorded as a long-term receivable (by the lessee) and liability (by the lessor) unless it is not expected to be returned. A prepayment of the last period's rent is recorded as prepaid rent and allocated to rent expense/rent revenue during the last period of the lease term.

At times, lease agreements call for uneven rent payments during the term of the lease. One way this can occur is when the initial payment (or maybe several payments) is waived. This is called a **rent abatement or rent holiday**. Alternatively, rent payments may be scheduled to increase periodically over the lease term. But, there is no such thing as free rent. Instead, later rent payments are high enough to compensate the lessor for receiving no payments or low payments early in the life of the lease. In response, we account for these arrangements by summing the total payments over the life of the lease and then expensing them in each period of the lease on a straight-line basis. This means the rent expense will be

A *rent abatement* occurs when the initial payment (or maybe several payments) is waived.

[12]FASB ASC 840–20–25: Leases–Operating Leases–Recognition (previously "Accounting for Operating Leases with Scheduled Rent Increases," *FASB Technical Bulletin 85-3* (Stamford, Conn.: FASB, 1985), par. 1).

[13]We see later in the chapter that sometimes this is not the case, particularly when the lease is a "sales-type" lease. Even when the two sides are not mirror images there are many similarities, so the comparison still is helpful.

the same amount for all periods of the lease, even those in which no rent is actually paid. The (temporarily) unpaid portion of rent expense early in the life of the lease must be credited to a liability, deferred rent expense payable, until later in the lease term, and then the liability is reduced to zero later in the lease term when rent payments exceed rent expense.

Leasehold Improvements

Sometimes a lessee will make improvements to leased property that reverts back to the lessor at the end of the lease. If a lessee constructs a new building or makes modifications to existing structures, that cost represents an asset just like any other capital expenditure. Like other assets, its cost is allocated as depreciation expense over its useful life to the lessee, which will be the shorter of the physical life of the asset or the lease term.[14] Theoretically, such assets can be recorded in accounts descriptive of their nature, such as buildings or plant. In practice, the traditional account title used is **leasehold improvements**.[15] In any case, the undepreciated cost usually is reported in the balance sheet under the caption *property, plant, and equipment.* Movable assets like office furniture and equipment that are not attached to the leased property are not considered leasehold improvements.

The cost of a *leasehold improvement* is depreciated over its useful life to the lessee.

A few years ago, hundreds of companies, particularly in the retail and restaurant industries, underwent one of the most widespread accounting correction events ever. Corrections were in the way these companies, including **Pep Boys**, **Ann Taylor**, **Target**, and **Domino's Pizza**, had allocated the cost of leasehold improvements. Rather than expensing leasehold improvements properly over the lease terms, these firms for years had inappropriately expensed the cost over the longer estimated useful lives of the properties. Prompting the sweeping revisions was a Securities and Exchange Commission letter, urging companies to follow long-standing accounting standards in this area. A result of the improper practices was to defer expense, thereby accelerating earnings. For instance, **McDonald's Corp.** recorded a charge of $139 million to adjust for the difference.

Hundreds of firms corrected the way they accounted for leases.

Let's turn our attention now to accounting for leases that meet the criteria and conditions for classification as capital leases by both the lessee and the lessor.

Capital Leases—Lessee and Lessor

LO15–5

In the operating lease illustration, we assumed Sans Serif leased equipment directly from the manufacturer. Now, in Illustration 15–6, let's assume a financial intermediary provided financing by acquiring the equipment and leasing it to the user.

The amount recorded (capitalized) by the lessee is the present value of the minimum lease payments. However, if the fair value of the asset is lower than this amount, the recorded value of the asset should be limited to fair value. Unless the lessor is a manufacturer or dealer, the fair value typically will be the lessor's cost ($479,079 in this case). However, if considerable time has elapsed between the purchase of the property by the lessor and the inception of the lease, the fair value might be different. When the lessor is a manufacturer or dealer, the fair value of the property at the inception of the lease ordinarily will be its normal selling price (reduced by any volume or trade discounts). We study this situation (a sales-type lease) later. In unusual cases, market conditions may cause fair value to be less than the normal selling price.[16]

A leased asset is recorded by the lessee at the *present value of the minimum lease payments* or the asset's fair value, whichever is lower.

Be sure to note that the entire $100,000 first rental payment is applied to principal reduction.[17] Because it occurred at the inception of the lease, no interest had yet accrued. Subsequent rental payments include interest on the outstanding balance as well as a portion that reduces that outstanding balance. As of the second rental payment date, one year's interest has accrued on the $379,079 balance outstanding during 2017, recorded as in Illustration 15–6A.

Interest is a function of time. It accrues at the effective rate on the balance outstanding during the period.

[14]If the agreement contains an option to renew, and the likelihood of renewal is uncertain, the renewal period is ignored.

[15]Also, traditionally, depreciation sometimes is labeled amortization when in connection with leased assets and leasehold improvements. This is of little consequence. Remember, both depreciation and amortization refer to the process of allocating an asset's cost over its useful life.

[16]FASB ASC 840–10: Leases–Overall (previously "Accounting for Leases," *Statement of Financial Accounting Standards No. 13* (Stamford, Conn.: FASB, 1980)).

[17]Another way to view this is to think of the first $100,000 as a down payment with the remaining $379,079 financed by 5 (i.e., 6–1) *year-end* lease payments.

Illustration 15–6
Capital Leases

On January 1, 2016, Sans Serif Publishers, Inc., leased printing equipment from First LeaseCorp. First LeaseCorp purchased the equipment from CompuDec Corporation at a cost of $479,079.

The lease agreement specifies annual payments beginning January 1, 2016, the inception of the lease, and at each December 31 thereafter through 2020. The six-year lease term ending December 31, 2021, is equal to the estimated useful life of the equipment.

First LeaseCorp routinely acquires electronic equipment for lease to other firms. The interest rate in these financing arrangements is 10%.

Since the lease term is equal to the expected useful life of the equipment (>75%), the transaction must be recorded by the lessee as a **capital lease**.[18] If we assume also that collectibility of the lease payments and any costs to the lessor that are yet to be incurred are reasonably predictable, this qualifies also as a **direct financing lease** to First LeaseCorp. To achieve its objectives, First LeaseCorp must (a) recover its $479,079 investment as well as (b) generate interest revenue at a rate of 10%. So, the lessor determined that annual rental payments would be $100,000:

$479,079	÷ 4.79079* =	$100,000
Lessor's cost		Rental payments

*Present value of an annuity due of $1: $n = 6$, $i = 10\%$.

Using Excel, enter:
= PMT(.10,6,479079,1)
Output: 100000

Of course, Sans Serif Publishers, Inc., views the transaction from the other side. The price the lessee pays for the equipment is the present value of the rental payments:

$100,000	× 4.79079* =	$479,079
Rental payments		Lessee's cost

*Present value of an annuity due of $1: $n = 6$, $i = 10\%$.

Using a calculator:
enter: BEG mode N 6
I 10
PV – 479079 FV
Output: PMT 100000

Direct Financing Lease (January 1, 2016)

	Debit	Credit
Sans Serif Publishers, Inc. (Lessee)		
Leased equipment (present value of lease payments)	479,079	
Lease payable (present value of lease payments)		479,079
First LeaseCorp (Lessor)		
Lease receivable (present value of lease payments)	479,079	
Inventory of equipment (lessor's cost)		479,079

Notice that the lessor's entries are the flip side or mirror image of the lessee's entries.

First Lease Payment (January 1, 2016)*

	Debit	Credit
Sans Serif Publishers, Inc. (Lessee)		
Lease payable	100,000	
Cash		100,000
First LeaseCorp (Lessor)		
Cash	100,000	
Lease receivable		100,000

*Of course, the entries to record the lease and the first payment could be combined into a single entry since they occur at the same time.

The first lease payment reduces the balances in the lease payable and the lease receivable by $100,000 to $379,079.

Illustration 15–6A
Journal Entries for the Second Lease Payment

Second Lease Payment (December 31, 2016)

	Debit	Credit
Sans Serif Publishers, Inc. (Lessee)		
Interest expense [10% × ($479,079 – 100,000)]	37,908	
Lease payable (difference)	62,092	
Cash (lease payment)		100,000
First LeaseCorp (Lessor)		
Cash (lease payment)	100,000	
Lease receivable		62,092
Interest revenue [10% × ($479,079 – 100,000)]		37,908

LESSEE
Lease Payable

$479,079
(100,000)
$379,079
(62,092)
$316,987

LESSOR
Lease Receivable

$479,079
(100,000)
$379,079
(62,092)
$316,987

Notice that the outstanding balance is reduced by $62,092—the portion of the $100,000 payment remaining after interest is covered.

[18]The fourth criterion also is met. The present value of lease payments ($479,079) is 100% (>90%) of the fair value of the equipment ($479,079). Meeting any one of the four criteria is sufficient.

Additional Consideration

Some lessors use what's called the "gross method" to record the receivable in a capital lease. By this method, the lessor debits lease receivable for the gross sum of the lease payments and credits *deferred interest revenue* for the difference between the total of the payments and the present value of the payments since that's the amount that eventually will be recorded as interest revenue over the term of the lease. In Illustration 15–6, the lessor's entry by the gross method at the inception of the lease would be:

Lease receivable ($100,000 × 6)	600,000	
Deferred interest revenue (difference)		120,921
Inventory of equipment (lessor's cost)		479,079

The same ultimate result is achieved either way. We use the net method in our illustrations to more easily demonstrate the lessee's entries and the lessor's entries being "two sides of the same coin." Whichever method is used, both the lessee and the lessor must report in the disclosure notes both the net and gross amounts of the lease.

The amortization schedule in Illustration 15–6B shows how the lease balance and the effective interest change over the six-year lease term. Each rental payment after the first includes both an amount that represents interest and an amount that represents a reduction of principal. The periodic reduction of principal is sufficient that, at the end of the lease term, the outstanding balance is zero.

Illustration 15–6B
Lease Amortization Schedule

The first rental payment includes no interest.

The total of the cash payments ($600,000) provides for:
1. **Payment for the equipment ($479,079).**
2. **Interest ($120,921) at an effective rate of 10%.**

	Payments	Effective Interest	Decrease in Balance	Outstanding Balance
		(10% × Outstanding balance)		
1/1/16				479,079
1/1/16	100,000		100,000	379,079
12/31/16	100,000	.10 (379,079) = 37,908	62,092	316,987
12/31/17	100,000	.10 (316,987) = 31,699	68,301	248,686
12/31/18	100,000	.10 (248,686) = 24,869	75,131	173,555
12/31/19	100,000	.10 (173,555) = 17,355	82,645	90,910
12/31/20	100,000	.10 (90,910) = 9,090*	90,910	0
	600,000	120,921*	479,079	

*Adjusted for rounding of other numbers in the schedule.

An interesting aspect of the amortization schedule that you may want to note at this point relates to a disclosure requirement that we discuss at the end of the chapter. Among other things, the lessee and lessor must report separately the current and noncurrent portions of the outstanding lease balance. Both amounts are provided by the amortization schedule. For example, if we want the amounts to report on the 2016 balance sheet, refer to the next row of the schedule. The portion of the 2017 payment that represents principal ($68,301) is the *current* (as of December 31, 2016) balance. The *noncurrent* amount is the balance outstanding after the 2017 reduction ($248,686). These amounts are the current and noncurrent lease liability for the lessee and the current and noncurrent net investment for the lessor.

Depreciation

Depreciation is recorded for leased assets in a manner consistent with the lessee's usual policy for depreciating its depreciable assets.

End of Each Year		
Sans Serif Publishers, Inc. (Lessee)		
Depreciation expense ($479,079 ÷ 6 years*)	79,847	
Accumulated depreciation		79,847

*If the lessee depreciates assets by the straight-line method.

Because a capital lease assumes the lessee purchased the asset, the lessee depreciates its cost.

DEPRECIATION PERIOD. The lessee normally should depreciate a leased asset over the term of the lease. However, if ownership transfers or a bargain purchase option is present (i.e., either of the first two classification criteria is met), the asset should be depreciated over its useful life. This means depreciation is recorded over the useful life of the asset *to the lessee* whether or not that useful life is limited by the term of the lease.

The depreciation period is restricted to the lease term unless the lease provides for transfer of title or a BPO.

A description of leased assets and related depreciation provided in a recent disclosure note (Illustration 15–7) of **Kroger Company** is representative of leased asset disclosures.

Illustration 15–7

Disclosure of Leased Assets—Kroger Company

Real World Financials

3. PROPERTY, PLANT AND EQUIPMENT, NET

Property, plant and equipment, net consists of:

$ in millions	Feb. 1, 2014	Feb. 2, 2013
Land	$ 2,639	$ 2,450
Buildings and land improvements	8,848	8,249
Equipment	11,037	10,267
Leasehold improvements	7,644	6,545
Construction-in-progress	1,520	1,239
Leased property under capital leases and financing obligations	691	593
Total property, plant and equipment	32,379	29,343
Accumulated depreciation and amortization	(15,486)	(14,495)
Property, plant and equipment, net	$ 16,893	$ 14,848

Accumulated depreciation for leased property under capital leases was $339 at February 1, 2014, and $321 at February 2, 2013.

Accrued Interest

If a company's reporting period ends at any time between payment dates, it's necessary to record (as an adjusting entry) any interest that has accrued since interest was last recorded. We purposely avoided this step in the previous illustration by assuming that the lease agreement specified rental payments on December 31—the end of the reporting period. But if payments were made on another date, or if the company's fiscal year ended on a date other than December 31, accrued interest would be recorded prior to preparing financial statements. For example, if lease payments were made on January 1 of each year, the effective interest amounts shown in the lease amortization schedule still would be appropriate but would be recorded one day prior to the actual rental payment. For instance, the second cash payment of $100,000 would occur on January 1, 2017, but the interest component of that payment ($37,908) would be accrued a day earlier as shown in Illustration 15–6C.

At each financial statement date, any interest that has accrued since interest was last recorded must be accrued for all liabilities and receivables, including those relating to leases.

Notice that this is consistent with recording accrued interest on any debt, whether in the form of a note, a bond, or a lease.

We assumed in this illustration that First LeaseCorp bought the equipment for $479,079 and then leased it for the same price. There was no profit on the "sale" itself. The only income derived by the lessor was interest revenue recognized over the lease term. In effect, First LeaseCorp financed the purchase of the equipment by Sans Serif Publishers. This type of lease is a direct financing lease. This kind of leasing is a thriving industry. It is a profitable part of operations for banks and other financial institutions (**Citicorp** is one of the largest). Some leasing companies do nothing else. Often leasing companies, like **IBM Credit Corporation**, are subsidiaries of larger corporations, formed for the sole purpose of conducting financing activities for their parent corporations.

Illustration 15–6C

Journal Entries When Interest Is Accrued Prior to the Lease Payment

December 31, 2016 (to accrue interest)		
Sans Serif Publishers, Inc. (Lessee)		
Interest expense [10% × ($479,079 − 100,000)]	37,908	
Interest payable		37,908
First LeaseCorp (Lessor)		
Interest receivable	37,908	
Interest revenue [10% × ($479,079 − 100,000)]		37,908
Second Lease Payment (January 1, 2017)		
Sans Serif Publishers, Inc. (Lessee)		
Interest payable (from adjusting entry above)	37,908	
Lease payable (difference)	62,092	
Cash (lease payment)		100,000
First LeaseCorp (Lessor)		
Cash (lease payment)	100,000	
Lease receivable (difference)		62,092
Interest receivable (from adjusting entry above)		37,908

Concept Review Exercise

DIRECT FINANCING LEASE

United Cellular Systems leased a satellite transmission device from Pinnacle Leasing Services on January 1, 2017. Pinnacle paid $625,483 for the transmission device. Its fair value is $625,483.

Terms of the Lease Agreement and Related Information:	
Lease term	3 years (6 semiannual periods)
Semiannual rental payments	$120,000 at beginning of each period
Economic life of asset	3 years
Interest rate	12%

Required:

1. Prepare the appropriate entries for both United Cellular Systems and Pinnacle Leasing Services on January 1, the inception of the lease.
2. Prepare an amortization schedule that shows the pattern of interest expense for United Cellular Systems and interest revenue for Pinnacle Leasing Services over the lease term.
3. Prepare the appropriate entries to record the second lease payment on July 1, 2017, and adjusting entries on December 31, 2017 (the end of both companies' fiscal years).

Solution:

1. Prepare the appropriate entries for both United Cellular Systems and Pinnacle Leasing Services on January 1, the inception of the lease.

Calculation of the present value of minimum lease payments.

Present value of periodic rental payments:

($120,000 × 5.21236*) = **$625,483**

*Present value of an annuity due of $1: $n = 6$, $i = 6\%$.

January 1, 2017		
United Cellular Systems (Lessee)		
Leased equipment (calculated above)	625,483	
Lease payable (calculated above)		625,483
Lease payable	120,000	
Cash (lease payment)		120,000

(continued)

(concluded)

Pinnacle Leasing Services (Lessor)

Lease receivable (calculated above)	625,483	
Inventory of equipment (lessor's cost)		625,483
Cash (lease payment)	120,000	
Lease receivable		120,000

2. Prepare an amortization schedule that shows the pattern of interest expense for United Cellular Systems and interest revenue for Pinnacle Leasing Services over the lease term.

Date	Payments	Effective Interest (6% × Outstanding balance)	Decrease in Balance	Outstanding Balance
1/1/17				625,483
1/1/17	120,000		120,000	505,483
7/1/17	120,000	.06 (505,483) = 30,329	89,671	415,812
1/1/18	120,000	.06 (415,812) = 24,949	95,051	320,761
7/1/18	120,000	.06 (320,761) = 19,246	100,754	220,007
1/1/19	120,000	.06 (220,007) = 13,200	106,800	113,207
7/1/19	120,000	.06 (113,207) = 6,793*	113,207	0
	720,000	94,517	625,483	

*Adjusted for rounding of other numbers in the schedule.

3. Prepare the appropriate entries to record the second lease payment on July 1, 2017, and adjusting entries on December 31, 2017 (the end of both companies' fiscal years).

July 1, 2017

United Cellular Systems (Lessee)

Interest expense [6% × ($625,483 − 120,000)]	30,329	
Lease payable (difference)	89,671	
Cash (lease payment)		120,000

Pinnacle Leasing Services (Lessor)

Cash (lease payment)	120,000	
Lease receivable (difference)		89,671
Interest revenue [6% × ($625,483 − 120,000)]		30,329

December 31, 2017

United Cellular Systems (Lessee)

Interest expense (6% × $415,812: from schedule)	24,949	
Interest payable		24,949
Depreciation expense ($625,483 ÷ 3 years)	208,494	
Accumulated depreciation		208,494

Pinnacle Leasing Services (Lessor)

Interest receivable	24,949	
Interest revenue (6% × $415,812: from schedule)		24,949

Let's turn our attention now to situations in which the lessors are manufacturers or retailers and use lease arrangements as a means of selling their products.

Sales-Type Leases

LO15–6

A **sales-type lease** differs from a direct financing lease in only one respect. In addition to interest revenue generated over the lease term, the lessor receives a manufacturer's or dealer's profit on the "sale" of the asset.[19] This additional profit exists when the fair value of the

[19]A lessor need not be a manufacturer or a dealer for the arrangement to qualify as a sales-type lease. The existence of a profit (or loss) on the sale is the distinguishing factor.

FINANCIAL Reporting Case

Q2, p. 853

asset (usually the present value of the minimum lease payments, or "selling price") exceeds the cost or book value of the asset sold. Accounting for a sales-type lease is the same as for a direct financing lease except for recognizing the profit at the inception of the lease.[20]

To illustrate, let's modify our previous illustration. Assume all facts are the same except Sans Serif Publishers leased the equipment directly from CompuDec Corporation, rather than through the financing intermediary. Also assume CompuDec's cost of the equipment was $300,000. If you recall that the lease payments (their present value) provide a selling price of $479,079, you see that CompuDec recognizes a gross profit on the sale of $479,079 − 300,000 = $179,079. This sales-type lease is demonstrated in Illustration 15–8.

Illustration 15–8

Sales-Type Lease

Sales revenue	$479,079
− COGS	300,000
Dealer's profit	$179,079

On January 1, 2016, Sans Serif Publishers, Inc., leased printing equipment from CompuDec Corporation at a price of $479,079.

The lease agreement specifies annual payments of $100,000 beginning January 1, 2016, the inception of the lease, and at each December 31 thereafter through 2020. The six-year lease term ending December 31, 2021, (a year after the final payment) is equal to the estimated useful life of the equipment.

CompuDec manufactured the equipment at a cost of $300,000.

CompuDec's interest rate for financing the transaction is 10%.

Sales-Type Lease*

CompuDec Corporation (Lessor)

Lease receivable (present value of lease payments)	479,079	
Cost of goods sold (lessor's cost)	300,000	
Sales revenue (present value of lease payments)		479,079
Inventory of equipment (lessor's cost)		300,000

Remember, no interest has accrued when the first payment is made at the inception of the lease.

First Lease Payment*

CompuDec Corporation (Lessor)

Cash	100,000	
Lease receivable		100,000

*Of course, the entries to record the lease and the first payment could be combined into a single entry:

Lease receivable ($479,079 − $100,000)	379,079	
Cost of goods sold	300,000	
Cash	100,000	
Sales revenue		479,079
Inventory of equipment		300,000

Recording a sales-type lease is similar to recording a sale of merchandise on account:

A/R	{price}	
Sales rev		{price}
COGS	{cost}	
Inventory		{cost}

You should recognize the similarity between recording both the revenue and cost components of this sale by lease and recording the same components of other sales transactions. As in the sale of any product, gross profit is the difference between sales revenue and cost of goods sold. **Hewlett-Packard Company** "sells" some of its products using sales-type leases and disclosed the following in a recent annual report:

Real World Financials

Note 1 (in part)

HP records revenue from the sale of equipment under sales-type leases as product revenue at the inception of the lease.

All entries other than the entry at the inception of the lease, which includes the gross profit on the sale, are the same for a sales-type lease and a direct financing lease.

Accounting by the lessee is not affected by how the lessor classifies the lease. All lessee entries are precisely the same as in the previous illustration of a direct financing lease.

[20]It is possible that the asset's book value will exceed its fair value, in which case a dealer's loss should be recorded.

Illustration 15–9 shows the relationships among various lease components, using dollar amounts from the previous illustration.

Illustration 15–9
Lease Payment Relationships

The difference between the total payments and their present value (selling price of the asset) represents interest.

If the price is higher than the cost to the lessor, the lessor realizes a profit on the sale.

Lessor:		**Lessee:**
SALES-TYPE LEASE		**CAPITAL LEASE**
Gross Investment in Lease*	**$600,000**	**Minimum Lease Payments**
	Less:	
	Interest during lease term	
	($120,921)	
	Equals:	
Selling Price (present value of payments)	**$479,079**	**Purchase Price** (present value of payments)
	Less:	
	Profit on sale†	
	($179,079)	
	Equals:	
Cost to Lessor	**$300,000**	**(irrelevant to lessee)**

*The lessor's gross investment in the lease also would include any *unguaranteed* residual value in addition to the minimum lease payments. Any residual value *guaranteed* by the lessee is included in the minimum lease payments (both companies). We address these issues later in the chapter.
†If profit is zero, this would be a direct financing lease.

Where We're Headed

● LO15–11

The FASB and IASB are working together on a standard that would dramatically impact the way we account for leases, perhaps eliminating the concept of operating leases.

IFRS ILLUSTRATION

The IASB and FASB are collaborating on a joint project for a revision of lease accounting standards. The Boards have agreed on a "right of use" model by which the lessee recognizes an asset representing the right to use the leased asset for the lease term and also recognizes a corresponding liability for the present value of the lease payments, regardless of the term of the lease. Many people expect the new standard to result in most leases being recorded as an asset for the right of use and a liability for the present value of the lease payments. Thus, the notion of operating leases will disappear.

For an example, let's revisit Sans Serif's operating lease in Illustration 15–5 on p. 862. None of the four criteria was met that would have caused it to be a capital lease, including Criterion 4:

Is the present value of the minimum lease payments equal to or greater than 90% of the fair value of the asset: NO
($348,685 < 90% of $479,079)

$100,000 × 3.48685 =	$348,685
Lease payments	Present value

Accordingly, under existing standards, we recorded no asset and no liability for this operating lease. Under the new standard update, on the other hand, Sans Serif would be deemed to have received the "right of use" of the asset and would record an asset for the right of use and a liability for the present value of the lease payments:

Right-of-use asset	348,685	
Lease payable (present value of lease payments)		348,685

The impact of any changes will be significant; U.S. companies alone have over $1.25 *trillion* in operating lease obligations. The new leases standard update is being finalized at the time this text is being written. We provide a more detailed discussion of the new standard update in the Chapter Supplement.

PART B

Bargain Purchase Options and Residual Value

Bargain Purchase Options

LO15–7

We mentioned earlier that a **bargain purchase option (BPO)** is a provision of some lease contracts that gives the lessee the option of purchasing the leased property at a bargain price. We have discussed BPOs in the context of how they affect the classification of leases, but none of our earlier illustrations included a situation in which a BPO was present. You should have noted that a bargain price is defined in such a way that an additional cash payment is expected when a BPO is included in the agreement. Remember, a bargain price is one that is sufficiently below the property's expected fair value that the exercise of the option appears reasonably assured. Because exercise of the option appears at the inception of the lease to be reasonably assured, payment of the option price is expected to occur when the option becomes exercisable.

When a BPO is present, both the lessee and the lessor view the option price as an additional cash payment.

The expectation that the option price will be paid effectively adds an additional cash flow to the lease for both the lessee and the lessor. That additional payment is included as a component of minimum lease payments for both the lessor and the lessee. It therefore (a) is included in the computation of the amount to be capitalized (as an asset and a liability) by the *lessee* and recorded as a receivable by the *lessor,* but (b) reduces the amount of the periodic rent payments the *lessor* will need to receive from the lessee to recover the desired "selling price." This is indicated in Illustration 15–10.

Illustration 15–10
Effect of a Bargain Purchase Option

- The **lessee** *adds* the present value of the BPO price to the present value of periodic rental payments when computing the amount to be recorded as a leased asset and a lease liability.
- The **lessor,** when computing periodic rental payments, *subtracts* the present value of the BPO price from the amount to be recovered (fair value) to determine the amount that must be recovered from the lessee through the periodic rental payments.

For demonstration, let's suppose the equipment leased in Illustration 15–7 could be purchased by Sans Serif for an option price of **$60,000** at the conclusion of the lease. To make this a "bargain" purchase option, assume the residual value at the conclusion of the lease is expected to be $75,000. This situation is assumed in Illustration 15–11.

Illustration 15–11
Bargain Purchase Option

On January 1, 2016, Sans Serif Publishers, Inc., leased printing equipment from CompuDec Corporation at a price of $479,079. The lease agreement specifies annual payments beginning January 1, 2016, the inception of the lease, and at each December 31 thereafter through 2020. On December 31, 2021, at the end of the six-year lease term, the equipment is expected to be worth $75,000, and Sans Serif has the option to purchase it for $60,000 on that date. The estimated useful life of the equipment is seven years. The residual value after seven years is zero.[21] CompuDec manufactured the equipment at a cost of $300,000 and its interest rate for financing the transaction is 10%.

The lessee *adds* the PV of the BPO price to determine its asset and liability.

Lessee's calculation of PV of minimum lease payments:

Present value of periodic rental payments ($92,931 × 4.79079†)	$445,211
Plus: Present value of the BPO price ($60,000 × .56447*)	33,868
Present value of minimum lease payments (Recorded as a leased asset and a lease liability)	$479,079

(continued)

[21]Our discussion of the effect of a bargain purchase option would be precisely the same if our illustration were of a direct financing lease (for instance, if the lessor's cost were $479,079) except that neither sales revenue nor cost of goods sold would be recorded in a direct financing lease.

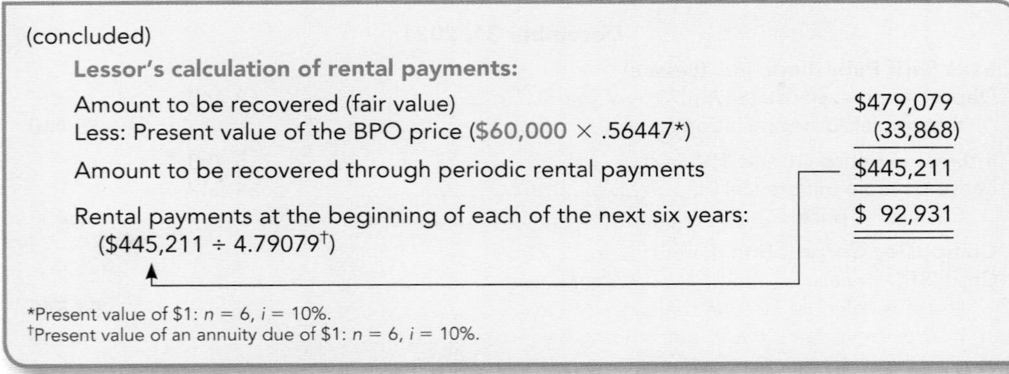

(concluded)

Lessor's calculation of rental payments:

Amount to be recovered (fair value)	$479,079
Less: Present value of the BPO price ($60,000 × .56447*)	(33,868)
Amount to be recovered through periodic rental payments	$445,211
Rental payments at the beginning of each of the next six years: ($445,211 ÷ 4.79079†)	$ 92,931

*Present value of $1: $n = 6$, $i = 10\%$.
†Present value of an annuity due of $1: $n = 6$, $i = 10\%$.

The lessor *subtracts* the PV of the BPO price to determine rental payments.

The lease amortization schedule for CompuDec and Sans Serif when a BPO is included in the lease agreement is shown in Illustration 15–11A.

Illustration 15–11A

Amortization Schedule—with BPO

	Payments	Effective Interest (10% × Outstanding balance)	Decrease in Balance	Outstanding Balance
1/1/16				479,079
1/1/16	92,931		92,931	386,148
12/31/16	92,931	.10 (386,148) = 38,615	54,316	331,832
12/31/17	92,931	.10 (331,832) = 33,183	59,748	272,084
12/31/18	92,931	.10 (272,084) = 27,208	65,723	206,361
12/31/19	92,931	.10 (206,361) = 20,636	72,295	134,066
12/31/20	92,931	.10 (134,066) = 13,407	79,524	54,542
12/31/21	60,000	.10 (54,542) = 5,458*	54,542	0
	617,586	138,507	479,079	

*Adjusted for rounding of other numbers in the schedule.

Both the lessor and lessee view the BPO price ($60,000) as an additional cash payment.

Be aware of several points the amortization schedule reveals. First, the six periodic cash payments are now $92,931 as we calculated in Illustration 15–11. Notice also that we now include the **$60,000** BPO price as an additional lease payment. Despite the different composition of the minimum lease payments, their present value ($479,079) is the same as when we assumed $100,000 periodic payments and no residual value. However, the effective interest that will be recorded over the lease term (as interest expense by the lessee and interest revenue by the lessor) now is more: $138,507. (It was $120,921 before.) The higher interest reflects the fact that payments are farther in the future, causing the outstanding lease balances (and interest on those balances) to be higher during the lease term. Also, note that the total of the lease payments now is more: $617,586. (It was $600,000 before.) This total is referred to as the lessor's **gross investment in the lease** and is disclosed in the lessor's disclosure note about leases.

The lessor's *gross investment in the lease* is the total of periodic rental payments and any residual value.

Recording the exercise of the option is similar to recording the periodic rent payments. That is, a portion of the payment covers interest for the year, and the remaining portion reduces the outstanding liability/receivable balance (to zero with this last payment), as shown in Illustration 15–11B.

Note that depreciation also is affected by the BPO. As pointed out earlier, the lessee normally depreciates a leased asset over the term of the lease. But if ownership transfers by contract or by the expected exercise of a bargain purchase option, the asset should be depreciated over the asset's useful life. This reflects the fact that the lessee anticipates using the

Illustration 15–11B
Journal Entries—with BPO

The cash payment expected when the BPO is exercised represents part interest and part principal just like the other cash payments.

December 31, 2021		
Sans Serif Publishers, Inc. (Lessee)		
Depreciation expense ($479,079* ÷ 7 years)	68,440	
Accumulated depreciation		68,440
Interest expense (10% × $54,542)	5,458	
Lease payable (difference)	54,542	
Cash (BPO price)		60,000
CompuDec Corporation (Lessor)		
Cash (BPO price)	60,000	
Lease receivable (account balance)		54,542
Interest revenue (10% × outstanding balance)		5,458

*The residual value is zero after the full seven-year useful life.

leased asset for its full useful life. In this illustration, the equipment is expected to be useful for seven years, so depreciation is $68,440 ($479,079 ÷ 7 years).

When a BPO Is Exercisable Before the End of the Lease Term

The length of the lease term is limited to the time up to when a bargain purchase option becomes exercisable.

In Illustration 15–11 we assumed that the BPO was exercisable on December 31, 2021—the end of the lease term. Sometimes, though, the lease contract specifies that a BPO becomes exercisable before the designated lease term ends. Since a BPO is expected to be exercised, the lease term ends for accounting purposes when the option becomes exercisable. For example, let's say the BPO in the illustration could be exercised a year earlier—at the end of the fifth year. The effect this would have on accounting for the lease is to change the lease term from six years to five. All calculations would be modified accordingly. Stated differently, minimum lease payments include only the periodic cash payments specified in the agreement that occur prior to the date a BPO becomes exercisable. (We assume the option is exercised at that time and the lease ends.)

Ethical Dilemma

"I know we had discussed that they're supposed to be worth $24,000 when our purchase option becomes exercisable," Ferris insisted. "That's why we agreed to the lease terms. But, Jenkins, you know how fast computers become dated. We can make a good case that they'll be worth only $10,000 in three years."

The computers to which Ferris referred were acquired by lease. The lease meets none of the criteria for classification as a capital lease except that it would contain a bargain purchase option if the computers could be purchased for $10,000 after three years.

"We could avoid running up our debt that way," Jenkins agreed.

How could debt be avoided?

Do you perceive an ethical problem?

Residual Value

The **residual value** of leased property is an estimate of what its commercial value will be at the end of the lease term. In our previous examples of capital leases for which no BPOs were present, we assumed that the residual value was negligible. Now let's consider the economic effect of a leased asset that does have a material residual value and how that will affect the way both the lessee and the lessor account for the lease agreement.

Suppose the equipment leased in Illustration 15–11 was expected to be worth $60,000 at the end of the six-year lease term. Should this influence the lessor's (CompuDec) calculation of periodic rental payments? Other than the possible influence on rental payments, should the lessee (Sans Serif Publishers) be concerned with the residual value of the leased asset? The answer to both questions is maybe. We'll use Illustration 15–12 to see why.

● LO15–8

Illustration 15–12
Residual Value

On January 1, 2016, Sans Serif Publishers, Inc., leased printing equipment from CompuDec Corporation at a price of $479,079. The lease agreement specifies annual payments beginning January 1, 2016, the inception of the lease, and at each December 31 thereafter through 2020. The estimated useful life of the equipment is seven years. On December 31, 2021, at the end of the six-year lease term, the equipment is expected to be worth $60,000. CompuDec manufactured the equipment at a cost of $300,000* and its interest rate for financing the transaction is 10%.

*This provision is for consistency with Illustration 15–8, which described a sales-type lease. However, our discussion of the effect of a residual value would be precisely the same if our illustration were of a direct financing lease (for instance, if the lessor's cost is $479,079) except that neither sales revenue nor cost of goods sold would be recorded in a direct financing lease.

We consider the lessee first.

Effect on the Lessee of a Residual Value

Should the lessee view the residual value as an additional "payment" by the lessee as it did for the BPO price in the previous section? That depends on whether the lessee *guarantees* the residual value to be a particular amount at the end of the lease term.

GUARANTEED RESIDUAL VALUE. Sometimes the lease agreement includes a guarantee by the lessee that the lessor will recover a specified residual value when custody of the asset reverts back to the lessor at the end of the lease term. This not only reduces the lessor's risk but also provides incentive for the lessee to exercise a higher degree of care in maintaining the leased asset to preserve the residual value. The lessee promises to return not only the property but also sufficient cash to provide the lessor with a minimum combined value. In effect, the guaranteed residual value is an additional lease payment that is to be paid in property, or cash, or both. As such, it is included in the minimum lease payments and affects the amount the lessee records as both a leased asset and a lease liability, as shown in Illustration 15–12A.

The guaranteed residual value is considered an additional lease payment that is to be paid in property, or cash, or both.

Illustration 15–12A
Lessee's Calculation of the Present Value of Minimum Lease Payments Including a Guaranteed Residual Value

Present value of periodic rental payments ($92,931 × 4.79079*)	$445,211
Plus: Present value of the residual value ($60,000 × .56447†)	33,868
Present value of minimum lease payments (recorded as a leased asset and a lease liability)	$479,079

*Present value of an annuity due of $1: $n = 6$, $i = 10\%$.
†Present value of $1: $n = 6$, $i = 10\%$.

You should recognize this as the same calculation we used in the previous section when we had a BPO, and so the BPO price was considered an additional lease payment. In fact, the amortization schedule is precisely the same as in Illustration 15–11A on page 871 when we had a BPO.

If the lessee obtains title, the lessor's computation of rental payments is unaffected by any residual value.

A question you might have at this point is: Earlier, when we had a BPO, why didn't we also view the residual value at the end of the lease term as an additional payment when calculating the present value of lease payments? The reason is obvious when you recall an essential characteristic of a BPO is that it's expected to be exercised. So, when it is exercised, title to the leased asset passes to the lessee and, with title, any residual value. When that happens, the residual value cannot be considered an additional lease payment to the lessor, and it therefore is not incorporated into the computation of lease payments.

Unguaranteed residual value. The previous example demonstrates that when the residual value is guaranteed, the lessee views it as a component of minimum lease payments. But what if the lessee does *not* guarantee the residual value? In that case, the lessee is not obligated to make any payments other than the periodic rental payments. As a result, the present value of the minimum lease payments—recorded as a leased asset and a lease liability—is simply the present value of periodic rental payments ($445,211). The same is true when the residual value is guaranteed by a third-party guarantor. (Insurance companies sometimes assume this role.)

Effect on the Lessor of a Residual Value

The lessor *subtracts* the PV of the residual value to determine rental payments, but includes it in the lease receivable.

Guaranteed residual value. When the residual value is guaranteed, the lessor as well as the lessee views it as a component of minimum lease payments. If CompuDec retains title to the asset at the end of the lease term, then it would anticipate receiving the $60,000 residual value at the conclusion of the lease term. That amount would contribute to the total amount to be recovered by the lessor and would reduce the amount needed to be recovered from the lessee through periodic rental payments. The amount of each payment would be reduced from $100,000 to $92,931, calculated in Illustration 15–12B.

Illustration 15–12B

Lessor's Calculation of Rental Payments When Lessor Retains Residual Value

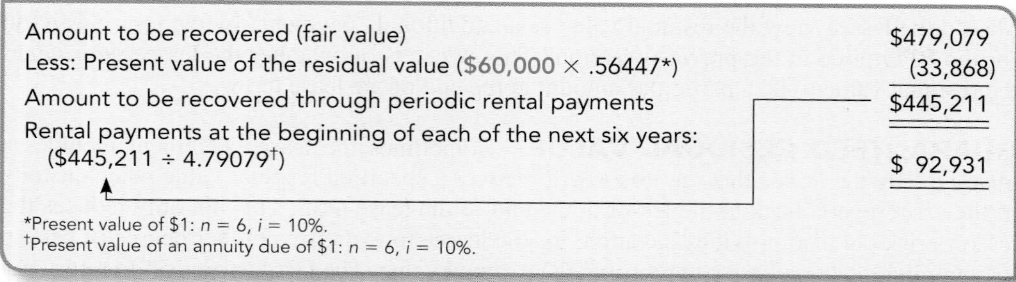

Amount to be recovered (fair value)	$479,079
Less: Present value of the residual value ($60,000 × .56447*)	(33,868)
Amount to be recovered through periodic rental payments	$445,211
Rental payments at the beginning of each of the next six years: ($445,211 ÷ 4.79079†)	$ 92,931

*Present value of $1: $n = 6$, $i = 10\%$.
†Present value of an annuity due of $1: $n = 6$, $i = 10\%$.

You should notice that the lessor's calculation of periodic rental payments is precisely the same as when we had the $60,000 BPO price in a previous section. It also is precisely the reverse of the *lessee's* calculation of the amount to capitalize when the residual value is guaranteed. This is because when the residual value is guaranteed, both view it as an additional lease payment. In accordance with GAAP, the guaranteed residual value is a component of the minimum lease payments for both the lessor and lessee.[22] In fact, the amortization schedule is precisely the same as in Illustration 15–11A on page 871 when we had a BPO.

If CompuDec had acquired the equipment for the $479,079 "selling price," it would be a direct financing lease recorded as follows:

Lease receivable (present value of minimum lease payments)	479,079	
Inventory of equipment (lessor's cost)		479,079

Illustration 15–12, though, states that CompuDec manufactured it at a cost of $300,000, making it a sales-type lease. In Illustration 15–12C, we see the lessor's entries for this sales-type lease along with the lessee's entries for comparison. Only the lessor's initial entry on January 1, 2016, is different. All other entries in Illustration 15–12C are the same whether it's a sales-type lease or a direct financing lease.

[22] Later you will see that when the residual value is not guaranteed, it is not considered a component of minimum lease payments for either the lessor or the lessee; but it still affects the amount of periodic lease payments.

Sales-Type Lease, January 1, 2016

Sans Serif Publishers, Inc. (Lessee)		
Leased equipment (present value of lease payments)	479,079	
Lease payable (present value of lease payments)		479,079
CompuDec Corporation (Lessor)		
Lease receivable (present value of minimum lease payments*)	479,079	
Cost of goods sold (lessor's cost)	300,000	
Sales revenue (present value of minimum lease payments*)		479,079
Inventory of equipment (lessor's cost)		300,000

First Lease Payment, January 1, 2016

Sans Serif Publishers, Inc. (Lessee)		
Lease payable	92,931	
Cash		92,931
CompuDec Corporation (Lessor)		
Cash	92,931	
Lease receivable		92,931

*Minimum lease payments include the $60,000 residual value because it's guaranteed.

Illustration 15–12C

Sales-Type Lease with Guaranteed Residual Value

Sales revenue	$479,079
− COGS	300,000
Dealer's profit	$179,079

The lessor's minimum lease payments include a residual value only if it is guaranteed (by either the lessee or a third-party guarantor).

Notice, too, that the timing of the **$60,000** payment is December 31, 2021, the end of the lease term. Remember, the final periodic cash payment on December 31, 2020, is at the beginning of the final year. The journal entries that accompany this final cash payment are shown in Illustration 15–12D.

December 31, 2020

Sans Serif Publishers, Inc. (Lessee)		
Depreciation expense [($479,079 − 60,000)* ÷ 6 *years*]	69,847	
Accumulated depreciation		69,847
Interest expense (10% × outstanding balance)	13,407	
Lease payable (difference)	79,524	
Cash (lease payment)		92,931
CompuDec Corporation (Lessor)		
Cash (lease payment)	92,931	
Lease receivable		79,524
Interest revenue (10% × outstanding balance)		13,407

*The depreciable cost is reduced by the lessee-guaranteed residual value.

Illustration 15–12D

Entries to Accompany Final Periodic Payment

The residual value reduces the asset's depreciable cost to $419,079.

As the outstanding balance becomes less toward the end of the lease term, the portion of each payment that represents interest also becomes less.

At December 31, 2021, the lessee's book value, sometimes called carrying value or carrying amount, of the fully depreciated equipment is its $60,000 estimated residual value. If we assume that the actual residual value also is at least $60,000, then the lessee is not obligated to pay cash in addition to returning the equipment to the lessor (demonstrated in Illustration 15–12E).[23]

However, if we assume that the actual residual value at December 31, 2021, is only $25,000, then the lessee is required to pay $35,000 cash to the lessor in addition to returning the equipment. The lessee records this payment as a loss.[24]

[23]If the actual value is *more* than the guaranteed residual value, the lessor may realize a gain if and when the asset subsequently is sold. Alternatively, the lessee could sell the asset, make the required $60,000 payment to the lessor, and realize the gain. Regardless, the potential gain does not affect the entries at the end of the lease term.

[24]Sometimes by mutual agreement the lessee will sell the leased asset at the end of the lease term and remit the proceeds (plus any deficiency under the guarantee) to the lessor.

Illustration 15–12E

End of Lease Term—Actual Residual Value Equals the Guaranteed Amount

The sixth and final depreciation charge increases the balance in accumulated depreciation to $419,079.

The equipment is reinstated on the books of the lessor at its fair value at the end of the lease term.

December 31, 2021		
Sans Serif Publishers, Inc. (Lessee)		
Depreciation expense [($479,079 − 60,000)* ÷ 6 years]	69,847	
Accumulated depreciation		69,847
Interest expense (10% × outstanding balance)	5,458	
Lease payable (difference)	54,542	
Accumulated depreciation (account balance)	419,079	
Leased equipment (account balance)		479,079
CompuDec Corporation (Lessor)		
Inventory of equipment (residual value)	60,000	
Lease receivable (account balance)		54,542
Interest revenue (10% × outstanding balance)		5,458

*The depreciable cost is reduced by the lessee-guaranteed residual value.

The lessor's minimum lease payments include a residual value only if it is guaranteed (by either the lessee or a third-party guarantor).

UNGUARANTEED RESIDUAL VALUE. The previous example demonstrates that when the residual value is guaranteed, both the lessor and lessee view it as a component of minimum lease payments. But what if the lessee does *not* guarantee the residual value? From the lessor's perspective, the residual value is a component of *minimum lease payments* only if it is guaranteed (by either the lessee or a third-party guarantor). Yet, even if it is not guaranteed, the lessor still expects to receive it. So, if we modify the previous illustration to assume the residual value is not guaranteed, the lessor's receivable still is $479,079, the present value of the lease payments, including the residual value, so a direct financing lease would be the same as if the residual value is guaranteed.

When the lessee doesn't guarantee the residual value, the lessee's net liability ($445,211) and the lessor's net receivable ($479,079) will differ because the lessee does not include the unguaranteed residual amount.

However, the sales revenue is only $445,211—the present value of the minimum lease payments *not* including the residual value. In other words, sales revenue includes the present value only of the periodic rental payments, not the unguaranteed residual value. Cost of goods sold is similarly reduced by the present value of the unguaranteed residual value, so the initial lessor entry would be modified as follows:

Sans Serif Publishers, Inc. (Lessee)		
Leased equipment (present value of lease payments)	445,211	
Lease payable (present value of lease payments)		445,211
CompuDec Corporation (Lessor)		
Lease receivable (PV of lease payments plus PV of $60,000 residual value)	479,079	
Cost of goods sold ($300,000 − 33,868)	266,132	
Sales revenue ($479,079 − 33,868)*		445,211
Inventory of equipment (lessor's cost)		300,000

*Also can be calculated as the present value of the lessor's minimum lease payments, which does not include the unguaranteed residual value.

Sales revenue does not include the unguaranteed residual value because the revenue to be recovered from the lessee is lease payments only. The remainder of the lessor's investment is to be recovered—not from payment by the lessee (as is presumed when the residual value is guaranteed), but by selling, re-leasing, or otherwise obtaining value from the asset when it reverts back to the lessor. You might want to view the situation this way: The portion of the asset sold is the portion not represented by the unguaranteed residual value. So, both the asset's cost and its selling price are reduced by the present value of the portion not sold.

When the residual value is not guaranteed, the lessor bears any loss that results from the actual residual value of the leased asset being less than the original estimate. The lessor would record (a) any cash received as well as (b) the returned asset at its actual residual value. It then would record a loss or gain if that total differs from the anticipated residual value.

Illustration 15–13 summarizes the effect of the residual value of a leased asset for each of the various possibilities regarding the nature of the residual value.

Illustration 15–13

Effect of a Residual Value: A Summary

Is the residual value of a leased asset included in:

	the Lessor's		the Lessee's
	(a) Computation of Lease Payments	(b) Minimum Lease Payments	(c) Minimum Lease Payments
Lessee gets the residual value (by transfer of title or the expected exercise of a bargain purchase option)	No	No	No
Lessor gets the residual value (title does not transfer; no bargain purchase option)			
• Residual value is *not* guaranteed	Yes	No	No
• Residual value *is* guaranteed by the lessee.	Yes	Yes	Yes
• Residual value is guaranteed by a *third party* guarantor.	Yes	Yes	No

(a) The lessor, when computing periodic rental payments, subtracts the present value of the residual value from the amount to be recovered (fair value) to determine the amount that must be recovered from the lessee through the periodic rent payments.
(b) The present value of the lessor's minimum lease payments is the lease receivable and, in a sales-type lease, the sales revenue.
(c) The present value of the lessee's minimum lease payments is the amount to be capitalized as an asset and a liability.

We have seen how minimum lease payments are affected by a residual value and by a bargain purchase option. Let's now consider how maintenance, insurance, taxes, and other costs usually associated with ownership (called *executory costs*) affect minimum lease payments.

Other Lease Accounting Issues

PART C

Executory Costs

● LO15–9

One of the responsibilities of ownership that is transferred to the lessee in a capital lease is the responsibility to pay for maintenance, insurance, taxes, and any other costs usually associated with ownership. These are referred to as **executory costs**. Lease agreements usually are written in such a way that these costs are borne by the lessee. These expenditures simply are expensed by the lessee as incurred: repair expense, insurance expense, property tax expense, and so on. Let's return, for example, to Illustration 15–6 on page 863. Now, suppose that a $2,000 per year maintenance agreement was arranged with an outside service for the leased equipment. Sans Serif (the lessee) would expense this fee each year as incurred:

The lessee simply expenses executory costs as incurred.

Maintenance expense	2,000	
Cash (annual fee)		2,000

The lessor is unaffected by executory costs paid by the lessee.

Any portion of rental payments that represents maintenance, insurance, taxes, or other executory costs is not considered when calculating the PV of lease payments.

Sometimes, as an expediency, a lease contract will specify that the lessor is to pay executory costs, but that the lessee will reimburse the lessor through higher periodic rental payments. When rental payments are inflated for this reason, these executory costs are excluded in determining the present value of the minimum lease payments. They still are expensed by the lessee, even though paid through the lessor. For demonstration, let's modify Illustration 15–6 to assume the periodic rental payments were increased to $102,000 with the provision the lessor (First LeaseCorp) pays the maintenance fee. We do this in Illustration 15–14.

Illustration 15–14

Rental Payments Including Executory Costs Paid by the Lessor

On January 1, 2016, Sans Serif Publishers, Inc., leased printing equipment from First LeaseCorp. First LeaseCorp purchased the equipment from CompuDec Corporation at a cost of $479,079.

Additional information:

- Six annual payments of $102,000 beginning January 1, 2016.
- Payments include $2,000 which First LeaseCorp will use to pay an annual maintenance fee.
- The interest rate in these financing arrangements is 10%.
- Capital lease to Sans Serif.
- Direct financing lease to First LeaseCorp.

Executory costs that are included in periodic rental payments to be paid by the lessor are, in effect, indirectly paid by the lessee—and expensed by the lessee.

First Payment (January 1, 2016)

Sans Serif Publishers, Inc. (Lessee)		
Maintenance expense (2013 fee)	2,000	
Lease payable	100,000	
Cash (lease payment)		102,000
First LeaseCorp (Lessor)		
Cash (rental payment)	102,000	
Lease receivable		100,000
Maintenance fee payable*		2,000

*This assumes the $2,000 maintenance fee has not yet been paid to the outside maintenance service.

Discount Rate

An important factor in the overall lease equation that we've glossed over until now is the discount rate used in present value calculations. Because lease payments occur in future periods, we must consider the time value of money when evaluating their present value. The rate is important because it influences virtually every amount reported by both the lessor and the lessee in connection with the lease.

One rate is implicit in the lease agreement. This is the effective interest rate the lease payments provide the lessor over and above the price at which the asset is sold under the lease. It is the desired rate of return the lessor has in mind when deciding the size of the lease payments. (Refer to our earlier calculations of the periodic rental payments.) Usually the lessee is aware of the lessor's implicit rate or can infer it from the asset's fair value.[25] When the lessor's implicit rate is unknown, the lessee should use its own incremental borrowing rate.

The lessee uses the lower of the interest rate implicit in the lease or the lessee's own incremental borrowing rate.

This is the rate the lessee would expect to pay a bank if funds were borrowed to buy the asset. When the lessor's implicit rate is known, the lessee should use the lower of the two rates.[26]

[25]The corporation laws of some states, Florida for instance, actually require the interest rate to be expressly stated in the lease agreement.
[26]*Incremental borrowing rate* refers to the fact that lending institutions tend to view debt as being increasingly risky as the level of debt increases. Thus, additional (i.e., incremental) debt is likely to be loaned at a higher interest rate than existing debt, other things being equal.

When the Lessee's Incremental Borrowing Rate Is Less Than the Lessor's Implicit Rate

Instances are few in which the lessee actually would use its incremental borrowing rate. Here's why. We noted earlier that, like any other asset, a leased asset should not be recorded at more than its fair value. Look what happens to the present value payments if Sans Serif uses a discount rate less than the 10% rate implicit in Illustration 15–6 (let's say 9%):

$100,000 × 4.88965*	=	$488,965
Rental payments		Lessee's cost

*Present value of an annuity due of $1: $n = 6$, $i = 9\%$.

But remember, the fair value of the equipment was $479,079. The $100,000 amount for the rental payments was derived by the lessor, contemplating a fair value of $479,079 and a desired rate of return (implicit rate) of 10%. So, using a discount rate lower than the lessor's implicit rate usually would result in the present value of minimum lease payments being more than the fair value, and we record the lease at the fair value.

This conclusion does not hold when the leased asset has an unguaranteed residual value. You will recall that the lessor's determinations always include any residual value that accrues to the lessor; but when the lessee doesn't guarantee the residual value, it is *not* included in the lessee's present value calculations. Combining two previous examples, let's modify our demonstration of an unguaranteed residual value to assume the lessee's incremental borrowing rate was 9%. Because the residual value was expected to contribute to the lessor's recovery of the $479,079 fair value, the rental payments were only $92,931. But, the lessee would ignore the unguaranteed residual value and calculate its cost of the leased asset to be $454,400.

$92,931 × 4.88965*	=	$454,400
Rental payments		Lessee's cost

*Present value of an annuity due of $1: $n = 6$, $i = 9\%$.

In this case, the present value of minimum lease payments would be less than the fair value even though a lower discount rate is used. But again, if there is no residual value, or if the lessee guarantees the residual value, or if the unguaranteed residual value is relatively small, a discount rate lower than the lessor's implicit rate will result in the present value of minimum lease payments being more than the fair value.

When the Lessor's Implicit Rate Is Unknown

What if the lessee is unaware of the lessor's implicit rate? This is a logical question in light of the rule that says the lessee should use its own incremental borrowing rate when the lessor's implicit rate is unknown to the lessee. But in practice the lessor's implicit rate usually is known. Even if the lessor chooses not to explicitly disclose the rate, the lessee usually can deduce the rate using information he knows about the value of the leased asset and the lease payments. After all, in making the decision to lease rather than buy, the lessee typically becomes quite knowledgeable about the asset.

Even so, it is possible that a lessee might be unable to derive the lessor's implicit rate. This might happen, for example, if the leased asset has a relatively high residual value. Remember, a residual value (guaranteed or not) is an ingredient in the lessor's calculation of the rental payments. Sometimes it may be hard for the lessee to identify the residual value estimated by the lessor if the lessor chooses not to make it known.[27] As the lease term and risk of obsolescence increase, the residual value typically is less of a factor.

[27]Disclosure requirements provide that the lessor company must disclose the components of its investments in nonoperating leases, which would include any estimated residual values. But the disclosures are aggregate amounts, not amounts of individual leased assets.

Additional Consideration

As pointed out earlier, the management of a lessee company sometimes will try to structure a lease to avoid the criteria that would cause the lease to be classified as a capital lease in order to gain the questionable advantages of off-balance-sheet financing. On the other hand, a lessor normally would prefer recording a capital lease, other things being equal. Two ways sometimes used to structure a lease to qualify as an operating lease by the lessee, but as a capital lease by the lessor are: (1) cause the two parties to use different interest rates and (2) avoid including the residual value in the lessee's minimum lease payments. Let's see how they work:

1. Cause the Two Parties to Use Different Interest Rates.

It was pointed out earlier that a lessee sometimes can claim to be unable to determine the lessor's implicit rate. Not knowing the lessor's implicit rate would permit the lessee to use its own incremental borrowing rate. If higher than the lessor's implicit rate, the present value it produces may cause the 90% of fair value criterion not to be met for the lessee (thus an operating lease) even though the criterion is met for the lessor (thus a capital lease).

2. Avoid Including the Residual Value in the Lessee's Minimum Lease Payments.

The residual value, if guaranteed by the lessee or by a third party guarantor, is included in the minimum lease payments by the lessor when applying the 90% of fair value criterion and thus increases the likelihood that a capital lease will be recorded. However, when the residual value is guaranteed by a third-party guarantor and not by the lessee, it is not included in the lessee's minimum lease payments. So, if a residual value is sufficiently large and guaranteed by a third-party guarantor, it may cause the 90% of fair value criterion to be met by the lessor, but not by the lessee.

Both schemes are unintentionally encouraged by lease accounting rules. As long as arbitrary cutoff points are used (90% of fair value in this case), maneuvers will be devised to circumvent them.

International Financial Reporting Standards

● LO15–11

Present Value of Minimum Lease Payments. Under *IAS No. 17,* both parties to a lease generally use the rate implicit in the lease to discount minimum lease payments.[28] Under U.S. GAAP, lessors use the implicit rate and lessees use the incremental borrowing rate unless the implicit rate is known and is the lower rate.

Lessor's Initial Direct Costs

The costs incurred by the lessor that are associated directly with originating a lease and are essential to acquire that lease are referred to as **initial direct costs**. They include legal fees, commissions, evaluating the prospective lessee's financial condition, and preparing and processing lease documents. The method of accounting for initial direct costs depends on the nature of the lease. Remember, a lessor can classify a lease as (1) an operating lease, (2) a direct financing lease, or (3) a sales-type lease. The accounting treatment for initial direct costs by each of the three possible lease types is summarized next.

1. For *operating leases,* initial direct costs are recorded as assets and amortized over the term of the lease. Since the only revenue an operating lease produces is rental revenue, and that

[28] "Leases," *International Accounting Standard No. 17* (IASCF), as amended effective January 1, 2014.

revenue is recognized over the lease term, initial direct costs also are automatically recognized over the lease term to match these costs with the rent revenues they help generate.

2. In *direct financing leases,* interest revenue is recognized over the lease term, so initial direct costs are recorded at the same time as the interest revenues they help generate. Therefore, initial direct costs are not expensed at the outset but are deferred and recognized over the lease term. This can be accomplished by increasing the lessor's *lease receivable* by the total of initial direct costs. Then, as interest revenue is recognized over the lease term at a constant effective rate, the initial direct costs are recognized at the same rate (that is, proportionally).
3. For *sales-type leases,* initial direct costs are expensed at the inception of the lease. Since the usual reason for a sales-type lease is for a manufacturer or a dealer to sell its product, it's reasonable to recognize the costs of creating the transaction as a selling expense in the period of the sale.

Contingent Rentals

Sometimes rental payments may be increased (or decreased) at some future time during the lease term, depending on whether or not some specified event occurs. Usually the contingency is related to revenues, profitability, or usage above some designated level. For example, a quarterly report of **Wal-Mart Stores, Inc.**, included the note re-created in Illustration 15–15.

> Certain of the Company's leases provide for the payment of contingent rentals based on a percentage of sales. Such contingent rentals were immaterial for fiscal 2014, 2013, and 2012.

Illustration 15–15

Disclosure of Contingent Rentals—Walmart

Real World Financials

Contingent rentals are *not* included in the minimum lease payments because they are not determinable at the inception of the lease. Instead, they are included as components of income when (and if) they occur or when they are considered probable. Increases or decreases in rental payments that are dependent only on the passage of time are not contingent rentals; these are part of minimum lease payments.

Although contingent rentals are not included in minimum lease payments, they are reported in disclosure notes by both the lessor and lessee.

A Brief Summary

Leasing arrangements often are complex. In studying this chapter you've encountered several features of lease agreements that alter the way we make several of the calculations needed to account for leases. Illustration 15–16 on the next page provides a concise review of the essential lease accounting components, using calculations from a hypothetical lease situation to provide a numerical perspective.

Lease Disclosures

Lease disclosure requirements are quite extensive for both the lessor and lessee. Virtually all aspects of the lease agreement must be disclosed. For *all* leases (a) a general description of the leasing arrangement is required as well as (b) minimum future payments, in the aggregate and for each of the five succeeding fiscal years. Other required disclosures are specific to the type of lease and include: residual values, contingent rentals, sublease rentals, and executory costs. The lessor must disclose its **net investment in the lease**. This amount is the present value of the **gross investment in the lease**, which is the total of the minimum lease

The lessor's net investment in the lease is the present value of the gross investment, which is the total of the minimum lease payments (plus any unguaranteed residual value).

Illustration 15–16 Lease Terms and Concepts: A Comprehensive Summary

Lease Situation for Calculations

($ in 000s)

Lease term (years)	4	Lessor's cost	$300
Asset's useful life (years)	5	Residual value (Total: $8 + 6 + 5 = $19):	
Lessor's implicit rate (known by lessee)	12%	Guaranteed by lessee	$8
Lessee's incremental borrowing rate	13%	Guaranteed by third party[a]	$6
Rental payments (including executory costs) at the beginning of each year	$102	Unguaranteed	$5
		Executory costs paid annually by lessor	$2
		Bargain purchase option	none

Amount	Description	Calculation
Lessee's:		
Minimum lease payments	Total of periodic rental payments[b] plus residual value guaranteed by lessee or plus BPO price[d]	($100 × 4) + $8 = $408
Leased asset	Present value of minimum lease payments (using lower of lessor's rate and lessee's incremental borrowing rate); cannot exceed fair value	($100 × 3.40183[e]) + ($8 × .63552[f]) = $345
Lease liability at inception	Same as leased asset	($100 × 3.40183[e]) + ($8 × .63552[f]) = $345
Lessor's:		
Minimum lease payments	Total of periodic rental payments[b] plus guaranteed[c] residual value or plus BPO price[d]	($100 × 4) + ($8 + 6) = $414
Lease receivable	Present value of periodic rental payments[b] plus any residual value that reverts to the lessor (guaranteed or not) or plus any BPO price[d] (discounted at the lessor's rate) plus any initial direct costs in a direct financing lease	($100 × 3.40183[e]) + ($19 × .63552[f]) = $352
If sales-type lease:		
Sales revenue	Present value of lessor's minimum lease payments	($100 × 3.40183[e]) + ([$19 − 5] × .63552[f]) = $349
Cost of goods sold	Lessor's cost − present value of unguaranteed residual value	$300 − ($5 × .63552[f]) = $297
Dealer's profit	Sales revenue − cost of goods sold	$349 − 297 = $52

[a]Beyond any amount guaranteed by the lessee ($8 + 6 minus any amount paid by the lessee).
[b]Any portion of rental payments that represents maintenance, insurance, taxes, or other executory costs is not considered part of minimum lease payments. In this case, rentals are reduced as follows: $102 − 2 = $100.
[c]By lessee and/or by third party.
[d]In this context, a residual value and a BPO price are mutually exclusive: if a BPO exists, any residual value is expected to remain with the lessee and is not considered an additional payment.
[e]Present value of annuity due of $1: $n = 4$, $i = 12\%$.
[f]Present value of $1: $n = 4$, $i = 12\%$.

payments (plus any unguaranteed residual value). Some representative disclosure examples are shown in Illustrations 15–17 (lessor) and 15–18 (lessee).

IBM is a manufacturer that relies heavily on leasing as a means of selling its products. Its disclosure of sales-type leases is shown in Illustration 15–17.

Illustration 15–17

Lessor Disclosure of Sales-Type Leases—IBM Corporation

Real World Financials

F Financing Receivables (in part)
(dollars in millions)

At December 31:	2013	2012
Current:		
Net investment in sales-type and direct financing leases	$ 4,004	$ 3,862
Commercial financing receivables	8,541	7,750
Client loan receivables	5,854	5,395
Installment payment receivables	1,389	1,031
Total	$19,787	$18,038
Noncurrent:		
Net investment in sales-type and direct financing leases	$ 5,700	$ 6,107
Commercial financing receivables	—	5
Client loan receivables	6,360	5,966
Installment payment receivables	695	733
Total	$12,755	$12,812

Net investment in sales-type and direct financing leases relates principally to the company's systems products and are for terms ranging generally from two to six years. Net investment in sales-type and direct financing leases includes unguaranteed residual values of $737 million and $794 million at December 31, 2013 and 2012, respectively, and is reflected net of unearned income of $672 million and $728 million, and net of the allowance for credit losses of $123 million and $114 million at those dates, respectively.

Note: Totals may not equal the sum of the numbers reported due to rounding of those individual numbers.

Walmart leases facilities under both operating and capital leases. Its long-term obligations under these lease agreements are disclosed in a note to its financial statements (see Illustration 15–18).

Illustration 15–18

Lessee Disclosure of Leases—Walmart

Real World Financials

Note 11 Commitments (in part)

The Company has long-term leases for stores and equipment. Rentals (including amounts applicable to taxes, insurance, maintenance, other operating expenses and contingent rentals) under operating leases and other short-term rental arrangements were $2.8 billion, $2.6 billion and $2.4 billion in fiscal 2014, 2013 and 2012, respectively. Aggregate minimum annual rentals at January 31, 2014, under non-cancelable leases are as follows:

(Amounts in millions)

Fiscal Year	Operating Leases	Capital Leases
2015	$ 1,734	$ 586
2016	1,632	558
2017	1,462	519
2018	1,314	479
2019	1,192	438
Thereafter	9,836	3,711
Total minimum rentals	$17,170	$ 6,291
Less estimated executory costs		(60)
Net minimum lease payments		6,231
Less imputed interest		(3,134)
Present value of minimum lease payments		$ 3,097

Decision Makers' Perspective—Financial Statement Impact

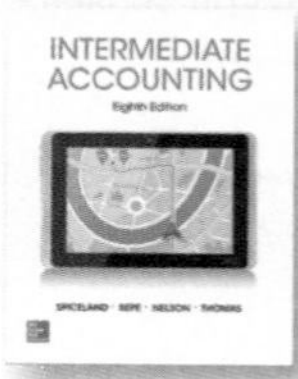

As indicated in the Decision Makers' Perspective at the beginning of the chapter, leasing can allow a firm to conserve assets, to avoid some risks of owning assets, and to obtain favorable tax benefits. These advantages are desirable. It also was pointed out earlier that some firms try to obscure the realities of their financial position through off-balance-sheet financing or by avoiding violating terms of contracts that limit the amount of debt a company can have. Accounting guidelines are designed to limit the ability of firms to hide financial realities. Nevertheless, investors and creditors should be alert to the impact leases can have on a company's financial position and on its risk. ●

Leasing sometimes is used as a means of off-balance-sheet financing.

Balance Sheet and Income Statement

Lease liabilities affect the debt to equity ratio and the rate of return on assets.

Capital lease transactions impact several of a firm's financial ratios. Because we record liabilities for capital leases, the debt-equity ratio (liabilities divided by shareholders' equity) is immediately impacted. Because we also record leased assets, the immediate impact on the rate of return on assets (net income divided by assets) is negative, but the lasting effect depends on how leased assets are utilized to enhance future net income. As illustrated in this chapter, the financial statement impact of a capital lease is no different from that of an installment purchase.

Do operating leases create long-term commitments equivalent to liabilities?

Even operating leases, though, can significantly affect risk. Operating leases represent long-term commitments that can become a problem if business declines and cash inflows drop off. For example, in 2009 the economic crisis caught many companies with a deadly combination of declining cash inflows and cash outflow commitments for lease agreements. Nearly four billion dollars in off-balance sheet obligations related to operating lease commitments was a major contributor to Circuit City's demise after a 60-year history as a leader in the electronics industry.

Operating lease commitments create problems during an economic downturn.

The net income difference between treating a lease as a capital lease versus an operating lease generally is not significant.

Whether leases are capitalized or treated as operating leases affects the income statement as well as the balance sheet. However, the impact on the income statement generally is not significant. Over the life of a lease, total expenses are equal regardless of the accounting treatment of a lease. If the lease is capitalized, total expenses comprise interest and depreciation. The total of these equals the total amount of rental payments, which would constitute rent expense if not capitalized. There is, however, a timing difference between lease capitalization and operating lease treatment, but the timing difference usually isn't great.

The difference in impact on the balance sheet between capital leases and operating leases is significant.

The more significant difference between capital leases and operating leases is the impact on the balance sheet. As mentioned above, a capital lease adds to both the asset and liability side of the balance sheet; operating leases do not affect the balance sheet at all. How can external financial statement users adjust their analysis to incorporate the balance sheet differences between capital and operating leases? A frequently offered suggestion is to capitalize all noncancelable lease commitments, including those related to operating leases. Some financial analysts, in fact, do this on their own to get a better feel for a company's actual debt position.

To illustrate, refer to Illustration 15–18 on the previous page, which reveals the operating lease commitments disclosed by Walmart. If these arrangements were considered capital leases, these payments would be capitalized (reported at the present value of all future payments). By making some reasonable assumptions, we can estimate the present value of all future payments to be made on existing operating leases. For example, the interest rates used by Walmart to discount rental payments on capital leases range from 3.0% to 13.6%. If we use the approximate average rate of 10%, and make certain other assumptions, we can determine the debt equivalent of the operating lease commitments as shown in Illustration 15–19.

If capitalized, these operating lease commitments would add $9,456 million to Walmart's liabilities and approximately $9,456 million to the company's assets.[29] Let's look at the

[29]If these operating leases were capitalized, both assets and liabilities would increase by the same amount at inception of the lease. However, in later years, the leased asset account balance and the lease liability account will, generally, not be equal. The leased asset account is reduced by depreciation and the lease liability account is reduced (amortized) to zero using the effective interest method.

Illustration 15–19

Estimating the Debt Equivalent of Operating Lease Commitments; Walmart

Real World Financials

Capitalized Value or Debt Equivalent of Walmart's Operating Leases
($ in millions)

Fiscal Years	Operating Leases	PV Factor 10%	Present Value
2015	$ 1,734	.909	$1,576
2016	1,632	.826	1,348
2017	1,462	.751	1,098
2018	1,314	.683	897
2019	1,192	.621	740
Thereafter	9,836	.386*	3,797
Total minimum rentals	$17,170		$9,456

*This is the PV factor for $i = 10\%$, $n = 10$, which treats payments after 2019 as occurring in 2024, an assumption due to not knowing precise dates of specific payments after 2019.

impact this would have on the company's debt to equity ratio and its return on assets ratio using selected financial statement information taken from Walmart's annual report for the fiscal year ending January 31, 2014, shown next:

	($ in millions)
Total assets	$204,751
Total liabilities	123,412
Total shareholders' equity	81,339
Net income	16,695

The debt to equity and return on assets ratios are calculated in Illustration 15–20 without considering the capitalization of operating leases and then again after adding **$9,456** million to both total assets and total liabilities. In the calculation of return on assets, we use only the year-end total assets rather than the average total assets for the year. Also, we assume no impact on net income.

Illustration 15–20

Ratios with and without Capitalization of Operating Leases; Walmart

Real World Financials

	($ in millions) Without Capitalization	With Capitalization
Debt to equity ratio	$\frac{\$123,412}{\$81,339} = 1.52$	$\frac{\$132,868}{\$81,339} = 1.63$
Return on assets	$\frac{\$16,695}{\$204,751} = 8.2\%$	$\frac{\$16,695}{\$214,207} = 7.8\%$

The debt to equity ratio rises from 1.52 to 1.63, and the return on assets ratio declines from 8.2% to 7.8%.

Statement of Cash Flow Impact

OPERATING LEASES. Remember, lease payments for operating leases represent rent—expense to the lessee, revenue for the lessor. These amounts are included in net income, so both the lessee and lessor report cash payments for operating leases in a statement of cash flows as cash flows from operating activities.

Operating leases are not reported in a statement of cash flows at the lease's inception.

CAPITAL LEASES AND DIRECT FINANCING LEASES. You've learned in this chapter that capital leases are agreements that we identify as being formulated outwardly as leases, but which are in reality installment purchases, so we account for them as such. Each rental payment (except the first if paid at inception) includes both an amount that represents interest and an amount that represents a reduction of principal. In a statement of

The interest portion of a capital lease payment is a cash flow from operating activities and the principal portion is a cash flow from financing activities.

cash flows, then, the lessee reports the interest portion as a cash outflow from operating activities and the principal portion as a cash outflow from financing activities. On the other side of the transaction, the lessor in a direct financing lease reports the interest portion as a cash inflow from operating activities and the principal portion as a cash inflow from investing activities. Both the lessee and lessor report the lease at its inception as a noncash investing/financing activity.

Cash receipts from a sales-type lease are cash flows from operating activities.

SALES-TYPE LEASES. A sales-type lease differs from a direct-financing lease for the lessor in that we assume the lessor is actually selling its product. Consistent with reporting sales of products under installment sales agreements rather than lease agreements, the lessor reports cash receipts from a sales-type lease as cash inflows from operating activities.

Concept Review Exercise

VARIOUS LEASE ACCOUNTING ISSUES

(This is an extension of the previous Concept Review Exercise.)
United Cellular Systems leased a satellite transmission device from Satellite Technology Corporation on January 1, 2017. Satellite Technology paid $500,000 for the transmission device. Its retail value is $653,681.

Terms of the Lease Agreement and Related Information:

Lease term	3 years (6 semiannual periods)
Semiannual rental payments	$123,000 at the beginning of each period
Economic life of asset	4 years
Implicit interest rate (Also lessee's incremental borrowing rate)	12%
Unguaranteed residual value	$40,000
Regulatory fees paid by lessor	$3,000/twice each year (included in rentals)
Lessor's initial direct costs	$4,500
Contingent rental payments	Additional $4,000 if revenues exceed a specified base

Required:

1. Prepare an amortization schedule that describes the pattern of interest expense over the lease term for United Cellular Systems.
2. Prepare an amortization schedule that describes the pattern of interest revenue over the lease term for Satellite Technology.
3. Prepare the appropriate entries for both United Cellular Systems and Satellite Technology on January 1 and June 30, 2017.
4. Prepare the appropriate entries for both United Cellular Systems and Satellite Technology on December 31, 2019 (the end of the lease term), assuming the device is returned to the lessor and its actual residual value is $14,000 on that date.

Solution:

1. Prepare an amortization schedule that describes the pattern of interest expense over the lease term for United Cellular Systems.

Calculation of the Present Value of Minimum Lease Payments:
Present value of periodic rental payments excluding executory costs of $3,000:

$$(\$120,000 \times 5.21236^{*}) = \$625,483$$

*Present value of an annuity due of $1: $n = 6$, $i = 6\%$.
Note: The *unguaranteed* residual value is excluded from minimum lease payments for both the lessee and lessor.

Date	Payments	Effective Interest	Decrease in Balance	Outstanding Balance
		(6% × Outstanding balance)		
1/1/17				625,483
1/1/17	120,000		120,000	505,483
6/30/17	120,000	.06 (505,483) = 30,329	89,671	415,812
1/1/18	120,000	.06 (415,812) = 24,949	95,051	320,761
6/30/18	120,000	.06 (320,761) = 19,246	100,754	220,007
1/1/19	120,000	.06 (220,007) = 13,200	106,800	113,207
6/30/19	120,000	.06 (113,207) = 6,793*	113,207	0
	720,000	94,517	625,483	

*Adjusted for rounding of other numbers in the schedule.

2. Prepare an amortization schedule that describes the pattern of interest revenue over the lease term for Satellite Technology.

Calculation of the Lessor's Net Investment:

Present value of periodic rental payments excluding executory costs of $3,000 ($120,000 × 5.21236*)	$625,483
Plus: Present value of the unguaranteed residual value ($40,000 × .70496†)	28,198
Lessor's net investment in lease	$653,681

*Present value of an annuity due of $1: $n = 6$, $i = 6\%$.
†Present value of $1: $n = 6$, $i = 6\%$.
Note: The unguaranteed residual value is excluded from minimum lease payments, but is part of the lessor's gross and net investment in the lease.

Date	Payments	Effective Interest	Decrease in Balance	Outstanding Balance
		(6% × Outstanding balance)		
1/1/17				653,681
1/1/17	120,000		120,000	533,681
6/30/17	120,000	.06 (533,681) = 32,021	87,979	445,702
1/1/18	120,000	.06 (445,702) = 26,742	93,258	352,444
6/30/18	120,000	.06 (352,444) = 21,147	98,853	253,591
1/1/19	120,000	.06 (253,591) = 15,215	104,785	148,806
6/30/19	120,000	.06 (148,806) = 8,928	111,072	37,734
12/31/19	40,000	.06 (37,734) = 2,266*	37,734	0
	760,000	106,319	653,681	

*Adjusted for rounding of other numbers in the schedule.

3. Prepare the appropriate entries for both United Cellular Systems and Satellite Technology on January 1 and June 30, 2017.

January 1, 2017

United Cellular Systems (Lessee)

	Debit	Credit
Leased equipment (calculated above)	625,483	
Lease payable (calculated above)		625,483
Lease payable (payment less executory costs)	120,000	
Regulatory fees expense (executory costs)	3,000	
Cash (lease payment)		123,000

Satellite Technology (Lessor)

Lease receivable (PV of lease payments + PV **$40,000** residual value)[a]	653,681	
Cost of goods sold [**$500,000** – (**$40,000**[a] × **.70496**)]	471,802	
Sales revenue (present value of minimum lease payments[b])		625,483
Inventory of equipment (lessor's cost)		500,000
Selling expense	4,500	
Cash (initial direct costs)		4,500
Cash (lease payment)	123,000	
Regulatory fees payable (or cash)		3,000
Lease receivable (payment less executory costs)		120,000

[a]This is the unguaranteed residual value.
[b]Also, $653,681 – ($40,000[a] × .70496).

June 30, 2017

United Cellular Systems (Lessee)

Interest expense [6% × ($625,483 – 120,000)]	30,329	
Lease payable (difference)	89,671	
Regulatory fees expense (annual fee)	3,000	
Cash (lease payment)		123,000

Satellite Technology (Lessor)

Cash (lease payment)	123,000	
Regulatory fees payable (or cash)		3,000
Lease receivable (to balance)		87,979
Interest revenue [6% × (**$653,681** – **120,000**)]		32,021

4. Prepare the appropriate entries for both United Cellular Systems and Satellite Technology on December 31, 2019 (the end of the lease term), assuming the device is returned to the lessor and its actual residual value is $14,000 on that date.

December 31, 2019

United Cellular Systems (Lessee)

Depreciation expense ($625,483 ÷ 3 years)	208,494	
Accumulated depreciation		208,494
Accumulated depreciation (account balance)	625,483	
Leased equipment (account balance)		625,483

Satellite Technology (Lessor)

Inventory of equipment (actual residual value)	14,000	
Loss on leased assets (**$40,000** – **14,000**)	26,000	
Lease receivable (account balance)		37,734
Interest revenue (**6%** × **$37,734**: from schedule)		2,266

PART D Special Leasing Arrangements

Sale-Leaseback Arrangements

LO15–10

In a **sale-leaseback transaction**, the owner of an asset sells it and immediately leases it back from the new owner. Sound strange? Maybe, but this arrangement is common. In a sale-leaseback transaction two things happen:

1. The seller-lessee receives cash from the sale of the asset.

2. The seller-lessee pays periodic rent payments to the buyer-lessor to retain the use of the asset.

What motivates this kind of arrangement? The two most common reasons are: (1) If the asset had been financed originally with debt and interest rates have fallen, the sale-leaseback transaction can be used to effectively refinance at a lower rate. (2) The most likely motivation for a sale-leaseback transaction is to generate cash.

Capital Leases

Illustration 15–21 demonstrates a sale-leaseback involving a capital lease for warehouses. The sale and simultaneous leaseback of the warehouses should be viewed as a single borrowing transaction. Although there appear to be two separate transactions, look closer at the substance of the agreement. Teledyne still retains the use of the warehouses that it had prior to the sale and leaseback. What is different? Teledyne has $900,000 cash and a noncancelable obligation to make annual payments of $133,155. In substance, Teledyne simply has borrowed $900,000 to be repaid over 10 years along with 10% interest. From the perspective of substance over form, we do not immediately recognize the $300,000 gain on the sale of the warehouses but defer the gain to be recognized over the term of the lease (or the useful life of the asset if title is expected to transfer outright or by the exercise of a BPO).

Recording a sale-leaseback transaction follows the basic accounting concept of substance over form.

Illustration 15–21

Sale-Leaseback

Teledyne Distribution Center was in need of cash. Its solution: sell its four warehouses for $900,000, and then lease back the warehouses to obtain their continued use. The warehouses had a carrying value on Teledyne's books of $600,000 (original cost $950,000). Other information:

1. The sale date is December 31, 2016.
2. The noncancelable lease term is 10 years and requires annual payments of $133,155 beginning December 31, 2016. The estimated remaining useful life of the warehouses is 10 years.
3. The annual rental payments (present value $900,000) provides the lessor with a 10% rate of return on the financing arrangement.* Teledyne's incremental borrowing rate is 10%.
4. Teledyne depreciates its warehouses on a straight-line basis.

December 31, 2016

Cash	900,000	
Accumulated depreciation ($950,000 – 600,000)	350,000	
Warehouses (cost)		950,000
Deferred gain on sale-leaseback (difference)		300,000
Leased warehouses (present value of lease payments)	900,000	
Lease payable (present value of lease payments)		900,000
Lease payable	133,155	
Cash		133,155

December 31, 2017

Interest expense [10% × ($900,000 – 133,155)]	76,685	
Lease payable (difference)	56,470	
Cash (rental payment)		133,155
Depreciation expense ($900,000 ÷ 10 years)	90,000	
Accumulated depreciation		90,000
Deferred gain on sale-leaseback (**$300,000** ÷ **10** years)	30,000	
Depreciation expense		30,000

The gain on sale-leaseback is deferred and recognized over the lease term as a reduction of depreciation expense.

*$133,155 × 6.75902 = $900,000 ($899,997.31 rounded)
Rent payments; (from Table 6) $n = 10, i = 10\%$; Present value

Since the lease term is equal to the expected useful life of the warehouses (>75%), the leaseback must be recorded by the lessee as a capital lease.[30] There typically is interdependency between the lease terms and the price at which the asset is sold. We view the sale and the leaseback as a single transaction. Look closely at the 2017 entries to see the net effect of recording the sale-leaseback this way. Amortizing the deferred gain over the lease term as a reduction of depreciation expense decreases depreciation each year to $60,000.[31] Interest expense is $76,685. If Teledyne had *not* sold the warehouses ($600,000 book value) and had borrowed $900,000 cash by issuing an installment note, the 2017 effect would have been virtually identical:

Depreciating the book value of the warehouses over their remaining useful life produces depreciation equal to the net depreciation recorded in a sale-leaseback.

December 31, 2017		
Interest expense [10% × ($900,000 − 133,155)]	76,685	
Note payable (difference)	56,470	
Cash (installment payment)		133,155
Depreciation expense ($600,000 ÷ 10 years)	60,000	
Accumulated depreciation		60,000

The deferred gain is reported in the balance sheet as a valuation (contra) account, offsetting the leased asset. The 2017 balance sheet effect of the sale-leaseback transaction and a $900,000 installment note are compared in Illustration 15–22. Once again, the effect is virtually identical.

Illustration 15–22

Comparison of a Sale-Leaseback and a Purchase

	Sale-Leaseback	Retain Asset; Borrow Cash
Assets		
Leased asset	$900,000	$950,000
Less: Accumulated depreciation	(90,000)	(410,000)
Less: Deferred gain ($300,000 − 30,000)	(270,000)	
	$540,000	$540,000
Liabilities		
Lease payable ($900,000 − 133,155 − 56,470)	$710,375	
Note payable ($900,000 − 133,155 − 56,470)		$710,375

Accounting by the buyer/lessor is no different in a sale-leaseback transaction than another lease transaction. That is, it records a lease in accordance with the usual lease guidelines.

Operating Leases

If the leaseback portion of the previous sale-leaseback transaction were classified as an operating lease, the gain still would be deferred but would be recognized as a reduction of rent expense rather than depreciation. There is no leased asset to depreciate.[32]

December 31, 2017		
Deferred gain on sale-leaseback ($300,000 ÷ 10 years)	30,000	
Rent expense		30,000

Those of you with a healthy sense of skepticism will question whether the leaseback portion of our sale-leaseback situation could qualify as an operating lease. After all, the 10-year lease term is equal to the 10-year remaining useful life. But when you remember that neither the third (75% of economic life) nor the fourth (90% recovery of fair value) capital lease classification

[30]The fourth criterion also is met. The present value of lease payments ($900,000) is 100% (> 90%) of the fair value of the warehouses ($900,000). Meeting any one of the four criteria is sufficient.

[31]If depreciation is over the useful life of the leased asset rather than the lease term because ownership is expected to transfer to the lessee, amortization of the deferred gain also would be over the useful life. If a leaseback of land is a capital lease, the amortization of the deferred gain is recorded as revenue.

[32]The deferred gain would be reported as a liability since it could not be offset against a leased asset.

criterion applies if the inception of the lease occurs during the last 25% of an asset's economic life, you see the possibility of an operating lease. Suppose, for instance, that the original useful life of the warehouses was 40 years. In that case, the current lease term would occur during the last 25% of an asset's economic life and we would have an operating lease.

Losses on Sale-Leasebacks

In a sale-leaseback, any gain on the sale of the asset is deferred and amortized. However, a real loss on the sale of the property is recognized immediately—not deferred. A real loss means the fair value is less than the book value of the asset. On the other hand, if the fair value exceeds the book value, but the asset is sold to the buyer/lessor for less than the book value, an artificial loss is produced that is probably in substance a prepayment of rent and should be deferred and amortized.

International Financial Reporting Standards

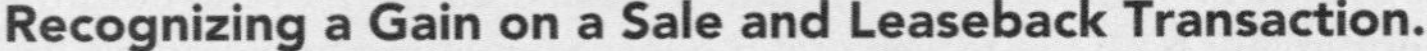

● LO15–11

IFRS ILLUSTRATION

Recognizing a Gain on a Sale and Leaseback Transaction.

Operating Lease:

When the leaseback is an operating lease (as long as the lease payments and sales price are at fair value), under *IAS No. 17,* any gain on the sale is recognized immediately but is amortized over the lease term using U.S. GAAP.[33]

For example, suppose Madison Storage sold its warehouse to an insurance company on January 1, 2016, for $400,000 and immediately leased the building back. The operating lease calls for annual rental payments of $25,000 for 12 years of the building's estimated 50-year useful life. The building has a fair value of $400,000 and a book value of $325,000 (its original cost was $500,000). The rental payments of $25,000 are payable to the insurance company each December 31. Here's a comparison:

	U.S. GAAP		IFRS	
January 1, 2016				
Cash (given)	400,000		400,000	
Accumulated depreciation (cost minus book value)	175,000		175,000	
Building (original cost)		500,000		500,000
Deferred gain on sale-leaseback		75,000		
Gain on sale-leaseback (difference)				75,000
December 31, 2016				
Rent expense	25,000		25,000	
Cash (lease payment)		25,000		25,000
Deferred gain on sale-leaseback	6,250			
Rent expense ($75,000 ÷ 12 years)		6,250		

Finance (Capital) Lease:

When the leaseback is a finance (capital) lease, under *IAS No. 17,* the gain is recognized over the lease term, but is recognized over the useful life of the asset under U.S. GAAP. When debiting the deferred gain each period, by either set of standards, the credit is to depreciation expense.

Real Estate Leases

Some leases involve land—exclusively or in part. The concepts we discussed in the chapter also relate to **real estate leases**. But the fact that land has an unlimited life causes us to modify how we account for some leases involving real estate.

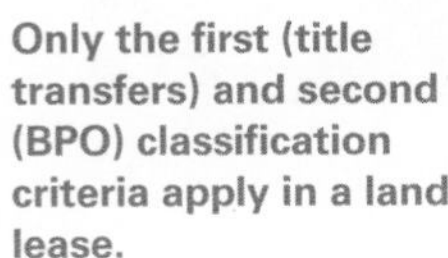
Only the first (title transfers) and second (BPO) classification criteria apply in a land lease.

[33]"Leases," *International Accounting Standard No. 17* (IASCF), as amended effective January 1, 2014.

Leases of Land Only

Because the useful life of land is indefinite, the risks and rewards of ownership cannot be presumed transferred from the lessor to the lessee unless title to the land is expected to transfer—outright or by the expected exercise of a bargain purchase option (criterion 1 or criterion 2). Since the useful life is undefined, the third and fourth criteria are not applicable. Relatedly, because the leased asset is land, depreciation is inappropriate.

Leases of Land and Building

When (a) the leased property includes both land and a building, (b) neither of the first two criteria is met, and (c) the fair value of the land is 25% or more of the combined fair value, both the lessee and the lessor treat the land as an operating lease and the building as any other lease.

When the leased property includes both land and a building and the lease transfers ownership or is expected to by exercise of a BPO, the lessee should record each leased asset separately. The present value of the minimum lease payments is allocated between the leased land and leased building accounts on the basis of their relative fair values.

When neither of the first two capital lease criteria is met, the question arises as to whether the third and fourth criteria apply. Because they logically should apply to the building (because its life is limited) but not to the land (because its life is unlimited), the profession employs an arbitrary guideline. If the fair value of the land is less than 25% of the combined fair value, it is in effect ignored and both the lessee and the lessor treat the land and building as a single unit. The single leased asset is depreciated as if land were not involved. If the fair value of the land is 25% or more of the combined fair value, both the lessee and the lessor treat the land and building as two separate leases. Thus, the land lease is an operating lease, and the building lease is classified and accounted for in the manner described in the chapter.

Leases of Only Part of a Building

Usual lease accounting procedures apply to leases that involve only part of a building, although extra effort may be needed to arrive at reasonable estimates of cost and fair value.

Some of the most common of leases involve leasing only part of a building. For instance, businesses frequently lease space in an office building or individual stores in a shopping mall. Practical difficulties arise when applying lease accounting procedures in these situations. What is the cost of the third shop from the entrance in a $14 million mall? What is the fair value of a sixth floor office suite in a 40-floor office complex? Despite practical difficulties, usual lease accounting treatment applies. It may, however, be necessary to employ real estate appraisals or replacement cost information to arrive at reasonable estimates of cost or fair value.

International Financial Reporting Standards

LO15–11

Leases of Land and Buildings. Under *IAS No. 17*, land and building elements are considered *separately* unless the land element is not material.[34] This often results in classification of the land component as an operating lease.

Under U.S. GAAP, land and building elements generally are accounted for as a single unit, unless land represents more than 25% of the total fair value of the leased property.

[34] "Leases," *International Accounting Standard No. 17* (IASCF), as amended effective January 1, 2014.

Financial Reporting Case Solution

1. **How would HG's revenues "take a hit" as a result of more customers leasing than buying labeling machines?** *(p. 860)* When HG leases machines under operating leases, it reports revenue as it collects "rent" over the lease term. When HG sells machines, on the other hand, it recognizes revenue "up front" in the year of sales. Actually, total revenues are not necessarily less with a lease, but are spread out over the several

years of the lease term. This delays the recognition of revenues, creating the "hit" in the reporting periods in which a shift to leasing occurs.

2. **Under what kind of leasing arrangements would the "hit" not occur?** *(p. 868)* The hit will not occur when HG leases its machines under sales-type leases. In those cases, despite the fact that the contract specifies a lease, in effect, HG actually sells its machines under the arrangement. Consequently, HG will recognize sales revenue (and cost of goods sold) at the inception of the lease. The amount recognized is roughly the same as if customers actually buy the machines. As a result, the income statement will not receive the hit created by the substitution of operating leases for outright sales. ●

The Bottom Line

- **LO15–1** Leasing is used as a means of financing assets as well as achieving operational and tax objectives. (*p. 854*)
- **LO15–2** In keeping with the concept of substance over form, a lease is accounted for as either a rental agreement or a purchase/sale accompanied by debt financing. (*p. 855*)
- **LO15–3** A lessee should classify a lease transaction as a capital lease if it is noncancelable and if one or more of four classification criteria are met. Otherwise, it is an operating lease. A lessor records a lease as a direct financing lease or a sales-type lease only if two conditions relating to revenue realization are met in addition to one of the four classification criteria. (*p. 856*)
- **LO15–4** In an operating lease a sale is not recorded by the lessor; a purchase is not recorded by the lessee. Instead, the periodic rental payments are accounted for as rent revenue by the lessor and rent expense by the lessee. (*p. 860*)
- **LO15–5** In a capital lease the lessee records a leased asset at the present value of the minimum lease payments. A capital lease is recorded by the lessor as a sales-type lease or direct financing lease, depending on whether the lease provides the lessor a dealer's profit. (*p. 862*)
- **LO15–6** A sales-type lease requires recording sales revenue and cost of goods sold by the lessor at the inception of the lease. All other entries are the same as in a direct financing lease. (*p. 867*)
- **LO15–7** A bargain purchase option is included as a component of minimum lease payments for both the lessor and the lessee. The lease term effectively ends when the BPO is exercisable. (*p. 870*)
- **LO15–8** A lessee-guaranteed residual value is included as a component of minimum lease payments for both the lessor and the lessee. An unguaranteed residual value is not (but is part of the lessor's gross investment in the lease). (*p. 873*)
- **LO15–9** Executory costs (maintenance, insurance, taxes, and any other costs usually associated with ownership) are expenses of the lessee. Any costs incurred by the lessor that are associated directly with originating a lease and are essential to acquire that lease are called *initial direct costs* and are expensed in accordance with the matching principle. To find the present value of minimum lease payments to capitalize as an asset and liability, the lessee usually uses a discount rate equal to the lower of the rate implicit in the lease agreement and its own incremental borrowing rate. Contingent rentals are *not* included in the minimum lease payments because they are not determinable at the inception of the lease. (*p. 877*)
- **LO15–10** A gain on the sale of an asset in a sale leaseback arrangement is deferred and amortized over the lease term (or asset life if title is expected to transfer to the lessee). The lease portion of the transaction is evaluated and accounted for like any lease. (*p. 888*)
- **LO15–11** In general, IFRS is considered to be more principles-based while U.S. GAAP is more rules-based. This difference is evident in accounting for leases. To distinguish between a capital lease and an operating lease U.S. GAAP uses four specific classification criteria, whereas IFRS uses a variety of "indicators" of a capital (finance) lease. We also often see differences in the discount rate used and how we account for sale-leasebacks and leases of land and buildings. (*pp. 859, 869, 880, 891*, and *892*) ●

Questions For Review of Key Topics

Q 15–1 The basic concept of "substance over form" influences lease accounting. Explain.

Q 15–2 How is interest determined in a capital lease transaction? How does the approach compare to other forms of debt (say bonds payable or notes payable)?

Q 15–3 How are leases and installment notes the same? How do they differ?

IFRS **Q 15–4** Former IASB chairman David Tweedie has noted that current GAAP allows airlines' balance sheets to appear as if the companies don't have airplanes. How can this be true?

Q 15–5 A lessee should classify a lease transaction as a capital lease if it is noncancelable and one or more of four classification criteria are met. Otherwise, it is an operating lease. What are these criteria?

Q 15–6 What is a bargain purchase option? How does it differ from other purchase options?

Q 15–7 Lukawitz Industries leased equipment to Seminole Corporation for a four-year period, at which time possession of the leased asset will revert back to Lukawitz. The equipment cost Lukawitz $4 million and has an expected useful life of six years. Its normal sales price is $5.6 million. The present value of the minimum lease payments for both the lessor and lessee is $5.2 million. The first payment was made at the inception of the lease. Collectibility of the remaining lease payments is reasonably assured, and Lukawitz has no material cost uncertainties. How should this lease be classified (a) by Lukawitz Industries (the lessor) and (b) by Seminole Corporation (the lessee)? Why?

Q 15–8 Can the present value of minimum lease payments differ between the lessor and lessee? If so, how?

Q 15–9 Compare the way a bargain purchase option and a residual value are treated by the lessee when determining minimum lease payments.

Q 15–10 What are executory costs? How are they accounted for by the lessee in a capital lease when paid by the lessee? When paid by the lessor? Explain.

Q 15–11 The discount rate influences virtually every amount reported in connection with a lease by both the lessor and the lessee. What is the lessor's discount rate when determining the present value of minimum lease payments? What is the lessee's discount rate?

Q 15–12 A lease might specify that rental payments may be increased (or decreased) at some future time during the lease term depending on whether or not some specified event occurs such as revenues or profits exceeding some designated level. Under what circumstances are contingent rentals included or excluded from minimum lease payments? If excluded, how are they recognized in income determination?

Q 15–13 The lessor's initial direct costs often are substantial. What are initial direct costs?

Q 15–14 When are initial direct costs recognized in an operating lease? In a direct financing lease? In a sales-type lease? Why?

Q 15–15 What are the required lease disclosures for the lessor and lessee?

Q 15–16 In a sale-leaseback transaction the owner of an asset sells it and immediately leases it back from the new owner. This dual transaction should be viewed as a single borrowing transaction. Why?

Q 15–17 Explain how the general classification criteria are applied to leases that involve land.

Q 15–18 What are the guidelines for determining when a material amount of land is involved in a lease?

Q 15–19 How does a leveraged lease differ from a nonleveraged lease?

IFRS **Q 15–20** Where can we find authoritative guidance for accounting for leases under IFRS?

IFRS **Q 15–21** Could a finance (capital) lease under IFRS be classified as an operating lease under U.S. GAAP? Explain.

IFRS **Q 15–22** Describe the primary differences between IFRS and U.S. GAAP in the way leases are classified as either operating or finance (capital) leases.

IFRS **Q 15–23** The IASB and FASB are collaborating on a joint project to revise accounting standards for leases. Briefly describe the direction the project is taking.

Brief Exercises

BE 15–1
Operating lease
● LO15–4

At the beginning of its fiscal year, Lakeside Inc. leased office space to LTT Corporation under a seven-year operating lease agreement. The contract calls for quarterly rent payments of $25,000 each. The office building was acquired by Lakeside at a cost of $2 million and was expected to have a useful life of 25 years with no residual value. What will be the effect of the lease on LTT's earnings for the first year (ignore taxes)?

BE 15–2
Operating lease
● LO15–4

In the situation described in BE 15–1, what will be the effect of the lease on Lakeside's earnings for the first year (ignore taxes)?

BE 15–3
Operating lease; advance payment
● LO15–4

Ward Products leased office space under a 10-year operating lease agreement. The lease specified 120 monthly rent payments of $5,000 each, beginning at the inception of the lease. In addition to the first rent payment, Ward also paid a $100,000 advance payment at the lease's inception. What will be the effect of the lease on Ward's earnings for the first year (ignore taxes)?

BE 15–4
Lease classification
● LO15–3, LO15–5

Corinth Co. leased equipment to Athens Corporation for an eight-year period, at which time possession of the leased asset will revert back to Corinth. The equipment cost Corinth $16 million and has an expected useful life of 12 years. Its normal sales price is $22.4 million. The present value of the minimum lease payments for both the lessor and lessee is $20.4 million. The first payment was made at the inception of the lease. Collectibility of the remaining lease payments is reasonably assured, and Corinth has no material cost uncertainties. How should Athens classify this lease? Why?

BE 15–5
Lease classification
● LO15–3, LO15–5

In the situation described in BE 15–4, how should Corinth classify this lease? Why?

BE 15–6
Net investment in leases; Sonic
● LO15–5
Real World Financials

The 2013 annual report of the **Sonic Corporation** reported minimum lease payments receivable of $1,701,000 and a net investment in direct financing leases of $1,531,000. What accounts for the difference between these two amounts? Explain.

BE 15–7
Capital lease; calculate interest
● LO15–5

A lease agreement calls for quarterly lease payments of $5,376 over a 10-year lease term, with the first payment at July 1, the lease's inception. The interest rate is 8%. Both the fair value and the cost of the asset to the lessor are $150,000. What would be the amount of interest expense the lessee would record in conjunction with the second quarterly payment at October 1? What would be the amount of interest revenue the lessor would record in conjunction with the second quarterly payment at October 1?

BE 15–8
Capital lease; lessee; balance sheet effects
● LO15–5

A lease agreement that qualifies as a capital lease calls for annual lease payments of $26,269 over a six-year lease term, with the first payment at January 1, the lease's inception. The interest rate is 5%. If lessee's fiscal year is the calendar year, what would be the amount of the lease liability that the lessee would report in its balance sheet at the end of the first year? What would be the interest payable?

BE 15–9
Capital lease; lessee; income statement effects
● LO15–5

In the situation described in BE 15–8, what would be the pretax amounts related to the lease that the lessee would report in its income statement for the year ended December 31?

BE 15–10
Sales-type lease; lessor; income statement effects
● LO15–6

In the situation described in BE 15–8, assume the asset being leased cost the lessor $125,000 to produce. Determine the price at which the lessor is "selling" the asset (present value of the lease payments). What would be the amounts related to the lease that the lessor would report in its income statement for the year ended December 31 (ignore taxes)?

BE 15–11
Sales-type lease; lessor; calculate lease payments
● LO15–6

Manning Imports is contemplating an agreement to lease equipment to a customer for five years. Manning normally sells the asset for a cash price of $100,000. Assuming that 8% is a reasonable rate of interest, what must be the amount of quarterly lease payments (beginning at the inception of the lease) in order for Manning to recover its normal selling price as well as be compensated for financing the asset over the lease term?

BE 15–12
Bargain purchase option; lessor; direct financing lease
● LO15–5, LO15–6, LO15–7

Ace Leasing acquires equipment and leases it to customers under long-term direct financing leases. Ace earns interest under these arrangements at a 6% annual rate. Ace leased a machine it purchased for $600,000 under an arrangement that specified annual payments beginning at the inception of the lease for five years. The lessee had the option to purchase the machine at the end of the lease term for $100,000 when it was expected to have a residual value of $160,000. Calculate the amount of the annual lease payments.

BE 15–13
Guaranteed residual value; direct financing lease
● LO15–5 through LO15–6, LO15–8

On January 1, James Industries leased equipment to a customer for a four-year period, at which time possession of the leased asset will revert back to James. The equipment cost James $700,000 and has an expected useful life of six years. Its normal sales price is $700,000. The residual value after four years, guaranteed by the lessee, is $100,000. Lease payments are due on December 31 of each year, beginning with the first payment at the end of the first year. Collectibility of the remaining lease payments is reasonably assured, and there are no material cost uncertainties. The interest rate is 5%. Calculate the amount of the annual lease payments.

BE 15–14
IFRS; lease classification
● LO15–3, LO15–11
IFRS

Adams Storage and Appraisal leased equipment to OAC Corporation for an eight-year period, at which time possession of the leased asset will revert back to Adams. The equipment cost Adams $32 million and has an expected useful life of 11 years. Its normal sales price is $45 million. The present value of the minimum lease payments for both the lessor and lessee is $40 million. The first payment was made at the inception of the lease. How would OAC classify this lease if it prepares its financial statements using IFRS? Why?

Exercises

An alternate exercise and problem set is available in the Connect library

E 15–1
Operating lease
● LO15–4

On January 1, 2016, Nath-Langstrom Services, Inc., a computer software training firm, leased several computers from ComputerWorld Corporation under a two-year operating lease agreement. The contract calls for four rent payments of $10,000 each, payable semiannually on June 30 and December 31 each year. The computers were acquired by ComputerWorld at a cost of $90,000 and were expected to have a useful life of six years with no residual value.

Required:
Prepare the appropriate entries for both (a) the lessee and (b) the lessor from the inception of the lease through the end of 2016. (Use straight-line depreciation.)

E 15–2
Operating lease; advance payment; leasehold improvement
● LO15–4

On January 1, 2016, Winn Heat Transfer leased office space under a three-year operating lease agreement. The arrangement specified three annual rent payments of $80,000 each, beginning January 1, 2016, the inception of the lease, and at each January 1 through 2018. Winn also paid a $96,000 advance payment at the inception of the lease in addition to the first $80,000 rent payment. With permission of the owner, Winn made structural modifications to the building before occupying the space at a cost of $180,000. The useful life of the building and the structural modifications were estimated to be 30 years with no residual value.

Required:
Prepare the appropriate entries for Winn Heat Transfer from the inception of the lease through the end of 2016. Winn's fiscal year is the calendar year. Winn uses straight-line depreciation.

E 15–3
Capital lease; lessee
● LO15–5

(Note: Exercises 15–3, 15–4, and 15–5 are three variations of the same basic situation.)
Manufacturers Southern leased high-tech electronic equipment from Edison Leasing on January 1, 2016. Edison purchased the equipment from International Machines at a cost of $112,080.

Related Information:	
Lease term	2 years (8 quarterly periods)
Quarterly rental payments	$15,000 at the beginning of each period
Economic life of asset	2 years
Fair value of asset	$112,080
Implicit interest rate (Also lessee's incremental borrowing rate)	8%

Required:
Prepare a lease amortization schedule and appropriate entries for Manufacturers Southern from the inception of the lease through January 1, 2017. Depreciation is recorded at the end of each fiscal year (December 31) on a straight-line basis.

E 15–4
Direct financing lease; lessor
● LO15–5

Edison Leasing leased high-tech electronic equipment to Manufacturers Southern on January 1, 2016. Edison purchased the equipment from International Machines at a cost of $112,080.

Related Information:

Lease term	2 years (8 quarterly periods)
Quarterly rental payments	$15,000 at the beginning of each period
Economic life of asset	2 years
Fair value of asset	$112,080
Implicit interest rate	8%
(Also lessee's incremental borrowing rate)	

Required:

Prepare a lease amortization schedule and appropriate entries for Edison Leasing from the inception of the lease through January 1, 2017. Edison's fiscal year ends December 31.

E 15–5
Sales-type lease; lessor
● LO15–6

Manufacturers Southern leased high-tech electronic equipment from International Machines on January 1, 2016. International Machines manufactured the equipment at a cost of $85,000.

Related Information:

Lease term	2 years (8 quarterly periods)
Quarterly rental payments	$15,000 at the beginning of each period
Economic life of asset	2 years
Fair value of asset	$112,080
Implicit interest rate	8%
(Also lessee's incremental borrowing rate)	

Required:

1. Show how International Machines determined the $15,000 quarterly rental payments.
2. Prepare appropriate entries for International Machines to record the lease at its inception, January 1, 2016, and the second rental payment on April 1, 2016.

E 15–6
Lease classification
● LO15–3

Each of the four independent situations below describes a lease requiring annual lease payments of $10,000. For each situation, determine the appropriate lease classification by the lessee and indicate why.

	Situation			
	1	**2**	**3**	**4**
Lease term (years)	4	4	4	4
Asset's useful life (years)	6	5	6	6
Asset's fair value	$44,000	$43,000	$41,000	$39,000
Bargain purchase option?	No	Yes	No	No
Annual lease payments	Beg. of yr.	End of yr.	Beg. of yr.	End of yr.
Lessor's implicit rate (known by lessee)	5%	6%	5%	6%
Lessee's incremental borrowing rate	5%	5%	5%	5%

E 15–7
Capital lease
● LO15–5

American Food Services, Inc., leased a packaging machine from Barton and Barton Corporation. Barton and Barton completed construction of the machine on January 1, 2016. The lease agreement for the $4 million (fair value and present value of the lease payments) machine specified four equal payments at the end of each year. The useful life of the machine was expected to be four years with no residual value. Barton and Barton's implicit interest rate was 10% (also American Food Services' incremental borrowing rate).

Required:

1. Prepare the journal entry for American Food Services at the inception of the lease on January 1, 2016.
2. Prepare an amortization schedule for the four-year term of the lease.
3. Prepare the journal entry for the first lease payment on December 31, 2016.
4. Prepare the journal entry for the third lease payment on December 31, 2018.

(Note: You may wish to compare your solution to this exercise with that of Exercise 14–20 which deals with a parallel situation in which the packaging machine was acquired with an installment note.)

E 15–8
Capital lease; lessee; balance sheet and income statement effects
● LO15–5

(Note: Exercises 15–8, 15–9, and 15–10 are three variations of the same situation.)

On June 30, 2016, Georgia-Atlantic, Inc., leased a warehouse facility from IC Leasing Corporation. The lease agreement calls for Georgia-Atlantic to make semiannual lease payments of $562,907 over a three-year lease term, payable each June 30 and December 31, with the first payment at June 30, 2016. Georgia-Atlantic's incremental borrowing rate is 10%, the same rate IC uses to calculate lease payment amounts. Depreciation is recorded on a straight-line basis at the end of each fiscal year. The fair value of the warehouse is $3 million.

Required:

1. Determine the present value of the lease payments at June 30, 2016 (to the nearest $000) that Georgia-Atlantic uses to record the leased asset and lease liability.

2. What amounts related to the lease would Georgia-Atlantic report in its balance sheet at December 31, 2016 (ignore taxes)?
3. What amounts related to the lease would Georgia-Atlantic report in its income statement for the year ended December 31, 2016 (ignore taxes)?

E 15–9
Direct financing lease; lessor; balance sheet and income statement effects
● LO15–5

On June 30, 2016, Georgia-Atlantic, Inc., leased a warehouse facility from IC Leasing Corporation. The lease agreement calls for Georgia-Atlantic to make semiannual lease payments of $562,907 over a three-year lease term, payable each June 30 and December 31, with the first payment at June 30, 2016. Georgia-Atlantic's incremental borrowing rate is 10%, the same rate IC used to calculate lease payment amounts. IC purchased the warehouse from Builders, Inc. at a cost of $3 million.

Required:
1. What amounts related to the lease would IC report in its balance sheet at December 31, 2016 (ignore taxes)?
2. What amounts related to the lease would IC report in its income statement for the year ended December 31, 2016 (ignore taxes)?

E 15–10
Sales-type lease; lessor; balance sheet and income statement effects
● LO15–6

On June 30, 2016, Georgia-Atlantic, Inc., leased a warehouse facility from Builders, Inc. The lease agreement calls for Georgia-Atlantic to make semiannual lease payments of $562,907 over a three-year lease term, payable each June 30 and December 31, with the first payment at June 30, 2016. Georgia-Atlantic's incremental borrowing rate is 10%, the same rate Builders used to calculate lease payment amounts. Builders constructed the warehouse at a cost of $2.5 million.

Required:
1. Determine the price at which Builders is "selling" the warehouse (present value of the lease payments) at June 30, 2016 (to the nearest $000).
2. What amounts related to the lease would Builders report in its balance sheet at December 31, 2016 (ignore taxes)?
3. What amounts related to the lease would Builders report in its income statement for the year ended December 31, 2016 (ignore taxes)?

E 15–11
IFRS; lease classification
● LO15–3, LO15–11

IFRS

Airway Leasing entered into an agreement to lease aircraft to Ouachita Airlines. Consider each of the following, *a–e,* to be independent scenarios.

a. The agreement calls for ownership of the aircraft to be transferred to Ouachita Airlines at the end of the lease term.
b. The fair value of the aircraft is expected to be $500,000 at the end of the lease term. Ouachita has the option to purchase the aircraft at the end of the lease term for $90,000.
c. The aircraft has a useful life of 20 years, and the term of the lease is 14 years.
d. The present value of the lease payments is $8,900,000 and the fair value of the leased aircraft is $10,000,000.
e. The aircraft was manufactured to meet specifications provided by Ouachita to optimize the exclusively regional nature of its flights.

Required:
1. In each scenario, indicate whether Ouachita would classify the lease as an operating lease or capital lease under U.S. GAAP. Assume the lease agreement has not met any of the other criteria of a capital lease. Provide brief explanations.
2. In each scenario, indicate whether Ouachita would classify the lease as an operating lease or finance lease under IFRS. Assume the lease agreement has not met any of the other indicators of a finance lease. Provide brief explanations.

E 15–12
Lessor calculation of annual lease payments; lessee calculation of asset and liability
● LO15–5

Each of the three independent situations below describes a capital lease in which annual lease payments are payable at the beginning of each year. The lessee is aware of the lessor's implicit rate of return.

	Situation		
	1	2	3
Lease term (years)	10	20	4
Lessor's rate of return (known by lessee)	11%	9%	12%
Lessee's incremental borrowing rate	12%	10%	11%
Fair value of leased asset	$600,000	$980,000	$185,000

Required:
For each situation, determine:
a. The amount of the annual lease payments as calculated by the lessor.
b. The amount the lessee would record as a leased asset and a lease liability.

E 15–13
Lessor calculation of annual lease payments; lessee calculation of asset and liability
● LO15–5

(Note: This is a variation of the Exercise 15–12 modified to assume lease payments are at the end of each period.) Each of the three independent situations below describes a capital lease in which annual lease payments are payable at the *end* of each year. The lessee is aware of the lessor's implicit rate of return.

	Situation		
	1	2	3
Lease term (years)	10	20	4
Lessor's rate of return	11%	9%	12%
Lessee's incremental borrowing rate	12%	10%	11%
Fair value of leased asset	$600,000	$980,000	$185,000

Required:
For each situation, determine:
a. The amount of the annual lease payments as calculated by the lessor.
b. The amount the lessee would record as a leased asset and a lease liability.

E 15–14
Calculation of annual lease payments; residual value
● LO15–5, LO15–6, LO15–8

Each of the four independent situations below describes a capital lease in which annual lease payments are payable at the beginning of each year. Determine the annual lease payments for each:

	Situation			
	1	2	3	4
Lease term (years)	4	7	5	8
Lessor's rate of return	10%	11%	9%	12%
Fair value of leased asset	$50,000	$350,000	$75,000	$465,000
Lessor's cost of leased asset	$50,000	$350,000	$45,000	$465,000
Residual value:				
Guaranteed by lessee	0	$ 50,000	0	$ 30,000
Unguaranteed	0	0	$ 7,000	$ 15,000

E 15–15
Lease concepts; direct financing leases; guaranteed and unguaranteed residual value
● LO15–5, LO15–6, LO15–8

Each of the four independent situations below describes a direct financing lease in which annual lease payments of $100,000 are payable at the beginning of each year. Each is a capital lease for the lessee. Determine the following amounts at the inception of the lease:

A. The lessor's:
1. Minimum lease payments
2. Gross investment in the lease
3. Net investment in the lease

B. The lessee's:
4. Minimum lease payments
5. Leased asset
6. Lease liability

	Situation			
	1	2	3	4
Lease term (years)	7	7	8	8
Lessor's and lessee's discount rate	9%	11%	10%	12%
Residual value:				
Guaranteed by lessee	0	$50,000	0	$40,000
Unguaranteed	0	0	$50,000	$60,000

E 15–16
Calculation of annual lease payments; BPO
● LO15–5, LO15–6, LO15–7

For each of the three independent situations below determine the amount of the annual lease payments. Each describes a capital lease in which annual lease payments are payable at the beginning of each year. Each lease agreement contains an option that permits the lessee to acquire the leased asset at an option price that is sufficiently lower than the expected fair value that the exercise of the option appears reasonably certain.

	Situation		
	1	2	3
Lease term (years)	5	12	4
Lessor's rate of return	12%	11%	9%
Fair value of leased asset	$60,000	$420,000	$185,000
Lessor's cost of leased asset	$50,000	$420,000	$145,000
Bargain purchase option:			
Option price	$10,000	$ 50,000	$ 22,000
Exercisable at end of year:	5	5	3

E 15–17
Capital lease; bargain purchase options; lessee
● LO15–5, LO15–6, LO15–7

Federated Fabrications leased a tooling machine on January 1, 2016, for a three-year period ending December 31, 2018. The lease agreement specified annual payments of $36,000 beginning with the first payment at the inception of the lease, and each December 31 through 2017. The company had the option to purchase the machine on December 30, 2018, for $45,000 when its fair value was expected to be $60,000. The machine's estimated useful life was six years with no salvage value. Federated depreciates assets by the straight-line method. The company was aware that the lessor's implicit rate of return was 12%, which was less than Federated's incremental borrowing rate.

Required:

1. Calculate the amount Federated should record as a leased asset and lease liability for this capital lease.
2. Prepare an amortization schedule that describes the pattern of interest expense for Federated over the lease term.
3. Prepare the appropriate entries for Federated from the inception of the lease through the end of the lease term.

E 15–18
Bargain purchase option; lessor; direct financing lease
● LO15–5, LO15–6, LO15–7

Universal Leasing leases electronic equipment to a variety of businesses. The company's primary service is providing alternate financing by acquiring equipment and leasing it to customers under long-term direct financing leases. Universal earns interest under these arrangements at a 10% annual rate.

The company leased an electronic typesetting machine it purchased for $30,900 to a local publisher, Desktop Inc., on December 31, 2015. The lease contract specified annual payments of $8,000 beginning January 1, 2016, the inception of the lease, and each December 31 through 2017 (three-year lease term). The publisher had the option to purchase the machine on December 30, 2018, the end of the lease term, for $12,000 when it was expected to have a residual value of $16,000.

Required:

1. Show how Universal calculated the $8,000 annual lease payments for this direct financing lease.
2. Prepare an amortization schedule that describes the pattern of interest revenue for Universal Leasing over the lease term.
3. Prepare the appropriate entries for Universal Leasing from the inception of the lease through the end of the lease term.

E 15–19
Executory costs; lessor and lessee
● LO15–5, LO15–6, LO15–8, LO15–9

On January 1, 2016, NRC Credit Corporation leased equipment to Brand Services under a direct financing lease designed to earn NRC a 12% rate of return for providing long-term financing. The lease agreement specified:

a. Ten annual payments of $55,000 (including executory costs) beginning January 1, 2016, the inception of the lease and each December 31 thereafter through 2024.
b. The estimated useful life of the leased equipment is 10 years with no residual value. Its cost to NRC was $316,412.
c. The lease qualifies as a capital lease to Brand.
d. A 10-year service agreement with Quality Maintenance Company was negotiated to provide maintenance of the equipment as required. Payments of $5,000 per year are specified, beginning January 1, 2016. NRC was to pay this executory cost as incurred, but lease payments reflect this expenditure.
e. A partial amortization schedule, appropriate for both the lessee and lessor, follows:

	Payments	Effective Interest	Decrease in Balance	Outstanding Balance
		(12% × Outstanding balance)		
				316,412
1/1/16	50,000		50,000	266,412
12/31/16	50,000	.12 (266,412) = 31,969	18,031	248,381
12/31/17	50,000	.12 (248,381) = 29,806	20,194	228,187

Required:

Prepare the appropriate entries for both the lessee and lessor to record:

1. The lease at its inception.
2. The second lease payment and depreciation (straight line) on December 31, 2016.

E 15–20
Executory costs plus management fee; lessor and lessee
● LO15–5, LO15–6, LO15–8, LO15–9

Refer to the lease agreement described in Exercise 15–19. Assume the contract specified that NRC (the lessor) was to pay, not only the $5,000 maintenance fees, but also insurance of $700 per year, and was to receive a $250 management fee for facilitating service and paying executory costs. The lessee's lease payments were increased to include an amount sufficient to reimburse executory costs plus NRC's fee.

Required:

Prepare the appropriate entries for both the lessee and lessor to record the **second** lease payment, executory costs, and depreciation (straight line) on December 31, 2016.

E 15–21
Lessor's initial direct costs; operating, direct financing and sales-type leases
● LO15–4, through LO15–6, LO15–9

Terms of a lease agreement and related facts were:

a. Leased asset had a retail cash selling price of $100,000. Its useful life was six years with no residual value (straight-line depreciation).
b. Annual lease payments at the beginning of each year were $20,873, beginning January 1.
c. Lessor's implicit rate when calculating annual rental payments was 10%.
d. Costs of negotiating and consummating the completed lease transaction incurred by the lessor were $2,062.
e. Collectibility of the lease payments by the lessor was reasonably predictable and there were no costs to the lessor that were yet to be incurred.

Required:

Prepare the appropriate entries for the lessor to record the lease, the initial payment at its inception, and at the December 31 fiscal year-end under each of the following three independent assumptions:

1. The lease term is three years and the lessor paid $100,000 to acquire the asset (operating lease).
2. The lease term is six years and the lessor paid $100,000 to acquire the asset (direct financing lease). Also assume that adjusting the net investment by initial direct costs reduces the effective rate of interest to 9%.
3. The lease term is six years and the lessor paid $85,000 to acquire the asset (sales-type lease).

E 15–22
Lessor's initial direct costs; operating, direct financing and sales-type leases
● LO15–9

The following relate to an operating lease agreement:

a. The lease term is 3 years, beginning January 1, 2016.
b. The leased asset cost the lessor $800,000 and had a useful life of eight years with no residual value. The lessor uses straight-line depreciation for its depreciable assets.
c. Annual lease payments at the beginning of each year were $137,000.
d. Costs of negotiating and consummating the completed lease transaction incurred by the lessor were $2,400.

Required:

Prepare the appropriate entries for the lessor from the inception of the lease through the end of the lease term.

E 15–23
Lessor's initial direct costs; direct financing lease
● LO15–9

Terms of a lease agreement and related facts were:

a. Costs of negotiating and consummating the completed lease transaction incurred by the lessor were $4,242.
b. The retail cash selling price of the leased asset was $500,000. Its useful life was three years with no residual value.
c. Collectibility of the lease payments by the lessor was reasonably predictable and there were no costs to the lessor that were yet to be incurred.
d. The lease term is three years and the lessor paid $500,000 to acquire the asset (direct financing lease).
e. Annual lease payments at the beginning of each year were $184,330.
f. Lessor's implicit rate when calculating annual rental payments was 11%.

Required:

1. Prepare the appropriate entries for the lessor to record the lease and related payments at its inception, January 1, 2016.
2. Calculate the effective rate of interest revenue after adjusting the net investment by initial direct costs.
3. Record any entry(s) necessary at December 31, 2016, the fiscal year-end.

E 15–24
Lessor's initial direct costs; sales-type lease
● LO15–9

The lease agreement and related facts indicate the following:

a. Leased equipment had a retail cash selling price of $300,000. Its useful life was five years with no residual value.
b. Collectibility of the lease payments by the lessor was reasonably predictable and there were no costs to the lessor that were yet to be incurred.
c. The lease term is five years and the lessor paid $265,000 to acquire the equipment (sales-type lease).
d. Lessor's implicit rate when calculating annual lease payments was 8%.
e. Annual lease payments beginning January 1, 2016, the inception of the lease, were $69,571.
f. Costs of negotiating and consummating the completed lease transaction incurred by the lessor were $7,500.

Required:

Prepare the appropriate entries for the lessor to record:

1. The lease and the initial payment at its inception.
2. Any entry(s) necessary at December 31, 2016, the fiscal year-end.

E 15–25
Concepts; terminology
● LO15–3 through LO15–9

Listed below are several terms and phrases associated with leases. Pair each item from List A with the item from List B (by letter) that is most appropriately associated with it.

	List A		List B
______	1. Effective rate times balance.	a.	PV of BPO price.
______	2. Revenue recognition issues.	b.	Lessor's net investment.
______	3. Minimum lease payments plus unguaranteed residual value.	c.	Lessor's gross investment.
______	4. Periodic lease payments plus lessee-guaranteed residual value.	d.	Operating lease.
______	5. PV of minimum lease payments plus PV of unguaranteed residual value.	e.	Depreciable assets.
______	6. Initial direct costs.	f.	Loss to lessee.
______	7. Rent revenue.	g.	Executory costs.
______	8. Bargain purchase option.	h.	Depreciation longer than lease term.
______	9. Leasehold improvements.	i.	Disclosure only.
______	10. Cash to satisfy residual value guarantee.	j.	Interest expense.
______	11. Capital lease expense.	k.	Additional lessor conditions.
______	12. Deducted in lessor's computation of lease payments.	l.	Lessee's minimum lease payments.
______	13. Title transfers to lessee.	m.	Purchase price less than fair value.
______	14. Contingent rentals.	n.	Sales-type lease selling expense.
______	15. Lease payments plus lessee-guaranteed and third-party-guaranteed residual value.	o.	Lessor's minimum lease payments.

E 15–26
Sale-leaseback; capital lease
● LO15–10

To raise operating funds, Signal Aviation sold an airplane on January 1, 2016, to a finance company for $770,000. Signal immediately leased the plane back for a 13-year period, at which time ownership of the airplane will transfer to Signal. The airplane has a fair value of $800,000. Its cost and its book value were $620,000. Its useful life is estimated to be 15 years. The lease requires Signal to make payments of $102,771 to the finance company each January 1. Signal depreciates assets on a straight-line basis. The lease has an implicit rate of 11%.

Required:
Prepare the appropriate entries for Signal on:
1. January 1, 2016, to record the sale-leaseback.
2. December 31, 2016, to record necessary adjustments.

E 15–27
IFRS; sale leaseback; capital lease
● LO15–10, LO15–11

IFRS

Refer to the situation described in Exercise 15–26.

Required:
How might your solution differ if Signal Aviation prepares its financial statements according to International Financial Reporting Standards? Include any appropriate journal entries in your response.

E 15–28
Sale-leaseback; operating lease
● LO15–10

To raise operating funds, National Distribution Center sold its office building to an insurance company on January 1, 2016, for $800,000 and immediately leased the building back. The operating lease is for the final 12 years of the building's estimated 50-year useful life. The building has a fair value of $800,000 and a book value of $650,000 (its original cost was $1 million). The rental payments of $100,000 are payable to the insurance company each December 31. The lease has an implicit rate of 9%.

Required:
Prepare the appropriate entries for National Distribution Center on:
1. January 1, 2016, to record the sale-leaseback.
2. December 31, 2016, to record necessary adjustments.

E 15–29
IFRS; sale leaseback; operating lease
● LO15–10, LO15–11

IFRS

Refer to the situation described in Exercise 15–28.

Required:
How might your solution differ if National Distribution Center prepares its financial statements according to International Financial Reporting Standards? Include any appropriate journal entries in your response.

E 15–30
FASB codification research; sale leaseback
● LO15–10

In a sale-leaseback transaction, the owner of an asset sells it and immediately leases it back from the new owner. The *FASB Accounting Standards Codification* represents the single source of authoritative U.S. generally accepted accounting principles.

Required:

1. Obtain the relevant authoritative literature on disclosure requirements pertaining to a seller-lessee in a sale-leaseback transaction. Use your institution's Academic Accounting Access to the *FASB Accounting Standards Codification* (www.fasb.org) or through your school library's subscription to a research database that includes the Codification. What is the specific citation that describes the guidelines for determining the disclosure requirements in the notes to the financial statements?
2. List the disclosure requirements.

E 15–31
Real estate lease; land and building
● LO15–10

On January 1, 2016, Cook Textiles leased a building with two acres of land from Peck Development. The lease is for 10 years at which time Cook has an option to purchase the property for $100,000. The building has an estimated life of 20 years with a residual value of $150,000. The lease calls for Cook to assume all costs of ownership and to make annual payments of $200,000 due at the beginning of each year. On January 1, 2016, the estimated value of the land was $400,000. Cook uses the straight-line method of depreciation and pays 10% interest on borrowed money. Peck's implicit rate is unknown.

Required:

Prepare Cook Company's journal entries related to the lease in 2016.

E 15–32
FASB codification research

● LO15–1
LO15–4,
LO15–7

Access the *FASB Accounting Standards Codification* at the FASB website (www.fasb.org). Determine the specific citation for accounting for each of the following items:

1. Definition of a bargain purchase option.
2. The calculation of the lessor's gross investment in a sales-type lease.
3. The disclosures required in the notes to the financial statements for an operating lease.
4. The additional disclosures necessary in the notes to the financial statements if the operating lease has a lease term greater than one year.

CPA and CMA Review Questions

CPA Exam Questions
KAPLAN CPA REVIEW

The following questions are adapted from a variety of sources including questions developed by the AICPA Board of Examiners and those used in the Kaplan CPA Review Course used to study lease accounting while preparing for the CPA examination. Determine the response that best completes the statements or questions.

● LO15–3

1. A company leases the following asset:
   - Fair value of $200,000.
   - Useful life of 5 years with no salvage value.
   - Lease term is 4 years.
   - Annual lease payment is $30,000 and the lease rate is 11%.
   - The company's overall borrowing rate is 9.5%.
   - The firm can purchase the equipment at the end of the lease period for $45,000.

   What type of lease is this?
   a. Operating.
   b. Capital.
   c. Financing.
   d. Long term.

● LO15–5

2. On January 1, 2016, Blaugh Co. signed a long-term lease for an office building. The terms of the lease required Blaugh to pay $10,000 annually, beginning December 30, 2016, and continuing each year for 30 years. The lease qualifies as a capital lease. On January 1, 2016, the present value of the lease payments is $112,500 at the 8% interest rate implicit in the lease. In Blaugh's December 31, 2016, balance sheet, the capital lease liability should be
   a. $102,500
   b. $111,500
   c. $112,500
   d. $290,000

● LO15–5

3. Glade Co. leases computer equipment to customers under direct-financing leases. The equipment has no residual value at the end of the lease and the leases do not contain bargain purchase options. Glade wishes to earn 8% interest on a five-year lease of equipment with a fair value of $323,400. The present value of an annuity due of $1 at 8% for five years is 4.312. What is the total amount of interest revenue that Glade will recognize over the life of the lease?
   a. $ 51,600
   b. $ 75,000
   c. $129,360
   d. $139,450

● LO15–6

4. Peg Co. leased equipment from Howe Corp. on July 1, 2016, for an eight-year period expiring June 30, 2024. Equal payments under the lease are $600,000 and are due on July 1 of each year. The first payment was made on July 1, 2016. The rate of interest contemplated by Peg and Howe is 10%. The cash selling price of the equipment is $3,520,000, and the cost of the equipment on Howe's accounting records is $2,800,000. The lease is appropriately recorded as a sales-type lease. What is the amount of profit on the sale and interest revenue that Howe should record for the year ended December 31, 2016?

	Profit on Sale	Interest Revenue
a.	$ 45,000	$146,000
b.	$ 45,000	$176,000
c.	$720,000	$146,000
d.	$720,000	$176,000

● LO15–6

5. On January 2, 2016, Nori Mining Co. (lessee) entered into a 5-year lease for drilling equipment. Nori accounted for the acquisition as a capital lease for $240,000, which includes a $10,000 bargain purchase option. At the end of the lease, Nori expects to exercise the bargain purchase option. Nori estimates that the equipment's fair value will be $20,000 at the end of its 8-year life. Nori regularly uses straight-line depreciation on similar equipment. For the year ended December 31, 2016, what amount should Nori recognize as depreciation expense on the leased asset?
   a. $27,500
   b. $30,000
   c. $48,000
   d. $46,000

● LO15–8

6. At the inception of a capital lease, the guaranteed residual value should be
   a. Included as part of minimum lease payments at present value.
   b. Included as part of minimum lease payments at future value.
   c. Included as part of minimum lease payments only to the extent that guaranteed residual value is expected to exceed estimated residual value.
   d. Excluded from minimum lease payments.

● LO15–9

7. Neal Corp. entered into a nine-year capital lease on a warehouse on December 31, 2016. Lease payments of $52,000, which includes real estate taxes of $2,000, are due annually, beginning on December 31, 2017, and every December 31 thereafter. Neal does not know the interest rate implicit in the lease; Neal's incremental borrowing rate is 9%. The rounded present value of an ordinary annuity for nine years at 9% is 6.0. What amount should Neal report as capitalized lease liability at December 31, 2016?
   a. $300,000
   b. $312,000
   c. $450,000
   d. $468,000

● LO15–10

8. On December 31, 2016, Bain Corp. sold a machine to Ryan and simultaneously leased it back for one year. Pertinent information at this date follows:

Sales price	$360,000
Book value	330,000
Present value of lease payments ($3,000 for 12 months at 12%)	34,100
Estimated remaining useful life	12 years

In Bain's December 31, 2016, balance sheet, the deferred revenue from the sale of this machine should be
   a. $ 0
   b. $ 4,100

c. $34,100
d. $30,000

 IFRS

International Financial Reporting Standards are tested on the CPA exam along with U.S. GAAP. The following questions deal with the application of IFRS in accounting for leases.

● LO15–11

9. For companies that prepare their financial statements in accordance with both U.S. GAAP and IFRS, a lease is deemed to be a capital lease (usually called a finance lease under IFRS) if substantially all risks and rewards of ownership are transferred. In making this distinction, less judgment, more specificity is applied using
   a. IFRS.
   b. U.S. GAAP.
   c. Either U.S. GAAP or IFRS.
   d. Neither U.S. GAAP nor IFRS.

● LO15–1

10. Blue Company is recording a capital lease (usually called a finance lease under IFRS) and is aware that the implicit interest rate used by the lessor to calculate lease payments is 8%. Blue's incremental borrowing rate is 7%. Blue should record the leased asset and lease liability at the present value of the lease payments discounted at
   a. 7% if using either U.S. GAAP or IFRS.
   b. 7% if using IFRS.
   c. 8% if using U.S. GAAP.
   d. 8% if using IFRS.

● LO15–1

11. When a sale-leaseback transaction occurs, if the leaseback is considered to be an operating lease, and the lease payments and sales price are at fair value, any gain on the sale
   a. Is amortized over the lease term by a company using IFRS.
   b. Is recognized immediately by a company using IFRS.
   c. Is amortized over the lease term by a company using either U.S. GAAP or IFRS.
   d. Is not recorded by a company using IFRS.

CPA Exam Questions

The following questions dealing with leases are adapted from questions that previously appeared on Certified Management Accountant (CMA) examinations. The CMA designation sponsored by the Institute of Management Accountants (**www.imanet.org**) provides members with an objective measure of knowledge and competence in the field of management accounting. Determine the response that best completes the statements or questions.

● LO15–5

1. For a direct-financing lease, the gross investment of the lessor is equal to the
   a. Present value of the minimum lease payments minus the unguaranteed residual value accruing to the lessor at the end of the lease term.
   b. Lower of 90% of the present value of the minimum lease payments or the fair value of the leased asset.
   c. Difference between the fair value of the leased asset and the deferred interest revenue.
   d. Minimum lease payments plus the unguaranteed residual value accruing to the lessor at the end of the lease term.

● LO15–7

2. Howell Corporation, a publicly traded corporation, is the lessee in a leasing agreement with Brandon Inc. to lease land and a building. If the lease contains a bargain purchase option, Howell should record the land and the building as a(n)
   a. Operating lease and capital lease, respectively.
   b. Capital lease and operating lease, respectively.
   c. Capital lease but recorded as a single unit.
   d. Capital lease but separately classified.

● LO15–9

3. Initial direct costs incurred by the lessor under a sales-type lease should be
   a. Deferred and allocated over the economic life of the leased property.
   b. Expensed in the period incurred.
   c. Deferred and allocated over the term of the lease in proportion to the recognition of rental income.
   d. Added to the gross investment in the lease and amortized over the term of the lease as a yield adjustment.

Problems

An alternate exercise and problem set is available in the Connect library.

P 15–1
Operating lease; scheduled rent increases
● LO15–4

On January 1, 2016, Sweetwater Furniture Company leased office space under a 21-year operating lease agreement. The contract calls for annual rent payments on December 31 of each year. The payments are $10,000 the first year and increase by $500 per year. Benefits expected from using the office space are expected to remain constant over the lease term.

Required:

Record Sweetwater's rent payment at December 31, 2020 (the fifth rent payment) and December 31, 2030 (the 15th rent payment).

P 15–2
Lease amortization schedule
● LO15–5, LO15–8

On January 1, 2016, National Insulation Corporation (NIC) leased office space under a capital lease. Lease payments are made annually. Title does not transfer to the lessee and there is no bargain purchase option. Portions of the lessee's lease amortization schedule appear below:

Jan. 1	Payments	Effective Interest	Decrease in Balance	Outstanding Balance
2016				192,501
2016	20,000		20,000	172,501
2017	20,000	17,250	2,750	169,751
2018	20,000	16,975	3,025	166,726
2019	20,000	16,673	3,327	163,399
2020	20,000	16,340	3,660	159,739
2021	20,000	15,974	4,026	155,713
—	—	—	—	—
—	—	—	—	—
—	—	—	—	—
2033	20,000	7,364	12,636	61,006
2034	20,000	6,101	13,899	47,107
2035	20,000	4,711	15,289	31,818
2036	35,000	3,182	31,818	0

Required:

1. What is NIC's lease liability at the inception of the lease (after the first payment)?
2. What amount would NIC record as a leased asset?
3. What is the lease term in years?
4. What is the asset's residual value expected at the end of the lease term?
5. How much of the residual value is guaranteed by the lessee?
6. What is the effective annual interest rate?
7. What is the total amount of minimum lease payments?
8. What is the total effective interest expense recorded over the term of the lease?

P 15–3
Direct financing and sales-type lease; lessee and lessor
● LO15–3, LO15–5, LO15–6

Rand Medical manufactures lithotripters. Lithotripsy uses shock waves instead of surgery to eliminate kidney stones. Physicians' Leasing purchased a lithotripter from Rand for $2,000,000 and leased it to Mid-South Urologists Group, Inc., on January 1, 2016.

Lease Description:	
Quarterly lease payments	$130,516—beginning of each period
Lease term	5 years (20 quarters)
No residual value; no BPO	
Economic life of lithotripter	5 years
Implicit interest rate and lessee's incremental borrowing rate	12%
Fair value of asset	$2,000,000

Collectibility of the lease payments is reasonably assured, and there are no lessor costs yet to be incurred.

Required:

1. How should this lease be classified by Mid-South Urologists Group and by Physicians' Leasing?
2. Prepare appropriate entries for both Mid-South Urologists Group and Physicians' Leasing from the inception of the lease through the second rental payment on April 1, 2016. Depreciation is recorded at the end of each fiscal year (December 31).
3. Assume Mid-South Urologists Group leased the lithotripter directly from the manufacturer, Rand Medical, which produced the machine at a cost of $1.7 million. Prepare appropriate entries for Rand Medical from the inception of the lease through the second lease payment on April 1, 2016.

P 15–4
Capital lease
● LO15–5

At the beginning of 2016, VHF Industries acquired a machine with a fair value of $6,074,700 by signing a four-year lease. The lease is payable in four annual payments of $2 million at the end of each year.

Required:

1. What is the effective rate of interest implicit in the agreement?
2. Prepare the lessee's journal entry at the inception of the lease.
3. Prepare the journal entry to record the first lease payment at December 31, 2016.
4. Prepare the journal entry to record the second lease payment at December 31, 2017.
5. Suppose the fair value of the machine and the lessor's implicit rate were unknown at the time of the lease, but that the lessee's incremental borrowing rate of interest for notes of similar risk was 11%. Prepare the lessee's entry at the inception of the lease.

(Note: You may wish to compare your solution to Problem 15–4 with that of Problem 14–12, which deals with a parallel situation in which the machine was acquired with an installment note.)

P 15–5
Capital lease; lessee; financial statement effects
● LO15–5

(Note: Problems 15–5, 15–6, and 15–7 are three variations of the same basic situation.)
Werner Chemical, Inc., leased a protein analyzer on September 30, 2016. The five-year lease agreement calls for Werner to make quarterly lease payments of $391,548, payable each September 30, December 31, March 31, June 30, with the first payment at September 30, 2016. Werner's incremental borrowing rate is 12%. Depreciation is recorded on a straight-line basis at the end of each fiscal year. The useful life of the equipment is five years.

Required:

1. Determine the present value of the lease payments at September 30, 2016 (to the nearest $000).
2. What amounts related to the lease would Werner report in its balance sheet at December 31, 2016 (ignore taxes)?
3. What amounts related to the lease would Werner report in its income statement for the year ended December 31, 2016 (ignore taxes)?
4. What amounts related to the lease would Werner report in its statement of cash flows for the year ended December 31, 2016 (ignore taxes)?

P 15–6
Direct financing lease; lessor; financial statement effects
● LO15–5

Abbott Equipment leased a protein analyzer to Werner Chemical, Inc., on September 30, 2016. Abbott purchased the machine from NutraLabs, Inc., at a cost of $6 million. The five-year lease agreement calls for Werner to make quarterly lease payments of $391,548, payable each September 30, December 31, March 31, June 30, with the first payment at September 30, 2016. Abbot's implicit interest rate is 12%.

Required:

1. What amounts related to the lease would Abbott report in its balance sheet at December 31, 2016 (ignore taxes)?
2. What amounts related to the lease would Abbott report in its income statement for the year ended December 31, 2016 (ignore taxes)?
3. What amounts related to the lease would Abbott report in its statement of cash flows for the year ended December 31, 2016 (ignore taxes)?

P 15–7
Sales-type lease; lessor; financial statement effects
● LO15–6

NutraLabs, Inc., leased a protein analyzer to Werner Chemical, Inc., on September 30, 2016. NutraLabs manufactured the machine at a cost of $5 million. The five-year lease agreement calls for Werner to make quarterly lease payments of $391,548, payable each September 30, December 31, March 31, June 30, with the first payment at September 30, 2016. NutraLabs' implicit interest rate is 12%.

Required:

1. Determine the price at which NutraLabs is "selling" the equipment (present value of the lease payments) at September 30, 2016 (to the nearest $000).
2. What amounts related to the lease would NutraLabs report in its balance sheet at December 31, 2016 (ignore taxes)?
3. What amounts related to the lease would NutraLabs report in its income statement for the year ended December 31, 2016 (ignore taxes)?
4. What amounts related to the lease would NutraLabs report in its statement of cash flows for the year ended December 31, 2016 (ignore taxes)?

P 15–8
Guaranteed residual value; direct financing lease
● LO15–3, LO15–5, LO15–8

(Note: Problems 15–8, 15–9, and 15–10 are three variations of the same basic situation.)
On December 31, 2016, Rhone-Metro Industries leased equipment to Western Soya Co. for a four-year period ending December 31, 2020, at which time possession of the leased asset will revert back to Rhone-Metro. The equipment cost Rhone-Metro $365,760 and has an expected useful life of six years. Its normal sales price is $365,760. The lessee-guaranteed residual value at December 31, 2020, is $25,000. Equal payments under the lease are $100,000 and are due on December 31 of each year. The first payment was made on December 31, 2016. Collectibility of the remaining lease payments is reasonably assured, and Rhone-Metro has no material

cost uncertainties. Western Soya's incremental borrowing rate is 12%. Western Soya knows the interest rate implicit in the lease payments is 10%. Both companies use straight-line depreciation.

Required:

1. Show how Rhone-Metro calculated the $100,000 annual lease payments.
2. How should this lease be classified (a) by Western Soya Co. (the lessee) and (b) by Rhone-Metro Industries (the lessor)? Why?
3. Prepare the appropriate entries for both Western Soya Co. and Rhone-Metro on December 31, 2016.
4. Prepare an amortization schedule(s) describing the pattern of interest over the lease term for the lessee and the lessor.
5. Prepare all appropriate entries for both Western Soya and Rhone-Metro on December 31, 2017 (the second lease payment and depreciation).
6. Prepare the appropriate entries for both Western Soya and Rhone-Metro on December 31, 2020 assuming the equipment is returned to Rhone-Metro and the actual residual value on that date is $1,500.

P 15–9
Unguaranteed residual value; executory costs; sales-type lease
● LO15–6, LO15–8, LO15–9

Rhone-Metro Industries manufactures equipment that is sold or leased. On December 31, 2016, Rhone-Metro leased equipment to Western Soya Co. for a four-year period ending December 31, 2020, at which time possession of the leased asset will revert back to Rhone-Metro. The equipment cost $300,000 to manufacture and has an expected useful life of six years. Its normal sales price is $365,760. The expected residual value of $25,000 at December 31, 2020, is not guaranteed. Equal payments under the lease are $104,000 (including $4,000 executory costs) and are due on December 31 of each year. The first payment was made on December 31, 2016. Collectibility of the remaining lease payments is reasonably assured, and Rhone-Metro has no material cost uncertainties. Western Soya's incremental borrowing rate is 12%. Western Soya knows the interest rate implicit in the lease payments is 10%. Both companies use straight-line depreciation.

Required:

1. Show how Rhone-Metro calculated the $104,000 annual lease payments.
2. How should this lease be classified (a) by Western Soya Co. (the lessee) and (b) by Rhone-Metro Industries (the lessor)? Why?
3. Prepare the appropriate entries for both Western Soya Co. and Rhone-Metro on December 31, 2016.
4. Prepare an amortization schedule(s) describing the pattern of interest over the lease term for the lessee and the lessor.
5. Prepare the appropriate entries for both Western Soya and Rhone-Metro on December 31, 2017 (the second lease payment and depreciation).
6. Prepare the appropriate entries for both Western Soya and Rhone-Metro on December 31, 2020, assuming the equipment is returned to Rhone-Metro and the actual residual value on that date is $1,500.

P 15–10
Bargain purchase option exercisable before lease term ends; executor costs; sales-type lease
● LO15–3, LO15–6, LO15–7, LO15–9

Rhone-Metro Industries manufactures equipment that is sold or leased. On December 31, 2016, Rhone-Metro leased equipment to Western Soya Co. for a noncancelable stated lease term of four years ending December 31, 2020, at which time possession of the leased asset will revert back to Rhone-Metro. The equipment cost $300,000 to manufacture and has an expected useful life of six years. Its normal sales price is $365,760. The expected residual value of $25,000 at December 31, 2020, is not guaranteed. Western Soya Co. can exercise a bargain purchase option on December 30, 2019, at an option price of $10,000. Equal payments under the lease are $134,960 (including $4,000 annual executory costs) and are due on December 31 of each year. The first payment was made on December 31, 2016. Collectibility of the remaining lease payments is reasonably assured, and Rhone-Metro has no material cost uncertainties. Western Soya's incremental borrowing rate is 12%. Western Soya knows the interest rate implicit in the lease payments is 10%. Both companies use straight-line depreciation.

Hint: A lease term ends for accounting purposes when an option becomes exercisable if it's expected to be exercised (i.e., a BPO).

Required:

1. Show how Rhone-Metro calculated the $134,960 annual lease payments.
2. How should this lease be classified (a) by Western Soya Co. (the lessee) and (b) by Rhone-Metro Industries (the lessor)? Why?
3. Prepare the appropriate entries for both Western Soya Co. and Rhone-Metro on December 31, 2016.
4. Prepare an amortization schedule(s) describing the pattern of interest over the lease term for the lessee and the lessor.
5. Prepare the appropriate entries for both Western Soya and Rhone-Metro on December 31, 2017 (the second rent payment and depreciation).

6. Prepare the appropriate entries for both Western Soya and Rhone-Metro on December 30, 2019, assuming the BPO is exercised on that date.

P 15–11
Operating lease to lessee—capital lease to lessor
● LO15–3, LO15–4, LO15–5, LO15–8

Allied Industries manufactures high-performance conveyers that often are leased to industrial customers. On December 31, 2016, Allied leased a conveyer to Poole Carrier Corporation for a three-year period ending December 31, 2019, at which time possession of the leased asset will revert back to Allied. Equal payments under the lease are $200,000 and are due on December 31 of each year. The first payment was made on December 31, 2016. Collectibility of the remaining lease payments is reasonably assured, and Allied has no material cost uncertainties. The conveyer cost $450,000 to manufacture and has an expected useful life of six years. Its normal sales price is $659,805. The expected residual value of $150,000 at December 31, 2019, is guaranteed by United Assurance Group. Poole Carrier's incremental borrowing rate and the interest rate implicit in the lease payments are 10%.

Required:

1. Show how Allied Industries calculated the $200,000 annual lease payments.
2. How should this lease be classified (a) by Allied (the lessor) and (b) by Poole (the lessee)? Why?
3. Prepare the appropriate entries for both Poole and Allied on December 31, 2016.
4. Prepare an amortization schedule(s) describing the pattern of interest over the lease term.
5. Prepare the appropriate entries for both Poole and Allied on December 31, 2017, 2018, and 2019, assuming the conveyer is returned to Allied at the end of the lease and the actual residual value on that date is $105,000.

P 15–12
Lease concepts; direct financing leases; guaranteed and unguaranteed residual value
● LO15–3, LO15–5, LO15–8

Each of the four independent situations below describes a direct financing lease in which annual lease payments of $10,000 are payable at the beginning of each year. Each is a capital lease for the lessee. Determine the following amounts at the inception of the lease:

A. The lessor's:
   1. Minimum lease payments
   2. Gross investment in the lease
   3. Net investment in the lease

B. The lessee's:
   4. Minimum lease payments
   5. Leased asset
   6. Lease liability

	Situation			
	1	2	3	4
Lease term (years)	4	4	4	4
Asset's useful life (years)	4	5	5	5
Lessor's implicit rate (known by lessee)	11%	11%	11%	11%
Lessee's incremental borrowing rate	11%	12%	11%	12%
Residual value:				
Guaranteed by lessee	0	$4,000	0	0
Guaranteed by third party	0	0	$4,000	0
Unguaranteed	0	0	0	$4,000

P 15–13
Lease concepts
● LO15–3, LO15–5, LO15–8

Four independent situations are described below. For each, annual lease payments of $100,000 (not including any executory costs paid by lessor) are payable at the beginning of each year. Each is a capital lease for both the lessor and lessee. Determine the following amounts at the inception of the lease:

A. The lessor's:
   1. Minimum lease payments
   2. Gross investment in the lease
   3. Net investment in the lease
   4. Sales revenue
   5. Cost of goods sold
   6. Dealer's profit

B. The lessee's:
   7. Minimum lease payments
   8. Leased asset
   9. Lease liability

	Situation			
	1	2	3	4
Lease term (years)	4	5	6	4
Lessor's cost	$369,175	$449,896	$500,000	$400,000
Asset's useful life (years)	6	7	7	5
Lessor's implicit rate (known by lessee)	10%	12%	9%	10%
Lessee's incremental borrowing rate	9%	10%	11%	12%
Residual value:				
Guaranteed by lessee	0	$ 53,000	$ 40,000	$ 60,000
Guaranteed by third party*	0	0	0	$ 50,000
Unguaranteed	$ 30,000	0	$ 35,000	$ 40,000
Executory costs paid annually by lessor	$ 1,000	$ 8,000	$ 5,000	$ 10,000

*Over and above any amount guaranteed by the lessee (after a deductible equal to any amount guaranteed by the lessee).

P 15–14
Executory costs; lessor and lessee
● LO15–3, LO15–5, LO15–9

Branif Leasing leases mechanical equipment to industrial consumers under direct financing leases that earn Branif a 10% rate of return for providing long-term financing. A lease agreement with Branson Construction specified 20 annual payments of $100,000 beginning December 31, 2016, the inception of the lease. The estimated useful life of the leased equipment is 20 years with no residual value. Its cost to Branif was $936,500. The lease qualifies as a capital lease to Branson. Maintenance of the equipment was contracted for through a 20-year service agreement with Midway Service Company requiring 20 annual payments of $3,000 beginning December 31, 2016. Both companies use straight-line depreciation.

Required:

Prepare the appropriate entries for both the lessee and lessor to record the second lease payment and depreciation on December 31, 2017, under each of three independent assumptions:

1. The lessee pays executory costs as incurred.
2. The contract specifies that the lessor pays executory costs as incurred. The lessee's lease payments were increased to $103,000 to include an amount sufficient to reimburse these costs.
3. The contract specifies that the lessor pays executory costs as incurred. The lessee's lease payments were increased to $103,300 to include an amount sufficient to reimburse these costs plus a 10% management fee for Branif.

P 15–15
Sales-type lease; bargain purchase option exercisable before lease term ends; lessor and lessee
● LO15–3, LO15–5, LO15–6, LO15–7, LO15–8

Mid-South Auto Leasing leases vehicles to consumers. The attraction to customers is that the company can offer competitive prices due to volume buying and requires an interest rate implicit in the lease that is one percent below alternate methods of financing. On September 30, 2016, the company leased a delivery truck to a local florist, Anything Grows.

The lease agreement specified quarterly payments of $3,000 beginning September 30, 2016, the inception of the lease, and each quarter (December 31, March 31, and June 30) through June 30, 2019 (three-year lease term). The florist had the option to purchase the truck on September 29, 2018, for $6,000 when it was expected to have a residual value of $10,000. The estimated useful life of the truck is four years. Mid-South Auto Leasing's quarterly interest rate for determining payments was 3% (approximately 12% annually). Mid-South paid $25,000 for the truck. Both companies use straight-line depreciation. Anything Grows' incremental interest rate is 12%.

Hint: A lease term ends for accounting purposes when an option becomes exercisable if it's expected to be exercised (i.e., a BPO).

Required:

1. Calculate the amount of dealer's profit that Mid-South would recognize in this sales-type lease. (Be careful to note that, although payments occur on the last calendar day of each quarter, since the first payment was at the inception of the lease, payments represent an annuity due.)
2. Prepare the appropriate entries for Anything Grows and Mid-South on September 30, 2016.
3. Prepare an amortization schedule(s) describing the pattern of interest expense for Anything Grows and interest revenue for Mid-South Auto Leasing over the lease term.
4. Prepare the appropriate entries for Anything Grows and Mid-South Auto Leasing on December 31, 2016.
5. Prepare the appropriate entries for Anything Grows and Mid-South on September 29, 2018, assuming the bargain purchase option was exercised on that date.

P 15–16
Lessee-guaranteed residual value; third-party-guaranteed residual value; unguaranteed residual value; executory costs; different interest rates for lessor and lessee
● LO15–3, LO15–5, LO15–8, LO15–9

On December 31, 2016, Yard Art Landscaping leased a delivery truck from Branch Motors. Branch paid $40,000 for the truck. Its retail value is $45,114.

The lease agreement specified annual payments of $11,000 beginning December 31, 2016, the inception of the lease, and at each December 31 through 2019. Branch Motors' interest rate for determining payments was 10%. At the end of the four-year lease term (December 31, 2020) the truck was expected to be worth $15,000. The estimated useful life of the truck is five years with no salvage value. Both companies use straight-line depreciation.

Yard Art guaranteed a residual value of $6,000. Guarantor Assurance Corporation was engaged to guarantee a residual value of $11,000, but with a deductible equal to any amount paid by the lessee ($11,000 reduced by any amount paid by the lessee). Yard Art's incremental borrowing rate is 9%.

A $1,000 per year maintenance agreement was arranged for the truck with an outside service firm. As an expediency, Branch Motors agreed to pay this fee. It is, however, reflected in the $11,000 lease payments.

Collectibility of the lease payments by Yard Art is reasonably predictable and there are no costs to the lessor that are yet to be incurred.

Required:

1. How should this lease be classified by Yard Art Landscaping (the lessee)? Why?
2. Calculate the amount Yard Art Landscaping would record as a leased asset and a lease liability.
3. How should this lease be classified by Branch Motors (the lessor)? Why?
4. Show how Branch Motors calculated the $11,000 annual lease payments.
5. Calculate the amount Branch Motors would record as sales revenue.
6. Prepare the appropriate entries for both Yard Art and Branch Motors on December 31, 2016.
7. Prepare an amortization schedule that describes the pattern of interest expense over the lease term for Yard Art.
8. Prepare an amortization schedule that describes the pattern of interest revenue over the lease term for Branch Motors.
9. Prepare the appropriate entries for both Yard Art and Branch Motors on December 31, 2017.
10. Prepare the appropriate entries for both Yard Art and Branch Motors on December 31, 2019 (the final lease payment).
11. Prepare the appropriate entries for both Yard Art and Branch Motors on December 31, 2020 (the end of the lease term), assuming the truck is returned to the lessor and the actual residual value of the truck was $4,000 on that date.

P 15–17
Integrating problem; bonds; note; lease
● LO15–5

You are the new controller for Moonlight Bay Resorts. The company CFO has asked you to determine the company's interest expense for the year ended December 31, 2016. Your accounting group provided you the following information on the company's debt:

1. On July 1, 2016, Moonlight Bay issued bonds with a face amount of $2,000,000. The bonds mature in 20 years and interest of 9% is payable semiannually on June 30 and December 31. The bonds were issued at a price to yield investors 10%. Moonlight Bay records interest at the effective rate.
2. At December 31, 2015, Moonlight Bay had a 10% installment note payable to Third Mercantile Bank with a balance of $500,000. The annual payment is $60,000, payable each June 30.
3. On January 1, 2016, Moonlight Bay leased a building under a capital lease calling for four annual lease payments of $40,000 beginning January 1, 2016. Moonlight Bay's incremental borrowing rate on the date of the lease was 11% and the lessor's implicit rate, which was known by Moonlight Bay, was 10%.

Required:

Calculate interest expense for the year ended December 31, 2016.

P 15–18
Initial direct costs; direct financing lease
● LO15–3, LO15–5, LO15–9

Bidwell Leasing purchased a single-engine plane for its fair value of $645,526 and leased it to Red Baron Flying Club on January 1, 2016.

Terms of the lease agreement and related facts were:

a. Eight annual payments of $110,000 beginning January 1, 2016, the inception of the lease, and at each December 31 through 2022. Bidwell Leasing's implicit interest rate was 10%. The estimated useful life of the plane is eight years. Payments were calculated as follows:

Amount to be recovered (fair value)	$645,526
Lease payments at the beginning of each of the next eight years: ($645,526 ÷ 5.86842*)	 $110,000

*Present value of an annuity due of $1: n = 8, i = 10%.

b. Red Baron's incremental borrowing rate is 11%.

c. Costs of negotiating and consummating the completed lease transaction incurred by Bidwell Leasing were $18,099.

d. Collectibility of the lease payments by Bidwell Leasing is reasonably predictable and there are no costs to the lessor that are yet to be incurred.

Required:

1. How should this lease be classified (a) by Bidwell Leasing (the lessor) and (b) by Red Baron (the lessee)?
2. Prepare the appropriate entries for both Red Baron Flying Club and Bidwell Leasing on January 1, 2016.
3. Prepare an amortization schedule that describes the pattern of interest expense over the lease term for Red Baron Flying Club.
4. Determine the effective rate of interest for Bidwell Leasing for the purpose of recognizing interest revenue over the lease term.
5. Prepare an amortization schedule that describes the pattern of interest revenue over the lease term for Bidwell Leasing.
6. Prepare the appropriate entries for both Red Baron and Bidwell Leasing on December 31, 2016 (the second lease payment). Both companies use straight-line depreciation.
7. Prepare the appropriate entries for both Red Baron and Bidwell Leasing on December 31, 2022 (the final lease payment).

P 15–19
Initial direct costs; sales-type lease
● LO15–3, LO15–6, LO15–9

(Note: This problem is a variation of P 15–18 modified to cause the lease to be a sales-type lease.)
Bidwell Leasing purchased a single-engine plane for $400,000 and leased it to Red Baron Flying Club for its fair value of $645,526 on January 1, 2016.

Terms of the lease agreement and related facts were:

a. Eight annual payments of $110,000 beginning January 1, 2016, the inception of the lease, and at each December 31 through 2022. Bidwell Leasing's implicit interest rate was 10%. The estimated useful life of the plane is eight years. Payments were calculated as follows:

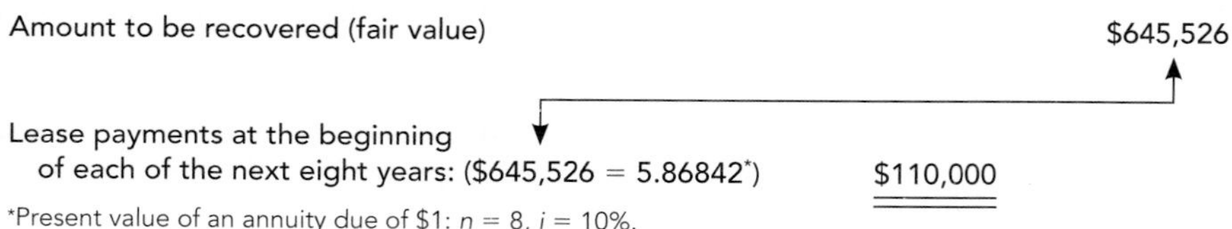

Amount to be recovered (fair value)		$645,526
Lease payments at the beginning of each of the next eight years: ($645,526 = 5.86842*)	$110,000	

*Present value of an annuity due of $1: $n = 8$, $i = 10\%$.

b. Red Baron's incremental borrowing rate is 11%.

c. Costs of negotiating and consummating the completed lease transaction incurred by Bidwell Leasing were $18,099.

d. Collectibility of the lease payments by Bidwell Leasing is reasonably predictable and there are no costs to the lessor that are yet to be incurred.

Required:

1. How should this lease be classified (a) by Bidwell Leasing (the lessor) and (b) by Red Baron (the lessee)?
2. Prepare the appropriate entries for both Red Baron Flying Club and Bidwell Leasing on January 1, 2016.
3. Prepare an amortization schedule that describes the pattern of interest expense over the lease term for Red Baron Flying Club.
4. Prepare the appropriate entries for both Red Baron and Bidwell Leasing on December 31, 2016 (the second lease payment). Both companies use straight-line depreciation.
5. Prepare the appropriate entries for both Red Baron and Bidwell Leasing on December 31, 2022 (the final lease payment).

15–20
Sale-leaseback
● LO15–5, LO15–10

To raise operating funds, North American Courier Corporation sold its building on January 1, 2016, to an insurance company for $500,000 and immediately leased the building back. The lease is for a 10-year period ending December 31, 2025, at which time ownership of the building will revert to North American Courier. The building has a book value of $400,000 (original cost $1,000,000). The lease requires North American to make payments of $88,492 to the insurance company each December 31. The building had a total original useful life of 30 years with no residual value and is being depreciated on a straight-line basis. The lease has an implicit rate of 12%.

Required:

1. Prepare the appropriate entries for North American on (a) January 1, 2016, to record the sale-leaseback and (b) December 31, 2016, to record necessary adjustments.
2. Show how North American's December 31, 2016, balance sheet and income statement would reflect the sale-leaseback.

P 15–21
Real estate lease; land and building
● LO15–10

On January 1, 2016, Cook Textiles leased a building with two acres of land from Peck Development. The lease is for 10 years. No purchase option exists and the property will revert to Peck at the end of the lease. The building and land combined have a fair market value on January 1, 2016, of $1,450,000 and the building has an estimated life of 20 years with a residual value of $150,000. The lease calls for Cook to assume all costs of ownership and to make annual payments of $200,000 due at the beginning of each year. On January 1, 2016, the estimated value of the land was $400,000. Cook uses the straight-line method of depreciation and pays 10% interest on borrowed money. Peck's implicit rate is unknown.

Required:

1. Prepare journal entries for Cook Textiles for 2016. Assume the land could be leased without the building for $59,000 each year.
2. Assuming the land had a fair value on January 1, 2016, of $200,000 and could be leased alone for $30,000, prepare journal entries for Cook Textiles for 2016.

P 15–22
IFRS; real estate lease; land and building
● LO15–10, LO15–11

IFRS

Refer to the situation described in Problem 15–21.

Required:

How might your solution differ if Cook Textiles prepares its financial statements according to International Financial Reporting Standards?

Broaden Your Perspective

Apply your critical-thinking ability to the knowledge you've gained. These cases will provide you an opportunity to develop your research, analysis, judgment, and communication skills. You also will work with other students, integrate what you've learned, apply it in real-world situations, and consider its global and ethical ramifications. This practice will broaden your knowledge and further develop your decision-making abilities.

Analysis Case 15–1
Capitalizing operating leases; financial statement effects
● LO15–1 through LO15–5

PetSmart

Refer to the financial statements and related disclosure notes of **PetSmart, Inc.**, located in the company's financial statements and related disclosure notes for the year ended February 2, 2014, in Appendix B located at the back of the text. You also can locate the report online at the PetSmart website, **petsmart.com**.

Required:

1. See the note on "Financing Arrangements and Lease Obligations" in the disclosure notes. What is PetSmart's capital lease liability?
2. If the operating leases were capitalized, approximately how much would that increase the capital lease liability?
3. What effect would that have on the company's debt to equity ratio? (Refer to the balance sheet.)

Research Case 15–2
FASB codification; locate and extract relevant information and authoritative support for a financial reporting issue; capital lease; sublease of a leased asset
● LO15–1 through LO15–5

"I don't see that in my intermediate accounting text I saved from college," you explain to another member of the accounting division of Dowell Chemical Corporation. "This will take some research." Your comments pertain to the appropriate accounting treatment of a proposed sublease of warehouses Dowell has used for product storage.

Dowell leased the warehouses one year ago on December 31. The five-year lease agreement called for Dowell to make quarterly lease payments of $2,398,303, payable each December 31, March 31, June 30, and September 30, with the first payment at the lease's inception. As a capital lease, Dowell had recorded the leased asset and liability at $40 million, the present value of the lease payments at 8%. Dowell records depreciation on a straight-line basis at the end of each fiscal year.

Today, Jason True, Dowell's controller, explained a proposal to sublease the underused warehouses to American Tankers, Inc. for the remaining four years of the lease term. American Tankers would be substituted as lessee under the original lease agreement. As the new lessee, it would become the primary obligor under the

agreement, and Dowell would not be secondarily liable for fulfilling the obligations under the lease agreement. "Check on how we would need to account for this and get back to me," he had said.

Required:

1. After the first full year under the warehouse lease, what is the balance in Dowell's lease liability? An amortization schedule will be helpful in determining this amount.
2. After the first full year under the warehouse lease, what is the book value (after accumulated depreciation) of Dowell's leased warehouses?
3. Obtain the relevant authoritative literature on accounting for derecognition of capital leases by lessees using the *FASB Accounting Standards Codification*. You might gain access from the FASB website (www.fasb.org), from your school library, or some other source. Determine the appropriate accounting treatment for the proposed sublease. What is the specific Codification citation that Dowell would rely on to determine:
   a. if the proposal to sublease will qualify as a termination of a capital lease, and
   b. the appropriate accounting treatment for the sublease?
4. What, if any, journal entry would Dowell record in connection with the sublease?

Communication Case 15–3
Classification issues; lessee accounting; group interaction
● LO15–3, LO15–7, LO15–8

Interstate Automobiles Corporation leased 40 vans to VIP Transport under a four-year noncancelable lease on January 1, 2016. Information concerning the lease and the vans follows:

a. Equal annual lease payments of $300,000 are due on January 1, 2016, and thereafter on December 31 each year. The first payment was made January 1, 2016. Interstate's implicit interest rate is 10% and known by VIP.
b. VIP has the option to purchase all of the vans at the end of the lease for a total of $290,000. The vans' estimated residual value is $300,000 at the end of the lease term and $50,000 at the end of 7 years, the estimated life of each van.
c. VIP estimates the fair value of the vans to be $1,240,000. Interstate's cost was $1,050,000.
d. VIP's incremental borrowing rate is 11%.
e. VIP will pay the executory costs (maintenance, insurance, and other fees not included in the annual lease payments) of $1,000 per year. The depreciation method is straight-line.
f. The collectibility of the lease payments is reasonably predictable, and there are no important cost uncertainties.

Your instructor will divide the class into two to six groups depending on the size of the class. The mission of your group is to assess the proper recording and reporting of the lease described.

Required:

1. Each group member should deliberate the situation independently and draft a tentative argument prior to the class session for which the case is assigned.
2. In class, each group will meet for 10 to 15 minutes in different areas of the classroom. During that meeting, group members will take turns sharing their suggestions for the purpose of arriving at a single group treatment.
3. After the allotted time, a spokesperson for each group (selected during the group meetings) will share the group's solution with the class. The goal of the class is to incorporate the views of each group into a consensus approach to the situation.

Specifically, you should address:

a. Identify potential advantages to VIP of leasing the vans rather than purchasing them.
b. How should the lease be classified by VIP? by Interstate?
c. Regardless of your response to previous requirements, suppose VIP recorded the lease on January 1, 2016, as a capital lease in the amount of $1,100,000. What would be the appropriate journal entries related to the capital lease for the second lease payment on December 31, 2016?

Ethics Case 15–4
Leasehold improvements
● LO15–3

American Movieplex, a large movie theater chain, leases most of its theater facilities. In conjunction with recent operating leases, the company spent $28 million for seats and carpeting. The question being discussed over breakfast on Wednesday morning was the length of the depreciation period for these leasehold improvements. The company controller, Sarah Keene, was surprised by the suggestion of Larry Person, her new assistant.

Keene: Why 25 years? We've never depreciated leasehold improvements for such a long period.

Person: I noticed that in my review of back records. But during our expansion to the Midwest, we don't need expenses to be any higher than necessary.

Keene: But isn't that a pretty rosy estimate of these assets' actual life? Trade publications show an average depreciation period of 12 years.

Required:
1. How would increasing the depreciation period affect American Movieplex's earnings?
2. Does revising the estimate pose an ethical dilemma?
3. Who would be affected if Person's suggestion is followed?

Real World Case 15–5
Lease concepts; Walmart
● LO15–1 through LO15–6

Real World Financials

Wal-Mart Stores, Inc., is the world's largest retailer. A large portion of the premises that the company occupies are leased. Its financial statements and disclosure notes revealed the following information:

Balance Sheet
($ in millions)

	2014	2013
Assets		
Property:		
Property under capital lease	$5,589	$5,889
Less: Accumulated amortization	(3,046)	(3,147)
Liabilities		
Current liabilities:		
Obligations under capital leases due within one year	309	327
Long-term debt:		
Long-term obligations under capital leases	2,788	3,023

Required:
1. Discuss some possible reasons why Walmart leases rather than purchases most of its premises.
2. The net asset "property under capital lease" has a 2014 balance of $2,543 million ($5,589 − 3,046). Liabilities for capital leases total $3,097 ($309 + 2,788). Why do the asset and liability amounts differ?
3. Prepare a 2014 summary entry to record Walmart's lease payments, which were $600 million.
4. What is the approximate average interest rate on Walmart's capital leases? (Hint: See requirement 3)

Real World Case 15–6
Sale-leaseback; FedEx
● LO15–10

Real World Financials

FedEx Corporation, the world's largest express transportation company, leases much of its aircraft, land, facilities, and equipment. A portion of those leases are part of sale and leaseback arrangements. An excerpt from FedEx's 2013 disclosure notes describes the company's handling of gains from those arrangements:

Deferred Gains

Gains on the sale and leaseback of aircraft and other property and equipment are deferred and amortized ratably over the life of the lease as a reduction of rent expense.

Required:
1. Why should companies defer gains from sale-leaseback arrangements?
2. Based on the information provided in the disclosure note, determine whether the leases in the leaseback portion of the arrangements are considered by FedEx to be capital leases or operating leases. Explain.

Communication Case 15–7
Where's the gain?
● LO15–1
LO15–2
LO15–3
LO15–10

General Tools is seeking ways to maintain and improve cash balances. As company controller, you have proposed the sale and leaseback of much of the company's equipment. As seller-lessee, General Tools would retain the right to essentially all of the remaining use of the equipment. The term of the lease would be six years. A gain would result on the sale portion of the transaction. The lease portion would be classified appropriately as a capital lease.

You previously convinced your CFO of the cash flow benefits of the arrangement, but now he doesn't understand the way you will account for the transaction. "I really had counted on that gain to bolster this period's earnings. What gives?" he wondered. "Put it in a memo, will you? I'm having trouble following what you're saying to me."

Required:
Write a memo to your CFO. Include discussion of each of these points:
1. How the sale portion of the sale-leaseback transaction should be accounted for at the lease's inception.
2. How the gain on the sale portion of the sale-leaseback transaction should be accounted for during the lease.
3. How the leaseback portion of the sale-leaseback transaction should be accounted for at the lease's inception.
4. The conceptual basis for capitalizing certain long-term leases.

Trueblood Case 15–8
Lease classification issues; U.S. GAAP and IFRS
● LO15–3

IFRS

The following Trueblood case is recommended for use with this chapter. The case provides an excellent opportunity for class discussion, group projects, and writing assignments. The case, along with Professor's Discussion Material, can be obtained by searching for "Trueblood Cases" on the Deloitte Foundation website: www.deloitte.com.

Case 11–6: Lessee, Ltd.

This case gives students the opportunity to extend their knowledge beyond chapter coverage by determining the appropriate classification and accounting for a lease arrangement under U.S. GAAP and IFRS.

IFRS Case 15–9
Lease classification; U.S. GAAP
● LO15–1
LO15–2
LO15–3
LO15–11

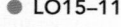

IFRS

Security Devices Inc. (SDI) needs additional office space to accommodate expansion. SDI wants to avoid additional debt in its balance sheet.

Required:

1. What lease classification would management prefer? Explain.
2. If SDI follows U.S. GAAP, how might SDI structure the lease agreement to avoid the additional debt? Explain.
3. Would avoiding the additional debt be more or less difficult under IFRS? Explain.

Air France–KLM Case

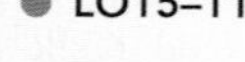
● LO15–11

IFRS

Air France–KLM (AF), a Franco-Dutch company, prepares its financial statements according to International Financial Reporting Standards. AF's financial statements and disclosure notes for the year ended December 31, 2013, are provided with all new textbooks. This material also is available at www.airfranceklm-finance.com.

Required:

1. In Note 4: Summary of accounting policies, part 4.13.4: Leases, AF states that "leases are classified as finance leases when the lease arrangement transfers substantially all the risks and rewards of ownership to the lessee." Is this the policy companies using U.S. GAAP follow in accounting for capital leases? Explain.
2. Look at AF's Note 32.4: Financial debt: Capital lease commitments and Note 35: Lease commitments. Does AF obtain use of its aircraft more using operating leases or finance leases? Do lessees report operating and finance lease commitments the same way? Explain.

CPA Simulation 15–1

GA Company
Leases

KAPLAN
CPA REVIEW

Test your knowledge of the concepts discussed in this chapter, practice critical professional skills necessary for career success, and prepare for the computer-based CPA exam by accessing our CPA simulations in the Connect library.

The GA Company simulation tests your knowledge of (a) the way we account for and report leases from the perspective of both the lessor and lessee, (b) how lease accounting is influenced by bargain purchase options and guaranteed residual value, and (c) accounting for sale-leaseback arrangements.

LEASES:

Where We're Headed

A Chapter Supplement

The FASB and the IASB are collaborating on several major new standards designed in part to move U.S. GAAP and IFRS closer together (convergence). This Supplement is based on their most recent joint Exposure Draft of the new leases standard update (Topic 842), modified by more recent "tentative decisions."[35] At the time this text went to press, the Boards were considering several alternative responses to comments they received on the Exposure Draft. Despite some unsettled specifics, there is broad agreement regarding the fundamental aspects of the proposed guidance for lease accounting. Accordingly, our focus in this supplement is on the broad accounting issues.

Even after a new Accounting Standard Update (ASU) is issued, previous GAAP will be relevant until the new ASU becomes effective (likely not before 2018), and students taking the CPA or CMA exams will be responsible for the previous GAAP until six months after that effective date. Additionally, prior to the effective date of the new ASU, it is useful for soon-to-be graduates to have an understanding of the new guidance on the horizon.

Overview of the Proposed Guidance

Underlying the new ASU is a dual concept of leases:

We account for leases differently for Type A and Type B leases.

Type A: The lease transfers substantially all the *risks and rewards of ownership* of the underlying asset.

Type B: The lease does *not* transfer substantially all the risks and rewards of ownership.

When we think about the way we classify leases under current GAAP, a Type A lease sounds like a capital lease, and a Type B lease sounds like an operating lease. However, the way we *account* for Type A and Type B leases is not the same as the way we account for capital leases and operating leases.

GAAP Change

The new guidance for lease accounting eliminates the concept of operating leases.

For **lessees** (the users of the asset), a fundamental difference between current GAAP and the proposed approach is that, under the proposed approach, the lessee reports both an asset and a liability for *both* Type A and Type B leases. Under current GAAP, the lessee reports an asset and a liability only for capital leases. Expense recognition for both types of leases is similar to current GAAP, with Type A leases producing more expense early in the life of the lease (as capital leases do currently), and Type B leases producing an equal amount of expense each period (as operating leases do currently).

[35]Because an ASU had not been finalized as of the date this text went to press, some aspects of the eventual ASU may be different from what we show in this Supplement. Check the book's FASB Updates page (**http://lsb.scu.edu/jsepe/fasb-update-8e.htm**) to see if any changes have occurred.

Lessor accounting under the new guidance is substantially the same as under current GAAP.

For **lessors** (the owners of the asset), there are fewer differences between current GAAP and the proposed approach. A lessor will apply an approach to all Type A leases that's substantially equivalent to existing capital lease accounting (direct financing and sales-type), and will apply to all Type B leases an approach that's substantially equivalent to existing operating leases. One change is that a lessor cannot recognize sales profit (or revenue) at the beginning of any lease (as we do currently for a sales-type lease) that doesn't transfer "control"[36] of the underlying asset to the lessee. This restriction is consistent with the concept of what constitutes a sale in the new revenue recognition standard, as we saw described in Chapter 5. Illustration 15–23 summarizes the new lease guidance.

Illustration 15–23
Lessee and Lessor Accounting Under the Proposed Lease Accounting Standards Update

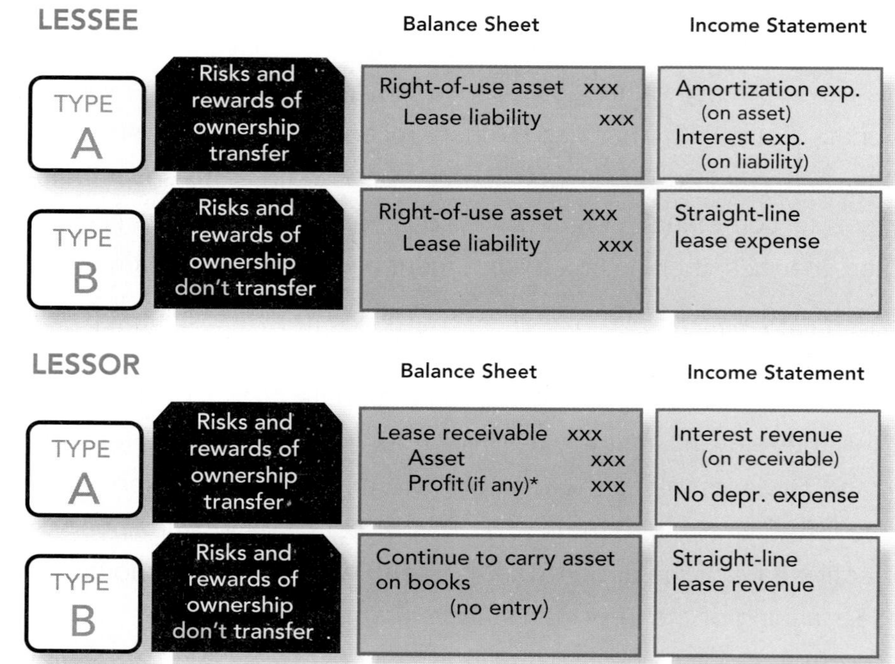

*If the lease receivable exceeds the asset's book value and "control" of the asset is transferred to the lessee

Right-of-Use Model

From your own experience of leasing an apartment or a car, or knowing someone who has, you know that a lease is a contractual arrangement by which a **lessor** provides a **lessee** the right to use an asset for a specified period of time. In return for this right, the lessee agrees to make periodic cash payments during the term of the lease.

Even when risks and rewards of ownership don't transfer to the lessee, the lessee obtains an asset—the right to use the property being leased.

GAAP Change

As we saw in the main chapter, under current GAAP many leases qualify as *operating* leases and therefore do not create an asset and a liability for the lessee, even though the right to use the leased asset can be a significant benefit, and the promise to make the lease payments can be a significant obligation. As a result, many financial statement users complain that current accounting for operating leases does not provide a faithful representation of leasing transactions. The new ASU proposes to eliminate the concept of operating leases and instead require a right-of-use model by which lessees record *all leases as an asset and a liability in the balance sheet*

"The proposal is responsive to the widespread view of investors that leases are liabilities that belong on the balance sheet."
Leslie Seidman, former Chairman of the FASB

[36]As explained in more detail in Chapter 5, "control" means that the customer has direct influence over the use of the good or service and obtains its benefits. That's a bit more restrictive than transferring the risks and rewards of ownership.

(with the exception of short-term leases as described later). This is the primary change in lease accounting provided by the guidance. It achieves the objective that motivated the reconsideration of lease accounting.

The lessee records both a right-of-use asset and a liability to pay for that right.

Type A Leases: Risks and Rewards of Ownership Transferred

Some agreements are called leases, but when we look beyond the "form" of the transactions and focus on their "substance," we find them to be, in reality, more like purchases of assets to be paid for with installment payments.[37] Sometimes the true nature of an arrangement is obvious. For example, a 10-year lease of a computer with a 10-year useful life, by which title passes to the lessee at the end of the lease term, obviously more nearly represents a purchase than a rental agreement. But what if the terms of the contract do not transfer title, and the lease term is for only seven years of the asset's 10-year life? Suppose contractual terms permit the lessee to obtain title under certain prearranged conditions? What if compensation provided by the lease contract is nearly equal to the value of the asset under lease? These situations are less clear-cut.

Professional judgment is needed to differentiate between leases that represent rental agreements and those that in essence are installment purchases/sales. It's important to note that from an accounting perspective legal ownership is irrelevant in the decision. The essential question is whether the usual risks and rewards of ownership have been transferred to the lessee.

Accounting for leases attempts to see through the legal form of the agreements to determine their economic substance.

In Illustration 15–24 we have the same straightforward lease agreement we saw in the main chapter in Illustration 15–6. Let's first think about this arrangement from the perspective of Sans Serif, the lessee. Because Sans Serif leases the asset for its entire useful life, it would classify the lease as a capital lease under current GAAP and record a leased asset and lease payable. Under the new lease guidance, Sans Serif would classify this arrangement as

Illustration 15–24

Type A Lease: Lessee Attains Risk and Rewards of Ownership

On January 1, 2016, Sans Serif Publishers, Inc., leased printing equipment from First LeaseCorp. First LeaseCorp purchased the equipment from CompuDec Corporation at a cost of $479,079.

The lease agreement specifies annual payments beginning January 1, 2016, the beginning of the lease, and at each December 31 thereafter through 2020. The six-year lease term ending December 31, 2021, is equal to the estimated useful life of the equipment. Sans Serif's borrowing rate for similar transactions is 10%.

The price Sans Serif pays for the right to use the equipment is the present value of the lease payments:

$100,000	× 4.79079*	= $479,079
Lease Payments		Lessee's cost

*Present value of an annuity due of $1: $n = 6$, $i = 10\%$.

Using Excel, enter:
= PV(.10,6,100000,1)
Output: 479079

Using a calculator:
enter: BEG mode N 6
I 10
PMT −100000 FV
Output: PV 479079

Beginning of the Lease (January 1, 2016)

Sans Serif (Lessee)

	Debit	Credit
Right-of-use asset (present value of lease payments)	479,079	
Lease payable (present value of lease payments)		479,079

First LeaseCorp (Lessor: *no profit* on the "sale") First LeaseCorp accounts for this *Type A* lease the same way it recorded a direct financing lease in the main chapter:[38]

	Debit	Credit
Lease receivable (present value of lease payments)	479,079	
Inventory of equipment (lessor's cost: book value)		479,079

CompuDec (Lessor: *profit on the "sale")* If Sans Serif had leased the equipment directly from CompuDec, which had produced it at a cost of $300,000, CompuDec would account for this ***Type A*** lease the same way it recorded a sales-type lease in the main chapter:[39]

(continued)

An asset and liability are recorded by the lessee at the *present value of the lease payments.*

[37]Like the installment notes we discussed in the previous chapter.

[38]Illustration 15–6.

[39]Illustration 15–8.

Illustration 15–24
(concluded)

Lease receivable (present value of lease payments)	479,079	
Inventory of equipment (lessor's cost: book value)		300,000
Profit (difference)		179,079[40]

GAAP Change

a *Type A* lease, and the accounting would be quite similar to current GAAP. Conceptually, though, we think of the asset that Sans Serif "purchases" to be, not printing equipment, but the *right to use* the printing equipment, in this case, for its entire useful life. That's why Sans Serif records a "right-of-use asset."

First LeaseCorp, the lessor, also would classify this arrangement as a Type A lease and record it as if it were an installment sale (like a capital lease under current GAAP). That is, it would record a lease receivable for the present value of the payments and remove from its balance sheet the asset being leased.

RECORDING INTEREST EXPENSE / INTEREST REVENUE

Interest accrues at the effective rate on the balance outstanding during the period.

As lease payments are made over the term of the lease, both the lessee and lessor record interest at the effective interest rate. The lessee, Sans Serif, also will record amortization expense on its right-of-use asset over the term of the lease. Let's first consider interest.

As shown in Illustration 15–24A, the entire $100,000 first lease payment is applied to principal (lease payable/receivable) reduction.[41] That's because the payment occurred at the beginning of the lease, so no interest had yet accrued. Subsequent lease payments, though, include interest of 10% on the outstanding balance as well as a portion that reduces that outstanding balance. As of the second lease payment date, one year's interest of $37,908 has accrued on the $379,079 ($479,079 − 100,000) balance outstanding during 2016. After recording that interest, the outstanding balance is reduced by $62,092, the portion of the $100,000 payment remaining after interest is covered.

Illustration 15–24A
Journal Entries for the First and Second Lease Payment

First Lease Payment (January 1, 2016)		
Sans Serif (Lessee)		
Lease payable	100,000	
Cash (lease payment)		100,000
First LeaseCorp (Lessor)		
Cash (lease payment)	100,000	
Lease receivable		100,000
Second Lease Payment (December 31, 2016)		
Sans Serif (Lessee)		
Interest expense [10% × ($479,079 − 100,000)]	37,908	
Lease payable (difference)	62,092	
Cash (lease payment)		100,000
First LeaseCorp (Lessor)		
Cash (lease payment)	100,000	
Lease receivable		62,092
Interest revenue [10% × ($479,079 − 100,000)]		37,908

Lease payable/receivable

$479,079	
(100,000)	1st payment
$379,079	
(62,092)	2nd payment
$316,987	

[40]Companies might choose to separate this profit into its two components: Sales revenue ($479,079) and cost of goods sold ($300,000), which is the gross method demonstrated for "sales-type" leases in the main chapter:

Lease receivable (present value of lease payments)	479,079	
Cost of goods sold	300,000	
Sales revenue		479,079
Inventory of equipment (lessor's cost: book value)		300,000

Exception: A lessor cannot recognize sales profit (or revenue) at the beginning of any lease that doesn't transfer "control" of the underlying asset to the lessee.

[41]Another way to view this is to think of the first $100,000 as a down payment with the remaining $379,079 financed by 5 (i.e., 6 – 1) *year-end* lease payments.

We see the amortization schedule for the lease payable/receivable in Illustration 15–24B. That amortization schedule is no different from what we would use under current GAAP if we were to record this arrangement as a capital lease. It shows how the lease balance and the effective interest change over the six-year lease term, using an effective interest rate of 10%. Each lease payment after the first one includes both an amount that represents interest and an amount that represents a reduction of the outstanding balance. The periodic reduction is sufficient that, at the end of the lease term, the outstanding balance is zero.

Illustration 15–24B

Lease Amortization Schedule

	Payments	Effective Interest	Decrease in Balance	Outstanding Balance
		(10% × Outstanding balance)		
1/1/16				479,079
1/1/16	100,000		100,000	379,079
12/31/16	100,000	.10 (379,079) = 37,908	62,092	316,987
12/31/17	100,000	.10 (316,987) = 31,699	68,301	248,686
12/31/18	100,000	.10 (248,686) = 24,869	75,131	173,555
12/31/19	100,000	.10 (173,555) = 17,355	82,645	90,910
12/31/20	100,000	.10 (90,910) = 9,090*	90,910	0
	600,000	120,921*	479,079	

*Adjusted for rounding of other numbers in the schedule.

The first rental payment includes no interest.

The total of the cash payments ($600,000) provides for:

1. **Payment for the equipment's use ($479,079).**
2. **Interest ($120,921) at an effective rate of 10%.**

Both the lessee and lessor would use this amortization schedule. The lessee amortizes its lease *payable* and records interest *expense.* Similarly, the lessor amortizes its lease *receivable* and records interest *revenue,* reflecting the opposite side of the same transaction.

Now, let's see how the lessee amortizes its right-of-use asset over the term of the lease.

RECORDING AMORTIZATION OF THE RIGHT-OF-USE ASSET

Like other noncurrent assets, the lessee's right-of-use asset provides an economic benefit (the right to use a productive asset) over the period covered by the lease term. Consistent with a reduction in that benefit over time, the lessee amortizes its right-of-use asset over the lease term (or the useful life of the asset if that is shorter). The amortization process usually is on a straight-line basis unless the lessee's pattern of using the asset is different.[42] That results in an *expense* for the lessee. In our example, the lessee amortizes its right-of-use asset over a six-year lease term.

December 31, 2016 and End of Next Five Years		
Amortization expense ($479,079 ÷ 6 years)	79,847*	
Right-of-use asset		79,847

*rounded

The lessee incurs an expense as it uses the asset.

Because the lessor, First LeaseCorp, removed the asset from its records at the beginning of the lease, it would not have depreciation to record. Note that, as with capital leases in current GAAP, the lessee records more expense and the lessor records more revenue early in the life of the lease. This "front loading" of lease expense occurs due to the fact that *interest is higher initially* than it is in the later stages of a lease, while amortization expense for the right-of-use asset remains the same each period. A key objective of Type B lease accounting we discuss next is to avoid this front loading when the lessee doesn't attain the usual risks and rewards of ownership and just "rents" the asset for a while.

[42]Output measures such as units produced or input measures such as hours used might provide a better indication of the reduction in some leased assets.

Type B Leases: Risks and Rewards of Ownership Not Transferred

In many lease agreements, the lessor retains the usual risks and rewards of ownership and merely "rents" the asset to the lessee for a period of time. We consider these arrangements to be *Type B* leases.

In the previous illustration, the lease term is equal to the expected useful life of the asset (six years). Now, in Illustration 15–25, we apply the right-of-use model to another situation (Illustration 15–5 in the main chapter) in which the lease term is only four years of the asset's six-year life. We'll assume that the shorter lease term indicates that the risks and rewards of ownership have been retained by the lessor, so the arrangement is classified as a Type B lease. Lessee accounting for this situation under the proposed ASU is a significant departure from current GAAP.

Under current GAAP, this lease would be considered an "operating lease" because none of the four criteria for capital lease classification is met, and thus no asset or liability would be recorded at the beginning of the lease. Instead, as we saw in the main chapter, we would simply record lease payments as lease expense on a straight-line basis over the lease term.

GAAP Change
The notion of operating leases is eliminated.

Under the new lease guidance, though, Sans Serif is deemed to have purchased the *right to use the asset* for four years of the asset's six-year useful life and records a "right-of-use asset" as well as a liability to pay for that right. So, just as for our prior example in which the asset was leased for its entire life, Sans Serif still recognizes a right-of-use asset and lease liability. The only difference is that, because the lease includes fewer payments, a smaller present value is recorded at the beginning of the lease.

Illustration 15–25

Type B Lease: Lessee Does Not Attain Risk and Rewards of Ownership

On January 1, 2016, Sans Serif Publishers leased printing equipment from First LeaseCorp. First LeaseCorp purchased the equipment from CompuDec Corporation at a cost of $479,079. Sans Serif's borrowing rate for similar transactions is 10%.

The lease agreement specifies four annual payments of $100,000 beginning January 1, 2016, the beginning of the lease, and at each December 31 thereafter through 2018. The useful life of the equipment is estimated to be six years, but the lessee will use the asset only until the end of 2019. The present value of those four payments at a discount rate of 10% is $348,685:

$100,000 × 3.48685* = $348,685
Lease Payments — Lessor's cost

*Present value of an annuity due of $1: $n = 4$, $i = 10\%$.

Beginning of the Lease (January 1, 2016)

Sans Serif (Lessee)

Right-of-use asset (present value of lease payments)	348,685	
Lease payable (present value of lease payments)		348,685

First LeaseCorp (Lessor)

[No entry to record receivable or to derecognize (remove from the balance sheet) the asset][43]

The lessee acquires an asset—the right to use the equipment—and records a liability to pay for it.

The lessor records *no* lease receivable.

RECORDING LEASE EXPENSE / LEASE REVENUE

In a Type B lease, both the lessee and lessor record total lease expense (lessee) and lease revenue (lessor) on a straight-line basis.

In a Type B lease, the lessee reports ***lease expense on a straight-line basis*** and the lessor reports ***lease revenue on a straight-line basis*** over the lease term. That's because in a Type B lease, the risks and rewards of ownership are deemed not to have been transferred to the lessee, so we view the arrangement as essentially a rental agreement. Consistent with that perspective, the lessee and the lessor will report straight-line rental of $100,000 during each of the four years. However, while the lessor's lease revenue is simply the $100,000 lease payment each year, the lessee has two lease-related expenses—*interest* expense on its lease

[43]This is like we recorded an operating lease in the main chapter. See Illustration 15–5A.

payable and *amortization* expense for its right-of-use asset. In its income statement, the lessee combines these two accounts into a single *lease expense* and reports a single straight-line amount each period. Let's look first at the interest component. Sans Serif determines interest on the lease payable the same way as in a Type A lease as demonstrated in Illustration 15–25A.

First Lease Payment (January 1, 2016)		
Lease payable	100,000	
Cash (lease payment)		100,000
Second Lease Payment (December 31, 2016)		
Interest expense [10% × ($348,685 − 100,000)]	24,869	
Lease payable (difference)	75,131	
Cash (lease payment)		100,000

Illustration 15–25A

Journal Entries for the First and Second Lease Payment

Lease payable
$348,685
(100,000) 1st payment
$248,685
(75,131) 2nd payment
$173,554

The amortization schedule in Illustration 15–25B shows how the lease balance and the effective interest change over the four-year lease term.

	Payments	Effective Interest		Decrease in Balance	Outstanding Balance
		(10% × Outstanding balance)			
1/1/16					348,685
1/1/16	100,000			100,000	248,685
12/31/16	100,000	.10 (248,685) =	24,869	75,131	173,554
12/31/17	100,000	.10 (173,554) =	17,355	82,645	90,909
12/31/18	100,000	.10 (90,909) =	9,091	90,909	0
	400,000		**51,315**	**348,685**	

Illustration 15–25B

Lease Amortization Schedule

The first lease payment includes no interest.

The total of the cash payments ($400,000) provides for:

1. **Payment for the equipment's use ($348,685).**
2. **Interest ($51,315) at an effective rate of 10%.**

In the next section, we see how the right-of-use asset is amortized to provide a straight-line total lease expense of $100,000 each year.

RECORDING AMORTIZATION OF THE RIGHT-OF-USE ASSET

We can say that recording lease expense in a *Type A lease* should reflect (a) the right to use the asset (amortization) plus (b) the financing of that right (interest). On the other hand, in a *Type B lease,* recording lease expense should simply reflect straight-line rental of the asset during the lease term. The way the lessee does that is to determine interest expense as in Illustration 15–25A and 15–25B above, but then determine amortization of the right-of-use asset as the amount needed to cause the *total* lease expense (interest plus amortization) to be an equal, straight-line amount over the lease term. Illustration 15–25C shows us how total lease expense (amortization plus interest) for Sans Serif will equal $100,000 each year over the lease term. The lessor reports *lease revenue* on a straight-line basis for a Type B lease as well, but because it records no entry at the beginning of the lease, it simply records the annual $100,000 lease receipts as lease revenue. This, too, is demonstrated in the illustration.

In a Type B lease, the lessee records interest the normal way and then "plugs" the right-of-use asset amortization at whatever amount is needed for interest plus amortization to equal the *straight-line* lease payment.

The lessor in a Type B lease does not record a lease receivable at the beginning of the lease and does not remove from its balance sheet (derecognize) the asset being leased. With no receivable to accrue interest, the First LeaseCorp simply records straight-line revenue as a single lease revenue amount equal to the $100,000 lease payments and equal to the $100,000 amount the lessee reports as lease expense as demonstrated in Illustration 15–25C.

We should take note of several aspects of these journal entries. First, at the beginning of the Type B lease, as in a Type A lease, the lessee records an asset for the right to use the equipment for four years as well as an obligation to pay for that right. However, in a Type B lease, unlike in a Type A lease, the *lessor* does not record a lease receivable, nor does it

A right-of-use asset is recorded by the lessee at the *present value of the lease payments.*

Illustration 15–25C Type B Lease—Determining Lease Expenses and Revenue

	Jan. 1, 2016		Dec. 31, 2016		Dec. 31, 2017		Dec. 31, 2018		Dec. 31, 2019	
Sans Serif (Lessee)										
Right-of-use asset	348,685									
Lease payable		348,685								
Interest expense	0		24,869		17,355		9,091		0	
Lease payable	100,000		75,131		82,645		90,909		0	
Cash		100,000		100,000		100,000		100,000		0
Amortization expense[φ]			75,131		82,645		90,909		100,000	
Right-of-use asset				75,131		82,645		90,909		100,000
Total lease expenses each year =			100,000		100,000		100,000		100,000	
First LeaseCorp (Lessor)										
[No entry to record receivable or to derecognize asset]										
Cash	100,000		100,000		100,000		100,000			
Deferred revenue[τ]		100,000		100,000		100,000		100,000		
Deferred revenue[τ]			100,000		100,000		100,000		100,000	
Lease revenue				100,000		100,000		100,000		100,000
Depreciation expense ($479,079 / 6)[Ψ]			79,847		79,847		79,847		79,847	
Accumulated depreciation				79,847		79,847		79,847		79,847

[φ]plug to cause the *total* lease expense to equal the straight-line amount: $100,000 minus interest

[τ]When the $100,000 is received at the beginning of the lease year, it is not yet earned and should be recorded as deferred lease revenue. When it has been earned by the end of the year, it becomes lease revenue.

[Ψ]also in 2020 and 2021 (rounded).

The lessor retains the equipment on its books.

remove the asset from its balance sheet. Instead, each $100,000 lease payment it receives is viewed as lease revenue for letting the lessee use the equipment. Second, straight-line recognition in the income statement is the key difference when recording a Type B lease. This avoids the so-called front loading of lease expense and lease revenue that occurs in a Type A lease.

In a Type B lease, the lessee records lease expense and the lessor records lease revenue on a straight-line basis over the lease term.

The lessor records lease revenue as $100,000 in each of the four years, and the lessee also records lease expense as $100,000 in each of the four years. But when looking at the journal entries in Illustration 15–25C, you'll see that the lessee's lease expense is separated into two parts. One part is the interest on the lease payable, which is calculated in the same way as we do for Type A leases. (See the amortization schedule in Illustration 15–24B for confirmation.) The second component of lease expense is the amortization of the right-of-use asset. This part requires some additional explanation.

The lessee's lease expense is separated into two parts, interest and an amortization amount that is a "plug" to cause the total expense to be $100,000 each year.

As is apparent in the journal entries, we don't simply amortize the lessee's right-of-use asset on a straight-line basis as we did for a Type A lease. To understand why, we need to remember that our primary objective here is to cause the total lease expense to be the straight-line amount of $100,000 each year. We can ensure that happens by having the *amortization* component be simply a "plug" amount that is the difference between $100,000 and the *interest* component determined first. So, for instance, when we determine the interest the first year to be 10% of $348,685 − 100,000,[44] or $24,869, we can simply subtract that amount from $100,000 to get the amortization amount of $75,131.

Notice, too, that we reduce both the asset and the liability by the same amount. In 2016, $75,131 is the amortization of the right-of-use asset, and it also is the reduction of the lease liability. The liability is accounted for the same way as in a Type A lease, and the amortization is adjusted to ensure that the asset is equal to the liability. This results in the total lease

[44]Remember, the interest for 2016 is the effective rate times the original liability reduced by the first $100,000 paid on the first day.

expense being the same for all four years and equal to what would have been recognized using operating lease accounting. Illustration 15–25D compares the front-loading effect of a Type A lease with the straight-line effect of a Type B lease.

Illustration 15–25D

Comparison of Lessee's Expense Recognition between Type A and Type B Leases

	Type A Lease Financing Approach			Type B Lease Straight-Line Approach		
	Interest Expense	**Amortization Expense**	**Total Expense**	**Interest Expense**	**Amortization Expense**	**Total Expense**
2016	24,869	87,171	112,040	24,869	75,131	100,000
2017	17,355	87,171	104,526	17,355	82,645	100,000
2018	9,091	87,171	96,262	9,091	90,909	100,000
2019	0	87,171	87,171	0	100,000	100,000
	51,315	348,685*	400,000*	51,315	348,685	400,000

*Adjusted for rounding of other numbers in the schedule.

It's the amortization of the leased asset that differs under a Type A lease from a Type B lease. In a Type A lease, the lessee amortizes its right-of-use asset on a straight-line basis. In a Type B lease, on the other hand, it's the *total* lease expense, not the amortization component, that's a straight-line amount. To make that happen, we "plug" the amortization as the difference between the desired straight-line amount and the interest component as we saw demonstrated in Illustration 15–25D.

REPORTING LEASE EXPENSE AND LEASE REVENUE

After recording these entries for Sans Serif, the lessee, will have two lease-related expenses—interest expense and amortization expense. However, the lessee combines these two accounts into a single *lease expense* and reports a single $100,000 amount each year in its income statement. This is consistent with the key objective of reporting a straight-line lease expense for a Type B lease. In a Type A lease, the lessee will report interest expense and amortization expense separately in the income statement. First LeaseCorp, the lessor, has only a single lease revenue account in a Type B lease and reports that straight-line amount, $100,000, each year in its income statement.

In a Type B lease, the lessee combines interest expense and amortization expense to report a single lease expense in the income statement.

Additional Consideration

If the annual lease payments are at the *end* of each year rather than the beginning of each year, the present value of the payments would be:

$100,000 × 3.16987* = $316,987
Lease Payments — Lessor's cost

*Present value of an ***ordinary*** annuity of $1: $n = 4$, $i = 10\%$.

The amortization schedule and journal entries would be:

	Payments	**Effective Interest**		**Decrease in Balance**	**Outstanding Balance**
		(10% × Outstanding balance)			
1/1/16					316,987
12/31/16	100,000	.10 (316,987) =	31,699	68,301	248,685
12/31/17	100,000	.10 (248,685) =	24,869	75,131	173,554
12/31/18	100,000	.10 (173,554) =	17,355	82,645	90,909
12/31/19	100,000	.10 (90,909) =	9,091	90,909	0
	400,000		**83,013**	**316,987**	

(continued)

(concluded)

	Jan. 1, 2016		Dec. 31, 2016		Dec. 31, 2017		Dec. 31, 2018		Dec. 31, 2019	
Sans Serif (Lessee)										
Right-of-use asset	316,987									
Lease payable		316,987								
Interest expense			31,699		24,869		17,355		9,901	
Lease payable			68,301		75,131		82,645		90,909	
Cash				100,000		100,000		100,000		100,000
Amortization expense^φ			68,301		75,131		82,645		90,909	
Right-of-use asset				68,301		75,131		82,645		90,909
First LeaseCorp (Lessor)										
[No entry to record receivable or to derecognize asset]										
Cash			100,000		100,000		100,000		100,000	
Deferred revenue^τ				100,000		100,000		100,000		100,000
Deferred revenue^τ			100,000		100,000		100,000		100,000	
Lease revenue				100,000		100,000		100,000		100,000
Depreciation expense ($479,079 / 6)^Ψ			79,846		79,846		79,846		79,846	
Accumulated depreciation				79,846		79,846		79,846		79,849

^τ plug to cause the total lease expense to equal the straight-line amount: $100,000 minus interest
^Ψ also in 2020 and 2021

Here's a comparison of the Lessee's expenses depending on whether it's a Type A lease or a Type B lease:

The lessee records interest at the effective interest rate and then "plugs" the right-of-use asset amortization at whatever amount is needed for interest plus amortization to equal the straight-line lease payment.

	Type A Lease Financing Approach			Type B Lease Straight-Line Approach		
	Interest Expense	Amortization Expense	Total Expense	Interest Expense	Amortization Expense	Total Expense
2016	31,699	79,247	110,946	31,699	68,301	100,000
2017	24,869	79,247	104,116	24,869	75,131	100,000
2018	17,355	79,247	96,602	17,355	82,645	100,000
2019	9,091	79,247	88,338	9,091	90,909	100,000
	83,014	316,987*	400,000*	83,014	316,987*	400,000*

*Adjusted for rounding of other numbers in the schedule.

Short-Term Leases—A Short-Cut Method

In a short-term lease, the lessee can elect not to record a right-of-use asset and lease payable at the beginning of the lease term, but instead to simply record lease payments as expense as they occur.

It's not unusual to simplify accounting for situations in which doing so has no material effect on the financial statements. You might recognize this as the concept of "materiality." One such situation that permits a simpler application is a short-term lease. A lease is considered a "short-term lease" if it has a maximum possible lease term (including any options to renew or extend) of twelve months or less and does not contain an option for the lessee to purchase the asset. For a short-term lease, the lessee has a lease-by-lease option to choose a short-cut approach.

The short-cut approach permits the lessee to choose ***not*** to record the lease transaction at the beginning of the lease term. Instead, the lessee can simply record lease payments as rent expense over the lease term. Yes, this is the approach used under current GAAP for operating leases.

Let's look at an example that illustrates the relatively straightforward accounting for short-term leases. To do this, in Illustration 15–26 we modify Illustration 15–25 to assume the lease term is *twelve months.*

Illustration 15–26
Short-Term Lease

On January 1, 2016, Sans Serif Publishers leased printing equipment from First LeaseCorp. The lease agreement specifies four **quarterly** payments of $25,000 beginning January 1, 2016, the beginning of the lease, and at the first day of each of the next three quarters. The useful life of the equipment is estimated to be six years.

Beginning of the Lease (January 1, 2016)

No entry to record a right-of-use asset and liability

Lease Payments (January 1, April 1, July 1, October 1, 2016)

Lease expense	25,000	
Cash		25,000

If the short-cut option is chosen, the lessee recognizes lease payments as lease expense over the lease term.

At the time this text was written, the FASB was deliberating several issues related to uncertainty in lease transactions that impact lessee and lessor accounting under the proposed ASU. Among those issues were variable lease terms and variable lease payments, guaranteed residual values, purchase options, and termination penalties.

Respond to the questions, brief exercises, exercises, and problems in this supplement with the presumption that the guidance provided by the new Accounting Standards Update is being applied.

Questions For Review of Key Topics

Q 15–24 Distinguish between a Type A lease and a Type B lease.

Q 15–25 At the beginning of a Type B lease, the *lessee* will record what asset and liability, if any?

Q 15–26 At the beginning of a Type B lease, the *lessor* will record what asset and liability, if any?

Q 15–27 In accounting for a Type A lease, how are the lessee's and lessor's income statements affected?

Q 15–28 In accounting for a Type B lease, how are the lessee's and lessor's income statements affected?

Q 15–29 In a Type A lease, "front loading" of lease expense and lease revenue occurs. What does this mean, and how is it avoided in a Type B lease?

Q 15–30 Briefly describe the conceptual basis for asset and liability recognition under the right-of-use approach used by the lessee in a lease transaction.

Q 15–31 A lease that has a lease term (including any options to terminate or renew that are reasonably certain) of twelve months or less is considered a "short-term lease." How does a lessee record a lease using the short-cut approach available as an option for short-term leases?

Brief Exercises

BE 15–15
Lessee; effect on earnings; Type A lease

At January 1, 2016, Café Med leased restaurant equipment from Crescent Corporation under a nine-year lease agreement. The lease agreement specifies annual payments of $25,000 beginning January 1, 2016, the beginning of the lease, and at each December 31 thereafter through 2023. The equipment was acquired recently by Crescent at a cost of $176,000 (its fair value) and was expected to have a useful life of 12 years with no residual value. The company seeks a 10% return on its lease investments. By this arrangement, the risks and rewards of ownership are deemed to have been transferred to the lessee. What will be the effect of the lease on Café Med's earnings for the first year (ignore taxes)?

BE 15–16
Lessee; effect on earnings; Type B lease

In the situation described in BE 15–15, assume that the risks and rewards of ownership are deemed *not* to have been transferred to the lessee. What will be the effect of the lease on Café Med's earnings for the first year (ignore taxes)?

BE 15–17
Lessor; effect on earnings; Type B lease

In the situation described in BE 15–16, what will be the effect of the lease on Crescent's (lessor's) earnings for the first year (ignore taxes)?

BE 15–18
Lessee; effect on balance sheet; Type A lease

In the situation described in BE 15–15, what will be the balances in the balance sheet accounts related to the lease at the end of the first year for Café Med (ignore taxes)?

BE 15–19
Lessee; effect on balance sheet; Type B lease

In the situation described in BE 15–16, what will be the balances in the balance sheet accounts related to the lease at the end of the first year for Café Med (ignore taxes)?

BE 15–20
Lessee; accrued interest; balance sheet effects; Type A lease

A Type A lease agreement calls for annual lease payments of $26,269 over a six-year lease term, with the first payment at January 1, the beginning of the lease, and subsequent payments at January 1 in each of the following five years. The interest rate is 5%. If the lessee's fiscal year is the calendar year, what would be the amount of the lease payable that the lessee would report in its balance sheet at the end of the first year? What would be the interest payable?

BE 15–21
Lessee; accrued interest; income statement effects; Type A lease

In the situation described in BE 15–20, what would be the amounts related to the lease that the lessee would report in its income statement for the first year ended December 31 (ignore taxes)?

BE 15–22
Lessor profit; income statement effects; Type A lease

In the situation described in BE 15–20, assume the asset being leased cost the lessor $125,000 to manufacture and that the agreement causes the lessee to obtain "control" of the leased asset. Determine the price at which the lessor is "selling" the right to use the asset (present value of the lease payments). What would be the amounts related to the lease that the lessor would report in its income statement for the first year ended December 31 (ignore taxes)?

BE 15–23
Lessee and lessor; calculate interest; Type A lease

A Type A lease agreement calls for quarterly lease payments of $5,376 over a 10-year lease term, with the first payment on July 1, the beginning of the lease. The annual interest rate is 8%. Both the fair value and the cost of the asset to the lessor are $150,000. What would be the amount of interest expense the lessee would record in conjunction with the second quarterly payment on October 1? What would be the amount of interest revenue the lessor would record in conjunction with the second quarterly payment on October 1?

BE 15–24
Short-term lease

King Cones leased ice cream-making equipment from Ace Leasing. Ace earns interest under such arrangements at a 6% annual rate. The lease term is eight months with monthly payments of $10,000 due at the end of each month. King Cones elected the short-term lease option. What is the effect of the lease on King Cones' earnings during the eight-month term (ignore taxes)?

Exercises

E 15–33
Lessee; amortization schedule; journal entries; Type A lease

(Note: Exercises 15–33 through 15–36 are variations of the same basic lease situation.)
Manufacturers Southern leased high-tech electronic equipment from Edison Leasing on January 1, 2016. Edison purchased the equipment from International Machines at a cost of $112,080.

Related Information:	
Lease term	2 years (8 quarterly periods)
Quarterly lease payments	$15,000 at Jan. 1, 2016, and at Mar. 31, June 30, Sept. 30, and Dec. 31 thereafter
Economic life of asset	2 years
Interest rate charged by the lessor	8%

Required:
Prepare a lease amortization schedule for the two-year term of the lease and appropriate entries for Manufacturers Southern from the beginning of the lease through December 31, 2016. The company's fiscal year-end is December 31. Appropriate adjusting entries are recorded at the end of each quarter.

E 15–34
Lessor; amortization schedule; journal entries; Type A lease

Refer to the situation described in E15–33.

Required:

Prepare a lease amortization schedule for the two-year term of the lease and appropriate entries for Edison Leasing from the beginning of the lease through December 31, 2016. December 31 is the fiscal year-end. Appropriate adjusting entries are recorded at the end of each quarter.

E 15–35
Lessee; journal entries; Type B lease

Manufacturers Southern leased high-tech electronic equipment from Edison Leasing on January 1, 2016. Edison purchased the equipment from International Machines at a cost of $250,177.

Related Information:	
Lease term	2 years (8 quarterly periods)
Quarterly lease payments	$15,000 at Jan. 1, 2016, and at Mar. 31, June 30, Sept. 30, and Dec. 31 thereafter
Economic life of asset	5 years
Interest rate charged by the lessor	8%

Required:

Prepare appropriate entries for Manufacturers Southern from the beginning of the lease through March 31, 2016. Appropriate adjusting entries are made quarterly.

E 15–36
Lessor; journal entries; Type B lease

Refer to the situation described in E15–35.

Required:

Prepare appropriate entries for Edison Leasing from the beginning of the lease through March 31, 2016. Appropriate adjusting entries are made quarterly.

E 15–37
Lessee; amortization schedule and journal entries; Type A lease

American Food Services, Inc., leased a packaging machine from Barton and Barton Corporation. Barton and Barton completed construction of the machine on January 1, 2016. The lease agreement for the $4 million (fair value and present value of the lease payments) machine specified four equal payments at the end of each year. The useful life of the machine was expected to be four years with no residual value. Barton and Barton's implicit interest rate was is 10%.

Required:

1. Prepare the journal entry for American Food Services at the beginning of the lease on January 1, 2016.
2. Prepare an amortization schedule for the four-year term of the lease.
3. Prepare the appropriate journal entries on December 31, 2016.
4. Prepare the appropriate journal entries on December 31, 2018.

E 15–38
Short-term lease

Manufacturers Southern leased high-tech electronic equipment from Edison Leasing on January 1, 2016. Edison purchased the equipment from International Machines at a cost of $250,177. Manufacturers Southern elected the short-term lease option. Appropriate adjusting entries are made annually.

Related Information:	
Lease term	1 years (4 quarterly periods)
Quarterly lease payments	$15,000 at Jan. 1, 2016, and at Mar. 31, June 30, Sept. 30
Economic life of asset	5 years
Interest rate charged by the lessor	8%

Required:

1. Prepare appropriate entries for Manufacturers Southern from the beginning of the lease through December 31, 2016.

Problems

P 15–23
Lessee and lessor; Type A lease; profit on sale

The Antonescu Sporting Goods leased equipment from Chapman Industries on January 1, 2016. The agreement causes the lessee to obtain "control" of the leased asset. Chapman Industries had manufactured the equipment at a cost of $800,000. Its cash selling price and fair value is $1,000,000.

Other Information:

Lease term	4 years
Annual payments	$279,556 beginning Jan.1, 2016, and at Dec. 31, 2016, 2017, and 2018
Life of asset	4 years
Rate the lessor charges	8%

Required:

1. Prepare the appropriate entries for Antonescu Sporting Goods (lessee) on January 1, 2016, and December 31, 2016. Round to nearest dollar.
2. Prepare the appropriate entries for Chapman Industries (lessor) on January 1, 2016, and December 31, 2016. Round to nearest dollar.

P 15–24
Lessee; effect on financial statements; Type B lease

On January 1, at the beginning of its fiscal year, Lakeside Inc. leased office space to LTT Corporation under a ten-year lease agreement. The contract calls for quarterly lease payments of $25,000 each at the end of each quarter. The office building was acquired by Lakeside at a cost of $1 million and was expected to have a useful life of 25 years with no residual value. Lakeside seeks a 10% return on its lease investments. Appropriate adjusting entries are made quarterly.

Required:

1. What amounts related to the lease would LTT report in its balance sheet at December 31, 2016?
2. What amounts related to the lease would LTT report in its income statement for the year ended December 31, 2016 (ignore taxes)?

P 15–25
Lessee; balance sheet and income statement effects; Type A lease; Type B lease

On June 30, 2016, Papa Phil Inc. leased 200 pizza ovens for its chain of restaurants from IC Leasing Corporation. The lease agreement calls for Papa Phil to make semiannual lease payments of $562,907 over a three-year lease term, payable each June 30 and December 31, with the first payment on June 30, 2016. IC calculated lease payment amounts using a 10% interest rate. IC purchased the 200 pizza ovens from Pizza Inc. at their retail price of $3 million.

Required:

1. Determine the present value of the lease payments at June 30, 2016 (to the nearest $000) that Papa Phil uses to record the right-of-use asset and lease payable.
2. What amounts related to the lease would Papa Phil report in its balance sheet at December 31, 2016 (ignore taxes)?
3. What pretax amounts related to the lease would Papa Phil report in its income statement for the year ended December 31, 2016 (ignore taxes)?
4. Assume the retail price is $5 million, so we assume the risks and rewards are not transferred to the lessee. What amounts related to the lease would Papa Phil report in its income statement for the year ended December 31, 2016 (ignore taxes)?

CHAPTER

16 Accounting for Income Taxes

OVERVIEW

In this chapter we explore financial accounting and reporting for the effects of income taxes. The discussion defines and illustrates temporary differences, which are the basis for recognizing deferred tax assets and deferred tax liabilities, as well as permanent differences, which have no deferred tax consequences. You will learn how to adjust deferred tax assets and deferred tax liabilities when tax laws or rates change. We also discuss accounting for net operating loss carrybacks and carryforwards as well as intraperiod tax allocation.

LEARNING OBJECTIVES

After studying this chapter, you should be able to:

- **LO16–1** Describe the types of temporary differences that cause deferred tax liabilities and determine the amounts needed to record periodic income taxes. (*p. 934*)
- **LO16–2** Describe the types of temporary differences that cause deferred tax assets and determine the amounts needed to record periodic income taxes. (*p. 941*)
- **LO16–3** Describe when and how a valuation allowance is recorded for deferred tax assets. (*p. 946*)
- **LO16–4** Explain why permanent differences have no deferred tax consequences. (*p. 947*)
- **LO16–5** Explain how a change in tax rates affects the measurement of deferred tax amounts. (*p. 951*)
- **LO16–6** Determine income tax amounts when multiple temporary differences exist. (*p. 954*)
- **LO16–7** Describe when and how a net operating loss carryforward and a net operating loss carryback are recognized in the financial statements. (*p. 955*)
- **LO16–8** Explain how deferred tax assets and deferred tax liabilities are classified and reported in a classified balance sheet and describe related disclosures. (*p. 959*)
- **LO16–9** Demonstrate how to account for uncertainty in income tax decisions. (*p. 961*)
- **LO16–10** Explain intraperiod tax allocation. (*p. 965*).
- **LO16–11** Discuss the primary differences between U.S. GAAP and IFRS with respect to accounting for income taxes. (*p. 950*).

FINANCIAL REPORTING CASE

What's the Difference?

The board of directors for Times-Lehrer Industries is meeting for the first time since Laura Drake was asked to join the board. Laura was the director of the regional office of United Charities. Although she has broad experience with the tax advantages of charitable giving and the vast array of investment vehicles available to donors, her 15 years of experience with not-for-profit organizations has not exposed her to the issues involved with corporate taxation. This gap in her considerable business knowledge causes her to turn to you, Times-Lehrer's CFO and a long-time friend, who recommended Laura for appointment to the board.

"I must say," Laura confided, "I've looked long and hard at these statements, and I can't quite grasp why the amount reported for income tax expense is not the same as the amount of income taxes we paid. What's the difference?"

QUESTIONS

By the time you finish this chapter, you should be able to respond appropriately to the questions posed in this case. Compare your response to the solution provided at the end of the chapter.

1. What's the difference? Explain to Laura how differences between financial reporting standards and income tax rules might cause the income tax expense and the amount of income tax paid to differ. *(p. 933)*
2. What is the conceptual advantage of determining income tax expense as we do? *(p. 934)*
3. Are there differences between financial reporting standards and income tax rules that will not cause a difference between income tax expense and the amount of income taxes paid? *(p. 948)*

Deferred Tax Assets and Deferred Tax Liabilities

PART A

FINANCIAL Reporting Case

Q1, p. 933

A manufacturer of leather accessories in the Midwest is obligated to pay the Internal Revenue Service $24 million in income taxes as determined by its 2016 income tax return. Another $9 million in income taxes also is attributable to 2016 activities. Conveniently, though, tax laws permit the company to defer paying the additional $9 million until subsequent tax years by reporting certain revenues and expenses on the tax return in years other than when those amounts are reported in the income statement. Does the company have only a current income tax liability of $24 million? Or does it also have a deferred income tax liability for the other $9 million? To phrase the question differently: Should the company report a 2016 income tax expense of the $24 million tax payable for the current year, or $33 million to include the future tax effects of events already recognized? For perspective on this question, we should look closer at the circumstances that might create the situation. Such circumstances are called *temporary differences*.

Conceptual Underpinning

FINANCIAL Reporting Case

Q2, p. 933

The goals of financial accounting and tax accounting are not the same.

Accounting for income taxes is consistent with the accrual concept of accounting.

When a company prepares its tax return for a particular year, the revenues and expenses (and gains and losses) included on the return are, by and large, the same as those reported on the company's income statement for the same year. However, in some instances tax laws and financial accounting standards differ. The reason they differ is that the fundamental objectives of financial reporting and those of taxing authorities are not the same. Financial accounting standards are established to provide useful information to investors and creditors. Congress, on the other hand, establishes tax regulations to allow it to raise funds in a socially acceptable manner, as well as to influence the behavior of taxpayers. In pursuing the latter objective, Congress uses tax laws to encourage activities it deems desirable, such as investment in productive assets, and to discourage activities it deems undesirable, such as violations of law.

A consequence of differences between GAAP and tax rules is that tax payments frequently occur in years different from when the revenues and expenses that cause the taxes are generated. One way to deal with these timing differences would be to ignore them, and simply report tax expense in the income statement each period equal to whatever tax is paid in that period. However, that approach would not communicate to investors that the company's current activities have resulted in future tax consequences. Companies should recognize income tax expense based on the "accrual concept," just like other expenses. That is, income tax expense reported each period should be the amount caused by that period's activities, regardless of *when* the tax laws require that the tax be paid. If tax laws allow a company to avoid a current tax payment by postponing when an amount is included in taxable income, the company must report a **deferred tax liability** based on the **future taxable amount**. On the other hand, if tax laws require the company to wait until a future period to take a tax deduction that *reduces* taxable income, the company reports a **deferred tax asset** reflecting the benefit of that **future deductible amount**. That means that tax expense includes not only current tax payable but also changes in the deferred tax assets and liabilities that represent taxes due in other periods but that resulted from the current period's operations.

To understand how that works, let's consider deferred tax liabilities and deferred tax assets in more detail, as well as the "temporary differences" that give rise to them.

Temporary Differences

● LO16–1

The differences in the rules for computing taxable income and those for financial reporting often cause amounts to be included in taxable income in a year later—or earlier—than the year in which they are recognized for financial reporting purposes. For example, you learned in Chapter 4 that income from selling properties on an installment basis is reported for financial reporting purposes in the year of the sale. But tax laws permit installment income to be reported on the tax return as it actually is received. This means taxable income might be less than accounting income in the year of an installment sale but higher than accounting income in later years when installment income is collected.

Temporary differences **arise when tax rules and accounting rules recognize income in different periods.**

The situation just described creates what's referred to as a **temporary difference** between pretax *accounting* income and *taxable* income and, consequently, between the amount of an asset or liability that is reported in the financial statements and the equivalent amount, called the *tax basis* of an asset or a liability, that is included in the company's tax records. In our example, the asset for which the temporary difference exists is the installment receivable that's recognized for financial reporting purposes, but not for tax purposes.

Deferred Tax Liabilities

It's important to understand that a temporary difference *originates* in one period and *reverses*, or turns around, in one or more subsequent periods. The temporary difference described above originates in the year the installment sales are made and are reported in the *income statement*. The temporary difference reverses in a future period when the installments are collected and income is reported on the *tax return*. An example is provided in Illustration 16–1.

Kent Land Management reported pretax accounting income in 2016, 2017, and 2018 of $100 million, plus additional 2016 income of $40 million from installment sales of property. However, the installment sales income is reported on the tax return when collected, in 2017 ($10 million) and 2018 ($30 million).* The enacted tax rate is 40% each year.†

($ in millions)	Temporary Difference			
	Originates	Reverses		
	2016	2017	2018	Total
Pretax accounting income	$140	$100	$100	$340
Installment sale income on the income statement	(40)	0	0	(40)
Installment sale income on the tax return	0	10	30	40
Taxable income (tax return)	$100	$110	$130	$340

*The installment method is not available to accrual method taxpayers. H.R. 1180, sec. 536, 1999.
†The enacted rate refers to the tax rate indicated by currently enacted tax legislation (as distinguished from anticipated legislation). This is discussed later in the chapter.

Illustration 16–1
Revenue Reported on the Tax Return *after* the Income Statement

In 2016, taxable income is less than accounting income because income from installment sales is not reported on the tax return until 2017–2018.

Notice that pretax accounting income and taxable income total the same amount over the three-year period but are different in each individual year. In 2016, taxable income is $40 million *less* than accounting income because it does not include income from installment sales. The difference is temporary, though. That situation reverses over the next two years. In 2017 and 2018 taxable income is *more* than accounting income because income from the installment sales, reported in the income statement in 2016, becomes taxable during the next two years as installments are collected.

The 2016 deferred tax liability will become tax payable in the next two years.

Because tax laws permit the company to delay reporting this income as part of taxable income, the company is able to defer paying the tax on that income. As shown in Illustration 16–1A, that tax is not avoided, just deferred.

Illustration 16–1A
Determining and Recording Income Taxes—2016

($ in millions)	Current Year	Future Taxable Amounts		Future Taxable Amounts
	2016	2017	2018	(total)
Pretax accounting income	$140			
Temporary difference:				
Installment income	(40)	$10	$30	$40
Taxable income (tax return)	$100			
Enacted tax rate	40%			40%
Tax payable currently	$ 40			

Reported in the income statement, not on the tax return

Deferred Tax Liability	
	0 beg. bal.
	16
	16 end. bal.

Deferred Tax Liability	
Desired ending balance	$ 16
Less: Beginning balance	0
Change in balance	$16

Journal Entry at the End of 2016

Income tax expense (to balance)	56	
Income tax payable (determined above)		40
Deferred tax liability (determined above)		16

With **future taxable amounts** of $40 million, taxable at 40%, a $16 million **deferred tax liability** should be recognized as of the end of 2016. Because no previous balance exists, we credit deferred tax liability for the entire $16 million.

Each year, income tax expense comprises both the current and the deferred tax consequences of events and transactions already recognized. This means we:

1. Calculate the income tax that is payable currently.
2. Calculate what the ending balance in the deferred tax liability (or asset) should be.
3. Determine the change (debit or credit) in the deferred tax liability (or asset) necessary to reach that ending balance.
4. Combine that change with tax payable to determine income tax expense.

Notice that, under this approach, tax expense is not calculated directly, but rather is the result of the combination of income tax payable and any changes in deferred tax assets and liabilities. In other words, tax expense is debited or credited to make the rest of the journal entry balance. That perspective will be important throughout this chapter.

Using the 2017 and 2018 income numbers, the journal entries to record income taxes for those years would be:

Deferred tax liability

1/1/2017	16 beg. bal.
change 4	
12/31/2017	12 ending bal.

2017	($ in millions)	
Income tax expense (to balance)	40	
Deferred tax liability [($30 million × 40%) − 16 million]	4	
Income tax payable ($110 million × 40%)		44

Deferred tax liability

1/1/2018	12 beg. bal.
change 12	
12/31/2018	0 ending bal.

2018		
Income tax expense (to balance)	40	
Deferred tax liability ($0 million − 12 million)	12	
Income tax payable ($130 million × 40%)		52

Now look at the activity in the deferred tax liability account over the life of the installment receivable. See how the temporary difference originates in 2016 and reverses in 2017 and 2018?

Deferred Tax Liability

($ in millions)			
		16	2016 ($40 × 40%)
2017 ($10 × 40%)	4		
2018 ($30 × 40%)	12		
		0	Balance after 3 years

At the end of 2017, the deferred tax liability should have a balance of $12 million. Because the balance from 2016 is $16 million, we reduce it by $4 million.

At the end of 2018, the deferred tax liability should have a balance of zero. So, we eliminate the $12 million balance.

Balance Sheet and Income Statement Perspectives

Our perspective in this example so far has centered around the income effects of the installment sales and thus on the changes in the deferred tax liability as the temporary difference reverses. Another perspective starts with the balance sheet effect. An assumption underlying a balance sheet is that assets will be recovered (used or sold to produce cash) and liabilities will be settled (typically paid with cash). So, for example, receivables will be collected, machines will be used or sold, and liabilities will be paid when they are due. Those assets and liabilities typically create taxable or deductible amounts in the future when they are recovered (an installment receivable is collected and taxable income is increased; a machine is used and depreciation is deducted) or settled (a warranty liability is paid and warranty expense is deducted). Before that occurs, there is a temporary difference between the *book value* (also called the *carrying value* or *carrying amount*) of those assets and liabilities on the balance sheet and the tax basis of those assets and liabilities for the tax return. The **tax basis** of an asset or liability is its original value for tax purposes reduced by any amounts included to date on tax returns. We can calculate the related deferred tax asset or liability balance by multiplying the *temporary book-tax difference* by the applicable tax rate.

Deferred tax assets and liabilities can be computed from temporary book-tax differences.

The *tax basis* of an asset or liability is its original value for tax purposes reduced by any amounts included to date on tax returns.

In our example, the company reports an installment receivable in the balance sheet in 2016 when it makes an installment sale. However, the tax return doesn't recognize a sale until cash has been collected, so there is no receivable for 2016 tax purposes. Therefore, as shown in Illustration 16–1B, we have a temporary book-tax difference in 2016 between the receivable's book value ($40) and its tax basis ($0), so we recognize a deferred tax liability to reflect the tax that will be paid when that difference reverses in the future. The book-tax difference (and the deferred tax liability) declines in 2017 and 2018 as the receivable is collected.

An installment receivable has no tax basis.

Illustration 16–1B

Temporary Book-Tax Difference

December 31 ($ in millions)	2016		2017		2018	
Receivable from installment sales:						
Accounting book value	$40	$40	$(10)	$30	$(30)	$0
Tax basis	(0)	(0)	(0)	(0)	(0)	(0)
Temporary difference	$40	$40	$(10)	$30	$(30)	$0
Tax rate	↑	× 40%	↑	× 40%	↑	× 40%
Deferred tax liability		$16		$12		$0
	Originating Difference		Reversing Differences			

The deferred tax liability each year is the tax rate times the temporary difference between the financial statement book value of the receivable and its tax basis.

Of course, we should get to the same deferred tax asset or liability if we base our calculations on (a) future deductible and taxable amounts or (b) present temporary book-tax differences. They are two different perspectives of the same basic event. We consider both perspectives in subsequent examples in this chapter.

Types of Temporary Differences

Examples of temporary differences are provided in Illustration 16–2.

Illustration 16–2

Types of Temporary Differences

	Revenues (or gains)	Expenses (or losses)
Reported in the income statement now, but on the tax return later	• Installment sales of property (installment method for taxes) • Unrealized gain from recording investments at fair value (taxable when asset is sold)	• Estimated expenses and losses (tax-deductible when paid) • Unrealized loss from recording investments at fair value or inventory at LCM (tax-deductible when asset is sold)
Reported on the tax return now, but in the income statement later	• Rent collected in advance • Subscriptions collected in advance • Other revenue collected in advance	• Accelerated depreciation on the tax return in excess of straight-line depreciation in the income statement • Prepaid expenses (tax-deductible when paid)

- The temporary differences shown in the diagonal purple areas create *deferred tax liabilities* because they result in *taxable* amounts in some future year(s) when the related assets are recovered or the related liabilities are settled (when the temporary differences reverse).
- The temporary differences in the opposite diagonal blue areas create *deferred tax assets* because they result in *deductible* amounts in some future year(s) when the related assets are recovered or the related liabilities are settled (when the temporary differences reverse).

Additional Consideration

As shown in Illustration 16–2, temporary differences between the reported amount of an asset or liability in the financial statements and its tax basis are primarily caused by revenues, expenses, gains, and losses being included in taxable income in a year other than the year in which they are recognized for financial reporting purposes. Other events also can cause temporary differences between the reported amount of an asset or liability in the financial statements and its tax basis. Other such events that are beyond the scope of this textbook are briefly described in FASB ASC 740–10–25: Income Taxes–Overall–Recognition (previously "Accounting for Income Taxes," *Statement of Financial Accounting Standards No. 109* (Norwalk, Conn.: FASB, 1992), par. 11 e–h). Our discussions in this chapter focus on temporary differences caused by the timing of revenue and expense recognition, but it's important to realize that the concept of temporary differences embraces all differences that will result in taxable or deductible amounts in future years.

Be sure to notice that deferred tax liabilities can arise from either (a) a revenue being reported on the tax return after the income statement or (b) an expense being reported on the tax return before the income statement. Illustration 16–1 was of the first type. We look at the second type in Illustration 16–3, which examines deferred tax liabilities associated with depreciation.

Illustration 16–3

Expense Reported on the Tax Return before the Income Statement

Courts Temporary Services reported pretax accounting income in 2016, 2017, 2018, and 2019 of $100 million. In 2016, an asset was acquired for $100 million. The asset is depreciated for financial reporting purposes over four years on a straight-line basis (no residual value). For tax purposes the asset's cost is deducted (by MACRS) over 2016–2019 as follows: $33 million, $44 million, $15 million, and $8 million. No other depreciable assets were acquired. The enacted tax rate is 40% each year.

To determine taxable income, we add back to accounting income the actual depreciation taken in the income statement and then subtract the depreciation deduction allowed on the tax return.

($ in millions)	Temporary Difference				
	Originates		Reverses		
	2016	**2017**	**2018**	**2019**	**Total**
Pretax accounting income	$100	$100	$100	$100	$400
Depreciation on the income statement	25	25	25	25	100
Depreciation on the tax return	(33)	(44)	(15)	(8)	(100)
Taxable income (tax return)	$ 92	$ 81	$110	$117	$400

Notice that the temporary difference shown in Illustration 16–3 originates during more than a single year before it begins to reverse. This usually is true when depreciation is the cause of the temporary difference. Tax laws typically permit the cost of a depreciable asset to be deducted on the tax return sooner than it is reported as depreciation in the income statement.[1] This means taxable income will be less than pretax accounting income in the income statement during the years the tax deduction is higher than income statement depreciation, but higher than pretax accounting income in later years when the situation reverses. 2016 income taxes would be recorded as shown in Illustration 16–3A.

Let's follow the determination of income taxes for this illustration all the way through the complete reversal of the temporary difference. We assume accounting income is $100 million each year and that the only difference between pretax accounting income and taxable

[1]The accelerated depreciation method prescribed by the tax code is the modified accelerated cost recovery system (MACRS). The method is described in the Chapter 11 appendix.

Illustration 16–3A
Determining and Recording Income Taxes—2016

($ in millions)

	Current Year 2016	Future Taxable Amounts 2017	2018	2019	Future Taxable Amounts (total)
Pretax accounting income	$ 100				
Temporary difference:					
Depreciation	(8)	$(19)	$10	$17	$ 8
Taxable income	$ 92				
Enacted tax rate	40%				40%
Tax payable currently	$36.8				

Tax depreciation is $8 million more than in the income statement.

Deferred Tax Liability	
	0 beg. bal.
	3.2
	3.2 end. bal.

Deferred Tax Liability	
Ending balance needed	$3.2
Less: Beginning balance	0
Change in balance	$3.2

Journal Entry at the End of 2016

Income tax expense (to balance)	40	
Income tax payable (determined above)		36.8
Deferred tax liability (determined above)		3.2

Taxable income is $8 million less than accounting income because that much more depreciation is deducted on the 2016 tax return ($33 million) than is reported in the income statement ($25 million).

Income tax expense is comprised of two components: the amount payable currently and the amount deferred until later.

income is caused by depreciation. 2017 income taxes would be determined as shown in Illustration 16–3B.

Notice that each year the appropriate balance is determined for the deferred tax liability. That amount is compared with any existing balance to determine whether the account must be either increased or decreased.

Illustration 16–3B
Determining and Recording Income Taxes—2017

($ in millions)

	2016	Current Year 2017	Future Taxable Amounts 2018	2019	Future Taxable Amounts (total)
Pretax accounting income		$ 100			
Temporary difference:					
Depreciation	$(8)	(19)	$10	$17	$ 27
Taxable income (tax return)		81			
Enacted tax rate		40%			40%
Tax payable currently		$32.4			

Deferred Tax Liability	
	3.2 beg. bal.
	7.6
	10.8 end. bal.

Deferred Tax Liability	
Ending balance needed	$ 10.8
Less: Beginning balance	(3.2)
Change in balance	$ 7.6

Journal Entry at the End of 2017

Income tax expense (to balance)	40	
Income tax payable (determined above)		32.4
Deferred tax liability (determined above)		7.6

The cumulative temporary difference ($27 million) is both (a) the sum of the amounts originating in 2016 ($8 million) and in 2017 ($19 million) and (b) the sum of the amounts reversing in 2018 ($10 million) and in 2019 ($17 million).

Since a balance of $3.2 million already exists, $7.6 million must be added.

Income taxes for 2018 would be recorded as shown in Illustration 16–3C.

Illustration 16–3C

Determining and Recording Income Taxes—2018

A credit balance of $6.8 million is needed in the deferred tax liability account.

Since a credit balance of $10.8 million already exists, $4 million must be deducted (debited).

A portion of the tax deferred from 2016 and 2017 is now payable in 2018.

($ in millions)

	2016	2017	Current Year 2018	Future Taxable Amounts 2019	Future Taxable Amounts (total)
Pretax accounting income			$100		
Temporary difference:					
Depreciation	$(8)	$(19)	10	$17	$ 17
Taxable income (tax return)			$110		
Enacted tax rate			40%		40%
Tax payable currently			$ 44		

Deferred Tax Liability	
	10.8 beg. bal.
4.0	
	6.8 end. bal.

Deferred Tax Liability	
Ending balance needed	$ 6.8
Less: Beginning balance	(10.8)
Change in balance	$ (4.0)

Journal Entry at the End of 2018

Income tax expense (to balance)	40	
Deferred tax liability (determined above)	4	
Income tax payable (determined above)		44

Income taxes for 2019 would be recorded as shown in Illustration 16–3D.

Illustration 16–3D

Determining and Recording Income Taxes—2019

Because the entire temporary difference has now reversed, there is a zero cumulative temporary difference, and the balance in the deferred tax liability should be zero.

Since a credit balance of $6.8 million exists, that amount must be deducted (debited). The final portion of the tax deferred from 2016 and 2017 is payable in 2019.

($ in millions)

	2016	2017	2018	Current Year 2019	Future Taxable Amounts (total)
Pretax accounting income				$ 100	
Temporary difference:					
Depreciation	$(8)	$(19)	$10	17	$ 0
Taxable income (tax return)				$ 117	
Enacted tax rate				40%	40%
Tax payable currently				$46.8	

Deferred Tax Liability	
	6.8 beg. bal.
6.8	
	0 end. bal.

Deferred Tax Liability	
Ending balance needed	$ 0.0
Less: Beginning balance	(6.8)
Change in balance	$(6.8)

Journal Entry at the End of 2019

Income tax expense (to balance)	40.0	
Deferred tax liability (determined above)	6.8	
Income tax payable (determined above)		46.8

Notice that the deferred tax liability is increased in 2016–2017 and decreased in 2018–2019.

Deferred Tax Liability

($ in millions)			
		3.2	2016 ($ 8 × 40%)
2018 ($10 × 40%)	4.0	7.6	2017 ($19 × 40%)
2019 ($17 × 40%)	6.8		
		0	Balance after 4 years

The deferred tax liability increases the first two years and becomes tax payable over the next two years.

We also can calculate this deferred tax liability each year using the alternate perspective of looking at the temporary book–tax difference that exists for the depreciable asset. Its book value is its cost minus accumulated straight-line depreciation. Its tax basis is its cost minus accumulated depreciation deductions taken on its tax return.

($ in millions)			December 31						
			2016		2017		2018		2019
Depreciable asset:									
Accounting book value	$100	$(25)	$ 75	$(25)	$ 50	$(25)	$ 25	$(25)	$ 0
Tax basis	100	(33)	67	(44)	23	(15)	8	(8)	0
Temporary difference		$ 8	$ 8	$ 19	$ 27	$(10)	$ 17	$(17)	$ 0
Tax rate			40%		40%		40%		40%
Deferred tax liability			$3.2		$10.8		$6.8		$ 0
		Originating Differences				Reversing Differences			

Deferred Tax Assets

● LO16–2

The temporary differences illustrated to this point produce future taxable amounts when the temporary differences reverse. Future taxable amounts mean taxable income will be increased relative to pretax accounting income in one or more future years, so we recognize a deferred tax liability to reflect the tax that will be due in those years. Sometimes, though, the future tax consequence of a temporary difference will be to *decrease* taxable income relative to accounting income. Such situations produce what's referred to as **future deductible amounts**. These have favorable future tax consequences that are recognized as **deferred tax assets**. Be sure to note, though, that unlike most assets, management views deferred tax assets to be *less* desirable than deferred tax liabilities. The reason is that deferred tax liabilities result from having lower taxable income (and thus lower tax) now. As we see in this section, deferred tax assets result from taxable income (and tax) being higher now than later. It's more desirable to delay paying taxes as long as possible.

Deferred tax assets are recognized for the future tax benefits of temporary differences that create future deductible amounts.

As noted in Illustration 16–2, one circumstance that requires recognition of a deferred tax asset is when estimated expenses are recognized in income statements when incurred but deducted on tax returns in later years when the expenses are actually paid. Illustration 16–4 provides an example: a quality-assurance warranty.

Illustration 16–4

Expense Reported on the Tax Return after the Income Statement

RDP Networking reported pretax accounting income in 2016, 2017, and 2018 of $70 million, $100 million, and $100 million, respectively. The 2016 income statement includes a $30 million warranty expense that is deducted for tax purposes when paid in 2017 ($15 million) and 2018 ($15 million). The income tax rate is 40% each year.

($ in millions)	Temporary Difference			
	Originates	Reverses		
	2016	2017	2018	Total
Pretax accounting income	$ 70	$100	$100	$270
Warranty expense in the income statement	30			30
Warranty expense on the tax return		(15)	(15)	(30)
Taxable income (tax return)	$100	$ 85	$ 85	$270

In 2016, taxable income is more than pretax accounting income because the warranty expense is not deducted on the tax return until paid.

At the end of 2016, the amounts needed to record income tax for 2016 would be determined as shown in Illustration 16–4A.

Illustration 16–4A

Determining and Recording Income Taxes—2016

Because the warranty expense is subtracted in the 2016 income statement but isn't deductible on the 2016 tax return, it is added back to pretax accounting income to find taxable income.

The amounts deductible in 2017 and 2018 will later produce tax benefits that are recognized now as a deferred tax asset.

($ in millions)

	Current Year 2016	Future Deductible Amounts 2017	Future Deductible Amounts 2018	Future Taxable Amounts (total)
Pretax accounting income	$ 70			
Temporary difference:				
Warranty expense in the income statement	30	$(15)	$(15)	$(30)
Taxable income (tax return)	$100			
Enacted tax rate	40%			40%
Tax payable currently	$ 40			

Deferred Tax Asset	
beg. bal. 0	
12	
end. bal. 12	

Deferred Tax Asset	
Ending balance needed	$ 12
Less: Beginning balance	0
Change in balance	$ 12

Journal Entry at the End of 2016

Income tax expense (to balance)	28	
Deferred tax asset (determined above)	12	
Income tax payable (determined above)		40

If we continue the assumption of $85 million taxable income in each of 2017 and 2018, income tax those years would be recorded this way:

2017		
Income tax expense (to balance)	40	
Deferred tax asset ($15 million × 40%)		6
Income tax payable ($85 million × 40%)		34
2018		
Income tax expense (to balance)	40	
Deferred tax asset ($15 million × 40%)		6
Income tax payable ($85 million × 40%)		34

At the end of 2016 and 2017, the company reports a deferred tax asset for future income tax benefits. That deferred tax asset is reduced to zero by the end of 2018.

Income taxes payable in 2017 and 2018 are less because of the taxes prepaid in 2016.

Deferred Tax Asset

			($ in millions)
2016 ($30 × 40%)	12		
		6	2017 ($15 × 40%)
		6	2018 ($15 × 40%)
Balance after 3 years	0		

We also can calculate this deferred tax asset each year using the alternative perspective of looking at the "temporary book-tax difference" that exists for the warranty liability. The warranty liability starts with a book value of $30 in the balance sheet, but a tax basis of $0.

That temporary book-tax difference of $30 in 2016 falls to $15 in 2017 and then $0 in 2018 as the warranty liability is satisfied.

($ in millions)	December 31					
	2016		2017		2018	
Warranty liability:						
Accounting book value	$30	$30	$(15)	$15	$(15)	$0
Tax basis	(0)	(0)	(0)	(0)	(0)	(0)
Temporary difference	$30	$30	$(15)	$15	$(15)	$0
Tax rate		× 40%		× 40%		× 40%
Deferred tax asset	↑	$12	↑	$ 6	↑	$0
	Originating Difference		Reversing Differences			

A warranty liability is recognized for financial reporting purposes when the product is sold:

2016	Warr. exp	30	
	Liability		30

and reduced when the expense is paid:

2017	Liability	15	
	Cash		15
2018	Liability	15	
	Cash		15

The preceding is an illustration of an estimated expense that is reported in the income statement when incurred but deducted on tax returns in later years when actually paid. A second type of temporary difference that gives rise to a deferred tax asset is a *revenue* that is taxed when collected but recognized on income statements in later years when actually earned. Illustration 16–5 demonstrates this second type with a common example: deferred revenue.

Illustration 16–5

Revenue Reported on the Tax Return *before* the Income Statement

Tomorrow Publications reported pretax accounting income in 2016, 2017, and 2018 of $80 million, $115 million, and $105 million, respectively. The 2016 income statement does *not* include $20 million of magazine subscriptions received that year for one- and two-year subscriptions. The subscription revenue is reported for tax purposes in 2016. The revenue will be recognized in 2017 ($15 million) and 2018 ($5 million). The income tax rate is 40% each year.

($ in millions)	Temporary Difference			
	Originates	Reverses		
	2016	2017	2018	Total
Pretax accounting income	$ 80	$115	$105	$300
Subscription revenue in the income statement		(15)	(5)	(20)
Subscription revenue on the tax return	20	0	0	20
Taxable income (tax return)	$100	$100	$100	$300

In 2016, taxable income is more than accounting income because subscription revenue is not reported in the income statement until 2017 and 2018.

Notice that this temporary difference produces future *deductible* amounts. In 2016, taxable income is $20 million *more* than pretax accounting income because it includes the deferred subscription revenue not yet reported in the income statement. However, in 2017 and 2018 taxable income is *less* than accounting income because the subscription revenue is recognized and reported in the income statements but not on the tax returns of those two years.

A deferred tax asset is recognized when an existing temporary difference will produce future deductible amounts.

In effect, tax laws require the company to prepay the income tax on this revenue, which is a sacrifice now but will benefit the company later when the revenue is recognized but not taxed. In the meantime, the company has an asset representing this future income tax benefit.

At the end of 2016, the amounts needed to record income tax for 2016 would be determined as shown in Illustration 16–5A.

At the end of 2016 and 2017, the company reports a deferred tax asset for future tax benefits. That deferred tax asset is reduced to zero by the end of 2018.

Deferred Tax Asset

			($ in millions)
2016 ($20 × 40%)	8		
		6	2017 ($15 × 40%)
		2	2018 ($ 5 × 40%)
Balance after 3 years	0		

Income taxes payable in 2017 and 2018 are less because of the taxes prepaid in 2016.

Illustration 16–5A

Determining and Recording Income Taxes—2016

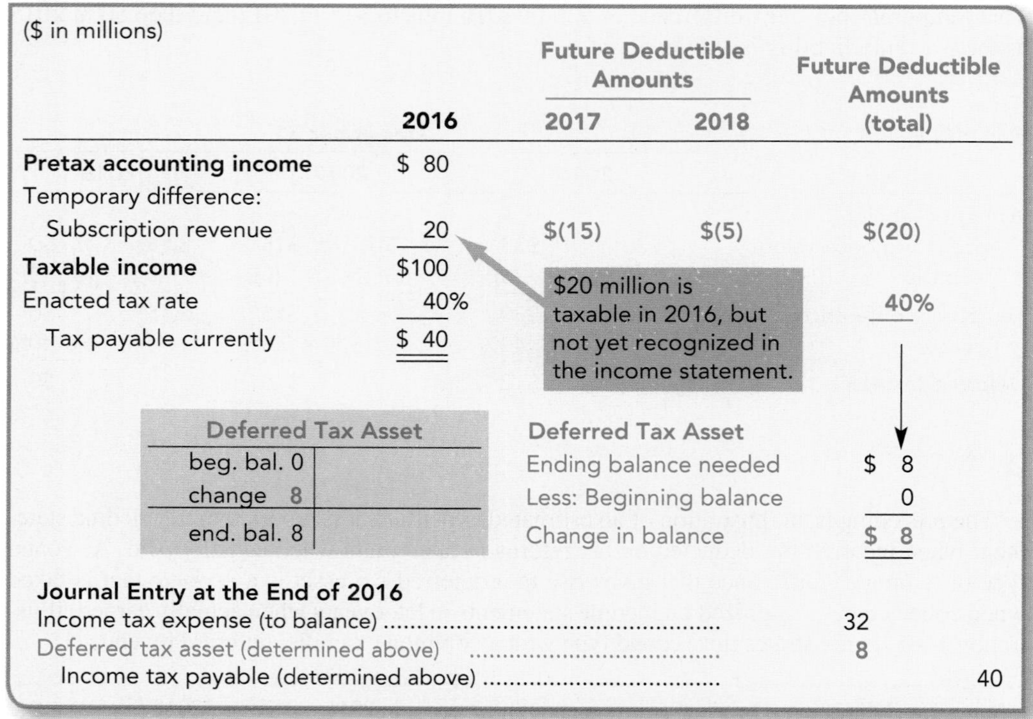

($ in millions)

	2016	Future Deductible Amounts 2017	Future Deductible Amounts 2018	Future Deductible Amounts (total)
Pretax accounting income	$ 80			
Temporary difference:				
Subscription revenue	20	$(15)	$(5)	$(20)
Taxable income	$100			
Enacted tax rate	40%			40%
Tax payable currently	$ 40			

$20 million is taxable in 2016, but not yet recognized in the income statement.

Deferred Tax Asset	
beg. bal. 0	
change 8	
end. bal. 8	

Deferred Tax Asset	
Ending balance needed	$ 8
Less: Beginning balance	0
Change in balance	$ 8

Journal Entry at the End of 2016

Income tax expense (to balance)	32	
Deferred tax asset (determined above)	8	
Income tax payable (determined above)		40

Again, we instead could determine the deferred tax asset as the future tax benefit from the reversal of a temporary difference between the balance sheet's book value of the subscription liability (a deferred revenue account) and its tax basis.[2]

A liability is recognized for financial reporting purposes when the cash is received:

2016	Cash	20	
	Liability		20

and reduced when the revenue is recognized:

2017	Liability	15	
	Revenue		15
2018	Liability	5	
	Revenue		5

From a tax perspective, there is no liability.

($ in millions)	December 31 2016		2017		2018	
Liability—subscriptions:						
Accounting book value	$20	$20	$(15)	$ 5	$(5)	$ 0
Tax basis	(0)	(0)	(0)	(0)	(0)	(0)
Temporary difference	$20	$20	$(15)	$ 5	$(5)	$ 0
Tax rate		× 40%		× 40%		× 40%
Deferred tax asset	↑ Originating Difference	$ 8	↑ Reversing Differences	$ 2	↑	$ 0

We've now worked through four examples that illustrate revenue-related and expense-related deferred tax assets and deferred tax liabilities. In each example, the journal entry to recognize tax expense included three items: income tax payable, the change in the deferred tax asset or liability, and (to balance) the debit to tax expense (or credit to tax benefit). Companies provide disclosure in the notes that help investors see these relationships. As an example, Illustrations 16–6A and 16–6B include two tables in the tax note that appeared in the February 1, 2014, annual report of **Shoe Carnival, Inc.**, a large footwear retailer.

This part of Shoe Carnival's tax note provides enough information to reproduce a journal entry that summarizes the company's 2013 tax expense. We just have to understand that

[2]It is less intuitive to view deferred revenue (Illustration 16–5) as producing future deductible amounts when the deferred revenue liability is settled than it is to view the future deductibility of an estimated expense (Illustration 16–4) as a future deductible amount. Nevertheless, the recognition of deferred tax assets for the future tax benefits of deferred revenue liability temporary differences is consistent with GAAP because these deferred revenue liabilities are reported as if they represent future refundable amounts and therefore future deductible amounts.

Illustration 16–6A

Disclosure of Tax Expense—Shoe Carnival, Inc.

Real World Financials

Note 7 - Income Taxes (in part)

The provision for income taxes consisted of:

(In thousands)	2013	2012	2011
Current:			
Federal	$15,366	$19,581	$11,318
State	1,805	2,601	1,210
Puerto Rico	185	79	0
Total current	17,356	22,261	12,528
Deferred:			
Federal	(139)	(2,692)	2,918
State	(138)	(304)	122
Puerto Rico	(444)	(350)	0
Total deferred	**(721)**	(3,346)	3,040
Total provision	$16,635	$18,915	$15,568

"total current" refers to income tax payable, "total deferred" refers to the total change in deferred tax assets and liabilities, and "total provision" refers to income tax expense:

Income tax expense	16,635	
Deferred tax assets and liabilities	721	
Income tax payable		17,356

We can see that Shoe Carnival's operations caused total deferred tax assets and liabilities to change by a debit of **$721** during 2013. Let's verify that change by comparing the 2013 fiscal year-end (February 1, 2014) and 2012 fiscal year-end (February 2, 2013) balances of Shoe Carnival's deferred tax assets and liabilities, shown in Illustration 16–6B.

Illustration 16–6B

Disclosure of Deferred Tax Assets and Liabilities—Shoe Carnival, Inc.

Real World Financials

Note 7 - Income Taxes (in part)

Deferred income taxes are the result of temporary differences in the recognition of revenue and expense for tax and financial reporting purposes. The sources of these differences and the tax effect of each are as follows:

(In thousands)	February 1, 2014		February 2, 2013	
Deferred tax assets:				
Accrued rent	$ 3,543		$ 2,878	
Accrued compensation	5,625		5,191	
Accrued employee benefits	506		479	
Inventory	411		916	
Self-insurance reserves	593		494	
Lease incentives	10,003		7,438	
Net operating loss carryforward	449		359	
Other	396		337	
Total deferred tax assets	21,526		18,092	
Deferred tax liabilities:				
Depreciation	15,265		12,801	
Capitalized costs	1,180		1,017	
Puerto Rico net operating loss carryforward	444		350	
Other	3		11	
Total deferred tax liabilities	16,892		14,179	
Net deferred tax asset	4,634	−	3,913	= **$721**
Less current deferred income tax benefit	(1,208)		(2,914)	
Long-term deferred income taxes	$ 3,426		$ 999	

We can see from Illustration 16–6B that Shoe Carnival has a net deferred tax asset of $4,634 as of February 1, 2014 (the end of its 2013 fiscal year), equal to its total deferred tax asset of $21,526 less its total deferred tax liability of $16,892. Compared to the net deferred tax asset of $3,913 at February 2, 2013, we see that the net deferred tax asset has increased by $4,634 − 3,913 = **$721**. That's the amount of change in deferred taxes we saw in Illustration 16–6A.

Additional Consideration

The amount of change in deferred taxes reconciles perfectly between the tables shown in Illustrations 16–6A and 16–6B. That won't always be the case in practice because the table shown in Illustration 16–6A focuses on taxes from *continuing operations*, but the deferred tax assets and liabilities listed in Illustration 16–6B relate to all aspects of the company. For example, if Shoe Carnival had deferred taxes associated with discontinued operations or other comprehensive income items, or if it had added deferred tax assets and liabilities from an acquisition during the year, the change in deferred taxes from continuing operations wouldn't capture everything that affected deferred tax assets and liabilities.

Valuation Allowance

LO16–3

We recognize deferred tax assets for all deductible temporary differences.[3] However, we then reduce a deferred tax asset by a valuation allowance if it is "more likely than not" that some portion or all of the deferred tax asset will not be realized.[4] Remember, a future deductible amount reduces taxable income in the future and saves taxes only if there is taxable income to be reduced when that deduction is available. So, a **valuation allowance** is needed if taxable income is anticipated to be insufficient to realize the tax benefit.

For example, let's say that in the previous illustration management determines that it's more likely than not that $3 million of the deferred tax asset ultimately will not be realized. The deferred tax asset would be reduced by the creation of a valuation allowance as follows:

A valuation allowance is needed if it is more likely than not that some portion or all of a deferred tax asset will not be realized.

	($ in millions)	
Income tax expense	3	
Valuation allowance—deferred tax asset		3

The effect is to increase the income tax expense as a result of reduced expectations of future tax savings. In the 2016 balance sheet, the deferred tax asset would be reported at its estimated net realizable value:

Deferred tax asset	$8
Less: Valuation allowance—deferred tax asset	(3)
	$5

This is not a new concept for you. You've reduced assets before using a valuation allowance. Suppose, for example, that you have accounts receivable of $8 million but expect that $3 million of that amount will not ultimately be collected from your customers. You would reduce the asset indirectly using a valuation allowance:

Accounts receivable	$8
Less: Allowance for uncollectible accounts	(3)
	$5

[3]Unless the deductibility itself is uncertain. In that case, whether we recognize a deferred tax asset (and if so, its amount) is determined in accordance with FASB ASC 740–10–25: Income Taxes–Overall–Recognition (previously FIN 48) discussed later in the chapter.

[4]"More likely than not" means a likelihood of more than 50%, FASB ASC 740–10–30: Income Taxes–Overall–Initial Measurement (previously "Accounting for Income Taxes," Statement of Financial Accounting Standards No. 109 (Norwalk, Conn.: FASB, 1992), par. 17).

Additional Consideration

The decision as to whether a valuation allowance is needed should be based on the weight of all available evidence. The real question is whether or not there will be sufficient taxable income in future years for the anticipated tax benefit to be realized. The benefit of future deductible amounts can be realized only if future income is at least equal to the deferred deductions. After all, a deduction reduces taxes only if it reduces taxable income.

All evidence—both positive and negative—should be considered. For instance, operating losses in recent years or anticipated circumstances that would adversely affect future operations would constitute negative evidence. On the other hand, a strong history of profitable operations or sizable, existing contracts would constitute positive evidence of sufficient taxable income to be able to realize the deferred tax asset.

Managerial actions that could be taken to reduce or eliminate a valuation allowance when deferred tax assets are not otherwise expected to be realized must be considered. These tax-planning strategies include any prudent and feasible actions management might take to realize a tax benefit while it is available.

This having been said, it should be clear that the decision as to whether or not a valuation allowance is used, as well as how large the allowance should be, rests squarely on managerial judgment. Because that decision directly impacts the amount of income tax expense and therefore reported income, it has obvious implications for earnings quality assessment from an analyst's perspective.

At the end of each reporting period, the valuation allowance is reevaluated. The appropriate balance is decided on and the valuation allowance is adjusted—up or down—to create that balance. For instance, let's say that at the end of the following year, 2017, available evidence now indicates that **$500,000** of the deferred tax asset at the end of 2017 ultimately will not be realized. We would adjust the valuation allowance to reflect the indicated amount:

	($ in millions)	
Valuation allowance—deferred tax asset ($3 million − 0.5 million).........	2.5	
Income tax expense		2.5

Valuation Allowance—Deferred Tax Asset

	Debit	Credit
1/1/2017		3
	2.5	
12/31/2017		0.5

The disclosure note shown in Illustration 16–7 accompanied the February 1, 2014, annual report of **Sears Holdings Corporation**, which operates a variety of retailers including Sears, Kmart, and Lands' End. Sears disclosed that it had deferred tax assets of $3.7 billion, offset by a valuation allowance of $3.4 billion. Why such a large valuation allowance? Illustration 16–7 provides Sears's depressing explanation.

Note 10 - Income Taxes (in part)
Management assesses the available positive and negative evidence to estimate if sufficient future taxable income will be generated to use the existing deferred tax assets. A significant piece of objective negative evidence evaluated was the cumulative loss incurred over the three-year periods ended February 1, 2014, February 2, 2013 and January 28, 2012.

Illustration 16–7
Explanation for Valuation Allowance—Sears Holding Corporation

Real World Financials

Given its large recent losses, Sears cannot argue that it's more likely than not that it will have sufficient future income to utilize its deferred tax assets, so it must record a large valuation allowance.

Permanent Differences

LO16–4

So far, we've dealt with temporary differences between the reported amount of an asset or liability in the financial statements and its tax basis. However, some differences aren't temporary. Rather, they are caused by transactions and events that under existing tax law will *never* affect taxable income or taxes payable. Interest received from investments in

FINANCIAL Reporting Case

Q3, p. 933

bonds issued by state and municipal governments, for instance, is exempt from taxation. Interest revenue of this type is, of course, reported as revenue on the recipient's income statement but not on its tax return—not now, not later. So, there is a permanent difference between pretax accounting income and taxable income. This situation will *not* reverse in a later year—the tax-free income will *never* be reported on the tax return.

Illustration 16–8 provides examples of permanent differences that commonly occur in practice.

Illustration 16–8

Differences without Deferred Tax Consequences

Provisions of the tax laws, in some instances, dictate that the amount of a revenue that is taxable or expense that is deductible permanently differs from the amount reported in the income statement.

- Interest received from investments in bonds issued by state and municipal governments (not taxable).
- Investment expenses incurred to obtain tax-exempt income (not tax deductible).
- Life insurance proceeds on the death of an insured executive (not taxable).
- Premiums paid for life insurance policies when the payer is the beneficiary (not tax deductible).
- Compensation expense pertaining to some employee stock option plans (not tax deductible).
- Expenses due to violations of the law (not tax deductible).
- Difference in tax paid on foreign income permanently reinvested in the foreign country and the amount that would have been paid if taxed at U.S. rates.
- Portion of dividends received from U.S. corporations that is not taxable due to the dividends received deduction.[5]
- Tax deduction for depletion of natural resources (percentage depletion) that permanently exceeds the income statement depletion expense (cost depletion).[6]

It's easy to account for permanent differences. We calculate taxes payable according to the tax law, and since permanent differences are never taxable, we don't create a deferred tax asset or liability. Therefore, tax expense is determined by tax payable. The term *permanent difference* doesn't refer to a difference between tax payable and tax expense—those are the same with respect to this item. Rather, it refers to a difference between taxable income and pretax accounting income. That's why we adjust pretax accounting income in the illustrations that follow to eliminate permanent differences when calculating tax payable.

To compare temporary and **permanent differences**, we can modify Illustration 16–1 to include nontaxable income in Kent Land Management's 2017 pretax accounting income. We do this in Illustration 16–9 on the next page.

Permanent differences affect a company's effective tax rate.

The *effective tax rate* equals tax expense divided by pretax accounting income.

A company's **effective tax rate** is calculated by dividing the company's tax expense by its pretax accounting income. Permanent differences affect the effective tax rate because they affect pretax accounting income. Let's look at Illustration 16–9 to understand why that's the case. In Illustration 16–9, the effective tax rate is \$56 million ÷ \$145 million, or 38.6%. That's with \$5 million of municipal bond interest included in the \$145 million of pretax accounting income. If, instead, pretax accounting income hadn't included the \$5 million of municipal bond interest, it would have been only \$140 million, and the effective tax rate would have been \$56 million ÷ \$140 million, or 40%. Including the municipal bond interest in pretax accounting income increased the denominator of the effective tax rate, so it produced a lower effective tax rate.

More generally, nontaxable revenues and gains like municipal bond interest are permanent differences that result in *higher* pretax accounting income, so they produce effective tax rates that are *lower* than the statutory tax rate. Likewise, nondeductible expenses and losses are permanent differences that result in *lower* pretax accounting income, so they produce effective tax rates that are *higher* than the statutory tax rate. Companies are required to report a reconciliation between their effective and statutory tax rates in disclosure notes, as shown in Illustration 16–10's example from **Walmart**'s financial statements for the fiscal year ended January 31, 2014.

[5]When a corporation owns shares of another U.S. corporation, a percentage of the dividends from those shares is exempt from taxation due to the dividends received deduction. The percentage is 70% if the investor owns less than 20% of the investee's shares, 80% for 20% to 80% ownership, and 100% for more than 80% ownership.

[6]The cost of natural resources is reported as depletion expense over their extraction period for financial reporting purposes; but tax rules prescribe sometimes different percentages of cost to be deducted for tax purposes. There usually is a difference between the cost depletion and percentage depletion that doesn't eventually reverse.

Illustration 16–9

Temporary and Permanent Differences

Kent Land Management reported pretax accounting income in 2016 of $100 million except for additional income of $40 million from installment sales of property and $5 million interest from investments in municipal bonds in 2016. The installment sales income is reported for tax purposes in 2017 ($10 million) and 2018 ($30 million). The enacted tax rate is 40% each year.

($ in millions)	Current Year 2016	Future Taxable Amounts 2017	2018	Future Taxable Amounts (total)
Pretax accounting income	$145			
Permanent difference:				
Municipal bond interest	(5)			
Temporary difference:				
Installment income	(40)	$10	$30	$40
Taxable income (tax return)	$100			
Enacted tax rate	40%			40%
Tax payable currently	$ 40			

Deferred Tax Liability	
	0 beg. bal.
	16
	16 end. bal.

Deferred Tax Liability	
Ending balance needed	$16
Less: Beginning balance	0
Change in balance	$16

Journal Entry at the End of 2016

Income tax expense (to balance)	56	
Income tax payable (determined above)		40
Deferred tax liability (determined above)		16

Because interest on municipal bonds is tax exempt, it is reported only in the income statement. This difference between pretax accounting income and taxable income does not reverse later.

Illustration 16–10

Effective Tax Rate—Walmart

Real World Financials

Note 9: Taxes (in part)

Effective Tax Rate Reconciliation

	Fiscal Year Ended January 31, 2014	2013	2012
U.S. statutory tax rate	35.0%	35.0%	35.0%
U.S. state income taxes, net of federal income tax benefit	2.0%	1.7%	2.0%
Income taxed outside the U.S.	(2.8)%	(2.6)%	(2.8)%
Net impact of repatriated international earnings	(1.4)%	(2.5)%	(0.3)%
Other, net	0.1%	(0.6)%	(1.3)%
Effective income tax rate	32.9%	31.0%	32.6%

Additional Consideration

Accounting for taxes on unrepatriated foreign earnings. The biggest "permanent difference" in many companies' effective tax rate reconciliation relates to taxes on foreign earnings. Companies often seek to minimize their tax bills by arranging their operations so their income is recognized outside the United States in jurisdictions that have low

(continued)

(concluded)

tax rates. Those lower tax bills are viewed as creating permanent differences so long as the company does not intend to "repatriate" the foreign earnings by transferring those earnings back to the United States. A company still must include the foreign income in pretax accounting income on the income statement, but that income is taxed at the lower foreign rate, so income tax payable is lower, tax expense is lower, and the company's effective tax rate is lower.

What if management changes its mind and decides to repatriate foreign earnings? In that case, the company must pay tax at the higher U.S. rate, making up the tax previously avoided. Companies usually don't want to pay that tax, so you will hear companies talk about having cash "trapped" overseas and needing to raise cash in other ways. For example, in 2013 Apple announced that it would be returning $60 billion to shareholders by repurchasing stock. Apple had $145 billion of cash and short-term investments at its disposal, so no problem, right? Wrong. Only $45 billion of Apple's cash was in the United States, so it issued $17 billion in bonds to make up the shortfall instead of paying tax to repatriate cash from foreign operations.

If a company does repatriate foreign earnings and repatriates cash, they have a higher tax bill and higher tax expense. Pretax accounting income is unaffected (remember, that income was recognized in the period in which it was earned), so the higher tax expense results in a higher effective tax rate. The company's original choice not to repatriate created a "permanent" difference that reduced the effective tax rate, and the company's later decision to repatriate creates an offsetting "permanent" difference that goes in the other direction.

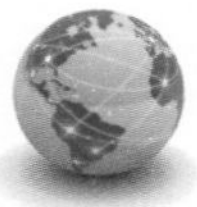

International Financial Reporting Standards

● LO16–11

Non-Tax Differences Affect Taxes. Despite the similar approaches for accounting for taxation under *IAS No. 12,* "Income Tax,"[7] and U.S. GAAP, differences in reported amounts for deferred taxes are among the most frequent between the two reporting approaches. The reason is that a great many of the nontax differences between IFRS and U.S. GAAP affect deferred taxes as well.

For example, we noted in Chapter 13 that we accrue a loss contingency under U.S. GAAP if it's both probable and can be reasonably estimated and that IFRS guidelines are similar, but the threshold is "more likely than not." This is a lower threshold than "probable." In this chapter, we noted that accruing a loss contingency (like warranty expense) in the income statement leads to a deferred tax asset if it can't be deducted on the tax return until a later period. As a result, under the lower threshold of IFRS, we might record a loss contingency and thus a deferred tax asset, but under U.S. GAAP we might record neither. So, even though accounting for deferred taxes is the same, accounting for loss contingencies is different, causing a difference in the reported amounts of deferred taxes under IFRS and U.S. GAAP.

Concept Review Exercise

TEMPORARY AND PERMANENT DIFFERENCES

Mid-South Cellular Systems began operations in 2016. That year the company reported pretax accounting income of $70 million, which included the following amounts:

1. Compensation expense of $3 million related to employee stock option plans granted to organizers was reported in the 2016 income statement. This expense is not deductible for tax purposes.
2. An asset with a four-year useful life was acquired last year. It is depreciated by the straight-line method in the income statement. MACRS is used on the tax return, causing

[7]"Income Taxes," International Accounting Standard No. 12 (IASCF), as amended effective January 1, 2014.

deductions for depreciation to be more than straight-line depreciation the first two years but less than straight-line depreciation the next two years ($ in millions):

	Depreciation		
	Income Statement	**Tax Return**	**Difference**
2016	$150	$198	$ (48)
2017	150	264	(114)
2018	150	90	60
2019	150	48	102
	$600	$600	$ 0

The enacted tax rate is 40%.

Required:

Prepare the journal entry to record Mid-South Cellular's income taxes for 2016.

Solution

($ in millions)

		Future Taxable Amounts			
	Current Year 2016	**2017**	**2018**	**2019**	**Future Taxable Amounts (total)**
Pretax accounting income	$70				
Permanent difference:					
Compensation expense	3				
Temporary difference:					
Depreciation	(48)	$(114)	$60	$102	$ 48
Taxable income (tax return)	$25				
Enacted tax rate	40%				40%
Tax payable currently	$10				

Because the compensation expense is not tax deductible, taxable income does not include the $3 million deduction and is higher than accounting income by that amount.

Deferred Tax Liability	
	0 beg. bal.
	19.2
	19.2 end. bal.

Deferred Tax Liability	
Ending balance needed	$19.2
Less: Beginning balance	0.0
Change in balance	$19.2

Journal Entry at the End of 2016

Income tax expense (to balance)	29.2	
Income tax payable (determined above)		10.0
Deferred tax liability (determined above)		19.2

Income tax expense is composed of: (1) the tax payable currently and (2) the tax deferred until later.

Other Tax Accounting Issues

PART B

Tax Rate Considerations

To measure the deferred tax liability or asset, we multiply the temporary difference by the currently *enacted* tax rate that will be effective in the year(s) the temporary difference reverses.[8] We do not base calculations on *anticipated* legislation that would alter the

● LO16–5

[8]The current U.S. corporate tax rate is 34%, or 35% for corporations with taxable income over $75,000. Most states tax corporate income at rates less than 10%. We use 40% in most of our illustrations to simplify calculations.

company's tax rate. A conceptual case can be made that expected rate changes should be anticipated when measuring the deferred tax liability or asset. However, this is one of many examples of the frequent trade-off between relevance and reliability. In this case, the FASB chose to favor reliability by waiting until an anticipated change actually is enacted into law before recognizing its tax consequences.

When Enacted Tax Rates Differ

A deferred tax liability (or asset) is based on enacted tax rates and laws.

Existing tax laws may call for enacted tax rates to be different in future years in which a temporary difference is expected to reverse. When a phased-in change in rates is scheduled to occur, the specific tax rates of each future year are multiplied by the amounts reversing in each of those years. The total is the deferred tax liability or asset.

To illustrate, let's again modify our Kent Land Management illustration, this time to assume a scheduled change in tax rates. See Illustration 16–11.

Illustration 16–11

Scheduled Change in Tax Rates

Kent Land Management reported pretax accounting income in 2016 of $100 million except for additional income of $40 million from installment sales of property and $5 million interest from investments in municipal bonds in 2016. The installment sales income is reported for tax purposes in 2017 ($10 million) and 2018 ($30 million). The enacted tax rates are 40% for 2016 and 2017, and 35% for 2018.

The tax effects of the future taxable amounts depend on the tax rates at which those amounts will be taxed.

($ in millions)	Current Year	Future Taxable Amounts			
	2016	**2017**	**2018**		**(total)**
Pretax accounting income	$145				
Permanent difference:					
Municipal bond interest	(5)				
Temporary difference:					
Installment income	(40)	$10	$ 30		
Taxable income (tax return)	$100				
Enacted tax rate	40%	40%	35%		
Tax payable currently	$ 40				
Deferred tax liability		$ 4 +	$10.5	=	$14.5

Deferred Tax Liability	
	0 beg. bal.
	14.5
	14.5 end. bal.

Deferred Tax Liability	
Ending balance needed	$14.5
Less: Beginning balance	0.0
Change in balance	$14.5

Journal Entry at the End of 2016

Income tax expense (to balance)	54.5	
Income tax payable (determined above)		40.0
Deferred tax liability (determined above)		14.5

Be sure to note that the 2017 rate (40%) as well as the 2018 rate (35%) already is enacted into law as of 2016 when the deferred tax liability is established. In the next section we discuss how to handle a change resulting from new legislation.

Changes in Tax Laws or Rates

As a result of a change [in tax law or rate] deferred tax consequences become larger or smaller.

Tax laws sometimes change. If a change in a tax law or rate occurs, any existing tax liability or asset must be adjusted. Remember, the deferred tax liability or asset is meant to reflect the amount to be paid or recovered in the future. When legislation changes that amount, the deferred tax liability or asset also should change. The effect is reflected in operating income in the year of the enactment of the change in the tax law or rate.[9]

For clarification, reconsider the previous illustration. Without a change in tax rates and assuming that pretax accounting income reported in the income statement in 2017 is $100 million (with no additional temporary or permanent differences), the 2017 income tax amounts would be determined as shown in Illustration 16–11A.

Illustration 16–11A
Reversal of Temporary Difference *without* a Tax Rate Change

($ in millions)	2016	Current Year 2017	Future Taxable Amount 2018
Pretax accounting income		$100	
Temporary difference:			
Installment income	(40)	10	$30
Taxable income (tax return)		$110	
Enacted tax rate		40%	35%
Tax payable currently		$ 44	

The 40% 2017 rate and the 35% 2018 rate are established by previously enacted legislation.

Deferred Tax Liability	
	14.5 beg. bal.
4	
	10.5 end. bal.

Deferred Tax Liability	
Ending balance needed	$10.5
Less: Beginning balance	(14.5)
Change in balance	$ (4.0)

Journal Entry at the End of 2017

Income tax expense (to balance)	40	
Deferred tax liability (determined above)	4	
Income tax payable (determined above)		44

Now assume Congress passed a new tax law in 2017 that will cause the 2018 tax rate to be 30% instead of the previously scheduled 35% rate. Because a deferred tax liability was established in 2016 with the expectation that the 2018 taxable amount would be taxed at 35%, it would now be adjusted to reflect taxation at 30%, instead. This is demonstrated in Illustration 16–11B.

When a tax rate changes, the deferred tax liability or asset should be adjusted with the effect reflected in operating income in the year of the change.

Notice that the methods used to determine the deferred tax liability and the change in that balance are the same as without the rate change—the calculation merely uses the new rate (30%) rather than the old rate (35%). So, recalculating the balance needed in the deferred tax liability each period and comparing that amount with any previously existing balance automatically takes into account tax rate changes.

Also notice that the income tax expense ($38.5 million) is $1.5 million less than it would have been without the tax rate change ($40 million). The effect of the change is included in income tax expense. In fact, this is highlighted if we separate the previous entry into its component parts: (1) record the income tax expense without the tax rate change and (2) separately record the adjustment of the deferred tax liability for the change.

Journal Entry at the End of 2017	($ in millions)	
Income tax expense	40	
Deferred tax liability	4	
Income tax payable		44
Deferred tax liability [$30 million × (35% − 30%)]	1.5	
Income tax expense		1.5

[9]FASB ASC 740–10–35: Income Taxes–Overall–Subsequent Measurement (previously "Accounting for Income Taxes," Statement of Financial Accounting Standards No. 109 (Norwalk, Conn.: FASB, 1992)).

Illustration 16–11B

Reversal of Temporary Difference with a Tax Rate Change

The deferred tax liability would have been $10.5 million (30 million × 35%) if the tax rate had not changed.

($ in millions)

	2016	Current Year 2017	Future Taxable Amount 2018
Pretax accounting income		$100	
Temporary difference:			
Installment income	(40)	10	$ 30
Taxable income (tax return)		$110	
Enacted tax rate		40%	30%*
Tax payable currently		$ 44	

*2018 rate enacted into law in 2014.

Deferred Tax Liability	
	14.5 beg. bal.
5.5	
	9 end. bal.

Deferred Tax Liability	
Ending balance	$ 9.0
Less: Beginning balance	(14.5)
Change in balance	$ (5.5)

Journal Entry at the End of 2017

	Debit	Credit
Income tax expense (to balance)	38.5	
Deferred tax liability (determined above)	5.5	
Income tax payable (determined above)		44.0

The tax consequence of a change in a tax law or rate is recognized in the period the change is enacted. In this case, the consequence of a lower tax rate is a reduced deferred tax liability, recognized as a reduction in income tax expense in 2017 when the change occurs.

Multiple Temporary Differences

LO16–6 It would be unusual for any but a very small company to have only a single temporary difference in any given year. Having multiple temporary differences, though, doesn't change any of the principles you've learned so far in connection with single differences. We categorize all temporary differences according to whether they create (a) future taxable amounts or (b) future deductible amounts. The total of the future taxable amounts then is multiplied by the future tax rate to determine the appropriate balance for the deferred tax liability, and the total of the future deductible amounts is multiplied by the future tax rate to determine the appropriate balance for the deferred tax asset. This is demonstrated in Illustration 16–12.

Look at Illustration 16–12A to see how Eli-Wallace determines the income tax amounts for 2016. Then turn to Illustration 16–12B on page 956 to see how those amounts are determined for 2017.

Illustration 16–12

Multiple Temporary Differences

2016

During 2016, its first year of operations, Eli-Wallace Distributors reported pretax accounting income of $200 million which included the following amounts:

1. Income (net) from installment sales of warehouses in 2016 of $9 million will be reported for tax purposes in 2017 ($5 million) and 2018 ($4 million).
2. Depreciation is reported by the straight-line method on an asset with a four-year useful life. On the tax return, deductions for depreciation will be more than straight-line depreciation the first two years but less than straight-line depreciation the next two years ($ in millions):

	Income Statement	Tax Return	Difference
2016	$ 50	$ 66	$(16)
2017	50	88	(38)
2018	50	30	20
2019	50	16	34
	$200	$200	$ 0

(continued)

(concluded)

3. Estimated warranty expense will be deductible on the tax return when actually paid during the next two years. Estimated deductions are as follows ($ in millions):

	Income Statement	Tax Return	Difference
2016	$7		$7
2017		$4	(4)
2018		3	(3)
	$7	$7	$0

2017

During 2017, pretax accounting income of $200 million included an estimated loss of $1 million from having accrued a loss contingency. The loss is expected to be paid in 2019 at which time it will be tax deductible.

The enacted tax rate is 40% each year.

Illustration 16–12A

Multiple Temporary Differences—2016

($ in millions)

	Current Year 2016	Future Taxable (Deductible) Amounts 2017	2018	2019	Future Taxable Amounts (total)	Future Deductible Amounts (total)
Pretax accounting income	$ 200					
Temporary differences:						
Installment sales	(9)	$ 5	$ 4		$ 9	
Depreciation	(16)	(38)	20	$34	16	
Warranty expense	7	(4)	(3)			$ (7)
Taxable income (tax return)	$ 182				$25	(7)
Enacted tax rate	40%				40%	40%
Tax payable currently	$72.8					
Deferred tax liability					$10	
Deferred tax asset						$(2.8)

Deferred Tax Liability	
	0 beg. bal.
	10
	10 end. bal.

Deferred Tax Asset	
beg. bal. 0	
2.8	
end. bal. 2.8	

	Deferred Tax Liability	Deferred Tax Asset
Ending balances:	$10	$ 2.8
Less: Beginning balances:	(0)	(0.0)
Change in balances	$10	$ 2.8

Journal Entry at the End of 2016

	Debit	Credit
Income tax expense (to balance)	80.0	
Deferred tax asset (determined above)	2.8	
Deferred tax liability (determined above)		10.0
Income tax payable (determined above)		72.8

Temporary differences are grouped according to whether they create future *taxable* amounts or future *deductible* amounts.

The balances needed in the deferred tax liability and the deferred tax asset are separately determined.

Income tax expense is composed of three components: (1) the tax payable currently plus (2) the tax deferred until later, reduced by (3) the deferred tax benefit.

Of course, if a phased-in change in rates is scheduled to occur, it would be necessary to determine the total of the future taxable amounts and the total of the future deductible amounts for each future year as outlined previously. Then the specific tax rates of each future year would be multiplied by the two totals in each of those years. Those annual tax effects would then be summed to find the balances for the deferred tax liability and the deferred tax asset.

Net Operating Losses

A **net operating loss** (NOL) is negative taxable income: tax-deductible expenses exceed taxable revenues. Of course, there is no tax payable for the year a net operating loss occurs because there's no taxable income. In addition, tax laws permit a net operating loss to be used

● LO16–7

Illustration 16–12B
Multiple Temporary Differences—2017

The future taxable amount of installment sales ($4 million) is equal to the cumulative temporary difference ($9 million – 5 million).

Similarly, the total of other future taxable and deductible amounts is equal to the cumulative temporary differences in the related assets and liabilities.

Analysis indicates that the deferred tax liability should be increased further and the deferred tax asset should be reduced.

($ in millions)

	2016	Current Year 2017	Future Taxable (Deductible) Amounts 2018	2019	Future Taxable Amounts (total)*	Future Deductible Amounts (total)*
Pretax accounting income		$200				
Temporary differences:						
Installment sales	$ (9)	$ 5	$ 4		$ 4	
Depreciation	(16)	(38)	20	$34	54	
Warranty expense	7	(4)	(3)			$ (3)
Estimated loss		1		(1)		(1)
Taxable income (tax return)		$164			$58	$ (4)
Enacted tax rate		40%			40%	40%
Tax payable currently		$ 65.6				
			Deferred tax liability		$23.2	
			Deferred tax asset		↓	$(1.6)

Deferred Tax Liability		Deferred Tax Asset	
	10.0 beg. bal.	beg. bal. 2.8	
	13.2		1.2
	23.2 end. bal.	end. bal. 1.6	

Deferred Tax Liability	Deferred Tax Liability	Deferred Tax Asset
Ending balance:	$23.2	$ 1.6
Less: Beginning balance:	(10.0)	(2.8)
Change in balances	$13.2	$(1.2)

Journal Entry at the End of 2017

Income tax expense (to balance)	80.0	
Deferred tax asset (determined above)		1.2
Deferred tax liability (determined above)		13.2
Deferred tax payable (determined above)		65.6

*Total future taxable and deductible amounts also are equal to the cumulative temporary differences in the related assets and liabilities.

to reduce taxable income in other, profitable years. Why do the tax laws permit that offsetting? Well, let's consider two imaginary companies. Volatile Co. has negative income some years and positive income other years that averages out to $0 income over time. Stable Co. has $0 income each year. It wouldn't be fair to tax Volatile in the good years and provide no relief in the bad years, while not taxing Stable at all, because Volatile and Stable generate the same total amount of income over time. It's more fair to allow Volatile to offset the income in its good years with the losses in its bad years when determining how much tax it should pay.

Offsetting operating profits with NOLs is achieved by either a carryback of the NOL to prior years or a carryforward of the NOL to later years, or both. In essence, the tax deductible expenses that can't be deducted this year because they exceed taxable revenues can be deducted in other years. An net operating loss can be carried back 2 years and forward for up to 20 years:

Carryforward ⟶ Up to 20 Years

2014	2015	LOSS	2017	2018	2019	⟶	2035	2036

2 years ⟵ Carryback

Tax laws permit a choice. A company can use a **net operating loss carryback** if taxable income was reported in either of the two previous years.[10] By reducing taxable income of a previous year, the company can receive an immediate refund of taxes paid that year.

[10]Actually, a carryback is automatic unless a company elects to forgo the carryback in favor of a carryforward.

If taxable income was not reported in either of the two previous years or higher tax rates are anticipated in the future, a company might elect to forgo the net operating loss carryback and carry the NOL forward for up to 20 years to offset taxable income of those years. Even if an NOL carryback is used, any NOL that remains after the two-year carryback can be carried forward. The carryforward election is a choice that must be made in the year the NOL occurs, and the choice is irrevocable. It usually is advantageous to carry back NOLs because by filing an amended tax return to get a refund, a company can realize the benefit much sooner than if the NOL is carried forward.

The accounting question is: *When* should the tax benefit created by a net operating loss be recognized in the income statement? The answer is: In the year the loss occurs.

Net Operating Loss Carryforward

First consider an NOL carryforward. You have learned in this chapter that a deferred tax asset is recognized for the future tax benefit of temporary differences that create future deductible amounts. A net operating loss carryforward also creates future deductible amounts. Logically, then, a deferred tax asset is recognized for a net operating loss carryforward also. This is demonstrated in Illustration 16–13.

Illustration 16–13
Net Operating Loss Carryforward

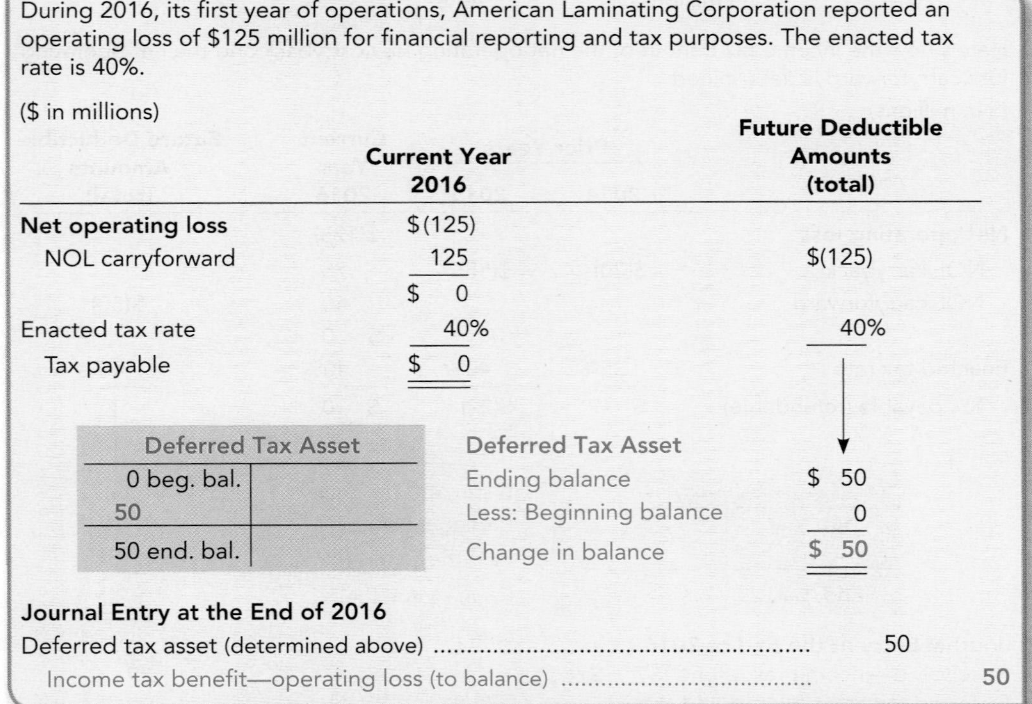

During 2016, its first year of operations, American Laminating Corporation reported an operating loss of $125 million for financial reporting and tax purposes. The enacted tax rate is 40%.

($ in millions)

	Current Year 2016	Future Deductible Amounts (total)
Net operating loss	$(125)	
NOL carryforward	125	$(125)
	$ 0	
Enacted tax rate	40%	40%
Tax payable	$ 0	

Deferred Tax Asset	
0 beg. bal.	
50	
50 end. bal.	

Deferred Tax Asset	
Ending balance	$ 50
Less: Beginning balance	0
Change in balance	$ 50

Journal Entry at the End of 2016

Deferred tax asset (determined above)	50	
Income tax benefit—operating loss (to balance)		50

A *net operating loss (NOL) carryforward* can be deducted from taxable income in future years.

The tax benefit of being able to deduct amounts in the future represents a deferred tax asset.

The income tax benefit of a net operating loss carryforward is recognized for accounting purposes in the year the net operating loss occurs. Just as we reduce pretax income by tax expense to calculate net income, we reduce a pretax loss by its tax benefit to calculate a net loss. That way, the net after-tax operating loss shown on the income statement reflects the tax savings that the operating loss is expected to create.

Income Statement (partial)

	($ in millions)
Operating loss before income taxes	$(125)
Less: Income tax benefit—net operating loss	50
Net loss	$ (75)

The income tax benefit of a net operating loss carryback, like a carryforward, is recognized in the year the net operating loss occurs.

VALUATION ALLOWANCE. Just as for all deductible temporary differences, deferred tax assets are recognized for any net operating loss without regard to the likelihood of having taxable income in future years sufficient to absorb future deductible amounts.

However, the deferred tax asset is then reduced by a valuation allowance if it is more likely than not that some portion or all of the deferred tax asset will not be realized. Remember, a valuation allowance both reduces the net deferred tax asset and increases the income tax expense just as if that portion of the deferred tax asset had not been recognized.

Net Operating Loss Carryback

A net operating loss must be applied to the earlier year first and then brought forward to the next year.

To compare the treatment of a net operating loss carryback, let's modify the illustration to assume that there was taxable income in the two years prior to the net operating loss and that American Laminating will utilize the NOL carryback (see Illustration 16–14). Note

Illustration 16–14

Net Operating Loss Carryback and Carryforward

A *net operating loss (NOL) carryback* can be deducted from taxable income in the two prior years, creating a refund of taxes paid for those years.

The portion of a net operating loss that remains after a carryback is carried forward.

The income tax benefit of a net operating loss carryforward is recognized in the year the operating loss occurs.

During 2016, American Laminating Corporation reported a net operating loss of $125 million for financial reporting and tax purposes. The enacted tax rate is 40% for 2016. Taxable income, tax rates, and income taxes paid in the two previous years were as follows:

	Taxable Income	Taxable Rates	Income Taxes Paid
2014	$20 million	35%	$ 7 million
2015	55 million	40%	22 million

Here's how the income tax benefit of the net operating loss carryback and the net operating loss carryforward is determined:
($ in millions)

	Prior Years		Current Year	Future Deductible Amounts
	2014	2015	2016	(total)
Net operating loss			$(125)	
NOL carryback	$(20)	$(55)	75	
NOL carryforward			50	$(50)
			$ 0	
Enacted tax rate	35%	40%	40%	40%
Tax payable (refundable)	$ (7)	$(22)	$ 0	

Deferred Tax Asset	
beg. bal. 0	
20	
end. bal. 20	

Deferred Tax Asset	
Ending balance	$ 20
Less: Beginning balance	0
Change in balance	$ 20

Journal Entry at the End of 2016

Receivable—income tax refund ($7 + 22)	29	
Deferred tax asset (determined above)	20	
Income tax benefit—operating loss (to balance)		49

that the net operating loss must be applied to the earlier year first and then brought forward to the next year. If any of the NOL remains after reducing taxable income to zero in the two previous years, the remainder is carried forward to future years as a net operating loss carryforward.

		($ in millions)
Operating loss before income taxes		$(125)
Income tax benefit:		
Tax refund from net operating loss carryback	$29	
Future tax savings from net operating loss carryforward	20	49
Net loss		$ (76)

The income tax benefit of both a net operating loss carryback and a net operating loss carry forward is recognized for accounting purposes in the year the NOL occurs. The net after-tax loss reflects the reduction of past taxes from the NOL carryback and future tax savings that the NOL carryforward is expected to create.

Notice that the income tax benefit ($49 million) is less than it was when we assumed a carryforward only ($50 million). This is because the tax rate in one of the carryback years (2014) was lower than the carryforward rate (40%).

Let's carry the illustration forward one year (see Illustration 16–14A) and assume a performance turnaround in 2017 resulted in pretax accounting income of $15 million.

Illustration 16–14A

Determining and Recording Income Taxes—2017

($ in millions)	2016	Current Year 2017	Future Deductible Amounts (total)
Pretax accounting income		$15	
Temporary difference:			
NOL carryforward	$50	(15)	$(35)
Taxable income (tax return)		$ 0	
Enacted tax rate		40%	40%
Tax payable currently		$ 0	

Deferred Tax Asset	
beg. bal. 20	
	6
end. bal. 14	

Deferred Tax Asset	
Ending balance	$ 14.0
Less: Beginning balance	(20.0)
Change in balance	$ (6.0)

Journal Entry at the End of 2017

Income tax expense (to balance)	6	
Deferred tax asset (determined above)		6

$15 million of the NOL carryforward can be used to offset 2017 income. The remaining $35 million is carried forward up to 19 more years.

The $20 million deferred tax asset is reduced to $14 million.

Financial Statement Presentation

Balance Sheet Classification

● LO16–8

In a classified balance sheet, deferred tax assets and deferred tax liabilities are classified as either current or noncurrent according to how the related assets or liabilities are classified for financial reporting. For instance, a deferred tax liability arising from different depreciation methods being used for tax and book purposes would be classified as noncurrent because depreciable assets are reported as noncurrent. A deferred tax asset or deferred tax liability is considered to be related to an asset or liability if reduction (including amortization) of that asset or liability will cause the temporary difference to reverse.

A net current amount and a net noncurrent amount are reported as either an asset or a liability.

Most companies will have several different types of temporary differences that give rise to deferred tax amounts. The several deferred tax assets and liabilities should not be reported individually but combined instead into two summary amounts. Current deferred tax assets and liabilities should be offset (netted together). The resulting *net current* amount is then reported as either a current asset (if deferred tax assets exceed deferred tax liabilities) or current liability (if deferred tax liabilities exceed deferred tax assets). Similarly, a single *net noncurrent* amount should be reported as a net noncurrent asset or a net noncurrent liability. This is demonstrated in Illustration 16–15.

DEFERRED TAX AMOUNT NOT RELATED TO A SPECIFIC ASSET OR LIABILITY. Sometimes, a deferred tax asset or a deferred tax liability cannot be identified with a specific asset or liability. When that's the case, classification should be according to when the underlying temporary difference is expected to reverse. For instance, some organization costs are recognized as expenses for financial reporting purposes when incurred, but

Illustration 16–15

Balance Sheet Classification and Presentation

Warren Properties, Inc., had future taxable amounts and future deductible amounts relating to temporary differences between the tax bases of the assets and liabilities indicated below and their financial reporting amounts:

($ in millions)

Related Balance Sheet Account	Classification Current—C Noncurrent—N	Future Taxable (Deductible) Amounts	Tax Rate	Deferred Tax (Asset) Liability C	N
Receivable—installment sales of land	C	$ 10	× 40%	$ 4	
Receivable—installment sales of land	N	5	× 40%		$ 2
Depreciable assets	N	105	× 40%		42
Allowance—uncollectible accounts	C	(15)	× 40%	(6)	
Liability—subscriptions received	C	(20)	× 40%	(8)	
Estimated warranty liability	C	(30)	× 40%	(12)	
Net current liability (asset)				$(22)	
Net noncurrent liability (asset)					$ 44
Balance Sheet Presentation					
Current Assets:					
Deferred tax asset	$22				
Long-Term Liabilities:					
Deferred tax liability	$44				

Note: Before offsetting assets and liabilities within the current and noncurrent categories, the **total** of deferred tax assets is $26 ($6 + 8 + 12) and the **total** of deferred tax liabilities is $48 ($4 + 2 + 42).

The current or noncurrent classification of deferred tax assets and deferred tax liabilities is the same as that of the related assets or liabilities.

A deferred tax asset or liability that is not related to a specific asset or liability should be classified according to when the underlying temporary difference is expected to reverse.

are deducted for tax purposes in later years. When such expenditures are made, an expense is recorded, but no asset or liability is recognized on the balance sheet. The deferred tax asset recognized for the future deductible amounts is classified as a current asset for the tax effect of the deduction expected next year, and as a noncurrent asset for the tax effect of the deductions expected in later years.

Net operating loss (NOL) carryforwards also are unrelated to a specific asset or liability and so are classified as current or noncurrent according to when future income is expected to be sufficient to realize the benefit of the carryforward.

A valuation allowance is allocated between current and noncurrent on a pro rata basis.

VALUATION ALLOWANCE. Any valuation allowance for deferred tax assets should be allocated between the current and noncurrent amount in proportion to the amounts of deferred tax assets that are classified as current and noncurrent. In our illustration, all three deferred tax assets were classified as current, so any valuation allowance would be reported with the net current deferred tax asset.

Disclosure Notes

We've already seen many of the disclosures that companies have to present in the tax note, but there are a few we haven't yet covered.

INCOME TAX EXPENSE. Illustration 16–6A shows Shoe Carnival's disclosure of current tax payable, deferred tax, and tax expense. More generally, disclosure notes should indicate the following:

- Current portion of the tax expense (or tax benefit).
- Deferred portion of the tax expense (or tax benefit), with separate disclosure of amounts attributable to:
  - Portions that do not include the effect of separately disclosed amounts.
  - Operating loss carryforwards.

- Adjustments due to changes in tax laws or rates.
- Adjustments to the beginning-of-the-year valuation allowance due to revised estimates.
- Tax credits.

DEFERRED TAX ASSETS AND DEFERRED TAX LIABILITIES. Illustration 16–6B shows Shoe Carnival's disclosure of its deferred tax assets and deferred tax liabilities. It shows a total net deferred tax asset of $4,634 for 2013, classified into a *current* net deferred tax asset of $1,208 and a *noncurrent* net deferred tax asset of $3,426. Those two amounts appear in Shoe Carnival's 2013 balance sheet in the current asset and noncurrent asset sections. More generally, companies must disclose the following:

- Total of all deferred tax liabilities.
- Total of all deferred tax assets.
- Total valuation allowance recognized for deferred tax assets.
- Net change in the valuation allowance.
- Approximate tax effect of each type of temporary difference (and carryforward).

EFFECTIVE TAX RATE RECONCILIATION. Illustration 16–10 shows Walmart's effective tax rate reconciliation. Companies are required to provide that reconciliation, indicating the amount and nature of each significant reconciling item.

NET OPERATING LOSS (NOL) CARRYFORWARDS. The amounts and expiration dates should be revealed for any net operating loss carryforwards. Remember, net operating losses can be carried forward for reduction of future taxable income for 20 years. This potential tax benefit can foreshadow desirable cash savings for the company if earnings sufficient to absorb the NOL carryforwards are anticipated before their expiration date. The presence of large net operating loss carryforwards also can make an unprofitable company an attractive target for acquisition by a company that could use those NOL carryforwards to shelter its own earnings from taxes with that loss deduction. If the IRS determines that an acquisition is made solely to obtain the tax benefits of net operating loss carryforwards, the deductions will not be allowed. However, motivation is difficult to determine, so it is not uncommon for companies to purchase other companies to obtain their net operating loss carryforwards.

Coping with Uncertainty in Income Taxes

Few expense items in the income statement rival the size of the income tax expense line, and few are subject to the complexities and differing interpretations inherent in reporting income tax expense. As you might imagine, most companies strive to legitimately reduce their overall tax burden and to reduce or delay cash outflows for taxes.

● LO16–9

Even without additional efforts to reduce taxes, most companies' tax returns will include many tax positions that are subject to multiple interpretations. That is, the position management takes with respect to an element of tax expense might differ from the position the IRS or the tax court might take on that same item. Despite good faith positions taken in preparing tax returns, those judgments may not ultimately prevail if challenged by the IRS. Managements' tax positions frequently are subjected to legal scrutiny before the uncertainty ultimately is resolved.

The IRS frequently disagrees with the position a company takes on its tax return.

For example, assume that if Derrick Company claims on its tax return a particular deduction it believes is legitimate, that position will save the company $8 million in 2016 income taxes. Derrick knows that, historically, the IRS has challenged many deductions of this type. Since tax returns usually aren't examined for one, two, or more years, uncertainty exists.

TWO-STEP DECISION PROCESS. To deal with that uncertainty, companies are allowed to recognize in the financial statements the tax benefit of a position it takes, such as the reduction in tax expense from Derrick's decision to take the 2016 deduction, only if it is "more likely than not" (greater than 50% chance) to be sustained if challenged.[11] Guidance also prescribes how to *measure* the amount to be recognized if, in fact, it can be recognized. The decision, then, is a "two-step" process.

The identified tax position must have a "more-likely-than-not" probability—a more than 50 percent chance—of being sustained on examination.

Step 1. A tax benefit may be reflected in the financial statements only if it is "more likely than not" that the company will be able to sustain the tax return position, based on its technical merits.

Step 2. A tax benefit should be measured as the largest amount of benefit that is "cumulatively greater than 50 percent likely to be realized" (demonstrated later).

For the Step 1 decision as to whether the position can be sustained, companies must assume that the position will be reviewed by the IRS or other taxing authority and litigated to the "highest court possible," and that the taxing authority has knowledge of all relevant facts.

If there's a 50% chance or less of the company's position being sustained on examination, the tax expense can't reflect the tax benefit.

NOT "MORE LIKELY THAN NOT." Let's say that in the Step 1 decision, Derrick believes the more-likely-than-not criterion is *not* met. This means that none of the tax benefit (reduction in tax expense) can be recorded in 2016. The income tax expense must be recorded at the same amount as if the tax deduction was not taken.

Suppose, for instance, that Derricks's current income tax payable is $24 million after being reduced by the full $8 million tax benefit.[12] However, if it's *more likely than not* that the tax benefit isn't sustainable upon examination, the benefit can't be recognized as a reduction of tax expense. So, Derrick would record (a) current income tax payable that reflects the entire $8 million benefit of the deduction, (b) an additional tax liability that represents the obligation to pay an additional $8 million of taxes under the assumption that the deduction ultimately will not be upheld, and (c) tax expense as if the deduction had never been taken.

The $8 million liability can be viewed as a "reserve" to cover the possibility that tax officials might disallow the tax treatment the income tax payable presumes.

	($ in millions)	
Income tax expense (without $8 tax benefit)	32	
Income tax payable (with $8 tax benefit)		24
Liability—projected additional tax		8

The $8 million difference is the tax not paid because Derrick took the deduction, but potentially due if the deduction is not upheld later. Because the ultimate outcome probably won't be determined within the upcoming year, the *Liability—projected additional tax* is reported as a long-term liability unless it's known to be current.[13]

MEASURING THE TAX BENEFIT. Now, let's say that even though Derrick is aware of the IRS's tendency to challenge deductions of this sort, management believes the more-likely-than-not criterion *is* met. Since we determine in Step 1 that—yes—a tax benefit can be recognized, we now need to decide how much. That's Step 2.

Suppose the following table represents management's estimates of the likelihood of various amounts of tax benefit that would be upheld:

The largest amount that has a cumulative greater-than-50%-chance of being realized is $6 million (10% + 20% + 25% = 55%).

Likelihood Table **($ in millions)**

Amount of the tax benefit that management expects to be sustained	$8	$7	$6	$5	$4
Percentage likelihood that the tax position will be sustained at this level	10%	20%	25%	25%	20%
Cumulative probability that the tax position will be sustained	10%	30%	55%	80%	100%

[11] FASB ASC 740: Income Taxes–Overall (previously "Accounting for Uncertainty in Income Taxes, an Interpretation of FASB Statement No. 109," FASB Interpretation No. 48 (Norwalk, Conn.: FASB, June 2006)), commonly called FIN 48.

[12] For illustration, if pretax accounting income is $80 million, the tax rate is 40%, and the questionable deduction is $20 million, income tax payable would be [$80 million − 20 million] × 40% = $24 million.

[13] If a company has any deferred tax assets from net operating loss carryforwards, it generally nets the liability for uncertain tax positions against those deferred tax assets for presentation in the balance sheet, rather than presenting the liability separately. Why? The liability indicates that future tax will be *paid,* and the operating loss carryforward indicates that future tax will be *saved,* so the two are netted.

The amount of tax benefit that Derrick can recognize in the financial statements (reduce tax expense) is $6 million because it represents the largest amount of benefit that is more than 50 percent (55%) likely to be the end result. So, Derrick would record (a) current income tax payable that reflects the entire $8 million benefit of the deduction, (b) an additional tax liability that represents the obligation to pay an additional $2 million of taxes under the assumption that $6 million of tax benefit ultimately will be upheld, and (c) tax expense as if there is a $6 million tax benefit.

	($ in millions)	
Income tax expense (with $6 tax benefit)	26	
Income tax payable (with $8 tax benefit)		24
Liability—projected additional tax ($8 – 6)		2

Only $6 million of the tax benefit is recognized in income tax expense

In summary, the highest amount Derrick might have to pay is the full $8 million benefit of the 2016 deduction; the least amount, of course, is zero. What's the most likely amount? We began to answer that question when we calculated the most likely eventual benefit. That's the largest amount of benefit that is "cumulatively greater than 50 percent likely to be realized," which is $6 million.

Because the most likely amount not to be paid is $6 million, the most likely additional liability is $2 million ($8 − 6 = $2). That's the amount we record as a *Liability—projected additional tax,* along with the current income tax payable of $24 million.

RESOLUTION OF THE UNCERTAINTY. Now let's consider alternative possibilities for resolution of the uncertainty associated with the tax position. Note that, in each case, the "Liability—projected additional tax" gets reduced to zero in the period in which the uncertainty is resolved.

1. **Worst case scenario.** The entire position is disallowed, such that Derrick owes $8 million tax (plus any interest and penalties, which we are ignoring).

	($ in millions)	
Income tax expense	6	
Liability—projected additional tax	2	
Income tax payable (or cash)		8

2. **Best case scenario.** The entire position is upheld, so Derrick owes no additional tax.

	($ in millions)	
Liability—projected additional tax	2	
Income tax expense		2

3. **Expected scenario.** The $6 million position is allowed as expected, so Derrick owes the expected $2 million tax (plus any interest and penalties, which we are ignoring).

	($ in millions)	
Liability—projected additional tax	2	
Income tax payable (or cash)		2

Companies are required to include in the disclosure notes a clear reconciliation of the beginning and ending balance of their liability for unrecognized tax benefits. As an example, Illustration 16–16 includes an excerpt from the tax note of **Staples, Inc.**, for its fiscal year ended February 1, 2014.

Illustration 16–16

Disclosure of Deferred Taxes—Staples, Inc.

Real World Financials

The following summarizes the activity related to the Company's unrecognized tax benefits, including those related to discontinued operations (in thousands):

	2013	2012	2011
Balance at beginning of fiscal year	$254,724	$250,397	$254,167
Additions for tax positions related to current year	28,390	39,989	48,032
Additions for tax positions of prior years	4,350	11,058	15,361
Reduction for statute of limitations expiration	(6,240)	(30,116)	(13,441)
Settlements	(265)	(16,604)	(53,722)
Balance at end of fiscal year	$280,959	$254,724	$250,397

Additional Consideration

The Balance Sheet Focus of Income Tax Accounting. The way we account for income taxes is a useful example of the FASB's balance sheet emphasis. Rather than calculating tax expense directly, it always is calculated as whatever amount is implied by the combination of income tax payable and the changes that occurred during the period in deferred tax assets, deferred tax liabilities, the valuation allowance for deferred tax assets, and the liability for uncertain tax positions. In fact, we can summarize virtually everything in this chapter by visualizing the journal entry implied by the changes in those accounts. Let's draw some T-accounts to see how that works:

	Deferred Tax Assets		**Val. Allowance— Deferred Tax Assets**		**Deferred Tax Liabilities**		**Liability for Uncertain Tax Positions**	
Beg. bal.	S			U		W		Y
	B	or B	C	or C	D	or D	E	or E
End. Bal.	T			V		X		Z

With these T-accounts in mind, think of a company's tax accounting as including the following steps:

1. Determine income tax payable (tax rate times taxable income). We'll call that number "A".
2. Determine T, V, X and Z, the ending balances needed in the tax-related balance sheet accounts, as we do in the chapter.
3. Determine whatever changes in those accounts, B, C, D, and E, are needed to reach their required ending balances. We already know the beginning balances in those accounts, because they are the same as the ending balances reported in the prior period.
4. Finally, calculate tax expense, F, as the amount necessary to balance the journal entry. For example:

Tax expense (to balance)	F	
Deferred tax asset (amount needed to achieve needed balance)	B	
Deferred tax liability (amount needed to achieve needed balance)		D
Valuation allowance—deferred tax asset (amount needed to achieve needed balance)		C
Liability for uncertain tax positions (amount needed to achieve needed balance)		E
Taxes payable (tax rate x taxable income)		A

Tax expense (F) always is a "plug" figure (rarely, we need a credit to recognize a tax benefit) to make the journal entry balance. Depending on a company's particular circumstances, a debit or a credit could be required to reach the appropriate ending balance in each of the tax-related balance sheet accounts, B, C, D, and E. To the extent these accounts changed because of other transactions (for example, an acquisition), we would account for those effects first and then determine the amounts necessary to reach the appropriate ending balances.

Intraperiod Tax Allocation

You should recall that an income statement reports certain items separately from income (or loss) from continuing operations when such items are present. Specifically, discontinued operations are given a place of their own in the income statement to better allow the user of the statement to isolate irregular components of net income from those that represent recurring business operations.[14] Presumably, this permits the user to more accurately project future operations without neglecting events that affect current performance. Following this logic, each component of net income should reflect the income tax effect directly associated with that component.

LO16–10

Consequently, the total income tax expense for a reporting period should be allocated among the income statement items that gave rise to it. Each of the following items should be reported net of its respective income tax effects:

- Income (or loss) from continuing operations.
- Discontinued operations.

The related tax effect can be either a tax expense or a tax benefit. For example, a gain on disposal of a discontinued operation adds to a company's tax expense, while a loss on disposal produces a tax reduction because it reduces taxable income and therefore reduces income taxes.[15] So a company with a tax rate of 40% would report $100 million pretax income that includes a $10 million gain on disposal of a discontinued operation this way:

	($ in millions)
Income before tax and discontinued operation ($100 − 10)	$ 90
Less: Income tax expense ($90 × 40%)	(36)
Income before discontinued operation	54
Gain on disposal of discontinued operation (net of $4 income tax expense)	6
Net income	$ 60

A gain causes an increase in taxes.

If the $100 million pretax income included a $10 million loss, the loss would be reported net of associated tax savings:

	($ in millions)
Income before tax and discontinued operation ($100 + 10)	$110
Less: Income tax expense ($110 × 40%)	(44)
Income before discontinued operation	66
Loss on disposal of discontinued operation (net of $4 income tax benefit)	(6)
Net income	$ 60

A loss causes a reduction in taxes.

Additional Consideration

If the gain in the earlier example had been of a type taxable at a capital gains tax rate of 30%, it would have been reported net of the specific tax associated with that gain:

Gain on disposal of discontinued operation (net of $3 income tax expense)	$7

[14]Until recently, GAAP included another category, extraordinary items, for which income was shown separately net of tax. To be considered extraordinary, an event had to be both unusual and infrequent, so that category was used very rarely. The FASB issued an exposure draft (ED) in July 2014 eliminating the extraordinary items category. As of the time this text went to print, a final Accounting Standards Update (ASU) had not yet been issued, but it appears very unlikely that the ASU will differ from the ED, so this discussion is based on the ED.

[15]As discussed in Chapter 4, companies separately report (a) any gain or loss from running a discontinued operation prior to disposal, and (b) any gain or loss on disposal of a discontinued operation's assets. For simplicity we focus on reporting taxes for (b), but the same separate net-of-tax presentation is used for (a).

Allocating income taxes within a particular reporting period is intraperiod tax allocation.

Allocating income taxes among financial statement components in this way within a particular reporting period is referred to as *intraperiod tax allocation.* You should recognize the contrast with *inter*period tax allocation—terminology sometimes used to describe allocating income taxes between two or more reporting periods by recognizing deferred tax assets and liabilities. While interperiod tax allocation is challenging and controversial, intraperiod tax allocation is relatively straightforward and substantially free from controversy.

OTHER COMPREHENSIVE INCOME. Allocating income tax expense or benefit also applies to components of comprehensive income reported separately from net income. You should recall from our discussions in Chapters 4 and 12 that "comprehensive income" extends our view of income beyond conventional net income to include four types of gains and losses that traditionally haven't been included in income statements. The other comprehensive income (OCI) items relate to investments, postretirement benefit plans, derivatives, and foreign currency translation. When these OCI items are reported in a statement of comprehensive income and then accumulated in shareholders' equity, they are reported net of their respective income tax effects.[16]

Decision Makers' Perspective

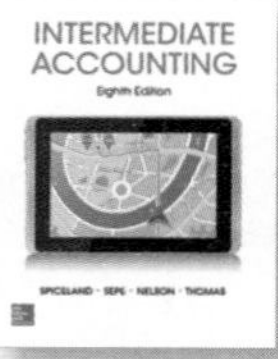

Income taxes represent one of the largest expenditures that many firms incur. When state, local, and foreign taxes are considered along with federal taxes, the total bite can easily consume 40% of income. A key factor, then, in any decision that managers make should be the impact on taxes. Decision makers must constantly be alert to options that minimize or delay taxes. During the course of this chapter, we encountered situations that avoid taxes (for example, interest on municipal bonds) and those that delay taxes (for example, using accelerated depreciation on the tax return). Astute managers make investment decisions that consider the tax effect of available alternatives. Similarly, outside analysts should consider how effectively management has managed its tax exposure and monitor the current and prospective impact of taxes on their interests in the company.

Investment patterns and other disclosures can indicate potential tax expenditures.

Consider an example. Large, capital-intensive companies with significant investments in buildings and equipment often have sizable deferred tax liabilities from temporary differences in depreciation. If new investments cause the level of depreciable assets to at least remain the same over time, the deferred tax liability can be effectively delayed indefinitely. Investors and creditors should be watchful for situations that might cause material paydowns of that deferred tax liability, such as impending plant closings or investment patterns that suggest declining levels of depreciable assets. Unexpected additional tax expenditures can severely diminish an otherwise attractive prospective rate of return.

Net operating loss carryforwards can indicate significant future tax savings.

You also learned in the chapter that deferred tax assets represent future tax benefits. One such deferred tax asset that often reflects sizable future tax deductions is a net operating loss (NOL) carryforward. When a company has a large net operating loss carryforward, a large amount of future income can be earned tax-free. This tax shelter can be a huge advantage, not to be overlooked by careful analysts.

Managers and outsiders are aware that increasing debt increases risk. Deferred tax liabilities increase reported debt. As discussed and demonstrated in the previous chapter, financial risk often is measured by the debt to equity ratio, total liabilities divided by shareholders' equity. Other things being equal, the higher the debt to equity ratio, the higher the risk. Should the deferred tax liability be included in the computation of this ratio? Some analysts

[16]This can be accomplished by (a) presenting components of other comprehensive income net of related income tax effects or (b) presenting a single tax amount for all, and individual components shown before income tax effects with disclosure of the income taxes allocated to each component either in a disclosure note or parenthetically in the statement.

will argue that it should be excluded, observing that in many cases the deferred tax liability account remains the same or continually grows larger. Their contention is that no future tax payment will be required. Others, though, contend that is no different from the common situation in which long-term borrowings tend to remain the same or continually grow larger. Research supports the notion that deferred tax liabilities are, in fact, viewed by investors as real liabilities and investors appear to discount them according to the timing and likelihood of the liabilities' settlement.[17]

Deferred tax liabilities increase risk as measured by the debt to equity ratio.

Whenever managerial discretion can materially impact reported earnings, analysts should be wary of the implications for earnings quality assessment. We indicated earlier that the decision as to whether or not a valuation allowance is used, as well as the size of the allowance, is largely discretionary. Research indicates that an increase in a valuation allowance provides useful information, signaling that management is pessimistic about its ability to generate enough future income to benefit from the tax deductions provided by deferred tax assets.[18] However, research also indicates that some companies do use the deferred tax asset valuation allowance account to manage earnings upward to meet analyst forecasts.[19] More generally, a recent survey of nearly 600 corporate tax executives provides evidence that most top management care at least as much about tax expense and its effect on earnings per share as they do about the actual cash taxes that are paid by their companies, and that an important consideration in tax planning is increasing earnings per share.[20] Alert investors should not overlook the potential for companies using tax expense to manage their earnings.

In short, managers who make decisions based on estimated pretax cash flows and outside investors and creditors who make decisions based on pretax income numbers are perilously ignoring one of the most important aspects of those decisions. Taxes should be a primary consideration in any business decision. ●

Concept Review Exercise

MULTIPLE DIFFERENCES AND NET OPERATING LOSS

Mid-South Cellular Systems began operations in 2016. That year the company reported taxable income of $25 million. In 2017, its second year of operations, pretax accounting income was $88 million, which included the following amounts:

1. Insurance expense of $14 million, representing one-third of a $42 million, three-year casualty and liability insurance policy that is deducted for tax purposes entirely in 2017.
2. Insurance expense for a $1 million premium on a life insurance policy for the company president. This is not deductible for tax purposes.
3. An asset with a four-year useful life was acquired last year. It is depreciated by the straight-line method in the income statement. MACRS is used on the tax return, causing deductions for depreciation to be more than straight-line depreciation the first two years but less than straight-line depreciation the next two years ($ in millions):

	Income Statement	Tax Return	Difference
2016	$150	$198	$ (48)
2017	150	264	(114)
2018	150	90	60
2019	150	48	102
	$600	$600	0

[17]See Dan Givoly and Carla Hayn, "The Valuation of the Deferred Tax Liability: Evidence from the Stock Market," *The Accounting Review*, April 1992, pp. 394–410.

[18]See Greg Miller and Doug Skinner, "Determinants of the Valuation Allowance for Deferred Tax Assets under SFAS No. 109," *The Accounting Review*, April 1998, pp. 213–233.

[19]See Sonia O. Rego and Mary Margaret Frank, "Do Managers Use the Valuation Allowance Account to Manage Earnings Around Certain Earnings Targets?" *Journal of the American Taxation Association 28 (1)*, 2006, pp. 43–65.

[20]See John Graham, Michelle Hanlon, Terry Shevlin, and Nemit Shroff, "Incentives for Tax Planning and Avoidance: Evidence from the Field," *The Accounting Review*, May 2014, pp. 999–1023.

4. Equipment rental revenue of $80 million, which does not include an additional $20 million of advance payment for 2018 rent. $100 million of rental revenue is reported on the 2017 income tax return.

The enacted tax rate is 40%.

Required:

1. Prepare the journal entry to record Mid-South Cellular's income taxes for 2017.
2. What is Mid-South Cellular's 2017 net income?
3. Show how any deferred tax amount(s) should be reported in the 2017 balance sheet. Assume taxable income is expected in 2018 sufficient to absorb any deductible amounts carried forward from 2017.

Solution

1. Prepare the journal entry to record Mid-South Cellular's income taxes for 2017.

($ in millions)

Differences in tax reporting and financial reporting of both the prepaid insurance and the depreciation create future taxable amounts.

Both the advance rent and the net operating loss carryforward create future deductible amounts.

	2016	Current Year 2017	Future Taxable (Deductible) Amounts 2018	2019	Future Taxable Amounts (total)	Future Deductible Amounts (total)
Pretax accounting income		$ 88				
Permanent difference:						
Life insurance premium		1				
Temporary differences:						
Prepaid insurance		(28)	$ 14	$ 14	$ 28	
Depreciation	$(48)	(114)	60	102	162	
Advance rent received		20	(20)			$ (20)
Net operating loss		$ (33)				
Loss carryback	(25)	← 25				
Loss carryforward		8 →				(8)
		$ 0			$190	$ (28)
Enacted tax rate	40%	40%			40%	40%
Tax payable (refundable)	$(10)	$ 0				
Deferred tax liability					$ 76.0	
Deferred tax asset						$(11.2)

	Deferred Tax Liability	Deferred Tax Asset
Ending balances:	$76.0	$ 11.2
Less: Beginning balance ($48* × 40%)	(19.2)	(0.0)
Change in balances	$56.8	$ 11.2

*2016's only temporary difference.

Income tax expense is composed of three components: (1) the tax deferred until later, reduced by (2) the deferred tax benefit and (3) the refund receivable of 2016 taxes paid.

Journal Entry at the End of 2017

Income tax expense (to balance)	35.6	
Receivable—income tax refund (determined above)	10.0	
Deferred tax asset (determined above)	11.2	
Deferred tax liability (determined above)		56.8

Note: Adjusting pretax accounting income by the permanent difference and the three temporary differences creates a negative taxable income, which is a net operating loss.

2. What is Mid-South Cellular's 2017 net income?

Pretax accounting income	$88.0
Income tax expense	(35.6)
Net income	$52.4

3. Show how any deferred tax amount(s) should be reported in the 2017 balance sheet. Assume taxable income is expected in 2018 sufficient to absorb any deductible amounts carried forward from 2017.

($ in millions)

	Classification Current—C Noncurrent—N	Future Taxable (Deductible) Amounts	Tax Rate	Deferred Tax (Asset) Liability C	Deferred Tax (Asset) Liability N
Related balance sheet account					
Prepaid insurance	C	28	× 40%	11.2	
Depreciable assets	N	162	× 40%		64.8
Liability—rent received in advance	C	(20)	× 40%	(8.0)	
Unrelated to any balance sheet account					
Operating loss carryforward	C*	(8)	× 40%	(3.2)	
Net current liability (asset)				0.0	
Net noncurrent liability (asset)					64.8

*Deferred tax asset classified entirely as current because 2018 income is expected to be sufficient to realize the benefit of the carryforward.

No net current amount
Long-term liabilities:

Deferred tax liability	$64.8

Note: These net amounts ($0.0 + 64.8 = $64.8) sum to the net **total** deferred tax liabilities and deferred tax assets from requirement 1 ($76.0 − 11.2 = $64.8).

Financial Reporting Case Solution

1. **What's the difference? Explain to Laura how differences between financial reporting standards and income tax rules might cause the income tax expense and the amount of income tax paid to differ.** *(p. 933)* The differences in the rules for computing taxable income and those for financial reporting often cause amounts to be included in taxable income in a different year(s) from the year in which they are recognized for financial reporting purposes. Temporary differences result in future taxable or deductible amounts when the temporary differences reverse. As a result, tax payments frequently occur in years different from the years in which the revenues and expenses that cause the taxes are generated.
2. **What is the conceptual advantage of determining income tax expense as we do?** *(p. 934)* Income tax expense is the combination of the current tax effect and the deferred tax consequences of the period's activities. Under the asset-liability approach, the objective of accounting for income taxes is to recognize a deferred tax liability or deferred tax asset for the tax consequences of amounts that will become taxable or deductible in future years as a result of transactions or events that already have occurred. A result is to recognize both the current and the deferred tax consequences of the operations of a reporting period.

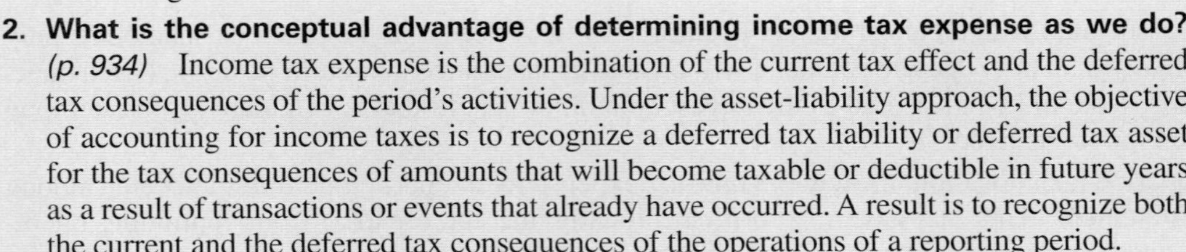

3. **Are there differences between financial reporting standards and income tax rules that will not cause a difference between income tax expense and the amount**

of income taxes paid? *(p. 948)* Yes. Some differences between accounting income and taxable income are caused by transactions and events that will never affect taxable income or taxes payable. These differences between accounting income and taxable income do not reverse later. These are permanent differences that are disregarded when determining (a) the tax payable currently, (b) the deferred tax effect, and therefore (c) the income tax expense. ●

The Bottom Line

- **LO16–1** Temporary differences produce future taxable amounts when the taxable income will be increased relative to pretax accounting income in one or more future years. These produce deferred tax liabilities for the taxes to be paid on the future taxable amounts. Income tax expense for the year includes an amount for which payment (or receipt) is deferred in addition to the amount for which payment is due currently. The deferred amount is the change in the tax liability (or asset). *(p. 934)*
- **LO16–2** When the future tax consequence of a temporary difference will be to decrease taxable income relative to pretax accounting income, future deductible amounts are created. These have favorable tax consequences that are recognized as deferred tax assets. *(p. 941)*
- **LO16–3** Deferred tax assets are recognized for all deductible temporary differences. However, a deferred tax asset is then reduced by a valuation allowance if it is more likely than not that some portion or all of the deferred tax asset will not be realized. *(p. 946)*
- **LO16–4** Permanent differences between the reported amount of an asset or liability in the financial statements and its tax basis are those caused by transactions and events that under existing tax law will never affect taxable income or taxes payable. These are disregarded when determining both the tax payable currently, the deferred tax effect, and tax expense. *(p. 947)*
- **LO16–5** Deferred tax liabilities (and assets) are calculated by multiplying future taxable (and deductible) amounts by the currently enacted tax rates that will apply to them. If a change in a tax law or rate occurs, the deferred tax liability or asset is adjusted to reflect the change in the amount to be paid or recovered. That effect is reflected in tax expense in the year of the enactment of the change in the tax law or rate. *(p. 951)*
- **LO16–6** When multiple temporary differences exist, the total of the future *taxable* amounts is multiplied by the future tax rate to determine the appropriate balance for the deferred tax liability, and the total of the future *deductible* amounts is multiplied by the future tax rate to determine the appropriate balance for the deferred tax asset. *(p. 954)*
- **LO16–7** Tax laws permit a net operating loss (NOL) to be used to reduce taxable income in other, profitable years by either a carryback of the loss to up to two prior years or a carryforward of the loss to up to 20 later years. The tax benefit of a net operating loss carryback or a net operating loss carryforward is recognized in the year of the loss. *(p. 955)*
- **LO16–8** Deferred tax assets and deferred tax liabilities are classified as either current or noncurrent according to how the related assets or liabilities are classified for financial reporting. Disclosure notes should reveal additional relevant information needed for full disclosure pertaining to deferred tax amounts reported on the balance sheet, the components of income tax expense, and available operating loss carryforwards. *(p. 959)*
- **LO16–9** A tax benefit associated with an uncertain tax position may be reflected in the financial statements only if it is "more likely than not" that the company will be able to sustain the tax return position, based on its technical merits. It should be measured as the largest amount of benefit that is cumulatively greater than 50 percent likely to be realized. *(p. 961)*
- **LO16–10** Through intraperiod tax allocation, the total income tax expense for a reporting period is allocated among the financial statement items that gave rise to it; specifically, income (or loss) from continuing operations, discontinued operations, and prior period adjustments (to the beginning retained earnings balance). *(p. 965)*
- **LO16–11** Despite the similar approaches for accounting for taxation under IFRS and U.S. GAAP, differences in reported amounts for deferred taxes are among the most frequent between the two approaches because a great many of the *nontax* differences between IFRS and U.S. GAAP affect deferred taxes. *(p. 950)* ●

Questions For Review of Key Topics

Q 16–1 A member of the board of directors is concerned that the company's income statement reports income tax expense of $12.3 million, but the income tax obligation to the government for the year is only $7.9 million. How might the corporate controller explain this difference?

Q 16–2 A deferred tax liability (or asset) is described as the tax effect of the temporary difference between the financial statement carrying amount (book value) of an asset or liability and its tax basis. Explain this tax effect of the temporary difference. How might it produce a deferred tax liability? A deferred tax asset?

Q 16–3 Sometimes a temporary difference will produce future deductible amounts. Explain what is meant by future deductible amounts. Describe two general situations that have this effect. How are such situations recognized in the financial statements?

Q 16–4 The benefit of future deductible amounts can be achieved only if future income is sufficient to take advantage of the deferred deductions. For that reason, not all deferred tax assets will ultimately be realized. How is this possibility reflected in the way we recognize deferred tax assets?

Q 16–5 Temporary differences result in future taxable or deductible amounts when the related asset or liability is recovered or settled. Some differences, though, are not temporary. What events create permanent differences? What effect do these have on the determination of income taxes payable? Of deferred income taxes? Of tax expense?

Q 16–6 Identify three examples of differences with no deferred tax consequences.

Q 16–7 The income tax rate for Hudson Refinery has been 35% for each of its 12 years of operation. Company forecasters expect a much-debated tax reform bill to be passed by Congress early next year. The new tax measure would increase Hudson's tax rate to 42%. When measuring this year's deferred tax liability, which rate should Hudson use?

Q 16–8 Suppose a tax reform bill is enacted that causes the corporate tax rate to change from 34% to 36%. How would this affect an existing deferred tax liability? How would the change be reflected in income?

Q 16–9 A net operating loss occurs when tax-deductible expenses exceed taxable revenues. Tax laws permit the net operating loss to be used to reduce taxable income in other, profitable years by either a carryback of the loss to prior years or a carryforward of the loss to later years. How are loss carrybacks and loss carryforwards recognized for financial reporting purposes?

Q 16–10 How are deferred tax assets and deferred tax liabilities reported in a classified balance sheet?

Q 16–11 Additional disclosures are required pertaining to deferred tax amounts reported on the balance sheet. What are the needed disclosures?

Q 16–12 Additional disclosures are required pertaining to the income tax expense reported in the income statement. What are the needed disclosures?

Q 16–13 Accounting for uncertainty in tax positions is prescribed by GAAP in FASB ASC 740–10: Income Taxes–Overall (previously *FASB Interpretation No. 48 (FIN 48))*. Describe the two-step process required by GAAP.

Q 16–14 What is intraperiod tax allocation?

IFRS **Q 16–15** IFRS and U.S. GAAP follow similar approaches for accounting for taxation. Nevertheless, differences in reported amounts for deferred taxes are among the most frequent between IFRS and U.S. GAAP. Why?

Brief Exercises

BE 16–1
Temporary difference
● LO16–1

A company reports *pretax accounting income* of $10 million, but because of a single temporary difference, *taxable income* is only $7 million. No temporary differences existed at the beginning of the year, and the tax rate is 40%. Prepare the appropriate journal entry to record income taxes.

BE 16–2
Temporary difference; determine taxable income; determine prior year deferred tax amount
● LO16–1

Kara Fashions uses straight-line depreciation for financial statement reporting and MACRS for income tax reporting. Three years after its purchase, one of Kara's buildings has a book value of $400,000 and a tax basis of $300,000. There were no other temporary differences and no permanent differences. Taxable income was $4 million and Kara's tax rate is 40%. What is the deferred tax liability to be reported in the balance sheet? Assuming that the deferred tax liability balance was $32,000 the previous year, prepare the appropriate journal entry to record income taxes this year.

BE 16–3
Temporary difference
● LO16–2

A company reports *pretax accounting income* of $10 million, but because of a single temporary difference, *taxable income* is $12 million. No temporary differences existed at the beginning of the year, and the tax rate is 40%. prepare the appropriate journal entry to record income taxes.

BE 16–4
Temporary difference; income tax payable given
● LO16–2

In 2016, Ryan Management collected rent revenue for 2017 tenant occupancy. For financial reporting, the rent is recorded as deferred revenue and then recognized as income in the period tenants occupy rental property, but for income tax reporting it is taxed when collected. The deferred portion of the rent collected in 2016 was $50 million. Taxable income is $180 million. No temporary differences existed at the beginning of the year, and the tax rate is 40%. Prepare the appropriate journal entry to record income taxes.

BE 16–5
Temporary difference; income tax payable given
● LO16–2

Refer to the situation described in BE 16–4. Suppose the deferred portion of the rent collected was $40 million at the end of 2017. Taxable income is $200 million. Prepare the appropriate journal entry to record income taxes.

BE 16–6
Valuation allowance
● LO16–2, LO16–3

At the end of the year, the deferred tax asset account had a balance of $12 million attributable to a cumulative temporary difference of $30 million in a liability for estimated expenses. Taxable income is $35 million. No temporary differences existed at the beginning of the year, and the tax rate is 40%. Prepare the journal entry(s) to record income taxes assuming it is more likely than not that one-fourth of the deferred tax asset will not ultimately be realized.

BE 16–7
Valuation allowance
● LO16–2, LO16–3
Real World Financials

VeriFone Systems is a provider of electronic card payment terminals, peripherals, network products, and software. In its 2013 annual report, the company reported current and long-term deferred tax assets totaling about $513 million. The company also reported valuation allowances totaling about $418 million. What would motivate VeriFone to have a valuation allowance almost equal to its deferred tax assets?

BE 16–8
Temporary and permanent differences; determine deferred tax consequences
● LO16–1, LO16–4

Differences between financial statement and taxable income were as follows:

	($ in millions)
Pretax accounting income	$300
Permanent difference	(24)
	276
Temporary difference	(18)
Taxable income	$258

The cumulative temporary difference to date is $40 million (also the future taxable amount). The enacted tax rate is 40%. What is deferred tax asset or liability to be reported in the balance sheet?

BE 16–9
Calculate taxable income
● LO16–1, LO16–4

Shannon Polymers uses straight-line depreciation for financial reporting purposes for equipment costing $800,000 and with an expected useful life of four years and no residual value. For tax purposes, the deduction is 40%, 30%, 20%, and 10% in those years. Pretax accounting income the first year the equipment was used was $900,000, which includes interest revenue of $20,000 from municipal bonds. Other than the two described, there are no differences between accounting income and taxable income. The enacted tax rate is 40%. Prepare the journal entry to record income taxes.

BE 16–10
Multiple tax rates
● LO16–5

J-Matt, Inc., had pretax accounting income of $291,000 and taxable income of $300,000 in 2016. The only difference between accounting and taxable income is estimated product warranty costs for sales this year. Warranty payments are expected to be in equal amounts over the next three years. Recent tax legislation will change the tax rate from the current 40% to 30% in 2018. Determine the amounts necessary to record J-Matt's income taxes for 2016 and prepare the appropriate journal entry.

BE 16–11
Change in tax rate
● LO16–5

Superior Developers sells lots for residential development. When lots are sold, Superior recognizes income for financial reporting purposes in the year of the sale. For some lots, Superior recognizes income for tax purposes when collected. In the *prior* year, income recognized for financial reporting purposes for lots sold this way was

$20 million, which would be collected equally over the next two years. The enacted tax rate was 40%. This year, a new tax law was enacted, revising the tax rate from 40% to 35% beginning next year. Calculate the amount by which Superior should reduce its deferred tax liability this year.

BE 16–12
Net operating loss carryforward
● LO16–7

During its first year of operations, **Nile.com** reported a net operating loss of $15 million for financial reporting and tax purposes. The enacted tax rate is 40%. Prepare the journal entry to recognize the income tax benefit of the net operating loss.

BE 16–13
Net operating loss carryback
● LO16–7

AirParts Corporation reported a net operating loss of $25 million for financial reporting and tax purposes. Taxable income last year and the previous year, respectively, was $20 million and $15 million. The enacted tax rate each year is 40%. Prepare the journal entry to recognize the income tax benefit of the net operating loss. AirParts elects the carryback option.

BE 16–14
Tax uncertainty
● LO16–9

First Bank has some question as to the tax-free nature of $5 million of its municipal bond portfolio. This amount is excluded from First Bank's taxable income of $55 million. Management has determined that there is a 65% chance that the tax-free status of this interest can't withstand scrutiny of taxing authorities. Assuming a 40% tax rate, what amount of income tax expense should the bank report?

BE 16–15
Intraperiod tax allocation
● LO16–10

Southeast Airlines had pretax earnings of $65 million, including a gain on disposal of a discontinued operation of $10 million. The company's tax rate is 40%. What is the amount of income tax expense that Southeast should report in its income statement? How should the gain on disposal of a discontinued operation be reported?

Exercises

An alternate exercise and problem set is available in the Connect library.

E 16–1
Temporary difference; taxable income given
● LO16–1

Alvis Corporation reports *pretax accounting income* of $400,000, but due to a single temporary difference, *taxable income* is only $250,000. At the beginning of the year, no temporary differences existed.

Required:
1. Assuming a tax rate of 35%, what will be Alvis's net income?
2. What will Alvis report in the balance sheet pertaining to income taxes?

E 16–2
Determine taxable income; determine prior year deferred tax amount
● LO16–1

On January 1, 2013, Ameen Company purchased a building for $36 million. Ameen uses straight-line depreciation for financial statement reporting and MACRS for income tax reporting. At December 31, 2015, the book value of the building was $30 million and its tax basis was $20 million. At December 31, 2016, the book value of the building was $28 million and its tax basis was $13 million. There were no other temporary differences and no permanent differences. Pretax accounting income for 2016 was $45 million.

Required:
1. Prepare the appropriate journal entry to record Ameen's 2016 income taxes. Assume an income tax rate of 40%.
2. What is Ameen's 2016 net income?

E 16–3
Taxable income given; calculate deferred tax liability
● LO16–1

Ayres Services acquired an asset for $80 million in 2016. The asset is depreciated for financial reporting purposes over four years on a straight-line basis (no residual value). For tax purposes the asset's cost is depreciated by MACRS. The enacted tax rate is 40%. Amounts for pretax accounting income, depreciation, and taxable income in 2016, 2017, 2018, and 2019 are as follows:

	($ in millions)			
	2016	**2017**	**2018**	**2019**
Pretax accounting income	$330	$350	$365	$400
Depreciation on the income statement	20	20	20	20
Depreciation on the tax return	(25)	(33)	(15)	(7)
Taxable income	$325	$337	$370	$413

Required:
For December 31 of each year, determine (a) the temporary book–tax difference for the depreciable asset and (b) the balance to be reported in the deferred tax liability account.

E 16–4
Temporary difference; income tax payable given
● LO16–2

In 2016, DFS Medical Supply collected rent revenue for 2017 tenant occupancy. For income tax reporting, the rent is taxed when collected. For financial statement reporting, the rent is recorded as deferred revenue and then recognized as income in the period tenants occupy the rental property. The deferred portion of the rent collected in 2016 amounted to $300,000 at December 31, 2016. DFS had no temporary differences at the beginning of the year.

Required:
Assuming an income tax rate of 40% and 2016 income tax payable of $950,000, prepare the journal entry to record income taxes for 2016.

E 16–5
Temporary difference; future deductible amounts; taxable income given
● LO16–2

Lance Lawn Services reports warranty expense by estimating the amount that eventually will be paid to satisfy warranties on its product sales. For tax purposes, the expense is deducted when the cost is incurred. At December 31, 2016, Lance has a warranty liability of $1 million and taxable income of $75 million. At December 31, 2015, Lance reported a deferred tax asset of $435,000 related to this difference in reporting warranties, its only temporary difference. The enacted tax rate is 40% each year.

Required:
Prepare the appropriate journal entry to record Lance's income tax provision for 2016.

E 16–6
Identify future taxable amounts and future deductible amounts
● LO16–1, LO16–2

Listed below are 10 causes of temporary differences. For each temporary difference, indicate (by letter) whether it will create future deductible amounts (D) or future taxable amounts (T).

Temporary Difference

____ 1. Accrual of loss contingency, tax-deductible when paid.
____ 2. Newspaper subscriptions; taxable when received, recognized for financial reporting when earned.
____ 3. Prepaid rent, tax-deductible when paid.
____ 4. Accrued bond interest expense, tax-deductible when paid.
____ 5. Prepaid insurance, tax-deductible when paid.
____ 6 Unrealized loss from recording investments at fair value (tax-deductible when investments are sold).
____ 7. Warranty expense; estimated for financial reporting when products are sold; deducted for tax purposes when paid.
____ 8. Advance rent receipts on an operating lease (as the lessor), taxable when received.
____ 9. Straight-line depreciation for financial reporting; accelerated depreciation for tax purposes.
____10. Accrued expense for employee postretirement benefits, tax-deductible when subsequent payments are made.

E 16–7
Identify future taxable amounts and future deductible amounts
● LO16–1, LO16–2

(This is a variation of E 16-6, modified to focus on the balance sheet accounts related to the deferred tax amounts.)

Listed below are 10 causes of temporary differences. For each temporary difference indicate the balance sheet account for which the situation creates a temporary difference.

Temporary Difference

____ 1. Accrual of loss contingency, tax-deductible when paid.
____ 2. Newspaper subscriptions; taxable when received, recognized for financial reporting when earned.
____ 3. Prepaid rent, tax-deductible when paid.
____ 4. Accrued bond interest expense, tax-deductible when paid.
____ 5. Prepaid insurance, tax-deductible when paid.
____ 6. Unrealized loss from recording investments at fair value (tax-deductible when investments are sold).
____ 7. Warranty expense; estimated for financial reporting when products are sold; deducted for tax purposes when paid.
____ 8. Advance rent receipts on an operating lease (as the lessor), taxable when received.
____ 9. Straight-line depreciation for financial reporting; accelerated depreciation for tax purposes.
____10. Accrued expense for employee postretirement benefits, tax-deductible when subsequent payments are made.

E 16–8
Calculate income tax amounts under various circumstances
● LO16–1, LO16–2

Four independent situations are described below. Each involves future deductible amounts and/or future taxable amounts produced by temporary differences:

	($ in thousands) Situation			
	1	**2**	**3**	**4**
Taxable income	$85	$215	$195	$260
Future deductible amounts	15		20	20
Future taxable amounts		15	15	30
Balance(s) at beginning of the year:				
Deferred tax asset	2		9	4
Deferred tax liability		2	2	

The enacted tax rate is 40%.

Required:
For each situation, determine the:
a. Income tax payable currently.
b. Deferred tax asset—balance.
c. Deferred tax asset—change (dr) cr.
d. Deferred tax liability—balance.
e. Deferred tax liability—change (dr) cr.
f. Income tax expense.

E 16–9
Determine taxable income
● LO16–1, LO16–2

Eight independent situations are described below. Each involves future deductible amounts and/or future taxable amounts produced by:

	($ in millions) Temporary Differences Reported First on:			
	The Income Statement		**The Tax Return**	
	Revenue	**Expense**	**Revenue**	**Expense**
1.		$20		
2.	$20			
3.			$20	
4.				$20
5.	15	20		
6.		20	15	
7.	15	20		10
8.	15	20	5	10

Required:
For each situation, determine taxable income assuming pretax accounting income is $100 million.

E 16–10
Deferred tax asset; taxable income given; valuation allowance
● LO16–3

At the end of 2015, Payne Industries had a deferred tax asset account with a balance of $30 million attributable to a temporary book–tax difference of $75 million in a liability for estimated expenses. At the end of 2016, the temporary difference is $70 million. Payne has no other temporary differences and no valuation allowance for the deferred tax asset. Taxable income for 2016 is $180 million and the tax rate is 40%.

Required:
1. Prepare the journal entry(s) to record Payne's income taxes for 2016, assuming it is more likely than not that the deferred tax asset will be realized.
2. Prepare the journal entry(s) to record Payne's income taxes for 2016, assuming it is more likely than not that one-fourth of the deferred tax asset will ultimately be realized.

E 16–11
Deferred tax asset; income tax payable given; previous balance in valuation allowance
● LO16–3

(This is a variation of Exercise 16–10, modified to assume a previous balance in the valuation allowance.)
At the end of 2015, Payne Industries had a deferred tax asset account with a balance of $30 million attributable to a temporary book-tax difference of $75 million in a liability for estimated expenses. At the end of 2016, the temporary difference is $70 million. Payne has no other temporary differences. Taxable income for 2016 is $180 million and the tax rate is 40%.

Payne has a valuation allowance of $10 million for the deferred tax asset at the beginning of 2016.

Required:
1. Prepare the journal entry(s) to record Payne's income taxes for 2016, assuming it is more likely than not that the deferred tax asset will be realized.
2. Prepare the journal entry(s) to record Payne's income taxes for 2016, assuming it is more likely than not that one-fourth of the deferred tax asset will ultimately be realized.

E 16–12
FASB codification research; valuation allowance
● LO16–3

CODE

When a company records a deferred tax asset, it may need to also report a valuation allowance if it is "more likely than not" that some portion or all of the deferred tax asset will not be realized. The *FASB Accounting Standards Codification* represents the single source of authoritative U.S. generally accepted accounting principles.

Required:
1. Obtain the relevant authoritative literature on disclosure requirements pertaining to how a firm should determine whether a valuation allowance for deferred tax assets is needed using the FASB's Codification Research System at the FASB website (www.fasb.org). What is the specific citation that describes the guidelines for determining the disclosure requirements?
2. What are the guidelines?

E 16–13
Multiple differences; calculate taxable income
● LO16–1, LO16–4

Southern Atlantic Distributors began operations in January 2016 and purchased a delivery truck for $40,000. Southern Atlantic plans to use straight-line depreciation over a four-year expected useful life for financial reporting purposes. For tax purposes, the deduction is 50% of cost in 2016, 30% in 2017, and 20% in 2018. Pretax accounting income for 2016 was $300,000, which includes interest revenue of $40,000 from municipal bonds. The enacted tax rate is 40%.

Required:
Assuming no differences between accounting income and taxable income other than those described above:
1. Prepare the journal entry to record income taxes in 2016.
2. What is Southern Atlantic's 2016 net income?

E 16–14
Multiple differences
● LO16–4, LO16–6

For the year ended December 31, 2016, Fidelity Engineering reported pretax accounting income of $977,000. Selected information for 2016 from Fidelity's records follows:

Interest income on municipal bonds	$32,000
Depreciation claimed on the 2016 tax return in excess of depreciation on the income statement	55,000
Carrying amount of depreciable assets in excess of their tax basis at year-end	85,000
Warranty expense reported on the income statement	26,000
Actual warranty expenditures in 2016	16,000

Fidelity's income tax rate is 40%. At January 1, 2016, Fidelity's records indicated balances of zero and $12,000 in its deferred tax asset and deferred tax liability accounts, respectively.

Required:
1. Determine the amounts necessary to record income taxes for 2016 and prepare the appropriate journal entry.
2. What is Fidelity's 2016 net income?

E 16–15
Multiple tax rates
● LO16–2, LO16–5

Allmond Corporation, organized on January 3, 2016, had pretax accounting income of $14 million and taxable income of $20 million for the year ended December 31, 2016. The 2016 tax rate is 35%. The only difference between accounting income and taxable income is estimated product warranty costs. Expected payments and scheduled tax rates (based on recent tax legislation) are as follows:

2017	$2 million	30%
2018	1 million	30%
2019	1 million	30%
2020	2 million	25%

Required:
1. Determine the amounts necessary to record Allmond's income taxes for 2016 and prepare the appropriate journal entry.
2. What is Allmond's 2016 net income?

E 16–16
Change in tax rates; calculate taxable income
● LO16–1, LO16–5

Arnold Industries has pretax accounting income of $33 million for the year ended December 31, 2016. The tax rate is 40%. The only difference between accounting income and taxable income relates to an operating lease in which Arnold is the lessee. The inception of the lease was December 28, 2016. An $8 million advance rent payment at the inception of the lease is tax-deductible in 2016 but, for financial reporting purposes, represents prepaid rent expense to be recognized equally over the four-year lease term.

Required:

1. Determine the amounts necessary to record Arnold's income taxes for 2016 and prepare the appropriate journal entry.
2. Determine the amounts necessary to record Arnold's income taxes for 2017 and prepare the appropriate journal entry. Pretax accounting income was $50 million for the year ended December 31, 2017.
3. Assume a new tax law is enacted in 2017 that causes the tax rate to change from 40% to 30% beginning in 2018. Determine the amounts necessary to record Arnold's income taxes for 2017 and prepare the appropriate journal entry.
4. Why is Arnold's 2017 income tax expense different when the tax rate change occurs from what it would be without the change?

E 16–17
Deferred taxes; change in tax rates
● LO16–1, LO16–5

Bronson Industries reported a deferred tax liability of $8 million for the year ended December 31, 2015, related to a temporary difference of $20 million. The tax rate was 40%. The temporary difference is expected to reverse in 2017 at which time the deferred tax liability will become payable. There are no other temporary differences in 2015–2017. Assume a new tax law is enacted in 2016 that causes the tax rate to change from 40% to 30% beginning in 2017. (The rate remains 40% for 2016 taxes.) Taxable income in 2016 is $30 million.

Required:
Determine the effect of the change and prepare the appropriate journal entry to record Bronson's income tax expense in 2016. What adjustment, if any, is needed to revise retained earnings as a result of the change?

E 16–18
Multiple temporary differences; record income taxes
● LO16–6

The information that follows pertains to Esther Food Products:

a. At December 31, 2016, temporary differences were associated with the following future taxable (deductible) amounts:

Depreciation	$60,000
Prepaid expenses	17,000
Warranty expenses	(12,000)

b. No temporary differences existed at the beginning of 2016.

c. Pretax accounting income was $80,000 and taxable income was $15,000 for the year ended December 31, 2016.

d. The tax rate is 40%.

Required:
Determine the amounts necessary to record income taxes for 2016 and prepare the appropriate journal entry.

E 16–19
Multiple temporary differences; record income taxes
● LO16–6

The information that follows pertains to Richards Refrigeration, Inc.:

a. At December 31, 2016, temporary differences existed between the financial statement carrying amounts and the tax bases of the following:

	($ in millions)		
	Carrying Amount	Tax Basis	Future Taxable (Deductible) Amount
Buildings and equipment (net of accumulated depreciation)	$120	$90	$30
Prepaid insurance	50	0	50
Liability—loss contingency	25	0	(25)

b. No temporary differences existed at the beginning of 2016.

c. Pretax accounting income was $200 million and taxable income was $145 million for the year ended December 31, 2016. The tax rate is 40%.

Required:

1. Determine the amounts necessary to record income taxes for 2016 and prepare the appropriate journal entry.
2. What is the 2016 net income?

E 16–20
Net operating loss carryforward
● LO16–7

During 2016, its first year of operations, Baginski Steel Corporation reported a net operating loss of $375,000 for financial reporting and tax purposes. The enacted tax rate is 40%.

Required:

1. Prepare the journal entry to recognize the income tax benefit of the net operating loss. Assume the weight of available evidence suggests future taxable income sufficient to benefit from future deductible amounts from the net operating loss carryforward.
2. Show the lower portion of the 2016 income statement that reports the income tax benefit of the net operating loss.

E 16–21
Net operating loss carryback
● LO16–7

Wynn Sheet Metal reported a net operating loss of $100,000 for financial reporting and tax purposes in 2016. The enacted tax rate is 40%. Taxable income, tax rates, and income taxes paid in Wynn's first four years of operation were as follows:

	Taxable Income	Tax Rates	Income Taxes Paid
2012	$60,000	30%	$18,000
2013	70,000	30	21,000
2014	80,000	40	32,000
2015	60,000	45	27,000

Required:

1. Prepare the journal entry to recognize the income tax benefit of the net operating loss. Wynn elects the carryback option.
2. Show the lower portion of the 2016 income statement that reports the income tax benefit of the net operating loss.

E 16–22
Net operating loss carryback and carryforward
● LO16–7

(This exercise is based on the situation described in E 16–21, modified to include a carryforward in addition to a carryback.)

Wynn Sheet Metal reported a net operating loss of $160,000 for financial reporting and tax purposes in 2016. The enacted tax rate is 40%. Taxable income, tax rates, and income taxes paid in Wynn's first four years of operation were as follows:

	Taxable Income	Tax Rates	Income Taxes Paid
2012	$60,000	30%	$18,000
2013	70,000	30	21,000
2014	80,000	40	32,000
2015	60,000	45	27,000

Required:

1. Prepare the journal entry to recognize the income tax benefit of the net operating loss. Wynn elects the carryback option.
2. Show the lower portion of the 2016 income statement that reports the income tax benefit of the net operating loss.

E 16–23
Identifying income tax deferrals
● LO16–1, LO16–2, LO16–4, LO16–7

Listed below are ten independent situations. For each situation indicate (by letter) whether it will create a deferred tax asset (A), a deferred tax liability (L), or neither (N).

Situation

_____ 1. Advance payments on insurance deductible when paid.
_____ 2. Estimated warranty costs, tax deductible when paid.
_____ 3. Rent revenue collected in advance; cash basis for tax purposes.
_____ 4. Interest received from investments in municipal bonds.
_____ 5. Prepaid expenses tax deductible when paid.
_____ 6. Net operating loss carryforward.
_____ 7. Net operating loss carryback.
_____ 8. Straight-line depreciation for financial reporting; MACRS for tax purposes.
_____ 9. Organization costs expensed when incurred, tax deductible over 15 years.
_____ 10. Life insurance proceeds received upon the death of the company president.

E 16–24
Balance sheet classification
● LO16–4, LO16–5, LO16–6, LO16–8

At December 31, DePaul Corporation had a $16 million balance in its deferred tax asset account and a $68 million balance in its deferred tax liability account. The balances were due to the following cumulative temporary differences:

1. Estimated warranty expense, $15 million: expense recorded in the year of the sale; tax-deductible when paid (one-year warranty).
2. Depreciation expense, $120 million: straight-line in the income statement; MACRS on the tax return.
3. Income from installment sales of properties, $50 million: income recorded in the year of the sale; taxable when received equally over the next five years.
4. Rent revenue collected in advance, $25 million; taxable in the year collected; recorded as income when earned the following year.

Required:

Show how any deferred tax amounts should be classified and reported in the December 31 balance sheet. The tax rate is 40%.

E 16–25
Multiple tax rates; balance sheet classification
● LO16–1, LO16–4, LO16–5, LO16–8

Case Development began operations in December 2016. When property is sold on an installment basis, Case recognizes installment income for financial reporting purposes in the year of the sale. For tax purposes, installment income is reported by the installment method. 2016 installment income was $600,000 and will be collected over the next three years. Scheduled collections and enacted tax rates for 2017–2019 are as follows:

2017	$150,000	30%
2018	250,000	40
2019	200,000	40

Pretax accounting income for 2016 was $810,000, which includes interest revenue of $10,000 from municipal bonds. The enacted tax rate for 2016 is 30%.

Required:

1. Assuming no differences between accounting income and taxable income other than those described above, prepare the appropriate journal entry to record Case's 2016 income taxes.
2. What is Case's 2016 net income?
3. How should the deferred tax amount be classified in a classified balance sheet?

E 16–26
Multiple differences; multiple tax rates; balance sheet classification
● LO16–1, LO16–2, LO16–4, LO16–5, LO16–6, LO16–8

(This exercise is a variation of E 16–25, modified to include a second temporary difference.)
Case Development began operations in December 2016. When property is sold on an installment basis, Case recognizes installment income for financial reporting purposes in the year of the sale. For tax purposes, installment income is reported by the installment method. 2016 installment income was $600,000 and will be collected over the next three years. Scheduled collections and enacted tax rates for 2017–2019 are as follows:

2017	$150,000	30%
2018	250,000	40
2019	200,000	40

Case also had product warranty costs of $80,000 expensed for financial reporting purposes in 2016. For tax purposes, only the $20,000 of warranty costs actually paid in 2016 was deducted. The remaining $60,000 will be deducted for tax purposes when paid over the next three years as follows:

2017	$20,000
2018	25,000
2019	15,000

Pretax *accounting* income for 2016 was $810,000, which includes interest revenue of $10,000 from municipal bonds. The enacted tax rate for 2016 is 30%.

Required:

1. Assuming no differences between accounting income and taxable income other than those described above, prepare the appropriate journal entry to record Case's 2016 income taxes.
2. What is Case's 2016 net income?
3. How should the deferred tax amounts be classified in a classified balance sheet?

E 16–27
Concepts; terminology
● LO16–1 through LO16–8

Listed below are several terms and phrases associated with accounting for income taxes. Pair each item from List A with the item from List B (by letter) that is most appropriately associated with it.

List A	List B
____ 1. No tax consequences.	a. Deferred tax liability.
____ 2. Originates, then reverses.	b. Deferred tax asset.
____ 3. Revise deferred tax amounts.	c. 2 years.
____ 4. Operating loss.	d. Current and deferred tax consequence combined.
____ 5. Future tax effect of prepaid expenses tax deductible when paid.	e. Temporary difference.
____ 6. Loss carryback.	f. Specific tax rates times amounts reversing each year.
____ 7. Future tax effect of estimated warranty expense.	g. Nontemporary differences.
____ 8. Valuation allowance.	h. When enacted tax rate changes.
____ 9. Phased-in change in rates.	i. Same as related asset or liability.
____ 10. Balance sheet classifications.	j. "More likely than not" test.
____ 11. Individual tax consequences of financial statement components.	k. Intraperiod tax allocation.
____ 12. Income tax expense.	l. Negative taxable income.

E 16–28
Tax credit; uncertainty regarding sustainability
● LO16–9

Delta Catfish Company has taken a position in its tax return to claim a tax credit of $10 million (direct reduction in taxes payable) and has determined that its sustainability is "more likely than not," based on its technical merits. Delta has developed the probability table shown below of all possible material outcomes:

Probability Table ($ in millions)

Amount of the tax benefit that management expects to receive	$10	$ 8	$ 6	$ 4	$ 2
Percentage likelihood that the tax benefit will be sustained at this level	10%	20%	25%	20%	25%

Delta's taxable income is $85 million for the year. Its effective tax rate is 40%. The tax credit would be a direct reduction in current taxes payable.

Required:

1. At what amount would Delta measure the tax benefit in its income statement?
2. Prepare the appropriate journal entry for Delta to record its income taxes for the year.

E 16–29
Intraperiod tax allocation
● LO16–10

The following income statement does not reflect intraperiod tax allocation.

Required:

Recast the income statement to reflect intraperiod tax allocation.

INCOME STATEMENT
For the Fiscal Year Ended March 31, 2016
($ in millions)

Revenues	$830
Cost of goods sold	(350)
Gross profit	480
Operating expenses	(180)
Income tax expense	(86)
Income before discontinued operations and extraordinary item	214
Loss from discontinued operations	(85)
Net income	$129

The company's tax rate is 40%.

E 16–30
FASB codification research
● LO16–5, LO16–8, LO16–10

Access the *FASB Accounting Standards Codification* at the FASB website (www.fasb.org). Determine the specific citation for accounting for each of the following items:

1. The specific items to which income tax expense is allocated for intraperiod tax allocation.
2. The tax rate used to calculate deferred tax assets and liabilities.
3. The required disclosures in the notes to financial statements for the components of income tax expense.

CPA and CMA Review Questions

CPA Exam Questions

KAPLAN CPA REVIEW

● LO16–1

The following questions are adapted from a variety of sources including questions developed by the AICPA Board of Examiners and those used in the Kaplan CPA Review Course to study accounting for income taxes while preparing for the CPA examination. Determine the response that best completes the statements or questions.

1. Scott Corp. received cash of $20,000 that was included in revenues in its 2016 financial statements, of which $12,000 will not be taxable until 2017. Scott's enacted tax rate is 30% for 2016, and 25% for 2017. What amount should Scott report in its 2016 balance sheet for deferred income tax liability?
   a. $2,000
   b. $2,400
   c. $3,000
   d. $3,600

● LO16–2

2. West Corp. leased a building and received the $36,000 annual rental payment on June 15, 2016. The beginning of the lease was July 1, 2016. Rental income is taxable when received. West's tax rates are 30% for 2016 and 40% thereafter. West had no other permanent or temporary differences. West determined that no valuation allowance was needed. What amount of deferred tax asset should West report in its December 31, 2016, balance sheet?
   a. $ 5,400
   b. $ 7,200
   c. $10,800
   d. $14,400

● LO16–3

3. In its December 31, 2016, balance sheet, Shin Co. had income taxes payable of $13,000 and a current deferred tax asset of $20,000 before determining the need for a valuation account. Shin had reported a current deferred tax asset of $15,000 at December 31, 2015. No estimated tax payments were made during 2016.

   At December 31, 2016, Shin determined that it was more likely than not that 10% of the deferred tax asset would not be realized. In its 2016 income statement, what amount should Shin report as total income tax expense?
   a. $ 8,000
   b. $ 8,500
   c. $10,000
   d. $13,000

● LO16–5

4. Stone Co. began operations in 2016 and reported $225,000 in income before income taxes for the year. Stone's 2016 tax depreciation exceeded its book depreciation by $25,000. Stone also had nondeductible book expenses of $10,000 related to permanent differences. Stone's tax rate for 2016 was 40%, and the enacted rate for years after 2016 is 35%. In its December 31, 2016, balance sheet, what amount of deferred income tax liability should Stone report?
   a. $ 8,750
   b. $10,000
   c. $12,250
   d. $14,000

● LO16–5

5. Black Co. organized on January 2, 2016, had pretax financial statement income of $500,000 and taxable income of $800,000 for the year ended December 31, 2016. The only temporary differences are accrued product warranty costs, which Black expects to pay as follows:

2017	$100,000
2018	$ 50,000
2019	$ 50,000
2020	$100,000

The enacted income tax rates are 25% for 2016, 30% for 2017 through 2019, and 35% for 2020. Black believes that future years' operations will produce profits. In its December 31, 2016, balance sheet, what amount should Black report as deferred tax asset?
   a. $50,000
   b. $75,000
   c. $90,000
   d. $95,000

● LO16–7

6. Dix, Inc., a calendar-year corporation, reported the following operating income (loss) before income tax for its first three years of operations:

2014	$100,000
2015	(200,000)
2016	400,000

There are no permanent or temporary differences between operating income (loss) for financial and income tax reporting purposes. When filing its 2015 tax return, Dix did not elect to forego the carryback of its loss for 2015. Assume a 40% tax rate for all years. What amount should Dix report as its income tax liability at December 31, 2016?
   a. $ 60,000
   b. $ 80,000
   c. $120,000
   d. $160,000

● LO16–10

7. An example of intraperiod income tax allocation is
   a. Reporting an extraordinary item in the income statement, net of direct tax effects.
   b. Interest income on municipal obligations.
   c. Estimated expenses for major repairs accrued for financial statement purposes in one year, but deducted for income tax purposes when paid in a subsequent year.
   d. Rental income included in income for income tax purposes when collected, but deferred for financial statement purposes until earned in a subsequent year.

CMA Exam Questions

The following questions dealing with accounting for income taxes are adapted from questions that previously appeared on Certified Management Accountant (CMA) examinations. The CMA designation sponsored by the Institute of Management Accountants (**www.imanet.org**) provides members with an objective measure of knowledge and competence in the field of management accounting. Determine the response that best completes the statements or questions.

● LO16–2

1. Which one of the following temporary differences will result in a deferred tax asset?
   a. Use of the straight-line depreciation method for financial statement purposes and the modified Accelerated Cost Recovery System (MACRS) for income tax purposes.
   b. Installment sale profits accounted for on the accrual basis for financial statement purposes and on a cash basis for income tax purposes.
   c. Advance rental receipts accounted for on the accrual basis for financial statement purposes and on a cash basis for tax purposes.
   d. Investment gains accounted for under the equity method for financial statement purposes and under the cost method for income tax purposes.

Questions 2 and 3 are based on the following information. Bearings Manufacturing Company Inc. purchased a new machine on January 1, 2017 for $100,000. The company uses the straight-line depreciation method with an estimated equipment life of 5 years and a zero salvage value for financial statement purposes, and uses the 3-year Modified Accelerated Cost Recovery System (MACRS) with an estimated equipment life of 3 years for income tax reporting purposes. Bearings is subject to a 35% marginal income tax rate. Assume that the deferred tax liability at the beginning of the year is zero and that Bearings has a positive earnings tax position. The MACRS depreciation rates for 3-year equipment are shown below.

Year	Rate
1	33.33%
2	44.45
3	14.81
4	7.41

● LO16–1

2. What is the deferred tax liability at December 31, 2017 (rounded to the nearest whole dollar)?
   a. $ 7,000
   b. $33,330
   c. $11,667
   d. $ 4,667

● LO16–5

3. For Bearings Manufacturing Company Inc., assume that the following new corporate income tax rates will go into effect:

2018–2020	40%
2021	45%

   What is the amount of the deferred tax asset/liability at December 31, 2017 (rounded to the nearest whole dollar)?
   a. $0
   b. $9,000
   c. $2,668
   d. $6,332

Problems

An alternate exercise and problem set is available in the Connect library.

P 16–1
Single temporary difference originates each year for four years
● LO16–1

Alsup Consulting sometimes performs services for which it receives payment at the conclusion of the engagement, up to six months after services commence. Alsup recognizes service revenue for financial reporting purposes when the services are performed. For tax purposes, revenue is reported when fees are collected. Service revenue, collections, and pretax accounting income for 2015–2018 are as follows:

	Service Revenue	Collections	Pretax Accounting Income
2015	$650,000	$620,000	$186,000
2016	750,000	770,000	250,000
2017	715,000	700,000	220,000
2018	700,000	720,000	200,000

There are no differences between accounting income and taxable income other than the temporary difference described above. The enacted tax rate for each year is 40%.

Required:
1. Prepare the appropriate journal entry to record Alsup's 2016 income taxes.
2. Prepare the appropriate journal entry to record Alsup's 2017 income taxes.
3. Prepare the appropriate journal entry to record Alsup's 2018 income taxes.

(Hint: You may find it helpful to prepare a schedule that shows the balances in service revenue receivable at December 31, 2015–2018.)

P 16–2
Temporary difference; determine deferred tax amount for three years; balance sheet classification
● LO16–2, LO16–8

Times-Roman Publishing Company reports the following amounts in its first three years of operation:

($ in 000s)	2016	2017	2018
Pretax accounting income	$250	$240	$230
Taxable income	290	220	260

The difference between pretax accounting income and taxable income is due to subscription revenue for one-year magazine subscriptions being reported for tax purposes in the year received, but reported in the income statement in later years when earned. The income tax rate is 40% each year. Times-Roman anticipates profitable operations in the future.

Required:
1. What is the balance sheet account for which a temporary difference is created by this situation?
2. For each year, indicate the cumulative amount of the temporary difference at year-end.
3. Determine the balance in the related deferred tax account at the end of each year. Is it a deferred tax asset or a deferred tax liability?
4. How should the deferred tax amount be classified and reported in the balance sheet?

P 16–3
Change in tax rate; single temporary difference
● LO16–1, LO16–5

Dixon Development began operations in December 2016. When lots for industrial development are sold, Dixon recognizes income for financial reporting purposes in the year of the sale. For some lots, Dixon recognizes income for tax purposes when collected. Income recognized for financial reporting purposes in 2016 for lots sold this way was $12 million, which will be collected over the next three years. Scheduled collections for 2017–2019 are as follows:

2017	$ 4 million
2018	5 million
2019	3 million
	$12 million

Pretax accounting income for 2016 was $16 million. The enacted tax rate is 40%.

Required:

1. Assuming no differences between accounting income and taxable income other than those described above, prepare the journal entry to record income taxes in 2016.
2. Suppose a new tax law, revising the tax rate from 40% to 35%, beginning in 2018, is enacted in 2017, when pretax accounting income was $15 million. No 2017 lot sales qualified for the special tax treatment. Prepare the appropriate journal entry to record income taxes in 2017.
3. If the new tax rate had not been enacted, what would have been the appropriate balance in the deferred tax liability account at the end of 2017? Why?

P 16–4
Change in tax rate; record taxes for four years
● LO16–1, LO16–5

Zekany Corporation would have had identical income before taxes on both its income tax returns and income statements for the years 2016 through 2019 except for differences in depreciation on an operational asset. The asset cost $120,000 and is depreciated for income tax purposes in the following amounts:

2016	$39,600
2017	52,800
2018	18,000
2019	9,600

The operational asset has a four-year life and no residual value. The straight-line method is used for financial reporting purposes.

Income amounts before depreciation expense and income taxes for each of the four years were as follows.

	2016	2017	2018	2019
Accounting income before taxes and depreciation	$60,000	$80,000	$70,000	$70,000

Assume the average and marginal income tax rate for 2016 and 2017 was 30%; however, during 2017 tax legislation was passed to raise the tax rate to 40% beginning in 2018. The 40% rate remained in effect through the years 2018 and 2019. Both the accounting and income tax periods end December 31.

Required:

Prepare the journal entries to record income taxes for the years 2016 through 2019.

P 16–5
Change in tax rate; record taxes for four years
● LO16–1, LO16–4, LO16–5

The DeVille Company reported pretax accounting income on its income statement as follows:

2016	$350,000
2017	270,000
2018	340,000
2019	380,000

Included in the income of 2016 was an installment sale of property in the amount of $50,000. However, for tax purposes, DeVille reported the income in the year cash was collected. Cash collected on the installment sale was $20,000 in 2017, $25,000 in 2018, and $5,000 in 2019.

Included in the 2018 income was $15,000 interest from investments in municipal bonds.

The enacted tax rate for 2016 and 2017 was 30%, but during 2017 new tax legislation was passed reducing the tax rate to 25% for the years 2018 and beyond.

Required:

Prepare the year-end journal entries to record income taxes for the years 2016–2019.

P 16–6
Multiple differences; temporary difference yet to originate; multiple tax rates; classification
● LO16–5, LO16–6, LO16–8

You are the new accounting manager at the Barry Transport Company. Your CFO has asked you to provide input on the company's income tax position based on the following:

1. Pretax accounting income was $41 million and taxable income was $8 million for the year ended December 31, 2016.
2. The difference was due to three items:
   a. Tax depreciation exceeds book depreciation by $30 million in 2016 for the business complex acquired that year. This amount is scheduled to be $60 million in 2017 and to reverse as ($50 million) and ($40 million) in 2018, and 2019, respectively.
   b. Insurance of $9 million was paid in 2016 for 2017 coverage.
   c. A $6 million loss contingency was accrued in 2016, to be paid in 2018.
3. No temporary differences existed at the beginning of 2016.
4. The tax rate is 40%.

Required:

1. Determine the amounts necessary to record income taxes for 2016 and prepare the appropriate journal entry.
2. How should the deferred tax amounts be classified in a classified balance sheet?
3. Assume the enacted federal income tax law specifies that the tax rate will change from 40% to 35% in 2018. When scheduling the reversal of the depreciation difference, you were uncertain as to how to deal with the fact that the difference will continue to originate in 2017 before reversing the next two years. Upon consulting **PricewaterhouseCoopers'** *Comperio* database, you found:

.441 Depreciable and amortizable assets

Only the reversals of the temporary difference at the balance sheet date would be scheduled. Future originations are not considered in determining the reversal pattern of temporary differences for depreciable assets. *FAS 109* [FASB ASC 740–Income Taxes] is silent as to how the balance sheet date temporary differences are deemed to reverse, but the FIFO pattern is intended.

You interpret that to mean that, when future taxable amounts are being scheduled, and a portion of a temporary difference has yet to originate, only the reversals of the *temporary difference at the balance sheet date* can be scheduled and multiplied by the tax rate that will be in effect when the difference reverses. Future originations (like the depreciation difference the second year) are not considered when determining the timing of the reversal. For the existing temporary difference, it is assumed that the difference will reverse the first year the difference begins reversing.

Determine the amounts necessary to record income taxes for 2016 and prepare the appropriate journal entry.

P 16–7
Multiple differences; calculate taxable income; balance sheet classification
● LO16–4, LO16–6, LO16–8

Sherrod, Inc., reported pretax accounting income of $76 million for 2016. The following information relates to differences between pretax accounting income and taxable income:

a. Income from installment sales of properties included in pretax accounting income in 2016 exceeded that reported for tax purposes by $3 million. The installment receivable account at year-end had a balance of $4 million (representing portions of 2015 and 2016 installment sales), expected to be collected equally in 2017 and 2018.

b. Sherrod was assessed a penalty of $2 million by the Environmental Protection Agency for violation of a federal law in 2016. The fine is to be paid in equal amounts in 2016 and 2017.

c. Sherrod rents its operating facilities but owns one asset acquired in 2015 at a cost of $80 million. Depreciation is reported by the straight-line method assuming a four-year useful life. On the tax return, deductions for depreciation will be more than straight-line depreciation the first two years but less than straight-line depreciation the next two years ($ in millions):

	Income Statement	Tax Return	Difference
2015	$20	$26	$ (6)
2016	20	35	(15)
2017	20	12	8
2018	20	7	13
	$80	$80	$ 0

d. Warranty expense of $3 million is reported in 2016. For tax purposes, the expense is deducted when costs are incurred, $2 million in 2016. At December 31, 2016, the warranty liability was $2 million (after adjusting entries). The balance was $1 million at the end of 2015.

e. In 2016, Sherrod accrued an expense and related liability for estimated paid future absences of $7 million relating to the company's new paid vacation program. Future compensation will be deductible on the tax return when actually paid during the next two years ($4 million in 2017; $3 million in 2018).

f. During 2015, accounting income included an estimated loss of $2 million from having accrued a loss contingency. The loss is paid in 2016 at which time it is tax deductible.

Balances in the deferred tax asset and deferred tax liability accounts at January 1, 2016, were $1.2 million and $2.8 million, respectively. The enacted tax rate is 40% each year.

Required:

1. Determine the amounts necessary to record income taxes for 2016 and prepare the appropriate journal entry.
2. What is the 2016 net income?
3. Show how any deferred tax amounts should be classified and reported in the 2016 balance sheet.

P 16–8
Multiple differences; taxable income given; two years; balance sheet classification; change in tax rate
● LO16–4, LO16–6, LO16–8

Arndt, Inc., reported the following for 2016 and 2017 ($ in millions):

	2016	2017
Revenues	$888	$983
Expenses	760	800
Pretax accounting income (income statement)	$128	$183
Taxable income (tax return)	$120	$200
Tax rate: 40%		

a. Expenses each year include $30 million from a two-year casualty insurance policy purchased in 2016 for $60 million. The cost is tax deductible in 2016.

b. Expenses include $2 million insurance premiums each year for life insurance on key executives.

c. Arndt sells one-year subscriptions to a weekly journal. Subscription sales collected and taxable in 2016 and 2017 were $33 million and $35 million, respectively. Subscriptions included in 2016 and 2017 financial reporting revenues were $25 million ($10 million collected in 2015 but not earned until 2016) and $33 million, respectively. Hint: View this as two temporary differences—one reversing in 2016; one originating in 2016.

d. 2016 expenses included a $17 million unrealized loss from reducing investments (classified as trading securities) to fair value. The investments were sold in 2017.

e. During 2015, accounting income included an estimated loss of $5 million from having accrued a loss contingency. The loss was paid in 2016 at which time it is tax deductible.

f. At January 1, 2016, Arndt had a deferred tax asset of $6 million and no deferred tax liability.

Required:

1. Which of the five differences described are temporary and which are permanent differences? Why?
2. Prepare a schedule that (a) reconciles the difference between pretax accounting income and taxable income and (b) determines the amounts necessary to record income taxes for 2016. Prepare the appropriate journal entry.
3. Show how any 2016 deferred tax amounts should be classified and reported on the 2016 balance sheet.
4. Prepare a schedule that (a) reconciles the difference between pretax accounting income and taxable income and (b) determines the amounts necessary to record income taxes for 2017. Prepare the appropriate journal entry.
5. Explain how any 2017 deferred tax amounts should be classified and reported on the 2017 balance sheet.
6. Suppose that during 2017, tax legislation was passed that will lower Arndt's effective tax rate to 35% beginning in 2018. Repeat requirement 4.

P 16–9
Determine deferred tax assets and liabilities
● LO16–6

Corning-Howell reported taxable income in 2016 of $120 million. At December 31, 2016, the reported amount of some assets and liabilities in the financial statements differed from their tax bases as indicated below:

	Carrying Amount	Tax Basis
Assets		
Current		
Net accounts receivable	$ 10 million	$ 12 million
Prepaid insurance	20 million	0
Prepaid advertising	6 million	0
Noncurrent		
Investments at fair value with changes in OCI*	4 million	0
Buildings and equipment (net)	360 million	280 million
Liabilities		
Current		
Liability—subscriptions received	14 million	0
Long-term		
Liability—postretirement benefits	594 million	0

*Gains and losses taxable when investments are sold.

The total deferred tax asset and deferred tax liability amounts at January 1, 2016, were $250 million and $40 million, respectively. The enacted tax rate is 40% each year.

Required:

1. Determine the total deferred tax asset and deferred tax liability amounts at December 31, 2016.
2. Determine the increase (decrease) in the deferred tax asset and deferred tax liability accounts at December 31, 2016.

3. Determine the income tax payable currently for the year ended December 31, 2016.
4. Prepare the journal entry to record income taxes for 2016.
5. Show how the deferred tax amounts should be classified and reported in the 2016 balance sheet.

P 16–10
Net operating loss carryback and carryforward; multiple differences
● LO16–2, LO16–4, LO16–7

Fores Construction Company reported a pretax operating loss of $135 million for financial reporting purposes in 2016. Contributing to the loss were (a) a penalty of $5 million assessed by the Environmental Protection Agency for violation of a federal law and paid in 2016 and (b) an estimated loss of $10 million from accruing a loss contingency. The loss will be tax deductible when paid in 2017.

The enacted tax rate is 40%. There were no temporary differences at the beginning of the year and none originating in 2016 other than those described above. Taxable income in Fores's two previous years of operation was as follows:

2014	$75 million
2015	30 million

Required:

1. Prepare the journal entry to recognize the income tax benefit of the net operating loss in 2016. Fores elects the carryback option.
2. Show the lower portion of the 2016 income statement that reports the income tax benefit of the net operating loss.
3. Prepare the journal entry to record income taxes in 2017 assuming pretax accounting income is $60 million. No additional temporary differences originate in 2017.

P 16–11
Valuation allowance; Delta Air Lines
● LO16–3, LO16–8
Real World Financials

Delta Air Lines revealed in its 10-K filing that its valuation allowance for deferred tax assets at the end of 2013 was $177 million, dramatically lower than the over $10 billion recorded at the end of 2012. Here is an excerpt from a press report from Bloomberg in January 2014, regarding this allowance:

> Delta Air Lines Inc. (DAL) led shares of U.S. carriers higher after posting fourth-quarter profit that topped analysts' estimates and forecasting an operating margin of as much as 8 percent in this year's initial three months. . . . Airlines are benefiting from lower fuel prices, constraints on capacity growth, controls on operating costs and demand that's keeping planes full, said Ray Neidl of Nexa Capital Partners LLC, a Washington-based aerospace and transportation consulting firm. . . . Net income was $8.48 billion, including an $8 billion non-cash gain from the reversal of a tax valuation allowance.
>
> Mary Schlangenstein, "Delta Leads Airline Stock Gains as Profit Beats Estimates," Bloomberg, January 21, 2014.

The following is an excerpt from a disclosure note to Delta's 2013 financial statements:

NOTE 12. INCOME TAXES *(In part)*
Deferred Taxes

The components of deferred tax assets and liabilities at December 31 were as follows (in millions):

	December 31,	
	2013	2012
Deferred tax assets:		
Net operating loss carryforwards	$ 6,024	$ 6,414
Pension, postretirement and other benefits	4,982	6,415
AMT credit carryforward	378	402
Deferred revenue	1,965	2,133
Other	698	881
Valuation allowance	(177)	(10,963)
Total deferred tax assets	$13,870	$ 5,282
Deferred tax liabilities:		
Depreciation	$ 4,799	$ 4,851
Intangible assets	1,704	1,730
Other	639	285
Total deferred tax liabilities	$ 7,142	$ 6,866

Required:

1. As indicated in the note, Delta had both deferred tax assets and deferred tax liabilities at the end of 2013. Some of each were current, some noncurrent. The balance sheet that year, though, reported only noncurrent deferred tax assets and current deferred tax assets. Explain why Delta's current deferred tax liabilities and noncurrent deferred tax liabilities were not explicitly reported. Explain what the current and noncurrent deferred tax assets represent.
2. What is a valuation allowance against deferred tax assets? When must such an allowance be recorded? Use Delta's situation to help illustrate your response.
3. Is an amount recorded in a valuation allowance for a deferred tax asset permanent? Explain why Delta is able to reclaim its valuation allowance.
4. Consider the excerpt from Bloomberg's press release. Recalculate the effect on Delta's 2013 net income of the change in Delta's valuation allowance for its deferred tax assets.

P 16–12
Integrating problem—bonds, leases, taxes
● LO16–1, LO16–5, LO16–8

The long-term liabilities section of CPS Transportation's December 31, 2015, balance sheet included the following:

a. A lease liability with 15 remaining lease payments of $10,000 each, due annually on January 1:

Lease liability	$76,061
Less: current portion	2,394
	$73,667

The incremental borrowing rate at the inception of the lease was 11% and the lessor's implicit rate, which was known by CPS Transportation, was 10%.

b. A deferred income tax liability due to a single temporary difference. The only difference between CPS Transportation's taxable income and pretax accounting income is depreciation on a machine acquired on January 1, 2015, for $500,000. The machine's estimated useful life is five years, with no salvage value. Depreciation is computed using the straight-line method for financial reporting purposes and the MACRS method for tax purposes. Depreciation expense for tax and financial reporting purposes for 2016 through 2019 is as follows:

Year	MACRS Depreciation	Straight-line Depreciation	Difference
2016	$160,000	$100,000	$60,000
2017	80,000	100,000	(20,000)
2018	70,000	100,000	(30,000)
2019	60,000	100,000	(40,000)

The enacted federal income tax rates are 35% for 2015 and 40% for 2016 through 2019. For the year ended December 31, 2016, CPS's income before income taxes was $900,000.

On July 1, 2016, CPS Transportation issued $800,000 of 9% bonds. The bonds mature in 20 years and interest is payable each January 1 and July 1. The bonds were issued at a price to yield the investors 10%. CPS records interest at the effective interest rate.

Required:

1. Determine CPS Transportation's income tax expense and net income for the year ended December 31, 2016.
2. Determine CPS Transportation's interest expense for the year ended December 31, 2016.
3. Prepare the long-term liabilities section of CPS Transportation's December 31, 2016, balance sheet.

P 16–13
Multiple differences; uncertain tax position
● LO16–3, LO16–4, LO16–6, LO16–9

Tru Developers, Inc., sells plots of land for industrial development. Tru recognizes income for financial reporting purposes in the year it sells the plots. For some of the plots sold this year, Tru took the position that it could recognize the income for tax purposes when the installments are collected. Income that Tru recognized for financial reporting purposes in 2016 for plots in this category was $60 million. The company expected to collect 60% of each sale in 2017 and 40% in 2018. This amount over the next two years is as follows:

2017	$36 million
2018	24 million
	$60 million

Tru's pretax accounting income for 2016 was $90 million. In its income statement, Tru reported interest income of $15 million, unrelated to the land sales, for which the company's position is that the interest is not taxable. Accordingly, the interest was not reported on the tax return. There are no differences between accounting income and taxable income other than those described above. The enacted tax rate is 40 percent.

Management believes the tax position taken on the land sales has a greater than 50% chance of being upheld based on its technical merits, but the position taken on the interest has a less than 50% chance of being upheld. It is further believed that the following likelihood percentages apply to the tax treatment of the land sales ($ in millions):

Amount Qualifying for Installment Sales Treatment	Percentage Likelihood of Tax Treatment Being Sustained
$60	20%
50	20%
40	20%
30	20%
20	20%

Required:

1. What portion of the tax benefit of tax-free interest will Tru recognize on its 2016 tax return?
2. What portion of the tax benefit of tax-free interest will Tru recognize on its 2016 financial statements?
3. What portion of the tax on the $60 million income from the plots sold on an installment basis will Tru defer on its 2016 tax return? What portion of the tax on the $60 million income from the plots sold on an installment basis will Tru defer in its 2016 financial statements? How is the difference between these two amounts reported?
4. Prepare the journal entry to record income taxes in 2016 assuming full recognition of the tax benefits in the financial statements of both differences between pretax accounting income and taxable income.
5. Prepare the journal entry to record income taxes in 2016 assuming the recognition of the tax benefits in the financial statements you indicated in requirements 1–3.

Broaden Your Perspective

Apply your critical-thinking ability to the knowledge you've gained. These cases will provide you an opportunity to develop your research, analysis, judgment, and communication skills. You also will work with other students, integrate what you've learned, apply it in real-world situations, and consider its global and ethical ramifications. This practice will broaden your knowledge and further develop your decision-making abilities.

Analysis Case 16–1
Basic concepts
● LO16–1 through LO16–8

One of the longest debates in accounting history is the issue of deferred taxes. The controversy began in the 1940s and has continued, even after the FASB issued *Statement of Financial Accounting Standards No. 109* [FASB ASC 740: Income Taxes] in 1992. At issue is the appropriate treatment of tax consequences of economic events that occur in years other than that of the events themselves.

Required:

1. Distinguish between temporary differences and permanent differences. Provide an example of each.
2. Distinguish between *intraperiod* tax allocation and *interperiod* tax allocation (deferred tax accounting). Provide an example of each.
3. How are deferred tax assets and deferred tax liabilities classified and reported in the financial statements?

Integrating Case 16–2
Postretirement benefits
● LO16–2

FASB ASC 715–60: Compensation–Retirement Benefits–Defined Benefit Plans–Other Postretirement (previously *Statement of Financial Accounting Standards No. 106)* establishes accounting standards for postretirement benefits other than pensions, most notably postretirement health care benefits. Essentially, the standard requires companies to accrue compensation expense each year employees perform services, for the expected cost of providing future postretirement benefits that can be attributed to that service. Typically, companies do not prefund these costs for two reasons: (a) unlike pension liabilities, no federal law requires companies to fund nonpension postretirement benefits and (b) funding contributions, again unlike for pension liabilities, are not tax deductible. (The costs aren't tax deductible until paid to, or on behalf of, employees.)

Required:

1. As a result of being required to record the periodic postretirement expense and related liability, most companies now report lower earnings and higher liabilities. How might many companies also report higher assets as a result of GAAP for postretirement plans?
2. One objection to current GAAP as cited in the chapter is the omission of requirements to discount deferred tax amounts to their present values. This objection is inappropriate in the context of deferred tax amounts necessitated by accounting for postretirement benefits. Why?

Real World Case 16–3
Income taxes and investment securities; Dominion Resources
● LO16–1, LO16–2, LO16–8

Real World Financials

Dominion Resources, Inc., is one of the nation's largest producers of energy. Corporate headquarters are in Richmond, VA. The following is an excerpt from a recent annual report.

INVESTMENTS (*IN PART*)
For all other available-for-sale securities, including those held in Dominion's merchant generation nuclear decommissioning trusts, net realized gains and losses (including any other-than-temporary impairments) are included in other income and unrealized gains and losses are reported as a component of AOCI, after-tax.

In fiscal 2013, Dominion's statement of comprehensive income reported an unrealized gain on investment securities of $203 million, net of $136 tax expense.

Required:
What would have been Dominion's journal entry to reflect the fair value of the investments?

Integrating Case 16–4
Tax effects of accounting changes and error correction; six situations
● LO16–1, LO16–2, LO16–8

Williams-Santana Inc. is a manufacturer of high-tech industrial parts that was started in 2002 by two talented engineers with little business training. In 2016, the company was acquired by one of its major customers. As part of an internal audit, the following facts were discovered. The audit occurred during 2016 before any adjusting entries or closing entries were prepared. The income tax rate is 40% for all years.

a. A five-year casualty insurance policy was purchased at the beginning of 2014 for $35,000. The full amount was debited to insurance expense at the time.
b. On December 31, 2015, merchandise inventory was overstated by $25,000 due to a mistake in the physical inventory count using the periodic inventory system.
c. The company changed inventory cost methods to FIFO from LIFO at the end of 2016 for both financial statement and income tax purposes. The change will cause a $960,000 increase in the beginning inventory at January 1, 2015.
d. At the end of 2015, the company failed to accrue $15,500 of sales commissions earned by employees during 2015. The expense was recorded when the commissions were paid in early 2016.
e. At the beginning of 2014, the company purchased a machine at a cost of $720,000. Its useful life was estimated to be 10 years with no salvage value. The machine has been depreciated by the double declining-balance method. Its carrying amount on December 31, 2015, was $460,800. On January 1, 2016, the company changed to the straight-line method.
f. Additional industrial robots were acquired at the beginning of 2013 and added to the company's assembly process. The $1,000,000 cost of the equipment was inadvertently recorded as repair expense. Robots have 10-year useful lives and no material salvage value. This class of equipment is depreciated by the straight-line method for both financial reporting and income tax reporting.

Required:
For each situation:
1. Identify whether it represents an accounting change or an error. If an accounting change, identify the type of change.
2. Prepare any journal entry necessary as a direct result of the change or error correction as well as any adjusting entry for 2016 related to the situation described. Any tax effects should be adjusted for through the deferred tax liability account.
3. Briefly describe any other steps that should be taken to appropriately report the situation.

Communication Case 16–5
Deferred taxes, changing rates; write a memo
● LO16–1, LO16–4, LO16–5

You are the new controller for Engineered Solutions. The company treasurer, Randy Patey, believes that as a result of pending legislation, the current 40% income tax rate will be decreased for 2017 to 35% and is uncertain which tax rate to apply in determining deferred taxes for 2016. Patey also is uncertain which differences should be included in that determination and has solicited your help. Your accounting group provided you the following information.

Two items are relevant to the decisions. One is the $50,000 insurance premium the company pays annually for the CEO's life insurance policy for which the company is the beneficiary. The second is that Engineered Solutions purchased a building on January 1, 2015, for $6,000,000. The building's estimated useful life is 30 years from the date of purchase, with no salvage value. Depreciation is computed using the straight-line method for financial reporting purposes and the MACRS method for tax purposes. As a result, the building's tax basis is $5,200,000 at December 31, 2016.

Required:
Write a memo to Patey that:
a. Identifies the objectives of accounting for income taxes.
b. Differentiates temporary differences and permanent differences.
c. Explains which tax rate to use.
d. Calculates the deferred tax liability at December 31, 2016.

Real World Case 16–6
Disclosure issues; balance sheet classifications; Walmart
● LO16–1, LO16–2, LO16–8

Real World Financials

The income tax disclosure note accompanying the January 31, 2014, financial statements of **Walmart** is reproduced below:

Note 9. Taxes (in part)
Income from Continuing Operations

	Fiscal Year Ended January 31,		
(Amounts in millions)	**2014**	**2013**	**2012**
Current:			
U.S. federal	$6,377	$5,611	$4,596
U.S. state and local	719	622	743
International	1,523	1,743	1,383
Total current tax provision	8,619	7,976	6,722
Deferred:			
U.S. federal	(72)	38	1,444
U.S. state and local	37	(8)	57
International	(479)	(48)	(299)
Total deferred tax expense (benefit)	(514)	(18)	1,202
Total provision for income taxes	$8,105	$7,958	$7,924

Deferred Taxes
The significant components of the Company's deferred tax account balances are as follows:

	January 31,	
(Amounts in millions)	**2014**	**2013**
Deferred tax assets:		
Loss and tax credit carryforwards	$ 3,566	$ 3,525
Accrued liabilities	2,986	2,683
Share-based compensation	126	204
Other	1,573	1,500
Total deferred tax assets	8,251	7,912
Valuation allowances	(1,801)	(2,225)
Deferred tax assets, net of valuation allowance	$ 6,450	$ 5,687
Deferred tax liabilities:		
Property and equipment	$ 6,295	$ 5,830
Inventories	1,641	1,912
Other	1,827	1,157
Total deferred tax liabilities	9,763	8,899
Net deferred tax liabilities	$ 3,313	$ 3,212

Required:

1. Focusing on only the first part of Note 9, relating current, deferred, and total provision for income taxes, prepare a summary journal entry that records Walmart's 2014 tax expense associated with income from continuing operations.
2. Compare the change in deferred taxes you recorded in your summary journal entry to the actual change in Walmart's net deferred tax liability for fiscal 2014. Do they reconcile? What besides continuing operations might affect deferred taxes?

Research Case 16–7
Researching the way tax deductions are reported on a corporation tax return; retrieving a tax form from the Internet
● LO16–1, LO16–2, LO16–3, LO16–8

The U.S. Treasury maintains an information site on the Internet. As part of this site the Internal Revenue Service provides tax information and services. Among those services is a server for publications and forms which allows a visitor to download a variety of IRS forms and publications.

Required:

1. Access the Treasury site on the Internet. The web address is **www.ustreas.gov**. After exploring the information available there, navigate to the IRS server for forms and publications via the IRS home page.
2. Download the corporation tax return, Form 1120.
3. Note the specific deductions listed that are deductible from total income to arrive at taxable income. Are any deductions listed that might not also be included among expenses in the income statement?
4. One of the deductions indicated is "net operating loss deduction." Under what circumstances might a company report an amount for this item?

5. Based on how taxable income is determined, how might temporary differences be created between taxable income and pretax income in the income statement?

Analysis Case 16–8
Reporting deferred taxes; Ford Motor Company
● LO16–1, LO16–2, LO16–3, LO16–7, LO16–8
Real World Financials

Access the financial statements and related disclosure notes of **Ford Motor Company** from its website at **corporate.ford.com**. In Ford's balance sheet, deferred income taxes in 2013 are reported as both a current asset ($13,315 million) and a noncurrent liability ($598 million).

Required:

1. Explain why deferred income taxes can be reported as both an asset and a liability. Is that the case for Ford in 2013?
2. Note 22 in the disclosure notes indicates that net deferred tax assets are $20,101 million and deferred tax liabilities are $7,384 million as of December 31, 2013. How can that be explained in light of the two amounts reported in the balance sheet?
3. Does Ford feel the need to record a valuation allowance for its deferred tax assets?

Analysis Case 16–9
Reporting deferred taxes; Kroger Co.
● LO16–1, LO16–2, LO16–3, LO16–7, LO16–8
Real World Financials

Kroger Co. is one of the largest retail food companies in the United States as measured by total annual sales. The Kroger Co. operates supermarkets, convenience stores, and manufactures and processes food that its supermarkets sell. Kroger's stores operate under names such as Dillon Food Stores, City Market, Kroger Kwik Shop, and Ralphs Grocery Company.

Like most corporations, Kroger has significant deferred tax assets and liabilities. Using Edgar (**www.sec.gov**) or the company's website, check the company's annual report for the year ended February 1, 2014.

Required:

1. From the income statement, determine the income tax expense for the most recent year. Tie that number to the first table in disclosure Note 5: "Taxes Based on Income," and prepare a summary journal entry that records Kroger's tax expense from continuing operations in the most recent year.
2. How are deferred taxes classified in Kroger's balance sheet? See the "Taxes Based on Income" note in the Notes to Consolidated Financial Statements. Considering disclosure Note 5: "Taxes Based on Income," what amounts are reported among current assets or liabilities and among noncurrent assets or liabilities?

Judgment Case 16–10
Analysing the effect of deferred tax liabilities on firm risk; Macy's, Inc.
● LO16–8
Real World Financials

The following is a portion of the February 2014 and 2013 balance sheets of **Macy's, Inc.**:

	February 1, 2014	February 2, 2013
LIABILITIES AND SHAREHOLDERS' EQUITY		
Current Liabilities:		
Short-term debt	$ 463	$ 124
Merchandise accounts payable	1,691	1,579
Accounts payable and accrued liabilities	2,810	2,610
Income taxes	362	355
Deferred income taxes	400	407
Total Current Liabilities	5,726	5,075
Long-Term debt	6,728	6,806
Deferred Income Taxes	1,273	1,238
Other Liabilities	1,658	1,821
Shareholders' Equity		
Common stock (364.9 and 387.7 shares outstanding)	4	4
Additional paid-in capital	2,522	3,872
Accumulated equity	6,235	5,108
Treasury stock	(1,847)	(2,002)
Accumulated other comprehensive loss	(665)	(931)
Total Shareholders' Equity	6,249	6,051
Total Liabilities and Shareholders' Equity	$21,634	$20,991

Macy's debt to equity ratio for the year ended February 1, 2014, was 2.46, calculated as ($21,634 − 6,249) ÷ 6,249. Some analysts argue that long-term deferred tax liabilities should be excluded from liabilities when computing the debt to equity ratio.

Required:

1. What is the rationale for the argument that long-term deferred tax liabilities should be excluded from liabilities when computing the debt to equity ratio?
2. What would be the effect on Macy's debt to equity ratio of excluding deferred tax liabilities from its calculation? What would be the percentage change?
3. What might be the rationale for not excluding long-term deferred tax liabilities from liabilities when computing the debt to equity ratio?

Trueblood Accounting Case 16–11
Valuation allowances against deferred tax assets
● LO16–3

The following Trueblood case is recommended for use with this chapter. The case provides an excellent opportunity for class discussion, group projects, and writing assignments. The case, along with Professor's Discussion material, can be obtained from the Deloitte foundation at its website: www.deloitte.com/us/truebloodcases.

Case 13-10: LOL – Income Taxes.

This case gives students an opportunity to better understand how valuation allowances against deferred tax assets are estimated and calculated. Students consider the sources of taxable income that can be used to determine whether a deferred tax asset is more likely than not to be realized in the future.

Trueblood Accounting Case 16–12
Uncertain tax positions
● LO16–9

The following Trueblood case is recommended for use with this chapter. The case provides an excellent opportunity for class discussion, group projects, and writing assignments. The case, along with Professor's Discussion Material, can be obtained from the Deloitte Foundation at its website: www.deloitte.com/us/truebloodcases.

Case 09-9: Bricks & Morta

This case gives the students an opportunity to better understand accounting for uncertain tax positions. The case illustrates the judgments involved in applying FASB ASC 740 (formerly FIN 48).

Judgment Case 16–13
Intraperiod tax allocation
● LO16–10

Russell-James Corporation is a diversified consumer products company. During 2016, Russell-James discontinued its line of cosmetics, which constituted discontinued operations for financial reporting purposes. As vice president of the food products division, you are interested in the effect of the discontinuance on the company's profitability. One item of information you requested was an income statement. The income statement you received was labeled *preliminary* and *unaudited:*

RUSSELL-JAMES CORPORATION
Income Statement
For the Year Ended December 31, 2016
($ in millions, except per share amounts)

Revenues		$ 300
Cost of goods sold		90
Gross profit		210
Selling and administrative expenses		(60)
Income from continuing operations before income taxes		150
Income taxes		(22)
Income from continuing operations		128
Discontinued operations:		
Loss from operations of cosmetics division	$(100)	
Gain from disposal of cosmetics division	15	(85)
Net income		$ 43
Per Share of Common Stock (100 million shares):		
Income from continuing operations		$1.28
Loss from operations of cosmetics division		(1.00)
Gain from disposal of cosmetics division		.15
Net income		$ .43

You are somewhat surprised at the magnitude of the loss incurred by the cosmetics division prior to its disposal. Another item that draws your attention is the apparently low tax rate indicated by the statement ($22 ÷ 150 = 15%). Upon further investigation you are told the company's tax rate is 40%.

Required:

1. Recast the income statement to reflect intraperiod tax allocation.
2. How would you reconcile the income tax expense shown on the statement above with the amount your recast statement reports?

Air France–KLM Case

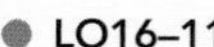

Air France–KLM (AF), a Franco-Dutch company, prepares its financial statements according to International Financial Reporting Standards. AF's financial statements and disclosure notes for the year ended December 31, 2013, are provided with all new textbooks. This material also is available at www.airfranceklm-finance.com.

Required:

1. Where in its December 31, 2013, balance sheet does AF report deferred taxes? How does this approach differ from the way deferred taxes are reported using U.S. GAAP? Using the Internet, determine how deferred taxes would be reported using IFRS at the time of your research. Explain why that approach might differ from the way AF reported deferred taxes at December 31, 2013.
2. Here's an excerpt from AF's notes to its financial statements:

> **Deferred taxes (in part)**
>
> The Group records deferred taxes using the balance sheet liability method, providing for any temporary differences between the carrying amounts of assets and liabilities for financial reporting purposes and the amounts used for taxation purposes, except for exceptions described in IAS 12 "Income taxes." The tax rates used are those enacted or substantively enacted at the balance sheet date.

   Is this policy consistent with U.S. GAAP? Explain.

3. Here's an excerpt from one of AF's notes to its financial statements:

> **Deferred taxes (in part)**
>
> Deferred tax assets related to temporary differences and tax losses carried forward are recognized only to the extent it is probable that a future taxable profit will be available against which the asset can be utilized at the tax entity level.

   Is this policy consistent with U.S. GAAP? Explain.

CPA Simulation 16–1

ABC, Inc.
Deferred Taxes
KAPLAN
CPA REVIEW

Test your knowledge of the concepts discussed in this chapter, practice critical professional skills necessary for career success, and prepare for the computer-based CPA exam by accessing our CPA simulations in the Connect Library.

The ABC simulation tests your ability to research authoritative accounting literature as to whether changes in tax laws and rates during the current year would affect the computation of ABC's deferred tax liabilities and deferred tax assets.

Specific tasks in the simulation include:

- Demonstrating an understanding of temporary and permanent differences.
- Analyzing transactions for their deferred tax reporting implications.
- Calculating the current and deferred tax components of income tax expense for multiple temporary differences.
- Applying judgment in deciding the deferred tax effects of a variety of transactions.
- Communicating the deferred tax effects of the two deferred tax reporting issues.
- Researching factors that might influence whether a valuation allowance might not be required in spite of evidence to the contrary.

CHAPTER

17 Pensions and Other Postretirement Benefits

OVERVIEW

Employee compensation comes in many forms. Salaries and wages, of course, provide direct and current payment for services provided. However, it's commonplace for compensation also to include benefits payable after retirement. We discuss pension benefits and other postretirement benefits in this chapter. Accounting for pension benefits recognizes that they represent deferred compensation for current service. Accordingly, the cost of these benefits is recognized on an accrual basis during the years that employees earn the benefits.

LEARNING OBJECTIVES

After studying this chapter, you should be able to:

- **LO17–1** Explain the fundamental differences between a defined contribution pension plan and a defined benefit pension plan. (*p. 999*)
- **LO17–2** Distinguish among the vested benefit obligation, the accumulated benefit obligation, and the projected benefit obligation (PBO). (*p. 1003*)
- **LO17–3** Describe the five events that might change the balance of the PBO. (*p. 1004*)
- **LO17–4** Explain how plan assets accumulate to provide retiree benefits and understand the role of the trustee in administering the fund. (*p. 1009*)
- **LO17–5** Describe the funded status of pension plans and how that amount is reported. (*p. 1011*)
- **LO17–6** Describe how pension expense is a composite of periodic changes that occur in both the pension obligation and the plan assets. (*p. 1011*)
- **LO17–7** Record for pension plans the periodic expense and funding as well as new gains and losses and new prior service cost as they occur. (*p. 1017*)
- **LO17–8** Understand the interrelationships among the elements that constitute a defined benefit pension plan. (*p. 1023*)
- **LO17–9** Describe the nature of postretirement benefit plans other than pensions and identify the similarities and differences in accounting for those plans and pensions. (*p. 1028*)
- **LO17–10** Explain how the obligation for postretirement benefits is measured and how the obligation changes. (*p. 1030*)
- **LO17–11** Determine the components of postretirement benefit expense. (*p. 1031*)
- **LO17–12** Discuss the primary differences between U.S. GAAP and IFRS with respect to accounting for postretirement benefit plans. (*pp. 1017, 1020, 1024,* and *1025*)

FINANCIAL REPORTING CASE

United Dynamics

You read yesterday that many companies in the United States have pension plans that are severely underfunded in the wake of the recent economic crisis. This caught your attention in part because you have your office interview tomorrow with United Dynamics. You hadn't really thought that much about the pension plan of your potential future employer, in part because your current employer has a defined contribution 401K plan, for which funding is not a concern. However, United Dynamics is an older firm with a defined benefit plan, for which funding is the employer's responsibility.

To prepare for your interview, you obtained a copy of United Dynamics' financial statements. Unfortunately, the financial statements themselves are of little help. You are unable to find any pension liability in the balance sheet, but the statement does report a relatively small "pension asset." The income statement reports pension expense for each of the years reported. For help, you search the disclosure notes. In part, the pension disclosure note reads as follows:

Note 7: Pension Plan

United Dynamics has a defined benefit pension plan covering substantially all of its employees. Plan benefits are based on years of service and the employee's compensation during the last three years of employment. The company's funding policy is consistent with the funding requirements of federal law and regulations. The net periodic pension expense for the company included the following components. The company's pension expense was as follows ($ in millions):

	2016	2015	2014
Current service costs	$ 43	$ 47	$ 42
Interest cost on projected benefit obligation	178	164	152
Return on assets	(213)	(194)	(187)
Amortization of prior service cost	43	43	43
Amortization of net gain	(2)	(1)	—
Net pension costs	$ 49	$ 59	$ 50

The following table describes the change in projected benefit obligation for the plan years ended December 31, 2016, and December 31, 2015 ($ in millions):

	2016	2015
Projected benefit obligation at beginning of year	$2,194	$2,121
Service cost	43	47
Interest cost	178	164
Actuarial (gain) loss	319	(40)
Benefits paid	(106)	(98)
Projected benefit obligation at end of year	$2,628	$2,194

The weighted-average discount rate and rate of increase in future compensation levels used in determining the actuarial present value of the projected benefit obligations in the above table were 8.1% and 4.3%, respectively, at December 31, 2016, and 7.73% and 4.7%, respectively, at December 31, 2015. The expected long-term rate of return on assets was 9.1% at December 31, 2016 and 2015.

(continued)

(continued)

The following table describes the change in the fair value of plan assets for the plan years ended December 31, 2016 and 2015 ($ in millions):

	2016	2015
Fair value of plan assets at beginning of year	$2,340	$2,133
Actual return on plan assets	215	178
Employer contributions	358	127
Benefits paid	(106)	(98)
Fair value of plan assets at end of year	$2,807	$2,340

"Ouch! I can't believe how much of my accounting I forgot," you complain to yourself. "I'd better get out my old intermediate accounting book."

QUESTION

By the time you finish this chapter, you should be able to respond appropriately to the questions posed in this case. Compare your response to the solution provided at the end of the chapter.

1. Why is pension plan underfunding not a concern in your present employment? (*p. 1001*)
2. Were you correct that the pension liability is not reported in the balance sheet? What is the liability? (*p. 1003*)
3. What is the amount of the plan assets available to pay benefits? What are the factors that can cause that amount to change? (*p. 1010*)
4. What does the "pension asset" represent? Are you interviewing with a company whose pension plan is severely underfunded? (*p. 1011*)
5. How is the pension expense influenced by changes in the pension liability and plan assets? (*p. 1012*)

PART A The Nature of Pension Plans

Over 125 million American workers are covered by pension plans. The United States' pension funds tripled in size during the previous two decades and now are roughly the size of Japan's gross national product. This powerful investment base now controls a sizable portion of the stock market. At the company level, the enormous size of pension funds is reflected in a periodic pension cost that constitutes one of the largest expenses many companies report. The corporate liability for providing pension benefits is huge. Obviously, then, the financial reporting responsibility for pensions has important social and economic implications.

Pension plans are designed to provide income to individuals during their retirement years. This is accomplished by setting aside funds during an employee's working years so that at retirement the accumulated funds plus earnings from investing those funds are available to replace wages. Actually, an individual who periodically invests in stocks, bonds, certificates of deposit (CDs), or other investments for the purpose of saving for retirement is establishing a personal pension fund. Often, such individual plans take the form of individual retirement accounts (IRAs) to take advantage of tax breaks offered by that arrangement. In employer plans, some or all of the periodic contributions to the retirement fund often are provided by the employer.

Pension plans often enhance productivity, reduce turnover, satisfy union demands, and allow employers to compete in the labor market.

Corporations establish pension plans for a variety of reasons. Sponsorship of pension plans provides employees with a degree of retirement security and fulfills a moral obligation felt by many employers. This security also can induce a degree of job satisfaction and perhaps loyalty that might enhance productivity and reduce turnover. Motivation to sponsor a plan sometimes comes from union demands and often relates to being competitive in the labor market.

Additional Consideration

When established according to tight guidelines, a pension plan gains important tax advantages. Such arrangements are called *qualified plans* because they qualify for favorable tax treatment. In a qualified plan, the employer is permitted an immediate tax deduction for amounts paid into the pension fund (within specified limits). The employees, on the other hand, are not taxed at the time employer contributions are made—only when retirement benefits are received. Moreover, earnings on the funds set aside by the employer are not taxed while in the pension fund, so the earnings accumulate tax free. If you are familiar with the tax advantages of IRAs, you probably recognize the similarity between those individual plans and corporate pension arrangements.

Qualified pension plans offer important tax benefits.

For a pension plan to be qualified for special tax treatment it must meet these general requirements.

1. It must cover at least 70% of employees.
2. It cannot discriminate in favor of highly compensated employees.
3. It must be funded in advance of retirement through contributions to an irrevocable trust fund.
4. Benefits must vest after a specified period of service, commonly five years. (We discuss this in more detail later.)
5. It complies with specific restrictions on the timing and amount of contributions and benefits.

● LO17–1

Sometimes, employers agree to annually contribute a specific (defined) amount to a pension fund on behalf of employees but make no commitment regarding benefit amounts at retirement. In other arrangements, employers don't specify the amount of annual contributions but promise to provide determinable (defined) amounts at retirement. These two arrangements describe defined contribution pension plans and defined benefit pension plans, respectively:

- **Defined contribution pension plans** promise fixed annual contributions to a pension fund (say, 5% of the employees' pay). Employees choose (from designated options) where funds are invested—usually stocks or fixed-income securities. Retirement pay depends on the size of the fund at retirement.
- **Defined benefit pension plans** promise fixed retirement benefits defined by a designated formula. Typically, the pension formula bases retirement pay on the employees' (a) years of service, (b) annual compensation (often final pay or an average for the last few years), and sometimes (c) age. Employers are responsible for ensuring that sufficient funds are available to provide promised benefits.

Today, approximately three-fourths of workers covered by pension plans are covered by defined contribution plans, roughly one-fourth by defined benefit plans. This represents a radical shift from previous years when the traditional defined benefit plan was far more common. However, very few new pension plans are of the defined benefit variety. In fact, many companies are terminating long-standing defined benefit plans and substituting defined contribution plans. Why the shift? There are three main reasons:

Virtually all *new* pension plans are defined contribution plans.

1. Government regulations make defined benefit plans cumbersome and costly to administer.
2. Employers are increasingly unwilling to bear the risk of defined benefit plans; with defined contribution plans, the company's obligation ends when contributions are made.
3. There has been a shift among many employers from trying to "buy long-term loyalty" (with defined benefit plans) to trying to attract new talent (with more mobile defined contribution plans).

The two categories of pension plans are depicted in Illustration 17–1.

Illustration 17–1
Defined Contribution and Defined Benefit Pension Plans

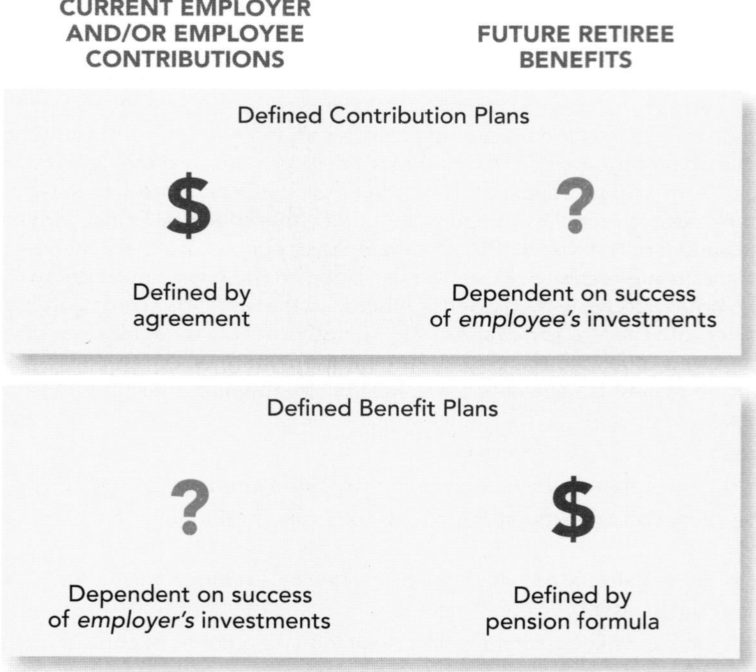

Both types of plans have a common goal: to provide income to employees during their retirement years. Still, the two types of plans differ regarding who bears the risk—the employer or the employees—for whether the retirement objectives are achieved. The two types of plans also have entirely different implications for accounting and financial reporting. Our discussion of defined contribution plans will be brief. Although these are now the most popular type of corporate pension plan, their relative simplicity permits a rather straightforward accounting treatment that requires little explanation. On the other hand, defined benefit plans require considerably more complex accounting treatment and constitute the primary focus of this chapter.

Defined Contribution Pension Plans

Defined contribution plans **promise defined periodic contributions to a pension fund, without further commitment regarding benefit amounts at retirement.**

Defined contribution pension plans are becoming increasingly popular vehicles for employers to provide retirement income without the paperwork, cost, and risk generated by the more traditional defined benefit plans. Defined contribution plans promise fixed periodic contributions to a pension fund. Retirement income depends on the size of the fund at retirement. No further commitment is made by the employer regarding benefit amounts at retirement.

These plans have several variations. In money purchase plans, employers contribute a fixed percentage of employees' salaries. Thrift plans, savings plans, and 401(k) plans (named after the Tax Code section that specifies the conditions for the favorable tax treatment of these plans) permit voluntary contributions by employees. These contributions typically are matched to a specified extent by employers. Most employers match up to 50% of employee contributions up to the first 6% of salary.

Approximately two-thirds of American workers participate in 401(k) plans. More than two trillion dollars are invested in these plans.

When plans link the amount of contributions to company performance, labels include profit-sharing plans, incentive savings plans, 401(k) profit-sharing plans, and similar titles. When employees make contributions to the plan in addition to employer contributions, it's called a *contributory* plan. Sometimes the amount the employer contributes is tied to the amount of the employee contribution.[1] Variations are seemingly endless. An example from a recent annual report of **Microsoft Corporation** is shown in Illustration 17–2.

Note 20 (in part)
Savings plan
We have a savings plan in the United States that qualifies under Section 401(k) of the Internal Revenue Code, and a number of savings plans in international locations. Participating U.S. employees may contribute up to 75% of their salary, but not more than statutory limits. We contribute fifty cents for each dollar a participant contributes in this plan, with a maximum contribution of 3% of a participant's earnings. Matching contributions for all plans were $393 million, $373 million, and $282 million in fiscal years 2013, 2012, and 2011, respectively, and were expensed as contributed.

Illustration 17–2
Defined Contribution Plan—Microsoft Corporation

Real World Financials

Accounting for these plans is quite easy. Each year, the employer simply records pension expense equal to the amount of the annual contribution. Suppose a plan promises an annual contribution equal to 3% of an employee's salary. If an employee's salary is $110,000 in a particular year, the employer would simply recognize pension expense in the amount of the contribution:

FINANCIAL Reporting Case

Q1, p. 998

Pension expense	3,300	
Cash ($110,000 × 3%)		3,300

For defined contribution plans, the employer simply records pension expense equal to the cash contribution.

The employee's retirement benefits are totally dependent upon how well investments perform. Who bears the risk (or reward) of that uncertainty? The employee would bear the risk of uncertain investment returns and, potentially, settle for far less at retirement than at first expected.[2] On the other hand, the employer would be free of any further obligation. Because the actual investments are held by an independent investment firm, the employer is free of that recordkeeping responsibility as well.

Risk is reversed in a defined benefit plan. Because specific benefits are promised at retirement, the employer would be responsible for making up the difference when investment performance is less than expected. We look at defined benefit plans next.

Defined Benefit Pension Plans

When setting aside cash to fund a pension plan, the uncertainty surrounding the rate of return on plan assets is but one of several uncertainties inherent in a defined benefit plan. Employee turnover affects the number of employees who ultimately will become eligible for retirement benefits. The age at which employees will choose to retire as well as life expectancies will impact both the length of the retirement period and the amount of the benefits. Inflation, future compensation levels, and interest rates also have obvious influence on eventual benefits.

***Defined benefit plans* promise fixed retirement benefits defined by a designated formula.**

Uncertainties complicate determining how much to set aside each year to ensure that sufficient funds are available to provide promised benefits.

This is particularly true when pension benefits are defined by a pension formula, as usually is the case. A typical formula might specify that a retiree will receive annual retirement benefits based on the employee's years of service and annual pay at retirement (say, pay level in the final year, highest pay achieved, or average pay in the last two or more years). For example, a pension formula might define annual retirement benefits as:

$$1\tfrac{1}{2}\% \times \text{Years of service} \times \text{Final year's salary}$$

By this formula, the annual benefits to an employee who retires after 30 years of service, with a final salary of $100,000, would be:

$$1\tfrac{1}{2}\% \times 30 \text{ years} \times \$100{,}000 = \$45{,}000$$

[1]One popular way for employer companies to provide contributions is with shares of its own common stock. If so, the arrangements usually are designed to comply with government requirements to be designated an employee stock ownership plan (ESOP).

[2]Of course, this is not entirely unappealing to the employee. Defined contribution plans allow an employee to select investments in line with his or her own risk preferences and often provide greater retirement benefits and flexibility than defined benefit plans.

A pension formula typically defines retirement pay based on the employees' (a) years of service, (b) annual compensation, and sometimes (c) age.

Pension gains and losses occur when the *pension obligation* is lower or higher than expected.

Pension gains and losses occur when the *return on plan assets* is higher or lower than expected.

Typically, a firm will hire an actuary, a professional trained in a particular branch of statistics and mathematics, to assess the various uncertainties (employee turnover, salary levels, mortality, etc.) and to estimate the company's obligation to employees in connection with its pension plan. Such estimates are inherently subjective, so regardless of the skill of the actuary, estimates invariably deviate from the actual outcome to one degree or another.[3] For instance, the return on assets can turn out to be more or less than expected. These deviations are referred to as *gains* and *losses* on pension assets. When it's necessary to revise estimates related to the pension obligation because it's determined to be more or less than previously thought, these revisions are referred to as *losses* and *gains,* respectively, on the pension liability. Later, we will discuss the accounting treatment of gains and losses from either source. The point here is that the risk of the pension obligation changing unexpectedly or the pension funds being inadequate to meet the obligation is borne by the employer with a defined benefit pension plan.

The key elements of a defined benefit pension plan are:

1. The *employer's obligation* to pay retirement benefits in the future.
2. The *plan assets* set aside by the employer from which to pay the retirement benefits in the future.
3. The *periodic expense* of having a pension plan.

Neither the pension obligation nor the plan assets are reported individually in the balance sheet.

The pension expense is a direct composite of periodic changes that occur in both the pension obligation and the plan assets.

As you will learn in this chapter, the first two of these elements are not reported individually in the employer's financial statements. This may seem confusing at first because it is inconsistent with the way you're accustomed to treating assets and liabilities. Even though they are not separately reported, it's critical that you understand the composition of both the pension obligation and the plan assets because (a) they are reported as a net amount in the balance sheet, and (b) their balances are reported in disclosure notes. And, importantly, the pension expense reported in the income statement is a direct composite of periodic changes that occur in both the pension obligation and the plan assets.

For this reason, we will devote a considerable portion of our early discussion to understanding the composition of the pension obligation and the plan assets before focusing on the derivation of pension expense and required financial statement disclosures. We will begin with a quick overview of how periodic changes that occur in both the pension obligation and the plan assets affect pension expense. Next we will explore how those changes occur, beginning with changes in the pension obligation followed by changes in plan assets. We'll then return to pension expense for a closer look at how those changes influence its calculation. After that, we will bring together the separate but related parts by using a simple spreadsheet to demonstrate how each element of the pension plan articulates with the other elements.

Current GAAP retains three fundamental aspects of past pension accounting: *delayed recognition* of certain events, reporting *net cost,* and *offsetting* liabilities and assets. Those three features of practice have shaped financial reporting for many years . . . and they conflict in some respects with accounting principles applied elsewhere.[4]

Pension Expense—An Overview

The annual pension expense reflects changes in both the pension obligation and the plan assets. Illustration 17–3 provides a brief overview of how these changes are included in pension expense. After the overview, we'll look closer at each of the components.

Next we explore each of these pension expense components in the context of its being a part of either (a) the pension obligation or (b) the plan assets. After you learn how the expense components relate to these elements of the pension plan, we'll return to explore further how they are included in the pension expense.

[3]We discuss changes in more detail in Chapter 20.

[4]FASB ASC 715: Compensation–Retirement Benefits (previously "Employers' Accounting for Pensions," *Statement of Financial Accounting Standards No. 87* (Stamford, Conn.: FASB, 1985)).

Components of Pension Expense

+	**Service cost** ascribed to employee service during the period
+	**Interest** accrued on the pension liability
−	**Return** on the plan assets*
	Amortized portion of:
+	**Prior service cost** attributed to employee service before an amendment to the pension plan
+ or (−)	**Losses or (gains)** from revisions in the pension liability or from investing plan assets
=	**Pension expense**

*The actual return is adjusted for any difference between actual and expected return, resulting in the expected return being reflected in pension expense. This loss or gain from investing plan assets is combined with losses and gains from revisions in the pension liability for deferred inclusion in pension expense. (See the last component of pension expense.)

Illustration 17–3

Components of Pension Expense—Overview (More Later)

Interest and investment return are financing aspects of the pension cost.

The recognition of some elements of the pension expense is delayed.

PART B

The Pension Obligation and Plan Assets

The Pension Obligation

FINANCIAL Reporting Case

Q2, p. 998

Now we consider more precisely what is meant by the pension obligation. Unfortunately, there's not just one definition, nor is there uniformity concerning which definition is most appropriate for pension accounting. Actually, three different ways to measure the pension obligation have meaning in pension accounting, as shown in Illustration 17–4.

1. **Accumulated benefit obligation (ABO)** The actuary's estimate of the total retirement benefits (at their discounted present value) earned so far by employees, applying the pension formula using **existing** compensation levels.
2. **Vested benefit obligation (VBO)** The portion of the accumulated benefit obligation that plan participants are entitled to receive regardless of their continued employment.
3. **Projected benefit obligation (PBO)** The actuary's estimate of the total retirement benefits (at their discounted present value) earned so far by employees, applying the pension formula using **estimated future** compensation levels. (If the pension formula does not include future compensation levels, the PBO and the ABO are the same.)

Illustration 17–4

Ways to Measure the Pension Obligation

● LO17–2

Later you will learn that the projected benefit obligation is the basis for some elements of the periodic pension expense. Remember, there is but one obligation; these are three ways to measure it. The relationship among the three is depicted in Illustration 17–5 on the next page.

Now let's look closer at how the obligation is measured in each of these three ways. Keep in mind, though, that it's not the accountant's responsibility to actually derive the measurement; a professional actuary provides these numbers. However, for the accountant to effectively use the numbers provided, she or he must understand their derivation.

Accumulated Benefit Obligation

The **accumulated benefit obligation (ABO)** is an estimate of the discounted present value of the retirement benefits earned so far by employees, applying the plan's pension formula using existing compensation levels. When we look at a detailed calculation of the projected benefit obligation later, keep in mind that simply substituting the employee's existing compensation in the pension formula for her projected salary at retirement would give us the accumulated benefit obligation.

The *accumulated benefit obligation* ignores possible pay increases in the future.

Illustration 17–5
Alternative Measures of the Pension Obligation

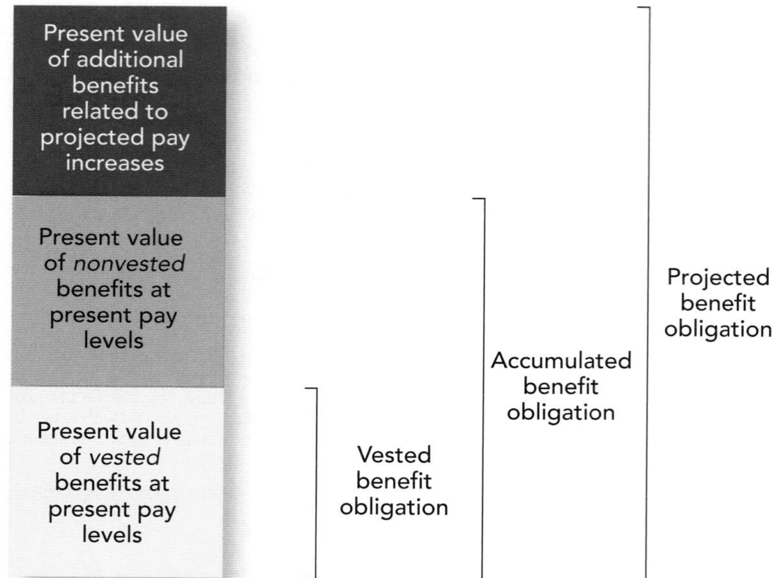

Vested Benefit Obligation

Suppose an employee leaves the company to take another job. Will she still get earned benefits at retirement? The answer depends on whether the benefits are vested under the terms of this particular pension plan. If benefits are fully vested—yes. **Vested benefits** are those that employees have the right to receive even if their employment were to cease today.

The benefits of most pension plans vest after five years.

Pension plans typically require some minimum period of employment before benefits vest. Before the Employee Retirement Income Security Act (ERISA) was passed in 1974, horror stories relating to lost benefits were commonplace. It was possible, for example, for an employee to be dismissed a week before retirement and be left with no pension benefits. Vesting requirements were tightened drastically to protect employees. These requirements have been changed periodically since then. Today, benefits must vest (a) fully within five years or (b) 20% within three years with another 20% vesting each subsequent year until fully vested after seven years. Five-year vesting is most common. ERISA also established the Pension Benefit Guaranty Corporation (PBGC) to impose liens on corporate assets for unfunded pension liabilities in certain instances and to administer terminated pension plans. The PBGC provides a form of insurance for employees similar to the role of the FDIC for bank accounts and is financed by premiums from employers equal to specified amounts for each covered employee. It makes retirement payments for terminated plans and guarantees basic vested benefits when pension liabilities exceed assets. The vested benefit obligation is actually a subset of the ABO, the portion attributable to benefits that have vested.

Projected Benefit Obligation

● LO17–3

The *PBO* estimates retirement benefits by applying the pension formula using projected future compensation levels.

As described earlier, when the ABO is estimated, the most recent salary is included in the pension formula to estimate future benefits, even if the pension formula specifies the final year's salary. No attempt is made to forecast what that salary would be the year before retirement. Of course, the most recent salary certainly offers an objective number to measure the obligation, but is it realistic? Since it's unlikely that there will be no salary increases between now and retirement, a more meaningful measurement should include a projection of what the salary might be at retirement.[5] Measured this way, the liability is referred to as the **projected benefit obligation (PBO)**. Hereafter in the chapter, when we mention the "pension obligation," we are referring to the PBO. The PBO measurement may be less reliable than the ABO but is more relevant and representationally faithful.

[5]To project future salaries for a group of employees, actuaries usually assume some percentage rate of increase in compensation levels in upcoming years. Recent estimates of the rate of compensation increase have ranged from 2.3% to 6% with 4% being the most commonly reported expectation (Pension/OPEB 2013 Assumption and Disclosure Survey, PWC, 2013).

To understand the concepts involved, it's helpful to look at a numerical example. We'll simplify the example (Illustration 17–6) by looking at how pension amounts would be determined for a single employee. Keep in mind though, that in actuality, calculations would be made (by the actuary) for the entire employee pool rather than on an individual-by-individual basis.

Illustration 17–6

Projected Benefit Obligation

Jessica Farrow was hired by Global Communications in 2005. The company has a defined benefit pension plan that specifies annual retirement benefits equal to:

1.5% × Service years × Final year's salary

Farrow is expected to retire in 2044 after 40 years service. Her retirement period is expected to be 20 years. At the end of 2014, 10 years after being hired, her salary is $100,000. The interest rate is 6%. The company's actuary projects Farrow's salary to be $400,000 at retirement.*

What is the company's projected benefit obligation with respect to Jessica Farrow?

Steps to calculate the projected benefit obligation:

1. Use the pension formula (including a projection of future salary levels) to determine the retirement benefits earned to date.
2. Find the present value of the retirement benefits as of the retirement date.
3. Find the present value of retirement benefits as of the current date.

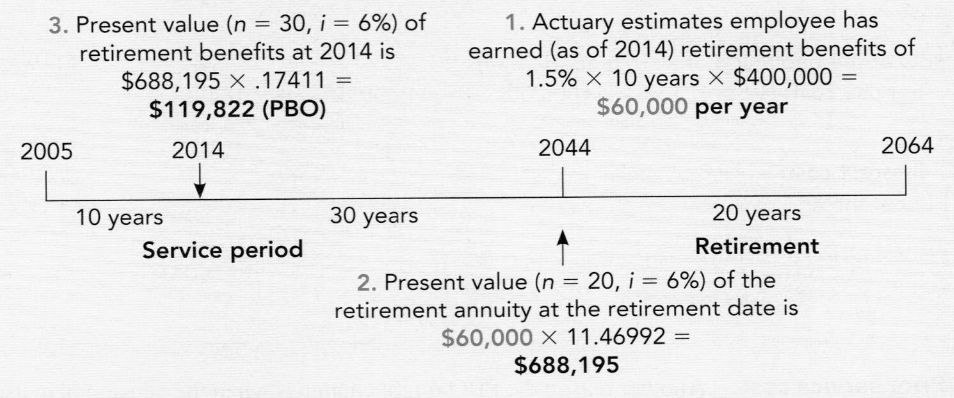
3. Present value (n = 30, i = 6%) of
retirement benefits at 2014 is
$688,195 × .17411 =
$119,822 (PBO)
1. Actuary estimates employee has
earned (as of 2014) retirement benefits of
1.5% × 10 years × $400,000 =
$60,000 **per year**
2005
2014
2044
2064
10 years
30 years
20 years
Service period
Retirement
2. Present value (n = 20, i = 6%) of the
retirement annuity at the retirement date is
$60,000 × 11.46992 =
$688,195

*This salary reflects an estimated compound rate of increase of about 5% and should take into account expectations concerning inflation, promotions, productivity gains, and other factors that might influence salary levels.

The actual includes projected salaries in the pension formula. The projected benefit obligation is the present value of those benefits.

Using Excel, enter:
= PV(.06,20,60000)
Output: 688195

Using a calculator:
enter: N 20 I 6
PMT – 60000 FV
Output: PV 688195

If the actuary's estimate of the final salary hasn't changed, the PBO a year later at the end of 2015 would be $139,715 as demonstrated in Illustration 17–6A.

Illustration 17–6A

PBO in 2015

3. Present value (n = 29, i = 6%) of retirement benefits at 2015 is $757,015 × .18456 = **$139,715 (PBO)**

1. Actuary estimates employee has earned (as of 2015) retirement benefits of 1.5% × 11 years × $400,000 = **$66,000 per year**

2005 — 2015 — 2044 — 2064

11 years | 29 years | 20 years

Service period | **Retirement**

2. Present value (n = 20, i = 6%) of the retirement annuity at the retirement date is $66,000 × 11.46992 = **$757,015**

In 2015 the pension formula includes one more service year.

Also, 2015 is one year closer to the retirement date for the purpose of calculating the present value.

CHANGES IN THE PBO. Notice that the PBO increased during 2015 (Illustration 17–6A) from $119,822 to $139,715 for two reasons:

1. One more service year is included in the pension formula calculation (service cost).
2. The employee is one year closer to retirement, causing the present value of benefits to increase due to the time value of future benefits (interest cost).

These represent two of the events that might possibly cause the balance of the PBO to change. Let's elaborate on these and the three other events that might change the balance of the PBO. The five events are (1) service cost, (2) interest cost, (3) prior service cost, (4) gains and losses, and (5) payments to retired employees.

Each year's service adds to the obligation to pay benefits.

1. Service cost. As we just witnessed in the illustration, the PBO increases each year by the amount of that year's service cost. This represents the increase in the projected benefit obligation attributable to employee service performed during the period. As we explain later, it also is the primary component of the annual pension expense.

Interest accrues on the PBO each year.

2. Interest cost. The second reason the PBO increases is called the interest cost. Even though the projected benefit obligation is not formally recognized as a liability in the company's balance sheet, it is a liability nevertheless. And, as with other liabilities, interest accrues on its balance as time passes. The amount can be calculated directly as the assumed discount rate multiplied by the projected benefit obligation at the beginning of the year.[6]

Additional Consideration

We can verify the increase in the PBO as being caused by the service cost and interest cost as follows:

PBO at the beginning of 2015 (end of 2014)					$119,822
Service cost: (1.5% × 1 yr. × $400,000) Annual retirement benefits from 2015 service	×	11.46992* To discount to 2044	×	.18456† To discount to 2015	12,701
Interest cost: $119,822 × 6%					7,189
PBO at the end of 2015					$139,712‡

*Present value of an ordinary annuity of $1: $n = 20$, $i = 6\%$.
†Present value of $1: $n = 29$, $i = 6\%$.
‡Differs from $139,715 due to rounding.

3. Prior service cost. Another reason the PBO might change is when the pension plan itself is *amended* to revise the way benefits are determined. For example, Global Communications in our illustration might choose to revise the pension formula by which benefits are calculated. Let's back up and assume the formula's salary percentage is increased in 2015 from 1.5% to 1.7%:

1.7% × Service years × Final year's salary
(revised pension formula)

Obviously, the annual service cost from this date forward will be higher than it would have been without the amendment. This will cause a more rapid future expansion of the PBO. But it also might cause an immediate increase in the PBO as well. Here's why.

When a pension plan is amended, credit often is given for employee service rendered in prior years. The cost of doing so is called *prior service cost*.

Suppose the amendment becomes effective for future years' service only, without consideration of employee service to date. As you might imagine, the morale and dedication of long-time employees of the company could be expected to suffer. So, for economic as well as ethical reasons, most companies choose to make amendments retroactive to prior years. In other words, the more beneficial terms of the revised pension formula are not applied just to future service years, but benefits attributable to all prior service years also are recomputed under the more favorable terms. Obviously, this decision is not without cost to the company. Making the amendment retroactive to prior years adds an extra layer of retirement benefits, increasing the company's benefit obligation. The increase in the PBO attributable to making a plan amendment retroactive is referred to as prior service cost.[7]

[6]Assumed discount rates should reflect rates used currently in annuity contracts. Discount rates recently reported have ranged from 3.44% to 4.4% with 4% being the most commonly assumed rate (Pension/OPEB 2013 Assumption and Disclosure Survey, PWC, 2013).
[7]Prior service cost also is created if a defined benefit pension plan is initially adopted by a company that previously did not have one, and the plan itself is made retroactive to give credit for prior years' service. Prior service cost is created by plan amendments far more often than by plan adoptions because most companies already have pension plans, and new pension plans in recent years have predominantly been defined contribution plans.

For instance, Illustration 17–7 presents an excerpt from an annual report of **Ecolab, Inc.** describing the increase in its PBO as a result of making an amendment retroactive:

Note 1: Retirement Plans (in part)

. . . The Company amended its U.S. pension plan to change the formula for pension benefits and to provide a more rapid vesting schedule. The plan amendments resulted in a $6 million increase in the projected benefits obligation.

Illustration 17–7

Prior Service Cost—Ecolab, Inc.

Real World Financials

Let's put prior service cost in the context of our illustration.

At the end of 2014, and therefore the beginning of 2015, the PBO is $119,822. If the plan is amended on January 3, 2015, the PBO for that date could be recomputed as:

Retroactive benefits from an amendment add additional costs, increasing the company's PBO. This increase is the prior service cost.

	PBO without Amendment		PBO with Amendment	
1.	1.5% × 10 yrs. × $400,000	= $ 60,000	1.7% × 10 yrs. × $400,000	= $ 68,000
2.	$60,000 × 11.46992	= 688,195	$68,000 × 11.46992	= 779,955
3.	$688,195 × .17411	= 119,822	$779,955 × .17411	= 135,798

$15,976
Prior service cost

The **$15,976** increase in the PBO attributable to applying the more generous terms of the amendment to prior service years is the prior service cost. And, because we assumed the amendment occurred at the beginning of 2015, both the 2015 service cost and the 2015 interest cost would change as a result of the prior service cost. This is how:

Prior service cost increased the PBO at the beginning of the year.

PBO at the beginning of 2015 (end of 2014)			$119,822
Prior service cost (determined above)			15,976
PBO including prior service cost at the beginning of 2015			135,798
Service cost: (1.7% × 1 yr. × $400,000) Annual retirement benefits from 2015 service	× 11.46992* To discount to 2044	× .18456† To discount to 2015	14,395
Interest cost: $135,798‡ × 6%			8,148
PBO at the end of 2015			$158,341

*Present value of an ordinary annuity of $1: $n = 20$, $i = 6\%$.
†Present value of $1: $n = 29$, $i = 6\%$.
‡Includes the beginning balance plus the prior service cost because the amendment occurred at the beginning of the year.

Additional Consideration

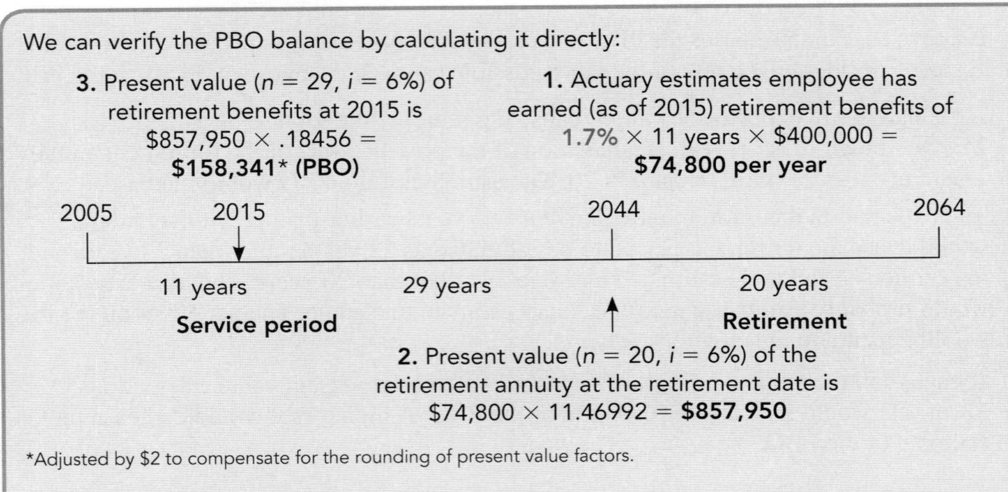

We can verify the PBO balance by calculating it directly:
3. Present value (n = 29, i = 6%) of retirement benefits at 2015 is $857,950 × .18456 = $158,341* (PBO)
1. Actuary estimates employee has earned (as of 2015) retirement benefits of 1.7% × 11 years × $400,000 = $74,800 per year
2005
2015
2044
2064
11 years
29 years
20 years
Service period
Retirement
2. Present value (n = 20, i = 6%) of the retirement annuity at the retirement date is $74,800 × 11.46992 = $857,950
*Adjusted by $2 to compensate for the rounding of present value factors.

The pension formula reflects the plan amendment.

The plan amendment would affect not only the year in which it occurs, but also each subsequent year because the revised pension formula determines each year's service cost. Continuing our illustration to 2016 demonstrates this:

PBO at the beginning of 2016 (end of 2015)			$158,341
Service cost: (1.7% × 1 yr. × $400,000) Annual retirement benefits from 2016 service	× 11.46992* To discount to 2044	× .19563† To discount to 2016	15,258
Interest cost: $158,341 × 6%			9,500
PBO at the end of 2016			$183,099

*Present value of an ordinary annuity of $1: $n = 20$, $i = 6\%$.
†Present value of $1: $n = 28$, $i = 6\%$.

During 2016, the PBO increased as a result of service cost and interest cost.

Decreases and increases in estimates of the PBO because of periodic re-evaluation of uncertainties are called gains and losses.

4. Gain or loss on the PBO. We mentioned earlier that a number of estimates are necessary to derive the PBO. When one or more of these estimates requires revision, the estimate of the PBO also will require revision. The resulting decrease or increase in the PBO is referred to as a *gain* or *loss*, respectively. Let's modify our illustration to imitate the effect of revising one of the several possible estimates involved. Suppose, for instance, that new information at the end of 2016 about inflation and compensation trends suggests that the estimate of Farrow's final salary should be increased by 5% to $420,000. This would affect the estimate of the PBO as follows:

Changing the final salary estimate changes the PBO.

	PBO *without* Revised Estimate		PBO *with* Revised Estimate	
1.	1.7% × 12 yrs. × $400,000	= $ 81,600	1.7% × 12 yrs. × $420,000	= $ 85,680
2.	$81,600 × 11.46992	= 935,945	$85,680 × 11.46992	= 982,743
3.	$935,945 × .19563	= 183,099	$982,743 × .19563	= 192,254

$9,155
Loss on PBO

The difference of $9,155 represents a loss on the PBO because the obligation turned out to be higher than previously expected. Now there would be three elements of the increase in the PBO during 2016.[8]

The revised estimate caused the PBO to increase.

PBO at the beginning of 2016	$158,341
Service cost (calculated above)	15,258
Interest cost (calculated above)	9,500
Loss on PBO (calculated above)	9,155
PBO at the end of 2016	$192,254

If a revised estimate causes the PBO to be lower than previously expected, a gain would be indicated. Consider how a few of the other possible estimate changes would affect the PBO:

- A change in life expectancies might cause the retirement period to be estimated as 21 years rather than 20 years. Calculation of the present value of the retirement annuity would use $n = 21$, rather than $n = 20$. The estimate of the PBO would increase.
- The expectation that retirement will occur two years earlier than previously thought would cause the retirement period to be estimated as 22 years rather than 20 years and the service period to be estimated as 28 years rather than 30 years. The new expectation would probably also cause the final salary estimate to change. The net effect on the PBO would depend on the circumstances.
- A change in the assumed discount rate would affect the present value calculations. A lower rate would increase the estimate of the PBO. A higher rate would decrease the estimate of the PBO.

[8]The increase in the PBO due to amending the pension formula (prior service cost) occurred in 2015.

5. Payment of retirement benefits. We've seen how the PBO will change due to the accumulation of service cost from year to year, the accrual of interest as time passes, making plan amendments retroactive to prior years, and periodic adjustments when estimates change. Another change in the PBO occurs when the obligation is reduced as benefits actually are paid to retired employees.

Payment of retirement benefits reduces the PBO.

The payment of such benefits is not applicable in our present illustration because we've limited the situation to calculations concerning an individual employee who is several years from retirement. Remember, though, in reality the actuary would make these calculations for the entire pool of employees covered by the pension plan. But the concepts involved would be the same. Illustration 17–8 summarizes the five ways the PBO can change.

Illustration 17–8

Components of Change in the PBO

The Projected Benefits Obligation Changes as a Result of:

Cause	Effect	Frequency
Service cost	+	Each period
Interest cost	+	Each period (except the first period of the plan, when no obligation exists to accrue interest)
Prior service cost	+	Only if the plan is amended (or initiated) that period
Loss or gain on PBO	+ or −	Whenever revisions are made in the pension liability estimate
Retiree benefits paid	−	Each period (unless no employees have yet retired under the plan)

Illustration Expanded to Consider the Entire Employee Pool

For our single employee, the PBO at the end of 2016 is $192,254. Let's say now that Global Communications has 2,000 active employees covered by the pension plan and 100 retired employees receiving retirement benefits. Illustration 17–9 expands the numbers to represent all covered employees.

The PBO is not formally recognized in the balance sheet.

Illustration 17–9

The PBO Expanded to Include All Employees

The changes in the PBO for Global Communications during 2016 were as follows:

	($ in millions)*
PBO at the beginning of 2016† (amount assumed)	$400
Service cost, 2016 (amount assumed)	41
Interest cost: $400 × 6%	24
Loss (gain) on PBO (amount assumed)	23
Less: Retiree benefits paid (amount assumed)	(38)
PBO at the end of 2016	$450

*Of course, these expanded amounts are not simply the amounts for Jessica Farrow multiplied by 2,000 employees because her years of service, expected retirement date, and salary are not necessarily representative of other employees. Also, the expanded amounts take into account expected employee turnover and current retirees.
†Includes the prior service cost that increased the PBO when the plan was amended in 2015.

Pension Plan Assets

● LO17-4

So far our focus has been on the employer's obligation to provide retirement benefits in the future. We turn our attention now to the resources with which the company will satisfy that obligation—the **pension plan assets**. Like the PBO, the pension plan assets are not reported separately in the employer's balance sheet but are netted together with the PBO to report either a net pension asset (debit balance) or a net pension liability (credit balance). Its separate balance, too, must be reported in the disclosure notes to the financial statements (as does the separate PBO balance), and as explained below, the return on these assets is included in the calculation of the periodic pension expense.

FINANCIAL Reporting Case

Q3, p. 998

We assumed in the previous section that Global Communications' obligation is $450 million for service performed to date. When employees retire, will there be sufficient funds to provide the anticipated benefits? To ensure sufficient funding, Global will contribute cash each year to a pension fund.

A *trustee* manages pension plan assets.

The assets of a pension fund must be held by a **trustee**. A trustee accepts employer contributions, invests the contributions, accumulates the earnings on the investments, and pays benefits from the plan assets to retired employees or their beneficiaries. The trustee can be an individual, a bank, or a trust company. Plan assets are invested in stocks, bonds, and other income-producing assets. The accumulated balance of the annual employer contributions plus the return on the investments (dividends, interest, market price appreciation) must be sufficient to pay benefits as they come due.

When an employer estimates how much it must set aside each year to accumulate sufficient funds to pay retirement benefits as they come due, it's necessary to estimate the return those investments will produce. This is the **expected return on plan assets**. The higher the return, the less the employer must actually contribute. On the other hand, a relatively low return means the difference must be made up by higher contributions. In practice, recent estimates of the rate of return have ranged from 4.8% to 9%, with 7.75% being the most commonly reported expectation.[9] In Illustration 17–10, we shift the focus of our numerical illustration to emphasize Global's pension plan assets.

Illustration 17–10
How Plan Assets Change

A trustee accepts employer contributions, invests the contributions, accumulates the earnings on the investments, and pays benefits from the plan assets.

Global Communications funds its defined benefit pension plan by contributing each year the year's service cost plus a portion of the prior service cost. Cash of $48 million was contributed to the pension fund at the end of 2016.

Plan assets at the beginning of 2016 were valued at $300 million. The expected rate of return on the investment of those assets was 9%, but the actual return in 2016 was 10%. Retirement benefits of $38 million were paid at the end of 2016 to retired employees.

What is the value of the company's pension plan assets at the end of 2016?

	($ in millions)
Plan assets at the beginning of 2016	$300
Actual return on plan assets (10% × $300)	30
Cash contributions	48
Less: Retiree benefits paid	(38)
Plan assets at the end of 2016	$340

An *underfunded* pension plan means the PBO exceeds plan assets.

Recall that Global's PBO at the end of 2016 is $450 million. Because the plan assets are only $340 million, the pension plan is said to be *underfunded*. One reason is that we assumed Global incurred a $60 million prior service cost from amending the pension plan at the beginning of 2015, and that cost is being funded over several years. Another factor is the loss from increasing the PBO due to the estimate revision, since funding has been based on the previous estimate. Later, we'll assume earlier revisions also have increased the PBO. Of course, actual performance of the investments also impacts a plan's funded status.

An *overfunded* pension plan means plan assets exceed the PBO.

It is not unusual for pension plans today to be underfunded. Historically the funded status of pension plans has varied considerably. Prior to the Employee Retirement Income Security Act (ERISA) in 1974, many plans were grossly underfunded. The law established minimum funding standards among other matters designed to protect plan participants. The new standards brought most plans closer to full funding. Then the stock market boom of the 1980s caused the value of plan assets for many pension funds to swell to well in excess of their projected benefit obligations. More than 80% of pension plans were overfunded. As a result, managers explored ways to divert funds to other areas of operations. Today a majority of plans again are underfunded. The economic crisis has taken its toll. Stock market declines reduced the funded status of pension plans from 108% at the end of 2007 to 79% at the end of 2008.[10] In 2009, pension plans of the country's 500 largest companies were

[9] Pension/OPEB 2013 Assumption and Disclosure Survey, PWC, 2013.

[10] Goldman Sachs, "Global Markets Institute Accounting Policy Update: Pension review 2009–Fallout from funded status decline just beginning," Global Markets Institute, June 4, 2009.

underfunded by $200 billion. Partly in response to the severe underfunding and partly spurred by attractive stock prices, unusually high cash contributions to plan assets reduced the underfunded status during 2009.[11] Then, despite positive stock market returns in 2012, the funded status for plans at the 500 largest U.S. companies tracked by Standard & Poor's dropped to 76.9% at the end of 2012, down from 84% in 2009.[12] One culprit was low interest rates. Low interest rates hurt plans' funded status because the pension obligation is a present value calculation that increases with a lower discount rate. Even small interest rate changes have big effects on funded status. Many of the underfunded plans are with troubled companies, placing employees at risk. The PBGC guarantees are limited to about $4,900 per month, often less than promised pension benefits.

Reporting the Funded Status of the Pension Plan

● LO17–5

FINANCIAL Reporting Case

Q4, p. 998

A company's PBO is not reported separately among liabilities in the balance sheet. Similarly, the plan assets a company sets aside to pay those benefits are not separately reported among assets in the balance sheet. However, firms do report the net difference between those two amounts, referred to as the "funded status" of the plan.[13] From our previous discussion, we see the funded status for Global to be the following at December 31, 2016, and December 31, 2015:

A company must report in its balance sheet a liability for the underfunded (or asset for the overfunded) status of its postretirement plans.

	($ in millions)	
	2016	**2015**
Projected benefit obligation (PBO)	$450	$400
Fair value of plan assets	340	300
Underfunded status	$110	$100

Because the plan is underfunded, Global reports a net pension liability of $110 million in its 2016 balance sheet and $100 million in 2015. Be sure to note that the "net pension liability" is not an actual account balance. Instead, it's the PBO account balance and the Plan assets account balance simply reported in the balance sheet as a single net amount. If the plan becomes overfunded in the future, Global will report a net pension asset instead.

Now, let's look at all the ways that changes in the PBO and the pension plan assets affect pension expense.

PART C

Determining Pension Expense

The Relationship between Pension Expense and Changes in the PBO and Plan Assets

● LO17–6

Like wages, salaries, commissions, and other forms of pay, pension expense is part of a company's compensation for employee services each year. Accordingly, the accounting objective is to achieve a matching of the costs of providing this form of compensation with the benefits of the services performed. However, the fact that this form of compensation actually is paid to employees many years after the service is performed means that other elements in addition to the annual service cost will affect the ultimate pension cost. These other elements are related to changes that occur over time in both the pension obligation and the pension plan assets. Illustration 17–11 provides a summary of how some of these changes influence pension expense.

The matching principle and the time period assumption dictate that the costs be allocated to the periods the services are performed.

We've examined each of the components of pension expense from the viewpoint of its effect on the PBO or on plan assets, using the Global Communications illustration to

[11]Goldman Sachs, "Notable Contributions Boost Funded Levels," Global Markets Institute, December 15, 2009.

[12]Wilshire Associates, Inc., as quoted in "Pension Liabilities Exceed Assets," *The Commercial Appeal,* June 4, 2013.

[13]FASB 715–30–25: Compensation–Retirement Benefits–Defined Benefit Plans–Pension–Recognition (previously "Employers' Accounting for Defined Benefit Pension and Other Postretirement Plans—an amendment of FASB Statements No. 87, 88, 106, and 132(R)," *Statement of Financial Accounting Standards No. 158* (Stamford, Conn.: FASB, 2006)).

Illustration 17–11
Components of the Periodic Pension Expense

FINANCIAL Reporting Case

Q5, p. 998

The pension expense reported in the income statement is a composite of periodic changes that occur in both the pension obligation and the plan assets.

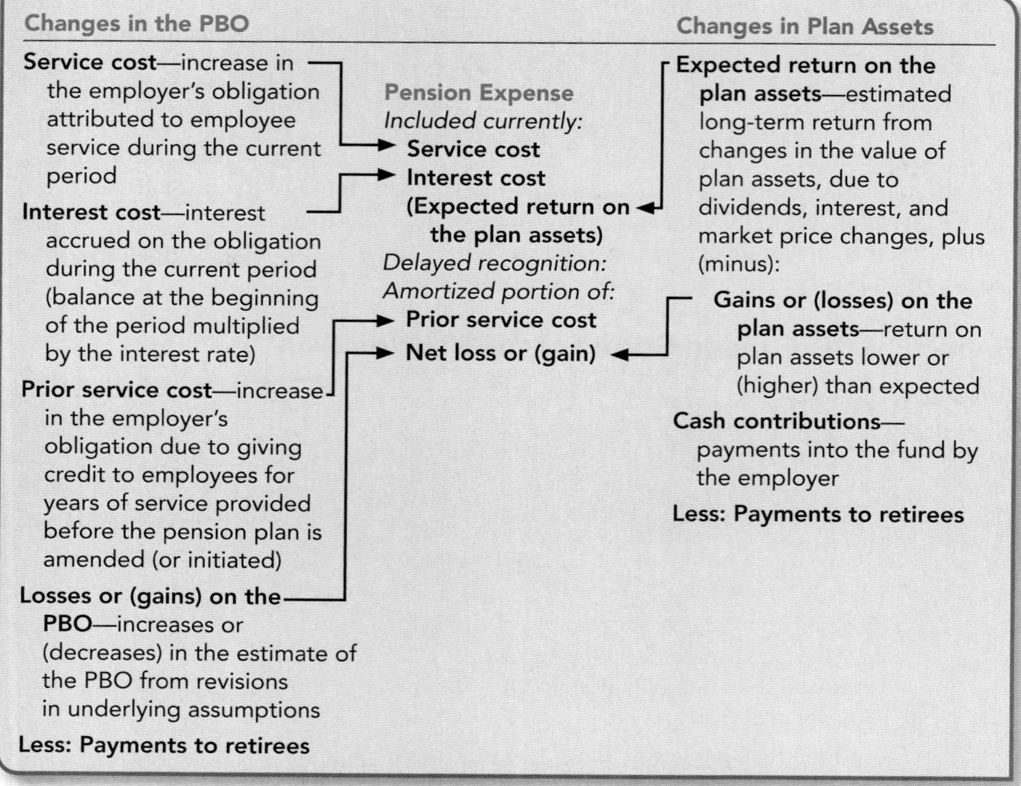

demonstrate that effect. Now, let's expand the same illustration to see how these changes affect *pension expense.* Illustration 17–12 provides this expanded example.

Changes in the PBO
Service cost—increase in the employer's obligation attributed to employee service during the current period
Interest cost—interest accrued on the obligation during the current period (balance at the beginning of the period multiplied by the interest rate)
Prior service cost—increase in the employer's obligation due to giving credit to employees for years of service provided before the pension plan is amended (or initiated)
Losses or (gains) on the PBO—increases or (decreases) in the estimate of the PBO from revisions in underlying assumptions
Less: Payments to retirees
Pension Expense
Included currently:
Service cost
Interest cost
(Expected return on the plan assets)
Delayed recognition:
Amortized portion of:
Prior service cost
Net loss or (gain)
Changes in Plan Assets
Expected return on the plan assets—estimated long-term return from changes in the value of plan assets, due to dividends, interest, and market price changes, plus (minus):
Gains or (losses) on the plan assets—return on plan assets lower or (higher) than expected
Cash contributions—payments into the fund by the employer
Less: Payments to retirees

Illustration 17–12
Pension Expense

These are the changes in the PBO and in the plan assets we previously discussed (Illustration 17–9 and Illustration 17–10).

Reports from the actuary and the trustee of plan assets indicate the following changes during 2016 in the PBO and plan assets of Global Communications.

($ in millions)	PBO		Plan Assets
Beginning of 2016	$400	*Beginning* of 2016	$300
Service cost	41	Actual return on plan assets,* 10% (9% expected)	30
Interest cost, 6%	24		
Loss (gain) on PBO	23	Cash contributions	48
Less: Retiree benefits	(38)	Less: Retiree benefits	(38)
End of 2016	$450	*End* of 2016	$340

Assume a *prior service cost* of $60 million was incurred at the beginning of the previous year (2015) due to a plan amendment increasing the PBO. Also assume that at the beginning of 2016 Global had a *net loss* of $55 million (previous losses exceeded previous gains). The average remaining service life of employees is estimated at 15 years.

2016 Pension Expense

Global's 2016 Pension Expense Is Determined as Follows:	($ in millions)
Service cost	$41
Interest cost	24
Expected return on the plan assets ($30 actual, less $3 gain)	(27)
Amortization of prior service cost (calculated later)	4
Amortization of net loss (calculated later)	1
Pension expense	$43

*Expected rates of return anticipate the performance of various investments of plan assets. This is not necessarily the same as the discount rate used by the actuary to estimate the pension obligation. Assumed rates of return recently reported have ranged from 4.8% to 9%, with 7.75% being the most commonly assumed rate (Pension/OPEB 2013 Assumption and Disclosure Survey, PWC, 2013).

Components of Pension Expense

Illustration 17–12 demonstrates the relationship between some of the changes in the PBO and in plan assets and the components of pension expense: service cost, interest cost, the return on plan assets, prior service cost amortization, and net gain or loss amortization. Let's look at these five components of pension expense one at a time.

1. SERVICE COST. The $41 million service cost represents the increase in the projected benefit obligation attributable to employee service performed during 2016 (benefits earned by employees during the year). Each year this is the first component of the pension expense.

2. INTEREST COST. The interest cost is calculated as the interest rate (discount rate) multiplied by the projected benefit obligation at the beginning of the year. In 2016, this is 6% times $400 million, or $24 million.

Interest cost is the discount rate times the PBO balance at the beginning of the year.

The PBO balance is not separately reported as a liability in the company's balance sheet,[14] but it is a liability nevertheless. The interest expense that accrues on its balance is not separately reported in the income statement but instead becomes the second component of the annual pension expense.

3. RETURN ON PLAN ASSETS. Remember, plan assets comprise funds invested in stocks, bonds, and other securities that presumably will generate dividends, interest, and capital gains. Each year these earnings represent the return on plan assets during that year. When accounting for the return, we need to differentiate between its two modes: the *expected* return and the *actual* return.

The return earned on investment securities increases the plan asset balance.

Actual versus expected return. We've assumed Global's expected rate of return is 9%, so its expected return on plan assets in 2016 was 9% times $300 million, or $27 million. But, as previously indicated, the actual rate of return in 2016 was 10%, producing an actual return on plan assets of 10% times $300 million, or $30 million.

The interest and return-on-assets components are financial items created rather than direct employee compensation.

Obviously, investing plan assets in income-producing assets lessens the amounts employers must contribute to the fund. So, the return on plan assets reduces the net cost of having a pension plan. Accordingly, the return on plan assets each year *reduces* the amount recorded as pension expense. Just as the interest expense that accrues on the PBO is included as a component of pension expense rather than being separately reported, the investment revenue on plan assets is not separately reported either. In actuality, both the interest and return-on-assets components of pension expense do not directly represent employee compensation. Instead, they are financial items created only because the future obligation to retirees must be funded currently.

Adjustment for loss or gain. A controversial question is *when* differences between the actual and expected return should be recognized in pension expense. It seems logical that since the net cost of having a pension plan is reduced by the actual return on plan assets, the charge to pension expense should be the actual return on plan assets. However, the FASB concluded that the actual return should first be adjusted by any difference between that return and the return amount that had been expected. So, it's actually the *expected* return that is included in the calculation of pension expense. In our illustration, Global's pension expense is reduced by the expected return of $27 million.

The return on plan assets reduces the net *cost of having a* pension plan.

The difference between the actual and expected return is considered a loss or gain on plan assets. Although we don't include these losses and gains as part of pension expense when they occur, it's possible they will affect pension expense at a later time. On the next page, we will discuss how that might happen.

Any loss or gain is not included in pension expense right away.

4. AMORTIZATION OF PRIOR SERVICE COST. Recall that the $60 million increase in Global's PBO due to recalculating benefits employees earned in prior years as a result of a plan amendment is referred to as the prior service cost. Obviously, prior service cost adds to the cost of having a pension plan. But when should this cost be recognized as

[14]As we discussed earlier and will revisit later, the PBO is combined with pension assets with the net difference reported in the balance sheet as either a net pension liability or a net pension asset.

pension expense? An argument can be made that the cost should be recognized as expense in the year of the amendment when the cost increases the company's pension obligation. In fact, some members of the FASB have advocated this approach. At present, though, we amortize the cost gradually to pension expense. Here's the rationalization.

Prior service cost is recognized as pension expense over the future service period of the employees whose benefits are recalculated.

Amending a pension plan, and especially choosing to make that amendment retroactive, typically is done with the idea that future operations will benefit from those choices. For that reason, the cost is not recognized as pension expense in the year the plan is amended. Instead, it is recognized as pension expense over the time that the employees who benefited from the retroactive amendment will work for the company in the future. Presumably, this future service period is when the company will receive the benefits of its actions.

In our illustration, the amendment occurred in 2015, increasing the PBO at that time. For the individual employee, Jessica Farrow, the prior service cost was calculated to be $15,976. Our illustration assumes that, for *all* plan participants, the prior service cost was $60 million at the beginning of 2015. The prior service cost at the beginning of 2016 is $56 million. The following section explains how this amount was computed.

One assumption in our illustration is that the average remaining service life of the active employee group is 15 years. To recognize the $60 million prior service cost in equal annual amounts over this period, the amount amortized as an increase in pension expense each year is $4 million:[15]

By the straight-line method, prior service cost is recognized over the average remaining service life of the active employee group.

Amortization of Prior Service Cost:	($ in millions)
Service cost	$41
Interest cost	24
Expected return on the plan assets	(27)
Amortization of prior service cost–AOCI	4
Amortization of net loss–AOCI	1
Pension expense	$43

Prior service cost is not expensed as it is incurred. Instead, it is reported as a component of AOCI to be amortized over time.

Be sure to note that, even though we're amortizing it, the prior service cost is not an asset, but instead a part of *accumulated other comprehensive income* (AOCI), a shareholders' equity account. This is a result of the FASB's disinclination to treat the cost as an expense as it is incurred. The Board, instead, prefers to consider it to be *other comprehensive income* (OCI) like the handful of losses and gains also categorized the same way and not reported among the gains and losses in the traditional income statement. You first learned about comprehensive income in Chapter 4 and again in Chapter 12. We'll revisit it again later in this chapter.

The prior service cost balance in AOCI declines by $4 million each year:

Prior Service Cost–AOCI	($ in millions)
Prior service cost at the beginning of 2016	$56
Less: 2016 amortization	(4)
Prior service cost at the end of 2016	$52

5. AMORTIZATION OF A NET LOSS OR NET GAIN. You learned previously that gains and losses can occur when expectations are revised concerning either the PBO or the return on plan assets. Illustration 17–13 summarizes the possibilities.

We report gains and losses as OCI in the statement of comprehensive income.

Like the prior service cost we just discussed, we don't include these gains and losses as part of pension expense in the income statement, but instead report them as OCI in the statement of comprehensive income as they occur. We then report the gains and losses (net of subsequent amortization) on a cumulative basis as a net loss–AOCI or a net gain–AOCI, depending on whether we have greater losses or gains over time. We report this amount in the balance sheet as a part of *accumulated other comprehensive income* (AOCI), a shareholders' equity account.

[15]An alternative to this straight-line approach, called the *service method,* attempts to allocate the prior service cost to each year in proportion to the fraction of the total remaining service years worked in each of those years. This method is described in the chapter appendix.

Illustration 17–13

Gains and Losses

	Projected Benefit Obligation	Return on Plan Assets
Higher than expected	Loss	Gain
Lower than expected	Gain	Loss

Gains and losses occur when either the PBO or the return on plan assets turns out to be different than expected.

There is no conceptual justification for not including losses and gains in earnings. After all, these increases and decreases in either the PBO or plan assets immediately impact the net cost of providing a pension plan and, conceptually, should be included in pension expense as they occur.

Nevertheless, the FASB requires that income statement recognition of gains and losses from either source be delayed. Why?—for practical reasons.

Income Smoothing

The FASB acknowledged the conceptual shortcoming of delaying the recognition of a gain or a loss while opting for this more politically acceptable approach. Delayed recognition was favored by a dominant segment of corporate America that was concerned with the effect of allowing gains and losses to immediately impact reported earnings.

> The Board believes that it would be conceptually appropriate and preferable to [have] . . . no delay in recognition of gains and losses, or perhaps [to have] . . . gains and losses reported currently in comprehensive income but not in earnings. However, it concluded that those approaches would be too great a change from past practice to be adopted at the present time.[16]

The practical justification for delayed recognition is that, over time, gains and losses might cancel one another out. Given this possibility, why create unnecessary fluctuations in reported income by letting temporary gains and losses decrease and increase (respectively) pension expense? Of course, as years pass there may be more gains than losses, or vice versa, preventing their offsetting one another completely. So, if a net gain or a net loss gets "too large," pension expense must be adjusted.

> The Board acknowledges that the delayed recognition included in this Statement results in excluding the most current and most relevant information.[17]

The FASB defines too large rather arbitrarily as being when a net gain or a net loss at the beginning of a year exceeds an amount equal to 10% of the PBO, or 10% of plan assets, whichever is higher.[18] This threshold amount is referred to as the "corridor." When the corridor is exceeded, the excess is not charged to pension expense all at once. Instead, as a further concession to income smoothing, only a portion of the excess is included in pension expense. The minimum amount that should be included is the excess divided by the average remaining service period of active employees expected to receive benefits under the plan.[19]

A net gain or a net loss affects pension expense only if it exceeds an amount equal to 10% of the PBO, or 10% of plan assets, whichever is higher.

In our illustration, we're assuming a net loss–AOCI of $55 million at the beginning of 2016. Also recall that the PBO and plan assets are $400 million and $300 million,

[16]FASB, "Employers' Accounting for Pension and Other Postretirement Benefits," *Preliminary Views,* November 1982, par. 107.

[17]Ibid., par. 88.

[18]For this purpose the FASB specifies the market-related value of plan assets. This can be either the fair value or a weighted-average fair value over a period not to exceed five years. We will uniformly assume fair value in this chapter.

[19]Companies are permitted to amortize the entire net loss (or gain) rather than just the excess, but few choose that option. (FASB ASC 715–30–35–25: Compensation–Retirement Benefits–Defined Benefit Plans–Pension–Subsequent Measurement–Gains and Losses (previously "Employers' Accounting for Pensions," *Statement of Financial Accounting Standards No. 87* (Stamford, Conn.: FASB, 1985))).

respectively, at that time. The amount amortized to 2016 pension expense is $1 million, calculated as follows:

Because the net loss exceeds an amount equal to the greater of 10% of the PBO or 10% of plan assets, part of the excess is amortized to pension expense.

Determining Net Loss Amortization—2016	($ in millions)
Net loss (previous losses exceeded previous gains)	$55
10% of $400 ($400 is greater than $300): the "corridor"	(40)
Excess at the beginning of the year	$15
Average remaining service period	÷ 15 years
Amount amortized to 2016 pension expense	$ 1

The pension expense is increased because a net loss is being amortized. If a net *gain* were being amortized, the amount would be *deducted* from pension expense because a gain would indicate that balance of the net cost of providing the pension plan had decreased.

Amortization of a net gain would decrease pension expense.

Amortization of a net loss increases pension expense.

Amortization of the Net Loss–AOCI:	($ in millions)
Service cost	$41
Interest cost	24
Expected return on the plan assets	(27)
Amortization of prior service cost–AOCI	4
Amortization of net loss–AOCI	1
Pension expense	$43

This amortization reduces the net loss–AOCI in 2016 by $1 million. Also recall that Global incurred (a) a $23 million loss in 2016 from revising estimates relating to the PBO and (b) a $3 million gain when the 2016 return on plan assets was higher than expected. These three changes affected the net loss–AOCI in 2016 as follows:

New losses add to a net loss; new gains reduce a net loss.

Net Loss–AOCI	($ in millions)
Net loss–AOCI at the beginning of 2016	$55
Less: 2016 amortization	(1)
Plus: 2016 loss on PBO	23
Less: 2016 gain on plan assets	(3)
Net loss–AOCI at the end of 2016	$74

Additional Consideration

The $74 million balance at the end of 2016 would be the beginning balance in 2017. It would be compared with the 2017 beginning balances in the PBO and plan assets to determine whether amortization would be necessary in 2017. If you were to look back to our analyses of the changes in those two balances, you would see the 2017 beginning balances in the PBO and plan assets to be $450 million and $340 million, respectively. The amount amortized to 2017 pension expense will be $1.93 million, calculated as follows:

	($ in millions)
Net loss (previous losses exceeded previous gains)	$ 74
10% of $450 ($450 is greater than $340)	(45)
Excess at the beginning of the year	$ 29
Average remaining service period	÷ 15 years*
Amount amortized to 2017 pension expense	**$1.93**

*Assumes the average remaining service period of active employees is still 15 years in 2017 due to new employees joining the firm.

Reporting Issues

PART D

Recording Gains and Losses

● LO17–7

As we discussed earlier, gains and losses (either from changing assumptions regarding the PBO or from the return on assets being higher or lower than expected) are deferred and not immediately included in pension expense and net income. Instead, we report them as *other comprehensive income (OCI)* in the statement of comprehensive income. So Global records a *loss–OCI* for the $23 million loss that occurs in 2017 when it revises its estimate of future salary levels causing its PBO estimate to increase. Global also records a $3 million *gain–OCI* that occurred when the $30 million actual return on plan assets exceeded the $27 million expected return. Here's the entry:

To Record Gains and Losses	($ in millions)	
Loss–OCI (from change in assumption)	23	
PBO		23
Plan assets	3	
Gain–OCI ($30 actual return on assets − $27 expected return)		3

Losses and gains (as well as any new prior service cost should it occur) are reported as OCI.

The loss is an increase in the PBO due to a change in an assumption. In this entry, we are recording that increase in the PBO account balance. If the change in assumption had caused the PBO to be reduced instead, we would debit the PBO here and credit a gain–OCI.

Similarly, the gain due to the actual return on plan assets exceeding the expected return is an increase in plan assets. In the next section, we increase plan assets for the expected return (as a component of pension expense) so the two adjustments together cause the plan assets account balance to reflect the actual return (expected increase plus the additional increase represented by the gain). Of course, if the actual return had been less than expected, we would debit a loss–OCI and credit plan assets here.

Additional Consideration

Just as we record new losses and gains as they occur, we also will record a change in the prior service cost account for any new prior service cost should it occur. For instance, if Global revised its pension formula again and recalculated its PBO using the more generous formula, causing a $40 million increase in the PBO, the company would record the new prior service cost this way:

To Record New Prior Service Cost	($ in millions)	
Prior service cost–OCI (increase in PBO due to plan amendment)	40	
PBO		40

If an amendment *reduces* rather than increases the PBO, the *negative prior service cost* would reduce both the prior service cost and pension liability.

International Financial Reporting Standards

● LO17–12

Accounting for Gains and Losses. Accounting for gains and losses in defined benefit plans (called "remeasurement" gains and losses under IFRS) under *IAS No. 19* is similar to U.S. GAAP, but there are two important differences.

(continued)

IFRS ILLUSTRATION

(concluded)

The first difference relates to the make-up of the gain or loss on plan assets. As we know from the chapter, this amount under U.S. GAAP is the difference between the actual and expected returns, where the expected return is different from company to company and usually different from the interest rate used to determine the interest cost. Not so under IFRS, which requires that we use the same rate (the rate for "high grade corporate bonds") for both the interest cost on the defined benefit obligation (called projected benefit obligation or PBO under U.S. GAAP) and the interest revenue on the plan assets. In fact, under IFRS, we multiply that rate, say 6%, times the net difference between the defined benefit obligation (DBO) and plan assets and report the net interest cost/income:

	($ in millions)	
Net interest cost (6% × [$400 − 300])	6	
Plan assets (6% × $300: interest income)	18	
DBO (6% × $400: interest cost)		24

As a result, the remeasurement gain (or loss) under IFRS usually is an amount different from the gain (or loss) on plan assets under GAAP:

Under IFRS, we have a *remeasurement* gain when the actual return on plan assets exceeds the "high grade corporate bond rate" we use to determine the net interest cost/income.

To Record Gains and Losses

U.S. GAAP

Actual return = 10% | Expected return = 9%

Plan assets	3	
Gain–OCI ([10% − 9%] × $300)		3

IFRS

Plan assets (actual interest income in excess of 6%)	12	
Remeasurement gain–OCI ([10% − 6%] × $300)		12

Actual return = 10% | High grade corporate bond rate = 6%

Remeasurement gains and losses under IFRS are reported as OCI but, unlike under U.S. GAAP, are *not subsequently amortized to expense* and recycled into net income.

A second difference relates to the treatment of gains and losses *after* they are initially recorded in OCI. We've seen that U.S. GAAP requires that gains and losses (either from the actual return exceeding an assumed amount [*entries above*] or from changing assumptions regarding the pension obligation [*entries below*]) are to be (a) included among OCI items in the statement of comprehensive income when they first arise and then (b) gradually amortized or recycled out of OCI and into expense (when the accumulated net gain or net loss exceeds the 10% threshold). Similar to U.S. GAAP, under IFRS these gains and losses are included in OCI when they first arise, but unlike U.S. GAAP those amounts are *not subsequently amortized out of OCI and into expense.*[20] Instead, under IFRS those amounts remain in the balance sheet as accumulated other comprehensive income. The initial entries, then, are the same:

U.S. GAAP

Loss–OCI[a]	23	
PBO		23

IFRS

Remeasurement loss–OCI[b]	23	
DBO		23

[a]subsequently amortized to expense and recycled from other comprehensive income to net income
[b]not subsequently amortized to expense; remains in accumulated other comprehensive income

[20]"Employee Benefits," *International Accounting Standard No. 19* (IASCF), as amended effective January 1, 2014.

Recording the Pension Expense

Recall from Illustration 17–12 that Global's 2016 pension expense is $43 million. The expense includes the $41 million service cost and the $24 million interest cost, both of which, as we learned earlier, add to Global's PBO. Similarly, the expense includes a $27 million expected return on plan assets, which adds to the plan assets.[21] These changes are reflected in the following entry:

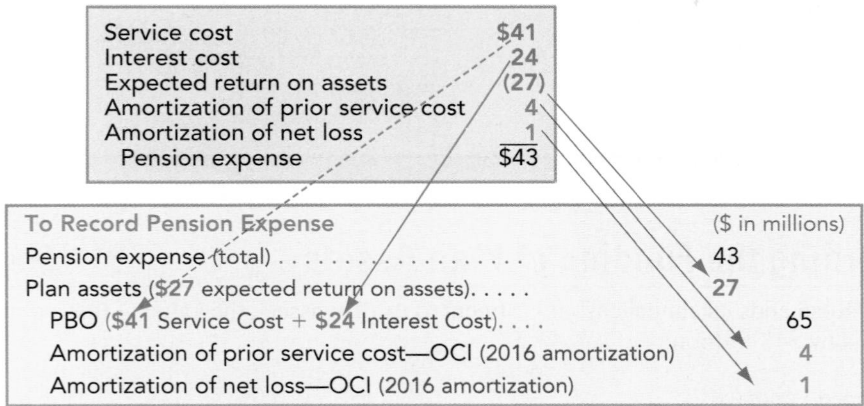

Service cost	$41
Interest cost	24
Expected return on assets	(27)
Amortization of prior service cost	4
Amortization of net loss	1
Pension expense	$43

To Record Pension Expense	($ in millions)	
Pension expense (total)	43	
Plan assets ($27 expected return on assets).	27	
PBO ($41 Service Cost + $24 Interest Cost). . . .		65
Amortization of prior service cost—OCI (2016 amortization)		4
Amortization of net loss—OCI (2016 amortization)		1

Each component of the pension expense is recorded in the journal entry to record pension expense.

Service cost and interest cost increase the PBO. The return on assets increases plan assets.

The pension expense also includes the $4 million amortization of the prior service cost and the $1 million amortization of the net loss. As we discussed earlier, we report prior service cost when it arises as well as gains and losses as they occur as *other comprehensive income (OCI)* in the statement of comprehensive income. These OCI items accumulate as Prior service cost–AOCI and Net loss (or gain)–AOCI. So, when we amortize these AOCI accounts, we report the amortization amounts as OCI items in the statement of comprehensive income as well (see p. 1023). These amortized amounts are being "reclassified" from OCI to net income.

Amortization reduces the Prior service cost–AOCI and the Net loss–AOCI. Since these accounts have debit balances, we credit the accounts for the amortization. If we were amortizing a net gain, we would *debit* the account because a net gain has a credit balance.

New gains and losses and prior service cost are reported as OCI. So is the amortization of their accumulated balances.

Remember, we report the funded status of the plan in the balance sheet. That's the difference between the PBO and plan assets. In this case, it's a net pension liability since the plan is underfunded; that is, the PBO exceeds plan assets.

The pension expense is, of course, reported in the income statement. In addition, the composition of that amount must be reported in disclosure notes. For instance, **General Mills, Inc.**, described the composition of its pension expense in the disclosure note in its 2013 annual report, shown in Illustration 17–14.

Components of Pension Expense

In Millions	2013	2012	2011
Service cost	$124.4	$114.3	$101.4
Interest cost	237.3	237.9	230.9
Expected return on plan assets	(428.0)	(440.3)	(408.5)
Amortization of losses	136.0	108.1	81.4
Amortization of prior service costs (credits)	6.2	8.6	9.0
Net expense	$ 75.9	$ 28.6	$ 14.2

Illustration 17–14

Disclosure of Pension Expense—**General Mills, Inc.**

The components of pension expense are itemized in the disclosure note.

Real World Financials

[21]The increase in plan assets is the $30 million *actual* return, but the $27 million *expected* return is the component of pension expense because the $3 million gain isn't included in expense. We saw in the previous section that the $3 million gain also increases plan assets.

International Financial Reporting Standards

LO17–12

Prior Service Cost. Under *IAS No. 19,* prior service cost (called past service cost under IFRS) is combined with the current service cost and reported within the income statement rather than as a component of other comprehensive income as it is under U.S. GAAP.[22] For Global, the service cost would be recorded under IFRS in 2015 when the plan amendment occurred as follows ($ in millions):

Service cost (service cost-2015 plus $60)	xxx	
DBO (service cost-2015)		xxx
DBO (past service cost)		60*

* from Illustration 17–12

Recording the Funding of Plan Assets

When Global adds its annual cash investment to its plan assets, the value of those plan assets increases by $48 million:

To Record Funding	($ in millions)	
Plan assets	48	
Cash (contribution to plan assets)		48

It's not unusual for the cash contribution to differ from that year's pension expense. After all, determining the periodic pension expense and the funding of the pension plan are two separate processes. Pension expense is an accounting decision. How much to contribute each year is a financing decision affected by cash flow and tax considerations, as well as minimum funding requirements. The Pension Protection Act of 2006 and the Employee Retirement Income Security Act of 1974 (ERISA) establish the pension funding requirements. Subject to these considerations, cash contributions are actuarially determined with the objective of accumulating (along with investment returns) sufficient funds to provide promised retirement benefits.

We saw earlier that when pension benefits are paid to retired employees, those payments reduce the plan assets established to pay the benefits and also reduce the obligation to pay the benefits, the PBO:

To Record Payment of Benefits	($ in millions)	
PBO	38	
Plan assets (payments to retired employees)		38

Now that we've recorded these entries for the funding of the pension plan and payment of benefits, we have recorded all the changes in the PBO and plan assets:

($ in millions)

PBO (debit)		PBO (credit)		Plan Assets (debit)		Plan Assets (credit)	
		400	Balance	Balance	300		
		23	Loss	Gain	3		
		41	Service cost	Expected return	27		
		24	Interest cost	Funding	48		
Benefits paid	38					38	Benefits paid
		450	Balance	Balance	340		

Remember, though, we don't report either of these balances separately in the balance sheet. Instead, we combine the two and report a net pension liability of $450 − 340 = $110 million, the funded status of the pension plan.

[22]"Employee Benefits," *International Accounting Standard No. 19* (IASCF), as amended effective January 1, 2014.

Additional Consideration

Rather than recording each of these changes in the PBO and Plan Asset accounts, we could have recorded them in a single Net pension (liability) asset account. For example, we could have recorded the gains and losses, pension expense, and funding as follows:

	($ in millions)	
Loss–OCI (from change in assumption)	23	
Net pension (liability) asset		23
Net pension (liability) asset	3	
Gain–OCI ($30 actual return on assets − $27 expected return)		3
Pension expense	43	
Net pension (liability) asset		38
Amortization of prior service cost—OCI*		4
Amortization of net loss—OCI*		1
Net pension (liability) asset	48	
Cash		48

In fact many companies use this abbreviated approach. However, recording the changes in the accounts they affect (PBO and Plan assets) and then combining the two accounts for balance sheet reporting as we do in our illustrations has two advantages. First, we need the separate balances for the required disclosure in the pension disclosure note. Second, it is a more logical approach. It's easier to see that the return on plan assets is an increase in plan assets than it is to see it as a reduction in Net pension (liability) asset.

*Because Prior service cost—OCI and Net loss—OCI have debit balances, we amortize them with credits. We would amortize a Net gain—OCI (credit balance) with a debit.

Comprehensive Income

Comprehensive income, as you may recall from Chapter 4, is a more expansive view of income than traditional net income. In fact, it encompasses all changes in equity other than from transactions with owners.[23] So, in addition to net income, comprehensive income includes up to four other changes in equity. A statement of comprehensive income is demonstrated in Illustration 17–15, highlighting the presentation of the components of OCI pertaining to Global's pension plan.

Illustration 17–15
Statement of Comprehensive Income

Gains and losses, as well as any new prior service cost should it arise, are among the OCI items reported in the period they occur.

	($ in millions)	
Net income		$xxx
Other comprehensive income:		
Unrealized holding gains (losses) on investments[24]	$ x	
Pension plan:		
Loss—due to revising a PBO estimate*	(23)	
Gain—return on plan assets exceeds expected*	3	
Amortization of net loss	1	
Amortization of prior service cost	4	
Deferred gains (losses) from derivatives	x	
Gains (losses) from foreign currency transactions and exchange rate adjustments	x	xx
Comprehensive income		$xxx

*From Illustration 17–12 on p. 1014.
Note: These amounts are shown without considering taxes. Actually each of the elements of comprehensive income should be reported net of tax. For instance, if the tax rate is 40%, the loss would be reported as $13.8 million: $23 million less a $9.2 million tax benefit.

[23]Transactions with owners primarily include dividends and the sale or purchase of shares of the company's stock.

[24]An unrealized loss also might occur from recording an impairment of a debt security investment as described in Chapter 12 and, as discussed in Chapter 14, applying the "fair value option" to a liability entails reporting in OCI any part of the change in the liability's fair value that's due to the liability's credit risk.

Other comprehensive income (OCI) items are reported both (a) as they occur and then (b) as an accumulated balance within shareholder's equity in the balance sheet as shown in Illustration 17–16.[25]

Reporting OCI as it occurs and also as an accumulated balance is consistent with the way we report net income and its accumulated counterpart, retained earnings.

In addition to reporting the gains or losses (and other elements of comprehensive income) that occur in the current reporting period, we also report these amounts on a *cumulative* basis in the balance sheet. Comprehensive income includes (a) net income and (b) OCI. Remember that we report net income that occurs in the current reporting period in the income statement and also report accumulated net income (that hasn't been distributed as dividends) in the balance sheet as retained earnings. Similarly, we report OCI as it occurs in the current reporting period (see Illustration 17–15) and also report *accumulated other comprehensive income* in the balance sheet. In its 2016 balance sheet, Global will report the amounts as shown in Illustration 17–16.

Illustration 17–16
Balance Sheet Presentation of Pension Amounts

If the plan had been overfunded, Global would have reported a pension asset among its assets rather than this pension liability.

The net loss and prior service cost *reduce* shareholders' equity.

Global Communication
Balance Sheets
For Years Ended December 31

	2016	2015
Assets		
Current assets	$xxx	$xxx
Property, plant, and equipment	xxx	xxx
Liabilities		
Current Liabilities	$xxx	$xxx
Net pension liability	110	100
Other long-term liabilities	xxx	xxx
Shareholders' Equity		
Common stock	$xxx	$xxx
Retained earnings	xxx	xxx
Accumulated other comprehensive income:		
Net unrealized holding gains and losses on investments—AOCI	xxx	xxx
Net loss–AOCI*	(74)	(55)
Prior service cost—AOCI*	(52)	(56)

*These are debit balances and therefore negative components of accumulated other comprehensive income; a net gain–AOCI would have a credit balance and be a positive component of accumulated other comprehensive income.

Look back to the schedule on page 1016 to see how the net loss–AOCI increased from $55 million to $74 million during 2016 and the schedule on page 1014 to see how the prior service cost–AOCI decreased from $56 million to $52 million. The pension liability represents the underfunded status of Global's pension plan on the two dates.

Income Tax Considerations

OCI items are reported net of tax, in both the (a) statement of comprehensive income and (b) AOCI.

We have ignored the income tax effects of the amounts in order to focus on the core issues. Note, though, that as gains and losses occur, they are reported along with their tax effects (tax expense for a gain, tax savings for a loss) in the statement of comprehensive income. This can be accomplished by presenting components of other comprehensive income either net of related income tax effects or *before* income tax effects with disclosure of the income taxes allocated to each component either in a disclosure note or parenthetically in the statement.[26] Likewise, AOCI in the balance sheet also is reported net of tax.

[25]Companies can present net income and other comprehensive income either in a single continuous statement of comprehensive income or in two separate, but consecutive, statements.

[26]Similarly, if any new prior service cost should arise due to a plan amendment, it too would be reported net of tax or with tax effects shown parenthetically.

Putting the Pieces Together

● LO17–8

In preceding sections, we've discussed (1) the projected benefit obligation (including changes due to periodic service cost, accrued interest, revised estimates, plan amendments, and the payment of benefits); (2) the plan assets (including changes due to investment returns, employer contributions, and the payment of benefits); (3) prior service cost; (4) gains and losses; (5) the periodic pension expense (comprising components of each of these); and (6) the funded status of the plan. These elements of a pension plan are interrelated. It's helpful to see how each element relates to the others. One way is to bring each part together in a *pension spreadsheet.* We do this for our 2016 Global Communications Illustration in Illustration 17–17.

Illustration 17–17
Pension Spreadsheet

	Recorded in Accounts						Reported Only
	PBO	Plan Assets	Prior Service Cost –AOCI	Net Loss –AOCI	Pension Expense	Cash	Net Pension (Liability)/ Asset
Balance, Jan. 1, 2016	(400)	300	56	55			(100)
Service cost	(41)				41		(41)
Interest cost	(24)				24		(24)
Expected return on assets		27			(27)		27
Adjust for: Gain on assets		3		(3)			3
Amortization of:							
Prior service cost–AOCI			(4)		4		
Net loss–AOCI				(1)	1		
Loss on PBO	(23)			23			(23)
Prior service cost (new)*	0		0				0
Contributions to fund		48				(48)	48
Retiree benefits paid	38	(38)					
Balance, Dec. 31, 2016	(450)	340	52	74	43		(110)

Note: ( )s represent credits to accounts, not necessarily decreases.
*This amount was $60 million in the 2015 pension spreadsheet.

When the PBO exceeds plan assets, we have a net pension liability. If plan assets exceed the PBO we have a net pension asset.

The net pension liability (or net pension asset) is not recorded in a journal entry but is the amount reported in the balance sheet as the PBO and plan assets combined.

You should spend several minutes studying this spreadsheet, focusing on the relationships among the elements that constitute a pension plan. Notice that the first numerical column simply repeats the actuary's report of how the PBO changed during the year, as explained previously (Illustration 17–9). Likewise, the second column reproduces the changes in plan assets we discussed earlier (Illustration 17–10). We've also previously noted the changes in the prior service cost–AOCI (page 1014) and the net loss–AOCI (page 1016) that are duplicated in the third and fourth columns. The fifth column repeats the calculation of the 2016 pension expense we determined earlier (page 1012), and the cash contribution to the pension fund is the sole item in the next column.

The last column shows the changes in the funded status of the plan. Be sure to notice that the funded status is the difference between the PBO (column 1) and the plan assets (column 2). That means that each of the changes we see in either of the first two columns also is reflected as a change in the funded status in the last column. The net pension liability (or net pension asset) balance is not carried in company records. Instead, we use this label to report the PBO and plan assets in the balance sheet as a single net amount.

Rather than report the PBO and plan asset balances separately, we combine those balances and report a single net pension liability or net pension asset in the balance sheet.

Notice that each change in a formal account (light-shaded columns) is reflected in exactly two of those columns with one debit and one credit.

International Financial Reporting Standards

● LO17–12

Reporting Pension Expense. Under IFRS we don't report pension expense as a single net amount. Instead, we separately report (a) the service cost component (including past service cost) and (b) the net interest cost/income component in the *income statement* and (c) remeasurement gains and losses as *other comprehensive income.*

Decision Makers' Perspective

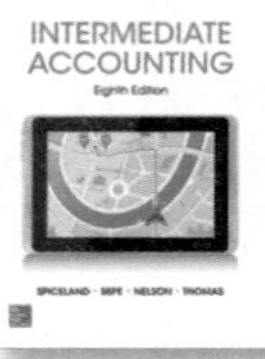

Pension amounts reported in the disclosure notes fill a reporting gap left by the minimal disclosures in the primary financial statements.

Although financial statement items are casualties of the political compromises of GAAP guidance, information provided in the disclosure notes fortunately makes up for some of the deficiencies.[27] Foremost among the useful disclosures are changes in the projected benefit obligation, changes in the fair value of plan assets, and a breakdown of the components of the annual pension expense. Other information also is made available to make it possible for interested analysts to reconstruct the financial statements with pension assets and liabilities included. We'll look at specific disclosures after we discuss postretirement benefits other than pensions because the two types of plans are reported together.

Investors and creditors must be cautious of the nontraditional treatment of pension information when developing financial ratios as part of an analysis of financial statements. The various elements of pensions that are not reported separately on the balance sheet and income statement (PBO, plan assets, gains and losses) can be included in ratios such as the debt to equity ratio or return on assets, but only by deliberately obtaining those numbers from the disclosure notes and adjusting the computation of the ratios. Similarly, without adjustment, profitability ratios and the times interest earned ratio will be distorted because pension expense includes the financial components of interest and return on assets.

Earnings quality (as defined in Chapter 4 and discussed in other chapters) also can be influenced by amounts reported in pension disclosures. Companies with relatively sizeable unrecognized pension costs (prior service cost, net gain or loss) can be expected to exhibit a relatively high "transitory" earnings component. Recall that transitory earnings are expected to be less predictive of future earnings than the "permanent" earnings component. ●

Settlement or Curtailment of Pension Plans

Companies sometimes terminate defined benefit plans to reduce costs and lessen risk.

To cut down on cumbersome paperwork and lessen their exposure to the risk posed by defined benefit plans, many companies are providing defined contribution plans instead. When a plan is terminated, GAAP requires a gain or loss to be reported at that time.[28] For instance, **Melville Corporation** described the termination of its pension plan in the following disclosure note:

Illustration 17–18

Gain on the Termination of a Defined Benefit Plan—Melville Corporation

Real World Financials

Retirement Plans (in part)

. . . As a result of the termination of the defined benefit plans, and after the settlement of the liability to plan participants through the purchase of nonparticipating annuity contracts or lump-sum rollovers into the new 401(k) Profit Sharing Plan, the Company recorded a nonrecurring gain of approximately $4,000,000 which was the amount of plan assets that reverted to the Company. This was accounted for in accordance with Statement of Financial Accounting Standards No. 88, "Employers' Accounting for Settlements and Curtailments of Defined Benefit Pension Plans and for Termination Benefits." [FASB ASC 715–30–35]

[27]FASB ASC 715–20–50: Compensation–Retirement Benefits–Defined Benefit Plans–General–Disclosure (previously "Employers' Disclosures about Pensions and Other Postretirement Benefits," *Statement of Financial Accounting Standards No. 132* (revised 2003), (Stamford, Conn.: FASB, 2003)).

[28]FASB ASC 715–30–35: Compensation–Retirement Benefits–Defined Benefit Plans–Pension–Subsequent Measurement (previously "Employers' Accounting for Settlements and Curtailments of Defined Benefit Pension Plans and for Termination Benefits," *Statement of Financial Accounting Standards No. 88* (Stamford, Conn.: FASB, 1985)).

Concept Review Exercise

PENSION PLANS

Allied Services, Inc., has a noncontributory, defined benefit pension plan. Pension plan assets had a fair value of $900 million at December 31, 2015.

On January 3, 2016, Allied amended the pension formula to increase benefits for each service year. By making the amendment retroactive to prior years, Allied incurred a prior service cost of $75 million, adding to the previous projected benefit obligation of $875 million. The prior service cost is to be amortized (expensed) over 15 years. The service cost is $31 million for 2016. Both the actuary's discount rate and the expected rate of return on plan assets were 8%. The actual rate of return on plan assets was 10%.

At December 31, 2016, $16 million was contributed to the pension fund and $22 million was paid to retired employees. Also, at that time, the actuary revised a previous assumption, increasing the PBO estimate by $10 million. The net loss AOCI at the beginning of the year was $13 million.

Required:

Determine each of the following amounts as of December 31, 2016, the fiscal year-end for Allied: (1) projected benefit obligation; (2) plan assets; and (3) pension expense.

Solution:

($ in millions)	Projected Benefit Obligation	Plan Assets	Pension Expense
Balances at Jan. 1	$ 875	$900	$ 0
Prior service cost	75		
Service cost	31		31
Interest cost [($875 + 75)* × 8%]	76		76
Return on plan assets:			
Actual ($900 × 10%)		90	
Expected ($900 × 8%)			(72)
Amortization of prior service cost ($75 ÷ 15)			5
Amortization of net loss			0†
Loss on PBO	10		
Cash contribution		16	
Retirement payments	(22)	(22)	
Balance at Dec. 31	$1,045	$984	$40

Note: The $18 million gain on plan assets ($90 − 72 million) is not recognized yet; it is carried forward to be combined with previous and future gains and losses, which will be recognized only if the net gain or net loss exceeds 10% of the higher of the PBO or plan assets.

*Since the plan was amended at the beginning of the year, the prior service cost increased the PBO at that time.

†Since the net loss ($13) does not exceed 10% of $900 (higher than $875), no amortization is required for 2016.

International Financial Reporting Standards

LO17–12

Accounting for pensions and other postretirement benefits under IFRS is specified in a recent IASB amendment to its postemployment benefit standard, *IAS No. 19.*

Under the update the changes that constitute the components of the net pension cost are separated into (a) the cost of service, (b) the cost of financing that cost, and (c) gains or losses from occasional remeasurement of the cost:

Components	Include:	Recognized immediately in:
Service cost	• Current service costs. • Past service costs (if any).	• the balance sheet • income statement
Net interest cost/income	• Net interest cost/income. (Interest rate* times net pension liability/ asset)	• the balance sheet • income statement

(continued)

(concluded)

Remeasurement cost	• Remeasurements of service costs caused by changes in assumptions (i.e., assumptions like salary expectations, length of service, length of retirement, etc.). • Gains and losses arising from experience differing from what was assumed. • Investment gains and losses on plan assets.	• the balance sheet • statement of comprehensive income as OCI

*High-quality corporate bond rate.

Classifying the Components of the Net Pension Cost

IFRS ILLUSTRATION

Using the amounts from our Global Communications illustration, the changes in 2016 would be classified as follows:

Profit & Loss (Income Statement):

		($ in millions)
Service cost:		
Service cost—2016	$41	
Past service cost	0*	$41
Net interest cost/income:		
Net interest cost (6% × [$400 − 300])		6
		$47

Other Comprehensive Income (OCI):

Remeasurement cost:		
Loss (gain) on DBO—change in salary estimate	$23	
Loss (gain) on plan assets: (10% − 6%) × $300	(12)	11
Net pension cost		$58

*Last year (2015) this amount was $60 million.

Notice that there is no separate interest cost and there is no "expected" return on plan assets. Instead, those two are essentially combined into a single measure, net interest cost/income. Because they're combined, the same rate (6% in this case) is used for both, rather than having one rate for interest cost and another for expected return on assets.

Recording the Components of the Net Pension Cost

We report the (a) service cost and (b) net interest cost/income in *net income* and (c) remeasurement costs in *OCI*, as each of those amounts occurs. By recording each component, we record the total pension expense. Remember, each component is a change in either plan assets (the return on assets) or the defined benefit obligation (all others), so as we record each component we also record its effect on plan assets and the defined benefit obligation, as follows:

We record (a) individual components of the net pension cost (in net income or OCI) and (b) the balance sheet accounts they affect.

To Record Net Pension Cost	($ in millions)	
Service cost	41	
DBO (service cost-2016)		41
DBO (past service cost: none in 2016)		0
Net interest cost (6% × [$400 − 300])	6	
Plan assets (6% × $300: interest income)	18	
DBO (6% × $400: interest cost)		24

(continued)

(concluded)

Plan assets (actual return in excess of 6%)	12	
Remeasurement gain on plan assets–OCI ([10% − 6%] × $300)		12
Remeasurement loss from change in assumption–OCI	23	
DBO (change in future salary estimate)		23

When Global adds its annual cash investment to its plan assets, the value of those plan assets increases by $48 million:

To Record Funding	($ in millions)	
Plan assets	48	
Cash (contribution to plan assets)		48

In our illustration, Global's retired employees were paid benefits of $38 million in 2016. Paying those benefits, of course, reduces the obligation to pay benefits (the DBO), and since the payments are made from the plan assets, that balance is reduced as well:

To Record Payment of Benefits	($ in millions)	
DBO	38	
Plan assets		38

Reporting the Components of the Net Pension Cost

We report the components of the total pension cost in the **statement of comprehensive** income as follows:

Revenue	$xxx
Operating expenses (including **$41 pension service cost**)	(xx)
Finance costs (including **$6 net interest cost on pensions**)	xx
Profit before tax	$xxx
Tax expense	(xx)
Net income	$xxx
Other comprehensive income	
Remeasurement loss arising from change in pension assumption	$ 23
Remeasurement gain from the return on plan assets exceeding the interest rate	(12)
Comprehensive income	$xxx

Notice in the journal entries that we have no "pension expense" being recorded as we had using U.S. GAAP in the chapter. Instead, individual components of the net pension cost are recorded. The reason is that the amendment calls for components, not the net total, to be reported in the income statement and statement of comprehensive income.

We report separately the three costs of having a defined benefit plan:

In net income:
- **service cost**
- **net interest cost**

In OCI:
- **remeasurement cost**

Postretirement Benefits Other Than Pensions

PART E

As we just discussed, most companies have pension plans that provide for the future payments of retirement benefits to compensate employees for their current services. Many companies also furnish *other postretirement benefits* to their retired employees. These may include medical coverage, dental coverage, life insurance, group legal services, and other benefits. By far the most common is health care benefits. One of every three U.S. workers in medium- and large-size companies participates in health care plans that provide for coverage that continues into retirement. The aggregate impact is considerable; the total obligation for all U.S. corporations is about $500 billion.

Prior to 1993, employers accounted for postretirement benefit costs on a pay-as-you-go basis, meaning the expense each year was simply the amount of insurance premiums or medical claims paid, depending on the way the company provided health care benefits. The FASB revised GAAP to require a completely different approach. The expected future health care costs for retirees now must be recognized as an expense over the years necessary for employees to become entitled to the benefits.[29] This is the accrual basis that also is the basis for pension accounting.

● LO17–9

In fact, accounting for postretirement benefits is similar in most respects to accounting for pension benefits. This is because the two forms of benefits are fundamentally similar. Each is a form of deferred compensation earned during the employee's service life and each can be estimated as the present value of the cost of providing the expected future benefits. **General Motors** described its plan as shown in Illustration 17–19.

Illustration 17–19

Disclosures—General Motors

Real World Financials

Note 5: Other Postretirement Benefits (in part)
The Corporation and certain of its domestic subsidiaries maintain hourly and salaried benefit plans that provide postretirement medical, dental, vision, and life insurance to retirees and eligible dependents. . . . [GAAP] requires that the cost of such benefits be recognized in the financial statements during the period employees provide service to the Corporation.

Despite the similarities, though, there are a few differences in the characteristics of the benefits that necessitate differences in accounting treatment. Because accounting for the two types of retiree benefits is so nearly the same, our discussion in this portion of the chapter will emphasize the differences. This will allow you to use what you learned earlier in the chapter regarding pension accounting as a foundation for learning how to account for other postretirement benefits, supplementing that common base only when necessary. Focusing on the differences also will reinforce your understanding of pension accounting.

What Is a Postretirement Benefit Plan?

Before addressing the accounting ramifications, let's look at a typical retiree health care plan.[30] First, it's important to distinguish retiree health care benefits from health care benefits provided during an employee's working years. The annual cost of providing *preretirement* benefits is simply part of the annual compensation expense. However, many companies offer coverage that continues into retirement. It is the deferred aspect of these *postretirement* benefits that creates an accounting issue.

Eligibility usually is based on age and/or years of service.

Usually a plan promises benefits in exchange for services performed over a designated number of years, or reaching a particular age, or both. For instance, a plan might specify that employees are eligible for postretirement benefits after both working 20 years and reaching age 62 while in service. Eligibility requirements and the nature of benefits usually are specified by a written plan, or sometimes only by company practice.

Postretirement Health Benefits and Pension Benefits Compared

Keep in mind that retiree health benefits differ fundamentally from pension benefits in some important respects:

1. The amount of *pension* benefits generally is based on the number of years an employee works for the company so that the longer the employee works, the higher are the benefits. On the other hand, the amount of *postretirement health care* benefits typically is unrelated to service. It's usually an all-or-nothing plan in which a certain level of coverage is promised upon retirement, independent of the length of service beyond that necessary for eligibility.

[29]FASB ASC 715–60: Compensation–Retirement Benefits–Defined Benefit Plans–Postretirement (previously "Employers' Accounting for Postretirement Benefits Other Than Pensions," *Statement of Financial Accounting Standards No. 106* (Norwalk, Conn.: FASB, 1990)). The Standard became effective (with some exceptions) in 1993.

[30]For convenience, our discussion focuses on health care benefits because these are by far the most common type of postretirement benefits other than pensions. But the concepts we discuss apply equally to other forms of postretirement benefits.

2. Although coverage might be identical, the cost of providing the coverage might vary significantly from retiree to retiree and from year to year because of differing medical needs.
3. Postretirement health care plans often require the retiree to share in the cost of coverage through monthly contribution payments. For instance, a company might pay 80% of insurance premiums, with the retiree paying 20%. The net cost of providing coverage is reduced by these contributions as well as by any portion of the cost paid by Medicare or other insurance.
4. Coverage often is provided to spouses and eligible dependents.

Determining the Net Cost of Benefits

To determine the postretirement benefit obligation and the postretirement benefit expense, the company's actuary first must make estimates of what the postretirement benefit costs will be for current employees. Then, as illustrated in Illustration 17–20, contributions to those costs by employees are deducted, as well as Medicare's share of the costs (for retirement years when the retiree will be 65 or older), to determine the estimated net cost of benefits to the employer:

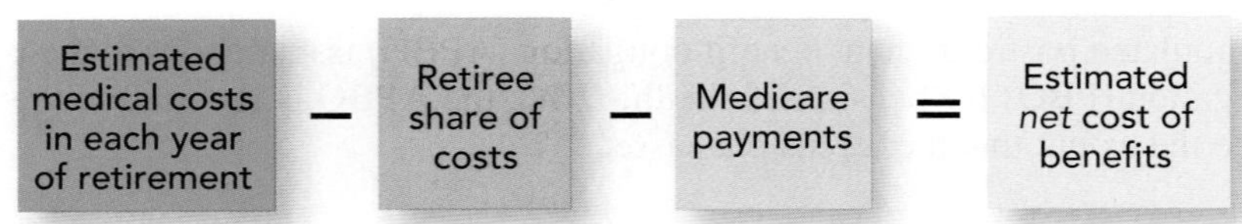

Illustration 17–20
Estimating the Net Cost of Benefits

Remember, postretirement health care benefits are anticipated actual costs of providing the promised health care, rather than an amount estimated by a defined benefit formula. This makes these estimates inherently more intricate, particularly because health care costs in general are notoriously difficult to forecast. And, since postretirement health care benefits are partially paid by the retiree and by Medicare, these cost-sharing amounts must be estimated as well.

On the other hand, estimating postretirement benefits costs is similar in many ways to estimating pension costs. Both estimates entail a variety of assumptions to be made by the company's actuary. Many of these assumptions are the same; for instance, both require estimates of:

Many of the assumptions needed to estimate postretirement health care benefits are the same as those needed to estimate pension benefits.

1. A discount rate.
2. Expected return on plan assets (if the plan is funded).
3. Employee turnover.
4. Expected retirement age.
5. Expected compensation increases (if the plan is pay-related).
6. Expected age of death.
7. Number and ages of beneficiaries and dependents.

Of course, the relative importance of some estimates is different from that for pension plans. Dependency status, turnover, and retirement age, for example, take on much greater significance. Also, additional assumptions become necessary as a result of differences between pension plans and other postretirement benefit plans. Specifically, it's necessary to estimate:

Some additional assumptions are needed to estimate postretirement health care benefits besides those needed to estimate pension benefits.

1. The current cost of providing health care benefits at each age that participants might receive benefits.
2. Demographic characteristics of plan participants that might affect the amount and timing of benefits.

3. Benefit coverage provided by Medicare, other insurance, or other sources that will reduce the net cost of employer-provided benefits.
4. The expected health care cost trend rate.[31]

The postretirement benefit obligation is the discounted present value of the benefits during retirement.

Taking these assumptions into account, the company's actuary estimates what the net cost of postretirement benefits will be for current employees in each year of their expected retirement. The discounted present value of those costs is the expected postretirement benefit obligation.

Postretirement Benefit Obligation

● LO17–10

There are two related obligation amounts. As indicated in Illustration 17–21, one measures the total obligation and the other refers to a specific portion of the total:

Illustration 17–21

Two Views of the Obligation for Postretirement Benefits Other Than Pensions

1. **Expected postretirement benefit obligation (EPBO):** The actuary's estimate of the total postretirement benefits (at their discounted present value) expected to be received by plan participants.
2. **Accumulated postretirement benefit obligation (APBO):** The portion of the EPBO attributed to employee service to date.

The accumulated postretirement benefit obligation (APBO) is analogous to the projected benefit obligation (PBO) for pensions. Like the PBO, the APBO is reported in the balance sheet only to the extent that it exceeds plan assets.

Measuring the Obligation

To illustrate, assume the actuary estimates that the net cost of providing health care benefits to Jessica Farrow (our illustration employee from earlier in the chapter) during her retirement years has a present value of $10,842 as of the end of 2014. This is the EPBO. If the benefits (and therefore the costs) relate to an estimated 35 years of service[32] and 10 of those years have been completed, the APBO would be:

$3,098 represents the portion of the EPBO related to the first 10 years of the 35-year service period.

$10,842	×	10/35	=	$3,098
EPBO		Fraction attributed to service to date		APBO

If the assumed discount rate is 6%, a year later the EPBO will have grown to $11,493 simply because of a year's interest accruing at that rate ($10,842 × 1.06 = $11,493). Notice that there is no increase in the EPBO for service because, unlike the obligation in most pension plans, the total obligation is not increased by an additional year's service.

The APBO, however, is the portion of the EPBO related to service up to a particular date. Consequently, the APBO will have increased both because of interest and because the service fraction will be higher (service cost):

$3,612 represents the portion of the EPBO related to the first 11 years of the 35-year service period.

$11,493	×	11/35	=	$3,612
EPBO		Fraction attributed to service to date		APBO

The two elements of the increase in 2015 can be separated as follows:

The APBO increases each year due to (a) interest accrued on the APBO and (b) the portion of the EPBO attributed to that year.

APBO at the beginning of the year	$3,098
Interest cost: $3,098 × 6%	186
Service cost: ($11,493 × 1/35) portion of EPBO attributed to the year	328
APBO at the end of the year	$3,612

[31]Health care cost trend rates recently reported have ranged from 3% to 9.7%, with 7.5% being the most commonly assumed rate. (Pension/OPEB 2013 Assumption and Disclosure Survey, PWC, 2013).

[32]Assigning the costs to particular service years is referred to as the *attribution* of the costs to the years the benefits are assumed earned. We discuss attribution in the next section.

Attribution

Attribution is the process of assigning the cost of benefits to the years during which those benefits are assumed to be earned by employees. We accomplish this by assigning an equal fraction of the EPBO to each year of service from the employee's date of hire to the employee's full eligibility date.[33] This is the date the employee has performed all the service necessary to have earned all the retiree benefits estimated to be received by the employee.[34] In our earlier example, we assumed the attribution period was 35 years and accordingly accrued 1/35 of the EPBO each year. The amount accrued each year increases both the APBO and the postretirement benefit expense. In Illustration 17–22 we see how the 35-year attribution (accrual) period was determined.

The cost of benefits is attributed to the years during which those benefits are assumed to be earned by employees.

Illustration 17–22
Determining the Attribution Period

Jessica Farrow was hired by Global Communications at age 22 at the beginning of 2005 and is expected to retire at the end of 2044 at age 61. The retirement period is estimated to be 20 years.*

Global's employees are eligible for postretirement health care benefits after both reaching age 56 while in service and having worked 20 years.

Since Farrow becomes fully eligible at age 56 (the end of 2039), retiree benefits are attributed to the 35-year period from her date of hire through that date. Graphically, the situation can be described as follows:

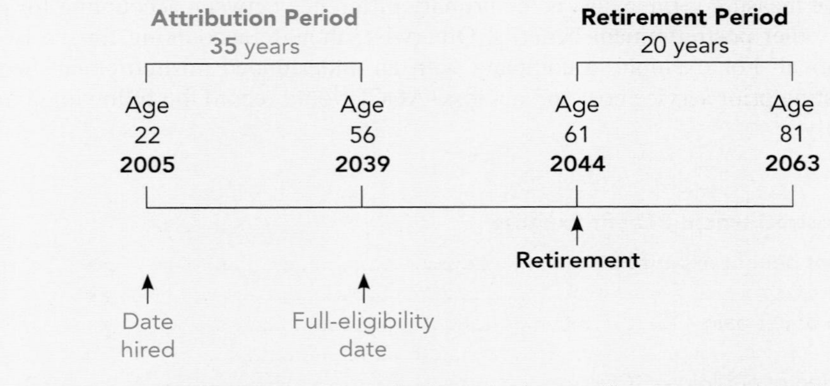

*You probably recognize this as the situation used earlier in the chapter to illustrate pension accounting.

The attribution period spans each year of service from the employee's date of hire to the employee's full eligibility date.

Some critics of this approach feel there is a fundamental inconsistency between the way we measure the benefits and the way we assign the benefits to specific service periods. The benefits (EPBO) are measured with the concession that the employee may work beyond the full eligibility date; however, the attribution period does not include years of service after that date. The counterargument is the fact that at the full eligibility date the employee will have earned the right to receive the full benefits expected under the plan and the amount of the benefits will not increase with service beyond that date.[35]

The attribution period does not include years of service beyond the full eligibility date even if the employee is expected to work after that date.

Accounting for Postretirement Benefit Plans Other Than Pensions

● LO17–11

We account for pensions and for other postretirement benefits essentially the same way.

As we just discussed, it's necessary to attribute a portion of the accumulated postretirement benefit obligation to each year as the service cost for that year as opposed to measuring the actual benefits employees earn during the year as we did for pension plans. That's due to the fundamental nature of these other postretirement plans under which employees are

[33]If the plan specifically grants credit only for service from a date after employee's date of hire, the beginning of the attribution period is considered to be the beginning of that credited service period, rather than the employee's date of hire.

[34]Or any beneficiaries and covered dependents.

[35]FASB ASC 715–60: Compensation–Retirement Benefits–Defined Benefit Plans–Other Postretirement (previously "Employers' Accounting for Postretirement Benefits Other Than Pensions," *Statement of Financial Accounting Standards No. 106* (Norwalk, Conn.: FASB, 1990), par. 219–239. These specific paragraphs are not codified in the FASB Research System as they contain bases for conclusions and are therefore what codifiers consider "nonessential" material.

ineligible for benefits until specific eligibility criteria are met, at which time they become 100% eligible. This contrasts with pension plans under which employees earn additional benefits each year until they retire.

Illustration 17–23
Measuring Service Cost

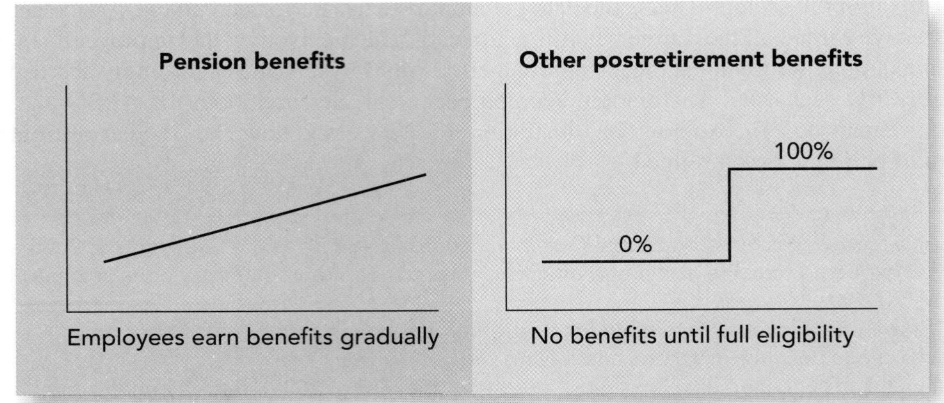

Measuring the service cost differs, though, due to a fundamental difference in the way employees acquire benefits under the two types of plans.

The way we measure service cost is the primary difference between accounting for pensions and for other postretirement benefits. Otherwise, though, accounting for the two is virtually identical. For example, a company with an underfunded postretirement benefit plan with existing prior service cost and net loss–AOCI would record the following journal entries annually:

We record the annual expense and funding for other postretirement benefit plans the same way we do for pensions.

We record losses and gains (as well as any new prior service cost should it occur) the same way we do for pensions.

To Record Postretirement Benefit Expense		
Postretirement benefit expense (total)	xx	
Plan assets (expected return on assets)	xx	
Amortization of net gain–OCI (current amortization)	xx	
APBO (service cost + interest cost)		xx
Amortization of net loss—OCI (current amortization)		xx
Amortization of prior service cost—OCI[36] (current amortization)		xx
To Record Cash Funding of Plan Assets		
Plan assets	xx	
Cash (contribution to plan assets)		xx
To Record Gains and Losses		
Loss–OCI (from change in assumption)	xx	
APBO		xx
or		
APBO	xx	
Gain–OCI (from change in assumption)		xx
Plan assets	xx	
Gain–OCI (actual return on assets − expected return)		xx
or		
Loss–OCI (expected return on assets − actual return)	xx	
Plan assets		xx

[36]The prior service cost for other postretirement benefits is amortized over the average remaining time until "full eligibility" for employees rather than until retirement as is the case for pension plans. This is consistent with recording "regular" service cost over the time to full eligibility.

Ethical Dilemma

Earlier this year, you were elected to the board of directors of Champion International, Inc. Champion has offered its employees postretirement health care benefits for 35 years. The practice of extending health care benefits to retirees began modestly. Most employees retired after age 65, when most benefits were covered by Medicare. Costs also were lower because life expectancies were shorter and medical care was less expensive. Because costs were so low, little attention was paid to accounting for these benefits. The company simply recorded an expense when benefits were provided to retirees. The FASB changed all that. Now, the obligation for these benefits must be anticipated and reported in the annual report. Worse yet, the magnitude of the obligation has grown enormously, almost unnoticed. Health care costs have soared in recent years. Medical technology and other factors have extended life expectancies. Of course, the value to employees of this benefit has grown parallel to the growth of the burden to the company.

Without being required to anticipate future costs, many within Champion's management were caught by surprise at the enormity of the company's obligation. Equally disconcerting was the fact that such a huge liability now must be exposed to public view. Now you find that several board members are urging the dismantling of the postretirement plan altogether.

A Comprehensive Illustration

We assumed earlier that the EPBO at the end of 2014 was determined by the actuary to be \$10,842. This was the present value on that date of all anticipated future benefits. Then we noted that the EPBO at the end of the next year would have grown by 6% to \$11,493. This amount, too, would represent the present value of the same anticipated future benefits, but as of a year later. The APBO, remember, is the portion of the EPBO attributed to service performed to a particular date. So, we determined the APBO at the end of 2015 to be \$11,493 × $^{11}/_{35}$, or \$3,612. We determined the \$328 service cost noted earlier for 2015 as the portion of the EPBO attributed to that year: \$11,493 × $^{1}/_{35}$.

Now, let's review our previous discussion of how the EPBO, the APBO, and the postretirement benefit expense are determined by calculating those amounts a year later, at the end of 2016. Before doing so, however, we can anticipate (a) the EPBO to be \$11,493 × 1.06, or \$12,182, (b) the APBO to be $^{12}/_{35}$ of that amount, or \$4,177, and (c) the 2016 service cost to be $^{1}/_{35}$ of that amount, or \$348. In Illustration 17–24 we see if our expectations are borne out by direct calculation.

Illustration 17–24
Determining the Postretirement Benefit Obligation

Assume the actuary has estimated the net cost of retiree benefits in each year of Jessica Farrow's 20-year expected retirement period to be the amounts shown in the calculation below. She is fully eligible for benefits at the end of 2039 and is expected to retire at the end of 2044.

Calculating the APBO and the postretirement benefit expense at the end of 2016, 12 years after being hired, begins with estimating the EPBO.

Steps to calculate (a) the EPBO, (b) the APBO, and (c) the annual service cost at the end of 2016, 12 years after being hired, are:

(a). 1. Estimate the cost of retiree benefits in each year of the expected retirement period and deduct anticipated Medicare reimbursements and retiree cost-sharing to derive the net cost to the employer in each year of the expected retirement period.
2. Find the present value of each year's net benefit cost as of the retirement date.
3. Find the present value of the total net benefit cost as of the current date. This is the EPBO.

(b). Multiply the EPBO by the attribution factor, (service to date/total attribution period). This is the APBO. The service cost in any year is simply one year's worth of the EPBO.

(c). Multiply the EPBO by $^{1}/_{\text{total attribution period}}$.

The EPBO is the discounted present value of the total benefits expected to be earned.

The fraction of the EPBO considered to be earned this year is the service cost.

The fraction of the EPBO considered to be earned so far is the APBO.

The steps are demonstrated in Illustration 17–24A.

Illustration 17–24A
EPBO, APBO, and Service Cost in 2016

The actuary estimates the net cost to the employer in each year the retiree is expected to receive benefits.

As of the retirement date, the lump-sum equivalent of the expected yearly costs is $62,269.

The EPBO in 2016 is the present value of those benefits.

The APBO is the portion of the EPBO attributed to service to date.

The service cost is the portion of the EPBO attributed to a particular year's service.

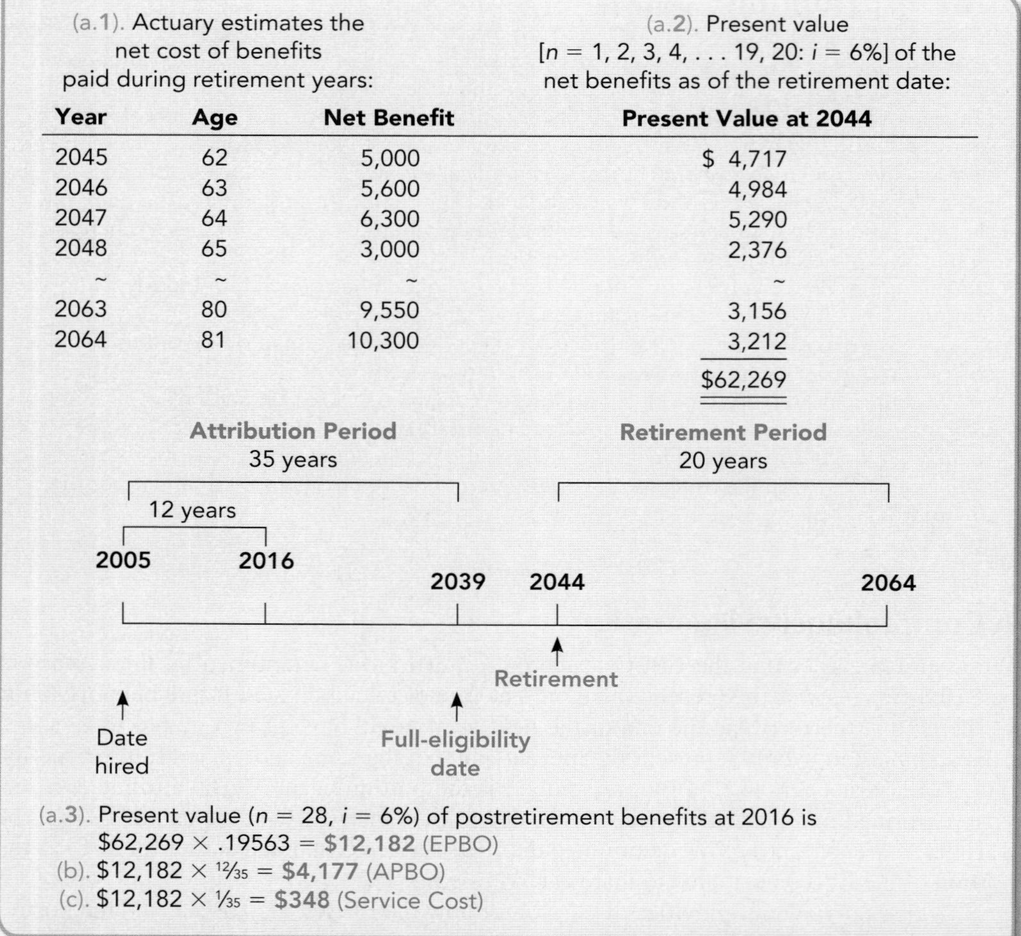

(a.1). Actuary estimates the net cost of benefits paid during retirement years:

(a.2). Present value [n = 1, 2, 3, 4, . . . 19, 20: i = 6%] of the net benefits as of the retirement date:

Year	Age	Net Benefit	Present Value at 2044
2045	62	5,000	$ 4,717
2046	63	5,600	4,984
2047	64	6,300	5,290
2048	65	3,000	2,376
~	~	~	~
2063	80	9,550	3,156
2064	81	10,300	3,212
			$62,269

(a.3). Present value (n = 28, i = 6%) of postretirement benefits at 2016 is $62,269 × .19563 = $12,182 (EPBO)
(b). $12,182 × 12/35 = $4,177 (APBO)
(c). $12,182 × 1/35 = $348 (Service Cost)

Decision Makers' Perspective

Postretirement benefit amounts reported in the disclosure notes fill a reporting gap left by the minimal disclosures in the primary financial statements.

When they analyze financial statements, investors and creditors should be wary of the nonstandard way companies report pension and other postretirement information. Recall that in the balance sheet, firms do not separately report the benefit obligation and the plan assets. Also, companies have considerable latitude in making the several assumptions needed to estimate the components of postretirement benefit plans. Fortunately, information provided in the disclosure notes makes up for some of the deficiency in balance sheet information and makes it possible for interested analysts to modify their analysis. As for pensions, the choices companies make for the discount rate, expected return on plan assets, and the compensation growth rate can greatly impact postretirement benefit expense and earnings quality. The disclosures required are very similar to pension disclosures. In fact, disclosures for the two types of retiree benefits typically are combined.[37] Disclosures include:

- Descriptions of the plans.
- Estimates of the obligations (PBO, ABO, vested benefit obligation, EPBO, and APBO).
- The percentage of total plan assets for each major category of assets (equity securities, debt securities, real estate, other) as well as a description of investment strategies, including any target asset allocations and risk management practices.

[37]FASB ASC 715–60–50: Compensation–Retirement Benefits–Defined Benefit Plans–Other Postretirement–Disclosure (previously "Employers' Disclosures about Pensions and Other Postretirement Benefits," *Statement of Financial Accounting Standards No. 132* (Stamford, Conn.: FASB, 1998))

- A breakdown of the components of the annual pension and postretirement benefit expenses for the years reported.
- The discount rates, the assumed rate of compensation increases used to measure the PBO, the expected long-term rate of return on plan assets, and the expected rate of increase in future medical and dental benefit costs.
- Estimated benefit payments presented separately for the next five years and in the aggregate for years 6–10.
- Estimate of expected contributions to fund the plan for the next year.
- Disclosures also include (a) any changes to the net gain or net loss and prior service cost arising during the period, (b) the accumulated amounts of these components of accumulated other comprehensive income, and (c) the amounts of those balances expected to be amortized in the next year.
- Other information to make it possible for interested analysts to reconstruct the financial statements with plan assets and liabilities included. ●

Concept Review Exercise

OTHER POSTRETIREMENT BENEFITS

Technology Group, Inc., has an unfunded retiree health care plan. The actuary estimates the net cost of providing health care benefits to a particular employee during his retirement years to have a present value of $24,000 as of the end of 2016 (the EPBO). The benefits and therefore the expected postretirement benefit obligation relate to an estimated 36 years of service and 12 of those years have been completed. The interest rate is 6%.

Required:

Pertaining to the one employee only:

1. What is the accumulated postretirement benefit obligation at the end of 2016?
2. What is the expected postretirement benefit obligation at the end of 2017?
3. What is the service cost to be included in 2017 postretirement benefit expense?
4. What is the interest cost to be included in 2017 postretirement benefit expense?
5. What is the accumulated postretirement benefit obligation at the end of 2017?
6. Show how the APBO changed during 2017 by reconciling the beginning and ending balances.
7. What is the 2017 postretirement benefit expense, assuming no net gains or losses and no prior service cost?

Solution:

1. What is the accumulated postretirement benefit obligation at the end of 2016?

$24,000	×	12/36	=	$8,000
EPBO 2016		Fraction earned		APBO 2016

2. What is the expected postretirement benefit obligation at the end of 2017?

$24,000	×	1.06	=	$25,440
EPBO 2016		To accrue interest		EPBO 2017

3. What is the service cost to be included in 2017 postretirement benefit expense?

$25,440	×	1/36	=	$707
EPBO 2017		Attributed to 2017		Service cost

4. What is the interest cost to be included in 2017 postretirement benefit expense?

$8,000 (beginning APBO) × 6% = $480

5. What is the accumulated postretirement benefit obligation at the end of 2017?

$25,440	×	13⁄36	=	$9,187
EPBO 2017		Fraction attributed to service to date		APBO 2017

6. Show how the APBO changed during 2017 by reconciling the beginning and ending balances.

APBO at the beginning of 2017 (from req. 1)	$8,000
Service cost: (from req. 3)	707
Interest cost: (from req. 4)	480
APBO at the end of 2017 (from req. 5)	$9,187

7. What is the 2017 postretirement benefit expense, assuming no net gains or losses and no prior service cost?

Service cost	$ 707
Interest cost	480
Actual return on the plan assets	(not funded)
Adjusted for: gain or loss on the plan assets	(not funded)
Amortization of prior service cost	none
Amortization of net gain or loss	none
Postretirement benefit expense	$1,187

Financial Reporting Case Solution

1. **Why is pension plan underfunding not a concern in your present employment?** *(p. 1001)* In a defined contribution plan, the employer is not obliged to provide benefits beyond the annual contribution to the employees' plan. No liability is created. Unlike retirement benefits paid in a defined benefit plan, the employee's retirement benefits in a defined contribution plan are totally dependent on how well invested assets perform in the marketplace.
2. **Were you correct that the pension liability is not reported in the balance sheet? What is the liability?** *(p. 1003)* Yes and no. The pension liability is not reported separately in the balance sheet. It is, however, combined with pension assets with the net difference reported in the balance sheet. The separate balance is disclosed, though, in the notes. For United Dynamics, the PBO at the end of 2016 is $2,628 million.
3. **What is the amount of the plan assets available to pay benefits? What are the factors that can cause that amount to change?** *(p. 1010)* The plan assets at the end of total $2,807 million. A trustee accepts employer contributions, invests the contributions, accumulates the earnings on the investments, and pays benefits from the plan assets. So the amount is increased each year by employer cash contributions and (hopefully) a return on assets invested. It is decreased by amounts paid out to retired employees.
4. **What does the "pension asset" represent? Are you interviewing with a company whose pension plan is severely underfunded?** *(p. 1011)* The pension asset is not the plan assets available to pay pension benefits. Instead, it's the net difference between those assets and the pension obligation. United Dynamics' plan assets exceed the pension obligation in each year presented and therefore is one of the few companies whose pension plan is overfunded.

5. **How is the pension expense influenced by changes in the pension liability and plan assets?** *(p. 1012)* The pension expense reported on the income statement is a composite of periodic changes that occur in both the pension obligation and the plan assets. For United Dynamics in 2016, the pension expense included the service cost and interest cost, which are changes in the PBO, and the return on plan assets. It also included an amortized portion of prior service costs (a previous change in the PBO) and of net gains (gains and losses result from changes in both the PBO and plan assets). ●

The Bottom Line

- **LO17–1** Pension plans are arrangements designed to provide income to individuals during their retirement years. *Defined contribution* plans promise fixed annual contributions to a pension fund, without further commitment regarding benefit amounts at retirement. *Defined benefit* plans promise fixed retirement benefits defined by a designated formula. The employer sets aside cash each year to provide sufficient funds to pay promised benefits. (*p. 999*)
- **LO17–2** The *accumulated benefit obligation* is an estimate of the discounted present value of the retirement benefits earned so far by employees, applying the plan's pension formula to *existing* compensation levels. The vested benefit obligation is the portion of the accumulated benefit obligation that plan participants are entitled to receive regardless of their continued employment. The *projected benefit obligation* estimates retirement benefits by applying the pension formula to *projected future* compensation levels. (*p. 1003*)
- **LO17–3** The PBO can change due to the accumulation of *service cost* from year to year, the accrual of *interest* as time passes, making plan amendments retroactive to prior years (prior service cost), and periodic adjustments when estimates change (gains and losses). The obligation is reduced as benefits actually are paid to retired employees. (*p. 1004*)
- **LO17–4** The plan assets consist of the accumulated balance of the annual employer contributions plus the return on the investments less benefits paid to retirees. (*p. 1009*)
- **LO17–5** The difference between an employer's obligation (PBO for pensions, APBO for other postretirement benefit plans) and the resources available to satisfy that obligation (plan assets) is the funded status of the pension plan. The employer must report the "funded status" of the plan in the balance sheet as a net pension liability if the obligation exceeds the plan assets or as a net pension asset if the plan assets exceed the obligation. (*p. 1011*)
- **LO17–6** The pension expense is a composite of periodic changes in both the projected benefit obligation and the plan assets. Service cost is the increase in the PBO attributable to employee service and is the primary component of pension expense. The interest and return-on-assets components are financial items created only because the pension payment is delayed and the obligation is funded currently. Prior service cost is recognized over employees' future service period. Also, neither a loss (gain) on the PBO nor a loss (gain) on plan assets is immediately recognized in pension expense; they are recognized on a delayed basis to achieve income smoothing. (*p. 1011*)
- **LO17–7** Recording pension expense causes the net pension liability/asset to change by the service cost, the interest cost, and the expected return on plan assets. Any amortization amounts included in the expense will reduce the *accumulated other comprehensive income* balances being amortized, e.g., net loss—AOCI and prior service cost–AOCI. Similarly, the plan assets are increased by the annual cash investment. New losses and gains (as well as any new prior service cost should it occur) are recognized as other comprehensive income. (*p. 1017*)
- **LO17–8** The various elements of a pension plan—projected benefit obligation, plan assets, prior service cost, gains and losses, pension expense, and the funded status of the plan—are interrelated. One way to see how each element relates to the other is to bring each part together in a *pension spreadsheet.* (*p. 1023*)
- **LO17–9** Accounting for postretirement benefits is similar in most respects to accounting for pension benefits. Like pensions, other postretirement benefits are a form of deferred compensation. Unlike pensions, their cost is attributed to the years from the employee's date of hire to the full eligibility date. (*p. 1028*)
- **LO17–10** The expected postretirement benefit obligation (EPBO) is the actuary's estimate of the total postretirement benefits (at their discounted present value) expected to be received by plan participants. The

accumulated postretirement benefit obligation (APBO) is the portion of the EPBO attributed to employee service to date. *(p. 1030)*

- **LO17–11** The components of postretirement benefit expense are essentially the same as those for pension expense. *(p. 1031)*
- **LO17–12** Under both U.S. GAAP and IFRS we report all changes in the obligation and in the value of plan assets as they occur. The ways the changes are determined and reported are different, though, for some of the changes. The changes that constitute the components of the net pension cost are reported separately as (a) the service cost, (b) the net interest cost/income, and (c) remeasurement gains or losses. Under IFRS, *past service cost* is combined with current service cost and reported as service cost within the income statement rather than as a component of other comprehensive income as it is under U.S. GAAP. Under IFRS, gains and losses are not recycled from other comprehensive income as is required under U.S. GAAP (when the accumulated net gain or net loss exceeds the 10% threshold). Also, the interest cost and return on plan assets are replaced by net interest cost/income (interest rate times the difference between the DBO and plan assets). *(pp. 1017, 1020, 1024, and 1025)*

APPENDIX 17 Service Method of Allocating Prior Service Cost

When amortizing prior service cost, our objective is to match the cost with employee service. The straight-line method described in this chapter allocates an equal amount of the prior service cost to each year of the 15-year average service period of affected employees. But consider this: fewer of the affected employees will be working for the company toward the end of that period than at the beginning. Some probably will retire or quit in each year following the amendment.

An allocation approach that reflects the declining service pattern is called the **service method**. This method allocates the prior service cost to each year in proportion to the fraction of the total remaining service years worked in each of those years. To do this, it's necessary to estimate how many of the 2,000 employees working at the beginning of 2015 when the amendment is made will still be employed in each year after the amendment.

Let's suppose, for example, that the actuary estimates that a declining number of these employees still will be employed in each of the next 28 years as indicated in the abbreviated schedule below. The portion of the prior service cost amortized to pension expense each year is $60 million times a declining fraction. Each year's fraction is that year's service divided by the 28-year total (30,000). This is demonstrated in Illustration 17A–1.

Illustration 17A–1
Service Method of Amortizing Prior Service Cost

By the service method, prior service cost is recognized each year in proportion to the fraction of the total remaining service years worked that year.

Year	Number of Employees Still Employed (assumed for the illustration)	Fraction of Total Service Years		Prior Service Cost ($ in millions)		Amount Amortized ($ in millions)
2015	2,000	2,000/30,000	×	$60	=	$ 4.0
2016	2,000	2,000/30,000	×	60	=	4.0
2017	1,850	1,850/30,000	×	60	=	3.7
2018	1,700	1,700/30,000	×	60	=	3.4
2019	1,550	1,550/30,000	×	60	=	3.1
—	—	—	×	—	=	—
2040	400	400/30,000	×	60	=	.8
2041	250	250/30,000	×	60	=	.5
2042	100	100/30,000	×	60	=	.2
Totals	30,000	30,000/30,000				$60.0
	Total number of service years					Total amount amortized

Conceptually, the service method achieves a better matching of the cost and benefits. In fact, this is the FASB's recommended approach. However, GAAP permits the consistent use of any method that amortizes the prior service cost at least as quickly.[38] The straight-line method meets this condition and is the approach most often used in practice. In our illustration, the cost is completely amortized over 15 years rather than the 28 years required by the service method. The 15-year average service life is simply the total estimated service years divided by the total number of employees in the group:

The service method amortized an equal amount *per employee* each year.

30,000 years	÷	2,000	=	15 years
Total number of service years		Total number of employees		Average service years

[38]FASB ASC 715–30–35–13: Compensation–Retirement Benefits–Defined Benefit Plans–Pension–Subsequent Measurement–Prior Service Costs (previously "Employers' Accounting for Pensions," *Statement of Financial Accounting Standards No. 87* (Stamford, Conn.: FASB, 1985), par. 26).

Questions For Review of Key Topics

Q 17–1 What is a pension plan? What motivates a corporation to offer a pension plan for its employees?

Q 17–2 Qualified pension plans offer important tax benefits. What is the special tax treatment and what qualifies a pension plan for these benefits?

Q 17–3 Lamont Corporation has a pension plan in which the corporation makes all contributions and employees receive benefits at retirement based on the balance in their accumulated pension fund. What type of pension plan does Lamont have?

Q 17–4 What is the vested benefit obligation?

Q 17–5 Differentiate between the accumulated benefit obligation and the projected benefit obligation.

Q 17–6 Name five events that might change the balance of the PBO.

Q 17–7 Name three events that might change the balance of the plan assets.

Q 17–8 What are the components that might be included in the calculation of net pension cost recognized for a period by an employer sponsoring a defined benefit pension plan?

Q 17–9 Define the service cost component of the periodic pension expense.

Q 17–10 Define the interest cost component of the periodic pension expense.

Q 17–11 The return on plan assets is the increase in plan assets (at fair value), adjusted for contributions to the plan and benefits paid during the period. How is the return included in the calculation of the periodic pension expense?

Q 17–12 Define prior service cost. How is it reported in the financial statements? How is it included in pension expense?

Q 17–13 How should gains or losses related to pension plan assets be recognized? How does this treatment compare to that for gains or losses related to the pension obligation?

Q 17–14 Is a company's PBO reported in the balance sheet? Its plan assets? Explain.

Q 17–15 What two components of pension expense may be negative (i.e., reduce pension expense)?

Q 17–16 Which are the components of pension expense that involve delayed recognition?

Q 17–17 Evaluate this statement: The excess of the actual return on plan assets over the expected return decreases the employer's pension cost.

Q 17–18 When accounting for pension costs, how should the payment into the pension fund be recorded? How does it affect the funded status of the plan?

Q 17–19 TFC Inc. revises its estimate of future salary levels, causing its PBO estimate to increase by $3 million. How is the $3 reflected in TFC's financial statements?

Q 17–20 A pension plan is underfunded when the employer's obligation (PBO) exceeds the resources available to satisfy that obligation (plan assets) and overfunded when the opposite is the case. How is this funded status reported on the balance sheet if plan assets exceed the PBO? If the PBO exceeds plan assets?

Q 17–21 What are two ways to measure the obligation for postretirement benefits other than pensions? Define these measurement approaches.

Q 17–22 How are the costs of providing postretirement benefits other than pensions expensed?

Q 17–23 The components of postretirement benefit expense are similar to the components of pension expense. In what fundamental way does the service cost component differ between these two expenses?

Q 17–24 The EPBO for Branch Industries at the end of 2016 was determined by the actuary to be $20,000 as it relates to employee Will Lawson. Lawson was hired at the beginning of 2002. He will be fully eligible to retire with health care benefits after 15 more years but is expected to retire in 25 years. What is the APBO as it relates to Will Lawson?

IFRS **Q 17–25** The income statement of Mid-South Logistics includes $12 million for amortized prior service cost. Does Mid-South Logistics prepare its financial statements according to U.S. GAAP or IFRS? Explain.

IFRS **Q 17–26** How do U.S. GAAP and IFRS differ with regard to reporting gains and losses from changing assumptions used to measure the pension obligation?

Brief Exercises

BE 17–1
Changes in the projected benefit obligation
● LO17–3

The projected benefit obligation was $80 million at the beginning of the year. Service cost for the year was $10 million. At the end of the year, pension benefits paid by the trustee were $6 million and there were no pension-related other comprehensive income accounts requiring amortization. The actuary's discount rate was 5%. What was the amount of the projected benefit obligation at year-end?

BE 17–2
Changes in the projected benefit obligation
● LO17–3

The projected benefit obligation was $80 million at the beginning of the year and $85 million at the end of the year. At the end of the year, pension benefits paid by the trustee were $6 million and there were no pension-related other comprehensive income accounts requiring amortization. The actuary's discount rate was 5%. What was the amount of the service cost for the year?

BE 17–3
Changes in the projected benefit obligation
● LO17–3

The projected benefit obligation was $80 million at the beginning of the year and $85 million at the end of the year. Service cost for the year was $10 million. At the end of the year, there was no prior service cost and a negligible net loss–AOCI. The actuary's discount rate was 5%. What was the amount of the retiree benefits paid by the trustee?

BE 17–4
Changes in the projected benefit obligation
● LO17–3

The projected benefit obligation was $80 million at the beginning of the year and $85 million at the end of the year. Service cost for the year was $10 million. At the end of the year, pension benefits paid by the trustee were $6 million. The actuary's discount rate was 5%. At the end of the year, the actuary revised the estimate of the percentage rate of increase in compensation levels in upcoming years. What was the amount of the gain or loss the estimate change caused?

BE 17–5
Changes in pension plan assets
● LO17–4

Pension plan assets were $80 million at the beginning of the year. The return on plan assets was 5%. At the end of the year, retiree benefits paid by the trustee were $6 million and cash invested in the pension fund was $7 million. What was the amount of the pension plan assets at year-end?

BE 17–6
Changes in pension plan assets
● LO17–4

Pension plan assets were $80 million at the beginning of the year and $83 million at the end of the year. The return on plan assets was 5%. At the end of the year, cash invested in the pension fund was $7 million. What was the amount of the retiree benefits paid by the trustee?

BE 17–7
Changes in pension plan assets
● LO17–4

Pension plan assets were $100 million at the beginning of the year and $104 million at the end of the year. At the end of the year, retiree benefits paid by the trustee were $6 million and cash invested in the pension fund was $7 million. What was the percentage rate of return on plan assets?

BE 17–8
Reporting the funded status of pension plans
● LO17–5

JDS Foods' projected benefit obligation, accumulated benefit obligation, and plan assets were $40 million, $30 million, and $25 million, respectively, at the end of the year. What, if any, pension liability must be reported in the balance sheet? What would JDS report if the plan assets were $45 million instead?

BE 17–9
Pension expense
● LO17–6

The projected benefit obligation was $80 million at the beginning of the year. Service cost for the year was $10 million. At the end of the year, pension benefits paid by the trustee were $6 million and there were no pension-related other comprehensive income accounts requiring amortization. The actuary's discount rate was 5%. The actual return on plan assets was $5 million although it was expected to be only $4 million. What was the pension expense for the year?

BE 17–10
Pension expense; prior service cost
● LO17–6

The pension plan was amended last year, creating a prior service cost of $20 million. Service cost and interest cost for the year were $10 million and $4 million, respectively. At the end of the year, there was a negligible balance in the net gain–pensions account. The actual return on plan assets was $4 million although it was expected to be $6 million. On average, employees' remaining service life with the company is 10 years. What was the pension expense for the year?

BE 17–11
Net gain
● LO17–6

The projected benefit obligation and plan assets were $80 million and $100 million, respectively, at the beginning of the year. Due primarily to favorable stock market performance in recent years, there also was a net gain of $30 million. On average, employees' remaining service life with the company is 10 years. As a result of the net gain, what was the increase or decrease in pension expense for the year?

BE 17–12
Recording pension expense
● LO17–7

The Warren Group's pension expense is $67 million. This amount includes a $70 million service cost, a $50 million interest cost, a $55 million reduction for the expected return on plan assets, and a $2 million amortization of a prior service cost. How is the net pension liability affected when the pension expense is recorded?

BE 17–13
Recording pension expense
● LO17–7

Andrews Medical reported a net loss–AOCI in last year's balance sheet. This year, the company revised its estimate of future salary levels causing its PBO estimate to decline by $4 million. Also, the $8 million actual return on plan assets fell short of the $9 million expected return. How does this gain and loss affect Andrews' income statement, statement of comprehensive income, and balance sheet?

BE 17–14
Postretirement benefits; determine the APBO and service cost
● LO17–9, LO17–10

Prince Distribution Inc. has an unfunded postretirement benefit plan. Medical care and life insurance benefits are provided to employees who render 10 years service and attain age 55 while in service. At the end of 2016, Jim Lukawitz is 31. He was hired by Prince at age 25 (6 years ago) and is expected to retire at age 62. The expected postretirement benefit obligation for Lukawitz at the end of 2016 is $50,000 and $54,000 at the end of 2017. Calculate the accumulated postretirement benefit obligation at the end of 2016 and 2017 and the service cost for 2016 and 2017 as pertaining to Lukawitz.

BE 17–15
Postretirement benefits; changes in the APBO
● LO17–11

On January 1, 2016, Medical Transport Company's accumulated postretirement benefit obligation was $25 million. At the end of 2016, retiree benefits paid were $3 million. Service cost for 2016 is $7 million. Assumptions regarding the trend of future health care costs were revised at the end of 2016, causing the actuary to revise downward the estimate of the APBO by $1 million. The actuary's discount rate is 8%. Determine the amount of the accumulated postretirement benefit obligation at December 31, 2016.

Exercises

An alternate exercise and problem set is available in the Connect library.

E 17–1
Changes in the PBO
● LO17–3

Indicate by letter whether each of the events listed below increases (**I**), decreases (**D**), or has no effect (**N**) on an employer's projected benefit obligation.

Events

____ 1. Interest cost.
____ 2. Amortization of prior service cost.
____ 3. A decrease in the average life expectancy of employees.
____ 4. An increase in the average life expectancy of employees.
____ 5. A plan amendment that increases benefits is made retroactive to prior years.
____ 6. An increase in the actuary's assumed discount rate.
____ 7. Cash contributions to the pension fund by the employer.
____ 8. Benefits are paid to retired employees.
____ 9. Service cost.
____ 10. Return on plan assets during the year are lower than expected.
____ 11. Return on plan assets during the year are higher than expected.

E 17–2
Determine the projected benefit obligation
● LO17–3

On January 1, 2016, Burleson Corporation's projected benefit obligation was $30 million. During 2016 pension benefits paid by the trustee were $4 million. Service cost for 2016 is $12 million. Pension plan assets (at fair value) increased during 2016 by $6 million as expected. At the end of 2016, there was no prior service cost and a negligible balance in net loss–AOCI. The actuary's discount rate was 10%.

Required:
Determine the amount of the projected benefit obligation at December 31, 2016.

E 17–3
Components of pension expense
● LO17–6

Indicate by letter whether each of the events listed below increases (**I**), decreases (**D**), or has no effect (**N**) on an employer's periodic pension expense in the year the event occurs.

Events

____ 1. Interest cost.
____ 2. Amortization of prior service cost–AOCI.
____ 3. Excess of the expected return on plan assets over the actual return.
____ 4. Expected return on plan assets.
____ 5. A plan amendment that increases benefits is made retroactive to prior years.
____ 6. Actuary's estimate of the PBO is increased.
____ 7. Cash contributions to the pension fund by the employer.
____ 8. Benefits are paid to retired employees.
____ 9. Service cost.
____ 10. Excess of the actual return on plan assets over the expected return.
____ 11. Amortization of net loss–AOCI.
____ 12. Amortization of net gain–AOCI.

E 17–4
Recording pension expense
● LO17–6, LO17–7

Harrison Forklift's pension expense includes a service cost of $10 million. Harrison began the year with a pension liability of $28 million (underfunded pension plan).

Required:
Prepare the appropriate general journal entries to record Harrison's pension expense in each of the following independent situations regarding the other components of pension expense ($ in millions):

1. Interest cost, $6; expected return on assets, $4; amortization of net loss, $2.
2. Interest cost, $6; expected return on assets, $4; amortization of net gain, $2.
3. Interest cost, $6; expected return on assets, $4; amortization of net loss, $2; amortization of prior service cost, $3 million.

E 17–5
Determine pension plan assets
● LO17–4

The following data relate to Voltaire Company's defined benefit pension plan:

	($ in millions)
Plan assets at fair value, January 1	$600
Expected return on plan assets	60
Actual return on plan assets	48
Contributions to the pension fund (end of year)	100
Amortization of net loss	10
Pension benefits paid (end of year)	11
Pension expense	72

Required:
Determine the amount of pension plan assets at fair value on December 31.

E 17–6
Changes in the pension obligation; determine service cost
● LO17–3, LO17–6

Pension data for Millington Enterprises include the following:

	($ in millions)
Discount rate, 10%	
Projected benefit obligation, January 1	$360
Projected benefit obligation, December 31	465
Accumulated benefit obligation, January 1	300
Accumulated benefit obligation, December 31	415
Cash contributions to pension fund, December 31	150
Benefit payments to retirees, December 31	54

Required:
Assuming no change in actuarial assumptions and estimates, determine the service cost component of pension expense for the year ended December 31.

E 17–7
Changes in plan assets; determine cash contributions
● LO17–4

Pension data for Fahy Transportation Inc. include the following:

	($ in millions)
Discount rate, 7%	
Expected return on plan assets, 10%	
Actual return on plan assets, 11%	
Projected benefit obligation, January 1	$730
Plan assets (fair value), January 1	700
Plan assets (fair value), December 31	750
Benefit payments to retirees, December 31	66

Required:
Assuming cash contributions were made at the end of the year, what was the amount of those contributions?

E 17–8
Components of pension expense
● LO17–6

Pension data for Sterling Properties include the following:

	($ in 000s)
Service cost, 2016	$112
Projected benefit obligation, January 1, 2016	850
Plan assets (fair value), January 1, 2016	900
Prior service cost–AOCI (2016 amortization, $8)	80
Net loss–AOCI (2016 amortization, $1)	101
Interest rate, 6%	
Expected return on plan assets, 10%	
Actual return on plan assets, 11%	

Required:
Determine pension expense for 2016.

E 17–9
Components of pension expense; IFRS
● LO17–6, LO17–12

IFRS

Refer to the situation described in Exercise 17–8.

Required:
How might your answer differ if we assume Sterling Properties prepares its financial statements according to International Financial Reporting Standards? 6% is the interest rate on high grade corporate bonds.

E 17–10
Determine pension expense
● LO17–6, LO17–7

Abbott and Abbott has a noncontributory, defined benefit pension plan. At December 31, 2016, Abbott and Abbott received the following information:

Projected Benefit Obligation	($ in millions)
Balance, January 1	$120
Service cost	20
Interest cost	12
Benefits paid	(9)
Balance, December 31	$143
Plan Assets	
Balance, January 1	$ 80
Actual return on plan assets	9
Contributions 2016	20
Benefits paid	(9)
Balance, December 31	$100

The expected long-term rate of return on plan assets was 10%. There was no prior service cost and a negligible net loss–AOCI on January 1, 2016.

Required:
1. Determine Abbott and Abbott's pension expense for 2016.
2. Prepare the journal entries to record Abbott and Abbott's pension expense, funding, and payment for 2016.

E 17–11
Components of pension expense; journal entries
● LO17–6, LO17–7

Pension data for Barry Financial Services Inc. include the following:

	($ in 000s)
Discount rate, 7%	
Expected return on plan assets, 10%	
Actual return on plan assets, 9%	
Service cost, 2016	$ 310
January 1, 2016:	
Projected benefit obligation	2,300
Accumulated benefit obligation	2,000
Plan assets (fair value)	2,400
Prior service cost–AOCI (2016 amortization, $25)	325
Net gain–AOCI (2016 amortization, $6)	330
There were no changes in actuarial assumptions.	

(continued)

(concluded)

December 31, 2016:	
Cash contributions to pension fund, December 31, 2016	245
Benefit payments to retirees, December 31, 2016	270

Required:

1. Determine pension expense for 2016.
2. Prepare the journal entries to record pension expense, gains and losses (if any), funding, and retiree benefits for 2016.

E 17–12
PBO calculations; ABO calculations; present value concepts
● LO17–1, LO17–2, LO17–3

Clark Industries has a defined benefit pension plan that specifies annual retirement benefits equal to:

$$1.2\% \times \text{Service years} \times \text{Final year's salary}$$

Stanley Mills was hired by Clark at the beginning of 1997. Mills is expected to retire at the end of 2041 after 45 years of service. His retirement is expected to span 15 years. At the end of 2016, 20 years after being hired, his salary is $80,000. The company's actuary projects Mills's salary to be $270,000 at retirement. The actuary's discount rate is 7%.

Required:

1. Estimate the amount of Stanley Mills's annual retirement payments for the 15 retirement years earned as of the end of 2016.
2. Suppose Clark's pension plan permits a lump-sum payment at retirement in lieu of annuity payments. Determine the lump-sum equivalent as the present value as of the retirement date of annuity payments during the retirement period.
3. What is the company's projected benefit obligation at the end of 2016 with respect to Stanley Mills?
4. Even though pension accounting centers on the PBO calculation, the ABO still must be disclosed in the pension disclosure note. What is the company's accumulated benefit obligation at the end of 2016 with respect to Stanley Mills?
5. If we assume no estimates change in the meantime, what is the company's projected benefit obligation at the end of 2017 with respect to Stanley Mills?
6. What portion of the 2017 increase in the PBO is attributable to 2017 service (the service cost component of pension expense) and to accrued interest (the interest cost component of pension expense)?

E 17–13
Determining the amortization of net loss or net gain
● LO17–6

Hicks Cable Company has a defined benefit pension plan. Three alternative possibilities for pension-related data at January 1, 2016, are shown below:

		($ in 000s)	
	Case 1	**Case 2**	**Case 3**
Net loss (gain)–AOCI, Jan. 1	$ 320	$ (330)	$ 260
2016 loss (gain) on plan assets	(11)	(8)	2
2016 loss (gain) on PBO	(23)	16	(265)
Accumulated benefit obligation, Jan. 1	(2,950)	(2,550)	(1,450)
Projected benefit obligation, Jan. 1	(3,310)	(2,670)	(1,700)
Fair value of plan assets, Jan. 1	2,800	2,700	1,550
Average remaining service period of active employees (years)	12	15	10

Required:

1. For each independent case, calculate any amortization of the net loss or gain that should be included as a component of pension expense for 2016.
2. For each independent case, determine the net loss–AOCI or net gain–AOCI as of January 1, 2017.

E 17–14
Effect of pension expense components on balance sheet accounts
● LO17–7, LO17–8

Warrick Boards calculated pension expense for its underfunded pension plan as follows:

	($ in millions)
Service cost	$224
Interest cost	150
Expected return on the plan assets ($100 actual, less $10 gain)	(90)
Amortization of prior service cost	8
Amortization of net loss	2
Pension expense	$294

Required:
Which elements of Warrick's balance sheet are affected by the components of pension expense? What are the specific changes in these accounts?

E 17–15
Pension spreadsheet
● LO17–8

A partially completed pension spreadsheet showing the relationships among the elements that comprise the defined benefit pension plan of Universal Products is given below. The actuary's discount rate is 5%. At the end of 2014, the pension formula was amended, creating a prior service cost of $120,000. The expected rate of return on assets was 8%, and the average remaining service life of the active employee group is 20 years in the current year as well as the previous two years.

Required:
Copy the incomplete spreadsheet and fill in the missing amounts.

( )s indicate credits; debits otherwise ($ in 000s)	PBO	Plan Assets	Prior Service Cost	Net Loss	Pension Expense	Cash	Net Pension (Liability)/ Asset
Balance, Jan. 1, 2016	(800)	600	114	80			(200)
Service cost					84		
Interest cost, 5%	(40)						
Expected return on assets					(48)		
Adjust for:							
Loss on assets				6			
Amortization:							
Prior service cost							
Amortization:							
Net loss							
Gain on PBO							12
Prior service cost	0						
Cash funding						(68)	
Retiree benefits							
Balance, Dec. 31, 2016	(862)		108				

E 17–16
Determine and record pension expense and gains and losses; funding and retiree benefits
● LO17–6, LO17–7

Actuary and trustee reports indicate the following changes in the PBO and plan assets of Douglas-Roberts Industries during 2016:

Prior service cost at Jan. 1, 2016, from plan amendment at the beginning of 2013 (amortization: $4 million per year)	$28 million
Net loss–AOCI at Jan.1, 2016 (previous losses exceeded previous gains)	$80 million
Average remaining service life of the active employee group	10 years
Actuary's discount rate	7%

($ in millions) PBO			Plan Assets
Beginning of 2016	$600	*Beginning* of 2016	$400
Service cost	80	Return on plan assets,	
Interest cost, 7%	42	8% (10% expected)	32
Loss (gain) on PBO	(14)	Cash contributions	90
Less: Retiree benefits	(38)	Less: Retiree benefits	(38)
End of 2016	$670	*End* of 2016	$484

Required:
1. Determine Douglas-Roberts' pension expense for 2016 and prepare the appropriate journal entries to record the expense.
2. Prepare the appropriate journal entry(s) to record any 2016 gains and losses.
3. Prepare the appropriate journal entry to record the cash contribution to plan assets.
4. Prepare the appropriate journal entry to record retiree benefits.

E 17–17
Concepts; terminology
● LO17–2 through LO17–8

Listed below are several terms and phrases associated with pensions. Pair each item from List A with the item from List B (by letter) that is most appropriately associated with it.

List A	List B
____ 1. Future compensation levels estimated.	a. Actual return exceeds expected
____ 2. All funding provided by the employer.	b. Net gain–AOCI
____ 3. Credit to OCI and debit to plan assets.	c. Vested benefit obligation
____ 4. Retirement benefits specified by formula.	d. Projected benefit obligation
____ 5. Trade-off between relevance and reliability.	e. Choice between PBO and ABO
____ 6. Cumulative gains in excess of losses.	f. Noncontributory pension plan
____ 7. Current pay levels implicitly assumed.	g. Accumulated benefit obligation
____ 8. Created by the passage of time.	h. Plan assets
____ 9. Not contingent on future employment.	i. Interest cost
____ 10. Risk borne by employee.	j. Delayed recognition in earnings
____ 11. Increased by employer contributions.	k. Defined contribution plan
____ 12. Caused by plan amendment.	l. Defined benefit plan
____ 13. Loss on plan assets.	m. Prior service cost
____ 14. Excess over 10% of plan assets or PBO.	n. Amortize net loss–AOCI

E 17–18
IFRS; actuarial gains and losses
● LO17–7, LO17–12

IFRS

Patel Industries has a noncontributory, defined benefit pension plan. Since the inception of the plan, the actuary has used as the discount rate the rate on high quality corporate bonds, which recently has been 7%. During 2016, changing economic conditions caused the rate to change to 6% and the actuary decided that 6% is the appropriate rate.

Required:

1. Does the change in discount rate create a gain or does it create a loss for Patel under U.S. GAAP? Why?
2. Assume the magnitude of the change is $13 million. Prepare the appropriate journal entry to record any 2016 gain or loss under U.S. GAAP. If Patel prepares its financial statements according to U.S. GAAP, how will the company report the gain or loss?
3. Would your response to requirement 2 differ if Patel prepares its financial statements according to International Financial Reporting Standards?

E 17–19
Record pension expense, funding, and gains and losses; determine account balances
● LO17–6, LO17–7, LO17–8

Beale Management has a noncontributory, defined benefit pension plan. On December 31, 2016 (the end of Beale's fiscal year), the following pension-related data were available:

Projected Benefit Obligation	($ in millions)
Balance, January 1, 2016	$480
Service cost	82
Interest cost, discount rate, 5%	24
Gain due to changes in actuarial assumptions in 2016	(10)
Pension benefits paid	(40)
Balance, December 31, 2016	$536
Plan Assets	
Balance, January 1, 2016	$500
Actual return on plan assets	40
(Expected return on plan assets, $45)	
Cash contributions	70
Pension benefits paid	(40)
Balance, December 31, 2016	$570
January 1, 2016, balances:	
Pension asset	$ 20
Prior service cost–AOCI (amortization $8 per year)	48
Net gain–AOCI (any amortization over 15 years)	80

Required:

1. Prepare the 2016 journal entry to record pension expense.
2. Prepare the journal entry(s) to record any 2016 gains and losses.
3. Prepare the 2016 journal entries to record the contribution to plan assets and benefit payments to retirees.
4. Determine the balances at December 31, 2016, in the PBO, plan assets, the net gain–AOCI, and prior service cost–AOCI and show how the balances changed during 2016. [Hint: You might find T-accounts useful.]
5. What amount will Beale report in its 2016 balance sheet as a net pension asset or net pension liability for the funded status of the plan?

E 17–20
Pension spreadsheet
● LO17–8

Refer to the data provided in Exercise 17–19.

Required:
Prepare a pension spreadsheet to show the relationship among the PBO, plan assets, prior service cost, the net gain, pension expense, and the net pension asset.

E 17–21
Determine pension expense; prior service cost
● LO17–6, LO17–7

Lacy Construction has a noncontributory, defined benefit pension plan. At December 31, 2016, Lacy received the following information:

Projected Benefit Obligation	($ in millions)
Balance, January 1	$360
Service cost	60
Prior service cost	12
Interest cost (7.5%)	27
Benefits paid	(37)
Balance, December 31	$422
Plan Assets	
Balance, January 1	$240
Actual return on plan assets	27
Contributions 2016	60
Benefits paid	(37)
Balance, December 31	$290

The expected long-term rate of return on plan assets was 10%. There were no AOCI balances related to pensions on January 1, 2016. At the end of 2016, Lacy amended the pension formula creating a prior service cost of $12 million.

Required:
1. Determine Lacy's pension expense for 2016.
2. Prepare the journal entry(s) to record Lacy's pension expense, gains or losses, prior service cost, funding, and payment of retiree benefits for 2016.

E 17–22
IFRS; prior service cost
● LO17–7, LO17–12

 **IFRS**

Refer to the situation described in Exercise 17–21.

Required:
How might your solution differ if Lacy Construction prepares its financial statements according to International Financial Reporting Standards? Assume the actuary's discount rate is the rate on high quality corporate bonds. Include any appropriate journal entries in your response.

E 17–23
Classifying accounting changes and errors
● LO17–8

Indicate with the appropriate letter the nature of each adjustment described below:

Type of Adjustment

A. Change in principle
B. Change in estimate
C. Correction of an error
D. Neither an accounting change nor an error

_____ 1. Change in actuarial assumptions for a defined benefit pension plan.
_____ 2. Determination that the projected benefit obligation under a pension plan exceeded the fair value of plan assets at the end of the previous year by $17,000. The only pension-related amount on the balance sheet was a net pension liability of $30,000.
_____ 3. Pension plan assets for a defined benefit pension plan achieving a rate of return in excess of the amount anticipated.
_____ 4. Instituting a pension plan for the first time and adopting GAAP for employers' accounting for defined benefit pension and other postretirement plans.

E 17–24
Postretirement benefits; determine APBO, EPBO
● LO17–10

Classified Electronics has an unfunded retiree health care plan. Each of the company's three employees has been with the firm since its inception at the beginning of 2015. As of the end of 2016, the actuary estimates the total net cost of providing health care benefits to employees during their retirement years to have a present value of $72,000. Each of the employees will become fully eligible for benefits after 28 more years of service but aren't expected to retire for 35 more years. The interest rate is 6%.

Required:

1. What is the expected postretirement benefit obligation at the end of 2016?
2. What is the accumulated postretirement benefit obligation at the end of 2016?
3. What is the expected postretirement benefit obligation at the end of 2017?
4. What is the accumulated postretirement benefit obligation at the end of 2017?

E 17–25
Postretirement benefits; determine APBO, service cost, interest cost; prepare journal entry
● LO17–10, LO17–11

The following data are available pertaining to Household Appliance Company's retiree health care plan for 2016:

Number of employees covered	2
Years employed as of January 1, 2016	3 [each]
Attribution period	25 years
Expected postretirement benefit obligation, Jan. 1	$50,000
Expected postretirement benefit obligation, Dec. 31	$53,000
Interest rate	6%
Funding	none

Required:

1. What is the accumulated postretirement benefit obligation at the beginning of 2016?
2. What is interest cost to be included in 2016 postretirement benefit expense?
3. What is service cost to be included in 2016 postretirement benefit expense?
4. Prepare the journal entry to record the postretirement benefit expense for 2016.

E 17–26
Postretirement benefits; determine EPBO; attribution period
● LO17–10, LO17–11

Lorin Management Services has an unfunded postretirement benefit plan. On December 31, 2016, the following data were available concerning changes in the plan's accumulated postretirement benefit obligation with respect to one of Lorin's employees:

APBO at the beginning of 2016	$16,364
Interest cost: ($16,364 × 10%)	1,636
Service cost: ($44,000 × 1/22)	2,000
Portion of EPBO attributed to 2016	
APBO at the end of 2016	$20,000

Required:

1. Over how many years is the expected postretirement benefit obligation being expensed (attribution period)?
2. What is the expected postretirement benefit obligation at the *end* of 2016?
3. When was the employee hired by Lorin?
4. What is the expected postretirement benefit obligation at the *beginning* of 2016?

E 17–27
Postretirement benefits; components of postretirement benefit expense
● LO17–11

Data pertaining to the postretirement health care benefit plan of Sterling Properties include the following for 2016:

	($ in 000s)
Service cost	$124
Accumulated postretirement benefit obligation, January 1	700
Plan assets (fair value), January 1	50
Prior service cost–AOCI	none
Net gain–AOCI (2016 amortization, $1)	91
Retiree benefits paid (end of year)	87
Contribution to health care benefit fund (end of year)	185
Discount rate, 7%	
Return on plan assets (actual and expected), 10%	

Required:

1. Determine the postretirement benefit expense for 2016.
2. Prepare the appropriate journal entries to record the postretirement benefit expense, funding, and retiree benefits for 2016.

E 17–28
Postretirement benefits; amortization of net loss
● LO17–11

Cahal-Michael Company has a postretirement health care benefit plan. On January 1, 2016, the following plan-related data were available:

	($ in 000s)
Net loss–AOCI	$ 336
Accumulated postretirement benefit obligation	2,800
Fair value of plan assets	500
Average remaining service period to retirement	14 years (same in previous 10 yrs.)

The rate of return on plan assets during 2016 was 10%, although it was expected to be 9%. The actuary revised assumptions regarding the APBO at the end of the year, resulting in a $39,000 increase in the estimate of that obligation.

Required:
1. Calculate any amortization of the net loss that should be included as a component of postretirement benefit expense for 2016.
2. Assume the postretirement benefit expense for 2016, not including the amortization of the net loss component, is $212,000. What is the expense for the year?
3. Determine the net loss or gain as of December 31, 2016.

E 17–29
Postretirement benefits; determine and record expense
● LO17–11

Gorky-Park Corporation provides postretirement health care benefits to employees who provide at least 12 years of service and reach age 62 while in service. On January 1, 2016, the following plan-related data were available:

	($ in millions)
Accumulated postretirement benefit obligation	$130
Fair value of plan assets	none
Average remaining service period to retirement	25 years (same in previous 10 yrs.)
Average remaining service period to full eligibility	20 years (same in previous 10 yrs.)

On January 1, 2016, Gorky-Park amends the plan to provide certain dental benefits in addition to previously provided medical benefits. The actuary determines that the cost of making the amendment retroactive increases the APBO by $20 million. Management chooses to amortize the prior service cost on a straight-line basis. The service cost for 2016 is $34 million. The interest rate is 8%.

Required:
1. Calculate the postretirement benefit expense for 2016.
2. Prepare the journal entry to record the expense.

E 17–30
Postretirement benefits; negative plan amendment
● LO17–11

Southeast Technology provides postretirement health care benefits to employees. On January 1, 2016, the following plan-related data were available:

	($ in 000s)
Prior service cost—originated in 2011	$ 50
Accumulated postretirement benefit obligation	530
Fair value of plan assets	none
Average remaining service period to retirement	20 years (same in previous 10 yrs.)
Average remaining service period to full eligibility	15 years (same in previous 10 yrs.)

On January 1, 2016, Southeast amends the plan in response to spiraling health care costs. The amendment establishes an annual maximum of $3,000 for medical benefits that the plan will provide. The actuary determines that the effect of this amendment is to decrease the APBO by $80,000. Management amortizes prior service cost on a straight-line basis. The interest rate is 8%. The service cost for 2016 is $114,000.

Required:
1. Calculate the prior service cost amortization for 2016.
2. Calculate the postretirement benefit expense for 2016.

E 17–31
Prior service cost; service method; straight-line method (Based on Appendix)

Frazier Refrigeration amended its defined benefit pension plan on December 31, 2016, to increase retirement benefits earned with each service year. The consulting actuary estimated the prior service cost incurred by making the amendment retroactive to prior years to be $110,000. Frazier's 100 present employees are expected to retire at the rate of approximately 10 each year at the end of each of the next 10 years.

Required:

1. Using the service method, calculate the amount of prior service cost to be amortized to pension expense in each of the next 10 years.
2. Using the straight-line method, calculate the amount of prior service cost to be amortized to pension expense in each of the next 10 years.

E 17–32
FASB codification research; postretirement benefit plan
● LO17–11

When a company sponsors a postretirement benefit plan other than a pension plan, benefits typically are not earned by employees on the basis of a formula, so assigning the service cost to specific periods is more difficult. The *FASB Accounting Standards Codification* represents the single source of authoritative U.S. generally accepted accounting principles.

Required:

1. Obtain the relevant authoritative literature on how a firm should attribute the expected postretirement benefit obligation to years of service using the *FASB Accounting Standards Codification* at the FASB website (**asc.fasb.org**). Find the specific citations that describe the guidelines for each of the following questions:
   a. What is the objective for attributing expected postretirement benefit obligations to years of service?
   b. When does the attribution period for expected postretirement benefits begin for an employee?
   c. When does the attribution period for expected postretirement benefits end for an employee?
2. What are the guidelines for each?

E 17–33
FASB codification research
● LO17–1, LO17–2, LO17–5

Access the *FASB Accounting Standards Codification* at the FASB website (**asc.fasb.org**). Determine the specific citation for accounting for each of the following items:

1. The disclosure required in the notes to the financial statements for pension plan assets.
2. Recognition of the net pension asset or net pension liability.
3. Disclosures required in the notes to the financial statements for pension cost for a defined contribution plan.

CPA and CMA Review Questions

CPA Exam Questions

KAPLAN CPA REVIEW

The following questions are adapted from a variety of sources including questions developed by the AICPA Board of Examiners and those used in the Kaplan CPA Review Course to study pensions and other postretirement benefits while preparing for the CPA examination. Determine the response that best completes the statements or questions.

● LO17–5

1. Wolf Inc. began a defined benefit pension plan for its employees on January 1, 2016. The following data are provided for 2016 as of December 31, 2016:

Projected benefit obligation	$385,000
Accumulated benefit obligation	340,000
Plan assets at fair value	255,000
Pension expense	95,000
Employer's cash contribution (end of year)	255,000

What amount should Wolf report as a net pension liability at December 31, 2016?
   a. $ 0
   b. $ 45,000
   c. $ 85,000
   d. $130,000

● LO17–7

2. A statement of comprehensive income for a company with a defined benefit pension plan does *not* include
   a. net income.
   b. the return on plan assets.
   c. gains from the return on assets exceeding expectations.
   d. losses from changes in estimates regarding the pension obligation.

● LO17–8

3. JWS Corporation has a defined benefit pension plan. JWS reported a net pension liability in last year's balance sheet. This year, the company revised its estimate of future salary levels causing its projected benefit obligation estimate to decline by $8 million. Also, the $16 million actual return on plan assets was less than the $18 million expected return. As a result
   a. the net pension liability will decrease by $8 million.
   b. the statement of comprehensive income will report a $2 million gain and an $8 million loss.
   c. the net pension liability will increase by $6 million.
   d. accumulated other comprehensive income will increase by $6 million.

● LO17–8

4. Amortizing a net gain for pensions and other postretirement benefit plans will
   a. decrease retained earnings and decrease accumulated other comprehensive income.
   b. increase retained earnings and increase accumulated other comprehensive income.
   c. decrease retained earnings and increase accumulated other comprehensive income.
   d. increase retained earnings and decrease accumulated other comprehensive income.

● LO17–11

5. At December 31, 2015, Johnston and Johnston reported in its balance sheet as part of accumulated other comprehensive income a net loss of $37 million related to its postretirement benefit plan. The actuary for J&J increased her estimate of J&J's future health care costs at the end of 2016. J&J's entry to record the effect of this change will include
   a. a debit to other comprehensive income and a credit to postretirement benefit liability.
   b. a debit to postretirement benefit liability and a credit to other comprehensive income.
   c. a debit to pension expense and a credit to postretirement benefit liability.
   d. a debit to pension expense and a credit to other comprehensive income.

International Financial Reporting Standards are tested on the CPA exam along with U.S. GAAP. The following questions deal with the application of IFRS to pensions.

● LO17–12

IFRS

6. Actuarial (Remeasurement) gains and losses are reported as OCI as they occur using
   a. U.S. GAAP.
   b. IFRS.
   c. Both U.S. GAAP and IFRS.
   d. Neither U.S. GAAP nor IFRS.

● LO17–12

IFRS

7. Prior (Past) service cost is included among OCI items in the statement of comprehensive income and thus subsequently becomes part of AOCI where it is amortized over the average remaining service period using
   a. U.S. GAAP.
   b. IFRS.
   c. Both U.S. GAAP and IFRS.
   d. Neither U.S. GAAP nor IFRS.

● LO17–12

IFRS

8. Prior (Past) service cost is expensed immediately using
   a. U.S. GAAP.
   b. IFRS.
   c. Both U.S. GAAP and IFRS.
   d. Neither U.S. GAAP nor IFRS.

CMA Exam Questions

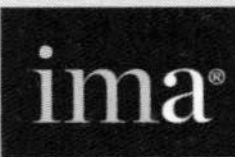

The following questions dealing with pensions and other postretirement benefits are adapted from questions that previously appeared on Certified Management Accountant (CMA) examinations. The CMA designation sponsored by the Institute of Management Accountants (**www.imanet.org**) provides members with an objective measure of knowledge and competence in the field of management accounting. Determine the response that best completes the statements or questions.

● LO17–3

1. The projected benefit obligation (PBO) is best described as the
   a. Present value of benefits accrued to date based on future salary levels.
   b. Present value of benefits accrued to date based on current salary levels.
   c. Increase in retroactive benefits at the date of the amendment of the plan.
   d. Amount of the adjustment necessary to reflect the difference between actual and estimated actuarial returns.

● LO17–6

2. On November 30, the Board of Directors of Baldwin Corporation amended its pension plan giving retroactive benefits to its employees. The information below is provided at November 30.

Accumulated benefit obligation (ABO)	$825,000
Projected benefit obligation (PBO)	900,000
Plan assets (fair value)	307,500
Market-related asset value	301,150
Prior service cost	190,000
Average remaining service life of employees	10 years
Useful life of pension goodwill	20 years

Using the straight-line method of amortization, the amount of prior service cost charged to expense during the year ended November 30 is

a. $9,500
b. $19,000
c. $30,250
d. $190,000

Problems

An alternate exercise and problem set is available in the Connect library.

(Note: Problems 1–5 are variations of the same situation, designed to focus on different elements of the pension plan.)

P 17–1
ABO calculations; present value concepts
● LO17–2, LO17–3

Sachs Brands' defined benefit pension plan specifies annual retirement benefits equal to: 1.6% × service years × final year's salary, payable at the end of each year. Angela Davenport was hired by Sachs at the beginning of 2002 and is expected to retire at the end of 2036 after 35 years' service. Her retirement is expected to span 18 years. Davenport's salary is $90,000 at the end of 2016 and the company's actuary projects her salary to be $240,000 at retirement. The actuary's discount rate is 7%.

Required:

1. Draw a time line that depicts Davenport's expected service period, retirement period, and a 2016 measurement date for the pension obligation.
2. Estimate by the accumulated benefits approach the amount of Davenport's annual retirement payments earned as of the end of 2016.
3. What is the company's accumulated benefit obligation at the end of 2016 with respect to Davenport?
4. If no estimates are changed in the meantime, what will be the accumulated benefit obligation at the end of 2019 (three years later) when Davenport's salary is $100,000?

P 17–2
PBO calculations; present value concepts
● LO17–3

Sachs Brands' defined benefit pension plan specifies annual retirement benefits equal to: 1.6% × service years × final year's salary, payable at the end of each year. Angela Davenport was hired by Sachs at the beginning of 2002 and is expected to retire at the end of 2036 after 35 years' service. Her retirement is expected to span 18 years. Davenport's salary is $90,000 at the end of 2016 and the company's actuary projects her salary to be $240,000 at retirement. The actuary's discount rate is 7%.

Required:

1. Draw a time line that depicts Davenport's expected service period, retirement period, and a 2016 measurement date for the pension obligation.
2. Estimate by the projected benefits approach the amount of Davenport's annual retirement payments earned as of the end of 2016.
3. What is the company's projected benefit obligation at the end of 2016 with respect to Davenport?
4. If no estimates are changed in the meantime, what will be the company's projected benefit obligation at the end of 2019 (three years later) with respect to Davenport?

P 17–3
Service cost, interest, and PBO calculations; present value concepts
● LO17–3

Sachs Brands' defined benefit pension plan specifies annual retirement benefits equal to: 1.6% × service years × final year's salary, payable at the end of each year. Angela Davenport was hired by Sachs at the beginning of 2002 and is expected to retire at the end of 2036 after 35 years' service. Her retirement is expected to span 18 years. Davenport's salary is $90,000 at the end of 2016 and the company's actuary projects her salary to be $240,000 at retirement. The actuary's discount rate is 7%.

Required:

1. What is the company's projected benefit obligation at the beginning of 2016 (after 14 years' service) with respect to Davenport?
2. Estimate by the projected benefits approach the portion of Davenport's annual retirement payments attributable to 2016 service.
3. What is the company's service cost for 2016 with respect to Davenport?
4. What is the company's interest cost for 2016 with respect to Davenport?
5. Combine your answers to requirements 1, 3, and 4 to determine the company's projected benefit obligation at the end of 2016 (after 15 years' service) with respect to Davenport.

P 17–4
Prior service cost; components of pension expense; present value concepts
● LO17–3, LO17–6

Sachs Brands' defined benefit pension plan specifies annual retirement benefits equal to: 1.6% × service years × final year's salary, payable at the end of each year. Angela Davenport was hired by Sachs at the beginning of 2002 and is expected to retire at the end of 2036 after 35 years' service. Her retirement is expected to span 18 years. Davenport's salary is $90,000 at the end of 2016 and the company's actuary projects her salary to be $240,000 at retirement. The actuary's discount rate is 7%.

At the beginning of 2017, the pension formula was amended to:

1.75% × Service years × Final year's salary

The amendment was made retroactive to apply the increased benefits to prior service years.

Required:

1. What is the company's prior service cost at the beginning of 2017 with respect to Davenport after the amendment described above?
2. Since the amendment occurred at the *beginning* of 2017, amortization of the prior service cost begins in 2017. What is the prior service cost amortization that would be included in pension expense?
3. What is the service cost for 2017 with respect to Davenport?
4. What is the interest cost for 2017 with respect to Davenport?
5. Calculate pension expense for 2017 with respect to Davenport, assuming plan assets attributable to her of $150,000 and a rate of return (actual and expected) of 10%.

P 17–5
Gain on PBO; present value concepts
● LO17–3, LO17–6

Sachs Brands' defined benefit pension plan specifies annual retirement benefits equal to: 1.6% × service years × final year's salary, payable at the end of each year. Angela Davenport was hired by Sachs at the beginning of 2002 and is expected to retire at the end of 2036 after 35 years' service. Her retirement is expected to span 18 years. Davenport's salary is $90,000 at the end of 2016 and the company's actuary projects her salary to be $240,000 at retirement. The actuary's discount rate is 7%.

At the beginning of 2017, changing economic conditions caused the actuary to reassess the applicable discount rate. It was decided that 8% is the appropriate rate.

Required:

Calculate the effect of the change in the assumed discount rate on the PBO at the beginning of 2017 with respect to Davenport.

P 17–6
Determine the PBO; plan assets; pension expense; two years
● LO17–3, LO17–4, LO17–6

Stanley-Morgan Industries adopted a defined benefit pension plan on April 12, 2016. The provisions of the plan were not made retroactive to prior years. A local bank, engaged as trustee for the plan assets, expects plan assets to earn a 10% rate of return. A consulting firm, engaged as actuary, recommends 6% as the appropriate discount rate. The service cost is $150,000 for 2016 and $200,000 for 2017. Year-end funding is $160,000 for 2016 and $170,000 for 2017. No assumptions or estimates were revised during 2016.

Required:

Calculate each of the following amounts as of both December 31, 2016, and December 31, 2017:

1. Projected benefit obligation
2. Plan assets
3. Pension expense
4. Net pension asset or net pension liability

P 17–7
Determining the amortization of net gain
● LO17–6

Herring Wholesale Company has a defined benefit pension plan. On January 1, 2016, the following pension-related data were available:

	($ in 000s)
Net gain–AOCI	$ 170
Accumulated benefit obligation	1,170
Projected benefit obligation	1,400
Fair value of plan assets	1,100
Average remaining service period of active employees (expected to remain constant for the next several years)	15 years

The rate of return on plan assets during 2016 was 9%, although it was expected to be 10%. The actuary revised assumptions regarding the PBO at the end of the year, resulting in a $23,000 decrease in the estimate of that obligation.

Required:

1. Calculate any amortization of the net gain that should be included as a component of net pension expense for 2016.
2. Assume the net pension expense for 2016, not including the amortization of the net gain component, is $325,000. What is pension expense for the year?
3. Determine the net loss—AOCI or net gain—AOCI as of January 1, 2017.

P 17–8
Pension spreadsheet; record pension expense and funding; new gains and losses
● LO17–7, LO17–8

A partially completed pension spreadsheet showing the relationships among the elements that constitute Carney, Inc.'s defined benefit pension plan follows. Six years earlier, Carney revised its pension formula and recalculated benefits earned by employees in prior years using the more generous formula. The prior service cost created by the recalculation is being amortized at the rate of $5 million per year. At the end of 2016, the pension formula was amended again, creating an additional prior service cost of $40 million. The expected rate of return on assets and the actuary's discount rate were 10%, and the average remaining service life of the active employee group is 10 years.

( )s indicate credits; debits otherwise ($ in millions)	PBO	Plan Assets	Prior Service Cost	Net Loss	Pension Expense	Cash	Net Pension (Liability) / Asset
Balance, Jan. 1, 2016	(830)	680	20	93			(150)
Service cost	?				74		?
Interest cost	?				?		?
Expected return on asset		?			?		?
Adjust for:							
Loss on assets		(7)		?			?
Amortization of:							
Prior service cost			?		?		
Net loss				?	?		
Loss on PBO	?			?			(13)
Prior service cost	?		?				?
Cash funding		?				?	84
Retiree benefits	?	?					
Balance, Dec. 31, 2016	?	775	?	?	?		?

Required:

1. Copy the incomplete spreadsheet and fill in the missing amounts.
2. Prepare the 2016 journal entry to record pension expense.
3. Prepare the journal entry(s) to record any 2016 gains and losses and new prior service cost in 2016.
4. Prepare the 2016 journal entries to record the cash contribution to plan assets and payment of retiree benefits.

P 17–9
Determine pension expense; PBO; plan assets; net pension asset or liability; journal entries
● LO17–3 through LO17–8

U.S. Metallurgical Inc. reported the following balances in its financial statements and disclosure notes at December 31, 2015.

Plan assets	$ 400,000
Projected benefit obligation	320,000

U.S.M.'s actuary determined that 2016 service cost is $60,000. Both the expected and actual rate of return on plan assets are 9%. The interest (discount) rate is 5%. U.S.M. contributed $120,000 to the pension fund at the end of 2016, and retirees were paid $44,000 from plan assets.

Required:

Determine the following amounts at the end of 2016.

1. Pension expense
2. Projected benefit obligation
3. Plan assets
4. Net pension asset or net pension liability
5. Prepare journal entries to record the pension expense, funding of plan assets, and retiree benefit payments.

P 17–10
Prior service cost; calculate pension expense; journal entries; determine net pension asset or liability
● LO17–5 through LO17–7

Electronic Distribution has a defined benefit pension plan. Characteristics of the plan during 2016 are as follows:

	($ millions):
PBO balance, January 1	$480
Plan assets balance, January 1	300
Service cost	75
Interest cost	45
Gain from change in actuarial assumption	22
Benefits paid	(36)
Actual return on plan assets	20
Contributions 2016	60

The expected long-term rate of return on plan assets was 8%. There were no AOCI balances related to pensions on January 1, 2016, but at the end of 2016, the company amended the pension formula creating a prior service cost of $12 million.

Required:
1. Calculate the pension expense for 2016.
2. Prepare the journal entry to record pension expense, gains or losses, prior service cost, funding, and payment of benefits for 2016.
3. What amount will Electronic Distribution report in its 2016 balance sheet as a net pension asset or net pension liability?

P 17–11
IFRS; calculate pension expense; journal entries; determine net pension asset or liability
● LO17–5 through LO17–7, LO17–12

IFRS

Refer to the situation described in Problem 17–10. Assume Electronic Distribution prepares its financial statements according to International Financial Reporting Standards. Also assume that 10% is the current interest rate on high-quality corporate bonds.

Required:
1. Calculate the net pension cost for 2016, separating its components into appropriate categories for reporting.
2. Prepare the journal entry to record the components of net pension cost, gains or losses, past service cost, funding, and payment of benefits for 2016.
3. What amount will Electronic Distribution report in its 2016 balance sheet as a net pension asset or net pension liability?

P 17–12
Determine pension expense; journal entries; two years
● LO17–3 through LO17–8

The Kollar Company has a defined benefit pension plan. Pension information concerning the fiscal years 2016 and 2017 are presented below ($ in millions):

Information Provided by Pension Plan Actuary:
a. Projected benefit obligation as of December 31, 2015 = $1,800.
b. Prior service cost from plan amendment on January 2, 2016 = $400 (straight-line amortization for 10-year average remaining service period).
c. Service cost for 2016 = $520.
d. Service cost for 2017 = $570.
e. Discount rate used by actuary on projected benefit obligation for 2016 and 2017 = 10%.
f. Payments to retirees in 2016 = $380.
g. Payments to retirees in 2017 = $450.
h. No changes in actuarial assumptions or estimates.
i. Net gain—AOCI on January 1, 2016 = $230.
j. Net gains and losses are amortized for 10 years in 2016 and 2017.

Information Provided by Pension Fund Trustee:
a. Plan asset balance at fair value on January 1, 2016 = $1,600.
b. 2016 contributions = $540.
c. 2017 contributions = $590.
d. Expected long-term rate of return on plan assets = 12%.
e. 2016 actual return on plan assets = $180.
f. 2017 actual return on plan assets = $210.

Required:

1. Calculate pension expense for 2016 and 2017.
2. Prepare the journal entries for 2016 and 2017 to record pension expense.
3. Prepare the journal entries for 2016 and 2017 to record any gains and losses and new prior service cost.
4. Prepare the journal entries for 2016 and 2017 to record the cash contribution to plan assets and benefit payments to retirees.

P 17–13
Determine the PBO, plan assets, pension expense; prior service cost
● LO17–3, LO17–4, LO17–6

Lewis Industries adopted a defined benefit pension plan on January 1, 2016. By making the provisions of the plan retroactive to prior years, Lewis incurred a prior service cost of $2 million. The prior service cost was funded immediately by a $2 million cash payment to the fund trustee on January 2, 2016. However, the cost is to be amortized (expensed) over 10 years. The service cost—$250,000 for 2016—is fully funded at the end of each year. Both the actuary's discount rate and the expected rate of return on plan assets were 9%. The actual rate of return on plan assets was 11%. At December 31, the trustee paid $16,000 to an employee who retired during 2016.

Required:

Determine each of the following amounts as of December 31, 2016, the fiscal year-end for Lewis:

1. Projected benefit obligation
2. Plan assets
3. Pension expense

P 17–14
Relationship among pension elements
● LO17–3 through LO17–8

The funded status of Hilton Paneling Inc.'s defined benefit pension plan and the balances in prior service cost and the net gain–pensions, are given below.

	($ in 000s)	
	2016 Beginning Balances	**2016 Ending Balances**
Projected benefit obligation	$2,300	$2,501
Plan assets	2,400	2,591
Funded status	100	90
Prior service cost–AOCI	325	300
Net gain–AOCI	330	300

Retirees were paid $270,000 and the employer contribution to the pension fund was $245,000 at the end of 2016. The expected rate of return on plan assets was 10%, and the actuary's discount rate is 7%. There were no changes in actuarial estimates and assumptions regarding the PBO.

Required:

Determine the following amounts for 2016:

1. Actual return on plan assets
2. Loss or gain on plan assets
3. Service cost
4. Pension expense
5. Average remaining service life of active employees (used to determine amortization of the net gain)

P 17–15
Comprehensive—pension elements; spreadsheet
● LO17–8

The following pension-related data pertain to Metro Recreation's noncontributory, defined benefit pension plan for 2016:

	($ in 000s)	
	Jan. 1	**Dec. 31**
Projected benefit obligation	$4,100	$4,380
Accumulated benefit obligation	3,715	3,950
Plan assets (fair value)	4,530	4,975
Interest (discount) rate, 7%		
Expected return on plan assets, 10%		
Prior service cost–AOCI		
(from Dec. 31, 2015, amendment)	840	
Net loss–AOCI	477	
Average remaining service life: 12 years		
Gain due to changes in actuarial assumptions		44
Contributions to pension fund (end of year)		340
Pension benefits paid (end of year)		295

Required:

Prepare a pension spreadsheet that shows the relationships among the various pension balances, shows the changes in those balances, and computes pension expense for 2016.

P 17–16
Comprehensive—reporting a pension plan; pension spreadsheet; determine changes in balances; two years
● LO17–3 through LO17–8

Actuary and trustee reports indicate the following changes in the PBO and plan assets of Lakeside Cable during 2016:

Prior service cost at Jan. 1, 2016, from plan amendment at the beginning of 2014 (amortization: $4 million per year)	$32 million
Net loss–pensions at Jan.1, 2016 (previous losses exceeded previous gains)	$40 million
Average remaining service life of the active employee group	10 years
Actuary's discount rate	8%

($ in millions)	PBO		Plan Assets
Beginning of 2016	$300	*Beginning* of 2016	$200
Service cost	48	Return on plan assets,	
Interest cost, 8%	24	7.5% (10% expected)	15
Loss (gain) on PBO	(2)	Cash contributions	45
Less: Retiree benefits	(20)	Less: Retiree benefits	(20)
End of 2016	$350	*End* of 2016	$240

Required:

1. Determine Lakeside's pension expense for 2016 and prepare the appropriate journal entries to record the expense as well as the cash contribution to plan assets and payment of benefits to retirees.
2. Determine the new gains and/or losses in 2016 and prepare the appropriate journal entry(s) to record them.
3. Prepare a pension spreadsheet to assist you in determining end of 2016 balances in the PBO, plan assets, prior service cost—AOCI, the net loss—AOCI, and the pension liability.
4. Assume the following actuary and trustee reports indicating changes in the PBO and plan assets of Lakeside Cable during 2017:

($ in millions)	PBO		Plan Assets
Beginning of 2017	$350	*Beginning* of 2017	$240
Service cost	38	Return on plan assets,	
Interest cost at 8%	28	15% (10% expected)	36
Loss (gain) on PBO	5	Cash contributions	30
Less: Retiree benefits	(16)	Less: Retiree benefits	(16)
End of 2017	$405	*End* of 2017	$290

Determine Lakeside's pension expense for 2017 and prepare the appropriate journal entries to record the expense, the cash funding of plan assets, and payment of benefits to retirees.

5. Determine the new gains and/or losses in 2017 and prepare the appropriate journal entry(s) to record them.
6. Using T-accounts, determine the balances at December 31, 2017, in the net loss–AOCI and prior service cost–AOCI.
7. Confirm the balances determined in Requirement 6 by preparing a pension spreadsheet.

P 17–17
Integrating Problem—Deferred tax effects of pension entries; integrate concepts learned in Chapter 16
● LO17–7

To focus on the core issues, we ignored the income tax effects of the pension amounts we recorded in the chapter. Reproduced below are the journal entries from the chapter that Global Communications used to record its pension expense and funding in 2016 and the new gain and loss that occurred that year.

	($ in millions)	
To Record Pension Expense		
Pension expense (total)	43	
Plan assets (expected return on plan assets)	27	
PBO ($41 service cost + $24 interest cost)		65
Amortization of prior service cost—OCI (2016 amortization)		4
Amortization of net loss—OCI (2016 amortization)		1
To Record Funding		
Plan assets	48	
Cash (contribution to plan assets)		48
To Record Payment of Benefits		
PBO	38	
Plan assets (retiree benefits)		38
To Record Gains and Losses		
Loss–OCI (from change in assumption)	23	
PBO		23
Plan assets	3	
Gain–OCI (from actual return exceeding expected return)		3

Required:

1. Recast these journal entries to include the income tax effects of the events being recorded. Assume that Global's tax rate is 40%. [Hint: Costs are incurred and recognized for financial reporting purposes now, but the tax impact comes much later—when these amounts are deducted for tax purposes as actual payments for retiree benefits occur in the future. As a result, the tax effects are deferred, creating the need to record deferred tax assets and deferred tax liabilities. So, you may want to refer back to Chapter 16 to refresh your memory on these concepts.]
2. Prepare a statement of comprehensive income for 2016 assuming Global's only other sources of comprehensive income were net income of $300 million and a $30 million unrealized holding gain on investments in securities available for sale.

P 17–18
Postretirement benefits; EPBO calculations; APBO calculations; components of postretirement benefit expense; present value concepts
● LO17–9, LO17–10

Century-Fox Corporation's employees are eligible for postretirement health care benefits after both being employed at the end of the year in which age 60 is attained and having worked 20 years. Jason Snyder was hired at the end of 1993 by Century-Fox at age 34 and is expected to retire at the end of 2021 (age 62). His retirement is expected to span five years (unrealistically short in order to simplify calculations). The company's actuary has estimated the net cost of retiree benefits in each retirement year as shown below. The discount rate is 6%. The plan is not prefunded. Assume costs are incurred at the end of each year.

Year	Expected Age	Net Cost
2022	63	$4,000
2023	64	4,400
2024	65	2,300
2025	66	2,500
2026	67	2,800

Required:

1. Draw a time line that depicts Snyder's attribution period for retiree benefits and expected retirement period.
2. Calculate the present value of the net benefits as of the expected retirement date.
3. With respect to Snyder, what is the company's expected postretirement benefit obligation at the end of 2016?
4. With respect to Snyder, what is the company's accumulated postretirement benefit obligation at the end of 2016?
5. With respect to Snyder, what is the company's accumulated postretirement benefit obligation at the end of 2017?
6. What is the service cost to be included in 2017 postretirement benefit expense?
7. What is the interest cost to be included in 2017 postretirement benefit expense?
8. Show how the APBO changed during 2017 by reconciling the beginning and ending balances.

P 17–19
Postretirement benefits; schedule of postretirement benefit costs
● LO17–9 through LO17–11

Stockton Labeling Company has a retiree health care plan. Employees become fully eligible for benefits after working for the company eight years. Stockton hired Misty Newburn on January 1, 2016. As of the end of 2016, the actuary estimates the total net cost of providing health care benefits to Newburn during her retirement years to have a present value of $18,000. The actuary's discount rate is 10%.

Required:

Prepare a schedule that shows the EPBO, the APBO, the service cost, the interest cost, and the postretirement benefit expense for each of the years 2016–2023.

P 17–20
Postretirement benefits; relationship among elements of postretirement benefit plan
● LO17–9 through LO17–11

The information below pertains to the retiree health care plan of Thompson Technologies:

	($ in 000s)	
	2016 Beginning Balances	**2016 Ending Balances**
Accumulated postretirement benefit obligation	$460	$485
Plan assets	0	75
Funded status	(460)	(410)
Prior service cost–AOCI	120	110
Net gain–AOCI	(50)	(49)

Thompson began funding the plan in 2016 with a contribution of $127,000 to the benefit fund at the end of the year. Retirees were paid $52,000. The actuary's discount rate is 5%. There were no changes in actuarial estimates and assumptions.

Required:

Determine the following amounts for 2016:

1. Service cost.
2. Postretirement benefit expense.
3. Net postretirement benefit liability.

P 17–21
Pension disclosure; amortization of actuarial gain or loss; Toys R Us, Inc.
● LO17–3 through LO17–7

Real World Financials

The **Toys R Us, Inc.**, is a leader in the retail toy industry. The following is an excerpt from a disclosure note in the company's annual report for the fiscal year ended February 1, 2014:

Note 12—Defined Benefit Pension Plans(in part)
($ in millions):

(In millions)	Year Ended February 1, 2014	February 2, 2013
Change in projected benefit obligation:		
Projected benefit obligation at beginning of year	$128	$118
Service cost	5	5
Interest cost	5	5
Employee contributions	1	1
Benefits paid	(2)	(2)
Actuarial (gain) loss	(1)	6
Foreign currency impact	1	(5)
Projected benefit obligation at end of year	$137	$128
Change in fair value of plan assets:		
Fair value of plan assets at beginning of year	$105	$93
Actual return on plan assets	5	10
Employer contributions	7	7
Employee contributions	1	1
Benefits paid	(2)	(2)
Foreign currency impact	2	(4)
Fair value of plan assets at end of year	$118	$105

Weighted-Average Assumptions Used to Determine Net Periodic Benefit Costs at Fiscal Year End:

	February 1, 2014	February 2, 2013	January 28, 2012
Discount rate	4.1%	4.0%	4.4%
Expected rate of return on plan assets	4.9%	4.6%	5.1%
Rate of compensation increase	2.7%	2.8%	2.8%

Required:

1. What amount did Toys R Us report in its balance sheet related to the pension plan at February 1, 2014?
2. When calculating pension expense at February 1, what amount did Toys R Us include as the amortization of unrecognized net actuarial loss (net loss–AOCI), which was $9 million at the beginning of the year? The average remaining service life of employees was 10 years.
3. There was no unrecognized prior service cost at the beginning of the year. What was the pension expense?
4. What were the appropriate journal entries to record Toys R Us's pension expense and to record gains and/or losses related to the pension plan?

Broaden Your Perspective

Apply your critical-thinking ability to the knowledge you've gained. These cases will provide you an opportunity to develop your research, analysis, judgment, and communication skills. You also will work with other students, integrate what you've learned, apply it in real-world situations, and consider its global and ethical ramifications. This practice will broaden your knowledge and further develop your decision-making abilities.

Judgment Case 17–1
Choose your retirement option
● LO17–1, LO17–3, LO17–4, LO17–5

"I only get one shot at this?" you wonder aloud. Mrs. Montgomery, human resources manager at Covington State University, has just explained that newly hired assistant professors must choose between two retirement plan options. "Yes, I'm afraid so," she concedes. "But you do have a week to decide."

Mrs. Montgomery's explanation was that your two alternatives are: (1) the state's defined benefit plan and (2) a defined contribution plan under which the university will contribute each year an amount equal to 8% of your salary. The defined benefit plan will provide annual retirement benefits determined by the following formula: 1.5% × years of service × salary at retirement.

"It's a good thing I studied pensions in my accounting program," you tell her. "Now let's see. You say the state is currently assuming our salaries will rise about 3% a year, and the interest rate they use in their calculations is 6%? And, for someone my age, you say they assume I'll retire after 40 years and draw retirement pay for 20 years. I'll do some research and get back to you."

Required:

1. You were hired at the beginning of 2016 at a salary of $100,000. If you choose the state's defined benefit plan and projections hold true, what will be your annual retirement pay? What is the present value of your retirement annuity as of the anticipated retirement date (end of 2055)?
2. Suppose instead that you choose the defined contribution plan. Assuming that the rate of increase in salary is the same as the state assumes and that the rate of return on your retirement plan assets will be 6% compounded annually, what will be the future value of your plan assets as of the anticipated retirement date (end of 2055)? What will be your annual retirement pay (assuming continuing investment of remaining assets at 6%)?
3. Based on this numerical comparison, which plan would you choose? What other factors must you also consider in making the choice?

Hint: The calculations are greatly simplified using an electronic spreadsheet such as Excel. There are many ways to set up the spreadsheet. One relatively easy way is to set up the first few rows with the formulas as shown below, then use the "fill down" function to fill in the remaining 38 rows, and use the Insert: Name: Define: function to name column B "n". Since contributions are assumed made at the end of each year, there are 39 years remaining to maturity at the end of 2016. Note that multiplying each contribution by $(1.06)^n$, where n equals the remaining number of years to retirement, calculates the future value of each contribution invested at 6% until retirement.

	A	B	C	D	E
1	End of	Years to			Future Value
2	Year:	Retirement	Salary	Contribution	at Retirement
3	2016	39	100,000	=C3*0.08	=D3*1.06^n
4	=A3+1	=B3−1	=C3*1.03	=C4*0.08	=D4*1.06^n

Communication Case 17–2
Pension concepts
● LO17–2 through LO17–8

Noel Zoeller is the newly hired assistant controller of Kemp Industries, a regional supplier of hardwood derivative products. The company sponsors a defined benefit pension plan that covers its 420 employees. On reviewing last year's financial statements, Zoeller was concerned about some items reported in the disclosure notes relating to the pension plan. Portions of the relevant note follow:

Note 8: Pensions

The company has a defined benefit pension plan covering substantially all of its employees. Pension benefits are based on employee service years and the employee's compensation during the last two years of employment. The company contributes annually the maximum amount permitted by the federal tax code. Plan contributions provide for benefits expected to be earned in the future as well as those earned to date. The following reconciles the plan's funded status and amount recognized in the balance sheet at December 31, 2016 ($ in 000s).

Actuarial Present Value Benefit Obligations:	
Accumulated benefit obligation (including vested benefits of $318)	$(1,305)
Projected benefit obligation	(1,800)
Plan assets at fair value	1,575
Projected benefit obligation in excess of plan assets	$ (225)

Kemp's comparative income statements reported net periodic pension expense of $108,000 in 2016 and $86,520 in 2015. Since employment has remained fairly constant in recent years, Zoeller expressed concern over the increase in the pension expense. He expressed his concern to you, a three-year senior accountant at Kemp. "I'm also interested in the differences in these liability measurements," he mentioned.

Required:

Write a memo to Zoeller. In the memo:

1. Explain to Zoeller how the composition of the net periodic pension expense can create the situation he sees. Briefly describe the components of pension expense.

2. Briefly explain how pension gains and losses are recognized in earnings.
3. Describe for him the differences and similarities between the accumulated benefit obligation and the projected benefit obligation.
4. Explain how the "Projected benefit obligation in excess of plan assets" is reported in the financial statements.

Judgment Case 17–3
Barlow's wife; relationship among pension elements
● LO17–8

LGD Consulting is a medium-sized provider of environmental engineering services. The corporation sponsors a noncontributory, defined benefit pension plan. Alan Barlow, a new employee and participant in the pension plan, obtained a copy of the 2016 financial statements, partly to obtain additional information about his new employer's obligation under the plan. In part, the pension disclosure note reads as follows:

Note 8: Retirement Benefits

The Company has a defined benefit pension plan covering substantially all of its employees. The benefits are based on years of service and the employee's compensation during the last two years of employment. The company's funding policy is consistent with the funding requirements of federal law and regulations. Generally, pension costs accrued are funded. Plan assets consist primarily of stocks, bonds, commingled trust funds, and cash.

The change in projected benefit obligation for the plan years ended December 31, 2016, and December 31, 2015:

($ in 000s)	2016	2015
Projected benefit obligation at beginning of year	$3,786	$3,715
Service cost	103	94
Interest cost	287	284
Actuarial (gain) loss	302	(23)
Benefits paid	(324)	(284)
Projected benefit obligation at end of year	$4,154	$3,786

The weighted average discount rate and rate of increase in future compensation levels used in determining the actuarial present value of the projected benefit obligations in the above table were 7.0% and 4.3%, respectively, at December 31, 2016, and 7.75% and 4.7%, respectively, at December 31, 2015. The expected long-term rate of return on assets was 10.0% at December 31, 2016 and 2015.

The change in the fair value of plan assets for the plan years ended December 31, 2016 and 2015:

($ in 000s)	2016	2015
Fair value of plan assets at beginning of year	$3,756	$3,616
Actual return on plan assets	1,100	372
Employer contributions	27	52
Benefits paid	(324)	(284)
Fair value of plan assets at end of year	$4,559	$3,756

Included in the Consolidated Balance Sheets are the following components of accumulated other comprehensive income:

($ in 000s)	2016	2015
Net actuarial gain	$(620)	$(165)
Prior service cost	44	46

Net periodic defined benefit pension cost for fiscal 2016, 2015, and 2014 included the following components:

($ in 000s)	2016	2015	2014
Service cost	$ 103	$ 94	$ 112
Interest cost	287	284	263
Expected return on plan assets	(342)	(326)	(296)
Amortization of prior service cost	2	2	1
Recognized net actuarial (gain) loss	(2)	2	4
Net periodic pension cost	$ 48	$ 56	$ 84

In attempting to reconcile amounts reported in the disclosure note with amounts reported in the income statement and balance sheet, Barlow became confused. He was able to find the pension expense on the income statement but was unable to make sense of the balance sheet amounts. Expressing his frustration to his wife, Barlow said, "It appears to me that the company has calculated pension expense as if they have the pension liability and pension assets they include in the note, but I can't seem to find those amounts in the balance sheet. In fact, there are several amounts here I can't seem to account for. They also say they've made some assumptions about interest rates, pay increases, and profits on invested assets. I wonder what difference it would make if they assumed other numbers,"

Barlow's wife took accounting courses in college and remembers most of what she learned about pension accounting. She attempts to clear up her husband's confusion.

Required:

Assume the role of Barlow's wife. Answer the following questions for your husband.

1. Is Barlow's observation correct that the company has calculated pension expense on the basis of amounts not reported in the balance sheet?
2. What amount would the company report as a pension liability in the balance sheet?
3. What amount would the company report as a pension asset in the balance sheet?
4. Which of the other amounts reported in the disclosure note would the company report in the balance sheet?
5. The disclosure note reports a net actuarial gain as well as an actuarial loss. How are these related? What do the amounts mean?
6. Which components of the pension expense represent deferred recognition? Where are these deferred amounts reported prior to amortization?

Communication Case 17–4
Barlow's wife; relationship among pension elements
● LO17–8

The focus of this case is question 1 in the previous case. Your instructor will divide the class into two to six groups, depending on the size of the class. The mission of your group is to assess the correctness of Barlow's observation and to suggest the appropriate treatment of the pension obligation. The suggested treatment need not be that required by GAAP.

Required:

1. Each group member should deliberate the situation independently and draft a tentative argument prior to the class session for which the case is assigned.
2. In class, each group will meet for 10 to 15 minutes in different areas of the classroom. During that meeting, group members will take turns sharing their suggestions for the purpose of arriving at a single group treatment.
3. After the allotted time, a spokesperson for each group (selected during the group meetings) will share the group's solution with the class. The goal of the class is to incorporate the views of each group into a consensus approach to the situation.

Real World Case 17–5
Types of pension plans; disclosures
● LO17–1

Real World Financials

PetSmart

Refer to the financial statements and related disclosure notes of **PetSmart Inc.** in Appendix B located at the back of the text. **www.petsmart.com**.

Required:

1. What type of pension plan does PetSmart sponsor for its employees? Explain.
2. Who bears the "risk" of factors that might reduce retirement benefits in this type of plan? Explain.
3. Assuming that employee and employer contributions vest immediately, suppose a PetSmart employee contributes $1,000 to the pension plan during her first year of employment and directs investments to a municipal bond mutual fund. If she leaves PetSmart early in her second year, after the mutual fund's value has increased by 2%, how much will she be entitled to roll over into an Individual Retirement Account (IRA)?
4. How did PetSmart account for its participation in the pension plan in fiscal 2013?

Ethics Case 17–6
401(k) plan contributions
● LO17–1

You are in your third year as internal auditor with VXI International, manufacturer of parts and supplies for jet aircraft. VXI began a defined contribution pension plan three years ago. The plan is a so-called 401(k) plan (named after the Tax Code section that specifies the conditions for the favorable tax treatment of these plans) that permits voluntary contributions by employees. Employees' contributions are matched with one dollar of employer contribution for every two dollars of employee contribution. Approximately $500,000 of contributions is deducted from employee paychecks each month for investment in one of three employer-sponsored mutual funds.

While performing some preliminary audit tests, you happen to notice that employee contributions to these plans usually do not show up on mutual fund statements for up to two months following the end of pay periods from which the deductions are drawn. On further investigation, you discover that when the plan was first begun, contributions were invested within one week of receipt of the funds. When you question the firm's investment manager about the apparent change in the timing of investments, you are told, "Last year Mr. Maxwell (the CFO) directed me to initially deposit the contributions in the corporate investment account. At the close of each quarter, we add the employer matching contribution and deposit the combined amount in specific employee mutual funds."

Required:

1. What is Mr. Maxwell's apparent motivation for the change in the way contributions are handled?
2. Do you perceive an ethical dilemma?

Research Case 17–7
Codification research; researching pension disclosures; retrieving information from the Internet
● LO17–1, LO17–3, LO17–4

All publicly traded domestic companies use EDGAR, the Electronic Data Gathering, Analysis, and Retrieval system, to electronically file annual reports, quarterly reports, and other filings with the SEC. You usually can access these reports on the Internet for a company by visiting the Investor Relations section of the company's website and clicking on SEC Filings or at www.sec.gov.

Required:

1. Search for a company with which you are familiar and which you believe is likely to have a pension plan. (Older, established firms are good candidates.) Access the company's most recent 10-K filing (annual report). Search or scroll to find the financial statements and related notes.
2. From the disclosure notes, determine the type of pension plan(s) the company has.
3. For any defined contribution plans, determine the contributions the company made to the plans on behalf of employees during the most recent three years.
4. For any defined benefit plans, what interest (discount) rate was used in estimating the PBO? Access the *FASB Accounting Standards Codification* at the FASB website (acs.fasb.org). Determine the specific citation for accounting for the requirement to disclose the discount rate used to estimate the PBO.
5. Repeat steps 2 through 4 for a second firm. Compare and contrast the types of pension plans offered. Are actuarial assumptions the same for defined benefit plans?

Real World Case 17–8
Types of pension plans; reporting postretirement plans; disclosures
● LO17–5, LO17–8

Real World Financials

Refer to the most recent financial statements and related disclosure notes of FedEx Corporation. The financial statements can be found at the company's website: www.fedex.com.

Required:

1. What pension and other postretirement benefit plans do FedEx sponsor for its employees? Explain.
2. What amount does FedEx report in its balance sheet for its pension and other postretirement benefit plans? Explain.
3. FedEx reports three actuarial assumptions used in its pension calculations. Did reported changes in those assumptions from the previous year increase or decrease the projected benefit obligation? Why?

Real World Case 17–9
Pension amendment
● LO17–5, LO17–8

Real World Financials

Charles Rubin is a 30-year employee of General Motors. Charles was pleased with recent negotiations between his employer and the United Auto Workers. Among other favorable provisions of the new agreement, the pact also includes a 13% increase in pension payments for workers under 62 with 30 years of service who retire during the agreement. Although the elimination of a cap on outside income earned by retirees has been generally viewed as an incentive for older workers to retire, Charles sees promise for his dream of becoming a part-time engineering consultant after retirement. What has caught Charles's attention is the following excerpt from an article in the financial press:

> General Motors Corp. will record a $170 million charge due to increases in retirement benefits for hourly United Auto Workers employees.
>
> The charge stems from GM's new tentative labor contract with the UAW. According to a filing with the Securities and Exchange Commission, the charge amounts to 22 cents a share and is tied to the earnings of GM's Hughes Electronics unit.
>
> The company warned that its "unfunded pension obligation and pension expense are expected to be unfavorably impacted as a result of the recently completed labor negotiations."

Taking advantage of an employee stock purchase plan, Charles has become an active GM stockholder as well as employee. His stockholder side is moderately concerned by the article's reference to the unfavorable impact of the recently completed labor negotiations.

Required:

1. When a company modifies its pension benefits the way General Motors did, what name do we give the added cost? How is it accounted for?
2. What does GM mean when it says its "unfunded pension obligation and pension expense are expected to be unfavorably impacted as a result of the recently completed labor negotiations"?

Analysis Case 17–10
Effect of pensions on earnings
● LO17–7

While doing some online research concerning a possible investment you come across an article that mentions in passing that a representative of Morgan Stanley had indicated that a company's pension plan had benefited its reported earnings. Curiosity piqued, you seek your old Intermediate Accounting text.

Required:

1. Can the net periodic pension "cost" cause a company's reported earnings to increase? Explain.
2. Companies must report the actuarial assumptions used to make estimates concerning pension plans. Which estimate influences the earnings effect in requirement 1? Can any of the other estimates influence earnings? Explain.

Research Case 17–11
Researching the way employee benefits are tested on the CPA Exam; retrieving information from the Internet
● LO17–9, LO17–10, LO17–11

The board of examiners of the American Institute of Certified Public Accountants (AICPA) is responsible for preparing the CPA examination. The boards of accountancy of all 50 states, the District of Columbia, Guam, Puerto Rico, the U.S. Virgin Islands, and the Mariana Islands use the examination as the primary way to measure the technical competence of CPA candidates. The content for each examination section is specified by the AICPA and described in outline form.

Required:

1. Access the AICPA website on the Internet. The web address is www.aicpa.org.
2. Access the CPA exam section within the site. Locate the exam content portion of the section.
3. In which of the four separately graded sections of the exam are postretirement benefits tested?
4. From the AICPA site, access the Board of Accountancy for your state. What are the education requirements in your state to sit for the CPA exam?

Analysis Case 17–12
Pensions and other postretirement benefit plans; analysis of disclosure notes
● LO17–6, LO17–11
Real World Financials

Macy's, Inc., operates about 840 Macy's and Bloomingdale's department stores and furniture galleries in 48 states and U.S. territories and 13 Bloomingdale's Outlet stores, macys.com, and bloomingdales.com. Refer to the 2013 financial statements and related disclosure notes of the company. The financial statements can be found at the company's website: www.macys.com.

Required:

1. From the information provided in various portions of Note 9, reconcile the beginning balance ($1,186) and ending balances for Net loss–AOCI associated with Macy's pension plan. Clearly label each reconciling amount.
2. Macy's was required to amortize a portion of its Net loss–AOCI associated with its pension plan in 2013. Based on the calculation of that amount, determine the average remaining service life of the company's employees used in that calculation.
3. From the information provided in various portions of Note 10, reconcile the beginning balance ($38) and ending balances for Net gain–AOCI associated with Macy's Other postretirement employee benefit plan. Clearly label each reconciling amount.
4. Suppose you believe that Macy's should have assumed a 1% lower healthcare cost trend during 2013. What would 2013 net income have been under that assumption? Assume a 35% income tax rate.

Air France–KLM Case

● LO17–12

IFRS

Air France–KLM (AF), a Franco-Dutch company, prepares its financial statements according to International Financial Reporting Standards. AF's financial statements and disclosure notes for the year ended December 31, 2013, are provided with all new textbooks. This material also is available at www.airfranceklm-finance.com.

Required:

1. Air France reported past service cost (called prior service cost under U.S. GAAP) in its income statement as part of net periodic pension cost. Is that reporting method the same or different from the way we report prior service cost under U.S. GAAP?
2. Look at note 31.1, "Retirement Benefits." AF incorporates estimates regarding staff turnover, life expectancy, salary increase, retirement age, and discount rates. How did AF report changes in these assumptions? Is that reporting method the same or different from the way we report changes under U.S. GAAP?
3. AF does not report remeasurement gains and losses in its income statement. Where did AF report these amounts? Is that reporting method the same or different from the way we report pension expense under U.S. GAAP?
4. See Note 23. Did AF report net interest cost or net interest income in 2013? How is that amount determined?

CHAPTER

18 Shareholders' Equity

OVERVIEW

We turn our attention from liabilities, which represent the creditors' interests in the assets of a corporation, to the shareholders' residual interest in those assets. The discussions distinguish between the two basic sources of shareholders' equity: (1) *invested capital* and (2) *earned capital.* We explore the expansion of corporate capital through the issuance of shares and the contraction caused by the retirement of shares or the purchase of treasury shares. In our discussions of retained earnings, we examine cash dividends, property dividends, stock dividends, and stock splits.

LEARNING OBJECTIVES

After studying this chapter, you should be able to:

- **LO18–1** Describe the components of shareholders' equity and explain how they are reported in a statement of shareholders' equity. (*p. 1068*)
- **LO18–2** Describe comprehensive income and its components. (*p. 1070*)
- **LO18–3** Understand the corporate form of organization and the nature of stock. (*p. 1073*)
- **LO18–4** Record the issuance of shares when sold for cash and for noncash consideration. (*p. 1079*)
- **LO18–5** Distinguish between accounting for retired shares and for treasury shares. (*p. 1083*)
- **LO18–6** Describe retained earnings and distinguish it from paid-in capital. (*p. 1089*)
- **LO18–7** Explain the basis of corporate dividends, including the similarities and differences between cash and property dividends. (*p. 1089*)
- **LO18–8** Explain stock dividends and stock splits and how we account for them. (*p. 1091*)
- **LO18–9** Discuss the primary differences between U.S. GAAP and IFRS with respect to accounting for shareholders' equity. (*pp. 1072* and *1078*)

FINANCIAL REPORTING CASE

MasterCard, Incorporated

Finally, you have some uninterrupted time to get back on the net. Earlier today you noticed on the Internet that the market price of MasterCard's common stock was up almost 10%. You've been eager to look into why this happened, but have had one meeting after another all day.

You've been a stockholder of **MasterCard** since the beginning of the year when you became a server at Ruth's Chris to help pay tuition and saw how many steak dinners were charged to MasterCard each night. The dividends of 60 cents a share that you receive quarterly are nice, but that's not why you bought the stock; you were convinced at the time that the stock price was poised to rise rapidly. A few well-placed clicks of the mouse and you come across the following news article:

> PURCHASE, N.Y.—(BUSINESS WIRE)—Dec. 10, 2013—MasterCard Incorporated (NYSE:MA) today announced that its Board of Directors has approved several capital actions.
>
> Among those actions were:
>
> - A 10-for-1 stock split " to be effected through a stock dividend"
> - An 83% increase in the quarterly cash dividend (to $1.10 per share)
> - A $3.5 billion share repurchase program
>
> MasterCard's president and chief executive officer, Ajay Banga, said these actions "reflect our ongoing commitment to deliver shareholder value as well as our confidence in the long-term growth and financial performance of our Company."
>
> The 10-for-1 stock split has a record date of January 9, 2014, and a share distribution date of January 21, 2014. Shareholders will receive nine additional shares of MasterCard common stock for each share held as of the record date. The stock split will cause total shares of common stock outstanding to increase from 120 million to 1.2 billion shares.
>
> The increased quarterly dividend of $1.10 per share is to be paid February 10, 2014 to shareholders of record as of January 9, 2014.

By the time you finish this chapter, you should be able to respond appropriately to the questions posed in this case. Compare your response to the solution provided at the end of the chapter.

QUESTIONS

1. Do you think the stock price increase is related to MasterCard's share repurchase plan? *(p. 1083)*
2. What are MasterCard's choices in accounting for the share repurchases? *(p. 1084)*
3. What effect does the quarterly cash dividend of $1.10 a share have on MasterCard's assets? Its liabilities? Its shareholders' equity? *(p. 1090)*
4. What effect does the stock split have on MasterCard's assets? Its liabilities? Its shareholders' equity? *(p. 1093)*

PART A The Nature of Shareholders' Equity

A corporation raises money to fund its business operations by some mix of debt and equity financing. In earlier chapters, we examined debt financing in the form of notes, bonds, leases, and other liabilities. Amounts representing those liabilities denote *creditors' interest* in the company's assets. Now we focus on various forms of equity financing. Specifically, in this chapter we consider transactions that affect shareholders' equity—those accounts that represent the *ownership interests* of shareholders.

● LO18–1

In principle, shareholders' equity is a relatively straightforward concept. Shareholders' equity is a residual amount—what's left over after creditor claims have been subtracted from assets (in other words, net assets). You probably recall the residual nature of shareholders' equity from the basic accounting equation:

Net assets equal shareholders' equity.

$$\underbrace{\text{Assets} - \text{Liabilities}}_{\text{Net Assets}} = \text{Shareholders' equity}$$

Shareholders' equity accounts denote the ownership interests of shareholders.

Ownership interests of shareholders arise primarily from two sources: (1) amounts *invested* by shareholders in the corporation and (2) amounts *earned* by the corporation on behalf of its shareholders. These two sources are reported as (1) paid-in capital and (2) retained earnings.

Despite being a seemingly clear-cut concept, shareholders' equity and its component accounts often are misunderstood and misinterpreted. As we explore the transactions that affect shareholders' equity and its component accounts, try not to allow yourself to be overwhelmed by unfamiliar terminology or to be overly concerned with precise account titles. Terminology pertaining to shareholders' equity accounts is notoriously diverse. Every shareholders' equity account has several aliases. Indeed, shareholders' equity itself is often referred to as *stockholders' equity* (**WalMart**), *shareowners' equity* (**General Electric**), *shareholders' investment* (**Target**), *stockholders' investment* (**FedEx**), *shareholders' equity* (**Apple**), *equity* (**AirFrance**), and many other similar titles.

Complicating matters, transactions that affect shareholders' equity are influenced by corporation laws of individual states in which companies are located. And, as we see later, generally accepted accounting principles provide companies with considerable latitude when choosing accounting methods in this area.

Legal requirements and disclosure objectives make it preferable to separate a corporation's capital into several separate shareholders' equity accounts.

Keeping this perspective in mind while you study the chapter should aid you in understanding the essential concepts. At a very basic level, each transaction we examine can be viewed simply as an increase or decrease in shareholders' equity, per se, without regard to specific shareholders' equity accounts. In fact, for a business organized as a single proprietorship, all capital changes are recorded in a single owner's equity account. The same concepts apply to a corporation. But for corporations, additional considerations make it desirable to separate owners' equity into several separate shareholders' equity accounts. These additional considerations—legal requirements and disclosure objectives—are discussed in later sections of this chapter. So, as you study the separate effects of transactions on retained earnings and specific paid-in capital accounts, you may find it helpful to ask yourself frequently "What is the net effect of this transaction on shareholders' equity?" or, equivalently, "By how much are net assets (assets minus liabilities) affected by this transaction?"

Financial Reporting Overview

Before we examine the events that underlie specific shareholders' equity accounts, let's overview how individual accounts relate to each other. The condensed balance sheet in Illustration 18–1 of Exposition Corporation, a hypothetical company, provides that perspective.

Illustration 18–1 depicts a rather comprehensive situation. It's unlikely that any one company would have shareholders' equity from all of these sources at any one time. Remember that, at this point, our objective is only to get a general perspective of the items constituting shareholders' equity. Although company records would include separate accounts for each of these components of shareholders' equity in the balance sheet, in practice Exposition

Illustration 18–1
Detailed Shareholders' Equity Presentation

EXPOSITION CORPORATION Balance Sheet December 31, 2016		
($ in millions)		
Assets		
$3,000		
Liabilities		
$1,000		
Shareholders' Equity		
Paid-in capital:		
Capital stock (par):		
Preferred stock, 10%, $10 par, cumulative, nonparticipating	$100	
Common stock, $1 par	55	
Common stock dividends distributable	5	
Additional paid-in capital:		
Paid-in capital—excess of par, preferred	50	
Paid-in capital—excess of par, common	260	
Paid-in capital—share repurchase	8	
Paid-in capital—conversion of bonds	7	
Paid-in capital—stock options	9	
Paid-in capital—restricted stock	5	
Paid-in capital—lapse of stock options	1	
Total paid-in capital		$ 500
Retained earnings		1,670
Accumulated other comprehensive income:		
Net unrealized holding gains (losses) on investments	(85)	
Net unrecognized gain (loss) on pensions	(75)	
Deferred gains (losses) on derivatives*	(4)	
Adjustments from foreign currency rates**	–0–	(164)
Treasury stock (at cost)		(6)
Total shareholders' equity		$2,000

*When a derivative designated as a cash flow hedge is adjusted to fair value, the gain or loss is deferred as a component of other comprehensive income and included in earnings later, at the same time as earnings are affected by the hedged transaction (described in Appendix A at the end of this textbook).
**Changes in foreign currency exchange rates are discussed elsewhere in your accounting curriculum. The amount could be an addition to or reduction in shareholders' equity.

Assets *minus* Liabilities equals Shareholders' Equity.

The primary source of paid-in capital is the investment made by shareholders when buying preferred and common stock.

Several other events also affect paid-in capital.

Retained earnings represents earned capital.

would report a more condensed version similar to that in Illustration 18–1A on page 1070 and the one we will see later in the chapter when we look at the presentation by Abercrombie & Fitch (in Illustration 18–3).

The four classifications within shareholders' equity are paid-in capital, retained earnings, accumulated other comprehensive income, and treasury stock. We discuss these now in the context of Exposition Corporation.

Paid-in Capital

Paid-in capital consists primarily of amounts invested by shareholders when they purchase shares of stock from the corporation or arise from the company buying back some of those shares or from share-based compensation activities. Later in this chapter and the next, we consider in more detail the events and transactions that affect paid-in capital.

Illustration 18–1A

Typical Shareholders' Equity Presentation

Preferred stock, 10%	$ 100
Common stock	60
Additional paid-in capital	340
Retained earnings	1,670
Accumulated other comprehensive income:	
Net unrealized holding losses on investments	(85)
Net unrealized loss on pensions	(75)
Deferred losses on derivatives	(4)
Treasury stock	(6)
Total shareholders' equity	$2,000

Retained Earnings

Retained earnings is reported as a single amount, $1,670 million. We discuss retained earnings in Part C of this chapter.

Treasury Stock

We discuss the final component of shareholders' equity—treasury stock—later in the chapter. It indicates that some of the shares previously sold were bought back by the corporation from shareholders.

● LO18–2

Accumulated Other Comprehensive Income

Also notice that shareholders' equity of Exposition Corporation is adjusted for three events that are not included in net income and so don't affect retained earnings but are part of "other comprehensive income" and therefore are included as a separate component of shareholders' equity, accumulated comprehensive income.[1] **Comprehensive income** provides a more expansive view of the change in shareholders' equity than does traditional net income. It is the total *nonowner* change in equity for a reporting period. In fact, it encompasses all changes in equity other than those from transactions with *owners*. Transactions between the corporation and its shareholders primarily include dividends and the issuance or purchase of shares of the company's stock. Most nonowner changes are reported in the income statement. So, the nonowner changes other than those that are part of traditional net income are the ones reported as "other comprehensive income."

Comprehensive income includes net income as well as other gains, losses, and other adjustments that change shareholders' equity but are not included in traditional net income.

Comprehensive income extends our view of income beyond net income reported in an income statement to include four types of gains and losses not included in income statements:

1. Net holding gains (losses) on investments.
2. Gains (losses) from and amendments to postretirement benefit plans.
3. Deferred gains (losses) on derivatives.
4. Adjustments from foreign currency translation.

The first of these are the gains and losses on some securities that occur when the fair values of these investments increase or decrease. As you learned in Chapters 12 and 14, some gains and losses aren't included in earnings until they are realized through the sale of the securities but are considered a component of *other comprehensive income (OCI)* in the meantime. Similarly, as we discussed in Chapter 17, net gains and losses as well as "prior service cost" on pensions sometimes affect other comprehensive income rather than net income as they occur. You have not yet studied the third and fourth potential components of other comprehensive income. As described in Appendix A, "Derivatives," at the back of this textbook, when a derivative designated as a "*cash flow hedge*" is adjusted to fair value, the gain or loss is deferred as a component of other comprehensive income and included in earnings later, at

[1]Comprehensive income was introduced in Chapter 4 and revisited in Chapters 12 and 17.

the same time as earnings are affected by the hedged transaction. Adjustments from changes in foreign currency exchange rates are discussed elsewhere in your accounting curriculum. These, too, are included in other comprehensive income (OCI) but not net income.

OCI shares another trait with net income. Just as net income is reported periodically in the income statement and also on a *cumulative* basis as part of retained earnings, OCI too, is reported periodically in the statement of comprehensive income and also as **accumulated other comprehensive income (AOCI)** in the balance sheet along with retained earnings. In other words, we report two attributes of OCI: (1) components of comprehensive income *created during the reporting period* and (2) the comprehensive income *accumulated* over the current and prior periods.

OCI is reported in the statement of comprehensive income.

AOCI is reported in the balance sheet.

The first attribute—components of comprehensive income *created during the reporting period*—can be reported either as (a) an expanded version of the income statement or (b) a separate statement immediately following the income statement. Regardless of the placement a company chooses, the presentation is similar. It will report net income, other components of comprehensive income, and total comprehensive income, similar to the presentation in Illustration 18–2. Note that each component is reported net of its related income tax expense or income tax benefit.[2]

Illustration 18–2

Comprehensive Income

	($ in millions)	
Net income		$xxx
Other comprehensive income:		
Net unrealized holding gains (losses) on some securities (net of tax)*	$ x	
Gains (losses) from and amendments to postretirement benefit plans (net of tax)†	(x)	
Deferred gains (losses) on derivatives (net of tax)‡	(x)	
Adjustments from foreign currency translation (net of tax)§	x	xx
Comprehensive income		$xxx

*Changes in the fair value of some investments (described in Chapter 12). An unrealized loss also might occur from recording an "other than temporary" impairment in excess of a credit loss for a debt investment. And, as discussed in Chapter 14, applying the "fair value option" to a liability entails reporting in OCI any part of the change in the liability's fair value that's due to the liability's credit risk.

†Gains and losses due to revising assumptions or market returns differing from expectations and prior service cost from amending the plan (described in Chapter 17).

‡When a derivative designated as a cash flow hedge is adjusted to fair value, the gain or loss is deferred as a component of comprehensive income and included in earnings later, at the same time as earnings are affected by the hedged transaction (described in the Derivatives Appendix to the text).

§Changes in foreign currency exchange rates when translating financial statements of foreign subsidiaries to U.S. dollars. The amount could be an addition to or reduction in shareholders' equity. (This item is discussed elsewhere in your accounting curriculum.)

The second measure—the comprehensive income *accumulated* over the current and prior periods—is reported as a separate component of shareholders' equity following retained earnings, similar to the presentation by Exposition Corporation in Illustration 18–1. Note that amounts reported here—accumulated other comprehensive income (AOCI)—represent the *cumulative* sum of the changes in each component created during each reporting period (Illustration 18–2) throughout all prior years.

Reporting Shareholders' Equity

You seldom, if ever, will see the degree of detail shown in Illustration 18–1 reported in the presentation of paid-in capital. Instead, companies keep track of individual additional paid-in capital accounts in company records but ordinarily report these amounts as a single subtotal—additional paid-in capital. Pertinent rights and privileges of various securities outstanding such as dividend and liquidation preferences, call and conversion information, and

[2]This can be accomplished by presenting components of other comprehensive income either net of related income tax effects (as in this presentation) or before income tax effects with disclosure of the income taxes allocated to each component either in a disclosure note or parenthetically in the statement.

voting rights are summarized in disclosure notes.[3] The shareholders' equity portion of the balance sheet of **Abercrombie & Fitch**, shown in Illustration 18–3, is a typical presentation format.

Illustration 18–3
Typical Presentation Format—Abercrombie & Fitch

Real World Financials

Details of each class of stock are reported on the face of the balance sheet or in disclosure notes.

ABERCROMBIE & FITCH CO.
Consolidated Balance Sheets
(Thousands, except par value amounts)

	February 1, 2014	February 1, 2013
Stockholders' Equity:		
Class A common stock—$0.01 par value: 150,000 shares authorized and 103,300 shares issued at each of February 1, 2014, and February 2, 2013	1,033	1,033
Paid-in capital	433,620	403,271
Retained earnings	2,556,270	2,567,261
Accumulated other comprehensive (loss), net of tax	(20,917)	(13,288)
Treasury stock, at average cost—26,898 and 24,855 shares at February 1, 2014, and February 2, 2013, respectively	(1,240,513)	(1,140,009)
Total Stockholders' Equity	1,729,493	1,818,268

International Financial Reporting Standards

● LO18–9

Use of the term "reserves" and other terminology differences. Shareholders' equity is classified under IFRS into two categories: share capital and "reserves." The term reserves is considered misleading and thus is discouraged under U.S. GAAP. Here are some other differences in equity terminology:

U.S. GAAP	IFRS
Capital stock:	Share capital:
Common stock	Ordinary shares
Preferred stock	Preference shares
Paid-in capital—excess of par, common	Share premium, ordinary shares
Paid-in capital—excess of par, preferred	Share premium, preference shares
Accumulated other comprehensive income:	Reserves:
Net gains (losses) on investments—AOCI	Investment revaluation reserve
Net gains (losses) foreign currency translation—AOCI	Translation reserve
{N/A: adjusting P,P, & E to fair value not permitted}	Revaluation reserve
Retained earnings	Retained earnings
Total shareholders' equity	**Total equity**
Presented after Liabilities	Often presented before Liabilities

***A statement of shareholders' equity* reports the transactions that cause changes in its shareholders' equity account balances.**

The balance sheet reports annual balances of shareholders' equity accounts. However, companies also should disclose the sources of the changes in those accounts.[4] This is the purpose of the **statement of shareholders' equity**. To illustrate, Illustration 18–4 on the next page shows how **Walmart** reported the changes in its shareholders' equity balances.

[3]FASB ACS 505–10–50: Equity–Overall–Disclosure (previously "Disclosure of Information about Capital Structure," *Statement of Financial Accounting Standards No. 129* (Norwalk, Conn.: FASB, 1997)).

[4]FASB ASC 505–10–50–2: Equity–Overall–Disclosure (previously "Omnibus Opinion," *APB Opinion No. 12* (New York: AICPA, 1967)).

Illustration 18—4 Changes in Stockholders' Equity—Walmart

Real World Financials

WAL-MART STORES, INC.
Consolidated Statements of Shareholders' Equity[5]

(Amounts in millions, except per share data)	Number of Shares	Common Stock	Capital in Excess of Par Value	Retained Earnings	Accumulated Other Comprehensive Income (Loss)	Total Walmart Shareholders' Equity
Balances as of February 1, 2011	3,516	$352	$3,577	$63,967	$ 646	$68,542
Consolidated net income	—	—	—	15,699	—	15,699
Other comprehensive loss, net of income taxes	—	—	—	—	(2,056)	(2,056)
Cash dividends declared ($1.46 per share)	—	—	—	(5,048)	—	(5,048)
Purchase of Company stock	(113)	(11)	(229)	(5,930)	—	(6,170)
Other	15	1	344	3	—	348
Balances as of January 31, 2012	3,418	342	3,692	68,691	(1,410)	71,315
Consolidated net income	—	—	—	16,999	—	16,999
Other comprehensive income, net of income taxes	—	—	—	—	823	823
Cash dividends declared ($1.59 per share)	—	—	—	(5,361)	—	(5,361)
Purchase of Company stock	(115)	(11)	(357)	(7,341)	—	(7,709)
Other	11	1	285	(10)	—	276
Balances as of January 31, 2013	3,314	332	3,620	72,978	(587)	76,343
Consolidated net income	—	—	—	16,022	—	16,022
Other comprehensive loss, net of income taxes	—	—	—	—	(2,409)	(2,409)
Cash dividends declared ($1.88 per share)	—	—	—	(6,139)	—	(6,139)
Purchase of Company stock	(87)	(9)	(294)	(6,254)	—	(6,557)
Redemption value adjustment of redeemable noncontrolling interest	—	—	(1,019)	—	—	(1,019)
Other	6	—	55	(41)	—	14
Balances as of January 31, 2014	3,233	$323	$2,362	$76,566	$(2,996)	$76,255

The current year changes that Walmart statements of shareholders' equity reveal are net income, other comprehensive income, the retirement of common stock, and dividends declared.

The Corporate Organization

A company may be organized in any of three ways: (1) a sole proprietorship, (2) a partnership, or (3) a corporation. In your introductory accounting course, you studied each form. In this course we focus exclusively on the corporate form of organization.

LO18–3

Most well-known companies, such as **Microsoft**, **Google**, and **General Electric**, are corporations. Also, many smaller companies—even one-owner businesses—are corporations. Although fewer in number than proprietorships and partnerships, in terms of business volume, corporations are the predominant form of business organization.

Corporations are the dominant form of business organization.

In most respects, transactions are accounted for in the same way regardless of the form of business organization. Assets and liabilities are unaffected by the way a company is organized. The exception is the method of accounting for capital, the ownership interest in the company. Rather than recording all changes in ownership interests in a single capital

Accounting for most transactions is the same regardless of the form of business organization.

[5]Excerpted for instructional clarity.

account for each owner, as we do for sole proprietorships and partnerships, we use the several capital accounts overviewed in the previous section to record those changes for a corporation. Before discussing how we account for specific ownership changes, let's look at the characteristics of a corporation that make this form of organization distinctive and require special accounting treatment.

Limited Liability

The owners are not personally liable for debts of a corporation. Unlike a proprietorship or a partnership, a corporation is a separate legal entity, responsible for its own debts. Shareholders' liability is limited to the amounts they invest in the company when they purchase shares (unless the shareholder also is an officer of the corporation). The limited liability of shareholders is perhaps the single most important advantage of corporate organization. In other forms of business, creditors may look to the personal assets of owners for satisfaction of business debt.

Ease of Raising Capital

A corporation is a separate legal entity—separate and distinct from its owners.

Ownership interest in a corporation is easily transferred.

A corporation is better suited to raising capital than is a proprietorship or a partnership. All companies can raise funds by operating at a profit or by borrowing. However, attracting equity capital is easier for a corporation. Because corporations sell ownership interest in the form of shares of stock, ownership rights are easily transferred. An investor can sell his/her ownership interest at any time and without affecting the corporation or its operations.

From the viewpoint of a potential investor, another favorable aspect of investing in a corporation is the lack of mutual agency. Individual partners in a partnership have the power to bind the business to a contract. Therefore, an investor in a partnership must be careful regarding the character and business savvy of fellow co-owners. On the other hand, shareholders' participation in the affairs of a corporation is limited to voting at shareholders' meetings (unless the shareholder also is a member of management). Consequently, a shareholder needn't exercise the same degree of care that partners must in selecting co-owners.

Shareholders do not have a mutual agency relationship.

Obviously, then, a corporation offers advantages over the other forms of organization, particularly in its ability to raise investment capital. As you might guess, though, these benefits do not come without a price.

Disadvantages

Paperwork! To protect the rights of those who buy a corporation's stock or who loan money to a corporation, the state in which the company is incorporated and the federal government impose expensive reporting requirements. Primarily the required paperwork is intended to ensure adequate disclosure of information needed by investors and creditors.

Corporations are subject to expensive government regulation.

You read earlier that corporations are separate legal entities. As such, they also are separate taxable entities. Often this causes what is referred to as *double taxation.* Corporations first pay income taxes on their earnings. Then, when those earnings are distributed as cash dividends, shareholders pay personal income taxes on the previously taxed earnings. Proprietorships and partnerships are not taxed at the business level; each owner's share of profits is taxed only as personal income.

Corporations create double taxation.

Types of Corporations

When referring to corporations in this text, we are referring to corporations formed by private individuals for the purpose of generating profits. These corporations raise capital by selling stock. There are, however, other types of corporations.

Not-for-profit corporations may be owned:
1. **By the public sector.**
2. **By a governmental unit.**

Some corporations such as churches, hospitals, universities, and charities do not sell stock and are not organized for profit. Also, some not-for-profit corporations are government-owned—the **Federal Deposit Insurance Corporation (FDIC)**, for instance. Accounting for not-for-profit corporations is discussed elsewhere in the accounting curriculum.

Corporations organized for profit may be publicly held or privately (or closely) held. The stock of publicly held corporations is available for purchase by the general public. You can buy shares of **General Electric**, **Ford Motor Company**, or **Walmart** through a stockbroker. These shares are traded on the New York Stock Exchange. Other publicly held stock, like **Intel** and **Microsoft**, are available through Nasdaq (National Association of Securities Dealers Automated Quotations).

Corporations organized for profit may be:
1. Publicly held and traded:
   a. On an exchange.
   b. Over-the-counter.
2. Privately held.

On the other hand, shares of privately held companies are owned by only a few individuals (perhaps a family) and are not available to the general public. Corporations whose stock is privately held do not need to register those shares with the Securities and Exchange Commission and are spared the voluminous, annual reporting requirements of the SEC. Of course, new sources of equity financing are limited when shares are privately held, as is the market for selling existing shares.

Frequently, companies begin as smaller, privately held corporations. Then as success broadens opportunities for expansion, the corporation goes public. For example, in 2012, the shareholders of **Facebook** decided to take public the privately held company. The result was the largest initial public offering since Visa in 2008.

Privately held companies' shares are held by only a few individuals and are not available to the general public.

Hybrid Organizations

A corporation can elect to comply with a special set of tax rules and be designated an **S corporation**. S corporations have characteristics of both regular corporations and partnerships. Owners have the limited liability protection of a corporation, but income and expenses are passed through to the owners as in a partnership, avoiding double taxation.

Two particular business structures have evolved in response to liability issues and tax treatment—limited liability companies and limited liability partnerships.

A **limited liability company** offers several advantages. Owners are not liable for the debts of the business, except to the extent of their investment. Unlike a limited partnership, all members of a limited liability company can be involved with managing the business without losing liability protection. Like an S corporation, income and expenses are passed through to the owners as in a partnership, avoiding double taxation, but there are no limitations on the number of owners as in an S corporation.

A **limited liability partnership** is similar to a limited liability company, except it doesn't offer all the liability protection available in the limited liability company structure. Partners are liable for their own actions but not entirely liable for the actions of other partners.

The Model Business Corporation Act

Corporations are formed in accordance with the corporation laws of individual states. State laws are not uniform, but share many similarities, thanks to the widespread adoption of the **Model Business Corporation Act**.[6] This act is designed to serve as a guide to states in the development of their corporation statutes. It presently serves as the model for the majority of states.

The *Model Business Corporation Act* serves as the model for the corporation statutes of most states.

State laws regarding the nature of shares that can be authorized, the issuance and repurchase of those shares, and conditions for distributions to shareholders obviously influence actions of corporations. Naturally, differences among state laws affect how we account for many of the shareholders' equity transactions discussed in this chapter. For that reason, we will focus on the normal case, as described by the Model Business Corporation Act, and note situations where variations in state law might require different accounting. Your goal is not to learn diverse procedures caused by peculiarities of state laws, but to understand the broad concepts of accounting for shareholders' equity that can be applied to any specific circumstance.

Variations among state laws influence GAAP pertaining to shareholders' equity transactions.

The process of incorporating a business is similar in all states. The **articles of incorporation** (sometimes called the *corporate charter*) describe (a) the nature of the firm's business activities, (b) the shares to be issued, and (c) the composition of the initial **board of directors**. The board of directors establishes corporate policies and appoints officers who manage the corporation.

The number of shares authorized is the maximum number of shares that a corporation is legally permitted to issue, as specified in its articles of incorporation. The number of authorized shares is determined at the company's creation and can only be increased by a vote of

[6] *Model Business Corporation Act*, the American Bar Association, 2011.

the shareholders. At least some of the shares authorized by the articles of incorporation are sold (issued) at the inception of the corporation. Frequently, the initial shareholders include members of the board of directors or officers (who may be one and the same). Ultimately, it is the corporation's shareholders that control the company. Shareholders are the owners of the corporation. By voting their shares, it is they who determine the makeup of the board of directors—who in turn appoint officers, who in turn manage the company.

Shareholders' investment in a corporation ordinarily is referred to as paid-in capital. In the next section, we examine the methods normally used to maintain records of shareholders' investment and to report such paid-in capital in financial statements.

PART B Paid-in Capital

Fundamental Share Rights

In reading the previous paragraphs, you noted that corporations raise equity funds by selling shares of the corporation. Shareholders are the owners of a corporation. If a corporation has only one class of shares, no designation of the shares is necessary, but they typically are labeled *common shares.* Ownership rights held by common shareholders, unless specifically withheld by agreement with the shareholders, are:

a. The right to vote on matters that come before the shareholders, including the election of corporate directors. Each share represents one vote.
b. The right to share in profits when dividends are declared. The percentage of shares owned by a shareholder determines his/her share of dividends distributed.
c. The right to share in the distribution of assets if the company is liquidated. The percentage of shares owned by a shareholder determines his/her share of assets after creditors and preferred shareholders are paid.

Another right sometimes given to common shareholders is the right to maintain one's percentage share of ownership when new shares are issued. This is referred to as a *preemptive right.* Each shareholder is offered the opportunity to buy a percentage of any new shares issued equal to the percentage of shares he/she owns at the time. In most states this right must be specifically granted; in others, it is presumed unless contractually excluded.

However, this right usually is not explicitly stated because of the inconvenience it causes corporations when they issue new shares. The exclusion of the preemptive right ordinarily is inconsequential because few shareholders own enough stock to be concerned about their ownership percentage.

Distinguishing Classes of Shares

It is not uncommon for a firm to have more than one, and perhaps several, classes of shares, each with different rights and limitations. To attract investors, companies have devised quite a variety of ownership securities.

If more than one class of shares is authorized by the articles of incorporation, the specific rights of each (for instance, the right to vote, residual interest in assets, and dividend rights) must be stated. Also, some designation must be given to distinguish each class.

Some of the distinguishing designations often used are:

Terminology varies in the way companies differentiate among share types.

1. Class A, class B, and so on (**Tyson Foods**).
2. Preferred stock, common stock, and class B stock (**Hershey's**).
3. Common and preferred (**Hewlett-Packard**).
4. Capital stock (**Reader's Digest**).
5. Common and serial preferred (**Smucker's**).

In your introductory study of accounting, you probably became most familiar with the common stock–preferred stock distinction. That terminology has deep roots in tradition. Early English corporate charters provided for shares that were preferred over others as to dividends and liquidation rights. These provisions were reflected in early American corporation laws. But as our economy developed, corporations increasingly felt the need for innovative ways of attracting investment capital. The result has been a gradual development of a wide range of share classifications that cannot easily be identified by these historical designations.

It often is difficult to predict the rights and privileges of shares on the basis of whether they are labeled *common* or *preferred*.

To reflect the flexibility that now exists in the creation of equity shares, the Model Business Corporation Act, and thus many state statutes, no longer mention the words common and preferred. But the influence of tradition lingers. Most corporations still designate shares as common or preferred. For consistency with practice, the illustrations you study in this chapter use those designations. As you consider the examples, keep in mind that the same concepts apply regardless of the language used to distinguish shares.

Typical Rights of Preferred Shares

An issue of shares with certain preferences or features that distinguish it from the class of shares customarily called common shares may be assigned any of the several labels mentioned earlier. Very often the distinguishing designation is **preferred shares**. The special rights of preferred shareholders usually include one or both of the following:

a. Preferred shareholders typically have a preference to a specified amount of dividends (stated dollar amount per share or % of par value per share). That is, if the board of directors declares dividends, preferred shareholders will receive the designated dividend before any dividends are paid to common shareholders.
b. Preferred shareholders customarily have a preference (over common shareholders) as to the distribution of assets in the event the corporation is dissolved.

Preferred shareholders sometimes have the **right of conversion** which allows them to exchange shares of preferred stock for common stock at a specified conversion ratio. Alternatively, a **redemption privilege** might allow preferred shareholders the option, under specified conditions, to return their shares for a predetermined redemption price. For instance, in 2014, **Xerox Corporation** had outstanding 300,000 shares of convertible preferred stock. Preferred shareholders have preference over common stockholders in dividends and liquidation rights. Each Xerox preferred share is convertible into 90 common shares. Similarly, shares may be redeemable at the option of the issuing corporation (sometimes referred to as *callable*).

Shares may be:
1. *Convertible* into a specified number of another class of shares.
2. *Redeemable* at the option of:
   a. Shareholders.
   b. The corporation.

Preferred shares may be **cumulative** or **noncumulative**. Typically, preferred shares are cumulative, which means that if the specified dividend is not paid for a given year, the unpaid dividends (called *dividends* in *arrears*) accumulate and must be made up in a later dividend year before any dividends are paid on common shares. Illustration 18–5 provides an example.

Illustration 18–5
Distribution of Dividends to Preferred Shareholders

The shareholders' equity of Corbin Enterprises includes the items shown below. The board of directors declared cash dividends of $360,000, $500,000, and $700,000 in its first three years of operation—2015, 2016, and 2017, respectively.

Common stock	$3,000,000
Paid-in capital—excess of par, common	9,800,000
Preferred stock, 8%	6,000,000
Paid-in capital—excess of par, preferred	780,000

Determine the amount of dividends to be paid to preferred and common shareholders in each of the three years, assuming that the preferred stock is cumulative and nonparticipating.

	Preferred	Common
2015	$360,000*	$0
2016	500,000**	0
2017	580,000***	120,000 (remainder)

* The preferred shareholders are entitled to dividends of $480,000 (8% × $6,000,000), but only $360,000 dividends are declared in 2015 so dividends in arrears are $120,000.
** $120,000 dividends in arrears plus $380,000 of the $480,000 current preference.
*** $100,000 dividends in arrears ($480,000 − 380,000) plus the $480,000 current preference.

If preferred shares are not cumulative, dividends not declared in any given year need never be paid.

Preferred shares may be **participating** or **nonparticipating**. A participating feature allows preferred shareholders to receive additional dividends beyond the stated amount. If the preferred shares are fully participating, the distribution of dividends to common and preferred shareholders is a pro rata allocation based on the relative par value amounts of common and preferred stock outstanding. Participating preferred stock, previously quite common, is rare today.

Remember that the designations of common and preferred imply no necessary rights, privileges, or limitations of the shares so designated. Such relative rights must be specified by the contract with shareholders. A corporation can create classes of preferred shares that are indistinguishable from common shares in voting rights and/or the right to participate in assets (distributed as dividends or distributed upon liquidation). Likewise, it is possible to devise classes of common shares that possess preferential rights, superior to those of preferred shares.

Is It Equity or Is It Debt?

The line between debt and equity is hard to draw.

You probably also can imagine an issue of preferred shares that is almost indistinguishable from a bond issue. Let's say, for instance, that preferred shares call for annual cash dividends of 10% of the par value, dividends are cumulative, and the shares must be redeemed for cash in 10 years. Although the declaration of dividends rests in the discretion of the board of directors, the contract with preferred shareholders can be worded in such a way that directors are compelled to declare dividends each year the company is profitable. For a profitable company, it would be difficult to draw the line between this issue of preferred shares and a 10%, 10-year bond issue. Even in a more typical situation, preferred shares are somewhat hybrid securities—a cross between equity and debt.

International Financial Reporting Standards

● LO18–9

Distinction between Debt and Equity for Preferred Stock. Differences in the definitions and requirements can result in the same instrument being classified differently between debt and equity under IFRS and U.S. GAAP. Under U.S. GAAP, preferred stock normally is reported as equity, but is reported as debt with the dividends reported in the income statement as interest expense if it is "mandatorily redeemable" preferred stock. Under IFRS, most non-mandatorily redeemable preferred stock (preference shares) also is reported as debt as well as some preference shares that aren't redeemable. Under IFRS (*IAS No. 32*), the critical feature that distinguishes a liability is if the issuer is or can be required to deliver cash (or another financial instrument) to the holder.[7] Unilever describes such a difference in a disclosure note:

> **Additional Information for U.S. Investors [in part]**
>
> **Preference Shares**
>
> Under IAS 32, Unilever recognises preference shares that provide a fixed preference dividend as borrowings with preference dividends recognised in the income statement. Under U.S. GAAP such preference shares are classified in shareholders' equity with dividends treated as a deduction to shareholder's equity.

Mandatorily redeemable shares are classified as liabilities.

Sometimes the similarity to debt is even more obvious. Suppose shares are mandatorily redeemable—the company is obligated to buy back the shares at a specified future date. The fact that the company is obligated to pay cash (or other assets) at a fixed or determinable date in the future makes this financial instrument tantamount to debt. A mandatorily redeemable financial instrument must be reported in the balance sheet as a liability, not as shareholders' equity.[8] **Revlon**, for instance, reported its mandatorily redeemable preferred shares as a liability in its 2014 balance sheet.

[7] "Financial Instruments: Presentation," *International Accounting Standard No. 32* (IASCF), as amended effective January 1, 2014.

[8] "FASB ASC 480–10–25–4: Distinguishing Liabilities from Equity–Overall–Recognition (previously Accounting for Certain Financial Instruments with Characteristics of Both Liabilities and Equity," *Statement of Financial Accounting Standards No. 150* (Norwalk, Conn.: FASB, 2005)).

The Concept of Par Value

Another prevalent practice (besides labeling shares as common and preferred) that has little significance other than historical is assigning a par value to shares. The concept of par value dates back as far as the concept of owning shares of a business. Par value originally indicated the real value of shares. All shares were issued at that price.

We have inherited the archaic concept of par value from early corporate law.

During the late 19th and early 20th centuries, many cases of selling shares for less than par value—known as *watered shares*—received a great deal of attention and were the subject of a number of lawsuits. Investors and creditors contended that they relied on the par value as the permanent investment in the corporation and therefore net assets must always be at least that amount. Not only was par value assumed to be the amount invested by shareholders, but it also was defined by early corporation laws as the amount of net assets not available for distribution to shareholders (as dividends or otherwise).

Many companies began turning to par value shares with very low par values—often pennies—to escape the watered shares liability of issuing shares below an arbitrary par value and to limit the restrictions on distributions. This practice is common today.

Shares with nominal par value became common to dodge elaborate statutory rules pertaining to par value shares.

Accountants and attorneys have been aware for decades that laws pertaining to par value and legal capital not only are bewildering but fail in their intent to safeguard creditors from payments to shareholders. Actually, to the extent that creditors are led to believe that they are afforded protection, they are misled. Like the designations of common and preferred shares, the concepts of par value and legal capital have been eliminated entirely from the Model Business Corporation Act.[9]

Many states already have adopted these provisions of the Model Act. But most established corporations issued shares prior to changes in the state statutes. Consequently, most companies have par value shares outstanding and continue to issue previously authorized par value shares. The evolution will be gradual to the simpler, more meaningful provisions of the Model Act.

In the meantime, accountants must be familiar with the outdated concepts of par value and legal capital in order to properly record and report transactions related to par value shares. For that reason, most of the discussion in this chapter centers on par value shares. Largely, this means only that proceeds from shareholders' investment is allocated between stated capital and additional paid-in capital. Be aware, though, that in the absence of archaic laws that prompted the creation of par value shares, there is no theoretical reason to do so.

Most shares continue to bear arbitrarily designated par values.

Accounting for the Issuance of Shares

Shares Issued For Cash

● LO18–4

When shares are sold for cash (see Illustration 18–6), the capital stock account (usually common or preferred) is credited for the amount representing stated capital. When shares have a designated par value, that amount denotes stated capital and is credited to the stock account. Proceeds in excess of this amount are credited to paid-in capital—excess of par (also called additional paid-in capital).

Illustration 18–6

Shares Sold for Cash

Dow Industrial sells 100,000 of its common shares, $1 par per share, for $10 per share:

	($ in 000s)	
Cash (100,000 shares at $10 price per share)	1,000	
Common stock (100,000 shares at $1 par per share)		100
Paid-in capital—excess of par (remainder)		900

The entire proceeds from the sale of no-par stock are deemed stated capital and recorded in the stock account. If the shares are no-par, the entry is as follows:

Cash (100,000 shares at $10 price per share)	1,000	
Common stock		1,000

The total amount received from the sale of no-par shares is credited to the stock account.

[9]American Bar Association, official comment to Section 6.21 of the *Model Business Corporation Act*, 2011.

Shares Issued for Noncash Consideration

Occasionally, a company might issue its shares for consideration other than cash. It is not uncommon for a new company, yet to establish a reliable cash flow, to pay for promotional and legal services with shares rather than with cash. Similarly, shares might be given in payment for land, or for equipment, or for some other noncash asset.

Shares should be issued at fair value.

Even without a receipt of cash to establish the fair value of the shares at the time of the exchange, the transaction still should be recorded at fair value. Best evidence of fair value might be:

- A quoted market price for the shares.
- A selling price established in a recent issue of shares for cash.
- The amount of cash that would have been paid in a cash purchase of the asset or service.
- An independent appraisal of the value of the asset received.
- Other available evidence.

Whichever evidence of fair value seems more clearly evident should be used.[10]

Illustration 18–7 demonstrates a situation where the quoted market price is the best evidence of fair value.

Illustration 18–7

Shares Sold for Noncash Consideration

The quoted market price for the shares issued might be the best evidence of fair value.

DuMont Chemicals issues 1 million of its common shares, $1 par per share, in exchange for a custom-built factory for which no cash price is available. Today's issue of *The Wall Street Journal* lists DuMont's stock at $10 per share:

	($ in millions)	
Property, plant, and equipment (1 million shares at $10 per share)	10	
Common stock (1 million shares at $1 par per share)		1
Paid-in capital—excess of par (remainder)		9

More Than One Security Issued for a Single Price

Although uncommon, a company might sell more than one security—perhaps common shares and preferred shares—for a single price. As you might expect, the cash received usually is the sum of the separate market values of the two securities. Of course, each is then recorded at its market value. However, if only one security's value is known, the second security's market value is inferred from the total selling price as demonstrated in Illustration 18–8.

Illustration 18–8

More than One Security Sold for a Single Price

When only one security's value is known ($40 million), the second security's market value ($60 million) is assumed from the total selling price ($100 million).

AP&P issues 4 million of its common shares, $1 par per share, and 4 million of its preferred shares, $10 par, for $100 million. Today's issue of *The Wall Street Journal* lists AP&P's common at $10 per share. There is no established market for the preferred shares:

	($ in millions)	
Cash	100	
Common stock (4 million shares × $1 par)		4
Paid-in capital—excess of par, common		36
Preferred stock (4 million shares × $10 par)		40
Paid-in capital—excess of par, preferred		20

[10]Although stock issuances are not specifically mentioned in FASB ASC 845–10–30: Nonmonetary Transactions–Overall–Initial Measurement (previously *APB Opinion No. 29*), this treatment is consistent with the general rule for accounting for noncash transactions as described in that pronouncement, pars. 18 and 25.

Because the shares sell for a total of $100 million, and the market value of the common shares is known to be $40 million (4 million × $10), the preferred shares are inferred to have a market value of $60 million.

Additional Consideration

In the unlikely event that the total selling price is not equal to the sum of the two market prices (when both market values are known), the total selling price is allocated between the two securities, in proportion to their relative market values. You should note that this is the same approach we use (a) when more than one asset is purchased for a single purchase price to allocate the single price to the various assets acquired, (b) when detachable warrants and bonds are issued for a single price, and (c) in any other situation when more than one item is associated with a single purchase price or selling price.

Share Issue Costs

When a company sells shares, it obtains the legal, promotional, and accounting services necessary to effect the sale. The cost of these services reduces the net proceeds from selling the shares. Since paid-in capital—excess of par is credited for the excess of the proceeds over the par value of the shares sold, the effect of share issue costs is to reduce the amount credited to that account. For example, the Internet search site Local.com noted in its financial statements: ". . . we completed an underwritten public offering of 4,600,000 shares of our common stock at $4.25 per share (the "Offering"), resulting in net proceeds to us of $18.2 million after deducting underwriting discounts and commissions and other related expenses." Local.com's entry to record the sale was:

Share issue costs reduce the net cash proceeds from selling the shares and thus paid-in capital—excess of par.

Real World Financials

	($ in millions)	
Cash	18.2	
Common stock (4,600,000 shares at $.00001 par per share)		.1
Paid-in capital—excess of par (remainder)		18.1

The cash proceeds is the net amount received after paying share issue costs.

You should notice that not separately reporting share issue costs differs from how *debt* issue costs are recorded. In Chapter 14 you learned that the costs associated with a debt issue are recorded in a separate debt issue costs account and amortized to expense over the life of the debt.

It can be argued that share issue costs and debt issue costs are fundamentally different. That view would argue that a debt issue has a fixed maturity and, like interest expense, debt issue costs are part of the expense of borrowing funds for that period of time (even though it's reported in a separate expense account—debt issue expense—as it's amortized). Selling shares, on the other hand, represents a perpetual equity interest. Dividends paid on that capital investment are not an expense; neither are the costs of obtaining that capital investment (share issue costs).

Like dividends, share issue costs are not an expense.

Although expensing debt issue costs presently is required by GAAP, the FASB has suggested in *Concept Statement 6* that those costs should be treated the same way as share issue costs. That is, the recorded amount of the debt would be reduced by the debt issue costs instead of recording the costs separately as an asset. Remember, though, that concept statements do not constitute GAAP, so until a new FASB standard is issued to supersede FASB ASC 835–30–45: Interest–Imputation of Interest–Other Presentation Matters (previously *APB Opinion 21*), the prescribed practice is to record debt issue costs as assets and expense the asset over the maturity of the debt.

Concept Review Exercise

EXPANSION OF CORPORATE CAPITAL

Situation: The shareholders' equity section of the balance sheet of National Foods, Inc., included the following accounts at December 31, 2014:

Shareholders' Equity	($ in millions)
Paid-in capital:	
Common stock, 120 million shares at $1 par	$ 120
Paid-in capital—excess of par	836
Retained earnings	2,449
Total shareholders' equity	$3,405

Required:

1. During 2015, several transactions affected the stock of National Foods. Prepare the appropriate entries for these events.
   a. On March 11, National Foods issued 10 million of its 9.2% preferred shares, $1 par per share, for $44 per share.
   b. On November 22, 1 million common shares, $1 par per share, were issued in exchange for eight labeling machines. Each machine was built to custom specifications so no cash price was available. National Food's stock was listed at $10 per share.
   c. On November 23, 1 million of the common shares and 1 million preferred shares were sold for $60 million. The preferred shares had not traded since March and their market value was uncertain.
2. Prepare the shareholders' equity section of the comparative balance sheets for National Foods at December 31, 2015 and 2014. Assume that net income for 2015 was $400 million and the only other transaction affecting shareholders' equity was the payment of the 9.2% dividend on the 11 million preferred shares ($1 million).

Solution:

1. During 2015 several transactions affected the stock of National Foods. Prepare the appropriate entries for these events.
   a. On March 11, National Foods issued 10 million of its preferred shares, $1 par per share, for $44 per share.

	($ in millions)	
Cash	440	
Preferred stock (10 million shares × $1 par per share)		10
Paid-in capital—excess of par, preferred		430

   b. On November 22, 1 million common shares, $1 par per share, were issued in exchange for 8 labeling machines:

The transaction was recorded at the fair value of the shares exchanged for the machinery.

Machinery (fair value of shares)	10	
Common stock (1 million shares × $1 par per share)		1
Paid-in capital—excess of par, common (1 million shares × $9)		9

   c. On November 23, 1 million of the common shares and 1 million preferred shares were sold for $60 million:

Since the value of only the common stock was known, the preferred stock's market value ($50/share) was inferred from the total selling price.

Cash	60	
Common stock (1 million shares × $1 par per share)		1
Paid-in capital—excess of par, common		9
Preferred stock (1 million shares × $1 par per share)		1
Paid-in capital—excess of par, preferred (to balance)		49

2. Prepare the shareholders' equity section of the comparative balance sheets for National Foods at December 31, 2015 and 2014.

NATIONAL FOODS, INC.
Balance Sheet
[Shareholders' Equity Section]

	($ in millions)	
	2015	**2014**
Shareholders' Equity		
Preferred stock, 9.2%, $1 par (2015: $10 million + 1 million)	$ 11	$ —
Common stock, $1 par (2015: $120 million + 1 million + 1 million)	122	120
Paid-in capital—excess of par, preferred (2015: $430 million + 49 million)	479	—
Paid-in capital—excess of par, common (2015: $836 million + 9 million + 9 million)	854	836
Retained earnings (2014: $2,449 million + 400 million − 1 million)	2,848	2,449
Total shareholders' equity	$4,314	$3,405

Note: This situation is continued in the next Concept Review Exercise on page 1087.

Share Buybacks

● LO18–5

In the previous section we examined various ways stock might be issued. In this section, we look at situations in which companies reacquire shares previously sold. Most medium- and large-size companies buy back their own shares. Many have formal share repurchase plans to buy back stock over a series of years.

Decision Maker's Perspective

When a company's management feels the market price of its stock is undervalued, it may attempt to support the price by decreasing the supply of stock in the marketplace. A **Johnson & Johnson** announcement that it planned to buy back up to $5 billion of its outstanding shares triggered a buying spree that pushed the stock price up by more than 3 percent.

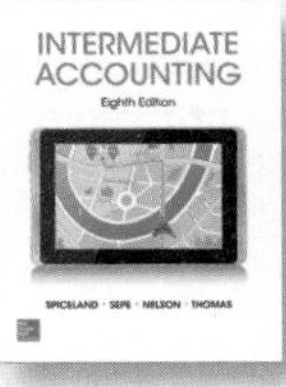

Decreasing the supply of shares in the marketplace supports the price of remaining shares.

When announcing plans to expand its stock buyback program to $90 billion, **Apple** chief executive Tim Cook said it "views its shares as undervalued."[11] Although clearly a company may attempt to increase net assets by buying its shares at a low price and selling them back later at a higher price, that investment is not viewed as an asset. Similarly, increases and decreases in net assets from that activity are not reported as gains and losses in the company's income statement. Instead, buying and selling its shares are transactions between the corporation and its owners, analogous to retiring shares and then selling previously unissued shares. You should note the contrast between a company's purchasing of its own shares and its purchasing of shares in another corporation as an investment.

FINANCIAL Reporting Case

Q1, p. 1067

Unlike an investment in another firm's shares, the acquisition of a company's own shares does not create an asset.

Though not considered an investment, the repurchase of shares often is a judicious use of a company's cash. By increasing per share earnings and supporting share price, shareholders benefit. To the extent this strategy is effective, a share buyback can be viewed as a way to "distribute" company profits without paying dividends. Capital gains from any stock price increase are taxed at lower capital gains tax rates than ordinary income tax rates on dividends.

Companies buy back shares to offset the increase in shares issued to employees.

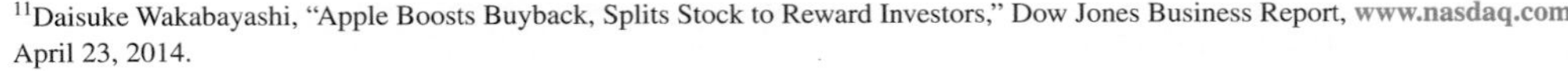

[11]Daisuke Wakabayashi, "Apple Boosts Buyback, Splits Stock to Reward Investors," Dow Jones Business Report, www.nasdaq.com, April 23, 2014.

Perhaps the primary motivation for most stock repurchases is to offset the increase in shares that routinely are issued to employees under stock award and stock option compensation programs. **Microsoft** reported its stock buyback program designed to offset the effect of its stock option and stock purchase plans as shown in Illustration 18–9.

Illustration 18–9
Disclosure of Share Repurchase Program—Microsoft

Real World Financials

> **Note 11: Stockholders' Equity (in part)**
> Our board of directors has approved a program to repurchase shares of our common stock to reduce the dilutive effect of our stock option and stock purchase plans.

Similarly, shares might be reacquired to distribute in a stock dividend, a proposed merger, or as a defense against a hostile takeover.[12]

The usual pattern of stock buybacks was interrupted by the recent economic decline. With corporate profits down and cash in short supply, companies drastically reduced their share repurchases. For some companies, the decision was a choice between cutting buybacks or cutting dividends, and dividend reductions are more obvious and less palatable than curtailing a buyback program.

Whatever the reason shares are repurchased, a company has a choice of how to account for the buyback:

1. The shares can be formally retired.
2. The shares can be called treasury stock.

Unfortunately, the choice is not dictated by the nature of the buyback, but by practical motivations of the company. ●

Shares Formally Retired or Viewed as Treasury Stock

FINANCIAL Reporting Case

Q2, p. 1067

When a corporation retires its own shares, those shares assume the same status as authorized but unissued shares, just the same as if they never had been issued. We saw earlier in the chapter that when shares are sold, both cash (usually) and shareholders' equity are increased; the company becomes larger. Conversely, when cash is paid to **retire stock**, the effect is to decrease both cash and shareholders' equity; the size of the company literally is reduced.

Reacquired shares are equivalent to authorized but unissued shares.

Out of tradition and for practical reasons, companies usually reacquire shares of previously issued stock without formally retiring them.[13] Shares repurchased and not retired are referred to as **treasury stock**. Because reacquired shares are essentially the same as shares that never were issued at all, treasury shares have no voting rights nor do they receive cash dividends. As demonstrated in Illustration 18–10 on the next page, when shares are repurchased as treasury stock, we reduce shareholders' equity with a debit to a negative (or contra) shareholders' equity account labeled treasury stock. That entry is reversed later through a credit to treasury stock when the treasury stock is resold. Like the concepts of par value and legal capital, the concept of treasury shares no longer is recognized in most state statutes.[14] Some companies, in fact, are eliminating treasury shares from their financial statements as corporate statutes are modernized. **Microsoft** retires the shares it buys back rather than labeling them treasury stock. Still, you will see treasury shares reported in the balance sheets of many companies.

[12]A corporate takeover occurs when an individual or group of individuals acquires a majority of a company's outstanding common stock from present shareholders. Corporations that are the object of a hostile takeover attempt—a public bid for control of a company's stock against the company's wishes—often take evasive action involving the reacquisition of shares.

[13]The concept of treasury shares originated long ago when new companies found they could sell shares at an unrealistically low price equal to par value to incorporators, who then donated those shares back to the company. Since these shares already had been issued (though not outstanding), they could be sold at whatever the real market price was without adjusting stated capital.Because treasury shares are already issued, different rules apply to their purchase and resale than to unissued shares. Companies can:

a. Issue shares without regard to preemptive rights of shareholders.
b. Distribute shares as a dividend to shareholders even without a balance in retained earnings.

[14]*The Revised Model Business Corporation Act* eliminated the concept of treasury shares in 1984 after 1980 revisions had eliminated the concepts of par value and legal capital. Most state laws have since followed suit.

American Semiconductor's balance sheet included the following:

Shareholders' Equity	($ in millions)
Common stock, 100 million shares at $1 par	$ 100
Paid-in capital—excess of par	900
Paid-in capital—share repurchase	2
Retained earnings	2,000

Retirement			Treasury Stock		
Reacquired 1 million of its common shares					
Case 1: Shares repurchased at $7 per share					
Common stock ($1 par × 1 million shares)	1		Treasury stock (cost)	7	
Paid-in capital—excess of par ($9 per sh.)	9				
Paid-in capital—share repurchase (difference)		3			
Cash		7	Cash		7
OR					
Case 2: Shares repurchased at $13 per share					
Common stock ($1 par × 1 million shares)	1		Treasury stock (cost)	13	
Paid-in capital—excess of par ($9 per sh.)	9				
Paid-in capital—share repurchase	2*				
Retained earnings (difference)	1				
Cash		13	Cash		13

*Because there is a $2 million credit balance.

Illustration 18–10

Comparison of Share Retirement and Treasury Stock Accounting—Share Buybacks

Formally retiring shares restores the balances in both the Common stock account and Paid-in capital—excess of par to what those balances would have been if the shares never had been issued.

When we view a buyback as treasury stock the cost of acquiring the shares is debited to the treasury stock account.

Accounting for Retired Shares

When shares are formally retired, we should reduce precisely the same accounts that previously were increased when the shares were sold, namely, common (or preferred) stock and paid-in capital—excess of par. The first column of Illustration 18–10 demonstrates this. The paid-in capital—excess of par account for American Semiconductor shows a balance of $900 million while the common stock account shows a balance of $100 million. Thus the 100 million outstanding shares were originally sold for an average of $9 per share above par, or $10 per share. Consequently, when 1 million shares are retired (regardless of the retirement price), American Semiconductor should reduce its common stock account by $1 per share and its paid-in capital—excess of par by $9 per share. Another way to view the reduction is that because 1% of the shares are retired, both share account balances (common stock and paid-in capital—excess of par) are reduced by 1%.

How we treat the difference between the cash paid to buy the shares and the amount the shares originally sold for (amounts debited to common stock and paid-in capital—excess of par) depends on whether the cash paid is *less* than the original issue price (credit difference) or the cash paid is *more* than the original issue price (debit difference):

1. If a *credit* difference is created (as in Case 1 of Illustration 18–10), we credit paid-in capital—share repurchase.
2. If a *debit* difference is created (as in Case 2 of Illustration 18–10), we debit paid-in capital—share repurchase, but only if that account already has a credit balance. Otherwise, we debit retained earnings. (Reducing the account beyond its previous balance would create a negative balance.)

***Paid-in capital—share repurchase* is debited to the extent of its credit balance before debiting retained earnings.**

Why is paid-in capital credited in Case 1 and retained earnings debited in Case 2? The answer lies in the fact that the payments made by a corporation to repurchase its own shares are a distribution of corporate assets to shareholders.

Payments made by a corporation to retire its own shares are viewed as a distribution of corporate assets to shareholders.

In Case 1, only $7 million is distributed to shareholders to retire shares that originally provided $10 million of paid-in capital. Thus, some of the original investment ($3 million in this case) remains and is labeled *paid-in capital—share repurchase.*

In Case 2, more cash ($13 million) is distributed to shareholders to retire shares than originally was paid in. The amount paid in comprises the original investment of $10 million for the shares being retired plus $2 million of paid-in capital created by previous repurchase transactions—$12 million total. Thirteen million is returned to shareholders. The additional $1 million paid is viewed as a dividend on the shareholders' investment, and thus a reduction of retained earnings.[15]

Accounting for Treasury Stock

We view the purchase of treasury stock as a temporary reduction of shareholders' equity, to be reversed later when the treasury stock is resold. The cost of acquiring the shares is "temporarily" debited to the treasury stock account (second column of Illustration 18–10). At this point, the shares are considered to be *issued, but not outstanding.*

Recording the effects on specific shareholders' equity accounts is delayed until later when the shares are reissued. In the meantime, the shares assume the fictional status we discussed earlier of being neither unissued nor outstanding. Effectively, we consider the purchase of treasury stock and its subsequent resale to be a "single transaction."

Additional Consideration

The approach to accounting for treasury stock we discuss in this chapter is referred to as the "cost method." Another permissible approach is the "par value method." It is essentially identical to formally retiring shares, which is why it sometimes is referred to as the *retirement method of accounting for treasury stock.* In fact, if we substitute Treasury stock for Common stock in each of the journal entries we used to account for retirement of shares in Illustrations 18–10 and 18–12, we have the par value method. Because the method has virtually disappeared from practice, we do not discuss it further in this chapter.

BALANCE SHEET EFFECT. Formally retiring shares restores the balances in both the Common stock account and Paid-in capital—excess of par to what those balances would have been if the shares never had been issued at all. As discussed above, any net increase in assets resulting from the sale and subsequent repurchase is reflected as Paid-in capital—share repurchase. On the other hand, any net decrease in assets resulting from the sale and subsequent repurchase is reflected as a reduction in retained earnings.

In contrast, when a share repurchase is viewed as treasury stock, the cost of the treasury stock is simply reported as a reduction in total shareholders' equity. Reporting under the two approaches is compared in Illustration 18–11 using the situation described above for American Semiconductor after the purchase of treasury stock in Illustration 18–10 (Case 2) on page 1085. Notice that either way total shareholders' equity is the same.

Illustration 18–11
Reporting Share Buyback in the Balance Sheet

Retirement reduces common stock and associated shareholders' equity accounts.

	($ in millions)	
	Shares Retired	**Treasury Stock**
Shareholders' Equity		
Paid-in capital:		
Common stock, 100 million shares at $1 par	$ 99	$ 100
Paid-in capital—excess of par	891	900
Paid-in capital—share repurchase		2
Retained earnings	1,999	2,000
Less: Treasury stock, 1 million shares (at cost)		(13)
Total shareholders' equity	$2,989	$2,989

[15]In the next section of this chapter, you will be reminded that dividends reduce retained earnings. (You first learned this in your introductory accounting course.)

Resale of Shares

After shares are formally retired, any subsequent sale of shares is simply the sale of new, unissued shares and is accounted for accordingly. This is demonstrated in the first column of Illustration 18–12.

Illustration 18–12
Comparison of Share Retirement and Treasury Stock Accounting—Subsequent Sale of Shares

American Semiconductor sold 1 million shares after reacquiring shares at $13 per share (Case 2 in Illustration 18–10).

Retirement			Treasury Stock		
Sold 1 million shares					
Case A: Shares sold at $14 per share					
Cash	14		Cash	14	
Common stock (par)		1	Treasury stock (cost)		13
Paid-in capital—excess of par		13	Paid-in capital—share repurchase		1
OR					
Case B: Shares sold at $10 per share					
Cash	10		Cash	10	
Common stock (par)		1	Retained earnings (to balance)	1	
Paid-in capital—excess of par		9	Paid-in capital—share repurchase	2*	
			Treasury stock (cost)		13

*Because there is a $2 million credit balance.

After formally retiring shares, we record a subsequent sale of shares exactly like any sale of shares.

The resale of treasury shares is viewed as the consummation of the "single transaction" begun when the treasury shares were purchased.

The resale of treasury shares is viewed as the consummation of the single transaction begun when the treasury shares were repurchased. The effect of the single transaction of purchasing treasury stock and reselling it for more than cost (Case 2 of Illustration 18–10 and Case A of Illustration 18–12) is to *increase* both cash and shareholders' equity (by $1 million). The effect of the single transaction of purchasing treasury stock and reselling it for less than cost (Case 2 of Illustration 18–10 and Case B of Illustration 18–12) is to *decrease* both cash and shareholders' equity (by $3 million).

Allocating the cost of treasury shares occurs when the shares are resold.

Note that retained earnings may be debited in a treasury stock transaction, but not credited. Also notice that transactions involving treasury stock have no impact on the income statement. This follows the reasoning discussed earlier that a corporation's buying and selling of its own shares are transactions between the corporation and its owners and not part of the earnings process.

Additional Consideration

Treasury Shares Acquired at Different Costs

Notice that the treasury stock account always is credited for the cost of the reissued shares ($13 million in Illustration 18–12). When shares are reissued, if treasury stock on hand has been purchased at different per share prices, the cost of the shares sold must be determined using a cost flow assumption—FIFO, LIFO, or weighted average—similar to determining the cost of goods sold when inventory items are acquired at different unit costs.

Determining the cost of treasury stock sold is similar to determining the cost of goods sold.

Concept Review Exercise

TREASURY STOCK

Situation: The shareholders' equity section of the balance sheet of National Foods, Inc. included the following accounts at December 31, 2015.

Shareholders' Equity	($ in millions)
Paid-in capital:	
Preferred stock, 11 million shares at $1 par	$ 11
Common stock, 122 million shares at $1 par	122
Paid-in capital—excess of par, preferred	479
Paid-in capital—excess of par, common	854
Retained earnings	2,848
Total shareholders' equity	$4,314

Required:

1. National Foods reacquired common shares during 2016 and sold shares in two separate transactions later that year. Prepare the entries for both the purchase and subsequent sale of shares during 2016 assuming that the shares were (a) retired and (b) considered to be treasury stock.
   a. National Foods purchased 6 million shares at $10 per share.
   b. National Foods sold 2 million shares at $12 per share.
   c. National Foods sold 2 million shares at $7 per share.
2. Prepare the shareholders' equity section of National Foods' balance sheet at December 31, 2016, assuming the shares were both (a) retired and (b) viewed as treasury stock. Net income for 2016 was $400 million, and preferred shareholders were paid $1 million cash dividends.

Solution:

1. National Foods reacquired common shares during 2016 and sold shares in two separate transactions later that year. Prepare the entries for both the purchase and subsequent sale of shares during 2016 assuming that the shares were (a) retired and (b) considered to be treasury stock.
   a. National Foods **purchased** 6 million shares at **$10** per share:

Retirement ($ in millions)			**Treasury Stock** ($ in millions)		
Common stock (6 million shares × $1)	6		Treasury stock (6 million shares × $10)	60	
Paid-in capital—excess of par (6 million shares × $7*)	42		Cash		60
Retained earnings (to balance)	12				
Cash		60			

*$854 million ÷ 122 million shares

b. National Foods **sold** 2 million shares at **$12** per share: ($ in millions)

Cash	24		Cash	24	
Common stock (2 million shares × $1)		2	Treasury stock (2 million shares × $10)		20
Paid-in capital—excess of par		22	Paid-in capital—share repurchase		4

c. National Foods **sold** 2 million shares at **$7** per share: ($ in millions)

Cash	14		Cash	14	
Common stock (2 million shares × $1 par)		2	Paid-in capital—share repurchase	4	
Paid-in capital—excess of par		12	Retained earnings (to balance)	2	
			Treasury stock (2 million shares × $10)		20

2. Prepare the shareholders' equity section of National Foods' balance sheet at December 31, 2016, assuming the shares were both (a) retired and (b) viewed as treasury stock.

NATIONAL FOODS, INC.
Balance Sheet
[Shareholders' Equity Section]
At December 31, 2016

	($ in millions)	
	Shares Retired	**Treasury Stock**
Shareholders' Equity		
Preferred stock, 11 million shares at $1 par	$ 11	$ 11
Common stock, 122 million shares at $1 par	120	122
Paid-in capital—excess of par, preferred	479	479
Paid-in capital—excess of par, common	846*	854
Retained earnings	3,235†	3,245‡
Treasury stock, at cost; 2 million common shares	—	(20)
Total shareholders' equity	$4,691	$4,691

*$854 − 42 + 22 + 12
†$2,848 − 12 + 400 − 1
‡$2,848 − 2 + 400 − 1

Note: This situation is continued in the next Concept Review Exercise on page 1097.

PART C

Retained Earnings

Characteristics of Retained Earnings

LO18–6

In the previous section we examined *invested* capital. Now we consider *earned* capital, that is, retained earnings. In general, retained earnings represents a corporation's accumulated, undistributed net income (or net loss). A more descriptive title used by some companies is reinvested earnings. A credit balance in this account indicates a dollar amount of assets previously earned by the firm but not distributed as dividends to shareholders. We refer to a debit balance in retained earnings as a **deficit**. **Microsoft** reported a deficit for several years until retained earnings grew to a positive balance in 2013.

Real World Financials

You saw in the previous section that the buyback of shares (as well as the resale of treasury shares in some cases) can decrease retained earnings. We examine in this section the effect on retained earnings of dividends and stock splits.

Dividends

LO18–7

Shareholders' initial investments in a corporation are represented by amounts reported as paid-in capital. One way a corporation provides a return to its shareholders on their investments is to pay them a **dividend**, typically cash.[16]

Dividends are distributions of assets the company has earned on behalf of its shareholders. If dividends are paid that exceed the amount of assets earned by the company, then management is, in effect, returning to shareholders a portion of their investments, rather than providing them a return on that investment. So most companies view retained earnings as the amount available for dividends.[17]

Liquidating Dividend

Any dividend not representing a distribution of earnings should be debited to paid-in capital.

In unusual instances in which a dividend exceeds the balance in retained earnings, the excess is referred to as a **liquidating dividend** because some of the invested capital is being liquidated.

[16]Dividends are not the only return shareholders earn; when market prices of their shares rise, shareholders benefit also. Indeed, many companies have adopted policies of never paying dividends but reinvesting all assets they earn. The motivation is to accommodate more rapid expansion and thus, presumably, increases in the market price of the stock.

[17]Ordinarily, this is not the legal limitation. Most states permit a company to pay dividends so long as, after the dividend, its assets would not be "less than the sum of its total liabilities plus the amount that would be needed, if the corporation were to be dissolved at the time of the distribution, to satisfy the preferential rights upon dissolution of shareholders whose preferential rights are superior to those receiving the distribution." (Revised Model Business Corporation Act, American Bar Association, 2011.) Thus, legally, a corporation can distribute amounts equal to total shareholders' equity less dissolution preferences of senior equity securities (usually preferred stock).

This might occur when a corporation is being dissolved and assets (not subject to a superior claim by creditors) are distributed to shareholders. Any portion of a dividend not representing a distribution of earnings should be debited to additional paid-in capital rather than retained earnings.

Retained Earnings Restrictions

A restriction of retained earnings communicates management's intention to withhold assets represented by a specified portion of the retained earnings balance.

Sometimes the amount available for dividends purposely is reduced by management. A restriction of retained earnings designates a portion of the balance in retained earnings as being *unavailable for dividends.* A company might restrict retained earnings to indicate management's intention to withhold for some specific purpose the assets represented by that portion of the retained earnings balance. For example, management might anticipate the need for a specific amount of assets in upcoming years to repay a maturing debt, to cover a contingent loss, or to finance expansion of the facilities. Be sure to understand that the restriction itself does not set aside cash for the designated event but merely communicates management's intention not to distribute the stated amount as a dividend.

Normally a restriction of retained earnings is indicated by a disclosure note.

A restriction of retained earnings normally is indicated by a disclosure note to the financial statements. Although instances are rare, a formal journal entry may be used to reclassify a portion of retained earnings to an "appropriated" retained earnings account.

Cash Dividends

You learned in Chapter 14 that paying interest to creditors is a contractual obligation. No such legal obligation exists for paying dividends to shareholders. A liability is not recorded until a company's board of directors votes to declare a dividend. In practice, though, corporations ordinarily try to maintain a stable dividend pattern over time.

> **Microsoft Corp.** announced that its Board of Directors declared a quarterly dividend of 28 cents per share. The dividend is payable June 12, 2014, to shareholders of record on May 15, 2014.[18]

When directors declare a cash dividend, we reduce retained earnings and record a liability. Before the payment actually can be made, a listing must be assembled of shareholders entitled to receive the dividend. A specific date is stated as to when the determination will be made of the recipients of the dividend. This date is called the **date of record**. Registered owners of shares of stock on this date are entitled to receive the dividend—even if they sell those shares prior to the actual cash payment. To be a registered owner of shares on the date of record, an investor must purchase the shares before the **ex-dividend date**. This date usually is two business days before the date of record. Shares purchased on or after that date are purchased ex dividend—without the right to receive the declared dividend. As a result, the market price of a share typically will decline by the amount of the dividend, other things being equal, on the ex-dividend date. Consider Illustration 18–13.

FINANCIAL Reporting Case

Q3, p. 1067

Illustration 18–13
Cash Dividends

On June 1, the board of directors of Craft Industries declares a cash dividend of $2 per share on its 100 million shares, payable to shareholders of record June 15, to be paid July 1:

	($ in millions)	
June 1—Declaration Date		
Retained earnings	200	
Cash dividends payable (100 million shares at $2/share)		200
June 13—Ex-Dividend Date		
No entry		
June 15—Date of Record		
No entry		
July 1—Payment Date		
Cash dividends payable	200	
Cash		200

At the declaration date, retained earnings is reduced and a liability is recorded.

Registered owners of shares on the date of record are entitled to receive the dividend.

[18]"Microsoft Expands Board, Announces Quarterly Dividend," SeattleTimes.com, March 11, 2014.

A sufficient balance in retained earnings permits a dividend to be declared. Remember, though, that retained earnings is a shareholders' equity account representing a dollar claim on assets in general, but not on any specific asset in particular. Sufficient retained earnings does not ensure sufficient cash to make payment. These are two separate accounts having no necessary connection with one another. When a dividend is "paid from retained earnings," this simply means that sufficient assets previously have been earned to pay the dividend without returning invested assets to shareholders.

Property Dividends

Because cash is the asset most easily divided and distributed to shareholders, most corporate dividends are cash dividends. In concept, though, any asset can be distributed to shareholders as a dividend. When a noncash asset is distributed, it is referred to as a **property dividend** (often called a *dividend in kind* or a *nonreciprocal transfer to owners*). **Gold Resource Corp.**, a Colorado gold mining company, announced in 2014 that it would make dividend payments in gold bullion instead of cash.

The *fair value* of the assets to be distributed is the amount recorded for a property dividend.

RFM Corporation conferred a property dividend to its shareholders when it distributed shares of **Philipine Townships, Inc.**, stock that RFM was holding as an investment. Securities held as investments are the assets most often distributed in a property dividend due to the relative ease of dividing these assets among shareholders and determining their fair values.

Real World Financials

A property dividend should be recorded at the fair value of the assets to be distributed, measured at the date of declaration. This may require revaluing the asset to fair value prior to recording the dividend. If so, a gain or loss is recognized for the difference between book value and fair value. This is demonstrated in Illustration 18–14.

Illustration 18–14
Property Dividends

On October 1 the board of directors of Craft Industries declares a property dividend of 2 million shares of Beaman Corporation's preferred stock that Craft had purchased in March as an investment (book value: $9 million). The investment shares have a fair value of $5 per share, **$10 million**, and are payable to shareholders of record October 15, to be distributed November 1:

October 1—Declaration Date	($ in millions)	
Investment in Beaman Corporation preferred stock	1	
Gain on appreciation of investment ($10 − 9)		1
Retained earnings (2 million shares at $5 per share)	10	
Property dividends payable		10
October 15—Date of Record		
No entry		
November 1—Payment Date		
Property dividends payable	10	
Investment in Beaman Corporation preferred stock		10

Before recording the property dividend, the asset first must be written up to fair value.

Stock Dividends and Splits

Stock Dividends

A **stock dividend** is the distribution of additional shares of stock to current shareholders of the corporation. Be sure to note the contrast between a stock dividend and either a cash or property dividend. A stock dividend affects neither the assets nor the liabilities of the firm. Also, because each shareholder receives the same percentage increase in shares, shareholders' proportional interest in (percentage ownership of) the firm remains unchanged.

● LO18–8

The prescribed accounting treatment of a stock dividend requires that shareholders' equity items be reclassified by reducing one or more shareholders' equity accounts and simultaneously increasing one or more paid-in capital accounts. The amount reclassified depends on the size of the stock dividend. For a small stock dividend, typically less than

25%, the fair value of the additional shares distributed is transferred from retained earnings to paid-in capital as demonstrated in Illustration 18–15.[19]

Illustration 18–15
Stock Dividend

A small stock dividend requires reclassification to paid-in capital of retained earnings equal to the fair value of the additional shares distributed.

Craft declares and distributes a 10% common stock dividend (10 million shares) when the market value of the $1 par common stock is $12 per share.

	($ in millions)	
Retained earnings (10 million shares at $12 per share)	120	
Common stock (10 million shares at $1 par per share)		10
Paid-in capital—excess of par (remainder)		110

Additional Consideration

The entry above is recorded on the declaration date. Since the additional shares are not yet issued, some accountants would prefer to credit "common stock dividends issuable" at this point, instead of common stock. In that case, when the shares are issued, common stock dividends issuable is debited and common stock credited. The choice really is inconsequential; either way the $10 million amount would be reported as part of paid-in capital on a balance sheet prepared between the declaration and distribution of the shares.

STOCK MARKET REACTION TO STOCK DISTRIBUTIONS. As a Craft shareholder owning 10 shares at the time of the 10% stock dividend, you would receive an 11th share. Since each is worth $12, would you benefit by $12 when you receive the additional share from Craft? Of course not. If the value of each share were to remain $12 when the 10 million new shares are distributed, the total market value of the company would grow by $120 million (10 million shares × $12 per share).

The market price per share will decline in proportion to the increase in the number of shares distributed in a stock dividend.

A corporation cannot increase its market value simply by distributing additional stock certificates. Because all shareholders receive the same percentage increase in their respective holdings, you, and all other shareholders, still would own the same percentage of the company as before the distribution. Accordingly, the per share value of your shares should decline from $12 to $10.91 so that your 11 shares would be worth $120—precisely what your 10 shares were worth prior to the stock dividend. You might compare Craft Industries to a pizza. Cutting the pizza into 16 slices instead of 12 doesn't create more to eat; you still have the same pizza, just a higher number of smaller slices. Any failure of the stock price to actually adjust in proportion to the additional shares issued probably would be due to information other than the distribution reaching shareholders at the same time.

Early rule-makers felt that per share market prices do not adjust in response to an increase in the number of shares.

Then, what justification is there for recording the additional shares at market value? In 1941 (and reaffirmed in 1953), accounting rule-makers felt that many shareholders are deceived by small stock dividends, believing they benefit by the market value of their additional shares. Furthermore they erroneously felt that these individual beliefs are collectively reflected in the stock market by per share prices that remain unchanged by stock dividends. Consequently, their prescribed accounting treatment is to reduce retained earnings by the same amount as if cash dividends were paid equal to the market value of the shares issued.[20]

[19]FASB ASC 505–20: Equity–Stock Dividends and Stock Splits (previously "Restatement and Revision of Accounting Research Bulletins," *Accounting Research Bulletin No. 43* (New York: AICPA, 1961), Chap. 7, sec. B, pars. 10–14). In this pronouncement, a small stock dividend is defined as one 20% to 25% or less. For filings with that agency, the SEC has refined the definition to comprise stock distributions of less than 25%.

[20]FASB ASC 505–20–30–3: Equity–Stock Dividends and Stock Splits–Initial Measurement (previously "Restatement and Revision of Accounting Research Bulletins," *Accounting Research Bulletin No. 43* (New York: AICPA, 1961), chap. 7).

This obsolete reasoning is inconsistent with our earlier conclusion that the market price per share *will* decline in approximate proportion to the increase in the number of shares distributed. Our intuitive conclusion is supported also by formal research.[21]

Besides being based on fallacious reasoning, accounting for stock dividends by artificially reclassifying "earned" capital as "invested" capital conflicts with the reporting objective of reporting shareholders' equity by source. Despite these limitations, this outdated accounting standard still applies.

Capitalizing retained earnings for a stock dividend artificially reclassifies earned capital as invested capital.

REASONS FOR STOCK DIVIDENDS. Since neither the corporation nor its shareholders apparently benefits from stock dividends, why do companies declare them?[22] Occasionally, a company tries to give shareholders the illusion that they are receiving a real dividend.

Companies sometimes declare a stock dividend in lieu of a real dividend.

Another reason is merely to enable the corporation to take advantage of the accepted accounting practice of capitalizing retained earnings. Specifically, a company might wish to reduce an existing balance in retained earnings—otherwise available for *cash* dividends—so it can reinvest the earned assets represented by that balance without carrying a large balance in retained earnings.

Companies sometimes declare a stock dividend so they can capitalize retained earnings.

Stock Splits

A frequent reason for issuing a stock dividend is actually to induce the per share market price decline that follows. For instance, after a company declares a 100% stock dividend on 100 million shares of common stock, with a per share market price of $12, it then has 200 million shares, each with an approximate market value of $6. The motivation for reducing the per share market price is to increase the stock's *marketability* by making it attractive to a larger number of potential investors.

FINANCIAL Reporting Case

Q4, p. 1067

Additional Consideration

No cash dividends are paid on treasury shares. Usually stock dividends aren't paid on treasury shares either. Treasury shares are essentially equivalent to shares that never have been issued. In some circumstances, though, the intended use of the repurchased shares will give reason for the treasury shares to participate in a stock dividend. For instance, if the treasury shares have been specifically designated for issuance to executives in a stock option plan or stock award plan it would be appropriate to adjust the number of shares by the stock distribution.

A stock distribution of 25% or higher can be accounted for in one of two ways: (1) as a "large" stock dividend or (2) as a **stock split**.[23] Thus, a 100% stock dividend could be labeled a 2-for-1 stock split and accounted for as such. Conceptually, the proper accounting treatment of a stock distribution is to make no journal entry. This, in fact, is the prescribed accounting treatment for a stock split.

A large stock dividend is known as a stock *split*.

> Apple's stock would be trading at around $5,100 a share without its four stock splits. Amazon, which did three stock splits, would have been trading at nearly $4,000 a share and Microsoft, which has done nine stock splits over the years, . . . $12,000 a share.[24]

Since the same common stock account balance (total par) represents twice as many shares in a 2-for-1 stock split, the par value per share will be reduced by one-half. In the previous example, if the par were $1 per share before the stock distribution, then after the 2-for-1 stock split, the par would be $.50 per share.

[21]Foster and Vickrey, "The Information Content of Stock Dividend Announcements," *Accounting Review* (April 1978); and Spiceland and Winters, "The Market Reaction to Stock Distributions: The Effect of Market Anticipation and Cash Returns," *Accounting and Business Research* (Summer 1986).

[22]After hitting a high in the 1940s, the number of stock dividends has declined significantly. Currently, about 3% of companies declare stock dividends in any given year.

[23]FASB ASC 505–20–25–2: Equity–Stock Dividends and Stock Splits–Recognition (previously "Restatement and Revision of Accounting Research Bulletins," *Accounting Research Bulletin No. 43* (New York: AICPA, 1961), Chap. 7, sec. B, par. 11).

[24]Seth Fiegerman, "Why Some Big Tech Companies Still Split Their Stocks," Mashable.com, June 9, 2014.

As you might expect, having the par value per share change in this way is cumbersome and expensive. All records, printed or electronic, that refer to the previous amount must be changed to reflect the new amount. The practical solution is to account for the large stock distribution as a stock dividend rather than a stock split.

Stock Splits Effected in the Form of Stock Dividends (Large Stock Dividends)

To avoid changing the per share par value of the shares, the stock distribution is referred to as a *stock split effected in the form of a stock dividend,* or simply a *stock dividend.* In that case, a journal entry increases the common stock account by the par value of the additional shares. To avoid reducing retained earnings in these instances, most companies reduce (debit) paid-in capital—excess of par to offset the credit to common stock (Illustration 18–16).

Illustration 18–16
Stock Split Effected in the Form of a Stock Dividend

If a *stock split* is effected in the form of a stock dividend, a journal entry prevents the par per share from changing.

Craft declares and distributes a 2-for-1 stock split effected in the form of a 100% stock dividend (100 million shares) when the market value of the $1 par common stock is $12 per share:

	($ in millions)	
Paid-in capital—excess of par	100	
Common stock (100 million shares at $1 par per share)		100

Notice that this entry does not reclassify earned capital as invested capital. Some companies, though, choose to debit retained earnings instead.

Some companies capitalize retained earnings when recording a stock split effected in the form of a stock dividend.

	($ in millions)	
Retained earnings	100	
Common stock (10 million shares × $1 par per share)		100

Nike, Inc., described a stock split in its disclosure notes as shown in Illustration 18–17.

Illustration 18–17
Stock Split Disclosure—Nike, Inc.

Real World Financials

Note 1—Summary of Significant Accounting Policies
Stock Split
On February 15 the Board of Directors declared a two-for-one stock split of the Company's Class A and Class B common shares, which was effected in the form of a 100% common stock dividend distributed on April 2. All references to share and per share amounts in the consolidated financial statements and accompanying notes to the consolidated financial statements have been retroactively restated to reflect the two-for-one stock split.

In 2014, **Apple Inc.** distributed a rare 7-for-1 stock split that dropped the price of Apple shares from about $600 all the way down to about $86.

Additional Consideration

A company choosing to capitalize retained earnings when recording a stock split effected in the form of a stock dividend may elect to capitalize an amount other than par value. Accounting guidelines are vague in this regard, stating only that legal amounts are minimum requirements and do not prevent the capitalization of a larger amount per share.

Source: FASB ASC 505–20–30–4: Equity–Stock Dividends and Stock Splits–Initial Measurement (previously "Restatement and Revision of Accounting Research Bulletins," *Accounting Research Bulletin No. 43* (New York: AICPA, 1961), Chap. 7, sec. B, par. 14).

REVERSE STOCK SPLIT. A **reverse stock split** occurs when a company decreases, rather than increases, its outstanding shares. After a 1-for-4 reverse stock split, for example, 100 million shares, $1 par per share, would become 25 million shares, $4 par per share. No journal entry is necessary. Of course the market price per share theoretically would quadruple, which usually is the motivation for declaring a reverse stock split. Companies that reverse split their shares frequently are struggling companies trying to accomplish with the split what the market has been unwilling to do—increase the stock price. Often this is to prevent the stock's price from becoming so low that it is delisted from a market exchange. Reverse splits are not unusual occurrences, particularly during stock market downturns. In 2014, Great American Group declared a 1-for-20 reverse split.

FRACTIONAL SHARES. Typically, a stock dividend or stock split results in some shareholders being entitled to fractions of whole shares. For example, if a company declares a 25% stock dividend, or equivalently a 5-for-4 stock split, a shareholder owning 10 shares would be entitled to 2½ shares. Another shareholder with 15 shares would be entitled to 3¾ shares.

Cash payments usually are made when shareholders are entitled to fractions of whole shares.

Cash payments usually are made to shareholders for **fractional** shares and are called "cash in lieu of payments." In the situation described above, for instance, if the market price at declaration is $12 per share, the shareholder with 15 shares would receive 3 additional shares and $9 in cash ($12 × ¾).

Decision Maker's Perspective

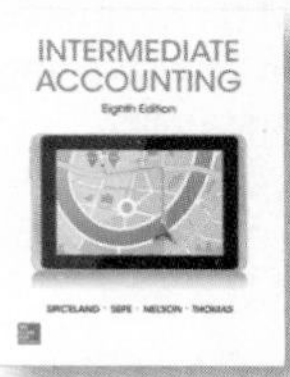

Profitability is the key to a company's long-run survival. A summary measure of profitability often used by investors and potential investors, particularly common shareholders, is the return on shareholders' equity. This ratio measures the ability of company management to generate net income from the resources that owners provide. The ratio is computed by dividing net income by average shareholders' equity. A variation of this ratio often is used when a company has both preferred and common stock outstanding. The return to common shareholders' equity is calculated by subtracting dividends to preferred shareholders from the numerator and using average common shareholders' equity as the denominator. The modified ratio focuses on the profits generated on the assets provided by common shareholders.

The return on shareholders' equity is a popular measure of profitability.

Although the ratio is useful when evaluating the effectiveness of management in employing resources provided by owners, analysts must be careful not to view it in isolation or without considering how the ratio is derived. Keep in mind that shareholders' equity is a measure of the book value of equity, equivalent to the book value of net assets. Book value measures quickly become out of line with market values. An asset's book value usually equals its market value on the date it's purchased; the two aren't necessarily the same after that. Equivalently, the market value of a share of stock (or of total shareholders' equity) usually is different from its book value. As a result, to supplement the return on shareholders' equity ratio, analysts often relate earnings to the market value of equity, calculating the earnings-price ratio. This ratio is simply the earnings per share divided by the market price per share.

Book value measures have limited use in financial analysis.

To better understand the differences between the book value ratio and the market value ratio, let's consider the following condensed information reported by Sharp-Novell Industries for 2016 and 2015:

($ in 000s except per share amounts)	2016	2015
Sales	$3,500	$3,100
Net income	125	114
Current assets	$ 750	$ 720
Property, plant, and equipment (net)	900	850
Total assets	$1,650	$1,570
Current liabilities	$ 550	$ 530
Long-term liabilities	540	520
Paid-in capital	210	210
Retained earnings	350	310
Liabilities and shareholders' equity	$1,650	$1,570
Shares outstanding	50,000	50,000
Stock price (average)	$42.50	$42.50

The 2016 return on shareholders' equity is computed by dividing net income by average shareholders' equity:

$$\$125 \div [(\$560 + 520)/2] = \underline{\underline{23.1\%}}$$

The earnings-price ratio is the earnings per share divided by the market price per share:

$$\text{Earnings per share (2016)} = \$125 \div 50 = \$2.50$$
$$\text{Earnings-price ratio} = \$2.50 \div 42.50 = \underline{\underline{5.9\%}}$$

Share retirement and treasury stock transactions can affect the return to owners.

Obviously, the return on the market value of equity is much lower than on the book value of equity. This points out the importance of looking at more than a single ratio when making decisions. While 23.1% may seem like a desirable return, 5.9% is not nearly so attractive. Companies often emphasize the return on shareholders' equity in their annual reports. Alert investors should not accept this measure of achievement at face value. For some companies this is a meaningful measure of performance; but for others, the market-based ratio means more, particularly for a mature firm whose book value and market value are more divergent.

Dividend decisions should be evaluated in light of prevailing circumstances.

Decisions managers make with regard to shareholders' equity transactions can significantly impact the return to shareholders. For example, when a company buys back shares of its own stock, the return on shareholders' equity goes up. Net income is divided by a smaller amount of shareholders' equity. On the other hand, the share buyback uses assets, reducing the resources available to earn net income in the future. So, managers as well as outside analysts must carefully consider the decision to reacquire shares in light of the current economic environment, the firm's investment opportunities, and cost of capital to decide whether such a transaction is in the long-term best interests of owners. Investors should be wary of buybacks during down times because the resulting decrease in shares and increase in earnings per share can be used to mask a slowdown in earnings growth.

The decision to pay dividends requires similar considerations. When earnings are high, are shareholders better off receiving substantial cash dividends or having management reinvest those funds to finance future growth (and future dividends)? The answer, of course, depends on the particular circumstances involved. Dividend decisions should reflect managerial strategy concerning the mix of internal versus external financing, alternative investment opportunities, and industry conditions. High dividends often are found in mature industries and low dividends in growth industries. ●

Ethical Dilemma

Interworld Distributors has paid quarterly cash dividends since 1980. The dividends have steadily increased from $.25 per share to the latest dividend declaration of $2.00 per share. The board of directors is eager to continue this trend despite the fact that revenues fell significantly during recent months as a result of worsening economic conditions and increased competition. The company founder and member of the board proposes a solution. He suggests a 5% stock dividend in lieu of a cash dividend to be accompanied by the following press announcement:

"In lieu of our regular $2.00 per share cash dividend, Interworld will distribute a 5% stock dividend on its common shares, currently trading at $40 per share. Changing the form of the dividend will permit the Company to direct available cash resources to the modernization of physical facilities in preparation for competing in the 21st century."

What do you think?

Concept Review Exercise

CHANGES IN RETAINED EARNINGS

Situation: The shareholders' equity section of the balance sheet of National Foods, Inc., included the following accounts at December 31, 2016:

Shareholders' Equity	($ in millions)
Paid-in capital	
Preferred stock, 9.09%, 11 million shares at $1 par	$ 11
Common stock, 122 million shares at $1 par	122
Paid-in capital—excess of par, preferred	479
Paid-in capital—excess of par, common	854
Retained earnings	3,245
Treasury stock, at cost, 2 million common shares	(20)
Total shareholders' equity	$4,691

Required:

1. During 2017, several events and transactions affected the retained earnings of National Foods. Prepare the appropriate entries for these events.
   a. On March 1, the board of directors declared a cash dividend of $1 per share on its 120 million outstanding shares (122 million − 2 million treasury shares), payable on April 3 to shareholders of record March 11.
   b. On March 5, the board of directors declared a property dividend of 120 million shares of **Kroger** common stock that National Foods had purchased in February as an investment (book value: $900 million). The investment shares had a fair value of $8 per share and were distributed March 30 to shareholders of record March 15.
   c. On April 13, a 3-for-2 stock split was declared and distributed. The stock split was effected in the form of a 50% stock dividend. The market value of the $1 par common stock was $20 per share.
   d. On October 13, a 10% common stock dividend was declared and distributed when the market value of the $1 par common stock was $12 per share. Cash in lieu of payments was distributed for fractional shares equivalent to 1 million whole shares.
   e. On December 1, the board of directors declared the 9.09% cash dividend on the 11 million preferred shares, payable on December 23 to shareholders of record December 11.
2. Prepare a statement of shareholders' equity for National Foods reporting the changes in shareholders' equity accounts for 2015, 2016, and 2017. Refer to the previous two Concept Reviews in this chapter for the 2015 and 2016 changes. For 2016, assume that shares were reacquired as treasury stock. Also, look back to the statement of shareholders' equity in Illustration 18–4 on page 1073 for the format of the statement. Assume that net income for 2017 is $225 million.

Solution:

1. During 2017, several events and transactions affected the retained earnings of National Foods. Prepare the appropriate entries for these events.
   a. Cash dividend of $1 per share on its 120 million *outstanding* common shares (122 million − 2 million treasury shares), payable on April 3 to shareholders of record March 11 (Note: Dividends aren't paid on treasury shares.):

March 1—Declaration Date	($ in millions)	
Retained earnings	120	
Cash dividends payable (120 million shares at $1/share)		120
March 11—Date of Record		
No entry		
April 3—Payment Date		
Cash dividends payable	120	
Cash		120

The declaration of a dividend reduces retained earnings and creates a liability.

b. Property dividend of 120 million shares of Kroger common stock:

The investment first must be written up to the $960 million fair value ($8 × 120 million shares).

The liability is satisfied when the Kroger shares are distributed to shareholders.

	($ in millions)	
March 5—Declaration Date		
Investment in Kroger common stock	60	
Gain on appreciation of investment ($960 − 900)		60
Retained earnings (fair value of asset to be distributed)	960	
Property dividends payable		960
March 15—Date of Record		
No entry		
March 30—Payment Date		
Property dividends payable	960	
Investment in Kroger common stock		960

c. 3-for-2 stock split effected in the form of a 50% stock dividend:

120 million shares times 50% equals 60 million new shares—recorded at par.

April 13		
Paid-in capital—excess of par*	60	
Common stock (60 million shares at $1 par per share)		60

*Alternatively, retained earnings may be debited.

d. 10% common stock dividend—with cash in lieu of payments for shares equivalent to 1 million whole shares:

The stock dividend occurs after the 3-for-2 stock split; thus 18 million shares are distributed.

The $12 fair value of the additional shares is capitalized in this small stock dividend.

October 13		
Retained earnings (18 million shares* at $12 per share)	216	
Common stock (17 million shares at $1 par per share)		17
Paid-in capital—excess of par		
(17 million shares at $11 per share above par)		187
Cash (1 million equivalent shares at $12 market price per share)		12

*(120 million + 60 million) × 10% = 18 million shares

e. 9.09% cash dividend on the 11 million preferred shares, payable on December 23 to shareholders of record December 11:

Preferred shareholders annually receive the designated percentage (9.09%) of the preferred's par value ($1 million), if dividends are declared.

	($ in millions)	
December 1—Declaration Date		
Retained earnings	1	
Cash dividends payable ($11 million par × 9.09%)		1
December 11—Date of Record		
No entry		
December 23—Payment Date		
Cash dividends payable	1	
Cash		1

2. Prepare a statement of shareholders' equity for National Foods reporting the changes in shareholders' equity accounts for 2015, 2016, and 2017.

These are the transactions from Concept Review Exercise—Expansion of Corporate Capital.

NATIONAL FOODS
Statement of Shareholders' Equity
For the Years Ended December 31, 2017, 2016, and 2015

($ in millions)

	Preferred Stock	Common Stock	Additional Paid-In Capital	Retained Earnings	Treasury Stock (at cost)	Total Shareholders' Equity
Balance at January 1, 2015		120	836	2,449		3,405
Sale of preferred shares	10		430			440
Issuance of common shares		1	9			10

(continued)

(concluded)

	Preferred Stock	Common Stock	Additional Paid-In Capital	Retained Earnings	Treasury Stock (at cost)	Total Share-holders' Equity
Issuance of common and preferred shares	1	1	58			60
Net income				400		400
Cash dividends, preferred	—	—	—	—	—	(1)
Balance at December 31, 2015	11	122	1,333	2,848		4,314
Purchase of treasury shares					(60)	(60)
Sale of treasury shares			4		20	24
Sale of treasury shares			(4)	(2)	20	14
Net income				400		400
Cash dividends, preferred	—	—	—	(1)	—	(1)
Balance at December 31, 2016	11	122	1,333	3,245	(20)	4,691
Cash dividends, common				(120)		(120)
Property dividends, common				(960)		(960)
3-for-2 split effected in the form of a stock dividend		60	(60)			
10% stock dividend		17	187	(216)		(12)
Preferred dividends				(1)		(1)
Net income	—	—	—	225	—	225
Balance at December 31, 2017	11	199	1,460	2,173	(20)	3,823

These are the transactions from Concept Review Exercise—Treasury Stock.

These are the transactions from Concept Review Exercise—Changes in Retained Earnings.

Financial Reporting Case Solution

1. **Do you think the stock price increase is related to MasterCard's share repurchase plan?** *(p. 1083)* The stock price increase probably is related to MasterCard's buyback plan. The marketplace realizes that decreasing the supply of shares supports the price of remaining shares. However, the repurchase of shares is not necessarily the best use of a company's cash. Whether it is in the shareholders' best interests depends on what other opportunities the company has for the cash available.
2. **What are MasterCard's choices in accounting for the share repurchases?** *(p. 1084)* When a corporation reacquires its own shares, those shares assume the same status as authorized but unissued shares, just as if they never had been issued. However, for exactly the same transaction, companies can choose between two accounting alternatives: (a) formally retiring them or (b) accounting for the shares repurchased as treasury stock. In actuality, MasterCard's uses alternative (b).
3. **What effect does the quarterly cash dividend of $1.10 share have on MasterCard's assets? Its liabilities? Its shareholders' equity?** *(p. 1090)* Each quarter, when directors declare a cash dividend, retained earnings are reduced and a liability is recorded. The liability is paid with cash on the payment date. So, the net effect is a decrease in MasterCard's assets and its shareholders' equity. The effect on liabilities is temporary.
4. **What effect does the stock split have on MasterCard's assets? Its liabilities? Its shareholders' equity?** *(p. 1093)* Conceptually, the proper accounting treatment of a stock split is to make no journal entry. However, since MasterCard refers to the stock distribution as a "stock split effected through a stock dividend," a journal entry would increase the common stock account by the par value of the additional shares and would reduce paid-in capital—excess of par. This merely moves an amount from one part of shareholders' equity to another. Regardless of the accounting method, there is no change in MasterCard's assets, liabilities, or total shareholders' equity. ●

The Bottom Line

- **LO18–1** Shareholders' equity is the owners' residual interest in a corporation's assets. It arises primarily from (1) amounts invested by shareholders and (2) amounts earned by the corporation on behalf of its shareholders. These are reported as (1) paid-in capital and (2) retained earnings in a balance sheet. A statement of shareholders' equity reports the sources of the changes in individual shareholders' equity accounts. (*p. 1068*)
- **LO18–2** Comprehensive income encompasses all changes in equity except those caused by transactions with owners (like dividends and the sale or purchase of shares). It includes traditional net income as well as "other comprehensive income." (*p. 1070*)
- **LO18–3** A corporation is a separate legal entity—separate and distinct from its owners. A corporation is well suited to raising capital and has limited liability. However, it is subject to "double taxation." Common shareholders usually have voting rights; preferred shareholders usually have a preference to a specified amount of dividends and to assets in the event of liquidation. (*p. 1073*)
- **LO18–4** Shares sold for consideration other than cash (maybe services or a noncash asset) should be recorded at the fair value of the shares or the noncash consideration, whichever seems more clearly evident. (*p. 1079*)
- **LO18–5** When a corporation retires previously issued shares, those shares assume the same status as authorized but unissued shares—just the same as if they had never been issued. Payments made to retire shares are viewed as a distribution of corporate assets to shareholders. When reacquired shares are viewed as treasury stock, the cost of acquiring the shares is temporarily debited to the treasury stock account. Recording the effects on specific shareholders' equity accounts is delayed until later when the shares are reissued. (*p. 1083*)
- **LO18–6** Retained earnings represents, in general, a corporation's accumulated, undistributed or reinvested net income (or net loss). Distributions of earned assets are dividends. (*p. 1089*)
- **LO18–7** Most corporate dividends are paid in cash. When a noncash asset is distributed, it is referred to as a property dividend. The fair value of the assets to be distributed is the amount recorded for a property dividend. (*p. 1089*)
- **LO18–8** A stock dividend is the distribution of additional shares of stock to current shareholders. For a small stock dividend (25% or less), the fair value of the additional shares distributed is transferred from retained earnings to paid-in capital. For a stock distribution of 25% or higher, the par value of the additional shares is reclassified within shareholders' equity if referred to as a stock split effected in the form of a stock dividend, but if referred to merely as a stock split, no journal entry is recorded. (*p. 1091*)
- **LO18–9** U.S. GAAP and IFRS are generally compatible with respect to accounting for shareholders' equity. Some differences exist in presentation format and terminology. (*pp. 1072* and *1078*)

APPENDIX 18 Quasi Reorganizations

A firm undergoing financial difficulties, but with favorable future prospects, may use a **quasi reorganization** to write down inflated asset values and eliminate an accumulated deficit (debit balance in retained earnings). To effect the reorganization the following procedures are followed:

1. The firm's assets (and perhaps liabilities) are revalued (up or down) to reflect fair values, with corresponding credits or debits to retained earnings. This process typically increases the deficit.
2. The debit balance in retained earnings (deficit) is eliminated against additional paid-in capital. If additional paid-in capital is not sufficient to absorb the entire deficit, a reduction in stock may be necessary (with an appropriate restating of the par amount per share).
3. Retained earnings is dated. That is, disclosure is provided to indicate the date the deficit was eliminated and when the new accumulation of earnings began.

The procedure is demonstrated in Illustration 18A–1. The shareholders approved the quasi reorganization effective January 1, 2016. The plan was to be accomplished by a reduction of inventory by $75 million, a reduction in property, plant, and equipment (net) of $175 million, and appropriate adjustments to shareholders' equity.

Illustration 18A–1
Quasi Reorganization

The Emerson-Walsch Corporation has incurred operating losses for several years. A newly elected board of directors voted to implement a quasi reorganization, subject to shareholder approval. The balance sheet, on December 31, 2015, immediately prior to the restatement, includes the data shown below.

	($ in millions)
Cash	$ 75
Receivables	200
Inventory	375
Property, plant, and equipment (net)	400
	$1,050
Liabilities	$ 400
Common stock (800 million shares at $1 par)	800
Additional paid-in capital	150
Retained earnings (deficit)	(300)
	$1,050

To Revalue Assets:

Retained earnings	75	
Inventory		75
Retained earnings	175	
Property, plant, and equipment		175

When assets are revalued to reflect fair values, the process often increases the deficit.

To Eliminate a Portion of the Deficit against Available Additional Paid-In Capital:

Additional paid-in capital	150	
Retained earnings		150

The deficit, $550 ($300 + 75 + 175), can be only partially absorbed by the balance of additional paid-in capital.

To Eliminate the Remainder of the Deficit against Common Stock:

Common stock	400	
Retained earnings		400

The remaining deficit, $400 ($300 + 75 + 175 − 150), must be absorbed by reducing the balance in common stock.

The balance sheet immediately after the restatement would include the following:

	($ in millions)
Cash	$ 75
Receivables	200
Inventory	300
Property, plant, and equipment (net)	225
	$800
Liabilities	$400
Common stock (800 million shares at $.50 par)	400
Additional paid-in capital	0
Retained earnings (deficit)	0
	$800

Assets and liabilities reflect current values.

Because a reduced balance represents the same 800 million shares, the par amount per share must be reduced.

The deficit is eliminated.

Note A: Upon the recommendation of the board of directors and approval by shareholders a quasi reorganization was implemented January 1, 2016. The plan was accomplished by a reduction of inventory by $75 million, a reduction in property, plant, and equipment (net) of $175 million, and appropriate adjustments to shareholders' equity. The balance in retained earnings reflects the elimination of a $300 million deficit on that date.

Questions For Review of Key Topics

Q 18–1 Identify and briefly describe the two primary sources of shareholders' equity.

Q 18–2 Identify the three common forms of business organization and the primary difference between the way they are accounted for.

Q 18–3 Corporations offer the advantage of limited liability. Explain what is meant by that statement.

Q 18–4 Distinguish between not-for-profit and for-profit corporations.

Q 18–5 Distinguish between publicly held and privately (or closely) held corporations.

Q 18–6 How does the Model Business Corporation Act affect the way corporations operate?

Q 18–7 The owners of a corporation are its shareholders. If a corporation has only one class of shares, they typically are labeled common shares. Indicate the ownership rights held by common shareholders, unless specifically withheld by agreement.

Q 18–8 What is meant by a shareholder's preemptive right?

Q 18–9 Terminology varies in the way companies differentiate among share types. But many corporations designate shares as common or preferred. What are the two special rights usually given to preferred shareholders?

Q 18–10 Most preferred shares are cumulative. Explain what this means.

Q 18–11 The par value of shares historically indicated the real value of shares and all shares were issued at that price. The concept has changed with time. Describe the meaning of par value as it has evolved to today.

Q 18–12 What is comprehensive income? How does comprehensive income differ from net income? Where do companies report it in a balance sheet?

Q 18–13 How do we report components of comprehensive income *created during the reporting period?*

Q 18–14 The balance sheet reports the balances of shareholders' equity accounts. What additional information is provided by the statement of shareholders' equity?

Q 18–15 At times, companies issue their shares for consideration other than cash. What is the measurement objective in those cases?

Q 18–16 Companies occasionally sell more than one security for a single price. How is the issue price allocated among the separate securities?

Q 18–17 The costs of legal, promotional, and accounting services necessary to effect the sale of shares are referred to as share issue costs. How are these costs recorded? Compare this approach to the way debt issue costs are recorded.

Q 18–18 When a corporation acquires its own shares, those shares assume the same status as authorized but unissued shares, as if they never had been issued. Explain how this is reflected in the accounting records if the shares are formally retired.

Q 18–19 Discuss the conceptual basis for accounting for a share buyback as treasury stock.

Q 18–20 The prescribed accounting treatment for stock dividends implicitly assumes that shareholders are fooled by small stock dividends and benefit by the market value of their additional shares. Explain this statement. Is it logical?

Q 18–21 Brandon Components declares a 2-for-1 stock split. What will be the effects of the split, and how should it be recorded?

Q 18–22 What is a reverse stock split? What would be the effect of a reverse stock split on one million $1 par shares? On the accounting records?

Q 18–23 Suppose you own 80 shares of **Facebook** common stock when the company declares a 4% stock dividend. What will you receive as a result?

Q 18–24 (Based on Appendix 18) A quasi reorganization is sometimes employed by a firm undergoing financial difficulties, but with favorable future prospects. What are two objectives of this procedure? Briefly describe the procedural steps.

Brief Exercises

BE 18–1
Comprehensive income
● LO18–1

Schaeffer Corporation reports $50 million accumulated other comprehensive income in its balance sheet as a component of shareholders' equity. In a related statement reporting comprehensive income for the year, the company reveals net income of $400 million and other comprehensive income of $15 million. What was the balance in accumulated other comprehensive income in last year's balance sheet?

BE 18–2
Stock issued
● LO18–4

Penne Pharmaceuticals sold 8 million shares of its $1 par common stock to provide funds for research and development. If the issue price is $12 per share, what is the journal entry to record the sale of the shares?

BE 18–3
Stock issued
● LO18–4

Lewelling Company issued 100,000 shares of its $1 par common stock to the Michael Morgan law firm as compensation for 4,000 hours of legal services performed. Morgan's usual rate is $240 per hour. By what amount should Lewelling's paid-in capital—excess of par increase as a result of this transaction?

BE 18–4
Stock issued
● LO18–4

Hamilton Boats issued 175,000 shares of its no par common stock to Sudoku Motors in exchange for 1,000 four-stroke outboard motors that normally sell in quantity for $3,500 each. By what amount should Hamilton's shareholders' equity increase as a result of this transaction?

BE 18–5
Effect of preferred stock on dividends
● LO18–4

The shareholders' equity of MLS Enterprises includes $200 million of no par common stock and $400 million of 6% cumulative preferred stock. The board of directors of MLS declared cash dividends of $50 million in 2016 after paying $20 million cash dividends in both 2015 and 2014. What is the amount of dividends common shareholders will receive in 2016?

BE 18–6
Retirement of shares
● LO18–5

Horton Industries' shareholders' equity included 100 million shares of $1 par common stock and a balance in paid-in capital—excess of par of $900 million. Assuming that Horton retires shares it reacquires (restores their status to that of authorized but unissued shares), by what amount will Horton's total paid-in capital decline if it reacquires 2 million shares at $8.50 per share?

BE 18–7
Retirement of shares
● LO18–5

Agee Storage issued 35 million shares of its $1 par common stock at $16 per share several years ago. Last year, for the first time, Agee reacquired 1 million shares at $14 per share. Assuming that Agee retires shares it reacquires (restores their status to that of authorized but unissued shares), by what amount will Agee's total paid-in capital decline if it now reacquires 1 million shares at $19 per share?

BE 18–8
Treasury stock
● LO18–5

The Jennings Group reacquired 2 million of its shares at $70 per share as treasury stock. Last year, for the first time, Jennings sold 1 million treasury shares at $71 per share. By what amount will Jennings' retained earnings decline if it now sells the remaining 1 million treasury shares at $67 per share?

BE 18–9
Treasury stock
● LO18–5

In previous years, Cox Transport reacquired 2 million treasury shares at $20 per share and, later, 1 million treasury shares at $26 per share. By what amount will Cox's paid-in capital—share repurchase increase if it now sells 1 million treasury shares at $29 per share and determines cost as the weighted-average cost of treasury shares?

BE 18–10
Treasury stock
● LO18–5

Refer to the situation described in BE 18–9. By what amount will Cox's paid-in capital—share repurchase increase if it determines the cost of treasury shares by the FIFO method?

BE 18–11
Cash dividend
● LO18–8
Real World Financials

Following is a recent **Microsoft** press release:

REDMOND, Wash.—March 15, 2014— Microsoft Corp. today announced that its board of directors declared a quarterly dividend of $0.28 per share. The dividend is payable June 12, 2014 to shareholders of record on May 15, 2014.

Prepare the journal entries Microsoft used to record the declaration and payment of the cash dividend for its 8,260 million shares.

BE 18–12
Property dividend
● LO18–7

Adams Moving and Storage, a family-owned corporation, declared a property dividend of 1,000 shares of **GE** common stock that Adams had purchased in February for $37,000 as an investment. GE's shares had a market value of $35 per share on the declaration date. Prepare the journal entries to record the property dividend on the declaration and payment dates.

BE 18–13
Stock dividend
● LO18–8

On June 13, the board of directors of Siewert Inc. declared a 5% stock dividend on its 60 million, $1 par, common shares, to be distributed on July 1. The market price of Siewert common stock was $25 on June 13. Prepare the journal entry to record the stock dividend.

BE 18–14
Stock split
● LO18–8

Refer to the situation described in BE 18–13, but assume a 2-for-1 stock split instead of the 5% stock dividend. Prepare the journal entry to record the stock split if it is *not* to be effected in the form of a stock dividend. What is the par per share after the split?

BE 18–15
Stock split
● LO18–8

Refer to the situation described in BE 18–13, but assume a 2-for-1 stock split instead of the 5% stock dividend. Prepare the journal entry to record the stock split if it is to be effected in the form of a 100% stock dividend. What is the par per share after the split?

BE 18–16
IFRS; reporting shareholders' equity
● LO18–9

Nestlé S.A., the largest food and beverage company in the world, prepares its financial statements according to International Financial Reporting Standards. Its financial statements include ordinary share capital, translation reserve, and share premium. If Nestlé used U.S. GAAP, what would be the likely account titles for these accounts?

Exercises

An alternate exercise and problem set is available in the Connect library.

E 18–1
Comprehensive income
● LO18–2

The following is from the 2016 annual report of Kaufman Chemicals, Inc.:

Statements of Comprehensive Income

Years Ended December 31	2016	2015	2014
Net income	$856	$766	$594
Other comprehensive income:			
Change in net unrealized gains on investments, net of tax of $22, ($14), and $15 in 2016, 2015, and 2014, respectively	34	(21)	23
Other	(2)	(1)	1
Total comprehensive income	$888	$744	$618

Kaufman reports accumulated other comprehensive income in its balance sheet as a component of shareholders' equity as follows:

	($ in millions)	
	2016	**2015**
Shareholders' equity:		
Common stock	355	355
Additional paid-in capital	8,567	8,567
Retained earnings	6,544	5,988
Accumulated other comprehensive income	107	75
Total shareholders' equity	$15,573	$14,985

Required:

1. What is comprehensive income and how does it differ from net income?
2. How is comprehensive income reported in a balance sheet?
3. Why is Kaufman's 2016 balance sheet amount different from the 2016 amount reported in the disclosure note? Explain.
4. From the information provided, determine how Kaufman calculated the $107 million accumulated other comprehensive income in 2016.

E 18–2
FASB codification research; reporting other comprehensive income in shareholders' equity
● LO18–2

Companies are required to transfer "other comprehensive income" each period to shareholders' equity. The *FASB Accounting Standards Codification* represents the single source of authoritative U.S. generally accepted accounting principles.

Required:

1. Obtain the relevant authoritative literature on reporting other comprehensive income in shareholders' equity using the *FASB Accounting Standards Codification* at the FASB website (asc.fasb.org). What is the specific citation that describes the guidelines for reporting that component of shareholders' equity?

2. What is the specific citation that describes the guidelines for presenting accumulated other comprehensive income on the statement of shareholders' equity?

E 18–3
Earnings or OCI?
● LO18–2

Indicate by letter whether each of the items listed below most likely is reported in the income statement as Net Income (**NI**) or in the statement of comprehensive income as Other Comprehensive Income (**OCI**).

Items

______ 1. Increase in the fair value of investments in available-for-sale securities
______ 2. Gain on sale of land
______ 3. Loss on pension plan assets (actual return less than expected)
______ 4. Gain from foreign currency translation
______ 5. Increase in the fair value of investments in trading securities
______ 6. Loss from revising an assumption related to a pension plan
______ 7. Loss on sale of patent
______ 8. Prior service cost
______ 9. Increase in the fair value of bonds outstanding due to change in general interest rates; fair value option
______ 10. Gain on postretirement plan assets (actual return more than expected)

E 18–4
Stock issued for cash; Wright Medical Group
● LO18–4
Real World Financials

The following is a news item reported by Reuters:

WASHINGTON, Jan 29 (Reuters)—**Wright Medical Group**, a maker of reconstructive implants for knees and hips, on Tuesday filed to sell 3 million shares of common stock.

In a filing with the U.S. Securities and Exchange Commission, it said it plans to use the proceeds from the offering for general corporate purposes, working capital, research and development, and acquisitions.

After the sale there will be about 31.5 million shares outstanding in the Arlington, Tennessee-based company, according to the SEC filing.

Wright shares closed at $17.15 on Nasdaq.

The common stock of Wright Medical Group has a par of $.01 per share.

Required:
Prepare the journal entry to record the sale of the shares assuming the price existing when the announcement was made and ignoring share issue costs.

E 18–5
Issuance of shares; noncash consideration
● LO18–4

During its first year of operations, Eastern Data Links Corporation entered into the following transactions relating to shareholders' equity. The articles of incorporation authorized the issue of 8 million common shares, $1 par per share, and 1 million preferred shares, $50 par per share.

Required:
Prepare the appropriate journal entries to record each transaction.

Feb. 12	Sold 2 million common shares, for $9 per share.
13	Issued 40,000 common shares to attorneys in exchange for legal services.
13	Sold 80,000 of its common shares and 4,000 preferred shares for a total of $945,000.
Nov. 15	Issued 380,000 of its common shares in exchange for equipment for which the cash price was known to be $3,688,000.

E 18–6
Redeemable shares
● LO18–4

Williams Industries has outstanding 30 million common shares, 20 million Class A shares, and 20 million Class B shares. Williams has the right but not the obligation to repurchase the Class A shares if a change in ownership of the voting common shares causes J. P. Williams, founder and CEO, to have less than 50% ownership. Williams has the unconditional obligation to repurchase the Class B shares upon the death of J. P. Williams.

Required:
Which, if any, of the shares should be reported in Williams' balance sheet as liabilities? Explain.

E 18–7
Share issue costs; issuance
● LO18–4

ICOT Industries issued 15 million of its $1 par common shares for $424 million on April 11. Legal, promotional, and accounting services necessary to effect the sale cost $2 million.

Required:
1. Prepare the journal entry to record the issuance of the shares.
2. Explain how recording the share issue costs differs from the way debt issue costs are recorded.

E 18–8
Reporting preferred shares
● LO18–4

Ozark Distributing Company is primarily engaged in the wholesale distribution of consumer products in the Ozark Mountain regions. The following disclosure note appeared in the company's 2016 annual report:

Note 5. Convertible Preferred Stock (in part):
The Company has the following Convertible Preferred Stock outstanding as of September 2016:

Date of issuance:	June 17, 2013
Optionally redeemable beginning	June 18, 2015
Par value (gross proceeds):	$2,500,000
Number of shares:	100,000
Liquidation preference per share:	$25.00
Conversion price per share:	$30.31
Number of common shares in which to be converted:	82,481
Dividend rate:	6.785%

The Preferred Stock is convertible at any time by the holders into a number of shares of Ozark's common stock equal to the number of preferred shares being converted times a fraction equal to $25.00 divided by the conversion price. The conversion prices for the Preferred Stock are subject to customary adjustments in the event of stock splits, stock dividends and certain other distributions on the Common Stock. Cumulative dividends for the Preferred Stock are payable in arrears, when, as and if declared by the Board of Directors, on March 31, June 30, September 30, and December 31 of each year.

The Preferred Stock is optionally redeemable by the Company beginning on various dates, as listed above, at redemption prices equal to 112% of the liquidation preference. The redemption prices decrease 1% annually thereafter until the redemption price equals the liquidation preference after which date it remains the liquidation preference.

Required:

1. What amount of dividends is paid annually to a preferred shareholder owning 100 shares of the Series A preferred stock?
2. If dividends are not paid in 2017 and 2018, but are paid in 2019, what amount of dividends will the shareholder receive?
3. If the investor chooses to convert the shares in 2017, how many shares of common stock will the investor receive for his/her 100 shares?
4. If Ozark chooses to redeem the shares on June 18, 2017, what amount will the investor be paid for his/her 100 shares?

E 18–9
New equity issues; offerings announcements
● LO18–4

When companies offer new equity security issues, they publicize the offerings in the financial press and on Internet sites. Assume the following were among the equity offerings reported in December 2016:

New Securities Issues

Equity

American Materials Transfer Corporation (AMTC)—7.5 million common shares, $.001 par, priced at $13.546 each through underwriters led by Second Tennessee Bank N.A. and Morgan, Dunavant & Co., according to a syndicate official.

Proactive Solutions Inc. (PSI)—Offering of nine million common shares, $.01 par, was priced at $15.20 a share via lead manager Stanley Brothers, Inc., according to a syndicate official.

Required:

Prepare the appropriate journal entries to record the sale of both issues to underwriters. Ignore share issue costs.

E 18–10
Effect of cumulative, nonparticipating preferred stock on dividends—3 years
● LO18–4

The shareholders' equity of WBL Industries includes the items shown below. The board of directors of WBL declared cash dividends of $8 million, $20 million, and $150 million in its first three years of operation—2016, 2017, and 2018, respectively.

	($ in millions)
Common stock	$100
Paid-in capital—excess of par, common	980
Preferred stock, 8%	200
Paid-in capital—excess of par, preferred	555

Required:
Determine the amount of dividends to be paid to preferred and common shareholders in each of the three years, assuming that the preferred stock is cumulative and nonparticipating.

	Preferred	Common
2016		
2017		
2018		

E 18–11
Retirement of shares
● LO18–5

Borner Communications' articles of incorporation authorized the issuance of 130 million common shares. The transactions described below effected changes in Borner's outstanding shares. Prior to the transactions, Borner's shareholders' equity included the following:

Shareholders' Equity	($ in millions)
Common stock, 100 million shares at $1 par	$100
Paid-in capital—excess of par	300
Retained earnings	210

Required:
Assuming that Borner Communications retires shares it reacquires (restores their status to that of authorized but unissued shares), record the appropriate journal entry for each of the following transactions:
1. On January 7, 2016, Borner reacquired 2 million shares at $5.00 per share.
2. On August 23, 2016, Borner reacquired 4 million shares at $3.50 per share.
3. On July 25, 2017, Borner sold 3 million common shares at $6 per share.

E 18–12
Retirement of shares
● LO18–5

In 2016, Borland Semiconductors entered into the transactions described below. In 2013, Borland had issued 170 million shares of its $1 par common stock at $34 per share.

Required:
Assuming that Borland retires shares it reacquires, record the appropriate journal entry for each of the following transactions:
1. On January 2, 2016, Borland reacquired 10 million shares at $32.50 per share.
2. On March 3, 2016, Borland reacquired 10 million shares at $36 per share.
3. On August 13, 2016, Borland sold 1 million shares at $42 per share.
4. On December 15, 2016, Borland sold 2 million shares at $36 per share.

E 18–13
Treasury stock
● LO18–5

In 2016, Western Transport Company entered into the treasury stock transactions described below. In 2014, Western Transport had issued 140 million shares of its $1 par common stock at $17 per share.

Required:
Prepare the appropriate journal entry for each of the following transactions:
1. On January 23, 2016, Western Transport reacquired 10 million shares at $20 per share.
2. On September 3, 2016, Western Transport sold 1 million treasury shares at $21 per share.
3. On November 4, 2016, Western Transport sold 1 million treasury shares at $18 per share.

E 18–14
Treasury stock; weighted-average and FIFO cost
● LO18–5

At December 31, 2015, the balance sheet of Meca International included the following shareholders' equity accounts:

Shareholders' Equity	($ in millions)
Common stock, 60 million shares at $1 par	$ 60
Paid-in capital—excess of par	300
Retained earnings	410

Required:
Assuming that Meca International views its share buybacks as treasury stock, record the appropriate journal entry for each of the following transactions:
1. On February 12, 2016, Meca reacquired 1 million common shares at $13 per share.
2. On June 9, 2017, Meca reacquired 2 million common shares at $10 per share.
3. On May 25, 2018, Meca sold 2 million treasury shares at $15 per share—determine cost as the weighted-average cost of treasury shares.
4. For the previous transaction, assume Meca determines the cost of treasury shares by the FIFO method.

E 18–15
Reporting shareholders' equity after share repurchase
● LO18–5

On two previous occasions, the management of Dennison and Company, Inc., repurchased some of its common shares. Between buyback transactions, the corporation issued common shares under its management incentive plan. Shown below is shareholders' equity following these share transactions, as reported by two different methods of accounting for reacquired shares.

	($ in millions)	
	Method A	**Method B**
Shareholders' equity		
Paid-in capital:		
Preferred stock, $10 par	$ 150	$ 150
Common stock, $1 par	200	197
Additional paid-in capital	1,204	1,201
Retained earnings	2,994	2,979
Less: Treasury stock	(21)	
Total shareholders' equity	$4,527	$4,527

Required:

1. Infer from the presentation which method of accounting for reacquired shares is represented by each of the two columns.
2. Explain why presentation formats are different and why some account balances are different for the two methods.

E 18–16
Change from treasury stock to retired stock
● LO18–5

In keeping with a modernization of corporate statutes in its home state, UMC Corporation decided in 2016 to discontinue accounting for reacquired shares as treasury stock. Instead, shares repurchased will be viewed as having been retired, reassuming the status of unissued shares. As part of the change, treasury shares held were reclassified as retired stock. At December 31, 2015, UMC's balance sheet reported the following shareholders' equity:

	($ in millions)
Common stock, $1 par	$ 200
Paid-in capital—excess of par	800
Retained earnings	956
Treasury stock (4 million shares at cost)	(25)
Total shareholders' equity	$1,931

Required:

Identify the type of accounting change this decision represents, and prepare the journal entry to effect the reclassification of treasury shares as retired shares.

E 18–17
Stock buyback; Ford press announcement
● LO18–5

Real World Financials

The following excerpt is from an article reported in the May 7, 2014, online issue of **Bloomberg**.

(Blomberg) **Ford Motor Co.** (F) said it will repurchase $1.8 billion of its shares to reduce dilution from recent stock grants to executives.

The par amount per share for Ford's common stock is $0.01. Paid-in capital—excess of par is $5.39 per share on average. The market price was $16.

Required:

1. Suppose Ford reacquires 112 million shares through repurchase on the open market at $16 per share. Prepare the appropriate journal entry to record the purchase. Ford considers the shares it buys back to be treasury stock.
2. Suppose Ford considers the shares it buys back to be retired rather than treated as treasury stock. Prepare the appropriate journal entry to record the purchase.
3. What does the company mean by saying that the buyback will serve "to offset dilution from executive compensation"?

E 18–18
Transactions affecting retained earnings
● LO18–6, LO18–7

Shown below in T-account format are the changes affecting the retained earnings of Brenner-Jude Corporation during 2016. At January 1, 2016, the corporation had outstanding 105 million common shares, $1 par per share.

Retained Earnings ($ in millions)

		90	Beginning balance
Retirement of 5 million common shares for $22 million	2		
		88	Net income for the year
Declaration and payment of a $.33 per share cash dividend	33		
Declaration and distribution of a 4% stock dividend	20		
		123	Ending balance

Required:

1. From the information provided by the account changes you should be able to recreate the transactions that affected Brenner-Jude's retained earnings during 2016. Prepare the journal entries that Brenner-Jude must have recorded during the year for these transactions.
2. Prepare a statement of retained earnings for Brenner-Jude for the year ended 2016.

E 18–19
Stock dividend
● LO18–8

The shareholders' equity of Core Technologies Company on June 30, 2015, included the following:

Common stock, $1 par; authorized, 8 million shares; issued and outstanding, 3 million shares	$ 3,000,000
Paid-in capital—excess of par	12,000,000
Retained earnings	14,000,000

On April 1, 2016, the board of directors of Core Technologies declared a 10% stock dividend on common shares, to be distributed on June 1. The market price of Core Technologies' common stock was $30 on April 1, 2016, and $40 on June 1, 2016.

Required:

Prepare the journal entry to record the declaration and distribution of the stock dividend on the declaration date.

E 18–20
Stock split; Hanmi Financial Corporation
● LO18–8
Real World Financials

Hanmi Financial Corporation is the parent company of Hanmi Bank. The company's stock split was announced in the following Business Wire:

> LOS ANGELES (BUSINESS WIRE) Jan. 20—Hanmi Financial Corporation (Nasdaq), announced that the Board of Directors has approved a two-for-one stock split, to be effected in the form of a 100 percent common stock dividend. Hanmi Financial Corporation stockholders of record at the close of business on January 31 will receive one additional share of common stock for every share of common stock then held. Distribution of additional shares issued as a result of the split is expected to occur on or about February 15.

At the time of the stock split, 24.5 million shares of common stock, $.001 par per share, were outstanding.

Required:

1. Prepare the journal entry, if any, that Hanmi recorded at the time of the stock split.
2. What is the probable motivation for declaring the 2-for-1 stock split to be effected by a dividend payable in shares of common stock?
3. If Hanmi's stock price had been $36 at the time of the split, what would be its approximate value after the split (other things equal)?

E 18–21
Cash in lieu of fractional share rights
● LO18–8

Douglas McDonald Company's balance sheet included the following shareholders' equity accounts at December 31, 2015:

	($ in millions)
Paid-in capital:	
Common stock, 900 million shares at $1 par	$ 900
Paid-in capital—excess of par	15,800
Retained earnings	14,888
Total shareholders' equity	$31,588

On March 16, 2016, a 4% common stock dividend was declared and distributed. The market value of the common stock was $21 per share. Fractional share rights represented 2 million equivalent whole shares. Cash was paid in lieu of the fractional share rights.

Required:
1. What is a fractional share right?
2. Prepare the appropriate entries for the declaration and distribution of the stock dividend.

E 18–22
FASB codification research
● LO18–1, LO18–5, LO18–8

Access the *FASB Accounting Standards Codification* at the FASB website (asc.fasb.org). Determine the specific citation for accounting for each of the following items:
1. Requirements to disclose within the financial statements the pertinent rights and privileges of the various securities outstanding.
2. Requirement to record a "small" stock dividend at the fair value of the shares issued.
3. Requirement to exclude from the determination of net income gains and losses on transactions in a company's own stock.

E 18–23
Transactions affecting retained earnings
● LO18–6 through LO18–8

The balance sheet of Consolidated Paper, Inc., included the following shareholders' equity accounts at December 31, 2015:

	($ in millions)
Paid-in capital:	
Preferred stock, 8.8%, 90,000 shares at $1 par	$ 90,000
Common stock, 364,000 shares at $1 par	364,000
Paid-in capital—excess of par, preferred	1,437,000
Paid-in capital—excess of par, common	2,574,000
Retained earnings	9,735,000
Treasury stock, at cost; 4,000 common shares	(44,000)
Total shareholders' equity	$14,156,000

During 2016, several events and transactions affected the retained earnings of Consolidated Paper.

Required:
1. Prepare the appropriate entries for these events:
   a. On March 3 the board of directors declared a property dividend of 240,000 shares of Leasco International common stock that Consolidated Paper had purchased in January as an investment (book value: $700,000). The investment shares had a fair value of $3 per share and were distributed March 31 to shareholders of record March 15.
   b. On May 3 a 5-for-4 stock split was declared and distributed. The stock split was effected in the form of a 25% stock dividend. The market value of the $1 par common stock was $11 per share.
   c. On July 5 a 2% common stock dividend was declared and distributed. The market value of the common stock was $11 per share.
   d. On December 1 the board of directors declared the 8.8% cash dividend on the 90,000 preferred shares, payable on December 28 to shareholders of record December 20.
   e. On December 1 the board of directors declared a cash dividend of $.50 per share on its common shares, payable on December 28 to shareholders of record December 20.
2. Prepare the shareholders' equity section of the balance sheet for Consolidated Paper, Inc., at December 31, 2016. Net income for the year was $810,000.

E 18–24
Profitability ratio
● LO18–1

Comparative balance sheets for Softech Canvas Goods for 2016 and 2015 are shown below. Softech pays no dividends, and instead reinvests all earnings for future growth.

Comparative Balance Sheets
($ in 000s)

	December 31	
	2016	**2015**
Assets:		
Cash	$ 50	$ 40
Accounts receivable	100	120
Short-term investments	50	40
Inventory	200	140
Property, plant, and equipment (net)	600	550
	$1,000	$890

(continued)

(concluded)

Liabilities and Shareholders' Equity:		
Current liabilities	$ 240	$210
Bonds payable	160	160
Paid-in capital	400	400
Retained earnings	200	120
	$1,000	$890

Required:

1. Determine the return on shareholders' equity for 2016.
2. What does the ratio measure?

E 18–25
IFRS; equity terminology
● LO18–9

IFRS

Indicate by letter whether each of the terms or phrases listed below is more associated with financial statements prepared in accordance with U.S. GAAP (**U**) or International Financial Reporting Standards (**I**).

Terms and phrases

_____ 1. Common stock
_____ 2. Preference shares
_____ 3. Liabilities often listed before equity in the balance sheet (statement of financial position)
_____ 4. Asset revaluation reserve
_____ 5. Accumulated other comprehensive income
_____ 6. Share premium
_____ 7. Equity often listed before liabilities in the balance sheet (statement of financial position)
_____ 8. Translation reserve
_____ 9. Ordinary shares
_____ 10. Paid-in capital—excess of par
_____ 11. Net gains (losses) on investments—AOCI
_____ 12. Investment revaluation reserve
_____ 13. Preferred stock

CPA and CMA Review Questions

CPA Exam Questions

KAPLAN CPA REVIEW

The following questions are adapted from a variety of sources including questions developed by the AICPA Board of Examiners and those used in the Kaplan CPA Review Course to study shareholders' equity while preparing for the CPA examination. Determine the response that best completes the statements or questions.

● LO18–5

1. In 2014, Fogg, Inc., issued $10 par value common stock for $25 per share. No other common stock transactions occurred until March 31, 2016, when Fogg acquired some of the issued shares for $20 per share and retired them. Which of the following statements correctly states an effect of this acquisition and retirement?
   a. 2016 net income is decreased.
   b. Additional paid-in capital is decreased.
   c. 2016 net income is increased.
   d. Retained earnings is increased.

● LO18–5

2. Copper, Inc., initially issued 100,000 shares of $1 par value stock for $500,000 in 2013. In 2015, the company repurchased 10,000 shares for $100,000. In 2016, 5,000 of the repurchased shares were resold for $80,000. In its balance sheet dated December 31, 2016, Copper, Inc.'s Treasury Stock account shows a balance of:
   a. $ 0
   b. $ 20,000
   c. $ 50,000
   d. $100,000

● LO18–7

3. On June 27, 2016, Brite Co. distributed to its common stockholders 100,000 outstanding common shares of its investment in Quik, Inc., an unrelated party. The carrying amount on Brite's books of Quik's $1 par common stock was $2 per share. Immediately after the distribution, the market price of Quik's stock was $2.50 per share. In its income statement for the year ended June 30, 2016, what amount should Brite report as gain before income taxes on disposal of the stock?
   a. $ 0
   b. $ 50,000
   c. $200,000
   d. $250,000

● LO18–7

4. Whipple Company has 1,000,000 shares of common stock authorized with a par value of $3 per share, of which 600,000 shares are outstanding. When the market value was $8 per share, Whipple issued a stock dividend whereby for each six shares held one share was issued as a stock dividend. The par value of the stock was not changed. What entry should Whipple make to record this transaction?

a. Retained earnings	$300,000	
Common stock		$300,000
b. Additional paid-in capital	300,000	
Common stock		300,000
c. Retained earnings	800,000	
Common stock		300,000
Additional paid-in capital		500,000
d. Additional paid-in capital	800,000	
Common stock		300,000
Retained earnings		500,000

● LO18–8

5. When a company issues a stock dividend which of the following would be affected?
   a. Earnings per share.
   b. Total assets.
   c. Total liabilities.
   d. Total stockholders' equity.

● LO18–8

6. Long Co. had 100,000 shares of common stock issued and outstanding at January 1, 2016. During 2016, Long took the following actions:

March 15	Declared a 2-for-1 stock split, when the fair value of the stock was $80 per share.
December 15	Declared a $0.50 per share cash dividend.

In Long's statement of shareholders' equity for 2016, what amount should Long report as dividends?
   a. $ 50,000
   b. $100,000
   c. $850,000
   d. $950,000

International Financial Reporting Standards are tested on the CPA exam along with U.S. GAAP. The following questions deal with the application of IFRS in accounting for shareholders' equity.

● LO18–9

 IFRS

7. Mandatorily redeemable preferred stock (preference shares) is reported among liabilities and their dividends are reported in the income statement as interest expense using
   a. U.S. GAAP.
   b. IFRS.
   c. Both U.S. GAAP and IFRS.
   d. Neither U.S. GAAP nor IFRS.

● LO18–9

 IFRS

8. Revenues, expenses, and components of other comprehensive income can be reported in a single statement of comprehensive income using
   a. U.S. GAAP.
   b. IFRS.
   c. Both U.S. GAAP and IFRS.
   d. Neither U.S. GAAP nor IFRS.

CMA Exam Questions

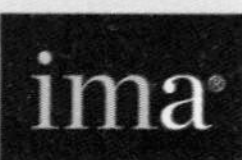

The following questions dealing with shareholders' equity are adapted from questions that previously appeared on Certified Management Accountant (CMA) examinations. The CMA designation sponsored by the Institute of Management Accountants (**www.imanet.org**) provides members with an objective measure of knowledge and competence in the field of management accounting. Determine the response that best completes the statements or questions.

● LO18–1

1. The par value of common stock represents
   a. the estimated fair value of the stock when it was issued.
   b. the liability ceiling of a shareholder when a company undergoes bankruptcy proceedings.
   c. the total value of the stock that must be entered in the issuing corporation's records.
   d. the amount that must be recorded on the issuing corporation's record as paid-in capital.

● LO18–1

2. The equity section of Smith Corporation's statement of financial position is presented below.

Preferred stock, $100 par	$12,000,000
Common stock, $5 par	10,000,000
Paid-in capital in excess of par	18,000,000
Retained earnings	9,000,000
Shareholders' equity	$49,000,000

The common shareholders of Smith Corporation have preemptive rights. If Smith Corporation issues 400,000 additional shares of common stock at $6 per share, a current holder of 20,000 shares of Smith Corporation's common stock must be given the option to buy

a. 1,000 additional shares.
b. 3,774 additional shares.
c. 4,000 additional shares.
d. 3,333 additional shares.

● LO18–8

3. A stock dividend

a. increases the debt to equity ratio of a firm.
b. decreases future earnings per share.
c. decreases the size of the firm.
d. increases shareholders' wealth.

Problems

An alternate exercise and problem set is available in the Connect library.

P 18–1
Various stock transactions; correction of journal entries
● LO18–4

Part A
During its first year of operations, the McCollum Corporation entered into the following transactions relating to shareholders' equity. The corporation was authorized to issue 100 million common shares, $1 par per share.

Required:
Prepare the appropriate journal entries to record each transaction.

Jan. 9	Issued 40 million common shares for $20 per share.
Mar. 11	Issued 5,000 shares in exchange for custom-made equipment. McCollum's shares have traded recently on the stock exchange at $20 per share.

Part B
A new staff accountant for the McCollum Corporation recorded the following journal entries during the second year of operations. McCollum retires shares that it reacquires (restores their status to that of authorized but unissued shares).

		($ in millions)	
Jan. 12	Land	2	
	Paid-in capital—donation of land		2
Sept. 1	Common stock	2	
	Retained earnings	48	
	Cash		50
Dec. 1	Cash	26	
	Common stock		1
	Gain on sale of previously issued shares		25

Required:
Prepare the journal entries that should have been recorded for each of the transactions.

P 18–2
Share buyback—comparison of retirement and treasury stock treatment
● LO18–5

The shareholders' equity section of the balance sheet of TNL Systems Inc. included the following accounts at December 31, 2015:

Shareholders' Equity	($ in millions)
Common stock, 240 million shares at $1 par	$ 240
Paid-in capital—excess of par	1,680
Paid-in capital—share repurchase	1
Retained earnings	1,100

Required:
1. During 2016, TNL Systems reacquired shares of its common stock and later sold shares in two separate transactions. Prepare the entries for both the purchase and subsequent resale of the shares assuming the shares are (a) retired and (b) viewed as treasury stock.

a. On February 5, 2016, TNL Systems purchased 6 million shares at $10 per share.
b. On July 9, 2016, the corporation sold 2 million shares at $12 per share.
c. On November 14, 2018, the corporation sold 2 million shares at $7 per share.

2. Prepare the shareholders' equity section of TNL Systems' balance sheet at December 31, 2018, comparing the two approaches. Assume all net income earned in 2016–2018 was distributed to shareholders as cash dividends.

P 18–3
Reacquired shares—comparison of retired shares and treasury shares
● LO18–5

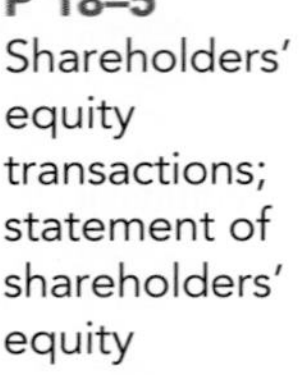

National Supply's shareholders' equity included the following accounts at December 31, 2015:

Shareholders' Equity	($ in millions)
Common stock, 6 million shares at $1 par	$ 6,000,000
Paid-in capital—excess of par	30,000,000
Retained earnings	86,500,000

Required:

1. National Supply reacquired shares of its common stock in two separate transactions and later sold shares. Prepare the entries for each of the transactions under each of two separate assumptions: the shares are (a) retired and (b) accounted for as treasury stock.

February 15, 2016	Reacquired 300,000 shares at $8 per share.
February 17, 2017	Reacquired 300,000 shares at $5.50 per share.
November 9, 2018	Sold 200,000 shares at $7 per share (assume FIFO cost).

2. Prepare the shareholders' equity section of National Supply's balance sheet at December 31, 2018, assuming the shares are (a) retired and (b) accounted for as treasury stock. Net income was $14 million in 2016, $15 million in 2017, and $16 million in 2018. No dividends were paid during the three-year period.

P 18–4
Statement of retained earnings
● LO18–5, LO18–7

Comparative statements of retained earnings for Renn-Dever Corporation were reported in its 2016 annual report as follows.

RENN-DEVER CORPORATION
Statements of Retained Earnings

For the Years Ended December 31,	2016	2015	2014
Balance at beginning of year	**$6,794,292**	**$5,464,052**	**$5,624,552**
Net income (loss)	3,308,700	2,240,900	(160,500)
Deductions:			
Stock dividend (34,900 shares)	242,000		
Common shares retired (110,000 shares)		212,660	
Common stock cash dividends	889,950	698,000	0
Balance at end of year	**$8,971,042**	**$6,794,292**	**$5,464,052**

At December 31, 2013, common shares consisted of the following:

Common stock, 1,855,000 shares at $1 par	$1,855,000
Paid-in capital—excess of par	7,420,000

Required:
Infer from the reports the events and transactions that affected Renn-Dever Corporation's retained earnings during 2014, 2015, and 2016. Prepare the journal entries that reflect those events and transactions.

P 18–5
Shareholders' equity transactions; statement of shareholders' equity
● LO18–6 through LO18–8

Listed below are the transactions that affected the shareholders' equity of Branch-Rickie Corporation during the period 2016–2018. At December 31, 2015, the corporation's accounts included:

	($ in 000s)
Common stock, 105 million shares at $1 par	$105,000
Paid-in capital—excess of par	630,000
Retained earnings	970,000

a. November 1, 2016, the board of directors declared a cash dividend of $.80 per share on its common shares, payable to shareholders of record November 15, to be paid December 1.
b. On March 1, 2017, the board of directors declared a property dividend consisting of corporate bonds of Warner Corporation that Branch-Rickie was holding as an investment. The bonds had a fair value of $1.6 million, but were purchased two years previously for $1.3 million. Because they were intended to be held to maturity, the bonds had not been previously written up. The property dividend was payable to shareholders of record March 13, to be distributed April 5.

c. On July 12, 2017, the corporation declared and distributed a 5% common stock dividend (when the market value of the common stock was $21 per share). Cash was paid in lieu of fractional shares representing 250,000 equivalent whole shares.

d. On November 1, 2017, the board of directors declared a cash dividend of $.80 per share on its common shares, payable to shareholders of record November 15, to be paid December 1.

e. On January 15, 2018, the board of directors declared and distributed a 3-for-2 stock split effected in the form of a 50% stock dividend when the market value of the common stock was $22 per share.

f. On November 1, 2018, the board of directors declared a cash dividend of $.65 per share on its common shares, payable to shareholders of record November 15, to be paid December 1.

Required:

1. Prepare the journal entries that Branch-Rickie recorded during the three-year period for these transactions.
2. Prepare comparative statements of shareholders' equity for Branch-Rickie for the three-year period ($ in 000s). Net income was $330 million, $395 million, and $455 million for 2016, 2017, and 2018, respectively.

P 18–6
Statement of shareholders' equity
● LO18–1, LO18–3 through LO18–8

Comparative statements of shareholders' equity for Anaconda International Corporation were reported as follows for the fiscal years ending December 31, 2016, 2017, and 2018.

ANACONDA INTERNATIONAL CORPORATION
Statements of Shareholders' Equity
For the Years Ended Dec. 31, 2016, 2017, and 2018
($ in millions)

	Preferred Stock $10 par	Common Stock $1 par	Additional Paid-In Capital	Retained Earnings	Total Shareholders' Equity
Balance at January 1, 2016		55	495	1,878	2,428
Sale of preferred shares	10		470		480
Sale of common shares		7	63		70
Cash dividend, preferred				(1)	(1)
Cash dividend, common				(16)	(16)
Net income	—	—	—	290	290
Balance at December 31, 2016	10	62	1,028	2,151	3,251
Retirement of shares		(3)	(27)	(20)	(50)
Cash dividend, preferred				(1)	(1)
Cash dividend, common				(20)	(20)
3-for-2 split effected in the form of a dividend	5		(5)		
Net income	—	—	—	380	380
Balance at December 31, 2017	15	59	996	2,490	3,560
Common stock dividend		6	59	(65)	
Cash dividend, preferred				(1)	(1)
Cash dividend, common				(22)	(22)
Net income	—	—	—	412	412
Balance at December 31, 2018	15	65	1,055	2,814	3,949

Required:

1. Infer from the statements the events and transactions that affected Anaconda International Corporation's shareholders' equity during 2016, 2017, and 2018. Prepare the journal entries that reflect those events and transactions.
2. Prepare the shareholders' equity section of Anaconda's comparative balance sheets at December 31, 2018 and 2017.

P 18–7
Reporting shareholders' equity; comprehensive income; Cisco Systems
● LO18–1 through LO18–4

The following is a portion of the Statement of Shareholders' Equity from Cisco Systems' January 25, 2014, quarterly report. Remember that comparative purposes, three years are reported in these statements. The 2013 and 2012 portions of the statement are not shown here for brevity of presentation.

Real World Financials

CISCO SYSTEMS, INC.
Consolidated Statements of Equity (in part)

($ in millions)	Shares of Common Stock	Common Stock and Additional Paid-In Capital	Retained Earnings	Accumulated Other Comprehensive Income	Total Shareholders' Equity
Balance at July 27, 2013	5,389	$42,297	$16,215	$608	$59,120
Net income			3,425		3,425
Other comprehensive income				95	95
Issuance of common stock	84	837			837
Repurchase of common stock	(282)	(2,427)	(3,902)		(6,329)
Cash dividends declared			(1,810)		(1,810)
Tax effects from employee stock incentive plans		29			29
Purchase acquisitions		46			46
Share-based compensation expense		656			656
Balance at January 25, 2014	5,191	$41,438	$13,928	$703	$56,069

Required:

1. What is the purpose of the statement of shareholders' equity?
2. How does Cisco account for its share buybacks?
3. For its share buybacks in the period shown, was the price Cisco paid for the shares repurchased more or less than the average price at which Cisco had sold the shares previously? Reconstruct the journal entry Cisco used to record the buyback. The par amount of Cisco's shares is $0.001.
4. What is comprehensive income? What is other comprehensive income?
5. What caused the change in Cisco's comprehensive income for the period shown? What was the amount of Accumulated other comprehensive income (loss) that Cisco reported in its January 25, 2014, balance sheet? Be specific.

P 18–8
Share issue costs; issuance; dividends; early retirement
● LO18–3, LO18–4, LO18–7

During its first year of operations, Cupola Fan Corporation issued 30,000 of $1 par Class B shares for $385,000 on June 30, 2016. Share issue costs were $1,500. One year from the issue date (July 1, 2017), the corporation retired 10% of the shares for $39,500.

Required:

1. Prepare the journal entry to record the issuance of the shares.
2. Prepare the journal entry to record the declaration of a $2 per share dividend on December 1, 2016.
3. Prepare the journal entry to record the payment of the dividend on December 31, 2016.
4. Prepare the journal entry to record the retirement of the shares.

(Note: You may wish to compare your solution to this problem with that of Problem 14–16, which deals with parallel issues of debt issue costs and the retirement of debt.)

P 18–9
Effect of preferred stock characteristics on dividends
● LO18–7

The shareholders' equity of Kramer Industries includes the data shown below. During 2017, cash dividends of $150 million were declared. Dividends were not declared in 2015 or 2016.

	($ in millions)
Common stock	$200
Paid-in capital—excess of par, common	800
Preferred stock, 10%, nonparticipating	100
Paid-in capital—excess of par, preferred	270

Required:

Determine the amount of dividends payable to preferred shareholders and to common shareholders under each of the following two assumptions regarding the characteristics of the preferred stock.

Assumption A—The preferred stock is noncumulative.
Assumption B—The preferred stock is cumulative.

P 18–10
Transactions affecting retained earnings
● LO18–4 through LO18–8

Indicate by letter whether each of the transactions listed below increases (**I**), decreases (**D**), or has no effect (**N**) on retained earnings. Assume the shareholders' equity of the transacting company includes only common stock, paid-in capital—excess of par, and retained earnings at the time of each transaction. (Some transactions have two possible answers. Indicate both.)

Transactions

Example

	Transactions
N	1. Sale of common stock
_____	2. Purchase of treasury stock at a cost *less* than the original issue price
_____	3. Purchase of treasury stock at a cost *greater* than the original issue price
_____	4. Declaration of a property dividend
_____	5. Sale of treasury stock for *more* than cost
_____	6. Sale of treasury stock for *less* than cost
_____	7. Net income for the year
_____	8. Declaration of a cash dividend
_____	9. Payment of a previously declared cash dividend
_____	10. Issuance of convertible bonds for cash
_____	11. Declaration and distribution of a 5% stock dividend
_____	12. Retirement of common stock at a cost *less* than the original issue price
_____	13. Retirement of common stock at a cost *greater* than the original issue price
_____	14. A stock split effected in the form of a stock dividend
_____	15. A stock split in which the par value per share is reduced (not effected in the form of a stock dividend)
_____	16. A net loss for the year

P 18–11
Stock dividends received on investments; integrative problem
● LO18–8

Ellis Transport Company acquired 1.2 million shares of stock in L&K Corporation at $44 per share. They are classified by Ellis as "available for sale." Ellis sold 200,000 shares at $46, received a 10% stock dividend, and then later in the year sold another 100,000 shares at $43.

Hint: There is no entry for the stock dividend, but a new investment per share must be calculated for use later when the shares are sold.

Required:
Prepare journal entries to record these transactions.

P 18–12
Various shareholders' equity topics; comprehensive
● LO18–1, LO18–4 through LO18–8

Part A
In late 2015, the Nicklaus Corporation was formed. The corporate charter authorizes the issuance of 5,000,000 shares of common stock carrying a $1 par value, and 1,000,000 shares of $5 par value, noncumulative, nonparticipating preferred stock. On January 2, 2016, 3,000,000 shares of the common stock are issued in exchange for cash at an average price of $10 per share. Also on January 2, all 1,000,000 shares of preferred stock are issued at $20 per share.

Required:
1. Prepare journal entries to record these transactions.
2. Prepare the shareholders' equity section of the Nicklaus balance sheet as of March 31, 2016. (Assume net income for the first quarter 2016 was $1,000,000.)

Part B
During 2016, the Nicklaus Corporation participated in three treasury stock transactions:

a. On June 30, 2016, the corporation reacquires 200,000 shares for the treasury at a price of $12 per share.
b. On July 31, 2016, 50,000 treasury shares are reissued at $15 per share.
c. On September 30, 2016, 50,000 treasury shares are reissued at $10 per share.

Required:
1. Prepare journal entries to record these transactions.
2. Prepare the Nicklaus Corporation shareholders' equity section as it would appear in a balance sheet prepared at September 30, 2016. (Assume net income for the second and third quarter was $3,000,000.)

Part C
On October 1, 2016, Nicklaus Corporation receives permission to replace its $1 par value common stock (5,000,000 shares authorized, 3,000,000 shares issued, and 2,900,000 shares outstanding) with a new common stock issue having a $.50 par value. Since the new par value is one-half the amount of the old, this represents a 2-for-1 stock split. That is, the shareholders will receive two shares of the $.50 par stock in exchange for each share of the $1 par stock they own. The $1 par stock will be collected and destroyed by the issuing corporation.

On November 1, 2016, the Nicklaus Corporation declares a $.05 per share cash dividend on common stock and a $.25 per share cash dividend on preferred stock. Payment is scheduled for December 1, 2016, to shareholders of record on November 15, 2016.

On December 2, 2016, the Nicklaus Corporation declares a 1% stock dividend payable on December 28, 2016, to shareholders of record on December 14. At the date of declaration, the common stock was selling in the open market at $10 per share. The dividend will result in 58,000 (.01 × 5,800,000) additional shares being issued to shareholders.

Required:

1. Prepare journal entries to record the declaration and payment of these stock and cash dividends.
2. Prepare the December 31, 2016, shareholders' equity section of the balance sheet for the Nicklaus Corporation. (Assume net income for the fourth quarter was $2,500,000.)
3. Prepare a statement of shareholders' equity for Nicklaus Corporation for 2016.

P 18–13
Quasi reorganization (based on Appendix 18)
● **Appendix**

A new CEO was hired to revive the floundering Champion Chemical Corporation. The company had endured operating losses for several years, but confidence was emerging that better times were ahead. The board of directors and shareholders approved a quasi reorganization for the corporation. The reorganization included devaluing inventory for obsolescence by $105 million and increasing land by $5 million. Immediately prior to the restatement, at December 31, 2016, Champion Chemical Corporation's balance sheet appeared as follows (in condensed form):

CHAMPION CHEMICAL CORPORATION
Balance Sheet
At December 31, 2016
($ in millions)

Cash	$ 20
Receivables	40
Inventory	230
Land	40
Buildings and equipment (net)	90
	$420
Liabilities	$240
Common stock (320 million shares at $1 par)	320
Additional paid-in capital	60
Retained earnings (deficit)	(200)
	$420

Required:

1. Prepare the journal entries appropriate to record the quasi reorganization on January 1, 2017.
2. Prepare a balance sheet as it would appear immediately after the restatement.

Broaden Your Perspective

Apply your critical-thinking ability to the knowledge you've gained. These cases will provide you an opportunity to develop your research, analysis, judgment, and communication skills. You also will work with other students, integrate what you've learned, apply it in real-world situations, and consider its global and ethical ramifications. This practice will broaden your knowledge and further develop your decision-making abilities.

Real World Case 18–1
Initial public offering of common stock; Dolby Laboratories
● LO18–4

Real World Financials

Ray Dolby started **Dolby Laboratories** and since then has been a leader in the entertainment industry and consumer electronics. Closely held since its founding in 1965, Dolby decided to go public. Here's an AP news report:

DOLBY'S IPO EXPECTED TO PLAY SWEET MUSIC

The initial public offering market is hoping for a big bang this week from Dolby Laboratories Inc. The San Francisco company, whose sound systems and double-D logo are ubiquitous in the movie industry as well as in consumer electronics, plans to sell 27.5 million shares for $13.50 to $15.50 each. Founded by Cambridge-trained scientist Ray Dolby 39 years ago, the company started out manufacturing noise-reduction equipment for the music industry that eliminated the background "hiss" on recordings, and has since expanded to encompass everything from digital audio systems to Dolby Surround sound. The company's IPO, which is lead-managed by underwriters Morgan Stanley and Goldman Sachs Group Inc., is expected to do well not only because of its brand recognition, but also because of its strong financials. (*AP*)

Required:

1. Assuming the shares are issued at the midpoint of the price range indicated, how much capital did the IPO raise for Dolby Laboratories before any underwriting discount and offering expenses?
2. If the par amount is $.01 per share, what journal entry did Dolby use to record the sale?

Analysis Case 18–2
Statement of shareholders' equity
● LO18–1, LO18–3, LO18–6, LO18–7

The shareholders' equity portion of the balance sheet of Sessel's Department Stores, Inc., a large regional specialty retailer, is as follows:

SESSEL'S DEPARTMENT STORES, INC.
Comparative Balance Sheets
Shareholders' Equity Section

($ in 000s, except per share amounts)	Dec. 31, 2017	Dec. 31, 2016
Shareholders' Equity		
Preferred stock—$1 par value; 20,000 total shares authorized,		
Series A—600 shares authorized, issued, and outstanding, $50 per share liquidation preference	$ 57,700	$ —
Series B—33 shares authorized, no shares outstanding		
Common stock—$.10 par; 200,000 shares authorized, 19,940 and 18,580 shares issued and outstanding at Dec. 31, 2017, and Dec. 31, 2016, respectively	1,994	1,858
Additional paid-in capital	227,992	201,430
Retained income	73,666	44,798
Total shareholders' equity	$361,352	$248,086

Disclosures elsewhere in Sessel's annual report revealed the following changes in shareholders' equity accounts for 2017, 2016, 2015:

2017:

1. The only changes in retained earnings during 2017 were preferred dividends on preferred stock of $3,388,000 and net income.
2. The preferred stock is convertible. During the year, 6,592 shares were issued. All shares were converted into 320,000 shares of common stock. No gain or loss was recorded on the conversion.
3. Common shares were issued in a public offering and upon the exercise of stock options. On the statement of shareholders' equity, Sessel's reports these two items on a single line entitled: "Issuance of shares."

2016:

1. Net income: $12,126,000.
2. Issuance of common stock: 5,580,000 shares at $112,706,000.

2015:

1. Net income: $13,494,000.
2. Issuance of common stock: 120,000 shares at $826,000.

Required:

From these disclosures, prepare comparative statements of shareholders' equity for 2017, 2016, and 2015.

Communication Case 18–3
IFRS; Is preferred stock debt or equity? Group interaction
● LO18–1, LO18–9

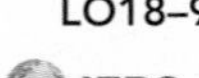
IFRS

An unsettled question in accounting for stock is: Should preferred stock be recognized as a liability, or should it be considered equity? Under International Financial Reporting Standards, preferred stock (preference shares) often is reported as debt with the dividends reported in the income statement as interest expense. Under U.S. GAAP, that is the case only for "mandatorily redeemable" preferred stock.

Two opposing viewpoints are:

View 1: Preferred stock should be considered equity.

View 2: Preferred stock should be reported as a liability.

In considering this question, focus on conceptual issues regarding the practicable and theoretically appropriate treatment, unconstrained by GAAP.

Required:

1. Which view do you favor? Develop a list of arguments in support of your view prior to the class session for which the case is assigned.

2. In class, your instructor will pair you (and everyone else) with a classmate (who also has independently developed an argument).
   a. You will be given three minutes to argue your view to your partner. Your partner likewise will be given three minutes to argue his or her view to you. During these three-minute presentations, the listening partner is not permitted to speak.
   b. Then after each person has had a turn attempting to convince his or her partner, the two partners will have a three-minute discussion in which they will decide which view is more convincing and arguments will be merged into a single view for each pair.
3. After the allotted time, a spokesperson for each of the two views will be selected by the instructor. Each spokesperson will field arguments from the class in support of that view's position and list the arguments on the board. The class then will discuss the merits of the two lists of arguments and attempt to reach a consensus view, though a consensus is not necessary.

Research Case 18–4
FASB codification; comprehensive income; locate and extract relevant information and authoritative support for a financial reporting issue; integrative; Cisco Systems
● LO18–2

Real World Financials

Titan Networking became a public company through an IPO (initial public offering) two weeks ago. You are looking forward to the challenges of being assistant controller for a publicly owned corporation. One such challenge came in the form of a memo in this morning's in-box. "We need to start reporting comprehensive income in our financials," the message from your boss said. "Do some research on that, will you? That concept didn't exist when I went to school." In response, you sought out the financial statements of Cisco Systems, the networking industry leader. The following are excerpts from disclosure notes from Cisco's 2013 annual report:

Consolidated Statements of Comprehensive Income (in part)

	Years Ended		
	July 27, 2013	**July 28, 2012**	**July 30, 2011**
Net income	$9,983	$8,041	$6,490
Other comprehensive income (loss):			
Change in unrealized gains on investments net of tax benefit	(37)	(96)	169
Change in hedging instruments net of tax benefit (expense)	61	(59)	(21)
Change in cumulative translation adjustment and other net of tax benefit (expense)	(84)	(496)	538
Comprehensive income	$9,923	$7,390	$7,176

Required:

1. Locate the financial statements of Cisco at www.sec.gov or Cisco's website. Search the 2013 annual report for information about how Cisco accounts for comprehensive income. What does Cisco report in its balance sheet regarding comprehensive income?
2. Access the *FASB Accounting Standards Codification* at the FASB website (asc.fasb.org). Identify the specific citation from the authoritative literature that describes the three alternative formats for reporting comprehensive income.
3. What is comprehensive income? How does it differ from net income? Where is it reported in a balance sheet?
4. One component of Other comprehensive income for Cisco is "net unrealized gains on investments." What does this mean? From the information Cisco's financial statements provide, determine how the company calculated the $608 million accumulated other comprehensive income at the end of fiscal 2013.
5. What might be possible causes for the "Other" component of Cisco's Other comprehensive income?

Judgment Case 18–5
Treasury stock; stock split; cash dividends; Alcoa
● LO18–5 through LO18–8

Real World Financials

Alcoa is the world's leading producer of primary aluminum, fabricated aluminum, and alumina. The following is a press release from the company:

ALCOA ANNOUNCES 33% INCREASE IN BASE DIVIDEND, 2-FOR-1 STOCK SPLIT

PITTSBURGH—Alcoa today announced that its Board of Directors approved a base quarterly dividend increase of 33.3%.

Alcoa's announcement indicated that the new quarterly dividend would be 25 cents per share. It also stated that the Board of Directors declared a two-for-one stock split and reaffirmed its commitment to a share repurchase program.

Required:

1. What are the two primary reporting alternatives Alcoa has in accounting for the repurchase of its shares? What would be the effect of the optional courses of action on total shareholders' equity? Explain. What would be the effect of the optional courses of action on how stock would be presented in Alcoa's balance sheet? If the shares are later resold for an amount greater than cost, how should Alcoa account for the sale?
2. What are the two primary courses of action Alcoa has in accounting for the stock split, and how would the choice affect Alcoa's shareholders' equity? Why?
3. How should Alcoa account for the cash dividend, and how would it affect Alcoa's balance sheet? Why?

Communication Case 18–6
Issuance of shares; share issue costs; prepare a report
● LO18–4

You are the newest member of the staff of Brinks & Company, a medium-size investment management firm. You are supervised by Les Kramer, an employee of two years. Les has a reputation as being technically sound but has a noticeable gap in his accounting education. Knowing you are knowledgeable about accounting issues, he requested you provide him with a synopsis of accounting for share issue costs.

"I thought the cost of issuing securities is recorded separately and expensed over time," he stated in a handwritten memo. "But I don't see that for IBR's underwriting expenses. What gives?"

He apparently was referring to a disclosure note on a page of IBR's annual report, photocopied and attached to his memo. To raise funds for expansion, the company sold additional shares of its $.10 par common stock. The following disclosure note appeared in the company's most recent annual report:

NOTES TO CONSOLIDATED FINANCIAL STATEMENTS

Note 10—Stock Transactions (in part)

In February and March, the Company sold 2,395,000 shares of Common Stock at $22.25 per share in a public offering. Net proceeds to the Company were approximately $50.2 million after the underwriting discount and offering expenses.

Required:

Write a formal memo to your supervisor. Briefly explain how share issue costs are accounted for and how that accounting differs from that of debt issue costs. To make sure your explanation is understood in context of the footnote, include in your memo the following:

a. At what total amount did the shares sell to the public? How is the difference between this amount and the $50.2 million net proceeds accounted for?
b. The appropriate journal entry to record the sale of the shares.

Analysis Case 18–7
Analyzing financial statements; price-earnings ratio; dividend payout ratio
● LO18–1

AGF Foods Company is a large, primarily domestic, consumer foods company involved in the manufacture, distribution, and sale of a variety of food products. Industry averages are derived from Troy's *The Almanac of Business and Industrial Financial Ratios* and Dun and Bradstreet's *Industry Norms and Key Business Ratios.* Following are the 2016 and 2015 comparative income statements and balance sheets for AGF. The market price of AGF's common stock is $47 during 2016. (The financial data we use are from actual financial statements of a well-known corporation, but the company name used in our illustration is fictitious and the numbers and dates have been modified slightly to disguise the company's identity.)

Profitability is the key to a company's long-run survival. Profitability measures focus on a company's ability to provide an adequate return relative to resources devoted to company operations.

AGF FOODS COMPANY
Years Ended December 31, 2016 and 2015

($ in millions)	2016	2015
Comparative Income Statements		
Net sales	$6,440	$5,800
Cost of goods sold	(3,667)	(3,389)
Gross profit	2,773	2,411
Operating expenses	(1,916)	(1,629)

(continued)

(concluded)

Operating income	857	782
Interest expense	(54)	(53)
Income from operations before tax	803	729
Income taxes	(316)	(287)
Net income	$ 487	$ 442
Net income per share	$ 2.69	$2.44
Average shares outstanding	181 million	181 million

Comparative Balance Sheets

Assets		
Current assets:		
Cash	$ 48	$ 142
Accounts receivable	347	320
Marketable securities	358	—
Inventories	914	874
Prepaid expenses	212	154
Total current assets	$1,879	$1,490
Property, plant, and equipment (net)	2,592	2,291
Intangibles (net)	800	843
Other assets	74	60
Total assets	$5,345	$4,684
Liabilities and Shareholders' Equity		
Current liabilities:		
Accounts payable	$ 254	$ 276
Accrued liabilities	493	496
Notes payable	518	115
Current portion of long-term debt	208	54
Total current liabilities	1,473	941
Long-term debt	534	728
Deferred income taxes	407	344
Total liabilities	2,414	2,013
Shareholders' equity:		
Common stock, $1 par	180	180
Additional paid-in capital	21	63
Retained earnings	2,730	2,428
Total shareholders' equity	2,931	2,671
Total liabilities and shareholders' equity	$5,345	$4,684

Required:

1. Calculate the return on shareholders' equity for AGF. The average return for the stocks listed on the New York Stock Exchange in a comparable period was 18.8%. What information does your calculation provide an investor?
2. Calculate AGF's earnings per share and earnings-price ratio. The average return for the stocks listed on the New York Stock Exchange in a comparable time period was 5.4%. What does your calculation indicate about AGF's earnings?

Ethics Case 18–8
The Swiss label maker; value of shares issued for equipment
● LO18–4

Bricker Graphics is a privately held company specializing in package labels. Representatives of the firm have just returned from Switzerland, where a Swiss firm is manufacturing a custom-made high speed, color labeling machine. Confidence is high that the new machine will help rescue Bricker from sharply declining profitability. Bricker's chief operating officer, Don Benson, has been under fire for not reaching the company's performance goals of achieving a rate of return on assets of at least 12%.

The afternoon of his return from Switzerland, Benson called Susan Sharp into his office. Susan is Bricker's Controller.

Benson: I wish you had been able to go. We have some accounting issues to consider.
Sharp: I wish I'd been there, too. I understand the food was marvelous. What are the accounting issues?

Benson: They discussed accepting our notes at the going rate for a face amount of $12.5 million. We also discussed financing with stock.

Sharp: I thought we agreed; debt is the way to go for us now.

Benson: Yes, but I've been thinking. We can issue shares for a total of $10 million. The labeler is custom-made and doesn't have a quoted selling price, but the domestic labelers we considered went for around $10 million. It sure would help our rate of return if we keep the asset base as low as possible.

Required:

1. How will Benson's plan affect the return measure? What accounting issue is involved?
2. Is the proposal ethical?
3. Who would be affected if the proposal is implemented?

Research Case 18–9
Researching the way shareholders' equity transactions are reported; retrieving financial statements from the Internet
● LO18–1, LO18–6

EDGAR, the Electronic Data Gathering, Analysis, and Retrieval system, performs automated collection, validation, indexing, and forwarding of submissions by companies and others who are required by law to file forms with the U.S. Securities and Exchange Commission (SEC). All publicly traded domestic companies use EDGAR to make the majority of their filings. (Filings by foreign companies are not required to be filed on EDGAR, but some of these companies do so voluntarily.) Form 10-K, which includes the annual report, is required to be filed on EDGAR. The SEC makes this information available on the Internet.

Required:

1. Access EDGAR on the Internet at **www.sec.gov**.
2. Search for a public company with which you are familiar. Access its most recent 10-K filing. Search or scroll to find the statement of shareholders' equity and related note(s). If a statement of shareholders' equity is not provided, try another company.
3. Determine from the statement the transactions that occurred during the most recent three years that affected retained earnings.
4. Determine from the statement the transactions that occurred during the most recent three years that affected common stock. Were any of these transactions identified in requirement 3 also?
5. Cross-reference your findings with amounts reported on the balance sheet. How do these two statements articulate with one another?

Communication Case 18–10
Should the present two-category distinction between liabilities and equity be retained? Group interaction.
● LO18–1

The current conceptual distinction between liabilities and equity defines liabilities independently of assets and equity, with equity defined as a residual amount. The present proliferation of financial instruments that combine features of both debt and equity and the difficulty of drawing a distinction have led many to conclude that the present two-category distinction between liabilities and equity should be eliminated. Two opposing viewpoints are:

View 1: The distinction should be maintained.

View 2: The distinction should be eliminated and financial instruments should instead be reported in accordance with the priority of their claims to enterprise assets.

One type of security that often is mentioned in the debate is convertible bonds. Although stock in many ways, such a security also obligates the issuer to transfer assets at a specified price and redemption date. Thus it also has features of debt. In considering this question, focus on conceptual issues regarding the practicable and theoretically appropriate treatment, unconstrained by GAAP.

Required:

1. Which view do you favor? Develop a list of arguments in support of your view prior to the class session for which the case is assigned.
2. In class, your instructor will pair you (and everyone else) with a classmate (who also has independently developed an argument).
   a. You will be given three minutes to argue your view to your partner. Your partner likewise will be given three minutes to argue his or her view to you. During these three-minute presentations, the listening partner is not permitted to speak.
   b. Then after each person has had a turn attempting to convince his or her partner, the two partners will have a three-minute discussion in which they will decide which view is more convincing and arguments will be merged into a single view for each pair.
3. After the allotted time, a spokesperson for each of the two views will be selected by the instructor. Each spokesperson will field arguments from the class in support of that view's position and list the arguments on the board. The class then will discuss the merits of the two lists of arguments and attempt to reach a consensus view, though a consensus is not necessary.

Air France—KLM Case

AIRFRANCE / KLM

● LO18–9

IFRS

Air France–KLM (AF), a Franco-Dutch company, prepares its financial statements according to International Financial Reporting Standards. AF's financial statements and disclosure notes for the year ended December 31, 2013, are provided with all new textbooks. This material also is available at **www.airfranceklm-finance.com**.

Required:

1. Air France–KLM lists four items in the shareholders' equity section of its balance sheet. If AF used U.S. GAAP, what would be the likely account titles for the first and fourth of those components?
2. Locate Note 29.4 in AF's financial statements. What items comprise "Reserves and retained earnings" as reported in the balance sheet? If Air France–KLM used U.S. GAAP, what would be different for the reporting of these items?
3. Describe the apparent differences in the order of presentation of the components of liabilities and shareholders' equity between IFRS as applied by AF and a typical balance sheet prepared in accordance with U.S. GAAP.

CPA Simulation 18–1

Hanson Corporation
Shareholders' Equity

KAPLAN CPA REVIEW

Test your knowledge of the concepts discussed in this chapter, practice critical professional skills necessary for career success, and prepare for the computer-based CPA exam by accessing our CPA simulations in the Connect library.

The Hansen Corporation simulation tests your knowledge of a variety of shareholders' equity reporting issues.

CHAPTER

19 Share-Based Compensation and Earnings Per Share

OVERVIEW

We've discussed a variety of employee compensation plans in prior chapters, including pension and other postretirement benefits in Chapter 17. In this chapter we look at some common forms of compensation in which the amount of the compensation employees receive is tied to the market price of company stock. We will see that these *share-based* compensation plans—stock awards, stock options, and stock appreciation rights—create shareholders' equity, which was the topic of the previous chapter, and which also often affects the way we calculate earnings per share, the topic of the second part of the current chapter. Specifically, we view these as *potential common shares* along with convertible securities, and we calculate earnings per share as if the securities already had been exercised or converted into additional common shares.

LEARNING OBJECTIVES

After studying this chapter, you should be able to:

- **LO19–1** Explain and implement the accounting for restricted stock plans. *(p. 1128)*
- **LO19–2** Explain and implement the accounting for stock options. *(p. 1130)*
- **LO19–3** Explain and implement the accounting for employee share purchase plans. *(p. 1139)*
- **LO19–4** Distinguish between a simple and a complex capital structure. *(p. 1142)*
- **LO19–5** Describe what is meant by the weighted-average number of common shares. *(p. 1142)*
- **LO19–6** Differentiate the effect on EPS of the sale of new shares, a stock dividend or stock split, and the reacquisition of shares. *(p. 1143)*
- **LO19–7** Describe how preferred dividends affect the calculation of EPS. *(p. 1145)*
- **LO19–8** Describe how options, rights, and warrants are incorporated in the calculation of EPS. *(p. 1146)*
- **LO19–9** Describe how convertible securities are incorporated in the calculation of EPS. *(p. 1147)*
- **LO19–10** Determine whether potential common shares are antidilutive. *(p. 1151)*
- **LO19–11** Determine the three components of the proceeds used in the treasury stock method. *(p. 1155)*
- **LO19–12** Explain the way contingently issuable shares are incorporated in the calculation of EPS. *(p. 1157)*
- **LO19–13** Describe the way EPS information should be reported in an income statement. *(p. 1159)*
- **LO19–14** Discuss the primary differences between U.S. GAAP and IFRS with respect to accounting for share-based compensation and earnings per share. *(pp. 1135, 1136, and 1141)*

FINANCIAL REPORTING CASE

Proper Motivation?

The coffee room discussion Thursday morning was particularly lively. Yesterday's press release describing National Electronic Ventures' choice of Sandra Veres as its president and chief operating officer was today's hot topic in all the company's departments. The press release noted that Ms. Veres's compensation package includes elements beyond salary that are intended to not only motivate her to accept the offer, but also to remain with the company and work to increase shareholder value. Excerpts from the release follow:

> National Electronic Ventures, Inc., today announced it had attracted G. Sandra Veres, respected executive from the wireless communications industry, to succeed chairman Walter Kovac. Veres will assume the new role as CEO on Jan. 1, 2016. Ms. Veres will receive a compensation package at NEV of more than $1 million in salary, stock options to buy more than 800,000 shares of NEV stock and a grant of restricted stock.

QUESTIONS

By the time you finish this chapter, you should be able to respond appropriately to the questions posed in this case. Compare your response to the solution provided at the end of the chapter.

1. How can a compensation package such as this serve as an incentive to Ms. Veres? *(p. 1127)*
2. Ms. Veres received a "grant of restricted stock." How should NEV account for the grant? *(p. 1128)*
3. Included were stock options to buy more than 800,000 shares of NEV stock. How will the options affect NEV's compensation expense? *(p. 1130)*
4. How will the presence of these and other similar stock options affect NEV's earnings per share? *(p. 1146)*

PART A

Share-Based Compensation

Employee compensation plans frequently include share-based awards. These awards are forms of payment whose value is dependent on the value of the company's stock. These may be outright awards of shares, stock options, or cash payments tied to the market price of shares. Sometimes only key executives participate in a stock benefit plan. Typically, an executive compensation plan is tied to performance in a strategy that uses compensation to motivate its recipients. Some firms pay their directors entirely in shares. Actual compensation depends on the market value of the shares. Obviously, that's quite an incentive to act in the best interests of shareholders.

Although the variations of share-based compensation plans are seemingly endless, each shares common goals. Whether the plan is a stock award plan, a stock option plan, a stock appreciation rights (SARs) plan, or one of the several similar plans, the goals are to provide compensation to designated employees, while sometimes providing those employees with some sort of performance incentive. Likewise, our goals in accounting for each of these plans are the same for each: (1) to determine the fair value of the compensation and (2) to expense that compensation over the periods in which participants perform services. The issue is not trivial. Salary often is a minor portion of executive pay relative to stock awards and stock options.

FINANCIAL Reporting Case

Q1, p. 1127

The accounting objective is to record compensation expense over the periods in which related services are performed.

Restricted Stock Plans

● LO19–1

Executive compensation sometimes includes a grant of shares of stock or the right to receive shares. Usually, such shares are restricted in such a way as to provide some incentive to the recipient. Typically, restricted stock award plans are tied to continued employment. The two primary types of restricted stock plans are (a) restricted stock awards and (b) restricted stock units. Let's compare the two.

Restricted Stock Awards

Usually, restricted shares are subject to forfeiture if the employee doesn't remain with the company.

In a **restricted stock award**, shares actually are awarded in the name of the employee, although the company might retain physical possession of the shares. The employee has all rights of a shareholder, subject to certain restrictions or forfeiture. Ordinarily, the shares are subject to forfeiture by the employee if employment is terminated within some specified number of years from the date of grant. The employee usually is not free to sell the shares during the restriction period and a statement to that effect often is inscribed on the stock certificates. These restrictions give the employee incentive to remain with the company until rights to the shares vest.

FINANCIAL Reporting Case

Q2, p. 1127

The compensation associated with a share of restricted stock is the market price at the grant date of an unrestricted share of the same stock. This amount is accrued as compensation expense over the service period for which participants receive the shares, usually from the date of grant to when restrictions are lifted (the vesting date).[1] Once the shares vest and the restrictions are lifted, paid-in capital—restricted stock is replaced by common stock and paid-in capital—excess of par. The amount of the compensation is measured at the date of grant—at the market price on that date. Any market price changes that might occur after that don't affect the total compensation. This is essentially the same as accounting for restricted stock units to be settled in shares as demonstrated in Illustration 19–2 on the next page.

Restricted Stock Units

An increasingly popular variation of restricted stock awards is **restricted stock units (RSUs)**. In fact, RSUs have become a much more popular form of compensation than their restricted stock award cousins. A restricted stock unit is a right to receive a specified number of shares of company stock. After the recipient of RSUs satisfies the vesting requirement, the company distributes the shares.[2] So, like restricted stock awards, the recipient benefits by the value of the shares at the end of the vesting period. Unlike restricted stock awards, though, the shares are not issued at the time of the grant. Delaying the increase in outstanding shares is more acceptable to other shareholders. As part of its share-based compensation plan, **Apple Inc.** provides compensation to executives in the form of RSUs as we see in Illustration 19–1.

Although both types of plans are becoming more popular with employers, RSUs are beginning to eclipse their counterparts because of their greater simplicity and deferment of share issuance.[3]

Illustration 19–1

Restricted Stock Units (RSUs); Apple Inc.

Real World Financials

Share-Based Compensation (in part)
Share-based compensation cost for RSUs is measured based on the closing fair market value of the Company's common stock on the date of grant. . . . The Company recognizes share-based compensation cost over the award's requisite service period on a straight-line basis.

Terms of RSUs vary.[4] Sometimes, the recipient is given the *cash equivalent* of the number of shares used to value the RSUs. Or, the terms might stipulate that either the recipient or the company is allowed to choose whether to settle in stock or cash.

[1]Restricted stock plans usually are designed to comply with Tax Code Section 83 to allow employee compensation to be nontaxable to the employee until the date the shares become substantially vested, which is when the restrictions are lifted. Likewise, the employer gets no tax deduction until the compensation becomes taxable to the employee.

[2]Sometimes, the shares to be issued depend upon achieving specific performance targets.

[3]Mark Cussen, "What Are Restricted Stocks & Restricted Stock Units (RSUs)," MoneyCrashes.com, April 14, 2014.

[4]Typically, but not always, RSUs have no voting privileges and receive no dividends until the shares are issued at vesting. Sometimes, restricted stock does have voting privileges and receives dividends during the vesting period even though recipients are restricted from selling the shares until vesting.

Although RSUs delay the issuance of shares and avoid some administrative complexities of outright awards of restricted stock, accounting for RSUs to be settled in stock is essentially the same as for restricted stock awards as we see demonstrated in Illustration 19–2.

Illustration 19–2

Restricted Stock Award Plans or Restricted Stock Units (RSUs)

Under its restricted stock unit (RSU) plan, Universal Communications grants RSUs representing five million of its $1 par common shares to certain key executives at January 1, 2016. The shares are subject to forfeiture if employment is terminated within four years. Shares have a current market price of $12 per share.

January 1, 2016

No entry

Calculate total compensation expense:

$12	Fair value per share
× 5 million	Shares awarded
= $60 million	Total compensation

The total compensation is to be allocated to expense over the four-year service (vesting) period: 2016–2019.

$60 million ÷ 4 years = $15 million per year

	($ in millions)	
December 31, 2016, 2017, 2018, 2019		
Compensation expense ($60 million ÷ 4 years)	15	
Paid-in capital—restricted stock		15
December 31, 2019		
Paid-in capital—restricted stock (5 million shares at $12)	60	
Common stock (5 million shares at $1 par)		5
Paid-in capital—excess of par (difference)		55

The total compensation is the market value of the shares ($12) times five million shares.

The $60 million is accrued to compensation expense over the four-year service period.

When restrictions are lifted, paid-in capital—restricted stock, is replaced by common stock and paid-in capital—excess of par.

On the other hand, *if the employee will receive cash* or can elect to receive cash, we consider the award to be a *liability* rather than equity as is the case in Illustration 19–2. When an RSU is considered to be a liability, we determine its fair value at the grant date and recognize that amount as compensation expense over the requisite service period consistent with the way we account for restricted stock awards, RSUs, and other share-based compensation. However, because these plans are considered to be liabilities payable in cash, the credit portion of the entry as we recognize compensation expense each year is to a liability—restricted stock account. And, it's necessary to periodically adjust the liability (and corresponding compensation) based on the change in the stock's fair value until the liability is paid. Note that this is consistent with the way we account for other liabilities. Accounting for share-based compensation considered to be a liability is demonstrated in Appendix B of the chapter.

If restricted stock shares or RSUs are forfeited because, say, the employee leaves the company, entries previously made related to that specific employee would simply be reversed. This would result in a decrease in compensation expense in the year of forfeiture. The total compensation, adjusted for the forfeited amount, is then allocated over the remaining service period.

Additional Consideration

An alternative way of accomplishing the same result is to debit deferred compensation for the full value of the RSUs ($60 million in the illustration) on the date they are granted:

Deferred compensation (5 million shares at $12)	60	
Common stock (5 million shares at $1 par)		5
Paid-in capital—excess of par (difference)		55

If so, deferred compensation is reported as a reduction in shareholders' equity, resulting in a zero net effect on shareholders' equity. Then, deferred compensation is credited when compensation expense is debited over the service period. Just as in Illustration 19–2, the result is an increase in both compensation expense and shareholders' equity each year over the vesting period.

Stock Option Plans

LO19–2

More commonly, employees aren't actually awarded shares, but rather are given the option to buy shares in the future. In fact, stock options have become an integral part of the total compensation package for key officers of most medium and large companies. As with any compensation plan, the accounting objective is to report compensation expense during the period of service for which the compensation is given.

Expense—The Great Debate

Stock option plans give employees the option to purchase (a) a specified number of shares of the firm's stock, (b) at a specified price, (c) during a specified period of time. One of the most heated controversies in standard-setting history has been the debate over the amount of compensation to be recognized as expense for stock options. At issue is how the value of stock options is measured, which for most options determines whether any expense at all is recognized.

Historically, options have been measured at their intrinsic values—the simple difference between the market price of the shares and the option price at which they can be acquired. For instance, an option that permits an employee to buy $25 stock for $10 has an intrinsic value of $15. However, plans in which the exercise price equals the market value of the underlying stock at the date of grant (which describes most executive stock option plans) have no intrinsic value and therefore result in zero compensation when measured this way, even though the fair value of the options can be quite significant. Facebook CEO Mark Zuckerberg reaped a $3.3 billion gain in 2013 alone by exercising stock options.[5] To many, it seems counterintuitive to not recognize compensation expense for plans that routinely provide executives with a substantial part of their total compensation.

FINANCIAL Reporting Case

Q3, p. 1127

After lengthy debate, the FASB consented to encourage, rather than require, that the fair value of options be recognized as expense.

FAILED ATTEMPT TO REQUIRE EXPENSING. This is where the controversy ensues. In 1993, the FASB issued an Exposure Draft of a new standard that would have required companies to measure options at their *fair values* at the time they are granted and to expense that amount over the appropriate service period. To jump straight to the punch line, the FASB bowed to public pressure and agreed to withdraw the requirement before it became a standard. The FASB consented to encourage, rather than require, that fair value compensation be recognized as expense. Companies were permitted to continue accounting under prior GAAP (the intrinsic value method referred to in the previous paragraph).[6] Before we discuss the details of accounting for stock options, it's helpful to look back at what led the FASB to first propose fair value accounting and later rescind that proposal.

As the 1990s began, the public was becoming increasingly aware of the enormity of executive compensation in general and compensation in the form of stock options in particular. The lack of accounting for this compensation was apparent, prompting the SEC to encourage the FASB to move forward on its stock option project. Even Congress got into the fray when, in 1992, a bill was introduced that would require firms to report compensation expense based on the fair value of options. Motivated by this encouragement, the FASB issued its exposure draft in 1993. The real disharmony began then. Opposition to the proposed standard was broad and vehement; and that perhaps is an understatement. Critics based their opposition on one or more of three objections:

1. *Options with no intrinsic value at issue have zero fair value and should not give rise to expense recognition.* The FASB, and even some critics of the proposal, were adamant that options provide valuable compensation at the grant date to recipients.
2. *It is impossible to measure the fair value of the compensation on the grant date.* The FASB argued vigorously that value can be approximated using one of several option pricing models. These are statistical models that use computers to incorporate information about a company's stock and the terms of the stock option to estimate the options'

[5] *San Jose Mercury News*, April 1, 2014.

[6] "Accounting for Stock Issued to Employees," *Opinions of the Accounting Principles Board No. 25* (New York: AICPA, 1972). This pronouncement is superseded and therefore is not codified in the *FASB Accounting Standards Codification*®.

fair value. We might say the FASB position is that it's better to be approximately right than precisely wrong.

3. *The proposed standard would have unacceptable economic consequences.* Essentially, this argument asserted that requiring this popular means of compensation to be expensed would cause companies to discontinue the use of options.

The opposition included corporate executives, auditors, members of Congress, and the SEC.[7] Ironically, the very groups that provided the most impetus for the rule change initially—the SEC and Congress—were among the most effective detractors in the end. The only group that offered much support at all was the academic community, and that was by-and-large nonvocal support. In reversing its decision, the FASB was not swayed by any of the specific arguments of any opposition group. Dennis Beresford, chair of the FASB at the time, indicated that it was fear of government control of the standard-setting process that prompted the Board to modify its position. The Board remained steadfast that the proposed change was appropriate.

There were consistent criticisms of the FASB's requirement to expense option compensation.

VOLUNTARY EXPENSING. Prior to 2002, only two companies—**Boeing** and **Winn-Dixie**—reported stock option compensation expense at fair value. However, in 2002 public outrage mounted amid high-profile accounting scandals at **Enron**, **WorldCom**, **Tyco**, and others. Some degree of consensus emerged that greed on the part of some corporate executives contributed to the fraudulent and misleading financial reporting at the time. In fact, many in the media were pointing to the proliferation of stock options as a primary form of compensation as a culprit in fueling that greed. An episode of the PBS series *Frontline* argued that not expensing the value of stock options contributed to the collapse of Enron. For these reasons, renewed interest surfaced in requiring stock option compensation to be reported in income statements.

Frank Partnoy—Author, Infectious Greed
. . . the increase in the use of stock options coincided with a massive increase in accounting fraud by corporate executives, who benefited from short-term increases in their stock prices.[8]

CURRENT REQUIREMENT TO EXPENSE. Emerging from the rekindled debate was a GAAP revision that now requires fair value accounting for employee stock options, eliminating altogether the intrinsic value approach.[9] As you might expect, the proposal did not come without opposition. Many of the same groups that successfully blocked the FASB from enacting a similar requirement in 1995 led the opposition. Not surprisingly, at the forefront of the resistance were the high-tech companies that extensively use stock options as a primary form of compensating employees and thus are most susceptible to a reduction in reported earnings when that compensation is included in income statements. For example, consider **Apple Inc.**'s earnings for the 12 months ending March 27, 2004. Reported net income of $179 million would have been only $56 million, or 69% less, if the GAAP revision had been in effect then.[10]

Current GAAP now requires companies to record the value of options in their income statements.

It's important to note that the way we account for stock options has no effect whatsoever on cash flows, only on whether the value of stock options is included among expenses. This is not to say that companies haven't altered their compensation strategies. Already, we have seen a shift in the way some companies compensate their employees. Partly due to the negative connotation that has become associated with executive stock options, we've seen fewer options and more bonuses and restricted stock awards. Let's examine the way stock options are accounted for now.

We've witnessed a discernable shift in the way executives are compensated—fewer options, more stock awards and bonuses.

Recognizing the Fair Value of Options

Accounting for stock options parallels the accounting for restricted stock we discussed in the first part of this chapter. That is, we measure compensation as the fair value of the stock

[7]All of the then "Big Six" CPA firms lobbied against the proposal. Senator Lieberman of Connecticut introduced a bill in Congress that if passed would have forbidden the FASB from passing a requirement to expense stock option compensation.

[8]Frank Partnoy, *Infectious Greed: How Deceit and Risk Corrupted the Financial Markets* (New York: Henry Holt/Times Books, Spring 2003), p. 159.

[9]FASB ASC 718–Compensation (previously "Share-Based Payment," *Statement of Financial Accounting Standards No. 123 (revised 2004)*, (Norwalk, Conn.: FASB 2004)).

[10]Alex Salkever, "What Could Crunch Apple Shares," *BusinessWeek*, July 12, 2004, p. 11.

The fair value of a stock option can be determined by employing a recognized option pricing model.

options at the grant date and then record that amount as compensation expense over the service period for which employees receive the options. Estimating the fair value requires the use of one of several option pricing models. These mathematical models assimilate a variety of information about a company's stock and the terms of the stock option to estimate the option's fair value. The model should take into account the:

An option pricing model takes into account several variables.

- Exercise price of the option.
- Expected term of the option.
- Current market price of the stock.
- Expected dividends.
- Expected risk-free rate of return during the term of the option.
- Expected volatility of the stock.

The techniques for estimating fair value have been among the most controversial issues in the debate.

The current GAAP for accounting for employee stock options modified the way companies actually measure fair value. It calls for using models that permit greater flexibility in modeling the ways employees are expected to exercise options and their expected employment termination patterns after options vest.[11] Option-pricing theory, on which the pricing models are based, is a topic explored in depth in finance courses and is subject to active empirical investigation and development. A simplified discussion is provided in Appendix 19A.[12]

The total compensation as estimated by the options' fair value is reported as compensation expense over the period of service for which the options are given. Recipients normally are not allowed to exercise their options for a specified number of years. This delay provides added incentive to remain with the company. The time between the date options are granted and the first date they can be exercised is the vesting period and usually is considered to be the service period over which the compensation expense is reported. The process is demonstrated in Illustration 19–3.

Illustration 19–3
Stock Options

At January 1, 2016, Universal Communications grants options that permit key executives to acquire 10 million of the company's $1 par common shares within the next eight years, but not before December 31, 2019 (the vesting date). The exercise price is the market price of the shares on the date of grant, $35 per share. The fair value of the options, estimated by an appropriate option pricing model, is $8 per option.

January 1, 2016
No entry

Fair value is estimated at the date of grant.

Calculate total compensation expense:

$ 8	Estimated fair value per option
× 10 million	Options granted
= $80 million	Total compensation

The value of the award is expensed over the service period for which the compensation is provided.

The total compensation is to be allocated to expense over the four-year service (vesting) period: 2016–2019.

$80 million ÷ 4 years = $20 million per year

December 31, 2016, 2017, 2018, 2019	($ in millions)	
Compensation expense ($80 million ÷ 4 years)	20	
Paid-in capital—stock options		20

Option compensation expense is based on the number of options expected to vest.

ESTIMATED FORFEITURES. If previous experience indicates that a material number of the options will be forfeited before they vest (due to employee turnover or violation of other terms of the options), we adjust the fair value estimate made on the grant date to reflect that expectation. For instance, if a forfeiture rate of 5% is expected, Universal's

[11]FASB ASC 718–10–55–30 to 32: Compensation–Stock Compensation–Overall–Implementation and Guidance Illustrations–Selecting or Estimating the Expected Term (previously "Share-Based Payment," *Statement of Financial Accounting Standards No. 123 (revised 2004)*, (Norwalk, Conn.: FASB 2004), par. A27–A29)).

[12]An expanded discussion is provided in FASB ASC 718–10–55: Compensation–Stock Compensation–Overall–Implementation and Guidance Illustrations (previously *SFAS No. 123 (revised 2004)*).

estimated total compensation would be 95% of $80 million, or $76 million. In that case, the annual compensation expense in Illustration 19–3 would have been **$19** million ($76/4) instead of $20 million. We see the effect of that possibility in Illustration 19–3A.

Illustration 19–3A
Estimates with Revisions

	($ in millions)	
2016		
Compensation expense ($80 × 95% ÷ 4)	19	
Paid-in capital—stock options		19
2017		
Compensation expense ($80 × 95% ÷ 4)	19	
Paid-in capital—stock options		19
2018		
Compensation expense [($80 × 90% × ¾) − ($19 + 19)]	16	
Paid-in capital—stock options		16
2019		
Compensation expense [($80 × 90% × 4/4) − ($19 + 19 + 16)]	18	
Paid-in capital—stock options		18

The value of the compensation is originally estimated to be $76 million, or $19 million per year.

The expense each year is the current estimate of total compensation that should have been recorded to date less the amount already recorded.

What if that expectation changes later? Universal should adjust the cumulative amount of compensation expense recorded to date in the year the estimate changes.[13] Suppose, for instance, that during the third year, Universal revises its estimate of forfeitures from 5% to 10%. The new estimate of total compensation would then be $80 million × 90%, or $72 million. For the first three years, the portion of the total compensation that should have been reported would be $72 million × ¾, or $54 million, and since $38 million (**$19** × 2) of that was recorded in 2016–2017 before the estimate changed, an additional $16 million would now be recorded in 2018. Then if the estimate isn't changed again, the remaining $18 million ($72 − 54) would be recorded in 2019.

When forfeiture estimates change, the cumulative effect on compensation is reflected in current earnings.

Additional Consideration

Notice that the $18 million in 2019 is the amount that would have been reported in each of the four years if Universal had assumed a 10% forfeiture rate from the beginning. Also be aware that this approach is contrary to the usual way companies account for changes in estimates. For instance, assume a company acquires a four-year depreciable asset having an estimated residual value of 5% of cost. The $76 million depreciable cost would be depreciated straight line at $19 million over the four-year useful life. If the estimated residual value changes after two years to 10%, the new estimated depreciable cost of $72 would be reduced by the $38 million depreciation recorded the first two years, and the remaining $34 million would be depreciated equally, $17 million per year, over the remaining two years.

When Options are Exercised

If half the options in Illustration 19–3 (five million shares) are exercised on July 11, 2022, when the market price is $50 per share, the following journal entry is recorded:

July 11, 2022	($ in millions)	
Cash ($35 exercise price × 5 million shares)	175	
Paid-in capital—stock options (½ account balance)	40	
Common stock (5 million shares at $1 par per share)		5
Paid-in capital—excess of par (to balance)		210

Recording the exercise of options is not affected by the market price on the exercise date.

[13]FASB ASC 718–10–35–3: Compensation–Stock Compensation–Overall–Subsequent Measurement (previously "Share-Based Payment," *Statement of Financial Accounting Standards No. 123 (revised 2004)*, (Norwalk, Conn.: FASB 2004), par. 43).

Notice that the market price at exercise is irrelevant. Changes in the market price of underlying shares do not influence the previously measured fair value of options.

When Unexercised Options Expire

If options that have vested expire without being exercised, the following journal entry is made (assuming the remaining 5 million options in our illustration are allowed to expire):

Paid-in capital—stock options becomes paid-in capital—expiration of stock options, **when options expire without being exercised.**

	($ in millions)	
Paid-in capital—stock options (account balance)	40	
Paid-in capital—expiration of stock options		40

In effect, we rename the paid-in capital attributable to the stock option plan. Compensation expense for the four years' service, as of the measurement date, is not affected.

Additional Consideration

Tax Consequences of Stock-Based Compensation Plans

In Illustration 19–3 we ignored the tax effect. To illustrate the effect of taxes, let's assume Universal Communications' income tax rate is 40%.

Tax treatment favors the employer in a nonqualified stock option plan.

For tax purposes, plans can either qualify as "incentive stock option plans" under the Tax Code or be "nonqualified plans." Among the requirements of a qualified option plan is that the exercise price be equal to the market price at the grant date. Under a qualified incentive plan, the recipient pays no income tax until any shares acquired from exercise of stock options are subsequently sold. On the other hand, the company gets no tax deduction at all. With a nonqualified plan the employee can't delay paying income tax, but the employer is permitted to deduct the difference between the exercise price and the market price at the exercise date. Let's consider both.

Because an incentive plan provides no tax deduction, it has no deferred tax consequences.

Case 1. With an incentive plan, the employer receives no tax deduction at all. If Universal's plan qualifies as an incentive plan, the company will receive no tax deduction upon exercise of the options and thus no tax consequences.

Case 2. On the other hand, if we assume the plan does not qualify as an incentive plan, Universal will deduct from taxable income the difference between the exercise price and the market price at the exercise date. Recall from Chapter 16 that this creates a temporary difference between accounting income (for which compensation expense is recorded currently) and taxable income (for which the tax deduction is taken later upon the exercise of the options). We assume the temporary difference is the cumulative amount expensed for the options. The following entries would be recorded on the dates shown:

A deferred tax asset is recognized now for the future tax savings from the tax deduction when the nonqualified stock options are exercised.

December 31, 2016, 2017, 2018, 2019	($ in millions)	
Compensation expense ($80 million ÷ 4 years)	20	
Paid-in capital—stock options		20
Deferred tax asset (40% × $20 million)	8	
Income tax expense		8

The after-tax effect on earnings is thus $12 million each year ($20 − 8).

If all of the options (ten million shares) are exercised on April 4, 2021:

Cash ($35 exercise price × 10 million shares)	350	
Paid-in capital—stock options (account balance)	80	
Common stock (10 million shares at $1 par per share)		10
Paid-in capital—excess of par (to balance)		420

(continued)

(concluded)

a. Options exercised when the tax benefit *exceeds* the deferred tax asset:
If the market price on April 4, 2021, is $50 per share:

Income taxes payable [(\$50 − 35) × 10 million shares × 40%]	60	
Deferred tax asset (4 years × \$8 million)		32
Paid-in capital—tax effect of stock options (remainder)*		28

If the eventual tax savings exceed the deferred tax asset, the difference is recognized as equity.

b. Options exercised when the tax benefit is *less than* the deferred tax asset:
If the market price on April 4, 2021, is $40 per share:

Income taxes payable [(\$40 − 35) × 10 million shares × 40%]	20	
Paid-in capital—tax effect of stock options or retained earnings† (remainder)	12	
Deferred tax asset (4 years × \$8 million)		32

The tax consequences of all nonqualifying stock options as well as restricted stock plans also are accounted for in the manner demonstrated above.

*This treatment is consistent with a provision of FASB ASC 740–20–45–11d that requires the tax effect of an increase or decrease in equity (paid-in capital—stock options, in this case) be allocated to equity.
†Paid-in capital—tax effect of stock options is debited only if that account has a sufficient credit balance from previous transactions in which the tax benefit exceeded the deferred tax asset.

International Financial Reporting Standards

Recognition of Deferred Tax Asset for Stock Options. Under U.S. GAAP, a deferred tax asset (DTA) is created for the cumulative amount of the fair value of the options the company has recorded for compensation expense. The DTA is the tax rate times the amount of compensation.

● LO19–14

Under IFRS, the deferred tax asset isn't created until the award is "in the money;" that is, it has intrinsic value. When it is in the money, the addition to the DTA is the portion of the intrinsic value earned to date times the tax rate.

IFRS ILLUSTRATION

For illustration, refer to Case 2 in the Additional Consideration example on the previous page. Now assume the share price, which was equal to the \$35 exercise price on January 1, 2016, was \$35, \$37, \$37, and \$37.50 on December 31, 2016, 2017, 2018, and 2019, respectively. We need this information to determine the intrinsic value for IFRS.

The addition to the DTA and reduction in the tax expense (tax benefit) is calculated in the following table for both U.S. GAAP and IFRS (\$ in millions):

Dec. 31	Compensation expense	Addition to DTA and reduction in tax expense at 40% U.S. GAAP	Cumulative reduction in tax expense	Intrinsic value (price − \$35) × 10M shares	Cumulative percent of services received	Percent × Intrinsic value	Addition to DTA and reduction in tax expense at 40%* IFRS
2016	\$20	\$ 8	\$ 8	\$ 0	25%	\$ 0	\$ 0
2017	20	8	16	20	50%	10	4
2018	20	8	24	20	75%	15	2
2019	20	8	32	25	100%	25	4

December 31, 2016, 2017, 2018, 2019 (\$ in millions)	**U.S. GAAP**		**IFRS**	
Compensation expense (\$80 million ÷ 4 years)	20		20	
Paid-in capital—stock options		20		20
Deferred tax asset	8		0	
Income tax expense		8		0

(continued)

(concluded)

Deferred tax asset	8		4	
Income tax expense		8		4
Deferred tax asset	8		2	
Income tax expense		8		2
Deferred tax asset	8		4	
Income tax expense		8		4

*The tax benefit recorded in earnings (cumulative amount in this column) cannot exceed the cumulative tax effect of the compensation (4th column). Any tax benefit in excess of that amount is recorded in equity. In 2019, $10 ($0 + 4 + 2 + 4) does not exceed $32.

Plans with Graded Vesting

The stock option plans we've discussed so far vest (become exercisable) on one single date (e.g., four years from date of grant). This is referred to as *cliff vesting*. More frequently, though, awards specify that recipients gradually become eligible to exercise their options rather than all at once. This is called *graded vesting*. For instance, a company might award stock options that vest 25% the first year, 25% the second year, and 50% the third year, or maybe 25% each year for four years.

In such a case, the company can choose to account for the options essentially the same as the cliff-vesting plans we've discussed to this point. It can estimate a single fair value for each of the options, even though they vest over different time periods, using a single weighted-average expected life of the options. The company then allocates that total compensation cost (fair value per option times number of options) over the entire vesting period.

Most companies, though, choose a slightly more complex method because it usually results in a lower expense.[14] In this approach, we view each vesting group (or tranche) separately, as if it were a separate award. See Illustration 19–4.

International Financial Reporting Standards

When options have graded vesting, U.S. GAAP permits companies to account for each vesting amount separately, for instance as if there were three separate awards as in the previous illustration, but also allows companies the option to account for the entire award on a straight-line basis over the entire vesting period. Either way, the company must recognize at least the amount of the award that has vested by that date.

LO19–14

Under IFRS, the straight-line choice is not permitted. Also, there's no requirement that the company must recognize at least the amount of the award that has vested by each reporting date.

Plans with Performance or Market Conditions

The terms of performance options vary with some measure of performance that ties rewards to productivity.

Stock option (and other share-based) plans often specify a performance condition or a market condition that must be satisfied before employees are allowed the benefits of the award. The objective is to provide employees with additional incentive for managerial achievement. For instance, an option might not be exercisable until a performance target is met. The target could be divisional revenue, earnings per share, sales growth, or rate of return on assets. The possibilities are limitless. On the other hand, the target might be market-related, perhaps a specified stock price or a stock price change exceeding a particular index. The way we account for such plans depends on whether the condition is performance-based or market-based.

PLANS WITH PERFORMANCE CONDITIONS. Whether we recognize compensation expense for performance-based options depends (a) initially on whether it's

[14]The fair value of the options usually is higher when estimated using a single weighted-average expected life of the options rather than when estimated as the total of fair values of the multiple vesting groups.

Illustration 19–4

Stock Options; Graded Vesting; Separate Valuation Approach

Taggart Mobility issued 10 million executive stock options permitting executives to buy 10 million shares of stock for $25. The vesting schedule is 20% the first year, 30% the second year, and 50% the third year (graded vesting). The value of the options that vest over the 3-year period is estimated at January 1, 2016, by separating the total award into three groups (or tranches) according to the year in which they vest (because the expected life for each group differs). The fair value of the options is estimated as follows:

Vesting Date	Amount Vesting	Fair Value per Option
Dec. 31, 2016	20%	$3.50
Dec. 31, 2017	30%	$4.00
Dec. 31, 2018	50%	$6.00

The compensation expense related to the options to be recorded each year 2016–2018 is:

Vesting Date	Number Vesting (shares in millions)	Fair Value per Option	Compensation Cost ($ in millions)
Dec. 31, 2016	2	$3.50	$ 7
Dec. 31, 2017	3	$4.00	12
Dec. 31, 2018	5	$6.00	30
Total	10		$49

We allocate the compensation cost for each of the three groups (tranches) evenly over its individual vesting (service) period:

	Compensation Expense Recorded in: ($ in millions)			
Shares Vesting at:	**2016**	**2017**	**2018**	**Total**
Dec. 31, 2016	$ 7			$ 7
Dec. 31, 2017	6	$ 6		12
Dec. 31, 2018	10	10	$10	30
	$23	$16	$10	= $49

At any given date, a company must have recognized at least the amount vested by that date. The allocation in this instance meets that constraint:

- The $23 million recognized in 2016 exceeds the $7 million vested.
- The $39 million ($23 + $16) recognized by 2017 exceeds the $19 million ($7 + $12) vested by the same time.

Companies also can choose to use the straight-line method, which would allocate the $49 million total compensation cost equally to 2016, 2017, and 2018 at $16.333 million per year.

probable[15] that the performance target will be met and (b) ultimately on whether the performance target actually is met. Accounting is as described earlier for other stock options. Initial estimates of compensation cost as well as subsequent revisions of that estimate take into account the likelihood of both forfeitures and achieving performance targets. For example, in Illustration 19–3, if the options described also had included a condition that the options would become exercisable only if sales increase by 10% after four years, we would estimate the likelihood of that occurring; specifically, is it probable? Let's say we initially estimate that it is probable that sales will increase by 10% after four years. Then, our initial estimate of the total compensation would have been unchanged at

If compensation from a stock option depends on meeting a performance target, compensation is recorded only if we feel it's probable the target will be met.

$10 million	×	$8	=	$80 million
Options expected to vest		Fair value		Estimated total compensation

[15] "Probable" means the same as it did in Chapter 13 when we were estimating the likelihood that payment would be made for a loss contingency and elsewhere when making accounting estimates. Probable is a matter of professional judgement (often 70–75%).

Suppose, though, that after two years, we estimate that it is *not* probable that sales will increase by 10% after four years. Then, our new estimate of the total compensation would change to

If it later becomes probable that a performance target will not be met, we reverse any compensation expense already recorded.

0	×	$8	=	0
Options expected to vest		Fair value		Estimated total compensation

In that case, we would reverse the $40 million expensed in 2016–2017. No compensation can be recognized for options that don't vest due to performance targets not being met, and that's our expectation.

When we revise our estimate of total compensation because our expectation of probability changes, we record the effect of the change in the current period.

Conversely, assume that our initial expectation is that it is *not* probable that sales will increase by 10% after four years and so we record no annual compensation expense. But then, in the third year, we estimate that it *is* probable that sales will increase by 10% after four years. At that point, our revised estimate of the total compensation would change to $80 million, and we would reflect the cumulative effect on compensation in 2018 earnings and record compensation thereafter:

If we had begun with our new estimate of total compensation, $20 million would have been expensed in each of the first three years.

2018		
Compensation expense [($80 ×¾) − $0]	60	
Paid-in capital—stock options		60
2019		
Compensation expense [($80 ×4/4) − $60]	20	
Paid-in capital—stock options		20

Additional **Consideration**

Suppose an executive who is granted some of the performance-based options in this example is eligible to retire on January 1, 2016. So, when the options are granted she would be eligible to receive the options even if the performance target (sales increase by 10%) is met after she retires. In that case, the service period needed to receive compensation effectively is one day. Should compensation for her be measured and expensed over the vesting period as in the example, or should that compensation be measured and recorded all at once (full amount if probable, zero otherwise) on the grant date?

It should be treated the same as the compensation for the other options. It should be treated as a performance condition consistent with those for which the requisite service period is not met prior to the performance target being met. So, we would record no compensation expense until meeting the performance target is probable, even if this is not until *after* the requisite vesting period is completed. An important secondary benefit of this treatment is that the employer doesn't need to assess at the grant date whether certain employees are retirement-eligible or will become retirement-eligible during the performance period in order to value the awards.[16]

This treatment differs from that of International Financial Reporting Standards, which specifies that if the performance target can be met *after* the requisite vesting period is completed, compensation for the recipients in this category, their compensation should be measured and recorded all at once (full amount if probable, zero otherwise) on the grant date.

[16]FASB Emerging Issues Task Force, *Accounting Standards Update No. 2014-12,* "Compensation—Stock Compensation (Topic 718): Accounting for Share-Based Payments When the Terms of an Award Provide That a Performance Target Could Be Achieved after the Requisite Service Period," June 2014.

PLANS WITH MARKET CONDITIONS. If the award contains a market condition (e.g., a share option with an exercisability requirement based on the stock price reaching a specified level), then no special accounting is required. The fair value estimate of the share option already implicitly reflects market conditions due to the nature of share option pricing models. So, we recognize compensation expense regardless of when, if ever, the market condition is met.

If the target is based on changes in the market rather than on performance, we record compensation as if there were no target.

DECLINE IN POPULARITY OF OPTIONS. Recent years have witnessed a steady shift in the way companies compensate their top executives. In the wake of recent accounting scandals, the image of stock options has been tarnished in the view of many who believe that the potential to garner millions in stock option gains created incentives for executives to boost company stock prices through risky or fraudulent behavior. That image has motivated many firms to move away from stock options in favor of other forms of share-based compensation, particularly restricted stock awards and, increasingly, restricted stock units. Also contributing to the rise of restricted stock is the feeling by many that it better aligns pay with performance. From the executive's perspective, restricted stock is a more certain, though potentially less lucrative, form of compensation.

At their peak in 1999, stock options represented about 78% of the average executive's incentive pay. In 2013, they accounted for just 31%, expected to shrink to 25% by 2015.[17]

Employee Share Purchase Plans

Employee share purchase plans often permit all employees to buy shares directly from their company at favorable terms. The primary intent of these plans is to encourage employee ownership of the company's shares. Presumably loyalty is enhanced among employee-shareholders. The employee also benefits because, typically, these plans allow employees to buy shares from their employer without brokerage fees and, perhaps, at a slight discount. Some companies even encourage participation by matching or partially matching employee purchases.

● LO19–3

Share purchase plans permit employees to buy shares directly from the corporation.

As long as (a) substantially all employees can participate, (b) employees have no longer than one month after the price is fixed to decide whether to participate, and (c) the discount is no greater than 5% (or can be justified as reasonable), accounting is straightforward. Simply record the sale of new shares as employees buy shares and do not record compensation expense.

If these criteria for the plan being noncompensatory are not met, say the discount is 15%, accounting is similar to other share-based plans. The 15% discount to employees, then, is considered to be compensation, and that amount is recorded as expense.[18] Compensation expense replaces the cash debit for any employer-provided portion. Say an employee buys shares (no par) under the plan for $850 rather than the current market price of $1,000. The $150 discount is recorded as compensation expense.

Cash (discounted price)	850	
Compensation expense ($1,000 × 15%)	150	
Common stock (market value)		1,000

Decision Makers' Perspective

In several previous chapters, we have revisited the concept of "earnings quality" (as first defined in Chapter 4). We also have noted that one rather common practice that negatively influences earnings quality is earnings management, which refers to companies' use of one or more of several techniques designed to artificially increase (or decrease) earnings. A frequent objective of earnings management is to meet analysts' expectations regarding

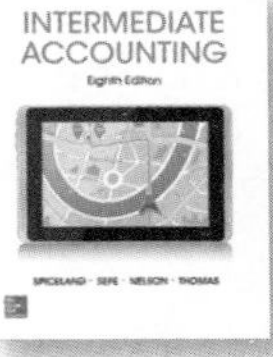

[17]According to an analysis of the 200 largest U.S. public companies by compensation consulting firm James F. Reda & Associates, as reported by Emily Chasan, "Last Gasp for Stock Options?" *USA Today,* August 26, 2013.

[18]FASB ASC 718–50–25–1 and 2: Compensation–Stock Compensation–Employee Share Purchase Plans–Recognition (previously "Share-Based Payment," *Statement of Financial Accounting Standards No. 123 (revised 2004),* (Norwalk, Conn.: FASB 2004), par. 12–13).

projections of income. The share-based compensation plans we discuss in this chapter suggest another motive managers sometimes have to manipulate income. If a manager's personal compensation includes company stock, stock options, or other compensation based on the value of the firm's stock, it's not hard to imagine an increased desire to ensure that market expectations are met and that reported earnings have a positive effect on stock prices. In fact, as we discussed earlier, that is precisely the reaction these incentive compensation plans are designed to elicit. Investors and creditors, though, should be alert to indications of attempts to artificially manipulate income and realize that the likelihood of earnings management is probably higher for companies with generous share-based compensation plans.

Analysts should be aware of the possibility of earnings management as a way to increase managers' compensation.

One way managers might manipulate numbers is to low-ball the data that go into the option-pricing models. The models used to estimate fair value are built largely around subjective assumptions. That possibility emphasizes the need for investors to look closely at the assumptions used as reported in the stock option disclosure note, and particularly at how those assumptions change from year to year. ●

Concept Review Exercise

SHARE-BASED COMPENSATION PLANS

Listed below are transactions dealing with various stock benefit plans of Fortune-Time Corporation during the period 2016–2018. The market price of the stock is $45 at January 1, 2016.

a. On January 1, 2016, the company issued 10 million common shares to divisional managers under its restricted stock award plan. The shares are subject to forfeiture if employment is terminated within three years.
b. On January 1, 2016, the company granted incentive stock options to its senior management exercisable for 1.5 million common shares. The options must be exercised within five years, but not before January 1, 2018. The exercise price of the stock options is equal to the fair value of the common stock on the date the options are granted. An option pricing model estimates the fair value of the options to be $4 per option. All recipients are expected to remain employed through the vesting date.
c. Recorded compensation expense on December 31, 2016.
d. A divisional manager holding 1 million of the restricted shares left the company to become CEO of a competitor on September 15, 2017, before the required service period ended.
e. Recorded compensation expense on December 31, 2017.

Required:

Prepare the journal entries that Fortune-Time recorded for each of these transactions. (Ignore any tax effects.)

Solution:

January 1, 2016

Restricted Stock Award Plan

No entry.

Total compensation is measured as 10 million shares × $45 = $450 million

Stock Options

No entry.

Total compensation is measured as 1.5 million shares × $4 = $6 million

December 31, 2016

Restricted Stock	($ in millions)	
Compensation expense ($450 million ÷ 3 years)	150	
Paid-in capital—restricted stock		150
Stock Options		
Compensation expense ($6 million ÷ 2 years)	3	
Paid-in capital—stock options		3

(continued)

(continued)

September 15, 2017

Restricted Stock

Paid-in capital—restricted stock (10% × $150)	15	
Compensation expense		15

December 31, 2017

Restricted Stock

Compensation expense [$450 − (.10 × $450) − 150 + 15] ÷ 2 years	135	
Paid-in capital—restricted stock		135

Stock Options

Compensation expense ($6 million ÷ 2 years)	3	
Paid-in capital—stock options		3

Earnings Per Share

PART B

A typical corporate annual report contains four comparative financial statements, an extensive list of disclosure notes and schedules, and several pages of charts, tables, and textual descriptions. Of these myriad facts and figures, the single accounting number that is reported most frequently in the media and receives by far the most attention by investors and creditors is **earnings per share** (EPS). The reasons for the considerable attention paid to earnings per share certainly include the desire to find a way to summarize the performance of business enterprises into a single number.

> Users' decisions involve choosing between alternatives . . . . . .Consequently, information about a reporting entity is more useful if it can be compared with similar information about other entities and with similar information about the same entity for another period or another date.[19]

***Earnings per share* is the single accounting number that receives the most media attention.**

Summarizing performance in a way that permits comparisons is difficult because the companies that report the numbers are different from one another. And yet, the desire to condense performance to a single number has created a demand for EPS information. The profession has responded with rules designed to maximize the comparability of EPS numbers by minimizing the inconsistencies in their calculation from one company to the next.[20]

Comparability is an enhancing characteristic of relevant accounting information *(Conceptual Framework)*.

Keep in mind as you study the requirements that a primary goal is comparability. As a result, many of the rules devised to achieve consistency are unavoidably arbitrary, meaning that other choices the FASB might have made in many instances would be equally adequate.

International Financial Reporting Standards

Earnings per Share. The earnings per share requirements of U.S. GAAP, *FASB ASC 260: Earnings per Share*, are a result of the FASB's cooperation with the IASB to narrow the differences between IFRS and U.S. GAAP. A few differences remain. The differences that remain are the result of differences in the application of the treasury stock method, the treatment of contracts that may be settled in shares or cash, and contingently issuable shares.

● LO19–14

[19]*SFAC 8, AQC 20, Conceptual Framework for Financial Reporting: Chapter 1, The Objective of General Purpose Reporting and Chapter 3, Qualitative Characteristics of Useful Financial Information,* (Norwalk, Conn.: FASB, September, 2010).

[20]FASB ASC 260: Earnings per Share (previously "Earnings per Share," *Statement of Financial Accounting Standards No. 128* (Norwalk, Conn.: FASB, 1997)). The guidance is applicable only for public companies.

Basic Earnings Per Share

A firm has a simple capital structure if it has no *potential common shares.*

A firm is said to have a **simple capital structure** if it has no outstanding securities that could potentially dilute earnings per share. In this context, to dilute means to *reduce* earnings per share. For instance, if a firm has convertible bonds outstanding and those bonds are converted, the resulting increase in common shares could decrease (or dilute) earnings per share. That is, the new shares replaced by the converted bonds might participate in future earnings. So convertible bonds are referred to as **potential common shares**. Other potential common shares are convertible preferred stock, stock options, and contingently issuable shares. We will see how the potentially dilutive effects of these securities are included in the calculation of EPS later in this chapter. Now, though, our focus is on the calculation of EPS for a simple capital structure—when no potential common shares are present. In these cases, the calculation is referred to as **basic EPS**, and is simply earnings available to common shareholders divided by the weighted-average number of common shares outstanding.

● LO19–4

Basic EPS reflects no dilution, only shares now outstanding.

In the most elemental setting, earnings per share (or net loss per share) is merely a firm's net income (or net loss) divided by the number of shares of common stock outstanding throughout the year. The calculation becomes more demanding (a) when the number of shares has changed during the reporting period, (b) when the earnings available to common shareholders are diminished by dividends to preferred shareholders, or (c) when we attempt to take into account the impending effect of potential common shares (which we do in a later section of the chapter). To illustrate the calculation of EPS in each of its dimensions, we will use only one example in this chapter. We'll start with the most basic situation and then add one new element at a time until we have considered all the principal ways the calculation can be affected. In this way you can see the effect of each component of earnings per share, not just in isolation, but in relation to the effects of other components as well. The basic calculation is shown in Illustration 19–5.

EPS expresses a firm's profitability on a per share basis.

Illustration 19–5
Fundamental Calculation

In the most elemental setting, earnings per share is simply a company's earnings divided by the number of shares outstanding.

Sovran Financial Corporation reported net income of $154 million in 2016 (tax rate 40%). Its capital structure consisted of:

Common Stock

Jan. 1 60 million common shares were outstanding
(amounts in millions, except per share amount)

Basic EPS:

$$\frac{\overset{\text{Net income}}{\$154}}{\underset{\text{Shares outstanding}}{60}} = \$2.57$$

Issuance of New Shares

Because the shares discussed in Illustration 19–5 remained unchanged throughout the year, the denominator of the EPS calculation is simply the number of shares outstanding. But if the number of shares has changed, it's necessary to find the *weighted average* of the shares outstanding during the period the earnings were generated. For instance, if an additional 12 million shares had been issued on March 1 of the year just ended, we calculate the weighted-average number of shares to be 70 million as demonstrated in Illustration 19–6 on the next page.

● LO19–5

Because the new shares were outstanding only 10 months, or $^{10}/_{12}$ of the year, we increase the 60 million shares already outstanding by the additional shares—weighted by the fraction of the year ($^{10}/_{12}$) they were outstanding. The weighted average is $60 + 12\ (^{10}/_{12}) = 60 + 10 = 70$ shares. The reason for time-weighting the shares issued is that the resources the stock sale provides the company are available for generating income only after the date the shares are sold. So, weighting is necessary to make the shares in the fraction's denominator consistent with the income in its numerator (see Illustration 19–6).

Illustration 19–6
Weighted Average

Sovran Financial Corporation reported net income of $154 million for 2016 (tax rate 40%). Its capital structure included:

Common Stock

Jan. 1	60 million common shares were outstanding
Mar. 1	12 million new shares were sold
	(amounts in millions, except per share amount)

Basic EPS:

Net income

$$\frac{\$154}{\underset{\text{Shares at Jan. 1}}{60} + \underset{\text{New shares}}{12\,(^{10}\!/_{12})}} = \frac{\$154}{70} = \$2.20$$

Any new shares issued are time-weighted by the fraction of the period they were outstanding and then added to the number of shares outstanding for the entire period.

Stock Dividends and Stock Splits

● LO19–6

Recall that a stock dividend or a stock split is a distribution of additional shares to existing shareholders. But there's an important and fundamental difference between the increase in shares caused by a stock dividend and an increase from selling new shares. When new shares are sold, both assets and shareholders' equity are increased by an additional investment in the firm by shareholders. On the other hand, a stock dividend or stock split merely increases the number of shares without affecting the firm's assets. In effect, the same pie is divided into more pieces. The result is a larger number of less valuable shares. This fundamental change in the nature of the shares is reflected in a calculation of EPS by simply increasing the number of shares.

In Illustration 19–7, notice that the additional shares created by the stock dividend are *not* weighted for the time period they were outstanding. Instead, the increase is treated as if it occurred at the beginning of the year.

Illustration 19–7
Stock Dividends and Stock Splits

Sovran Financial Corporation reported net income of $154 million in 2016 (tax rate 40%). Its capital structure included:

Common Stock

Jan. 1	60 million common shares were outstanding
Mar. 1	12 million new shares were sold
June 17	A 10% stock dividend was distributed
	(amounts in millions, except per share amount)

Basic EPS:

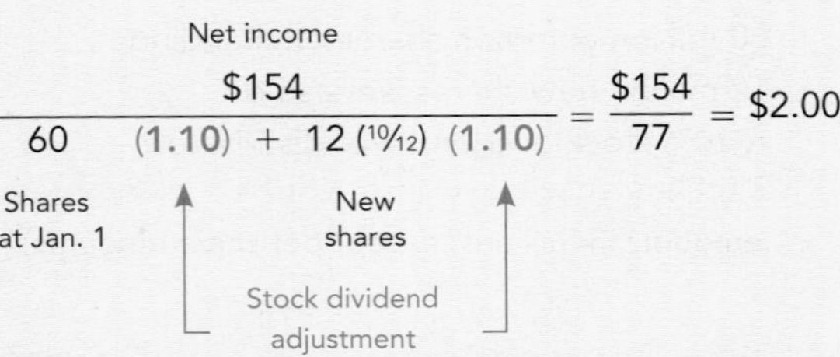

Net income

$$\frac{\$154}{60\,(1.10) + 12\,(^{10}\!/_{12})\,(1.10)} = \frac{\$154}{77} = \$2.00$$

Shares outstanding prior to the stock dividend are retroactively restated to reflect the 10% increase in shares—that is, treated as if the distribution occurred at the beginning of the period.

The number of shares outstanding after a 10% stock dividend is 1.10 times higher than before. This multiple is applied to both the beginning shares and the new shares sold before the stock distribution. If this had been a 25% stock dividend, the multiple would have been 1.25; a 2-for-1 stock split means a multiple of 2; and so on.

Notice that EPS without the 10% stock dividend ($2.20) is 10% more than it is with the stock distribution ($2). This is caused by the increase in the number of shares. But, unlike a sale of new shares, this should not be interpreted as a "dilution" of earnings per share.

Shareholders' interests in their company's earnings have not been diluted. Instead, each shareholder's interest is represented by more—though less valuable—shares.

A simplistic but convenient way to view the effect is to think of the predistribution shares as having been "blue." After the stock dividend, the more valuable "blue" shares are gone, replaced by a larger number of, let's say, "green" shares. From now on, we compute the earnings per "green" share, whereas we previously calculated earnings per "blue" share. We restate the number of shares retroactively to reflect the stock dividend, as if the shares always had been "green." After all, our intent is to let the calculation reflect the fundamental change in the nature of the shares.

Additional Consideration

When last year's EPS is reported in the current year's comparative income statements, it too should reflect the increased shares from the stock dividend. For instance, suppose EPS was $2.09 for 2015: $115 million net income divided by 55 million weighted-average shares. When reported again for comparison purposes in the 2016 comparative income statements, that figure would be restated to reflect the 10% stock dividend [$115 ÷ (55 × 1.10) = $1.90]:

Earnings per Share:	**2016**	**2015**
	$2.00	$1.90

The EPS numbers now are comparable—both reflect the stock dividend. Otherwise we would be comparing earnings per "green" share with earnings per "blue" share; this way both are earnings per "green" share.

Reacquired Shares

If shares were reacquired during the period (either retired or as treasury stock), the weighted-average number of shares is reduced. The number of reacquired shares is time-weighted for the *fraction of the year they were **not** outstanding,* prior to being *subtracted* from the number of shares outstanding during the period. Let's modify our continuing illustration to assume 8 million shares were reacquired on October 1 as treasury stock (Illustration 19–8).

Illustration 19–8
Reacquired Shares

Sovran Financial Corporation reported net income of $154 million in 2016 (tax rate 40%). Its capital structure included:

Common Stock

Jan. 1	60 million common shares outstanding
Mar. 1	12 million new shares were sold
June 17	A 10% stock dividend was distributed
Oct. 1	8 million shares were reacquired as treasury stock

(amounts in millions, except per share amounts)

Basic EPS:

The 8 million shares reacquired as treasury stock are weighted by (3/12) to reflect the fact they were not outstanding the last three months of the year.

$$\frac{\overset{\text{Net income}}{\$154}}{\underset{\text{Shares at Jan. 1}}{60}\,(1.10) + \underset{\text{New shares}}{12\,(^{10}/_{12})}\,(1.10) - \underset{\text{Treasury shares}}{8\,(^{3}/_{12})}} = \frac{\$154}{75} = \$2.05$$

(1.10): Stock dividend adjustment*

*Not necessary for the treasury shares since they were reacquired after the stock dividend and thus already reflect the adjustment (that is, the shares repurchased are 8 million "new green" shares).

Compare the adjustment for treasury shares with the adjustment for new shares sold. Each is time-weighted for the fraction of the year the shares were or were not outstanding. But also notice two differences. The new shares are added, while the reacquired shares are subtracted. The second difference is that the reacquired shares are not multiplied by 1.10 to adjust for the 10% stock dividend. The reason is the shares were repurchased after the June 17 stock dividend; the reacquired shares are 8 million of the new post-distribution shares. (To use our earlier representation, these are 8 million "green" shares.) To generalize, when a stock distribution occurs during the reporting period, any sales or purchases of shares that occur *before* the distribution are increased by the distribution. But the stock distribution does not increase the number of shares sold or purchased, if any, *after* the distribution.

The adjustment for reacquired shares is the same as for new shares sold except the shares are deducted rather than added.

Any sales or purchases of shares that occur before, but not after, a stock dividend or split are affected by the distribution.

Earnings Available to Common Shareholders

● LO19–7

The denominator in an EPS calculation is the weighted-average number of common shares outstanding. Logically, the numerator should similarly represent earnings available to common shareholders. This was automatic in our illustrations to this point because the only shares outstanding were common shares. But when a senior class of shareholders (like preferred shareholders) is entitled to a specified allocation of earnings (like preferred dividends), those amounts are subtracted from earnings before calculating earnings per share.[21] This is demonstrated in Illustration 19–9.

Illustration 19–9
Preferred Dividends

Sovran Financial Corporation reported net income of $154 million in 2016 (tax rate 40%). Its capital structure included:

Common Stock

January 1	60 million common shares were outstanding
March 1	12 million new shares were sold
June 17	A 10% stock dividend was distributed
October 1	8 million shares were reacquired as treasury stock

Preferred Stock Nonconvertible

January 1–December 31 5 million shares 8%, $10 par

(amounts in millions, except per share amount)

Basic EPS:

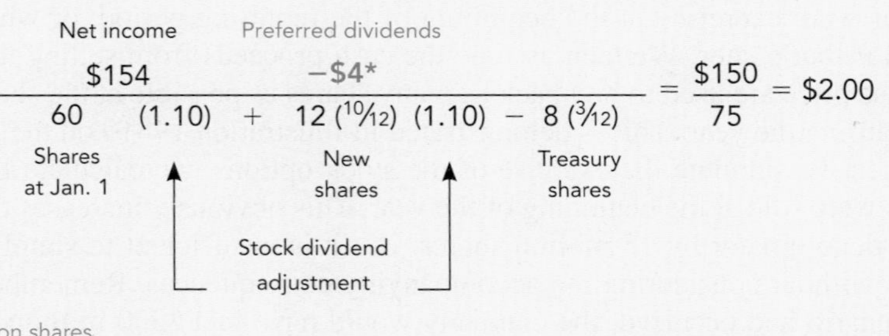

Net income
Preferred dividends
$154
−$4*
60 (1.10) + 12 (10/12) (1.10) − 8 (3/12)
=
$150
75
= $2.00
Shares at Jan. 1
New shares
Treasury shares
Stock dividend adjustment

*8% × $10 par × 5 million shares.

Preferred dividends are subtracted from net income so that "earnings available to common shareholders" is divided by the weighted-average number of common shares.

Suppose no dividends were declared for the year. Should we adjust for preferred dividends? Yes, if the preferred stock is cumulative—and most preferred stock is. This means that when dividends are not declared, the unpaid dividends accumulate to be paid in a future year when (if) dividends are subsequently declared. Obviously, the presumption is that, although the year's dividend preference isn't distributed this year, it eventually will be paid.

Preferred dividends reduce earnings available to common shareholders unless the preferred stock is noncumulative and no dividends were declared that year.

We have encountered no potential common shares to this point in our continuing illustration. As a result, we have what is referred to as a simple capital structure. (Although, at

[21]You learned in Chapter 18 that when dividends are declared, preferred shareholders have a preference (over common shareholders) to a specified amount.

this point, you may question this label.) For a simple capital structure, a single presentation of basic earnings per common share is appropriate. We turn our attention now to situations described as complex capital structures. In these situations, two separate presentations are required: basic EPS and diluted EPS.

Diluted Earnings Per Share

Potential Common Shares

Imagine a situation in which convertible bonds are outstanding that will significantly increase the number of common shares if bondholders exercise their options to exchange their bonds for shares of common stock. Should these potential shares be ignored when earnings per share is calculated? After all, they haven't been converted as yet, so to assume an increase in shares for a conversion that may never occur might mislead investors and creditors. On the other hand, if conversion is imminent, not taking into account the dilutive effect of the share increase might mislead investors and creditors. The profession's solution to the dilemma is to calculate earnings per share twice.

In a complex capital structure, a second EPS computation takes into account the assumed effect of *potential common* shares, essentially a "worst case scenario."

Securities such as these convertible bonds, while not being common stock, may become common stock through their exercise or conversion. Therefore, they may dilute (reduce) earnings per share and are called **potential common shares**. A firm is said to have a **complex capital structure** if potential common shares are outstanding. Besides convertible bonds, other potential common shares are convertible preferred stock, stock options, and contingently issuable securities. (We'll discuss each of these shortly.) A firm with a complex capital structure reports two EPS calculations. **Basic EPS** ignores the dilutive effect of such securities, **diluted EPS** incorporates the dilutive effect of all potential common shares.

Options, Rights, and Warrants

● LO19–8

Stock options, stock rights, and stock warrants are similar. Each gives its holders the right to exercise their option to purchase common stock, usually at a specified exercise price. The dilution that would result from their exercise should be reflected in the calculation of diluted EPS, but not basic EPS.

Stock options are assumed to have been exercised when calculating diluted EPS.

To include the dilutive effect of a security means to calculate EPS *as if* the potential increase in shares already has occurred (even though it hasn't yet). So, for stock options (or rights, or warrants), we pretend the options have been exercised. In fact, we assume the options were exercised at the beginning of the reporting period, or when the options were issued if that's later. We then assume the cash proceeds from selling the new shares at the exercise price are used to buy back as many shares as possible at the shares' average market price during the year. This is demonstrated in Illustration 19–10 on the next page.

FINANCIAL Reporting Case

Q4, p. 1127

When we simulate the exercise of the stock options, we calculate EPS as if 15 million shares were sold at the beginning of the year. This obviously increases the number of shares in the denominator by 15 million shares. But it is insufficient to simply add the additional shares without considering the accompanying consequences. Remember, if this hypothetical scenario had occurred, the company would have had \$300 million cash proceeds from the exercise of the options (15 million shares × \$20 exercise price per share). What would have been the effect on earnings per share? This depends on what the company would have done with the \$300 million cash proceeds. Would the proceeds have been used to buy more equipment? Increase the sales force? Expand facilities? Pay dividends?

Obviously, there are literally hundreds of choices, and it's unlikely that any two firms would spend the \$300 million exactly the same way. But remember, our objective is to create some degree of uniformity in the way firms determine earnings per share so the resulting numbers are comparable. So, standard-setters decided on a single assumption for all firms to provide some degree of comparability.

For diluted EPS, we assume the proceeds from exercise of the options were used to reacquire shares as treasury stock at the average market price of the common stock during the reporting period. Consequently, the weighted-average number of shares is increased by the difference between the shares assumed issued and those assumed reacquired—in

Illustration 19–10
Stock Options

Sovran Financial Corporation reported net income of $154 million in 2016 (tax rate 40%). Its capital structure included:

Common Stock

January 1	60 million common shares outstanding
March 1	12 million new shares were sold
June 17	A 10% stock dividend was distributed
October 1	8 million shares were reacquired as treasury stock

(The average market price of the common shares during 2016 was $25 per share.)

Preferred Stock Nonconvertible

January 1–December 31 5 million shares 8%, $10 par

Incentive Stock Options

Executive stock options granted in 2011, exercisable after 2015 for 15 million common shares* at an exercise price of $20 per share

(amounts in millions, except per share amounts)

Basic EPS (unchanged)

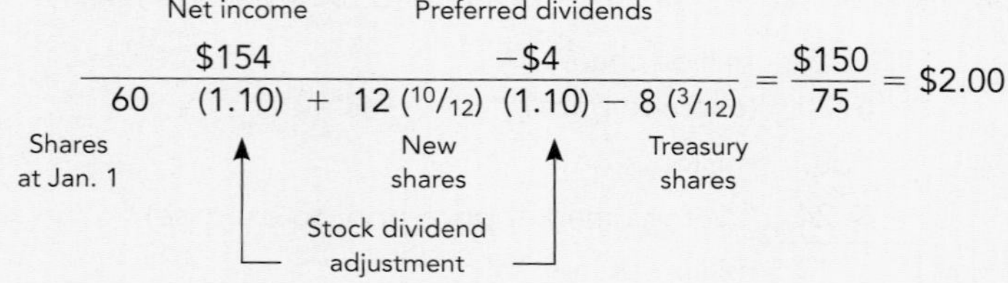

$$\frac{\$154 \quad -\$4}{60 \quad (1.10) + 12\,(^{10}/_{12})\,(1.10) - 8\,(^{3}/_{12})} = \frac{\$150}{75} = \$2.00$$

Diluted EPS

Net income — Preferred dividends

$$\frac{\$154 \quad -\$4}{60 \quad (1.10) + 12\,(^{10}/_{12})\,(1.10) - 8\,(^{3}/_{12}) + (15^{*} - 12^{\dagger})} = \frac{\$150}{78} = \$1.92$$

Shares at Jan. 1 — New shares — Treasury shares — Exercise of options — Stock dividend adjustment

*Adjusted for the stock dividend. Prior to the stock dividend, the options were exercisable for 13 7/11 million of the "old" shares. Upon the stock dividend, the new equivalent of 13 7/11 became 15 million (13 7/11 × 1.10) of the "new" shares.

†Shares Assumed Reacquired for Diluted EPS

15	million shares
× $ 20	(exercise price)
$300	million
÷ $ 25	(average market price)
12	million shares reacquired

Stock options give their holders (company executives in this case) the right to purchase common stock at a specified exercise price ($20 in this case).

The stock options do not affect the calculation of *basic* EPS.

The calculation of diluted EPS assumes that the shares specified by stock options were issued at the exercise price and that the proceeds were used to buy back (as treasury stock) as many of those shares as can be purchased at the market price during the period.

our illustration: 15 million shares issued minus 12 million shares reacquired ($300 million × $25 per share) equals 3 million net increase in shares.

The way we take into account the dilutive effect of stock options is called the *treasury stock method* because of our assumption that treasury shares are purchased with the cash proceeds of the exercise of the options. Besides providing comparability, this assumption actually is plausible because, if the options were exercised, more shares would be needed to issue to option-holders. And, as discussed in the previous chapter, many firms routinely buy back shares either to issue to option-holders or, equivalently, to offset the issuance of new shares.

Convertible Securities

● LO19–9

Sometimes corporations include a conversion feature as part of a bond offering, a note payable, or an issue of preferred stock. Convertible securities can be converted into (exchanged

Additional Consideration

Actual Exercise of Options

What if options are actually exercised during the reporting period? In that case, we include in the denominator of both basic and diluted EPS the actual shares issued upon the exercise of the options, time-weighted for the fraction of the year the new shares actually are outstanding. This is consistent with the way we include new shares sold under any circumstances.

In addition, we include in diluted EPS only, the incremental shares that would have been issued prior to the actual exercise of the options if we pretend the options were exercised at the beginning of the period. We time-weight those shares by the fraction of the year the shares would be outstanding prior to the actual exercise of the options.

Let's say the options in our illustration were exercised on September 1 and that the average per-share price of the stock from the beginning of the year until September 1 was \$24. In that case, we add 5 million shares to the denominator of both basic and diluted EPS: the 15 million shares actually issued × 4/12 of the year actually outstanding = 5 million shares. Then, for *diluted EPS only,* we add the incremental shares that would have been issued *prior to* the actual exercise of the options if we pretend the options were exercised at the beginning of the period. We assume the proceeds (15 million shares × \$20 = \$300 million) are used to buy shares back at \$24:

15	million shares
× \$ 20	(exercise price)
\$300	million
÷ \$ 24	(average market price prior to exercise)
12.5	million shares

The incremental number of shares to be included in the computation of diluted EPS, then, are weighted for the period the options were outstanding prior to exercise, the 8 months from January 1 to September 1, or 8/12 of a year.

$$\frac{\text{No adjustment to the numerator}}{+ (15 - 12.5)(8/12)}$$

for) shares of stock at the option of the holder of the security. For that reason, convertible securities are potentially dilutive. EPS will be affected if and when such securities are converted and new shares of common stock are issued. In the previous section you learned that the potentially dilutive effect of stock options is reflected in diluted EPS calculations by assuming the options were exercised. Similarly, the potentially dilutive effect of convertible securities is reflected in diluted EPS calculations by assuming they were converted.

When we assume conversion, the denominator of the EPS fraction is increased by the additional common shares that would have been issued upon conversion.

By the *if converted method* as it's called, we assume the conversion into common stock occurred at the beginning of the period (or at the time the convertible security is issued, if that's later). We increase the denominator of the EPS fraction by the additional common shares that would have been issued upon conversion. We increase the numerator by the interest (after-tax) on bonds or other debt or the preferred dividends that would have been avoided if the convertible securities had not been outstanding due to having been converted.

The numerator is increased by the after-tax interest that would have been avoided.

CONVERTIBLE BONDS. Now, let's return to our continuing illustration and modify it to include the existence of convertible bonds (Illustration 19–11). We increase the denominator by the 12 million shares that would have been issued if the bonds had been converted. However, if that hypothetical conversion had occurred, the bonds would not have been outstanding during the year. What effect would the absence of the bonds have had on income? Obviously, the bond interest expense (10% × \$300 million = \$30 million) would have been saved, causing income to be higher. But saving the interest paid would also have meant losing a \$30 million tax deduction on the income tax return. With a 40% tax rate that would mean paying \$12 million more income taxes. So, to reflect in earnings the \$18 million after-tax interest that would have been avoided in the event of conversion, we add back the \$30 million of interest expense, but deduct 40% × \$30 million for the higher tax expense.

Illustration 19–11
Convertible Bonds

Sovran Financial Corporation reported net income of $154 million in 2016 (tax rate 40%). Its capital structure included:

Common Stock

Jan. 1	60 million common shares were outstanding
Mar. 1	12 million new shares were sold
June 17	A 10% stock dividend was distributed
Oct. 1	8 million shares were reacquired as treasury stock

(The average market price of the common shares during 2016 was $25 per share.)

Preferred Stock, Nonconvertible

January 1–December 31 5 million shares 8%, $10 par

Incentive Stock Options

Executive stock options granted in 2011, exercisable after 2015 for 15 million common shares* at an exercise price of $20 per share

Convertible Bonds

10%, $300 million face amount issued in 2015, convertible into 12 million common shares

(amounts in millions, except per share amounts)

Basic EPS (unchanged)

$$\frac{\underset{\text{Net income}}{\$154} \quad \underset{\text{Preferred dividends}}{-\$4}}{\underset{\text{Shares at Jan. 1}}{60}\ (1.10) + \underset{\text{New shares}}{12}\ (10/12)\ (1.10) - \underset{\text{Treasury shares}}{8}\ (3/12)} = \frac{\$150}{75} = \$2.00$$

(1.10: Stock dividend adjustment)

The convertible bonds do not affect the calculation of *basic* EPS.

Diluted EPS

$$\frac{\underset{\text{Net income}}{\$154} \quad \underset{\text{Preferred dividends}}{-\$4} \quad \underset{\text{After-tax interest savings}}{+\ \$30 - 40\%\ (30)}}{\underset{\text{Shares at Jan. 1}}{60}\ (1.10) + \underset{\text{New shares}}{12}\ (10/12)\ (1.10) - \underset{\text{Treasury shares}}{8}\ (3/12) + \underset{\text{Exercise of options}}{(15^* - 12)} \quad \underset{\text{Conversion of bonds}}{+12^*}} = \frac{\$168}{90} = \$1.87$$

(1.10: Stock dividend adjustment)

If the bonds had been converted, 12 million more common shares would have been issued, and net income would have been higher by the interest saved (after tax) from not having the bonds outstanding.

*Adjusted for the stock dividend. For example, prior to the stock dividend, the bonds were exercisable for $10^{10}/_{11}$ million of the "old" shares which became 12 million ($10^{10}/_{11} \times 1.10$) of the "new" shares after the stock dividend.

Additional Consideration

The $300 million of convertible bonds in our illustration were issued at face value. Suppose the bonds had been issued for $282 million. In that case, the adjustment to earnings would be modified to include the amortization of the $18 million bond discount. Assuming straight-line amortization and a 10-year maturity, the adjustment to the diluted EPS calculation would have been

$$\frac{+\ [\$30 + (\$18 \div 10 \text{ years})] \times (1 - 40\%)^*}{+\ 12}$$

to reflect the fact that the interest expense would include the $30 million stated interest plus one-tenth of the bond discount.†

*This is an alternative way to represent the after-tax adjustment to interest since subtracting 40% of the interest expense is the same as multiplying interest expense by 60%.

†See Chapter 14 if you need to refresh your memory about bond discount amortization.

Our illustration describes the treatment of convertible bonds. The same treatment pertains to other debt that is convertible into common shares such as convertible notes payable. Remember from our discussion of debt in earlier chapters that all debt is similar whether in the form of bonds, notes, or other configurations.

Additional Consideration

We assume convertible securities were converted (or options exercised) at the beginning of the reporting period or at the time the securities are issued, if later.

Notice that we assumed the bonds were converted at the beginning of the reporting period since they were outstanding all year. However, if the convertible bonds had been issued during the reporting period, we would assume their conversion occurred on the date of issue. It would be illogical to assume they were converted before they were issued. If the convertible bonds in our illustration had been sold on September 1, for instance, the adjustment to the EPS calculation would have been

$$\frac{+ [\$30 - 40\% (\$30)] (4/12)}{+ 12 (4/12)}$$

to reflect the fact that the net increase in shares would have been effective for only four months of the year.

CONVERTIBLE PREFERRED STOCK. The potentially dilutive effect of convertible preferred stock is reflected in EPS calculations in much the same way as convertible debt. That is, we calculate EPS as if conversion already had occurred. Specifically, we add shares to the denominator of the EPS fraction. We do not subtract the preferred dividends in the numerator because those dividends would have been avoided if the preferred stock had been converted. In Illustration 19–12 we assume our preferred stock is convertible into 3 million shares of common stock.

The adjustment for the conversion of the preferred stock is applied only to diluted EPS computations. Basic EPS is unaffected.

Illustration 19–12
Convertible Preferred Stock

Sovran Financial Corporation reported net income of $154 million in 2016 (tax rate 40%). Its capital structure included:

Common Stock

Jan. 1	60 million common shares were outstanding
Mar. 1	12 million new shares were sold
June 17	A 10% stock dividend was distributed
Oct. 1	8 million shares were reacquired as treasury stock

(The average market price of the common shares during 2016 was $25 per share.)

Preferred Stock, Convertible into 3 million common shares*
January 1–December 31 5 million shares 8%, $10 par

Incentive Stock Options
Executive stock options granted in 2011, exercisable after 2015 for 15 million common shares* at an exercise price of $20 per share

Convertible Bonds
10%, $300 million face amount issued in 2015, convertible into 12 million common shares

(amounts in millions, except per share amounts)

Basic EPS

$$\frac{\underset{\text{Net income}}{\$154} \quad \underset{\text{Preferred dividends}}{-\$4}}{\underset{\text{Shares at Jan. 1}}{60} (1.10) + \underset{\text{New shares}}{12 (10/12)} (1.10) - \underset{\text{Treasury shares}}{8 (3/12)}} = \frac{\$150}{75} = \$2.00$$

(1.10): Stock dividend adjustment

(continued)

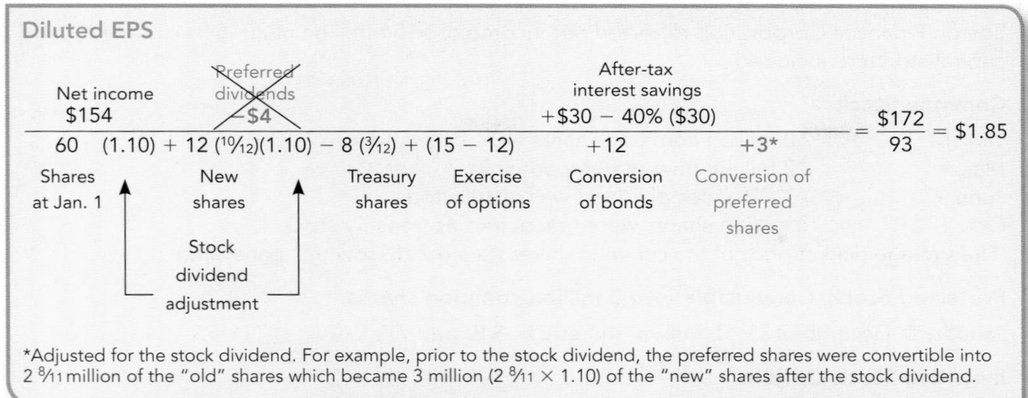

Diluted EPS
Net income
$154
Preferred dividends
−$4
After-tax interest savings
+$30 − 40% ($30)
60 (1.10) + 12 (10⁄12)(1.10) − 8 (3⁄12) + (15 − 12) +12 +3*
= $172 / 93 = $1.85
Shares at Jan. 1
New shares
Treasury shares
Exercise of options
Conversion of bonds
Conversion of preferred shares
Stock dividend adjustment
*Adjusted for the stock dividend. For example, prior to the stock dividend, the preferred shares were convertible into 2 8⁄11 million of the "old" shares which became 3 million (2 8⁄11 × 1.10) of the "new" shares after the stock dividend.

Illustration 19–12 (concluded)

Since diluted EPS is calculated as if the preferred shares had been converted, there are no dividends.

However, when diluted EPS is calculated, we hypothetically assume the convertible preferred stock was *not* outstanding. Accordingly, no preferred dividends on these shares would have been paid.

Antidilutive Securities

At times, the effect of the conversion or exercise of potential common shares would be to increase, rather than decrease, EPS. These we refer to as **antidilutive securities**. Such securities are ignored when calculating both basic and diluted EPS.

Options, Warrants, Rights

LO19–10

For illustration, recall the way we treated the stock options in our continuing illustration. In applying the treasury stock method, the number of shares assumed repurchased is fewer than the number of shares assumed sold. This is the case any time the buyback (average market) price is higher than the exercise price. Consequently, there will be a net increase in the number of shares, so earnings per share will decline.

On the other hand, when the exercise price is *higher* than the market price, to assume shares are sold at the exercise price and repurchased at the market price would mean buying back *more* shares than were sold. This would produce a net decrease in the number of shares. EPS would increase, not decrease. These would have an antidilutive effect and would not be considered exercised. In fact, a rational investor would not exercise options at an exercise price higher than the current market price anyway. Let's look at the example provided by Illustration 19–13.

> The computation of dilutive shares outstanding excludes the out-of-the-money stock options because such outstanding options' exercise prices were greater than the average market price of our common shares and, therefore, the effect would be antidilutive (i.e., including such options would result in higher earnings per share).[22]

Antidilutive securities are ignored when calculating both basic and diluted EPS.

To assume 4 million shares were sold at the $32.50 exercise price and repurchased at the lower market price ($25) would mean reacquiring 5.2 million shares. That's more shares than were assumed sold. Because the effect would be antidilutive, we would simply ignore the warrants in the calculations.

In our continuing illustration, only the stock warrants were antidilutive. The other potential common shares caused EPS to decline when we considered them exercised or converted. In the case of the executive stock options, it was readily apparent that their effect would be dilutive because the exercise price was less than the market price, indicating that fewer shares could be repurchased (at the average market price) than were assumed issued (at the exercise price). As a result, the denominator increased. When only the denominator of a fraction increases, the fraction itself decreases. On the other hand, in the case of the warrants, it was apparent that their effect would be antidilutive because the exercise price was higher than the market price, which would have decreased the denominator and therefore increased the fraction.

When a company has a net loss, rather than net income, it reports a loss per share. In that situation, stock options that otherwise are dilutive will be antidilutive. Here's why. Suppose we have a

[22]Best Buy Co., Inc., *Form 10-Q* for the quarter ended August 3, 2013.

Illustration 19–13
Antidilutive Warrants

Sovran Financial Corporation reported net income of $154 million in 2016 (tax rate 40%). Its capital structure included:

Common Stock

Jan. 1	60 million common shares were outstanding
Mar. 1	12 million new shares were sold
June 17	A 10% stock dividend was distributed
Oct. 1	8 million shares were reacquired as treasury stock

(The average market price of the common shares during 2016 was $25 per share.)

Preferred Stock, Convertible into 3 million common shares.

January 1–December 31 5 million shares 8%, $10 par

Incentive Stock Options

Executive stock options granted in 2011, exercisable after 2015 for 15 million common shares at an exercise price of $20 per share

Convertible Bonds

10%, $300 million face amount issued in 2015, convertible into 12 million common shares

Stock Warrants

Warrants granted in 2015, exercisable for 4 million common shares* at an exercise price of $32.50 per share

Calculations:

The calculations of both basic and diluted EPS are unaffected by the warrants because the effect of exercising the warrants would be antidilutive.

*Adjusted for the stock dividend. For example, prior to the stock dividend, the warrants were exercisable for $3\frac{7}{11}$ million of the "old" shares which became 4 million ($3\frac{7}{11} \times 1.10$) of the "new" shares after the stock dividend.

The $32.50 exercise price is higher than the market price, $25, so to assume shares are sold at the exercise price and repurchased at the market price would mean reacquiring more shares than were sold.

loss per share of $2.00 calculated as ($150 million) ÷ 75 million shares = ($2.00). Now suppose stock options are outstanding that, if exercised, will increase the number of shares by 5 million. If that increase is included in the calculation, the loss per share will be $1.88 calculated as ($150 million) ÷ 80 million shares = ($1.88). The *loss* per share *declines*. This represents an *increase* in performance—not a dilution of performance. The options would be considered antidilutive, then, and not included in the calculation of the net loss per share. Any potential common shares not included in dilutive EPS because they are antidilutive should be revealed in the disclosure notes.

Convertible Securities

For convertible securities, though, it's not immediately obvious whether the effect of their conversion would be dilutive or antidilutive because the assumed conversion would affect both the numerator and the denominator of the EPS fraction. We discovered each was dilutive only after including the effect in the calculation and observing the result—a decline in EPS. But there's an easier way.

To determine whether convertible securities are dilutive and should be included in a diluted EPS calculation, we can compare the "incremental effect" of the conversion (expressed as a fraction) with the EPS fraction before the effect of any convertible security is considered. This, of course is our basic EPS. Recall from Illustration 19–12 that basic EPS is $2.00.

For comparison, we determine the "earnings per incremental share" of the two convertible securities.

Conversion of bonds.

After-tax interest savings

$$\frac{+\$30 - 40\%\ (\$30)}{+12} = \frac{\$18}{12} = \$1.50$$

Conversion of bonds

The incremental effect (of conversion) of the bonds is the after-tax interest saved divided by the additional common shares from conversion.

Conversion of preferred stock.

$$\frac{+\$4 \text{ (Preferred dividends)}}{+\ 3 \text{ (Conversion of preferred shares)}} = \$1.33$$

The incremental effect (of conversion) of the preferred stock is the dividends that wouldn't be paid divided by the additional common shares from conversion.

If the incremental effect of a security is *higher* than basic EPS, it is antidilutive. That's not the case in our illustration.

Order of Entry for Multiple Convertible Securities

A convertible security might seem to be dilutive when looked at individually but, in fact, may be antidilutive when included in combination with other convertible securities. This is because the *order of entry* for including their effects in the EPS calculation determines by how much, or even whether, EPS decreases as a result of their assumed conversion. Because our goal is to reveal the maximum potential dilution that might result, theoretically we should calculate diluted EPS using every possible combination of potential common shares to find the combination that yields the lowest EPS. But that's not necessary.

We can use the earnings per incremental share we calculated to determine the sequence of including securities' effects in the calculation. We include the securities in reverse order, beginning with the lowest incremental effect (that is, most dilutive), followed by the next lowest, and so on. This is, in fact, the order in which we included the securities in our continuing illustration.

Additional Consideration

Actually, the order of inclusion made no difference in our example, but would in many instances. For example, suppose the preferred stock had been convertible into 2.1 million shares, rather than 3 million shares. The incremental effect of its conversion would have been:

Conversion of Preferred Stock

$$\frac{\text{Preferred dividends } +\$4}{+2.1 \text{ Conversion of preferred shares}} = \$1.90$$

On the surface, the effect would seem to be dilutive because $1.90 is less than $2.00, basic EPS. In fact, if this were the only convertible security, it would be dilutive. But, after the convertible bonds are assumed converted first, then the assumed conversion of the preferred stock would be *antidilutive:*

With Conversion of Bonds

$$\frac{\underset{\text{Net income}}{\$154} \ \underset{\text{Preferred dividends}}{-\$4} \ \underset{\text{After-tax interest savings}}{+\ \$30 - 40\%\ (\$30)}}{\underset{\text{Shares at Jan. 1}}{60}\ (1.10) + \underset{\text{New shares}}{12\ (^{10}\!/_{12})}\ (1.10) - \underset{\text{Treasury shares}}{8\ (^{3}\!/_{12})} + \underset{\text{Exercise of options}}{(15 - 12)} + \underset{\text{Conversion of bonds}}{12}} = \frac{\$168}{90} = \$1.867$$

(The (1.10) factors are the stock dividend adjustment.)

Because the incremental effect of the convertible bonds ($1.50) is lower than the incremental effect of the convertible preferred stock ($1.90), it is included first.

(continued)

A convertible security might seem to be dilutive when looked at individually but may be antidilutive when included in combination with other convertible securities.

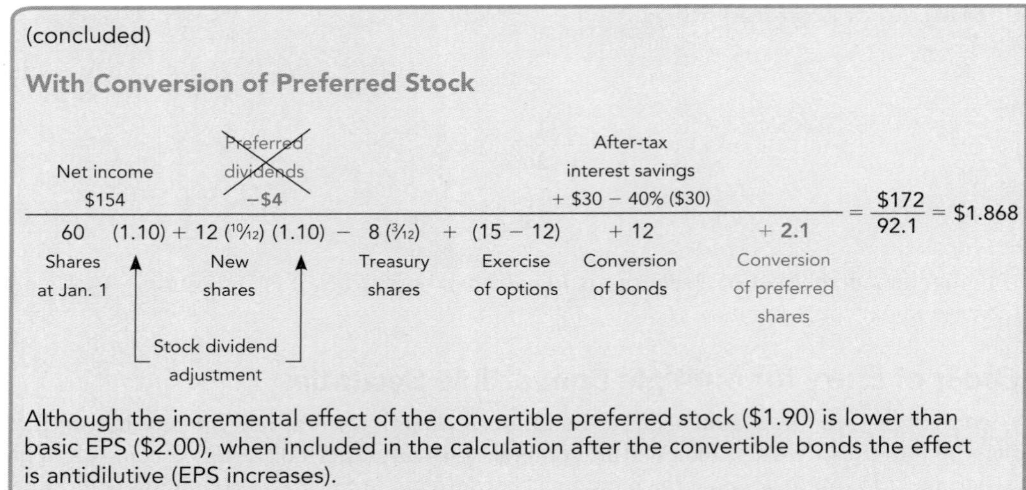

Concept Review Exercise

BASIC AND DILUTED EPS

At December 31, 2016, the financial statements of Clevenger Casting Corporation included the following:

Net income for 2016	$500 million
Common stock, $1 par:	
Shares outstanding on January 1	150 million shares
Shares retired for cash on February 1	24 million shares
Shares sold for cash on September 1	18 million shares
2-for-1 split on July 23	
Preferred stock, 10%, $70 par, cumulative, nonconvertible	$ 70 million
Preferred stock, 8%, $50 par, cumulative, convertible into 4 million shares of common stock	$100 million
Incentive stock options outstanding, fully vested, for 4 million shares of common stock; the exercise price is $15	
Bonds payable, 12.5%, convertible into 20 million shares of common stock	$200 million

Additional data:
The market price of the common stock averaged $20 during 2016.
The convertible preferred stock and the bonds payable had been issued at par in 2014. The tax rate for the year was 40%.

Required:
Compute basic and diluted earnings per share for the year ended December 31, 2016.

(amounts in millions, except per share amounts)

Solution:
Basic EPS

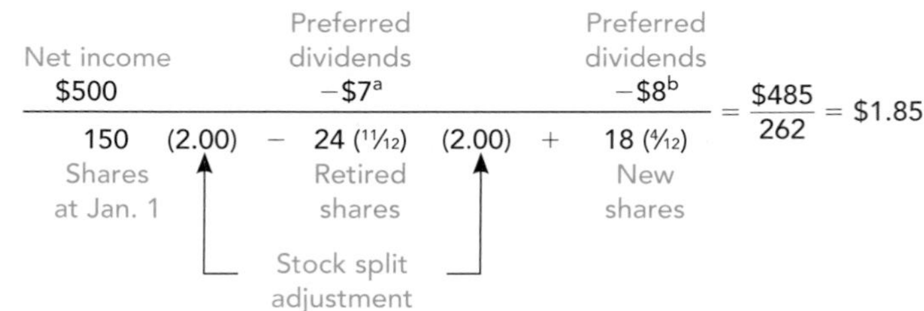

Diluted EPS

$$\frac{\overset{\text{Net income}}{\$500} - \overset{\text{Preferred dividends}}{\$7^{a}} - \overset{\text{Preferred dividends}}{\$8^{b}} + \overset{\text{After-tax interest savings}}{25^{d} - 40\%(\$25^{d})}}{\underset{\text{Shares at Jan. 1}}{150}\ (2.00) - \underset{\text{Retired shares}}{24\ (^{11}\!/_{12})}\ (2.00) + \underset{\text{New shares}}{18\ (^{4}\!/_{12})} + \underset{\text{Exercise of warrants}}{(4-3)^{c}} + \underset{\text{Conversion of bonds}}{20}} = \frac{\$500}{283} = \$1.77$$

(2.00) — Stock split adjustment

[a]10% × $70 million = $7 million
[b]8% × $100 million = $8 million

[c]Exercise of warrants:

4 million shares
× $15 (exercise price)
$60 million
÷ $20 (average market price)
3 million shares

[d]12.5% × $200 million = $25 million

Dilution:

Conversion of Bonds	Conversion of 8% Preferred Stock
$\dfrac{\overset{\text{After-tax interest savings}}{+\$25 - 40\%(\$25)}}{\underset{\text{Conversion of bonds}}{+20}} = \$0.75$	$\dfrac{\overset{\text{Preferred dividends}}{+\$8}}{\underset{\text{Conversion of preferred shares}}{+4}} = \$2.00^{*}$

*Because the incremental effect of conversion of the preferred stock ($2) is higher than EPS without the conversion of the preferred stock, the conversion would be *antidilutive* and is *not* considered in the calculation of diluted EPS.

Additional EPS Issues

Components of the "Proceeds" in the Treasury Stock Method

● LO19–11

For the treasury stock method, "proceeds" include:

1. The amount, if any, received from the hypothetical exercise of options or vesting of restricted stock.

2. The total compensation from the award that's not yet expensed.

In calculating diluted EPS when stock options are outstanding, we assume the options have been exercised. That is, we pretend the company sold the shares specified by the options at the exercise price and that the "proceeds" were used to buy back (as treasury stock) as many shares as can be purchased at the average market price of the stock during the year. The proceeds for the calculation should include the amount received from the hypothetical exercise of the options ($300 million in Illustration 19–10 in the chapter). But that's only the first of three possible components.

The second component of the proceeds is the total compensation from the award that's not yet expensed. If the fair value of an option had been $4 at the grant date, the total compensation would have been 15 million shares times $4, or $60 million. In our illustration, though, we assumed the options were fully vested before 2016, so all $60 million already had been expensed and this second component of the proceeds was zero. If the options had been only half vested, half the compensation would have been unexpensed and $30 million would have been added to the $300 million proceeds.

The third component of the proceeds is what's called the *excess tax benefit.* We expense the fair value of stock options at the date of grant. If the options were nonqualified options, rather than incentive stock options, the corporation receives a tax deduction at exercise equal to the difference between the stock's market value and its exercise price. That amount usually is higher than the fair value of the options at the grant date, and the difference times the tax rate is the excess tax benefit. In our illustration, though, we assumed the options were incentive stock options, hence no tax benefit. Had they been nonqualified options, the proceeds also would have included a $6 million excess tax benefit:

$ 25	market price during 2016 (and price at hypothetical exercise)
(20)	exercise price
$ 5	tax deduction at hypothetical exercise
(4)	fair value at grant date (and amount expensed over the vesting period)
$ 1	excess tax deduction per option
× 15	million options
$ 15	million excess tax deduction
× 40%	tax rate
$ 6	million excess tax benefit[23]

3. The difference between the eventual tax benefit and the amount recognized in expense.

Why do the proceeds include these three components? We might think of it like this. The "proceeds" include everything the firm will receive from the award: (1) cash, if any, at exercise, (2) services from the recipient (value of award given as compensation), and (3) tax savings. The reason we *exclude the expensed portion* is that, when it's expensed, earnings are reduced, and that dilution is reflected in EPS. Excluding that expensed portion from the proceeds avoids the additional dilution that would occur if more proceeds are available in our hypothetical buyback of shares. Hence, we avoid double-counting the dilutive effect of the compensation.

RESTRICTED STOCK AWARDS IN EPS CALCULATIONS. As we discussed earlier, restricted stock awards and restricted stock units (RSUs) are quickly replacing stock options as the share-based compensation plan of choice. Like stock options, they represent potential common shares and their dilutive effect is included in diluted EPS. In fact, they too are included using the treasury stock method. That is, the shares are added to the denominator and then reduced by the number of shares that can be bought back with the "proceeds" at the average market price of the company's stock during the year. Unlike stock options, though, the first component of the proceeds usually is absent; employees don't pay to acquire their shares.

Also, only *unvested* restricted stock award shares and RSU shares are included in hypothetical EPS calculations; fully vested shares are actually distributed and thus outstanding. The proceeds for the EPS calculation include the total compensation from the unvested restricted stock that's not yet expensed, the second component. For an example, refer back to the restricted stock in Illustration 19–2 on page 1129. The total compensation for the award is $60 million ($12 market price per share × 5 million shares). Because the restricted stock vests over four years, it is expensed as $15 million each year for four years. At the end of 2016, the first year, $45 million remains unexpensed, so $45 million would be the assumed proceeds in an EPS calculation.[24] If we assume the market price remains at $12, the $45 million will buy back 3.75 million shares and we would add to the denominator of diluted EPS 1.25 million common shares:

$$\frac{\text{No adjustment to the numerator}}{5 \text{ million} - 3.75^{*} \text{ million} = \mathbf{1.25 \text{ million}}}$$

*Assumed purchase of treasury shares

$45	million
÷ $12	average market price
3.75	million shares

[23]Journal entries for the tax benefit are described in the Additional Consideration on p. 1136.

[24]The proceeds also must be increased (or decreased) by any tax benefits that would be added to (or deducted from) paid-in capital when the eventual tax deduction differs from the amount expensed as described for the stock options above and in the Additional Consideration on p. 1136. Because that occurs when the stock price at vesting differs from the stock price at the grant date, our assumption above that the market price remained at $12 avoided that complexity.

At the end of 2017, the *second* year, $30 million remains unexpensed, so assuming the average market price again is $12, we would add to the denominator of diluted EPS 2.5 million common shares:

$$\frac{\text{No adjustment to the numerator}}{5 \text{ million} - 2.5^{*} \text{ million} = \mathbf{2.5\ million}}$$

*Assumed purchase of treasury shares

$30	million
÷ $12	average market price
2.5	million shares

Contingently Issuable Shares

Sometimes an agreement specifies that additional shares of common stock will be issued, contingent on the occurrence of some future circumstance. For instance, in the disclosure note reproduced in Illustration 19–14, **Hunt Manufacturing Co.** reported contingent shares in connection with its acquisition of **Feeny Manufacturing Company**.

● LO19–12

Note 12: Acquisitions (in part)

The Company acquired Feeny Manufacturing Company of Muncie, Indiana, for 135,000 shares of restricted common stock with a value of $7.71 per share. Feeny Manufacturing Company is a manufacturer of kitchen storage products. The purchase agreement calls for the issuance of up to 135,000 additional shares of common stock in the next fiscal year based on the earnings of Feeny Manufacturing Company. . . .

Illustration 19–14

Contingently Issuable Shares—Hunt Manufacturing Company

Real World Financials

At times, contingent shares are issuable to shareholders of an acquired company, certain key executives, or others in the event a certain level of performance is achieved. Contingent performance may be a desired level of income, a target stock price, or some other measurable activity level.

When calculating EPS, **contingently issuable shares** are considered to be outstanding in the computation of diluted EPS if the target performance level already is being met (assumed to remain at existing levels until the end of the contingency period). For example, if shares will be issued at a future date if a certain level of income is achieved and that level of income or more was already reported this year, those additional shares are simply added to the denominator of the diluted EPS fraction.[25]

Contingently issuable shares are considered outstanding in the computation of diluted EPS.

For clarification, refer to our continuing illustration of diluted EPS and assume 3 million additional shares will become issuable to certain executives in the following year (2017) if net income that year is $150 million or more. Recall that net income for Sovran Finanical in 2016 was $154 million, so the additional shares would be considered outstanding in the computation of diluted EPS by simply adding **3 million** additional shares to the denominator of the EPS fraction. Obviously, the 2017 condition ($150 million net income or more) has not been met yet since it's only year 2016. But because that level of income was achieved in 2016, the presumption is it's likely to be achieved in 2017 as well.

If a level of income must be attained before the shares will be issued, and income already is that amount or more, the additional shares are simply added to the denominator.

Assumed Issuance of Contingently Issuable Shares (diluted EPS):

$$\frac{\text{No adjustment to the numerator}}{+3}$$

Additional shares

On the other hand, if the target income next year is $160 million, the contingent shares would simply be ignored in our calculation.

[25]The shares should be included in both basic and diluted EPS if all conditions have actually been met so that there is no *circumstance* under which those shares would not be issued. In essence, these *are no longer contingent shares.*

Summary of the Effect of Potential Common Shares on Earnings Per Share

You have seen that under certain circumstances, securities that have the potential of reducing earnings per share by becoming common stock are assumed already to have become common stock for the purpose of calculating EPS. The table in Illustration 19–15 summarizes the circumstances under which the dilutive effect of these securities is reflected in the calculation of basic and diluted EPS.

Illustration 19–15

When Potential Common Shares Are Reflected in EPS

	Is the Dilutive Effect Reflected in the Calculation of EPS?*	
Potential Common Shares	**Basic EPS**	**Diluted EPS**
• Stock options (or warrants, rights)	no	yes
• Restricted stock	no	yes
• Convertible securities (bonds, notes, preferred stock)	no	yes
• Contingently issuable shares	no	yes†

*The effect is not included for any security if its effect is antidilutive.
†Unless shares are contingent upon some level of performance not yet achieved.

Illustration 19–16 summarizes the specific effects on the diluted EPS fraction when the dilutive effect of a potentially dilutive security is reflected in the calculation.

Illustration 19–16

How Potential Common Shares Are Reflected in a Diluted EPS Calculation

	Modification to the Diluted EPS Fractions:	
Potential Common Shares	Numerator	Denominator
• Stock options (or warrants, rights)	None	Add the shares that would be created by their exercise,* reduced by shares repurchased at the average share price.
• Restricted stock	None	Add shares that would be created by their vesting,* reduced by shares repurchased at the average share price.
• Convertible bonds (or notes)	Add the interest (after-tax) that would have been avoided if the debt had been converted.	Add shares that would be created by the conversion* of the bonds (or notes).
• Convertible preferred stock	Do not deduct the dividends that would have been avoided if the preferred stock had been converted.	Add shares that would have been created by the conversion* of the preferred stock.
• Contingently issuable shares: Issuable when specified conditions are met, and those conditions currently are being met	None	Add shares that are issuable.
• Contingently issuable shares: Issuable when specified conditions are met, and those conditions are **not** currently being met	None	None

*At the beginning of the year or when potential common shares were issued, whichever is later (time-weight the increase in shares if assumed exercised or converted in midyear).

Actual Conversions

When calculating EPS in our example, we "pretended" the convertible bonds had been converted at the beginning of the year. What if they actually had been converted, let's say on November 1? Interestingly, diluted EPS would be precisely the same. Here's why:

1. The actual conversion would cause an actual increase in shares of 12 million on November 1. These would be time-weighted so the denominator would increase by 12 ($\frac{2}{12}$) Also, the numerator would be higher because net income actually would be increased by the after-tax interest saved on the bonds for the last two months, [\$30 − 40% (\$30)] × ($\frac{2}{12}$). Be sure to note that this would not be an adjustment in the EPS calculation. Instead, net income would actually have been higher by [\$30 − 40% (\$30)] × ($\frac{2}{12}$) = \$3. That is, reported net income would have been \$157 rather than \$154.
2. We would assume conversion for the period before November 1 because they were potentially dilutive during that period. The 12 million shares assumed outstanding from January 1 to November 1 would be time-weighted for that 10-month period: 12 ($\frac{10}{12}$) Also, the numerator would be increased by the after-tax interest assumed saved on the bonds for the first 10 months, [\$30 − 40% (\$30)] × ($\frac{10}{12}$).

   Notice that the incremental effect on diluted EPS is the same either way.

Not Actually Converted: **Converted on November 1:**

Not Actually Converted		Converted on November 1		
Assumed after-tax interest savings		Actual after-tax interest savings		Assumed after-tax interest savings
+ \$30 − 40% (\$30)	=	+[\$30 − 40% (\$30)] × ($\frac{2}{12}$)	+	[\$30 − 40% (\$30)] × ($\frac{10}{12}$)
+ 12		+ 12 ($\frac{2}{12}$)		+ 12 ($\frac{10}{12}$)
Assumed conversion of bonds		Actual conversion of bonds		Assumed conversion of bonds

$$\frac{\$18}{12} = \frac{\$3 + \$15}{2 + 10}$$

EPS would be precisely the same whether convertible securities were actually converted or not.

Illustration 19–17 shows the disclosure note **Clorox Company** reported after the conversion of convertible notes during the year.

Illustration 19–17
Conversion of Notes—The Clorox Company

Real World Financials

> **Note 1: Significant Accounting Policies—Earnings Per Common Share (in part)**
> A \$9,000,000 note payable to Henkel Corporation was converted into 1,200,000 shares of common stock on August 1. . . . Earnings per common share and weighted-average shares outstanding reflect this conversion as if it were effective during all periods presented.

● LO19–13

Financial Statement Presentation of Earnings Per Share Data

Recall from Chapter 4 that if a company disposes of a component of its operations, the company will report "discontinued operations" as a separate item within the income statement as follows:

Income from Continuing Operations
Discontinued operations
Net income

When the income statement includes discontinued operations, EPS data (both basic and diluted) must also be reported separately for income from continuing operations and net income. Per share amounts for discontinued operations would be disclosed either on the face of the income statement or in the notes to financial statements. Presentation on the face of the income statement is illustrated by the partial income statements of **H&R Block, Inc.**, from its annual report for the year ended April 30, 2014, and exhibited in Illustration 19–18.

Illustration 19–18
EPS Disclosure—H&R Block

Real World Financials

Consolidated Income Statements (partial)
For the Years Ended April 30, 2014 and 2013

	2014	2013
Net income from continuing operations	$500,097	$465,158
Net loss from discontinued operations	(24,940)	(31,210)
Net income	$475,157	$433,948
Basic Earnings (Loss) Per Share:		
Continuing operations	$ 1.82	$ 1.70
Discontinued operations	(0.09)	(0.11)
Consolidated	$ 1.73	$ 1.59
Diluted Earnings (Loss) Per Share:		
Continuing operations	$ 1.81	$ 1.69
Discontinued operations	(0.09)	(0.11)
Consolidated	$ 1.72	$ 1.58

Basic and diluted EPS data should be reported on the face of the income statement for all reporting periods presented in the comparative statements. Businesses without potential common shares present basic EPS only. Disclosure notes should provide additional disclosures including:

1. A reconciliation of the numerator and denominator used in the basic EPS computations to the numerator and the denominator used in the diluted EPS computations. An example of this is presented in Illustration 19–19 using the situation described in Illustration 19–12.
2. Any adjustments to the numerator for preferred dividends.
3. Any potential common shares that weren't included because they were antidilutive.
4. Any transactions that occurred after the end of the most recent period that would materially affect earnings per share.

Illustration 19–19
Reconciliation of Basic EPS Computations to Diluted EPS Computations

Earnings per Share Reconciliation:

	Income (Numerator)	Share (Denominator)	Per Share Amount
Net income	$ 154		
Preferred dividends	(4)		
Basic earnings per share	150	75	$2.00
Stock options	None	3*	
Convertible debt	18	12	
Convertible preferred stock	4	3	
Diluted earnings per share	$ 172	93	$1.85

Note: Stock warrants to purchase an additional 4 million shares at $32.50 per share were outstanding throughout the year but were not included in diluted EPS because the warrants' exercise price is greater than the average market price of the common shares.
*15 million − [(15 million × $20) ÷ $25] = 3 million net additional shares

Additional Consideration

It is possible that potential common shares would have a dilutive effect on one component of net income but an antidilutive effect on another. When the inclusion of the potential common shares has a dilutive effect on "income from continuing operations," the effect should be included in all calculations of diluted EPS. In other words, the same number of potential common shares used in computing the diluted per-share amount for income from continuing operations is used in computing all other diluted per-share amounts, even when amounts are antidilutive to the individual per-share amounts.

Decision Makers' Perspective

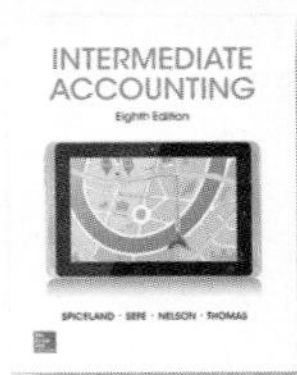

We noted earlier in the chapter that investors and creditors pay a great deal of attention to earnings per share information. Because of the importance analysts attach to earnings announcements, companies are particularly eager to meet earnings expectations. As we first noted in Chapter 4, this desire has contributed to a relatively recent trend, especially among technology firms, to report pro forma earnings per share. What exactly are pro forma earnings? Unfortunately there is no answer to that question. Essentially, pro forma earnings are actual (GAAP) earnings reduced by any expenses the reporting company feels are unusual and should be excluded. Always, though, the pro forma results of a company look better than the real results. Broadcom Corporation, a provider of broadband and network products, reported pro forma *earnings* of $0.49 per share. However on a GAAP basis, it actually had a *loss* of $3.29 per share. This is not an isolated example.

Make sure you pay lots of attention to the man behind the curtain. If any earnings figure says pro forma, you should immediately look for a footnote or explanation telling you just what is and is not included in the calculation.

When companies report pro forma results, they argue they are trying to help investors by giving them numbers that more accurately reflect their normal business activities, because they exclude unusual expenses. Analysts should be skeptical, though. Because of the purely discretionary nature of pro forma reporting and several noted instances of abuse, analysts should, at a minimum, find out precisely what expenses are excluded and what the actual GAAP numbers are.

Another way management might enhance the appearance of EPS numbers is by massaging the denominator of the calculation. Reducing the number of shares increases earnings *per share.* Some companies judiciously use share buyback programs to manipulate the number of shares and therefore EPS. There is nothing inherently wrong with share buybacks and, as we noted in Chapter 18, they can benefit shareholders. The motivation for buybacks, though, can sometimes be detected in the year-to-year pattern of net income and EPS. Companies whose growth rates in earnings per share routinely exceed their growth in net income may be using buybacks to artificially increase EPS.

One way analysts use EPS data is in connection with the price-earnings ratio. This ratio is simply the market price per share divided by the earnings per share. It measures the market's perception of the quality of a company's earnings by indicating the price multiple the capital market is willing to pay for the company's earnings. Presumably, this ratio reflects the information provided by all financial information in that the market price reflects analysts' perceptions of the company's growth potential, stability, and relative risk. The price-earnings ratio relates these performance measures with the external judgment of the marketplace concerning the value of the firm.

The price-earnings ratio measures the quality of a company's earnings.

The ratio measures the quality of earnings in the sense that it represents the market's expectation of future earnings as indicated by current earnings. Caution is called for in comparing price-earnings ratios. For instance, a ratio might be low, not because earnings expectations are low, but because of abnormally elevated current earnings. On the contrary, the ratio might be high, not because earnings expectations are high, but because the company's current earnings are temporarily depressed. Similarly, an analyst should be alert to differences among accounting methods used to measure earnings from company to company when making comparisons.

The dividend payout ratio indicates the percentage of earnings that is distributed to shareholders as dividends.

Another ratio frequently calculated by shareholders and potential shareholders is the dividend payout ratio. This ratio expresses the percentage of earnings that is distributed to shareholders as dividends. The ratio is calculated by dividing dividends per common share by the earnings per share.

This ratio provides an indication of a firm's reinvestment strategy. A low payout ratio suggests that a company is retaining a large portion of earnings for reinvestment for new facilities and other operating needs. Low payouts often are found in growth industries and high payouts in mature industries. Often, though, the ratio is merely a reflection of managerial strategy concerning the mix of internal versus external financing. The ratio also is considered by investors who, for tax or other reasons, prefer current income over market price appreciation, or vice versa. ●

Concept Review Exercise

ADDITIONAL EPS ISSUES

At December 31, 2016, the financial statements of Bahnson General, Inc., included the following:

Net income for 2016 (including a net-of-tax loss from discontinued operations of $10 million)	$180 million
Common stock, $1 par:	
Shares outstanding on January 1	44 million
The share price was $25 and $28 at the beginning and end of the year, respectively.	

Additional data:

- At January 1, 2016, $200 million of 10% convertible notes were outstanding. The notes were converted on April 1 into 16 million shares of common stock.
- An agreement with company executives calls for the issuance of up to 12 million additional shares of common stock in 2017 and 2018 based on Bahnson's net income in those years. Executives will receive 2 million shares at the end of each of those two years if the company's stock price is at least $26 and another 4 million shares each year if the stock price is at least $29.50.

The tax rate is 40%.

Required:

Compute basic and diluted earnings per share for the year ended December 31, 2016.

Solution:

(amounts in millions, except per share amounts)

Basic EPS

$$\frac{\overset{\text{Net income}}{\$180}}{\underset{\text{Shares at Jan. 1}}{44} + \underset{\text{Actual conversion of notes}}{16\,(9/12)}} = \frac{\$180}{56} = \$3.21$$

Diluted EPS

$$\frac{\overset{\text{Net income}}{\$180} + [\$20 - 40\%\,(\$20)] \times (3/12)}{\underset{\text{Shares at Jan. 1}}{44} + \underset{\text{Actual conversion of notes}}{16\,(9/12)} + \underset{\text{Assumed conversion of notes}}{16\,(3/12)} + \underset{\text{Contingent shares}}{(2 + 2)}} = \frac{\$183}{64} = \$2.86$$

Convertible Notes: Notice that the effect on diluted EPS would be precisely the same whether the convertible notes were actually converted or not.

Converted on April 1:

$$\frac{\underset{\text{Net income including actual after-tax interest savings}}{\$180} + \underset{\text{Assumed after-tax interest savings}}{[\$20 - 40\% (\$20)] \times (3/12)}}{\underset{\text{Shares at Jan. 1}}{44} + \underset{\text{Actual conversion of notes}}{16 (9/12)} + \underset{\text{Assumed conversion of notes}}{16 (3/12)}} = \frac{\$183}{60}$$

Not Actually Converted:

$$\frac{\underset{\text{Net income without actual after-tax interest savings}}{\$171^*} + \underset{\text{Assumed after-tax interest savings}}{[\$20 - 40\% (\$20)]}}{\underset{\text{Shares at Jan. 1}}{44} + \underset{\text{Assumed conversion of notes}}{16}} = \frac{\$183}{60}$$

*$180 – {[$20 – 40% ($20)] × (9/12)} = $171
After-tax interest from Apr. 1 to Dec. 31

Contingently Issuable Shares:
Because the conditions are met for issuing 4 million shares (2 million for each of two years), those shares are simply added to the denominator of diluted EPS. The current share price ($28) is projected to remain the same throughout the contingency period, so the other 8 million shares (4 million for each of two years) are excluded.

Income Statement Presentation:
To determine the per share amounts for income before discontinued operations, we substitute that amount for net income in the numerator (in this case, that means adding back the $10 million loss from discontinued operations):

$$\text{Basic: } \frac{\$180 + 10}{56} = \$3.39 \qquad \text{Diluted: } \frac{\$183 + 10}{64} = \$3.02$$

Earnings per Share:	**Basic***	**Diluted**
Income before discontinued operations	$3.39	$3.02
Loss from discontinued operations	(.18)	(.16)
Net income	$3.21	$2.86

*Only diluted EPS is required on the face of the income statement. Basic EPS is reported in the EPS reconciliation shown in the disclosure note (below).

Disclosure Note:

Earnings per Share Reconciliation:

	Income (Numerator)	**Shares (Denominator)**	**Per Share Amount**
Basic Earnings per Share			
Income before discontinued operations	$190	56	$3.39
Loss from discontinued opeations	(10)	56	(.18)
Net income	$180	56	$3.21
Convertible debt	3	4	
Contingently issuable shares	—	4	
Diluted Earnings per Share			
Income before disontinued operations	$193	64	$3.02
Loss from discontinued operations	(10)	64	(.16)
Net income	$183	64	$2.86

Financial Reporting Case Solution

1. **How can a compensation package such as this serve as an incentive to Ms. Veres?** *(p. 1127)* Stock-based plans like the restricted stock and stock options that Ms. Veres is receiving are designed to motivate recipients. If the shares awarded are restricted so that Ms. Veres is not free to sell the shares during the restriction period, she has an incentive to remain with the company until rights to the shares vest. Likewise, stock options can be made exercisable only after a specified period of employment. An additional incentive of stock-based plans is that the recipient will be motivated to take actions that will maximize the value of the shares.
2. **Ms. Veres received a "grant of restricted stock." How should NEV account for the grant?** *(p. 1128)* The compensation associated with restricted stock is the market price of unrestricted shares of the same stock. NEV will accrue this amount as compensation expense over the service period from the date of grant to when restrictions are lifted.
3. **Included were stock options to buy more than 800,000 shares of NEV stock. How will the options affect NEV's compensation expense?** *(p. 1130)* Similar to the method used for restricted stock, the value of the options is recorded as compensation over the service period, usually the vesting period.
4. **How will the presence of these and other similar stock options affect NEV's earnings per share?** *(p. 1146)* If outstanding stock options were exercised, the resulting increase in shares would reduce or dilute EPS. If we don't take into account the dilutive effect of the share increase, we might mislead investors and creditors. So, in addition to basic EPS, we also calculate diluted EPS to include the dilutive effect of options and other potential common shares. This means calculating EPS as if the potential increase in shares already has occurred (even though it hasn't yet). ●

The Bottom Line

- **LO19–1** We measure the fair value of stock issued in a restricted stock plan and expense it over the service period, usually from the date of grant to the vesting date. (*p. 1128*)
- **LO19–2** Similarly, we estimate the fair value of stock options at the grant date and expense it over the service period, usually from the date of grant to the vesting date. Fair value is estimated at the grant date using an option-pricing model that considers the exercise price and expected term of the option, the current market price of the underlying stock and its expected volatility, expected dividends, and the expected risk-free rate of return. (*p. 1130*)
- **LO19–3** Employee share purchase plans allow employees to buy company stock under convenient or favorable terms. Most such plans are considered compensatory and require any discount to be recorded as compensation expense. (*p. 1139*)
- **LO19–4** A company has a simple capital structure if it has no outstanding securities that could potentially dilute earnings per share. For such a firm, EPS is simply earnings available to common shareholders divided by the weighted-average number of common shares outstanding. When potential common shares are outstanding, the company is said to have a complex capital structure. In that case, two EPS calculations are reported. Basic EPS assumes no dilution. Diluted EPS assumes maximum potential dilution. (*p. 1142*)
- **LO19–5** EPS calculations are based on the weighted-average number of shares outstanding during the period. Any new shares issued during the period are time-weighted by the fraction of the period they were outstanding and then added to the number of shares outstanding for the period. (*p. 1142*)
- **LO19–6** For a stock dividend or stock split, shares outstanding prior to the stock distribution are retroactively restated to reflect the increase in shares. When shares are reacquired, as treasury stock or to be retired, they are time-weighted for the fraction of the period they were not outstanding, prior to being subtracted from the number of shares outstanding during the reporting period. (*p. 1143*)

- **LO19–7** The numerator in the EPS calculation should reflect earnings available to common shareholders. So, any dividends on preferred stock outstanding should be subtracted from reported net income. This adjustment is made for cumulative preferred stock whether or not dividends are declared that period. (*p. 1145*)
- **LO19–8** For diluted EPS, it is assumed that stock options, rights, and warrants are exercised at the beginning of the period (or at the time the options are issued, if later) and the cash proceeds received are used to buy back (as treasury stock) as many of those shares as can be acquired at the average market price during the period. (*p. 1146*)
- **LO19–9** To incorporate convertible securities into the calculation of diluted EPS, the conversion is assumed to have occurred at the beginning of the period (or at the time the convertible security is issued, if later). The denominator of the EPS fraction is adjusted for the additional common shares assumed and the numerator is increased by the interest (after-tax) on bonds and not reduced by the preferred dividends that would have been avoided in the event of conversion. (*p. 1147*)
- **LO19–10** If including potential common shares in the EPS calculation causes EPS to *increase* rather than decrease, then those potential common shares are considered *antidilutive* and are omitted from the calculation. (*p. 1151*)
- **LO19–11** For the treasury stock method, "proceeds" include (1) the amount, if any, received from the hypothetical exercise of options or vesting of restricted stock, (2) the total compensation from the award that's not yet expensed, and (3) the difference between the eventual tax benefit and the amount recognized in expense. (*p. 1155*)
- **LO19–12** Contingently issuable shares are considered outstanding in the computation of diluted EPS when they will later be issued upon the mere passage of time or because of conditions that currently are met. (*p. 1157*)
- **LO19–13** EPS data (both basic and diluted) must be reported for (a) income before any discontinued operations, (b) the discontinued operations, and (c) net income. Disclosures also should include a reconciliation of the numerator and denominator used in the computations. (*p. 1159*)
- **LO19–14** When options have graded vesting, unlike under U.S. GAAP, IFRS does not permit the straight-line method for allocating compensation or require that the company recognize at least the amount of the award that has vested by each reporting date. The earnings per share requirements of IFRS and U.S. GAAP are similar. The few differences that remain are the result of differences in the application of the treasury stock method, the treatment of contracts that may be settled in shares or cash, and contingently issuable shares. (*pp. 1135, 1136*, and *1141*)

Option-Pricing Theory

APPENDIX 19A

Option values have two essential components: (1) intrinsic value and (2) time value.

Intrinsic Value

Intrinsic value is the benefit the holder of an option would realize by exercising the option rather than buying the underlying stock directly. An option that permits an employee to buy $25 stock for $10 has an intrinsic value of $15. An option that has an exercise price equal to or exceeding the market price of the underlying stock has zero intrinsic value.

Time Value

In addition to their intrinsic value, options also have a time value due to the fact that (a) the holder of an option does not have to pay the exercise price until the option is exercised and (b) the market price of the underlying stock may yet rise and create additional intrinsic value. All options have time value so long as time remains before expiration. The longer the time until expiration, other things being equal, the greater the time value. For instance, the option described above with an intrinsic value of $15, might have a fair value of, say, $22 if time still remains until the option expires. The $7 difference represents the time value of the option. Time value can be subdivided into two components: (1) the effects of time value of money and (2) volatility value.

TIME VALUE OF MONEY

An option's value is enhanced by the delay in paying cash for the shares.

The time value of money component arises because the holder of an option does not have to pay the exercise price until the option is exercised. Instead, the holder can invest funds elsewhere while waiting to exercise the option. For measurement purposes, the time value of money component is assumed to be the rate of return available on risk-free U.S. Treasury Securities. The higher the time value of money, the higher the value of being able to delay payment of the exercise price.

When the underlying stock pays no dividends, the time value of money component is the difference between the exercise price (a future amount) and its discounted present value. Let's say the exercise price is $30. If the present value (discounted at the risk-free rate) is $24, the time value of money component is $6. On the other hand, if the stock pays a dividend (or is expected to during the life of the option), the time value of money component is lower. The value of being able to delay payment of the exercise price would be partially off-set by the cost of forgoing the dividend in the meantime. For instance, if the stock underlying the options just described were expected to pay dividends and the discounted present value of the expected dividends were $2, the time value of money component in that example would be reduced from $6 to $4.

The time value of money component is the difference between the exercise price and its discounted present value minus the present value of expected dividends.

VOLATILITY VALUE

The volatility value represents the possibility that the option holder might profit from market price appreciation of the underlying stock while being exposed to the loss of only the value of the option, rather than the full market value of the stock. For example, fair value of an option to buy a share at an exercise price of $30 might be measured as $7. The potential profit from market price appreciation is conceptually unlimited. And yet, the potential loss from the stock's value failing to appreciate is only $7.

Volatility enhances the likelihood of stock price appreciation.

A stock's volatility is the amount by which its price has fluctuated previously or is expected to fluctuate in the future. The greater a stock's volatility, the greater the potential profit. It usually is measured as one standard deviation of a statistical distribution. Statistically, if the expected annualized volatility is 25%, the probability is approximately 67% that the stock's year-end price will fall within roughly plus or minus 25% of its beginning-of-year price. Stated differently, the probability is approximately 33% that the year-end stock price will fall outside that range.

Option-pricing models make assumptions about the likelihood of various future stock prices by making assumptions about the statistical distribution of future stock prices that take into account the expected volatility of the stock price. One popular option pricing model, the Black–Scholes model, for instance, assumes a log-normal distribution. This assumption posits that the stock price is as likely to fall by half as it is to double and that large price movements are less likely than small price movements. The higher a stock's volatility, the higher the probability of large increases or decreases in market price. Because the cost of large decreases is limited to the option's current value, but the profitability from large increases is unlimited, an option on a highly volatile stock has a higher probability of a large profit than does an option on a less volatile stock.

Summary

In summary, the fair value of an option is (a) its intrinsic value plus (b) its time value of money component plus (c) its volatility component. The variables that affect an option's fair value and the effect of each are indicated in Illustration 19A–1.

Illustration 19A–1

Effect of Variables on an Option's Fair Value

All Other Factors Being Equal, If the:	The Option Value Will Be:
Exercise price is higher	Lower
Term of the option is longer	Higher
Market price of the stock is higher	Higher
Dividends are higher	Lower
Risk-free rate of return is higher	Higher
Volatility of the stock is higher	Higher

APPENDIX 19B

Stock Appreciation Rights

Stock appreciation rights (SARs) overcome a major disadvantage of stock option plans that require employees to actually buy shares when the options are exercised. Even though the options' exercise price may be significantly lower than the market value of the shares, the employee still must come up with enough cash to take advantage of the bargain. This can be quite a burden if the award is sizable. In a nonqualified stock option plan, income taxes also would have to be paid when the options are exercised.[26]

SARs offer a solution. Unlike stock options, these awards enable an employee to benefit by the amount that the market price of the company's stock rises without having to buy shares. Instead, the employee is awarded the share appreciation, which is the amount by which the market price on the exercise date exceeds a prespecified price (usually the market price at the date of grant). For instance, if the share price rises from $35 to $50, the employee receives $15 cash for each SAR held. The share appreciation usually is payable in cash or the recipient has the choice between cash and shares. A plan of this type offered by **IBM** is described in Illustration 19B–1.

In an SAR plan, the employer pays compensation equal to the increase in share price from a specified level.

Illustration 19B–1
Stock Appreciation Rights—IBM Corporation

Real World Financials

Long-Term Performance Plan (in part)

SARs offer eligible optionees the alternative of electing not to exercise the related stock option, but to receive payment in cash and/or stock, equivalent to the difference between the option price and the average market price of IBM stock on the date of exercising the right.

IS IT DEBT OR IS IT EQUITY?

In some plans, the employer chooses whether to issue shares or cash at exercise. In other plans, the choice belongs to the employee.[27] Who has the choice determines the way it's accounted for. More specifically, the accounting treatment depends on whether the award is considered an equity instrument or a liability. If the employer can elect to settle in shares of stock rather than cash, the award is considered to be equity. On the other hand, if the employee will receive cash or can elect to receive cash, the award is considered to be a liability.

If an employer can elect to settle in shares of stock rather than cash, the award is considered to be equity.

The distinction between share-based awards that are considered equity and those that are considered liabilities is based on whether the employer is obligated to transfer assets to the employee. A cash SAR requires the transfer of assets, and therefore is a liability. A stock option, on the other hand, is an equity instrument if it requires only the issuance of stock. This does not mean that a stock option whose issuer may later choose to settle in cash is not an equity instrument. Instead, cash settlement would be considered equivalent to repurchasing an equity instrument for cash.

If an employee can elect to receive cash, the award is considered to be a liability.

SARS PAYABLE IN SHARES (EQUITY)

When a SAR is considered to be equity (because the employer can elect to settle in shares of stock rather than cash), we estimate the fair value of the SARs at the grant date and accrue that compensation to expense over the service period. Normally, the fair value of a SAR is the same as the fair value of a stock option with the same terms. The fair value is determined at the grant date and accrued to compensation expense over the service period the same way as for other share-based compensation plans. The total compensation is not revised for subsequent changes in the price of the underlying stock. This is demonstrated in Case 1 of Illustration 19–B2 on the next page.

The cash settlement of an equity award is considered the repurchase of an equity instrument.

Compensation expense reported to date is the estimated total compensation multiplied by the fraction of the service period that has expired.

SARS PAYABLE IN CASH (LIABILITY)

When a SAR is considered to be a liability (because the employee can elect to receive cash upon settlement), we estimate the fair value of the SARs and recognize that amount as compensation expense over the requisite service period consistent with the way we account for

[26]The tax treatment of share-based plans is discussed the Additional Consideration on page 1134.

[27]Many such plans are called tandem plans and award an employee both a cash SAR and an SAR that calls for settlement in an equivalent amount of shares. The exercise of one cancels the other.

options and other share-based compensation. However, because these plans are considered to be liabilities, it's necessary to periodically re-estimate the fair value in order to continually adjust the liability (and corresponding compensation) until it is paid. Be sure to note that this is consistent with the way we account for other liabilities. Recall from our discussions in Chapter 16, for instance, that when a tax rate change causes a change in the eventual liability for deferred income taxes, we adjust that liability.

We make up for incorrect previous estimates by adjusting expense in the period the estimate is revised.

The periodic expense (and adjustment to the liability) is the fraction of the total compensation earned to date by recipients of the SARs (based on the elapsed fraction of the service period) reduced by any amounts expensed in prior periods. For example, if the fair value of SARs at the end of a period is $8, the total compensation would be $80 million if 10 million SARs are expected to vest. Let's say two years of a four-year service period have elapsed, and $21 million was expensed the first year. Then, compensation expense the second year would be $19 million, calculated as (2⁄4 of $80 million) minus $21. An example spanning several years is provided in Illustration 19B–2, case 2.

Illustration 19B–2

Stock Appreciation Rights

Case 1: Equity

At January 1, 2016, Universal Communications issued SARs that, upon exercise, entitle key executives to receive compensation equal in value to the excess of the market price at exercise over the share price at the date of grant. The SARs vest at the end of 2016 (cannot be exercised until then) and expire at the end of 2020. The fair value of the SARs, estimated by an appropriate option pricing model, is $8 per SAR at January 1, 2016. The fair value re-estimated at December 31, 2016, 2017, 2018, 2019, and 2020, is $8.40, $8, $6, $4.30, and $5, respectively.

Case 1: SARs considered to be equity because Universal can elect to settle in shares of Universal stock at exercise

January 1, 2016

No entry

Calculate total compensation expense:

$ 8	Estimated fair value per SAR
× 10 million	SARs granted
= $80 million	Total compensation

Fair value is estimated at the date of grant.

The total compensation is allocated to expense over the four-year service (vesting) period: 2016–2019

$80 million ÷ 4 years = $20 million per year

The value of the award is expensed over the service period for which the compensation is provided.

December 31, 2016, 2017, 2018, 2019	($ in millions)	
Compensation expense ($80 million ÷ 4 years)	20	
Paid-in capital—SAR plan		20

Case 2: SARs considered to be a liability because employees can elect to receive cash at exercise

The value of the compensation is estimated each year at the fair value of the SARs.

January 1, 2016

No entry

The expense each year is the current estimate of total compensation that should have been recorded to date less the amount already recorded.

	($ in millions)	
December 31, 2016		
Compensation expense ($8.40 × 10 million × 1⁄4)	21	
Liability—SAR plan		21
December 31, 2017		
Compensation expense [($8 × 10 million × 2⁄4) − 21]	19	
Liability—SAR plan		19
December 31, 2018		
Compensation expense [($6 × 10 million × 3⁄4) − 21 − 19]	5	
Liability—SAR plan		5
December 31, 2019		
Liability—SAR plan	2	
Compensation expense [($4.30 × 10 million × 4⁄4) − 21 − 19 − 5]		2

If the fair value falls below the amount expensed to date, both the liability and expense are reduced.

Note that the way we treat changes in compensation estimates entails a catch-up adjustment in the period of change, *inconsistent* with the usual treatment of a change in estimate. Remember that for most changes in estimate, revisions are allocated over remaining periods, rather than all at once in the period of change. The treatment is, however, consistent with the way we treat changes in forfeiture rate estimates as we discussed earlier in the chapter.

The liability continues to be adjusted after the service period if the rights haven't been exercised yet.

December 31, 2020	($ in millions)	
Compensation expense [($5 × 10 million × all) − 21 − 19 − 5 + 2]	7	
Liability—SAR plan		7

Compensation expense and the liability continue to be adjusted until the SARs expire or are exercised.

It's necessary to continue to adjust both compensation expense and the liability until the SARs ultimately either are exercised or lapse.[28] Assume for example that the SARs are exercised on October 11, 2021, when their fair value is $4.50, and executives choose to receive the market price appreciation in cash:

October 11, 2021	($ in millions)	
Liability—SAR plan	5	
Compensation expense [($4.50 × 10 million × all) − 50]		5
Liability—SAR plan (balance)	45	
Cash		45

Adjustment continues after the service period if the SARs have not yet been exercised.

Let's look at the changes in the liability—SAR plan account during the 2016–2021 period:

Liability—SAR Plan

		($ in millions)	
		21	2016
		19	2017
		5	2018
2019	2		
		7	2020
2021	5		
2021	45		
		0	Balance after exercise

The liability is adjusted each period as changes in the fair value estimates cause changes in the liability.

RESTRICTED STOCK UNITS PAYABLE IN CASH (LIABILITY)

Recall from our discussion in the chapter that restricted stock units (RSUs) give the recipient the right to receive a set number of shares of company stock after the vesting requirement is satisfied. But, sometimes the recipient is given the *cash equivalent* of those shares instead. *If the employee will receive cash* or can elect to receive cash, as in the case of an SAR, we consider the award to be a *liability*. We determine its fair value at the grant date and recognize that amount as compensation expense over the requisite service period and, like SARs payable in cash, we periodically adjust the liability (and corresponding compensation) based on the change in the stock's fair value until the liability is paid. Accounting for RSUs payable in cash is quite similar to accounting for the SARs payable in cash in case 2 of Illustration 19B–2. Of course, though, we would label the liability "Liability—restricted stock." And, we would determine the periodic value of the liability (and compensation) as the actual fair value of the shares, rather than an *estimated* fair value as is necessary when valuing SARs. ●

Accounting for RSUs payable in cash is essentially the same as accounting for the SARs payable in cash.

[28]Except that the cumulative compensation expense cannot be negative; that is, the liability cannot be reduced below zero.

Questions For Review of Key Topics

Q 19–1 What is restricted stock? How do restricted stock awards differ from restricted stock units (RSUs)? Describe how compensation expense is determined and recorded for a restricted stock award plan.

Q 19–2 Stock option plans provide employees the option to purchase: (a) a specified number of shares of the firm's stock, (b) at a specified price, (c) during a specified period of time. One of the most controversial aspects of accounting for stock-based compensation is how the fair value of stock options should be measured. Describe the general approach to measuring fair value.

Q 19–3 The Tax Code differentiates between qualified option plans, including incentive plans, and nonqualified plans. What are the major differences in tax treatment between incentive plans and nonqualified plans?

Q 19–4 Stock option (and other share-based) plans often specify a performance condition or a market condition that must be satisfied before employees are allowed the benefits of the award. Describe the general approach we use to account for performance-based options and options with market-related conditions.

Q 19–5 What is a simple capital structure? How is EPS determined for a company with a simple capital structure?

Q 19–6 When calculating the weighted average number of common shares, how are stock dividends and stock splits treated? Compare this treatment with that of additional shares sold for cash in midyear.

Q 19–7 Blake Distributors had 100,000 common shares outstanding at the beginning of the year, January 1. On May 13, Blake distributed a 5% stock dividend. On August 1, 1,200 shares were retired. What is the weighted average number of shares for calculating EPS?

Q 19–8 Why are preferred dividends deducted from net income when calculating EPS? Are there circumstances when this deduction is not made?

Q 19–9 Distinguish between basic and diluted EPS.

Q 19–10 The treasury stock method is used to incorporate the dilutive effect of stock options, stock warrants, and similar securities. Describe this method as it applies to diluted EPS.

Q 19–11 The potentially dilutive effect of convertible securities is reflected in EPS calculations by the if-converted method. Describe this method as it relates to convertible bonds.

Q 19–12 How is the potentially dilutive effect of convertible preferred stock reflected in EPS calculations by the if-converted method? How is this different from the way convertible bonds are considered?

Q 19–13 A convertible security may appear to be dilutive when looked at individually but might be antidilutive when included in combination with other convertible securities. How should the order be determined for inclusion of convertible securities in an EPS calculation to avoid including an antidilutive security?

Q 19–14 If stock options and restricted stock are outstanding when calculating diluted EPS, what are the components of the "proceeds" available for the repurchase of shares under the treasury stock method?

Q 19–15 Wiseman Electronics has an agreement with certain of its division managers that 50,000 contingently issuable shares will be issued next year in the event operating income exceeds $2.1 million that year. In what way, if any, is the calculation of EPS affected by these contingently issuable shares assuming this year's operating income was $2.2 million? $2.0 million?

Q 19–16 Diluted EPS would be precisely the same whether convertible securities were actually converted or not. Why?

Q 19–17 When the income statement includes discontinued operations, which amounts require per share presentation?

Q 19–18 In addition to EPS numbers themselves, what additional disclosures should be provided concerning the EPS information?

Q 19–19 (Based on Appendix A) The fair value of stock options can be considered to comprise two main components. What are they?

Q 19–20 (Based on Appendix B) LTV Corporation grants SARs to key executives. Upon exercise, the SARs entitle executives to receive either cash or stock equal in value to the excess of the market price at exercise over the share price at the date of grant. How should LTV account for the awards?

Brief Exercises

BE 19–1
Restricted stock award
● LO19–1

First Link Services granted 8 million of its $1 par common shares to executives, subject to forfeiture if employment is terminated within three years. The common shares have a market price of $6 per share on the grant date of the restricted stock award. Ignoring taxes, what is the total compensation cost pertaining to the restricted shares? What is the effect on earnings in the year after the shares are granted to executives?

BE 19–2
Restricted stock units
● LO19–1

Second Link Services granted restricted stock units (RSUs) representing 16 million of its $1 par common shares to executives, subject to forfeiture if employment is terminated within four years. After the recipients of the RSUs satisfy the vesting requirement, the company will distribute the shares. The common shares had a market price of $10 per share on the grant date. Ignoring taxes, what is the total compensation cost pertaining to the restricted stock units? What is the effect on earnings in the year after the shares are granted to executives?

BE 19–3
Stock options
● LO19–2

Under its executive stock option plan, National Corporation granted options on January 1, 2016, that permit executives to purchase 12 million of the company's $1 par common shares within the next six years, but not before December 31, 2018 (the vesting date). The exercise price is the market price of the shares on the date of grant, $17 per share. The fair value of the options, estimated by an appropriate option pricing model, is $5 per option. No forfeitures are anticipated. Ignoring taxes, what is the total compensation cost pertaining to the stock options? What is the effect on earnings in the year after the options are granted to executives?

BE 19–4
Stock options; forfeiture
● LO19–2

Refer to the situation described in BE 19–3. Suppose that unexpected turnover during 2017 caused the forfeiture of 5% of the stock options. Ignoring taxes, what is the effect on earnings in 2017? In 2018?

BE 19–5
Stock options; exercise
● LO19–2

Refer to the situation described in BE 19–3. Suppose that the options are exercised on April 3, 2019, when the market price is $19 per share. Ignoring taxes, what journal entry will National record?

BE 19–6
Stock options; expiration
● LO19–2

Refer to the situation described in BE 19–3. Suppose that the options expire without being exercised. Ignoring taxes, what journal entry will National record?

BE 19–7
Performance-based options
● LO19–2

On October 1, 2016, Farmer Fabrication issued stock options for 100,000 shares to a division manager. The options have an estimated fair value of $6 each. To provide additional incentive for managerial achievement, the options are not exercisable unless divisional revenue increases by 5% in three years. Farmer initially estimates that it is probable the goal will be achieved. How much compensation will be recorded in each of the next three years?

BE 19–8
Performance-based options
● LO19–2

Refer to the situation described in BE 19–7. Suppose that after one year, Farmer estimates that it is *not* probable that divisional revenue will increase by 5% in three years. What action will be taken to account for the options in 2017?

BE 19–9
Performance-based options
● LO19–2

Refer to the situation described in BE 19–7. Suppose that Farmer initially estimates that it is *not* probable the goal will be achieved, but then after one year, Farmer estimates that it *is* probable that divisional revenue will increase by 5% by the end of 2018. What action will be taken to account for the options in 2017 and thereafter?

BE 19–10
Options with market-based conditions
● LO19–2

On October 1, 2016, Farmer Fabrication issued stock options for 100,000 shares to a division manager. The options have an estimated fair value of $6 each. To provide additional incentive for managerial achievement, the options are not exercisable unless Farmer Fabrication's stock price increases by 5% in three years. Farmer initially estimates that it is not probable the goal will be achieved. How much compensation will be recorded in each of the next three years?

BE 19–11
EPS; shares issued, shares retired
● LO19–5, LO19–6

McDonnell-Myer Corporation reported net income of $741 million. The company had 544 million common shares outstanding at January 1 and sold 36 million shares on Feb. 28. As part of an annual share repurchase plan, 6 million shares were retired on April 30 for $47 per share. Calculate McDonnell-Myer's earnings per share for the year.

BE 19–12
EPS; nonconvertible preferred shares
● LO19–7

At December 31, 2015 and 2016, Funk & Noble Corporation had outstanding 820 million shares of common stock and 2 million shares of 8%, $100 par value cumulative preferred stock. No dividends were declared on either the preferred or common stock in 2015 or 2016. Net income for 2016 was $426 million. The income tax rate is 40%. Calculate earnings per share for the year ended December 31, 2016.

BE 19–13
EPS; stock options
● LO19–8

Fully vested incentive stock options exercisable at $50 per share to obtain 24,000 shares of common stock were outstanding during a period when the average market price of the common stock was $60 and the ending market price was $60. By how many shares will the assumed exercise of these options increase the weighted-average number of shares outstanding when calculating diluted earnings per share?

BE 19–14
EPS; convertible preferred shares
● LO19–9

Ahnberg Corporation had 800,000 shares of common stock issued and outstanding at January 1. No common shares were issued during the year, but on January 1 Ahnberg issued 100,000 shares of convertible preferred stock. The preferred shares are convertible into 200,000 shares of common stock. During the year Ahnberg paid $60,000 cash dividends on the preferred stock. Net income was $1,500,000. What were Ahnberg's basic and diluted earnings per share for the year?

BE 19–15
EPS; restricted stock award
● LO19–11

Niles Company granted 9 million of its no par common shares to executives, subject to forfeiture if employment is terminated within three years. The common shares have a market price of $5 per share on January 1, 2015, the grant date of the restricted stock award. When calculating diluted EPS at December 31, 2016, what will be the net increase in the denominator of the EPS fraction if the market price of the common shares averaged $5 per share during 2016?

Exercises

An alternate exercise and problem set is available in the Connect library.

E 19–1
Restricted stock award plan
● LO19–1

Allied Paper Products, Inc. offers a restricted stock award plan to its vice presidents. On January 1, 2016, the company granted 16 million of its $1 par common shares, subject to forfeiture if employment is terminated within two years. The common shares have a market price of $5 per share on the grant date.

Required:
1. Determine the total compensation cost pertaining to the restricted shares.
2. Prepare the appropriate journal entries related to the restricted stock through December 31, 2017.

E 19–2
Restricted stock units
● LO19–1

On January 1, 2016, VKI Corporation awarded restricted stock units (RSUs) representing 12 million of its $1 par common shares to key personnel, subject to forfeiture if employment is terminated within three years. After the recipients of the RSUs satisfy the vesting requirement, the company will distribute the shares. On the grant date, the shares had a market price of $2.50 per share.

Required:
1. Determine the total compensation cost pertaining to the RSUs.
2. Prepare the appropriate journal entry to record the award of RSUs on January 1, 2016.
3. Prepare the appropriate journal entry to record compensation expense on December 31, 2016.
4. Prepare the appropriate journal entry to record compensation expense on December 31, 2017.
5. Prepare the appropriate journal entry to record compensation expense on December 31, 2018.
6. Prepare the appropriate journal entry to record the lifting of restrictions on the RSUs and issuing shares at December 31, 2018.

E 19–3
Restricted stock units; Facebook
● LO19–1
Real World Financials

Facebook Inc. included the following disclosure note in an annual report:

Share-Based Compensation (in part)
. . . compensation expense related to these grants is based on the grant date fair value of the RSUs and is recognized on a straight-line basis over the applicable service period.

The following table summarizes the activities for our unvested RSUs for the year ended December 31, 2013:

	Number of Shares (in thousands)	**Weighted Average Grant Date Fair Value**
Unvested at December 31, 2012	113,044	$21.38
Granted	53,344	29.98
Vested	(47,550)	16.96
Forfeited	(14,867)	25.31
Unvested at December 31, 2013	103,971	$27.30

Required:

1. Assuming a four-year vesting period, how much compensation expense did Facebook report in the year ended December 31, 2014, for the restricted stock units granted during the year ended December 31, 2013? (Round dollar amounts to the nearest million.)
2. Based on the information provided in the disclosure note, prepare the journal entry that summarizes the vesting of RSUs during the year ended December 31, 2013. (Facebook's common shares have a par amount per share of $0.000006. Round dollar amounts to the nearest million.)

E 19–4
Restricted stock award plan; forfeitures anticipated
● LO19–1

Magnetic-Optical Corporation offers a variety of share-based compensation plans to employees. Under its restricted stock award plan, the company on January 1, 2016, granted 4 million of its $1 par common shares to various division managers. The shares are subject to forfeiture if employment is terminated within three years. The common shares have a market price of $22.50 per share on the grant date.

Required:

1. Determine the total compensation cost pertaining to the restricted shares.
2. Prepare the appropriate journal entry to record the award of restricted shares on January 1, 2016.
3. Prepare the appropriate journal entry to record compensation expense on December 31, 2016.
4. Suppose Magnetic-Optical expected a 10% forfeiture rate on the restricted shares prior to vesting. Determine the total compensation cost.

E 19–5
Stock options
● LO19–2

American Optical Corporation provides a variety of share-based compensation plans to its employees. Under its executive stock option plan, the company granted options on January 1, 2016, that permit executives to acquire 4 million of the company's $1 par common shares within the next five years, but not before December 31, 2017 (the vesting date). The exercise price is the market price of the shares on the date of grant, $14 per share. The fair value of the 4 million options, estimated by an appropriate option pricing model, is $3 per option. No forfeitures are anticipated. Ignore taxes.

Required:

1. Determine the total compensation cost pertaining to the options.
2. Prepare the appropriate journal entry to record the award of options on January 1, 2016.
3. Prepare the appropriate journal entry to record compensation expense on December 31, 2016.
4. Prepare the appropriate journal entry to record compensation expense on December 31, 2017.

E 19–6
Stock options; forfeiture of options
● LO19–2

On January 1, 2016, Adams-Meneke Corporation granted 25 million incentive stock options to division managers, each permitting holders to purchase one share of the company's $1 par common shares within the next six years, but not before December 31, 2018 (the vesting date). The exercise price is the market price of the shares on the date of grant, currently $10 per share. The fair value of the options, estimated by an appropriate option pricing model, is $3 per option.

Required:

1. Determine the total compensation cost pertaining to the options on January 1, 2016.
2. Prepare the appropriate journal entry to record compensation expense on December 31, 2016.
3. Unexpected turnover during 2017 caused the forfeiture of 6% of the stock options. Determine the adjusted compensation cost, and prepare the appropriate journal entry(s) on December 31, 2017 and 2018.

E 19–7
Stock options exercise; forfeitures
● LO19–2

Walters Audio Visual Inc. offers an incentive stock option plan to its regional managers. On January 1, 2016, options were granted for 40 million $1 par common shares. The exercise price is the market price on the grant date—$8 per share. Options cannot be exercised prior to January 1, 2018, and expire December 31, 2022. The fair value of the 40 million options, estimated by an appropriate option pricing model, is $1 per option.

Required:

1. Determine the total compensation cost pertaining to the incentive stock option plan.
2. Prepare the appropriate journal entry to record compensation expense on December 31, 2016.
3. Prepare the appropriate journal entry to record compensation expense on December 31, 2017.
4. Prepare the appropriate journal entry to record the exercise of 75% of the options on March 12, 2018, when the market price is $9 per share.
5. Prepare the appropriate journal entry on December 31, 2022, when the remaining options that have vested expire without being exercised.

E 19–8
Stock options
● LO19–2

SSG Cycles manufactures and distributes motorcycle parts and supplies. Employees are offered a variety of share-based compensation plans. Under its nonqualified stock option plan, SSG granted options to key officers on January 1, 2016.

The options permit holders to acquire 12 million of the company's $1 par common shares for $11 within the next six years, but not before January 1, 2019 (the vesting date). The market price of the shares on the date of grant is $13 per share. The fair value of the 12 million options, estimated by an appropriate option pricing model, is $3 per option.

Required:

1. Determine the total compensation cost pertaining to the incentive stock option plan.
2. Prepare the appropriate journal entries to record compensation expense on December 31, 2016, 2017, and 2018.
3. Record the exercise of the options if all of the options are exercised on May 11, 2020, when the market price is $14 per share.

E 19–9
Employee share purchase plan
● LO19–3

In order to encourage employee ownership of the company's $1 par common shares, Washington Distribution permits any of its employees to buy shares directly from the company through payroll deduction. There are no brokerage fees and shares can be purchased at a 15% discount. During March, employees purchased 50,000 shares at a time when the market price of the shares on the New York Stock Exchange was $12 per share.

Required:
Prepare the appropriate journal entry to record the March purchases of shares under the employee share purchase plan.

E 19–10
EPS; shares issued; stock dividend
● LO19–5, LO19–6

For the year ended December 31, 2016, Norstar Industries reported net income of $655,000. At January 1, 2016, the company had 900,000 common shares outstanding. The following changes in the number of shares occurred during 2016:

Apr. 30	Sold 60,000 shares in a public offering.
May 24	Declared and distributed a 5% stock dividend.
June 1	Issued 72,000 shares as part of the consideration for the purchase of assets from a subsidiary.

Required:
Compute Norstar's earnings per share for the year ended December 31, 2016.

E 19–11
EPS; treasury stock; new shares; stock dividends; two years
● LO19–5, LO19–6

The Alford Group had 202,000 shares of common stock outstanding at January 1, 2016. The following activities affected common shares during the year. There are no potential common shares outstanding.

2016	
Feb. 28	Purchased 6,000 shares of treasury stock.
Oct. 31	Sold the treasury shares purchased on February 28.
Nov. 30	Issued 24,000 new shares.
Dec. 31	Net income for 2016 is $400,000.
2017	
Jan. 15	Declared and issued a 2-for-1 stock split.
Dec. 31	Net income for 2017 is $400,000.

Required:

1. Determine the 2016 EPS.
2. Determine the 2017 EPS.
3. At what amount will the 2016 EPS be presented in the 2017 comparative financial statements?

E 19–12
EPS; stock dividend; nonconvertible preferred stock
● LO19–5, LO19–6, LO19–7

Hardaway Fixtures' balance sheet at December 31, 2015, included the following:

Shares issued and outstanding:	
Common stock, $1 par	$800,000
Nonconvertible preferred stock, $50 par	20,000

On July 21, 2016, Hardaway issued a 25% stock dividend on its common stock. On December 12 it paid $50,000 cash dividends on the preferred stock. Net income for the year ended December 31, 2016, was $2,000,000.

Required:
Compute Hardaway's earnings per share for the year ended December 31, 2016.

E 19–13
EPS; net loss; nonconvertible preferred stock; shares sold
● LO19–5, LO19–6, LO19–7

At December 31, 2015, Albrecht Corporation had outstanding 373,000 shares of common stock and 8,000 shares of 9.5%, $100 par value cumulative, nonconvertible preferred stock. On May 31, 2016, Albrecht sold for cash 12,000 shares of its common stock. No cash dividends were declared for 2016. For the year ended December 31, 2016, Albrecht reported a net loss of $114,000.

Required:
Calculate Albrecht's net loss per share for the year ended December 31, 2016.

E 19–14
EPS; stock dividend; nonconvertible preferred stock; treasury shares; shares sold
● LO19–5, LO19–6, LO19–7

On December 31, 2015, Berclair Inc. had 200 million shares of common stock and 3 million shares of 9%, $100 par value cumulative preferred stock issued and outstanding. On March 1, 2016, Berclair purchased 24 million shares of its common stock as treasury stock. Berclair issued a 5% common stock dividend on July 1, 2016. Four million treasury shares were sold on October 1. Net income for the year ended December 31, 2016, was $150 million.

Required:
Compute Berclair's earnings per share for the year ended December 31, 2016.

E 19–15
EPS; stock dividend; nonconvertible preferred stock; treasury shares; shares sold; stock options
● LO19–5 through LO19–8

(Note: This is a variation of E19–14, modified to include stock options.) On December 31, 2015, Berclair Inc. had 200 million shares of common stock and 3 million shares of 9%, $100 par value cumulative preferred stock issued and outstanding. On March 1, 2016, Berclair purchased 24 million shares of its common stock as treasury stock. Berclair issued a 5% common stock dividend on July 1, 2016. Four million treasury shares were sold on October 1. Net income for the year ended December 31, 2016, was $150 million.

Also outstanding at December 31 were incentive stock options granted to key executives on September 13, 2011. The options were exercisable as of September 13, 2015, for 30 million common shares at an exercise price of $56 per share. During 2016, the market price of the common shares averaged $70 per share.

Required:
Compute Berclair's basic and diluted earnings per share for the year ended December 31, 2016.

E 19–16
EPS; stock dividend; nonconvertible preferred stock; treasury shares; shares sold; stock options exercised
● LO19–5 through LO19–8

(Note: This is a variation of E19–14, modified to include the exercise of stock options.)
On December 31, 2015, Berclair Inc. had 200 million shares of common stock and 3 million shares of 9%, $100 par value cumulative preferred stock issued and outstanding. On March 1, 2016, Berclair purchased 24 million shares of its common stock as treasury stock. Berclair issued a 5% common stock dividend on July 1, 2016. Four million treasury shares were sold on October 1. Net income for the year ended December 31, 2016, was $150 million.

Also outstanding at December 31 were incentive stock options granted to key executives on September 13, 2011. The options were exercisable as of September 13, 2015, for 30 million common shares at an exercise price of $56 per share. During 2016, the market price of the common shares averaged $70 per share.

The options were exercised on September 1, 2016.

Required:
Compute Berclair's basic and diluted earnings per share for the year ended December 31, 2016.

E 19–17
EPS; stock dividend; nonconvertible preferred stock; treasury shares; shares sold; stock options; convertible bonds
● LO19–5 through LO19–9

(Note: This is a variation of E 19–15 modified to include convertible bonds).
On December 31, 2015, Berclair Inc. had 200 million shares of common stock and 3 million shares of 9%, $100 par value cumulative preferred stock issued and outstanding. On March 1, 2016, Berclair purchased 24 million shares of its common stock as treasury stock. Berclair issued a 5% common stock dividend on July 1, 2016. Four million treasury shares were sold on October 1. Net income for the year ended December 31, 2016, was $150 million. The income tax rate is 40%.

Also outstanding at December 31 were incentive stock options granted to key executives on September 13, 2011. The options are exercisable as of September 13, 2015, for 30 million common shares at an exercise price of $56 per share. During 2016, the market price of the common shares averaged $70 per share.

In 2012 $62.5 million of 8% bonds, convertible into 6 million common shares, were issued at face value.

Required:
Compute Berclair's basic and diluted earnings per share for the year ended December 31, 2016.

E 19–18
EPS; shares issued; stock options
● LO19–6 through LO19–9

Stanley Department Stores reported net income of $720,000 for the year ended December 31, 2016.

Additional Information:

Common shares outstanding at Jan. 1, 2016	80,000
Incentive stock options (vested in 2015) outstanding throughout 2016	24,000
(Each option is exercisable for one common share at an exercise price of $37.50)	
During the year, the market price of Stanley's common stock averaged $45 per share.	
On Aug. 30 Stanley sold 15,000 common shares.	
Stanley's only debt consisted of $50,000 of 10% short term bank notes.	
The company's income tax rate is 40%.	

Required:
Compute Stanley's basic and diluted earnings per share for the year ended December 31, 2016.

E 19–19
EPS; convertible preferred stock; convertible bonds; order of entry
● LO19–7, LO19–9

Information from the financial statements of Ames Fabricators, Inc., included the following:

	December 31	
	2016	**2015**
Common shares	100,000	100,000
Convertible preferred shares (convertible into 32,000 shares of common)	12,000	12,000
10% convertible bonds (convertible into 30,000 shares of common)	$1,000,000	$1,000,000

Ames's net income for the year ended December 31, 2016, is $500,000. The income tax rate is 40%. Ames paid dividends of $5 per share on its preferred stock during 2016.

Required:
Compute basic and diluted earnings per share for the year ended December 31, 2016.

E 19–20
EPS; restricted stock
● LO19–11

As part of its executive compensation plan, Vertovec Inc. granted 54,000 of its no par common shares to executives, subject to forfeiture if employment is terminated within three years. Vertovec's common shares have a market price of $5 per share on January 1, 2015, the grant date of the restricted stock award, as well as on December 31, 2016. 800,000 shares were outstanding at January 1, 2016. Net income for 2016 was $120,000.

Required:
Compute Vertovec's basic and diluted earnings per share for the year ended December 31, 2016.

E 19–21
Record restricted stock; effect on EPS
● LO19–1, LO19–11

PHN Foods granted 18 million of its no par common shares to executives, subject to forfeiture if employment is terminated within three years. The common shares have a market price of $5 per share on January 1, 2015, the grant date.

Required:
1. What journal entry will PHN Foods prepare to record executive compensation regarding these restricted shares at December 31, 2015 and December 31, 2016?
2. When calculating diluted EPS at December 31, 2016, what will be the net increase in the denominator of the EPS fraction if the market price of the common shares averages $5 per share during 2016?

E 19–22
New shares; contingently issuable shares
● LO19–6, LO19–12

During its first year of operations, McCollum Tool Works entered into the following transactions relating to shareholders' equity. The corporation was authorized to issue 100 million common shares, $1 par per share.

Jan. 2	Issued 35 million common shares for cash.
3	Entered an agreement with the company president to issue up to 2 million additional shares of common stock in 2017 based on the earnings of McCollum in 2017. If net income exceeds $140 million, the president will receive 1 million shares; 2 million shares if net income exceeds $150 million.
Mar. 31	Issued 4 million shares in exchange for plant facilities.

Net income for 2016 was $148 million.

Required:
Compute basic and diluted earnings per share for the year ended December 31, 2016.

E 19–23
EPS; new shares; contingent agreements
● LO19–6, LO19–12

Anderson Steel Company began 2016 with 600,000 shares of common stock outstanding. On March 31, 2016, 100,000 new shares were sold at a price of $45 per share. The market price has risen steadily since that time to a high of $50 per share at December 31. No other changes in shares occurred during 2016, and no securities are outstanding that can become common stock. However, there are two agreements with officers of the company for future issuance of common stock. Both agreements relate to compensation arrangements reached in 2015. The first agreement grants to the company president a right to 10,000 shares of stock each year the closing market price is at least $48. The agreement begins in 2017 and expires in 2020. The second agreement grants to the controller a right to 15,000 shares of stock if she is still with the firm at the end of 2024. Net income for 2016 was $2,000,000.

Required:
Compute Anderson Steel Company's basic and diluted EPS for the year ended December 31, 2016.

E 19–24
EPS; concepts; terminology
● LO19–5 through LO19–13

Listed below are several terms and phrases associated with earnings per share. Pair each item from List A with the item from List B (by letter) that is most appropriately associated with it.

List A

____ 1. Subtract preferred dividends.
____ 2. Time-weighted by $5/12$.
____ 3. Time-weighted shares assumed issued plus time-weighted actual shares.
____ 4. Midyear event treated as if it occurred at the beginning of the reporting period.
____ 5. Preferred dividends do not reduce earnings.
____ 6. Single EPS presentation.
____ 7. Stock split.
____ 8. Potential common shares.
____ 9. Exercise price exceeds market price.
____ 10. No dilution assumed.
____ 11. Convertible bonds.
____ 12. Contingently issuable shares.
____ 13. Maximum potential dilution.
____ 14. Shown between per share amounts for net income and for income from continuing operations.

List B

a. Options exercised.
b. Simple capital structure.
c. Basic EPS.
d. Convertible preferred stock.
e. Earnings available to common shareholders.
f. Antidilutiv[illegible].
g. Increased m[illegible]rketability.
h. Discontinued [illegible]erations.
i. Stock dividend.
j. Add after-tax inte[illegible] numerator.
k. Diluted EPS.
l. Noncumulative, undec[illegible]eferred dividends.
m. Common shares retired a[illegible]inning of August.
n. Include in diluted EPS when co[illegible]or issuance are met.

E 19–25
FASB codification research
● LO19–2

The *FASB Accounting Standards Codification* represents the single source of authoritative U.S. generally accounting principles.

Required:

1. Obtain the relevant authoritative literature on stock compensation using the *FASB Accounting Standards Codification* at the FASB website (asc.fasb.org). What is the specific citation that describes the information that companies must disclose about the exercise prices for their stock option plans?
2. List the disclosure requirements.

E 19–26
FASB codification research
● LO19–2, LO19–3, LO19–7, LO19–13

Access the *FASB Accounting Standards Codification* at the FASB website (asc.fasb.org). Determine the specific citation for accounting for each of the following items:

1. Initial measurement of stock options.
2. The measurement date for share-based payments classified as liabilities.
3. The formula to calculate diluted earnings per share.
4. The way stock dividends or stock splits in the current year affect the presentation of EPS in the income statement.

E 19–27
Stock appreciation rights; settlement in shares
● (Appendix B)

As part of its stock-based compensation package, International Electronics granted 24 million stock appreciation rights (SARs) to top officers on January 1, 2016. At exercise, holders of the SARs are entitled to receive stock equal in value to the excess of the market price at exercise over the share price at the date of grant. The SARs cannot be exercised until the end of 2019 (vesting date) and expire at the end of 2021. The $1 par common shares have a market price of $46 per share on the grant date. The fair value of the SARs, estimated by an appropriate option pricing model, is $3 per SAR at January 1, 2016. The fair value reestimated at December 31, 2016, 2017, 2018, 2019, and 2020, is $4, $3, $4, $2.50, and $3, respectively. All recipients are expected to remain employed through the vesting date.

Required:

1. Prepare the appropriate journal entry to record the award of SARs on January 1, 2016. Will the SARs be reported as debt or equity?
2. Prepare the appropriate journal entries pertaining to the SARs on December 31, 2016–December 31, 2019.
3. The SARs remain unexercised on December 31, 2020. Prepare the appropriate journal entry on that date.
4. The SARs are exercised on June 6, 2021, when the share price is $50. Prepare the appropriate journal entry(s) on that date.

E 19–28
Stock appreciation rights; cash settlement
● (Appendix B)

(Note: This is a variation of the E19–27, modified to allow settlement in cash.)
As part of its stock-based compensation package, International Electronics granted 24 million stock appreciation rights (SARs) to top officers on January 1, 2016. At exercise, holders of the SARs are entitled to receive cash or stock equal in value to the excess of the market price at exercise over the share price at the date of grant. The SARs cannot be exercised until the end of 2019 (vesting date) and expire at the end of 2021. The $1 par common shares

have a market price of $46 per share on the grant date. The fair value of the SARs, estimated by an appropriate option pricing model, is $3 per SAR at January 1, 2016. The fair value re-estimated at December 31, 2016, 2017, 2018, 2019, and 2020, is $4, $3, $4, $2.50, and $3, respectively. All recipients are expected to remain employed through the vesting date.

Required:

1. Prepare the appropriate journal entry to record the award of SARs on January 1, 2016.
2. Prepare the appropriate journal entries pertaining to the SARs on December 31, 2016–December 31, 2019.
3. The SARs remain unexercised on December 31, 2020. Prepare the appropriate journal entry on that date.
4. The SARs are exercised on June 6, 2021, when the share price is $50, and executives choose to receive the market price appreciation in cash. Prepare the appropriate journal entry(s) on that date.

E 19–29
Restricted stock units; cash settlement

As part of its stock-based compensation package, on January 1, 2016, International Electronics granted restricted stock units (RSUs) representing 50 million $1 par common shares. At exercise, holders of the RSUs are entitled to receive cash or stock equal in value to the market price of those shares at exercise. The RSUs cannot be exercised until the end of 2019 (vesting date) and expire at the end of 2021. The $1 par common shares have a market price of $6 per share on the grant date. The fair value at December 31, 2016, 2017, 2018, 2019, and 2020, is $8, $6, $8, $5, and $6, respectively. All recipients are expected to remain employed through the vesting date.

Required:

1. Prepare the appropriate journal entry to record the award of RSUs on January 1, 2016.
2. Prepare the appropriate journal entries pertaining to the RSUs on December 31, 2016–December 31, 2019.
3. The RSUs remain unexercised on December 31, 2020. Prepare the appropriate journal entry on that date.
4. The RSUs are exercised on June 6, 2021, when the share price is $6.50, and executives choose to receive cash. Prepare the appropriate journal entry(s) on that date.

After the recipients of the RSUs satisfy the vesting requirement, the company will distribute the shares.

CPA and CMA Review Questions

CPA Exam Questions

KAPLAN CPA REVIEW

The following questions are adapted from a variety of sources including questions developed by the AICPA Board of Examiners and those used in the Kaplan CPA Review Course to study accounting for share-based compensation and earnings per share while preparing for the CPA examination. Determine the response that best completes the statements or questions.

● LO19–2

1. On January 1, 2016, Pall Corp. granted stock options to key employees for the purchase of 40,000 shares of the company's common stock at $25 per share. The options are intended to compensate employees for the next two years. The options are exercisable within a four-year period beginning January 1, 2018, by the grantees still in the employ of the company. No options were terminated during 2016, but the company does have an experience of 4% forfeitures over the life of the stock options. The market price of the common stock was $32 per share at the date of the grant. Pall Corp. used the binomial pricing model and estimated the fair value of each of the options at $10. What amount should Pall charge to compensation expense for the year ended December 31, 2016?
   a. $153,600
   b. $160,000
   c. $192,000
   d. $200,000

● LO19–2

2. On January 1, 2016, Doro Corp. granted an employee an option to purchase 3,000 shares of Doro's $5 par value common stock at $20 per share. The options became exercisable on December 31, 2017, after the employee completed two years of service. The options were exercised on January 10, 2018. The market prices of Doro's stock were as follows: January 1, 2016, $30; December 31, 2017, $50; and January 10, 2018, $45. The Black-Scholes-Merton option pricing model estimated the value of the options at $8 each on the grant date. For 2016, Doro should recognize compensation expense of
   a. $ 0
   b. $12,000
   c. $15,000
   d. $45,000

● LO19–6

3. The following information pertains to Jet Corp.'s outstanding stock for 2016:

Common stock, $5 par value	
Shares outstanding, 1/1/2016	20,000
2-for-1 stock split, 4/1/2016	20,000
Shares issued, 7/1/2016	10,000
Preferred stock, $10 par value, 5% cumulative	
Shares outstanding, 1/1/2016	4,000

What is the number of shares Jet should use to calculate 2016 basic earnings per share?

a. 40,000
b. 45,000
c. 50,000
d. 54,000

● LO19–7

4. At December 31, 2016 and 2015, Gow Corp. had 100,000 shares of common stock and 10,000 shares of 5%, $100 par value cumulative preferred stock outstanding. No dividends were declared on either the preferred or common stock in 2016 or 2015. Net income for 2016 was $1,000,000. For 2016, basic earnings per common share amounted to

a. $ 5.00
b. $ 9.50
c. $ 9.00
d. $10.00

● LO19–8

5. January 1, 2016, Hage Corporation granted options to purchase 9,000 of its common shares at $7 each. The market price of common stock was $9 per share on March 31, 2016, and averaged $9 per share during the quarter then ended. There was no change in the 50,000 shares of outstanding common stock during the quarter ended March 31, 2016. Net income for the quarter was $8,268. The number of shares to be used in computing diluted earnings per share for the quarter is

a. 50,000
b. 52,000
c. 53,000
d. 59,000

● LO19–9

6. During 2016, Moore Corp. had the following two classes of stock issued and outstanding for the entire year:

- 100,000 shares of common stock, $1 par.
- 1,000 shares of 4% preferred stock, $100 par, convertible share for share into common stock.

Moore's 2016 net income was $900,000, and its income tax rate for the year was 30%. In the computation of diluted earnings per share for 2016, the amount to be used in the numerator is

a. $896,000
b. $898,800
c. $900,000
d. $901,200

● LO19–9

7. On January 2, 2016, Lang Co. issued at par $10,000 of 4% bonds convertible in total into 1,000 shares of Lang's common stock. No bonds were converted during 2016.

Throughout 2016, Lang had 1,000 shares of common stock outstanding. Lang's 2016 net income was $1,000. Lang's income tax rate is 50%.

No potential common shares other than the convertible bonds were outstanding during 2016. Lang's diluted earnings per share for 2016 would be

a. $ .50
b. $ .60
c. $ .70
d. $1.00

International Financial Reporting Standards are tested on the CPA exam along with U.S. GAAP. The following questions deal with the application of IFRS in accounting for share-based compensation.

● LO19–14

IFRS

8. M Company prepares its financial statements using IFRS. M will record a deferred tax asset for stock options

a. for the cumulative amount of the fair value of the options M has recorded for compensation expense.
b. for the portion of the options' intrinsic value earned to date times the tax rate.
c. for the tax rate times the amount of compensation.
d. unless the award is "in the money;" that is, it has intrinsic value.

● LO19–14

9. N Company had issued 80,000 executive stock options as of January 1, 2016, permitting executives to buy 80,000 shares of stock for $60 per share. N's vesting schedule is 20% the first year, 30% the second year, and 50% the third year (graded-vesting). The fair value of the options is estimated as follows:

Vesting Date	Amount Vesting	Fair Value per Option
Dec. 31, 2016	20%	$5
Dec. 31, 2017	30%	$6
Dec. 31, 2018	50%	$9

Assuming N prepares its financial statements in accordance with International Financial Reporting Standards, what is the compensation expense related to the options to be recorded in 2017?

a. $ 72,000
b. $144,000
c. $192,000
d. $195,000

CMA Exam Questions

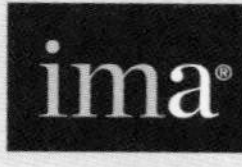

The following questions dealing with share-based compensation and earnings per share are adapted from questions that previously appeared on Certified Management Accountant (CMA) examinations. The CMA designation sponsored by the Institute of Management Accountants (**www.imanet.org**) provides members with an objective measure of knowledge and competence in the field of management accounting. Determine the response that best completes the statements or questions.

● LO19–2

1. Noncompensatory stock option plans have all of the following characteristics except
   a. participation by substantially all full-time employees who meet limited employment qualifications.
   b. equal offers of stock to all eligible employees.
   c. a limited amount of time permitted to exercise the option.
   d. a provision related to the achievement of certain performance criteria.

● LO19–2

2. A stock option plan may or may not be intended to compensate employees for their work. The compensation expense for compensatory stock option plans should be recognized in the periods the
   a. employees become eligible to exercise the options.
   b. employees perform services.
   c. stock is issued.
   d. options are granted.

Problems

An alternate exercise and problem set is available at the Connect library.

P 19–1
Stock options; forfeiture; exercise
● LO19–2

On October 15, 2015, the board of directors of Ensor Materials Corporation approved a stock option plan for key executives. On January 1, 2016, 20 million stock options were granted, exercisable for 20 million shares of Ensor's $1 par common stock. The options are exercisable between January 1, 2019, and December 31, 2021, at 80% of the quoted market price on January 1, 2016, which was $15. The fair value of the 20 million options, estimated by an appropriate option pricing model, is $6 per option.

Two million options were forfeited when an executive resigned in 2017. All other options were exercised on July 12, 2020, when the stock's price jumped unexpectedly to $19 per share.

Required:

1. When is Ensor's stock option measurement date?
2. Determine the compensation expense for the stock option plan in 2016. (Ignore taxes.)
3. What is the effect of forfeiture of the stock options on Ensor's financial statements for 2017 and 2018?
4. Is this effect consistent with the general approach for accounting for changes in estimates? Explain.
5. How should Ensor account for the exercise of the options in 2020?

P 19–2
Stock options; graded vesting
● LO19–2

Pastner Brands is a calendar-year firm with operations in several countries. As part of its executive compensation plan, at January 1, 2016, the company issued 400,000 executive stock options permitting executives to buy 400,000 shares of Pastner stock for $34 per share. One-fourth of the options vest in each of the next four years beginning at December 31, 2016 (graded vesting). Pastner elects to separate the total award into four groups (or tranches) according to the year in which they vest and measures the compensation cost for each vesting date as a separate award. The fair value of each tranche is estimated at January 1, 2016, as follows:

Vesting Date	Amount Vesting	Fair Value per Option
Dec. 31, 2016	25%	$3.50
Dec. 31, 2017	25%	$4.00
Dec. 31, 2018	25%	$4.50
Dec. 31, 2019	25%	$5.00

Required:

1. Determine the compensation expense related to the options to be recorded each year 2016–2019, assuming Pastner allocates the compensation cost for each of the four groups (tranches) separately.
2. Determine the compensation expense related to the options to be recorded each year 2016–2019, assuming Pastner uses the straight-line method to allocate the total compensation cost.

P 19–3
Stock options; graded vesting; measurement using a single fair value per option
● LO19–2

Refer to the situation described in P19–2. Assume Pastner measures the fair value of all options on January 1, 2016, to be $4.50 per option using a single weighted-average expected life of the options assumption.

Required:

1. Determine the compensation expense related to the options to be recorded each year 2016–2019, assuming Pastner allocates the compensation cost for each of the four groups (tranches) separately.
2. Determine the compensation expense related to the options to be recorded each year 2016–2019, assuming Pastner uses the straight-line method to allocate the total compensation cost.

P 19–4
Stock options; graded vesting; IFRS
● LO19–2, LO19–14

IFRS

Refer to the situation described in P19–2. Assume Pastner prepares its financial statements using International Financial Reporting Standards.

Required:

How might your responses to requirement 1 and requirement 2 differ using IFRS? Explain.

P 19–5
Stock option plan; deferred tax effect recognized
● LO19–2

Walters Audio Visual, Inc., offers a stock option plan to its regional managers. On January 1, 2016, options were granted for 40 million $1 par common shares. The exercise price is the market price on the grant date, $8 per share. Options cannot be exercised prior to January 1, 2018, and expire December 31, 2022. The fair value of the options, estimated by an appropriate option pricing model, is $2 per option. Because the plan does not qualify as an incentive plan, Walters will receive a tax deduction upon exercise of the options equal to the excess of the market price at exercise over the exercise price. The income tax rate is 40%.

Required:

1. Determine the total compensation cost pertaining to the stock option plan.
2. Prepare the appropriate journal entries to record compensation expense and its tax effect on December 31, 2016.
3. Prepare the appropriate journal entries to record compensation expense and its tax effect on December 31, 2017.
4. Record the exercise of the options and their tax effect if *all* of the options are exercised on March 20, 2021, when the market price is $12 per share.
5. Assume the option plan qualifies as an incentive plan. Prepare the appropriate journal entries to record compensation expense and its tax effect on December 31, 2016.
6. Assuming the option plan qualifies as an incentive plan, record the exercise of the options and their tax effect if *all* of the options are exercised on March 20, 2021, when the market price is $11 per share.

P 19–6
Stock option plan; deferred tax effect of a non-qualifying plan
● LO19–2

JBL Aircraft manufactures and distributes aircraft parts and supplies. Employees are offered a variety of share-based compensation plans. Under its nonqualified stock option plan, JBL granted options to key officers on January 1, 2016. The options permit holders to acquire six million of the company's $1 par common shares for $22 within the next six years, but not before January 1, 2019 (the vesting date). The market price of the shares on the date of grant is $26 per share. The fair value of the 6 million options, estimated by an appropriate option pricing model, is $6 per option. Because the plan does not qualify as an incentive plan, JBL will receive a tax deduction upon exercise of the options equal to the excess of the market price at exercise over the exercise price. The tax rate is 40%.

Required:

1. Determine the total compensation cost pertaining to the incentive stock option plan.
2. Prepare the appropriate journal entries to record compensation expense and its tax effect on December 31, 2016, 2017, and 2018.
3. Record the exercise of the options and their tax effect if *all* of the options are exercised on August 21, 2020, when the market price is $27 per share.

P 19–7
Performance option plan
● LO19–2

LCI Cable Company grants 1 million performance stock options to key executives at January 1, 2016. The options entitle executives to receive 1 million of LCI $1 par common shares, subject to the achievement of specific financial goals over the next four years. Attainment of these goals is considered probable initially and throughout the service period. The options have a current fair value of $12 per option.

Required:

1. Prepare the appropriate entry when the options are awarded on January 1, 2016.
2. Prepare the appropriate entries on December 31 of each year 2016–2019.
3. Suppose at the beginning of 2018, LCI decided it is not probable that the performance objectives will be met. Prepare the appropriate entries on December 31 of 2018 and 2019.

P 19–8
Net loss; stock dividend; nonconvertible preferred stock; treasury shares; shares sold; discontinued operations
● LO19–5 through LO19–7, LO19–13

On December 31, 2015, Ainsworth, Inc., had 600 million shares of common stock outstanding. Twenty million shares of 8%, $100 par value cumulative, nonconvertible preferred stock were sold on January 2, 2016. On April 30, 2016, Ainsworth purchased 30 million shares of its common stock as treasury stock. Twelve million treasury shares were sold on August 31. Ainsworth issued a 5% common stock dividend on June 12, 2016. No cash dividends were declared in 2016. For the year ended December 31, 2016, Ainsworth reported a net loss of $140 million, including an after-tax loss from discontinued operations of $400 million.

Required:

1. Determine Ainsworth's net loss per share for the year ended December 31, 2016.
2. Determine the per share amount of income or loss from continuing operations for the year ended December 31, 2016.
3. Prepare an EPS presentation that would be appropriate to appear on Ainsworth's 2016 and 2015 comparative income statements. Assume EPS was reported in 2015 as $.75, based on net income (no discontinued operations) of $450 million and a weighted-average number of common shares of 600 million.

P 19–9
EPS from statement of retained earnings
● LO19–4 through LO19–6

(Note: This problem is based on the same situation described in P18–4 in Chapter 18, modified to focus on EPS rather than recording the events that affected retained earnings.)
Comparative Statements of Retained Earnings for Renn-Dever Corporation were reported as follows for the fiscal years ending December 31, 2014, 2015, and 2016.

RENN-DEVER CORPORATION
Statements of Retained Earnings

For the Years Ended December 31	2016	2015	2014
Balance at beginning of year	$6,794,292	$5,464,052	$5,624,552
Net income (loss)	3,308,700	2,240,900	(160,500)
Deductions:			
Stock dividend (34,900 shares)	242,000		
Common shares retired, September 30 (110,000 shares)		212,660	
Common stock cash dividends	889,950	698,000	0
Balance at end of year	$8,971,042	$6,794,292	$5,464,052

At December 31, 2013, paid-in capital consisted of the following:

Common stock, 1,855,000 shares at $1 par,	$1,855,000
Paid in capital—excess of par	7,420,000

No preferred stock or potential common shares were outstanding during any of the periods shown.

Required:

Compute Renn-Dever's earnings per share as it would have appeared in income statements for the years ended December 31, 2014, 2015, and 2016.

P 19–10
EPS from statement of shareholders' equity
● LO19–4 through LO19–6

Comparative Statements of Shareholders' Equity for Locke Intertechnology Corporation were reported as follows for the fiscal years ending December 31, 2014, 2015, and 2016.

LOCKE INTERTECHNOLOGY CORPORATION
Statements of Shareholders' Equity
For the Years Ended Dec. 31, 2014, 2015, and 2016
($ in millions)

	Preferred Stock, $10 par	Common Stock, $1 par	Additional Paid-In Capital	Retained Earnings	Total Shareholders' Equity
Balance at January 1, 2014		$ 55	$ 495	$1,878	$2,428
Sale of preferred shares	10		470		480
Sale of common shares, 7/1		9	81		90
Cash dividend, preferred				(1)	(1)
Cash dividend, common				(16)	(16)
Net income				290	290
Balance at December 31, 2014	10	64	1,046	2,151	3,271
Retirement of common shares, 4/1		(4)	(36)	(20)	(60)
Cash dividend, preferred				(1)	(1)
Cash dividend, common				(20)	(20)
3-for-2 split effected in the form of a common stock dividend, 8/12		30	(30)		
Net income				380	380
Balance at December 31, 2015	10	90	980	2,490	3,570
10% common stock dividend, 5/1		9	90	(99)	
Sale of common shares, 9/1		3	31		34
Cash dividend, preferred				(2)	(2)
Cash dividend, common				(22)	(22)
Net income				412	412
Balance at December 31, 2016	$10	$102	$1,101	$2,779	$3,992

Required:
Infer from the statements the events and transactions that affected Locke Intertechnology Corporation's shareholders' equity and compute earnings per share as it would have appeared on the income statements for the years ended December 31, 2014, 2015, and 2016. No potential common shares were outstanding during any of the periods shown.

P 19–11
EPS; nonconvertible preferred stock; treasury shares; shares sold; stock dividend
● LO19–4 through LO19–7

On December 31, 2015, Dow Steel Corporation had 600,000 shares of common stock and 300,000 shares of 8%, noncumulative, nonconvertible preferred stock issued and outstanding. Dow issued a 4% common stock dividend on May 15 and paid cash dividends of $400,000 and $75,000 to common and preferred shareholders, respectively, on December 15, 2016.

On February 28, 2016, Dow sold 60,000 common shares. In keeping with its long-term share repurchase plan, 2,000 shares were retired on July 1. Dow's net income for the year ended December 31, 2016, was $2,100,000. The income tax rate is 40%.

Required:
Compute Dow's earnings per share for the year ended December 31, 2016.

P 19–12
EPS; nonconvertible preferred stock; treasury shares; shares sold; stock dividend; options
● LO19–4 through LO19–8, LO19–10

(Note: This is a variation of P19–12, modified to include stock options.)
On December 31, 2015, Dow Steel Corporation had 600,000 shares of common stock and 300,000 shares of 8%, noncumulative, nonconvertible preferred stock issued and outstanding. Dow issued a 4% common stock dividend on May 15 and paid cash dividends of $400,000 and $75,000 to common and preferred shareholders, respectively, on December 15, 2016.

On February 28, 2016, Dow sold 60,000 common shares. In keeping with its long-term share repurchase plan, 2,000 shares were retired on July 1. Dow's net income for the year ended December 31, 2016, was $2,100,000. The income tax rate is 40%.

As part of an incentive compensation plan, Dow granted incentive stock options to division managers at December 31 of the current and each of the previous two years. Each option permits its holder to buy one share of common stock at an exercise price equal to market value at the date of grant and can be exercised one year from that date. Information concerning the number of options granted and common share prices follows:

Date Granted	Options Granted	Share Price
	(adjusted for the stock dividend)	
December 31, 2014	8,000	$24
December 31, 2015	3,000	$33
December 31, 2016	6,500	$32

The market price of the common stock averaged $32 per share during 2016.

Required:

Compute Dow's earnings per share for the year ended December 31, 2016.

P 19–13
EPS; nonconvertible preferred stock; treasury shares; shares sold; stock dividend; options; convertible bonds; contingently issuable shares
● LO19–4 through LO19–11

(Note: This is a variation of P19–13, modified to include convertible bonds and contingently issuable shares.) On December 31, 2015, Dow Steel Corporation had 600,000 shares of common stock and 300,000 shares of 8%, noncumulative, nonconvertible preferred stock issued and outstanding. Dow issued a 4% common stock dividend on May 15 and paid cash dividends of $400,000 and $75,000 to common and preferred shareholders, respectively, on December 15, 2016.

On February 28, 2016, Dow sold 60,000 common shares. In keeping with its long-term share repurchase plan, 2,000 shares were retired on July 1. Dow's net income for the year ended December 31, 2016, was $2,100,000. The income tax rate is 40%. Also, as a part of a 2015 agreement for the acquisition of Merrill Cable Company, another 23,000 shares (already adjusted for the stock dividend) are to be issued to former Merrill shareholders on December 31, 2017, if Merrill's 2017 net income is at least $500,000. In 2016, Merrill's net income was $630,000.

As part of an incentive compensation plan, Dow granted incentive stock options to division managers at December 31 of the current and each of the previous two years. Each option permits its holder to buy one share of common stock at an exercise price equal to market value at the date of grant and can be exercised one year from that date. Information concerning the number of options granted and common share prices follows:

Date Granted	Options Granted	Share Price
	(adjusted for the stock dividend)	
December 31, 2014	8,000	$24
December 31, 2015	3,000	$33
December 31, 2016	6,500	$32

The market price of the common stock averaged $32 per share during 2016.

On July 12, 2014, Dow issued $800,000 of convertible 10% bonds at face value. Each $1,000 bond is convertible into 30 common shares (adjusted for the stock dividend).

Required:

Compute Dow's basic and diluted earnings per share for the year ended December 31, 2016.

P 19–14
EPS; convertible preferred stock; convertible bonds; order of entry
● LO19–7, LO19–9, LO19–10

Information from the financial statements of Henderson-Niles Industries included the following at December 31, 2016:

Common shares outstanding throughout the year	100 million
Convertible preferred shares (convertible into 32 million shares of common)	60 million
Convertible 10% bonds (convertible into 13.5 million shares of common)	$900 million

Henderson-Niles' net income for the year ended December 31, 2016, is $520 million. The income tax rate is 40%. Henderson-Niles paid dividends of $2 per share on its preferred stock during 2016.

Required:

Compute basic and diluted earnings per share for the year ended December 31, 2016.

P 19–15
EPS; antidilution
● LO19–4 through LO19–10, LO19–13

Alciatore Company reported a net income of $150,000 in 2016. The weighted-average number of common shares outstanding for 2016 was 40,000. The average stock price for 2016 was $33. Assume an income tax rate of 40%.

Required:

For each of the following independent situations, indicate whether the effect of the security is antidilutive for diluted EPS.

1. 10,000 shares of 7.7% of $100 par convertible, cumulative preferred stock. Each share may be converted into two common shares.
2. 8% convertible 10-year, $500,000 of bonds, issued at face value. The bonds are convertible to 5,000 shares of common stock.

3. Stock options exercisable at $30 per share after January 1, 2018.
4. Warrants for 1,000 common shares with an exercise price of $35 per share.
5. A contingent agreement to issue 5,000 shares of stock to the company president if net income is at least $125,000 in 2017.

P 19–16
EPS; convertible bonds; treasury shares
● LO19–4 through LO19–6, LO19–9

At December 31, 2016, the financial statements of Hollingsworth Industries included the following:

Net income for 2016	$560 million
Bonds payable, 10%, convertible into 36 million shares of common stock	$300 million
Common stock:	
Shares outstanding on January 1	400 million
Treasury shares purchased for cash on September 1	30 million

Additional data:

The bonds payable were issued at par in 2014. The tax rate for 2016 was 40%.

Required:
Compute basic and diluted EPS for the year ended December 31, 2016.

P 19–17
EPS; options; convertible preferred; additional shares
● LO19–4 through LO19–9

On January 1, 2016, Tonge Industries had outstanding 440,000 common shares (par $1) that originally sold for $20 per share, and 4,000 shares of 10% cumulative preferred stock (par $100), convertible into 40,000 common shares.

On October 1, 2016, Tonge sold and issued an additional 16,000 shares of common stock at $33. At December 31, 2016, there were incentive stock options outstanding, issued in 2015, and exercisable after one year for 20,000 shares of common stock at an exercise price of $30. The market price of the common stock at year-end was $48. During the year the price of the common shares had averaged $40.

Net income was $650,000. The tax rate for the year was 40%.

Required:
Compute basic and diluted EPS for the year ended December 31, 2016.

P 19–18
EPS; stock options; nonconvertible preferred; convertible bonds; shares sold
● LO19–4 through LO19–9

At January 1, 2016, Canaday Corporation had outstanding the following securities:

600 million common shares
20 million 6% cumulative preferred shares, $50 par
8% convertible bonds, $2,000 million face amount, convertible into 80 million common shares

The following additional information is available:

- On September 1, 2016, Canaday sold 72 million additional shares of common stock.
- Incentive stock options to purchase 60 million shares of common stock after July 1, 2015, at $12 per share were outstanding at the beginning and end of 2016. The average market price of Canaday's common stock was $18 per share during 2016.
- Canaday's net income for the year ended December 31, 2016, was $1,476 million. The effective income tax rate was 40%.

Required:
1. Calculate basic earnings per common share for the year ended December 31, 2016.
2. Calculate the diluted earnings per common share for the year ended December 31, 2016.

P 19–19
EPS; options; restricted stock; additional components for "proceeds" in treasury stock method
● LO19–1, LO19–2, LO19–4, LO19–8, LO19–11

Witter House is a calendar-year firm with 300 million common shares outstanding throughout 2016 and 2017. As part of its executive compensation plan, at January 1, 2015, the company had issued 30 million executive stock options permitting executives to buy 30 million shares of stock for $10 within the next eight years, but not prior to January 1, 2018. The fair value of the options was estimated on the grant date to be $3 per option.

In 2016, Witter House began granting employees stock awards rather than stock options as part of its equity compensation plans and granted 15 million restricted common shares to senior executives at January 1, 2016. The shares vest four years later. The fair value of the stock was $12 per share on the grant date. The average price of the common shares was $12 and $15 during 2016 and 2017, respectively.

The stock options qualify for tax purposes as an incentive plan. The restricted stock does not. The company's net income was $150 million and $160 million in 2016 and 2017, respectively. Its income tax rate is 40%.

Required:
1. Determine basic and diluted earnings per share for Witter House in 2016.
2. Determine basic and diluted earnings per share for Witter House in 2017.

Broaden Your Perspective

Apply your critical-thinking ability to the knowledge you've gained. These cases will provide you an opportunity to develop your research, analysis, judgment, and communication skills. You also will work with other students, integrate what you've learned, apply it in real-world situations, and consider its global and ethical ramifications. This practice will broaden your knowledge and further develop your decision-making abilities.

Real World Case 19–1
Restricted stock awards; Microsoft
● LO19–1

Real World Financials

Microsoft provides compensation to executives in the form of a variety of incentive compensation plans including restricted stock award grants. The following is an excerpt from a disclosure note from Microsoft's 2013 annual report:

Note 20 Employee Stock and Savings Plans (in part)
Stock awards are grants that entitle the holder to shares of common stock as the award vests. Our stock awards generally vest over a five-year period. . . . During fiscal year 2013, the following activity occurred under our plans:

	Shares (in millions)	**Weighted Average Grant-Date Fair Value**
Stock awards:		
Nonvested balance, beginning of year	281	$ 23.91
Granted	104	28.37
Vested	(90)	24.49
Forfeited	(22)	25.10
Nonvested balance, end of year	**273**	**$25.50**

Required:

1. What is the "incentive" provided by Microsoft's restricted stock grants?
2. If all awards are granted, vested, and forfeited evenly throughout the year, what is the compensation expense in fiscal 2013 pertaining to the previous and current stock awards? Explain. Assume forfeited shares were granted evenly throughout the three previous years.

Communication Case 19–2
Stock options; basic concepts; prepare a memo
● LO19–2

You are assistant controller of Stamos & Company, a medium-size manufacturer of machine parts. On October 22, 2015, the board of directors approved a stock option plan for key executives. On January 1, 2016, a specific number of stock options were granted. The options were exercisable between January 1, 2018, and December 31, 2022, at 100% of the quoted market price at the grant date. The service period is for 2016 through 2018.

Your boss, the controller, is one of the executives to receive options. Neither he nor you have had occasion to deal with GAAP on accounting for stock options. He and you are aware of the traditional approach your company used years ago but do not know the newer method. Your boss understands how options might benefit him personally but wants to be aware also of how the options will be reported in the financial statements. He has asked you for a one-page synopsis of accounting for stock options under the fair value approach. He instructed you, "I don't care about the effect on taxes or earnings per share—just the basics, please."

Required:

Prepare such a report that includes the following:

1. At what point should the compensation cost be measured? How should it be measured?
2. How should compensation expense be measured for the stock option plan in 2016 and later?
3. If options are forfeited because an executive resigns before vesting, what is the effect of that forfeiture of the stock options on the financial statements?
4. If options are allowed to lapse after vesting, what is the effect on the financial statements?

Ethics Case 19–3
Stock options
● LO19–2

You are in your second year as an auditor with Dantly and Regis, a regional CPA firm. One of the firm's long-time clients is Mayberry-Cleaver Industries, a national company involved in the manufacturing, marketing, and sales of hydraulic devices used in specialized manufacturing applications. Early in this year's audit you discover that Mayberry-Cleaver has changed its method of determining inventory from LIFO to FIFO. Your client's explanation is that FIFO is consistent with the method used by some other companies in the industry. Upon further investigation, you discover an executive stock option plan whose terms call for a significant increase in the shares available to executives if net income this year exceeds $44 million. Some quick calculations convince you that without the change in inventory methods, the target will not be reached; with the change, it will.

Required:
Do you perceive an ethical dilemma? What would be the likely impact of following the controller's suggestions? Who would benefit? Who would be injured?

Trueblood Accounting Case 19–4
Share-based awards
● LO19–1, LO19–2

The following Trueblood case is recommended for use with this chapter. The case provides an excellent opportunity for class discussion, group projects, and writing assignments. The case, along with Professor's Discussion Material, can be obtained from the Deloitte Foundation at its website: **www.deloitte.com/us/truebloodcases**.

Case 13-5: *Occupy Mall Street*

This case gives students the opportunity to consider the accounting treatment for different aspects of a share-based compensation plan.

Real World Case 19–5
Share-based plans; Walmart
● LO19–1, LO19–2

Real World Financials

Walmart offers its employees a variety of share-based compensation plans including stock options, performance share awards, restricted stock, and restricted stock units. The following is an excerpt from a disclosure note from Walmart's 2013 financial statements:

Note 3. Share-Based Compensation
The Company has awarded share-based compensation to associates and nonemployee directors of the Company. The compensation cost recognized for all plans was $378 million, $355 million and $371 million for fiscal 2013, 2012 and 2011, respectively. . . . The following table summarizes our share-based compensation expense by award type:

	Fiscal Years Ended January 31,		
(Amounts in millions)	**2013**	**2012**	**2011**
Restricted stock and performance share awards	$152	$142	$162
Restricted stock rights	195	184	157
Stock options	31	29	52
Share-based compensation expense	$378	$355	$371

Required:
1. Walmart's share-based compensation includes stock options, restricted stock units, restricted stock awards, and performance-based awards. What is the general financial reporting objective when recording compensation expense for these forms of compensation?
2. Walmart reported share-based expense of $378 million in 2013. Without referring to specific numbers and ignoring other forms of share-based compensation, describe how this amount reflects the value of stock options.

Analysis Case 19–6
Share-based compensation
● LO19–1, LO19–2

Real World Financials

Refer to the financial statements and related disclosure notes of **PetSmart** in Appendix B located at the back of this textbook. PetSmart's share-based compensation includes several long-term incentive plans.

Required:
1. How many stock options did PetSmart grant during the year ending February 2, 2014? What is the total compensation of those options granted during the year? Over how many years will that total compensation be expensed?
2. Over how many years is the compensation associated with restricted stock awards expensed? What was the total fair value of restricted stock that vested during the most recent three years?

Real World Case 19–7
Employee share purchase plan; PetSmart
● LO19–3

Real World Financials

Refer to the financial statements and related disclosure notes of **PetSmart** in Appendix B located at the back of this textbook. PetSmart's share-based compensation includes several long-term incentive plans.

Required:
Describe the way "Compensation expense for the employee stock purchase plan is recognized" by PetSmart. Include in your explanation the journal entry that summarizes employee share purchases for the year ending February 2, 2014.

Ethics Case 19–8
International Network Solutions
● LO19–6

International Network Solutions provides products and services related to remote access networking. The company has grown rapidly during its first 10 years of operations. As its segment of the industry has begun to mature, though, the fast growth of previous years has begun to slow. In fact, this year revenues and profits are roughly the same as last year.

One morning, nine weeks before the close of the fiscal year, Rob Mashburn, CFO, and Jessica Lane, controller, were sharing coffee and ideas in Lane's office.

Lane: About the Board meeting Thursday. You may be right. This may be the time to suggest a share buyback program.

Mashburn: To begin this year, you mean?

Lane: Right! I know Barber will be lobbying to use the funds for our European expansion. She's probably right about the best use of our funds, but we can always issue more notes next year. Right now, we need a quick fix for our EPS numbers.

Mashburn: Our shareholders are accustomed to increases every year.

Required:

1. How will a buyback of shares provide a "quick fix" for EPS?
2. Is the proposal ethical?
3. Who would be affected if the proposal is implemented?

Real World Case 19–9
Per share data; stock options; antidilutive securities; Best Buy Co.
● LO19–8

Real World Financials

The 2013 annual report of **Best Buy Co., Inc.**, reported profitable operations for the year. However, the company suffered a net loss in 2012. Best Buy reported the following for the twelve months ended March 3, 2012:

Basic (loss) earnings per share:	
Continuing operations	$(2.89)
Discontinued operations	(0.47)
Basic (loss) earnings per share	$(3.36)
Diluted (loss) earnings per share:	
Continuing operations	$(2.89)
Discontinued operations	(0.47)
Diluted (loss) earnings per share	$(3.36)
Dividends declared per Best Buy Co., Inc. common share	$ 0.62
Weighted average common shares outstanding (in millions)	
Basic	366.3
Diluted	366.3

Note: The calculation of diluted earnings per share assumes the conversion of the company's previously outstanding convertible debentures due in 2022 into 8.8 million shares common stock . . . and adds back the related after-tax interest expense of $1.5. . . . The calculation of diluted (loss) per share for the twelve months ended March 3, 2012, does not include potential dilutive shares of common stock because their inclusion would be antidilutive (i.e., reduce the net loss per share).

Required:

1. The note indicates that Best Buy does not include potentially dilutive shares when calculating EPS for the twelve months ended March 3, 2012. What are potentially dilutive shares?
2. The note indicates that "diluted earnings per share assumes the conversion of the company's **previously outstanding** convertible debentures due in 2022 into 8.8 million shares common stock . . . and adds back the related after-tax interest expense of $1.5." Apparently, these bonds were actually converted during the year. Would diluted EPS have been different if the bonds had not been converted and were still outstanding? Explain.
3. Best Buy does not include potentially dilutive shares when calculating EPS for the twelve months ended March 3, 2012. Why not? Assume Best Buy had 40 million common equivalent shares and included them in the calculation, what would have been the amount of diluted loss per share for the twelve months ended March 3, 2012?

Analysis Case 19–10
EPS concepts
● LO19–4 through LO19–8

The shareholders' equity of Proactive Solutions, Inc., included the following at December 31, 2016:

Common stock, $1 par
Paid-in capital—excess of par on common stock
7% cumulative convertible preferred stock, $100 par value
Paid-in capital—excess of par on preferred stock
Retained earnings

Additional Information:

- Proactive had 7 million shares of preferred stock authorized of which 2 million were outstanding. All 2 million shares outstanding were issued in 2010 for $112 a share. The preferred stock is convertible into common stock on a two-for-one basis until December 31, 2018, after which the preferred stock no longer is convertible. None of the preferred stock has been converted into common stock at December 31, 2016. There were no dividends in arrears.

- Of the 13 million common shares authorized, there were 8 million shares outstanding at January 1, 2016. Proactive also sold 3 million shares at the beginning of September 2016 at a price of $52 a share.
- The company has an employee stock option plan in which certain key employees and officers may purchase shares of common stock at the market price at the date of the option grant. All options are exercisable beginning one year after the date of the grant and expire if not exercised within five years of the grant date. On January 1, 2016, options for 2 million shares were outstanding at prices ranging from $45 to $53 a share. Options for 1 million shares were exercised at $49 a share at the end of June 2016. No options expired during 2016. Additional options for 1.5 million shares were granted at $55 a share during the year. The 2.5 million options outstanding at December 31, 2016, were exercisable at $45 to $55 a share.

The only changes in the shareholders' equity for 2016 were those described above, 2016 net income, and cash dividends paid.

Required:

Explain how each of the following amounts should be determined when computing earnings per share for presentation in the income statements. For each, be specific as to the treatment of each item.

1. Numerator for basic EPS.
2. Denominator for basic EPS.
3. Numerator for diluted EPS.
4. Denominator for diluted EPS.

Analysis Case 19–11
EPS; AIG
● LO19–5 through LO19–8

Real World Financials

"I guess I'll win that bet!" you announced to no one in particular.

"What bet?" Renee asked. Renee Patey was close enough to overhear you.

"When I bought my **AIG** stock last year Randy insisted it was a mistake, that they were going to collapse. I bet him a Coke he was wrong. This press release says they have positive earnings," you bragged. Renee was looking over your shoulder now at the article you were pointing at:

(BUSINESS WIRE)—Aug. 1, 2013—American International Group, Inc. (NYSE: AIG) today reported net income attributable to AIG of $2.7 billion for the quarter ended June 30, 2013, . . . Diluted earnings per share attributable to AIG were $1.84 for the second quarter of 2013, compared with $1.33 for the second quarter of 2012.

Our Board of Directors . . . authorized the repurchase of shares of AIG Common Stock, with an aggregate purchase price of up to $1.0 billion.

(a) Share and per share amounts prior to the second quarter of 2011 have been restated to reflect the 1-for-20 reverse stock split effective June 30, 2011.

Excerpt from: "AIG Reports Second Quarter 2013 Net Income Attributable to AIG of $2.7 Billion and Diluted Earnings Per Share of $1.84," August 1, 2013.

"A dollar eighty-four a share, huh?" Renee asked. "How many shares do you have? When do you get the check?"

Required:

1. Renee's questions imply that she thinks you will get cash dividends of $1.84 a share. What does earnings per share really tell you?
2. A previous press release indicated that "Share and per share amounts prior to the second quarter of 2009 have been restated to reflect the 1-for-20 reverse stock split effective June 30, 2009." What does that mean?
3. The press release indicates plans to repurchase shares of its own stock. Would the reduction in shares from a stock repurchase be taken into account when EPS is calculated? How?

Judgment Case 19–12
Where are the profits?
● LO19–4 through LO19–7, LO19–9

Del Conte Construction Company has experienced generally steady growth since its inception in 1953. Management is proud of its record of having maintained or increased its earnings per share in each year of its existence.

The economic downturn has led to disturbing dips in revenues the past two years. Despite concerted cost-cutting efforts, profits have declined in each of the two previous years. Net income in 2014, 2015, and 2016 was as follows:

2014	$145 million
2015	$134 million
2016	$ 95 million

A major shareholder has hired you to provide advice on whether to continue her present investment position or to curtail that position. Of particular concern is the declining profitability, despite the fact that earnings per share has continued a pattern of growth:

	Basic	Diluted
2014	$2.15	$1.91
2015	$2.44	$2.12
2016	$2.50	$2.50

She specifically asks you to explain this apparent paradox. During the course of your investigation you discover the following events:

- For the decade ending December 31, 2013, Del Conte had 60 million common shares and 20 million shares of 8%, $10 par nonconvertible preferred stock outstanding. Cash dividends have been paid quarterly on both.
- On July 1, 2015, half the preferred shares were retired in the open market. The remaining shares were retired on December 30, 2015.
- $55 million of 8% nonconvertible bonds were issued at the beginning of 2016 and a portion of the proceeds were used to call and retire $50 million of 10% debentures (outstanding since 2011) that were convertible into 9 million common shares.
- In 2014 management announced a share repurchase plan by which up to 24 million common shares would be retired. 12 million shares were retired on March 1 of both 2014 and 2015.
- Del Conte's income tax rate is 40% and has been for the last several years.

Required:

Explain the apparent paradox to which your client refers. Include calculations that demonstrate your explanation.

Communication Case 19–13
Dilution
● LO19–9

"I thought I understood earnings per share," lamented Brad Dawson, "but you're telling me we need to pretend our convertible bonds have been converted! Or maybe not?"

Dawson, your boss, is the new manager of the Fabricating division of BVT Corporation. His background is engineering and he has only a basic understanding of earnings per share. Knowing you are an accounting graduate, he asks you to explain the questions he has about the calculation of the company's EPS. His reaction is to your explanation that the company's convertible bonds might be included in this year's calculation.

"Put it in a memo!" he grumbled as he left your office.

Required:

Write a memo to Dawson. Explain the effect on earnings per share of each of the following:

1. Convertible securities.
2. Antidilutive securities.

Real World Case 19–14
Earnings per share; PetSmart
● LO19–8, LO19–10, LO19–12

Real World Financials

Refer to the financial statements and related disclosure notes of **PetSmart** in Appendix B located at the back of this textbook.

Required:

1. What were PetSmart's basic and diluted earnings per share for the year ending February 2, 2014?
2. How many shares were included in diluted earnings per share but not basic earnings per share due to stock-based compensation awards? How many shares of common stock representing due to stock-based compensation awards were not included in the calculation of diluted earnings per common share? Why?

Real World Case 19–15
Reporting EPS; discontinued operations; Kaman Corporation
● LO19–13

Real World Financials

Kaman Corporation, headquartered in Bloomfield, Connecticut, was incorporated in 1945. It is a diversified company that conducts business in the aerospace and distribution markets. The following is an excerpt from the comparative income statements (beginning with earnings from continuing operations) from Kaman's 2013 annual report ($ in thousands):

An income statement sometimes includes discontinued operations. Kaman Corporation reports income from discontinued operations.

A disclosure note from Kaman's 2013 annual report is shown below:

18. COMPUTATION OF EARNINGS PER SHARE (in part)

The computation of basic earnings per share is based on net earnings divided by the weighted average number of shares of common stock outstanding for each year. The computation of diluted earnings per share includes the common stock equivalency of dilutive options granted to employees under the Stock Incentive Plan.

Excluded from the diluted earnings per share calculation for the years ended December 31, 2013, 2012 and 2011, respectively, are 391,717, 338,248 and 265,026 shares associated with equity awards granted to employees that are anti-dilutive based on the average stock price.

	For the year ended December 31,		
	2013	**2012**	**2011**
(In thousands, except per share amounts)			
Earnings from continuing operations	$56,699	$53,928	$49,928
Earnings from discontinued operations, net of tax	(19)	(226)	1,214
Gain on disposal of discontinued operations, net of tax	420	1,323	—
Net earnings	$57,100	$55,025	$51,142
Basic:			
Weighted average number of shares outstanding	26,744	26,425	26,246
Diluted:			
Weighted average number of shares outstanding	26,744	26,425	26,246
Weighted average shares issuable on exercise of dilutive stock options	159	162	223
Weighted average shares issuable on exercise of convertible notes	240	35	31
Total	27,143	26,622	26,500

Required:

1. The disclosure note shows adjustments for "the common stock equivalency of dilutive options granted to employees under the Stock Incentive Plan." What other adjustments might be needed? Explain why and how these adjustments are made to the weighted-average shares outstanding.
2. The disclosure note indicates that the effect of some of the equity awards granted to employees were not included because they would be antidilutive. What does that mean? Why not include antidilutive securities?
3. Based on the information provided, prepare the presentation of basic and diluted earnings per share for 2013, 2012, and 2011 that Kaman reports in its 2013 annual report.

Analysis Case 19–16
Analyzing financial statements; price-earnings ratio; dividend payout ratio
● LO19–13

IGF Foods Company is a large, primarily domestic, consumer foods company involved in the manufacture, distribution, and sale of a variety of food products. Industry averages are derived from Troy's *The Almanac of Business and Industrial Financial Ratios* and Dun and Bradstreet's *Industry Norms and Key Business Ratios.* Following are the 2016 and 2015 comparative income statements and balance sheets for IGF. The market price of IGF's common stock is $47 during 2016. (The financial data we use are from actual financial statements of a well-known corporation, but the company name used in our illustration is fictitious and the numbers and dates have been modified slightly to disguise the company's identity.)

IGF FOODS COMPANY
Years Ended December 31, 2016 and 2015

($ in millions)	2016	2015
Comparative Income Statements		
Net sales	$6,440	$5,800
Cost of goods sold	(3,667)	(3,389)
Gross profit	2,773	2,411
Operating expenses	(1,916)	(1,629)
Operating income	857	782
Interest expense	(54)	(53)
Income from operations before tax	803	729
Income taxes	(316)	(287)
Net income	$ 487	$ 442
Net income per share	$ 2.69	$ 2.44
Average shares outstanding	181 million	181 million

(continued)

(concluded)

($ in millions)	2016	2015
Comparative Balance Sheets		
Assets		
Total current assets	$1,879	$1,490
Property, plant, and equipment (net)	2,592	2,291
Intangibles (net)	800	843
Other assets	74	60
Total assets	$5,345	$4,684
Liabilities and Shareholders' Equity		
Total current liabilities	$1,473	$ 941
Long term debt	534	728
Deferred income taxes	407	344
Total liabilities	2,414	2,013
Shareholders' equity:		
Common stock	180	180
Additional paid-in capital	21	63
Retained earnings	2,730	2,428
Total shareholders' equity	2,931	2,671
Total liabilities and shareholders' equity	$5,345	$4,684

Some ratios express income, dividends, and market prices on a per share basis. As such, these ratios appeal primarily to common shareholders, particularly when weighing investment possibilities. These ratios focus less on the fundamental soundness of a company and more on its investment characteristics.

Required:

1. Earnings per share expresses a firm's profitability on a per share basis. Calculate 2016 earnings per share for IGF.
2. Calculate IGF's 2016 price-earnings ratio. The average price-earnings ratio for the stocks listed on the New York Stock Exchange in a comparable time period was 18.5. What does your calculation indicate about IGF's earnings?
3. Calculate IGF's 2016 dividend payout ratio. What information does the calculation provide an investor?

Research Case 19–17
Determining and comparing price-earnings ratios; retrieving stock prices and earnings per share numbers from the Internet
● LO19–13

Many sites on the Internet allow the retrieval of current stock price information. Among those sites are Marketwatch (cbs.marketwatch.com) and Quicken (www.quicken.com).

Required:

1. Access any site on the Internet that permits you to get a current stock quote. Determine the current price of Microsoft Corporation's common stock (MSFT) and that of Intel Corporation (INTC).
2. Access EDGAR on the Internet at www.sec.gov. Search for Microsoft and access its most recent 10-K filing. Search or scroll to find the income statement and related note(s). Determine the most recent earnings per share. Repeat this step for Intel.
3. Calculate the price-earnings ratio for each company.
4. Compare the PE ratios of Microsoft and Intel. What information might be gleaned from your comparison?

Analysis Case 19–18
Kellogg's EPS; PE ratio; dividend payout
● LO19–13

Real World Financials

While eating his Kellogg's Frosted Flakes one January morning, Tony noticed the following article in his local paper:

Kellogg Company Reports Fourth-Quarter and Full-Year Results and Provides Guidance For 2014 (in part)

BATTLE CREEK, Mich., Feb. 6, 2014 /PRNewswire/—Kellogg Company (NYSE: K) Reported full-year 2013 net earnings were $1.8 billion, or $4.94 per diluted share.

As a shareholder, Tony is well aware that Kellogg pays a regular cash dividend of $0.46 per share quarterly. A quick click on a price quote service indicated that Kellogg's shares closed at $61.07 on December 31.

Required:

1. Using the numbers provided, determine the price/earnings ratio for Kellogg Company for 2013. What information does this ratio impart?
2. What is the dividend payout ratio for Kellogg? What does it indicate?

Research Case 19–19
FASB codification; locate and extract relevant information and cite authoritative support for a financial reporting issue; change in classification of a share-based compensation instrument
● LO19–13

"Now what do I do?" moaned your colleague, Matt. "This is a first for me," he confided. You and Matt are recent hires in the Accounting Division of National Paper. A top executive in the company has been given share-based incentive instruments that permit her to receive shares of National Paper equal in value to the amount the company shares rise above the shares' value two years ago when the instruments were issued to her as compensation. The instruments vest in three years. A clause was included in the compensation agreement that would permit her to receive cash rather than shares upon exercise if sales revenue in her division were to double by that time. Because that contingency was considered unlikely, the instruments have been accounted for as equity, with the grant date fair value being expensed over the five-year vesting period.

Now, though, surging sales of her division indicate that the contingent event has become probable, and the instruments should be accounted for as a liability rather than equity. The fair value of the award was estimated at $5 million on the grant date, but now is $8 million. Matt has asked your help in deciding what to recommend to your controller as the appropriate action to take at this point.

Required:

1. Obtain the relevant authoritative literature on accounting for a change in classification due to a change in probable settlement outcome using the *FASB Accounting Standards Codification* at the FASB website (**asc.fasb.org**). Explain to Matt the basic treatment of the situation described. What is the specific citation that you would rely on in applying that accounting treatment?
2. Prepare the journal entry to record the change in circumstance.

Air France–KLM Case

● LO19–9

Air France–KLM (AF), a Franco-Dutch company, prepares its financial statements according to International Financial Reporting Standards. AF's financial statements and disclosure notes for the year ended December 31, 2013, are provided with all new textbooks. This material also is available at **www.airfranceklm-finance.com**.

Required:

1. What is the amount that AF reports in its income statement for its stock options for the year ended December 31, 2013? [Hint: See Note 30: "Share-Based Compensation."] Are AF's share options cliff vesting or graded vesting? How does accounting differ between U.S. GAAP and IFRS for graded-vesting plans?
2. What amount(s) of earnings per share did AF report in its income statement for the year ended December 31, 2013? If AF used U.S. GAAP would it have reported EPS using the same classification?

CPA Simulation 19–1

Tork Corporation
Researching Share-Based Compensation Disclosure Requirements

KAPLAN
CPA REVIEW

Test your knowledge of the concepts discussed in this chapter, practice critical professional skills necessary for career success, and prepare for the computer-based CPA exam by accessing our CPA simulations in the Connect library.

The Tork Corporation simulation tests your ability to search the authoritative literature to determine the disclosure requirements for Tork Corporation's share-based compensation.

CHAPTER

20 Accounting Changes and Error Corrections

OVERVIEW

Chapter 4 provided a brief overview of accounting changes and error correction. Later, we discussed changes encountered in connection with specific assets and liabilities as we dealt with those topics in subsequent chapters.

Here we revisit accounting changes and error correction to synthesize the way these are handled in a variety of situations that might be encountered in practice. We see that most changes in accounting principle are reported retrospectively. Changes in estimates are accounted for prospectively. A change in depreciation methods is considered a change in estimate resulting from a change in principle. Both changes in reporting entities and the correction of errors are reported retrospectively.

LEARNING OBJECTIVES

After studying this chapter, you should be able to:

- **LO20–1** Differentiate among the three types of accounting changes and distinguish between the retrospective and prospective approaches to accounting for and reporting accounting changes. (*p. 1196*)
- **LO20–2** Describe how changes in accounting principle typically are reported. (*p. 1198*)
- **LO20–3** Explain how and why some changes in accounting principle are reported prospectively. (*p. 1202*)
- **LO20–4** Explain how and why changes in estimates are reported prospectively. (*p. 1205*)
- **LO20–5** Describe the situations that constitute a change in reporting entity. (*p. 1207*)
- **LO20–6** Understand and apply the four-step process of correcting and reporting errors, regardless of the type of error or the timing of its discovery. (*p. 1210*)
- **LO20–7** Discuss the primary differences between U.S. GAAP and IFRS with respect to accounting changes and error corrections. (*pp. 1203, 1210,* and *1217*)

FINANCIAL REPORTING CASE

In a Jam

"What the heck!" Martin yelped as he handed you the annual report of **J.M. Smucker** he'd received in the mail today. "It looks like Smucker found a bunch of lost jelly. It says here that their inventory was $54 million last year. I distinctly remember them reporting that number last year as $52 million because my dad was born in '52, and I did a little wordplay in my mind about him 'taking inventory' of his life when he bought the red Mustang." He had circled the number in the comparative balance sheets. "When I bought Smucker shares last year, I promised myself I would monitor things pretty closely, but it's not as easy as I thought it would be."

As an accounting graduate, you can understand Martin's confusion. Flipping to the disclosure note on accounting changes, you proceed to clear things up for him.

QUESTIONS

By the time you finish this chapter, you should be able to respond appropriately to the questions posed in this case. Compare your response to the solution provided at the end of the chapter.

1. How can an accounting change cause a company to increase a previously reported inventory amount? *(p. 1199)*
2. Are all accounting changes reported this way? *(p. 1206)*

You learned early in your study of accounting that two of the qualitative characteristics of accounting information that contribute to its relevance and representational faithfulness are *consistency* and *comparability*. Though we strive to achieve and maintain these financial reporting attributes, we cannot ignore the forces of change. Ours is a dynamic business environment. The economy is increasingly a global one. Technological advances constantly transform both day-to-day operations and the flow of information about those operations. The accounting profession's response to the fluid environment often means issuing new standards that require companies to change accounting methods. Often, developments within an industry or the economy will prompt a company to voluntarily switch methods of accounting or to revise estimates or expectations. In short, change is inevitable. The question then becomes a matter of how best to address change when reporting financial information from year to year.

In the first part of this chapter, we differentiate among the various types of accounting changes that businesses face, with a focus on the most meaningful and least disruptive ways to report those changes. Then, in the second part of the chapter, we direct our attention to a closely related circumstance—the correction of errors.

PART A

Accounting Changes

Accounting changes fall into one of the three categories listed in Illustration 20–1.[1]

Illustration 20–1
Types of Accounting Changes

● LO20–1

Type of Change	Description	Examples
Change in accounting principle	Change from one generally accepted accounting principle to another.	• Adopt a new Accounting Standard. • Change methods of inventory costing. • Change from cost method to equity method, or vice versa.
Change in accounting estimate	Revision of an estimate because of new information or new experience.	• Change depreciation methods.* • Change estimate of useful life of depreciable asset. • Change estimate of residual value of depreciable asset. • Change estimate of periods benefited by intangible assets. • Change actuarial estimates pertaining to a pension plan.
Change in reporting entity	Change from reporting as one type of entity to another type of entity.	• Consolidate a subsidiary not previously included in consolidated financial statements. • Report consolidated financial statements in place of individual statements.

*A change in depreciation methods is a change in estimate that is achieved by a change in accounting principle.

The correction of an error is another adjustment sometimes made to financial statements that is not actually an accounting change but is accounted for similarly. Errors occur when transactions are either recorded incorrectly or not recorded at all as shown in Illustration 20–2.

Illustration 20–2
Correction of Errors

Type of Change	Description	Examples
Error correction	Correction of an error caused by a transaction being recorded incorrectly or not at all.	• Mathematical mistakes. • Inaccurate physical count of inventory. • Change from the cash basis of accounting to the accrual basis. • Failure to record an adjusting entry. • Recording an asset as an expense, or vice versa. • Fraud or gross negligence.

Two approaches to reporting accounting changes and error corrections are used, depending on the situation.

The retrospective approach offers consistency and comparability.

1. Using the **retrospective approach**, financial statements issued in previous years are revised to reflect the impact of the change whenever those statements are presented again for comparative purposes. An advantage of this approach is that it achieves comparability among financial statements. All financial statements presented are prepared on the same basis. However, some argue that public confidence in the integrity of

[1]FASB ASC 250: Accounting Changes and Error Corrections (previously "Accounting Changes and Error Corrections—A Replacement of APB Opinion No. 20 and FASB Statement No. 3," *Statement of Financial Accounting Standards No. 154,* (Norwalk, Conn: FASB, 2005)).

financial data suffers when numbers previously reported as correct are later superseded. On the other hand, proponents argue the opposite—that it's impossible to maintain public confidence unless the financial statements are comparable.

For each year reported in the comparative statements reported, the balance of each account affected is revised. In other words, those statements are made to appear as if the newly adopted accounting method had been applied all along or that the error had never occurred. Then, a journal entry is created to adjust all account balances affected to what those amounts would have been. In addition, if retained earnings is one of the accounts that requires adjustment, that adjustment is made to the beginning balance of retained earnings for the earliest period reported in the comparative statements of shareholders' equity.

2. The **prospective approach** requires neither a modification of prior years' financial statements nor a journal entry to adjust account balances. Instead, the change is simply implemented now, and its effects are reflected in the financial statements of the current and future years only.

The effects of a change are reflected in the financial statements of only the current and future years under the *prospective approach*.

Now, let's look at each type of accounting change, one at a time, focusing on the selective application of these approaches.

Change in Accounting Principle

Accounting is not an exact science. Professional judgment is required to apply a set of principles, concepts, and objectives to specific sets of circumstances. This means choices must be made. In your study of accounting to date, you've encountered many areas where choices are necessary. For example, management must choose whether to use accelerated or straight-line depreciation. Is FIFO, LIFO, or average cost most appropriate to measure inventories? Should we adopt a new accounting standard early or wait until it's mandatory? These are but a few of the accounting choices management makes.

You also probably recall that comparability is an enhancing qualitative characteristic of financial reporting. To achieve this attribute of information, accounting choices, once made, should be consistently followed from year to year. This doesn't mean, though, that methods can never be changed. Changing circumstances might make a new method more appropriate. A change in economic conditions, for instance, might prompt a company to change accounting methods. The most extensive voluntary accounting change ever—a switch by hundreds of companies from FIFO to LIFO in the mid-1970s, for example—was a result of heightened inflation. Changes within a specific industry, too, can lead a company to switch methods, often to adapt to new technology or to be consistent with others in the industry. And, of course, a change might be mandated when the FASB codifies a new accounting standard. For these reasons, it's not uncommon for a company to switch from one accounting method to another. This is called a **change in accounting principle**.

Although consistency and comparability are desirable, changing to a new method sometimes is appropriate.

Decision Makers' Perspective—Motivation for Accounting Choices

It would be nice to think that all accounting choices are made by management in the best interest of fair and consistent financial reporting. Unfortunately, other motives influence the choices among accounting methods and whether to change methods. It has been suggested that the effect of choices on management compensation, on existing debt agreements, and on union negotiations each can affect management's selection of accounting methods.[2] For instance, research has suggested that managers of companies with bonus plans are more likely to choose accounting methods that maximize their bonuses (often those that increase net income).[3] Other research has indicated that the existence and nature of debt agreements

[2] R. L. Watts and J. L. Zimmerman, "Towards a Positive Theory of the Determination of Accounting Standards," *The Accounting Review*, January 1978, and "Positive Accounting Theory: A Ten Year Perspective," *The Accounting Review*, January 1990.

[3] For example, see P. M. Healy, "The Effect of Bonus Schemes on Accounting Decisions," *Journal of Accounting and Economics*, April 1985; and D. Dhaliwal, G. Salamon, and E. Smith, "The Effect of Owner versus Management Control on the Choice of Accounting Methods," *Journal of Accounting and Economics*, July 1992.

and other aspects of a firm's capital structure can influence accounting choices.[4] Whether a company is forbidden from paying dividends if retained earnings fall below a certain level, for example, can affect the choice of accounting methods.

A financial analyst must be aware that different accounting methods used by different firms and by the same firm in different years complicate comparisons. Financial ratios, for example, will differ when different accounting methods are used, even when there are no differences in attributes being compared.

Investors and creditors also should be alert to instances in which companies change accounting methods. They must consider not only the effect on comparability but also possible hidden motivations for making the changes. Are managers trying to compensate for a downturn in actual performance with a switch to methods that artificially inflate reported earnings? Is the firm in danger of violating debt covenants or other contractual agreements regarding financial position? Are executive compensation plans tied to reported performance measures? Fortunately, the nature and effect of changes are reported in the financial statements. Although a justification for a change is provided by management, analysts should be wary of accepting the reported justification at face value without considering a possible hidden agenda.

Choices are not always those that tend to increase income. As you learned in Chapter 8, many companies use the LIFO inventory method because it reduces income and therefore reduces the amount of income taxes that must be paid currently. Also, some very large and visible companies might be reluctant to report high income that might render them vulnerable to union demands, government regulations, or higher taxes.[5]

Another reason managers sometimes choose accounting methods that don't necessarily increase earnings was mentioned earlier. Most managers tend to prefer to report earnings that follow a regular, smooth trend from year to year. The desire to "smooth" earnings means that any attempt to manipulate earnings by choosing accounting methods is not always in the direction of higher income. Instead, the choice might be to avoid irregular earnings, particularly those with wide variations from year to year, a pattern that might be interpreted by analysts as denoting a risky situation.

Obviously, any time managers make accounting choices for any of the reasons discussed here, when the motivation is an objective other than to provide useful information, earnings quality suffers. As mentioned frequently throughout this text, earnings quality refers to the ability of reported earnings (income) to predict a company's future earnings.

A notable example of alleged "cooking the books" involved **General Electric**. The company was often suspected of using "cookie jar accounting," the practice of using unrealistic estimates and strategic choices of accounting methods to smooth out its earnings. In 2009 GE appeared to get its hand caught in the cookie jar for going beyond acceptable limits. GE paid a $50 million civil penalty to settle charges by the Securities and Exchange Commission accusing the company of violating U.S. securities laws four times between 2002 and 2003 to help it maintain a succession of earnings reports that beat Wall Street expectations each quarter from 1995 through 2004.

Let's turn our attention now to situations involving changes in methods and how we account for those changes. ●

The Retrospective Approach: Most Changes in Accounting Principle

● LO20–2 We report most voluntary changes in accounting principles retrospectively.[6] This means reporting all previous period's financial statements as if the new method had been used in all prior periods. An example is provided in Illustration 20–3.

[4]R. M. Bowen, E. W. Noreen, and J. M. Lacy, "Determinants of the Corporate Decision to Capitalize Interest," *Journal of Accounting and Economics*, August 1981.

[5]This political cost motive is suggested by R. L. Watts and J. L. Zimmerman, "Positive Accounting Theory: A Ten Year Perspective," *The Accounting Review*, January 1990, and M. Zmijewski and R. Hagerman, "An Income Strategy Approach to the Positive Theory of Accounting Standard Setting/Choice," *Journal of Accounting and Economics*, August 1981.

[6]FASB ASC 250–10–45: Accounting Changes and Error Corrections–Overall–Other Presentation Matters (previously "Accounting Changes and Error Corrections—A Replacement of APB Opinion No. 20 and FASB Statement No. 3," *Statement of Financial Accounting Standards No. 154*, (Norwalk, Conn: FASB, 2005)).

Air Parts Corporation used the LIFO inventory costing method. At the beginning of 2016, Air Parts decided to change to the FIFO method. Income components for 2016 and prior years were as follows ($ in millions):

	2016	2015	2014	Previous Years
Cost of goods sold (LIFO)	$430	$420	$405	$2,000
Cost of goods sold (FIFO)	370	365	360	1,700
Difference	$ 60	$ 55	$ 45	$ 300
Revenues	$950	$900	$875	$4,500
Operating expenses	230	210	205	1,000

Air Parts has paid dividends of $40 million each year beginning in 2009. Its income tax rate is 40%. Retained earnings on January 1, 2014, was $700 million; inventory was $500 million.

Illustration 20–3
Change in Accounting Principle

LIFO usually produces higher cost of goods sold than does FIFO because more recently purchased goods (usually higher priced) are assumed sold first.

1. REVISE COMPARATIVE FINANCIAL STATEMENTS. For each year reported in the comparative statements, Air Parts makes those statements appear as if the newly adopted accounting method (FIFO) had been applied all along. As you learned in Chapter 1, comparability is one of the important qualitative characteristics of accounting information.

When accounting changes occur, the usefulness of the comparative financial statements is enhanced with retrospective application of those changes.

FINANCIAL Reporting Case

Q1, p. 1195

Income statements.

($ in millions)	2016	2015	2014
Revenues	$950	$900	$875
Cost of goods sold (FIFO)	(370)	(365)	(360)
Operating expenses	(230)	(210)	(205)
Income before tax	$350	$325	$310
Income tax expense (40%)	(140)	(130)	(124)
Net income	$210	$195	$186

The company recasts the comparative statements to appear as if the accounting method adopted in 2016 (FIFO) had been used in 2015 and 2014 as well.

Earnings per share each year, of course, also will be based on the revised net income numbers.

Balance sheets.

Inventory. In its comparative balance sheets, Air Parts will report 2016 inventory by its newly adopted method, FIFO, and also will revise the amounts it reported last year for its 2015 and 2014 inventory. Each year, inventory will be higher than it would have been by LIFO. Here's why:

Since the cost of goods *available for sale* each period is the sum of the cost of goods *sold* and the cost of goods *unsold* (inventory), a difference in cost of goods sold resulting from having used LIFO rather than FIFO means there also is an opposite difference in inventory. Because cost of goods sold by the FIFO method is *less* than by LIFO, inventory by FIFO is *greater* than by LIFO. The amounts of the differences and also the cumulative differences over the years are calculated in Illustration 20–3A.

FIFO usually produces *lower* cost of goods sold and thus *higher* inventory than does LIFO.

Retained earnings. Similarly, Air Parts will report retained earnings by FIFO each year as well. Retained earnings is different because the two inventory methods affect income differently. Because cost of goods sold by FIFO is *less* than by LIFO, income and therefore retained earnings by FIFO are *greater* than by LIFO.

Comparative balance sheets, then, will report retained earnings for 2016, 2015, and 2014 at amounts $276, $240, and $207 million higher than would have been reported if the switch from LIFO had not occurred. These are the cumulative net income differences shown in Illustration 20–3A.

When costs are rising, FIFO produces *lower* cost of goods sold than does LIFO and thus *higher* net income and retained earnings.

Retained earnings is revised each year to reflect FIFO.

Illustration 20–3A
Effects of Switch to FIFO

By FIFO, cost of goods sold is lower.

The cumulative income effect increases each year by the annual after-tax difference in COGS.

Inventory, pretax income, income taxes, net income, and retained earnings all are higher.

($ in millions)	Years Ending Dec. 31: 2016	2015	2014	Previous Years
Cost of goods sold (LIFO)	$430	$420	$405	$2,000
Cost of goods sold (FIFO)	370	365	360	1,700
Differences	$ 60	$ 55	$ 45	$ 300
Cumulative differences:				
Cost of goods sold	$460	$400	$345	$ 300
Income taxes (40%)	184	160	138	120
Net income and retained earnings	$276	$240	$207	$ 180

Comparative balance sheets, then, will report 2014 inventory $345 million higher than it was reported in last year's statements. Likewise, 2015 inventory will be increased by $400 million. Inventory for 2016, being reported for the first time, is $460 million higher than it would have been if the switch from LIFO had not occurred.

Statements of shareholders' equity. Recall that a statement of shareholders' equity reports changes that occur in each shareholders' equity account starting with the beginning balances in the earliest year reported.

Because it's the earliest year reported, 2014's beginning retained earnings is increased by the $180 million cumulative income effect of the difference in inventory methods that occurred before 2014.

So, if retained earnings is one of the accounts whose balance requires adjustment due to a change in accounting principle (and it usually is), we must adjust the beginning balance of retained earnings for the earliest period reported in the comparative statements of shareholders' equity. The amount of the revision is the cumulative effect of the change on years prior to that date. Air Parts will revise its 2014 beginning retained earnings since that's the earliest year in its comparative statements. That balance had been reported in prior statements as $700 million. If FIFO had been used for inventory rather than LIFO, that amount would have been higher by $180 million as calculated in Illustration 20–3A. The disclosure note pertaining to the inventory change should point out the amount of the adjustment. The January 1, 2014, retained earnings balance reported in the comparative statements of shareholders' equity in Illustration 20–3B has been adjusted from $700 million to $880 million.

Illustration 20–3B
Comparative Statements of Shareholders' Equity

A disclosure note should indicate that the beginning retained earnings balance has been increased by $180 million from $700 million to $880 million.

($ in millions)	Common Stock	Additional Paid-In Capital	Retained Earnings	Total Shareholders' Equity
Jan. 1, 2014			$ 880	
Net income (revised to FIFO)			186	
Dividends			(40)	
Dec. 31, 2014			$1,026	
Net income (revised to FIFO)			195	
Dividends			(40)	
Dec. 31, 2015			$1,181	
Net income (using FIFO)			210	
Dividends			(40)	
Dec. 31, 2016			$1,351	

2. ADJUST ACCOUNTS FOR THE CHANGE. Besides reporting revised amounts in the comparative financial statements, Air Parts must also adjust the book balances of affected accounts. It does so by creating a journal entry to change those balances from their current amounts (from using LIFO) to what those balances would have been using the newly adopted method (FIFO). As discussed in the previous section, differences in cost of goods sold and income are reflected in retained earnings, as are the income tax effects of changes in income. So, the journal entry updates inventory, retained earnings, and the income tax liability for revisions resulting from differences in the LIFO and FIFO methods prior to the switch, pre-2016. Repeating a portion of the calculation we made in Illustration 20–3A, we determine the difference in cost of goods sold and therefore in inventory.

Cost of goods sold would have been $400 million *less* if FIFO rather than LIFO had been used in years before the change.

($ in millions)

	2015	2014	Cumulative Difference pre-2014	Cumulative Difference pre-2016
Cost of goods sold (LIFO)	$420	$405	$1,000	
Cost of goods sold (FIFO)	365	360	700	
Difference	$ 55	$ 45	$ 300	$400

The $400 million cumulative difference in cost of goods sold also is the difference between the balance in inventory and what that balance would have been if the FIFO method, rather than LIFO, had been used before 2016. Inventory must be increased by that amount. Retained earnings must be increased also, but by only 60% of that amount because income taxes would have been higher by 40% of the change in pretax income.

Inventory would have been $400 million more and cumulative prior earnings $240 more if FIFO rather than LIFO had been used.

Journal entry to record the change in principle.

January 1, 2016		
Inventory (additional inventory if FIFO had been used)	400	
Retained earnings (additional net income if FIFO had been used)		240
Income tax payable ($400 × 40%)		160

Notice that the income tax effect is reflected in the income tax payable account. The reason is that, unlike for other accounting method changes, the Internal Revenue Code requires that the inventory costing method used for tax purposes must be the same as that used for financial reporting. For that reason, the tax code allows a retrospective change in an inventory method, but then requires that taxes saved previously ($160 million in this case) from having used another inventory method must now be repaid. However, taxpayers are given up to six years to pay the tax due. As a result, this liability has both a current portion (payable within one year) and a noncurrent portion (payable after one year), but is not a deferred tax liability.

Additional **Consideration**

What if the tax law did not require a recapture of the tax difference? Then there would be a credit to a deferred tax liability. That's because retrospectively increasing accounting income, but not taxable income, creates a temporary difference between the two that will reverse over time as the unsold inventory becomes cost of goods sold. Recall from Chapter 16 that in the meantime, there is a temporary difference, reflected in the deferred tax liability.

If we were switching from FIFO to, say, the average method, we would record a deferred tax asset instead. For financial reporting purposes, but not for tax, we would be retrospectively decreasing accounting income, but not taxable income. This creates a temporary difference between the two that will reverse over time as the unsold inventory becomes cost of goods sold. When that happens, taxable income will be less than accounting income. When taxable income will be less than accounting income as a temporary difference reverses, we have a "future deductible amount" and record a deferred tax asset.

3. DISCLOSURE NOTES. To achieve consistency and comparability, accounting choices once made should be consistently followed from year to year. Any change, then, requires that the new method be justified as clearly more appropriate. In the first set of financial statements after the change, a disclosure note is needed to provide that justification. The note also should point out that comparative information has been revised, or that retrospective revision has not been made because it is impracticable, and report any per share amounts affected for the current period and all prior periods presented. Disclosure

Note disclosure explains why the change was needed as well as its effects on items not reported on the face of the primary statements.

of a recent change by **Abercrombie & Fitch** in a recent annual report provides us the example shown in Illustration 20–4.

Illustration 20–4
Disclosure of a Change in Inventory Method—Abercrombie & Fitch

Real World Financials

4. CHANGE IN ACCOUNTING PRINCIPLE
The Company elected to change its method of accounting for inventory from the lower of cost or market utilizing the retail method to the weighted average cost method effective February 2, 2013. In accordance with generally accepted accounting principles, all periods have been retroactively adjusted to reflect the period-specific effects of the change to the weighted average cost method. The Company believes that accounting under the weighted average cost method is preferable as it better aligns with the Company's focus on realized selling margin and improves the comparability of the Company's financial results with those of its competitors. Additionally, it will improve the matching of cost of goods sold with the related net sales and reflect the acquisition cost of inventory outstanding at each balance sheet date. The cumulative adjustment as of January 30, 2010, was an increase in its inventory of $73.6 million and an increase in retained earnings of $47.3 million.

The Prospective Approach

Although we usually report voluntary changes in accounting principles retrospectively, it's not always practicable or appropriate to do so.

● LO20–3

THE PROSPECTIVE APPROACH: WHEN RETROSPECTIVE APPLICATION IS IMPRACTICABLE. For some changes in principle, insufficient information is available for retrospective application to be practicable. Revising balances in prior years means knowing what those balances should be. But suppose we're switching from the FIFO method of inventory costing to the LIFO method. Recall from your study of inventory costing methods that LIFO inventory consists of "layers" added in prior years at costs existing in those years. If another method has been used, though, the company likely hasn't kept track of those costs. So, accounting records of prior years usually are inadequate to report the change retrospectively. In that case, a company changing *to* LIFO usually reports the change prospectively, and the beginning inventory in the year the LIFO method is adopted becomes the base year inventory for all future LIFO calculations. A disclosure note should indicate reasons why retrospective application was impracticable. Prospective changes usually are accounted for as of the beginning of the year of change.

Sometimes a lack of information makes it impracticable to report a change retrospectively so the new method is simply applied prospectively.

When **Books A Million, Inc.**, adopted the LIFO cost flow assumption for valuing its inventories, the change was reported in a disclosure note as shown in Illustration 20–5.

Illustration 20–5
Disclosure of a Change to LIFO—Books A Million, Inc.

Real World Financials

Inventories (in part)
. . . the Company changed from the first-in, first-out (FIFO) method of accounting for inventories to the last-in, first-out (LIFO) method. Management believes this change was preferable in that it achieves a more appropriate matching of revenues and expenses. The impact of this accounting change was to increase "Costs of Products Sold" in the consolidated statements of operations by $0.7 million for the fiscal year. . . . The cumulative effect of a change in accounting principle from the FIFO method to LIFO method is not determinable. Accordingly, such change has been accounted for prospectively.

When it is impracticable to determine some period-specific effects. A company may have some, but not all, the information it needs to account for a change retrospectively. For instance, let's say a company changes to the LIFO inventory method effective as of the beginning of 2016. It has information that would allow it to revise all assets and liabilities on the basis of the newly adopted method for 2015 in its comparative statements, but not for 2014. In that case, the company should report 2015 statement amounts (revised) and 2016 statement amounts (reported without restatement for the first time) based on LIFO, but not revise 2014 numbers. Then, account balances should be retrospectively adjusted at the beginning of 2015 since that's the earliest date it's practicable to do so.

If it's impracticable to adjust each year reported, the change is applied retrospectively as of the earliest year practicable.

When it is impracticable to determine the cumulative effect of prior years. Another possibility is that the company doesn't have the information necessary to retrospectively adjust retained earnings, but does have information that would allow it to revise all assets and liabilities for one or more specific years. Let's say the records of inventory purchases and sales are not available for some previous years, which would have allowed it to determine the cumulative effect of applying this change to LIFO retrospectively. However, it does have all of the information necessary to apply the LIFO method on a prospective basis beginning in, say, 2014. In that case, the company should report numbers for years beginning in 2014 as if it had carried forward the 2013 ending balance in inventory (measured on the previous inventory costing basis) and then had begun applying LIFO as of January 1, 2014. Of course there would be no adjustment to retained earnings for the cumulative income effect of not using LIFO prior to that.

If full retrospective application isn't possible, the new method is applied prospectively beginning in the earliest year practicable.

THE PROSPECTIVE APPROACH: WHEN MANDATED BY AUTHORITATIVE ACCOUNTING LITERATURE. Another exception to retrospective application of voluntary changes in accounting principle is when authoritative literature requires prospective application for specific changes in accounting methods. For instance, for a change from the equity method to another method of accounting for long-term investments, GAAP requires the prospective application of the new method.[7] Recall from Chapter 12 that when an investor's level of influence changes, it may be necessary to change from the equity method to another method. This could happen, for instance, if a sale of shares causes the investor's ownership interest to fall from, say, 25% to 15%, resulting in the equity method no longer being appropriate. When this situation happens, no adjustment is made to the remaining book value, sometimes called carrying value or carrying amount of the investment. Instead, the equity method is simply discontinued and the new method applied from then on. The balance in the investment account when the equity method is discontinued would serve as the new "cost" basis for writing the investment up or down to fair value on the next set of financial statements.

If a new accounting standards update specifically requires prospective accounting, that requirement is followed.

International Financial Reporting Standards

● LO20–7

In previous chapters we discussed the possibility that U.S. companies will be required to or may choose to switch from U.S. GAAP to international financial reporting standards. When a company moves for the first time from U.S. GAAP to IFRS it should follow the requirements of *IFRS No. 1:* "First-time Adoption of International Financial Reporting Standards."

The basic requirement is full retrospective application of IFRS for the company's first IFRS financial statements. A company's first IFRS financial statements must include at least three balance sheets and two of each of the other financial statements. For instance, if the company's first IFRS reporting period is for the year ended December 31, 2018, the first balance sheet will be the opening balance sheet of 2017, which is the ending balance sheet of 2016. The other two balance sheets and each of the other statements—income statement, statement of comprehensive income, statement of cash flows, statements of changes in equity—are for the years ended December 31, 2017, and December 31, 2018. The date of transition to IFRS is the date of the opening balance sheet, January 1, 2017, in this situation.

First-time application of IFRS entails:

√ Recording some assets and liabilities not permitted under U.S. GAAP such as some provisions (contingent liabilities) permitted under IFRS but not U.S. GAAP.

√ *Not* recording (derecognizing) some assets and liabilities, for example, an intangible asset for research expenditures, permitted under U.S. GAAP but not IFRS.

(continued)

[7]FASB ACS 323–10–35–35: Investments–Equity Method and Joint Ventures–Overall–Subsequent Measurement–Decrease in Level of Ownership or Degree of Influence (previously "The Equity Method of Accounting for Investments in Common Stock," *Accounting Principles Board Opinion No. 18* (New York: AICPA, 1971)).

(concluded)

√ Reclassifying items that are classified differently under the two sets of standards, for instance, reclassifying some preferred shares from shareholder equity classification under U.S. GAAP to liability classification under IFRS.

√ Providing disclosures (in notes to the financial statements) required under IFRS but not U.S. GAAP.

√ Providing extensive disclosures to explain how the transition to IFRS affected the company's financial position, financial performance, and cash flows. These disclosures include (a) providing explanations of material adjustments to the balance sheet, income statement, and cash flow statement; and (b) reconciliations of equity and total comprehensive income reported under previous GAAP to equity under IFRS.

Although the basic requirement is full retrospective application of IFRS, there are several optional *exemptions* and five mandatory *exceptions* to the requirement for retrospective application.

The exemptions are designed to allow companies to avoid excessive costs or difficulties expected for retrospective application of certain standards. For example, if an adopter chooses to report assets such as property, plant, and equipment at fair value as permitted by IFRS, it can measure that fair value at the opening IFRS balance sheet date rather than having to do so retrospectively. Fair value becomes the "deemed cost" going forward under IFRS. Also, consistent with the fair value option under IFRS, fair value is permissible for intangible assets only if they are traded in an active market. The optional exemptions relate to:

a. Business combinations.
b. Fair value or revaluation as deemed cost for property, plant and equipment and other assets.
c. Employee benefits.
d. Cumulative translation differences.
e. Compound financial instruments.
f. Assets and liabilities of subsidiaries.
g. Associates and joint ventures.
h. Designation of previously recognized financial instruments.
i. Share-based payment transactions.
j. Insurance contracts.
k. Decommissioning liabilities.
l. Arrangements containing leases.
m. Fair value measurement of no-active market financial instruments at initial recognition.
n. Service concession arrangements.
o. Borrowing costs.

The five exceptions cover areas in which retrospective application of IFRS is considered inappropriate and relate to:

1. Derecognition of financial assets and financial liabilities (mandatory).
2. Hedge accounting (mandatory).
3. Noncontrolling interests (mandatory).
4. Full-cost oil and gas assets (optional).
5. Determining whether an arrangement contains a lease (mandatory).

Almost all adjustments arising from the first-time application of IFRS are against opening retained earnings of the first period that is presented on an IFRS basis.

THE PROSPECTIVE APPROACH: CHANGING DEPRECIATION, AMORTIZATION, AND DEPLETION METHODS. A change in depreciation methods is considered to be a change in accounting estimate that is achieved by a change in accounting principle. As a result, we account for such a change prospectively—precisely the way we account for changes in estimates. We discuss that approach in the next section.

Change in Accounting Estimate

You've encountered many instances during your study of accounting in which it's necessary to make estimates of uncertain future events. Depreciation, for example, entails estimates not only of the useful lives of depreciable assets, but their anticipated residual values as well. Anticipating uncollectible accounts receivable, predicting warranty expenses, amortizing intangible assets, and making actuarial assumptions for pension benefits are but a few of the accounting tasks that require estimates.

● LO20–4

Accordingly, estimates are an inherent aspect of accounting. Unfortunately, though, estimates routinely turn out to be wrong. No matter how carefully known facts are considered and forecasts are prepared, new information and experience frequently force the revision of estimates. Of course, if the original estimate was based on erroneous information or calculations or was not made in good faith, the revision of that estimate constitutes the correction of an error.

Revisions are viewed as a natural consequence of making estimates.

Changes in accounting estimates are accounted for prospectively. When a company revises a previous estimate, prior financial statements are *not* revised. Instead, the company merely incorporates the new estimate in any related accounting determinations from then on. So, it usually will affect some aspects of both the balance sheet and the income statement in the current period and future periods. A disclosure note should describe the effect of a change in estimate on income from continuing operations, net income, and related per share amounts for the current period.

A change in estimate is reflected in the financial statements of the current period and future periods.

When **Owens-Corning Fiberglass** revised estimates of the useful lives of some of its depreciable assets, the change was disclosed in its annual report as shown in Illustration 20–6.

Note 6: Depreciation of Plant and Equipment (in part)
. . . the Company completed a review of its fixed asset lives. The Company determined that as a result of actions taken to increase its preventative maintenance and programs initiated with its equipment suppliers to increase the quality of their products, actual lives for certain asset categories were generally longer than the useful lives for depreciation purposes. Therefore, the Company extended the estimated useful lives of certain categories of plant and equipment, effective . . . The effect of this change in estimate reduced depreciation expense for the year ended . . ., by $14 million and increased income before cumulative effect of accounting change by $8 million ($.19 per share).

Illustration 20–6

Change in Estimate—Owens-Corning Fiberglass Corporation

Real World Financials

An example of another change in estimate is provided in Illustration 20–7.

Universal Semiconductors estimates warranty expense as 2% of sales. After a review during 2016, Universal determined that 3% of sales is a more realistic estimate of its payment experience. Sales in 2016 are $300 million. The effective income tax rate is 40%.

No account balances are adjusted. The cumulative effect of the estimate change is not reported in current income. Rather, in 2016 and later years, the adjusting entry to record warranty expense simply will reflect the new percentage. In 2016, the entry would be:

	($ in millions)	
Warranty expense (3% × $300 million)	9	
Warranty liability		9

Illustration 20–7

Change in Accounting Estimate

The after-tax effect of the change in estimate is $1.8 million [$300 million × (3% − 2%) = $3 million, less 40% of $3 million]. Assuming 100 million outstanding shares of common stock, the effect is described in a disclosure note to the financial statements as follows:

Note A: Warranties
In 2016, the company revised the percentage used to estimate warranty expense. The change provides a better indication of cost experience. The effect of the change was to decrease 2016 net income by $1.8 million, or $.018 per share.

Changing Depreciation, Amortization, and Depletion Methods

FINANCIAL Reporting Case

Q2, p. 1195

When a company acquires an asset that will provide benefits for several years, it allocates the cost of the asset over the asset's useful life. If the asset is a building, equipment, or other tangible asset, the allocation process is called *depreciation.* It's referred to as *amortization* if an intangible asset or *depletion* if a natural resource. In each case, estimates are essential to the allocation process. How long will benefits accrue? What will be the value of the asset when its use is discontinued? Will the benefits be realized evenly over the asset's life or will they be higher in some years than in others?

The choice of depreciation method and application reflects these estimates. Likewise, when a company changes the way it depreciates an asset in midstream, the change would be made to reflect a change in (a) estimated future benefits from the asset, (b) the pattern of receiving those benefits, or (c) the company's knowledge about those benefits. For instance, suppose Universal Semiconductors originally chose an accelerated depreciation method because it expected greater benefits in the earlier years of an asset's life. Then, two years later, when it became apparent that remaining benefits would be realized approximately evenly over the remaining useful life, Universal Semiconductor switched to straight-line depreciation. Even though the company is changing its depreciation method, it is doing so to reflect changes in its estimates of future benefits. As a result, we report a change in depreciation method as a change in estimate, rather than as a change in accounting principle.

An exception to retrospective application of a change in accounting principle is a change in the method of depreciation (or amortization or depletion).

For this reason, a company reports a change in depreciation method (say to straight-line) prospectively; previous financial statements are not revised. Instead, the company simply employs the straight-line method from then on. The undepreciated cost remaining at the time of the change would be depreciated straight-line over the remaining useful life. Illustration 20–8 provides an example.

Companies report a change in depreciation prospectively.

Illustration 20–8

Change in Depreciation Methods

Universal Semiconductors switched from the SYD depreciation method to straight-line depreciation in 2016. The change affects its precision equipment purchased at the beginning of 2014 at a cost of $63 million. The machinery has an expected useful life of five years and an estimated residual value of $3 million.

The depreciation prior to the change is as follows ($ in millions):

Sum-of-the-Years'-Digits Depreciation:		
2014 depreciation	$20	($60 × 5/15)
2015 depreciation	16	($60 × 4/15)
Accumulated depreciation	$36	

A change in depreciation method is considered a change in accounting estimate resulting from a change in accounting principle. So, Universal Semiconductors reports the change prospectively; previous financial statements are not revised. Instead, the company simply employs the straight-line method from 2016 on. The undepreciated cost remaining at the time of the change is depreciated straight-line over the remaining useful life.

Calculation of Straight-Line Depreciation:	($ in millions)
Asset's cost	$63
Accumulated depreciation to date (calculated above)	(36)
Undepreciated cost, Jan. 1, 2016	$27
Estimated residual value	(3)
To be depreciated over remaining 3 years	$24
	3 years
Annual straight-line depreciation 2016–2018	$ 8

The $24 million depreciable cost not yet depreciated is spread over the asset's remaining three years.

Adjusting entry (2016, 2017, and 2018 depreciation):	($ in millions)	
Depreciation expense (calculated above)	8	
Accumulated depreciation		8

Is a change in depreciation method a change in accounting principle, or is it a change in estimate? As we've seen, it's both. Even though it's considered to reflect a change in estimate and is accounted for as such, a change to a new depreciation method requires the company to justify the new method as being preferable to the previous method, just as for any other change in principle. A disclosure note should justify that the change is preferable and describe the effect of a change on any financial statement line items and per share amounts affected for all periods reported.

A company must justify any change in principle as preferable to the previous method.

In practice, the situation arises infrequently. Most companies changing depreciation methods do not apply the change to existing assets, but instead to assets placed in service after that date. In those cases, of course, the new method is simply applied prospectively (see Illustration 20–9).

Note 12: Land, Buildings, and Equipment, Net (in part)
. . . the company changed its method of depreciation for newly acquired buildings and equipment to the straight-line method. The change had no cumulative effect on prior years' earnings but did increase [current year] net earnings by $9 million, or $.14 per share . . .

Illustration 20–9
Change in Depreciation Method for Newly Acquired Assets—Rohm and Haas Company

Real World Financials

Sometimes, it's not easy to distinguish between a change in principle and a change in estimate. For example, if a company begins to capitalize rather than expense the cost of tools because their benefits beyond one year become apparent, the change could be construed as either a change in principle or a change in the estimated life of the asset. When the distinction is not possible, the change should be treated as a change in estimate. This treatment also is appropriate when both a change in principle and a change in estimate occur simultaneously.

When it's not possible to distinguish between a change in principle and a change in estimate, the change should be treated as a change in estimate.

Change in Reporting Entity

● LO20–5

A reporting entity can be a single company, or it can be a group of companies that reports a single set of financial statements. For example, the consolidated financial statements of **PepsiCo Inc.** report the financial position and results of operations not only for the parent company but also for its subsidiaries which include **Frito-Lay** and **Gatorade**. A **change in reporting entity** occurs as a result of (1) presenting consolidated financial statements in place of statements of individual companies or (2) changing specific companies that constitute the group for which consolidated or combined statements are prepared.[8]

Some changes in reporting entity are a result of changes in accounting rules. For example, companies like **Ford**, **General Motors**, and **General Electric** must consolidate their manufacturing operations with their financial subsidiaries, creating a new entity that includes them both.[9] For those changes in entity, the prior-period financial statements that are presented for comparative purposes must be restated to appear as if the new entity existed in those periods.

However, the more frequent change in entity occurs when one company acquires another one. In those circumstances, the financial statements of the acquirer include the acquiree as of the date of acquisition, and the acquirer's prior-period financial statements that are presented for comparative purposes are not restated. This makes it difficult to make year-to-year comparisons for a company that frequently acquires other companies. Acquiring companies are required to provide a footnote that presents key financial statement information as if the acquisition had occurred before the beginning of the previous year. At a minimum, the supplemental pro forma information should display revenue, income from continuing operations, net income, and earnings per share.

A change in reporting entity is reported by recasting all previous periods' financial statements as if the new reporting entity existed in those periods.[10] In the first set of financial statements after the change, a disclosure note should describe the nature of the change and the reason it occurred. Also, the effect of the change on net income, income from continuing operations, and related per share amounts should be indicated for all periods presented. These disclosures aren't necessary in subsequent financial statements. **Hartford Life Insurance Company**, a financial services company, changed the composition of its reporting entity and described it this way (see Illustration 20–10):

A change in reporting entity requires that financial statements of prior periods be retrospectively revised to report the financial information for the new reporting entity in all periods.

[8]FASB ASC 810: Consolidation and 840: Leases (previously "Consolidation of All Majority-Owned Subsidiaries," *Statement of Financial Accounting Standards No. 94* (Stamford, Conn.: FASB, 1987)).

[9]The issuance of *SFAS No. 94*, "Consolidation of All Majority-Owned Subsidiaries," [FASB ASC 810: Consolidation and 840: Leases] resulted in hundreds of entities consolidating previously unconsolidated finance subsidiaries.

[10]Any prior periods' statements are recast when those statements are presented again for comparative purposes.

Illustration 20–10
Change in Reporting Entity—Hartford Life Insurance

Real World Financials

1. Basis of Presentation and Accounting Policies (in part)
Hartford Life changed its reporting entity structure to contribute certain wholly owned subsidiaries, including Hartford Life's European insurance operations, several broker dealer entities and investment advisory and service entities from Hartford Life and Accident to the Company. The contribution of subsidiaries was effected to more closely align servicing entities with the writing company issuing the business they service as well as to more efficiently deploy capital across the organization. The change in reporting entity was retrospectively applied to the financial statements of the Company for all periods presented. The contributed subsidiaries resulted in an increase in stockholder's equity of approximately $1.3 billion.

Error Correction

The correction of an error is not actually an accounting change but is accounted for similarly. In fact, it's accounted for retrospectively like a change in reporting entity and like most changes in accounting principle.

More specifically, previous years' financial statements that were incorrect as a result of the error are retrospectively restated to reflect the correction. And, of course, any account balances that are incorrect as a result of the error are corrected by a journal entry. If retained earnings is one of the incorrect accounts, the correction is reported as a prior period adjustment to the beginning balance in a statement of shareholders' equity (or statement of retained earnings if that's presented instead).[11] And, as for accounting changes, a disclosure note is needed to describe the nature of the error and the impact of its correction on operations. We discuss the correction of errors in more detail in Part B of this chapter. But first, let's compare the two approaches for reporting accounting changes and error corrections (Illustration 20–11).

Previous years' financial statements are retrospectively restated to reflect the correction of an error.

Illustration 20–11
Approaches to Reporting Accounting Changes and Error Corrections

Previous Years	Current Year	Later Years

← Retrospective:
Most changes in accounting principle
Change in reporting entity
Corrections of errors

Prospective →
Changes in estimate including changes in depreciation method
Changes in accounting principle when retrospective application is impractical
Changes in accounting principle when prospective application is mandated

A comparison of accounting treatments is provided by Illustration 20–12.

Illustration 20–12 Accounting Changes and Errors: A Summary

	Change in Accounting Principle		Change in Estimate (including depreciation changes)	Change in Reporting Entity	Error
	Most Changes*	Exceptions†			
Method of accounting:	Retrospective	Prospective	Prospective	Retrospective	Retrospective
• Restate prior years' statements?	Yes	No	No	Yes	Yes
• Cumulative effect on prior years' income reported:	As adjustment to retained earnings of earliest year reported.‡	Not reported.	Not reported.	Not reported.	As adjustment to retained earnings of earliest year reported.‡

(continued)

[11]FASB ASC 250–10–45: Accounting Changes and Error Corrections–Overall–Other Presentation Matters (previously "Prior Period Adjustments," *Statement of Financial Accounting Standards No. 16* (Stamford, CT: FASB, 1977)).

Illustration 20–12 (concluded)

• Journal entry:	To adjust affected balances to new method.	None, but subsequent accounting is affected by the change.	None, but subsequent accounting is affected by the new estimate.	Involves consolidated financial statements discussed in other courses.	To correct any balances that are incorrect as a result of the error.
• Disclosure note?	Yes	Yes	Yes	Yes	Yes

*Changes in depreciation, amortization, and depletion methods are considered changes in estimates.
†When retrospective application is impracticable such as most changes to LIFO and certain mandated changes.
‡In the statement of shareholders' equity or statement of retained earnings.

Concept Review Exercise

ACCOUNTING CHANGES

Modern Business Machines recently conducted an extensive review of its accounting and reporting policies. The following accounting changes are an outgrowth of that review:

1. MBM has a patent on a copier design. The patent has been amortized on a straight-line basis since it was acquired at a cost of $400,000 in 2013. During 2016, MBM decided that the benefits from the patent would be experienced over a total of 13 years rather than the 20-year legal life now being used to amortize its cost.
2. At the beginning of 2016, MBM changed its method of valuing inventory from the FIFO cost method to the average cost method. At December 31, 2015 and 2014, MBM's inventories were $560 and $540 million, respectively, on a FIFO cost basis but would have totaled $500 and $490 million, respectively, if determined on an average cost basis. MBM's income tax rate is 40%.

Required:

Prepare all journal entries needed in 2016 related to each change. Also, briefly describe any other measures MBM would take in connection with reporting the changes.

Solution:

1. **Change in estimate**

	($ in 000s)	
Patent amortization expense (determined below)	34	
Patent		34

Calculation of Annual Amortization after the Estimate Change

	$400,000	Cost
$20,000		Old annual amortization ($400,000 ÷ 20 years)
× 3 years	(60,000)	Amortization to date (2013, 2014, 2015)
	340,000	Unamortized cost
	÷ 10	Estimated remaining life (13 years − 3 years)
	$ 34,000	New annual amortization

A disclosure note should describe the effect of a change in estimate on income from continuing operations, net income, and related per-share amounts for the current period.

2. **Change in principle**

MBM creates a journal entry to bring up to date all account balances affected.

	($ in millions)	
Retained earnings (The difference in net income before 2016)	36	
Deferred tax asset ($60 million × 40%)	24	
Inventory ($560 million − $500 million)		60

Prior years' financial statements are revised to reflect the use of the new accounting method.

For financial reporting purposes, but not for tax, MBM is retrospectively *decreasing* accounting income, but not taxable income. This creates a temporary difference between the two that will reverse over time as the unsold inventory becomes cost of goods sold. When that happens, taxable income will be less than accounting income. When taxable income will be less than accounting income as a temporary difference reverses, we have a "future deductible amount" and record a deferred tax asset.

Also, MBM will revise all previous periods' financial statements (in this case 2015) as if the new method (average cost) were used in those periods. In other words, for each year in the comparative statements reported, the balance of each account affected will be revised to appear as if the average method had been applied all along.

Since it's the earliest year reported, 2015's beginning retained earnings is adjusted for the portion of the cumulative income effect of the change attributable to prior years.

Since retained earnings is one of the accounts whose balance requires adjustment (and it usually is), MBM makes an adjustment to the beginning balance of retained earnings for the earliest period (2015) reported in the comparative statements of shareholders' equity. Also, in the first set of financial statements after the change, a *disclosure note* describes the nature of the change, justifies management's decision to make the change, and indicates its effect on each item affected in the financial statements.

International Financial Reporting Standards

● LO20–7

The FASB and the International Accounting Standards Board have a continuing commitment to converge their accounting standards. As part of their short-term convergence effort, they identified how companies report accounting changes as an area in which the FASB could improve its guidance by converging it with the provisions of *IAS No. 8*, "Accounting Policies, Changes in Accounting Estimates and Errors."[12] The product of this effort was new FASB guidance issued in 2005.[13] Few differences remain, so it's unlikely we will see much change in this area.

PART B

Correction of Accounting Errors

● LO20–6

Nobody's perfect. People make mistakes, even accountants. When errors are discovered, they should be corrected.[14] Illustration 20–13 describes the steps to be taken to correct an error, if the effect of the error is material.[15]

Prior Period Adjustments

Before we see these steps applied to the **correction of an error**, one of the steps requires elaboration. As discussed in Chapter 4, the correction of errors is the situation that creates prior period adjustments. A **prior period adjustment** refers to an addition to or reduction in the beginning retained earnings balance in a statement of shareholders' equity (or statement of retained earnings if that's presented instead).

[12]"Accounting Policies, Changes in Accounting Estimates and Errors, "*International Accounting Standard No. 8* (IASCF), as amended effective January 1, 2011.

[13]FASB ASC 250: Accounting Changes and Error Corrections (previously "Accounting Changes and Error Corrections—A Replacement of APB Opinion No. 20 and FASB Statement No. 3," *Statement of Financial Accounting Standards No. 154,* (Norwalk, Conn: FASB, 2005)).

[14]Interestingly, it appears that not all accounting errors are unintentional. Research has shown that firms with errors that overstate income are more likely "to have diffuse ownership, lower growth in earnings and fewer income-increasing GAAP alternatives available, and are less likely to have audit committees," suggesting that "overstatement errors are the result of managers responding to economic incentives." M. L. DeFond and J. Jiambaolvo, "Incidence and Circumstances of Accounting Errors," *The Accounting Review,* July 1991.

[15]In practice, the vast majority of errors are not material with respect to their effect on the financial statements and are, therefore, simply corrected in the year discovered (step 1 only).

Illustration 20–13
Steps to Correct an Error

Step 1. A journal entry is made to correct any account balances that are incorrect as a result of the error.
Step 2. Previous years' financial statements that were incorrect as a result of the error are retrospectively restated to reflect the correction (for all years reported for comparative purposes).
Step 3. If retained earnings is one of the accounts incorrect as a result of the error, the correction is reported as a prior period adjustment to the beginning balance in a statement of shareholders' equity (or statement of retained earnings if that's presented instead).
Step 4. A disclosure note should describe the nature of the error and the impact of its correction on net income.

The retrospective approach is used for the correction of errors.

The correction of an error is treated as a prior period adjustment.

In an earlier chapter we saw that a statement of shareholders' equity is the most commonly used way to report the events that cause components of shareholders' equity to change during a particular reporting period. Some companies, though, choose to report the changes that occur in the balance of retained earnings separately in a statement of retained earnings. When it's discovered that the ending balance of retained earnings in the period prior to the discovery of an error was incorrect as a result of that error, the balance must be corrected when it appears as the beginning balance the following year. However, simply reporting a corrected amount might cause misunderstanding for someone familiar with the previously reported amount. Explicitly reporting a prior period adjustment on the statement itself avoids this confusion. Assume, for example, the following comparative statements of retained earnings:

STATEMENTS OF RETAINED EARNINGS
For the Years Ended December 31, 2015 and 2014

	2015	2014
Balance at beginning of year	$600,000	$450,000
Net income	400,000	350,000
Less: Dividends	(200,000)	(200,000)
Balance at end of year	$800,000	$600,000

A statement of retained earnings reports the events that cause changes in retained earnings.

Now suppose that in 2016 it's discovered that an error in 2014 caused that year's net income to be overstated by $20,000 (it should have been $330,000). This means retained earnings in both prior years were overstated. Because comparative financial statements are presented and the current year is the year in which the error was discovered, the prior year would include a prior period adjustment as shown below:

STATEMENTS OF RETAINED EARNINGS
For the Years Ended December 31, 2016 and 2015

	2016	2015
Balance at beginning of year	$ 780,000	$600,000
Prior period adjustment		(20,000)
Corrected balance		$580,000
Net Income	500,000	400,000
Less: Dividends	(200,000)	(200,000)
Balance at end of year	$1,080,000	$780,000

The incorrect balance as previously reported is corrected by the prior period adjustment.

At least two years' (as in our example) and often three years' statements are reported in comparative financial statements. The prior period adjustment is applied to beginning retained earnings for the year following the error, or for the earliest year being reported in the comparative financial statements when the error occurs prior to the earliest year presented.[16]

[16]The retained earnings balances in years after the first year also are adjusted to what those balances would be if the error had not occurred, but a company may choose not to explicitly report those adjustments as separate line items.

Error Correction Illustrated

You shouldn't try to memorize how specific errors are corrected; you should learn the process needed to analyze whatever errors you might encounter.

Now, let's discuss these procedures to correct errors in the context of a variety of the most common types of errors. Since there are literally thousands of possibilities, it's not practical to describe every error in every stage of its discovery. However, by applying the process to the situations described below, you should become sufficiently comfortable with the *process* that you could apply it to whatever situation you might encounter.

As you study these examples, be sure to notice that it's significantly more complicated to deal with an error if (a) it affected net income in the reporting period in which it occurred and (b) it is not discovered until a later period.

Error Discovered in the Same Reporting Period That It Occurred

If an accounting error is made and discovered in the same accounting period, the original erroneous entry should simply be reversed and the appropriate entry recorded. The possibilities are limitless. Let's look at the one in Illustration 20–14.

Illustration 20–14
Error Discovered in the Same Reporting Period That It Occurred

G. H. Little, Inc. paid $3 million for replacement computers and recorded the expenditure as maintenance expense. The error was discovered a week later.

To Reverse Erroneous Entry	($ in millions)	
Cash	3	
Maintenance expense		3
To Record Correct Entry		
Equipment	3	
Cash		3

Note: These entries can, of course, be combined.

Error Affecting Previous Financial Statements, but Not Net Income

If an error did *not* affect net income in the year it occurred, it's relatively easy to correct. Examples are incorrectly recording salaries payable as accounts payable, recording a loss as an expense, or classifying a cash flow as an investing activity rather than a financing activity on the statement of cash flows. A disclosure note in the 2013 financial statements of **Barnes & Noble**, reproduced in Illustration 20–15, provides an example. Illustration 20–16 provides another.

Illustration 20–15
Error Correction; Barnes & Noble

Real World Financials

2. Restatement of Prior Period Financial Statements (in part)
The Company has restated its previously reported consolidated financial statements for the years ended April 28, 2012 and April 30, 2011, including the opening stockholders' equity balance, in order to correct certain previously reported amounts.

In fiscal 2013, management determined that the Company had incorrectly overstated certain accruals for the periods prior to April 27, 2013, as a result of inadequate controls over its Distribution Center accrual reconciliation process. . . . the Company recorded an adjustment to decrease cost of sales by $6,700 ($4,027 after tax) and $8,460 ($5,084 after tax) to correctly present the statement of operations for fiscal 2012 and 2011, respectively. The Company also decreased accounts payable by $89,500 and $96,200 at April 30, 2011 and April 28, 2012, respectively; increased income taxes payable included in Accrued Liabilities in the consolidated Balance Sheets by $14,939 and $18,598 at April 30, 2011 and April 28, 2012, respectively; and increased retained earnings by $74,561 and $78,588, net of tax at April 30, 2011 and April 28, 2012, respectively.

Illustration 20–16

Error Affecting Previous Financial Statements, but Not Net Income

MDS Transportation incorrectly recorded a $2 million note receivable as accounts receivable. The error was discovered a year later.

To Correct Incorrect Accounts	($ in millions)	
Note receivable	2	
Accounts receivable		2

Step 1

When reported for comparative purposes in the current year's annual report, last year's balance sheet would be restated to report the note as it should have been reported last year.

Step 2

Since last year's net income was not affected by the error, the balance in retained earnings was not incorrect. So no prior period adjustment to that account is necessary.

Step 3

A disclosure note would describe the nature of the error, but there would be no impact on net income, income from continuing operations, and earnings per share to report.

Step 4

Error Affecting a Prior Year's Net Income

Most errors affect net income in some way. When they do, they affect the balance sheet as well. Both statements must be retrospectively restated; the statement of cash flows sometimes is affected, too. As with any error, all incorrect account balances must be corrected. Because these errors affect income, one of the balances that will require correction is retained earnings. Complicating matters, income taxes often are affected by income errors. In those cases, amended tax returns are prepared either to pay additional taxes or to claim a tax refund for taxes overpaid.

In Illustration 20–17 (except as indicated), we ignore the tax effects of the errors and their correction to allow us to focus on the errors themselves rather than their tax aspects.

Illustration 20–17

Error Affecting Net Income: Recording an Asset as an Expense

In 2016, internal auditors discovered that Seidman Distribution, Inc., had debited an expense account for the $7 million cost of sorting equipment purchased at the beginning of 2014. The equipment's useful life was expected to be five years with no residual value. Straight-line depreciation is used by Seidman.

Analysis:

($ in millions)

	Correct (Should have been recorded)			Incorrect (As recorded)		
2014	Equipment	7.0		Expense	7.0	
	Cash		7.0	Cash		7.0
2014	Expense	1.4		Depreciation entry omitted		
	Accum. deprec.		1.4			
2015	Expense	1.4		Depreciation entry omitted		
	Accum. deprec.		1.4			

Sometimes, the analysis is easier if you re-create the entries actually recorded incorrectly and those that would have been recorded if the error hadn't occurred and then compare them.

During the two-year period, depreciation expense was understated by $2.8 million, but other expenses were overstated by $7 million, so net income during the period was understated by $4.2 million. This means retained earnings is currently understated by that amount.

Accumulated depreciation is understated by $2.8 million.

To Correct Incorrect Accounts	($ in millions)	
Equipment	7.0	
Accumulated depreciation		2.8
Retained earnings		4.2

Step 1

The 2014 and 2015 financial statements that were incorrect as a result of the error are retrospectively restated to report the equipment acquired and to reflect the correct amount of depreciation expense and accumulated depreciation, assuming both statements are reported again for comparative purposes in the 2016 annual report.

Step 2

Because retained earnings is one of the accounts that is incorrect as a result of the error, a correction to that account of $4.2 million is reported as a prior period adjustment to

(continued)

Illustration 20–17
(concluded)

Step 3

the 2016 beginning retained earnings balance in Seidman's comparative statements of shareholders' equity. A correction would be made also to the 2015 beginning retained earnings balance. That prior period adjustment, though, would be for the pre-2015 difference: $7 million − 1.4 million = $5.6 million. If 2014 statements also are included in the comparative report, no adjustment would be necessary for that period because the error didn't occur until after the beginning of 2014.

Step 4

Also, a disclosure note accompanying Seidman's 2016 financial statements should describe the nature of the error and the impact of its correction on each year's net income (understated by $5.6 million in 2014 and overstated by $1.4 million in 2015), income from continuing operations (same as net income), and earnings per share.

The effect of most errors is different, depending on ***when*** the error is discovered. For example, if the error in Illustration 20–17 is not discovered until 2017, rather than 2016, accumulated depreciation would be understated by another $1.4 million, or a total of $4.2 million. If not discovered until 2019 or after, no correcting entry at all would be needed. By then, the sum of the omitted depreciation amounts ($1.4 million × 5 years) would equal the expense incorrectly recorded in 2014 ($7 million), so the retained earnings balance would be the same as if the error never had occurred. Also, the asset may have been disposed of—if the useful life estimate was correct—so neither the equipment nor accumulated depreciation would need to be recorded. Of course, any statements of prior years that were affected and are reported again in comparative statements still would be restated, and a disclosure note would describe the error.

Most errors, in fact, eventually self-correct. An example of an uncommon instance in which an error never self-corrects would be an expense account debited for the cost of land. Because land doesn't depreciate, the error would continue until the land is sold.

Even errors that eventually correct themselves cause financial statements to be misstated in the meantime.

Some errors correct themselves the following year. For instance, if a company's ending inventory is incorrectly counted or otherwise misstated, the income statement would be in error for the year of the error and the following year, but the balance sheet would be incorrect only for the year the error occurs. After that, all account balances will be correct. This is demonstrated in Illustration 20–18 on the next page.

Additional Consideration

We ignored the tax impact of the error and its correction in Illustration 20–17. To consider taxes, we need to know whether depreciation was also omitted from the tax return and the depreciation methods used for tax reporting. Let's say that depreciation was omitted from the tax return also, and that straight-line depreciation is used by Seidman for both tax and financial reporting. The tax rate is 40%.

Total operating expenses (nontax) still would have been overstated by $4.2 million over the two-year period. But that would have caused taxable income to be understated and the tax liability and income tax expense to be understated by 40% of $4.2 million, or $1.68 million. So net income and retained earnings would have been understated by only $2.52 million:

Operating expenses *overstated*	$4.20 million
Income tax expense *understated*	(1.68) million
Net income (and retained earnings) *understated*	$2.52 million

To Correct Incorrect Accounts:	($ in millions)	
Equipment	7.00	
Accumulated depreciation		2.80
Income tax payable (40% × $4.2 million)		1.68
Retained earnings		2.52

If depreciation had been omitted from the income statement but not from the tax return, or if accelerated depreciation was used for tax reporting but straight-line depreciation for financial reporting, the credit to income tax payable in the correcting entry would be replaced by a credit to deferred tax liability.

Illustration 20–18
Error Affecting Net Income: Inventory Misstated

In early 2016, Overseas Wholesale Supply discovered that $1 million of inventory had been inadvertently excluded from its 2014 ending inventory count.

Analysis:

U = Understated O = Overstated

2014		**2015**	
Beginning inventory		Beginning inventory	U
Plus: Net purchases		Plus: Net purchases	
Less: Ending inventory	U	Less: Ending inventory	
Cost of goods sold	O	Cost of goods sold	U
Revenues		Revenues	
Less: Cost of goods sold	O	Less: Cost of goods sold	U
Less: Other expenses		Less: Other expenses	
Net income	U	Net income	O
↓		↓	
Retained earnings	U	Retained earnings	*corrected*

When analyzing inventory errors or other errors that affect cost of goods sold, you may find it helpful to visualize the determination of cost of goods sold, net income, and retained earnings.

If Error Is Discovered in 2015 (before closing):

Step 1

	($ in millions)	
Inventory	1	
Retained earnings		1

If Error Discovered in 2016 or Later:
No correcting entry needed

Step 2

If the error is discovered in 2015, the 2014 financial statements that were incorrect as a result of the error are retrospectively restated to reflect the correct inventory amounts, cost of goods sold, and retained earnings when those statements are reported again for comparative purposes in the 2015 annual report. If the error is discovered in 2016, the 2015 financial statements also are retrospectively restated to reflect the correct inventory amounts and cost of goods sold (retained earnings would not require adjustment), even though no correcting entry would be needed at that point.

Step 3

Because retained earnings is one of the accounts incorrect if the error is discovered in 2015, the correction to that account is reported as a prior period adjustment to the 2015 beginning retained earnings balance in Overseas' statement of shareholders' equity. Of course, no prior period adjustment is needed if the error isn't discovered until 2017 or later.

Step 4

Also, a disclosure note in Overseas' annual report should describe the nature of the error and the impact of its correction on each year's net income (understated by $1 million in 2014, overstated by $1 million in 2015), income from continuing operations (same as net income), and earnings per share.

Other error corrections that benefit from a similar analysis are the overstatement of ending inventory, the overstatement or understatement of beginning inventory, and errors in recording merchandise purchases (or returns).

An error also would occur if a revenue or an expense is recorded in the wrong accounting period. Illustration 20–19 offers an example.

Illustration 20–19
Error Affecting Net Income: Failure to Record Sales Revenue

In 2016, General Paper Company discovered that $3,000 of merchandise (credit) sales the last week of 2015 were not recorded until the first week of 2016. The merchandise sold was appropriately excluded from 2015 ending inventory.

Analysis:

($ in 000s)

	Correct (Should have been recorded)			Incorrect (As recorded)		
2015	Accounts receivable	3		No entry		
	Sales revenue		3			
2016	No entry			Accounts receivable	3	
				Sales revenue		3

(continued)

Illustration 20–19 (concluded)

2015 sales revenue was incorrectly recorded in 2016, so 2015 net income was understated. Retained earnings is currently understated in 2016. 2016 sales revenue is overstated.

Step 1

To Correct Incorrect Accounts	($ in 000s)	
Sales revenue	3	
Retained earnings		3

Note: If the sales revenue had not been recorded at all, the correcting entry would include a debit to accounts receivable rather than sales revenue.

Step 2

The 2015 financial statements that were incorrect as a result of the error are retroactively restated to reflect the correct amount of sales revenue and accounts receivable when those statements are reported again for comparative purposes in the 2016 annual report.

Step 3

Because retained earnings is one of the accounts incorrect as a result of the error, the correction to that account is reported as a prior period adjustment to the 2015 beginning retained earnings balance in General Paper's comparative statements of shareholders' equity.

Step 4

Also, a disclosure note in General Paper's 2016 annual report should describe the nature of the error and the impact of its correction on each year's net income ($3,000 in 2015), income from continuing operations ($3,000 in 2015), and earnings per share.

Ethical Dilemma

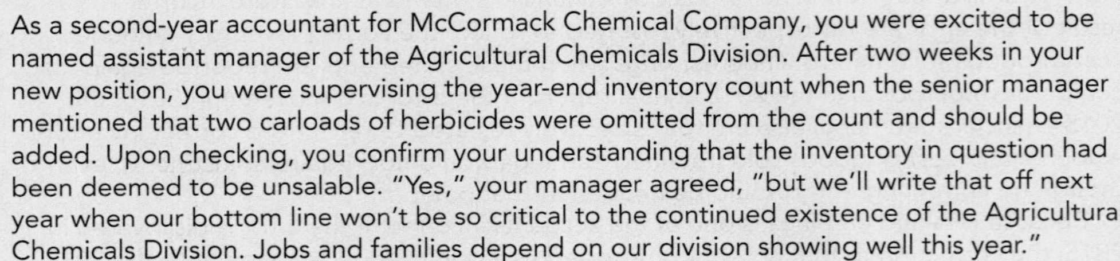

As a second-year accountant for McCormack Chemical Company, you were excited to be named assistant manager of the Agricultural Chemicals Division. After two weeks in your new position, you were supervising the year-end inventory count when the senior manager mentioned that two carloads of herbicides were omitted from the count and should be added. Upon checking, you confirm your understanding that the inventory in question had been deemed to be unsalable. "Yes," your manager agreed, "but we'll write that off next year when our bottom line won't be so critical to the continued existence of the Agricultural Chemicals Division. Jobs and families depend on our division showing well this year."

Illustration 20–20 shows how **Benihana, Inc.**, corrected its financial statements for having incorrectly expensed leasehold improvements and assets on leased properties in past years. Benihana was one of hundreds of firms making similar correction in 2007 following a Securities and Exchange Commission letter on February 7, 2007, urging companies to follow long-standing accounting standards in this area. As the note indicates, Benihana's previous earnings had been overstated by $2.2 million as a result of the error and the balance in retained earnings was accordingly decreased in the correcting journal entry. At about the same time, **McDonald's Corp.** recorded a similar charge of $139 million.

Illustration 20–20
Error Correction; Benihana, Inc.

Real World Financials

2. Restatement of Previously Issued Financial Statements (in part)
Following a February 2005 review . . . we have restated our consolidated financial statements for the fiscal years through 2004 and for the third quarter of fiscal 2004 included herein. Previously, when accounting for leases with renewal options, we recorded rent expense on a straight-line basis over the initial noncancelable lease term, with the term commencing when actual rent payments began. We depreciate our buildings, leasehold improvements and other long-lived assets on those properties over a period that includes both the initial noncancelable lease term and all option periods provided for in the lease (or the useful life of the assets if shorter). We previously believed that these long-standing accounting treatments were appropriate under generally accepted accounting principles. We now have restated our financial statements to recognize rent expense on a straight-line basis over the expected lease term, including cancelable option periods where failure

(continued)

to exercise such options would result in an economic penalty and including the period that commences when the underlying property is made available to us for construction.

The cumulative effect of the Restatement through fiscal 2004 is an increase in deferred rent liability of $3.6 million and a decrease in deferred income tax liability of $1.4 million. As a result, retained earnings at the end of fiscal 2004 decreased by $2.2 million. Rent expense for fiscal year ended 2004 and for the three and ten periods ended January 4, 2004 increased by $0.4 million, and $0.1 million and $0.3, respectively. The Restatement decreased reported diluted net earnings per share $0.01 and $0.03 for the three and ten periods ended January 4, 2004, respectively.

Illustration 20–20
(concluded)

As mentioned at the outset, we've made no attempt to demonstrate the correction process for every kind of error in every stage of its discovery. However, after seeing the process applied to the few situations described, you should feel comfortable that the process is the same regardless of the specific situation you might encounter.

International Financial Reporting Standards

Accounting Changes and Error Corrections. U.S. GAAP and International standards are largely converged regarding accounting changes and error corrections, but one difference concerns error corrections. When correcting errors in previously issued financial statements, IFRS (*IAS No. 8*[17]) permits the effect of the error to be reported in the current period if it's not considered practicable to report it retrospectively as is required by U.S. GAAP.

● LO20–7

Concept Review Exercise

CORRECTION OF ERRORS

In 2016, the following errors were discovered by the internal auditors of Development Technologies, Inc.

1. 2015 accrued wages of $2 million were not recognized until they were paid in 2016.
2. A $3 million purchase of merchandise in 2016 was recorded in 2015 instead. The physical inventory count at the end of 2015 was correct.

Required:
Prepare the journal entries needed in 2016 to correct each error. Also, briefly describe any other measures Development Technologies would take in connection with correcting the errors. (Ignore income taxes.)

Solution:

Step 1:

1. To reduce 2016 wages expense and reduce retained earnings to what it would have been if the expense had reduced net income in 2015.

	($ in millions)	
Retained earnings	2	
Wages expense		2

2. To include the $3 million in 2016 purchases and increase retained earnings to what it would have been if 2015 cost of goods sold had not included the $3 million purchases.

[17]"Accounting Policies, Changes in Accounting Estimates and Errors," *International Accounting Standard No. 8* (IASCF), as amended effective January 1, 2014.

Analysis

U = Understated O = Overstated

2015		2016	
Beginning inventory		Beginning inventory	
Purchases	O	Purchases	U
Less: Ending inventory			
Cost of goods sold	O		
Revenues			
Less: Cost of goods sold	O		
Less: Other expenses			
Net income	U		
Retained earnings	U		

	($ in millions)	
Purchases	3	
Retained earnings		3

Step 2:

The 2015 financial statements that were incorrect as a result of the errors would be *retrospectively restated* to reflect the correct wages expense, cost of goods sold (income tax expense if taxes are considered), net income, and retained earnings when those statements are reported again for comparative purposes in the 2016 annual report.

Step 3:

Because retained earnings is one of the accounts that is incorrect, the correction to that account is reported as a "*prior period adjustment*" to the 2016 beginning retained earnings balance in the comparative Statements of Shareholders' Equity.

Step 4:

Also, a *disclosure note* should describe the nature of the error and the impact of its correction on each year's net income, income from continuing operations, and earnings per share.

Financial Reporting Case Solution

1. **How can an accounting change cause a company to increase a previously reported inventory amount?** *(p. 1199)* Smucker didn't find any lost jelly. The company increased last year's inventory number by $2 million to reflect its change from **LIFO** to **FIFO** this year. If it had not revised the number, last year's inventory would be based on **LIFO** and this year's inventory on **FIFO.** Analysts would be comparing apples and oranges (or apple jelly and orange jelly). Retrospective application of an accounting change provides better comparability in accounting information.
2. **Are all accounting changes reported this way?** *(p. 1206)* Not all accounting changes are reported retrospectively. Besides most changes in accounting principle, changes in reporting entity and the correction of errors are reported that way, but some changes are reported prospectively instead. Changes in depreciation method, changes in accounting estimate, and some changes for which retrospective application is either impracticable or prohibited are reported prospectively in current and future periods only. ●

The Bottom Line

- **LO20–1** Accounting changes are categorized as:
  a. Changes in *principle,*
  b. Changes in *estimates,* or
  c. Changes in *reporting entity.*

  Accounting changes can be accounted for retrospectively (prior years revised) or prospectively (only current and future years affected). (*p. 1196*)
- **LO20–2** Most voluntary changes in accounting principles are reported retrospectively. This means revising all previous periods' financial statements to appear as if the newly adopted accounting method had been applied all along. A journal entry is created to adjust all account balances affected as of the date of the change. In the first set of financial statements after the change, a disclosure note describes the change and justifies the new method as preferable. It also describes the effects of the change on all items affected, including the fact that the retained earnings balance was revised in the statement of shareholders' equity. (*p. 1198*)
- **LO20–3** Some changes are reported prospectively. These include (a) changes in the method of depreciation, amortization, or depletion, (b) some changes in principle for which retrospective application is impracticable, and (c) a few changes for which an authoritative pronouncement requires prospective application. (*p. 1202*)
- **LO20–4** Changes in estimates are accounted for prospectively. When a company revises a previous estimate, prior financial statements are not revised. Instead, the company merely incorporates the new estimate in any related accounting determinations from then on. (*p. 1205*)
- **LO20–5** A change in reporting entity requires that financial statements of prior periods be retrospectively revised to report the financial information for the new reporting entity in all periods. (*p. 1207*)
- **LO20–6** When errors are discovered, they should be corrected and accounted for retrospectively. Previous years' financial statements that were incorrect as a result of an error are retrospectively restated, and any account balances that are incorrect are corrected by a journal entry. If retained earnings is one of the incorrect accounts, the correction is reported as a prior period adjustment to the beginning balance in a statement of shareholders' equity. And, a disclosure note should describe the nature of the error and the impact of its correction on operations. (*p. 1210*)
- **LO20–7** U.S. GAAP and International standards are largely converged with respect to accounting changes and error corrections. One remaining difference is that when correcting errors in previously issued financial statements, IFRS permits the effect of the error to be reported in the current period if it's not considered practicable to report it retrospectively as is required by U.S. GAAP. (*pp. 1203, 1210,* and *1217*)

Questions For Review of Key Topics

Q 20–1 For accounting purposes, we classify accounting changes into three categories. What are they? Provide a short description of each.

Q 20–2 There are two basic accounting approaches to reporting accounting changes. What are they?

Q 20–3 We report most changes in accounting principle retrospectively. Describe this general way of recording and reporting changes in accounting principle.

Q 20–4 Lynch Corporation changes from the sum-of-the-years'-digits method of depreciation for existing assets to the straight-line method. How should the change be reported? Explain.

Q 20–5 Sugarbaker Designs, Inc., changed from the FIFO inventory costing method to the average cost method during 2016. Which items from the 2015 financial statements should be restated on the basis of the average cost method when reported in the 2016 comparative financial statements?

Q 20–6 Most changes in accounting principles are recorded and reported retrospectively. In a few situations, though, the changes should be reported prospectively. When is prospective application appropriate? Provide examples.

Q 20–7 Southeast Steel, Inc., changed from the FIFO inventory costing method to the LIFO method during 2015. How would this change likely be reported in the 2016 comparative financial statements?

Q 20–8 Direct Assurance Company revised the estimates of the useful life of a trademark it had acquired three years earlier. How should Direct account for the change?

Q 20–9 It's not easy sometimes to distinguish between a change in principle and a change in estimate. In these cases, how should the change be accounted for?

Q 20–10 For financial reporting, a reporting entity can be a single company, or it can be a group of companies that reports a single set of financial statements. When changes occur that cause the financial statements to be those of a different reporting entity, we account for the situation as a change in reporting entity. What are the situations deemed to constitute a change in reporting entity?

Q 20–11 The issuance of FASB guidance regarding consolidation of all majority-owned subsidiaries required Ford Motors to include a previously unconsolidated finance subsidiary as part of the reporting entity. How did Ford report the change?

Q 20–12 Describe the process of correcting an error when it's discovered in a subsequent reporting period.

Q 20–13 If merchandise inventory is understated at the end of 2015, and the error is not discovered, how will net income be affected in 2016?

Q 20–14 If it is discovered that an extraordinary repair in the previous year was incorrectly debited to repair expense, how will retained earnings be reported in the current year's statement of shareholders' equity?

Q 20–15 What action is required when it is discovered that a five-year insurance premium payment of $50,000 two years ago was debited to insurance expense? (Ignore taxes.)

Q 20–16 Suppose the error described in the previous question is not discovered until six years later. What action will the discovery of this error require?

Q 20–17 With regard to the correction of accounting errors, what is the difference between U.S. GAAP and IFRS?

Brief Exercises

BE 20–1
Change in inventory methods
● LO20–2

In 2016, the Barton and Barton Company changed its method of valuing inventory from the FIFO method to the average cost method. At December 31, 2015, B & B's inventories were $32 million (FIFO). B & B's records indicated that the inventories would have totaled $23.8 million at December 31, 2015, if determined on an average cost basis. Ignoring income taxes, what journal entry will B & B use to record the adjustment in 2016? Briefly describe other steps B & B should take to report the change.

BE 20–2
Change in inventory methods
● LO20–2

In 2016, Adonis Industries changed its method of valuing inventory from the average cost method to the FIFO method. At December 31, 2015, Adonis's inventories were $47.6 million (average cost). Adonis's records indicated that the inventories would have totaled $64 million at December 31, 2015, if determined on a FIFO basis. Ignoring income taxes, what journal entry will Adonis use to record the adjustment in 2016?

BE 20–3
Change in inventory methods
● LO20–3

In 2016, J J Dishes changed its method of valuing inventory from the FIFO method to the LIFO method. At December 31, 2015, J J's inventories were $96 million (FIFO). J J's records were insufficient to determine what inventories would have totaled if determined on a LIFO cost basis. Briefly describe the steps J J should take to report the change.

BE 20–4
Change in depreciation methods
● LO20–3

Irwin, Inc., constructed a machine at a total cost of $35 million. Construction was completed at the end of 2012 and the machine was placed in service at the beginning of 2013. The machine was being depreciated over a 10-year life using the sum-of-the-years'-digits method. The residual value is expected to be $2 million. At the beginning of 2016, Irwin decided to change to the straight-line method. Ignoring income taxes, what journal entry(s) should Irwin record relating to the machine for 2016?

BE 20–5
Change in depreciation methods
● LO20–3

Refer to the situation described in BE 20–4. Suppose Irwin has been using the straight-line method and switches to the sum-of-the-years'-digits method. Ignoring income taxes, what journal entry(s) should Irwin record relating to the machine for 2016?

BE 20–6
Book royalties
● LO20–4

Three programmers at Feenix Computer Storage, Inc., write an operating systems control manual for Hill-McGraw Publishing, Inc., for which Feenix receives royalties equal to 12% of net sales. Royalties are payable annually on February 1 for sales the previous year. The editor indicated to Feenix on December 31, 2016, that book sales subject to royalties for the year just ended are expected to be $300,000. Accordingly, Feenix accrued royalty revenue of $36,000 at December 31 and received royalties of $36,500 on February 1, 2017. What adjustments, if any, should be made to retained earnings or to the 2016 financial statements? Explain.

BE 20–7
Warranty expense
● LO20–4

In 2015, Quapau Products introduced a new line of hot water heaters that carry a one-year warranty against manufacturer's defects. Based on industry experience, warranty costs were expected to approximate 5% of sales revenue. First-year sales of the heaters were $300,000. An evaluation of the company's claims experience in late 2016 indicated that actual claims were less than expected—4% of sales rather than 5%. Assuming sales of the heaters in 2016 were $350,000 and warranty expenditures in 2016 totaled $12,000, what is the 2016 warranty expense?

BE 20–8
Change in estimate; useful life of patent
● LO20–4

Van Frank Telecommunications has a patent on a cellular transmission process. The company has amortized the $18 million cost of the patent on a straight-line basis since it was acquired at the beginning of 2012. Due to rapid technological advances in the industry, management decided that the patent would benefit the company over a total of six years rather than the nine-year life being used to amortize its cost. The decision was made at the end of 2016 (before adjusting and closing entries). What is the appropriate adjusting entry for patent amortization in 2016 to reflect the revised estimate?

BE 20–9
Error correction
● LO20–6

When DeSoto Water Works purchased a machine at the end of 2015 at a cost of $65,000, the company debited Buildings and credited Cash $65,000. The error was discovered in 2016. What journal entry will DeSoto use to correct the error? What other step(s) would be taken in connection with the error?

BE 20–10
Error correction
● LO20–6

In 2016, internal auditors discovered that PKE Displays, Inc., had debited an expense account for the $350,000 cost of a machine purchased on January 1, 2013. The machine's useful life was expected to be five years with no residual value. Straight-line depreciation is used by PKE. Ignoring income taxes, what journal entry will PKE use to correct the error?

BE 20–11
Error correction
● LO20–6

Refer to the situation described in BE 20–10. Assume the error was discovered in 2018 after the 2017 financial statements are issued. Ignoring income taxes, what journal entry will PKE use to correct the error?

BE 20–12
Error correction
● LO20–6

In 2016, the internal auditors of Development Technologies, Inc., discovered that (a) 2015 accrued wages of $2 million were not recognized until they were paid in 2016 and (b) a $3 million purchase of merchandise in 2016 was recorded in 2015 instead. The physical inventory count at the end of 2015 was correct. Ignoring income taxes, what journal entries are needed in 2016 to correct each error? Also, briefly describe any other measures Development Technologies would take in connection with correcting the errors.

Exercises

An alternate exercise and problem set is available in the Connect library.

E 20–1
Change in principle; change in inventory methods
● LO20–2

During 2014 (its first year of operations) and 2015, Batali Foods used the FIFO inventory costing method for both financial reporting and tax purposes. At the beginning of 2016, Batali decided to change to the average method for both financial reporting and tax purposes.

Income components before income tax for 2016, 2015, and 2014 were as follows ($ in millions):

	2016	2015	2014
Revenues	$420	$390	$380
Cost of goods sold (FIFO)	(46)	(40)	(38)
Cost of goods sold (average)	(62)	(56)	(52)
Operating expenses	(254)	(250)	(242)

Dividends of $20 million were paid each year. Batali's fiscal year ends December 31.

Required:

1. Prepare the journal entry at the beginning of 2016 to record the change in accounting principle. (Ignore income taxes.)
2. Prepare the 2016–2015 comparative income statements.
3. Determine the balance in retained earnings at January 1, 2015, as Batali reported previously using the FIFO method.
4. Determine the adjustment to the January 1, 2015, balance in retained earnings that Batali would include in the 2016–2015 comparative statements of retained earnings or retained earnings column of the statements of shareholders' equity to revise it to the amount it would have been if Batali had used the average method.

E 20–2
Change in principle; change in inventory methods
● LO20–2

Aquatic Equipment Corporation decided to switch from the LIFO method of costing inventories to the FIFO method at the beginning of 2016. The inventory as reported at the end of 2015 using LIFO would have been $60,000 higher using FIFO. Retained earnings at the end of 2015 was reported as $780,000 (reflecting the LIFO method). The tax rate is 40%.

Required:

1. Calculate the balance in retained earnings at the time of the change (beginning of 2016) as it would have been reported if FIFO had been used in prior years.
2. Prepare the journal entry at the beginning of 2016 to record the change in accounting principle.

E 20–3
Change from the treasury stock method to retired stock
● LO20–2

In keeping with a modernization of corporate statutes in its home state, UMC Corporation decided in 2016 to discontinue accounting for reacquired shares as treasury stock. Instead, shares repurchased will be viewed as having been retired, reassuming the status of unissued shares. As part of the change, treasury shares held were reclassified as retired stock. At December 31, 2015, UMC's balance sheet reported the following shareholders' equity:

	($ in millions)
Common stock, $1 par	$ 200
Paid-in capital—excess of par	800
Retained earnings	956
Treasury stock (4 million shares at cost)	(25)
Total shareholders' equity	$1,931

Required:

Identify the type of accounting change this decision represents and prepare the journal entry to effect the reclassification of treasury shares as retired shares.

E 20–4
Change in principle; change to the equity method
● LO20–2

The Trump Companies, Inc., has ownership interests in several public companies. At the beginning of 2016, the company's ownership interest in the common stock of Milken Properties increased to the point that it became appropriate to begin using the equity method of accounting for the investment. The balance in the investment account was $31 million at the time of the change. Accountants working with company records determined that the balance would have been $48 million if the account had been adjusted to reflect the equity method.

Required:

1. Prepare the journal entry to record the change in accounting principle. (Ignore income taxes.)
2. Briefly describe other steps Trump should take to report the change.
3. Suppose Trump is changing *from* the equity method rather than *to* the equity method. How would your answers to requirements 1 and 2 differ?

E 20–5
FASB codification research; change in accounting for investments
● LO20–2

Companies often invest in the common stock of other corporations. The way we report these investments depends on the nature of the investment and the investor's motivation for the investment. The *FASB Accounting Standards Codification* represents the single source of authoritative U.S. generally accepted accounting principles.

Required:

1. Obtain the relevant authoritative literature on accounting for a change from the cost method to the equity method for investments in common stock using the *FASB Accounting Standards Codification* at the FASB website (asc.fasb.org).
2. What is the specific citation that describes how to account for a change from the cost method to the equity method for investments in common stock?
3. What are the specific requirements?

E 20–6
FASB codification research
● LO20–2

Access the *FASB Accounting Standards Codification* at the FASB website (asc.fasb.org). Determine the specific citation for accounting for each of the following items:

1. Reporting most changes in accounting principle.
2. Disclosure requirements for a change in accounting principle.
3. Illustration of the application of a retrospective change in the method of accounting for inventory.

E 20–7
Change in principle; change in inventory cost method
● LO20–2

Millington Materials is a leading supplier of building equipment, building products, materials & timber for sale, with over 200 branches across the Mid-South. On January 1, 2016, management decided to change from the LIFO inventory costing method to the FIFO inventory costing method at each of its outlets.

The following table presents information concerning the change. The income tax rate for all years is 40%.

	Income before Income Tax		
	FIFO	**Average Cost**	**Difference**
Before 2015	$15 million	$8 million	$7 million
2015	8 million	5 million	3 million
2016	10 million	9 million	1 million

Required:

1. Prepare the journal entry to record the change in accounting principle. (All tax effects should be reflected in the deferred tax liability account.)
2. Determine the net income to be reported in the 2016–2015 comparative income statements.
3. Which other 2015 amounts would be reported differently in the 2016–2015 comparative income statements and 2016–2015 comparative balance sheets than they were reported the previous year?
4. How would the change be reflected in the 2016–2015 comparative statements of shareholders' equity? Cash dividends were $1 million each year. Assume no dividends were paid prior to 2015.

E 20–8
Change in inventory methods; incomplete information
● LO20–3

Flay Foods has always used the FIFO inventory costing method for both financial reporting and tax purposes. At the beginning of 2016, Flay decided to change to the LIFO method. As a result of the change, net income in 2016 was $80 million. If the company had used LIFO in 2015, its cost of goods sold would have been higher by $6 million that year. Flay's records of inventory purchases and sales are not available for 2014 and several previous years. Last year, Flay reported the following net income amounts in its comparative income statements:

($ in millions)	2015	2014	2013
Net income	$84	$82	$80

Required:

1. Prepare the journal entry at the beginning of 2016 to record the change in accounting principle. (Ignore income taxes.)
2. Briefly describe other steps Flay will take to report the change.
3. What amounts will Flay report for net income in its 2016–2014 comparative income statements?

E 20–9
Change in inventory methods; incomplete information
● LO20–3

Wolfgang Kitchens has always used the FIFO inventory costing method for both financial reporting and tax purposes. At the beginning of 2016, Wolfgang decided to change to the LIFO method. Net income in 2016 was correctly stated as $90 million. If the company had used LIFO in 2015, its cost of goods sold would have been higher by $7 million that year. Company accountants are able to determine that the cumulative net income for all years prior to 2015 would have been lower by $23 million if LIFO had been used all along, but have insufficient information to determine specific effects of using LIFO in 2014. Last year, Wolfgang reported the following net income amounts in its comparative income statements:

($ in millions)	2015	2014	2013
Net income	$94	$92	$90

Required:

1. Prepare the journal entry at the beginning of 2016 to record the change in accounting principle. (Ignore income taxes.)
2. Briefly describe other steps Wolfgang will take to report the change.
3. What amounts will Wolfgang report for net income in its 2016–2014 comparative income statements?

E 20–10
Change in depreciation methods
● LO20–3

For financial reporting, Clinton Poultry Farms has used the declining-balance method of depreciation for conveyor equipment acquired at the beginning of 2013 for $2,560,000. Its useful life was estimated to be six years with a $160,000 residual value. At the beginning of 2016, Clinton decides to change to the straight-line method. The effect of this change on depreciation for each year is as follows ($ in 000s):

Year	Straight-Line	Declining Balance	Difference
2013	$ 400	$ 853	$453
2014	400	569	169
2015	400	379	(21)
	$1,200	$1,801	$601

Required:

1. Briefly describe the way Clinton should report this accounting change in the 2015–2016 comparative financial statements.
2. Prepare any 2016 journal entry related to the change.

E 20–11
Change in depreciation methods
● LO20–3

The Canliss Milling Company purchased machinery on January 2, 2014, for $800,000. A five-year life was estimated and no residual value was anticipated. Canliss decided to use the straight-line depreciation method and recorded $160,000 in depreciation in 2014 and 2015. Early in 2016, the company changed its depreciation method to the sum-of-the-years'-digits (SYD) method.

Required:

1. Briefly describe the way Canliss should report this accounting change in the 2015–2016 comparative financial statements.
2. Prepare any 2016 journal entry related to the change.

E 20–12
Book royalties
● LO20–4

Dreighton Engineering Group receives royalties on a technical manual written by two of its engineers and sold to William B. Irving Publishing, Inc. Royalties are 10% of net sales, receivable on October 1 for sales in January through June and on April 1 for sales in July through December of the prior year. Sales of the manual began in July 2015, and Dreighton accrued royalty revenue of $31,000 at December 31, 2015, as follows:

Receivable—royalty revenue	31,000	
Royalty revenue		31,000

Dreighton received royalties of $36,000 on April 1, 2016, and $40,000 on October 1, 2016. Irving indicated to Dreighton on December 31 that book sales subject to royalties for the second half of 2016 are expected to be $500,000.

Required:

1. Prepare any journal entries Dreighton should record during 2016 related to the royalty revenue.
2. What adjustments, if any, should be made to retained earnings or to the 2015 financial statements? Explain.

E 20–13
Loss contingency
● LO20–4

The Commonwealth of Virginia filed suit in October 2014, against Northern Timber Corporation seeking civil penalties and injunctive relief for violations of environmental laws regulating forest conservation. When the financial statements were issued in 2015, Northern had not reached a settlement with state authorities, but legal counsel advised Northern Timber that it was probable the ultimate settlement would be $1,000,000 in penalties. The following entry was recorded:

Loss—litigation	1,000,000	
Liability—litigation		1,000,000

Late in 2016, a settlement was reached with state authorities to pay a total of $600,000 to cover the cost of violations.

Required:

1. Prepare any journal entries related to the change.
2. Briefly describe other steps Northern should take to report the change.

E 20–14
Warranty expense
● LO20–4

Woodmier Lawn Products introduced a new line of commercial sprinklers in 2015 that carry a one-year warranty against manufacturer's defects. Because this was the first product for which the company offered a warranty, trade publications were consulted to determine the experience of others in the industry. Based on that experience, warranty costs were expected to approximate 2% of sales. Sales of the sprinklers in 2015 were $2,500,000. Accordingly, the following entries relating to the contingency for warranty costs were recorded during the first year of selling the product:

Accrued liability and expense

Warranty expense (2% × $2,500,000)	50,000	
Estimated warranty liability		50,000

Actual expenditures (summary entry)

Estimated warranty liability	23,000	
Cash, wages payable, parts and supplies, etc		23,000

In late 2016, the company's claims experience was evaluated and it was determined that claims were far more than expected—3% of sales rather than 2%.

Required:

1. Assuming sales of the sprinklers in 2016 were $3,600,000 and warranty expenditures in 2016 totaled $88,000, prepare any journal entries related to the warranty.
2. Assuming sales of the sprinklers were discontinued after 2015, prepare any journal entry(s) in 2016 related to the warranty.

E 20–15
Deferred taxes; change in tax rates
● LO20–4

Bronson Industries reported a deferred tax liability of $8 million for the year ended December 31, 2015, related to a temporary difference of $20 million. The tax rate was 40%. The temporary difference is expected to reverse in 2017 at which time the deferred tax liability will become payable. There are no other temporary differences in 2015–2017. Assume a new tax law is enacted in 2016 that causes the tax rate to change from 40% to 30% beginning in 2017. (The rate remains 40% for 2016 taxes.) Taxable income in 2016 is $30 million.

Required:

1. Determine the effect of the change and prepare the appropriate journal entry to record Bronson's income tax expense in 2016.
2. What adjustment, if any, is needed to revise retained earnings as a result of the change?

E 20–16
Accounting change
● LO20–4

The Peridot Company purchased machinery on January 2, 2014, for $800,000. A five-year life was estimated and no residual value was anticipated. Peridot decided to use the straight-line depreciation method and recorded $160,000 in depreciation in 2014 and 2015. Early in 2016, the company revised the total estimated life of the machinery to eight years.

Required:

1. What type of change is this?
2. Briefly describe the accounting treatment for this change.
3. Determine depreciation for 2016.

E 20–17
Change in estimate; useful life and residual value of equipment
● LO20–4

Wardell Company purchased a mini computer on January 1, 2014, at a cost of $40,000. The computer has been depreciated using the straight-line method over an estimated five-year useful life with an estimated residual value of $4,000. On January 1, 2016, the estimate of useful life was changed to a total of 10 years, and the estimate of residual value was changed to $900.

Required:

1. Prepare the appropriate adjusting entry for depreciation in 2016 to reflect the revised estimate.
2. Repeat requirement 1 assuming that the company uses the sum-of-the-years'-digits method instead of the straight-line method.

E 20–18
Classifying accounting changes
● LO20–1 through LO20–5

Indicate with the appropriate letter the nature of each situation described below:

Type of Change

PR	Change in principle reported retrospectively
PP	Change in principle reported prospectively
E	Change in estimate
EP	Change in estimate resulting from a change in principle
R	Change in reporting entity
N	Not an accounting change

_____ 1. Change from declining balance depreciation to straight-line.
_____ 2. Change in the estimated useful life of office equipment.
_____ 3. Technological advance that renders worthless a patent with an unamortized cost of $45,00.
_____ 4. Change from determining lower of cost or market for the inventories by the individual item approach to the aggregate approach.
_____ 5. Change from LIFO inventory costing to the weighted-average inventory costing.
_____ 6. Settling a lawsuit for less than the amount accrued previously as a loss contingency.
_____ 7. Including in the consolidated financial statements a subsidiary acquired several years earlier that was appropriately not included in previous years.
_____ 8. Change by a retail store from reporting warranty expense on a pay-as-you-go basis to estimating the expense in the period of sale.
_____ 9. A shift of certain manufacturing overhead costs to inventory that previously were expensed as incurred to more accurately measure cost of goods sold. (Either method is generally acceptable.)
_____ 10. Pension plan assets for a defined benefit pension plan achieving a rate of return in excess of the amount anticipated.

E 20–19
Error correction; inventory error
● LO20–6

During 2016, WMC Corporation discovered that its ending inventories reported on its financial statements were misstated by the following amounts:

2014	understated by	$120,000
2015	overstated by	150,000

WMC uses the periodic inventory system and the FIFO cost method.

Required:

1. Determine the effect of these errors on retained earnings at January 1, 2016, before any adjustments. Explain your answer. (Ignore income taxes.)
2. Prepare a journal entry to correct the error.
3. What other step(s) would be taken in connection with the error?

E 20–20
Error corrections; investment
● LO20–6

On December 12, 2016, an investment costing $80,000 was sold for $100,000. The total of the sale proceeds was credited to the investment account.

Required:

1. Prepare the journal entry to correct the error assuming it is discovered before the books are adjusted or closed in 2016. (Ignore income taxes.)
2. Prepare the journal entry to correct the error assuming it is not discovered until early 2017. (Ignore income taxes.)

E 20–21
Error in amortization schedule
● LO20–6

Wilkins Food Products Inc. acquired a packaging machine from Lawrence Specialists Corporation. Lawrence completed construction of the machine on January 1, 2014. In payment for the machine Wilkins issued a three-year installment note to be paid in three equal payments at the end of each year. The payments include interest at the rate of 10%. Lawrence made a conceptual error in preparing the amortization schedule which Wilkins failed to discover until 2016. As a result of the error, Wilkins understated interest expense by $45,000 in 2014 and $40,000 in 2015.

Required:

1. Determine which accounts are incorrect as a result of these errors at January 1, 2016, before any adjustments. Explain your answer. (Ignore income taxes.)
2. Prepare a journal entry to correct the error.
3. What other step(s) would be taken in connection with the error?

E 20–22
Error correction; accrued interest on bonds
● LO20–6

At the end of 2015, Majors Furniture Company failed to accrue $61,000 of interest expense that accrued during the last five months of 2015 on bonds payable. The bonds mature in 2027. The discount on the bonds is amortized by the straight-line method. The following entry was recorded on February 1, 2016, when the semiannual interest was paid:

Interest expense	73,200	
Discount on bonds payable		1,200
Cash		72,000

Required:

Prepare any journal entry necessary to correct the error as well as any adjusting entry for 2016 related to the situation described. (Ignore income taxes.)

E 20–23
Error correction; three errors
● LO20–6

Below are three independent and unrelated errors.

a. On December 31, 2015, Wolfe-Bache Corporation failed to accrue office supplies expense of $1,800. In January 2016, when it received the bill from its supplier, Wolfe-Bache made the following entry:

Office supplies expense	1,800	
Cash		1,800

b. On the last day of 2015, Midwest Importers received a $90,000 prepayment from a tenant for 2016 rent of a building. Midwest recorded the receipt as rent revenue.

c. At the end of 2015, Dinkins-Lowery Corporation failed to accrue interest of $8,000 on a note receivable. At the beginning of 2016, when the company received the cash, it was recorded as interest revenue.

Required:

For each error:

1. What would be the effect of each error on the income statement and the balance sheet in the 2015 financial statements?
2. Prepare any journal entries each company should record in 2016 to correct the errors.

E 20–24
Inventory errors
● LO20–6

For each of the following inventory errors occurring in 2016, determine the effect of the error on 2016's cost of goods sold, net income, and retained earnings. Assume that the error is not discovered until 2017 and that a periodic inventory system is used. Ignore income taxes.

U = Understated O = Overstated NE = No effect

	Cost of Goods Sold	Net Income	Retained Earnings
(Example) 1. Overstatement of ending inventory	U	O	O
2. Overstatement of purchases			
3. Understatement of beginning inventory			
4. Freight-in charges are understated			
5. Understatement of ending inventory			
6. Understatement of purchases			
7. Overstatement of beginning inventory			
8. Understatement of purchases and understatement of ending inventory, by the same amount			

E 20–25
Classifying accounting changes and errors
● LO20–1 through LO20–6

Indicate with the appropriate letter the nature of each adjustment described below:

Type of Adjustment	
A.	Change in accounting principle (reported retrospectively)
B.	Change in accounting principle (exception reported prospectively)
C.	Change in estimate
D.	Change in estimate resulting from a change in principle
E.	Change in reporting entity
F.	Correction of an error

_____ 1. Change from expensing extraordinary repairs to capitalizing the expenditures.
_____ 2. Change in the residual value of machinery.
_____ 3. Change from FIFO inventory costing to LIFO inventory costing.
_____ 4. Change in the percentage used to determine warranty expense.
_____ 5. Change from LIFO inventory costing to FIFO inventory costing.
_____ 6. Change from reporting an investment by the equity method due to a reduction in the percentage of shares owned.
_____ 7. Change in the composition of a group of firms reporting on a consolidated basis.
_____ 8. Change from sum-of-the-years'-digits depreciation to straight-line.
_____ 9. Change from FIFO inventory costing to average inventory costing.
_____ 10. Change in actuarial assumptions for a defined benefit pension plan.

CPA and CMA Review Questions

CPA Exam Questions

KAPLAN CPA REVIEW

The following questions are adapted from a variety of sources including questions developed by the AICPA Board of Examiners and those used in the Kaplan CPA Review Course to study accounting changes and errors while preparing for the CPA examination. Determine the response that best completes the statements or questions.

● LO20–3

1. Kap Company switched from the sum-of-the-years-digits depreciation method to straight-line depreciation in 2016. The change affects machinery purchased at the beginning of 2014 at a cost of $36,000. The machinery has an estimated life of five years and an estimated residual value of $1,800. What is Kap's 2016 depreciation expense?
   a. $4,200
   b. $4,560
   c. $4,800
   d. $7,920

● LO20–4

2. Retrospective restatement usually is appropriate for a change in

	Accounting Principle	Accounting Estimate
a.	Yes	Yes
b.	Yes	No
c.	No	Yes
d.	No	No

● LO20–4

3. For 2015, Pac Co. estimated its two-year equipment warranty costs based on $100 per unit sold in 2015. Experience during 2016 indicated that the estimate should have been based on $110 per unit. The effect of this $10 difference from the estimate is reported
   a. in 2016 income from continuing operations.
   b. as an accounting change, net of tax, below 2016 income from continuing operations.
   c. as an accounting change requiring 2015 financial statements to be restated.
   d. as a correction of an error requiring 2015 financial statements to be restated.

● LO20–5

4. A company has included in its consolidated financial statements this year a subsidiary acquired several years ago that was appropriately excluded from consolidation last year. This results in
   a. an accounting change that should be reported prospectively.
   b. an accounting change that should be reported by restating the financial statements of all prior periods presented.
   c. a correction of an error.
   d. neither an accounting change nor a correction of an error.

● LO20–6

5. Conn Co. reported a retained earnings balance of $400,000 at December 31, 2015. In August 2016, Conn determined that insurance premiums of $60,000 for the three-year period beginning January 1, 2015, had been paid and fully expensed in 2015. Conn has a 30% income tax rate. What amount should Conn report as adjusted beginning retained earnings in its 2016 statement of retained earnings?
   a. $420,000
   b. $428,000
   c. $440,000
   d. $442,000

● LO20–6

6. During 2017, Paul Company discovered that the ending inventories reported on its financial statements were incorrect by the following amounts:

2015	$ 60,000 understated
2016	75,000 overstated

   Paul uses the periodic inventory system to ascertain year-end quantities that are converted to dollar amounts using the FIFO cost method. Prior to any adjustments for these errors and ignoring income taxes, Paul's retained earnings at January 1, 2017, would be
   a. correct.
   b. $15,000 overstated.
   c. $75,000 overstated.
   d. $135,000 overstated.

International Financial Reporting Standards are tested on the CPA exam along with U.S. GAAP. The following questions deal with the application of IFRS in accounting for accounting changes and errors.

● LO20–7 IFRS

7. Under IFRS, how should changes in accounting policy be recognized in the financial statements?
   a. Prospectively.
   b. Retroactively for all periods presented.
   c. In the statement of cash flows.
   d. In the statement of comprehensive income.

● LO20–7 IFRS

8. According to IAS 8, how should prior period errors that are discovered in a subsequent reporting period be recognized in the financial statements?
   a. As an adjustment to beginning retained earnings for the reporting period in which the error was discovered.
   b. As a note in the financial statements that the error was previously made but has since been corrected.
   c. In the statement of comprehensive income.
   d. Retroactively for all periods presented.

● LO20–7 IFRS

9. Using IFRS, a change in accounting policy for which a standard does not include specific transitional provisions should be applied
   a. prospectively.
   b. practicably.
   c. in accordance with management's judgment.
   d. retrospectively.

● LO20–7 IFRS

10. Using IFRS, how should prior period errors that are discovered in a subsequent reporting period be recognized in the financial statements?
   a. As an adjustment to beginning retained earnings for the reporting period in which the error was discovered.
   b. As a note in the financial statements that the error was previously made but has since been corrected.
   c. In the current period if it's not considered practicable to report it retrospectively.
   d. In the statement of comprehensive income.

● LO20–7 IFRS

11. Under IFRS, changes in accounting policies are
   a. permitted if the change will result in a more reliable and more relevant presentation of the financial statements.
   b. permitted if the entity encounters new transactions, events, or conditions that are substantively different from existing or previous transactions.
   c. required on material transactions, if the entity had previously accounted for similar, though immaterial, transactions under an unacceptable accounting method.
   d. required if an alternate accounting policy gives rise to a material change in assets, liabilities, or the current-year net income.

● LO20–7 IFRS

12. Upon first-time adoption of IFRS, an entity may elect to use fair value as deemed cost for
   a. biological assets related to agricultural activity for which there is *no* active market.
   b. intangible assets for which there is *no* active market.
   c. any individual item of property, plant, and equipment.
   d. financial liabilities that are *not* held for trading.

● LO20–7 IFRS

13. On July 1, year 2, a company decided to adopt IFRS. The company's first IFRS reporting period is as of and for the year ended December 31, year 2. The company will present one year of comparative information. What is the company's date of transition to IFRS?
   a. January 1, year 1.
   b. January 1, year 2.
   c. July 1, year 2.
   d. December 31, year 2.

● LO20–7 IFRS

14. Which of the following statements is true regarding correcting errors in previously issued financial statements prepared in accordance with International Financial Reporting Standards?
   a. The error can be reported in the current period if it's not considered practicable to report it retrospectively.
   b. The error can be reported in the current period if it's not considered practicable to report it prospectively.
   c. The error can be reported prospectively if it's not considered practicable to report it retrospectively.
   d. Retrospective application is required with no exception.

● LO20–7

15. Which of the accounting changes listed below is more associated with financial statements prepared in accordance with U.S. GAAP than with International Financial Reporting Standards?

a. Change in reporting entity.
b. Change to the LIFO method from the FIFO method.
c. Change in accounting estimate.
d. Change in depreciation methods.

CMA Exam Questions

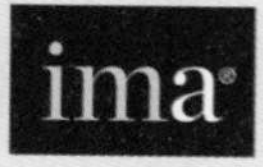

The following questions dealing with accounting changes and errors are adapted from questions that previously appeared on Certified Management Accountant (CMA) examinations. The CMA designation sponsored by the Institute of Management Accountants (**www.imanet.org**) provides members with an objective measure of knowledge and competence in the field of management accounting. Determine the response that best completes the statements or questions.

● LO20–4

1. A change in the liability for warranty costs requires
   a. presenting prior-period financial statements as previously reported.
   b. presenting the effect of pro forma data on income and earnings per share for all prior periods presented.
   c. reporting an adjustment to the beginning retained earnings balance in the statement of retained earnings.
   d. reporting current and future financial statements on the new basis.

● LO20–6

2. In a review of the May 31, 2016, financial statements during the normal year-end closing process, it was discovered that the interest income accrual on Simpson Company's notes receivable was omitted. The amounts omitted were calculated as follows:

May 31, 2015	$ 91,800
May 31, 2016	100,200

   The May 31, 2016, entry to correct for these errors, ignoring the effect of income taxes, includes a
   a. credit to retained earnings for $91,800.
   b. credit to interest revenue for $91,800.
   c. debit to interest revenue for $100,200.
   d. credit to interest receivable for $100,200.

● LO20–6

3. An example of an item that should be reported as a prior-period adjustment in a company's annual financial statements is
   a. a settlement resulting from litigation.
   b. an adjustment of income taxes.
   c. a correction of an error that occurred in a prior period.
   d. an adjustment of utility revenue because of rate revisions ordered by a regulatory commission.

Problems

An alternate exercise and problem set is available at the Connect library.

P 20–1
Change in inventory costing methods; comparative income statements
● LO20–2

The Cecil-Booker Vending Company changed its method of valuing inventory from the average cost method to the FIFO cost method at the beginning of 2016. At December 31, 2015, inventories were $120,000 (average cost basis) and were $124,000 a year earlier. Cecil-Booker's accountants determined that the inventories would have totaled $155,000 at December 31, 2015, and $160,000 at December 31, 2014, if determined on a FIFO basis. A tax rate of 40% is in effect for all years.

One hundred thousand common shares were outstanding each year. Income from continuing operations was $400,000 in 2015 and $525,000 in 2016. There were no discontinued operations either year.

Required:

1. Prepare the journal entry to record the change in accounting principle. (All tax effects should be reflected in the deferred tax liability account.)
2. Prepare the 2016–2015 comparative income statements beginning with income from continuing operations. Include per share amounts.

P 20–2
Change in principle; change in method of accounting for long-term construction
● LO20–2

The Pyramid Construction Company has used the completed-contract method of accounting for construction contracts during its first two years of operation, 2014 and 2015. At the beginning of 2016, Pyramid decided to change to the percentage-of-completion method for both tax and financial reporting purposes. The following table presents information concerning the change for 2014–2016. The income tax rate for all years is 40%.

	Income before Income Tax				
	Percentage of Completion Method	Completed Contract Method	Difference	Income Tax Effect	Difference after Tax
2014	$ 90,000	$60,000	$30,000	$12,000	$18,000
2015	45,000	36,000	9,000	3,600	5,400
Total	$135,000	$96,000	$39,000	$15,600	$23,400
2016	$ 51,000	$46,000	$ 5,000	$ 2,000	$ 3,000

Pyramid issued 50,000 $1 par, common shares for $230,000 when the business began, and there have been no changes in paid-in capital since then. Dividends were not paid the first year, but $10,000 cash dividends were paid in both 2015 and 2016.

Required:

1. Prepare the journal entry to record the change in accounting principle. (All tax effects except those resulting from inventory method changes should be reflected in the deferred tax liability account.)
2. Prepare the 2016–2015 comparative income statements beginning with income before income taxes.
3. Prepare the 2016–2015 comparative statements of shareholders' equity. (Hint: The 2014 statements reported retained earnings of $36,000. This is $60,000 − [$60,000 × 40%].

P 20–3
Change in inventory costing methods; comparative income statements
● LO20–2, LO20–3

Shown below are net income amounts as they would be determined by Weihrich Steel Company by each of three different inventory costing methods ($ in 000s).

	FIFO	Average Cost	LIFO
Pre-2015	$2,800	$2,540	$2,280
2015	750	600	540
	$3,550	$3,140	$2,820

Required:

1. Assume that Weihrich used FIFO before 2016, and then in 2016 decided to switch to average cost. Prepare the journal entry to record the change in accounting principle and briefly describe any other steps Weihrich should take to appropriately report the situation. (Ignore income tax effects.)
2. Assume that Weihrich used FIFO before 2016, and then in 2016 decided to switch to LIFO. Assume accounting records are inadequate to determine LIFO information prior to 2016. Therefore, the 2015 ($540) and pre-2015 ($2,280) data are not available. Prepare the journal entry to record the change in accounting principle and briefly describe any other steps Weihrich should take to appropriately report the situation. (Ignore income tax effects.)
3. Assume that Weihrich used FIFO before 2016, and then in 2016 decided to switch to LIFO cost. Weihrich's records of inventory purchases and sales are not available for several previous years. Therefore, the pre-2015 LIFO information ($2,280) is not available. However, Weihrich does have the information needed to apply LIFO on a prospective basis beginning in 2015. Prepare the journal entry to record the change in accounting principle and briefly describe any other steps Weihrich should take to appropriately report the situation. (Ignore income tax effects.)

P 20–4
Change in inventory methods
● LO20–2

The Rockwell Corporation uses a periodic inventory system and has used the FIFO cost method since inception of the company in 1977. In 2016, the company decided to change to the average cost method. Data for 2016 are as follows:

Beginning inventory, FIFO (5,000 units @ $30.00)		$150,000
Purchases:		
5,000 units @ $36.00	$180,000	
5,000 units @ $40.00	200,000	380,000
Cost of goods available for sale		$530,000
Sales for 2016 (8,000 units @ $70.00)		$560,000

Additional Information:

1. The company's effective income tax rate is 40% for all years.
2. If the company had used the average cost method prior to 2016, ending inventory for 2015 would have been $130,000.
3. 7,000 units remained in inventory at the end of 2016.

Required:

1. Prepare the journal entry at the beginning of 2016 to record the change in principle.
2. In the 2016–2014 comparative financial statements, what will be the amounts of cost of goods sold and inventory reported for 2016?

P 20–5
Change in inventory methods
● LO20–2

Fantasy Fashions had used the LIFO method of costing inventories, but at the beginning of 2016 decided to change to the FIFO method. The inventory as reported at the end of 2015 using LIFO would have been $20 million higher using FIFO.

Retained earnings reported at the end of 2014 and 2015 was $240 million and $260 million, respectively (reflecting the LIFO method). Those amounts reflecting the FIFO method would have been $250 million and $272 million, respectively. 2015 net income reported at the end of 2015 was $28 million (LIFO method) but would have been $30 million using FIFO. After changing to FIFO, 2016 net income was $36 million. Dividends of $8 million were paid each year. The tax rate is 40%.

Required:

1. Prepare the journal entry at the beginning of 2016 to record the change in accounting principle.
2. In the 2016–2015 comparative income statements, what will be the amounts of net income reported for 2015 and 2016?
3. Prepare the 2016–2015 retained earnings column of the comparative statements of shareholders' equity.

P 20–6
Change in principle; change in depreciation methods
● LO20–3

During 2014 and 2015, Faulkner Manufacturing used the sum-of-the-years'-digits (SYD) method of depreciation for its depreciable assets, for both financial reporting and tax purposes. At the beginning of 2016, Faulkner decided to change to the straight-line method for both financial reporting and tax purposes. A tax rate of 40% is in effect for all years.

For an asset that cost $21,000 with an estimated residual value of $1,000 and an estimated useful life of 10 years, the depreciation under different methods is as follows:

Year	Straight Line	SYD	Difference
2014	$2,000	$3,636	$1,636
2015	2,000	3,273	1,273
	$4,000	$6,909	$2,909

Required:

1. Describe the way Faulkner should account for the change described. Include in your answer any journal entry Faulkner will record in 2016 related to the change and any required footnote disclosures.
2. Suppose instead that Faulkner previously used straight-line depreciation and changed to sum-of-the-years'-digits in 2016. Describe the way Faulkner should account for the change. Include in your answer any journal entry Faulkner will record in 2016 related to the change and any required note disclosures.

P 20–7
Depletion; change in estimate
● LO20–4

In 2016, the Marion Company purchased land containing a mineral mine for $1,600,000. Additional costs of $600,000 were incurred to develop the mine. Geologists estimated that 400,000 tons of ore would be extracted. After the ore is removed, the land will have a resale value of $100,000.

To aid in the extraction, Marion built various structures and small storage buildings on the site at a cost of $150,000. These structures have a useful life of 10 years. The structures cannot be moved after the ore has been removed and will be left at the site. In addition, new equipment costing $80,000 was purchased and installed at the site. Marion does not plan to move the equipment to another site, but estimates that it can be sold at auction for $4,000 after the mining project is completed.

In 2016, 50,000 tons of ore were extracted and sold. In 2017, the estimate of total tons of ore in the mine was revised from 400,000 to 487,500. During 2017, 80,000 tons were extracted.

Required:

1. Compute depletion and depreciation of the mine and the mining facilities and equipment for 2016 and 2017. Marion uses the units-of-production method to determine depreciation on mining facilities and equipment.
2. Compute the book value of the mineral mine, structures, and equipment as of December 31, 2017.

P 20–8
Accounting changes; six situations
● LO20–1, LO20–3, LO20–4

Described below are six independent and unrelated situations involving accounting changes. Each change occurs during 2016 before any adjusting entries or closing entries were prepared. Assume the tax rate for each company is 40% in all years. Any tax effects should be adjusted through the deferred tax liability account.

a. Fleming Home Products introduced a new line of commercial awnings in 2015 that carry a one-year warranty against manufacturer's defects. Based on industry experience, warranty costs were expected to approximate 3% of sales. Sales of the awnings in 2015 were $3,500,000. Accordingly, warranty expense and a warranty liability of $105,000 were recorded in 2015. In late 2016, the company's claims experience was evaluated and it was determined that claims were far fewer than expected: 2% of sales rather than 3%. Sales of the awnings in 2016 were $4,000,000 and warranty expenditures in 2016 totaled $91,000.

b. On December 30, 2012, Rival Industries acquired its office building at a cost of $1,000,000. It was depreciated on a straight-line basis assuming a useful life of 40 years and no salvage value. However, plans were finalized in 2016 to relocate the company headquarters at the end of 2020. The vacated office building will have a salvage value at that time of $700,000.

c. Hobbs-Barto Merchandising, Inc., changed inventory cost methods to LIFO from FIFO at the end of 2016 for both financial statement and income tax purposes. Under FIFO, the inventory at January 1, 2016, is $690,000.

d. At the beginning of 2013, the Hoffman Group purchased office equipment at a cost of $330,000. Its useful life was estimated to be 10 years with no salvage value. The equipment was depreciated by the sum-of-the-years'-digits method. On January 1, 2016, the company changed to the straight-line method.

e. In November 2014, the State of Minnesota filed suit against Huggins Manufacturing Company, seeking penalties for violations of clean air laws. When the financial statements were issued in 2015, Huggins had not reached a settlement with state authorities, but legal counsel advised Huggins that it was probable the company would have to pay $200,000 in penalties. Accordingly, the following entry was recorded:

Loss—litigation	200,000	
Liability—litigation		200,000

Late in 2016, a settlement was reached with state authorities to pay a total of $350,000 in penalties.

f. At the beginning of 2016, Jantzen Specialties, which uses the sum-of-the-years'-digits method, changed to the straight-line method for newly acquired buildings and equipment. The change increased current year net earnings by $445,000.

Required:

For each situation

1. Identify the type of change.
2. Prepare any journal entry necessary as a direct result of the change as well as any adjusting entry for 2016 related to the situation described.
3. Briefly describe any other steps that should be taken to appropriately report the situation.

P 20–9
Accounting changes; identify type and reporting approach
● LO20–1 through LO20–4

At the beginning of 2016, Wagner Implements undertook a variety of changes in accounting methods, corrected several errors, and instituted new accounting policies.

Required:

On a sheet of paper numbered from 1 to 10, indicate for each item below the type of change and the reporting approach Wagner would use.

Type of Change (choose one)	Reporting Approach (choose one)
P. Change in accounting principle	R. Retrospective approach
E. Change in accounting estimate	P. Prospective approach
EP. Change in estimate resulting from a change in principle	
X. Correction of an error	
N. Neither an accounting change nor an accounting error.	

Change:

1. By acquiring additional stock, Wagner increased its investment in Wise, Inc., from a 12% interest to 25% and changed its method of accounting for the investment to the equity method.
2. Wagner instituted a postretirement benefit plan for its employees in 2016. Wagner did not previously have such a plan.
3. Wagner changed its method of depreciating computer equipment from the SYD method to the straight-line method.

4. Wagner determined that a liability insurance premium it both paid and expensed in 2015 covered the 2015–2017 period.
5. Wagner custom-manufactures farming equipment on a contract basis. Wagner switched its accounting for these long-term contracts from the completed-contract method to the percentage-of-completion method.
6. Due to an unexpected relocation, Wagner determined that its office building, previously depreciated using a 45-year life, should be depreciated using an 18-year life.
7. Wagner offers a three-year warranty on the farming equipment it sells. Manufacturing efficiencies caused Wagner to reduce its expectation of warranty costs from 2% of sales to 1% of sales.
8. Wagner changed from LIFO to FIFO to account for its materials and work-in-process inventories.
9. Wagner changed from FIFO to average cost to account for its equipment inventory.
10. Wagner sells extended service contracts on some of its equipment sold. Wagner performs services related to these contracts over several years, so in 2016 Wagner changed from recognizing revenue from these service contracts on a cash basis to the accrual basis.

P 20–10
Inventory errors
● LO20–6

You have been hired as the new controller for the Ralston Company. Shortly after joining the company in 2016, you discover the following errors related to the 2014 and 2015 financial statements:

a. Inventory at 12/31/2014 was understated by $6,000.
b. Inventory at 12/31/2015 was overstated by $9,000.
c. On 12/31/2015, inventory was purchased for $3,000. The company did not record the purchase until the inventory was paid for early in 2016. At that time, the purchase was recorded by a debit to purchases and a credit to cash.

The company uses a periodic inventory system.

Required:

1. Assuming that the errors were discovered after the 2015 financial statements were issued, analyze the effect of the errors on 2015 and 2014 cost of goods sold, net income, and retained earnings. (Ignore income taxes.)
2. Prepare a journal entry to correct the errors.
3. What other step(s) would be taken in connection with the error?

P 20–11
Error correction; change in depreciation method
● LO20–6

The Collins Corporation purchased office equipment at the beginning of 2014 and capitalized a cost of $2,000,000. This cost included the following expenditures:

Purchase price	$1,850,000
Freight charges	30,000
Installation charges	20,000
Annual maintenance charge	100,000
Total	$2,000,000

The company estimated an eight-year useful life for the equipment. No residual value is anticipated. The double-declining-balance method was used to determine depreciation expense for 2014 and 2015.

In 2016, after the 2015 financial statements were issued, the company decided to switch to the straight-line depreciation method for this equipment. At that time, the company's controller discovered that the original cost of the equipment incorrectly included one year of annual maintenance charges for the equipment.

Required:

1. Ignoring income taxes, prepare the appropriate correcting entry for the equipment capitalization error discovered in 2016.
2. Ignoring income taxes, prepare any 2016 journal entry(s) related to the change in depreciation methods.

P 20–12
Accounting changes and error correction; eight situations; tax effects ignored
● LO20–1 through LO20–4, LO20–6

Williams-Santana, Inc., is a manufacturer of high-tech industrial parts that was started in 2004 by two talented engineers with little business training. In 2016, the company was acquired by one of its major customers. As part of an internal audit, the following facts were discovered. The audit occurred during 2016 before any adjusting entries or closing entries were prepared.

a. A five-year casualty insurance policy was purchased at the beginning of 2014 for $35,000. The full amount was debited to insurance expense at the time.
b. Effective January 1, 2016, the company changed the salvage value used in calculating depreciation for its office building. The building cost $600,000 on December 29, 2005, and has been depreciated on a straight-line basis assuming a useful life of 40 years and a salvage value of $100,000. Declining real estate values in the area indicate that the salvage value will be no more than $25,000.

c. On December 31, 2015, merchandise inventory was overstated by $25,000 due to a mistake in the physical inventory count using the periodic inventory system.

d. The company changed inventory cost methods to FIFO from LIFO at the end of 2016 for both financial statement and income tax purposes. The change will cause a $960,000 increase in the beginning inventory at January 1, 2017.

e. At the end of 2015, the company failed to accrue $15,500 of sales commissions earned by employees during 2015. The expense was recorded when the commissions were paid in early 2016.

f. At the beginning of 2014, the company purchased a machine at a cost of $720,000. Its useful life was estimated to be 10 years with no salvage value. The machine has been depreciated by the double-declining balance method. Its book value on December 31, 2015, was $460,800. On January 1, 2016, the company changed to the straight-line method.

g. Warranty expense is determined each year as 1% of sales. Actual payment experience of recent years indicates that 0.75% is a better indication of the actual cost. Management effects the change in 2016. Credit sales for 2016 are $4,000,000; in 2015 they were $3,700,000.

Required:

For each situation

1. Identify whether it represents an accounting change or an error. If an accounting change, identify the type of change.
2. Prepare any journal entry necessary as a direct result of the change or error correction as well as any adjusting entry for 2016 related to the situation described. (Ignore tax effects.)
3. Briefly describe any other steps that should be taken to appropriately report the situation.

P 20–13
Accounting changes and error correction; eight situations; tax effects considered
● **LO20–1 through LO20–4, LO20–6**

(Note: This problem is a variation of P 20–12, modified to consider income tax effects.) Williams-Santana, Inc., is a manufacturer of high-tech industrial parts that was started in 2004 by two talented engineers with little business training. In 2016, the company was acquired by one of its major customers. As part of an internal audit, the following facts were discovered. The audit occurred during 2016 before any adjusting entries or closing entries were prepared. The income tax rate is 40% for all years.

a. A five-year casualty insurance policy was purchased at the beginning of 2014 for $35,000. The full amount was debited to insurance expense at the time.

b. Effective January 1, 2016, the company changed the salvage values used in calculating depreciation for its office building. The building cost $600,000 on December 29, 2005, and has been depreciated on a straight-line basis assuming a useful life of 40 years and a salvage value of $100,000. Declining real estate values in the area indicate that the salvage value will be no more than $25,000.

c. On December 31, 2015, merchandise inventory was overstated by $25,000 due to a mistake in the physical inventory count using the periodic inventory system.

d. The company changed inventory cost methods to FIFO from LIFO at the end of 2016 for both financial statement and income tax purposes. The change will cause a $960,000 increase in the beginning inventory at January 1, 2017.

e. At the end of 2015, the company failed to accrue $15,500 of sales commissions earned by employees during 2015. The expense was recorded when the commissions were paid in early 2016.

f. At the beginning of 2014, the company purchased a machine at a cost of $720,000. Its useful life was estimated to be ten years with no salvage value. The machine has been depreciated by the double-declining balance method. Its book value on December 31, 2015, was $460,800. On January 1, 2016, the company changed to the straight-line method.

g. Warranty expense is determined each year as 1% of sales. Actual payment experience of recent years indicates that 0.75% is a better indication of the actual cost. Management effects the change in 2016. Credit sales for 2016 are $4,000,000; in 2015 they were $3,700,000.

Required:

For each situation

1. Identify whether it represents an accounting change or an error. If an accounting change, identify the type of change.
2. Prepare any journal entry necessary as a direct result of the change or error correction as well as any adjusting entry for 2016 related to the situation described. Any tax effects should be adjusted for through Income tax payable or Refund-income tax.
3. Briefly describe any other steps that should be taken to appropriately report the situation.

P 20–14
Errors; change in estimate; change in principle; restatement of previous financial statements
● LO20–1, LO20–3, LO20–4, LO20–6

Whaley Distributors is a wholesale distributor of electronic components. Financial statements for the years ended December 31, 2014 and 2015, reported the following amounts and subtotals ($ in millions):

	Assets	Liabilities	Shareholders' Equity	Net Income	Expenses
2014	$740	$330	$410	$210	$150
2015	820	400	420	230	175

In 2016 the following situations occurred or came to light:

a. Internal auditors discovered that ending inventories reported on the financial statements the two previous years were misstated due to faulty internal controls. The errors were in the following amounts:

2014 inventory	Overstated by $12 million
2015 inventory	Understated by $10 million

b. A liability was accrued in 2014 for a probable payment of $7 million in connection with a lawsuit ultimately settled in December 2016 for $4 million.

c. A patent costing $18 million at the beginning of 2014, expected to benefit operations for a total of six years, has not been amortized since acquired.

d. Whaley's conveyer equipment was depreciated by the sum-of-the-years'-digits (SYD) basis since it was acquired at the beginning of 2014 at a cost of $30 million. It has an expected useful life of five years and no expected residual value. At the beginning of 2016, Whaley decided to switch to straight-line depreciation.

Required:

For each situation

1. Prepare any journal entry necessary as a direct result of the change or error correction as well as any adjusting entry for 2016 related to the situation described. (Ignore tax effects.)
2. Determine the amounts to be reported for each of the five items shown above from the 2014 and 2015 financial statements when those amounts are reported again in the 2014–2016 comparative financial statements.

P 20–15
Correction of errors; six errors
● LO20–6

Conrad Playground Supply underwent a restructuring in 2016. The company conducted a thorough internal audit, during which the following facts were discovered. The audit occurred during 2016 before any adjusting entries or closing entries are prepared.

a. Additional computers were acquired at the beginning of 2014 and added to the company's office network. The $45,000 cost of the computers was inadvertently recorded as maintenance expense. Computers have five-year useful lives and no material salvage value. This class of equipment is depreciated by the straight-line method.

b. Two weeks prior to the audit, the company paid $17,000 for assembly tools and recorded the expenditure as office supplies. The error was discovered a week later.

c. On December 31, 2015, merchandise inventory was understated by $78,000 due to a mistake in the physical inventory count. The company uses the periodic inventory system.

d. Two years earlier, the company recorded a 4% stock dividend (2,000 common shares, $1 par) as follows:

Retained earnings	2,000	
Common stock		2,000

The shares had a market price at the time of $12 per share.

e. At the end of 2015, the company failed to accrue $104,000 of interest expense that accrued during the last four months of 2015 on bonds payable. The bonds, which were issued at face value, mature in 2020. The following entry was recorded on March 1, 2016, when the semiannual interest was paid:

Interest expense	156,000	
Cash		156,000

f. A three-year liability insurance policy was purchased at the beginning of 2015 for $72,000. The full premium was debited to insurance expense at the time.

Required:

For each error, prepare any journal entry necessary to correct the error as well as any year-end adjusting entry for 2016 related to the situation described. (Ignore income taxes.)

P 20–16
Integrating problem; errors; deferred taxes; contingency; change in tax rates
● LO20–6

You are internal auditor for Shannon Supplies, Inc., and are reviewing the company's preliminary financial statements. The statements, prepared after making the adjusting entries, but before closing entries for the year ended December 31, 2016, are as follows:

SHANNON SUPPLIES, INC.
Balance Sheet
December 31, 2016

Assets	($ in 000s)
Cash	$2,400
Investments	250
Accounts receivable, net	810
Inventory	1,060
Property, plant, and equipment	1,240
Less: Accumulated depreciation	(560)
Total assets	$5,200
Liabilities and Stockholders' Equity	
Accounts payable and accrued expenses	$3,320
Income tax payable	220
Common stock, $1 par	200
Additional paid-in capital	750
Retained earnings	710
Total liabilities and shareholders' equity	$5,200

SHANNON SUPPLIES, INC.
Income Statement
For the Year Ended December 31, 2016

Sales revenue		$3,400
Operating expenses:		
Cost of goods sold	$1,140	
Selling and administrative	896	
Depreciation	84	2,120
Income before income tax		$1,280
Income tax expense		(512)
Net income		$ 768

Shannon's income tax rate was 40% in 2016 and previous years. During the course of the audit, the following additional information (not considered when the above statements were prepared) was obtained:

a. Shannon's investment portfolio consists of blue chip stocks held for long-term appreciation. To raise working capital, some of the shares with an original cost of $180,000 were sold in May 2016. Shannon accountants debited cash and credited investments for the $220,000 proceeds of the sale.

b. At December 31, 2016, the fair value of the remaining securities in the portfolio was $274,000.

c. The state of Alabama filed suit against Shannon in October 2014 seeking civil penalties and injunctive relief for violations of environmental regulations regulating emissions. Shannon's legal counsel previously believed that an unfavorable outcome was not probable, but based on negotiations with state attorneys in 2016, now believe eventual payment to the state of $130,000 is probable, most likely to be paid in 2019.

d. The $1,060,000 inventory total, which was based on a physical count at December 31, 2016, was priced at cost. Based on your conversations with company accountants, you determined that the inventory cost was overstated by $132,000.

e. Electronic counters costing $80,000 were added to the equipment on December 29, 2015. The cost was charged to repairs.

f. Shannon's equipment on which the counters were installed had a remaining useful life of four years on December 29, 2015, and is being depreciated by the straight-line method for both financial and tax reporting.

g. A new tax law was enacted in 2016 which will cause Shannon's income tax rate to change from 40% to 35% beginning in 2017.

Required:

Prepare journal entries to record the effects on Shannon's accounting records at December 31, 2016, for each of the items described above. Show all calculations.

P 20–17
Integrating problem; error; depreciation; deferred taxes
● LO20–6

George Young Industries (GYI) acquired industrial robots at the beginning of 2013 and added them to the company's assembly process. During 2016, management became aware that the $1 million cost of the machinery was inadvertently recorded as repair expense on GYI's books and on its income tax return. The industrial robots have 10-year useful lives and no material salvage value. This class of equipment is depreciated by the straight-line method for financial reporting purposes and for tax purposes it is considered to be MACRS 7-year property (cost deducted over 7 years by the modified accelerated recovery system as follows):

Year	MACRS Deductions
2013	$ 142,900
2014	244,900
2015	174,900
2016	124,900
2017	89,300
2018	89,200
2019	89,300
2020	44,600
Totals	$ 1,000,000

The tax rate is 40% for all years involved.

Required:

1. Prepare any journal entry necessary as a direct result of the error described.
2. Briefly describe any other steps GYI would take to appropriately report the situation.
3. Prepare the adjusting entry for 2016 depreciation.

Broaden Your Perspective

Apply your critical-thinking ability to the knowledge you've gained. These cases will provide you an opportunity to develop your research, analysis, judgment, and communication skills. You also will work with other students, integrate what you've learned, apply it in real-world situations, and consider its global and ethical ramifications. This practice will broaden your knowledge and further develop your decision-making abilities.

Integrating Case 20–1
Change to dollar-value LIFO
● LO20–3

Webster Products, Inc., adopted the dollar-value LIFO method of determining inventory costs for financial and income tax reporting on January 1, 2016. Webster continues to use the FIFO method for internal decision-making purposes. Webster's FIFO inventories at December 31, 2016, 2017, and 2018, were $300,000, $412,500, and $585,000, respectively. Internally generated cost indexes are used to convert FIFO inventory amounts to dollar-value LIFO amounts. Webster estimated these indexes as follows:

2016	1.00
2017	1.25
2018	1.50

Required:

1. Determine Webster's dollar-value LIFO inventory at December 31, 2017 and 2018.
2. Describe how the change should have been reported in Webster's 2016 financial statements.

Communication Case 20–2
Change in inventory method; disclosure note
● LO20–2

Mayfair Department Stores, Inc., operates over 30 retail stores in the Pacific Northwest. Prior to 2016, the company used the FIFO method to value its inventory. In 2016, Mayfair decided to switch to the dollar-value LIFO retail inventory method. One of your responsibilities as assistant controller is to prepare the disclosure note describing the change in method that will be included in the company's 2016 financial statements. Kenneth Meier, the controller, provided the following information:

- Internally developed retail price indexes are used to adjust for the effects of changing prices.
- If the change had not been made, cost of goods sold for the year would have been $22 million lower. The company's income tax rate is 40% and there were 100 million shares of common stock outstanding during 2016.
- The cumulative effect of the change on prior years' income is not determinable.
- The reasons for the change were (a) to provide a more consistent matching of merchandise costs with sales revenue, and (b) the new method provides a more comparable basis of accounting with competitors that also use the LIFO method.

Required:

1. Prepare for Kenneth Meier the disclosure note that will be included in the 2016 financial statements.
2. Explain why the "cumulative effect of the change on prior years' income is not determinable."

Ethics Case 20–3
Softening the blow
● LO20–1, LO20–2, LO20–3

Late one Thursday afternoon, Joy Martin, a veteran audit manager with a regional CPA firm, was reviewing documents for a long-time client of the firm, AMT Transport. The year-end audit was scheduled to begin Monday.

For three months, the economy had been in a down cycle and the transportation industry was particularly hard hit. As a result, Joy expected AMT's financial results would not be pleasant news to shareholders. However, what Joy saw in the preliminary statements made her sigh aloud. Results were much worse than she feared.

"Larry (the company president) already is in the doghouse with shareholders," Joy thought to herself. "When they see these numbers, they'll hang him out to dry."

"I wonder if he's considered some strategic accounting changes," she thought, after reflecting on the situation. "The bad news could be softened quite a bit by changing inventory methods from LIFO to FIFO or reconsidering some of the estimates used in other areas."

Required:

1. How would the actions contemplated contribute toward "softening" the bad news?
2. Do you perceive an ethical dilemma? What would be the likely impact of following up on Joy's thoughts? Who would benefit? Who would be injured?

Analysis Case 20–4
Change in inventory methods; concepts
● LO20–2, LO20–3

Generally accepted accounting principles should be applied consistently from period to period. However, changes within a company, as well as changes in the external economic environment, may force a company to change an accounting method. The specific reporting requirements when a company changes from one generally accepted inventory method to another depend on the methods involved.

Required:

Explain the accounting treatment for a change in inventory method (a) not involving LIFO, (b) from the LIFO method, and (c) to the LIFO method. Explain the logic underlying those treatments. Also, describe how disclosure requirements are designed to address the departure from consistency and comparability of changes in accounting principle.

Communication Case 20–5
Change in loss contingency; write a memo
● LO20–4

Late in 2016, you and two other officers of Curbo Fabrications Corporation just returned from a meeting with officials of The City of Jackson. The meeting was unexpectedly favorable even though it culminated in a settlement with city authorities that your company pay a total of $475,000 to cover the cost of violations of city construction codes. Jackson filed suit in November 2014 against Curbo Fabrications Corporation, seeking civil penalties and injunctive relief for violations of city construction codes regulating earthquake damage standards. Alleged violations involved several construction projects completed during the previous three years. When the financial statements were issued in 2015, Curbo had not reached a settlement with state authorities, but legal counsel had advised the company that it was probable the ultimate settlement would be $750,000 in penalties. The following entry was recorded:

Loss—litigation	750,000	
Liability—litigation		750,000

The final settlement, therefore, was a pleasant surprise. While returning from the meeting, conversation turned to reporting the settlement in the 2016 financial statements. You drew the short straw and were selected to write a memo to Janet Zeno, the financial vice president, advising the proper course of action.

Required:

Write the memo. Include descriptions of any journal entries related to the change in amounts. Briefly describe other steps Curbo should take to report the settlement.

Analysis Case 20–6
Two wrongs make a right?
● LO20–4

Early one Wednesday afternoon, Ken and Larry studied in the dormitory room they shared at Fogelman College. Ken, an accounting major, was advising Larry, a management major, regarding a project for Larry's Business Policy class. One aspect of the project involved analyzing the 2016 annual report of Craft Paper Company. Though not central to his business policy case, a footnote had caught Larry's attention.

Depreciation and Cost of Timber Harvested (in part)
($ in millions)

	2016	2015	2014
Depreciation of buildings, machinery and equipment	$260.9	$329.8	$322.5
Cost of timber harvested and amortization of logging roads	4.9	4.9	4.9
	$265.8	$334.7	$327.4

(continued)

Beginning in 2016, the Company revised the estimated average useful lives used to compute depreciation for most of its pulp and paper mill equipment from 16 years to 20 years and for most of its finishing and converting equipment from 12 years to 15 years. These revisions were made to more properly reflect the true economic lives of the assets and to better align the Company's depreciable lives with the predominant practice in the industry. The change had the effect of increasing net income by approximately $55 million.

"If I understand this right, Ken, the company is not going back and recalculating a lower depreciation for earlier years. Instead they seem to be leaving depreciation overstated in earlier years and making up for that by understating it in current and future years," Larry mused. "Is that the way it is in accounting? Two wrongs make a right?"

Required:

What are the two wrongs to which Larry refers? Is he right?

Research Case 20–7
FASB codification; researching the way changes in postretirement benefit estimates are reported; retrieving disclosures from the Internet
● LO20–4

CODE

It's financial statements preparation time at Center Industries where you have been assistant controller for two months. Ben Huddler, the controller, seems to be pleasant but unpredictable. Today, although your schedule is filled with meetings with internal and outside auditors and two members of the board of directors, Ben made a request. "As you know, we're decreasing the rate at which we assume health care costs will rise when measuring our postretirement benefit obligation. I'd like to know how others have reported similar changes. Can you find me an example?" he asked. "I'd bet you could get one off the Internet." As a matter of fact, you often use EDGAR, the Electronic Data Gathering, Analysis, and Retrieval system (www.sec.gov) to access financial statements filed with the U.S. Securities and Exchange Commission (SEC).

Required:

1. Access EDGAR on the Internet. Access a recent 10-K filing of a firm you think might have a postretirement health care plan. You may need to look up several companies before you find what you're looking for. Older, established companies are most likely to have such benefit plans.

   (Note: You may be able to focus your search by searching with key words and phrases in Google on the Internet.)
2. Find the portion of the disclosures that reports the effect of a change in health care cost trends.
3. What information is provided about the effect of the change on the company's estimated benefit obligation?
4. Obtain the relevant authoritative literature on disclosure requirements for health care cost trends using the FASB's *Codification* Research System. Access the *FASB Accounting Standards Codification* at the FASB website (asc.fasb.org). What authoritative literature do companies rely on when disclosing the effect of a change in health care cost trends?

Analysis Case 20–8
Various changes
● LO20–1 through LO20–4

DRS Corporation changed the way it depreciates its computers from the sum-of-the-year's-digits method to the straight-line method beginning January 1, 2016. DRS also changed its estimated residual value used in computing depreciation for its office building. At the end of 2016, DRS changed the specific subsidiaries constituting the group of companies for which its consolidated financial statements are prepared.

Required:

1. For each accounting change DRS undertook, indicate the type of change and how DRS should report the change. Be specific.
2. Why should companies disclose changes in accounting principles?

Analysis Case 20–9
Various changes
● LO20–1 through LO20–4

Ray Solutions decided to make the following changes in its accounting policies on January 1, 2016:

a. Changed from the cash to the accrual basis of accounting for recognizing revenue on its service contracts.
b. Adopted straight-line depreciation for all future equipment purchases, but continued to use accelerated depreciation for all equipment acquired before 2016.
c. Changed from the LIFO inventory method to the FIFO inventory method.

Required:

For each accounting change Ray undertook, indicate the type of change and how Ray should report the change. Be specific.

Judgment Case 20–10
Accounting changes; independent situations
● LO20–1 through LO20–5

Sometimes a business entity will change its method of accounting for certain items. The change may be classified as a change in accounting principle, a change in accounting estimate, or a change in reporting entity.

Listed below are three independent, unrelated sets of facts relating to accounting changes.

Situation I: A company determined that the depreciable lives of its fixed assets are presently too long to fairly match the cost of the fixed assets with the revenue produced. The company decided at the beginning of the current year to reduce the depreciable lives of all of its existing fixed assets by five years.

Situation II: On December 31, 2015, Gary Company owned 51% of Allen Company, at which time Gary reported its investment on a nonconsolidated basis due to political uncertainties in the country in which Allen was located. On January 2, 2016, the management of Gary Company was satisfied that the political uncertainties were resolved and the assets of the company were in no danger of nationalization. Accordingly, Gary will prepare consolidated financial statements for Gary and Allen for the year ended December 31, 2016.

Situation III: A company decides in January 2016 to adopt the straight-line method of depreciation for plant equipment. The straight-line method will be used for new acquisitions as well as for previously acquired plant equipment for which depreciation had been provided on an accelerated basis.

Required:
For each of the situations described above, provide the information indicated below. Complete your discussion of each situation before going on to the next situation.

1. Type of accounting change.
2. Manner of reporting the change under current generally accepted accounting principles including a discussion, where applicable, of how amounts are computed.
3. Effect of the change on the balance sheet and income statement.
4. Footnote disclosures that would be necessary.

Judgment Case 20–11
Inventory errors
● LO20–6

Some inventory errors are said to be "self-correcting" in that the error has the opposite financial statement effect in the period following the error, thereby "correcting" the original account balance errors.

Required:
Despite this self-correcting feature, discuss why these errors should not be ignored and describe the steps required to account for the error correction.

Ethics Case 20–12
Overstatement of ending inventory
● LO20–6

Danville Bottlers is a wholesale beverage company. Danville uses the FIFO inventory method to determine the cost of its ending inventory. Ending inventory quantities are determined by a physical count. For the fiscal year-end June 30, 2016, ending inventory was originally determined to be $3,265,000. However, on July 17, 2016, John Howard, the company's controller, discovered an error in the ending inventory count. He determined that the correct ending inventory amount should be $2,600,000.

Danville is a privately owned corporation with significant financing provided by a local bank. The bank requires annual audited financial statements as a condition of the loan. By July 17, the auditors had completed their review of the financial statements which are scheduled to be issued on July 25. They did not discover the inventory error.

John's first reaction was to communicate his finding to the auditors and to revise the financial statements before they are issued. However, he knows that his and his fellow workers' profit-sharing plans are based on annual pretax earnings and that if he revises the statements, everyone's profit sharing bonus will be significantly reduced.

Required:

1. Why will bonuses be negatively affected? What is the effect on pretax earnings?
2. If the error is not corrected in the current year and is discovered by the auditors during the following year's audit, how will the error be reported in the company's financial statements?
3. Discuss the ethical dilemma Howard faces.

CPA Simulation 20–1

QuickTab
Accounting changes

KAPLAN CPA REVIEW

Test your knowledge of the concepts discussed in this chapter, practice critical professional skills necessary for career success, and prepare for the computer-based CPA exam by accessing our CPA simulations in the Connect Library.

The QuickTab simulation tests your knowledge of appropriate recognition of types of accounting changes and how we should account for them.

CHAPTER

21 The Statement of Cash Flows Revisited

OVERVIEW

The objective of financial reporting is to provide investors and creditors with useful information, primarily in the form of financial statements. The balance sheet and the income statement—the focus of your study in earlier chapters—do not provide all the information needed by these decision makers. Here you will learn how the statement of cash flows fills the information gap left by the other financial statements.

The statement lists all cash inflows and cash outflows, and classifies them as cash flows from (a) operating, (b) investing, or (c) financing activities. Investing and financing activities that do not directly affect cash also are reported.

LEARNING OBJECTIVES

After studying this chapter, you should be able to:

- **LO21–1** Explain the usefulness of the statement of cash flows. *(p. 1243)*
- **LO21–2** Define cash equivalents. *(p. 1247)*
- **LO21–3** Determine cash flows from operating activities by the direct method. *(p. 1248)*
- **LO21–4** Determine cash flows from operating activities by the indirect method. *(p. 1249)*
- **LO21–5** Identify transactions that are classified as investing activities. *(p. 1250)*
- **LO21–6** Identify transactions that are classified as financing activities. *(p. 1251)*
- **LO21–7** Identify transactions that represent noncash investing and financing activities. *(p. 1252)*
- **LO21–8** Prepare a statement of cash flows with the aid of a spreadsheet or T-accounts. *(p. 1253)*
- **LO21–9** Discuss the primary differences between U.S. GAAP and IFRS with respect to the statement of cash flows. *(p. 1272)*

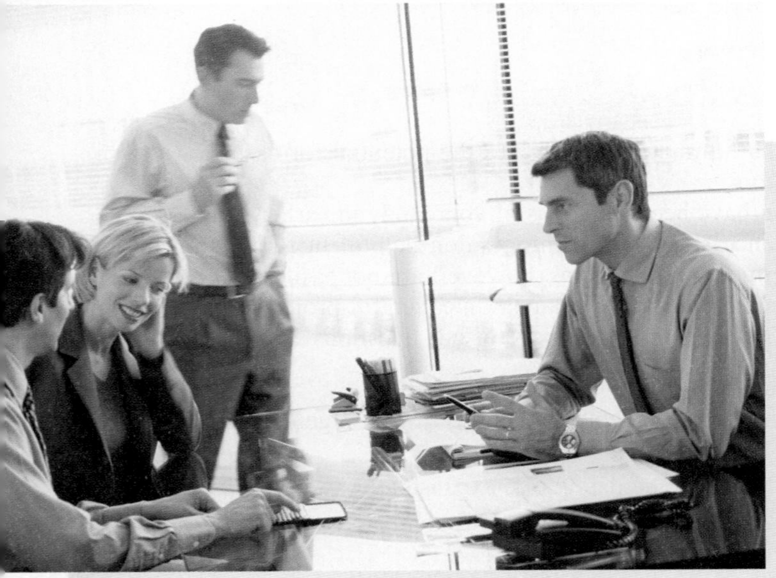

FINANCIAL REPORTING CASE

Where's the Cash?

"What do you mean you can't afford a wage increase?" union negotiator Vince Barr insisted. "We've all seen your income statement. You had record earnings this year."

This is the first day of company negotiations with union representatives. As company controller, you know it's going to be up to you to explain the company's position on the financial aspects of the negotiations. In fact, you've known for some time that a critical point of contention would be the moderate increase in this year's profits after three years of level or slightly declining earnings. Not helping the situation is that the company has always used accelerated depreciation on its equipment which it began replacing this year at considerably higher prices than it cost several years back.

QUESTIONS

By the time you finish this chapter, you should be able to respond appropriately to the questions posed in this case. Compare your response to the solution provided at the end of the chapter.

1. What are the cash flow aspects of the situation that Mr. Barr may be overlooking in making his case for a wage increase? How can a company's operations generate a healthy profit and yet produce meager or even negative cash flows? (*p. 1248*)
2. What information can a statement of cash flows provide about a company's investing activities that can be useful in decisions such as this? (*p. 1250*)
3. What information can a statement of cash flows provide about a company's financing activities that can be useful in decisions such as this? (*p. 1251*)

The Content and Value of the Statement of Cash Flows — PART A

Decision Makers' Perspective—Usefulness of Cash Flow Information

A fund manager of a major insurance company, considering investing $8,000,000 in the common stock of **The Coca-Cola Company**, asks herself: "What are the prospects of future dividends and market-price appreciation? Will we get a return commensurate with the cost and risk of our investment?" A bank officer, examining an application for a business loan, asks himself: "If I approve this loan, what is the likelihood of the borrower making interest payments on time and repaying the loan when due?" Investors and creditors continually face these and similar decisions that require projections of the relative ability of a business to generate future cash flows and of the risk associated with those forecasts.

● LO21–1

Investors and creditors require cash flows from the corporation.

To make these projections, decision makers rely heavily on the information reported in periodic financial statements. In the final analysis, cash flows into and out of a business enterprise are the most fundamental events on which investors and creditors base their decisions. Naturally, these decisions focus on the prospects of the decision makers receiving cash returns from their dealings with the firm. However, it is the ability of the firm to

Cash flows to investors and creditors depend on the corporation generating cash flows to itself.

generate cash flows to itself that ultimately determines the potential for cash flows from the firm to investors and creditors.

The financial statements that have been the focus of your study in earlier chapters—the income statement and the balance sheet—offer information helpful in forecasting future cash-generating ability. Some important questions, however, are not easily answered from the information these statements provide. For example, meaningful projections of a company's future profitability and risk depend on answers to such questions as:

- In what types of activities is the company investing?
- Are these activities being financed with debt? with equity? by cash generated from operations?
- Are facilities being acquired to accommodate future expansion?
- How does the amount of cash generated from operations compare with net income over time?
- Why isn't the increase in retained earnings reflected as an increase in dividends?
- What happens to the cash received from the sale of assets?
- By what means is debt being retired?

Many decisions benefit from information about the company's underlying cash flow process.

The information needed to answer these and similar questions is found in the continuous series of cash flows that the income statement and the balance sheet describe only indirectly. This underlying cash flow process is considered next. ●

Cash Inflows and Outflows

Cash continually flows into and out of an active business. Businesses disburse cash to acquire property and equipment to maintain or expand productive capacity. When no longer needed, these assets may be sold for cash. Cash is paid to produce or purchase inventory for resale, as well as to pay for the expenses of selling these goods. The ultimate outcome of these selling activities is an inflow of cash. Cash might be invested in securities of other firms. These investments provide cash inflows during the investment period in the form of dividends or interest and at the end of the investment period when the securities are sold. To raise cash to finance their operations, firms sell stock and/or acquire debt. Cash payments are made as dividends to shareholders and interest to creditors. When debt is repaid or stock repurchased, cash flows out of the firm. To help you visualize the continual process of cash receipts and cash payments, that process is diagrammed in Illustration 21–1. The diagram also previews the way we will later classify the cash flows in a statement of cash flows.

Illustration 21–1

Cash Inflows and Cash Outflows

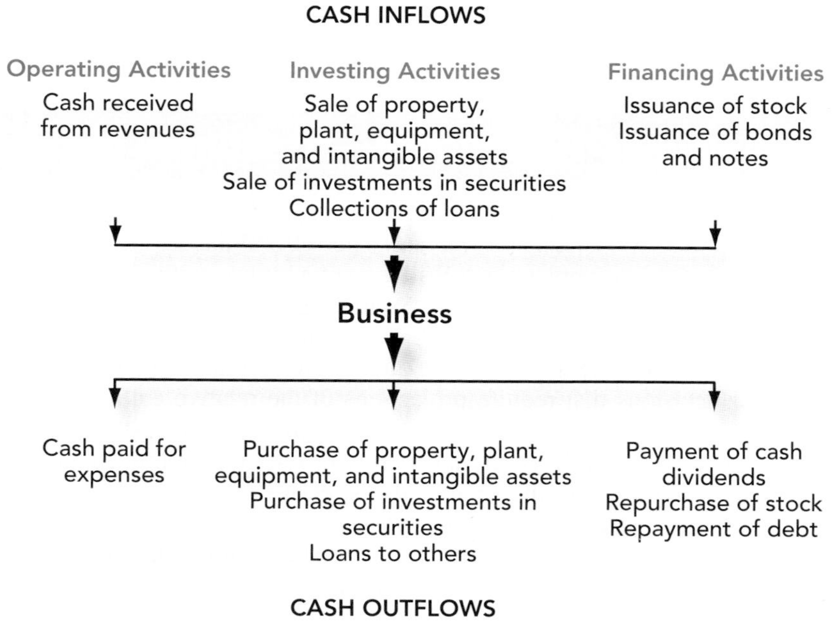

CASH INFLOWS

Operating Activities	Investing Activities	Financing Activities
Cash received from revenues	Sale of property, plant, equipment, and intangible assets Sale of investments in securities Collections of loans	Issuance of stock Issuance of bonds and notes

↓

Business

↓

Cash paid for expenses	Purchase of property, plant, equipment, and intangible assets Purchase of investments in securities Loans to others	Payment of cash dividends Repurchase of stock Repayment of debt

CASH OUTFLOWS

Embodied in this assortment of cash flows is a wealth of information that investors and creditors require to make educated decisions. Much of the value of the underlying information provided by the cash flows is lost when reported only indirectly by the balance sheet and the income statement. Each cash flow eventually impacts decision makers by affecting the balances of various accounts in the balance sheet. Also, many of the cash flows—those related to income-producing activities—are represented in the income statement. However, they are not necessarily reported in the period the cash flows occur because the income statement measures activities on an accrual basis. The statement of cash flows fills the information gap by reporting the cash flows directly.

The statement of cash flows provides information about cash flows that is lost when reported only indirectly by the balance sheet and the income statement.

Role of the Statement of Cash Flows

A statement of cash flows is shown in Illustration 21–2 on the next page. The statement lists all cash inflows and cash outflows during the reporting period. To enhance the informational value of the presentation, the cash flows are classified according to the nature of the activities that bring about the cash flows. The three primary categories of cash flows are (1) cash flows from operating activities, (2) cash flows from investing activities, and (3) cash flows from financing activities. Classifying each cash flow by source (operating, investing, or financing activities) is more informative than simply listing the various cash flows. Notice, too, that the noncash investing and financing activities—investing and financing activities that do not directly increase or decrease cash—also are reported. The GAAP requirement for the statement of cash flows was issued in direct response to *FASB Concept Statement 1,* which stated that the primary objective of financial reporting is to "provide information to help investors and creditors, and others assess the amounts, timing, and uncertainty of prospective net cash inflows to the related enterprise."[1]

Many companies suffered bankruptcy because they were unable to generate sufficient cash to satisfy their obligations. Doubtless, many investors in the stock of these firms would have been spared substantial losses if the financial statements had been designed to foresee the cash flow problems the companies were experiencing. A noted illustration is the demise of **W. T. Grant** during the 1970s. Grant, a general retailer in the days before malls, was a blue chip stock of its time. Grant's statement of changes in financial position (the predecessor of the statement of cash flows) reported working capital from operations of $46 million in 1972. Yet, if presented, a statement of cash flows would have reported cash flows from operating activities of negative $10 million. In fact, the unreported cash flow deficiency grew to $114 million in 1973, while working capital from operations was reported as having increased by $1 million. That year, without the benefit of cash flow information, investors were buying Grant's stock at prices that represented up to 20 times its earnings.[2]

More recently, even with cash flow information available, cash flow problems can go unnoticed. An example is the rapid growth and subsequent bankruptcy of the **Wicks 'N' Sticks** franchise. The company's drive for rapid growth led to a dependence on the sale of new franchises in order to generate cash flow instead of doing so in a more healthy way internally through its operations. As we see shortly, a statement of cash flows can indicate not just the amount of cash flows, but also whether those cash flows are coming from internal operations or from outside sources. Wicks 'N' Sticks was able to emerge from bankruptcy through restructuring and a new perspective on cash flow management.

Realize, too, that an unprofitable company with good cash flow can survive. **Amazon.com** provides an excellent example. Founded as an online seller of books in 1995, Amazon.com didn't actually make a profit for a decade, but it did raise huge amounts of cash by selling stock, so much so that it was able to weather 10 years of sizable losses. The financing cash inflows funded expansion into many new lines of business and made up for the continual losses. Amazon now has positive operating cash flows and is profitable.

[1]FASB Concepts Statement No. 8, Conceptual Framework for Financial Reporting—Chapter 1, *The Objective of General Purpose Financial Reporting,* and Chapter 3, *Qualitative Characteristics of Useful Financial Information* (a replacement of FASB Concepts Statements No. 1 and No. 2), *September 2010.*

[2]Cheryl A. Zega, "The New Statement of Cash Flows," *Management Accounting,* September 1988.

Illustration 21–2
Statement of Cash Flows

UNITED BRANDS CORPORATION
Statement of Cash Flows
For Year Ended December 31, 2016
($ in millions)

Cash Flows from Operating Activities		
Cash inflows:		
From customers	$98	
From investment revenue	3	
Cash outflows:		
To suppliers of goods	(50)	
To employees	(11)	
For interest	(3)	
For insurance	(4)	
For income taxes	(11)	
Net cash flows from operating activities		$22
Cash Flows from Investing Activities		
Purchase of land	(30)	
Purchase of short-term investment	(12)	
Sale of land	18	
Sale of equipment	5	
Net cash flows from investing activities		(19)
Cash Flows from Financing Activities		
Sale of common shares	26	
Retirement of bonds payable	(15)	
Payment of cash dividends	(5)	
Net cash flows from financing activities		6
Net increase in cash		9
Cash balance, January 1		20
Cash balance, December 31		$29

Note X:

Noncash Investing and Financing Activities	
Acquired $20 million of equipment by issuing a 12%, 5-year note.	$20
Reconciliation of Net Income to Cash Flows from Operating Activities:	
Net income	$12
Adjustments for noncash effects:	
Gain on sale of land	(8)
Depreciation expense	3
Loss on sale of equipment	2
Changes in operating assets and liabilities:	
Increase in accounts receivable	(2)
Decrease in inventory	4
Increase in accounts payable	6
Increase in salaries payable	2
Discount on bonds payable	2
Decrease in prepaid insurance	3
Decrease in income tax payable	(2)
Net cash flows from operating activities	$22

The Importance of Cash Flows in an Economic Decline

The near-collapse of **Bear Stearns** in the Spring of 2008 likely will be remembered as the single most dramatic event in exposing the fragility of Wall Street and precipitating the most severe financial crisis since the Great Depression. At the heart of Bear's calamity and the subsequent worldwide economic decline was a shortage of cash flows. First Bear Stearns; then Lehman Brothers; then AIG, Citigroup, Fannie Mae, and Freddie Mac. As we know, it didn't stop there. Each of these meltdowns involved a lack of measuring and monitoring the ebb and flow of cash.

When the financial industry is burdened with enormous amounts of uncollectible debt, as during the recent credit crisis, banks and others are reluctant to lend money. Cash becomes scarce. It's critical for companies to monitor their cash flows.

Let's say Lucky Strike Lures, Inc., manufactures fishing lures and sells them to a distributor. The distributor warehouses them before selling them to Bubba's Bait Shop, where they are put on display awaiting customers to buy them. During an economic downturn, the customers may delay buying the lures or not buy them at all. So, the lures stay in the store gathering dust, and Bubba's Bait can't pay for the lures that haven't sold. The distributor is then slow to pay Lucky Strike. Lucky Strike has bills to pay but no cash. In normal times, the company would go to the bank and borrow money. But in hard times, the bank is reluctant to lend. There is no quick fix as normal financing options are closed. Lucky Strike has cash flowing out, but not flowing in.

The survival and success of every business depends on its ability to create or otherwise attain cash. You can be profitable and still go broke. Companies must closely plan and monitor their cash flows to stay in business. During the recent economic decline, even some of the most well-known companies suffered the consequences of not following this principle.

Cash is king! Especially during an economic downturn.

The statement of cash flows for United Brands Corporation (UBC), shown in Illustration 21–2, is intended at this point in the discussion to illustrate the basic structure and composition of the statement. Later we will see how the statement of cash flows for UBC is prepared from the information typically available for this purpose. We will refer to UBC's statement of cash flows frequently throughout the chapter as the discussion becomes more specific regarding the criteria for classifying cash flows in the three primary categories and as we identify the specific cash flows to be reported on the statement. We will examine the content of the statement in more detail following a look at how this relatively recent financial statement has evolved to its present form over the course of the last several decades.

Cash and Cash Equivalents

● LO21–2

Skilled cash managers will invest temporarily idle cash in short-term investments to earn interest on those funds, rather than maintain an unnecessarily large balance in a checking account. The FASB views short-term, highly liquid investments that can be readily converted to cash, with little risk of loss, as cash equivalents. Amounts held as investments of this type are essentially equivalent to cash because they are quickly available for use as cash. Therefore, on the statement of cash flows there is no differentiation between amounts held as cash (e.g., currency and checking accounts) and amounts held in cash equivalent investments. So, when we refer in this chapter to cash, we are referring to the total of cash and cash equivalents.

There is no differentiation between amounts held as cash and amounts held in cash equivalent investments.

Examples of cash equivalents are money market funds, Treasury bills, and commercial paper. To be classified as cash equivalents, these investments must have a maturity date not longer than three months from the date of purchase. Flexibility is permitted in designating cash equivalents. Each company must establish a policy regarding which short-term, highly liquid investments it classifies as cash equivalents. The policy should be consistent with the company's customary motivation for acquiring various investments and should be disclosed in the notes to the statement.[3] A recent annual report of ExxonMobil Corporation provides this description of its cash equivalents (Illustration 21–3):

Each firm's policy regarding which short-term, highly liquid investments it classifies as cash equivalents should be disclosed in the notes to the financial statements.

Illustration 21–3

Disclosure of Cash Equivalents—ExxonMobil Corporation

Real World Financials

Note 4: Cash Flow Information (in part)
The consolidated statement of cash flows provides information about changes in cash and cash equivalents. Highly liquid investments with maturities of three months or less when acquired are classified as cash equivalents.

[3]A change in that policy is treated as a change in accounting principle.

Transactions that involve merely transfers from cash to cash equivalents (such as the purchase of a three-month Treasury bill), or from cash equivalents to cash (such as the sale of a Treasury bill), should not be reported on the statement of cash flows. The total of cash and cash equivalents is not altered by such transactions.[4] The cash balance reported in the balance sheet also represents the total of cash and cash equivalents, which allows us to compare the change in that balance with the net increase or decrease in the cash flows reported on the statement of cash flows.

Primary Elements of the Statement of Cash Flows

This section describes the three primary activity classifications: (1) operating activities, (2) investing activities, and (3) financing activities; and two other requirements of the statement of cash flows: (4) the reconciliation of the net increase or decrease in cash with the change in the balance of the cash account and (5) noncash investing and financing activities.

FINANCIAL Reporting Case

Q1, p. 1243

● LO21–3

CASH FLOWS FROM OPERATING ACTIVITIES. The income statement reports the success of a business in generating a profit from its operations. Net income (or loss) is the result of netting together the revenues recognized during the reporting period, regardless of when cash is received, and the expenses incurred in generating those revenues, regardless of when cash is paid. This is the accrual concept of accounting that has been emphasized throughout your study of accounting. Information about net income and its components, measured by the accrual concept, generally provides a better indication of current operating performance than does information about current cash receipts and payments.[5] Nevertheless, as indicated earlier, the cash effects of earning activities also provide useful information that is not directly accessible from the income statement. The first cash flow classification in the statement of cash flows reports that information.

The cash effects of the elements of net income are reported as cash flows from operating activities.

Cash flows from operating activities are both inflows and outflows of cash that result from activities reported in the income statement. In other words, this classification of cash flows includes the elements of net income, but reported on a cash basis. The components of this section of the statement of cash flows, and their relationship with the elements of the income statement, are illustrated in Illustration 21–4.

Illustration 21–4

Relationship between the Income Statement and Cash Flows from Operating Activities (Direct Method)

Income Statement	Cash Flows from Operating Activities
Revenues:	Cash inflows:
Sales and service revenue	Cash received from customers
Investment revenue	Cash revenue received (e.g., dividends, interest)
Noncash revenues and gains (e.g., gain on sale of assets)	(Not reported)
Less: Expenses:	Less: Cash outflows:
Cost of goods sold	Cash paid to suppliers of inventory
Salaries expense	Cash paid to employees
Noncash expenses and losses (e.g., depreciation, amortization, loss on sale of assets)	(Not reported)
Interest expense	Cash paid to creditors
Other operating expenses	Cash paid to insurance companies and others
Income tax expense	Cash paid to the government
Net income	*Net cash flows from operating activities*

[4]An exception is the sale of a cash equivalent at a gain or loss. This exception is described in more detail later in the chapter.

[5]FASB Concepts Statement No. 8, Conceptual Framework for Financial Reporting—Chapter 1, *The Objective of General Purpose Financial Reporting*, and Chapter 3, *Qualitative Characteristics of Useful Financial Information* (a replacement of FASB Concepts Statements No. 1 and No. 2), *September 2010*.

To see the concept applied, let's look again at the cash flows from operating activities reported by United Brands Corporation. That section of the statement of cash flows is extracted from Illustration 21–2 and reproduced in Illustration 21–5.

Illustration 21–5
Cash Flows from Operating Activities; Direct Method

Cash Flows from Operating Activities:		
Cash inflows:		
From customers	$98	
From investment revenue	3	
Cash outflows:		
To suppliers of goods	(50)	
To employees	(11)	
For interest	(3)	
For insurance	(4)	
For income taxes	(11)	
Net cash flows from operating activities		$22

Cash flows from operating activities are the elements of net income, but reported on a cash basis.

Cash inflows from operating activities exceeded cash outflows for expenses by $22 million. We'll see later (in Illustration 21–9) that UBC's net income from the same operating activities was only $12 million. Why did operating activities produce net cash inflows greater than net income? The reason will become apparent when we determine, in a later section, the specific amounts of these cash flows.

You also should be aware that the generalization stated earlier that cash flows from operating activities include the elements of net income reported on a cash basis is not strictly true for all elements of the income statement. Notice in Illustration 21–5 that no cash effects are reported for depreciation and amortization of property, plant, and equipment, and intangibles, nor for gains and losses from the sale of those assets. Cash outflows occur when these assets are acquired, and cash inflows occur when the assets are sold. However, as described later, the acquisition and subsequent resale of these assets are classified as investing activities, rather than as operating activities.

Quite the opposite, the purchase and the sale of inventory are considered operating activities. The cash effects of these transactions—namely, (1) cash payments to suppliers and (2) cash receipts from customers—are included in the determination of cash flows from operating activities. Why are inventories treated differently from property, plant, equipment, and intangible assets when classifying their cash effects if they all are acquired for the purpose of producing revenues? The essential difference is that inventory typically is purchased for the purpose of being sold as part of the firm's current operations, while the other assets are purchased as investments to benefit the business over a relatively long period of time.

DIRECT METHOD OR INDIRECT METHOD OF REPORTING CASH FLOWS FROM OPERATING ACTIVITIES. The presentation by UBC of cash flows from operating activities illustrated in Illustration 21–2 and reproduced in Illustration 21–5 is referred to as the **direct method**. The method is named for the fact that the cash effect of each operating activity (i.e., income statement item) is reported *directly* on the statement of cash flows. For instance, UBC reports "cash received from customers" as the cash effect of sales activities, "cash paid to suppliers" as the cash effect of cost of goods sold, and so on. Then, UBC simply omits from the presentation any income statement items that do not affect cash at all, such as depreciation expense.

● LO21–4

Another way UBC might have reported cash flows from operating activities is by the **indirect method**. By this approach, the net cash increase or decrease from operating activities ($22 million in our example) would be derived *indirectly* by starting with reported net income and working backwards to convert that amount to a cash basis. As we see later in the chapter, UBC's net income is $12 million. Using the indirect method, UBC would replace the previous presentation of net cash flows from operating activities with the one shown in Illustration 21–6.

Illustration 21–6

Cash Flows from Operating Activities; Indirect Method

By the indirect method, UBC derives the net cash increase or decrease from operating activities indirectly, by starting with reported net income and working backwards to convert that amount to a cash basis.

Cash Flows from Operating Activities:		
Net income		$12
Adjustments for noncash effects:		
Gain on sale of land	(8)	
Depreciation expense	3	
Loss on sale of equipment	2	
Changes in operating assets and liabilities:		
Increase in accounts receivable	(2)	
Decrease in inventory	4	
Increase in accounts payable	6	
Increase in salaries payable	2	
Decrease in discount on bonds payable	2	
Decrease in prepaid insurance	3	
Decrease in income tax payable	(2)	
Net cash flows from operating activities		$22

Be sure to note that the indirect method generates the same $22 million net cash flows from operating activities as the direct method. Rather than directly reporting only the components of the income statement that *do* represent increases or decreases in cash, by the indirect method we begin with net income—which includes both cash and noncash components—and back out all amounts that *don't* reflect increases or decreases in cash. Later in the chapter, we explore the specific adjustments made to net income to achieve this result. At this point it is sufficient to realize that two alternative methods are permitted for reporting net cash flows from operating activities. Either way, we convert accrual-based income to cash flows produced by those same operating activities.

Notice also that the indirect method presentation is identical to what UBC reported earlier as the "Reconciliation of Net Income to Cash Flows from Operating Activities" in Note X of Illustration 21–2. Whether cash flows from operating activities are reported by the direct method or by the indirect method, the financial statements must reconcile the difference between net income and cash flows from operating activities. When a company uses the *direct method,* the company presents the reconciliation in a separate schedule as UBC does. That presentation is precisely the same as the presentation of net cash flows from operating activities by the indirect method. On the other hand, a company choosing to use the indirect method is not required to provide a separate reconciliation schedule because the "cash flows from operating activities" section of the statement of cash flows serves that purpose. Most companies use the indirect method.[6]

It's important to understand, too, that regardless of which method a company chooses to report *operating* activities, that choice has no effect on the way it identifies and reports cash flows from *investing* and *financing* activities. We turn our attention now to those two sections of the statement of cash flows. Later in Part C, we'll return for a more thorough discussion of the alternative methods of reporting the operating activities section.

FINANCIAL Reporting Case

Q2, p. 1243

● LO21–5

CASH FLOWS FROM INVESTING ACTIVITIES. Companies periodically invest cash to replace or expand productive facilities such as property, plant, and equipment. Investments might also be made in other assets, such as securities of other firms, with the expectation of a return on those investments. Information concerning these investing activities can provide valuable insight to decision makers regarding the nature and magnitude of assets being acquired for future use, as well as provide clues concerning the company's ambitions for the future.

[6]According to the *AICPA, U.S. GAAP Financial Statements—Best Practices in Presentation and Disclosure—2013,* a recent survey of 500 companies showed that 495 companies chose to use the indirect method, only 5 the direct method.

Cash flows from investing activities are both outflows and inflows of cash caused by the acquisition and disposition of assets. Included in this classification are cash payments to acquire (1) property, plant, and equipment and other productive assets (except inventories), (2) investments in securities (except cash equivalents and trading securities[7]), and (3) nontrade receivables.[8] When these assets later are liquidated, any cash receipts from their disposition also are classified as investing activities. For instance, cash received from the sale of the assets or from the collection of a note receivable (principal amount only) represents cash inflows from investing activities. Be sure to realize that, unlike the label might imply, any investment revenue like interest, dividends, or other cash return from these investments is not an investing activity. The reason, remember, is that investment revenue is an income statement item and therefore is an operating activity.

Cash outflows and cash inflows due to the acquisition and disposition of assets (other than inventory and assets classified as cash equivalents) are reported as cash flows from investing activities.

For illustration, notice the cash flows reported as investing activities by UBC. That section of the statement of cash flows is extracted from the complete statement in Illustration 21–2 and reproduced in Illustration 21–7.

Illustration 21–7

Cash Flows from Investing Activities

Cash Flows from Investing Activities:		
Purchase of land	$(30)	
Purchase of short-term investment	(12)	
Sale of land	18	
Sale of equipment	5	
Net cash flows from investing activities		$(19)

Cash flows from investing activities include investments in assets and their subsequent sale.

UBC reports as investing activities the cash paid to purchase both land and a short-term investment. The other two investing activities reported are cash receipts for the sale of assets—equipment and land—that were acquired in earlier years. The specific transactions creating these cash flows are described in a later section of this chapter.

The purchase and sale of inventories are not considered investing activities. Inventories are purchased for the purpose of being sold as part of the firm's primary operations, so their purchase and sale are classified as operating activities.

Also, the purchase and sale of assets classified as cash equivalents are not reported as investing activities. In fact, these activities usually are not reported on the statement of cash flows. For example, when temporarily idle cash is invested in a money market fund considered to be a cash equivalent, the total of cash and cash equivalents does not change. Likewise, when the cash is later withdrawn from the money market fund, the total remains unchanged. The exception is when cash equivalents are sold at a gain or a loss. In that case, the total of cash and cash equivalents actually increases or decreases in the process of transferring from one cash equivalent account to another cash equivalent account. As a result, the change in cash would be reported as a cash flow from operating activities. This is illustrated later in the chapter.

FINANCIAL Reporting Case

Q3, p. 1243

● LO21–6

CASH FLOWS FROM FINANCING ACTIVITIES. Not only is it important for investors and creditors to be informed about how a company is investing its funds, but also how its investing activities are being financed. Hopefully, the primary operations of the firm provide a source of internal financing. Information revealed in the cash flows from operating activities section of the statement of cash flows lets statement users know the extent of available internal financing. However, a major portion of financing for many companies is provided by external sources, specifically by shareholders and creditors.

[7]Inflows and outflows of cash from buying and selling trading securities typically are considered operating activities because financial institutions that routinely transact in trading securities consider them an appropriate part of their normal operations.

[8]A nontrade receivable differs from a trade receivable in that it is not one associated with the company's normal trade; that is, it's not received from a customer. A trade receivable, or accounts receivable, is an *operating asset*. A nontrade receivable, on the other hand, might be a loan to an affiliate company or to an officer of the firm. To understand how the creation of a nontrade receivable is an *investing* activity, you might view such a loan as an investment in the receivable.

Cash inflows and cash outflows due to the external financing of a business are reported as cash flows from financing activities.

Cash flows from financing activities are both inflows and outflows of cash resulting from the external financing of a business. We include in this classification cash inflows from (a) the sale of common and preferred stock and (b) the issuance of bonds and other debt securities. Subsequent transactions related to these financing transactions, such as a buyback of stock (to retire the stock or as treasury stock), the repayment of debt, and the payment of cash dividends to shareholders, also are classified as financing activities.

For illustration, refer to Illustration 21–8 excerpted from the complete statement of cash flows of UBC in Illustration 21–2.

Illustration 21–8
Cash Flows from Financing Activities

Cash Flows from Financing Activities:		
Sale of common shares	$26	
Retirement of bonds payable	(15)	
Payment of cash dividends	(5)	
Net cash flows from financing activities		$6

Cash flows from financing activities include the sale or repurchase of shares, the issuance or repayment of debt securities, and the payment of cash dividends.

The cash received from the sale of common stock is reported as a financing activity. Since the sale of common stock is a financing activity, providing a cash return (dividend) to common shareholders also is a financing activity. Similarly, when the bonds being retired were issued in a prior year, that cash inflow was reported as a financing activity. In the current year, when the bonds are retired, that same amount of the resulting cash outflow is likewise classified as a financing activity.

Interest, unlike dividends, is a determinant of net income and therefore an operating activity.

At first glance, it may appear inconsistent to classify the payment of cash dividends to shareholders as a financing activity when, as stated earlier, paying interest to creditors is classified as an operating activity. But remember, cash flows from operating activities should reflect the cash effects of items that enter into the determination of net income. Interest expense is a determinant of net income. A dividend, on the other hand, is a distribution of net income and not an expense.

RECONCILIATION WITH CHANGE IN CASH BALANCE. One of the first items you may have noticed about UBC's statement of cash flows is that there is a net change in cash of $9 million. Is this a significant item of information provided by the statement? The primary objective of the statement of cash flows is not to tell us that cash increased by $9 million. We can readily see the increase or decrease in cash by comparing the beginning and ending balances in the cash account in comparative balance sheets. Instead, the purpose of the statement of cash flows is to explain *why* cash increased by $9 million.

To reinforce the fact that the net amount of cash inflows and outflows explains the change in the cash balance, the statement of cash flows includes a reconciliation of the net increase (or decrease) in cash with the company's beginning and ending cash balances. Notice, for instance, that on UBC's statement of cash flows, the reconciliation appears as:

The net amount of cash inflows and outflows reconciles the change in the company's beginning and ending cash balances.

Net Increase in Cash	$ 9
Cash balance, January 1	20
Cash balance, December 31	$29

NONCASH INVESTING AND FINANCING ACTIVITIES. Suppose UBC were to borrow $20 million cash from a bank, issuing a long-term note payable for that amount. This transaction would be reported on a statement of cash flows as a financing activity. Now suppose UBC used that $20 million cash to purchase new equipment. This second transaction would be reported as an investing activity.

● LO21–7

Instead of two separate transactions, as indicated by Illustration 21–2, UBC acquired $20 million of new equipment by issuing a $20 million long-term note payable in a single transaction. Undertaking a significant investing activity and a significant financing activity as two parts of a single transaction does not diminish the value of reporting these activities. For that reason, transactions that do not increase or decrease cash, but which result in significant investing and financing activities, must be reported in related disclosures.

These **noncash investing and financing activities**, such as UBC's acquiring equipment (an investing activity) by issuing a long-term note payable (a financing activity), are reported in a separate disclosure schedule or note. UBC reported this transaction in the following manner:

Noncash Investing and Financing Activities:
Acquired $20 million of equipment by issuing a 12%, 5-year note.

Significant noncash investing and financing activities are reported also.

It's convenient to report noncash investing and financing activities on the same page as the statement of cash flows as did UBC only if there are few such transactions. Otherwise, precisely the same information would be reported in disclosure notes to the financial statements.[9]

Examples of noncash transactions that would be reported in this manner are:

1. Acquiring an asset by incurring a debt payable to the seller.
2. Acquiring use of an asset by entering into a lease agreement.
3. Converting debt into common stock or other equity securities.
4. Exchanging noncash assets or liabilities for other noncash assets or liabilities.

Noncash transactions that do not affect a company's assets or liabilities, such as the distribution of stock dividends, are not considered investing or financing activities and are not reported. Recall from Chapter 18 that stock dividends merely increase the number of shares of stock owned by existing shareholders. From an accounting standpoint, the stock dividend causes a dollar amount to be transferred from one part of shareholders' equity (retained earnings) to another part of shareholders' equity (paid-in capital). Neither assets nor liabilities are affected; therefore, no investing or financing activity has occurred.

Preparation of the Statement of Cash Flows

LO21–8

The objective in preparing the statement of cash flows is to identify all transactions and events that represent operating, investing, or financing activities and to list and classify those activities in proper statement format. A difficulty in preparing a statement of cash flows is that typical accounting systems are not designed to produce the specific information we need for the statement. At the end of a reporting cycle, balances exist in accounts reported in the income statement (sales revenue, cost of goods sold, etc.) and the balance sheet (accounts receivable, common stock, etc.). However, the ledger contains no balances for cash paid to acquire equipment, or cash received from sale of land, or any other cash flow needed for the statement. As a result, it's necessary to find a way of using available information to reconstruct the various cash flows that occurred during the reporting period. Typically, the information available to assist the statement preparer includes an income statement for the year and balance sheets for both the current and preceding years (comparative statements). The accounting records also can provide additional information about transactions that caused changes in account balances during the year.

Additional Consideration

A transaction involving an investing and financing activity may be part cash and part noncash. For example, a company might pay cash for a part of the purchase price of new equipment and issue a long-term note for the remaining amount. In our previous

(continued)

[9]FASB ASC 230–10–50–6: Statement of Cash Flows–Overall–Disclosure–Noncash Investing and Financing Activities (previously "Statement of Cash Flows," *Statement of Financial Accounting Standards No. 95* (Stamford, Conn.: FASB, 1987), par. 74).

(concluded)

illustration, UBC issued a note payable for the $20 million cost of the equipment it acquired. Suppose the equipment were purchased in the following manner:

Equipment	20	
Cash		6
Note payable		14

In that case, $6 million would be reported under the caption "Cash flows from investing activities," and the noncash portion of the transaction—issuing a $14 million note payable for $14 million of equipment—would be reported as a "noncash investing and financing activity." UBC's statement of cash flows, if modified by the assumption of a part cash/part noncash transaction, would report these two elements of the transaction as follows:

Cash Flows from Investing Activities:		
Purchase of land	$(30)	
Purchase of short-term investments	(12)	
Sale of land	18	
Sale of equipment	5	
Purchase of equipment	(6)	
Net cash flows from investing activities		$(25)

Noncash Investing and Financing Activities:

Acquired $20 million of equipment by paying cash and issuing a 12%, 5-year note as follows:

Cost of equipment	$20 million
Cash paid	(6 million)
Note issued	$14 million

The typical year-end data is provided for UBC in Illustration 21–9 on the next page. We have referred frequently to the statement of cash flows of UBC to illustrate the nature of the activities the statement reports. Now we will see how that statement is developed from the data provided in that illustration.

In situations involving relatively few transactions, it is possible to prepare the statement of cash flows by merely inspecting the available data and logically determining the reportable activities. Few real-life situations are sufficiently simple to be solved this way. Usually, it is more practical to use some systematic method of analyzing the available data to ensure that all operating, investing, and financing activities are detected. A common approach is to use either a manual or electronic spreadsheet to organize and analyze the information used to prepare the statement.[10]

Reconstructing the events and transactions that occurred during the period helps identify the operating, investing, and financing activities to be reported.

Whether the statement of cash flows is prepared by an unaided inspection and analysis or with the aid of a systematic technique such as spreadsheet analysis, the analytical process is the same. To identify the activities to be reported on the statement, we use available data to reconstruct the events and transactions that involved operating, investing, and financing activities during the year. It is helpful to reproduce the journal entries that were recorded at the time of the transaction. Examining reconstructed journal entries makes it easier to visualize whether a reportable activity is involved and how that activity is to be classified.

Next, in Part B, we see how a spreadsheet simplifies the process of preparing a statement of cash flows. Even if you choose not to use a spreadsheet, the summary entries described can be used to help you find the cash inflows and outflows you need to prepare a statement of cash flows. For this demonstration, we assume the direct method is used to determine and report cash flows from operating activities. Appreciation of the direct method provides the backdrop for a thorough understanding of the indirect method that we explore in Part C.

[10]The T-account method is a second systematic approach to the preparation of the statement of cash flows. This method is identical in concept and similar in application to the spreadsheet method. The T-account method is used to prepare the statement of cash flows for UBC in Appendix 21B.

Illustration 21–9

Comparative Balance Sheets and Income Statement

UNITED BRANDS CORPORATION
Comparative Balance Sheets
December 31, 2016 and 2015
($ in millions)

Assets	2016	2015
Cash	$ 29	$ 20
Accounts receivable	32	30
Short-term investments	12	0
Inventory	46	50
Prepaid insurance	3	6
Land	80	60
Buildings and equipment	81	75
Less: Accumulated depreciation	(16)	(20)
	$267	$221
Liabilities		
Accounts payable	$ 26	$ 20
Salaries payable	3	1
Income tax payable	6	8
Notes payable	20	0
Bonds payable	35	50
Less: Discount on bonds	(1)	(3)
Shareholders' Equity		
Common stock	130	100
Paid-in capital—excess of par	29	20
Retained earnings	19	25
	$267	$221

Income Statement

Revenues		
Sales revenue	$100	
Investment revenue	3	
Gain on sale of land	8	$111
Expenses		
Cost of goods sold	60	
Salaries expense	13	
Depreciation expense	3	
Bond interest expense	5	
Insurance expense	7	
Loss on sale of equipment	2	
Income tax expense	9	99
Net income		$ 12

Additional Information from the Accounting Records

a. Company land, purchased in a previous year for $10 million, was sold for $18 million.
b. Equipment that originally cost $14 million, and which was one-half depreciated, was sold for $5 million cash.
c. The common shares of Mazuma Corporation were purchased for $12 million as a short-term investment.
d. Property was purchased for $30 million cash for use as a parking lot.
e. On December 30, 2016, new equipment was acquired by issuing a 12%, five-year, $20 million note payable to the seller.
f. On January 1, 2016, $15 million of bonds (issued 20 years ago at their face amount) were retired at maturity.
g. The increase in the common stock account is attributable to the issuance of a 10% stock dividend (1 million shares) and the subsequent sale of 2 million shares of common stock. The market price of the $10 par value common stock was $13 per share on the dates of both transactions.
h. Cash dividends of $5 million were paid to shareholders.

PART B

Preparing the SCF: Direct Method of Reporting Cash Flows from Operating Activities

Using a Spreadsheet

There can be no cash inflow or cash outflow without a corresponding change in a noncash account.

An important advantage gained by using a spreadsheet is that it ensures that no reportable activities are inadvertently overlooked. Spreadsheet analysis relies on the fact that, in order for cash to increase or decrease, there must be a corresponding change in an account other than cash. Therefore, if we can identify the events and transactions that caused the change in each noncash account during the year, we will have identified all the operating, investing, and financing activities that are to be included in the statement of cash flows.

Recording spreadsheet entries that explain account balance changes simultaneously identifies and classifies the activities to be reported on the statement of cash flows.

The beginning and ending balances of each account are entered on the spreadsheet. Then, as journal entries are reconstructed in our analysis of the data, those entries are recorded on the spreadsheet so that the debits and credits of the spreadsheet entries explain the changes in the account balances. Only after spreadsheet entries have explained the changes in all account balances, can we feel confident that all operating, investing, and financing activities have been identified. The spreadsheet is designed in such a way that, as we record spreadsheet entries that explain account balance changes, we are simultaneously identifying and classifying the activities to be reported on the statement of cash flows.

We begin by transferring the comparative balance sheets and income statement to a blank spreadsheet. For illustration, refer to the 2016 and 2015 balances in the completed spreadsheet for UBC, shown in Illustration 21–9A on the next two pages. Notice that the amounts for elements of the income statement are ending balances resulting from accumulations during the year. Beginning balances in each of these accounts are always zero.

Following the balance sheets and income statement, we allocate space on the spreadsheet for the statement of cash flows. Although at this point we have not yet identified the specific cash flow activities shown in the completed spreadsheet, we can include headings for the major categories of activities: cash flows from operating activities, cash flows from investing activities, and cash flows from financing activities. Leaving several lines between headings allows adequate space to include the specific cash flows identified in subsequent analysis.

Spreadsheet entries duplicate the actual journal entries used to record the transactions as they occurred during the year.

The spreadsheet entries shown in the two changes columns, which separate the beginning and ending balances, explain the increase or decrease in each account balance. You will see in the next section how these entries were reconstructed. Although spreadsheet entries are in the form of debits and credits like journal entries, they are entered on the spreadsheet only. They are not recorded in the formal accounting records. In effect, these entries duplicate, frequently in summary form, the actual journal entries used to record the transactions as they occurred during the year.

To reconstruct the journal entries, we analyze each account, one at a time, deciding at each step what transaction or event caused the change in that account. Often, the reason for the change in an account balance is readily apparent from viewing the change in conjunction with that of a related account elsewhere in the financial statements. Sometimes it is necessary to consult the accounting records for additional information to help explain the transaction that resulted in the change.

You may find it helpful to diagram in T-account format the relationship between accounts to better visualize certain changes, particularly in your initial study of the chapter. The analysis that follows is occasionally supplemented with such diagrams to emphasize *why,* rather than merely *how,* specific cash flow amounts emerge from the analysis.

Although there is no mandatory order in which to analyze the accounts, it is convenient to begin with the income statement accounts, followed by the balance sheet accounts. We analyze the accounts of UBC in that order below. Although our analysis of each account culminates in a spreadsheet entry, keep in mind that the analysis described also is appropriate to identify reportable activities when a spreadsheet is not used.[11]

[11]The spreadsheet entries also are used to record the same transactions when the T-account method is used. We refer again to these entries when that method is described in Appendix 21B.

Illustration 21–9A

Spreadsheet—Direct Method

UNITED BRANDS CORPORATION
Spreadsheet for the Statement of Cash Flows

	Dec. 31 2015	Changes: Debits		Changes: Credits		Dec. 31 2016
Balance Sheet						
Assets:						
Cash	20	(19)	9			29
Accounts receivable	30	(1)	2			32
Short-term investments	0	(12)	12			12
Inventory	50			(4)	4	46
Prepaid insurance	6			(8)	3	3
Land	60	(13)	30	(3)	10	80
Buildings and equipment	75	(14)	20X	(9)	14	81
Less: Accumulated depreciation	(20)	(9)	7	(6)	3	(16)
	221					267
Liabilities:						
Accounts payable	20			(4)	6	26
Salaries payable	1			(5)	2	3
Income tax payable	8	(10)	2			6
Notes payable	0			(14)	20X	20
Bonds payable	50	(15)	15			35
Less: Discount on bonds	(3)			(7)	2	(1)
Shareholders' Equity:						
Common stock	100			(16)	10	
				(17)	20	130
Paid-in capital—excess of par	20			(16)	3	
				(17)	6	29
Retained earnings	25	(16)	13			
		(18)	5	(11)	12	19
	221					267
Income Statement						
Revenues:						
Sales revenue				(1)	100	100
Investment revenue				(2)	3	3
Gain on sale of land				(3)	8	8
Expenses:						
Cost of goods sold		(4)	60			(60)
Salaries expense		(5)	13			(13)
Depreciation expense		(6)	3			(3)
Bond interest expense		(7)	5			(5)
Insurance expense		(8)	7			(7)
Loss on sale of equipment		(9)	2			(2)
Income tax expense		(10)	9			(9)
Net income		(11)	**12**			**12**
Statement of Cash Flows						
Operating Activities:						
Cash inflows:						
From customers		(1)	98			
From investment revenue		(2)	3			
Cash outflows:						
To suppliers of goods				(4)	50	
To employees				(5)	11	
To bondholders				(7)	3	
For insurance expense				(8)	4	
For income taxes				(10)	11	
Net cash flows						22

(continued)

Illustration 21–9A
(concluded)

	Dec. 31 2015	Changes Debits		Changes Credits		Dec. 31 2016
Investing Activities:						
Sale of land		(3)	18			
Sale of equipment		(9)	5			
Purchase of S-T investment				(12)	12	
Purchase of land				(13)	30	
Net cash flows						(19)
Financing Activities:						
Retirement of bonds payable				(15)	15	
Sale of common shares		(17)	26			
Payment of cash dividends				(18)	5	
Net cash flows						6
Net increase in cash				(19)	9	9
Totals			376		376	

X—As explained later, the X's serve as a reminder to report this noncash transaction.

Income Statement Accounts

Amounts reported in the income statement usually are not the same as the cash effects of the items reported.

As described in an earlier section, cash flows from operating activities are inflows and outflows of cash that result from activities reported in the income statement. Thus, to identify those cash inflows and outflows, we begin by analyzing the components of the income statement. It is important to keep in mind that the amounts reported in the income statement usually do not represent the cash effects of the items reported. For example, UBC reports sales revenue of $100 million. This does not mean, however, that it collected $100 million cash from customers during the year. In fact, by referring to the beginning and ending balances in accounts receivable, we see that cash received from customers could not have been $100 million. Since accounts receivable increased during the year, some of the sales revenue earned must not yet have been collected. This is explained further in the next section.

The cash effects of other income statement elements can be similarly discerned by referring to changes in the balances of the balance sheet accounts that are directly related to those elements. So, to identify cash flows from operating activities we examine, one at a time, the elements of the income statement in conjunction with any balance sheet accounts affected by each element.

1. SALES REVENUE. Accounts receivable is the balance sheet account that is affected by sales revenue. Specifically, accounts receivable is increased by credit sales and is decreased as cash is received from customers. We can compare sales and the change in accounts receivable during the year to determine the amount of cash received from customers. This relationship can be viewed in T-account format as follows:

Accounts Receivable

Beginning balance	30		
Credit sales *(increases A/R)*	100	?	Cash received *(decreases A/R)*
Ending balance	32		

We see from this analysis that cash received from customers must have been $98 million. Note that even if some of the year's sales were cash sales, say $40 million cash sales and $60 million credit sales, the result is the same:

Accounts Receivable

Beginning balance	30		Cash sales	$40
Credit sales	60	58 →	Received on account	58
Ending balance	32		Cash received	$98

Thus, cash flows from operating activities should include cash received from customers of $98 million. The net effect of sales revenue activity during the year can be summarized in the following entry.

	($ in millions)	
Entry (1) Cash (received from customers)	98	
Accounts receivable (given)	2	
Sales revenue ($100 − 0)		100

Relating sales and the *change* in accounts receivable during the period helps determine the amount of cash received from customers.

The entry above appears as entry (1) in the completed spreadsheet for UBC, shown in Illustration 21–9A. The entry explains the changes in two account balances—accounts receivable and sales revenue. Since the entry affects cash, it also identifies a cash flow to be reported on the statement of cash flows. The $98 million debit to cash is therefore entered in the statement of cash flows section of the spreadsheet under the heading of cash flows from operating activities.

Additional Consideration

The preceding discussion describes the most common situation—companies earn revenue by selling goods and services, increase accounts receivable, and then collect the cash and decrease accounts receivable later. Some companies, though, often collect the cash in advance of earning it, record deferred revenue, and then later record revenue and decrease deferred revenue. In those cases, we need to analyze any changes in the deferred revenue account for differences between revenue reported and cash collected. For instance, if UBC also had a $1 million increase in deferred revenue, the summary entry would be modified as follows:

	($ in millions)	
Entry (1) Cash (received from customers)	99	
Accounts receivable (given)	2	
Deferred revenue (given)		1
Sales revenue ($100 − 0)		100

Notice that we enter the cash portion of entry (1) as one of several cash flows on the statement of cash flows rather than as a debit to the cash account. Only after all cash inflows and outflows have been identified will the net change in cash be entered as a debit to the cash account. In fact, the entry to reconcile the $9 million increase in the cash account and the $9 million net increase in cash on the statement of cash flows will serve as a final check of the accuracy of our spreadsheet analysis.

The remaining summary entries are described in subsections 2 through 19. When including the entries on the spreadsheet, it is helpful to number the entries sequentially to provide a means of retracing the steps taken in the analysis if the need arises. You also may find it helpful to put a check mark (✔) to the right of the ending balance when the change in that balance has been explained. Then, once you have check marks next to every noncash account, you will know you are finished.

2. INVESTMENT REVENUE. The income statement reports investment revenue of $3 million. Before concluding that this amount was received in cash, we first refer to the balance sheets to see whether a change in an account there indicates otherwise. A change in either of two balance sheet accounts, (a) investment revenue receivable or (b) long-term investments, might indicate that cash received from investment revenue differs from the amount reported in the income statement.

Changes in related accounts might indicate that investment revenue reported in the income statement is a different amount from cash received from the investment.

a. If we observe either an increase or a decrease in an *investment revenue receivable* account (e.g., interest receivable, dividends receivable), we would conclude that the amount of cash received during the year was less than (if an increase) or more than (if a decrease) the amount of revenue reported. The analysis would be identical to that of sales revenue and accounts receivable.

b. Also, an unexplained increase in a *long-term investment* account might indicate that a portion of investment revenue has not yet been received in cash. Recall from Chapter 12 that when using the equity method to account for investments in the stock of another corporation, investment revenue is recognized as the investor's percentage share of the investee's income, whether or not the revenue is received currently as cash dividends. For example, assume the investor owns 25% of the common stock of a corporation that reports net income of $12 million and pays dividends of $4 million. This situation would have produced a $2 million increase in long-term investments, which can be demonstrated by reconstructing the journal entries for the recognition of investment and the receipt of cash dividends:

	($ in millions)	
Long-term investments	3	
Investment revenue ($12 × 25%)		3
Cash ($4 × 25%)	1	
Long-term investments		1

A combined entry would produce the same results:

Long-term investments	2	
Cash ($4 × 25%)	1	
Investment revenue ($12 × 25%)		3

The $2 million net increase in long-term investments would represent the investment revenue not received in cash. This would also explain why there is a $3 million increase (credit) in investment revenue. If these events had occurred, we would prepare a spreadsheet entry identical to the combined entry above. The spreadsheet entry would (a) explain the $2 million increase in long-term investments, (b) explain the $3 million increase in investment revenue, and (c) identify a $1 million cash inflow from operating activities.

However, because neither an investment revenue receivable account nor a long-term investment account appears on the comparative balance sheets, we can conclude that $3 million of investment revenue was collected in cash. Entry (2) on the spreadsheet is as follows:

Because no other transactions are apparent that would have caused a change in investment revenue, we can conclude that $3 million of investment revenue was collected in cash.

	($ in millions)	
Entry (2) Cash (received from investment revenue)	3	
Investment revenue ($3 − 0)		3

3. GAIN ON SALE OF LAND. The third item reported in the income statement is an $8 million gain on the sale of land. Recall that our objective in analyzing each element of the statement is to determine the cash effect of that element. To do so, we need additional information about the transaction that caused this gain. The accounting records—item (a) in Illustration 21–9—indicate that land that originally cost $10 million was sold for $18 million. The entry recorded in the journal when the land was sold also serves as our summary entry:

A gain (or loss) is simply the difference between cash received in the sale of an asset and the book value of the asset—not a cash flow.

	($ in millions)	
Entry (3) Cash (received from sale of land)	18	
Land (given)		10
Gain on sale of land ($8 − 0)		8

The cash effect of this transaction is a cash increase of $18 million. We therefore include the debit as a cash inflow in the statement of cash flows section of the spreadsheet. However, unlike the cash effect of the previous two spreadsheet entries, it is not reported as an operating activity. The sale of land is an *investing* activity, so this cash inflow is listed under that heading of the spreadsheet. The entry also accounts for the $8 million gain on sale of land. The $10 million credit to land does not, by itself, explain the $20 million increase in that account. As we will later discover, another transaction also affected the land account.

It is important to understand that the gain is simply the difference between cash received in the sale of land (reported as an investing activity) and the book value of the land. To report the $8 million gain as a cash flow from operating activities, in addition to reporting $18 million as a cash flow from investing activities, would be to report the $8 million twice.

4. COST OF GOODS SOLD. During the year UBC sold goods that had cost $60 million. This does not necessarily indicate that $60 million cash was paid to suppliers of those goods. To determine the amount of cash paid to suppliers, we look to the two current accounts affected by merchandise purchases—inventory and accounts payable. The analysis can be viewed as a two-step process.

First, we compare cost of goods sold with the change in inventory to determine the cost of goods *purchased* (not necessarily cash paid) during the year. To facilitate our analysis, we can examine the relationship in T-account format:

Inventory

Beginning balance	50		
Cost of goods purchased *(increases inventory)*	?	60	Cost of goods sold *(decreases inventory)*
Ending balance	46		

From this analysis, we see that $56 million of goods were *purchased* during the year. It is not necessarily true, though, that $56 million cash was paid to suppliers of these goods. By looking in accounts payable, we can determine the cash paid to suppliers:

Determining the amount of cash paid to suppliers means looking at not only the cost of goods sold, but also the changes in both inventory and accounts payable.

Accounts Payable

		20	Beginning balance
Cash paid to suppliers *(decreases A/P)*	?	56	Cost of goods purchased *(increases A/P)*
		26	Ending Balance

We now see that cash paid to suppliers was $50 million. The entry that summarizes merchandise acquisitions is as follows:

	($ in millions)	
Entry (4) Cost of goods sold ($60 – 0)	60	
Inventory ($46 – 50)		4
Accounts payable ($26 – 20)		6
Cash (paid to suppliers of goods)		50

Although $60 million of goods were sold during the year, only $50 million cash was paid to suppliers of these goods.

5. SALARIES EXPENSE. The balance sheet account affected by salaries expense is salaries payable. By analyzing salaries expense in relation to the change in salaries payable, we can determine the amount of cash paid to employees:

Salaries Payable

		1	Beginning balance
Cash paid to employees *(decreases salaries payable)*	?	13	Salaries expense *(increases salaries payable)*
		3	Ending Balance

This analysis indicates that only $11 million cash was paid to employees; the remaining $2 million of salaries expense is reflected as an increase in salaries payable.

Viewing the relationship in journal entry format provides the same conclusion and also gives us the entry in our spreadsheet analysis:

Although salaries expense was $13 million, only $11 million cash was paid to employees.

	($ in millions)	
Entry (5) Salaries expense ($13 – 0)	13	
Salaries payable ($3 – 1)		2
Cash (paid to employees)		11

6. DEPRECIATION EXPENSE. The income statement reports depreciation expense of $3 million. The entry used to record depreciation, which also serves as our summary entry, is

Depreciation expense does not require a current cash expenditure.

	($ in millions)	
Entry (6) Depreciation expense ($3 – 0)	3	
Accumulated depreciation		3

Depreciation is a noncash expense. It is merely an allocation in the current period of a prior cash expenditure (for the depreciable asset). Therefore, unlike the other entries to this point, the depreciation entry has no effect on the statement of cash flows. However, it does explain the change in the depreciation expense account and a portion of the change in accumulated depreciation.

7. INTEREST EXPENSE. Recall from Chapter 14 that bond interest expense differs from the amount of cash paid to bondholders when bonds are issued at either a premium or a discount. The difference between the two amounts is the reduction of the premium or discount. By referring to the balance sheet, we see that UBC's bonds were issued at a discount. Since we know that bond interest expense is $5 million and that $2 million of the discount was reduced in 2016, we can determine that $3 million cash was paid to bondholders by recreating the entry that summarizes the recording of bond interest expense.

Bond interest expense is not the same as the amount of cash paid to bondholders when bonds are issued at either a premium or a discount.

	($ in millions)	
Entry (7) Interest expense ($5 – 0)	5	
Discount on bonds payable ($1 – 3)		2
Cash (paid to bondholders)		3

Recording this entry on the spreadsheet explains the change in both the bond interest expense and discount on bonds payable accounts. It also provides us with another cash outflow from operating activities. Of course, if a premium were being reduced, rather than a discount, the cash outflow would be *greater* than the expense.

8. INSURANCE EXPENSE. A decrease of $3 million in the prepaid insurance account indicates that cash paid for insurance coverage was $3 million less than the $7 million insurance expense for the year. Viewing prepaid insurance in T-account format clarifies this point.

Additional Consideration

If the balance sheet had revealed an increase or decrease in an accrued bond interest payable account, the entry calculating cash paid to bondholders would require modification. For example, if UBC had a bond interest payable account, and that account had increased (a credit) by $1 million, the entry would have been:

	($ in millions)	
Entry (7) Interest expense	5	
(revised) Discount on bonds payable		2
Interest payable		1
Cash (paid to bondholders)		2

(continued)

(concluded)

If the amount owed to bondholders increased by $1 million, they obviously were paid $1 million less cash than if there had been no change in the amount owed them. Similarly, if bond interest payable decreased by $1 million, the opposite would be true; that is, cash paid to them would have been $1 million more.

Prepaid Insurance

Beginning balance	6		
Cash paid for insurance *(increases prepaid insurance)*	?	7	Insurance expense *(decreases prepaid insurance)*
Ending balance	3		

From this analysis, we can conclude that $4 million was paid for insurance. We reach the same conclusion by preparing the following spreadsheet entry:

	($ in millions)	
Entry (8) Insurance expense ($7 – 0)	7	
Prepaid insurance ($3 – 6)		3
Cash (paid for insurance)		4

Since $3 million of prepaid insurance was allocated to insurance expense, only $4 million of the expense was paid in cash during the period.

The entry accounts for the change in both the insurance expense and prepaid insurance accounts and also identifies a cash outflow from operating activities.

9. LOSS ON SALE OF EQUIPMENT. A $2 million loss on the sale of equipment is the next item reported in the income statement. To determine the cash effect of the sale of equipment, we need additional information about the transaction. The information we need is provided in item (b) of Illustration 21–9. Recreating the journal entry for the transaction described gives us the following entry:

	($ in millions)	
Entry (9) Cash (from the sale of equipment)	5	
Loss on sale of equipment ($2 – 0)	2	
Accumulated depreciation ($14 × 50%)	7	
Buildings and equipment (given)		14

Recreating the journal entry for the sale of equipment reveals a $5 million cash inflow from investing activities.

The $5 million cash inflow is entered in the statement of cash flows section of the spreadsheet as an investing activity. The $2 million debit to the loss on sale of equipment explains the change in that account balance. Referring to the spreadsheet, we see that a portion of the change in accumulated depreciation was accounted for in entry (6). The debit to accumulated depreciation in the entry above completes the explanation for the change in that account. However, the credit to buildings and equipment only partially justifies the change in that account. We must assume that the analysis of a subsequent transaction will account for the unexplained portion of the change.

Recognize too that the loss, like the gain in entry (3), has no cash effect in the current period. Therefore, it is not reported in the statement of cash flows when using the direct method.

10. INCOME TAX EXPENSE. The final expense reported in the income statement is income tax expense. Since income taxes payable is the balance sheet account affected by this expense, we look to the change in that account to help determine the cash paid for income taxes. A T-account analysis can be used to find the cash effect as follows:

Income Tax Payable

		8	Beginning balance
Cash paid for income tax *(decreases the liability)*	?	9	Income tax expense
		6	Ending Balance

This analysis reveals that $11 million cash was paid for income taxes, $2 million more than the year's expense. The overpayment explains why the liability for income taxes decreased by $2 million.

The same conclusion can be reached from the following summary entry, which represents the net effect of income taxes on UBC's accounts.

	($ in millions)	
Entry (10) Income tax expense ($9 − 0)	9	
Income tax payable ($6 − 8)	2	
Cash (paid for income taxes)		11

Additional Consideration

Entry (10) would require modification in the situation described below.

Note that UBC does not have a deferred income tax account. Recall from Chapter 16 that temporary differences between taxable income and pretax accounting income give rise to deferred taxes. If temporary differences had been present, which would be evidenced by a change in a deferred income taxes account, the calculation of cash paid for income taxes would require modification. Assume, for example, that a deferred income tax liability account had experienced a credit change of $1 million for the year. In that case, the previous spreadsheet entry would be revised as follows:

	($ in millions)	
Entry (10) Interest tax expense	9	
(revised) Income tax payable	2	
Deferred income tax liability		1
Cash (paid for income taxes)		10

As the revised entry indicates, only $10 million cash would have been paid in this situation, rather than $11 million. The $1 million difference represents the portion of the income tax expense whose payment is deferred to a later year.

11. NET INCOME. The balance in the retained earnings account at the end of the year includes an increase due to net income. If we are to account for all changes in each of the accounts, we must include the following entry on the spreadsheet, which represents the closing of net income to retained earnings.

This entry partially explains the change in the retained earnings account.

	($ in millions)	
Entry (11) Net income	12	
Retained earnings		12

This entry does not affect amounts reported on the statement of cash flows. We include the entry in the spreadsheet analysis only to help explain account balance changes.

Balance Sheet Accounts

To identify all the operating, investing, and financing activities when using a spreadsheet, we must account for the changes in each account on both the income statement and the balance sheet. Thus far, we have explained the change in each income statement account. Since the transactions that gave rise to some of those changes involved balance sheet accounts as well, some changes in balance sheet accounts have already been explained. We now reconstruct the transactions that caused changes in the remaining balances.

With the exception of the cash account, the accounts are analyzed in the order of their presentation in the balance sheet. As noted earlier, we save the entry that reconciles the change in the cash account with the net change in cash from the statement of cash flows as a final check on the accuracy of the spreadsheet.

12. SHORT-TERM INVESTMENTS. Since the change in accounts receivable was explained previously [in entry (1)], we proceed to the next asset in the balance sheet. The balance in short-term investments increased from zero to $12 million. In the absence of evidence to the contrary, we could assume that the increase is due to the purchase of short-term investments during the year. This assumption is confirmed by item (c) of Illustration 21–9.

The entry to record the investment and our summary entry is as follows:

	($ in millions)	
Entry (12) Short-term investment ($12 – 0)	12	
Cash (purchase of short-term investment)		12

The $12 million increase in the short-term investments account is due to the purchase of short-term investments during the year.

The $12 million cash outflow is entered in the statement of cash flows section of the spreadsheet as an investing activity. An exception is when an investment is classified as a "trading security," in which case the cash outflow is reported as an operating activity.

Additional Consideration

Recall that some highly liquid, short-term investments such as money market funds, Treasury bills, or commercial paper might be classified as cash equivalents. If the short-term investment above were classified as a cash equivalent, its purchase would have no effect on the total of cash and cash equivalents. In other words, since cash would include this investment, its purchase would constitute both a debit and a credit to cash. We would neither prepare a spreadsheet entry nor report the transaction on the statement of cash flows.

Likewise, a sale of a cash equivalent would not affect the total of cash and cash equivalents and would not be reported.

An exception would be if the cash equivalent investment were sold for either more or less than its acquisition cost. For example, assume a Treasury bill classified as a cash equivalent was sold for $1 million more than its $2 million cost. The sale would constitute both a $3 million increase and a $2 million decrease in cash. We see the effect more clearly if we reconstruct the transaction in journal entry format:

	($ in millions)	
Cash	3	
Gain on sale of cash equivalent		1
Cash (cash equivalent investment)		2

The spreadsheet entry to reflect the net increase in cash would be:

Entry (X) Cash (from sale of cash equivalents)	1	
Gain on sale of cash equivalent		1

The $1 million net increase in cash and cash equivalents would be reported as a cash inflow from *operating* activities.

When we discuss the "indirect method" of reporting operating activities later in the chapter, we will be adding noncash losses and subtracting noncash gains when adjusting net income for noncash income items. Unlike most losses and gains, though, we would not add a loss or deduct a gain on cash equivalents because they *do* affect "cash" as defined.

13. LAND. The changes in the balances of both inventory and prepaid insurance were accounted for in previous summary entries: (4) and (8). Land is the next account whose change has yet to be fully explained. We discovered in a previous transaction that a sale of land caused a $10 million reduction in the account. Yet, the account shows a net *increase* of $20 million. It would be logical to assume that the unexplained increase of $30 million was due to a purchase of land. The transaction described in item (d) of Illustration 21–9 supports that assumption and is portrayed in the following summary entry:

A $30 million purchase of land accounts for the portion of the $20 million increase in the account that was not previously explained by the sale of land.

	($ in millions)	
Entry (13) Land (given)	30	
Cash (purchase of land)		30

The $30 million payment is reported as a cash outflow from investing activities.

14. BUILDINGS AND EQUIPMENT. When examining a previous transaction [entry (9)], we determined that the buildings and equipment account was reduced by $14 million from the sale of used equipment. And yet the account shows a net *increase* of $6 million for the year. The accounting records [item (e) of Illustration 21–9] reveal the remaining unexplained cause of the net increase. New equipment costing $20 million was purchased by issuing a $20 million note payable. Recall from the discussion in a previous section of this chapter that, although this is a noncash transaction, it represents both a significant investing activity (investing in new equipment) and a significant financing activity (financing the acquisition with long-term debt).

The journal entry used to record the transaction when the equipment was acquired also serves as our summary entry:

Investing in new equipment is a significant investing activity and financing the acquisition with long-term debt is a significant financing activity.

	($ in millions)	
Entry (14) Buildings and equipment (given)	20	
Note payable (given)		20

Remember that the statement of cash flows section of the spreadsheet will serve as the basis for our preparation of the formal statement. But the noncash entry above will not affect the cash flows section of the spreadsheet. Because we want to report this noncash investing and financing activity when we prepare the statement of cash flows, it is helpful to "mark" the spreadsheet entry as a reminder not to overlook this transaction when the statement is prepared. Crosses (*X*) serve this purpose on the spreadsheet in Illustration 21–9A.

Additional Consideration

Leases

When a lessee acquires an asset and related liability as a result of a lease agreement, there is no inflow or outflow of cash. However, because a primary purpose of the statement of cash flows is to report significant operating, investing, and financing activities, the initial transaction is reported in the disclosure notes as a significant noncash investing activity (investing in the asset) and financing activity (financing it with debt). Then the lessee's cash payments for leases are classified as financing activities in its statement of cash flows and presented separately from other financing cash flows. The lessor classifies its cash receipts from lease payments as operating activities in its statement of cash flows after initially reporting its acquisition of a lease receivable and derecognition of the asset under lease as a significant noncash investing and financing activity in its cash flow disclosure note.

15. BONDS PAYABLE. The balance in the bonds payable account decreased during the year by $15 million. Illustration 21–9, item (f), reveals the cause. Cash was paid to retire $15 million face value of bonds. The spreadsheet entry that duplicates the journal entry that was recorded when the bonds were retired is:

	($ in millions)	
Entry (15) Bonds payable ($35 − 50)	15	
Cash (retirement of bonds payable)		15

The cash outflow is reported as a financing activity.

Additional Consideration

Statement of Cash Flows: Reporting a Bond Discount or Premium

Conceptually, the way we report cash flows for bonds depends on whether the bonds were issued at face amount, at a discount, or at a premium.[12] As we look at these three possibilities, note that in each case:

- √ The same total amount that is borrowed (lent) and reported as a financing (investing) activity is the amount that should be reported later as a *financing* (*investing*) activity as the loan is repaid.
- √ All other amounts paid during or at the end of the term to maturity represent interest and should be reported among *operating* activities.

Though not codified in the *FASB Accounting Standards Codification*®, this treatment is a preference of the SEC, though anecdotal evidence suggests that many firms do not follow this procedure in practice.

Bonds Issued at Face Amount

If bonds are issued at their face amount, the cash inflow at issuance ($15 million in the illustration) is a financing activity as is the cash outflow at maturity to repay the amount borrowed ($15 million in the illustration). The periodic cash interest payments in the meantime are operating activities.

Bonds Issued at a Discount

If bonds are issued at a discount, the cash inflow at issuance is a financing activity, but that discounted price is less than the cash outflow for the face amount at maturity. The portion of the face amount paid at maturity to be reported as a financing activity, then, is limited to the amount borrowed (discounted price at issuance). The remaining portion of the payment (equal to the discount) represents interest and thus should be reported as an operating activity. This "extra" amount paid at maturity, together with the periodic cash interest payments during the term to maturity, comprise the total interest paid to borrow the cash received at issuance. This total amount of interest reported among operating activities is equal to the total interest expense reported during the term to maturity.

In Chapter 14's Illustration 14–3, for instance, $700,000 of bonds were issued at $666,633. That discounted price is the amount the issuer borrowed and the amount reported as a financing activity. When the $700,000 face amount is paid at maturity, $666,633 of that amount represents repayment of the borrowing and also is reported as a financing activity. The remaining $33,367 (the discount) represents interest (as do the periodic cash payments) and is reported among operating activities.

(continued)

[12]Source: Lisa Koonce, "SCF Insights," Financial Accounting Standards Research Initiative, October 6, 2011.

(concluded)

We can better visualize this if we look again at the amortization schedule we saw earlier for the bonds issued at a discount:

Date	Cash Interest	Effective Interest	Increase in Balance	Outstanding Balance
	(6% × Face amount)	(7% × Outstanding balance)	(Discount reduction)	
1/1/16				666,633
6/30/16	42,000	.07 (666,633) = 46,664	4,664	671,297
12/31/16	42,000	.07 (671,297) = 46,991	4,991	676,288
6/30/17	42,000	.07 (676,288) = 47,340	5,340	681,628
12/31/17	42,000	.07 (681,628) = 47,714	5,714	687,342
6/30/18	42,000	.07 (687,342) = 48,114	6,114	693,456
12/31/18	42,000	.07 (693,456) = 48,544	6,544	700,000
	252,000	**285,367**	33,367	

Operating

$700,000	Payment
– 33,367	Operating
$666,633	Financing

You may remember from Chapter 14 that the *total* interest, $285,367, is the $252,000 *cash* interest paid during the term to maturity plus the "extra" amount paid at maturity. The $33,367 extra amount is necessary for the bonds to pay an effective interest rate equal to what the market demanded when the bonds were purchased (which was higher than the rate at which the bonds made periodic interest payments).

To summarize, bonds issued at a discount are treated as follows on a statement of cash flows:

	Financing Activities	Operating Activities
INFLOWS:		
At issuance	Face Amount minus Discount	
OUTFLOWS:		
During term to maturity		Cash Interest Payments
At maturity	Face Amount minus Discount	Discount

Bonds Issued at a Premium

If the bonds are issued at a premium, the cash repaid at maturity is less than the cash received at issuance. So, when does the rest of the amount received at issuance get repaid? To see the answer, remember that when bonds are issued at a premium, it's because the stated interest rate at issuance is higher than the market interest rate. That means that the cash interest payments each period are higher than the interest expense amounts reported each period. The remainder of each payment is a repayment of the extra amount received at issuance. Similar to installment payments that include both (a) an amount for interest and (b) an amount that reduces the debt, we can think of these bond interest payments the same way. The cash payments cover the interest expense, and the remainder of each payment (the premium amortization) goes toward paying a portion of the amount borrowed. The interest expense portions of the cash payments are operating activities and the repayment portions are reported as financing activities each period. That means that the total amount of financing *outflows,* including payment of the face amount at maturity and the premium amortization over the life of the bonds, equals the total amount of financing *inflow* received when the bonds are issued.

(continued)

(concluded)

To see this more clearly, let's look again at the amortization schedule we saw in Chapter 14 for bonds issued at a premium:

Date	Cash Interest	Effective Interest		Decrease in Balance	Outstanding Balance
	(6% × Face amount)	(5% × Outstanding balance)		(Premium reduction)	
1/1/16					735,533
6/30/16	42,000	.05 (735,533) =	36,777	5,223	730,310
12/31/16	42,000	.05 (730,310) =	36,516	5,484	724,826
6/30/17	42,000	.05 (724,826) =	36,241	5,759	719,067
12/31/17	42,000	.05 (719,067) =	35,953	6,047	713,020
6/30/18	42,000	.05 (713,020) =	35,651	6,349	706,671
12/31/18	42,000	.05 (706,671) =	35,329	6,671	700,000
	252,000		**216,467**	**35,533**	

Operating

$700,000	Payment
+ 35,533	Financing
$735,533	Financing

To summarize, bonds issued at a premium are treated as follows on a statement of cash flows:

	Financing Activities	Operating Activities
INFLOWS:		
At issuance	Face Amount plus Premium	
OUTFLOWS:		
During term to maturity	Premium Amortization	Interest Expense
At maturity	Face Amount	

Remember that when using the ***indirect method,*** we add any discount amortization back to net income each period. That's in order to adjust the interest expense that's subtracted within net income to cash interest paid, which is the amount we want to report as an operating activity. When we have a premium, though, the amount we want to report as an operating activity is interest expense, as we just saw. As a result, we do *not* adjust net income for premium amortization as we do for discount amortization.

Early Extinguishment of Debt

The description of the transaction stipulated that $15 million of bonds were retired at their maturity on the first day of the year. Thus, any discount or premium on the bonds would have been completely amortized before the start of the year. If bonds are retired prior to their scheduled maturity, any unamortized discount or premium would be removed from the accounts at that time. For instance, assume that the bonds above were callable at $16 million and that $1 million of unamortized discount remained when they were retired by a call at that price. The summary entry would be revised as follows:

		($ in millions)	
Entry (15)	Bonds payable	15	
(revised)	Loss on early extinguishment of bonds	2	
	Discount on bonds payable		1
	Cash (retirement of bonds payable)		16

The loss, of course, would not be reported in the statement of cash flows. The amortization of the discount, however, would affect a previous summary entry. In entry (7) we concluded that the decrease in discount on bonds payable was due to the amortization of $2 million of the discount when recording bond interest expense. However, if the early

(continued)

(concluded)

retirement assumed above had occurred, that transaction would have accounted for $1 million of the $2 million decrease in the discount. Entry (7) would be modified as follows:

		($ in millions)	
Entry (7)	Interest expense	5	
(revised)	Discount on bonds payable		1
	Cash (paid to bondholders)		4

16–17. COMMON STOCK. The comparative balance sheets indicate that the common stock account balance increased by $30 million. We look to the accounting records— Illustration 21–9, item (g)—for an explanation. Two transactions, a stock dividend and a sale of new shares of common stock, combined to cause the increase. To create the summary entries for our analysis, we replicate the journal entries for the two transactions as described below.

Remember from Chapter 18 that to record a small stock dividend, we capitalize retained earnings for the market value of the shares distributed—in this case, 1 million shares times $13 per share, or $13 million. The entry is as follows:

Although this transaction does not identify a cash flow, nor does it represent an investing or financing activity, we include the summary entry to help explain changes in the three account balances affected.

		($ in millions)	
Entry (16)	Retained earnings (1 million shares × $13)	13	
	Common stock (1 million shares × $10 par)		10
	Paid-in capital—excess of par (difference)		3

Also recall from the discussion of noncash investing and financing activities earlier in the chapter, that stock dividends do not represent a significant investing or financing activity. Therefore, this transaction is not reported in the statement of cash flows. We include the entry in our spreadsheet analysis only to help explain changes in the account balances affected.

The sale of 2 million shares of common stock at $13 per share is represented by the following spreadsheet entry:

The sale of common shares explains the remaining increase in the common stock account and the remaining increase in paid-in capital—excess of par.

		($ in millions)	
Entry (17)	Cash (from sale of common stock)	26	
	Common stock ([$130 − 100] − 10)		20
	Paid-in capital—excess of par ([$29 − 20] − 3)		6

The cash inflow is reported in the statement of cash flows as a financing activity.

Additional Consideration

If cash is paid to retire outstanding shares of stock or to purchase those shares as treasury stock, the cash outflow would be reported in a statement of cash flows as a financing activity.

Together, the two entries above account for both the $30 million increase in the common stock account and the $9 million increase in paid-in capital—excess of par.

18. RETAINED EARNINGS. The stock dividend in entry (16) above includes a $13 million reduction of retained earnings. Previously, we saw in entry (11) that net income increased retained earnings by $12 million. The net reduction of $1 million accounted for by these two entries leaves $5 million of the $6 million net decrease in the account unexplained.

Retained Earnings

		25	Beginning balance
(16) Stock dividend	13	12	Net income (11)
(18) ?	?		
		19	Ending balance

Without additional information about the $5 million decrease in retained earnings, we might assume it was due to a $5 million cash dividend. This assumption is unnecessary, though, because the cash dividend is described in Illustration 21–9, item (h).

Retained Earnings

		25	Beginning balance
(16) Stock dividend	13	12	Net income (11)
(18) Cash dividend	5		
		19	Ending balance

The summary entry for the spreadsheet is as follows:

	($ in millions)	
Entry (18) Retained earnings	5	
Cash (payment of cash dividends)		5

The cash dividend accounts for the previously unexplained change in retained earnings.

19. COMPLETING THE SPREADSHEET. In preparing the spreadsheet to this point, we have analyzed each noncash account on both the income statement and the balance sheet. Our purpose was to identify the transactions that, during the year, had affected each account. By recreating each transaction in the form of a summary entry—in effect, duplicating the journal entry that had been used to record the transaction—we were able to explain the change in the balance of each account. That is, the debits and credits in the changes columns of the spreadsheet account for the increase or decrease in each noncash account. When a transaction being entered on the spreadsheet included an operating, investing, or financing activity, we entered that portion of the entry under the corresponding heading of the statement of cash flows section of the spreadsheet. Since, as noted earlier, there can be no operating, investing, or financing activity without a corresponding change in one or more of the noncash accounts, we should feel confident at this point that we have identified all of the activities that should be reported on the statement of cash flows.

To check the accuracy of the analysis, we compare the change in the balance of the cash account with the net change in cash flows produced by the activities listed in the statement of cash flows section of the spreadsheet. The net increase or decrease in cash flows from each of the statement of cash flows categories is extended to the extreme right column of the spreadsheet. By reference to Illustration 21–9A, we see that net cash flows from operating, investing, and financing activities are: $22 million; ($19 million); and $6 million, respectively. Together these activities provide a net increase in cash of $9 million. This amount corresponds to the increase in the balance of the cash account from $20 million to $29 million. To complete the spreadsheet, we include the final summary entry:

The cash flows section of the spreadsheet provides the information to be reported in the statement of cash flows.

	($ in millions)	
Entry (19) Cash	9	
Net increase in cash (from statement of cash flows activities)		9

As a final check of accuracy, we can confirm that the total of the debits is equal to the total of the credits in the changes columns of the spreadsheet.[13]

[13]The mechanical and computational aspects of the spreadsheet analysis are simplified greatly when performed on an electronic spreadsheet such as Microsoft Excel.

Ethical Dilemma

"We must get it," Courtney Lowell, president of Industrial Fasteners, roared. "Without it we're in big trouble." The "it" Mr. Lowell referred to is the renewal of a $14 million loan with Community First Bank. The big trouble he fears is the lack of funds necessary to repay the existing debt and few, if any, prospects for raising the funds elsewhere.

Mr. Lowell had just hung up the phone after a conversation with a bank vice-president in which it was made clear that this year's statement of cash flows must look better than last year's. Mr. Lowell knows that improvements are not on course to happen. In fact, cash flow projections were dismal.

Later that day, Tim Cratchet, assistant controller, was summoned to Mr. Lowell's office. "Cratchet," Lowell barked, "I've looked at our accounts receivable. I think we can generate quite a bit of cash by selling or factoring most of those receivables. I know it will cost us more than if we collect them ourselves, but it sure will make our cash flow picture look better."

Is there an ethical question facing Cratchet?

International Financial Reporting Standards

● LO21–9

Classification of Cash Flows. Like U.S. GAAP, international standards also require a statement of cash flows. Consistent with U.S. GAAP, cash flows are classified as operating, investing, or financing. However, the U.S. standard designates cash outflows for interest payments and cash inflows from interest and dividends received as operating cash flows. Dividends paid to shareholders are classified as financing cash flows.

IAS No. 7, on the other hand, allows more flexibility. Companies can report interest and dividends paid as either operating or financing cash flows and interest and dividends received as either operating or investing cash flows. Interest and dividend payments usually are reported as financing activities. Interest and dividends received normally are classified as investing activities.

IFRS ILLUSTRATION

Typical Classification of Cash Flows from Interest and Dividends

U.S. GAAP	IFRS
Operating Activities	***Operating Activities***
Dividends received	
Interest received	
Interest paid	
Investing Activities	***Investing Activities***
	Dividends received
	Interest received
Financing Activities	***Financing Activities***
Dividends paid	Dividends paid
	Interest paid

The spreadsheet is now complete. The statement of cash flows can now be prepared directly from the spreadsheet simply by presenting the items included in the statement of cash flows section of the spreadsheet in the appropriate format of the statement.

The statements of cash flows from an annual report of **CVS Caremark Corp.** are shown in Illustration 21–10. Notice that the reconciliation schedule was reported by CVS in the statement of cash flows itself. Many companies report the schedule separately in the disclosure notes.

Illustration 21–10 Statement of Cash Flows—CVS Caremark Corp.

Real Company Financials

CVS CAREMARK CORP.
Consolidated Statements of Cash Flows

	December 31,		
In millions	**2013**	**2012**	**2011**
Cash flows from operating activities:			
Cash receipts from customers	$114,993	113,205	$97,688
Cash paid for inventory and prescriptions dispensed by retail network pharmacies	(91,178)	(90,032)	(75,148)
Cash paid to other suppliers and employees	(14,295)	(13,643)	(13,635)
Interest received	8	4	4
Interest paid	(534)	(581)	(647)
Income taxes paid	(3,211)	(2,282)	(2,406)
Net cash provided by operating activities	5,783	6,671	5,856
Cash flows from investing activities:			
Purchases of property and equipment	(1,984)	(2,030)	(1,872)
Proceeds from sale-leaseback transactions	600	529	592
Proceeds from sale of property and equipment and other assets	54	23	4
Acquisitions (net of cash acquired) and other investments	(415)	(378)	(1,441)
Purchase of available-for-sale investments	(226)	—	(3)
Maturity of available-for-sale investments	136	—	60
Proceeds from sale of subsidiary	—	7	250
Net cash used in investing activities	(1,835)	(1,849)	(2,410)
Cash flows from financing activities:			
Increase (decrease) in short-term debt	(690)	(60)	450
Proceeds from issuance of long-term debt	3,964	1,239	1,463
Repayments of long-term debt	—	(1,718)	(2,122)
Purchase of noncontrolling interest in subsidiary	—	(26)	—
Dividends paid	(1,097)	(829)	(674)
Derivative settlements	—	—	(19)
Proceeds from exercise of stock options	500	836	431
Excess tax benefits from stock-based compensation	62	28	21
Repurchase of common stock	(3,976)	(4,330)	(3,001)
Other	—	—	(9)
Net cash used in financing activities	(1,237)	(4,860)	(3,460)
Effect of exchange rate changes on cash and cash equivalents	3	—	—
Net increase (decrease) in cash and cash equivalents	**2,714**	**(38)**	**(14)**
Cash and cash equivalents at the beginning of the year	1,375	1,413	1,427
Cash and cash equivalents at the end of the year	$ 4,089	1,375	$ 1,413
Reconciliation of net income to net cash provided by operating activities:			
Net income	$ 4,592	3,862	$ 3,458
Adjustments required to reconcile net income to net cash provided by operating activities:			
Depreciation and amortization	1,870	1,753	1,568
Stock-based compensation	141	132	135
Loss on early extinguishment of debt	—	348	—
Gain on sale of subsidiary	—	—	(53)
Deferred income taxes and other noncash items	(86)	(111)	144
Change in operating assets and liabilities, net of effects from acquisitions:			
Accounts receivable, net	(2,210)	(387)	(748)
Inventories	12	(853)	586
Other current assets	105	3	(420)
Other assets	(135)	(99)	(49)
Accounts payable and claims and discounts payable	1,024	1,147	1,128
Accrued expenses	471	766	105
Other long-term liabilities	(1)	110	2
Net cash provided by operating activities	$ 5,783	6,671	$ 5,856

Concept Review Exercise

COMPREHENSIVE REVIEW

The comparative balance sheets for 2016 and 2015 and the income statement for 2016 are given below for Beneficial Drill Company. Additional information from Beneficial Drill's accounting records is provided also.

Required:

Prepare the statement of cash flows of Beneficial Drill Company for the year ended December 31, 2016. Present cash flows from operating activities by the direct method and use a spreadsheet to assist in your analysis.

BENEFICIAL DRILL COMPANY
Comparative Balance Sheets
December 31, 2016 and 2015
($ in millions)

Assets	2016	2015
Cash	$ 24	$ 41
Accounts receivable	94	96
Investment revenue receivable	3	2
Inventory	115	110
Prepaid insurance	2	3
Long-term investments	77	60
Land	110	80
Buildings and equipment	220	240
Less: Accumulated depreciation	(35)	(60)
Patent	15	16
	$625	$588
Liabilities		
Accounts payable	$ 23	$ 30
Salaries payable	2	5
Bond interest payable	4	2
Income tax payable	6	8
Deferred income tax liability	5	4
Notes payable	15	0
Bonds payable	150	130
Less: Discount on bonds	(9)	(10)
Shareholders' Equity		
Common stock	210	200
Paid-in capital—excess of par	44	40
Retained earnings	182	179
Less: Treasury stock (at cost)	(7)	0
	$625	$588

BENEFICIAL DRILL COMPANY
Income Statement
For Year Ended December 31, 2016
($ in millions)

Revenues		
Sales revenue	$200	
Investment revenue	6	
Investment revenue—sale of treasury bills	1	$207

(continued)

Expenses and losses		
Cost of goods sold	110	
Salaries expense	30	
Depreciation expense	5	
Patent amortization expense	1	
Insurance expense	3	
Bond interest expense	14	
Loss on destruction of equipment	10	
Income tax expense	7	(180)
Net income		$ 27

Additional information from the accounting records:

a. Investment revenue includes Beneficial Drill Company's $3 million share of the net income of Hammer Company, an equity method investee.

b. Treasury bills were sold during 2016 at a gain of $1 million. Beneficial Drill Company classifies its investments in Treasury bills as cash equivalents.

c. Equipment that originally cost $60 million and was one-half depreciated was rendered unusable by a bolt of lightning. Most major components of the machine were unharmed and were sold for $20 million.

d. Temporary differences between pretax accounting income and taxable income caused the deferred income tax liability to increase by $1 million.

e. The common stock of Wrench Corporation was purchased for $14 million as a long-term investment.

f. Land costing $30 million was acquired by paying $15 million cash and issuing a 13%, seven-year, $15 million note payable to the seller.

g. New equipment was purchased for $40 million cash.

h. $20 million of bonds were sold at face value.

i. On January 19, Beneficial issued a 5% stock dividend (1 million shares). The market price of the $10 par value common stock was $14 per share at that time.

j. Cash dividends of $10 million were paid to shareholders.

k. In November, 500,000 common shares were repurchased as treasury stock at a cost of $7 million.

Solution:

BENEFICIAL DRILL COMPANY
Spreadsheet for the Statement of Cash Flows

	Dec. 31 2015	Changes Debits		Credits		Dec. 31 2016
Balance Sheet						
Assets						
Cash	41			(20)	17	24
Accounts receivable	96			(1)	2	94
Investment revenue receivable	2	(2)	1			3
Inventory	110	(4)	5			115
Prepaid insurance	3			(8)	1	2
Long-term investments	60	(2)	3			
		(13)	14			77
Land	80	(14)	30X			110
Buildings and equipment	240	(15)	40	(10)	60	220
Less: Accumulated depreciation	(60)	(10)	30	(6)	5	(35)
Patent	16			(7)	1	15
	588					625

(continued)

(concluded)

BENEFICIAL DRILL COMPANY
Spreadsheet for the Statement of Cash Flows

	Dec. 31 2015	Changes Debits		Credits		Dec. 31 2016
Liabilities						
Accounts payable	30	(4)	7			23
Salaries payable	5	(5)	3			2
Bond interest payable	2			(9)	2	4
Income tax payable	8	(11)	2			6
Deferred income tax liability	4			(11)	1	5
Notes payable	0			(14)	15X	15
Bonds payable	130			(16)	20	150
Less: Discount on bonds	(10)			(9)	1	(9)
Shareholders' Equity						
Common stock	200			(17)	10	210
Paid-in capital—excess of par	40			(17)	4	44
Retained earnings	179	(17)	14			
		(18)	10	(12)	27	182
Less: Treasury stock	0	(19)	7			(7)
	588					625
Income Statement						
Revenues:						
Sales revenue				(1)	200	200
Investment revenue				(2)	6	6
Investment revenue—sale of Treasury bills				(3)	1	1
Expenses:						
Cost of goods sold		(4)	110			(110)
Salaries expense		(5)	30			(30)
Depreciation expense		(6)	5			(5)
Patent amortization expense		(7)	1			(1)
Insurance expense		(8)	3			(3)
Bond interest expense		(9)	14			(14)
Loss on destruction of equipment		(10)	10			(10)
Income tax expense		(11)	7			(7)
Net income		(12)	27			27
Statement of Cash Flows						
Operating Activities:						
Cash inflows:						
From customers		(1)	202			
From investment revenue		(2)	2			
From sale of Treasury bills		(3)	1			
Cash outflows:						
To suppliers of goods				(4)	122	
To employees				(5)	33	
For insurance expense				(8)	2	
For bond interest expense				(9)	11	
For income taxes				(11)	7	
Net cash flows						29
Investing Activities:						
Sale of equipment		(10)	20			
Purchase of LT investments				(13)	14	
Purchase of land				(14)	15	
Purchase of equipment				(15)	40	
Net cash flows						(49)
Financing Activities:						
Sale of bonds payable		(16)	20			
Payment of cash dividends				(18)	10	
Purchase of treasury stock				(19)	7	
Net cash flows						3
Net decrease in cash		(20)	17			(17)
Totals			635		635	

BENEFICIAL DRILL COMPANY
Statement of Cash Flows
For Year Ended December 31, 2016
($ in millions)

Cash Flows from Operating Activities		
Cash inflows:		
From customers	$202	
From investment revenue	2	
From sale of Treasury bills	1	
Cash outflows:		
To suppliers of goods	(122)	
To employees	(33)	
For insurance expense	(2)	
For bond interest expense	(11)	
For income taxes	(8)	
Net cash flows from operating activities		$29
Cash Flows from Investing Activities		
Sale of equipment	$ 20	
Purchase of long-term investments	(14)	
Purchase of land	(15)	
Purchase of equipment	(40)	
Net cash flows from investing activities		(49)
Cash Flows from Financing Activities		
Sale of bonds payable	$ 20	
Payment of cash dividends	(10)	
Purchase of treasury stock	(7)	
Net cash flows from financing activities		3
Net decrease in cash		($17)
Cash balance, January 1		41
Cash balance, December 31		$24
Noncash Investing and Financing Activities		
Acquired $30 million of land by paying cash and issuing a 13%, 7-year note as follows:		
Cost of land	$ 30	
Cash paid	15	
Note issued	$ 15	

Preparing the SCF: Indirect Method of Reporting Cash Flows from Operating Activities

PART C

Getting There through the Back Door

The presentation of cash flows from operating activities illustrated in Part B is referred to as the *direct method.* By this method, the cash effect of each operating activity (i.e., income statement item) is reported directly on the statement of cash flows. For instance, cash received from customers is reported as the cash effect of sales activities, and cash paid to suppliers is reported as the cash effect of cost of goods sold. Income statement items that have *no* cash effect, such as depreciation expense, gains, and losses, are simply not reported.

As pointed out previously, a permissible alternative is the *indirect method,* by which the net cash increase or decrease from operating activities is derived indirectly by starting with reported net income and working backwards to convert that amount to a cash basis. The derivation by the indirect method of net cash flows from operating activities for UBC is shown in Illustration 21–9B. For the adjustment amounts, you may wish to refer back to UBC's balance sheets and income statement presented in Illustration 21–9.

Illustration 21–9B
Indirect Method

The indirect method derives the net cash increase or decrease from operating activities indirectly, by starting with reported net income and "working backwards" to convert that amount to a cash basis.

Cash Flows from Operating Activities—Indirect Method *and* Reconciliation of Net Income to Net Cash Flows from Operating Activities	
Net Income	$12
Adjustments for noncash effects:	
Gain on sale of land	(8)
Depreciation expense	3
Loss on sale of equipment	2
Changes in operating assets and liabilities:	
Increase in accounts receivable	(2)
Decrease in inventory	4
Increase in accounts payable	6
Increase in salaries payable	2
Decrease in discount on bonds payable	2
Decrease in prepaid insurance	3
Decrease in income tax payable	(2)
Net cash flows from operating activities	$22

Notice that the indirect method yields the same $22 million net cash flows from operating activities as does the direct method. This is understandable when you consider that the indirect method simply reverses the differences between the accrual-based income statement and cash flows from operating activities. We accomplish this as described in the next two sections.

Components of Net Income That Do Not Increase or Decrease Cash

Amounts that were subtracted in determining net income but did not reduce cash are *added back* to net income to reverse the effect of their having been subtracted. For example, depreciation expense and the loss on sale of equipment are added back to net income. Other things being equal, this restores net income to what it would have been had depreciation and the loss not been subtracted at all.

Similarly, amounts that were added in determining net income but did not increase cash are subtracted from net income to reverse the effect of their having been added. For example, UBC's gain on sale of land is deducted from net income. Here's why. UBC sold for $18 million land that originally cost $10 million. Recording the sale produced a gain of $8 million, which UBC appropriately included in its income statement. But did this gain increase UBC's cash? No. Certainly selling the land increased cash—by $18 million. We therefore include the $18 million as a cash inflow in the statement of cash flows. However, the sale of land is an investing activity. The gain itself, though, is simply the difference between cash received in the sale of land (reported as an investing activity) and the original cost of the land. If UBC also reported the $8 million gain as a cash flow from operating activities, in addition to reporting $18 million as a cash flow from investing activities, UBC would report the $8 million twice. So, because UBC added the gain in determining its net income but the gain had no effect on cash, the gain must now be subtracted from net income to reverse the effect of its having been added.

Components of Net Income That Do Increase or Decrease Cash

For components of net income that increase or decrease cash, but by an amount different from that reported in the income statement, net income is adjusted for changes in the balances of related balance sheet accounts to *convert the effects of those items to a cash basis.*

For example, sales of $100 million are included in the income statement as a component of net income, and yet, since accounts receivable increased by $2 million, only $98 million cash was collected from customers during the reporting period. Sales are converted to a cash basis by subtracting the $2 million increase in accounts receivable. Here's another example:

The income statement reports salaries expense as $13 million. Just because employees earned $13 million during the reporting period, though, doesn't necessarily mean UBC paid those employees $13 million in cash during the same period. In fact, we see in the comparative balance sheets that salaries payable increased from $1 million to $3 million; UBC owes its employees $2 million more than before the year started. The company must not have paid the entire $13 million expense. By analyzing salaries expense in relation to the change in salaries payable, we can determine the amount of cash paid to employees:

Salaries Payable

		1	Beginning balance
Cash paid to employees *(decreases salaries payable)*	?	13	Salaries expense *(increases salaries payable)*
		3	Ending balance

This inspection indicates that UBC paid only $11 million cash to its employees; the remaining $2 million of salaries expense is reflected as an increase in salaries payable. From a cash perspective, then, by subtracting $13 million for salaries in the income statement, UBC has subtracted $2 million more than the reduction in cash. Adding back the $2 million leaves UBC in the same position as if it had deducted only the $11 million cash paid to employees.

Following a similar analysis of the cash effects of the remaining components of net income, those items are likewise converted to a cash basis by adjusting net income for increases and decreases in related accounts.

For components of net income that increase or decrease cash by an amount exactly the same as that reported in the income statement, no adjustment of net income is required. For example, investment revenue of $3 million is included in UBC's $12 million net income amount. Because $3 million also is the amount of cash received from that activity, this element of net income already represents its cash effect and needs no adjustment.[14]

Comparison with the Direct Method

The indirect method is compared with the direct method in Illustration 21–11, using the data of UBC. To better illustrate the relationship between the two methods, the adjustments to net income using the indirect method are presented parallel to the related cash inflows and cash outflows of the direct method. The income statement is included in the graphic to demonstrate that the indirect method also serves to reconcile differences between the elements of that statement and the cash flows reported by the direct method.

As a practical consideration, you might notice that the adjustments to net income using the indirect method follow a convenient pattern. *Increases* in related assets are deducted from net income (i.e., the increase in accounts receivable) when converting to cash from operating activities. Conversely, *decreases* in assets are added (inventory and prepaid insurance in this case). Changes in related liabilities are handled in just the opposite way. Increases in related liabilities are *added* to net income (i.e., the increases in accounts payable and salaries payable) while decreases in liabilities are subtracted (i.e., decrease in income tax payable).[15]

Of course, these are adjustments to net income that effectively convert components of income from reported accrual amounts to a cash basis. The other adjustments to net income (gain, depreciation, loss) as pointed out earlier are to remove the three income statement components that have no effect at all on cash. This pattern is summarized in Illustration 21–12 on the next page.

[14]We determined in Part B (subsection 2) that there is no evidence that cash received from investments differs from investment revenue.

[15]The adjustment for the decrease in bond discount is logically consistent with this pattern as well. Bond discount is a contra liability. It's logical, then, that an adjustment for a decrease in this account be added—the opposite of the way a decrease in a liability is treated.

Illustration 21–11 Comparison of the Indirect Method and the Direct Method of Determining Cash Flows from Operating Activities

Income Statement		Cash Flows from Operating Activities: Indirect Method		Direct Method	
		Net income	$12		
		Adjustments:			
Sales	$100	Increase in accounts receivable	(2)	Cash received from customers	$98
Investment revenue	3	*(No adjustment—no investment revenue receivable or long-term investments)*		Cash received from investments	3
Gain on sale of land	8	Gain on sale of land	(8)	*(Not reported—no cash effect)*	
Cost of goods sold	(60)	Decrease in inventory	4		
		Increase in accounts payable	6	Cash paid to suppliers	(50)
Salaries expense	(13)	Increase in salaries payable	2	Cash paid to employees	(11)
Depreciation expense	(3)	Depreciation expense	3	*(Not reported—no cash effect)*	
Interest expense	(5)	Decrease in bond discount	2	Cash paid for interest	(3)
Insurance expense	(7)	Decrease in prepaid insurance	3	Cash paid for insurance	(4)
Loss on sale of equipment	(2)	Loss on sale of equipment	2	*(Not reported—no cash effect)*	
Income tax expense	(9)	Decrease in income tax payable	(2)	Cash paid for income taxes	(11)
Net Income	$ 12	**Net cash flows from operating activities**	**$22**	**Net cash flows from operating activities**	**$22**

Illustration 21–12

Adjustments to Convert Net Income to a Cash Basis—Indirect Method

Type of Adjustment	To Adjust for Noncash Effect
Adjustments for Noncash Effects:	
Income statement components that have *no effect* at all on cash but are *additions* to income	Deduct from net income
Income statement components that have *no effect* at all on cash but are *deductions* from income	Add to net income
Changes in Operating Assets and Liabilities:	
Increases in assets related to an income statement component	Deduct from net income
Decreases in assets related to an income statement component	Add to net income
Increases in liabilities related to an income statement component	Add to net income
Decreases in liabilities related to an income statement component	Deduct from net income

Although either the direct method or the indirect method is permitted, the FASB strongly encourages companies to report cash flows from operating activities by the direct method. The obvious appeal of this approach is that it reports specific operating cash receipts and operating cash payments, which is consistent with the primary objective of the statement of cash flows. Investors and creditors gain additional insight into the specific sources of cash receipts and payments from operating activities revealed by this reporting method. Also, statement users can more readily interpret and understand the information presented because the direct method avoids the confusion caused by reporting noncash items and other reconciling adjustments under the caption *cash flows from operating activities.* Nonetheless, the vast majority of companies choose to use the indirect method. Reasons for this choice range from longstanding tradition to the desire to withhold as much information as possible from competitors.[16]

[16]As indicated earlier, a recent Staff Draft of an Exposure Draft from the IASB and FASB advocates requiring the direct method and disallowing the indirect method for the proposed new Financial Statement Presentation format.

Reconciliation of Net Income to Cash Flows from Operating Activities

As we discussed earlier, whether cash flows from operating activities are reported by the direct method or by the indirect method, the financial statements must report a reconciliation of net income to net cash flows from operating activities. When the direct method is used, the reconciliation is presented in a separate schedule and is identical to the presentation of net cash flows from operating activities by the indirect method. In other words, Illustration 21–9B also serves as the reconciliation schedule to accompany a statement of cash flows using the direct method. Obviously, a separate reconciliation schedule is not required when using the indirect method because the cash flows from operating activities section of the statement of cash flows *is* a reconciliation of net income to net cash flows from operating activities.[17]

Remember that the direct and indirect methods are alternative approaches to deriving net cash flows from *operating* activities only. The choice of which method is used for that purpose does not affect the way cash flows from *investing* and *financing* activities are identified and reported.

The statements of cash flows from the annual report of **Toys "R" Us, Inc.**, which uses the indirect method, are shown in Illustration 21–13.

Illustration 21–13 Statement of Cash Flows—Indirect Method; Toys "R" Us, Inc. Real World Financials

TOYS "R" US, INC. AND SUBSIDIARIES
Consolidated Statements of Cash Flows

	Fiscal Years Ended		
(In millions)	**February 1, 2014**	**February 2, 2013**	**January 28, 2012**
Cash Flows from Operating Activities:			
Net (loss) earnings	**$(1,036)**	$ 39	$ 151
Adjustments to reconcile Net (loss) earnings to Net cash provided by operating activities:			
Depreciation and amortization	**388**	407	403
Amortization and write-off of debt issuance costs	**51**	36	35
Net gains on sales of properties	**(8)**	(4)	(3)
Deferred income taxes	**133**	36	(43)
Non-cash portion of asset impairments, restructuring and other charges	**49**	22	18
Goodwill impairment	**378**	—	—
Other	**37**	6	(5)
Changes in operating assets and liabilities:			
Accounts and other receivables	**(1)**	(9)	1
Merchandise inventories	**13**	(32)	(92)
Prepaid expenses and other operating assets	**21**	13	45
Accounts payable, Accrued expenses and other liabilities	**160**	(4)	(182)
Income taxes payable and receivable	**(41)**	27	(9)
Net cash provided by operating activities	**144**	537	319
Cash Flows from Investing Activities:			
Capital expenditures	**(238)**	(286)	(380)
(Increase) decrease in restricted cash	**(34)**	14	(14)
Proceeds from sales of fixed assets	**35**	20	24
Purchases of debt securities	**(20)**	—	(26)
Proceeds from redemption of debt securities	**52**	—	—
Acquisitions	—	(15)	(70)
Cash effect of the consolidation of Labuan	—	—	12
Net cash used in investing activities	**(205)**	(267)	(454)

(continued)

[17]It is permissible to present the reconciliation in a separate schedule and to report the net cash flows from operating activities as a single line item on the statement of cash flows.

Illustration 21–13 (concluded)

(In millions)	February 1, 2014	February 2, 2013	January 28, 2012
	Fiscal Years Ended		
Cash Flows from Financing Activities:			
Long-term debt borrowings	3,159	1,972	2,236
Long-term debt repayments	(3,491)	(1,802)	(2,396)
Short-term debt borrowings, net	(2)	5	(11)
Capitalized debt issuance costs	(47)	(25)	(14)
Purchase of Toys-Japan shares	—	—	(1)
Other	(7)	(3)	1
Net cash (used in) provided by financing activities	(388)	147	(185)
Effect of exchange rate changes on Cash and cash equivalents	(25)	—	8
Cash and cash equivalents:			
Net (decrease) increase during period	(474)	417	(312)
Cash and cash equivalents at beginning of period	1,118	701	1,013
Cash and cash equivalents at end of period	$ 644	$1,118	$ 701
Supplemental Disclosures of Cash Flow Information:			
Interest paid	$ 458	$ 432	$ 432
Net income tax payments (refunds)	$ 71	$ (4)	$ 66
Non-Cash Operating Information:			
Purchases of property and equipment included in Accounts payable and Accrued expenses and other current liabilities	$ 24	$ 26	$ 28

For most companies, expenditures for interest and for taxes are significant. Cash payments for interest and for taxes usually are specifically indicated when the direct method is employed as is the case for **CVS Caremark Corp.** reported earlier in Illustration 21–10. When the indirect method is used, those amounts aren't readily apparent and must be *separately reported* either on the face of the statement or in an accompanying disclosure note as Toys "R" Us does.

We use a spreadsheet to help prepare a statement of cash flows by the indirect method in Appendix 21A.

Decision Makers' Perspective—Cash Flow Ratios

We have emphasized the analysis of financial statements from a decision maker's perspective throughout this text. Often that analysis included the development and comparison of financial ratios. Ratios based on income statement and balance sheet amounts enjoy a long tradition of acceptance from which several standard ratios, including those described in earlier chapters, have evolved. To gain another viewpoint, some analysts supplement their investigation with cash flow ratios. Some cash flow ratios are derived by simply substituting cash flow from operations (CFFO) from the statement of cash flows in place of net income in many ratios, not to replace those ratios but to complement them. For example, the times interest earned ratio can be modified to reflect the number of times the cash outflow for interest is provided by cash inflow from operations and any of the profitability ratios can be modified to determine the cash generated from assets, shareholders' equity, sales, etc. Illustration 21–14 summarizes the calculation and usefulness of several representative cash flow ratios.

Cash flow ratios have received limited acceptance to date, due in large part to the long tradition of accrual-based ratios coupled with the relatively brief time that all companies have published statements of cash flows. A lack of consensus on cash flow ratios by which to make comparisons also has slowed their acceptance. In fact, companies are prohibited

Illustration 21–14
Cash Flow Ratios

	Calculation	Measures
Performance Ratios		
Cash flow to sales	CFFO / Net sales	Cash generated by each sales dollar
Cash return on assets	CFFO / Average total assets	Cash generated from all resources
Cash return on shareholders' equity	CFFO / Average shareholders' equity	Cash generated from owner-provided resources
Cash to income	CFFO / Income from continuing operations	Cash-generating ability of continuing operations
Cash flow per share	(CFFO − preferred dividends) / Weighted-average shares	Operating cash flow on a per share basis
Sufficiency Ratios		
Debt coverage	Total liabilities / CFFO	Financial risk and financial leverage
Interest coverage	(CFFO + interest + taxes) / Interest	Ability to satisfy fixed obligations
Reinvestment	CFFO / Cash outflow for noncurrent assets	Ability to acquire assets with operating cash flows
Debt payment	CFFO / Cash outflow for LT debt repayment	Ability to pay debts with operating cash flows
Dividend payment	CFFO / Cash outflow for dividends	Ability to pay dividends with operating cash flows
Investing and financing activity	CFFO / Cash outflows for investing and financing activities	Ability to acquire assets, pay debts, and make distributions to owners

from reporting cash flow per share in the statement of cash flows. Nevertheless, cash flow ratios offer insight in the evaluation of a company's profitability and financial strength.[18] ●

Financial Reporting Case Solution

1. **What are the cash flow aspects of the situation that Mr. Barr may be overlooking in making his case for a wage increase? How can a company's operations generate a healthy profit and yet produce meager or even negative cash flows?** *(p. 1248)* Positive net income does not necessarily indicate a healthy cash position. A statement of cash flows provides information about cash flows not seen when looking only at the balance sheet and the income statement. Although cash flows from operating activities result from the same activities that are reported in the income statement, the income statement reports the activities on an accrual basis. That is, revenues reported are those earned during the reporting period, regardless of when cash is received, and the expenses incurred in generating those revenues, regardless of when cash is paid. Thus, the very same operations can generate a healthy profit and yet produce meager or even negative cash flows.
2. **What information can a statement of cash flows provide about a company's investing activities that can be useful in decisions such as this?** *(p. 1250)* Cash flows from investing activities result from the acquisition and disposition of assets. Information about

[18]Proposals for informative sets of cash flow ratios are offered by Charles Carslaw and John Mills, "Developing Ratios for Effective Cash Flow Analysis," *Journal of Accountancy,* November 1991; Don Giacomino and David Mielke, "Cash Flows: Another Approach to Ratio Analysis," *Journal of Accountancy,* March 1993; and John Mills and Jeanne Yamamura, "The Power of Cash Flows Ratios," *Journal of Accountancy,* October 1998.

investing activities is useful to decision makers regarding the nature and magnitude of productive assets being acquired for future use. In the union negotiations, for instance, Mr. Barr may not be aware of the substantial investments under way to replace and update equipment and the cash requirements of those investments. Relatedly, the relatively low depreciation charges accelerated depreciation provides in the later years of assets' lives may cause profits to seem artificially high given the necessity to replace those assets at higher prices.

3. **What information can a statement of cash flows provide about a company's financing activities that can be useful in decisions such as this?** *(p. 1251)* Information about financing activities provides insights into sources of a company's external financing. Recent debt issues, for instance, might indicate a need for higher cash flows to maintain higher interest charges. Similarly, recent external financing activity may suggest that a company might be near its practical limits from external sources and, therefore, may need a greater reliance on internal financing through operations. ●

The Bottom Line

- **LO21–1** Decision makers focus on the prospects of receiving a cash return from their dealings with a firm. But it is the ability of the firm to generate cash flows to itself that ultimately determines the potential for cash flows to investors and creditors. The statement of cash flows fills an information gap left by the balance sheet and the income statement by presenting information about cash flows that the other statements either do not provide or provide only indirectly. *(p. 1243)*
- **LO21–2** Cash includes cash equivalents. These are short-term, highly liquid investments that can readily be converted to cash with little risk of loss. *(p. 1247)*
- **LO21–3** Cash flows from operating activities are both inflows and outflows of cash that result from activities reported in the income statement. *(p. 1248)*
- **LO21–4** Unlike the direct method, which directly lists cash inflows and outflows, the indirect method derives cash flows indirectly, by starting with reported net income and working backwards to convert that amount to a cash basis. *(p. 1249)*
- **LO21–5** Cash flows from investing activities are related to the acquisition and disposition of assets, other than inventory and assets classified as cash equivalents. *(p. 1250)*
- **LO21–6** Cash flows from financing activities result from the external financing of a business. *(p. 1251)*
- **LO21–7** Noncash investing and financing activities, such as acquiring equipment (an investing activity) by issuing a long-term note payable (a financing activity), are reported in a related disclosure schedule or note. *(p. 1252)*
- **LO21–8** A spreadsheet provides a systematic method of preparing a statement of cash flows by analyzing available data to insure that all operating, investing, and financing activities are detected. Recording spreadsheet entries that explain account balance changes simultaneously identifies and classifies the activities to be reported on the statement of cash flows. *(p. 1253)*
- **LO21–9** IFRS allows more flexibility than U.S. GAAP in the classification of cash flows. Companies can report interest and dividends paid as either operating or financing cash flows and interest and dividends received as either operating or investing cash flows. *(p. 1272)* ●

APPENDIX 21A Spreadsheet for the Indirect Method

A spreadsheet is equally useful in preparing a statement of cash flows whether we use the direct or the indirect method of determining cash flows from operating activities. The format of the spreadsheet differs only with respect to operating activities. The analysis of transactions for the purpose of identifying cash flows to be reported is the same. To illustrate, Illustration 21A–1 on the next page provides a spreadsheet analysis of the data for UBC.

Two differences should be noted between the spreadsheet in Illustration 21A–1 and the spreadsheet we used earlier for the direct method. First, in the statement of cash flows section of the spreadsheet, under the heading of "cash flows from operating activities,"

Illustration 21A–1

Indirect Method

UNITED BRANDS CORPORATION
Spreadsheet for the Statement of Cash Flows

	Dec. 31 2015	Changes: Debits		Changes: Credits		Dec. 31 2016
Balance Sheet						
Assets						
Cash	20	(19)	9			29
Accounts receivable	30	(5)	2			32
Short-term investments	0	(12)	12			12
Inventory	50			(6)	4	46
Prepaid insurance	6			(8)	3	3
Land	60	(13)	30	(2)	10	80
Buildings and equipment	75	(14)	20X	(3)	14	81
Less: Accumulated depreciation	(20)	(3)	7	(4)	3	(16)
	221					267
Liabilities						
Accounts payable	20			(7)	6	26
Salaries payable	1			(9)	2	3
Income tax payable	8	(11)	2			6
Notes payable	0			(14)	20X	20
Bonds payable	50	(15)	15			35
Less: Discount on bonds	(3)			(10)	2	(1)
Shareholders' Equity						
Common stock	100			(16)	10	
				(17)	20	130
Paid-in capital—excess of par	20			(16)	3	
				(17)	6	29
Retained earnings	25	(16)	13			
		(18)	5	(1)	12	19
	221					267
Statement of Cash Flows						
Operating activities:						
Net income		(1)	12			
Adjustments for noncash effects:						
Gain on sale of land				(2)	8	
Depreciation expense		(4)	3			
Loss on sale of equipment		(3)	2			
Increase in accounts receivable				(5)	2	
Decrease in inventory		(6)	4			
Decrease in prepaid insurance		(8)	3			
Increase in accounts payable		(7)	6			
Increase in salaries payable		(9)	2			
Decrease in income tax payable				(11)	2	
Amortization of discount		(10)	2			
Net cash flows						22
Investing activities:						
Purchase of land				(13)	30	
Purchase of S-T investment				(12)	12	
Sale of land		(2)	18			
Sale of equipment		(3)	5			
Net cash flows						(19)
Financing activities:						
Sale of common shares		(17)	26			
Retirement of bonds payable				(15)	15	
Payment of cash dividends				(18)	5	
Net cash flows						6
Net increase in cash				(19)	9	9
Totals			198		198	

specific cash inflows and cash outflows are replaced by net income and the required adjustments for noncash effects. Second, we do not include an income statement section. This section is unnecessary because, using the indirect method, we are not interested in identifying specific operating activities that cause increases and decreases in cash. Instead, we need from the income statement only the amount of net income, which is converted to a cash basis by adjusting for any noncash amounts included in net income. The spreadsheet entries in journal entry form for the indirect method are illustrated in Illustration 21A–2.

Remember that there is no mandatory order in which the account changes must be analyzed. However, since we determine net cash flows from operating activities by working backwards from net income when using the indirect method, it is convenient to start with the spreadsheet entry that represents the credit to retained earnings due to net income. This entry corresponds to summary entry (11) using the direct method. By entering the debit portion of the entry as the first item under the cash flows from operating activities (CFOA), we establish net income as the initial amount of cash flows from operating activities, which is then adjusted to a cash basis by subsequent entries. Entries (2)–(4) duplicate the transactions that involve noncash components of net income. Changes in current assets and current liabilities that represent differences between revenues and expenses and the cash effects of those revenues and expenses are accounted for by entries (5)–(11). Summary entries (12)–(19) explain the changes in the balance sheet not already accounted for by previous entries, and are identical to entries (12)–(19) recorded using the direct method.

Illustration 21A–2
Spreadsheet Entries for the Indirect Method

Entry (1)	Net income—CFOA	12	
	Retained earnings		12
	Establishes net income as the initial amount of cash flows from operating activities, to be adjusted to a cash basis by subsequent entries.		
Entry (2)	Cash (received from sale of land)	18	
	Land		10
	Gain on sale of land—CFOA		8
	Deducts the noncash gain added in determining net income, explains a portion of the change in land, and identifies a cash inflow from investing activities.		
Entry (3)	Cash (received from sale of equipment)	5	
	Loss on sale of equipment—CFOA	2	
	Accumulated depreciation	7	
	Buildings and equipment		14
	Adds back the noncash loss subtracted in determining net income, explains portions of the changes in accumulated depreciation and buildings and equipment, and identifies a cash inflow from investing activities.		
Entry (4)	Depreciation expense—CFOA	3	
	Accumulated depreciation		3
	Adds back the noncash expense subtracted in determining net income.		
Entry (5)	Accounts receivable	2	
	Increase in accounts receivable—CFOA		2
	Reduces net income to reflect $98 million cash received from customers rather than $100 million sales.		
Entry (6)	Decrease in inventory—CFOA	4	
	Inventory		4
	Increases net income to reflect a deduction of $56 million cost of goods purchased rather than $60 million cost of goods sold.		
Entry (7)	Increase in accounts payable—CFOA	6	
	Accounts payable		6
	Increases net income to reflect a deduction of $50 million cash paid to suppliers rather than $56 million cost of goods purchased.		

(continued)

Illustration 21A–2
(concluded)

		Debit	Credit
Entry (8)	Decrease in prepaid insurance—CFOA	3	
	Prepaid insurance		3
	Increases net income to reflect a deduction of $4 million cash paid for insurance rather than $7 million insurance expense.		
Entry (9)	Increase in salaries payable—CFOA	2	
	Salaries payable		2
	Increases net income to reflect a deduction of $11 million cash paid to employees rather than $13 million salaries expense.		
Entry (10)	Amortization of discount on bonds—CFOA	2	
	Discount on bonds		2
	Increases net income to reflect a deduction of $3 million cash paid for bond interest rather than $5 million bond interest expense.		
Entry (11)	Income taxes payable	2	
	Decrease in income taxes payable—CFOA		2
	Reduces net income to reflect a deduction of $11 million cash paid for income taxes rather than $9 million income tax expense.		
Entry (12)	Short-term investment	12	
	Cash (purchase of short-term investment)		12
	Explains the increase in the short-term investment account and identifies a cash outflow from investing activities.		
Entry (13)	Land	30	
	Cash (purchase of land)		30
	Explains a portion of the change in the land account and identifies a cash outflow from investing activities.		
Entry (14)	Buildings and equipment	20	
	Note payable		20
	Partially explains the changes in the buildings and equipment and notes payable accounts and identifies a significant noncash investing and financing activity.		
Entry (15)	Bonds payable	15	
	Cash (retirement of bonds payable)		15
	Explains the decrease in the bonds payable account and identifies a cash outflow from financing activities.		
Entry (16)	Retained earnings	13	
	Common stock		10
	Paid-in capital—excess of par		3
	Partially explains the changes in the retained earnings, common stock, and paid-in capital—excess of par accounts.		
Entry (17)	Cash (from sale of common stock)	26	
	Common stock		20
	Paid-in capital—excess of par		6
	Partially explains the changes in the common stock and paid-in capital—excess of par accounts and identifies a cash inflow from financing activities.		
Entry (18)	Retained earnings	5	
	Cash (payment of cash dividends)		5
	Partially explains the change in the retained earnings account and identifies a cash outflow from financing activities.		
Entry (19)	Cash	9	
	Net increase in cash (from statement of cash flows activities)		9
	Reconciles the net increase in cash from operating, investing, and financing activities to the increase in the cash balance.		

The statement of cash flows presenting net cash flows from operating activities by the indirect method is illustrated in Illustration 21A–3.

Illustration 21A–3

Statement of Cash flows—Indirect Method

All parts of the statement of cash flows except operating activities are precisely the same as in the direct method.

UNITED BRANDS CORPORATION
Statement of Cash Flows
For Year Ended December 31, 2016
($ in millions)

Cash Flows from Operating Activities		
Net income	$12	
Adjustments for noncash effects:		
Gain on sale of land	(8)	
Depreciation expense	3	
Loss on sale of equipment	2	
Changes in operating assets and liabilities:		
Increase in accounts receivable	(2)	
Decrease in inventory	4	
Decrease in prepaid insurance	3	
Increase in accounts payable	6	
Increase in salaries payable	2	
Decrease in income tax payable	(2)	
Decrease in discount on bonds payable	2	
Net cash flows from operating activities		$22
Cash Flows from Investing Activities		
Purchase of land	(30)	
Purchase of short-term investment	(12)	
Sale of land	18	
Sale of equipment	5	
Net cash from investing activities		(19)
Cash Flows from Financing Activities		
Sale of common shares	26	
Retirement of bonds payable	(15)	
Payment of cash dividends	(5)	
Net cash flows from financing activities		6
Net increase in cash		9
Cash balance, January 1		20
Cash balance, December 31		$29
Note X:		
Noncash Investing and Financing Activities		
Acquired $20 million of equipment by issuing a 12%, 5-year note		$20

APPENDIX 21B The T-Account Method of Preparing the Statement of Cash Flows

The T-account method serves the same purpose as a spreadsheet in assisting in the preparation of a statement of cash flows.

This chapter demonstrates the use of a spreadsheet to prepare the statement of cash flows. A second systematic approach to the preparation of the statement is referred to as the T-account method. The two methods are identical in concept. Both approaches reconstruct the transactions that caused changes in each account balance during the year, simultaneously identifying the operating, investing, and financing activities to be reported on the statement of cash flows. The form of the two methods differs only by whether the entries for those transactions are recorded on a spreadsheet or in T-accounts. In both cases, entries are recorded until the net change in each account balance has been explained.

Some accountants feel that the T-account method is less time-consuming than preparing a spreadsheet but accomplishes precisely the same goal. Since both methods are simply analytical techniques to assist in statement preparation, the choice is a matter of personal preference. The following five steps outline the T-account method:

1. Draw T-accounts for each income statement and balance sheet account.
2. The T-account for cash should be drawn considerably larger than other T-accounts because more space is required to accommodate the numerous debits and credits to cash. Also, the cash T-account will serve the same purpose as the statement of cash flows section of the spreadsheet in that the formal statement of cash flows is developed from the cash flows reported there. Therefore, it is convenient to partition the cash T-account with headings for "Operating Activities," "Investing Activities," and "Financing Activities" before entries are recorded.
3. Enter each account's net change on the appropriate side (debit or credit) of the uppermost portion of each T-account. These changes will serve as individual check figures for determining whether the increase or decrease in each account balance has been explained. These first three steps establish the basic work form for the T-account method.
4. Reconstruct the transactions that caused changes in each account balance during the year and record the entries for those transactions directly in the T-accounts. Again using UBC as an example, the entries we record in the T-accounts are exactly the same as the spreadsheet entries we created in the chapter when using the spreadsheet method. The analysis we used in creating those spreadsheet entries is equally applicable to the T-account method. For that reason, that analysis is not repeated here. The complete T-account work form for UBC is presented below. Account balance changes are provided from balances given in Illustration 21–9.
5. After all account balances have been explained by T-account entries, prepare the statement of cash flows from the cash T-account, being careful also to report noncash investing and financing activities. The statement of cash flows for UBC appears in Illustration 21–2 on page 1246.

BALANCE SHEET ACCOUNTS

Cash (statement of cash flows)

		Debit	Credit		
		9			
Operating Activities:					
From customers	(1)	98	50	(4)	To suppliers of goods
From investment revenue	(2)	3	11	(5)	To employees
			3	(7)	For interest
			4	(8)	For insurance
			11	(10)	For income taxes
Investing Activities:					
Sale of land	(3)	18	12	(12)	Purchase of short-term investment
Sale of equipment	(9)	5	30	(13)	Purchase of land
Financing Activities:					
Sale of common stock	(17)	26	15	(15)	Retirement of bonds payable
			5	(18)	Payment of cash dividends

Accounts Receivable

	Debit	Credit
	2	
(1)	2	

Short-Term Investments

	Debit	Credit
	12	
(12)	12	

Inventory

Debit	Credit	
	4	
	4	(4)

Prepaid Insurance

Debit	Credit	
	3	
	3	(8)

Land

	Debit	Credit	
	20		
(13)	30	10	(3)

(continued)

(concluded)

	Buildings and Equipment		
	6		
X(14)	20	14	(9)

	Accumulated Depreciation		
	4		
(9)	7	3	(6)

	Accounts Payable		
		6	
		6	(4)

	Salaries Payable		
		2	
		2	(5)

	Income Tax Payable		
	2		
(10)	2		

	Notes Payable		
		20	
		20	(14)X

	Bonds Payable		
	15		
(15)	15		

	Discount on Bonds		
		2	
		2	(7)

	Common Stock		
		30	
		10	(16)
		20	(17)

	Paid-in Capital—excess of par		
		9	
		3	(16)
		6	(17)

	Retained Earnings		
	6		
(16)	13		
(18)	5	12	(11)

X Noncash Investing and Financing Activity

INCOME STATEMENT ACCOUNTS

	Sales Revenue		
		100	
		100	(1)

	Investment Revenue		
		3	
		3	(2)

	Gain on Sale of Land		
		8	
		8	(3)

	Cost of Goods Sold		
	60		
(4)	60		

	Salaries Expense		
	13		
(5)	13		

	Depreciation Expense		
	3		
(6)	3		

	Interest Expense		
	5		
(7)	5		

	Insurance Expense		
	7		
(8)	7		

	Loss on Sale of Equipment		
	2		
(9)	2		

	Income Tax Expense		
	9		
(10)	9		

	Net Income (Income Summary)		
	12		
(11)	12		

Questions For Review of Key Topics

Q 21–1 Effects of all cash flows affect the balances of various accounts reported in the balance sheet. Also, the activities that cause some of these cash flows are reported in the income statement. What, then, is the need for an additional financial statement that reports cash flows?

Q 21–2 The statement of cash flows provides a list of all the cash inflows and cash outflows during the reporting period. To make the list more informative, the cash flows are classified according to the nature of the activities that create the cash flows. What are the three primary classifications?

Q 21–3 Is an investment in Treasury bills always classified as a cash equivalent? Explain.

Q 21–4 Transactions that involve merely purchases or sales of cash equivalents generally are not reported in a statement of cash flows. Describe an exception to this generalization. What is the essential characteristic of the transaction that qualifies as an exception?

Q 21–5 What are the differences between cash flows from operating activities and the elements of an income statement?

Q 21–6 Do cash flows from operating activities report all the elements of the income statement on a cash basis? Explain.

Q 21–7 Investing activities include the acquisition and disposition of assets. Provide four specific examples. Identify two exceptions.

Q 21–8 The sale of stock and the sale of bonds are reported as financing activities. Are payments of dividends to shareholders and payments of interest to bondholders also reported as financing activities? Explain.

Q 21–9 Does the statement of cash flows report only transactions that cause an increase or a decrease in cash? Explain.

Q 21–10 How would the acquisition of a building be reported on a statement of cash flows if purchased by issuing a mortgage note payable in addition to a significant cash down payment?

Q 21–11 Perhaps the most noteworthy item reported on an income statement is net income—the amount by which revenues exceed expenses. The most noteworthy item reported on a statement of cash flows is *not* the amount of net cash flows. Explain.

Q 21–12 What is the purpose of the "changes" columns of a spreadsheet to prepare a statement of cash flows?

Q 21–13 Given sales revenue of $200,000, how can it be determined whether or not $200,000 cash was received from customers?

Q 21–14 When an asset is sold at a gain, why is the gain not reported as a cash inflow from operating activities?

Q 21–15 When determining the amount of cash paid for income taxes, what would be indicated by an increase in the deferred income tax liability account?

Q 21–16 When using the indirect method of determining net cash flows from operating activities, how is warranty expense reported? Why? What other expenses are reported in a like manner?

Q 21–17 When using the indirect method of determining net cash flows from operating activities, how are revenues and expenses reported on the statement of cash flows if their cash effects are identical to the amounts reported in the income statement?

Q 21–18 Why does the FASB recommend the direct method over the indirect method?

Q 21–19 Compare the manner in which investing activities are reported on a statement of cash flows prepared by the direct method and by the indirect method.

IFRS **Q 21–20** Where can we find authoritative guidance for the statement of cash flows under IFRS?

IFRS **Q 21–21** U.S. GAAP designates cash outflows for interest payments and cash inflows from interest and dividends received as operating cash flows. Dividends paid to shareholders are classified as financing cash flows. How are these cash flows reported under IFRS?

Brief Exercises

BE 21–1
Determine cash received from customers
● LO21–3

Horton Housewares' accounts receivable decreased during the year by $5 million. What is the amount of cash Horton received from customers during the reporting period if its sales were $33 million? Prepare a summary entry that represents the net effect of the selling and collection activities during the reporting period.

BE 21–2
Determine cash received from customers
● LO21–3

April Wood Products' accounts receivable increased during the year by $4 million. What is the amount of cash April Wood Products received from customers during the reporting period if its sales were $44 million? Prepare a summary entry that represents the net effect of the selling and collection activities during the reporting period.

BE 21–3
Determine cash paid to suppliers
● LO21–3

LaRoe Lawns' inventory increased during the year by $6 million. Its accounts payable increased by $5 million during the same period. What is the amount of cash LaRoe paid to suppliers of merchandise during the reporting period if its cost of goods sold was $25 million? Prepare a summary entry that represents the net effect of merchandise purchases during the reporting period.

BE 21–4
Determine cash paid to employees
● LO21–3

Sherriane Baby Products' salaries expense was $17 million. What is the amount of cash Sherriane paid to employees during the reporting period if its salaries payable increased by $3 million? Prepare a summary entry that represents the net effect of salaries expense incurred and paid during the reporting period.

BE 21–5
Bond interest and discount
● LO21–3, LO21–6

Agee Technology, Inc., issued 9% bonds, dated January 1, with a face amount of $400 million on July 1, 2016, at a price of $380 million. For bonds of similar risk and maturity, the market yield is 10%. Interest is paid semi-annually on June 30 and December 31. Prepare the journal entry to record interest at the effective interest rate at December 31. What would be the amount(s) related to the bonds that Agee would report in its statement of cash flows for the year ended December 31, 2016, if it uses the direct method?

BE 21–6
Bond interest and discount
● LO21–4, LO21–6

Refer to the situation described in BE 21–5. What would be the amount(s) related to the bonds that Agee would report in its statement of cash flows for the year ended December 31, 2016, if it uses the indirect method?

BE 21–7
Installment note
● LO21–3, LO21–6

On January 1, 2016, the Merit Group issued to its bank a $41 million, five-year installment note to be paid in five equal payments at the end of each year. Installment payments of $10 million annually include interest at the rate of 7%. What would be the amount(s) related to the note that Merit would report in its statement of cash flows for the year ended December 31, 2016?

BE 21–8
Sale of land
● LO21–3, LO21–4, LO21–5

On July 15, 2016, M.W. Morgan Distribution sold land for $35 million that it had purchased in 2011 for $22 million. What would be the amount(s) related to the sale that Morgan would report in its statement of cash flows for the year ended December 31, 2016, using the direct method? The indirect method?

BE 21–9
Investing activities
● LO21–5

Carter Containers sold marketable securities, land, and common stock for $30 million, $15 million, and $40 million, respectively. Carter also purchased treasury stock, equipment, and a patent for $21 million, $25 million, and $12 million, respectively. What amount should Carter report as net cash from investing activities?

BE 21–10
Financing activities
● LO21–6

Refer to the situation described in BE 21–9. What amount should Carter report as net cash from financing activities?

BE 21–11
Indirect method
● LO21–4

Sheen Awnings reported net income of $90 million. Included in that number were depreciation expense of $3 million and a loss on the sale of equipment of $2 million. Records reveal increases in accounts receivable, accounts payable, and inventory of $1 million, $4 million, and $3 million, respectively. What were Sheen's cash flows from operating activities?

BE 21–12
Indirect method
● LO21–4

Sunset Acres reported net income of $60 million. Included in that number were trademark amortization expense of $2 million and a gain on the sale of land of $1 million. Records reveal decreases in accounts receivable, accounts payable, and inventory of $2 million, $5 million, and $4 million, respectively. What were Sunset's cash flows from operating activities?

Exercises

An alternate exercise and problem set is available in the Connect library.

E 21–1
Classification of cash flows
● LO21–3 through LO21–6

Listed below are several transactions that typically produce either an increase or a decrease in cash. Indicate by letter whether the cash effect of each transaction is reported on a statement of cash flows as an operating (**O**), investing (**I**), or financing (**F**) activity.

Transactions

F	1. Sale of common stock
____	2. Sale of land
____	3. Purchase of treasury stock
____	4. Merchandise sales
____	5. Issuance of a long-term note payable
____	6. Purchase of merchandise
____	7. Repayment of note payable

(continued)

(concluded)

____ 8. Employee salaries
____ 9. Sale of equipment at a gain
____ 10. Issuance of bonds
____ 11. Acquisition of bonds of another corporation
____ 12. Payment of semiannual interest on bonds payable
____ 13. Payment of a cash dividend
____ 14. Purchase of a building
____ 15. Collection of nontrade note receivable (principal amount)
____ 16. Loan to another firm
____ 17. Retirement of common stock
____ 18. Income taxes
____ 19. Issuance of a short-term note payable
____ 20. Sale of a copyright

E 21–2
Determine cash paid to suppliers of merchandise
● LO21–3, LO21–6

Shown below in T-account format are the beginning and ending balances ($ in millions) of both inventory and accounts payable.

Inventory

Beginning balance	90		
Ending balance	93		

Accounts Payable

		14	Beginning balance
		16	Ending balance

Required:

1. Use a T-account analysis to determine the amount of cash paid to suppliers of merchandise during the reporting period if cost of goods sold was $300 million.
2. Prepare a summary entry that represents the net effect of merchandise purchases during the reporting period.

E 21–3
Determine cash received from customers
● LO21–3

Determine the amount of cash received from customers for each of the three independent situations below. All dollars are in millions.

Situation	Sales Revenue	Accounts Receivable Increase (Decrease)	Cash Received from Customers
1	100	–0–	?
2	100	5	?
3	100	(5)	?

E 21–4
Summary entries for cash received from customers
● LO21–3

For each of the three independent situations below, prepare journal entries that summarize the selling and collection activities for the reporting period in order to determine the amount of cash received from customers and to explain the change in each account shown. All dollars are in millions.

Situation	Sales Revenue	Accounts Receivable Increase (Decrease)	Cash Received from Customers
1	200	–0–	?
2	200	10	?
3	200	(10)	?

E 21–5
Determine cash paid to suppliers of merchandise
● LO21–3

Determine the amount of cash paid to suppliers of merchandise for each of the nine independent situations below. All dollars are in millions.

Situation	Cost of Goods Sold	Inventory Increase (Decrease)	Accounts Payable Increase (Decrease)	Cash Paid to Suppliers
1	100	0	0	?
2	100	3	0	?
3	100	(3)	0	?
4	100	0	7	?
5	100	0	(7)	?
6	100	3	7	?
7	100	3	(7)	?
8	100	(3)	(7)	?
9	100	(3)	7	?

E 21–6
Summary entries for cash paid to suppliers of merchandise
● LO21–3

For each of the five independent situations below, prepare a journal entry that summarizes the purchases, sales, and payments related to inventories in order to determine the amount of cash paid to suppliers and explain the change in each account shown. All dollars are in millions.

Situation	Cost of Goods Sold	Inventory Increase (Decrease)	Accounts Payable Increase (Decrease)	Cash Paid to Suppliers
1	200	0	0	?
2	200	6	0	?
3	200	0	14	?
4	200	6	14	?
5	200	(6)	(14)	?

E 21–7
Determine cash paid for bond interest
● LO21–3

Determine the amount of cash paid to bondholders for bond interest for each of the six independent situations below. All dollars are in millions.

Situation	Bond Interest Expense	Bond Interest Payable Increase (Decrease)	Unamortized Discount Increase (Decrease)	Cash Paid for Interest
1	10	0	0	?
2	10	2	0	?
3	10	(2)	0	?
4	10	0	(3)	?
5	10	2	(3)	?
6	10	(2)	(3)	?

E 21–8
Determine cash paid for bond interest
● LO21–3

For each of the four independent situations below, prepare a single journal entry that summarizes the recording and payment of interest in order to determine the amount of cash paid for bond interest and explain the change (if any) in each of the accounts shown. All dollars are in millions.

Situation	Bond Interest Expense	Bond Interest Payable Increase (Decrease)	Unamortized Discount Increase (Decrease)	Cash Paid for Interest
1	20	0	0	?
2	20	4	0	?
3	20	0	(6)	?
4	20	(4)	(6)	?

E 21–9
Determine cash paid for income taxes
● LO21–3

Determine the amount of cash paid for income taxes in each of the nine independent situations below. All dollars are in millions.

Situation	Income Tax Expense	Income Tax Payable Increase (Decrease)	Deferred Tax Liability Increase (Decrease)	Cash Paid for Taxes
1	10	0	0	?
2	10	3	0	?
3	10	(3)	0	?
4	10	0	2	?
5	10	0	(2)	?
6	10	3	2	?
7	10	3	(2)	?
8	10	(3)	(2)	?
9	10	(3)	2	?

E 21–10
Summary entries for cash paid for income taxes
● LO21–3

For each of the five independent situations below, prepare a single journal entry that summarizes the recording and payment of income taxes in order to determine the amount of cash paid for income taxes and explain the change (if any) in each of the accounts shown. All dollars are in millions.

Situation	Income Tax Expense	Income Tax Payable Increase (Decrease)	Deferred Tax Liability Increase (Decrease)	Cash Paid for Taxes
1	10	0	0	?
2	10	3	0	?
3	10	0	(2)	?
4	10	3	2	?
5	10	(3)	(2)	?

E 21–11
Bonds; statement of cash flow effects
● LO21–3

Most Solutions, Inc., issued 10% bonds, dated January 1, with a face amount of $640 million on January 1, 2016. The bonds mature in 2026 (10 years). For bonds of similar risk and maturity the market yield is 12%. Interest expense is recorded at the effective interest rate. Interest is paid semiannually on June 30 and December 31. Most recorded the sale as follows:

January 1, 2016		
Cash (price)	566,589,440	
Discount on bonds (difference)	73,410,560	
Bonds payable (face amount)		640,000,000

Required:
What would be the amount(s) related to the bonds that Most would report in its statement of cash flows for the year ended December 31, 2016?

E 21–12
Installment note; statement of cash flow effects
● LO21–3, LO21–6

National Food Services, Inc., borrowed $4 million from its local bank on January 1, 2016, and issued a 4-year installment note to be paid in four equal payments at the end of each year. The payments include interest at the rate of 10%. Installment payments are $1,261,881 annually.

Required:
What would be the amount(s) related to the note that National would report in its statement of cash flows for the year ended December 31, 2016?

E 21–13
Identifying cash flows from investing activities and financing activities
● LO21–5, LO21–6

In preparation for developing its statement of cash flows for the year ended December 31, 2016, Rapid Pac, Inc., collected the following information:

	($ in millions)
Fair value of shares issued in a stock dividend	$ 65
Payment for the early extinguishment of long-term bonds (book value: $97 million)	102
Proceeds from the sale of treasury stock (cost: $17 million)	22
Gain on sale of land	4
Proceeds from sale of land	12
Purchase of Microsoft common stock	160
Declaration of cash dividends	44
Distribution of cash dividends declared in 2015	40

Required:
1. In Rapid Pac's statement of cash flows, what were net cash inflows (or outflows) from investing activities for 2016?
2. In Rapid Pac's statement of cash flows, what were net cash inflows (or outflows) from financing activities for 2016?

E 21–14
Identifying cash flows from investing activities and financing activities
● LO21–5, LO21–6

In preparation for developing its statement of cash flows for the year ended December 31, 2016, Millennium Solutions, Inc., collected the following information ($ in millions):

Payment for the early extinguishments of long-term notes (book value: $50 million)	$ 54
Sale of common shares	176
Retirement of common shares	122
Loss on sale of equipment	2
Proceeds from sale of equipment	8
Issuance of short-term note payable for cash	10
Acquisition of building for cash	7
Purchase of marketable securities (not a cash equivalent)	5
Purchase of marketable securities (considered a cash equivalent)	1
Cash payment for 3-year insurance policy	3
Collection of note receivable with interest (principal amount, $11)	13
Declaration of cash dividends	33
Distribution of cash dividends declared in 2015	30

Required:
1. In Millennium's statement of cash flows, what were net cash inflows (or outflows) from investing activities for 2016?
2. In Millennium's statement of cash flows, what were net cash inflows (or outflows) from financing activities for 2016?

E 21–15
Lease; lessee; statement of cash flows effects
● LO21–3, LO21–5, LO21–6

Wilson Foods Corporation leased a commercial food processor on September 30, 2016. The five-year lease agreement calls for Wilson to make quarterly lease payments of $195,774, payable each September 30, December 31, March 31, June 30, with the first payment at September 30, 2016. Wilson's incremental borrowing rate is 12%. Wilson records depreciation on a straight-line basis at the end of each fiscal year. Wilson recorded the lease as follows:

September 30, 2016		
Asset (calculated below)	3,000,000	
Lease payable (calculated below)		3,000,000
Lease payable	195,774	
Cash (first payment)		195,774

Calculation of the present value of lease payments

$195,774 × 15.32380* = $3,000,000 (rounded)

*Present value of an annuity due of $1: n = 20, i = 3% (from Table 6)

Required:
What would be the pretax amounts related to the lease that Wilson would report in its statement of cash flows for the year ended December 31, 2016?

E 21–16
Equity method investment; statement of cash flow effects
● LO21–3, LO21–5

On January 1, 2016, Beilich Enterprises bought 20% of the outstanding common stock of Wolfe Construction Company for $600 million cash. Wolfe's net income for the year ended December 31, 2016, was $300 million. During 2016, Wolfe declared and paid cash dividends of $60 million. Beilich recorded the investment as follows:

	($ in millions)	
Purchase		
Investment in Wolfe Construction shares	600	
Cash		600
Net income		
Investment in Wolfe Construction shares (20% × $300 million)	60	
Investment revenue		60
Dividends		
Cash (20% × $60 million)	12	
Investment in Wolfe Construction shares		12

Required:
What would be the pretax amounts related to the investment that Beilich would report in its statement of cash flows for the year ended December 31, 2016?

E 21–17
Indirect method; reconciliation of net income to net cash flows from operating activities
● LO21–4

The accounting records of EZ Company provided the data below. Prepare a reconciliation of net income to net cash flows from operating activities.

Net income	$50,000
Depreciation expense	7,000
Increase in inventory	1,500
Decrease in salaries payable	800
Decrease in accounts receivable	2,000
Amortization of patent	500
Amortization of premium on bonds	1,000
Increase in accounts payable	4,000
Cash dividends	12,000

E 21–18
Spreadsheet entries from statement of retained earnings
● LO21–3 through LO21–8

The statement of retained earnings of Gary Larson Publishers is presented below.

GARY LARSON PUBLISHERS
Statement of Retained Earnings
For the Year Ended December 31, 2016
($ in millions)

Retained earnings, January 1		$200
Add:	Net income	75
Deduct:	Cash dividend	(25)
	Stock dividend (1 million shares of $1 par common stock)	(16)
	Property dividend (Garfield Company preferred stock held as a short-term investment)	(12)
	Sale of treasury stock (cost $53 million)	(10)
Retained earnings, December 31		$212

Required:
For the transactions that affected Larson's retained earnings, reconstruct the journal entries for the transactions that affected retained earnings and that can be used to determine cash flows to be reported in a statement of cash flows. Also indicate any investing and financing activities you identify from this analysis that should be reported on the statement of cash flows.

E 21–19
Relationship between the income statement and cash flows from operating activities (direct method and indirect method)
● LO21–3, LO21–4

The following schedule relates the income statement with cash flows from operating activities, derived by both the direct and indirect methods, in the format illustrated by Illustration 21–11 in the chapter. The amounts for income statement elements are missing.

Income Statement		**Cash Flows from Operating Activities** **Indirect Method**		**Direct Method**	
		Net income	$?		
		Adjustments:			
Sales	$?	Decrease in accounts receivable	12	Cash received from customers	$612
Cost of goods sold	?	Increase in inventory	(24)		
		Decrease in accounts payable	(36)	Cash paid to suppliers	(420)
Salaries expense	?	Increase in salaries payable	12	Cash paid to employees	(66)
Depreciation expense	?	Depreciation expense	18	(Not reported—no cash effect)	
Insurance expense	?	Decrease in prepaid insurance	18	Cash paid for insurance	(24)
Loss on sale of land	?	Loss on sale of land	12	(Not reported—no cash effect)	
Income tax expense	?	Increase in income tax payable	12	Cash paid for income taxes	(42)
Net income	$?	**Net cash flows from operating activities**	$60	**Net cash flows from operating activities**	$ 60

Required:
Deduce the missing amounts and prepare the income statement.

E 21–20
Reconciliation of net cash flows from operating activities to net income
● LO21–3, LO21–4

The income statement and the cash flows from the operating activities section of the statement of cash flows are provided below for Syntric Company. The merchandise inventory account balance neither increased nor decreased during the reporting period. Syntric had no liability for insurance, deferred income taxes, or interest at any time during the period.

SYNTRIC COMPANY
Income Statement
For the Year Ended December 31, 2016
($ in 000s)

Sales		$312
Cost of goods sold		(188)
Gross margin		124
Salaries expense	$41	
Insurance expense	22	
Depreciation expense	11	
Depletion expense	5	
Bond interest expense	10	(89)
Gains and losses:		
Gain on sale of equipment		25
Loss on sale of land		(8)
Income before tax		52
Income tax expense		(26)
Net income		$ 26
Cash Flows from Operating Activities:		
Cash received from customers		$258
Cash paid to suppliers		(175)
Cash paid to employees		(37)
Cash paid for interest		(9)
Cash paid for insurance		(16)
Cash paid for income taxes		(14)
Net cash flows from operating activities		$ 7

Required:
Prepare a schedule to reconcile net income to net cash flows from operating activities.

E 21–21
Cash flows from operating activities (direct method) derived from an income statement and cash flows from operating activities indirect method)
● LO21–3, LO21–4

The income statement and a schedule reconciling cash flows from operating activities to net income are provided below ($ in 000s) for Peach Computers.

PEACH COMPUTERS
Income Statement
For the Year Ended December 31, 2016

Sales		$305
Cost of goods sold		185
Gross margin		120
Salaries expense	$41	
Insurance expense	19	
Depreciation expense	11	
Loss on sale of land	5	76
Income before tax		44
Income tax expense		22
Net income		$ 22

Reconciliation of Net Income
To Net Cash Flows from Operating Activities

Net income	$22
Adjustments for Noncash Effects	
Depreciation expense	11
Loss on sale of land	5
Changes in operating assets and liabilities:	
Decrease in accounts receivable	6
Increase in inventory	(13)
Decrease in accounts payable	(8)
Increase in salaries payable	5
Decrease in prepaid insurance	9
Increase in income tax payable	20
Net cash flows from operating activities	$57

Required:
1. Calculate each of the following amounts for Peach Computers:
   a. Cash received from customers during the reporting period.
   b. Cash paid to suppliers of goods during the reporting period.
   c. Cash paid to employees during the reporting period.
   d. Cash paid for insurance during the reporting period.
   e. Cash paid for income taxes during the reporting period.
2. Prepare the cash flows from operating activities section of the statement of cash flows (direct method).

E 21–22
Indirect method; reconciliation of net income to net cash flows from operating activities
● LO21–4

The accounting records of Baddour Company provided the data below. Prepare a reconciliation of net income to net cash flows from operating activities.

Net loss	$5,000
Depreciation expense	6,000
Increase in salaries payable	500
Decrease in accounts receivable	2,000
Increase in inventory	2,300
Amortization of patent	300
Reduction in discount on bonds	200

E 21–23
Cash flows from operating activities (direct method)
● LO21–3

Portions of the financial statements for Myriad Products are provided below.

MYRIAD PRODUCTS COMPANY
Income Statement
For the Year Ended December 31, 2016
($ in millions)

Sales		$ 660
Cost of goods sold		250
Gross margin		410
Salaries expense	$110	
Depreciation expense	90	
Patent amortization expense	5	
Interest expense	20	
Loss on sale of land	3	228
Income before taxes		182
Income tax expense		91
Net Income		$ 91

MYRIAD PRODUCTS COMPANY
Selected Accounts from Comparative Balance Sheets
December 31, 2016 and 2015
($ in millions)

	Year		
	2016	**2015**	**Change**
Cash	$102	$100	$ 2
Accounts receivable	220	232	(12)
Inventory	440	450	(10)
Accounts payable	140	134	6
Salaries payable	80	86	(6)
Interest payable	25	20	5
Income taxes payable	15	10	5

Required:
Prepare the cash flows from operating activities section of the statement of cash flows for Myriad Products Company using the *direct method.*

E 21–24
Cash flows from operating activities (indirect method)
● LO21–4

Refer to the data provided in E21–23 for Myriad Products Company.

Required:
Prepare the cash flows from operating activities section of the statement of cash flows for Myriad Products Company using the *indirect method.*

E 21–25
Cash flows from operating activities (direct method)—includes sale of cash equivalent
● LO21–3

Portions of the financial statements for Clear Transmissions Company are provided below.

CLEAR TRANSMISSIONS COMPANY
Income Statement
For the Year Ended December 31, 2016 ($ in 000s)

Sales		$1,320
Cost of goods sold		500
Gross margin		820
Salaries expense	$220	
Depreciation expense	180	
Patent amortization expense	10	
Interest expense	40	
Loss on sale of cash equivalents	6	456
Income before taxes		364
Income tax expense		182
Net Income		$ 182

CLEAR TRANSMISSIONS COMPANY
Selected Accounts from Comparative Balance Sheets
December 31, 2016 and 2015 ($ in 000s)

	Year		
	2016	2015	Change
Cash	$102	$100	$ 2
Accounts receivable	220	232	(12)
Inventory	440	450	(10)
Accounts payable	140	134	6
Salaries payable	80	86	(6)
Interest payable	25	20	5
Income taxes payable	15	10	5

Required:
Prepare the cash flows from operating activities section of the statement of cash flows for Clear Transmissions Company using the *direct method.*

E 21–26
Cash flows from operating activities (indirect method)—includes sale of cash equivalent
● LO21–4

Refer to the data provided in E21–25 for Clear Transmissions Company.

Required:
Prepare the cash flows from operating activities section of the statement of cash flows for Clear Transmissions Company using the *indirect method.*

E 21–27
Statement of cash flows; direct method
● LO21–3, LO21–5, LO21–6, LO21–8

Comparative balance sheets for 2016 and 2015, a statement of income for 2016, and additional information from the accounting records of Red, Inc., are provided below.

RED, INC.
Comparative Balance Sheets
December 31, 2016 and 2015 ($ in millions)

	2016	2015
Assets		
Cash	$ 24	$110
Accounts receivable	178	132
Prepaid insurance	7	3
Inventory	285	175
Buildings and equipment	400	350
Less: Accumulated depreciation	(119)	(240)
	$775	$530
Liabilities		
Accounts payable	$ 87	$100
Accrued expenses payable	6	11
Notes payable	50	0
Bonds payable	160	0
Shareholders' Equity		
Common stock	400	400
Retained earnings	72	19
	$775	$530

RED, INC.
Statement of Income
For Year Ended December 31, 2016 ($ in millions)

Revenues		
Sales revenue		$2,000
Expenses		
Cost of goods sold	$1,400	
Depreciation expense	50	
Operating expenses	447	1,897
Net income		$ 103

Additional information from the accounting records:

a. During 2016, $230 million of equipment was purchased to replace $180 million of equipment (95% depreciated) sold at book value.
b. In order to maintain the usual policy of paying cash dividends of $50 million, it was necessary for Red to borrow $50 million from its bank.

Required:
Prepare the statement of cash flows of Red, Inc., for the year ended December 31, 2016. Present cash flows from operating activities by the direct method. (You may omit the schedule to reconcile net income with cash flows from operating activities.)

E 21–28
Pension plan funding
● LO21–3

Mayer Corporation has a defined benefit pension plan. Mayer's policy is to fund the plan annually, cash payments being made at the end of each year. Data relating to the pension plan for 2016 are as follows:

	December 31 ($ in millions)	
	2016	**2015**
Plan assets	$1,080	$900
Net Pension Expense for 2016:		
Service cost	$ 112	
Interest cost (6% × $850)	51	
Actual return on the plan assets (11% × $900 = $99)		
Adjusted for: $9 gain on the plan assets*	(90)	
Amortization of prior service cost	8	
Amortization of net loss	1	
	$ 82	

*(11% × $900) − (10% − $900)

Required:
Recreate the journal entries used to record Mayer's 2016 pension expense, gain on plan assets, and funding of plan assets in order to determine the cash paid to the pension trustee as reported in the statement of cash flows.

E 21–29
FASB codification research
● LO21–2

The statement of cash flows (as well as the balance sheet) includes within cash the notion of cash equivalents. The *FASB Accounting Standards Codification* represents the single source of authoritative U.S. generally accepted accounting principles.

Required:
1. Obtain the relevant authoritative literature on cash equivalents using the *FASB Accounting Standards Codification* at the FASB website (asc.fasb.org). What is the specific citation that describes the guidelines for determining what items should be deemed cash equivalents?
2. List the guidelines.

E 21–30
FASB codification research
● LO21–1, LO21–4, LO21–7

Access the *FASB Accounting Standards Codification* at the FASB website (asc.fasb.org). Determine the specific citation for accounting for each of the following items:
1. Disclosure of interest and income taxes paid if the indirect method is used.
2. Primary objectives of a statement of cash flows.
3. Disclosure of noncash investing and financing activities.

E 21–31
Statement of cash flows; indirect method
● LO21–4, LO21–5, LO21–6, LO21–8, Appendix A

Refer to the data provided in E21–27 for Red, Inc.

Required:
Prepare the statement of cash flows for Red, Inc., using the indirect method to report operating activities.

E 21–32
Statement of cash flows; T-account method
● LO21–8, Appendix B

Refer to the data provided in E21–27 for Red, Inc.

Required:
Prepare the statement of cash flows (direct method) for Red, Inc. Use the T-account method to assist in your analysis.

CPA and CMA Review Questions

CPA Exam Questions

KAPLAN CPA REVIEW

The following questions are adapted from a variety of sources including questions developed by the AICPA Board of Examiners and those used in the Kaplan CPA Review Course to study the statement of cash flows while preparing for the CPA examination. Determine the response that best completes the statements or questions.

● LO21–3

1. In a statement of cash flows in which operating activities are reported by the direct method, which of the following would increase reported cash flows from operating activities?
   a. Gain on sale of land.
   b. Interest revenue.
   c. Gain on early extinguishment of bonds.
   d. Proceeds from sale of equipment.

● LO21–6

2. During 2016, TEL Company engaged in the following activities:

Distribution of cash dividends declared in 2015	$ 24
Fair value of shares issued in a stock dividend	110
Payment to retire bonds	226
Proceeds from the sale of treasury stock (cost: $26)	30

   In TEL's statement of cash flows, what were net cash outflows from financing activities for 2016?
   a. $196
   b. $220
   c. $280
   d. $366

● LO21–4

3. SOL Company reported net income for 2016 in the amount of $200,000. The company's financial statements also included the following:

Increase in accounts receivable	$ 40,000
Decrease in inventory	30,000
Increase in accounts payable	100,000
Depreciation expense	52,000
Gain on sale of land	74,000

   What is net cash provided by operating activities under the indirect method?
   a. $216,000
   b. $268,000
   c. $290,000
   d. $416,000

● LO21–3

4. Which of the following does *not* represent a cash flow relating to operating activities?
   a. Dividends paid to stockholders.
   b. Cash received from customers.
   c. Interest paid to bondholders.
   d. Cash paid for salaries.

● LO21–5

5. Which of the following would *not* be a component of cash flows from investing activities?
   a. Sale of land.
   b. Purchase of securities.
   c. Purchase of equipment.
   d. Dividends paid.

● LO21–4

6. An analyst compiled the following information for Universe, Inc., for the year ended December 31, 2016:
   - Net income was $850,000.
   - Depreciation expense was $200,000.
   - Interest paid was $100,000.
   - Income taxes paid were $50,000.
   - Common stock was sold for $100,000.
   - Preferred stock (8% annual dividend) was sold at par value of $125,000.
   - Common stock dividends of $25,000 were paid.
   - Preferred stock dividends of $10,000 were paid.
   - Equipment with a book value of $50,000 was sold for $100,000.

   Using the indirect method, what was Universe, Inc.'s net cash flow from operating activities for the year ended December 31, 2016?
   a. $1,000,000
   b. $1,015,000
   c. $1,040,000
   d. $1,050,000

International Financial Reporting Standards are tested on the CPA exam along with U.S. GAAP. The following questions deal with the application of IFRS in the statement of cash flows.

● LO21–7

IFRS

7. Consistent with U.S GAAP, we classify cash flows as operating, investing, or financing activities under IFRS. However, with regard to interest and dividend inflows and outflows, IFRS
   a. permits companies to report cash outflows from interest payments as either operating *or* investing cash flows.
   b. permits companies to report cash inflows from interest and dividends as either operating *or* financing cash flows.
   c. permits companies to report dividends paid as either financing *or* operating cash flows.
   d. requires companies to report cash outflows for interest payments and cash inflows from interest and dividends received as operating cash flows.

● LO21–7

IFRS

8. Interest received and interest payments must be reported as operating cash flows using
   a. IFRS.
   b. U.S. GAAP.
   c. both U.S. GAAP and IFRS.
   d. neither U.S. GAAP nor IFRS.

● LO21–7

IFRS

9. Gee Company's accounting records and financial statements reported the following:

Cash paid to acquire machinery	$70,000
Proceeds from sale of land	80,000
Loss from the sale of land	5,000
Cash paid to acquire a trademark	38,000
Treasury stock purchased for cash	50,000
Dividend revenue received	20,000

   Gee prepares its financial statements in accordance with IFRS. In its statement of cash flows, Gee most likely reports net cash outflows from investing activities of
   a. $ 8,000.
   b. $11,000.
   c. $28,000.
   d. $33,000.

CMA Exam Questions

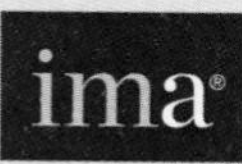

The following questions dealing with the statement of cash flows are adapted from questions that previously appeared on Certified Management Accountant (CMA) examinations. The CMA designation sponsored by the Institute of Management Accountants (**www.imanet.org**) provides members with an objective measure of knowledge and competence in the field of management accounting. Determine the response that best completes the statements or questions.

● LO21–3

1. When preparing the statement of cash flows, companies are required to report separately as operating cash flows all of the following except
   a. interest received on investments in bonds.
   b. interest paid on the company's bonds.
   c. cash collected from customers.
   d. cash dividends paid on the company's stock.

● LO21–5, LO21–6

2. The following information was taken from the accounting records of Oak Corporation for the year ended December 31:

Proceeds from issuance of preferred stock	$4,000,000
Dividends paid on preferred stock	400,000
Bonds payable converted to common stock	2,000,000
Payment for purchase of machinery	500,000
Proceeds from sale of plant building	1,200,000
2% stock dividend on common stock	300,000
Gain on sale of plant building	200,000

   The net cash flows from investing and financing activities that should be presented on Oak's statement of cash flows for the year ended December 31 are, respectively
   a. $700,000 and $3,600,000.
   b. $700,000 and $3,900,000.
   c. $900,000 and $3,900,000.
   d. $900,000 and $3,600,000.

● LO21–4

3. The net income for Cypress Inc. was $3,000,000 for the year ended December 31. Additional information is as follows:

Depreciation on fixed assets	$1,500,000
Gain from cash sale of land	200,000
Increase in accounts payable	300,000
Dividends paid on preferred stock	400,000

   The net cash provided by operating activities in the statement of cash flows for the year ended December 31 should be
   a. $4,200,000.
   b. $4,500,000.
   c. $4,600,000.
   d. $4,800,000.

Problems

An alternate exercise and problem set is available in the Connect library.

P 21–1
Classification of cash flows from investing and financing activities
● LO21–2, LO21–5 through LO21–7

Listed below are transactions that might be reported as investing and/or financing activities on a statement of cash flows. Possible reporting classifications of those transactions are provided also.

Required:
Indicate the reporting classification of each transaction by entering the appropriate classification code.

	Classifications
+I	Investing activity (cash inflow)
−I	Investing activity (cash outflow)
+F	Financing activity (cash inflow)
−F	Financing activity (cash outflow)
N	Noncash investing and financing activity
X	Not reported as an investing and/or a financing activity

Transactions

Example

+I 1. Sale of land.
_____ 2. Issuance of common stock for cash.
_____ 3. Purchase of treasury stock.
_____ 4. Conversion of bonds payable to common stock.
_____ 5. Lease of equipment.
_____ 6. Sale of patent.
_____ 7. Acquisition of building for cash.
_____ 8. Issuance of common stock for land.
_____ 9. Collection of note receivable (principal amount).
_____ 10. Issuance of bonds.
_____ 11. Issuance of stock dividend.
_____ 12. Payment of property dividend.
_____ 13. Payment of cash dividends.
_____ 14. Issuance of short-term note payable for cash.
_____ 15. Issuance of long-term note payable for cash.
_____ 16. Purchase of marketable securities ("available for sale").
_____ 17. Payment of note payable.
_____ 18. Cash payment for 5-year insurance policy.
_____ 19. Sale of equipment.
_____ 20. Issuance of note payable for equipment.
_____ 21. Acquisition of common stock of another corporation.
_____ 22. Repayment of long-term debt by issuing common stock.
_____ 23. Payment of semiannual interest on bonds payable.
_____ 24. Retirement of preferred stock.
_____ 25. Loan to another firm.
_____ 26. Sale of inventory to customers.
_____ 27. Purchase of marketable securities (cash equivalents).

P 21–2
Statement of cash flows; direct method
● LO21–3, LO21–8

The comparative balance sheets for 2016 and 2015 and the statement of income for 2016 are given below for Wright Company. Additional information from Wright's accounting records is provided also.

WRIGHT COMPANY
Comparative Balance Sheets
December 31, 2016 and 2015
($ in 000s)

	2016	2015
Assets		
Cash	$ 42	$ 30
Accounts receivable	73	75
Short-term investment	40	15
Inventory	75	70
Land	50	60
Buildings and equipment	550	400
Less: Accumulated depreciation	(115)	(75)
	$ 715	$575
Liabilities		
Accounts payable	$ 28	$ 35
Salaries payable	2	5
Interest payable	5	3
Income tax payable	9	12
Notes payable	0	30
Bonds payable	160	100
Shareholders' Equity		
Common stock	250	200
Paid-in capital—excess of par	126	100
Retained earnings	135	90
	$ 715	$575

WRIGHT COMPANY
Income Statement
For Year Ended December 31, 2016
($ in 000s)

Revenues:		
Sales revenue		$380
Expenses:		
Cost of goods sold	$130	
Salaries expense	45	
Depreciation expense	40	
Interest expense	12	
Loss on sale of land	3	
Income tax expense	70	300
Net income		$ 80

Additional information from the accounting records:

a. Land that originally cost $10,000 was sold for $7,000.

b. The common stock of Microsoft Corporation was purchased for $25,000 as a short-term investment not classified as a cash equivalent.

c. New equipment was purchased for $150,000 cash.

d. A $30,000 note was paid at maturity on January 1.

e. On January 1, 2016, bonds were sold at their $60,000 face value.

f. Common stock ($50,000 par) was sold for $76,000.

g. Net income was $80,000 and cash dividends of $35,000 were paid to shareholders.

Required:

Prepare the statement of cash flows of Wright Company for the year ended December 31, 2016. Present cash flows from operating activities by the direct method. (You may omit the schedule to reconcile net income with cash flows from operating activities.)

P 21–3
Statement of cash flows; direct method
● LO21–3, LO21–8

The comparative balance sheets for 2016 and 2015 and the statement of income for 2016 are given below for National Intercable Company. Additional information from NIC's accounting records is provided also.

NATIONAL INTERCABLE COMPANY
Comparative Balance Sheets
December 31, 2016 and 2015
($ in millions)

	2016	2015
Assets		
Cash	$ 69	$ 55
Accounts receivable	173	164
Prepaid insurance	7	12
Inventory	170	165
Long-term investment	66	90
Land	150	150
Buildings and equipment	290	270
Less: Accumulated depreciation	(85)	(75)
Trademark	24	25
	$864	$856
Liabilities		
Accounts payable	$ 30	$ 45
Salaries payable	3	8
Deferred income tax liability	18	15
Lease liability	80	0
Bonds payable	145	275
Less: Discount on bonds	(22)	(25)
Shareholders' Equity		
Common stock	310	290
Paid-in capital—excess of par	95	85
Preferred stock	50	0
Retained earnings	155	163
	$864	$856

NATIONAL INTERCABLE COMPANY
Income Statement
For Year Ended December 31, 2016
($ in millions)

Revenues		
Sales revenue	$320	
Investment revenue	15	
Gain on sale of investments	5	$ 340
Expenses		
Cost of goods sold	125	
Salaries expense	55	
Depreciation expense	25	
Trademark amortization expense	1	
Insurance expense	20	
Bond interest expense	30	
Loss on building fire	42	298
Income before tax		42
Income tax expense		20
Net income		$ 22

Additional information from the accounting records:

a. Investment revenue includes National Intercable Company's $6 million share of the net income of Central Fiber Optics Corporation, an equity method investee.
b. A long-term investment in bonds, originally purchased for $30 million, was sold for $35 million.
c. Pretax accounting income exceeded taxable income causing the deferred income tax liability to increase by $3 million.
d. A building that originally cost $60 million, and which was one-fourth depreciated, was destroyed by fire. Some undamaged parts were sold for $3 million.
e. The right to use a building was acquired with a seven-year lease agreement; present value of lease payments, $80 million.
f. $130 million of bonds were retired at maturity.
g. $20 million par value of common stock was sold for $30 million, and $50 million of preferred stock was sold at par.
h. Shareholders were paid cash dividends of $30 million.

Required:

1. Prepare a spreadsheet for preparation of the statement of cash flows (direct method) of National Intercable Company for the year ended December 31, 2016.
2. Prepare the statement of cash flows. (A reconciliation schedule is not required.)

P 21–4
Statement of cash flows; direct method
● LO21–3, LO21–8

The comparative balance sheets for 2016 and 2015 and the statement of income for 2016 are given below for Dux Company. Additional information from Dux's accounting records is provided also.

DUX COMPANY
Comparative Balance Sheets
December 31, 2016 and 2015
($ in 000s)

	2016	2015
Assets		
Cash	$ 33	$ 20
Accounts receivable	44	47
Dividends receivable	3	2
Inventory	55	50
Long-term investment	15	10
Land	70	40
Buildings and equipment	225	250
Less: Accumulated depreciation	(25)	(50)
	$420	$369

(continued)

(concluded)

Liabilities		
Accounts payable	$ 13	$ 20
Salaries payable	2	5
Interest payable	4	2
Income tax payable	7	8
Notes payable	30	0
Bonds payable	95	70
Less: Discount on bonds	(2)	(3)
Shareholders' Equity		
Common stock	210	200
Paid-in capital—excess of par	24	20
Retained earnings	45	47
Less: Treasury stock	(8)	0
	$420	$369

DUX COMPANY
Income Statement
For the Year Ended December 31, 2016
($ in 000s)

Revenues		
Sales revenue	$200	
Dividend revenue	3	$203
Expenses		
Cost of goods sold	120	
Salaries expense	25	
Depreciation expense	5	
Interest expense	8	
Loss on sale of building	3	
Income tax expense	17	178
Net income		$ 25

Additional information from the accounting records:

a. A building that originally cost $40,000, and which was three-fourths depreciated, was sold for $7,000.
b. The common stock of Byrd Corporation was purchased for $5,000 as a long-term investment.
c. Property was acquired by issuing a 13%, seven-year, $30,000 note payable to the seller.
d. New equipment was purchased for $15,000 cash.
e. On January 1, 2016, bonds were sold at their $25,000 face value.
f. On January 19, Dux issued a 5% stock dividend (1,000 shares). The market price of the $10 par value common stock was $14 per share at that time.
g. Cash dividends of $13,000 were paid to shareholders.
h. On November 12, 500 shares of common stock were repurchased as treasury stock at a cost of $8,000.

Required:
Prepare the statement of cash flows of Dux Company for the year ended December 31, 2016. Present cash flows from operating activities by the direct method. (You may omit the schedule to reconcile net income to cash flows from operating activities.)

P 21–5
Statement of cash flows; direct method
● LO21–3, LO21–8

Comparative balance sheets for 2016 and 2015 and a statement of income for 2016 are given below for Metagrobolize Industries. Additional information from the accounting records of Metagrobolize also is provided.

METAGROBOLIZE INDUSTRIES
Comparative Balance Sheets
December 31, 2016 and 2015
($ in 000s)

	2016	2015
Assets		
Cash	$ 600	$ 375
Accounts receivable	600	450
Inventory	900	525
Land	675	600
Building	900	900
Less: Accumulated depreciation	(300)	(270)

(continued)

(concluded)

Equipment	2,850	2,250
Less: Accumulated depreciation	(525)	(480)
Patent	1,200	1,500
	$6,900	$5,850
Liabilities		
Accounts payable	$ 750	$ 450
Accrued expenses payable	300	225
Lease liability—land	150	0
Shareholders' Equity		
Common stock	3,150	3,000
Paid-in capital—excess of par	750	675
Retained earnings	1,800	1,500
	$6,900	$5,850

METAGROBOLIZE INDUSTRIES
Income Statement
For the Year Ended December 31, 2016
($ in 000s)

Revenues		
Sales revenue	$2,645	
Gain on sale of land	90	$2,735
Expenses		
Cost of goods sold	$ 600	
Depreciation expense—building	30	
Depreciation expense—equipment	315	
Loss on sale of equipment	15	
Amortization of patent	300	
Operating expenses	500	1,760
Net income		$ 975

Additional information from the accounting records:

a. During 2016, equipment with a cost of $300,000 (90% depreciated) was sold.

b. The statement of shareholders' equity reveals reductions of $225,000 and $450,000 for stock dividends and cash dividends, respectively.

Required:

Prepare the statement of cash flows of Metagrobolize for the year ended December 31, 2016. Present cash flows from operating activities by the direct method. (You may omit the schedule to reconcile net income to cash flows from operating activities.)

P 21–6
Cash flows from operating activities (direct method) derived from an income statement and cash flows from operating activities (indirect method)
● LO21–3, LO21–4

The income statement and a schedule reconciling cash flows from operating activities to net income are provided below ($ in millions) for Mike Roe Computers.

MIKE ROE COMPUTERS
Income Statement
For the Year Ended December 31, 2016

Sales		$150
Cost of goods sold		90
Gross margin		60
Salaries expense	$20	
Insurance expense	12	
Depreciation expense	5	
Interest expense	6	(43)
Gains and losses:		
Gain on sale of equipment		12
Loss on sale of land		(3)
Income before tax		26
Income tax expense		(13)
Net income		$ 13

Reconciliation of Net Income to Net Cash Flows from Operating Activities

Net income	$13
Adjustments for noncash effects:	
Decrease in accounts receivable	5
Gain on sale of equipment	(12)
Increase in inventory	(6)
Increase in accounts payable	9
Increase in salaries payable	3
Depreciation expense	5
Decrease in bond discount	3
Decrease in prepaid insurance	2
Loss on sale of land	3
Increase in income tax payable	6
Net cash flows from operating activities	$31

Required:

1. Calculate each of the following amounts for Mike Roe Computers:
   a. Cash received from customers during the reporting period.
   b. Cash paid to suppliers of goods during the reporting period.
   c. Cash paid to employees during the reporting period.
   d. Cash paid for interest during the reporting period.
   e. Cash paid for insurance during the reporting period.
   f. Cash paid for income taxes during the reporting period.
2. Prepare the cash flows from operating activities section of the statement of cash flows (direct method).

P 21–7
Cash flows from operating activities (direct method) derived from an income statement and cash flows from operating activities (indirect method)
● LO21–3, LO21–4

The income statement and a schedule reconciling cash flows from operating activities to net income are provided below for Macrosoft Corporation.

MACROSOFT CORPORATION
Income Statement
For the Year Ended December 31, 2016
($ in millions)

Revenues and gains:		
Sales	$310	
Gain on sale of cash equivalents	2	
Gain on sale of investments	24	$336
Expenses and loss:		
Cost of goods sold	$120	
Salaries	40	
Interest expense	12	
Insurance	20	
Depreciation	10	
Patent amortization	4	
Loss on sale of land	6	212
Income before tax		124
Income tax expense		62
Net income		$ 62

Reconciliation of Net Income to Net Cash Flows from Operating Activities

Net income	$62
Adjustments for noncash effects:	
Depreciation expense	10
Patent amortization expense	4
Loss on sale of land	6
Gain on sale of investment	(24)
Decrease in accounts receivable	6
Increase in inventory	(12)
Increase in accounts payable	18
Decrease in bond discount	1
Increase in salaries payable	6
Decrease in prepaid insurance	4
Increase in income tax payable	10
Net cash flows from operating activities	$91

Required:

Prepare the cash flows from operating activities section of the statement of cash flows (direct method).

P 21–8
Cash flows from operating activities (direct method and indirect method)—deferred income tax liability and amortization of bond discount
● LO21–3, LO21–4

Portions of the financial statements for Parnell Company are provided below.

PARNELL COMPANY
Income Statement
For the Year Ended December 31, 2016
($ in 000s)

Revenues and gains:		
Sales	$800	
Gain on sale of buildings	11	$811
Expenses and loss:		
Cost of goods sold	$300	
Salaries	120	
Insurance	40	
Depreciation	123	
Interest expense	50	
Loss on sale of machinery	12	645
Income before tax		166
Income tax expense		78
Net income		$ 88

PARNELL COMPANY
Selected Accounts from Comparative Balance Sheets
December 31, 2016 and 2015
($ in 000s)

	Year		
	2016	**2015**	**Change**
Cash	$134	$100	$ 34
Accounts receivable	324	216	108
Inventory	321	425	(104)
Prepaid insurance	66	88	(22)
Accounts payable	210	117	93
Salaries payable	102	93	9
Deferred income tax liability	60	52	8
Bond discount	190	200	(10)

Required:

1. Prepare the cash flows from operating activities section of the statement of cash flows for Parnell Company using the direct method.
2. Prepare the cash flows from operating activities section of the statement of cash flows for Parnell Company using the indirect method.

P 21–9
Cash flows from operating activities (direct method and indirect method)—cash equivalent
● LO21–3, LO21–4

Portions of the financial statements for Hawkeye Company are provided below.

HAWKEYE COMPANY
Income Statement
For the Year Ended December 31, 2016

Sales		$900
Cost of goods sold		350
Gross margin		550
Operating expenses:		
Salaries	$232	
Depreciation	190	
Inventory loss from water damage	12	
Total operating expenses		434
Operating income		116
Other income (expense):		
Gain on sale of cash equivalents		4
Interest expense		(40)
Income before tax		80
Income tax expense		40
Net income		$ 40

HAWKEYE COMPANY
Selected Accounts from Comparative Balance Sheets
December 31, 2016 and 2015

	Year		
	2016	**2015**	**Change**
Cash	$212	$200	$ 12
Accounts receivable	395	421	(26)
Inventory	860	850	10
Accounts payable	210	234	(24)
Salaries payable	180	188	(8)
Interest payable	55	50	5
Income taxes payable	90	104	(14)

Required:

1. Prepare the cash flows from operating activities section of the statement of cash flows for Hawkeye Company using the direct method.
2. Prepare the cash flows from operating activities section of the statement of cash flows for Hawkeye Company using the indirect method.

P 21–10
Relationship between the income statement and cash flows from operating activities (direct method and indirect method)
● LO21–3, LO21–4

The following schedule relates the income statement with cash flows from operating activities, derived by both the direct and indirect methods, in the format illustrated by Illustration 21–11 in the chapter. Some elements necessary to complete the schedule are missing.

Income Statement		Cash Flows from Operating Activities Indirect Method		Direct Method	
		Net income	$?		
		Adjustments:			
Sales	$300	Decrease in accounts receivable	6	Cash received from customers	$?
Gain on sale of equipment	24	Gain on sale of equipment	(24)	(Not reported—no cash effect)	
		Increase in inventory	(12)		
Cost of goods sold	(?)	Increase in accounts payable	18	Cash paid to suppliers	(174)
Salaries expense	(42)	? in salaries payable	6	Cash paid to employees	(36)
Depreciation expense	(9)	Depreciation expense	9	Cash paid for depreciation	?
Interest expense	(?)	Decrease in bond discount	3	Cash paid for interest	(9)
Insurance expense	(21)	Decrease in prepaid insurance	9	Cash paid for insurance	(?)
Loss on sale of land	(6)	Loss on sale of land	6	(Not reported—no cash effect)	
Income tax expense	(27)	Increase in income tax payable	?	Cash paid for income taxes	(21)
Net Income	$?	**Net cash flows from operating activities**	$ 54	**Net cash flows from operating activities**	$ 54

Required:

Complete the schedule by determining each of the following missing elements:

1. Cash received from customers
2. Cost of goods sold
3. ? in salaries payable (Increase? or decrease?)
4. Cash paid for depreciation
5. Interest expense
6. Cash paid for insurance
7. Increase in income tax payable
8. Net income

P 21–11
Prepare a statement of cash flows; direct method
● LO21–3, LO21–8

The comparative balance sheets for 2016 and 2015 and the income statement for 2016 are given below for Arduous Company. Additional information from Arduous's accounting records is provided also.

ARDUOUS COMPANY
Comparative Balance Sheets
December 31, 2016 and 2015
($ in millions)

	2016	2015
Assets		
Cash	$ 116	$ 81
Accounts receivable	190	194
Investment revenue receivable	6	4
Inventory	205	200
Prepaid insurance	4	8
Long-term investment	156	125
Land	196	150
Buildings and equipment	412	400
Less: Accumulated depreciation	(97)	(120)
Patent	30	32
	$1,218	$1,074
Liabilities		
Accounts payable	$ 50	$ 65
Salaries payable	6	11
Bond interest payable	8	4
Income tax payable	12	14
Deferred income tax liability	11	8
Notes payable	23	0
Lease liability	82	0
Bonds payable	215	275
Less: Discount on bonds	(22)	(25)

Shareholders' Equity		
Common stock	430	410
Paid-in capital—excess of par	95	85
Preferred stock	75	0
Retained earnings	242	227
Less: Treasury stock	(9)	0
	$1,218	$1,074

ARDUOUS COMPANY
Income Statement
For Year Ended December 31, 2016
($ in millions)

Revenues and gain:		
Sales revenue	$410	
Investment revenue	11	
Gain on sale of treasury bills	2	$423
Expenses and loss:		
Cost of goods sold	180	
Salaries expense	73	
Depreciation expense	12	
Patent amortization expense	2	
Insurance expense	7	
Bond interest expense	28	
Loss on machine damage	18	
Income tax expense	36	356
Net income		$ 67

Additional information from the accounting records:

a. Investment revenue includes Arduous Company's $6 million share of the net income of Demur Company, an equity method investee.

b. Treasury bills were sold during 2016 at a gain of $2 million. Arduous Company classifies its investments in Treasury bills as cash equivalents.

c. A machine originally costing $70 million that was one-half depreciated was rendered unusable by a flood. Most major components of the machine were unharmed and were sold for $17 million.

d. Temporary differences between pretax accounting income and taxable income caused the deferred income tax liability to increase by $3 million.

e. The preferred stock of Tory Corporation was purchased for $25 million as a long-term investment.

f. Land costing $46 million was acquired by issuing $23 million cash and a 15%, four-year, $23 million note payable to the seller.

g. The right to use a building was acquired with a 15-year lease agreement; present value of lease payments, $82 million.

h. $60 million of bonds were retired at maturity.

i. In February, Arduous issued a 4% stock dividend (4 million shares). The market price of the $5 par value common stock was $7.50 per share at that time.

j. In April, 1 million shares of common stock were repurchased as treasury stock at a cost of $9 million.

Required:

Prepare the statement of cash flows of Arduous Company for the year ended December 31, 2016. Present cash flows from operating activities by the direct method. (A reconciliation schedule is not required.)

P 21–12
Transactions affecting retained earnings
● LO21–5, LO21–6, LO21–8

Shown below in T-account format are the changes affecting the retained earnings of Brenner-Jude Corporation during 2016. At January 1, 2016, the corporation had outstanding 105 million common shares, $1 par per share.

Retained Earnings ($ in millions)

Debit		Credit	
		90	Beginning balance
Retirement of 5 million common shares for $22 million	2		
		88	Net income for the year
Declaration and payment of a $.33 per share cash dividend	33		
Declaration and distribution of a 4% stock dividend	20		
		123	Ending balance

Required:

1. From the information provided by the account changes you should be able to re-create the transactions that affected Brenner-Jude's retained earnings during 2016. Reconstruct the journal entries which can be used as spreadsheet entries in the preparation of a statement of cash flows. Also indicate any investing and financing activities you identify from this analysis that should be reported on the statement of cash flows.
2. Prepare a statement of retained earnings for Brenner-Jude for the year ended 2016. (You may wish to compare your solution to this problem with the parallel situation described in Exercise 18–18.)

P 21–13
Various cash flows
● LO21–3 through LO21–8

Following are selected balance sheet accounts of Del Conte Corp. at December 31, 2016 and 2015, and the increases or decreases in each account from 2015 to 2016. Also presented is selected income statement information for the year ended December 31, 2016, and additional information.

Selected Balance Sheet Accounts	2016	2015	Increase (Decrease)
Assets			
Accounts receivable	$ 34,000	$ 24,000	$ 10,000
Property, plant, and equipment	277,000	247,000	30,000
Accumulated depreciation	(178,000)	(167,000)	11,000
Liabilities and Stockholders' Equity			
Bonds payable	49,000	46,000	3,000
Dividends payable	8,000	5,000	3,000
Common stock, $1 par	22,000	19,000	3,000
Additional paid-in capital	9,000	3,000	6,000
Retained earnings	104,000	91,000	13,000

Selected Income Statement Information for the Year Ended December 31, 2016

Sales revenue	$ 155,000
Depreciation	33,000
Gain on sale of equipment	13,000
Net income	28,000

Additional Information:

a. Accounts receivable relate to sales of merchandise.

b. During 2016, equipment costing $40,000 was sold for cash.

c. During 2016, bonds payable with a face value of $20,000 were issued in exchange for property, plant, and equipment. There was no amortization of bond discount or premium.

Required:

Items 1 through 5 represent activities that will be reported in Del Conte's statement of cash flows for the year ended December 31, 2016. The following two responses are required for each item:

- Determine the amount that should be reported in Del Conte's 2016 statement of cash flows.
- Using the list below, determine the category in which the amount should be reported in the statement of cash flows.
  O. Operating activity
  I. Investing activity
  F. Financing activity

	Amount	Category
1. Cash collections from customers (direct method).	____	____
2. Payments for purchase of property, plant, and equipment.	____	____
3. Proceeds from sale of equipment.	____	____
4. Cash dividends paid.	____	____
5. Redemption of bonds payable.	____	____

(AICPA adapted)

P 21–14
Statement of cash flows; indirect method; limited information
● LO21–4, LO21–8

The comparative balance sheets for 2016 and 2015 are given below for Surmise Company. Net income for 2016 was $50 million.

SURMISE COMPANY
Comparative Balance Sheets
December 31, 2016 and 2015
($ in millions)

	2016	2015
Assets		
Cash	$ 45	$ 40
Accounts receivable	92	96
Less: Allowance for uncollectible accounts	(12)	(4)
Prepaid expenses	8	5
Inventory	145	130
Long-term investment	80	40
Land	100	100
Buildings and equipment	411	300
Less: Accumulated depreciation	(142)	(120)
Patent	16	17
	$ 743	$ 604
Liabilities		
Accounts payable	$ 17	$ 32
Accrued liabilities	(2)	10
Notes payable	35	0
Lease liability	111	0
Bonds payable	65	125
Shareholders' Equity		
Common stock	60	50
Paid-in capital—excess of par	245	205
Retained earnings	212	182
	$ 743	$ 604

Required:

Prepare the statement of cash flows of Surmise Company for the year ended December 31, 2016. Use the indirect method to present cash flows from operating activities because you do not have sufficient information to use the direct method. You will need to make reasonable assumptions concerning the reasons for changes in some account balances. A spreadsheet or T-account analysis will be helpful.

P 21–15
Integrating problem; bonds; lease transactions; lessee and lessor; statement of cash flow effects
● LO21–3, LO21–5, LO21–6

Digital Telephony issued 10% bonds, dated January 1, with a face amount of $32 million on January 1, 2016. The bonds mature in 2026 (10 years). For bonds of similar risk and maturity the market yield is 12%. Interest is paid semiannually on June 30 and December 31. Digital recorded the issue as follows:

Cash	28,329,472	
Discount on bonds	3,670,528	
Bonds payable		32,000,000

Digital also leased switching equipment to Midsouth Communications, Inc., on September 30, 2016. Digital purchased the equipment from MDS Corp. at a cost of $6 million. The five-year lease agreement calls for Midsouth to make quarterly lease payments of $391,548, payable each September 30, December 31, March 31, and June 30, with the first payment on September 30, 2016. Digital's implicit interest rate is 12%.

Required:

Part A

Respond to the following questions assuming neither company applies the proposed Accounting Standards Update for lease accounting described in the Chapter 15 Supplement.

1. What would be the amount(s) related to the bonds that Digital would report in its statement of cash flows for the year ended December 31, 2016, if Digital uses the direct method? The indirect method?
2. What would be the amounts related to the lease that *Midsouth* would report in its statement of cash flows for the year ended December 31, 2016?
3. What would be the amounts related to the lease that *Digital* would report in its statement of cash flows for the year ended December 31, 2016?
4. Assume MDS manufactured the equipment at a cost of $5 million and that Midsouth leased the equipment directly from MDS. What would be the amounts related to the lease that *MDS* would report in its statement of cash flows for the year ended December 31, 2016?

Part B

Respond to the preceding questions assuming both companies use the proposed Accounting Standards Update for lease accounting described in the Chapter 15 Supplement.

P 21–16
Statement of cash flows; indirect method
● LO21–4, LO21–8

Refer to the data provided in the P21–4 for Dux Company.

Required:
Prepare the statement of cash flows for Dux Company using the *indirect method.*

P 21–17
Statement of cash flows; indirect method
● LO21–4, LO21–8

Refer to the data provided in the P21–5 for Metagrobolize Industries.

Required:
Prepare the statement of cash flows for Metagrobolize Industries using the *indirect method.*

P 21–18
Statement of cash flows; indirect method
● LO21–4, LO21–8

Refer to the data provided in the P21–11 for Arduous Company.

Required:
Prepare the statement of cash flows for Arduous Company using the *indirect method.*

(Note: The following problems use the technique learned in Appendix 21B.)

P 21–19
Statement of cash flows; T-account method
● LO21–3, LO21–8

Refer to the data provided in the P21–4 for Dux Company.

Required:
Prepare the statement of cash flows for Dux Company. Use the T-account method to assist in your analysis.

P 21–20
Statement of cash flows; T-account method
● LO21–3, LO21–8

Refer to the data provided in the P21–5 for Metagrobolize Industries.

Required:
Prepare the statement of cash flows for Metagrobolize Industries. Use the T-account method to assist in your analysis.

P 21–21
Statement of cash flows; T-account method
● LO21–3, LO21–8

Refer to the data provided in the P21–11 for Arduous Company.

Required:
Prepare the statement of cash flows for Arduous Company. Use the T-account method to assist in your analysis.

Broaden Your Perspective

Apply your critical-thinking ability to the knowledge you've gained. These cases will provide you an opportunity to develop your research, analysis, judgment, and communication skills. You also will work with other students, integrate what you've learned, apply it in real-world situations, and consider its global and ethical ramifications. This practice will broaden your knowledge and further develop your decision-making abilities.

Communication Case 21–1
Distinguish income and cash flows
● LO21–1, LO21–3, LO21–4

"Why can't we pay our shareholders a dividend?" shouted your new boss. "This income statement you prepared for me says we earned $5 million in our first half-year!"

You were hired last month as the chief accountant for Enigma Corporation which was organized on July 1 of the year just ended. You recently prepared the financial statements below.

ENIGMA CORPORATION
Income Statement
For the Six Months Ended December 31, 2016
($ in millions)

Sales revenue	$ 75
Cost of goods sold	(30)
Depreciation expense	(5)
Remaining expenses	(35)
Net income	$ 5

ENIGMA CORPORATION
Balance Sheet
December 31, 2016 ($ in millions)

Cash	$ 1
Accounts receivable (net)	20
Merchandise inventory	15
Machinery (net)	44
Total	$80
Accounts payable	$ 2
Accrued expenses payable	7
Notes payable	36
Common stock	30
Retained earnings	5
Total	$80

You have just explained to your boss, Robert James, that although net income was $5 million, operating activities produced a net decrease in cash. Unable to understand your verbal explanation, he has asked you to prepare a written report.

Required:
Prepare a report explaining the apparent discrepancy between Enigma's profitability and its cash flows. To increase the chances of your boss's understanding the situation, include in your report a determination of net cash flows from operating activities by both the direct and indirect methods. Your report should also include a narrative explanation of how it is possible for operating activities to simultaneously produce a positive net income and negative net cash flows.

Judgment Case 21–2
Distinguish income and cash flows
● LO21–3, LO21–8

You are a loan officer for First Benevolent Bank. You have an uneasy feeling as you examine a loan application from Daring Corporation. The application included the following financial statements.

DARING CORPORATION
Income Statement
For the Year Ended December 31, 2016

Sales revenue	$100,000
Cost of goods sold	(50,000)
Depreciation expense	(5,000)
Remaining expenses	(25,000)
Net income	$ 20,000

DARING CORPORATION
Balance Sheet
December 31, 2016

Cash	$ 5,000
Accounts receivable	25,000
Inventory	20,000
Operational assets	55,000
Accumulated depreciation	(5,000)
Total	$100,000
Accounts payable	$ 10,000
Interest payable	5,000
Note payable	45,000
Common stock	20,000
Retained earnings	20,000
Total	$100,000

It is not Daring's profitability that worries you. The income statement submitted with the application shows net income of $20,000 in Daring's first year of operations. By referring to the balance sheet, you see that this net income represents a 20% rate of return on assets of $100,000. Your concern stems from the recollection that the note payable reported on Daring's balance sheet is a two-year loan you approved earlier in the year.

You also recall another promising new company that, just last year, defaulted on another of your bank's loans when it failed due to its inability to generate sufficient cash flows to meet its obligations. Before requesting additional information from Daring, you decide to test your memory of the intermediate accounting class you took in night school by attempting to prepare a statement of cash flows from the information available in the loan application.

Research Case 21–3
Information from cash flow activities; FedEx
● **LO21–3 through LO21–8**

Real World Financials

Locate the most recent financial statements and related disclosure notes of **FedEx Corporation**. You can locate the report online at www.fedex.com.

Required:

1. From the information provided in the statement of cash flows, explain what allows FedEx Corporation to expand its business as evidenced by the investing activities, while at the same time not raising as much cash through financing activities.
2. Describe the activities listed under financing activities for the most recent fiscal year. [*Hint:* FedEx's Statement of Changes in Common Stockholders' Investment (statement of shareholders' equity) will help you determine the nature of the stock activity.] What is the most notable financing activity reported?
3. What are the cash payments FedEx made for interest and for income taxes in the three years reported? (*Hint:* See the disclosure notes.)
4. Obtain the relevant authoritative literature on disclosure of interest and income taxes using the *FASB Accounting Standards Codification*. You might gain access at the FASB website (asc.fasb.org). What is the specific citation that specifies the way FedEx reports interest and income taxes separately that enabled you to answer requirement 3?

Trueblood Accounting Case 21–4
Presentation issues
● **LO21–5, LO21–6,**

The following Trueblood case is recommended for use with this chapter. The case provides an excellent opportunity for class discussion, group projects, and writing assignments. The case, along with Professor's Discussion Material, can be obtained from the Deloitte Foundation at its website: www.deloitte.com/us/truebloodcases.

Case 13-2: Buck's Dilemma: Gross or Net

This case gives students the opportunity to consider when borrowings and payments under a revolving line of credit may be presented on a net (versus gross) basis within the statement of cash flows.

Analysis Case 21–5
Smudged ink; find missing amounts
● **LO21–3, LO21–4**

"Be careful with that coffee!" Your roommate is staring in disbelief at the papers in front of her. "This was my contribution to our team project," she moaned. "When you spilled your coffee, it splashed on this page. Now I can't recognize some of these numbers, and Craig has my source documents."

Knowing how important this afternoon's presentation is to your roommate, you're eager to see what can be done. "Let me see that," you offer. "I think we can figure this out." The statement of cash flows and income statement are intact. The reconciliation schedule and the comparative balance sheets are coffee casualties.

DISTINCTIVE INDUSTRIES
Statement of Cash Flows
For the Year Ended December 31, 2016
($ in millions)

Cash Flows from Operating Activities:		
Collections from customers	$213	
Payment to suppliers	(90)	
Payment of general & administrative expenses	(54)	
Payment of income taxes	(27)	
Net cash flows from operating activities		$ 42
Cash Flows from Investing Activities:		
Sale of equipment		120
Cash Flows from Financing Activities:		
Issuance of common stock	30	
Payment of dividends	(9)	
Net cash flows from financing activities		21
Net increase in cash		$183
Reconciliation of net income to cash flows from operating activities:		
Net income	$ 84	
Adjustments for noncash items:		
Depreciation expense	☐	
☐	☐	
☐	☐	
☐	☐	
☐	☐	
☐	☐	
Net cash flows from operating activities		☐

DISTINCTIVE INDUSTRIES
Income Statement
For the Year Ended December 31, 2016

Sales revenue		$240
Cost of goods sold		96
Gross profit		144
Operating expenses:		
General and administrative	$54	
Depreciation	30	
Total operating expenses		84
Operating income		60
Other income:		
Gain on sale of equipment		45
Income before income taxes		105
Income tax expense		21
Net income		$ 84

DISTINCTIVE INDUSTRIES
Comparative Balance Sheets
At December 31

	2016	**2015**
Assets:		
Cash	$360	☐
Accounts receivable (net)	☐	252
Inventory	180	☐
Property, plant, & equipment	450	600
Less: Accumulated depreciation	(120)	☐
Total assets	☐	☐

(continued)

(concluded)

Liabilities and shareholders' equity:		
Accounts payable	$120	$ 90
General and administrative expenses payable	27	27
Income taxes payable	66	☐
Common stock	720	690
Retained earnings	☐	141
Total liabilities and shareholders' equity	☐	☐

Required:

1. Determine the missing amounts.
2. Reconstruct the reconciliation of net income to cash flows from operating activities (operating cash flows using the indirect method).

Real World Case 21–6
Analyze cash flow activities; Staples, Inc.
● LO21–1 through LO21–8

Real World Financials

Staples, Inc., is the world's leading office products company. Locate the statement of cash flows of Staples for the fiscal year ended February 1, 2014 on the Internet.

Required:

1. In the three years reported, what was Staples' primary investing activity? How was this activity financed? Be specific.
2. During the most recent fiscal year, Staples purchased certificates of deposit. How were these purchases reported in the statement of cash flows? (Note: This is not an investing activity.)
3. How are issuances of debt securities and issuances of equity securities classified in a statement of cash flows?
4. How are payments to investors in debt securities (interest) and payments to investors in equity securities (dividends) classified in a statement of cash flows? Is this a conceptual inconsistency? Explain.
5. Staples' statement of cash flows reports expenditures for acquisition of businesses. It also reports additions to long-term debt. Suppose the businesses had been acquired, not with cash, but by exchange for debt securities. Would such a transaction be reported? Explain.

Ethics Case 21–7
Where's the cash?
● LO21–1, LO21–3

After graduating near the top of his class, Ben Naegle was hired by the local office of a Big 4 CPA firm in his hometown. Two years later, impressed with his technical skills and experience, Park Electronics, a large regional consumer electronics chain, hired Ben as assistant controller. This was last week. Now Ben's initial excitement has turned to distress.

The cause of Ben's distress is the set of financial statements he's stared at for the last four hours. For some time prior to his recruitment, he had been aware of the long trend of moderate profitability of his new employer. The reports on his desk confirm the slight, but steady, improvements in net income in recent years. The trend he was just now becoming aware of, though, was the decline in cash flows from operations.

Ben had sketched out the following comparison ($ in millions):

	2016	2015	2014	2013
Income from operations	$140.0	$132.0	$127.5	$127.0
Net income	38.5	35.0	34.5	29.5
Cash flow from operations	1.6	17.0	12.0	15.5

Profits? Yes. Increasing profits? Yes. The cause of his distress? The ominous trend in cash flow which is consistently lower than net income.

Upon closer review, Ben noticed three events in the last two years that, unfortunately, seemed related:

a. Park's credit policy had been loosened; credit terms were relaxed and payment periods were lengthened.
b. Accounts receivable balances had increased dramatically.
c. Several of the company's compensation arrangements, including that of the controller and the company president, were based on reported net income.

Required:

1. What is so ominous about the combination of events Ben sees?
2. What course of action, if any, should Ben take?

Real World Case 21–8
Disparity between net income and cash flows; PetSmart
● LO21–3, LO21–4

Real World Financials

"I've been reading that the pet care and product industry is somewhat recession-resistant," said Bee Del Conte as you walked with her to the library. "How is it, then, that I hear on the radio this morning that although PetSmart's net income has increased steadily over the previous three years, its cash flows from its operations last year were down significantly from prior years?" Curious, the two of you stop by a computer terminal on the way to the reference section and do a quick search. A few clicks later you're looking at PetSmart's income statements and cash flow statements for the fiscal year ended February 2, 2014. These are reproduced in the financial statements and related disclosure notes of PetSmart in Appendix B located at the back of this textbook. They also can be found at www.PetSmart.com.

PetSmart

Required:

1. Without regard to PetSmart specifically, explain to Bee the difference between net income and the cash flows from operating activities.
2. Why did PetSmart add $235.4 million in the determination of cash flows from operating activities for depreciation and amortization?
3. A contributor to the difference in PetSmart's net income and cash flows from operating activities and net income in each of the three years presented is a sizable reduction in the amount PetSmart owes its suppliers. If PetSmart had used the direct rather than the indirect method of reporting operating activities, how would this reduction in accounts payable have affected cash from operating activities?
4. Cash outflows for financing activities during each of the three years presented exceeded cash inflows from financing activities. In fact, investing activities also produced net cash outflows in each of the three years. How is that possible? What is the major contributor from year to year in the amount of cash used in financing activities? What are the next two highest contributors to that difference?

Research Case 21–9
Researching the way cash flows are reported; retrieving information from the Internet
● LO21–3 through LO21–8

Corporate financial statements are readily available on the Internet.

Required:

1. Search the Internet for a public company with which you are familiar. Access its most recent annual report or 10-K filing. Search or scroll to find the statement of cash flows and related note(s).
2. Is the direct or indirect method used to report operating activities? What is the largest adjustment to net income in reconciling net income and cash flows from operations in the most recent year?
3. What are the cash payments for interest and for taxes?
4. What has been the most significant investing activity for the company in the most recent three years?
5. What has been the most significant financing activity for the company in requirements 1–4 for another company?

Analysis Case 21–10
Information from cash flow activities; PetSmart
● LO21–3 through LO21–8

Real World Financials

PetSmart

Refer to the financial statements and related disclosure notes of **PetSmart Inc.** located in the company's annual report for the fiscal year ending February 2, 2014 included with all new copies of this textbook. You also can locate the report online at **www.PetSmart.com**.

Notice that PetSmart's net income has increased over the three years reported. To supplement their analysis of profitability, many analysts like to look at "free cash flow." A popular way to measure this metric is "structural free cash flow" (or as Warren Buffett calls it "owner's earnings"), which is calculated as net income from operations plus depreciation and amortization minus capital expenditures.

Required:

Determine free cash flows for PetSmart in each of the three years reported. Compare that amount with net income each year. What pattern do you detect?

Research Case 21–11
FASB codification; locate and extract relevant information and cite authoritative support for a financial reporting issue; cash flow classification
● LO21–4 through LO21–6

"This one's got me stumped," you say to no one in particular. "First day on the job; I'd better get it right." It's the classification of notes payable in the statement of cash flows that has you in doubt. Having received an "A" in Intermediate Accounting, you know that a note payable representing a bank loan is a financing activity, but this one is a note payable to your employer's primary merchandise supplier. "I wonder if the accounting is the same."

Required:

1. Obtain the relevant authoritative literature on cash flow classification using the *FASB Accounting Standards Codification*. You might gain access at the FASB website (**asc.fasb.org**). What is the specific citation that specifies the classification of notes payable to suppliers?
2. Is accounting the same as for notes payable to banks? Explain.
3. Is accounting the same for both short-term and long-term notes payable to suppliers?

IFRS Case 21–12
Statement of cash flows presentation, British Telecommunications
● LO21–3 through LO21–6, LO21–9

Real World Financials

British Telecommunications Plc (BT), a U.K. company, is the world's oldest communications company. The company prepares its financial statements in accordance with International Financial Reporting Standards. Locate BT's statement of cash flows from it's website at www.btplc.com.

Required:

1. What are the primary classifications into which BT's cash inflows and cash outflows are separated? Is this classification the same as or different from cash flow statements prepared in accordance with U.S. GAAP?
2. How are cash inflows from dividends and interest and cash outflows for dividends and interest classified in BT's cash flow statements? Is this classification the same as or different from cash flow statements prepared in accordance with U.S. GAAP?

Air France–KLM Case

AIRFRANCE / KLM
● LO21–9

Air France–KLM (AF), a Franco-Dutch company, prepares its financial statements according to International Financial Reporting Standards. AF's financial statements and disclosure notes for the year ended December 31, 2013, are provided with all new textbooks. This material also is available at www.airfranceklm-finance.com.

Required:

1. What are the primary classifications into which AF's cash inflows and cash outflows are separated? Is this classification the same as or different from cash flow statements prepared in accordance with U.S. GAAP?
2. How are cash inflows from dividends and interest and cash outflows for dividends and interest classified in AF's cash flow statements? Is this classification the same as or different from cash flow statements prepared in accordance with U.S. GAAP?

CPA Simulation 21–1

Alpha Company
Classification of Cash Flows

KAPLAN
CPA REVIEW

Test your knowledge of the concepts discussed in this chapter, practice critical professional skills necessary for career success, and prepare for the computer-based CPA exam by accessing our CPA simulations in the Connect Library.

The Alpha Company simulation tests your ability to select the appropriate classification for a variety of cash flows.

APPENDIX

A

Derivatives

"... derivatives are financial weapons of mass destruction ..."

— WarrenBuffett, Berkshire Hathaway CEO

"... the growing use of complex financial instruments known as derivatives does not pose a threat to the country's financial system ..."

— AlanGreenspan, Federal Reserve Chairman

"Total world derivatives are $1000 trillion or 19 times the total world GDP of $54 trillion."

— ChuckBurr, *Culture Change*

In today's global economy and evolving financial markets, businesses are increasingly exposed to a variety of risks, which, unmanaged, can have major impacts on earnings or even threaten a company's very existence. Risk management, then, has become critical. Derivative financial instruments have become the key tools of risk management.[1]

Derivatives are financial instruments that "derive" their values or contractually required cash flows from some other security or index. For instance, a contract allowing a company to buy a particular asset (say steel, gold, or flour) at a designated future date at a predetermined price is a financial instrument that derives its value from expected and actual changes in the price of the underlying asset. Financial futures, forward contracts, options, and interest rate swaps are the most frequently used derivatives. Derivatives are valued as tools to manage or hedge companies' increasing exposures to risk, including interest rate risk, price risk, and foreign exchange risk. The variety, complexity, and magnitude of derivatives have grown rapidly in recent years. Accounting standard-setters have scrambled to keep pace.

Derivatives are financial instruments that "derive" their values from some other security or _index_.

A persistent stream of headline stories has alerted us to multimillion-dollar losses by many companies and the financial collapse of Bear Stearns and AIG.[2] Focusing on these headlines, it would be tempting to conclude that derivatives are risky business indeed. Certainly they can be quite risky, if misused, but the fact is, these financial instruments exist to lessen, not increase, risk. Properly used, they serve as a form of "insurance" against risk. In fact, if a company is exposed to a substantial risk and does not hedge that risk, it is taking a gamble. On the other hand, if a derivative is used improperly, it can be a huge gamble itself.

Derivatives serve as a form of "insurance" against risk.

The notional amount of the derivatives market vastly exceeds the total value of the assets they are intended to mimic or mirror. This implies that firms are using derivatives for purposes other than risk management. Many observers are fearful that the size of the derivatives market poses significant risk to the economy. Some caution that the vast derivatives market could even cause the entire global financial system to crash. Why? If interest rates rise, then many speculative interest rate swaps would incur losses. But it's the size of the interest rate swap market and thus the size of the resultant losses that prompts the anxiety. At the start of 2014, the over-the-counter derivatives market was $702 trillion. Yes, that's 702 with twelve zeroes ($702,000,000,000,000). And, that's over 30 times the U.S. Gross Domestic product. Eighty-two percent of those derivatives ($584 trillion) are interest rate swaps.[3] Our focus here, though, is not on the risk posed by the speculative use of derivatives, but instead on the use of derivatives to reduce company risk.

[1]Almost all financial institutions and over half of all nonfinancial companies use derivatives.

[2]Bear Sterns has since been sold at a bargain basement price to JP Morgan, and AIG has since recovered from its difficulties.

[3]Bank for International Settlements, *BIS Quarterly Review*, June 2014.

Derivatives Used to Hedge Risk

Hedging means taking a risk position that is opposite to an actual position that is exposed to risk.

Hedging means taking an action that is expected to produce exposure to a particular type of risk that is precisely the *opposite* of an actual risk to which the company already is exposed. For instance, the volatility of interest rates creates exposure to interest-rate risk for companies that issue debt—which, of course, includes most companies. So, a company that frequently arranges short-term loans from its bank under a floating (variable) interest rate agreement is exposed to the risk that interest rates might increase and adversely affect borrowing costs. Similarly, a company that regularly reissues commercial paper as it matures faces the possibility that new rates will be higher and cut into forecasted income. When borrowings are large, the potential cost can be substantial. So, the firm might choose to hedge its position by entering into a transaction that would produce a *gain* of roughly the same amount as the potential loss if interest rates do, in fact, increase.

Hedging is used to deal with three areas of risk exposure: fair value risk, cash flow risk, and foreign currency risk. Let's look at some of the more common derivatives.

A *futures contract* allows a firm to sell (or buy) a financial instrument at a designated future date, at today's price.

FINANCIAL FUTURES A futures contract is an agreement between a seller and a buyer that requires the seller to deliver a particular commodity (say corn, gold, or pork bellies) at a designated future date, at a *predetermined* price. These contracts are actively traded on regulated futures exchanges. When the "commodity" is a *financial instrument,* such as a Treasury bond, Treasury bill, commercial paper, or a certificate of deposit, the agreement is referred to as a *financial futures contract.*[4]

To appreciate the way these hedges work, you need to remember that when interest rates rise, the market price of interest-bearing securities goes down. For instance, if you have an investment in a 10% bond and market interest rates go up to, say, 12%, your 10% bond is less valuable relative to other bonds paying the higher rate. Conversely, when interest rates decline, the market price of interest-bearing securities goes up. This risk that the investment's value might change is referred to as *fair value risk.* The company that issued the securities is faced with fair value risk also. If interest rates decline, the fair value of that company's debt would rise, a risk the borrower may want to hedge against. Later in this section, we'll look at an illustration of how the borrower would account for and report such a hedge.

The seller in a financial futures contract realizes a gain (loss) when interest rates rise (decline).

Now let's look at the effect on a contract to sell or buy securities (or any asset for that matter) at preset prices. One who is contracted to *sell* securities at a *preset* price after their market price has fallen benefits from the rise in interest rates. Consequently, the value of the contract that gives one the right to sell securities at a preset price goes up as the market price declines. The seller in a futures contract derives a gain (loss) when interest rates rise (decline).[5] Conversely, the one obligated to buy securities at a preset price experiences a loss. This risk of having to pay more cash or receive less cash is referred to as *cash flow risk.*

Another example of cash flow risk would be borrowing money by issuing a variable (floating) rate note. If market interest rates rise, the borrower would have to pay more interest. Similarly, the lender (investor) in the variable (floating) rate note transaction would face cash flow risk that interest rates would decline, resulting in lower cash interest receipts.

Let's look closer at how a futures contract can mitigate cash flow risk. Consider a company in April that will replace its $10 million of 8.5% bank notes with a bond issue when the notes mature in June. The company is exposed to the risk that interest rates in June will have risen, increasing borrowing costs. To counteract that possibility, the firm might enter a contract in April to deliver (sell) bonds in June at their *current* price. Since there are no corporate bond futures contracts, the company buys Treasury bond futures, which will accomplish essentially the same purpose. In essence, the firm agrees to sell Treasury bonds in June at a price established now (April). Let's say it's April 6 and the price of Treasury bond futures on the International Monetary Market of the Chicago Mercantile Exchange is quoted as 95.24.[6] Since the trading unit of Treasury bond futures is a 15-year, $100,000, 8% Treasury bond,

[4]Note that a financial futures contract meets the definition of a financial instrument because it entails the exchange of financial instruments (cash for Treasury bonds, for instance). But, a futures contract for the sale or purchase of a nonfinancial commodity like corn or gold does not meet the definition because one of the items to be exchanged is not a financial instrument.

[5]The seller of a futures contract is obligated to sell the bonds at a future date. The buyer of a futures contract is obligated to buy the bonds at a future date. The company in our example, then, is the seller of the futures contract.

[6]Price quotes are expressed as a percentage of par.

the company might sell 105 Treasury bond futures to hedge the June issuance of debt. This would effectively provide a hedge of 105 × \$100,000 × 95.24% = \$10,000,200.[7]

Here's what happens then. If interest rates rise, borrowing costs will go up for our example company because it will have to sell debt securities at a higher interest cost (or lower price). But that loss will be offset (approximately) by the gain produced by being in the opposite position on Treasury bond futures. Take note, though, this works both ways. If interest rates go down causing debt security prices to rise, the potential benefit of being able to issue debt at that lower interest rate (higher price) will be offset by a loss on the futures position.

A very important point about futures contracts is that the seller does not need to have actual possession of the commodity (the Treasury bonds, in this case), nor is the purchaser of the contract required to take possession of the commodity. In fact, virtually all financial futures contracts are "netted out" before the actual transaction is to take place. This is simply a matter of reversing the original position. A seller closes out his transaction with a purchase. Likewise, a purchaser would close out her transaction with a sale. After all, the objective is not to actually buy or sell Treasury bonds (or whatever the commodity might be), but to incur the financial impact of movements in interest rates as reflected in changes in Treasury bond prices. Specifically, it will buy at the lower price (to reverse the original seller position) at the same time it's selling its new bond issue at that same lower price. The financial futures market is an "artificial" exchange in that its reason for existing is to provide a mechanism to transfer risk from those exposed to it to those willing to accept the risk, not to actually buy and sell the underlying financial instruments.

If the impending debt issue being hedged is a short-term issue, the company may attain a more effective hedge by selling Treasury *bill* futures since Treasury bills are 90-day securities, or maybe certificate of deposit (CD) futures that also are traded in futures markets. The object is to get the closest association between the financial effects of interest rate movements on the actual transaction and the effects on the financial instrument used as a hedge.

The effectiveness of a hedge is influenced by the closeness of the match between the item being hedged and the financial instrument chosen as a hedge.

FINANCIAL FORWARD CONTRACTS A **forward contract** is similar to a futures contract but differs in three ways:

1. A forward contract calls for delivery on a specific date, whereas a futures contract permits the seller to decide later which specific day within the specified month will be the delivery date (if it gets as far as actual delivery before it is closed out).
2. Unlike a futures contract, a forward contract usually is not traded on a market exchange.
3. Unlike a futures contract, a forward contract does not call for a daily cash settlement for price changes in the underlying contract. Gains and losses on forward contracts are paid only when they are closed out.

OPTIONS **Options** frequently are purchased to hedge exposure to the effects of changing interest rates. Options serve the same purpose as futures in that respect but are fundamentally different. An option on a financial instrument—say a Treasury bill—gives its holder the right either to buy or to sell the Treasury bill at a specified price and within a given time period. Importantly, though, the option holder has no obligation to exercise the option. On the other hand, the holder of a futures contract must buy or sell within a specified period unless the contract is closed out before delivery comes due.

FOREIGN CURRENCY FUTURES Foreign loans frequently are denominated in the currency of the lender (Japanese yen, Swiss franc, Euro, and so on). When loans must be repaid in foreign currencies, a new element of risk is introduced. This is because if exchange rates change, the dollar equivalent of the foreign currency that must be repaid differs from the dollar equivalent of the foreign currency borrowed.

To hedge against "foreign exchange risk" exposure, some firms buy or sell **foreign currency futures** contracts. These are similar to financial futures except specific foreign

Foreign exchange risk often is hedged in the same manner as interest rate risk.

[7]This is a simplification of the more sophisticated way financial managers determine the optimal number of futures.

currencies are specified in the futures contracts rather than specific debt instruments. They work the same way to protect against foreign exchange risk as financial futures protect against fair value or cash flow risk.

***Interest rate swaps* exchange fixed interest payments for floating rate payments, or vice versa, without exchanging the underlying notional amounts.**

INTEREST RATE SWAPS Over 82% of derivatives are **interest rate swaps**. These contracts exchange fixed interest payments for floating rate payments, or vice versa, without exchanging the underlying principal amounts. For example, suppose you owe $100,000 on a 10% fixed rate home loan. You envy your neighbor who also is paying 10% on her $100,000 mortgage, but hers is a floating rate loan, so if market rates fall, so will her loan rate. To the contrary, she is envious of your fixed rate, fearful that rates will rise, increasing her payments. A solution would be for the two of you to effectively swap interest payments using an interest rate swap agreement. The way a swap works, you both would continue to actually make your own interest payments, but would exchange the net cash difference between payments at specified intervals. So, in this case, if market rates (and thus floating payments) increase, you would pay your neighbor; if rates fall, she pays you. The net effect is to exchange the consequences of rate changes. In other words, you have effectively converted your fixed-rate debt to floating-rate debt; your neighbor has done the opposite.

Of course, this technique is not dependent on happening into such a fortuitous pairing of two borrowers with opposite philosophies on interest rate risk. Instead, banks or other intermediaries offer, for a fee, one-sided swap agreements to companies desiring to be either fixed-rate payers or variable-rate payers. Intermediaries usually strive to maintain a balanced portfolio of matched, offsetting swap agreements.

Theoretically, the two parties to such a transaction exchange principal amounts, say the $100,000 amount above, in addition to the interest on those amounts. It makes no practical sense, though, for the companies to send each other $100,000. So, instead, the principal amount is not actually exchanged, but serves merely as the computational base for interest calculations and is called the *notional amount.* Similarly, the fixed-rate payer doesn't usually send the entire fixed interest amount (say 10% × $100,000 = $10,000) and receive the entire variable interest amount (say 9% × $100,000 = $9,000). Generally, only the net amount ($1,000 in this case) is exchanged. This is illustrated in Illustration A–1.

Illustration A–1

Interest Rate Swap—Shortcut Method

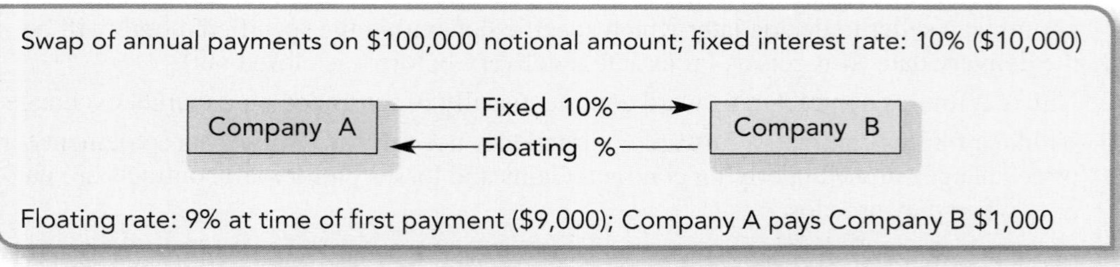

From an accounting standpoint, the central issue is not the operational differences among various hedge instruments, but their similarities in functioning as hedges against risk.

Accounting for Derivatives

A key to accounting for derivatives is knowing the purpose for which a company holds them and whether the company is effective in serving that purpose. Derivatives, for instance, may be held for risk management (hedging activities). The desired effect, and often the real effect, is a reduction in risk. On the other hand, derivatives sometimes are held for speculative position taking, hoping for large profits. The effect of this activity usually is to *increase* risk. Perhaps more important, derivatives acquired as hedges and intended to reduce risk may, in fact, unintentionally increase risk instead.

Derivatives not serving as hedges are extremely speculative due to the high leverage inherent in such investments.

It's important to understand that, serving as investments rather than as hedges, derivatives are extremely speculative. This is due to the high leverage inherent in derivatives. Here's why. The investment outlay usually is negligible, but, the potential gain or loss on the investment usually is quite high. A small change in interest rates or another underlying event can trigger a large change in the fair value of the derivative. Because the initial investment was minimal, the change in value relative to the investment itself represents a huge percentage gain or loss. Their extraordinarily risky nature prompted Warren Buffett, one of the country's most celebrated financiers, to refer to derivatives as "financial weapons of mass destruction." Accounting for derivatives is designed to treat differently (a) derivatives designated as hedges and those not designated as hedges as well as (b) the effective portion and the ineffective portion of gains and losses from intended hedges.

The basic approach to accounting for derivatives is fairly straightforward, although implementation can be quite cumbersome. All derivatives, no exceptions, are carried on the balance sheet as either assets or liabilities at fair (or market) value.[8] The reasoning is that (a) derivatives create either rights or obligations that meet the definition of assets or liabilities, and (b) fair value is the most meaningful measurement.

Each derivative contract has a "fair value," which is an amount that one side owes the other at a particular moment.

Accounting for the gain or loss on a derivative depends on how it is used. Specifically, if the derivative is not designated as a hedging instrument, or doesn't qualify as one, any gain or loss from fair value changes is recognized immediately in earnings. On the other hand, if a derivative is used to hedge against exposure to risk, any gain or loss from fair value changes is either (a) recognized immediately in earnings along with an offsetting loss or gain on the item being hedged or (b) deferred in comprehensive income until it can be recognized in earnings at the same time as earnings are affected by a hedged transaction. Which way depends on whether the derivative is designated as a (a) fair value hedge, (b) cash flow hedge, or (c) foreign currency hedge. Let's look now at each of the three hedge designations.

FAIR VALUE HEDGES A company can be adversely affected when a change in either prices or interest rates causes a change in the fair value of one of its assets, its liabilities, or a commitment to buy or sell assets or liabilities. If a derivative is used to hedge against the exposure to changes in the fair value of an asset or liability or a firm commitment, it can be designated as a **fair value hedge**. In that case, when the derivative is adjusted to reflect changes in fair value, the other side of the entry recognizes a gain or loss to be included *currently* in earnings. At the same time, though, the loss or gain from changes in the fair value (due to the risk being hedged)[9] of the item being hedged also is included currently in earnings. This means that, to the extent the hedge is effective in serving its purpose, the gain or loss on the derivative will be offset by the loss or gain on the item being hedged. In fact, this is precisely the concept behind the procedure.

A gain or loss from a *fair value hedge* is recognized immediately in earnings along with the loss or gain from the item being hedged.

The reasoning is that as interest rates or other underlying events change, a hedge instrument will produce a gain approximately equal to a loss on the item being hedged (or vice versa). These income effects are interrelated and offsetting, so it would be improper to report the income effects in different periods. More critically, the intent and effect of having the hedge instrument is to *lessen* risk. And yet, recognizing gains in one period and counterbalancing losses in another period would tend to cause fluctuations in income that convey an *increase* in risk. However, to the extent that a hedge is ineffective and produces gains or losses different from the losses or gains being hedged, the ineffective portion is recognized in earnings immediately.

The income effects of the hedge instrument and the income effects of the item being hedged should affect earnings at the same time.

Some of the more common fair value hedges use:

- An interest rate swap to synthetically convert fixed-rate debt (for which interest rate changes could change the fair value of the debt) into floating-rate debt.
- A futures contract to hedge changes in the fair value (due to price changes) of aluminum, sugar, or some other type of inventory.
- A futures contract to hedge the fair value (due to price changes) of a firm commitment to sell natural gas or some other asset.

ILLUSTRATION Because interest rate swaps comprise over 82% of derivatives in use, we will use swaps to illustrate accounting for derivatives. Let's look at the example in Illustration A–2 on the next page.

[8]FASB ASC 815–10: Derivatives and Hedging–Overall (previously "Accounting for Derivative Instruments and Hedging Activities," *Statement of Financial Accounting Standards No. 133* (Norwalk, Conn.: FASB, 1998)).

[9]The fair value of a hedged item might also change for reasons other than from effects of the risk being hedged. For instance, the hedged risk may be that a change in interest rates will cause the fair value of a bond to change. The bond price might also change, though, if the market perceives that the bond's default risk has changed.

When the floating rate declined from 10% to 9%, the fair values of both the derivative (swap) and the note increased. This created an offsetting gain on the derivative and a holding loss on the note. Both are recognized in earnings at the same time (at June 30, 2016).

Illustration A–2

Interest Rate Swap—Shortcut Method

Wintel Semiconductors issued $1 million of 18-month, 10% bank notes on January 1, 2016. Wintel is exposed to the risk that general interest rates will decline, causing the fair value of its debt to rise. (If the fair value of Wintel's debt increases, its effective borrowing cost is higher relative to the market.) To hedge against this fair value risk, the firm entered into an 18-month interest rate swap agreement on January 1 and designated the swap as a hedge against changes in the fair value of the note. The swap calls for the company to *receive payment* based on a 10% fixed interest rate on a notional amount of $1 million and to *make payment* based on a floating interest rate tied to changes in general rates.[10] As the Illustration will show, this effectively converts Wintel's fixed-rate debt to floating-rate debt. Cash settlement of the net interest amount is made semiannually at June 30 and December 31 of each year with the net interest being the difference between the $50,000 fixed interest [$1 million × (10% × ½)] and the floating interest rate times $1 million at those dates.

Floating (market) settlement rates were 9% at June 30, 2016, 8% at December 31, 2016, and 9% at June 30, 2017. Net interest receipts can be calculated as shown below. Fair values of both the derivative and the note resulting from those market rate changes are assumed to be quotes obtained from securities dealers.

	1/1/16	6/30/16	12/31/16	6/30/17
Fixed rate	10%	10%	10%	10%
Floating rate	10%	9%	8%	9%
Fixed payments ($1 million × [10% × ½])		$ 50,000	$ 50,000	$ 50,000
Floating payments ($1 million × ½ floating rate)		45,000	40,000	45,000
Net interest receipts		$ 5,000	$ 10,000	$ 5,000
Fair value of interest rate swap	0	$ 9,363	$ 9,615	0
Fair value of note payable	$1,000,000	$1,009,363	$1,009,615	$1,000,000

The interest rate swap is designated as a fair value hedge on this note at issuance.

January 1, 2016		
Cash	1,000,000	
Notes payable		1,000,000
To record the issuance of the note.		
June 30, 2016		
Interest expense (10% × ½ × $1 million)	50,000	
Cash		50,000
To record interest.		
Cash ($50,000 − [9% × ½ × $1 million])	5,000	
Interest expense		5,000
To record the net cash settlement.		
Interest rate swap[11] ($9,363 − 0)	9,363	
Holding gain—interest rate swap		9,363
To record change in fair value of the derivative.		
Holding loss—hedged note	9,363	
Note payable ($1,009,363 − 1,000,000)		9,363
To record change in fair value of the note due to interest rate changes.		

The swap settlement is the difference between the fixed interest (5%) and variable interest (4.5%).

The fair value of derivatives is recognized in the balance sheet.

The hedged liability (or asset) is adjusted to fair value as well.

The net interest settlement on June 30, 2016, is $5,000 because the fixed rate is 5% (half of the 10% annual rate) and the floating rate is 4.5% (half of the 9% annual rate).

[10] A common measure for benchmarking variable interest rates is LIBOR, the London Interbank Offered Rate, a base rate at which large international banks lend funds to each other.

[11] This would be a liability rather than an investment (asset) if the fair value had declined.

December 31, 2016		
Interest expense	50,000	
Cash (10% × ½ × $1,000,000)		50,000
To record interest.		
Cash ($50,000 − [8% × ½ × $1 million])	10,000	
Interest expense		10,000
To record the net cash settlement.		
Interest rate swap ($9,615 − 9,363)	252	
Holding gain—interest rate swap		252
To record the change in fair value of the derivative.		
Holding loss—hedged note	252	
Note payable ($1,009,615 − 1,009,363)		252
To record the change in fair value of the note due to interest rate changes.		

As with any debt, interest expense is the effective rate times the outstanding balance.

The settlement is the difference between the fixed interest (5%) and variable interest (4%).

The derivative is increased by the change in fair value. The note is increased by the change in fair value.

The fair value of the swap increased by $252 (from $9,363 to $9,615). Similarly, we adjust the note's book value by the amount necessary to increase it to fair value. This produces a holding loss on the note that exactly offsets the gain on the swap. This result is the hedging effect that motivated Wintel to enter the fair value hedging arrangement in the first place.

At June 30, 2017, Wintel repeats the process of adjusting to fair value both the derivative investment and the note being hedged.

June 30, 2017		
Interest expense	50,000	
Cash (10% × ½ × $1,000,000)		50,000
To record interest.		
Cash [$50,000 − (9% × ½ × $1 million)]	5,000	
Interest expense		5,000
To record the net cash settlement.		
Holding loss—interest rate swap	9,615	
Interest rate swap ($0 − 9,615)		9,615
To record the change in fair value of the derivative.		
Note payable ($1,000,000 − 1,009,615)	9,615	
Holding gain—hedged note		9,615
To record the change in fair value of the note due to interest rate changes.		
Note payable	1,000,000	
Cash		1,000,000
To repay the loan.		

The net interest received is the difference between the fixed interest (5%) and floating interest (4.5%).

The swap's fair value now is zero.

The net interest received is the difference between the fixed rate (5%) and floating rate (4.5%) times $1 million. The fair value of the swap decreased by $9,615 (from $9,615 to zero).[12] That decline represents a holding *loss* that we recognize in earnings. Similarly, we record an offsetting holding gain on the note for the change in its fair value.

Now let's see how the book values changed for the swap account and the note:

	Swap (Dr)	Swap (Cr)	Note (Dr)	Note (Cr)
Jan. 1, 2016				1,000,000
June 30, 2016	9,363			9,363
Dec. 31, 2016	252			252
June 30, 2017		9,615	9,615 1,000,000	
	0			0

[12]Because there are no future cash receipts from the swap arrangement at this point, the fair value of the swap is zero.

The income statement is affected as follows:

	Income Statement + (−)	
June 30, 2016	(50,000)	Interest expense—fixed payment
	5,000	Interest expense—net cash settlement
	9,363	Holding gain—interest rate swap
	(9,363)	Holding loss—hedged note
	(45,000)	Net effect—same as floating interest payment
Dec. 31, 2016	(50,000)	Interest expense—fixed payment
	10,000	Interest expense—net cash settlement
	252	Holding gain—interest rate swap
	(252)	Holding loss—hedged note
	(40,000)	Net effect—same as floating interest payment
June 30, 2017	(50,000)	Interest expense—fixed payment
	5,000	Interest expense—net cash settlement
	9,615	Holding gain—interest rate swap
	(9,615)	Holding loss—hedged note
	(45,000)	Net effect—same as floating interest payment

As this demonstrates, the swap effectively converts fixed-interest debt to floating-interest debt.

Additional Consideration

Fair Value of the Swap

The fair value of a derivative typically is based on a quote obtained from a derivatives dealer. That fair value will approximate the present value of the expected net interest settlement receipts for the remaining term of the swap. In fact, we can actually calculate the fair value of the swap that we accepted as given in our illustration.

Since the June 30, 2016, floating rate of 9% caused the cash settlement on that date to be $5,000, it's reasonable to look at 9% as the best estimate of future floating rates and therefore assume the remaining two cash settlements also will be $5,000 each. We can then calculate at June 30, 2016, the present value of those expected net interest settlement receipts for the remaining term of the swap:

Fixed interest	10% × ½ × $1 million	$ 50,000
Expected floating interest	9% × ½ × $1 million	45,000
Expected cash receipts for both Dec. 31, 2016 and June 30, 2017		$ 5,000
		× 1.87267*
Present value		$ 9,363

*Present value of an ordinary annuity of $1: $n = 2$, $i = 4.5\%$ (½ of 9%) (from Table 4)

Fair Value of the Notes

The fair value of the note payable will be the present value of principal and remaining interest payments discounted at the *market rate*. The market rate will vary with the designated floating rate but might differ due to changes in default (credit) risk and the term structure of interest rates. Assuming it's 9% at June 30, 2016, we can calculate the fair value (present value) of the notes:

Interest	$50,000* × 1.87267† =	$ 93,633
Principal	$1,000,000 × .91573‡ =	915,730
		$1,009,363

*½ of 10% × $1,000,000
†Present value of an ordinary annuity of $1: $n = 2$, $i = 4.5\%$ (from Table 4)
‡Present value of $1: $n = 2$, $i = 4.5\%$ (from Table 2)

(continued)

(concluded)

Note: Often the cash settlement rate is "reset" as of each cash settlement date (thus the floating rate actually used at the end of each period to determine the payment is the floating market rate as of the *beginning* of the same period). In our illustration, for instance, there would have been no cash settlement at June 30, 2016, since we would use the beginning floating rate of 10% to determine payment. Similarly, we would have used the 9% floating rate at June 30, 2016, to determine the cash settlement six months later at December 31. In effect, each cash settlement would be delayed six months. Had this arrangement been in effect in the current illustration, there would have been one fewer cash settlement payments (two rather than three), but would not have affected the fair value calculations above because, either way, our expectation would be cash receipts of $5,000 for both Dec. 31, 2016, and June 30, 2017.

CASH FLOW HEDGES The risk in some transactions or events is the risk of a change in cash flows, rather than a change in fair values. We noted earlier, for instance, that *fixed-rate* debt subjects a company to the risk that interest rate changes could change the fair value of the debt. On the other hand, if the obligation is *floating-rate* debt, the fair value of the debt will not change when interest rates do, but cash flows will. If a derivative is used to hedge against the exposure to changes in cash inflows or cash outflows of an asset or liability or a forecasted transaction (like a future purchase or sale), it can be designated as a cash flow hedge. In that case, when the derivative is adjusted to reflect changes in fair value, the other side of the entry is a gain or loss to be deferred as a component of other comprehensive income and included in earnings later, at the same time as earnings are affected by the hedged transaction. Once again, the effect is matching the earnings effect of the derivative with the earnings effect of the item being hedged, precisely the concept behind hedge accounting.

A gain or loss from a *cash flow hedge* is deferred as other comprehensive income until it can be recognized in earnings along with the earnings effect of the item being hedged.

To understand the deferral of the gain or loss, we need to revisit the concept of comprehensive income. Comprehensive income, as you may recall from Chapters 4, 12, 17, and 18, is a more expansive view of the change in shareholders' equity than traditional net income. In fact, it encompasses all changes in equity other than from transactions with owners.[13] So, in addition to net income itself, comprehensive income includes up to four other changes in equity that don't (yet) belong in net income, namely, net holding gains (losses) on investments (Chapter 12), gains (losses) from and amendments to postretirement benefit plans (Chapter 17), gains (losses) from foreign currency translation, and deferred gains (losses) from derivatives designated as cash flow hedges.[14]

Some of the more commonly used cash flow hedges are:

- An interest rate swap to synthetically convert floating rate debt (for which interest rate changes could change the cash interest payments) into fixed rate debt.
- A futures contract to hedge a forecasted sale (for which price changes could change the cash receipts) of natural gas, crude oil, or some other asset.

FOREIGN CURRENCY HEDGES Today's economy is increasingly a global one. The majority of large "U.S." companies are, in truth, multinational companies that may receive only a fraction of their revenues from U.S. operations. Many operations of those companies are located abroad. Foreign operations often are denominated in the currency of the foreign country (the Euro, Japanese yen, Russian rubles, and so on). Even companies without foreign operations sometimes hold investments, issue debt, or conduct other transactions denominated in foreign currencies. As exchange rates change, the dollar equivalent of the

The possibility that foreign currency exchange rates might change exposes many companies to foreign currency risk.

[13]Transactions with owners primarily include dividends and the sale or purchase of shares of the company's stock.

[14]FASB ASC 220–10–55–2: Comprehensive Income–Overall–Implementation Guidance and Illustrations (previously "Reporting Comprehensive Income," *Statement of Financial Accounting Standards No. 130* (Norwalk, Conn.: FASB, 1997)).

foreign currency changes. The possibility of currency rate changes exposes these companies to the risk that some transactions require settlement in a currency other than the entities' functional currency or that foreign operations will require translation adjustments to reported amounts.

A **foreign currency hedge** can be a hedge of foreign currency exposure of:

- A firm commitment—treated as a fair value hedge.
- An available-for-sale security—treated as a fair value hedge.
- A forecasted transaction—treated as a cash flow hedge.
- A company's net investment in a foreign operation—the gain or loss is reported in *other comprehensive income* as part of unrealized gains and losses from foreign currency translation.[15]

To qualify as a hedge, the hedging relationship must be highly effective in achieving offsetting changes in fair values or cash flows.

HEDGE EFFECTIVENESS When a company elects to apply hedge accounting, it must establish at the inception of the hedge the method it will use to assess the effectiveness of the hedging derivative as well as the measurement approach it will use to determine the ineffective portion of the hedge.[16] The key criterion for qualifying as a hedge is that the hedging relationship must be "highly effective" in achieving offsetting changes in fair values or cash flows based on the hedging company's specified risk management objective and strategy.

An assessment of this effectiveness must be made at least every three months and whenever financial statements are issued. There are no precise guidelines for assessing effectiveness, but it generally means a high correlation between changes in the fair value or cash flows of the derivative and of the item being hedged, not necessarily a specific reduction in risk. Hedge accounting must be terminated for hedging relationships that no longer are highly effective.

Imperfect hedges result in part of the derivative gain or loss being included in current earnings.

HEDGE INEFFECTIVENESS In Illustration A–2, the loss on the hedged note exactly offset the gain on the swap. This is because the swap in this instance was highly effective in hedging the risk due to interest rate changes. However, the loss and gain would not have exactly offset each other if the hedging arrangement had been ineffective. For instance, suppose the swap's term had been different from that of the note (say a three-year swap term compared with the 18-month term of the note) or if the notional amount of the swap differed from that of the note (say $500,000 rather than $1 million). In that case, changes in the fair value of the swap and changes in the fair value of the note would not be the same. The result would be a greater (or lesser) amount recognized in earnings for the swap than for the note. Because there would not be an exact offset, earnings would be affected, an effect resulting from hedge ineffectiveness. That is a desired effect of hedge accounting; to the extent that a hedge is effective, the earnings effect of a derivative cancels out the earnings effect of the item being hedged. However, even if a hedge is highly effective, all ineffectiveness is recognized currently in earnings.

FAIR VALUE CHANGES UNRELATED TO THE RISK BEING HEDGED In Illustration A–2, the fair value of the hedged note and the fair value of the swap changed by the same amounts each year because we assumed the fair values changed only due to interest rate changes. It's also possible, though, that the note's fair value would change by an amount different from that of the swap for reasons unrelated to interest rates. Remember from our earlier discussion that the market's perception of a company's creditworthiness, and thus

[15]This is the same treatment previously prescribed for these translation adjustments by FASB ASC 830: Foreign Currency Matters (previously *Statement of Financial Accounting Standards No. 52*).

[16]Remember, if a derivative is not designated as a hedge, any gains or losses from changes in its fair value are recognized immediately in earnings.

its ability to pay interest and principal when due, also can affect the value of debt, whether interest rates change or not. In hedge accounting, we ignore those changes. We recognize only the fair value changes in the hedged item that we can attribute to the risk being hedged (interest rate risk in this case). For example, if a changing perception of default risk had caused the note's fair value to increase by an additional, say $5,000, our journal entries in Illustration A–2 would have been unaffected. Notice, then, that although we always mark a *derivative* to fair value, the reported amount of the *item being hedged* may not be its fair value. We mark a hedged item to fair value only to the extent that its fair value changed due to the risk being hedged.

Fair value changes unrelated to the risk being hedged are ignored.

Disclosure of Derivatives and Risk

To be adequately informed about the effectiveness of a company's risk management, investors and creditors need information about strategies for holding derivatives and specific hedging activities. Toward that end, extensive disclosure requirements provide information that includes:

- Objectives and strategies for holding and issuing derivatives.
- A description of the items for which risks are being hedged.
- For forecasted transactions: a description, time before the transaction is expected to occur, the gains and losses accumulated in other comprehensive income, and the events that will trigger their recognition in earnings.
- Beginning balance of, changes in, and ending balance of the derivative component of other comprehensive income.
- The net amount of gain or loss reported in earnings (representing aggregate hedge ineffectiveness).
- Qualitative and quantitative information about failed hedges: canceled commitments or previously hedged forecasted transactions no longer expected to occur.

The intent is to provide information about the company's success in reducing risks and consequently about risks not managed successfully. Remember, too, that when derivatives are employed ineffectively, risks can escalate. Ample disclosures about derivatives are essential to maintain awareness of potential opportunities and problems with risk management.

In addition, GAAP requires companies to provide enhanced disclosures indicating (a) how and why the company uses derivative instruments, (b) how the company accounts for derivative instruments and related hedged items, and (c) how derivative instruments and related hedged items affect the company's balance sheet, income statement, and cash flows.[17] The required disclosures include two tables, one that highlights the location and fair values of derivative instruments in the balance sheet, and another that indicates the location and amounts of gains and losses on derivative instruments in the income statement. The two tables distinguish between derivative instruments that are designated as hedging instruments and those that are not. The tables also categorize derivative instruments by each major type—interest rate contracts, foreign exchange contracts, equity contracts, commodity contracts, credit contracts and other types of contracts.

Even for some traditional liabilities, the amounts reported on the face of the financial statements provide inadequate disclosure about the degree to which a company is exposed to risk of loss. To provide adequate disclosure about a company's exposure to risk, additional information must be provided about (a) concentrations of credit risk and (b) the fair value of all financial instruments.[18]

[17]FASB ASC 815: Derivatives and Hedging (previously "Disclosures about Derivative Instruments and Hedging Activities—an amendment of FASB Statement No. 133," *Statement of Financial Accounting Standards No. 161* (Stamford, Conn.: FASB, 2008)).

[18]FASB ASC 825–10–50–1: Financial Instruments–Overall–Disclosure (previously "Disclosures About Fair Values of Financial Instruments," *Statement of Financial Accounting Standards No. 107* (Norwalk, Conn.: FASB, 1991), as amended by *Statement of Financial Accounting Standards No. 133,* "Accounting for Derivative Instruments and Hedging Activities" (Norwalk, Conn.: FASB, 1998)).

Extended Method for Interest Rate Swap Accounting

A shortcut method for accounting for an interest rate swap is permitted when a hedge meets certain criteria. In general, the criteria are designed to see if the hedge supports the assumption of "no ineffectiveness." Illustration A–2 of a fair value hedge met those criteria, in particular, (a) the swap's notional amount matches the note's principal amount, (b) the swap's expiration date matches the note's maturity date, (c) the fair value of the swap is zero at inception, and (d) the floating payment is at the market rate.[19] Because Wintel can conclude that the swap will be highly effective in offsetting changes in the fair value of the debt, it can use the changes in the fair value of the swap to measure the offsetting changes in the fair value of the debt. That's the essence of the shortcut method used in Illustration A–2. The extended method required when the criteria are *not* met for the short-cut method is described in this section (Illustration A–3 begins by describing the same scenario as in Illustration A–2). It produces the same effect on earnings and in the balance sheet as does the procedure shown in Illustration A–2.

Illustration A–3
Interest Rate Swap—Extended Method

Wintel Semiconductors issued $1 million of 18-month, 10% bank notes on January 1, 2016. Wintel is exposed to the risk that general interest rates will decline, causing the fair value of its debt to rise. (If the fair value of Wintel's debt increases, its effective borrowing cost is higher relative to the market.) To hedge against this fair value risk, the firm entered into an 18-month interest rate swap agreement on January 1 and designated the swap as a hedge against changes in the fair value of the note. The swap calls for the company to *receive payment* based on a 10% fixed interest rate on a notional amount of $1 million and to *make payment* based on a floating interest rate tied to changes in general rates. Cash settlement of the net interest amount is made semiannually at June 30 and December 31 of each year with the net interest being the difference between the $50,000 fixed interest [$1 million × (10% × ½)] and the floating interest rate times $1 million at those dates.

Floating (market) settlement rates were 9% at June 30, 2016, 8% at December 31, 2016, and 8% at June 30, 2017. Net interest receipts can be calculated as shown below. Fair values of both the derivative and the note resulting from those market rate changes are assumed to be quotes obtained from securities dealers.

	1/1/16	6/30/16	12/31/16	6/30/17
Fixed rate	10%	10%	10%	10%
Floating rate	10%	9%	8%	9%
Fixed payments [$1 million × (10% × ½)]		$ 50,000	$ 50,000	$ 50,000
Floating payments ($1 million × ½ floating rate)		45,000	40,000	45,000
Net interest receipts		$ 5,000	$ 10,000	$ 5,000
Fair value of interest rate swap	0	$ 9,363	$ 9,615	0
Fair value of note payable	$1,000,000	$1,009,363	$1,009,615	$1,000,000

When the floating rate declined in Illustration A–3 from 10% to 9%, the fair values of both the derivative (swap) and the note increased. This created an offsetting gain on the derivative and holding loss on the note. Both are recognized in earnings the same period (June 30, 2016).

The interest rate swap is designated as a fair value hedge on this note at issuance.

January 1, 2016		
Cash	1,000,000	
Notes payable		1,000,000
To record the issuance of the note.		

[19]There is no precise minimum interval, though it generally is three to six months or less. Other criteria are specified by previously FASB ASC 815–20–25–104: Derivatives and Hedging–Hedging-General–Recognition–Shortcut Method, *SFAS No. 133* (para. 68) in addition to the key conditions listed here.

June 30, 2016		
Interest expense (10% × ½ × $1 million)	50,000	
Cash		50,000
To record interest.		
Cash ($50,000 − [9% × ½ × $1 million])	5,000	
Interest rate swap ($9,363 − 0)	9,363	
Interest revenue (10% × ½ × $0)		0
Holding gain—interest rate swap (to balance)		14,363
To record the net cash settlement, accrued interest on the swap, and change in the fair value of the derivative.		
Holding loss—hedged note	9,363	
Notes payable ($1,009,363 − 1,000,000)		9,363
To record change in fair value of the note due to interest rate changes.		

The swap settlement is the difference between the fixed interest (5%) and variable interest (4.5%).

The fair value of derivatives is recognized in the balance sheet.

The hedged liability (or asset) is adjusted to fair value as well.

The net interest settlement on June 30, 2016, is $5,000 because the fixed rate is 5% (half of the 10% annual rate) and the floating rate is 4.5% (half of the 9% annual rate). A holding gain ($14,363) is produced by holding the derivative security during a time when an interest rate decline caused an increase in the value of that asset. A portion ($5,000) of the gain was received in cash and another portion ($9,363) is reflected as an increase in the value of the asset.

We also have holding loss of the same amount. This is because we also held a liability during the same time period, and the interest rate change caused its fair value to increase as well.

December 31, 2016		
Interest expense (9% × ½ × $1,009,363)	45,421	
Notes payable (difference)*	4,579	
Cash (10% × ½ × $1,000,000)		50,000
To record interest.		
Cash [$50,000 − (8% × ½ × $1 million)]	10,000	
Interest rate swap ($9,615 − 9,363)	252	
Interest revenue (9% × ½ × $9,363)		421
Holding gain—interest rate swap (to balance)		9,831
To record the net cash settlement, accrued interest on the swap, and change in the fair value of the derivative.		
Holding loss—hedged note	4,831	
Notes payable ($1,009,615 − 1,009,363 + 4,579)		4,831
To record the change in fair value of the note due to interest rate changes.		

*We could use a premium on the note to adjust its book value.

As with any debt, interest expense is the effective rate times the outstanding balance.

The cash settlement is the difference between the fixed interest (5%) and variable interest (4%).

Interest ($421) accrues on the asset.

The note is increased by the change in fair value.

We determine interest on the note the same way we do for any liability, as you learned earlier—at the effective rate (9% × ½) times the outstanding balance ($1,009,363). This results in reducing the note's book value for the cash interest paid in excess of the interest expense.

The fair value of the swap increased due to the interest rate decline by $252 (from $9,363 to $9,615). The holding gain we recognize in earnings consists of that increase (a) plus the $10,000 cash settlement also created by the interest rate decline and (b) minus the $421 increase that results not from the interest rate decline, but from interest accruing on the asset.[20] Similarly, we adjust the note's book value by the amount necessary to increase it to fair value, allowing for the $4,579 reduction in the note in the earlier entry to record interest.

At June 30, 2017, Wintel repeats the process of adjusting to fair value both the derivative investment and the note being hedged.

[20]The investment in the interest rate swap represents the present value of expected future net interest receipts. As with other such assets, interest accrues at the effective rate times the outstanding balance. You also can think of the accrued interest mathematically as the increase in present value of the future cash flows as we get one period nearer to the dates when the cash will be received.

Interest expense is the effective rate times the outstanding balance.

The net interest received is the difference between the fixed interest (5%) and floating interest (4.5%).

The swap's fair value now is zero.

June 30, 2017		
Interest expense (8% × ½ × $1,009,615)	40,385	
Notes payable (difference)	9,615	
Cash (10% × ½ × $1,000,000)		50,000
To record interest.		
Cash [$50,000 − (9% × ½ × $1 million)]	5,000	
Holding loss—interest rate swap (to balance)	5,000	
Interest rate swap ($0 − $9,615)		9,615
Interest revenue (8% × ½ × $9,615)		385
To record the net cash settlement, accrued interest on the swap, and change in the fair value of the derivative.		
Notes payable ($1,000,000 − 1,009,615 + 9,615)	0	
Holding gain—hedged note		0
To record the change in fair value of the note due to interest rate changes.		
Note payable	1,000,000	
Cash		1,000,000
To repay the loan		

The net interest received is the difference between the fixed rate (5%) and floating rate (4.5%) times $1 million. The fair value of the swap decreased by $9,615 (from $9,615 to zero).[21] The holding loss we recognize in earnings consists of that decline (a) minus the $5,000 portion of the decline resulting from it being realized in cash settlement and (b) plus the $385 increase that results not from the interest rate change, but from interest accruing on the asset.

Now let's see how the book values changed for the swap account and the note:

	Swap (Dr)	Swap (Cr)	Note (Dr)	Note (Cr)
Jan. 1, 2016				1,000,000
June 30, 2016	9,363			9,363
Dec. 31, 2016	252		4,579	4,831
June 30, 2017		9,615	9,615	
			1,000,000	
	0			0

The income statement is affected as follows:

	Income Statement + (−)	
June 30, 2016	(50,000)	Interest expense
	0	Interest revenue (no time has passed)
	14,363	Holding gain interest rate swap
	(9,363)	Holding loss—hedged note
	(45,000)	Net effect—same as floating interest payment
Dec. 31, 2016	(45,421)	Interest expense
	421	Interest revenue
	9,831	Holding gain—interest rate swap
	(4,831)	Holding loss—hedged note
	(40,000)	Net effect—same as floating interest payment
June 30, 2017	(40,385)	Interest expense
	385	Interest revenue
	(5,000)	Holding gain—interest rate swap
	0	Holding loss—hedged note
	(45,000)	Net effect—same as floating interest payment

As this demonstrates, the swap effectively converts Wintel's fixed-interest debt to floating interest debt.

[21]Because there are no future cash receipts or payments from the swap arrangement at this point, the fair value of the swap is zero.

Additional Consideration

Private Company GAAP – Derivatives and Hedging. The Private Company Council (PCC) sought feedback from private company stakeholders and found that most users of private company financial statements find it difficult to obtain fixed-rate borrowing and often enter into an interest rate swap to economically convert their variable-rate borrowing into a fixed-rate borrowing, which under GAAP caused significant variability in the income statements. As a result, the PCC concluded that the cost and complexity of hedge accounting outweigh the benefits for private companies.

In response to the PCC's conclusion, the FASB issued an Accounting Standards Update in 2014 that allows an accounting alternative to make it easier for certain interest rate swaps to qualify for hedge accounting for private companies that is quite different from what is required for public companies.[22] This alternative allows a nonpublic company (that's not a financial institution) to apply hedge accounting to its interest rate swaps as long as the terms of the swap and the related debt are aligned. If the conditions are met, the company can assume the cash flow hedge is fully effective. Those applying the simplified hedge accounting approach will be able to recognize the swap at its settlement value, instead of at its fair value.

This alternative should significantly reduce the cost and complexity of accounting for derivatives and hedging transactions of private companies.

Where We're Headed

One phase of the FASB's *Financial Instruments* project aspires to improve, simplify, and converge the financial reporting requirements for hedging activities. In May 2010, the FASB proposed revisions of standards for hedge accounting in its proposed Accounting Standards Update (Update), *Accounting for Financial Instruments and Revisions to the Accounting for Derivative Instruments and Hedging Activities—Financial Instruments (Topic 825) and Derivatives and Hedging (Topic 815).*

In July 2014, the International Accounting Standards Board (IASB) issued a revision of IFRS 9 *Financial Instruments.* This guidance differs significantly from the FASB's proposal.

At the time this textbook was written, the FASB's strategy was to conduct research and consider feedback from comment letters and outreach activities to decide the best path forward for the hedge accounting phase of its financial instruments project. During this research and redeliberations, the FASB also will consider the viability of the IASB's hedge accounting standard.

The Bottom Line

- **LOA–1** All derivatives are reported in the balance sheet at fair value.
- **LOA–2** *Hedging* means taking a risk position that is opposite to an actual position that is exposed to risk. For a derivative used to hedge against exposure to risk, treatment of any gain or loss from fair value changes depends on whether the derivative is designated as (a) a fair value hedge, (b) a cash flow hedge, or (c) a foreign currency hedge.
- **LOA–3** We recognize a gain or loss from a *fair value hedge* immediately in earnings along with the loss or gain from the item being hedged. This is so the income effects of the hedge instrument and the income effects of the item being hedged will affect earnings at the same time.

[22] *Accounting Standards Update No. 2014-03,* "Derivatives and Hedging (Topic 815): Accounting for Certain Receive-Variable, Pay-Fixed Interest Rate Swaps—Simplified Hedge Accounting Approach (a consensus of the Private Comapny Council)," (Norwalk, Conn.: FASB, January 2014).

- LOA–4 We defer a gain or loss from a cash *flow hedge* as part of other comprehensive income until it can be recognized in earnings along with the earnings effect of the item being hedged.
- LOA–5 Imperfect hedges result in part of the derivative gain or loss being included in current earnings. We ignore market value changes unrelated to the risk being hedged.
- LOA–6 Extensive disclosure requirements about derivatives are designed to provide investors and creditors information about the adequacy of a company's risk management and the company's success in reducing risks, including risks not managed successfully.

Questions For Review of Key Topics

Q A–1 Some financial instruments are called derivatives. Why?

Q A–2 Should gains and losses on a fair value hedge be recorded as they occur, or should they be recorded to coincide with losses and gains on the item being hedged?

Q A–3 Hines Moving Company held a fixed-rate debt of $2 million. The company wanted to hedge its fair value exposure with an interest rate swap. However, the only notional available at the time, on the type of swap it desired, was $2.5 million. What will be the effect of any gain or loss on the $500,000 notional difference?

Q A–4 What is a futures contract?

Q A–5 What is the effect on interest of an interest rate swap?

Q A–6 How are derivatives reported on the balance sheet? Why?

Q A–7 When is a gain or a loss from a cash flow hedge reported in earnings?

Exercises

E A–1
Derivatives-hedge classification

Indicate (by abbreviation) the type of hedge each activity described below would represent.

Hedge Type

FV	Fair value hedge
CF	Cash flow hedge
FC	Foreign currency hedge
N	Would not qualify as a hedge

Activity

____ 1. An options contract to hedge possible future price changes of inventory.

____ 2. A futures contract to hedge exposure to interest rate changes prior to replacing bank notes when they mature.

____ 3. An interest rate swap to synthetically convert floating rate debt into fixed rate debt.

____ 4. An interest rate swap to synthetically convert fixed rate debt into floating rate debt.

____ 5. A futures contract to hedge possible future price changes of timber covered by a firm commitment to sell.

____ 6. A futures contract to hedge possible future price changes of a forecasted sale of tin.

____ 7. ExxonMobil's net investment in a Kuwait oil field.

____ 8. An interest rate swap to synthetically convert floating rate interest on a stock investment into fixed rate interest.

____ 9. An interest rate swap to synthetically convert fixed rate interest on a held-to-maturity debt investment into floating rate interest.

____ 10. An interest rate swap to synthetically convert floating rate interest on a held-to-maturity debt investment into fixed rate interest.

____ 11. An interest rate swap to synthetically convert fixed rate interest on a stock investment into floating rate interest.

E A–2
Derivatives; interest rate swap; fixed rate debt

On January 1, 2016, LLB Industries borrowed $200,000 from Trust Bank by issuing a two-year, 10% note, with interest payable quarterly. LLB entered into a two-year interest rate swap agreement on January 1, 2016, and designated the swap as a fair value hedge. Its intent was to hedge the risk that general interest rates will decline, causing the fair value of its debt to increase. The agreement called for the company to receive payment based on a 10% fixed interest rate on a notional amount of $200,000 and to pay interest based on a floating interest rate. The contract called for cash settlement of the net interest amount quarterly.

Floating (LIBOR) settlement rates were 10% at January 1, 8% at March 31, and 6% June 30, 2016. The fair values of the swap are quotes obtained from a derivatives dealer. Those quotes and the fair values of the note are as indicated below.

	January 1	March 31	June 30
Fair value of interest rate swap	0	$ 6,472	$ 11,394
Fair value of note payable	$200,000	$206,472	$211,394

Required:

1. Calculate the net cash settlement at March 31 and June 30, 2016.
2. Prepare the journal entries through June 30, 2016, to record the issuance of the note, interest, and necessary adjustments for changes in fair value.

E A–3
Derivatives; interest rate swap; fixed rate investment

(This is a variation of Exercise A–2, modified to consider an investment in debt securities.)

On January 1, 2016, S&S Corporation invested in LLB Industries' negotiable two-year, 10% notes, with interest receivable quarterly. The company classified the investment as available-for-sale. S&S entered into a two-year interest rate swap agreement on January 1, 2016, and designated the swap as a fair value hedge. Its intent was to hedge the risk that general interest rates will decline, causing the fair value of its investment to increase. The agreement called for the company to make payment based on a 10% fixed interest rate on a notional amount of $200,000 and to receive interest based on a floating interest rate. The contract called for cash settlement of the net interest amount quarterly.

Floating (LIBOR) settlement rates were 10% at January 1, 8% at March 31, and 6% June 30, 2016. The fair values of the swap are quotes obtained from a derivatives dealer. Those quotes and the fair values of the investment in notes are as follows:

	January 1	March 31	June 30
Fair value of interest rate swap	0	$ 6,472	$ 11,394
Fair value of the investment in notes	$200,000	$206,472	$211,394

Required:

1. Calculate the net cash settlement at March 31 and June 30, 2016.
2. Prepare the journal entries through June 30, 2016, to record the investment in notes, interest, and necessary adjustments for changes in fair value.

E A–4
Derivatives; interest rate swap; fixed rate debt; fair value change unrelated to hedged risk

(This is a variation of Exercise A–2, modified to consider fair value change unrelated to hedged risk.)

LLB Industries borrowed $200,000 from Trust Bank by issuing a two-year, 10% note, with interest payable quarterly. LLB entered into a two-year interest rate swap agreement on January 1, 2016 and designated the swap as a fair value hedge. Its intent was to hedge the risk that general interest rates will decline, causing the fair value of its debt to increase. The agreement called for the company to receive payment based on a 10% fixed interest rate on a notional amount of $200,000 and to pay interest based on a floating interest rate.

Floating (LIBOR) settlement rates were 10% at January 1, 8% at March 31, and 6% at June 30, 2016. The fair values of the swap are quotes obtained from a derivatives dealer. Those quotes and the fair values of the note are as indicated below. The additional rise in the fair value of the note (higher than that of the swap) on June 30 was due to investors' perceptions that the creditworthiness of LLB was improving.

	January 1	March 31	June 30
Fair value of interest rate swap	0	$ 6,472	$ 11,394
Fair value of note payable	$200,000	$206,472	$220,000

Required:

1. Calculate the net cash settlement at June 30, 2016.
2. Prepare the journal entries on June 30, 2016, to record the interest and necessary adjustments for changes in fair value.

E A–5
Derivatives; interest rate swap; fixed rate debt; extended method

(This is a variation of Exercise A–2, modified to consider the extended method.)

On January 1, 2016, LLB Industries borrowed $200,000 from Trust Bank by issuing a two-year, 10% note, with interest payable quarterly. LLB entered into a two-year interest rate swap agreement on January 1, 2016, and designated the swap as a fair value hedge. Its intent was to hedge the risk that general interest rates will decline, causing the fair value of its debt to increase. The agreement called for the company to receive payment based on a 10% fixed interest rate on a notional amount of $200,000 and to pay interest based on a floating interest rate. The contract called for cash settlement of the net interest amount quarterly.

Floating (LIBOR) settlement rates were 10% at January 1, 8% at March 31, and 6% at June 30, 2016. The fair values of the swap are quotes obtained from a derivatives dealer. Those quotes and the fair values of the note are as follows:

	January 1	March 31	June 30
Fair value of interest rate swap	0	$ 6,472	$ 11,394
Fair value of note payable	$200,000	$206,472	$211,394

Required:

Prepare the journal entries through June 30, 2016, to record the issuance of the note, interest, and necessary adjustments for changes in fair value. Use the extended method demonstrated in Illustration A–3.

E A–6
Derivatives; interest rate swap; fixed-rate debt; fair value change unrelated to hedged risk; extended method

(Note: This is a variation of Exercise A–5, modified to consider fair value change unrelated to hedged risk.)

On January 1, 2016, LLB Industries borrowed $200,000 from trust Bank by issuing a two-year, 10% note, with interest payable quarterly. LLB entered into a two-year interest rate swap agreement on January 1, 2016, and designated the swap as a fair value hedge. Its intent was to hedge the risk that general interest rates will decline, causing the fair value of its debt to increase. The agreement called for the company to receive payment based on a 10% fixed interest rate on a notional amount of $200,000 and to pay interest based on a floating interest rate. The contract called for cash settlement of the net interest amount quarterly.

Floating (LIBOR) settlement rates were 10% at January 1, 8% at March 31, and 6% June 30, 2016. The fair values of the swap are quotes obtained from a derivatives dealer. Those quotes and the fair values of the note are as indicated below. The additional rise in the fair value of the note (higher than that of the swap) on June 30 was due to investors' perceptions that the creditworthiness of LLB was improving.

	January 1	March 31	June 30
Fair value of interest rate swap	0	$ 6,472	$ 11,394
Fair value of note payable	$200,000	206,472	220,000

Required:

1. Calculate the net cash settlement at June 30, 2016.
2. Prepare the journal entries on June 30, 2016, to record the interest and necessary adjustments for changes in fair value. Use the extended method demonstrated in Illustration A–3.

Problems

P A–1
Derivatives—interest rate swap

On January 1, 2016, Labtech Circuits borrowed $100,000 from First Bank by issuing a three-year, 8% note, payable on December 31, 2018. Labtech wanted to hedge the risk that general interest rates will decline, causing the fair value of its debt to increase. Therefore, Labtech entered into a three-year interest rate swap agreement on January 1, 2016, and designated the swap as a fair value hedge. The agreement called for the company to receive payment based on an 8% fixed interest rate on a notional amount of $100,000 and to pay interest based on a floating interest rate tied to LIBOR. The contract called for cash settlement of the net interest amount on December 31 of each year.

Floating (LIBOR) settlement rates were 8% at inception and 9%, 7%, and 7% at the end of 2016, 2017, and 2018, respectively. The fair values of the swap are quotes obtained from a derivatives dealer. These quotes and the fair values of the note are as follows:

	January 1	December 31		
	2016	2016	2017	2018
Fair value of interest rate swap	0	$ (1,759)	$ 935	0
Fair value of note payable	$100,000	$98,241	$100,935	$100,000

Required:

1. Calculate the net cash settlement at the end of 2016, 2017, and 2018.
2. Prepare the journal entries during 2016 to record the issuance of the note, interest, and necessary adjustments for changes in fair value.
3. Prepare the journal entries during 2017 to record interest, net cash interest settlement for the interest rate swap, and necessary adjustments for changes in fair value.
4. Prepare the journal entries during 2018 to record interest, net cash interest settlement for the interest rate swap, necessary adjustments for changes in fair value, and repayment of the debt.

5. Calculate the book values of both the swap account and the note in each of the three years.
6. Calculate the net effect on earnings of the hedging arrangement in each of the three years. (Ignore income taxes.)
7. Suppose the fair value of the note at December 31, 2016, had been $97,000 rather than $98,241 with the additional decline in fair value due to investors' perceptions that the creditworthiness of Labtech was worsening. How would that affect your entries to record changes in the fair values?

P A–2
Derivatives; interest rate swap; comprehensive

CMOS Chips is hedging a 20-year, $10 million, 7% bond payable with a 20-year interest rate swap and has designated the swap as a fair value hedge. The agreement called for CMOS to receive payment based on a 7% fixed interest rate on a notional amount of $10 million and to pay interest based on a floating interest rate tied to LIBOR. The contract calls for cash settlement of the net interest amount on December 31 of each year.

At December 31, 2016, the fair value of the derivative and of the hedged bonds has increased by $100,000 because interest rates declined during the reporting period.

Required:

1. Does CMOS have an unrealized gain or loss on the derivative for the period? On the bonds? Will earnings increase or decrease due to the hedging arrangement? Why?
2. Suppose interest rates increased, rather than decreased, causing the fair value of both the derivative and of the hedged bonds to decrease by $100,000. Would CMOS have an unrealized gain or loss on the derivative for the period? On the bonds? Would earnings increase or decrease due to the hedging arrangement? Why?
3. Suppose the fair value of the bonds at December 31, 2016, had increased by $110,000 rather than $100,000, with the additional increase in fair value due to investors' perceptions that the creditworthiness of CMOS was improving. Would CMOS have an unrealized gain or loss on the derivative for the period? On the bonds? Would earnings increase or decrease due to the hedging arrangement? Why?
4. Suppose the notional amount of the swap had been $12 million, rather than the $10 million principal amount of the bonds. As a result, at December 31, 2016, the swap's fair value had increased by $120,000 rather than $100,000. Would CMOS have an unrealized gain or loss on the derivative for the period? On the bonds? Would earnings increase or decrease due to the hedging arrangement? Why?
5. Suppose BIOS Corporation is an investor having purchased all $10 million of the bonds issued by CMOS as described in the original situation above. BIOS is hedging its investment, classified as available-for-sale, with a 20-year interest rate swap and has designated the swap as a fair value hedge. The agreement called for BIOS to make *payment* based on a 7% fixed interest rate on a notional amount of $10 million and to *receive* interest based on a floating interest rate tied to LIBOR. Would BIOS have an unrealized gain or loss on the derivative for the period due to interest rates having declined? On the bonds? Would earnings increase or decrease due to the hedging arrangement? Why?

P A–3
Derivatives; interest rate swap; fixed rate debt; extended method

(Note: This is a variation of Problem A–1, modified to consider the extended method demonstrated in Illustration A–3.)

On January 1, 2016, Labtech Circuits borrowed $100,000 from First Bank by issuing a three-year, 8% note, payable on December 31, 2018. Labtech wanted to hedge the risk that general interest rates will decline, causing the fair value of its debt to increase. Therefore, Labtech entered into a three-year interest rate swap agreement on January 1, 2016, and designated the swap as a fair value hedge. The agreement called for the company to receive payment based on an 8% fixed interest rate on a notional amount of $100,000 and to pay interest based on a floating interest rate tied to LIBOR. The contract called for cash settlement of the net interest amount on December 31 of each year.

Floating (LIBOR) settlement rates were 8% at inception and 9%, 7%, and 7% at the end of 2016, 2017, and 2018, respectively. The fair values of the swap are quotes obtained from a derivatives dealer. Those quotes and the fair values of the note are as follows:

	January 1	December 31		
	2016	2016	2017	2018
Fair value of interest rate swap	0	$ (1,759)	$ 935	0
Fair value of note payable	$100,000	$ 98,241	100,935	$100,000

Required:

Use the extended method demonstrated in Illustration A–3.

1. Calculate the net cash settlement at the end of 2016, 2017, and 2018.
2. Prepare the journal entries during 2016 to record the issuance of the note, interest, and necessary adjustments for changes in fair value.
3. Prepare the journal entries during 2017 to record interest, net cash interest settlement for the interest rate swap, and necessary adjustments for changes in fair value.

4. Prepare the journal entries during 2018 to record interest, net cash interest settlement for the interest rate swap, necessary adjustments for changes in fair value, and repayment of the debt.
5. Calculate the book values of both the swap account and the note in each of the three years.
6. Calculate the net effect on earnings of the hedging arrangement in each of the three years. (Ignore income taxes.)
7. Suppose the fair value of the note at December 31, 2016, had been $97,000 rather than $98,241 with the additional decline in fair value due to investors' perceptions that the creditworthiness of Labtech was worsening. How would that affect your entries to record changes in the fair values?

Broaden Your Perspective

Apply your critical-thinking ability to the knowledge you've gained. These cases will provide you an opportunity to develop your research, analysis, judgment, and communication skills. You also will work with other students, integrate what you've learned, apply it in real-world situations, and consider its global and ethical ramifications. This practice will broaden your knowledge and further develop your decision-making abilities.

Real World Case A–1
Derivative losses; recognition in earnings

The following is an excerpt from a disclosure note of **Johnson & Johnson**:

6. Fair Value Measurements (in part)
As of January 2, 2011, the balance of deferred net gains on derivatives included in accumulated other comprehensive income was $100 million after-tax. The Company expects that substantially all the amount related to foreign exchange contracts will be reclassified into earnings over the next 12 months as a result of transactions that are expected to occur over that period.

Required:

1. Johnson & Johnson indicates that it expects that substantially all of the balance of deferred net gains on derivatives will be reclassified into earnings over the next 12 months as a result of transactions that are expected to occur over that period. What is meant by "reclassified into earnings"?
2. What type(s) of hedging transaction might be accounted for in this way?

Communication Case A–2
Derivatives; hedge accounting

A conceptual question in accounting for derivatives is: Should gains and losses on a hedge instrument be recorded as they occur, or should they be recorded to coincide (match) with income effects of the item being hedged?

ABI Wholesalers plans to issue long-term notes in May that will replace its $20 million of 9.5% bonds when they mature in July. ABI is exposed to the risk that interest rates in July will have risen, increasing borrowing costs (reducing the selling price of its notes). To hedge that possibility, ABI entered a (Treasury bond) futures contract in May to deliver (sell) bonds in July at their *current* price.

As a result, if interest rates rise, borrowing costs will go up for ABI because it will sell notes at a higher interest cost (or lower price). But that loss will be offset (approximately) by the gain produced by being in the opposite position on Treasury bond futures.

Two opposing viewpoints are:

View 1: Gains and losses on instruments designed to hedge anticipated transactions should be recorded as they occur.

View 2: Gains and losses on instruments designed to hedge anticipated transactions should be recorded to coincide (match) with income effects of the item being hedged.

In considering this question, focus on conceptual issues regarding the practicable and theoretically appropriate treatment, unconstrained by GAAP. Your instructor will divide the class into two to six groups depending on the size of the class. The mission of your group is to reach consensus on the appropriate accounting for the gains and losses on instruments designed to hedge anticipated transactions.

Required:

1. Each group member should deliberate the situation independently and draft a tentative argument prior to the class session for which the case is assigned.
2. In class, each group will meet for 10 to 15 minutes in different areas of the classroom. During that meeting, group members will take turns sharing their suggestions for the purpose of arriving at a single group treatment.
3. After the allotted time, a spokesperson for each group (selected during the group meetings) will share the group's solution with the class. The goal of the class is to incorporate the views of each group into a consensus approach to the situation.

Real World Case A–3
Researching the way interest rate futures prices are quoted on the Chicago Mercantile Exchange; retrieving information from the Internet

The **Chicago Mercantile Exchange**, or Merc, at 30 S. Wacker Drive in Chicago, is the world's largest financial exchange, an international marketplace enabling institutions and businesses to trade futures and options contracts including currencies, interest rates, stock indices, and agricultural commodities.

Required:

1. Access the Merc on the Internet. The web address is **www.cmegroup.com**
2. Access the daily settlements within the site. In the Search box, enter "13-week t-bill." Choose 13-week t-bill.
3. What are the settlement prices for September futures contracts?

Research Case A–4
Issue related to the derivatives standard; research an article

In an effort to keep up with the rapidly changing global financial markets, the FASB issued standards on accounting for and disclosure of derivative financial instruments. A *Journal of Accountancy* article that discusses this standard is "The Decision on Derivatives," by Arlette C. Wilson, Gary Waters, and Barry J. Bryan, November 1998.

Required:

On the Internet, go to the AICPA site at **www.aicpa.org** and find the article mentioned.

1. What are the primary problems or issues the FASB attempts to address regarding accounting for derivative financial instruments?
2. In considering the issues, the FASB made four fundamental decisions that became the cornerstones of the statement issued in 1998. What are those fundamental decisions? Which do you think is most critical to fair financial reporting?

APPENDIX

B PetSmart Annual Report (selected pages)

UNITED STATES
SECURITIES AND EXCHANGE COMMISSION
Washington, D.C. 20549

Form 10-K

(Mark One)

☒ **ANNUAL REPORT PURSUANT TO SECTION 13 OR 15(d) OF THE SECURITIES EXCHANGE ACT OF 1934**

For the Fiscal Year Ended February 2, 2014

or

☐ **TRANSITION REPORT PURSUANT TO SECTION 13 OR 15(d) OF THE SECURITIES EXCHANGE ACT OF 1934**

For the transition period from to

Commission file number 0-21888

PetSmart, Inc.

(Exact name of registrant as specified in its charter)

Delaware	**94-3024325**
(State or other jurisdiction of incorporation or organization)	*(I.R.S. Employer Identification No.)*
19601 N. 27th Avenue **Phoenix, Arizona**	**85027**
(Address of principal executive offices)	*(Zip Code)*

Registrant's telephone number, including area code:
(623) 580-6100
Securities registered pursuant to Section 12(b) of the Act:

Title of Each Class	Name of Each Exchange on Which Registered
Common Stock, $.0001 par value	The NASDAQ Stock Market LLC (NASDAQ Global Select Market)

Securities registered pursuant to Section 12(g) of the Act:
None

Indicate by check mark if the registrant is a well-known seasoned issuer, as defined in Rule 405 of the Securities Act. Yes ☒ No ☐

Indicate by check mark if the registrant is not required to file reports pursuant to Section 13 or Section 15(d) of the Act. Yes ☐ No ☒

Indicate by check mark whether the registrant (1) has filed all reports required to be filed by Section 13 or 15(d) of the Securities Exchange Act of 1934 during the preceding 12 months (or for such shorter period that the registrant was required to file such reports), and (2) has been subject to such filing requirements for the past 90 days. Yes ☒ No ☐

Indicate by check mark whether the registrant has submitted electronically and posted on its corporate Web site, if any, every Interactive Data File required to be submitted and posted pursuant to Rule 405 of Regulation S-T (§232.405 of this chapter) during the preceding 12 months (or for such shorter period that the registrant was required to submit and post such files). Yes ☒ No ☐

Indicate by check mark if disclosure of delinquent filers pursuant to Item 405 of Regulation S-K (§229.405 of this chapter) is not contained herein, and will not be contained, to the best of registrant's knowledge, in definitive proxy or information statements incorporated by reference in Part III of this Form 10-K or any amendment to this Form 10-K. ☐

Indicate by check mark whether the registrant is a large accelerated filer, an accelerated filer, a non-accelerated filer, or a smaller reporting company. See the definitions of "large accelerated filer," "accelerated filer" and "smaller reporting company" in Rule 12b-2 of the Exchange Act.

Large accelerated filer ☒ Accelerated filer ☐ Non-accelerated filer ☐ Smaller reporting company ☐
(Do not check if a smaller reporting company)

Indicate by check mark whether the registrant is a shell company (as defined in Rule 12b-2 of the Act). Yes ☐ No ☒

The aggregate market value of the common stock held by non-affiliates of the registrant, based on the closing sale price of the registrant's common stock on August 4, 2013, the last business day of the registrant's most recently completed second fiscal quarter, as reported on the NASDAQ Global Select Market was approximately $7,730,027,000. This calculation excludes approximately 404,000 shares held by directors and executive officers of the registrant. This calculation does not exclude shares held by such organizations whose ownership exceeds 5% of the registrant's outstanding common stock as of December 31, 2013, that have represented to the registrant that they are registered investment advisers or investment companies registered under Section 8 of the Investment Company Act of 1940.

The number of shares of the registrant's common stock outstanding as of March 13, 2014, was 98,654,676.

DOCUMENTS INCORPORATED BY REFERENCE

Portions of the Proxy Statement for the 2014 Annual Meeting of Stockholders to be held on June 18, 2014, to be filed on or about May 8, 2014, have been incorporated by reference into Part III of this Annual Report on Form 10-K.

REPORT OF INDEPENDENT REGISTERED PUBLIC ACCOUNTING FIRM

To the Board of Directors and Stockholders of
PetSmart, Inc.
Phoenix, Arizona

We have audited the accompanying consolidated balance sheets of PetSmart, Inc. and subsidiaries (the "Company") as of February 2, 2014 and February 3, 2013, and the related consolidated statements of income and comprehensive income, stockholders' equity, and cash flows for each of the three years in the period ended February 2, 2014. These financial statements are the responsibility of the Company's management. Our responsibility is to express an opinion on these financial statements based on our audits.

We conducted our audits in accordance with the standards of the Public Company Accounting Oversight Board (United States). Those standards require that we plan and perform the audit to obtain reasonable assurance about whether the financial statements are free of material misstatement. An audit includes examining, on a test basis, evidence supporting the amounts and disclosures in the financial statements. An audit also includes assessing the accounting principles used and significant estimates made by management, as well as evaluating the overall financial statement presentation. We believe that our audits provide a reasonable basis for our opinion.

In our opinion, such consolidated financial statements present fairly, in all material respects, the financial position of PetSmart, Inc. and subsidiaries as of February 2, 2014 and February 3, 2013, and the results of their operations and their cash flows for each of the three years in the period ended February 2, 2014, in conformity with accounting principles generally accepted in the United States of America.

We have also audited, in accordance with the standards of the Public Company Accounting Oversight Board (United States), the Company's internal control over financial reporting as of February 2, 2014, based on the criteria established in *Internal Control-Integrated Framework (1992)* issued by the Committee of Sponsoring Organizations of the Treadway Commission and our report dated March 27, 2014 expressed an unqualified opinion on the Company's internal control over financial reporting.

/s/ DELOITTE & TOUCHE LLP

Phoenix, Arizona
March 27, 2014

PetSmart, Inc. and Subsidiaries

Consolidated Balance Sheets
(In thousands, except par value)

	February 2, 2014	February 3, 2013
ASSETS		
Cash and cash equivalents	$ 285,622	$ 335,155
Short-term investments	—	9,150
Restricted cash	71,226	71,916
Receivables, net	72,685	72,198
Merchandise inventories	740,302	679,090
Deferred income taxes	71,945	62,859
Prepaid expenses and other current assets	76,463	86,768
Total current assets	1,318,243	1,317,136
Property and equipment, net	952,955	985,707
Equity investment in Banfield	33,577	39,934
Deferred income taxes	110,408	102,992
Goodwill	41,140	44,242
Other noncurrent assets	65,645	46,970
Total assets	$ 2,521,968	$ 2,536,981
LIABILITIES AND STOCKHOLDERS' EQUITY		
Accounts payable and bank overdraft	$ 255,251	$ 202,122
Accrued payroll, bonus, and employee benefits	160,008	176,082
Accrued occupancy expenses and deferred rents	81,867	70,671
Current maturities of capital lease obligations	66,887	61,581
Other current liabilities	230,332	244,436
Total current liabilities	794,345	754,892
Capital lease obligations	451,597	464,578
Deferred rents	65,932	73,855
Other noncurrent liabilities	116,312	120,064
Total liabilities	1,428,186	1,413,389
Commitments and contingencies		
Stockholders' equity:		
Preferred stock; $.0001 par value; 10,000 shares authorized, none issued and outstanding	—	—
Common stock; $.0001 par value; 625,000 shares authorized, 169,178 and 167,209 shares issued	17	17
Additional paid-in capital	1,515,333	1,418,411
Retained earnings	2,173,005	1,827,996
Accumulated other comprehensive (loss) income	(2,159)	5,506
Less: Treasury stock, at cost, 68,520 and 61,879 shares	(2,592,414)	(2,128,338)
Total stockholders' equity	1,093,782	1,123,592
Total liabilities and stockholders' equity	$ 2,521,968	$ 2,536,981

The accompanying notes are an integral part of these consolidated financial statements.

PetSmart, Inc. and Subsidiaries

Consolidated Statements of Income and Comprehensive Income
(In thousands, except per share data)

	Year Ended		
	February 2, 2014 (52 weeks)	February 3, 2013 (53 weeks)	January 29, 2012 (52 weeks)
Merchandise sales	$ 6,111,702	$ 5,979,604	$ 5,401,731
Services sales	766,006	740,471	674,859
Other revenue	38,919	38,162	36,714
Net sales	6,916,627	6,758,237	6,113,304
Cost of merchandise sales	4,222,542	4,124,432	3,783,951
Cost of services sales	539,229	533,504	488,216
Cost of other revenue	38,919	38,162	36,714
Total cost of sales	4,800,690	4,696,098	4,308,881
Gross profit	2,115,937	2,062,139	1,804,423
Operating, general, and administrative expenses	1,422,619	1,410,922	1,301,304
Operating income	693,318	651,217	503,119
Interest expense, net	(51,779)	(54,329)	(56,842)
Income before income tax expense and equity income from Banfield	641,539	596,888	446,277
Income tax expense	(239,444)	(223,329)	(166,960)
Equity income from Banfield	17,425	15,970	10,926
Net income	419,520	389,529	290,243
Other comprehensive (loss) income, net of income tax:			
Foreign currency translation adjustments	(7,645)	36	77
Other	(20)	(20)	33
Comprehensive income	$ 411,855	$ 389,545	$ 290,353
Earnings per common share:			
Basic	$ 4.06	$ 3.61	$ 2.59
Diluted	$ 4.02	$ 3.55	$ 2.55
Weighted average shares outstanding:			
Basic	103,203	107,819	111,909
Diluted	104,316	109,611	113,993

The accompanying notes are an integral part of these consolidated financial statements.

PetSmart, Inc. and Subsidiaries

Consolidated Statements of Stockholders' Equity
(In thousands, except per share data)

	Shares							
	Common Stock	Treasury Stock	Common Stock	Additional Paid-in Capital	Retained Earnings	Accumulated Other Comprehensive Income (Loss)	Treasury Stock	Total
BALANCE AT JANUARY 30, 2011	162,586	(47,094)	$ 16	$ 1,222,340	$ 1,277,803	$ 5,380	$ (1,334,897)	$ 1,170,642
Net Income					290,243			290,243
Issuance of common stock under stock incentive plans	2,215		—	46,378				46,378
Stock-based compensation expense				27,989				27,989
Excess tax benefits from stock-based compensation				16,289				16,289
Dividends declared ($0.545 per share)					(60,992)			(60,992)
Other comprehensive income (loss), net of income tax						110		110
Purchase of treasury stock, at cost		(7,592)					(336,830)	(336,830)
BALANCE AT JANUARY 29, 2012	164,801	(54,686)	16	1,312,996	1,507,054	5,490	(1,671,727)	1,153,829
Net Income					389,529			389,529
Issuance of common stock under stock incentive plans	2,408		1	32,273				32,274
Stock-based compensation expense				29,957				29,957
Excess tax benefits from stock-based compensation				43,185				43,185
Dividends declared ($0.635 per share)					(68,587)			(68,587)
Other comprehensive income (loss), net of income tax						16		16
Purchase of treasury stock, at cost		(7,193)					(456,611)	(456,611)
BALANCE AT FEBRUARY 3, 2013	167,209	(61,879)	17	1,418,411	1,827,996	5,506	(2,128,338)	1,123,592
Net Income					419,520			419,520
Issuance of common stock under stock incentive plans	1,969		—	43,816				43,816
Stock-based compensation expense				28,300				28,300
Excess tax benefits from stock-based compensation				24,806				24,806
Dividends declared ($0.72 per share)					(74,511)			(74,511)
Other comprehensive income (loss), net of income tax						(7,665)		(7,665)
Purchase of treasury stock, at cost		(6,641)					(464,076)	(464,076)
BALANCE AT FEBRUARY 2, 2014	169,178	(68,520)	$ 17	$ 1,515,333	$ 2,173,005	$ (2,159)	$ (2,592,414)	$ 1,093,782

The accompanying notes are an integral part of these consolidated financial statements.

PetSmart, Inc. and Subsidiaries

Consolidated Statements of Cash Flows
(In thousands)

	Year Ended		
	February 2, 2014 (52 weeks)	February 3, 2013 (53 weeks)	January 29, 2012 (52 weeks)
CASH FLOWS FROM OPERATING ACTIVITIES:			
Net income	$ 419,520	$ 389,529	$ 290,243
Adjustments to reconcile net income to net cash provided by operating activities:			
Depreciation and amortization	235,431	238,406	236,974
Loss on disposal of property and equipment	3,927	5,742	6,882
Stock-based compensation expense	28,300	29,957	27,989
Deferred income taxes	(11,973)	(21,009)	(3,702)
Equity income from Banfield	(17,425)	(15,970)	(10,926)
Dividend received from Banfield	23,782	13,860	15,960
Excess tax benefits from stock-based compensation	(24,970)	(43,196)	(14,223)
Non-cash interest expense	608	962	782
Changes in assets and liabilities:			
Merchandise inventories	(64,473)	(34,015)	(29,220)
Other assets	2,234	(46,932)	(26,703)
Accounts payable	37,118	40,653	9,135
Accrued payroll, bonus, and employee benefits	(15,578)	18,042	18,707
Other liabilities	(1,321)	76,978	53,522
Net cash provided by operating activities	615,180	653,007	575,420
CASH FLOWS FROM INVESTING ACTIVITIES:			
Purchases of investments	(14,446)	(4,027)	(38,738)
Proceeds from maturities of investments	12,801	23,230	10,215
Proceeds from sales of investments	580	3,695	2,304
Decrease (Increase) in restricted cash	690	(1,727)	(8,750)
Cash paid for property and equipment	(146,822)	(138,467)	(120,720)
Proceeds from sales of property and equipment	9,006	2,685	331
Net cash used in investing activities	(138,191)	(114,611)	(155,358)
CASH FLOWS FROM FINANCING ACTIVITIES:			
Net proceeds from common stock issued under stock incentive plans	49,506	55,197	53,439
Minimum statutory withholding requirements	(5,792)	(23,172)	(7,061)
Cash paid for treasury stock	(485,404)	(435,283)	(336,830)
Payments of capital lease obligations	(72,986)	(64,462)	(54,437)
Change in bank overdraft and other financing activities	23,847	(37,728)	21,269
Excess tax benefits from stock-based compensation	24,970	43,196	14,223
Cash dividends paid to stockholders	(54,374)	(83,661)	(60,011)
Net cash used in financing activities	(520,233)	(545,913)	(369,408)
EFFECT OF EXCHANGE RATE CHANGES ON CASH AND CASH EQUIVALENTS	(6,289)	(220)	289
(DECREASE) INCREASE IN CASH AND CASH EQUIVALENTS	(49,533)	(7,737)	50,943
CASH AND CASH EQUIVALENTS AT BEGINNING OF PERIOD	335,155	342,892	291,949
CASH AND CASH EQUIVALENTS AT END OF PERIOD	$ 285,622	$ 335,155	$ 342,892
SUPPLEMENTAL DISCLOSURE OF CASH FLOW INFORMATION:			
Interest paid	$ 52,144	$ 54,659	$ 57,692
Income taxes paid, net of refunds	$ 250,958	$ 192,629	$ 156,234
Assets acquired using capital lease obligations	$ 65,816	$ 28,830	$ 46,704
Accruals and accounts payable for capital expenditures	$ 18,000	$ 39,075	$ 40,308
Treasury stock purchased, not yet settled	$ —	$ 21,328	$ —
Dividends declared but unpaid	$ 20,479	$ 342	$ 15,417
Non-cash construction in progress acquired with note payable	$ 16,000	$ —	$ —

The accompanying notes are an integral part of these consolidated financial statements.

PetSmart, Inc. and Subsidiaries

Notes to the Consolidated Financial Statements

Note 1 — The Company and its Significant Accounting Policies

Business

PetSmart, Inc., including its wholly owned subsidiaries (the "Company," "PetSmart," "we," or "us"), is the leading specialty provider of products, services, and solutions for the lifetime needs of pets in North America. We offer a broad selection of products for all the life stages of pets, as well as various services including professional grooming and boarding, as well as training and day camp for dogs. We also offer pet products through PetSmart.com. As of February 2, 2014, we operated 1,333 stores and had full-service veterinary hospitals in 844 of our stores. We have a 21.0% investment in MMI Holdings, Inc., which is accounted for under the equity method of accounting. MMI Holdings, Inc., through a wholly owned subsidiary, Medical Management International, Inc., collectively referred to as "Banfield," operated 837 of the veterinary hospitals under the registered trade name of "Banfield, The Pet Hospital." The remaining 7 hospitals are operated by other third parties in Canada.

Principles of Consolidation

Our consolidated financial statements include the accounts of PetSmart and our wholly owned subsidiaries. We have eliminated all intercompany accounts and transactions.

Fiscal Year

Our fiscal year consists of 52 or 53 weeks and ends on the Sunday nearest January 31. The 2013 fiscal year ended on February 2, 2014, and was a 52-week year. Fiscal years 2012 and 2011 consisted of 53 weeks and 52 weeks, respectively. Unless otherwise specified, all references to years in these consolidated financial statements are to fiscal years.

Use of Estimates

The preparation of financial statements in conformity with accounting principles generally accepted in the United States of America, or "GAAP," requires management to make estimates and assumptions that affect the reported amounts of assets and liabilities, disclosure of contingent assets and liabilities at the date of the consolidated financial statements, and the reported amounts of revenues and expenses during the reporting period. Management bases its estimates on historical experience and on various other assumptions it believes to be reasonable under the circumstances, the results of which form the basis for making judgments about the carrying values of assets and liabilities that are not readily apparent from other sources. Under different assumptions or conditions, actual results could differ from these estimates.

Segment Reporting

We have identified two operating segments, Merchandise and Services. These operating segments have similar long-term economic characteristics, include sales to the same types of customers, have the same distribution method, and include sales similar in nature; therefore, they have been aggregated into one reportable segment.

Net sales in the United States and Puerto Rico were $6.5 billion, $6.4 billion, and $5.8 billion for 2013, 2012, and 2011, respectively. Net sales in Canada, denominated in United States dollars, were $0.4 billion, $0.4 billion, and $0.3 billion for 2013, 2012, and 2011, respectively. Substantially all our long-lived assets are located in the United States.

Financial Instruments

Our financial instruments consist primarily of cash and cash equivalents, restricted cash, receivables and accounts payable. These balances, as presented in the consolidated financial statements at February 2, 2014, and February 3, 2013, approximate fair value because of the short-term nature. Our short-term investments in municipal bonds are recorded at fair value using quoted prices in active markets for identical assets or liabilities as detailed in Note 4. We also have investments in negotiable certificates of deposit, which are carried at their amortized cost basis as detailed in Note 4. From time to time, we have entered into foreign currency exchange forward contracts, or "Foreign Exchange Contracts." We did not designate these Foreign Exchange Contracts as hedges, and accordingly, they were recorded at fair value using quoted prices for similar assets or liabilities in active markets. The changes in the fair value were recognized in operating, general, and administrative expenses in the Consolidated Statements of Income and Comprehensive Income. We did not enter into Foreign Exchange Contracts during 2013 or 2012. The recorded gains and losses were immaterial for 2011.

Cash and Cash Equivalents

We consider any liquid investments with a maturity of three months or less at purchase to be cash equivalents. Included in cash and cash equivalents are credit and debit card receivables from banks, which typically settle within five business days, of $61.5 million and $58.9 million as of February 2, 2014, and February 3, 2013, respectively.

Under our cash management system, a bank overdraft balance exists for our primary disbursement accounts. This overdraft represents uncleared checks in excess of cash balances in the related bank accounts. Our funds are transferred on an as-needed basis to pay for clearing checks. As of February 2, 2014, and February 3, 2013, bank overdrafts of $32.8 million and $16.1 million, respectively, were included in accounts payable and bank overdraft in the Consolidated Balance Sheets.

PetSmart, Inc. and Subsidiaries

Notes to the Consolidated Financial Statements — (Continued)

Restricted Cash

Our stand-alone letter of credit facility agreement allows us to issue letters of credit for guarantees provided for insurance programs. We are required to maintain a cash deposit with the lender for outstanding letter of credit issuances, as detailed in Note 11.

Vendor Allowances

We receive vendor allowances from agreements made with certain merchandise suppliers, primarily in the form of advertising funding agreements. These vendor allowances are specifically related to identifiable advertising costs incurred to promote and sell vendor products. We also receive vendor allowances as reimbursement of costs incurred for fixtures used to display and sell our suppliers' products. Vendor allowances for advertising and fixtures are recorded as a reduction of operating, general, and administrative expenses in the Consolidated Statements of Income and Comprehensive Income. Excess cash consideration received is recorded as a reduction to cost of goods sold, rather than operating, general, and administrative expenses. Vendor allowances that we receive prior to the period that they relate to are considered unearned vendor consideration and are recorded in accounts payable in the Consolidated Balance Sheets. We establish a receivable for vendor allowances that are earned but not yet received. Vendor allowances remaining in receivables in the Consolidated Balance Sheets were not material as of February 2, 2014, and February 3, 2013.

Merchandise Inventories and Valuation Reserves

Merchandise inventories represent finished goods and are recorded at the lower of cost or market. Cost is determined by the moving average cost method and includes inbound freight, as well as certain procurement and distribution costs related to the processing of merchandise.

We have established reserves for estimated inventory shrinkage between physical inventories. Physical inventory counts are taken on a regular basis, and inventory is adjusted accordingly. Distribution centers perform cycle counts using a velocity based system that determines whether the inventory should be counted every 30, 90, 180, or 365 days. Stores generally perform physical inventories at least once per year, and count certain inventory items between physical inventories. For each reporting period presented, we estimate the inventory shrinkage based on a two-year historical trend analysis. Changes in shrink results or market conditions could cause actual results to vary from estimates used to establish the reserves.

We also have reserves for estimated obsolescence and to reduce merchandise inventory to the lower of cost or market. We evaluate inventory for excess, obsolescence, or other factors that may render inventories unmarketable at historical cost. Factors used in determining obsolescence reserves, which are recorded to reflect approximate net realizable value of our inventories, include current and anticipated demand, customer preferences, age of merchandise, seasonal trends, and decisions to discontinue certain products. If assumptions about future demand change, or actual market conditions are less favorable than those projected by management, we may require additional reserves.

As of February 2, 2014, and February 3, 2013, our inventory valuation reserves were $12.7 million and $11.8 million, respectively.

Property and Equipment

Property and equipment are recorded at cost less accumulated depreciation and amortization. Depreciation is provided on buildings, furniture, fixtures, equipment, and computer software using the straight-line method over the estimated useful lives of the related assets. Leasehold improvements and capital lease assets are amortized using the straight-line method over the shorter of the lease term or the estimated useful lives of the related assets. Computer software consists primarily of third-party software purchased for internal use. Costs associated with the preliminary stage of a project are expensed as incurred. In the development phase, project costs that we capitalize include external consulting costs, as well as qualifying internal labor costs. Training costs, data conversion costs, and maintenance costs are expensed as incurred. Maintenance and repairs to furniture, fixtures, and equipment are expensed as incurred.

We review long-lived assets for impairment based on undiscounted cash flows on a quarterly basis, and whenever events or changes in circumstances indicate that the carrying amount of such assets may not be recoverable. If this review indicates that the carrying amount of the long-lived assets is not recoverable, we recognize an impairment loss, measured at fair value by estimated discounted cash flows or market appraisals. No material asset impairments were identified during 2013, 2012, or 2011.

Our property and equipment are depreciated using the following estimated useful lives:

Capital lease assets	Shorter of the lease term or estimated useful life
Furniture, fixtures, and equipment	2 — 7 years
Leasehold improvements	1 — 20 years
Computer software	3 — 7 years

Goodwill

The carrying value of goodwill of $41.1 million and $44.2 million as of February 2, 2014, and February 3, 2013, respectively, represents the excess of the cost of acquired businesses over the fair market value of their net assets. Other than the effects of foreign currency translation, no other changes were made to goodwill during 2013, 2012, or 2011.

PetSmart, Inc. and Subsidiaries

Notes to the Consolidated Financial Statements — (Continued)

Insurance Liabilities and Reserves

We maintain workers' compensation, general liability, product liability, and property insurance on all our operations, properties, and leasehold interests. We utilize high deductible plans for each of these areas including a self-insured health plan for our eligible associates. Workers' compensation deductibles generally carry a $1.0 million per occurrence risk of claim liability. Our general liability plan specifies a $0.5 million per occurrence risk of claim liability. We establish reserves for claims under workers' compensation and general liability plans based on periodic actuarial estimates of the amount of loss for all pending claims, including estimates for claims that have been incurred but not reported. Our loss estimates rely on actuarial observations of ultimate loss experience for similar historical events and changes in such assumptions could result in an adjustment, favorable or adverse, to our reserves. As of February 2, 2014, and February 3, 2013, we had approximately $102.1 million and $107.2 million, respectively, in reserves related to workers' compensation, general liability, and self-insured health plans, of which $68.2 million and $74.0 million were classified as other noncurrent liabilities in the Consolidated Balance Sheets.

Reserve for Closed Stores

We continuously evaluate the performance of our stores and periodically close those that are under-performing. Closed stores are generally replaced by a new store in a nearby location. We establish reserves for future occupancy payments on closed stores in the period the store closes. The costs for future occupancy payments are reported in operating, general, and administrative expenses in the Consolidated Statements of Income and Comprehensive Income. We calculate the cost for future occupancy payments, net of expected sublease income, associated with closed stores using the net present value method at a credit-adjusted risk-free interest rate over the remaining life of the lease. Judgment is used to estimate the underlying real estate market related to the expected sublease income, and we can make no assurances that additional charges will not be required based on the changing real estate environment.

Property and equipment retirement losses at closed stores are recorded as operating, general, and administrative expenses in the Consolidated Statements of Income and Comprehensive Income.

Income Taxes

We establish deferred income tax assets and liabilities for temporary differences between the financial reporting bases and the income tax bases of our assets and liabilities at enacted tax rates expected to be in effect when such assets or liabilities are realized or settled. We generally do not materially adjust deferred income taxes at interim periods. We record a valuation allowance on the deferred income tax assets to reduce the total to an amount we believe is more likely than not to be realized. Valuation allowances at February 2, 2014, and February 3, 2013, were principally to offset certain deferred income tax assets for net operating loss carryforwards.

We recognize the tax benefit from an uncertain tax position only if it is more likely than not that the tax position will be sustained on examination by the taxing authorities. The determination is based on the technical merits of the position and presumes that each uncertain tax position will be examined by the relevant taxing authority that has full knowledge of all relevant information. Although we believe the estimates are reasonable, no assurance can be given that the final outcome of these matters will be consistent with what is reflected in the historical income tax provisions and accruals.

We operate in multiple tax jurisdictions and could be subject to audit in any of these jurisdictions. These audits can involve complex issues that may require an extended period of time to resolve and may cover multiple years. To the extent we prevail in matters for which reserves have been established, or are required to pay amounts in excess of our reserves, our effective income tax rate in a given fiscal period could be materially affected. An unfavorable tax settlement would require use of our cash and could result in an increase in our effective income tax rate in the period of resolution. A favorable tax settlement could result in a reduction in our effective income tax rate in the period of resolution.

At the end of each interim period, we estimate the annual effective tax rate and apply that rate to our quarterly earnings. The tax expense or benefit related to significant, unusual, or extraordinary items is recognized in the interim period in which those items occur. In addition, the effect of changes in enacted tax laws, rates, or tax status is recognized in the interim period in which the change occurs.

Although we believe that the judgments and estimates discussed herein are reasonable, actual results could differ, and we may be exposed to losses or gains that could be material.

Other Current Liabilities

Other current liabilities consisted of the following (in thousands):

	February 2, 2014	February 3, 2013
Accrued income and sales tax	$ 29,847	$ 72,435
Non-trade accounts payable	46,776	47,714
Other(1)	153,709	124,287
	$ 230,332	$ 244,436

(1) There were no other individual items within other current liabilities greater than 5% of total current liabilities.

PetSmart, Inc. and Subsidiaries

Notes to the Consolidated Financial Statements — (Continued)

Revenue Recognition

Revenue is recognized net of applicable sales tax in the Consolidated Statements of Income and Comprehensive Income. We record the sales tax liability in other current liabilities in the Consolidated Balance Sheets. We recognize revenue for store merchandise sales when the customer receives and pays for the merchandise at the register. We recognize revenue from professional grooming, boarding, and dog training when the services are performed. Internet sales are recognized at the time that the customer receives the product. We defer revenue and the related product costs for shipments that are in transit to the customer. Customers typically receive goods within a few days of shipment. Such amounts were immaterial as of February 2, 2014, and February 3, 2013. Amounts related to shipping and handling that are billed to customers are reflected in merchandise sales, and the related costs are reflected in cost of merchandise sales.

We record deferred revenue for the sale of gift cards and recognize this revenue in net sales when cards are redeemed. Gift card breakage income is recognized over two years based upon historical redemption patterns and represents the balance of gift cards for which we believe the likelihood of redemption by the customer is remote. We recognized $3.0 million, $2.0 million, and $1.8 million of gift card breakage income during 2013, 2012, and 2011, respectively. Gift card breakage is recorded monthly and is included in the Consolidated Statements of Income and Comprehensive Income as a reduction of operating, general, and administrative expenses.

We record allowances for estimated returns based on historical return patterns. These allowances were not material during 2013, 2012, and 2011.

In accordance with our master operating agreement with Banfield, we charge Banfield license fees for the space used by the veterinary hospitals and for its portion of specific operating expenses. License fees and the reimbursements for specific operating expenses are included in other revenue in the Consolidated Statements of Income and Comprehensive Income.

Cost of Merchandise Sales

Cost of merchandise sales includes the following types of expenses:

- Purchase price of inventory sold;
- Transportation costs associated with inventory;
- Inventory shrinkage costs and valuation adjustments;
- Costs associated with operating our distribution network, including payroll and benefit costs, occupancy costs, utilities costs, and depreciation;
- Procurement costs, including merchandising and other costs directly associated with the procurement, storage, and handling of inventory;
- Store occupancy costs, including rent, common area maintenance, real estate taxes, utilities, and depreciation of leasehold improvements and capitalized lease assets; and
- Reductions for promotions and discounts, as well as vendor funding for temporary price reductions.

Cost of Services Sales

Cost of services sales primarily relates to payroll and benefit expenses related to PetSmart-employed groomers, trainers, and PetsHotel associates. Also included in cost of services sales are services-related costs for supplies and repairs, as well as professional fees for the training of groomers, trainers, and PetsHotel associates.

Cost of Other Revenue

Cost of other revenue includes the costs related to license fees and specific operating expenses charged to Banfield.

Vendor Concentration Risk

We purchase merchandise inventories from several hundred vendors worldwide. Sales of products from our two largest vendors represented approximately 19.0%, 20.5%, and 20.7% of our net sales for 2013, 2012, and 2011, respectively.

Advertising

Advertising costs are expensed as incurred, and are classified within operating, general, and administrative expenses in the Consolidated Statements of Income and Comprehensive Income. Total advertising expenditures, net of vendor allowances for advertising agreements, and including direct response advertising, were $139.9 million, $117.6 million, and $95.9 million for 2013, 2012, and 2011, respectively. Vendor allowances for advertising agreements reduced total advertising expense by $38.8 million, $35.8 million, and $33.0 million for 2013, 2012, and 2011, respectively.

Stock-based Compensation

We recognize stock-based compensation expense based on the fair value of the awards at the grant date for all awards except management equity units which are evaluated quarterly based upon the current market value of our common stock. We use option pricing methods that require the input of highly subjective assumptions, including the expected stock price volatility. Compensation cost is recognized on a straight-line basis over the vesting period of the related stock-based compensation award, with the exception of certain retirement provisions.

PetSmart, Inc. and Subsidiaries

Notes to the Consolidated Financial Statements — (Continued)

Foreign Currency

The local currency is used as the functional currency in Canada. We translate assets and liabilities denominated in foreign currency into United States dollars at the current rate of exchange at year-end, and translate revenues and expenses at the average exchange rate during the year. Foreign currency translation adjustments are included in other comprehensive income and are reported in stockholders' equity in the Consolidated Balance Sheets. Transaction gains and losses are included in net income in the Consolidated Statements of Income and Comprehensive Income.

Activities related to foreign currency adjustments were as follows (in thousands):

	Year Ended		
	February 2, 2014 (52 weeks)	February 3, 2013 (53 weeks)	January 29, 2012 (52 weeks)
Deferred tax (benefit) expense on translation adjustments	$ (4,529)	$ 23	$ 50
Transaction loss	889	454	817

Earnings Per Common Share

Basic earnings per common share is calculated by dividing net income by the weighted average of shares outstanding during each period. Diluted earnings per common share reflects the potential dilution of securities that could share in earnings, such as potentially dilutive common shares that may be issuable under our stock incentive plans, and is calculated by dividing net income by the weighted average shares, including dilutive securities, outstanding during the period.

Note 2 — Recently Issued Accounting Pronouncements

In July 2013, the Financial Accounting Standards Board, or "FASB," issued an accounting standards update on the presentation of unrecognized tax benefits. The update clarifies that unrecognized tax benefits related to a net operating loss carryforward, or similar tax loss, or tax credit carryforward, should generally be presented in the financial statements as a reduction to a deferred tax asset. The amendments in this update are effective for fiscal years, and interim periods within those years, beginning after December 15, 2013. The update allows for early adoption. We have accordingly presented applicable uncertain tax positions as reductions to deferred income tax assets in the Consolidated Balance Sheet as of February 2, 2014. These amounts are presented in other current liabilities and other noncurrent liabilities in the Consolidated Balance Sheet as of February 3, 2013. The adoption of the new guidance did not have a material impact on our consolidated financial statements.

Note 3 — Income Taxes

Income before income tax expense and equity income from Banfield was as follows (in thousands):

	Year Ended		
	February 2, 2014 (52 weeks)	February 3, 2013 (53 weeks)	January 29, 2012 (52 weeks)
United States and Puerto Rico	$ 626,634	$ 580,672	$ 433,633
Foreign	14,905	16,216	12,644
	$ 641,539	$ 596,888	$ 446,277

Income tax expense consisted of the following (in thousands):

	Year Ended		
	February 2, 2014 (52 weeks)	February 3, 2013 (53 weeks)	January 29, 2012 (52 weeks)
Current provision:			
Federal	$ 219,617	$ 218,469	$ 147,728
State	31,800	25,869	22,934
	251,417	244,338	170,662
Deferred:			
Federal	(8,440)	(19,687)	574
State	(3,533)	(1,322)	(4,276)
	(11,973)	(21,009)	(3,702)
Income tax expense	$ 239,444	$ 223,329	$ 166,960

PetSmart, Inc. and Subsidiaries

Notes to the Consolidated Financial Statements — (Continued)

A reconciliation of the federal statutory income tax rate to our effective tax rate is as follows (dollars in thousands):

	Year Ended					
	February 2, 2014 (52 weeks)		February 3, 2013 (53 weeks)		January 29, 2012 (52 weeks)	
Provision at federal statutory tax rate	$ 224,544	35.0%	$ 208,911	35.0%	$ 156,197	35.0%
State income taxes, net of federal income tax benefit	15,518	2.4	15,724	2.6	10,423	2.3
Tax on equity income from Banfield	(560)	(0.1)	1,709	0.3	(645)	(0.2)
Other	(58)	—	(3,015)	(0.5)	985	0.3
	$ 239,444	37.3%	$ 223,329	37.4%	$ 166,960	37.4%

The components of the net deferred income tax assets (liabilities) included in the Consolidated Balance Sheets are as follows (in thousands):

	February 2, 2014	February 3, 2013
Deferred income tax assets:		
Capital lease obligations	$ 170,155	$ 185,137
Employee benefit expense	91,367	102,063
Deferred rents	30,687	33,086
Net operating loss carryforwards	14,482	15,534
Other	45,259	38,047
Total deferred income tax assets	351,950	373,867
Valuation allowance	(8,592)	(8,250)
Deferred income tax assets, net of valuation allowance	343,358	365,617
Deferred income tax liabilities:		
Property and equipment	(130,800)	(167,428)
Inventory	(9,952)	(10,771)
Other	(20,253)	(21,567)
Total deferred income tax liabilities	(161,005)	(199,766)
Net deferred income tax assets	$ 182,353	$ 165,851

As of February 2, 2014, we had, for income tax reporting purposes, federal net operating loss carryforwards of $41.4 million which expire in varying amounts between 2019 and 2020. The federal net operating loss carryforwards are subject to certain limitations on their utilization pursuant to the Internal Revenue Code. We also had a Canadian capital loss carryforward of $11.6 million and state tax credit carryforwards of $4.6 million which expire in varying amounts between 2017 and 2023.

A reconciliation of the beginning and ending amount of unrecognized tax benefits is as follows (in thousands):

	Year Ended		
	February 2, 2014 (52 weeks)	February 3, 2013 (53 weeks)	January 29, 2012 (52 weeks)
Unrecognized tax benefits, beginning balance	$ 15,679	$ 20,940	$ 16,735
Gross increases - tax positions related to the current year	2,067	1,757	1,938
Gross increases - tax positions in prior periods	4,321	1,362	3,730
Gross decreases - tax positions in prior periods	(393)	(4,854)	(146)
Gross settlements	(3,610)	(2,819)	(922)
Lapse of statute of limitations	—	(719)	(393)
Gross (decreases) increases - foreign currency translation	(237)	12	(2)
Unrecognized tax benefits, ending balance	$ 17,827	$ 15,679	$ 20,940

Included in the balance of unrecognized tax benefits at February 2, 2014, February 3, 2013, and January 29, 2012, were $8.9 million, $7.9 million, and $11.1 million, respectively, of tax benefits that, if recognized, would affect the effective tax rate.

PetSmart, Inc. and Subsidiaries

Notes to the Consolidated Financial Statements — (Continued)

We continue to recognize penalties and interest accrued related to unrecognized tax benefits as income tax expense. During 2013, 2012, and 2011, the impact of accrued interest and penalties related to unrecognized tax benefits on the Consolidated Statements of Income and Comprehensive Income was immaterial. In total, as of February 2, 2014, we had recognized a liability for penalties of $1.3 million and interest of $2.5 million. As of February 3, 2013, we had recognized a liability for penalties of $0.9 million and interest of $2.0 million.

Our unrecognized tax benefits largely include state exposures from filing positions taken on state tax returns and characterization of income and timing of deductions on federal and state tax returns. We believe that it is reasonably possible that approximately $0.8 million of our currently remaining unrecognized tax positions, each of which are individually insignificant, may be recognized by the end of 2014 as a result of settlements or a lapse of the statute of limitations.

We have substantially settled all federal income tax matters through 2008, state and local jurisdictions through 2005, and foreign jurisdictions through 2003. We could be subject to audits in these jurisdictions for the subsequent years.

Note 4 — Investments

Short-term Investments

Our short-term investments consisted of municipal bonds with various maturities, representing funds available for current operations. These short-term investments are classified as available-for-sale and are carried at fair value using quoted prices in active markets for identical assets or liabilities (Level 1). Accrued interest was immaterial at February 3, 2013. The amortized cost basis at February 3, 2013 was $9.1 million. Unrealized gains and losses are included in other comprehensive income in the Consolidated Statements of Income and Comprehensive Income. We did not have short-term investments at February 2, 2014.

Investments in Negotiable Certificates of Deposit

At February 2, 2014, and February 3, 2013, we had investments in negotiable certificates of deposit, or "NCDs," with various maturities. These investments are classified as held-to-maturity and are carried at their amortized cost basis.

The amortized cost basis of our investments in NCDs was classified in the Consolidated Balance Sheets as follows (in thousands):

	February 2, 2014	February 3, 2013
Prepaid expenses and other current assets	$ 7,045	$ 2,571
Noncurrent assets	5,760	240

The aggregate fair value of our investments in NCDs was $12.8 million and $2.8 million at February 2, 2014, and February 3, 2013, respectively. The fair value is determined using pricing models which use inputs based on observable market data (Level 2). The inputs of the pricing models are issuer spreads and reported trades. Unrecognized gains for 2013, 2012, and 2011 were immaterial.

Equity Investment in Banfield

We have an investment in Banfield which is accounted for using the equity method of accounting. We record our equity income from our investment in Banfield one month in arrears. As of February 2, 2014, and February 3, 2013, our investment represented 21.4% of the voting common stock and 21.0% of the combined voting and non-voting stock of Banfield. Our investment includes goodwill of $15.9 million. The goodwill is calculated as the excess of the purchase price for each step of the acquisition of our ownership interest in Banfield relative to that step's portion of Banfield's net assets at the respective acquisition date.

As of February 2, 2014, we held 4.7 million shares of Banfield voting stock, consisting of:

- 2.9 million shares of voting preferred stock that may be converted into voting common stock at any time at our option; and
- 1.8 million shares of voting common stock.

PetSmart, Inc. and Subsidiaries

Notes to the Consolidated Financial Statements — (Continued)

Banfield's financial data is summarized as follows (in thousands):

	February 2, 2014	February 3, 2013
Current assets	$ 450,657	$ 429,787
Noncurrent assets	160,268	141,209
Current liabilities	448,665	388,729
Noncurrent liabilities	26,776	16,508

	Year Ended		
	February 2, 2014 (52 weeks)	February 3, 2013 (53 weeks)	January 29, 2012 (52 weeks)
Net sales	$ 1,005,629	$ 884,324	$ 747,705
Income from operations	138,589	128,234	89,569
Net income	82,975	76,052	52,019

We recognized license fees and reimbursements for specific operating expenses from Banfield of $38.9 million, $38.2 million, and $36.7 million during 2013, 2012, and 2011, respectively, in other revenue in the Consolidated Statements of Income and Comprehensive Income. The related costs are included in cost of other revenue in the Consolidated Statements of Income and Comprehensive Income. Receivables from Banfield totaled $3.3 million and $3.2 million at February 2, 2014, and February 3, 2013, respectively, and were included in receivables, net in the Consolidated Balance Sheets.

Our master operating agreement with Banfield also includes a provision for the sharing of profits on the sale of therapeutic pet foods sold in all stores with an operating Banfield hospital. The net sales and gross profit on the sale of therapeutic pet food are not material to our consolidated financial statements.

Note 5 — Property and Equipment

Property and equipment consisted of the following (in thousands):

	February 2, 2014	February 3, 2013
Buildings	$ —	$ 9,568
Furniture, fixtures, and equipment	1,084,047	1,051,821
Leasehold improvements	714,888	683,358
Computer software	138,613	122,377
Buildings under capital leases	805,627	765,517
	2,743,175	2,632,641
Less: accumulated depreciation and amortization	1,860,674	1,700,715
	882,501	931,926
Construction in progress	70,454	53,781
Property and equipment, net	$ 952,955	$ 985,707

Note 6 — Reserve for Closed Stores

The components of the reserve for closed stores were as follows (in thousands):

	February 2, 2014	February 3, 2013
Total remaining gross occupancy costs	$ 13,180	$ 22,699
Less:		
Expected sublease income	(8,922)	(13,117)
Interest costs	(312)	(856)
Reserve for closed stores	$ 3,946	$ 8,726
Current portion, included in other current liabilities	1,690	3,466
Noncurrent portion, included in other noncurrent liabilities	2,256	5,260
Reserve for closed stores	$ 3,946	$ 8,726

PetSmart, Inc. and Subsidiaries

Notes to the Consolidated Financial Statements — (Continued)

Activities related to the reserve for closed stores were as follows (in thousands):

	Year Ended		
	February 2, 2014 (52 weeks)	**February 3, 2013 (53 weeks)**	**January 29, 2012 (52 weeks)**
Opening balance	$ 8,726	$ 10,007	$ 9,764
Provision for new store closures	1,171	5,180	1,297
Lease terminations	(236)	(584)	—
Changes in sublease assumptions	(197)	228	3,338
Other charges	290	353	606
Payments	(5,808)	(6,458)	(4,998)
Ending balance	$ 3,946	$ 8,726	$ 10,007

We record charges for new closures and adjustments related to changes in subtenant assumptions and other occupancy payments in operating, general, and administrative expenses in the Consolidated Statements of Income and Comprehensive Income. We can make no assurances that additional charges related to closed stores will not be required based on the changing real estate environment.

Note 7 — Earnings per Common Share

The following table presents a reconciliation of the weighted average shares outstanding used in the earnings per common share calculations (in thousands):

	Year Ended		
	February 2, 2014 (52 weeks)	**February 3, 2013 (53 weeks)**	**January 29, 2012 (52 weeks)**
Basic	103,203	107,819	111,909
Dilutive stock-based compensation awards	1,113	1,792	2,084
Diluted	104,316	109,611	113,993

Certain stock-based compensation awards representing 0.3 million, 0.5 million, and 1.3 million shares of common stock in 2013, 2012, and 2011, respectively, were not included in the calculation of diluted earnings per common share because the inclusion of such awards would have been antidilutive for the periods presented.

Note 8 — Stockholders' Equity

Share Purchase Programs

In September 2013, the Board of Directors approved a share purchase program authorizing the purchase of up to $535.0 million through January 31, 2015. The $535.0 million program commenced on October 1, 2013, and was in addition to any unused amount remaining under the previous$525.0 million program. We completed the $525.0 million program during the thirteen weeks ended February 2, 2014. As of February 2, 2014, $417.9 million remained available under the $535.0 million program.

The following table presents our purchases of our common stock under the respective share purchase programs (in thousands):

Share Purchase Program			Year Ended					
			February 2, 2014 (52 weeks)		**February 3, 2013 (53 weeks)**		**January 29, 2012 (52 weeks)**	
Authorized Amount	**Date Approved by Board**	**Program Termination Date**	**Shares Purchased**	**Purchase Value**	**Shares Purchased**	**Purchase Value**	**Shares Purchased**	**Purchase Value**
$ 400,000	June 2010	July 31, 2011	—	$ —	—	$ —	3,909	$ 165,383
$ 450,000	June 2011	January 31, 2013	—	—	4,594	278,553	3,683	171,447
$ 525,000	June 2012	January 31, 2014	5,025	346,942	2,599	178,058	—	—
$ 535,000	September 2013	January 31, 2015	1,616	117,134	—	—	—	—
			6,641	$ 464,076	7,193	$ 456,611	7,592	$ 336,830

PetSmart, Inc. and Subsidiaries

Notes to the Consolidated Financial Statements — (Continued)

Dividends

In 2013 and 2012, the Board of Directors declared the following dividends:

Date Declared	Dividend Amount per Share	Stockholders of Record Date	Payment Date
March 26, 2013	$0.165	May 3, 2013	May 17, 2013
June 14, 2013	$0.165	August 2, 2013	August 16, 2013
September 25, 2013	$0.195	November 1, 2013	November 15, 2013
December 4, 2013	$0.195	January 31, 2014	February 14, 2014
March 14, 2012	$0.14	April 27, 2012	May 11, 2012
June 13, 2012	$0.165	July 27, 2012	August 10, 2012
September 26, 2012	$0.165	October 26, 2012	November 9, 2012
December 7, 2012	$0.165	December 19, 2012	December 31, 2012

On March 19, 2014, the Board of Directors declared a quarterly cash dividend of $0.195 per share payable on May 16, 2014, to stockholders of record on May 2, 2014.

Note 9 — Stock-based Compensation

We have several long-term incentive plans, including plans for stock options, restricted stock, performance share units, management equity units, and employee stock purchases. Shares issued under our long-term incentive plans are issued from new shares.

Stock Options

At February 2, 2014, stock option grants representing 2.0 million shares of common stock were outstanding under all of the stock option plans, and 22.8 million of additional stock options or awards may be issued under the 2011 Equity Incentive Plan. These grants are made to employees, including officers. Stock options, which are subject to time-based, graduated vesting at 25% per year, are fully vested on the fourth anniversary of the initial grant date and expire seven years after the grant date.

Activities in all of our stock option plans were as follows (in thousands, except per share data):

	Year Ended February 2, 2014 (52 weeks)			
	Shares	Weighted-Average Exercise Price	Weighted-Average Remaining Contractual Term	Aggregate Intrinsic Value
Outstanding at beginning of year	3,414	$35.53		
Granted	609	$62.77		
Exercised	(1,603)	$27.99		$ 66,682
Forfeited/canceled	(462)	$52.27		
Outstanding at end of year	1,958	$46.22	4.35	$ 33,317
Vested and expected to vest at end of year	1,924	$46.00	4.33	$ 33,161
Exercisable at end of year	491	$34.86	3.15	$ 13,823

PetSmart, Inc. and Subsidiaries

Notes to the Consolidated Financial Statements — (Continued)

	Year Ended February 3, 2013 (53 weeks)			
	Shares	Weighted-Average Exercise Price	Weighted-Average Remaining Contractual Term	Aggregate Intrinsic Value
Outstanding at beginning of year	4,838	$28.66		
Granted	649	$58.00		
Exercised	(1,907)	$25.58		$ 70,917
Forfeited/canceled	(166)	$37.37		
Outstanding at end of year	3,414	$35.53	4.28	$ 97,182
Vested and expected to vest at end of year	3,307	$35.10	4.23	$ 95,558
Exercisable at end of year	1,042	$25.73	2.94	$ 39,839

	Year Ended January 29, 2012 (52 weeks)			
	Shares	Weighted-Average Exercise Price	Weighted-Average Remaining Contractual Term	Aggregate Intrinsic Value
Outstanding at beginning of year	5,985	$23.07		
Granted	1,384	$40.82		
Exercised	(2,306)	$21.48		$ 55,431
Forfeited/canceled	(225)	$28.47		
Outstanding at end of year	4,838	$28.66	4.39	$ 120,299
Vested and expected to vest at end of year	4,661	$28.35	4.34	$ 117,289
Exercisable at end of year	1,552	$23.57	2.80	$ 46,489

Restricted Stock Awards and Restricted Stock Units

We may grant restricted stock awards or restricted stock units under the 2011 Equity Incentive Plan. Under the terms of the plan, employees may be awarded shares or units of our common stock, subject to approval by the Board of Directors. The shares or units of common stock awarded under the plan are subject to a reacquisition right held by us. In the event that the award recipient's employment by, or service to, us is terminated for any reason other than death or disability, we are entitled to simultaneously and automatically reacquire for no consideration all of the unvested shares or units of restricted common stock previously awarded to the recipient. Restricted stock awards cliff vest after the requisite service period, which is four years for restricted stock awards and one year for restricted stock awarded to Directors. The shares for restricted stock units are not issued until cliff vesting on the third anniversary of the grant date.

Activities in our restricted stock awards and restricted stock units plan were as follows (in thousands, except per share data):

	Year Ended					
	February 2, 2014 (52 weeks)		February 3, 2013 (53 weeks)		January 29, 2012 (52 weeks)	
	Shares	Weighted-Average Grant Date Fair Value	Shares	Weighted-Average Grant Date Fair Value	Shares	Weighted-Average Grant Date Fair Value
Nonvested at beginning of year	220	$57.52	612	$20.20	1,188	$24.85
Granted	236	$62.08	237	$57.83	24	$40.78
Vested	(26)	$57.44	(604)	$20.10	(543)	$31.35
Forfeited	(44)	$60.06	(25)	$50.87	(57)	$19.89
Nonvested at end of year	386	$60.08	220	$57.52	612	$20.20

PetSmart, Inc. and Subsidiaries

Notes to the Consolidated Financial Statements — (Continued)

The total fair value of restricted stock which vested during 2013, 2012, and 2011 was $1.7 million, $35.7 million, and $22.7 million, respectively.

Performance Share Units

The 2009 Performance Share Unit Program, approved by the Board of Directors in January 2009, provides for the issuance of Performance Share Units, or "PSUs," under our equity incentive plans, to executive officers and certain other members of our management team based upon an established performance goal. The PSUs are subject to time-based vesting, cliff vesting on the third anniversary of the initial grant date, and settle in shares at that time.

For units granted in 2013 and 2012, the performance goal was defined as a specified cumulative three-year annualized, compound growth of income before income tax expense and equity income from Banfield for the performance period, as compared to the fiscal year prior to the grant date. The actual number of PSUs awarded to each participant was set at a minimum threshold of 0% of the participant's target number of PSUs and could increase up to 200% based upon performance results. Actual performance against the performance goal will be measured at the end of the performance period, which coincides with the vesting period, and approved by the Board in March 2015 for awards granted in 2012, and in March 2016 for awards granted in 2013.

For units granted in 2011, the performance goal was defined as a specified growth of income before income tax expense and equity income from Banfield as compared to 2010. The actual number of PSUs awarded to each participant was set at a minimum threshold of 50% of the participant's target number of PSUs, regardless of performance results, and could increase up to 150% based upon performance results. Actual performance against the 2011 performance goal was approved by the Board in March 2012, and qualified participants achieved 150% of their target awards. The 2011 PSUs vested in March 2014.

Activities for PSUs in 2013, 2012, and 2011 were as follows (in thousands, except per share data):

	Year Ended					
	February 2, 2014 (52 weeks)		February 3, 2013 (53 weeks)		January 29, 2012 (52 weeks)	
	Shares	Weighted-Average Grant Date Fair Value	Shares	Weighted-Average Grant Date Fair Value	Shares	Weighted-Average Grant Date Fair Value
Nonvested at beginning of year	835	$41.14	1,337	$25.17	1,065	$22.14
Granted	211	$62.64	213	$58.32	228	$40.80
Additional units granted for performance achievement	—	$—	109	$40.80	139	$31.77
Vested	(362)	$62.34	(760)	$17.97	(5)	$20.73
Forfeited	(147)	$52.57	(64)	$38.98	(90)	$24.08
Nonvested at end of year	537	$52.74	835	$41.14	1,337	$25.17

The total fair value of PSUs which vested during 2013 and 2012 was $22.6 million and $44.7 million, respectively.

Management Equity Units

From 2009 to 2011, certain members of management received Management Equity Units, or "MEUs." The value of one MEU is equal to the value of one share of our common stock and cliff vests on the third anniversary of the grant date. The payout value of the vested MEU grants is determined using our closing stock price on the vest date and is paid out in cash.

As of February 2, 2014, and February 3, 2013, the total liability included in other current liabilities and other non-current liabilities in the Consolidated Balance Sheets was $9.2 million and $16.7 million, respectively. The 2009 management equity unit grant vested on March 9, 2012, and $11.9 million was paid in cash in March 2012. The 2010 management equity unit grant vested on March 29, 2013, and $10.8 million was paid in cash in April 2013. The 2011 management equity unit grant vests on March 28, 2014. No additional MEUs were granted in 2012 or thereafter.

Employee Stock Purchase Plan

We have an Employee Stock Purchase Plan, or "ESPP," that allows essentially all employees who meet certain service requirements to purchase our common stock on semi-annual offering dates at 95% of the fair market value of the shares on the purchase date. A maximum of 4.0 million shares was authorized for purchase under the 2002 ESPP until the plan termination date of July 31, 2012. The 2012 ESPP commenced on August 1, 2012, replacing the 2002 ESPP. A maximum of 2.5 million shares is authorized for purchase under the 2012 ESPP until the plan termination date of July 31, 2022.

PetSmart, Inc. and Subsidiaries

Notes to the Consolidated Financial Statements — (Continued)

Share purchases and proceeds were as follows (in thousands):

	Year Ended		
	February 2, 2014 (52 weeks)	February 3, 2013 (53 weeks)	January 29, 2012 (52 weeks)
Shares purchased	73	114	99
Aggregate proceeds	$ 4,720	$ 6,664	$ 3,918

Stock-based Compensation Expense

Stock-based compensation expense, net of forfeitures, and the total income tax benefit recognized in the Consolidated Statements of Income and Comprehensive Income were as follows (in thousands):

	Year Ended		
	February 2, 2014 (52 weeks)	February 3, 2013 (53 weeks)	January 29, 2012 (52 weeks)
Stock options expense	$ 10,850	$ 11,159	$ 11,435
Restricted stock expense	7,214	4,885	4,624
Performance share unit expense	10,236	13,913	11,930
Stock-based compensation expense – equity awards	28,300	29,957	27,989
Management equity unit expense	3,387	10,242	11,457
Total stock-based compensation expense	$ 31,687	$ 40,199	$ 39,446
Tax benefit	$ 12,404	$ 15,010	$ 14,764

At February 2, 2014, the total unrecognized stock-based compensation expense for equity awards, net of estimated forfeitures, was $32.8 million and is expected to be recognized over a weighted average period of 1.9 years. At February 2, 2014, the total unrecognized stock-based compensation expense for liability awards, net of estimated forfeitures, was $0.5 million and is expected to be recognized over a weighted average period of 0.2 years.

We estimated the fair value of stock options issued using a lattice option pricing model. Expected volatilities are based on implied volatilities from traded call options on our stock, historical volatility of our stock, and other factors. We use historical data to estimate option exercises and employee terminations within the valuation model. The expected term of options granted is derived from the output of the option valuation model and represents the period of time we expect options granted to be outstanding. The risk-free rates for the periods within the contractual life of the option are based on the monthly United States Treasury yield curve in effect at the time of the option grant using the expected life of the option. Stock options are amortized straight-line over the vesting period net of estimated forfeitures by a charge to income. Actual values of grants could vary significantly from the results of the calculations.

The following assumptions were used to value stock option grants:

	Year Ended		
	February 2, 2014	February 3, 2013	January 29, 2012
Dividend yield	1.00%	1.20%	1.40%
Expected volatility	30.2%	28.8%	31.6%
Risk-free interest rate	1.33%	1.70%	1.24%
Forfeiture rate	13.4%	13.8%	14.3%
Expected lives	5.1 years	5.6 years	5.1 years
Vesting periods	4.0 years	4.0 years	4.0 years
Term	7.0 years	7.0 years	7.0 years
Weighted average fair value	$ 15.62	$ 14.54	$ 10.76

Restricted stock expense reflects the fair market value on the date of the grant, net of forfeitures, and is amortized on a straight-line basis by a charge to income over the requisite service period.

PSU expense, net of forfeitures, is recognized on a straight-line basis over the requisite service period based upon the fair market value on the date of grant, adjusted for the anticipated or actual achievement against the established performance goal.

Compensation expense, net of forfeitures, for MEUs is recognized on a straight-line basis over the requisite service period and is evaluated quarterly based upon the current market value of our common stock.

PetSmart, Inc. and Subsidiaries

Notes to the Consolidated Financial Statements — (Continued)

Note 10 — Employee Benefit Plans

We have a defined contribution plan, or the "Plan," pursuant to Section 401(k) of the Internal Revenue Code. The Plan covers all employees that meet certain service requirements. We match employee contributions, up to specified percentages of those contributions, as approved by the Board of Directors. In addition, certain employees can elect to defer receipt of certain salary and cash bonus payments pursuant to our Non-Qualified Deferred Compensation Plan. We match employee contributions up to certain amounts as defined in the Non-Qualified Deferred Compensation Plan documents. During 2013, 2012, and 2011, we recognized expense related to matching contributions under these Plans of $7.6 million, $8.5 million, and $7.1 million, respectively.

Note 11 — Financing Arrangements and Lease Obligations

Credit Facilities

We have a $100.0 million revolving credit facility agreement, or "Revolving Credit Facility," which expires on March 23, 2017. Borrowings under this Revolving Credit Facility are subject to a borrowing base and bear interest, at our option, at LIBOR plus 1.25% or Base Rate plus 0.25%. The Base Rate is defined as the highest of the following rates: the Federal Funds Rate plus 0.5%, the Adjusted LIBOR plus 1.0%, or the Prime Rate.

We are subject to fees payable each month at an annual rate of 0.20% of the unused amount of the Revolving Credit Facility. The Revolving Credit Facility also gives us the ability to issue letters of credit, which reduce the amount available under the Revolving Credit Facility. Letter of credit issuances under the Revolving Credit Facility are subject to interest payable and bear interest of 0.625% for standby letters of credit and commercial letters of credit.

We had no borrowings under our Revolving Credit Facility at February 2, 2014, and February 3, 2013. We had $14.3 million and $17.9 million in stand-by letter of credit issuances under our Revolving Credit Facility as of February 2, 2014, and February 3, 2013, respectively.

We also have a $100.0 million stand-alone letter of credit facility agreement, or "Stand-alone Letter of Credit Facility," which expires on March 23, 2017. We are subject to fees payable each month at an annual rate of 0.175% of the average daily face amount of the letters of credit outstanding during the preceding month. In addition, we are required to maintain a cash deposit with the lender equal to 103% of the amount of outstanding letters of credit.

We had $69.2 million and $69.8 million in outstanding letters of credit, issued for guarantees provided for insurance programs, under our Stand-alone Letter of Credit Facility as of February 2, 2014, and February 3, 2013, respectively. We had $71.2 million and $71.9 million in restricted cash on deposit as of February 2, 2014, and February 3, 2013, respectively.

Our Revolving Credit Facility and Stand-alone Letter of Credit Facility permit the payment of dividends if we are not in default and payment conditions as defined in the agreement are satisfied. As of February 2, 2014, we were in compliance with the terms and covenants of our Revolving Credit Facility and Stand-alone Letter of Credit Facility. The Revolving Credit Facility and Stand-alone Letter of Credit Facility are secured by substantially all our financial assets.

Operating and Capital Leases

We lease all our stores, distribution centers, and corporate offices under noncancelable leases. The terms of the store leases generally range from 10 to 15 years and typically allow us to renew for two to four additional five-year terms. Store leases, excluding renewal options, expire at various dates through 2026. Generally, the leases require payment of property taxes, utilities, common area maintenance, insurance, and if annual sales at certain stores exceed specified amounts, provide for additional rents. We also lease certain equipment under operating leases and capital leases. Total operating lease expense incurred, net of sublease income, during 2013, 2012, and 2011 was $331.3 million, $325.4 million, and $319.9 million, respectively. Additional rent included in those amounts was not material.

At February 2, 2014, the future minimum annual rental commitments under all noncancelable leases were as follows (in thousands):

	Operating Leases	Capital Leases
2014	$ 325,830	$ 115,340
2015	334,756	120,018
2016	301,162	107,652
2017	264,995	98,141
2018	210,121	80,262
Thereafter	491,633	204,548
Total minimum rental commitments	$ 1,928,497	725,961
Less: amounts representing interest		(207,477)
Present value of minimum lease payments		518,484
Less: current portion		(66,887)
Long-term obligations		$ 451,597

PetSmart, Inc. and Subsidiaries

Notes to the Consolidated Financial Statements — (Continued)

The rental commitments schedule includes all locations for which we have the right to control the use of the property and includes open stores, closed stores, stores to be opened in the future, distribution centers, and corporate offices. We have recorded accrued rent of $0.7 million and $0.7 million in the Consolidated Balance Sheets as of February 2, 2014, and February 3, 2013, respectively. In addition to the commitments scheduled above, we have executed lease agreements with total minimum lease payments of $157.4 million.The typical lease term for these agreements is 10 years. We do not have the right to control the use of the property under these leases as of February 2, 2014, because we have not taken physical possession of the property.

Future minimum annual rental commitments have not been reduced by amounts expected to be received from subtenants. At February 2, 2014, the future annual payments expected to be collected from subtenants were as follows (in thousands):

2014	$	3,248
2015		3,289
2016		2,430
2017		1,542
2018		1,025
Thereafter		1,367
	$	12,901

Note 12 — Commitments and Contingencies

Advertising Purchase Commitments

As of February 2, 2014, we had obligations to purchase $42.4 million of advertising in 2014.

Product Purchase Commitments

As of February 2, 2014, we had various commitments to purchase $24.8 million of merchandise from certain vendors in 2014, and $103.5 million in 2015 through 2017.

Litigation and Settlements

We are involved in the legal proceedings described below and are subject to other claims and litigation arising in the normal course of our business. We have made accruals with respect to certain of these matters, where appropriate, that are reflected in our consolidated financial statements but are not, individually or in the aggregate, considered material. For other matters, we have not made accruals because we have not yet determined that a loss is probable or because the amount of loss cannot be reasonably estimated. While the ultimate outcome of the matters described below cannot be determined, we currently do not expect that these proceedings and claims, individually or in the aggregate, will have a material effect on our consolidated financial position, results of operations, or cash flows. The outcome of any litigation is inherently uncertain, however, and if decided adversely to us, or if we determine that settlement of particular litigation is appropriate, we may be subject to liability that could have a material adverse effect on our consolidated financial position, results of operations, or cash flows. Accordingly, we disclose matters below for which a material loss is reasonably possible. In each case, however, we have either determined that the range of loss is not reasonably estimable or that any reasonably estimable range of loss is not material to our consolidated financial statements.

In May 2012, we were named as a defendant in *Moore, et al. v. PetSmart, Inc., et al.*, a lawsuit originally filed in the California Superior Court for the County of Alameda. PetSmart removed the case to the United States District Court for the Northern District of California. The complaint brings both individual and class action claims, first alleging that PetSmart failed to engage in the interactive process and failed to accommodate the disabilities of four current and former named associates. The complaint also alleges on behalf of current and former hourly store associates that PetSmart failed to provide pay for all hours worked, failed to properly reimburse associates for business expenses, failed to properly calculate and pay vacation, failed to provide suitable seating, and failed to provide timely and uninterrupted meal and rest periods. The lawsuit seeks compensatory damages, statutory penalties, and other relief, including attorneys' fees, costs, and injunctive relief. In January 2014, the parties entered a proposed settlement agreement to resolve this matter in line with reserves that were established for this case in the first and second quarters of 2013. The motion for preliminary approval of the settlement was filed on January 31, 2014, and the hearing on the motion, initially scheduled for March 2014, was continued until April 2014.

In September 2012, a former associate named us as a defendant in *McKee, et al. v. PetSmart, Inc.*, which is currently pending before the United States District Court for the District of Delaware. The case seeks to assert a Fair Labor Standards Act collective action on behalf of PetSmart's operations managers nationwide. The complaint alleges that PetSmart has misclassified operations managers as exempt and as a result failed to pay them overtime for hours worked in excess of forty hours per week. The plaintiffs seek compensatory damages, liquidated damages, and other relief, including attorneys' fees, costs, and injunctive relief. The plaintiffs filed a motion for conditional certification in September 2013, which was granted. The Court conditionally certified a collective action consisting of all current and former operations managers employed by PetSmart at any time in the preceding three-year period. Notices were sent to potential class members in February 2014, and the Court has established a 60-day period within which recipients may consent to join the lawsuit.

PetSmart, Inc. and Subsidiaries

Notes to the Consolidated Financial Statements — (Continued)

Also in September 2012, a former groomer filed a lawsuit against us captioned *Negrete, et al. v. PetSmart, Inc.* in the California Superior Court for the County of Shasta. The plaintiff seeks to assert claims on behalf of current and former California groomers that PetSmart failed to provide pay for all hours worked, failed to properly reimburse associates for business expenses, failed to provide proper wage statements, failed to properly calculate and pay vacation, and failed to provide timely and uninterrupted meal and rest periods. The lawsuit seeks compensatory damages, statutory penalties, and other relief, including attorneys' fees, costs, and injunctive relief. On June 14, 2013, we removed the case to the United States District Court for the Eastern District of California and subsequently filed a motion to transfer the case to the United States District Court for the Northern District of California. On November 1, 2013, the court deemed the *Negrete* and the *Moore* actions related and the *Negrete* action was reassigned to the same judge overseeing the *Moore* action. All deadlines have been stayed until the case management conference currently scheduled for April 2014.

On December 22, 2012, a customer filed a lawsuit against us captioned *Matin, et al. v. Nestle Purina PetCare Company, et al.* in the United States District Court for the Northern District of California. The plaintiff claims he purchased jerky treats containing duck or chicken imported from China that caused injury to his pet, and he seeks to assert claims on behalf of a nationwide class of consumers. We tendered the claim to Nestle Purina, and Nestle Purina is currently defending the case on our behalf. In May 2013, the case was transferred to the Northern District of Illinois and consolidated with another case involving the same products, *Adkins, et al. v. Nestle Purina PetCare Company, et al.* Mediation discussions are ongoing.

On February 20, 2013, a former groomer in California filed a complaint in the Superior Court of California for the County of Orange captioned *Pace v. PetSmart, Inc.* PetSmart removed the case to the United States District Court for the Central District of California. The plaintiff seeks to certify a class of all former PetSmart employees in California since February 20, 2010, who were not paid all wages owed within 72 hours of their separations. The plaintiff challenges PetSmart's use of pay cards for separation payments and seeks waiting time penalties, attorneys' fees, and other relief. The plaintiff also asserts claims under California's Private Attorney General Act as well as individual claims for wrongful termination and disability discrimination. The plaintiff filed a motion for class certification on January 31, 2014 which is currently scheduled for hearing in March 2014.

We are involved in the defense of various other legal proceedings that we do not believe are material to our consolidated financial statements.

PetSmart, Inc. and Subsidiaries

Notes to the Consolidated Financial Statements — (Continued)

Note 13 — Selected Quarterly Financial Data (Unaudited)

Summarized quarterly financial information for 2013 and 2012 is as follows:

Year Ended February 2, 2014	First Quarter (13 weeks)	Second Quarter (13 weeks)	Third Quarter (13 weeks)	Fourth Quarter (13 weeks)
	(In thousands, except per share data)			
Merchandise sales	$ 1,509,372	$ 1,492,457	$ 1,500,443	$ 1,609,430
Services sales	191,577	204,707	184,190	185,532
Other revenue	9,647	8,833	10,535	9,904
Net sales	1,710,596	1,705,997	1,695,168	1,804,866
Gross profit	529,746	515,220	504,973	565,998
Operating income	167,518	156,550	152,669	216,581
Income before income tax expense and equity income from Banfield	154,350	143,722	139,739	203,728
Net income	102,415	93,368	92,221	131,516
Earnings per common share:				
Basic	$ 0.99	$ 0.90	$ 0.89	$ 1.29
Diluted	$ 0.98	$ 0.89	$ 0.88	$ 1.28
Weighted average shares outstanding:				
Basic	103,305	103,474	103,957	102,076
Diluted	104,583	104,512	104,753	102,992

Year Ended February 3, 2013	First Quarter (13 weeks)	Second Quarter (13 weeks)	Third Quarter (13 weeks)	Fourth Quarter (1) (14 weeks)
	(In thousands, except per share data)			
Merchandise sales	$ 1,439,559	$ 1,419,383	$ 1,444,683	$ 1,675,979
Services sales	181,014	190,867	175,018	193,572
Other revenue	9,320	9,417	9,810	9,615
Net sales	1,629,893	1,619,667	1,629,511	1,879,166
Gross profit	497,374	488,815	482,512	593,438
Operating income	154,351	136,060	139,554	221,252
Income before income tax expense and equity income from Banfield	140,222	122,510	126,179	207,977
Net income	94,683	78,520	82,316	134,010
Earnings per common share:				
Basic	$ 0.87	$ 0.73	$ 0.76	$ 1.26
Diluted	$ 0.85	$ 0.71	$ 0.75	$ 1.24
Weighted average shares outstanding:				
Basic	108,930	108,260	107,719	106,470
Diluted	111,030	109,934	109,333	108,071

(1) The estimated impact of the additional week in the fourth quarter of 2012 was: net sales, $126.0 million; gross profit, $48.3 million; operating income, $29.9 million; income before income tax expense and equity income from Banfield, $29.9 million; net income, $18.6 million; and diluted earnings per common share, $0.17.

The full annual report can be downloaded from sec.gov or the investor relations section of the company's website.

APPENDIX C

IFRS Comprehensive Case

AIRFRANCE / KLM

Air France–KLM (AF), a Franco-Dutch company, prepares its financial statements according to International Financial Reporting Standards. AF's financial statements and disclosure notes for the year ended December 31, 2013, are provided with all new textbooks. This material also is available at **www.airfranceklm-finance.com**. This case addresses a variety of characteristics of financial statements prepared using IFRS often comparing and contrasting those attributes of statements prepared under U.S. GAAP. Questions are grouped in parts according to various sections of the textbook.

Part A: Financial Statements, Income Measurement, and Current Assets

A1. What amounts did AF report for the following items for the fiscal year ended December 31, 2013?

a. Total revenues
b. Income from current operations
c. Net income or net loss (AF equity holders)
d. Total assets
e. Total equity

A2. What was AF's basic earnings or loss per share for the 2013 fiscal year?

A3. Examine Note 4.1.1 of AF's annual report. What accounting principles were used to prepare AF's financial statements? Under those accounting principles, could AF's financial information differ from that of a company that exactly followed IFRS as published by the IASB? Explain.

A4. Describe the apparent differences in the order of presentation of the components of the balance sheet between IFRS as applied by Air France–KLM (AF) and a typical balance sheet prepared in accordance with U.S. GAAP.

A5. How does AF classify operating expenses in its income statement? How are these expenses typically classified in a U.S. company income statement?

A6. How does AF classify interest paid, interest received, and dividends received in its statement of cash flows? What other alternatives, if any, does the company have for the classification of these items? How are these items classified under U.S. GAAP?

A7. In note 4.6, AF indicates that "Both passenger and cargo tickets are recorded as "Deferred revenue on ticket sales" and that "Sales related to air transportation are recognized when the transportation service is provided."

a. Examine AF's balance sheet. What is the total amount of deferred revenue on ticket sales as of December 31, 2013?
b. When transportation services are provided with respect to the deferred revenue on ticket sales, what journal entry would AF make to reduce deferred revenue?
c. Does AF's treatment of deferred revenue under IFRS appear consistent with how these transactions would be handled under U.S. GAAP? Explain.

A8. AF has a frequent flyer program, "Flying Blue," which allows members to acquire "miles" as they fly on Air France or partner airlines that are redeemable for free flights or other benefits.

a. How does AF account for these miles?
b. Does AF report any liability associated with these miles as of December 31, 2013?
c. Is AF's accounting approach under IFRS consistent with how U.S. GAAP accounts for contracts with multiple performance obligations? Explain.

A9. In note 4.10.1, AF describes how it values trade receivables. How does the approach used by AF compare to U.S. GAAP?

A10. In note 26, AF reconciles the beginning and ending balances of its valuation allowance for trade accounts receivable. Prepare a T-account for the valuation allowance and include entries for the beginning and ending balances and any reconciling items that affected the account during 2013.

A11. Examine note 28. Does AF have any bank overdrafts? If so, are the overdrafts shown in the balance sheet the same way they would be shown under U.S. GAAP?

A12. What method does the company use to value its inventory? What other alternatives are available under IFRS? Under U.S. GAAP?

A13. AF's inventories are valued at the lower of cost and net realizable value. Does this approach differ from U.S. GAAP?

Part B: Property, Plant, and Equipment and Intangible Assets

B1. What method does AF use to amortize the cost of computer software development costs? How does this approach differ from U.S. GAAP?

B2. AF does not report any research and development expenditures. If it did, its approach to accounting for research and development would be significantly different from U.S. GAAP. Describe the differences between IFRS and U.S. GAAP in accounting for research and development expenditures.

B3. AF does not report the receipt of any governments grants. If it did, its approach to accounting for government grants would be significantly different from U.S. GAAP. Describe the differences between IFRS and U.S. GAAP in accounting for government grants. If AF received a grant for the purchase of assets, what alternative accounting treatments are available under IFRS?

B4. AF's property, plant, and equipment is reported at cost. The company has a policy of not revaluing property, plant, and equipment. Suppose AF decided to revalue its flight equipment on December 31, 2013 and that the fair value of the equipment on that date was €10,000 million. Prepare the journal entry to record the revaluation assuming that the journal entry to record annual depreciation had already been recorded. (Hint: you will need to locate the original cost and accumulated depreciation of the equipment at the end of the year in the appropriate disclosure note.)

B5. Under U.S. GAAP, what alternatives do companies have to value their property, plant, and equipment?

B6. AF calculates depreciation of plant and equipment on a straight-line basis, over the useful life of the asset. Describe any differences between IFRS and U.S. GAAP in the calculation of depreciation.

B7. When does AF test for the possible impairment of fixed assets? How does this approach differ from U.S. GAAP?

B8. Describe the approach AF uses to determine fixed asset impairment losses. (Hint: see Note 4.14) How does this approach differ from U.S. GAAP?

B9. The following is included in AF's disclosure note 4.12: "Intangible assets are held at initial cost less accumulated amortization and any accumulated impairment losses." Assume that on December 31, 2013, AF decided to revalue its Other intangible assets (see Note 18) and that the fair value on that date was determined to be €580 million. Amortization expense for the year already has been recorded. Prepare the journal entry to record the revaluation.

Part C: Investments

C1. Read Notes 4.10.2, 4.10.5, 24, 34.3, and 34.4. Focusing on investments accounted for at fair value through profit and loss (FVTPL):

a. As of December 31, 2013, what is the balance of those investments in the balance sheet? Be specific regarding which line of the balance sheet includes the balance.
b. How much of that balance is classified as current and how much as noncurrent?
c. Is that balance stated at fair value? How do you know?
d. How much of the fair value of those investments is accounted for using level 1, level 2, and level 3 inputs of the fair value hierarchy? Given that information, assess the reliability (representational faithfulness) of this fair value estimate.

C2. Complete Requirement 1 again, but for investments accounted for as available for sale.

C3. Read Notes 4.3.2, 11, and 22.

a. When AF can exercise significant influence over an investee, what accounting approach do they use to account for the investment? How does AF determine if it can exercise significant influence?
b. If AF exercises joint control over an investee by virtue of a contractual agreement, what accounting method does it use?
c. What is the carrying value of AF's equity-method investments in its December 31, 2013, balance sheet?
d. How did AF's equity-method investments affect AF's 2013 net income from continuing operations?

Part D: Liabilities

D1. Read Notes 4.6 and 33. What do you think gave rise to total deferred income of €126 as of the end of fiscal 2013? Would transactions of this type be handled similarly under U.S. GAAP?

D2. Is the threshold for recognizing a provision under IFRS different than it is under U.S. GAAP? Explain.

D3. Note 31 lists "provisions and retirement benefits."

a. Do the beginning and ending balances of total provisions and retirement benefits shown in Note 31 for fiscal 2013 tie to the balance sheet? By how much has the total amount of the AF's "provisions and retirement benefits" increased or decreased during fiscal 2013?
b. Write journal entries for the following changes in the litigation provision that occurred during fiscal 2013, assuming any amounts recorded on the income statement are recorded as "provision expense", and any use of provisions is paid for in cash. In each case, provide a brief explanation of the event your journal entry is capturing.
   i. New provision.
   ii. Use of provision.
c. Is AF's treatment of litigation provision under IFRS similar to how it would be treated under U.S. GAAP?

D4. Note 31.3 lists a number of contingent liabilities. Are amounts for those items recognized as a liability on AF's balance sheet? Explain.

D5. **Sealy Corporation** reported the following line items in its statement of cash flows:

Amortization of discount on secured notes	382,000
Amortization of debt issuance costs and other	1,175,000

In AF's financial statements, Note 32: "Financial Debt" describes the company's long-term debt. Neither of the two items above is reported in the financial statements of Air France, and neither is likely to appear there in the future. Why?

D6. Examine the long-term borrowings in AF's balance sheet and the related note. Note that AF has convertible bonds outstanding that it issued in 2005. Prepare the journal entry AF would use to record the issue of convertible bonds. Prepare the journal entry AF would use to record the issue of the convertible bonds if AF used U.S. GAAP.

D7. AF does not elect the fair value option (FVO) to report its financial liabilities. Examine Note 34.3. "Market value of financial instruments." If the company had elected the FVO for all of its debt measured at amortized cost, what would be the balance at December 31, 2013, in the fair value adjustment account?

Part E: Leases, Income Taxes, and Pensions

E1. In Note 4: Summary of accounting policies, part 4.13.4: Leases, AF states that "leases are classified as finance leases when the lease arrangement transfers substantially all the risks and rewards of ownership to the lessee." Is this the policy companies using U.S. GAAP follow in accounting for capital leases? Explain.

E2. Look at AF's Note 32: Financial debt and Note 33: Lease commitments. Does AF obtain use of its aircraft more using operating leases or finance leases? Do lessees report operating and finance lease commitments the same way? Explain.

E3. Where in its December 31, 2013, balance sheet does AF report deferred taxes? How does this approach differ from the way deferred taxes are reported using U.S. GAAP? Using the Internet, determine how deferred taxes would be reported using IFRS at the time of your research.

E4. Here's an excerpt from one of AF's notes to its financial statements:

> **Deferred taxes (in part)**
>
> The Group records deferred taxes using the balance sheet liability method, providing for any temporary differences between the carrying amounts of assets and liabilities for financial reporting purposes and the amounts used for taxation purposes. . . . The tax rates used are those enacted or substantively enacted at the balance sheet date.

Is this policy consistent with U.S. GAAP? Explain.

E5. Here's an excerpt from one AF's notes to its financial statements:

> **Deferred taxes (in part)**
>
> Deferred tax assets related to temporary differences and carry forwards are recognized only to the extent it is probable that a future taxable profit will be available against which the asset can be utilized at the tax entity level.

Is this policy consistent with U.S. GAAP? Explain.

E6. Air France reported past service cost (called prior service cost under U.S. GAAP) in its income statement as part of net periodic pension cost. Is that reporting method the same or different from the way we report prior service cost under U.S. GAAP?

E7. Look at note 31.1, "Retirement Benefits." AF incorporates estimates regarding staff turnover, life expectancy, salary increase, retirement age and discount rates. How did AF report changes in these assumptions? Is that reporting method the same or different from the way we report changes under U.S. GAAP?

E8. AF does not report remeasurement gains and losses in its income statement. Where did AF report these amounts? Is that reporting method the same or different from the way we report pension expense under U.S. GAAP?

E9. See Note 23. Did AF report Net interest cost or Net interest income in 2013? How is that amount determined?

Part F: Shareholders' Equity and Additional Financial Reporting Issues

F1. Air France-KLM lists four items in the shareholders' equity section of its balance sheet. If AF used U.S. GAAP, what would be the likely account titles for the first and fourth of those components?

F2. Locate Note 29.4 in AF's financial statements. What items comprise "Reserves and retained earnings" as reported in the balance sheet? If Air France-KLM used U.S. GAAP, what would be different for the reporting of these items?

F3. Describe the apparent differences in the order of presentation of the components of liabilities and shareholders' equity between IFRS as applied by AF and a typical balance sheet prepared in accordance with U.S. GAAP.

F4. What is the amount that AF reports in its income statement for its stock options for the year ended December 31, 2013? [*Hint:* See Note 30: "Share-Based Compensation."] Are AF's share options cliff vesting or graded vesting? How does accounting differ between U.S. GAAP and IFRS for graded-vesting plans?

F5. What amount(s) of earnings per share did AF report in its income statement for the year ended December 31, 2013? If AF used U.S. GAAP would it have reported EPS using the same classification?

F6. What are the primary classifications into which AF's cash inflows and cash outflows are separated? Is this classification the same as or different from cash flow statements prepared in accordance with U.S. GAAP?

F7. How are cash inflows from dividends and interest and cash outflows for dividends and interest classified in AF's cash flow statements? Is this classification the same as or different from cash flow statements prepared in accordance with U.S. GAAP?

Glossary

Accounting equation the process used to capture the effect of economic events; Assets = Liabilities + Owner's Equity.

Accounting Principles Board (APB) the second private sector body delegated the task of setting accounting standards.

Accounts storage areas to keep track of the increases and decreases in financial position elements.

Accounts payable obligations to suppliers of merchandise or of services purchased on open account.

Accounts receivable receivables resulting from the sale of goods or services on account.

Accounts receivable aging schedule applying different percentages to accounts receivable balances depending on the length of time outstanding.

Accretion increase in the carrying value of an asset or liability.

Accretion expense the increase in an asset retirement obligation that accrues as an operating expense.

Accretion revenue the increase in a lessor's residual asset that accrues as revenue.

Accruals when the cash flow comes after either expense or revenue recognition.

Accrual accounting measurement of the entity's accomplishments and resource sacrifices during the period, regardless of when cash is received or paid.

Accrued interest interest that has accrued since the last interest date.

Accrued liabilities expenses already incurred but not yet paid (accrued expenses).

Accrued receivables the recognition of revenue earned before cash is received.

Accumulated benefit obligation (ABO) the discounted present value of estimated retirement benefits earned so far by employees, applying the plan's pension formula using existing compensation levels.

Accumulated other comprehensive income amount of other comprehensive income (nonowner changes in equity other than net income) accumulated over the current and prior periods.

Accumulated postretirement benefit obligation (APBO) portion of the EPBO attributed to employee service up to a particular date.

Acid-test ratio current assets, excluding inventories and prepaid items, divided by current liabilities.

Acquisition costs the amounts paid to acquire the rights to explore for undiscovered natural resources or to extract proven natural resources.

Activity-based method allocation of an asset's cost base using a measure of the asset's input or output.

Actuary a professional trained in a particular branch of statistics and mathematics to assess the various uncertainties and to estimate the company's obligation to employees in connection with its pension plan.

Additions the adding of a new major component to an existing asset.

Adjusted trial balance trial balance after adjusting entries have been recorded.

Adjusting entries internal transactions recorded at the end of any period when financial statements are prepared.

Agent facilitates transfers of goods and services between sellers and customers.

Allocation base the value of the usefulness that is expected to be consumed.

Allocation method the pattern in which the usefulness is expected to be consumed.

Allowance method recording bad debt expense and reducing accounts receivable indirectly by crediting a contra account (allowance for uncollectible accounts) to accounts receivable for an estimate of the amount that eventually will prove uncollectible.

American Institute of Accountants (AIA)/American Institute of Certified Public Accountants (AICPA) national organization of professional public accountants.

Amortization cost allocation for intangibles.

Amortization schedule schedule that reflects the changes in the debt over its term to maturity.

Annuity cash flows received or paid in the same amount each period.

Annuity due cash flows occurring at the beginning of each period.

Antidilutive securities the effect of the conversion or exercise of potential common shares would be to increase rather than decrease, EPS.

Articles of incorporation statement of the nature of the firm's business activities, the shares to be issued, and the composition of the initial board of directors.

Asset retirement obligations (AROs) obligations associated with the disposition of an operational asset.

Assets probable future economic benefits obtained or controlled by a particular entity as a result of past transactions or events.

Asset turnover ratio measure of a company's efficiency in using assets to generate revenue.

Assigning using receivables as collateral for loans; nonpayment of a debt will require the proceeds from collecting the assigned receivables to go directly toward repayment of the debt.

Attribution process of assigning the cost of benefits to the years during which those benefits are assumed to be earned by employees.

Auditors independent intermediaries who help ensure that management has appropriately applied GAAP in preparing the company's financial statements.

Auditor's report report issued by CPAs who audit the financial statements that informs users of the audit findings.

Average collection period indication of the average age of accounts receivable.

Average cost method assumes cost of goods sold and ending inventory consist of a mixture of all the goods available for sale.

Average days in inventory indicates the average number of days it normally takes to sell inventory.

Bad debt expense an operating expense incurred to boost sales; inherent cost of granting credit.

Balance sheet a position statement that presents an organized list of assets, liabilities, and equity at a particular point in time.

Balance sheet approach determination of bad debt expense by estimating the net realizable value of accounts receivable to be reported in the balance sheet.

Bank reconciliation comparison of the bank balance with the balance in the company's own records.

Bargain purchase option (BPO) provision in the lease contract that gives the lessee the option of purchasing the leased property at a bargain price.

Bargain renewal option gives the lessee the option to renew the lease at a bargain rate.

Basic EPS computed by dividing income available to common stockholders (net income less any preferred stock dividends) by the weighted-average number of common shares outstanding for the period.

Billings on construction contract contra account to the asset construction in progress; subtracted from construction in progress to determine balance sheet presentation.

Board of directors establishes corporate policies and appoints officers who manage the corporation.

Bond indenture document that describes specific promises made to bondholders.

Bonds A form of debt consisting of separable units (bonds) that obligates the issuing corporation to repay a stated amount at a specified maturity date and to pay interest to bondholders between the issue date and maturity.

Book value assets minus liabilities as shown in the balance sheet.

Callable allows the issuing company to buy back, or call, outstanding bonds from the bondholders before their scheduled maturity date.

Capital budgeting The process of evaluating the purchase of operational assets.

Capital leases installment purchases/sales that are formulated outwardly as leases.

Capital markets mechanisms that foster the allocation of resources efficiently.

Cash currency and coins, balances in checking accounts, and items acceptable for deposit in these accounts, such as checks and money orders received from customers.

Cash basis accounting/net operating cash flow difference between cash receipts and cash disbursements during a reporting period from transactions related to providing goods and services to customers.

Cash disbursements journal record of cash disbursements.

Cash discounts sales discounts; represent reductions not in the selling price of a good or service but in the amount to be paid by a credit customer if paid within a specific period of time.

Cash equivalents certain negotiable items such as commercial paper, money market funds, and U.S. Treasury bills that are highly liquid investments quickly convertible to cash.

Cash equivalents short-term, highly liquid investments that can be readily converted to cash with little risk of loss.

Cash flow hedge a derivative used to hedge against the exposure to changes in cash inflows or cash outflows of an asset or liability or a forecasted transaction (like a future purchase or sale).

Cash flows from financing activities both inflows and outflows of cash resulting from the external financing of a business.

Cash flows from investing activities both outflows and inflows of cash caused by the acquisition and disposition of assets.

Cash flows from operating activities both inflows and outflows of cash that result from activities reported on the income statement.

Cash receipts journal record of cash receipts.

Certified Public Accountants (CPAs) licensed individuals who can represent that the financial statements have been audited in accordance with generally accepted auditing standards.

Change in accounting estimate a change in an estimate when new information comes to light.

Change in accounting principle switch by a company from one accounting method to another.

Change in reporting entity presentation of consolidated financial statements in place of statements of individual companies, or a change in the specific companies that constitute the group for which consolidated or combined statements are prepared.

Closing process the temporary accounts are reduced to zero balances, and these temporary account balances are closed (transferred) to retained earnings to reflect the changes that have occurred in that account during the period.

Commercial paper unsecured notes sold in minimum denominations of $25,000 with maturities ranging from 30 to 270 days.

Committee on Accounting Procedure (CAP) the first private sector body that was delegated the task of setting accounting standards.

Comparability the ability to help users see similarities and differences among events and conditions.

Comparative financial statements corresponding financial statements from the previous years accompanying the issued financial statements.

Compensating balance a specified balance (usually some percentage of the committee amount) a borrower of a loan is asked to maintain in a low-interest or noninterest-bearing account at the bank.

Completed contract method recognition of revenue for a long-term contract when the project is complete.

Complex capital structure potential common shares are outstanding.

Complex debt debt that lacks one or more of the characteristics of simple debt.

Composite depreciation method physically dissimilar assets are aggregated to gain the convenience of group depreciation.

Compound interest interest computed not only on the initial investment but also on the accumulated interest in previous periods.

Comprehensive income traditional net income plus other nonowner changes in equity.

Conceptual framework deals with theoretical and conceptual issues and provides an underlying structure for current and future accounting and reporting standards.

Conservatism practice followed in an attempt to ensure that uncertainties and risks inherent in business situations are adequately considered.

Consignment the consignor physically transfers the goods to the other company (the consignee), but the consignor retains legal title.

Consistency permits valid comparisons between different periods.

Consolidated financial statements combination of the separate financial statements of the parent and subsidiary each period into a single aggregate set of financial statements as if there were only one company.

Construction in progress asset account equivalent to the asset work-in-progress inventory in a manufacturing company.

Contingently issuable shares additional shares of common stock to be issued, contingent on the occurrence of some future circumstance.

Contract an agreement that creates legally enforceable rights and obligations. Contracts can be explicit or implicit.

Contract liability a label given to deferred revenue or unearned revenue accounts.

Conventional retail method applying the retail inventory method in such a way that LCM is approximated.

Convertible bonds bonds for which bondholders have the option to convert the bonds into shares of stock.

Copyright exclusive right of protection given to a creator of a published work, such as a song, painting, photograph, or book.

Corporation the dominant form of business organization that acquires capital from investors in exchange for ownership interest and from creditors by borrowing.

Correction of an error an adjustment a company makes due to an error made.

Cost effectiveness the perceived benefit of increased decision usefulness exceeds the anticipated cost of providing that information.

Cost of goods sold cost of the inventory sold during the period.

Cost recovery method deferral of all gross profit recognition until the cost of the item sold has been recovered.

Cost-to-cost ratio ratio found by calculating the percentage of estimated total cost that has been incurred to date.

Cost-to-retail percentage ratio found by dividing goods available for sale at cost by goods available for sale at retail.

Coupons bonds name of the owner was not registered; the holder actually clipped an attached coupon and redeemed it in accordance with instructions on the indenture.

Credits represent the right side of the account.

Cumulative if the specified dividend is not paid in a given year, the unpaid dividends accumulate and must be made up in a later dividend year before any dividends are paid on common shares.

Current assets includes assets that are cash, will be converted into cash, or will be used up within one year or the operating cycle, whichever is longer.

Current liabilities expected to require current assets and usually are payable within one year.

Current maturities of long-term debt the current installment due on long-term debt, reported as a current liability.

Current ratio current assets divided by current liabilities.

Date of record specific date stated as to when the determination will be made of the recipient of the dividend.

Debenture bond secured only by the "full faith and credit" of the issuing corporation.

Debits represent the left side of the account.

Debt issue cost with either publicly or privately sold debt, the issuing company will incur costs in connection with issuing bonds or notes, such as legal and accounting fees and printing costs, in addition to registration and underwriting fees.

Debt to equity ratio compares resources provided by creditors with resources provided by owners.

Decision usefulness the quality of being useful to decision making.

Default risk a company's ability to pay its obligations when they come due.

Deferred annuity the first cash flow occurs more than the one period after the date the agreement begins.

Deferred tax asset taxes to be saved in the future when future deductible amounts reduce taxable income (when the temporary differences reverse).

Deferred tax liability taxes to be paid in the future when future taxable amounts become taxable (when the temporary differences reverse).

Deficit debit balance in retained earnings.

Defined benefit pension plans fixed retirement benefits defined by a designated formula, based on employees' years of service and annual compensation.

Defined contribution pension plans fixed annual contributions to a pension fund; employees choose where funds are invested-usually stocks or fixed-income securities.

Depletion allocation of the cost of natural resources.

Depreciation cost allocation for plant and equipment.

Derivatives financial instruments usually created to hedge against risks created by other financial instruments or by transactions that have yet to occur but are anticipated and that "derive" their values or contractually required cash flows from some other security or index.

Detachable stock purchase warrants the investor has the option to purchase a stated number of shares of common stock at a specified option price, within a given period of time.

Development costs for natural resources, costs incurred after the resource has been discovered but before production begins.

Diluted EPS incorporates the dilutive effect of all potential common shares.

Direct financing lease lease in which the lessor finances the asset for the lessee and earns interest revenue over the lease term.

Direct method the cash effect of each operating activity (i.e., income statement item) is reported directly on the statement of cash flows.

Direct write-off method an allowance for uncollectible accounts is not used; instead bad debts that do arise are written off as bad debt expense.

Disclosure notes additional insights about company operations, accounting principles, contractual agreements, and pending litigation.

Discontinued operations the discontinuance of a component of an entity whose operations and cash flows can be clearly distinguished from the rest of the entity.

Discount arises when bonds are sold for less than face amount.

Discounting the transfer of a note receivable to a financial institution.

Distinct A good or service is *distinct* if it is both *capable of being distinct* (the customer could use the good or service on its own or in combination with other goods and services it could obtain elsewhere), and *separately identifiable from other goods or services in the contract* (the good or service is distinct in the context of the contract because it is not highly interrelated with other goods and services in the contract.)

Distributions to owners decreases in equity resulting from transfers to owners.

Dividend distribution to shareholders of a portion of assets earned.

Dollar-value LIFO (DVL) Inventory is viewed as a quantity of value instead of a physical quantity of goods. Instead of layers of units from different purchases, the DVL inventory pool is viewed as comprising layers of dollar value from different years.

Dollar-value LIFO retail method LIFO retail method combined with dollar-value LIFO.

Double-declining-balance (DDB) method 200% of the straight-line rate is multiplied by book value.

Double-entry system dual effect that each transaction has on the accounting equation when recorded.

DuPont framework depict return on equity as determined by profit margin (representing profitability), asset turnover (representing efficiency), and the equity multiplier (representing leverage).

Early extinguishment of debt debt is retired prior to its scheduled maturity date.

Earnings per share (EPS) the amount of income earned by a company expressed on a per share basis.

Earnings quality refers to the ability of reported earnings (income) to predict a company's future earnings.

Economic events any event that directly affects the financial position of the company.

Effective interest method calculates interest revenue as the market rate of interest multiplied by the outstanding balance of the investment.

Effective rate the actual rate at which money grows per year.

Effective tax rate equals tax expense divided by pretax accounting income.

Emerging Issues Task Force (EITF) responsible for providing more timely responses to emerging financial reporting issues.

Employee share purchase plans permit all employees to buy shares directly from their company, often at favorable terms.

Equity method used when an investor can't control, but can significantly influence, the investee.

Equity multiplier depicts leverage as total assets divided by total equity.

Equity/net assets called shareholders' equity or stockholders' equity for a corporation; the residual interest in the assets of an entity that remains after deducting liabilities.

Estimates prediction of future events.

Ethics a code or moral system that provides criteria for evaluating right and wrong.

Ex-dividend date date usually two business days before the date of the record and is the first day the stock trades without the right to receive the declared dividend.

Executory costs maintenance, insurance, taxes, and any other costs usually associated with ownership.

Expected cash flow approach adjusts the cash flows, not the discount rate, for the uncertainty or risk of those cash flows.

Expected economic life useful life of an asset.

Expected postretirement benefit obligation (EPBO) discounted present value of the total net cost to the employer of postretirement benefits.

Expected return on plan assets estimated long-term return on invested assets.

Expenses outflows or other using up of assets or incurrences of liabilities during a period from delivering or producing good, rendering services, or other activities that constitute the entity's ongoing major, or central, operations.

Exploration costs for natural resources, expenditures such as drilling a well, or excavating a mine, or any other costs of searching for natural resources.

Extended warranties an additional, extended service that covers new problems arising after the buyer takes control of the product.

External events exchange between the company and a separate economic entity.

Extraordinary items material events and transactions that are both unusual in nature and infrequent in occurrence.

F.O.B. (free on board) shipping point legal title to the goods changes hands at the point of shipment when the seller delivers the goods to the common carrier, and the purchaser is responsible for shipping costs and transit insurance.

F.O.B. destination the seller is responsible for shipping and the legal title does not pass until the goods arrive at their destination.

Factor financial institution that buys receivables for cash, handles the billing and collection of the receivables, and charges a fee for this service.

Fair value hedge a derivative is used to hedge against the exposure to changes in the fair value of an asset or liability or a firm commitment.

Fair value hierarchy prioritizes the inputs companies should use when determinig fair value.

Fair value option allows companies to report their financial assets and liabilities at fair value.

Faithful representation exists when there is agreement between a measure or description and the phenomenon it purports to represent.

Financial accounting provides relevant financial information to various external users.

Financial Accounting Foundation (FAF) responsible for selecting the members of the FASB and its Advisory Council, ensuring adequate funding of FASB activities, and exercising general oversight of the FASB's activities.

Financial Accounting Standards Board (FASB) the current private sector body that has been delegated the task of setting accounting standards.

Financial activities cash inflows and outflows from transactions with creditors and owners.

Financial instrument cash; evidence of an ownership interest in an entity; a contract that imposes on one entity an obligation to deliver cash or another financial instrument, and conveys to the second entity a right to receive cash or another financial instrument; and a contract that imposes on one entity an obligation to exchange financial instruments on potentially unfavorable terms and conveys to a second entity a right to exchange other financial instruments on potentially favorable terms.

Financial leverage by earning a return on borrowed funds that exceeds the cost of borrowing the funds, a company can provide its shareholders with a total return higher than it could achieve by employing equity funds alone.

Financial reporting process of providing financial statement information to external users.

Financial statements primary means of communicating financial information to external parties.

Finished goods costs that have accumulated in work-in-process are transferred to finished goods once the manufacturing process is completed.

First-in, first-out (FIFO) method assumes that items sold are those that were acquired first.

Fiscal year the annual time period used to report to external users.

Fixed-asset turnover ratio used to measure how effectively managers used PP&E.

$$\text{Fixed-asset turnover ratio} = \frac{\text{Net sales}}{\text{Average-fixed assets}}$$

Foreign currency futures contract agreement that requires the seller to deliver a specific foreign currency at a designated future date at a specific price.

Foreign currency hedge if a derivative is used to hedge the risk that some transactions require settlement in a currency other than the entities' functional currency or that foreign operations will require translation adjustments to reported amounts.

Forward contract calls for delivery on a specific date; is not traded on a market exchange; does not call for a daily cash settlement for price changes in the underlying contract.

Fractional shares a stock dividend or stock split results in some shareholders being entitled to fractions of whole shares.

Franchise contractual arrangement under which the franchisor grants the franchisee the exclusive right to use the franchisor's trademark or tradename within a geographical area, usually for specified period of time.

Franchisee individual or corporation given the right to sell the franchisor's products and use its name for a specified period of time.

Fraud an intentional act by one or more individuals among management, those charged with governance, employees, or third parties, involving the use of deception that results in a misstatement in the financial statements that are the subject of an audit.

Franchisor grants to the franchisee the right to sell the franchisor's products and use its name for a specific period of time.

Freight-in transportation-in; in a periodic system, freight costs generally are added to this temporary account, which is added to purchases in determining net purchases.

Full-cost method allows costs incurred in searching for oil and gas within a large geographical area to be capitalized as assets and expensed in the future as oil and gas from the successful wells are removed from that area.

Full-disclosure principle the financial reports should include any information that could affect the decisions made by external users.

Funded status difference between the employer's obligation (PBO) and the resources available to satisfy that obligation (plan assets).

Future deductible amounts the future tax consequence of a temporary difference will be to decrease taxable income relative to accounting income.

Futures contract agreement that requires the seller to deliver a particular commodity at a designated future date at a specified price.

Future taxable amounts the future tax consequence of temporary difference will be to increase taxable income relative to accounting income.

Future value amount of money that a dollar will grow to at some point in the future.

Gain or loss on the PBO the decrease or increase in the PBO when one or more estimates used in determining the PBO require revision.

Gains increases in equity from peripheral, or incidental, transactions of an entity.

General journal used to record any type of transaction.

General ledger collection of accounts.

Generally Accepted Accounting Principles (GAAP) set of both broad and specific guidelines that companies should follow when measuring and reporting the information in their financial statements and related notes.

Going concern assumption in the absence of information to the contrary, it is anticipated that a business entity will continue to operate indefinitely.

Goodwill unique intangible asset in that its cost can't be directly associated with any specifically identifiable right and it is not separable from the company itself.

Government Accounting Standards Board (GASB) responsible for developing accounting standards for governmental units such as states and cities.

Gross investment in the lease total of periodic rental payments and residual value.

Gross method For the buyer, views a discount not taken as part of the cost of inventory. For the seller, views a discount not taken by the customer as part of sales of revenue.

Gross profit method (gross margin method) estimates cost of goods sold which is then subtracted from cost of goods available for sale to estimate ending inventory.

Gross profit/ratio highlights the important relationship between net sales revenue and cost of goods sold.

$$\text{Gross profit ratio} = \frac{\text{Gross profit}}{\text{Net sales}}$$

Group depreciation method collection of assets defined as depreciable assets that share similar service lives and other attributes.

Half-year convention record one-half of a full year's depreciation in the year of acquisition and another half year in the year of disposal.

Hedging taking an action that is expected to produce exposure to a particular type of risk that is precisely the opposite of an actual risk to which the company already is exposed.

Historical costs original transaction value.

Horizontal analysis comparison by expressing each item as a percentage of that same item in the financial statements of another year (base amount) in order to more easily see year-to-year changes.

Illegal acts violations of the law, such as bribes, kickbacks, and illegal contributions to political candidates.

Impairment of value operational assets should be written down if there has been a significant impairment (fair value less than book value) of value.

Implicit rate of interest rate implicit in the agreement.

Improvements replacement of a major component of an operational asset.

Income from continuing operations revenues, expenses (including income taxes), gain, and losses, excluding those related to discontinued operations and extraordinary items.

Income statement statement of operations or statement of earnings is used to summarize the profit-generating activities that occurred during a particular reporting period.

Income statement approach estimating bad debt expense as a percentage of each period's net credit sales; usually determined by reviewing the company's recent history of the relationship between credit sales and actual bad debts.

Income summary account that is a bookkeeping convenience used in the closing process that provides a check that all temporary accounts have been properly closed.

Income tax expense provision for income taxes; reported as a separate expense in corporate income statements.

Indirect method the net cash increase or decrease from operating activities is derived indirectly by starting with reported net income and working backwards to convert that amount to a cash basis.

Initial direct costs costs incurred by the lessor that are associated directly with originating a lease and are essential to acquire the lease.

Initial market transactions provide for new cash by the issuance of stocks and bonds by the corporation.

In-process research and development the amount of the purchase price in a business acquisition that is allocated to projects that have not yet reached technological feasibility.

Installment notes notes payable for which equal installment payments include both an amount that represents interest and an amount that represents a reduction of the outstanding balance so that at maturity the note is completely paid.

Installment sales method recognizes revenue and costs only when cash payments are received.

Institute of Internal Auditors national organization of accountants providing internal auditing services for their own organizations.

Institute of Management Accountants (IMA) primary national organization of accountants working in industry and government.

Intangible assets operational assets that lack physical substance; examples include patents, copyrights, franchises, and goodwill.

Interest "rent" paid for the use of money for some period of time.

Interest cost interest accrued on the projected benefit obligation calculated as the discount rate multiplied by the projected benefit obligation at the beginning of the year.

Interest rate swap agreement to exchange fixed interest payments for floating rate payments, or vice versa, without exchanging the underlying principal amounts.

Internal control a company's plan to encourage adherence to company policies and procedures, promote operational efficiency, minimize errors and theft, and enhance the reliability and accuracy of accounting data.

Internal events events that directly affect the financial position of the company but don't involve an exchange transaction with another entity.

International Accounting Standards Board (IASB) objectives are to develop a single set of high-quality, understandable global accounting standards, to promote the use of those standards, and to bring about the convergence of national accounting standards and International Accounting Standards.

International Accounting Standards Committee (IASC) umbrella organization formed to develop global accounting standards.

International Financial Reporting Standards (IFRS) developed by the IASB and used by more than 100 countries.

Intraperiod tax allocation associates (allocates) income tax expense (or income tax gross profit net sales benefit if there is a loss) with each major component of income that causes it.

Intrinsic value the difference between the market price of the shares and the option price at which they can be acquired.

Inventories goods awaiting sale (finished goods), goods in the course of production (work in process), and goods to be consumed directly or indirectly in production (raw materials).

Inventory goods acquired, manufactured, or in the process of being manufactured for sale.

Inventory turnover ratio measures a company's efficiency in managing its investment in inventory.

Investing activities involve the acquisition and sale of long-term assets used in the business and non-operating investment assets.

Investments by owners increases in equity resulting from transfers of resources (usually cash) to a company in exchange for ownership interest.

Journal a chronological record of all economic events affecting financial position.

Journal entry captures the effect of a transaction on financial position in debit/credit form.

Just-in-time (JIT) system a system used by a manufacturer to coordinate production with suppliers so that raw materials or components arrive just as they are needed in the production process.

Land improvements the cost of parking lots, driveways, and private roads and the costs of fences and lawn and garden sprinkler systems.

Last-in, first-out (LIFO) method assumes units sold are the most recent units purchased.

Leasehold improvements account title when a lessee makes improvements to leased property that reverts back to the lessor at the end of the lease.

Lessee user of a leased asset.

Lessor owner of a leased asset.

Leveraged lease a third-party, long-term creditor provides nonrecourse financing for a lease agreement between a lessor and a lessee.

Liabilities probable future sacrifices of economic benefits arising from present obligations of a particular entity to transfer assets or provide services to other entities in the future as a result of past transactions or events.

Licenses allow the customer to use seller's intellectual property.

LIFO conformity rule if a company uses LIFO to measure taxable income, the company also must use LIFO for external financial reporting.

LIFO inventory pools simplifies recordkeeping and reduces the risk of LIFO liquidation by grouping inventory units into pools based on physical similarities of the individual units.

LIFO liquidation the decline in inventory quantity during the period.

LIFO reserve contra account to inventory used to record the difference between the internal method and LIFO.

Limited liability company owners are not liable for the debts of the business, except to the extent of their investment; all members can be involved with managing the business without losing liability protection; no limitations on the number of owners.

Limited liability partnership similar to a limited liability company, except it doesn't offer all the liability protection available in the limited liability company structure.

Line of credit allows a company to borrow cash without having to follow formal loan procedures and paperwork.

Liquidating dividend when a dividend exceeds the balance in retained earnings.

Liquidity period of time before an asset is converted to cash or until a liability is paid.

Long-term solvency the riskiness of a company with regard to the amount of liabilities in its capital structure.

Loss contingency existing, uncertain situation involving potential loss depending on whether some future event occurs.

Losses decreases in equity arising from peripheral, or incidental, transactions of the entity.

Lower-of-cost-or-market (LCM) recognizes losses in the period that the value of inventory declines below its cost.

Management discussion and analysis (MDA) provides a biased but informed perspective of a company's operations, liquidity, and capital resources.

Managerial accounting deals with the concepts and methods used to provide information to an organization's internal users (i.e., its managers).

Matching principle expenses are recognized in the same period as the related revenues.

Materiality if a more costly way of providing information is not expected to have a material effect on decisions made by those using the information, the less costly method may be acceptable.

Measurement process of associating numerical amounts to the elements.

Minimum lease payments payments the lessee is required to make in connection with the lease.

Minimum pension liability an employer must report a pension liability at least equal to the amount by which its ABO exceeds its plan assets.

Model Business Corporation Act designed to serve as a guide to states in the development of their corporation statutes.

Modified accelerated cost recovery system (MACRS) The federal income tax code allows taxpayers to compute depreciation for their tax returns using this method.

Monetary assets money and claims to receive money, the amount of which is fixed or determinable.

Monetary liabilities obligations to pay amounts of cash, the amount of which is fixed or determinable.

Mortgage bond backed by a lien on specified real estate owned by the issuer.

Multiple-deliverable arrangements require allocation of revenue to multiple elements that qualify for separate revenue recognition.

Multiple-step income statement format that includes a number of intermediate subtotals before arriving at income from continuing operations.

Natural resources oil and gas deposits, timber tracts, and mineral deposits.

Net income/net loss revenue + gains − (expenses and losses for a period) income statement bottom line.

Net interest cost/income interest rate times the net difference between the defined benefit obligation (DBO) and plan assets using IFRS.

Net markdown net effect of the change in selling price (increase, decrease, increase).

Net markup net effect of the change in selling price (increase, increase, decrease).

Net method For the buyer, considers the cost of inventory to include the net, after-discount amount, and any discounts not taken are reported as interest expense. For the seller, considers sales revenue to be the net amount, after discount, and any discounts not taken by the customer as interest revenue.

Net operating loss negative taxable income because tax-deductible expenses exceed taxable revenues.

Net realizable less a normal profit margin (NRV − NP) lower limit of market.

Net realizable value the amount of cash the company expects to actually collect from customers.

Net realizable value (NRV) upper limit of market.

Neutrality neutral with respect to parties potentially affected.

Noncash investing and financing activities transactions that do not increase or decrease cash but that result in significant investing and financing activities.

Noninterest-bearing note notes that bear interest, but the interest is deducted (or discounted) from the face amount to determine the cash proceeds made available to the borrower at the outset.

Nonoperating income includes gains and losses and revenues and expenses related to peripheral or incidental activities of the company.

Note payable promissory note (essentially an IOU) that obligates the issuing corporation to repay a stated amount at or by a specified maturity date and to pay interest to the lender between the issue date and maturity.

Notes receivable receivables supported by a formal agreement or note that specifies payment terms.

Objectives-oriented/principles-based accounting standards approach to standard setting stresses professional judgment, as opposed to following a list of rules.

Onerous performance obligation The proposed ASU on revenue recognition may require the seller to recognize a liability and expense for an unprofitable performance obligation satisfied over a period of time greater than one year.

Operating activities inflows and outflows of cash related to transactions entering into the determination of net income.

Operating cycle period of time necessary to convert cash to raw materials, raw materials to finished product, the finished product to receivables, and then finally receivables back to cash.

Operating income includes revenues and expenses directly related to the principal revenue-generating activities of the company.

Operating leases fundamental rights and responsibilities of ownership are retained by the lessor and that the lessee merely is using the asset temporarily.

Operating loss carryback reduction of prior (up to two) years' taxable income by a current net operating loss.

Operating loss forward reduction of future (up to 20) years' taxable income by a current net operating loss.

Operating segment a component of an enterprise that engages in business activities from which it may earn revenues and incur expenses (including revenues and expenses relating to transactions with other companies of the same enterprise); whose operating results are regularly reviewed by the enterprise's chief operating decision maker to make decisions about resources to be allocated to the segment and assess its performance; for which discrete financial information is available.

Operational assets property, plant, and equipment, along with intangible assets.

Operational risk how adept a company is at withstanding various events and circumstances that might impair its ability to earn profits.

Option gives the holder the right either to buy or sell a financial instrument at a specified price.

Option pricing models statistical models that incorporate information about a company's stock and the terms of the stock option to estimate the option's fair value.

Ordinary annuity cash flows occur at the end of each period.

Other comprehensive income certain gains and losses that are excluded from the calculation of net income, but included in the calculation of comprehensive income.

Paid-in capital invested capital consisting primarily of amounts invested by shareholders when they purchase shares of stock from the corporation.

Parenthetical comments/modifying comments supplemental information disclosed on the face of financial statements.

Participating preferred shareholders are allowed to receive additional dividends beyond the stated amount.

Patent exclusive right to manufacture a product or to use a process.

Pension plan assets employer contributions and accumulated earnings on the investment of those contributions to be used to pay retirement benefits to retired employees.

Percentage-of-completion method recognizes revenue over time as progress on the contract occurs.

Performance obligations promises to transfer goods and services to a customer. They are satisfied when the seller transfers *control* of goods or services to the customer.

Periodic inventory system the merchandise inventory account balance is not adjusted as purchases and sales are made but only periodically at the end of a reporting period when a physical count of the period's ending inventory is made and costs are assigned to the quantities determined.

Periodicity assumption allows the life of a company to be divided into artificial time periods to provide timely information.

Permanent accounts represent assets, liabilities, and shareholders' equity at a point in time.

Permanent difference difference between pretax accounting income and taxable income and, consequently, between the reported amount of an asset or liability in the financial statements and its tax basis that will not "reverse" resulting from transactions and events that under existing tax law will never affect taxable income or taxes payable.

Perpetual inventory system account inventory is continually adjusted for each change in inventory, whether it's caused by a purchase, a sale, or a return of merchandise by the company to its supplier.

Pledging trade receivables in general rather than specific receivables are pledged as collateral; the responsibility for collection of the receivables remains solely with the company.

Point-of-sale the goods or services sold to the buyer are delivered (the title is transferred).

Post-closing trial balance verifies that the closing entries were prepared and posted correctly and that the accounts are now ready for next year's transactions.

Posting transferring debits and credits recorded in individual journal entries to the specific accounts affected.

Postretirement benefits all types of retiree benefits; may include medical coverage, dental coverage, life insurance, group legal services, and other benefits.

Potential common shares Securities that, while not being common stock may become common stock through their exercise, conversion, or issuance and therefore dilute (reduce) earnings per share.

Predictive value/confirmatory value confirmation of investor expectations about future cash-generating ability.

Preferred stock typically has a preference (a) to a specified amount of dividends (stated dollar amount per share or percentage of par value per share) and (b) to distribution of assets in the event the corporation is dissolved.

Premium arises when bonds are sold for more than face amount.

Prepaid expense represents an asset recorded when an expense is paid in advance, creating benefits beyond the current period.

Prepayments/deferrals the cash flow precedes either expense or revenue recognition.

Principal controls goods or services and is responsible for providing them to the customer.

Present value today's equivalent to a particular amount in the future.

Prior period adjustment addition to or reduction in the beginning retained earnings balance in a statement of shareholders' equity due to a correction of an error.

Prior service cost the cost of credit given for an amendment to a pension plan to employee service rendered in prior years.

Product costs costs associated with products and expensed as cost of goods sold only when the related products are sold.

Profit margin on sales net income divided by net sales; measures the amount of net income achieved per sales dollar.

Pro forma earnings actual (GAAP) earnings reduced by any expenses the reporting company feels are unusual and should be excluded.

Projected benefit obligation (PBO) the discounted present value of estimated retirement benefits earned so far by employees, applying the plan's pension formula using projected future compensation levels.

Property dividend when a noncash asset is distributed.

Property, plant, and equipment land, buildings, equipment, machinery, autos, and trucks.

Prospective approach the accounting change is implemented in the present, and its effects are reflected in the financial statements of the current and future years only.

Proxy statement contains disclosures on compensation to directors and executives; sent to all shareholders each year.

Purchase commitments contracts that obligate a company to purchase a specified amount of merchandise or raw materials at specified prices on or before specified dates.

Purchase discounts reductions in the amount to be paid if remittance is made within a designated period of time.

Purchase option a provision of some lease contracts that gives the lessee the option of purchasing the leased property during, or at the end of, the lease term at a specified price.

Purchase return a reduction in both inventory and accounts payable (if the account has not yet been paid) at the time of the return.

Purchases journal records the purchase of merchandise on account.

Quality-assurance warranty obligation by the seller to make repairs or replace products that are later demonstrated to be defective for some period of time after the sale.

Quasi reorganization a firm undergoing financial difficulties, but with favorable future prospects, may use a quasi reorganization to write down inflated asset values and eliminate an accumulated deficit.

Rate of return on stock investment

$$\frac{\text{Dividends} + \text{Share price appreciation}}{\text{Initial investment}}$$

Ratio analysis comparison of accounting numbers to evaluate the performance and risk of a firm.

Raw materials cost of components purchased from other manufacturers that will become part of the finished product.

Real estate lease involves land—exclusively or in part.

Rearrangements expenditures made to restructure an asset without addition, replacement, or improvement.

Reasonably assured to be entitled seller's experience indicates that it will be entitled to receive an amount of uncertain consideration.

Receivables a company's claims to the future collection of cash, other assets, or services.

Receivables turnover ratio indicates how quickly a company is able to collect its accounts receivable.

Recognition process of admitting information into the basic financial statements.

Redemption privilege might allow preferred shareholders the option, under specified conditions, to return their shares for a predetermined redemption price.

Related-party transactions transactions with owners, management, families of owners or management, affiliated companies, and other parties that can significantly influence or be influenced by the company.

Relevance one of the primary decision-specific qualities that make accounting information useful; made up of predictive value and/or feedback value, and timeliness.

Reliability the extent to which information is verifiable, representationally faithful, and neutral.

Remeasurement gains gains from changes in pension assumptions or actual return on plan assets exceeding the interest rate.

Remeasurement losses losses from changes in pension assumptions or actual return on plan assets being less than the interest rate.

Rent abatement lease agreements may call for uneven rent payments during the term of the lease, e.g., when the initial payment (or maybe several payments) is waived.

Replacement cost (RC) the cost to replace the item by purchase or manufacture.

Replacement depreciation method depreciation is recorded when assets are replaced.

Representational faithfulness agreement between a measure or description and the phenomenon it purports to represent.

Residual asset the carrying amount of a leased asset not transferred to the lessee.

Residual value or salvage value, the amount the company expects to receive for the asset at the end of its service life less any anticipated disposal costs.

Restoration costs costs to restore land or other property to its original condition after extraction of the natural resource ends.

Restricted stock shares subject to forfeiture by the employee if employment is terminated within some specified number of years from the date of grant.

Retail inventory method relies on the relationship between cost and selling price to estimate ending inventory and cost of goods sold; provides a more accurate estimate than the gross profit method.

Retained earnings amounts earned by the corporation on behalf of its shareholders and not (yet) distributed to them as dividends.

Retired stock shares repurchased and not designated as treasury stock.

Retirement depreciation method records depreciation when assets are disposed of and measures depreciation as the difference between the proceeds received and cost.

Retrospective approach financial statements issued in previous years are revised to reflect the impact of an accounting change whenever those statements are presented again for comparative purpose.

Return on assets (ROA) indicates a company's overall profitability.

Return on shareholders' equity (ROE) amount of profit management can generate from the assets that owners provide.

Revenues inflows or other enhancements of assets or settlements of liabilities from delivering or producing goods, rendering services, or other activities that constitute the entity's ongoing major, or central, operations.

Reverse stock split when a company decreases, rather than increases, its outstanding shares.

Reversing entries optional entries that remove the effects of some of the adjusting entries made at the end of the previous reporting period for the sole purpose of simplifying journal entries made during the new period.

Right of conversion shareholders' right to exchange shares of preferred stock for common stock at specified conversion ratio.

Right of return customers' right to return merchandise to retailers if they are not satisfied.

Right-of-use asset the right to use an asset for a specified period of time.

Rules-based accounting standards a list of rules for choosing the appropriate accounting treatment for a transaction.

S corporation characteristics of both regular corporations and partnerships.

SAB No. 101 *Staff Accounting Bulletin 101 summarizes* the SEC's views on revenue recognition.

Sale-leaseback transaction the owner of an asset sells it and immediately leases it back from the new owner.

Sales journal records credit sales.

Sales return the return of merchandise for a refund or for credit to be applied to other purchases.

Sales-type lease in addition to interest revenue earned over the lease term, the lessor receives a manufacturer's or dealer's profit on the sale of the asset.

Sarbanes-Oxley Act law provides for the regulation of the key players in the financial reporting process.

Secondary market transactions provide for the transfer of stocks and bonds among individuals and institutions.

Securities and Exchange Commission (SEC) responsible for setting accounting and reporting standards for companies whose securities are publicly traded.

Securities available-for-sale equity or debt securities the investor acquires, not for an active trading account or to be held to maturity.

Securities to be held-to-maturity debt securities for which the investor has the "positive intent and ability" to hold the securities to maturity.

Securitization the company creates a special purpose entity (SPE), usually a trust or a subsidiary; the SPE buys a pool of trade receivables, credit card receivables, or loans from the company and then sells related securities.

Separation of duties an internal control technique in which various functions are distributed amongst employees to provide cross-checking that encourages accuracy and discourages fraud.

Serial bonds more structured (and less popular) way to retire bonds on a piecemeal basis.

Service cost increase in the projected benefit obligation attributable to employee service performed during the period.

Service life (useful life) the estimated use that the company expects to receive from the asset.

Service method allocation approach that reflects the declining service pattern of the prior service cost.

Share purchase contract shares ordinarily are sold in exchange for a promissory note from the subscriber-in essence, shares are sold on credit.

Short-term investments investments not classified as cash equivalents that will be liquidated in the coming year or operating cycle, whichever is longer.

Significant influence effective control is absent but the investor is able to exercise significant influence over the operating and financial policies of the investee (usually between 20% and 50% of the investee's voting shares are held).

Simple capital structure a firm that has no potential common shares (outstanding securities that could potentially dilute earnings per share).

Simple debt (1) involves a lender providing an amount up front that eventually must be repaid, (2) doesn't permit the borrower to prepay or settle the debt unless the lender allows it, and (3) is not a derivative.

Simple interest computed by multiplying an initial investment times both the applicable interest rate and the period of time for which the money is used.

Single-step income statement format that groups all revenues and gains together and all expenses and losses together.

Sinking fund debentures bonds that must be redeemed on a prespecified year-by-year basis; administered by a trustee who repurchases bonds in the open market.

Source documents relay essential information about each transaction to the accountant, e.g., sales invoices, bills from suppliers, cash register tapes.

Special journal record of a repetitive type of transaction, e.g., a sales journal.

Specific identification method each unit sold during the period or each unit on hand at the end of the period to be matched with its actual cost.

Specific interest method for interest capitalization, rates from specific construction loans to the extent of specific borrowings are used before using the average rate of other debt.

Stand-alone selling price the amount at which the good or service is sold separately under similar circumstances.

Start-up costs whenever a company introduces a new product or service, or commences business in a new territory or with a new customer, it incurs one-time costs that are expensed in the period incurred.

Statement of cash flows change statement summarizing the transactions that caused cash to change during the period.

Statement of shareholders' equity statement disclosing the source of changes in the shareholders' equity accounts.

Stock appreciation rights (SARs) awards that enable an employee to benefit by the amount that the market price of the company's stock rises above a specified amount without having to buy shares.

Stock dividend distribution of additional shares of stock to current shareholders of the corporation.

Stock options employees aren't actually awarded shares, but rather are given the option to buy shares at a specified exercise price within some specified number of years from the date of grant.

Stock split stock distribution of 25% or higher, sometimes called a *large* stock dividend.

Straight line an equal amount of depreciable base is allocated to each year of the asset's service life.

Straight-line method recording interest each period at the same dollar amount.

Subordinated debenture the holder is not entitled to receive any liquidation payments until the claims of other specified debt issues are satisfied.

Subsequent event a significant development that takes place after the company's fiscal year-end but before the financial statements are issued.

Subsidiary ledger record of a group of subsidiary accounts associated with a particular general ledger control account.

Successful efforts method requires that exploration costs that are known not to have resulted in the discovery of oil or gas be included as expense in the period the expenditures are made.

Sum-of-the-years'-digits (SYD) method systematic acceleration of depreciation by multiplying the depreciable base by a fraction that declines each year.

Supplemental financial statements reports containing more detailed information than is shown in the primary financial statements.

T-account account with space at the top for the account title and two sides for recording increases and decreases.

Tax basis of an asset or liability is its original value for tax purposes reduced by any amounts included to date on tax returns.

Taxable income comprises revenues, expenses, gains, and losses as measured according to the regulations of the appropriate taxing authority.

Technological feasibility established when the enterprise has completed all planning, designing, coding, and testing activities that are necessary to establish that the product can be produced to meet its design specifications including functions, features, and technical performance requirements.

Temporary accounts represent changes in the retained earnings component of shareholders' equity for a corporation caused by revenue, expense, gain, and loss transactions.

Temporary difference difference between pretax accounting income and taxable income and, consequently, between the reported amount of an asset or liability in the financial statements and its tax basis which will "reverse" in later years.

Time-based methods allocates the cost base according to the passage of time.

Timeliness information that is available to users early enough to allow its use in the decision process.

Times interest earned ratio a way to gauge the ability of a company to satisfy its fixed debt obligations by comparing interest charges with the income available to pay those charges.

Time value of money money can be invested today to earn interest and grow to a larger dollar amount in the future.

Trade discounts percentage reduction from the list price.

Trademark (tradename) exclusive right to display a word, a slogan, a symbol, or an emblem that distinctively identifies a company, a product, or a service.

Trade notes payable formally recognized by a written promissory note.

Trading securities equity or debt securities the investor (usually a financial institution) acquires principally for the purpose of selling in the near term.

Transaction analysis process of reviewing the source documents to determine the dual effect on the accounting equation and the specific elements involved.

Transaction obligation the unfunded accumulated postretirement benefit obligation existing when *SFAS 106* was adopted.

Transaction price the amount the seller expects to be entitled to receive from the customer in exchange for providing goods and services.

Transactions economic events.

Treasury stock shares repurchased and not retired.

Troubled debt restructuring the original terms of a debt agreement are changed as a result of financial difficulties experienced by the debtor (borrower).

Trustee person who accepts employer contributions, invests the contributions, accumulates the earnings on the investments, and pays benefits from the plan assets to retired employees or their beneficiaries.

Unadjusted trial balance a list of the general ledger accounts and their balances at a particular date.

Understandability users must understand the information within the context of the decision being made.

Unearned revenues cash received from a customer in one period for goods or services that are to be provided in a future period.

Units-of-production method computes a depreciation rate per measure of activity and then multiplies this rate by actual activity to determine periodic depreciation.

Unqualified opinion auditors are satisfied that the financial statements present fairly the company's financial position, results of operations, and cash flows and are in conformity with generally accepted accounting principles.

Variable consideration transaction price is uncertain because some of the price is to be paid to the seller depending on the outcome of future events.

Valuation allowance indirect reduction (contra account) in a deferred tax asset when it is more likely than not that some portion or all of the deferred tax asset will not be realized.

Verifiability implies a consensus among different measurers.

Vertical analysis expression of each item in the financial statements as a percentage of an appropriate corresponding total, or base amount, but within the same year.

Vested benefits benefits that employees have the right to receive even if their employment were to cease today.

Weighted-average interest method for interest capitalization, weighted-average rate on all interest-bearing debt, including all construction loans, is used.

Without recourse the buyer assumes the risk of bad debts.

With recourse the seller retains the risk of uncollectibility.

Working capital differences between current assets and current liabilities.

Work-in-process inventory products that are not yet complete.

Worksheet used to organize the accounting information needed to prepare adjusting and closing entries and the financial statements.

Photo Credits

Image researcher: Editorial Image, LLC

Chapter 1
Page 3: © Lev Dolgachov/Syda Productions/AGE Fotostock.

Chapter 2
Page 51: © Image Source/Getty Images.

Chapter 3
Page 113: © James Woodson/Digital Vision/Getty Images.

Chapter 4
Page 171: © Onoky/SuperStock.

Chapter 5
Page 231: © Hero Images/Getty Images.

Chapter 6
Page 323: © Jay Paul/Bloomberg via Getty Images.

Chapter 7
Page 361: © Cultura Creative/Alamy.

Chapter 8
Page 425: © John Anthony Rizzo/Getty Images.

Chapter 9
Page 479: © PRNewsFoto/Sears, Roebuck and Co./AP Images.

Chapter 10
Page 527: © Preston Mack/Disney Parks via Getty Images.

Chapter 11
Page 587: © fStop/Getty Images.

Chapter 12
Page 655: © Paul Sakuma/AP Images.

Chapter 13
Page 731: © mediaphotos/Getty Images.

Chapter 14
Page 789: © Klaus Vedfelt/Getty Images.

Chapter 15
Page 853: © Blend Images/Alamy.

Chapter 16
Page 933: © Image Source.

Chapter 17
Page 997: © Stockbyte/PunchStock.

Chapter 18
Page 1067: © Andrew Harrer/Bloomberg via Getty Images.

Chapter 19
Page 1127: © Comstock/PunchStock.

Chapter 20
Page 1195: © Richard Levine/Alamy.

Chapter 21
Page 1243: © E. Audras/PhotoAlto.

Text Credits

Chapter 1
Page 48: © Air France.

Chapter 3
Page 168: © Air France.

Chapter 4
Page 219: © Kaplan, Inc.; p. 231: © Air France.

Chapter 5
Page 305: © Air France; p. 321 © Institute of Management Accountants, Inc.

Chapter 7
Page 416: Sam Antar, "Is Green Mountain Coffee Roasters Shuffling the Beans to Beat Earnings Expectations?" Phil's Stock World delivered by Newstex, May 9, 2011. © 2011 by Sam Antar. All rights reserved. Used with permission; p. 425: © Air France.

Chapter 8
Page 478: © Air France.

Chapter 9
Page 527: © Air France.

Chapter 10
Page 586: © Air France.

Chapter 11
Page 653: © Air France.

Chapter 12
Page 730: © Air France.

Chapter 13
Page 788: © Air France; p. 791: Michael J. Moore, Joel Rosenblatt, and Patricia Hurtado, "JPMorgan Joins Morgan Stanley in Settling U.S. Mortgage Lawsuits," *Bloomberg,* February 5, 2014. © 2014 by Bloomberg. All rights reserved. Used with permission.

Chapter 14
Page 851: © Air France.

Chapter 15
Page 918: © Air France.

Chapter 16
Page 996: © Air France.

Chapter 17
Page 1066: © Air France.

Chapter 18
Page 1106: Seth Fiegerman, "Why Some Big Tech Companies Still Split Their Stocks," Mashable.com, June 9, 2014; p. 1126: © Air France; p. 1131: "Dolby's IPO expected to play sweet music," AP news report, Feb. 14, 2005. © 2005 The Associated Press. All rights reserved. Used with permission; p. 1133: © Alcoa Inc. Used with permission.

Subject Index

Note: Page numbers followed by *n* indicate material in footnotes. General information about standards and standart-setting organizations may be found in this index. Specific standards and pronouncements are listed in the Accounting Standards Index.

C

D

N

Q

U

Accounting Standards Index

Notes: Page numbers followed by *n* indicate material in footnotes. Specific standards and pronouncements are found in this index; general information about standards and standard-setting organizations is found in the Subject Index. Unless otherwise noted, standards will be found under the name of the issuing organization.

Present and Future Value Tables

This table shows the future value of $1 at various interest rates (i) and time periods (n). It is used to calculate the future value of any single amount.

TABLE 1 Future Value of $1

$FV = \$1\,(1 + i)^n$

n/i	1.0%	1.5%	2.0%	2.5%	3.0%	3.5%	4.0%	4.5%	5.0%	5.5%	6.0%	7.0%	8.0%	9.0%	10.0%	11.0%	12.0%	20.0%
1	1.01000	1.01500	1.02000	1.02500	1.03000	1.03500	1.04000	1.04500	1.05000	1.05500	1.06000	1.07000	1.08000	1.09000	1.10000	1.11000	1.12000	1.20000
2	1.02010	1.03022	1.04040	1.05063	1.06090	1.07123	1.08160	1.09203	1.10250	1.11303	1.12360	1.14490	1.16640	1.18810	1.21000	1.23210	1.25440	1.44000
3	1.03030	1.04568	1.06121	1.07689	1.09273	1.10872	1.12486	1.14117	1.15763	1.17424	1.19102	1.22504	1.25971	1.29503	1.33100	1.36763	1.40493	1.72800
4	1.04060	1.06136	1.08243	1.10381	1.12551	1.14752	1.16986	1.19252	1.21551	1.23882	1.26248	1.31080	1.36049	1.41158	1.46410	1.51807	1.57352	2.07360
5	1.05101	1.07728	1.10408	1.13141	1.15927	1.18769	1.21665	1.24618	1.27628	1.30696	1.33823	1.40255	1.46933	1.53862	1.61051	1.68506	1.76234	2.48832
6	1.06152	1.09344	1.12616	1.15969	1.19405	1.22926	1.26532	1.30226	1.34010	1.37884	1.41852	1.50073	1.58687	1.67710	1.77156	1.87041	1.97382	2.98598
7	1.07214	1.10984	1.14869	1.18869	1.22987	1.27228	1.31593	1.36086	1.40710	1.45468	1.50363	1.60578	1.71382	1.82804	1.94872	2.07616	2.21068	3.58318
8	1.08286	1.12649	1.17166	1.21840	1.26677	1.31681	1.36857	1.42210	1.47746	1.53469	1.59385	1.71819	1.85093	1.99256	2.14359	2.30454	2.47596	4.29982
9	1.09369	1.14339	1.19509	1.24886	1.30477	1.36290	1.42331	1.48610	1.55133	1.61909	1.68948	1.83846	1.99900	2.17189	2.35795	2.55804	2.77308	5.15978
10	1.10462	1.16054	1.21899	1.28008	1.34392	1.41060	1.48024	1.55297	1.62889	1.70814	1.79085	1.96715	2.15892	2.36736	2.59374	2.83942	3.10585	6.19174
11	1.11567	1.17795	1.24337	1.31209	1.38423	1.45997	1.53945	1.62285	1.71034	1.80209	1.89830	2.10485	2.33164	2.58043	2.85312	3.15176	3.47855	7.43008
12	1.12683	1.19562	1.26824	1.34489	1.42576	1.51107	1.60103	1.69588	1.79586	1.90121	2.01220	2.25219	2.51817	2.81266	3.13843	3.49845	3.89598	8.91610
13	1.13809	1.21355	1.29361	1.37851	1.46853	1.56396	1.66507	1.77220	1.88565	2.00577	2.13293	2.40985	2.71962	3.06580	3.45227	3.88328	4.36349	10.69932
14	1.14947	1.23176	1.31948	1.41297	1.51259	1.61869	1.73168	1.85194	1.97993	2.11609	2.26090	2.57853	2.93719	3.34173	3.79750	4.31044	4.88711	12.83918
15	1.16097	1.25023	1.34587	1.44830	1.55797	1.67535	1.80094	1.93528	2.07893	2.23248	2.39656	2.75903	3.17217	3.64248	4.17725	4.78459	5.47357	15.40702
16	1.17258	1.26899	1.37279	1.48451	1.60471	1.73399	1.87298	2.02237	2.18287	2.35526	2.54035	2.95216	3.42594	3.97031	4.59497	5.31089	6.13039	18.48843
17	1.18430	1.28802	1.40024	1.52162	1.65285	1.79468	1.94790	2.11338	2.29202	2.48480	2.69277	3.15882	3.70002	4.32763	5.05447	5.89509	6.86604	22.18611
18	1.19615	1.30734	1.42825	1.55966	1.70243	1.85749	2.02582	2.20848	2.40662	2.62147	2.85434	3.37993	3.99602	4.71712	5.55992	6.54355	7.68997	26.62333
19	1.20811	1.32695	1.45681	1.59865	1.75351	1.92250	2.10685	2.30786	2.52695	2.76565	3.02560	3.61653	4.31570	5.14166	6.11591	7.26334	8.61276	31.94800
20	1.22019	1.34686	1.48595	1.63862	1.80611	1.98979	2.19112	2.41171	2.65330	2.91776	3.20714	3.86968	4.66096	5.60441	6.72750	8.06231	9.64629	38.33760
21	1.23239	1.36706	1.51567	1.67958	1.86029	2.05943	2.27877	2.52024	2.78596	3.07823	3.39956	4.14056	5.03383	6.10881	7.40025	8.94917	10.80385	46.00512
25	1.28243	1.45095	1.64061	1.85394	2.09378	2.36324	2.66584	3.00543	3.38635	3.81339	4.29187	5.42743	6.84848	8.62308	10.83471	13.58546	17.00006	95.39622
30	1.34785	1.56308	1.81136	2.09757	2.42726	2.80679	3.24340	3.74532	4.32194	4.98395	5.74349	7.61226	10.06266	13.26768	17.44940	22.89230	29.95992	237.37631
40	1.48886	1.81402	2.20804	2.68506	3.26204	3.95926	4.80102	5.81636	7.03999	8.51331	10.28572	14.97446	21.72452	31.40942	45.25926	65.00087	93.05097	1469.77160

This table shows the present value of $1 at various interest rates (i) and time periods (n). It is used to calculate the present value of any single amount.

TABLE 2 Present Value of $1

$$PV = \frac{\$1}{(1+i)^n}$$

n/i	1.0%	1.5%	2.0%	2.5%	3.0%	3.5%	4.0%	4.5%	5.0%	5.5%	6.0%	7.0%	8.0%	9.0%	10.0%	11.0%	12.0%	20.0%
1	0.99010	0.98522	0.98039	0.97561	0.97087	0.96618	0.96154	0.95694	0.95238	0.94787	0.94340	0.93458	0.92593	0.91743	0.90909	0.90090	0.89286	0.83333
2	0.98030	0.97066	0.96117	0.95181	0.94260	0.93351	0.92456	0.91573	0.90703	0.89845	0.89000	0.87344	0.85734	0.84168	0.82645	0.81162	0.79719	0.69444
3	0.97059	0.95632	0.94232	0.92860	0.91514	0.90194	0.88900	0.87630	0.86384	0.85161	0.83962	0.81630	0.79383	0.77218	0.75131	0.73119	0.71178	0.57870
4	0.96098	0.94218	0.92385	0.90595	0.88849	0.87144	0.85480	0.83856	0.82270	0.80722	0.79209	0.76290	0.73503	0.70843	0.68301	0.65873	0.63552	0.48225
5	0.95147	0.92826	0.90573	0.88385	0.86261	0.84197	0.82193	0.80245	0.78353	0.76513	0.74726	0.71299	0.68058	0.64993	0.62092	0.59345	0.56743	0.40188
6	0.94205	0.91454	0.88797	0.86230	0.83748	0.81350	0.79031	0.76790	0.74622	0.72525	0.70496	0.66634	0.63017	0.59627	0.56447	0.53464	0.50663	0.33490
7	0.93272	0.90103	0.87056	0.84127	0.81309	0.78599	0.75992	0.73483	0.71068	0.68744	0.66506	0.62275	0.58349	0.54703	0.51316	0.48166	0.45235	0.27908
8	0.92348	0.88771	0.85349	0.82075	0.78941	0.75941	0.73069	0.70319	0.67684	0.65160	0.62741	0.58201	0.54027	0.50187	0.46651	0.43393	0.40388	0.23257
9	0.91434	0.87459	0.83676	0.80073	0.76642	0.73373	0.70259	0.67290	0.64461	0.61763	0.59190	0.54393	0.50025	0.46043	0.42410	0.39092	0.36061	0.19381
10	0.90529	0.86167	0.82035	0.78120	0.74409	0.70892	0.67556	0.64393	0.61391	0.58543	0.55839	0.50835	0.46319	0.42241	0.38554	0.35218	0.32197	0.16151
11	0.89632	0.84893	0.80426	0.76214	0.72242	0.68495	0.64958	0.61620	0.58468	0.55491	0.52679	0.47509	0.42888	0.38753	0.35049	0.31728	0.28748	0.13459
12	0.88745	0.83639	0.78849	0.74356	0.70138	0.66178	0.62460	0.58966	0.55684	0.52598	0.49697	0.44401	0.39711	0.35553	0.31863	0.28584	0.25668	0.11216
13	0.87866	0.82403	0.77303	0.72542	0.68095	0.63940	0.60057	0.56427	0.53032	0.49856	0.46884	0.41496	0.36770	0.32618	0.28966	0.25751	0.22917	0.09346
14	0.86996	0.81185	0.75788	0.70773	0.66112	0.61778	0.57748	0.53997	0.50507	0.47257	0.44230	0.38782	0.34046	0.29925	0.26333	0.23199	0.20462	0.07789
15	0.86135	0.79985	0.74301	0.69047	0.64186	0.59689	0.55526	0.51672	0.48102	0.44793	0.41727	0.36245	0.31524	0.27454	0.23939	0.20900	0.18270	0.06491
16	0.85282	0.78803	0.72845	0.67362	0.62317	0.57671	0.53391	0.49447	0.45811	0.42458	0.39365	0.33873	0.29189	0.25187	0.21763	0.18829	0.16312	0.05409
17	0.84438	0.77639	0.71416	0.65720	0.60502	0.55720	0.51337	0.47318	0.43630	0.40245	0.37136	0.31657	0.27027	0.23107	0.19784	0.16963	0.14564	0.04507
18	0.83602	0.76491	0.70016	0.64117	0.58739	0.53836	0.49363	0.45280	0.41552	0.38147	0.35034	0.29586	0.25025	0.21199	0.17986	0.15282	0.13004	0.03756
19	0.82774	0.75361	0.68643	0.62553	0.57029	0.52016	0.47464	0.43330	0.39573	0.36158	0.33051	0.27651	0.23171	0.19449	0.16351	0.13768	0.11611	0.03130
20	0.81954	0.74247	0.67297	0.61027	0.55368	0.50257	0.45639	0.41464	0.37689	0.34273	0.31180	0.25842	0.21455	0.17843	0.14864	0.12403	0.10367	0.02608
21	0.81143	0.73150	0.65978	0.59539	0.53755	0.48557	0.43883	0.39679	0.35894	0.32486	0.29416	0.24151	0.19866	0.16370	0.13513	0.11174	0.09256	0.02174
24	0.78757	0.69954	0.62172	0.55288	0.49193	0.43796	0.39012	0.34770	0.31007	0.27666	0.24698	0.19715	0.15770	0.12640	0.10153	0.08170	0.06588	0.01258
25	0.77977	0.68921	0.60953	0.53939	0.47761	0.42315	0.37512	0.33273	0.29530	0.26223	0.23300	0.18425	0.14602	0.11597	0.09230	0.07361	0.05882	0.01048
28	0.75684	0.65910	0.57437	0.50088	0.43708	0.38165	0.33348	0.29157	0.25509	0.22332	0.19563	0.15040	0.11591	0.08955	0.06934	0.05382	0.04187	0.00607
29	0.74934	0.64936	0.56311	0.48866	0.42435	0.36875	0.32065	0.27902	0.24295	0.21168	0.18456	0.14056	0.10733	0.08215	0.06304	0.04849	0.03738	0.00506
30	0.74192	0.63976	0.55207	0.47674	0.41199	0.35628	0.30832	0.26700	0.23138	0.20064	0.17411	0.13137	0.09938	0.07537	0.05731	0.04368	0.03338	0.00421
31	0.73458	0.63031	0.54125	0.46511	0.39999	0.34423	0.29646	0.25550	0.22036	0.19018	0.16425	0.12277	0.09202	0.06915	0.05210	0.03935	0.02980	0.00351
40	0.67165	0.55126	0.45289	0.37243	0.30656	0.25257	0.20829	0.17193	0.14205	0.11746	0.09722	0.06678	0.04603	0.03184	0.02209	0.01538	0.01075	0.00068

This table shows the future value of an ordinary annuity of $1 at various interest rates (i) and time periods (n). It is used to calculate the future value of any series of equal payments made at the *end* of each compounding period.

TABLE 3 Future Value of an Ordinary Annuity of $1

$$FVA = \frac{(1+i)^n - 1}{i}$$

n/i	1.0%	1.5%	2.0%	2.5%	3.0%	3.5%	4.0%	4.5%	5.0%	5.5%	6.0%	7.0%	8.0%	9.0%	10.0%	11.0%	12.0%	20.0%
1	1.0000	1.0000	1.0000	1.0000	1.0000	1.0000	1.0000	1.0000	1.0000	1.0000	1.0000	1.0000	1.0000	1.0000	1.0000	1.0000	1.0000	1.0000
2	2.0100	2.0150	2.0200	2.0250	2.0300	2.0350	2.0400	2.0450	2.0500	2.0550	2.0600	2.0700	2.0800	2.0900	2.1000	2.1100	2.1200	2.2000
3	3.0301	3.0452	3.0604	3.0756	3.0909	3.1062	3.1216	3.1370	3.1525	3.1680	3.1836	3.2149	3.2464	3.2781	3.3100	3.3421	3.3744	3.6400
4	4.0604	4.0909	4.1216	4.1525	4.1836	4.2149	4.2465	4.2782	4.3101	4.3423	4.3746	4.4399	4.5061	4.5731	4.6410	4.7097	4.7793	5.3680
5	5.1010	5.1523	5.2040	5.2563	5.3091	5.3625	5.4163	5.4707	5.5256	5.5811	5.6371	5.7507	5.8666	5.9847	6.1051	6.2278	6.3528	7.4416
6	6.1520	6.2296	6.3081	6.3877	6.4684	6.5502	6.6330	6.7169	6.8019	6.8881	6.9753	7.1533	7.3359	7.5233	7.7156	7.9129	8.1152	9.9299
7	7.2135	7.3230	7.4343	7.5474	7.6625	7.7794	7.8983	8.0192	8.1420	8.2669	8.3938	8.6540	8.9228	9.2004	9.4872	9.7833	10.0890	12.9159
8	8.2857	8.4328	8.5830	8.7361	8.8923	9.0517	9.2142	9.3800	9.5491	9.7216	9.8975	10.2598	10.6366	11.0285	11.4359	11.8594	12.2997	16.4991
9	9.3685	9.5593	9.7546	9.9545	10.1591	10.3685	10.5828	10.8021	11.0266	11.2563	11.4913	11.9780	12.4876	13.0210	13.5795	14.1640	14.7757	20.7989
10	10.4622	10.7027	10.9497	11.2034	11.4639	11.7314	12.0061	12.2882	12.5779	12.8754	13.1808	13.8164	14.4866	15.1929	15.9374	16.7220	17.5487	25.9587
11	11.5668	11.8633	12.1687	12.4835	12.8078	13.1420	13.4864	13.8412	14.2068	14.5835	14.9716	15.7836	16.6455	17.5603	18.5312	19.5614	20.6546	32.1504
12	12.6825	13.0412	13.4121	13.7956	14.1920	14.6020	15.0258	15.4640	15.9171	16.3856	16.8699	17.8885	18.9771	20.1407	21.3843	22.7132	24.1331	39.5805
13	13.8093	14.2368	14.6803	15.1404	15.6178	16.1130	16.6268	17.1599	17.7130	18.2868	18.8821	20.1406	21.4953	22.9534	24.5227	26.2116	28.0291	48.4966
14	14.9474	15.4504	15.9739	16.5190	17.0863	17.6770	18.2919	18.9321	19.5986	20.2926	21.0151	22.5505	24.2149	26.0192	27.9750	30.0949	32.3926	59.1959
15	16.0969	16.6821	17.2934	17.9319	18.5989	19.2957	20.0236	20.7841	21.5786	22.4087	23.2760	25.1290	27.1521	29.3609	31.7725	34.4054	37.2797	72.0351
16	17.2579	17.9324	18.6393	19.3802	20.1569	20.9710	21.8245	22.7193	23.6575	24.6411	25.6725	27.8881	30.3243	33.0034	35.9497	39.1899	42.7533	87.4421
17	18.4304	19.2014	20.0121	20.8647	21.7616	22.7050	23.6975	24.7417	25.8404	26.9964	28.2129	30.8402	33.7502	36.9737	40.5447	44.5008	48.8837	105.9306
18	19.6147	20.4894	21.4123	22.3863	23.4144	24.4997	25.6454	26.8551	28.1324	29.4812	30.9057	33.9990	37.4502	41.3013	45.5992	50.3959	55.7497	128.1167
19	20.8109	21.7967	22.8406	23.9460	25.1169	26.3572	27.6712	29.0636	30.5390	32.1027	33.7600	37.3790	41.4463	46.0185	51.1591	56.9395	63.4397	154.7400
20	22.0190	23.1237	24.2974	25.5447	26.8704	28.2797	29.7781	31.3714	33.0660	34.8683	36.7856	40.9955	45.7620	51.1601	57.2750	64.2028	72.0524	186.6880
21	23.2392	24.4705	25.7833	27.1833	28.6765	30.2695	31.9692	33.7831	35.7193	37.7861	39.9927	44.8652	50.4229	56.7645	64.0025	72.2651	81.6987	225.0256
30	34.7849	37.5387	40.5681	43.9027	47.5754	51.6227	56.0849	61.0071	66.4388	72.4355	79.0582	94.4608	113.2832	136.3075	164.4940	199.0209	241.3327	1181.8816
40	48.8864	54.2679	60.4020	67.4026	75.4013	84.5503	95.0255	107.0303	120.7998	136.6056	154.7620	199.6351	259.0565	337.8824	442.5926	581.8261	767.0914	7343.8578

This table shows the present value of an ordinary annuity of $1 at various interest rates (i) and time periods (n). It is used to calculate the present value of any series of equal payments made at the *end* of each compounding period.

TABLE 4 Present Value of an Ordinary Annuity of $1

$$PVA = \frac{1 - \frac{1}{(1+i)^n}}{i}$$

n/i	1.0%	1.5%	2.0%	2.5%	3.0%	3.5%	4.0%	4.5%	5.0%	5.5%	6.0%	7.0%	8.0%	9.0%	10.0%	11.0%	12.0%	20.0%
1	0.99010	0.98522	0.98039	0.97561	0.97087	0.96618	0.96154	0.95694	0.95238	0.94787	0.94340	0.93458	0.92593	0.91743	0.90909	0.90090	0.89286	0.83333
2	1.97040	1.95588	1.94156	1.92742	1.91347	1.89969	1.88609	1.87267	1.85941	1.84632	1.83339	1.80802	1.78326	1.75911	1.73554	1.71252	1.69005	1.52778
3	2.94099	2.91220	2.88388	2.85602	2.82861	2.80164	2.77509	2.74896	2.72325	2.69793	2.67301	2.62432	2.57710	2.53129	2.48685	2.44371	2.40183	2.10648
4	3.90197	3.85438	3.80773	3.76197	3.71710	3.67308	3.62990	3.58753	3.54595	3.50515	3.46511	3.38721	3.31213	3.23972	3.16987	3.10245	3.03735	2.58873
5	4.85343	4.78264	4.71346	4.64583	4.57971	4.51505	4.45182	4.38998	4.32948	4.27028	4.21236	4.10020	3.99271	3.88965	3.79079	3.69590	3.60478	2.99061
6	5.79548	5.69719	5.60143	5.50813	5.41719	5.32855	5.24214	5.15787	5.07569	4.99553	4.91732	4.76654	4.62288	4.48592	4.35526	4.23054	4.11141	3.32551
7	6.72819	6.59821	6.47199	6.34939	6.23028	6.11454	6.00205	5.89270	5.78637	5.68297	5.58238	5.38929	5.20637	5.03295	4.86842	4.71220	4.56376	3.60459
8	7.65168	7.48593	7.32548	7.17014	7.01969	6.87396	6.73274	6.59589	6.46321	6.33457	6.20979	5.97130	5.74664	5.53482	5.33493	5.14612	4.96764	3.83716
9	8.56602	8.36052	8.16224	7.97087	7.78611	7.60769	7.43533	7.26879	7.10782	6.95220	6.80169	6.51523	6.24689	5.99525	5.75902	5.53705	5.32825	4.03097
10	9.47130	9.22218	8.98259	8.75206	8.53020	8.31661	8.11090	7.91272	7.72173	7.53763	7.36009	7.02358	6.71008	6.41766	6.14457	5.88923	5.65022	4.19247
11	10.36763	10.07112	9.78685	9.51421	9.25262	9.00155	8.76048	8.52892	8.30641	8.09254	7.88687	7.49867	7.13896	6.80519	6.49506	6.20652	5.93770	4.32706
12	11.25508	10.90751	10.57534	10.25776	9.95400	9.66333	9.38507	9.11858	8.86325	8.61852	8.38384	7.94269	7.53608	7.16073	6.81369	6.49236	6.19437	4.43922
13	12.13374	11.73153	11.34837	10.98319	10.63496	10.30274	9.98565	9.68285	9.39357	9.11708	8.85268	8.35765	7.90378	7.48690	7.10336	6.74987	6.42355	4.53268
14	13.00370	12.54338	12.10625	11.69091	11.29607	10.92052	10.56312	10.22283	9.89864	9.58965	9.29498	8.74547	8.24424	7.78615	7.36669	6.98187	6.62817	4.61057
15	13.86505	13.34323	12.84926	12.38138	11.93794	11.51741	11.11839	10.73955	10.37966	10.03758	9.71225	9.10791	8.55948	8.06069	7.60608	7.19087	6.81086	4.67547
16	14.71787	14.13126	13.57771	13.05500	12.56110	12.09412	11.65230	11.23402	10.83777	10.46216	10.10590	9.44665	8.85137	8.31256	7.82371	7.37916	6.97399	4.72956
17	15.56225	14.90765	14.29187	13.71220	13.16612	12.65132	12.16567	11.70719	11.27407	10.86461	10.47726	9.76322	9.12164	8.54363	8.02155	7.54879	7.11963	4.77463
18	16.39827	15.67256	14.99203	14.35336	13.75351	13.18968	12.65930	12.15999	11.68959	11.24607	10.82760	10.05909	9.37189	8.75563	8.20141	7.70162	7.24967	4.81219
19	17.22601	16.42617	15.67846	14.97889	14.32380	13.70984	13.13394	12.59329	12.08532	11.60765	11.15812	10.33560	9.60360	8.95011	8.36492	7.83929	7.36578	4.84350
20	18.04555	17.16864	16.35143	15.58916	14.87747	14.21240	13.59033	13.00794	12.46221	11.95038	11.46992	10.59401	9.81815	9.12855	8.51356	7.96333	7.46944	4.86958
21	18.85698	17.90014	17.01121	16.18455	15.41502	14.69797	14.02916	13.40472	12.82115	12.27524	11.76408	10.83553	10.01680	9.29224	8.64869	8.07507	7.56200	4.89132
25	22.02316	20.71961	19.52346	18.42438	17.41315	16.48151	15.62208	14.82821	14.09394	13.41393	12.78336	11.65358	10.67478	9.82258	9.07704	8.42174	7.84314	4.94759
30	25.80771	24.01584	22.39646	20.93029	19.60044	18.39205	17.29203	16.28889	15.37245	14.53375	13.76483	12.40904	11.25778	10.27365	9.42691	8.69379	8.05518	4.97894
40	32.83469	29.91585	27.35548	25.10278	23.11477	21.35507	19.79277	18.40158	17.15909	16.04612	15.04630	13.33171	11.92461	10.75736	9.77905	8.95105	8.24378	4.99660

This table shows the future value of an annuity due of $1 at various interest rates (i) and time periods (n). It is used to calculate the future value of any series of equal payments made at the *beginning* of each compounding period.

TABLE 5 Future Value of an Annuity Due of $1

$$FVAD = \left[\frac{(1+i)^n - 1}{i}\right] \times (1+i)$$

n/i	1.0%	1.5%	2.0%	2.5%	3.0%	3.5%	4.0%	4.5%	5.0%	5.5%	6.0%	7.0%	8.0%	9.0%	10.0%	11.0%	12.0%	20.0%
1	1.0100	1.0150	1.0200	1.0250	1.0300	1.0350	1.0400	1.0450	1.0500	1.0550	1.0600	1.0700	1.0800	1.0900	1.1000	1.1100	1.1200	1.2000
2	2.0301	2.0452	2.0604	2.0756	2.0909	2.1062	2.1216	2.1370	2.1525	2.1680	2.1836	2.2149	2.2464	2.2781	2.3100	2.3421	2.3744	2.6400
3	3.0604	3.0909	3.1216	3.1525	3.1836	3.2149	3.2465	3.2782	3.3101	3.3423	3.3746	3.4399	3.5061	3.5731	3.6410	3.7097	3.7793	4.3680
4	4.1010	4.1523	4.2040	4.2563	4.3091	4.3625	4.4163	4.4707	4.5256	4.5811	4.6371	4.7507	4.8666	4.9847	5.1051	5.2278	5.3528	6.4416
5	5.1520	5.2296	5.3081	5.3877	5.4684	5.5502	5.6330	5.7169	5.8019	5.8881	5.9753	6.1533	6.3359	6.5233	6.7156	6.9129	7.1152	8.9299
6	6.2135	6.3230	6.4343	6.5474	6.6625	6.7794	6.8983	7.0192	7.1420	7.2669	7.3938	7.6540	7.9228	8.2004	8.4872	8.7833	9.0890	11.9159
7	7.2857	7.4328	7.5830	7.7361	7.8923	8.0517	8.2142	8.3800	8.5491	8.7216	8.8975	9.2598	9.6366	10.0285	10.4359	10.8594	11.2997	15.4991
8	8.3685	8.5593	8.7546	8.9545	9.1591	9.3685	9.5828	9.8021	10.0266	10.2563	10.4913	10.9780	11.4876	12.0210	12.5795	13.1640	13.7757	19.7989
9	9.4622	9.7027	9.9497	10.2034	10.4639	10.7314	11.0061	11.2882	11.5779	11.8754	12.1808	12.8164	13.4866	14.1929	14.9374	15.7220	16.5487	24.9587
10	10.5668	10.8633	11.1687	11.4835	11.8078	12.1420	12.4864	12.8412	13.2068	13.5835	13.9716	14.7836	15.6455	16.5603	17.5312	18.5614	19.6546	31.1504
11	11.6825	12.0412	12.4121	12.7956	13.1920	13.6020	14.0258	14.4640	14.9171	15.3856	15.8699	16.8885	17.9771	19.1407	20.3843	21.7132	23.1331	38.5805
12	12.8093	13.2368	13.6803	14.1404	14.6178	15.1130	15.6268	16.1599	16.7130	17.2868	17.8821	19.1406	20.4953	21.9534	23.5227	25.2116	27.0291	47.4966
13	13.9474	14.4504	14.9739	15.5190	16.0863	16.6770	17.2919	17.9321	18.5986	19.2926	20.0151	21.5505	23.2149	25.0192	26.9750	29.0949	31.3926	58.1959
14	15.0969	15.6821	16.2934	16.9319	17.5989	18.2957	19.0236	19.7841	20.5786	21.4087	22.2760	24.1290	26.1521	28.3609	30.7725	33.4054	36.2797	71.0351
15	16.2579	16.9324	17.6393	18.3802	19.1569	19.9710	20.8245	21.7193	22.6575	23.6411	24.6725	26.8881	29.3243	32.0034	34.9497	38.1899	41.7533	86.4421
16	17.4304	18.2014	19.0121	19.8647	20.7616	21.7050	22.6975	23.7417	24.8404	25.9964	27.2129	29.8402	32.7502	35.9737	39.5447	43.5008	47.8837	104.9306
17	18.6147	19.4894	20.4123	21.3863	22.4144	23.4997	24.6454	25.8551	27.1324	28.4812	29.9057	32.9990	36.4502	40.3013	44.5992	49.3959	54.7497	127.1167
18	19.8109	20.7967	21.8406	22.9460	24.1169	25.3572	26.6712	28.0636	29.5390	31.1027	32.7600	36.3790	40.4463	45.0185	50.1591	55.9395	62.4397	153.7400
19	21.0190	22.1237	23.2974	24.5447	25.8704	27.2797	28.7781	30.3714	32.0660	33.8683	35.7856	39.9955	44.7620	50.1601	56.2750	63.2028	71.0524	185.6880
20	22.2392	23.4705	24.7833	26.1833	27.6765	29.2695	30.9692	32.7831	34.7193	36.7861	38.9927	43.8652	49.4229	55.7645	63.0025	71.2651	80.6987	224.0256
21	23.4716	24.8376	26.2990	27.8629	29.5368	31.3289	33.2480	35.3034	37.5052	39.8643	42.3923	48.0057	54.4568	61.8733	70.4027	80.2143	91.5026	270.0307
25	28.5256	30.5140	32.6709	35.0117	37.5530	40.3131	43.3117	46.5706	50.1135	53.9660	58.1564	67.6765	78.9544	92.3240	108.1818	126.9988	149.3339	566.3773
30	35.1327	38.1018	41.3794	45.0003	49.0027	53.4295	58.3283	63.7524	69.7608	76.4194	83.8017	101.0730	122.3459	148.5752	180.9434	220.9132	270.2926	1418.2579
40	49.3752	55.0819	61.6100	69.0876	77.6633	87.5095	98.8265	111.8467	126.8398	144.1189	164.0477	213.6096	279.7810	368.2919	486.8518	645.8269	859.1424	8812.6294

This table shows the present value of an annuity due of $1 at various interest rates (i) and time periods (n). It is used to calculate the present value of any series of equal payments made at the *beginning* of each compounding period.

TABLE 6 Present Value of an Annuity Due of $1

$$PVAD = \left[\frac{1 - \frac{1}{(1+i)^n}}{i}\right] \times (1+i)$$

n/i	1.0%	1.5%	2.0%	2.5%	3.0%	3.5%	4.0%	4.5%	5.0%	5.5%	6.0%	7.0%	8.0%	9.0%	10.0%	11.0%	12.0%	20.0%
1	1.00000	1.00000	1.00000	1.00000	1.00000	1.00000	1.00000	1.00000	1.00000	1.00000	1.00000	1.00000	1.00000	1.00000	1.00000	1.00000	1.00000	1.00000
2	1.99010	1.98522	1.98039	1.97561	1.97087	1.96618	1.96154	1.95694	1.95238	1.94787	1.94340	1.93458	1.92593	1.91743	1.90909	1.90090	1.89286	1.83333
3	2.97040	2.95588	2.94156	2.92742	2.91347	2.89969	2.88609	2.87267	2.85941	2.84632	2.83339	2.80802	2.78326	2.75911	2.73554	2.71252	2.69005	2.52778
4	3.94099	3.91220	3.88388	3.85602	3.82861	3.80164	3.77509	3.74896	3.72325	3.69793	3.67301	3.62432	3.57710	3.53129	3.48685	3.44371	3.40183	3.10648
5	4.90197	4.85438	4.80773	4.76197	4.71710	4.67308	4.62990	4.58753	4.54595	4.50515	4.46511	4.38721	4.31213	4.23972	4.16987	4.10245	4.03735	3.58873
6	5.85343	5.78264	5.71346	5.64583	5.57971	5.51505	5.45182	5.38998	5.32948	5.27028	5.21236	5.10020	4.99271	4.88965	4.79079	4.69590	4.60478	3.99061
7	6.79548	6.69719	6.60143	6.50813	6.41719	6.32855	6.24214	6.15787	6.07569	5.99553	5.91732	5.76654	5.62288	5.48592	5.35526	5.23054	5.11141	4.32551
8	7.72819	7.59821	7.47199	7.34939	7.23028	7.11454	7.00205	6.89270	6.78637	6.68297	6.58238	6.38929	6.20637	6.03295	5.86842	5.71220	5.56376	4.60459
9	8.65168	8.48593	8.32548	8.17014	8.01969	7.87396	7.73274	7.59589	7.46321	7.33457	7.20979	6.97130	6.74664	6.53482	6.33493	6.14612	5.96764	4.83716
10	9.56602	9.36052	9.16224	8.97087	8.78611	8.60769	8.43533	8.26879	8.10782	7.95220	7.80169	7.51523	7.24689	6.99525	6.75902	6.53705	6.32825	5.03097
11	10.47130	10.22218	9.98259	9.75206	9.53020	9.31661	9.11090	8.91272	8.72173	8.53763	8.36009	8.02358	7.71008	7.41766	7.14457	6.88923	6.65022	5.19247
12	11.36763	11.07112	10.78685	10.51421	10.25262	10.00155	9.76048	9.52892	9.30641	9.09254	8.88687	8.49867	8.13896	7.80519	7.49506	7.20652	6.93770	5.32706
13	12.25508	11.90751	11.57534	11.25776	10.95400	10.66333	10.38507	10.11858	9.86325	9.61852	9.38384	8.94269	8.53608	8.16073	7.81369	7.49236	7.19437	5.43922
14	13.13374	12.73153	12.34837	11.98318	11.63496	11.30274	10.98565	10.68285	10.39357	10.11708	9.85268	9.35765	8.90378	8.48690	8.10336	7.74987	7.42355	5.53268
15	14.00370	13.54338	13.10625	12.69091	12.29607	11.92052	11.56312	11.22283	10.89864	10.58965	10.29498	9.74547	9.24424	8.78615	8.36669	7.98187	7.62817	5.61057
16	14.86505	14.34323	13.84926	13.38138	12.93794	12.51741	12.11839	11.73955	11.37966	11.03758	10.71225	10.10791	9.55948	9.06069	8.60608	8.19087	7.81086	5.67547
17	15.71787	15.13126	14.57771	14.05500	13.56110	13.09412	12.65230	12.23402	11.83777	11.46216	11.10590	10.44665	9.85137	9.31256	8.82371	8.37916	7.97399	5.72956
18	16.56225	15.90765	15.29187	14.71220	14.16612	13.65132	13.16567	12.70719	12.27407	11.86461	11.47726	10.76322	10.12164	9.54363	9.02155	8.54879	8.11963	5.77463
19	17.39827	16.67256	15.99203	15.35336	14.75351	14.18968	13.65930	13.15999	12.68959	12.24607	11.82760	11.05909	10.37189	9.75563	9.20141	8.70162	8.24967	5.81219
20	18.22601	17.42617	16.67846	15.97889	15.32380	14.70984	14.13394	13.59329	13.08532	12.60765	12.15812	11.33560	10.60360	9.95011	9.36492	8.83929	8.36578	5.84350
21	19.04555	18.16864	17.35143	16.58916	15.87747	15.21240	14.59033	14.00794	13.46221	12.95038	12.46992	11.59401	10.81815	10.12855	9.51356	8.96333	8.46944	5.86958
25	22.24339	21.03041	19.91393	18.88499	17.93554	17.05837	16.24696	15.49548	14.79864	14.15170	13.55036	12.46933	11.52876	10.70661	9.98474	9.34814	8.78432	5.93710
30	26.06579	24.37608	22.84438	21.45355	20.18845	19.03577	17.98371	17.02189	16.14107	15.33310	14.59072	13.27767	12.15841	11.19828	10.36961	9.65011	9.02181	5.97472
40	33.16303	30.36458	27.90259	25.73034	23.80822	22.10250	20.58448	19.22966	18.01704	16.92866	15.94907	14.26493	12.87858	11.72552	10.75696	9.93567	9.23303	5.99592

Contents

5.5 Consolidated financial statements

5.6 Notes to the consolidated financial statements

5.5 Consolidated financial statements

Financial year ended December 31, 2013

5.5.1 Consolidated income statement

Period from January 1 to December 31 *(In € million)*	**Notes**	**2013**	**2012 Pro forma***
Sales	*6*	*25,520*	*25,423*
Other revenues		10	16
Revenues		*25,530*	*25,439*
External expenses	7	(15,997)	(16,272)
Salaries and related costs	8	(7,482)	(7,662)
Taxes other than income taxes		(186)	(184)
Amortization	9	(1,566)	(1,576)
Depreciation and provisions	9	(159)	(154)
Other income and expenses	10	(10)	73
Income from current operations		*130*	*(336)*
Sales of aircraft equipment	11	(12)	8
Other non-current income and expenses	11	(345)	(403)
Income from operating activities		*(227)*	*(731)*
Cost of financial debt		(481)	(436)
Income from cash and cash equivalents		77	83
Net cost of financial debt	*12*	*(404)*	*(353)*
Other financial income and expenses	12	103	144
Income before tax		*(528)*	*(940)*
Income taxes	13	(957)	(17)
Net income of consolidated companies		*(1,485)*	*(957)*
Share of profits (losses) of associates	22	(211)	(66)
Net income from continuing operations		*(1,696)*	*(1,023)*
Net income from discontinued operations	14	(122)	(197)
Net income for the period		*(1,818)*	*(1,220)*
Equity holders of Air France-KLM		*(1,827)*	*(1,225)*
Non controlling interests		9	5
Earnings per share – Equity holders of Air France-KLM *(in euros)*			
• Basic and diluted	16.1	(6.17)	(4.14)
Net income from continuing operations - Equity holders of Air France-KLM *(in euros)*			
• Basic and diluted	16.1	(5.76)	(3.47)
Net income from discontinued operations - Equity holders of Air France-KLM *(in euros)*			
• Basic and diluted	16.1	(0.41)	(0.67)

* *See Note 2 "Restatement of the 2012 financial statements" in notes to the consolidated financial statements.*

The accompanying notes are an integral part of these consolidated financial statements.

5.5.2 Consolidated statement of recognized income and expenses

(In € million)	**December 31, 2013**	**December 31, 2012 Pro forma***
Net income for the period	***(1,818)***	***(1,220)***
Fair value adjustment on available-for-sale securities		
• Change in fair value recognized directly in other comprehensive income	420	269
• Change in fair value transferred to profit or loss	-	(97)
Fair value hedges		
Effective portion of changes in fair value hedge recognized directly in other comprehensive income	(101)	-
Cash flow hedges		
• Effective portion of changes in fair value hedge recognized directly in other comprehensive income	213	124
• Change in fair value transferred to profit or loss	(120)	(251)
Currency translation adjustment	**(2)**	**-**
Deferred tax on items of comprehensive income that will be reclassified to profit or loss	**(10)**	**30**
Items of the recognized income and expenses of equity shares, net of tax	**(4)**	**(7)**
Total of other comprehensive income that will be reclassified to profit or loss	***396***	***68***
Remeasurements of defined benefit pension plans	**26**	**(313)**
Deferred tax on items of comprehensive income that will not be reclassified to profit or loss	**(18)**	**95**
Remeasurements of defined benefit pension plans of equity shares, net of tax	**(1)**	**(2)**
Total of other comprehensive income that will not be reclassified to profit or loss	***7***	***(220)***
Total of other comprehensive income, after tax	***403***	***(152)***
Recognized income and expenses	***(1,415)***	***(1,372)***
• ***Equity holders of Air France-KLM***	**(1,423)**	**(1,376)**
• Non-controlling interests	8	4

* *See Note 2 "Restatement of the 2012 financial statements" in notes to the consolidated financial statements.*

The accompanying notes are an integral part of these consolidated financial statements.

5.5.3 Consolidated balance sheet

Assets *(In € million)*	Notes	December 31, 2013	December 31, 2012 Pro forma*	January 1, 2012 Pro forma*
Goodwill	17	237	252	426
Intangible assets	18	896	842	774
Flight equipment	20	9,391	10,048	10,689
Other property, plant and equipment	20	1,819	1,932	2,055
Investments in equity associates	22	177	381	422
Pension assets	23	2,454	2,477	2,336
Other financial assets**	24	1,963	1,665	2,015
Deferred tax assets	13.4	436	1,392	1,322
Other non-current assets	27	113	152	168
Total non-current assets		***17,486***	***19,141***	***20,207***
Assets held for sale	15	91	7	10
Other short-term financial assets**	24	1,031	933	751
Inventories	25	511	521	585
Trade accounts receivables	26	1,775	1,859	1,774
Income tax receivables		23	11	10
Other current assets	27	822	828	995
Cash and cash equivalents	28	3,684	3,420	2,283
Total current assets		***7,937***	***7,579***	***6,408***
Total assets		**25,423**	**26,720**	**26,615**

* *See Note 2 "Restatement of the 2012 financial statements" in notes to the consolidated financial statements.*

** *Including:*

(In € million)	*December 31, 2013*	*December 31, 2012 Pro forma**	*January 1, 2012 Pro forma**
Deposits related to financial debts	*780*	*806*	*656*
Marketable securities (including cash secured)	*951*	*956*	*987*

The accompanying notes are an integral part of these consolidated financial statements.

Liabilities and equity *(In € million)*	**Notes**	**December 31, 2013**	**December 31, 2012 Pro forma***	**January 1, 2012 Pro forma***
Issued capital	**29.1**	300	300	300
Additional paid-in capital	**29.2**	2,971	2,971	2,971
Treasury shares	**29.3**	(85)	(85)	(89)
Reserves and retained earnings	**29.4**	(944)	403	1,775
Equity attributable to equity holders of Air France-KLM		***2,242***	***3,589***	***4,957***
Non-controlling interests		48	48	47
Total equity		***2,290***	***3,637***	***5,004***
Provisions and retirement benefits	**31**	3,102	3,158	2,692
Long-term debt	**32**	8,596	9,565	9,228
Deferred tax liabilities	**13.4**	178	149	223
Other non-current liabilities	**33**	397	384	321
Total non-current liabilities		***12,273***	***13,256***	***12,464***
Liabilities relating to assets held for sale	**15**	58	-	-
Provisions	**31**	670	555	156
Current portion of long-term debt	**32**	2,137	1,434	1,174
Trade accounts payables		2,369	2,219	2,599
Deferred revenue on ticket sales		2,371	2,115	1,885
Frequent flyer programs		755	770	784
Current tax liabilities		2	3	6
Other current liabilities	**33**	2,332	2,474	2,386
Bank overdrafts	**28**	166	257	157
Total current liabilities		***10,860***	***9,827***	***9,147***
Total liabilities		**23,133**	**23,083**	**21,611**
Total liabilities and equity		**25,423**	**26,720**	**26,615**

* *See Note 2 "Restatement of the 2012 financial statements" in notes to the consolidated financial statements.*

The accompanying notes are an integral part of these consolidated financial statements.

5.5.4 Consolidated statement of changes in stockholders' equity

(In € million)	Number of shares	Issued capital	Additional paid-in capital	Treasury shares	Reserves and retained earnings	Equity attributable to holders of Air France-KLM	Non controlling interests	Total equity
January 1, 2012	*300,219,278*	*300*	*2,971*	*(89)*	*2,858*	*6,040*	*54*	*6,094*
First application of IAS 19 Revised " Employee Benefits" (Note 2)	-	-	-	-	(1,083)	**(1,083)**	(7)	**(1,090)**
January 1, 2012 (Pro forma) *	*300,219,278*	*300*	*2,971*	*(89)*	*1,775*	*4,957*	*47*	*5,004*
Fair value adjustment on available for sale securities	-	-	-	-	168	**168**	-	**168**
Gain/ (loss) on cash flow hedges	-	-	-	-	(100)	**(100)**	-	**(100)**
Remeasurements of defined benefit pension plans	-	-	-	-	(219)	**(219)**	(1)	**(220)**
Other comprehensive income	-	-	-	-	*(151)*	*(151)*	*(1)*	*(152)*
Net income for the year	-	-	-	-	(1,225)	(1,225)	5	(1,220)
Total of income and expenses recognized	**-**	**-**	**-**	**-**	**(1,376)**	**(1,376)**	**4**	**(1,372)**
Stock based compensation (ESA) and stock option	-	-	-	-	3	**3**	-	**3**
Dividends paid	-	-	-	-	-	**-**	(2)	**(2)**
Treasury shares	-	-	-	4	-	**4**	-	**4**
Change in consolidation scope	-	-	-	-	1	**1**	(1)	**-**
December 31, 2012 (Pro forma) *	*300,219,278*	*300*	*2,971*	*(85)*	*403*	*3,589*	*48*	*3,637*
Fair value adjustment on available for sale securities	-	-	-	-	402	**402**	-	**402**
Gain / (loss) on cash flow hedges	-	-	-	-	62	**62**	-	**62**
Gain /(loss) on fair value hedges	-	-	-	-	(66)	**(66)**	-	**(66)**
Remeasurements of defined benefit pension plans	-	-	-	-	8	**8**	(1)	**7**
Currency translation adjustment	-	-	-	-	(2)	**(2)**	-	**(2)**
Other comprehensive income	-	-	-	-	*404*	*404*	*(1)*	*403*
Net income for the year	-	-	-	-	(1,827)	**(1,827)**	9	**(1,818)**
Total of income and expenses recognized	**-**	**-**	**-**	**-**	**(1,423)**	**(1,423)**	**8**	**(1,415)**
Stock based compensation (ESA) and stock option	-	-	-	-	3	**3**	-	**3**
OCEANE	-	-	-	-	70	**70**	-	**70**
Treasury shares	-	-	-	-	(1)	**(1)**	-	**(1)**
Dividends paid	-	-	-	-	-	**-**	(4)	**(4)**
Change in consolidation scope	-	-	-	-	4	**4**	(4)	**-**
December 31, 2013	*300,219,278*	*300*	*2,971*	*(85)*	*(944)*	*2,242*	*48*	*2,290*

* *See Note 2 "Restatement of the 2012 financial statements" in notes to the consolidated financial statements.*

The accompanying notes are an integral part of these consolidated financial statements.

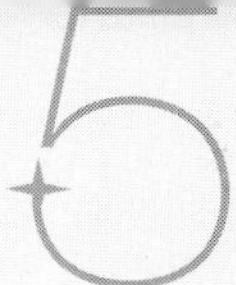

5.5.5 Consolidated statements of cash flows

(In € million) **Period from January 1 to December 31**	**Notes**	**2013**	**2012 Pro forma***
Net income from continuing operations		(1,696)	(1,023)
Net income from discontinued operations	**14**	(122)	(197)
Amortization, depreciation and operating provisions	**9**	1,735	1,748
Financial provisions	**12**	28	(15)
Gain on disposals of tangible and intangible assets		12	(24)
Loss / (gain) on disposals of subsidiaries and associates	**11**	(6)	(97)
Derivatives – non monetary result		(61)	(86)
Unrealized foreign exchange gains and losses, net		(114)	(94)
Share of (profits) losses of associates	**22**	211	66
Deferred taxes	**13**	916	(21)
Impairment	**39.1**	79	173
Other non-monetary	**39.1**	127	372
Subtotal		***1,109***	***802***
Of which discontinued operations		***(19)***	***(5)***
(Increase) / decrease in inventories		1	65
(Increase) / decrease in trade receivables		59	(142)
Increase / (decrease) in trade payables		55	(299)
Change in other receivables and payables		228	416
Change in working capital from discontinued operations		27	9
Net cash flow from operating activities		***1,479***	***851***
Acquisition of subsidiaries, of shares in non-controlled entities	**39.2**	(27)	(39)
Purchase of property, plant and equipment and intangible assets	**21**	(1,186)	(1,465)
Loss of subsidiaries, of disposal of shares in non-controlled entities	**11**	27	467
Proceeds on disposal of property, plant and equipment and intangible assets		245	742
Dividends received		17	24
Decrease (increase) in net investments, between 3 months and 1 year		5	30
Net cash flow used in investing activities of discontinued operations		(5)	(4)
Net cash flow used in investing activities		***(924)***	***(245)***

(In € million) **Period from January 1 to December 31**	**Notes**	**2013**	**2012 Pro forma***
Increase in capital		6	-
Disposal of subsidiaries without loss of control, of owned shares	**39.3**	-	7
Issuance of debt		1,887	1,780
Repayment on debt		(1,480)	(847)
Payment of debt resulting from finance lease liabilities		(588)	(514)
New loans		(136)	(90)
Repayment on loans		157	100
Dividends paid		(4)	(2)
Net cash flow from financing activities		***(158)***	***434***
Effect of exchange rate on cash and cash equivalents and bank overdrafts		(36)	(1)
Effect of exchange rate on cash and cash equivalents and bank overdrafts of discontinued operations		1	(2)
Change in cash and cash equivalents and bank overdrafts		***362***	***1,037***
Cash and cash equivalents and bank overdrafts at beginning of period	**28**	3,160	2,121
Cash and cash equivalents and bank overdrafts at end of period	**28**	3,518	3,160
Change in cash of discontinued operations		4	(2)
Income tax (paid) / reimbursed (flow included in operating activities)		(48)	(45)
Interest paid (flow included in operating activities)		(403)	(414)
Interest received (flow included in operating activities)		41	35

* *See Note 2 "Restatement of the 2012 financial statements" in notes to the consolidated financial statements.*

The accompanying notes are an integral part of these consolidated financial statements.

5.6 Notes to the consolidated financial statements

Note 1 Business description

As used herein, the term "Air France-KLM" refers to Air France-KLM SA, a limited liability company organized under French law.

The term "Group" is represented by the economic definition of Air France-KLM and its subsidiaries. The Group is headquartered in France and is one of the largest airlines in the world. The Group's core business is passenger transportation. The Group's activities also include cargo, aeronautics maintenance and other air-transport-related activities including, principally, catering and charter services.

The limited company Air France-KLM, domiciled at 2 rue Robert Esnault-Pelterie 75007 Paris, France, is the parent company of the Air France-KLM Group. Air France-KLM is listed for trading in Paris (Euronext) and Amsterdam (Euronext).

The presentation currency used in the Group's financial statements is the euro, which is also Air France-KLM's functional currency.

Note 2 Restatements of the 2012 financial statements

2.1 Application of IAS 19 Revised

Since January 1, 2013, the IAS 19 Revised "Employee Benefits" standard, published by the IASB in June 2011, has been applicable. The main changes for the Group are as follows:

- the option previously used by the Group, allowing the amortization of actuarial differences with the «corridor» method, has been deleted. Actuarial gains and losses are now recognized immediately in other comprehensive income;
- non-vested past service costs, previously amortized, are now fully recognized in the income statement;
- the return on assets, previously determined from an expected rate of return, is now assessed on the basis of the discount rate used to value the benefit obligations.

The consolidated financial statements as of December 31, 2012 have been restated to facilitate comparison. The restated balance sheet as of January 1, 2012 is also presented.

The impacts of the revision in the standard are summarized below:

➤ Impacts on the consolidated income statement

(In € million)	**December 31, 2012**
Salaries and related costs	(53)
Other non-current income and expenses	13
Income taxes	7
Net income for the period	***(33)***
• *Equity holders of Air France-KLM*	(33)
• *Non-controlling interests*	-
Earnings per share – Equity holders of Air France-KLM (in euros)	
• *Basic*	*(0.11)*
• *Diluted*	*(0.11)*

➤ **Impacts on the consolidated statement of recognized income and expenses**

(In € million)	**December 31, 2012**
Net income for the period	***(33)***
Remeasurements of defined benefit pension plans	(313)
Items of the recognized income and expenses of equity shares	(2)
Tax on items of other comprehensive income that will not be reclassified to profit or loss	95
Recognized income and expenses	***(253)***
◆ *Equity holders of Air France-KLM*	*(252)*
◆ *Non-controlling interests*	*(1)*

➤ **Impacts on the consolidated balance sheet**

(In € million)	**January 1, 2012**	**December 31, 2012**
Investments in equity associates	-	(2)
Pension assets	(881)	(993)
Deferred tax assets	179	241
Provisions and retirement benefits	631	871
Deferred tax liabilities	(243)	(282)
Net impacts on equity	(1,090)	(1,343)
◆ *Equity holders of Air France-KLM*	*(1,083)*	*(1,335)*
◆ *Non-controlling interests*	*(7)*	*(8)*

2.2 Presentation of the CityJet Group's financial statements as a discontinued operation

On December 20, 2013, Air France received a firm offer from Intro Aviation GmbH to purchase its subsidiaries CityJet and VLM. The employee representative bodies of the relevant companies need to be informed and consulted to enable the disposal to be finalized. The CityJet Group, who has always dealed on its own trademark, comprises the only airlines in the Group that operate:

- outside the short/medium-haul scope defined by the Transform 2015 plan;
- mainly on the basis of London City which appears non-complementary to the Group activities;
- with few operational links or "businesses" with the rest of the company (maintenance, information systems, etc.).

This unit represents a clearly identifiable component, with limited links to the rest of the Group but nevertheless significant in term of business.

As result, the planned disposal justifies the discontinued operations treatment, as defined in the standard IFRS 5. The detail on the net income from discontinued operations is given in Note 14.

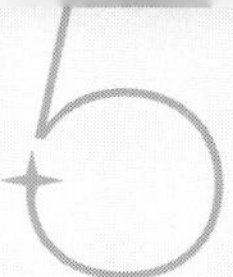

Note 3 Significant events

3.1 Change in the scope of consolidation

Within the framework of the Transform 2015 project, the Air France Group decided to regroup its French regional activities Britair, Régional and Airlinair within a holding company known as *HOP! (see Note 5)*, and, during the third quarter, announced the deployment of additional measures to reduce costs concerning the restructuring plan launched in 2012. Based on the measures presented to the different bodies officially representing the Air France Group, the Group has made, to date, its best estimate of the new costs involved and has booked an additional provision for restructuring *(see Note 11)*.

On March 28, 2013, Air France-KLM issued 53,398,058 bonds convertible and/or exchangeable for new or existing Air France-KLM shares (OCEANE) maturing on February 15, 2023 for an amount of €550 million *(see Note 32)*.

On June 19, 2013, the Group finalized the firm order for 25 Airbus A350s, in accordance with the letter of intention signed on May 27, 2013.

Following its decision not to participate in the Alitalia capital increase of October 2013, and after conversion into equity of the €23.8 million shareholder loan subscribed in February 25, 2013, the Air France-KLM Group saw its shareholding in Alitalia decrease from 25% to 7.08% *(see Notes 5, 11, 22 and 24)*.

3.2 Subsequent events

There has been no significant event since the closing of the financial year.

Note 4 Rules and accounting principles

4.1 Accounting principles

4.1.1 Accounting principles used for consolidated financial statements

Pursuant to the European Regulation 1606/2002, July 19, 2002, the consolidated financial statements as of December 31, 2013 have been prepared in accordance with International Financial Reporting Standards ("IFRS") as adopted by the European Commission ("EU") and applicable on the date these consolidated financial statements were established.

IFRS as adopted by the EU differ in certain respects from IFRS as published by the International Accounting Standards Board ("IASB"). The Group has, however, determined that the financial information for the periods presented would not differ substantially if the Group had applied IFRS as published by the IASB.

The consolidated financial statements were approved by the Board of Directors on February 19, 2014.

4.1.2 Change in accounting principles

▮ *IFRS standards, amendments and IFRIC interpretations (IFRS Interpretation Committee) applicable on a mandatory basis to the 2013 financial statements*

The texts whose application became mandatory during the accounting period ended December 31, 2013 are the following:

- standard IFRS 13 " Fair Value Measurement";
- amendment to IFRS 7 "Disclosures – Offsetting Financial assets and Financial liabilities";
- amendment to IAS 1 on presentation of other comprehensive income;
- standard IAS 19 Revised" Employee Benefit";
- annual improvements to IFRS 2009-11.

The impacts of IAS 19 Revised on the Group's consolidated financial statements are detailed in Note 2 "Restatements of the 2012 financial statements". The other standards and amendments mentioned above did not have any significant impact on the Group's consolidated financial statements as of December 31, 2013.

The other texts whose application became mandatory during the year ended December 31, 2013 had no impact on the Group's consolidated financial statements.

▮ *IFRS standards, amendments and IFRIC interpretations which are not applicable on a mandatory basis to the 2013 financial statements*

- Standard IFRS 10 "Consolidated Financial Statements" which will replace IAS 27 "Consolidated and Separate Financial Statements" for the part concerning the consolidated financial statements and also the SIC 12 interpretation "Consolidation – Special Purpose Entities" (applicable on a mandatory basis from fiscal years starting on January 1, 2014).
- Standard IFRS 11 "Joint Arrangements" which will replace IAS 31 "Interests in Joint Ventures" and also the SIC 13 interpretation "Jointly Controlled Entities – Non-Monetary Contributions by Venturers (applicable on a mandatory basis from fiscal years starting on January 1, 2014).
- Standard IFRS 12 "Disclosure on Interests in Other Entities (applicable on a mandatory basis from fiscal years starting on January 1, 2014).
- Standard IAS 28 (2011) "Investments in Associates (applicable on a mandatory basis from fiscal years starting on January 1, 2014).
- Amendment to IAS 32 "Presentation - Offsetting Financial assets and Financial liabilities (applicable on a mandatory basis from fiscal years starting on January 1, 2014).

The application of IFRS 10 and IFRS 11 is currently being considered. Nevertheless, the Group does not expect any significant changes in its consolidation scope.

- ***IFRS standards and IFRIC interpretations which are applicable on a mandatory basis to the 2014 financial statements***
  - Amendment to IAS 36 "Recoverable Amount Disclosures for Non Financial Assets".
  - Amendment to IAS 39 "Novation of Derivatives and Continuation of Hedge Accounting".

- ***Other texts potentially applicable to the Group, published by the IASB but not yet adopted by the European Union, are described below***
  - Interpretation IFRIC 21 "Levies" applicable from January 1, 2014.
  - Standard IFRS 9 "Financial instruments - Classification and measurement of financial assets and liabilities", applicable not earlier than January 2017 because the IASB has postponed the initial effective date from January 2015 to another as-yet-unset date.

4.2 Use of estimates

The preparation of the consolidated financial statements in conformity with IFRS requires management to make estimates and use assumptions that affect the reported amounts of assets and liabilities and the disclosures of contingent assets and liabilities at the date of the consolidated financial statements and the reported amounts of revenues and expenses. The main estimates are described in the following notes:

- Note 4.6 – Revenue recognition related to deferred revenue on ticket sales;
- Notes 4.13 and 4.12 – Tangible and intangible assets;
- Note 4.10 – Financial instruments;
- Note 4.22 – Deferred taxes;
- Note 4.7 – "Flying Blue" frequent flyer program;
- Notes 4.17, 4.18 and 4.19 – Provisions (including employee benefits).

The Group's management makes these estimates and assessments continuously on the basis of its past experience and various other factors considered to be reasonable.

The consolidated financial statements for the financial year have thus been established taking into account the economic and financial crisis unfolding since 2008 and on the basis of financial parameters available at the closing date. The immediate effects of the crisis have been taken into account, in particular the valuation of current assets and liabilities. Concerning the longer-term assets, i.e. the non-current assets, the assumptions are based on limited growth.

The future results could differ from these estimates depending on changes in the assumptions used or different conditions.

4.3 Consolidation principles

4.3.1 Subsidiaries

Companies over which the Group exercises control are fully consolidated. Control is defined as the power to govern the financial and operating policies of an entity so as to obtain benefits from its activities. The financial statements of subsidiaries are included in the consolidated financial statements from the date that control begins until the date this control ceases.

Non-controlling interests are presented within equity and on the income statement separately from Group stockholders' equity and the Group's net income, under the line "non-controlling interests".

The effects of a buyout of non-controlling interests in a subsidiary already controlled by the Group and divestment of a percentage interest without loss of control are recognized in equity.

In a partial disposal resulting in loss of control, the retained equity interest is remeasured at fair value at the date of loss of control. The gain or loss on the disposal will include the effect of this remeasurement and the gain or loss on the sale of the equity interest, including all the items initially recognized in equity and reclassified to profit and loss.

4.3.2 Interest in associates and joint-ventures

Companies in which the Group has the ability to exercise significant influence on financial and operating policy decisions are accounted for using the equity method; the ability to exercise significant influence is presumed to exist when the Group holds more than 20% of the voting rights.

In addition, companies in which the Group exercises joint control according to a contractual agreement are accounted for using the equity method.

The consolidated financial statements include the Group's share of the total recognized global result of associates and joint-ventures from the date the ability to exercise significant influence begins to the date it ceases, adjusted for any impairment loss.

The Group's share of losses of an associate that exceed the value of the Group's interest and net investment (long-term receivables for which no reimbursement is scheduled or likely) in this entity are not accounted for, unless:

- the Group has incurred contractual obligations; or
- the Group has made payments on behalf of the associate.

Any surplus of the investment cost over the Group's share in the fair value of the identifiable assets, liabilities and contingent liabilities of the associate company on the date of acquisition is accounted for as goodwill and included in the book value of the investment accounted for using the equity method.

The investments in which the Group has ceased to exercise significant influence or joint control are no longer accounted for by the equity method and are valued at their fair value on the date of loss of significant influence or joint control.

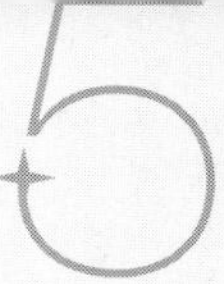

4.3.3 Intra-group operations

All intra-group balances and transactions, including income, expenses and dividends are fully eliminated. Profits and losses resulting from intra-group transactions that are recognized in assets are also eliminated.

Gains and losses realized on internal sales with associates and jointly-controlled entities are eliminated, to the extent of the Group's interest in the entity, providing there is no impairment.

4.4 Translation of foreign companies' financial statements and transactions in foreign currencies

4.4.1 Translation of foreign companies' financial statements

The financial statements of foreign subsidiaries are translated into euros on the following basis:

- except for the equity for which historical prices are applied, balance sheet items are converted on the basis of the foreign currency exchange rates in effect at the closing date;
- the income statement and the statement of cash flows are converted on the basis of the average foreign currency exchange rates for the period;
- the resulting foreign currency exchange adjustment is recorded in the «Translation adjustments» item included within equity.

Goodwill is expressed in the functional currency of the entity acquired and is converted into euros using the foreign exchange rate in effect at the closing date.

4.4.2 Translation of foreign currency transactions

Foreign currency transactions are translated using the exchange rate prevailing on the date of the transaction.

Monetary assets and liabilities denominated in foreign currencies are translated at the rate in effect at the closing date or at the rate of the related hedge if any.

Non-monetary assets and liabilities denominated in foreign currencies assessed on an historical cost basis are translated using the rate in effect at the transaction date or using the hedged rate where necessary *(see 4.13.2)*.

The corresponding exchange rate differences are recorded in the Group's consolidated income statement. Changes in fair value of the hedging instruments are recorded using the accounting treatment described in Note 4.10 "Financial instruments, valuation of financial assets and liabilities".

4.5 Business combinations

4.5.1 Business combinations completed on or after April 1, 2010

Business combinations completed on or after April 1, 2010 are accounted for using the purchase method in accordance with IFRS 3 (2008) "Business combinations". In accordance with this standard, all assets and liabilities assumed are measured at fair value at the acquisition date. The time period for adjustments to goodwill/negative goodwill is limited to 12 months from the date of acquisition, except for non-current assets classified as assets held for sale which are measured at fair value less costs to sell.

Goodwill corresponding, at the acquisition date, to the aggregate of the consideration transferred and the amount of any non-controlling interest in the acquiree minus the net amounts (usually at fair value) of the identifiable assets acquired and the liabilities assumed at the acquisition date, is subject to annual impairment tests or more frequently if events or changes in circumstances indicate that goodwill might be impaired.

Costs other than those related to the issuance of debt or equity securities are recognized immediately as an expense when incurred.

For each acquisition, the Group has the option of using the "full" goodwill method, where goodwill is calculated by taking into account the fair value of non-controlling interests at the acquisition date rather than their proportionate interest in the fair value of the assets and liabilities of the acquiree.

Should the fair value of identifiable assets acquired and liabilities assumed exceed the consideration transferred, the resulting negative goodwill is recognized immediately in the income statement.

Contingent considerations or earn-outs are recorded in equity if contingent payment is settled by delivery of a fixed number of the acquirer's equity instruments (according to IAS 32). In all other cases, they are recognized in liabilities related to business combinations. Contingent payments or earn-outs are measured at fair value at the acquisition date. This initial measurement is subsequently adjusted through goodwill only when additional information is obtained after the acquisition date about facts and circumstances that existed at that date. Such adjustments are made only during the 12-month measurement period that follows the acquisition date. Any other subsequent adjustments which do not meet these criteria are recorded as receivables or payables through the income statement.

In a step acquisition, the previously-held equity interest in the acquiree is remeasured at its acquisition-date fair value. The difference between the fair value and the net book value must be accounted in profit or loss as well as elements previously recognized in other comprehensive income.

4.5.2 Business combination carried out before April 1, 2010

Business combinations carried out before April 1, 2010 are accounted for using the purchase method in accordance with IFRS 3 (2004) "Business combinations". In accordance with this standard, all assets, liabilities assumed and contingent liabilities are measured at fair value at the acquisition date. The time period for adjustments to goodwill/negative goodwill is limited to 12 months from the date of acquisition.

Assets meeting the criteria of IFRS 5 "Non-current assets held for sale and discontinued operations", as described in Note 4.23, are recorded at the lower of their net book value and their fair value less costs to sell.

Goodwill arising from the difference between the acquisition cost, which includes the potential equity instruments issued by the Group to gain control over the acquired entity and other costs potentially dedicated to the business combination, and the Group's interest in the fair value of the identifiable assets and liabilities acquired, is subject to annual impairment tests or more frequently if events or changes in circumstances indicate that goodwill might be impaired.

Should the fair value of identifiable assets acquired and liabilities assumed exceed the cost of acquisition, the resulting negative goodwill is recognized immediately in the income statement.

4.6 Sales

Sales related to air transportation operations are recognized when the transportation service is provided, net of any discounts granted. Transportation service is also the trigger for the recognition of external expenses, such as the commissions paid to agents.

Both passenger and cargo tickets are consequently recorded as "Deferred revenue on ticket sales".

Sales relating to the value of tickets that have been issued, but never be used, are recognized as revenues at issuance. The amounts recognized are based on a statistical analysis, which is regularly updated.

Sales on third-party maintenance contracts are recorded on the basis of completion method.

4.7 Loyalty programs

The two sub-groups Air France and KLM have a common frequent flyer program *Flying Blue*. This program enables members to acquire "miles" as they fly with airlines partners or transactions with non airline partners (credit cards, hotels, car rental agencies). These miles entitle members to a variety of benefits such as free flights with the two companies or other free services with non flying partners.

In accordance with IFRIC 13 "Loyalty programs", these "miles" are considered as distinct elements from a sale with multiple elements and one part of the price of the initial sale of the airfare is allocated to these "miles" and deferred until the Group's commitments relating to these "miles" have been met. The deferred amount due in relation to the acquisition of miles by members is estimated:

- according to the fair value of the "miles", defined as the amount at which the benefits can be sold separately;
- after taking into account the redemption rate, corresponding to the probability that the miles will be used by members, using a statistical method.

With regards to the invoicing of other partners in the program, the margins realized on sales of "miles" by the sub-groups Air France and KLM to other partners are recorded immediately in the income statement.

4.8 Distinction between income from current operations and income from operating activities

The Group considers it is relevant to the understanding of its financial performance to present in the income statement a subtotal within the income from operating activities. This subtotal, entitled "Income from current operations", excludes unusual elements that do not have predictive value due to their nature, frequency and/or materiality, as defined in the recommendation no. 2009-R.03 from the National Accounting Council.

Such elements are as follows:

- sales of aircraft equipment and disposals of other assets;
- income from the disposal of subsidiaries and affiliates;
- restructuring costs when they are significant;
- significant and infrequent elements such as the recognition of badwill in the income statement, recording an impairment loss on goodwill and significant provisions for litigation.

4.9 Earnings per share

Earnings per share are calculated by dividing net income attributable to the equity holders of Air France-KLM by the average number of shares outstanding during the period. The average number of shares outstanding does not include treasury shares.

Diluted earnings per share are calculated by dividing the net income attributable to the equity holders of Air France-KLM adjusted for the effects of dilutive instrument exercise, by the average number of shares outstanding during the period, adjusted for the effect of all potentially-dilutive ordinary shares.

4.10 Financial instruments, valuation of financial assets and liabilities

4.10.1 Valuation of trade receivables and non-current financial assets

Trade receivables, loans and other non-current financial assets are considered to be assets issued by the Group and are recorded at fair value then, subsequently, using the amortized cost method less impairment losses, if any. The purchases and sales of financial assets are accounted for as of the transaction date.

4.10.2 Investments in equity securities

Investments in equity securities qualifying as assets available for sale are stated at fair value in the Group's balance sheet. For publicly-traded securities, the fair value is considered to be the market price at the closing date. For other securities, if the fair value cannot be reliably estimated, the Group uses the exception of accounting at costs (i.e acquisition cost less impairment, if any).

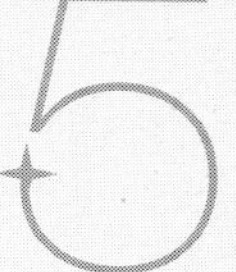

Potential gains and losses, except for impairment charges, are recorded in a specific component of other comprehensive income "Derivatives and available for sale securities reserves". If there is an indication of impairment of the financial asset, the amount of the loss resulting from the impairment test is recorded in the income statement for the period.

4.10.3 Derivative financial instruments

The Group uses various derivative financial instruments to hedge its exposure to the risks incurred on shares, exchange rates, changes in interest rates or fuel prices.

Forward currency contracts and options are used to cover exposure to exchange rates. For firm commitments, the unrealized gains and losses on these financial instruments are included in the carrying value of the hedged asset or liability.

The Group also uses rate swaps to manage its exposure to interest rate risk. Most of the swaps traded convert floating-rate debt to fixed-rate debt.

Finally, exposure to the fuel risk is hedged by swaps or options on jet fuel, diesel or Brent.

Most of these derivatives are classified as hedging instruments if the derivative is eligible as a hedging instrument and if the hedging contracts are documented as required by IAS 39 "Financial instruments: recognition and measurement".

These derivative instruments are recorded on the Group's consolidated balance sheet at their fair value taken into account the market value of the credit risk of the Group (DVA) and the credit risk of the counterpart (CVA). The calculation of credit risk follows a common model based on default probabilities from CDS counterparts.

The method of accounting for changes in fair value depends on the classification of the derivative instruments. There are three classifications:

- *derivatives classified as fair value hedge*: changes in the derivative fair value are recorded through the income statement and offset within the limit of its effective portion against the changes in the fair value of the underlying item (assets, liability or firm commitment), which are also recognized as earnings;
- *derivatives classified as cash flow hedge*: the changes in fair value are recorded in other comprehensive income for the effective portion and are reclassified as income when the hedged element affects earnings. The ineffective portion is recorded as financial income or losses;
- *derivatives classified as trading*: changes in the derivative fair value are recorded as financial income or losses.

4.10.4 Convertible bonds

Convertible bonds are financial instruments comprising two components: a bond component recorded as debt and a stock component recorded in equity. The bond component is equal to the discounted value of all coupons due for the bond at the rate of a simple bond that would have been issued at the same time as the convertible bond. The value of the stock component recorded in the Group's equity is calculated by the difference between such value and the bond's nominal value at issue. The difference between the financial expense recorded and the amounts effectively paid out is added, at each closing date, to the amount of the debt component so that, at maturity, the amount to be repaid if there is no conversion equals the redemption price.

4.10.5 Financial assets, cash and cash equivalents

Financial assets at fair value through profit and loss

Financial assets include financial assets at fair value through profit and loss (French mutual funds such as SICAVs and FCPs, certificates, etc.) that the Group intends to sell in the near term to realize a capital gain, or that are part of a portfolio of identified financial instruments managed collectively and for which there is evidence of a practice of short-term profit taking. They are classified in the balance sheet as current financial assets. Furthermore, the Group opted not to designate any assets at fair value through the income statement.

Cash and cash equivalents

Cash and cash equivalents are short-term, highly liquid investments that are readily convertible to known amounts of cash and which are subject to an insignificant risk of change in value.

4.10.6 Long-term debt

Long-term debt is recognized initially at fair value. Subsequent to the initial measurement, long-term debt is recorded at amortized cost calculated using the effective interest rate. Under this principle, any redemption and issue premiums are recorded as debt in the balance sheet and amortized as financial income or expense over the life of the loans.

In addition, long-term debt documented in the context of fair value hedging relationships is revalued at the fair value for the risk hedged, i.e. the risk related to the fluctuation in interest rates. Changes in fair value of the hedged debt are recorded symmetrically in the income statement for the period with the change in fair value of the hedging swaps.

4.10.7 Fair value hierarchy

The table presenting a breakdown of financial assets and liabilities categorized by value *(see Note 34.4)* meets the amended requirements of IFRS 7 "Financial instruments: Disclosures". The fair values are classified using a scale which reflects the nature of the market data used to make the valuations.

This scale has three levels of fair value.

- **Level 1**: fair value calculated from the exchange rate/price quoted on the active market for identical instruments;
- **Level 2**: fair value calculated from valuation methods based on observable data such as the prices of similar assets and liabilities or scopes quoted on the active market;
- **Level 3**: fair value calculated from valuation methods which rely completely or in part on non-observable data such as prices on an inactive market or the valuation on a multiples basis for non-quoted securities.

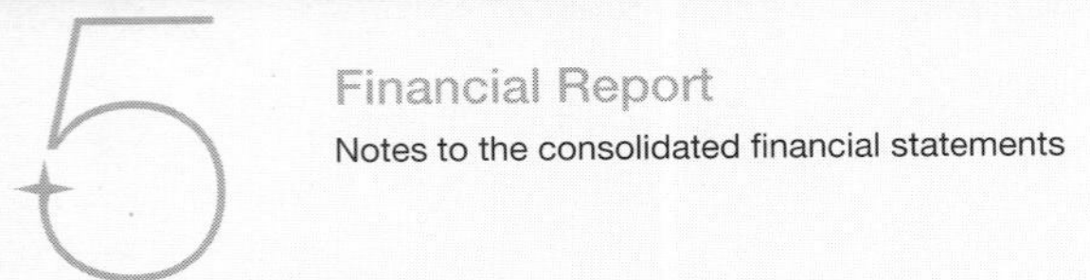

4.11 Goodwill

Goodwill corresponds, at the acquisition date, to the aggregation of the consideration transferred and the amount of any non-controlling interest in the acquiree minus the net amounts (usually at fair value) of the identifiable amounts acquired and the liabilities assumed at the acquisition-date.

For acquisitions prior to April 1, 2004, goodwill is included on the basis of its deemed cost, which represents the amount recorded under French GAAP. The classification and accounting treatment of business combinations that occurred prior to April 1, 2004 was not modified at the time international standards were adopted, on April 1, 2004, in accordance with IFRS 1 "First-time adoption of international financial reporting standards".

Goodwill is valued in the functional currency of the entity acquired. It is recorded as an asset in the balance sheet.

It is not amortized and is tested for impairment annually and at any point during the year when an indicator of impairment exists. As discussed in Note 4.14, once recorded the impairment may not subsequently be reversed.

When the acquirer's interest in the net fair value of the identifiable assets and liabilities acquired exceeds the consideration transferred, there is negative goodwill which is recognized and immediately reversed in the Group's income statement.

At the time of the sale of a subsidiary or an equity affiliate, the amount of the goodwill attributable to the entity sold is included in the calculation of the income from the sale.

4.12 Intangible assets

Intangible assets are recorded at initial cost less accumulated amortization and any accumulated impairment losses.

Software development costs are capitalized and amortized over their useful lives. The Group has the necessary tools to enable the tracking by project of all the stages of development, and particularly the internal and external costs directly related to each project during its development phase.

Identifiable intangible assets acquired with a finite useful life are amortized over their useful lives from the date they are available for use.

Identifiable intangible assets acquired with an indefinite useful life are not amortized but tested annually for impairment or whenever there is an indication that the intangible asset may be impaired. If necessary, an impairment as described in Note 4.14 is recorded.

Since January 1, 2012, airlines have been subject to the ETS (Emission Trading Scheme) market regulations as described in Note 4.20 and the "Risks on carbon credit" paragraph in Note 34.1. As such, the Group is required to purchase CO_2 quotas to offset its emissions. The Group records the CO_2 quotas as intangible assets. These assets are not depreciable.

Intangible assets with a definite useful life are amortized on a straight line basis over the following periods:

- software — 1 to 5 years
- customer relationships — 5 to 12 years

4.13 Property, plant and equipment

4.13.1 Principles applicable

Property, plant and equipment are recorded at the acquisition or manufacturing cost, less accumulated depreciation and any accumulated impairment losses.

The financial interest attributed to progress payments made on account of aircraft and other significant assets under construction is capitalized and added to the cost of the asset concerned. As prepayments on investment are not financed by specific loans, the Group uses the average interest rate on the current unallocated loans of the period.

Maintenance costs are recorded as expenses during the period when incurred, with the exception of programs that extend the useful life of the asset or increase its value, which are then capitalized (e.g. maintenance on airframes and engines, excluding parts with limited useful lives).

4.13.2 Flight equipment

The purchase price of aircraft equipment is denominated in foreign currencies. It is translated at the exchange rate at the date of the transaction or, if applicable, at the hedging price assigned to it. Manufacturers' discounts, if any, are deducted from the value of the related asset.

Aircraft are depreciated using the straight-line method over their average estimated useful life of 20 years, assuming no residual value for most of the aircraft in the fleet. This useful life can, however, be extended to 25 years for some aircraft.

During the operating cycle, and when establishing fleet replacement plans, the Group reviews whether the amortizable base or the useful life should be adjusted and, if necessary, determines whether a residual value should be recognized.

Any major airframes and engines (excluding parts with limited useful lives) are treated as a separate asset component with the cost capitalized and depreciated over the period between the date of acquisition and the next major overhaul.

Aircraft components which enable the use of the fleet are recorded as fixed assets and are amortized on a straight-line basis over the estimated residual lifetime of the aircraft/engine type on the world market. The useful life is limited to a maximum of 30 years.

4.13.3 Other property, plant and equipment

Other property, plant and equipment are depreciated using the straight line method over their useful life. Such useful lives are as follows:

- buildings — 20 to 50 years
- fixtures and fittings — 8 to 15 years
- flight simulators — 10 to 20 years
- equipment and tooling — 5 to 15 years

4.13.4 Leases

In accordance with IAS 17 «Leases», leases are classified as finance leases when the lease arrangement transfers substantially all the risks and rewards of ownership to the lessee.

All other leases are classified as operating leases.

The assets held under a finance lease are recognized as assets at the lower of the following two values: the present value of the minimum lease payments under the lease arrangement or their fair value determined at inception of the lease. The corresponding obligation to the lessor is accounted for as long-term debt.

These assets are depreciated over the shorter of the useful life of the assets and the lease term when there is no reasonable certainty that the lessee will obtain ownership by the end of the lease term.

In the context of sale and operating leaseback transactions, the related profit or losses are accounted for as follows:

- they are recognized immediately when it is clear that the transaction has been realized at fair value;
- if the sale price is below fair value, any profit or loss is recognized immediately except that, if the loss is compensated for by future lease payments at below market price, it is deferred and amortized in proportion to the lease payments over the period for which the asset is expected to be used;
- if the sale price is above fair value, the excess over fair value is deferred and amortized over the period for which the asset is expected to be used.

In the context of sale and finance leaseback transactions, the asset remains in the Group's balance sheet with the same net book value. Such transactions are a means whereby the lessor provides finance to the lessee, with the asset as security.

4.14 Impairment test

In accordance with the standard IAS 36 "Impairment of Assets", tangible fixed assets, intangible assets and goodwill are tested for depreciation if there is an indication of impairment, and those with an indefinite useful life are tested at least once a year on September 30.

For this test, the Group deems the recoverable value of the asset to be the higher of the market value less cost of disposal and its value in use. The latter is determined according to the discounted future cash flow method, estimated based on budgetary assumptions approved by management, using an actuarial rate which corresponds to the weighted average cost of the Group's capital and a growth rate which reflects the market hypotheses for the appropriate activity.

The depreciation tests are carried out individually for each asset, except for those assets to which it is not possible to attach independent cash flows. In this case, these assets are regrouped within the CGU to which they belong and it is this which is tested. The CGU relates to different activity sectors of the Group: passenger business, cargo, maintenance, leisure and others.

When the recoverable value of an asset or CGU is inferior to its net book value, an impairment is realized. The impairment of a CGU is charged in the first instance to goodwill, the remainder being charged to the other assets which comprise the CGU, prorated to their net book value.

4.15 Inventories

Inventories are measured at the lower of cost and net realizable value.

The cost of inventories comprises all costs of purchase, costs of conversion and other costs incurred in bringing the inventories to their present condition and location. These costs include the direct and indirect production costs incurred under normal operating conditions.

Inventories are valued on a weighted average basis.

The net realizable value of the inventories is the estimated selling price in the ordinary course of business less the estimated costs of completion and selling expenses.

4.16 Treasury shares

Air-France-KLM shares held by the Group are recorded as a deduction from the Group's consolidated equity at the acquisition cost. Subsequent sales are recorded directly in equity. No gains or losses are recognized in the Group's income statement.

4.17 Employee benefits

The Group's obligations in respect of defined benefit pension plans, including the termination indemnities, are calculated in accordance with IAS 19 Revised "Employee benefits", using the projected units of credit method based on actuarial assumptions and considering the specific economic conditions in each country concerned. The commitments are covered either by insurance or pension funds or by provisions recorded on the balance sheet as and when rights are acquired by employees.

The Group recognizes in Other Comprehensive Income the actuarial gains or losses relating to post-employment plans, the differential between the actual return and the expected return on the pension assets and the impact of any plan curtailment. The gains or losses relating to termination benefits are booked in the income statement.

The Group books all the costs linked to pensions (defined benefit plans and net periodic pension costs) in the income from current operations (salaries and related costs).

Specific information related to the recognition of some pension plan assets

Pension plans in the Netherlands are generally subject to minimum funding requirements ("MFR") that can involve the recognition of pension surpluses.

These pension surpluses constituted by the KLM sub group are recognized in the balance sheet according to the IFRIC 14 interpretation IAS 19 "The Limit on a Defined Benefit Asset, Minimum Funding Requirements and their Interaction".

4.18 Provisions for restitution of aircraft under operating leases

For certain operating leases, the Group is contractually committed to restitute aircraft to a defined level of potential.

The Group accrues for restitution costs related to aircraft under operating leases.

When the condition of aircraft exceeds the return condition as set per the lease arrangement, the Group capitalizes the related amount in excess under "Flight equipment". Such amounts are subsequently amortized on a straight-line basis over the period during which the potential exceeds the restitution condition. Any remaining capitalized excess potential upon termination of a lease is reimbursable by the lessor.

4.19 Other provisions

The Group recognizes a provision in the balance sheet when the Group has an existing legal or implicit obligation to a third party as a result of a past event, and it is probable that an outflow of economic benefits will be required to settle the obligation. The amounts recorded as provisions are discounted when the effect of the passage of time is material.

The effect of the time value of money is presented as a component of financial income.

Restructuring provisions are recognized once the Group has established a detailed and formal restructuring plan which has been announced to the parties concerned.

4.20 Emission Trading Scheme

Since January 2012, European airlines have been included in the scope of companies subject to the Emission Trading Scheme (ETS).

In the absence of an IFRS standard or interpretation regarding ETS accounting, the Group has adopted the accounting treatment known as the "netting approach".

According to this approach, the quotas are recognized as intangible assets:

- free quotas allocated by the State are valued at nil; and
- quotas purchased on the market are accounted at their acquisition cost.

These intangible assets are not amortized.

If the difference between recognized quotas and real emissions is negative then the Group recognizes a provision. This provision is assessed at the acquisition cost for the acquired rights and, for the non-hedged portion, with reference to the market price as of each closing date.

At the date of the restitution to the State of the quotas corresponding to real emissions, the provision is written-off in exchange for the intangible assets returned.

4.21 Equity and debt issuance costs

Debt issuance costs are mainly amortized as financial expenses over the term of the loans using the actuarial method.

The capital increase costs are deducted from paid-in capital.

4.22 Deferred taxes

The Group records deferred taxes using the balance sheet liability method, providing for any temporary differences between the carrying amounts of assets and liabilities for financial reporting purposes and the amounts used for taxation purposes, except for exceptions described in IAS 12 "Income taxes".

The tax rates used are those enacted or substantively enacted at the balance sheet date.

Net deferred tax balances are determined on the basis of each entity's tax position.

Deferred tax assets related to temporary differences and tax losses carried forward are recognized only to the extent it is probable that a future taxable profit will be available against which the asset can be utilized at the tax entity level.

Deferred tax assets corresponding to fiscal losses are recognized as assets given the prospects of recoverability resulting from budgets and medium term plans prepared by the Group. The assumptions used are similar to those used for testing the value of assets *(see Note 4.14)*.

A deferred tax liability is also recognized for the undistributed reserves of the equity affiliates.

Taxes payable and/or deferred are recognized in the income statement for the period, unless they are generated by a transaction or event recorded directly in other comprehensive income. In such a case, they are recorded directly in other comprehensive income.

Impact of the Territorial Economic Contribution

The 2010 Finance Law voted on December 30, 2009, removed the business tax liability for French fiscal entities from January 1, 2010 and replaced it with the new TEC (Territorial Economic Contribution/ Contribution Economique Territoriale – CET) comprising two contributions: the LDE (land tax of enterprises/Cotisation Foncière des Entreprises - CFE) and the CAVE (Contribution on Added Value of Enterprises/Cotisation sur la Valeur Ajoutée des Entreprises – CVAE). The latter is calculated by the application of a rate to the added value

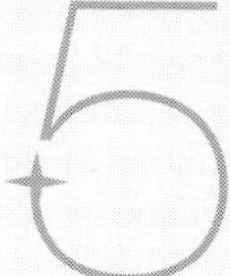

generated by the company during the year. As the added value is a net amount of income and expenses, the CAVE meets the definition of a tax on profits as set out in IAS 12.2. Consequently, the expense relating to the CAVE is presented under the line "tax".

4.23 Non-current assets held for sale and discontinued operations

Assets or groups of assets held for sale meet the criteria of such a classification if their carrying amount is recovered principally through a sale rather than through their continuing use. This condition is considered to be met when the sale is highly probable and the asset (or the group of assets intended for sale) is available for immediate sale in its present condition. Management must be committed to a plan to sell, with the expectation that the sale will be realized within a period of twelve months from the date on which the asset or group of assets were classified as assets held for sale.

The Group determines on each closing date whether any assets or groups of assets meet the above criteria and presents such assets, if any, as "non-current assets held for sale".

Any liabilities related to these assets are also presented on a separate line in liabilities on the balance sheet.

Assets and groups of assets held for sale are valued at the lower of their book value or their fair value minus exit costs. As of the date of such a classification, the asset is no longer depreciated.

The results from discontinued operations are presented separately from the results from continuing operations in the income statement.

4.24 Share-based compensation

Stock subscription or purchase option schemes are valued at the fair value on the date the plans are awarded.

The fair value of the stock option schemes is determined using the Black-Scholes model. This model takes into account the features of the plan (exercise price, exercise period) and the market data at the time they are granted (risk-free interest rate, market value of the share, volatility and expected dividends).

This fair value is the fair value of the services rendered by the employees in consideration for the options received. It is recognized over the vesting period as salary cost with a corresponding increase to equity for transactions paid with shares and with a corresponding increase of liabilities for transactions paid in cash. During the vesting period, this salary cost is adjusted, if applicable, to take into account the number of options effectively vested.

Note 5 Change in the consolidation scope

Within the framework of the establishment of *HOP!*, the Group acquired Airlinair. This operation took place as follows:

- the sale, on February 28, 2013, of the shareholding in Financière LMP (39.86%), the parent company which owned Airlinair *(see Note 11)*;
- the acquisition, on February 28, 2013, of 100% of the Airlinair share capital for €17 million. The goodwill relating to this operation amounts to €3 million.

On May 15, 2013, the Group sold its Italian subsidiary Servair Airchef, specialized in airline catering.

As of December 31, 2013, following the Air France-KLM Group's decision not to subscribe to the capital increase requested in October 2013, the Alitalia entity is no longer consolidated by the equity method. The Group's remaining equity interest in Alitalia (7.08%) is recorded under other financial assets *(see Notes 3, 11, 22 and 24)*.

Note 6 Segment information

Business segments

The segment information by activity and geographical area presented below is prepared on the basis of internal management data communicated to the Executive Committee, the Group's principal operational decision-making body.

The Group is organized around the following segments:

- **Passenger**: Passenger operating revenues primarily come from passenger transportation services on scheduled flights with the Group's airline code, including flights operated by other airlines under code-sharing agreements. They also include commissions paid by SkyTeam alliance partners, code-sharing revenues, revenues from excess baggage, airport services supplied by the Group to third-party airlines and services linked to IT systems;
- **Cargo**: Cargo operating revenues come from freight transport on flights under the companies' codes, including flights operated by other partner airlines under code-sharing agreements. Other cargo revenues are derived principally from sales of cargo capacity to third parties.

- **Maintenance**: Maintenance operating revenues are generated through maintenance services provided to other airlines and customers globally;
- **Other**: The revenues from this segment come primarily from catering supplied by the Group to third-party airlines and from charter flights operated primarily by Transavia.

The results, assets and liabilities allocated to the business segments correspond to those attributable directly and indirectly. Amounts allocated to business segments mainly correspond, for the income statement, to the income from operating activities and for the balance sheet, to the goodwill, intangible assets, flight equipment and other tangible assets, the share in equity affiliates, some account receivables, deferred revenue on ticket sales and a portion of provisions and retirement benefits. Other elements of the income statement and balance sheet are presented in the "non-allocated" column.

Inter-segment transactions are evaluated based on normal market conditions.

Geographical segments

The Group's activities are broken down into six geographical regions:

- Metropolitan France;
- Europe (excluding France) and North Africa;
- Caribbean, French Guiana and Indian Ocean;
- Africa, Middle East;
- Americas, Polynesia;
- Asia and New Caledonia.

Only segment revenue is allocated by geographical sales area.

The carrying amount of segment assets by geographical location and the costs incurred to acquire segment assets are not presented, since most of the Group's assets (flight equipment) cannot be allocated to a geographical area.

6.1 Information by business segment

Year ended December 31, 2013

(In € million)	Passenger	Cargo	Maintenance	Other	Non-allocated	Total
Total sales	21,578	2,849	3,280	1,980	-	29,687
Inter-segment sales	(1,466)	(33)	(2,055)	(613)	-	(4,167)
External sales	***20,112***	***2,816***	***1,225***	***1,367***	***-***	***25,520***
Income from current operations	174	(202)	159	(1)	-	130
Income from operating activities	(39)	(343)	146	9	-	(227)
Share of profits (losses) of associates	(215)	-	2	2	-	(211)
Net cost of financial debt and other financial income and expenses	-	-	-	-	(301)	(301)
Income taxes	-	-	-	-	(957)	(957)
Net income from continuing operations	***(254)***	***(343)***	***148***	***11***	***(1,258)***	***(1,696)***
Depreciation and amortization for the period	(1,062)	(71)	(277)	(156)	-	(1,566)
Other non monetary items	(385)	(78)	(43)	(200)	(835)	(1,541)
Total assets	**11,089**	**1,052**	**2,671**	**862**	**9,749**	**25,423**
Segment liabilities	6,341	281	713	367	4,532	12,234
Financial debt, bank overdraft and equity	-	-	-	-	13,189	13,189
Total liabilities	**6,341**	**281**	**713**	**367**	**17,721**	**25,423**
Purchase of property, plant and equipment and intangible assets (continuing operations)	***829***	***44***	***188***	***125***	***-***	***1,186***

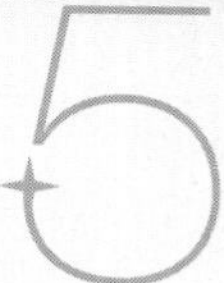

Non-allocated assets, amounting to €9.7 billion, are mainly financial assets held by the Group. They especially comprise cash and cash equivalent for €3.7 billion, pension assets for €2.5 billion, financial assets for €2.7 billion, deferred tax for €0.4 billion and derivatives for €0.4 billion.

Non-allocated liabilities, amounting to €4.5 billion, mainly comprise a portion of provisions and retirement benefits for €2.3 billion, tax and employee-related liabilities for €1.2 billion, deferred tax for €0.2 billion and derivatives for €0.4 billion.

Financial debts, bank overdrafts and equity are not allocated.

➤ **Year ended December 31, 2012 (pro forma)**

(In € million)	Passenger	Cargo	Maintenance	Other	Non-allocated	Total
Total sales	21,495	3,084	3,134	1,901	-	29,614
Inter-segment sales	(1,519)	(27)	(2,038)	(607)	-	(4,191)
External sales	***19,976***	***3,057***	***1,096***	***1,294***	**-**	***25,423***
Income from current operations	(260)	(230)	140	14	-	(336)
Income from operating activities	(518)	(333)	104	16	-	(731)
Share of profits (losses) of associates	(72)	1	1	4	-	(66)
Net cost of financial debt and other financial income and expenses	-	-	-	-	(209)	(209)
Income taxes	-	-	-	-	(17)	(17)
Net income from continuing operations	***(590)***	***(332)***	***105***	***20***	***(226)***	***(1,023)***
Depreciation and amortization for the period	(1,079)	(69)	(278)	(150)	-	(1,576)
Other non monetary items	(1,521)	(106)	(61)	5	160	(1,523)
Total assets	**11,386**	**1,177**	**2,679**	**1,499**	**9,979**	**26,720**
Segment liabilities	6,034	276	713	835	3,969	11,827
Financial debt, bank overdraft and equity	-	-	-	-	14,893	14,893
Total liabilities	**6,034**	**276**	**713**	**835**	**18,862**	**26,720**
Purchase of property, plant and equipment and intangible assets (continuing operations)	***1,105***	***36***	***201***	***123***	**-**	***1,465***

Non-allocated assets, amounting to €10 billion, were mainly financial assets held by the Group. They comprise marketable securities for €3.8 billion, pension assets for €2.5 billion, financial assets for €1.4 billion, deferred tax for €1.4 billion, cash for €0.6 billion and derivatives for €0.3 billion.

Non-allocated liabilities, amounting to €4 billion, mainly comprised a portion of provisions and retirement benefits for €2.4 billion, tax and employee-related liabilities for €1.1 billion, deferred tax for €0.1 billion and derivatives for €0.4 billion.

Financial debts, bank overdrafts and equity are not allocated.

6.2 Information by geographical area

Sales by geographical area

➤ Year ended December 31, 2013

(In € million)	Metropolitan France	Europe (except France) North Africa	Caribbean, French Guiana, Indian Ocean	Africa, Middle East	Americas, Polynesia	Asia, New Caledonia	Total
Scheduled passenger	5,818	6,002	364	1,286	3,596	2,110	19,176
Other passenger sales	399	302	15	56	64	100	936
Total passenger	***6,217***	***6,304***	***379***	***1,342***	***3,660***	***2,210***	***20,112***
Scheduled cargo	388	1,026	26	177	443	559	2,619
Other cargo sales	55	33	4	17	47	41	197
Total cargo	***443***	***1,059***	***30***	***194***	***490***	***600***	***2,816***
Maintenance	749	442	-	-	34	-	1,225
Other	466	803	33	65	-	-	1,367
Total	**7,875**	**8,608**	**442**	**1,601**	**4,184**	**2,810**	**25,520**

➤ Year ended December 31, 2012 (pro forma)

(In € million)	Metropolitan France	Europe (except France) North Africa	Caribbean, French Guiana, Indian Ocean	Africa, Middle East	Americas, Polynesia	Asia, New Caledonia	Total
Scheduled passenger	5,799	6,171	365	1,263	3,403	2,064	19,065
Other passenger sales	359	303	14	61	60	114	911
Total passenger	***6,158***	***6,474***	***379***	***1,324***	***3,463***	***2,178***	***19,976***
Scheduled cargo	372	1,123	30	206	524	617	2,872
Other cargo sales	51	49	4	10	41	30	185
Total cargo	***423***	***1,172***	***34***	***216***	***565***	***647***	***3,057***
Maintenance	709	351	-	-	36	-	1,096
Other	400	805	29	59	-	1	1,294
Total	**7,690**	**8,802**	**442**	**1,599**	**4,064**	**2,826**	**25,423**

Traffic sales by geographical area of destination

➤ Year ended December 31, 2013

(In € million)	Metropolitan France	Europe (except France) North Africa	Caribbean, French Guiana, Indian Ocean	Africa, Middle East	Americas, Polynesia	Asia, New Caledonia	Total
Scheduled passenger	1,932	4,466	1,421	2,538	5,397	3,422	19,176
Scheduled cargo	5	46	142	524	1,053	849	2,619
Total	**1,937**	**4,512**	**1,563**	**3,062**	**6,450**	**4,271**	**21,795**

➤ Year ended December 31, 2012 (pro forma)

(In € million)	Metropolitan France	Europe (except France) North Africa	Caribbean, French Guiana, Indian Ocean	Africa, Middle East	Americas, Polynesia	Asia, New Caledonia	Total
Scheduled passenger	1,970	4,438	1,401	2,567	5,248	3,441	19,065
Scheduled cargo	5	49	148	603	1,168	899	2,872
Total	**1,975**	**4,487**	**1,549**	**3,170**	**6,416**	**4,340**	**21,937**

Note 7 External expenses

Period from 1 January to 31 December *(In € million)*	2013	2012 Pro forma
Aircraft fuel	6,897	7,278
Chartering costs	455	551
Aircraft operating lease costs	913	949
Landing fees and en route charges	1,839	1,832
Catering	589	591
Handling charges and other operating costs	1,405	1,368
Aircraft maintenance costs	1,303	1,131
Commercial and distribution costs	852	866
Other external expenses	1,744	1,706
Total	**15,997**	**16,272**
Excluding aircraft fuel	*9,100*	*8,994*

Note 8 Salaries and number of employees

Salaries and related costs

Period from January 1 to December 31 *(In € million)*	2013	2012 Pro forma
Wages and salaries	5,424	5,514
Costs linked to defined contribution plans	603	610
Net periodic pension cost	379	359
Social contributions	1,171	1,207
Expenses related to share-based compensation	3	5
Other expenses	(98)	(33)
Total	**7,482**	**7,662**

The Group pays contributions to a multi-employer plan in France, the CRPN (public pension fund for crew). This multi-employer plan being assimilated with a French State plan, it is accounted for as a defined contribution plan in "social contributions".

The "other expenses" notably comprise:

- the CICE tax credit amounting to €43 million as of December 31, 2013;
- the capitalization of salary costs on aircraft and engine overhaul.

Average number of employees on continuing operations

Year ended December 31	2013	2012 Pro forma
Flight deck crew	8,103	8,157
Cabin crew	21,779	22,104
Ground staff	66,535	69,639
Total	**96,417**	**99,900**

Note 9 Amortization, depreciation and provisions

Period from January 1 to December 31 *(In € million)*	2013	2012 Pro forma
Intangible assets	80	67
Flight equipment	1,227	1,238
Other property, plant and equipment	259	271
Amortization	***1,566***	***1,576***
Inventories	(1)	-
Trade receivables	5	(1)
Risks and contingencies	155	155
Depreciation and provisions	***159***	***154***
Total	**1,725**	**1,730**

The impact of the review of the useful lives of some aircraft on the value of amortization amounted to €(29) million as of December 31, 2012.

The amortization changes for intangible and tangible assets are presented in Notes 18 and 20.

The changes in impairment relating to inventories and trade receivables are presented in Notes 25, 26 and 27.

The movements in provisions for risks and charges are detailed in Note 31.

Note 10 Other income and expenses

Period from January 1 to December 31 *(In € million)*	2013	2012 Pro forma
Joint operation of routes	(84)	(39)
Operations-related currency hedges	65	117
Other	9	(5)
Total	**(10)**	**73**

Note 11 Other non-current income and expenses

Period from January 1 to December 31 *(In € million)*	2013	2012 Pro forma
Sales of aircraft equipment	*(12)*	8
Restructuring costs	(209)	(455)
Depreciation of assets available for sale	(102)	-
Disposals of subsidiaries and affiliates	7	97
Impairment on goodwill	-	(5)
Other	(41)	(40)
Total	***(345)***	***(403)***

Period from January 1 to December 31, 2013

Restructuring costs

During the third quarter 2013, the Group announced the implementation of additional measures to reduce Air France's salary costs. The overstaffing was estimated at 2,880 employees, including 1,826 for ground staff. In this context, a voluntary departure plan is proposed to ground staff and cabin crew, whose application period will open in 2014.

During the financial year, the Group also adjusted the amount of the net provision booked as of December 31, 2012 concerning the initial voluntary departure plan and the resizing of the fleet.

The Group has consequently made its best estimate of the costs incurred by the measures mentioned above and has recorded a restructuring provision for a total amount of €200 million as of December 31, 2013.

A provision for an onerous lease contract on a Martinair Boeing B747 has also been recorded for an amount of €9 million.

Depreciation of assets available for sale

As part of the review of its fleet plan, the Air France Group has decided to sell two Boeing B747s freighters. The impact of the revaluation of these non-operated aircraft on their sale amounts to €82 million *(see Note 15)*.

For its part, the KLM Group has revalued seven Fokker F70s, two MD11s, one Fokker F100 and several engines at their sale value, representing a total amount of €20 million.

Disposal of subsidiaries and affiliates

This line includes:

- the sale of the shareholding in Financière LMP (39.86%) *(see Note 5)*;
- the sale of the shareholding in Servair Airchef (50%) *(see Note 5)*;
- the impact of dilution on the Alitalia shareholding *(see Notes 3, 5, 22 and 24)*.

Other

This line mainly includes:

- a provision of €18 million relating to crew disputes;
- an additional provision related to anti-competitive cargo practices amounting to €14 million *(see Note 31.3)*;
- an exceptional tax on salaries in the Netherlands, linked to the economic crisis in Europe, amounting to €7 million.

Period from January 1 to December 31, 2012

Restructuring costs

The Group initiated a restructuring plan concerning all the Group companies, comprising mostly two parts: a fleet capacity adjustment and a plan to reduce staff.

Concerning the Air France Group, the plan's conditions were presented to the employee representative bodies of Air France in June 2012 and to its affiliates during the fourth quarter of 2012.

Concerning the resizing of the fleet, the modalities may result, for the equipment involved, in the disposal, sale or dismantling of aircraft or the termination of operating lease contracts.

The Air France staff reduction plan concerning 5,122 positions included assistance for voluntary retirement and a voluntary departure plan whose period of application had opened during the fourth quarter of 2012.

Concerning KLM, a resizing of the fleet was carried out, resulting in the booking of fair value for the MD11 aircraft which were withdrawn from operation.

Given the items mentioned above, the Group had made its best estimate of the costs incurred by these measures and had recorded a provision for restructuring amounting to €408 million as of December 31, 2012.

This provision has been updated as the conditions modalities evolved.

A provision for onerous lease contracts on three Martinair Boeing B747s had also been recorded amounting to €50 million.

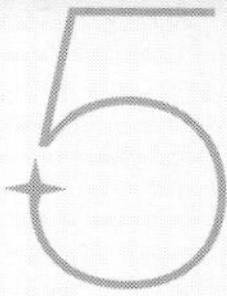

Disposals of subsidiaries and affiliates

The "disposals of subsidiaries and affiliates" line included €97 million corresponding to the gain on disposal realised by the Group on March 1, 2012 concerning a private placement of Amadeus IT Holding SA shares, whose sale proceeds amounted to €466 million.

Other

The "other" line mainly included:

- an exceptional tax on salaries in the Netherlands, linked to the economic crisis in Europe, amounting to €17 million;
- an additional provision related to anti-competitive cargo practices in Switzerland, Brazil and the United States amounting to €20 million *(see Note 31.3)*.

Note 12 Net cost of financial debt and other financial income and expenses

Period from January 1 to December 31 *(In € million)*	**2013**	**2012**
Income from marketable securities	26	28
Other financial income	51	55
Financial income	***77***	***83***
Loan interests	(290)	(269)
Lease interests	(75)	(87)
Capitalized interests	9	14
Other financial expenses	(125)	(94)
Cost of financial debt	***(481)***	***(436)***
Net cost of financial debt	***(404)***	***(353)***
Foreign exchange gains (losses), net	74	64
Change in fair value of financial assets and liabilities	57	63
• *Including fuel derivatives*	*84*	*61*
• *Including currency derivatives*	*(30)*	*(27)*
• *Including interest rates derivatives*	*4*	*(10)*
• *Including other derivatives*	*(1)*	*39*
Net charge release to provisions	(30)	15
Other	2	2
Other financial income and expenses	***103***	***144***
Total	**(301)**	**(209)**

The interest rate used in the calculation of capitalized interest is 3.8% for the year ended December 31, 2013 versus 4% for the year ended December 31, 2012.

Financial income mainly comprises interest income and gains on the sale of financial assets at fair value through profit and loss.

As of December 31, 2013, the cost of financial debt includes an amount of €41 million corresponding to the difference between the nominal interest rate and the effective interest rate (after split accounting of the OCEANEs bonds issued), against €24 million as of December 31, 2012.

As of December 31, 2012, the Group had recorded under change in fair value of financial assets and liabilities (line "Other derivatives") a financial income amounting to €38 million linked to the swap on the OCEANE 2005 *(see Note 32.2.1)*.

Note 13 Income taxes

13.1 Income tax expense

Current income tax expenses and deferred income tax are detailed as follows:

Period from January 1 to December 31 *(In € million)*	2013	2012 Pro forma
(Expense) / income for the year	(41)	(41)
Current tax (expense) / income	***(41)***	***(41)***
Change in temporary differences	20	(50)
CAVE impact	3	3
Tax loss carryforwards	(939)	71
Deferred tax income / (expense) from continuing operations	***(916)***	***24***
Total	**(957)**	**(17)**

The current tax expense relates to the amounts paid or payable in the short term to the tax authorities in respect of the financial year, in accordance with the regulations prevailing in the different countries and any applicable treaties.

In France, tax losses can be carried forward for an unlimited period. However, the 2011 and 2012 Finance Acts limited the amount of the fiscal loss recoverable each year to 50% of the profit for the period beyond the first million. The period for recovering these losses against future profits having also been extended within the context of prevailing economic crisis and a highly competitive global market, the Group decided, for reasons of prudence, to limit on an appropriate period its recoverability horizon relating to the French fiscal group. The amount of deferred tax assets relating to tax losses has consequently been reduced to €708 million as of December 31, 2013, against €1,645 million as of December 31, 2012.

In the Netherlands, tax losses can be carried forward for a period of nine years, without any limit on the amount that can be recovered in any one year.

During the year ended December 31, 2012, the Group had recognized deferred tax assets on fiscal losses of €71 million, mainly relating to the Dutch fiscal group.

13.2 Deferred tax recorded directly in equity – Group

Period from January 1 to December 31 *(In € million)*	2013	2012 Pro forma
Treasury shares	-	(3)
OCEANE	(37)	-
Other comprehensive income that will be reclassified to profit or loss	(10)	30
♦ *Assets available for sale*	*(18)*	*(4)*
♦ *Derivatives*	*8*	*34*
Other comprehensive income that will not be reclassified to profit or loss	(18)	95
♦ *Pensions*	*(18)*	*95*
Total	**(65)**	**122**

13.3 Effective tax rate

The difference between the standard tax rate in France and the effective tax rate is detailed as follows:

Period from January 1 to December 31 *(In € million)*	**2013**	**2012 Pro forma**
Income before tax	(528)	(940)
Standard tax rate in France	34.43%	34.43%
Theoretical tax calculated with the standard tax rate in France	182	324
Differences in French / foreign tax rates	16	(2)
Non deductible expenses or non taxable income	(20)	2
Variation of unrecognized deferred tax assets	(1,135)	(317)
CAVE impact	(24)	(21)
Other	24	(3)
Income tax expenses	**(957)**	**(17)**
Effective tax rate	NS	NS

The current tax rate applicable in France is 38% within 2014 including additional contributions. Since the French fiscal group realized a fiscal deficit as of December 31, 2013, the taxproof has been established using the rate excluding additional contributions, i.e. 34.43%. Deferred tax has been calculated on the same basis.

The current tax rate applicable in the Netherlands is 25%.

13.4 Deferred tax recorded on the balance sheet

(In € million)	**January 1, 2013**	**Amounts recorded in income**	**Amounts recorded in OCI**	**Amounts recorded in equity**	**Currency translation adjustment**	**Reclassification and other**	**December 31, 2013**
Flight equipment	(1,257)	(15)	-	-	-	(5)	(1,277)
Pension assets	(566)	(47)	14	-	-	(9)	(608)
Financial debt	758	60	-	(37)	-	(1)	780
Deferred revenue on ticket sales	166	11	-	-	-	-	177
Others	(14)	14	(42)	-	-	(1)	(43)
Deferred tax corresponding to fiscal losses	2,156	(939)	-	-	-	12	1,229
Deferred tax asset / (liability)	**1,243**	**(916)**	**(28)**	**(37)**	**-**	**(4)**	**258**

Deferred taxes recognized on fiscal losses for the French and Dutch fiscal perimeters amount to €1,178 million as of December 31, 2013 (€708 million for the French fiscal group and €470 million for the Dutch fiscal group).

The recognition of this asset for each of the two perimeters is based on the prospects for taxable income established by the Group's three-year plan and based on the same assumptions as those outlined in Note 19 "Impairment" to these consolidated financial statements.

Based on these prospects for taxable income, the recoverability horizon is suitable as for the French perimeter than for the Dutch perimeter. The non realization of these assumptions could have a significant impact on the recoverability horizon for these deferred tax assets.

(In € million)	January 1, 2012 Pro forma	Amounts recorded in income	Amounts recorded in OCI	Amounts recorded in equity	Currency translation adjustment	Reclassification and other	December 31, 2012 Pro forma
Flight equipment	(1,147)	(110)	-	-	-	-	(1,257)
Pension assets	(530)	(43)	7	-	-	-	(566)
Financial debt	614	144	-	-	-	-	758
Other liabilities	84	(55)	44	-	-	-	73
Deferred revenue on ticket sales	170	(4)	-	-	-	-	166
Others	(176)	18	74	(3)	-	-	(87)
Deferred tax corresponding to fiscal losses	2,085	71	-	-	-	-	2,156
Deferred tax asset / (liability)	**1,100**	**21**	**125**	**(3)**	**-**	**-**	**1,243**

Deferred tax recognized on fiscal losses for the French and Dutch fiscal perimeters amounted to €2,100 million as of December 31, 2012 (€1,645 million for the French fiscal group and €455 million for the Dutch fiscal group).

13.5 Unrecognized deferred tax assets

(In € million)	December 31, 2013		December 31, 2012	
	Basis	Tax	Basis	Tax
Temporary differences	476	164	469	159
Tax losses	4,025	1,386	755	260
Total	**4,501**	**1,550**	**1,224**	**419**

As of December 31, 2013, the cumulative effect of the limitation the French fiscal group's deferred tax assets results in the non-recognition of a deferred tax asset amounting to €1,525 million (corresponding to a basis of €4,429 million), including €1,362 million relating to tax losses and €163 million relating to temporary differences (non-recognition of deferred tax assets relating to restructuration provisions). The amount of deferred tax on tax losses non recognized during the period includes €937 million relating to the limitation of the recoverability horizon *(see Note 13.1)*.

As of December 31, 2012, the cumulative effect of the limitation the French fiscal group's deferred tax assets resulted in the non-recognition of a deferred tax asset amounting to €394 million (corresponding to a basis of €1,144 million), including €239 million relating to tax losses and €155 million relating to temporary differences (non-recognition of deferred tax assets relating to restructuration provisions).

Other unrecognized deferred tax assets mainly correspond to a portion of the tax loss carry-forwards of the Air France Group subsidiaries, as well as tax loss carryforwards in some subsidiairies in the United Kingdom.

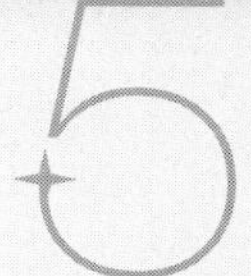

Note 14 Net income from discontinued operations

The line "Net income from discontinued operations" corresponds to the contribution of the all CityJet and VLM

Period from January 1 to December 31 *(In millions of euros)*	2013	2012 Pro forma
Sales	*150*	*210*
Income from current operations	***(19)***	***(17)***
Impairment	(77)	(168)
Other non current items	(25)	(4)
Income from operating activities	***(121)***	***(189)***
Financial income	(1)	(5)
Income before taxes	(122)	(194)
Income taxes	-	(3)
Net income from discontinued operations	**(122)**	**(197)**

Period from January 1 to December 31, 2013

Impairment

Within the framework of the valuation of the Irish and Belgian "regional" companies, the Group recorded an additional provision of €77 million, to align the net assets of the CityJet and VLM Group with its expected sale value.

Other non current items

The other non current items include provisions regarding a breach of contract and disputes relating to the payment of social contributions in France.

Period from January 1 to December 31, 2012

Impairment

Within the framework of the "Transform 2015" restructuring plan as presented at the end of August 2012 to the Works Councils of the relevant companies, the Air France Group decided to reorganize its "regional" activity by regrouping the French subsidiaries in Hop! and separating them from the other regional airlines, particularly in Ireland and Belgium.

Within this framework, the Group reviewed the assets of CityJet and its subsidiary VLM, which are now valued on a stand-alone basis. In 2012, this review prompted the Group to depreciate all the goodwill attached to VLM, amounting to €168 million.

Note 15 Assets held for sale and liabilities related to assets held for sale

Year ended December 31, 2013

As of December 31, 2013, the "Assets held for sale" and "Liabilities related to assets held for sale" correspond, for a respective €34 million and €58 million, to the assets and liabilities of the CityJet Group held for sale *(see Notes 2 and 14)*.

Furthermore, the line "Assets held for sale" includes the fair value of six aircraft held for sale for an amount of €57 million, including two Boeing B747 freighters in the Air France Group for €51 million *(see Note 11)*.

Year ended December 31, 2012

As of December 31, 2012, the line "assets held for sale" included the fair value of six aircraft held for sale for an amount of €7 million.

Note 16 Earnings per share

16.1 Income for the period – Equity holders of Air France-KLM per share

Reconciliation of income used to calculate earnings per share

The result used to calculate earnings per share are as follows:

As of January 1 to December 31 *(In € million)*	**2013**	**2012 Pro forma**
Net income- Equity holders of Air France-KLM	(1,827)	(1,225)
Net income from continuing operations - Equity holders of Air France-KLM	(1,705)	(1,028)
Net income from discontinued operations - Equity holders of Air France-KLM	(122)	(197)

Since the Group does not pay dividends to preferred stockholders, there is no difference with the results appearing in the financial statements. The results being losses for the periods presented, the results used to calculate diluted earnings per share are to the same as the results used to calculate earnings per share.

Reconciliation of the number of shares used to calculate earnings per share

Year ended to December 31	**2013**	**2012**
Weighted average number of:		
• Ordinary shares issued	300,219,278	300,219,278
• Treasury stock held regarding stock option plan	(1,116,420)	(1,116,420)
• Treasury stock held in stock buyback plan	-	(159,712)
• Other treasury stock	(3,067,607)	(3,073,029)
Number of shares used to calculate basic earnings per share	***296,035,251***	***295,870,117***
OCEANE conversion	-	-
Number of ordinary and potential ordinary shares used to calculate diluted earnings per share	***296,035,251***	***295,870,117***

16.2 Non dilutive instruments

The Air France-KLM Group did not own any non dilutive instrument as of December 31, 2013.

16.3 Instruments issued after the closing date

No instruments were issued after the closing date.

Note 17 Goodwill

Detail of consolidated goodwill

As of December 31 *(In € million)*	2013			2012		
	Gross value	Impairment	Net value	Gross value	Impairment	Net value
VLM	-	-	-	168	(168)	-
UTA	112	-	112	112	-	112
Régional	60	-	60	60	-	60
Aeromaintenance Group	20	(3)	17	21	(4)	17
Britair	20	-	20	20	-	20
CityJet	-	-	-	11	-	11
NAS Airport Services Limited	22	-	22	24	(1)	23
Other	7	(1)	6	10	(1)	9
Total	**241**	**(4)**	**237**	**426**	**(174)**	**252**

The goodwill concerns mainly the “Passenger” business.

Movement in net book value of goodwill

As of December 31 *(In € million)*	2013	2012
Opening balance	**252**	**426**
Acquisitions	3	-
Disposals	(6)	-
Impairment	(11)	(173)
Currency translation adjustment	(1)	(1)
Closing balance	**237**	**252**

As of December 31, 2013, the impairment recorded concerns CityJet, following the writing down of its net asset value on its reclassification under assets available for sale *(see Note 2.2)*.

As of December 31, 2012, the impairment recorded mainly concerned the VLM goodwill. Within the framework of the «Transform 2015» restructuring plan, the Group proceeded to review the assets of CityJet and its subsidiary VLM as described in Note 14. This review had led the Group to depreciate all the goodwill attached to VLM amounting to €168 million. The related expense was recognized in non-current expenses in the income statement.

Note 18 Intangible assets

(In € million)	Trademarks and slots	Customer relationships	Other intangible assets	Total
Gross value				
Amount as of December 31, 2011	*297*	*107*	*825*	*1,229*
Additions	-	-	146	**146**
Change in scope	-	-	-	**-**
Disposals	-	-	(25)	**(25)**
Transfer	-	-	(4)	**(4)**
Amount as of December 31, 2012	*297*	*107*	*942*	*1,346*
Additions	-	-	166	**166**
Change in scope	-	-	(6)	**(6)**
Disposals	-	-	(32)	**(32)**
Transfer	(4)	-	(4)	**(8)**
Amount as of December 31, 2013	*293*	*107*	*1,066*	*1,466*
Depreciation				
Amount as of December 31, 2011	*(2)*	*(102)*	*(351)*	*(455)*
Charge to depreciation	-	-	(68)	**(68)**
Releases on disposal	-	-	19	**19**
Transfer	-	-	-	**-**
Amount as of December 31, 2012	*(2)*	*(102)*	*(400)*	*(504)*
Charge to depreciation	(1)	(2)	(73)	**(76)**
Releases on disposal	-	-	5	**5**
Change in scope	-	-	5	**5**
Amount as of December 31, 2013	*(3)*	*(104)*	*(463)*	*(570)*
Net value				
As of December 31, 2012	295	5	542	**842**
As of December 31, 2013	290	3	603	**896**

Intangible assets mainly comprise:

- the KLM and Transavia brands and slots (takeoff and landing) acquired by the Group as part of the acquisition of KLM. These intangible assets have an indefinite useful life as the nature of the assets means they have no time limit;
- software and capitalized IT costs.

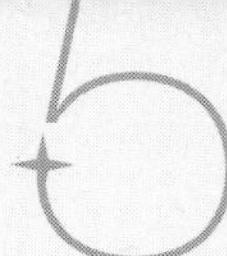

Note 19 Impairment

Concerning the methodology followed to test impairment, the Group has allocated each item of goodwill and each intangible fixed asset with an indefinite useful life to Cash Generating Units (CGU), corresponding to their business segments (see "Accounting Policies").

As of December 31, 2013, goodwill and intangible fixed assets with an indefinite useful life were attached principally to the "Passenger" CGU for €194 million and €288 million respectively.

The recoverable value of the CGU assets has been determined by reference to their value in use as of September 30, 2013, except for the Cargo CGU for which an additional test has been made as of December 31, 2013. The tests were realized for all the CGUs on the basis of a three-year Group plan, approved by the management, including a recovery hypothesis after the economic slowdown, enabling the achievement of the medium-term forecasts made by the Group before the emergence of the crisis.

The discount rate used for the test corresponds to the Group's weighted average cost of capital (WACC). It amounts to 7.4% at December 31, 2013 against 7.7% at December 31, 2012.

After this test, no impairment was observed on the Group's CGUs.

The Cargo CGU being loss-making, the Group has also tested all the tangible assets of this business as of December 31, 2013. No impairment was observed.

The asset value of Cargo CGU, which amounts to €715 millions, is covered by its future free cash flows. A decrease of 50 basis points in the percentage of the current operations margin target would lead to record an impairment loss of approximately €100 million. An increase of 50 basis points of the discount rate would lead to record an impairment loss of approximately €60 million.

Note 20 Tangible assets

	Flight equipment					Other tangible assets					
(In € million)	Owned aircraft	Leased aircraft	Assets in progress	Other	Total	Land and buildings	Equip-ment and machi-nery	Assets in progress	Other	Total	Total
Gross value											
As of December 31, 2011	***10,872***	***5,216***	***728***	***2,143***	***18,959***	***2,673***	***1,288***	***100***	***908***	***4,969***	***23,928***
Acquisitions	351	161	764	105	1,381	46	51	55	29	181	**1,562**
Disposals	(922)	(77)	(63)	(150)	(1,212)	(41)	(23)	-	(27)	(91)	**(1,303)**
Fair value	-	-	48	-	48	-	-	-	-	-	**48**
Transfer	(480)	883	(1,130)	37	(690)	64	10	(100)	15	(11)	**(701)**
As of December 31, 2012	***9,821***	***6,183***	***347***	***2,135***	***18,486***	***2,742***	***1,326***	***55***	***925***	***5,048***	***23,534***
Acquisitions	133	4	705	109	951	48	22	70	20	160	**1,111**
Disposals	(732)	(79)	-	(188)	(999)	(16)	(16)	-	(15)	(47)	**(1,046)**
Scope variation	20	36	-	-	56	-	-	-	(6)	(6)	**50**
Fair value	-	-	54	-	54	-	-	-	-	-	**54**
Transfer	(380)	588	(706)	107	(391)	54	-	(30)	(41)	(17)	**(408)**
Currency translation adjustment	-	-	-	-	-	-	(1)	-	(1)	(2)	**(2)**
As of December 31, 2013	***8,862***	***6,732***	***400***	***2,163***	***18,157***	***2,828***	***1,331***	***95***	***882***	***5,136***	***23,293***
Depreciation											
As of December 31, 2011	***(5,695)***	***(1,645)***	***-***	***(930)***	***(8,270)***	***(1,422)***	***(834)***	***-***	***(658)***	***(2,914)***	***(11,184)***
Charge to depreciation	(800)	(364)	-	(128)	(1,292)	(134)	(82)	-	(56)	(272)	**(1,564)**
Releases on disposal	286	73	-	134	493	34	20	-	15	69	**562**
Transfer	721	(111)	-	21	631	(1)	-	-	2	1	**632**
As of December 31, 2012	***(5,488)***	***(2,047)***	***-***	***(903)***	***(8,438)***	***(1,523)***	***(896)***	***-***	***(697)***	***(3,116)***	***(11,554)***
Charge to depreciation	(788)	(405)	-	(144)	(1,337)	(132)	(80)	-	(48)	(260)	**(1,597)**
Releases on disposal	518	76	-	162	756	15	13	-	8	36	**792**
Scope variation	-	-	-	-	-	-	-	-	3	3	**3**
Transfer	423	(113)	-	(57)	253	(28)	13	-	34	19	**272**
Currency translation adjustment	-	-	-	-	-	-	1	-	-	1	**1**
As of December 31, 2013	***(5,335)***	***(2,489)***	***-***	***(942)***	***(8,766)***	***(1,668)***	***(949)***	***-***	***(700)***	***(3,317)***	***(12,083)***
Net value											
As of December 31, 2012	4,333	4,136	347	1,232	**10,048**	1,219	430	55	228	**1,932**	**11,980**
As of December 31, 2013	3,527	4,243	400	1,221	**9,391**	1,160	382	95	182	**1,819**	**11,210**

Aeronautical assets under construction mainly include advance payments, maintenance work in progress concerning engines and aircraft modifications.

Note 37 details the amount of pledged tangible assets.

Commitments to property purchases are detailed in Notes 37 and 38.

The net book value of tangible assets financed under capital lease amounts to €4,762 million as of December 31, 2013 versus €4,618 million as of December 31, 2012.

The charge to depreciation as of December 31, 2013 includes €102 million of depreciation booked in non current charges *(see Note 11)*.

The charge to depreciation as of December 31, 2012 included €40 million relating to the resizing of the Group's fleet, booked in restructuring costs *(see Note 11)*.

Note 21 Capital expenditure

The detail of capital expenditures on tangible and intangible assets presented in the consolidated cash flow statements is as follows:

As of December 31 *(In € million)*	**2013**	**2012**
Acquisition of tangible assets	1,046	1,351
Acquisition of intangible assets	166	146
Accounts payable on acquisitions and capitalized interest	(26)	(32)
Total	**1,186**	**1,465**

Note 22 Equity affiliates

Movements over the period

The table below presents the movement in equity affiliates:

(In € million)	Alitalia	Kenya Airways	Other	Total
Carrying value of share in investment as of December 31, 2011	***274***	***57***	***91***	***422***
Share in net income of equity affiliates	(61)	(12)	7	(66)
Distributions	-	(1)	(3)	(4)
Change in consolidation scope	-	1	2	3
Fair value adjustment	(6)	(2)	-	(8)
Other variations	-	36	1	37
Currency translation adjustment	-	(3)	-	(3)
Carrying value of share in investment as of December 31, 2012 (pro forma)	***207***	***76***	***98***	***381***
Share in net income of equity affiliates	(202)	(8)	(1)	(211)
Distributions	-	-	(2)	(2)
Change in consolidation scope	-	-	(11)	(11)
Other variations	-	4	7	11
Fair value adjustment	(5)	-	-	(5)
Capital increase	-	-	16	16
Currency translation adjustment	-	(2)	-	(2)
Carrying value of share in investment as of December 31, 2013	***-***	***70***	***107***	***177***
Market value for listed companies		***45***		

Following the dilution in its shareholding during the last quarter of 2013, the Group no longer accounts for Alitalia as an equity affiliate, but now recognizes its equity interest under other financial assets *(see Notes 3, 5, 11 and 24)*.

Given the uncertainties overhanging Alitalia's situation prior to this dilution in its shareholding, the Group decided, during the third quarter, to totally depreciate its shareholding in Alitalia. The share of losses and a provision for impairment have consequently been booked amounting to a total of €202 million.

Simplified financial statements of the main equity affiliates

The investments in equity affiliates as of December 31, 2013 mainly concern the company Kenya Airways, a Kenyan airline based in Nairobi, over which the Group exercises a significant influence.

As of December 31, 2012, besides Kenya Airways, investments in equity affiliates also included the company Alitalia Aerea Italiana Spa. This entity, which began operations on January 12, 2009, is derived from the contribution of the transition from the old Alitalia and redemption of Air One activity. It was removed from the equity affiliates scope during the last quarter of 2013 following the Group's decision not to subscribe to the requested capital increase. Since this date, Alitalia's shares are recognized in other financial assets.

The financial statements of the main equity affiliates are presented below.

They correspond to 100% of the financial data for the years 2013 and 2012, prepared in accordance with the local standards of the relevant host countries.

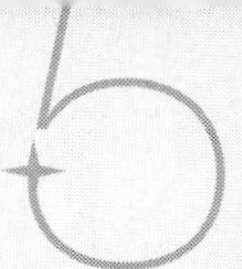

(In € million)	Alitalia 12/31/2012	Kenya Airways 03/31/2012
% holding as of December 31, 2012	25%	26.7%
Operating revenues	3,594	949
Operating income	(119)	11
Net income / loss	(280)	14
Stockholders' equity	201	203
Total assets	**2,634**	**681**
Total liabilities and stockholders' equity	**2,634**	**681**
	12/31/2013	**03/31/2013**
% holding as of December 31, 2013		26.7%
Operating revenues		902
Operating income		(82)
Net income / loss		(72)
Stockholders' equity		281
Total assets		**1,104**
Total liabilities and stockholders' equity		**1,104**

Note 23 Pension assets

(In € million)	December 31, 2013	December 31, 2012 Pro forma	January 1, 2012 Pro forma
Opening balance	**2,477**	**2,336**	**2,995**
Net periodic pension (cost) / income for the period	(277)	(190)	(36)
Contributions paid to the funds	342	359	258
First application of IAS 19 Revised " Employee Benefits" (Note 2)	-	-	(881)
Fair value revaluation	(138)	(29)	-
Reclassification	-	1	-
Closing balance	**2,454**	**2,477**	**2,336**

The detail of these pension assets is presented in Note 31.1.

Note 24 Other financial assets

As of December 31 *(In € million)*	2013		2012	
	Current	Non current	Current	Non current
Financial assets available for sale				
Available shares	-	762	-	475
Shares secured	-	373	-	229
Assets at fair value through profit and loss				
Marketable securities	106	20	235	85
Cash secured	825	-	636	-
Loans and receivables				
Financial lease deposit (bonds)	12	142	31	125
Financial lease deposit (others)	65	560	11	639
Loans and receivables	23	125	20	124
Gross value	***1,031***	***1,982***	***933***	***1,677***
Impairment at opening date	-	*(12)*	-	*(11)*
New impairment charge	-	(7)	-	(11)
Use of provision	-	-	-	10
Impairment at closing date	-	*(19)*	-	*(12)*
Total	**1,031**	**1,963**	**933**	**1,665**

Financial assets available for sale are as follows:

(In € million)	Fair Value	% interest	Stockholder's equity	Net income	Stock price *(in €)*	Closing date
As of December 31, 2013						
Amadeus*	1,076	7.73%	ND**	ND**	31.10	December 2013
Alitalia	22	7.08%	ND**	ND**	NA***	December 2013
Other	37	-	-	-	-	-
Total	**1,135**					
As of December 31, 2012						
Amadeus*	659	7.73%	1,531	496	19.05	December 2012
Other	45	-	-	-	-	-
Total	**704**					

* *Listed company.*
** *Non-available.*
*** *Non-applicable.*

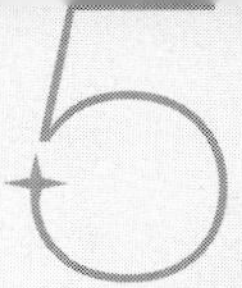

Assets at fair value through profit and loss mainly comprise shares in mutual funds that do not meet the “cash equivalents” definition and cash account secured, mainly within the framework of the swap contract with Natixis on the OCEANE 2005 *(see Note 32)* and the guarantee given to the European Union concerning the anti-trust litigation *(see Note 31)*.

Concerning the Amadeus shares, on November 13, 2012, the Group entered into a hedging transaction with Société Générale to hedge the value of one third of its stake, i.e 12 million shares. The hedging instrument implemented was a collar. As part of this transaction, a loan of the same number of shares was set up with Société Générale. The collar was qualified as a fair value hedge. Its fair value amounts to €108 million as of December 31, 2013 (against €0.2 million as of December 31, 2012).

Loans and receivables mainly include deposits on flight equipment made within the framework of operating and capital leases.

Transfer of financial assets that are not derecognized in their entirety

Transfer of receivables agreement

The Group entered into a loan agreement secured by Air France's 1% housing loans. For each of the CILs (Comités interprofessionnels du logement), Air France and the bank concluded a tripartite receivables delegation agreement with reference to the loan agreement. Through this agreement, the CILs commit to repaying the bank directly on each payment date. These are imperfect delegations: in the event of non repayment by the CILs, Air France remains liable to the bank for the loan repayments and interest. As of December 31, 2013, the amount of transferred receivables stood at €111 million (against €112 million as of December 31, 2012). The associated loan stood at €81 million as of December 31, 2013 (against €80 million as of December 31, 2012).

Loan of shares agreement

On November 13, 2012, the Group signed a loan of shares agreement on Amadeus shares, within the framework of the hedging transaction to protect the value of Amadeus shares, as described above. As of December 31, 2013, the amount of the loan, excluding hedge effect, amounts to €373 million (against €229 million as of December 31, 2012).

Transfer of financial assets that are derecognized in their entirety

Since 2011, the Group has established non recourse transfert agreements concerning trade passenger, cargo and airlines receivables.

These agreements apply to receivables originating in France and other European countries for a total transferred amount of €211 million as of December 31, 2013, against €246 million as of December 31, 2012.

As of December 31, 2013, the link retained by the Group with the transferred assets represents a risk of dilution for which guarantee funds have been secured for €10 million, against €9 million as of December 31, 2012.

End of December 2013, the Group concluded a contract with a bank transfer without recourse by way of discount on the entire Receivable Tax Credit for Competitiveness Employment (CICE) 2013 with a notional amount of €42 million. The contract of assignment transferring substantially all the risks and rewards of the debt to the bank, the debt has been fully derecognised. As of December 31, 2013 the Group has a receivable from the bank corresponding to 5% of the nominal value of the assigned receivable, payable when the specific CICE statement will be sent to the tax administration in 2014.

Note 25 Inventories

As of December 31 *(In € million)*	2013	2012
Aeronautical spare parts	510	508
Other supplies	158	176
Production work in progress	7	7
Gross value	***675***	***691***
Opening valuation allowance	***(170)***	***(173)***
Charge to allowance	(11)	(18)
Use of allowance	11	18
Releases of allowance no longer required	-	-
Reclassification	6	3
Closing valuation allowance	***(164)***	***(170)***
Net value of inventory	***511***	***521***

Note 26 Trade accounts receivables

As of December 31 *(In € million)*	2013	2012
Airlines	399	495
Other clients:		
♦ Passenger	681	625
♦ Cargo	353	378
♦ Maintenance	377	364
♦ Other	52	82
Gross value	***1,862***	***1,944***
Opening valuation allowance	***(85)***	***(88)***
Charge to allowance	(21)	(18)
Use of allowance	16	19
Change of scope	2	-
Reclassification	1	2
Closing valuation allowance	***(87)***	***(85)***
Net value	***1,775***	***1,859***

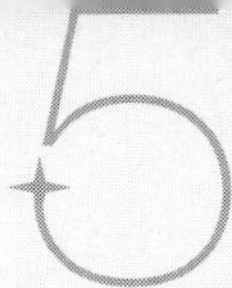

Note 27 Other assets

As of December 31 *(In € million)*	2013		2012	
	Current	Non current	Current	Non current
Suppliers with debit balances	140	-	161	-
State receivable	72	-	71	-
Derivative instruments	267	97	201	103
Prepaid expenses	164	16	156	49
Other debtors	181	-	241	-
Gross value	***824***	***113***	***830***	***152***
Opening valuation allowance	***(2)***	**-**	***(2)***	**-**
Charge to allowance	(1)	-	-	-
Use of allowance	1	-	-	-
Closing valuation allowance	**(2)**	**-**	**(2)**	**-**
Net realizable value of other assets	***822***	***113***	***828***	***152***

As of December 31, 2012, non-current derivatives comprised an amount of €9 million relating to currency hedges on financial debt.

Note 28 Cash, cash equivalents and bank overdrafts

As of December 31 *(In € million)*	2013	2012
Liquidity funds (SICAV) (assets at fair value through profit and loss)	1,563	2,467
Bank deposits and term accounts (assets at fair value through profit and loss)	1,141	334
Cash in hand	980	619
Total cash and cash equivalents	***3,684***	***3,420***
Bank overdrafts	(166)	(257)
Cash, cash equivalents and bank overdrafts	***3,518***	***3,163***

The Group holds €3,684 million in cash as of December 31, 2013, including €199 million placed on bank accounts in Venezuela.This amount comes from the sale of airline tickets made locally during the period from December 2012 to December 2013. Under the exchange control, monthly requests for money transfers have been made to the Commission of Currency Administration *(Comisión de Administración de-Divisas - CADIVI)*. Given the economic and political context of Venezuela, these requests did not give rise to currency transfers (the last transfer tooking place in October 2013).

Note 29 Equity attributable to equity holders of Air France-KLM SA

29.1 Issued capital

As of December 31, 2013, the issued capital of Air France-KLM comprised 300,219,278 fully paid-up shares. Each share with a nominal value of one euro is entitled to one vote.

The change in the number of issued shares is as follows:

As of December 31 *(In number of shares)*	2013	2012
At the beginning of the period	***300,219,278***	***300,219,278***
Issuance of shares for OCEANE conversion	-	-
At the end of the period	***300,219,278***	***300,219,278***
Of which:		
• number of shares issued and paid up	300,219,278	300,219,278
• number of shares issued and not paid up	-	-

The shares comprising the issued capital of Air France-KLM are subject to no restriction or priority concerning dividend distribution or reimbursement of the issued capital.

Authorized stock

The Combined Ordinary and Extraordinary Shareholders' Meeting of May 16, 2013 authorized the Board of Directors, for a period of 26 months from the date of the Meeting, to issue shares and/or other securities conferring immediate or future rights to Air France-KLM's capital limited to a total maximum nominal amount of €120 million.

Breakdown of the share capital and voting rights

The breakdown of the share capital and voting rights is as follows:

As of December 31	% of capital		% of voting rights	
	2013	2012	2013	2012
French State	16%	16%	16%	16%
Employees and former employees	7%	10%	7%	10%
Treasury shares	1%	1%	-	-
Other	76%	73%	77%	74%
Total	**100%**	**100%**	**100%**	**100%**

The item "Employees and former employees" includes shares held by employees and former employees identified in funds or by a Sicovam code.

Other securities giving access to common stock

OCEANE

See Note 32.2.

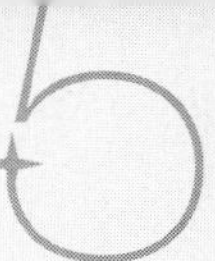

29.2 Additional paid-in capital

Additional paid-in capital represents the difference between the nominal value of equity securities issued and the value of contributions in cash or in kind received by Air France-KLM.

29.3 Treasury shares

	Treasury shares	
	Number	**(In € million)**
December 31, 2011	*5,639,477*	*(89)*
Change in the period	(1,450,072)	4
December 31, 2012	*4,189 405*	*(85)*
Change in the period	(9,601)	-
December 31, 2013	*4,179,804*	*(85)*

As of December 31, 2013, Air France-KLM held 3,063,384 of its own shares acquired pursuant to the annual authorizations granted by the Shareholders' Meeting. As of December 31, 2013, the Group also held 1,116,420 of its own shares in respect of KLM stock option programs. All these treasury shares are classified as a reduction of equity.

29.4 Reserves and retained earnings

(In € million)	December 31, 2013	December 31, 2012 Pro forma	January 1, 2012 Pro forma
Legal reserve	70	70	70
Distributable reserves	734	850	962
Pension defined benefit reserves	(1,193)	(1,203)	(1,083)
Derivatives reserves	(47)	(43)	55
Available for sale securities reserves	655	253	86
Other reserves	664	1,701	2,127
Net income (loss) – Group share	(1,827)	(1,225)	(442)
Total	**(944)**	**403**	**1,775**

As of December 31, 2013, the legal reserve of €70 million represented 23% of Air France-KLM's issued capital. French company law requires that a limited company *(société anonyme)* allocates 5% of its unconsolidated statutory net income each year to this legal reserve until it reaches 10% of the Group's issued capital. The amount allocated to this legal reserve is deducted from the distributable income for the current year.

The legal reserve of any company subject to this requirement may only be distributed to shareholders upon liquidation of the company.

Note 30 Share-based compensation

30.1 Outstanding share-based compensation plans and other plans as of December 31, 2013

As of December 31, 2013, there were no outstanding share-based compensation plans in the Air France-KLM Group.

Changes in options

	Average exercise price (€)	Number of options
Options outstanding as of December 31, 2011	*34.21*	*390,517*
Of which: options exercisable at December 31, 2011	*34.21*	*390,517*
Options forfeited during the period	34.21	(390,517)
Options exercised during the period	-	-
Options granted during the period	-	-
Options outstanding as of December 31, 2012	-	-
Of which: options exercisable at December 31, 2012	-	-
Options forfeited during the period	-	
Options exercised during the period	-	
Options granted during the period	-	
Options outstanding as of December 31, 2013	-	-
Of which: options exercisable at December 31, 2013	-	-

Description of KLM stock-option plans

Prior to the combination with Air France, members of the Management Board and the key executives of KLM had been granted KLM stock options. Within the combination agreement between KLM and Air France, stock-options and SAR (Share Appreciation Rights) that were not exercised during the operation were modified on May 4, 2004 so that their holders could purchase Air France-KLM shares and SARs attached to Air France-KLM shares. The shares held by KLM within this plan were converted into Air France-KLM shares and transferred to a foundation whose sole purpose is their retention until the stock options are exercised or forfeited.

The vesting conditions of the stock-option plan granted by KLM in July 2007 are such that one third of the options vest at grant date with a further one third after one and two years, respectively. Vesting was conditional on KLM achieving predetermined non-market-dependent performance criteria.

30.2 KLM PPSs plan

During the periods ending December 31, 2013 and December 31, 2012, cash-settled share-based compensation plans index-linked to the change in the Air France-KLM share price were granted by KLM. They correspond to share-based plans with settlement in cash (PPS).

Plans	Grant date	Number of PPSs granted	Start date for PPSs exercise	Date of expiry	Number of PPSs exercised as of 12/31/2013
KLM	01/07/2008	153,080	01/07/2008	01/07/2013	68,451
KLM	01/07/2009	136,569	01/07/2009	01/07/2014	23,615
KLM	01/07/2010	145,450	01/07/2010	01/07/2015	12,189
KLM	01/07/2011	144,235	01/07/2011	01/07/2016	-
KLM	01/04/2012	146,004	01/04/2012	01/04/2017	-
KLM	01/04/2013	150,031	01/04/2013	01/04/2018	-

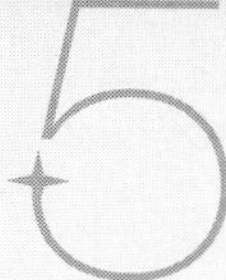

The changes in PPSs were as follows:

	Number of PPSs
PPSs outstanding as of December 31, 2011	***465,497***
Of which: SARs exercisable at December 31, 2011	***270,908***
PPSs granted during the period	146,004
PPSs exercised during the period	(51,348)
PPSs forfeited during the period	13,493
PPSs outstanding as of December 31, 2012	***573,646***
Of which: PPSs exercisable at December 31, 2012	***357,687***
PPSs granted during the period	150,031
PPSs exercised during the period	(104,255)
PPSs forfeited during the period	(99,064)
PPSs outstanding as of December 31, 2013	***520,358***
Of which: PPSs exercisable at December 31, 2013	***330,807***

The vesting conditions of the PPSs plans granted by KLM are such that one third of the options vest at grant date, with a further one third after one and two years, respectively. Vesting is conditional on KLM achieving predetermined non-market-dependent performance criteria.

The fair value of the services provided under the PPSs plan has been determined according to the market value of the Air France-KLM share at the closing date i.e €7.58:

PPSs	Fair value as of December 31, 2013 *(In € million)*
01/07/2009	0.4
01/07/2010	0.6
01/07/2011	0.9
01/04/2012	0.9
01/04/2013	1.1

30.3 Salary expenses related to share-based compensation

Period from January 1 to December 31	2013	2012
(In € million)		
2005 Shares-for-Salary Exchange	2	3
Stock option plan	1	2
Salary expenses (Note 8)	***3***	***5***

Note 31 Provisions and retirement benefits

(In € million)	Retirement benefits Note 31.1	Restitution of aircraft	Restructuring	Litigation	Others	Total
Amount as of January 1, 2012 (pro forma)	***1,687***	***575***	***12***	***404***	***170***	***2,848***
Of which:						
• Non-current	*1,687*	*459*	*-*	*390*	*156*	*2,692*
• Current	*-*	*116*	*12*	*14*	*14*	*156*
New provision	84	259	442	51	103	**939**
Use of provision	(91)	(119)	(26)	(15)	(39)	**(290)**
Reversal of unnecessary provisions	-	(3)	-	(1)	-	**(4)**
Fair value revaluation	283	-	-	-	-	**283**
Currency translation adjustment	1	1	-	-	1	**3**
Discount/Accretion impact	-	(25)	-	-	-	**(25)**
Reclassification	1	(47)	-	-	5	**(41)**
Amount as of December 31, 2012 (pro forma)	***1,965***	***641***	***428***	***439***	***240***	***3,713***
Of which:						
• Non-current	*1,965*	*545*	*4*	*429*	*215*	*3,158*
• Current	*-*	*96*	*424*	*10*	*25*	*555*
New provision	99	272	282	76	97	**826**
Use of provision	(39)	(123)	(233)	(43)	(79)	**(517)**
Reversal of unnecessary provisions	-	(18)	(34)	-	(6)	**(58)**
Fair value revaluation	(162)	-	-	-	-	**(162)**
Currency translation adjustment	(9)	(1)	-	-	(1)	**(11)**
Change in scope	2	-	-	-	(2)	**-**
Discount/Accretion impact	-	(2)	-	-	-	**(2)**
Reclassification	(3)	(15)	(1)	2	-	**(17)**
Amount as of December 31, 2013	***1,853***	***754***	***442***	***474***	***249***	***3,772***
Of which:						
• Non-current	*1,853*	*606*	*-*	*439*	*204*	*3,102*
• Current	*-*	*148*	*442*	*35*	*45*	*670*

As of December 31, 2013, the impact on the net periodic pension cost, amounting to €54 million, linked to the restructuring plans of Air France and its regional subsidiaries has been recorded in "Other non-current income and expenses" *(see Note 11)*.

As of December 31, 2012, the impact was about €81 million and was also recorded in "Other non-current income and expenses".

Movements in provisions for restructuring which have an impact on the income statement are recorded in "other non-current income and expenses" when the plans concerned have a material impact *(see Note 11)*.

Movements in provisions for restitution of aircraft which have an impact on the income statement are recorded in "provisions" except for the discount/accretion impact which is recorded in "other financial income and expenses".

Movements in provisions for litigation and in provisions for other risks and charges which have an impact on the income statement are recorded, depending on their nature, in the different lines of the income statement.

31.1 Retirement benefits

The Group has a large number of retirement and other long-term benefits plans for its employees, several of which are defined benefit plans. The specific characteristics (benefit formulas, funding policies and types of assets held) of the plans vary according to the regulations

and laws in the particular country in which the employees are located. As indicated in Notes 2 and 4, since January 1, 2013, the Group has applied the standard IAS 19 Revised "Employee benefits". To facilitate comparison, the financial statements as of December 31, 2012 have been restated in accordance with the new rules.

31.1.1 Characteristics of the main defined benefit plans

Pension plan related to flight deck crew - Netherlands

The pension plan related to the flight deck crew in the KLM entity is a defined benefit plan with a reversion to the spouse on the beneficiary's death.

The retirement age defined in the plan is 56 years.

The Board of the pension fund comprises members appointed by the employer and employees and has full responsibility for the administration and management of the plan. KLM can only control the financing agreement between KLM and the pension fund. The financing agreement is part of the Collective Labor Agreement between KLM and the Unions/Works Council.

To satisfy the requirements of the Dutch regulations and the agreements defined between the employer and the pension fund Board, the plan has a minimum mandatory funding ratio of 105% of the projected short-term obligation, and approximately 115% to 120% of the projected long-term obligation. The projection of these commitments is calculated based on the local funding rules.

If the coverage ratio is under the funding agreement detailed above, the company is required to make additional contributions: within the current year for non-compliance with the 105% threshold or within 10 years for non-compliance with the 115% to 120% threshold. The amount of normal and additional employer contributions is not limited. The employee contributions cannot be increased in the event of non-compliance with these minimum funding rules.

A reduction in the employer contribution is possible if the indexation of pensions is fully funded. This reduction is not capped and can be realised either via a reimbursement of contributions, or by a reduction in future contributions.

The return on plan assets, the discount rate used to value the obligations and the longevity and characteristics of the active population are the main factors liable to influence the coverage ratio and lead to a risk of additional contributions for KLM.

The funds, which are fully dedicated to the KLM Group companies, are mainly invested in bonds, equities and real estate.

The management of most assets is outsourced to a private institution, under a service contract.

The required funding of this pension plan also includes a buffer against the following risks: interest rate risks, equity risks, currency risks, credit risks, actuarial risks and real estate risks.

For example, about 90% of the currency risk is hedged. Put options are in place, which cover a decrease of about 25% of the value of the equity portfolio.

Pension plan related to ground staff - Netherlands

The pension plan related to the ground staff in the KLM entity is a defined benefit plan with a reversion to the spouse on the beneficiary's death.

The retirement age defined in the plan was 65 years until December 31, 2013 and 67 years after this date.

The Board of the pension fund comprises members appointed by the employer and employees and has full responsibility for the administration and management of the plan. KLM can only control the financing agreement between KLM and the pension fund. The financing agreement is part of the Collective Labor Agreement between KLM and the Unions/Works Council.

To satisfy the requirements of Dutch regulations and the agreements defined between the employer and the pension fund Board, the plan has a minimum mandatory funding ratio of 105% of the projected short-term obligation, and approximately 115% to 120% of the projected long-term obligation. The projection of these commitments is calculated based on the local funding rules.

If the coverage ratio is under the funding agreement detailed above, the company and the employee are required to make additional contributions: within the current year for non-compliance with the 105% threshold or within 15 years for non-compliance with the 115% to 120% threshold. The amount of basic and additional employer contributions is not limited. Any additional employee contributions are limited to 2% of the pension basis.

A reduction in contributions is possible if the indexation of pensions is fully funded. This reduction is not capped and can be realised either via a reimbursement of contributions, or by a reduction in future contributions.

The return on plan assets, the discount rate used to value the obligations and the longevity and characteristics of the active population are the main factors liable to both influence the coverage ratio and the level of the normal contribution for future pension accrual. The normal contributions are limited to 24% of the pension base.

The funds, which are fully dedicated to the KLM Group companies, are mainly invested in bonds, equities and real estate. The management of most assets is outsourced to a private institution, under a service contract.

The required funding of this pension plan also includes a buffer against the following risks: interest rate risks, equity risks, currency risks, credit risks, actuarial risks and real estate risks. For example, an interest hedge is foreseen to halve the potential impact of the sensitivity to an interest rate decrease. Similarly, about 90% of the currency risk is hedged. Put options are in place, which cover a decrease of about 25% of the value of the equity portfolio.

Pension plan related to cabin crew - Netherlands

The pension plan related to the cabin crew in the KLM entity is a defined benefit plan with a reversion to the spouse on the beneficiary's death.

The pension is calculated based on their final salaries for employees hired since 2009, and based on average salaries for their entire careers for the other employees.

The retirement age defined in the plan is 60 years.

The Board of the pension fund comprises members appointed by the employer and employees and has full responsibility for the administration and management of the plan. KLM can only control the financing agreement between KLM and the pension fund. The financing agreement is part of the Collective Labor Agreement between KLM and the Unions/Works Council.

To satisfy the requirements of Dutch regulations and the agreements defined between the employer and the pension fund Board, the plan has a minimum mandatory funding ratio of 105% of the projected short-term obligation, and approximately 115% to 120% of the projected long-term obligation. The projection of these commitments is calculated based on the local funding rules.

If the coverage ratio is under the funding agreement detailed above, the company and the employee have to pay additional contributions: within three years for non-compliance with the 105% threshold or within 15 years for non-compliance with the 115% to 120% threshold. The amount of normal and additional employer contributions is capped at 48% of the pension basis. Any additional employee contributions are limited to 0.7% of the pension basis.

A reduction in contributions is possible if the indexation of pensions is fully funded. This reduction is limited to twice the normal annual contribution.

The return on plan assets, the discount rate used to value the obligations and the longevity and characteristics of the active population are the main factors liable to both influence the coverage ratio and the level of the normal contribution for future pension accrual.

The funds, which are fully dedicated to the KLM Group companies, are mainly invested in bonds, equities and real estate. The management of most assets is outsourced to a private institution, under a service contract.

The required funding of this pension plan also includes a buffer against the following risks: interest rate risks, equity risks, currency risks, credit risks, actuarial risks and real estate risks.

For example, an interest hedge is foreseen to halve the potential impact of the sensitivity to an interest rate decrease.

Similarly, about 90% of the currency risk is hedged. Put options are in place, which cover a decrease of about 25% of the value of the equity portfolio.

Air France pension plan (CRAF) – France

The employees covered by this plan are the Air France ground staff affiliated to the CRAF until December 31, 1992. The participants receive, or will receive on retirement, an additional pension paid monthly and permanently calculated based on the data known as of December 31, 1992 and expressed in the form of points. The value of each point is reevaluated every year based on the weighted increases seen in the CNAV and ARRCO schemes over the last twelve months.

Until 2009, the CRAF had the legal form of a supplementary pension institution (pursuant to the "Sécurité sociale" Code). With this status, the CRAF was responsible, on behalf of the Air France ground staff employed in France, for managing the pension plan resulting from the merging of the Air France ground staff plan with the mandatory pension plan for the private sector.

Following the 2003 law on pension reform, foreseeing the disappearance of supplementary pension institutions as of December 31, 2008, the CRAF's Board of Directors opted to transform it into an institution managing supplementary pensions. The CRAF is now responsible for the administrative functions linked to the plan. The pension rights were not amended by this reform. Air France is directly responsible for the pension obligations.

As of December 31, 2008, all the funds managed by the CRAF had been transferred to two insurance companies. On December 31, 2012, one of the insurance contracts was terminated and its funds were transferred to the other, which thus became the only insurer.

This insurance company guarantees a capital equal to the amount of capital invested in units of account in its collective fund, which represents a little more than 5% of the amount of funds, this percentage being automatically set to increase over time.

The annual payments made by Air France to the insurance company are governed by the agreement signed with the employee representative bodies on December 14, 2009. The minimum annual payment defined by this agreement amounts to €32.5 million. If the value of the funds falls below 50% of the total obligations calculated for funding purposes, Air France is required to make an additional payment to achieve a minimum 50% coverage rate.

The funds are invested in bonds, equities and general assets of the insurance company. Studies of assets/liabilities allocation are carried out regularly, to verify the relevance of the investment strategy.

Air France end of service benefit plan (ICS) - France

Pursuant to French regulations and the company agreements, every employee receives an end of service indemnity when leaving the company for retirement.

In France, this indemnity depends on the number of years of service, the professional category of the employee (flight deck crew, cabin crew, ground staff, agent, technician and executive) and, in some cases, on the age of the employee at retirement.

On retirement, employees consequently receive an end of service indemnity based on their final salaries over the last twelve-months and on their seniority.

The indemnity is only payable to employees on their retirement date.

There is no mandatory minimum funding requirement for this scheme.

Air France has nevertheless signed contracts with three insurance companies to pre-finance the plan. The company has sole responsibility for payment of the indemnities, but remains free to make payments to the insurance companies.

The relevant outsourced funds are invested in bonds and equities.

As of December 31, 2013, the three Dutch plans and the two French plans presented above represent a respective 79% and 12% of the Group's pension liabilities and 91% and 4% of the Group's pension assets.

31.1.2 Description of the actuarial assumptions and related sensitivities

Actuarial valuations of the Group's benefit obligation have been made as of December 31, 2013 and December 31, 2012. These calculations include:

- assumptions on staff turnover and life expectancy of the beneficiaries of the plan;
- assumptions on salary and pension increases;
- assumptions of retirement ages varying from 55 to 67 depending on the localization and the applicable laws;
- discount rates used to determine the actuarial present value of the projected benefit obligations.

The discount rates for the different geographical areas are thus determined based on the duration of each plans, taking into account the average trend in interest rates on high quality bonds, observed on the main available indices. In some countries, where the market regarding this type of bond is not broad enough, the discount rate is determined with reference to government bonds. Most of the Group's benefit obligations are located in the Euro zone, where the discount rates used are as follows:

As of December 31	2013	2012
Euro zone - Duration 10 to 15 years	3.00%	3.00%
Euro zone - Duration 15 years and more	3.65%	3.65%

The duration between 10 and 15 years mainly concerns the plans located in France while the duration of 15 years and beyond mainly concerns plans located in the Netherlands.

On an average basis, the main assumptions used to value the liabilities are summarized below:

- the rate of salary increase (excluding inflation) is 1.75% for the Group as of December 31, 2013 against 1.69% as of December 31, 2012;
- the rate of pension increase (excluding inflation) is 1.36% for the Group as of December 31, 2013 against 1.46% as of December 31, 2012.

The sensitivity of the pension obligations to a change in assumptions, based on actuarial calculations, is as follows:

Sensitivity to changes in the discount rate

(In € million)	Sensitivity of the assumptions for the year ended December 31, 2013	Sensitivity of the assumptions for the year ended December 31, 2012 (pro forma)
0.25% increase in the discount rate	(688)	(667)
0.25% decrease in the discount rate	792	825

Sensitivity to changes in salary increase

(In € million)	Sensitivity of the assumptions for the year ended December 31, 2013	Sensitivity of the assumptions for the year ended December 31, 2012 (pro forma)
0.25% increase in the salary increase rate	142	146
0.25% decrease in the salary increase rate	(127)	(133)

Sensitivity to changes in pension increase

(In € million)	Sensitivity of the assumptions for the year ended December 31, 2013	Sensitivity of the assumptions for the year ended December 31, 2012 (pro forma)
0.25% increase in the pension increase rate	629	505
0.25% decrease in the pension increase rate	(538)	(489)

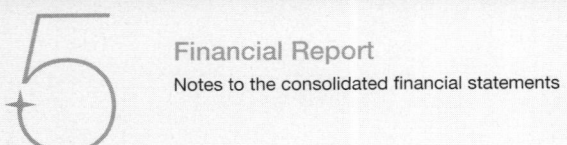

31.1.3 Evolution of commitments

The following table details the reconciliation between the benefits obligation and plan assets of the Group and the amounts recorded in the financial statements for the years ended December 31, 2013 and December 31, 2012 (pro forma).

(In € million)	As of December 31, 2013			As of December 31, 2012		
	Netherlands	France	Others	Netherlands	France	Others
Benefit obligation at beginning of year	***13,258***	***2,191***	***870***	***11,411***	***2,016***	***706***
Service cost	386	65	13	340	53	21
Interest cost	478	64	31	556	94	34
Employees' contribution	45	-	1	54	-	1
Plan amendments and curtailment	(41)	(56)	(5)	-	(82)	(3)
Change in consolidation scope	-	2	-	-	-	-
Benefits paid	(383)	(101)	(28)	(360)	(114)	(39)
Transfers of assets/liability through balance sheet	2	(5)	-	-	-	-
Actuarial loss / (gain) demographic assumptions	(16)	(3)	(1)	103	-	-
Actuarial loss / (gain) financial assumptions	(203)	(25)	(43)	1,193	247	136
Actuarial loss / (gain) experience gap	133	(16)	(6)	(22)	(23)	4
Currency translation adjustment	10	-	(35)	-	-	11
Other	-	-	-	(17)	-	(1)
Benefit obligation at end of year	***13,669***	***2,116***	***797***	***13,258***	***2,191***	***870***
Including benefit obligation resulting from schemes totally or partly funded	*13,575*	*2,055*	*690*	*13,167*	*2,131*	*729*
Including unfunded benefit obligation	*94*	*61*	*107*	*91*	*60*	*141*
Fair value of plan assets at beginning of year	***15,528***	***787***	***515***	***13,563***	***768***	***450***
Actual return on plan assets	346	71	38	1,904	96	60
Employers' contributions	361	(11)	14	384	37	2
Employees' contributions	45	-	1	54	-	1
Change in consolidation scope	(1)	-	1	-	-	-
Settlements	-	-	(1)	-	-	-
Transfers of assets/liability through balance sheet	-	-	-	-	-	1
Benefits paid	(375)	(99)	(21)	(360)	(114)	(8)
Currency translation adjustment	(1)	-	(15)	-	-	10
Other	-	-	-	(17)	-	(1)
Fair value of plan assets at end of year	***15,903***	***748***	***532***	***15,528***	***787***	***515***

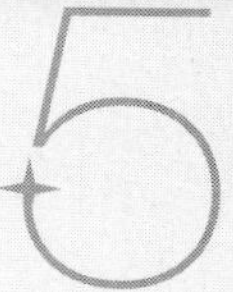

(In € million)	As of December 31, 2013			As of December 31, 2012		
	Netherlands	France	Others	Netherlands	France	Others
Amounts recorded in the balance sheet*:						
Pension asset (Note 23)	2,452	-	2	2,477	-	-
Provision for retirement benefits	(220)	(1,368)	(265)	(207)	(1,404)	(354)
Net amount recognized	***2,232***	***(1,368)***	***(263)***	***2,270***	***(1,404)***	***(354)***
Net periodic cost:						
Service cost	386	65	13	340	53	21
Interest cost	(90)	41	12	(123)	59	11
Plan amendments and curtailment	(40)	(57)	(5)	-	(82)	(1)
Settlement	-	-	1	-	-	-
Net periodic cost	**256**	**49**	**21**	**217**	**30**	**31**

* *All the obligations are recorded as non-current liabilities, except for the pension plans for which the balance is a net asset fully recorded as a non-current asset.*

Amendments and curtailment of pension plans

As of December 31, 2013, a curtailment has been booked by Air France and its subsidiaries for an amount of €54 million, relating to the voluntary departure plan *(see Note 11)*.

By KLM, the amendments of pension plans led to a decrease of €40 million of the defined benefit obligation: €25 million further to the modification of the retirement age from 65 to 67 years concerning the ground staff pension plan and €15 million further to the decrease of the annual accrual rates on cabin crew and ground staff pension plans.

As of December 31, 2012, a curtailment was booked by Air France and its subsidiaries for an amount of €81 million, relating to the voluntary departure plan *(see Note 11)*.

31.1.4 Asset allocation

The weighted average allocation of the funds invested in the Group's pension and other long-term benefit plans is as follows:

Funds invested	As of December 31, 2013		As of December 31, 2012	
	France	Netherlands	France	Netherlands
Equities	41%	38%	40%	38%
Bonds	46%	50%	49%	51%
Real estate	-	10%	-	10%
Others	13%	2%	11%	1%
Total	**100%**	**100%**	**100%**	**100%**

Equities are mainly invested in active markets in Europe, United States and emerging countries.

Bonds are primarily composed of government bonds, at least rated BBB, and invested in Europe, United States and emerging countries.

Real estate assets are mainly located in Europe and in the United States.

The Group's pension assets do not include assets occupied or used by the Group.

31.1.5 Expected cash flows and risks linked to the pension obligations

The expected cash flows relative to the defined benefit pension plans will amount to €435 million for the year ending as of December 31, 2014. The weighted average duration of the obligation is 18 years.

The funding, capitalization and matching strategies implemented by the Group are presented in paragraph 30.1.

According to this description, the Group has no obligation to recapitalize the plans for which a minimum funding is required over the short or long term.

31.2 Provisions for restructuring

As of December 31, 2013 and December 31, 2012, provision for restructuring mainly includes the provision for the voluntary departure plans of Air France and its regional affiliates *(see Note 11)*.

31.3 Provisions for litigation

31.3.1 Provision for litigation with third parties

An assessment of litigation risks with third parties was carried out with the Group's attorneys and provisions have been recorded whenever circumstances required.

Provisions for litigation with third parties also include provisions for tax risks. Such provisions are set up when the Group considers that the tax authorities could challenge a tax position adopted by the Group or one of its subsidiaries.

In the normal course of its activities, the Air France-KLM Group and its subsidiaries Air France and KLM (and their subsidiaries) are involved in litigation, some of which may be significant.

31.3.2 Provision for litigation concerning anti-trust laws in the air-freight industry

Air France, KLM and Martinair, a wholly-owned subsidiary of KLM since January 1, 2009, have been involved, since February 2006, with up to twenty-five other airlines in investigations initiated by the anti-trust authorities in several countries, with respect to allegations of anti-competitive agreements or concerted actions in the air-freight industry.

As of December 31, 2013 most of these proceedings had resulted in Plea Agreements made by Air France, KLM and Martinair with the appropriate agencies, and the payment of settlement amounts which ended procedures.

In Europe, the European Commission announced, on November 9, 2010, its decision to impose fines on 14 airlines including Air France, KLM and Martinair related to anti-competition practices - mainly concerning fuel surcharges in the air freight industry. The Commission imposed an overall fine of €340 million on the Air France-KLM Group companies.

As the Group's parent company, Air France-KLM was considered by the European Commission to be jointly and severally liable for the anti-competitive practices of which the Group companies were found guilty.

On January 24 and 25, 2011, the Group companies filed an appeal against the decision before the General Court of the European Union.

Since the appeal does not suspend the payment of the fines, the Group companies chose not to pay the fine immediately, but to provide bank guarantees until a definitive ruling by the European Courts.

On January 10, 2014 the Swiss anti-trust authority (COMCO) imposed a fine of €3.2 million on Air France and KLM. The Group companies intend to file an appeal on this decision before the Federal Administrative Tribunal.

In South Korea on November 29, 2010, the Korean antitrust authority (KFTC) imposed on Air France-KLM, Air France and KLM a total fine of €8.8 million which was paid in January 2011. The Group companies filed an appeal before the competent Seoul High Court in December 2010.

On May 16, 2012 the 6th chamber of the Seoul High Court vacated the KFTC's decision against Air France-KLM on the grounds that Air France-KLM was not engaged in the air freight transportation business after it converted to a holding company on September 15, 2004. With regard to the appeals of Air France and KLM, the Court found in favour of the KFTC. Appeal filings against the Court decisions were submitted to the Supreme Court by both Air France and KLM in June 2012. Generally, the Supreme Court appeal process will take 1-2 years to conclude.

Since January 10, 2014 (the imposition of a fine by the Swiss antitrust authorities), the Group companies have no longer been exposed to anti-trust proceedings with respect to alleged of concerted actions in the air freight industry.

As of December 31, 2013, the total amount of provisions amounts to €372 million in respect of all the proceedings which have not yet been concluded by a final decision.

31.3.3 Other provisions

Other provisions are mainly provisions for power-by-hour contracts (maintenance activity of the Group), provisions for onerous leases, provisions for the portion of CO_2 emissions not covered by the free allocation of quotas and provisions for the dismantling of buildings.

31.4 Contingent liabilities

The Group is involved in a number of governmental, legal and arbitrage procedures for which provisions have not been recorded in the financial statements.

31.4.1 Litigations concerning anti-trust laws in the air-freight industry

These litigations have not been provisioned given that the Group is unable, given the current status of proceedings, to evaluate its exposure.

Pursuant to the initiation in February 2006 of the various competition authority investigations, class actions were brought by forwarding agents and air-freight shippers in several countries against Air France, KLM and Martinair, and the other freight carriers. In addition, civil suits have been filed in Europe by shippers following the European Commission's decision of November 9, 2010. The Group companies vigorously oppose all such civil actions.

United States

In the United States, the Group concluded a Settlement Agreement with the representatives of the class action in July 2010, bringing to an end all claims and, court proceedings in connection with unlawful practices for cargo transportation to, from and within the United States.

With respect to those Air France, KLM and Martinair customers who chose to be excluded, a portion of the settlement proportional to the revenue Air France, KLM and Martinair received from those parties over the relevant period as compared with the overall revenue for this same period has been segregated in a separate escrow account. The parties who opted out are free to sue Air France, KLM and Martinair individually.

Netherlands

a) Litigation vehicle Equilib has initiated two largely overlapping proceedings before the Amsterdam District Court aimed at establishing liability on behalf of 184 groups, whereby the actual amounts are to be determined in follow-up proceedings. Following the annulment by the Amsterdam Court of Appeal of the interim decision of the District Court to stay the proceedings, Air France, KLM and Martinair are due to file their statement of defence on April 2, 2014 in the first proceeding. The second proceeding will be introduced during the second half of 2014.
Air France, KLM and Martinair initiated contribution proceedings before the Amsterdam District Court against the other airlines included in the European Commission decision, which were stayed with the main proceedings. As the annulment of this stay by the Amsterdam Court of Appeal did not affect the stay of the contribution proceedings, Air France, KLM and Martinair asked the Court of Appeal in a separate appeal to annul the stay of the contribution proceedings, which would again synchronize the main and contribution proceedings.

b) A second litigation vehicle, East West Debt ("EWD"), also initiated proceedings before the Amsterdam District Court to obtain compensation from the Group, as well as two other European airlines, for the claims of 8 individual shippers. Following the annulment by the Amsterdam Court of Appeal of the interim decision of the District Court to stay the proceedings, the case is expected to resume at the District Court where a date will be set for filing the statement of defence.
The Group has also initiated contribution proceedings at the Amsterdam District Court against the other airlines included in the decision.

c) A third litigation vehicle Stichting Cartel Compensation ("SCC") initiated proceedings before the Amsterdam District Court to obtain compensation from the Goup and several other European and Asian airlines, for the claims of 877 individual shippers. The proceedings will be introduced on April 2, 2014.

United Kingdom

In the United Kingdom, a civil suit has been filed against British Airways with the competent court by two flower importers.

British Airways issued contribution proceedings against all the airlines fined by the European Commission including entities of the Group. To date, British Airways has neither quantified nor substantiated its purported claims. These contribution proceedings have been stayed.

In the main proceedings, the plaintiffs were granted permission to add parties to the proceedings, resulting in over 500 plaintiffs.

Australia

Within the context of ongoing class action proceedings instituted in 2007 against seven airlines (excluding the Air France-KLM Group) in the Australian Federal Court, cross claims have been filed against Air France, KLM and Martinair by Singapore Airlines (August 15, 2011), Cathay Pacific (August 15, 2011), Lufthansa (November 4, 2011), Air New Zealand (December 5, 2011) and British Airways (December 19, 2011). In the cross claims, the respondent airlines claim that if, despite their denial of the claims of wrongdoing in the class action, they are ordered to pay damages, they will seek contributions from the cross respondents. The Group companies have filed defences to these cross claims in which they deny that the respondent airlines are entitled to any contribution from them. As of December 31, 2013 this proceeding was still pending.

Norway

On May 25, 2012, a civil suit was filed by a company named Marine Harvest before the Norwegian court on the grounds of allegedly additional costs caused by anti-competitive practices. The Group companies have requested a stay of the proceeding upon which the court has not ruled yet.

31.4.2 Legislation concerning anti-trust laws in the passenger sector

Canada

A civil class action was reinitiated in 2013 by claimants in Ontario against seven airlines including Air France and KLM. The plaintiffs allege that the defendants participated in a conspiracy to increase the price of passenger services by an adjustment in fuel surcharges to and from Canada and on transatlantic destinations, for which they are claiming damages. Air France and KLM strongly deny any participation in such a conspiracy and intend to file a motion to dismiss.

31.4.3 Other litigations

a) *Pretory*

Company Air France, as a legal entity, was placed under investigation on July 20, 2006 on charges of concealed employment and as an accessory to misuse of corporate assets in connection with a judicial investigation initiated against the officers of Pretory, a company with which Air France, pursuant to the September 2001 attacks, had entered into an agreement for the provision of safety officers on certain flights. Despite a non prosecution decision by the Public Prosecutor, the investigating magistrate decided, on February 7, 2012, to bring the case to court on charges of concealed employment.

On July 9, 2013, the court imposed a €0.15 million fine on the company. Air France has filed an appeal against this decision which it deems to be without grounds.

b) *KLM minority shareholders*

On December 31, 2012, two KLM minority shareholders filed a request with the Enterprise Chamber of the Amsterdam Court of Appeal to order an enquiry into, amongst other matters, the KLM's dividend policy in respect of the years 2004-05 to 2010-11 periods. This file relates to a claim for higher dividend for the fiscal year 2007-08 by these shareholders together with the Vereniging van Effectenbezitters (VEB) initiated in January 2008 against KLM and Air France-KLM. In this last proceeding, a final decision ruling from the Dutch Supreme Court on July 2013 definitively rejected all claims against KLM.

The Enterprise Chamber did, however, uphold the request for an enquiry into the dividend policy for the period under consideration. The main focus of the enquiry is the manner in which Air France-KLM, in its capacity as the sole priority shareholder, and KLM's Management and Supervisory Boards executed clause 32 of KLM's Articles of Association. This provides that the priority shareholder may reserve part of the profits after consulting with the Management Board and the Supervisory Board of KLM.

c) *Rio-Paris AF447 flight*

Following to the crash of the Rio-Paris AF447 flight in the South Atlantic, a number of legal actions have been brought in the United States and Brazil and, more recently, in France by the victims' heirs.

All these proceedings are aimed at receiving damages as reparation for the losses suffered by the heirs of the passengers who died in the crash.

In the United States, all the proceedings have been consolidated in California before the Northern District Court.

On October 4, 2010, the District judge granted the defendants' motion for dismissal on grounds of "forum non convenience" and suggested that they pursue their claim in France.

On March 17 and 18, 2011 respectively, Airbus and Air France were indicted for manslaughter by the investigating magistrate and incur the penalties of fines prescribed by law. Air France intends to challenge its implication in this case.

These penalties should not have a material effect on the financial situation of Air France.

The damages as reparation for the losses suffered by the heirs of the passengers who died in the crash are covered by Air France's third-party liability insurance policy.

Except for the matters specified under the paragraphs 31.3, 31.4, the Group is not aware of any dispute or governmental, judicial and arbitration proceedings (including any proceedings of which the issuer is aware, or that are pending or threatened against it) that could have or have recently had a significant impact on the Group's financial position, earnings, assets, liabilities or profitability, during a period including at least the past twelve months.

Note 32 Financial debt

As of December 31 *(In € million)*	**2013**	**2012**
Non current financial debt		
Perpetual subordinated loan stock in Yen	211	256
Perpetual subordinated loan stock in Swiss francs	341	347
OCEANE (convertible bonds)	1,478	988
Bonds	1,200	1,950
Capital lease obligations	3,808	3,919
Other debt	1,558	2,105
Total	**8,596**	**9,565**
Current financial debt		
Bonds	741	-
Capital lease obligations	599	588
Other debt	653	734
Accrued interest	144	112
Total	**2,137**	**1,434**

32.1 Perpetual subordinated bond

32.1.1 Perpetual subordinated bond in Japanese Yen

The perpetual subordinated bond in Japanese Yen was issued by KLM in 1999 for a total amount of JPY 30 billion, i.e. €211 million as of December 31, 2013.

Until 2019, this perpetual subordinated bond is subject to the payment of a 5.28% coupon on a notional of USD 248 million.

The debt is perpetual. It is nevertheless reimbursable at its nominal value at the Group's discretion as of August 28, 2019. This reimbursement does not involve a premium. A premium would be due if the debt were to be reimbursed in a currency other than the yen.

This debt is subordinated to all other existing and future KLM debts.

32.1.2 Perpetual subordinated bond in Swiss francs

The perpetual subordinated bond in Swiss francs was issued by KLM in two installments in 1985 and 1986 for a total original amount of CHF 500 million. Following the purchases made by KLM, the outstanding subordinated bond amounts to CHF 419 million, i.e. €341 million as of December 31, 2013.

The bonds are reimbursable on certain dates at the Group's discretion at a price between nominal value and 101.25% (depending on the bond and date of early repayment).

This loan is subject to the payment of a coupon considered to be fixed-rate (5.75% on a CHF 270 million portion and 2.125% on a CHF 149 million portion) for the years ended December 31, 2013 and December 31, 2012.

This debt is subordinated to all other existing and future KLM debts.

32.2 OCEANE

32.2.1 OCEANE issued in 2005

In April 2005, the company Air France, a subsidiary of the Air France-KLM Group, issued convertible bonds maturing in 15 years. The conversion option allows for conversion and/or exchange at any time into new or existing Air France-KLM shares (OCEANE). 21,951,219 bonds were issued for a total amount of €450 million. Each bond has a nominal value of €20.50. As of December 31, 2013, the conversion ratio is 1.03 Air France-KLM shares for one bond.

The maturity date for this convertible bond is April 1, 2020. Bond holders could request reimbursement as of April 1, 2012 and will also be able to do this as of April 1, 2016. Air France holds a call option triggering early cash reimbursement which can be exercised starting April 1, 2010 and, under certain conditions, encouraging OCEANE holders to convert into Air France-KLM shares. The annual coupon is 2.75% payable in arrears at the end of each period ended April 1.

The conversion period of these bonds runs from June 1, 2005 to March 23, 2020, except in the event of early reimbursement.

On December 6, 2011, to optimize its debt repayment schedule by neutralizing the exercise of the OCEANE repayment option on April 1, 2012, Air France signed a swap agreement relating to these OCEANEs (total return swap) with Natixis expiring on April 1, 2016 at the latest. In order to hedge this contract, Natixis launched a contractual acquisition procedure to purchase the aforementioned OCEANEs.

This contract was thus reflected in the following operations:

- the purchase by Natixis of 18,692,474 OCEANEs (i.e. 85.16% of the amount initially issued) at a fixed price of €21 following a contractual acquisition procedure open between December 7 and December 13, 2011. Natixis is the owner of the acquired OCEANEs and did not exercise its early repayment option on April 1, 2012;
- the entry into force effective December 14, 2011 of a swap contract expiring on April 1, 2016 whose notional amounts to €392.5 million (number of OCEANEs acquired by Natixis multiplied by the purchase price of €21). Regarding this swap, Air France receives the coupon on the OCEANEs i.e. 2.75% and pays variable interest indexed to Euribor 6 months. At the swap termination, Air France and Natixis will also exchange the difference between the OCEANE price at that date and the initial price of €21;
- Air France has a termination option on the swap starting December 19, 2012 and expiring on February 1, 2016;
- the contract is the subject of a guarantee for 100% of the notional of the swap *(see Note 24)*. From April 1, 2012, the guarantee can partially comprise securities provided this portion does not exceed 50% of the notional amount of the swap.

Of the 3,258,150 OCEANEs not purchased by Natixis within the framework of the contractual acquisition procedure, 1,501,475 OCEANEs were reimbursed on April 2, 2012, for an amount of €31 million, following exercice of the repayment option by some holders.

As of December 31, 2013, the debt value amounts to €390 million.

32.2.2 OCEANE issued in 2009

As of June 26, 2009, Air France-KLM issued a bond with an option of conversion and/or exchange for new or existing Air France-KLM shares (OCEANE) with a maturity date fixed at April 1, 2015. 56,016,949 bonds were issued for a total amount of €661 million. Each bond has a nominal value of €11.80. The annual coupon amounts to 4.97%.

The conversion period of these bonds runs from August 6, 2009 to the seventh working day preceding the normal or early reimbursement date.

Since April 1, 2013 Air France-KLM has had the option to impose the cash reimbursement of these bonds by exercising a call if the share price exceeds 130% of the nominal, i.e. €15.34, encouraging OCEANE owners to convert their bonds into Air France-KLM shares.

Upon issue of this convertible debt, Air France-KLM recorded a debt of €556 million, corresponding to the present value of future payments of interest and nominal discounted at the rate of a similar bond without a conversion option. As of December 31, 2013, the debt value amounts to €633 million.

The option value was evaluated by deducting this debt value from the total nominal amount (i.e. €661 million) and was recorded in equity.

32.2.3 OCEANE issued in 2013

On March 28, 2013, Air France-KLM issued 53,398,058 bonds convertible and/or exchangeable for new or existing Air France-KLM shares (OCEANE) with a maturity date fixed at February 15, 2023 for a total nominal amount of €550 million. Each bond has a nominal value of €10.30. The annual coupon amounts to 2.03%.

The conversion period of these bonds runs from May 7, 2013 to the seventh working day preceding the normal or early reimbursement date. The conversion ratio is one share for one bond.

Repayment at par, plus accrued interest, will be possible as of February 15, 2019 at the request of the bond holders. Air France-KLM can impose the cash reimbursement of these bonds by exercising a call from September 28, 2016 if the share price exceeds 130% of nominal, amounting to €13.39, encouraging OCEANE owners to convert their bonds into Air France-KLM shares.

Upon issue of this convertible debt, Air France-KLM recorded a debt of €443 million, corresponding to the present value of future payments of interest and nominal discounted at the rate of a similar bond without a conversion option. As of December 31, 2013, the debt value amounts to €455 million.

The option value was evaluated by deducting this debt value from the total nominal amount (i.e. €550 million) and was recorded in equity.

32.3 Bonds

32.3.1 Bonds issued in 2006 and 2007

On September 2006 and April 2007, the company Air France, a subsidiary of the Air France-KLM Group, issued bonds for a total amount of €750 million, maturing on January 22, 2014 and bearing an annual interest rate of 4.75%.

On July 3, 2013, Air France redeemed a portion of these bonds amounting to €9 million.

32.3.2 Bonds issued in 2009

As of October 27, 2009, Air France-KLM issued bonds for a total amount of €700 million, maturing on October 27, 2016 and bearing an annual interest rate of 6.75%.

32.3.3 Bonds issued in 2012

As of December 14, 2012, Air France-KLM issued bonds for a total amount of €500 million, maturing on January 18, 2018 and bearing an annual interest rate of 6.25%.

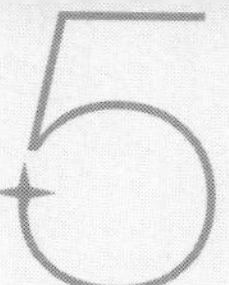

32.4 Capital lease commitments

The breakdown of total future minimum lease payments related to capital leases is as follows:

As of December 31, *(In € million)*	2013	2012
Aircraft		
Future minimum lease payments – due dates		
Y+1	637	651
Y+2	612	605
Y+3	549	576
Y+4	526	510
Y+5	469	489
Over 5 years	1,560	1,760
Total	**4,353**	**4,591**
Including:		
• Principal	3,893	4,015
• Interest	460	576
Buildings		
Future minimum lease payments – due dates		
Y+1	65	58
Y+2	67	59
Y+3	51	59
Y+4	55	44
Y+5	58	49
Over 5 years	288	212
Total	**584**	**481**
Including:		
• Principal	426	401
• Interest	158	80
Other property, plant and equipment		
Future minimum lease payments – due dates		
Y+1	13	13
Y+2	12	12
Y+3	10	11
Y+4	10	9
Y+5	10	9
Over 5 years	78	87
Total	**133**	**141**
Including:		
• Principal	88	91
• Interest	45	50

The lease expenses over the period do not include contingent leases. Deposits made on purchase options are presented in Note 24.

32.5 Other debt

Other debt breaks down as follows:

As of December 31 *(In € million)*	2013	2012
Reservation of ownership clause and mortgage debt	1,321	1,773
Other debt	890	1,066
Total	**2,211**	**2,839**

Other debt corresponds mainly to bank borrowings.

Mortgage debt is a debt secured by a mortgage on an aircraft. The mortgage is filed at the national civil aviation authority (the DGAC in France) in order to be publicly available to third parties. A mortgage grants to the mortgagee a right to enforce the security (by order of a judge), the sale of the asset and a priority claim on the sale proceeds in line with the amount of the loan, the balance reverting to the other creditors.

32.6 Maturity analysis

The financial debt maturities break down as follows:

As of December 31 *(In € million)*	2013	2012
Maturities in		
Y+1	2,500	1,817
Y+2	1,871	2,256
Y+3	2,095	1,815
Y+4	1,034	2,095
Y+5	1,291	920
Over 5 years	3,491	4,081
Total	**12,282**	**12,984**
Including:		
♦ Principal	10,733	10,999
♦ Interest	1,549	1,985

As of December 31, 2013, the expected financial costs amount to €363 million for the 2014 financial year, €811 million for the financial years 2015 to 2018, and €375 million thereafter.

As of December 31, 2013, it has been considered that the perpetual subordinated loan stocks and the OCEANEs would be reimbursed according to their most probable maturity:

- probable exercice date of the issuer call for the perpetual subordinated loans;
- second exercice date of the investor put, i.e April 1, 2016, for the majority of the OCEANEs issued in 2005 *(see Note 32.2.1)*;
- probable exercice date of the investor put, i.e February 15, 2019, for the majority of the OCEANEs issued in 2013 *(see Note 32.2.3)*;
- contractual maturity date for the OCEANE issued in 2009.

Repayable bonds issued in 2006, 2007, 2009 and 2012 will be reimbursed at their contractual maturity date *(see Notes 32.2 and 32.3)*.

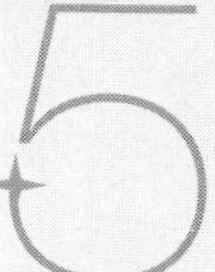

32.7 Currency analysis

The breakdown of financial debt by currency after impact of derivative instruments is as follows:

As of December 31 *(In € million)*	2013	2012
Euro	9,131	9,059
US dollar	587	867
Swiss franc	351	357
Yen	664	716
Total	**10,733**	**10,999**

32.8 Credit lines

As of December 31, 2013, the Group had credit lines amounting to €1,806 million, of which only €4 million have been drawn down. The three main credit lines amounted, respectively, to €1,060 million for Air France, €540 million for KLM and €200 million for the holding company Air France-KLM.

On April 4, 2011, Air France renewed its credit facility maturing on April 7, 2013 with a €1,060 million revolving credit facility maturing on April 4, 2016, subject to the following financial covenants based on the Air France Group's consolidated financial statements:

- EBITDAR must not be lower than two and a half times the net interest charges increased by one third of operating lease payments;
- tangible and financial assets in the balance sheet, not pledged as collateral, must be at least equal to unsecured financial net debts.

These ratios are calculated every six months based on Air France Group's consolidated financial statements and were respected at December 31, 2013.

KLM's credit facility, which amounts to €540 million with a maturity in 2016, is subject to the company respecting the following financial covenants:

- EBITDAR must not be lower than two and a half times the sum of net interest charges and one third of operating lease payments;
- tangible and financial assets in the balance sheet, not pledged as collateral, must be at least equal to unsecured net debts.

These ratios are calculated every six months based on KLM Group's consolidated financial statements and were respected at December 31, 2013.

Air France-KLM's credit facility, with a maturity as of October 4, 2017, amounts to €200 million as of December 31, 2013. It will be reduced by €50 million every year on its October 4 anniversary, and, is subject to respect of the following financial covenants calculated based on the Air France-KLM consolidated financial statements:

- EBITDAR must be at least equal to one and a half times net interest charges added to one third of operating lease payments;
- tangible and financial assets in the balance sheet, not pledged as collateral, must be at least equal to unsecured financial net debt.

These ratios are calculated every six months and were respected at December 31, 2013.

Note 33 Other liabilities

As of December 31 *(In € million)*	2013		2012	
	Current	Non current	Current	Non current
Tax liabilities	707	-	502	-
Employee-related liabilities	832	-	844	-
Non current assets' payables	87	-	48	-
Derivative instruments	118	319	85	279
Deferred income	120	6	122	32
Other	468	72	873	73
Total	**2,332**	**397**	**2,474**	**384**

Derivative instruments comprise €88 million of currency hedges on financial debts as of December 31, 2013, including €86 million as non current liability and €2 million as current liability (against €13 million as of December 31, 2012, all non current liability).

Note 34 Financial instruments

34.1 Risk management

Market risk management

Market risk coordination and management is the responsibility of the Risk Management Committee (RMC) which comprises the Chief Executive Officer of Air France-KLM, the Chief Executive Officers of Air France and of KLM, the Chief Financial Officer of Air France-KLM, and the Chief Financial Officers of Air France and of KLM. The RMC meets each quarter to review Group reporting of the risks relating to the fuel price, the principal currency exchange rates, interest rates and carbon quota prices, and to decide on the hedging to be implemented: targets for hedging ratios, the time periods for the respect of these targets and, potentially, the preferred types of hedging instrument. The aim is to reduce the exposure of Air France-KLM to the market fluctuations. The RMC also defines the counterparty-risk policy.

The decisions made by the RMC are implemented by the treasury and fuel purchasing departments within each company. In-house procedures governing risk management prohibit speculation.

The instruments used are swaps, futures and options.

Regular meetings are held between the fuel purchasing and treasury departments of both companies in order to exchange information concerning matters such as hedging instruments used, strategies planned and counterparties.

The treasury management departments of each company circulate information on the level of cash and cash equivalents to their respective executive managements on a daily basis. Every month, a detailed report including, amongst other information, interest rate and currency positions, the portfolio of hedging instruments, a summary of investments and financing by currency and the monitoring of risk by counterparty is transmitted to the executive managements.

The implementation of the policy on fuel hedging is the responsibility of the fuel purchasing departments, which are also in charge of purchasing fuel for physical delivery. A weekly report, enabling the evaluation of the net-hedged fuel cost of the current fiscal year and the two following years, is sent to the executive management. This mainly covers the transactions carried out during the week, the valuation of all the positions, the hedge percentages as well as the breakdown of instruments and the underlyings used, average hedge levels, the resulting net prices and stress scenarii, as well as market commentary. Furthermore, the fuel purchasing department issues a weekly Air France-KLM Group report (known as the GEC Report) which consolidates the figures from the two companies relating to fuel hedging and physical cost.

Lastly, a monthly report, which is submitted to the executive management by the fuel purchasing department, indicates the level of advancement on carbon quota purchases and the forecast related expenditure.

Currency risk

Most of the Group's revenues are generated in euros. However, because of its international activities, the Group incurs a foreign exchange risk. The principal exposure is to the US dollar.

With regard to the US dollar, since expenditure on items such as fuel, operating leases and component costs exceed the level of revenues, the Group is a net buyer. This means that any significant appreciation in the dollar against the euro could result in a negative impact on the Group's activity and financial results.

Conversely, Air France-KLM is a net seller of other currencies, the level of revenues exceeding expenditure. The main exposure concerns the yen and sterling. As a result, any significant decline in these currencies

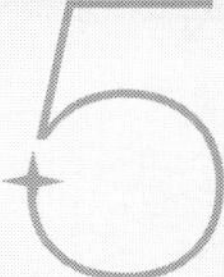

relative to the euro could have a negative effect on the Group's activity and financial results.

In order to reduce its currency exposure, the Group has adopted hedging strategies.

Both companies progressively hedge their net exposure over a rolling 24-month period.

Aircraft are mainly purchased in US dollars, meaning that the Group is highly exposed to a rise in the dollar against the euro for its aeronautics investments. The hedging policy plans the progressive and systematic implementation of hedging between the date of the aircraft order and their delivery date.

The exchange rate risk on the Group's financial debt is limited. At December 31, 2013, 87% of the Group's gross debt, after taking into account derivative instruments, was issued in or converted into euros, thereby markedly reducing the risk of currency fluctuation on the debt. The exposure of the debt to other currencies mainly concerns yen, US dollar and Swiss Franc.

Despite this active hedging policy, all exchange rate risks are not covered, especially in the event of significant variation of currencies in which debts are denominated. The Group and its subsidiaries might then encounter difficulties in managing currency risks, which could have a negative impact on the Group's business and financial results.

Interest rate risk

At both Air France and KLM, most financial debt is contracted in floating-rate instruments in line with market practice. However, given the historically low level of interest rates, Air France and KLM have used swap strategies and options to hedge a significant proportion of their debt. After hedging, the Air France-KLM Group's gross debt contracted at fixed rates represents 69% of the overall total.

Fuel price risk

Risks linked to the jet fuel price are hedged within the framework of a hedging strategy for the whole of the Air France-KLM Group and approved by the executive management. The RMC reconsider the hedging strategy quarterly and can change the hedge percentage or underlyings.

Main characteristics of the hedge strategy

- *Hedge horizon:* 2 years
- *Minimum hedge percentage:*
  - quarter underway: 60% of the volumes consumed,
  - quarter 1 to quarter 3: 60% of the volumes consumed,
  - quarter 4: 50% of the volumes consumed,
  - quarter 5: 40% of the volumes consumed,
  - quarter 6: 30% of the volumes consumed,
  - quarter 7: 20% of the volumes consumed,
  - quarter 8: 10% of the volumes consumed.
- *Increment of coverage ratios:* 10% by quarter
- *Underlyings:* Brent, Diesel and Jet Fuel
  The strategy of the Group recommends to use three underlying instruments which are Brent, Diesel and Jet Fuel. Currently, the volumes are mainly hegded with Brent given the few attractive prices of Diesel and Jet Fuel.
- *Instruments:*
  Swap, call, call spread, three ways, four ways and collar.
- *IAS 39 rule:*
  The instruments and underlyings used within the framework of the strategy must be compliant with IAS 39.
- *Implementation of monitoring indicators on positions:*
  To ensure more effective monitoring of the marked-to-market positions and a dynamic management of its exposure, the Air France-KLM Group uses the VAR (value at risk) metric to help measure the risk incurred by its portfolio. This monitoring is also reinforced by taking into account the maximum loss and maximum gain which limit the scale of variation of this same portfolio and enable the appropriate reaction.

Risks on carbon credit

To meet its regulatory obligations, the CO_2 emission quota acquisition strategy has been monitored and reviewed during every RMC meeting since October 2011. Its implementation led to the progressive hedging of the requirement for the current year (2013) and to anticipate the needs of the following year (2014), by hedging a portion of the later based on an applicable scope similar to that of 2012.

The European Commission had effectively announced the suspension of the application of its CO_2 emission permit system for intercontinental flights and had maintained its application for intra-European flights in respect of 2012 compliance.

Following the triennial assembly of the ICAO in autumn 2013, the change in applicable scope was also announced by the European Commission for 2013 and the following years. The scope applicable for 2013 compliance should therefore concern intra-European flights. The scope applicable for 2014 still needs to be clearly defined and remains under discussion.

- *Underlyings:* EUA quotas
- *Instruments:* Forwards, delivery and payment during the quarter preceding the compliance application date.

Investment risks

The cash resources of Air France, KLM and Air France-KLM are currently invested in short term, primarily money market mutual funds and certificates mainly rated A1/P1, the other lines being rated A2/P2.

Lastly, in order to reduce the currency risk on the debt, a portion of KLM's liquid assets is invested in foreign-currency rated as high quality bonds.

Equity risks

The Air France-KLM Group holds a limited number of shares which are listed for trading.

The value of these investments may vary during their period of ownership. These investments are accounted for using either the equity method (associates) if the Group has the ability to exercise significant influence, or at their fair value. If the fair value cannot be determined from a practical point of view, the value of the investment is measured at its acquisition cost.

The Group is exposed to the risk of significant and unexpected change in the fair value of its shares in Amadeus IT Holding. The Group consequently entered into a hedge agreement with Société Générale for approximately one third of its stake (12 million Amadeus shares) via a collar in November 2012, enabling the value of these shares to be protected *(see Note 24)*.

Treasury shares held by Air France-KLM are not deemed to be investments. Furthermore, treasury shares are not deemed to be exposed to risk, since any variation in the value of these shares is only recognized directly in equity when they are sold in the market, with no impact on the net result.

Counterparty risk management

The transactions involving potential counterparty risk are as follows:

- financial investments;
- derivative instruments;
- trade receivables.

Counterparty risk linked to financial investments and derivative instruments is managed by the Risk Management Committee which establishes limits by counterparty, for all instruments except investments in money market funds (OPCVM) for which the counterparty risk is deemed not to be significant. The Group's counterparty-risk reporting is circulated each month to the executive managements, the risk being measured at the fair market value of the various instruments. Any exceeding of a limit immediately results in the implementation of corrective measures,

The counterparty risk linked to derivative instruments is taken into account in the valuation of their market value as described in the Note 4.10.3. Derivative instruments are guided by framework compensation agreements ISDA and FBF. In these agreements, the compensation (in case of default) has to be made by counterparty for all the derivative guided by each agreement,

Counterparty risk relating to trade receivables is limited due to the large number and geographical diversity of the customers comprising the trade receivables portfolio.

The Group has identified the following exposure to counterparty risk:

	Total exposure in € millions	
LT Rating (Standards & Poors)	**As of December 31, 2013**	**As of December 31, 2012**
AAA	145	104
AA	196	303
A	1,880	1,539
BBB	96	94
Total	**2,317**	**2,040**

Liquidity risk

The liquidity risk is associated to the credit lines held by the Group, as described in Note 32.8.

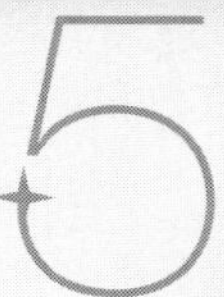

34.2 Derivative instruments

As of December 31, 2013 the fair value of the Group's derivative instruments and their expected maturities are as follows:

(In € million)		Total	Y+1	Y+2	Y+3	Y+4	Y+5	> Y+5
Commodities derivative instruments	Asset	255	205	50	-	-	-	-
	Liability	(10)	(9)	(1)	-	-	-	-
Interest rate derivative instruments	Asset	14	1	-	1	-	-	12
	Liability	(129)	(4)	(11)	(19)	(14)	(18)	(63)
Currency exchange derivative instruments	Asset	95	61	26	-	2	3	3
	Liability	(182)	(105)	(48)	(8)	(7)	(5)	(9)
OCEANE swap instrument *(see Note 32.2.1)*	Asset	-	-	-	-	-	-	-
	Liability	(8)	-	-	(8)	-	-	-
Amadeus shares derivative instrument	Asset	-	-	-	-	-	-	-
	Liability	(108)	-	(72)	(36)	-	-	-
Carbon credit derivative instruments	Asset	-	-	-	-	-	-	-
	Liability	-	-	-	-	-	-	-
Total	**Asset**	**364**	**267**	**76**	**1**	**2**	**3**	**15**
	Liability	**(437)**	**(118)**	**(132)**	**(71)**	**(21)**	**(23)**	**(72)**

As of December 31, 2012 the fair value of the Group's derivative instruments and their expected maturities are as follows:

(In € million)		Total	Y+1	Y+2	Y+3	Y+4	Y+5	> Y+5
Commodities derivative instruments	Asset	146	113	33	-	-	-	-
	Liability	(35)	(24)	(11)	-	-	-	-
Interest rate derivative instruments	Asset	24	4	1	-	3	-	16
	Liability	(200)	(7)	(17)	(14)	(19)	(29)	(114)
Currency exchange derivative instruments	Asset	134	84	34	4	-	5	7
	Liability	(105)	(44)	(33)	(11)	(2)	(6)	(9)
Carbon credit derivative instruments	Asset	-	-	-	-	-	-	-
	Liability	(10)	(10)	-	-	-	-	-
OCEANE swap instrument *(see Note 32.2.1)*	Asset	-	-	-	-	-	-	-
	Liability	(14)	-	-	-	(14)	-	-
Total	**Asset**	**304**	**201**	**68**	**4**	**3**	**5**	**23**
	Liability	**(364)**	**(85)**	**(61)**	**(25)**	**(35)**	**(35)**	**(123)**

The value of the derivatives used by the Group to hedge the Amadeus equity risk does not figure in this table since it is below €1 million.

34.2.1 Commodity risk linked to fuel prices

The Group's commitments on Brent, Diesel and Jet CIF are presented below, at their nominal value:

➤ Year ended December 31, 2013

(In € million)	Nominal	Maturity below 1 year	Maturities between 1 and 5 years					Fair value
			1-2 years	2-3 years	3-4 years	4-5 years	+ 5 years	
Commodity risk (cash flow hedging operating flows)								
Swap	617	617	-	-	-	-	-	38
Options	4,931	3,377	1,554	-	-	-	-	207
Total	**5,548**	**3,994**	**1,554**	**-**	**-**	**-**	**-**	**245**

➤ Year ended December 31, 2012

(In € million)	Nominal	Maturity below 1 year	Maturities between 1 and 5 years					Fair value
			1-2 years	2-3 years	3-4 years	4-5 years	+ 5 years	
Commodity risk (cash flow hedging operating flows)								
Swap	451	224	227	-	-	-	-	16
Options	5,831	4,387	1,444	-	-	-	-	95
Total	**6,282**	**4,611**	**1,671**	**-**	**-**	**-**	**-**	**111**

Fuel hedge sensitivity

The impact on "income before tax" and on "gains/(losses) taken to equity" of a variation in the fair value of the fuel hedges following a +/- USD 10 variation in the price of a barrel of Brent is as follows:

(In € million)	2013		2012	
As of December 31	Increase of USD 10 per barrel of Brent	Decrease of USD 10 per barrel of Brent	Increase of USD 10 per barrel of Brent	Decrease of USD 10 per barrel of Brent
Income before tax	(66)	(187)	123	(194)
Gains / (losses) taken to equity	477	(181)	290	(213)

34.2.2 Exposure to interest rate risk

To manage the interest rate risk on its short and long-term borrowings, the Group uses instruments with the following nominal values:

➤ Year ended December 31, 2013

(In € million)	Nominal	Maturity below 1 year	Maturity between 1 and 5 years					Fair value
			1-2 years	2-3 years	3-4 years	4-5 years	+ 5 years	
Operations qualified as cash flow hedging	***2,272***	***294***	***184***	***461***	***251***	***316***	***766***	***(112)***
Interest rate swaps	1,983	201	154	319	251	292	766	(107)
Options	289	93	30	142	-	24	-	(5)
Operations qualified as fair value hedging	***261***	***28***	***17***	***35***	***-***	***-***	***181***	***1***
Interest rate swaps	261	28	17	35	-	-	181	1
Operations qualified as fair value through profit and loss	***117***	***-***	***-***	***48***	***-***	***-***	***69***	***(4)***
Interest rate swaps	83	-	-	14	-	-	69	(10)
Others	34	-	-	34	-	-	-	6
TOTAL	**2,650**	**322**	**201**	**544**	**251**	**316**	**1,016**	**(115)**

➤ Year ended December 31, 2012

(In € million)	Nominal	Maturity below 1 year	Maturity between 1 and 5 years					Fair value
			1-2 years	2-3 years	3-4 years	4-5 years	+ 5 years	
Operations qualified as cash flow hedging	***2,766***	***146***	***367***	***280***	***244***	***545***	***1,184***	***(155)***
Interest rate swaps	2,307	70	321	182	214	336	1,184	(145)
Options	459	76	46	98	30	209	-	(10)
Operations qualified as fair value hedging	***593***	***-***	***30***	***32***	***60***	***-***	***471***	***(8)***
Interest rate swaps	593	-	30	32	60	-	471	(8)
Operations qualified as fair value through profit and loss	***146***	***-***	***-***	***-***	***-***	***58***	***88***	***(13)***
Interest rate swaps	104	-	-	-	-	16	88	(13)
Others	42	-	-	-	-	42	-	-
TOTAL	**3,505**	**146**	**397**	**312**	**304**	**603**	**1,743**	**(176)**

Based on the hedging operations, the Group's exposure to interest rate risks breaks down as follows:

As of December 31 *(In € million)*	2013				2012			
	Before hedging		After hedging		Before hedging		After hedging	
	Base	Average interest rate	Base	Average interest rate	Base	Average interest rate	Base	Average interest rate
Fixed-rate financial assets and liabilities								
Fixed-rate financial assets	2,052	2.8%	2,052	2.8%	2,198	2.2%	2,198	2.2%
Fixed-rate financial liabilities	5,965	4.4%	7,486	4.1%	5,673	4.5%	7,752	4.2%
Floating-rate financial assets and liabilities								
Floating-rate financial assets	2,400	0.5%	2,400	0.5%	2,299	1.1%	2,299	1.1%
Floating-rate financial liabilities	4,934	1.7%	3,413	2.1%	5,583	2.2%	3,504	1.9%
Without-rate financial assets	**2,226**	**-**	**2,226**	**-**	**1,521**	**-**	**1,521**	**-**

As of December 31, 2013 and December 31, 2012, without-rate financial assets mainly include cash and the revaluation of Amadeus' shares at their fair value.

Interest rate sensitivity

The Group is exposed to the risk of interest rate variation. A 100 basis point variation (increase or decrease) in interest rates would have an impact of €12 million on the financial income for the year ended December 31, 2013 versus €6 million for the year ended December 31, 2012.

34.2.3 Exposure to exchange rate risk

The nominal amount of futures and swaps linked to exchange rate are detailed below given the nature of the hedging operations:

➤ Year ended December 31, 2013

(In € million)	Nominal	Maturity below 1 year	Maturities between 1 and 5 years					Fair value
			1-2 years	2-3 years	3-4 years	4-5 years	+ 5 years	
Exchange risk (cash flow hedging of operating flows)	***4,143***	***2,785***	***1,347***	***11***	***-***	***-***	***-***	***(33)***
Exchange rate options	2,222	1,511	711	-	-	-	-	(15)
Forward purchases	1,509	1,003	495	11	-	-	-	(57)
Forward sales	412	271	141	-	-	-	-	39
Exchange risk (Fair value hedging of flight equipment acquisition)	***1,338***	***429***	***408***	***251***	***120***	***81***	***49***	***(54)***
Forward purchases	1,338	429	408	251	120	81	49	(54)
Exchange risk (trading)	***438***	***72***	***62***	***-***	***98***	***110***	***96***	***-***
Forward purchases	219	36	31	-	49	55	48	3
Forward sales	219	36	31	-	49	55	48	(3)
Total	**5,919**	**3,286**	**1,817**	**262**	**218**	**191**	**145**	**(87)**

➤ Year ended December 31, 2012

(In € million)	Nominal	Maturity below 1 year	Maturities between 1 and 5 years					Fair value
			1-2 years	2-3 years	3-4 years	4-5 years	+ 5 years	
Exchange risk (cash flow hedging of operating flows)	***4,414***	***2,949***	***1,460***	***4***	***1***	***-***	***-***	***19***
Exchange rate options	2,278	1,508	770	-	-	-	-	12
Forward purchases	1,717	1,170	542	4	1	-	-	(14)
Forward sales	419	271	148	-	-	-	-	21
Exchange risk (Fair value hedging of flight equipment acquisition)	**1,360**	**471**	**336**	**249**	**105**	**79**	**120**	**10**
Forward purchases	1,322	433	336	249	105	79	120	7
Forward sales	38	38	-	-	-	-	-	3
Exchange risk (trading)	***540***	***82***	***76***	***64***	***-***	***102***	***216***	***-***
Forward purchases	270	41	38	32	-	51	108	14
Forward sales	270	41	38	32	-	51	108	(14)
Total	**6,314**	**3,502**	**1,872**	**317**	**106**	**181**	**336**	**29**

Currency hedge sensitivity

The value in euros of the monetary assets and liabilities is presented below:

As of December 31 *(In € million)*	Monetary assets		Monetary liabilities	
	2013	2012	2013	2012
US dollar	143	228	519	432
Pound sterling	23	26	-	1
Yen	8	8	727	819
Swiss franc	11	8	341	347

The amount of monetary assets and liabilities disclosed above does not include the effect of the revaluation of assets and liabilities documented in fair value hedge.

The impact on "income before tax" and on "gains/(losses) taken to equity" of a 10% appreciation in foreign currencies relative to the euro is presented below:

As of December 31 *(In € million)*	US dollar		Pound Sterling		Yen	
	2013	2012	2013	2012	2013	2012
Income before tax	37	9	(8)	(7)	(70)	(79)
Gains / (losses) taken to equity	312	392	(24)	(22)	(37)	(44)

The impact of the change in fair value of currency derivatives on "income before tax" and on "gains/(losses) taken to equity" of a 10% depreciation in foreign currencies relative to the euro is presented below:

As of December 31 *(In € million)*	US dollar		Pound Sterling		Yen	
	2013	2012	2013	2012	2013	2012
Income before tax	(108)	(60)	-	(1)	62	68
Gains / (losses) taken to equity	(220)	(266)	23	22	34	45

34.2.4 Carbon credit risk

As of December 31, 2013, the Group has hedged its future purchases of CO_2 quotas via forward purchase for a nominal of €15 million whose fair value is nil, versus, respectively, €16 million and €(10) million as of December 31, 2012.

These contracts mostly expire within less than 2 years.

34.3 Market value of financial instruments

Market values are estimated for most of the Group's financial instruments using a variety of valuation methods, such as discounted future cash flows. However, the methods and assumptions used to provide the information set out below are theoretical in nature. They bear the following inherent limitations:

- estimated market values cannot take into consideration the effect of subsequent fluctuations in interest or exchange rates;
- estimated amounts as of December 31, 2013 and December 31, 2012 are not indicative of gains and/or losses arising upon maturity or in the event of cancellation of a financial instrument.

The application of alternative methods and assumptions may, therefore, have a significant impact on the estimated market values.

The methods used are as follows:

- *Cash, trade receivables, other receivables, short-term bank facilities, trade payables and other payables:*
  The Group believes that, due to its short-term nature, net book value can be deemed a reasonable approximation of market value.

- *Marketable securities, investments and other securities:*
The market value of securities is determined based mainly on the market price or the prices available on other similar securities. Securities classified under "Assets available for sale" are recorded at their stock market value.
Where no comparable exists, the Group uses their book value, which is deemed a reasonable approximation of market value in this instance.
- *Borrowings, other financial debts and loans:*
The market value of fixed and floating-rate loans and financial debts is determined based on discounted future cash flows at market interest rates for instruments with similar features.
- *Derivative instruments:*
The market value of derivative instruments corresponds to the amounts payable or receivable were the positions to be closed out as of December 31, 2013 and December 31, 2012 calculated using the year-end market rate.

Only the financial assets and liabilities whose fair value differs from their net book value are presented in the following table:

As of December 31 *(In € million)*	2013		2012	
	Net book value	Estimated market value	Net book value	Estimated market value
Financial assets				
Loans	164	167	160	171
Financial liabilities				
Debt measured at amortized cost				
Bonds	3,419	3,788	2,938	3,201
OCEANE 2005	*390*	*428*	*419*	*433*
OCEANE 2009	*633*	*717*	*569*	*718*
OCEANE 2013	*455*	*588*	*-*	*-*
Bond 2006/2007	*741*	*743*	*750*	*767*
Bond 2009	*700*	*765*	*700*	*757*
Bond 2012	*500*	*547*	*500*	*526*
Perpetual subordinated loans	552	248	603	306
Other borrowings and financial debt	1,857	1,770	2,061	1 881

34.4 Valuation methods for financial assets and liabilities at their fair value

The breakdown of the Group's financial assets and liabilities is as follows based on the three classification levels *(see Note 4.10.7):*

As of December 31 *(In € million)*	Level 1		Level 2		Level 3		Total	
	2013	2012	2013	2012	2013	2012	2013	2012
Financial assets available for sale								
Shares	1,100	684	35	20	-	-	**1,135**	**704**
Assets at fair value through profit and loss								
Marketable securities and cash secured	31	36	920	920	-	-	**951**	**956**
Cash equivalents	1,552	2,653	1,152	148	-	-	**2,704**	**2,801**
Derivative instruments asset								
Interest rate derivatives	-	-	14	24	-	-	**14**	**24**
Currency exchange derivatives	-	-	95	134	-	-	**95**	**134**
Commodity derivatives	-	-	255	146	-	-	**255**	**146**

Financial liabilities at fair value comprise the fair value of interest rate, foreign exchange and commodity derivative instruments. These valuations are classified as level 2.

Note 35 Lease commitments

35.1 Capital leases

The debt related to capital leases is detailed in Note 32.

35.2 Operating leases

The minimum future payments on operating leases are as follows:

As of December 31 *(In € million)*	Minimum lease payments	
	2013	**2012**
Flight equipment		
Due dates		
Y+1	912	913
Y+2	816	841
Y+3	754	717
Y+4	727	615
Y+5	606	513
Over 5 years	1,872	1,423
Total	**5,687**	**5,022**
Buildings		
Due dates		
Y+1	221	221
Y+2	152	169
Y+3	136	148
Y+4	108	134
Y+5	94	107
Over 5 years	878	956
Total	**1,589**	**1,735**

The Group may sub-lease flight equipment and buildings. The revenue generated by this activity is not significant for the Group.

Note 36 Flight equipment orders

Due dates for commitments in respect of flight equipment orders are as follows:

As of December 31 *(In € million)*	2013	2012
Y+1	381	511
Y+2	436	431
Y+3	616	434
Y+4	536	354
Y+5	931	248
> Y+5	3,828	2,162
Total	**6,728**	**4,140**

These commitments relate to amounts in US dollars, converted into euros at the closing date exchange rate. Furthermore these amounts are hedged.

The number of aircraft under firm order as of December 31, 2013 increased by 21 units compared with December 31, 2012 and stood at 64 aircraft.

The changes are explained by the order for 25 aircraft, the delivery of five aircraft over the period and the conversion of one option into a firm order over the period.

Long-haul fleet

Passenger

The Group ordered 25 Airbus A350s.

The Group took delivery of one Airbus A380, one Airbus A330 and one Boeing B777.

Moreover, a Boeing B777 on option has been transformed into firm order.

Cargo

The Group did not take any deliveries.

Medium-haul fleet

The Group took delivery of 2 Boeing B737s.

Regional fleet

The Group did not take any deliveries.

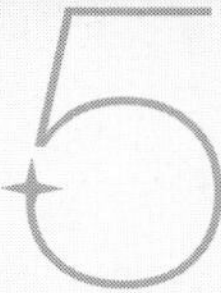

The Group's commitments concern the following aircraft:

Aircraft type	To be delivered in year	Y+1	Y+2	Y+3	Y+4	Y+5	Beyond Y+5	Total
Long-haul fleet – passenger								
A380	***As of December 31, 2013***	***1***	***-***	***-***	***-***	***2***	***-***	***3***
	As of December 31, 2012	2	2	-	-	-	-	4
A350	***As of December 31, 2013***	***-***	***-***	***-***	***-***	***2***	***23***	***25***
	As of December 31, 2012	-	-	-	-	-	-	-
A330	***As of December 31, 2013***	***-***	***-***	***-***	***-***	***-***	***-***	***-***
	As of December 31, 2012	1	-	-	-	-	-	1
B787	***As of December 31, 2013***	***-***	***-***	***3***	***5***	***3***	***14***	***25***
	As of December 31, 2012	-	-	-	3	3	19	25
B777	***As of December 31, 2013***	***-***	***3***	***2***	***-***	***-***	***-***	***5***
	As of December 31, 2012	1	-	3	1	-	-	5
Medium-haul fleet								
A320	***As of December 31, 2013***	***-***	***-***	***3***	***-***	***-***	***-***	***3***
	As of December 31, 2012	-	-	3	-	-	-	3
B737	***As of December 31, 2013***	***2***	***-***	***-***	***-***	***-***	***-***	***2***
	As of December 31, 2012	2	2	-	-	-	-	4
Regional fleet								
CRJ 1000	***As of December 31, 2013***	***-***	***1***	***-***	***-***	***-***	***-***	***1***
	As of December 31, 2012	-	-	1	-	-	-	1

Note 37 Other commitments

37.1 Commitments made

As of December 31 *(In € million)*	**2013**	**2012**
Call on investment securities	3	3
Warranties, sureties and guarantees	288	284
Secured debts	5,756	6,279
Other purchase commitments	155	106

The restrictions and pledges as of December 31, 2013 were as follows:

(In € million)	Starting date of pledge	End of pledge	Amount pledged	NBV of balance sheet entry concerned	Corresponding %
Intangible assets			-	896	-
Tangible assets	March 1999	September 2027	7,022	11,210	62.7%
Other financial assets	November 1999	May 2027	1,824	2,994	60.9%
Total			**8,846**	**15,100**	**-**

37.2 Commitments received

As of December 31 *(In € million)*	2013	2012
Warranties, sureties and guarantees	135	142

Warranties, sureties and guarantees principally comprise letters of credit from financial institutions.

Note 38 Related parties

38.1 Transactions with the principal executives

As of December 31, 2013, directors and their relatives hold less than 0.01% of the voting rights.

Short term benefits granted to the principal company officers and booked in expenses amounts to €0.6 million as of December 31, 2013 against €0.4 million as of December 31, 2012.

During these two periods, there were no payments of post employment benefits.

Directors' fees paid during the financial year ended December 31, 2013 for attendance of Board meetings during the financial year ended December 31, 2012 amounted to €0.3 million. To join the efforts required under the recovery plan Transform 2015, the directors had decided to give up half of fees concerning the year 2012.

Concerning the financial year ended December 31, 2013, €0.6 million was also paid for attendance of Board meetings.

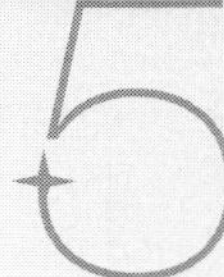

38.2 Transactions with other related parties

The total amounts of transactions with related parties for the financial years ended December 31, 2013 and December 31, 2012 are as follows:

As of December 31 *(In € million)*	2013	2012
Assets		
Net trade accounts receivable	126	128
Other current assets	25	12
Other non-current assets	7	21
Total	**158**	**161**
Liabilities		
Trade accounts payable	114	183
Other current liabilities	56	66
Other long-term liabilities	72	35
Total	**242**	**284**

As of December 31 *(In € million)*	2013	2012
Net sales	244	215
Landing fees and other rents	(394)	(415)
Other selling expenses	(153)	(158)
Passenger service	(53)	(43)
Other	(49)	(56)
Total	**(405)**	**(457)**

As a part of its normal business, the Group enters into transactions with related parties including transactions with State-owned and governmental entities such as the Defense Ministry, the Paris Airport Authority ("Aéroports de Paris", or "ADP") and the French civil aviation regulator ("DGAC"). Air France-KLM considers that such transactions are concluded on terms equivalent to those on transactions with third parties. The most significant transactions are described below:

Aéroports De Paris (ADP)

- land and property rental agreements;
- airport and passenger-related fee arrangements.

In addition, ADP collects airport landing fees on behalf of the French State.

Total expenses incurred by the Group in connection with the above-mentioned arrangements amounted to a respective €372 million and €373 million for the periods ended December 31, 2013 and December 31, 2012.

Defense Ministry

Air France-KLM has entered into contracts with the French Defense Ministry concerning the maintenance of aircraft in the French Air Force. The net revenue derived from this activity amounted to €42 million for the year ended December 31, 2013 versus €67 million as of December 31, 2012.

Direction Générale de l'Aviation Civile (DGAC)

This civil aviation regulator is under the authority of the French Ministry of Transport, which manages security and safety in the French air space and at airport. As a result, the DGAC charges fees to Air France-KLM for the use of installations and services which amounted to €105 million as of December 31, 2013 versus €115 million for the year ended December 31, 2012.

Amadeus

For the year ended December 31, 2013, total transactions with Amadeus amounted to an expense of €132 million for the Group, compared with €141 million for the year ended December 31, 2012.

Alitalia

For the year ended December 31, 2013, the amount of transactions realized with Alitalia represents revenues of €81 million for the Group (compared with €53 million for the year ended December 31, 2012) and a cost of €12 million (compared with €14 million for the year ended December 31, 2012).

Note 39 Consolidated statement of cash flow

39.1 Other non-monetary items and impairment

Other non-monetary items and impairment can be analyzed as follows:

As of December 31 *(In € million)*	Notes	2013	2012 Pro forma
Variation of provisions relating to restructuring plan	**11**	17	375
Variation of provisions relating to pension and pension assets		(51)	(91)
Variation of provisions relating to goodwill	**17**	11	173
Impairment of Cityjet VLM Group	**14**	66	-
Variation of provisions relating to onerous contracts	**11**	(4)	50
Depreciation of assets available for sale	**11**	102	-
Other		65	38
Total		**206**	**545**

39.2 Acquisitions of subsidiaries, of shares in non-controlled entities

Net cash disbursements related to the acquisition of subsidiaries and investments in associates were as follows:

As of December 31 *(In € million)*	2013	2012
Cash disbursement for acquisitions	(33)	(39)
Cash from acquired subsidiaries	6	-
Net cash disbursement	***(27)***	***(39)***

There were no significant acquisitions of subsidiaries and investments for the periods presented.

39.3 Disposal of subsidiaries without loss of control, of owned shares

As of December 31, 2013, no cash proceeds have been recorded on this line.

As of December 31, 2012, the net cash proceeds corresponded to profits of disposal of owned shares for €7 million.

39.4 Non cash transactions

During the financial year ended December 31, 2013, the Group renewed a lease contract for a car park with Aéroport de Paris. This contract is classified as a financial lease.

A lease contract on A340 aircraft, classified as a financial lease in 2012, has also been reclassified as an operational lease.

During the financial year ended December 31, 2012, the Group had entered into a financial lease for the acquisition of an A380 aircraft and for the acquisition of a building dedicated to handling delayed luggage. The Group had also renewed a lease contract for a B747-400 aircraft and reclassified under financial lease the contract on an A340 aircraft.

These operations have no impact on the cash flow statement.

Note 40 Fees of Statutory Auditors

As of 31 December 31 (In € million)	KPMG			
	2013		2012	
	Amount	%	Amount	%
Audit				
Statutory audit, certification, review of stand-alone and consolidated accounts	3.7	88%	3.8	85%
Air France-KLM SA	*0.7*	-	*0.7*	-
Consolidated subsidiaries	*3.0*	-	*3.1*	-
Other ancillary services and audit services	0.2	5%	0.6	13%
Air France-KLM SA	*0.1*	-	*0.1*	-
Consolidated subsidiaries	*0.1*	-	*0.5*	-
Sub-total	**3.9**	**93%**	**4.4**	**98%**
Other services				
Legal, tax and corporate	0.3	7%	0.1	2%
Information technology	-	-	-	-
Internal audit	-	-	-	-
Others	-	-	-	-
Total Air France-KLM Group	**4.2**	**100%**	**4.5**	**100%**

As of December 31 (In € million)	Deloitte & Associés			
	2013		2012	
	Amount	%	Amount	%
Audit				
Statutory audit, certification, review of stand-alone and consolidated accounts	3.7	90%	3.8	87%
Air France-KLM SA	*0.7*	-	*0.7*	-
Consolidated subsidiaries	*3.0*	-	*3.1*	-
Other ancillary services and audit services	0.3	8%	0.5	11%
Air France-KLM SA	*0.1*	-	*0.1*	-
Consolidated subsidiaries	*0.2*	-	*0.4*	-
Sub-total	**4.0**	**98%**	**4.3**	**98%**
Other services				
Legal, tax and corporate	0.1	2%	0.1	2%
Information technology	-	-	-	-
Internal audit	-	-	-	-
Others	-	-	-	-
Total Air France-KLM Group	**4.1**	**100%**	**4.4**	**100%**

Note 41 Consolidation scope as of December 31, 2013

The scope includes 162 fully-consolidated entities and 41 equity affiliates.

Based on the Air France-KLM ownership in terms of both voting rights and equity interest and on the functioning mode of the Group's Executive Committee, Air France-KLM has the power to manage the KLM Group's financial and operational strategies and controls KLM. As a result, KLM is fully consolidated in Air France-KLM's consolidated financial statements.

41.1 Consolidated entities

Entity	Country	Segment	% interest	% control
AIR FRANCE SA	France	Multisegment	100	100
KONINKLIJKE LUCHTVAART MAATSCHAPPIJ N.V.	Netherlands	Multisegment	99	49
MARTINAIR HOLLAND N.V.	Netherlands	Multisegment	99	49
AIR FRANCE GROUND HANDLING INDIA PVT LTD	India	Passenger	51	51
AIRLINAIR	France	Passenger	100	100
BLUE LINK	France	Passenger	100	100
BLUE LINK INTERNATIONAL	France	Passenger	100	100
BLUELINK INTERNATIONAL AUSTRALIA	Australia	Passenger	100	100
BLUELINK INTERNATIONAL CZ	Czech Rep.	Passenger	100	100
BLUELINK INTERNATIONAL MAURITIUS	Mauritius	Passenger	100	100
BLUE CONNECT	Mauritius	Passenger	70	70
HOP BRIT AIR	France	Passenger	100	100
CITY JET	Ireland	Passenger	100	100
COBALT GROUND SOLUTIONS LIMITED	United Kingdom	Passenger	99	49
CONSTELLATION FINANCE LIMITED	Ireland	Passenger	100	100
CYGNIFIC B.V.	Netherlands	Passenger	99	49
HEATHROW AIRPORT HANDLING LTD	United Kingdom	Passenger	99	49
HOP	France	Passenger	100	100
IAS ASIA INCORPORATED	Philippines	Passenger	99	49
IASA INCORPORATED	Philippines	Passenger	99	49
ICARE	France	Passenger	100	100
INTERNATIONAL AIRLINE SERVICES EUROPE LIMITED	United Kingdom	Passenger	99	49
INTERNATIONAL AIRLINE SERVICES LIMITED	United Kingdom	Passenger	99	49
INTERNATIONAL MARINE AIRLINE SERVICES LIMITED	United Kingdom	Passenger	99	49
INTERNATIONAL AIRLINE SERVICES AMERICAS L.P	United States	Passenger	99	49
KLM CITYHOPPER B.V.	Netherlands	Passenger	99	49
KLM CITYHOPPER UK LTD	United Kingdom	Passenger	99	49
KLM EQUIPMENT SERVICES B.V.	Netherlands	Passenger	99	49
KLM FLIGHT ACADEMY B.V.	Netherlands	Passenger	99	49
LYON MAINTENANCE	France	Passenger	100	100
MILESHOUSE	France	Passenger	100	100

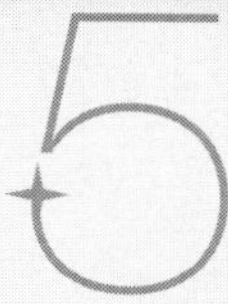

Entity	Country	Segment	% interest	% control
HOP REGIONAL	France	Passenger	100	100
STICHTING STUDENTENHUISVESTING VLIEGVELD EELDE	Netherlands	Passenger	99	49
VLM AIRLINES N.V.	Belgium	Passenger	100	100
BLUE CROWN B.V.	Netherlands	Cargo	99	49
MEXICO CARGO HANDLING	Mexico	Cargo	100	100
SODEXI	France	Cargo	65	65
AEROMAINTENANCE GROUP	United States	Maintenance	100	100
AIR FRANCE INDUSTRIE US	United States	Maintenance	100	100
AIR FRANCE KLM COMPONENT SERVICES CO LTD	Chine	Maintenance	100	100
AIR ORIENT SERVICES	France	Maintenance	100	100
CRMA	France	Maintenance	100	100
EUROPEAN PNEUMATIC COMPONENT OVERHAUL AND REPAIR (EPCOR) B.V.	Netherlands	Maintenance	99	49
KLM E&M MALAYSIA SDN BHD	Malaysia	Maintenance	99	49
KLM UK ENGINEERING LIMITED	United Kingdom	Maintenance	99	49
ACNA	France	Other	98	100
ACSAIR	France	Other	50	51
SERVAIR FORMATION	France	Other	98	100
AFRIQUE CATERING	France	Other	50	51
AIDA	Mauritius	Other	77	77
AIR FRANCE FINANCE	France	Other	100	100
AIR FRANCE FINANCE IRELAND	Ireland	Other	100	100
AIR FRANCE KLM FINANCE	France	Other	100	100
AIRPORT MEDICAL SERVICES B.V.	Netherlands	Other	79	39
AIRPORT MEDICAL SERVICES C.V.	Netherlands	Other	79	39
ALL AFRICA AIRWAYS	Mauritius	Other	80	80
AMSTERDAM SCHIPOL PIJPLEIDING BEHEER B.V.	Netherlands	Other	59	49
AMSTERDAM SCHIPOL PIJPLEIDING C.V.	Netherlands	Other	75	49
BLUE YONDER IX B.V.	Netherlands	Other	99	49
BLUE YONDER X B.V.	Netherlands	Other	99	49
BLUE YONDER XIV B.V.	Netherlands	Other	99	49
BLUE YONDER XV B.V.	Netherlands	Other	99	49
B.V. KANTOORGEBOUW MARTINAIR	Netherlands	Other	99	49
CATERING FDF	France	Other	98	100
CATERING PTP	France	Other	98	100
CELL K16 INSURANCE COMPANY	United Kingdom	Other	99	0
DAKAR CATERING	Senegal	Other	64	65
ETS SCHIPHOL B.V.	Netherlands	Other	99	49
EUROPEAN CATERING SERVICES	United States	Other	98	100

Entity	Country	Segment	% interest	% control
GIE JEAN BART	France	Other	10	10
GIE SERVCENTER	France	Other	98	100
GIE SURCOUF	France	Other	100	100
GUINEENNE DE SERVICES AEROPORTUAIRES S.A.	Guinea	Other	30	60
HEESWIJK HOLDING B.V.	Netherlands	Other	99	49
INTERNATIONALE FINANCIERING EN MANAGEMENT MAATSCHAPPIJ B.V.	Netherlands	Other	99	49
KES AIRPORT EQUIPMENT FUELLING B.V.	Netherlands	Other	99	49
KES AIRPORT EQUIPMENT LEASING B.V.	Netherlands	Other	99	49
KLM AIRL CHARTER B.V.	Netherlands	Other	99	49
KLM CATERING SERVICES SCHIPOL B.V.	Netherlands	Other	99	49
KLM FINANCIAL SERVICES B.V.	Netherlands	Other	99	49
KLM HEALTH SERVICES B.V.	Netherlands	Other	99	49
KLM INTERNATIONAL CHARTER B.V.	Netherlands	Other	99	49
KLM INTERNATIONAL FINANCE COMPANY B.V.	Netherlands	Other	99	49
KLM OLIEMAATSCHAPPIJ B.V.	Netherlands	Other	99	49
KLM UNTERSTUTZUNGSKASSEN GMBH	Germany	Other	99	49
KROONDUIF B.V.	Netherlands	Other	99	49
LYON AIR TRAITEUR	France	Other	98	100
MALI CATERING	Mali	Other	70	99
MARTINAIR AFRICA LTD.	Kenya	Other	99	49
MARTINAIR FAR EAST LTD.	Hong Kong	Other	99	49
MARTINAIR HK LTD.	Hong Kong	Other	99	49
MARTINAIR VESTIGING VLIEGVELD LELYSTAD B.V.	Netherlands	Other	99	49
MARTINIQUE CATERING	France	Other	91	93
MAURITANIE CATERING	Mauritania	Other	25	51
NAS AIRPORT SERVICES LIMITED	Kenya	Other	58	100
O'FIONNAGAIN HOLDING COMPANY LIMITED	Ireland	Other	100	100
ORION-STAETE B.V.	Netherlands	Other	99	49
ORLY AIR TRAITEUR	France	Other	98	100
SERVAIR BURKINA FASO	Burkina Faso	Other	84	86
PARIS AIR CATERING	France	Other	98	100
PASSERELLE CDG	France	Other	64	66
PELICAN	Luxembourg	Other	100	100
PMAIR	France	Other	50	51
PRESTAIR	France	Other	98	100
PYRHELIO-STAETE B.V.	Netherlands	Other	99	49
QUASAR-STAETE B.V.	Netherlands	Other	99	49
RIGEL-STAETE B.V.	Netherlands	Other	99	49

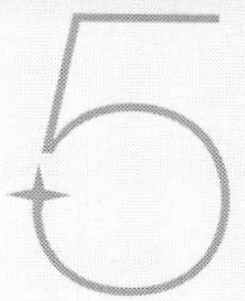

Entity	Country	Segment	% interest	% control
SENCA	Senegal	Other	32	51
SEREP	Senegal	Other	57	59
SERVAIR (Cie d'exploitation des services auxiliaires aériens)	France	Other	98	98
SERVAIR ABIDJAN	Ivory Coast	Other	84	86
SERVAIR CARAIBES	France	Other	98	98
SERVAIR GHANA	Ghana	Other	56	57
SERVAIR RETAIL FORT DE France	France	Other	50	51
SERVAIR SATS	Singapore	Other	50	51
SERVAIR SOLUTION ITALIA S.R.L.	Italy	Other	98	100
SERVANTAGE	France	Other	98	100
SERVASCO	Macao	Other	59	60
SERVAIR SOLUTIONS	France	Other	98	100
SERVAIR GABON	Gabon	Other	54	55
SERVLOGISTIC	France	Other	98	100
SIA AFRIQUE	France	Other	98	98
SIA COMMERCES ET SERVICES	France	Other	98	98
SIA INTERNATIONAL	France	Other	98	98
SIA KENYA HOLDING LIMITED	Kenya	Other	58	59
SIEGA LOGISTICS (PROPRIETARY) PTY	South Africa	Other	99	49
SISALOGISTIC NETHERLANDS B.V.	Netherlands	Other	99	49
SISALOGISTIC U.S. LTD.	United States	Other	99	49
SKYCHEF	Seychelles	Other	54	55
SKYLOGISTIC	France	Other	98	100
SKYLOGISTIQUE AFRIQUE	France	Other	64	66
SOCIETE IMMOBILIERE AEROPORTUAIRE	France	Other	98	100
SOGRI	France	Other	95	97
SORI	France	Other	49	50
SPECIAL MEALS CATERING	France	Other	98	100
SPICA-STAETE B.V.	Netherlands	Other	99	49
STICHTING GARANTIEFONDS KLM LUCHTVAARTSCHOOL	Netherlands	Other	99	49
SVRL@LA REUNION	France	Other	49	50
TAKEOFF 1 LIMITED	Ireland	Other	100	100
TAKEOFF 2 LIMITED	Ireland	Other	100	100
TAKEOFF 3 LIMITED	Ireland	Other	100	100
TAKEOFF 4 LIMITED	Ireland	Other	100	100
TAKEOFF 5 LIMITED	Ireland	Other	100	100
TAKEOFF 6 LIMITED	Ireland	Other	100	100
TAKEOFF 7 LIMITED	Ireland	Other	100	100
TAKEOFF 8 LIMITED	Ireland	Other	100	100

Entity	Country	Segment	% interest	% control
TAKEOFF 9 LIMITED	Ireland	Other	100	100
TAKEOFF 10 LIMITED	Ireland	Other	100	100
TAKEOFF 11 LIMITED	Ireland	Other	100	100
TAKEOFF 12 LIMITED	Ireland	Other	100	100
TAKEOFF 13 LIMITED	Ireland	Other	100	100
TAKEOFF 14 LIMITED	Ireland	Other	100	100
TAKEOFF 15 LIMITED	Ireland	Other	100	100
TAKEOFF 16 LIMITED	Ireland	Other	100	100
TRANSAVIA AIRLINES B.V.	Netherlands	Other	99	49
TRANSAVIA AIRLINES C.V.	Netherlands	Other	99	49
TRANSAVIA AIRLINES LTD.	Bermuda	Other	99	49
TRANSAVIA FINANCE B.V.	Netherlands	Other	99	49
TRANSAVIA FRANCE S.A.S.	France	Other	100	100
TRAVEL INDUSTRY SYSTEMS B.V.	Netherlands	Other	99	49
UILEAG HOLDING COMPANY LIMITED	Ireland	Other	100	100
WEBLOK B.V.	Netherlands	Other	99	49

41.2 Equity affiliates

Entity	Country	Segment	% interest	% control
AIR COTE D'IVOIRE	Ivory Coast	Passenger	20	20
AEROLIS	France	Passenger	50	50
HEATHROW CARGO HANDLING	United Kingdom	Cargo	50	50
SPAIRLINERS	Germany	Maintenance	50	50
AAF SPARES	Ireland	Maintenance	50	50
AEROSTRUCTURES MIDDLE EAST SERVICES	United Arab Emirates	Maintenance	50	50
AEROTECHNIC INDUSTRIES	Morocco	Maintenance	50	50
MAX MRO SERVICE	India	Maintenance	26	26
NEW TSI	United States	Maintenance	50	50
ACAS – ATLAS CATERING AIRLINES SERVICES	Morocco	Other	39	40
AIRCRAFT CAPITAL LTD	United Kingdom	Other	40	40
CITY LOUNGE SERVICES	France	Other	17	35
COTONOU CATERING	Benin	Other	24	49
DOUAL'AIR	Cameroon	Other	25	25
FLYING FOOD CATERING	United States	Other	48	49
FLYNG FOOD JFK	United States	Other	48	49
FLYING FOOD MIAMI	United States	Other	48	49
FLYING FOOD SAN FRANCISCO	United States	Other	48	49

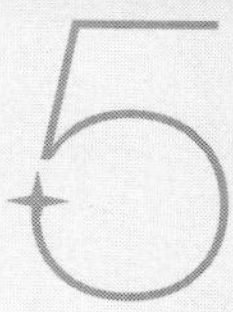

Entity	Country	Segment	% interest	% control
FLYING FOOD SERVICES	United States	Other	48	49
FLYING FOOD SERVICES USA	United States	Other	49	49
GUANGHOU NANLAND CATERING COMPANY	China	Other	24	25
GUEST LOUNGE SERVICES	France	Other	17	35
INTERNATIONAL AEROSPACE MANAGEMENT COMPANY S.C.R.L.	Italy	Other	25	25
KENYA AIRWAYS LIMITED	Kenya	Other	26	27
DUTYFLY SOLUTIONS	France	Other	49	50
DUTYFLY SOLUTIONS ESPAGNE	Spain	Other	49	50
DUTYFLY SOLUTIONS ITALIE	Italy	Other	49	50
LOME CATERING SA	Togo	Other	17	35
MACAU CATERING SERVICES	Macao	Other	17	34
MAINPORT INNOVATION FUND B.V.	Netherlands	Other	25	25
NEWREST SERVAIR UK LTD	United Kingdom	Other	39	40
OVID	France	Other	32	33
PRIORIS	France	Other	33	34
SCHIPHOL LOGISTICS PARK B.V.	Netherlands	Other	45	45
SCHIPHOL LOGISTICS PARK C.V.	Netherlands	Other	52	45
SERVAIR CONGO	Congo	Other	49	50
SERVAIR EUREST	Spain	Other	34	35
SHELTAIR	France	Other	50	50
SKYENERGY B.V.	Netherlands	Other	30	30
SIA MAROC INVEST	Morocco	Other	50	51
TERMINAL ONE GROUP ASSOCIATION	United States	Other	25	25

5.7 Statutory auditors' report on the consolidated financial statements

Year ended December 31, 2013

To the Shareholders,

In compliance with the assignment entrusted by your Annual General Meetings, we hereby report to you, for the year ended December 31, 2013, on:

- the audit of the accompanying consolidated financial statements of Air France-KLM S.A.;
- the justification of our assessments;
- the specific verification required by law.

These consolidated financial statements have been approved by the Board of Directors. Our role is to express an opinion on these financial statements based on our audit.

1. Opinion on the consolidated financial statements

We conducted our audit in accordance with professional standards applicable in France. Those standards require that we plan and perform the audit to obtain reasonable assurance about whether the consolidated financial statements are free of material misstatement. An audit involves performing procedures, using sampling techniques or other methods of selection, to obtain evidence about the amounts and disclosures in the consolidated financial statements. An audit also includes evaluating the appropriateness of accounting policies used and the reasonableness of accounting estimates made, as well as the overall presentation of the consolidated financial statements. We believe that the audit evidence we have obtained is sufficient and appropriate to provide a basis for our audit opinion.

In our opinion, the consolidated financial statements give a true and fair view of the assets and liabilities and of the financial position of the Group as at December 31, 2013 and of the results of its operations for the year then ended in accordance with International Financial Reporting Standards as adopted by the European Union.

Without qualifying our opinion, we draw your attention to the note 2.1 to the consolidated financial statements which sets out the change in accounting policy relating to the application of IAS 19 revised "Employee Benefits" effective as from January 1st, 2013.

2. Justification of assessments

The accounting estimates used in the preparation of the consolidated financial statements were made in a context of an economic downturn raising certain difficulties to apprehend future economic perspectives. These conditions are described in Note 4.2 to the consolidated financial statements. Such is the context in which we made our own assessments that we bring to your attention in accordance with the requirements of Article L. 823-9 of the French Commercial Code (Code de commerce):

- the company recognized deferred tax assets based on the future taxable income determined based on medium and long term business plans as described in notes 4.2, 4.22 and 13 to the consolidated financial statements. Our procedures consisted in analyzing the data and assumptions used by Air France-KLM's management in order to verify the recoverability of these deferred tax assets;
- notes 4.2, 4.17 and 31.1 to the consolidated financial statements specify the accounting policies for employee benefits. These benefits and obligations were evaluated by external actuaries. Our procedures consisted in examining the data used, assessing the assumptions made and verifying that the information included in note 31.1 to the consolidated financial statements was appropriate. In addition, we verified that the accounting policy used for the recognition of the pension fund surplus as outlined in Note 4.17 to the consolidated financial statements was appropriate. Lastly, as mentioned in the first part of this report, note 2.1 to the consolidated financial statements describes the change in the accounting policy done this year relating to the accounting of employee benefits. As part of assessment of accounting principles applied by your company, we have verified the correct application of this change in the accounting policy and the information disclosed on it;
- Air France-KLM's management is required to adopt judgment and estimates concerning determination of the provisions for risk and charges which are described in Notes 3.1, 11, 31.2, 31.3 and 31.4 to the consolidated financial statements. We have examined particularly the estimates and the assumptions used regarding the restructuring provision booked in 2013 and linked to the Transform 2015 plan and the provisions accounted for the anti-trust litigations to which the Company is exposed. We have also verified that the information as disclosed in the notes to the consolidated financial statements was appropriate;
- notes 4.2, 4.14 and 19 to the consolidated financial statements describe the estimates and assumptions that Air France-KLM's management was required to make regarding the impairment tests of tangible and intangible assets. We have examined the data and assumptions on which these impairment tests were based as well as the procedures for implementing impairment tests, as described in the notes;

Registration Document 2013

Air France-KLM

including the annual financial report

This Registration Document is an unofficial translation of the French Document de Référence, which was filed with the French Autorité des Marchés Financiers on Tuesday April 8, 2014, pursuant to article 212-13 of the AMF General Regulations. This unofficial translation has been prepared by Air France-KLM for the information and convenience of English-speaking readers and has not been reviewed or registered with the AMF. No assurances are given as to the accuracy or completeness of this translation, nor any responsibility assumed for any misstatement or omission that may be contained therein. The French Document de Référence may be used for the purposes of a financial transaction if supplemented with an offering memorandum approved by the AMF. In the event of any ambiguity or discrepancy between this unofficial translation and the French Document de Référence, the French version shall prevail.

This page has been intentionally left blank

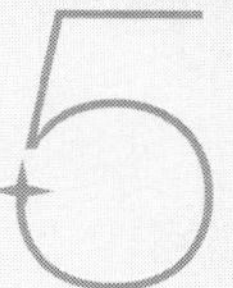

- Air France-KLM's management is required to make estimates and assumptions relating to the recognition of revenue arising from issued but unused tickets and its Frequent Flyer Program, in accordance with the terms and conditions described in Notes 4.2, 4.6 and 4.7 to the consolidated financial statements. Our procedures consisted in analyzing the data used, assessing the assumptions made and reviewing the calculations performed.

These assessments were made as part of our audit of the consolidated financial statements taken as a whole and therefore contributed to the opinion we formed which is expressed in the first part of this report.

3. Specific procedures

As required by law we have also verified, in accordance with professional standards applicable in France, the information presented in the Group's management report.

We have no matters to report as to its fair presentation and its consistency with the consolidated financial statements.

Paris La Défense and Neuilly-sur-Seine, February 24, 2014

The Statutory Auditors

KPMG Audit

Division of KPMG S.A.

Valérie Besson

Partner

Michel Piette

Partner

Deloitte & Associés

Dominique Jumaucourt

Partner

This is a free translation into English of the statutory auditors' reports on the consolidated financial statements issued in the French language and is provided solely for the convenience of English speaking readers.

The statutory auditors' report includes information specifically required by French law in such report, whether qualified or not. This information is presented below the audit opinion on consolidated financial statements and includes explanatory paragraph discussing the auditors' assessments of certain significant accounting and auditing matters. These assessments were made for the purpose of issuing an audit opinion on the consolidated financial statements taken as a whole and not to provide separate assurance on individual account captions or on information taken outside of the consolidated financial statements.

This report also includes information relating to the specific verification of information given in the Group's management report. This report should be read in conjunction with and construed in accordance with French law and professional auditing standards applicable in France.

This page has been intentionally left blank

Glossaries

Air transport glossary

AEA

Association of European Airlines. Created in 1952, notably by Air France and KLM, the AEA represents the interests of its members within the European Union institutions, the European Civil Aviation Conference and other organizations and associations.

Available seat-kilometers (ASK)

Total number of seats available for the transportation of passengers multiplied by the number of kilometres traveled.

Available ton-kilometers (ATK)

Total number of tons available for the transportation of cargo, multiplied by the number of kilometres traveled.

Biometry

Technique enabling the identity of an individual to be verified, while crossing a national border for example, through the automatic recognition of certain pre-recorded physical characteristics.

Coordinated airport

Airport where a coordinator has been appointed to allocate landing and take off slots according to rules established in advance. All large European Union airports are coordinated.

Cabotage

Airline cabotage is the carriage of air traffic that originates and terminates within the boundaries of a given country by an air carrier of another country.

Capacity

Capacity is measured in available seat-kilometers.

Catering

In-flight catering involves the planning and preparation of meals and the assembly of meal trays destined to be served on board an aircraft.

Code share

In accordance with a code share agreement, two partner airlines offer services on the same aircraft, each under their own brand, their own IATA code and their own flight number. Code sharing may take two forms. In the first case, the two airlines purchase and sell seats to and from each other at an agreed price. The airline which has purchased the seats then markets them under its brand and at its fares. In the second case, under the system known as free flow, the two airlines are allowed to sell all the seats on the flights involved. Each airline retains the revenues generated on the flight it operates and remunerates the other airline for the number of seats the latter has sold on its aircraft.

Combi

Aircraft whose main deck is equipped for the transportation of both passengers and cargo. The freight is stored at the back of the aircraft and is accessed by a specially-fitted cargo door.

Connecting traffic

Traffic between two destinations which are not linked by a direct flight.

DGAC

Direction Générale de l'Aviation Civile. Under the authority of the French Ministry of Transport, the DGAC is in charge of the security of air transport and of air space in France.

DGTL

Directoraat-Generaal Transport en Luchtvaart. Under the authority of the Dutch Ministry of Traffic and Public Works, the DGTL is in charge of the security of air transport and of air space in the Netherlands.

E-services

Range of ground services offered by Air France and KLM to their passengers, based on the new information technologies. E-services notably enable passengers to check in using self-service kiosks or *via* the airlines' websites as well as the use of electronic tickets.

EASA

European Aviation Safety Agency. EASA develops safety and environmental protection expertise in civil aviation in order to assist the European institutions to establish legislation and implement measures regarding aircraft security, organizations and associated staff.

Electronic ticket

All the journey information for one or several passengers which, instead of being printed, is recorded in an airline's IT database, once the reservation has been made and paid for. An electronic or e-ticket replaces a traditional paper ticket.

Equivalent available seat-kilometer (EASK)

Overall measure of production for the Air France-KLM group after conversion of cargo tons into equivalent available seats.

Equivalent revenue passenger-kilometers (ERPK)

Overall measure of the Air France-KLM group's traffic after conversion of cargo tons into equivalent revenue passenger-kilometers.

Fare combinability

System which, on destinations served by both Air France and KLM, enables customers to choose between a journey with an onward flight connection at KLM's Schiphol hub and a journey with an onward flight connection at Air France's Roissy-Charles de Gaulle hub. With fare combinability, customers benefit from a choice of more frequencies *via* one or other of the hubs, for both the inbound and outbound trips. The fare is based on two half return tickets.

FAA

Federal Aviation Administration. Body responsible for civil aviation security in the United States.

Handling

Preparation of the aircraft, involving loading and unloading, as well as the associated logistics such as management and storage of hotel products.

High contribution

Fare classes corresponding to business or first class.

Hub

Term used for a transfer platform where departures and arrivals are scheduled to minimize transit times. Air France-KLM disposes of two of the four major European hubs: Roissy-Charles de Gaulle and Amsterdam-Schiphol. The Air France and KLM hubs are organized into successive waves for arrivals and departures each day in order to increase the transfer opportunities for customers.

IATA

International Air Transport Association. Created in 1945, IATA establishes regulations for the air transport industry and provides its members with a framework for the coordination and proper implementation of tariffs, together with various commercial and financial support services.

IATA year

Financial year which runs from April 1 to March 31 of the following year.

ICAO

The International Civil Aviation Organisation, a UN Specialized Agency, promotes the safe, secure and sustainable development of civil aviation world-wide. It establishes the standards and regulations required to ensure the safety, security, efficiency and continuity of aviation operations as well as the protection of the environment.

Joint-venture

Joint company with two partners, often held equally with 50% each. This type of shareholder structure notably allows the implementation of technological or industrial alliances in order to undertake specific projects common to both partner companies.

Load factor

Revenue passenger-kilometers (RPK) divided by available seat-kilometers (ASK). In the cargo activity this is revenue ton-kilometers (RTK) divided by available ton-kilometers (ATK).

Multi-hub

System linking several hubs, allowing customers to access the networks developed from each hub, thus multiplying the round-trip offer to and from world-wide destinations.

Over-reservation or over-booking

Over-reservation or over-booking consists of accepting more bookings than seats available. Practiced by all airline companies and permitted by European legislation, over-booking enables management of the fact that some passengers cancel their trips but not their reservations. It thus allows many passengers to find a seat on board flights that could have departed with available seats. Airlines usually have a passenger compensation policy.

Point-to-point traffic

Traffic between two airports, excluding passengers prolonging their trip with a connecting flight.

Revenue management

Technique designed to optimize revenue on flights, by constantly seeking a better balance between the load factor and the fares offered.

Revenue passenger-kilometer (RPK)

Total number of paying passengers carried multiplied by the number of kilometers traveled.

Revenue ton-kilometer (RTK)

Total number of tons of paid cargo multiplied by the number of kilometers that this cargo is carried.

Safety and security

Airline safety includes all the measures implemented by air transport professionals aimed at ensuring the reliable operation and maintenance of aircraft.

Airline security involves all the measures taken by air transport professionals to prevent any illicit or malicious act. Air transport is particularly exposed to terrorist acts due to the considerable media impact offered by such activity. Airline security notably includes baggage screening, and the screening and questioning of passengers.

Summer season

Defined by IATA as the period running from the last Saturday in March to the last Saturday in October. The summer season corresponds to a schedule of summer flights over a period of seven months.

Self-service check-in kiosk

Self-service check-in kiosks, available in airport departure halls, allow passengers to check in and print their own boarding cards, without having to go to a check-in counter.

Segment

Section of a flight between two destinations. The number of passengers is calculated by segment carried.

Slot

A slot represents clearance given for a carrier to land at or take off from an airport at a specified time and date.

Sub-fleet

All the aircraft of the same type, with identical technical and commercial characteristics (engines, cabin configuration, etc.).

Ton-kilometers transported

Total number of tons transported multiplied by the number of kilometer covered.

Traffic

Traffic is measured in Revenue Passenger-Kilometers (RPK).

Unit revenue

In the passenger business, corresponds to the revenue for one available seat or for one paying passenger transported over one kilometer. In the cargo business, corresponds to the revenue for one available ton or one ton transported over one kilometer.

Winter season

Defined by IATA as the period running from the first Sunday following the last Saturday in October to the Friday before the last Saturday in March. The winter season corresponds to a schedule of winter flights over five months.

Financial Glossary

Adjusted operating income

Adjusted operating income corresponds to income from current operations increased for the portion of operating leases deemed to be interest charges.

Adjusted operating margin

The adjusted operating margin is the percentage of revenues represented by operating income adjusted for the portion of operating leases (34%) deemed to be financial charges. The adjusted operating margin calculation is detailed in section 5.4, page 159.

Adjusted net debt

Adjusted net debt comprises net debt and the amount resulting from the capitalization of operating leases (7x the annual charge).

ADR

American Depositary Receipt. ADRs are negotiable certificates representing a specific number of shares with a nominal value in dollars. The Air France-KLM level 1 ADR program is traded on the OTCQX Market.

Earnings per share

Net income divided by the average number of shares for the period.

EASK (revenue and cost)

The EASK or equivalent available seat-kilometer is an overall indicator of the Group's air transport activity. Given the weight of the passenger business (including the leisure business), the indicators for the cargo business (ATK and RTK) are converted into the ASK and RPK "equivalents", the indicators used in the passenger business. Unit revenue per EASK corresponds to the revenues generated by the passenger and cargo businesses divided by the number of EASK. Unit cost per EASK corresponds to the net costs divided by the number of EASKs. The calculation of the unit cost per EASK is detailed in section 5.4, page 159.

EBITDA

Earnings before interest, taxation, depreciation and amortization. The calculation method is detailed in section 5.4, page 159.

EBITDAR

Earnings before interest, taxation, depreciation, amortization and operating leases. This metric facilitates comparison between companies with different aircraft financing policies.

Fuel hedging

Financial mechanism aimed at protecting Air France-KLM from the risk of a rise in the fuel price. Involves purchasing financial instruments, mostly in the form of options, whose value fluctuates as a function of the jet fuel price and the related oil products (oil, diesel). The hedging strategy is detailed in section 3.3, page 91.

Gearing ratio

The gearing ratio reflects the respective proportions of Group net debt and stockholders' equity at a given time. This ratio gives a measure of the company's financial independence: the lower it is, the greater the company's room for manoeuvre.

IFRS

International Financial Reporting Standards. International accounting standards used by European Union listed companies to establish their consolidated financial statements. Adopted on January 1, 2005, they allow investors to compare European companies more easily.

ISIN

International Securities Identification Number. Attributed to securities listed for trading on the Euronext market.

Market capitalization

The market capitalization corresponds to the share price multiplied by the number of shares comprising the company's capital.

Net adjusted interest costs

Net interest costs are adjusted for the portion (34%) of operating leases deemed to be financial costs.

Net income, Group share

Corresponds to net income, minus the share reverting to the minority shareholders in fully consolidated subsidiaries.

OCÉANE

Acronym of Obligations Convertibles En Actions Nouvelles ou Existantes or bonds convertible and/or exchangeable into new or existing shares.

OPE

Offre Publique d'Échange. A public exchange offer (PEO) is an offer to purchase shares in a target company in exchange for shares in the company initiating the offer.

Operating income

Operating income is the amount remaining after operating expenses (external expenses, payroll costs, amortization and provisions) have been deducted from revenues. It shows what the company earns from its principal activity before the impact of financial and exceptional items.

ORS

Offre Réservée aux Salariés or offer reserved for employees. Within the context of privatizations, the State sells a tranche of shares to employees of the company at preferential conditions.

Return on capital employed (ROCE)

A measure of the returns that a company is making on the capital employed to ensure its business activity. The calculation is detailed in section 5.4, page 159.

Revenues

Revenues corresponds to the total sales generated by the Air France-KLM group in its three core businesses (passenger, cargo, maintenance) and in its ancillary activities. The revenues from airline operations are recognized on realization of the transportation, net of any potential discounts granted. Consequently, when passenger and cargo tickets are issued, they are recorded in balance sheet liabilities under deferred revenue on ticket sales.

Share capital

Corresponds to the total contributions either financial or in kind made by the shareholders either at the time the company is created or during capital increases. It is equal to the number of shares multiplied by the nominal value of the share.

SSE

Shares-for-Salary Exchange. In connection with the French State's sale of Air France-KLM shares, employees were offered shares in exchange for a salary reduction over a six-year period.

Stockholders' equity

Stockholders' equity represents accounting value of the capital contributed by the shareholders to establish the company or subsequently, or left at the disposal of the company as income not distributed in the form of dividends. Corresponds to total balance sheet assets, net of total debt.

TPI

Titre au Porteur Identifiable or identifiable bearer shares. TPI analysis enables a company to identify its shareholders holding stock in bearer form.